G000139502

Street by Street

LONDON

Extended Coverage of the Capital

Ist edition May 2001

© Automobile Association Developments Limited 2001

This product includes map data licensed from Ordnance Survey® with the permission of the Controller of Her Majesty's Stationery Office. © Crown copyright 2000. All rights reserved. Licence No: 399221.

All rights reserved. No part of this publication may be reproduced, stored in a retrieval system, or transmitted in any form or by any means– electronic, mechanical, photocopying, recording or otherwise – unless the permission of the publisher has been given beforehand.

Published by AA Publishing (a trading name of Automobile Association Developments Limited, whose registered office is Norfolk House, Priestley Road, Basingstoke, Hampshire, RG24 9NY.Registered number 1878835).

Mapping produced by the Cartographic Department of The Automobile Association.

ISBN 0 7495 2360 3

A CIP Catalogue record for this book is available from the British Library.

Printed by G. Canale & C. s.p.a., Torino, Italy

The contents of this atlas are believed to be correct at the time of the latest revision. However, the publishers cannot be held responsible for loss occasioned to any person acting or refraining from action as a result of any material in this atlas, nor for any errors, omissions or changes in such material. The publishers would welcome information to correct any errors or omissions and to keep this atlas up to date. Please write to Publishing, The Automobile Association, Fanum House, Basing View, Basingstoke, Hampshire, RG21 4EA.

Ref: MX039

Key to map pages	ii-iii
Key to map symbols	iv-1
Enlarged scale pages	2-19
Street by Street	20-187
Index – towns & villages	188-189
Index – streets	190-277
Index – featured places	278-299

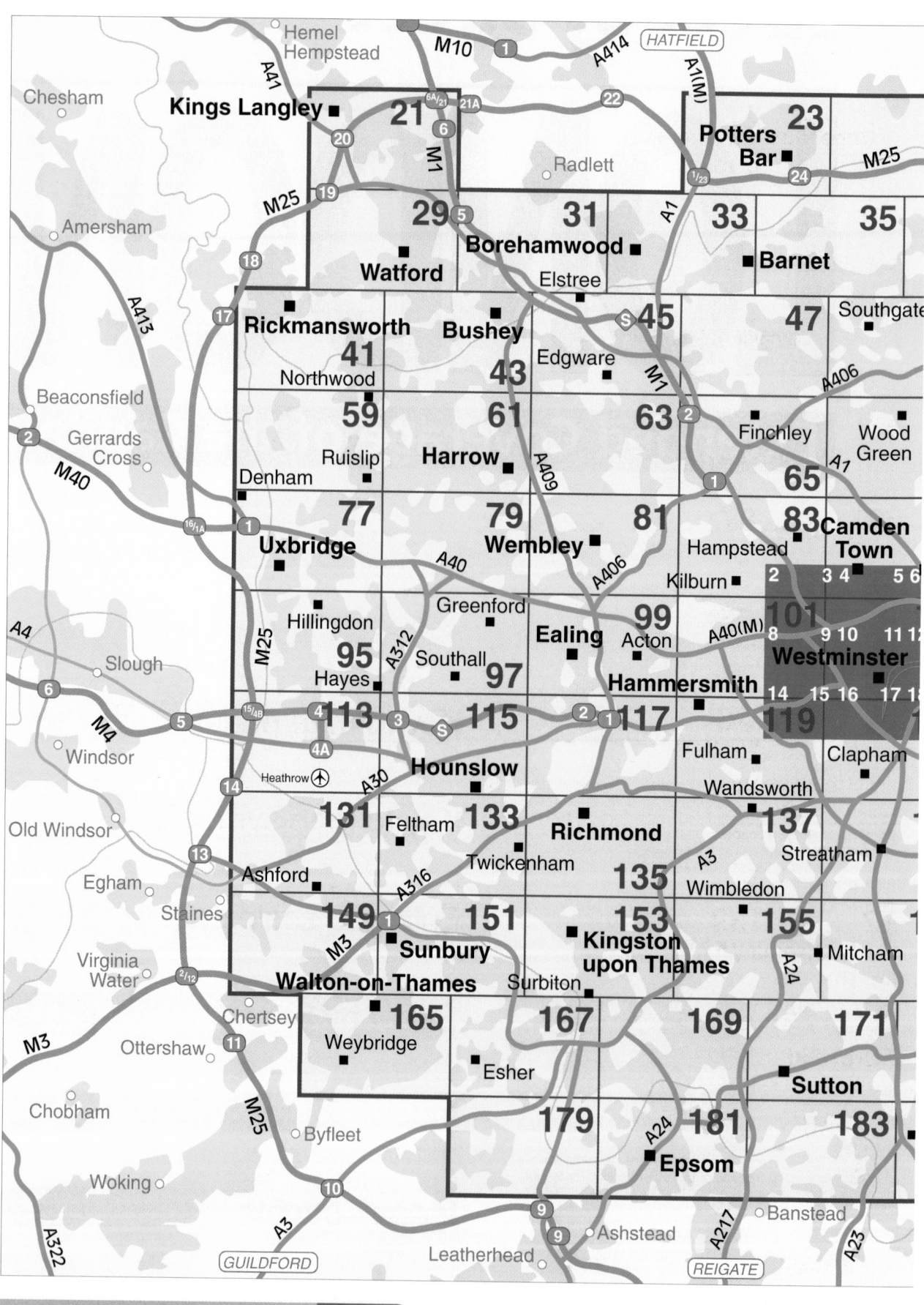

Enlarged scale pages 1:10,000 6.3 inches to 1 mile

miles: 0 — 1/4 — 1/2 — 3/4

kilometres: 0 — 1/4 — 1/2 — 3/4 — 1 — 1 1/4

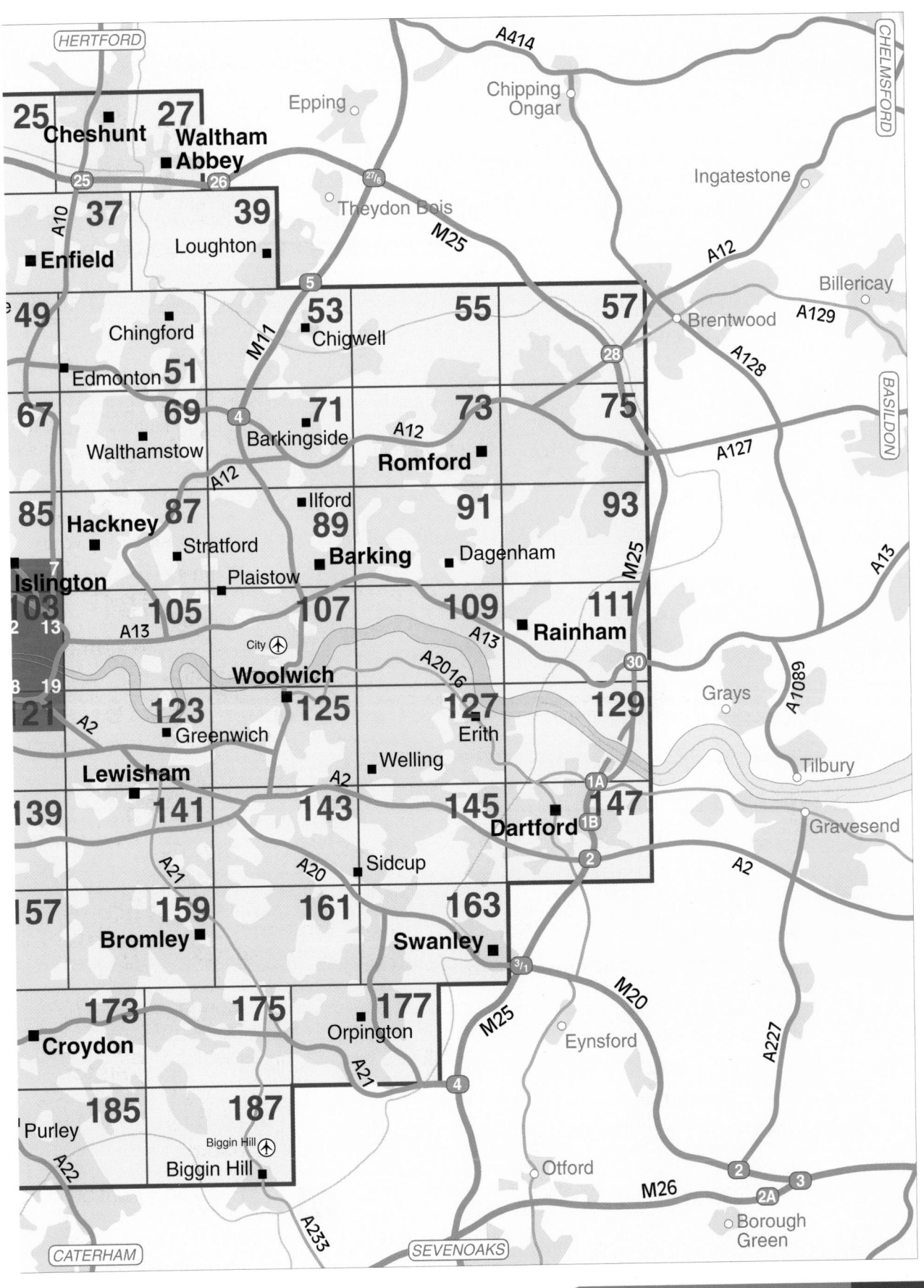

Junction 9	Motorway & junction
Services	Motorway service area
	Primary road single/dual carriageway
Services	Primary road service area
	A road single/dual carriageway
	B road single/dual carriageway
	Other road single/dual carriageway
	Restricted road
	Private road
← ←	One way street
	Pedestrian street
	Track/footpath
	Road under construction
	Road tunnel
P	Parking

P+	Park & Ride
	Bus/coach station
	Railway & main railway station
	Railway & minor railway station
⊖	Underground station
⊖	Light railway & station
	Preserved private railway
LC	Level crossing
• • • •	Tramway
- - - -	Ferry route
....	Airport runway
-·-·-·-	Boundaries- borough/district
▼▼▼▼	Mounds
93	Page continuation 1:17,500
7	Page continuation to enlarged scale 1:10,000

River/canal
lake, pier

Toilet with
disabled facilities

Aqueduct
lock, weir

Petrol station

465
▲
Winter Hill

Peak (with
height in
metres)

PH   Public house

Beach

PO   Post Office

Coniferous
woodland

Public library

Broadleaved
woodland

Tourist Information
Centre

Mixed
woodland

Castle

Park

Historic house/
building

Cemetery

Wakehurst
Place NT

National Trust
property

Built-up
area

M   Museum/
art gallery

Featured building

†   Church/chapel

ⴰⴰⴰⴰⴰⴰⴰ City wall

Country park

A&E

Accident &
Emergency
hospital

Theatre/
performing arts

Toilet

Cinema

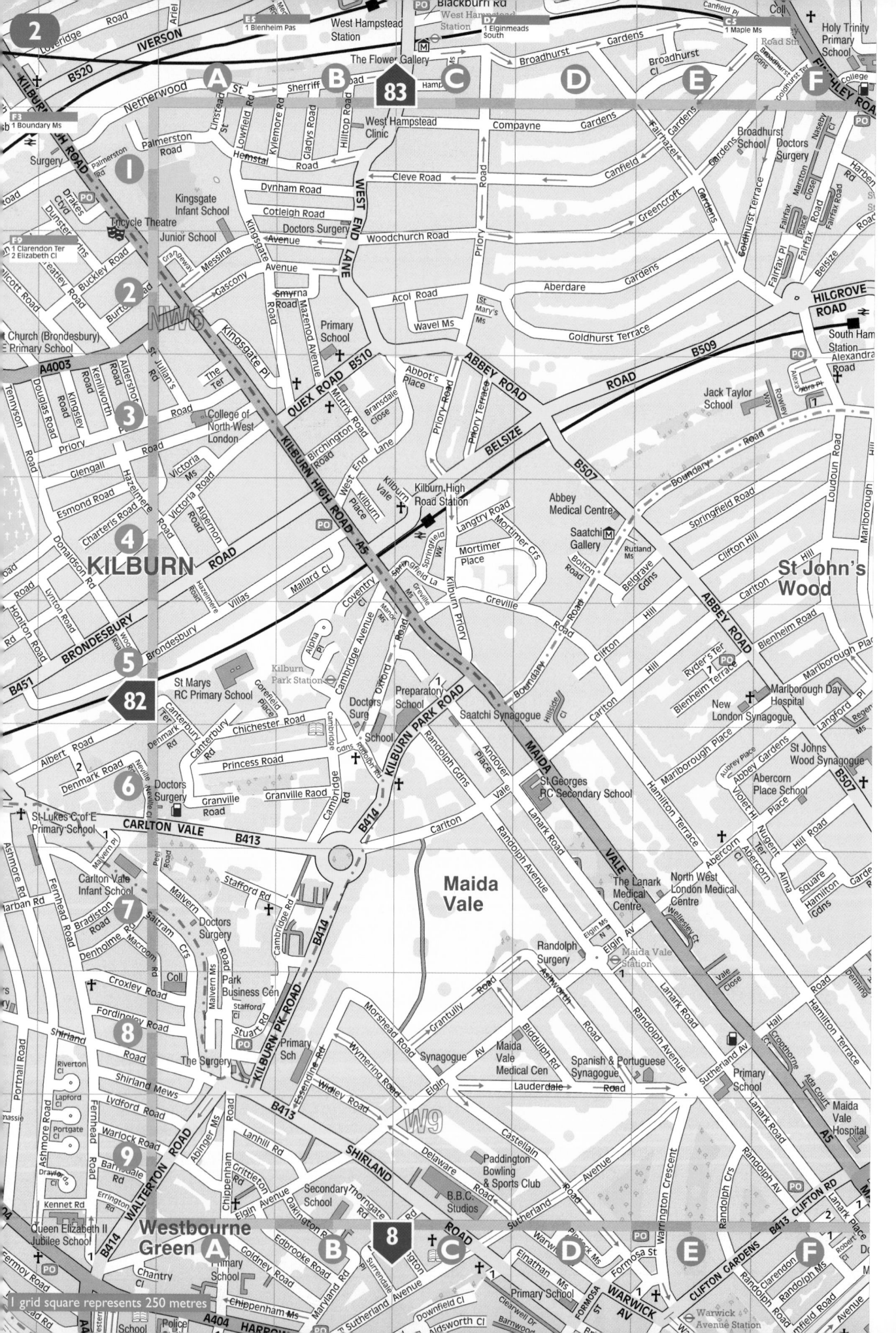

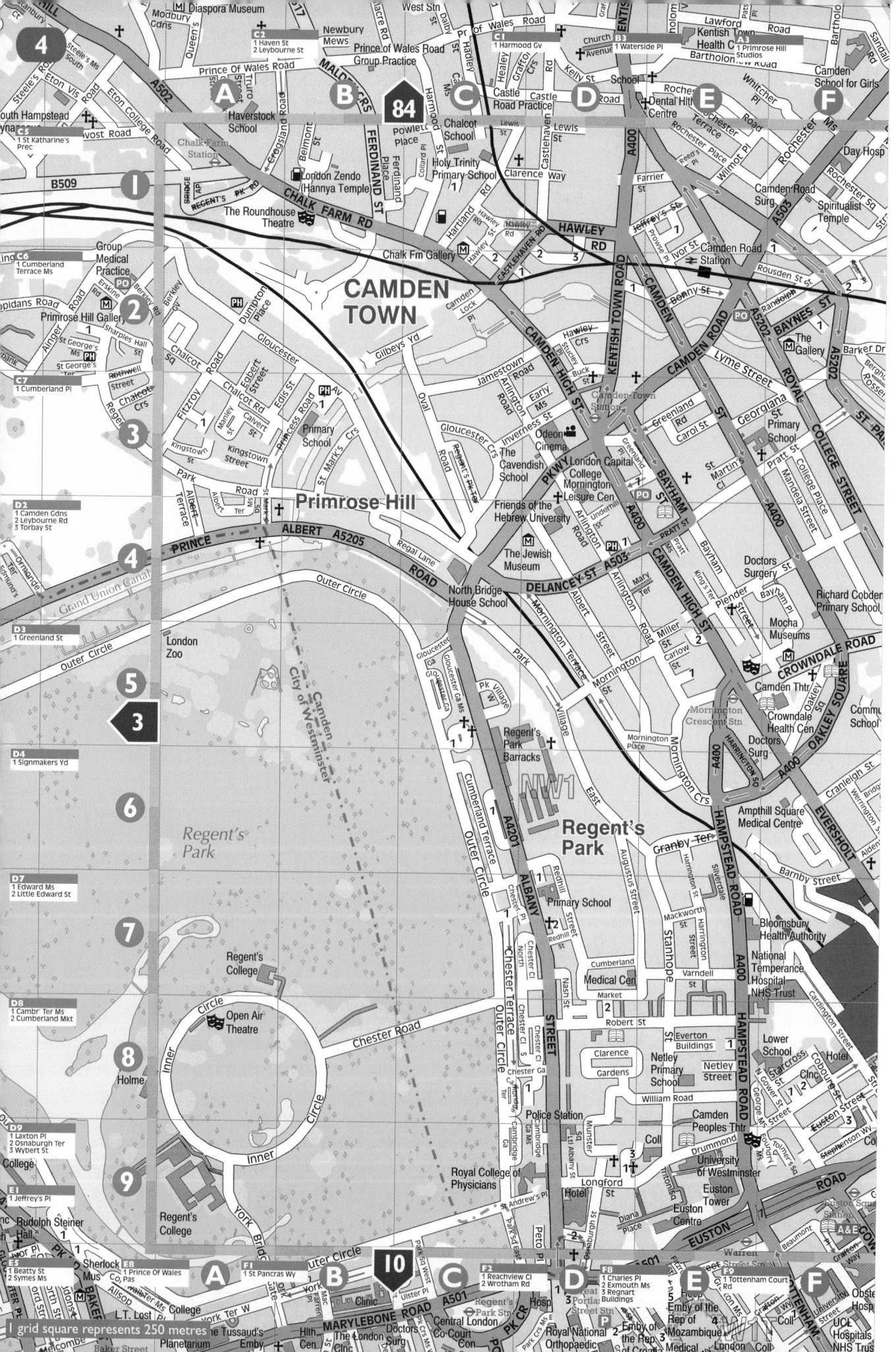

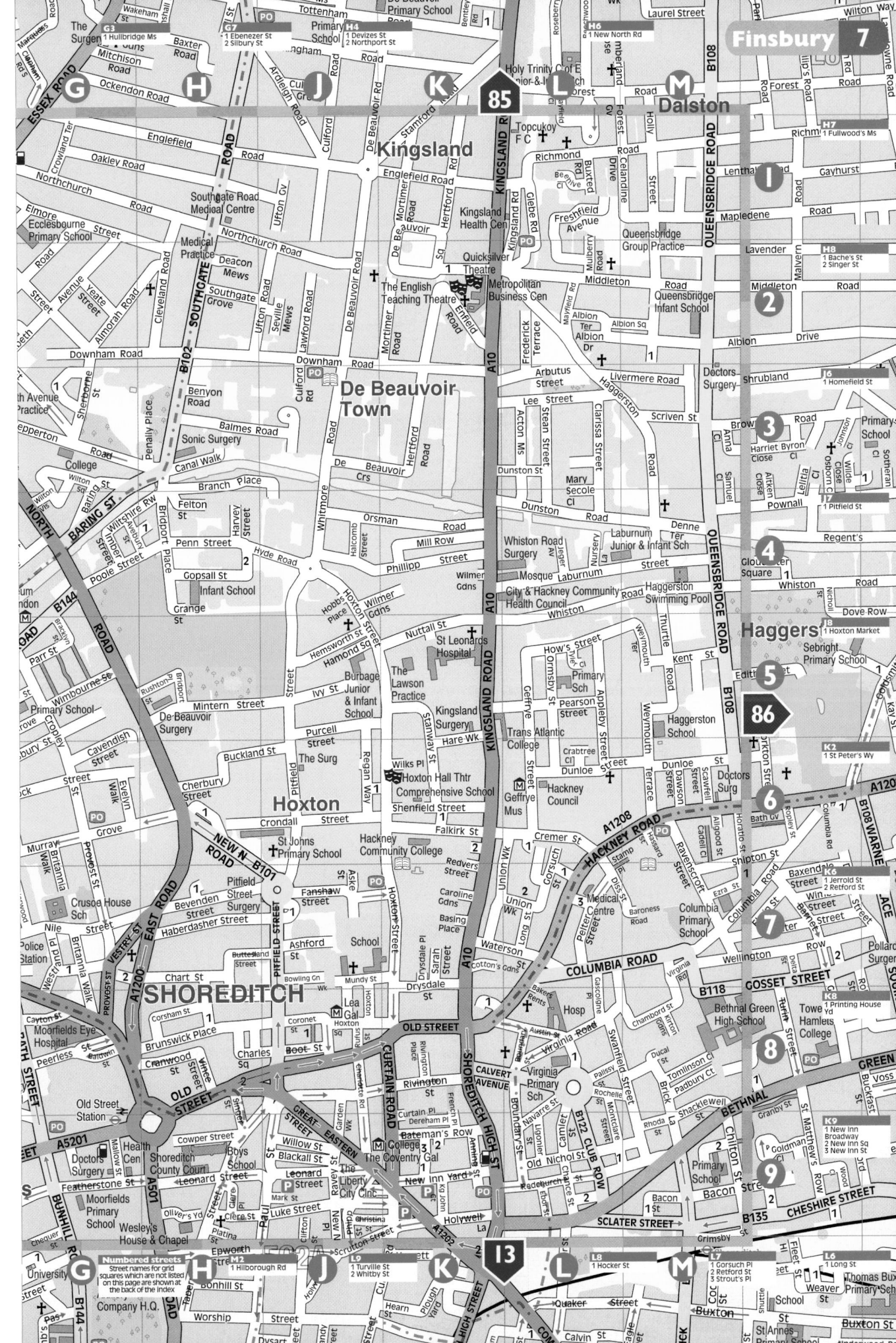

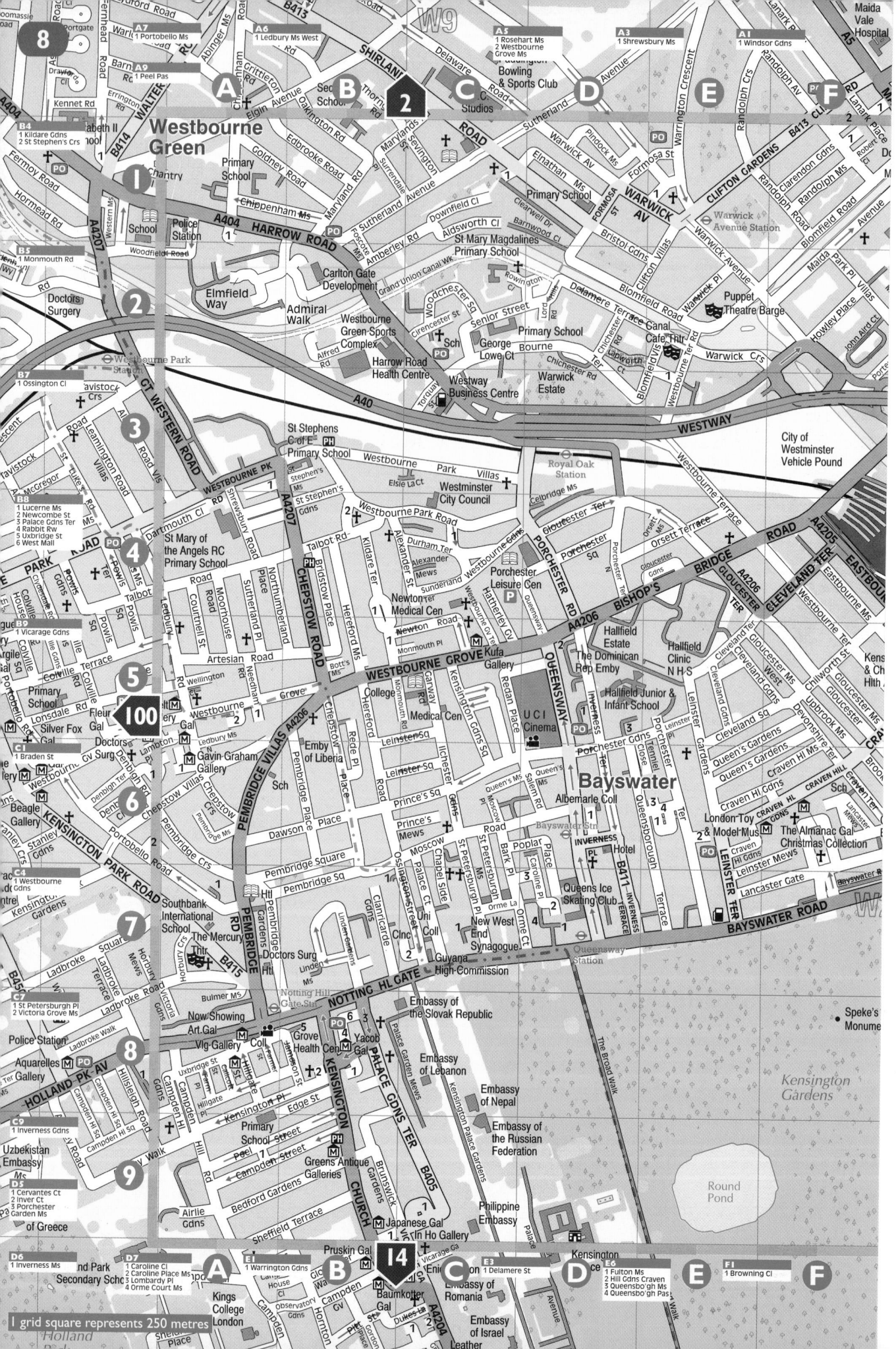

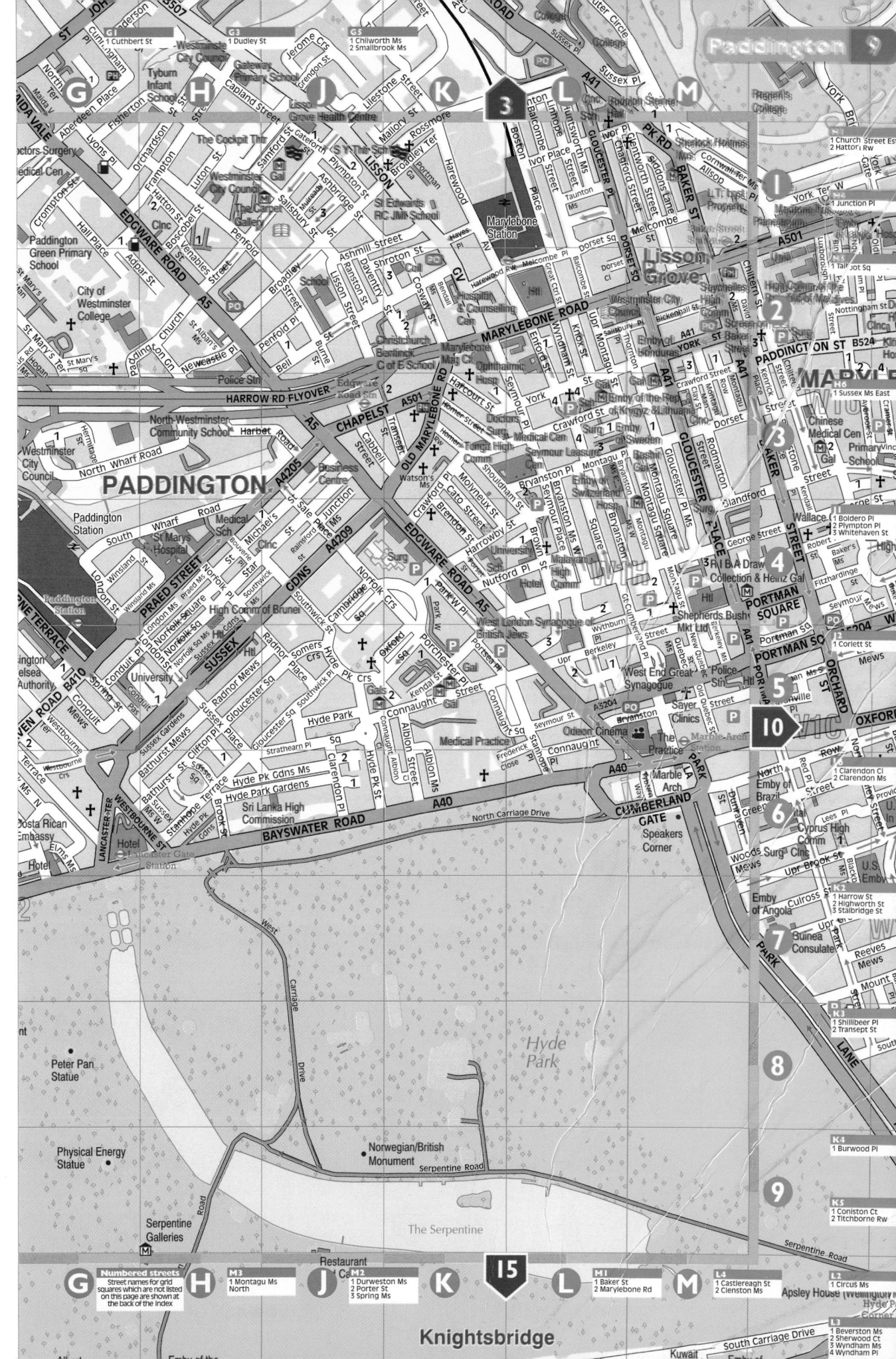

16

1 grid square represents 250 metres

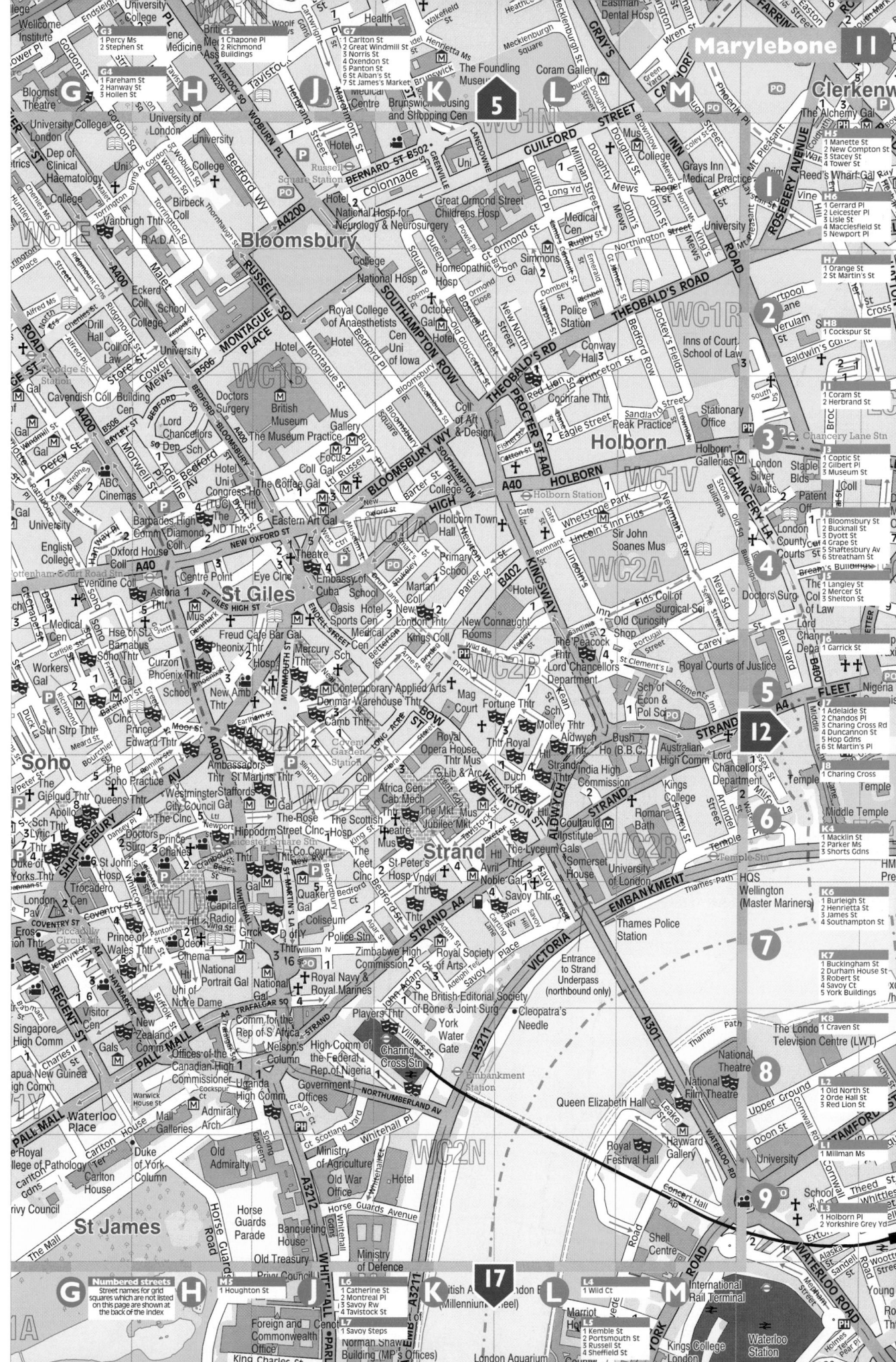

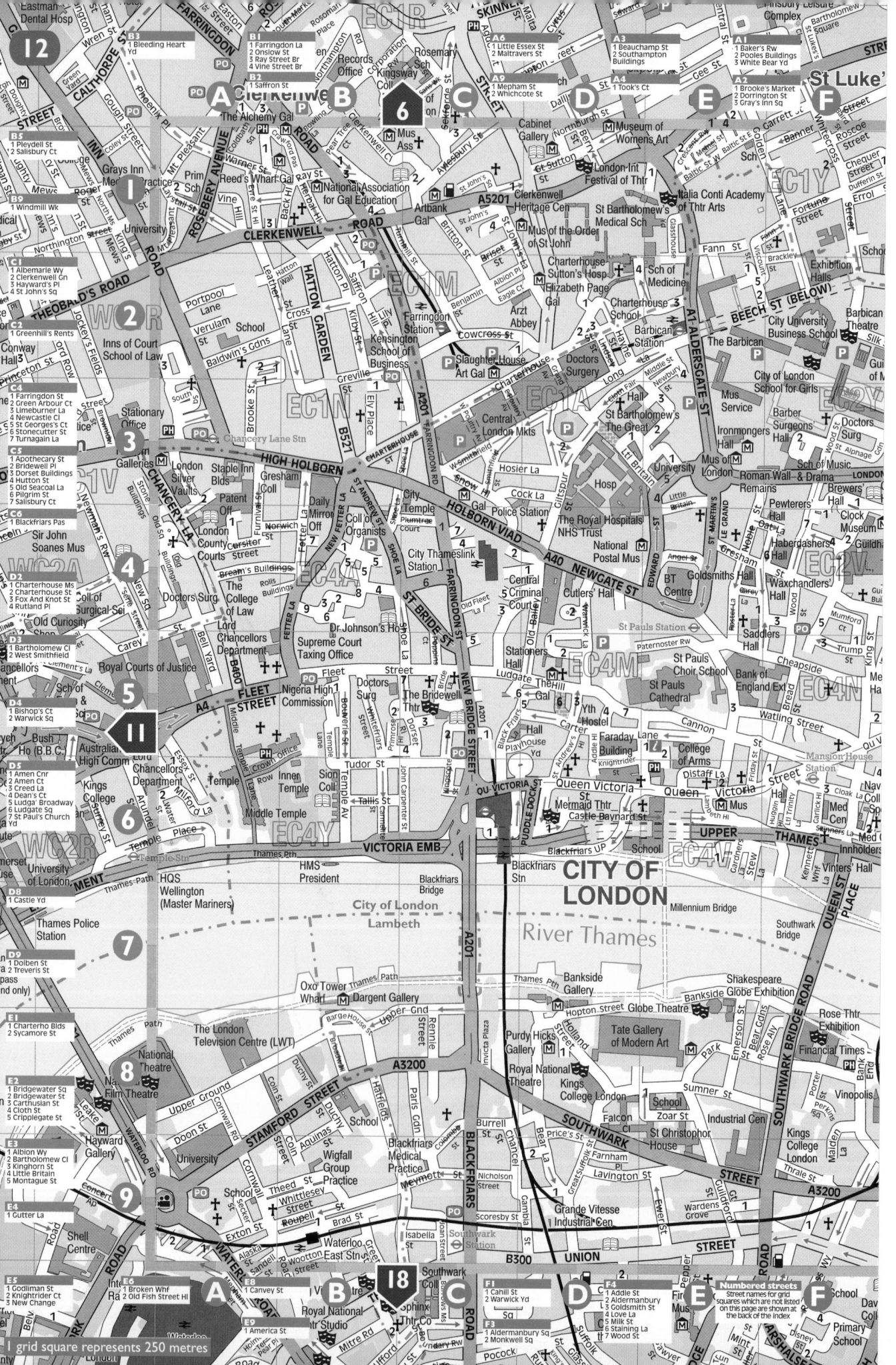

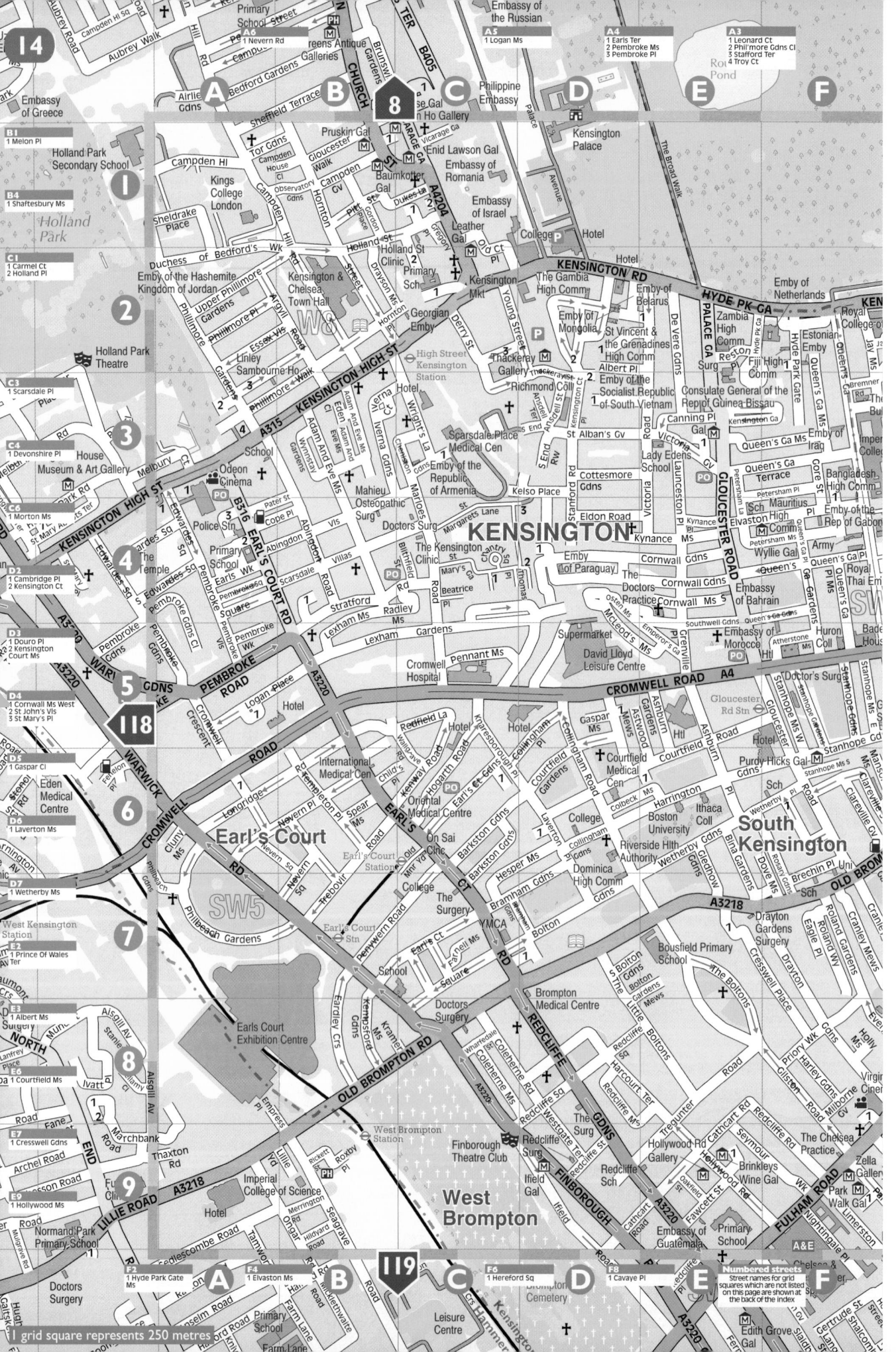

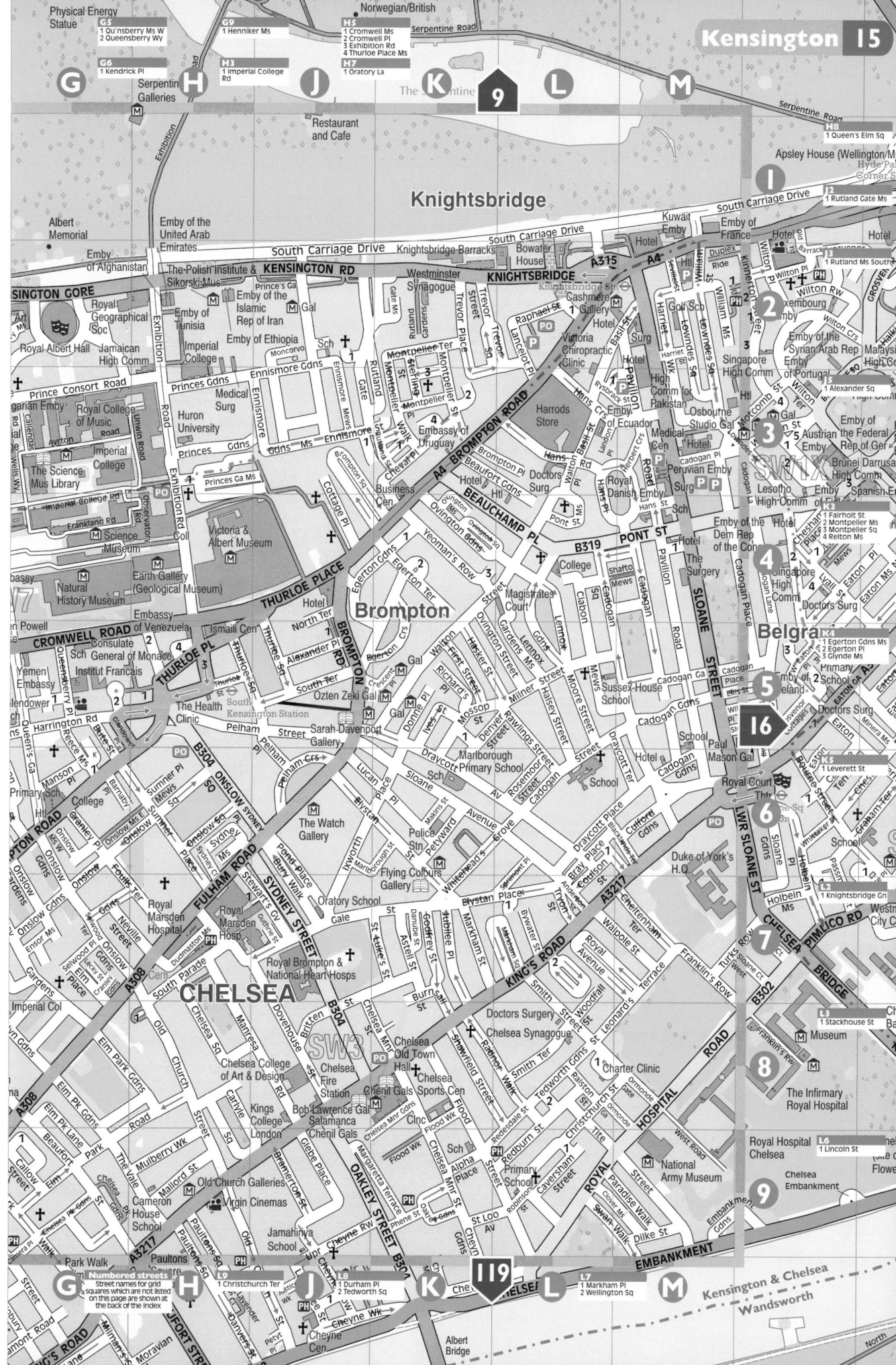

Physical Energy Statue

G5
1 Qu'nsberry Ms W
2 Queensberry Wy

G9
1 Henniker Ms

H5
1 Cromwell Ms
2 Cromwell Pl
3 Exhibition Rd
4 Thurloe Place Ms

Norwegian/British

G6
1 Kendrick Pl

H3
1 Imperial College Rd

H7
1 Oratory La

H8
1 Queen's Elm Sq

Serpentine Road

G H J K 9 L M

Serpentine Galleries

The Serpentine

Restaurant and Cafe

Knightsbridge

Apsley House (Wellington/Mu...
Hyde Par
Corner Hou...

Albert Memorial

Emby of the United Arab Emirates

South Carriage Drive

I
1 Rutland Gate Ms

KSINGTON GORE

Emby of Afghanistan

South Carriage Drive
Knightsbridge Barracks
KENSINGTON RD
Westminster Synagogue

South Carriage Drive
Bowater House

Kuwait Emby
Hotel

Emby of France
Hotel
Hotel

The Polish Institute & Sikorski-Mus
Prince's Ga
Emby of the Islamic Rep of Iran

Gate Ms
Trevor Pl
Raphael St
KNIGHTSBRIDGE
Knightsbridge Stn
A315
A4

Duplex

Htl
Ride

Wilton Pl
PH

2
Luxembourg Emby

Royal Geographical Soc
Art Ms
Royal Albert Hall
Jamaican High Comm

Emby of Tunisia
Emby of Ethiopia
Imperial College

Prince's Ga
Gal
Sch
Montpelier Ter
Trevor Sq
Lancelot Pl

Victoria Chiropractic Clinic
Hotel
Surg

Golf Sch
Harriet Wk

Wilton Cres
Wilton RW
PH
Emby of the Syrian Arab Rep
Emby of Portugal

Prince Consort Road
Royal College of Music
arian Emby
Ayrton
Rd
Imperial College

Princes Gdns
Medical Surg
Ennismore Gdns
Huron University
Princes

Ennismore Mews
Montpelier Sq
Montpelier Pl
Montpelier
Pl
Embassy of Uruguay

Brompton Rd
Hans Rd
Harrods Store

Singapore High Comm
High Comm for Pakistan
Osbourne Studio Gal
Medical Cen
Hotel

Norcomb
Wilton
1 Alexander Sq

3
Emby of Ecuador
Peruvian Emby
Surg
Lesotho High Comm

4 5 Austrian Emby
Emby of the Federal Rep of Ger
Brunei Darrusal High Comm
Spanish Em

SW1X

The Science Mus Library
Imperial College
Frankland Rd
Science Museum

Exhibition Rd
Observatory
Princes Ga Ms
Cottage Pl

Business Cen
BEAUCHAMP PL
Ovington Gdns
Beaufort Gdns
Hotel
Yeoman's Row

Hans St
PONT ST
B319
Royal Danish Emby
Cadogan Pl
Doctors Surg
Surg
P P

Cadogan Pl
Emby Spanish En
Emby of the Dem Rep of the Con

3
4
5
Emby of the Syrian Arab Rep

1 Fairholt St
2 Montpelier Ms
3 Montpelier Sq
4 Relton Ms

K4

Natural History Museum
Earth Gallery (Geological Museum)

THURLOE PLACE
Hotel
North Ter
Egerton Gdns
Egerton Ter
Walton St

Gardens Ms
Lennox Gdns
Clabon Ms

College
Shafto Mews
Pavilion

The Surgery
Logan Lane
Cadogan Place

Singapore High Comm
Doctors Surg

Belgra
1 Egerton Gdns Ms
2 Egerton Pl
3 Glynde Ms

Embassy of Venezuela
CROMWELL ROAD
Consulate General of Monaco
Institut Francais
Ismaili Cen
Gal
THURLOE PL
Alexander Ter
South Ter

Brompton
BROMPTON RD
Egerton Crs
Crescent Pl
Gal
Walton St
Richard's Pl
Mossop St

First Street
Hasker St
Halsey Street
Milner Street
Moore Street

Cadogan Gdns
Sussex House School
Cadogan Gdns
School

SLOANE STREET
Cadogan Place
Hotel
Paul Mason Gal

Primary School
Emby of Ireland

K4

Yemen Embassy
Glendower
Harrington Rd
Reece Ms

The Health Clinic
South Kensington Station
Ozten Zeki Gal
Gal
Donne Pl

Pelham Street
Pelham Crs
Lucan Place
Sloane Ave
Marlborough Primary School
Draycott
Avenue
Rosemoor Street
Cadogan Gdns
Draycott Ter

5
Doctors Surg
Eaton
Eaton Ms N
Minera Ms

16

5
6
1 Leverett St

K5

Primary Sch
Manson Pl
Selwood Ter
B304
ONSLOW SQ
SYDNEY
Sumner Pl
Sumner Mews
Onslow Ms
Onslow Sq
Sydney Ms
The Watch Gallery

Ixworth Pl
Denyer Street
Rawlings Street
Cadogan
St

Blacklands Ter
Police Stn
Petyward
Draycott Place
Bray Pl
Cadogan Gdns
Hotel
Holbein Pl
Royal Court Thtr

Sloane Sq
Graham Ter
Graham Ter
School

6
LWR SLOANE ST

1 Knightsbridge Gn

N ROAD
Onslow Gdns
College
Onslow Ms W
Burnaby
Sydney Cl
Pond Place
Stewart's Gv
Bury Walk

Elystan St
Makins St
Marlborough St
Whitehead's Gr
Flying Colours Gallery
Oratory School
Gale
Elystan Place

Duke of York's H.Q.

Holbein Ms
CHELSEA BRIDGE
Sloane Gdns
Whitaker Ms
Passmo

7
PIMLICO RD

7

Royal Marsden Hospital
Royal Marsden Hosp
Dudmaston Ms
PH
Neville St
Onslow Gdns

FULHAM ROAD
SYDNEY STREET
Royal Brompton & National Heart Hosps
Danube St
A StelI St
Godfrey St
Hobbe St
Markham St
Bywater St

KING'S ROAD
Tryon St
Smith Ter
Smith St
St Leonard's Ter

Walpole St
Royal
Avenue
Cheltenham Ter
Franklin's Row

Turk's Row
West
Franklin's Rw

Museum

L3
1 Stackhouse St

CHELSEA
SW3
Chelsea College of Art & Design
Kings College London
Manresa Rd
Dovehouse St
B304
Chelsea Mnr St
PO
Chelsea Fire Station
Bob Lawrence Gal
Salamanca
Chenil Gals

Chelsea Old Town Hall
Chenil Gals
Chelsea Sports Cen
Clnc
Doctors Surgery
Chelsea Synagogue
Woodfall Street
Ralston St
Tedworth Gdns
Charter Clinic
Ormonde Gate
Ormonde

HOSPITAL ROAD
West Road
National Army Museum

8
The Infirmary Royal Hospital

Imperial Col
A308
Elm Park Gdns
Old Church
Carlyle Sq
Mulberry Wk
Mallord St
Old Church Galleries
Virgin Cinemas

Glebe Place
Bramerton St
OAKLEY STREET
Margaretta Terrace
Redesdale St
Flood Walk
Sch
Redburn St
Alpha Place
Caversham Street
Tite Street
Christchurch Street
Paradise Walk
Royal Hospital Road
Swan Walk
Dilke St

Royal Hospital Chelsea
Chelsea Embankment

L6
1 Lincoln St

Elm Pk Gdns
Beaufort St
The Vale
Cameron House School
Chelsea Pk Gdns
Paultons Sq
Jamahiriya School
Upr Cheyne Rw
Cheyne Rw
Petyt PI
Cheyne Wk
Cheyne Cen

EMBANKMENT
Kensington & Chelsea
Wandsworth

A3217
KING'S LANE
Park Walk
Paultons Square
PH
Christchurch Ter
Lavender
Danvers St
Cheyne Wk
CHELSEA
Albert Bridge

G H J K L119 L M

Numbered streets
Street names for grid squares which are not listed on this page are shown at the back of the index

L9
1 Christchurch Ter

L8
1 Durham Pl
2 Tedworth Sq

L7
1 Markham Pl
2 Wellington Sq

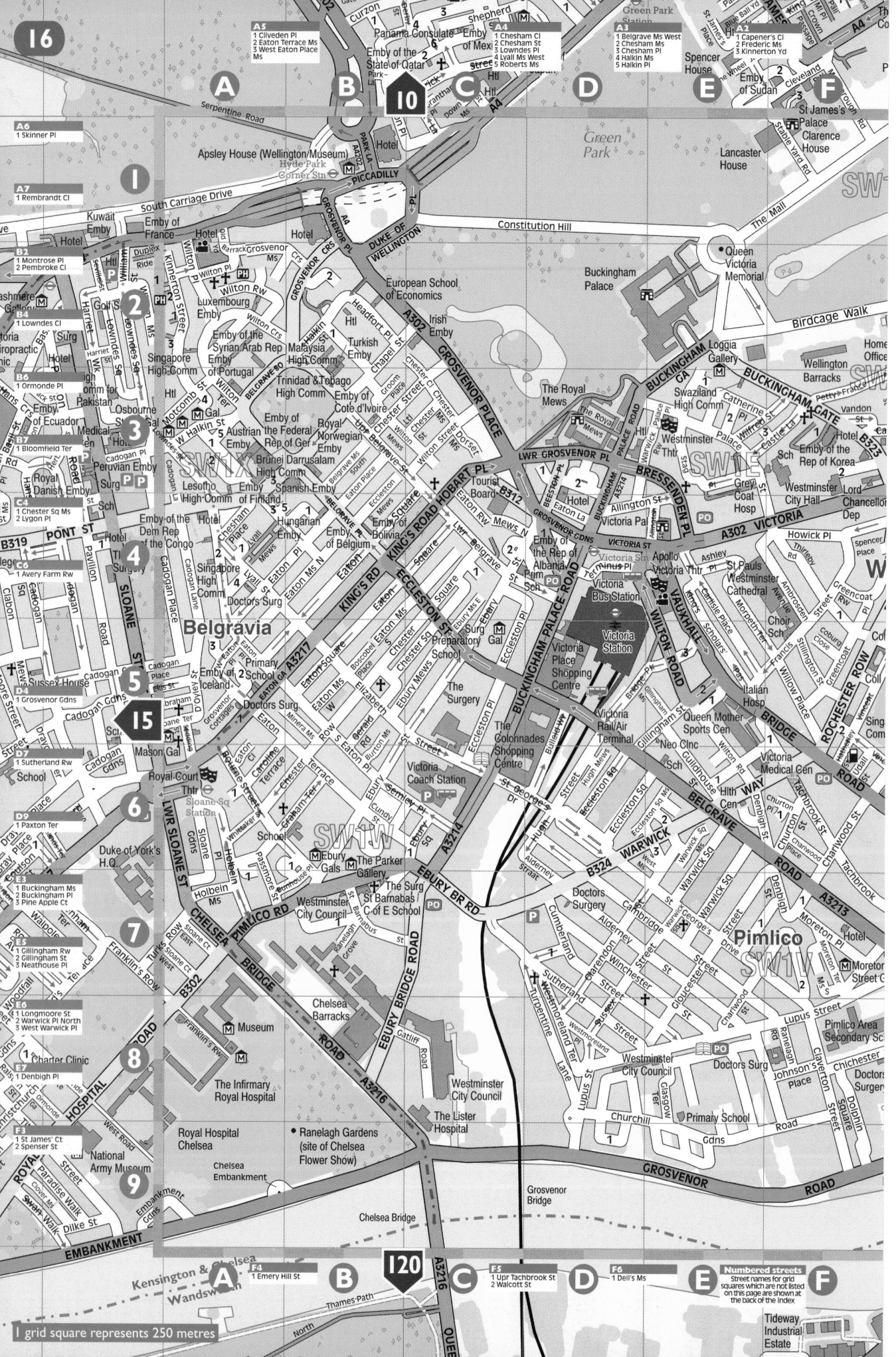

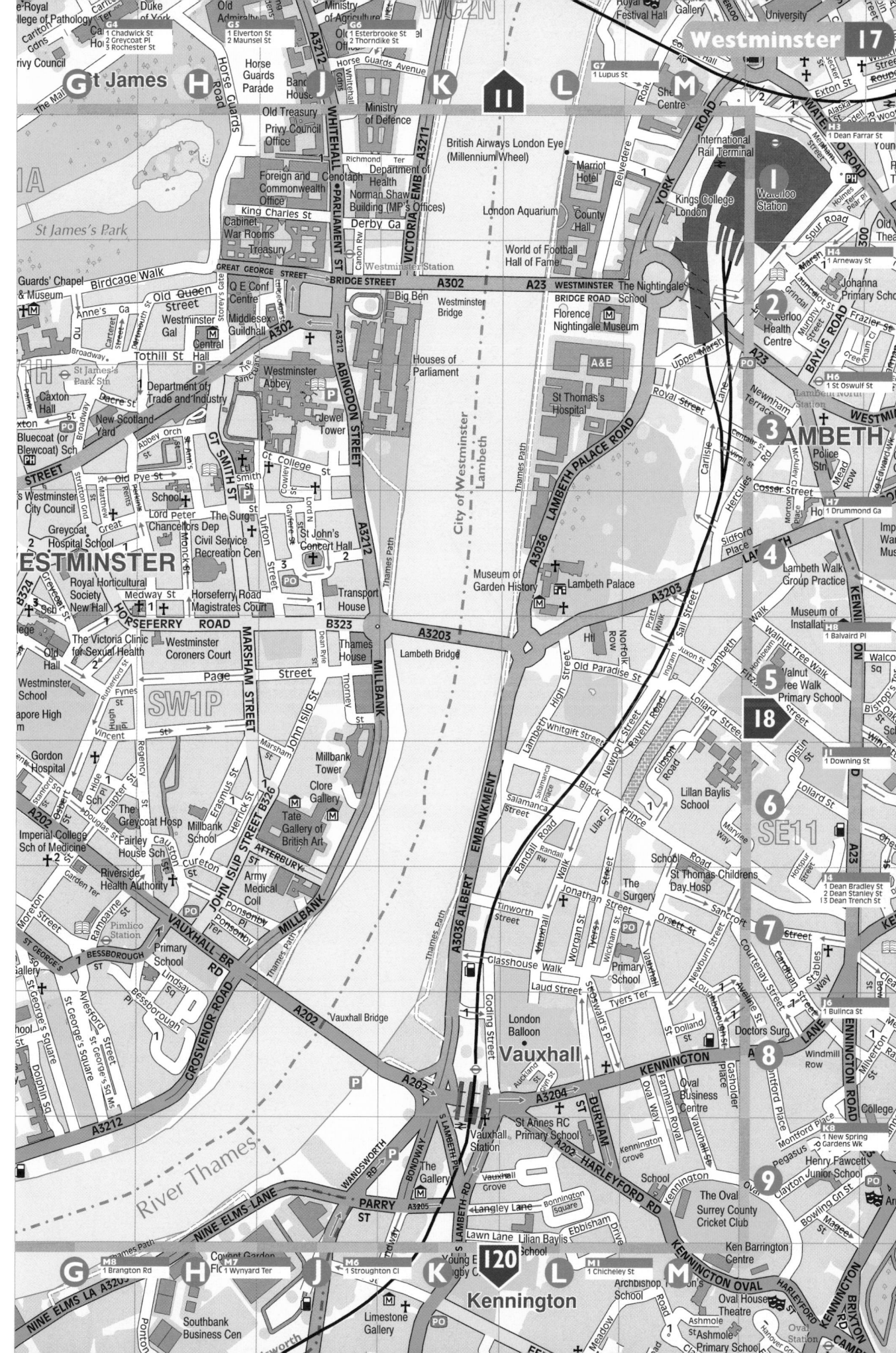

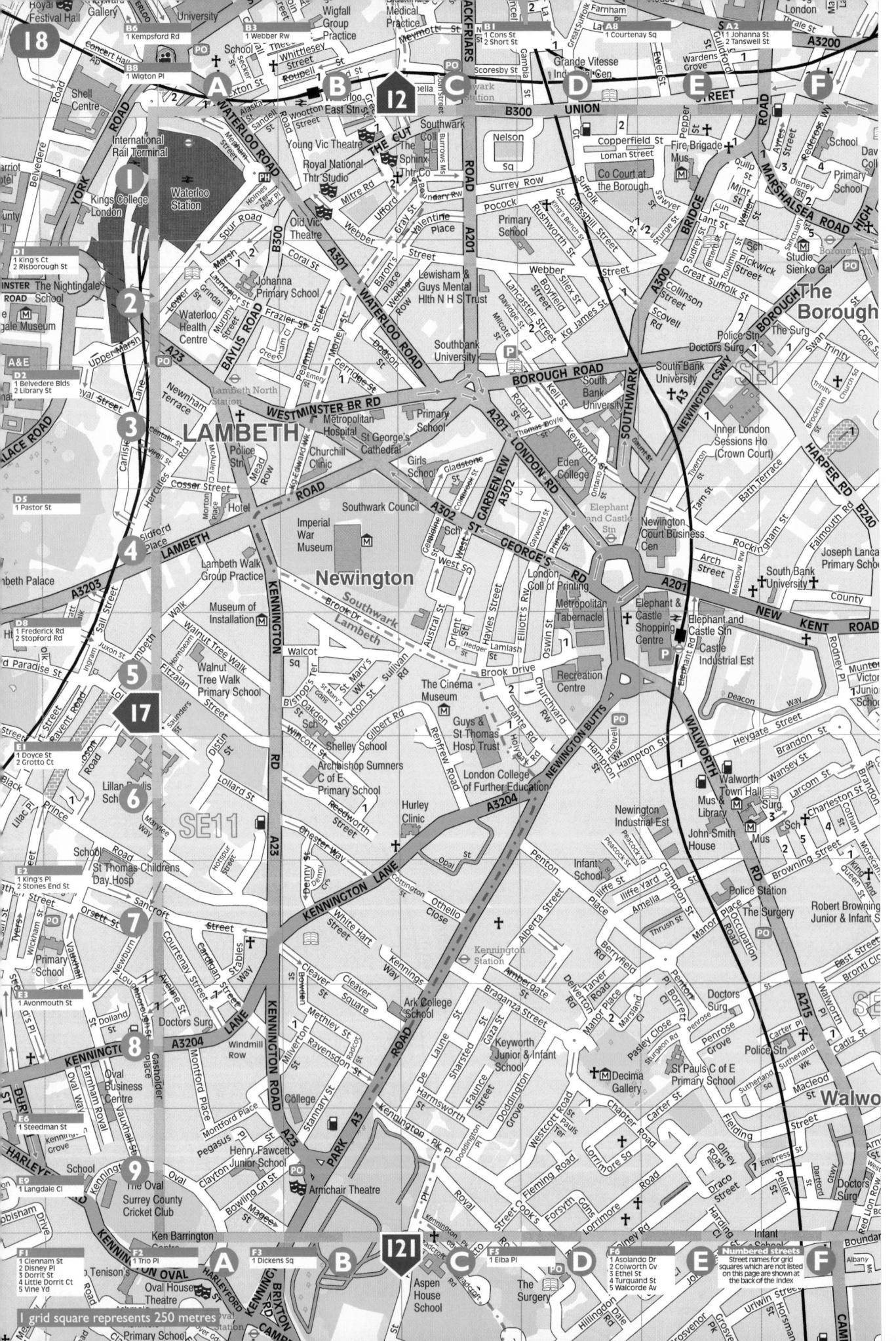

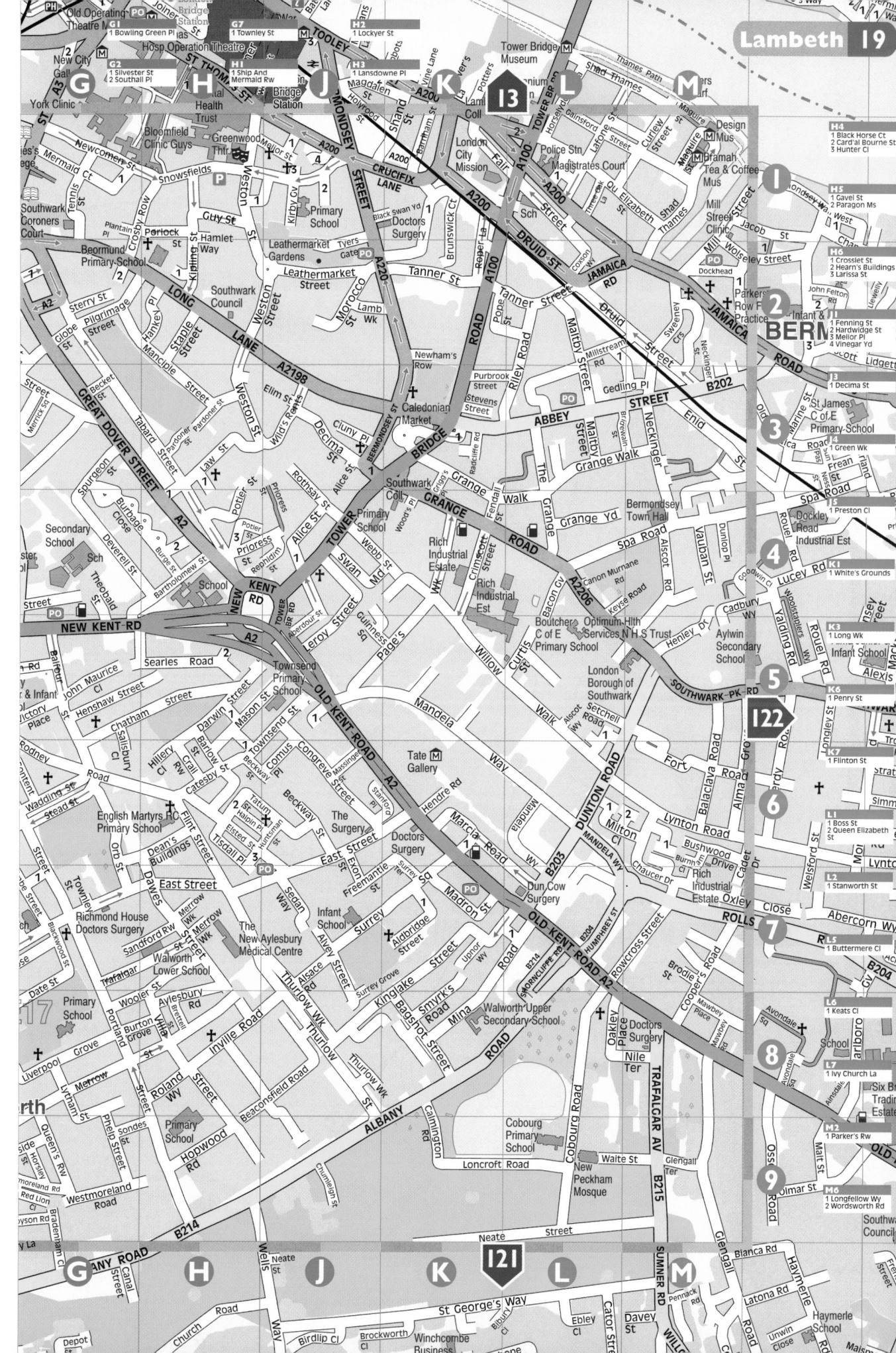

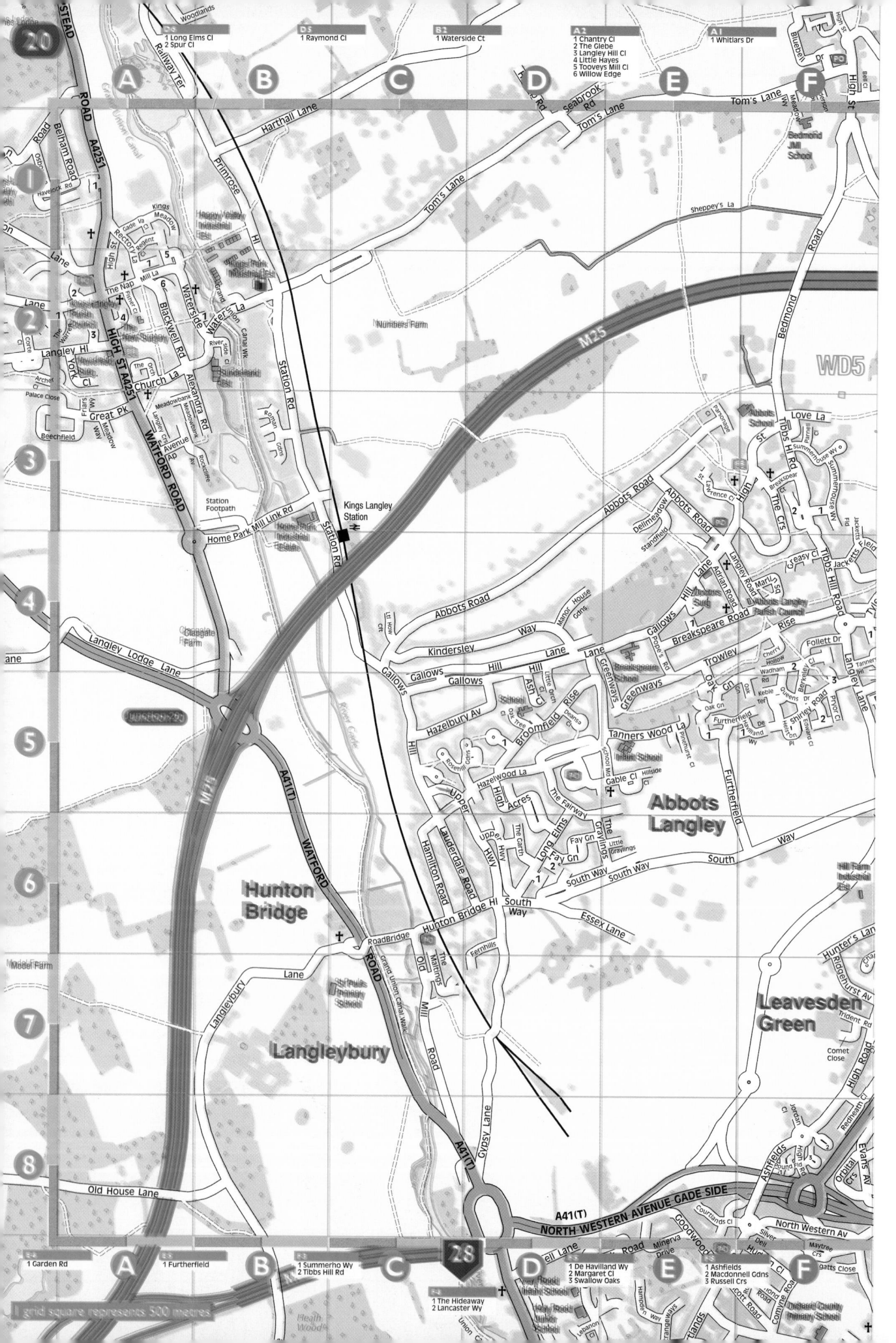

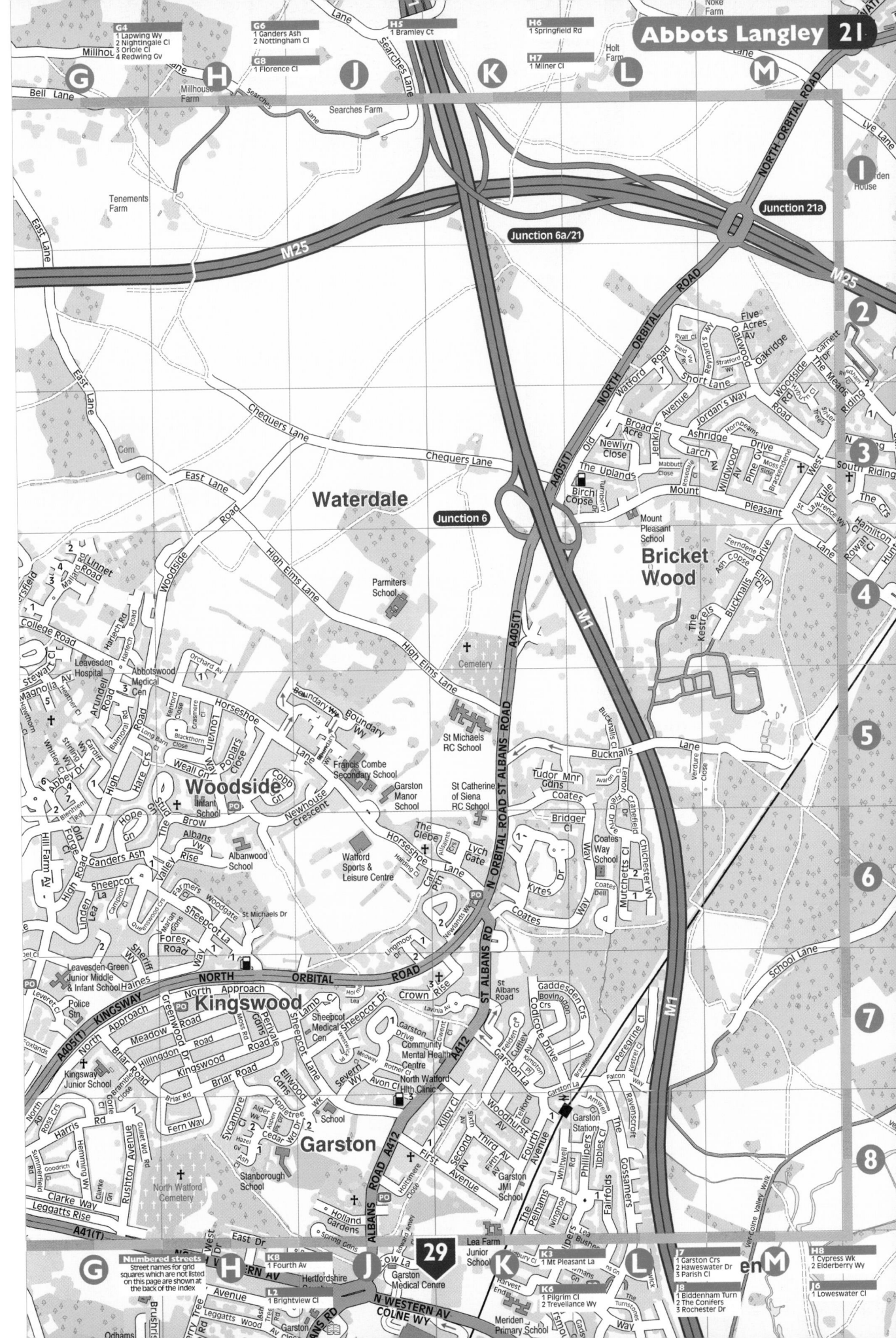

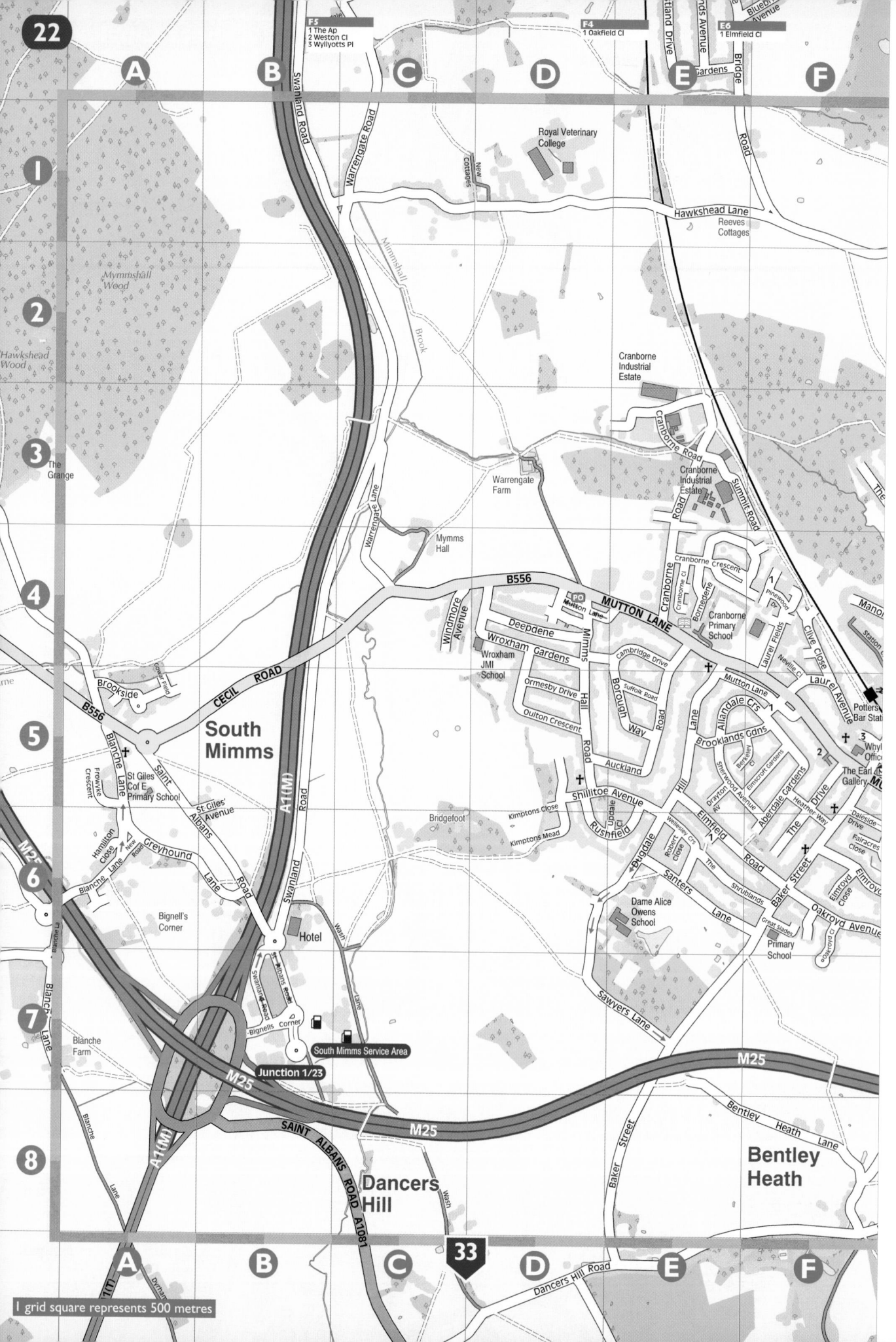

A B C D E F

1

Hawkshead Wood

Mymmshall Wood

2

The Grange

3

Royal Veterinary College

New Cottages

Hawkshead Lane

Reeves Cottages

Mimmshall Brook

Warrengate Road

Swanland Road

Cranborne Industrial Estate

Cranborne Road

Summit Road

Warrengate Lane

Warrengate Farm

4

Mymms Hall

B556

Windmore Avenue

Deepdene

Wroxham Gardens

Wroxham JMI School

Ormesby Drive

Oulton Crescent

PO Mutton

MUTTON LANE

Cranborne Crescent

Cranborne Primary School

Cambridge Drive

Mutton Lane

Laurel Fields

Neville Cl

Clive Close

Station Road

Manor

5

South Mimms

CECIL ROAD

Brookside

Cowl Field

B556

Blanche Lane

Frowyke Crescent

St Giles Cof E Primary School

St Giles' Avenue

Saint Albans

A1(M) Road

Bridgefoot

Kimptons Close

Kimptons Mead

Mimms Hall Road

Borough Way

Suffolk Road

Auckland

Shillitoe Avenue

Rushfield

Brooklands Gdns

Berkeley Cl

Sherwood Avenue

Drayton Av

Wellesley Crs

Elmscroft Gardens

Allandale Crs

Laurel Avenue

Potters Bar Stati

Whyl

The Earl Gallery

2

3

The Drive

Heather Way

Daleside

1 grid square represents 500 metres

6

M25

Hamilton Close

Blanche Lane

New Road

Greyhound Lane

Bignell's Corner

Swanland Road

Hotel

Albans Road

Wash Lane

Dame Alice Owens School

Dugdale

Robert Close

Santers Lane

The

shrublands

Great slades

Primary School

Eimfield Road

Baker Street

Elmroyd Close

Fairacres Close

Elmroyd

Oakroyd Avenue

7

Blanche Lane

Blanche Farm

Bignells Corner

South Mimms Service Area

Sawyers Lane

Oakroyd

8

A1(M)

M25

Junction 1/23

SAINT ALBANS ROAD

M25

Bentley Heath Lane

Bentley Heath

Blanche Lane

Dytham

Wash

Dancers Hill

Dancers Hill Road

A1081

Baker Street

A B C D E F

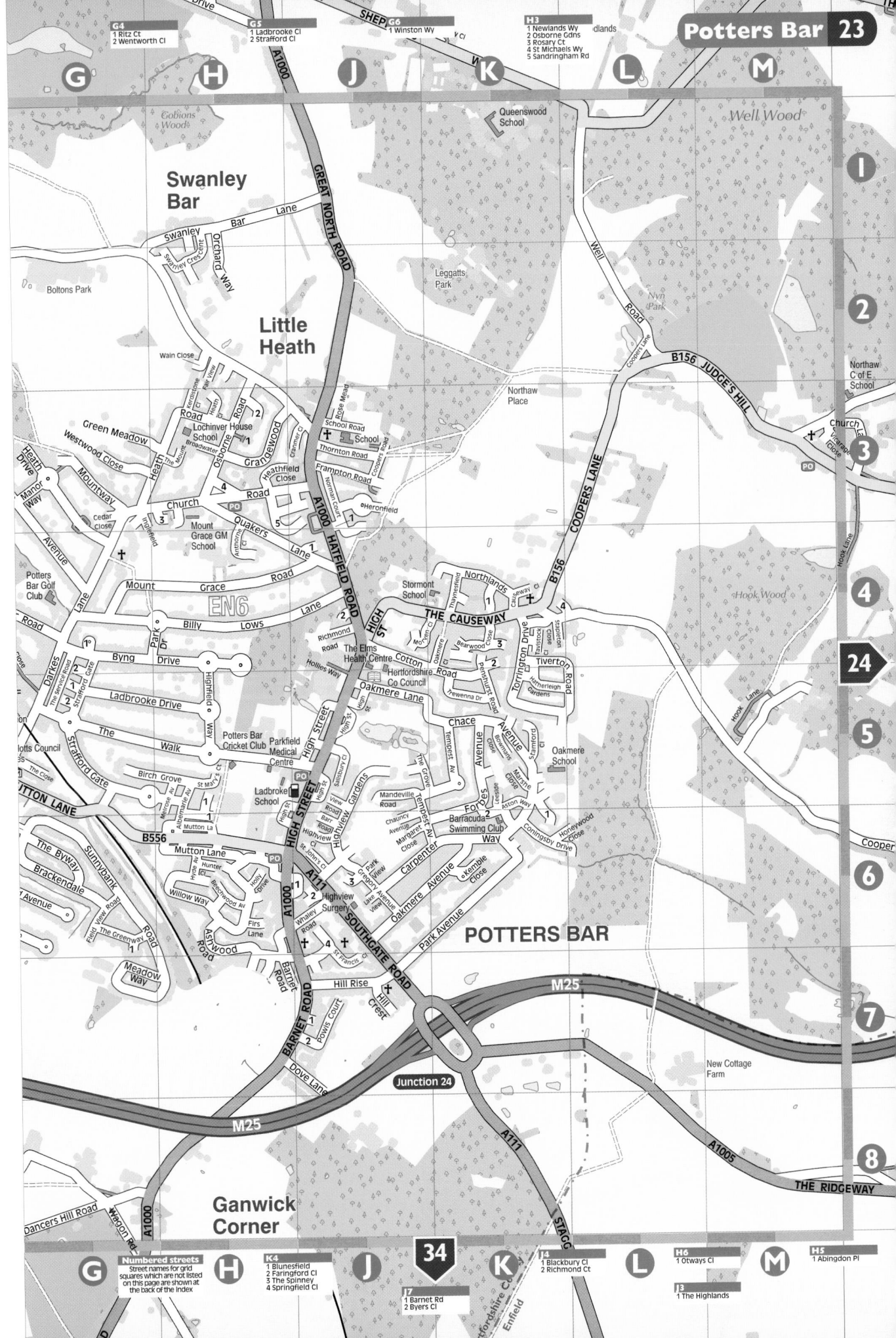

Swanley
Bar

Gobions
Wood

Well Wood

Boltons Park

Queenswood
School

Little
Heath

Leggatts
Park

Nyn
Park

Northaw C of E
School

Wain Close

Northaw
Place

Church Mead Close

PO

Green Meadow

Lochinver House
School

Broadwater

School Road

School

Thornton Road

Frampton Road

Heronfield

Hook Wood

Church Road Close

B156 JUDGE'S HILL

COOPERS LANE

Heath Drive

Manor Way

Westwood Close

Cedar Close

Mountway

Church Road

Heathfield Close

Mount Grace GM School

Quakers Lane

Northlands

Stormont School

THE CAUSEWAY

Hook Lane

Potters Bar Golf Club

Mount Grace Road

EN6

Lane

High St

Richmond Road

Hollies Way

The Elms Health Centre

Cotton Road

Oakmere Lane

Torrington Drive

Tiverton Road

Hook Lane

Byng Drive

Park Drive

Billy Lows Lane

Highfield Way

Potters Bar Cricket Club

Parkfield Medical Centre

Hertfordshire Co Council

Chace Avenue

Oakmere School

Darkes Lane

Ladbrooke Drive

The Walk

High Street

PO

Ladbroke School

Highview Gardens

Forbes Avenue

Coningsby Drive

Honeywood Close

MUTTON LANE

Birch Grove

St Mary

B556

Mutton Lane

PO

Mandeville Road

Chauncy Avenue

Barracuda Swimming Club

Willow Way

Firs Lane

Highview Surgery

SOUTHGATE ROAD

Oakmere Avenue

Kemble Close

Park Avenue

POTTERS BAR

Brackendale

The Byway

Sunnybank

Meadow Way

Ashwood Road

Barnet Road

St Francis Cl

Hill Rise

M25

New Cottage Farm

Dancers Hill Road

Ganwick
Corner

Junction 24

M25

A111

A1005

THE RIDGEWAY

I grid square represents 500 metres

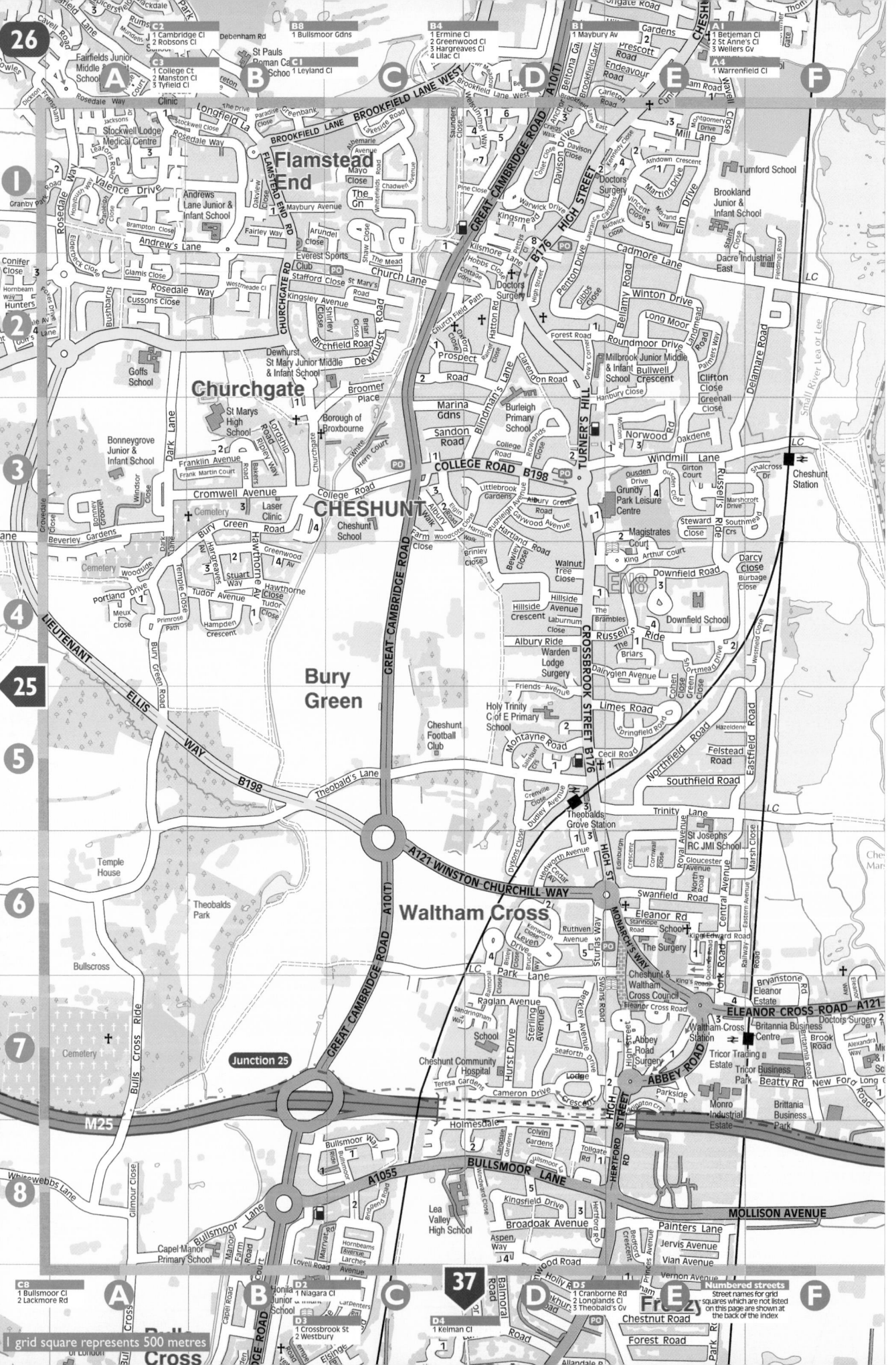

G7
1 Berwick Cl

J5
1 Hereward Cl

J6
1 Church St
2 Darby Dr
3 Greenyard
4 Mile Cl

J7
1 Fountain Pl
2 King George Rd
3 Milton Ct
4 Paradise Rd
5 Rue De St
Lawrence
6 Silver St

G H J K L M I

Lee Valley
Park

Hayes Hill
Farm

Holyfield

**Aimes
Green**

HOLYFIELD   ROAD   B194

Claverhambury Road

2

Monkhams
Hall

Fishers
Green

EN9

Dallance
House

CROOKED   MILE   B194

3

Breaches
Farm

Galleyhill Road

4

Old River Lea or Lee Loop Road

Powdermill Way

Hazelmill Stream

Cornmill Stream

5

Marie Gardens

Valley Close

**WALTHAM
ABBEY**

Parklands

Paternoster Hill

Upshire
Road

Hertfordshire County

Essex County

Harold
Crescent

Parvills

Newteswell
Drive

Drayson   Close

The
Coppins

Congreve
Road

Ninefields

6

The Struts

ABBEYVIEW   A121

CROOKED   MILE

South Weald
Dr

Waltham
Holy Cross
Junior School

Over Thaxted Way
Quendon

Tudor Way

Monkswood   Avenue

Broomstick Hall Road

King Harold
Comprehensive
School

Mallion
Court

Cullings
Court

St Lawrence
C of E School

Shingle
Ct

Beaulieu Drive

Flagstaff Close
Cannon
Mews
Warton
Gdns
Leavy

Highbridge Street

Town Hall

Llewelyn
Surgery
The
Surgery

Romeland
PO
Sun street

Halfhides

Rounton Road
Eastbrook Road

Mason Way

Thomas
Tallis
School

STATION ROAD   HIGHBRIDGE STREET

Waltham Holy
Cross Council
Health Centre

Leverton Way

Essex Co.
Council
Mus
M

FARM HILL ROAD   A121

PO

Woodbrook
Gardens

Honey
Brook

Charwell
Mead

Shernbroke Road

Queen's Drive

Fishers

Barbel
Close
River Close

Grove
Road

Abbey
Court

Mead
Court

Quaker Lane

Woollard
Street

Cleall Av
Victoria Road

Howard
Business
Park

Oak Close
Howard Close

A121   SEWARDSTONE   ROAD

Rochford Avenue

Rosebank

Stonyshotts

Meadowcross

Morris Court

Shernbroke
Road

Hayward
Court

7

Middle
Infant
School
Croft Drive

Gordon
Road

Industrial
Park

Orchard Gardens

Brooker Rd
Harveyfields
Greenfield St

Audley
Gardens

Denny Avenue

Cattersfield Road

Cemetery

Elm Close

Roundhills

Ruskin
Avenue

Ferguson
Avenue

Caldeck

HONEY   LANE   A121

Windmill
Lane

Gant Court

Caterham
Court

Pinnacles

The
Dales

Roundhills

Holecroft

Hotel

Cattersfield Road
Cemetery

A112

Waltham Abbey
Swimming Pool

Gilsland

Wren Dr

Quinton   Way

Lodge Lane

M25

8

Lower   Island   Way

Centre   Way

Beechfield Wy

Numbered streets
Street names for grid
squares which are not listed
on this page are shown at
the back of the index

H7
1 Downlands
2 Patmore Rd

Ditch Ro

J7
Ditch

Sewardston
Way

South Way

L5
1 Brookside
2 Galleyhill Rd
3 Old Oaks
4 Smeaton Cl

K6
1 Margaret Cl
2 Pasfield
3 St Pauls Wy
4 Takeley Cl

K5
1 Willinghall Cl

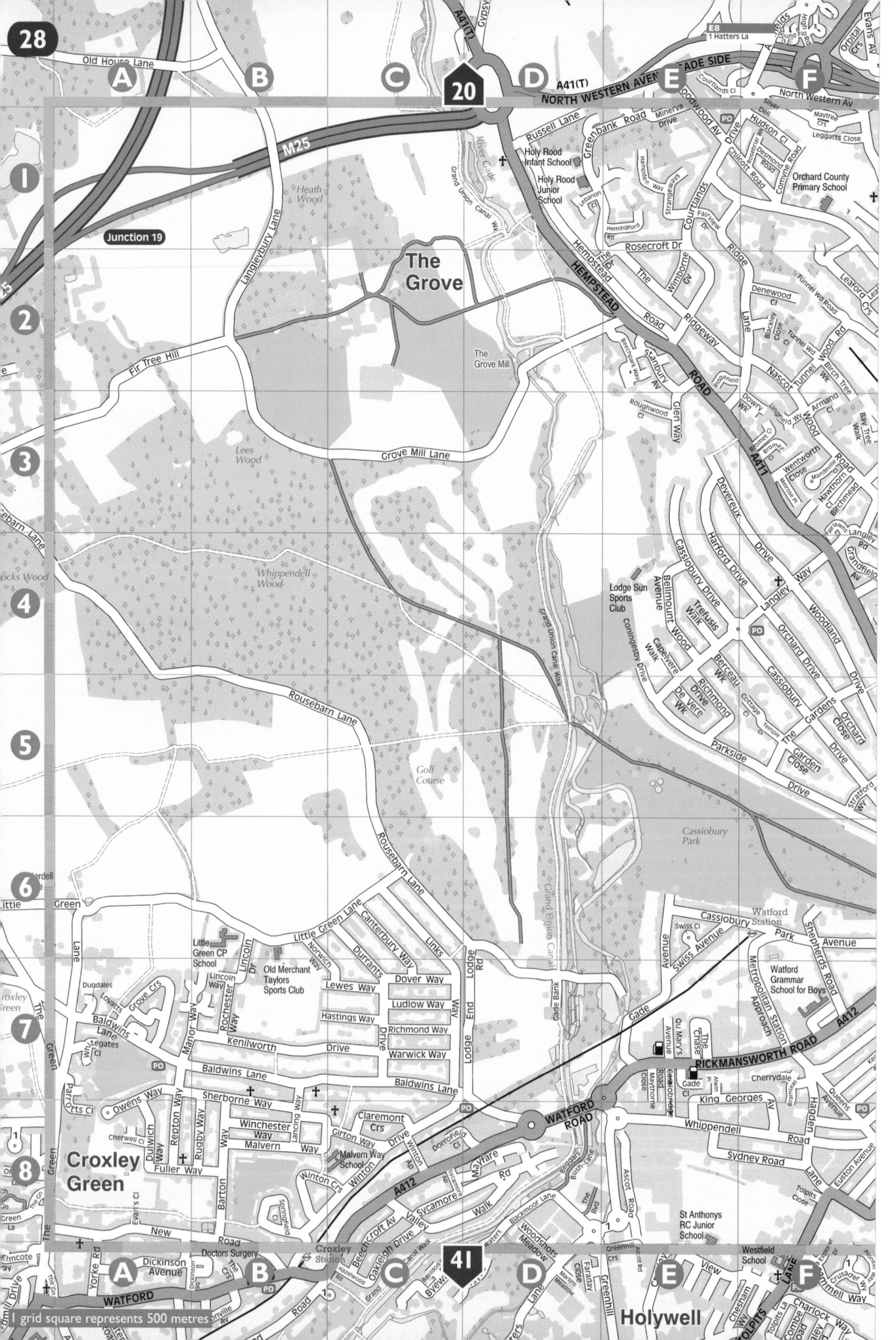

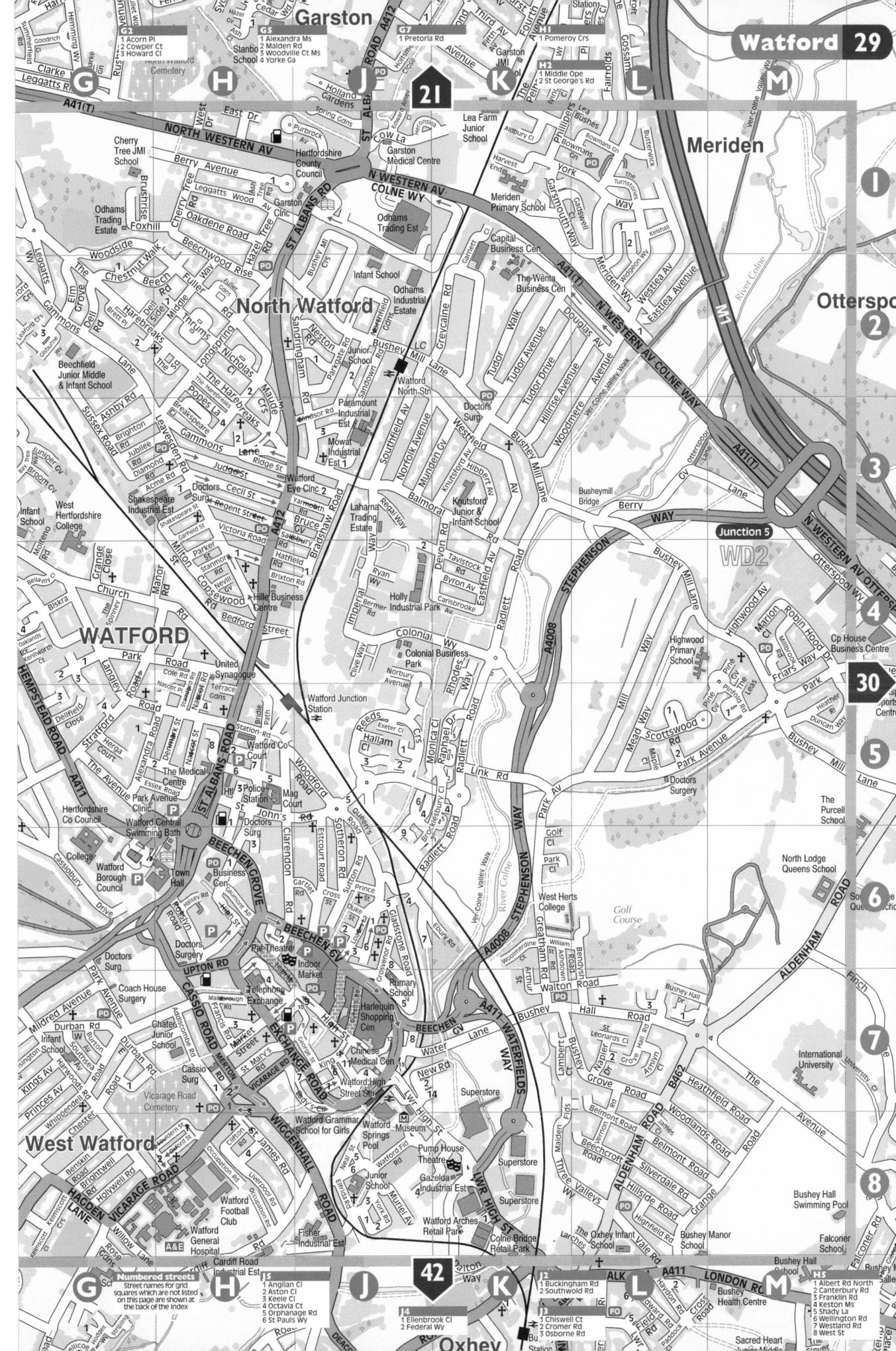

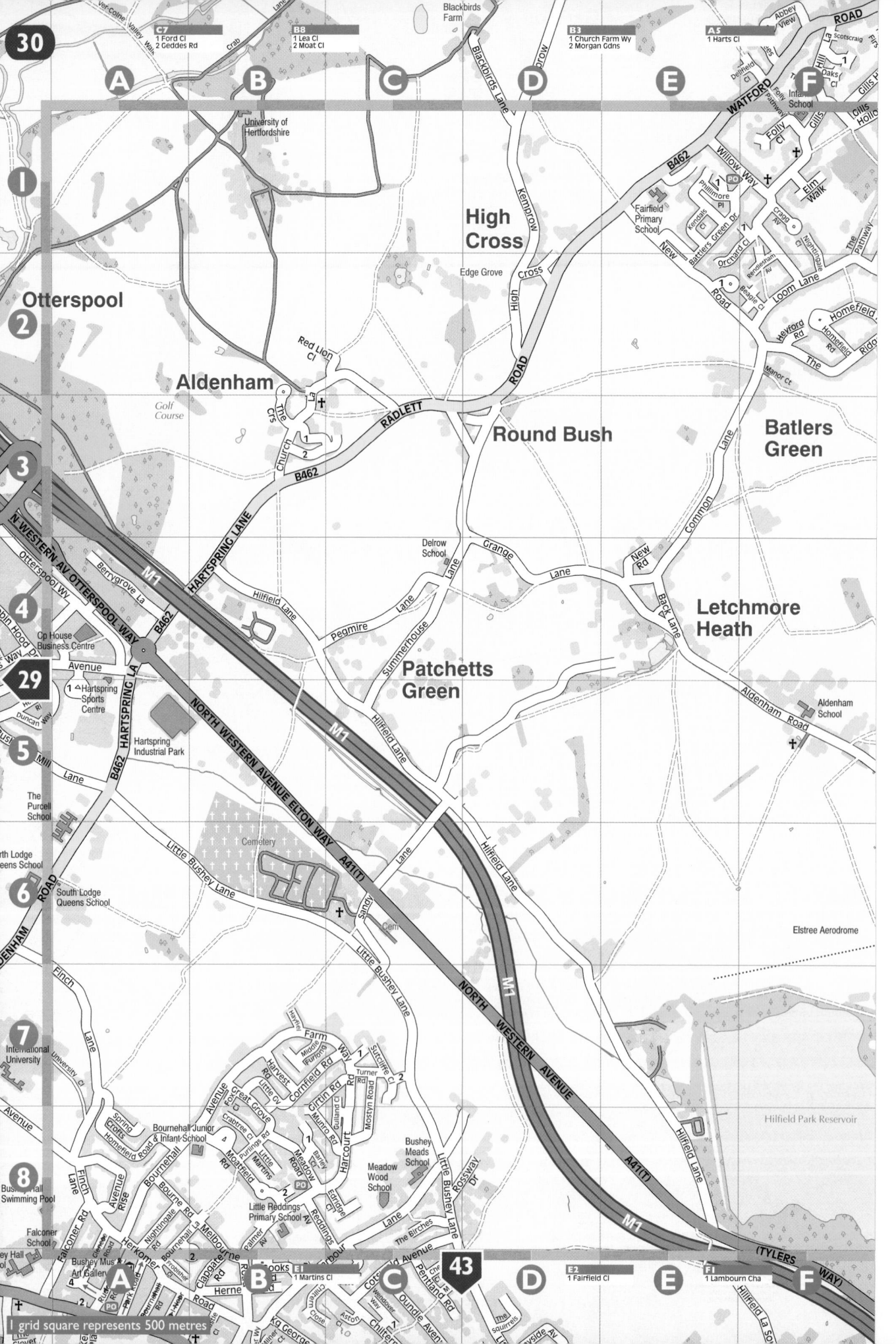

30

A   B   C   D   E   F

Green
Street

Well
End

Rowley
Green

Elstree Studios

Borehamwood Football Club

Borehamwood Industrial Park

Hertsmere Borough Council

Oaklands College

BARNET BY-PASS

ELSTREE WY   A5135   ELSTREE WAY

NEWARK GN

Hertfordshire County
Barnet

Laings
Sports
Ground

BARNET LANE

A   B   C   D   E   F

grid square represents 500 metres

G H J K L M

Dancers Hill

Bentley Hea

J8
1 Malins Cl
2 Well Ap

K8
1 Eleanor Gdns
2 Palmer Gdns
3 St Anna Rd

L6
1 Bruce Rd
2 Chipping Cl

22

Dancers Hill Road

Dancers Hill Road

Kitt's End Road

1 I
2
3
4
34
5
6
Hadle
7
8

Kitt's End

Trotters Bottom

Galley Lane

A1081

Hadley Highstone

Langley Row

Beaumont Place

Old Fold Manor Golf Club

Monken Hadley

SAINT ALBANS ROAD

A1000

HADLEY GREEN

Monken Had C of E Prima

Dury Rd

Hadley Green Rd

EN5

High Barnet

Christ Church C of E Primary School

Cavendish Road

Old Fold View

Grimsdyke Crescent

Galley Lane

Arkley Lane

Jennings Way

Kings Road

Grimsdyke Crescent

Granville Road

Argyle Road

Byng Rd

Wentworth Road

Cecil Rd

Foulds Primary School

Queen Elizabeths School

Elizabeth Close

Queens Rd

Blenheim Rd

Calvert

Puller Road

Puller Road

Cemetery

Sunset Vw

Falkland Rd

Wrotham Road

Christ Church

Hadley Grove

Hadley Green W

Gladsmuir Rd

Hadley Green Rd

East View

Christ Church Lane

Hadley Green Rd

Belgravia

Wyborn Avenue

Hyde Close

East View

South Close

Lucan Rd

Alston Rd

Strafford Rd

Carnarvon Rd

Salisbury Rd

Marriott Rd

Thornton Rd

Ravenscroft Park

Chinese Medical Cen

The Spires Shopping Centre

The Drive

Stapylton Rd

Longrove Surg

Moxon Street

Victor's Way

PO

Monken Hadley

WOOD STREET

A411

Wellhouse Lane

West End Lane

Lingholm

Cartley Close

Manor Cl

The Surgery

The Bull Park

Road

Barnet College of Further Education

The Bull Theatre

Girls School

HIGH ST

High Bar Station

Gordon Way

Chipping Barnet

Orchard Av

Normandy Av

Fitzjohn Av

Bedford Avenue

Milton Avenue

Elton Avenue

BARNET HILL

Barnet Health Centre

Barnet Magistrates Court

Barnet Road

A411

Wood Street

Barnet Hospital Chest Clinic

A&E

Barnet General Hospital

Cemetery

West End Lane

The Croft

Hill

Dunster Close

Lexington Way

Newlands Place

Sutton Crescent

Leecroft Road

Hillside

Pinecroft Crs

Manorside

Sutherland Rd

Cedar Lawn

Willow Dr.

Boardman Close

Mays Lane

The Print Room Museum

Primary School

PO

Dollis Valley

Woodfall Avenue

Vale Drive

May's Lane

Bre PI

Carrington Close

Chartridge Close

Rowley Green Road

Hazel Mead

Arkley Drive

Arkley View

Oaklands

Stonecroft Close

Garden Close

Kern Close

Elmbank Avenue

Vyse Close

Wellside

Garthland Drive

Nottingham Road

Endersby Drive

Denton Close

Escot Way

Well Road

Trinder Road

Pepys Crs

Spring Close

Redwood

St Stephens

Whittings Hill School

Chesterfield Rd

Jarvis Cl

Sellwood

Juniper Close

Kenerne Drive

Mays Lane

Underhill Junior & Infant School

Northbrook

Hardy Cl

Leeside

Eastham

Fields

Bryant Cl

Cross Cl

Glebe Lane

Meadowbanks

Arkley

St Peters Gardens

Raeburn Gardens

Hackforth Close

Ryecroft Crescent

Farm Close

Brett Road

Whittings Road

46

J

K

M7
1 Newlyn Rd

L

M6
1 Moon La
2 Tapster St

M4
1 Boundary Cl
2 Old Fold Cl
3 Taylor's La

G H

Under

London Loo

G8
1 Balmore Crs

J8
1 Belgrave Cl
2 Catherine Ct
3 Conisbee Ct

K7
1 South Lodge Crs

G   H   J   **24**   K   L   M

Botany Bay

THE RIDGEWAY A1005

Botany Bay Cricket Club

1

London Loop

London Loop

THE RIDGEWAY

The Kings C Private Hos

2

3

Hotel

Mount View High Oaks

Oak Avenue

Hadley Road

Hadley Road

Spring Cou Road

Ridge Crest

Cha Hos

4

36

London Loop

University of Middlesex

5

Grafton Road

Trentwood Side

Elmer Close

Park
Slades Gardens
Windmill Gardens

Trent Country Park

Merryhills Clinic

Linksid Gardens
Linkside Close

6

Snakes Lane

Bincote Road

Merryhills Primary School

Cotswold Wy

Links Side

rs Sports

Trent Park Cemetery

hgate
npton Cricket Club

Cockfosters Station

Enfield & Haringey Hlth Authority

A110 ENFIELD RD

Lowther Drive

Glenbrook S

7

Lonsdale

South Lodge Dr
Greydale Gdns

Netherby Culbaith Gardens

Lonsdale Drive North

Silverdale

Roundhill Dr
Rushey Hill

Laidlaw Gdns
Hamber Dr

Grang Primar

Norton Close
West Close
East Close

Calvert
Close

Mount Close
Doctors Surgery

Gloucester Gardens

Kent Drive

Westpole Avenue

Merryhills Drive

Brantwood Gardens
Clifton Gardens

Lonsdale Drive

Lindal Crescent

Sydenham

Tresilian Av

8

Gerrards Chase

Belgrave Gdns

Grosvenor Gdns

Carlton Av

George Av

Braxton Gdns
Curthwaite Gdns

Barnes

Pennington Dr

Treves

Kaplan

Highlands Av

Newsholme Dr

reston Gardens

Leys Gdns

Southgate School

Sussex

Way

Prince

Oakwood Medical Cen

Harper Cl

Priory Close

Stafford Cl

Tregenna Close

Doctors Surgery

Lakenheath

South Lodge Drive

South Lodg Dr

Chaseville Park Road

Eversley Primary School

Chasevillet Clinic

A110

Bramley Close
De Bohun School

Homestead Paddock

Reservoir Road

Ashmead

Wolverton Wy
Chester Cl

The Vineries

Merrivale

Overton Road Dr

Green

Cadogan

M8
1 Anderson Cl
2 Banting Dr
3 Buchanan Cl
4 Corfield Rd
5 Macleod Rd

Mansfield Avenue

Vernon Crs

Saracens

G

The Fairway

H

The
Hood
Tre

Cowper Gardens

M8
1 Chadwick Av
2 Cotswold Gn

Southgate

J

Linden Court

Wayside Cl

Highmead Court

48

Saxon Wy

K

Oakwood

Kenwood Av

sheri Aver

M3
1 Aragon Cl
2 Roundhedge Wy
3 William Covell Cl

Willow Walk

L

lolly Hill

Eversley Rd

L8
1 Fothergill Dr
2 Lwr Kenwood Av
3 Macleod Rd
4 Moynihan Dr
5 Simpson Cl
6 South Lodge Dr
7 Tarnbank

M

Callus C

EVERSLEY RD

L7
1 Bewcastle Gdns
2 Clifton Gdns
3 Corby Crs
4 Woodend Gdns

C6
1 Chapel St
2 Chase Hl
3 Gresham Cl
4 Horseshoe La

C4
1 Radcliffe Av
2 St Faith's Cl
3 Tippetts Cl

C3
1 Bedale Rd
2 York Ter

B5
1 Heather Dr
2 Hermitage Cl
3 Mcadam Dr
4 Wellesley Park Ms

A4
1 Woodridge Cl

C5
1 Christchurch Cl
2 Cricketers Arms Rd
3 Lambs Wk

A **B** **C** **D** **E** **F**

25

St Johns C of E
Junior & Infant School
Strayfield Road

Clay Hill

EN2

Cemetery

The Kings Oak
Private Hospital

Chase Farm
Hospitals N H S Trust

35

World's
End

Enfield
Town

ENFIELD

Grange Park
Primary School

Grange Park

Worcesters Infant &
Primary School

Forty
Hill

EN1

49

D4
1 College Gdns
2 Walton St

D6
1 Burleigh Wy
2 Sarnesfield Rd
3 Wilford Cl

D8
1 Brooklands Ct

E3
1 Adelaide Cl
2 Henry Cl
3 Portland Dr

Numbered streets
Street names for grid
squares which are not listed
on this page are shown at
the back of the index

Bush Hill Park

1 grid square represents 500 metres

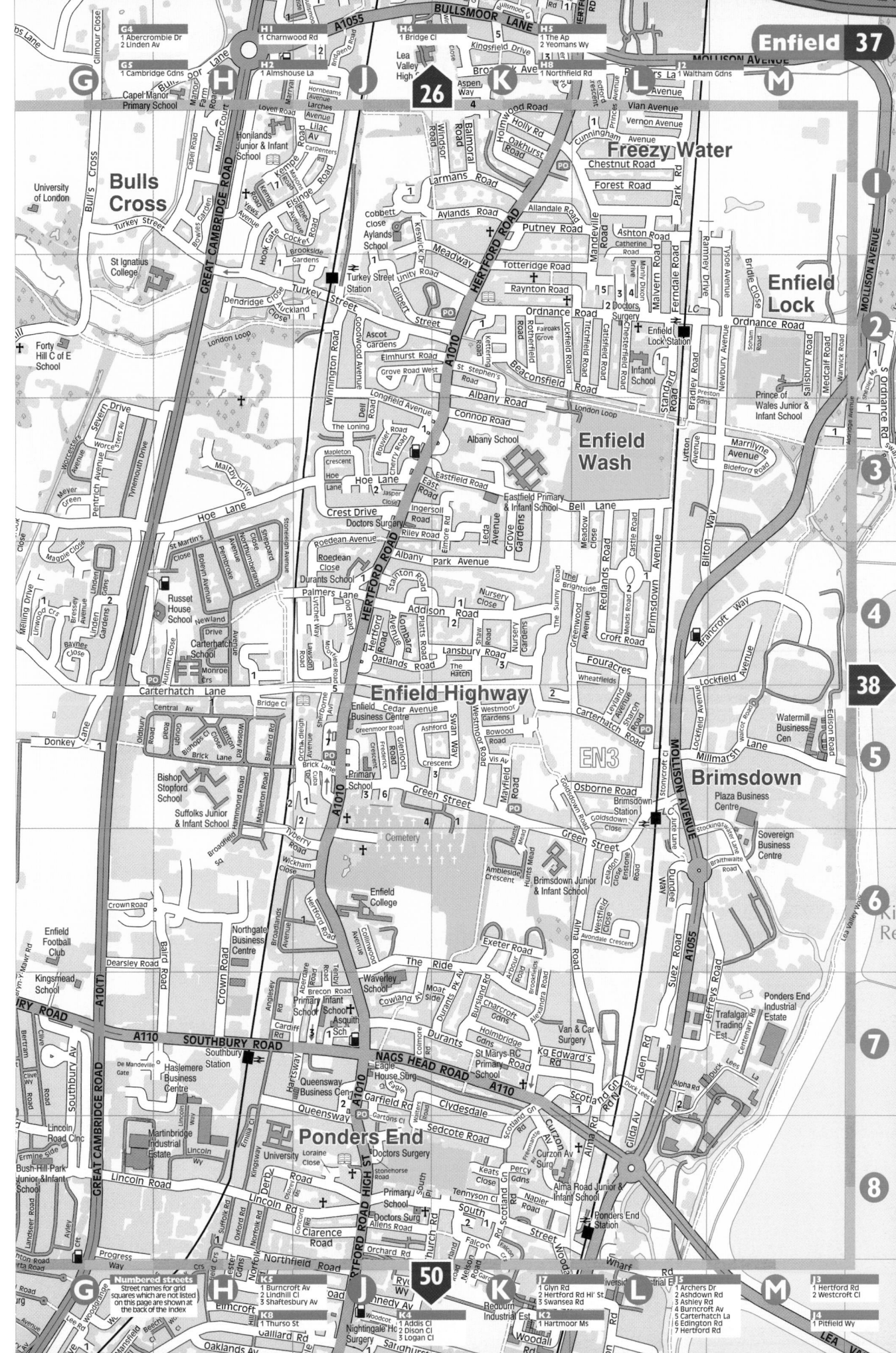

38

A B C 27 D E F

1 Yardley Cl
B8
Quinton Way
Lodge Lane
M25
A3 1 Somerset Rd
2 Soper Ms
A2 1 King Henry's Ms
Beechfield Wd

Black Ditch Way
Black Ditch Road
Sewardstone Way

I

South Way

MOLLISON AVENUE
Lea Valley Walk
Government Row
Enfield
Essex County
West Way
South Way

2
Medcalf Road
Warwick Road
Shipley Ms
1
S Ordnance Rd
Smeaton Road
Swan And Pike Road
Aldridge Avenue
1
Harston Drive
Brunswick Road

field
ck
Salisbury Road

Avey Lane

SEWARDSTONE ROAD

Hawes Lane

3
Joslyn Close
2

Butlers Drive

London Loop
Godwin Close

4

Mott Street

37

Lippitts Hill

Sewardstone

5
Edison Road
ermill
iness

Lippitts
Hill

London Loop

6
Lea Valley Walk

King George's
Reservoir

Mill Lane   A112
SEWARDSTONE ROAD
Daws Hill

Gilwell
Park

7
's End
al

Enfield
Essex County
Sewardstone
Road
Gilwell Cl

Gilwell Lane
Bury Road

London Loop

8
Boardman Av
Antlers Hill
Deanesid
Antlers Hill La
Yardley
Hawkswood School & Centre

Farm End
Woodman Lane
Hornbeam Lane
Bury Road

Sewardstonebury

Essex County
Waltham Forest
London Loop

A B C 51 D E F
Hawkwood Crescent
Avenue
Hawkdene
Epping Glade
Yardley Primary School
Epping Way

Golf Course

1 grid square represents 500 metres

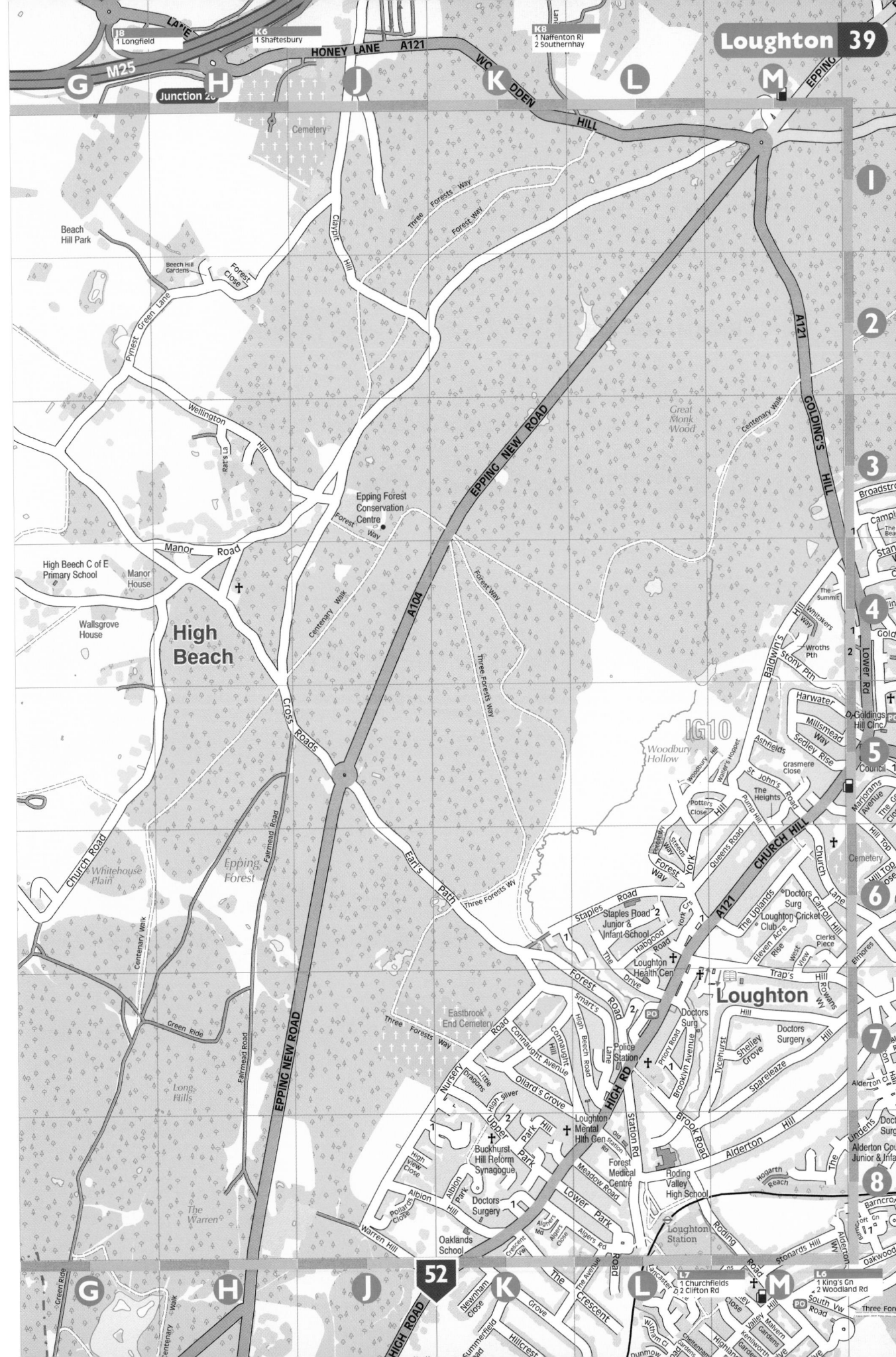

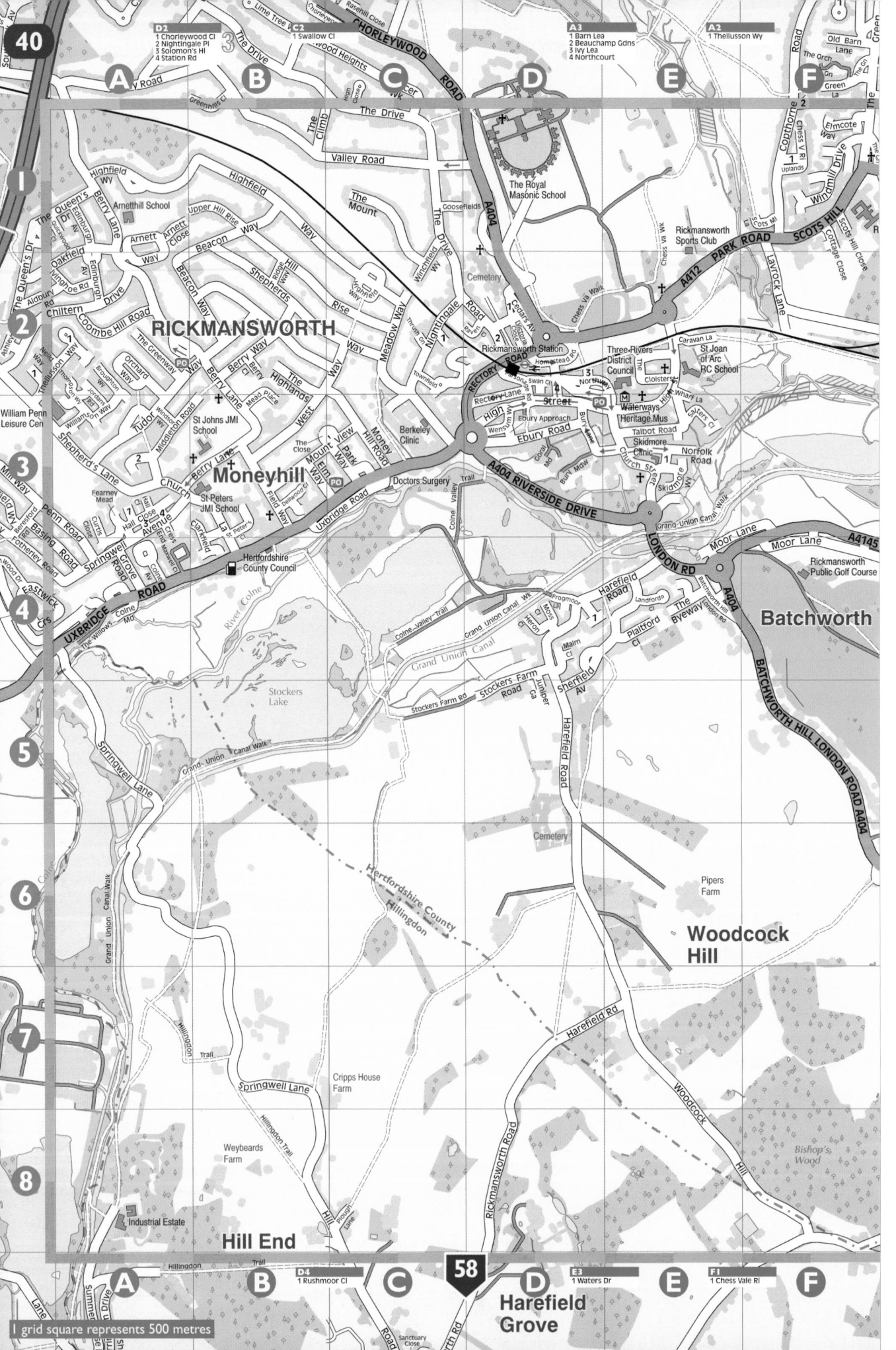

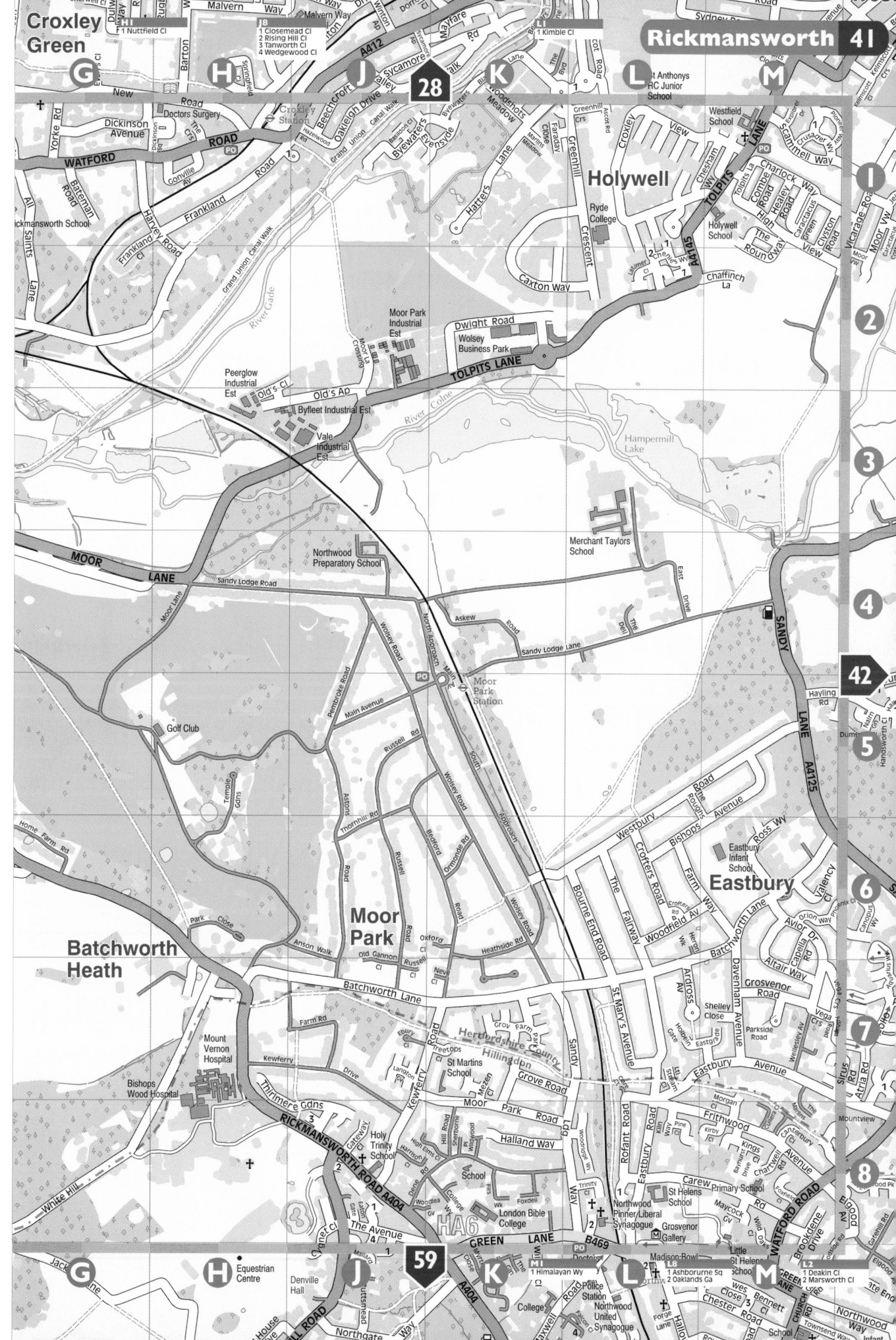

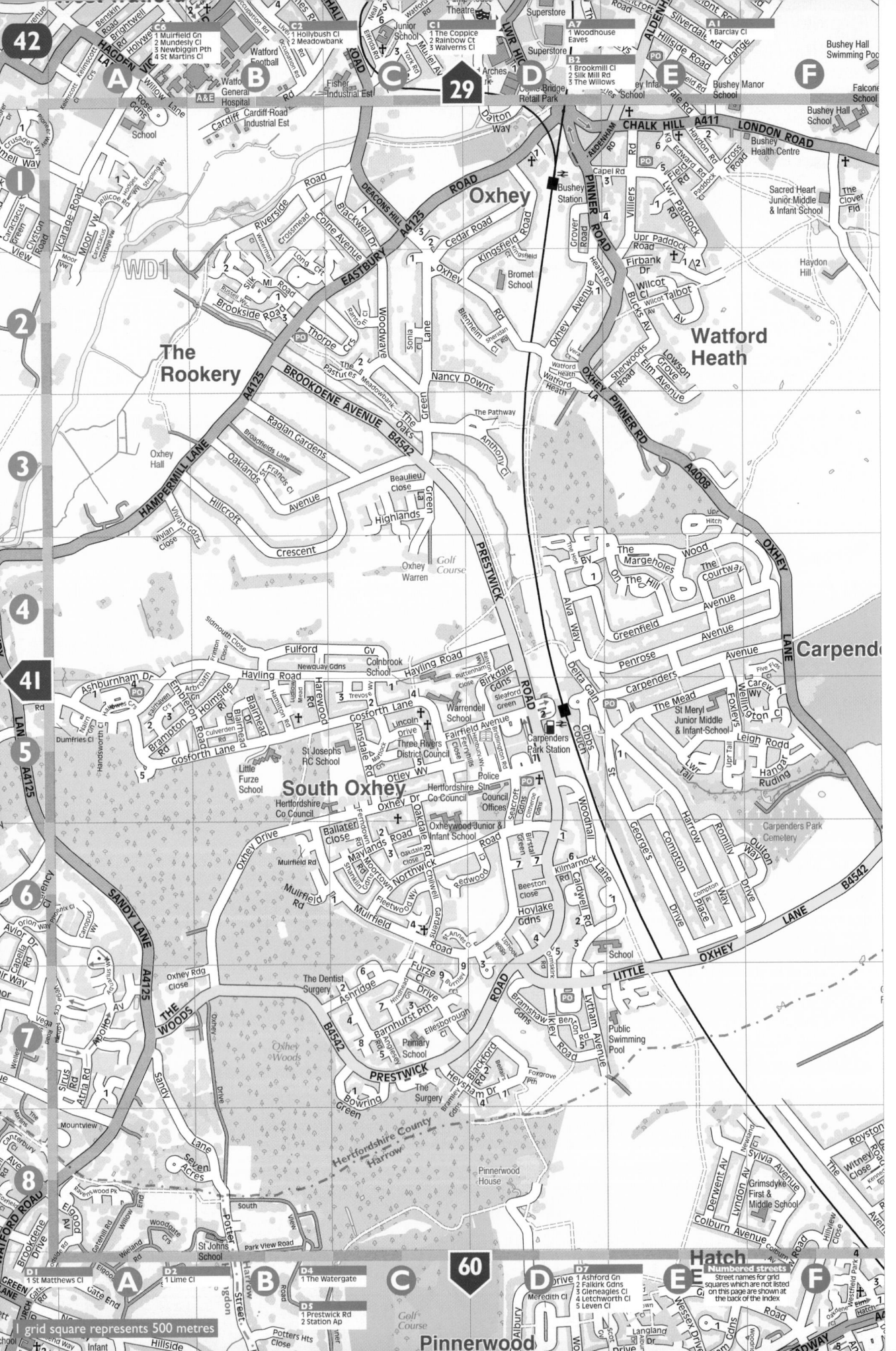

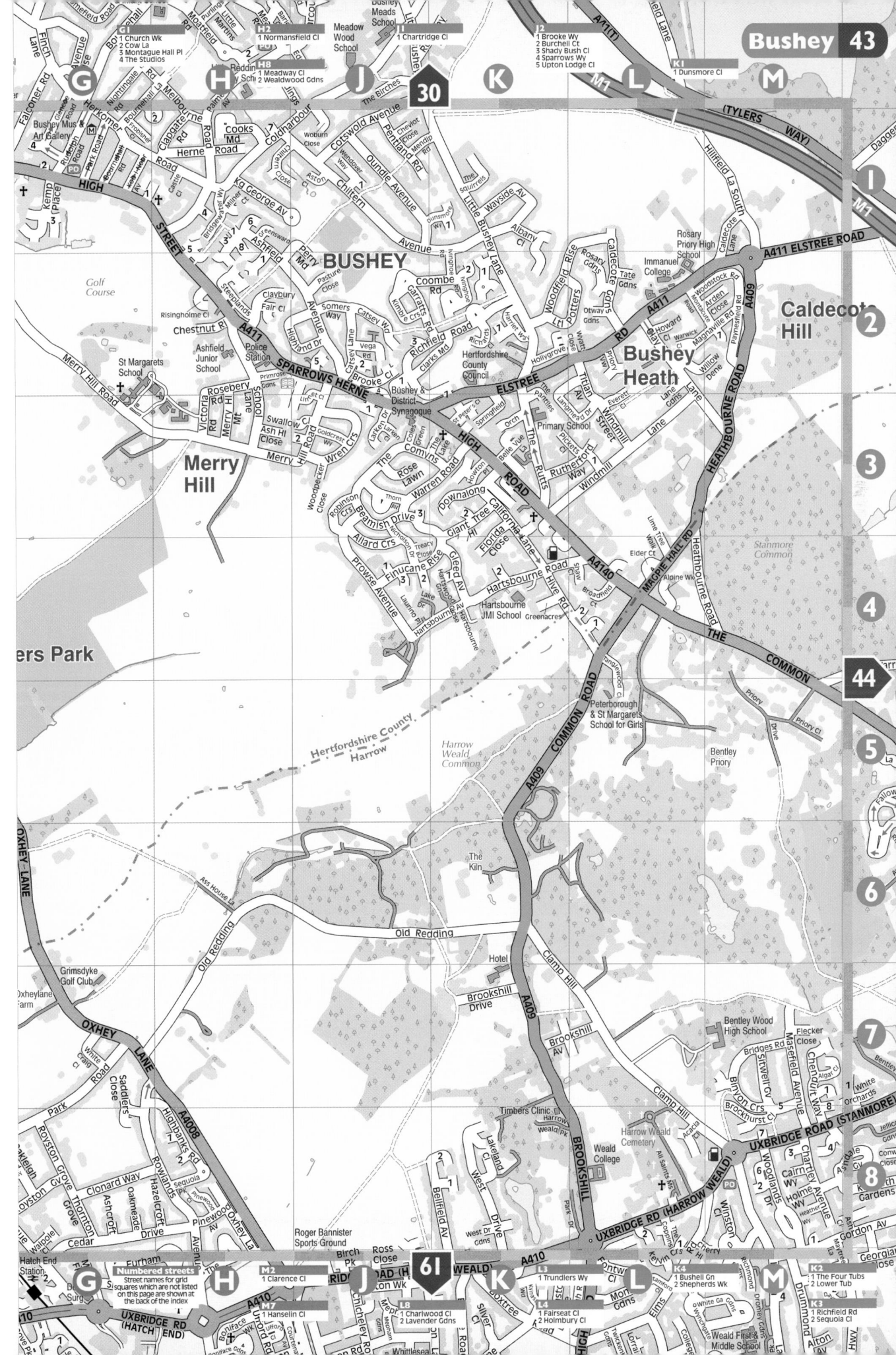

G
H
J
K
L
M

G1 1 Church Wk
2 Cow La
3 Montague Hall Pl
4 The Studios

H2 1 Normansfield Cl

H8 1 Meadway Cl
2 Wealdwood Gdns

J1 1 Chartridge Cl

J2 1 Brooke Wy
2 Burchell Ct
3 Shady Bush Cl
4 Sparrows Wy
5 Upton Lodge Cl

K1 1 Dunsmore Cl

1

30

Meadow Wood School

Bushey Meads School

I

Golf Course

BUSHEY

Caldecot Hill

2

Merry Hill Road

Merry Hill

St Margarets School

Ashfield Junior School

Police Station

SPARROWS HERNE

Bushey & District Synagogue

Hertfordshire County Council

ELSTREE

Bushey Heath

Rosary Priory High School

Immanuel College

Primary School

3

HIGH ROAD

Stanmore Common

4

HEATHBOURNE ROAD

A4140

Hartsbourne JMI School

Greenacres

THE COMMON

44

ers Park

Hertfordshire County Harrow

Harrow Weald Common

Peterborough & St Margarets School for Girls

Bentley Priory

5

COMMON ROAD

A409

6

The Kiln

Old Redding

Hotel

Brookshill Drive

Clamp Hill

Bentley Wood High School

Flecker Close

7

OXHEY LANE

Grimsdyke Golf Club

Oxheylane Farm

A4008

Saddlers Close

Highbanks Rd

Brookshill AV

BROOKSHILL

Timbers Clinic

Harrow Weald College

Harrow Weald Cemetery

Weald College

UXBRIDGE ROAD (STANMORE)

8

Roger Bannister Sports Ground

Hatch End Station

G
H
J
K
L
M

Numbered streets
Street names for grid squares which are not listed on this page are shown at the back of the index

61

UXBRIDGE RD (HARROW WEALD)

A410

UXBRIDGE RD (HATCH END)

A410

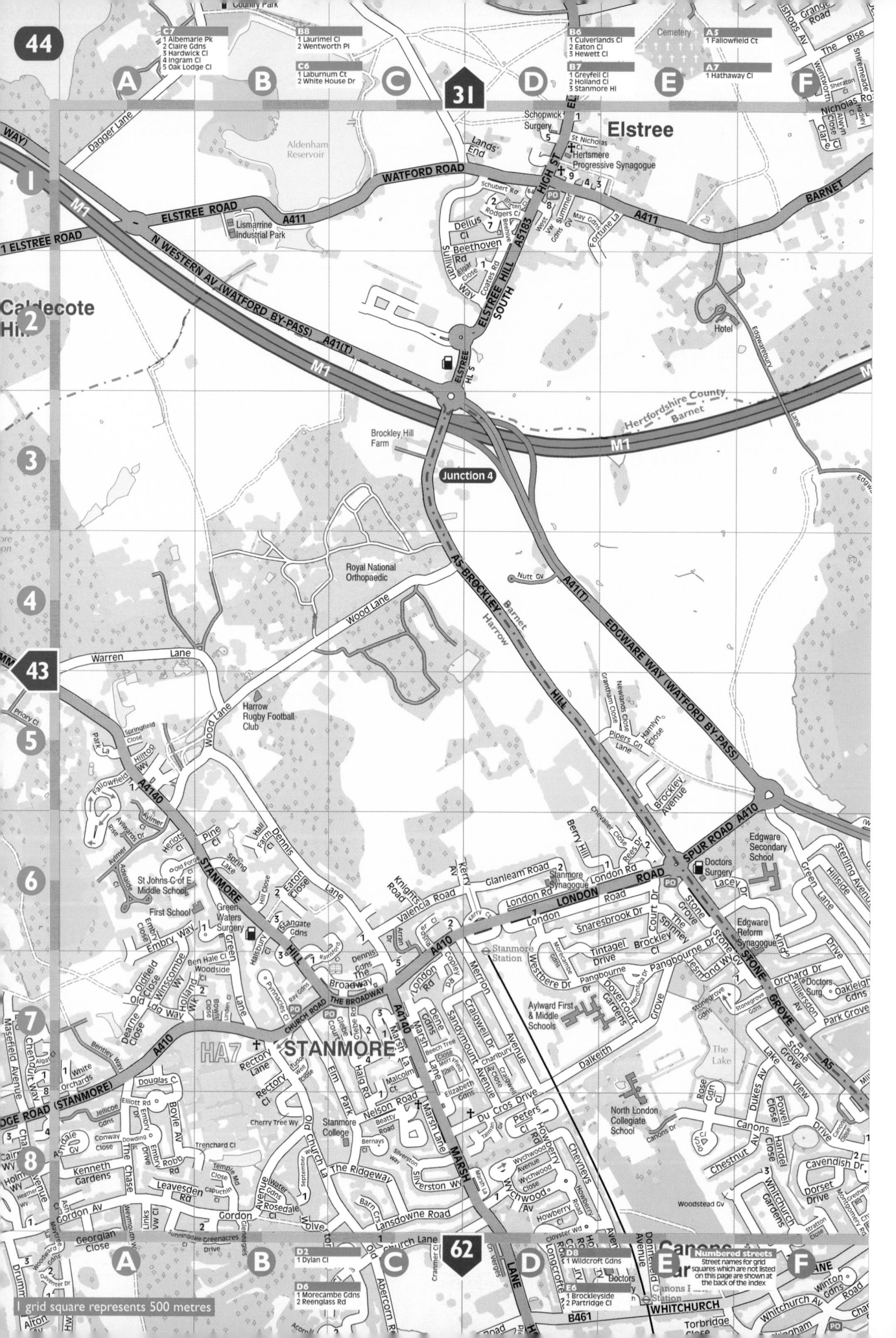

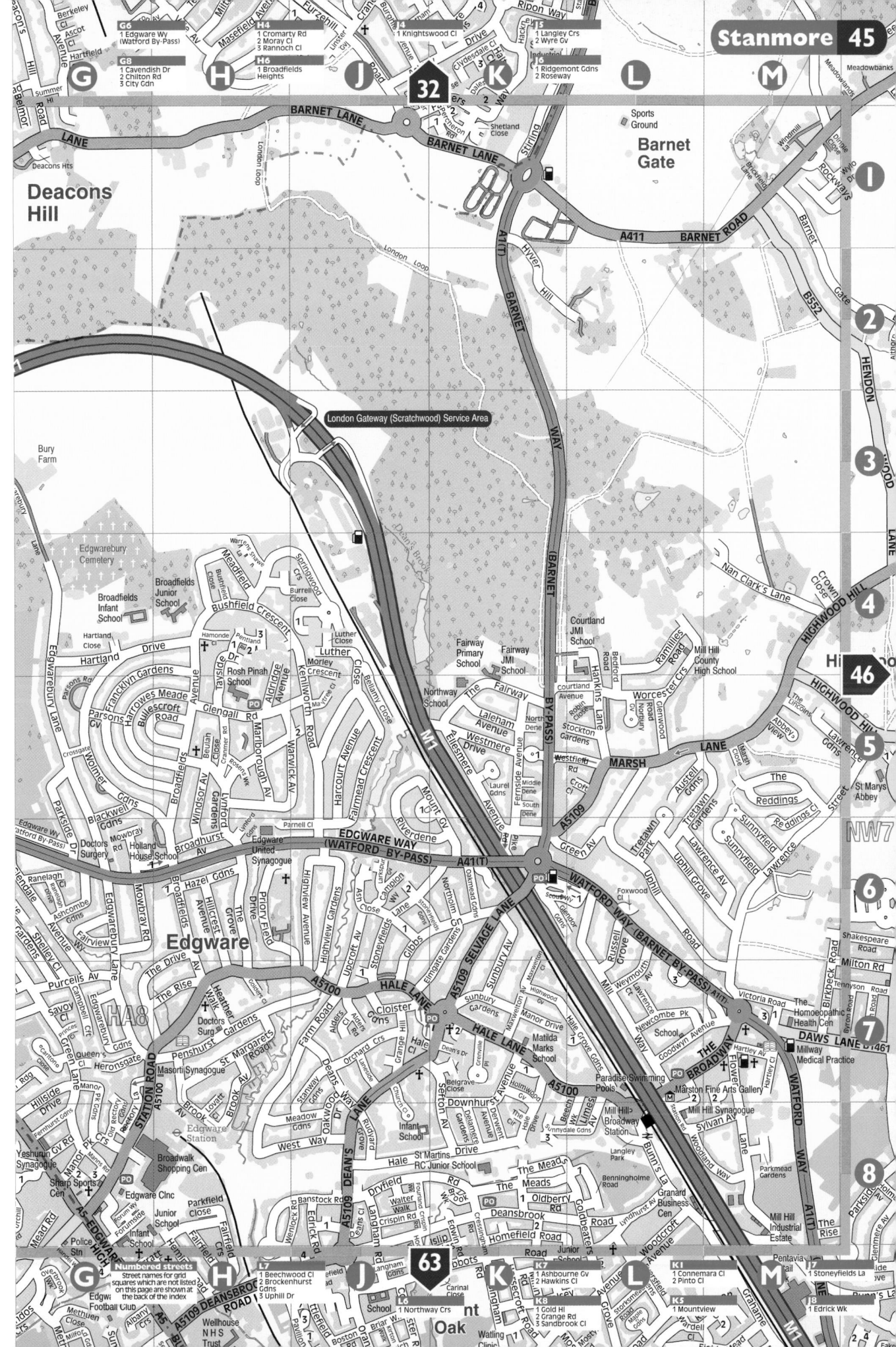

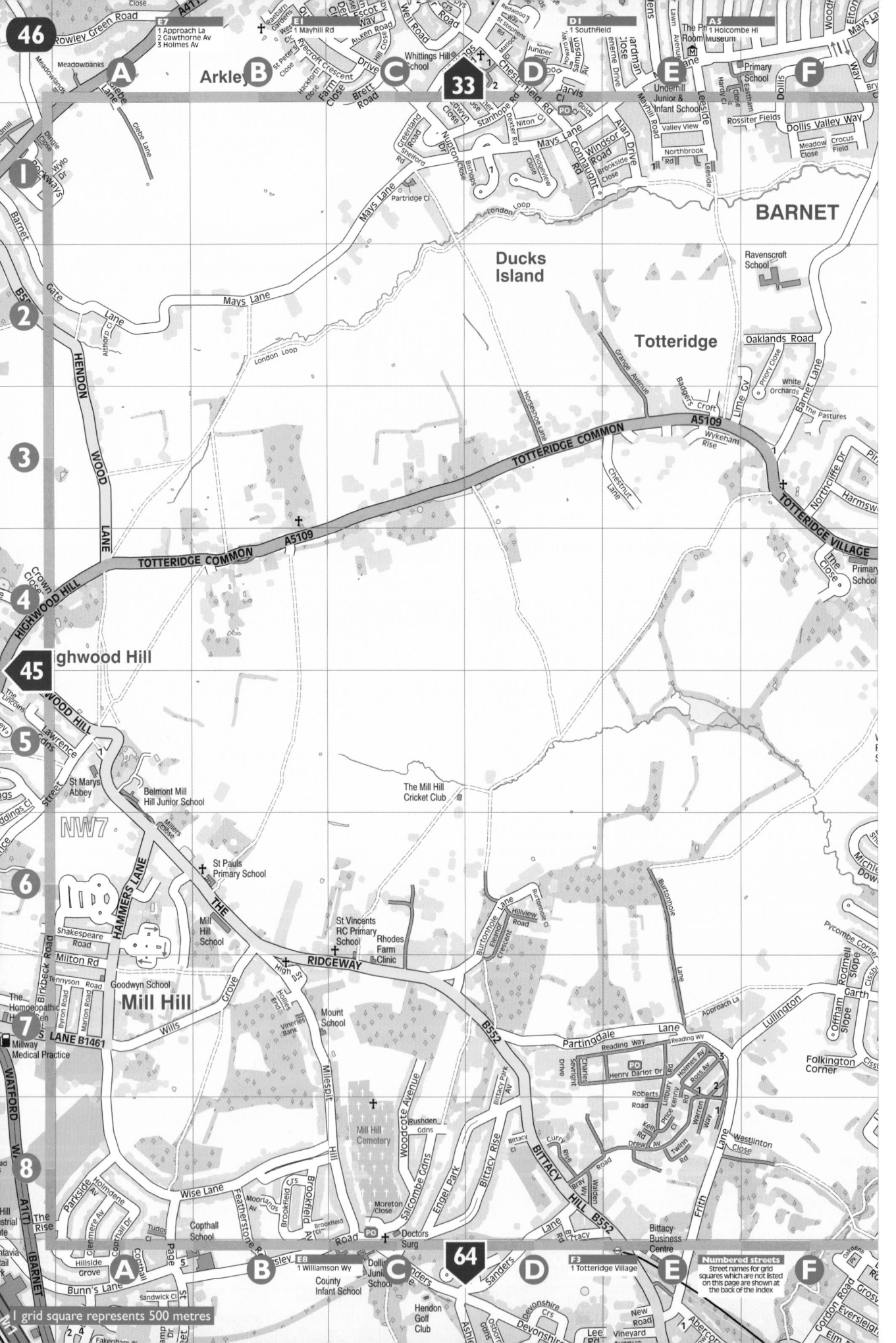

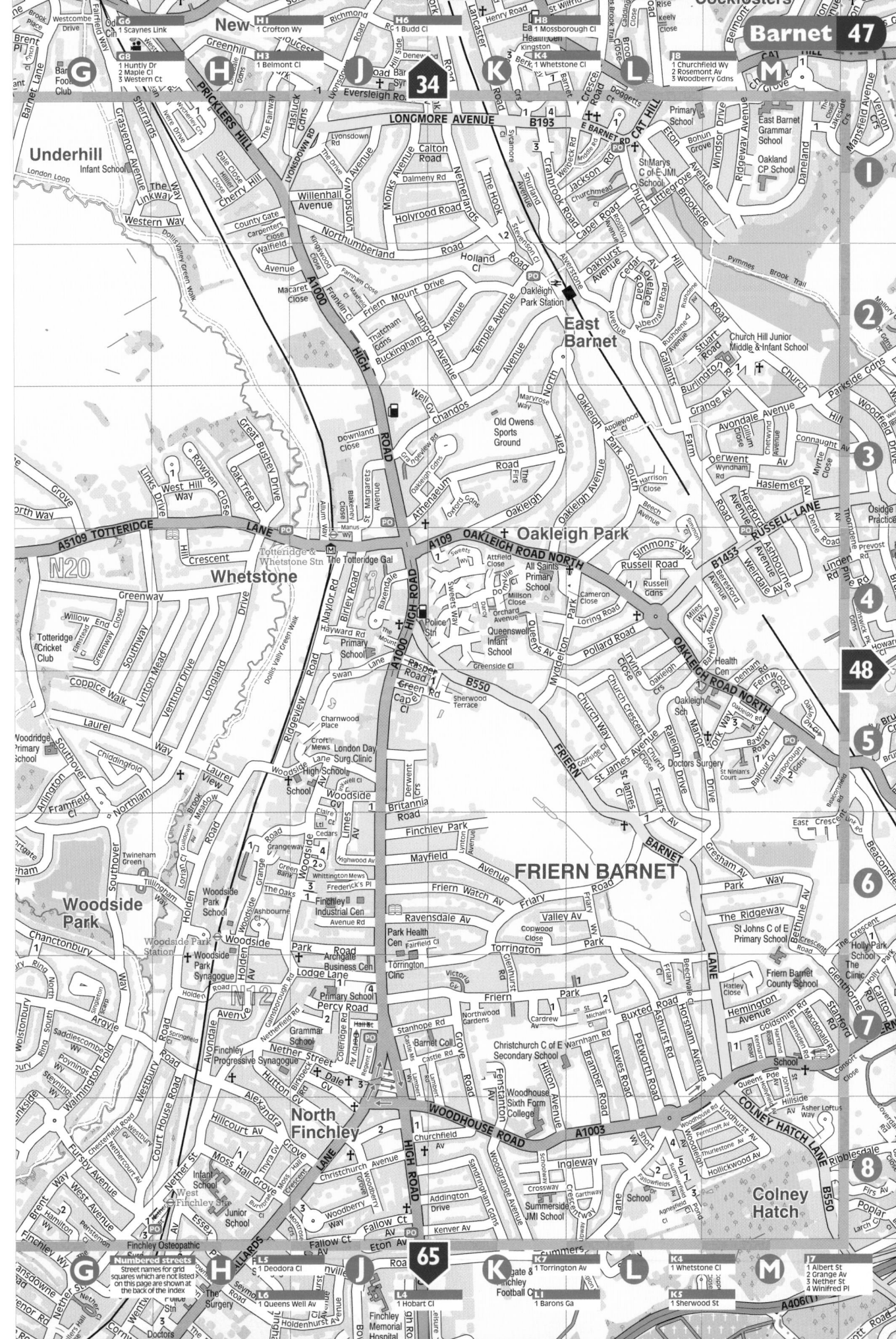

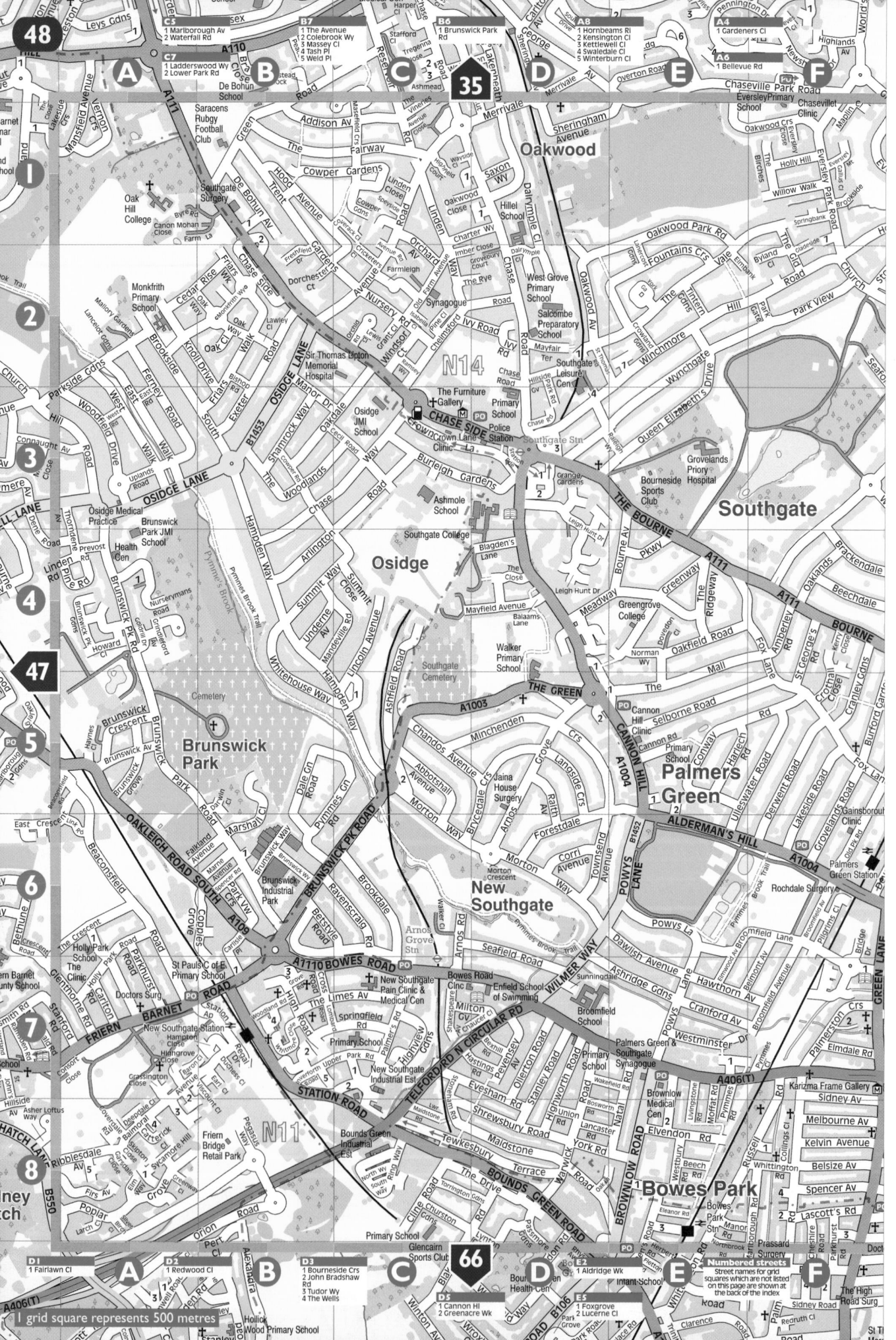

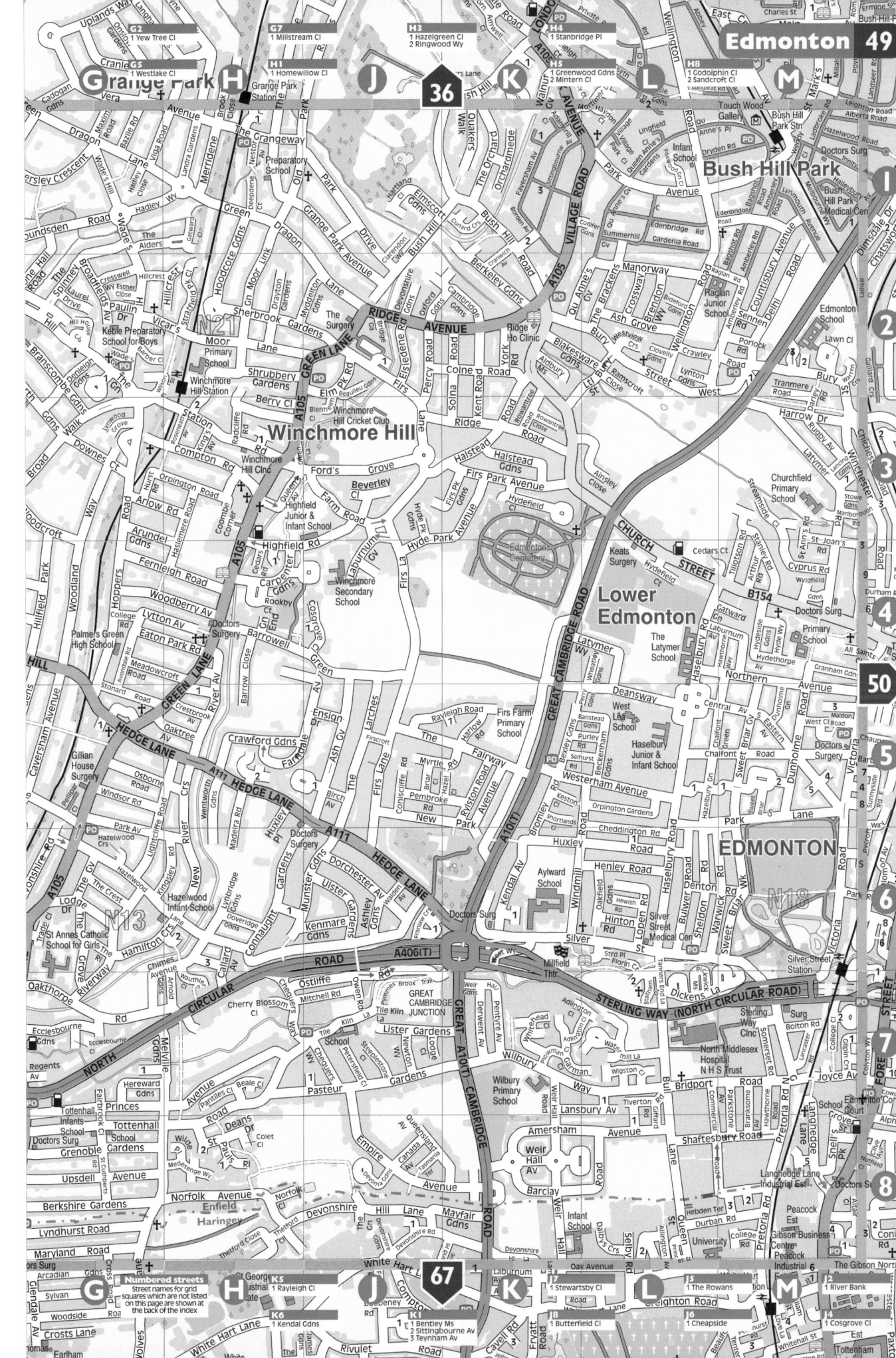

G · H · J · 38 · K · L · M

I

2

3

4

52

5

6

7

8

Chingford Green

Chingford

Friday Hill

Chingford Hatch

Hale End

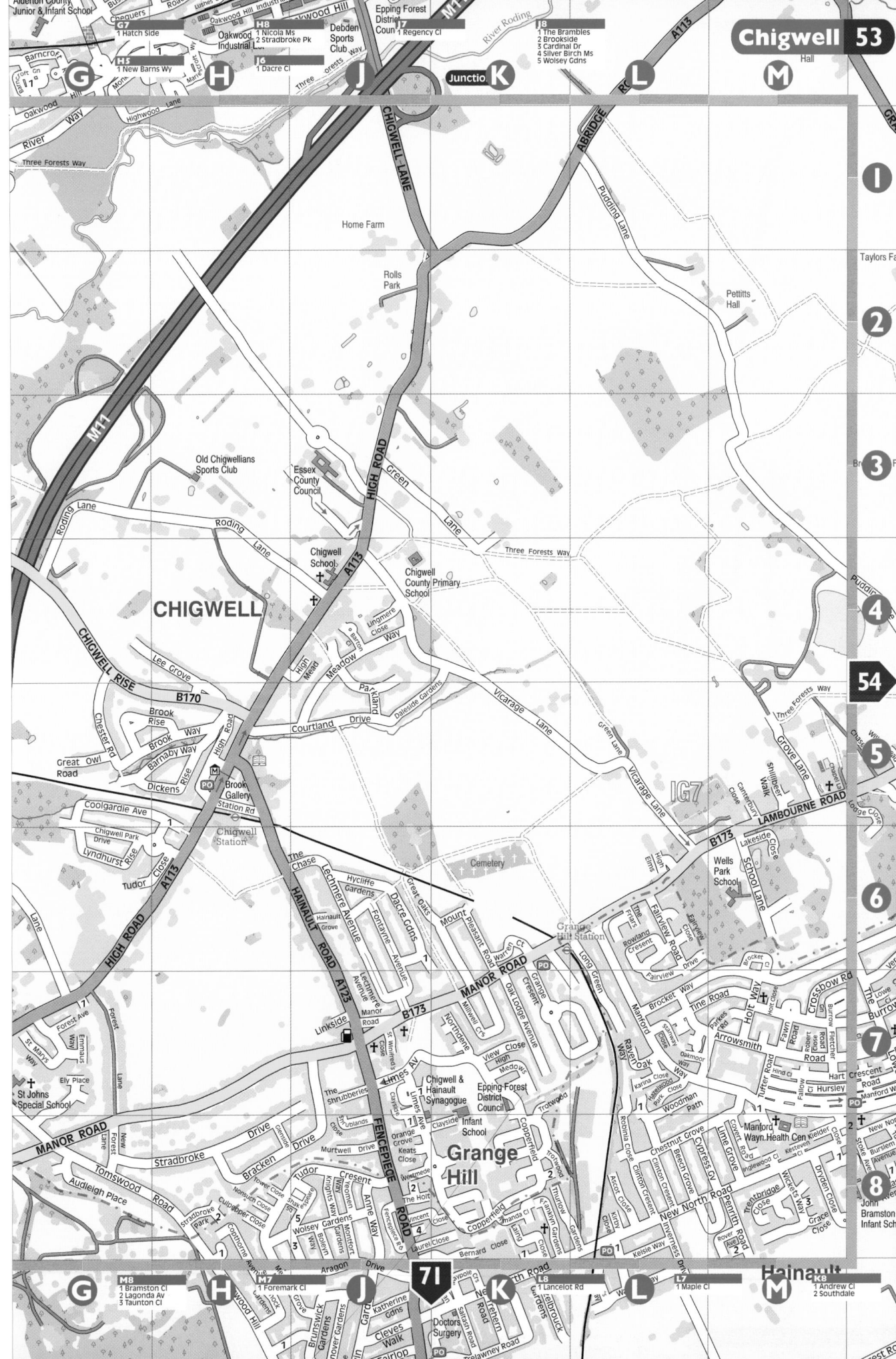

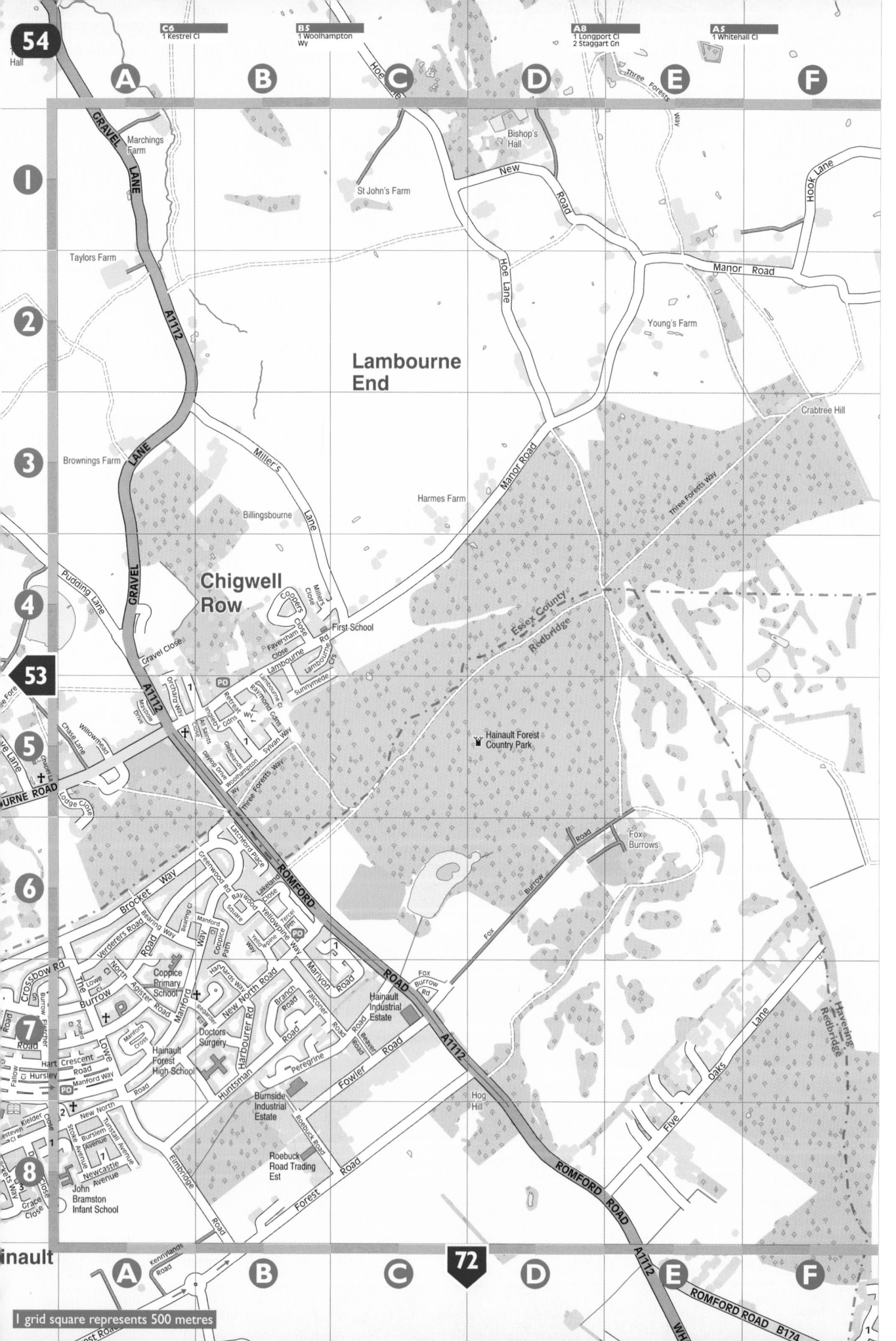

A   B   C   D   E   F

I

2

3

4

53

5

6

7

8

A   B   C   **72**   D   E   F

Hall

GRAVEL LANE

Marchings Farm

St John's Farm

Bishop's Hall

New Road

Hoe Lane

Three Forests Way

Manor Road

Hook Lane

Taylors Farm

Young's Farm

Crabtree Hill

Lambourne End

A1112

Brownings Farm

GRAVEL LANE

Miller's Lane

Billingsbourne

Harmes Farm

Manor Road

Three Forests Way

Pudding Lane

Chigwell Row

Cooper's Close

Miller's Lane

First School

Faversham Close

Lambourne Rd

Lambourne Cl

Essex County
Redbridge

Gravel Close

PO

Orchard Way

Raymond Gdns

Intlesty

All Saints

Sunnymede

Chase Lane

Willowmead

Maxdale Drive

A1112

Wychbury

Woodhampton Way

Sylvan Way

Three Forests Way

Hainault Forest
Country Park

Church Close

Lodge Close

BOURNE ROAD

ye Fore

Tye Lane

Road

Fox-
Burrows

Latchford Place

ROMFORD

Brocket Way

Greenwood Rd

Baywood

Lakeland Cl

Yellowpine Way

Fox
Burrow

Manford Way

Bearing Way

Coppice Path

Yellowpine Way

PO

Fox
Burrow
Rd

ROAD

A1112

Crossdow Rd

Burrow

The

Lowe

Burrow

North

Alister
Road

Manford

Way

Coppice Primary School

Hanards Way

New North Road

Branch Road

Manyon
Road

Falconer Road

Beaver Road

Hainault
Industrial
Estate

Fox
Burrow
Rd

Havering
Redbridge

Road

Furrier

Verderers Road

Manford Cross

Poynol

Lowe
Road

Doctors Surgery

Embers

Harbourer Rd

Huntsman

Peregrine

Hainault
Forest
High School

Oaks Lane

Hart Crescent

Fallow
Cl   Hursley

Manford Way

PO

Burnside
Industrial
Estate

Fowler Road

Hog
Hill

Five Oaks Lane

Kielder Close

New North
Road

Bursiem
Avenue

Stone Avenue

Newcastle
Avenue

Tunstall Avenue

Roebuck Road

Roebuck
Road Trading
Est

ROMFORD ROAD

Grace
Close

kets Way

John Bramston Infant School

Elmbridge
Road

Forest Road

Road

A1112

ROMFORD ROAD B174

WHIT

Hainault

G8
1 Pennington Cl

H7
1 Conifer Av

H8
1 Owen Cl

Abbotts County
Primary School

G **H** **J** **K** **L** **M**

Hook Lane

Grove House

Cutteridge Lane

Stapleford
Hall Farm

Curtis Mill

Tyseahill Farm

The Paddocks

I

High House Farm

Brook Farm
Industrial
Estate

**Stapleford
Abbotts**

Tysea Hill

Tysea Hill

2

Ashet
Farm

Knolls Hill
Farm

Bournebridge Lane

Crown Park
Farm

**Nuper's
Hatch**

OAK

PO

HILL

ROAD

Tysea Hill

3

B175 NORTH ROAD

4

56

Bower Farm

Bower

Farm

Road

Dame Tipping
School

**Havering-
atte-Bower**

5

Park Farm

Wellingtonia
Avenue

Elmer Av

B175

6

Havering
Country
Park

Pinewood

Road

Bower House

ORANGE TREE HILL

7

River Rom

Carter Drive

Lodge Lane

Craven Gdns

Mozart Gardens

Patmore Way

Thistledene Av

Pinewood
Primary School

Lulworth Drive

Ray Road

Cornell Way

Firbank Road

Saint

Johns

Road

Bedfords
Park

Wensley Cl

Oates Road

Bamford Way

Fox Close

Ravenswood
Close

Hunter's
Grove

Silvermere Ave

Warden Av

Tresco Gdns

Clitheroe Road

Boxmoor Road

Prestwood Cl

JO Prestwood

Vernon Road

Ashvale Gdns

Havering Court
Nursing Home

Portmore Gdns

Navarre Gdns

Charlotte Gardens

Victoria Avenue

Larchwood Avenue

Kingshill Lane

Larchwood Close

Harlow Gdns

Highfield Close

Hillrise

Hendon Gdns

Highfield

Avenue

Mount Pleasant Rd

Hawkhurst Close

Cornelia Link

Avelon Road

Merlin Road

Merlin
Gdns

Merlin
Close

Merlin Gdns

Gobions
JMI
School

Immanuel School

Bower
Park
School

**Chase
Cross**

8

Abridge Gardens

Stapleford
Gardens

Fry Close

Defoe W

Turpin Av

Dominion Drive

RM5

Udall Gardens

Bacon Link

Judith
Avenue

Clockhouse
Junior School

Lynwood
Drive

Clockhouse Lane

Burland Road

Felstead

Belle Vue Road

Chelmsford Avenue

Ascension Road

Robin Close

Bower Road

Campbell
Close

Heck Way

Denton

Glenton

Nevis
Close

Helmsdale Rd

Risebridge Chase

K8
1 Galleywood Crs
2 Merlin Gdns
3 Paceheath Cl

Frinton Road

Lodge Lane

Penn Close

Mayor Close

Downham Way

Doctors Surgery

Riversdale Road

Gelsthorpe Rd

Doctors
Chakrabarti Surg

G **H** **J** `73` **K** **L** **M**

CHASE

Gabriel Cl

Berkeley Avenue

Faircross Av

Iron

B1459

Carry Way

Helmsdale
Close

L8
1 Chaseside Cl

A   B   C   D   E   F

E5
1 Priory Pth

D8
1 Cloudberry Rd
2 Dewsbury Gdns
3 Honeysuckle Cl

D7
1 Bridgwater Wk
2 Chip'ham Gdns
3 Newbury Wk

C8
1 Charlbury Cl
2 Okehampton Sq
3 Saddleworth Sq

D6
1 Woodbridge Cl

Waterhales

I

Watton's
Green

Horseman side

M25

Weald Brook

Tysea Hill

2

Asheton
Farm

Goatswood

Lane

Navestock
Common

Havering
Plain

3

Essex County
Havering

Church

Road

Paternoster Row

Barnskins

Wrightsbridge Ro

Home Farm

4

Widdrington
Farm

Schoolhouse

Noak
Hill

Cheqers Road

Lower

Noke

Close

55

Cummings Hall La

Manor Farm

Broxhill Road

5

Greenbank
Cl

The Mount

Castle
Close

Wincanton Road

Noak Hill Road

Priory Road

Priory Grove

Havering College
of Further &
Higher Education

6

Kynance
Close

Ingrebourne CP
School

Ashbourne Road

North Lane

Preston Road

Woodbridge La

Woodbridge Dr

Drive

Whitchurch

Wigton Rd

Wigton Way

Tring Gardens

Tring Close

Sedgefield Crescent

Hitchin
Cl

Taunton
Rd

Lewes
Rd

Avisham
Rd

Troopers
Dr

Dorking

Dorking

PO

Broseley
Gdns

Broseley Road

Hitchin
Cl

Sevenoaks
Close

Sevenoaks

Chudleigh Rd

Lindfield Road

7

Stanwyck
Gardens

Appleby
Dr

Hailsham
Road

Stephens Cl

Halsham
Close

Barnstaple Road

Montgomery Crs

Darlington
Gardens

Dorking
Wk
Drive

Infant
School

Central Park
Swimming
Pool

Dagnam Park Drive

Harkness
Close

Swindon Lane

Wickford Dr

Redruth Rd

Recar Rd

Harold
Hill

Doctors
Surgery

Bedfords
Park

Lower Bedfords Road

Straight Road

Daventry Rd

Longtown Rd
End

Daventry
Gdns

Edenhall Rd

Hilldene

Bridgwater
Rd

Avenue

Farnham Rd

Den
Dr

The
Health
Centre

PO

Road

Trowbridge
Rd

Tansy
Cl

Gooshays Dr

Gooshays Gdns

Petersfield Av

Colne

Drive

Paines

Brook Way

Oxford

Rd

Hucknall
Cl

RM3

Amersham

PO

Mead
Infant
School

8

St Ursulas
Junior and
Infant
School

Grange

Hale
End

Road

Charlbury

Crescent

Chippenham

Road

Newbury
Gdns

Kings Lynn
Dr

Chatter's

Dunstable
Rd

Dudley

Dartfields
Rd

Dukerton Rd

Guildford Rd

Dewsbury Road

Kingsbridge Road

Halesworth
Rd

Amersham

Road

Archway

Hilldene Junior and Infant
School

Myrtle

Tulip
Wy

Lucerne
Wy

Coltsfoote Pth

Cricklade Av

Broadford
Primary
School

Kingsbridge Road

Harlesden Gdns

RM3

St Ives Close

Chaucer Road

Heaton

Av

Heaton
Way

Briar Cl

Rose Cl

Briar
Rd

Veronica

Tonbridge
Rd

Camborne

Spilsby Rd

Stoke

Sunnydene

The Business
Cen

Guardian

Sussex Cl

ER ROAD

E6
1 Whitchurch Rd

74

E8
1 Dewsbury Rd
2 Halesworth Cl
3 Kingsbridge Rd

F7
1 Swindon Gdns

F8
1 Amersham Wk

1 grid square represents 500 metres

A B **40** C D E F

Weybeards Farm

Bishop's Wood

Hill End

Hillingdon Trail

Harefield Grove

Shepherds Hill House

Mount Pleasant

Harefield Hospital

Colney Farm

Harefield Health Centre

Harefield Junior School

Harefield Infant School

John Penrose School

Ash Grove

Hospital Annexe

Newdigate Road

Vernon Drive

Olivia Gdns

Gilbert Road

Sullivan Crescent

Harefield Cricket Club

Harefield

Knightscote Farm

Breakspear Road North

Bourne Farm

Breakspear House

St Mary's Close

St Anne's Road

Church Road

Church Hill

Broadwater Lane

Broadwater Gdns

Sedley Gv

Priory Gdns

Peerless Drive

Harvil Road

Truesdale Drive

Park Lodge Farm

Hillingdon Trail

South Harefield

Dellside

Hillside

Harvil Road

Bayhurst Wood Country Park

Moorhall Road

Grand Union Canal Walk

Savay Farm

St Francis Road

St Mary's Road

Penn Drive

Moorfield Road

James Martin Close

Savay Close

Savay Lane

UB9

Highway Farm

Station Pde

Denham Station

Martin Baker Sports Ground

South Bucks Way

Buckinghamshire County

A B **76** C D E F

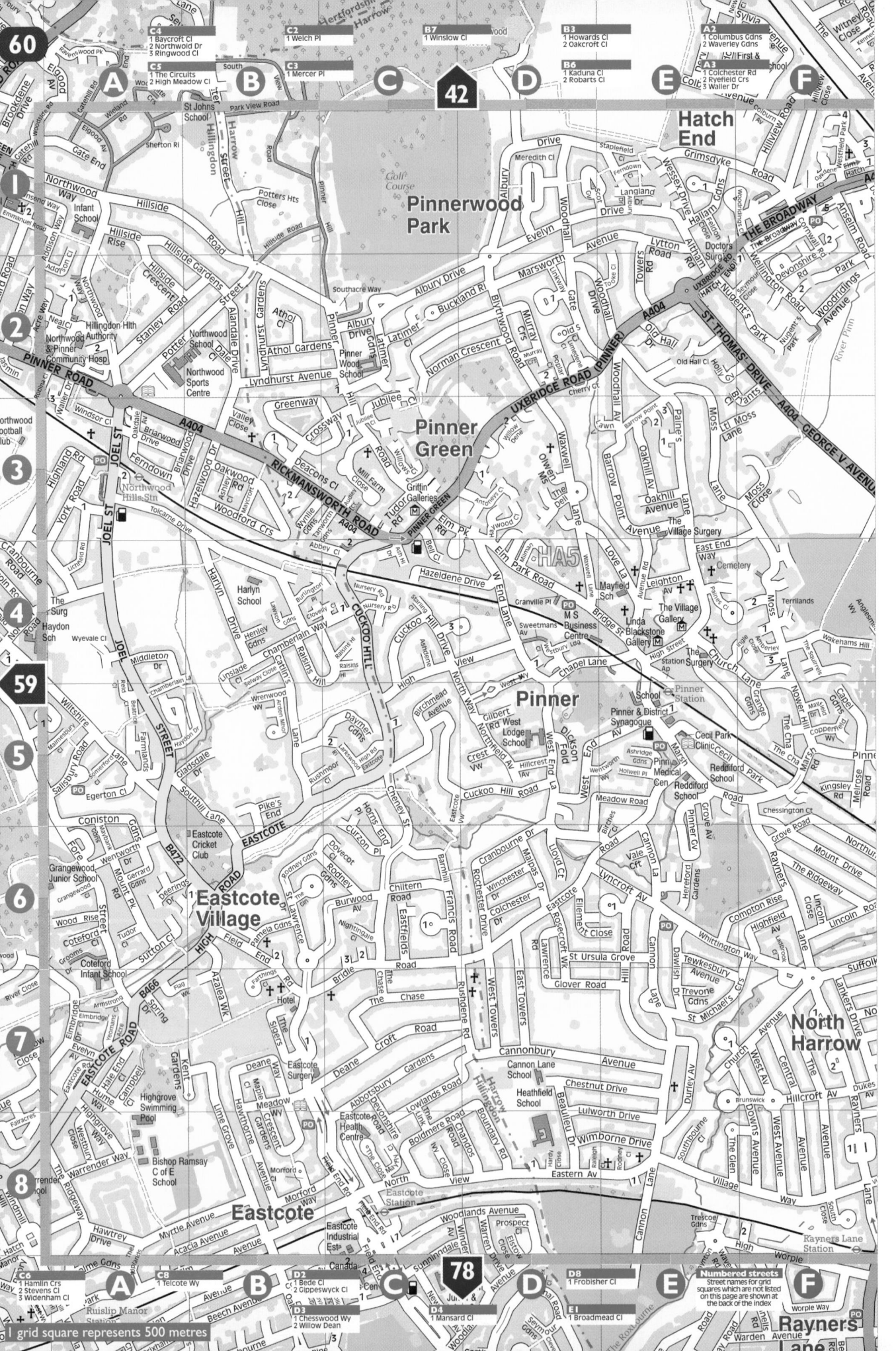

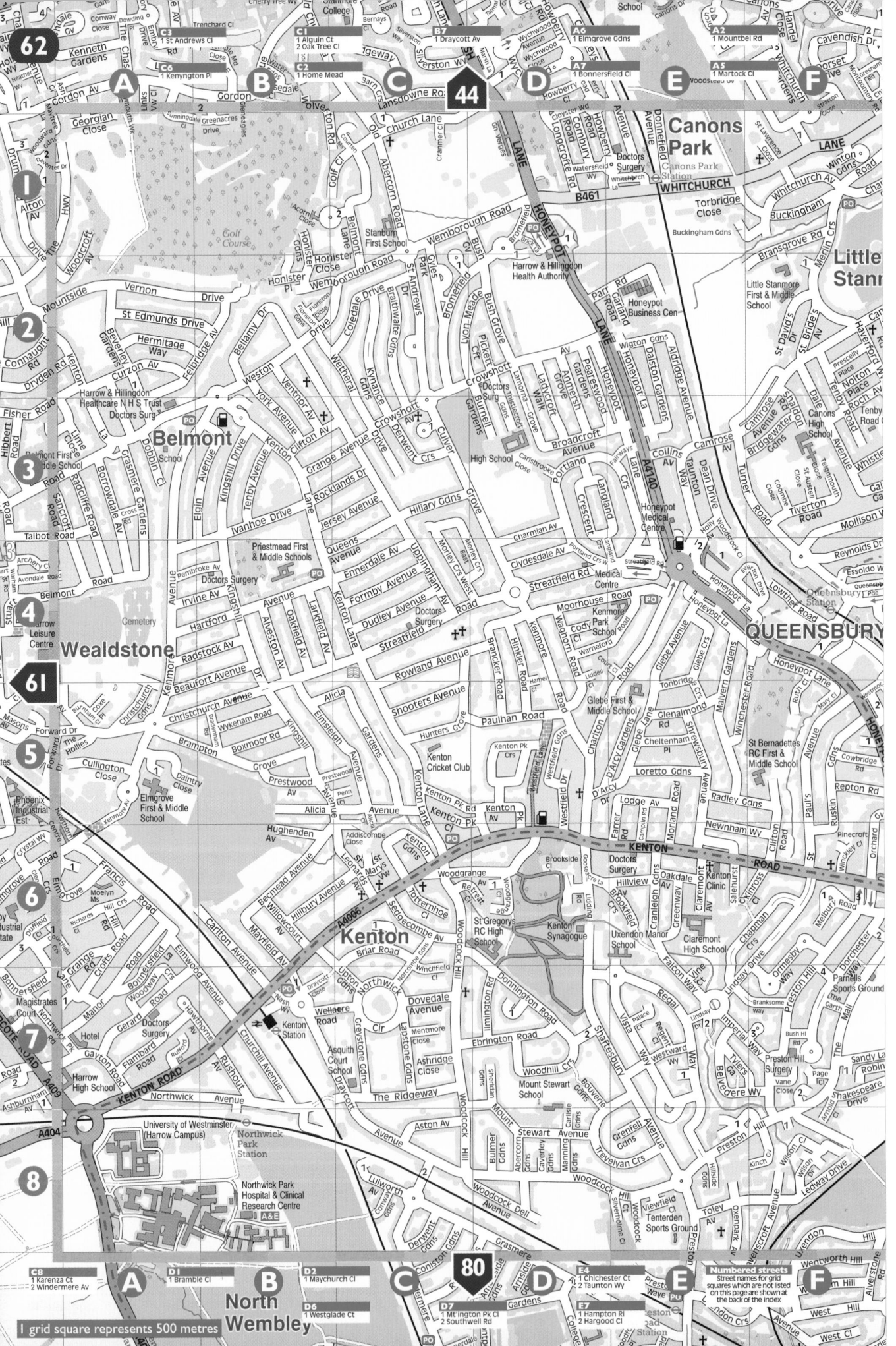

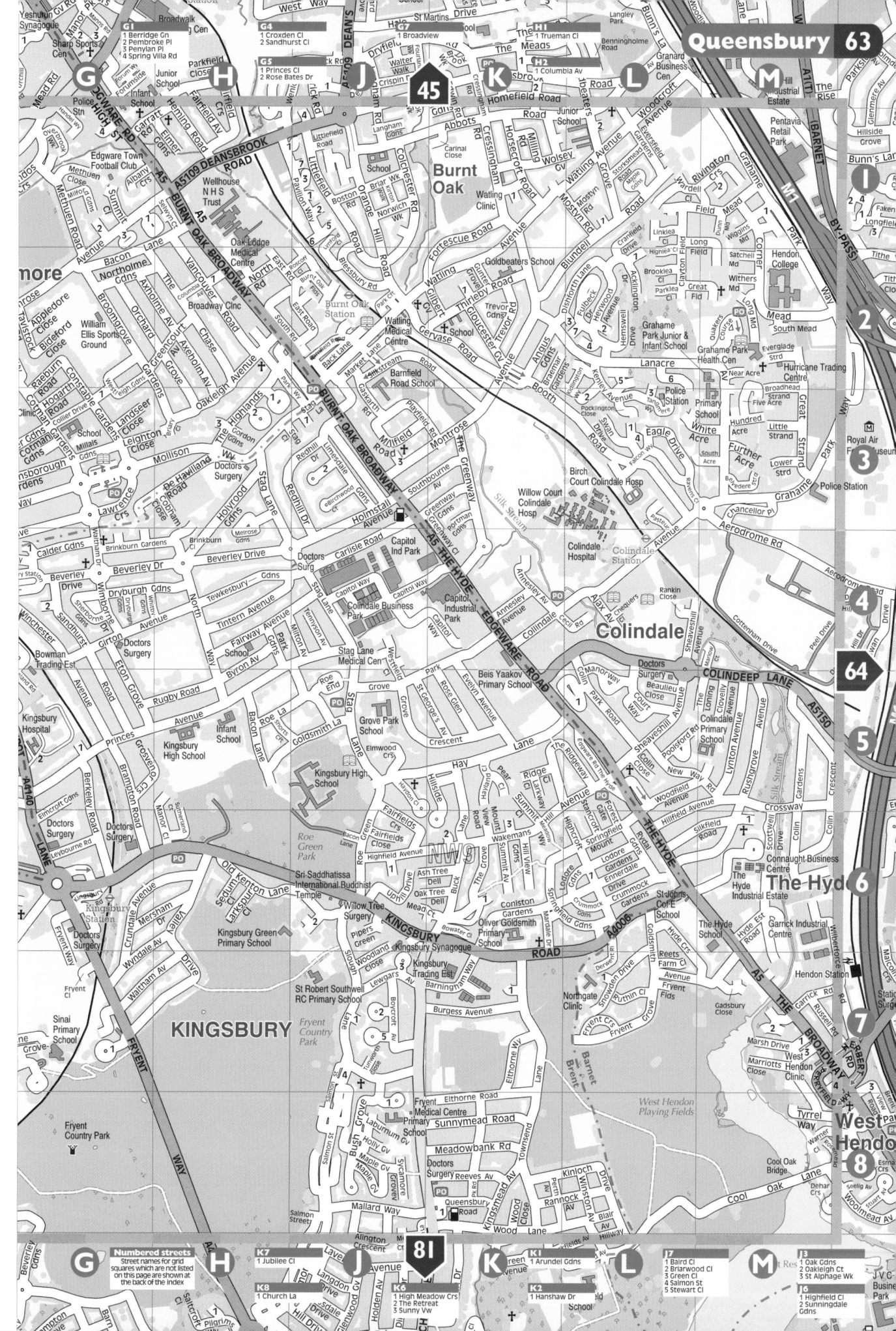

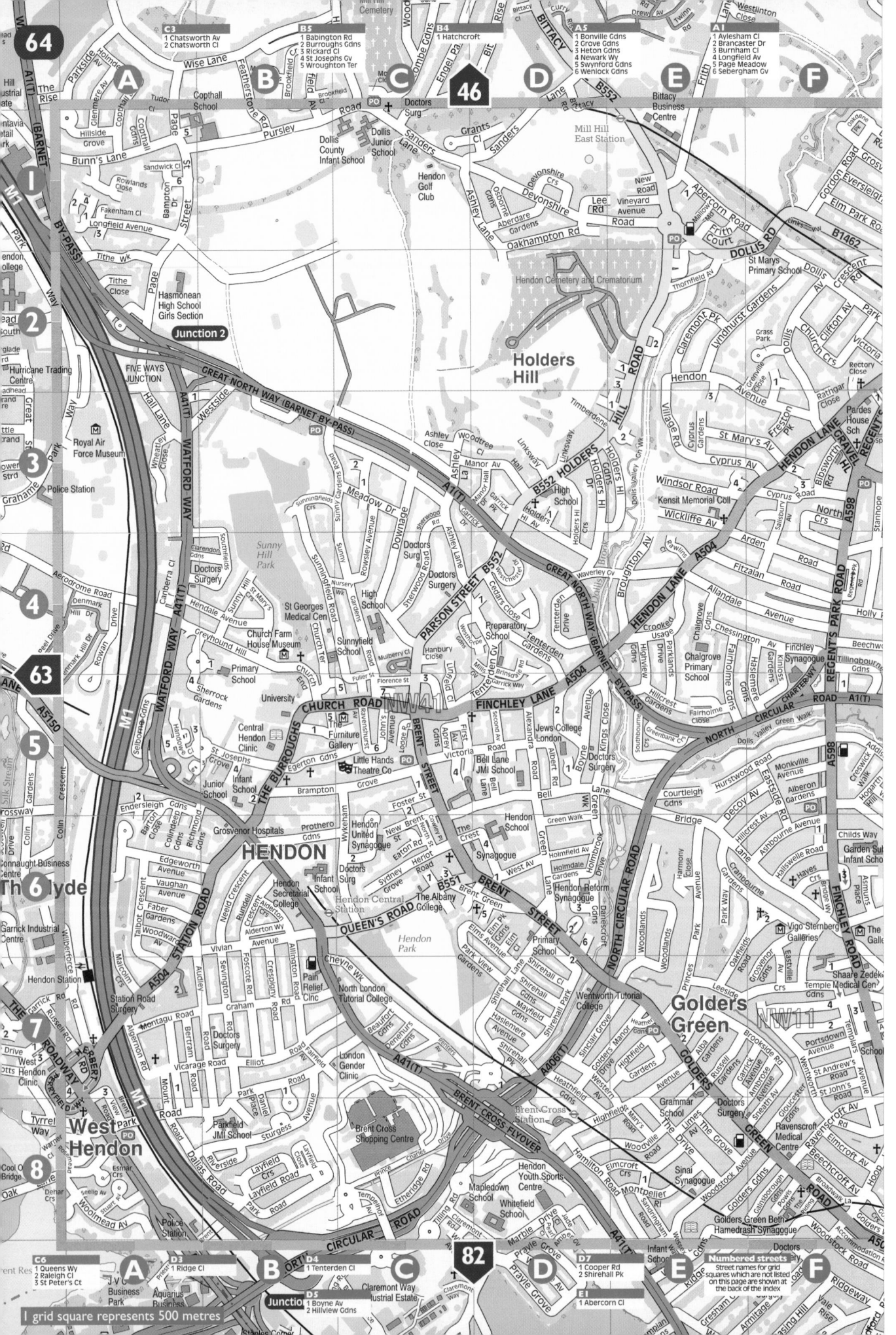

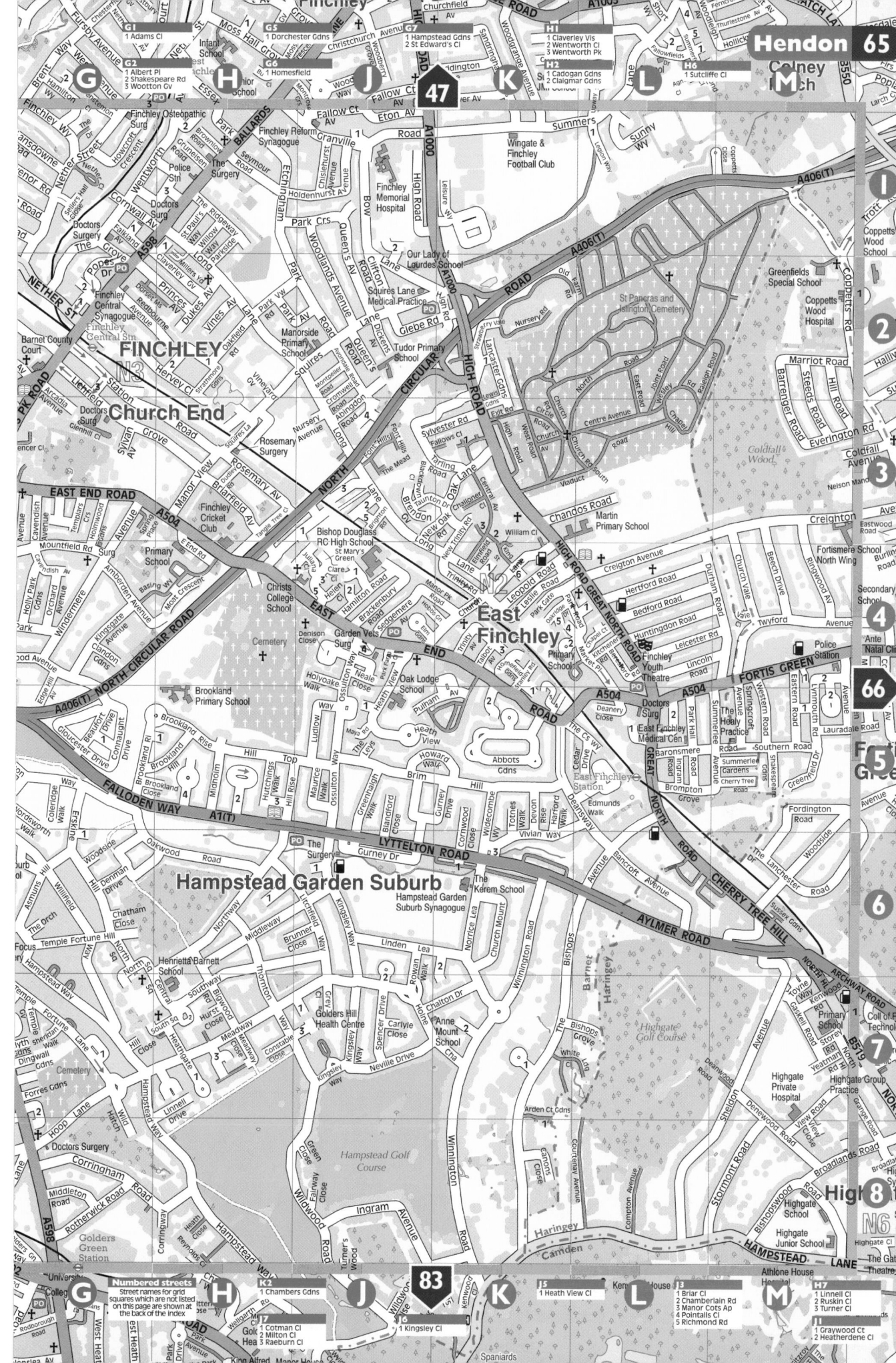

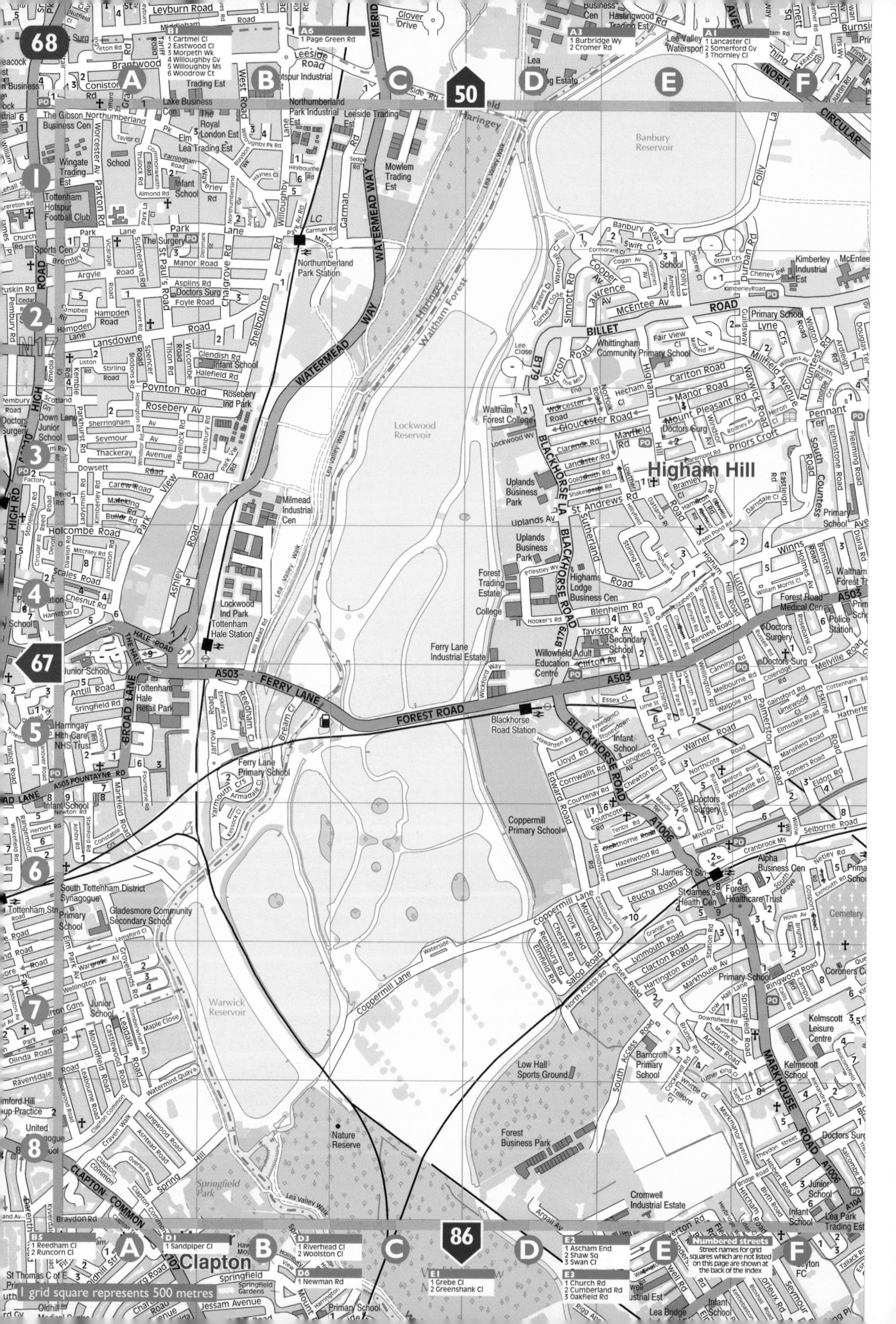

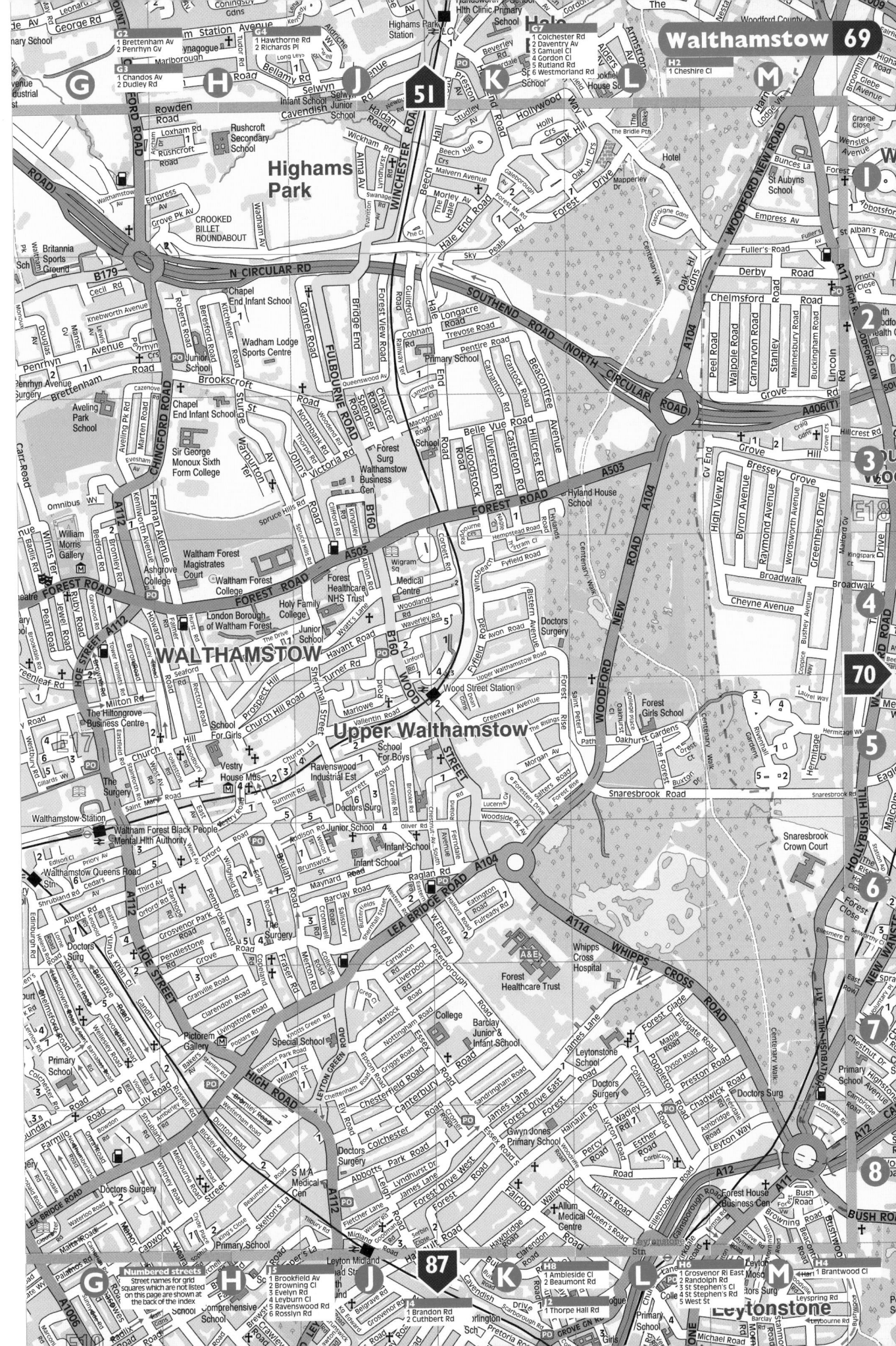

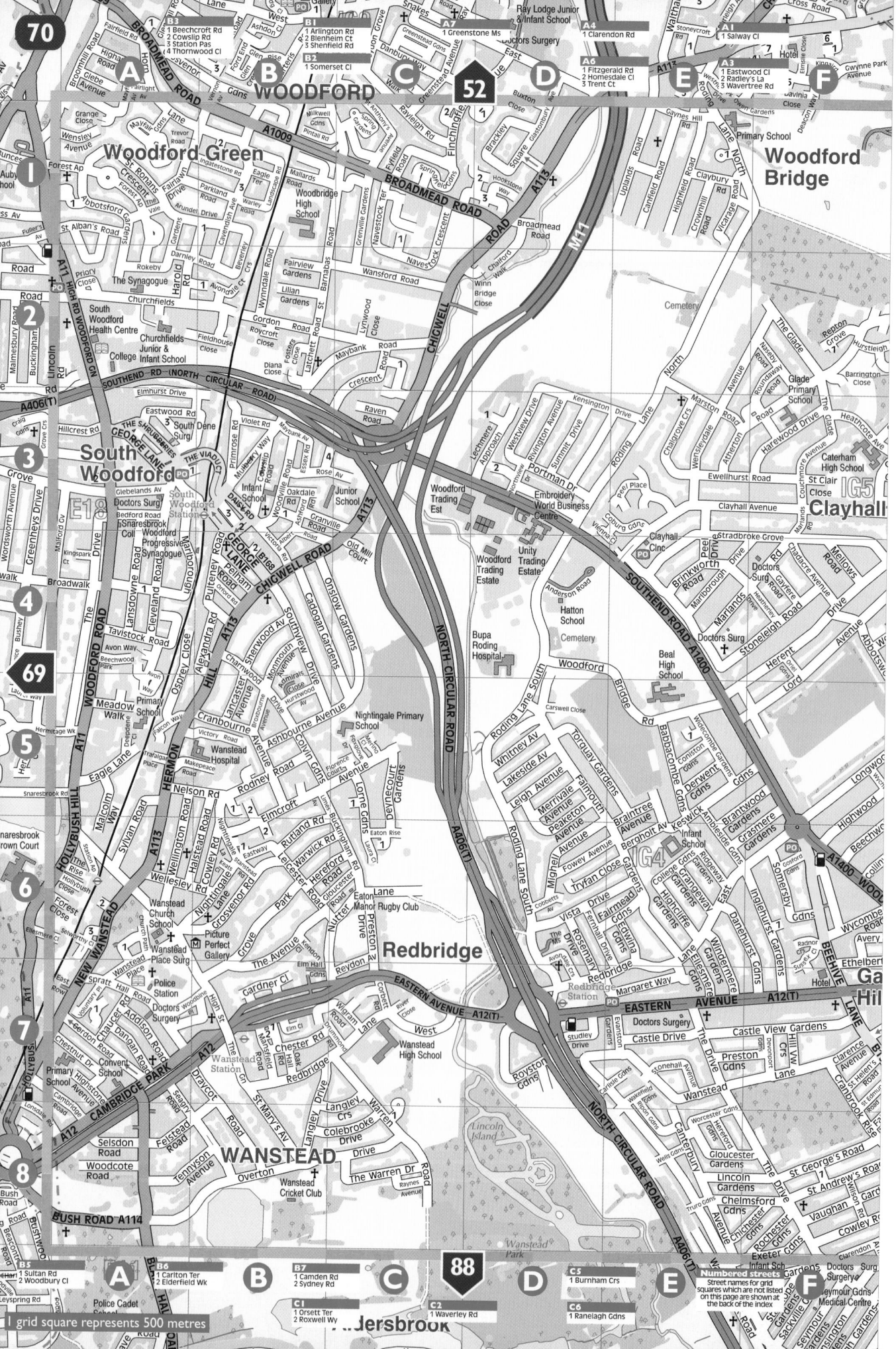

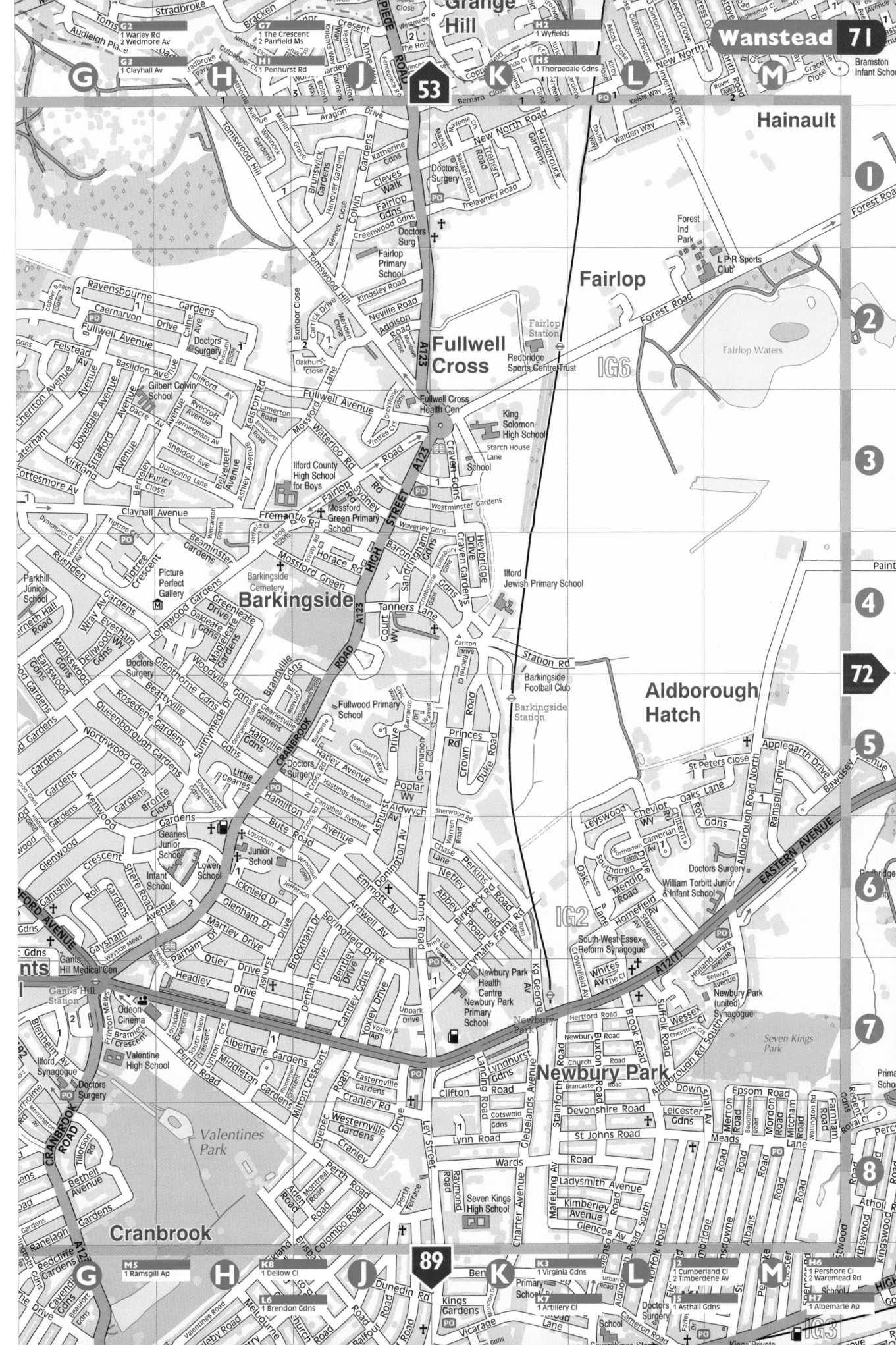

G H J 53 K L M

Grange Hill

1 Wyfields

1 Thorpedale Gdns

New North Road

Bramston Infant School

Hainault

I

Forest Road

Forest Ind Park

L P R Sports Club

Fairlop Station

Redbridge Sports Centre Trust

Fairlop

Fairlop Waters

IG6

2

3

Fullwell Cross

A123

Ilford County High School for Boys

King Solomon High School

Starch House Lane School

Fullwell Cross Health Cen

Craven Gdns

Westminster Gardens

Ilford Jewish Primary School

Painte

4

Barkingside

Barkingside Cemetery

Picture Perfect Gallery

Mossford Green Primary School

Fullwood Primary School

Tanners Lane

Station Rd

Barkingside Football Club

Barkingside Station

Carlton Drive

Aldborough Hatch

St Peters Close

Applegarth Drive

Aldborough Road North

72

5

Cheviot Wy

Chiltern Gdns

Leyswood Drive

Oaks Lane

Ramsgill Drive

EASTERN AVENUE

Bawdsey Avenue

6

Doctors Surgery

William Torbitt Junior & Infant School

Mendip Road

Homefield

Stapleford

A12 (T)

IG2

South-West Essex Reform Synagogue

Whites Av

Newbury Park Health Centre

Newbury Park Primary School

Newbury Park

Holland Park Avenue

Selwyn Avenue

Newbury Park (united) Synagogue

Wessex Gdns

Seven Kings Park

7

Odeon Cinema

Valentine High School

Doctors Surgery

Gants Hill Medical Cen

Gant's Hill Station

Ilford Synagogue

Newbury Park

Hertford Road

Newbury Road

Buxton Road

Brook Road

Suffolk Road

Epsom Road

Merton Road

Mordon Road

Mitcham Road

Farnham Road

Primar School

8

Valentines Park

Seven Kings High School

Clifton Road

Devonshire Road

St Johns Road

Leicester Gdns

Ladysmith Avenue

Kimberley Avenue

Glencoe Av

Redbridge

Primar School

Cranbrook

CRANBROOK ROAD

A123

G 89 H J K L M

1 Ramsgill Ap

1 Dellow Cl

1 Virginia Gdns

1 Cumberland Cl
2 Timberdene Av

1 Pershore Cl
2 Waremead Rd

1 Albemarle Ap

1 Brendon Gdns

1 Artillery Cl

Doctors Surgery

1 Asthall Gdns

IG3

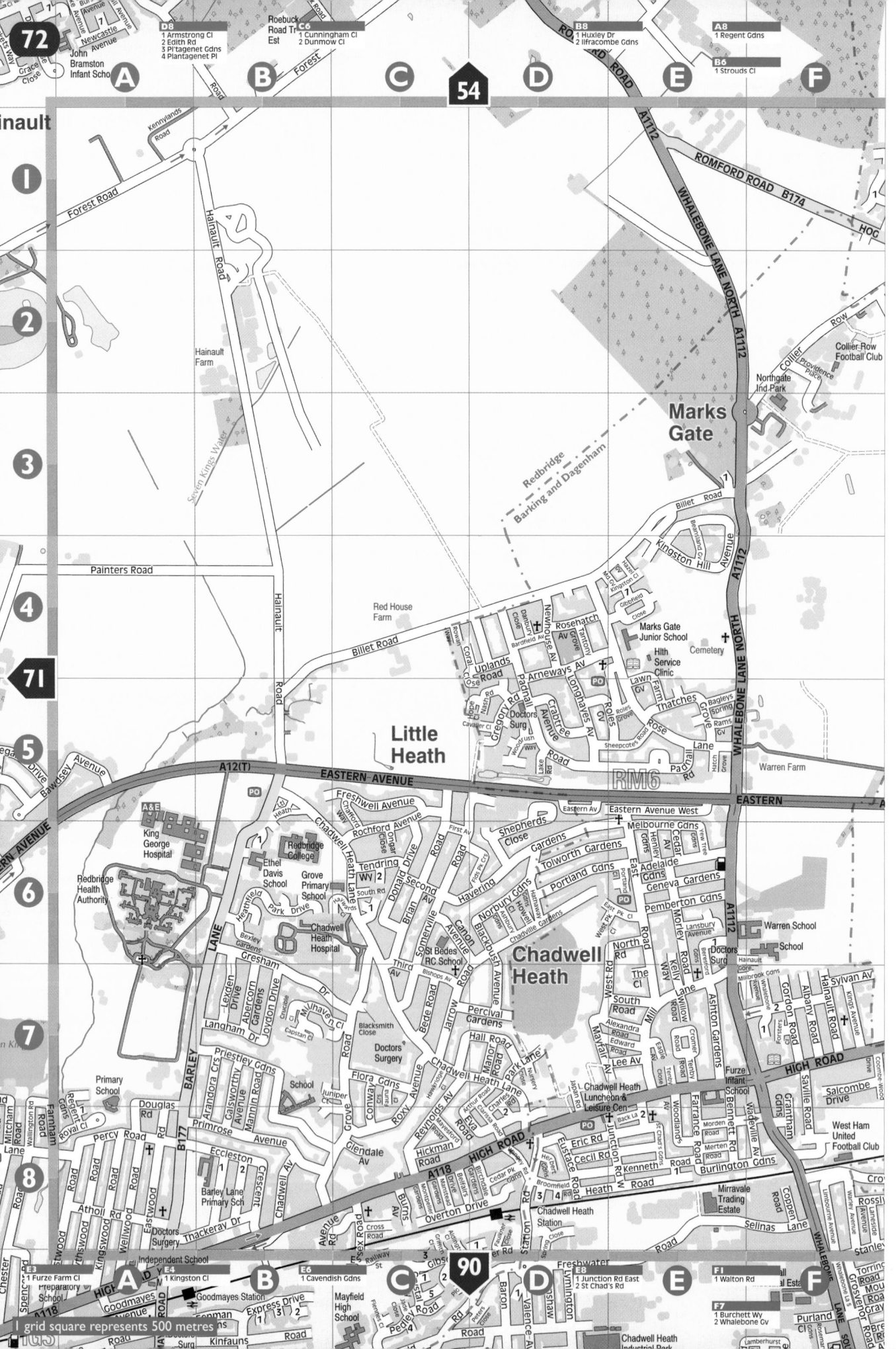

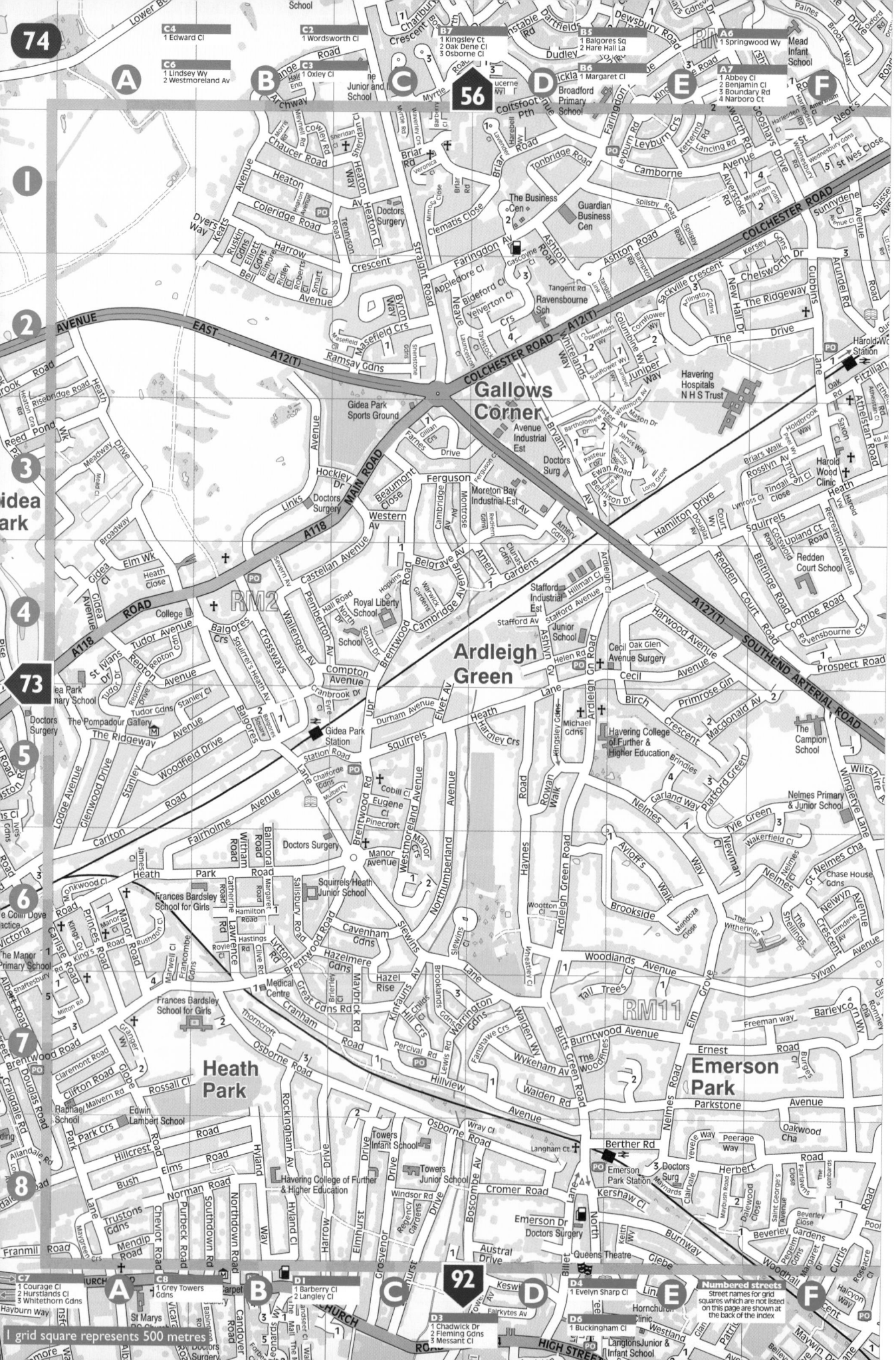

G1
1 Birkdale Av
2 Firham Park Av
3 Hoylake Gdns

G5
1 Cornwall Cl
2 Hampshire Rd
3 Pembroke Cl
4 Suffolk Wy

G6
1 Cheshire Cl

G7
1 Romney Cha
2 Wych Elm Cl

G **H** **J** 57 **K** **L** **M**

Essex County
Havering

Boyles
Court

I

Great
Warle

G 2

Harold Court
School

Harold
Court

Harold
Wood

Tylers
Common

Warley Road

Beredens Lane

combe

3

Shepherds

Hill

Phillida
Road

Hall

Lane

Harold
Wood JMI School

Nag's Head Lane

Hall Lane

Tomkyns

Lane

4

M25

Folkes Lane

5

Denbigh
Cl

Avenue

Oxford
Rd

Berkshire Way

Essex Gardens

Rutland

Drive

Lincoln

Hubbards Close

Hubbards Chase

Copthorne Gardens

A127(T)

Hall Lane

Hall

Lane

Chapmans
Farm

Bird

Lane

A127(T)

SOUTHEND ARTERIAL ROAD

6

Folkes Lane

Wingletye La

Lillyputts

River

Dr

Severn

Trent Avenue

Fleet Av

Fleet Cl

Dee Cl

Stour Wy

Tamar

Pentire
Cl

Front Lane

Griffin Av

Roseberry Cl.

Lexington Wy

Waycross Rd

Macon Wy

Queens Gdns

Roseberry Gardens

Moor Lane

Ferndown

Braemar
Gdns

Wych Elm Road

Wych Elm Cl

Fordyce
Close

Rayburn Rd

Bourne End

Emerson
Park School

River Drive

Avon Rd

Mersey
Av

Avon

Colne
Valley

Forth
Road

Tyne Cl

Isis Dr

Clyde
Crescent

Engayne
Junior School

Humber Dr

Kennet

Brunswick Av

The Crs

Gardens

The
Cobbles

Fairholme Gdns

Acacia
Gdns

Laburnham

Limerick Gdns

7

8

Wingletye Lane

Chelmer Rd

Tees

The
Leas

Ruskin Av

Drive

Masefie

Spenser Crs

Hall

Lane

Crouch valley

Eldred
Gdns

Cranham Health
Cen

Brookmans
Cl

Esdaile Gdns

Kings Gardens

Marlborough

Front Lane

Briarleas
Gdns

Doctors
Surgery

Cranham
Park Av

Kerry

Kerry
Drive

Cranham

Golf
Course

The Fairway

Holden
Way

Dorkins
Wy

Hall
Mead

Plough
Rise

G M8
1 Mallard Cl
H M7
1 Wingfield Gdns
J 93 **K** L7
1 Gadsden Cl
L K7
1 Dart Cl
M G8
1 Fordham Cl
2 Ingleglen

Benets
Road

Tiptree
Cl

Somerset Gdns

Ashburnham Gardens

Inglebourne

Gardens

Nightingale
Avenue

Chipperfield

Swan Av

Heron

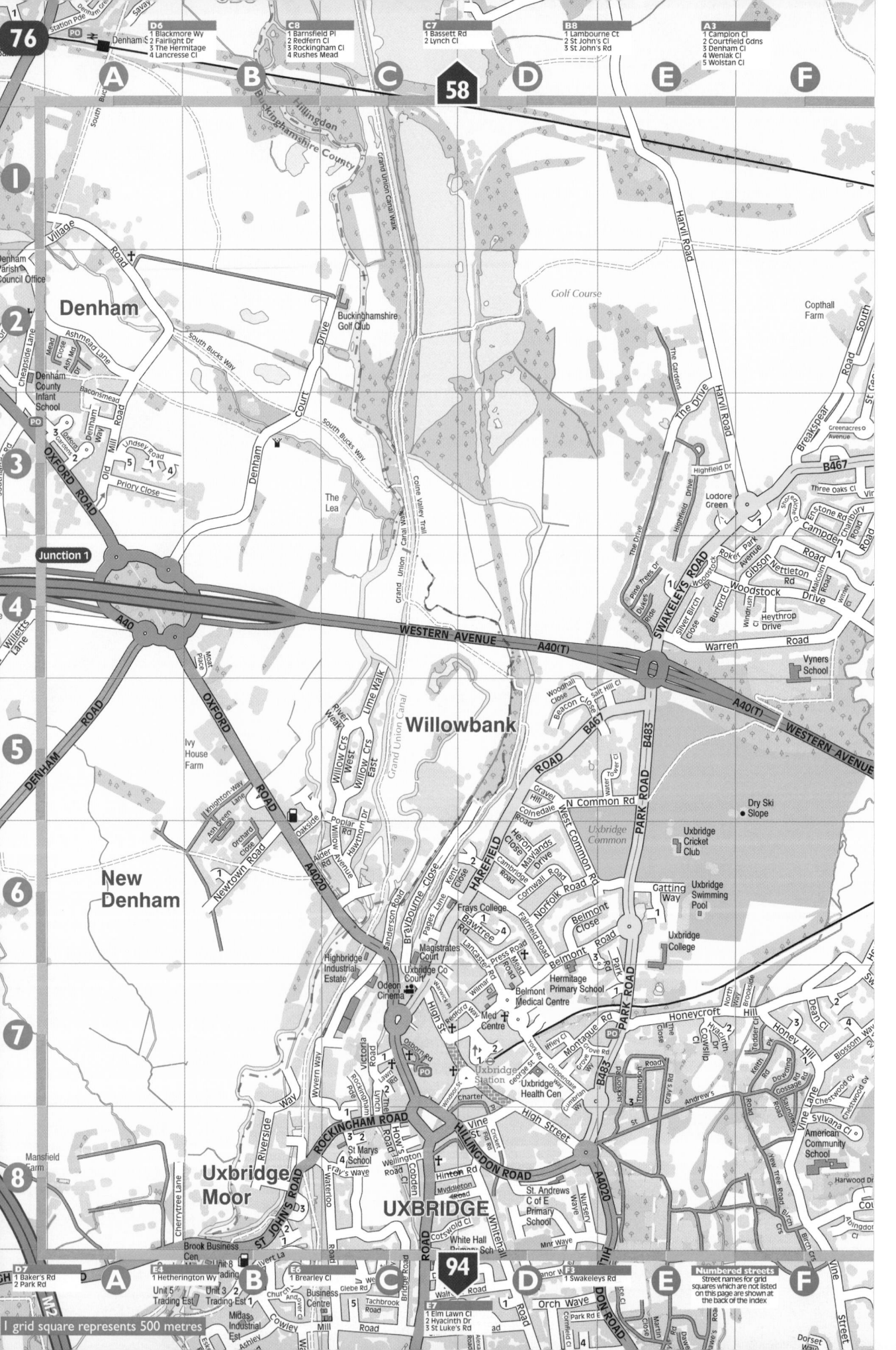

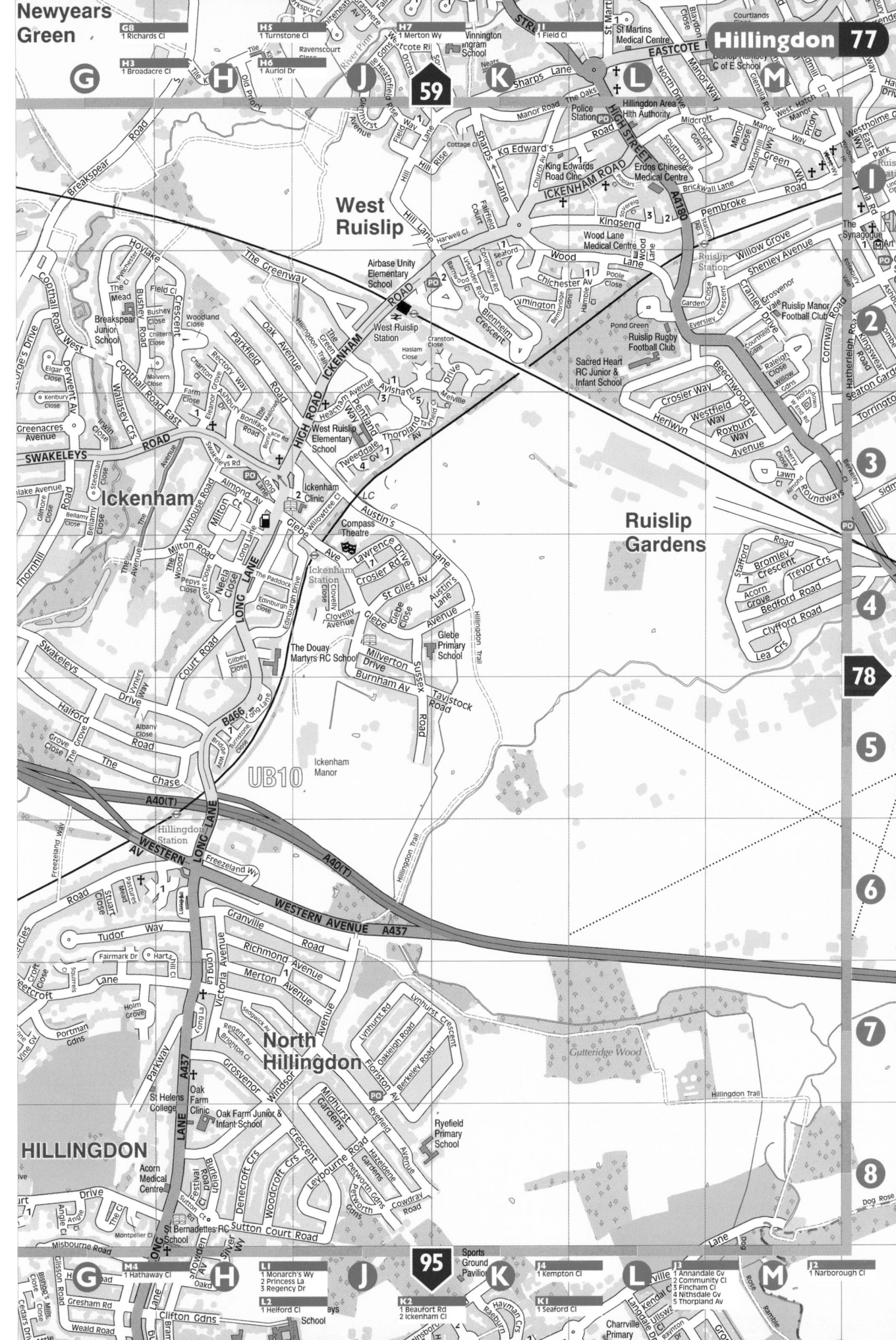

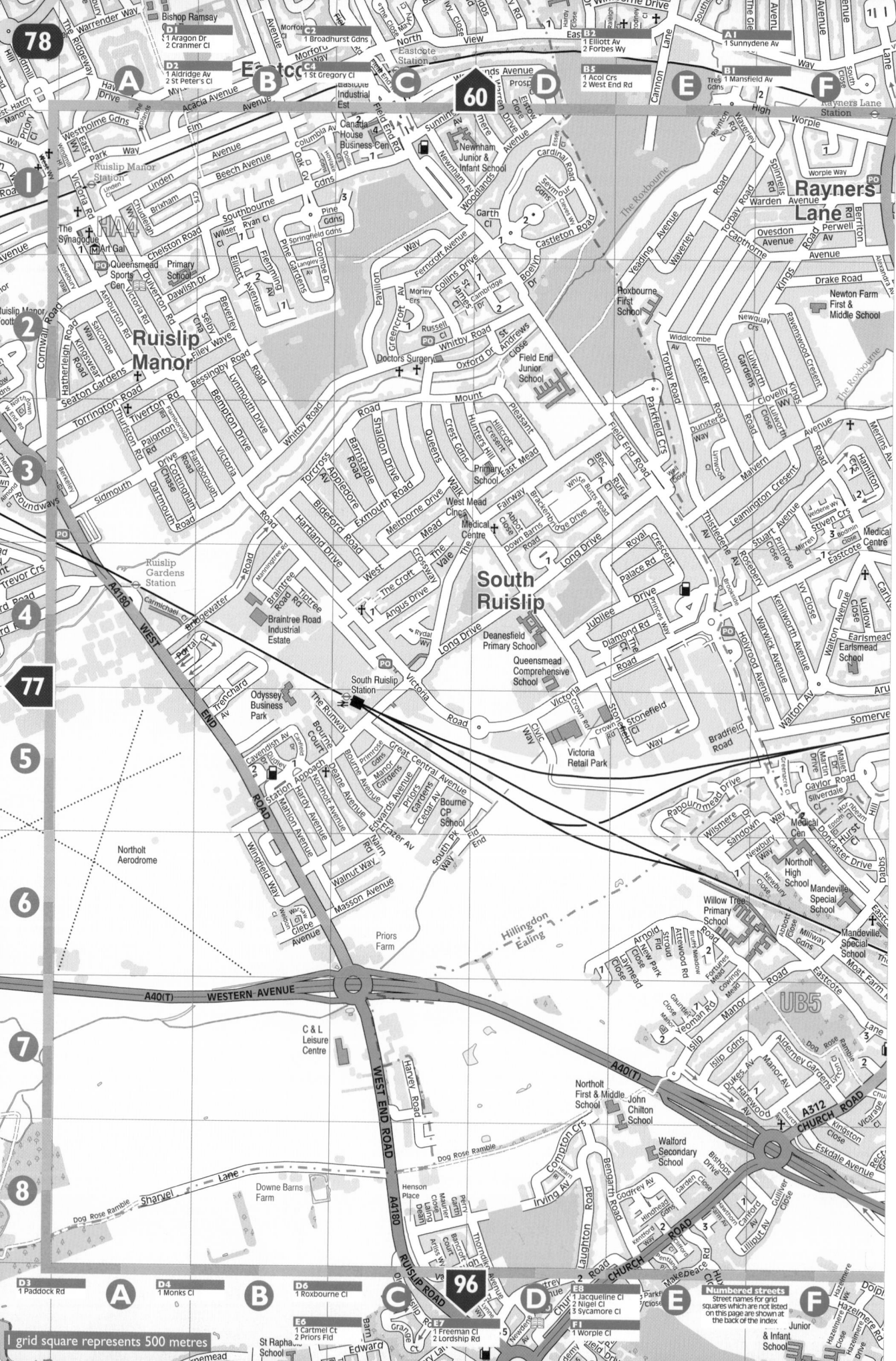

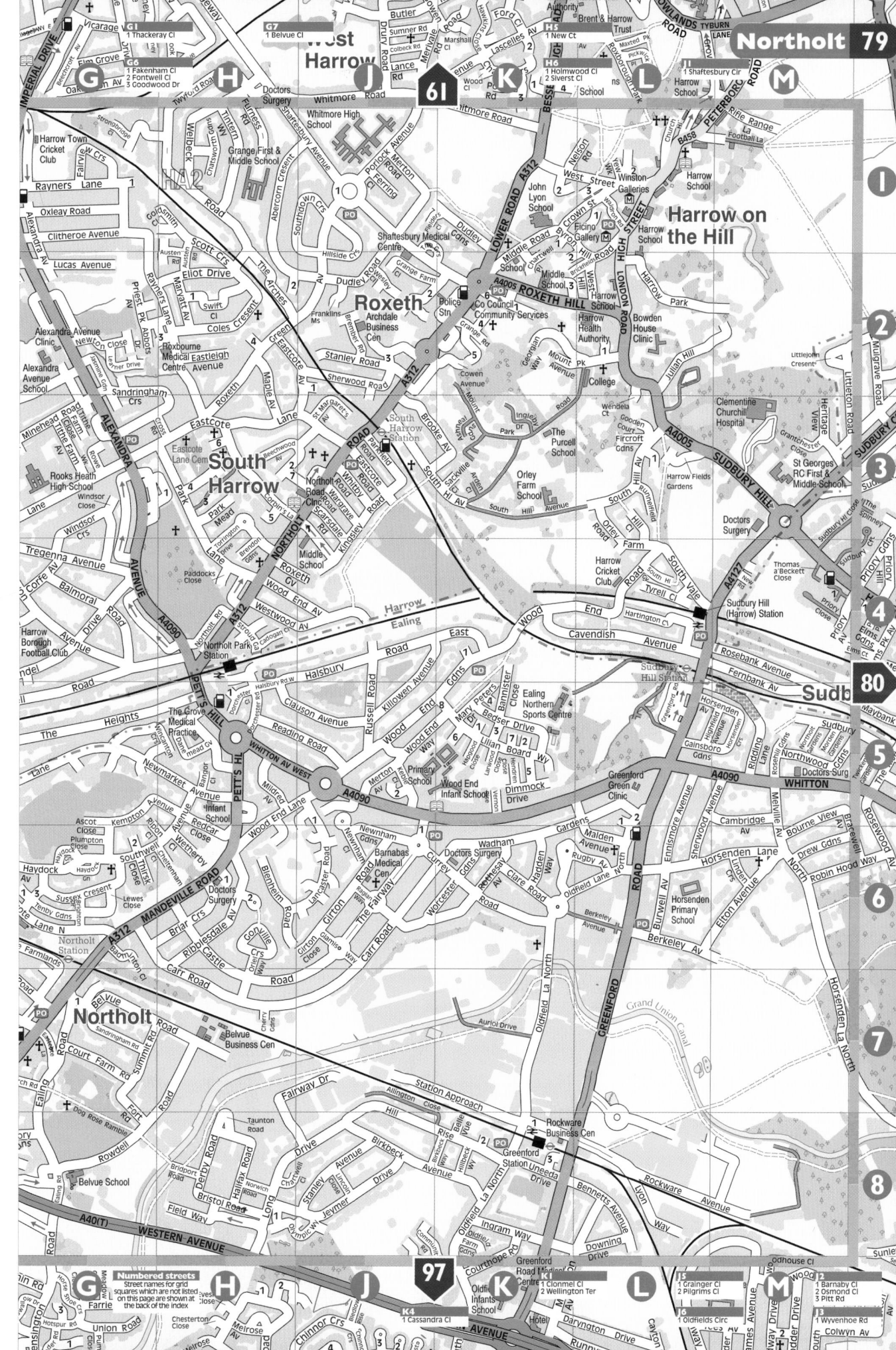

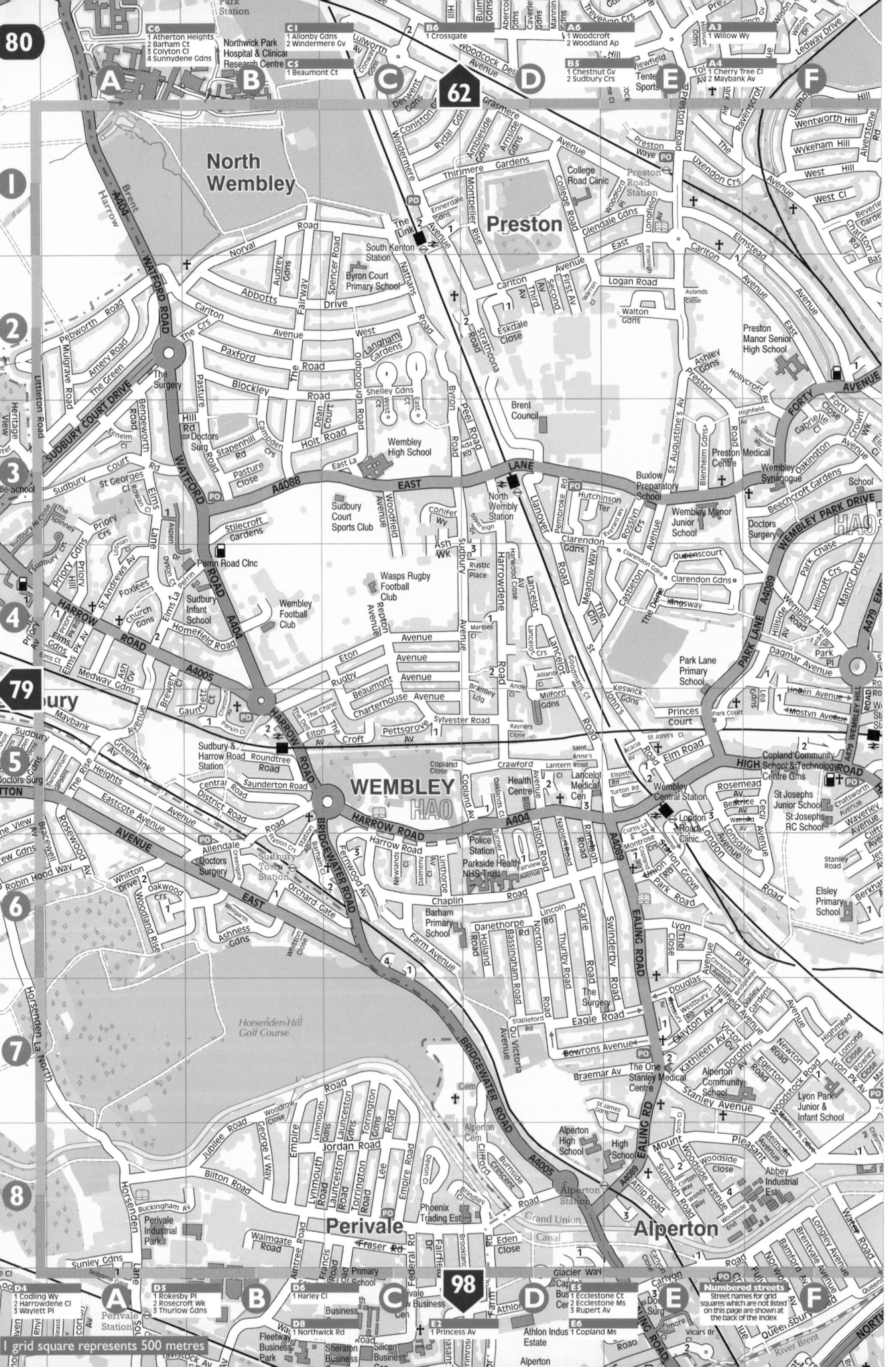

North
Wembley

Preston

WEMBLEY
HA0

Horsenden Hill
Golf Course

Perivale

Alperton

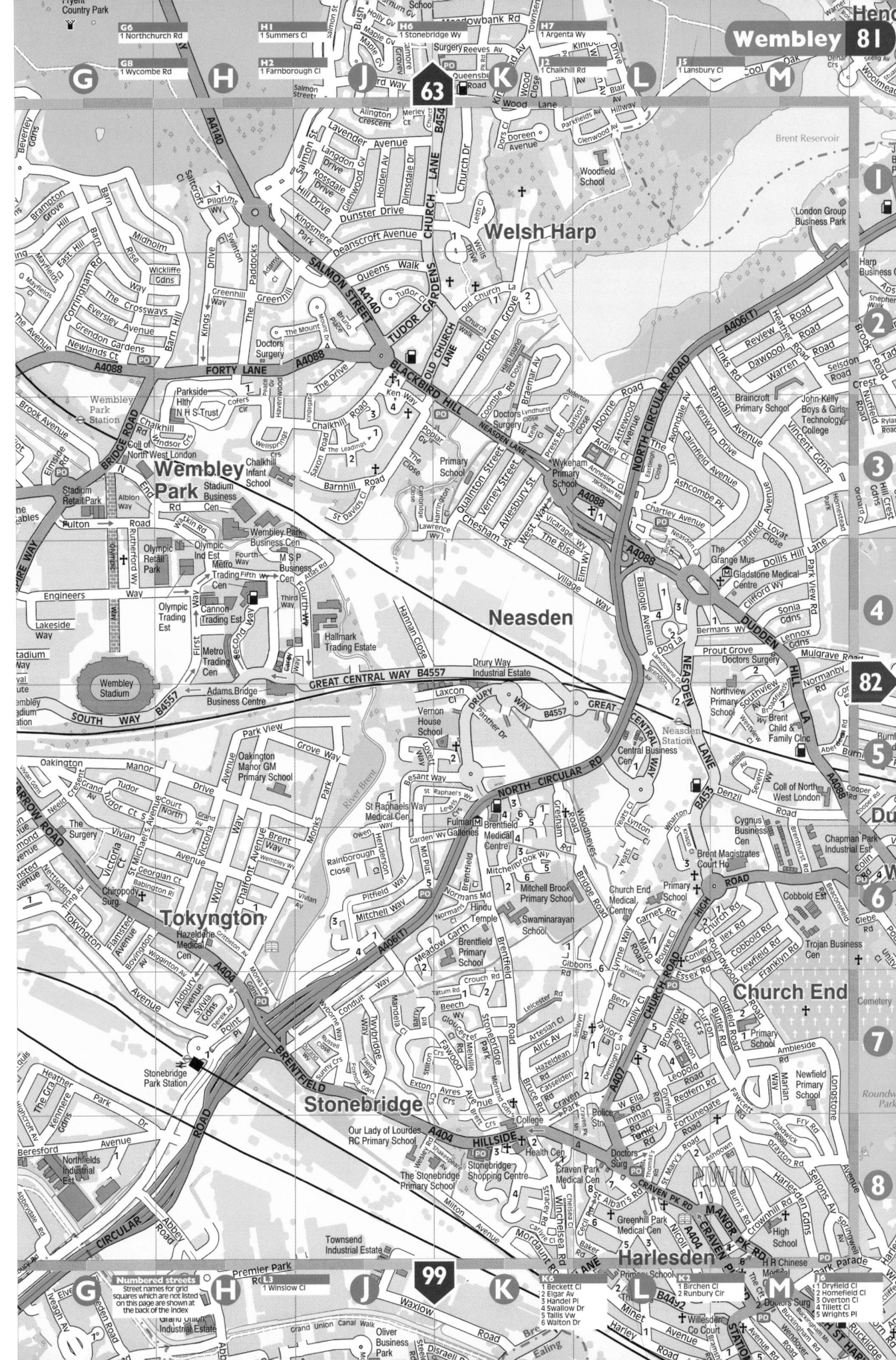

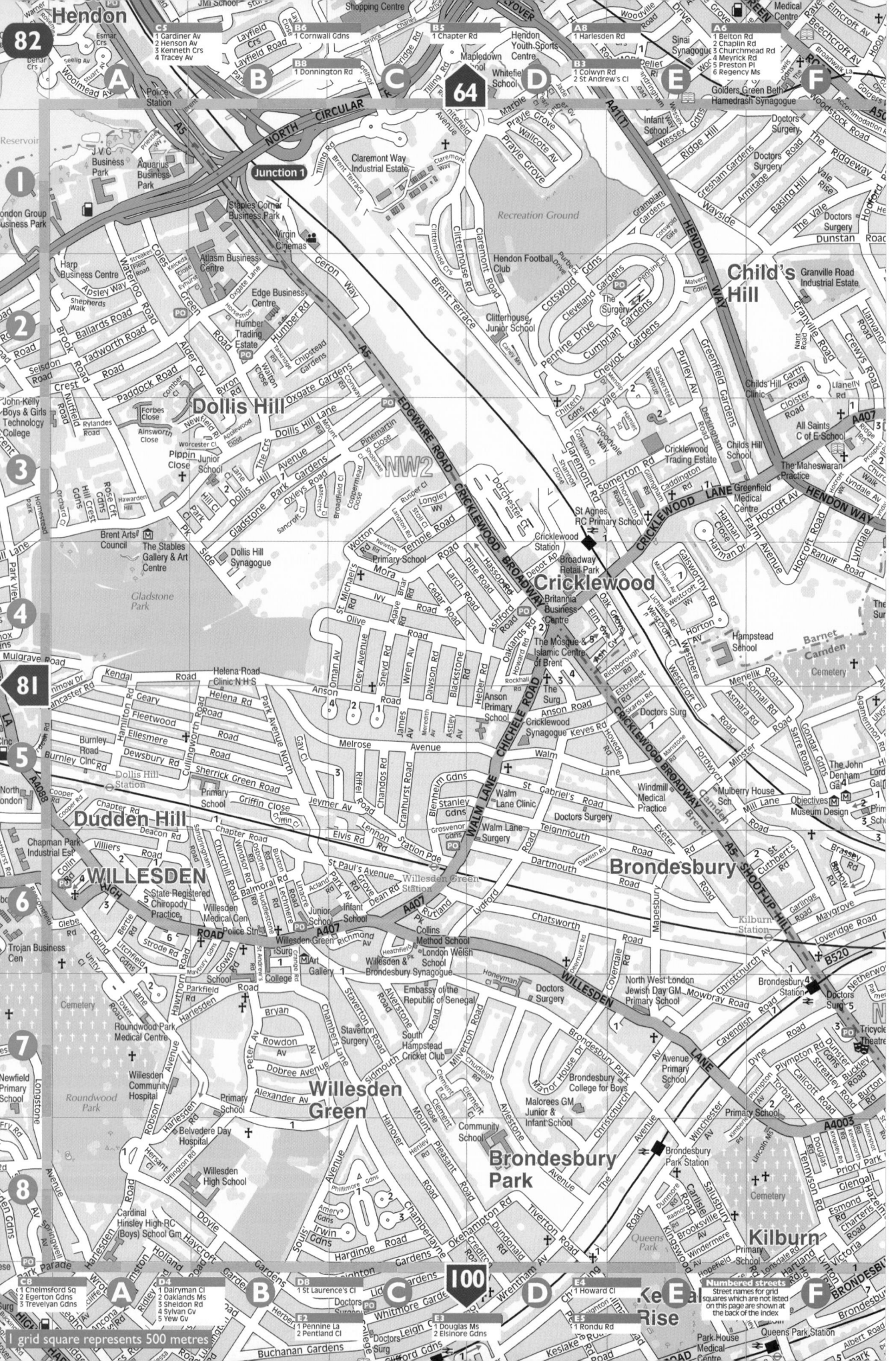

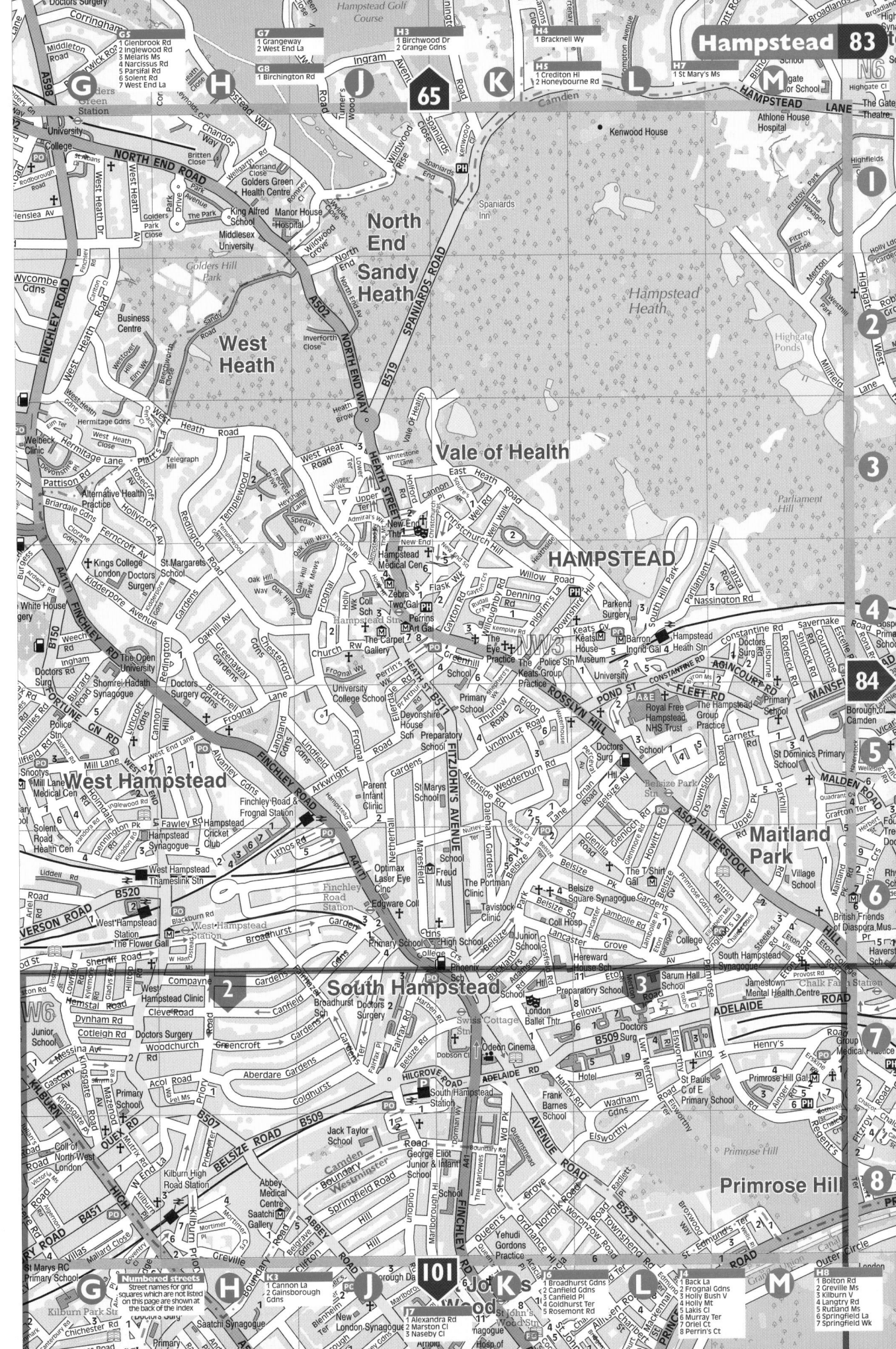

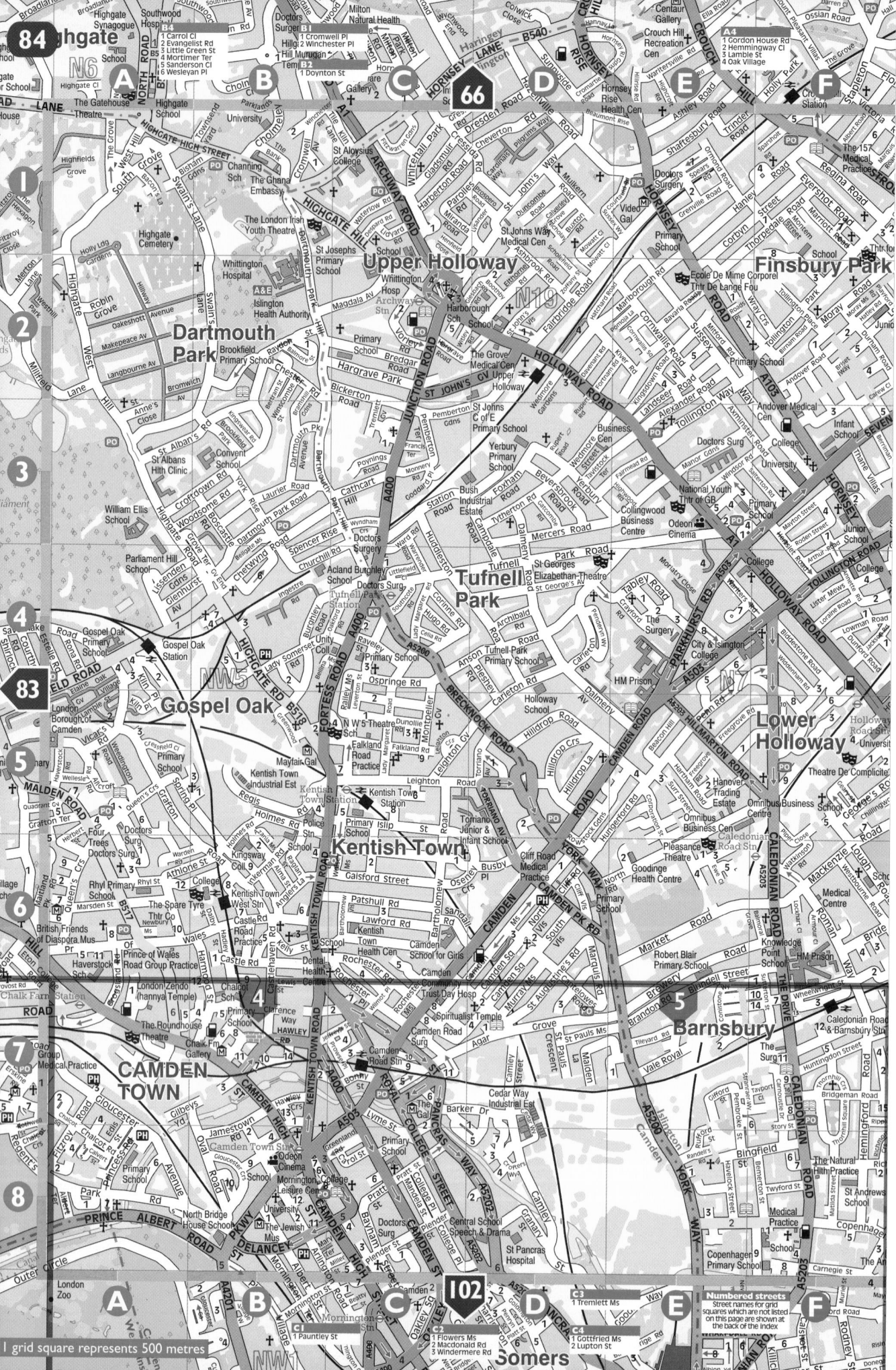

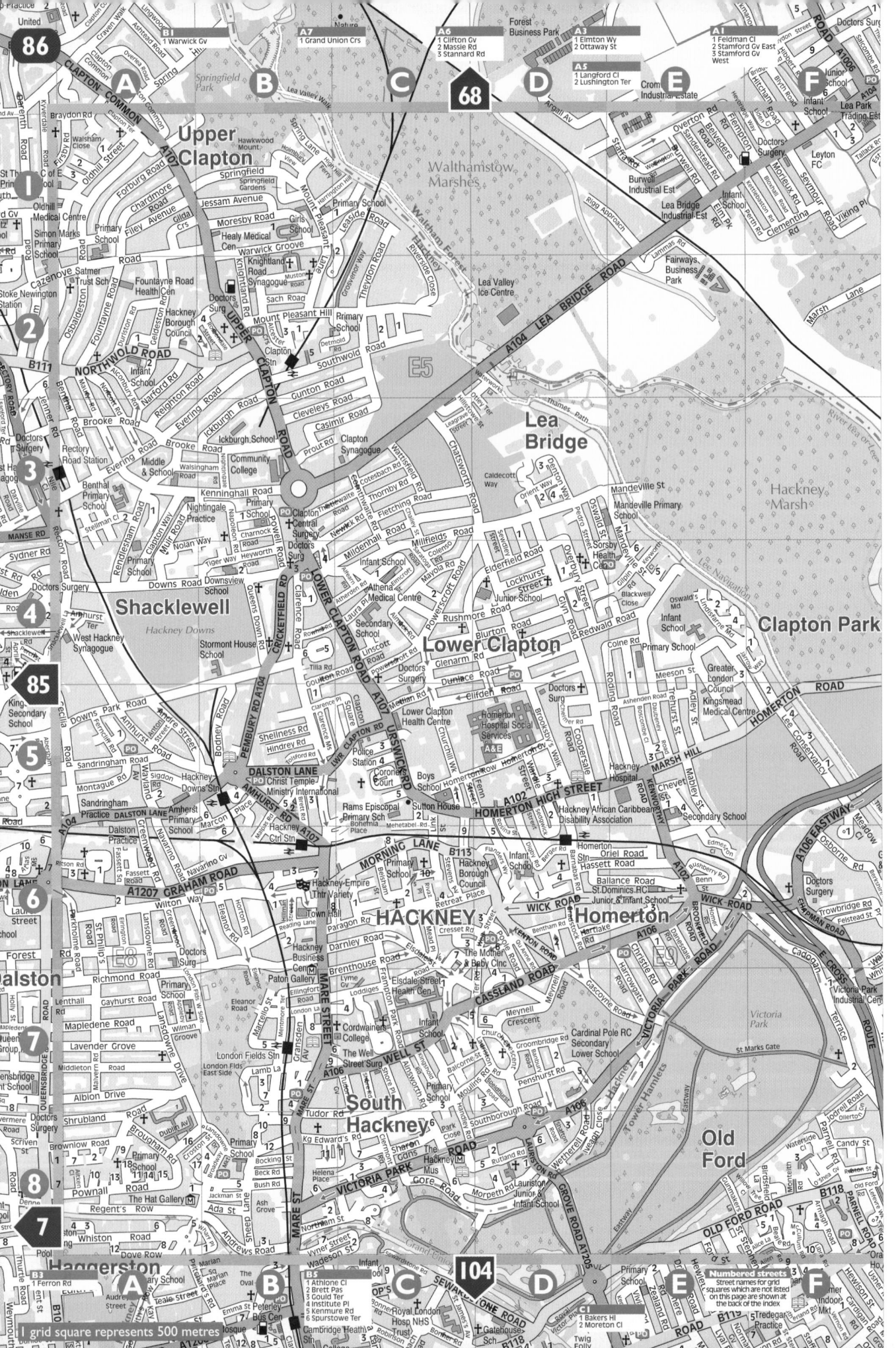

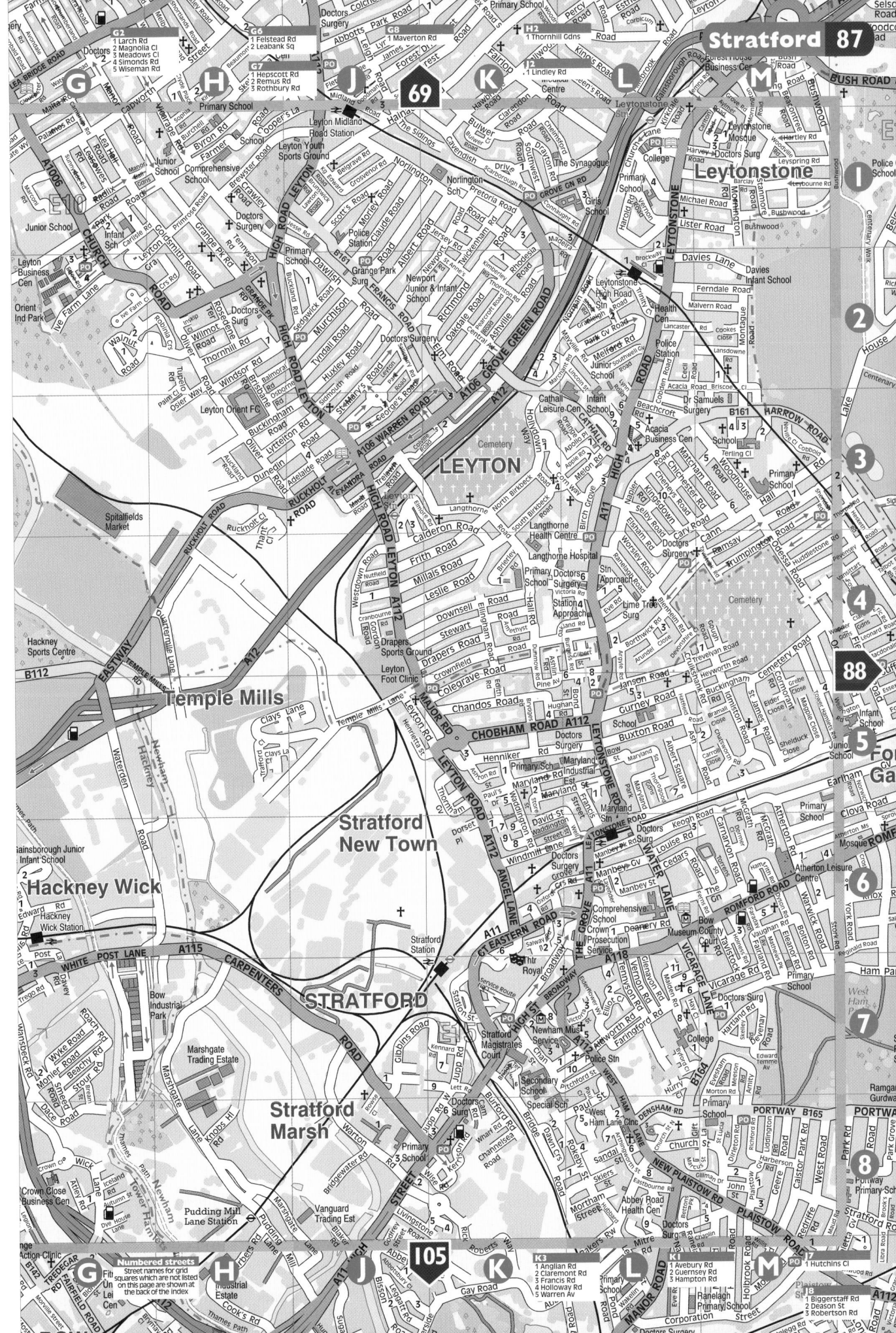

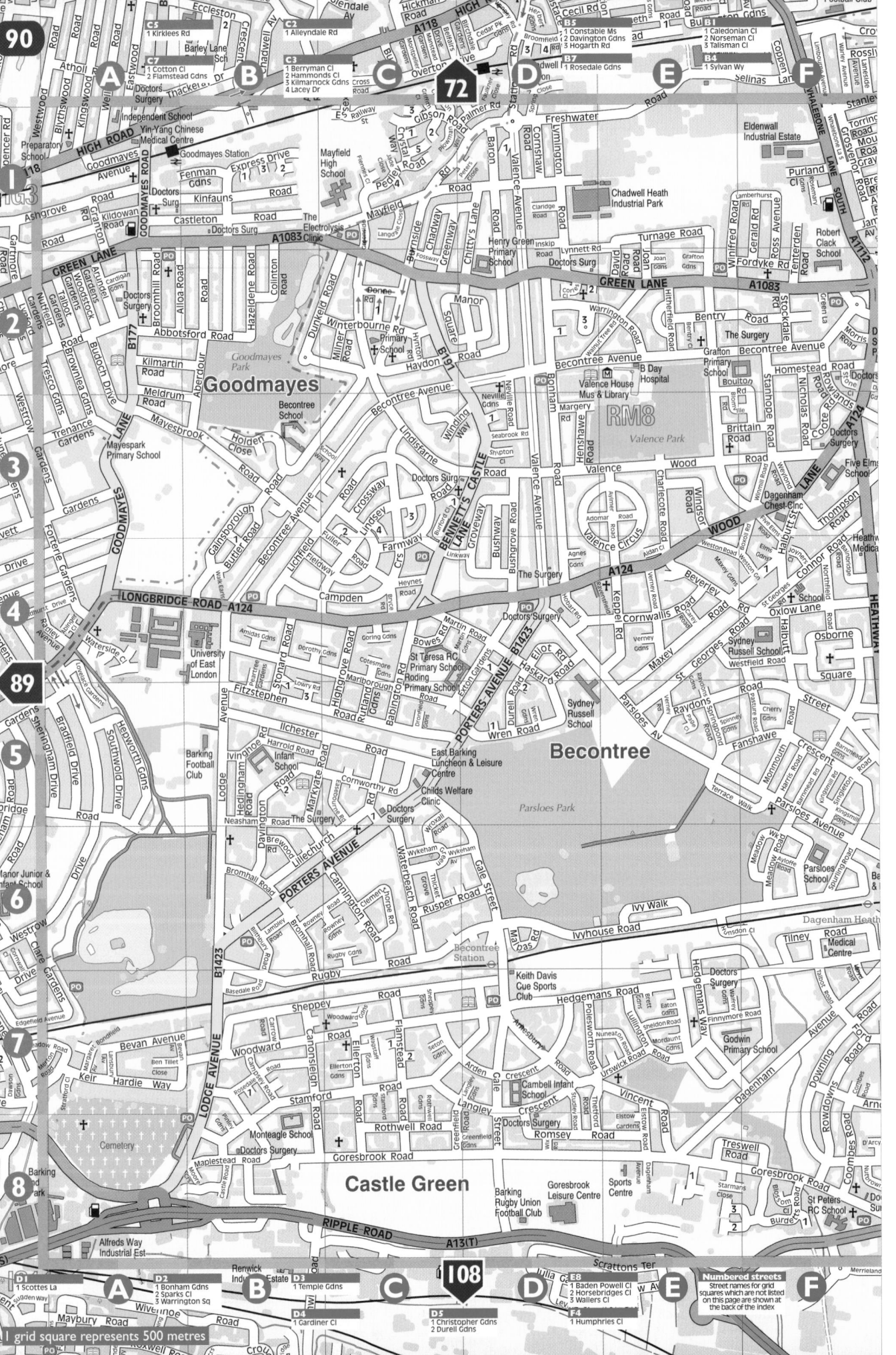

72

A   B   C   D   E   F

89

108

I grid square represents 500 metres

Goodmayes

Becontree

Castle Green

RM8

Valence Park

Parsloes Park

Chadwell Heath
Industrial Park

Eldenwall
Industrial Estate

Dagenham Heath

Numbered streets
Street names for grid
squares which are not listed
on this page are shown at
the back of the index

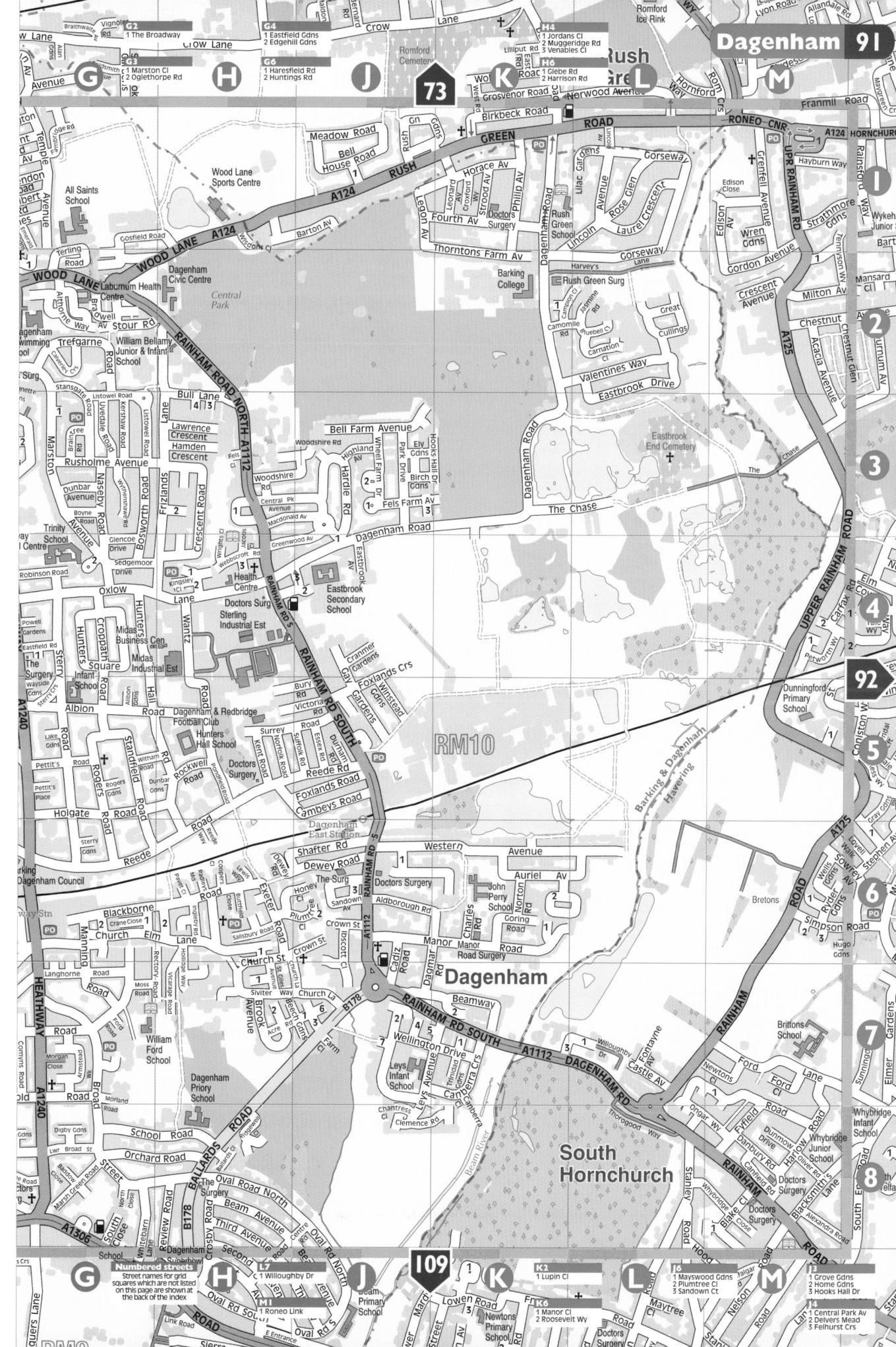

G1
1 Ashby Cl
2 Caernarvon Cl
3 Carisbrooke Cl
4 Lee Gardens Av

G4
1 Murfitt Wy
2 Park Rd

H2
1 Tyrelis Cl

H3
1 Brookdale Cl

G   H   J   **75**   K   **L** Cranham   M   Kerry Drive

Course

Wingletye
Rayburn Rd

Benets Road
Somerset Gdns
Hedingham Road
Tiptree Cl
Holme
Frimley Av
Falkirk
Way

Ashburnham Gardens
Engayne Gardens
Hall Lane
Courtenay Gardens
Grosvenor Gardens
Claremont Gdns
Eversleigh Gdns

Ingrebourne Gardens

Masefie
Spenser Crs
Holden
Marlborough
Hall
Mead
School
High Elms

Esdaile Gdns
Brookman
Doctors
Surgery
Dorkins
Wy
Rustic
Close
Chapperfield
Close

Kings Gardens
Briarleas Gdns
Front Lane
Plough
Rise

Nathan Ct
Heron

Nightingale
Avenue

Swan Av

I

Westbury
Farm

Peterborough AV
Canterbury
St Albans Av
Worcester Av
Winchester Av
Chester Av
Boyd Sch
Lichfield Ter

B187

2

Berkeley Drive
Gunster Crs
Berkeley Cl
Waldegrave Gdns
Deyncourt Gardens

Upminster Station
UPMINSTER

Rectory Gdns
Front Lane

Ashvale Gdns
Westbury Terrace
Ashvale

Oglethorpe
County Junior
& Infant School

Pike Lane

Upminster
Bridge Station
A124 ST MARY'S LANE
Hill Ri
Church
Highview Gdns
Carlton Cl
Cranborne Gdns
Branfill Rd
Howard   Road
Gaynes Rd
St Lawrence Road
B187
Eaton Road
The Chase

Norfolk Road
Clarence Av
Boundary
St Joseph's
School
Infant
School
The Sacred Heart
of Mary RC School
Upminster
Primary
School
Cedar Gdns
New Pl Gardens
Argyle
Derham Gardens
Doctors Surgery
Sunnyside   Gardens
Tudor Gardens

Cranham
Hall

3

Brookdale Av
Bridge Av
B1421
Stewart Avenue
Springfield
The Shrubbery
Gardens
Roxburgh Av
Ashleigh Gdns
Gardens

South
View
Drive
Oak Av
Maple Av
Beech Av
Elm Avenue
Meadow Way
Leasway
Fairfield Av
Rushmere Av
CORBETS
The Ap

Branfil Junior &
Infant School
Cedar Avenue
Acacia Drive
Sycamore Avenue
Beech
Avenue Surgery
Gaynes Park Road
Pine
Ct
Doctors
Surgery
Meistock Avenue
Coniston   Avenue
TEY
Brackendale Gdns

4

Hobbs
Hole

Gaynes
Park
Road
Little
Gaynes
Lane
Gaynes Ct
Little Gaynes Gardens
Doctors Surg
Cranston   Park   Avenue
The
Tawny Avenue
Freshfields Av
Longwood Close
Gaynes School

5

Grove
Clayton Avenue
Corbets Av
Parkland   Avenue
ROAD
Foxhall Road
Meadowside Rd
Huntsmans Dr
The Gld
Upminster
Cemetery

B1421

**Corbets
Tey**
Corbets
Tey Sch
B1421

Manor
Farm

6

Park
Farm
Road
Harwood   Hall   Lane
Harwood
Hall
OCKENDON ROAD
Stubbers (Outdoor
Pursuits Centre)

Show Jumping/
Equestrian Circuit

Gerpins Lane
Aveley Road
Sunnings Lane
Stubbers   Lane

7

Dennises La

8

Bramble
Farm
Bramble   Lane
Dennises   Lane
Dennises
Baldwins

 Kerr

Numbered streets
Street names for grid
squares which are not listed
on this page are shown at
the back of the index

L1
1 Blenheim Cl
2 Marlborough Cl
3 Swift Cl
4 Tern Gdns

J5
1 Hall Park Rd
2 Londons Cl

J2
1 Aylett Rd
2 Garbutt Rd

H5
1 Tadlows Cl

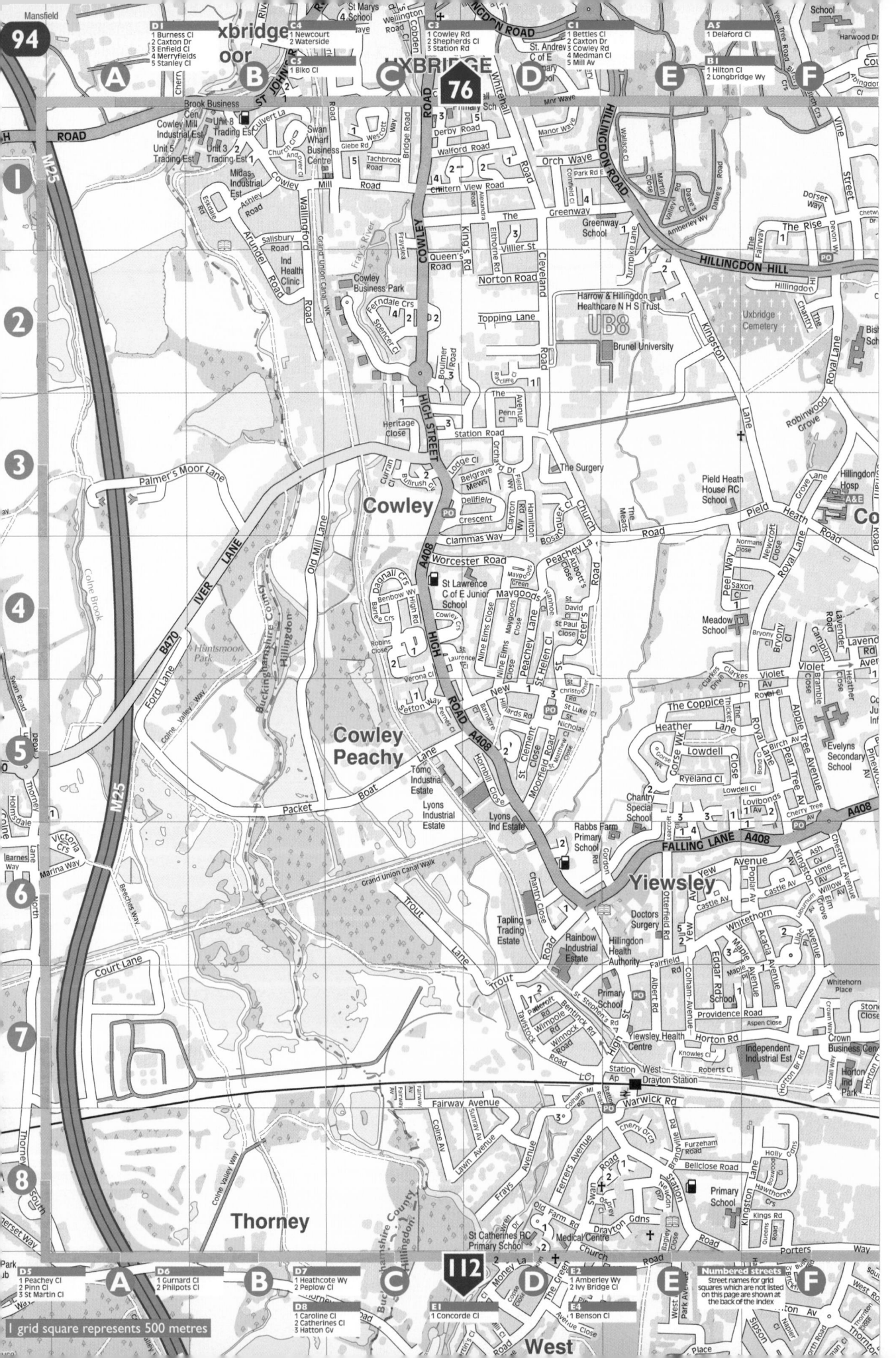

xbridge oor

UXBRIDGE

76

M25

ROAD

Mansfield

Brook Business Cen
Cowley Mill Industrial Est
Unit 8 Trading Est
Unit 5 Trading Est
Unit 3 Trading Est
Midas Industrial Est
Ashley Road
Salisbury Road
Ind Health Clinic

Culvert La
Andover
Church
Cowley
Wallingford Road
Arundel Road
Escdale Rd

St John's
St John's Rd

Wescott Way
Glebe Rd
Tachbrook Road
Swan Wharf Business Centre
Mill
Frays River
Cowley Business Park
Ferndale Crs
Spencer Cl
Bourne Road

HIGH STREET
COWLEY ROAD
BRIDGE

Wellington Road
Cobden
Derby Road
Walford Road
Chiltern View Road
Queen's Road
Norton Road
Topping Lane
The Villier St
Cleveland Road
Station Road

NORTON ROAD
Primary Sch
St. Andrew C of E
Manor Way
Orch Wave
King's Rd
Ethorne Rd
Alexandra
Hamilton Rd W

Hillingdon
Wallace Rd
Orch Wave
Park Rd E
Cornfield Cl
Greenway
Greenway School
Harrow & Hillingdon Healthcare N H S Trust
Brunel University
UB8

HILLINGDON ROAD
Martin Rd
Dawe's Road
Turnpike Lane
Amberley Wy
Kingston Lane
HILLINGDON HILL
Uxbridge Cemetery
Robinwood Grove

Delaford Cl
Harwood Dr
School
Vine Tree Road
The Fairway
The Rise
Dorset Way
Devon Wy
Hillingdon
Chantry
Royal Lane
Hillingdon Hosp
A&E
Co

I

2

3

Palmer's Moor Lane
Colne Brook
Huntsmoor Park
IVER LANE
B470
Ford Lane
Colne Valley Way
Hillingdon
Buckinghamshire County

Cowley

Heritage Close
Curran
Bullrush Cl
Lodge Cl
Belgrave Mews
Dellfield
Crescent
Clammas Way
Worcester Road
St Lawrence C of E Junior School
Dagnall Crs
Benbow Wy
Barrie Crs
High Rd
Robins Close
Verona Cl
Sefton Cl
Cowley Crs
St Lawrence
New
Hillards Rd
Barnakre
Clement Close
Moorfield Close
Matthews Close
Nicholas
St Luke
St Christopher Rd
St David
St Paul Close
Peters
Maygoods Close
Nine Elms Close
Maygoods Lane
Peachey Lane
Abbot's Close
Bosanquet Rd
Church Rd
St Helen Cl

The Surgery
The Meads
Pield Heath House RC School
Pield Heath Road
Peel Way
Saxon Cl
Meadow School
Bryony
Lavender Rd
Campion Cl
Violet Av
Violet Cl
The Coppice
Heather Lane
Royal Lane
Grove Lane
Newcourt Close
Normans Close
Evelyns Secondary School

4

5

Cowley Peachy

Boat
Packet
Trout Lane
Grand Union Canal Walk
Tomo Industrial Estate
Lyons Industrial Estate
Lyons Ind Estate
Hornbill Close
Sefton Cl
Fernie Cl

The Coppice
Heather
Lowdell
Ryeland Cl
Lowdell Cl
Chantry Special School
Lovibonds Av
Birch Av
Pear Tree Av
Apple Tree Avenue
Cherry Tree
Gorse Wk
GOSE WK
Royal Lane
A408
PO

5

6

Victoria Crs
Marina Way
Barnes Way
Beeches Way
M25
Holmsdale
Thornley
Colne

Court Lane

Rabbs Farm Primary School
Tapling Trading Estate
Rainbow Industrial Estate
Hillingdon Health Authority
Chantry Close
Gordon
FALLING LANE A408
Yiewsley
Doctors Surgery
Otterfield Rd
Yew Avenue
Poplar Av
Castle Av
Castle Av
Whitethorn
Acacia Avenue
Edgar Rd
Maple Avenue
Lilac
Labaurnum
Elm Grove
Willow
Fairfield Rd
Colham Avenue
Providence Road
Aspen Close
Ash
Kingston Lane
Chestnut Avenue
Lime
Crown Business Cen
Whitehorn Place

6

7

8

Thorney

Trout Lane
Fairway Av
Fairway
Coin
Coin Av
Lawn Avenue
Frays Avenue
Sunray Av
Ferrers Avenue
Fairway Avenue
Pattercroft
Wimpole Road
Winnock Road
Bentinck Rd
Tavistock
St Stephen's Rd
Primary School
Yiewsley Health Centre
Horton Rd
Knowles Cl
Roberts Cl
LC
Station Ap
West Drayton Station
Warwick Rd
Independent Industrial Est
Horton Br Rd
Horton Ind Park
Crown

7

8

St Catherines RC Primary School
Drayton Gdns
Frays Avenue
Old Farm Av
Money La
Coln
Coleridge
Coin
Swan Road
Station Road
Medical Centre
Church Road
Cherry Orch
Furzeham Rd
Bellclose Road
Holly
Hawthorne Crs
Kings Rd
Bagley Close
Kingston Road
Porters
West Way
Sipson

West

112

1 grid square represents 500 metres

A   B   C   D   E   F

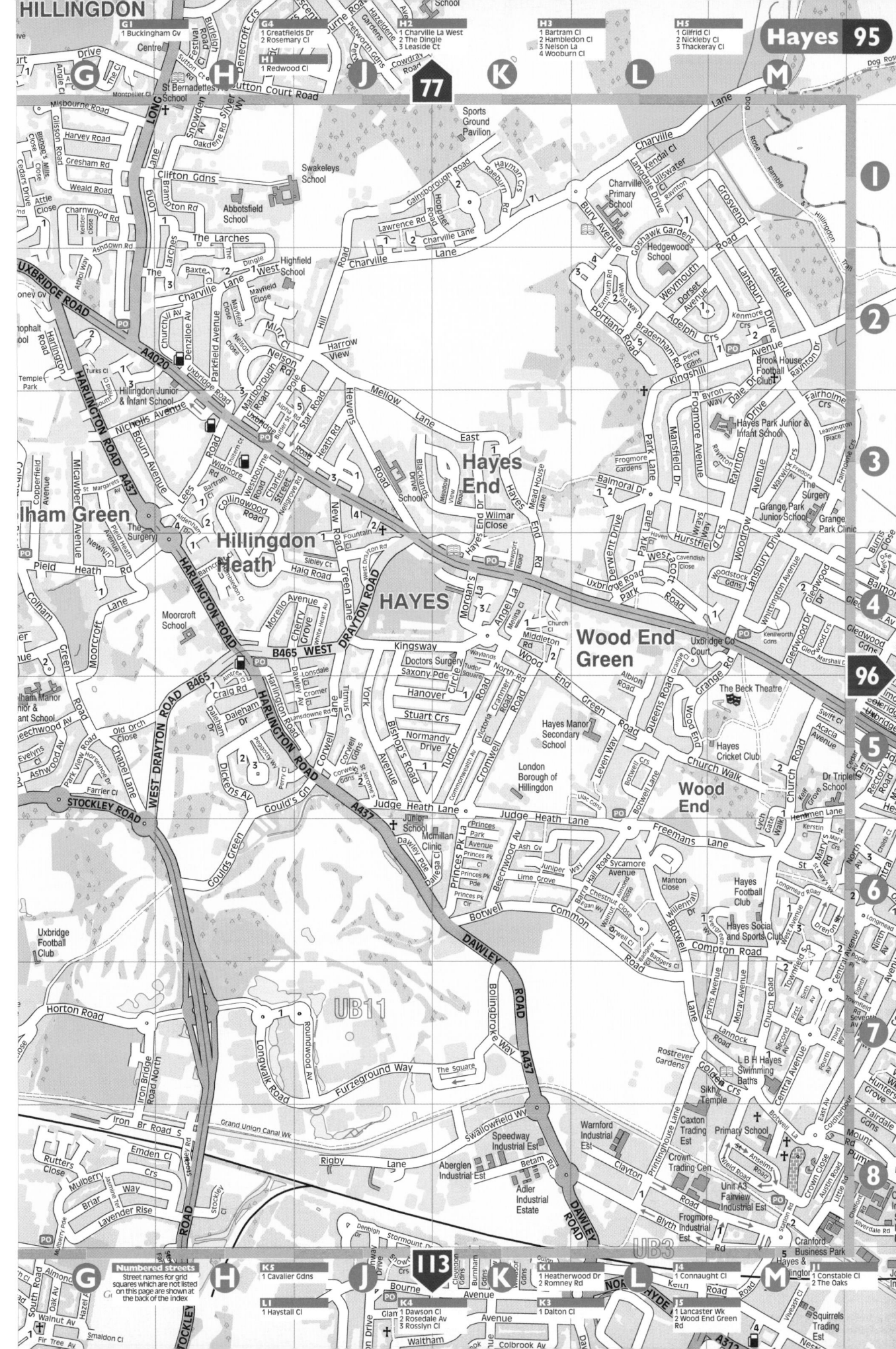

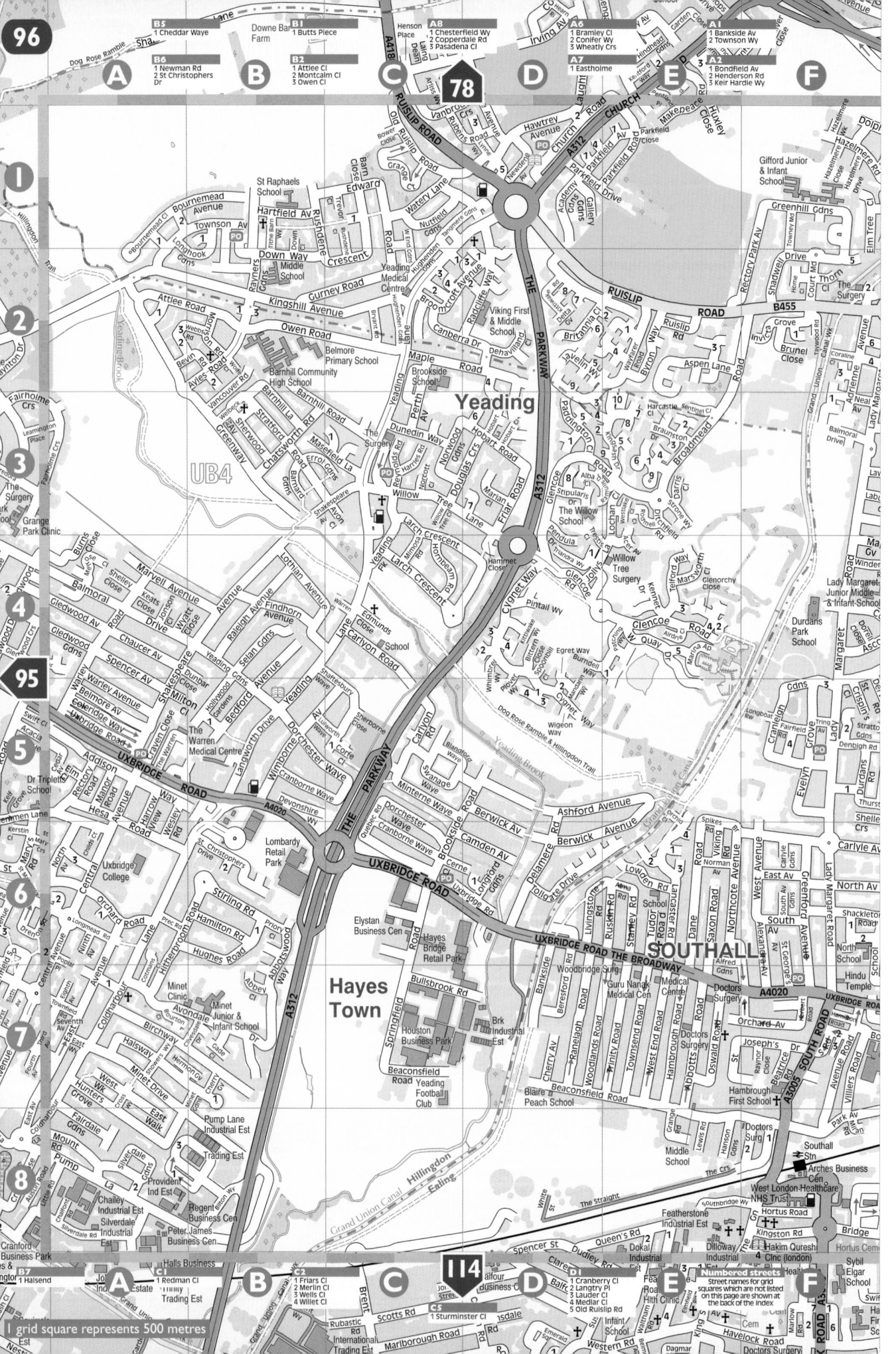

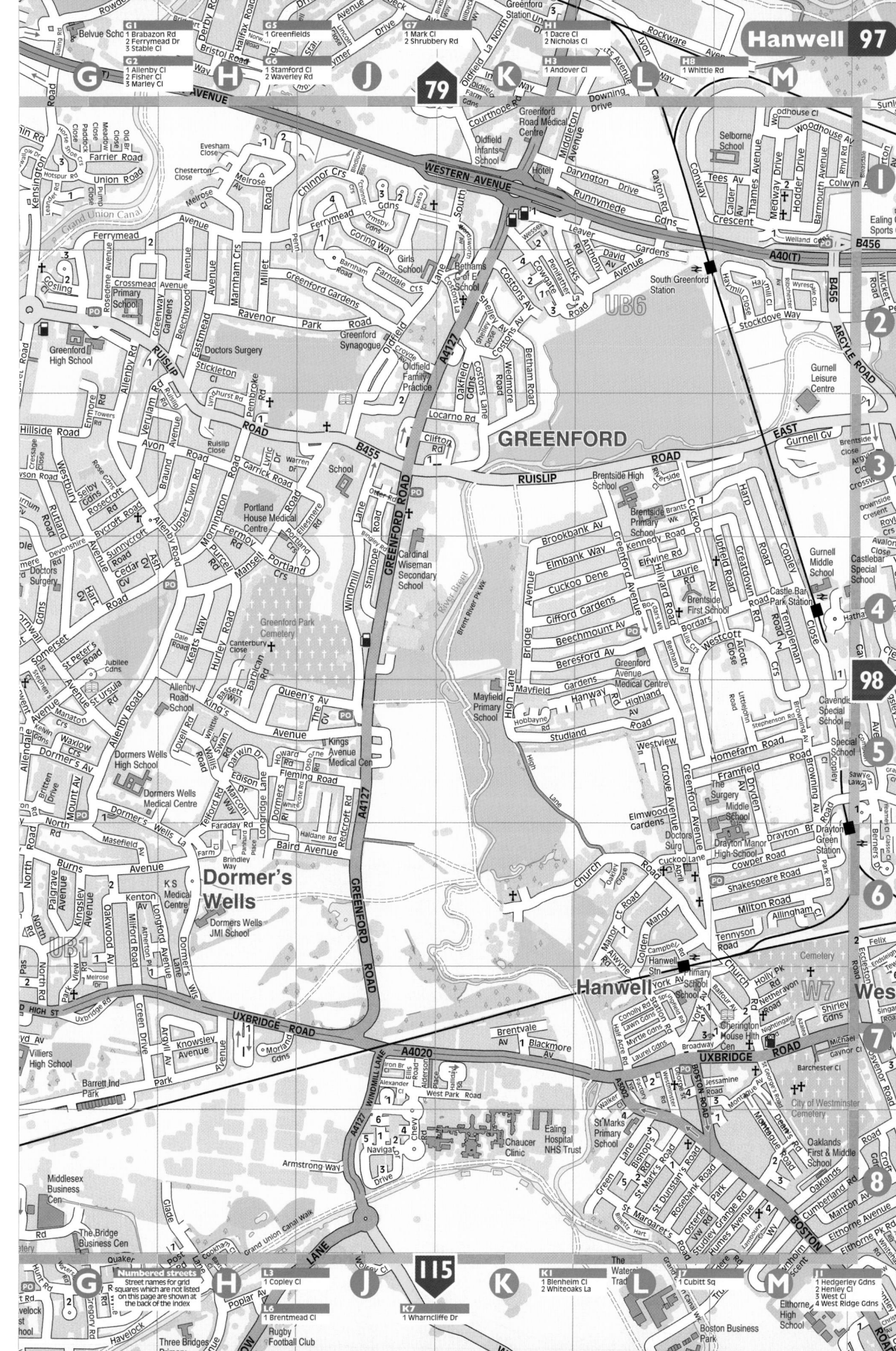

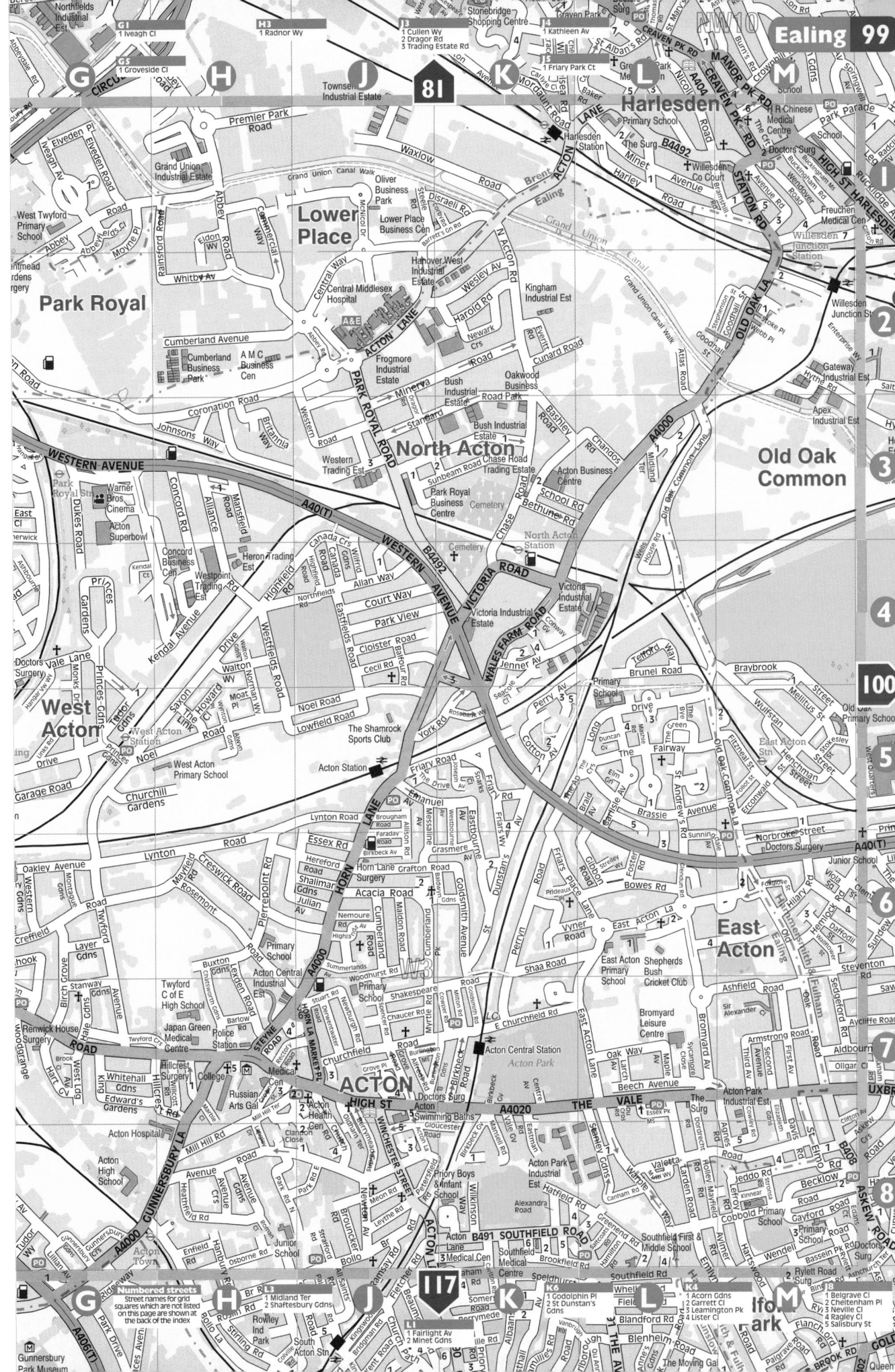

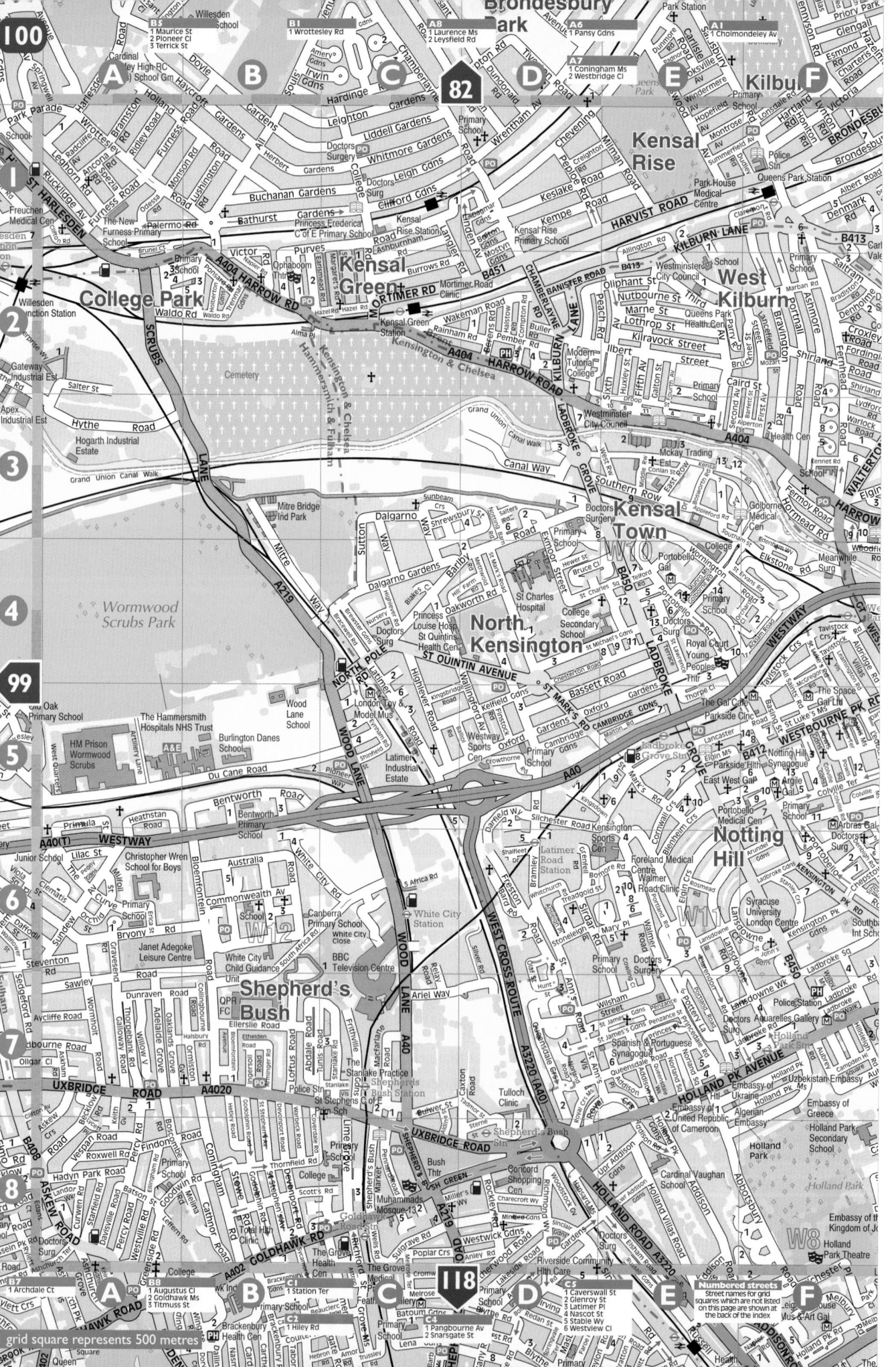

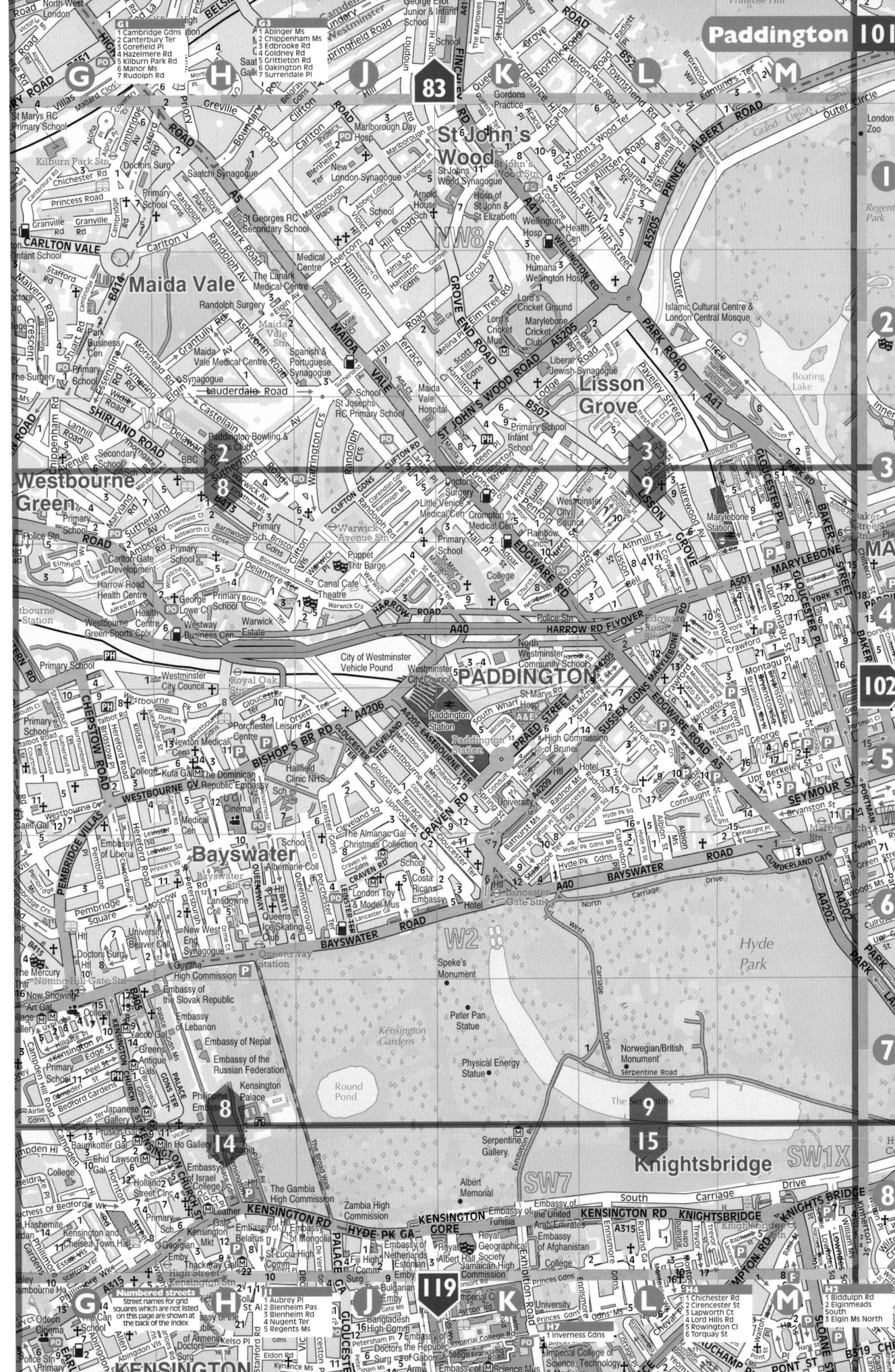

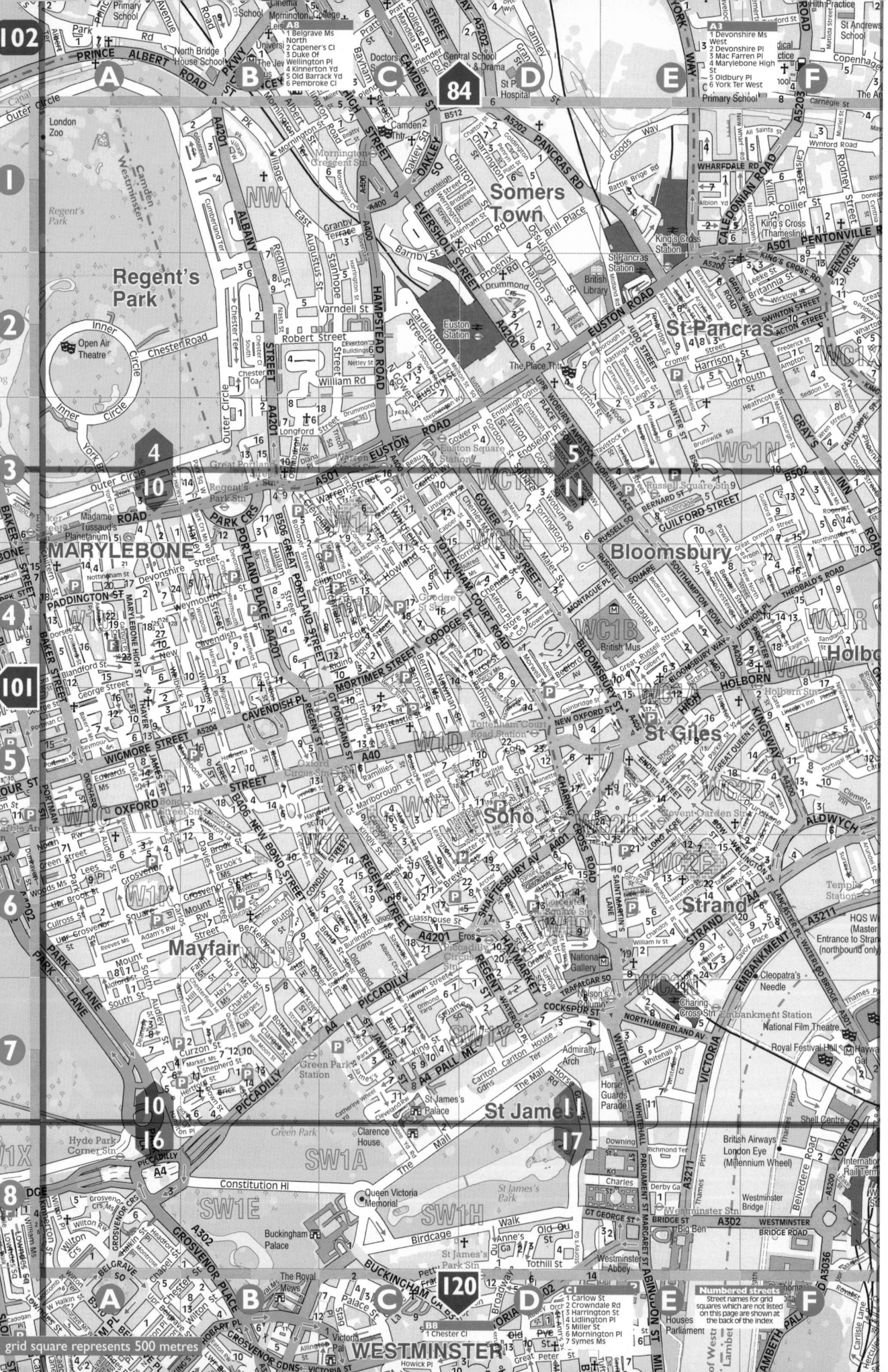

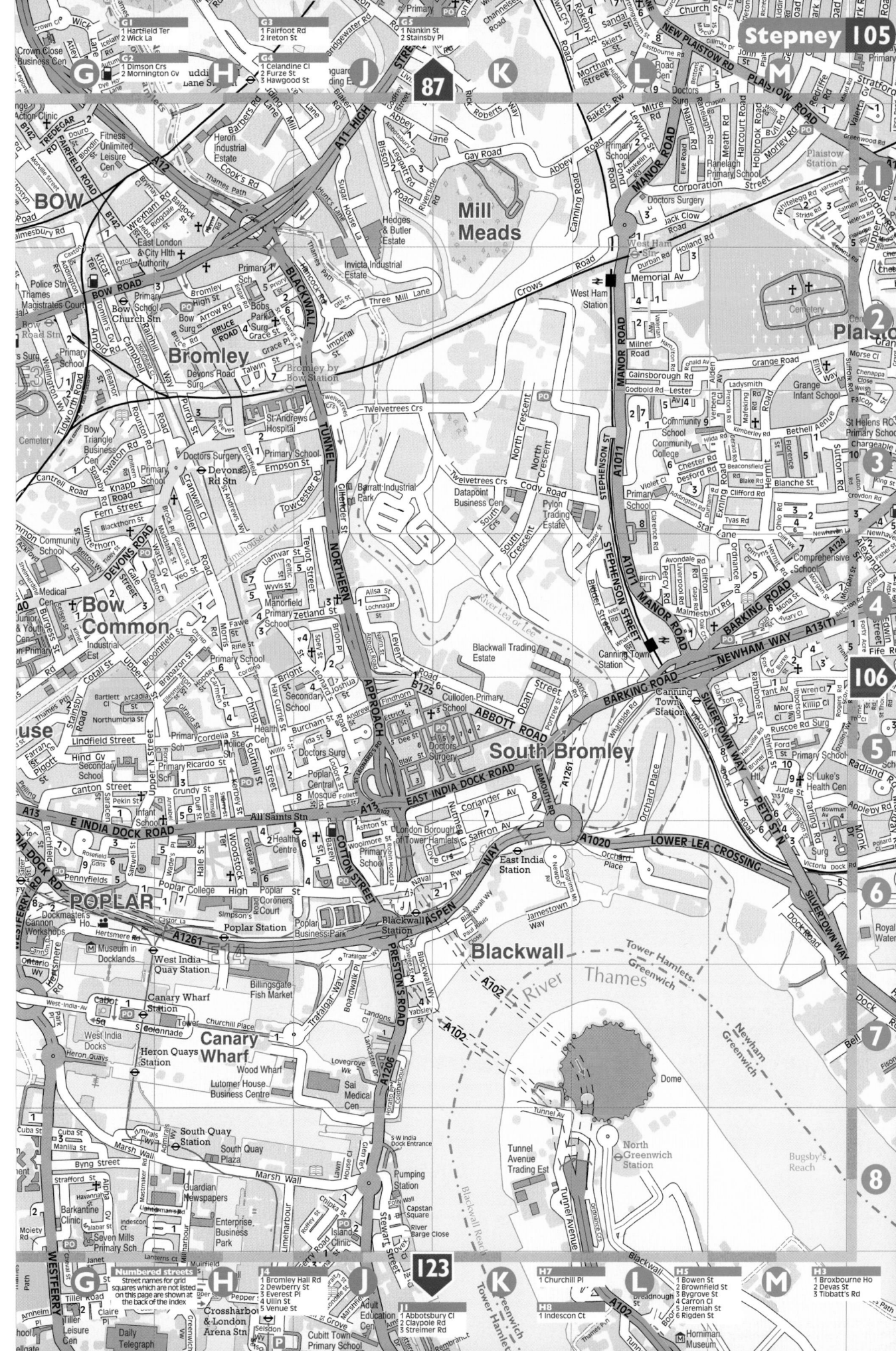

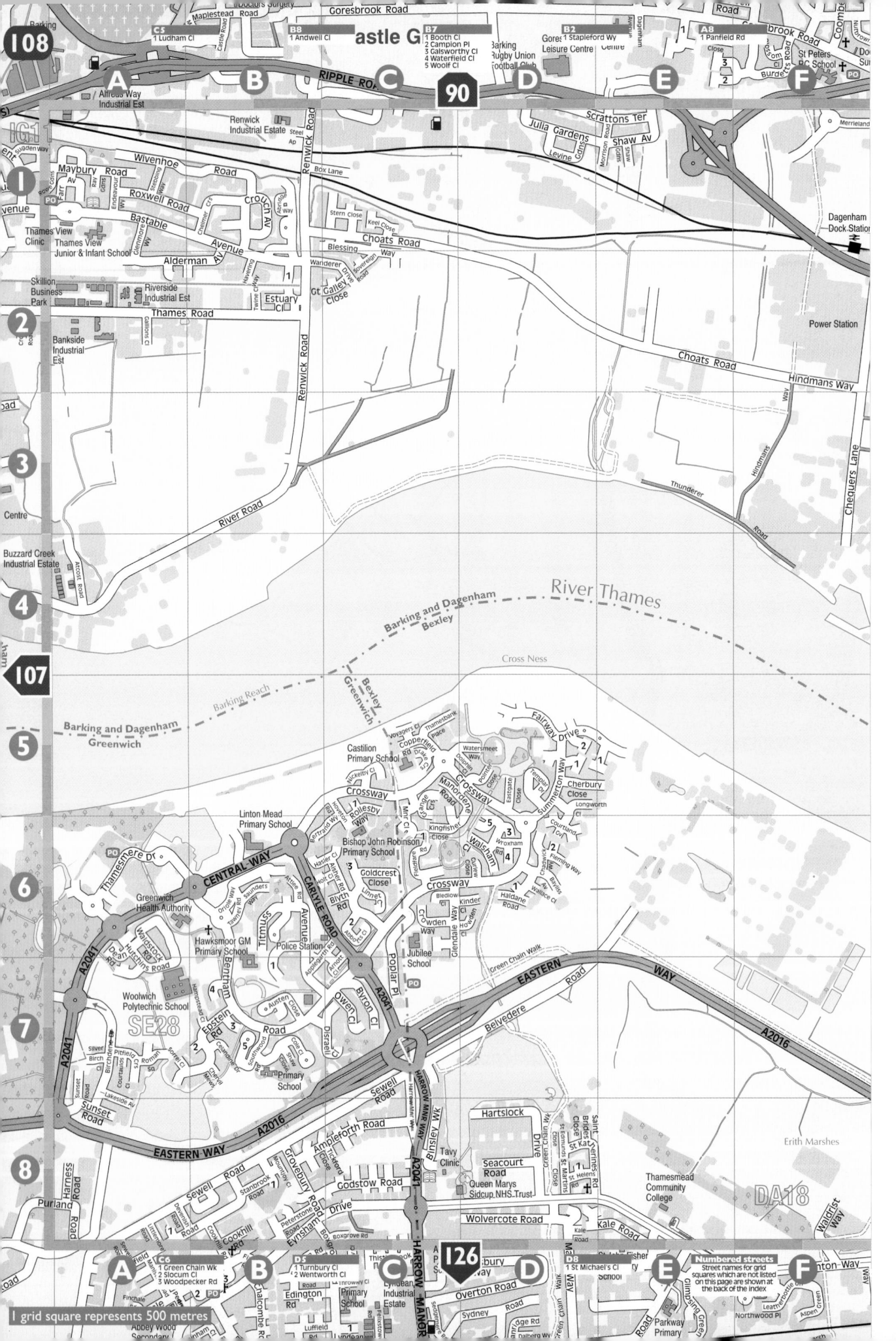

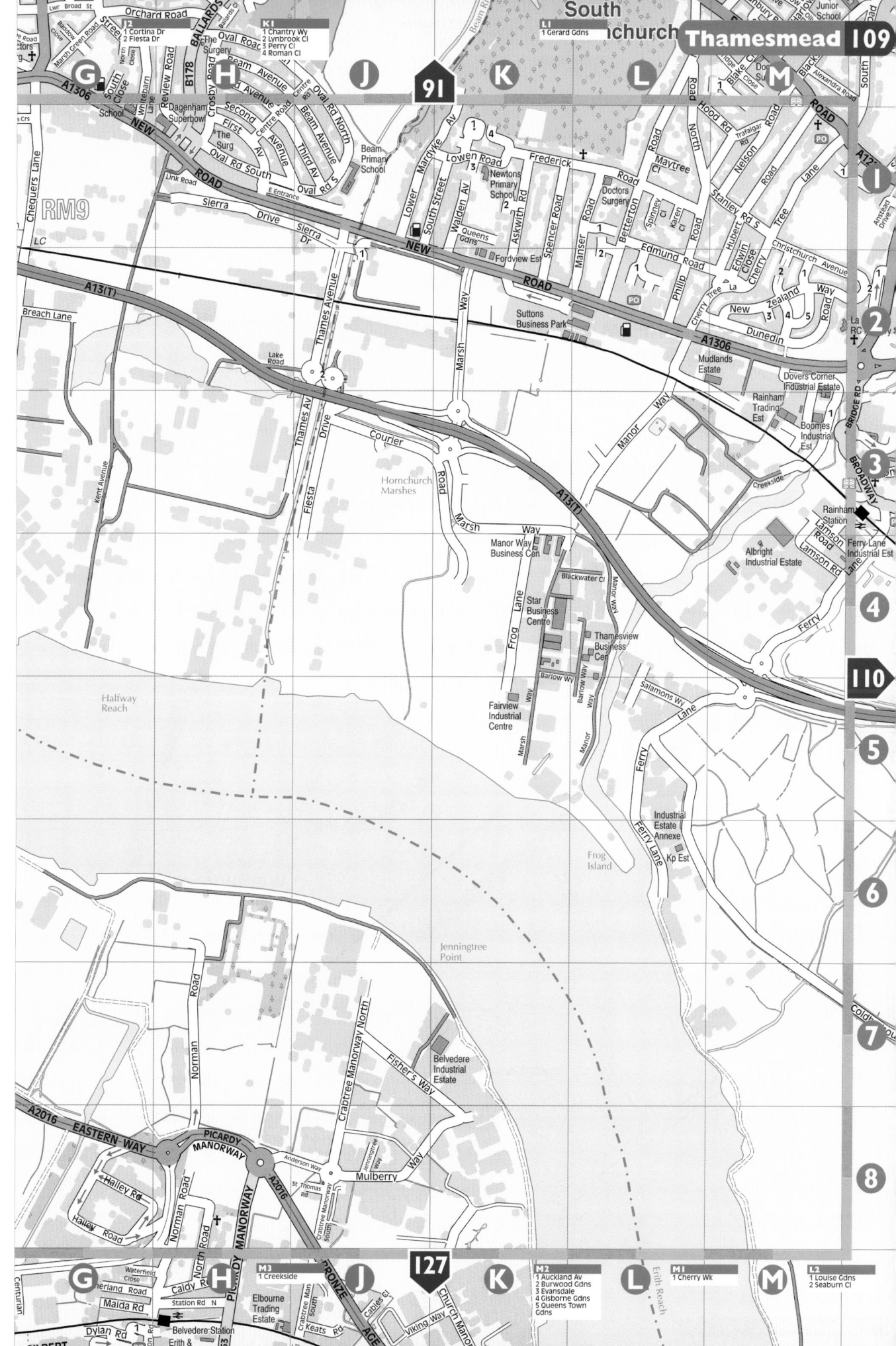

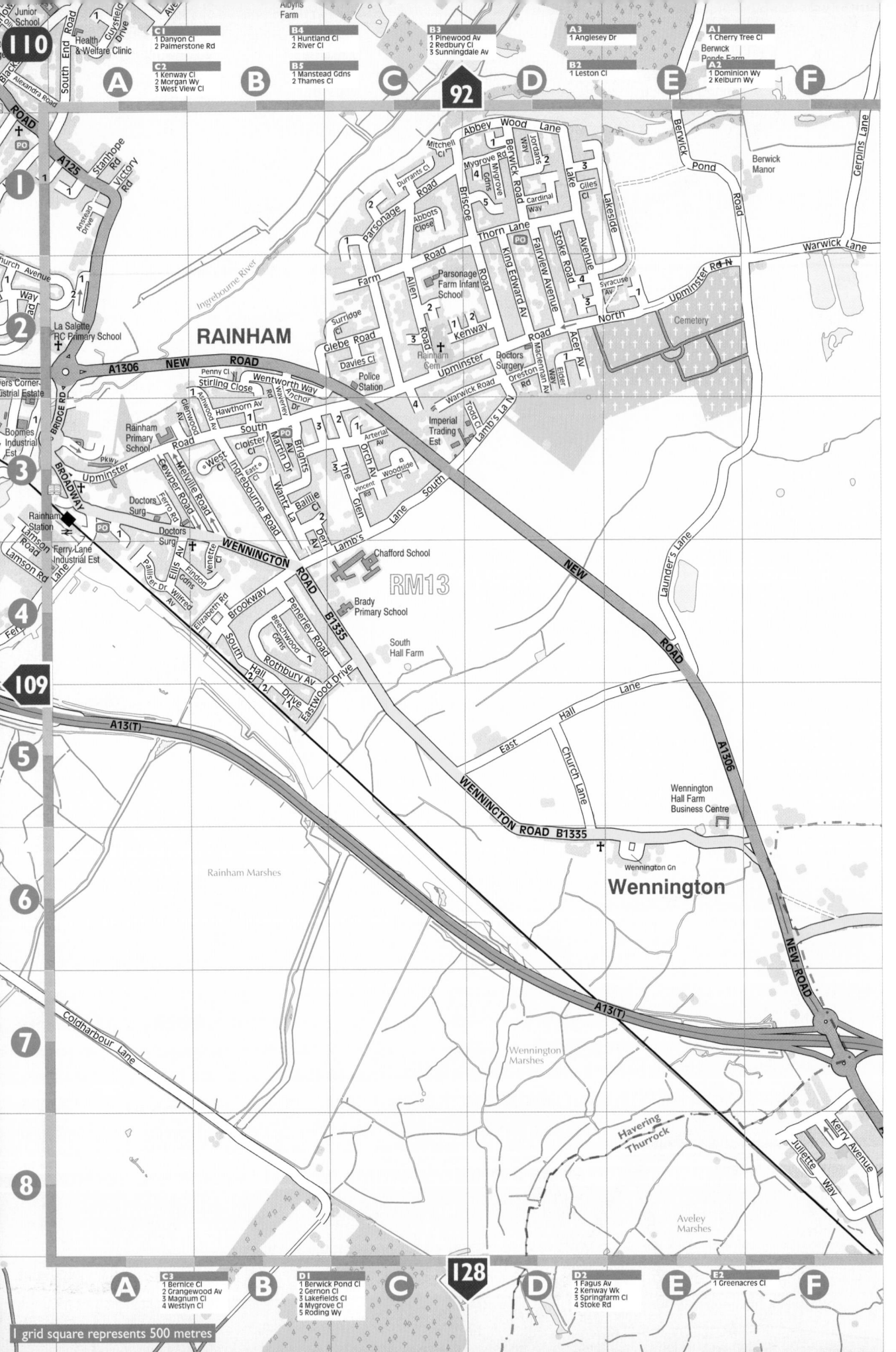

110

C1
1 Danyon Cl
2 Palmerstone Rd

B4
1 Huntland Cl
2 River Cl

B3
1 Pinewood Av
2 Redbury Cl
3 Sunningdale Av

A3
1 Anglesey Dr

A1
1 Cherry Tree Cl

C2
1 Kenway Cl
2 Morgan Wy
3 West View Cl

B5
1 Manstead Gdns
2 Thames Cl

B2
1 Leston Cl

F2
1 Dominion Wy
2 Kelburn Wy

A   **B**   **C**   **D**   **E**   **F**

I

2

RAINHAM

3

RM13

4

109

5

6

7

8

128

Wennington

C3
1 Bernice Cl
2 Grangewood Av
3 Magnum Cl
4 Westlyn Cl

D1
1 Berwick Pond Cl
2 Gernon Cl
3 Lakefields Cl
4 Mygrove Cl
5 Roding Wy

D2
1 Fagus Av
2 Kenway Wk
3 Springfarm Cl
4 Stoke Rd

E2
1 Greenacres Cl

A   **B**   **C**   **D**   **E**   **F**

I grid square represents 500 metres

J5
1 Shannon Wy
2 Swale Cl

J6
1 St Paul's Cl
2 St Paul's Pl
3 Tyne Gdns

J7
1 Alfred Rd
2 Buchanan Cl
3 Hanford Rd
4 The Rowans

Bramble
Farm

Bra... Lane

Warwick Lane

Aveley Road

Romford Road

93

Baldwins
Farm

Kemps...
Farm

G   H   J   K   L   M

I

2

3

Belhus Woods
Country Park

M25

4

Woodacre
School

Hamble
Lane

Humber Av

Fowle

Easing...

Dunkellin

Bretts
Farm

Kenningtons

Usk Road

Ravel
Gdns

Severn Rd

Ravel Road

Belhus
Park

Irvine
Gdns

Humber
Lane

†

3

Dilkes
CP School

Loman
Path

5

Doctors Surgery

PO

Usk

Primary
School

Tamar Drive

Teviot Avenue

Belhus Golf Club
& Leisure Centre

Humber Av

Caverny
Path

2

Garron
Drive

Gatehope

Fullarton Crs

Fowle Drive

Moor
Hall

2

1
Way

Shannon

Navarro †

Perry
Wy

3

Monnow
Drive

Rd

The Aveley
School

Park
Lane

2

1

Carron
Lane

Fairha...

Nethan

AVELEY

BY-PASS

Fyfield
Drive

Knightsmead
School

Fairha...

For...

6

SANDY   LANE   B1335

Sandy Lane
Farm

Mill Road

Rowan
Grove

2
1

St Michaels Cl

Aveley Football
Club

AVELEY

B1335

Fulbrook Lane

Stifford

B1335 STIFFORD ROAD

M25

7

Toplands Av

Grange Road

Manor
Close

Blenheim
Gdns

Lowlands
Road

3
2
1

Davis
Road

Martin Road

Dacre Crescent

Chick...ester

Elm Rd
1
Chick...

Dacre Avenue

Crescent Wy

Park
VW

Park Lane

1

Stanford
Gdns

Stifford Road

School House
Aveley School

†

Junction 30

A13(T)

Purfleet

Road

Arnhem Avenue

Manning St

Field Rd

Hall Avenue

Beech...

High   Street

PO

†

Doctors
Surgery

RW

Leonard

Aveley Cl

†
Aveley Primary
School

A13(T)

LONDON ROAD

A13(T)

Myrtle
Grove

Love
View

Kent
Lane

Central Av

Hall Crs

Eastern RW

Church View

Hall Road

Hall...ter

Crescent
Walk

Hall Road

Health Centre

Ship Lane

A13(T)

M25

8

Thurrock Service Area

...otel

Fanns Farm

LC

G   H   J   K   L   M

M6
1 Fusedale Wy
2 Groves Cl

129

M5
1 Frances Gdns
2 Fullarton Crs

K7
1 Broome Pl

The Caravan
Site

Causeway
Bridge

L8
1 Crescent Rd

ARTERIAL R...

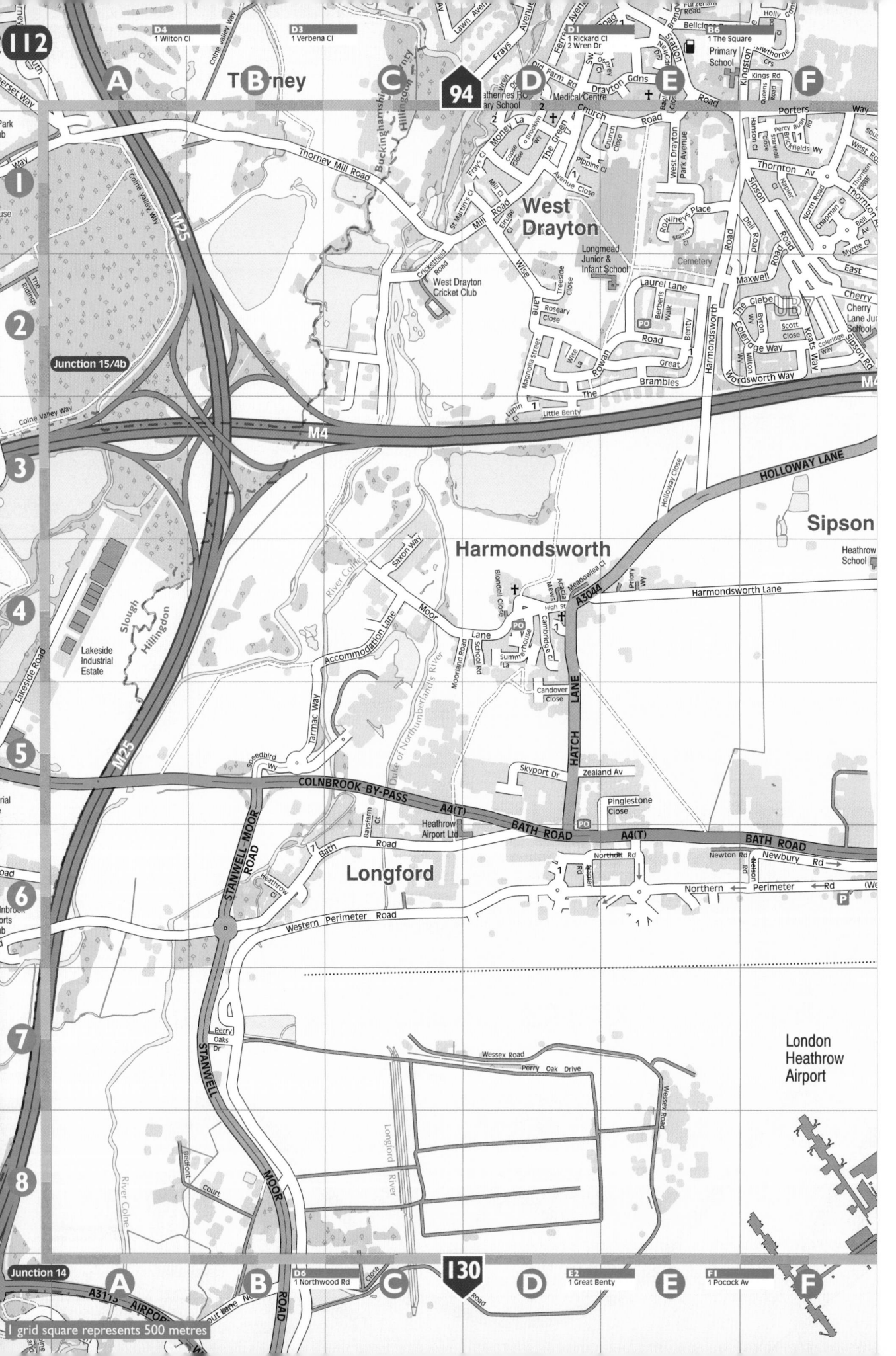

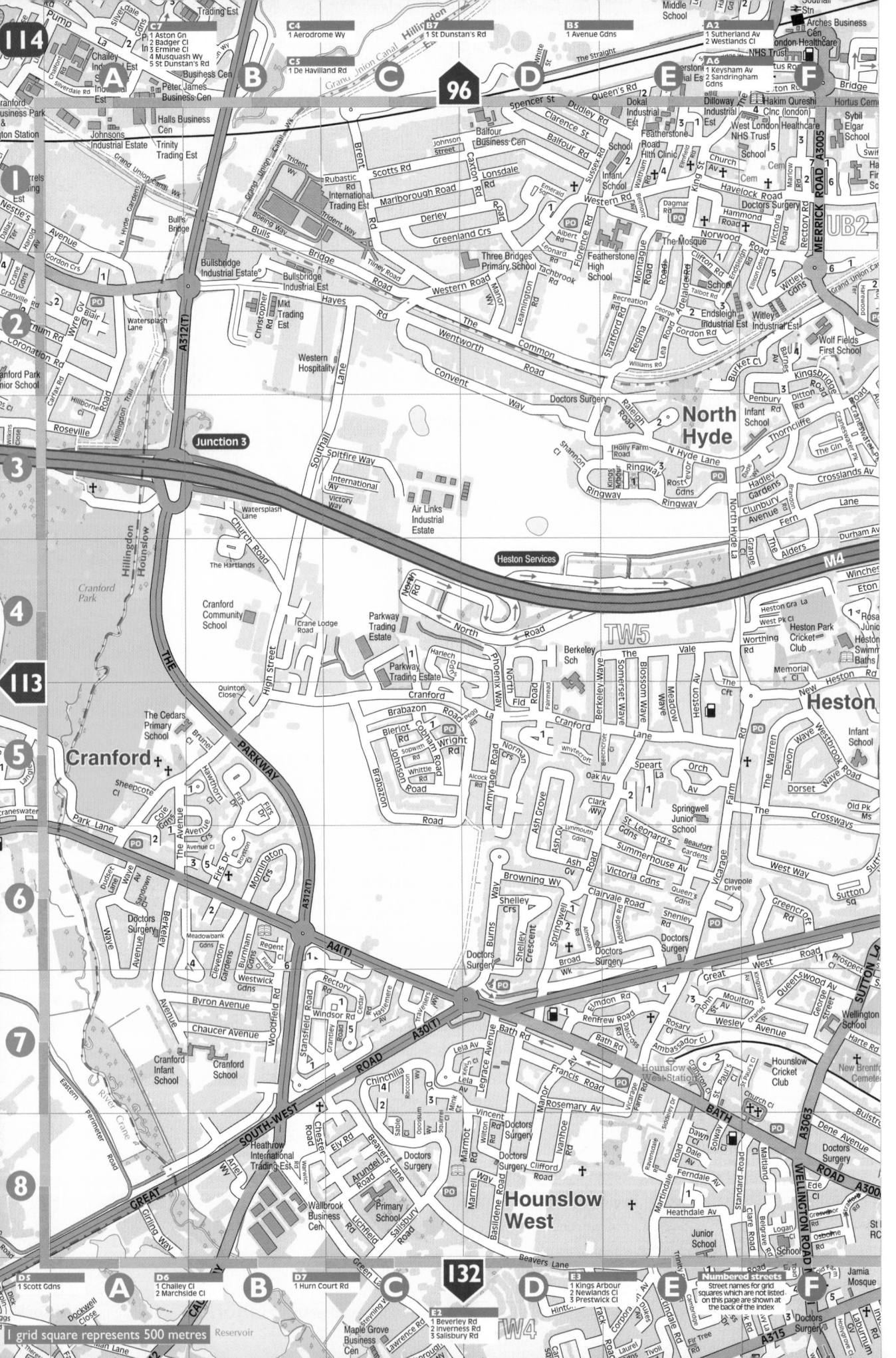

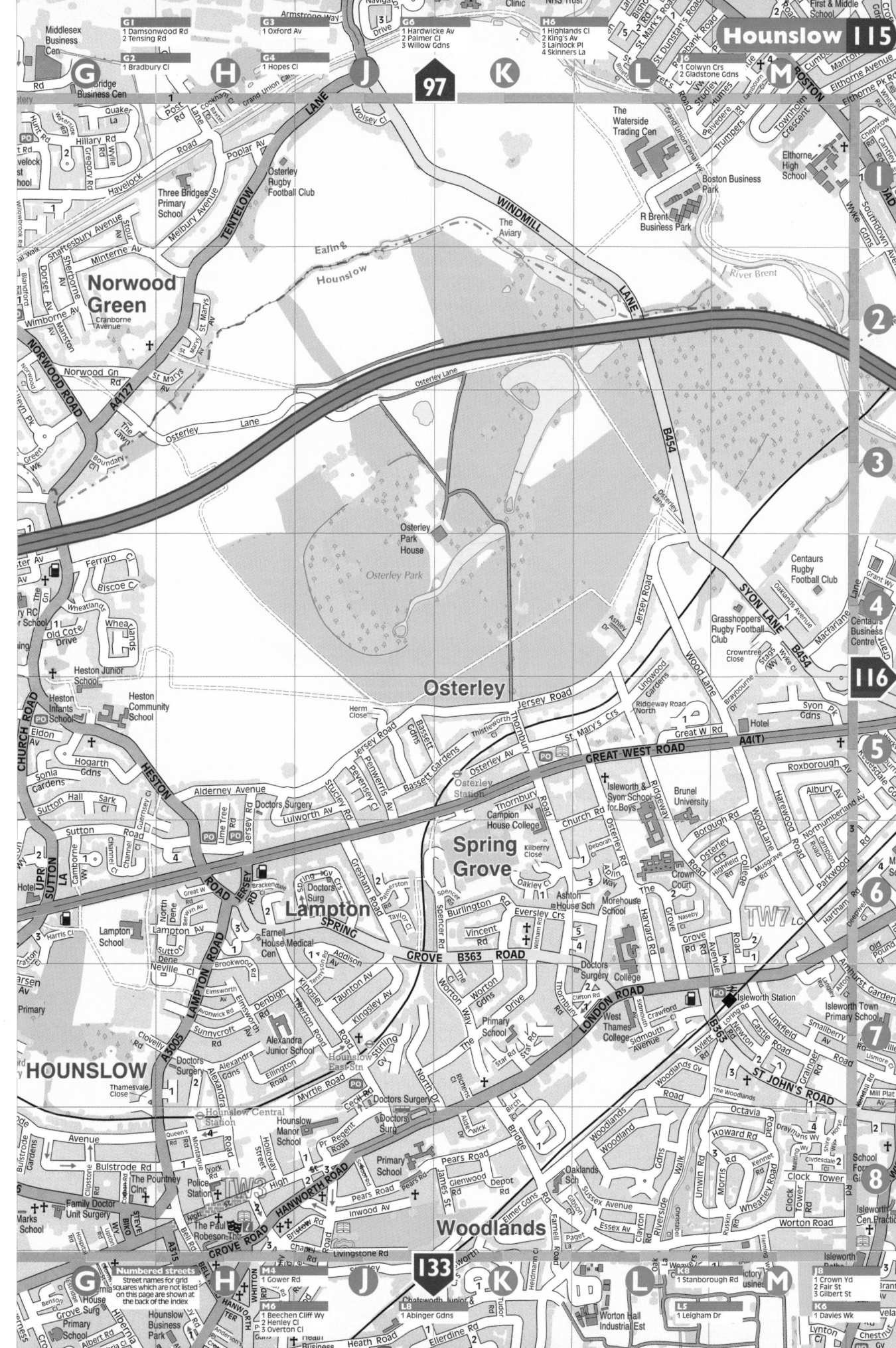

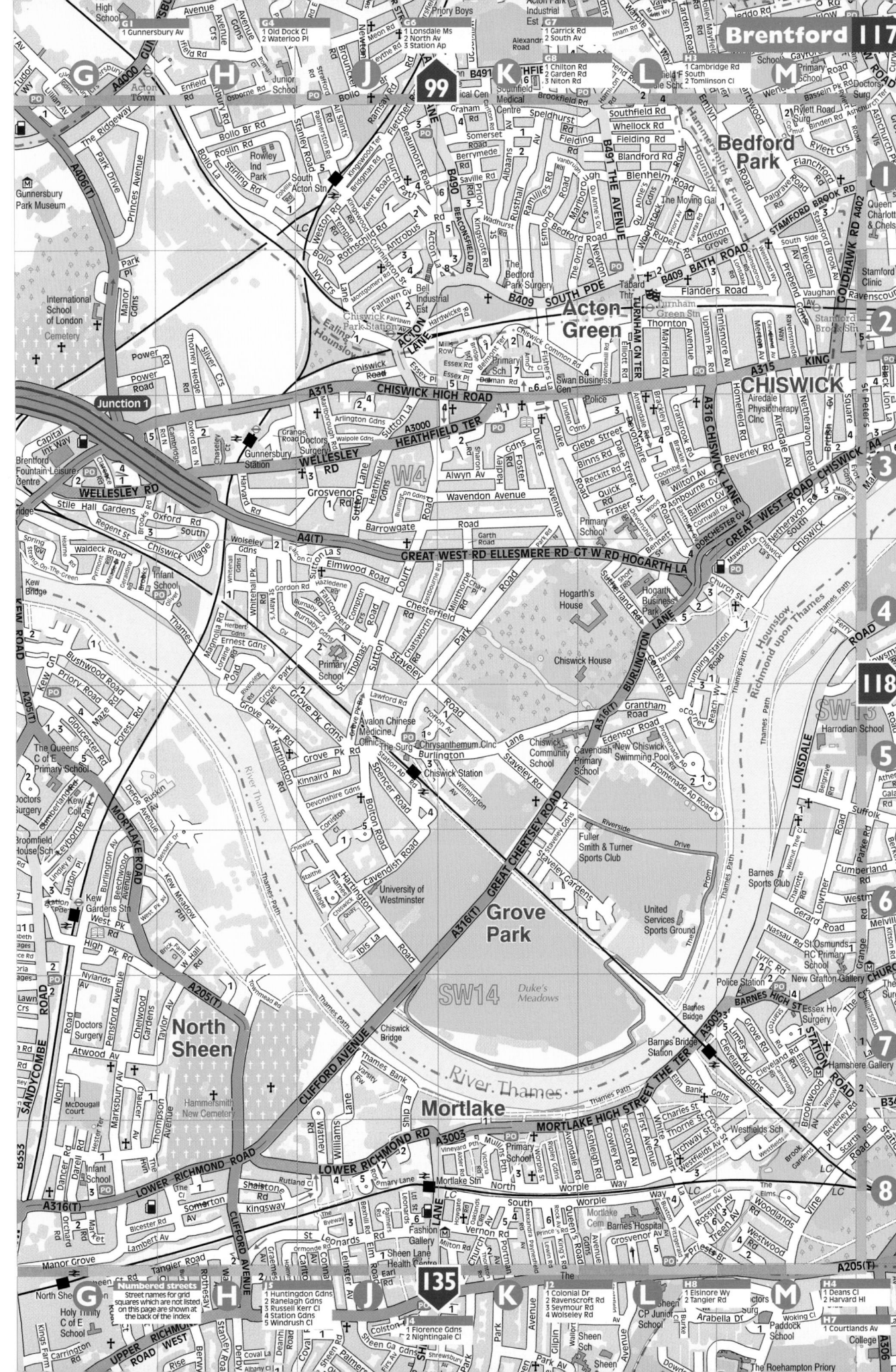

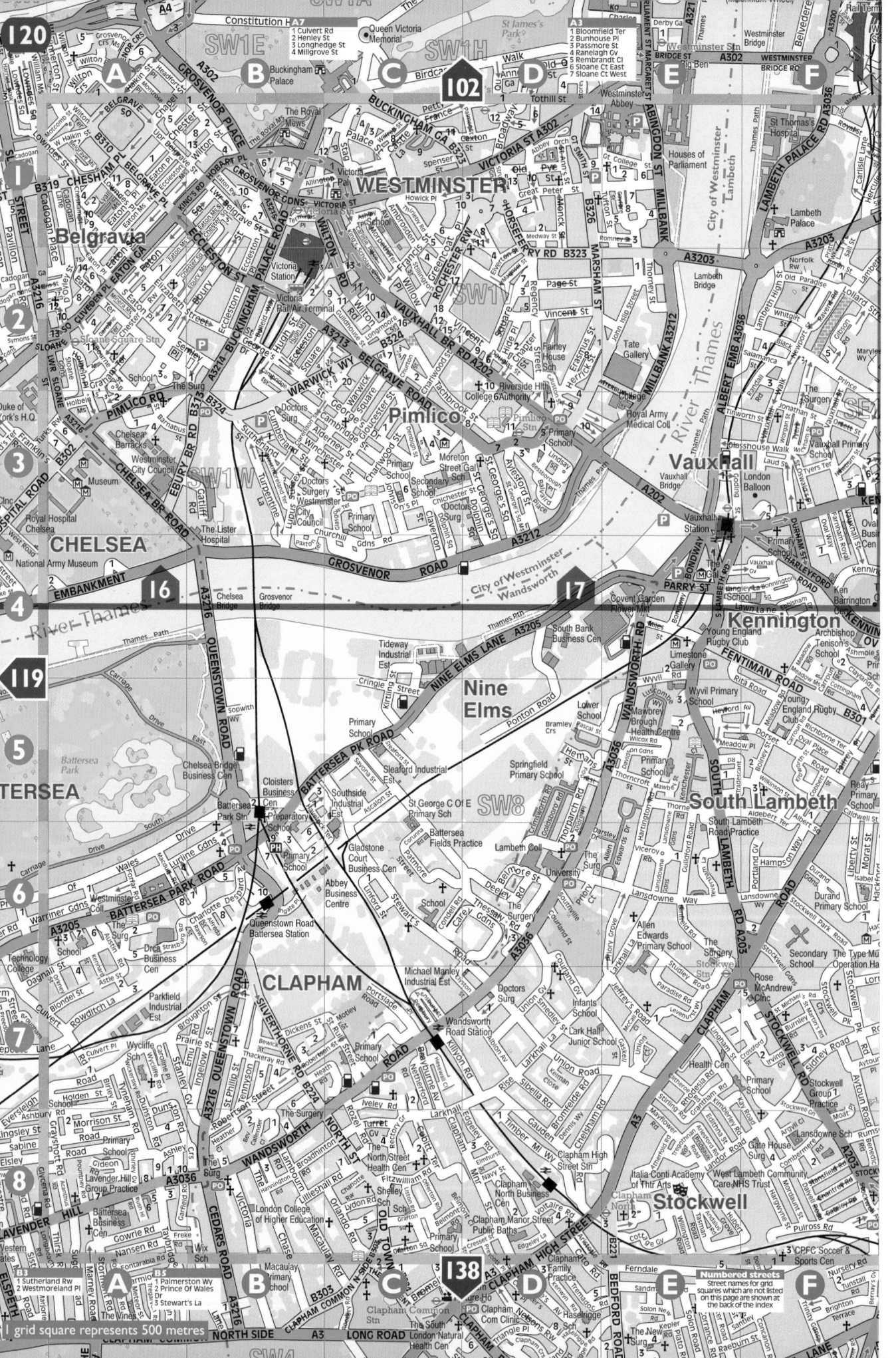

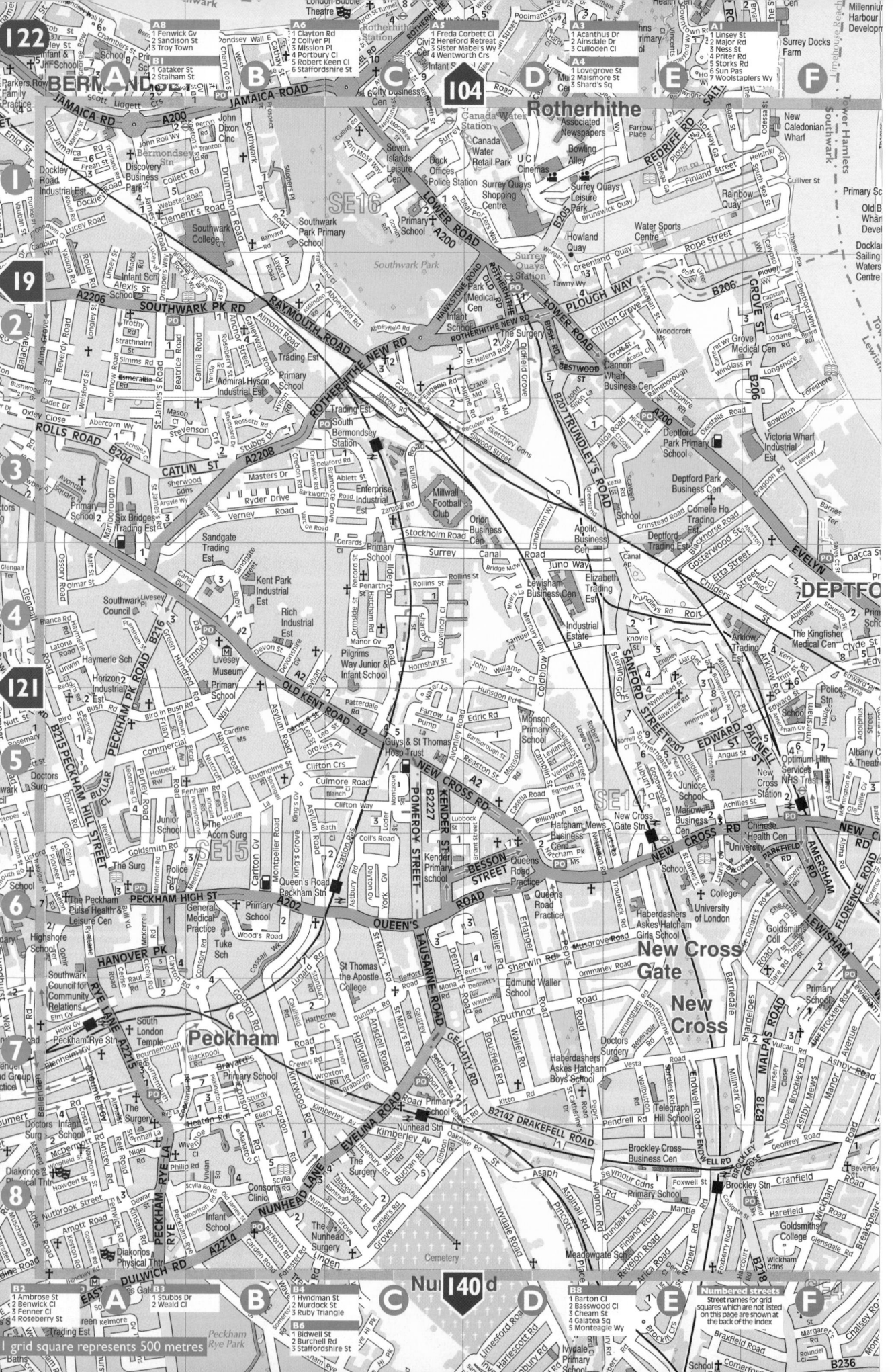

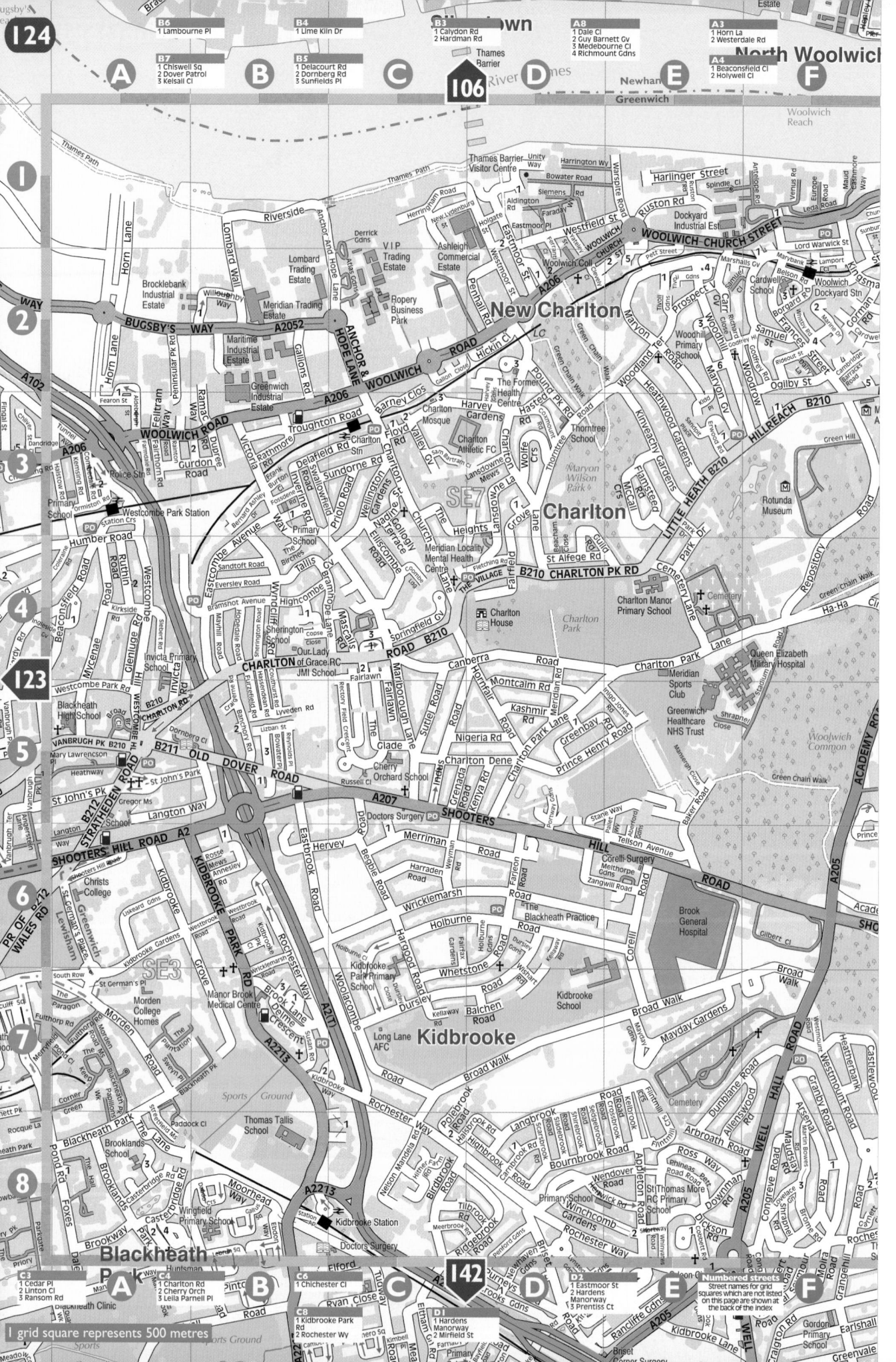

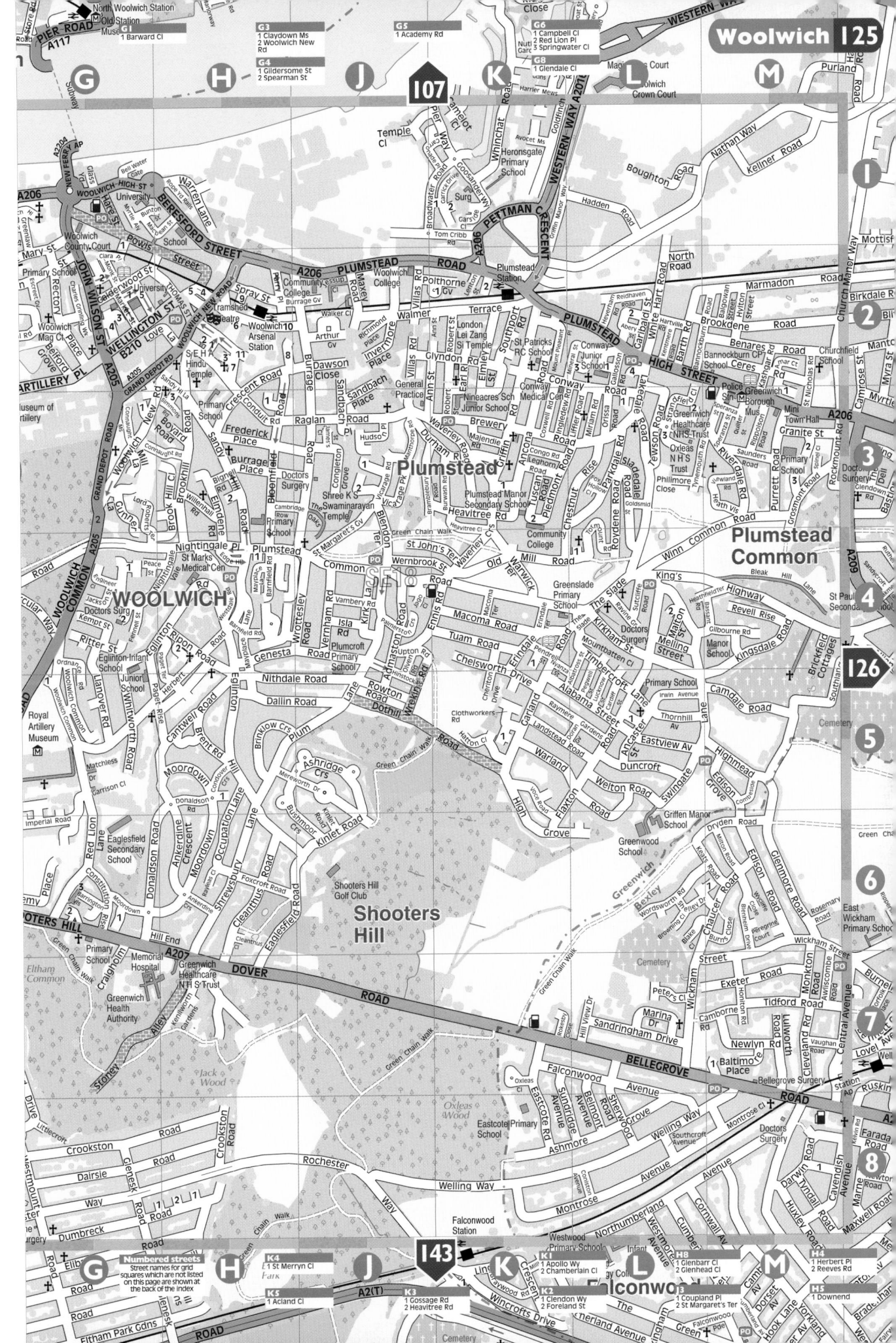

A   B   C   110   D   E   F

Coldharbour

Erith Rands

Havering
Bexley

Crayford
Ness

River Thames

Thurrock
Council

Marine
Court

Centurion
Mulberry Drive

1 Mannock Rd

B6
1 Watermeadow Cl

B5
1 Dabbling Cl
2 Lapwing Cl
3 Moorhen Cl
4 Stevenson Cl
5 Sunset Cl
6 Webber Cl

Landau Way
Dayton Drive
Maypole Crescent
Burnett Road
Ness Road

Manford
Industrial
Estate

Rav Lamb Way
Canada Road
Durlun Way
Jenningtree Road
Beacon Rd
Widgeon Rd
Sandpipe Dr
Sandpipe Cl

Bilton Road

Turpin Lane
Cornwallis Close
Wheatley Ter
Watt Way

Frobisher Road
Aperfield Road

127

Longreach
Shepdey
Alderney Road
Agra Wy

Church
Trading
Estate

School

Wallhouse Road

Hilden Dr   Brompton Dr

Hollywood Wy
Fern Cl
Rodeo
Dr

Slade Green Road
Green Road
Elm Road
Hazel Road
Hazel
Hazel Dr

Leycroft Gdns

Slade Green
Football Club

Dartford
Marshes

Darent Valley Path

Joyce Green Lane

Richmer Rd
Freeland Rd
Power Ind.
Estate
Cedar Rd
Willow Rd
PO
Clark Rd

Slade Rd
Shieling Cl
Larkswood Cl

**North
End**

Slade Green
Station

Moat Lane
Oak Rd

**Slade
Green**

Crayford
Marshes

Whitehall Lane
Dale View
Sun Ct
Coln Rd
Coln Road

Howbury Lane

Kent County
Bexley

Joyce Green
Hospital

A&E

Howbury Rd

Buckley Cl
Burritton Rd
Coyne Dr
Shearwood Crescent

Crayside
Industrial Estate

Kennet Road

A206
Thames
Road

University Way
A206

McCudden
Rd
Grove
Cornwall
Rd

Joyce Green Lane
Salmon
Av
Strickland Av
Strickland

Ravensbourne Rd
Shuttle Rd
Stour Rd
Maiden Lane

Medway Road
Russell Rd
Mayplace Avenue

Crayside
Industrial
Estate

DA1

Sandpit Rd

Swan
Business Park

Millside
Industrial Estate

Burnham
Trading Estate

Barnes Cray
Primary

Iron Mill Lane

Barnes

Temple Hill

Hall R
Wellcome

A   B   146   C   D   E   F

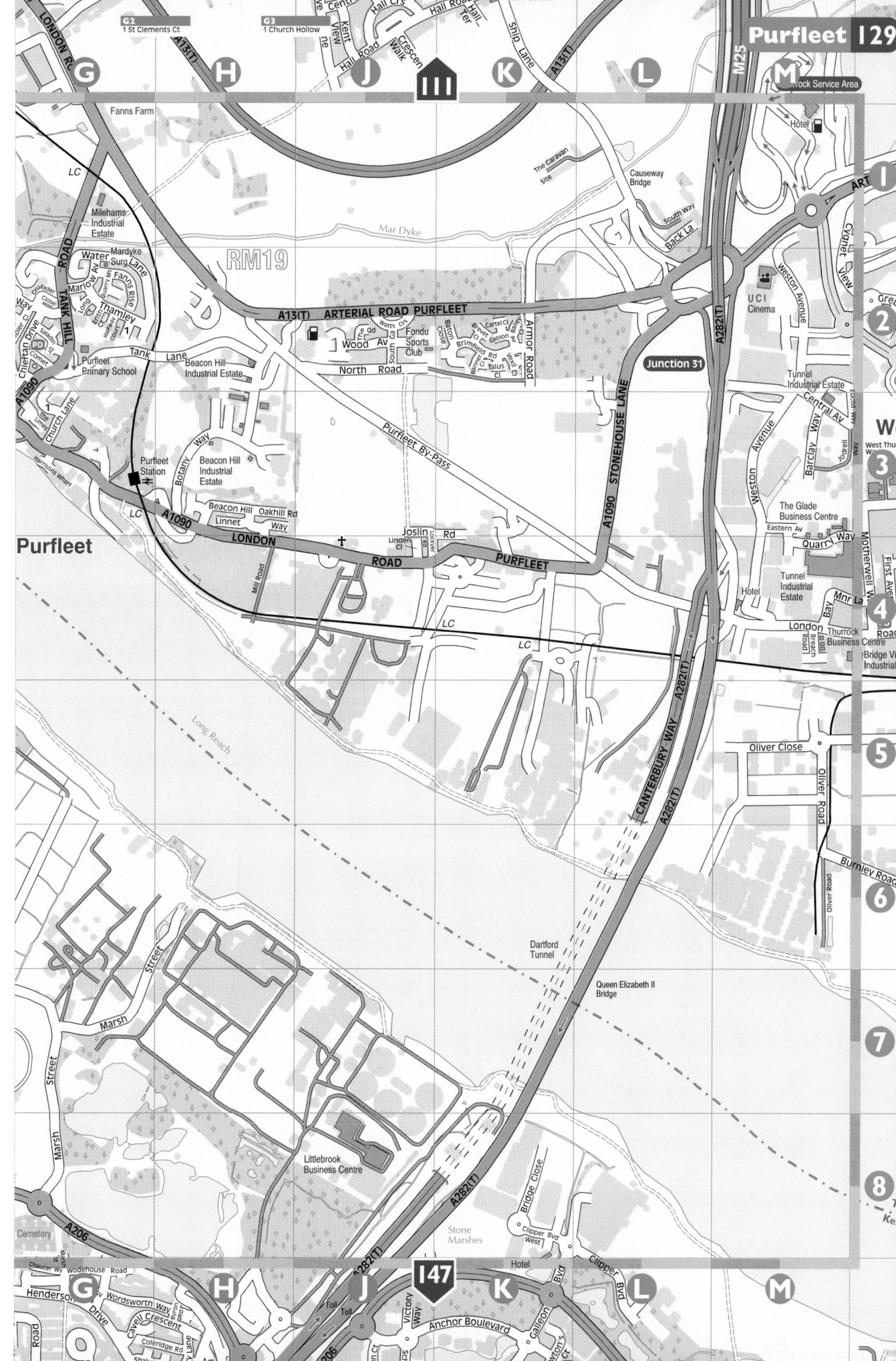

G   H   J   K   L   M   I

G2
1 St Clements Ct

G3
1 Church Hollow

LONDON RD.

A13(T)

Hall Crs

Hall Road

Hall Road

Ship Lane

A13(T)

M25

Thurrock Service Area

Hotel

Fanns Farm

Kent

Crescent Walk

The Caravan site

Causeway Bridge

Cygnet View

Grebe

LC

Mar Dyke

South Way

Back La

RM19

Milehams Industrial Estate

Water Surg
Mardyke Lane

Weston Avenue

UCI Cinema

Tunnel Industrial Estate

Central Av

West Thurrock

We

TANK HILL ROAD

Marlow Av

Fanns Rise

A13(T)   ARTERIAL ROAD PURFLEET

Wood Av

The Qd

Watts Crs

Fondu Sports Club

Baron Cl

Cartel Cl

Gabion Cl

Brinfield Rd

A282(T)

Junction 31

Barclay Way

Jodrell Way

Edith Way

Crusader Way

Thamley

Chieftan Drive

A1090

PO

Purfleet Primary School

Tank   Lane

North   Road

South Ca

Brimfield Cl

Balmer Cl

Talus Cl

Yeovil Cl

Armor Road

STONEHOUSE LANE

Weston Avenue

Tunnel Industrial Estate

The Glade Business Centre

Eastern Av

Quarry Way

First Av

Motherwell Way

Church Lane

Beacon Hill Industrial Estate

Botany Way

Beacon Hill Industrial Estate

Purfleet By-Pass

A1090

Purfleet

Harrisons Wharf

Purfleet Station

Beacon Hill Way

Oakhill Rd

Linnet Way

Joslin Rd

Locker Rd

Linden Cl

LONDON   ROAD   PURFLEET

A1090

A282(T)

Hotel

Bay

Mnr La

London Road

Thurrock Business Centre

Breach Rd

Hotel

Tunnel Industrial Estate

First Av

Thurrock Road

Bridge View Industrial E

Mill Road

LC

LC

LC

Long Reach

CANTERBURY WAY   A282(T)

Oliver Close

Oliver Road

Oliver Road

Burnley Road

A282(T)

Street

Marsh

Dartford Tunnel

Queen Elizabeth II Bridge

Marsh

Street

Littlebrook Business Centre

A282(T)

Cemetery

A206

Chaucer W

Wodehouse Road

Henderson Drive

Wordsworth Way

Calvey Crescent

Coleridge Rd

Shakes

A282(T)

Victory Way

Toll

Toll

147

Anchor Boulevard

Stone Marshes

Hotel

Clipper Blvd West

Galleon Blvd

Clipper Blvd

Bridge Close

A206

Sch

Lawton's

King

Thr
Kent

G   H   J   K   L   M

2   3   4   5   6   7   8

I

Heathrow Airport
Central Bus Stn

H1
1 Clifton Rd

H8
1 Chattern Hl
2 Reedsfield Rd
3 Wentworth Cl

J8
1 John's Cl

K2
1 Sheffield Wy

H7
1 Reedsfield Cl

J3
1 Swindon Rd

K3
1 Bishops Dr

K8
1 South Gate Av

Terminal 3

Terminal 2

G
H
J
113
K
L
M

Viscount Way

Hatton

Lithgow's Rd

Hatton Cross Stn

St Theresa's Road

St Anthony's Rd

Cem

Doctors Surgery

Terminal 4

The British Museum Shop

PO

Heathrow Terminal 4 Stn

Swindon Rd

Southern

Road West

Sheffield Rd

A30(T)

Stratford Rd

Swansea Rd

Shrewsbury Road

Great South-West Road

Perimeter

Road

Cain's Lane

Orchard Av

Edward Rd

The Marjory Kinnon School

Hatton Medical Practice

Bedfont Junior & Infant School

Wellington Rd

Myrtle Av

Hatton Road

I

2

3

Hazelmere Cl

Marriott

Peninsular Rd

Kingston Av

Northumberland Crs

Richmond

Longford

Avenue

Eimcroft

Staines Road

A315

Burn

Sea Country

World Centre

Tunnel Link Road

Sealand Road

Crane Road

Sanctuary Rd

Beacon

Southern

Perimeter

Road

Longford River

Scylla Rd Crs

Hillingdon

Stanwell

Surrey County

Road

East Bedfont

Hounslow

Bedfont Cl

Montrose Rd

Horsham Rd

Bedfont Cl

Hatton Road

West Road

East Road

New

Page

Road

Dorchester

Bethany Waye

Target Cl

Ruskin Av

Cassiobury Avenue

Staines Rd

Bedfont Lane

Longford School

Tachbrook Rd

Frien Rd

TW14

4

132

East Bedfont

West View

Spinney Drive

St Mary's Drive

Stanwell Rd

Longleat Wy

Burlington Cl

Pates Mnr Dr

Natalie Rd

Staines Rd

Staines Road

A315

Benedict

Doctors Surgery

Grovestile Waye

Elm Road

Sherborne Rd

Cedar Rd

Padbury

Lox

Beech Road

Imperial Rd

Colonial Rd

Monarch Cl

Southville Rd

Southville

Oak

Ash Gv

Bedfont Health Clinic

Staines Rd

Gould Rd

Warfield Rd

Bedfont Lane

Walker Cl

Beattie Cl

Chambers

Southville Junior School

5

Clockhouse Industrial Estate

A30(T)

Harrow Road

Ascot Road

B3003

Bedfont Green Close

Hatchett Rd

Fawns Manor

Dudley Road

Peacock Avenue

Fairholme Junior & Infant School

Elsworth Close

Santry Dr

Oak

Kinross Rd

Kilross Rd

Grove Village Medical Cen

Southville Crs

Golden Close

Water Mead

Westmacott Drive

Derwent Rd

Padstow Walk

Waterloo Cl

Guildford Rd

Hanover

6

Cemetery

Bedfont Road

Bedfont Lakes Country Park

Edward Pauling School

Redford Cl

Lancing Rd

Raleigh Rd

Vernon Road

Percival Road

Princes Road

Rochester Av

Westbourne Rd

Bedfont Road

Lower Feltham

St Dunstan's Rd

Francis Rd

7

Clockhouse Lane

Hounslow

Surrey County

Challenge Road

HM Young Offender Institution

Feltham Hill Junior School

High St

Ashford Rd

A244

Spring

Sunbury Road

Cemetery

Hayes

Cralgwer Avenue

Anglesey Cl

Reedsfield Road

Grays Lane

Portland Crs

Field Vw

Shield Rd

The Clumps

Ashford Road

Chertsey Road

A244

Walton Gdns

Shelson Avenue

Ryland Close

Ellington Road

Denison Rd

Harvest

8

Glen Av

Parkland Gv

Clifford Gv

Clclhouse La

Rosemary Gdns

Chattern Road

Fernhurst Rd

Duke's

Anderson Dr

Doctors Surgery

Chattern Hill

Feltham Road

Sandell's Av

Cranleigh Road

Hamilton

Highland Pk

Hamilton Close

Church

Feltham Rd

Margarets Rd

Lynegrove Av

149

M6

G
H
J
K
L
M

M4
1 Ruscombe Wy

M1
1 Steam Farm La

L4
1 Bridlepath Wy

M3
1 Turpin Rd
2 Welwyn Av

L7
1 Briarwood Cl
2 Larkham Cl

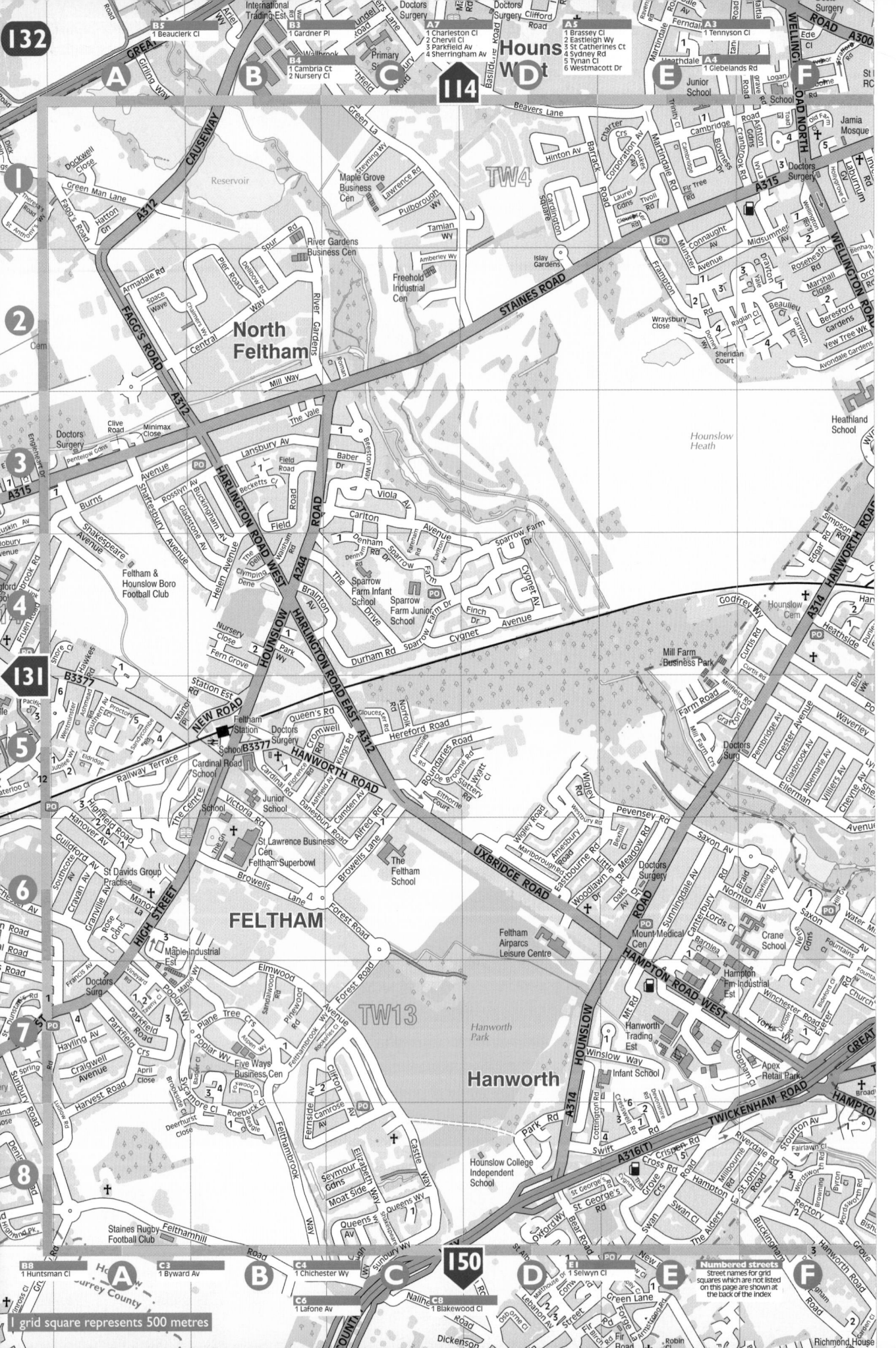

G **H** **J** **117** **K** **L** **M** **I**

2

3

136

5

6

7

8

G **153** **H** **J** **K** **L** **M** **I**

A316(T)

Manor Grove

UPPER RICHMOND ROAD WEST

A205(T)

LOWER RICH

RICHMOND ROAD

H1
1 Coval Gdns
2 Langdale Cl

H2
1 Uplands Cl

1 Medcroft Gdns
2 Penrhyn Crs
3 Wellside Gdns

J2
1 Martindale
2 Spencer Gdns

North Sheen Station

Holy Trinity
C of E
School

Sheen Mount
Primary School

Christchurch
Road

East Sheen
Cemetery

East Sheen
Common

Bog
Lodge

Hill

Richmond
Park

White
Lodge

Pen
Ponds

Isabella
Plantation

Richmond Park

M4
1 Mount Angelus
Rd

M1
1 Rockingham Cl

L8
1 Mary Adelaide Cl

K8
1 Ullswater Cl

K1
1 Larches Av

East
Sheen

Roehampton

Roehampton
Golf Course

Roehampton
Gate

Grove
House

Clarence Lane

Highcliffe
Drive South Thames
College / Wandsworth
Adult College

Ibstock
Place
School

Sherfield Gdns

Roehampton
Community
Council

The Roehampton Priory
Hospital

The Priory

Rosslyn Park
Rugby Football
Club

Froebel
College

Richmond
Park
Golf Course

Beverley Brook

Wandsworth

Richmond upon Thames

Roehampton
Recreation
Centre

ROEHAMPTON VALE

A3(T)

Friars Av

Stag Lane

Stroud Crescent

KINGSTON VALE

Robinwood
Place

Grasmere
Avenue

Ullswater Crs

Robin Hood
Road

ROBIN HOOD

A308

Kingston
Uni

Keswick Avenue

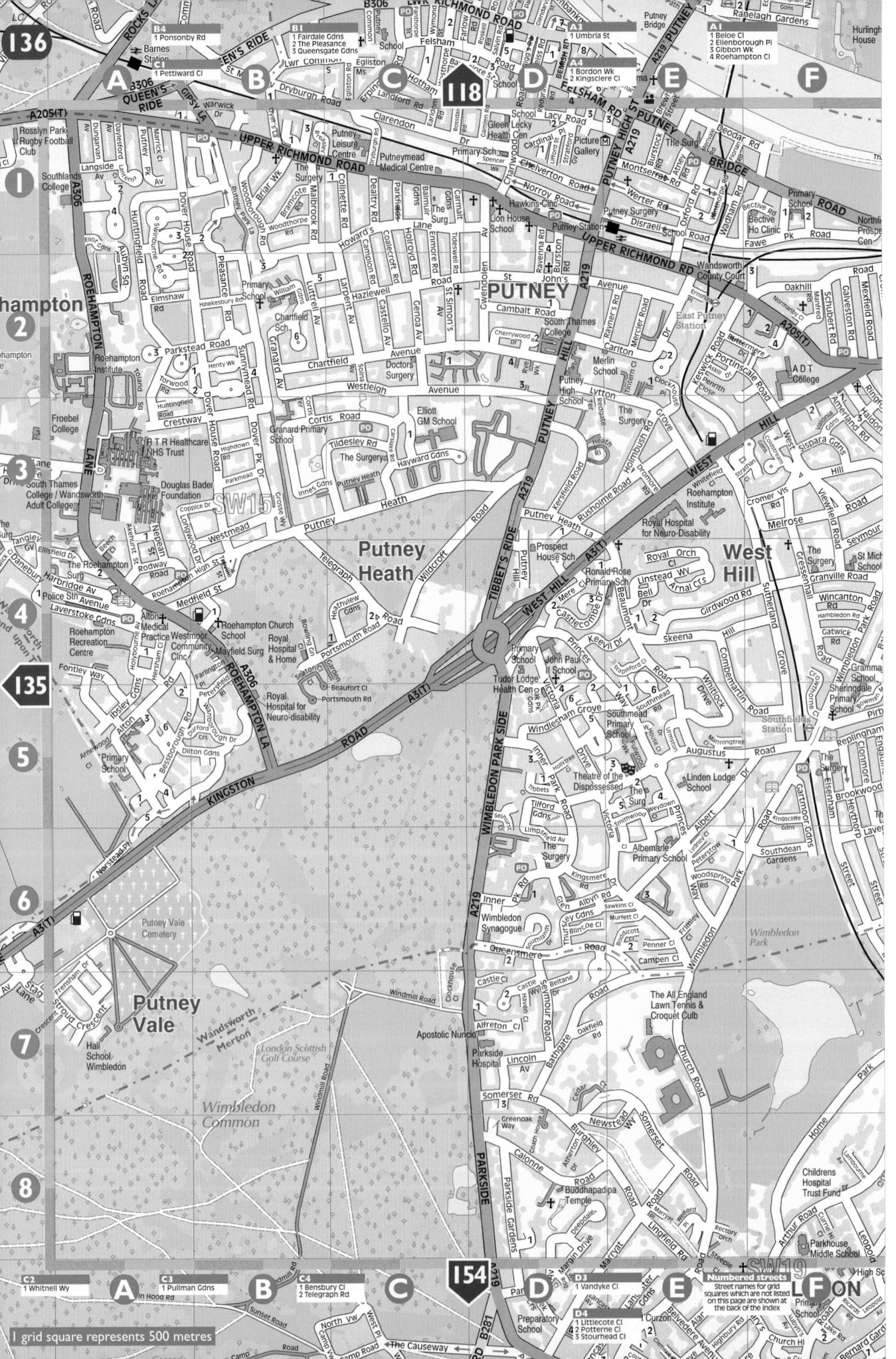

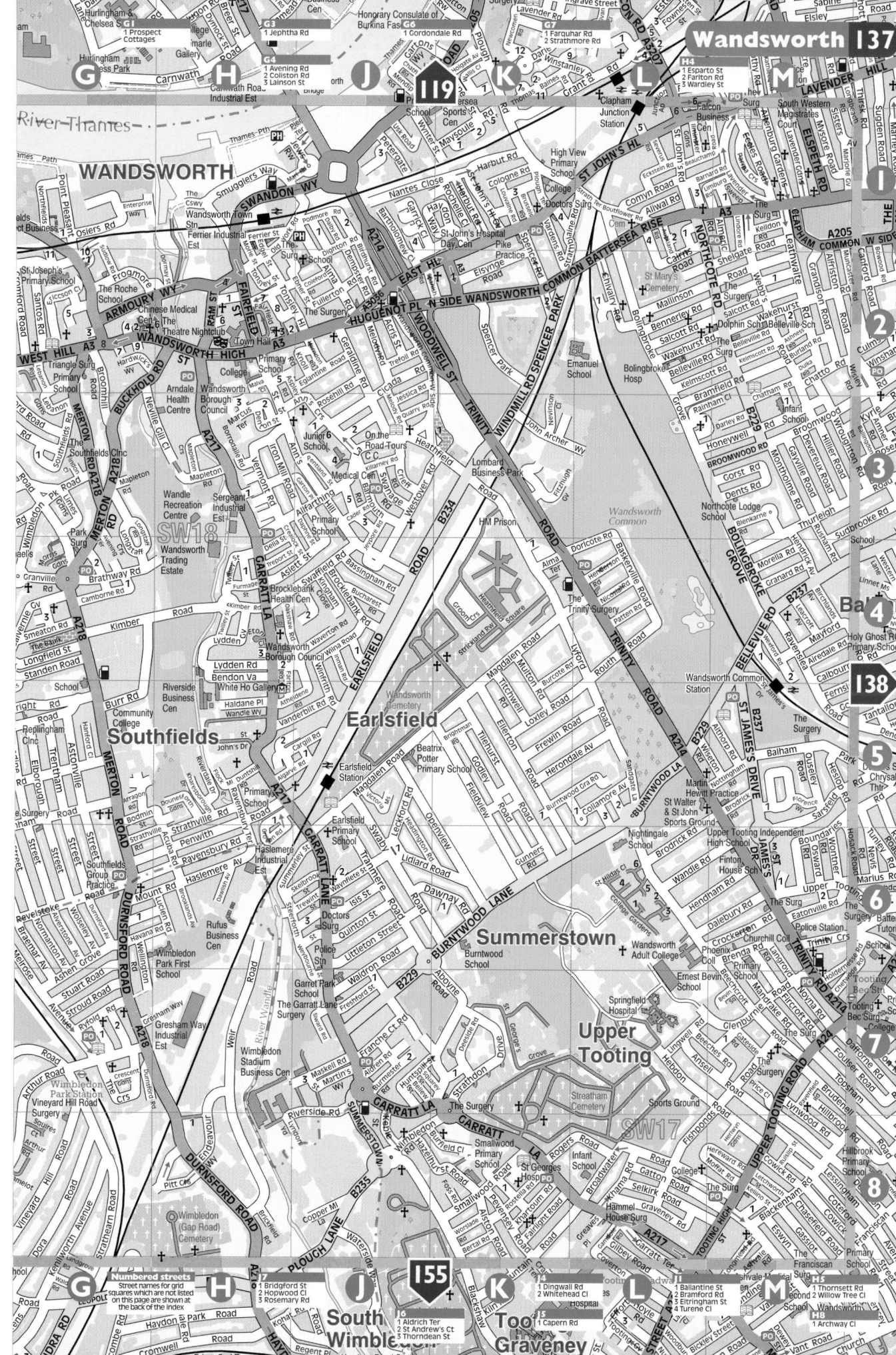

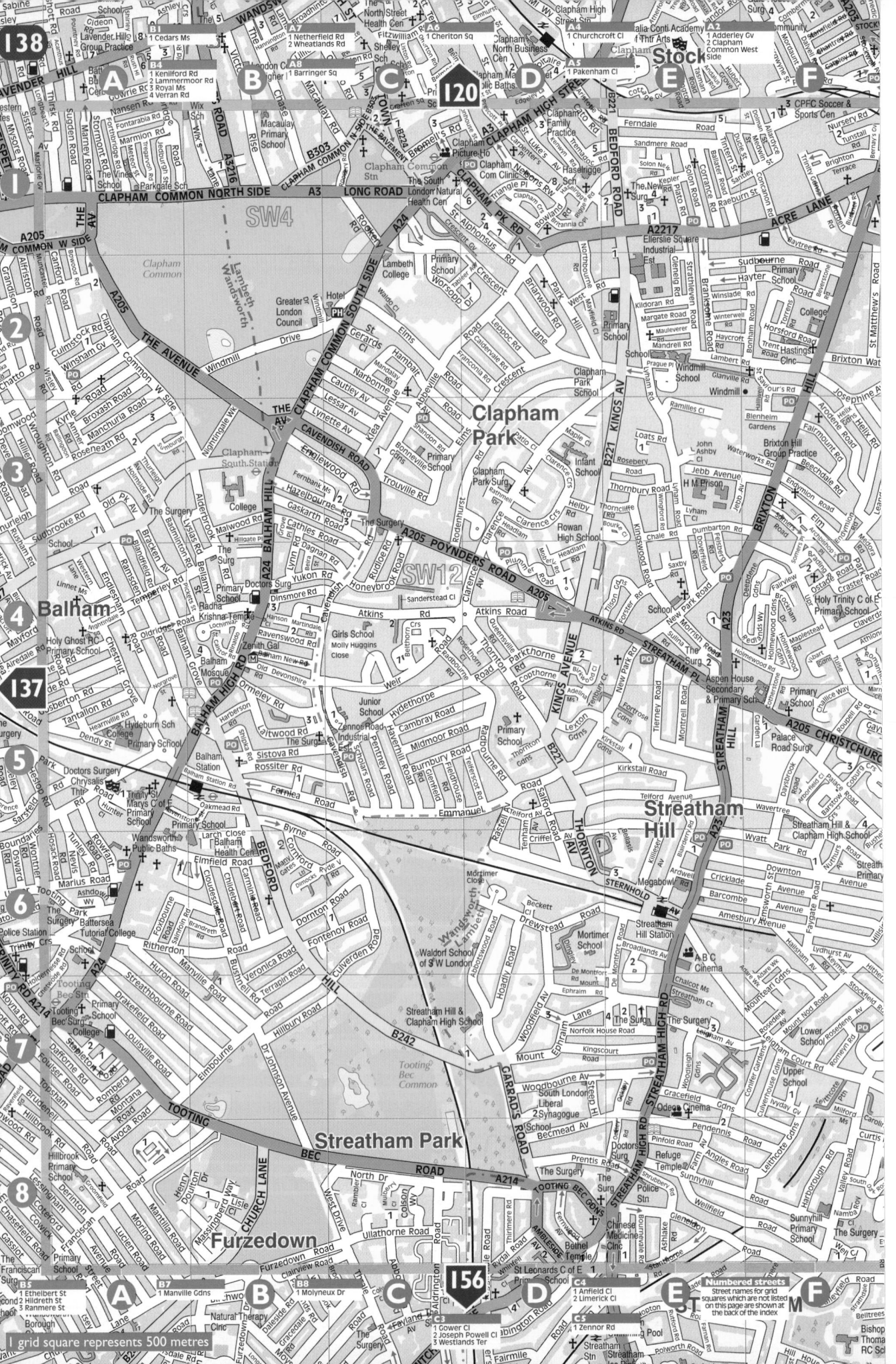

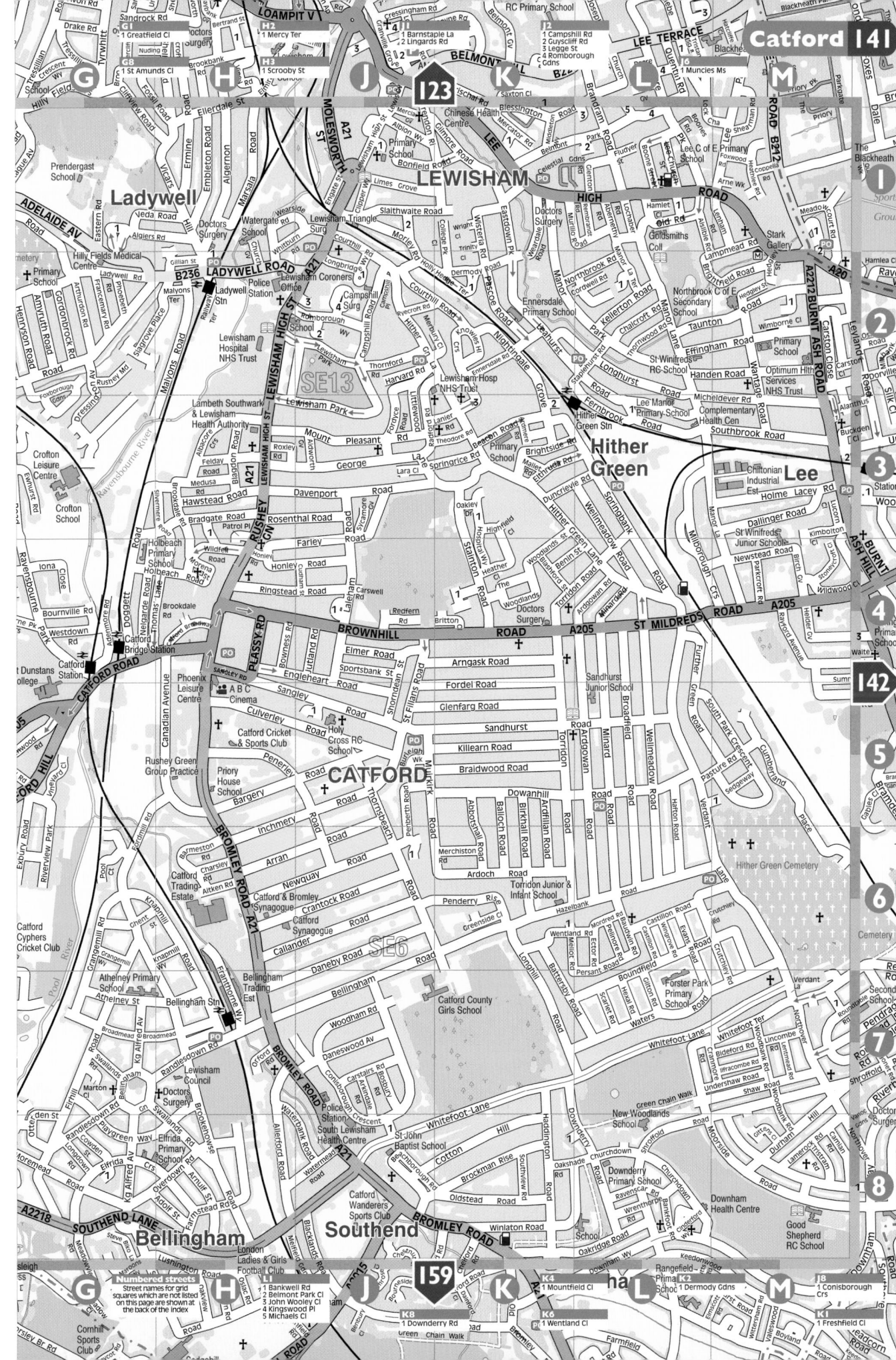

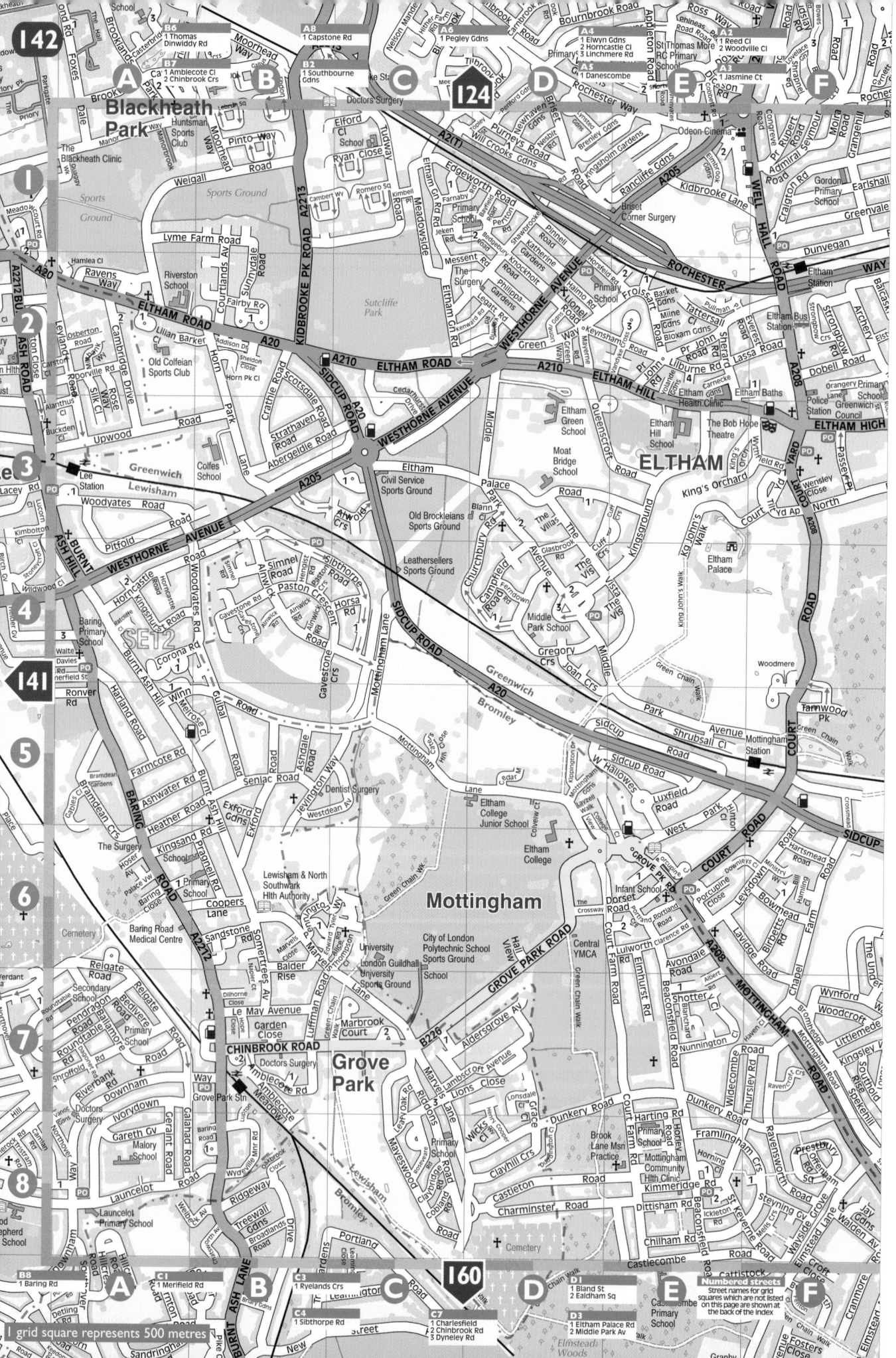

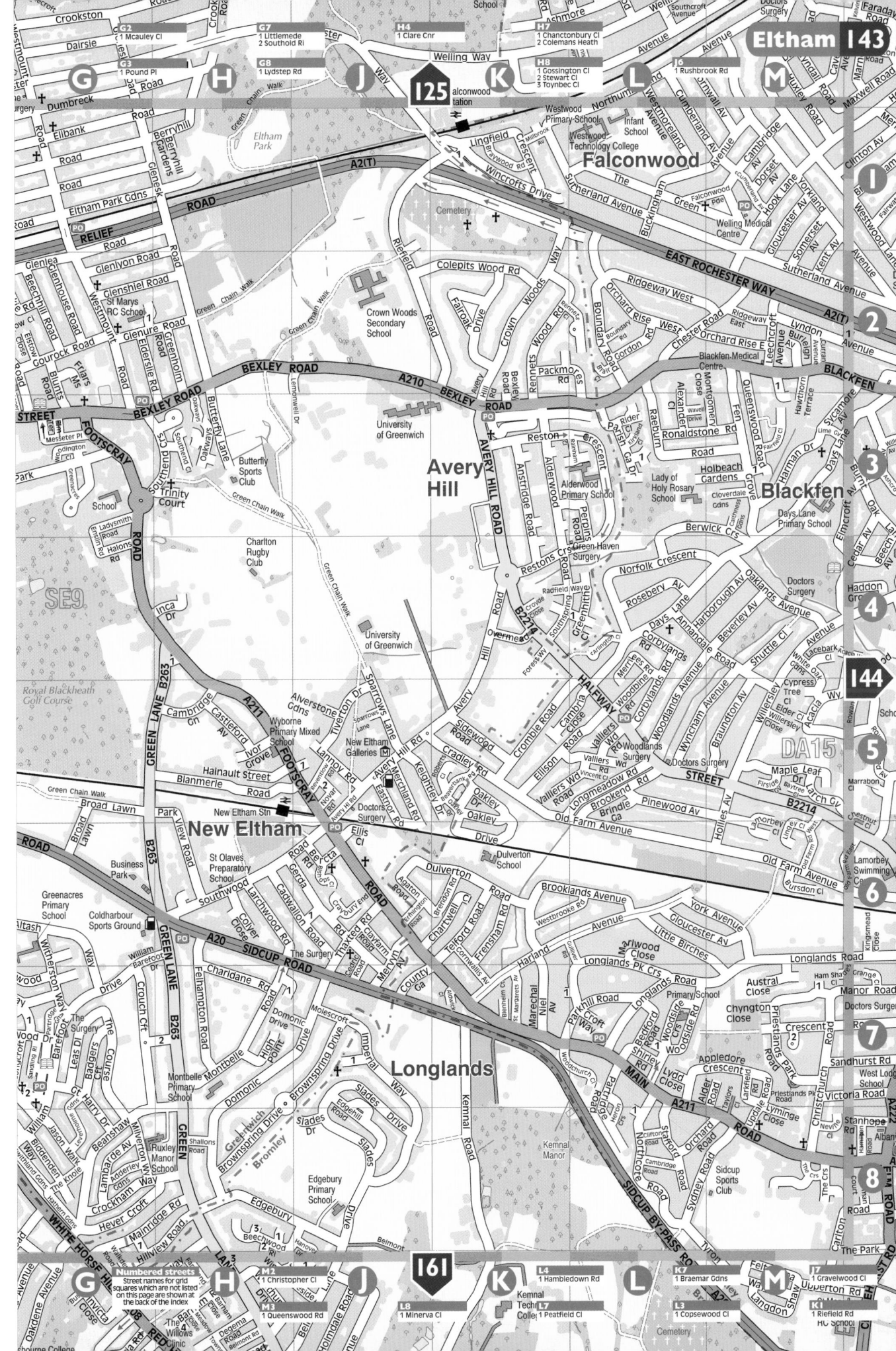

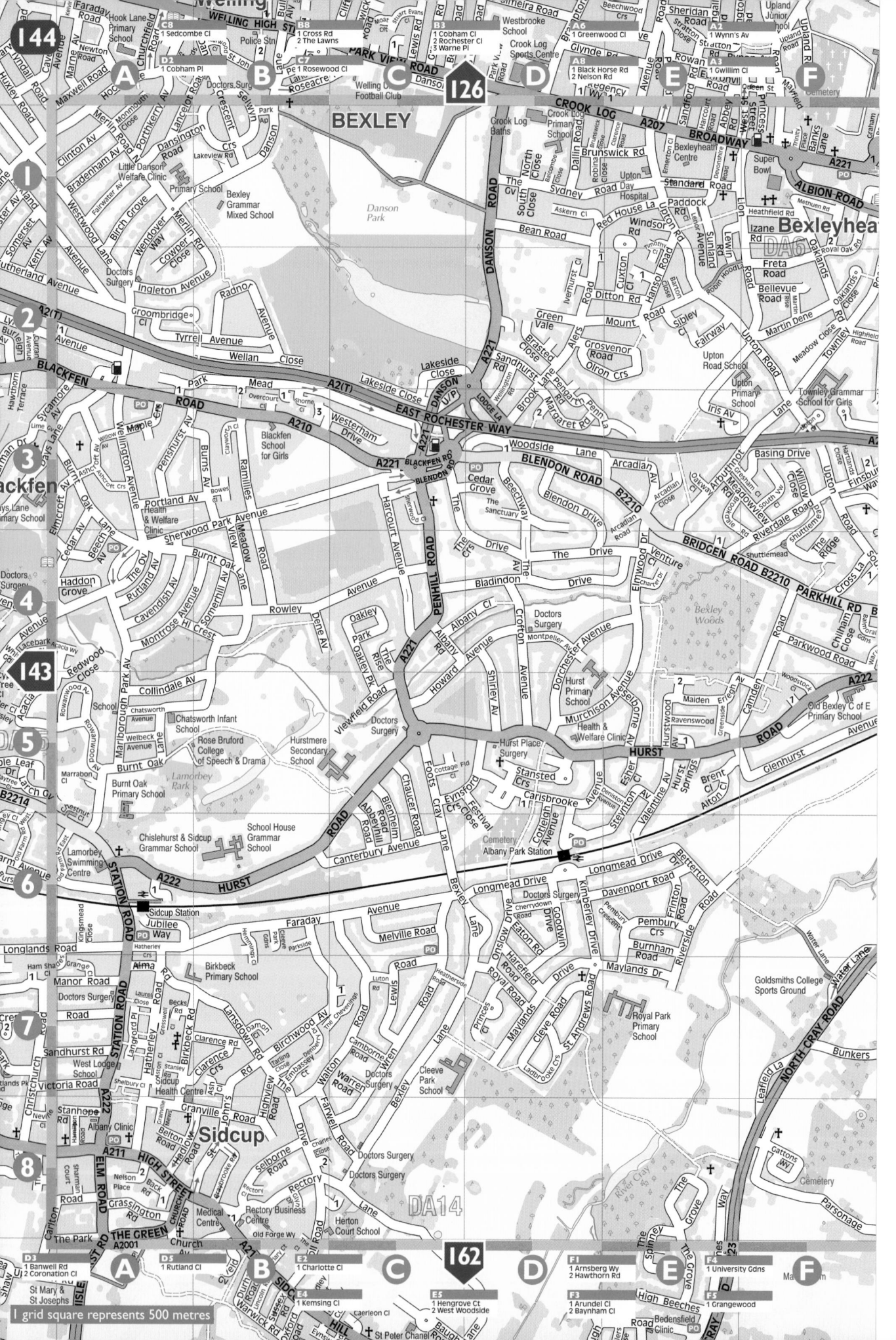

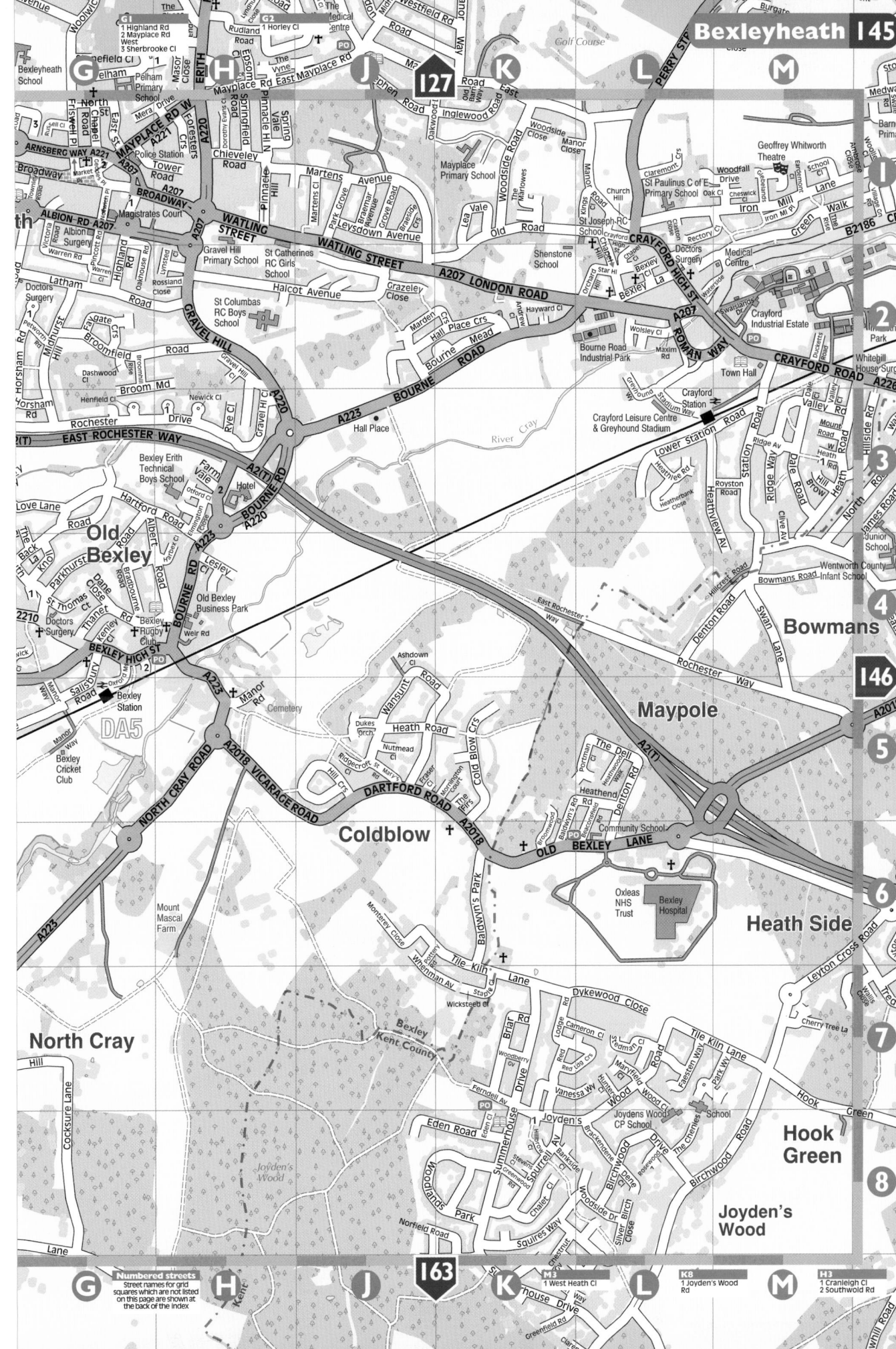

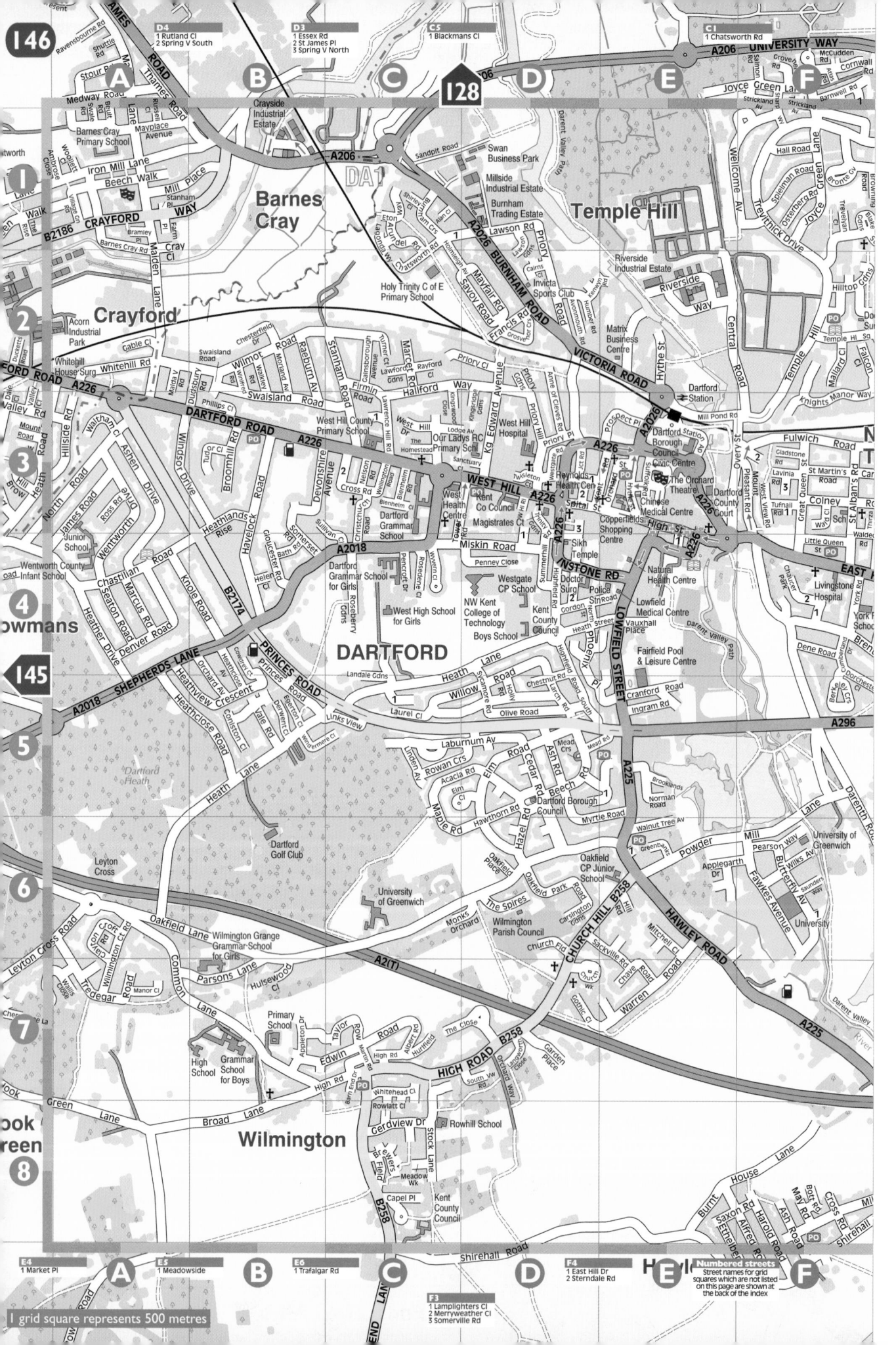

128

145

128

D4
1 Rutland Cl
2 Spring V South

D3
1 Essex Rd
2 St James Pl
3 Spring V North

C5
1 Blackmans Cl

C1
1 Chatsworth Rd

A206 **UNIVERSITY WAY**

CRAYFORD

Barnes
Cray

DA1

Crayford

Temple Hill

DARTFORD

owmans

Wilmington

E4
1 Market Pl

E5
1 Meadowside

E6
1 Trafalgar Rd

F3
1 Lamplighters Cl
2 Merryweather Cl
3 Somerville Rd

F4
1 East Hill Dr
2 Sterndale Rd

Numbered streets
Street names for grid
squares which are not listed
on this page are shown at
the back of the index

A   B   C   D   E   F

Shotton Hill

G8
1 Pool End Cl
2 Roseacre Cl
3 Thornhill Wy

H1
1 Hawley Wy
2 Worcester Dr

H2
1 The Coppice
2 Landon Wy

H8
1 Harrison Ct
2 Pearmain Cl
3 Shepperton Court Dr

1 Ashdene Cl
2 Cornerside
3 Oxford Cl
4 Thorne Rd

G7
1 Bancroft Cl
2 Elmcroft Dr
3 Fontmell Pk

G7
1 Barley Mow Wy
2 Burbidge Rd
3 Ford Cl

FELTHAM

131

Surrey

Felthamhill

HFORD

FELTHAM RD

Littleton Common

Ashford Common

STAINES ROAD WEST

Sunbury Common

Queen Mary Reservoir

Sunbury Stn.

150

Littleton

Charlton

Upper Halliford Station

Littleton Church of England Infant School

TW17

Upper Halliford

Shepperton Green

Shepperton Business Park

Shepperton Station

B3366

164

GREEN LANE

Shepperton

L2
1 Cardinals Wk
2 Marlin Cl

L3
1 Percy Bryant Rd
2 Saddlebrook Pk

1 King George Cl

K3
1 Alexandra Cl
2 Rowland Wy
3 Squires Wk

K1
1 Beaumont Dr

1 Crosswell Cl
2 Harrow Wy
3 Lodge Wy
4 Queen Mary Rd

Numbered streets
Street names for grid
squares which are not listed
on this page are shown at
the back of the Index

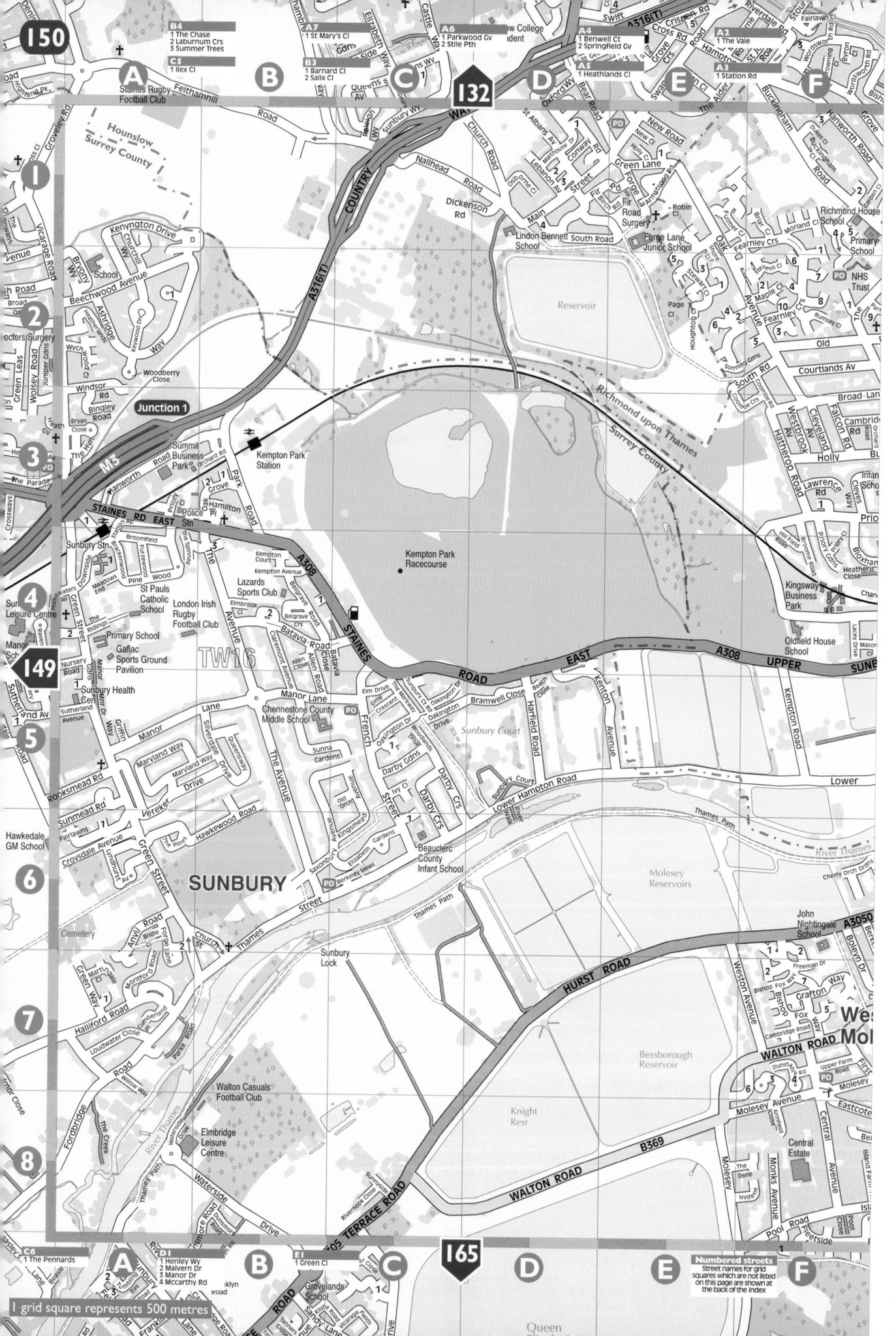

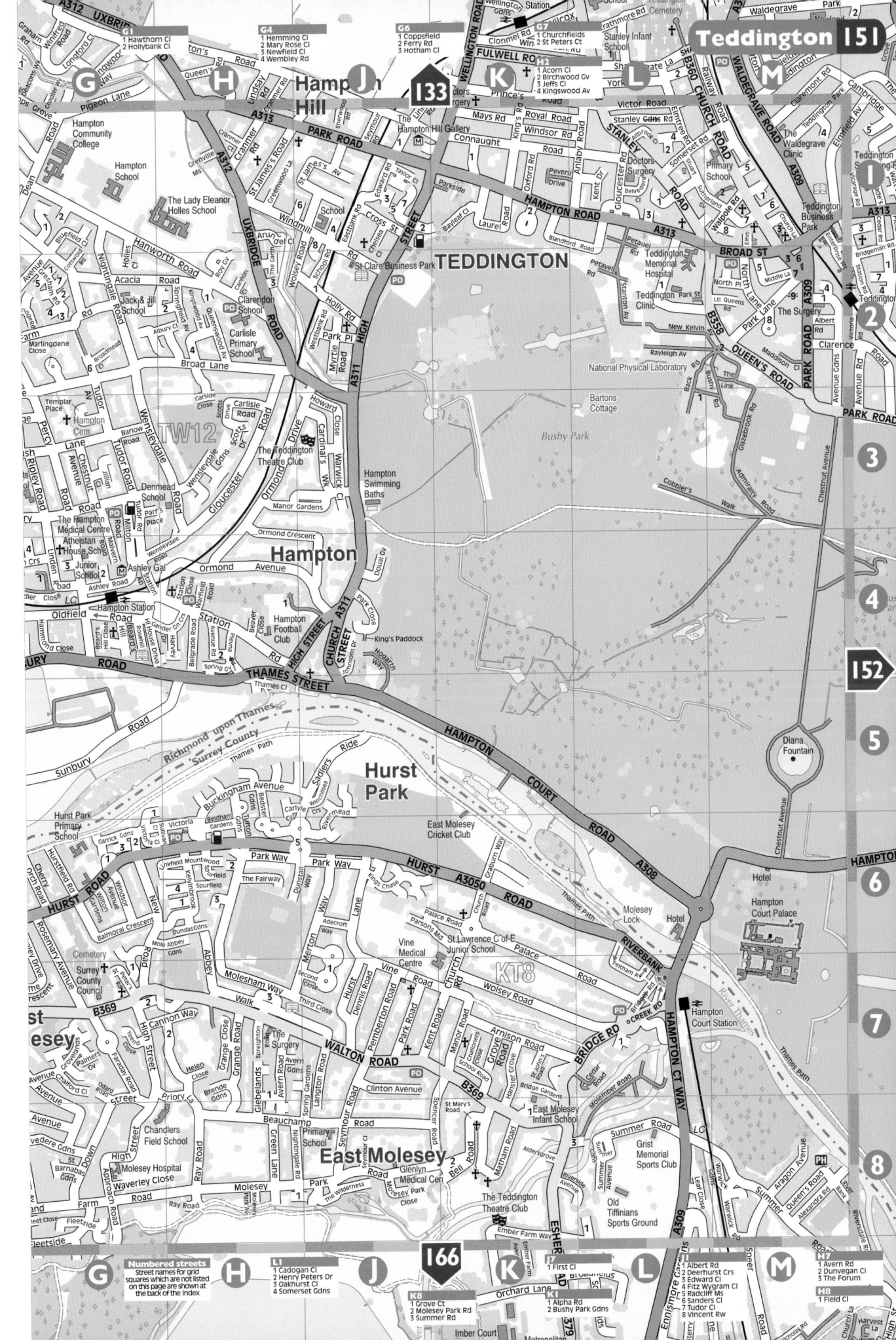

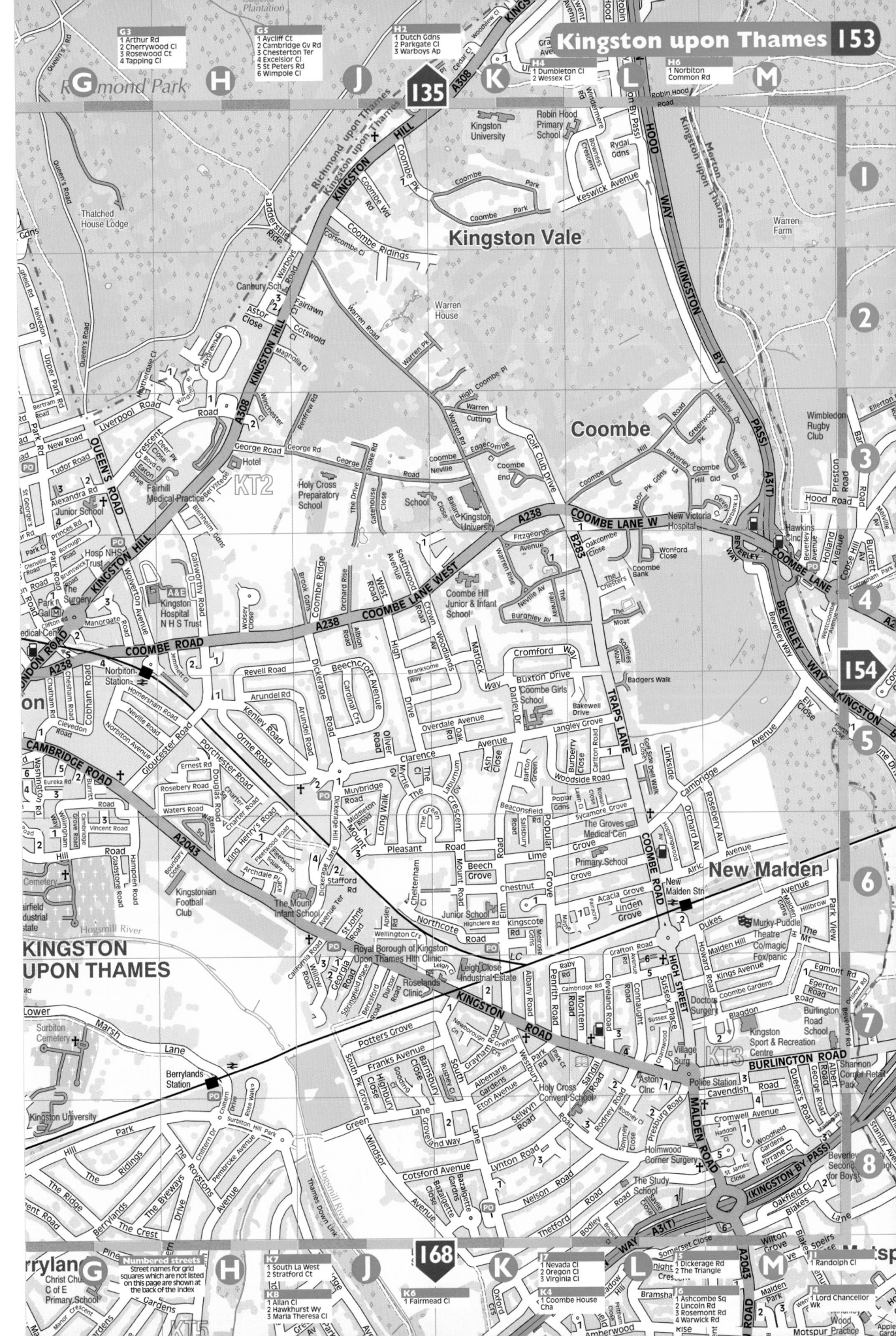

G3
1 Arthur Rd
2 Cherrywood Cl
3 Rosewood Ct
4 Tapping Cl

G5
1 Aycliff Ct
2 Cambridge Gv Rd
3 Chesterton Ter
4 Excelsior Cl
5 St Peters Rd
6 Wimpole Cl

H2
1 Dutch Gdns
2 Parkgate Cl
3 Warboys Ap

H4
1 Ul
2 Dumbleton Cl
3 Wessex Rd

H6
1 Norbiton
  Common Rd

Richmond upon Thames
Kingston upon Thames

135 A308

Kingston University

Robin Hood
Primary School

Kingston By Pass

Kingston upon Thames

Warren Farm

Kingston Vale

Coombe

Kingston University

Holy Cross
Preparatory School

KT2

Hotel

Kingston Hospital
N H S Trust

A238 COOMBE LANE WEST

Coombe Lane W

B283

New Victoria
Hospital

Wimbledon
Rugby Club

A3(T)

154

A238 COOMBE ROAD

Norbiton
Station

Coombe Hill
Junior & Infant School

Coombe Girls
School

TRAPS LANE

CAMBRIDGE ROAD

A2043

Kingstonian
Football Club

The Mount
Infant School

New
Malden Stn

New Malden

COOMBE ROAD

KINGSTON
UPON THAMES

Hogsmill River

Royal Borough of Kingston
upon Thames Hlth Clinic

Roselands
Clinic

Leigh Close
Industrial Estate

KINGSTON ROAD

Murky Puddle
Theatre
Co/magic
Fox/panic

KT3

Kingston
Sport & Recreation
Centre

BURLINGTON ROAD

Shannon
Corner Retail
Park

Surbiton
Cemetery

Berrylands
Station

Kingston University

Holy Cross
Convent School

Police Station

Doctors
Surgery

Holmwood
Corner Surgery

The Study
School

Beverley
Second
for Boys

A3(T)

(KINGSTON BY PASS)

Motspur

K5
1 Nevada Cl
2 Oregon Cl
3 Virginia Cl

K4
1 Dickerage Rd
2 The Triangle

M
1 Randolph Cl

Numbered streets
Street names for grid
squares which are not listed
on this page are shown at
the back of the index

K7
1 South La West
2 Stratford Ct

K6
1 Fairmead Cl

L
1 Coombe House
  Cha

M
1 Ashcombe Sq
2 Lincoln Rd
3 Rosemont Rd
4 Warwick Rd

M
1 Lord Chancellor
  Wk

K8
1 Allan Cl
2 Hawkhurst Wy
3 Maria Theresa Cl

Berrylands
Christ Church
C of E
Primary School

Motspur Practice

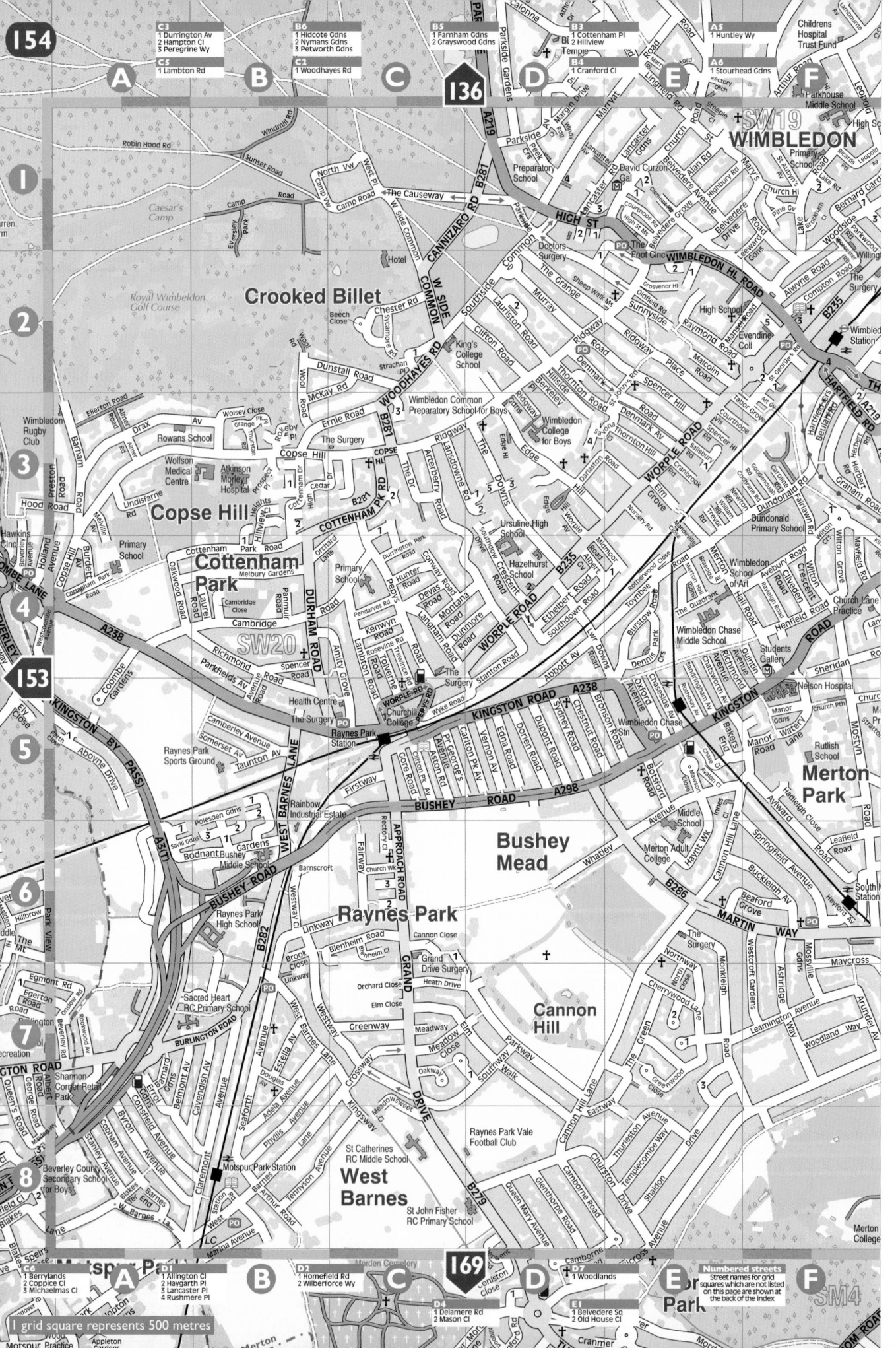

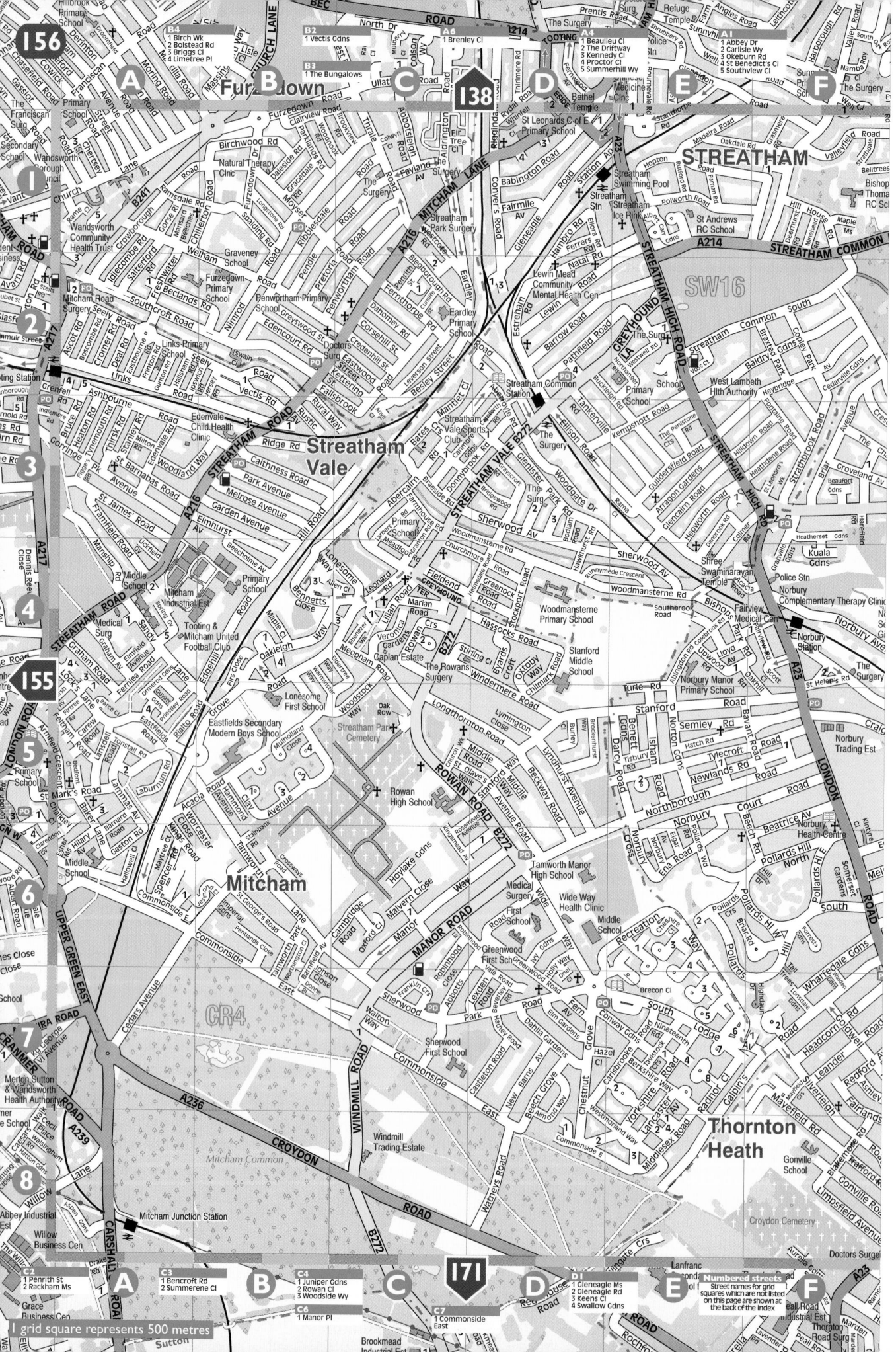

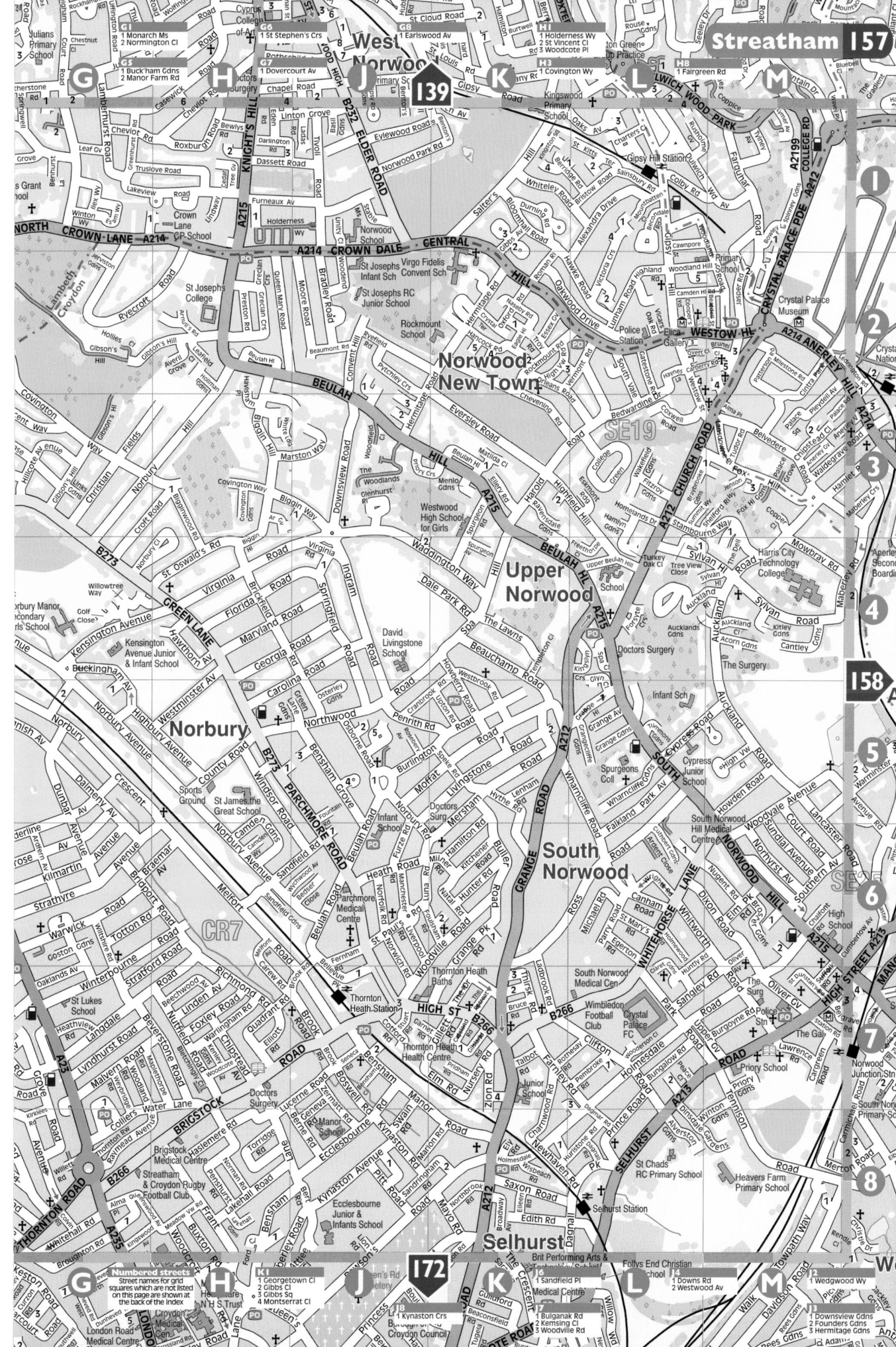

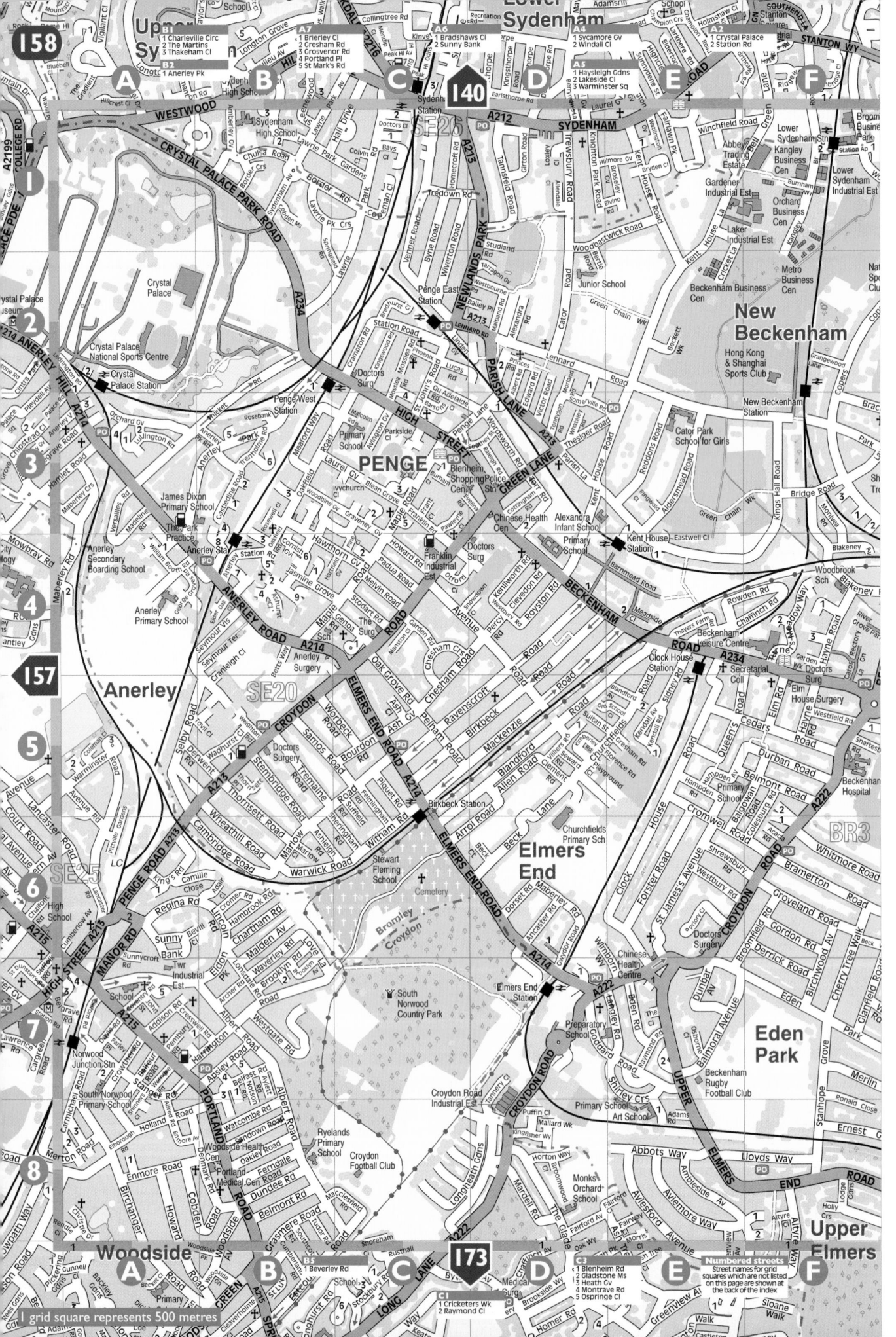

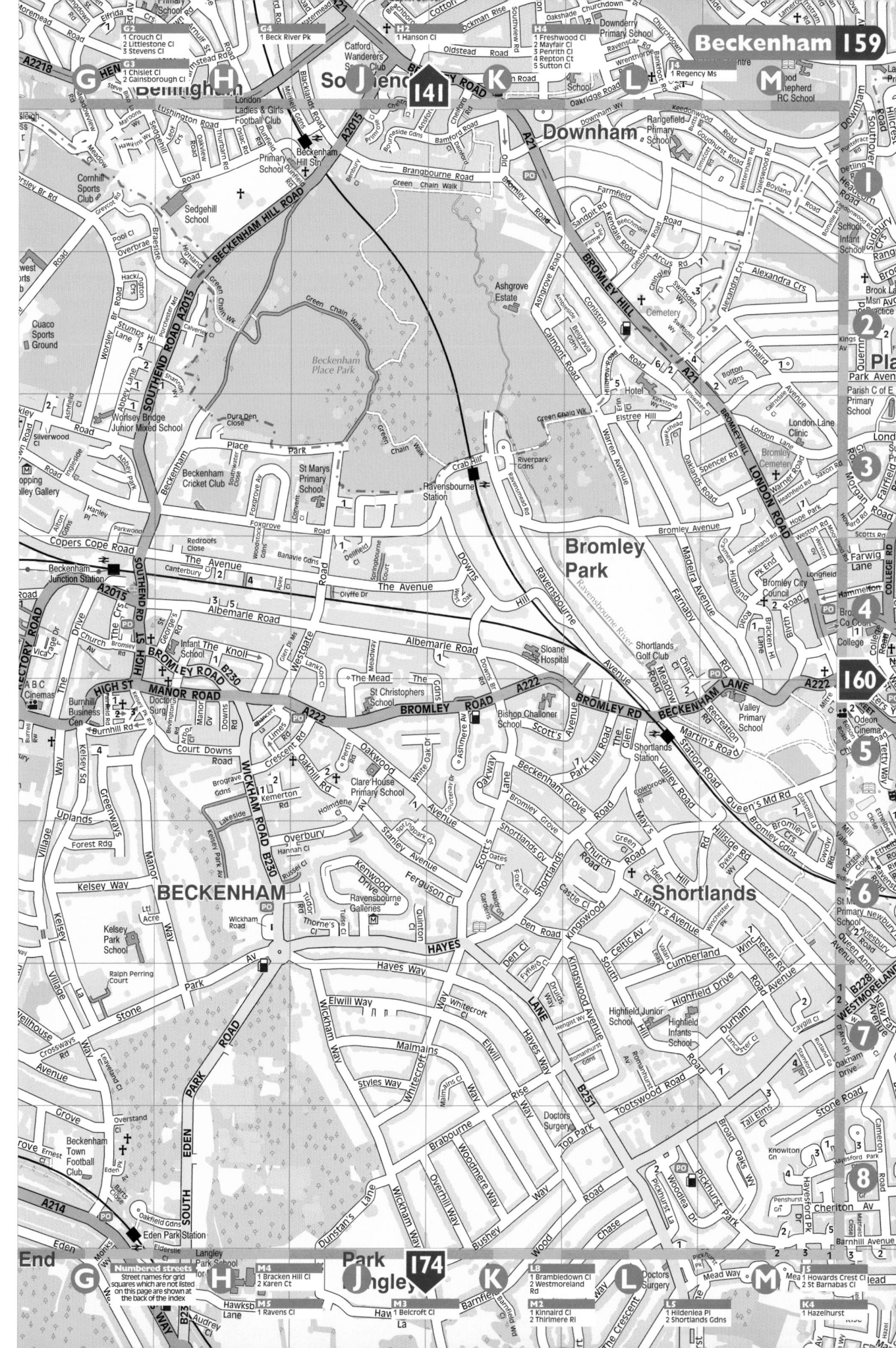

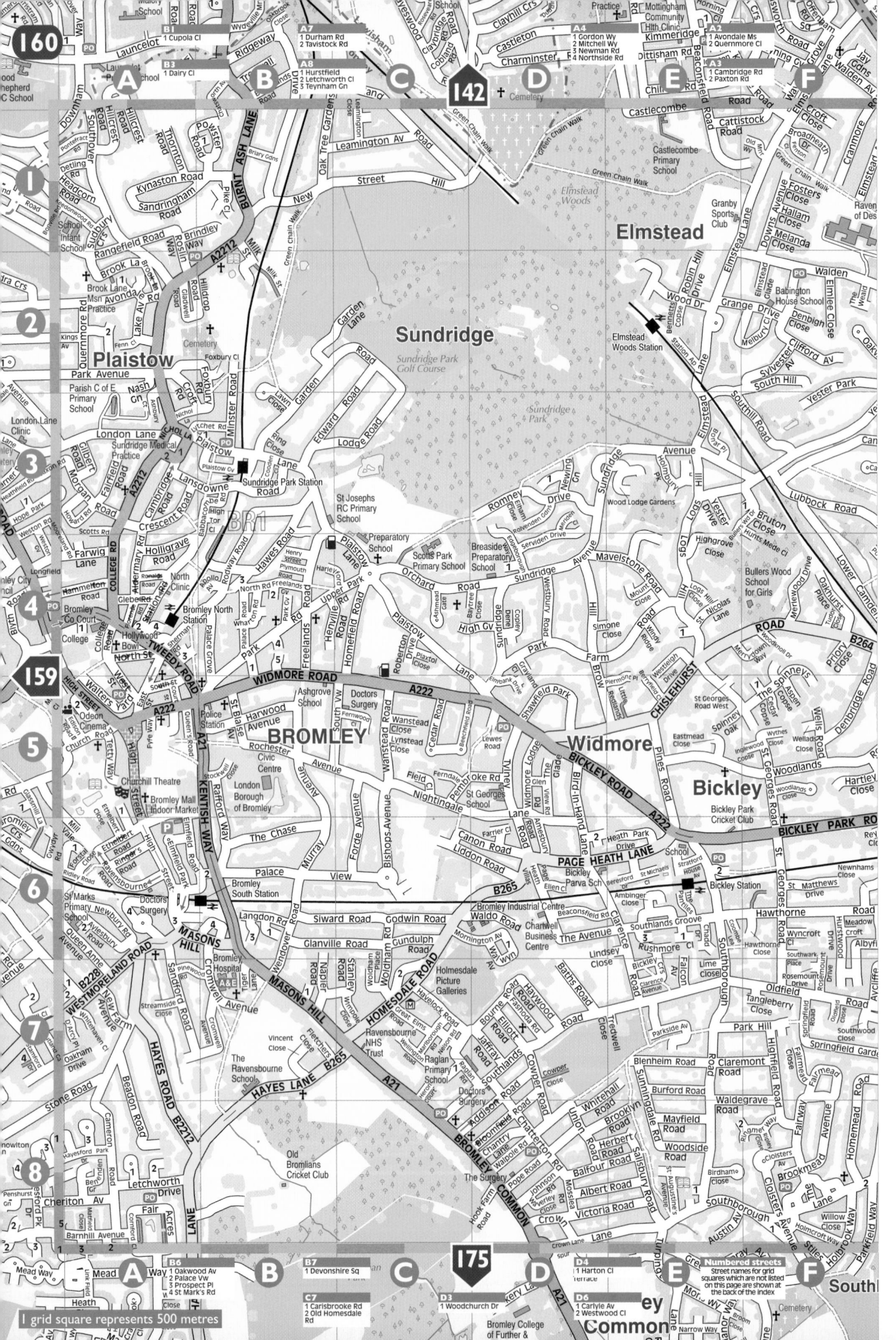

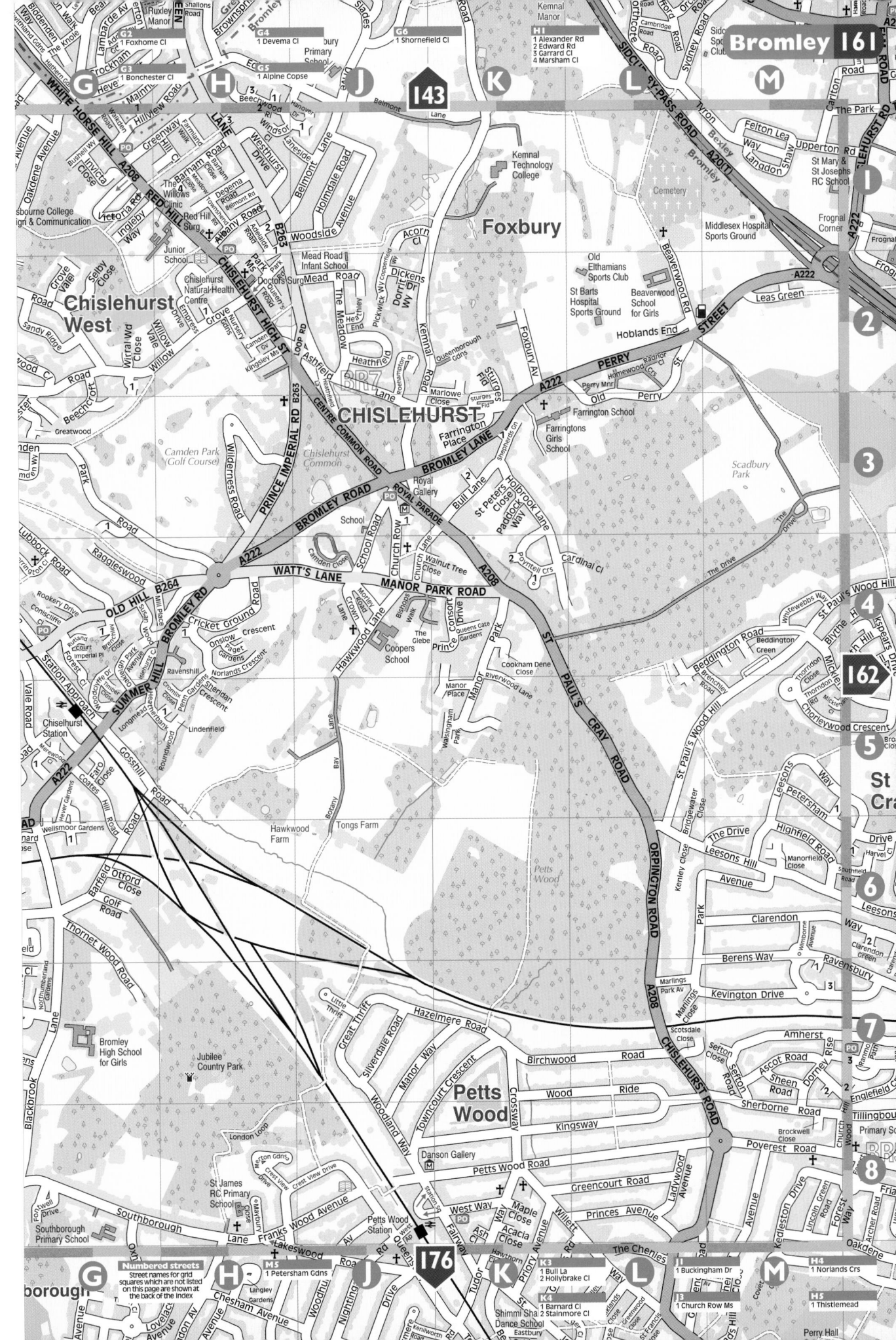

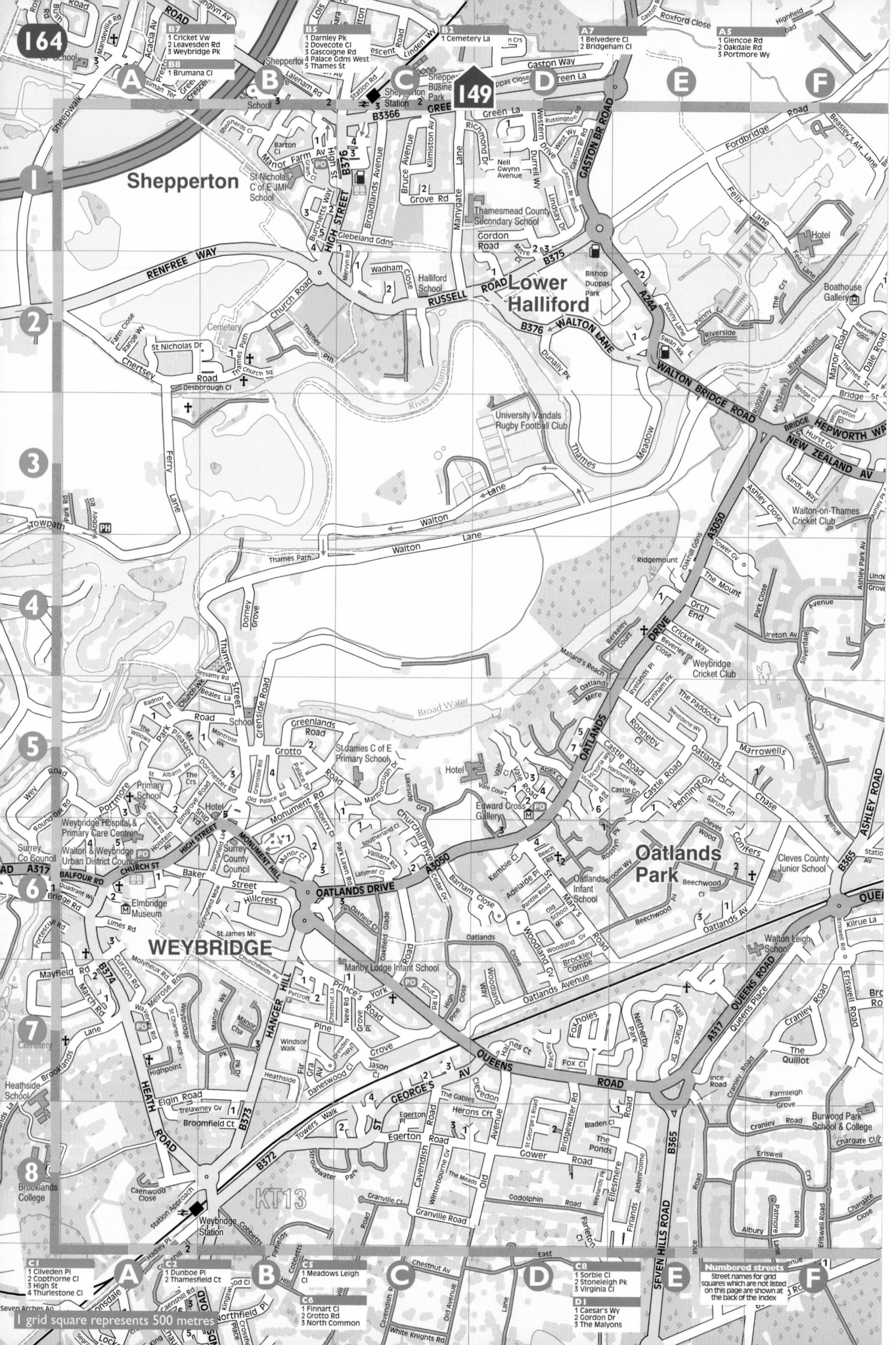

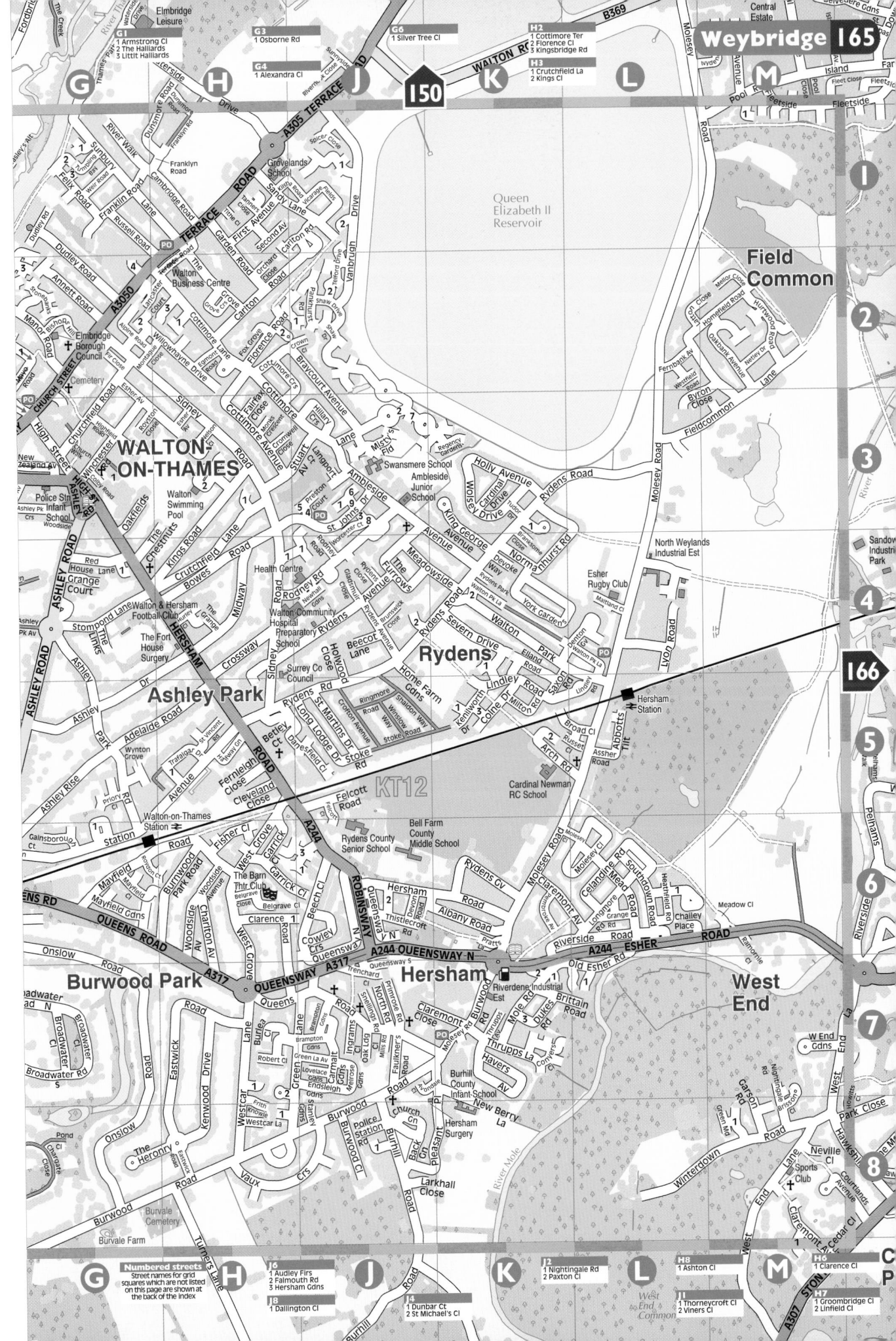

G
H
J
K
L
M

I
2
3
4
5
6
7
8

150
166

G1
1 Armstrong Cl
2 The Halliards
3 Littt Halliards

G3
1 Osborne Rd

G4
1 Alexandra Rd

G6
1 Silver Tree Cl

H2
1 Cottimore Ter
2 Florence Cl
3 Kingsbridge Rd

H3
1 Crutchfield La
2 Kings Cl

Queen
Elizabeth II
Reservoir

Field
Common

Sandow
Industrial
Park

WALTON-
ON-THAMES

Rydens

Ashley Park

KT12

Cardinal Newman
RC School

Hersham
Station

Burwood Park

Hersham

West
End

Walton-on-Thames
Station

Rydens County
Senior School

Bell Farm
County
Middle School

Numbered streets
Street names for grid
squares which are not listed
on this page are shown at
the back of the index

J6
1 Audley Firs
2 Falmouth Rd
3 Hersham Gdns

J8
1 Dallington Cl

J4
1 Dunbar Ct
2 St Michael's Cl

K2
1 Nightingale Rd
2 Paxton Cl

H8
1 Ashton Cl

H7
1 Thorneycroft Cl
2 Viners Cl

H6
1 Clarence Cl

H7
1 Groombridge Cl
2 Linfield Cl

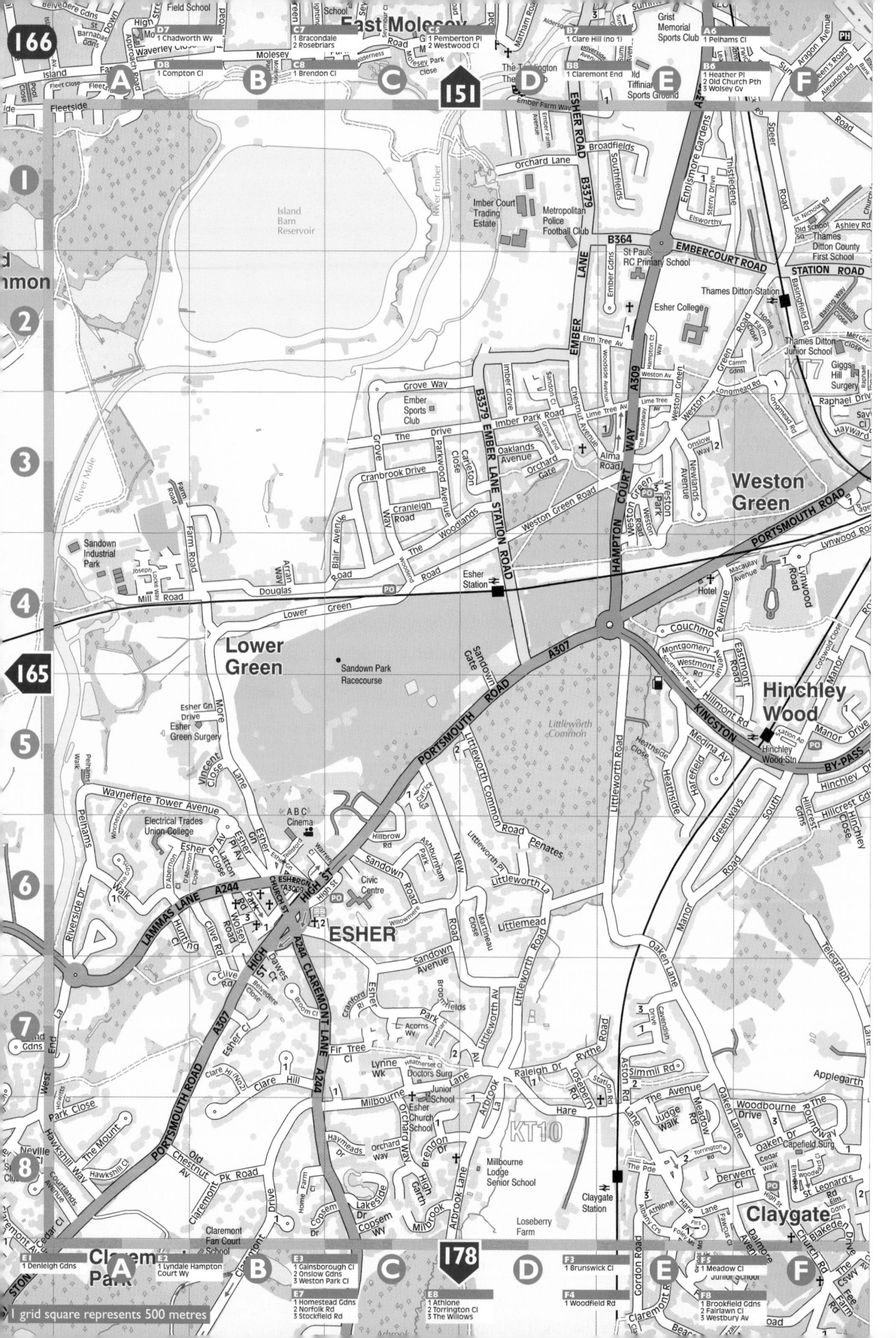

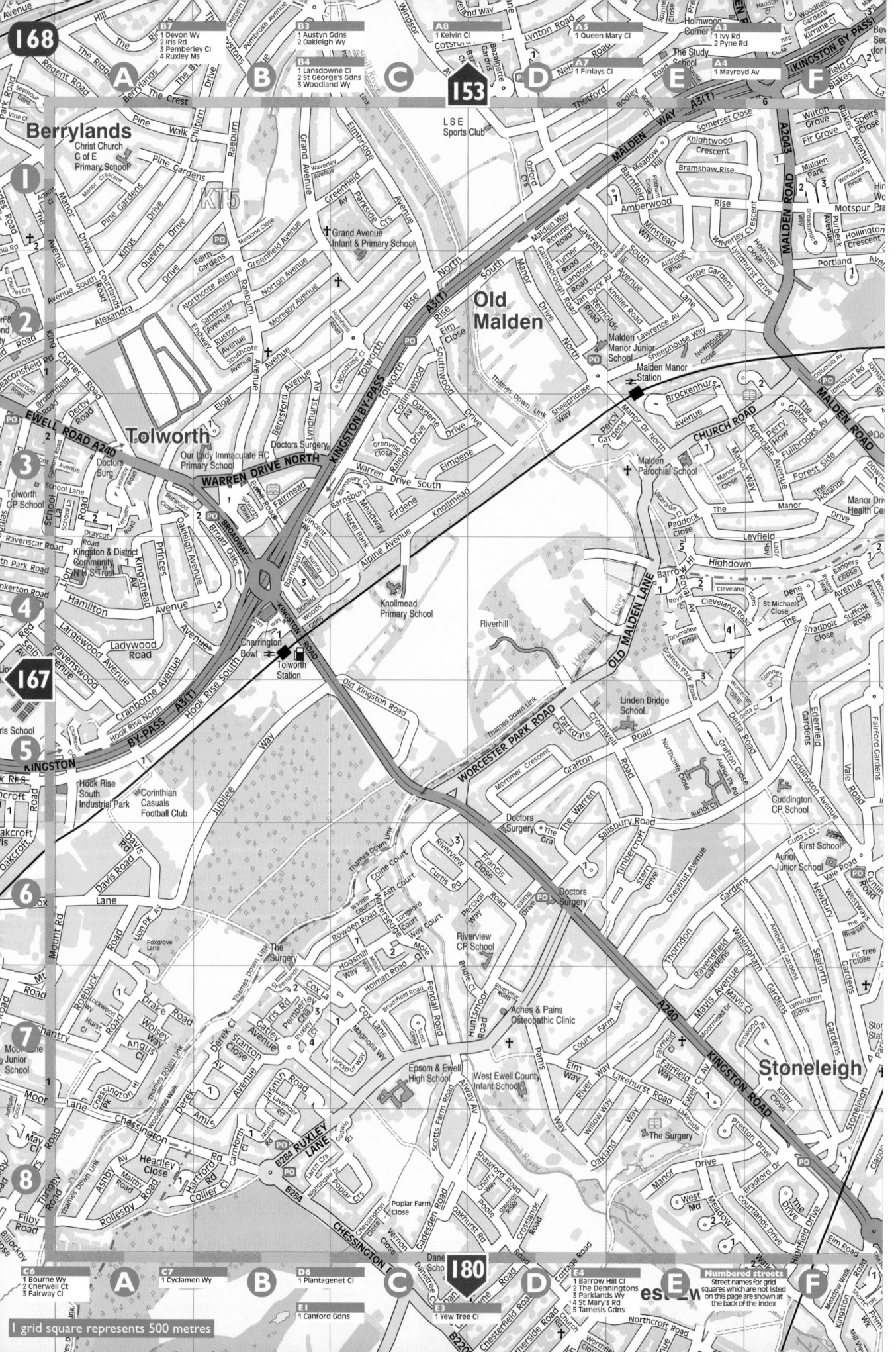

A   B   C   D   E   F

B2
1 Devon Wy
2 Iris Rd
3 Pemberley Cl
4 Ruxley Ms

B3
1 Austyn Gdns
2 Oakleigh Wy

A8
1 Kelvin Cl

A5
1 Queen Mary Cl

B4
1 Lansdowne Cl
2 St George's Gdns
3 Woodland Wy

153

A7
1 Finlays Cl

A4
1 Mayroyd Av

Berrylands

KT5

Old
Malden

Tolworth

167

Kingston

Stoneleigh

A   B   C   D   E   F

C6
1 Bourne Wy
2 Cherwell Ct
3 Fairway Cl

C7
1 Cyclamen Wy

D6
1 Plantagenet Cl

E1
1 Canford Gdns

E4
1 Barrow Hill Cl
2 The Denningtons
3 Parklands Wy
4 St Mary's Rd
5 Tamesis Gdns

E3
1 Yew Tree Cl

Numbered streets
Street names for grid
squares which are not listed
on this page are shown at
the back of the index

1 grid square represents 500 metres

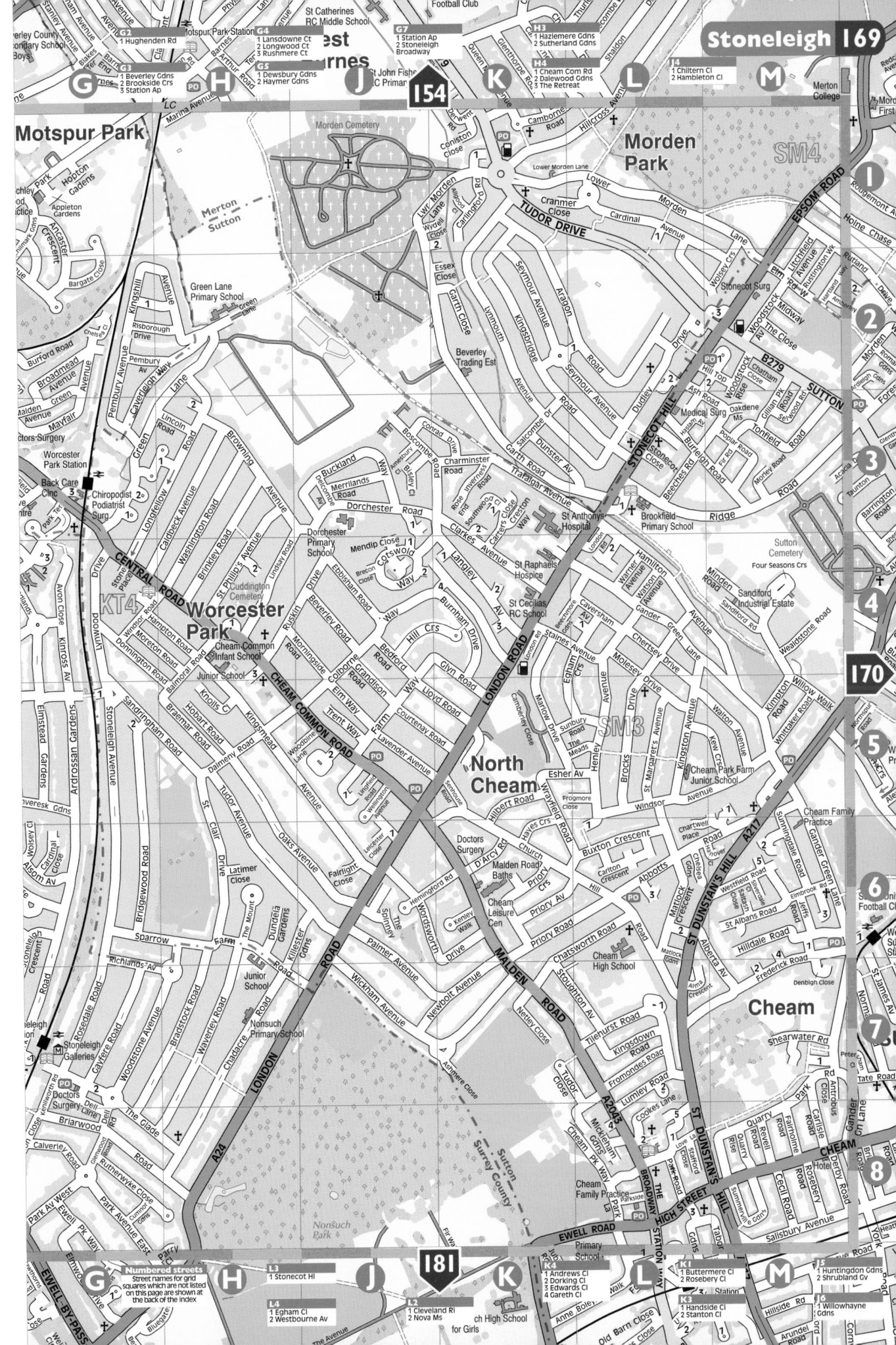

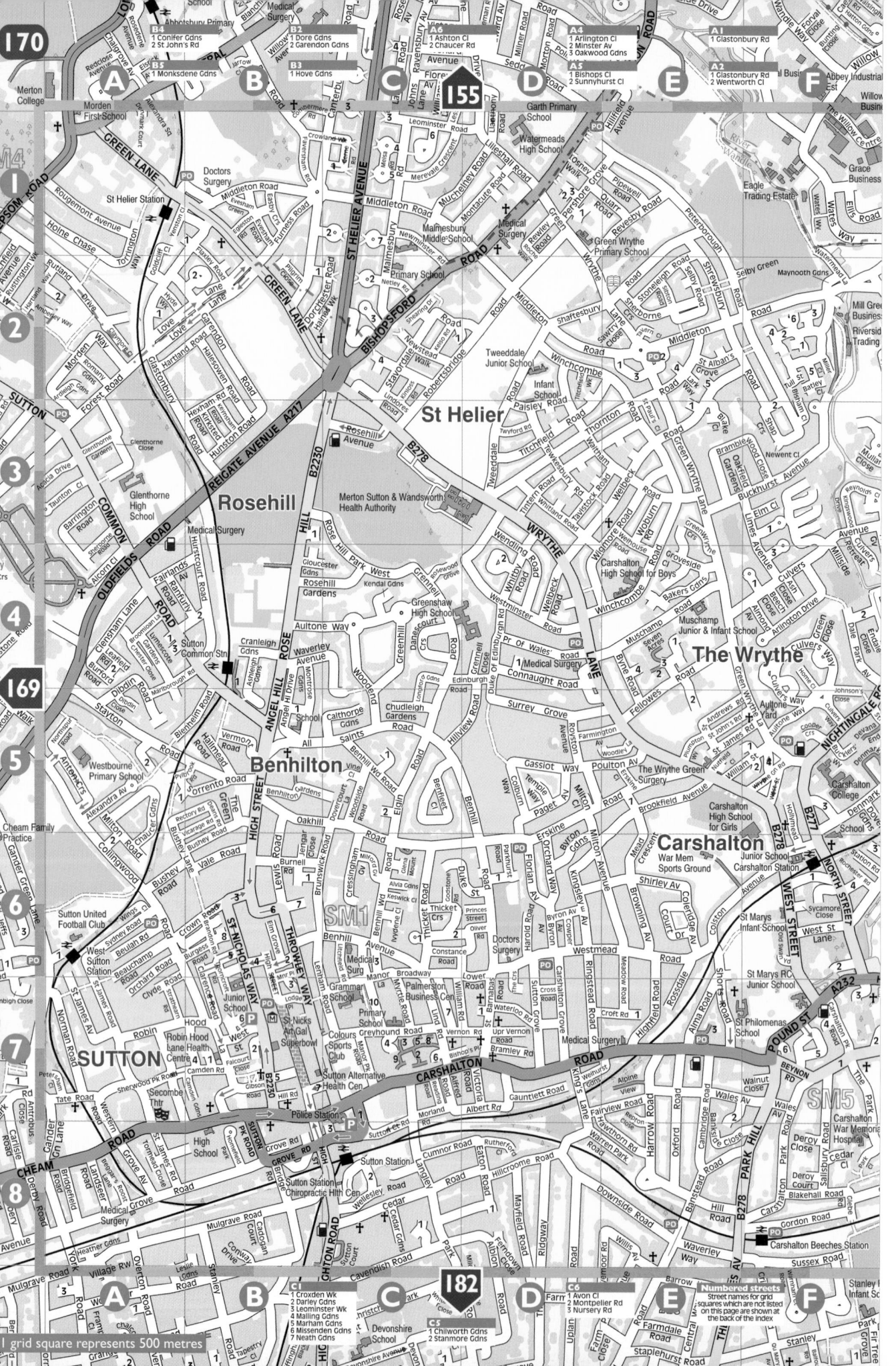

A4
1 Arlington Cl
2 Minster Av
3 Oakwood Gdns

A5
1 Bishops Cl
2 Sunnyhurst Cl

A1
1 Glastonbury Rd

A2
1 Glastonbury Rd
2 Wentworth Cl

A6
1 Ashton Cl
2 Chaucer Rd

B4
1 Conifer Gdns
2 St John's Rd

B5
1 Monksdene Gdns

B2
1 Dore Gdns
2 Garendon Gdns

B1
1 Hove Gdns

St Helier

Rosehill

Merton Sutton & Wandsworth
Health Authority

Benhilton

The Wrythe

Carshalton

SUTTON

SM1

SM5

C1
1 Croxden Wk
2 Darley Gdns
3 Leominster Wk
4 Malling Gdns
5 Marham Gdns
6 Missenden Gdns
7 Neath Gdns

C5
1 Chilworth Gdns
2 Stanmore Gdns

D2
1 Avon Cl
2 Montpelier Rd
3 Nursery Rd

Numbered streets
Street names for grid
squares which are not listed
on this page are shown at
the back of the index

I grid square represents 500 metres

A   B   C   D   E   F

1   2   3   4   5   6   7   8

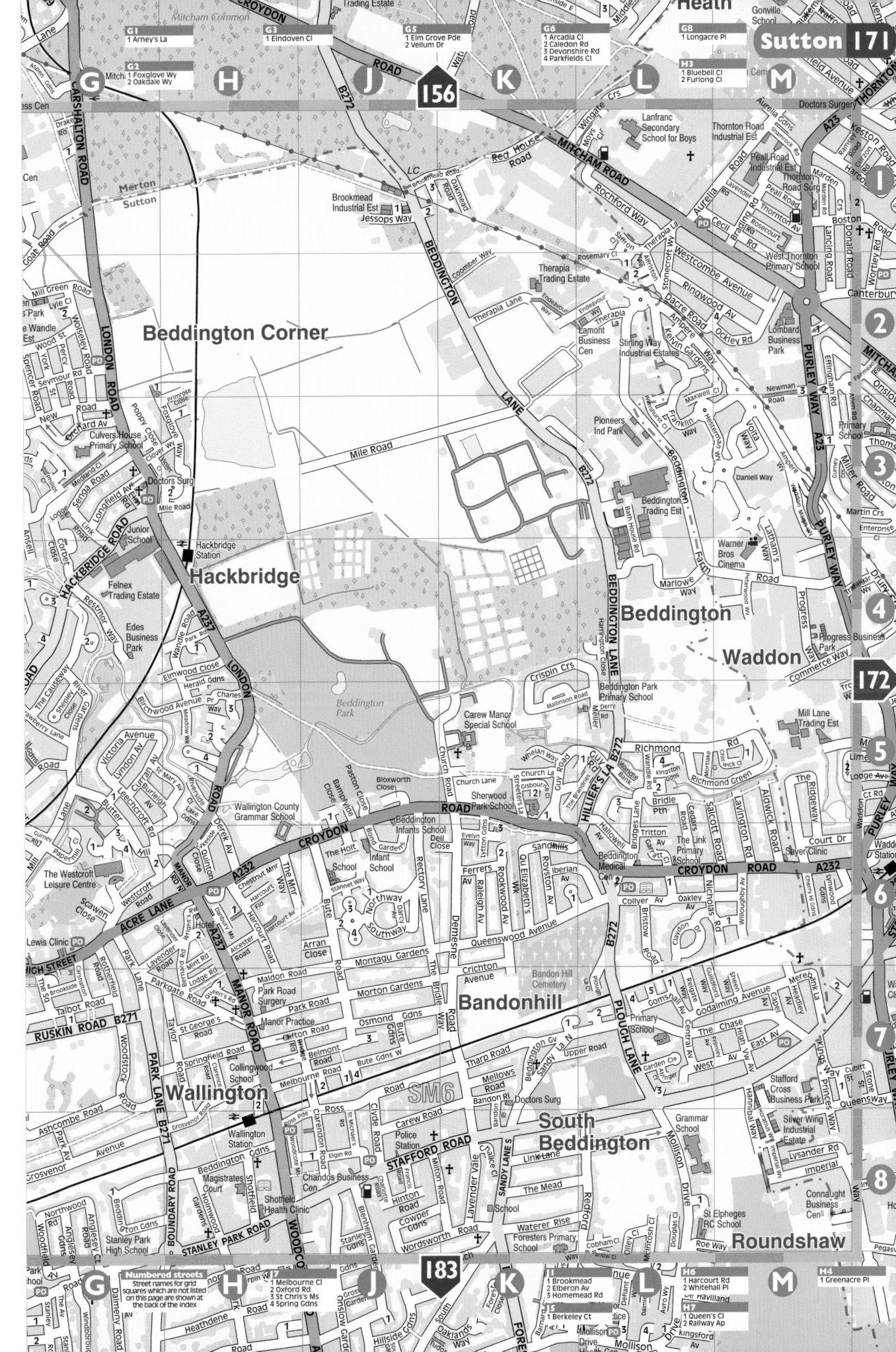

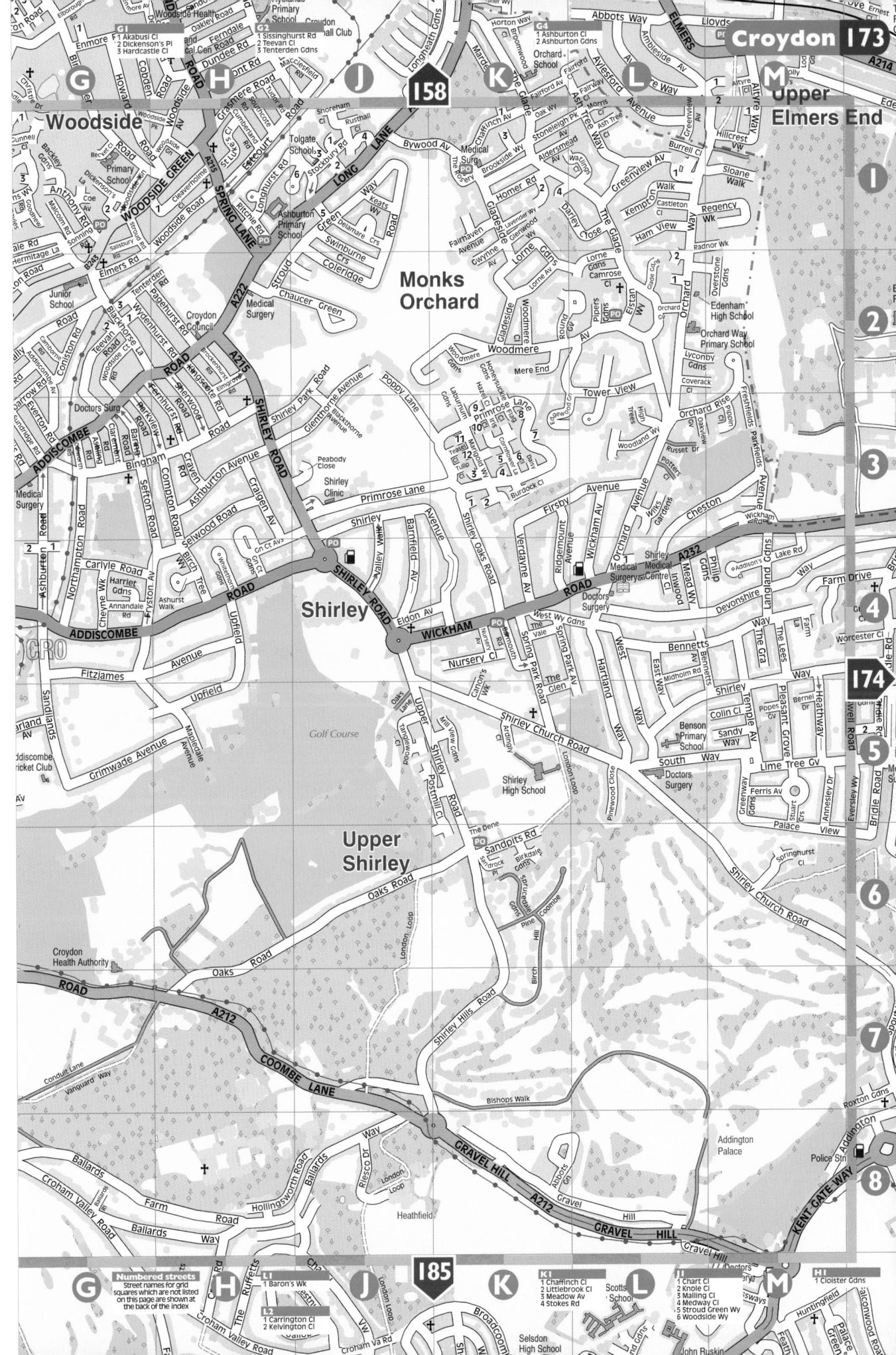

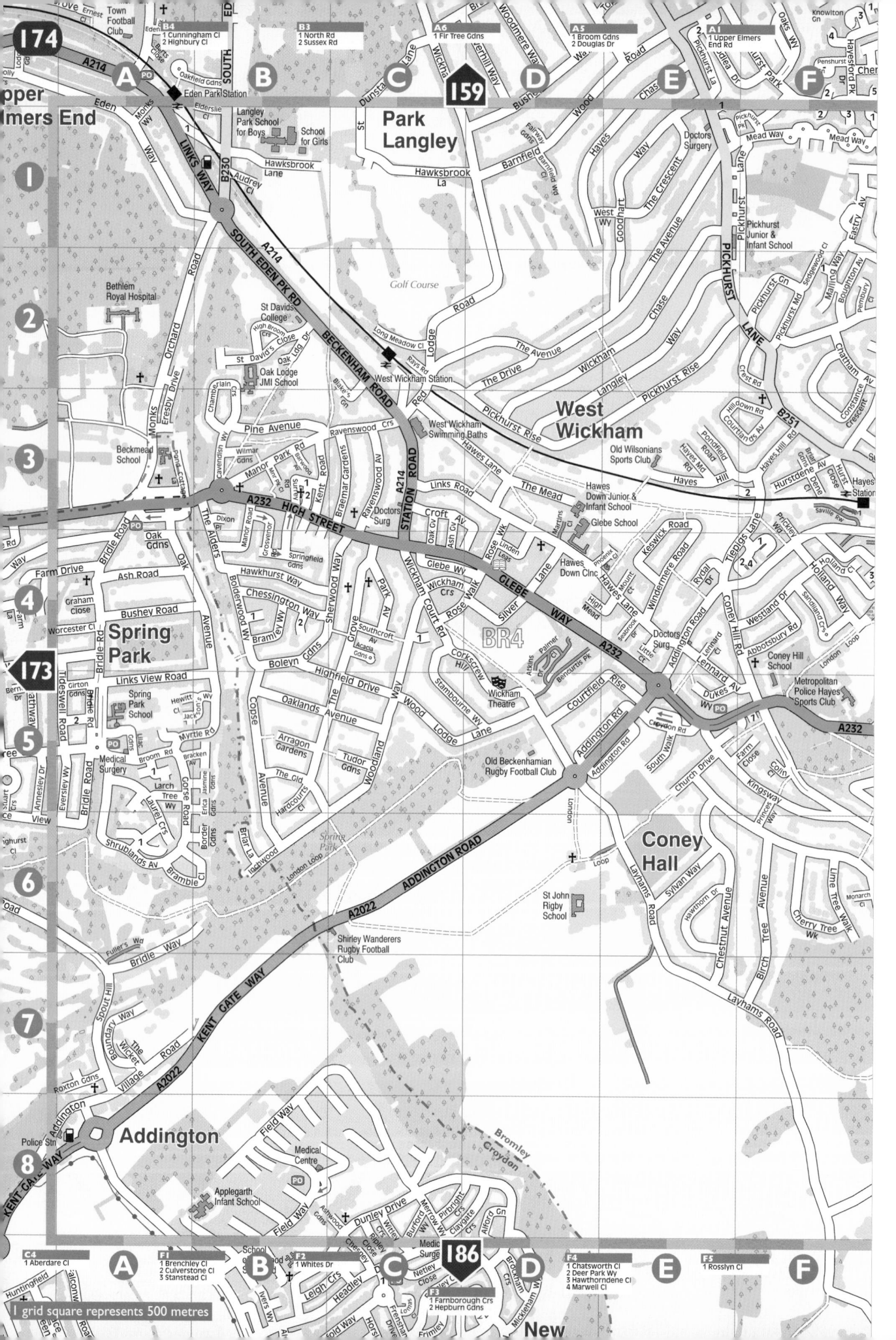

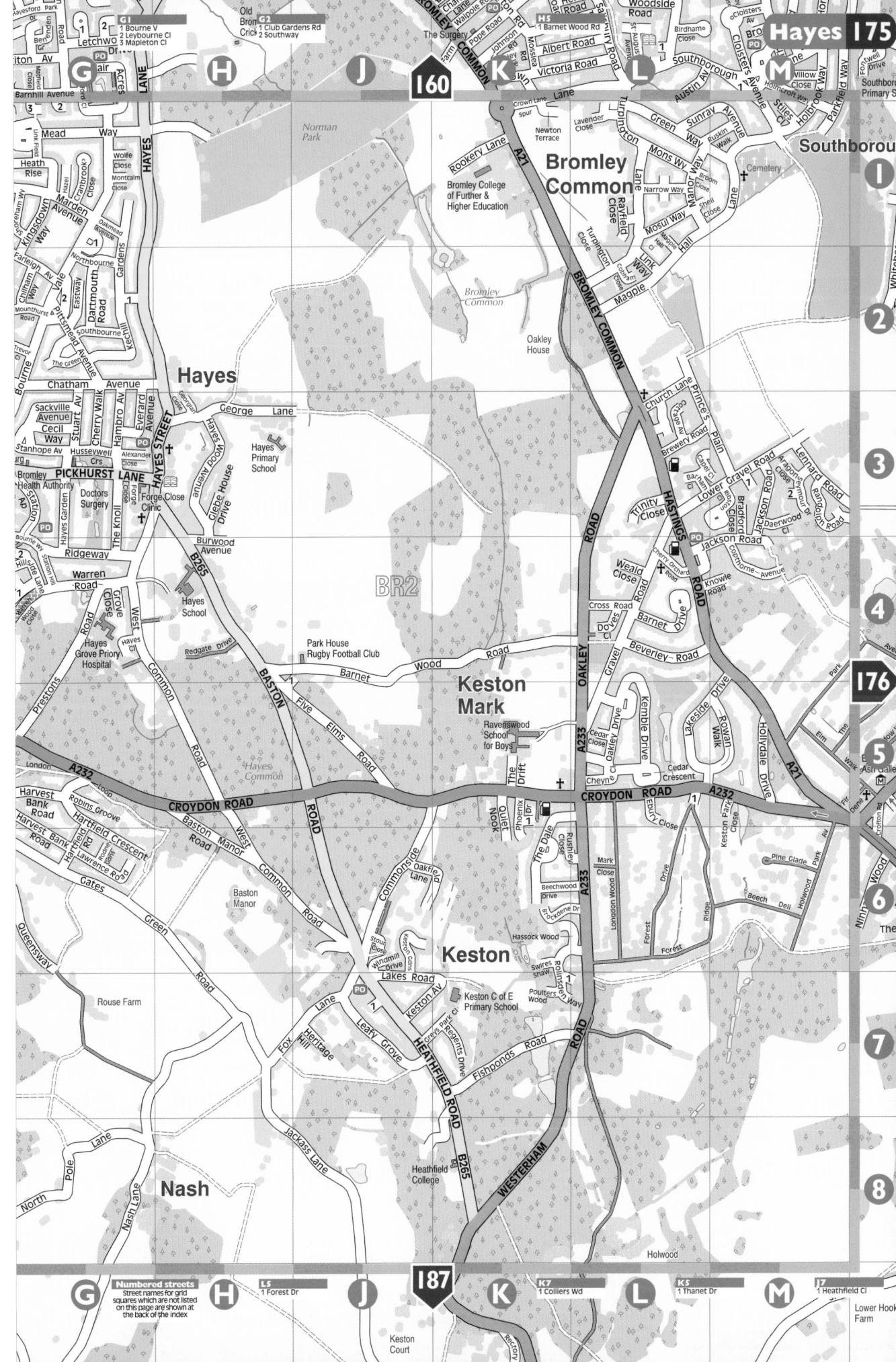

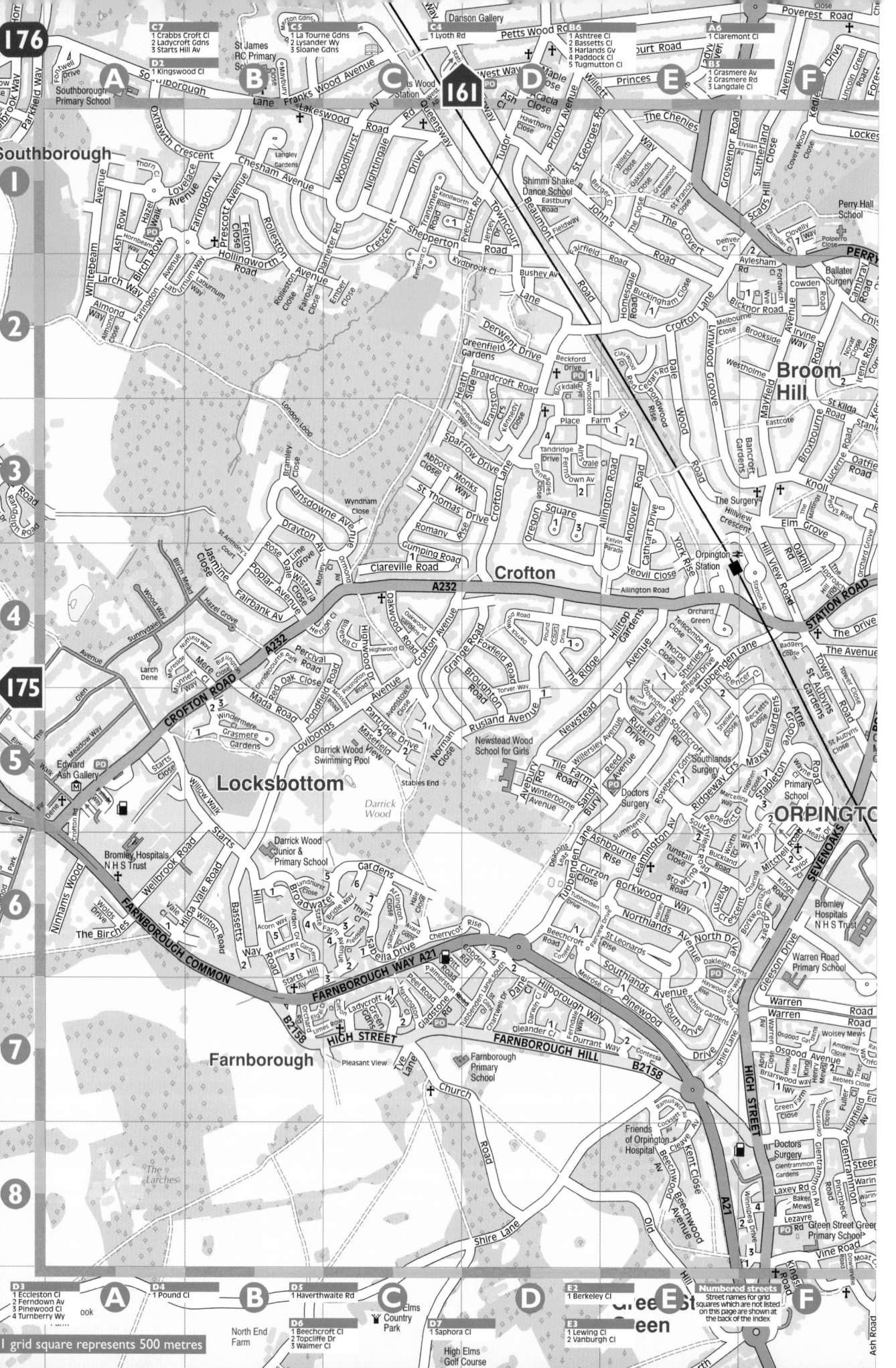

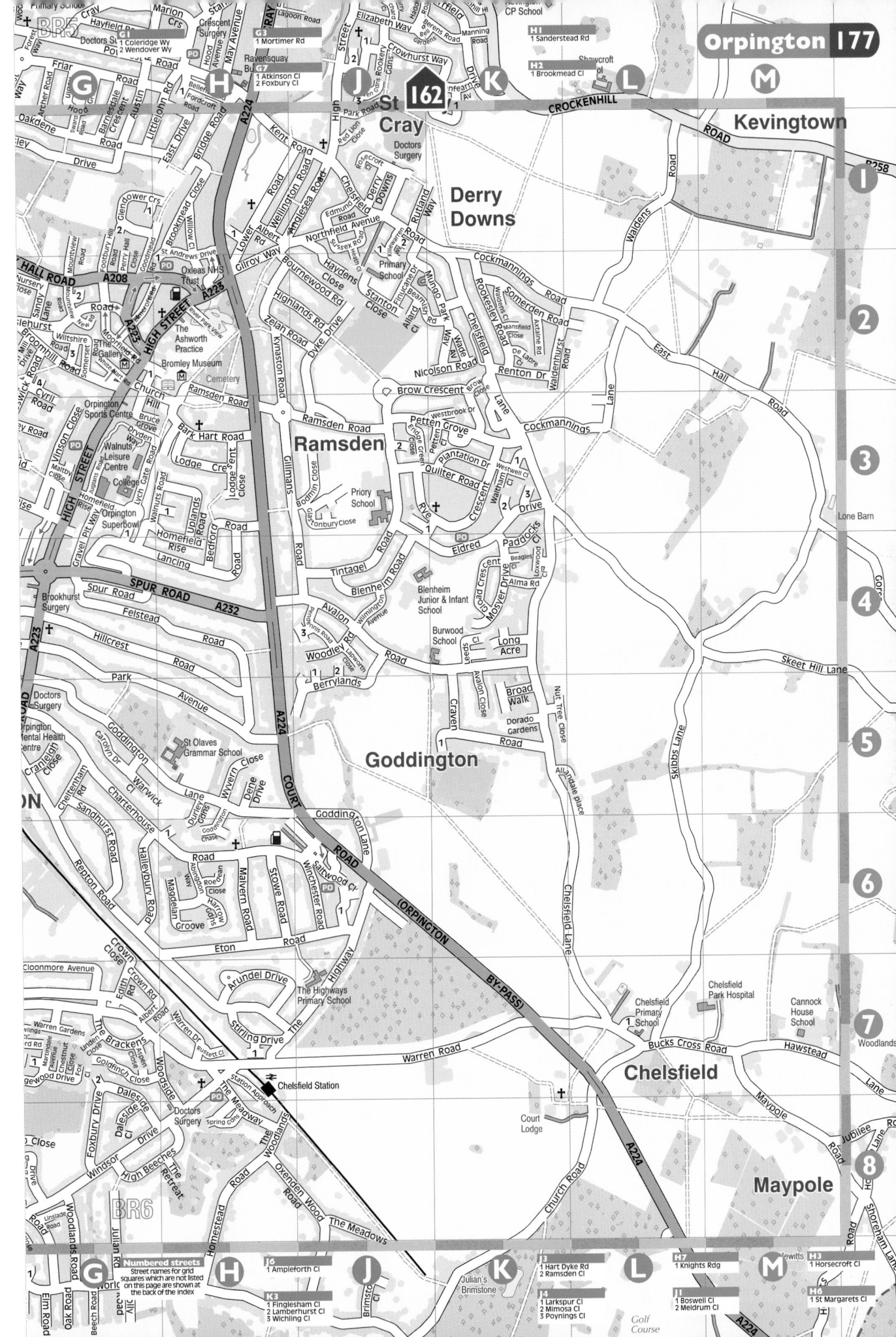

178

A B C **166** D E Clay F e

Claremont Park

1 Uplands Dr (D7) 1 Arnewood Cl (B7) 1 Sandroyd Wy (A6) 1 Beechwood Dr (A4)
2 Danesmead

Claremont Fan Court School

Millbourne Lodge Senior School

Claygate Station

Claygate Junior School

1

Claremont Landscape Garden (NT)

Esher Common

Black Pond

2 Blackhills

Arbrook Common

3

Arbrook Farm

A3(T)

A3(T)

A3(T)

Copsen Wd

Queens Drive

Stokesheath

Parkfields

Stokesheath Road

FAIROAK LANE

The Avenue

4 Beech Cl Ct

Spinney Cl

Sandy Dr

Brackenhill

Roundhill Wy

Sandy Lane

Queens Drive

The Spinney

Fair Oak Close

Moles Hill

Highfield

Prince's Coverts

5 Fairmile

Reeds School

Sandy Lane

The Ridings

Oxshott Heath

WARREN LANE

Heath

B280

Montrose Gdns

Broomfield

Leys Road

Spicer's Field

Prince's Drive

Stoke Wood

6 Fairmile Park Road

Lebanon Dr

Woodside Rd

Kimberley Ride

Goldrings Road

Oxshott Station

Holtwood Road

Oxshott

Birds Hill Rd

Furze Field

High Drive

Woodsway

7 Little Heath

Hawkhurst

Somerville Road

Richards Road

Webster Cl

Waverley Road

Oxshott Medical Practice

Websters Art Gallery

Oakshade Road

Royal Kent (C of E) First & Middle School

Danes Close

Broom Hall

LEATHERHEAD RD

Fernhill

Danes Way

Meadway

1 Woodlands Cl (F1) 1 Holroyd Rd (F2)

Danes Hill Preparatory School

Wren's Hill

Old Farmhouse Drive

Falconhurst

8

Bridle Lane

Manor Way

Charlwood Drive

Spinneycroft

LEATHERHEAD ROAD

A B C D E A244 F

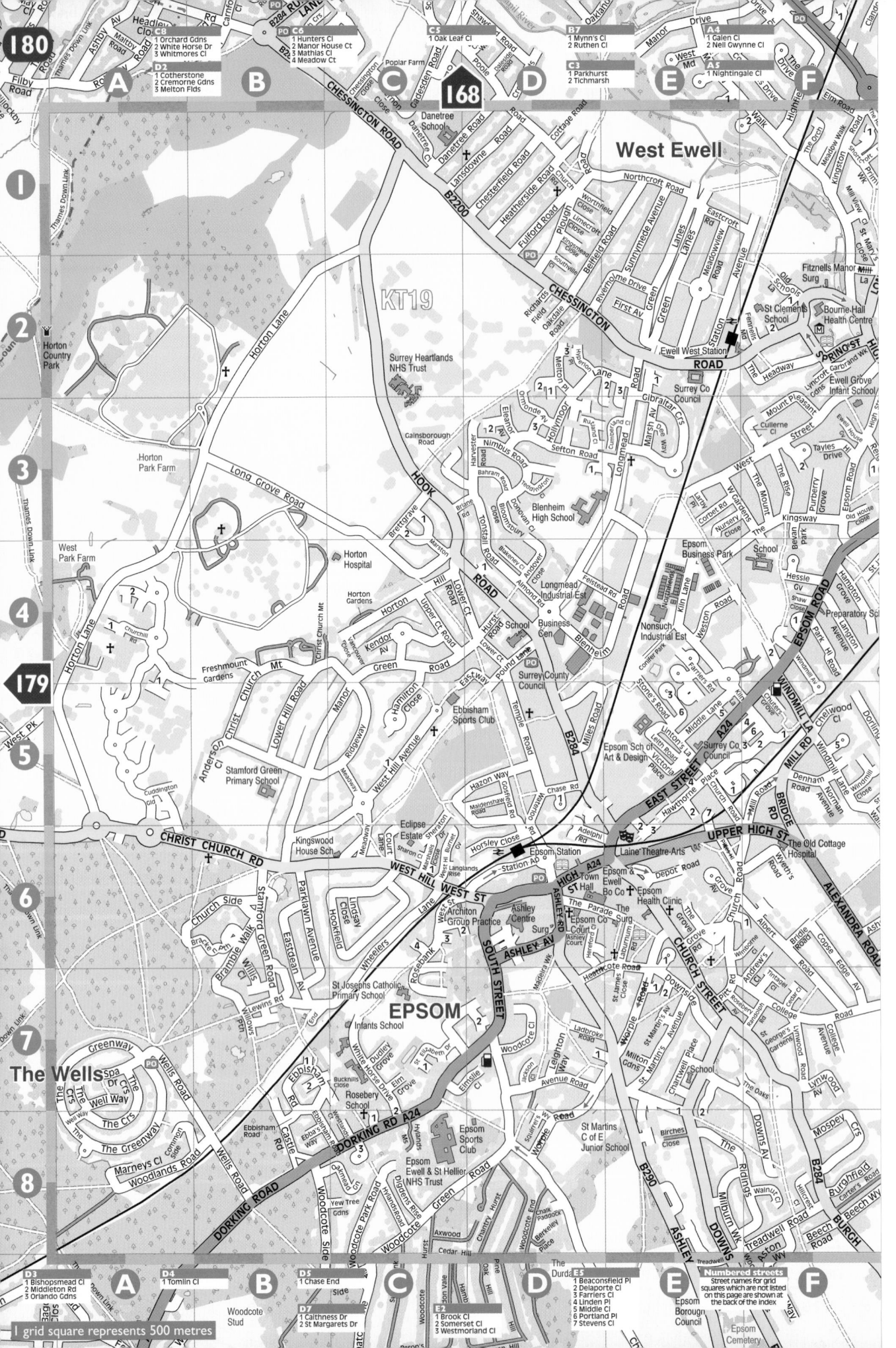

180

I

2

3

4

179

5

6

7

8

KT19

168

West Ewell

Horton Country Park

Horton Park Farm

West Park Farm

Surrey Heartlands NHS Trust

Blenheim High School

Epsom Business Park

Horton Hospital

Horton Gardens

Longmead Industrial Est

Nonsuch Industrial Est

Freshmount Gardens

Stamford Green Primary School

Ebbisham Sports Club

Surrey County Council

Epsom Sch of Art & Design

CHRIST CHURCH RD

Kingswood House Sch

Eclipse Estate

WEST HILL

WEST ST

Epsom Station

The Wells

EPSOM

St Josephs Catholic Primary School

Rosebery School

DORKING RD A24

Epsom Sports Club

Epsom Ewell & St Hellier NHS Trust

St Martins C of E Junior School

UPPER HIGH ST

The Old Cottage Hospital

Woodcote Stud

Epsom Borough Council

Epsom Cemetery

1 grid square represents 500 metres

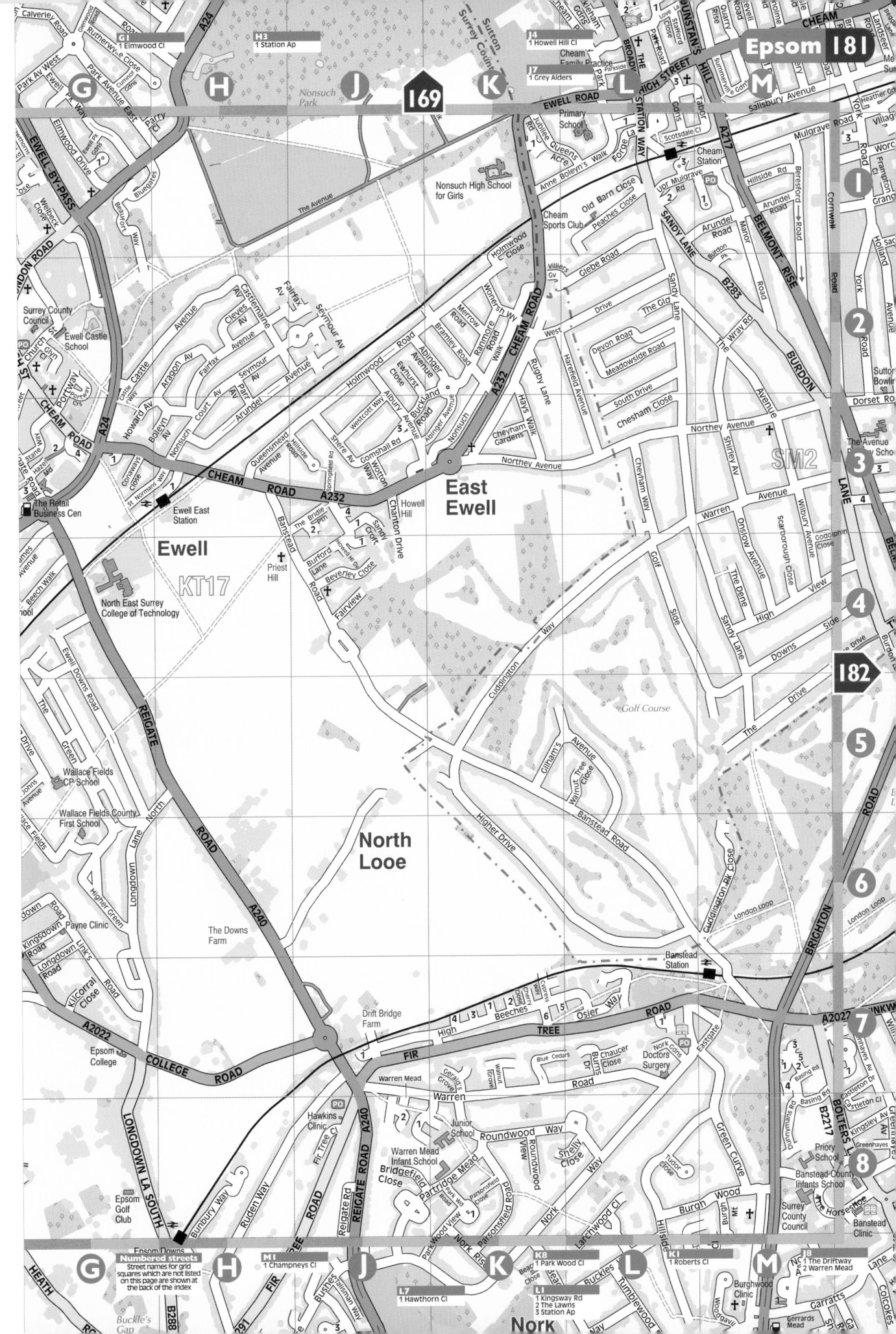

G **H** **J** **169** **K** **L** **M**

I

2

3

4

182

5

6

7

8

Calverley Road
Rutherwyke Close
Cunnor Gdns
Park Av West
Park Avenue East
Ewell Park Way
EWELL-BY-PASS
Elmwood Drive
Elmwood Close
Walbert Close
Beaufort Way
BURDON ROAD
Surrey County Council
Church
PO
Ewell Castle School
Ewell Castle
Castle Cp's
Portway
Thames
Stane
Hazel
CHEAM ROAD
A24
St Norman's
Conways Close
Castlemaine Av
Fairfax Av
Cleves Av
Castle Way
Howard Av
Aragon Av
Boleyn Av
Nonsuch Court Av
Fairfax
Seymour Av
Arundel
Seymour Av
Seymour Avenue
Avenue

Nonsuch Park
Party Rd
The Avenue

Holmwood Road
Holmwood
Holmwood Close
Merrow Road
Womersh Walk
Bramley Road
Ratmore Road
CHEAM ROAD
A232
West

Nonsuch High School for Girls

Ewell Road
Primary School
Jubilee Way
Queens Acre
Anne Boleyn's Walk
Forge La
Cheam Sports Club
Old Barn Close
Peaches Close
Villiers Gv
Glebe Road
Upr Mulgrave Rd
PO
Scotsdale Cl
Cheam Station
Burdon
Sandy Lane
SANDY LANE
Arundel Road
Manor
B283
BELMONT RISE
Cornwall Road
York Road
Hillside Rd
Beresford Road
Arundel Road
Holland Av
Frampton Rd
Worc

CHEAM
DUNSTAN'S HILL
THE BROADWAY
HIGH STREET
Tabor
Salisbury Avenue
Mulgrave Road
Heather Cl
Village

SM2
The Wray Rd
The Old
Devon Road
Meadowside Road
South Drive
Chesham Close
Northey Avenue
Shirley Av
Cheyham Way
Warren
Avenue
The Dene
Sandy Lane
High
Scarborough Close
Wilburn Avenue
Onslow Avenue
Godolphin Cl
The Avenue
Suy Scho
Suy Scho
Sutton Bowli
Dorset Rd
Harefield Avenue
Rugby Lane
Hays Walk
Cheyham Gardens
Northey Avenue
Chanton Drive
Hilside Road
Queensmead Avenue
Albury Avenue
Buckland Avenue
Abinger Avenue
Abinger Avenue
Westcott Way
Gomshall Rd
Shere Av
Wotton
Way
Ewhurst Close

East
Ewell

Howell Hill
Sandy Croft
The Bridle Pth
Burford Lane
Howell Hl Gv
Beverley Close
Fairview
Priest Hill
Banstead Road
Banstead Rd

Ewell

KT17

North East Surrey College of Technology

Beech Walk
hool
The Avenue
John's Avenue
The Green
The Drive
Ewell Downs Road
REIGATE ROAD
A240
Cuddington
Way
Golf Side
Side
The Downs
Golf Course

182

Walnut Tree Close
Gilnam's
Avenue
Banstead Road
London Loop
Cuddington Pk Close
London Loop
BRIGHTON ROAD
London Loop

Wallace Fields CP School
Wallace Fields County First School
Longdown Lane North
Higher Green
Higher Drive
Payne Clinic
Longdown Road
Kingsdown Road
Kilcorral Close
Links Road
Longdown Road

North
Looe

The Downs Farm

Higher Drive

Drift Bridge Farm
High
Beeches
Osler Way
TREE ROAD
Banstead Station
A2022

Cherry Way
Cypress Way
Nork Cons
Nork PO
Eastgate
Nork
Doctors Surgery

HNKW
B2217
Mayhaes Av
Willi
Basing Rd
Basing Rd
Castleton Dr
Streeton Cl
Greenhayes
Kingsley Av
Priory School
Greenhayes
The Horseshoe
Banstead County Infants School
Surrey County Council
Banstead Clinic

Epsom College
A2022 COLLEGE ROAD
FIR
Warren Mead
Gerard's Grove
Walnut Grove
Burns Close
Chaucer Close
Blue Cedars
Warren
Burns Close
WARREN
Hawkins Clinic
PO
Fir Tree Road
REIGATE ROAD
A240
Junior School
Roundwood Way
Roundwood View
Roundwood Way
Shelly Close
Way
Green Curve
Burgh Wood
Tudor Close

LONGDOWN LA SOUTH
Bunbury Way
Ruden Way
FIR TREE ROAD
Reigate Rd
Warren Mead Infant School
Bridgefield Close
Partridge Mead
Parsonsfield Close
Parsonsfield Road
Park Road
Nork Way
Nork Rise
Larchwood Close
Hillside Rd
Burgh Wood
Tumblewood
Burghwood Clinic

Epsom Golf Club

G **H** **J** **K** **L** **M**

M1
1 Champneys Cl

K8
1 Park Wood Cl

K1
1 Roberts Cl

NC
1 The Driftway
2 Warren Mead

L7
1 Hawthorn Cl

1 Kingsway Rd
2 The Lawns
3 Station Ap

HEATH
B288
Buckle's Gap
291
Bushes
Talisman Way

Nork

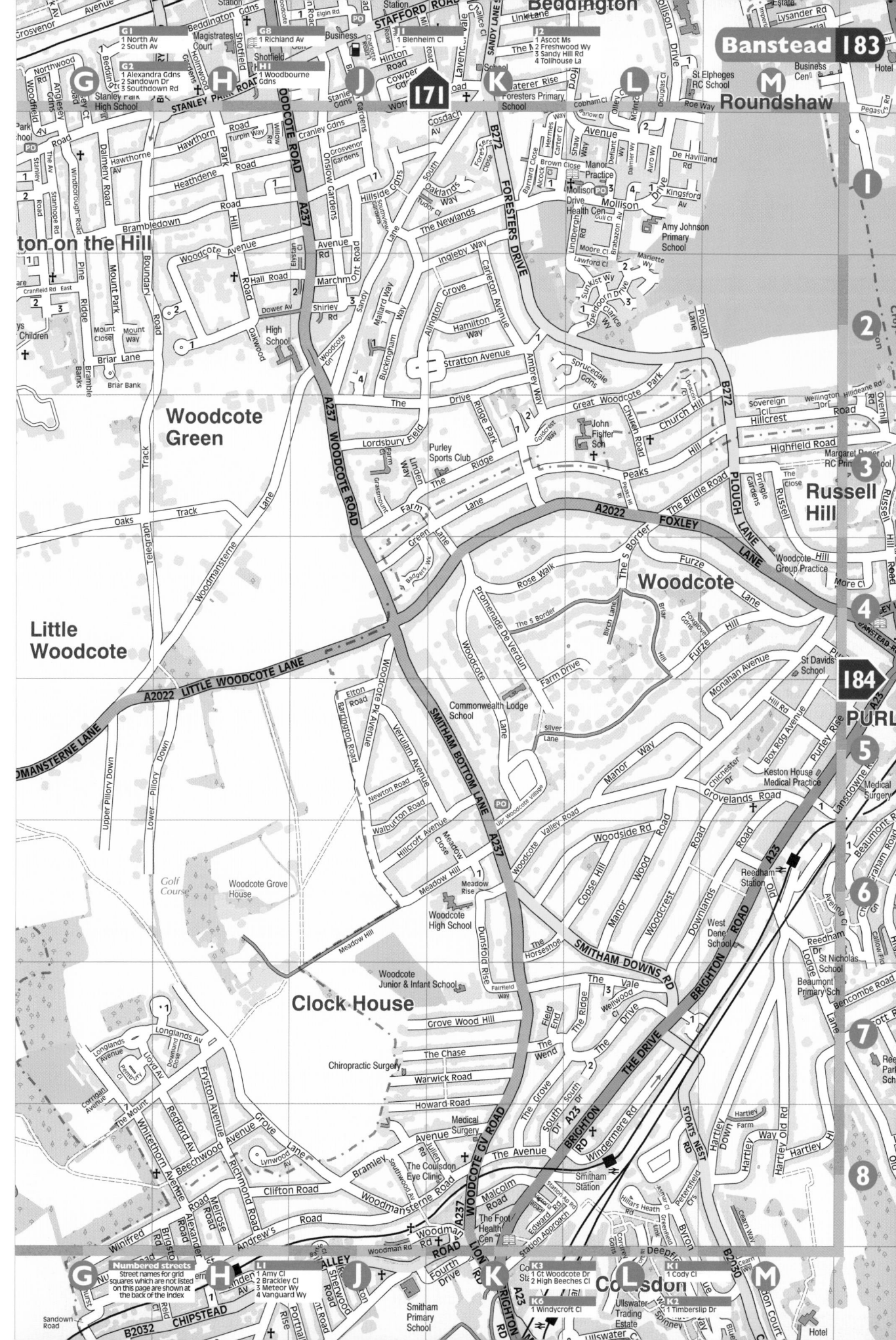

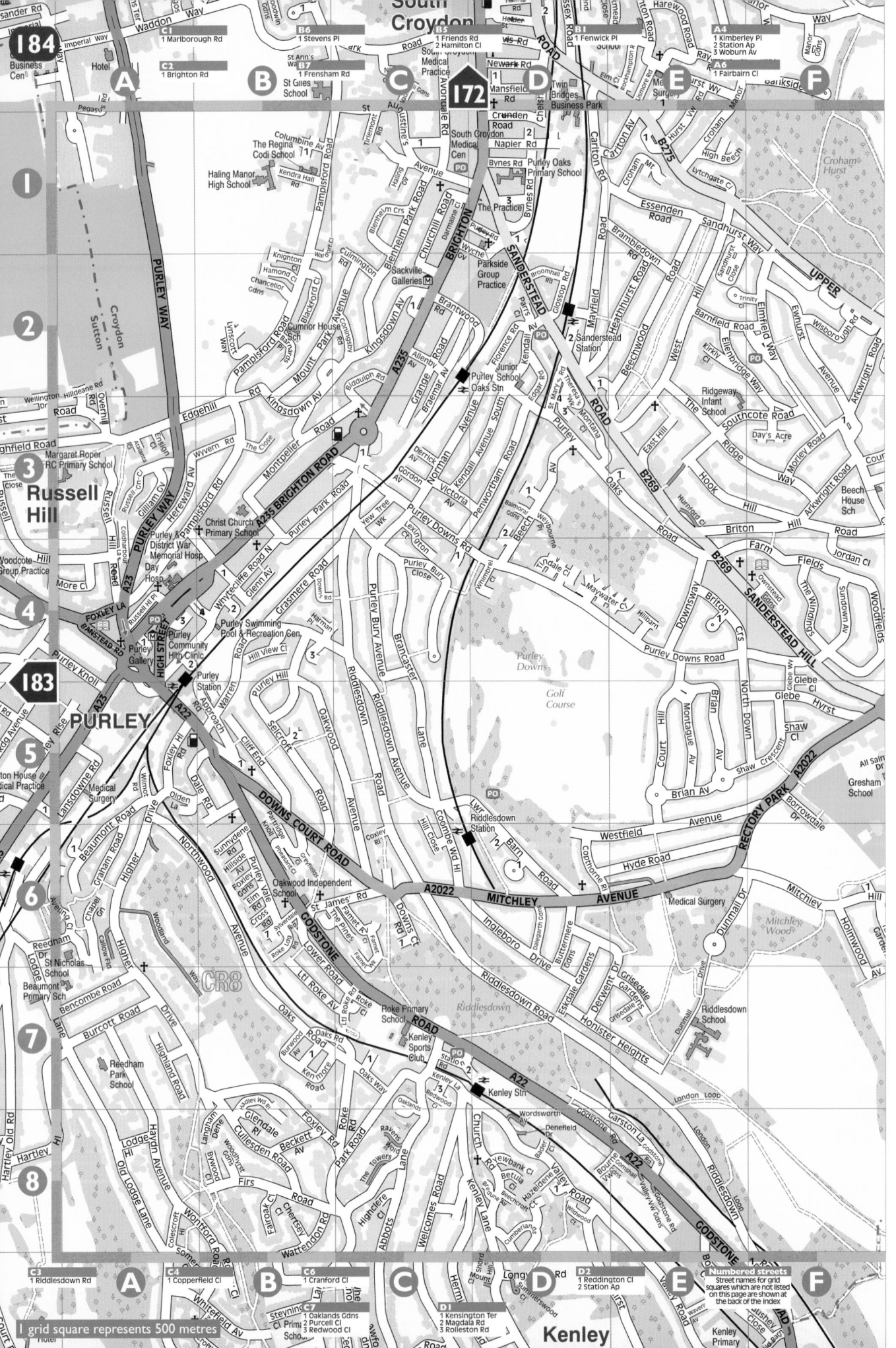

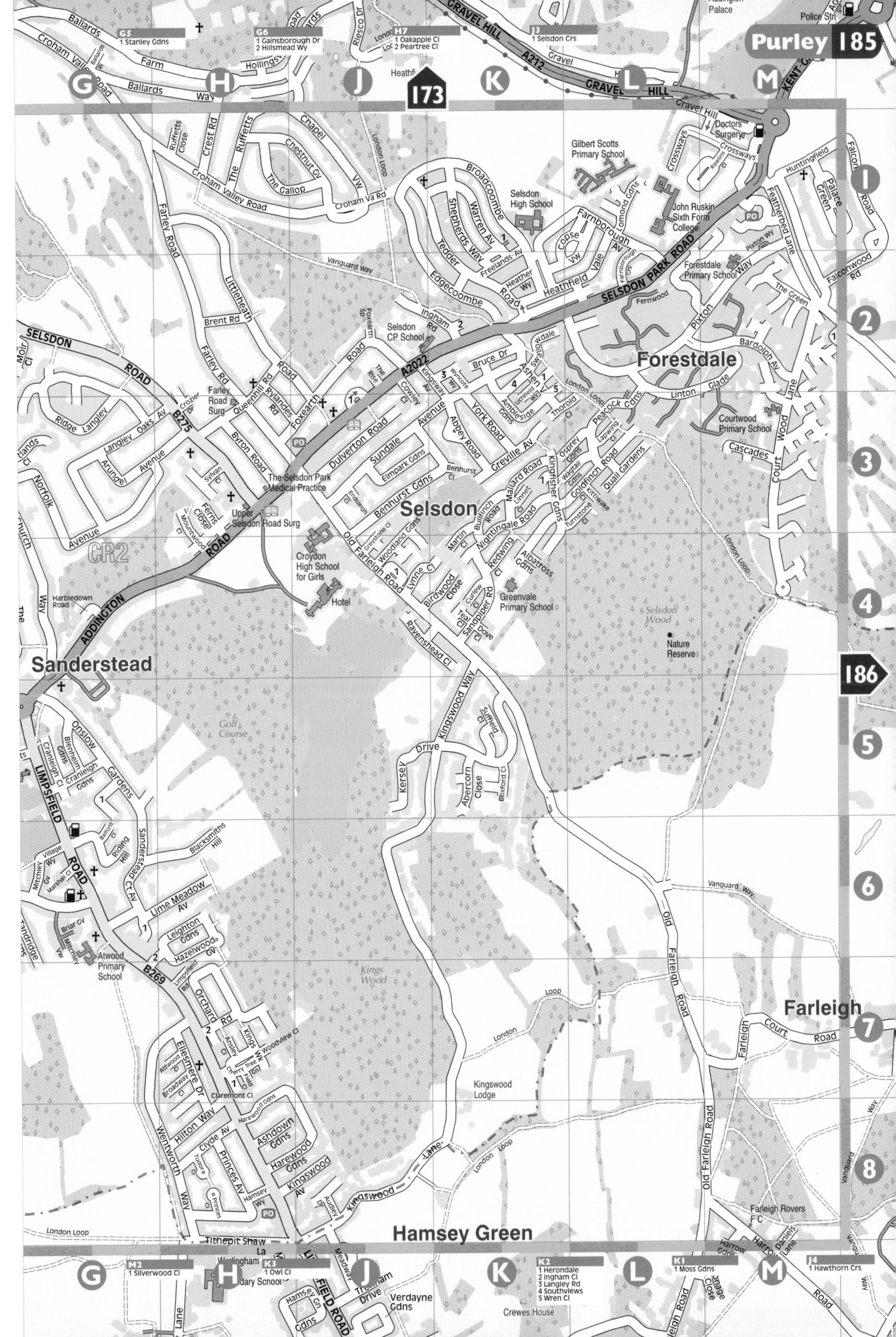

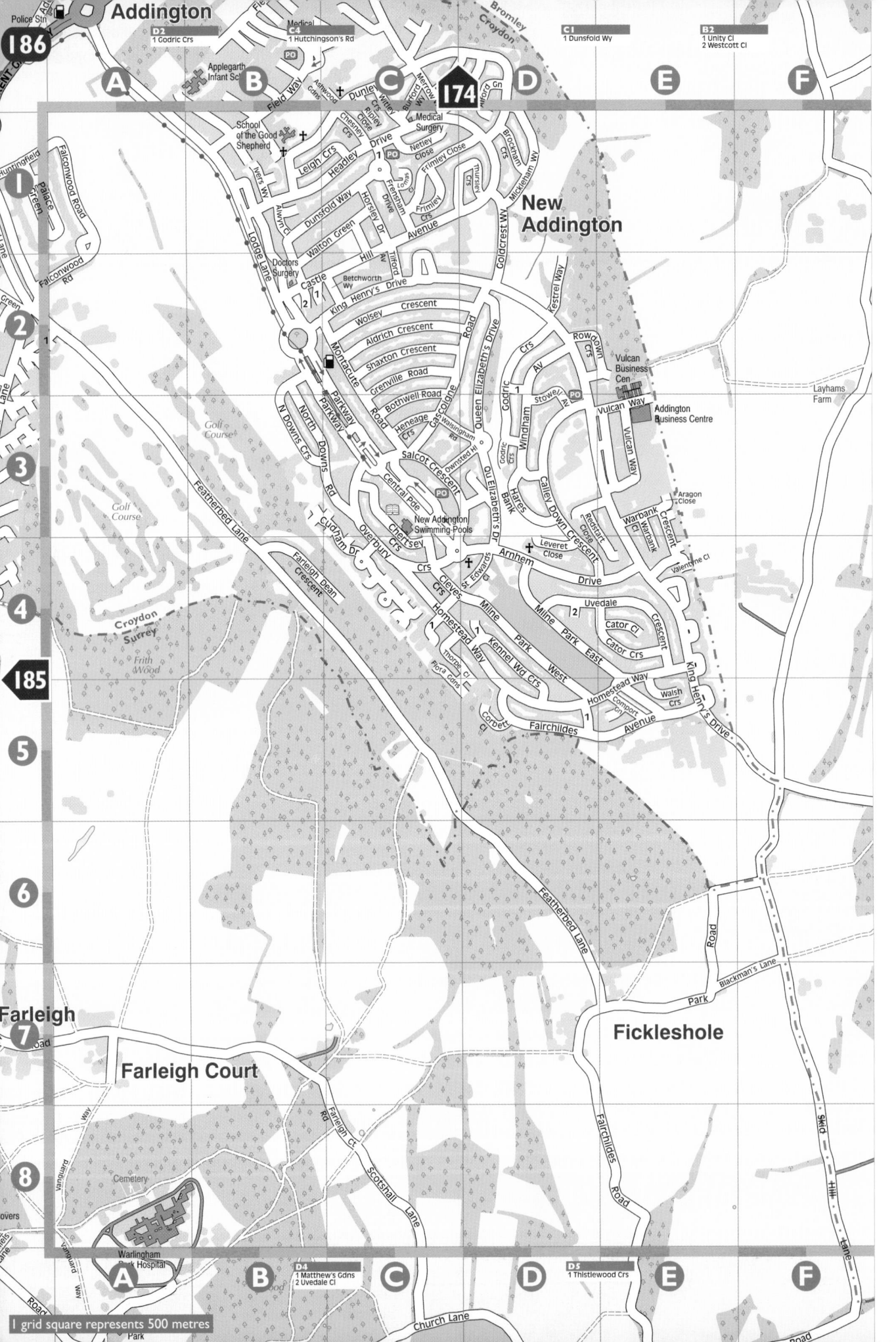

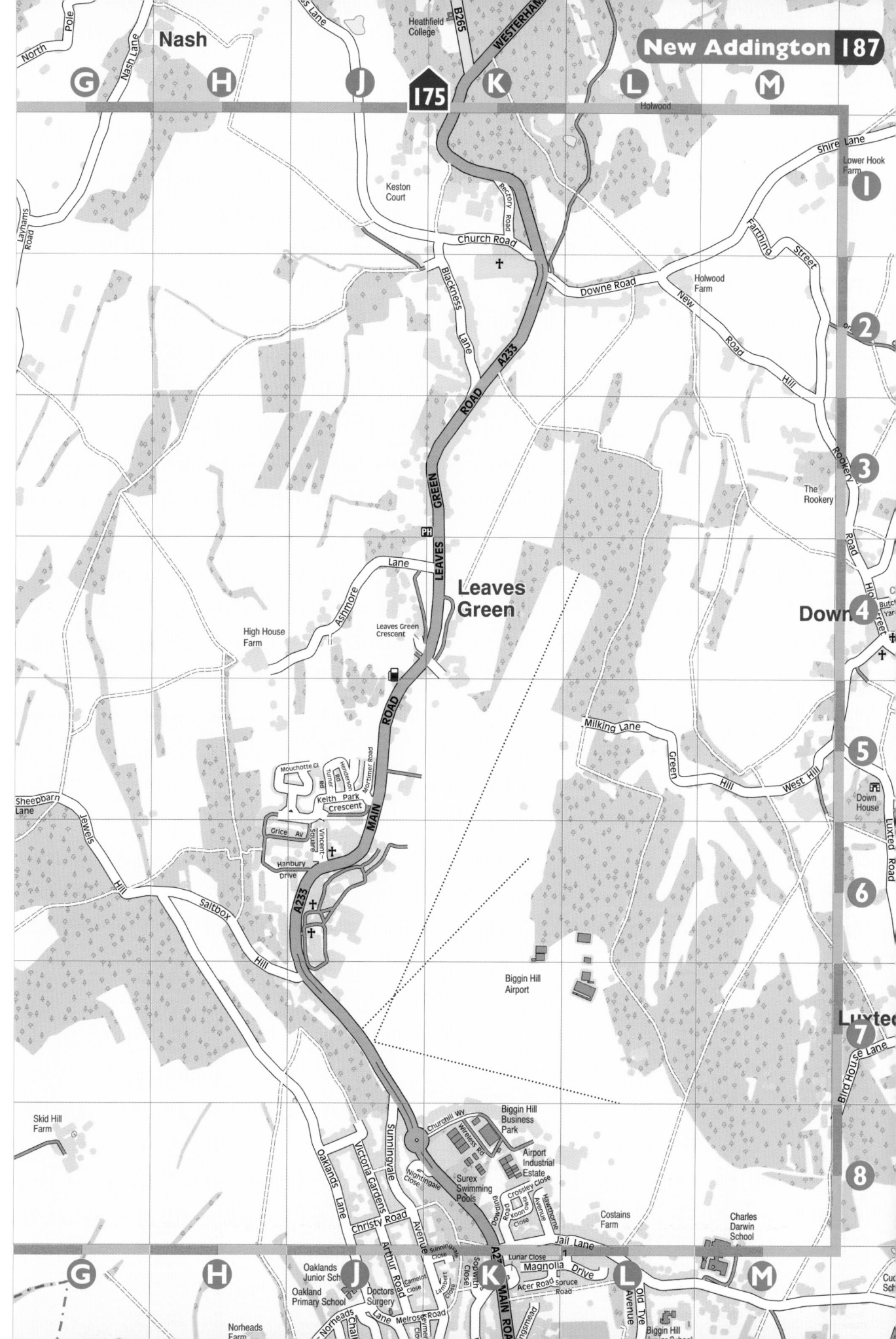

Nash

G H J 175 K L M

North Pole

Nash Lane

Layhams Road

Heathfield College

B265

WESTERHAM

Shire Lane

Lower Hook Farm

I

Keston Court

Rectory Road

Church Road

Downe Road

Holwood

Holwood Farm

New Road Hill

Farthing Street

2

Blackness Lane

A233 ROAD

3

The Rookery

Rookery Road

High Street

Down 4

Ashmore Lane

LEAVES GREEN

PH

Leaves Green

Leaves Green Crescent

High House Farm

Milking Lane

Green Hill

West Hill

5

Down House

Luxted Road

Sheepbarn Lane

Jewels Hill

Mouchotte Ci

Henderson Square

Keith Turner Ct

Keith Park Crescent

Grice Av

Vincent Rd

Mortimer Road

MAIN ROAD

6

Hanbury Drive

A233

saltbox

Hill

Biggin Hill Airport

Luxted

7

Bird House Lane

Skid Hill Farm

Oaklands Lane

Victoria Gardens

Sunningvale

Nightingale Close

Churchill Wy

Wireless Rd

Surex Swimming Pools

Biggin Hill Business Park

Airport Industrial Estate

Crossley Close

Costains Farm

Charles Darwin School

8

Oaklands Junior Sch

Oakland Primary School

Doctors Surgery

Christy Road

Arthur Road

Camelot Close

Lambert

Melrose Lane

Sopwith Close

A233 MAIN ROAD

Jail Lane

Lunar Close

Magnolia

Acer Road Spruce Road

Old Tye Avenue

Biggin Hill

G H J K L M

Norheads Farm

Abbey Wood 126 B2
Abbots Langley 20 E5
Acton 99 J7
Acton Green 117 K2
Addington 174 A8
Addiscombe 172 F3
Aimes Green 27 M1
Aldborough Hatch 71 L5
Aldenham 30 A2
Aldersbrook 88 C1
Alperton 80 E8
Anerley 158 A5
Ardleigh Green 74 C4
Arkley 33 H8
Ashford 148 F1
Ashford Common 149 K2
Ashley Park 165 G5
Aveley 111 K6
Avery Hill 143 J3
Balham 137 M4
Bandonhill 171 K7
Barking 89 K7
Barkingside 71 H4
Barnehurst 127 K8
Barnes 118 B6
Barnes Cray 146 B1
Barnet 46 F1
Barnet Gate 45 L1
Barnsbury 5 L1
Barwell 179 J1
Batchworth 40 F4
Batchworth Heath 41 G6
Batlers Green 30 F3
Battersea 119 M5
Bayswater 8 D6
Beckenham 159 H6
Beckton 106 F5
Becontree 90 D5
Beddington 171 L4
Beddington Corner 171 G2
Bedford Park 117 M1
Belgravia 16 A5
Bell Green 140 F7
Bellingham 141 G8
Belmont 62 A3
Belmont 182 A2
Belvedere 127 H3
Benhilton 170 B5
Bentley Heath 22 F8
Bermondsey 104 A8
Berrylands 167 M1
Bethnal Green 104 B2
Bexley 144 C1
Bexleyheath 144 F1
Bickley 160 E5
Blackfen 143 M3
Blackheath 123 M7
Blackheath Park 142 A1
Blackwall 105 K6
Bloomsbury 11 H1
Borehamwood 31 L6
The Borough 18 F2
Botany Bay 35 K1
Bow 105 G1
Bow Common 105 G4
Bowes Park 48 E8
Bowmans 145 M4
Brentford 116 D4
Brentford End 116 B4
Bricket Wood 21 L4
Brimsdown 37 L5
Brixton 139 G1
Broad Green 172 B2
Brockley 140 F2
Bromley 105 H2
Bromley 160 B5
Bromley Common 175 K1
Bromley Park 159 L4
Brompton 15 J4
Brondesbury 82 E6
Brondesbury Park 82 D8
Brook Green 118 C1
Brook Street 57 L6
Broom Hill 176 F2
Brunswick Park 48 A5
Buckhurst Hill 52 C5
Bulls Cross 37 G1
Burnt Oak 63 K1
Burwood Park 165 G7
Bury Green 26 B4
Bushey 43 J2
Bushey Heath 43 L2
Bushey Mead 154 D6
Bush Hill Park 49 L1
Caldecote Hill 43 M2
Camberwell 121 M6
Camden Town 4 B2
Canary Wharf 105 H7
Cannon Hill 154 D7
Canonbury 6 F1
Canons Park 62 E1
Carpenders Park 42 F4
Carshalton 170 E6
Carshalton Beeches 182 E2
Carshalton on the Hill 182 F1
Castle Green 90 C8
Catford 141 J5
Chadwell Heath 72 D6
Charlton 124 D3
Charlton 149 J5
Chase Cross 55 L8
Chattern Hill 131 H8
Cheam 169 M7
Chelsea 15 H8
Chelsfield 177 L7
Cheshunt 26 B3
Chessington 167 L8
Chigwell 53 H4
Chigwell Row 54 B4
Child's Hill 82 E2
Chingford 51 J4
Chingford Green 51 J3
Chingford Hatch 51 L6
Chipping Barnet 33 L7
Chislehurst 161 G1
Chislehurst West 161 G2
Chiswick 117 M2
Church End 65 G3

Church End 81 M7
Churchgate 26 B2
City of London 12 D6
Clapham 120 B7
Clapham Park 138 D3
Clapton Park 86 F4
Claremont Park 178 A1
Claygate 166 F8
Clayhall 70 F3
Clay Hill 36 C2
Clerkenwell 6 A9
Clock House 183 J7
Cockfosters 34 E8
Coldblow 145 J6
Coldharbour 128 A2
Cole Park 134 A3
Colham Green 94 F3
Colindale 63 L4
Collier Row 73 J2
Collier's Wood 155 K3
Colney Hatch 47 M8
Coney Hall 174 E6
Coombe 153 L3
Copse Hill 154 A3
Corbets Tey 93 H5
Cottenham Park 154 B4
Cowley 94 C3
Cowley Peachy 94 C5
Cranbrook 71 G8
Cranford 114 A5
Cranham 75 L8
Cranley Gardens 66 A5
Crayford 146 A2
Creekmouth 107 L4
Crews Hill 25 H8
Cricklewood 82 D4
Crofton 176 D4
Crooked Billet 154 B2
Crouch End 66 C7
Croxley Green 28 A8
Croydon 172 D5
Cubitt Town 123 J2
Cuffley 24 F1
Custom House 106 E6
Dagenham 91 K7
Dancers Hill 22 C8
Dartford 146 C4
Dartmouth Park 84 A2
Deacons Hill 45 G1
De Beauvoir Town 7 J3
Denham 76 A2
Deptford 122 F4
Derry Downs 177 K1
Dollis Hill 82 B3
Dormer's Wells 97 H6
Downe 187 M4
Downham 159 K1
Ducks Island 46 D2
Dudden Hill 82 A5
Dulwich 139 M6
Dulwich Village 139 L4
Ealing 98 C6
Earl's Court 14 A6
Earlsfield 137 J5
East Acton 99 L6
East Barnet 47 K2
East Bedfont 131 H4
Eastbury 41 M6
Eastcote 60 B8
Eastcote Village 60 B6
East Dulwich 140 A2
East Ewell 181 K3
East Finchley 65 K4
East Ham 106 E1
East Molesey 151 J8
East Sheen 135 K2
East Wickham 126 A6
Eden Park 158 F7
Edgware 45 H6
Edmonton 49 M6
Elmers End 158 D6
Elm Park 92 B5
Elmstead 160 E1
Elstree 44 L1
Eltham 142 E3
Emerson Park 74 E7
Enfield 36 C7
Enfield Highway 37 J5
Enfield Lock 37 M2
Enfield Town 36 D6
Enfield Wash 37 L3
Epsom 180 C7
Erith 127 M3
Esher 166 C6
Ewell 181 H4
Fair Cross 89 M5
Fairlop 71 L2
Falconwood 143 L1
Farleigh 185 M7
Farleigh Court 186 A7
Farnborough 176 B7
Feltham 132 B6
Felthamhill 149 L1
Ficklesole 186 E7
Field Common 165 M2
Finchley 65 G2
Finsbury 6 A7
Finsbury Park 84 F2
Flamstead End 26 B1
Fleet Downs 147 H6
Foots Cray 162 B2
Forestdale 185 L2
Forest Gate 88 A5
Forest Hill 140 D5
Fortis Green 66 A5
Forty Hill 36 F4
Foxbury 161 K1
Freezy Water 37 L1
Friday Hill 51 K5
Friern Barnet 47 K7
Fulham 118 D5
Fullwell Cross 71 K2
Furzedown 138 B8
Gallows Corner 74 D2
Gants Hill 71 F7
Ganwick Corner 23 H8
Garston 21 J8

Gidea Park 73 M3
Giggshill 167 G2
Gilwell Park 38 C6
Globe Town 104 D2
Goddington 177 J5
Goff's Oak 25 J4
Golders Green 64 E7
Goodmayes 90 B2
Gospel Oak 84 A5
Grange Hill 53 H8
Grange Park 36 A8
Greenford 97 K3
Greenhill 61 M6
Green Street 32 A2
Greenwich 123 K3
Grove Park 117 K6
Grove Park 142 C7
The Grove 28 C2
Hackbridge 171 H4
Hackney 86 C6
Hackney Wick 87 G6
Hacton 92 E5
Hadley 34 A6
Hadley Wood 34 D3
Haggerston 7 M5
Hainault 71 M1
Hale End 51 K8
Ham 134 D7
Hammersmith 118 B2
Hampstead 83 K4
Hampstead Garden Suburb ... 65 H6
Hampton 151 H4
Hampton Hill 133 J8
Hampton Wick 152 B4
Hamsey Green 185 J8
Hanwell 97 L7
Hanworth 132 D7
Harefield 58 C3
Harefield Grove 58 D1
Harlesden 99 L1
Harlington 113 J4
Harmondsworth 112 C4
Harold Hill 56 E7
Harold Park 57 H8
Harold Wood 75 G2
Harringay 67 G6
Harrow 61 K7
Harrow on the Hill 79 L1
Harrow Weald 61 L1
Hatch End 60 E1
Hatton 131 L1
Havering-atte-Bower 55 M5
Hayes 95 J4
Hayes 175 H2
Hayes End 95 K3
Hayes Town 96 C7
Headstone 61 H5
Heath Park 74 B7
Heath Side 145 M6
Hendon 64 B6
Herne Hill 139 J3
Hersham 165 J7
Heston 114 F5
Higham Hill 68 E3
Highams Park 69 H1
High Barnet 33 J6
High Beach 39 H4
Highbury Park 85 H4
Highbury 6 D1
High Cross 30 D1
Highgate 65 M8
Highwood Hill 45 M4
Hill End 40 B8
Hillingdon 77 G8
Hillingdon Heath 95 H4
Hinchley Wood 166 F5
Hither Green 141 L3
Hockenden 163 H6
Holborn 11 L3
Holders Hill 64 D2
Holloway 84 F3
Holyfield 27 J1
Holywell 41 L1
Homerton 86 D6
Honor Oak 140 D3
Honor Oak Park 140 E3
Hook 167 L7
Hook Green 145 M8
Hornchurch 92 D2
Hornsey 66 E5
Hornsey Vale 66 F6
Hounslow 115 G7
Hounslow West 114 D8
Hoxton 7 J6
Hunton Bridge 20 B6
Hurst Park 151 J5
The Hyde 63 M6
Ickenham 77 G3
Ilford 89 G3
Isle of Dogs 123 H2
Isleworth 116 B8
Islington 6 A3
Kennington 120 E4
Kensal Green 100 C2
Kensal Rise 100 E1
Kensal Town 100 E3
Kensington 14 C4
Kentish Town 84 C6
Kenton 62 C6
Keston 175 K6
Keston Mark 175 K5
Kevingtown 177 M1
Kew 116 F5
Kidbrooke 124 C7
Kilburn 82 F8
Kingsbury 63 H7
Kingsland 7 J1
Kingston upon Thames ... 152 F6
Kingston Vale 153 K1
Kingswood 21 H7
Kitt's End 33 L3
Knight's Hill 139 J5
Knowle Green 148 B1
Ladywell 141 G1
Laleham 148 C6
Lambeth 18 A3
Lambourne End 54 C2
Lampton 115 H6
Langleybury 20 B7

Lea Bridge 86 D3
Leavesden Green 20 F7
Leaves Green 187 K4
Lee 141 M3
Lessness Heath 127 H4
Letchmore Heath 30 E4
Lewisham 141 J1
Leyton 87 K3
Leytonstone 87 M1
Limehouse 104 F5
Lippitts Hill 38 F5
Lisson Grove 9 M2
Little Heath 23 H2
Little Heath 72 C5
Little Ilford 89 G5
Little Stanmore 62 F2
Littleton 149 H6
Littleton Common 149 H3
Little Woodcote 183 G4
Locksbottom 176 B5
Long Ditton 167 H3
Longford 112 C6
Longlands 143 J7
Loughton 39 M7
Lower Clapton 86 C4
Lower Edmonton 49 L4
Lower Feltham 131 L7
Lower Green 166 B4
Lower Halliford 164 D2
Lower Holloway 84 F5
Lower Place 99 J1
Lower Sydenham 140 D8
Loxford 89 J5
Maida Vale 2 C7
Maitland Park 83 M6
Malden Rushett 179 H5
Manor Park 88 E4
Marks Gate 72 E3
Marylebone 10 A3
Mayfair 10 C7
Maypole 145 L5
Maypole 177 M8
Meriden 29 L1
Merry Hill 43 H3
Merton 155 H4
Merton Park 154 F5
Mile End 104 E3
Mill Hill 46 A7
Mill Meads 105 K1
Millwall 123 G1
Mitcham 156 B6
Moneyhill 40 B3
Monken Hadley 33 L5
Monks Orchard 173 J2
Moor Park 41 J6
Morden 155 G7
Morden Park 169 L1
Mortlake 117 J7
Motspur Park 169 G1
Mottingham 142 C6
Mount Pleasant 58 B2
Muswell Hill 66 A3
Nash 175 H8
Neasden 81 K4
New Addington 186 D1
New Barnet 34 B8
New Beckenham 158 E2
Newbury Park 71 K7
New Charlton 124 D2
New Cross 122 E7
New Cross Gate 122 E6
New Denham 76 A6
New Eltham 143 H6
Newington 18 B4
New Malden 153 M6
New Southgate 48 C6
New Town 146 F3
Newyears Green 59 G8
Nine Elms 120 D5
Noak Hill 56 E4
Noel Park 67 H3
Norbiton 152 F5
Norbury 157 H5
Nork 181 L7
North Acton 99 J3
Northaw 24 A3
North Cheam 169 K5
North Cray 145 G7
North End 83 J1
North End 127 M6
North Feltham 132 B2
North Finchley 47 J8
North Harrow 60 F7
North Hillingdon 77 H7
North Hyde 114 E3
North Kensington 100 D4
North Looe 181 J6
Northolt 79 G7
North Sheen 117 H7
Northumberland Heath ... 127 H5
North Watford 29 H2
North Wembley 80 B1
Northwood 59 J2
Northwood Hills 59 K3
North Woolwich 106 E8
Norwood Green 115 G2
Norwood New Town 157 K2
Notting Hill 100 E6
Nunhead 140 C1
Nuper's Hatch 55 L2
Oakleigh Park 47 K4
Oakwood 48 D1
Oatlands Park 164 E6
Old Bexley 145 G4
Old Ford 86 E3
Old Malden 168 D2
Old Oak Common 99 M3
Orpington 176 F5
Osidge 48 C5
Osterley 115 J5
Otterspool 29 M2
Oxhey 42 D1
Oxshott 178 C5
Paddington 9 G3
Palmers Green 49 G5
Park Langley 174 C1
Park Royal 99 G2
Parsons Green 119 G6

Patchetts Green 30 C4
Peckham 122 B7
Penge 158 C3
Pentonville 5 M3
Perivale 80 C8
Petersham 134 E5
Petts Wood 161 K7
Pimlico 16 E7
Pinner 60 D5
Pinner Green 60 C3
Pinnerwood Park 60 C1
Plaistow 105 M2
Plaistow 160 A2
Plashet 88 D6
Plumstead 125 J3
Plumstead Common 125 M4
Ponders End 37 J8
Poplar 105 G6
Potter's Bar 23 K6
Poverest 162 A7
Preston 80 D1
Primrose Hill 4 B4
Puddledock 163 K2
Purfleet 129 G4
Purley 184 A5
Putney 136 D2
Putney Heath 136 C4
Putney Vale 136 A7
Queensbury 62 E4
Rainham 110 B2
Ramsden 177 J3
Ratcliff 104 E6
Rayners Lane 78 F1
Raynes Park 154 C6
Redbridge 70 C6
Regent's Park 4 A6
Richmond 134 E2
Richmond Hill 134 E3
Rickmansworth 40 A2
Rise Park 73 L2
Roehampton 135 M2
Romford 73 K6
The Rookery 42 A2
Rosedale 25 M1
Rosehill 170 B3
Rotherhithe 122 D1
Round Bush 30 D3
Roundshaw 171 M8
Rowley Green 32 F6
Roxeth 79 J2
Ruislip 59 L7
Ruislip Common 59 K5
Ruislip Gardens 77 L3
Ruislip Manor 78 A2
Rush Green 73 L8
Russell Hill 183 M3
Ruxley 162 E2
Rydens 165 L4
St George in the East 104 A6
St Giles 11 H4
St Helier 170 C3
St James 11 G9
St Johns 123 G7
St John's Wood 2 F1
St Luke's 6 F9
St Margarets 134 C3
St Mary Cray 162 C8
St Pancras 5 K8
St Paul's Cray 162 A5
St Vincent's Hamlet 57 G3
Sanderstead 184 F5
Sands End 119 J7
Seething Wells 167 H1
Selhurst 157 K6
Selsdon 185 J3
Seven Kings 89 L1
Sewardstone 38 D5
Sewardstonebury 38 E8
Shacklewell 86 A4
Shadwell 104 C6
Shepherd's Bush 100 B7
Shepperton 164 A1
Shepperton Green 149 G7
Shirley 173 J4
Shooters Hill 125 J6
Shoreditch 7 H8
Shortlands 159 L6
Sidcup 144 B8
Silvertown 106 C8
Sipson 112 F3
Slade Green 128 A7
Soho 11 G6
Somers Town 5 G6
Southall 96 E6
South Beddington 171 K8
Southborough 175 M1
South Bromley 105 K5
South Croydon 172 C8
Southend 141 J8
Southfields 137 G5
Southgate 48 E3
South Hackney 86 C7
South Hampstead 3 G1
South Harefield 58 D5
South Harrow 79 H3
South Hornchurch 91 K8
South Kensington 14 E6
South Lambeth 120 E5
South Mimms 22 B5
South Norwood 157 K6
South Oxhey 42 B5
South Ruislip 78 D4
South Tottenham 67 L6
South Weald 57 L4
South Wimbledon 155 J1
South Woodford 70 A3
Spitalfields 13 L2
Spring Grove 115 K5
Spring Park 174 A4
Stamford Hill 67 M8
Stanmore 44 B7
Stanwell 130 C3
Stanwell Moor 130 A3
Stapleford Abbotts 55 K1
Stepney 104 C4
Stockwell 120 E8
Stoke Newington 85 M2
Stone 147 M2

Stonebridge 81 J7
Stonehill Green 163 J2
Stoneleigh 168 F7
Strand 11 K6
Stratford 87 J7
Stratford Marsh 87 H8
Stratford New Town .. 87 J6
Strawberry Hill 133 L7
Streatham 156 E1
Streatham Hill 138 E5
Streatham Park 138 B8
Streatham Vale 156 B3
Stroud Green 67 G7
Sudbury 79 M5
Summerstown 137 K6
Sunbury 150 A6
Sunbury Common 149 M3
Sundridge 160 C2
Surbiton 167 K3
Sutton 170 A7
Swanley Bar 23 H1
Teddington 151 K2
Temple Hill 146 D1
Temple Mills 87 H5
Thames Ditton 167 G2
Thamesmead 107 M7
Thorney 94 B8
Thornton Heath 156 E8

Tokyngton 81 H6
Tolworth 168 A3
Tooting Graveney 155 K1
Tottenham 67 L3
Tottenham Hale 67 M4
Totteridge 46 E2
Tufnell Park 84 C4
Tulse Hill 139 H5
Twickenham 133 L4
Underhill 47 G1
Upminster 93 J2
Upper Clapton 86 A1
Upper Edmonton 50 A6
Upper Elmers End 158 F8
Upper Halliford 149 K7
Upper Holloway 84 C2
Upper Norwood 157 K4
Upper Shirley 173 J6
Upper Sydenham 140 A8
Upper Tooting 137 L7
Upper Walthamstow ... 69 J5
Upton 88 B7
Upton Park 88 C8
Uxbridge 76 C8
Uxbridge Moor 76 B8
Vale of Health 83 K3
Vauxhall 17 K8
Waddon 171 M4

Walham Green 118 F4
Wallend 89 C8
Wallington 171 H7
Waltham Abbey 27 K5
Waltham Cross 26 C6
Walthamstow 69 G4
Walton-on-Thames 165 G3
Walworth 18 F8
Wandle Park 172 A4
Wandsworth 137 G1
Wanstead 70 B8
Wapping 104 B7
Waterdale 21 J3
Waterhales 56 D1
Watford 29 G4
Watford Heath 42 E2
Watton's Green 56 B1
Wealdstone 62 A4
Well End 32 C3
Welling 126 B8
The Wells 179 M7
Welsh Harp 81 K1
Wembley 80 C5
Wembley Park 81 G3
Wennington 110 E6
West Acton 99 G5
West Barnes 154 C8
West Bedfont 130 F4

West Brompton 14 C9
West Drayton 112 D1
West Dulwich 139 K6
West Ealing 98 A7
West End 165 M7
West Green 67 J4
West Ewell 180 E1
West Hampstead 83 G5
West Harrow 61 J8
West Heath 83 H2
West Heath 126 D4
West Hendon 64 A8
West Hill 136 E4
West Kensington 118 D3
West Kilburn 100 E2
West Molesey 150 F7
West Norwood 139 J8
Weston Green 166 E3
West Ruislip 77 J1
West Watford 29 G8
West Wickham 174 D3
Weybridge 164 A6
Whetstone 47 H4
Whitechapel 13 M6
White Oak 163 L5
Whitton 133 J3
Widmore 160 D5

Willesden 82 A6
Willesden Green 82 B7
Willowbank 76 C5
Wilmington 146 B8
Wimbledon 154 E1
Winchmore Hill 49 H3
Woodcock Hill 40 E6
Woodcote 183 L4
Woodcote Green 183 H3
Wood End 95 L5
Wood End Green 95 L4
Woodford 52 B8
Woodford Bridge 70 F1
Woodford Green 70 A1
Woodford Wells 52 B5
Wood Green 67 G2
Woodlands 115 K8
Woodmansterne 182 D8
Woodside 21 H5
Woodside 173 G1
Woodside Park 47 G6
Woolwich 125 G4
Worcester Park 169 H4
World's End 36 A7
The Wrythe 170 E4
Yeading 96 C3
Yiewsley 94 E6

USING THE STREET INDEX

Street names are listed alphabetically. Each street name is followed by its postal town or area locality, the Postcode District, the page number, and the reference to the square in which the name is found.

Example: **Abbeville Ms** *CLAP* SW4 .... **138 D1** 🖪

Some entries are followed by a number in a blue box. This number indicates the location of the street within the referenced grid square. The full street name is listed at the side of the map page.

GENERAL ABBREVIATIONS

ACC......ACCESS; ALY......ALLEY; AP......APPROACH; AR......ARCADE; ASS......ASSOCIATION; AV......AVENUE; BCH......BEACH; BLDS......BUILDINGS; BND......BEND; BNK......BANK; BR......BRIDGE; BRK......BROOK; BTM......BOTTOM; BUS......BUSINESS; BVD......BOULEVARD; BY......BYPASS; CATH......CATHEDRAL; CEM......CEMETERY; CEN......CENTRE; CFT......CROFT; CH......CHURCH; CHA......CHASE; CHYD......CHURCHYARD; CIR......CIRCLE; CIRC......CIRCUS; CL......CLOSE; CLFS......CLIFFS; CMP......CAMP; CNR......CORNER; CO......COUNTY; COLL......COLLEGE; COM......COMMON; COMM......COMMISSION; CON......CONVENT; COT......COTTAGE; COTS......COTTAGES; CP......CAPE; CPS......COPSE; CR......CREEK; CREM......CREMATORIUM; CRS......CRESCENT; CSWY......CAUSEWAY; CT......COURT; CTRL......CENTRAL; CTS......COURTS

CTYD......COURTYARD; CUTT......CUTTINGS; CV......COVE; CYN......CANYON; DEPT......DEPARTMENT; DL......DALE; DM......DAM; DR......DRIVE; DRO......DROVE; DRY......DRIVEWAY; DWGS......DWELLINGS; E......EAST; EMB......EMBANKMENT; EMBY......EMBASSY; ESP......ESPLANADE; EST......ESTATE; EX......EXCHANGE; EXPY......EXPRESSWAY; EXT......EXTENSION; F/O......FLYOVER; FC......FOOTBALL CLUB; FK......FORK; FLD......FIELD; FLDS......FIELDS; FLS......FALLS; FLS......FLATS; FM......FARM; FT......FORT; FWY......FREEWAY; FY......FERRY; GA......GATE; GAL......GALLERY; GDN......GARDEN; GDNS......GARDENS; GLD......GLADE; GLN......GLEN; GN......GREEN; GND......GROUND; GRA......GRANGE; GRG......GARAGE; GT......GREAT; GTWY......GATEWAY; GV......GROVE; HGR......HIGHER; HL......HILL

HLS......HILLS; HO......HOUSE; HOL......HOLLOW; HOSP......HOSPITAL; HRB......HARBOUR; HTH......HEATH; HTS......HEIGHTS; HVN......HAVEN; HWY......HIGHWAY; IMP......IMPERIAL; IN......INLET; IND EST......INDUSTRIAL ESTATE; INF......INFIRMARY; INFO......INFORMATION; INT......INTERCHANGE; IS......ISLAND; JCT......JUNCTION; JTY......JETTY; KG......KING; KNL......KNOLL; L......LAKE; LA......LANE; LDG......LODGE; LGT......LIGHT; LK......LOCK; LKS......LAKES; LNDG......LANDING; LTL......LITTLE; LWR......LOWER; MAG......MAGISTRATE; MAN......MANSIONS; MD......MEAD; MDW......MEADOWS; MEM......MEMORIAL; MKT......MARKET; MKTS......MARKETS; ML......MALL; ML......MILL; MNR......MANOR; MS......MEWS; MSN......MISSION; MT......MOUNT; MTN......MOUNTAIN; MTS......MOUNTAINS; MUS......MUSEUM

MWY......MOTORWAY; N......NORTH; NE......NORTH EAST; NW......NORTH WEST; O/P......OVERPASS; OFF......OFFICE; ORCH......ORCHARD; OV......OVAL; PAL......PALACE; PAS......PASSAGE; PAV......PAVILION; PDE......PARADE; PH......PUBLIC HOUSE; PK......PARK; PKWY......PARKWAY; PL......PLACE; PLN......PLAIN; PLNS......PLAINS; PLZ......PLAZA; POL......POLICE STATION; PR......PRINCE; PREC......PRECINCT; PREP......PREPARATORY; PRIM......PRIMARY; PROM......PROMENADE; PRS......PRINCESS; PRT......PORT; PT......POINT; PTH......PATH; PZ......PIAZZA; QD......QUADRANT; QU......QUEEN; QY......QUAY; R......RIVER; RBT......ROUNDABOUT; RD......ROAD; RDG......RIDGE; REP......REPUBLIC; RES......RESERVOIR; RFC......RUGBY FOOTBALL CLUB; RI......RISE; RP......RAMP; RW......ROW; S......SOUTH; SCH......SCHOOL

SE......SOUTH EAST; SER......SERVICE AREA; SH......SHORE; SHOP......SHOPPING; SKWY......SKYWAY; SMT......SUMMIT; SOC......SOCIETY; SP......SPUR; SPR......SPRING; SQ......SQUARE; ST......STREET; STN......STATION; STR......STREAM; STRD......STRAND; SW......SOUTH WEST; TDG......TRADING; TER......TERRACE; THWY......THROUGHWAY; TNL......TUNNEL; TOLL......TOLLWAY; TPK......TURNPIKE; TR......TRACK; TRL......TRAIL; TWR......TOWER; U/P......UNDERPASS; UNI......UNIVERSITY; UPR......UPPER; V......VALE; VA......VALLEY; VIAD......VIADUCT; VIL......VILLA; VIS......VISTA; VLG......VILLAGE; VLS......VILLAS; VW......VIEW; W......WEST; WD......WOOD; WHF......WHARF; WK......WALK; WKS......WALKS; WLS......WELLS; WY......WAY; YD......YARD; YHA......YOUTH HOSTEL

POSTCODE TOWNS AND AREA ABBREVIATIONS

ABLGY......Abbots Langley; ABR/ST......Abridge/Stapleford Abbotts; ABYW......Abbey Wood; ACT......Acton; ALP/SUD......Alperton/Sudbury; ARCH......Archway; ASHF......Ashford (Surrey); ASHTD......Ashtead; BAL......Balham; BANK......Bank; BAR......Barnet; BARB......Barbican; BARK......Barking; BARK/HLT......Barkingside/Hainault; BARN......Barnes; BAY/PAD......Bayswater/Paddington; BCTR......Becontree; BECK......Beckenham; BELMT......Belmont; BELV......Belvedere; BERM/RHTH......Bermondsey/Rotherhithe; BETH......Bethnal Green; BFN/LL......Blackfen/Longlands; BGVA......Belgravia; BH/WHM......Biggin Hill/Westerham; BKHH......Buckhurst Hill; BKHTH/KID......Blackheath/Kidbrooke; BLKFR......Blackfriars; BMLY......Bromley; BMSBY......Bloomsbury; BNSTD......Banstead; BORE......Borehamwood; BOW......Bow; BRKMPK......Brookmans Park; BROCKY......Brockley; BRW......Brentwood; BRWN......Brentwood north; BRXN/ST......Brixton north/Stockwell; BRXS/STRHM......Brixton south/Streatham Hill; BRYLDS......Berrylands; BTFD......Brentford; BTSEA......Battersea

BUSH......Bushey; BXLY......Bexley; BXLYHN......Bexleyheath north; BXLYHS......Bexleyheath south; CAMTN......Camden Town; CAN/RD......Canning Town/Royal Docks; CANST......Cannon Street station; CAR......Carshalton; CAT......Catford; CAVSQ/HST......Cavendish Square/Harley Street; CDALE/KGS......Colindale/Kingsbury; CEND/HSY/TPKLN......Crouch End/Hornsey/Turnpike Lane; CHARL......Charlton; CHCR......Charing Cross; CHDH......Chadwell Heath; CHEAM......Cheam; CHEL......Chelsea; CHERT......Chertsey; CHES/WCR......Cheshunt/Waltham Cross; CHESW......Cheshunt west; CHIG......Chigwell; CHING......Chingford; CHSGTN......Chessington; CHST......Chislehurst; CHSWK......Chiswick; CITYW......City of London west; CLAP......Clapham; CLAY......Clayhall; CLKNW......Clerkenwell; CLPT......Clapton; CMBW......Camberwell; COB......Cobham; CONDST......Conduit Street; COUL/CHIP......Coulsdon/Chipstead; COVGDN......Covent Garden; CRICK......Cricklewood; CROY/NA......Croydon/New Addington; CRW......Collier Row; CTHM......Caterham; DAGE......Dagenham east; DAGW......Dagenham west

DART......Dartford; DEN/HRF......Denham/Harefield; DEPT......Deptford; DTCH/LGLY......Datchet/Langley; DUL......Dulwich; E/WMO/HCT......East & West Molesey/Hampton Court; EA......Ealing; EBAR......East Barnet; EBED/NFELT......East Bedfont/North Feltham; ECT......Earl's Court; ED......Edmonton; EDGW......Edgware; EDUL......East Dulwich; EFNCH......East Finchley; EHAM......East Ham; ELTH/MOT......Eltham/Mottingham; EMB......Embankment; EMPK......Emerson Park; EN......Enfield; ENC/FH......Enfield Chase/Forty Hill; EPP......Epping; EPSOM......Epsom; ERITH......Erith; ERITHM......Erith Marshes; ESH/CLAY......Esher/Claygate; EW......Ewell; FARR......Farringdon; FBAR/BDGN......Friern Barnet/Bounds Green; FELT......Feltham; FENCHST......Fenchurch Street; FITZ......Fitzrovia; FLST/FETLN......Fleet Street/Fetter Lane; FNCH......Finchley; FSBYE......Finsbury east; FSBYPK......Finsbury Park; FSBYW......Finsbury west; FSTGT......Forest Gate; FSTH......Forest Hill; FUL/PGN......Fulham/Parsons Green; GDMY/SEVK......Goodmayes/Seven Kings; GFD/PVL......Greenford/Perivale

GINN......Gray's Inn; GLDGN......Golders Green; GNTH/NBYPK......Gants Hill/Newbury Park; GNWCH......Greenwich; GPK......Gidea Park; GRH......Greenhithe; GSTN......Garston; GTPST......Great Portland Street; GWRST......Gower Street; HACK......Hackney; HAMP......Hampstead; HARH......Harold Hill; HAYES......Hayes; HBRY......Highbury; HCH......Hornchurch; HCIRC......Holborn Circus; HDN......Hendon; HDTCH......Houndsditch; HEST......Heston; HGDN/ICK......Hillingdon/Ickenham; HGT......Highgate; HHOL......High Holborn; HMSMTH......Hammersmith; HNHL......Herne Hill; HNWL......Hanwell; HOL/ALD......Holborn/Aldwych; HOLWY......Holloway; HOM......Homerton; HOR/WEW......Horton/West Ewell; HPTN......Hampton; HRW......Harrow; HSLW......Hounslow; HSLWW......Hounslow west; HTHAIR......Heathrow Airport; HYS/HAR......Hayes/Harlington; IL......Ilford; IS......Islington; ISLW......Isleworth; IVER......Iver; KENS......Kensington; KGLGY......Kings Langley; KIL/WHAMP......Kilburn/West Hampstead

KTBR......Knightsbridge; KTN/HRWW/WS......Kenton/Harrow Weald/Wealdstone; KTTN......Kentish Town; KUT......Kingston upon Thames; KUTN/CMB......Kingston upon Thames north/Coombe; LBTH......Lambeth; LEE/GVPK......Lee/Grove Park; LEW......Lewisham; LEY......Leyton; LHD/OX......Leatherhead/Oxshott; LINN......Lincoln's Inn; LOTH......Lothbury; LOU......Loughton; LSQ/SEVD......Leicester Square/Seven Dials; LVPST......Liverpool Street; MANHO......Mansion House; MBLAR......Marble Arch; MHST......Marylebone High Street; MLHL......Mill Hill; MNPK......Manor Park; MON......Monument; MORT/ESHN......Mortlake/East Sheen; MRDN......Morden; MTCM......Mitcham; MUSWH......Muswell Hill; MV/WKIL......Maida Vale/West Kilburn; MYFR/PICC......Mayfair/Piccadilly; MYFR/PKLN......Mayfair/Park Lane; NFNCH/WDSPK......North Finchley/Woodside Park; NKENS......North Kensington; NOXST/BSQ......New Oxford Street/Bloomsbury Square; NRWD......Norwood; NTGHL......Notting Hill; NTHLT......Northolt; NTHWD......Northwood; NWCR......New Cross; NWDGN......Norwood Green; NWMAL......New Malden; OBST......Old Broad Street

190

ORP ... Orpington
OXHEY ... Oxhey
OXSTW ... Oxford Street west
PECK ... Peckham
PEND ... Ponders End
PGE/AN ... Penge/Anerley
PIM ... Pimlico
PIN ... Pinner
PLMGR ... Palmers Green
PLSTW ... Plaistow
POP/IOD ... Poplar/Isle of Dogs
POTB/CUF ... Potters Bar/Cuffley
PUR ... Purfleet
PUR/KEN ... Purley/Kenley
PUT/ROE ... Putney/Roehampton
RAD ... Radlett
RAIN ... Rainham (Gt Lon)
RBRW/HUT ... Rural Brentwood/Hutton
RCH/KEW ... Richmond/Kew
RCHPK/HAM ... Richmond Park/Ham
RDART ... Rural Dartford
REDBR ... Redbridge
REGST ... Regent Street
RKW/CH/CXG ... Rickmansworth/Chorleywood/Croxley Green
ROM ... Romford
ROMW/RG ... Romford west/Rush Green
RSLP ... Ruislip
RSQ ... Russell Square
RYLN/HDSTN ... Rayners Lane/Headstone
RYNPK ... Raynes Park
SCUP ... Sidcup
SDTCH ... Shoreditch
SEVS/STOTM ... Seven Sisters/South Tottenham
SHB ... Shepherd's Bush
SHPTN ... Shepperton
SKENS ... South Kensington
SNWD ... South Norwood
SOCK/AV ... South Ockendon/Aveley
SOHO/CST ... Soho/Carnaby Street
SOHO/SHAV ... Soho/Shaftesbury Avenue
SRTFD ... Stratford
STA ... Staines
STALW/RED ... St Albans west/Redbourn
STAN ... Stanmore
STBT ... St Bart's
STHGT/OAK ... Southgate/Oakwood
STHL ... Southall
STHWK ... Southwark
STJS ... St James's
STJSPK ... St James's Park
STJWD ... St John's Wood
STKPK ... Stockley Park
STLK ... St Luke's
STMC/STPC ... St Mary Cray/St Paul's Cray
STNW/STAM ... Stoke Newington/Stamford Hill
STP ... St Paul's
STPAN ... St Pancras
STRHM/NOR ... Streatham/Norbury
STWL/WRAY ... Stanwell/Wraysbury
SUN ... Sunbury
SURB ... Surbiton
SUT ... Sutton
SWFD ... South Woodford
SWLY ... Swanley
SYD ... Sydenham
TEDD ... Teddington
THDIT ... Thames Ditton
THHTH ... Thornton Heath
THMD ... Thamesmead
TOOT ... Tooting
TOTM ... Tottenham
TPL/STR ... Temple/Strand
TRDG/WHET ... Totteridge/Whetstone
TWK ... Twickenham
TWRH ... Tower Hill
UED ... Upper Edmonton
UPMR ... Upminster
UX/CGN ... Uxbridge/Colham Green
VX/NE ... Vauxhall/Nine Elms
WAB ... Waltham Abbey
WALTH ... Walthamstow
WALW ... Walworth
WAN ... Wanstead
WAND/EARL ... Wandsworth/Earlsfield
WAP ... Wapping
WARL ... Warlingham
WAT ... Watford
WATN ... Watford North
WATW ... Watford West
WBLY ... Wembley
WBPTN ... West Brompton
WCHMH ... Winchmore Hill
WCHPL ... Whitechapel
WDGN ... Wood Green
WDR/YW ... West Drayton/Yiewsley
WEA ... West Ealing
WELL ... Welling
WEST ... Westminster
WESTW ... Westminster west
WEY ... Weybridge
WFD ... Woodford
WHALL ... Whitehall
WHTN ... Whitton
WIM/MER ... Wimbledon/Merton
WKENS ... West Kensington
WLGTN ... Wallington
WLSDN ... Willesden
WNWD ... West Norwood
WOOL/PLUM ... Woolwich/Plumstead
WOT/HER ... Walton-on-Thames/Hersham
WPK ... Worcester Park
WTHK ... West Thurrock
WWKM ... West Wickham
YEAD ... Yeading

Abb - Ais

Index - streets

A

Abbess Cl BRXS/STRHM SW2 ... 139 H5
Abbeville Ms CLAP SW4 ... 138 D1
Abbeville Rd CEND/HSY/T N8 ... 66 D5
CLAP SW4 ... 138 C3
Abbey Av ALP/SUD HA0 ... 98 E1
Abbey Cl HYS/HAR UB3 ... 96 B7
NTHLT UB5 ... 96 F2
PIN HA5 ... 60 B4
ROM RM1 ... 74 A7
Abbey Ct WAB EN9 ... 27 H7
Abbey Crs BELV DA17 ... 127 G2
Abbeydale Rd ALP/SUD HA0 ... 80 F8
Abbey Dr ABLGY WD5 ... 21 G5
STA TW18 ... 148 C7
TOOT SW17 ... 156 A1
Abbeyfield Rd
BERM/RHTH SE16 ... 122 C2
Abbeyfields Cl WLSDN NW10 ... 99 G2
Abbey Gdns HMSMTH W6 ... 118 E4
STJWD NW8 ... 2 E6
Abbey Gv ABYW SE2 ... 126 B2
Abbeyhill Rd BFN/LL DA15 ... 144 C5
Abbey La BECK BR3 ... 159 G3
SRTFD E15 ... 105 J1
Abbey Orchard St WEST SW1P ... 17 H3
Abbey Pk BECK BR3 ... 159 G3
Abbey Rd BARK IG11 ... 89 H7
BELV DA17 ... 126 D2
BXLYHS DA6 ... 144 E1
CHES/WCR EN8 ... 26 E7
CROY/NA CR0 ... 172 B5
EN EN1 ... 36 E8
GNTH/NBYPK IG2 ... 71 K6
KIL/WHAMP NW6 ... 2 C3
SAND/SEL CR2 ... 185 K3
SHPTN TW17 ... 164 A3
SRTFD E15 ... 105 K1
WIM/MER SW19 ... 155 J3
WLSDN NW10 ... 81 H8
WLSDN NW10 ... 99 H1
Abbey St PLSTW E13 ... 106 A3
STHWK SE1 ... 19 L3
Abbey Ter ABYW SE2 ... 126 C1
Abbey Vw MLHL NW7 ... 45 M5
Abbeyview WAB EN9 ... 27 H6
Abbey Wk E/WMO/HCT KT8 ... 151 H6
Abbey Wood La RAIN RM13 ... 110 D1
Abbey Wood Rd ABYW SE2 ... 126 B2
Abbot Cl RSLP HA4 ... 78 D3
STA TW18 ... 148 D3
Abbotsbury Cl SRTFD E15 ... 105 J1
WKENS W14 ... 100 F8
Abbotsbury Gdns PIN HA5 ... 60 C7
Abbotsbury Ms PECK SE15 ... 122 C8
Abbotsbury Rd MRDN SM4 ... 155 H7
WKENS W14 ... 100 E8
WWKM BR4 ... 174 F4
Abbots Cl RAIN RM13 ... 110 C1
STMC/STPC BR5 ... 176 C3
Abbots Dr RYLN/HDSTN HA2 ... 79 G2
Abbotsford Av SEVS/STOTM N15 ... 67 J5
Abbotsford Gdns WFD IG8 ... 70 A1
Abbotsford Rd GDMY/SEVK IG3 ... 90 A2
Abbots Gdns EFNCH N2 ... 65 K5
Abbots Gn CROY/NA CR0 ... 173 K8
Abbotshade Rd
BERM/RHTH SE16 ... 104 D7
Abbotshall Av STHGT/OAK N14 ... 48 C5
Abbotshall Rd CAT SE6 ... 141 K5
Abbots La PUR/KEN CR8 ... 184 C8
STHWK SE1 ... 13 K9
Abbotsleigh Cl BELMT SM2 ... 182 B1
Abbotsleigh Rd
STRHM/NOR SW16 ... 138 C8
Abbotsmede Cl TWK TW1 ... 133 M6
Abbots Pk BRXS/STRHM SW2 ... 139 G5
Abbot's Pl KIL/WHAMP NW6 ... 2 C3
Abbots Rd ABLGY WD5 ... 20 C4
EDGW HA8 ... 63 K1
EHAM E6 ... 88 D8
Abbots Ter CEND/HSY/T N8 ... 66 E7
Abbotstone Rd
PUT/ROE SW15 ... 118 C8
Abbot St HACK E8 ... 85 M6
Abbots Wy BECK BR3 ... 158 E8
Abbotswell Rd BROCKY SE4 ... 140 F2
Abbotswood Cl BELV DA17 ... 126 E1
Abbotswood Gdns CLAY IG5 ... 70 F4
Abbotswood Rd EDUL SE22 ... 139 L1
STRHM/NOR SW16 ... 138 D7
Abbotswood Wy HYS/HAR UB3 ... 96 B7
Abbott Av RYNPK SW20 ... 154 D5
Abbott Cl HPTN TW12 ... 150 E2
NTHLT UB5 ... 78 F6
Abbott Rd POP/IOD E14 ... 105 J4
Abbotts Cl ROMW/RG RM7 ... 73 H4
THMD SE28 ... 108 C6
UX/CGN UB8 ... 94 D4
Abbotts Crs CHING E4 ... 51 K6
ENC/FH EN2 ... 36 B5
Abbotts Dr ALP/SUD HA0 ... 80 B2
Abbotts Park Rd LEY E10 ... 69 J8
Abbotts Rd BAR EN5 ... 34 B7
CHEAM SM3 ... 169 L6
MTCM CR4 ... 156 C7
STHL UB1 ... 96 E7
Abbotts Tilt WOT/HER KT12 ... 165 L5
Abbott's Wk BXLYHN DA7 ... 126 D5
Abbs Cross Gdns HCH RM12 ... 92 C1
Abbs Cross La HCH RM12 ... 92 C3
Abchurch La MANHO EC4N ... 13 H5
Abdale Rd SHB W12 ... 100 B7
Aberavon Rd BOW E3 ... 104 E2
Abercairn Rd
STRHM/NOR SW16 ... 156 C3
Aberconway Rd MRDN SM4 ... 155 H6
Abercorn Cl MLHL NW7 ... 64 E1
SAND/SEL CR2 ... 185 K5
STJWD NW8 ... 2 E6
Abercorn Crs RYLN/HDSTN HA2 ... 79 H1
Abercorn Gdns CHDH RM6 ... 72 B7
KTN/HRWW/W HA3 ... 62 D8
Abercorn Gv RSLP HA4 ... 59 K5
Abercorn Pl STJWD NW8 ... 2 E7
Abercorn Rd MLHL NW7 ... 64 E1
STAN HA7 ... 62 C1
Abercorn Wy STHWK SE1 ... 122 A3
Abercrombie Dr EN EN1 ... 37 G4
Abercrombie St BTSEA SW11 ... 119 L7
Aberdale Gdns POTB/CUF EN6 ... 22 F6
Aberdare Cl WWKM BR4 ... 174 C4
Aberdare Gdns KIL/WHAMP NW6 ... 2 D2
MLHL NW7 ... 64 D1
Aberdare Rd PEND EN3 ... 37 J7
Aberdeen La HBRY N5 ... 85 H5
Aberdeen Pk HBRY N5 ... 85 H5
Aberdeen Pl STJWD NW8 ... 9 G1
Aberdeen Rd CROY/NA CR0 ... 172 C6
HBRY N5 ... 85 J4
KTN/HRWW/W HA3 ... 61 M4
UED N18 ... 50 B7
WLSDN NW10 ... 81 M5
Aberdeen Ter BKHTH/KID SE3 ... 123 K7
Aberdour Rd BCTR RM8 ... 90 B3
Aberdour St STHWK SE1 ... 19 J5
Aberfeldy St POP/IOD E14 ... 105 J5
POP/IOD E14 ... 105 J5
Aberford Gdns
WOOL/PLUM SE18 ... 124 E6
Aberford Rd BORE WD6 ... 32 A5
Aberfoyle Rd
STRHM/NOR SW16 ... 156 D2
Abergeldie Rd LEE/GVPK SE12 ... 142 B3
Abernethy Rd LEW SE13 ... 141 L1
Abersham Rd HACK E8 ... 85 M5
Abery St WOOL/PLUM SE18 ... 125 L2
Abingdon Cl HGDN/ICK UB10 ... 76 F8
WIM/MER SW19 ... 155 J2
Abingdon Pl POTB/CUF EN6 ... 23 H5
Abingdon Rd FNCH N3 ... 65 J3
KENS W8 ... 14 B4
STRHM/NOR SW16 ... 156 E4
Abingdon St WEST SW1P ... 17 J2
Abingdon Vls KENS W8 ... 14 A4
Abingdon Wy ORP BR6 ... 177 H6
Abinger Av BELMT SM2 ... 181 J2
Abinger Cl BMLY BR1 ... 160 E6
GDMY/SEVK IG3 ... 90 A4
WLGTN SM6 ... 171 L7
Abinger Gdns ISLW TW7 ... 115 L8
Abinger Gv DEPT SE8 ... 122 F4
Abinger Ms MV/WKIL W9 ... 2 A9
Abinger Rd CHSWK W4 ... 117 M1
Ablett St BERM/RHTH SE16 ... 122 C3
Aboyne Dr RYNPK SW20 ... 154 A5
Aboyne Rd TOOT SW17 ... 137 K7
WLSDN NW10 ... 81 L3
Abridge Cl CHES/WCR EN8 ... 26 D8
Abridge Gdns CRW RM5 ... 55 G8
Abridge Rd CHIG IG7 ... 53 L1
Abridge Wy BARK IG11 ... 108 B1
Abyssinia Cl BTSEA SW11 ... 137 L1
Abyssinia Rd BTSEA SW11 ... 137 L1
Acacia Av ALP/SUD HA0 ... 80 E5
BTFD TW8 ... 116 B5
HCH RM12 ... 91 M2
HYS/HAR UB3 ... 95 M5
RSLP HA4 ... 78 A1
SHPTN TW17 ... 149 G8
TOTM N17 ... 67 K3
WDR/YW UB7 ... 94 F6
Acacia Cl DEPT SE8 ... 122 E2
KTN/HRWW/W HA3 ... 43 L8
STMC/STPC BR5 ... 161 K8
Acacia Dr CHEAM SM3 ... 169 M3
EW KT17 ... 181 K7
UPMR RM14 ... 93 G4
Acacia Gdns STJWD NW8 ... 3 H5
UPMR RM14 ... 75 M8
WWKM BR4 ... 174 C4
Acacia Gv DUL SE21 ... 139 K6
NWMAL KT3 ... 153 L6
Acacia Ms WDR/YW UB7 ... 112 D4
Acacia Pl STJWD NW8 ... 3 H5
Acacia Rd ACT W3 ... 99 J6
BECK BR3 ... 158 F6
DART DA1 ... 146 C5
ENC/FH EN2 ... 36 D4
GRH DA9 ... 147 L3
HPTN TW12 ... 151 G2
MTCM CR4 ... 156 A5
STA TW18 ... 148 B1
STJWD NW8 ... 3 H5
STRHM/NOR SW16 ... 156 E4
WALTH E17 ... 68 E7
WAN E11 ... 87 L2
WDGN N22 ... 67 G2
Acacia Wy BFN/LL DA15 ... 143 M4
Academy Gdns CROY/NA CR0 ... 172 F3
NTHLT UB5 ... 96 D1
Academy Pl WOOL/PLUM SE18 ... 124 F6
Academy Rd
WOOL/PLUM SE18 ... 125 G5
Acanthus Dr STHWK SE1 ... 122 A3
Acanthus Rd BTSEA SW11 ... 120 A8
Accommodation La
WDR/YW UB7 ... 112 C4
Accommodation Rd
GLDGN NW11 ... 64 F8
Acer Av RAIN RM13 ... 110 D2
YEAD UB4 ... 96 E3
Acfold Rd FUL/PGN SW6 ... 119 H6
Achilles Cl STHWK SE1 ... 122 A3
Achilles Rd KIL/WHAMP NW6 ... 83 G5
Achilles St NWCR SE14 ... 122 E5
Acklam Rd NKENS W10 ... 100 F4
Acklington Dr CDALE/KGS NW9 ... 63 L2
Ackmar Rd FUL/PGN SW6 ... 119 G6
Ackroyd Dr BOW E3 ... 104 F4
Ackroyd Rd FSTH SE23 ... 140 D4
Acland Cl WOOL/PLUM SE18 ... 125 K5
Acland Crs CMBW SE5 ... 139 K1
Acland Rd CRICK NW2 ... 82 B6
Acme Rd WATN WD24 ... 29 G3
Acol Crs RSLP HA4 ... 78 B5
Acol Rd KIL/WHAMP NW6 ... 2 B2
Acorn Cl CHING E4 ... 51 H7
CHST BR7 ... 161 J1
ENC/FH EN2 ... 36 A4
HPTN TW12 ... 151 H2
STAN HA7 ... 62 B1
Acorn Gdns ACT W3 ... 99 K4
NRWD SE19 ... 157 M4
Acorn Gv HYS/HAR UB3 ... 113 M5
RSLP HA4 ... 77 M4
Acorn La POTB/CUF EN6 ... 24 E2
Acorn Pl WATN WD24 ... 29 G2
Acorns Wy ESH/CLAY KT10 ... 166 C7
Acorn Wy FSTH SE23 ... 140 D7
ORP BR6 ... 176 B6
Acre Dr EDUL SE22 ... 140 A1
Acre La BRXS/STRHM SW2 ... 138 F1
CAR SM5 ... 171 G6
Acre Rd DAGE RM10 ... 91 J7
KUTN/CMB KT2 ... 152 E4
WIM/MER SW19 ... 155 K2
Acre Wy NTHWD HA6 ... 59 M2
Acris St WAND/EARL SW18 ... 137 J2
Acton Cl CHES/WCR EN8 ... 26 E4
ED N9 ... 50 A4
Acton La ACT W3 ... 99 J8
CHSWK W4 ... 117 J1
WLSDN NW10 ... 99 K1
Acton Ms HACK E8 ... 7 L3
Acton St FSBYW WC1X ... 5 L8
Acuba Rd WAND/EARL SW18 ... 137 H6
Ada Ct MV/WKIL W9 ... 2 F8
Ada Gdns POP/IOD E14 ... 105 K5
SRTFD E15 ... 87 M8
Adair Cl SNWD SE25 ... 158 B6
Adair Rd NKENS W10 ... 100 E3
Adam And Eve Ms KENS W8 ... 14 B3
Adam Rd CHING E4 ... 50 F8
Adams Cl BRYLDS KT5 ... 167 M1
FNCH N3 ... 65 G1
WBLY HA9 ... 81 H2
Adams Ms WDGN N22 ... 66 F1
Adamson Rd CAN/RD E16 ... 106 A5
HAMP NW3 ... 3 H1
Adamsrill Cl WCHMH N21 ... 49 K1
Adamsrill Rd SYD SE26 ... 140 D8
Adams Rd BECK BR3 ... 158 E8
TOTM N17 ... 67 K3
Adam's Rw MYFR/PKLN W1K ... 10 B7
Adams Sq BXLYHN DA7 ... 126 E8
Adam St TPL/STR WC2R ... 11 K7
Adams Wy SNWD SE25 ... 172 F1
Ada Pl BETH E2 ... 86 B8
Adare Wk STRHM/NOR SW16 ... 138 F7
Ada Rd ALP/SUD HA0 ... 80 D3
CMBW SE5 ... 121 L5
Ada St HACK E8 ... 86 B8
Adderley Gdns ELTH/MOT SE9 ... 143 G8
Adderley Gv BTSEA SW11 ... 138 A2
Adderley Rd KTN/HRWW/W HA3 ... 61 M2
Adderley St POP/IOD E14 ... 105 J5
Addington Dr
NFNCH/WDSP N12 ... 47 K8
Addington Gv SYD SE26 ... 140 E8
Addington Rd BOW E3 ... 105 G2
CAN/RD E16 ... 105 L3
CROY/NA CR0 ... 172 A3
FSBYPK N4 ... 67 G7
SAND/SEL CR2 ... 185 G4
WWKM BR4 ... 174 D5
Addington Sq CMBW SE5 ... 121 J5
Addington Village Rd
CROY/NA CR0 ... 173 M8
Addis Cl PEND EN3 ... 37 K4
Addiscombe Av CROY/NA CR0 ... 173 G2
Addiscombe Cl
KTN/HRWW/W HA3 ... 62 C6
Addiscombe Court Rd
CROY/NA CR0 ... 172 E3
Addiscombe Gv CROY/NA CR0 ... 172 D4
Addiscombe Rd CROY/NA CR0 ... 172 E4
WATW WD18 ... 29 H7
Addison Av HSLW TW3 ... 115 J6
NTGHL W11 ... 100 E7
STHGT/OAK N14 ... 48 B1
Addison Bridge Pl
WKENS W14 ... 118 F2
Addison Cl NTHWD HA6 ... 60 A2
STMC/STPC BR5 ... 176 C1
Addison Crs WKENS W14 ... 118 E1
Addison Dr LEE/GVPK SE12 ... 142 B2
Addison Gdns BRYLDS KT5 ... 152 F7
WKENS W14 ... 118 D1
Addison Gv CHSWK W4 ... 117 L1
Addison Pl NTGHL W11 ... 100 E7
Addison Rd BARK/HLT IG6 ... 71 J2
HAYES BR2 ... 160 D8
NTGHL W11 ... 100 E8
PEND EN3 ... 37 J4
SNWD SE25 ... 158 A6
TEDD TW11 ... 152 B2
WALTH E17 ... 69 H6
WAN E11 ... 70 A7
WKENS W14 ... 100 E8
WKENS W14 ... 118 F1
Addison's Cl CROY/NA CR0 ... 173 M4
Addison Wy GLDGN NW11 ... 64 F5
HYS/HAR UB3 ... 96 A5
NTHWD HA6 ... 59 M2
Addle Hl BLKFR EC4V ... 12 D6
Addle St CITYW EC2V ... 12 F4
Adecroft Wy E/WMO/HCT KT8 ... 151 J6
Adela Av NWMAL KT3 ... 154 B8
Adelaide Av BROCKY SE4 ... 141 G2
Adelaide Cl EN EN1 ... 36 E3
STAN HA7 ... 44 A6
Adelaide Ct HNWL W7 ... 97 M8
Adelaide Gdns CHDH RM6 ... 72 E6
Adelaide Gv SHB W12 ... 100 A7
Adelaide Pl WEY KT13 ... 164 D6
Adelaide Rd ASHF TW15 ... 148 D1
CHST BR7 ... 161 H1
HAMP NW3 ... 3 J1
HEST TW5 ... 114 E6
IL IG1 ... 89 H2
LEY E10 ... 87 J3
NWDGN UB2 ... 114 E2
RCH/KEW TW9 ... 134 F1
SURB KT6 ... 152 E8
TEDD TW11 ... 151 M2
WAND/EARL SW18 ... 137 G2
WEA W13 ... 98 A8
WOT/HER KT12 ... 165 G5
Adelaide St CHCR WC2N ... 11 J7
Adela St NKENS W10 ... 100 E3
Adelina Gv WCHPL E1 ... 104 C4
Adelina Ms BAL SW12 ... 138 D5
Adeline Pl RSQ WC1B ... 11 H3
Adeliza Cl BARK IG11 ... 89 J7
Adelphi Crs HCH RM12 ... 92 A2
YEAD UB4 ... 95 L2
Adelphi Rd EW KT17 ... 180 D6
Adelphi Ter CHCR WC2N ... 11 K7
Adelphi Wy YEAD UB4 ... 95 M2
Adeney Cl HMSMTH W6 ... 118 D4
Aden Gv STNW/STAM N16 ... 85 K4
Adenmore Rd CAT SE6 ... 141 G4
Aden Rd IL IG1 ... 71 H8
PEND EN3 ... 37 L7
Adhara Rd NTHWD HA6 ... 41 M7
Adie Rd HMSMTH W6 ... 118 C1
Adine Rd PLSTW E13 ... 106 A3
Adler St WCHPL E1 ... 104 A4
Adley St CLPT E5 ... 86 E5
Adlington Cl UED N18 ... 49 K7
Admaston Rd
WOOL/PLUM SE18 ... 125 J5
Admiral Cl STMC/STPC BR5 ... 162 D7
Admiral Ms NKENS W10 ... 100 D3
Admirals Cl SWFD E18 ... 70 B5
Admiral Seymour Rd
ELTH/MOT SE9 ... 142 F1
Admiral's Ga GNWCH SE10 ... 123 H6
Admiral St DEPT SE8 ... 123 G6
Admiral's Wk HAMP NW3 ... 83 J3
Admirals Wy POP/IOD E14 ... 105 H8
Admiralty Rd TEDD TW11 ... 151 M3
Admiral Wk MV/WKIL W9 ... 8 B2
Adnams Wk RAIN RM13 ... 92 A6
Adolf St CAT SE6 ... 141 G8
Adolphus Rd FSBYPK N4 ... 85 H2
Adolphus St DEPT SE8 ... 122 F5
Adomar Rd BCTR RM8 ... 90 D3
Adpar St BAY/PAD W2 ... 9 G2
Adrian Cl DEN/HRF UB9 ... 58 D2
Adrian Rd ABLGY WD5 ... 20 E4
Adrienne Av STHL UB1 ... 96 F3
Advance Rd WNWD SE27 ... 139 J8
Advent Wy UED N18 ... 50 D7
Adys Rd PECK SE15 ... 121 M8
Aerodrome Rd CDALE/KGS NW9 ... 63 M4
Aerodrome Wy HEST TW5 ... 114 C4
Affleck St IS N1 ... 5 M6
Afghan Rd BTSEA SW11 ... 119 L7
Agamemnon Rd
KIL/WHAMP NW6 ... 82 F5
Agar Cl SURB KT6 ... 167 M4
Agar Gv CAMTN NW1 ... 5 H1
Agar Pl CAMTN NW1 ... 4 F2
Agar St CHCR WC2N ... 11 J7
Agate Cl CAN/RD E16 ... 106 D5
Agate Rd HMSMTH W6 ... 118 C1
Agatha Cl WAP E1W ... 104 B7
Agaton Rd ELTH/MOT SE9 ... 143 J6
Agave Rd CRICK NW2 ... 82 C4
Agdon St FSBYE EC1V ... 6 C9
Agincourt Rd HAMP NW3 ... 83 M4
Agister Rd CHIG IG7 ... 54 A7
Agnes Av IL IG1 ... 89 G4
Agnes Cl EHAM E6 ... 107 G6
Agnesfield Cl NFNCH/WDSP N12 ... 47 L8
Agnes Gdns BCTR RM8 ... 90 D4
Agnes Rd ACT W3 ... 99 M8
Agnes St POP/IOD E14 ... 104 F5
Agnew Rd FSTH SE23 ... 140 E4
Agricola Pl EN EN1 ... 36 F8
Aidan Cl DAGW RM9 ... 90 E4
Ailsa Av TWK TW1 ... 134 A2
Ailsa Rd TWK TW1 ... 134 B2
Ailsa St POP/IOD E14 ... 105 J4
Ainger Rd HAMP NW3 ... 3 M2
Ainsdale Cl ORP BR6 ... 176 D3
Ainsdale Crs PIN HA5 ... 61 G4
Ainsdale Dr STHWK SE1 ... 122 A3
Ainsdale Rd EA W5 ... 98 D3
OXHEY WD19 ... 42 C5
Ainsley Av ROMW/RG RM7 ... 73 J7
Ainsley Cl ED N9 ... 49 L3
Ainsley St BETH E2 ... 104 B2
Ainslie Wood Crs CHING E4 ... 51 H7
Ainslie Wood Gdns CHING E4 ... 51 H6
Ainslie Wood Rd CHING E4 ... 51 G7
Ainsworth Cl CMBW SE5 ... 121 L7
CRICK NW2 ... 82 A3
Ainsworth Rd CROY/NA CR0 ... 172 B4
HOM E9 ... 86 C7
Aintree Av EHAM E6 ... 88 E8
Aintree Cl UX/CGN UB8 ... 95 H5
Aintree Crs BARK/HLT IG6 ... 71 J3
Aintree Gv UPMR RM14 ... 92 F3
Aintree Rd GFD/PVL UB6 ... 98 B1
Aintree St FUL/PGN SW6 ... 118 E5
Airdrie Cl YEAD UB4 ... 96 E4
Airedale Av CHSWK W4 ... 117 M3
Airedale Av South
CHSWK W4 ... 117 M3
Airedale Cl RDART DA2 ... 147 J5
Airedale Rd BAL SW12 ... 137 M4
EA W5 ... 116 C1
Airfield Wy HCH RM12 ... 92 B6
Airlie Gdns IL IG1 ... 89 H1
KENS W8 ... 8 A9
Airport Wy STWL/WRAY TW19 ... 130 A1
Air St REGST W1B ... 10 F7
Aisgill Av ECT SW5 ... 118 F3
WKENS W14 ... 118 F3

Aisher Rd THMD SE28 108 C6
Aislibie Rd LEW SE13 141 L1
Aiten Pl HMSMTH W6 118 A2
Aitken Cl HACK E8 86 A8
MTCM CR4 170 F2
Aitken Rd BAR EN5 33 J8
CAT SE6 141 H6
Ajax Av CDALE/KGS NW9 63 L4
Ajax Rd KIL/WHAMP NW6 82 F4
Akabusi Cl SNWD SE25 173 G1
Akehurst St PUT/ROE SW15 136 A3
Akenside Rd HAMP NW3 83 K5
Akerman Rd CMBW SE5 121 H6
SURB KT6 167 J1
Alabama St WOOL/PLUM SE18 125 K5
Alacross Rd EA W5 98 C8
Alamein Gdns RDART DA2 147 K4
Alan Cl DART DA1 146 C1
Alandale Dr PIN HA5 60 B2
Alan Dr BAR EN5 46 E1
Alan Gdns ROMW/RG RM7 73 G8
Alan Hocken Wy SRTFD E15 105 L1
Alan Rd WIM/MER SW19 154 E1
Alanthus Cl LEE/GVPK SE12 141 M3
Alaska St STHWK SE1 12 A9
Alba Cl YEAD UB4 96 D3
Albacore Crs LEW SE13 141 H3
Alba Gdns GLDGN NW11 64 E7
Albain Crs ASHF TW15 130 E6
Alban Crs BORE WD6 32 B4
Albans Vw GSTN WD25 21 H6
Albany Cl BUSH WD23 43 K1
BXLY DA5 144 C4
ESH/CLAY KT10 178 A2
HGDN/ICK UB10 77 G5
MORT/ESHN SW14 135 H1
SEVS/STOTM N15 67 H5
Albany Ctyd MYFR/PICC W1J 10 F7
Albany Crs EDGW HA8 63 G1
ESH/CLAY KT10 166 E8
Albany Ms KUTN/CMB KT2 152 D2
KUTN/CMB KT2 152 D2
SUT SM1 170 B7
WALW SE17 121 J4
Albany Park Av PEND EN3 37 J4
Albany Park Rd KUTN/CMB KT2 152 D2
Albany Pl BTFD TW8 116 D4
HOLWY N7 85 G4
Albany Rd BELV DA17 126 F4
BTFD TW8 116 D4
BXLY DA5 144 C4
CHDH RM6 72 F7
CHST BR7 161 H1
CMBW SE5 19 J9
FSBYPK N4 66 F7
HCH RM12 92 A1
LEY E10 69 G8
MNPK E12 88 D4
NWMAL KT3 153 K7
PEND EN3 37 K2
RCHPK/HAM TW10 134 F2
UED N18 50 B7
WALTH E17 68 E7
WEA W13 98 B6
WIM/MER SW19 155 H1
WOT/HER KT12 165 K6
Albany St CAMTN NW1 4 D7
The Albany KUTN/CMB KT2 152 D2
Albany Vw BKHH IG9 52 A3
Alba Pl NTGHL W11 100 F5
Albatross Gdns SAND/SEL CR2 185 K4
Albatross St WOOL/PLUM SE18 125 L5
Albemarle Ap
GNTH/NBYPK IG2 71 H7
Albemarle Av CHES/WCR EN8 26 C1
POTB/CUF EN6 23 H6
WHTN TW2 132 F5
Albemarle Gdns
GNTH/NBYPK IG2 71 H7
NWMAL KT3 153 K7
Albemarle Pk STAN HA7 44 C7
Albemarle Rd BECK BR3 159 H4
EBAR EN4 47 L2
Albemarle St CONDST W1S 10 E7
Albemarle Wy FARR EC1M 12 C1
Alberon Gdns GLDGN NW11 64 F5
Alberta Av SUT SM1 169 L6
Alberta Rd BXLYHN DA7 127 J6
EN EN1 49 M1
Alberta St WALW SE17 18 D7
Albert Av CHERT KT16 148 A6
CHING E4 51 G6
VX/NE SW8 120 F5
Albert Br BTSEA SW11 119 L5
Albert Bridge Rd BTSEA SW11 119 L5
CHEL SW3 119 L4
Albert Carr Gdns
STRHM/NOR SW16 156 E1
Albert Cl HOM E9 86 B8
WDGN N22 66 D2
Albert Crs CHING E4 51 G6
Albert Dr WIM/MER SW19 136 E6
Albert Emb LBTH SE11 17 K7
Albert Gdns WCHPL E1 104 D5
Albert Gv RYNPK SW20 154 D4
Albert Ms KENS W8 14 E3
Albert Pl FNCH N3 65 G2
KENS W8 14 D2
Albert Rd ASHF TW15 148 F1
BCTR RM8 90 F1
BELV DA17 126 F3
BKHH IG9 52 D4
BXLY DA5 145 G3
CAN/RD E16 107 G8
EA W5 98 B3
EBAR EN4 34 C7
ELTH/MOT SE9 142 E7
EW KT17 180 F6
FSBYPK N4 84 F1
HAYES BR2 160 D8
HDN NW4 64 D5
HPTN TW12 151 J1
HSLW TW3 133 G1
HYS/HAR UB3 113 L1
IL IG1 89 J3
KIL/WHAMP NW6 100 F1
KUT KT1 152 F5
MLHL NW7 45 M7
MTCM CR4 155 M6
NWDGN UB2 114 D1
NWMAL KT3 153 M7
ORP BR6 177 G7
PGE/AN SE20 158 D3
RCHPK/HAM TW10 134 E2
RDART DA2 146 C7
ROM RM1 73 M7
RYLN/HDSTN HA2 61 J4
SEVS/STOTM N15 67 L7
SNWD SE25 158 B7
STMC/STPC BR5 177 H1
SUT SM1 170 D7
SWFD E18 70 B4
TEDD TW11 151 M2
TWK TW1 133 M5
WALTH E17 69 G6
WAN E11 87 J2
WDGN N22 66 D2
WDR/YW UB7 94 E7
Albert Rd North WAT WD17 29 H5
Albert Rd South WAT WD17 29 H6
Albert Sq SRTFD E15 87 L5
VX/NE SW8 120 F5
Albert St CAMTN NW1 4 D4
NFNCH/WDSP N12 47 J7
Albert Ter CAMTN NW1 4 A3
Albert Terrace Ms CAMTN NW1 4 A3
Albion Av MUSWH N10 66 A2
VX/NE SW8 120 D7
Albion Cl BAY/PAD W2 9 K6
ROMW/RG RM7 73 K7
Albion Dr HACK E8 7 L2
Albion Gdns HMSMTH W6 118 B2
Albion Gv STNW/STAM N16 85 L4
Albion Hl LOU IG10 39 J8
Albion Ms BAY/PAD W2 9 K5
IS N1 6 A2
Albion Pk LOU IG10 39 K8
Albion Pl FARR EC1M 12 C2
HMSMTH W6 118 B2
Albion Rd BELMT SM2 170 D8
BXLYHS DA6 144 F1
DAGE RM10 91 G5
HSLW TW3 133 G1
HYS/HAR UB3 95 L4
KUTN/CMB KT2 153 J4
STNW/STAM N16 85 K5
TOTM N17 67 M3
WALTH E17 69 J4
WHTN TW2 133 L5
Albion Sq HACK E8 7 L2
Albion St BAY/PAD W2 9 K5
BERM/RHTH SE16 104 C8
CROY/NA CR0 172 B3
Albion Ter HACK E8 7 L2
Albion Villas Rd FSTH SE23 140 C7
Albion Wy LEW SE13 141 J1
STBT EC1A 12 E3
WBLY HA9 81 G3
Albion Yd IS N1 5 K6
Albrighton Rd CMBW SE5 121 L8
CMBW SE5 121 L8
Albuhera Cl ENC/FH EN2 36 A4
Albury Av BELMT SM2 181 J2
BXLYHN DA7 126 E7
ISLW TW7 115 M5
Albury Cl HPTN TW12 151 G2
Albury Dr PIN HA5 60 C2
Albury Grove Rd CHES/WCR EN8 26 D3
Albury Ms MNPK E12 88 C1
Albury Ride CHES/WCR EN8 26 D4
Albury Rd CHSGTN KT9 167 L7
WOT/HER KT12 164 E8
Albury St DEPT SE8 123 G4
Albury Wk CHES/WCR EN8 26 C3
Albyfield BMLY BR1 160 F6
Albyn Rd DEPT SE8 123 G6
Alcester Crs CLPT E5 86 B2
Alcester Rd WLGTN SM6 171 H6
Alcock Cl WLGTN SM6 183 K1
Alcock Rd HEST TW5 114 D5
Alconbury Rd CLPT E5 86 A2
Alcorn Cl CHEAM SM3 170 A4
Alcott Cl HNWL W7 97 M4
Aldborough Rd DAGE RM10 91 J6
UPMR RM14 92 F2
Aldborough Rd North
GNTH/NBYPK IG2 71 M6
Aldborough Rd South
GDMY/SEVK IG3 89 L1
Aldbourne Rd ACT W3 99 M7
Aldbridge St WALW SE17 19 K7
Aldbury Av WBLY HA9 81 H7
Aldbury Cl GSTN WD25 29 K1
Aldbury Ms WCHMH N21 49 K2
Aldebert Ter VX/NE SW8 120 F5
Aldeburgh Pl WFD IG8 52 A6
Aldeburgh St GNWCH SE10 124 A3
Alden Av SRTFD E15 105 M2
Aldenham Av RAD WD7 31 G2
Aldenham Dr UX/CGN UB8 95 H3
Aldenham Rd BUSH WD23 29 M7
GSTN WD25 30 F5
OXHEY WD19 42 D1
Aldenham St CAMTN NW1 4 F6
Aldenholme WEY KT13 164 E8
Aldensley Rd HMSMTH W6 118 B1
Alder Av UPMR RM14 92 F4
Alderbrook Rd BAL SW12 138 B3
Alderbury Rd BARN SW13 118 A4
Alder Gv CRICK NW2 82 A2
Alderman Av BARK IG11 108 A2
Aldermanbury CITYW EC2V 12 F4
Aldermanbury Sq CITYW EC2V 12 F3
Alderman's Hl PLMGR N13 48 E6
Aldermary Rd BMLY BR1 160 A4
Aldermoor Rd CAT SE6 140 F7
Alderney Av HEST TW5 115 H5
Alderney Gdns NTHLT UB5 78 F7
Alderney Rd ERITH DA8 128 A5
WCHPL E1 104 D3
Alderney St PIM SW1V 16 D7
Alder Rd DEN/HRF UB9 76 B6
MORT/ESHN SW14 117 K8
SCUP DA14 143 L7
Alders Av WFD IG8 51 L8
Aldersbrook Av EN EN1 36 E5
Aldersbrook Dr KUTN/CMB KT2 152 F2
Aldersbrook La MNPK E12 88 F3
Aldersbrook Rd MNPK E12 88 C2
Alders Cl EA W5 116 D1
EDGW HA8 45 J7
WAN E11 88 B2
Aldersey Gdns BARK IG11 89 K6
Aldersford Cl BROCKY SE4 140 D1
Aldersgate St STBT EC1A 12 E2
Aldersgrove E/WMO/HCT KT8 151 K8
Aldersgrove Av LEE/GVPK SE12 142 C7
Aldershot Rd KIL/WHAMP NW6 82 F8
Aldersmead Av CROY/NA CR0 173 K1
Aldersmead Rd BECK BR3 158 E3
Alderson Pl STHL UB1 97 J7
Alderson St NKENS W10 100 E3
Alders Rd EDGW HA8 45 J7
The Alders FELT TW13 150 E1
NWDGN UB2 114 F4
WCHMH N21 49 G1
WWKM BR4 174 B3
Alderton Cl WLSDN NW10 81 K2
Alderton Crs HDN NW4 64 B6
Alderton Hl LOU IG10 39 M8
Alderton Rd CROY/NA CR0 172 F2
HNHL SE24 121 J8
Alderton Wy HDN NW4 64 B6
LOU IG10 39 M8
Alderville Rd FUL/PGN SW6 118 F7
Alder Wk GSTN WD25 21 H8
Alder Wy SWLY BR8 163 K5
Alderwick Dr HSLW TW3 115 K8
Alderwood Rd ELTH/MOT SE9 143 K3
Aldford St MYFR/PKLN W1K 10 A8
Aldgate FENCHST EC3M 13 K5
Aldgate High St TWRH EC3N 13 L5
Aldine St SHB W12 100 C8
Aldingham Gdns HCH RM12 92 A5
Aldington Cl CHDH RM6 72 C8
Aldington Rd
WOOL/PLUM SE18 124 D1
Aldis Ms TOOT SW17 155 L1
Aldis St TOOT SW17 155 L1
Aldred Rd KIL/WHAMP NW6 83 G5
Aldren Rd TOOT SW17 137 J7
Aldrich Crs CROY/NA CR0 186 C2
Aldriche Wy CHING E4 51 J8
Aldrich Gdns CHEAM SM3 169 M5
Aldrich Ter WAND/EARL SW18 137 J6
Aldridge Av EDGW HA8 45 H5
PEND EN3 38 A3
RSLP HA4 78 D2
STAN HA7 62 E2
Aldridge Ri NWMAL KT3 168 E2
Aldridge Road Vls NTGHL W11 100 F4
Aldridge Wk STHGT/OAK N14 48 E2
Aldrington Rd
STRHM/NOR SW16 156 C1
Aldsworth Cl MV/WKIL W9 8 C1
Aldwick Cl CHST BR7 143 K7
Aldwick Rd CROY/NA CR0 171 M5
Aldworth Gv LEW SE13 141 J3
Aldworth Rd SRTFD E15 87 L7
Aldwych TPL/STR WC2R 11 L6
Aldwych Av BARK/HLT IG6 71 J5
Aldwych Cl HCH RM12 92 A2
Alers Rd BXLYHS DA6 144 D2
Alesia Cl WDGN N22 66 E1
Alestan Beck Rd CAN/RD E16 106 D5
Alexander Av WLSDN NW10 82 B7
Alexander Cl BFN/LL DA15 143 L2
EBAR EN4 34 D7
HAYES BR2 175 G3
STHL UB1 97 J7
WHTN TW2 133 L6
Alexander Evans Ms
FSTH SE23 140 D6
Alexander Ms BAY/PAD W2 8 C4
Alexander Pl SKENS SW7 15 J5
Alexander Rd ARCH N19 84 E3
CHST BR7 161 H1
COUL/CHIP CR5 183 H8
WELL DA16 126 D7
Alexander Sq CHEL SW3 15 J5
Alexander St BAY/PAD W2 8 B4
Alexandra Av BTSEA SW11 120 A6
RYLN/HDSTN HA2 78 F1
STHL UB1 96 F6
SUT SM1 170 A5
WDGN N22 66 D2
Alexandra Cl ASHF TW15 149 K3
RYLN/HDSTN HA2 79 H3
STA TW18 148 D2
SWLY BR8 163 L5
WOT/HER KT12 165 G4
Alexandra Cottages
NWCR SE14 122 F6
Alexandra Ct ASHF TW15 149 K2
Alexandra Crs BMLY BR1 159 M2
Alexandra Dr BRYLDS KT5 168 A2
NRWD SE19 157 L1
Alexandra Gdns CAR SM5 183 G2
HSLW TW3 115 H7
MUSWH N10 66 B5
Alexandra Gv FSBYPK N4 85 H1
NFNCH/WDSP N12 47 H7
Alexandra Ms EFNCH N2 65 M4
WAT WD17 29 G5
Alexandra Palace Wy
CEND/HSY/T N8 66 C5
Alexandra Park Rd MUSWH N10 66 B3
WDGN N22 66 C2
Alexandra Pl CROY/NA CR0 172 E3
SNWD SE25 157 K8
STJWD NW8 2 F3
Alexandra Rd ASHF TW15 149 K3
BORE WD6 32 D3
BTFD TW8 116 D4
CEND/HSY/T N8 67 G4
CHDH RM6 72 D7
CHSWK W4 99 K8
CROY/NA CR0 172 E3
ED N9 50 B2
EHAM E6 107 G2
ERITH DA8 127 M4
EW KT17 180 F6
HDN NW4 64 D5
HSLW TW3 115 H7
KGLGY WD4 20 A2
KUTN/CMB KT2 153 G3
LEY E10 87 J3
MORT/ESHN SW14 117 K8
MUSWH N10 66 B2
PEND EN3 37 K7
RAIN RM13 91 M8
RCH/KEW TW9 116 F7
ROM RM1 73 M7
SEVS/STOTM N15 67 K6
STJWD NW8 2 F3
SWFD E18 70 B4
SYD SE26 158 D2
THDIT KT7 151 M8
TWK TW1 134 C3
UX/CGN UB8 94 D1
WALTH E17 68 F7
WAT WD17 29 G5
WIM/MER SW19 155 L3
WIM/MER SW19 155 G1
Alexandra Sq MRDN SM4 155 G8
Alexandra St CAN/RD E16 106 A4
NWCR SE14 122 E5
Alexandra Wy CHES/WCR EN8 26 F7
Alexandria Rd WEA W13 98 A6
Alexis St BERM/RHTH SE16 122 A2
Alfearn Rd CLPT E5 86 C4
Alford Gn CROY/NA CR0 174 D8
Alford Pl IS N1 6 F6
Alford Rd ERITH DA8 127 J3
Alfoxton Av SEVS/STOTM N15 67 H5
Alfreda St BTSEA SW11 120 B6
Alfred Cl CHSWK W4 117 K2
Alfred Gdns STHL UB1 96 E6
Alfred Ms FITZ W1T 11 G2
Alfred Pl FITZ W1T 11 G2
Alfred Rd ACT W3 99 J7
BAY/PAD W2 8 B2
BELV DA17 126 F3
BKHH IG9 52 D4
FELT TW13 132 C6
FSTGT E7 87 M5
KUT KT1 152 E6
RDART DA2 146 F8
SNWD SE25 158 A8
SOCK/AV RM15 111 J7
SUT SM1 170 C7
Alfred's Gdns BARK IG11 107 L1
Alfred St BOW E3 104 F2
Alfred's Wy (East Ham And Barking
By-pass) BARK IG11 107 K1
Alfreton Cl WIM/MER SW19 136 D7
Alfriston BRYLDS KT5 167 M1
Alfriston Av CROY/NA CR0 171 L2
RYLN/HDSTN HA2 61 G7
Alfriston Cl BRYLDS KT5 167 M1
Alfriston Rd BTSEA SW11 137 M2
Algar Cl STAN HA7 43 M7
Algar Rd ISLW TW7 116 A8
Algarve Rd WAND/EARL SW18 137 H5
Algernon Rd HDN NW4 64 A7
KIL/WHAMP NW6 2 A4
LEW SE13 141 H1
Algers Cl LOU IG10 39 K8
Algers Rd LOU IG10 39 L8
Alghers Md LOU IG10 39 K8
Algiers Rd LEW SE13 141 G1
Alguin Ct STAN HA7 62 C1
Alibon Gdns DAGE RM10 91 G5
Alice La BOW E3 86 F8
Alice Ms TEDD TW11 151 M1
Alice St STHWK SE1 19 J4
Alice Thompson Cl
LEE/GVPK SE12 142 C6
Alice Walker Cl HNHL SE24 139 H1
Alice Wy HSLW TW3 133 H1
Alicia Av KTN/HRWW/W HA3 62 B5
Alicia Cl KTN/HRWW/W HA3 62 C5
Alicia Gdns KTN/HRWW/W HA3 62 B5
Alie St WCHPL E1 13 M5
WCHPL E1 104 A5
Alington Crs CDALE/KGS NW9 81 J1
Alington Gv WLGTN SM6 183 K2
Alison Cl CROY/NA CR0 173 K3
EHAM E6 107 G5
Aliwal Rd BTSEA SW11 137 L1
Alkerden Rd CHSWK W4 117 L3
Alkham Rd STNW/STAM N16 85 M2
Allan Barclay Cl
STNW/STAM N16 67 M7
Allan Cl NWMAL KT3 153 K8
Allandale Av FNCH N3 64 E4
Allandale Crs POTB/CUF EN6 22 E5
Allandale Pl ORP BR6 177 K5
Allandale Rd EMPK RM11 73 M8
PEND EN3 37 K1
Allan Wy ACT W3 99 J4
Allard Cl STMC/STPC BR5 177 J2
Allard Crs BUSH WD23 43 J4
Allardyce St CLAP SW4 138 F1
Allbrook Cl TEDD TW11 151 L1
Allcot Cl EBED/NFELT TW14 131 M5
Allcroft Rd KTTN NW5 84 A6
Allenby Av SAND/SEL CR2 184 C2
Allenby Cl GFD/PVL UB6 97 G2
Allenby Dr EMPK RM11 92 E1
Allenby Rd FSTH SE23 140 E7
GFD/PVL UB6 97 G5
Allen Cl MTCM CR4 156 B4
SUN TW16 150 B4
Allendale Av STHL UB1 97 G5
Allendale Cl CMBW SE5 121 K7
RDART DA2 147 K5
SYD SE26 158 D1
Allendale Rd GFD/PVL UB6 80 B6
Allen Edwards Dr VX/NE SW8 120 E6
Allen Rd BECK BR3 158 D5
BOW E3 104 F1
CROY/NA CR0 171 M2
RAIN RM13 110 C2
STNW/STAM N16 85 L4
SUN TW16 150 B4
Allens Rd PEND EN3 37 J8
Allenswood Rd ELTH/MOT SE9 124 E8
Allerford Rd CAT SE6 141 H8
Allerton Cl BORE WD6 31 M3
Allerton Rd BORE WD6 31 L3
STNW/STAM N16 85 J2
Allestree Rd FUL/PGN SW6 118 E5
Alleyn Crs DUL SE21 139 K6
Alleyndale Rd BCTR RM8 90 C2
Alleyn Pk DUL SE21 139 K6
NWDGN UB2 114 F3
Alleyn Rd DUL SE21 139 K7
Allfarthing La
WAND/EARL SW18 137 J3
Allgood Cl MRDN SM4 169 K1
Allgood St BETH E2 7 M6
Allhallows La CANST EC4R 13 G6
Allhallows Rd EHAM E6 106 E5
All Hallows Rd TOTM N17 67 L2
Alliance Cl ALP/SUD HA0 80 D4
Alliance Rd ACT W3 99 H3
PLSTW E13 106 C3
WOOL/PLUM SE18 126 A4
Allingham Cl HNWL W7 97 M6
Allingham St IS N1 6 E5
Allington Av SHPTN TW17 149 L6
TOTM N17 49 L8
Allington Cl GFD/PVL UB6 79 J7
WIM/MER SW19 154 D1
Allington Rd HDN NW4 64 B6
NKENS W10 100 E2
ORP BR6 176 E3
RYLN/HDSTN HA2 61 J6
Allington St WESTW SW1E 16 D4
Allison Cl GNWCH SE10 123 J6
Allison Gv DUL SE21 139 L5
Allison Rd ACT W3 99 J5
CEND/HSY/T N8 67 G6
Allitsen Rd STJWD NW8 3 J6
Allnutt Wy CLAP SW4 138 D2
Alloa Rd DEPT SE8 122 D3
GDMY/SEVK IG3 90 B2
Allonby Dr RSLP HA4 59 H8
Allonby Gdns WBLY HA9 80 C1
Alloway Rd BOW E3 104 E2
All Saints Cl CHIG IG7 54 B5
ED N9 49 M4
Allsaints Crs GSTN WD25 21 K6
All Saints Dr BKHTH/KID SE3 123 M7
SAND/SEL CR2 184 F5
All Saints La RKW/CH/CXG WD3 41 G1
All Saints Ms KTN/HRWW/W HA3 43 L8
All Saints Pas
WAND/EARL SW18 137 G2
All Saints' Rd ACT W3 99 J8
NTGHL W11 100 F4
SUT SM1 170 B5
WIM/MER SW19 155 J3
All Saints St IS N1 5 L5
Allsop Pl CAMTN NW1 9 M1
All Souls' Av WLSDN NW10 100 B1
All Souls' Pl REGST W1B 10 D3
Allum La BORE WD6 31 L8
Allum Wy TRDG/WHET N20 47 J3
Allwood Cl SYD SE26 140 D8
Alma Av CHING E4 69 J1
HCH RM12 92 E3
Almack Rd CLPT E5 86 C4
Alma Crs SUT SM1 169 L7
Alma Gv STHWK SE1 19 M6
Alma Pl NRWD SE19 157 M3
THHTH CR7 157 G8
WLSDN NW10 100 B2
Alma Rd CAR SM5 170 E7
ESH/CLAY KT10 166 E3
MUSWH N10 66 A1
PEND EN3 37 L8
SCUP DA14 144 A7
STHL UB1 96 E6
STMC/STPC BR5 177 K4
WAND/EARL SW18 137 J2
Alma Rw KTN/HRWW/W HA3 61 K2
Alma Sq STJWD NW8 2 F7
Alma St KTTN NW5 84 B6
SRTFD E15 87 K6
Alma Ter BOW E3 86 F8
WAND/EARL SW18 137 K4
Almeida St IS N1 6 C3
Almeric Rd BTSEA SW11 137 M1
Almer Rd RYNPK SW20 154 A3
Almington St FSBYPK N4 84 F1
Almond Av CAR SM5 170 F4
EA W5 116 E1
HGDN/ICK UB10 77 H3
WDR/YW UB7 113 G1
Almond Cl HAYES BR2 176 A2
HYS/HAR UB3 95 L6
RSLP HA4 77 M3
SHPTN TW17 149 J5
Almond Dr SWLY BR8 163 K6
Almond Gv BTFD TW8 116 B5
Almond Rd BERM/RHTH SE16 122 B2
HOR/WEW KT19 180 D4
RDART DA2 147 J4
TOTM N17 68 A1
Almonds Av BKHH IG9 52 A4
Almond Wy BORE WD6 32 B7
HAYES BR2 176 A2
MTCM CR4 156 D8
RYLN/HDSTN HA2 61 J3
Almorah Rd HEST TW5 114 D6
IS N1 7 G2
Almshouse La CHSGTN KT9 179 J2
EN EN1 37 H2
Alnwick Gv MRDN SM4 155 H7
Alnwick Rd CAN/RD E16 106 C5
LEE/GVPK SE12 142 B4
Alperton La ALP/SUD HA0 98 D2
Alperton St NKENS W10 100 E3
Alphabet Gdns CAR SM5 170 D1
Alpha Cl CAMTN NW1 3 K9
Alpha Gv POP/IOD E14 105 G8
Alpha Pl CHEL SW3 15 K9
KIL/WHAMP NW6 2 B5
Alpha Rd BRYLDS KT5 167 M1
CHING E4 51 G5
CROY/NA CR0 172 E3
HGDN/ICK UB10 95 H3
HPTN TW12 151 K1
NWCR SE14 122 F6
UED N18 50 A8
Alpha St PECK SE15 122 A7
Alphea Cl WIM/MER SW19 155 L3
Alpine Av BRYLDS KT5 168 C4

Alpine Cl CROY/NA CR0 ...... 172 E5
Alpine Copse BMLY BR1 ...... 161 C5 ⓘ
Alpine Rd BERM/RTH SE16 .. 122 C2 ⓘ
  WOT/HER KT12 ...... 165 C2
Alpine Vw SUT TW1 ...... 170 E7
Alpine Wy EHAM E6 ...... 107 C4
Alric Av NWMAL KT3 ...... 153 L6
  WLSDN NW10 ...... 81 K7
Alroy Rd FSBYPK N4 ...... 67 C8
Alsace Rd WALW SE17 ...... 19 J7
Alscot Rd BERM/RTH SE16 .. 19 M4
Alscot Wy STHWK SE1 ...... 19 L5
Alsike Rd BELV DA17 ...... 126 D1
Alsom Av HOR/WEW KT19 .. 168 F6
Alston Cl THDIT KT7 ...... 167 H2
Alston Rd BAR EN5 ...... 33 L6
  TOOT SW17 ...... 137 K8
  UED N18 ...... 50 B7
Altair Cl UED N18 ...... 49 M8
Altair Wy NTHWD HA6 ...... 41 M7
Altash Wy ELTH/MOT SE9 .. 142 F6
Altenburg Av WEA W13 ...... 116 B1
Altenburg Gdns BTSEA SW11 137 M1
Alt Gv WIM/MER SW19 ...... 154 F3
Altham Rd PIN HA5 ...... 60 L1
Althea St FUL/PGN SW6 .. 119 H7
Althorne Gdns SWFD E18 .. 69 M5 ⓘ
Althorne Wy DAGE RM10 .. 91 C2
Althorp Cl TRDG/WHET N20 46 A2
Althorpe Rd HRW HA1 ...... 61 K6 ⓘ
Althorp Rd TOOT SW17 ...... 137 M5
Altmore Av EHAM E6 ...... 88 F7
Alton Av STAN HA7 ...... 61 M1
Alton Cl BXLY DA5 ...... 144 E5
  ISLW TW7 ...... 115 M7
Alton Gdns BECK BR3 ...... 159 C3
  WHTN TW2 ...... 133 K4
Alton Rd CROY/NA CR0 ...... 172 A5
  PUT/ROE SW15 ...... 136 A5
  RCH/KEW TW9 ...... 134 E1
  TOTM N17 ...... 67 H4
Alton St POP/IOD E14 ...... 105 H4
Altyre Cl BECK BR3 ...... 158 F8
Altyre Rd CROY/NA CR0 ...... 172 D4
Altyre Wy BECK BR3 ...... 158 F8
Alvanley Gdns KIL/WHAMP NW6 .. 83 H5
Alva Wy OXHEY WD19 ...... 42 D4
Alverstone Av EBAR EN4 ...... 47 K2
  WAND/EARL SW18 ...... 137 C6
Alverstone Gdns
  ELTH/MOT SE9 ...... 143 H5
Alverstone Rd CRICK NW2 .. 82 C7
  MNPK E12 ...... 89 C4
  NWMAL KT3 ...... 153 M7 ⓘ
  WBLY HA9 ...... 80 F1
Alverston Gdns SNWD SE25 157 L8
Alverton St DEPT SE8 ...... 122 F3
Alveston Av KTN/HRWW/W HA3 .. 62 B4
Alvey St WALW SE17 ...... 19 J7
Alvia Gdns SUT SM1 ...... 170 G6
Alvington Crs HACK E8 ...... 85 M5
Alwin Pl WATW WD18 ...... 28 E7
Alwold Crs LEE/GVPK SE12 142 C3
Alwyn Av CHSWK W4 ...... 117 K3
Alwyn Cl BORE WD6 ...... 44 F1
  CROY/NA CR0 ...... 186 B1
Alwyne La IS N1 ...... 6 D1
Alwyne Pl IS N1 ...... 6 E1
Alwyne Rd HNWL W7 ...... 97 L6
  IS N1 ...... 6 E1
  WIM/MER SW19 ...... 154 F2
Alwyne Sq IS N1 ...... 85 J6 ⓘ
Alwyne Vls IS N1 ...... 6 D1
Alwyn Gdns ACT W3 ...... 99 H5
Alyth Gdns GLDGN NW11 .. 64 F7
Amalgamated Dr BTFD TW8.. 116 A4
Amanda Cl CHIG IG7 ...... 53 K8
Amar Ct WOOL/PLUM SE18.. 125 M2
Amardeep Ct
  WOOL/PLUM SE18 ...... 125 M3 ⓘ
Amazon St WCHPL E1 ...... 104 A5 ⓘ
Ambassador Cl HSLW TW3 .. 114 E7
Ambassador Gdns EHAM E6 .. 106 F4 ⓘ
Ambassador Sq
  POP/IOD E14 ...... 123 H2 ⓘ
Amber Av WALTH E17 ...... 68 E2
Amberden Av FNCH N3 ...... 65 C4
Ambergate St WALW SE17 .. 18 C7
Amber Gv CRICK NW2 ...... 82 D1
Amberley Cl ORP BR6 ...... 176 F7
  PIN HA5 ...... 60 F4
Amberley Ct SCUP DA14 .. 162 C1
Amberley Gdns
  HOR/WEW KT19 ...... 168 F6
Amberley Gv CROY/NA CR0 172 F2 ⓘ
  SYD SE26 ...... 140 B8
Amberley Rd ABYW SE2 .. 126 D4
  BKHH IG9 ...... 52 C3
  EN EN1 ...... 49 M2
  LEY E10 ...... 69 C8
  MV/WKIL W9 ...... 8 B2
  PLMGR N13 ...... 48 F4
Amberley Wy HGDN/ICK UB10 .. 94 E1
  HSLWW TW4 ...... 132 C2
  MRDN SM4 ...... 169 M2
  ROMW/RG RM7 ...... 73 H5
  UX/CGN UB8 ...... 94 E2 ⓘ
Amberside Cl ISLW TW7 .. 133 K3
Amber St SRTFD E15 ...... 87 K6 ⓘ
Amberwood Ri NWMAL KT3 .. 168 L1
Amblecote Cl
  LEE/GVPK SE12 ...... 142 B7 ⓘ
Amblecote Meadow
  LEE/GVPK SE12 ...... 142 B7
Amblecote Rd LEE/GVPK SE12 .. 142 B7
Ambleside BMLY BR1 ...... 159 K2
Ambleside Av BECK BR3 .. 158 E8
  HCH RM12 ...... 92 B5
  STRHM/NOR SW16 ...... 138 D5
  WOT/HER KT12 ...... 165 J3
Ambleside Cl LEY E10 ...... 69 L8 ⓘ
Ambleside Crs PEND EN3 ...... 37 K6
Ambleside Dr
  EBED/NFELT TW14 ...... 131 M5 ⓘ

Ambleside Gdns BELMT SM2 .. 170 C8 ⓘ
  REDBR IG4 ...... 70 E5
  SAND/SEL CR2 ...... 185 K3
  WBLY HA9 ...... 80 D1
Ambleside Rd BXLYHN DA7.. 127 C7
  WLSDN NW10 ...... 81 M7
Ambrey Wy WLGTN SM6 .. 183 K2
Ambrook Rd BELV DA17 .. 127 C1
Ambrosden Av WEST SW1P .. 16 F4
Ambrose Av GLDGN NW11 .. 64 F7
Ambrose Cl DART DA1 ...... 145 M1
  ORP BR6 ...... 176 F5 ⓘ
Ambrose St
  BERM/RTH SE16 ...... 122 B2 ⓘ
Amelia St WALW SE17 ...... 18 D7
Amen Cnr STP EC4M ...... 12 D5 ⓘ
Amen Cr STP EC4M ...... 12 D5 ⓘ
America Sq TWRH EC3N .. 13 L6 ⓘ
America St STHWK SE1 .. 12 E9 ⓘ
Amerland Rd
  WAND/EARL SW18 ...... 136 F3
Amersham Av UED N18 .. 49 K8
Amersham Gv NWCR SE14 122 B8
Amersham Rd CROY/NA CR0 .. 172 D1 ⓘ
  HARH RM3 ...... 56 E8
  NWCR SE14 ...... 122 B8
Amersham V NWCR SE14 .. 122 F5 ⓘ
Amersham Wk HARH RM3 .. 56 F8 ⓘ
Amery Gdns GPK RM2 ...... 74 D4
  WLSDN NW10 ...... 82 B8
Amery Rd HRW HA1 ...... 80 A2
Amesbury Av
  BRXS/STRHM SW2 ...... 138 E6
Amesbury Cl WPK KT4 .. 153 M8
Amesbury Dr CHING E4 .. 51 H1 ⓘ
Amesbury Rd BMLY BR1 .. 160 D6
  DAGW RM9 ...... 90 D7
  FELT TW13 ...... 132 D6
Amethyst Rd WAN E11 ...... 87 K4
Amherst Av WEA W13 .. 98 C5
Amherst Cl STMC/STPC BR5 .. 162 A7
Amherst Dr STMC/STPC BR5.. 161 M7
Amherst Rd WEA W13 .. 98 C5
Amhurst Gdns ISLW TW7 .. 115 M6
Amhurst Pk STNW/STAM N16.. 67 L8
Amhurst Rd HACK E8 .. 86 A5
  STNW/STAM N16 ...... 85 M4
Amhurst Ter HACK E8 ...... 86 A4
Amidas Gdns BCTR RM8 .. 90 B4
Amiel St WCHPL E1 ...... 104 C3 ⓘ
Amies St BTSEA SW11 .. 119 M8
Amis Av HOR/WEW KT19 .. 168 A8
Amity Gv RYNPK SW20 .. 154 C4
Amity Rd SRTFD E15 .. 87 M7
Amner Rd BTSEA SW11 .. 138 A3
Amor Rd HMSMTH W6 .. 118 C1
Amott Rd PECK SE15 .. 122 A8
Ampere Wy CROY/NA CR0 171 L2
Amyand Cottages
  TWK TW1 ...... 134 B3 ⓘ
Amyand Park Gdns
  TWK TW1 ...... 134 B4 ⓘ
Amyand Park Rd TWK TW1.. 134 A4
Amy Cl WLGTN SM6 ...... 183 L1 ⓘ
Amyruth Rd BROCKY SE4 .. 141 C2
Amy Warne Cl EHAM E6 .. 106 A4
Ancaster Crs NWMAL KT3 .. 169 G1
Ancaster Rd BECK BR3 .. 158 D6
Ancaster St WOOL/PLUM SE18.. 125 L5
Anchorage Cl
  WIM/MER SW19 ...... 155 G1 ⓘ
Anchor And Hope La
  CHARL SE7 ...... 124 B1
Anchor Bvd GRH DA9 .. 147 J4
Anchor Cl CHES/WCR EN8.. 26 D1
Anchor Dr RAIN RM13 .. 110 B2
Anchor St BERM/RTH SE16 .. 122 B2
Anchor Yd FSBYE EC1V .. 6 F9 ⓘ
Ancill Cl HMSMTH W6 .. 118 D4
Ancona Rd WLSDN NW10 .. 100 A1
  WOOL/PLUM SE18 ...... 125 K3
Andalus Rd BRXN/ST SW9 120 E8
Ander Cl ALP/SUD HA0 .. 80 D1
Anderson Cl ACT W3 .. 99 K5 ⓘ
  DEN/HRF UB9 ...... 58 A2
  HOR/WEW KT19 ...... 180 B5
  WCHMH N21 ...... 35 M8 ⓘ
Anderson Dr ASHF TW15 .. 133 L4
Anderson Pl HSLW TW3 .. 133 H1 ⓘ
Anderson Rd CHEL SW3 .. 15 L7
Anderson Wy BELV DA17 .. 109 H8
Andover Av CAN/RD E16 .. 106 D5 ⓘ
Andover Cl
  EBED/NFELT TW14 ...... 131 M5 ⓘ
  GFD/PVL UB6 ...... 97 H3 ⓘ
  HOR/WEW KT19 ...... 180 D4
  UX/CGN UB8 ...... 94 B1
Andover Pl KIL/WHAMP NW6 .. 2 C6 ⓘ
  ORP BR6 ...... 176 E3 ⓘ
  WHTN TW2 ...... 133 K5
Andre St HACK E8 ...... 86 A5
Andrew Borde St
  LSQ/SEVD WC2H ...... 11 H4 ⓘ
Andrew Cl BARK/HLT IG6 .. 53 K8 ⓘ
  DART DA1 ...... 145 K2
Andrewes Gdns EHAM E6 .. 106 E5
Andrew Pl VX/NE SW8 .. 120 D6 ⓘ
Andrews Cl BKHH IG9 .. 109 F7
  EW KT17 ...... 180 F7
  HRW HA1 ...... 61 K8 ⓘ
  STMC/STPC BR5 ...... 162 D6 ⓘ
  WPK KT4 ...... 169 K4 ⓘ
Andrew's La CHESW EN7 .. 25 L1
Andrews Rd HACK E8 ...... 86 B8
Andrew St POP/IOD E14 .. 105 J5

Andwell Cl ABYW SE2 .. 108 B8
Anerley Gv NRWD SE19 .. 157 M3
Anerley Hl NRWD SE19 .. 157 M2
Anerley Pk PGE/AN SE20 .. 158 B2
Anerley Park Rd PGE/AN SE20.. 158 B3
Anerley Rd NRWD SE19 .. 158 A1
  PGE/AN SE20 ...... 158 B4
Anerley Station Rd
  PGE/AN SE20 ...... 158 B4
Anerley St BTSEA SW11 .. 119 M1
Anerley V NRWD SE19 .. 157 M3
Anfield Cl BAL SW12 .. 138 C4 ⓘ
Angel Cl UED N18 ...... 50 A7 ⓘ
Angelfield HSLW TW3 .. 133 H2 ⓘ
Angel Hl SUT SM1 ...... 170 B5
Angel Hill Dr SUT SM1 .. 170 B5
Angelica Cl WDR/YW UB7 .. 94 F5 ⓘ
Angelica Dr EHAM E6 ...... 107 C4
Angelica Gdns CROY/NA CR0.. 173 K3 ⓘ
Angel La HYS/HAR UB3 .. 95 K4
  SRTFD E15 ...... 87 K6 ⓘ
Angell Park Gdns
  BRXN/ST SW9 ...... 121 C8
Angell Rd BRXN/ST SW9 .. 121 H8
Angel Pas CANST EC4R .. 13 C7 ⓘ
Angel Rd HRW HA1 ...... 61 L7
  THDIT KT7 ...... 167 C3
Angel Rd (North Circular Road)
  UED N18 ...... 50 A7
Angel Wk HMSMTH W6 .. 118 C2 ⓘ
Angel Wy ROM RM1 ...... 73 L6 ⓘ
Angerstein La BKHTH/KID SE3.. 123 M5
Angle Cl HGDN/ICK UB10 .. 77 C8
Anglers La KTTN NW5 .. 84 B6
Anglesea Av
  WOOL/PLUM SE18 ...... 125 H2 ⓘ
Anglesea Rd KUT KT1 .. 152 D7
  STMC/STPC BR5 ...... 177 J1
  WOOL/PLUM SE18 ...... 125 H2 ⓘ
Anglesey Cl ASHF TW15 .. 131 C8
Anglesey Court Rd CAR SM5.. 171 C8
Anglesey Dr RAIN RM13 .. 110 A3 ⓘ
Anglesey Gdns CAR SM5 .. 171 C8
  PEND EN3 ...... 37 H7
Anglesmede Crs PIN HA5 .. 61 C4
Anglesmede Wy PIN HA5 .. 60 F4
Angles Rd STRHM/NOR SW16.. 138 E8
Anglia Cl TOTM N17 ...... 68 B1
Anglian Cl WATN WD24 .. 29 J5
Anglian Rd WAN E11 ...... 87 K3 ⓘ
Anglo Rd BOW E3 ...... 104 F1 ⓘ
Angus Cl CHSGTN KT9 .. 168 A7
Angus Dr RSLP HA4 ...... 78 C4
Angus Gdns CDALE/KGS NW9.. 63 K2
Angus Rd PLSTW E13 .. 106 C2 ⓘ
Angus St NWCR SE14 .. 122 E5
Anhalt Rd BTSEA SW11 .. 119 L5
Ankerdine Crs
  WOOL/PLUM SE18 ...... 125 H6
Anlaby Rd TEDD TW11 .. 151 L1
Anley Rd HMSMTH W6 .. 100 C8
Annabel Cl POP/IOD E14 .. 105 H5
Anna Cl HACK E8 ...... 7 M3
Annandale Gv HGDN/ICK UB10.. 77 J3 ⓘ
Annandale Rd BFN/LL DA15.. 143 L4
  CHSWK W4 ...... 117 J2
  CROY/NA CR0 ...... 173 G4
  GNWCH SE10 ...... 123 M3
Anna Neagle Cl FSTGT E7.. 88 A4 ⓘ
Annan Wy ROM RM1 .. 73 K2
Anne Boleyn's Wk BELMT SM2.. 181 K1
  KUTN/CMB KT2 ...... 152 E1
Anne of Cleves Rd DART DA1.. 146 D2
Annesley Av CDALE/KGS NW9.. 63 K4
Annesley Cl WLSDN NW10 .. 81 L3
Annesley Dr CROY/NA CR0.. 173 M5
Annesley Rd BKHTH/KID SE3.. 124 B6
Anne St PLSTW E13 ...... 106 A3
Annett Cl SHPTN TW17 .. 149 L2 ⓘ
Annett Cl KTN/HRWW/W HA3.. 61 L3 ⓘ
Annette Rd HOLWY N7 .. 84 F3 ⓘ
Annett Rd WOT/HER KT12.. 165 C2
Anne Wy BARK/HLT IG6 .. 53 J8
  THDIT KT7 ...... 151 M8
Annie Besant Cl BOW E3 .. 86 F8 ⓘ
Annington Rd EFNCH N2 .. 65 M4 ⓘ
Annis Rd HOM E9 ...... 86 E6 ⓘ
Ann La WBPTN SW10 .. 119 K5
Ann Moss Wy
  BERM/RTH SE16 ...... 122 F1
Ann St WOOL/PLUM SE18 .. 125 K2
Annsworthy Av THHTH CR7.. 157 K6 ⓘ
Ansar Gdns WALTH E17 .. 68 F6 ⓘ
Ansdell Rd PECK SE15 .. 122 C7
Ansdell St KENS W8 ...... 14 D3
Ansdell Ter KENS W8 .. 14 D3 ⓘ
Ansell Gv CAR SM5 ...... 170 F3
Ansell Rd TOOT SW17 .. 137 C4
Anselm Cl CROY/NA CR0.. 172 F5 ⓘ
Anselm Rd FUL/PGN SW6.. 119 C4
  PIN HA5 ...... 60 L1
Ansford Rd BMLY BR1 .. 159 J1
Ansleigh Pl NTGHL W11 .. 100 D6
Ansley Cl SAND/SEL CR2 .. 185 H7
Anson Cl ROMW/RG RM7 .. 73 H3
Anson Rd CRICK NW2 .. 82 B5
  HOLWY N7 ...... 84 C4
Anson Wk NTHWD HA6 .. 41 J6
Anstead Dr RAIN RM13 .. 110 A1
Anstey Rd PECK SE15 .. 142 A2
Anstice Cl CHSWK W4 .. 117 L5 ⓘ
Anstridge Rd ELTH/MOT SE9.. 143 K3
Antelope Rd WOOL/PLUM SE18.. 124 F1
Anthony Cl OXHEY WD19.. 42 D3
Anthony Rd BORE WD6 .. 31 L5
  GFD/PVL UB6 ...... 97 L1
  SNWD SE25 ...... 173 C1
  WELL DA16 ...... 126 A3
Anthony's Cl WAP E1W .. 104 A7 ⓘ
Anthus Ms NTHWD HA6 .. 59 K1
Antill Rd BOW E3 ...... 104 E2
  SEVS/STOTM N15 ...... 68 A5

Antill Ter WCHPL E1 ...... 104 D5
Antlers Hl CHING E4 ...... 38 C8
Anton Crs SUT SM1 ...... 170 A5
Antoneys Cl PIN HA5 ...... 60 D3
Anton St HACK E8 ...... 86 A5
Antrim Rd HAMP NW3 ...... 83 M6
Antrobus Cl SUT SM1 ...... 170 A5
Antrobus Rd CHSWK W4 .. 117 J2
Anvil Cl STRHM/NOR SW16.. 156 C3
Anvil Rd SUN TW16 ...... 150 A6
Apeldoorn Dr WLGTN SM6.. 183 L2
Aperfield Rd ERITH DA8 .. 127 M4
Apex Cl BECK BR3 ...... 159 H4
  WEY KT13 ...... 164 D5
Aplin Wy ISLW TW7 ...... 115 L6
Apollo Av BMLY BR1 ...... 160 B4
  NTHWD HA6 ...... 42 A7
Apollo Cl HCH RM12 ...... 92 B2
Apollo Pl WAN E11 ...... 87 L3 ⓘ
  WBPTN SW10 ...... 119 M6
Apollo Wy WOOL/PLUM SE18.. 125 K1 ⓘ
Apothecary St BLKFR EC4V.. 12 C5 ⓘ
Appach Rd BRXS/STRHM SW2.. 139 C2
Appleby Cl CHING E4 ...... 51 J8 ⓘ
  SEVS/STOTM N15 ...... 67 K6 ⓘ
  WHTN TW2 ...... 133 K6
Appleby Dr HARH RM3 .. 56 C7
Appleby Gdns
  EBED/NFELT TW14 ...... 131 M5 ⓘ
  HACK E8 ...... 86 A7
Appleby St BETH E2 ...... 7 L5
Appleby Rd CAN/RD E16 .. 106 A5
  HACK E8 ...... 86 A7
Appledore Av BXLYHN DA7.. 127 J6
  RSLP HA4 ...... 78 B3
Appledore Cl EDGW HA8 .. 63 G2
  HARH RM3 ...... 74 C2
  HAYES BR2 ...... 159 M8 ⓘ
  TOOT SW17 ...... 137 M6 ⓘ
Appledore Crs BFN/LL DA15.. 143 L7
Appleford Rd NKENS W10.. 100 D4
Apple Garth BTFD TW8 .. 116 D2
Applegarth CROY/NA CR0.. 180 A6
  ESH/CLAY KT10 ...... 166 F7
Applegarth Dr DART DA1.. 146 E6
  GNTH/NBYPK IG2 ...... 71 M5
Applegarth Rd THMD SE28.. 108 B7
  WKENS W14 ...... 118 D1 ⓘ
Apple Gv CHSGTN KT9 .. 167 L6
  EN EN1 ...... 36 E6
Apple Orch SWLY BR8 .. 163 K7 ⓘ
Apple Rd WAN E11 ...... 87 L3
Appleton Dr RDART DA2 .. 146 F5
Appleton Gdns NWMAL KT3.. 169 L1
Appleton Rd ELTH/MOT SE9.. 124 E8
  WFD IG8 ...... 92 D1
Apple Tree Av WDR/YW UB7.. 94 F5
Appletree Cl PGE/AN SE20.. 158 B4 ⓘ
Appletree Gdns EBAR EN4.. 34 E7
Appletree Wk GSTN WD25.. 21 H8
Applewood Cl CRICK NW2.. 82 B3
  TRDG/WHET N20 ...... 47 L3
Appold St BFN/LL DA15 .. 127 M4
  ERITH DA8 ...... 127 M4
  LVPST EC2M ...... 13 J2 ⓘ
  SDTCH EC2A 13 J2
Apprentice Wy CLPT E5 .. 86 B4 ⓘ
Approach La MLHL NW7 .. 46 E7 ⓘ
  NFNCH/WDSP N12 ...... 46 E7
Approach Rd ASHF TW15 .. 149 J2
  BAR EN5 ...... 34 D7 ⓘ
  BETH E2 ...... 104 C1
  E/WMO/HCT KT8 ...... 151 L8
  PUR/KEN CR8 ...... 184 B5
  RYNPK SW20 ...... 154 C6
The Approach ACT W3 .. 99 K5
  EN EN1 ...... 37 H5 ⓘ
  HDN NW4 ...... 64 D6 ⓘ
  ORP BR6 ...... 176 F4
  POTB/CUF EN6 ...... 22 F5 ⓘ
  UPMR RM14 ...... 93 H3
Aprey Gdns HDN NW4 .. 64 C5
April Cl FELT TW13 ...... 132 A7
  HNWL W7 ...... 97 J8
  ORP BR6 ...... 176 F7
April Gln FSTH SE23 .. 140 D7
April St STNW/STAM N16.. 85 M4
Apsley Cl HRW HA1 ...... 61 J6
Apsley Rd NWMAL KT3 .. 153 J6
  SNWD SE25 ...... 158 B7
Apsley Wy CRICK NW2 .. 82 A2
Aquarius Wy NTHWD HA6.. 42 A7
Aquila St STJWD NW8 .. 3 H5 ⓘ
Aquinas St STHWK SE1 .. 12 B9
Arabella Dr PUT/ROE SW15.. 135 L1
Arabia Cl CHING E4 ...... 51 J2
Arabin Rd BROCKY SE4 .. 140 E1
Aragon Av EW KT17 ...... 181 H2
  THDIT KT7 ...... 151 M8
Aragon Cl CROY/NA CR0.. 186 E3
  ENC/FH EN2 ...... 35 M3 ⓘ
  HAYES BR2 ...... 175 M3
  SUN TW16 ...... 149 M3
Aragon Dr BARK/HLT IG6 .. 71 J1
  RSLP HA4 ...... 78 D1 ⓘ
Aragon Rd KUTN/CMB KT2.. 152 E1
  MRDN SM4 ...... 169 K2

Archangel St BERM/RTH SE16.. 104 D8
Archbishop's Pl
  BRXS/STRHM SW2 ...... 138 F3
Archdale Ct SHB W12 .. 100 B7 ⓘ
Archdale Pl NWMAL KT3 .. 153 H6
Archdale Rd EDUL SE22 .. 139 M2
Archel Rd WKENS W14 .. 118 F4
Archer Cl KUTN/CMB KT2 .. 152 E3
Archer Rd SNWD SE25 .. 158 B7
  STMC/STPC BR5 ...... 177 G1
Archers Dr PEND EN3 .. 37 J5 ⓘ
Archer Sq DEPT SE8 ...... 122 E4 ⓘ
Archer St SOHO/SHAV W1D.. 11 G6 ⓘ
Archer Wy SWLY BR8 .. 163 M6
Archery Cl KTN/HRWW/W HA3.. 61 M4
Archery Rd ELTH/MOT SE9.. 142 F2
The Arches RYLN/HDSTN HA2.. 79 H2
Archibald Ms MYFR/PICC W1J.. 10 B7
Archibald Rd HARH RM3 .. 75 C3
  HOLWY N7 ...... 84 D4
Arch Rd WOT/HER KT12.. 165 K5
Arch St STHWK SE1 ...... 18 E4
Archway HARH RM3 ...... 56 B8
Archway Cl NKENS W10 .. 100 D4 ⓘ
  WIM/MER SW19 ...... 137 H8 ⓘ
  WLGTN SM6 ...... 171 L5 ⓘ
Archway Rd ARCH N19 .. 84 C1
  HGT N6 ...... 65 M6
Archway St BARN SW13 .. 117 L8
Arcola St HACK E8 ...... 85 M5
Arctic St KTTN NW5 ...... 84 B5 ⓘ
Arcus Rd BMLY BR1 ...... 159 L2 ⓘ
Ardbeg Rd HNHL SE24 .. 139 K3
Arden Cl BUSH WD23 ...... 43 M2
  HRW HA1 ...... 79 K3
Arden Court Gdns EFNCH N2.. 65 K3
Arden Crs DAGW RM9 .. 90 D7
  POP/IOD E14 ...... 123 G2
Arden Gv ORP BR6 ...... 176 B6
Arden Mhor PIN HA5 ...... 60 B5
Arden Rd FNCH N3 ...... 64 F4
  WEA W13 ...... 98 C6
Ardent Cl SNWD SE25 .. 157 L6
Ardesley Wd WEY KT13 .. 164 E6 ⓘ
Ardfern Av STRHM/NOR SW16.. 157 G6
Ardfillan Rd CAT SE6 .. 141 K5
Ardgowan Rd CAT SE6 .. 141 K5
Ardilaun Rd HBRY N5 .. 85 J4 ⓘ
Ardingly Cl CROY/NA CR0.. 173 K5
Ardleigh Cl EMPK RM11.. 74 D4
Ardleigh Gdns CHEAM SM3.. 170 A3
Ardleigh Green Rd EMPK RM11.. 74 D6
Ardleigh Rd IS N1 ...... 85 L3
  WALTH E17 ...... 68 F2 ⓘ
Ardleigh Ter WALTH E17 .. 68 F2 ⓘ
Ardley Cl FSTH SE23 .. 140 E7
  WLSDN NW10 ...... 81 L3
Ardlui Rd WNWD SE27 .. 139 J6
Ardmay Gdns SURB KT6.. 152 E7 ⓘ
  SURB KT6 ...... 152 E8 ⓘ
Ardmere Rd LEW SE13 .. 141 K3
Ardmore La BKHH IG9 .. 52 B3
Ardoch Rd CAT SE6 ...... 141 K6
Ardra Rd ED N9 ...... 50 D5
Ardrossan Gdns WPK KT4.. 169 G5
Ardross Av NTHWD HA6 .. 41 J7
Ardshiel Cl PUT/ROE SW15.. 118 D8 ⓘ
Ardwell Av BARK/HLT IG6 .. 71 J6
Ardwell Rd BRXS/STRHM SW2.. 138 E6
Ardwick Rd CRICK NW2 .. 83 G4
Argall Av LEY E10 ...... 68 D8
Argenta Wy WLSDN NW10.. 81 H7 ⓘ
Argon Ms FUL/PGN SW6.. 119 G5 ⓘ
Argon Rd UED N18 ...... 50 D7
Argosy La STWL/WRAY TW19.. 130 D4
Argus Cl ROMW/RG RM7 .. 73 H2
Argus Wy NTHLT UB5 .. 96 C2 ⓘ
Argyle Av HSLW TW3 .. 133 G3
  WHTN TW2 ...... 133 C3
Argyle Cl WEA W13 ...... 98 A3
Argyle Gdns UPMR RM14.. 93 K3
Argyle Pl HMSMTH W6 .. 118 B2 ⓘ
Argyle Rd BAR EN5 ...... 33 J4
  CAN/RD E16 ...... 106 B5
  GFD/PVL UB6 ...... 97 M2
  HSLW TW3 ...... 133 H2
  IL IG1 ...... 89 G2
  NFNCH/WDSP N12 ...... 47 G2
  RYLN/HDSTN HA2 ...... 61 H7
  SRTFD E15 ...... 87 L4
  TOTM N17 ...... 68 A2
  UED N18 ...... 50 A4
  WCHPL E1 ...... 104 D3
  WEA W13 ...... 98 A4
Argyle Sq STPAN WC1H .. 5 K7
Argyle St STPAN WC1H .. 5 K8
Argyle Wy BERM/RTH SE1.. 122 A3
Argyll Av STHL UB1 ...... 97 H7
Argyll Cl BRXN/ST SW9.. 120 F8
Argyll Gdns EDGW HA8 .. 63 H3 ⓘ
Argyll Rd KENS W8 ...... 14 A2
  WOOL/PLUM SE18 ...... 109 H7
Argyll St REGST W1B .. 10 E5
Arica Rd BROCKY SE4 .. 140 E1
Ariel Rd KIL/WHAMP NW6.. 83 G6
Ariel Wy HSLWW TW4 .. 114 B8
  SHB W12 ...... 100 C7
Aristotle Rd CLAP SW4 .. 120 E8
Arkell Gv STRHM/NOR SW16.. 157 H3
Arkindale Rd CAT SE6 .. 141 J7
Arkley Crs WALTH E17 .. 68 F6 ⓘ
Arkley Dr BAR EN5 ...... 33 G3
Arkley La BAR EN5 ...... 33 G6
Arkley Rd WALTH E17 .. 68 F6 ⓘ
Arkley Vw BAR EN5 ...... 33 H7
Arklow Rd NWCR SE14 .. 122 F4
Arkwright Rd HAMP NW3.. 83 J5
  SAND/SEL CR2 ...... 184 F3
Arlesford Rd BRXN/ST SW9.. 120 E8
Arlingford Rd
  BRXS/STRHM SW2 ...... 139 G2 ⓘ
Arlington NFNCH/WDSP N12.. 47 G5
Arlington Av IS N1 ...... 6 F4
Arlington Cl BFN/LL DA15.. 143 L4
  SUT SM1 ...... 170 A4 ⓘ
  TWK TW1 ...... 134 C2 ⓘ
Arlington Ct HYS/HAR UB3.. 113 K3 ⓘ
Arlington Crs CHES/WCR EN8.. 26 E7
Arlington Dr CAR SM5 .. 170 F4

RSLP HA4 59 K7
Arlington Gdns CHSWK W4 117 J3
HARH RM3 74 E2
IL IG1 70 F8
Arlington Ldg WEY KT13 164 B6
Arlington Rd ASHF TW15 148 F1
CAMTN NW1 4 D4
RCHPK/HAM TW10 134 D6
STHGT/OAK N14 48 B4
SURB KT6 167 K1
TEDD TW11 133 M8
TWK TW1 134 C3
WEA W13 98 B5
WFD IG8 70 B1
Arlington Sq IS N1 6 F4
Arlington St MYFR/PICC W1J 10 E8
Arlington Wy CLKNW EC1R 6 B7
Arliss Wy NTHLT UB5 78 C8
Arlow Rd WCHMH N21 49 G3
Armadale CI WALTH E17 68 B5
Armadale Rd
EBED/NFELT TW14 132 A2
FUL/PGN SW6 119 G4
Armada St DEPT SE8 123 C4
Armada Wy EHAM E6 107 J5
Armagh Rd BOW E3 86 F8
Armand CI WAT WD17 28 F3
Armfield CI E/WMO/HCT KT8 150 F8
Armfield Rd ENC/FH EN2 36 D4
Arminger Rd SHB W12 100 B7
Armitage Rd GLDGN NW11 82 C1
GNWCH SE10 123 M2
Armor Rd PUR RM19 129 K2
Armour CI HOLWY N7 84 F6
Armoury Rd DEPT SE8 123 H7
Armoury Wy WAND/EARL SW18 137 G2
Armstead Wy DAGE RM10 91 C7
Armstrong Av WFD IG8 51 L8
Armstrong CI BCTR RM8 72 D8
BMLY BR1 160 E6
EHAM E6 106 F5
RSLP HA4 60 A7
WOT/HER KT12 165 G1
Armstrong Crs EBAR EN4 34 D6
Armstrong Rd ACT W3 99 M7
FELT TW13 150 E1
Armstrong Wy STHL UB1 97 H8
Armytage Rd HEST TW5 114 D5
Arnal Crs WAND/EARL SW18 136 E4
Arne Gv ORP BR6 176 F5
Arne St LSQ/SEVD WC2H 11 K5
Arnett CI RKW/CH/CXG WD3 40 A8
Arnett Sq CHING E4 50 F8
Arnett Wy RKW/CH/CXG WD3 40 A1
Arne Wk BKHTH/KID SE3 141 M1
Arneways Av CHDH RM6 72 D5
Arneway St WEST SW1P 17 H4
Arnewood CI LHD/OX KT22 178 B7
PUT/ROE SW15 136 A5
Arney's La MTCM CR4 171 G1
Arngask Rd CAT SE6 141 K4
Arnheim PI POP/IOD E14 123 G1
Arnhem Av SOCK/AV RM15 111 J7
Arnhem Dr CROY/NA CR0 186 D4
Arnison Rd E/WMO/HCT KT8 151 K7
Arnold Av East PEND EN3 37 M3
Arnold Av West PEND EN3 37 M3
Arnold CI KTN/HRWW/W HA3 62 F8
Arnold Crs ISLW TW7 133 K2
Arnold Dr CHSGTN KT9 171 K8
Arnold Gdns PLMGR N13 49 H7
Arnold Rd BOW E3 105 G2
DAGW RM9 90 F7
NTHLT UB5 78 E6
STA TW18 148 C3
TOOT SW17 155 M3
TOTM N17 67 M4
Arnos Gv STHGT/OAK N14 48 D6
Arnos Rd FBAR/BDGN N11 48 C7
Arnott CI CHSWK W4 117 K2
THMD SE28 108 C7
Arnould Av CMBW SE5 139 K1
Arnsberg Wy BXLYHN DA7 145 G1
BXLYHS DA6 144 F1
Arnside Gdns WBLY HA9 80 D1
Arnside Rd BXLYHN DA7 127 G6
Arnside St WALW SE17 18 F9
Arnulf St CAT SE6 141 H8
Arnull's Rd STRHM/NOR SW16 157 H2
Arodene Rd BRXS/STRHM SW2 138 F3
Arosa Rd TWK TW1 134 D3
Arragon Gdns
STRHM/NOR SW16 156 E3
WWKM BR4 174 B5
Arragon Rd EHAM E6 88 D8
TWK TW1 134 A3
WAND/EARL SW18 137 C5
Arran CI ERITH DA8 127 K4
WLGTN SM6 171 J6
Arran Dr MNPK E12 88 D1
STAN HA7 44 C6
Arran Ms EA W5 98 F7
Arran Rd CAT SE6 141 H6
Arran Wk IS N1 6 E1
Arran Wy ESH/CLAY KT10 166 B4
Arras Av MRDN SM4 155 J8
Arrol Rd BECK BR3 158 C6
Arrow Rd BOW E3 105 H2
Arrowsmith Rd CHIG IG7 53 M7
Arsenal Rd ELTH/MOT SE9 124 F7
Arterberry Rd RYNPK SW20 154 C3
Arterial Rd RAIN RM13 110 C3
Arterial Road Purfleet
PUR RM19 129 J2
Arterial Road West Thurrock
WTHK RM20 129 M1
Artesian CI ROM RM1 73 M8
WLSDN NW10 81 K7
Artesian Gv BAR EN5 34 C7
Artesian Rd NTGHL W11 8 A5
Arthingworth St SRTFD E15 87 L8
Arthurdon Rd LEW SE13 141 H4
Arthur Gv WOOL/PLUM SE18 125 J2
Arthur Rd BH/WHM TN16 187 J8
CHDH RM6 72 C8
ED N9 49 M4
EHAM E6 106 F1
HOLWY N7 84 F4

KUTN/CMB KT2 153 G3
NWMAL KT3 154 B8
WIM/MER SW19 136 F8
Arthur St BUSH WD23 29 K6
CANST EC4R 13 H7
ERITH DA8 127 M5
Artichoke HI WAP E1W 104 B6
Artichoke PI CMBW SE5 121 K6
Artillery CI GNTH/NBYPK IG2 71 K7
Artillery La LVPST EC2M 13 K3
Artington CI ORP BR6 176 C6
Artizan St WCHPL E1 13 K4
Arundel Av EW KT17 181 H3
MRDN SM4 154 F7
SAND/SEL CR2 185 G3
Arundel CI BTSEA SW11 137 L2
BXLY DA5 144 F3
CHES/WCR EN8 26 B1
CROY/NA CR0 172 B5
HPTN TW12 151 H1
SRTFD E15 87 L4
Arundel Dr BORE WD6 32 C7
ORP BR6 177 H7
RYLN/HDSTN HA2 78 F4
WFD IG8 70 A1
Arundel Gdns EDGW HA8 63 K1
GDMY/SEVK IG3 90 A2
NTGHL W11 100 F6
WCHMH N21 49 G3
Arundel Gv STNW/STAM N16 85 L3
Arundell Rd ABLGY WD5 21 G5
Arundel PI IS N1 85 G6
Arundel Rd BELMT SM2 181 M1
CROY/NA CR0 172 D1
DART DA1 146 C1
EBAR EN4 34 E6
HARH RM3 74 F1
HSLWW TW4 114 C8
KUT KT1 153 H5
UX/CGN UB8 94 B1
Arundel Sq HOLWY N7 85 G6
Arundel St TPL/STR WC2R 11 M6
Arundel Ter BARN SW13 118 B4
Arvon Rd HBRY N5 85 G5
Asbaston Ter IL IG1 89 J6
Ascalon St VX/NE SW8 120 C5
Ascension Rd CRW RM5 55 J8
Ascham Dr CHING E4 69 H1
Ascham End WALTH E17 68 E2
Ascham St KTTN NW5 84 C5
Aschurch Rd CROY/NA CR0 172 F2
Ascot CI BARK/HLT IG6 53 L8
BORE WD6 32 A8
NTHLT UB5 79 C5
Ascot Gdns HCH RM12 92 E4
PEND EN3 37 J2
STHL UB1 96 F4
Ascot Ms WLGTN SM6 183 J2
Ascot Rd ASHF TW15 131 G5
EHAM E6 106 F2
SEVS/STOTM N15 67 K6
STMC/STPC BR5 161 M7
TOOT SW17 156 A2
UED N18 50 A6
WATW WD18 28 E8
Ascott Av EA W5 98 E8
Ashbourne Sq NTHWD HA6 41 L8
Ashbourne Av BXLYHN DA7 126 E5
GLDGN NW11 64 F6
RYLN/HDSTN HA2 79 K2
SWFD E18 70 B5
TRDG/WHET N20 47 M1
Ashbourne CI EA W5 99 C4
NFNCH/WDSP N12 47 H6
Ashbourne Gv CHSWK W4 117 L3
EDUL SE22 139 M2
MLHL NW7 45 K7
Ashbourne Ri ORP BR6 176 D6
Ashbourne Rd EA W5 99 C4
HARH RM3 56 C6
MTCM CR4 156 A2
Ashbourne Ter
WIM/MER SW19 155 C3
Ashbourne Wy GLDGN NW11 64 F6
Ashbridge Rd WAN E11 69 L8
Ashbridge St STJWD NW8 9 J1
Ashbrook Rd ARCH N19 84 D1
DAGE RM10 91 H5
Ashburn Gdns SKENS SW7 14 E5
Ashburnham Av HRW HA1 61 M8
Ashburnham CI EFNCH N2 65 K5
OXHEY WD19 42 A5
Ashburnham Dr OXHEY WD19 42 A5
Ashburnham Gdns HRW HA1 61 M7
UPMR RM14 93 H1
Ashburnham Gv GNWCH SE10 123 H5
Ashburnham Pk
ESH/CLAY KT10 166 C6
Ashburnham PI GNWCH SE10 123 H5
Ashburnham Retreat
GNWCH SE10 123 H5
Ashburnham Rd BELV DA17 127 J2
RCHPK/HAM TW10 134 D7
WBPTN SW10 119 J5
WLSDN NW10 100 C2
Ashburn PI SKENS SW7 14 E5
Ashburton Av CROY/NA CR0 173 H5
GDMY/SEVK IG3 89 M4
Ashburton CI CROY/NA CR0 173 G4
Ashburton Gdns
CROY/NA CR0 173 G4
Ashburton Gv HOLWY N7 85 G4
Ashburton Rd CAN/RD E16 106 C4
CROY/NA CR0 173 G4
RSLP HA4 78 A2
Ashbury Ct BMLY BR1 160 A3
Ashbury Dr HGDN/ICK UB10 77 H2
Ashbury Gdns CHDH RM6 72 D8
Ashbury PI WIM/MER SW19 155 J2
Ashbury Rd BTSEA SW11 119 M8
Ashby Av CHSGTN KT9 168 A8
Ashby CI EMPK RM11 93 G1
Ashby Gv IS N1 6 F1
Ashby Ms BROCKY SE4 122 F4
Ashby Rd BNSTD SM7 182 A7
SEVS/STOTM N15 68 A6
WATN WD24 29 G3

Ashby St FSBYE EC1V 6 D8
Ashby Wk CROY/NA CR0 172 C1
Ashby Wy WDR/YW UB7 113 G5
Ashchurch Gv SHB W12 100 A8
Ashchurch Park Vis SHB W12 118 A1
Ashchurch Ter SHB W12 117 M1
Ash CI ABLGY WD5 20 D5
CAR SM5 170 F4
DEN/HRF UB9 58 D2
EDGW HA8 45 J6
GSTN WD25 21 H3
PGE/AN SE20 158 C5
ROMW/RG RM7 73 H1
SCUP DA14 144 B7
STAN HA7 44 A8
STMC/STPC BR5 161 K8
SWLY BR8 163 J5
Ashcombe Av SURB KT6 167 K2
Ashcombe Gdns EDGW HA8 45 G6
Ashcombe Pk CRICK NW2 81 L3
Ashcombe Rd CAR SM5 171 G8
WIM/MER SW19 155 G1
Ashcombe Sq NWMAL KT3 153 J6
Ashcombe St FUL/PGN SW6 119 H7
Ash Copse LCOL/BKTW AL2 21 M4
Ash Ct HOR/WEW KT19 168 C6
Ashcroft PIN HA5 43 G8
Ashcroft Av BFN/LL DA15 144 A3
Ashcroft Crs BFN/LL DA15 144 A3
Ashcroft Rd BOW E3 104 E2
CHSGTN KT9 167 M5
Ashdale CI STWL/WRAY TW19 130 E6
WHTN TW2 133 H4
Ashdale Gv STAN HA7 43 M8
Ashdale Rd LEE/GVPK SE12 142 B5
Ashdene PIN HA5 60 C4
Ashdene CI ASHF TW15 149 J3
Ashdon CI WFD IG8 52 B8
Ashdown CI BECK BR3 159 H5
BXLY DA5 145 J4
Ashdown Crs CHES/WCR EN8 26 E1
KTTN NW5 84 A5
Ashdown Dr BORE WD6 31 M5
Ashdown Gdns SAND/SEL CR2 185 H8
Ashdown PI THDIT KT7 167 G1
Ashdown Rd BUSH WD23 29 K6
EW KT17 180 F6
HGDN/ICK UB10 95 G2
KUT KT1 152 E5
PEND EN3 37 J5
WLSDN NW10 81 L8
Ashdown Wk ROMW/RG RM7 73 H2
TOOT SW17 138 A6
Ashenden Rd CLPT E5 86 E5
Ashen Dr DART DA1 146 A3
Ashen Gv WIM/MER SW19 137 G7
Ashen V SAND/SEL CR2 185 K2
Asher Loftus Wy
FBAR/BDGN N11 47 M8
Asher Wy WAP E1W 104 B6
Ashfield Av BUSH WD23 43 H1
FELT TW13 132 B5
Ashfield CI BECK BR3 159 G3
RCHPK/HAM TW10 134 E5
Ashfield La CHST BR7 161 J2
Ashfield Rd ACT W3 99 M7
FSBYPK N4 67 J7
STHGT/OAK N14 48 C5
Ashfields GSTN WD25 20 F8
LOU IG10 39 M5
Ashfield St WCHPL E1 104 B4
Ashford Av ASHF TW15 149 H2
CEND/HSY/T N8 66 E5
YEAD UB4 96 D5
Ashford CI ASHF TW15 130 E8
WALTH E17 68 F7
Ashford Crs ASHF TW15 130 E7
PEND EN3 37 J5
Ashford Gn OXHEY WD19 42 D7
Ashford Rd CRICK NW2 82 D4
EHAM E6 88 F6
FELT TW13 131 K8
SHPTN TW17 149 J3
STA TW18 148 D4
SWFD E18 70 B3
Ashford St IS N1 7 J7
Ash Gn DEN/HRF UB9 76 B6
Ash Gv ALP/SUD HA0 80 A4
CRICK NW2 82 D4
DEN/HRF UB9 58 D2
EA W5 98 E8
EBED/NFELT TW14 131 L5
EN EN1 49 L2
HACK E8 86 D3
HEST TW5 114 D6
HYS/HAR UB3 95 K6
PGE/AN SE20 158 C5
PLMGR N13 49 J5
STA TW18 148 C2
STHL UB1 97 G4
WDR/YW UB7 94 F6
WWKM BR4 174 A4
Ashgrove Rd ASHF TW15 149 J1
BMLY BR1 159 K2
GDMY/SEVK IG3 89 M1
Ash Hill CI BUSH WD23 43 H5
Ash Hill Dr PIN HA5 60 C4
Ashingdon CI CHING E4 51 J5
Ashington Rd FUL/PGN SW6 119 J7
Ashlake Rd STRHM/NOR SW16 138 E8
Ashland PI MHST W1U 10 A2
Ashlar PI WOOL/PLUM SE18 125 H2
Ashleigh Gdns SUT SM1 170 B4
Ashleigh Rd MORT/ESHN SW14 117 J8
PGE/AN SE20 158 B6
Ashley Av BARK/HLT IG6 71 H3
EPSOM KT18 180 D6
MRDN SM4 155 J5
Ashley CI HDN NW4 64 C3
PIN HA5 60 D3
WEY KT13 164 E3
Ashley Crs BTSEA SW11 120 A8
WDGN N22 67 G3
Ashley Dr BNSTD SM7 182 A7
BORE WD6 32 C5
ISLW TW7 115 L4

WHTN TW2 133 H5
WOT/HER KT12 165 G5
Ashley Gdns ORP BR6 176 E7
PLMGR N13 49 J6
RCHPK/HAM TW10 134 D7
WBLY HA9 80 B2
Ashley La CROY/NA CR0 172 B6
HDN NW4 64 C4
MLHL NW7 64 C1
Ashley Park Av WOT/HER KT12 164 F3
Ashley Park Crs WOT/HER KT12 164 F3
Ashley Park Rd WOT/HER KT12 165 G4
Ashley PI WEST SW1P 16 E4
Ashley Ri WOT/HER KT12 165 G5
Ashley Rd ARCH N19 84 E1
CHING E4 51 G7
EW KT17 180 D6
FSTGT E7 88 C7
HPTN TW12 151 C4
PEND EN3 37 J5
RCH/KEW TW9 116 E8
THDIT KT7 166 F1
THHTH CR7 156 E5
TOTM N17 68 A4
WIM/MER SW19 155 H2
WOT/HER KT12 164 F6
Ashling Rd CROY/NA CR0 173 J3
Ashlin Rd SRTFD E15 87 K4
Ashlone Rd PUT/ROE SW15 118 D7
Ashlyn CI BUSH WD23 29 L7
Ashlyn Gv EMPK RM11 74 D4
Ashlyns Wy CHSGTN KT9 167 K8
Ashmead STHGT/OAK N14 35 J4
Ash Mead Dr DEN/HRF UB9 76 A2
Ashmead Ga BMLY BR1 160 C4
Ashmead La DEN/HRF UB9 76 A2
Ashmead Rd DEPT SE8 123 G7
EBED/NFELT TW14 132 A5
Ashmere Av BECK BR3 159 K5
Ashmere CI CHEAM SM3 169 K7
Ashmere Gv
BRXS/STRHM SW2 138 E1
Ash Ms EPSOM KT18 180 E6
Ashmill St CAMTN NW1 9 J2
Ashmole St VX/NE SW8 120 F4
Ashmore Gv WELL DA16 125 K8
Ashmore La HAYES BR2 187 J4
Ashmore Rd MV/WKIL W9 100 F2
Ashmount Rd ARCH N19 66 C8
Ashmour Gdns ROM RM1 73 K3
Ashness Gdns GFD/PVL UB6 80 B6
Ashness Rd BTSEA SW11 137 M2
Ash Ride ENC/FH EN2 25 M2
Ashridge Crs WOOL/PLUM SE18 125 J5
Ashridge Dr LCOL/BKTW AL2 21 L3
OXHEY WD19 42 C7
Ashridge Gdns PIN HA5 60 E5
PLMGR N13 48 E7
Ashridge Wy MRDN SM4 154 F7
SUN TW16 150 A2
Ash Rw CROY/NA CR0 174 A4
Ashtead Rd CLPT E5 68 B4
Ashton CI SUT SM1 170 A6
WOT/HER KT12 165 H8
Ashton Gdns CHDH RM6 72 E7
HSLWW TW4 132 F1
Ashton Rd HARH RM3 74 D1
PEND EN3 37 L1
SRTFD E15 87 K5
Ashton St POP/IOD E14 105 J3
Ashtree Av MTCM CR4 155 K5
Ash Tree CI CROY/NA CR0 173 L1
SURB KT6 167 L3
Ash Tree Dell CDALE/KGS NW9 63 G3
Ash Tree Wy WATN WD24 29 H1
Ash Tree Wy CROY/NA CR0 158 E8
Ashurst CI DART DA1 127 M8
NTHWD HA6 59 L1
PGE/AN SE20 158 A5
PUR/KEN CR8 184 D8
Ashurst Dr BARK/HLT IG6 71 J6
GNTH/NBYPK IG2 71 H7
SHPTN TW17 148 E8
Ashurst Rd EBAR EN4 34 F8
NFNCH/WDSP N12 47 L7
Ashurst Wk CROY/NA CR0 173 H4
Ashvale Dr UPMR RM14 93 L2
Ashvale Gdns CRW RM5 55 K7
UPMR RM14 93 L2
Ashvale Rd TOOT SW17 155 M1
Ashview CI ASHF TW15 148 E2
Ashview Gdns ASHF TW15 148 E1
Ashville Rd WAN E11 87 K2
Ash Wk ALP/SUD HA0 80 C4
Ashwater Rd LEE/GVPK SE12 142 A5
Ashwin St HACK E8 85 M6
Ashwood Av RAIN RM13 110 B2
UX/CGN UB8 95 G5
Ashwood Gdns CROY/NA CR0 174 B8
HYS/HAR UB3 113 M2
Ashwood Rd CHING E4 51 K5
POTB/CUF EN6 23 H6
Ashworth CI CMBW SE5 121 K7
Ashworth Rd MV/WKIL W9 2 D4
Askern CI BXLYHS DA6 144 D1
Aske St IS N1 7 J7
Askew Crs SHB W12 99 M8
Askew Rd NTHWD HA6 41 K4
SHB W12 99 M8
Askill Dr PUT/ROE SW15 136 A7
Askwith Rd RAIN RM13 109 K1
Asland Rd SRTFD E15 87 K1
Aslett St WAND/EARL SW18 137 H4
Asmara Rd CRICK NW2 82 E5
Asmar CI COUL/CHIP CR5 183 L8
Asmuns HI GLDGN NW11 65 G5

Asmuns PI GLDGN NW11 64 F5
Asolando Dr WALW SE17 18 F6
Aspen CI EA W5 98 F8
ORP BR6 177 G7
SWLY BR8 163 K4
WDR/YW UB7 94 F7
Aspen Copse BMLY BR1 160 F5
Aspen Dr ALP/SUD HA0 79 G4
Aspen Gdns MTCM CR4 156 A8
Aspen Gn ERITH DA8 126 F1
Aspen Gv UPMR RM14 93 G4
Aspen La NTHLT UB5 96 E2
Aspenlea Rd HMSMTH W6 118 D4
Aspen Park Dr GSTN WD25 21 H5
Aspen Wy EW KT17 181 K7
FELT TW13 132 B7
PEND EN3 26 D8
POP/IOD E14 105 K5
Aspern Gv HAMP NW3 83 L5
Aspinall Rd BROCKY SE4 122 B4
NWCR SE14 122 D8
Aspinden Rd BERM/RHTH SE16 123 B2
Aspley Rd WAND/EARL SW18 137 H2
Asplins Rd TOTM N17 68 A2
Asquith CI BCTR RM8 90 C1
Assam St WCHPL E1 104 A5
Assata Ms IS N1 85 H6
Assembly Pas WCHPL E1 104 C4
Assembly Wk CAR SM5 170 E2
Assher Rd WOT/HER KT12 165 L5
Ass House La
KTN/HRWW/W HA3 43 H6
Astall CI KTN/HRWW/W HA3 61 K2
Astbury Rd PECK SE15 122 C6
Astell St CHEL SW3 15 J7
The Asters CHESW EN7 25 K1
Asthall Gdns BARK/HLT IG6 71 J5
Astleham Wy SHPTN TW17 148 E6
Astle St BTSEA SW11 120 A7
Astley Av CRICK NW2 82 A3
Aston Av KTN/HRWW/W HA3 62 C8
Aston CI BUSH WD23 43 J1
SCUP DA14 144 A7
WATN WD24 29 J5
Aston Gn HEST TW5 114 C7
Aston Rd EA W5 98 D5
ESH/CLAY KT10 166 E7
RYNPK SW20 154 C5
Astons Rd NTHWD HA6 41 J5
Astonville St WAND/EARL SW18 137 G5
Aston Wy POTB/CUF EN6 23 K5
Astor Av ROMW/RG RM7 73 H7
Astor CI KUTN/CMB KT2 153 H2
Astoria Wk BRXN/ST SW9 121 G8
Astra CI HCH RM12 92 B6
Astral St STHL UB1 97 G6
Astrop Ms HMSMTH W6 118 C1
Astrop Ter HMSMTH W6 100 C8
Astwood Ms SKENS SW7 14 D5
Asylum Rd PECK SE15 122 B5
Atalanta CI PUR/KEN CR8 184 A3
Atalanta St FUL/PGN SW6 118 D6
Atbara Rd TEDD TW11 152 B2
Atcham Rd HSLW TW3 133 J1
Atcost Rd BARK IG11 108 A4
Athelbert Rd WAND/EARL SW18 137 H5
Athelney St CAT SE6 141 G7
Athelstane Gv BOW E3 104 F1
Athelstane Ms FSBYPK N4 85 G1
Athelstan Rd HARH RM3 74 F2
KUT KT1 152 F7
Athelstan Wy STMC/STPC BR5 162 A4
Athelstone Rd
KTN/HRWW/W HA3 61 K3
Athena CI KUT KT1 152 F6
RYLN/HDSTN HA2 79 K2
Athenaeum PI MUSWH N10 66 B4
Athenaeum Rd TRDG/WHET N20 47 J1
Athena PI NTHWD HA6 59 M2
Athenlay Rd PECK SE15 140 D2
Atherden Rd CLPT E5 86 C4
Atherfold Rd BRXN/ST SW9 120 E8
Atherley Wy HSLWW TW4 132 F4
Atherstone Ms SKENS SW7 14 F5
Atherton CI
STWL/WRAY TW19 130 D3
Atherton Dr WIM/MER SW19 136 D8
Atherton Hts ALP/SUD HA0 80 C6
Atherton Ms FSTGT E7 88 B6
Atherton PI RYLN/HDSTN HA2 61 J4
STHL UB1 97 G6
Atherton Rd BARN SW13 118 A5
CLAY IG5 70 E3
FSTGT E7 87 M5
Atherton St BTSEA SW11 119 M7
Athlone ESH/CLAY KT10 166 E8
Athlone CI CLPT E5 86 B5
RAD WD7 31 H1
Athlone Ct WALTH E17 69 K4
Athlone Rd BRXS/STRHM SW2 138 F4
Athlone St KTTN NW5 84 A6
Athlon Rd ALP/SUD HA0 98 D1
Athol CI PIN HA5 60 B2
Athole Gdns EN EN1 36 E8
Athol Gdns PIN HA5 60 B2
Atholl Rd GDMY/SEVK IG3 72 A8
Athol Rd ERITH DA8 127 J3
Athol Sq POP/IOD E14 105 J5
Athol Wy HGDN/ICK UB10 95 G2
Atkins Dr WWKM BR4 174 D5
Atkinson CI ORP BR6 177 G7
Atkinson Rd CAN/RD E16 106 C4
Atkins Rd BAL SW12 138 D4
CLAP SW4 138 D4
LEY E10 69 H7
Atlanta Bvd ROM RM1 73 L7
Atlantic Rd BRXN/ST SW9 139 C1
Atlas Gdns CHARL SE7 124 C2
Atlas Ms HACK E8 85 M6
Atlas Rd DART DA1 128 F8
PLSTW E13 107 G1
WBLY HA9 81 J4
WLSDN NW10 99 L2
Atley Rd BOW E3 87 C8
Atlip Rd ALP/SUD HA0 80 B8
Atney Rd PUT/ROE SW15 136 B2

Atria Rd *NTHWD* HA6 .... 42 A7
Attenborough Cl
 OXHEY WD19 .... 42 E5 🔲
Atterbury Rd *FSBYPK* N4 .... 67 H7 🔲
Atterbury St *WEST* SW1P 17 H6
Attewood Av *CRICK* NW2 .... 81 L6
Attewood Rd *NTHLT* UB5 .... 78 E6
Attfield Cl *TRDG/WHET* N20 .... 47 K4
Attle Cl *HGDN/ICK* UB10 .... 95 G1 🔲
Attlee Cl *CROY/NA* CR0 .... 172 C1
 YEAD UB4 .... 96 B2 🔲
Attlee Dr *DART* DA1 .... 147 G2
Attlee Rd *THMD* SE28 .... 108 B6
 YEAD UB4 .... 96 A2
Attneave St *FSBYW* WC1X 6 A9
Attwood Cl *SAND/SEL* CR2 .... 185 H7
Atwell Rd *PECK* SE15 .... 122 A7 🔲
Atwood Av *RCH/KEW* TW9 .... 117 C7
Atwood Rd *HMSMTH* W6 .... 118 B2
Aubert Pk *HBRY* N5 .... 85 G4
Aubert Rd *HBRY* N5 .... 85 H4
Aubrey Pl *STJWD* NW8 .... 2 E6
Aubrey Rd *CEND/HSY/T* N8 .... 66 E6 🔲
 KENS W8 .... 100 F7
 WALTH E17 .... 69 G4
Aubrey Wk *KENS* W8 .... 100 F7
Aubrietia Cl *HARH* RM3 .... 74 E2 🔲
Aubyn Hl *WNWD* SE27 .... 139 J8
Aubyn Sq *PUT/ROE* SW15 .... 136 A1
Auckland Av *RAIN* RM13 .... 109 N2 🔲
Auckland Cl *EN* EN1 .... 37 H2
 NRWD SE19 .... 157 M4
Auckland Hl *WNWD* SE27 .... 139 J8
Auckland Ri *NRWD* SE19 .... 157 L4
Auckland Rd *BTSEA* SW11 .... 137 L1
 IL IG1 .... 89 H1
 KUT KT1 .... 152 F7
 LEY E10 .... 87 H3
 NRWD SE19 .... 157 M4
 POTB/CUF EN6 .... 22 D5
Aucklands Gdns *NRWD* SE19 .... 157 L4
Auckland St *LBTH* SE11 .... 17 L8
Audleigh Pl *CHIG* IG7 .... 53 C8
 MUSWH N10 .... 66 B1
Audley Cl *BORE* WD6 .... 32 A6
 SWFD E18 .... 69 H5 🔲
Audley Ct *PIN* HA5 .... 60 C3
 SWFD E18 .... 69 H5 🔲
Audley Dr *CAN/RD* E16 .... 106 B7
 SAND/SEL CR2 .... 178 A7
Audley Firs *WOT/HER* KT12 .... 165 J6 🔲
 WAB EN9 .... 27 J7
Audley Pl *BELMT* SM2 .... 182 B1 🔲
Audley Rd *EA* W5 .... 98 F4
 ENC/FH EN2 .... 36 B5
 HDN NW4 .... 64 A7
 RCHPK/HAM TW10 .... 134 F2 🔲
Audrey Cl *BECK* BR3 .... 174 B1
Audrey Gdns *ALP/SUD* HA0 .... 80 B2
Audrey Rd *IL* IG1 .... 89 H3
Audrey St *BETH* E2 .... 104 A1
Audric Cl *KUTN/CMB* KT2 .... 153 G4 🔲
Audwick Cl *CHES/WCR* EN8 .... 26 D1
Augurs La *PLSTW* E13 .... 106 B2 🔲
Augusta Cl *E/WMO/HCT* KT8 .... 150 F6 🔲
Augusta Rd *WHTN* TW2 .... 133 J6
Augustine Rd *HMSMTH* W6 .... 118 D1 🔲
 KTN/HRWW/W HA3 .... 61 H2 🔲
 STMC/STPC BR5 .... 162 D6 🔲
Augustus Cl *BTFD* TW8 .... 116 D5 🔲
 HMSMTH W6 .... 100 B8 🔲
Augustus Rd *WIM/MER* SW19 .... 136 E5 🔲
Augustus St *CAMTN* NW1 .... 4 D6
Aultone Wy *CAR* SM5 .... 170 F5
 SUT SM1 .... 170 B4
Aurelia Gdns *THHTH* CR7 .... 156 F8
Aurelia Rd *CROY/NA* CR0 .... 171 L1
Auriel Av *DAGE* RM10 .... 91 K6
Auriga Ms *STNW/STAM* N16 .... 85 K5 🔲
Auriol Cl *HOR/WEW* KT19 .... 168 E5 🔲
Auriol Dr *GFD/PVL* UB6 .... 79 K7
 HGDN/ICK UB10 .... 77 H6 🔲
Auriol Park Rd *WPK* KT4 .... 168 E5 🔲
Auriol Rd *WKENS* W14 .... 118 C2
Austell Gdns *MLHL* NW7 .... 45 L5
Austen Cl *THMD* SE28 .... 108 B7
Austen Rd *ERITH* DA8 .... 127 H5
 RYLN/HDSTN HA2 .... 79 H2
Austin Av *HAYES* BR2 .... 175 L1
Austin Cl *CAT* SE6 .... 140 E4
Austin Friars *OBST* EC2N .... 13 H4 🔲
Austin Friars Sq *OBST* EC2N .... 13 H4 🔲
Austin Rd *BTSEA* SW11 .... 120 A6
 HYS/HAR UB3 .... 95 M8
 STMC/STPC BR5 .... 177 G1
Austin's La *HGDN/ICK* UB10 .... 77 K4
Austin St *BETH* E2 .... 7 L8
Austral Cl *BFN/LL* DA15 .... 143 M7
Austral Dr *EMPK* RM11 .... 74 D8
Australia Rd *SHB* W12 .... 100 B6
Austral St *LBTH* SE11 .... 18 C5
Austyn Gdns *BRYLDS* KT5 .... 168 B3 🔲
Autumn Cl *EN* EN1 .... 37 H5
 WIM/MER SW19 .... 155 J2
Autumn Dr *BELMT* SM2 .... 182 B2
Autumn St *BOW* E3 .... 87 G8
Avalon Cl *ENC/FH* EN2 .... 36 A5
 GSTN WD25 .... 21 L5
 ORP BR6 .... 177 K4
 RYNPK SW20 .... 154 E5
 WEA W13 .... 98 A4
Avalon Rd *FUL/PGN* SW6 .... 119 H6
 ORP BR6 .... 177 J4
 WEA W13 .... 98 A3
Avard Gdns *ORP* BR6 .... 176 C6
Avarn Rd *TOOT* SW17 .... 155 M2
Avebury Rd *ORP* BR6 .... 176 D5
 WAN E11 .... 87 K1 🔲
 WIM/MER SW19 .... 154 F4
Avebury St *IS* N1 .... 7 G4
Aveley By-pass *SOCK/AV* RM15 .... 111 J6 🔲
Aveley Cl *ERITH* DA8 .... 127 M4 🔲
Aveley Rd *ROM* RM1 .... 73 K5 🔲
 UPMR RM14 .... 93 H7
Aveline St *LBTH* SE11 .... 17 M7
Aveling Cl *PUR/KEN* CR8 .... 183 M6
Aveling Park Rd *WALTH* E17 .... 69 G3

Avelon Rd *CRW* RM5 .... 55 K8
 RAIN RM13 .... 92 A8
Avenell Rd *FSBYPK* N4 .... 85 H3
Avening Rd
 WAND/EARL SW18 .... 137 G4 🔲
Avening Ter *WAND/EARL* SW18 .... 137 G3
Avenue Ap *KGLGY* WD4 .... 20 A3
Avenue Cl *HARH* RM3 .... 74 F1
 STHGT/OAK N14 .... 28 C1
 WDR/YW UB7 .... 112 D1
Avenue Crs *ACT* W3 .... 99 H8
 HEST TW5 .... 114 A6
Avenue Gdns *ACT* W3 .... 99 H8
 HEST TW5 .... 114 B5 🔲
 MORT/ESHN SW14 .... 117 L8
 TEDD TW11 .... 151 M3
Avenue Ms *MUSWH* N10 .... 66 B4
Avenue Park Rd *WNWD* SE27 .... 139 H6
Avenue Ri *BUSH* WD23 .... 30 A8
Avenue Rd *ACT* W3 .... 99 H8
 BELMT SM2 .... 182 A3
 BNSTD SM7 .... 182 B8
 BXLYHS DA6 .... 126 E8
 EPSOM KT18 .... 180 D7
 ERITH DA8 .... 127 J5
 FELT TW13 .... 131 M7
 FSTGT E7 .... 88 B5
 GDMY/SEVK IG3 .... 72 B8
 HAMP NW3 .... 3 G1
 HARH RM3 .... 74 F1
 HGT N6 .... 66 C8
 HPTN TW12 .... 151 H4
 ISLW TW7 .... 115 L6
 KUT KT1 .... 152 E6
 NFNCH/WDSP N12 .... 47 J6
 NWMAL KT3 .... 153 L6
 PGE/AN SE20 .... 158 C4
 PIN HA5 .... 60 E4
 RYNPK SW20 .... 154 B5
 SEVS/STOTM N15 .... 67 K6
 SNWD SE25 .... 158 A5
 STHGT/OAK N14 .... 28 C1
 STHL UB1 .... 96 F7
 STJWD NW8 .... 3 K5
 STJWD NW8 .... 3 H2
 STRHM/NOR SW16 .... 156 D5
 TEDD TW11 .... 151 A3
 WFD IG8 .... 52 C8
 WLGTN SM6 .... 183 J1
 WWKM BR4 .... 99 M1
Avenue South *BRYLDS* KT5 .... 167 M2
Avenue Ter *NWMAL* KT3 .... 153 J6
 OXHEY WD19 .... 42 E1 🔲
The Avenue *BAR* EN5 .... 33 L6
 BECK BR3 .... 159 H4
 BELMT SM2 .... 181 M2
 BMLY BR1 .... 160 D6
 BRYLDS KT5 .... 167 M1
 BTSEA SW11 .... 138 A2
 BUSH WD23 .... 29 M7
 BXLY DA5 .... 144 D4
 CAR SM5 .... 183 G1
 CEND/HSY/T N8 .... 67 G4 🔲
 CHING E4 .... 51 K8
 CHSWK W4 .... 117 L1
 CLAP SW4 .... 138 B3
 CLAP SW4 .... 138 A1
 COUL/CHIP CR5 .... 183 K8
 CROY/NA CR0 .... 172 E5
 ESH/CLAY KT10 .... 166 E8
 EW KT17 .... 181 J1
 FBAR/BDGN N11 .... 48 B7 🔲
 GNWCH SE10 .... 123 K5
 HCH RM12 .... 92 D2
 HEST TW5 .... 114 A6
 HGDN/ICK UB10 .... 77 G3
 HPTN TW12 .... 150 F7
 HSLW TW3 .... 133 H2
 KIL/WHAMP NW6 .... 82 D8
 KTN/HRWW/W HA3 .... 61 M2
 LHD/OX KT22 .... 178 F5
 LOU IG10 .... 52 E1
 MUSWH N10 .... 66 C3
 NTHWD HA6 .... 41 J8
 ORP BR6 .... 176 F4
 PIN HA5 .... 42 F8
 PIN HA5 .... 60 F7
 POTB/CUF EN6 .... 22 F3
 RCH/KEW TW9 .... 116 F7
 ROM RM1 .... 73 K5
 STA TW18 .... 148 B4
 STMC/STPC BR5 .... 162 B3
 SUN TW16 .... 150 B4
 TOTM N17 .... 67 L3
 TWK TW1 .... 134 C2
 UX/CGN UB8 .... 94 D3
 WAN E11 .... 70 B7
 WAT WD17 .... 29 G5
 WBLY HA9 .... 80 F2
 WEA W13 .... 98 B6
 WPK KT4 .... 168 F4
 WWKM BR4 .... 174 D2
Averil Gv *STRHM/NOR* SW16 .... 157 H2
Averill St *HMSMTH* W6 .... 118 D4
Avern Gdns *E/WMO/HCT* KT8 .... 151 H7
Avernons Rd *PLSTW* E13 .... 106 A4
Avern Rd *E/WMO/HCT* KT8 .... 151 H7 🔲
Avery Farm Rw *BGVA* SW1W .... 16 C6 🔲
Avery Gdns *GNTH/NBYPK* IG2 .... 70 F6
Avery Hill Rd *ELTH/MOT* SE9 .... 143 K3
Avery Rw *MYFR/PKLN* W1K 10 C5
Avey La *LOU* IG10 .... 38 F2
Aviary Cl *CAN/RD* E16 .... 105 M4
Aviemore Cl *BECK* BR3 .... 158 F8 🔲
Aviemore Wy *BECK* BR3 .... 158 E8
Avignon Rd *BROCKY* SE4 .... 122 D8
Avington Gv *PGE/AN* SE20 .... 158 C3
Avior Dr *NTHWD* HA6 .... 41 M6
Avis Sq *WCHPL* E1 .... 104 D5
Avoca Rd *TOOT* SW17 .... 138 A8
Avocet Ms *THMD* SE28 .... 125 K1
Avon Cl *GSTN* WD25 .... 21 J7
 SUT SM1 .... 170 C6 🔲
 WPK KT4 .... 169 G4
 YEAD UB4 .... 96 C3
Avondale Av *CRICK* NW2 .... 81 L3

 EBAR EN4 .... 47 M3
 ESH/CLAY KT10 .... 167 C5
 NFNCH/WDSP N12 .... 47 H7
 WPK KT4 .... 168 F3
Avondale Cl *LOU* IG10 .... 52 F2
 WOT/HER KT12 .... 165 J7
Avondale Ct *WFD* IG8 .... 70 B2
Avondale Crs *PEND* EN3 .... 37 L6
 REDBR IG4 .... 70 D6
Avondale Dr *HYS/HAR* UB3 .... 96 A1
 LOU IG10 .... 52 F1
Avondale Ms *BMLY* BR1 .... 160 A2 🔲
Avondale Park Gdns
 NTGHL W11 .... 100 E6 🔲
Avondale Park Rd
 NTGHL W11 .... 100 E6 🔲
Avondale Rd *ASHF* TW15 .... 130 D7
 BMLY BR1 .... 159 L2 🔲
 CAN/RD E16 .... 105 L4
 ELTH/MOT SE9 .... 142 E6
 FNCH N3 .... 65 J2
 KTN/HRWW/W HA3 .... 61 M4
 MORT/ESHN SW14 .... 117 K8
 PLMGR N13 .... 49 G4
 SAND/SEL CR2 .... 172 C8
 SEVS/STOTM N15 .... 67 H6
 WALTH E17 .... 69 G8
 WELL DA16 .... 126 C7
 WIM/MER SW19 .... 155 H1
Avondale Sq *STHWK* SE1 .... 122 A3
Avonley Rd *NWCR* SE14 .... 122 C5
Avonmore Pl *WKENS* W14 .... 118 E2 🔲
Avonmore Rd *WKENS* W14 .... 118 E2 🔲
Avonmouth Rd *DART* DA1 .... 146 D2
Avonmouth St *STHWK* SE1 .... 18 E3 🔲
Avon Rd *BROCKY* SE4 .... 123 G8
 GFD/PVL UB6 .... 97 G3
 SUN TW16 .... 149 M3
 UPMR RM14 .... 75 J7
 WALTH E17 .... 69 K4
Avonstowe Cl *ORP* BR6 .... 176 C5
Avon Wy *SWFD* E18 .... 70 A4
Avonwick Rd *HSLW* TW3 .... 115 H7
Avril Wy *CHING* E4 .... 51 J7
Avro Wy *WLGTN* SM6 .... 183 L1
Awlfield Av *TOTM* N17 .... 67 K2
Awliscombe Rd *WELL* DA16 .... 125 M7
Axeholm Av *EDGW* HA8 .... 63 H2
Axe St *BARK* IG11 .... 89 J8
Axholme Av *EDGW* HA8 .... 63 G2
Axminster Crs *WELL* DA16 .... 126 C6
Axminster Rd *HOLWY* N7 .... 84 E3
Axtaine Rd *STMC/STPC* BR5 .... 177 K2
Axwood *EPSOM* KT18 .... 180 C8
Aybrook St *MHST* W1U 10 A3
Aycliff Ct *KUT* KT1 .... 153 G5 🔲
Aycliffe Cl *BMLY* BR1 .... 160 F7
Aycliffe Rd *BORE* WD6 .... 31 M4
 SHB W12 .... 99 M7
Aylands Cl *WBLY* HA9 .... 80 E2
Aylands Rd *PEND* EN3 .... 37 K1
Aylesbury Cl *FSTGT* E7 .... 87 M6 🔲
Aylesbury Rd *HAYES* BR2 .... 160 A6
 WALW SE17 .... 19 H8
Aylesbury St *CLKNW* EC1R 12 C1
 WLSDN NW10 .... 81 K3
Aylesford Av *BECK* BR3 .... 158 E8
Aylesford St *PIM* SW1V 17 G8
Aylesham Cl *MLHL* NW7 .... 64 A1 🔲
Aylesham Rd *ORP* BR6 .... 176 E2
Ayles Rd *YEAD* UB4 .... 96 B2
Aylestone Av *KIL/WHAMP* NW6 .... 82 D7
Aylett Rd *ISLW* TW7 .... 115 L7
 SNWD SE25 .... 158 B7
 UPMR RM14 .... 93 J7
Ayley Cft *EN* EN1 .... 37 G8
Ayliffe Cl *KUT* KT1 .... 153 G6 🔲
Aylmer Cl *STAN* HA7 .... 44 A4
Aylmer Dr *STAN* HA7 .... 44 A6
Aylmer Pde *BCTR* RM8 .... 90 E3
 EFNCH N2 .... 65 L6
 SHB W12 .... 99 L8
 WAN E11 .... 69 M8
Aylofte Rd *DAGW* RM9 .... 90 B4
Ayloffs Cl *EMPK* RM11 .... 74 E6 🔲
Ayloff's Wk *EMPK* RM11 .... 74 E6
Aylsham Dr *HGDN/ICK* UB10 .... 77 J2
Aylsham La *HARH* RM3 .... 56 C6
Aylton Est *BERM/RHTH* SE16 .... 🔲 *(not legible)*
Aylward Rd *FSTH* SE23 .... 140 F6
 RYNPK SW20 .... 154 F5
Aylwards Ri *STAN* HA7 .... 44 A6
Aylward St *WCHPL* E1 .... 104 D4 🔲
 WCHPL E1 .... 104 C5 🔲
 WCHPL E1 .... 104 C5 🔲
Aynhoe Rd *WKENS* W14 .... 118 D1 🔲
Aynho St *WATW* WD18 .... 29 H8 🔲
Aynscombe Angle *ORP* BR6 .... 177 G2 🔲
Ayres Cl *PLSTW* E13 .... 106 A2
Ayres Crs *WLSDN* NW10 .... 81 K7
Ayres St *STHWK* SE1 .... 18 F1
Ayr Gn *ROM* RM1 .... 73 L2
Ayrsome Rd *STNW/STAM* N16 .... 85 L3 🔲
Ayr Wy *ROM* RM1 .... 73 L2
Aysgarth Rd *DUL* SE21 .... 139 K3
Aytoun Pl *BRXN/ST* SW9 .... 120 F7
Aytoun Rd *BRXN/ST* SW9 .... 120 F7
Azalea Cl *HNWL* W7 .... 97 M7
 IL IG1 .... 89 H5
Azalea Dr *SWLY* BR8 .... 163 K7
Azalea Wk *PIN* HA5 .... 60 B7
Azania Ms *KTTN* NW5 .... 84 B5
Azenby Rd *PECK* SE15 .... 121 M7 🔲
Azof St *GNWCH* SE10 .... 123 L2

B

Baalbec Rd *HBRY* N5 .... 85 H5
Babbacombe Cl *CHSGTN* KT9 .... 167 K7 🔲
Babbacombe Gdns *REDBR* IG4 .... 70 E5
Babbacombe Rd *BMLY* BR1 .... 160 B4
Baber Dr *EBED/NFELT* TW14 .... 132 C3
Babington Rd *HNWL* W7 .... 81 G6 🔲
Babington Rd *BCTR* RM8 .... 90 C5
 HCH RM12 .... 92 B1
 HDN NW4 .... 64 B5 🔲

 STRHM/NOR SW16 .... 138 D8 🔲
Bache's St *IS* N1 .... 7 H8
Back Church La *WCHPL* E1 .... 104 A5
Back Gn *WOT/HER* KT12 .... 165 J8
Back Hl *CLKNW* EC1R 12 B1
Back La *BTFD* TW8 .... 116 D5
 BXLY DA5 .... 145 G4
 CEND/HSY/T N8 .... 66 E6 🔲
 CHDH RM6 .... 72 E8
 EDGW HA8 .... 63 J2
 GSTN WD25 .... 30 E4
 HAMP NW3 .... 83 J4 🔲
 PUR RM19 .... 129 L2
 RCHPK/HAM TW10 .... 134 C6
Backley Gdns *SNWD* SE25 .... 173 G1
Back Rd *SCUP* DA14 .... 144 A8
 TEDD TW11 .... 151 L3
Bacon Gv *STHWK* SE1 .... 19 L5
Bacon La *CDALE/KGS* NW9 .... 63 H5
 EDGW HA8 .... 63 G2
Bacon Link *CRW* RM5 .... 55 H8
Bacons Dr *POTB/CUF* EN6 .... 24 E1
Bacon's La *HGT* N6 .... 84 A1
Baconsmead *DEN/HRF* UB9 .... 76 A2
Bacon St *BETH* E2 .... 7 M9
 BETH E2 .... 104 A3 🔲
 WCHPL E1 .... 7 M9
Bacton St *BETH* E2 .... 104 C2 🔲
Badburgham Ct *WAB* EN9 .... 27 M6
Baddow Cl *DAGE* RM10 .... 91 G8
 WFD IG8 .... 52 D8
Baden Cl *STA* TW18 .... 149 L7
Baden Powell Cl *DAGW* RM9 .... 90 E8 🔲
 SURB KT6 .... 167 M4 🔲
Baden Rd *CEND/HSY/T* N8 .... 66 D5 🔲
 IL IG1 .... 89 H5
Bader Wy *RAIN* RM13 .... 92 A6
Badger Cl *FELT* TW13 .... 132 B7
 HSLWW TW4 .... 114 C7 🔲
Badgers Cl *ASHF* TW15 .... 148 F1 🔲
 BORE WD6 .... 31 M5 🔲
 ENC/FH EN2 .... 36 B6
 HRW HA1 .... 61 K7
 HYS/HAR UB3 .... 95 L7
Badgers Copse *ORP* BR6 .... 176 F4
 WPK KT4 .... 168 F4
Badgers Cft *ELTH/MOT* SE9 .... 143 G7
 TRDG/WHET N20 .... 46 E2
Badgers Wk *NWMAL* KT3 .... 153 L5
 PUR/KEN CR8 .... 183 J4
Badlis Rd *WALTH* E17 .... 69 G3
Badlow Cl *ERITH* DA8 .... 127 L5
Badminton Cl *BORE* WD6 .... 32 A5 🔲
 HRW HA1 .... 61 L5 🔲
 NTHLT UB5 .... 78 A5
Badminton Ms *CAN/RD* E16 .... 106 A7 🔲
Badminton Rd *BAL* SW12 .... 138 A3
Badsworth Rd *CMBW* SE5 .... 121 J5
Bagley Cl *WDR/YW* UB7 .... 94 E8
Bagley's La *FUL/PGN* SW6 .... 119 H6
Bagleys Spring *CHDH* RM6 .... 72 E5
Bagshot Rd *EN* EN1 .... 49 M2
Bagshot St *WALW* SE17 .... 19 K8
Bahram Rd *HOR/WEW* KT19 .... 180 D3
Baildon St *DEPT* SE8 .... 122 F5
Bailey Cl *PUR* RM19 .... 129 K2
 WDGN N22 .... 66 D2
Bailey Pl *SYD* SE26 .... 158 C2
Baillie Cl *RAIN* RM13 .... 110 B3
Baillies Wk *EA* W5 .... 116 B2
Bainbridge Cl *KUTN/CMB* KT2 .... 152 E1
Bainbridge Rd *DAGW* RM9 .... 90 B4
Bainbridge St
 NOXST/BSQ WC1A .... 11 H4 🔲
Baines Cl *SAND/SEL* CR2 .... 172 D7 🔲
Baird Av *STHL* UB1 .... 96 B6
Baird Cl *BUSH* WD23 .... 43 H1 🔲
 CDALE/KGS NW9 .... 63 J7 🔲
Baird Gdns *NRWD* SE19 .... 139 L8 🔲
Baird Rd *EN* EN1 .... 37 H6
Baird St *STLK* EC1Y 6 F9
Bairstow Cl *BORE* WD6 .... 31 L4
Baizdon Rd *BKHTH/KID* SE3 .... 123 L7
Baker La *MTCM* CR4 .... 156 A5
Baker Ms *ORP* BR6 .... 176 F8
Baker Rd *WLSDN* NW10 .... 81 L8
 WOOL/PLUM SE18 .... 124 E6
Bakers Av *LEY* E10 .... 69 H7
Bakers End *RYNPK* SW20 .... 154 E5
Bakers Gdns *CAR* SM5 .... 170 E4
Bakers Hl *BAR* EN5 .... 34 B5
 CLPT E5 .... 86 C1 🔲
Baker's Ms *MHST* W1U 10 A4
Bakers Rents *BETH* E2 .... 7 L8
Bakers Rd *CHESW* EN7 .... 26 B3
 UX/CGN UB8 .... 76 D7 🔲
Baker's Rw *CLKNW* EC1R .... 12 A1 🔲
 SRTFD E15 .... 105 L1
Baker St *CAMTN* NW1 .... 9 M1 🔲
 EN EN1 .... 36 D5
 MHST W1U 10 A3
 POTB/CUF EN6 .... 22 F6
 WEY KT13 .... 164 A6
Bakewell Dr *NWMAL* KT3 .... 153 L5
Balaams La *STHGT/OAK* N14 .... 48 D4
Balaam St *PLSTW* E13 .... 106 A2
Balaclava Rd *STHWK* SE1 .... 19 M6
 SURB KT6 .... 167 J3
Balcaskie Rd *ELTH/MOT* SE9 .... 142 F2
Balchen Rd *BKHTH/KID* SE3 .... 124 D7
Balchier Rd *EDUL* SE22 .... 140 B3
Balcombe Cl *BXLYHS* DA6 .... 144 D1
Balcombe St *CAMTN* NW1 .... 3 L9
Balcon Wy *BORE* WD6 .... 32 C4
Balcorne St *HOM* E9 .... 86 C7
Balder Ri *LEE/GVPK* SE12 .... 142 E8
Balderton St *MYFR/PKLN* W1K 10 B5
Baldock St *BOW* E3 .... 105 H1
Baldry Gdns *STRHM/NOR* SW16 .... 156 E2
Baldwin Crs *CMBW* SE5 .... 121 J6
Baldwins Gdns *FSBYW* WC1X 12 A2
Baldwin's Gdns *FSBYW* WC1X 7 G8
Baldwin's Hl *LOU* IG10 .... 39 M4
Baldwin La *RKW/CH/CXG* WD3 .... 28 A7
Baldwin St *FSBYE* EC1V 7 G8
Baldwin Ter *IS* N1 .... 6 E5 🔲
Baldwyn Gdns *ACT* W3 .... 99 J6

Baldwyn's Pk *BXLY* DA5 .... 145 K6
Baldwyn's Rd *BXLY* DA5 .... 145 K6
Balfern Gv *CHSWK* W4 .... 117 L3
Balfern St *BTSEA* SW11 .... 119 L7
Balfe St *IS* N1 .... 5 K6
Balfont Cl *SAND/SEL* CR2 .... 185 G6
Balfour Av *HNWL* W7 .... 97 M7
Balfour Gv *TRDG/WHET* N20 .... 47 M5
Balfour Ms *ED* N9 .... 50 A5 🔲
 MYFR/PKLN W1K 10 B8
Balfour Pl *MYFR/PKLN* W1K 10 B7
 PUT/ROE SW15 .... 🔲 *(not legible)*
Balfour Rd *ACT* W3 .... 99 J4
 CAR SM5 .... 182 F1
 HAYES BR2 .... 160 D8
 HBRY N5 .... 85 J4
 HRW HA1 .... 61 K6
 HSLW TW3 .... 115 H8 🔲
 IL IG1 .... 89 H2
 NWDGN UB2 .... 114 D1
 SNWD SE25 .... 158 A7
 WEA W13 .... 98 B8
 WIM/MER SW19 .... 155 H3
Balfour St *STHWK* SE1 .... 19 G5
Balgonie Rd *CHING* E4 .... 51 K3
Balgores Crs *GPK* RM2 .... 74 B4
Balgores La *GPK* RM2 .... 74 B5
Balgores Sq *GPK* RM2 .... 74 B5
Balgowan Cl *NWMAL* KT3 .... 153 L7 🔲
Balgowan Rd *BECK* BR3 .... 158 E6
Balgowan St *WOOL/PLUM* SE18 .... 125 M2
Balham Gv *BAL* SW12 .... 138 A4
Balham High Rd *BAL* SW12 .... 138 B5
Balham Hl *BAL* SW12 .... 138 B4
Balham New Rd *BAL* SW12 .... 138 B4
Balham Park Rd *TOOT* SW17 .... 137 M5
Balham Rd *ED* N9 .... 50 A4
Balham Station Rd *BAL* SW12 .... 138 A5
Balladier Wk *POP/IOD* E14 .... 105 H4 🔲
Ballamore Rd *BMLY* BR1 .... 142 A7
Ballance Rd *HOM* E9 .... 86 D6
Ballantine St
 WAND/EARL SW18 .... 137 J1 🔲
Ballard Cl *KUTN/CMB* KT2 .... 153 K3
Ballards Cl *DAGE* RM10 .... 91 H8
Ballards Farm Rd
 SAND/SEL CR2 .... 173 G5
Ballards La *FNCH* N3 .... 65 H1
Ballards Ri *SAND/SEL* CR2 .... 173 G5
Ballards Rd *CRICK* NW2 .... 82 A2
 DAGE RM10 .... 91 H8
Ballards Wy *SAND/SEL* CR2 .... 173 J8
 PUR/KEN CR8 .... 183 J4
Ballast Quay *GNWCH* SE10 .... 123 K3
Ballater Cl *OXHEY* WD19 .... 42 B6
Ballater Rd *CLAP* SW4 .... 138 C1
 SAND/SEL CR2 .... 172 F7
Ballina St *FSTH* SE23 .... 140 D4
Ballingdon Rd *BTSEA* SW11 .... 138 A3
Balliol Av *CHING* E4 .... 51 K6
Balliol Rd *NKENS* W10 .... 100 C5
 TOTM N17 .... 67 L2
 WELL DA16 .... 126 B7
Balloch Rd *CAT* SE6 .... 141 K5
Ballogie Av *WLSDN* NW10 .... 81 L4
Ball's Pond Pl *IS* N1 .... 85 K6 🔲
Ball's Pond Rd *IS* N1 .... 85 K6
Balmain Cl *EA* W5 .... 98 D7
Balmer Rd *BOW* E3 .... 104 F1 🔲
Balmes Rd *IS* N1 .... 7 H3
Balmoral Av *BECK* BR3 .... 158 E7
 FBAR/BDGN N11 .... 48 A8
Balmoral Cl *CHES/WCR* EN8 .... 26 D7
Balmoral Crs *E/WMO/HCT* KT8 .... 151 G6
Balmoral Dr *BORE* WD6 .... 32 D7
 STHL UB1 .... 96 F3
 YEAD UB4 .... 95 L3
Balmoral Gdns *BXLY* DA5 .... 144 F4
 HNWL W7 .... 116 A1
 SAND/SEL CR2 .... 184 D3
Balmoral Gv *HOLWY* N7 .... 84 F4
Balmoral Ms *SHB* W12 .... 117 M1 🔲
Balmoral Rd *CRICK* NW2 .... 82 B6
 FSTGT E7 .... 88 C4
 GPK RM2 .... 74 B5
 GSTN WD25 .... 21 G5
 HCH RM12 .... 92 D3
 KUT KT1 .... 152 F7
 LEY E10 .... 87 H2
 PEND EN3 .... 37 K1
 RYLN/HDSTN HA2 .... 79 G4
 WATN WD24 .... 29 J3
 WPK KT4 .... 169 H5
Balmoral Wy *BELMT* SM2 .... 182 A3
Balmore Crs *EBAR* EN4 .... 35 G8 🔲
Balmore St *KTTN* NW5 .... 84 B2
Balmuir Gdns *PUT/ROE* SW15 .... 136 C5
Balnacraig Av *WLSDN* NW10 .... 81 L4 🔲
Baltic Cl *WIM/MER* SW19 .... 155 K3
Baltic St East *STLK* EC1Y 12 E1
Baltic St West *FARR* EC1M 12 E1
Baltimore Pl *WELL* DA16 .... 125 M7 🔲
Balvaird Pl *PIM* SW1V .... 17 H8 🔲
Balvernie Gv *WAND/EARL* SW18 .... 136 F4
Bamborough Gdns *SHB* W12 .... 100 C8 🔲
Bamford Av *ALP/SUD* HA0 .... 80 F8
Bamford Rd *BMLY* BR1 .... 159 L1
Bamford Wy *CRW* RM5 .... 55 H1
Bampfylde Cl *WLGTN* SM6 .... 171 J3
Bampton Dr *MLHL* NW7 .... 64 A1
Bampton Rd *FSTH* SE23 .... 140 D7
 HARH RM3 .... 74 E1
Banavie Gdns *BECK* BR3 .... 159 H4
Banbury Cl *ENC/FH* EN2 .... 36 B4
Banbury Rd *HOM* E9 .... 86 D7
 WALTH E17 .... 68 L1
Banbury St *BTSEA* SW11 .... 119 L7 🔲
 WATW WD18 .... 29 H8 🔲
Banchory Rd *BKHTH/KID* SE3 .... 124 B5
Bancroft Av *EFNCH* N2 .... 65 L6
Bancroft Cl *ASHF* TW15 .... 149 L5 🔲
Bancroft Ct *NTHLT* UB5 .... 78 C3
Bancroft Gdns
 KTN/HRWW/W HA3 .... 61 J2 🔲
 ORP BR6 .... 176 F3
Bancroft Rd *KTN/HRWW/W* HA3 .... 61 J3
 WCHPL E1 .... 104 D2
Bandon Ri *WLGTN* SM6 .... 171 K8
Bangalore St *PUT/ROE* SW15 .... 118 C8
Bangor Cl *NTHLT* UB5 .... 79 H5

Banim St *HMSMTH* W6 ...... 118 B1
Banister Rd *WLSDN* NW10 ...... 100 D2
Bank Av *MTCM* CR4 ...... 155 K5
Bank End *STHWK* SE1 ...... 12 F8
Bankfoot Rd *BMLY* BR1 ...... 141 L8
Bankhurst Rd *CAT* SE6 ...... 140 F4
Bank La *KUTN/CMB* KT2 ...... 152 E3
  PUT/ROE SW15 ...... 135 L2
Banksia Rd *UED* N18 ...... 50 C7
Bankside *ENC/FH* EN2 ...... 36 B4
  SAND/SEL CR2 ...... 172 F8
  STHL UB1 ...... 96 D7
  STHWK SE1 ...... 12 E7
Bankside Av *NTHLT* UB5 ...... 96 A1
Bankside Cl *CAR* SM5 ...... 170 E7
  ISLW TW7 ...... 133 M1
  RDART DA2 ...... 145 K8
Bankside Dr *THDIT* KT7 ...... 167 H4
Bankside Rd *IL* IG1 ...... 89 J5
Banks La *BXLYHS* DA6 ...... 144 F1
Banks Rd *BORE* WD6 ...... 32 C5
The Bank *HGT* N6 ...... 84 B1
Bankton Rd *BRXS/STRHM* SW2 ...... 139 G1
Bankwell Rd *LEW* SE13 ...... 141 L1
Bank Willow
  RCHPK/HAM TW10 ...... 134 B7
Banner Cl *PUR* RM19 ...... 129 K2
Banner St *STLK* EC1Y 12 F1
Banning St *GNWCH* SE10 ...... 123 L3
Bannister Cl
  BRXS/STRHM SW2 ...... 139 G5
  NTHLT UB5 ...... 79 K5
Bannister Gdns
  STMC/STPC BR5 ...... 162 C6
Bannockburn Rd
  WOOL/PLUM SE18 ...... 125 L2
Banstead Gdns *ED* N9 ...... 49 K5
Banstead Rd *BELMT* SM2 ...... 182 D1
  BNSTD SM7 ...... 181 L6
  CAR SM5 ...... 170 E8
  EW KT17 ...... 181 H3
  PUR/KEN CR8 ...... 184 A4
Banstead Rd South
  BELMT SM2 ...... 182 C3
Banstead St *PECK* SE15 ...... 122 C8
Banstead Wy *WLGTN* SM6 ...... 171 L7
Banstock Rd *EDGW* HA8 ...... 45 J8
Banton Cl *EN* EN1 ...... 37 H5
Bantry St *CMBW* SE5 ...... 121 K5
Banwell Rd *BXLY* DA5 ...... 144 D5
Banyard Rd *BERM/RHTH* SE16 ...... 122 B3
Banyards *EMPK* RM11 ...... 74 E5
Bapchild Pl *STMC/STPC* BR5 ...... 162 C7
Baptist Gdns *KTTN* NW5 ...... 84 A6
Barbara Cl *SHPTN* TW17 ...... 149 H8
Barbauld Rd *STNW/STAM* N16 ...... 85 L3
Barbel Cl *CHES/WCR* EN8 ...... 27 C7
Barber Cl *WCHMH* N21 ...... 49 G2
Barberry Cl *HARH* RM3 ...... 74 D1
Barbers Rd *SRTFD* E15 ...... 105 H1
Barbican Rd *GFD/PVL* UB6 ...... 97 H5
Barb Ms *HMSMTH* W6 ...... 118 C1
Barbon Cl *BMSBY* WC1N 11 K2
Barbot Cl *ED* N9 ...... 49 M5
Barchard St
  WAND/EARL SW18 ...... 137 H2
Barchester Cl *HNWL* W7 ...... 97 M7
Barchester Rd
  KTN/HRWW/W HA3 ...... 61 K2
Barchester St *POP/IOD* E14 ...... 105 H4
Barclay Cl *WATW* WD18 ...... 42 A1
Barclay Ov *WFD* IG8 ...... 52 A6
Barclay Rd *CROY/NA* CR0 ...... 172 D5
  FUL/PGN SW6 ...... 119 G5
  PLSTW E13 ...... 106 C3
  UED N18 ...... 49 K8
  WALTH E17 ...... 69 J6
  WAN E11 ...... 87 M1
Barclay Wy *WTHK* RM20 ...... 129 M3
Barcombe Av
  BRXS/STRHM SW2 ...... 138 E6
Barcombe Cl *CHST* BR7 ...... 162 A6
Barden Cl *DEN/HRF* UB9 ...... 58 C2
Barden St *WOOL/PLUM* SE18 ...... 125 L5
Bardfield Av *CHDH* RM6 ...... 72 D4
Bardney Rd *MRDN* SM4 ...... 155 H7
Bardolph Av *CROY/NA* CR0 ...... 185 M2
Bardolph Rd *HOLWY* N7 ...... 84 E4
  RCH/KEW TW9 ...... 134 F1
Bardsey Pl *WCHPL* E1 ...... 104 C4
Bardsley Cl *CROY/NA* CR0 ...... 172 F5
Bardsley La *BRXS/STRHM* SW2 ...... 139 G1
  GNWCH SE10 ...... 123 J4
Barfett St *NKENS* W10 ...... 100 F3
Barfield Av *TRDG/WHET* N20 ...... 47 M4
Barfield Rd *BMLY* BR1 ...... 161 G6
  WAN E11 ...... 87 M1
Barford Cl *HDN* NW4 ...... 64 A3
Barford St *IS* N1 ...... 6 B4
Barforth Rd *PECK* SE15 ...... 141 J3
Barfreston Wy *PGE/AN* SE20 ...... 158 B4
Bargate Cl *NWMAL* KT3 ...... 169 G2
  WOOL/PLUM SE18 ...... 125 M3
Barge House Rd *CAN/RD* E16 ...... 107 H8
Barge House St *STHWK* SE1 ...... 12 B8
Bargery Rd *CAT* SE6 ...... 141 K5
Bargrove Cl *PGE/AN* SE20 ...... 158 A3
Bargrove Crs *CAT* SE6 ...... 140 F6
Barham Av *BORE* WD6 ...... 31 M6
Barham Cl *ALP/SUD* HA0 ...... 80 B6
  CHST BR7 ...... 161 H1
  HAYES BR2 ...... 175 L3
  ROMW/RG RM7 ...... 73 H3
  WEY KT13 ...... 164 C6
Barham Ct *ALP/SUD* HA0 ...... 80 C6
Barham Rd *CHST* BR7 ...... 161 H1
  CROY/NA CR0 ...... 172 C6
  DART DA1 ...... 147 G4
  RYNPK SW20 ...... 154 A3
Baring Cl *LEE/GVPK* SE12 ...... 142 H8
Baring Rd *BMLY* BR1 ...... 142 B8
  CROY/NA CR0 ...... 173 G3
  EBAR EN4 ...... 34 D6
  LEE/GVPK SE12 ...... 142 A5
Baring St *IS* N1 ...... 7 G4
Barker Dr *CAMTN* NW1 ...... 4 F2

Barkham Rd *TOTM* N17 ...... 67 K1
Bark Hart Rd *ORP* BR6 ...... 177 H3
Barking Rd *CAN/RD* E16 ...... 105 M4
  EHAM E6 ...... 88 F8
  PLSTW E13 ...... 106 B3
  POP/IOD E14 ...... 105 L5
Barkston Gdns *ECT* SW5 ...... 14 C6
Barkwood Cl *ROMW/RG* RM7 ...... 73 J6
Barkworth Rd
  BERM/RHTH SE16 ...... 122 B3
Barlborough St *NWCR* SE14 ...... 122 D5
Barlby Gdns *NKENS* W10 ...... 100 D3
Barlby Rd *NKENS* W10 ...... 100 C4
Barlee Crs *UX/CGN* UB8 ...... 94 C4
Barley Cl *BUSH* WD23 ...... 30 B8
Barleycorn Wy *EMPK* RM11 ...... 74 F7
Barley La *GDMY/SEVK* IG3 ...... 72 A7
Barley Mow Pas *CHSWK* W4 ...... 117 K3
Barley Mow Wy
  SHPTN TW17 ...... 149 G7
Barlow Cl *WLGTN* SM6 ...... 171 L8
Barlow Pl *MYFR/PICC* W1J 10 D7
Barlow Rd *ACT* W3 ...... 99 H7
  CRICK NW2 ...... 82 F6
  HPTN TW12 ...... 151 L3
Barlow St *WALW* SE17 ...... 19 H5
Barlow Wy *DAGW* RM9 ...... 109 K5
  RAIN RM13 ...... 109 L5
Barmeston Rd *CAT* SE6 ...... 141 H6
Barnaby Cl *RYLN/HDSTN* HA2 ...... 79 J2
Barnaby Pl *SKENS* SW7 ...... 15 C6
Barnabas Rd *HOM* E9 ...... 86 D6
Barnacre Cl *UX/CGN* UB8 ...... 94 D5
Barnard Cl *CHST* BR7 ...... 145 H5
  SUN TW16 ...... 150 B3
  WLGTN SM6 ...... 183 K1
Barnard Gdns *NWMAL* KT3 ...... 154 A7
  YEAD UB4 ...... 96 B3
Barnard Hl *MUSWH* N10 ...... 66 B3
Barnard Ms *BTSEA* SW11 ...... 137 L1
Barnardo Dr *BARK/HLT* IG6 ...... 71 J5
Barnardo St *WCHPL* E1 ...... 104 D5
Barnard Rd *BTSEA* SW11 ...... 137 L1
  EN EN1 ...... 37 H5
  MTCM CR4 ...... 156 A6
Barnards Pl *SAND/SEL* CR2 ...... 184 B2
Barnby Sq *SRTFD* E15 ...... 87 L8
Barn Cl *ASHF* TW15 ...... 149 H1
  BNSTD SM7 ...... 182 D8
  NTHLT UB5 ...... 77 M8
Barn Crs *PUR/KEN* CR8 ...... 184 D6
  STAN HA7 ...... 44 C8
Barncroft Cl *UX/CGN* UB8 ...... 95 H4
Barnehurst Av *BXLYHN* DA7 ...... 127 J6
Barnehurst Cl *ERITH* DA8 ...... 127 J6
Barnehurst Rd *BXLYHN* DA7 ...... 127 J7
Barn End Dr *RDART* DA2 ...... 146 C8
Barnes Av *BARN* SW13 ...... 118 A5
  NWDGN UB2 ...... 114 F2
Barnes Br *CHSWK* W4 ...... 117 L7
Barnes Cl *MNPK* E12 ...... 88 D4
Barnes Cray Rd *DART* DA1 ...... 146 A1
Barnesdale Crs
  STMC/STPC BR5 ...... 177 G1
Barnes End *NWMAL* KT3 ...... 154 A8
Barnes High St *BARN* SW13 ...... 117 M7
Barnes Rd *IL* IG1 ...... 89 J5
  UED N18 ...... 50 C6
Barnes St *POP/IOD* E14 ...... 104 E5
Barnes Ter *DEPT* SE8 ...... 122 F3
Barnet By-pass *BORE* WD6 ...... 32 E8
Barnet Dr *HAYES* BR2 ...... 175 L4
Barnet Gate La *BAR* EN5 ...... 45 M1
Barnet Hl *BAR* EN5 ...... 104 A2
Barnet Hl *BAR* EN5 ...... 33 M7
Barnet La *BORE* WD6 ...... 44 F1
  TRDG/WHET N20 ...... 46 F3
Barnet Rd *EBAR* EN4 ...... 34 A2
  MLHL NW7 ...... 45 L1
  POTB/CUF EN6 ...... 23 J6
  POTB/CUF EN6 ...... 23 J7
Barnett Cl *ERITH* DA8 ...... 127 M7
Barnett St *WCHPL* E1 ...... 104 B5
Barnet Wy (Barnet By-pass)
  MLHL NW7 ...... 45 K2
Barnet Wood Rd *HAYES* BR2 ...... 175 H5
Barney Cl *CHARL* SE7 ...... 124 B6
Barn Fld *BNSTD* SM7 ...... 182 B7
Barnfield Av *CROY/NA* CR0 ...... 173 J3
  KUTN/CMB KT2 ...... 134 D8
  MTCM CR4 ...... 156 B7
Barnfield Cl *GRH* DA9 ...... 147 M3
Barnfield Gdns *KUTN/CMB* KT2 ...... 152 E1
Barnfield Rd *BELV* DA17 ...... 126 F4
  EA W5 ...... 98 C3
  EDGW HA8 ...... 63 J2
  SAND/SEL CR2 ...... 184 C2
  STMC/STPC BR5 ...... 162 D6
  WOOL/PLUM SE18 ...... 125 H4
Barnfield Wood Cl *BECK* BR3 ...... 174 D1
Barnfield Wood Rd *BECK* BR3 ...... 174 C1
Barnham Rd *GFD/PVL* UB6 ...... 97 J2
Barnham St *STHWK* SE1 ...... 19 K1
Barnhill *PIN* HA5 ...... 60 C6
Barn Hl *WBLY* HA9 ...... 81 H2
Barnhill Av *HAYES* BR2 ...... 160 A8
Barnhill La *YEAD* UB4 ...... 96 B2
Barnhill Rd *WBLY* HA9 ...... 81 J3
  YEAD UB4 ...... 96 B3
Barnhurst Pth *OXHEY* WD19 ...... 42 C7
Barningham Wy
  CDALE/KGS NW9 ...... 63 J7
Barn Lea *RKW/CH/CXG* WD3 ...... 40 A3
Barnlea Cl *FELT* TW13 ...... 132 E6
Barnmead Gdns *DAGW* RM9 ...... 90 B3
Barnmead Rd *BECK* BR3 ...... 158 E4
  DAGW RM9 ...... 90 B3
Barn Ri *WBLY* HA9 ...... 81 C1
Barnsbury Cl *NWMAL* KT3 ...... 153 G5
Barnsbury Crs *BRYLDS* KT5 ...... 168 D2

Barnscroft *RYNPK* SW20 ...... 154 B6
Barnsbury Gv *HOLWY* N7 ...... 5 M1
Barnsbury La *BRYLDS* KT5 ...... 168 B4
Barnsbury Pk *IS* N1 ...... 6 A1
Barnsbury Rd *IS* N1 ...... 6 A2
Barnsbury Sq *IS* N1 ...... 6 A1
Barnsbury Ter *IS* N1 ...... 5 M2
Barnsdale Av *POP/IOD* E14 ...... 123 H2
Barnsdale Rd *MV/WKIL* W9 ...... 100 F3
Barnsfield Pl *UX/CGN* UB8 ...... 76 C8
Barnsley Rd *HARH* RM3 ...... 74 F1
Barnsley St *WCHPL* E1 ...... 104 B3
Barnstaple La *LEW* SE13 ...... 141 J1
Barnstaple Rd *HARH* RM3 ...... 56 C7
  RSLP HA4 ...... 77 G3
Barn Wy *WBLY* HA9 ...... 81 H1
Barnwell Rd *BRXS/STRHM* SW2 ...... 139 G2
  DART DA1 ...... 128 F8
Barnwood Cl *MV/WKIL* W9 ...... 8 C1
  RSLP HA4 ...... 77 K2
Baron Cl *BELMT* SM2 ...... 182 B5
  FBAR/BDGN N11 ...... 48 A7
Baroness Rd *BETH* E2 ...... 7 M7
Baronet Gv *TOTM* N17 ...... 68 A2
Baronet Rd *TOTM* N17 ...... 68 A2
Baron Gdns *BARK/HLT* IG6 ...... 71 J4
Baron Gv *MTCM* CR4 ...... 155 L7
Baron Rd *BCTR* RM8 ...... 90 D1
Baron's Cl *HMSMTH* W6 ...... 118 E3
Baronsfield Rd *TWK* TW1 ...... 134 B3
Barons Ga *EBAR* EN4 ...... 47 L1
Barons Md *HRW* HA1 ...... 61 L5
Baronsmead Rd *BARN* SW13 ...... 118 A6
Baronsmede *EA* W5 ...... 98 F8
Baronsmere Rd *EFNCH* N2 ...... 65 L5
Baron's Pl *STHWK* SE1 ...... 18 B2
The Barons *TWK* TW1 ...... 134 B3
Baron St *IS* N1 ...... 6 A6
Baron's Wk *CROY/NA* CR0 ...... 173 L1
Barque Ms *DEPT* SE8 ...... 123 G4
Barrack Rd *HSLWW* TW4 ...... 132 D1
Barra Hall Rd *HYS/HAR* UB3 ...... 95 L6
Barratt Av *WDGN* N22 ...... 66 F3
Barratt Wy *KTN/HRWW/W* HA3 ...... 61 K4
Barrenger Rd *MUSWH* N10 ...... 65 M2
Barrett Rd *WALTH* E17 ...... 69 J5
Barrett's Green Rd
  WLSDN NW10 ...... 99 J1
Barrett's Gv *STNW/STAM* N16 ...... 85 L7
Barrett St *MBLAR* W1H 10 B5
  MHST W1U 10 B5
Barrhill Rd
  BRXS/STRHM SW2 ...... 138 E6
Barriedale *NWCR* SE14 ...... 122 E6
Barringer Sq *TOOT* SW17 ...... 138 A8
Barrington Cl *CLAY* IG5 ...... 70 F2
Barrington Dr *DEN/HRF* UB9 ...... 58 A1
Barrington Ldg *WEY* KT13 ...... 164 C7
Barrington Rd *BRXN/ST* SW9 ...... 121 H8
  CEND/HSY/T N8 ...... 66 D6
  CHEAM SM3 ...... 170 A3
  MNPK E12 ...... 89 G6
  PUR/KEN CR8 ...... 183 J5
  WELL DA16 ...... 126 D7
Barrington Vls
  WOOL/PLUM SE18 ...... 125 G6
Barrow Av *CAR* SM5 ...... 182 F1
Barrow Cl *WCHMH* N21 ...... 49 H5
Barrowdene Cl *PIN* HA5 ...... 60 E3
Barrowell Gn *WCHMH* N21 ...... 49 H4
Barrowfield Cl *ED* N9 ...... 50 B5
Barrowgate Rd *CHSWK* W4 ...... 117 J3
Barrow Hedges Cl *CAR* SM5 ...... 182 E1
Barrow Hedges Wy *CAR* SM5 ...... 182 E1
Barrow Hl *WPK* KT4 ...... 168 E4
Barrow Hill Cl *WPK* KT4 ...... 168 E4
Barrow Hill Rd *STJWD* NW8 ...... 3 H6
Barrow La *CHESW* EN7 ...... 25 M4
Barrow Point Av *PIN* HA5 ...... 60 F3
Barrow Point La *PIN* HA5 ...... 60 F3
Barrow Rd *CROY/NA* CR0 ...... 172 A7
  STRHM/NOR SW16 ...... 156 D2
Barr Rd *POTB/CUF* EN6 ...... 23 J4
Barrs Rd *WLSDN* NW10 ...... 81 K7
Barry Av *BXLYHN* DA7 ...... 126 E5
  SEVS/STOTM N15 ...... 67 M7
Barry Cl *ORP* BR6 ...... 176 E5
Barry Rd *EDUL* SE22 ...... 140 A3
  EHAM E6 ...... 106 E5
  WLSDN NW10 ...... 81 J7
Barset Rd *PECK* SE15 ...... 122 C8
Barsons Cl *PGE/AN* SE20 ...... 158 C3
Barston Rd *WNWD* SE27 ...... 139 J6
Barstow Crs *BRXS/STRHM* SW2 ...... 138 F5
Barter St *NOXST/BSQ* WC1A 11 K3
Bartholomew Cl *STBT* EC1A 12 E3
  STBT EC1A 12 D3
  WAND/EARL SW18 ...... 137 J1
Bartholomew Dr *HARH* RM3 ...... 74 D3
Bartholomew La *OBST* EC2N 13 H5
Bartholomew Rd *KTTN* NW5 ...... 84 C6
Bartholomew Sq *FSBYE* EC1V 6 F9
Bartholomew St *STHWK* SE1 ...... 19 H4
Bartholomew Vls *KTTN* NW5 ...... 84 C6
Bartholomew Wy *SWLY* BR8 ...... 163 L6
Bartle Av *EHAM* E6 ...... 106 E1
Bartle Rd *NTGHL* W11 ...... 100 B5
Bartlett Cl *POP/IOD* E14 ...... 105 G5
Bartlett Ct *FLST/FETLN* EC4A 12 B4
Bartlett St *SAND/SEL* CR2 ...... 172 D7
Bartlow Gdns *CRW* RM5 ...... 73 K2
Barton Av *RAIN* RM13 ...... 109 G2
Barton Cl *BXLYHS* DA6 ...... 144 E2
  CHIG IG7 ...... 53 J4
  HDN NW4 ...... 64 A6
  PECK SE15 ...... 122 B8
  SHPTN TW17 ...... 164 B1
Barton Gn *NWMAL* KT3 ...... 153 K5
Barton Mdw *BARK/HLT* IG6 ...... 71 H5
Barton Rd *HCH* RM12 ...... 92 A1
  SCUP DA14 ...... 162 E2
  VX/NE SW8 ...... 120 D5
The Bartons *BORE* WD6 ...... 44 D1
Barton Wy *BORE* WD6 ...... 32 A5

RKW/CH/CXG WD3 ...... 28 B8
Bartram Cl *UX/CGN* UB8 ...... 95 H3
Bartram Rd *BROCKY* SE4 ...... 140 E2
Bartrams La *EBAR* EN4 ...... 34 C3
Bartrip St *HOM* E9 ...... 86 E6
Barts Cl *BECK* BR3 ...... 159 G8
Barward Cl
  WOOL/PLUM SE18 ...... 125 G1
Barwick Rd *FSTGT* E7 ...... 88 B4
Barwood Av *WKENS* W14 ...... 76 B8
Basden Gv *FELT* TW13 ...... 133 C6
Basedale Rd *DAGW* RM9 ...... 90 B7
Baseing Cl *EHAM* E6 ...... 107 G6
Bashley Rd *WLSDN* NW10 ...... 99 K3
Basil Av *EHAM* E6 ...... 106 E2
Basildene Rd *HSLWW* TW4 ...... 114 D8
Basildon Av *CLAY* IG5 ...... 71 G2
Basildon Cl *BELMT* SM2 ...... 182 B2
  WATW WD18 ...... 41 J1
Basildon Rd *ABYW* SE2 ...... 126 A2
Basil Gdns *CROY/NA* CR0 ...... 173 K3
  WNWD SE27 ...... 157 J1
Basilon Rd *BXLYHN* DA7 ...... 126 E7
Basil St *CHEL* SW3 ...... 15 L2
Basing Cl *THDIT* KT7 ...... 166 F7
Basing Dr *BXLY* DA5 ...... 144 F3
Basingfield Rd *THDIT* KT7 ...... 166 F2
Basinghall Av *CITYW* EC2V 13 G4
Basinghall Gdns *BELMT* SM2 ...... 182 B2
Basinghall St *CITYW* EC2V 13 G4
Basing Hl *GLDGN* NW11 ...... 82 F1
  WBLY HA9 ...... 80 F2
Basing Pl *BETH* E2 ...... 7 K7
Basing Rd *BNSTD* SM7 ...... 181 M8
Basing St *NTGHL* W11 ...... 100 F5
Basing Wy *FNCH* N3 ...... 65 G4
  THDIT KT7 ...... 166 F2
Basire St *IS* N1 ...... 6 F3
Baskerville Gdns
  WLSDN NW10 ...... 81 L4
Baskerville Rd
  WAND/EARL SW18 ...... 137 L4
Basket Gdns *ELTH/MOT* SE9 ...... 142 E2
Baslow Cl *KTN/HRWW/W* HA3 ...... 61 K2
Baslow Wk *CLPT* E5 ...... 86 D4
Basnett Rd *BTSEA* SW11 ...... 120 A8
Bassano St *EDUL* SE22 ...... 139 M2
Bassant Rd *WOOL/PLUM* SE18 ...... 125 M4
Bassein Park Rd *SHB* W12 ...... 99 M8
Bassett Cl *BELMT* SM2 ...... 182 B2
Bassett Gdns *ISLW* TW7 ...... 115 J5
Bassett Rd *NKENS* W10 ...... 100 D5
  UX/CGN UB8 ...... 76 C7
Bassetts Cl *ORP* BR6 ...... 176 B6
Bassetts Wy *ORP* BR6 ...... 176 B6
Bassett St *KTTN* NW5 ...... 84 A6
Bassett Wy *GFD/PVL* UB6 ...... 97 H5
Bassingham Rd *ALP/SUD* HA0 ...... 80 D6
  WAND/EARL SW18 ...... 137 J4
Basswood Cl *PECK* SE15 ...... 122 B8
Bastable Av *BARK* IG11 ...... 108 A1
Baston Manor Rd *WWKM* BR4 ...... 175 H5
Baston Rd *HAYES* BR2 ...... 175 H4
Bastwick St *FSBYE* EC1V 6 D9
Basuto Rd *FUL/PGN* SW6 ...... 119 G6
Batavia Cl *SUN* TW16 ...... 150 B4
Batavia Rd *NWCR* SE14 ...... 122 F2
  SUN TW16 ...... 150 B4
Batchelor St *IS* N1 ...... 6 B5
Batchwood Gn
  STMC/STPC BR5 ...... 162 A7
Batchworth Hill London Rd
  RKW/CH/CXG WD3 ...... 40 E4
Batchworth La *NTHWD* HA6 ...... 41 J7
Bateman Cl *BARK* IG11 ...... 89 J6
Bateman Rd *CHING* E4 ...... 51 C8
  RKW/CH/CXG WD3 ...... 41 G1
Bateman's Rw *SDTCH* EC2A 7 K9
Bateman St *SOHO/SHAV* W1D 11 G5
Bates Crs *CROY/NA* CR0 ...... 172 A8
  STRHM/NOR SW16 ...... 156 C3
Bates Rd *HARH* RM3 ...... 75 C1
Bate St *POP/IOD* E14 ...... 104 F6
Bathgate Rd *WIM/MER* SW19 ...... 136 D7
Bath Gv *BETH* E2 ...... 104 A1
Bath House Rd *CROY/NA* CR0 ...... 171 L3
Bath Pas *KUT* KT1 ...... 152 D5
Bath Rd *CHSWK* W4 ...... 117 L2
  DART DA1 ...... 146 B4
  ED N9 ...... 50 B4
  FSTGT E7 ...... 88 D6
  HEST TW5 ...... 114 B6
  HSLWW TW4 ...... 114 D7
  HTHAIR TW6 ...... 113 H6
  WDR/YW UB7 ...... 112 F6
Baths Ap *FUL/PGN* SW6 ...... 118 F5
Baths Rd *BMLY* BR1 ...... 160 D7
Bath St *FSBYE* EC1V 6 F8
Bath Ter *STHWK* SE1 ...... 18 E4
Bathurst Av *WIM/MER* SW19 ...... 155 H4
Bathurst Gdns *WLSDN* NW10 ...... 100 B1
Bathurst Ms *BAY/PAD* W2 ...... 9 H6
Bathurst Rd *IL* IG1 ...... 89 H1
Bathurst St *BAY/PAD* W2 ...... 9 H6
Bathway *WOOL/PLUM* SE18 ...... 125 G2
Batley Cl *MTCM* CR4 ...... 170 F2
Batley Pl *STNW/STAM* N16 ...... 85 M3
Batley Rd *STNW/STAM* N16 ...... 85 M3
Batman Cl *SHB* W12 ...... 100 C6
Baton Cl *PUR* RM19 ...... 129 K2
Batoum Gdns *HMSMTH* W6 ...... 118 C1
Batson St *SHB* W12 ...... 100 A8
Batsworth Rd *MTCM* CR4 ...... 155 K6
Batten Cl *EHAM* E6 ...... 106 E1
Batten St *BTSEA* SW11 ...... 119 L8
Battersby Rd *CAT* SE6 ...... 141 K6
Battersea Br *BTSEA* SW11 ...... 119 K5
Battersea Bridge Rd
  BTSEA SW11 ...... 119 L5
Battersea Church Rd
  BTSEA SW11 ...... 119 K6
Battersea High St *BTSEA* SW11 ...... 119 K6
Battersea Park Rd *BTSEA* SW11 ...... 120 A6
Battersea Ri *BTSEA* SW11 ...... 137 L2
Battery Rd *THMD* SE28 ...... 107 L8

Battishill St *IS* N1 ...... 6 C1
Battle Bridge La *STHWK* SE1 ...... 13 J3
Battle Bridge Rd *CAMTN* NW1 ...... 5 J6
Battle Cl *WIM/MER* SW19 ...... 155 J2
Battledean Rd *HBRY* N5 ...... 85 H5
Battle Rd *ERITH* DA8 ...... 127 J2
Batty St *WCHPL* E1 ...... 104 A5
Baudwin Rd *CAT* SE6 ...... 141 L6
Baugh Rd *SCUP* DA14 ...... 162 C1
The Baulk *WAND/EARL* SW18 ...... 137 G4
Bavant Rd *STRHM/NOR* SW16 ...... 156 E5
Bavaria Rd *ARCH* N19 ...... 84 E2
Bavent Rd *CMBW* SE5 ...... 121 J7
Bawdale Rd *EDUL* SE22 ...... 139 M4
Bawdsey Av *GNTH/NBYPK* IG2 ...... 71 M5
Bawtree Cl *BELMT* SM2 ...... 182 C3
Bawtree Rd *NWCR* SE14 ...... 122 E5
  UX/CGN UB8 ...... 76 D6
Bawtry Rd *TRDG/WHET* N20 ...... 47 M5
Baxendale *TRDG/WHET* N20 ...... 47 L4
Baxendale St *BETH* E2 ...... 104 A2
Baxter Cl *HGDN/ICK* UB10 ...... 95 H2
  NWDGN UB2 ...... 115 H1
Baxter Rd *CAN/RD* E16 ...... 106 C5
  IL IG1 ...... 89 H5
  IS N1 ...... 85 K6
  UED N18 ...... 50 B6
Baycroft Cl *PIN* HA5 ...... 60 C4
Bayfield Rd *ELTH/MOT* SE9 ...... 142 E3
Bayford Rd *WLSDN* NW10 ...... 100 D2
Bayford St *HACK* E8 ...... 86 B1
Bayham Pl *CAMTN* NW1 ...... 4 E4
Bayham Rd *CHSWK* W4 ...... 117 K1
  MRDN SM4 ...... 155 H7
  WEA W13 ...... 98 B6
Bayham St *CAMTN* NW1 ...... 4 E4
Bayhurst Dr *NTHWD* HA6 ...... 41 M8
Bayleaf Cl *HPTN* TW12 ...... 151 K1
Bayley St *FITZ* W1T 11 G3
Baylis Rd *STHWK* SE1 ...... 18 A3
Bayliss Av *THMD* SE28 ...... 108 D6
Bayliss Cl *STHGT/OAK* N14 ...... 35 L8
Bayly Rd *DART* DA1 ...... 147 G3
Bay Manor La *WTHK* RM20 ...... 129 M4
Bayne Cl *EHAM* E6 ...... 106 F5
Baynes Cl *EN* EN1 ...... 37 G4
Baynes Ms *HAMP* NW3 ...... 83 K6
Baynes St *CAMTN* NW1 ...... 4 E1
Baynham Cl *BXLY* DA5 ...... 144 F3
Bayonne Rd *FUL/PGN* SW6 ...... 118 K4
Bays Cl *SYD* SE26 ...... 158 C5
Baysfarm Ct *WDR/YW* UB7 ...... 112 C6
Bayston Rd *STNW/STAM* N16 ...... 85 M3
Bayswater Rd *BAY/PAD* W2 ...... 8 F7
Baythorne St *BOW* E3 ...... 104 F4
  BOW E3 ...... 104 F4
Baytree Cl *BFN/LL* DA15 ...... 143 H5
  BMLY BR1 ...... 160 D4
Baytree Rd *BRXS/STRHM* SW2 ...... 138 F1
Bay Tree Wk *WAT* WD17 ...... 28 F3
Baywood Sq *CHIG* IG7 ...... 54 B6
Bazalgette Cl *NWMAL* KT3 ...... 153 J8
Bazalgette Gdns *NWMAL* KT3 ...... 153 K8
Bazely St *POP/IOD* E14 ...... 105 K3
Bazile Rd *WCHMH* N21 ...... 49 G1
Beacham Cl *CHARL* SE7 ...... 124 D4
Beachborough Rd *BMLY* BR1 ...... 141 J8
Beachcroft Rd *WAN* E11 ...... 87 L3
Beach Gv *FELT* TW13 ...... 133 G7
Beachy Rd *BOW* E3 ...... 87 G7
Beacon Cl *UX/CGN* UB8 ...... 76 D5
Beacon Hl *HOLWY* N7 ...... 84 F5
  PUR RM19 ...... 129 H3
Beacon Rd *ERITH* DA8 ...... 128 B5
  HTHAIR TW6 ...... 131 G3
  LEW SE13 ...... 141 K3
Beaconsfield Cl
  BKHTH/KID SE3 ...... 124 A4
  CHSWK W4 ...... 117 J3
Beaconsfield Pl *EW* KT17 ...... 180 E5
Beaconsfield Rd
  BKHTH/KID SE3 ...... 124 A4
  BMLY BR1 ...... 160 E6
  BRYLDS KT5 ...... 167 M2
  BXLY DA5 ...... 145 L6
  CAN/RD E16 ...... 105 M3
  CHSWK W4 ...... 117 K1
  CROY/NA CR0 ...... 172 D1
  EA W5 ...... 98 C4
  ED N9 ...... 50 A5
  ELTH/MOT SE9 ...... 142 E7
  ESH/CLAY KT10 ...... 178 L1
  FBAR/BDGN N11 ...... 48 A6
  HYS/HAR UB3 ...... 96 C7
  LEY E10 ...... 87 J3
  NWMAL KT3 ...... 153 K5
  PEND EN3 ...... 37 K2
  SEVS/STOTM N15 ...... 67 L5
  TRDG/WHET N20 ...... 47 M5
  TWK TW1 ...... 134 B4
  WALTH E17 ...... 69 H6
  WALW SE17 ...... 19 H6
  WLSDN NW10 ...... 81 M6
Beaconsfield Terrace Rd
  WKENS W14 ...... 118 E1
Beaconsfield Wk
  FUL/PGN SW6 ...... 118 F6
Beacontree Av *WALTH* E17 ...... 69 K2
Beacontree Rd *WAN* E11 ...... 69 M8
Beacon Wy *RKW/CH/CXG* WD3 ...... 40 B2
Beadlow Cl *MRDN* SM4 ...... 170 D1
Beadman Pl *WNWD* SE27 ...... 139 H8
Beadman St *WNWD* SE27 ...... 139 H8
Beadnell Rd *FSTH* SE23 ...... 140 D5
Beadon Rd *HAYES* BR2 ...... 160 A7
  HMSMTH W6 ...... 118 C2
Beaford Gv *RYNPK* SW20 ...... 154 E6
Beagle Cl *FELT* TW13 ...... 132 B8
  RAD WD7 ...... 30 D2
Beagles Cl *STMC/STPC* BR5 ...... 177 K4
Beak St *REGST* W1B 10 F6
Beal Cl *WELL* DA16 ...... 126 A6
Beale Pl *BOW* E3 ...... 104 F1
Beale Rd *BOW* E3 ...... 86 F8
Beales La *WEY* KT13 ...... 164 B5
Beal Rd *IL* IG1 ...... 89 G2

Beam Av *DAGE* RM10 **91** H8
Beaminster Gdns *BARK/HLT* IG6 **71** H4
Beamish Dr *BUSH* WD23 **43** J3
Beamish Rd *ED* N9 **50** A3
STMC/STPC BR5 **177** J2
Beamway *DAGE* RM10 **91** K7
Bean Rd *BXLYHS* DA6 **144** D1
Beanshaw *ELTH/MOT* SE9 **143** G8
Beansland Gv *CHDH* RM6 **72** E3
Bear Cl *ROMW/RG* RM7 **73** H7
Beardell St *NRWD* SE19 **157** M2
Beard Rd *RCHPK/HAM* TW10 **152** F1
Beardsfield *PLSTW* E13 **106** A1
Beard's Hl *HPTN* TW12 **151** G4
Beards Hill Cl *HPTN* TW12 **151** G4
Beardsley Wy *ACT* W3 **99** K8
Beards Rd *ASHF* TW15 **149** L2
Bearfield Rd *KUTN/CMB* KT2 **152** E3
Bear Gdns *STHWK* SE1 **12** E8
Bearing Cl *CHIG* IG7 **54** A6
Bearing Wy *CHIG* IG7 **54** A6
Bear La *STHWK* SE1 **12** D8
Bear Rd *FELT* TW13 **132** D8
Bearstead Ri *BROCKY* SE4 **140** F2
Bear St *LSQ/SEVD* WC2H **11** H6
Bearwood Cl *POTB/CUF* EN6 **23** K4
Beasant House *WATN* WD24 **29** K5
Beasley's Ait *SHPTN* TW17 **164** F1
Beasley's Ait La *SUN* TW16 **164** F1
Beatrice Av *STRHM/NOR* SW16 **156** F6
WBLY HA9 **80** E5
Beatrice Cl *PIN* HA5 **60** A5
PLSTW E13 **106** A3
Beatrice Rd *ED* N9 **50** C2
FSBYPK N4 **67** G8
RCHPK/HAM TW10 **134** F2
STHL UB1 **96** F7
STHWK SE1 **122** A2
WALTH E17 **69** G6
Beattie Cl *EBED/NFELT* TW14 **131** M5
Beattock Ri *MUSWH* N10 **66** B5
Beatty Rd *CHES/WCR* EN8 **26** F7
STAN HA7 **44** C8
STNW/STAM N16 **85** L4
Beatty St *CAMTN* NW1 **4** E5
Beattyville Gdns *BARK/HLT* IG6 **71** G5
Beauchamp Gdns
RKW/CH/CXG WD3 **40** A3
Beauchamp Pl *BORE* WD6 **32** B2
CHEL SW3 **15** K3
Beauchamp Rd *BTSEA* SW11 **137** L1
E/WMO/HCT KT8 **151** H8
FSTGT E7 **88** B7
SUT SM1 **170** A7
THHTH CR7 **157** K4
TWK TW1 **134** A4
Beauchamp St *HCIRC* EC1N **12** A3
Beauchamp Ter
PUT/ROE SW15 **118** B8
Beauclerc Rd *HMSMTH* W6 **118** B1
Beauclerk Cl *FELT* TW13 **132** B5
Beaufort *EHAM* E6 **107** G4
Beaufort Av *KTN/HRWW/W* HA3 **62** A5
Beaufort Cl *CHING* E4 **51** H8
EA W5 **98** F4
PUT/ROE SW15 **136** C5
ROMW/RG RM7 **73** J5
Beaufort Dr *GLDGN* NW11 **65** G5
Beaufort Gdns *CHEL* SW3 **15** K3
HDN NW4 **64** C7
HEST TW5 **114** E6
IL IG1 **89** G1
STRHM/NOR SW16 **156** F3
Beaufort Rd *EA* W5 **98** F4
KUT KT1 **152** E7
RCHPK/HAM TW10 **134** C8
RSLP HA4 **77** K2
TWK TW1 **134** C4
Beaufort St *CHEL* SW3 **15** G9
Beaufort Wy *EW* KT17 **181** G1
Beaufoy Rd *TOTM* N17 **67** L1
Beaulieu Av *CAN/RD* E16 **106** B7
SYD SE26 **140** B8
Beaulieu Cl *CDALE/KGS* NW9 **63** L5
HSLWW TW4 **132** F2
MTCM CR4 **156** A4
OXHEY WD19 **42** C3
TWK TW1 **134** D3
Beaulieu Dr *PIN* HA5 **60** D7
WAB EN9 **27** H6
Beaulieu Gdns *WCHMH* N21 **49** J2
Beaulieu Pl *CHSWK* W4 **117** J1
Beauly Wy *ROM* RM1 **73** L2
Beaumont Av *ALP/SUD* HA0 **80** B5
RCH/KEW TW9 **116** F8
RYLN/HDSTN HA2 **61** H7
WKENS W14 **118** F3
Beaumont Cl *GPK* RM2 **74** C3
Beaumont Ct *ALP/SUD* HA0 **80** C5
Beaumont Crs *RAIN* RM13 **92** A6
WKENS W14 **118** F3
Beaumont Dr *ASHF* TW15 **149** K1
Beaumont Gv *WCHPL* E1 **104** D3
Beaumont Ms
CAVSQ/HST W1G **10** B2
Beaumont Pl *BAR* EN5 **33** M4
FITZ W1T **4** F9
ISLW TW7 **133** M2
Beaumont Ri *ARCH* N19 **84** D1
Beaumont Rd *CHSWK* W4 **117** J1
LEY E10 **69** J8
LEY E10 **69** H8
LEY E10 **69** H8
NRWD SE19 **157** J2
PLSTW E13 **106** B2
PUR/KEN CR8 **184** A6
STMC/STPC BR5 **176** D1
WIM/MER SW19 **136** E4
Beaumont Sq *WCHPL* E1 **104** D4
Beaumont St *MHST* W1U **10** B2
Beauvais Ter *NTHLT* UB5 **96** D2
Beauval Rd *EDUL* SE22 **139** M3
Beaverbank Rd *ELTH/MOT* SE9 **143** K5
Beaver Cl *HPTN* TW12 **151** H4
PGE/AN SE20 **158** A3
Beavers La *HSLWW* TW4 **114** C8
Beaverwood Rd *CHST* BR7 **161** L1
Beavor La *HMSMTH* W6 **118** A2
Bebbington Rd
WOOL/PLUM SE18 **125** L2
Beblets Cl *ORP* BR6 **176** F7
Beccles St *POP/IOD* E14 **104** F5
Bec Cl *RSLP* HA4 **78** D3
Beck Cl *LEW* SE13 **123** H6
Beck Ct *BECK* BR3 **158** D6
Beckenham Gdns *ED* N9 **49** L5
Beckenham Gv *HAYES* BR2 **159** K5
Beckenham Hill Rd *BECK* BR3 **159** H2
Beckenham La *HAYES* BR2 **159** L5
Beckenham Place Pk
BECK BR3 **159** H3
Beckenham Rd *BECK* BR3 **158** D4
WWKM BR4 **174** B2
Beckenshaw Gdns *BNSTD* SM7 **182** E8
Becket Av *EHAM* E6 **107** G2
Becket Cl *SNWD* SE25 **173** G1
Becket Fold *HRW* HA1 **61** M6
Becket Rd *UED* N18 **50** C6
Becket St *STHWK* SE1 **19** G3
Beckett Av *PUR/KEN* CR8 **184** B8
Beckett Cl *BELV* DA17 **126** E1
STRHM/NOR SW16 **138** D6
WLSDN NW10 **81** K6
Becketts Cl *EBED/NFELT* TW14 **132** B3
ORP BR6 **176** F5
Becketts Pl *KUT* KT1 **152** D4
Beckett Wk *BECK* BR3 **158** E2
Beckford Dr *STMC/STPC* BR5 **176** D2
Beckford Pl *WALW* SE17 **18** F8
Beckford Rd *CROY/NA* CR0 **172** F1
Beck La *BECK* BR3 **158** D6
Becklow Rd *SHB* W12 **99** M8
Beck River Pk *BECK* BR3 **159** G4
Beck Rd *HACK* E8 **86** B8
Becks Rd *SCUP* DA14 **144** A7
Beckton Rd *CAN/RD* E16 **105** M4
Beck Wy *BECK* BR3 **158** F6
Beckway Rd *STRHM/NOR* SW16 **156** D5
Beckway St *WALW* SE17 **19** H6
Beckwith Rd *HNHL* SE24 **139** K3
Beclands Rd *TOOT* SW17 **156** A2
Becmead Av *KTN/HRWW/W* HA3 **62** B6
STRHM/NOR SW16 **138** D8
Becondale Rd *NRWD* SE19 **157** L1
Becontree Av *BCTR* RM8 **90** D2
Bective Rd *FSTGT* E7 **88** A4
PUT/ROE SW15 **136** F1
Becton Pl *ERITH* DA8 **127** H5
Bedale Rd *ENC/FH* EN2 **36** C3
HARH RM3 **57** G7
Bedale St *STHWK* SE1 **13** G9
Beddington Farm Rd
CROY/NA CR0 **171** L3
Beddington Gdns *CAR* SM5 **171** G8
WLGTN SM6 **171** H8
Beddington Gn
STMC/STPC BR5 **161** M4
Beddington Gv *WLGTN* SM6 **171** K7
Beddington La *CROY/NA* CR0 **171** L4
MTCM CR4 **171** J1
Beddington Rd *GDMY/SEVK* IG3 **71** M8
STMC/STPC BR5 **161** L4
Bede Cl *PIN* HA5 **60** D2
Bedens Rd *SCUP* DA14 **162** E2
Bede Rd *CHDH* RM6 **72** C7
Bedfont Cl *EBED/NFELT* TW14 **131** J3
MTCM CR4 **156** A5
Bedfont Ct *STWL/WRAY* TW19 **112** A8
Bedfont Green Cl
EBED/NFELT TW14 **131** J5
Bedfont La *EBED/NFELT* TW14 **131** L4
Bedfont Rd *EBED/NFELT* TW14 **131** J5
FELT TW13 **131** M7
STWL/WRAY TW19 **130** F3
Bedford Av *BAR* EN5 **33** M8
RSQ WC1B **11** H3
YEAD UB4 **96** B5
Bedfordbury *CHCR* WC2N **11** J6
Bedford Cl *CHSWK* W4 **117** L4
MUSWH N10 **66** A1
Bedford Ct *CHCR* WC2N **11** J7
Bedford Crs *PEND* EN3 **26** E8
Bedford Gdns *HCH* RM12 **92** C2
KENS W8 **8** A9
Bedford Hl *BAL* SW12 **138** B6
Bedford Pk *CROY/NA* CR0 **172** C3
Bedford Pl *CROY/NA* CR0 **172** D3
RSQ WC1B **11** J2
Bedford Rd *BFN/LL* DA15 **143** L7
CEND/HSY/T N8 **66** D7
CHSWK W4 **117** K1
CLAP SW4 **138** E1
DART DA1 **147** G4
ED N9 **50** B2
EFNCH N2 **65** L4
EHAM E6 **89** G8
HRW HA1 **61** J7
IL IG1 **89** H3
MLHL NW7 **45** L4
NTHWD HA6 **41** J6
ORP BR6 **177** H4
RSLP HA4 **77** M4
SEVS/STOTM N15 **67** K5
SWFD E18 **70** A3
WALTH E17 **69** G3
WDGN N22 **66** E2
WEA W13 **98** B6
WHTN TW2 **133** K7
WPK KT4 **169** J4
Bedford Rw *FSBYW* WC1X **11** M2
Bedford Sq *RSQ* WC1B **11** H3
Bedford St *COVGDN* WC2E **11** J6
WATN WD24 **29** H4
Bedford Wy *STPAN* WC1H **11** H1
Bedgebury Gdns
WIM/MER SW19 **136** E6
Bedgebury Rd *ELTH/MOT* SE9 **142** D1
Bedivere Rd *BMLY* BR1 **142** A7
Bedlow Wy *CROY/NA* CR0 **171** M6
Bedmond Rd *ABLGY* WD5 **20** F2
Bedonwell Rd *BELV* DA17 **126** E4
BXLYHN DA7 **126** F4
Bedser Cl *THHTH* CR7 **157** J6
Bedser Dr *NTHLT* UB5 **79** K5
Bedster Gdns *E/WMO/HCT* KT8 **151** H5
Bedwardine Rd *NRWD* SE19 **157** L3
Bedwell Gdns *HYS/HAR* UB3 **113** L3
Bedwell Rd *BELV* DA17 **127** G3
TOTM N17 **67** L2
Beeby Rd *CAN/RD* E16 **106** B4
Beech Av *ACT* W3 **99** L7
BFN/LL DA15 **144** A4
BKHH IG9 **52** B4
BTFD TW8 **116** B5
ENC/FH EN2 **25** G8
RSLP HA4 **78** B1
SAND/SEL CR2 **184** D4
SWLY BR8 **163** M7
TRDG/WHET N20 **47** L3
UPMR RM14 **93** H3
Beech Cl *ASHF* TW15 **149** K1
CAR SM5 **170** F4
COB KT11 **178** A5
DEPT SE8 **122** F4
ED N9 **50** A1
HCH RM12 **92** B3
PUT/ROE SW15 **136** A4
RYNPK SW20 **154** C2
STWL/WRAY TW19 **130** D4
SUN TW16 **150** D5
WDR/YW UB7 **113** G1
WOT/HER KT12 **165** J6
Beech Copse *BMLY* BR1 **160** F5
SAND/SEL CR2 **172** E7
Beechcroft *CHST* BR7 **161** G3
Beechcroft Av *BXLYHN* DA7 **127** K6
GLDGN NW11 **64** F8
NWMAL KT3 **153** J4
PUR/KEN CR8 **184** D8
RKW/CH/CXG WD3 **41** J1
RYLN/HDSTN HA2 **61** G8
STHL UB1 **96** F7
Beechcroft Cl *HEST* TW5 **114** E5
ORP BR6 **176** D6
STRHM/NOR SW16 **156** F1
Beechcroft Gdns *WBLY* HA9 **80** F3
Beechcroft Rd *BUSH* WD23 **30** A8
CHSGTN KT9 **167** M5
MORT/ESHN SW14 **117** J8
ORP BR6 **176** D6
SWFD E18 **70** B3
TOOT SW17 **137** M7
Beechdale *WCHMH* N21 **48** F4
Beechdale Rd
BRXS/STRHM SW2 **138** F3
Beech Dell *HAYES* BR2 **175** M6
Beech Dr *BORE* WD6 **31** M3
EFNCH N2 **65** M4
Beechen Cliff Wy *ISLW* TW7 **115** M6
Beechengrove *PIN* HA5 **60** F4
Beechen Gv *WAT* WD17 **29** H6
Beechen Pl *FSTH* SE23 **140** C6
The Beeches Av *CAR* SM5 **182** E1
Beeches Cl *PGE/AN* SE20 **158** C4
Beeches Rd *CHEAM* SM3 **169** L3
TOOT SW17 **137** L7
Beeches Wk *CAR* SM5 **182** D2
Beechfield *BNSTD* SM7 **182** B6
Beechfield Gdns *ROMW/RG* RM7 **73** J8
Beechfield Rd *BMLY* BR1 **160** C5
CAT SE6 **140** F5
ERITH DA8 **127** L5
FSBYPK N4 **67** J7
Beechfield Wk *WAB* EN9 **27** K8
Beech Gdns *DAGE* RM10 **91** H7
EA W5 **98** E8
Beech Gv *BARK/HLT* IG6 **53** L8
MTCM CR4 **156** D8
NWMAL KT3 **153** K6
SOCK/AV RM15 **111** J8
Beech Hall Crs *CHING* E4 **69** K1
Beech Hall Rd *CHING* E4 **69** J1
Beech Hl *EBAR* EN4 **34** D3
Beech Hill Av *EBAR* EN4 **34** C4
Beech Hill Gdns *WAB* EN9 **39** H2
Beechhill Rd *ELTH/MOT* SE9 **143** G2
Beech House Rd *CROY/NA* CR0 **172** D5
Beechmont Cl *BMLY* BR1 **159** L1
Beechmore Gdns *CHEAM* SM3 **169** K4
Beechmore Rd *BTSEA* SW11 **119** M6
Beechmount Av *HNWL* W7 **97** K4
Beecholme Av *MTCM* CR4 **156** B4
Beechpark Wy *WAT* WD17 **28** E2
Beech Rd *DART* DA1 **146** D5
EBED/NFELT TW14 **131** L4
EPSOM KT18 **180** F8
FBAR/BDGN N11 **48** E8
STRHM/NOR SW16 **156** E5
WATN WD24 **29** G2
WEY KT13 **164** D6
Beechrow *KUTN/CMB* KT2 **134** E8
Beech St *ROMW/RG* RM7 **73** J5
Beech St (Below) *STBT* EC1A **12** E2
Beech Tree Cl *STAN* HA7 **44** C7
Beech Tree Gld *CHING* E4 **51** M3
Beech Tree La *STA* TW18 **148** B5
Beech Tree Pl *SUT* SM1 **170** B7
Beechvale Cl *NFNCH/WDSP* N12 **47** L7
Beech Wk *DART* DA1 **146** A1
EW KT17 **181** G4
MLHL NW7 **45** K8
Beechway *BXLY* DA5 **144** D3
Beech Wy *EW* KT17 **180** F8
FELT TW13 **133** G7
WLSDN NW10 **81** K7
Beechwood Av *COUL/CHIP* CR5 **183** H8
FNCH N3 **64** F4
GFD/PVL UB6 **97** H2
HYS/HAR UB3 **95** K6
ORP BR6 **176** E8
POTB/CUF EN6 **23** H6
RCH/KEW TW9 **117** G6
RSLP HA4 **77** M2
RYLN/HDSTN HA2 **79** H3
STA TW18 **148** B2
SUN TW16 **150** A2
THHTH CR7 **157** H7
UX/CGN UB8 **94** F5
WEY KT13 **164** E6
Beechwood Cl *MLHL* NW7 **45** L7
SURB KT6 **167** J2
WEY KT13 **164** E6
Beechwood Crs *BXLYHN* DA7 **144** C1
Beechwood Dr *COB* KT11 **178** A4
HAYES BR2 **175** K6
WFD IG8 **51** M7
Beechwood Gdns *CLAY* IG5 **70** F6
RAIN RM13 **110** B4
RYLN/HDSTN HA2 **79** H3
Beechwood Gv *ACT* W3 **99** L6
Beechwood Mnr *WEY* KT13 **164** E6
Beechwood Ms *ED* N9 **50** A4
Beechwood Pk *SWFD* E18 **70** A4
Beechwood Ri *CHST* BR7 **143** H8
WATN WD24 **29** H1
Beechwood Rd *CEND/HSY/T* N8 **66** D5
HACK E8 **85** M6
SAND/SEL CR2 **184** E2
Beechworth Cl *HAMP* NW3 **83** H2
Beecot La *WOT/HER* KT12 **165** J4
Beecroft Rd *BROCKY* SE4 **140** E2
Beehive Cl *BORE* WD6 **44** D1
HACK E8 **7** L1
HGDN/ICK UB10 **76** F7
Beehive La *REDBR* IG4 **70** F6
Beehive Pl *BRXN/ST* SW9 **121** G8
Beehive Rd *CHESW* EN7 **25** H1
Beeken Dene *ORP* BR6 **176** C6
Beeleigh Rd *MRDN* SM4 **155** H7
Beeston Cl *OXHEY* WD19 **42** D6
Beeston Pl *BGVA* SW1W **16** D4
Beeston Rd *EBAR* EN4 **47** K1
Beeston Wy *EBED/NFELT* TW14 **132** C3
Beethoven Rd *BORE* WD6 **44** C2
Beethoven St *NKENS* W10 **100** E2
Beeton Cl *PIN* HA5 **61** G1
Begbie Rd *BKTH/KID* SE3 **124** C6
Beggars Bush La *WATW* WD18 **28** D8
Beggar's Roost La *SUT* SM1 **170** A8
Begonia Cl *EHAM* E6 **106** E4
Begonia Pl *HPTN* TW12 **151** G2
Beira St *BAL* SW12 **138** B4
Bekesbourne St
POP/IOD E14 **104** E5
Belcroft Cl *BMLY* BR1 **159** M3
Beldham Gdns
E/WMO/HCT KT8 **151** H6
Belfairs *OXHEY* WD19 **42** D7
Belfairs Dr *CHDH* RM6 **72** C8
Belfast Rd *SNWD* SE25 **158** B7
STNW/STAM N16 **85** M2
Belfield Rd *HOR/WEW* KT19 **180** D2
Belford Gv *WOOL/PLUM* SE18 **125** G2
Belford Rd *BORE* WD6 **31** M3
Belfort Rd *PECK* SE15 **122** C7
Belfry Av *DEN/HRF* UB9 **58** A2
Belgrade Rd *HPTN* TW12 **151** H4
STNW/STAM N16 **85** L4
Belgrave Av *GPK* RM2 **74** C4
Belgrave Cl *ACT* W3 **99** J8
MLHL NW7 **45** K7
STHGT/OAK N14 **35** J8
STMC/STPC BR5 **162** C7
WOT/HER KT12 **165** H6
Belgrave Crs *SUN* TW16 **150** B4
Belgrave Gdns *STHGT/OAK* N14 **35** K8
STJWD NW8 **2** D4
Belgrave Ms *UX/CGN* UB8 **94** D7
Belgrave Ms South *KTBR* SW1X **16** B3
Belgrave Ms West *KTBR* SW1X **16** A3
Belgrave Pl *KTBR* SW1X **16** B4
Belgrave Rd *BARN* SW13 **117** M5
HSLWW TW4 **114** F8
IL IG1 **89** G2
LEY E10 **87** J1
MTCM CR4 **155** K6
PIM SW1V **16** E6
PLSTW E13 **106** C3
SNWD SE25 **157** M7
SUN TW16 **150** B4
WALTH E17 **69** G7
WAN E11 **88** A1
Belgrave Sq *KTBR* SW1X **16** A3
Belgrave St *WCHPL* E1 **104** D4
Belgrave Wk *MTCM* CR4 **155** K6
Belgravia Cl *BAR* EN5 **33** M6
Belgravia Gdns *BMLY* BR1 **159** L2
Belgravia Ms *KUT* KT1 **152** D7
Belgrove St *CAMTN* NW1 **5** J7
Belinda Rd *BRXN/ST* SW9 **121** H8
Belitha Vls *IS* N1 **5** M1
Bellamy Cl *ECT* SW5 **118** F3
EDGW HA8 **45** J5
HGDN/ICK UB10 **77** G3
WAT WD17 **29** G4
Bellamy Dr *STAN* HA7 **62** B2
Bellamy Rd *CHES/WCR* EN8 **26** E2
CHING E4 **51** H8
ENC/FH EN2 **36** D5
Bellamy St *BAL* SW12 **138** B4
Bellasis Av *BRXS/STRHM* SW2 **138** E5
Bell Av *HARH* RM3 **74** B2
WDR/YW UB7 **112** F1
Bell Cl *GRH* DA9 **147** M2
PIN HA5 **60** C4
Bellclose Rd *WDR/YW* UB7 **94** E8
Bell Dr *WAND/EARL* SW18 **136** E4
Bellefield Rd *STMC/STPC* BR5 **162** B8
Bellefields Rd *BRXN/ST* SW9 **120** F8
Bellegrove Cl *WELL* DA16 **125** M7
Bellegrove Rd *WELL* DA16 **125** L7
Bellenden Rd *PECK* SE15 **121** M7
Belle Staines Pleasaunce
CHING E4 **51** G4
Belleville Rd *BTSEA* SW11 **137** M2
Belle Vue *GFD/PVL* UB6 **79** K8
Belle Vue Cl *STA* TW18 **148** A4
Belle Vue La *BUSH* WD23 **43** K3
Bellevue Pk *THHTH* CR7 **157** J6
Belle Vue Rd *CRW* RM5 **55** J8
WALTH E17 **69** K3
Bellevue Rd *BARN* SW13 **118** A7
BXLYHS DA6 **144** F2
EMPK RM11 **92** F1
FBAR/BDGN N11 **48** A6
KUT KT1 **152** E6
TOOT SW17 **137** M4
WEA W13 **98** B3
Bellew St *TOOT* SW17 **137** J7
Bell Farm Av *DAGE* RM10 **91** J3
Bellfield Av *KTN/HRWW/W* HA3 **43** K8
Bell Gdns *STMC/STPC* BR5 **162** C8
Bellgate Ms *KTTN* NW5 **84** B4
Bell Gn *SYD* SE26 **140** E8
Bell Green La *SYD* SE26 **158** F1
Bell House Rd *ROMW/RG* RM7 **91** J1
Bellina Ms *KTTN* NW5 **84** B4
Bellingham Gn *CAT* SE6 **141** G7
Bellingham Rd *CAT* SE6 **141** J7
Bell La *CAN/RD* E16 **106** A7
HDN NW4 **64** D5
PEND EN3 **37** K3
TWK TW1 **134** A5
WCHPL E1 **13** L3
Bell Meadow *NRWD* SE19 **139** L8
Bellmount Wood Av *WAT* WD17 **28** E4
Bello Cl *BRXS/STRHM* SW2 **139** H5
Bellot St *GNWCH* SE10 **123** L3
Bellring Cl *BELV* DA17 **127** G4
Bell Rd *E/WMO/HCT* KT8 **151** K8
ENC/FH EN2 **36** D4
HSLW TW3 **115** H8
Bells Hl *BAR* EN5 **33** K8
Bell St *BAY/PAD* W2 **9** J2
Belltrees Gv *STRHM/NOR* SW16 **156** F1
Bell Water Ga
WOOL/PLUM SE18 **125** G1
Bellwood Rd *PECK* SE15 **140** D1
Bell Yd *LINN* WC2A **12** A5
Belmont Av *ALP/SUD* HA0 **80** F8
EBAR EN4 **34** F8
ED N9 **50** A3
NWDGN UB2 **114** E1
NWMAL KT3 **154** A8
PLMGR N13 **48** E7
TOTM N17 **67** J4
UPMR RM14 **92** F2
WELL DA16 **125** L7
Belmont Cl *CHING* E4 **51** K7
CLAP SW4 **120** C8
EBAR EN4 **34** F7
TRDG/WHET N20 **47** H3
UX/CGN UB8 **76** D6
WFD IG8 **52** B6
Belmont Gv *CHSWK* W4 **117** K2
LEW SE13 **123** K8
Belmont Hl *LEW* SE13 **123** K8
Belmont La *CHST* BR7 **143** J8
STAN HA7 **62** C1
Belmont Pk *LEW* SE13 **141** K1
Belmont Park Cl *LEW* SE13 **141** L1
Belmont Park Rd *LEY* E10 **69** H7
Belmont Ri *BELMT* SM2 **181** M1
Belmont Rd *BECK* BR3 **158** E5
BELMT SM2 **182** A3
BUSH WD23 **29** L7
CHST BR7 **161** H1
CLAP SW4 **120** C8
ERITH DA8 **127** G5
HCH RM12 **92** D3
IL IG1 **89** J3
KTN/HRWW/W HA3 **61** M4
SEVS/STOTM N15 **67** J5
SNWD SE25 **158** B8
UX/CGN UB8 **76** D7
WHTN TW2 **133** K6
WLGTN SM6 **171** J7
Belmont St *CAMTN* NW1 **4** B1
Belmont Ter *CHSWK* W4 **117** K2
Belmor *BORE* WD6 **32** A8
Belmore Av *YEAD* UB4 **96** A5
Belmore St *VX/NE* SW8 **120** D6
Beloe Cl *BARN* SW13 **136** A1
Belsham St *HOM* E9 **86** C6
Belsize Av *HAMP* NW3 **83** L5
PLMGR N13 **48** F8
WEA W13 **116** B1
Belsize Court Garages
HAMP NW3 **83** K5
Belsize Crs *HAMP* NW3 **83** K5
Belsize Gdns *SUT* SM1 **170** B6
Belsize Gv *HAMP* NW3 **83** L6
Belsize La *HAMP* NW3 **83** K6
Belsize Ms *HAMP* NW3 **83** K6
Belsize Pk *HAMP* NW3 **83** K6
Belsize Park Gdns *HAMP* NW3 **83** K6
Belsize Park Ms *HAMP* NW3 **83** K6
Belsize Pl *HAMP* NW3 **83** K5
Belsize Rd *KIL/WHAMP* NW6 **2** F2
KTN/HRWW/W HA3 **61** K1
Belsize Sq *HAMP* NW3 **83** K6
Belsize Ter *HAMP* NW3 **83** K6
Belson Rd *WOOL/PLUM* SE18 **124** F2
Beltane Dr *WIM/MER* SW19 **136** D7
Belthorn Crs *BAL* SW12 **138** C4
Beltinge Rd *HARH* RM3 **74** F4
Belton Rd *CRICK* NW2 **82** A6
FSTGT E7 **88** B7
SCUP DA14 **144** A8
TOTM N17 **67** L4
WAN E11 **87** L4
Belton Wy *BOW* E3 **105** G4
Beltran Rd *FUL/PGN* SW6 **119** H7
Beltwood Rd *BELV* DA17 **127** J2
Belvedere Av *CLAY* IG5 **71** H3
WIM/MER SW19 **154** E1
Belvedere Buildings
STHWK SE1 **18** D2
Belvedere Cl *ESH/CLAY* KT10 **166** B7
TEDD TW11 **151** L1
WEY KT13 **164** A7
Belvedere Ct *BELV* DA17 **126** F1
Belvedere Dr *WIM/MER* SW19 **154** E1
Belvedere Gdns
E/WMO/HCT KT8 **150** F8
Belvedere Gv *WIM/MER* SW19 **154** E1
Belvedere Ms *PECK* SE15 **122** C8
Belvedere Rd *BRW* CM14 **57** M5
BXLYHN DA7 **126** F8
HNWL W7 **115** L1
LEY E10 **86** E1
NRWD SE19 **157** M3
STHWK SE1 **17** L1
THMD SE28 **108** D7
Belvedere Sq
WIM/MER SW19 **154** E1
Belvedere Strd *CDALE/KGS* NW9 **63** M3
Belvedere Wy
KTN/HRWW/W HA3 **62** E7
Belvoir Rd *EDUL* SE22 **140** A4

Belvue Cl NTHLT UB5 ..... 79 G7
Belvue Rd NTHLT UB5 ..... 79 G7
Bembridge Cl
KIL/WHAMP NW6 ..... 82 E7
Bembridge Gdns RSLP HA4 ..... 77 K2
Bemerton St IS N1 ..... 5 L3
Bemish Rd PUT/ROE SW15 ..... 118 D8
Bempton Dr RSLP HA4 ..... 78 B2
Bemsted Rd WALTH E17 ..... 68 F4
Benares Rd WOOL/PLUM SE18 ..... 125 M2
Benbow Rd HMSMTH W6 ..... 118 B1
Benbow St DEPT SE8 ..... 123 G4
Benbow Wy UX/CGN UB8 ..... 94 C4
Benbury Cl BMLY BR1 ..... 159 J1
Bench Fld SAND/SEL CR2 ..... 172 F7
Bencombe Rd PUR/KEN CR8 ..... 184 A7
Bencroft Rd
STRHM/NOR SW16 ..... 156 C3
Bencurtis Pk WWKM BR4 ..... 174 D5
Bendall Ms CAMTN NW1 ..... 9 K2
Bendemeer Rd PUT/ROE SW15 ..... 118 D8
Bendish Rd EHAM E6 ..... 88 E7
Bendmore Av ABYW SE2 ..... 126 A3
Bendon Va WAND/EARL SW18 ..... 137 H4
Bendysh Rd BUSH WD23 ..... 29 L6
Benedict Cl ORP BR6 ..... 176 E5
Benedict Dr EBED/NFELT TW14 ..... 131 K4
Benedict Rd BRXN/ST SW9 ..... 120 F8
MTCM CR4 ..... 155 K6
Benedict Wy EFNCH N2 ..... 65 J4
Benedict Whf MTCM CR4 ..... 155 L6
Benenden Gn HAYES BR2 ..... 160 A8
Benen-stock Rd
STWL/WRAY TW19 ..... 130 A3
Benets Rd EMPK RM11 ..... 93 G1
Benett Gdns STRHM/NOR SW16 ..... 156 E5
Benfleet Cl SUT SM1 ..... 170 C5
Bengal Rd IL IG1 ..... 89 H4
Bengarth Dr KTN/HRWW/W HA3 ..... 61 K3
Bengarth Rd NTHLT UB5 ..... 78 D8
Bengeworth Rd HRW HA1 ..... 80 A2
Ben Hale Cl STAN HA7 ..... 44 A7
Benham Cl BTSEA SW11 ..... 119 K8
CHSGTN KT9 ..... 167 J8
Benham Gdns HSLWW TW4 ..... 132 F2
Benham Rd HNWL W7 ..... 97 L4
Benhill Av SUT SM1 ..... 170 B6
Benhill Rd CMBW SE5 ..... 121 K5
SUT SM1 ..... 170 D5
Benhill Wood Rd SUT SM1 ..... 170 C6
Benhilton Gdns SUT SM1 ..... 170 B5
Benhurst Av HCH RM12 ..... 92 B4
Benhurst Cl SAND/SEL CR2 ..... 185 K3
Benhurst Gdns SAND/SEL CR2 ..... 185 J3
Benhurst La STRHM/NOR SW16 ..... 157 G1
Benin St LEW SE13 ..... 141 K4
Benjafield Cl UED N18 ..... 50 B6
Benjamin Cl EMPK RM11 ..... 74 A7
HACK E8 ..... 86 A8
Benjamin St FARR EC1M 12 C2
Ben Jonson Rd WCHPL E1 ..... 104 E4
Benledi St POP/IOD E14 ..... 105 K5
Bennelong Cl SHB W12 ..... 100 B6
Bennerley Rd BTSEA SW11 ..... 137 M2
Bennet Cl KUT KT1 ..... 152 C4
Bennetsfield Rd STKPK UB11 ..... 95 H7
Bennett Cl NTHWD HA6 ..... 59 M1
WELL DA16 ..... 126 A7
Bennett Gv LEW SE13 ..... 123 H6
Bennett Pk BKHTH/KID SE3 ..... 123 M8
Bennett Rd CHDH RM6 ..... 72 E7
PLSTW E13 ..... 106 C3
Bennetts Av CROY/NA CR0 ..... 173 L4
GFD/PVL UB6 ..... 79 L8
Bennett's Castle La BCTR RM8 ..... 90 C4
Bennetts Cl MTCM CR4 ..... 156 B4
TOTM N17 ..... 49 M8
Bennetts Copse CHST BR7 ..... 160 E2
Bennett St CHSWK W4 ..... 117 L4
WHALL SW1A 10 E8
Bennetts Wy CROY/NA CR0 ..... 173 L4
Bennett Wy RDART DA2 ..... 147 K8
Benningholme Rd EDGW HA8 ..... 45 L8
Bennington Rd TOTM N17 ..... 67 L2
WFD IG8 ..... 69 L1
Bennions Cl HCH RM12 ..... 92 D6
Bennison Dr HARH RM3 ..... 74 D3
Benn St HOM E9 ..... 86 E6
Benrek Cl BARK/HLT IG6 ..... 71 J1
Bensbury Cl PUT/ROE SW15 ..... 136 C4
Bensham Cl THHTH CR7 ..... 157 J7
Bensham Gv THHTH CR7 ..... 157 J5
Bensham La CROY/NA CR0 ..... 172 B2
THHTH CR7 ..... 157 H8
Bensham Manor Rd
THHTH CR7 ..... 157 J7
Benskin Rd WATW WD18 ..... 29 G8
Benskins La ABR/ST RM4 ..... 56 D3
Benson Av PLSTW E13 ..... 106 C1
Benson Cl HSLW TW3 ..... 133 G1
UX/CGN UB8 ..... 94 E4
Benson Quay WAP E1W 104 C6
Benson Rd CROY/NA CR0 ..... 172 A5
FSTH SE23 ..... 140 C5
Benthal Rd STNW/STAM N16 ..... 85 M2
Bentham Rd HOM E9 ..... 86 D6
THMD SE28 ..... 108 B6
Ben Tillet Cl BARK IG11 ..... 90 A7
CAN/RD E16 ..... 106 F7
Bentinck Ms MHST W1U 10 B4
Bentinck Rd WDR/YW UB7 ..... 94 D7
Bentinck St MHST W1U 10 B4
Bentley Dr GNTH/NBYPK IG2 ..... 71 J7
Bentley Heath La BAR EN5 ..... 22 E8
Bentley Ms WCHMH N21 ..... 49 K1
Bentley Rd IS N1 ..... 85 L6
Bentley Wy STAN HA7 ..... 44 A7
WFD IG8 ..... 52 A5
Benton Rd IL IG1 ..... 89 K1
OXHEY WD19 ..... 42 D7
Benton's La WNWD SE27 ..... 139 J8
Benton's Ri WNWD SE27 ..... 157 K1
Bentry Cl BCTR RM8 ..... 90 E2
Bentry Rd BCTR RM8 ..... 90 E2
Bentworth Rd SHB W12 ..... 100 B5
Benwell Ct SUN TW16 ..... 150 A4
Benwell Rd HOLWY N7 ..... 85 G4
Benwick Cl
BERM/RHTH SE16 ..... 122 B2
Benworth St BOW E3 ..... 104 F2
Benyon Rd IS N1 ..... 7 H3
Berberis Wk WDR/YW UB7 ..... 112 E2
Berber Rd BTSEA SW11 ..... 137 M2
Berceau Wk WAT WD17 ..... 28 E4
Bercta Rd ELTH/MOT SE9 ..... 143 J6
Beredens La RBRW/HUT CM13 ..... 75 M3
Berens Rd STMC/STPC BR5 ..... 162 C8
WLSDN NW10 ..... 100 D2
Berens Wy CHST BR7 ..... 161 M7
Beresford Av ALP/SUD HA0 ..... 81 G8
BRYLDS KT5 ..... 168 B3
HNWL W7 ..... 97 K4
TRDG/WHET N20 ..... 47 M4
TWK TW1 ..... 134 C3
Beresford Dr BMLY BR1 ..... 160 D6
WFD IG8 ..... 52 C6
Beresford Gdns CHDH RM6 ..... 72 E6
EN EN1 ..... 36 E7
HSLWW TW4 ..... 132 F2
Beresford Rd BELMT SM2 ..... 181 M1
CEND/HSY/T N8 ..... 67 G6
CHING E4 ..... 51 L3
EFNCH N2 ..... 65 L4
HBRY N5 ..... 85 K5
HRW HA1 ..... 61 K6
KUTN/CMB KT2 ..... 152 F4
NWMAL KT3 ..... 153 J7
STHL UB1 ..... 96 D7
WALTH E17 ..... 69 H2
Beresford St WOOL/PLUM SE18 ..... 125 H1
Beresford Ter HBRY N5 ..... 85 J5
Berestede Rd HMSMTH W6 ..... 117 M3
Bere St WAP E1W 104 D6
Berger Cl STMC/STPC BR5 ..... 176 D1
Berger Rd HOM E9 ..... 86 D6
Berghem Ms WKENS W14 ..... 118 D1
Bergholt Av REDBR IG4 ..... 70 E6
Bergholt Crs STNW/STAM N16 ..... 67 L8
Bergholt Ms CAMTN NW1 ..... 4 F2
Bering Wk CAN/RD E16 ..... 106 D5
Berisford Ms
WAND/EARL SW18 ..... 137 J3
Berkeley Av CLAY IG5 ..... 71 G3
CRW RM5 ..... 73 J1
GFD/PVL UB6 ..... 79 L6
HEST TW5 ..... 114 A6
WELL DA16 ..... 126 D6
Berkeley Cl ABLGY WD5 ..... 20 F5
BORE WD6 ..... 32 A8
KUTN/CMB KT2 ..... 152 E3
ORP BR6 ..... 176 E2
POTB/CUF EN6 ..... 22 E5
RSLP HA4 ..... 78 A3
UPMR RM14 ..... 93 H2
Berkeley Ct WEY KT13 ..... 164 D4
WLGTN SM6 ..... 171 J5
Berkeley Crs DART DA1 ..... 146 F5
EBAR EN4 ..... 34 D8
Berkeley Dr E/WMO/HCT KT8 ..... 150 F6
EMPK RM11 ..... 93 G1
Berkeley Gdns ESH/CLAY KT10 ..... 179 G1
WCHMH N21 ..... 49 K2
WOT/HER KT12 ..... 164 F2
Berkeley Ms MBLAR W1H 9 M4
SUN TW16 ..... 150 C6
Berkeley Pl EPSOM KT18 ..... 180 D8
WIM/MER SW19 ..... 154 D2
Berkeley Rd BARN SW13 ..... 118 A6
CDALE/KGS NW9 ..... 63 G5
CEND/HSY/T N8 ..... 66 D6
HGDN/ICK UB10 ..... 77 J7
MNPK E12 ..... 88 E5
SEVS/STOTM N15 ..... 67 K7
Berkeley Sq MYFR/PICC W1J 10 D7
Berkeley St MYFR/PICC W1J 10 D7
Berkeley Waye HEST TW5 ..... 114 E5
Berkhampstead Rd BELV DA17 ..... 127 G3
Berkhamsted Av WBLY HA9 ..... 80 F6
Berkley Av CHES/WCR EN8 ..... 26 D7
Berkley Gv CAMTN NW1 ..... 4 A2
Berkley Rd CAMTN NW1 ..... 3 M2
Berkshire Gdns PLMGR N13 ..... 49 G8
UED N18 ..... 50 B7
Berkshire Rd HOM E9 ..... 86 F6
Berkshire Wy EMPK RM11 ..... 75 G6
MTCM CR4 ..... 156 E7
Bermans Wy WLSDN NW10 ..... 81 L4
Bermer Rd WATN WD24 ..... 29 J4
Bermondsey St STHWK SE1 ..... 13 J9
Bermondsey Wall East
BERM/RHTH SE16 ..... 104 B8
STHWK SE1 ..... 104 A8
Bermondsey Wall West
STHWK SE1 ..... 104 A8
Bernal Cl THMD SE28 ..... 108 D6
Bernard Ashley Dr CHARL SE7 ..... 124 B3
Bernard Av WEA W13 ..... 116 B1
Bernard Cassidy St
CAN/RD E16 ..... 105 M4
Bernard Cl BARK/HLT IG6 ..... 53 K8
Bernard Gdns
WIM/MER SW19 ..... 154 F1
Bernard Gv WAB EN9 ..... 27 H6
Bernard Rd ROMW/RG RM7 ..... 73 J8
SEVS/STOTM N15 ..... 67 M6
WLGTN SM6 ..... 171 H7
Bernard St BMSBY WC1N 11 J1
Bernays Cl STAN HA7 ..... 44 C8
Bernay's Gv BRXN/ST SW9 ..... 138 F1
Bernel Dr CROY/NA CR0 ..... 173 M5
Berne Rd THHTH CR7 ..... 157 H8
Berners Dr WEA W13 ..... 98 A6
Berners Ms FITZ W1T 10 F3
Berners Pl FITZ W1T 10 F4
Berners Rd IS N1 ..... 6 C4
WDGN N22 ..... 67 G2
Berners St FITZ W1T 10 F3
Berney Rd CROY/NA CR0 ..... 172 D2
Bernice Cl RAIN RM13 ..... 110 C3
Bernwell Rd CHING E4 ..... 51 L5
Berridge Gn EDGW HA8 ..... 63 G1
Berridge Rd NRWD SE19 ..... 157 K1
Berriman Rd HOLWY N7 ..... 84 F3
Berriton Raod RYLN/HDSTN HA2 ..... 78 F1
Berry Av WATN WD24 ..... 29 H1
Berrybank Cl CHING E4 ..... 51 J4
Berry Cl HCH RM12 ..... 92 D5
RKW/CH/CXG WD3 ..... 40 B2
WCHMH N21 ..... 49 H3
WLSDN NW10 ..... 81 L7
Berrydale Rd YEAD UB4 ..... 96 E3
Berryfield Cl BMLY BR1 ..... 160 E4
Berry Field Cl WALTH E17 ..... 69 H5
Berryfield Rd WALW SE17 ..... 18 D7
Berry Grove La BUSH WD23 ..... 29 L3
Berrygrove La GSTN WD25 ..... 30 A4
Berryhill ELTH/MOT SE9 ..... 143 H1
Berry Hl STAN HA7 ..... 44 D6
Berryhill Gdns ELTH/MOT SE9 ..... 143 H1
Berrylands BRYLDS KT5 ..... 153 G8
ORP BR6 ..... 177 J5
RYNPK SW20 ..... 154 C6
Berrylands Rd BRYLDS KT5 ..... 167 M1
Berry La DUL SE21 ..... 139 K8
RKW/CH/CXG WD3 ..... 40 B3
Berryman Cl BCTR RM8 ..... 90 C3
Berryman's La SYD SE26 ..... 140 D8
Berrymead Gdns ACT W3 ..... 99 J7
Berrymede Rd CHSWK W4 ..... 117 K1
Berry Pl FSBYE EC1V 6 D8
Berryscroft Rd STA TW18 ..... 148 C3
Berry St FSBYE EC1V 12 D1
Berry Wy EA W5 ..... 116 E1
RKW/CH/CXG WD3 ..... 40 B2
Bertal Rd TOOT SW17 ..... 137 K8
Berther Rd EMPK RM11 ..... 74 E8
Berthon St DEPT SE8 ..... 123 G5
Bertie Rd SYD SE26 ..... 158 D2
WLSDN NW10 ..... 82 A6
Bertram Rd EN EN1 ..... 37 G7
HDN NW4 ..... 64 A7
KUTN/CMB KT2 ..... 153 G3
Bertram St KTTN NW5 ..... 84 B3
Bertrand St LEW SE13 ..... 123 H8
Bertrand Wy THMD SE28 ..... 108 B6
Bert Rd THHTH CR7 ..... 157 J8
Bert Wy EN EN1 ..... 36 F7
Berwick Av YEAD UB4 ..... 96 D6
Berwick Cl CHES/WCR EN8 ..... 27 G7
STAN HA7 ..... 43 M8
Berwick Crs BFN/LL DA15 ..... 143 L3
Berwick Pond Cl RAIN RM13 ..... 110 D1
Berwick Pond Rd RAIN RM13 ..... 110 E1
UPMR RM14 ..... 92 F6
Berwick Rd BORE WD6 ..... 31 M3
CAN/RD E16 ..... 106 B5
RAIN RM13 ..... 110 D1
WDGN N22 ..... 67 H2
WELL DA16 ..... 126 B6
Berwick St SOHO/CST W1F 10 F5
Berwyn Av HSLW TW3 ..... 115 H6
Berwyn Rd HNHL SE24 ..... 139 H5
RCHPK/HAM TW10 ..... 135 H1
Beryl Av EHAM E6 ..... 106 E4
Beryl Rd HMSMTH W6 ..... 118 D3
Berystede KUTN/CMB KT2 ..... 153 H3
Besant Wy WLSDN NW10 ..... 81 J5
Besley St STRHM/NOR SW16 ..... 156 C2
Bessant Dr RCH/KEW TW9 ..... 117 H6
Bessborough Pl PIM SW1V 17 G8
Bessborough Rd HRW HA1 ..... 79 K1
PUT/ROE SW15 ..... 136 A5
Bessborough St PIM SW1V 17 G7
Bessemer Rd CMBW SE5 ..... 121 J7
Bessie Lansbury Cl EHAM E6 ..... 107 G5
Bessingby Rd RSLP HA4 ..... 78 A2
Besson St NWCR SE14 ..... 122 D6
Bessy St BETH E2 ..... 104 C2
Bestwood St DEPT SE8 ..... 122 D2
Beswick Ms HAMP NW3 ..... 83 H6
Betam Rd HYS/HAR UB3 ..... 95 K8
Betchworth Cl SUT SM1 ..... 170 D7
Betchworth Rd GDMY/SEVK IG3 ..... 89 L2
Betchworth Wy CROY/NA CR0 ..... 186 C2
Betham Rd GFD/PVL UB6 ..... 97 K2
Bethany Waye
EBED/NFELT TW14 ..... 131 L4
Bethecar Rd HRW HA1 ..... 61 L6
Bethell Av CAN/RD E16 ..... 105 M3
IL IG1 ..... 71 G8
Bethel Rd WELL DA16 ..... 126 C8
Bethersden Cl BECK BR3 ..... 158 F3
Bethnal Green Rd BETH E2 ..... 7 M9
Bethune Av FBAR/BDGN N11 ..... 47 M6
Bethune Rd STNW/STAM N16 ..... 67 K8
WLSDN NW10 ..... 99 K3
Bethwin Rd CMBW SE5 ..... 121 H5
Betjeman Cl CHESW EN7 ..... 26 A1
RYLN/HDSTN HA2 ..... 61 G5
Betley Ct WOT/HER KT12 ..... 165 H5
Betony Cl CROY/NA CR0 ..... 173 K3
Betoyne Av CHING E4 ..... 51 L6
Betsham Rd ERITH DA8 ..... 127 M5
Betstyle Rd FBAR/BDGN N11 ..... 48 B6
Betterton Dr SCUP DA14 ..... 144 E6
Betterton Rd RAIN RM13 ..... 109 L1
Betterton St LSQ/SEVD WC2H 11 J5
Bettles Cl UX/CGN UB8 ..... 94 C1
Bettons Pk SRTFD E15 ..... 87 L8
Bettridge Rd FUL/PGN SW6 ..... 118 F7
Betts Cl BECK BR3 ..... 158 E5
Betts Rd CAN/RD E16 ..... 106 B5
Betts St WCHPL E1 ..... 104 B6
Betts Wy PGE/AN SE20 ..... 158 B5
THDIT KT7 ..... 167 H3
Betula Cl PUR/KEN CR8 ..... 184 D8
Beulah Cl EDGW HA8 ..... 45 H5
Beulah Crs THHTH CR7 ..... 157 J5
Beulah Gv CROY/NA CR0 ..... 172 C1
Beulah Hl NRWD SE19 ..... 157 K4
Beulah Rd HCH RM12 ..... 92 C3
SUT SM1 ..... 170 A6
THHTH CR7 ..... 157 J6
WALTH E17 ..... 69 H6
WIM/MER SW19 ..... 154 F3
Beult Rd DART DA1 ..... 128 A8
Bevan Av BARK IG11 ..... 90 A7
Bevan Ct CROY/NA CR0 ..... 172 A7
Bevan House WATN WD24 ..... 29 K5
Bevan Pk EW KT17 ..... 180 F4
Bevan Pl SWLY BR8 ..... 163 M7
Bevan Rd ABYW SE2 ..... 126 B3
EBAR EN4 ..... 34 F7
Bevan St IS N1 ..... 6 F4
Bevan Wy HCH RM12 ..... 92 F3
Bev Callender Cl VX/NE SW8 ..... 120 B8
Bevenden St IS N1 ..... 7 H7
Beverley Av BFN/LL DA15 ..... 143 M4
HSLWW TW4 ..... 132 F1
RYNPK SW20 ..... 153 M4
Beverley Cl BARN SW13 ..... 118 A7
BTSEA SW11 ..... 137 K1
CHSGTN KT9 ..... 167 J6
EMPK RM11 ..... 74 F8
EW KT17 ..... 181 J4
WCHMH N21 ..... 49 J3
WEY KT13 ..... 164 E4
Beverley Ct BROCKY SE4 ..... 122 F8
Beverley Crs WFD IG8 ..... 70 B2
Beverley Dr EDGW HA8 ..... 63 H4
Beverley Gdns BARN SW13 ..... 117 M8
CHESW EN7 ..... 25 M4
EMPK RM11 ..... 74 E8
GLDGN NW11 ..... 64 E7
STAN HA7 ..... 62 A2
WBLY HA9 ..... 80 F1
WPK KT4 ..... 169 G3
Beverley La KUTN/CMB KT2 ..... 153 L3
Beverley Rd BARN SW13 ..... 117 M8
BXLYHN DA7 ..... 127 J7
CHING E4 ..... 51 K8
CHSWK W4 ..... 117 M3
DAGW RM9 ..... 90 E4
EHAM E6 ..... 106 D2
HAYES BR2 ..... 175 L4
KUT KT1 ..... 152 C4
MTCM CR4 ..... 156 D7
NWDGN UB2 ..... 114 E2
NWMAL KT3 ..... 154 A7
PGE/AN SE20 ..... 158 B5
RSLP HA4 ..... 78 B2
SUN TW16 ..... 149 M4
WPK KT4 ..... 169 J4
Beverley Wy NWMAL KT3 ..... 153 M4
Beverley Wy (Kingston by Pass)
NWMAL KT3 ..... 153 M4
Beversbrook Rd ARCH N19 ..... 84 D3
Beverstone Rd
BRXS/STRHM SW2 ..... 138 F2
THHTH CR7 ..... 157 G7
Beverston Ms MBLAR W1H 9 L3
Bevill Cl SNWD SE25 ..... 158 A6
Bevin Cl BERM/RHTH SE16 ..... 104 E7
Bevington Rd BECK BR3 ..... 159 H5
NKENS W10 ..... 100 E4
Bevington St
BERM/RHTH SE16 ..... 104 A8
Bevin Rd YEAD UB4 ..... 96 A2
Bevin Sq TOOT SW17 ..... 137 M7
Bevin Wy FSBYW WC1X 6 A6
Bevis Cl RDART DA2 ..... 147 J4
Bevis Marks HDTCH EC3A 13 K4
Bewcastle Gdns ENC/FH EN2 ..... 35 L7
Bewdley St IS N1 ..... 6 A1
Bewick St VX/NE SW8 ..... 120 B7
Bewley Cl CHES/WCR EN8 ..... 26 D4
Bewley St WCHPL E1 ..... 104 B6
Bewlys Rd WNWD SE27 ..... 157 H1
Bexhill Cl FELT TW13 ..... 132 E6
Bexhill Rd BROCKY SE4 ..... 140 F3
FBAR/BDGN N11 ..... 48 D7
MORT/ESHN SW14 ..... 117 J8
Bexley Cl DART DA1 ..... 145 L2
Bexley Gdns CHDH RM6 ..... 72 B6
ED N9 ..... 49 K5
Bexley High St BXLY DA5 ..... 145 G4
Bexley La DART DA1 ..... 145 L2
SCUP DA14 ..... 144 C8
Bexley Rd ELTH/MOT SE9 ..... 143 K2
ERITH DA8 ..... 127 M3
Beynon Rd CAR SM5 ..... 170 F7
Bianca Rd PECK SE15 ..... 121 M4
Bibsworth Rd FNCH N3 ..... 64 F3
Bibury Cl PECK SE15 ..... 121 L4
Bicester Rd RCH/KEW TW9 ..... 117 G8
Bickenhall St MBLAR W1H 9 M2
Bickersteth Rd TOOT SW17 ..... 155 M2
Bickerton Rd KTTN NW5 ..... 84 B2
Bickley Crs BMLY BR1 ..... 160 F7
Bickley Park Rd BMLY BR1 ..... 160 F6
Bickley Rd BMLY BR1 ..... 160 D5
LEY E10 ..... 69 H8
Bickley St TOOT SW17 ..... 155 L1
Bicknell Rd CMBW SE5 ..... 121 J8
Bicknoller Cl BELMT SM2 ..... 182 B3
Bicknoller Rd EN EN1 ..... 36 F4
Bicknor Rd ORP BR6 ..... 176 E2
Bidborough Cl HAYES BR2 ..... 159 M8
Bidborough St STPAN WC1H 5 J8
Biddenden Wy ELTH/MOT SE9 ..... 143 G8
Biddenham Turn GSTN WD25 ..... 21 J8
Bidder St CAN/RD E16 ..... 105 L4
Biddestone Rd HOLWY N7 ..... 84 F4
Biddulph Rd MV/WKIL W9 ..... 2 D8
SAND/SEL CR2 ..... 184 C2
Bideford Av GFD/PVL UB6 ..... 98 B2
Bideford Cl EDGW HA8 ..... 63 G2
FELT TW13 ..... 132 F7
HARH RM3 ..... 74 C2
Bideford Gdns EN EN1 ..... 49 L2
Bideford Rd BMLY BR1 ..... 141 M7
PEND EN3 ..... 37 M3
RSLP HA4 ..... 78 B3
WELL DA16 ..... 126 B5
Bidwell Gdns FBAR/BDGN N11 ..... 66 C2
Bidwell St PECK SE15 ..... 122 B6
Biggerstaff Rd SRTFD E15 ..... 87 J8
Biggerstaff St FSBYPK N4 ..... 85 G2
Biggin Av MTCM CR4 ..... 155 M4
Biggin Hl STRHM/NOR SW16 ..... 157 H4
Biggin Wy NRWD SE19 ..... 157 H3
Bigginwood Rd
STRHM/NOR SW16 ..... 157 H3
Bigg's Rw PUT/ROE SW15 ..... 118 D8
Bigland St WCHPL E1 ..... 104 B5
Bignell Rd WOOL/PLUM SE18 ..... 125 H3
Bignells Cnr POTB/CUF EN6 ..... 22 B7
Bignold Rd FSTGT E7 ..... 88 A4
Bigwood Rd GLDGN NW11 ..... 65 H7
Biko Cl UX/CGN UB8 ..... 94 C5
Billet La EMPK RM11 ..... 92 D1
Billet Rd CHDH RM6 ..... 72 C4
WALTH E17 ..... 68 D2
Billetts Hart Cl HNWL W7 ..... 97 L8
Bill Hamling Cl ELTH/MOT SE9 ..... 142 F6
Billingford Cl BROCKY SE4 ..... 140 D1
Billing Pl WBPTN SW10 ..... 119 H5
Billing Rd WBPTN SW10 ..... 119 H5
Billington Rd NWCR SE14 ..... 122 D5
Billiter Sq FENCHST EC3M 13 K5
Billiter St FENCHST EC3M 13 K5
Billockby Cl CHSGTN KT9 ..... 167 M8
Billson St POP/IOD E14 ..... 123 J2
Billy Lows La POTB/CUF EN6 ..... 23 H4
Bilton Rd GFD/PVL UB6 ..... 80 B8
Bilton Wy HYS/HAR UB3 ..... 96 B8
PEND EN3 ..... 37 M4
Bina Gdns ECT SW5 ..... 14 E6
Bincote Rd ENC/FH EN2 ..... 35 M6
Binden Rd SHB W12 ..... 117 M1
Binfield Rd SAND/SEL CR2 ..... 172 F7
VX/NE SW8 ..... 120 E6
Bingfield IS N1 ..... 5 K3
Bingfield St IS N1 ..... 5 L3
Bingham Dr STA TW18 ..... 148 D3
Bingham Pl MHST W1U 10 A1
Bingham Rd CROY/NA CR0 ..... 173 G3
Bingham St IS N1 ..... 85 K6
Bingley Rd CAN/RD E16 ..... 106 C5
GFD/PVL UB6 ..... 97 J3
SUN TW16 ..... 150 A3
Binney St MYFR/PKLN W1K 10 B6
Binns Rd CHSWK W4 ..... 117 L3
Binsey Wk ABYW SE2 ..... 108 C8
Binstead Cl YEAD UB4 ..... 96 E4
Binyon Crs STAN HA7 ..... 43 M7
Birbetts Rd ELTH/MOT SE9 ..... 142 F6
Birchanger Rd SNWD SE25 ..... 158 A8
Birch Av PLMGR N13 ..... 49 J5
WDR/YW UB7 ..... 94 F5
Birch Cl BKHH IG9 ..... 52 D5
BTFD TW8 ..... 116 B5
CAN/RD E16 ..... 105 L4
HSLW TW3 ..... 115 K8
ROMW/RG RM7 ..... 73 H4
TEDD TW11 ..... 152 A1
Birch Copse LCOL/BKTW AL2 ..... 21 L3
Birch Crs EMPK RM11 ..... 74 E5
HGDN/ICK UB10 ..... 76 F8
Birchdale Gdns CHDH RM6 ..... 72 D8
Birchdale Rd FSTGT E7 ..... 88 C5
Birchdene Dr THMD SE28 ..... 108 A7
Birchen Cl CDALE/KGS NW9 ..... 81 K2
Birchend Cl SAND/SEL CR2 ..... 172 D8
Birchen Gv CDALE/KGS NW9 ..... 81 K2
Birchen La BANK EC3V 13 H5
Birches Cl EPSOM KT18 ..... 180 E8
MTCM CR4 ..... 155 M6
PIN HA5 ..... 60 E6
The Birches BUSH WD23 ..... 30 C8
CHARL SE7 ..... 124 B4
ORP BR6 ..... 176 A6
STHGT/OAK N14 ..... 48 F1
SWLY BR8 ..... 163 L5
Birchfield Gv EW KT17 ..... 181 J3
Birchfield Rd CHES/WCR EN8 ..... 26 B2
Birchfield St POP/IOD E14 ..... 105 G6
Birch Gdns DAGE RM10 ..... 91 J3
Birch Gv ACT W3 ..... 99 G7
LEE/GVPK SE12 ..... 141 M4
POTB/CUF EN6 ..... 23 G5
SHPTN TW17 ..... 149 L5
WAN E11 ..... 87 L3
WELL DA16 ..... 144 A1
Birch Hl CROY/NA CR0 ..... 173 K7
Birchington Cl BXLYHN DA7 ..... 127 H6
Birchington Rd BRYLDS KT5 ..... 167 M2
CEND/HSY/T N8 ..... 66 D7
KIL/WHAMP NW6 ..... 2 B3
Birchlands Av BAL SW12 ..... 137 M4
Birch La PUR/KEN CR8 ..... 183 L4
Birch Md HAYES BR2 ..... 176 A4
Birchmead WAT WD17 ..... 28 F3
Birchmead Av PIN HA5 ..... 60 C5
Birchmore Wk HBRY N5 ..... 85 J3
Birch Pk KTN/HRWW/W HA3 ..... 61 J1
Birch Pl GRH DA9 ..... 147 L3
Birch Rd FELT TW13 ..... 150 D1
ROMW/RG RM7 ..... 73 H4
Birch Rw HAYES BR2 ..... 176 A2
Birch Tree Av WWKM BR4 ..... 174 F7
Birch Tree Wk WAT WD17 ..... 28 F2
Birch Tree Wy CROY/NA CR0 ..... 173 H4
Birch V COB KT11 ..... 178 A6
Birch Wk MTCM CR4 ..... 156 B4
Birchway HYS/HAR UB3 ..... 96 A7
Birchwood Av BECK BR3 ..... 158 F7
CAR SM5 ..... 171 G5
MUSWH N10 ..... 66 A4
SCUP DA14 ..... 144 B7
Birchwood Cl MRDN SM4 ..... 155 H7
Birchwood Ct EDGW HA8 ..... 63 J3
Birchwood Dr HAMP NW3 ..... 83 H3
RDART DA2 ..... 145 L8
Birchwood Gv HPTN TW12 ..... 151 H2
Birchwood Park Av SWLY BR8 ..... 163 L6
Birchwood Rd RDART DA2 ..... 145 L8
STMC/STPC BR5 ..... 161 K7
TOOT SW17 ..... 156 B1
Birdbrook Cl DAGE RM10 ..... 91 J7
Birdbrook Rd BKHTH/KID SE3 ..... 124 C8
Birdcage Wk STJSPK SW1H 16 F2
Birdham Cl BMLY BR1 ..... 160 E8
Birdhurst Av SAND/SEL CR2 ..... 172 D6
Birdhurst Gdns SAND/SEL CR2 ..... 172 D6
Birdhurst Ri SAND/SEL CR2 ..... 172 E7
Birdhurst Rd SAND/SEL CR2 ..... 172 E7
WAND/EARL SW18 ..... 137 J1
WIM/MER SW19 ..... 155 L2
Bird In Bush Rd PECK SE15 ..... 122 A5
Bird-in-hand La BMLY BR1 ..... 160 D5
Bird-in-hand Pas FSTH SE23 ..... 140 C6
Bird La UPMR RM14 ..... 75 K6
Birdlip Cl PECK SE15 ..... 121 L4
Birds Farm Av ROMW/RG RM7 ..... 73 H2
Birdsfield La HOM E9 ..... 86 F8
Birds Hill Dr LHD/OX KT22 ..... 178 D6
Birds Hill Ri LHD/OX KT22 ..... 178 D6
Birds Hill Rd LHD/OX KT22 ..... 178 D5

Bird St *MHST* W1U 10 B5
Bird Wk *WHTN* TW2 .... 132 F5
Birdwood Cl *SAND/SEL* CR2 .. 185 J4
TEDD TW11 .... 133 L8 🔲
Birkbeck Av *ACT* W3 .... 99 J6
GFD/PVL UB6 .... 79 J8
Birkbeck Gv *ACT* W3 .... 99 K8
Birkbeck Hl *DUL* SE21 .... 139 H6
Birkbeck Pl *DUL* SE21 .... 139 H5
Birkbeck Rd *ACT* W3 .... 99 K7
BECK BR3 .... 158 D5
CEND/HSY/T N8 .... 66 E5
EA W5 .... 116 C2
ENC/FH EN2 .... 36 D3
GNTH/NBYPK IG2 .... 71 K6
HACK E8 .... 85 M5
NFNCH/WDSP N12 .... 47 J7
ROMW RM7 .... 91 K1
SCUP DA14 .... 144 A7
TOTM N17 .... 67 M2
WIM/MER SW19 .... 155 H1
Birkbeck St *BETH* E2 .... 104 B2 🔲
Birkbeck Wy *GFD/PVL* UB6 .. 79 K8
PIN HA5 .... 61 G4
Birkdale Av *HARH* RM3 .... 75 K1 🔲
OXHEY WD19 .... 42 D5
Birkdale Cl *ORP* BR6 .... 176 D2
Birkdale Gdns *CROY/NA* CR0 173 K6
OXHEY WD19 .... 42 D5
Birkdale Rd *ABYW* SE2 .... 126 A2
EA W5 .... 98 E3
Birkenhead Av *KUTN/CMB* KT2 .. 152 F5
Birkenhead St *IS* N1 .... 5 K7
Birkhall Rd *CAT* SE6 .... 141 K5
Birkwood Cl *BAL* SW12 .... 138 D4
Birley Rd *TRDG/WHET* N20 .. 47 J4
Birley St *BTSEA* SW11 .... 120 A7
Birling Rd *ERITH* DA8 .... 127 K5
Birnam Rd *HOLWY* N7 .... 84 F2
Birse Crs *WLSDN* NW10 .... 81 L4
Birstal Gn *OXHEY* WD19 .... 42 D6
Birstall Rd *SEVS/STOTM* N15 .. 67 L6 🔲
Biscay Rd *HMSMTH* W6 .... 118 D3
Biscoe Cl *HEST* TW5 .... 115 G4
Biscoe Wy *LEW* SE13 .... 123 K8 🔲
Bisenden Rd *CROY/NA* CR0 .. 172 E4
Bisham Cl *MTCM* CR4 .... 170 F2
Bisham Gdns *HGT* N6 .... 84 A1
Bishop Butt Cl *ORP* BR6 .... 176 F5 🔲
Bishop Ken Rd *KTN/HRWW/W* HA3 .. 61 M3
Bishop King's Rd *WKENS* W14 .. 118 E2 🔲
Bishop Rd *STHGT/OAK* N14 .. 48 B2
Bishops Av *BMLY* BR1 .... 160 C6
BORE WD6 .... 31 M8
CHDH RM6 .... 72 C7
FUL/PGN SW6 .... 118 D7
NTHWD HA6 .... 41 L6
PLSTW E13 .... 88 B8 🔲
The Bishops Av *EFNCH* N2 .. 65 K7
Bishop's Bridge Rd *BAY/PAD* W2 .. 8 D4
Bishops Cl *BAR* EN5 .... 46 D1
CHSWK W4 .... 117 J3 🔲
ELTH/MOT SE9 .... 143 J6
EN EN1 .... 37 H5
HGDN/ICK UB10 .... 95 G1
SUT SM1 .... 170 A5 🔲
WALTH E17 .... 69 H5 🔲
Bishops Ct *GRH* DA9 .... 147 L2
STP EC4M .... 12 D4 🔲
Bishops Dr *EBED/NFELT* TW14 .. 131 K3 🔲
NTHLT UB5 .... 78 E8
Bishopsford Rd *MRDN* SM4 .. 170 C2
Bishops Gv *EFNCH* N2 .... 65 K7
HPTN TW12 .... 133 G8 🔲
Bishop's Hall *KUT* KT1 .... 152 D5 🔲
Bishops Hl *WOT/HER* KT12 .. 165 G2
Bishopsmead Cl
HOR/WEW KT19 .... 180 D3 🔲
Bishop's Park Rd
FUL/PGN SW6 .... 118 D7
STRHM/NOR SW16 .... 156 E4
Bishop's Pl *SUT* SM1 .... 170 C7
Bishop's Rd *CROY/NA* CR0 .. 172 B2
FUL/PGN SW6 .... 118 F6
HGT N6 .... 66 A7
HNWL W7 .... 97 L8
UX/CGN UB8 .... 95 J5
Bishop's Ter *LBTH* SE11 .... 18 B5
Bishopsthorpe Rd *SYD* SE26 .. 140 C8
Bishop St *IS* N1 .... 6 E3
Bishops Wk *CHST* BR7 .... 161 J4
CROY/NA CR0 .... 173 K7
Bishop's Wy *BETH* E2 .... 104 C1
Bishopswood Rd *HGT* N6 .. 65 M8
Bishop Wy *WLSDN* NW10 .. 81 L7 🔲
Biskra *WAT* WD17 .... 29 G4
Bisley Cl *CHES/WCR* EN8 .. 26 D6
WPK KT4 .... 169 J3
Bispham Rd *WLSDN* NW10 .. 98 F2
Bisson Rd *SRTFD* E15 .... 105 J1
Bistern Av *WALTH* E17 .... 69 K4
Bittacy Cl *MLHL* NW7 .... 46 D8
Bittacy Hl *MLHL* NW7 .... 46 D8
Bittacy Park Av *MLHL* NW7 .. 46 D8
Bittacy Ri *MLHL* NW7 .... 46 D8
Bittacy Rd *MLHL* NW7 .... 46 D8
Bittern Cl *YEAD* UB4 .... 96 D4
Bittern St *STHWK* SE1 .... 18 E2
The Bittoms *KUT* KT1 .... 152 D6
Bixley Cl *NWDGN* UB2 .... 114 F2 🔲
Blackall St *SDTCH* EC2A 7 J9
Blackberry Fld *SHPTN* TW17 149 L7 🔲
Blackberry Farm Cl
HEST TW5 .... 114 E5 🔲
Blackberry Fld
STMC/STPC BR5 .... 162 A4 🔲
Blackbird Hl *WBLY* HA9 .... 81 J2
Blackborne Rd *DAGE* RM10 .. 91 G6

Black Boy La *SEVS/STOTM* N15 .. 67 J6
Blackbrook La *HAYES* BR2 .. 161 G8
Blackburne's Ms
MYFR/PKLN W1K 10 A6
Blackburn Rd *KIL/WHAMP* NW6 .. 83 H6
Blackbury Cl *POTB/CUF* EN6 .. 23 J4 🔲
Blackbush Av *CHDH* RM6 .. 72 D6
Blackbush Cl *BELMT* SM2 .. 182 B1
Black Ditch Rd *WAB* EN9 .. 38 C1
Black Ditch Wy *WAB* EN9 .. 38 B1
Blackdown Cl *EFNCH* N2 .. 65 J3
EFNCH N2 .... 65 J6
ROMW/RG RM7 .... 73 H5
Blackenham Rd *TOOT* SW17 137 M8
Blackett St *PUT/ROE* SW15 118 D3
Black Fan Cl *ENC/FH* EN2 .. 36 C4
Blackfen Rd *BFN/LL* DA15 .. 143 M2
Blackford Cl *SAND/SEL* CR2 184 B2
Blackford Rd *OXHEY* WD19 .. 42 D7
Blackfriars Br *EMB* EC4Y .. 12 C6
Blackfriars Pas *BLKFR* EC4V 12 C6 🔲
Blackfriars Rd *STHWK* SE1 .. 12 C8
Blackfriars U/P *BLKFR* EC4V .. 12 D6
Black Friars La *BLKFR* EC4V .. 12 C6 🔲
Blackheath Av *GNWCH* SE10 .. 123 K5
Blackheath Gv *BKHTH/KID* SE3 .. 123 M7
Blackheath Hl *GNWCH* SE10 .. 123 J6
Blackheath Pk *BKHTH/KID* SE3 .. 123 M8
Blackheath Ri *LEW* SE13 .... 123 J7
Blackheath Rd *GNWCH* SE10 .. 123 H6
Blackheath V *BKHTH/KID* SE3 .. 123 L7
Blackhorse La *CROY/NA* CR0 .. 173 G2
WALTH E17 .... 68 D4
Blackhorse Rd *DEPT* SE8 .... 122 E4
Black Horse Rd *SCUP* DA14 .. 144 A8 🔲
Blackhorse Rd *WALTH* E17 .. 68 E6
Blacklands Dr *YEAD* UB4 .... 95 J3
Blacklands Rd *CAT* SE6 .... 141 J8
Blacklands Ter *CHEL* SW3 .. 15 L6
Blackley Cl *WAT* WD17 .... 28 F2
Black Lion La *HMSMTH* W6 .. 118 A2
Blackmans Cl *DART* DA1 .... 146 C5 🔲
Blackman's La *WARL* CR6 .. 186 E7
Blackmoor La *WATW* WD18 .. 28 D5
Blackmore Av *STHL* UB1 .... 97 K7
Blackmore's Gv *TEDD* TW11 .. 152 A2 🔲
Blackmore Rd *BKHH* IG9 .... 52 E2 🔲
Blackness La *HAYES* BR2 .... 187 K2
Blackpool Gdns *YEAD* UB4 .. 95 L3 🔲
Blackpool Rd *PECK* SE15 .... 122 B7
Black Prince Rd *LBTH* SE11 .. 17 L5
Black Rod Cl *HYS/HAR* UB3 .. 113 M1 🔲
Blackshaw Rd *TOOT* SW17 .. 155 K1
Blacksmiths Hl *SAND/SEL* CR2 .. 185 H6
Blacksmith's La *RAIN* RM13 .. 91 M8
STA TW18 .... 148 C6 🔲
STMC/STPC BR5 .... 162 C8
Black's Rd *HMSMTH* W6 .... 118 C3
Blackstock Rd *FSBYPK* N4 .. 85 H2
Blackstone Rd *CRICK* NW2 .. 82 C5
Blackthorn Av *WDR/YW* UB7 113 G2
Blackthorn Cl *GSTN* WD25 .. 21 H5
Blackthorne Av *CROY/NA* CR0 .. 173 J3
Blackthorne Dr *CHING* E4 .. 51 K6
Blackthorn Gv *BXLYHN* DA7 .. 126 E8
Blackthorn St *BOW* E3 .... 105 G3
Blackwall La *GNWCH* SE10 .. 123 L1
Blackwall Tunnel Northern Ap
BOW E3 .... 105 H2
Blackwall Wy *POP/IOD* E14 .. 105 K6
Blackwater Cl *RAIN* RM13 .. 109 K4
Blackwater St *EDUL* SE22 .. 139 M2
Blackwell Cl *CLPT* E5 .... 86 E4
KTN/HRWW/W HA3 .... 61 K1
Blackwell Dr *OXHEY* WD19 .. 42 C1
Blackwell Gdns *EDGW* HA8 .. 45 C6
Blackwell Rd *KGLGY* WD4 .. 20 A2
Blackwood St *WALW* SE17 .. 19 G7
Bladen Cl *WEY* KT13 .... 164 D8
Bladindon Dr *BXLY* DA5 .. 144 D4
Bladon Gdns *RYLN/HDSTN* HA2 .. 61 H7
Blagden's La *STHGT/OAK* N14 .. 48 D4
Blagdon Rd *LEW* SE13 .... 141 H5
NWMAL KT3 .... 153 M7
Blagdon Wk *TEDD* TW11 .. 152 D2
Blagrove Rd *NKENS* W10 .. 100 F4 🔲
Blair Av *CDALE/KGS* NW9 .. 63 L8
ESH/CLAY KT10 .... 166 C4
Blair Cl *BFN/LL* DA15 .... 143 L2
HYS/HAR UB3 .... 114 A2
Blairderry Rd
BRXS/STRHM SW2 .... 138 E6
Blairhead Dr *OXHEY* WD19 .. 42 B5
Blair St *POP/IOD* E14 .... 105 L5
Blake Av *BARK* IG11 .... 89 L8
Blake Cl *CAR* SM5 .... 170 E3
RAIN RM13 .... 91 M8
WELL DA16 .... 125 L6
Blakeden Dr *ESH/CLAY* KT10 .. 178 F1
Blake Gdns *DART* DA1 .... 146 F1
FUL/PGN SW6 .... 119 G6
Blakehall Rd *CAR* SM5 .... 170 F8
Blake Hall Rd *WAN* E11 .. 88 A1
Blakemore Rd
STRHM/NOR SW16 .... 138 E7 🔲
THHTH CR7 .... 156 F8
Blakemore Wy *BELV* DA17 .. 126 E1 🔲
Blakeney Av *BECK* BR3 .... 158 F8
Blakeney Cl *HOR/WEW* KT19 .. 180 D4
TRDG/WHET N20 .... 47 J3
Blakeney Rd *BECK* BR3 .... 158 F4
Blaker Rd *SRTFD* E15 .... 87 J8
Blakes Av *NWMAL* KT3 .... 153 M8
Blakes Cl *NKENS* W10 .... 100 C4
Blake's Gn *WWKM* BR4 .... 174 C2
Blakesley Av *EA* W5 .... 98 C5
Blake's Rd *PECK* SE15 .... 121 L5
Blakes Ter *NWMAL* KT3 .... 153 M8
Blakesware Gdns *WCHMH* N21 .. 49 K2
Blakewood Cl *FELT* TW13 .. 132 C8 🔲

Blanchard Cl *ELTH/MOT* SE9 .. 142 E7
HOR/WEW KT19 .... 180 D3
Blanch Cl *PECK* SE15 .... 122 C5
Blanchedowne *CMBW* SE5 .. 139 K1
Blanche La *POTB/CUF* EN6 .. 22 A6
Blanchland Rd *MRDN* SM4 .. 155 H8
Blanche St *CAN/RD* E16 .. 105 M3
Blanchland Rd *BECK* BR3 .. 158 E5
WHTN TW2 .... 133 H5
Blandfield Rd *BAL* SW12 .. 138 A3
Blandford Cl *CROY/NA* CR0 171 L5 🔲
EFNCH N2 .... 65 J6
ROMW/RG RM7 .... 73 H5
Blandford Crs *CHING* E4 .... 51 J2
Blandford Rd *BECK* BR3 .. 158 D5
CHSWK W4 .... 117 L1
EA W5 .... 98 D8
NWDGN UB2 .... 115 G2
TEDD TW11 .... 151 K1
Blandford Waye *YEAD* UB4 .. 96 C5
Bland St *ELTH/MOT* SE9 .... 142 D1 🔲
Blaney Crs *EHAM* E6 .... 107 H2
Blanmerle Rd *ELTH/MOT* SE9 143 H5
Blann Cl *ELTH/MOT* SE9 .. 142 D3
Blantyre St *WBPTN* SW10 .. 119 K5
Blashford St *LEW* SE13 .... 141 K4
Blattner Cl *BORE* WD6 .... 31 L7
Blawith Rd *HRW* HA1 .... 61 L3
Blaydon Cl *RSLP* HA4 .... 59 L8
Blaydon Wk *TOTM* N17 .... 68 B1
Bleak Hill La *WOOL/PLUM* SE18 .. 125 M4
Blean Gv *PGE/AN* SE20 .. 158 C3
Bleasdale Av *GFD/PVL* UB6 .. 98 A1
Blechynden St *NTGHL* W11 .. 100 D6 🔲
Bledlow Cl *THMD* SE28 .. 108 C6
Bledlow Ri *GFD/PVL* UB6 .. 97 J1
Bleeding Heart Yd
HCIRC EC1N .... 12 B3 🔲
Blegborough Rd
STRHM/NOR SW16 .... 156 C2
Blendon Dr *BXLY* DA5 .... 144 D3
Blendon Rd *BXLY* DA5 .... 144 D3
Blendon Ter *WOOL/PLUM* SE18 .. 125 J3
Blenheim Av *GNTH/NBYPK* IG2 .. 71 J7
GFD/PVL UB6 .... 97 L1
OXHEY WD19 .... 42 C2
ROMW/RG RM7 .... 73 J5
RYNPK SW20 .... 154 C6
UPMR RM14 .... 93 L1
WCHMH N21 .... 49 J3
WLGTN SM6 .... 183 J1
Blenheim Cl *DART* DA1 .... 146 C3
GFD/PVL UB6 .... 97 K1 🔲
OXHEY WD19 .... 42 C2
ROMW/RG RM7 .... 73 J5
RYNPK SW20 .... 154 C6
UPMR RM14 .... 93 L1
WGTN SM6 .... 183 J1
Blenheim Ct *BFN/LL* DA15 .. 143 K7
WFD IG8 .... 70 B1 🔲
TWK TW1 .... 133 M5 🔲
Blenheim Crs *NTGHL* W11 .. 100 F5 🔲
RSLP HA4 .... 77 K2
SAND/SEL CR2 .... 184 C1
Blenheim Dr *WELL* DA16 .. 125 M6
Blenheim Gdns
BRXS/STRHM SW2 .... 138 F3
CRICK NW2 .... 82 C5
KUTN/CMB KT2 .... 153 H3
SAND/SEL CR2 .... 185 G5
SOCK/AV RM15 .... 111 H7
WBLY HA9 .... 80 E3
WLGTN SM6 .... 171 J8
Blenheim Gv *PECK* SE15 .. 122 K7
Blenheim Park Rd
SAND/SEL CR2 .... 184 C2
Blenheim Pas *STJWD* NW8 .. 2 E5 🔲
Blenheim Rd *BAR* EN5 .... 33 K8
BFN/LL DA15 .... 144 C5
CHSWK W4 .... 117 L1
DART DA1 .... 146 C3
EHAM E6 .... 106 D2
FSTGT E7 .... 87 L4
HAYES BR2 .... 160 E7
HOR/WEW KT19 .... 180 D4
NTHLT UB5 .... 79 H6
ORP BR6 .... 177 J4
PGE/AN SE20 .... 158 C3 🔲
RYLN/HDSTN HA2 .... 60 A6
STJWD NW8 .... 2 E5
SUT SM1 .... 170 A5
WALTH E17 .... 68 D4
Blenheim Ter *STJWD* NW8 .. 2 E5
Blenheim Wy *ISLW* TW7 .. 116 A6
Blenkarne Rd *BTSEA* SW11 137 M3
Bleriot Rd *HEST* TW5 .... 114 C5
Blessbury Rd *EDGW* HA8 .. 63 J7
Blessington Rd *LEW* SE13 .. 141 K1
Blessing Wy *BARK* IG11 .. 108 C1
Bletchingley Cl *THHTH* CR7 .. 157 H7
Bletchingly Cl *IS* N1 .... 6 F6
Bletchmore Cl *HYS/HAR* UB3 .. 113 K3
Bletsoe Wk *IS* N1 .... 6 F5
Blincoe Cl *WIM/MER* SW19 .. 136 D6
Blindman's La *CHES/WCR* EN8 .. 26 D3
Blissett St *GNWCH* SE10 .. 123 H7
Blisworth Cl *YEAD* UB4 .. 96 E3 🔲
Blithbury Rd *DAGW* RM9 .. 90 B6
Blithdale Rd *ABYW* SE2 .. 126 A2
Blithfield St *KENS* W8 .. 14 C4
Blockley Rd *ALP/SUD* HA0 .. 80 B2
Bloemfontein Av *SHB* W12 .. 100 D7
Bloemfontein Rd *SHB* W12 100 B6
Blomfield Rd *BAY/PAD* W2 .. 8 D2
Blomfield St *LVPST* EC2M .. 13 H3
Blomfield Vls *BAY/PAD* W2 .. 8 D3
Blomville Rd *BCTR* RM8 .. 90 B2
Blondell Cl *WDR/YW* UB7 112 D4
Blondel St *BTSEA* SW11 .. 120 A7
Blondin Av *EA* W5 .... 116 C2
Blondin St *BOW* E3 .... 105 J1 🔲
Bloomfield Pl
MYFR/PKLN W1K .... 10 D6 🔲
Bloomfield Rd *HAYES* BR2 .. 160 D8
HGT N6 .... 66 A3
KUT KT1 .... 152 E7
WOOL/PLUM SE18 .... 125 H5
Bloomfield Ter *BGVA* SW1W 16 B7 🔲
Bloom Gv *WNWD* SE27 .. 139 H7 🔲
Bloomhall Rd *NRWD* SE19 .. 157 K1
Bloom Park Rd *FUL/PGN* SW6 .. 118 F5

Bloomsbury Cl *EA* W5 .... 98 F6
HOR/WEW KT19 .... 180 D3
Bloomsbury Pl
NOXST/BSQ WC1A 11 K3
Bloomsbury Sq
NOXST/BSQ WC1A 11 K3
Bloomsbury St
NOXST/BSQ WC1A .... 11 J4 🔲
RSQ WC1B 11 H3
Bloomsbury Wy
NOXST/BSQ WC1A 11 J3
Blore Cl *VX/NE* SW8 .... 120 D6 🔲
Blossom Cl *DAGW* RM9 .. 90 F8
EA W5 .... 98 E8 🔲
SAND/SEL CR2 .... 172 F7
Blossom La *ENC/FH* EN2 .. 36 C4
Blossom St *WCHPL* E1 .... 13 K2
Blossom Wy *HGDN/ICK* UB10 .. 76 F7
WDR/YW UB7 .... 113 G2
Blossom Waye *HEST* TW5 .. 114 E4
Blount St *POP/IOD* E14 .. 104 E5 🔲
Bloxam Gdns *ELTH/MOT* SE9 142 E2
Bloxhall Rd *LEY* E10 .... 86 F1
Bloxham Crs *HPTN* TW12 .. 150 F4
Bloxworth Cl *WLGTN* SM6 .. 171 J5
Blucher Rd *CMBW* SE5 .. 121 J5
Blue Anchor La
BERM/RHTH SE16 .... 122 A2
Blue Anchor Yd *WCHPL* E1 .. 104 A6
Blue Ball Yd *WHALL* SW1A .. 10 E9
Bluebell Av *FSTGT* E7 .... 88 D5
MNPK E12 .... 88 E5
Bluebell Cl *MTCM* CR4 .... 171 H3 🔲
ORP BR6 .... 176 C4
ROMW/RG RM7 .... 91 L2
SYD SE26 .... 139 M8
Bluebell Dr *CHESW* EN7 .. 25 K1
Bluebell Wy *IL* IG1 .... 89 H6
Blueberry Cl *WFD* IG8 .... 52 A8 🔲
Blue Cedars *BNSTD* SM7 .. 181 K7
Bluefield Cl *HPTN* TW12 .. 151 G1
Bluegates *EW* KT17 .... 181 G1
Bluehouse Rd *CHING* E4 .. 51 L5
Bluewater Pkwy *GRH* DA9 .. 147 M4
Blundel Cl *COB* KT11 .... 178 B7
Blundell Rd *EDGW* HA8 .... 63 L1 🔲
Blundell St *HOLWY* N7 .. 5 K1
Blunden Cl *BCTR* RM8 .... 90 C1 🔲
Blunesfield *POTB/CUF* EN6 .. 23 K4 🔲
Blunt Rd *CROY/NA* CR0 .. 172 D7 🔲
Blunts Av *WDR/YW* UB7 .. 113 G5
Blunts Rd *ELTH/MOT* SE9 .. 143 G2
Blurton Rd *CLPT* E5 .... 86 D4
Blyth Cl *BORE* WD6 .... 31 M4
TWK TW1 .... 133 M3 🔲
Blythe Cl *FSTH* SE23 .... 140 F4
Blythe Hl *FSTH* SE23 .... 140 F4
STMC/STPC BR5 .... 161 M4
Blythe Hill La *FSTH* SE23 .. 140 F4
Blythe Rd *WKENS* W14 .. 118 D1
Blythe V *FSTH* SE23 .... 140 D1
Blyth Rd *BMLY* BR1 .... 159 M4
HYS/HAR UB3 .... 95 L8
THMD SE28 .... 108 C6
WALTH E17 .... 68 F8
Blythswood Rd *GDMY/SEVK* IG3 .. 90 A1
Blyth Wk *UPMR* RM14 .... 75 L3
Blythwood Rd *FSBYPK* N4 .. 66 E8
PIN HA5 .... 60 D2
Boadicea St *IS* N1 .... 5 L4
Boardman Av *CHING* E4 .. 38 B8
Boardman Cl *BAR* EN5 .... 33 L8
Boardwalk Pl *POP/IOD* E14 105 J7
Boathouse Wk *PECK* SE15 121 M5 🔲
Boat Lifter Wy
BERM/RHTH SE16 .... 122 E2
Bob Anker Cl *PLSTW* E13 .. 106 A2 🔲
Bobbin Cl *CLAP* SW4 .... 120 C8 🔲
Bob Marley Wy *HNHL* SE24 .. 139 G1
Bockhampton Rd
KUTN/CMB KT2 .... 152 F3
Bocking St *HACK* E8 .... 86 B8
Boddicott Cl *WIM/MER* SW19 .. 136 E6
Bodiam Cl *EN* EN1 .... 36 D5
Bodiam Rd *STRHM/NOR* SW16 .. 156 D4
Bodley Cl *NWMAL* KT3 .... 153 L8
Bodley Rd *NWMAL* KT3 .. 168 E1
Bodmin Cl *RYLN/HDSTN* HA2 .. 78 F3
STMC/STPC BR5 .... 177 J3
Bodmin Gv *MRDN* SM4 .. 155 H7
Bodmin St *WAND/EARL* SW18 137 G5
Bodnant Gdns *RYNPK* SW20 154 A6
Bodney Rd *CLPT* E5 .... 86 D5
Boeing Wy *NWDGN* UB2 .. 114 B1
Boevey Path *BELV* DA17 .. 109 F6
Bognor Gdns *OXHEY* WD19 .. 42 C7 🔲
Bognor Rd *WELL* DA16 .. 126 D6
Bohemia Pl *HACK* E8 .... 86 C6
Bohun Gv *EBAR* EN4 .... 47 L1
Boileau Rd *BARN* SW13 .. 118 A5
EA W5 .... 98 F5
Bolden St *DEPT* SE8 .... 123 H7
Boldero Pl *STJWD* NW8 .. 9 J1 🔲
Bolderwood Wy *WWKM* BR4 174 B4
Boldmere Rd *PIN* HA5 .... 60 C8
Boleyn Av *EN* EN1 .... 37 H4
EW KT17 .... 181 G3
Boleyn Cl *BKHH* IG9 .... 52 A3
WALTH E17 .... 69 G5 🔲
Boleyn Dr *E/WMO/HCT* KT8 .. 150 F2
WWKM BR4 .... 174 B4
Boleyn Gdns *DAGE* RM10 .. 91 J7 🔲
WWKM BR4 .... 174 B4
Boleyn Rd *EHAM* E6 .... 106 D1
FSTGT E7 .... 88 F7 🔲
STNW/STAM N16 .... 85 L5
Boleyn Wy *BAR* EN5 .... 34 C5
BARK/HLT IG6 .... 53 J8
Bolina Rd *BERM/RHTH* SE16 122 C3
Bolingbroke Gv *BTSEA* SW11 137 L2
Bolingbroke Rd *WKENS* W14 .. 118 D1
Bolingbroke Wk *BTSEA* SW11 119 K6 🔲
Bolingbroke Wy *HYS/HAR* UB3 .. 95 K7
Bollo Bridge Rd *ACT* W3 .. 99 J3 🔲
Bollo La *ACT* W3 .... 117 H1
CHSWK W4 .... 117 J2 🔲
Bolney St *VX/NE* SW8 .... 120 F7
Bolney Wy *FELT* TW13 .. 150 E1
Bolsover St *GTPST* W1W .. 10 D1
Bolstead Rd *MTCM* CR4 .. 156 B4 🔲

Bolters La *BNSTD* SM7 .... 181 M8
Bolton Cl *CHSGTN* KT9 .... 167 K8
Bolton Crs *CMBW* SE5 .... 121 G4
Bolton Gdns *BMLY* BR1 .... 159 M2
ECT SW5 .... 14 D7
TEDD TW11 .... 152 A2
WLSDN NW10 .... 100 D1
Bolton Gardens Ms
WBPTN SW10 .... 14 D7
Bolton Rd *CHSGTN* KT9 .... 167 K8
CHSWK W4 .... 117 J5
FSTGT E7 .... 87 M6
HRW HA1 .... 61 J5
KIL/WHAMP NW6 .... 2 D4
UED N18 .... 49 M7
WLSDN NW10 .... 81 L8
Bolton's La *HYS/HAR* UB3 .. 113 J5
The Boltons *ALP/SUD* HA0 .. 79 M4 🔲
WBPTN SW10 .... 14 E7
Bolton St *MYFR/PICC* W1J .. 10 D8
Bombay St *BERM/RHTH* SE16 122 B2
Bomer Cl *WDR/YW* UB7 .. 113 G5
Bomore Rd *NTGHL* W11 .. 100 D6
Bonar Pl *CHST* BR7 .... 160 E3
Bonar Rd *PECK* SE15 .... 122 A5
Bonchester Cl *CHST* BR7 .. 161 G3 🔲
Bonchurch Cl *BELMT* SM2 .. 182 B1 🔲
Bonchurch Rd *NKENS* W10 .. 100 E4 🔲
WEA W13 .... 98 B7 🔲
Bond Cl *WDR/YW* UB7 .... 94 F5
Bondfield Av *YEAD* UB4 .. 96 A2 🔲
Bond Gdns *WLGTN* SM6 .. 171 J6
Bond Rd *MTCM* CR4 .... 155 M5
SURB KT6 .... 167 M4
Bond St *EA* W5 .... 98 D6
SRTFD E15 .... 87 L5
Bondway *VX/NE* SW8 .... 120 E4
Boneta Rd
WOOL/PLUM SE18 .... 124 F1 🔲
Bonfield Rd *LEW* SE13 .... 141 J1
Bonham Gdns *BCTR* RM8 .. 90 D2 🔲
Bonham Rd *BCTR* RM8 .... 90 D2
BRXS/STRHM SW2 .... 138 F2
Bonheur Rd *CHSWK* W4 .. 99 K8 🔲
Bonhill St *SDTCH* EC2A 13 H1
Boniface Gdns
KTN/HRWW/W HA3 .... 61 H1
Boniface Rd *HGDN/ICK* UB10 .. 77 H3
Boniface Wk *KTN/HRWW/W* HA3 .. 61 H1
Bonington Rd *HCH* RM12 .. 92 D3 🔲
Bonner Hill Rd *KUT* KT1 .. 152 F6
Bonner Rd *BETH* E2 .... 104 C1
Bonnersfield Cl *HRW* HA1 .. 62 A7 🔲
Bonnersfield La *HRW* HA1 .. 61 M7
Bonner St *BETH* E2 .... 104 D1
Bonneville Gdns *CLAP* SW4 138 C3
Bonney Gv *CHESW* EN7 .. 26 A3
Bonney Wy *SWLY* BR8 .... 163 L5
Bonnington Sq *VX/NE* SW8 .. 17 L9
Bonny St *CAMTN* NW1 .... 4 E2
Bonser Rd *TWK* TW1 .... 133 M6 🔲
Bonsor St *CMBW* SE5 .... 121 J6
Bonville Gdns *HDN* NW4 .. 64 A5 🔲
Bonville Rd *BMLY* BR1 .... 159 M1
Booker Cl *UED* N18 .... 50 A7 🔲
Boones Rd *LEW* SE13 .... 141 L1
Boone St *LEW* SE13 .... 141 L1
Boord St *GNWCH* SE10 .. 123 L1
Boothby Rd *ARCH* N19 .... 84 D7 🔲
Booth Cl *THMD* SE28 .... 108 B7 🔲
Booth Dr *STA* TW18 .... 148 D2
Booth Rd *CDALE/KGS* NW9 .. 63 K2
CROY/NA CR0 .... 172 B4 🔲
Boot St *IS* N1 .... 7 J8
Bordars Rd *HNWL* W7 .. 97 L4
Bordars Wk *HNWL* W7 .. 97 L4
Borden Av *WCHMH* N21 .. 49 K1
Border Crs *SYD* SE26 .... 158 B1
Border Gdns *CROY/NA* CR0 .. 174 B6
Border Ga *MTCM* CR4 .. 156 B1
Border Rd *SYD* SE26 .. 158 B1
Bordesley Rd *MRDN* SM4 .. 155 H7 🔲
Bordon Wk *PUT/ROE* SW15 .. 136 M4 🔲
Boreham Av *CAN/RD* E16 .. 106 A5
Boreham Rd *WDGN* N22 .. 67 J2
Borgard Rd *WOOL/PLUM* SE18 .. 124 F2
Borkwood Pk *ORP* BR6 .. 176 F6
Borkwood Wy *ORP* BR6 .. 176 E6
Borland Rd *PECK* SE15 .. 140 C1
TEDD TW11 .... 152 B2
Bornedene *POTB/CUF* EN6 .. 22 E4
Borneo St *PUT/ROE* SW15 .. 118 F8
Borough High St *STHWK* SE1 .. 13 G9 🔲
Borough Hl *CROY/NA* CR0 .. 172 B5
Borough Rd *ISLW* TW7 .. 115 L4
KUTN/CMB KT2 .... 153 G4
MTCM CR4 .... 155 L5
STHWK SE1 .... 18 C3
Borough Wy *POTB/CUF* EN6 .. 22 E5
Borrett Cl *WALW* SE17 .... 18 E8
Borrodaile Rd
WAND/EARL SW18 .... 137 H3
Borrowdale Av
KTN/HRWW/W HA3 .... 62 A3
Borrowdale Cl *REDBR* IG4 .. 70 E5 🔲
SAND/SEL CR2 .... 184 F6 🔲
Borrowdale Dr *SAND/SEL* CR2 .. 184 F5
Borthwick Ms *SRTFD* E15 .. 87 L4 🔲
Borthwick Rd
CDALE/KGS NW9 .... 63 M7 🔲
SRTFD E15 .... 87 L4
Borthwick St *DEPT* SE8 .. 123 G3
Borwick Av *WALTH* E17 .. 68 F4 🔲
Bosanquet Cl *UX/CGN* UB8 .. 94 D4
Bosbury Rd *CAT* SE6 .... 141 J7
Boscastle Rd *KTTN* NW5 .. 84 B3
Boscobel Pl *BGVA* SW1W .. 16 B5
Boscobel St *BAY/PAD* W2 .. 9 G2
Boscombe Av *EMPK* RM11 .. 74 D8
WAN E11 .... 69 K8 🔲
Boscombe Cl *CLPT* E5 .. 86 E5
Boscombe Rd *SHB* W12 .. 100 A8
TOOT SW17 .... 156 A2
WIM/MER SW19 .... 155 J1
WPK KT4 .... 169 J3
Bosgrove *CHING* E4 .... 51 J3
Boss St *STHWK* SE1 .... 19 L1 🔲
Bostall Hl *ABYW* SE2 .. 126 B3

Bostall La ABYW SE2 126 B2
Bostall Manorway ABYW SE2 126 B2
Bostall Park Av BXLYHN DA7 126 E5
Bostall Rd STMC/STPC BR5 162 B3
Boston Gdns BTFD TW8 116 A2
  CHSWK W4 117 L4
Boston Gv RSLP HA4 59 L1
Boston Manor Rd BTFD TW8 116 A2
Boston Park Rd BTFD TW8 116 C3
Boston Pl CAMTN NW1 9 L1
Boston Rd CROY/NA CR0 171 M1
  EDGW HA8 63 J1
  EHAM E6 106 E2
  HNWL W7 97 M8
Bostonthorpe Rd HNWL W7 97 L8
Boston V HNWL W7 116 A2
Boswell Rd THHTH CR7 157 J7
Boswell St BMSBY WC1N 11 K2
Bosworth Cl WALTH E17 68 F2
Bosworth Crs HARH RM3 56 C8
Bosworth Rd BAR EN5 34 A6
  DAGE RM10 91 G4
  FBAR/BDGN N11 48 D8
  NKENS W10 100 E3
Botany Bay La CHST BR7 161 J5
Botany Cl EBAR EN4 34 E7
Botany Wy PUR RM19 129 H3
Boteley Cl CHING E4 51 K4
Botham Cl EDGW HA8 63 J1
Botha Rd PLSTW E13 106 B4
Bothwell Cl CAN/RD E16 106 A4
Bothwell Rd CROY/NA CR0 186 C3
Bothwell St FUL/PGN SW6 118 D4
Botolph La MON EC3R 13 J7
Botsford Rd RYNPK SW20 154 E5
Bott Rd RDART DA2 146 F8
Bott's Ms BAY/PAD W2 8 B5
Botwell Common Rd
  HYS/HAR UB3 95 K6
Botwell Crs HYS/HAR UB3 95 L5
Botwell La HYS/HAR UB3 95 M8
Boucher Cl TEDD TW11 151 M1
Boughton Av HAYES BR2 174 F2
Boughton Rd THMD SE28 125 L1
Boulcott St WCHPL E1 104 D5
The Boulevard WATW WD18 28 D8
Boulmer Rd UX/CGN UB8 94 C2
Boulogne Rd CROY/NA CR0 172 C1
Boulter Gdns RAIN RM13 92 A6
Boulton Rd BCTR RM8 90 E2
Boultwood Rd EHAM E6 106 F5
Bounces La ED N9 50 B4
Bounces Rd ED N9 50 B4
Boundaries Rd BAL SW12 137 M6
  FELT TW13 132 C5
Boundary Av WALTH E17 68 F8
Boundary Cl BAR EN5 33 M4
  GDMY/SEVK IG3 89 L4
  KUT KT1 153 H6
  NWDGN UB2 115 G3
Boundary La PLSTW E13 106 D2
  WALW SE17 121 J4
Boundary Ms STJWD NW8 2 F5
Boundary Rd ASHF TW15 148 D3
  BARK IG11 89 K8
  BFN/LL DA15 143 L2
  ED N9 50 C1
  PIN HA5 60 D7
  PLSTW E13 106 C1
  ROM RM1 74 A7
  STJWD NW8 2 E4
  UPMR RM14 93 G3
  WALTH E17 68 F8
  WDGN N22 67 J3
  WIM/MER SW19 155 K2
  WLGTN SM6 171 H8
  WLGTN SM6 183 G2
Boundary Rw STHWK SE1 18 C1
Boundary Ms BETH E2 7 L8
  ERITH DA8 127 M5
Boundary Wy CROY/NA CR0 174 A2
  GSTN WD25 21 J5
Boundfield Rd CAT SE6 141 L7
Bounds Green Rd
  FBAR/BDGN N11 48 D8
  WDGN N22 66 E1
Bourchier St SOHO/CST W1F 11 G6
Bourdon Rd PGE/AN SE20 158 C5
Bourdon St MYFR/PKLN W1K 10 C7
Bourke Cl CLAP SW4 138 E3
  WLSDN NW10 81 L6
Bourlet Cl FITZ W1T 10 E3
Bourn Av EBAR EN4 34 D8
  SEVS/STOTM N15 67 K5
  UX/CGN UB8 95 G3
Bournbrook Rd BKHTH/KID SE3 124 D8
Bourne Av CHERT KT16 148 A6
  HYS/HAR UB3 113 J1
  RSLP HA4 78 C5
  STHGT/OAK N14 48 E4
Bournebridge La ABR/ST RM4 55 H2
Bourne Cl RSLP HA4 78 B5
Bourne Dr MTCM CR4 155 K5
Bourne End EMPK RM11 75 G4
Bourne End Rd NTHWD HA6 41 L6
Bourne Gdns CHING E4 51 H6
Bournehall Av BUSH WD23 30 A8
Bournehall La BUSH WD23 43 C1
Bournehall Rd BUSH WD23 43 C1
Bourne HI PLMGR N13 48 F1
Bourne Md BXLY DA5 145 J2
Bournemead Av NTHLT UB5 96 A1
Bournemead Cl NTHLT UB5 96 A2
Bournemouth Rd PECK SE15 122 A7
  WIM/MER SW19 155 K2
Bourne Rd BUSH WD23 30 A8
  BXLY DA5 145 H4
  CEND/HSY/T N8 66 E7
  FSTGT E7 87 M3
  HAYES BR2 160 D7
Bourneside Crs
  STHGT/OAK N14 48 D3
Bourneside Gdns CAT SE6 159 J1
Bourne St BGVA SW1W 16 A6
  CROY/NA CR0 172 B4

Bourne Ter BAY/PAD W2 8 C2
The Bourne STHGT/OAK N14 48 E3
Bourne V HAYES BR2 175 G1
Bournevale Rd
  STRHM/NOR SW16 138 E8
Bourne Vw GFD/PVL UB6 79 M6
  PUR/KEN CR8 184 D8
Bourne Wy HAYES BR2 175 G4
  HOR/WEW KT19 168 C6
  SUT SM1 169 M7
  SWLY BR8 163 J6
Bournewood Rd
  STMC/STPC BR5 177 H2
  WOOL/PLUM SE18 126 A5
Bournville Rd CAT SE6 141 G4
Bournwell Cl EBAR EN4 34 F6
Bourton Cl HYS/HAR UB3 96 A7
Bousfield Rd NWCR SE14 122 D7
Boutflower Rd BTSEA SW11 137 L1
Bouverie Gdns
  KTN/HRWW/W HA3 62 D7
  PUR/KEN CR8 183 L7
Bouverie Ms STNW/STAM N16 85 L2
Bouverie Pl BAY/PAD W2 9 H4
Bouverie Rd HRW HA1 61 J7
  STNW/STAM N16 85 L2
Bouverie St EMB EC4Y 12 B5
Bouvier Rd PEND EN3 37 J3
Boveney Rd FSTH SE23 140 D4
Bovill Rd FSTH SE23 140 D4
Bovingdon Av WBLY HA9 81 C6
Bovingdon Crs GSTN WD25 21 K7
Bovingdon La
  CDALE/KGS NW9 63 L2
Bovingdon Rd FUL/PGN SW6 119 H6
Bow Arrow La DART DA1 147 L3
  RDART DA2 147 H3
Bowater Cl CDALE/KGS NW9 63 K6
  CLAP SW4 138 E3
Bowater Pl BKHTH/KID SE3 124 F3
Bowater Rd WOOL/PLUM SE18 124 D1
Bow Common La BOW E3 104 F3
Bowden Cl EBED/NFELT TW14 131 L5
Bowden Dr EMPK RM11 92 E1
Bowden St LBTH SE11 18 B7
Bowditch DEPT SE8 122 F3
Bowdon Rd LEY E10 69 C8
Bowen Dr DUL SE21 139 L7
Bowen Rd HRW HA1 61 J6
Bowen St POP/IOD E14 105 H5
Bower Av GNWCH SE10 123 L6
Bower Cl CRW RM5 73 K1
  NTHLT UB5 96 C1
Bowerdean St FUL/PGN SW6 119 H6
Bower Farm Rd ABR/ST RM4 55 J5
Bowerman Av NWCR SE14 122 E4
Bower St WCHPL E1 104 D5
Bowes Cl BFN/LL DA15 144 B3
Bowes Rd ACT W3 99 L6
  BCTR RM8 90 C4
  FBAR/BDGN N11 48 B7
  WOT/HER KT12 165 H4
Bowes Rd (North Circular Road)
  PLMGR N13 48 E7
Bowfell Rd HMSMTH W6 118 C4
Bowford Av BXLYHN DA7 126 E6
Bowhill Cl BRXN/ST SW9 121 G5
Bowie Cl CLAP SW4 138 D4
Bowland Rd CLAP SW4 138 D1
  WFD IG8 52 C8
Bow La FNCH N3 65 J1
Bowles Gn EN EN1 37 H1
Bowley Cl NRWD SE19 157 M2
Bowley La NRWD SE19 157 M1
Bowley Rd POP/IOD E14 104 F6
Bowling Green Cl
  PUT/ROE SW15 136 B4
Bowling Green Ct WBLY HA9 80 F2
Bowling Green La CLKNW EC1R 12 B1
Bowling Green Pl STHWK SE1 19 G1
Bowling Green Rw
  WOOL/PLUM SE18 124 F2
Bowling Green St LBTH SE11 18 B8
Bowling Green Wk IS N1 7 J2
Bowls Cl STAN HA7 44 B7
Bowman Av CAN/RD E16 105 M6
Bowman Ms WAND/EARL SW18 136 F5
Bowmans Cl POTB/CUF EN6 23 K5
  WEA W13 98 B7
Bowmans Gn GSTN WD25 29 L1
Bowmans Lea FSTH SE23 140 C4
Bowman's Meadow
  WLGTN SM6 171 H5
Bowman's Ms HOLWY N7 84 E3
Bowman's Pl HOLWY N7 84 E3
Bowmans Rd DART DA1 145 M4
Bowmead ELTH/MOT SE9 142 F6
Bowness Crs PUT/ROE SW15 153 L1
Bowness Dr HSLWW TW4 132 E1
Bowness Rd BXLYHN DA7 127 H7
  CAT SE6 141 H4
Bowness Wy HCH RM12 92 A5
Bowood Rd BTSEA SW11 138 A1
  PEND EN3 37 K5
Bowring Gn OXHEY WD19 42 C7
Bow Rd BOW E3 105 G2
Bowrons Av ALP/SUD HA0 80 D7
Bowsley Ct FELT TW13 132 A6
Bow St COVGDN WC2E 11 K5
  SRTFD E15 87 L5
Bowyer Cl EHAM E6 106 F4
Bowyer Pl CMBW SE5 121 J5
Boxall Rd DUL SE21 139 L3
Boxford Cl SAND/SEL CR2 185 K5
Boxgrove Rd ABYW SE2 126 C1
Box La BARK IG11 108 B1
Boxley Rd MRDN SM4 155 J7
Boxley St CAN/RD E16 106 B7
Boxmoor Rd CRW RM5 73 K5
  KTN/HRWW/W HA3 62 B5
Boxoll Rd DAGW RM9 90 A4
Box Ridge Av PUR/KEN CR8 183 M5
Boxted Cl BKHH IG9 52 E3
Boxtree La KTN/HRWW/W HA3 61 J2
Boxtree Rd KTN/HRWW/W HA3 61 K1
Boxwood Cl WDR/YW UB7 94 F8
Boxworth Gv IS N1 5 M3
Boyard Rd WOOL/PLUM SE18 125 H3

Boyce Cl BORE WD6 31 L4
Boyce Wy PLSTW E13 106 A3
Boycroft Av CDALE/KGS NW9 63 J7
Boyd Cl KUTN/CMB KT2 153 G3
Boyd Ct STJWD NW8 3 G2
Boyd Rd WIM/MER SW19 155 K2
Boyd St WCHPL E1 104 A5
Boyfield St STHWK SE1 18 D2
Boyland Rd BMLY BR1 159 M1
Boyle Av STAN HA7 44 A8
Boyle Farm Rd THDIT KT7 167 G1
Boyne Av HDN NW4 64 D5
Boyne Rd DAGE RM10 91 G3
  LEW SE13 123 K8
Boyne Terrace Ms
  NTGHL W11 100 F7
Boyson Rd WALW SE17 18 F9
Boyton Cl CEND/HSY/T N8 66 E4
  WCHPL E1 104 C3
Boyton Rd CEND/HSY/T N8 66 E3
Brabant Rd WDGN N22 66 F3
Brabazon Av WLGTN SM6 183 L2
Brabazon Rd HEST TW5 114 C5
  NTHLT UB5 97 G1
Brabazon St POP/IOD E14 105 H5
Brabourne Cl NRWD SE19 157 L1
Brabourne Crs BXLYHN DA7 126 F4
Brabourne Ri BECK BR3 159 K8
Brabourn Gv PECK SE15 122 C7
Bracewell Av GFD/PVL UB6 79 M5
Bracewell Rd NKENS W10 100 C4
Bracewood Gdns
  CROY/NA CR0 172 F5
Bracey St ARCH N19 84 E2
Bracken Av BAL SW12 138 A3
  CROY/NA CR0 174 A5
Brackenbridge Dr RSLP HA4 78 D3
Brackenbury Gdns
  HMSMTH W6 118 E1
Brackenbury Rd EFNCH N2 65 J4
  HMSMTH W6 118 E1
Bracken Cl EHAM E6 106 F4
  HSLWW TW4 133 G4
  SUN TW16 149 M2
Brackendale POTB/CUF EN6 23 G6
  WCHMH N21 48 F4
Brackendale Cl HEST TW5 115 H6
Brackendale Gdns UPMR RM14 93 J4
Brackendene BXLY DA5 145 L8
  LCOL/BKTW AL2 21 M3
Bracken Dr CHIG IG7 53 H8
Bracken End ISLW TW7 133 K2
Bracken Gdns BARN SW13 118 A7
Brackenhill COB KT11 178 A4
Bracken Hill Cl BMLY BR1 159 M4
Bracken Hill La BMLY BR1 159 M4
Bracken Ms ROMW/RG RM7 73 G7
Bracken Pth EPSOM KT18 180 A6
The Brackens ED N9 49 L2
  ORP BR6 177 G7
The Bracken CHING E4 51 J4
Brackenwood SUN TW16 150 A4
Brackley WEY KT13 164 D7
Brackley Cl WLGTN SM6 183 L1
Brackley Rd BECK BR3 158 F3
  CHSWK W4 117 L2
Brackley Sq WFD IG8 70 D1
Brackley St BARB EC2Y 12 F2
Brackley Ter CHSWK W4 117 L3
Bracklyn St IS N1 7 G5
Bracknell Cl WDGN N22 66 F2
Bracknell Gdns HAMP NW3 83 H5
Bracknell Wy HAMP NW3 83 H4
Bracondale ESH/CLAY KT10 166 C7
Bracondale Rd ABYW SE2 126 A2
Bradbourne Rd BXLY DA5 145 G4
Bradbourne St FUL/PGN SW6 119 L7
Bradbury Cl BORE WD6 32 B4
  NWDGN UB2 115 G2
Bradbury St STNW/STAM N16 85 L3
Braddock Cl ISLW TW7 115 M8
Braddon Rd RCH/KEW TW9 116 F6
Braddyll St GNWCH SE10 123 L3
Bradenham Av WELL DA16 144 A1
Bradenham Cl WALW SE17 19 G9
Bradenham Rd
  KTN/HRWW/W HA3 62 B5
  YEAD UB4 95 L2
Braden St MV/WKIL W9 8 C1
Bradfield Dr BARK IG11 90 A5
Bradfield Rd CAN/RD E16 106 A8
  RSLP HA4 78 E5
Bradford Cl HAYES BR2 175 M3
  SYD SE26 140 B8
  UED N18 49 M8
Bradford Dr HOR/WEW KT19 168 F8
Bradford Rd ACT W3 99 L8
  IL IG1 89 K1
Bradgate Cl POTB/CUF EN6 26 C1
Bradgate Rd CAT SE6 141 H3
Brading Crs WAN E11 88 B2
Brading Rd BRXS/STRHM SW2 138 F4
  CROY/NA CR0 171 M1
Brading Ter SHB W12 118 A1
Bradiston Rd MV/WKIL W9 100 F2
Bradley Cl HOLWY N7 84 F6
Bradley Gdns WEA W13 98 B5
Bradley Rd NRWD SE19 157 J2
  PEND EN3 37 L3
  WDGN N22 66 F3
Bradley Stone Rd EHAM E6 106 F5
Bradmead VX/NE SW8 120 C5
Bradmore Park Rd
  HMSMTH W6 118 E1
Bradshaw Cl
  WIM/MER SW19 155 J1
Bradshaw Rd WATN WD24 29 J1
Bradshaws Cl SNWD SE25 158 A6
Bradstock Rd EW KT17 169 H7
  HOM E9 87 H4
Brad St STHWK SE1 12 B9
Bradwell Av DAGE RM10 91 G2
Bradwell Cl HCH RM12 92 B6
  SWFD E18 69 M5
Bradwell Ms UED N18 50 A6
Bradwell Rd BKHH IG9 52 E3
Bradymead EHAM E6 107 G5

Brady St WCHPL E1 104 B3
Braemar Av ALP/SUD HA0 80 D7
  BXLYHN DA7 145 J1
  SAND/SEL CR2 184 C3
  THHTH CR7 157 G6
  WDGN N22 66 E2
  WIM/MER SW19 137 G6
  WLSDN NW10 81 K1
Braemar Gdns BFN/LL DA15 143 K7
  CDALE/KGS NW9 63 K2
  EMPK RM11 75 C7
  WWKM BR4 160 A7
Braemar Rd BTFD TW8 116 D4
  PLSTW E13 106 A3
  SEVS/STOTM N15 67 L6
  WPK KT4 169 H5
Braeside BECK BR3 159 C1
Braeside Av WIM/MER SW19 154 E4
Braeside Cl PIN HA5 61 L1
Braeside Crs BXLYHN DA7 145 J1
Braeside Rd STRHM/NOR SW16 156 C3
Braes St IS N1 6 D2
Braesyde Cl BELV DA17 126 F2
Brafferton Rd CROY/NA CR0 172 C6
Braganza St WALW SE17 18 C8
Bragg Rd TEDD TW11 151 L3
Braham St WCHPL E1 13 M5
Braid Av ACT W3 99 L5
Braid Cl FELT TW13 132 F6
Braidwood Rd CAT SE6 141 K5
Brailsford Cl WIM/MER SW19 155 L3
Brailsford Rd
  BRXS/STRHM SW2 139 G3
Brainton Av EBED/NFELT TW14 132 B4
Braintree Av REDBR IG4 70 E6
Braintree Rd DAGE RM10 91 G3
  RSLP HA4 78 B4
Braintree St BETH E2 104 C2
Brair Bank CAR SM5 183 G2
Braithwaite Av ROMW/RG RM7 73 G8
Braithwaite Gdns STAN HA7 62 C2
Braithwaite Rd PEND EN3 37 M6
Bramall Cl FSTGT E7 87 M5
Bramber Rd FUL/PGN SW6 118 F4
  NFNCH/WDSP N12 47 L7
Bramble Acres Cl
  BELMT SM2 182 A1
Bramble Banks CAR SM5 183 G2
Bramblebury Rd
  WOOL/PLUM SE18 125 K3
Bramble Cl CROY/NA CR0 174 A6
  GSTN WD25 21 G7
  SEVS/STOTM N15 68 A5
  SHPTN TW17 149 K7
  STAN HA7 62 D1
  UX/CGN UB8 94 F4
Bramble Cft ERITH DA8 127 J2
Brambledown STA TW18 148 B4
Brambledown Rd CAR SM5 183 L8
  SAND/SEL CR2 184 E1
Bramble Gdns SHB W12 99 M6
Bramble La HPTN TW12 150 F2
  UPMR RM14 93 J8
Brambles Cl BTFD TW8 116 B5
Brambles Farm Dr
  UX/CGN UB8 95 G2
The Brambles CHES/WCR EN8 26 D5
  CHIG IG7 53 J8
  WDR/YW UB7 112 E3
Bramble Wk EPSOM KT18 180 B7
Bramblewood Cl CAR SM5 170 F3
The Bramblings CHING E4 51 K6
Bramcote Av MTCM CR4 155 M7
Bramcote Gv BERM/RHTH SE16 122 C3
Bramcote Rd PUT/ROE SW15 136 B1
Bramdean Crs LEE/GVPK SE12 142 A5
Bramdean Gdns
  LEE/GVPK SE12 142 A5
Bramerton Rd BECK BR3 158 F6
Bramerton St CHEL SW3 15 J9
Bramfield GSTN WD25 21 L7
Bramfield Rd BTSEA SW11 137 L5
Bramford Rd
  WAND/EARL SW18 137 J1
Bramham Gdns CHSGTN KT9 167 K6
  ECT SW5 14 C7
Bramhope La CHARL SE7 126 A5
Bramlands Cl BTSEA SW11 119 L8
Bramleas WATW WD18 28 F8
Bramley Av COUL/CHIP CR5 183 J8
  SHPTN TW17 149 L6
Bramley Cl HYS/HAR UB3 96 A6
  ORP BR6 176 B5
  SAND/SEL CR2 172 B7
  STA TW18 148 C2
  STHGT/OAK N14 33 H8
  SWLY BR8 163 L7
  WALTH E17 68 E3
  WHTN TW2 133 J3
Bramley Crs GSTN WD25 21 H5
  VX/NE SW8 120 D5
Bramley Gdns OXHEY WD19 42 C8
Bramley HI SAND/SEL CR2 172 C6
Bramley Ldg ALP/SUD HA0 80 C4
Bramley Pl DART DA1 146 A1
Bramley Rd BELMT SM2 181 K2
  EA W5 116 C1
  NKENS W10 100 D6
  STHGT/OAK N14 35 H8
  SUT SM1 170 D7
Bramley Shaw WAB EN9 27 M6
Bramley Wy HSLWW TW4 132 E4
  WWKM BR4 174 B4

  CROY/NA CR0 172 F2
  EHAM E6 106 D3
  FSBYPK N4 67 J6
  HGDN/ICK UB10 95 H1
  OXHEY WD19 42 A5
Brampton Ter BORE WD6 32 A3
Bramshaw Gdns OXHEY WD19 42 D7
Bramshaw Ri NWMAL KT3 168 E1
Bramshaw Rd HOM E9 86 D6
Bramshill Gdns KTTN NW5 84 B3
Bramshill Rd WLSDN NW10 99 L1
Bramshot Av CHARL SE7 125 M6
Bramston Cl BARK/HLT IG6 53 M8
Bramston Rd WLSDN NW10 100 A1
Bramwell Cl SUN TW16 150 D5
Brancaster Dr MLHL NW7 64 A1
Brancaster La PUR/KEN CR8 184 C4
Brancaster Rd GNTH/NBYPK IG2 71 K7
  STRHM/NOR SW16 138 E7
Branch Pl IS N1 7 H3
Branch Rd BARK/HLT IG6 54 B7
  POP/IOD E14 104 E6
  POP/IOD E14 104 E6
Branch St PECK SE15 121 M5
Brancker Rd KTN/HRWW/W HA3 62 D4
Brancroft Wy PEND EN3 37 L4
Brand Cl FSBYPK N4 85 H1
Brandlehow Rd
  PUT/ROE SW15 136 F1
Brandon Rd DART DA1 147 G4
  HOLWY N7 5 J1
  NWDGN UB2 114 F3
  SUT SM1 170 B6
  WALTH E17 69 J4
Brandon St WALW SE17 18 F6
Brandram Rd LEW SE13 123 L8
Brandreth Rd EHAM E6 106 F5
  TOOT SW17 138 B6
The Brandries WLGTN SM6 171 K5
Brand St GNWCH SE10 123 J5
Brandville Gdns BARK/HLT IG6 71 H5
Brandville Rd WDR/YW UB7 94 E8
Brandy Wy BELMT SM2 182 A1
Branfill Rd UPMR RM14 93 H2
Brangbourne Rd BMLY BR1 159 J4
Brangton Rd LBTH SE11 17 M8
Brangwyn Crs WIM/MER SW19 155 K5
Branksea St FUL/PGN SW6 118 E5
Branksome Av UED N18 49 M8
Branksome Cl WOT/HER KT12 165 K4
Branksome Rd
  BRXS/STRHM SW2 138 E2
  WIM/MER SW19 155 G4
Branksome Wy
  KTN/HRWW/W HA3 62 F1
  NWMAL KT3 153 J5
Bransby Rd CHSGTN KT9 179 L1
Branscombe Gdns WCHMH N21 49 G2
Branscombe St LEW SE13 123 H8
Bransdale Cl KIL/WHAMP NW6 2 B3
Bransgrove Rd EDGW HA8 62 F2
Branston Crs STMC/STPC BR5 176 D3
Branstone Rd RCH/KEW TW9 116 F6
Branton Rd GRH DA9 147 M3
Brants Wk HNWL W7 97 L3
Brantwood Av ERITH DA8 127 J5
  ISLW TW7 134 A1
Brantwood Cl WALTH E17 69 H4
Brantwood Gdns ENC/FH EN2 35 L7
  REDBR IG4 70 E6
Brantwood Rd BXLYHN DA7 127 H5
  HNHL SE24 139 J2
  SAND/SEL CR2 184 C2
  TOTM N17 50 A8
Brantwood Wy
  STMC/STPC BR5 162 C6
Brasher Cl NTHLT UB5 79 K5
Brassey Cl
  EBED/NFELT TW14 132 A5
Brassey Rd CRICK NW2 82 A2
Brassey Sq BTSEA SW11 120 A8
Brassie Av ACT W3 99 L5
Brasted Cl BELMT SM2 182 A3
  BXLYHS DA6 144 D2
  SYD SE26 140 C8
Brasted Rd ERITH DA8 127 L5
Brathway Rd
  WAND/EARL SW18 137 J1
Bratley St WCHPL E1 104 A3
Braund Av GFD/PVL UB6 97 H3
Braundton Av BFN/LL DA15 143 M5
Braunston Dr YEAD UB4 96 E3
Bravington Cl SHPTN TW17 148 C5
Bravington Pl MV/WKIL W9 100 F3
Bravington Rd MV/WKIL W9 100 F2
Braxfield Rd BROCKY SE4 140 E1
Braxted Pk STRHM/NOR SW16 156 F2
Brayard's Rd PECK SE15 122 B7
Braybourne Dr ISLW TW7 115 M5
Braybrook St SHB W12 99 M4
Braybrooke Gdns NRWD SE19 157 J3
Braybrook St SHB W12 99 M4
Brayburne Av VX/NE SW8 120 C7
Bray Cl BORE WD6 32 C4
Braycourt Av WOT/HER KT12 165 J2
Bray Crs BERM/RHTH SE16 104 D8
Braydon Rd STNW/STAM N16 85 M3
Brayfield Ter IS N1 6 A2
Bray Pl CHEL SW3 15 L7
Bray Rd MLHL NW7 46 D8
Brayton Gdns ENC/FH EN2 35 K7
Braywood Rd ELTH/MOT SE9 143 K1
Breach La DAGW RM9 109 G2
Breach Rd WTHK RM20 129 A4
Bread St BLKFR EC4V 12 F6
  STP EC4M 12 F5
Breakspear Ct ABLGY WD5 20 F3
Breakspeare Cl WATN WD24 29 H3
Breakspeare Rd ABLGY WD5 20 E3
Breakspear Rd RSLP HA4 59 H7
Breakspear Rd North
  DEN/HRF UB9
Breakspear Rd South
  HGDN/ICK UB10 76 F3
Breakspears Dr
  STMC/STPC BR5 162 A4
Breakspears Ms BROCKY SE4 123 G7

Breakspears Rd *BROCKY* SE4 ...... 122 F8
Bream Cl *WALTH* E17 .... 68 B5
Bream Gdns *EHAM* E6 .... 107 G2
Breamore Cl *PUT/ROE* SW15 ... 136 A5 1
Breamore Rd *GDMY/SEVK* IG3 ..... 89 M2
Bream's Buildings *LINN* WC2A 12 A4
Bream St *BOW* E3 .... 87 G7
Breamwater Gdns
RCHPK/HAM TW10 .... 134 B7
Brearley Cl *EDGW* HA8 .... 63 J1 2
HGDN/ICK UB10 .... 76 E6 1
Breasley Cl *PUT/ROE* SW15 .... 136 B1
Brechin Pl *SKENS* SW7 .... 14 F7
Brecknock Rd *ARCH* N19 .... 84 C4
Brecon Cl *MTCM* CR4 .... 156 E7
WPK KT4 .... 169 J4
Brecon Rd *HMSMTH* W6 .... 118 E4
PEND EN3 .... 37 J7
Brede Cl *EHAM* E6 .... 107 G2
Bredgar Rd *ARCH* N19 .... 84 C2
Bredhurst Cl *PGE/AN* SE20 .... 158 C2
Bredon Rd *CROY/NA* CR0 .... 172 F2
Bredune *PUR/KEN* CR8 .... 183 K6
Breer St *FUL/PGN* SW6 .... 119 H8
Breezer's Hl *WAP* E1W 104 A6 1
Brember Rd *RYLN/HDSTN* HA2 ...... 79 J2
Bremer Ms *WALTH* E17 .... 69 H5 3
Bremer Rd *STA* TW18 .... 130 A7 1
Bremner Rd *SKENS* SW7 .... 14 F3
Brenchley Cl *CHST* BR7 .... 161 G4
HAYES BR2 .... 174 F1 1
Brenchley Gdns *FSTH* SE23 .... 140 C3
Brenchley Rd *STMC/STPC* BR5 .... 161 L4
Brendans Cl *EMPK* RM11 .... 92 E1 2
Brenda Rd *TOOT* SW17 .... 137 M6
Brende Gdns *E/WMO/HCT* KT8 .... 151 H7
Brendon Av *WLSDN* NW10 .... 81 L4
Brendon Cl *BXLYHN* DA7 .... 127 L6
ESH/CLAY KT10 .... 166 C8 1
HYS/HAR UB3 .... 113 J5
Brendon Dr *ESH/CLAY* KT10 .... 166 C8
Brendon Gdns
GNTH/NBYPK IG2 .... 71 L6 1
RYLN/HDSTN HA2 .... 79 H4
Brendon Gv *EFNCH* N2 .... 65 J3
Brendon Rd *BCTR* RM8 .... 90 F1
CHST BR7 .... 143 K6
Brendon St *MBLAR* W1H 9 K4
Brendon Wy *EN* EN1 .... 49 L2
Brenley Cl *MTCM* CR4 .... 156 A6 1
Brenley Gdns *ELTH/MOT* SE9 ...... 142 D1
Brent Cl *BXLY* DA5 .... 144 E5
RDART DA2 .... 147 H3
Brentcot Cl *WEA* W13 .... 98 B3
Brent Crs *WLSDN* NW10 .... 98 F1
Brent Cross F/O *HDN* NW4 .... 64 C7
Brentfield *WLSDN* NW10 .... 81 H7
Brentfield Cl *WLSDN* NW10 .... 81 K6
Brentfield Rd *DART* DA1 .... 147 G3
WLSDN NW10 .... 81 K6
Brentford Cl *YEAD* UB4 .... 96 D3 1
Brent Gn *HDN* NW4 .... 64 C6
Brentham Wy *EA* W5 .... 98 D3
Brenthouse Rd *HACK* E8 .... 86 B7
Brenthurst Rd *WLSDN* NW10 .... 81 M6
Brentlands Dr *DART* DA1 .... 147 G5
Brent La *DART* DA1 .... 146 F4
Brent Lea *BTFD* TW8 .... 116 C5
Brentmead Cl *HNWL* W7 .... 97 L6 1
Brentmead Gdns *WLSDN* NW10 ...... 98 F1
Brenton St *POP/IOD* E14 .... 104 E5 1
Brent Park Rd *CDALE/KGS* NW9 .... 82 A1
Brent Pl *BAR* EN5 .... 34 A8
Brent River Park Wk *HNWL* W7 ..... 97 K4
WEA W13 .... 98 B2
Brent Rd *BTFD* TW8 .... 116 C4 1
CAN/RD E16 .... 106 A5
NWDGN UB2 .... 114 C1
SAND/SEL CR2 .... 185 H2
WOOL/PLUM SE18 .... 125 H5
Brentside *BTFD* TW8 .... 116 C4
Brentside Cl *WEA* W13 .... 97 M3
Brent St *HDN* NW4 .... 64 D6 2
Brent Ter *CRICK* NW2 .... 82 C1
The Brent *DART* DA1 .... 147 H4
Brentvale Av *ALP/SUD* HA0 .... 80 F8
STHL UB1 .... 97 K7
Brent View Rd *CDALE/KGS* NW9 .... 64 A7
Brent Wy *BTFD* TW8 .... 116 D5 2
DART DA1 .... 147 H3
FNCH N3 .... 47 G8
WBLY HA9 .... 81 H6
Brentwick Gdns *BTFD* TW8 .... 116 E2
Brentwood Cl *ELTH/MOT* SE9 .. 143 J5 1
Brentwood Rd *GPK* RM2 .... 74 C6
ROM RM1 .... 73 M7
Brereton Rd *TOTM* N17 .... 67 M1
Bressenden Pl *WESTW* SW1E 16 D3
Bressey Av *EN* EN1 .... 37 G4
Bressey Gv *SWFD* E18 .... 69 M3
Brett Cl *NTHLT* UB5 .... 96 D2 2
STNW/STAM N16 .... 85 L2
Brett Crs *WLSDN* NW10 .... 81 K7
Brettell St *WALW* SE17 .... 19 H8
Brettenham Av *WALTH* E17 .... 69 G2 1
Brettenham Rd *UED* N18 .... 50 A6
WALTH E17 .... 69 G3
Brett Gdns *DAGW* RM9 .... 90 E7
Brettgrave *HOR/WEW* KT19 .... 180 C3
Brett Pas *HACK* E8 .... 86 B5 2
Brett Pl *WATN* WD24 .... 29 G2
Brett Rd *BAR* EN5 .... 33 J8
HACK E8 .... 86 B5
Brevet Cl *PUR* RM19 .... 129 K2
Brewers Fld *RDART* DA2 .... 146 C8
Brewer St *REGST* W1B 10 F6
Brewery Cl *ALP/SUD* HA0 .... 80 A5
Brewery Rd *HAYES* BR2 .... 175 L3
WOOL/PLUM SE18 .... 125 K3
Brewhouse La *WAP* E1W 104 B7 2
Brewhouse Rd
WOOL/PLUM SE18 .... 124 F2 2
Brewhouse St *PUT/ROE* SW15 ...... 136 E1
Brewhouse Wk
BERM/RHTH SE16 .... 104 E7
Brewood Rd *BCTR* RM8 .... 90 B6
Brewster Gdns *NKENS* W10 .... 100 C4
Brewster Rd *LEY* E10 .... 87 H1
Brian Av *SAND/SEL* CR2 .... 184 E5
Brian Cl *HCH* RM12 .... 92 B4 1
Briane Rd *HOR/WEW* KT19 .... 180 C3
Brian Rd *CHDH* RM6 .... 72 C6
Briants Cl *PIN* HA5 .... 60 E2
Briant St *NWCR* SE14 .... 122 D6
Briar Av *STRHM/NOR* SW16 .... 156 F3
Briarbank Rd *WEA* W13 .... 98 A5
Briar Cl *BKHH* IG9 .... 52 D4
CHES/WCR EN8 .... 26 C2
EFNCH N2 .... 65 J3 1
HPTN TW12 .... 150 F1
ISLW TW7 .... 133 M2
PLMGR N13 .... 49 J5
Briar Crs *NTHLT* UB5 .... 79 H6
Briardale Gdns *HAMP* NW3 .... 83 G3
Briarfield Av *FNCH* N3 .... 65 H3
Briar Gdns *HAYES* BR2 .... 174 F3
Briar Gv *SAND/SEL* CR2 .... 185 G6
Briar Hl *PUR/KEN* CR8 .... 183 L4
Briar La *CAR* SM5 .... 183 G2
CROY/NA CR0 .... 174 B6
Briarleas Gdns *UPMR* RM14 .... 75 L8
Briar Rd *BXLY* DA5 .... 145 K7
CRICK NW2 .... 82 C4
GSTN WD25 .... 21 G7
HARH RM3 .... 74 C1
KTN/HRWW/W HA3 .... 62 C6
SHPTN TW17 .... 148 F8
STRHM/NOR SW16 .... 156 E6
WHTN TW2 .... 133 L5
Briars Ct *LHD/OX* KT22 .... 178 D7
The Briars *CHES/WCR* EN8 .... 26 E4
STWL/WRAY TW19 .... 130 A2 1
Briars Wk *HARH* RM3 .... 74 E3
Briarswood Wy *ORP* BR6 .... 176 F7
Briar Wk *EDGW* HA8 .... 63 J1
NKENS W10 .... 100 E3 2
PUT/ROE SW15 .... 136 B1
Briar Wy *WDR/YW* UB7 .... 95 G8
Briarwood Cl *CDALE/KGS* NW9 .. 63 J7 2
FELT TW13 .... 131 L7 1
Briarwood Dr *NTHWD* HA6 .... 60 A3
Briarwood Rd *CLAP* SW4 .... 138 D2
EW KT17 .... 169 G8
Briary Cl *EDGW* HA8 .... 63 H3
HAMP NW3 .... 3 J1
Briary Ct *SCUP* DA14 .... 162 B1
Briary Gdns *BMLY* BR1 .... 160 B1
Briary La *ED* N9 .... 49 M5 1
Brickett Cl *RSLP* HA4 .... 59 J6
Brick Farm Cl *RCH/KEW* TW9 ...... 117 H6
Brickfield Cl *BTFD* TW8 .... 116 C5 1
Brickfield Cottages
WOOL/PLUM SE18 .... 125 M5
Brickfield Farm Gdns
ORP BR6 .... 176 C6 2
Brickfield La *BAR* EN5 .... 45 M1
HYS/HAR UB3 .... 113 K4
Brickfield Rd *BOW* E3 .... 105 H3
THHTH CR7 .... 157 H4
WIM/MER SW19 .... 137 H8
Brickfields *RYLN/HDSTN* HA2 .... 79 K2 3
Brickfields Wy *WDR/YW* UB7 ...... 112 F1
Brick Kiln Cl *BUSH* WD23 .... 42 E1 2
Brick La *BETH* E2 .... 7 M8
EN EN1 .... 37 H5
PEND EN3 .... 37 J5
STAN HA7 .... 62 D1
WCHPL E1 .... 13 M1
Brick St *MYFR/PICC* W1J 10 C9
Brickwall La *RSLP* HA4 .... 77 L1
Brickwood Cl *SYD* SE26 .... 140 B7 1
Brickwood Rd *CROY/NA* CR0 .... 172 E4
Bride La *EMB* EC4Y 12 C5
Bride St *HOLWY* N7 .... 84 F6
Bridewain St *STHWK* SE1 .... 19 L3
Bridewell Pl *BLKFR* EC4V 12 C5 2
WAP E1W 104 B7 3
Bridford Ms *REGST* W1B 10 D2
Bridge Ap *CAMTN* NW1 .... 4 A1
Bridge Av *HMSMTH* W6 .... 118 C2 3
HNWL W7 .... 97 K4
UPMR RM14 .... 93 G3
Bridge Cl *EN* EN1 .... 37 H4 1
GRH DA9 .... 129 K8
NKENS W10 .... 100 D5 1
ROM RM1 .... 73 L7
WOT/HER KT12 .... 164 F2
Bridge Dr *PLMGR* N13 .... 48 F6
Bridge End *WALTH* E17 .... 69 J2
Bridgefield Cl *BNSTD* SM7 .... 181 J8
Bridgefield Rd *SUT* SM1 .... 170 A8
Bridge Gdns *ASHF* TW15 .... 149 J3
E/WMO/HCT KT8 .... 151 K7
Bridge Ga *WCHMH* N21 .... 49 J2
Bridgeham Cl *WEY* KT13 .... 164 A7 2
Bridge House Quay
POP/IOD E14 .... 105 J7 1
Bridgeland Rd *CAN/RD* E16 .... 106 A6
Bridge La *BTSEA* SW11 .... 119 L6
GLDGN NW11 .... 64 E6
Bridgeman Rd *IS* N1 .... 5 M2
TEDD TW11 .... 152 A2
Bridgeman St *STJWD* NW8 .... 3 J6
Bridge Mdw *NWCR* SE14 .... 122 D4
Bridgend Rd *EN* EN1 .... 26 C8
Bridgenhall Rd *EN* EN1 .... 36 F4
Bridgen Rd *BXLY* DA5 .... 144 E4
Bridge Pl *CROY/NA* CR0 .... 172 D3
PIM SW1V 16 D5
WAT WD17 .... 29 K8 1
Bridger Cl *GSTN* WD25 .... 21 K6
Bridge Rd *BECK* BR3 .... 158 F3
BELMT SM2 .... 170 B8
BXLYHN DA7 .... 126 E8
CHSGTN KT9 .... 167 L7
E/WMO/HCT KT8 .... 151 L7
ED N9 .... 50 A5 2
EHAM E6 .... 88 F7
ERITH DA8 .... 127 M6
EW KT17 .... 180 F5
HSLW TW3 .... 115 K8
KGLGY WD4 .... 20 C6
LEY E10 .... 68 F8
NWDGN UB2 .... 96 F8
RAIN RM13 .... 110 A3
SRTFD E15 .... 87 K8
STMC/STPC BR5 .... 177 H1
TWK TW1 .... 134 B3 3
UX/CGN UB8 .... 94 C1
WBLY HA9 .... 81 J3
WDGN N22 .... 66 E2
WLGTN SM6 .... 171 H7
WLSDN NW10 .... 81 L6
Bridge Rw *CROY/NA* CR0 .... 172 D3 1
Bridges Ct *BTSEA* SW11 .... 119 K8
Bridges Dr *DART* DA1 .... 147 H2
Bridges La *CROY/NA* CR0 .... 171 L6
Bridges Rd *STAN* HA7 .... 43 M7
Bridge St *CHSWK* W4 .... 117 K2
PIN HA5 .... 60 D4
TWK TW1 .... 134 D3
WEST SW1P 17 J2
WOT/HER KT12 .... 164 F3
Bridge Ter *SRTFD* E15 .... 87 K7
The Bridge *KTN/HRWW/W* HA3 .... 61 M4
Bridgetown Cl *NRWD* SE19 ...... 157 L1 2
Bridgeview *HMSMTH* W6 .... 118 C3 1
Bridgewater Cl *CHST* BR7 .... 161 L6
Bridgewater Gdns *EDGW* HA8 ...... 62 F3
Bridgewater Rd *ALP/SUD* HA0 ...... 80 C7
RSLP HA4 .... 78 A4
SRTFD E15 .... 87 J8
WEY KT13 .... 164 D8
Bridgewater Sq *BARB* EC2Y 12 E2 1
Bridgewater St *BARB* EC2Y 12 E2 2
Bridgewater Wy *BUSH* WD23 .... 43 H1
Bridge Wy *WHTN* TW2 .... 133 J4
GLDGN NW11 .... 64 F6
HGDN/ICK UB10 .... 77 H5
Bridgeway *ALP/SUD* HA0 .... 80 E7
BARK IG11 .... 89 M7 1
Bridgeway St *CAMTN* NW1 .... 4 F6
Bridgewood Cl *PGE/AN* SE20 .. 158 B3 1
Bridgewood Rd
STRHM/NOR SW16 .... 156 D3
WPK KT4 .... 169 G6
Bridgford St
WAND/EARL SW18 .... 137 J7 1
Bridgman Rd *CHSWK* W4 .... 117 J1
Bridgwater Rd *HARH* RM3 .... 56 C7
Bridgwater Wk *HARH* RM3 .... 56 D7 1
Bridle Cl *HOR/WEW* KT19 .... 168 C6
KUT KT1 .... 152 D7 1
PEND EN3 .... 37 M2
SUN TW16 .... 150 A6
Bridle La *COB* KT11 .... 178 B8
SOHO/CST W1F 10 F6
TWK TW1 .... 134 B3 1
Bridle Pth *CROY/NA* CR0 .... 171 L5
WAT WD17 .... 29 H5
The Bridle Pth *EW* KT17 .... 181 J3
WFD IG8 .... 69 L1
Bridlepath Wy
EBED/NFELT TW14 .... 131 L4 1
Bridle Rd *CROY/NA* CR0 .... 174 A4
ESH/CLAY KT10 .... 167 H8
EW KT17 .... 180 F6
PIN HA5 .... 60 C7
The Bridle Rd *PUR/KEN* CR8 .... 183 L3
Bridle Wy *CROY/NA* CR0 .... 174 A7
ORP BR6 .... 176 C6
Bridleway Cl *EW* KT17 .... 181 J3 2
The Bridle Wy *WLGTN* SM6 .... 171 J6
Bridlington Rd *ED* N9 .... 50 B2
OXHEY WD19 .... 42 D5
Bridport Av *ROMW/RG* RM7 .... 73 H7
Bridport Pl *IS* N1 .... 7 H5
Bridport Rd *NTHLT* UB5 .... 79 H8
THHTH CR7 .... 157 G6
UED N18 .... 49 L7
Bridstow Pl *BAY/PAD* W2 .... 8 B4
Brief St *CMBW* SE5 .... 121 H6
Brierley Av *ED* N9 .... 50 C3
Brierley Cl *EMPK* RM11 .... 74 C7
SNWD SE25 .... 158 A7 1
Brierley Rd *BAL* SW12 .... 138 C6 1
WAN E11 .... 87 K4
Brierly Gdns *BETH* E2 .... 104 C1 1
Brigade Cl *RYLN/HDSTN* HA2 ...... 79 K2 1
Brigade St *BKHTH/KID* SE3 ...... 123 M7 1
Brigadier Av *ENC/FH* EN2 .... 36 C4
Brigadier Hl *ENC/FH* EN2 .... 36 C3
Briggeford Cl *CLPT* E5 .... 86 A2 1
Briggs Cl *MTCM* CR4 .... 156 B4 1
Bright Cl *BELV* DA17 .... 126 D2
Brightfield Rd *LEW* SE13 .... 141 L2
Brightling Rd *BROCKY* SE4 .... 140 F3
Brightlingsea Pl
POP/IOD E14 .... 104 F6 2
Brightman Rd
WAND/EARL SW18 .... 137 K5
Brighton Av *WALTH* E17 .... 68 F6
Brighton Cl *HGDN/ICK* UB10 .... 77 H7
Brighton Dr *NTHLT* UB5 .... 79 G6
Brighton Rd *BELMT* SM2 .... 182 B3
BNSTD SM7 .... 181 M7
COUL/CHIP CR5 .... 183 L8
EFNCH N2 .... 65 J3
EHAM E6 .... 107 G2
PUR/KEN CR8 .... 183 L7
SAND/SEL CR2 .... 184 C2 1
STNW/STAM N16 .... 85 L4
SURB KT6 .... 167 J1
WATN WD24 .... 29 G3
Brighton Ter *BRXN/ST* SW9 .... 138 F1
Brights Av *RAIN* RM13 .... 110 B3
Brightside Av *STA* TW18 .... 148 C3
Brightside Rd *LEW* SE13 .... 141 K3
The Brightside *PEND* EN3 .... 37 K4
Bright St *POP/IOD* E14 .... 105 H5
Brightview Cl *LCOL/BKTW* AL2 .... 21 L2 1
Brightwell Cl *CROY/NA* CR0 ...... 172 A3 1
Brightwell Crs *TOOT* SW17 .... 155 M1
Brightwell Rd *WATW* WD18 .... 29 G8
Brig Ms *DEPT* SE8 .... 123 G4
Brigstock Rd *BELV* DA17 .... 127 H2
COUL/CHIP CR5 .... 183 H8
THHTH CR7 .... 157 H8
Brill Pl *CAMTN* NW1 .... 5 H6
Brimfield Rd *PUR* RM19 .... 129 K2
Brim Hl *EFNCH* N2 .... 65 J5
Brimpsfield Cl *ABYW* SE2 .... 126 B1 1
Brimsdown Av *PEND* EN3 .... 37 H4
Brindle Ga *BFN/LL* DA15 .... 143 L5
Brindles *EMPK* RM11 .... 74 E5
Brindley Cl *BXLYHN* DA7 .... 127 H8 1
GFD/PVL UB6 .... 80 C8
Brindley St *NWCR* SE14 .... 122 F6
Brindley Wy *BMLY* BR1 .... 160 A1
STHL UB1 .... 97 H6
Brindwood Rd *CHING* E4 .... 51 G5
Brinkburn Cl *ABYW* SE2 .... 126 A2 1
EDGW HA8 .... 63 H4
Brinkburn Gdns *EDGW* HA8 .... 63 G4
Brinkley Rd *WPK* KT4 .... 169 H4
Brinklow Crs *WOOL/PLUM* SE18 .. 125 H5
Brinkworth Rd *CLAY* IG5 .... 70 E4
Brinley Cl *CHES/WCR* EN8 .... 26 D4
Brinsdale Rd *HDN* NW4 .... 64 D4
Brinsley Rd *KTN/HRWW/W* HA3 .... 61 K3
Brinsley St *WCHPL* E1 .... 104 B5 3
Brinsmead Rd *HARH* RM3 .... 75 G3
Brinsworth Cl *WHTN* TW2 .... 133 K5
Brion Pl *POP/IOD* E14 .... 105 J4
Brisbane Av *WIM/MER* SW19 .... 155 H4
Brisbane Rd *IL* IG1 .... 71 J8
LEY E10 .... 87 H2
Brisbane St *CMBW* SE5 .... 121 K5
Briscoe Cl *WAN* E11 .... 87 M2
Briscoe Rd *RAIN* RM13 .... 110 C1
WIM/MER SW19 .... 155 K2
Briset Rd *ELTH/MOT* SE9 .... 124 D8
Briset St *FARR* EC1M 12 C2
Briset Wy *HOLWY* N7 .... 84 F2 1
Brisson Cl *ESH/CLAY* KT10 .... 165 M8
Bristol Cl *STWL/WRAY* TW19 ...... 130 E3 1
Bristol Gdns *MV/WKIL* W9 .... 8 D1
Bristol Park Rd *WALTH* E17 .... 68 E5 1
Bristol Rd *FSTGT* E7 .... 88 C6
GFD/PVL UB6 .... 79 H8
MRDN SM4 .... 155 J8
Briston Gv *CEND/HSY/T* N8 ...... 66 E7 1
Bristow Rd *BXLYHN* DA7 .... 126 E6
CROY/NA CR0 .... 171 L6
HSLW TW3 .... 115 H8
NRWD SE19 .... 157 L1
Britannia Cl *CLAP* SW4 .... 138 D1
NTHLT UB5 .... 96 D2
Britannia Ga *CAN/RD* E16 .... 106 A7 2
Britannia Rd *BRYLDS* KT5 .... 167 M2
CHES/WCR EN8 .... 26 F7
FUL/PGN SW6 .... 119 H5
IL IG1 .... 89 H3
NFNCH/WDSP N12 .... 47 J5
POP/IOD E14 .... 123 G2 1
Britannia Rw *IS* N1 .... 6 D3
Britannia St *FSBYW* WC1X 5 L7
Britannia Wk *IS* N1 .... 7 G7
Britannia Wy *FUL/PGN* SW6 .... 119 H5 2
STWL/WRAY TW19 .... 130 D4
WLSDN NW10 .... 99 H3
British Gv *CHSWK* W4 .... 117 M3
British Grove Pas
CHSWK W4 .... 117 M3 3
British Legion Rd *CHING* E4 ...... 51 M4 1
British St *BOW* E3 .... 104 F2
Briton Cl *SAND/SEL* CR2 .... 184 E4 1
Briton Crs *SAND/SEL* CR2 .... 184 E4
Briton Hill Rd *SAND/SEL* CR2 ...... 184 E3
Brittain Rd *BCTR* RM8 .... 90 E3
WOT/HER KT12 .... 165 K7
Britten Cl *BORE* WD6 .... 44 D1
GLDGN NW11 .... 83 H1
Britten Dr *STHL* UB1 .... 97 G5
Britten St *CHEL* SW3 .... 15 J8
Britton Cl *CAT* SE6 .... 141 K4
Britton St *FARR* EC1M 12 C1
Brixham Crs *RSLP* HA4 .... 78 A1
Brixham Gdns *GDMY/SEVK* IG3 ...... 89 L5
Brixham Rd *WELL* DA16 .... 126 D6
Brixham St *CAN/RD* E16 .... 106 F7
Brixton Hl *BRXS/STRHM* SW2 ...... 138 F3
Brixton Hill Pl
BRXS/STRHM SW2 .... 138 E4 1
Brixton Ov *BRXN/ST* SW9 .... 139 G1 1
Brixton Rd *BRXN/ST* SW9 .... 121 G7
CMBW SE5 .... 121 G4 1
WATN WD24 .... 29 H4
Brixton Station Rd
BRXN/ST SW9 .... 121 G8
Brixton Water La
BRXS/STRHM SW2 .... 138 F2
Broad Acre *LCOL/BKTW* AL2 .... 21 L3
Broadacre *STA* TW18 .... 148 A1 1
Broadacre Cl *HGDN/ICK* UB10 .... 77 H3 1
Broadbent St
MYFR/PKLN W1K 10 C6 1
Broad Bridge Cl
BKHTH/KID SE3 .... 124 A5
Broad Cl *WOT/HER* KT12 .... 165 K5
Broadcoombe *SAND/SEL* CR2 ...... 185 K1
Broadcroft Av *STAN* HA7 .... 62 D3
Broadcroft Rd *STMC/STPC* BR5 .. 176 D2
Broadfield Cl *CRICK* NW2 .... 82 C3
ROM RM1 .... 73 M6 1
Broadfield Ct *BUSH* WD23 .... 43 L4
Broadfield La *HOLWY* N7 .... 5 J2
Broadfield Rd *CAT* SE6 .... 141 L5
Broadfields *CHESW* EN7 .... 25 H2
E/WMO/HCT KT8 .... 166 D1
PIN HA5 .... 61 H3
RYLN/HDSTN HA2 .... 61 H3
Broadfields Av *EDGW* HA8 .... 45 H6
WCHMH N21 .... 49 G2
Broadfields Hts *EDGW* HA8 ...... 45 H6 1
Broadfields La *OXHEY* WD19 ...... 42 B3
Broadfield Sq *EN* EN1 .... 37 H6
Broadfields Wy *WLSDN* NW10 ...... 81 M5
Broadfield Wy *BKHH* IG9 .... 52 C5
Broadgate *WAB* EN9 .... 27 M6
Broadgates Av *EBAR* EN4 .... 34 B4
Broadgates Rd
WAND/EARL SW18 .... 137 K5 1
Broad Green Av *CROY/NA* CR0 .... 172 B2
Broadhead Strd
CDALE/KGS NW9 .... 63 M3
Broadheath Dr *CHST* BR7 .... 160 F1
Broadhinton Rd *CLAP* SW4 .... 120 B8
Broadhurst Av *EDGW* HA8 .... 45 H6
GDMY/SEVK IG3 .... 89 M4
Broadhurst Gdns
KIL/WHAMP NW6 .... 83 J6 1
RSLP HA4 .... 78 C2 1
Broadlands *FELT* TW13 .... 132 F7
Broadlands Av *PEND* EN3 .... 37 H6
SHPTN TW17 .... 164 C1
STRHM/NOR SW16 .... 138 E6
Broadlands Cl *HGT* N6 .... 66 A8
PEND EN3 .... 37 J6 1
STRHM/NOR SW16 .... 138 E6 2
Broadlands Rd *BMLY* BR1 .... 142 B8
HGT N6 .... 65 M8
Broadlands Wy *NWMAL* KT3 ...... 168 F1
Broad La *HPTN* TW12 .... 150 F3
RDART DA2 .... 146 B8
SEVS/STOTM N15 .... 67 M6
Broad Lawn *ELTH/MOT* SE9 .... 143 G5
Broadlawns Ct
KTN/HRWW/W HA3 .... 61 M2 1
Broadley St *STJWD* NW8 .... 9 J2
Broadley Ter *CAMTN* NW1 .... 9 K1
Broadmead *CAT* SE6 .... 141 G7
Broadmead Av *WPK* KT4 .... 169 G2
Broadmead Cl *HPTN* TW12 .... 151 G2
PIN HA5 .... 60 E1 1
Broadmead Rd *WFD* IG8 .... 52 A8
YEAD UB4 .... 96 E3
Broad Oak *SUN* TW16 .... 149 M2
WFD IG8 .... 52 B7
Broadoak Av *PEND* EN3 .... 26 D8
Broad Oak Cl *CHING* E4 .... 51 G7
STMC/STPC BR5 .... 162 A5
Broadoak Rd *ERITH* DA8 .... 127 K5
Broad Oaks *SURB* KT6 .... 168 B3
Broad Oaks Wy *HAYES* BR2 .... 159 M8
Broadstone Pl *MHST* W1U 10 A3
Broadstone Rd *HCH* RM12 .... 92 A2 2
Broad St *DAGE* RM10 .... 91 G7
TEDD TW11 .... 151 M2
Broad Street Av *LVPST* EC2M 13 J3
Broadview *WBLY* HA9 .... 63 G7 1
Broadview Rd
STRHM/NOR SW16 .... 156 D3 1
Broad Wk *WCHMH* N21 .... 49 G3
WOOL/PLUM SE18 .... 124 F7
BKHTH/KID SE3 .... 124 C7
HEST TW5 .... 114 D6
ORP BR6 .... 177 K5
RCH/KEW TW9 .... 116 F5
Broadwalk *SWFD* E18 .... 69 M4
Broadwalk La *GLDGN* NW11 .... 64 F8
The Broad Wk *KENS* W8 .... 8 D8
NTHWD HA6 .... 59 J3
Broadwall *STHWK* SE1 .... 12 B8
Broadwater *POTB/CUF* EN6 .... 23 H3
Broadwater Cl *WOT/HER* KT12 .... 165 G7
Broadwater Gdns *DEN/HRF* UB9 .. 58 B5
ORP BR6 .... 176 B6
Broadwater La *DEN/HRF* UB9 ...... 58 B5
Broadwater Rd *TOOT* SW17 .... 137 L8
TOTM N17 .... 67 L3
WOOL/PLUM SE18 .... 125 K1
Broadwater Rd North
WOT/HER KT12 .... 165 G7
Broadwater Rd South
WOT/HER KT12 .... 165 G7
Broadway *BARK* IG11 .... 89 J8
BXLYHS DA6 .... 144 E1
GPK RM2 .... 74 A4
HNWL W7 .... 97 L7
RAIN RM13 .... 110 A3
SRTFD E15 .... 87 K7
STJSPK SW1H 17 G3
SURB KT6 .... 168 B3
SUT SM1 .... 170 C6
Broadway Av *CROY/NA* CR0 .... 157 K8
TWK TW1 .... 134 B3
Broadway Cl *SAND/SEL* CR2 .... 185 H7
WFD IG8 .... 52 B8 2
Broadway Gdns *MTCM* CR4 .... 155 L7
Broadway Market *HACK* E8 .... 86 B8
Broadway Ms
STNW/STAM N16 .... 67 M8 1
The Broadway *BCTR* RM8 .... 91 G2 1
CDALE/KGS NW9 .... 63 M7
CEND/HSY/T N8 .... 66 E7
CHEAM SM3 .... 169 L8
EA W5 .... 98 D6
HCH RM12 .... 92 B4
KTN/HRWW/W HA3 .... 61 L3
MLHL NW7 .... 45 L7
PIN HA5 .... 60 F1
PLSTW E13 .... 106 A1
STA TW18 .... 148 C6
STAN HA7 .... 44 C7
THDIT KT7 .... 166 E3
WAT WD17 .... 29 J6 1
WFD IG8 .... 52 B8 1
WIM/MER SW19 .... 154 F2
Broadwick St *SOHO/CST* W1F 10 F5
Broadwood Av *RSLP* HA4 .... 59 L7
Brocas Cl *HAMP* NW3 .... 3 K1
Brockdene Dr *HAYES* BR2 .... 175 K6
Brockdish Av *BARK* IG11 .... 89 M5 1
Brockenhurst
E/WMO/HCT KT8 .... 165 M1 1
Brockenhurst Av *WPK* KT4 .... 168 E3
Brockenhurst Gdns *IL* IG1 .... 89 J5
MLHL NW7 .... 45 L7 2
Brockenhurst Rd *CROY/NA* CR0 .. 173 H2
Brockenhurst Wy
STRHM/NOR SW16 .... 156 D5
Brocket Cl *CHIG* IG7 .... 53 M6
Brocket Wy *CHIG* IG7 .... 53 L7
Brockham Cl *WIM/MER* SW19 ...... 154 F1
Brockham Crs *CROY/NA* CR0 .... 186 D1
Brockham Dr
BRXS/STRHM SW2 .... 138 F4
GNTH/NBYPK IG2 .... 71 J7
Brockham St *STHWK* SE1 .... 18 F3
Brockhurst Cl *STAN* HA7 .... 43 M8
Brockill Crs *BROCKY* SE4 .... 140 E1
Brocklebank Rd *CHARL* SE7 ...... 124 B2 1
WAND/EARL SW18 .... 137 J4
Brocklehurst St *NWCR* SE14 ...... 122 D5
Brocklesbury Cl *WATN* WD24 ...... 29 J6
Brocklesby Rd *SNWD* SE25 ...... 158 B7 1
Brockley Av *EDGW* HA8 .... 44 E5
Brockley Cl *STAN* HA7 .... 44 E6
Brockley Combe *WEY* KT13 .... 164 D7

Brockley Crs CRW RM5 73 J1
Brockley Cross BROCKY SE4 122 E8
Brockley Gv BROCKY SE4 140 F2
Brockley Hall Rd BROCKY SE4 140 E3
Brockley Hl STAN HA7 44 C4
Brockley Ms BROCKY SE4 140 E2
Brockley Pk FSTH SE23 140 E4
Brockley Ri FSTH SE23 140 E4
Brockley Rd BROCKY SE4 140 F2
Brockleyside STAN HA7 44 E6 1
Brockley Vw FSTH SE23 140 E4
Brockley Wy FSTH SE23 140 D2
Brockman Ri BMLY BR1 141 K8
Brock Pl BOW E3 105 H3
Brock Rd PLSTW E13 106 B4
Brocks Dr CHEAM SM3 169 L5
Brockshot Cl BTFD TW8 116 D4 5
Brock St PECK SE15 122 C8 4
Brockton Cl ROM RM1 73 M5 1
Brockway Cl WAN E11 87 L2
Brockwell Cl STMC/STPC BR5 161 M8
Brockwell Park Gdns
HNHL SE24 139 H4
Brockworth Cl PECK SE15 121 L4 2
Brodewater Rd BORE WD6 32 B5 1
Brodia Rd STNW/STAM N16 85 L3
Brodie Rd CHING E4 51 J3
ENC/FH EN2 36 C3
Brodie St STHWK SE1 19 M7
Brodlove La WAP E1W 104 D6
Brodrick Gv ABYW SE2 126 B2
Brodrick Rd TOOT SW17 137 M5
Brograve Gdns BECK BR3 159 H5
Broken Whf BLKFR EC4V 12 E6 1
Brokesley St BOW E3 104 F3
Bromar Rd CMBW SE5 121 L8
Bromborough Gn
OXHEY WD19 42 C7 2
Bromefield STAN HA7 62 C2
Bromehead St WCHPL E1 104 C5 2
Bromell's Rd CLAP SW4 138 C1
Brome Rd ELTH/MOT SE9 124 F8
Bromet Cl WAT WD17 28 F3
Bromfelde Rd CLAP SW4 120 D8
Bromfield St IS N1 6 B5
Bromhall Rd DAGW RM9 90 B6
Bromhedge ELTH/MOT SE9 142 F7
Bromholm Rd ABYW SE2 126 B1
Bromleigh Cl CHES/WCR EN8 26 E1 1
Bromley Av BMLY BR1 159 L3
Bromley Common HAYES BR2 175 L2
Bromley Crs HAYES BR2 159 M6
RSLP HA4 77 M4
Bromley Gdns HAYES BR2 159 M5
Bromley Gv HAYES BR2 159 K5
Bromley Hall Rd
POP/IOD E14 105 J4 1
Bromley High St BOW E3 105 H2 1
Bromley Hl BMLY BR1 159 L2
Bromley La CHST BR7 161 J3
Bromley Rd BECK BR3 159 H4
CAT SE6 141 H6
CHST BR7 161 H4
HAYES BR2 159 L5
LEY E10 69 H7
TOTM N17 67 M2
UED N18 49 K6
WALTH E17 69 G3
Bromley St WCHPL E1 104 D4
Brompton Cl HSLWW TW4 132 F2 2
Brompton Dr ERITH DA8 128 B5
Brompton Gv EFNCH N2 65 L5
Brompton Park Crs
FUL/PGN SW6 119 H4
Brompton Pl CHEL SW3 15 K3
Brompton Rd CHEL SW3 15 J5
Brompton Sq CHEL SW3 15 J3
Bromwich Av HGT N6 84 A2
Bromyard Av ACT W3 99 L7
Brondesbury Pk CRICK NW2 82 C7 1
KIL/WHAMP NW6 82 D7
Brondesbury Rd
KIL/WHAMP NW6 100 F1
Brondesbury Vls
KIL/WHAMP NW6 100 F1
Bronsart Rd FUL/PGN SW6 118 E5
Bronson Rd RYNPK SW20 154 D5
Bronte Cl ERITH DA8 127 H5
FSTGT E7 88 A4 2
GNTH/NBYPK IG2 71 G6
Bronte Gv DART DA1 146 F1
Bronti Cl WALW SE17 18 F7
Bronze Age Wy BELV DA17 127 J1
Bronze St DEPT SE8 123 G5
Brook Av DAGE RM10 91 H7
EDGW HA8 45 H8
WBLY HA9 81 G3
Brookbank Av HNWL W7 97 K4
Brookbank Rd LEW SE13 123 H8
Brook Cl ACT W3 99 G7
GPK RM2 73 M2
HOR/WEW KT19 180 E2 1
RSLP HA4 59 L8
RYNPK SW20 154 B6
STWL/WRAY TW19 130 F4
Brook Crs CHING E4 51 G6
UED N18 50 B6
Brookdale FBAR/BDGN N11 48 C6
Brookdale Av UPMR RM14 93 G3
Brookdale Cl UPMR RM14 93 H3 1
Brookdale Rd BXLY DA5 144 E3
CAT SE6 141 H4
LEW SE13 141 H3
WALTH E17 69 G4
Brookdene Av OXHEY WD19 42 B2
Brookdene Dr NTHWD HA6 59 M1
Brookdene Rd
WOOL/PLUM SE18 125 L2
Brook Dr RSLP HA4 59 L7
RYLN/HDSTN HA2 61 J5
STHWK SE1 18 B4
SUN TW16 149 L2
Brooke Av RYLN/HDSTN HA2 79 J3
Brooke Cl BUSH WD23 43 J2
Brookehowse Rd CAT SE6 141 H7
Brookend Rd BFN/LL DA15 143 L5
Brooke Rd CLPT E5 86 A3
STNW/STAM N16 85 M3
WALTH E17 69 J5
Brooker Rd WAB EN9 27 J7
Brooke's Market HCIRC EC1N 12 A2 1
Brooke St HCIRC EC1N 12 A3
Brooke Wy BUSH WD23 43 J2 1
Brookfield Av EA W5 98 D3
MLHL NW7 46 B8
SUT SM1 170 E5
WALTH E17 69 J5 1
Brookfield Cl MLHL NW7 46 B8
Brookfield Crs
KTN/HRWW/W HA3 62 E6
MLHL NW7 46 B8
Brookfield Gdns
ESH/CLAY KT10 166 F8 1
Brookfield La CHES/WCR EN8 26 B1
Brookfield La West
CHES/WCR EN8 26 C1
Brookfield Pk KTTN NW5 84 B3
Brookfield Pth CHING E4 51 K8
Brookfield Rd CHSWK W4 99 K8
ED N9 50 A5
HOM E9 86 E6
Brookfields PEND EN3 37 K7
Brookfields Av MTCM CR4 155 L8
Brook Gdns BARN SW13 117 M8
CHING E4 51 H6
KUTN/CMB KT2 153 J4
Brook Gn HMSMTH W6 118 C1
Brookhill Cl EBAR EN4 34 E8
Brook Hill Cl WOOL/PLUM SE18 125 H3
Brookhill Rd WOOL/PLUM SE18 125 H3
Brookhouse Gdns CHING E4 51 L6 2
Brooking Rd FSTGT E7 88 A5 1
Brookland Cl GLDGN NW11 65 G5
Brookland Garth
GLDGN NW11 65 H5 1
Brookland Hl GLDGN NW11 65 G5
Brookland Ri GLDGN NW11 65 G5
Brooklands DART DA1 146 E5
Brooklands Ap
ROMW/RG RM7 73 K5 2
Brooklands Av BFN/LL DA15 143 K6
WAND/EARL SW18 137 H6
Brooklands Cl ROMW/RG RM7 73 K5 3
SUN TW16 149 L4
Brooklands Ct
KIL/WHAMP NW6 82 F7 1
WCHMH N21 36 D8 1
Brooklands Dr GFD/PVL UB6 80 C8
Brooklands Gdns EMPK RM11 74 C6
POTB/CUF EN6 22 E5
Brooklands La
ROMW/RG RM7 73 K5 4
Brooklands Pk BKHTH/KID SE3 124 A8
Brooklands Rd ROMW/RG RM7 73 K5
THDIT KT7 167 G3 1
Brook La BKHTH/KID SE3 124 B7
BMLY BR1 160 A2
BXLY DA5 144 D3
Brook La North BTFD TW8 116 D4 3
Brooklea Cl CDALE/KGS NW9 63 L2
Brooklyn Av LOU IG10 39 L7
SNWD SE25 158 B7
Brooklyn Cl CAR SM5 170 E4 1
Brooklyn Gv SNWD SE25 158 B7 2
Brooklyn Rd HAYES BR2 160 D8
SNWD SE25 158 B7
Brooklyn Wy WDR/YW UB7 112 D1
Brookmans Cl UPMR RM14 75 L8
Brook Md HOR/WEW KT19 168 E8 1
Brookmead MTCM CR4 171 J1 1
Brookmead Av HAYES BR2 160 F8
Brookmead Cl ORP BR6 177 H2 1
Brook Meadow
NFNCH/WDSP N12 47 H6
Brook Meadow Cl WFD IG8 51 L8 1
Brookmead Rd CROY/NA CR0 171 J1
Brookmead Wy ORP BR6 177 H1
Brook Ms North BAY/PAD W2 8 F6
Brookmill Cl OXHEY WD19 42 B2 1
Brookmill Rd DEPT SE8 123 G6
Brook Park Cl WCHMH N21 49 H1
Brook Pl BAR EN5 34 A8
Brook Ri CHIG IG7 53 G5
Brook Rd BKHH IG9 52 A4
BORE WD6 32 A4
BRW CM14 57 M5
CEND/HSY/T N8 66 E5
CHES/WCR EN8 26 F7
CRICK NW2 82 A2
GNTH/NBYPK IG2 71 L7
GPK RM2 73 M3
LOU IG10 39 L8
SURB KT6 167 L4
SWLY BR8 163 K6
THHTH CR7 157 J7
TWK TW1 134 A3
WDGN N22 66 F3 2
Brook Rd South BTFD TW8 116 D3 1
BTFD TW8 116 E4 1
Brooks Av EHAM E6 106 F3
Brooksbank St HOM E9 86 D6 3
Brooksby Ms IS N1 6 A1
Brooksby St IS N1 6 A2
Brooksby's Wk HOM E9 86 D5
Brookscroft Rd WALTH E17 69 H2
Brookshill KTN/HRWW/W HA3 43 L8
Brookshill Av
KTN/HRWW/W HA3 43 K7
Brookshill Dr
KTN/HRWW/W HA3 43 K7
Brookside BARK/HLT IG6 53 J8 2
CAR SM5 171 G7
EBAR EN4 47 L1
EMPK RM11 74 E6
HGDN/ICK UB10 76 F7
ORP BR6 176 F2
POTB/CUF EN6 22 A5
WAB EN9 27 L5 1
WCHMH N21 48 F1
Brookside Av ASHF TW15 148 C1
Brookside Cl BAR EN5 46 D1
FELT TW13 132 A7
KTN/HRWW/W HA3 62 D6
RSLP HA4 78 E4
Brookside Crs WPK KT4 169 G3 2
Brookside Gdns EN EN1 37 H2
Brookside Rd ED N9 50 B6
GLDGN NW11 64 E7
OXHEY WD19 42 B2
UED N18 50 B6 2
YEAD UB4 96 C6
Brookside South EBAR EN4 48 A2
Brookside Wy CROY/NA CR0 173 K1
Brooks La CHSWK W4 117 G4
Brook's Ms MYFR/PKLN W1K 10 C6
Brooks Rd CHSWK W4 117 G3
PLSTW E13 88 A8
Brook St BAY/PAD W2 9 H6
BELV DA17 127 H3
BRW CM14 57 L6
KUT KT1 152 E5
MYFR/PKLN W1K 10 C6
Brooksville Av KIL/WHAMP NW6 82 E8
Brookview Rd
STRHM/NOR SW16 156 C1
Brookville Rd FUL/PGN SW6 118 F5
Brook Wk EDGW HA8 45 K8
Brook Wy CHIG IG7 53 G5
Brookway BKHTH/KID SE3 124 A8
RAIN RM13 110 B4
Brookwood Av BARN SW13 117 M8
Brookwood Cl HAYES BR2 159 M7 1
Brookwood Rd HSLW TW3 115 H7
WAND/EARL SW18 136 F5
Broom Av STMC/STPC BR5 162 B5
Broom Cl ESH/CLAY KT10 166 B7
HAYES BR2 175 L1
TEDD TW11 152 D3
Broomcroft Av NTHLT UB5 96 C2
Broome Pl SOCK/AV RM15 111 K7 1
Broome Rd HPTN TW12 150 F4
Broomer Pl CHES/WCR EN8 26 C2
Broome Wy CMBW SE5 121 K5 1
Broomfield SUN TW16 150 A4
WALTH E17 68 F8 2
Broomfield Av LOU IG10 52 F1
PLMGR N13 48 F7
Broomfield Cl CRW RM5 55 K8
Broomfield Ct WEY KT13 164 A8
Broomfield La PLMGR N13 48 F7 1
Broomfield Pl WEA W13 98 B7 3
Broomfield Ride LHD/OX KT22 178 D5
Broomfield Ri ABLGY WD5 20 D5
Broomfield Rd BECK BR3 158 E7
BRYLDS KT5 167 M3
BXLYHS DA6 145 G2
CHDH RM6 72 D8
PLMGR N13 48 E7 1
RCH/KEW TW9 116 F6
TEDD TW11 152 C2 2
WEA W13 98 B7
Broomfields ESH/CLAY KT10 166 C7
Broomfield St POP/IOD E14 105 G4
Broom Gdns CROY/NA CR0 174 A5 1
Broom Gv WAT WD17 29 G3
Broomgrove Gdns EDGW HA8 63 G2
Broomgrove Rd
BRXN/ST SW9 120 F7 1
Broom Hall LHD/OX KT22 178 C7
Broomhall Rd SAND/SEL CR2 184 D2
Broomhill Ri BXLYHS DA6 145 G2
Broomhill Rd DART DA1 146 B3
GDMY/SEVK IG3 90 A2
ORP BR6 177 G2
WAND/EARL SW18 137 G2
WFD IG8 52 A8
Broomhouse La FUL/PGN SW6 119 G7
Broomhouse Rd FUL/PGN SW6 119 G7
Broomloan La SUT SM1 170 A4
Broom Md BXLYHS DA6 145 G3
Broom Pk KUT KT1 152 D3
TEDD TW11 152 D3
Broom Rd CROY/NA CR0 174 A5
TEDD TW11 152 B1
Broomsleigh St
KIL/WHAMP NW6 82 F5 1
Broomstick Hall Rd WAB EN9 27 L6
Broom Water TEDD TW11 152 C2
Broom Water West TEDD TW11 152 C1
Broom Wy WEY KT13 164 D6
Broomwood Cl BXLY DA5 145 K6
CROY/NA CR0 158 D8
Broomwood Rd BTSEA SW11 137 M3
STMC/STPC BR5 162 B5
Broseley Gdns HARH RM3 56 E6
Broseley Gv SYD SE26 158 E1
Broseley Rd HARH RM3 56 E6
Broster Gdns SNWD SE25 157 M6
Brougham Rd ACT W3 99 J5
HACK E8 86 A8
Brougham St BTSEA SW11 119 M7
Broughinge Rd BORE WD6 32 B5
Broughton Av FNCH N3 64 E4
RCHPK/HAM TW10 134 C8
Broughton Dr BRXN/ST SW9 139 H1 2
Broughton Gdns HGT N6 66 C7 1
Broughton Rd FUL/PGN SW6 119 H7
ORP BR6 176 D4
THHTH CR7 172 A1
WEA W13 98 B6
Broughton Road Ap
FUL/PGN SW6 119 H7 2
Broughton St VX/NE SW8 120 B7 2
Broughton Wy
RKW/CH/CXG WD3 40 A2
Brouncker Rd ACT W3 99 J8
Brow Cl STMC/STPC BR5 177 K2
Brow Crs STMC/STPC BR5 177 J3
Browells La FELT TW13 132 C6
Brown Cl WLGTN SM6 183 K1
Brownfield St POP/IOD E14 105 H5 2
Browngraves Rd HYS/HAR UB3 113 J5
Brown Hart Gdns
MYFR/PKLN W1K 10 B6 1
Brownhill Rd CAT SE6 141 J4
Browning Av HNWL W7 97 M5
SUT SM1 170 E6
WPK KT4 169 H3
Browning Cl HPTN TW12 132 F8
MV/WKIL W9 8 F1 1
WALTH E17 69 J5 2
WELL DA16 125 L6
Browning Rd DART DA1 146 F1
ENC/FH EN2 36 D3
MNPK E12 88 F6
WAN E11 69 M8
Browning St WALW SE17 18 F7
Browning Wy HEST TW5 114 D6
Brownlea Gdns GDMY/SEVK IG3 90 A2
Brownlow Ms FSBYW WC1X 5 M9
Brownlow Rd BORE WD6 32 A7 1
CROY/NA CR0 172 E6
FBAR/BDGN N11 48 E8
FNCH N3 65 H1
FSTGT E7 88 A4 3
HACK E8 7 M3
WEA W13 98 A7 1
WLSDN NW10 81 L7
Brownlow St GINN WC1R 11 M3
Brownrigg Rd ASHF TW15 131 G8
Brownspring Dr ELTH/MOT SE9 143 H7
Brown's Rd BRYLDS KT5 167 M2
WALTH E17 69 G4
Brown St MBLAR W1H 9 L4
Brownswell Rd EFNCH N2 65 K3 1
Brownswood Rd FSBYPK N4 85 J2
The Brow GSTN WD25 21 H6
Broxash Rd BTSEA SW11 138 A3
Broxbourne Av WAN E11 70 B5
Broxbourne House BOW E3 105 H3 1
Broxbourne Rd FSTGT E7 88 A3 1
ORP BR6 176 F3
Broxhill Rd ABR/ST RM4 56 A5
Broxholm Rd WNWD SE27 139 G7
Broxted Rd FSTH SE23 140 F6
Broxwood Wy STJWD NW8 3 K4
Bruce Av HCH RM12 92 C1
SHPTN TW17 164 C1
Bruce Castle Rd TOTM N17 67 M2
Bruce Cl NKENS W10 100 D4
WELL DA16 126 B6
Bruce Dr SAND/SEL CR2 185 K2
Bruce Gdns TRDG/WHET N20 47 M5 1
Bruce Gv ORP BR6 177 G3
TOTM N17 67 M3
WATN WD24 29 H3
Bruce Rd BAR EN5 33 L6 1
BOW E3 105 H2
KTN/HRWW/W HA3 61 L3
MTCM CR4 156 A3
SNWD SE25 157 K7
WLSDN NW10 81 K7
Bruce Wy CHES/WCR EN8 26 D6
Bruckner St NKENS W10 100 E2
Brudenell Rd TOOT SW17 137 M7
Bruffs Meadow NTHLT UB5 78 E6
Brumana Cl WEY KT13 164 B8 1
Brumfield Rd HOR/WEW KT19 168 C7
Brunel Cl HEST TW5 114 B5
NRWD SE19 157 M2
NTHLT UB5 96 F2
ROM RM1 73 L5 1
Brunel Ct WLSDN NW10 100 A2
Brunel Rd ACT W3 99 L4
BERM/RHTH SE16 104 C7 1
WALTH E17 68 E7
WFD IG8 52 F7
Brunel St CAN/RD E16 105 M5
Brunel Wk HSLWW TW4 133 G4 2
Brune St WCHPL E1 13 L3
Brunner Cl GLDGN NW11 65 H6
Brunner Rd EA W5 98 D3
WALTH E17 68 F6 2
Bruno Pl WBLY HA9 81 J2
Brunswick Av FBAR/BDGN N11 48 A5
UPMR RM14 75 L8
Brunswick Cl BXLYHS DA6 144 D1
PIN HA5 60 E7
THDIT KT7 166 F3 1
WHTN TW2 133 K7
WOT/HER KT12 165 J4
Brunswick Ct STHWK SE1 19 K2
Brunswick Crs FBAR/BDGN N11 48 A5
Brunswick Gdns BARK/HLT IG6 71 J1
EA W5 98 E2
KENS W8 8 B9
Brunswick Gv FBAR/BDGN N11 48 A5
Brunswick Ms MBLAR W1H 9 M4 1
STRHM/NOR SW16 156 D2 1
Brunswick Pk CMBW SE5 121 K6
Brunswick Park Gdns
FBAR/BDGN N11 48 A4
Brunswick Park Rd
FBAR/BDGN N11 48 B6 1
Brunswick Pl IS N1 7 H8
NRWD SE19 158 A3 3
Brunswick Quay
BERM/RHTH SE16 122 D1
Brunswick Rd BXLYHS DA6 144 D1
EA W5 98 D3
KUTN/CMB KT2 152 G4
LEY E10 87 J1
SEVS/STOTM N15 67 L5 1
SEVS/STOTM N15 67 L6 2
SUT SM1 170 B6
WAB EN9 38 A3
Brunswick Sq BMSBY WC1N 5 K9
Brunswick St WALTH E17 69 J6
Brunswick Vls CMBW SE5 121 K6 1
Brunswick Wy FBAR/BDGN N11 48 A5
Brunton Pl POP/IOD E14 104 E5 3
Brushfield St WCHPL E1 13 K2
Brushrise WATN WD24 29 G1
Brussels Rd BTSEA SW11 137 K1
Bruton Cl CHST BR7 160 F3
Bruton La MYFR/PICC W1J 10 D7
Bruton Pl MYFR/PKLN W1K 10 D7
Bruton Rd MRDN SM4 155 J7
Bruton St MYFR/PICC W1J 10 D7
Bruton Wy WEA W13 98 A4
Bryan Av WLSDN NW10 82 B7
Bryan Cl SUN TW16 150 A3
Bryan Rd BERM/RHTH SE16 104 F8
Bryanston Av WHTN TW2 133 H5
Bryanston Cl NWDGN UB2 114 F2 2
Bryanstone Rd
CEND/HSY/T N8 66 D7 1
CHES/WCR EN8 26 F7
Bryanston Ms East MBLAR W1H 9 L3
Bryanston Ms West MBLAR W1H 9 L3
Bryanston Pl MBLAR W1H 9 L3
Bryanston Sq MBLAR W1H 9 L4
Bryanston St MBLAR W1H 9 L5
Bryant Av HARH RM3 74 D3
Bryant Cl BAR EN5 33 M8
Bryant Rd NTHLT UB5 96 C2
Bryant St SRTFD E15 87 K7 1
Bryantwood Rd HOLWY N7 85 G5
Brycedale Crs STHGT/OAK N14 48 D6
Bryce Rd BCTR RM8 90 C4
Bryden Cl SYD SE26 158 E1
Brydges Rd SRTFD E15 87 K5
Brymay Cl BOW E3 105 G1
Brynmaer Rd BTSEA SW11 119 M6
Bryn-y-mawr Rd EN EN1 37 G7
Bryony Cl UX/CGN UB8 94 F4
Bryony Rd SHB W12 100 A6
Bryony Wy SUN TW16 150 A2
Buchanan Cl SOCK/AV RM15 111 J7 2
WCHMH N21 35 M8 3
Buchanan Ct BORE WD6 32 C5 1
Buchanan Gdns WLSDN NW10 100 B1
Buchan Cl UX/CGN UB8 94 C2 1
Buchan Rd PECK SE15 122 C8
Bucharest Rd
WAND/EARL SW18 137 J4
Buckden Cl LEE/GVPK SE12 141 M3
Buckettsland La BORE WD6 32 D3
Buckfast Rd MRDN SM4 155 H7
Buckfast St BETH E2 104 A2
Buckhold Rd WAND/EARL SW18 137 G3
Buckhurst Av CAR SM5 170 E3
Buckhurst St WCHPL E1 104 B3
Buckhurst Wy BKHH IG9 52 D5
Buckingham Av
E/WMO/HCT KT8 151 H5
EBED/NFELT TW14 132 B3
GFD/PVL UB6 80 A8
THHTH CR7 157 G4
TRDG/WHET N20 47 J2
WELL DA16 143 L1
Buckingham Cl EA W5 98 C4
EMPK RM11 74 D6 1
EN EN1 36 E5
HPTN TW12 150 F1
STMC/STPC BR5 176 E2
Buckingham Dr CHST BR7 161 J1 1
Buckingham Gdns STAN HA7 62 E1
THHTH CR7 157 G5 1
Buckingham Ga WESTW SW1E 16 E3
Buckingham Gv
HGDN/ICK UB10 95 G1 1
Buckingham La FSTH SE23 140 E4 1
Buckingham Ms WESTW SW1E 16 E3 1
WLSDN NW10 99 M1
Buckingham Palace Rd
PIM SW1V 16 C5
WESTW SW1E 16 D4
Buckingham Pl WESTW SW1E 16 E3 2
Buckingham Rd BORE WD6 32 D7
EDGW HA8 62 F1
FELT TW13 132 F8
FSTGT E7 87 M5
HRW HA1 61 K6
IL IG1 89 K2
IS N1 85 L6
KUT KT1 152 F7
LEY E10 87 H3
MTCM CR4 156 E8 1
RCHPK/HAM TW10 134 D6
SWFD E18 69 M2
WAN E11 70 B5
WATN WD24 29 J2 1
WDGN N22 66 E2 1
WLSDN NW10 99 M1
Buckingham St CHCR WC2N 11 K7 1
Buckingham Wy WLGTN SM6 183 J2
Buckland Crs HAMP NW3 3 G1
Buckland Ri PIN HA5 60 C2
Buckland Rd BELMT SM2 181 J3
CHSGTN KT9 167 M7
LEY E10 87 J2
ORP BR6 176 E6
Bucklands Rd TEDD TW11 152 C2
Buckland St IS N1 7 H6
Buckland Wk MRDN SM4 155 J7 2
Buckland Wy WPK KT4 169 J3
Buck La CDALE/KGS NW9 63 K6
Buckleigh Av RYNPK SW20 154 F6
Buckleigh Rd
STRHM/NOR SW16 156 D2
Buckleigh Wy NRWD SE19 157 M3 1
Bucklersbury MANHO EC4N 13 G5 1
Bucklers' Wy CAR SM5 170 F5
Buckle St WCHPL E1 13 M4
Buckley Cl DART DA1 127 M7
Buckley Rd KIL/WHAMP NW6 82 F7
Buckmaster Rd BTSEA SW11 137 L1 4
Bucknalls Cl GSTN WD25 21 L5
Bucknalls Dr LCOL/BKTW AL2 21 M4
Bucknalls La GSTN WD25 21 L5
Bucknall St LSQ/SEVD WC2H 11 J4 2
Buckner Rd BRXS/STRHM SW2 138 F1
Bucknills Cl EPSOM KT18 180 B7
Buckrell Rd CHING E4 51 K4
Bucks Av OXHEY WD19 42 E2
Bucks Cross Rd ORP BR6 177 L7
Buckstone Cl FSTH SE23 140 C3
Buckstone Rd UED N18 50 A7 3
Buck St CAMTN NW1 4 D3
Buckters Rents
BERM/RHTH SE16 104 E7
Buckthorne Rd BROCKY SE4 140 E3
Buckton Rd BORE WD6 31 M3
Budd Cl NFNCH/WDSP N12 47 H6 1
Buddings Cir WBLY HA9 81 J3 1
Budge La MTCM CR4 170 F2 2
Budleigh Crs WELL DA16 126 C6
Budoch Dr GDMY/SEVK IG3 90 A2
Buer Rd FUL/PGN SW6 118 E7
Buff Av BNSTD SM7 182 B7
Bugsby's Wy GNWCH SE10 123 M2
Bulganak Rd THHTH CR7 157 J7 1
Bulinca St WEST SW1P 17 J6 1
Bullace Rw CMBW SE5 121 K6 2
Bull Aly WELL DA16 126 B8
Bullar Cl PECK SE15 122 A5
Bullard Rd TEDD TW11 151 M2 2
Bullards Pl BETH E2 104 D2 2
Bullbanks Rd BELV DA17 127 J2

Bulleid Wy PIM SW1V 16 D6
Bullen St BTSEA SW11 .... 119 L7
Buller Rd BARK IG11 .... 89 L7
  THHTH CR7 .... 157 K6
  TOTM N17 .... 68 A3
  WDGN N22 .... 67 G3
  WLSDN NW10 .... 100 D2
Bullers Cl SCUP DA14 .... 162 E1
Bullers Wood Dr CHST BR7 .... 160 E4
Bullescroft Rd EDGW HA8 .... 45 G5
Bullfinch Rd SAND/SEL CR2 .... 185 K3
Bullhead Rd BORE WD6 .... 32 C5
Bullivant St POP/IOD E14 .... 105 J6
Bull La CHST BR7 .... 161 K3
  DAGE RM10 .... 91 H3
  UED N18 .... 49 L1
Bull Rd SRTFD E15 .... 105 M1
Bullrush Cl CROY/NA CR0 .... 172 E1
Bullrush Gv UX/CGN UB8 .... 94 C3
Bulls Aly MORT/ESHN SW14 .... 117 K8
Bull's Br HYS/HAR UB3 .... 114 A1
Bulls Bridge Rd NWDGN UB2 .... 114 B1
Bullsbrook Rd HYS/HAR UB3 .... 96 C7
Bull Yd BORE WD6 .... 32 C5
Bullsmoor Cl CHES/WCR EN8 .... 26 C8
Bullsmoor Gdns
  CHES/WCR EN8 .... 26 B8
Bullsmoor La EN EN1 .... 26 B8
  PEND EN3 .... 26 D8
Bullsmoor Ride CHES/WCR EN8 .... 26 C8
Bullsmoor Wy CHES/WCR EN8 ...... 26 B8
Bullwell Crs CHES/WCR EN8 .... 26 E2
Bull Yd PECK SE15 .... 122 A6
Bulmer Gdns
  KTN/HRWW/W HA3 .... 62 D8
Bulmer Ms NTGHL W11 .... 8 A8
Bulstrode Av HSLW TW3 .... 114 F8
Bulstrode Gdns HSLW TW3 .... 115 G8
Bulstrode Pl MHST W1U 10 B3
Bulstrode Rd HSLW TW3 .... 115 G8
Bulstrode St MHST W1U 10 B4
Bulwer Court Rd WAN E11 .... 87 K1
Bulwer Gdns BAR EN5 .... 34 C7
  UED N18 .... 49 K1
  WAN E11 .... 87 K1
Bulwer St SHB W12 .... 100 C1
Bunces La WFD IG8 .... 69 M1
Bungalow Rd SNWD SE25 .... 157 L7
The Bungalows
  STRHM/NOR SW16 .... 156 B3
Bunhill Rw STLK EC1Y 7 G9
Bunkers Hl SCUP DA14 .... 144 F7
Bunning Wy HOLWY N7 .... 5 K1
Bunn's La MLHL NW7 .... 45 L8
Bunsen St BOW E3 .... 104 E1
Bunting Cl ED N9 .... 50 D3
  MTCM CR4 .... 155 M8
Bunton St WOOL/PLUM SE18 .... 125 G1
Bunyan Rd WALTH E17 .... 68 E4
Burbage Cl CHES/WCR EN8 .... 26 E4
  STHWK SE1 .... 19 G4
Burbage Rd HNHL SE24 .... 139 K3
Burberry Cl NWMAL KT3 .... 153 L5
Burbidge Rd SHPTN TW17 .... 149 G7
Burbridge Wy TOTM N17 .... 68 A3
Burcham St POP/IOD E14 .... 105 H5
Burcharbro Rd ABYW SE2 .... 126 D4
Burchell Ct BUSH WD23 .... 43 J2
Burchell Rd LEY E10 .... 87 H1
  PECK SE15 .... 122 B6
Burchetts Wy SHPTN TW17 .... 164 B1
Burchett Wy CHDH RM6 .... 72 F7
Burchwall Cl CRW RM5 .... 55 J8
Burcote Rd WAND/EARL SW18 .... 137 K5
Burcott Rd PUR/KEN CR8 .... 184 A7
Burden Cl BTFD TW8 .... 116 C3
Burdenshott Av
  RCHPK/HAM TW10 .... 135 H1
Burden Wy WAN E11 .... 88 B2
Burder Rd IS N1 .... 85 L6
Burdett Av RYNPK SW20 .... 154 A4
Burdett Cl HNWL W7 .... 97 M1
  SCUP DA14 .... 162 E1
Burdett Rd BOW E3 .... 104 F3
  CROY/NA CR0 .... 172 D1
  RCH/KEW TW9 .... 116 F7
Burdetts Rd DAGW RM9 .... 90 F8
Burdock Cl CROY/NA CR0 .... 173 K3
Burdock Rd TOTM N17 .... 68 A4
Burdon La BELMT SM2 .... 181 M2
Burdon Pk BELMT SM2 .... 181 M2
Burfield Cl TOOT SW17 .... 137 J8
Burford Cl BARK/HLT IG6 .... 71 J5
  BCTR RM8 .... 90 C3
  HGDN/ICK UB10 .... 76 E4
Burford La EW KT17 .... 181 J4
Burford Rd BMLY BR1 .... 160 E7
  BTFD TW8 .... 116 E3
  CAT SE6 .... 140 F6
  EHAM E6 .... 106 E2
  SRTFD E15 .... 87 K7
  SUT SM1 .... 170 A4
  WPK KT4 .... 169 G2
Burford Wy CROY/NA CR0 .... 186 C1
Burgate Cl DART DA1 .... 127 M8
Burges Cl EMPK RM11 .... 74 F7
Burges Gv BARN SW13 .... 118 B5
Burges Rd EHAM E6 .... 89 G7
  STA TW18 .... 148 A2
Burgess Av CDALE/KGS NW9 .... 63 K7
Burgess Cl FELT TW13 .... 132 E8
Burgess Rd SRTFD E15 .... 87 L4
  SUT SM1 .... 170 B6
Burgess St POP/IOD E14 .... 105 J2
Burge St STHWK SE1 .... 19 H4
Burghfield EW KT17 .... 180 F8
Burgh Heath Rd EW KT17 .... 180 F8
Burghill Rd SYD SE26 .... 140 D8
Burghley Av BORE WD6 .... 32 C8
  NWMAL KT3 .... 153 K4
Burghley Hall Cl
  WIM/MER SW19 .... 136 E5
Burghley Pl MTCM CR4 .... 155 M8
Burghley Rd CEND/HSY/T N8 .... 67 G4

KTTN NW5 .... 84 B4
  WAN E11 .... 87 L1
  WIM/MER SW19 .... 136 D8
Burgh Mt BNSTD SM7 .... 181 M8
Burgh St IS N1 .... 6 D5
Burgh Wd BNSTD SM7 .... 181 L8
Burgos Cl CROY/NA CR0 .... 172 A8
Burgos Gv GNWCH SE10 .... 123 H6
Burgoyne Rd BRXN/ST SW9 .... 120 F8
  FSBYPK N4 .... 67 H4
  SNWD SE25 .... 157 M7
  SUN TW16 .... 149 M2
Burham Cl PGE/AN SE20 .... 158 C3
Burhill Gv PIN HA5 .... 60 E3
Burhill Rd WOT/HER KT12 .... 165 H8
Burke Cl PUT/ROE SW15 .... 135 L1
Burke St CAN/RD E16 .... 105 M5
Burket Cl NWDGN UB2 .... 114 E2
Burland Rd BTSEA SW11 .... 137 M2
  CRW RM5 .... 55 J8
Burlea Cl WOT/HER KT12 .... 165 H7
Burleigh Av BFN/LL DA15 .... 143 M2
  WLGTN SM6 .... 171 G5
Burleigh Gdns ASHF TW15 .... 149 J1
  STHGT/OAK N14 .... 48 C3
Burleigh Pl PUT/ROE SW15 .... 136 D2
Burleigh Rd CHEAM SM3 .... 169 L3
  CHES/WCR EN8 .... 26 E5
  EN EN1 .... 36 E7
  HGDN/ICK UB10 .... 77 H8
Burleigh St COVGDN WC2E 11 K6
Burleigh Wk CAT SE6 .... 141 J5
Burleigh Wy ENC/FH EN2 .... 36 D6
  POTB/CUF EN6 .... 24 E3
Burley Cl CHING E4 .... 51 G7
  STRHM/NOR SW16 .... 156 D5
Burley Rd CAN/RD E16 .... 106 C5
Burlington Av RCH/KEW TW9 ...... 117 G6
  ROMW/RG RM7 .... 73 J7
Burlington Cl
  EBED/NFELT TW14 .... 131 K4
  EHAM E6 .... 106 E5
  ORP BR6 .... 176 B4
Burlington Gdns ACT W3 .... 99 J7
  CHDH RM6 .... 72 E8
  CHSWK W4 .... 117 J3
  MYFR/PICC W1J 10 E7
Burlington La CHSWK W4 .... 117 J5
Burlington Ms CHSWK W4 .... 117 J3
Burlington Pl FUL/PGN SW6 .... 118 E7
  PIN HA5 .... 60 B4
  WFD IG8 .... 52 A5
Burlington Ri EBAR EN4 .... 47 L3
Burlington Rd CHSWK W4 .... 117 J3
  ENC/FH EN2 .... 36 D4
  FUL/PGN SW6 .... 118 E7
  ISLW TW7 .... 115 K6
  MUSWH N10 .... 66 A4
  NWMAL KT3 .... 153 M7
  THHTH CR7 .... 157 J5
  TOTM N17 .... 68 A2
Burman Cl RDART DA2 .... 147 J4
Burma Rd STNW/STAM N16 .... 85 K4
Burmester Rd TOOT SW17 .... 137 J7
Burnaby Crs CHSWK W4 .... 117 H4
Burnaby Gdns CHSWK W4 .... 117 H4
Burnaby St WBPTN SW10 .... 119 J5
Burnbrae Cl NFNCH/WDSP N12 ... 47 H8
Burnbury Rd BAL SW12 .... 138 C3
Burn Cl LHD/OX KT22 .... 178 C8
Burncroft Av PEND EN3 .... 37 J5
  PEND EN3 .... 37 J5
Burndell Wy YEAD UB4 .... 96 D4
Burnell Av RCHPK/HAM TW10 .... 152 C1
  WELL DA16 .... 126 A7
Burnell Gdns STAN HA7 .... 62 D3
Burnell Rd SUT SM1 .... 170 B6
Burnels Av EHAM E6 .... 107 G2
Burness Cl UX/CGN UB8 .... 94 D1
Burne St CAMTN NW1 .... 9 J2
Burnet Gv HOR/WEW KT19 .... 180 C6
Burnett Rd ERITH DA8 .... 128 D4
Burney Av BRYLDS KT5 .... 152 F8
Burney St GNWCH SE10 .... 123 J5
Burnfoot Av FUL/PGN SW6 .... 118 E6
Burnham Cl ENC/FH EN2 .... 36 E3
  KTN/HRWW/W HA3 .... 62 A3
  MLHL NW7 .... 64 A1
  STHWK SE1 .... 19 M6
Burnham Crs DART DA1 .... 146 D1
  WAN E11 .... 70 C5
Burnham Dr WPK KT4 .... 169 K4
Burnham Gdns
  CROY/NA CR0 .... 172 F2
  HEST TW5 .... 114 B4
  HYS/HAR UB3 .... 113 K1
Burnham Rd CHING E4 .... 50 F7
  DART DA1 .... 146 D2
  MRDN SM4 .... 155 H8
  ROMW/RG RM7 .... 73 J4
  SCUP DA14 .... 144 E1
Burnham St BETH E2 .... 104 C2
  KUTN/CMB KT2 .... 153 L4
Burnham Wy SYD SE26 .... 158 F1
  WEA W13 .... 116 B2
Burnhill Rd BECK BR3 .... 159 G5
Burnley Cl OXHEY WD19 .... 42 C7
Burnley Rd BRXN/ST SW9 .... 120 F7
  WLSDN NW10 .... 81 M5
  WTHK RM20 .... 129 M6
Burnsall St CHEL SW3 .... 15 K7
Burns Av BFN/LL DA15 .... 144 B3
  CHDH RM6 .... 72 C8
  EBED/NFELT TW14 .... 132 A3
  STHL UB1 .... 97 G6
Burns Cl ERITH DA8 .... 127 M6
  TOOT SW17 .... 155 K2
  WELL DA16 .... 125 M6
  YEAD UB4 .... 96 A4
Burns Dr BNSTD SM7 .... 181 L7
Burnside Av CHING E4 .... 50 F8
Burnside Cl BAR EN5 .... 34 A6
  BERM/RHTH SE16 .... 104 D7
  TWK TW1 .... 134 A3
Burnside Crs ALP/SUD HA0 .... 80 D8
Burnside Rd BCTR RM8 .... 90 C2
Burns Rd ALP/SUD HA0 .... 98 E1

BTSEA SW11 .... 119 M7
  WEA W13 .... 98 B8
  WLSDN NW10 .... 81 M8
Burns Wy HEST TW5 .... 114 D6
Burnt Ash Hl LEE/GVPK SE12 ..... 141 M3
Burnt Ash La BMLY BR1 .... 160 B1
Burnt Ash Rd
  LEE/GVPK SE12 .... 141 M3
Burntfarm Ride CHESW EN7 .... 25 H5
Burnt House La RDART DA2 .... 146 E8
Burnthwaite Rd FUL/PGN SW6 ... 118 F5
Burnt Oak Broadway EDGW HA8 .. 63 H1
Burnt Oak Flds EDGW HA8 .... 63 J3
Burnt Oak La BFN/LL DA15 .... 144 A3
Burntwood Cl
  WAND/EARL SW18 .... 137 L5
Burntwood Grange Rd
  WAND/EARL SW18 .... 137 K5
Burntwood La TOOT SW17 .... 137 K6
Burntwood Vw NRWD SE19 .... 157 M1
Burnway EMPK RM11 .... 74 E8
Burnwood Park Rd
  WOT/HER KT12 .... 165 H6
Buross St WCHPL E1 .... 104 B5
Burrage Gv WOOL/PLUM SE18 ... 125 H5
Burrage Pl WOOL/PLUM SE18 .... 125 H3
Burrage Rd WOOL/PLUM SE18 ... 125 J5
Burrard Rd CAN/RD E16 .... 106 A5
  KIL/WHAMP NW6 .... 83 C5
Burr Cl BXLYHN DA7 .... 126 F8
Burrell Cl CROY/NA CR0 .... 173 L1
  EDGW HA8 .... 45 H4
Burrell Rw BECK BR3 .... 159 G5
Burrell St STHWK SE1 .... 12 C3
Burrfield Dr STMC/STPC BR5 ...... 162 D8
Burritt Rd KUT KT1 .... 153 L5
Burroughs Gdns HDN NW4 .... 64 B5
The Burroughs HDN NW4 .... 64 B5
Burrow Gn CHIG IG7 .... 53 M7
Burrow Rd CHIG IG7 .... 54 A7
  CMBW SE5 .... 139 L1
Burrows Hill Cl
  STWL/WRAY TW19 .... 130 B1
Burrows Ms STHWK SE1 .... 18 C1
Burrows Rd WLSDN NW10 .... 100 C2
Burr Rd WAND/EARL SW18 .... 137 G5
Bursar St STHWK SE1 .... 13 J9
Bursdon Cl BFN/LL DA15 .... 143 M6
Bursland Rd PEND EN3 .... 37 K7
Burslem Av BARK/HLT IG6 .... 54 A8
Burslem St WCHPL E1 .... 104 B5
Burstock Rd PUT/ROE SW15 ...... 136 E1
Burston Rd PUT/ROE SW15 .... 136 D2
Burstow Rd RYNPK SW20 .... 154 E4
Burtenshaw Rd THDIT KT7 .... 167 G2
Burtley Cl FSBYPK N4 .... 85 J1
Burton Av WATW WD18 .... 29 G7
Burton Cl CHSGTN KT9 .... 179 K1
Burton Gdns HEST TW5 .... 114 F6
Burton La BRXN/ST SW9 .... 121 G7
  KIL/WHAMP NW6 .... 82 F7
  KUTN/CMB KT2 .... 152 C3
  SWFD E18 .... 70 B4
Burtons Ct SRTFD E15 .... 87 K7
Burton's Rd HPTN TW12 .... 133 H8
Burton St STPAN WC1H 5 H9
Burt Rd CAN/RD E16 .... 106 C7
Burtwell La WNWD SE27 .... 138 E8
Burwash Rd WOOL/PLUM SE18 .. 125 K3
Burwash Rd WOOL/PLUM SE18 .. 125 K3
Burway Crs CHERT KT16 .... 148 A7
Burwell Av GFD/PVL UB6 .... 79 L6
Burwell Cl WCHPL E1 .... 104 B5
Burwell Rd LEY E10 .... 86 E1
Burwood Av HAYES BR2 .... 175 H4
  PIN HA5 .... 60 C6
  PUR/KEN CR8 .... 184 B7
Burwood Cl SURB KT6 .... 168 A3
  WOT/HER KT12 .... 165 K7
Burwood Gdns RAIN RM13 .... 109 M2
Burwood Pl BAY/PAD W2 .... 9 K4
Burwood Rd WOT/HER KT12 .... 165 K7
Bury Av RSLP HA4 .... 59 J7
  YEAD UB4 .... 95 L1
Bury Cl BERM/RHTH SE16 .... 104 D7
Bury Ct HDTCH EC3A 13 K4
Bury Green Rd CHESW EN7 .... 26 A4
Bury Gv MRDN SM4 .... 155 H8
Bury La RKW/CH/CXG WD3 .... 40 D3
Bury Mdw RKW/CH/CXG WD3 ...... 40 D3
Bury Pl NOXST/BSQ WC1A 11 J3
Bury Rd CHING E4 .... 38 D7
  DAGE RM10 .... 91 J5
  WDGN N22 .... 67 G4
Bury St ED N9 .... 49 M2
  ED N9 .... 49 M2
  HDTCH EC3A 13 K5
  RSLP HA4 .... 59 K7
  STJS SW1Y 10 E8
Bury St West ED N9 .... 49 M2
Bury Wk CHEL SW3 .... 15 J6
Busby Pl KTTN NW5 .... 84 D6
Busch Cl ISLW TW7 .... 116 B6
Bushbarns CHESW EN7 .... 26 A2
Bushberry Rd HOM E9 .... 86 E6
Bush Cl GNTH/NBYPK IG2 .... 71 K6
Bush Cottages
  WAND/EARL SW18 .... 137 G2
Bushell Cl BRXS/STRHM SW2 ..... 138 F6
Bushell Gn BUSH WD23 .... 43 K4
Bushell St WAP E1W 104 A7
Bushell Wy CHST BR7 .... 161 L5
Bush Elms Rd EMPK RM11 .... 74 A8
Bushey Av STMC/STPC BR5 .... 176 D2
  SWFD E18 .... 69 M4
Bushey Cl CHING E4 .... 51 J5
  HGDN/ICK UB10 .... 77 G2
Bushey Grove Rd BUSH WD23 ..... 29 K7
Bushey Hall Dr BUSH WD23 .... 29 L5
Bushey Hall Rd BUSH WD23 .... 29 K7

Bushey Hill Rd CMBW SE5 .... 121 M6
Bushey La SUT SM1 .... 170 A5
Busheymill Br BUSH WD23 .... 29 L3
Bushey Mill Crs WATN WD24 .... 29 J2
Bushey Mill La BUSH WD23 .... 29 M5
  WATN WD24 .... 29 J2
Bushey Rd CROY/NA CR0 .... 174 A4
  HYS/HAR UB3 .... 113 L2
  PLSTW E13 .... 106 C1
  RYNPK SW20 .... 154 C5
  SEVS/STOTM N15 .... 67 L7
  SUT SM1 .... 170 A6
Bushey Wy BECK BR3 .... 174 D1
Bushfield Cl EDGW HA8 .... 45 H4
Bushfield Crs EDGW HA8 .... 45 H4
Bush Gv CDALE/KGS NW9 .... 63 J8
  STAN HA7 .... 62 D2
Bushgrove Rd BCTR RM8 .... 90 A4
Bush Hl WCHMH N21 .... 49 J4
Bush Hill Rd KTN/HRWW/W HA3 .. 62 F7
  WCHMH N21 .... 49 K1
Bush La CANST EC4R 13 G6
Bushmead Cl
  SEVS/STOTM N15 .... 67 M5
Bushmoor Crs
  WOOL/PLUM SE18 .... 125 H5
Bushnell Rd TOOT SW17 .... 138 B6
Bush Rd BERM/RHTH SE16 .... 122 D2
  BKHH IG9 .... 52 D6
  HACK E8 .... 86 B8
  RCH/KEW TW9 .... 116 F4
  SHPTN TW17 .... 148 F8
  WAN E11 .... 69 M8
Bushway BCTR RM8 .... 90 A4
Bushwood WAN E11 .... 69 M8
Bushwood Dr STHWK SE1 .... 19 M6
Bushwood Rd RCH/KEW TW9 ..... 117 G4
Bushy Park Gdns
  HPTN TW12 .... 151 K1
Bushy Park Rd TEDD TW11 .... 152 B5
Bushy Rd TEDD TW11 .... 151 L2
Butcher Rw POP/IOD E14 .... 104 D5
Butchers Rd CAN/RD E16 .... 106 A5
Bute Av RCHPK/HAM TW10 .... 134 E6
Bute Gdns HMSMTH W6 .... 118 D2
  WLGTN SM6 .... 171 J7
Bute Gdns West WLGTN SM6 ...... 171 J7
Bute Rd BARK/HLT IG6 .... 71 H6
  CROY/NA CR0 .... 172 A3
  WLGTN SM6 .... 171 J6
Bute St SKENS SW7 .... 15 G5
Butler Av HRW HA1 .... 61 K8
Butler Rd BCTR RM8 .... 90 B4
  HRW HA1 .... 61 J8
  WLSDN NW10 .... 81 M7
Butlers Dr CHING E4 .... 38 C3
Butler St BETH E2 .... 104 D2
  BETH E2 .... 104 C2
  HGDN/ICK UB10 .... 95 H3
Buttercup Cl HARH RM3 .... 74 D2
Buttercup Sq
  STWL/WRAY TW19 .... 130 D5
Butterfield Cl TOTM N17 .... 49 J8
  TWK TW1 .... 133 M3
Butterfields WALTH E17 .... 69 J6
Butterfield Sq EHAM E6 .... 106 F5
Butterfly Av DART DA1 .... 146 F6
Butterfly La BORE WD6 .... 31 H6
  ELTH/MOT SE9 .... 143 H3
Butter Hl WLGTN SM6 .... 171 G5
Butteridges Cl DAGW RM9 .... 90 F8
Buttermere Cl
  EBED/NFELT TW14 .... 131 M5
  MRDN SM4 .... 169 K1
  STHWK SE1 .... 19 L5
Buttermere Dr PUT/ROE SW15 ... 136 E2
Buttermere Gdns
  PUR/KEN CR8 .... 184 D6
Buttermere Rd
  STMC/STPC BR5 .... 162 D7
Butterwick GSTN WD25 .... 29 L1
  HMSMTH W6 .... 118 C2
Butterworth Gdns WFD IG8 .... 52 A7
Buttesland St IS N1 .... 7 H7
Buttfield Cl DAGE RM10 .... 91 H6
Buttmarsh Cl
  WOOL/PLUM SE18 .... 125 H3
Buttsbury Rd IL IG1 .... 89 J5
Butts Crs FELT TW13 .... 133 C7
Butts Green Rd EMPK RM11 .... 74 D7
Buttsmead NTHWD HA6 .... 59 J1
Butts Piece NTHLT UB5 .... 96 B1
The Butts BTFD TW8 .... 116 D4
  BMLY BR1 .... 159 L1
Buxted Rd EDUL SE22 .... 139 L1
  HACK E8 .... 7 L1
  NFNCH/WDSP N12 .... 47 L7
Buxton Cl WFD IG8 .... 52 D8
Buxton Crs CHEAM SM3 .... 169 L6
Buxton Dr NWMAL KT3 .... 153 K5
  WAN E11 .... 70 C1
Buxton Gdns ACT W3 .... 99 H6
Buxton Pth OXHEY WD19 .... 42 C5
Buxton Rd ARCH N19 .... 84 D1
  ASHF TW15 .... 148 D1
  CHING E4 .... 51 K2
  CRICK NW2 .... 82 B6
  EHAM E6 .... 106 C2
  ERITH DA8 .... 127 K5
  GNTH/NBYPK IG2 .... 71 L7
  MORT/ESHN SW14 .... 117 L8
  SRTFD E15 .... 87 L5
  THHTH CR7 .... 157 H8
  WALTH E17 .... 69 J1
Buxton St WCHPL E1 .... 13 M1
Byam St FUL/PGN SW6 .... 119 M7
Byards Cft STRHM/NOR SW16 .... 156 D4
Bychurch End TEDD TW11 .... 151 M1
Bycroft Rd STHL UB1 .... 97 G4
Bycroft St PGE/AN SE20 .... 158 D3
Bycullah Av ENC/FH EN2 .... 36 B6
Bycullah Rd ENC/FH EN2 .... 36 B6
Byefield Cl BERM/RHTH SE16 ..... 104 E8
Byelands
  BERM/RHTH SE16 .... 104 D7
Byers Cl POTB/CUF EN6 .... 23 J7
The Bye ACT W3 .... 99 L5

Byewaters WATW WD18 .... 41 K1
Bye Ways WHTN TW2 .... 133 H7
The Byeways BRYLDS KT5 .... 153 G8
The Bye Wy KTN/HRWW/W HA3 .. 61 L2
The Byeway MORT/ESHN SW14 .. 117 J8
  RKW/CH/CXG WD3 .... 40 E4
Byfeld Gdns BARN SW13 .... 118 A6
Byfield Cl BERM/RHTH SE16 .... 104 E8
Byfield Rd ISLW TW7 .... 116 A3
Byford Cl SRTFD E15 .... 87 L7
Bygrove Rd WIM/MER SW19 .... 155 K2
Bygrove St POP/IOD E14 .... 105 H5
Byland Cl ABYW SE2 .... 126 B1
  UED N18 .... 48 F2
Byne Rd CAR SM5 .... 170 A4
  SYD SE26 .... 158 C2
Bynes Rd SAND/SEL CR2 .... 184 A5
Byng Dr POTB/CUF EN6 .... 23 G4
Byng Pl GWRST WC1E 11 H1
Byng Rd BAR EN5 .... 33 K6
Byng St POP/IOD E14 .... 105 G8
Bynon Av BXLYHN DA7 .... 126 E8
Byre Rd STHGT/OAK N14 .... 48 A1
Byrne Rd BAL SW12 .... 138 B5
Byron Av BORE WD6 .... 32 A8
  CDALE/KGS NW9 .... 63 H5
  COUL/CHIP CR5 .... 183 L8
  HSLWW TW4 .... 114 B7
  MNPK E12 .... 88 E6
  NWMAL KT3 .... 154 A8
  SUT SM1 .... 170 D6
  SWFD E18 .... 69 M3
  WATN WD24 .... 29 K4
Byron Av East SUT SM1 .... 170 D6
Byron Cl HACK E8 .... 86 A8
  HPTN TW12 .... 132 E6
  THMD SE28 .... 108 C7
  WALTH E17 .... 51 L3
Byron Ct ENC/FH EN2 .... 36 B5
Byron Dr EFNCH N2 .... 65 K7
  ERITH DA8 .... 127 H5
Byron Gdns SUT SM1 .... 170 D6
Byron Hill Rd RYLN/HDSTN HA2 .. 79 K3
Byron Ms HAMP NW3 .... 83 L5
Byron Rd ACT W3 .... 98 F7
  ALP/SUD HA0 .... 80 C2
  CRICK NW2 .... 82 B2
  DART DA1 .... 147 H1
  HRW HA1 .... 61 M4
  KTN/HRWW/W HA3 .... 61 M4
  LEY E10 .... 87 H1
  MLHL NW7 .... 46 H7
  SAND/SEL CR2 .... 185 H3
  WALTH E17 .... 69 G4
Byron St POP/IOD E14 .... 105 J5
Byron Wy HARH RM3 .... 74 C2
  NTHLT UB5 .... 96 E2
  WDR/YW UB7 .... 112 F2
  YEAD UB4 .... 95 L3
Bysouth Cl CLAY IG5 .... 71 H2
By the Wd OXHEY WD19 .... 42 D4
Bythorn St CLAP SW4 .... 120 F8
Byton Rd TOOT SW17 .... 155 M2
Byward Av
  EBED/NFELT TW14 .... 132 C3
Bywater Pl BERM/RHTH SE16 ..... 104 E7
Bywater St CHEL SW3 .... 15 L7
The Byways HOR/WEW KT19 ...... 168 B6
The Byway BELMT SM2 .... 182 D2
  POTB/CUF EN6 .... 23 G6
Bywell Pl GTPST W1W 10 E3
Bywood Av CROY/NA CR0 .... 173 J1
Bywood Cl PUR/KEN CR8 .... 184 B8

C

Cabbell St CAMTN NW1 .... 9 J3
Cabinet Wy CHING E4 .... 50 F8
Cable Pl GNWCH SE10 .... 123 J6
Cables Cl BELV DA17 .... 127 J1
Cable St WCHPL E1 .... 104 A6
Cabot Sq POP/IOD E14 .... 105 G7
Cabot Wy EHAM E6 .... 88 D8
Cabul Rd BTSEA SW11 .... 119 L7
Cactus Cl CMBW SE5 .... 121 L7
Cadbury Cl ISLW TW7 .... 116 A6
  SUN TW16 .... 149 L3
Cadbury Rd SUN TW16 .... 149 L3
Cadbury Wy BERM/RHTH SE16 .... 19 M4
Caddington Cl EBAR EN4 .... 34 E8
Caddington Rd CRICK NW2 .... 82 E3
Caddis Cl STAN HA7 .... 61 M1
Cadell Cl BETH E2 .... 7 M6
Cade Rd GNWCH SE10 .... 123 K6
Cader Rd WAND/EARL SW18 .... 137 J3
Cadet Dr STHWK SE1 .... 19 M7
Cadet Pl GNWCH SE10 .... 123 L5
Cadiz Rd DAGE RM10 .... 91 J7
Cadiz St WALW SE17 .... 18 F8
Cadman Cl BRXN/ST SW9 .... 121 H5
Cadmer Cl NWMAL KT3 .... 153 L2
Cadmore La CHES/WCR EN8 .... 26 E1
Cadogan Av RDART DA2 .... 147 K4
Cadogan Cl HOM E9 .... 86 F7
  RYLN/HDSTN HA2 .... 79 H4
  TEDD TW11 .... 151 L1
Cadogan Ct BELMT SM2 .... 170 B8
Cadogan Gdns CHEL SW3 .... 15 L6
  FNCH N3 .... 65 H2
  SWFD E18 .... 70 E1
  WCHMH N21 .... 36 A8
Cadogan Ga KTBR SW1X 15 L6
Cadogan La KTBR SW1X 16 A4
Cadogan Pl KTBR SW1X 15 L5
Cadogan Rd SURB KT6 .... 152 D8
Cadogan Sq KTBR SW1X 15 L5
Cadogan St CHEL SW3 .... 15 L6
Cadogan Ter HOM E9 .... 86 F6
Cadoxton Av SEVS/STOTM N15 .... 67 M7
Cadwallon Rd ELTH/MOT SE9 ..... 143 H6
Caedmon Rd HOLWY N7 .... 84 F1
Caenwood Cl WEY KT13 .... 164 A8
Caerleon Cl SCUP DA14 .... 162 C1
Caernarvon Cl EMPK RM11 .... 93 G1
  MTCM CR4 .... 156 E6

Caernarvon Dr *CLAY* IG5 .... 71 G2
Caesars Wk *MTCM* CR4 .... 155 M8
Caesar's Wy *SHPTN* TW17 .... 164 D1
Cahill St *STLK* EC1Y 12 F1
Cahir St *POP/IOD* E14 .... 123 H2
Cain's La *EBED/NFELT* TW14 ...... 131 K2
Cairn Av *EA* W5 .... 98 D7
Cairndale Cl *BMLY* BR1 .... 159 M3
Cairnfield Av *CRICK* NW2 .... 81 L3
Cairns Av *WFD* IG8 .... 52 F8
Cairns Cl *DART* DA1 .... 146 D2
Cairns Rd *BTSEA* SW11 .... 137 L2
Cairn Wy *STAN* HA7 .... 43 M8
Cairo New Rd *CROY/NA* CR0 .... 172 B4
Cairo Rd *WALTH* E17 .... 69 G5
Caishowe Rd *BORE* WD6 .... 32 B4
Caistor Park Rd *SRTFD* E15 .... 87 M8
Caistor Rd *BAL* SW12 .... 138 B4
Caithness Dr *EPSOM* KT18 .... 180 D7
Caithness Gdns *BFN/LL* DA15 ..... 143 M3
Caithness Rd *MTCM* CR4 .... 156 B3
WKENS W14 .... 118 D1
Calabria Rd *HBRY* N5 .... 85 H6
Calais St *CMBW* SE5 .... 121 H6
Calbourne Av *HCH* RM12 .... 92 B5
Calbourne Rd *BAL* SW12 .... 137 M4
Caldbeck *WAB* EN9 .... 27 K7
Caldbeck Av *WPK* KT4 .... 169 H4
Caldecote Av *CHESW* EN7 .... 25 M2
Caldecote Gdns *BUSH* WD23 ...... 43 L1
Caldecote La *BUSH* WD23 .... 44 A1
Caldecot Rd *CMBW* SE5 .... 121 J7
Caldecott Wy *CLPT* E5 .... 86 D3
Calder Av *GFD/PVL* UB6 .... 97 M1
Calder Gdns *EDGW* HA8 .... 63 G4
Calderon Rd *WAN* E11 .... 87 J4
Calder Rd *MRDN* SM4 .... 155 J8
Caldervale Rd *CLAP* SW4 .... 138 D2
Calderwood St
WOOL/PLUM SE18 .... 125 G2
Caldwell Rd *OXHEY* WD19 .... 42 D6
Caldwell St *BRXN/ST* SW9 .... 120 F5
Caldy Rd *BELV* DA17 .... 127 H1
Caledonian Cl *GDMY/SEVK* IG3 .. 90 B1
Caledonian Rd *HOLWY* N7 .... 84 F5
IS N1 .... 5 L2
Caledonian Wharf Rd
POP/IOD E14 .... 123 K2
Caledonia Rd
STWL/WRAY TW19 .... 130 C5
Caledonia St *IS* N1 .... 5 K6
EHAM E6 .... 88 F8
California La *BUSH* WD23 .... 43 K3
California Rd *NWMAL* KT3 .... 153 H7
Callander Rd *CAT* SE6 .... 141 H6
Callard Av *PLMGR* N13 .... 49 H7
Callcott Rd *KIL/WHAMP* NW6 ...... 82 F7
Callcott St *KENS* W8 .... 8 A8
Calley Down Crs *CROY/NA* CR0 .. 186 D3
Callingham Cl *POP/IOD* E14 .... 104 F4
Callis Farm Cl
STWL/WRAY TW19 .... 130 E3
Callis Rd *WALTH* E17 .... 68 F7
Callow Fld *PUR/KEN* CR8 .... 184 A6
Callowland Pl *WATN* WD24 .... 29 H3
Callow St *CHEL* SW3 .... 15 G9
Calmington Rd *CMBW* SE5 .... 19 K8
Calmont Rd *BMLY* BR1 .... 159 K2
Calmore Cl *HCH* RM12 .... 92 C5
Calne Av *CLAY* IG5 .... 71 H2
Calonne Rd *WIM/MER* SW19 ...... 136 D8
Calshot Rd *HTHAIR* TW6 .... 113 H7
Calshot St *IS* N1 .... 5 L5
Calshot Wy *ENC/FH* EN2 .... 36 B6
HTHAIR TW6 .... 113 G7
Calthorpe Gdns *EDGW* HA8 .... 44 E7
SUT SM1 .... 170 C5
Calthorpe St *FSBYW* WC1X 5 M9
Calton Av *DUL* SE21 .... 139 L3
Calton Rd *BAR* EN5 .... 47 J1
Calverley Rd *BECK* BR3 .... 159 H2
Calverley Crs *DAGE* RM10 .... 91 C2
Calverley Gv *ARCH* N19 .... 84 D1
Calverley Rd *EW* KT17 .... 169 G8
Calvert Av *BETH* E2 .... 7 K8
Calvert Cl *BELV* DA17 .... 127 C2
SCUP DA14 .... 162 E2
Calverton Rd *EHAM* E6 .... 89 C8
Calvert Rd *BAR* EN5 .... 33 K5
GNWCH SE10 .... 123 M3
Calvert St *CAMTN* NW1 .... 4 A3
Calvin St *STMC/STPC* BR5 .... 162 D6
Calvin St *WCHPL* E1 .... 13 L1
Calydon Rd *CHARL* SE7 .... 124 B3
Calypso Wy *BERM/RHTH* SE16 ... 122 F1
Camac Rd *WHTN* TW2 .... 133 K5
Cambalt Rd *PUT/ROE* SW15 ...... 136 D2
Camberley Av *EN* EN1 .... 36 E7
RYNPK SW20 .... 154 B5
Camberley Cl *CHEAM* SM3 .... 169 K5
Camberley Rd *HTHAIR* TW6 .... 113 G8
Cambert Wy *ELTH/MOT* SE9 ...... 142 B1
Camberwell Church St
CMBW SE5 .... 121 K6
Camberwell Glebe *CMBW* SE5 ... 121 K6
Camberwell Gn *CMBW* SE5 .... 121 K6
Camberwell Gv *CMBW* SE5 .... 121 K6
Camberwell New Rd
CMBW SE5 .... 121 H5
Camberwell Rd *CMBW* SE5 .... 121 J4
Camberwell Station Rd
CMBW SE5 .... 121 J6
Cambeys Rd *DAGE* RM10 .... 91 J5
Camborne Av *HARH* RM3 .... 74 E1
WEA W13 .... 98 B8
Camborne Cl *HTHAIR* TW6 .... 113 G8
Camborne Rd *BELMT* SM2 .... 182 A1
CROY/NA CR0 .... 173 G2
MRDN SM4 .... 154 D8
SCUP DA14 .... 144 C7
WAND/EARL SW18 .... 137 G4
WELL DA16 .... 125 M8
Camborne Wy *HARH* RM3 .... 74 F1
HEST TW5 .... 115 G4
Cambourne Av *ED* N9 .... 50 D2
Cambourne Ms *NTGHL* W11 .... 100 E5

Cambray Rd *BAL* SW12 .... 138 C5
ORP BR6 .... 176 F2
Cambria Cl *BFN/LL* DA15 .... 143 K5
HSLW TW3 .... 133 G1
Cambria Ct
EBED/NFELT TW14 .... 132 B4
Cambria Gdns
STWL/WRAY TW19 .... 130 E4
Cambrian Av *GNTH/NBYPK* IG2... 71 L6
Cambrian Cl *WNWD* SE27 .... 139 H7
Cambrian Rd *LEY* E10 .... 69 G8
RCHPK/HAM TW10 .... 134 F3
Cambria Rd *CMBW* SE5 .... 121 J8
Cambria St *FUL/PGN* SW6 .... 119 H5
Cambridge Av *GFD/PVL* UB6 .... 79 M5
GPK RM2 .... 74 C4
KIL/WHAMP NW6 .... 2 B5
NWMAL KT3 .... 153 L5
WELL DA16 .... 143 M1
Cambridge Barracks Rd
WOOL/PLUM SE18 .... 124 F2
Cambridge Cl *CHES/WCR* EN8 .... 26 C2
HSLWW TW4 .... 132 E1
RYNPK SW20 .... 154 B4
WDGN N22 .... 67 G2
WDR/YW UB7 .... 112 D4
WLSDN NW10 .... 81 J3
Cambridge Crs *BETH* E2 .... 104 B1
TEDD TW11 .... 152 A1
Cambridge Dr *LEE/GVPK* SE12 .. 142 A2
POTB/CUF EN6 .... 22 E4
RSLP HA4 .... 76 F2
Cambridge Gdns *EN* EN1 .... 37 G5
KIL/WHAMP NW6 .... 2 B5
MUSWH N10 .... 66 A2
NKENS W10 .... 100 E4
TOTM N17 .... 67 K1
WCHMH N21 .... 49 K2
Cambridge Ga *CAMTN* NW1 .... 4 C8
Cambridge Gate Ms *CAMTN* NW1 .. 4 D8
Cambridge Gn *ELTH/MOT* SE9 ... 143 H5
Cambridge Gv *HMSMTH* W6 ...... 118 E2
PGE/AN SE20 .... 158 B4
Cambridge Grove Rd
KUT KT1 .... 153 C5
Cambridge Heath Rd *BETH* E2.... 104 B2
Cambridge Pk *TWK* TW1 .... 134 D4
WAN E11 .... 70 A8
Cambridge Park Rd *WAN* E11...... 70 A8
Cambridge Pas *HOM* E9 .... 86 C7
Cambridge Pl *KENS* W8 .... 14 D2
Cambridge Rd *ASHF* TW15 .... 149 J5
BARK IG11 .... 89 J7
BARN SW13 .... 117 M7
BMLY BR1 .... 160 A3
BTSEA SW11 .... 119 M6
CAR SM5 .... 170 E8
CHING E4 .... 51 K3
E/WMO/HCT KT8 .... 150 F7
GDMY/SEVK IG3 .... 89 L1
HNWL W7 .... 97 M8
HPTN TW12 .... 150 F3
HSLWW TW4 .... 132 E1
KIL/WHAMP NW6 .... 2 B6
KUT KT1 .... 153 G5
MTCM CR4 .... 156 C6
NWMAL KT3 .... 153 K7
RCH/KEW TW9 .... 117 G5
RYLN/HDSTN HA2 .... 61 G6
RYNPK SW20 .... 154 B4
SCUP DA14 .... 143 L8
SNWD SE25 .... 156 D1
STHL UB1 .... 96 F7
TEDD TW11 .... 134 A8
TWK TW1 .... 134 D3
UX/CGN UB8 .... 76 D6
WAN E11 .... 70 A7
WATW WD18 .... 29 J7
WOT/HER KT12 .... 165 H1
Cambridge Rd North
CHSWK W4 .... 117 H3
Cambridge Rd South
CHSWK W4 .... 117 H3
Cambridge Rw
WOOL/PLUM SE18 .... 125 H3
Cambridge Sq *BAY/PAD* W2 .... 9 J4
Cambridge St *PIM* SW1V 16 D7
Cambridge Ter *CAMTN* NW1 .... 4 C8
Cambridge Terrace Ms
CAMTN NW1 .... 4 D8
Cambus Cl *YEAD* UB4 .... 96 E4
Cambus Rd *CAN/RD* E16 .... 106 A4
Camdale Rd *WOOL/PLUM* SE18 . 125 M5
Camden Av *FELT* TW13 .... 132 C6
YEAD UB4 .... 96 C6
Camden Cl *CHST* BR7 .... 161 J4
Camden Gdns *CAMTN* NW1 .... 4 D2
SUT SM1 .... 170 B7
THHTH CR7 .... 157 H6
Camden Gv *CHST* BR7 .... 161 H2
Camden High St *CAMTN* NW1 .... 4 D2
Camden Hill Rd *NRWD* SE19 ...... 157 L2
Camdenhurst St *POP/IOD* E14.... 104 E5
Camden Lock Pl *CAMTN* NW1 .... 4 C2
Camden Ms *CAMTN* NW1 .... 4 E1
HOLWY N7 .... 84 D6
Camden Park Rd *CAMTN* NW1 ..... 84 D6
CHST BR7 .... 160 F3
Camden Pas *IS* N1 .... 6 C5
Camden Rd *BXLY* DA5 .... 144 F5
CAMTN NW1 .... 5 G1
CAR SM5 .... 170 F6
HOLWY N7 .... 84 E4
SUT SM1 .... 170 B7
WALTH E17 .... 68 F7
WAN E11 .... 70 B7
Camden Rw *BKHTH/KID* SE3 ..... 123 L7
Camden Sq *CAMTN* NW1 .... 5 G1
CAMTN NW1 .... 84 D6
Camden St *CAMTN* NW1 .... 4 C4
Camden Wk *IS* N1 .... 6 C4
Camden Wy *CHST* BR7 .... 160 F3
THHTH CR7 .... 157 H6
Camel Gv *KUTN/CMB* KT2 .... 152 D1
Camellia La *HARH* RM3 .... 74 E2
Camellia Pl *WHTN* TW2 .... 133 H4
Camelot Cl *WIM/MER* SW19 .... 136 F8
WOOL/PLUM SE18 .... 107 K8

Camel Rd *CAN/RD* E16 .... 106 D7
Cameron Cl *BXLY* DA5 .... 145 K7
TRDG/WHET N20 .... 47 L4
UED N18 .... 50 B7
Cameron Dr *CHES/WCR* EN8 .... 26 D7
Cameron Rd *CAT* SE6 .... 140 F6
CROY/NA CR0 .... 172 B1
GDMY/SEVK IG3 .... 89 L1
HAYES BR2 .... 160 A8
Camilla Cl *SUN* TW16 .... 149 M2
Camilla Rd *BERM/RHTH* SE16 .... 122 E2
Camille Cl *SNWD* SE25 .... 158 A6
Camlan Rd *BMLY* BR1 .... 141 M8
Camlet St *BETH* E2 .... 7 L9
Camlet Wy *EBAR* EN4 .... 34 A5
Camley St *CAMTN* NW1 .... 5 G2
Camm Gdns *KUT* KT1 .... 152 F5
THDIT KT7 .... 166 F2
Camomile Av *MTCM* CR4 .... 155 M4
Camomile St *HDTCH* EC3A 13 K4
LVPST EC2M 13 J4
Camomile Wy *WDR/YW* UB7 .... 94 K5
Campana Rd *FUL/PGN* SW6 .... 119 G6
Campbell Av *BARK/HLT* IG6 .... 71 J5
RSLP HA4 .... 60 A7
STRHM/NOR SW16 .... 138 D8
WHTN TW2 .... 133 K5
WOOL/PLUM SE18 .... 125 G6
Campbell Cft *EDGW* HA8 .... 45 G7
Campbell Rd *BOW* E3 .... 105 G2
CROY/NA CR0 .... 172 B2
EHAM E6 .... 88 E8
FSTGT E7 .... 87 M4
HNWL W7 .... 97 L6
TOTM N17 .... 67 M2
WALTH E17 .... 68 F5
WHTN TW2 .... 133 K6
Campdale Rd *ARCH* N19 .... 84 D3
Campden Crs *ALP/SUD* HA0 .... 80 B3
BCTR RM8 .... 71 J8
Campden Gv *KENS* W8 .... 14 B1
Campden Hl *KENS* W8 .... 14 A1
Campden Hill Gdns *KENS* W8 .... 8 A8
Campden Hill Pl *KENS* W8 .... 100 F7
Campden Hill Rd *KENS* W8 .... 8 A8
Campden Hill Sq *KENS* W8 .... 100 F7
Campden House Cl *KENS* W8 .... 14 A1
Campden St *KENS* W8 .... 8 A9
Camperdown St *WCHPL* E1 .... 13 M5
Campfield Rd *ELTH/MOT* SE9 ..... 142 D4
Campine Cl *CHES/WCR* EN8 .... 26 D1
Campion Cl *DEN/HRF* UB9 .... 76 A3
EHAM E6 .... 106 F6
CSTN WD25 .... 21 G6
KTN/HRWW/W HA3 .... 62 F7
ROMW/RG RM7 .... 91 K2
SAND/SEL CR2 .... 172 E6
UX/CGN UB8 .... 94 F4
Campion Gdns *WFD* IG8 .... 52 A7
Campion Pl *THMD* SE28 .... 108 B7
Campion Rd *ISLW* TW7 .... 115 M6
PUT/ROE SW15 .... 136 C1
The Campions *BORE* WD6 .... 31 M3
Campion Wy *EDGW* HA8 .... 45 J6
Camplin Rd *KTN/HRWW/W* HA3 .. 62 E6
Camplin St *NWCR* SE14 .... 122 D5
Camp Rd *WIM/MER* SW19 .... 154 C1
Campsbourne Rd
CEND/HSY/T N8 .... 66 E4
The Campsbourne
CEND/HSY/T N8 .... 66 E5
Campsey Rd *DAGE* RM9 .... 90 B7
Campsfield Rd *CEND/HSY/T* N8 ... 66 E3
Campshill Pl *LEW* SE13 .... 141 J2
Campshill Rd *LEW* SE13 .... 141 J2
Campus Rd *WALTH* E17 .... 68 F7
Camp Vw *WIM/MER* SW19 .... 154 B1
Camrose Av *EDGW* HA8 .... 44 A5
ERITH DA8 .... 127 H4
FELT TW13 .... 132 B8
STAN HA7 .... 62 E3
Camrose Cl *CROY/NA* CR0 .... 173 L2
MRDN SM4 .... 155 G7
Camrose St *ABYW* SE2 .... 126 A3
Canada Av *UED* N18 .... 49 J8
Canada Crs *ACT* W3 .... 99 J4
Canada Rd *ACT* W3 .... 99 J4
ERITH DA8 .... 128 B5
Canada St *BERM/RHTH* SE16 .... 104 D8
Canada Wy *SHB* W12 .... 100 B6
Canadian Av *CAT* SE6 .... 141 H5
Canal Ap *DEPT* SE8 .... 122 E4
Canal Cl *NKENS* W10 .... 100 D3
WCHPL E1 .... 14 D3
Canal Gv *PECK* SE15 .... 122 A4
Canal Rd *WCHPL* E1 .... 104 E3
Canal St *CMBW* SE5 .... 121 K4
Canal Wk *CROY/NA* CR0 .... 172 L1
IS N1 .... 7 H3
Canal Wy *NKENS* W10 .... 100 D3
Canberra Cl *DAGE* RM10 .... 91 K7
HCH RM12 .... 92 C4
HDN NW4 .... 64 A4
Canberra Crs *DAGE* RM10 .... 91 K7
Canberra Dr *NTHLT* UB5 .... 96 C2
Canberra Rd *ABYW* SE2 .... 126 D4
CHARL SE7 .... 124 C4
EHAM E6 .... 88 F8
Canbury Av *KUTN/CMB* KT2 ...... 152 F4
Canbury Ms *SYD* SE26 .... 140 A7
Canbury Park Rd
KUTN/CMB KT2 .... 152 E4
Canbury Pth *STMC/STPC* BR5... 162 A7
Cancell Rd *BRXN/ST* SW9 .... 121 G6
Candahar Rd *BTSEA* SW11 .... 119 L7
Candler Ms *TWK* TW1 .... 134 A4
Candler St *SEVS/STOTM* N15 ...... 67 L7
Candover Cl *WDR/YW* UB7 .... 112 D5
Candover Rd *HCH* RM12 .... 92 B1
Candover St *GTPST* W1W 10 E3
Candy St *BOW* E3 .... 87 M1
Cane Hl *HARH* RM3 .... 74 D3
Caney Ms *CRICK* NW2 .... 82 D2

Canfield Dr *RSLP* HA4 .... 78 B5
Canfield Gdns *HAMP* NW3 .... 83 J6
KIL/WHAMP NW6 .... 2 D1
Canfield Pl *KIL/WHAMP* NW6 .... 83 J6
Canfield Rd *RAIN* RM13 .... 91 M8
WFD IG8 .... 70 E1
Canford Av *NTHLT* UB5 .... 78 E8
Canford Cl *ENC/FH* EN2 .... 36 A5
Canford Gdns *NWMAL* KT3 .... 168 E1
Canford Pl *TEDD* TW11 .... 152 C2
Canford Rd *BTSEA* SW11 .... 138 A1
Canham Rd *CHSWK* W4 .... 99 L8
SNWD SE25 .... 157 L6
Canmore Gdns
STRHM/NOR SW16 .... 156 C3
Cann Hall Rd *FSTGT* E7 .... 87 M4
Canning Crs *WDGN* N22 .... 66 F2
Canning Cross *CMBW* SE5 .... 121 L7
Canning Pl *KENS* W8 .... 14 E3
Canning Rd *CROY/NA* CR0 .... 172 F4
FSBYPK N4 .... 85 H3
KTN/HRWW/W HA3 .... 61 L4
SRTFD E15 .... 105 L1
WALTH E17 .... 68 E5
Cannington Rd *DAGW* RM9 .... 90 C6
Cannizaro Rd *WIM/MER* SW19 .. 154 C2
Cannonbury Av *PIN* HA5 .... 60 D7
Cannon Cl *HPTN* TW12 .... 151 H2
RYNPK SW20 .... 154 C6
Cannon Dr *POP/IOD* E14 .... 105 C6
Cannon Hl *KIL/WHAMP* NW6 .... 83 H5
STHGT/OAK N14 .... 48 D5
Cannon Hill La *MRDN* SM4 .... 154 D8
Cannon La *HAMP* NW3 .... 83 K3
PIN HA5 .... 60 E8
Cannon Ms *WAB* EN9 .... 27 H6
Cannon Pl *CHARL* SE7 .... 124 E5
HAMP NW3 .... 83 J3
Cannon Rd *BXLYHN* DA7 .... 126 E6
STHGT/OAK N14 .... 48 E5
WATW WD18 .... 29 J8
Cannon St *STP* EC4M 12 E5
Cannon Street Rd *WCHPL* E1 ..... 104 B5
Cannon Wy *E/WMO/HCT* KT8 .... 151 G7
Canon Av *CHDH* RM6 .... 72 C6
Canon Beck Rd
BERM/RHTH SE16 .... 104 C8
Canonbie Rd *FSTH* SE23 .... 140 C4
Canonbury Crs *IS* N1 .... 6 E1
Canonbury Gv *IS* N1 .... 6 E1
Canonbury La *IS* N1 .... 6 E1
Canonbury Pk North *IS* N1 .... 85 J6
Canonbury Pk South *IS* N1 .... 85 J6
Canonbury Rd *ENC/FH* EN2 .... 36 E4
IS N1 .... 6 D1
Canonbury Sq *IS* N1 .... 6 D1
Canonbury St *IS* N1 .... 6 E1
Canonbury Vls *IS* N1 .... 6 D2
Canon Mohan Cl *EBAR* EN4 .... 48 A1
Canon Murnane Rd *STHWK* SE1... 19 L4
Canon Rd *BMLY* BR1 .... 160 C6
Canon Rw *WHALL* SW1A 17 J2
Canons Cl *EDGW* HA8 .... 44 F8
EFNCH N2 .... 65 K8
Canons Dr *EDGW* HA8 .... 44 E8
Canonsleigh Rd *DAGW* RM9 .... 90 B7
Canon St *IS* N1 .... 6 E4
Canon's Wk *CROY/NA* CR0 .... 173 K5
Canopus Wy *NTHWD* HA6 .... 42 A6
STWL/WRAY TW19 .... 130 E4
Canrobert St *BETH* E2 .... 104 B1
BETH E2 .... 104 B2
Cantelowes Rd *CAMTN* NW1 .... 84 D6
Canterbury Av *BFN/LL* DA15 ...... 144 C4
IL IG1 .... 70 E8
UPMR RM14 .... 93 M1
Canterbury Cl *BECK* BR3 .... 159 H4
CHIG IG7 .... 53 M5
DART DA1 .... 147 G4
EHAM E6 .... 106 F5
GFD/PVL UB6 .... 96 B4
NTHWD HA6 .... 41 M8
Canterbury Crs *BRXN/ST* SW9 ... 121 G8
Canterbury Gv *WNWD* SE27 ...... 139 G7
Canterbury Rd *BORE* WD6 .... 32 B1
CROY/NA CR0 .... 171 M2
FELT TW13 .... 132 E6
HRW HA1 .... 61 H6
KIL/WHAMP NW6 .... 2 C5
LEY E10 .... 69 J8
MRDN SM4 .... 170 C1
RYLN/HDSTN HA2 .... 61 H6
WAT WD17 .... 29 H5
Canterbury Ter *KIL/WHAMP* NW6 .. 2 A5
Canterbury Wy *DART* DA1 .... 147 J1
RKW/CH/CXG WD3 .... 28 C6
WTHK RM20 .... 129 L5
Cantley Gdns *GNTH/NBYPK* IG2 .. 71 J7
NRWD SE19 .... 157 M4
Cantley Rd *HNWL* W7 .... 116 A1
Canton St *POP/IOD* E14 .... 105 G5
Cantrell Rd *BOW* E3 .... 105 H4
Cantwell Rd *WOOL/PLUM* SE18 . 125 H5
Canvey St *STHWK* SE1 .... 12 E8
Cape Cl *BARK* IG11 .... 89 H7
Capel Av *WLGTN* SM6 .... 171 M7
Capel Cl *HAYES* BR2 .... 175 L3
TRDG/WHET N20 .... 47 J5
Capel Gdns *GDMY/SEVK* IG3 ...... 89 M4
PIN HA5 .... 60 F5
Capella Rd *NTHWD* HA6 .... 41 M8
Capel Pl *RDART* DA2 .... 146 C8
Capel Rd *EBAR* EN4 .... 47 J1
EN EN1 .... 37 H1
FSTGT E7 .... 88 B4
OXHEY WD19 .... 42 D1
Capelvere Wk *WAT* WD17 .... 28 E4
Capener's Cl *KTBR* SW1X 16 A2
Capern Rd *WAND/EARL* SW18 ... 137 J5
Cape Rd *SEVS/STOTM* N15 .... 68 A4
Capital Interchange Wy
CHSWK W4 .... 117 G3
Capitol Wy *CDALE/KGS* NW9 .... 63 K4
Capland Rd *STJWD* NW8 .... 3 G9
Caple Rd *WLSDN* NW10 .... 99 H1
Caprea Cl *YEAD* UB4 .... 96 D4
Capri Rd *CROY/NA* CR0 .... 172 F3
Capstan Cl *CHDH* RM6 .... 72 B7

Capstan Ct *GRH* DA9 .... 147 J5
Capstan Ride *ENC/FH* EN2 .... 36 A5
Capstan Rd *DEPT* SE8 .... 122 F2
Capstan Sq *POP/IOD* E14 .... 105 J8
Capstan Wy *BERM/RHTH* SE16 .. 104 E7
Capstone Rd *BMLY* BR1 .... 142 A8
Capthorne Av *RYLN/HDSTN* HA2 .. 78 E1
Capuchin Cl *STAN* HA7 .... 44 B8
Capulet Ms *CAN/RD* E16 .... 106 A7
Capworth St *LEY* E10 .... 87 G1
Caractacus Cottage Vw
WATW WD18 .... 42 A2
Caractacus Gn *WATW* WD18 .... 41 M1
Caradoc St *GNWCH* SE10 .... 123 L3
Caradon Cl *WAN* E11 .... 87 L1
Caradon Wy *SEVS/STOTM* N15 ... 67 K5
SEVS/STOTM N15 .... 67 K5
Caravan La *RKW/CH/CXG* WD3 ... 40 E2
The Caravan Site
SOCK/AV RM15 .... 129 K1
Caravel Ms *DEPT* SE8 .... 123 C4
Caraway Cl *PLSTW* E13 .... 106 B4
Caraway Pl *WLGTN* SM6 .... 171 H5
Carbery Av *ACT* W3 .... 98 F8
Carbis Cl *CHING* E4 .... 51 K3
Carbis Rd *POP/IOD* E14 .... 104 F5
Carburton St *GTPST* W1W 10 C2
Carbury Cl *HCH* RM12 .... 92 C6
Cardale St *POP/IOD* E14 .... 123 J1
Carden Rd *PECK* SE15 .... 122 B8
Cardiff Rd *HNWL* W7 .... 116 A1
PEND EN3 .... 37 H7
WATW WD18 .... 42 B1
Cardiff St *WOOL/PLUM* SE18..... 125 L5
Cardiff Wy *ABLGY* WD5 .... 21 C5
Cardigan Gdns *GDMY/SEVK* IG3 . 90 A2
Cardigan Rd *BARN* SW13 .... 118 A7
BOW E3 .... 104 F1
RCHPK/HAM TW10 .... 134 E3
WIM/MER SW19 .... 155 J2
Cardigan St *LBTH* SE11 .... 18 A7
Cardinal Av *BORE* WD6 .... 32 B6
KUTN/CMB KT2 .... 152 E1
MRDN SM4 .... 169 H8
Cardinal Bourne St
STHWK SE1 .... 19 H4
Cardinal Cl *CHST* BR7 .... 161 K4
EDGW HA8 .... 45 J4
MRDN SM4 .... 169 L1
WPK KT4 .... 169 G6
Cardinal Crs *NWMAL* KT3 .... 153 J5
Cardinal Dr *BARK/HLT* IG6 .... 53 J8
WOT/HER KT12 .... 165 K3
Cardinal Pl *PUT/ROE* SW15 .... 136 D1
Cardinal Rd *FELT* TW13 .... 132 B5
RSLP HA4 .... 78 D1
Cardinal's Wk *HPTN* TW12 .... 151 J3
SUN TW16 .... 149 L2
Cardinals Wy *ARCH* N19 .... 84 D1
Cardinal Wy
KTN/HRWW/W HA3 .... 61 L4
RAIN RM13 .... 110 D1
Cardine Ms *PECK* SE15 .... 122 B5
Cardington Sq *HSLWW* TW4 .... 132 D1
Cardington St *CAMTN* NW1 .... 4 F7
Cardozo Rd *HOLWY* N7 .... 84 E3
Cardrew Av *NFNCH/WDSP* N12 .... 47 K7
Cardross St *HMSMTH* W6 .... 118 E3
Cardwell Rd *HOLWY* N7 .... 84 E3
WOOL/PLUM SE18 .... 124 F2
Carew Cl *HOLWY* N7 .... 84 F2
Carew Rd *ASHF* TW15 .... 149 J2
MTCM CR4 .... 156 A5
NTHWD HA6 .... 41 L8
THHTH CR7 .... 157 H6
TOTM N17 .... 68 A3
WEA W13 .... 98 C8
WLGTN SM6 .... 170 E6
Carew St *CMBW* SE5 .... 121 J7
Carew Wy *OXHEY* WD19 .... 42 F5
Carey Gdns *VX/NE* SW8 .... 120 C6
Carey La *CITYW* EC2V 12 E4
Carey Rd *DAGW* RM9 .... 90 A4
Carey St *LINN* WC2A 11 M5
Carey Wy *WBLY* HA9 .... 81 H4
Carfax Pl *CLAP* SW4 .... 138 D2
Carfax Rd *HCH* RM12 .... 91 M4
HYS/HAR UB3 .... 114 A3
Carfree Cl *IS* N1 .... 6 B1
Cargill Rd *WAND/EARL* SW18 .... 137 J5
Cargreen Rd *SNWD* SE25 .... 157 M7
Carholme Rd *FSTH* SE23 .... 140 F5
Carisbrook Cl *EN* EN1 .... 36 F4
WATN WD24 .... 29 G8
Carisbrooke Av *BXLY* DA5 .... 144 D5
Carisbrooke Cl *EMPK* RM11 .... 93 G1
STAN HA7 .... 62 D3
Carisbrooke Rd *HAYES* BR2 .... 160 C7
MTCM CR4 .... 156 A5
WALTH E17 .... 68 E6
Carleton Av *WLGTN* SM6 .... 183 K2
Carleton Cl *ESH/CLAY* KT10 ...... 166 D3
Carleton Rd *DART* DA1 .... 147 G4
HOLWY N7 .... 84 D5
Carlina Gdns *WFD* IG8 .... 52 E7
Carlingford Rd *HAMP* NW3 .... 83 K3
MRDN SM4 .... 169 K1
SEVS/STOTM N15 .... 67 H4
Carlisle Av *ACT* W3 .... 99 L5
TWRH EC3N 13 K5
Carlisle Cl *KUTN/CMB* KT2 .... 153 G3
Carlisle Gdns *IL* IG1 .... 70 D7
KTN/HRWW/W HA3 .... 62 D8
Carlisle La *STHWK* SE1 .... 17 M3
Carlisle Pl *FBAR/BDGN* N11 .... 48 B4
WEST SW1P 16 E4
Carlisle Rd *CDALE/KGS* NW9 .... 63 J4
DART DA1 .... 147 G3
FSBYPK N4 .... 85 G1
HPTN TW12 .... 151 H3
KIL/WHAMP NW6 .... 82 E8
LEY E10 .... 69 H5
ROM RM1 .... 73 M6
SUT SM1 .... 169 M8
Carlisle St *SOHO/CST* W1F 11 G5
Carlisle Wy *TOOT* SW17 .... 156 A1

Carlos Pl *MYFR/PKLN* W1K 10 B7
Carlow St *CAMTN* NW1 .... 4 E5
Carlton Av *EBED/NFELT* TW14 .. 132 C3
  GRH DA9 .... 147 L3
  HYS/HAR UB3 .... 113 L2
  KTN/HRWW/W HA3 .... 62 B6
  SAND/SEL CR2 .... 184 D1
  STHGT/OAK N14 .... 35 K8
Carlton Av East *WBLY* HA9 .... 80 B5
Carlton Av West *ALP/SUD* HA0 .. 80 B2
Carlton Cl *BORE* WD6 .... 32 D7
  CHSGTN KT9 .... 167 K8
  EDGW HA8 .... 45 G7
  HAMP NW3 .... 83 G2
  UPMR RM14 .... 93 H2
Carlton Crs *CHEAM* SM3 .... 169 L6
Carlton Dr *BARK/HLT* IG6 .... 71 K4
  PUT/ROE SW15 .... 136 D2
Carlton Gdns *EA* W5 .... 98 C5
  STJS SW1Y 11 G9
Carlton Gv *PECK* SE15 .... 122 B6
Carlton Hl *STJWD* NW8 .... 2 E4
Carlton House Ter *STJS* SW1Y .. 11 G9
Carlton Park Av *RYNPK* SW20.. 154 C5
Carlton Rd *CHSWK* W4 .... 99 K8
  EA W5 .... 98 C6
  ERITH DA8 .... 127 H4
  FBAR/BDGN N11 .... 48 A7
  FSBYPK N4 .... 67 G8
  GPK RM2 .... 74 A6
  MNPK E12 .... 88 D4
  MORT/ESHN SW14 .... 117 J8
  NWMAL KT3 .... 153 L5
  SAND/SEL CR2 .... 184 D1
  SCUP DA14 .... 161 M1
  SUN TW16 .... 149 M3
  WALTH E17 .... 68 C2
  WAN E11 .... 87 M1
  WELL DA16 .... 126 B8
  WOT/HER KT12 .... 165 H2
Carlton Sq *WCHPL* E1 .... 104 D3
Carlton St *STJS* SW1Y 11 G7
Carlton Ter *SYD* SE26 .... 140 C7
  WAN E11 .... 70 B6
Carlton V *KIL/WHAMP* NW6 .... 2 C6
Carlwell St *TOOT* SW17 .... 155 L1
Carlyle Av *BMLY* BR1 .... 160 D6
  STHL UB1 .... 96 F6
Carlyle Cl *E/WMO/HCT* KT8 .... 151 H5
  EFNCH N2 .... 65 J7
  WLSDN NW10 .... 81 K8
Carlyle Gdns *STHL* UB1 .... 96 F6
Carlyle Rd *CROY/NA* CR0 .... 173 G4
  EA W5 .... 116 C2
  MNPK E12 .... 88 E4
  THMD SE28 .... 108 B6
Carlyle Sq *CHEL* SW3 .... 15 H8
Carlyon Av *RYLN/HDSTN* HA2 .. 78 F4
Carlyon Cl *ALP/SUD* HA0 .... 80 E8
Carlyon Rd *ALP/SUD* HA0 .... 98 E1
  YEAD UB4 .... 96 C4
Carlys Cl *BECK* BR3 .... 158 D5
Carmalt Gdns *PUT/ROE* SW15 .. 136 C1
  WOT/HER KT12 .... 165 J7
Carmelite Rd *KTN/HRWW/W* HA3 .... 61 J2
Carmelite St *EMB* EC4Y 12 B6
Carmen St *POP/IOD* E14 .... 105 H5
Carmichael Cl *BTSEA* SW11 .... 78 A4
Carmichael Rd *SNWD* SE25 .... 158 A8
Carminia Rd *TOOT* SW17 .... 138 B6
Carnaby St *REGST* W1B 10 E6
Carnac St *WNWD* SE27 .... 139 K8
Carnanton Rd *WALTH* E17 .... 69 K2
Carnarvon Av *EN* EN1 .... 36 F5
Carnarvon Dr *HYS/HAR* UB3 .. 113 J1
Carnarvon Rd *BAR* EN5 .... 33 L6
  LEY E10 .... 69 J7
  SRTFD E15 .... 87 M6
  SWFD E18 .... 69 M2
Carnation Cl *ROMW/RG* RM7 .. 91 L2
Carnation St *ABYW* SE2 .... 126 B3
Carnbrook Rd *BKHTH/KID* SE3 .. 124 D8
Carnecke Gdns *ELTH/MOT* SE9 .. 142 E2
Carnegie Cl *SURB* KT6 .... 167 M4
Carnegie Pl *WIM/MER* SW19 .. 136 D7
Carnegie St *IS* N1 .... 5 L4
Carnforth Cl *HOR/WEW* KT19 .. 168 B8
Carnforth Gdns *HCH* RM12 .... 92 A5
Carnforth Rd *STRHM/NOR* SW16 .... 156 D3
Carnoustie Dr *IS* N1 .... 5 L2
Carnwath Rd *FUL/PGN* SW6 .. 119 G8
Carolina Cl *SRTFD* E15 .... 87 L5
Carolina Rd *THHTH* CR7 .... 157 H5
Caroline Cl *BAY/PAD* W2 .... 8 D7
  CROY/NA CR0 .... 172 E6
  STRHM/NOR SW16 .... 138 F8
  WDR/YW UB7 .... 94 B8
Caroline Place Ms *BAY/PAD* W2 .. 8 D7
Caroline Rd *WIM/MER* SW19 .. 154 F3
Caroline St *WCHPL* E1 .... 104 D5
Caroline Ter *BCVA* SW1W 16 A6
Caroline Wk *FUL/PGN* SW6 .. 118 E4
Carol St *CAMTN* NW1 .... 4 E3
Carolyn Dr *ORP* BR6 .... 177 G5
Carpenders Av *OXHEY* WD19 .. 42 E5
Carpenter Gdns *WCHMH* N21.. 49 H4
Carpenter's Cl *TRDG/WHET* N20.. 47 H1
Carpenter's Pl *CLAP* SW4 .... 138 D1
Carpenters Rd *EN* EN1 .... 37 J1
  SRTFD E15 .... 87 H7
Carpenter St *MYFR/PKLN* W1K .. 10 C7
Carpenter Wy *POTB/CUF* EN6 .. 23 J4
Carr Gv *WOOL/PLUM* SE18 .. 124 E2
Carriage Dr East *BTSEA* SW11 .. 120 A4
Carriage Dr North *BTSEA* SW11 .. 119 M5
Carriage Dr South *BTSEA* SW11 .. 119 M6
Carriage Dr West *BTSEA* SW11 .. 119 M5
Carriage Ms *IL* IG1 .... 89 J2

Carrick Cl *ISLW* TW7 .... 116 A8
Carrick Dr *BARK/HLT* IG6 .... 71 J2
Carrick Gdns *TOTM* N17 .... 67 L1
Carrill Wy *BELV* DA17 .... 126 D2
Carrington Av *BORE* WD6 .... 32 B8
  HSLW TW3 .... 133 H2
Carrington Cl *BAR* EN5 .... 33 G8
  CROY/NA CR0 .... 173 L2
Carrington Gdns *FSTGT* E7 .... 88 A4
Carrington Rd *DART* DA1 .... 146 F3
  RCHPK/HAM TW10 .... 135 G1
Carrington Sq *KTN/HRWW/W* HA3 .... 61 J1
Carrol Cl *KTTN* NW5 .... 84 B4
Carroll Cl *SRTFD* E15 .... 87 M5
Carroll Hl *LOU* IG10 .... 39 M6
Carron Cl *POP/IOD* E14 .... 105 H5
Carroun Rd *VX/NE* SW8 .... 120 F5
Carroway La *GFD/PVL* UB6 .... 97 K2
Carrow Rd *DAGW* RM9 .... 90 B7
  WOT/HER KT12 .... 165 K5
Carr Rd *NTHLT* UB5 .... 79 H7
  WALTH E17 .... 68 F3
Carrs La *WCHMH* N21 .... 36 D8
Carr St *POP/IOD* E14 .... 104 E5
Carshalton Gv *SUT* SM1 .... 170 D6
Carshalton Park Rd *CAR* SM5 .. 170 F7
Carshalton Pl *CAR* SM5 .... 171 G6
Carshalton Rd *BNSTD* SM7 .... 182 F6
  MTCM CR4 .... 156 A8
  SUT SM1 .... 170 C7
Carsington Gdns *DART* DA1 .... 146 D6
Carslake Rd *PUT/ROE* SW15 .... 136 C3
Carson Rd *CAN/RD* E16 .... 106 A4
  DUL SE21 .... 139 J6
  EBAR EN4 .... 34 F7
Carstairs Rd *CAT* SE6 .... 141 J7
Carston Cl *LEE/GVPK* SE12 .... 141 M2
Carswell Cl *REDBR* IG4 .... 70 D5
Carswell Rd *CAT* SE6 .... 141 J4
Cartel Ct *PUR* RM19 .... 129 K2
Carter Cl *CRW* RM5 .... 73 H1
  WLGTN SM6 .... 183 K1
Carter Dr *CRW* RM5 .... 55 H6
Carteret St *STJSPK* SW1H 17 G2
Carteret Wy *DEPT* SE8 .... 122 E2
Carterhatch La *EN* EN1 .... 36 F4
  PEND EN3 .... 37 J5
Carterhatch Rd *PEND* EN3 .... 37 L5
Carter La *BLKFR* EC4V 12 D5
Carter Pl *WALW* SE17 .... 18 F8
  WIM/MER SW19 .... 155 K2
Cartersfield Rd *WAB* EN9 .... 27 J7
Carters Hill Cl *ELTH/MOT* SE9 .. 142 C5
Carter's Rd *EW* KT17 .... 180 F8
Carter St *WALW* SE17 .... 18 E9
Carter's Yd *WAND/EARL* SW18 .. 137 G2
Carthew Rd *HMSMTH* W6 .... 118 B1
Carthew Vls *HMSMTH* W6 .... 118 B1
Carthusian St *FARR* EC1M 12 E2
Carting La *TPL/STR* WC2R 11 K7
Cart La *CHING* E4 .... 45 K2
Cartmel Cl *TOTM* N17 .... 68 B1
Cartmel Ct *NTHLT* UB5 .... 78 G6
Cartmel Gdns *MRDN* SM4 .... 155 J8
Cartmel Rd *BXLYHN* DA7 .... 127 G6
Cart Pth *GSTN* WD25 .... 21 J6
Cartwright Gdns *STPAN* WC1H .. 5 H8
Cartwright St *WHR* EC3N 13 M6
Cartwright Wy *BARN* SW13 .... 118 B5
Carver Rd *HNHL* SE24 .... 139 J3
Carville Crs *BTFD* TW8 .... 116 E2
Cary Rd *WAN* E11 .... 87 L4
Carysfort Rd *CEND/HSY/T* N8 .. 66 D6
  STNW/STAM N16 .... 85 K3
Cascade Av *MUSWH* N10 .... 66 C5
Cascade Cl *STMC/STPC* BR5 .. 162 C6
Cascade Rd *BKHH* IG9 .... 52 D4
Cascades *CROY/NA* CR0 .... 185 M3
Casella Rd *NWCR* SE14 .... 122 D5
Casewick Rd *WNWD* SE27 .... 157 H1
Casimir Rd *CLPT* E5 .... 86 B3
Casino Av *HNHL* SE24 .... 139 J2
Caspian Strret *CMBW* SE5 .... 121 K5
Caspian Wk *CAN/RD* E16 .... 106 D5
Cassandra Cl *NTHLT* UB5 .... 79 K4
Casselden Rd *WLSDN* NW10 .. 81 K7
Cassidy Rd *FUL/PGN* SW6 .... 119 G5
Cassilda Rd *ABYW* SE2 .... 126 A2
Cassilis Rd *TWK* TW1 .... 134 B3
Cassiobridge Rd *WATW* WD18.. 28 E7
Cassiobury Av *EBED/NFELT* TW14 .... 131 M4
Cassiobury Dr *WAT* WD17 .... 28 F1
Cassiobury Park Av *WATW* WD18.. 28 E6
Cassiobury Rd *WALTH* E17 .... 68 D6
Cassio Rd *WATW* WD18 .... 29 H7
Cassland Rd *HOM* E9 .... 86 D7
  THHTH CR7 .... 157 K7
Casslee Rd *CAT* SE6 .... 140 F4
Casson St *WCHPL* E1 .... 104 A4
Casstine Cl *SWLY* BR8 .... 163 M4
Castellain Rd *MV/WKIL* W9 .... 2 C9
Castellan Av *GPK* RM2 .... 74 B4
Castellane Cl *STAN* HA7 .... 61 M1
Castello Av *PUT/ROE* SW15 .. 136 C2
Castelnau *BARN* SW13 .... 118 B5
Casterbridge Rd *BKHTH/KID* SE3.. 124 A4
Casterton St *HACK* E8 .... 86 B6
Castile Rd *WOOL/PLUM* SE18 .. 125 G2
Castillon Rd *CAT* SE6 .... 141 M6
Castlands Rd *CAT* SE6 .... 140 F6
Castle Av *CHING* E4.. 51 K8
  EW KT17 .... 181 G2
  RAIN RM13 .... 91 L7
  WDR/YW UB7 .... 94 B6
Castlebar Hi *WEA* W13 .... 98 B4
Castlebar Ms *EA* W5 .... 98 B4
Castlebar Pk *EA* W5 .... 98 B4

Castlebar Rd *WEA* W13 .... 98 C5
Castle Baynard St *BLKFR* EC4V.. 12 D6
Castle Cl *BUSH* WD23 .... 43 H1
  HARH RM3 .... 56 C5
  HAYES BR2 .... 159 K6
  WIM/MER SW19 .... 136 D7
Castlecombe Dr *WIM/MER* SW19 .... 136 D4
Castlecombe Rd *ELTH/MOT* SE9 .... 160 E1
Castle Ct *SYD* SE26 .... 140 E8
Castledine Rd *PGE/AN* SE20 .. 158 B3
Castle Dr *REDBR* IG4.. 70 E7
Castleford Av *ELTH/MOT* SE9 .. 143 H5
Castleford Cl *UED* N18 .... 49 M8
Castlegate *RCH/KEW* TW9 .... 116 F8
Castle Gn *WEY* KT13 .... 164 E5
Castlehaven Rd *CAMTN* NW1 .. 4 D1
Castle Hill Av *CROY/NA* CR0 .. 186 B2
Castle La *WESTW* SW1E 16 E3
Castleleigh Ct *ENC/FH* EN2 .... 36 D8
  SAND/SEL CR2 .... 172 F7
Castlemaine Av *EW* KT17 .... 181 H2
  SAND/SEL CR2 .... 184 D1
Castle Ms *NFNCH/WDSP* N12 .. 47 J7
Castlereagh St *MBLAR* W1H .. 9 L4
Castle Rd *CAMTN* NW1 .... 84 B6
  DAGW RM9 .... 90 B8
  EPSOM KT18 .... 180 B8
  ISLW TW7 .... 115 M7
  NFNCH/WDSP N12 .... 47 J7
  NTHLT UB5 .... 79 H6
  NWDGN UB2 .... 114 F1
  PEND EN3 .... 37 L4
  WEY KT13 .... 164 D5
Castle St *EHAM* E6 .... 106 C1
  KUT KT1 .... 152 E5
Castleton Av *BXLYHN* DA7 .... 127 K6
  WBLY HA9 .... 80 E4
Castleton Cl *BNSTD* SM7 .... 182 A8
  CROY/NA CR0 .... 173 L1
Castleton Dr *BNSTD* SM7 .... 182 A8
Castleton Gdns *GDMY/SEVK* IG3.. 90 A1
Castleton Rd *GDMY/SEVK* IG3.. 90 A1
  LEE/GVPK SE12 .... 142 D8
  MTCM CR4 .... 156 D7
  RSLP HA4 .... 78 D1
  WALTH E17 .... 69 K3
Castletown Rd *WKENS* W14 .. 118 E3
Castleview Rd *FSBYPK* N4 .... 85 J1
Castle View Gdns *IL* IG1 .... 70 E7
Castle View Rd *WEY* KT13 .... 164 B6
Castle Wy *EW* KT17 .... 181 G3
  FELT TW13 .... 132 C8
Castlewood Dr *ELTH/MOT* SE9.. 124 F7
Castlewood Rd *EBAR* EN4.. 34 D6
  SEVS/STOTM N15 .... 68 A7
Castle Yd *HGT* N6 .... 66 A6
  RCHPK/HAM TW10 .... 134 D2
  STHWK SE1 .... 12 D8
Castor La *POP/IOD* E14 .... 105 H6
Catalina Rd *HTHAIR* TW6 .... 113 G8
Caterham Av *CLAY* IG5 .... 71 G3
Caterham Ct *WAB* EN9.. 27 M7
Caterham Rd *LEW* SE13 .... 123 J8
Catesby St *WALW* SE17 .... 19 H6
Catford Broadway *CAT* SE6 .. 141 H4
Catford Hl *CAT* SE6 .... 140 F5
Catford Rd *CAT* SE6 .... 141 G5
Cathall Rd *WAN* E11 .... 87 L1
Cathay St *BERM/RHTH* SE16 .. 104 B8
Cathcart Dr *ORP* BR6 .... 176 E4
Cathcart Hl *ARCH* N19 .... 84 C3
Cathcart Rd *WBPTN* SW10 .. 14 E9
Cathcart St *KTTN* NW5 .... 84 B6
Cathedral St *STHWK* SE1 .... 13 G8
Catherall Rd *HBRY* N5 .... 85 J3
Catherine Dr *RCH/KEW* TW9 .. 134 E1
  SUN TW16 .... 149 M3
Catherine Gdns *HSLW* TW3 .. 133 K1
Catherine Gv *GNWCH* SE10 .. 123 H6
Catherine Pl *WESTW* SW1E .. 16 E3
  PEND EN3 .... 37 L1
  SURB KT6 .... 152 D8
Catherines Cl *WDR/YW* UB7 .. 94 D8
Catherine St *HOL/ALD* WC2B.. 11 L6
Catherine Wheel Aly *LVPST* EC2M 13 K3
Catherine Wheel Yd *WHALL* SW1A 10 E9
Cat Hi *EBAR* EN4 .... 34 F8
Cathles Rd *BAL* SW12 .... 138 B3
Cathnor Rd *SHB* W12 .... 100 B8
Catisfield Rd *PEND* EN3.. 37 L2
Catlin Crs *SHPTN* TW17 .... 149 K8
Catling Cl *FSTH* SE23 .... 140 C7
Catlin's La *PIN* HA5 .... 60 B4
Catlin St *BERM/RHTH* SE16 .. 122 A3
Cator Cl *CROY/NA* CR0 .... 186 E4
Cator Crs *CROY/NA* CR0 .... 186 E4
Cator La *BECK* BR3 .... 158 F5
Cato Rd *CLAP* SW4 .... 120 D8
Cator Rd *CAR* SM5 .... 170 F7
  SYD SE26 .... 158 D2
Cator St *PECK* SE15 .... 121 M4
Cato St *MBLAR* W1H 9 L3
Catsey La *BUSH* WD23 .... 43 J2
Catsey Wd *BUSH* WD23 .... 43 J2
Catterick Cl *FBAR/BDGN* N11 .. 48 A8
Cattistock Rd *ELTH/MOT* SE9 .. 160 E1
Cattle Gate Rd *POTB/CUF* EN6 .. 24 C4
Cattlegate Rd Crews Hl *ENC/FH* EN2 .... 24 F7
Cattley Cl *BAR* EN5 .... 33 L7
Cattlins Cl *CHESW* EN7 .... 25 L2
Catton St *RSQ* WC1B 11 L3
Caulfield Rd *EHAM* E6 .... 88 F7
  PECK SE15.. 122 B7
Causeway *EBED/NFELT* TW14.. 132 B1
Causeway Br *SOCK/AV* RM15 .. 129 L1
Causeway Cl *POTB/CUF* EN6 .. 23 K4
The Causeway *BELMT* SM2 .. 182 C7
  CAR SM5 .... 171 G5
  CHSGTN KT9 .... 167 L6
  EFNCH N2 .... 65 K5

  ESH/CLAY KT10 .... 178 F1
  POTB/CUF EN6.. 23 J4
  TEDD TW11 .... 151 M2
  WAND/EARL SW18 .... 137 H1
  WIM/MER SW19 .... 154 C1
Causeyware Rd *ED* N9 .... 50 B2
Causton St *WEST* SW1P 17 H6
Cautley Av *CLAP* SW4 .... 138 C2
Cavalier Cl *CHDH* RM6 .... 72 C5
Cavalier Gdns *HYS/HAR* UB3 .. 95 K5
Cavalry Gdns *PUT/ROE* SW15 .. 136 F2
Cavaye Pl *WBPTN* SW10 .... 14 F8
Cavell Crs *DART* DA1 .... 147 L1
Cavell Dr *ENC/FH* EN2 .... 36 A5
Cavell Rd *TOTM* N17 .... 67 K1
Cavell St *WCHPL* E1 .... 104 B4
Cavendish Av *BFN/LL* DA15.. 144 A4
  ERITH DA8 .... 127 J4
  FNCH N3 .... 65 G2
  NTHLT UB5 .... 79 K4
  NWMAL KT3 .... 154 B8
  RAIN RM13 .... 92 B6
  RSLP HA4 .... 78 B5
  STJWD NW8 .... 3 H6
  WEA W13 .... 98 A4
  WELL DA16 .... 125 M8
  WFD IG8 .... 70 B1
Cavendish Cl *KIL/WHAMP* NW6 .. 82 F6
  STJWD NW8 .... 3 H7
  SUN TW16 .... 149 M2
  UED N18 .... 50 B7
  YEAD UB4 .... 95 L4
Cavendish Ct *SUN* TW16 .... 149 M2
Cavendish Crs *BORE* WD6 .... 32 A7
  RAIN RM13 .... 92 B6
Cavendish Dr *EDGW* HA8 .... 44 C3
  ESH/CLAY KT10 .... 166 E7
  WAN E11 .... 87 K1
Cavendish Gdns *BARK* IG11 .. 89 M5
  CHDH RM6 .... 72 C6
  RAIN RM13 .... 92 B6
  WELL DA16 .... 126 B1
Cavendish Ms North *REGST* W1B 10 D2
Cavendish Ms South *GTPST* W1W 10 D3
Cavendish Pl *CAVSQ/HST* W1G.. 10 D4
  MHST W1U 10 C4
Cavendish Rd *BAL* SW12 .... 138 C4
  BAR EN5 .... 33 J6
  BELMT SM2 .... 182 C1
  CHING E4 .... 69 H1
  CHSWK W4 .... 117 J6
  CLAP SW4 .... 138 B3
  CROY/NA CR0 .... 172 B3
  FSBYPK N4 .... 67 H7
  KIL/WHAMP NW6.. 82 E7
  NWMAL KT3 .... 153 M8
  SUN TW16 .... 149 M2
  UED N18 .... 50 B7
  WEY KT13 .... 164 C8
  WIM/MER SW19 .... 155 L3
Cavendish Sq *CAVSQ/HST* W1G 10 D4
Cavendish St *IS* N1 .... 7 G6
Cavendish Wy *WWKM* BR4 .. 174 B3
Cavenham Gdns *EMPK* RM11.. 74 C6
  IL IG1 .... 89 K3
Caverleigh Wy *WPK* KT4 .... 169 G3
Caversham Av *CHEAM* SM3 .. 169 L4
  PLMGR N13 .... 49 G5
Caversham Rd *KTTN* NW5 .... 84 C6
  SEVS/STOTM N15 .... 67 J5
Caversham St *CHEL* SW3 .... 15 L9
Caverswall St *SHB* W12 .... 100 C5
Cawdor Crs *HNWL* W7 .... 116 A2
Cawnpore St *NRWD* SE19 .... 157 L1
Caxton Dr *UX/CGN* UB8 .... 94 C1
  UX/CGN UB8 .... 94 D1
Caxton Gv *BOW* E3 .... 105 G2
Caxton Rd *NWDGN* UB2 .... 114 D1
  SHB W12 .... 100 D7
  WDGN N22 .... 66 F3
  WIM/MER SW19 .... 155 J1
Caxton St *STJSPK* SW1H 16 F3
Caxton St North *CAN/RD* E16 .... 105 M5
Caxton Wy *WATW* WD18 .... 41 K2
Caygill Cl *HAYES* BR2 .... 159 M7
Cayton Rd *GFD/PVL* UB6 .... 97 L1
Cayton St *FSBYE* EC1V 7 G8
Cazenove Rd *STNW/STAM* N16 .. 85 M2
  WALTH E17 .... 69 G2
Cearn Wy *COUL/CHIP* CR5.. 183 M8
Cecil Av *BARK* IG11 .... 89 K7
  EMPK RM11 .... 74 C4
  EN EN1 .... 36 F7
  WBLY HA9 .... 80 F5
Cecil Cl *ASHF* TW15 .... 149 J2
  CHSGTN KT9 .... 167 K6
Cecil Ct *BAR* EN5 .... 33 K6
Cecile Pk *CEND/HSY/T* N8 .... 66 E7
Cecilia Cl *EFNCH* N2 .... 65 J4
Cecilia Rd *HACK* E8 .... 85 M5
Cecil Pk *PIN* HA5 .... 61 K1
Cecil Pl *MTCM* CR4 .... 155 M8
Cecil Rd *ACT* W3 .... 99 J4
  ASHF TW15 .... 149 J3
  CDALE/KGS NW9 .... 63 K4
  CHDH RM6 .... 72 C5
  CHES/WCR EN8 .... 26 D5
  CROY/NA CR0 .... 171 L1
  ENC/FH EN2 .... 36 D7
  HSLW TW3 .... 115 J8
  IL IG1 .... 89 H4
  KTN/HRWW/W HA3 .... 61 L4
  MUSWH N10 .... 66 B3
  PLSTW E13 .... 88 F8
  POTB/CUF EN6 .... 22 B5
  STHGT/OAK N14 .... 48 B3
  SUT SM1 .... 169 M8
  WALTH E17 .... 69 J1

  WAN E11 .... 87 L2
  WIM/MER SW19 .... 155 H3
  WLSDN NW10 .... 81 L8
Cecil St *WATN* WD24 .... 29 H3
Cecil Wy *HAYES* BR2 .... 175 G3
Cedar Av *BARK/LL* DA15.. 144 A4
  CHDH RM6 .... 72 B6
  CHES/WCR EN8 .... 26 D6
  EBAR EN4 .... 47 L2
  HYS/HAR UB3 .... 96 A5
  PEND EN3 .... 37 J5
  RSLP HA4 .... 78 C5
  UPMR RM14 .... 93 G4
  WDR/YW UB7 .... 94 F7
  WHTN TW2 .... 133 H3
Cedar Cl *BKHH* IG9 .... 52 D4
  CAR SM5 .... 170 F8
  DUL SE21 .... 139 J5
  EW KT17 .... 180 F7
  HAYES BR2 .... 175 L5
  KUTN/CMB KT2 .... 135 K8
  POTB/CUF EN6 .... 23 J3
  ROMW/RG RM7 .... 73 J5
  STA TW18 .... 148 C6
  SWLY BR8 .... 163 J5
Cedar Copse *BMLY* BR1 .... 160 F5
Cedar Ct *WIM/MER* SW19 .. 136 D7
Cedar Crs *HAYES* BR2 .... 175 L5
Cedarcroft Rd *CHSGTN* KT9.. 167 M6
Cedar Dr *EFNCH* N2 .... 65 L5
  PIN HA5.. 43 G8
Cedar Gdns *BELMT* SM2.. 170 C8
  UPMR RM14 .... 93 J3
Cedar Gv *BXLY* DA5.. 144 D3
  EA W5 .... 116 D1
  STHL UB1 .... 97 G4
  WEY KT13 .... 164 F6
Cedar Hts *RCHPK/HAM* TW10.. 134 E5
Cedar Hl *EPSOM* KT18 .... 180 C8
Cedar Lawn Av *BAR* EN5 .... 33 L8
Cedar Mt *ELTH/MOT* SE9 .... 142 D5
Cedarne Rd *FUL/PGN* SW6 .. 119 G5
Cedar Park Gdns *CHDH* RM6.. 72 D8
Cedar Park Rd *ENC/FH* EN2 .. 36 A5
Cedar Pl *CHARL* SE7 .... 124 C3
Cedar Ri *STHGT/OAK* N14 .. 48 A2
Cedar Rd *BELMT* SM2.. 170 C8
  BMLY BR1 .... 160 C5
  CRICK NW2 .... 82 C4
  CROY/NA CR0 .... 172 E4
  DART DA1 .... 146 D5
  E/WMO/HCT KT8 .... 151 L7
  EBED/NFELT TW14 .... 131 K5
  ENC/FH EN2 .... 36 B3
  ERITH DA8 .... 128 A6
  HCH RM12 .... 92 C3
  HEST TW5 .... 114 C7
  OXHEY WD19 .... 42 C1
  ROMW/RG RM7 .... 73 J5
  TEDD TW11 .... 152 A1
  TOTM N17 .... 67 M2
  WEY KT13 .... 164 E5
Cedars *BNSTD* SM7 .... 182 F7
Cedars Av *MTCM* CR4 .... 156 A7
  RKW/CH/CXG WD3.. 40 D2
  WALTH E17 .... 69 G6
Cedars Cl *BORE* WD6.. 32 A7
  HDN NW4 .... 64 C4
  LEW SE13 .... 123 K8
Cedars Ct *ED* N9 .... 49 L4
Cedars Dr *HGDN/ICK* UB10.. 95 G1
Cedars Ms *CLAP* SW4 .... 138 F1
Cedars Rd *BARN* SW13 .... 118 A7
  BECK BR3 .... 158 E5
  CLAP SW4 .... 120 B8
  CROY/NA CR0 .... 171 L5
  E/WMO/HCT KT8 .... 152 C4
  ED N9 .... 50 A4
  MRDN SM4 .... 155 J5
  SRTFD E15 .... 87 L6
  WCHMH N21 .... 49 H4
The Cedars *BKHH* IG9 .... 52 A3
  TEDD TW11 .... 151 M2
Cedar Ter *RCH/KEW* TW9 .. 134 E1
Cedar Tree Gv *WNWD* SE27 .. 157 H1
Cedarville Gdns *STRHM/NOR* SW16 .... 156 F2
Cedar Wy *CAMTN* NW1 .... 5 G2
  SUN TW16 .... 149 L3
Cedar Wood Dr *GSTN* WD25 .. 21 H8
Cedric Av *ROM* RM1 .... 73 L4
Cedric Rd *ELTH/MOT* SE9 .... 143 J7
Celadon Cl *PEND* EN3 .... 37 L6
Celandine Cl *POP/IOD* E14 .. 105 G4
Celandine Dr *HACK* E8 .... 7 M1
  THMD SE28 .... 108 B7
Celandine Rd *WOT/HER* KT12.. 165 L6
Celandine Wy *SRTFD* E15 .. 105 L2
Celbridge Ms *BAY/PAD* W2 .. 8 D4
Celestial Gdns *LEW* SE13 .... 141 K1
Celia Crs *ASHF* TW15 .... 148 D2
Celia Rd *ARCH* N19 .... 84 C3
Celtic Av *HAYES* BR2 .... 159 L6
Celtic St *POP/IOD* E14 .... 105 H4
Cemetery La *CHARL* SE7 .... 124 E4
  SHPTN TW17 .... 164 B2
Cemetery Rd *ABYW* SE2 .... 126 B4
  FSTGT E7 .... 87 M5
  TOTM N17 .... 67 L1
Cenacle Cl *HAMP* NW3 .... 83 G3
Centaur Ct *BTFD* TW8 .... 116 E3
Centaur St *STHWK* SE1 .... 17 M3
Centenary Wk *LOU* IG10 .... 52 B7
  WALTH E17 .... 69 L4
  WAN E11 .... 88 A1
  WFD IG8 .... 51 L8
Central Av *CHES/WCR* EN8 .. 26 E6
  E/WMO/HCT KT8 .... 150 F6
  ED N9 .... 49 L5
  EFNCH N2 .... 65 J2
  EN EN1 .... 37 H5
  HSLW TW3 .... 133 J1
  HYS/HAR UB3 .... 95 M7
  PIN HA5 .... 60 F7
  SOCK/AV RM15 .... 111 J8
  WAN E11 .... 87 K2

WELL DA16 .... 126 A7
WLGTN SM6 .... 171 J7
WTHK RM20 .... 129 M3
Central Dr HCH RM12 .... 92 E3
Central HI NRWD SE19 .... 157 J1
Central Pde CROY/NA CR0 .... 186 C3
  HRW HA1 .... 61 M6
Central Park Av DAGE RM10 .... 91 J4
Central Park Rd EHAM E6 .... 106 E1
Central Rd ALP/SUD HA0 .... 80 B5
  DART DA1 .... 146 E2
  MRDN SM4 .... 155 H8
  WPK KT4 .... 169 C4
Central Sq E/WMO/HCT KT8 .... 150 F7
  GLDGN NW11 .... 65 C7
Central St FSBYE EC1V 6 E8
Central Wy CAR SM5 .... 182 E1
  EBED/NFELT TW14 .... 132 B2
  NTHWD HA6 .... 59 L1
  THMD SE28 .... 108 B6
  WLSDN NW10 .... 99 J2
Centre Av ACT W3 .... 99 K7
  EFNCH N2 .... 65 K3
Centre Common Rd CHST BR7 .... 161 J3
Centre Rd DAGE RM10 .... 91 J8
  WAN E11 .... 88 A2
Centre St BETH E2 .... 104 B1
The Centre FELT TW13 .... 132 A6
Centre Wy ED N9 .... 50 C4
  WAB EN9 .... 27 J8
Centurian Wy ERITHM DA18 .... 126 F1
Centurion CI HOLWY N7 .... 5 L1
Centurion La BOW E3 .... 104 F1
Centurion Wy PUR RM19 .... 128 F2
Century Rd WALTH E17 .... 68 E4
Cephas Av WCHPL E1 .... 104 C3
Cephas St WCHPL E1 .... 104 C3
Ceres Rd WOOL/PLUM SE18 .... 125 A2
Cerise Rd PECK SE15 .... 122 A6
Cerne CI YEAD UB4 .... 96 C6
Cerne Rd MRDN SM4 .... 170 C1
Cervantes Ct BAY/PAD W2 .... 8 C7
  NTHWD HA6 .... 59 M1
Ceylon Rd WKENS W14 .... 118 D1
Chace Av POTB/CUF EN6 .... 23 K5
Chadacre Av CLAY IG5 .... 70 F4
Chadacre Rd EW KT17 .... 169 H7
Chadbourn St POP/IOD E14 .... 105 H4
Chadd Dr BMLY BR1 .... 160 E6
Chadville Gdns CHDH RM6 .... 72 D6
Chadway BCTR RM8 .... 90 C2
Chadwell Av CHDH RM6 .... 72 B8
  CHES/WCR EN8 .... 26 C1
Chadwell Heath La CHDH RM6 .... 72 B5
Chadwell St CLKNW EC1R 6 B7
Chadwick Av CHING E4 .... 51 K6
  WCHMH N21 .... 35 M7
  WIM/MER SW19 .... 155 G2
Chadwick CI TEDD TW11 .... 152 A2
Chadwick Dr HARH RM3 .... 74 D3
Chadwick Rd CMBW SE5 .... 121 M7
  IL IG1 .... 89 J3
  WAN E11 .... 69 L8
  WLSDN NW10 .... 81 M8
Chadwick St WEST SW1P 17 C4
Chadwick Wy THMD SE28 .... 108 D6
Chadwin Rd PLSTW E13 .... 106 B4
Chadworth Wy
  ESH/CLAY KT10 .... 166 D7
Chaffinch Av CROY/NA CR0 .... 173 K1
Chaffinch CI CROY/NA CR0 .... 173 K1
  ED N9 .... 50 D3
  SURB KT6 .... 168 A5
Chaffinch La WATW WD18 .... 41 M2
Chaffinch Rd BECK BR3 .... 158 E4
Chafford Wy CHDH RM6 .... 72 C5
Chagford St CAMTN NW1 .... 9 L1
Chailey Av EN EN1 .... 36 F5
Chailey CI HEST TW5 .... 114 D6
Chailey PI WOT/HER KT12 .... 165 L6
Chailey St CLPT E5 .... 86 C3
Chain Wk CHESW EN7 .... 25 J3
  ENC/FH EN2 .... 36 A1
Chalcombe Rd ABYW SE2 .... 126 B3
Chalcot CI BELMT SM2 .... 182 A1
Chalcot Crs CAMTN NW1 .... 3 M3
Chalcot Gdns HAMP NW3 .... 83 M6
Chalcot Ms STRHM/NOR SW16 .... 138 E7
Chalcot Rd CAMTN NW1 .... 4 A3
Chalcot Sq CAMTN NW1 .... 4 A2
Chalcott Gdns SURB KT6 .... 167 J3
Chalcroft Rd LEW SE13 .... 141 L2
Chaldon Rd FUL/PGN SW6 .... 118 E5
Chale Rd BRXS/STRHM SW2 .... 138 E5
Chalet CI RDART DA2 .... 145 K8
Chalfont Av WBLY HA9 .... 81 H6
Chalfont Gn ED N9 .... 49 L5
Chalfont Rd ED N9 .... 49 L5
  HYS/HAR UB3 .... 96 A8
  SNWD SE25 .... 157 M6
Chalfont Wy WEA W13 .... 116 B1
Chalford CI E/WMO/HCT KT8 .... 151 C7
Chalford Rd DUL SE21 .... 139 K8
Chalford Wk WFD IG8 .... 70 D2
Chalgrove Av MRDN SM4 .... 155 C8
Chalgrove Crs CLAY IG5 .... 70 E3
Chalgrove Gdns FNCH N3 .... 64 E4
Chalgrove Rd BELMT SM2 .... 182 D1
  HOM E9 .... 86 C6
  TOTM N17 .... 68 B2
Chalice CI WLGTN SM6 .... 171 K8
Chalice Wy GRH DA9 .... 147 K7
Chalkenden CI PGE/AN SE20 .... 158 B3
Chalk Farm Rd CAMTN NW1 .... 4 A1
Chalk HI OXHEY WD19 .... 42 E1
Chalk Hill Rd HMSMTH W6 .... 118 D2
Chalkhill Rd WBLY HA9 .... 81 J3
Chalklands WBLY HA9 .... 81 J3
Chalk La EBAR EN4 .... 34 F6
Chalkley CI MTCM CR4 .... 155 M5
Chalk Paddock EPSOM KT18 .... 180 C8
Chalk Pit Av STMC/STPC BR5 .... 162 C6
Chalk Pit Rd SUT SM1 .... 170 C7
Chalk Rd PLSTW E13 .... 106 B4
Chalkstone CI WELL DA16 .... 126 A6
Chalkwell Park Av EN EN1 .... 36 E7
Chalky La CHSGTN KT9 .... 179 K2

Challenge Rd ASHF TW15 .... 131 J7
Challice Wy BRXS/STRHM SW2 .... 138 F5
Challin St PGE/AN SE20 .... 158 C4
Challis Rd BTFD TW8 .... 116 D3
Challoner CI EFNCH N2 .... 65 K3
Challoner Crs WKENS W14 .... 118 F5
Challoners CI E/WMO/HCT KT8 .... 151 K7
Challoner St WKENS W14 .... 118 F5
Chalmers Wy
  EBED/NFELT TW14 .... 132 B2
Chalsey Rd BROCKY SE4 .... 140 F1
Chalton Dr EFNCH N2 .... 65 J7
Chalton St CAMTN NW1 .... 5 G5
Chamberlain CI
  WOOL/PLUM SE18 .... 125 K1
Chamberlain Crs WWKM BR4 .... 174 B3
Chamberlain La PIN HA5 .... 60 C1
Chamberlain Rd ED N9 .... 50 A5
  EFNCH N2 .... 65 J3
  WEA W13 .... 98 A1
Chamberlain St CAMTN NW1 .... 3 M2
  SURB KT6 .... 167 L2
Chamberlayne Rd WLSDN NW10 .... 82 C8
Chambers CI GRH DA9 .... 147 M2
Chambers Gdns EFNCH N2 .... 65 K2
Chambers La WLSDN NW10 .... 82 B7
Chambers Rd HOLWY N7 .... 84 E4
Chambers St BERM/RHTH SE16 .... 104 A8
Chamber St WCHPL E1 .... 13 M6
Chambon PI HMSMTH W6 .... 118 A2
Chambord St BETH E2 .... 7 M8
Champion Crs SYD SE26 .... 140 E8
Champion Gv CMBW SE5 .... 121 K8
Champion HI CMBW SE5 .... 121 K8
Champion Pk CMBW SE5 .... 121 K8
Champion Rd SYD SE26 .... 140 E8
  UPMR RM14 .... 93 H2
Champions CI BORE WD6 .... 32 B3
Champness CI WNWD SE27 .... 139 K8
Champneys CI BELMT SM2 .... 181 M1
Chancellor Gdns SAND/SEL CR2 .... 184 B2
Chancellor Gv DUL SE21 .... 139 J6
Chancellor PI CDALE/KGS NW9 .... 63 J3
Chancellor's Rd HMSMTH W6 .... 118 C3
Chancellors St HMSMTH W6 .... 118 C3
Chancelot Rd ABYW SE2 .... 126 B2
Chancel St STHWK SE1 .... 12 C8
Chancery La BECK BR3 .... 159 H5
  LINN WC2A 11 M3
Chance St BETH E2 .... 7 L9
Chanctonbury CI
  ELTH/MOT SE9 .... 143 H7
Chanctonbury Gdns
  BELMT SM2 .... 182 B1
Chanctonbury Wy
  NFNCH/WDSP N12 .... 47 G6
Chandler Av CAN/RD E16 .... 106 A4
Chandler CI HPTN TW12 .... 150 A4
Chandlers CI EBED/NFELT TW14 .... 131 M4
Chandlers Dr ERITH DA8 .... 127 K2
Chandlers Ms POP/IOD E14 .... 105 H8
Chandler St WAP E1W 104 B7
Chandlers Wy ROM RM1 .... 75 L6
Chandler Wy PECK SE15 .... 121 M5
Chandos Av EA W5 .... 116 C2
  STHGT/OAK N14 .... 48 C5
  TRDG/WHET N20 .... 47 K3
  WALTH E17 .... 69 G3
Chandos CI BKHH IG9 .... 52 B4
Chandos Crs EDGW HA8 .... 62 F1
Chandos PI CHCR WC2N 11 J7
Chandos Rd BORE WD6 .... 31 M5
  CRICK NW2 .... 82 C5
  EFNCH N2 .... 65 K3
  HRW HA1 .... 61 J6
  PIN HA5 .... 60 C8
  SRTFD E15 .... 87 K5
  TOTM N17 .... 67 L3
  WLSDN NW10 .... 99 J3
Chandos St CAVSQ/HST W1G 10 D3
Chandos Wy GLDGN NW11 .... 83 H1
Channel CI HEST TW5 .... 115 G6
Channelsea Rd SRTFD E15 .... 87 K8
Channing CI EMPK RM11 .... 74 F8
Chanton Dr BELMT SM2 .... 181 J3
Chantress CI DAGE RM10 .... 91 J8
Chantrey CI SCUP DA14 .... 162 E1
Chantrey Rd BRXN/ST SW9 .... 120 F8
Chantry CI ENC/FH EN2 .... 36 C3
  KGLGY WD4 .... 20 A2
  KTN/HRWW/W HA3 .... 62 A2
  MV/WKIL W9 .... 100 F3
  WDR/YW UB7 .... 94 D6
Chantry Hurst EPSOM KT18 .... 180 C8
Chantry La HAYES BR2 .... 160 D8
Chantry PI RYLN/HDSTN HA2 .... 61 H2
Chantry Rd CHSGTN KT9 .... 167 M7
  KTN/HRWW/W HA3 .... 61 H2
Chantry St IS N1 .... 6 D4
The Chantry UX/CGN UB8 .... 94 F2
Chantry Wy MTCM CR4 .... 155 K6
  RAIN RM13 .... 109 K1
Chant Sq SRTFD E15 .... 87 K7
Chant St SRTFD E15 .... 87 K7
Chapel CI DART DA1 .... 145 L2
  GSTN WD25 .... 20 F7
Chapel Ct EFNCH N2 .... 65 L4
Chapel Farm Rd ELTH/MOT SE9 .... 142 F7
Chapel Gn PUR/KEN CR8 .... 184 A6
Chapel HI DART DA1 .... 145 L1
  EFNCH N2 .... 65 L3
Chapel House St POP/IOD E14 .... 123 H3
Chapel La CHIG IG7 .... 53 M5
  PIN HA5 .... 60 D4
  UX/CGN UB8 .... 95 D4
Chapel Market IS N1 .... 6 A5
Chapel PI CAVSQ/HST W1G 10 C4
  IS N1 .... 6 B5
  TOTM N17 .... 67 M1
Chapel Rd BXLYHN DA7 .... 145 G1
  HSLW TW3 .... 115 H8
  IL IG1 .... 89 D3
  TWK TW1 .... 134 B4

WEA W13 .... 98 B7
WNWD SE27 .... 139 H8
Chapel Rw DEN/HRF UB9 .... 58 C2
Chapel Side BAY/PAD W2 .... 8 C6
Chapel St BAY/PAD W2 .... 9 J3
  ENC/FH EN2 .... 36 C6
  KTBR SW1X 16 B3
Chaplaincy Gdns EMPK RM11 .... 92 E1
Chaplemount Rd WFD IG8 .... 52 F8
Chaplin Crs SUN TW16 .... 149 L2
Chaplin Rd ALP/SUD HA0 .... 80 C6
  CRICK NW2 .... 82 A6
  EHAM E6 .... 89 G5
  SRTFD E15 .... 105 L1
  TOTM N17 .... 67 M4
Chapman CI WDR/YW UB7 .... 112 F1
Chapman Crs
  KTN/HRWW/W HA3 .... 62 E6
Chapman Rd BELV DA17 .... 127 G3
  CROY/NA CR0 .... 172 A3
  HOM E9 .... 87 J5
Chapman's La STMC/STPC BR5 .... 162 D5
  SWLY BR8 .... 163 G5
Chapman St WCHPL E1 .... 104 B6
Chapmans La WAT WD17 .... 29 J7
Chapone PI SOHO/SHAV W1D 11 G5
Chapter CI CHSWK W4 .... 117 K3
  UX/CGN UB10 .... 76 F7
Chapter Rd CRICK NW2 .... 82 B5
  WALW SE17 .... 18 D8
Chapter St WEST SW1P 17 G6
Chara PI CHSWK W4 .... 117 K4
Charcroft Gdns PEND EN3 .... 37 K7
Chardin Rd CHSWK W4 .... 117 L2
Chardmore Rd STNW/STAM N16 .... 86 A1
Chardwell CI EHAM E6 .... 106 E5
Charecroft Wy WKENS W14 .... 100 D8
Charford Rd CAN/RD E16 .... 106 A4
Chargate CI WOT/HER KT12 .... 164 F8
Chargeable La PLSTW E13 .... 106 A3
Chargeable St CAN/RD E16 .... 105 M3
Charing CI ORP BR6 .... 176 F6
Charing Cross CHCR WC2N 11 J8
Charing Cross Rd
  LSQ/SEVD WC2H 11 J7
  SOHO/SHAV W1D 11 H5
Charlbert St STJWD NW8 .... 3 J5
Charlbury Av STAN HA7 .... 44 D7
Charlbury CI HARH RM3 .... 56 C8
Charlbury Crs HARH RM3 .... 56 C8
Charlbury Gdns GDMY/SEVK IG3 .... 89 M2
Charlbury Gv EA W5 .... 98 C5
Charldane Rd ELTH/MOT SE9 .... 143 H7
Charlecote Gv SYD SE26 .... 140 F6
Charlecote Rd BCTR RM8 .... 90 B3
Charlemont Rd EHAM E6 .... 106 F2
Charles Barry CI CLAP SW4 .... 120 C8
Charles CI SCUP DA14 .... 144 B8
Charles Coveney Rd
  PECK SE15 .... 121 M6
Charles Crs HRW HA1 .... 61 K8
Charlesfield LEE/GVPK SE12 .... 142 C7
Charles Flemwell Ms
  CAN/RD E16 .... 106 A7
Charles Grinling Wk
  WOOL/PLUM SE18 .... 125 G2
Charles Ii St STJS SW1Y 11 G8
Charles La STJWD NW8 .... 3 J6
Charles PI CAMTN NW1 .... 4 F8
Charles Rd CHDH RM6 .... 72 D8
  DAGE RM10 .... 91 K6
  FSTGT E7 .... 88 C7
  STA TW18 .... 148 D2
  WEA W13 .... 98 A5
  WIM/MER SW19 .... 155 G4
Charles Sevright Dr MLHL NW7 .... 46 D7
Charles Sq IS N1 .... 7 H8
Charles St BARN SW13 .... 117 L8
  CAN/RD E16 .... 106 C7
  CROY/NA CR0 .... 172 C5
  EN EN1 .... 36 F8
  GRH DA9 .... 147 M2
  HSLW TW3 .... 114 F7
  MYFR/PICC W1J 10 C8
  UX/CGN UB8 .... 95 H3
Charleston CI FELT TW13 .... 132 A7
Charleston St WALW SE17 .... 18 F6
Charleville Circ SYD SE26 .... 158 B1
Charleville Rd WKENS W14 .... 118 E5
Charlieville Rd ERITH DA8 .... 127 J5
Charlmont Rd TOOT SW17 .... 155 L2
Charlock Wy WATW WD18 .... 41 M1
Charlotte CI BXLYHS DA6 .... 144 E2
Charlotte Despard Av
  BTSEA SW11 .... 120 A6
Charlotte Gdns CRW RM5 .... 55 H8
Charlotte Ms FITZ W1T 10 F2
  NKENS W10 .... 100 B5
Charlotte Park Av BMLY BR1 .... 160 E6
Charlotte Rd BARN SW13 .... 117 M6
  IS N1 .... 7 J8
  WLGTN SM6 .... 171 J5
Charlotte Rw CLAP SW4 .... 120 C8
Charlotte St FITZ W1T 10 F2
Charlotte Ter IS N1 .... 5 M4
Charlow CI FUL/PGN SW6 .... 119 J7
Charlton Av WOT/HER KT12 .... 165 H6
Charlton Church La CHARL SE7 .... 124 C5
Charlton CI HGDN/ICK UB10 .... 77 H2
Charlton Crs BARK IG11 .... 107 M1
Charlton Dene CHARL SE7 .... 124 C5
Charlton Kings WEY KT13 .... 164 E5
Charlton King's Rd KTTN NW5 .... 84 D1
Charlton La CHARL SE7 .... 124 D4
  SHPTN TW17 .... 149 L2
Charlton Park La CHARL SE7 .... 124 D6
Charlton Park Rd CHARL SE7 .... 124 D6
Charlton PI IS N1 .... 6 C5
Charlton Rd BKHTH/KID SE3 .... 124 A5
  CHARL SE7 .... 124 C4
  ED N9 .... 50 D3
  KTN/HRWW/W HA3 .... 62 D3
  SHPTN TW17 .... 149 J5
  WBLY HA9 .... 80 F1
Charlton Wy BKHTH/KID SE3 .... 123 L6

Charlwood CI
  KTN/HRWW/W HA3 .... 43 L8
Charlwood Dr LHD/OX KT22 .... 178 D8
Charlwood PI PIM SW1V 16 F6
Charlwood Rd PUT/ROE SW15 .... 136 D1
Charlwood St PIM SW1V 16 F7
Charlwood Ter
  PUT/ROE SW15 .... 136 D1
Charman Av STAN HA7 .... 62 D4
Charminster Av
  WIM/MER SW19 .... 155 G5
Charminster Rd
  LEE/GVPK SE12 .... 142 D8
  WPK KT4 .... 169 K3
Charmouth Rd WELL DA16 .... 126 C6
Charnock SWLY BR8 .... 163 L7
Charnock Rd CLPT E5 .... 86 B3
Charnwood Av
  WIM/MER SW19 .... 155 G5
Charnwood CI NWMAL KT3 .... 153 L7
Charnwood Dr SWFD E18 .... 70 B4
Charnwood Gdns POP/IOD E14 .... 123 G3
Charnwood PI TRDG/WHET N20 .... 47 J3
  HGDN/ICK UB10 .... 95 G1
  SNWD SE25 .... 157 K8
Charnwood St CLPT E5 .... 86 B2
Charrington Rd
  CROY/NA CR0 .... 172 C4
Charrington St CAMTN NW1 .... 5 G4
Charsley Rd CAT SE6 .... 141 H6
Chart CI CROY/NA CR0 .... 173 J1
  HAYES BR2 .... 159 L4
  MTCM CR4 .... 155 M7
Charter Av GNTH/NBYPK IG2 .... 89 K7
Charter Crs HSLWW TW4 .... 132 E1
Charter Dr BXLY DA5 .... 144 E4
Charterhouse Av ALP/SUD HA0 .... 80 C5
Charterhouse Bldgs
  FARR EC1M 12 E1
Charterhouse Ms FARR EC1M 12 D2
Charterhouse Sq FARR EC1M 12 D2
Charterhouse St FARR EC1M 12 D2
  HCIRC EC1N 12 B3
Charteris Rd FSBYPK N4 .... 84 F1
  KIL/WHAMP NW6 .... 82 F8
  WFD IG8 .... 52 B8
Charter PI UX/CGN UB8 .... 76 D7
Charter Rd KUT KT1 .... 153 H6
The Charter Rd WFD IG8 .... 51 L8
Charters CI NRWD SE19 .... 157 L1
Charter Sq KUT KT1 .... 153 H5
Charter Wy GLDGN NW11 .... 64 F5
  STHGT/OAK N14 .... 48 C1
Chartfield Av PUT/ROE SW15 .... 136 E2
Chartfield Sq PUT/ROE SW15 .... 136 D2
Chartham Gv WNWD SE27 .... 139 H7
Chartham Rd SNWD SE25 .... 158 B6
Chartley Av CRICK NW2 .... 81 L3
  STAN HA7 .... 43 M8
Charton CI BELV DA17 .... 126 F4
Chartridge CI BAR EN5 .... 33 G8
  BUSH WD23 .... 43 J1
Chart St IS N1 .... 7 H7
Chartwell CI CHST BR7 .... 143 K6
  GFD/PVL UB6 .... 79 H8
  WAB EN9 .... 27 L6
Chartwell Dr ORP BR6 .... 176 D7
Chartwell PI CHEAM SM3 .... 169 G3
  EPSOM KT18 .... 180 E7
  RYLN/HDSTN HA2 .... 79 K2
Chartwell Rd NTHWD HA6 .... 40 E2
Chartwell Wy PGE/AN SE20 .... 158 B4
Charville La HGDN/ICK UB10 .... 95 L1
Charville La West
  HGDN/ICK UB10 .... 95 H2
Chase Ct RYNPK SW20 .... 154 E5
Chase Court Gdns ENC/FH EN2 .... 36 C6
Chase Cross Rd CRW RM5 .... 73 J1
Chase End Rd/WEW KT19 .... 180 D5
Chasefield Rd TOOT SW17 .... 137 M8
Chase Gdns CHING E4 .... 51 C6
  WHTN TW2 .... 133 K3
Chase Gn ENC/FH EN2 .... 36 C6
Chase Green Av ENC/FH EN2 .... 36 B5
Chase HI ENC/FH EN2 .... 36 C6
Chase House Gdns EMPK RM11 .... 74 F6
Chase La BARK/HLT IG6 .... 71 K6
  CHIG IG7 .... 54 A5
Chaseley Ct CHSWK W4 .... 117 H3
Chaseley Dr SAND/SEL CR2 .... 184 D3
Chaseley St POP/IOD E14 .... 104 E5
Chasemore CI MTCM CR4 .... 170 F2
Chasemore Gdns
  CROY/NA CR0 .... 172 A7
Chase Ridings ENC/FH EN2 .... 36 A5
Chase Rd ACT W3 .... 99 K3
  HOR/WEW KT19 .... 180 D5
  STHGT/OAK N14 .... 34 C8
Chase Side ENC/FH EN2 .... 36 C5
  STHGT/OAK N14 .... 34 C8
Chase Side Av ENC/FH EN2 .... 36 C5
  RYNPK SW20 .... 154 E4
Chaseside CI ROM RM1 .... 55 L8
Chase Side Crs ENC/FH EN2 .... 36 C4
The Chase BMLY BR1 .... 160 B6
  BXLYHN DA7 .... 127 H8
  CHESW EN7 .... 25 H1
  CHIG IG7 .... 53 H6
  CLAP SW4 .... 120 C5
  COUL/CHIP CR5 .... 183 J7
  DAGE RM10 .... 91 M3
  EDGW HA8 .... 63 H2
  HGDN/ICK UB10 .... 77 C5
  LHD/OX KT22 .... 178 C8
  LOU IG10 .... 52 D4
  MNPK E12 .... 88 D4
  PIN HA5 .... 60 C1
  ROM RM1 .... 73 J4
  STAN HA7 .... 44 A8
  STRHM/NOR SW16 .... 156 F3
  SUN TW16 .... 150 B4
  UPMR RM14 .... 93 L3
  WATW WD18 .... 28 E7
  WLGTN SM6 .... 171 J5
Chaseville Park Rd WCHMH N21 .... 35 L8
Chase Wy STHGT/OAK N14 .... 48 B3

Chasewood Av ENC/FH EN2 .... 36 B5
Chastilian Rd DART DA1 .... 146 A4
Chatfield Rd BTSEA SW11 .... 119 J8
  CROY/NA CR0 .... 172 B3
Chatham Av HAYES BR2 .... 174 F2
Chatham CI CHEAM SM3 .... 169 M2
  GLDGN NW11 .... 65 G6
Chatham PI HOM E9 .... 86 C6
Chatham Rd BTSEA SW11 .... 137 M3
  KUTN/CMB KT2 .... 153 J8
  SWFD E18 .... 69 M3
  WALTH E17 .... 68 E4
Chatham St WALW SE17 .... 19 G5
Chatsfield EW KT17 .... 181 G3
Chatsfield PI EA W5 .... 98 E5
Chatsworth Av BFN/LL DA15 .... 144 A5
  BMLY BR1 .... 160 B1
  HDN NW4 .... 64 C3
  RYNPK SW20 .... 154 E4
  WBLY HA9 .... 80 F5
Chatsworth CI BORE WD6 .... 32 A6
  HDN NW4 .... 64 C3
  WWKM BR4 .... 174 F4
Chatsworth Crs HSLW TW3 .... 133 K1
Chatsworth Dr EN EN1 .... 50 A2
Chatsworth Gdns ACT W3 .... 99 H6
  NWMAL KT3 .... 153 M8
  RYLN/HDSTN HA2 .... 79 H1
Chatsworth PI LHD/OX KT22 .... 178 D5
  MTCM CR4 .... 155 M6
  TEDD TW11 .... 134 A2
Chatsworth Ri EA W5 .... 98 F3
Chatsworth Rd CHEAM SM3 .... 169 K7
  CHSWK W4 .... 117 J4
  CLPT E5 .... 86 C3
  CRICK NW2 .... 82 D6
  CROY/NA CR0 .... 172 D6
  DART DA1 .... 146 C1
  EA W5 .... 98 F3
  FSTGT E7 .... 87 M5
  YEAD UB4 .... 96 B3
Chatsworth Wy WNWD SE27 .... 139 J6
Chatterton Av HARH RM3 .... 56 C8
Chattern HI ASHF TW15 .... 131 H8
Chattern Rd ASHF TW15 .... 131 J8
Chatterton Rd FSBYPK N4 .... 85 H3
  HAYES BR2 .... 160 B8
Chatto Rd BTSEA SW11 .... 137 M2
Chaucer Av HSLWW TW4 .... 114 B7
  RCH/KEW TW9 .... 117 G7
  YEAD UB4 .... 96 A4
Chaucer CI BNSTD SM7 .... 181 L7
  FBAR/BDGN N11 .... 48 C7
Chaucer Dr STHWK SE1 .... 19 M6
Chaucer Gdns SUT SM1 .... 170 A6
Chaucer Gn CROY/NA CR0 .... 173 H2
Chaucer Pk DART DA1 .... 146 F4
Chaucer Rd ACT W3 .... 99 J7
  ASHF TW15 .... 130 E8
  BFN/LL DA15 .... 144 C5
  FSTGT E7 .... 88 A6
  HARH RM3 .... 74 B1
  HNHL SE24 .... 139 H2
  SUT SM1 .... 170 A6
  WALTH E17 .... 69 J2
  WAN E11 .... 71 J4
  WELL DA16 .... 125 M1
Chaucer Wy DART DA1 .... 147 L1
Chauncey CI ED N9 .... 50 A5
Chauncy Av POTB/CUF EN6 .... 23 J6
Chaundrye CI ELTH/MOT SE9 .... 142 F7
Chauntler Rd CAN/RD E16 .... 106 B6
Chave Rd DART DA1 .... 146 E7
Cheam Common Rd
  WPK KT4 .... 169 H4
Cheam Park Wy CHEAM SM3 .... 169 K8
Cheam Rd BELMT SM2 .... 181 K2
  EW KT17 .... 181 G3
  SUT SM1 .... 169 M8
Cheam St PECK SE15 .... 122 B8
Cheapside CITYW EC2V 12 F5
  PLMGR N13 .... 49 J6
Cheddar Waye YEAD UB4 .... 96 B5
Cheddington Rd UED N18 .... 49 L6
Cheeseman CI HPTN TW12 .... 150 E2
Chelford Rd BMLY BR1 .... 159 K1
Chelmer Crs BARK IG11 .... 108 B1
Chelmer Rd HOM E9 .... 86 D5
  UPMR RM14 .... 75 K7
Chelmsford Av CRW RM5 .... 73 K1
Chelmsford CI BELMT SM2 .... 182 A2
  EHAM E6 .... 106 F5
  HMSMTH W6 .... 118 D4
Chelmsford Dr UPMR RM14 .... 92 F3
Chelmsford Gdns IL IG1 .... 70 E8
Chelmsford Rd STHGT/OAK N14 .... 48 C2
  SWFD E18 .... 69 M2
  WALTH E17 .... 69 G7
  WAN E11 .... 87 K1
Chelmsford Sq WLSDN NW10 .... 82 C8
Chelsea Br CHEL SW3 .... 16 B9
Chelsea Bridge Rd BGVA SW1W 16 A7
Chelsea CI HPTN TW12 .... 151 J2
  WLSDN NW10 .... 81 K8
  WPK KT4 .... 169 G2
Chelsea Emb CHEL SW3 .... 16 A9
Chelsea Gdns CHEAM SM3 .... 169 J6
Chelsea Harbour Dr
  WBPTN SW10 .... 119 J6
Chelsea Manor Gdns CHEL SW3 .... 15 J9
Chelsea Manor St CHEL SW3 .... 15 K9
Chelsea Park Gdns CHEL SW3 .... 15 G9
Chelsea Sq CHEL SW3 .... 15 H8
Chelsfield Av ED N9 .... 50 D2
Chelsfield Gdns SYD SE26 .... 140 F6
Chelsfield La ORP BR6 .... 177 K5
  STMC/STPC BR5 ....
Chelsfield Rd STMC/STPC BR5 .... 177 J1
Chelsham Rd CLAP SW4 .... 120 D8
  SAND/SEL CR2 .... 184 D1
Chelston Rd RSLP HA4 .... 78 A2
Chelsworth Dr HARH RM3 .... 74 E2
  WOOL/PLUM SE18 .... 125 L5
Cheltenham Av TWK TW1 .... 134 A4
Cheltenham CI NTHLT UB5 .... 79 H6
  NWMAL KT3 .... 153 G3
Cheltenham Gdns EHAM E6 .... 106 E1

LOU IG10 52 E1
Cheltenham PI ACT W3 99 J8
    KTN/HRWW/W HA3 62 E5
Cheltenham Rd LEY E10 69 J7
    ORP BR6 177 G5
    PECK SE15 140 C1
Cheltenham Ter CHEL SW3 15 M7
Chelverton Rd PUT/ROE SW15 136 D1
Chelwood Cl CHING E4 51 H1
    EW KT17 180 F5
    NTHWD HA6 59 J1
Chelwood Gdns RCH/KEW TW9 117 G7
Chenappa Cl PLSTW E13 106 A2
Chenduit Wy STAN HA7 43 M7
Cheney Rd CAMTN NW1 5 J6
Cheneys Rd WALTH E17 87 L3
Cheney Row WALTH E17 68 F2
Cheney St PIN HA5 60 C5
Chenies Ms GWRST WC1E 11 C1
Chenies PI CAMTN NW1 5 H5
Chenies St GWRST WC1E 11 C2
The Chenies ORP BR6 176 E1
    RDART DA2 145 L8
Chenies VIs NTGHL W11 100 F6
Chepstow Av HCH RM12 92 E3
Chepstow Cl PUT/ROE SW15 136 E2
Chepstow Crs GDMY/SEVK IG3 71 L7
    NTGHL W11 8 A6
Chepstow Gdns STHL UB1 96 F5
Chepstow PI BAY/PAD W2 8 B5
Chepstow Ri CROY/NA CRO 172 E5
Chepstow Rd BAY/PAD W2 8 B4
    CROY/NA CRO 172 E5
    HNWL W7 116 A1
Chepstow VIs NTGHL W11 100 F6
Chepstow Wy PECK SE15 121 M6
Chequers BKHH IG9 52 E5
Chequers Cl CDALE/KGS NW9 63 L4
    STMC/STPC BR5 161 M7
Chequers La DAGW RM9 108 F3
    GSTN WD25 21 H3
Chequers Rd ABR/ST RM4 56 E4
Chequer St STLK EC1Y 12 F1
Chequers Wy PLMGR N13 49 J7
Cherbury Cl THMD SE28 108 D5
Cherbury St IS N1 7 H6
Cherimoya Gdns
    E/WMO/HCT KT8 151 H6
Cherington Rd HNWL W7 97 M7
Cheriton Cl CLAY IG5 71 G3
    HAYES BR2 160 A8
Cheriton Ct EA W5 98 C4
    EBAR EN4 34 F7
Cheriton Dr WOOL/PLUM SE18 125 K5
Cheriton Sq TOOT SW17 138 A6
Cherry Cl STHL UB1 96 D7
    SWLY BR8 163 K6
Cherry Blossom Cl PLMGR N13 49 H7
Cherry Cl CAR SM5 170 F4
    EA W5 116 D1
    EW KT17 181 K7
    MRDN SM4 154 E7
    RSLP HA4 77 M3
Cherrycot Ri ORP BR6 176 C6
Cherry Crs BTFD TW8 116 B5
Cherry Croft Gdns PIN HA5 60 F1
Cherrydale WATW WD18 28 F7
Cherrydown Av CHING E4 50 F5
Cherrydown Cl CHING E4 50 F5
Cherrydown Rd SCUP DA14 144 D6
Cherrydown Wk
    ROMW/RG RM7 73 H3
Cherry Gdns DAGW RM9 90 F5
    NTHLT UB5 79 H7
Cherry Garden St
    BERM/RHTH SE16 104 B8
Cherry Garth BTFD TW8 116 D3
Cherry Gv HYS/HAR UB3 96 B7
    UX/CGN UB8 95 J4
Cherry Hl BAR EN5 47 H1
    KTN/HRWW/W HA3 43 L8
Cherry Hill Gdns CROY/NA CRO 171 M6
Cherry Hollow ABLGY WD5 20 F4
Cherry Orch CHARL SE7 124 C4
Cherry Orchard Cl
    STMC/STPC BR5 162 C8
Cherry Orchard Gdns
    E/WMO/HCT KT8 150 F6
Cherry Orchard Rd
    CROY/NA CRO 172 D3
    E/WMO/HCT KT8 151 G6
    HAYES BR2 175 L4
Cherry Rd PEND EN3 37 J3
Cherry Tree Av STA TW18 148 B2
    WDR/YW UB7 94 F5
Cherry Tree Cl ALP/SUD HA0 80 B2
    RAIN RM13 110 A1
Cherry Tree Dr
    STRHM/NOR SW16 138 E7
Cherry Tree Gn SAND/SEL CR2 185 H7
Cherry Tree HI EFNCH N2 65 L6
Cherry Tree La RAIN RM13 109 L2
    RDART DA2 145 M7
Cherrytree La IVER SL0 76 A3
Cherry Tree Ri BKHH IG9 52 D6
Cherry Tree Rd EFNCH N2 65 M5
    SRTFD E15 87 L5
    WATN WD24 29 H1
Cherry Tree Wk BECK BR3 158 F4
    WWKM BR4 174 F6
Cherry Tree Wy STAN HA7 43 J3
Cherry Wk HAYES BR2 175 L3
    RAIN RM13 109 M1
Cherry Wy HOR/WEW KT19 168 D8
    SHPTN TW17 149 K2
Cherrywood Cl BOW E3 104 E2
    KUTN/CMB KT2 153 G3
Cherrywood Dr PUT/ROE SW15 136 D2
Cherrywood La MRDN SM4 154 E7
Chertsey Crs CROY/NA CRO 186 C5
Chertsey Dr CHEAM SM3 169 L4

Chertsey Rd ASHF TW15 149 K3
    FELT TW13 131 L8
    IL IG1 89 K4
    SHPTN TW17 164 A2
    SUN TW16 149 L2
    TWK TW1 134 A3
    WAN E11 87 K2
    WHTN TW2 133 J5
Chertsey St TOOT SW17 156 A1
Chervil Cl FELT TW13 132 A7
Chervil Ms THMD SE28 108 B7
Cherwell Cl RKW/CH/CXG WD3 28 A8
Cherwell Ct HOR/WEW KT19 168 C6
Cherwell Wy RSLP HA4 59 J7
Cheryls Cl FUL/PGN SW6 119 H6
Cheseman St SYD SE26 140 B7
Chesfield Rd KUTN/CMB KT2 152 E3
    KTBR SW1X 16 A4
    ROMW/RG RM7 73 K5
Chesham Crs PGE/AN SE20 158 C4
Chesham Ms KTBR SW1X 16 A3
Chesham PI KTBR SW1X 16 A3
Chesham Rd KUTN/CMB KT2 153 G4
    PGE/AN SE20 158 C5
Chesham St KTBR SW1X 16 A4
    WLSDN NW10 81 K3
Chesham Ter WEA W13 98 B3
Cheshire Wy WATW WD18 41 L1
Cheshire Cl EMPK RM11 75 G6
    MTCM CR4 156 E6
    WALTH E17 69 H2
Cheshire Gdns CHSGTN KT9 167 K8
Cheshire Rd WDGN N22 66 F1
Cheshire St BETH E2 104 A3
Chesholm Rd STNW/STAM N16 85 L3
Cheshunt Rd BELV DA17 127 G3
    FSTGT E7 88 B6
Chesilton Rd FUL/PGN SW6 118 F6
Chesil Wy YEAD UB4 95 M2
Chesley Gdns EHAM E6 106 D1
Chesney Crs CROY/NA CRO 186 C1
Chesney St BTSEA SW11 120 A6
Chesnut Av North WALTH E17 69 K5
Chesnut Gv TOTM N17 67 M4
    TOTM N17 68 A4
    TOTM N17 68 A4
Chesnut Rd TOTM N17 68 A4
Chessholme Rd ASHF TW15 149 J3
Chessington Av BXLYHN DA7 126 E5
    FNCH N3 64 E4
Chessington Cl HOR/WEW KT19 168 C8
Chessington Ct PIN HA5 60 F5
Chessington Hall Gdns
    CHSGTN KT9 179 K1
Chessington Hill Pk
    CHSGTN KT9 168 A8
Chessington Rd CHSGTN KT9 168 A8
    HOR/WEW KT19 168 C8
Chessington Wy WWKM BR4 174 B4
Chesson Rd WKENS W14 119 K5
Chess Vale Ri
    RKW/CH/CXG WD3 40 F1
Chesswood Wy PIN HA5 60 D3
Chester Av RCHPK/HAM TW10 134 F3
    UPMR RM14 93 L2
    WHTN TW2 132 F5
Chester Cl ASHF TW15 149 K1
    KTBR SW1X 16 B2
    SUT SM1 170 A4
Chester Cl North CAMTN NW1 4 D7
Chester Cl South CAMTN NW1 4 D8
Chester Crs HACK E8 85 M5
Chester Dr RYLN/HDSTN HA2 61 G7
Chesterfield Cl STMC/STPC BR5 162 D7
Chesterfield Dr DART DA1 146 B2
    ESH/CLAY KT10 167 G4
Chesterfield Gdns FSBYPK N4 67 H6
    MYFR/PICC W1J 10 C8
Chesterfield Gv EDUL SE22 139 M2
Chesterfield HI MYFR/PICC W1J 10 C7
Chesterfield Rd ASHF TW15 148 L1
    BAR EN5 33 K8
    CHSWK W4 117 J4
    FNCH N3 47 G8
    HOR/WEW KT19 180 D1
    LEY E10 69 J8
    PEND EN3 37 L2
Chesterfield St
    MYFR/PICC W1J 10 C8
Chesterfield Wy
    HYS/HAR UB3 96 A8
    NWCR SE14 122 C5
Chesterford Gdns HAMP NW3 83 H4
Chesterford Rd MNPK E12 88 F5
Chester Gdns ED N9 50 B1
    MRDN SM4 155 J8
Chester Ga CAMTN NW1 4 C8
Chester Ms KTBR SW1X 16 C3
Chester PI CAMTN NW1 4 C7
Chester Rd BFN/LL DA15 143 L2
    BORE WD6 32 C6
    CAMTN NW1 4 B8
    CAN/RD E16 105 L3
    CHIG IG7 53 G5
    ED N9 50 B3
    FSTGT E7 88 D7
    GDMY/SEVK IG3 89 M1
    HSLWW TW4 114 B8
    HTHAIR TW6 113 G8
    KTTN NW5 84 B2
    NTHWD HA6 59 M1
    TOTM N17 67 K4
    WALTH E17 68 D6
    WAN E11 70 B7
    WATW WD18 29 G8
    WIM/MER SW19 154 C2
Chester Rw BGVA SW1W 16 A6
Chester Sq BGVA SW1W 16 B5
Chester Square Ms
    BGVA SW1W 16 C4
The Chesters NWMAL KT3 153 L4
Chester St BETH E2 86 A8
    BETH E2 104 A3
    KTBR SW1X 16 B3
Chester Ter CAMTN NW1 4 C7
Chesterton Cl GFD/PVL UB6 97 H1

WAND/EARL SW18 137 G2
Chesterton Dr
    STWL/WRAY TW19 130 F5
Chesterton Rd NKENS W10 100 A4
    PLSTW E13 106 A2
Chesterton Ter KUT KT1 153 G5
    PLSTW E13 106 A2
Chester Wy LBTH SE11 18 B6
Chesthunte Rd TOTM N17 67 J2
Chestnut Aly FUL/PGN SW6 118 F4
Chestnut Av ALP/SUD HA0 80 B5
    BKHH IG9 52 D5
    BTFD TW8 116 D3
    CEND/HSY/T N8 66 E6
    E/WMO/HCT KT8 151 M6
    EDGW HA8 44 E8
    ESH/CLAY KT10 166 D2
    FSTGT E7 88 B4
    GRH DA9 147 M4
    HCH RM12 91 M2
    HOR/WEW KT19 168 E6
    HPTN TW12 151 G3
    MORT/ESHN SW14 117 K8
    NTHWD HA6 59 M3
    TEDD TW11 151 M3
    WDR/YW UB7 94 F6
    WWKM BR4 174 F7
Chestnut Av South WALTH E17 69 J5
Chestnut Cl ASHF TW15 131 H8
    BFN/LL DA15 144 A5
    BKHH IG9 52 D4
    CAR SM5 170 F3
    CAT SE6 141 J8
    HCH RM12 92 C4
    HYS/HAR UB3 95 L6
    NWCR SE14 122 F6
    ORP BR6 177 G7
    STHGT/OAK N14 35 J8
    STRHM/NOR SW16 139 G8
    SUN TW16 149 M2
    WDR/YW UB7 113 H5
Chestnut Dr BXLYHN DA7 126 D8
    KTN/HRWW/W HA3 61 M1
    PIN HA5 60 D7
    WAN E11 70 A7
Chestnut Gln HCH RM12 91 M2
Chestnut Gv ALP/SUD HA0 80 B5
    BAL SW12 138 A4
    BARK/HLT IG6 53 L8
    EA W5 116 D1
    EBAR EN4 34 F8
    ISLW TW7 134 A1
    MTCM CR4 156 D8
    NWMAL KT3 153 K6
    RDART DA2 163 K1
    SAND/SEL CR2 185 H1
    STA TW18 148 C2
Chestnut La TRDG/WHET N20 46 E3
    WEY KT13 164 B7
Chestnut Mnr WLGTN SM6 171 H6
Chestnut Manor Cl STA TW18 148 B1
Chestnut Ri BUSH WD23 43 H2
    WOOL/PLUM SE18 125 L4
Chestnut Rd ASHF TW15 131 G8
    DART DA1 146 D5
    KUTN/CMB KT2 152 E3
    PEND EN3 37 L1
    RYNPK SW20 154 D5
    WHTN TW2 133 J4
    WNWD SE27 139 H7
The Chestnuts WOT/HER KT12 165 C4
    SHPTN TW17 149 L8
    WATN WD24 29 G2
Chestnut Wy FELT TW13 132 B7
Cheston Av CROY/NA CRO 173 L3
Chestwood Gv HGDN/ICK UB10 76 F8
Cheswick Cl DART DA1 145 M1
Chesworth Cl ERITH DA8 127 L6
Chetwode Rd TOOT SW17 137 M7
Chetwynd Av EBAR EN4 47 M3
Chetwynd Dr HGDN/ICK UB10 94 F1
Chetwynd Rd KTTN NW5 84 B3
Chevalier Cl STAN HA7 44 D5
Cheval PI SKENS SW7 15 K3
Cheval St POP/IOD E14 123 L3
Cheveney Wk HAYES BR2 160 A6
Chevening Rd GNWCH SE10 123 M3
    KIL/WHAMP NW6 100 D1
    NRWD SE19 157 K3
The Chevenings SCUP DA14 144 B7
Cheverton Rd ARCH N19 84 D1
Chevet St HOM E9 86 E5
Chevington Wy HCH RM12 92 D4
Cheviot Cl BELMT SM2 182 D2
    BNSTD SM7 182 B8
    BUSH WD23 43 J1
    BXLYHN DA7 127 L7
    ENC/FH EN2 36 D5
    HYS/HAR UB3 113 K5
Cheviot Gdns GLDGN NW11 82 D2
    WNWD SE27 157 H1
Cheviot Rd EMPK RM11 74 A3
    WNWD SE27 157 H1
Cheviot Wy GNTH/NBYPK IG2 71 L6
Chevron Cl CAN/RD E16 106 A5
Chevy Rd STHL UB1 97 J8
Chewton Rd WALTH E17 68 E5
Cheyham Gdns BELMT SM2 181 K3
Cheyham Wy BELMT SM2 181 L3
Cheyne Av SWFD E18 69 M4
    WHTN TW2 132 F5
Cheyne Cl HAYES BR2 175 L5
Cheyne Ct BNSTD SM7 182 B8
Cheyne Gdns CHEL SW3 15 K9
Cheyne HI BRYLDS KT5 152 F7
Cheyne Ms CHEL SW3 15 K9
Cheyne Pth WEA W13 98 C5
Cheyne Rd ASHF TW15 149 K2
Cheyne Rw CHEL SW3 15 J9
Cheyne Wk CHEL SW3 15 J9
    CROY/NA CRO 173 G4
    HDN NW4 64 B7
    WBPTN SW10 119 K5
    WIM/MER SW19 154 C2
Cheyneys Av EDGW HA8 44 D8
Chichele Gdns CROY/NA CRO 172 E6
Chichele Rd CRICK NW2 82 D5
Chicheley Rd
    KTN/HRWW/W HA3 61 J1
Chicheley St STHWK SE1 17 M1

Chichester Av RSLP HA4 77 K2
Chichester Cl BKHTH/KID SE3 124 C6
    EHAM E6 106 E5
    HPTN TW12 150 F2
    SOCK/AV RM15 111 J7
Chichester Ct EW KT17 180 F2
    STAN HA7 62 E4
Chichester Dr PUR/KEN CR8 183 M5
Chichester Gdns IL IG1 70 E8
Chichester Rd BAY/PAD W2 8 D2
    CROY/NA CRO 172 E5
    ED N9 49 M3
    GRH DA9 147 M2
    KIL/WHAMP NW6 2 A6
    WAN E11 87 L3
Chichester St PIM SW1V 16 F8
Chichester Wy
    EBED/NFELT TW14 132 C4
    GSTN WD25 21 L6
    POP/IOD E14 123 K2
    WCHPL E1 104 A4
Chicksand St WCHPL E1 13 M3
Chiddingfold NFNCH/WDSP N12 47 G5
Chiddingstone Av BXLYHN DA7 126 F4
Chiddingstone Cl
    BELMT SM2 182 A3
Chiddingstone St
    FUL/PGN SW6 119 G7
Chieftan Dr PUR RM19 129 G2
Chieveley Rd BXLYHN DA7 145 H1
Chignell PI WEA W13 98 A7
Chigwell HI WAP E1W 104 B6
Chigwell Park Dr CHIG IG7 53 G6
Chigwell Ri CHIG IG7 53 G4
Chigwell Rd SWFD E18 70 B4
    WFD IG8 52 E8
Chilcott Rd WATN WD24 28 E1
Childebert Rd TOOT SW17 138 B6
Childeric Rd NWCR SE14 122 C5
Childerley St FUL/PGN SW6 118 E6
Childers St DEPT SE8 122 C4
The Childers WFD IG8 52 F7
Childs Av DEN/HRF UB9 58 C3
Childs Cl EMPK RM11 74 C7
Childs Ct HYS/HAR UB3 96 A6
Childs La NRWD SE19 157 L2
Child's PI ECT SW5 14 B6
Childs Wy GLDGN NW11 64 F6
Chilham Cl BXLY DA5 144 F4
    GFD/PVL UB6 98 A1
Chilham Rd ELTH/MOT SE9 142 E8
Chilham Wy HAYES BR2 175 G2
Chillerton Rd TOOT SW17 156 A1
Chillingworth Gdns
    TWK TW1 133 M6
Chillingworth Rd HOLWY N7 85 G5
Chilmark Gdns NWMAL KT3 168 F1
Chilmark Rd STRHM/NOR SW16 156 F5
Chiltern Av BUSH WD23 43 J1
    WHTN TW2 133 G5
Chiltern Cl BORE WD6 31 M5
    BUSH WD23 43 H1
    BXLYHN DA7 127 L6
    CROY/NA CRO 172 E5
    HGDN/ICK UB10 77 G2
    STA TW18 148 A1
    WPK KT4 169 A4
Chiltern Ct UX/CGN UB8 95 H3
Chiltern Dene ENC/FH EN2 35 M7
Chiltern Dr BRYLDS KT5 153 H8
Chiltern Gdns CRICK NW2 82 D3
    HAYES BR2 159 M7
    HCH RM12 92 C3
Chiltern Rd BELMT SM2 182 C3
    BOW E3 105 G3
    GNTH/NBYPK IG2 71 L5
    PIN HA5 60 C6
Chiltern St MHST W1U 10 A1
Chiltern View Rd UX/CGN UB8 94 C1
Chiltern Wy WFD IG8 52 A5
Chilthorne Cl CAT SE6 140 F4
Chilton Av EA W5 116 D2
Chilton Gv DEPT SE8 122 D2
Chilton Rd EDGW HA8 45 G8
    RCH/KEW TW9 117 G8
Chiltons Cl BNSTD SM7 182 B8
Chilton St BETH E2 7 M9
Chilver St GNWCH SE10 123 M3
Chilwell Gdns OXHEY WD19 42 C6
Chilworth Gdns SUT SM1 170 C5
Chilworth Ms BAY/PAD W2 9 G5
Chilworth St BAY/PAD W2 8 F5
Chimes Av PLMGR N13 49 G6
Chinbrook Crs
    LEE/GVPK SE12 142 B7
Chinbrook Rd LEE/GVPK SE12 142 C7
Chinchilla Dr HSLWW TW4 114 C7
The Chine ALP/SUD HA0 80 B5
    MUSWH N10 66 C5
    WCHMH N21 49 H1
Chingdale Rd CHING E4 51 L5
Chingford Av CHING E4 51 H5
Chingford La WFD IG8 51 L6
Chingford Mount Rd CHING E4 51 G7
Chingford Rd CHING E4 51 G8
    WALTH E17 69 H3
Chingley Cl BMLY BR1 159 L2
Ching Wy WALTH E17 50 F8
Chinnery Cl EN EN1 36 F4
Chinnor Crs GFD/PVL UB6 97 H1
Chipka St POP/IOD E14 105 J8
Chipley St NWCR SE14 122 E4
Chippendale St CLPT E5 86 D3
Chippendale Waye UX/CGN UB8 76 D7
Chippenham Av WBLY HA9 80 E3
Chippenham Gdns
    KIL/WHAMP NW6 2 A9
    MV/WKIL W9 2 A9
Chippenham Ms MV/WKIL W9 8 A1
Chippenham Rd HARH RM3 56 D7
    MV/WKIL W9 2 A9
Chipperfield Rd
    STMC/STPC BR5 162 A5
Chipping Cl BAR EN5 33 L6
Chipstead Av THHTH CR7 157 H7
Chipstead Cl BELMT SM2 182 B2
    NRWD SE19 157 M3
Chipstead Gdns CRICK NW2 82 B2

Chipstead Rd ERITH DA8 127 L5
Chipstead St FUL/PGN SW6 119 G6
Chirk Cl YEAD UB4 96 E3
Chisenhale Rd BOW E3 104 E1
Chisholm Rd CROY/NA CRO 172 E4
    RCHPK/HAM TW10 134 F3
Chislehurst Av FNCH N3 65 H1
Chislehurst High St CHST BR7 161 H2
Chislehurst Rd BMLY BR1 160 E5
    ORP BR6 177 G7
    RCHPK/HAM TW10 134 E2
    SCUP DA14 162 A1
    STMC/STPC BR5 161 L7
Chislet Cl BECK BR3 159 G3
Chisley Rd SEVS/STOTM N15 67 L7
Chiswell Ct WATN WD24 29 J5
Chiswell Sq BKHTH/KID SE3 124 B7
Chiswell St STLK EC1Y 13 G2
Chiswick Br MORT/ESHN SW14 117 J7
Chiswick Cl CROY/NA CRO 171 M5
Chiswick Common Rd
    CHSWK W4 117 K2
Chiswick High Rd CHSWK W4 117 J2
Chiswick La CHSWK W4 117 L3
Chiswick La South CHSWK W4 117 M4
Chiswick MI CHSWK W4 117 M4
Chiswick Quay CHSWK W4 117 J6
Chiswick Rd CHSWK W4 117 J2
    ED N9 50 A4
Chiswick Staithe CHSWK W4 117 L4
Chiswick Village CHSWK W4 117 H6
Chiswick Wharf CHSWK W4 117 M4
Chitterfield Ga WDR/YW UB7 113 G5
Chitty's La BCTR RM8 90 D2
Chitty St FITZ W1T 10 F2
Chivalry Rd BTSEA SW11 137 L2
Chivenor Gv KUTN/CMB KT2 152 D1
Chivers Rd CHING E4 51 H5
Choats Rd BARK IG11 108 C1
Chobham Gdns
    WIM/MER SW19 136 D6
Chobham Rd SRTFD E15 87 K5
Cholmeley Crs HGT N6 66 B8
Cholmeley Pk HGT N6 84 B1
Cholmley Rd THDIT KT7 167 H1
Cholmondeley Av
    WLSDN NW10 100 A1
Chopwell Cl SRTFD E15 87 K7
Chorleywood Cl
    RKW/CH/CXG WD3 40 D2
Chorleywood Crs
    STMC/STPC BR5 161 M4
Choumert Gv PECK SE15 122 A7
Choumert Rd PECK SE15 121 M8
Chrislaine Cl
    STWL/WRAY TW19 130 D3
Chrisp St POP/IOD E14 105 H4
Christabel Cl ISLW TW7 115 L8
Christchurch Av ALP/SUD HA0 80 L6
Christ Church Av ERITH DA8 127 K4
Christchurch Av
    KIL/WHAMP NW6 82 D8
    KTN/HRWW/W HA3 61 M5
    NFNCH/WDSP N12 47 J8
    RAIN RM13 109 M1
    TEDD TW11 133 M2
Christchurch Cl ENC/FH EN2 36 C5
    WIM/MER SW19 155 K3
Christchurch Crs RAD WD7 31 L3
Christchurch Gdns
    KTN/HRWW/W HA3 62 A5
Christchurch HI HAMP NW3 83 K3
Christ Church La BAR EN5 33 L5
Christ Church Mt
    HOR/WEW KT19 180 B5
Christchurch Pk BELMT SM2 182 C1
Christchurch Pas HAMP NW3 83 K3
Christchurch Rd BECK BR3 159 G5
    BFN/LL DA15 143 M8
    BRXS/STRHM SW2 138 F5
Christ Church Rd
    BRYLDS KT5 167 M1
    CEND/HSY/T N8 66 E7
Christ Church Rd DART DA1 146 C4
    EPSOM KT18 179 L5
Christchurch Rd IL IG1 89 H1
    MORT/ESHN SW14 135 H2
    PUR/KEN CR8 184 B4
    WIM/MER SW19 155 K4
Christchurch St CHEL SW3 15 L9
Christchurch Ter CHEL SW3 15 L9
Christchurch Wy GNWCH SE10 123 L3
Christian Flds
    STRHM/NOR SW16 157 G3
Christian St WCHPL E1 104 A5
Christie Dr SNWD SE25 158 A8
Christie Rd HOM E9 86 E6
Christina Sq FSBYPK N4 85 H1
Christina St SDTCH EC2A 7 J4
Christopher Av HNWL W7 116 A1
Christopher Cl BFN/LL DA15 143 M2
    HCH RM12 92 E3
Christopher Gdns DAGW RM9 90 D5
Christopher PI CAMTN NW1 5 H7
Christopher Rd NWDGN UB2 114 B2
Christopher St SDTCH EC2A 13 H1
Christy Rd BH/WHM TN16 187 J8
Chryssell Rd BRXN/ST SW9 121 G5
Chubworthy St NWCR SE14 122 E4
Chudleigh Crs GDMY/SEVK IG3 89 L4
Chudleigh Gdns SUT SM1 170 C5
Chudleigh Rd BROCKY SE4 140 C2
    HARH RM3 56 E6
    KIL/WHAMP NW6 82 C7
    WHTN TW2 133 L3
Chudleigh St WCHPL E1 104 D5
Chudleigh Wy RSLP HA4 78 A1
Chulsa Rd SYD SE26 158 B1
Chumleigh St CMBW SE5 19 J9
Chumleigh Wk BRYLDS KT5 152 F7
Church Ap DUL SE21 139 K7
Church Av BECK BR3 159 G4
    CAMTN NW1 84 B6
    CHING E4 51 K8
    EFNCH N2 65 K3
    MORT/ESHN SW14 135 K1
    NTHLT UB5 78 F7
    NWDGN UB2 114 E1

PIN HA5.........60 E7
RSLP HA4.........77 K1
SCUP DA14.........162 A1
Churchbury Cl *EN* EN1.........36 E5
Churchbury La *EN* EN1.........36 F4
Churchbury Rd
 ELTH/MOT SE9.........142 D4
 EN EN1.........36 E5
Church Cl *EDGW* HA8.........45 J7
 HSLW TW3.........114 F7
 HYS/HAR UB3.........95 K4
 NTHWD HA6.........59 M1
 POTB/CUF EN6.........24 E2
 RAD WD7.........31 C1
 STA TW18.........148 C6
 TRDG/WHET N20.........47 L5
 UX/CGN UB8.........94 B1
 WDR/YW UB7.........112 E1
Church Crs *FNCH* N3.........64 F2
 HOM E9.........86 D7
 MUSWH N10.........66 B5
 TRDG/WHET N20.........47 L5
Churchcroft Cl *BAL* SW12.........138 A4
Churchdown *BMLY* BR1.........141 L8
Church Dr *CDALE/KGS* NW9.........81 K1
 RYLN/HDSTN HA2.........61 G7
 WWKM BR4.........174 E5
Church Elm La *DAGE* RM10.........91 G6
Church End *HDN* NW4.........64 B4
 WALTH E17.........69 H5
Church Farm La *CHEAM* SM3.........169 L8
Church Farm Wy *GSTN* WD25.........30 B3
Church Fld *DART* DA1.........146 D6
Churchfield Av
 NFNCH/WDSP N12.........47 J8
Churchfield Cl *HYS/HAR* UB3.........95 M6
 RYLN/HDSTN HA2.........61 J5
Church Field Pth
 CHES/WCR EN8.........26 C2
Churchfield Rd *ACT* W3.........99 J7
 HNWL W7.........97 L8
 WEA W13.........98 B7
 WELL DA16.........126 A8
 WEY KT13.........164 A6
 WOT/HER KT12.........165 G3
Churchfields
 E/WMO/HCT KT8.........151 G7
 GNWCH SE10.........123 J4
 LOU IG10.........39 L7
 SWFD E18.........70 A2
Churchfields Av *FELT* TW13.........132 F7
 WEY KT13.........164 B6
Churchfields Rd *BECK* BR3.........158 D5
Churchfield Wy
 NFNCH/WDSP N12.........47 J8
Church Gdns *ALP/SUD* HA0.........80 A4
 EA W5.........98 D8
Churchgate *CHES/WCR* EN8.........26 B3
Church Ga *FUL/PGN* SW6.........118 E8
Churchgate Rd *CHES/WCR* EN8.........26 B2
Church Gn *HYS/HAR* UB3.........95 M5
 WOT/HER KT12.........165 J8
Church Gv *KUT* KT1.........152 C4
 LEW SE13.........141 H1
Church HI *CAR* SM5.........170 F7
 DART DA1.........145 L4
 DART DA1.........146 D7
 DEN/HRF UB9.........58 C5
 GRH DA9.........147 L2
 HRW HA1.........79 L1
 LOU IG10.........39 M6
 ORP BR6.........177 G2
 PUR/KEN CR8.........183 L3
 WALTH E17.........69 G5
 WCHMH N21.........48 F2
 WIM/MER SW19.........154 F1
 WOOL/PLUM SE18.........124 F1
Church Hill Rd *CHEAM* SM3.........169 K6
 EBAR EN4.........47 M2
 SURB KT6.........152 E8
 WALTH E17.........69 H5
Church Hill Wd
 STMC/STPC BR5.........161 M8
Church Hollow *PUR* RM19.........129 G3
Church Hyde
 WOOL/PLUM SE18.........125 L4
Churchill Av *HGDN/ICK* UB10.........95 H3
 KTN/HRWW/W HA3.........62 B7
Churchill Cl *DART* DA1.........147 H5
 EBED/NFELT TW14.........131 M5
Churchill Dr *WEY* KT13.........164 C5
Churchill Gdns *ACT* W3.........99 G5
Churchill Gardens Rd *PIM* SW1V...16 D8
Churchill Pl *POP/IOD* E14.........105 H7
Churchill Rd *CAN/RD* E16.........106 C5
 CRICK NW2.........82 B6
 EDGW HA8.........44 F8
 HOR/WEW KT19.........180 A4
 KTTN NW5.........4 B1
 SAND/SEL CR2.........184 C2
Churchill Ter *CHING* E4.........51 G6
Churchill Wk *HOM* E9.........86 C5
Churchill Wy *BMLY* BR1.........160 A5
 SUN TW16.........150 A1
Church La *CDALE/KGS* NW9.........63 K8
 CDALE/KGS NW9.........81 J1
 CEND/HSY/T N8.........66 F5
 CHES/WCR EN8.........26 C2
 CHSGTN KT9.........167 M8
 CHST BR7.........161 J4
 DAGE RM10.........91 H6
 ED N9.........50 A4
 EFNCH N2.........65 K4
 ENC/FH EN2.........36 D6
 GSTN WD25.........30 B3
 HAYES BR2.........175 L3
 KGLGY WD4.........20 A3
 KTN/HRWW/W HA3.........61 M2
 LOU IG10.........39 M6
 PIN HA5.........60 E4
 POTB/CUF EN6.........23 M3
 PUR RM19.........129 G3
 RAIN RM13.........110 D5
 RKW/CH/CXG WD3.........40 A3
 ROM RM1.........73 L5
 TEDD TW11.........151 M1
 THDIT KT7.........166 F1
 TOOT SW17.........138 B8

TOTM N17.........67 L2
TWK TW1.........134 A5
WALTH E17.........69 L5
WAN E11.........87 L1
WEA W13.........98 C8
WEY KT13.........164 A6
WIM/MER SW19.........155 G5
WLGTN SM6.........171 K5
Churchley Rd *SYD* SE26.........140 B8
Church Manor Wy *ABYW* SE2.........126 A2
Church Manorway *ERITH* DA8.........127 K1
Churchmead Cl *EBAR* EN4.........47 L1
Church Meadow *SURB* KT6.........167 J4
Churchmead Rd
 WLSDN NW10.........82 A6
Churchmore Rd
 STRHM/NOR SW16.........156 C4
Church Mt *EFNCH* N2.........65 K6
Church Pth *CHSWK* W4.........117 J1
 CROY/NA CR0.........2 C6
 GRH DA9.........147 M3
 MTCM CR4.........155 L6
 RYNPK SW20.........154 F5
 WAN E11.........70 A6
 WIM/MER SW19.........154 F5
Church Pl *EA* W5.........98 D8
 MTCM CR4.........155 L6
Church Ri *CHSGTN* KT9.........167 M8
 FSTH SE23.........140 D5
Church Rd *ABR/ST* RM4.........56 D3
 ACT W3.........99 J8
 ASHF TW15.........130 F8
 BARK IG11.........89 J6
 BARN SW13.........118 A7
 BXLYHN DA7.........126 F7
 CHEAM SM3.........169 L8
 CROY/NA CR0.........172 C6
 DEN/HRF UB9.........58 C4
 E/WMO/HCT KT8.........151 K7
 EFNCH N2.........65 K2
 ERITH DA8.........127 J3
 ESH/CLAY KT10.........166 F8
 EW KT17.........180 E5
 FELT TW13.........150 C1
 GNTH/NBYPK IG2.........71 L7
 GRH DA9.........147 L2
 HARH RM3.........75 G1
 HAYES BR2.........159 L6
 HAYES BR2.........187 K1
 HDN NW4.........64 B5
 HEST TW5.........114 B3
 HEST TW5.........115 G5
 HNWL W7.........97 M6
 HOR/WEW KT19.........180 D1
 HYS/HAR UB3.........95 M7
 ISLW TW7.........115 K6
 KUT KT1.........152 F5
 LEY E10.........87 G1
 LOU IG10.........39 G6
 MNPK E12.........88 F5
 MTCM CR4.........155 K5
 NRWD SE19.........157 L3
 NTHLT UB5.........78 F7
 NTHLT UB5.........96 D1
 NTHWD HA6.........59 M1
 NWDGN UB2.........114 F1
 ORP BR6.........176 C7
 ORP BR6.........177 K8
 PEND EN3.........50 C1
 POTB/CUF EN6.........23 H3
 PUR/KEN CR8.........183 L3
 PUR/KEN CR8.........184 D8
 RCHPK/HAM TW10.........134 E8
 RCHPK/HAM TW10.........134 E2
 SCUP DA14.........144 A8
 SHPTN TW17.........164 B2
 STAN HA7.........44 B7
 SURB KT6.........167 J3
 TEDD TW11.........133 L8
 TOTM N17.........67 M1
 UX/CGN UB8.........94 D3
 WALTH E17.........68 E3
 WAT WD17.........29 G4
 WDR/YW UB7.........94 D8
 WELL DA16.........126 A7
 WIM/MER SW19.........154 E1
 WLGTN SM6.........171 J5
 WLSDN NW10.........81 L4
 WPK KT4.........168 E3
Church Rd South *EFNCH* N2.........65 K3
Church Rw *CHST* BR7.........161 J4
 HAMP NW3.........83 J4
 WAND/EARL SW18.........137 G2
Church Rw Ms *CHST* BR7.........161 J3
Church Side *EPSOM* KT18.........180 B6
Church Sq *SHPTN* TW17.........164 B2
Church St *BAY/PAD* W2.........9 H2
 CHSWK W4.........117 L4
 CROY/NA CR0.........172 B5
 DAGE RM10.........91 H7
 ED N9.........49 L3
 ENC/FH EN2.........36 C6
 EPSOM KT18.........180 E6
 ESH/CLAY KT10.........166 B6
 EW KT17.........181 G2
 HPTN TW12.........133 J2
 HSLW TW3.........116 B8
 ISLW TW7.........116 B3
 KUT KT1.........152 D5
 RKW/CH/CXG WD3.........40 E3
 SRTFD E15.........87 L3
 SUN TW16.........150 A6
 TWK TW1.........134 C5
 WAB EN9.........27 J6
 WATW WD18.........29 J7
 WEY KT13.........164 A6
 WOT/HER KT12.........165 K6
Church Street Est *STJWD* NW8.........9 H1
Church St North *SRTFD* E15.........87 L8
Church Ter *HDN* NW4.........64 B4
 LEW SE13.........123 L8
 RCHPK/HAM TW10.........134 D2
Church V *EFNCH* N2.........65 M4
 FSTH SE23.........140 C6
Church Vw *SOCK/AV* RM15.........111 J8
 UPMR RM14.........93 K2
Churchview Rd *WHTN* TW2.........133 K5
Church Wk *BTFD* TW8.........116 C4

BUSH WD23.........43 G1
CDALE/KGS NW9.........81 K2
CRICK NW2.........82 F3
DART DA1.........146 D7
HYS/HAR UB3.........95 L5
RYNPK SW20.........154 C6
STNW/STAM N16.........85 K4
STRHM/NOR SW16.........156 C5
WEY KT13.........164 A5
WOT/HER KT12.........165 G3
Churchway *CAMTN* NW1.........5 H8
Church Wy *SAND/SEL* CR2.........184 F5
 TRDG/WHET N20.........47 L5
Churchyard Rw *LBTH* SE11.........18 D5
Churston Av *PLSTW* E13.........88 B8
Churston Dr *MRDN* SM4.........154 D8
Churston Gdns *FBAR/BDGN* N11..48 C8
Churton Pl *PIM* SW1V.........16 F6
Churton St *PIM* SW1V.........16 F6
Chuters Gv *EW* KT17.........180 F5
Chyngton Cl *BFN/LL* DA15.........143 M7
Cibber Rd *FSTH* SE23.........140 D6
Cicada Rd *WAND/EARL* SW18.........137 J3
Cicely Rd *PECK* SE15.........122 A6
Cinderford Wy *BMLY* BR1.........141 L8
Cinnamon Cl *CROY/NA* CR0.........171 L2
Cinnamon St *WAP* E1W.........104 E7
Cintra Pk *NRWD* SE19.........157 M3
Circle Gdns *WIM/MER* SW19.........155 G6
Circle Rd *EFNCH* N2.........65 K3
The Circle *CRICK* NW2.........81 L3
 MLHL NW7.........45 K8
The Circuits *PIN* HA5.........60 C5
Circular Rd *TOTM* N17.........67 M4
Circular Wy *WOOL/PLUM* SE18...124 F4
Circus Ms *MBLAR* W1H.........9 L2
Circus Pl *LVPST* EC2M.........13 H3
Circus Rd *STJWD* NW8.........3 G7
Circus St *GNWCH* SE10.........123 J5
Cirencester St *BAY/PAD* W2.........8 C2
Cissbury Ring North
 NFNCH/WDSP N12.........46 F7
Cissbury Ring South
 NFNCH/WDSP N12.........46 F7
Cissbury Rd *SEVS/STOTM* N15....67 K6
Citizen Rd *HOLWY* N7.........85 G3
City Gdn *EDGW* HA8.........45 G8
City Garden Rw *IS* N1.........6 C6
City Rd *FSBYE* EC1V.........6 C6
 STLK EC1Y.........13 H1
Civic Wy *BARK/HLT* IG6.........71 J5
 RSLP HA4.........78 D5
Clabon Ms *KTBR* SW1X.........15 L4
Clack St *BERM/RHTH* SE16.........104 C8
Clacton Rd *TOTM* N17.........67 M4
 WALTH E17.........68 E7
Claigmar Gdns *FNCH* N3.........65 H2
Claire Ct *NFNCH/WDSP* N12.........47 J5
Claire Gdns *STAN* HA7.........44 C7
Claire Pl *POP/IOD* E14.........123 G1
Clairvale *EMPK* RM11.........74 E8
Clairvale Rd *HEST* TW5.........114 D6
Clairview Rd *TOOT* SW17.........156 B1
Clairville Gdns *HNWL* W7.........97 L7
Clammas Wy *UX/CGN* UB8.........94 C4
Clamp HI *KTN/HRWW/W* HA3.........43 K6
Clancarty Rd *FUL/PGN* SW6.........119 G7
Clandon Cl *ACT* W3.........99 H8
 EW KT17.........168 F8
Clandon Gdns *FNCH* N3.........65 G4
Clandon Rd *GDMY/SEVK* IG3.........89 L2
Clandon St *DEPT* SE8.........123 G7
Clanricarde Gdns *BAY/PAD* W2....8 B7
Clapgate Rd *BUSH* WD23.........43 H1
Clapham Common North Side
 CLAP SW4.........138 B1
Clapham Common South Side
 CLAP SW4.........138 B3
Clapham Common West Side
 BTSEA SW11.........138 A2
Clapham Crs *CLAP* SW4.........138 D1
Clapham High St *CLAP* SW4.........138 D1
Clapham Manor St *CLAP* SW4.........120 C8
Clapham Park Rd *CLAP* SW4.........138 C1
Clapham Rd *BRXN/ST* SW9.........120 E7
Clapham Rd South *IS* N1.........85 K6
Claps Gate La *EHAM* E6.........107 H3
Clapton Common *CLPT* E5.........68 A8
Clapton Sq *CLPT* E5.........86 C5
Clapton Ter *STNW/STAM* N16.....68 A8
Clapton Wy *CLPT* E5.........86 A4
Clara Pl *WOOL/PLUM* SE18.........125 G2
Clare Cl *BORE* WD6.........44 F1
Clare Cnr *ELTH/MOT* SE9.........143 H4
Clare Ct *NTHWD* HA6.........41 L7
Clare Gdns *BARK* IG11.........89 M6
 FSTGT E7.........88 A4
Clare HI *ESH/CLAY* KT10.........166 B7
Clare HI (No 1)
 ESH/CLAY KT10.........166 B7
Clare HI (No 2) *ESH/CLAY* KT10..166 B7
Clare La *IS* N1.........6 F2
Clare Lawn Av
 MORT/ESHN SW14.........135 K2
Claremont *CHESW* EN7.........25 M2
 IS N1.........6 A6
Claremont Av *ESH/CLAY* KT10....166 A5
 KTN/HRWW/W HA3.........62 B3
 NWMAL KT3.........154 B8
 SUN TW16.........150 B4
 WOT/HER KT12.........165 K6
Claremont Cl
 BRXS/STRHM SW2.........138 F5
 CAN/RD E16.........107 G2
 ORP BR6.........176 A6
 SAND/SEL CR2.........185 H7
 WLGTN SM6.........171 G5
Claremont End
 ESH/CLAY KT10.........166 B8
Claremont Gdns
 GDMY/SEVK IG3.........89 L2

SURB KT6.........152 E7
UPMR RM14.........93 K1
Claremont Gv *CHSWK* W4.........117 L5
 WFD IG8.........52 C8
Claremont La *ESH/CLAY* KT10....166 B8
Claremont Pk *FNCH* N3.........64 E2
Claremont Park Rd
 ESH/CLAY KT10.........166 B8
Claremont Rd *BMLY* BR1.........160 E7
 CRICK NW2.........64 C8
 CROY/NA CR0.........173 G3
 EBAR EN4.........34 C3
 EMPK RM11.........74 A7
 ESH/CLAY KT10.........178 E1
 FSTGT E7.........88 B5
 HGT N6.........66 B8
 KTN/HRWW/W HA3.........61 L3
 MV/WKIL W9.........100 E1
 SURB KT6.........152 E8
 SWLY BR8.........163 L3
 TEDD TW11.........151 M1
 TWK TW1.........134 B4
 WALTH E17.........68 E3
 WAN E11.........87 K3
 WEA W13.........98 A4
Claremont Sq *IS* N1.........6 A6
Claremont St *GNWCH* SE10.........123 H4
 UED N18.........50 A8
Claremont Wy *CRICK* NW2.........82 C1
Clarence Av *CLAP* SW4.........138 D4
 HAYES BR2.........160 E7
 IL IG1.........70 F7
 NWMAL KT3.........153 J5
 UPMR RM14.........93 G2
Clarence Cl *BUSH* WD23.........43 M2
 WOT/HER KT12.........165 H6
Clarence Crs *CLAP* SW4.........138 D3
 SCUP DA14.........144 B7
Clarence La *PUT/ROE* SW15.........135 M3
Clarence Ms *CLPT* E5.........86 B5
Clarence Pl *CLPT* E5.........86 B5
Clarence Rd *BMLY* BR1.........160 E6
 BXLYHS DA6.........144 E1
 CAN/RD E16.........105 L3
 CHSWK W4.........117 G3
 CLPT E5.........86 B4
 CROY/NA CR0.........172 D2
 ELTH/MOT SE9.........142 E6
 FSTGT E7.........88 C4
 KIL/WHAMP NW6.........82 F7
 PEND EN3.........37 J8
 RCH/KEW TW9.........116 F6
 SCUP DA14.........144 B7
 SEVS/STOTM N15.........67 J6
 SUT SM1.........170 B6
 TEDD TW11.........151 M2
 WALTH E17.........68 D3
 WDGN N22.........66 E1
 WIM/MER SW19.........155 L2
 WLGTN SM6.........171 H7
 WOT/HER KT12.........165 H6
Clarence St *KUT* KT1.........152 D5
 NWDGN UB2.........114 D1
 RCH/KEW TW9.........134 E1
Clarence Ter *CAMTN* NW1.........3 M8
 HSLW TW3.........133 H1
Clarence Wk *CLAP* SW4.........120 F7
Clarence Wy *CAMTN* NW1.........4 C1
Clarendon Cl *BAY/PAD* W2.........9 J6
 STMC/STPC BR5.........162 A6
Clarendon Crs *WHTN* TW2.........133 K7
Clarendon Cross *NTGHL* W11.....100 C6
Clarendon Dr *PUT/ROE* SW15....136 C1
Clarendon Gdns *HDN* NW4.........64 A4
 IL IG1.........88 F1
 MV/WKIL W9.........8 F1
 RDART DA2.........147 K5
 WBLY HA9.........80 E1
Clarendon Gn *STMC/STPC* BR5...162 A6
Clarendon Gv *MTCM* CR4.........155 M6
 STMC/STPC BR5.........162 A7
Clarendon Ms *BAY/PAD* W2.........9 J6
 BORE WD6.........32 A6
Clarendon Pth *STMC/STPC* BR5..162 A7
Clarendon Pl *BAY/PAD* W2.........9 J6
 RDART DA2.........163 K1
Clarendon Ri *LEW* SE13.........123 J8
Clarendon Rd *ASHF* TW15.........130 F8
 BORE WD6.........32 A6
 CEND/HSY/T N8.........66 F4
 CHES/WCR EN8.........26 D2
 CROY/NA CR0.........172 B4
 EA W5.........98 A4
 HRW HA1.........61 L7
 HYS/HAR UB3.........95 M8
 LEY E10.........69 H7
 NTGHL W11.........100 C6
 SEVS/STOTM N15.........67 H5
 SWFD E18.........70 A4
 UED N18.........50 A8
 WAN E11.........87 K1
 WAT WD17.........29 H6
 WDGN N22.........66 F3
 WIM/MER SW19.........155 L3
 WLGTN SM6.........171 J7
Clarendon St *PIM* SW1V.........16 D7
Clarendon Ter *MV/WKIL* W9.........2 F9
Clarendon Wy *CHST* BR7.........161 M6
 WCHMH N21.........49 J3
Clarens St *CAT* SE6.........140 F6
Clare Rd *HSLWW* TW4.........114 F8
 NTHLT UB5.........79 K6
 NWCR SE14.........122 F7
 STWL/WRAY TW19.........130 D5
 WAN E11.........69 K7
 WLSDN NW10.........82 A7
Clareville Gv *SKENS* SW7.........14 F6
Clareville Rd *STMC/STPC* BR5....176 C4
 STMC/STPC BR5.........28 C8
Clareville St *SKENS* SW7.........14 F6
Clare Wy *BXLYHN* DA7.........126 F6
Clarges Ms *MYFR/PICC* W1J.....10 D8
Clarges St *MYFR/PICC* W1J.....10 D8
Claribel Rd *BRXN/ST* SW9.........121 H7
Clarice Wy *WLGTN* SM6.........183 L2
Claridge Rd *BCTR* RM8.........90 D1
Clarissa Rd *CHDH* RM6.........72 D7

Clarissa St *HACK* E8.........7 L3
Clark Cl *ERITH* DA8.........128 A6
Clarkes Av *WPK* KT4.........169 K3
Clarkes Dr *WDR/YW* UB7.........94 E5
Clarkes Ms *CAVSO/HST* W1G.....10 B2
Clarke Wy *GSTN* WD25.........21 G8
Clarkfield *RKW/CH/CXG* WD3.....40 A3
Clarkson Rd *CAN/RD* E16.........105 M5
Clarkson St *BETH* E2.........104 B2
Clark's Rd *IL* IG1.........89 K2
Clark St *WCHPL* E1.........104 C5
Classon Cl *WDR/YW* UB7.........94 E8
Claston Cl *DART* DA1.........145 L1
Claude Rd *LEY* E10.........87 M1
 PECK SE15.........122 B7
 PLSTW E13.........88 B8
Claude St *POP/IOD* E14.........123 G2
Claudia Pl *WIM/MER* SW19.........136 E5
Claughton Rd *PLSTW* E13.........106 C1
Clauson Av *NTHLT* UB5.........79 H5
Clavell St *GNWCH* SE10.........123 J4
Claverdale Rd
 BRXS/STRHM SW2.........138 F4
Claverhambury Rd *WAB* EN9....27 M2
Clavering Av *BARN* SW13.........118 E1
Clavering Cl *TWK* TW1.........134 A8
Clavering Rd *MNPK* E12.........88 D1
Claverley Gv *FNCH* N3.........65 G2
Claverley Vls *FNCH* N3.........65 H1
Claverton St *PIM* SW1V.........16 F8
Clave St *WAP* E1W.........104 C7
Claxton Gv *HMSMTH* W6.........118 G5
Clay Av *MTCM* CR4.........156 B5
Claybank Gv *LEW* SE13.........123 H8
Claybridge Rd *LEE/GVPK* SE12...142 C8
Claybrook Cl *EFNCH* N2.........65 K4
Claybrook Rd *HMSMTH* W6.........118 D4
Claybury *BUSH* WD23.........43 H2
Claybury Rd *WFD* IG8.........70 E1
Claydon Dr *CROY/NA* CR0.........171 L6
Claydown Ms
 WOOL/PLUM SE18.........125 G3
Clayfarm Rd *ELTH/MOT* SE9.....143 J6
Claygate Cl *HCH* RM12.........92 A4
Claygate Crs *CROY/NA* CR0.....174 C8
Claygate La *ESH/CLAY* KT10.....167 G5
 THDIT KT7.........167 G3
Claygate Lodge Cl
 ESH/CLAY KT10.........178 E1
Claygate Rd *WEA* W13.........116 B1
Clayhall Av *CLAY* IG5.........71 G3
Clay HI *ENC/FH* EN2.........36 C2
Clayhill Crs *LEE/GVPK* SE12.....142 C8
Claylands Pl *VX/NE* SW8.........121 G5
Claylands Rd *VX/NE* SW8.........120 F4
Clay La *BUSH* WD23.........43 L2
Claymore Cl *MRDN* SM4.........170 A2
Claypit HI *WAB* EN9.........39 J1
Claypole Dr *HEST* TW5.........114 E6
Claypole Rd *SRTFD* E15.........105 J2
Claypoods Av *BTFD* TW8.........116 E2
Claypoods Gdns *BTFD* TW8.........116 D2
 EA W5.........116 D2
Claypoods La *BTFD* TW8.........116 E3
Clayside *CHIG* IG7.........53 K8
Clays La *SRTFD* E15.........87 H5
Clays Lane Cl *SRTFD* E15.........87 H5
Clay St *MHST* W1U.........9 M3
Clayton Av *ALP/SUD* HA0.........80 E7
 UPMR RM14.........93 H5
Clayton Cl *EHAM* E6.........106 F5
Clayton Crs *BTFD* TW8.........116 D3
Clayton Croft Rd *RDART* DA2....146 A6
Clayton Fld *CDALE/KGS* NW9.....45 G8
Clayton Ms *GNWCH* SE10.........123 K6
Clayton Rd *CHSGTN* KT9.........167 J6
 EW KT17.........180 E6
 HYS/HAR UB3.........95 L8
 ISLW TW7.........115 L8
 PECK SE15.........122 A6
 ROMW/RG RM7.........91 J1
Clayton St *LBTH* SE11.........18 A9
Clayton Wy *UX/CGN* UB8.........94 B3
Clay Wood Cl *ORP* BR6.........176 E2
Clayworth Cl *BFN/LL* DA15.....144 B3
Cleall Av *WAB* EN9.........27 J7
Cleanthus Cl *WOOL/PLUM* SE18..125 H6
Cleanthus Rd
 WOOL/PLUM SE18.........125 H6
Clearbrook Wy *WCHPL* E1.........104 C5
Clearwater Ter *WKENS* W14.....100 D8
Clearwell Dr *MV/WKIL* W9.........8 C1
Cleave Av *HYS/HAR* UB3.........113 L2
 ORP BR6.........177 K8
Cleaveland Rd *SURB* KT6.........152 D8
Cleaverholme Cl *SNWD* SE25.....173 H1
Cleaver Sq *LBTH* SE11.........18 B7
Cleaver St *LBTH* SE11.........18 B7
Cleeve HI *FSTH* SE23.........140 B5
Cleeve Park Gdns *SCUP* DA14....144 B6
Clegg St *PLSTW* E13.........106 A1
 WAP E1W.........104 E7
Clematis Cl *HARH* RM3.........74 C1
Clematis Gdns *WFD* IG8.........52 A7
Clematis St *SHB* W12.........99 H6
Clemence Rd *DAGE* RM10.........91 J8
Clemence St *POP/IOD* E14.........105 H8
Clement Av *CLAP* SW4.........138 D1
Clement Cl *CHSWK* W4.........117 K2
 KIL/WHAMP NW6.........82 C7
Clement Gdns *HYS/HAR* UB3....113 L2
Clementhorpe Rd *DAGW* RM9....90 C6
Clementina Rd *LEY* E10.........86 F1
Clementine Cl *WEA* W13.........98 B8
Clement Rd *BECK* BR3.........158 D5
 WIM/MER SW19.........154 C1
Clements Av *CAN/RD* E16.........106 A6
Clements Inn *LINN* WC2A.........11 M5
Clements La *IL* IG1.........89 H3
 MANHO EC4N.........13 H6
Clements Pl *BTFD* TW8.........116 D3

WOT/HER KT12 .... **165** H4 🔟
Clement Wy *HCH* RM12 ...... **92** F3
Clendon Wy
  WOOL/PLUM SE18 ...... **125** K2 🔟
Clennam St *STHWK* SE1 ...... **18** F1 🔟
Clenston Ms *MBLAR* W1H ...... **9** L4 🔟
Clephane Rd *IS* N1 ...... **85** J6
Clere PI *SDTCH* EC2A **7** H9
Clere St *SDTCH* EC2A **7** H9
Clerkenwell CI *CLKNW* EC1R ...... **6** B9 🔟
Clerkenwell Gn *CLKNW* EC1R ...... **12** C1 🔟
Clerkenwell Rd *CLKNW* EC1R ...... **12** A1 🔟
Clerks Piece *LOU* IG10 ...... **39** M6
Clermont Rd *HOM* E9 ...... **86** C8
Clevedon *WEY* KT13 ...... **164** D7
Clevedon Gdns *HEST* TW5 ...... **114** B7
  HYS/HAR UB3 ...... **113** K1
Clevedon Rd *KUT* KT1 ...... **153** C5
  PGE/AN SE20 ...... **158** D4
  TWK TW1 ...... **134** D3
Cleveland Av *CHSWK* W4 ...... **117** M2
  HPTN TW12 ...... **150** F3
Cleveland CI *WOT/HER* KT12 ...... **165** H5
Cleveland Crs *BORE* WD6 ...... **32** C8
Cleveland Dr *STA* TW18 ...... **148** B5
Cleveland Gdns *BARN* SW13 ...... **117** M7
  BAY/PAD W2 ...... **8** E5
  CRICK NW2 ...... **82** D2
  FSBYPK N4 ...... **67** J6 🔟
  WPK KT4 ...... **168** E4
Cleveland Ms *FITZ* W1T **10** E2
Cleveland Park Av *WALTH* E17 ...... **69** C5 🔟
Cleveland Park Crs
  WALTH E17 ...... **69** C5 🔟
Cleveland PI *STJS* SW1Y **10** F8
Cleveland Ri *MRDN* SM4 ...... **169** L2 🔟
Cleveland Rd *BARN* SW13 ...... **117** M7
  CHSWK W4 ...... **117** J1 🔟
  ED N9 ...... **50** B2 🔟
  IL IG1 ...... **89** H3
  IS N1 ...... **7** H1
  ISLW TW7 ...... **134** A1
  NWMAL KT3 ...... **153** L7
  SWFD E18 ...... **70** A4
  UX/CGN UB8 ...... **94** D2
  WEA W13 ...... **98** A4
  WELL DA16 ...... **125** M7
  WPK KT4 ...... **168** E4
Cleveland Rw *WHALL* SW1A **10** F9
Cleveland Sq *BAY/PAD* W2 ...... **8** E5
Cleveland St *CAMTN* NW1 ...... **10** D1
Cleveland Ter *BAY/PAD* W2 ...... **8** E5
Cleveland Wy *WCHPL* E1 ...... **104** C3
Cleveley Crs *EA* W5 ...... **98** C1
Cleveleys Rd *CLPT* E5 ...... **86** B3
Clevely CI *CHARL* SE7 ...... **124** D2
Cleve Rd *KIL/WHAMP* NW6 ...... **2** B1
  SCUP DA14 ...... **144** D7
Cleves Av *EW* KT17 ...... **181** H2
Cleves Crs *CROY/NA* CR0 ...... **186** C4
Cleves Rd *EHAM* E6 ...... **88** D8
  RCHPK/HAM TW10 ...... **134** C7
Cleves Wk *BARK/HLT* IG6 ...... **71** J1
Cleves Wy *HPTN* TW12 ...... **150** F3
  RSLP HA4 ...... **78** D1
  SUN TW16 ...... **149** M2
Cleves Wd *WEY* KT13 ...... **164** E5
Clewer Crs *KTN/HRWW/W* HA3 ...... **61** K2
Clifden Rd *BTFD* TW8 ...... **116** D4
  CLPT E5 ...... **86** C5
  TWK TW1 ...... **133** M5
Clifdens Dr *HYS/HAR* UB3 ...... **96** A7
Clive Wy *EN* EN1 ...... **37** G7
  WATN WD24 ...... **29** J4
Cloak La *BLKFR* EC4V **12** F6
Clockhouse Av *BARK* IG11 ...... **89** J8
Clockhouse La *ASHF* TW15 ...... **131** H7
  CRW RM5 ...... **73** J1
Clock House Md *COB* KT11 ...... **178** B7
Clockhouse PI *PUT/ROE* SW15 ...... **136** E2
Clock House Rd *BECK* BR3 ...... **158** E6
Clock Tower Rd *ISLW* TW7 ...... **115** M8
Cloister CI *RAIN* RM13 ...... **110** B3
  TEDD TW11 ...... **152** B1 🔟
Cloister Gdns *EDGW* HA8 ...... **45** J7
  SNWD SE25 ...... **173** H1 🔟
Cloister Rd *ACT* W3 ...... **99** J4
  CRICK NW2 ...... **82** F3
Cloisters Av *HAYES* BR2 ...... **160** F8
The Cloisters *RKW/CH/CXG* WD3 ...... **40** E2
Clonard Wy *PIN* HA5 ...... **43** G8
Clonbrock Rd *STNW/STAM* N16 ...... **85** L4
Cloncurry St *FUL/PGN* SW6 ...... **136** C1
Clonmel CI *RYLN/HDSTN* HA2 ...... **79** K1 🔟
Clonmell Rd *TOTM* N17 ...... **67** K4
Clonmel Rd *FUL/PGN* SW6 ...... **118** F5
  HPTN TW12 ...... **133** K8
Clonmore St *WAND/EARL* SW18 ...... **136** F5
Cloonmore Av *ORP* BR6 ...... **176** F7
Clorane Gdns *HAMP* NW3 ...... **83** G3
Closemead CI *NTHWD* HA6 ...... **41** J8 🔟
The Close *ALP/SUD* HA0 ...... **80** E6
  BECK BR3 ...... **158** E7
  BUSH WD23 ...... **43** H1 🔟
  BXLY DA5 ...... **145** G3
  CAR SM5 ...... **182** E2
  CHDH RM6 ...... **72** E7
  CHEAM SM3 ...... **169** M2
  CHING E4 ...... **69** J1
  EBAR EN4 ...... **47** M1
  GNTH/NBYPK IG2 ...... **71** L7
  HGDN/ICK UB10 ...... **76** E7
  HGDN/ICK UB10 ...... **77** G8
  ISLW TW7 ...... **115** K7
  MTCM CR4 ...... **155** M7
  NWMAL KT3 ...... **153** J5
  PIN HA5 ...... **59** J4
  PIN HA5 ...... **60** F8 🔟
  POTB/CUF EN6 ...... **23** G5
  PUR/KEN CR8 ...... **183** M3
  RCH/KEW TW9 ...... **117** H8
  RDART DA2 ...... **146** C2
  RKW/CH/CXG WD3 ...... **40** B3
  SCUP DA14 ...... **162** B1
  STHGT/OAK N14 ...... **48** D4
  SURB KT6 ...... **167** L2 🔟
  TRDG/WHET N20 ...... **46** F4

FNCH N3 ...... **65** J2
FSTGT E7 ...... **88** D6
GFD/PVL UB6 ...... **97** J3
GNTH/NBYPK IG2 ...... **71** K7
HTHAIR TW6 ...... **131** H1 🔟
ISLW TW7 ...... **115** J7
KTN/HRWW/W HA3 ...... **62** F6
KUTN/CMB KT2 ...... **152** F4
LOU IG10 ...... **39** L7 🔟
MV/WKIL W9 ...... **8** D2
NWDGN UB2 ...... **114** E2
SCUP DA14 ...... **143** L8
SNWD SE25 ...... **157** L7
TEDD TW11 ...... **133** L8 🔟
WATW WD18 ...... **29** H8
WDGN N22 ...... **66** C2
WELL DA16 ...... **126** C8
WIM/MER SW19 ...... **154** D2
WLGTN SM6 ...... **171** H7
WLSDN NW10 ...... **100** A1

Cloth Fair *STBT* EC1A **12** D3
Clothier St *HDTCH* EC3A ...... **13** K4 🔟
Cloth St *STBT* EC1A ...... **12** E2 🔟
Clothworkers Rd
  WOOL/PLUM SE18 ...... **125** K5
Cloudberry Rd *HARH* RM3 ...... **56** D8 🔟
Cloudesdale Rd *TOOT* SW17 ...... **138** B6
Cloudesley PI *IS* N1 ...... **6** B4
Cloudesley Rd *BXLYHN* DA7 ...... **126** F6
  ERITH DA8 ...... **127** M6
  IS N1 ...... **6** A4
Cloudesley Sq *IS* N1 ...... **6** B3
Cloudesley St *IS* N1 ...... **6** B4
Clouston CI *WLGTN* SM6 ...... **171** L7 🔟
Clova Rd *FSTGT* E7 ...... **88** A6
Clove Crs *POP/IOD* E14 ...... **105** K6
Clovelly Av *CDALE/KGS* NW9 ...... **63** M5
  HGDN/ICK UB10 ...... **77** J4
  PIN HA5 ...... **60** B4
Clovelly CI *HGDN/ICK* UB10 ...... **77** J4
  PIN HA5 ...... **60** B4
Clovelly Gdns *EN* EN1 ...... **49** L2
  ROMW/RG RM7 ...... **73** H2
Clovelly Rd *BXLYHN* DA7 ...... **126** E4
  CEND/HSY/T N8 ...... **66** D5
  CHSWK W4 ...... **99** K8 🔟
  HSLW TW3 ...... **115** G7
  WEA W13 ...... **98** C8
Clovelly Wy *ORP* BR6 ...... **176** F1
  RYLN/HDSTN HA2 ...... **78** F3
Clover CI *WAN* E11 ...... **87** K2 🔟
Cloverdale Gdns *BFN/LL* DA15 ...... **143** M3
The Clover Fld *BUSH* WD23 ...... **42** F1
Clover Ms *CHEL* SW3 ...... **15** L9
Clover Wy *MTCM* CR4 ...... **155** J1
Clove St *PLSTW* E13 ...... **106** A3 🔟
Clowders Rd *CAT* SE6 ...... **140** F7
Clowser CI *SUT* SM1 ...... **170** C7 🔟
Cloyster Wd *EDGW* HA8 ...... **62** D1
Club Gardens Rd *HAYES* BR2 ...... **175** G2 🔟
The Clumps *ASHF* TW15 ...... **131** K8
Clunas Gdns *GPK* RM2 ...... **74** D4
Clunbury Av *NWDGN* UB2 ...... **114** F3
Cluny Ms *ECT* SW5 ...... **14** A6
Cluny PI *STHWK* SE1 ...... **19** J3
Clutton St *POP/IOD* E14 ...... **105** H4 🔟
Clydach Rd *EN* EN1 ...... **36** F6 🔟
Clyde Av *SAND/SEL* CR2 ...... **185** H8
Clyde Circ *SEVS/STOTM* N15 ...... **67** L5 🔟
Clyde Crs *UPMR* RM14 ...... **75** L7
Clyde PI *LEY* E10 ...... **69** H8
Clyde Rd *CROY/NA* CR0 ...... **172** F4
  SEVS/STOTM N15 ...... **67** L5
  STWL/WRAY TW19 ...... **130** D5
  SUT SM1 ...... **170** A7
  WDGN N22 ...... **66** D2
  WLGTN SM6 ...... **171** J7
Clydesdale *PEND* EN3 ...... **37** K7
Clydesdale Av
  KTN/HRWW/W HA3 ...... **62** D4
Clydesdale CI *BORE* WD6 ...... **32** D8
  ISLW TW7 ...... **115** M8 🔟
Clydesdale Gdns
  RCHPK/HAM TW10 ...... **135** H1
Clydesdale Rd *EMPK* RM11 ...... **73** M8
  NTGHL W11 ...... **100** F5 🔟
Clyde St *DEPT* SE8 ...... **122** F4
Clyde Ter *FSTH* SE23 ...... **140** C6
Clyde V *FSTH* SE23 ...... **140** C6
Clyde Wy *ROM* RM1 ...... **73** L2
Clyfford Rd *RSLP* HA4 ...... **77** M4
Clymping Dene
  EBED/NFELT TW14 ...... **132** B4
Clyston Rd *WATW* WD18 ...... **41** M1
Clyston St *VX/NE* SW8 ...... **120** C7
Coach And Horses Yd
  CONDST W1S ...... **10** E6 🔟
Coach House La *HBRY* N5 ...... **85** H4 🔟
  WIM/MER SW19 ...... **136** D8
Coalecroft Rd *PUT/ROE* SW15 ...... **136** C1
Coates Dell *GSTN* WD25 ...... **21** L6
Coates Hill Rd *BMLY* BR1 ...... **161** G5
Coates Rd *BORE* WD6 ...... **44** D2
Coate St *BETH* E2 ...... **104** A1
Coates Wy *GSTN* WD25 ...... **21** K6
Cobbett CI *PEND* EN3 ...... **37** J1
Cobbett Rd *ELTH/MOT* SE9 ...... **124** E8
  WHTN TW2 ...... **133** C5
Cobbetts Av *REDBR* IG4 ...... **70** D6
Cobbett St *VX/NE* SW8 ...... **120** F5
Cobb Gn *GSTN* WD25 ...... **21** H5
The Cobbins *WAB* EN9 ...... **27** L5
Cobble La *IS* N1 ...... **6** B1
Cobble Ms *FSBYPK* N4 ...... **85** J3 🔟
Cobbler's Wk *TEDD* TW11 ...... **151** L3
The Cobbles *UPMR* RM14 ...... **75** M8
Cobblestone PI
  CROY/NA CR0 ...... **172** C3 🔟
Cobbold Ms *SHB* W12 ...... **99** M8 🔟
Cobbold Rd *SHB* W12 ...... **99** M8
  WAN E11 ...... **87** M3
  WLSDN NW10 ...... **81** J4
Cobb's Rd *HSLWW* TW4 ...... **132** F1 🔟
Cobb St *WCHPL* E1 ...... **13** L4
Cob CI *BORE* WD6 ...... **32** C8
Cobden Av *UX/CGN* UB8 ...... **76** C8
Cobden Hl *RAD* WD7 ...... **31** H1
Cobden Ms *SYD* SE26 ...... **158** B1
Cobden Rd *ORP* BR6 ...... **176** D6
  SNWD SE25 ...... **158** A8
  WAN E11 ...... **87** L3
Cobham Av *NWMAL* KT3 ...... **154** A8
Cobham CI *BFN/LL* DA15 ...... **144** B2 🔟
  BTSEA SW11 ...... **137** L3 🔟
  EDGW HA8 ...... **63** H3
  HAYES BR2 ...... **175** J3
  WLGTN SM6 ...... **171** L6
Cobham Ms *CAMTN* NW1 ...... **5** G1
Cobham PI *BXLYHS* DA6 ...... **144** D2 🔟
Cobham Rd *GDMY/SEVK* IG3 ...... **89** L2
  HEST TW5 ...... **114** C5
  KUT KT1 ...... **153** G5
  WALTH E17 ...... **69** J2
  WDGN N22 ...... **67** H4
Cobill CI *EMPK* RM11 ...... **74** C5
Cobland Rd *LEE/GVPK* SE12 ...... **142** C8

Coborn Rd *BOW* E3 ...... **104** F2
Coborn St *BOW* E3 ...... **104** F2
Cobourg Rd *CMBW* SE5 ...... **19** L9
Cobourg St *CAMTN* NW1 ...... **4** F8
Coburg CI *WEST* SW1P **16** F5
Coburg Crs *BRXS/STRHM* SW2 ...... **138** C5
Coburg Gdns *CLAY* IG5 ...... **70** D3
Coburg Rd *WDGN* N22 ...... **66** F3 🔟
Cochrane Ms *STJWD* NW8 ...... **3** H6
Cochrane Rd *WIM/MER* SW19 ...... **154** E3
Cochrane St *STJWD* NW8 ...... **3** H6
Cockerell Rd *WALTH* E17 ...... **68** E8
Cockfosters Rd *EBAR* EN4 ...... **34** F3
Cock La *STBT* EC1A **12** C3
Cockmannings La
  STMC/STPC BR5 ...... **177** K3
Cockmannings Rd
  STMC/STPC BR5 ...... **177** K2
Cocks Crs *NWMAL* KT3 ...... **153** M7 🔟
Cocksett Av *ORP* BR6 ...... **176** E8
Cockspur Ct *STJS* SW1Y **11** H8
Cockspur St *CHCR* WC2N ...... **11** H8 🔟
Cocksure La *SCUP* DA14 ...... **145** G8
Codicote Dr *GSTN* WD25 ...... **21** K7
Codling CI *WAP* E1W ...... **104** A7 🔟
Codling Wy *ALP/SUD* HA0 ...... **80** D4 🔟
Codrington HI *FSTH* SE23 ...... **140** E4
Codrington Ms *NTGHL* W11 ...... **100** E5 🔟
Cody CI *KTN/HRWW/W* HA3 ...... **62** D4
  WLGTN SM6 ...... **183** K1 🔟
Cody Rd *CAN/RD* E16 ...... **105** K3
Coe Av *SNWD* SE25 ...... **173** G1
Cofers Cir *WBLY* HA9 ...... **81** H3
Coffey St *DEPT* SE8 ...... **123** G5
Cogan Av *WALTH* E17 ...... **68** E2
Cohen CI *CHES/WCR* EN8 ...... **26** E5
Coin St *STHWK* SE1 ...... **12** A8
Coity Rd *KTTN* NW5 ...... **84** A6 🔟
Cokers La *DUL* SE21 ...... **139** J5
Coke St *WCHPL* E1 ...... **104** A5 🔟
Colbeck Ms *ECT* SW5 ...... **14** D6
Colbeck Rd *HRW* HA1 ...... **61** J8
Colberg PI *STNW/STAM* N16 ...... **67** L8 🔟
Colborne Wy *WPK* KT4 ...... **169** J5
Colbrook Av *HYS/HAR* UB3 ...... **113** K1
Colbrook CI *HYS/HAR* UB3 ...... **113** K1
Colburn Av *PIN* HA5 ...... **42** E8
Colburn Wy *SUT* SM1 ...... **170** D5
Colby Rd *NRWD* SE19 ...... **157** L1
  WOT/HER KT12 ...... **165** G3
Colchester Dr *PIN* HA5 ...... **60** D6
Colchester Rd *EDGW* HA8 ...... **63** J1
  HARH RM3 ...... **74** E1
  LEY E10 ...... **69** J8
  NTHWD HA6 ...... **60** A3 🔟
  WALTH E17 ...... **69** G7 🔟
Colchester St *WCHPL* E1 ...... **13** M4 🔟
Coldbath Sq *CLKNW* EC1R ...... **6** A9 🔟
Coldbath St *SE13* ...... **123** H7 🔟
Cold Blow Crs *BXLY* DA5 ...... **145** K5
Coldblow La *NWCR* SE14 ...... **122** D5
Coldershaw Rd *HNWL* W7 ...... **98** A8
Coldfall Av *MUSWH* N10 ...... **65** H3
Coldharbour *POP/IOD* E14 ...... **105** J7
Coldharbour La *BRXN/ST* SW9 ...... **139** C1
  BUSH WD23 ...... **43** H1
  HYS/HAR UB3 ...... **95** M8
  PUR/KEN CR8 ...... **184** A3
  RAIN RM13 ...... **110** A7
Coldharbour PI *CMBW* SE5 ...... **121** K7 🔟
Coldharbour Rd *CROY/NA* CR0 ...... **172** A7
Coldharbour Wy *CROY/NA* CR0 ...... **172** A7
Coldstream Gdns
  WAND/EARL SW18 ...... **136** F3
Colebeck Ms *IS* N1 ...... **85** H6 🔟
Colebert Av *WCHPL* E1 ...... **104** C3
Colebrooke Av *WEA* W13 ...... **98** B5
Colebrooke Dr *WAN* E11 ...... **70** B8
Colebrooke Rw *IS* N1 ...... **6** B6
Colebrook Ri *HAYES* BR2 ...... **159** L5
Colebrook Rd
  STRHM/NOR SW16 ...... **156** E4
Colebrook Wy
  FBAR/BDGN N11 ...... **48** B7 🔟
Cole CI *THMD* SE28 ...... **108** B7
Coledale Dr *STAN* HA7 ...... **62** J2
Coleford Rd *WAND/EARL* SW18 ...... **137** J2
Cole Gdns *HEST* TW5 ...... **114** A5
Colegrave Rd *SRTFD* E15 ...... **87** K5
Colegrove Rd *PECK* SE15 ...... **121** M4
Coleherne Ms *WBPTN* SW10 ...... **14** C8
Coleherne Rd *WBPTN* SW10 ...... **14** C8
Colehill Gdns *FUL/PGN* SW6 ...... **118** E6
Colehill La *FUL/PGN* SW6 ...... **118** E6
Coleman CI *SNWD* SE25 ...... **158** A5
Coleman Flds *IS* N1 ...... **6** F3
Coleman Rd *BELV* DA17 ...... **127** G1
  CMBW SE5 ...... **121** L5
Colemans Heath
  ELTH/MOT SE9 ...... **143** H7 🔟
Coleman St *LOTH* EC2R **13** G4
Colenso Rd *CLPT* E5 ...... **86** C4
  GNTH/NBYPK IG2 ...... **89** L1
Colepits Wood Rd
  ELTH/MOT SE9 ...... **143** K2
Coleraine Rd *BKHTH/KID* SE3 ...... **123** M4
  CEND/HSY/T N8 ...... **67** G4 🔟
Coleridge Av *MNPK* E12 ...... **88** E6
  SUT SM1 ...... **170** E6
Coleridge CI *VX/NE* SW8 ...... **120** B7 🔟
Coleridge Rd *ASHF* TW15 ...... **130** E8
  CEND/HSY/T N8 ...... **66** D7
  CROY/NA CR0 ...... **173** J2
  DART DA1 ...... **147** G1
  FSBYPK N4 ...... **85** G2 🔟
  HARH RM3 ...... **74** B1
  NFNCH/WDSP N12 ...... **47** J2
  WALTH E17 ...... **68** F5
Coleridge Sq *WEA* W13 ...... **98** A5 🔟
Coleridge Wk *GLDGN* NW11 ...... **65** G5
Coleridge Wy *ORP* BR6 ...... **177** G1 🔟
  WDR/YW UB7 ...... **112** F2
  YEAD UB4 ...... **96** A5
Cole Rd *TWK* TW1 ...... **134** A3

WAT WD17 ...... **29** H4
Colesburg Rd *BECK* BR3 ...... **158** F6
Coles Crs *RYLN/HDSTN* HA2 ...... **79** H2
Colescroft HI *PUR/KEN* CR8 ...... **184** A8
Colesdale *POTB/CUF* EN6 ...... **24** C3 🔟
Coles Gn *BUSH* WD23 ...... **43** J3
Coles Green Rd *CRICK* NW2 ...... **82** A1
Coleshill Rd *TEDD* TW11 ...... **151** L2 🔟
Colestown St *BTSEA* SW11 ...... **119** L7 🔟
Cole St *STHWK* SE1 ...... **18** F2
Colet CI *PLMGR* N13 ...... **49** H8
Colet Gdns *WKENS* W14 ...... **118** D3
Coley St *FSBYW* WC1X **11** M1
Colfe Rd *FSTH* SE23 ...... **140** E5
Colham Av *WDR/YW* UB7 ...... **94** E7
Colham Green Rd *UX/CGN* UB8 ...... **95** G4
Colham Mill Rd *WDR/YW* UB7 ...... **94** D8
Colham Rd *UX/CGN* UB8 ...... **94** F3
Colina Ms *SEVS/STOTM* N15 ...... **67** H5
Colina Rd *CEND/HSY/T* N8 ...... **67** H6
Colin CI *CDALE/KGS* NW9 ...... **63** L5
  CROY/NA CR0 ...... **173** M5
  RDART DA2 ...... **147** H3
  WWKM BR4 ...... **174** F5
Colin Crs *CDALE/KGS* NW9 ...... **63** M6
Colindale Av *CDALE/KGS* NW9 ...... **63** L3
Colindeep Gdns *HDN* NW4 ...... **64** A6
Colindeep La *CDALE/KGS* NW9 ...... **63** M5
Colinette Rd *PUT/ROE* SW15 ...... **136** C1
Colin Gdns *CDALE/KGS* NW9 ...... **63** M6
Colin Park Rd *CDALE/KGS* NW9 ...... **63** L4
Colinton Rd *WLSDN* NW10 ...... **82** A6
Colin Rd *BCTR* RM8 ...... **90** B2
Coliston Rd
  WAND/EARL SW18 ...... **137** G4 🔟
Collamore Av
  WAND/EARL SW18 ...... **137** L5
Collapit CI *RYLN/HDSTN* HA2 ...... **61** H7
Collard PI *CAMTN* NW1 ...... **4** C1
College Ap *GNWCH* SE10 ...... **123** J4 🔟
College Av *EW* KT17 ...... **180** F7
  KTN/HRWW/W HA3 ...... **61** L2
  UED N18 ...... **49** M7
  WHTN TW2 ...... **133** K5 🔟
College CI *CHES/WCR* EN8 ...... **26** C3 🔟
College Crs *KIL/WHAMP* NW6 ...... **83** J6
College Cross *IS* N1 ...... **6** B1
College Dr *CHING* E4 ...... **51** H2
  ENC/FH EN2 ...... **36** D4 🔟
  NWMAL KT3 ...... **153** M8 🔟
  REDBR IG4 ...... **70** E6
  TOOT SW17 ...... **137** L6
  UED N18 ...... **49** M7 🔟
College Gn *NRWD* SE19 ...... **157** L3
College Gv *CAMTN* NW1 ...... **5** G4
College HI *CANST* EC4R ...... **12** F6 🔟
College Hill Rd
  KTN/HRWW/W HA3 ...... **61** L1
College Ms *IS* N1 ...... **6** B2
College Park CI *LEW* SE13 ...... **141** K1
College PI *CAMTN* NW1 ...... **4** F3
  WALTH E17 ...... **69** L5
College Rd *ABLGY* WD5 ...... **21** G4
  BMLY BR1 ...... **160** A4
  CHES/WCR EN8 ...... **26** D3
  CHSWK EN7 ...... **26** B3
  CROY/NA CR0 ...... **172** D4
  DUL SE21 ...... **139** L4
  ENC/FH EN2 ...... **36** D5
  EW KT17 ...... **180** F7
  HRW HA1 ...... **61** L7
  ISLW TW7 ...... **115** M6
  KTN/HRWW/W HA3 ...... **61** L2
  LEY E10 ...... **69** J8
  NRWD SE19 ...... **157** M1
  SWLY BR8 ...... **163** L3
  TOTM N17 ...... **49** M8
  WBLY HA9 ...... **80** D1
  WCHMH N21 ...... **49** G4
  WEA W13 ...... **98** B5
  WIM/MER SW19 ...... **155** K2
  WLSDN NW10 ...... **100** C1
College Ter *FNCH* N3 ...... **64** F3 🔟
College Vw *ELTH/MOT* SE9 ...... **142** D5
College Wy *ASHF* TW15 ...... **130** F8 🔟
  NTHWD HA6 ...... **41** K8
Collent St *HOM* E9 ...... **86** D6 🔟
Colless Rd *SEVS/STOTM* N15 ...... **67** M6
Collet Cl *CHES/WCR* EN8 ...... **26** D1
Collett Rd *BERM/RHTH* SE16 ...... **122** A1
Collier CI *EHAM* E6 ...... **107** H6 🔟
  HOR/WEW KT19 ...... **168** A8
Collier Dr *EDGW* HA8 ...... **63** G3
Collier Row La *CRW* RM5 ...... **73** H2
Collier Row Rd *CRW* RM5 ...... **73** G2
  ROMW/RG RM7 ...... **72** F2
Collier St *IS* N1 ...... **5** L6
Colliers Water La *THHTH* CR7 ...... **157** G8
Colliers Wd *HAYES* BR2 ...... **175** K2 🔟
Collindale Av *BFN/LL* DA15 ...... **144** A5
  CDALE/KGS NW9 ...... **63** K4
  ERITH DA8 ...... **127** H4
Collingbourne Rd *SHB* W12 ...... **100** B7
Collingham Gdns *ECT* SW5 ...... **14** D6
Collingham PI *ECT* SW5 ...... **14** C6
Collingham Rd *ECT* SW5 ...... **14** D5
Collings CI *WDGN* N22 ...... **48** F8
Collington St *WCHPL* E1 ...... **104** B3
Collins Av *STAN* HA7 ...... **62** L3
Collins Dr *RSLP* HA4 ...... **78** C2
Collinson St *STHWK* SE1 ...... **18** E2
Collins Rd *HBRY* N5 ...... **85** J4
Collins St *BKHTH/KID* SE3 ...... **123** J7
Collinwood Av *PEND* EN3 ...... **37** J6
Collinwood Gdns
  GNTH/NBYPK IG2 ...... **70** F6

Coll's Rd PECK SE15 122 C6
Collyer Av CROY/NA CR0 171 L6
Collyer Pl PECK SE15 122 A6 2
Collyer Rd CROY/NA CR0 171 L6 1
Colman Rd CAN/RD E16 106 C4
Colmar Cl WCHPL E1 104 D3 3
Colmer Pl KTN/HRWW/W HA3 61 K1
Colmer Rd STRHM/NOR SW16 156 E3
Colmore Rd PEND EN3 37 J7
Colnbrook By-pass
WDR/YW UB7 112 B5
Colnbrook St STHWK SE1 18 C4
Colne Av OXHEY WD19 42 B1
RKW/CH/CXG WD3 40 A4
WDR/YW UB7 94 C8
Colne Ct HOR/WEW KT19 168 C6
Colnedale Rd UX/CGN UB8 76 D5
Colne Dr HARH RM3 56 F8
WOT/HER KT12 165 K5
Colne Md RKW/CH/CXG WD3 40 A4
Colne Rd CLPT E5 86 D4
WCHMH N21 49 K2
WHTN TW2 133 L5
Colne St PLSTW E13 106 A2
Colne Va UPMR RM14 75 L7
Colne Valley Trail
HGDN/ICK UB10 76 C3
RKW/CH/CXG WD3 40 C4
Colne Valley Wy IVER SL0 94 A5
Colney Hatch La
FBAR/BDGN N11 47 M8
MUSWH N10 66 A1
Colney Rd DART DA1 146 F3
Cologne Rd BTSEA SW11 137 K1
Colombo Rd IL IG1 89 J1
Colombo St STHWK SE1 12 C9
Colomb St GNWCH SE10 123 L3
Colonels Wk ENC/FH EN2 36 B5
Colonial Av WHTN TW2 133 J3
Colonial Dr CHSWK W4 117 J2 1
Colonial Rd EBED/NFELT TW14 131 L4
Colonial Wy WATN WD24 29 J4
Colonnade BMSBY WC1N 11 J1
The Colonnade
CHES/WCR EN8 26 D1 2
Colson Rd CROY/NA CR0 172 D4
Colson Wy STRHM/NOR SW16 138 C8
Colsterworth Rd
SEVS/STOTM N15 67 M5 2
Colston Av CAR SM5 170 E6
Colston Rd FSTGT E7 88 D6
MORT/ESHN SW14 135 J1
Colthurst Crs FSBYPK N4 85 H2
Coltishall Rd HCH RM12 92 C6
Coltness Crs ABYW SE2 126 B3
Colton Gdns TOTM N17 67 J4
Colton Rd HRW HA1 61 L6 1
Coltsfoot Dr WDR/YW UB7 94 E5 2
Coltsfoot Pth HARH RM3 74 D1
Columbia Av EDGW HA8 63 H2 1
RSLP HA4 78 B1
WPK KT4 168 F2
Columbia Rd BETH E2 7 M7
BETH E2 104 A1 2
PLSTW E13 105 M3 2
Columbine Av EHAM E6 106 E4
SAND/SEL CR2 184 B1
Columbine Wy HARH RM3 74 E2
Columbus Gdns NTHWD HA6 60 A2 1
Colveiw Ct ELTH/MOT SE9 142 D6
Colvestone Crs HACK E8 85 M5
Colville Gdns NTGHL W11 100 F5 1
Colville Ms NTGHL W11 100 F5
Colville Rd ACT W3 117 H1
ED N9 50 B3
NTGHL W11 100 F5
WALTH E17 68 E3
WAN E11 87 J3
Colville Sq NTGHL W11 100 F5 5
Colville Ter NTGHL W11 100 F5
Colvin Cl SYD SE26 158 C1
Colvin Gdns BARK/HLT IG6 71 J1
CHES/WCR EN8 26 D8
CHING E4 51 J5
SWFD E18 70 B5
Colvin Rd EHAM E6 88 E7
THHTH CR7 157 G8
Colwall Gdns WFD IG8 52 A7 2
Colwell Rd EDUL SE22 139 M2
Colwick Cl HGT N6 66 D8
Colwith Rd HMSMTH W6 118 C4
Colwood Gdns WIM/MER SW19 155 K3
Colworth Gv WALW SE17 18 F6 2
Colworth Rd CROY/NA CR0 173 G3
WAN E11 69 L7
Colwyn Av GFD/PVL UB6 97 M1
Colwyn Cl STRHM/NOR SW16 156 C1
Colwyn Crs HSLW TW3 115 J6 1
Colwyn Rd CRICK NW2 82 B3 1
Colyer Cl ELTH/MOT SE9 143 H6
Colyers Cl ERITH DA8 127 K6
Colyers La ERITH DA8 127 J6
Colyton Cl ALP/SUD HA0 80 C6 3
WELL DA16 126 D6
Colyton Rd EDUL SE22 140 B2
Colyton Wy UED N18 50 A7
Combe Av BKHTH/KID SE3 123 M5
Combedale Rd GNWCH SE10 124 A3
Combemartin Rd
WAND/EARL SW18 136 E4
Comber Cl CRICK NW2 82 A3
Comber Gv CMBW SE5 121 J5
Combermere Rd BRXN/ST SW9 120 F8
MRDN SM4 170 B1
Combe Rd WATW WD18 41 M1
Comberton Rd CLPT E5 86 B2 3
Combeside WOOL/PLUM SE18 125 M5
Combes Rd DAGW RM9 90 F7
Combwell Crs ABYW SE2 126 A1
Comely Bank Rd WALTH E17 69 J6 1
Comeragh Rd WKENS W14 118 E3
Comerford Rd BROCKY SE4 140 E1
Comet Cl GSTN WD25 20 F7
MNPK E12 88 D4
PUR RM19 129 G2
Comet Pl DEPT SE8 123 G5
Comet Rd STWL/WRAY TW19 130 D4
Comet St DEPT SE8 123 G5
Commerce Rd BTFD TW8 116 C4
WDGN N22 66 F2
Commerce Wy CROY/NA CR0 171 M5
Commercial Rd POP/IOD E14 104 E5
STA TW18 148 A2
UED N18 49 L7
WCHPL E1 13 M4 2
Commercial St WCHPL E1 13 L1
Commercial Wy PECK SE15 121 M6
WLSDN NW10 99 H1
Commerell Pl GNWCH SE10 123 M3 1
Commerell St GNWCH SE10 123 L3
Commodore St WCHPL E1 104 D4 3
Commondale PUT/ROE SW15 118 C7
Commonfield Rd BNSTD SM7 182 A7
Common La ESH/CLAY KT10 179 G1
GSTN WD25 30 E3
RDART DA2 146 A6
Common Rd BARN SW13 118 A8
ESH/CLAY KT10 167 G8
STAN HA7 43 K5
Common Side EPSOM KT18 180 A8
Commonside HAYES BR2 175 J6
Commonside Cl BELMT SM2 182 B4
Commonside East
MTCM CR4 156 C7 1
The Common EA W5 98 E7
NWDGN UB2 114 D2
STAN HA7 43 M4
Commonwealth Av
HYS/HAR UB3 95 K5
SHB W12 100 B6 3
Commonwealth Rd TOTM N17 68 A1
Commonwealth Wy ABYW SE2 126 B3
Community Cl HEST TW5 114 B6 2
HGDN/ICK UB10 77 J3 2
Community Rd GFD/PVL UB6 79 J8
SRTFD E15 87 K5 1
Como Rd FSTH SE23 140 E6
Como St ROMW/RG RM7 73 K6
Compass Hl
RCHPK/HAM TW10 134 D3 2
Compayne Gdns
KIL/WHAMP NW6 2 C1
Comport Gn CROY/NA CR0 186 E5
Compton Av EHAM E6 106 D1
GPK RM2 74 B4
HGT N6 65 L8
IS N1 85 H6
Compton Cl CRICK NW2 82 D3
EDGW HA8 63 J1 2
ESH/CLAY KT10 166 D8 1
WEA W13 98 A5
Compton Crs CHSGTN KT9 167 L8
CHSWK W4 117 J4
NTHLT UB5 78 D8
TOTM N17 67 J1
Compton Pl ERITH DA8 127 M4
OXHEY WD19 42 E6
STPAN WC1H 5 J9 1
Compton Ri PIN HA5 60 E6
Compton Rd CROY/NA CR0 173 H3
HYS/HAR UB3 95 L6
IS N1 85 H6
WCHMH N21 49 H3
WIM/MER SW19 154 F2
WLSDN NW10 100 D2
Compton St FSBYE EC1V 6 C9
Compton Ter IS N1 85 H6
Comreddy Cl ENC/FH EN2 36 B4
Comus Pl WALW SE17 19 J6
Comyne Rd WATN WD24 28 F1
Comyn Rd BTSEA SW11 137 L1
Comyns Cl CAN/RD E16 105 M4
Comyns Rd DAGW RM9 91 G7
The Comyns BUSH WD23 43 J3
Conaways Cl EW KT17 181 G3
Concanon Rd
BRXS/STRHM SW2 138 F1
Concert Hall Ap STHWK SE1 11 M9
Concord Cl NTHLT UB5 96 E2 2
Concorde Cl HSLW TW3 115 H7 1
UX/CGN UB8 94 E1 1
Concorde Dr EHAM E6 106 F4
Concord Rd ACT W3 99 H3
PEND EN3 37 J8
Condell Rd VX/NE SW8 120 C6
Conder St POP/IOD E14 104 E5 2
Condor Rd STA TW18 148 C6
Condover Crs
WOOL/PLUM SE18 125 H5
Condray Pl BTSEA SW11 119 L5
Conduit La SAND/SEL CR2 173 G7
UED N18 50 C7
Conduit Ms BAY/PAD W2 9 G5
Conduit Pas BAY/PAD W2 9 G5
Conduit Pl BAY/PAD W2 9 G5
Conduit Rd WOOL/PLUM SE18 125 H3
Conduit St CONDST W1S 10 D6
Conduit Wy WLSDN NW10 81 J7
Conewood St HBRY N5 85 H3
Coney Acre DUL SE21 139 J5 1
Coney Burrows CHING E4 51 L4 1
Coney Gv UX/CGN UB8 94 F2
Coney Hill Rd WWKM BR4 174 E4
Conference Cl CHING E4 51 J4 2
Conference Rd ABYW SE2 126 C2 1
Congleton Gv
WOOL/PLUM SE18 125 J3
Congo Rd WOOL/PLUM SE18 125 K3
Congress Rd ABYW SE2 126 C2
Congreve Rd ELTH/MOT SE9 124 F8
WAB EN9 27 L6
Congreve St WALW SE17 19 J6
Conical Cnr ENC/FH EN2 36 C5
Conifer Av CRW RM5 55 H7 1
Conifer Cl CHESW EN7 25 M2
ORP BR6 176 D6
Conifer Gdns EN EN1 49 K1
STRHM/NOR SW16 138 F7
SUT SM1 170 B4 1
Conifers WEY KT13 164 E6
Conifers Cl TEDD TW11 152 C3 1
The Conifers GSTN WD25 21 J8 2
Conifer Wy ALP/SUD HA0 80 C3
HYS/HAR UB3 96 A6 2
SWLY BR8 163 J4
Coniger Rd FUL/PGN SW6 119 G7
Coningesby Dr WAT WD17 28 E4
Coningham Ms SHB W12 100 A7 1
Coningham Rd SHB W12 100 B8
Coningsby Cottages EA W5 98 D8 1
Coningsby Dr POTB/CUF EN6 23 K6
Coningsby Gdns CHING E4 51 H8
Coningsby Rd EA W5 98 C8
FSBYPK N4 67 H8 1
SAND/SEL CR2 184 C2
Conington Rd LEW SE13 123 H7
Conisbee Ct STHGT/OAK N14 35 J8 3
Conisborough Crs CAT SE6 141 J8 1
Coniscliffe Cl CHST BR7 161 G4
Coniscliffe Rd PLMGR N13 49 J5
Coniston Av BARK IG11 89 L7
GFD/PVL UB6 98 B2
UPMR RM14 93 J4
WELL DA16 125 L8
Coniston Cl BARN SW13 117 M5 1
BXLYHN DA7 127 J6
CHSWK W4 117 J6
DART DA1 146 B5
ERITH DA8 127 L5
MRDN SM4 169 K1
Coniston Ct BAY/PAD W2 9 K5 1
Conistone Wy HOLWY N7 5 K1
Coniston Gdns BELMT SM2 170 D8 1
CDALE/KGS NW9 63 K6
ED N9 50 C3
PIN HA5 60 A5
REDBR IG4 70 E5
WBLY HA9 80 C1
Coniston Rd BMLY BR1 159 L2
BXLYHN DA7 127 J6
CROY/NA CR0 173 G2
MUSWH N10 66 B3
TOTM N17 50 A8
WHTN TW2 133 H3
Coniston Wy CHSGTN KT9 167 L5
HCH RM12 92 A5
Conlan St NKENS W10 100 E3
Conley Rd WLSDN NW10 81 L6
Conley St GNWCH SE10 123 L3 1
Connaught Av ASHF TW15 130 E8 2
CHING E4 51 K2
EBAR EN4 47 M3
EN EN1 36 E5
HSLWW TW4 132 E2
LOU IG10 39 K7
MORT/ESHN SW14 117 J8
Connaught Br CAN/RD E16 106 D7
Connaught Cl BAY/PAD W2 9 J5
EN EN1 36 E5 3
SUT SM1 170 D4 1
UX/CGN UB8 95 J4 1
Connaught Dr GLDGN NW11 65 G5
Connaught Gdns MRDN SM4 155 J8
MUSWH N10 66 B6
PLMGR N13 49 H6
Connaught Hl LOU IG10 39 K7
Connaught La IL IG1 89 J2
Connaught Ms
WOOL/PLUM SE18 125 G3
Connaught Pl BAY/PAD W2 9 L6
Connaught Rd BAR EN5 46 D1
CAN/RD E16 106 C6
CHING E4 51 L2 1
FSBYPK N4 67 G8
HCH RM12 92 D3
HPTN TW12 151 K1
IL IG1 89 K2
KTN/HRWW/W HA3 61 M2
NWMAL KT3 153 L7
RCHPK/HAM TW10 134 F2 1
SUT SM1 170 D4
WALTH E17 69 G6 1
WAN E11 87 K1
WEA W13 98 B6 2
WLSDN NW10 81 L8 3
WOOL/PLUM SE18 125 G3
Connaught Sq BAY/PAD W2 9 K5
Connaught St BAY/PAD W2 9 K5
Connaught Wy PLMGR N13 49 H6 1
Connell Crs EA W5 98 F3
Connemara Cl BORE WD6 45 K1 1
Connington Crs CHING E4 51 K5 1
Connop Rd PEND EN3 37 K3
Connor Rd DAGW RM9 90 F4
Connor St HOM E9 86 D8 1
Conolly Rd HNWL W7 97 L7
Conrad Dr WPK KT4 169 J3
Consfield Av NWMAL KT3 154 A7
Consort Cl FBAR/BDGN N11 47 M7
Consort Ms ISLW TW7 133 K3
Consort Rd PECK SE15 122 B7
Cons St STHWK SE1 18 B1 1
Constable Cl GLDGN NW11 65 H7
YEAD UB4 95 J1 1
Constable Crs SEVS/STOTM N15 68 A6
Constable Gdns EDGW HA8 63 G2
ISLW TW7 133 K2
Constable Ms BCTR RM8 90 B5 1
Constance Crs HAYES BR2 174 F3
Constance Rd CROY/NA CR0 172 B2
EN EN1 49 L1
SUT SM1 170 C6
WHTN TW2 133 H4
Constance St CAN/RD E16 106 E7 1
Constantine Rd HAMP NW3 83 M4
Constitution Hl WHALL SW1A 16 C1
Constitution Ri
WOOL/PLUM SE18 125 G6
Content St WALW SE17 18 F6
Contessa Cl ORP BR6 176 E7
Control Tower Rd HTHAIR TW6 113 G8
Convent Cl BECK BR3 159 J3
Convent Gdns EA W5 116 C2
NTGHL W11 100 F5 6
Convent Hl NRWD SE19 157 J2
Convent Rd ASHF TW15 149 H1
Convent Wy NWDGN UB2 114 C2
Conway Cl RAIN RM13 92 A7 1
STAN HA7 44 A8
Conway Crs CHDH RM6 72 C8
GFD/PVL UB6 97 L1
Conway Dr ASHF TW15 149 J2
BELMT SM2 170 B8
HYS/HAR UB3 113 J1
Conway Gdns ENC/FH EN2 36 E3
MTCM CR4 156 D7
WBLY HA9 62 C8
Conway Gv ACT W3 99 K4
Conway Ms FITZ W1T 10 E1 2
Conway Rd CRICK NW2 82 C2
FELT TW13 150 D1
HSLWW TW4 132 F4
RYNPK SW20 154 C4
SEVS/STOTM N15 67 J6 2
STHGT/OAK N14 48 E5
WOOL/PLUM SE18 125 L3 1
Conway St FITZ W1T 10 E1 2
FITZ W1T 10 E2 1
Conybeare HAMP NW3 3 K2 1
Conyers Cl WOT/HER KT12 165 K7
Conyer's Rd STRHM/NOR SW16 156 D1
Conyer St BOW E3 104 E1 1
Cooden Cl BMLY BR1 160 B3
Cookes Cl WAN E11 87 M2
Cookes La CHEAM SM3 169 L8
Cookham Cl NWDGN UB2 115 H1
Cookham Dene Cl CHST BR7 161 K4
Cookham Rd SWLY BR8 163 G4
Cookhill Rd ABYW SE2 108 B8
Cook's Cl CRW RM5 73 J2
Cooks Ferry Rbt UED N18 50 E7
Cook's Hole Rd ENC/FH EN2 36 B3
Cooks Md BUSH WD23 43 H1
Cookson Gv ERITH DA8 127 H5
Cook's Rd SRTFD E15 105 H1
WALW SE17 18 C9
Coolfin Rd CAN/RD E16 106 A5
Coolgardie Av CHIG IG7 53 G5
CHING E4 51 K7
Coolgardie Rd ASHF TW15 149 J1
Coolhurst Rd CEND/HSY/T N8 66 D7
Cool Oak Br CDALE/KGS NW9 63 M8
Cool Oak La CDALE/KGS NW9 63 M8
Coomassie Rd MV/WKIL W9 100 F3 1
Coombe Av CROY/NA CR0 172 E6
Coombe Bank NWMAL KT3 153 L4
Coombe Cl EDGW HA8 62 F3
HSLW TW3 133 G1
Coombe Cnr WCHMH N21 49 H3
Coombe Crs HPTN TW12 150 E3
Coombe Dr RSLP HA4 78 B1
Coombe End KUTN/CMB KT2 153 K3
Coombefield Cl NWMAL KT3 153 L8 1
Coombe Gdns NWMAL KT3 153 M7
RYNPK SW20 154 A5
Coombe Hill Gld
KUTN/CMB KT2 153 L3
Coombe Hill Rd KUTN/CMB KT2 153 L3
RKW/CH/CXG WD3 40 A2
Coombe House Cha
NWMAL KT3 153 K4 1
Coombehurst Cl EBAR EN4 34 F5
Coombe La CROY/NA CR0 173 H7
RYNPK SW20 153 M4
Coombe La West
KUTN/CMB KT2 153 J4
NWMAL KT3 153 L3 1
Coombe Lea BMLY BR1 160 E6
Coombe Ldg CHARL SE7 124 C4
Coombe Neville
KUTN/CMB KT2 153 J3
Coombe Pk KUTN/CMB KT2 153 J1
Coombe Ridings
KUTN/CMB KT2 153 J1
Coombe Ri KUTN/CMB KT2 153 J4
Coombe Rd BUSH WD23 43 J2
CHSWK W4 117 L3
CROY/NA CR0 172 F6
HARH RM3 74 F4
HPTN TW12 150 F2
KUTN/CMB KT2 153 G4
NWMAL KT3 153 L6
SAND/SEL CR2 172 E6
SYD SE26 140 B8
WDGN N22 67 G3 2
WEA W13 116 B1 1
WLSDN NW10 81 K3
Coombes Rd DAGW RM9 90 F8
Coombe-Wood Dr CHDH RM6 72 F7
Coombe Wood Hl
PUR/KEN CR8 184 C5
Coombe Wood Rd
KUTN/CMB KT2 153 J1
Coombfield Dr RDART DA2 147 K8
Coombs St IS N1 6 D6
Coomer Ms FUL/PGN SW6 118 F4 2
Coomer Pl FUL/PGN SW6 118 F4
Cooperage Cl TOTM N17 49 M8 1
Cooper Av WALTH E17 68 D2
Cooper Cl GRH DA9 147 L2
Cooper Crs CAR SM5 170 F5
Cooper Rd CRICK NW2 82 A5
CROY/NA CR0 172 A7
HDN NW4 64 D7 1
Coopersale Rd HOM E9 86 D5
Coopers Cl CHIG IG7 54 B4
DAGE RM10 91 H6
WCHPL E1 104 C3
Coopers Crs BORE WD6 32 C4
Coopers La LEE/GVPK SE12 142 B6
LEY E10 87 H1
POTB/CUF EN6 23 L2
Coopers Lane Rd POTB/CUF EN6 24 A6
Coopers Rd POTB/CUF EN6 23 J3
STHWK SE1 19 M8
Cooper's Rw TWRH EC3N 13 L6
Cooper St CAN/RD E16 105 M4 2
Cooper's Yd NRWD SE19 157 J2
Coote Rd BCTR RM8 90 F3
BXLYHN DA7 126 F6
Copeland Dr POP/IOD E14 123 G2 2
Copeland Rd LEY E10 69 H6
PECK SE15 122 A7
Copeman Cl SYD SE26 158 C1
Copenhagen Pl POP/IOD E14 104 F5
Copenhagen St IS N1 5 M4
Copenhagen Wy
WOT/HER KT12 165 H5 1
Cope Pl KENS W8 14 A4
Copers Cope Rd BECK BR3 158 F3
Cope St BERM/RHTH SE16 122 D2 1
Copland Av ALP/SUD HA0 80 D5
Copland Cl ALP/SUD HA0 80 C5
Copland Ms ALP/SUD HA0 80 E6 1
Copland Rd ALP/SUD HA0 80 E6
Copleston Rd PECK SE15 121 M8
Copley Cl HNWL W7 97 L3 1
WALW SE17 121 H4
Copley Dene BMLY BR1 160 D4
Copley Pk STRHM/NOR SW16 156 F2
Copley Rd STAN HA7 44 C7
Coppard Gdns CHSGTN KT9 167 J8
Coppelia Rd BKHTH/KID SE3 141 M1
Coppen Rd BCTR RM8 72 F8
Copperas St DEPT SE8 123 H4
Copper Beech Cl CLAY IG5 71 G2
STMC/STPC BR5 162 C8 2
Copper Cl NRWD SE19 157 M3
Copperdale Rd HYS/HAR UB3 96 A8 2
Copperfield CHIG IG7 53 K8
Copperfield Av UX/CGN UB8 95 G3
Copperfield Cl PUR/KEN CR8 184 C4 1
Copperfield Dr
SEVS/STOTM N15 67 M5 3
Copperfield Rd BOW E3 104 E3
THMD SE28 108 C5
Copperfield St STHWK SE1 18 D1
Copperfields Wy HARH RM3 74 D2 2
Copperfield Wy CHST BR7 161 J2
PIN HA5 60 F5
Coppermead Cl CRICK NW2 82 C3
Copper Mill Dr ISLW TW7 115 M7 1
Copper Mill La TOOT SW17 137 J8
Coppermill La WALTH E17 68 C7
Coppetts Cl NFNCH/WDSP N12 65 M1
Coppetts Rd MUSWH N10 65 M2
Coppice Cl
KTN/HRWW/W HA3 43 M8 2
RSLP HA4 59 K7 1
RYNPK SW20 154 C6 2
Coppice Dr PUT/ROE SW15 136 A3
Coppice Pth CHIG IG7 54 B6
The Coppice ASHF TW15 149 H2 1
ENC/FH EN2 36 B7
OXHEY WD19 42 C1 1
WDR/YW UB7 94 E5
Coppice Wk TRDG/WHET N20 47 G5
Coppice Wy SWFD E18 69 M5
Coppies Gv FBAR/BDGN N11 48 B6
Copping Cl CROY/NA CR0 172 E6
The Coppins KTN/HRWW/W HA3 43 L8
Coppock Cl BTSEA SW11 119 L7 3
Coppsfield E/WMO/HCT KT8 151 G6 1
Copse Av WWKM BR4 174 B5
Copse Cl CHARL SE7 124 B4
NTHWD HA6 59 J2
WDR/YW UB7 112 D1
Copse Edge Av EW KT17 180 F6
Copse Gld SURB KT6 167 K3
Copse Hl BELMT SM2 182 B1
PUR/KEN CR8 183 L6
RYNPK SW20 154 A4
Copsem Dr ESH/CLAY KT10 166 B8
Copsem La ESH/CLAY KT10 178 C2
LHD/OX KT22 178 C4
Copsem Wy ESH/CLAY KT10 166 C8
Copsen Wd LHD/OX KT22 178 C4
The Copse CHING E4 51 M3
Copse Vw SAND/SEL CR2 185 L2
Copsewood Cl BFN/LL DA15 143 L3 1
Copsewood Rd WATN WD24 29 H4
Copse Wood Wy NTHWD HA6 59 J2
Coptefield Dr BELV DA17 126 D1 1
Copthall Av LOTH EC2R 13 H4 3
Copthall Dr MLHL NW7 64 A1
Copthall Gdns MLHL NW7 64 A1
TWK TW1 134 A5 2
Copthall Rd East
HGDN/ICK UB10 77 G2
Copthall Rd West
HGDN/ICK UB10 77 G2
Copthorne Av BAL SW12 138 D4
BARK/HLT IG6 53 H8
HAYES BR2 175 M4
Copthorne Cl SHPTN TW17 164 C1 1
Copthorne Gdns EMPK RM11 75 G6
Copthorne Ms HYS/HAR UB3 113 L2
Copthorne Ri PUR/KEN CR8 184 D6
Copthorne Rd
RKW/CH/CXG WD3 40 F1
Coptic St NOXST/BSQ WC1A 11 J3 1
Copton Cl BOW E3 105 G4
Copwood Cl NFNCH/WDSP N12 47 K6
Coral Cl CHDH RM6 72 C4
Coraline Cl STHL UB1 96 F2
Coral St STHWK SE1 18 B2
Coram St BMSBY WC1N 11 J1 1
Coran Cl ED N9 50 D2
Corban Rd HSLW TW3 115 G8
Corbar Cl EBAR EN4 34 D3
Corbet Cl MTCM CR4 171 G3
Corbet Pl WCHPL E1 13 L2 1
Corbet Rd EW KT17 180 E3
Corbets Av UPMR RM14 93 H5
Corbets Tey Rd UPMR RM14 93 H3
Corbett Cl CROY/NA CR0 186 D5
Corbett Gv FBAR/BDGN N11 66 E1
Corbett Rd WALTH E17 69 K3
WAN E11 70 C7
Corbett's La
BERM/RHTH SE16 122 C2 2
Corbicum WAN E11 69 L8
Corbin's La RYLN/HDSTN HA2 79 H3
Corbridge Crs BETH E2 104 B1 3
Corby Crs ENC/FH EN2 35 L7 3
Corbylands Rd BFN/LL DA15 143 L4
Corbyn St FSBYPK N4 84 E1
Corby Rd WLSDN NW10 99 J1
Cordelia Cl HNHL SE24 139 H1 3
Cordelia Gdns
STWL/WRAY TW19 130 E4
Cordelia Rd STWL/WRAY TW19 130 E4
Cordelia St POP/IOD E14 105 H5
Cordell Cl CHES/WCR EN8 26 E1 2
Cordingley Rd RSLP HA4 77 K1
Cording St POP/IOD E14 105 H4
Cordova Rd BOW E3 104 E2
Cordrey Gdns COUL/CHIP CR5 183 L8
Cordwell Rd LEW SE13 141 K2
Corelli Rd BKHTH/KID SE3 124 E6

Corfe Av RYLN/HDSTN HA2 ...... 79 G4
Corfe CI YEAD UB4 ...... 96 C5
Corfield Rd WCHMH N21 ...... 35 M8
Corfield St BETH E2 ...... 104 B3 🔢
Corfton Rd W5 ...... 98 E5
Coriander Av POP/IOD E14 ...... 105 K5
Cories CI BCTR RM8 ...... 90 D2
Corinium CI WBLY HA9 ...... 80 F4 🔢
Corinne Rd ARCH N19 ...... 84 C4
Corinthian Manorway
 ERITH DA8 ...... 127 K2
Corinthian Rd ERITH DA8 ...... 127 K2 🔢
Corkran Rd SURB KT6 ...... 167 K2
Cork St Ms CONDST W1S ...... 10 E7 🔢
Cork St CONDST W1S ...... 10 E7 🔢
Cork Tree Wy CHING E4 ...... 50 E7 🔢
Corlett St CAMTN NW1 ...... 9 J2
Cormont Rd CMBW SE5 ...... 121 H6
Cormorant CI WALTH E17 ...... 68 D2
Cormorant Rd FSTGT E7 ...... 87 M5
Cornbury Rd EDGW HA8 ...... 62 D1
Cornelia St HOLWY N7 ...... 84 F6 🔢
Cornell CI SCUP DA14 ...... 162 E2
Cornell Wy CRW RM5 ...... 55 H7
Corner Gn BKHTH/KID SE3 ...... 124 A7
Corner Md CDALE/KGS NW9 ...... 63 H1
Cornerside ASHF TW15 ...... 149 J3 🔢
Corney Reach Wy CHSWK W4 ...... 117 L5
Corney Rd CHSWK W4 ...... 117 L5
Cornfield CI UX/CGN UB8 ...... 94 D1
Cornflower La CROY/NA CR0 ...... 173 K3
Cornfield Rd BUSH WD23 ...... 30 B7
Cornflower Ter EDUL SE22 ...... 140 B3
Cornflower Wy HARH RM3 ...... 74 E2
Cornford CI HAYES BR2 ...... 160 A8
Cornford Gv BAL SW12 ...... 138 B6
Cornhill BANK EC3V 13 H5
Cornhill Dr PEND EN3 ...... 37 L2 🔢
Cornish Gv PGE/AN SE20 ...... 158 B4
Cornmill La LEW SE13 ...... 123 H8
Cornmow Dr WLSDN NW10 ...... 81 M5
Cornshaw Rd BCTR RM8 ...... 90 D1
Cornthwaite Rd CLPT E5 ...... 86 C3
Cornwall Av BETH E2 ...... 104 C2 🔢
 ESH/CLAY KT10 ...... 178 F1
 FNCH N3 ...... 65 G1
 STHL UB1 ...... 96 F4
 WDGN N22 ...... 66 E2
 WELL DA16 ...... 125 L8
Cornwall CI BARK IG11 ...... 89 M6
 CHES/WCR EN8 ...... 26 E6
 EMPK RM11 ...... 75 G5 🔢
Cornwall Crs NTGHL W11 ...... 100 E6
Cornwall Dr STMC/STPC BR5 ...... 162 C3
Cornwall Gdns SKENS SW7 ...... 14 E4
 WLSDN NW10 ...... 82 B6 🔢
Cornwall Gv CHSWK W4 ...... 117 L3
Cornwall Ms South SKENS SW7 ...... 14 E4
Cornwall Ms West SKENS SW7 ...... 14 D4
Cornwall Rd BELMT SM2 ...... 181 M1
 CROY/NA CR0 ...... 172 B4
 DART DA1 ...... 128 F8
 FSBYPK N4 ...... 67 G8
 HRW HA1 ...... 61 J7
 PIN HA5 ...... 60 F1
 RSLP HA4 ...... 77 M2
 SEVS/STOTM N15 ...... 67 K6
 STHWK SE1 ...... 12 A3
 TWK TW1 ...... 134 A5 🔢
 UED N18 ...... 50 A7 🔢
 UX/CGN UB8 ...... 94 B7
Cornwall St WCHPL E1 ...... 104 B6 🔢
Cornwall Terrace Ms CAMTN NW1 ...... 9 M1
Corn Wy WAN E11 ...... 87 K3
Cornwood CI EFNCH N2 ...... 65 K6
Cornwood Dr WCHPL E1 ...... 104 C5
Cornworthy Rd BCTR RM8 ...... 90 C5
Corona Rd LEE/GVPK SE12 ...... 142 A4
Coronation CI BARK/HLT IG6 ...... 71 J5 🔢
 BXLY DA5 ...... 144 D3 🔢
Coronation Dr HCH RM12 ...... 92 B5
Coronation Rd HYS/HAR UB3 ...... 113 M2
 PLSTW E13 ...... 106 C2
 WLSDN NW10 ...... 98 F2
Coronet St IS N1 ...... 7 J8
Corporation Av HSLWW TW4 ...... 132 E1
Corporation Rw CLKNW EC1R 6 B9
Corporation St HOLWY N7 ...... 84 E5
 SRTFD E15 ...... 105 L1
Corrance Rd BRXS/STRHM SW2 ...... 138 E1
Corri Av STHGT/OAK N14 ...... 48 D6
Corrib Dr SUT SM1 ...... 170 E7 🔢
Corrigan Av COUL/CHIP CR5 ...... 183 G8
Corringham Rd GLDGN NW11 ...... 65 G8
 WBLY HA9 ...... 81 C2
Corringway EA W5 ...... 98 F4
 GLDGN NW11 ...... 65 H8
Corsair CI STWL/WRAY TW19 ...... 130 D4
Corsair Rd STWL/WRAY TW19 ...... 130 E4
Corscombe CI KUTN/CMB KT2 ...... 153 J1
Corsehill St STRHM/NOR SW16 ...... 156 C2
Corsham St IS N1 ...... 7 H8
Corsica St HBRY N5 ...... 85 H6
Cortayne Rd FUL/PGN SW6 ...... 118 F7 🔢
Cortis Rd PUT/ROE SW15 ...... 136 B3
Cortis Ter PUT/ROE SW15 ...... 136 B3
Corunna Rd VX/NE SW8 ...... 120 C6
Corunna Ter VX/NE SW8 ...... 120 C6 🔢
Corwell Gdns UX/CGN UB8 ...... 95 J5
Corwell La UX/CGN UB8 ...... 95 J5
Cosbycote Av HNHL SE24 ...... 139 J3
Cosdach Av WLGTN SM6 ...... 183 K1
Cosedge Crs CROY/NA CR0 ...... 172 A7
Cosgrove CI WCHMH N21 ...... 49 J4 🔢

YEAD UB4 ...... 96 D3 🔢
Cosmo PI RSQ WC1B 11 K2
Cosmur CI SHB W12 ...... 117 M1
Cossall Wk PECK SE15 ...... 122 B6
Cosser St STHWK SE1 ...... 18 A3
Costa St PECK SE15 ...... 122 A7
Costons Av GFD/PVL UB6 ...... 97 K2
Costons La GFD/PVL UB6 ...... 97 K2
Cotall St POP/IOD E14 ...... 105 G5
Coteford CI PIN HA5 ...... 60 A6
Coteford St TOOT SW17 ...... 137 M8
Cotelands CROY/NA CR0 ...... 172 E5
Cotesbach Rd CLPT E5 ...... 86 C3
Cotesmore Gdns BCTR RM8 ...... 90 C4
Cotford Rd THHTH CR7 ...... 157 J7
Cotham St WALW SE17 ...... 18 F6
Cotherstone
 HOR/WEW KT19 ...... 180 D2 🔢
Cotherstone Rd
 BRXS/STRHM SW2 ...... 138 F5
Cotleigh Av BXLY DA5 ...... 144 D6
Cotleigh Rd KIL/WHAMP NW6 ...... 2 A1
 ROMW/RG RM7 ...... 73 K7
Cotman CI EFNCH N2 ...... 65 J7 🔢
Cotmandene Crs
 STMC/STPC BR5 ...... 162 B5
Cotman Gdns EDGW HA8 ...... 63 G3
Cotmans CI HYS/HAR UB3 ...... 96 A7
Coton Rd WELL DA16 ...... 126 A8
Cotsford Av NWMAL KT3 ...... 153 J8
Cotswold Av BUSH WD23 ...... 43 J1
Cotswold CI BXLYHN DA7 ...... 127 L6
 ESH/CLAY KT10 ...... 166 F4
 KUTN/CMB KT2 ...... 153 J2
 STA TW18 ...... 148 A1 🔢
 UX/CGN UB8 ...... 76 C8
Cotswold Gdns CRICK NW2 ...... 82 D2
 GNTH/NBYPK IG2 ...... 71 K8
Cotswold Ga CRICK NW2 ...... 82 E1
Cotswold Gn ENC/FH EN2 ...... 35 M7 🔢
Cotswold Ri ORP BR6 ...... 176 F1 🔢
Cotswold Rd BELMT SM2 ...... 182 B3
 HARH RM3 ...... 74 F3
 HPTN TW12 ...... 151 G2
Cotswold St WNWD SE27 ...... 139 H8 🔢
 WPK KT4 ...... 169 J4
Cotswold Wy ENC/FH EN2 ...... 35 M6
Cottage Av HAYES BR2 ...... 175 L3
Cottage CI RKW/CH/CXG WD3 ...... 40 F1
 RSLP HA4 ...... 77 K1
 WAT WD17 ...... 28 F5
Cottage Field CI SCUP DA14 ...... 144 C5
Cottage Gdns CHES/WCR EN8 ...... 26 C2
Cottage Gn CMBW SE5 ...... 121 L5 🔢
Cottage Gv BRXN/ST SW9 ...... 120 E8 🔢
 CLAP SW4 ...... 120 E8
 SURB KT6 ...... 167 K1
Cottage PI SKENS SW7 ...... 15 J3
Cottage Rd HOR/WEW KT19 ...... 180 D1
Cottage St POP/IOD E14 ...... 105 H6
Cottenham Dr CDALE/KGS NW9 ...... 63 H4
 RYNPK SW20 ...... 154 B3
Cottenham Park Rd
 RYNPK SW20 ...... 154 B3 🔢
Cottenham PI RYNPK SW20 ...... 154 B3 🔢
Cottenham Rd WALTH E17 ...... 68 F5
Cotterill Rd SURB KT6 ...... 167 K4
Cottesbrook St NWCR SE14 ...... 122 E5 🔢
Cottesmore Av CLAY IG5 ...... 70 F3
Cottesmore Gdns KENS W8 ...... 14 D3
Cottimore Av WOT/HER KT12 ...... 165 H3
Cottimore Crs WOT/HER KT12 ...... 165 H2
Cottimore La WOT/HER KT12 ...... 165 J3 🔢
Cottimore Ter
 WOT/HER KT12 ...... 165 H2 🔢
Cottingham Cha RSLP HA4 ...... 78 A3
Cottingham Rd PGE/AN SE20 ...... 158 D3
 VX/NE SW8 ...... 120 F5
Cotton Av ACT W3 ...... 99 K5
Cotton CI DAGW RM9 ...... 90 C7 🔢
Cottongrass CI CROY/NA CR0 ...... 173 K3 🔢
Cotton HI BMLY BR1 ...... 141 K8
Cotton La GRH DA9 ...... 147 J2
Cotton Rd POTB/CUF EN6 ...... 23 J4
Cotton Rw BTSEA SW11 ...... 119 K8
Cottons Ap ROMW/RG RM7 ...... 73 K6
Cotton's Gdns BETH E2 ...... 7 K7
Cotton St POP/IOD E14 ...... 105 J6
Couchmore Av CLAY IG5 ...... 70 F3
 ESH/CLAY KT10 ...... 166 E4
Coulgate St BROCKY SE4 ...... 122 E8
Coulson CI BCTR RM8 ...... 90 C1 🔢
Coulson St CHEL SW3 ...... 15 L7
Coulter CI UED UB4 ...... 96 E3 🔢
Coulter Rd HMSMTH W6 ...... 118 B1
Councillor St CMBW SE5 ...... 121 J5
Countess CI DEN/HRF UB9 ...... 58 C3 🔢
Countess Rd KTTN NW5 ...... 84 C2
Countisbury Av EN EN1 ...... 49 M2
Country Wy FELT TW13 ...... 150 C1
 HNWL TW7 ...... 150 C1
County Ga CHST BR7 ...... 143 J7
 TRDG/WHET N20 ...... 47 H1
County Gv CMBW SE5 ...... 121 J6
County Rd EHAM E6 ...... 107 H4
 THHTH CR7 ...... 157 H5
County St STHWK SE1 ...... 18 F4
Coupland PI
 WOOL/PLUM SE18 ...... 125 J3 🔢
Courage CI EMPK RM11 ...... 74 C7 🔢
Courcy Rd CEND/HSY/T N8 ...... 67 G4
Courier Rd DAGW RM9 ...... 109 J3
Courland Gv VX/NE SW8 ...... 120 D6
Courland Rd VX/NE SW8 ...... 120 D6
The Course ELTH/MOT SE9 ...... 143 G7
Courtauld Rd ARCH N19 ...... 84 D1
Courtaulds CI THMD SE28 ...... 108 A7
Court Av BELV DA17 ...... 126 F3
 HARH RM3 ...... 75 G1
Court CI FELT TW13 ...... 133 H7
 KTN/HRWW/W HA3 ...... 62 A8
Court Close Av FELT TW13 ...... 133 H7
Court Crs CHSGTN KT9 ...... 167 K8
 SWLY BR8 ...... 163 L7
Court Downs Rd BECK BR3 ...... 159 H5
Court Dr CROY/NA CR0 ...... 171 M6

HGDN/ICK UB10 ...... 76 F8
 STAN HA7 ...... 44 E6
 SUT SM1 ...... 170 E6
Courtenay Av BELMT SM2 ...... 182 A2
 HGT N6 ...... 65 L8
Courtenay Dr BECK BR3 ...... 159 K5
Courtenay Gdns UPMR RM14 ...... 93 J2
Courtenay Ms WALTH E17 ...... 68 E6 🔢
Courtenay PI PGE/AN SE20 ...... 158 D2 🔢
 WALTH E17 ...... 68 D6
 WAN E11 ...... 87 M3 🔢
 WPK KT4 ...... 169 J5
Courtenay Sq LBTH SE11 ...... 18 A8 🔢
Courtenay St LBTH SE11 ...... 17 M7
Courten Ms STAN HA7 ...... 62 C1
Court Farm Av HOR/WEW KT19 ...... 168 D7
Court Farm Rd ELTH/MOT SE9 ...... 142 G7
 NTHLT UB5 ...... 79 G7
Courtfield Av HRW HA1 ...... 61 M6 🔢
Courtfield Crs HRW HA1 ...... 61 M6
Courtfield Gdns
 DEN/HRF UB9 ...... 76 A3 🔢
 ECT SW5 ...... 14 D6
 RSLP HA4 ...... 77 M2
 WEA W13 ...... 98 A5
Courtfield Ms SKENS SW7 ...... 14 E6
Courtfield Ri WWKM BR4 ...... 174 D5
Courtfield Rd ASHF TW15 ...... 149 H2
 SKENS SW7 ...... 14 E6
Court Gdns HOLWY N7 ...... 85 G6
Court Haw BNSTD SM7 ...... 182 E8
Court HI SAND/SEL CR2 ...... 184 E5
Courthill Rd LEW SE13 ...... 141 J1
Courthope Rd GFD/PVL UB6 ...... 97 K1
 HAMP NW3 ...... 83 M4
 WIM/MER SW19 ...... 154 E1
Courthope Vls WIM/MER SW19 ...... 154 E1
Court House Rd FNCH N3 ...... 47 H8
Courtland Av CHING E4 ...... 51 M4
 IL IG1 ...... 88 F2
 MLHL NW7 ...... 45 K5
 STRHM/NOR SW16 ...... 156 F5 🔢
Courtland Gv THMD SE28 ...... 108 D6
Courtland Rd EHAM E6 ...... 88 E8
Courtlands RCHPK/HAM TW10 ...... 135 C2
Courtlands Av ESH/CLAY KT10 ...... 165 M8
 HAYES BR2 ...... 174 E3
 HPTN TW12 ...... 150 F2
 LEE/GVPK SE12 ...... 142 B2
 RCH/KEW TW9 ...... 117 H7 🔢
Courtlands CI RSLP HA4 ...... 59 M8
 SAND/SEL CR2 ...... 184 F3
 WATN WD24 ...... 20 E8
Courtlands Dr HOR/WEW KT19 ...... 168 E8
Courtlands Rd BRYLDS KT5 ...... 168 A2
Court La DUL SE21 ...... 139 M4
 HOR/WEW KT19 ...... 180 C6
 IVER SL0 ...... 94 A7
Court Lane Gdns DUL SE21 ...... 139 L4
Courtleas COB KT11 ...... 178 A6
Courtleet Dr BXLYHN DA7 ...... 127 H6
Courtleigh Av EBAR EN4 ...... 34 D3
Courtleigh Gdns GLDGN NW11 ...... 64 E5
Court Md NTHLT UB5 ...... 96 F2
Courtmead CI HNHL SE24 ...... 139 J3 🔢
Courtnell St BAY/PAD W2 ...... 8 A4
Courtney Crs CAR SM5 ...... 182 F1 🔢
Courtney PI CROY/NA CR0 ...... 172 A5
 HOLWY N7 ...... 85 G3 🔢
 HTHAIR TW6 ...... 113 G8 🔢
 WIM/MER SW19 ...... 155 J3
Courtney Wy HTHAIR TW6 ...... 113 G8 🔢
Courtrai Rd BROCKY SE4 ...... 140 E3
Court Rd BNSTD SM7 ...... 182 A8
 ELTH/MOT SE9 ...... 142 F7
 HGDN/ICK UB10 ...... 77 H5
 NWDGN UB2 ...... 114 F2 🔢
 SNWD SE25 ...... 157 M5
Court Rd (Orpington By-pass)
 ORP BR6 ...... 177 H5
Courtside CEND/HSY/T N8 ...... 66 D7
Court St BMLY BR1 ...... 160 A5
 WCHPL E1 ...... 104 B4 🔢
The Court RSLP HA4 ...... 78 E4
Court Wy ACT W3 ...... 99 J4
 BARK/HLT IG6 ...... 71 J4
 CDALE/KGS NW9 ...... 63 L5
 HARH RM3 ...... 74 E3
 WHTN TW2 ...... 133 M4
The Courtway OXHEY WD19 ...... 42 E4
Court Wood La CROY/NA CR0 ...... 185 M3
Court Yd ELTH/MOT SE9 ...... 142 E3
The Courtyard IS N1 ...... 5 M1
Cousin La CANST EC4R 13 G7
Cousins CI WDR/YW UB7 ...... 94 E6 🔢
Couthurst Rd BKHTH/KID SE3 ...... 124 B4
Coutts Av CHSGTN KT9 ...... 167 L7 🔢
Coval Gdns
 MORT/ESHN SW14 ...... 135 H4 🔢
Coval La MORT/ESHN SW14 ...... 135 H1
Coval Rd MORT/ESHN SW14 ...... 135 J1
Covelees Wall EHAM E6 ...... 107 C5
Covent Gdn COVGDN WC2E 11 K6
Coventry CI EHAM E6 ...... 106 F5 🔢
 KIL/WHAMP NW6 ...... 2 B5
Coventry Rd BETH E2 ...... 104 B3 🔢
 IL IG1 ...... 89 H1
 SNWD SE25 ...... 157 H4
 WCHPL E1 ...... 104 B3 🔢
Coventry St MYFR/PICC W1J 11 G7
Coverack CI CROY/NA CR0 ...... 173 L2
 STHGT/OAK N14 ...... 48 C5
Coverdale Gdns
 CROY/NA CR0 ...... 172 F5 🔢
Coverdale Rd FBAR/BDGN N11 ...... 48 A8
 KIL/WHAMP NW6 ...... 82 E7
 SHB W12 ...... 100 B7
The Coverdales BARK IG11 ...... 107 K1
Coverley CI WCHPL E1 ...... 104 A4 🔢
Coverton Rd TOOT SW17 ...... 137 L8
Covert Rd BARK/HLT IG6 ...... 53 M8
Coverts Rd ESH/CLAY KT10 ...... 178 F1
The Covert NTHWD HA6 ...... 59 J7

ORP BR6 ...... 176 E1
Covert Wy EBAR EN4 ...... 34 C5
Covet Wood CI STMC/STPC BR5 ...... 176 F1
Covey CI WIM/MER SW19 ...... 155 H5
Covington Gdns
 STRHM/NOR SW16 ...... 157 H3
Covington Wy
 STRHM/NOR SW16 ...... 157 H3 🔢
Cowbridge La BARK IG11 ...... 89 H7
Cowbridge Rd
 KTN/HRWW/W HA3 ...... 62 F5
Cowcross St FARR EC1M 12 C2
Cowden Rd ORP BR6 ...... 176 F2
Cowden St CAT SE6 ...... 141 G8
Cowdray Rd HGDN/ICK UB10 ...... 77 J8
Cowdray Wy HCH RM12 ...... 92 A4
Cowdrey CI EN EN1 ...... 36 E5
Cowdrey Ct DART DA1 ...... 146 B4
Cowdrey Rd WIM/MER SW19 ...... 155 H2
Cowen Av HRW/HDSTN HA2 ...... 79 K2
Cowgate Rd GFD/PVL UB6 ...... 97 K2
Cowick Rd TOOT SW17 ...... 137 M8
Cowings Md NTHLT UB5 ...... 78 E7
Cowland Av PEND EN3 ...... 37 J7
Cow La BUSH WD23 ...... 43 G1 🔢
 GSTN WD25 ...... 29 J1
Cow Leaze EHAM E6 ...... 107 G5 🔢
Cowleaze Rd KUTN/CMB KT2 ...... 152 E4 🔢
Cowley Av GRH DA9 ...... 147 M2
Cowley CI SAND/SEL CR2 ...... 185 J2
Cowley Crs UX/CGN UB8 ...... 94 C4
 WOT/HER KT12 ...... 165 J6
Cowley La BORE WD6 ...... 32 B2
Cowley Mill Rd UX/CGN UB8 ...... 94 B1
Cowley PI HDN NW4 ...... 64 C6
Cowley Rd ACT W3 ...... 99 M7
 BRXN/ST SW9 ...... 121 G5 🔢
 HARH RM3 ...... 74 B1
 IL IG1 ...... 70 F8
 MORT/ESHN SW14 ...... 117 L8
 UX/CGN UB8 ...... 94 C2 🔢
 UX/CGN UB8 ...... 94 C2 🔢
 UX/CGN UB8 ...... 94 C3 🔢
 UX/CGN UB8 ...... 94 C1 🔢
 WAN E11 ...... 70 B6
Cowley St WEST SW1P 17 J4
Cowling CI NTGHL W11 ...... 100 E6
Cowper Av EHAM E6 ...... 88 E7
 SUT SM1 ...... 170 D6
Cowper CI HAYES BR2 ...... 160 D7
 WELL DA16 ...... 144 A2
Cowper Ct WATN WD24 ...... 29 G2 🔢
Cowper Gdns STHGT/OAK N14 ...... 48 C1
 WLGTN SM6 ...... 171 J8
Cowper Rd ACT W3 ...... 99 K7
 BELV DA17 ...... 126 F2
 HAYES BR2 ...... 160 D7
 HNWL W7 ...... 97 M6
 RAIN RM13 ...... 110 A3
 RCHPK/HAM TW10 ...... 152 F1
 STHGT/OAK N14 ...... 48 B3
 STNW/STAM N16 ...... 86 A3
 UED N18 ...... 50 A7
 WIM/MER SW19 ...... 155 J2
Cowper St STLK EC1Y 7 H9
Cowslip CI HGDN/ICK UB10 ...... 76 E7
Cowslip Rd SWFD E18 ...... 53 G1
Cowthorpe Rd VX/NE SW8 ...... 120 D6 🔢
Coxe PI KTN/HRWW/W HA3 ...... 62 A5
Cox La CHSGTN KT9 ...... 167 M6
 HOR/WEW KT19 ...... 168 B7
Coxley Ri PUR/KEN CR8 ...... 184 C6
Coxmount Rd CHARL SE7 ...... 124 D3
Coxs Av SHPTN TW17 ...... 149 L6 🔢
Coxson Wy STHWK SE1 ...... 19 L2
Coxtie Green Rd BRW CM14 ...... 57 G1
Coxwell Rd NRWD SE19 ...... 157 L3
 WOOL/PLUM SE18 ...... 125 K3
Crabbs Croft CI ORP BR6 ...... 176 C7 🔢
Crab HI BECK BR3 ...... 159 K3
Crabtree Av ALP/SUD HA0 ...... 98 E1
 CHDH RM6 ...... 72 D5
Crabtree CI BETH E2 ...... 7 L6
 BUSH WD23 ...... 30 B8
Crabtree La FUL/PGN SW6 ...... 118 D5
Crabtree Manorway North
 BELV DA17 ...... 109 J8
Crabtree Manorway South
 BELV DA17 ...... 109 J8
Craddock Rd EN EN1 ...... 36 F6
Craddock St CAMTN NW1 ...... 84 A6 🔢
Cradley Rd ELTH/MOT SE9 ...... 143 K5
Cragg Av RAD WD7 ...... 30 F1
Craigdale Rd ROM RM1 ...... 73 M7
Craigen Av CROY/NA CR0 ...... 173 H3
Craigerne Rd BKHTH/KID SE3 ...... 124 B5
Craig Gdns SWFD E18 ...... 69 M3
Craigholm WOOL/PLUM SE18 ...... 125 G7
Craigmuir Pk ALP/SUD HA0 ...... 80 F8
Craignair Rd BRXS/STRHM SW2 ...... 138 C4
Craigish Av STRHM/NOR SW16 ...... 156 F5
Craig Park Rd UED N18 ...... 50 B7 🔢
Craig Rd RCHPK/HAM TW10 ...... 134 C8
 UX/CGN UB8 ...... 95 H5
Craig's Ct WHALL SW1A 11 J8
Craigs Wk CHES/WCR EN8 ...... 26 D1
Craigton Rd ELTH/MOT SE9 ...... 142 F1
Craigweil CI STAN HA7 ...... 44 D7
Craigweil Dr STAN HA7 ...... 44 D7
Craigwell Av FELT TW13 ...... 132 A7
Crail Rw WALW SE17 ...... 19 H6
Cramer St MHST W1U 10 B3
Crammond CI HMSMTH W6 ...... 118 E4 🔢
Crampton Rd PGE/AN SE20 ...... 158 C2
Crampton St WALW SE17 ...... 18 E7
Cranberry CI NTHLT UB5 ...... 96 D1 🔢
Cranberry La CAN/RD E16 ...... 105 L3 🔢
 SURB KT6 ...... 168 A5
Cranborne Av NWDGN UB2 ...... 115 G2
 SURB KT6 ...... 168 A5
Cranborne Crs POTB/CUF EN6 ...... 22 E3
Cranborne Gdns UPMR RM14 ...... 93 H2
Cranborne Rd BARK IG11 ...... 89 K8
 CHES/WCR EN8 ...... 26 D5 🔢
 POTB/CUF EN6 ...... 22 E3
Cranborne Waye YEAD UB4 ...... 96 C6
Cranbourne Av WAN E11 ...... 70 B5

Cranbourne CI
 STRHM/NOR SW16 ...... 156 E6 🔢
Cranbourne Dr PIN HA5 ...... 60 D6
Cranbourne Rd BARK/HLT IG6 ...... 71 J4 🔢
 GLDGN NW11 ...... 64 F2 🔢
Cranbourne Rd MNPK E12 ...... 88 E5 🔢
 MUSWH N10 ...... 66 B4
 NTHWD HA6 ...... 59 M4
 SRTFD E15 ...... 87 J4
Cranburn St LSQ/SEVD WC2H ...... 11 D1 🔢
Cranbrook CI HAYES BR2 ...... 175 G1
Cranbrook Dr ESH/CLAY KT10 ...... 166 C3
 GPK RM2 ...... 74 B5
 WHTN TW2 ...... 133 H5 🔢
Cranbrook Ms WALTH E17 ...... 68 F6
Cranbrook Pk WDGN N22 ...... 67 G2
Cranbrook Ri IL IG1 ...... 70 F7
Cranbrook Rd BARK/HLT IG6 ...... 71 H5
 BXLYHN DA7 ...... 126 F6
 CHSWK W4 ...... 117 L3
 DEPT SE8 ...... 123 G6 🔢
 EBAR EN4 ...... 47 K1
 HSLWW TW4 ...... 132 F1
 IL IG1 ...... 71 G8
 THHTH CR7 ...... 157 J5
 WIM/MER SW19 ...... 154 E3
Cranbrook St BETH E2 ...... 104 D1 🔢
Cranbury Rd FUL/PGN SW6 ...... 119 H7
Crane Av ACT W3 ...... 99 J6 🔢
 ISLW TW7 ...... 134 A2
Cranebrook WHTN TW2 ...... 133 J6 🔢
Crane CI DAGE RM10 ...... 91 G6
Cranefield Dr GSTN WD25 ...... 21 L5
Craneford CI WHTN TW2 ...... 133 M4
Craneford Wy WHTN TW2 ...... 133 L4
Crane Gdns HYS/HAR UB3 ...... 113 M2
Crane Gv HOLWY N7 ...... 85 G6 🔢
Crane Lodge Rd HEST TW5 ...... 114 B4
Crane Md BERM/RHTH SE16 ...... 122 D2
Crane Park Rd WHTN TW2 ...... 133 H6
Crane Rd STWL/WRAY TW19 ...... 131 G3
 WHTN TW2 ...... 133 L5
Cranes Dr BRYLDS KT5 ...... 152 E7
Cranes Pk SURB KT6 ...... 152 E7
Cranes Park Av SURB KT6 ...... 152 E7
Cranes Park Crs BRYLDS KT5 ...... 152 F7
Crane St PECK SE15 ...... 121 M6 🔢
Craneswater HYS/HAR UB3 ...... 113 M5
Craneswater Pk NWDGN UB2 ...... 114 F3
Cranes Wy BORE WD6 ...... 32 C8
Crane Wy WHTN TW2 ...... 133 J4
Cranfield Crs POTB/CUF EN6 ...... 24 E2
Cranfield Dr CDALE/KGS NW9 ...... 63 L1
Cranfield Rd BROCKY SE4 ...... 122 F8
Cranfield Rd East CAR SM5 ...... 182 F2 🔢
Cranfield Rd West CAR SM5 ...... 182 F2 🔢
Cranford Av PLMGR N13 ...... 48 E7
 STWL/WRAY TW19 ...... 130 E4
Cranford CI PUR/KEN CR8 ...... 184 C6 🔢
 RYNPK SW20 ...... 154 B4 🔢
 STWL/WRAY TW19 ...... 130 E4
Cranford Dr HYS/HAR UB3 ...... 113 M2
Cranford La HEST TW5 ...... 114 D5
 HTHAIR TW6 ...... 113 M8
 HYS/HAR UB3 ...... 113 K4
Cranford Park Rd
 HYS/HAR UB3 ...... 113 M2 🔢
Cranford Ri ESH/CLAY KT10 ...... 166 C7
Cranford Rd DART DA1 ...... 146 E3
Cranford St WAP E1W ...... 104 D6 🔢
Cranford Wy CEND/HSY/T N8 ...... 66 F6
Cranham Gdns UPMR RM14 ...... 75 M8
Cranham Rd EMPK RM11 ...... 74 B7
Cranhurst Rd CRICK NW2 ...... 82 C5
Cranleigh CI BXLY DA5 ...... 145 K3
 CHESW EN7 ...... 26 A1
 ORP BR6 ...... 177 G5
 PGE/AN SE20 ...... 158 B5
 SAND/SEL CR2 ...... 185 G5
Cranleigh Dr SWLY BR8 ...... 163 G4
Cranleigh Gdns BARK IG11 ...... 89 K7
 KTN/HRWW/W HA3 ...... 62 B6
 KUTN/CMB KT2 ...... 152 F2
 LOU IG10 ...... 52 F1 🔢
 SAND/SEL CR2 ...... 185 G5
 SNWD SE25 ...... 157 L6 🔢
 STHL UB1 ...... 96 F5
 SUT SM1 ...... 170 B4
 WCHMH N21 ...... 36 A8
Cranleigh Ms BTSEA SW11 ...... 119 L7
Cranleigh Rd ESH/CLAY KT10 ...... 166 C3
 FELT TW13 ...... 131 M8
 SEVS/STOTM N15 ...... 67 J6
 WIM/MER SW19 ...... 155 G6
Cranleigh St CAMTN NW1 ...... 4 F6
Cranley Dr GNTH/NBYPK IG2 ...... 71 J8
 RSLP HA4 ...... 77 M2
Cranley Gdns CHEL SW3 ...... 15 G7
 MUSWH N10 ...... 66 B6
 PLMGR N13 ...... 48 F5
 SKENS SW7 ...... 14 F7
 WLGTN SM6 ...... 183 J1
Cranley Ms SKENS SW7 ...... 14 F7
Cranley PI SKENS SW7 ...... 15 G6
Cranley Rd GNTH/NBYPK IG2 ...... 71 J8
 PLSTW E13 ...... 106 F4 🔢
 WOT/HER KT12 ...... 164 F8
Cranmer Av WEA W13 ...... 116 B1
Cranmer CI MRDN SM4 ...... 169 K1
 POTB/CUF EN6 ...... 23 J3
 RSLP HA4 ...... 78 D1 🔢
 STAN HA7 ...... 62 C1
Cranmer Ct HPTN TW12 ...... 151 H1
Cranmer Farm CI MTCM CR4 ...... 155 M7 🔢
Cranmer Gdns DAGE RM10 ...... 91 J4
Cranmer Rd BRXN/ST SW9 ...... 121 G5
 CROY/NA CR0 ...... 172 B5
 EDGW HA8 ...... 45 H5
 FSTGT E7 ...... 88 B1
 HPTN TW12 ...... 151 H1
 HYS/HAR UB3 ...... 95 K5
 KUTN/CMB KT2 ...... 152 E1
 MTCM CR4 ...... 155 M7
Cranmer Ter TOOT SW17 ...... 155 K1
Cranmore Rd BMLY BR1 ...... 141 K7
 CHST BR7 ...... 160 F1
Cranston CI HGDN/ICK UB10 ...... 77 J2
 HSLW TW3 ...... 114 E7

Cranston Gdns CHING E4 ... 51 H8
Cranston Park Av UPMR RM14 ... 93 J4
Cranston Rd FSTH SE23 ... 140 E5
Cranswick Rd
　BERM/RHTH SE16 ... 122 B3
Crantock Rd CAT SE6 ... 141 H5
Cranwell Cl BOW E3 ... 105 H3
Cranwell Gv SHPTN TW17 ... 148 F7
Cranwich Av NFNCH N2 ... 49 K2
Cranwich Rd STNW/STAM N16 ... 67 L8
Cranwood St FSBYE EC1V ... 7 H8
Cranworth Crs CHING E4 ... 51 K3
Cranworth Gdns BRXN/ST SW9 ... 121 C6
Craster Rd BRXS/STRHM SW2 ... 138 F4
Crathie Rd LEE/GVPK SE12 ... 142 B3
Cravan Av FELT TW13 ... 132 A6
Craven Av WEA W13 ... 98 C6
Craven Cl YEAD UB4 ... 96 A5
Craven Gdns BARK IG11 ... 107 L1
　BARK/HLT IG6 ... 71 K3
　CRW RM5 ... 55 C7
　HARH RM3 ... 57 J8
　WIM/MER SW19 ... 155 H1
Craven HI BAY/PAD W2 ... 8 E6
Craven Hill Gdns BAY/PAD W2 ... 8 E6
Craven Hill Ms BAY/PAD W2 ... 8 E6
Craven Ms BTSEA SW11 ... 120 A8
Craven Pk WLSDN NW10 ... 81 L8
Craven Park Ms WLSDN NW10 ... 81 L7
Craven Park Rd
　STNW/STAM N16 ... 67 M7
　WLSDN NW10 ... 81 L8
Craven Rd BAY/PAD W2 ... 8 F6
　CROY/NA CR0 ... 173 H3
　KUTN/CMB KT2 ... 152 F4
　ORP BR6 ... 177 K5
　WEA W13 ... 98 C6
　WLSDN NW10 ... 81 K8
Craven St CHCR WC2N ... 11 K8
Craven Ter BAY/PAD W2 ... 8 F6
Craven Wk CLPT E5 ... 68 A8
Crawford Av ALP/SUD HA0 ... 80 D5
Crawford Cl ISLW TW7 ... 115 L7
Crawford Gdns GFD/PVL UB6 ... 96 F2
　PLMGR N13 ... 49 H5
Crawford Pas CLKNW EC1R ... 12 A1
Crawford Pl BAY/PAD W2 ... 9 K4
Crawford Rd CMBW SE5 ... 121 J7
Crawfords SWLY BR8 ... 163 L3
Crawford St MBLAR W1H ... 9 L3
Crawley Rd EN EN1 ... 49 L2
　LEY E10 ... 87 H1
　WDGN N22 ... 67 J3
Craword Compton Cl
　HCH RM12 ... 92 C6
Crawthew Gv EDUL SE22 ... 139 M1
Cray Av STMC/STPC BR5 ... 162 B8
Craybrooke Rd SCUP DA14 ... 144 B8
Craybury End ELTH/MOT SE9 ... 143 J6
Cray Cl DART DA1 ... 146 A2
Craydene Rd ERITH DA8 ... 127 M6
Crayford High St DART DA1 ... 145 L1
Crayford Rd DART DA1 ... 145 M2
　HOLWY N7 ... 84 E4
Crayford Wy DART DA1 ... 146 A1
Crayke HI CHSGTN KT9 ... 179 L1
Craylands STMC/STPC BR5 ... 162 C6
Cray Rd BELV DA17 ... 127 G4
　SCUP DA14 ... 162 C2
Cray Valley Rd STMC/STPC BR5 ... 162 A8
Crealock Gv WFD IG8 ... 51 M7
Crealock St WAND/EARL SW18 ... 137 K3
Creasey Cl HCH RM12 ... 92 B2
Crebor St EDUL SE22 ... 140 A3
Credenhall Dr HAYES BR2 ... 175 M3
Credenhill St
　STRHM/NOR SW16 ... 156 C2
Crediton HI KIL/WHAMP NW6 ... 83 H5
Crediton Rd WLSDN NW10 ... 82 D8
Crediton Wy ESH/CLAY KT10 ... 167 G7
Credon Rd BERM/RHTH SE16 ... 122 B3
　PLSTW E13 ... 89 H6
Creechurch La HDTCH EC3A ... 13 K4
Creechurch Pl HDTCH EC3A ... 13 K4
Creed La BLKFR EC4V ... 12 D5
Creek Rd BARK IG11 ... 107 M2
　DEPT SE8 ... 123 C4
　E/WMO/HCT KT8 ... 151 L7
　GNWCH SE10 ... 123 J4
Creekside DEPT SE8 ... 123 G5
　RAIN RM13 ... 109 M3
The Creek SUN TW16 ... 150 A8
Creeland Gv CAT SE6 ... 140 F5
Cree Wy ROM RM1 ... 73 L1
Crefeld Cl FUL/PGN SW6 ... 118 D4
Creffield Rd ACT W3 ... 99 C6
Creighton Av EFNCH N2 ... 65 M3
　EHAM E6 ... 106 D1
Creighton Rd EA W5 ... 116 D1
　KIL/WHAMP NW6 ... 100 D1
　TOTM N17 ... 67 L1
Creigton Av EFNCH N2 ... 65 L4
Cremer St BETH E2 ... 7 L6
Cremorne Gdns
　HOR/WEW KT19 ... 180 D2
Cremorne Rd WBPTN SW10 ... 119 J5
Crescent Av HCH RM12 ... 91 M2
Crescent Dr STMC/STPC BR5 ... 176 C1
Crescent East EBAR EN4 ... 34 C3
Crescent Gdns RSLP HA4 ... 60 B8
　SWLY BR8 ... 163 J5
　WIM/MER SW19 ... 137 G7
Crescent Gv CLAP SW4 ... 138 C1
　MTCM CR4 ... 155 L7
Crescent La CLAP SW4 ... 138 D2
Crescent Pl CHEL SW3 ... 15 J5
Crescent Ri EBAR EN4 ... 34 E8
　WDGN N22 ... 66 D2
Crescent Rd BECK BR3 ... 159 H5
　BFN/LL DA15 ... 143 M7
　BMLY BR1 ... 160 A3
　CEND/HSY/T N8 ... 66 D7
　CHING E4 ... 51 L2
　DAGE RM10 ... 92 H4
　EBAR EN4 ... 34 D7
　EBAR EN4 ... 47 L1
　ED N9 ... 50 A3
　ENC/FH EN2 ... 36 B7

ERITH DA8 ... 127 M4
FBAR/BDGN N11 ... 47 M6
FNCH N3 ... 64 F2
KUTN/CMB KT2 ... 153 G3
LEY E10 ... 87 H2
PLSTW E13 ... 88 A8
RYNPK SW20 ... 154 D4
SEVS/STOTM N15 ... 67 H4
SHPTN TW17 ... 149 J6
SOCK/AV RM15 ... 111 J8
SWFD IG8 ... 70 C2
WDGN N22 ... 66 D2
WOOL/PLUM SE18 ... 125 H3
Crescent Rw STLK EC1Y ... 12 E1
Crescent St IS N1 ... 5 M1
The Crescent ABLGY WD5 ... 20 F3
　ACT W3 ... 99 G5
　ALP/SUD HA0 ... 80 B2
　ASHF TW15 ... 148 F1
　BAR EN5 ... 34 B6
　BARN SW13 ... 117 M7
　BECK BR3 ... 159 G4
　BELMT SM2 ... 182 A4
　BXLY DA5 ... 144 C4
　CHERT KT16 ... 148 A6
　CRICK NW2 ... 82 B3
　E/WMO/HCT KT8 ... 150 F7
　EPSOM KT18 ... 180 A8
　FBAR/BDGN N11 ... 47 M6
　GNTH/NBYPK IG2 ... 71 C7
　GSTN WD25 ... 30 B3
　HYS/HAR UB3 ... 113 J5
　LOU IG10 ... 52 D1
　NWDGN UB2 ... 96 B5
　NWMAL KT3 ... 153 J5
　RKW/CH/CXG WD3 ... 41 H1
　RYLN/HDSTN HA2 ... 79 J1
　SCUP DA14 ... 143 M8
　SHPTN TW17 ... 164 F2
　SNWD SE25 ... 172 D1
　STHL UB1 ... 96 F8
　SURB KT6 ... 152 E8
　SUT SM1 ... 170 D7
　UPMR RM14 ... 75 L8
　WALTH E17 ... 68 E6
　WAT WD17 ... 29 J7
　WEY KT13 ... 164 A5
　WIM/MER SW19 ... 137 G7
　WWKM BR4 ... 174 E1
Crescent Vw LOU IG10 ... 52 D1
Crescent Wk SOCK/AV RM15 ... 111 J8
Crescent Wy BROCKY SE4 ... 123 G8
Crescentway NFNCH/WDSP N12 ... 47 L8
Crescent Wy ORP BR6 ... 176 E7
　SOCK/AV RM15 ... 111 K7
　STRHM/NOR SW16 ... 156 F3
Crescent West EBAR EN4 ... 34 C3
Crescent Wood Rd DUL SE21 ... 140 A7
Cresford Rd FUL/PGN SW6 ... 119 H6
Crespigny Rd HDN NW4 ... 64 B7
Cressage Cl STHL UB1 ... 97 G3
Cress End RKW/CH/CXG WD3 ... 40 A3
Cresset St HOM E9 ... 86 C6
Cresset St CLAP SW4 ... 120 D8
Cressfield Cl KTTN NW5 ... 84 A5
Cressida Rd ARCH N19 ... 84 C1
Cressingham Gv SUT SM1 ... 170 C6
Cressingham Rd EDGW HA8 ... 45 K8
　EDGW HA8 ... 63 K1
　LEW SE13 ... 123 J8
Cressington Cl
　STNW/STAM N16 ... 85 L5
Cresswell Gdns ECT SW5 ... 14 E7
Cresswell Pk BKHTH/KID SE3 ... 123 M8
Cresswell Pl ECT SW5 ... 14 E7
Cresswell Rd FELT TW13 ... 132 E7
　SNWD SE25 ... 158 A4
　TWK TW1 ... 134 D3
Cresswell Wy WCHMH N21 ... 49 G2
Cressy Ct HMSMTH W6 ... 118 B1
Cressy Pl WCHPL E1 ... 104 C4
Cressy Rd HAMP NW3 ... 83 M4
Crestbrook Av PLMGR N13 ... 49 H5
Crest Dr PEND EN3 ... 37 J3
Crestfield St CAMTN NW1 ... 5 K7
Crest Gdns RSLP HA4 ... 78 C3
Creston Wy WPK KT4 ... 169 K3
Crest Rd CRICK NW2 ... 82 A2
　HAYES BR2 ... 174 F2
　SAND/SEL CR2 ... 185 H1
The Crest BRYLDS KT5 ... 153 G8
　HDN NW4 ... 64 C6
　PLMGR N13 ... 49 G6
Crest Vw PIN HA5 ... 60 D5
Crest View Dr STMC/STPC BR5 ... 161 H8
Crestway PUT/ROE SW15 ... 136 K3
Crestwood Wy HSLWW TW4 ... 132 F2
Creswick Rd ACT W3 ... 99 H6
Creswick Wk GLDGN NW11 ... 64 F5
Crewdson Rd BRXN/ST SW9 ... 120 F5
Crewe Pl WLSDN NW10 ... 99 M2
Crews St POP/IOD E14 ... 123 C2
Crewys Rd CRICK NW2 ... 82 F2
　PECK SE15 ... 122 B7
Crichton Av WLGTN SM6 ... 171 K7
Crichton Rd CAR SM5 ... 183 J5
Crichton St VX/NE SW8 ... 120 C7
Cricketers Arms Rd
　ENC/FH EN2 ... 36 C5
Cricketers Cl CHSGTN KT9 ... 167 K7
　ERITH DA8 ... 127 L3
　STHGT/OAK N14 ... 48 C2
Cricketers Wk SYD SE26 ... 158 C1
Cricketfield Rd CLPT E5 ... 86 B4
Cricketfield Rd WDR/YW UB7 ... 112 C2
Cricket Gn MTCM CR4 ... 155 M6
Cricket Ground Rd CHST BR7 ... 161 H4
Cricket La BECK BR3 ... 158 E5
Cricket Vw WEY KT13 ... 164 B7
Cricket Wy WEY KT13 ... 164 E4
Cricklade Av BRXS/STRHM SW2 ... 138 E6
　HARH RM3 ... 56 D8
Cricklewood Broadway
　CRICK NW2 ... 82 C3
Cricklewood La CRICK NW2 ... 82 E4
Cridland St SRTFD E15 ... 87 M8
Crieff Rd WAND/EARL SW18 ... 137 J3

Criffel Av BRXS/STRHM SW2 ... 138 D6
Crimscott St STHWK SE1 ... 19 K4
Crimsworth Rd VX/NE SW8 ... 120 D6
Crinan St IS N1 ... 5 K5
Cringle St VX/NE SW8 ... 120 C5
Cripplegate St BARB EC2Y ... 12 E2
Crispen Rd FELT TW13 ... 132 E8
Crispian Cl WLSDN NW10 ... 81 L4
Crispin Crs WLGTN SM6 ... 171 K5
Crispin Rd EDGW HA8 ... 45 J8
Crispin St WCHPL E1 ... 13 L3
Crisp Rd HMSMTH W6 ... 118 C3
Cristowe Rd FUL/PGN SW6 ... 118 F7
Criterion Ms ARCH N19 ... 84 D2
Cricketers Ms
　WAND/EARL SW18 ... 137 H2
Crockenhill HI STMC/STPC BR5 ... 162 D8
Crockenhill Rd STMC/STPC BR5 ... 177 K1
Crockerton Rd TOOT SW17 ... 137 M6
Crockham Wy ELTH/MOT SE9 ... 143 G8
Crocus Cl CROY/NA CR0 ... 173 K5
Crocus Fld BAR EN5 ... 46 F1
Croft Av WWKM BR4 ... 174 C3
Croft Cl BELV DA17 ... 126 F3
　CHST BR7 ... 160 F1
　HGDN/ICK UB10 ... 77 C7
　HYS/HAR UB3 ... 113 J5
　MLHL NW7 ... 45 L5
Croftdown Rd KTTN NW5 ... 84 A3
Crofters Cl ISLW TW7 ... 133 K2
Crofters Rd NTHWD HA6 ... 41 L6
Crofters Wy CAMTN NW1 ... 5 G3
Croft Gdns HNWL W7 ... 98 A8
　RSLP HA4 ... 77 L1
Croft Lodge Cl WFD IG8 ... 52 B8
Croft Ms NFNCH/WDSP N12 ... 47 J5
The Crofts SHPTN TW17 ... 149 L7
Croft St DEPT SE8 ... 122 E2
　WCHPL E1 ... 104 A6
The Croft ALP/SUD HA0 ... 80 C5
　BAR EN5 ... 33 L7
　CHING E4 ... 51 L4
　EA W5 ... 98 E4
　HEST TW5 ... 114 E5
　RSLP HA4 ... 78 C4
　SWLY BR8 ... 163 J6
　WLSDN NW10 ... 99 M1
Croft Wy BFN/LL DA15 ... 143 L7
　RCHPK/HAM TW10 ... 134 B7
Crogsland Rd CAMTN NW1 ... 4 A1
Croham Cl SAND/SEL CR2 ... 172 E8
Croham Manor Rd
　SAND/SEL CR2 ... 184 E1
Croham Mt SAND/SEL CR2 ... 184 E1
Croham Park Av SAND/SEL CR2 ... 172 F7
Croham Rd SAND/SEL CR2 ... 172 E7
Croham Valley Rd
　SAND/SEL CR2 ... 173 G8
Croindene Rd
　STRHM/NOR SW16 ... 156 E4
Cromartie Rd ARCH N19 ... 66 D8
Cromarty Rd EDGW HA8 ... 45 H4
Crombie Cl REDBR IG4 ... 70 F6
Crombie Ms BTSEA SW11 ... 119 L7
Crombie Rd BFN/LL DA15 ... 143 K5
Cromer Cl UX/CGN UB8 ... 95 J5
Cromer Rd BAR EN5 ... 34 C7
　CHDH RM6 ... 72 E7
　EMPK RM11 ... 74 D8
　HTHAIR TW6 ... 113 G8
　LEY E10 ... 69 K8
　ROMW/RG RM7 ... 73 J7
　SNWD SE25 ... 158 B6
　TOOT SW17 ... 156 A2
　TOTM N17 ... 68 A3
　WATN WD24 ... 29 J3
Cromer St STPAN WC1H ... 5 K8
Cromer Villas Rd
　WAND/EARL SW18 ... 136 F3
Cromford Cl ORP BR6 ... 176 E5
Cromford Rd PUT/ROE SW15 ... 136 F2
Cromford Wy NWMAL KT3 ... 153 K4
Cromlix Cl CHST BR7 ... 161 H5
Crompton St BAY/PAD W2 ... 9 G1
Cromwell Av CHESW EN7 ... 26 B3
　HAYES BR2 ... 160 B6
　HGT N6 ... 84 B1
　HMSMTH W6 ... 118 B3
　NWMAL KT3 ... 153 M8
Cromwell Cl EFNCH N2 ... 65 K3
　WOT/HER KT12 ... 165 H3
Cromwell Ct ALP/SUD HA0 ... 98 E1
Cromwell Crs ECT SW5 ... 14 A5
Cromwell Gv HMSMTH W6 ... 118 C1
Cromwell Ms SKENS SW7 ... 15 H5
Cromwell Pl ACT W3 ... 99 J7
　HGT N6 ... 84 B1
　MORT/ESHN SW14 ... 117 J8
　SKENS SW7 ... 15 H5
Cromwell Rd ALP/SUD HA0 ... 98 D1
　BECK BR3 ... 158 E5
　BORE WD6 ... 31 L4
　BRXN/ST SW9 ... 121 H6
　CROY/NA CR0 ... 172 D2
　FELT TW13 ... 132 B5
　FNCH N3 ... 65 J3
　FSTGT E7 ... 88 D7
　HSLW TW3 ... 133 G1
　HYS/HAR UB3 ... 95 K5

Crouch HI ARCH N19 ... 66 E8
Crouchmans Cl DUL SE21 ... 139 M1
Crouch Rd WLSDN NW10 ... 81 K7
Crouch Va UPMR RM14 ... 75 L8
Crowborough Pth
　OXHEY WD19 ... 42 D6
Crowborough Rd TOOT SW17 ... 156 A1
Crowden Wy THMD SE28 ... 108 C6
Crowder St WCHPL E1 ... 104 B6
Crowfoot Cl HOM E9 ... 86 F5
Crowhurst Cl BRXN/ST SW9 ... 121 C2
Crowhurst Wy STMC/STPC BR5 ... 162 C8
Crowland Av HYS/HAR UB3 ... 113 J2
Crowland Gdns STHGT/OAK N14 ... 48 E2
Crowland Rd SEVS/STOTM N15 ... 67 M6
　THHTH CR7 ... 157 K7
Crowlands Av ROMW/RG RM7 ... 73 H7
Crowland Ter IS N1 ... 7 G1
Crowland Wk MRDN SM4 ... 170 B1
Crow La ROMW/RG RM7 ... 72 F8
　ROMW/RG RM7 ... 73 J8
Crowley Crs CROY/NA CR0 ... 172 A7
Crown Cl BOW E3 ... 87 C8
　HYS/HAR UB3 ... 95 M8
　KIL/WHAMP NW6 ... 83 H6
　MLHL NW7 ... 45 M4
　ORP BR6 ... 177 G6
　WOT/HER KT12 ... 165 J2
Crown Dl NRWD SE19 ... 157 J2
Crowndale Rd CAMTN NW1 ... 4 F5
Crownfield Av GNTH/NBYPK IG2 ... 71 L4
Crownfield Rd SRTFD E15 ... 87 K5
Crownhill Rd WFD IG8 ... 70 E1
　WLSDN NW10 ... 81 M8
Crown La CHST BR7 ... 161 J4
　HAYES BR2 ... 160 D8
　MRDN SM4 ... 155 G6
　STHGT/OAK N14 ... 48 C3
　STRHM/NOR SW16 ... 157 C1
　WIM/MER SW19 ... 155 G6
Crown Lane Sp HAYES BR2 ... 175 K1
Crown Office Rw EMB EC4Y ... 12 A6
Crown Pas STJS SW1Y ... 10 F7
Crown Pl KTTN NW5 ... 84 B2
Crown Ri GSTN WD25 ... 21 J7
Crown Rd BARK/HLT IG6 ... 71 K5
　BORE WD6 ... 32 A4
　EN N1 ... 37 G6
　MUSWH N10 ... 66 A1
　NWMAL KT3 ... 153 J4
　ORP BR6 ... 177 G7
　RSLP HA4 ... 78 D5
　SUT SM1 ... 170 B6
　TWK TW1 ... 134 B3
　WIM/MER SW19 ... 155 G7
Crownstone Rd
　BRXS/STRHM SW2 ... 139 G2
Crown St ACT W3 ... 99 H7
　CMBW SE5 ... 121 J5
　DAGE RM10 ... 91 M6
　RYLN/HDSTN HA2 ... 60 B8
Crown Ter RCH/KEW TW9 ... 134 F1
Crowntree Cl ISLW TW7 ... 115 M4
Crown Wk WBLY HA9 ... 80 F3
Crown Wy WDR/YW UB7 ... 94 F7
Crown Woods Wy
　ELTH/MOT SE9 ... 143 K2
Crown Yd HSLW TW3 ... 115 J8
Crowshott Av STAN HA7 ... 62 C3
Crows Rd BARK IG11 ... 89 H6
　SRTFD E15 ... 105 K2
Crowther Av BTFD TW8 ... 116 E3
Crowther Rd SNWD SE25 ... 158 A7
Crowthorne Cl
　WAND/EARL SW18 ... 136 F4
Crowthorne Rd NKENS W10 ... 100 D5
Croxdale Rd BORE WD6 ... 31 M5
Croxden Cl EDGW HA8 ... 63 G4
Croxden Wk MRDN SM4 ... 170 C1
Croxford Gdns WDGN N22 ... 67 H1
Croxford Wy ROMW/RG RM7 ... 91 K1
Croxley Cl STMC/STPC BR5 ... 162 B5
Croxley Gn STMC/STPC BR5 ... 162 B4
Croxley Rd MV/WKIL W9 ... 100 F2
Croxley Vw WATW WD18 ... 41 L1
Croxted Cl DUL SE21 ... 139 J4
Croxted Rd DUL SE21 ... 139 K6
Croyde Av GFD/PVL UB6 ... 97 J2
　HYS/HAR UB3 ... 113 L2
Croyde Cl ELTH/MOT SE9 ... 143 K4
The Croydon F/O CROY/NA CR0 ... 172 B6
Croydon Gv CROY/NA CR0 ... 172 B3
Croydon La BNSTD SM7 ... 182 D6
Croydon La South BNSTD SM7 ... 182 B7
Croydon Rd BECK BR3 ... 158 E6
　CROY/NA CR0 ... 158 D8
　CROY/NA CR0 ... 171 L6
　MTCM CR4 ... 156 B8
　PGE/AN SE20 ... 158 B5
　PLSTW E13 ... 106 A3
　WLGTN SM6 ... 171 K5
　WWKM BR4 ... 174 E5
Croyland Rd ED N9 ... 50 A3
Croylands Dr SURB KT6 ... 167 L2
Croysdale Av SUN TW16 ... 150 A6
Crozier Dr SAND/SEL CR2 ... 185 A8
Crozier Ter HOM E9 ... 86 D5
Crucible Cl CHDH RM6 ... 72 B7
Crucifix La STHWK SE1 ... 19 J1
Cruden St IS N1 ... 6 D4
Cruikshank St FSBYW WC1X ... 6 A7
Cruikshank Rd SRTFD E15 ... 87 L4
Crummock Gdns
　CDALE/KGS NW9 ... 63 L6
Crumpsall St ABYW SE2 ... 126 C2
Crundale Av CDALE/KGS NW9 ... 63 G6
Crunden Rd SAND/SEL CR2 ... 184 D1
Crusader Gdns CROY/NA CR0 ... 172 E5
Crusader Wy WATW WD18 ... 41 M1
Crusoe Ms STNW/STAM N16 ... 85 K2
Crusoe Rd ERITH DA8 ... 127 K3
　MTCM CR4 ... 155 M3
Crutched Friars MON EC3R ... 13 K6
Crutchfield La
　WOT/HER KT12 ... 165 H3
Crutchley Rd CAT SE6 ... 141 L6
Crystal Av HCH RM12 ... 92 E4

Crystal Palace *NRWD* SE19 ... 158 A2
Crystal Palace Pde *NRWD* SE19 ... 157 M2
Crystal Palace Park Rd *NRWD* SE19 ... 158 A1
Crystal Palace Rd *EDUL* SE22 ... 139 M3
Crystal Ter *NRWD* SE19 ... 157 K2
Crystal Wy *BCTR* RM8 ... 90 C1
  HRW HA1 ... 61 M6
Cuba Dr *PEND* EN3 ... 37 J5
Cuba St *POP/IOD* E14 ... 105 G8
Cubitt Sq *STHL* UB1 ... 97 J7
Cubitt St *CROY/NA* CR0 ... 171 M7
  FSBYW WC1X ... 5 M8
Cubitt Ter *CLAP* SW4 ... 120 C8
Cuckoo Av *HNWL* W7 ... 97 L3
Cuckoo Dene *HNWL* W7 ... 97 K4
Cuckoo Hall La *ED* N9 ... 50 C2
Cuckoo HI *PIN* HA5 ... 60 C4
Cuckoo Hill Dr *PIN* HA5 ... 60 C4
Cuckoo Hill Rd *PIN* HA5 ... 60 D5
Cuckoo La *HNWL* W7 ... 97 L6
Cuda's Cl *HOR/WEW* KT19 ... 168 F6
Cuddington Av *WPK* KT4 ... 168 F5
Cuddington Gld *BNSTD* SM7 ... 180 A5
Cuddington Park Cl *BNSTD* SM7 ... 181 M6
Cuddington Wy *BELMT* SM2 ... 181 K5
Cudham Cl *BELMT* SM2 ... 182 A3
Cudham Dr *CROY/NA* CR0 ... 186 B3
Cudham St *CAT* SE6 ... 141 J4
Cudworth St *WCHPL* E1 ... 104 B3
Cuff Crs *ELTH/MOT* SE9 ... 142 D4
Cuffley Av *GSTN* WD25 ... 21 K7
Cuffley HI *CHESW* EN7 ... 25 H2
Cugley Rd *RDART* DA2 ... 147 J4
Culford Gdns *CHEL* SW3 ... 15 M6
Culford Gv *IS* N1 ... 85 L6
Culford Ms *IS* N1 ... 85 K6
Culford Rd *IS* N1 ... 7 J3
Culgaith Gdns *ENC/FH* EN2 ... 35 L7
Cullen Wy *WLSDN* NW10 ... 99 J3
Cullera Cl *NTHWD* HA6 ... 41 M8
Cullerne Cl *EW* KT17 ... 180 F3
Cullesden Rd *PUR/KEN* CR8 ... 184 B8
Culling Rd *BERM/RHTH* SE16 ... 124 F3
Cullings Ct *WAB* EN9 ... 27 M6
Cullington Cl *KTN/HRWW/W* HA3 ... 62 A5
Cullingworth Rd *WLSDN* NW10 ... 82 A5
Culloden Cl *STHWK* SE1 ... 122 A3
Culloden Rd *ENC/FH* EN2 ... 36 B5
Culloden St *POP/IOD* E14 ... 105 J5
Cullum St *FENCHST* EC3M ... 13 J6
Culmington Rd *SAND/SEL* CR2 ... 184 C1
  WEA W13 ... 98 C7
Culmore Rd *PECK* SE15 ... 122 B5
Culmstock Rd *BTSEA* SW11 ... 138 A2
Culpepper Cl *CHIG* IG7 ... 53 H8
Culross Cl *SEVS/STOTM* N15 ... 67 J5
Culross St *MYFR/PKLN* W1K ... 10 A7
Culsac Rd *SURB* KT6 ... 167 L4
Culverden Rd *BAL* SW12 ... 138 C7
  OXHEY WD19 ... 42 B5
Culver Gv *STAN* HA7 ... 62 C3
Culverhouse Gdns *STRHM/NOR* SW16 ... 138 F8
Culverlands Cl *STAN* HA7 ... 44 B6
Culverley Rd *CAT* SE6 ... 141 H5
Culvers Av *CAR* SM5 ... 170 F4
Culvers Retreat *CAR* SM5 ... 170 F2
Culverstone Cl *HAYES* BR2 ... 174 F1
Culvers Wy *CAR* SM5 ... 170 F4
Culvert La *UX/CGN* UB8 ... 94 B1
Culvert Pl *BTSEA* SW11 ... 120 A7
  SEVS/STOTM N15 ... 67 L6
Culworth St *STJWD* NW8 ... 3 J4
Cumberland Av *HCH* RM12 ... 92 E3
  WELL DA16 ... 125 L8
  WLSDN NW10 ... 99 H2
Cumberland Cl *BARK/HLT* IG6 ... 71 J2
  HACK E8 ... 85 M6
  HOR/WEW KT19 ... 180 E3
  RYNPK SW20 ... 154 D3
  TWK TW1 ... 134 B3
Cumberland Crs *BXLYHN* DA7 ... 126 E5
  CHSGTN KT9 ... 167 L5
  DART DA1 ... 146 F4
  ESH/CLAY KT10 ... 167 G4
Cumberland Gdns *FSBYW* WC1X ... 5 M7
  HDN NW4 ... 64 E3
Cumberland Ga *BAY/PAD* W2 ... 9 L6
  MBLAR W1H ... 9 L6
Cumberland Market *CAMTN* NW1 ... 4 D8
Cumberland Pk *ACT* W3 ... 99 J6
Cumberland Pl *CAMTN* NW1 ... 4 C7
  CAT SE6 ... 141 M5
  SUN TW16 ... 150 A7
Cumberland Rd *ACT* W3 ... 99 J6
  ASHF TW15 ... 130 D7
  BARN SW13 ... 117 M6
  CDALE/KGS NW9 ... 62 F4
  ED N9 ... 50 C3
  HAYES BR2 ... 159 L7
  HNWL W7 ... 97 M8
  HRW HA1 ... 61 H6
  MNPK E12 ... 88 D4
  PLSTW E13 ... 106 B4
  RCH/KEW TW9 ... 117 G6
  SNWD SE25 ... 173 H1
  WALTH E17 ... 68 E3
  WDGN N22 ... 66 F3
Cumberlands *PUR/KEN* CR8 ... 184 D8
Cumberland St *PIM* SW1V ... 16 D7
Cumberland Ter *CAMTN* NW1 ... 4 C6
Cumberland Terrace Ms *CAMTN* NW1 ... 4 C6
Cumberlow Av *SNWD* SE25 ... 157 H8
Cumbernauld Gdns *SUN* TW16 ... 149 M1
Cumberton Rd *TOTM* N17 ... 67 K2
Cumbrae Gdns *SURB* KT6 ... 163 G7
Cumbrian Av *BXLYHN* DA7 ... 127 L7
Cumbrian Gdns *CRICK* NW2 ... 82 D2
Cumbrian Wy *UX/CGN* UB8 ... 76 D8
Cummings Hall La *ABR/ST* RM4 ... 56 C5
Cumming St *IS* N1 ... 5 M6

Cumnor Gdns *EW* KT17 ... 169 G8
Cumnor Rd *BELMT* SM2 ... 170 C8
Cunard Crs *WCHMH* N21 ... 49 K1
Cunard Rd *WLSDN* NW10 ... 99 K2
Cundy Rd *CAN/RD* E16 ... 106 C5
Cundy St *BGVA* SW1W ... 16 B6
Cunliffe Rd *HOR/WEW* KT19 ... 168 F6
Cunliffe St *STRHM/NOR* SW16 ... 156 C2
Cunningham Av *PEND* EN3 ... 37 L1
  WWKM BR4 ... 174 B4
Cunningham Cl *CHDH* RM6 ... 72 C6
  WWKM BR4 ... 174 B4
Cunningham Pk *HRW* HA1 ... 61 K6
Cunningham Pl *STJWD* NW8 ... 3 G9
Cunningham Rd *BNSTD* SM7 ... 182 D8
  SEVS/STOTM N15 ... 68 A5
Cunnington St *CHSWK* W4 ... 117 J1
Cupar Rd *BTSEA* SW11 ... 120 A6
Cupola Cl *BMLY* BR1 ... 160 B1
Cureton St *WEST* SW1P ... 17 H7
Curlew Cl *SAND/SEL* CR2 ... 185 K4
  THMD SE28 ... 108 D6
Curlew St *STHWK* SE1 ... 19 M1
Curlew Wy *YEAD* UB4 ... 96 D3
Curnick's La *WNWD* SE27 ... 139 J8
Curran Av *BFN/LL* DA15 ... 143 M2
  WLGTN SM6 ... 171 G5
Curran Cl *UX/CGN* UB8 ... 94 C3
Currey Rd *NTHLT* UB5 ... 79 J6
Curricle St *ACT* W3 ... 99 L7
Curry Ri *MLHL* NW7 ... 46 D8
Cursitor St *FLST/FETLN* EC4A ... 12 A4
Curtain Pl *SDTCH* EC2A ... 7 K9
Curtain Rd *IS* N1 ... 7 K8
  SDTCH EC2A ... 13 J1
Curthwaite Gdns *ENC/FH* EN2 ... 35 K7
Curtis Cl *RKW/CH/CXG* WD3 ... 40 A3
Curtis Dr *ACT* W3 ... 99 K5
Curtis Field Rd *STRHM/NOR* SW16 ... 138 F3
Curtis La *ALP/SUD* HA0 ... 80 E6
Curtismill Cl *STMC/STPC* BR5 ... 162 B6
Curtis Mill La *ABR/ST* RM4 ... 56 A1
Curtismill Wy *STMC/STPC* BR5 ... 162 B6
Curtis Rd *EMPK* RM11 ... 92 F1
  HOR/WEW KT19 ... 168 C6
  HSLWW TW4 ... 132 F4
Curtis St *STHWK* SE1 ... 19 L5
Curvan Cl *EW* KT17 ... 180 F3
The Curve *SHB* W12 ... 99 J6
Curwen Av *FSTGT* E7 ... 88 B4
Curwen Rd *SHB* W12 ... 100 A8
Curzon Av *PEND* EN3 ... 37 K8
  STAN HA7 ... 62 A2
Curzon Cl *ORP* BR6 ... 176 D6
  WEY KT13 ... 164 A6
Curzon Crs *BARK* IG11 ... 107 M2
  WLSDN NW10 ... 81 G7
Curzon Pl *MYFR/PKLN* W1K ... 10 B9
  PIN HA5 ... 60 C6
Curzon Rd *EA* W5 ... 98 B3
  MUSWH N10 ... 66 B3
  THHTH CR7 ... 172 A1
  WEY KT13 ... 164 A6
Curzon St *MYFR/PICC* W1J ... 10 D8
  MYFR/PKLN W1K ... 10 B9
Cusack Cl *TWK* TW1 ... 133 M1
Cussons Cl *CHESW* EN7 ... 26 A2
Cutcombe Rd *CMBW* SE5 ... 121 J7
Cuthberga Cl *BARK* IG11 ... 89 J7
Cuthbert Cl *CHESW* EN7 ... 25 M2
Cuthbert Gdns *SNWD* SE25 ... 157 L6
Cuthbert Rd *CROY/NA* CR0 ... 172 B4
  UED N18 ... 50 A7
  WALTH E17 ... 69 J4
Cuthbert St *BAY/PAD* W2 ... 9 G1
Cutler St *HDTCH* EC3A ... 13 K4
The Cut *STHWK* SE1 ... 18 B1
Cuxton Cl *BXLYHS* DA6 ... 144 E2
Cyclamen Cl *HPTN* TW12 ... 151 G2
Cyclamen Rd *SWLY* BR8 ... 163 K7
Cyclamen Wy *HOR/WEW* KT19 ... 168 C7
Cygnet Av *EBED/NFELT* TW14 ... 132 C4
Cygnet Cl *BORE* WD6 ... 32 C4
  NTHWD HA6 ... 40 C8
  WLSDN NW10 ... 81 K5
The Cygnets *FELT* TW13 ... 132 E8
Cygnet St *WCHPL* E1 ... 7 M9
Cygnet Vw *WTHK* RM20 ... 129 M1
Cygnet Wy *YEAD* UB4 ... 96 D5
Cynthia St *IS* N1 ... 5 M6
Cypress Av *ENC/FH* EN2 ... 25 G8
  WHTN TW2 ... 133 J4
Cypress Cl *WAB* EN9 ... 27 K7
Cypress Gdns *BROCKY* SE4 ... 140 E2
Cypress Gv *BARK/HLT* IG6 ... 53 L8
Cypress Pl *KTN/HRWW/W* HA3 ... 61 K3
  SNWD SE25 ... 157 L5
Cypress Tree Cl *BFN/LL* DA15 ... 143 M5
Cypress Wk *GSTN* WD25 ... 21 H8
Cypress Wy *EW* KT17 ... 181 K7
Cyprus Av *FNCH* N3 ... 64 E3
Cyprus Cl *FSBYPK* N4 ... 67 H7
Cyprus Gdns *FNCH* N3 ... 64 E3
Cyprus Pl *BETH* E2 ... 104 C1
  EHAM E6 ... 107 G6
Cyprus Rd *ED* N9 ... 49 M4
  FNCH N3 ... 64 F3
Cyprus St *BETH* E2 ... 104 C1
Cyrena Rd *EDUL* SE22 ... 139 M3
Cyril Rd *BXLYHN* DA7 ... 126 E7
  ORP BR6 ... 177 G2
Cyrus St *FSBYE* EC1V ... 6 D9
Czar St *DEPT* SE8 ... 123 G4

D

Dabbling Cl *ERITH* DA8 ... 128 B5
Dabbs Hill La *NTHLT* UB5 ... 78 F6
D'abernon Cl *ESH/CLAY* KT10 ... 166 A6
Dabin Crs *GNWCH* SE10 ... 123 H6
Dacca St *DEPT* SE8 ... 122 F4
Dace Rd *BOW* E3 ... 87 G8
Dacre Av *CLAY* IG5 ... 71 G3
  SOCK/AV RM15 ... 111 K7
Dacre Cl *CHIG* IG7 ... 53 J6
  GFD/PVL UB6 ... 97 H1
Dacre Gdns *SOCK/AV* RM15 ... 111 K7
Dacre Gdns *BORE* WD6 ... 32 D4
  CHIG IG7 ... 53 J6
Dacre Pk *LEW* SE13 ... 123 L8
Dacre Pl *LEW* SE13 ... 123 L8
Dacre Rd *CROY/NA* CR0 ... 171 L2
  PLSTW E13 ... 88 B8
  WAN E11 ... 87 M1
Dacres Rd *FSTH* SE23 ... 140 D7
Dacre St *STJSPK* SW1H ... 17 G3
Dade Wy *NWDGN* UB2 ... 114 F3
Daerwood Cl *HAYES* BR2 ... 175 M3
Daffodil Cl *CROY/NA* CR0 ... 173 K3
  HPTN TW12 ... 151 C2
Daffodil Gdns *IL* IG1 ... 89 H5
Daffodil St *SHB* W12 ... 99 M6
Dafforne Rd *TOOT* SW17 ... 137 M3
Dagenham Av *DAGW* RM9 ... 90 E8
Dagenham Rd *DAGE* RM10 ... 91 J4
  LEY E10 ... 86 F1
  RAIN RM13 ... 91 K7
  ROMW/RG RM7 ... 73 K8
Dagger La *BORE* WD6 ... 44 A1
Dagmar Av *WBLY* HA9 ... 80 F4
Dagmar Gdns *WLSDN* NW10 ... 100 D1
Dagmar Rd *CMBW* SE5 ... 121 L6
  DAGE RM10 ... 91 J7
  FSBYPK N4 ... 67 G8
  KUTN/CMB KT2 ... 152 F4
  NWDGN UB2 ... 114 E1
  SEVS/STOTM N15 ... 67 K5
  SNWD SE25 ... 157 L7
  WDGN N22 ... 66 D2
Dagmar Ter *IS* N1 ... 6 D3
Dagnall Crs *UX/CGN* UB8 ... 94 C4
Dagnall Pk *SNWD* SE25 ... 157 L8
Dagnall Rd *SNWD* SE25 ... 157 L8
Dagnall St *BTSEA* SW11 ... 119 M7
Dagnam Park Cl *HARH* RM3 ... 57 G7
Dagnam Park Dr *HARH* RM3 ... 56 F7
Dagnam Park Gdns *HARH* RM3 ... 57 G8
Dagnam Park Sq *HARH* RM3 ... 57 H8
Dagnan Rd *BAL* SW12 ... 138 B4
Dagonet Rd *BMLY* BR1 ... 142 A7
Dahlia Dr *SWLY* BR8 ... 163 M5
Dahlia Gdns *IL* IG1 ... 89 H6
  MTCM CR4 ... 156 D7
Dahlia Rd *ABYW* SE2 ... 126 B3
Dahomey Rd *STRHM/NOR* SW16 ... 156 C2
Daimler Wy *WLGTN* SM6 ... 183 L1
Daines Cl *MNPK* E12 ... 88 F3
Dainford Cl *BMLY* BR1 ... 159 K1
Daintry Cl *KTN/HRWW/W* HA3 ... 62 A1
Dairsie Rd *ELTH/MOT* SE9 ... 125 G8
Dairy Cl *BMLY* BR1 ... 160 B3
  THHTH CR7 ... 157 J5
Dairyglen Av *CHES/WCR* EN8 ... 26 D4
Dairy La *WOOL/PLUM* SE18 ... 124 F2
Dairyman Cl *CRICK* NW2 ... 82 D4
Daisy Cl *CROY/NA* CR0 ... 173 K3
Daisy La *FUL/PGN* SW6 ... 119 G8
Daisy Rd *SWFD* E18 ... 70 B3
Dakota Gdns *EHAM* E6 ... 106 E3
Dalberg Rd *BRXS/STRHM* SW2 ... 139 G2
Dalberg Wy *ABYW* SE2 ... 126 D1
Dalby Rd *WAND/EARL* SW18 ... 137 J1
Dalbys Crs *TOTM* N17 ... 49 L8
Dalby St *KTTN* NW5 ... 84 B4
Dalcross Rd *HEST* TW5 ... 114 E7
Dale Av *EDGW* HA8 ... 62 F2
  HSLWW TW4 ... 114 E8
Dalebury Rd *TOOT* SW17 ... 137 M6
Dale Cl *BAR* EN5 ... 47 H1
  BKHTH/KID SE3 ... 124 A8
  DART DA1 ... 145 M3
  PIN HA5 ... 60 B2
Dale Dr *YEAD* UB4 ... 95 M3
Dale Gdns *WFD* IG8 ... 52 B6
Dalegarth Gdns *PUR/KEN* CR8 ... 184 D6
Dale Green Rd *FBAR/BDGN* N11 ... 48 B5
Dale Gv *NFNCH/WDSP* N12 ... 47 J7
Daleham Dr *UX/CGN* UB8 ... 95 H5
Daleham Gdns *HAMP* NW3 ... 83 K5
Daleham Ms *HAMP* NW3 ... 83 K6
Dale Park Av *CAR* SM5 ... 170 F4
Dale Park Rd *NRWD* SE19 ... 157 J4
Dale Rd *DART* DA1 ... 145 M3
  GFD/PVL UB6 ... 97 H4
  KTTN NW5 ... 84 A5
  PUR/KEN CR8 ... 184 A5
  SUN TW16 ... 149 M3
  SUT SM1 ... 169 M6
  SWLY BR8 ... 163 J6
  WALW SE17 ... 121 H4
  WOT/HER KT12 ... 142 E6
Dale Rw *NTGHL* W11 ... 100 E5
Daleside *ORP* BR6 ... 177 G7
Daleside Cl *ORP* BR6 ... 177 G8
Daleside Dr *POTB/CUF* EN6 ... 22 F5
Daleside Gdns *CHIG* IG7 ... 53 J5
Daleside Rd *HOR/WEW* KT19 ... 168 D8
  TOOT SW17 ... 156 B1
Dales Rd *BORE* WD6 ... 32 D8
Dale St *CHSWK* W4 ... 117 L3
The Dale *HAYES* BR2 ... 175 K6
  WAB EN9 ... 27 L7
Dale Vw *ERITH* DA8 ... 128 A7
Dale View Av *CHING* E4 ... 51 J4
Dale View Crs *CHING* E4 ... 51 J4
Dale View Gdns *CHING* E4 ... 51 K5
Daleview Rd *SEVS/STOTM* N15 ... 67 L7
Dalewood Cl *EMPK* RM11 ... 74 E8
Dalewood Gdns *WPK* KT4 ... 169 H4
Dale Wood Rd *ORP* BR6 ... 176 D7
Daley St *HOM* E9 ... 86 D1
Daley Thompson Wy *VX/NE* SW8 ... 120 B8
Dalgarno Gdns *NKENS* W10 ... 100 C4
Dalgarno Wy *NKENS* W10 ... 100 C3
Dalkeith Gv *STAN* HA7 ... 44 D7
Dalkeith Rd *DUL* SE21 ... 139 J5
  IL IG1 ... 89 J3
Dallas Rd *CHEAM* SM3 ... 169 L8
  EA W5 ... 98 F4

  HDN NW4 ... 64 A8
  SYD SE26 ... 140 B8
Dallas Ter *HYS/HAR* UB3 ... 113 H1
Dallega Cl *HYS/HAR* UB3 ... 95 J6
Dallinger Rd *LEE/GVPK* SE12 ... 141 K3
Dalling Rd *HMSMTH* W6 ... 118 B1
Dallington St *FSBYE* EC1V ... 6 D9
Dallin Rd *BXLYHS* DA6 ... 144 D1
  WOOL/PLUM SE18 ... 125 H5
Dalmain Rd *FSTH* SE23 ... 140 D5
Dalmally Rd *CROY/NA* CR0 ... 172 F2
Dalmeny Av *HOLWY* N7 ... 84 D4
  STRHM/NOR SW16 ... 157 G5
Dalmeny Cl *ALP/SUD* HA0 ... 80 C6
Dalmeny Crs *HSLW* TW3 ... 133 K1
Dalmeny Rd *ARCH* N19 ... 84 D3
  BAR EN5 ... 47 J1
  CAR SM5 ... 183 G1
  ERITH DA8 ... 127 H6
  WPK KT4 ... 169 H5
Dalmore Av *ESH/CLAY* KT10 ... 166 F8
Dalmore Rd *DUL* SE21 ... 139 J6
Dalrymple Cl *STHGT/OAK* N14 ... 48 D2
Dalrymple Rd *BROCKY* SE4 ... 140 E1
Dalston Gdns *STAN* HA7 ... 44 A6
Dalston La *HACK* E8 ... 85 M6
Dalton Av *MTCM* CR4 ... 155 L5
Dalton Cl *ORP* BR6 ... 176 E5
  YEAD UB4 ... 95 K3
Dalton St *WNWD* SE27 ... 139 H6
Dalton Wy *WAT* WD17 ... 42 D1
Dalwood St *CMBW* SE5 ... 121 L6
Dalyell Rd *BRXN/ST* SW9 ... 120 F8
Damask Crs *CAN/RD* E16 ... 105 L3
Damer Ter *WBPTN* SW10 ... 119 J5
Dames Rd *FSTGT* E7 ... 88 A4
Dame St *IS* N1 ... 6 E5
Damien Cl *WCHPL* E1 ... 104 B4
Damon Cl *SCUP* DA14 ... 144 B7
Damsel Ct *BERM/RHTH* SE16 ... 104 A8
Damsonwood Rd *NWDGN* UB2 ... 115 G1
Danbrook Rd *STRHM/NOR* SW16 ... 156 E4
Danbury Cl *CHDH* RM6 ... 72 D4
Danbury Ms *CAR* SM5 ... 171 H6
Danbury Rd *LOU* IG10 ... 52 E1
  RAIN RM13 ... 91 M8
Danbury St *IS* N1 ... 6 D5
Danbury Wy *WFD* IG8 ... 52 C8
Danby St *PECK* SE15 ... 121 M8
Dancer Rd *FUL/PGN* SW6 ... 118 F6
  RCH/KEW TW9 ... 117 G8
Dancers Hill Rd *BAR* EN5 ... 33 K1
Dando Crs *BKHTH/KID* SE3 ... 124 B8
Dandridge Cl *GNWCH* SE10 ... 123 M3
Danebury Av *PUT/ROE* SW15 ... 135 M4
Daneby Rd *CAT* SE6 ... 141 J7
Dane Cl *BXLY* DA5 ... 145 G4
  ORP BR6 ... 176 F7
Danecourt Gdns *CROY/NA* CR0 ... 172 F5
Danecroft Rd *HNHL* SE24 ... 139 J2
Danehurst Gdns *REDBR* IG4 ... 70 E6
Danehurst St *FUL/PGN* SW6 ... 118 E6
Daneland *EBAR* EN4 ... 34 F8
Danemead Gv *NTHLT* UB5 ... 79 H5
Danemere St *PUT/ROE* SW15 ... 118 C8
Dane Pl *BOW* E3 ... 104 F1
Dane Rd *ASHF* TW15 ... 149 J2
  IL IG1 ... 89 J5
  STHL UB1 ... 96 E6
  UED N18 ... 50 C6
  WEA W13 ... 98 C6
  WIM/MER SW19 ... 155 J4
Danes Cl *LHD/OX* KT22 ... 178 C7
Danescombe *LEE/GVPK* SE12 ... 142 A5
Danescourt Crs *SUT* SM1 ... 170 C4
Danescroft Av *HDN* NW4 ... 64 D6
Danescroft Gdns *HDN* NW4 ... 64 D6
Danesdale Rd *HOM* E9 ... 86 E6
Danesfield *WOT/HER* KT12 ... 165 H1
Danes Ga *HRW* HA1 ... 61 L4
Danesmead *COB* KT11 ... 178 A4
Dane St *GINN* WC1R ... 11 L3
Danes Wy *LHD/OX* KT22 ... 178 D7
Daneswood Av *CAT* SE6 ... 141 J7
Daneswood Cl *WEY* KT13 ... 164 B7
Danethorpe Rd *ALP/SUD* HA0 ... 80 B6
Danetree Cl *HOR/WEW* KT19 ... 180 C1
Danetree Rd *HOR/WEW* KT19 ... 180 C1
Danette Gdns *DAGE* RM10 ... 90 F2
Daneville Rd *CMBW* SE5 ... 121 K6
Dangan Rd *WAN* E11 ... 70 A7
Daniel Bolt Cl *POP/IOD* E14 ... 105 H4
Daniel Cl *HSLWW* TW4 ... 132 F4
  UED N18 ... 50 C6
  WIM/MER SW19 ... 155 L2
Daniel Gdns *PECK* SE15 ... 121 M5
Daniell Wy *CROY/NA* CR0 ... 171 M3
Daniel Pl *HDN* NW4 ... 64 B7
Daniel Rd *ACT* W3 ... 98 F6
Daniel's Rd *PECK* SE15 ... 122 C8
Daniel Wy *BNSTD* SM7 ... 182 A7
Dan Leno Wk *FUL/PGN* SW6 ... 119 H5
Dansey Pl *SOHO/SHAV* W1D ... 11 G6
Dansington Rd *WELL* DA16 ... 144 A1
Danson Crs *WELL* DA16 ... 126 B8
Danson La *WELL* DA16 ... 144 B1
Danson Md *WELL* DA16 ... 144 D1
Danson Rd *BXLYHS* DA6 ... 144 D2
Danson U/P *BFN/LL* DA15 ... 144 B4
Dante Rd *LBTH* SE11 ... 18 C5
Danube Cl *CHEL* SW3 ... 15 K7
Danvers Rd *CEND/HSY/T* N8 ... 66 D5
Danvers St *CHEL* SW3 ... 119 K4
Danyon Cl *RAIN* RM13 ... 110 C1
Danziger Wy *BORE* WD6 ... 32 C4
Daphne Gdns *CHING* E4 ... 51 J5
Daphne Rd *WAND/EARL* SW18 ... 137 J3
Daplyn St *WCHPL* E1 ... 104 A4
D'arblay St *SOHO/CST* W1F ... 10 F5
Darby Crs *SUN* TW16 ... 150 C5
Darby Dr *WAB* EN9 ... 27 J6
Darby Gdns *SUN* TW16 ... 150 C5
Darcy Av *WLGTN* SM6 ... 171 J4

Darcy Cl *CHES/WCR* EN8 ... 26 E4
  TRDG/WHET N20 ... 47 K4
D'arcy Gdns *DAGW* RM9 ... 90 F8
  KTN/HRWW/W HA3 ... 62 E5
D'arcy Pl *HAYES* BR2 ... 160 A1
D'arcy Rd *CHEAM* SM3 ... 169 K6
  ISLW TW7 ... 116 A6
  STRHM/NOR SW16 ... 156 E5
Darell Rd *RCH/KEW* TW9 ... 117 G8
Darenth Park Av *RDART* DA2 ... 147 K6
Darenth Rd *DART* DA1 ... 146 F5
  STNW/STAM N16 ... 67 M8
  WELL DA16 ... 126 A6
Darenth Rd South *RDART* DA2 ... 147 K6
Darenth Wood Rd *RDART* DA2 ... 147 L5
Darent Valley Pth *DART* DA1 ... 128 D6
Darfield Rd *BROCKY* SE4 ... 140 F2
Darfield Wy *NKENS* W10 ... 100 D6
Darfur St *PUT/ROE* SW15 ... 118 D3
Dargate Cl *NRWD* SE19 ... 157 M3
Darien Rd *BTSEA* SW11 ... 119 K8
Darkes La *POTB/CUF* EN6 ... 23 G5
Dark La *CHESW* EN7 ... 26 A4
Darlan Rd *FUL/PGN* SW6 ... 118 F5
Darlaston Rd *WIM/MER* SW19 ... 154 D3
Darley Cl *CROY/NA* CR0 ... 173 K1
Darley Dr *NWMAL* KT3 ... 153 K5
Darley Gdns *MRDN* SM4 ... 170 C1
Darley Rd *BTSEA* SW11 ... 137 M3
  ED N9 ... 49 M3
Darling Rd *BROCKY* SE4 ... 123 G8
Darling Rw *WCHPL* E1 ... 104 B3
Darlington Gdns *HARH* RM3 ... 56 D7
Darlington Rd *WNWD* SE27 ... 157 H1
Darlton Cl *DART* DA1 ... 127 M7
Darmaine Cl *SAND/SEL* CR2 ... 184 C1
Darndale Cl *WALTH* E17 ... 68 F3
Darnley Pk *WEY* KT13 ... 164 B5
Darnley Rd *HACK* E8 ... 86 B6
  WFD IG8 ... 69 A2
Darnley Ter *NTGHL* W11 ... 100 D7
Darrell Rd *EDUL* SE22 ... 140 A2
Darren Cl *FSBYPK* N4 ... 66 F8
Darrick Wood Rd *ORP* BR6 ... 176 D4
Darrington Rd *BORE* WD6 ... 31 L4
Darris Cl *YEAD* UB4 ... 96 E3
Darsley Dr *VX/NE* SW8 ... 120 D6
Dart Cl *UPMR* RM14 ... 75 K7
Dartfields *HARH* RM3 ... 56 D8
Dartford Av *ED* N9 ... 50 C1
Dartford Rd *BXLY* DA5 ... 145 J5
  DART DA1 ... 146 A3
Dartford St *WALW* SE17 ... 122 G8
Dartmoor Wk *POP/IOD* E14 ... 123 G2
Dartmouth Cl *NTGHL* W11 ... 100 F5
Dartmouth Gv *GNWCH* SE10 ... 123 J6
Dartmouth HI *GNWCH* SE10 ... 123 J6
Dartmouth Park Av *KTTN* NW5 ... 84 B3
Dartmouth Park HI *ARCH* N19 ... 84 B1
  KTTN NW5 ... 84 B3
Dartmouth Park Rd *KTTN* NW5 ... 84 B3
Dartmouth Pl *CHSWK* W4 ... 117 L4
  FSTH SE23 ... 140 C6
Dartmouth Rd *CRICK* NW2 ... 82 C2
  HAYES BR2 ... 175 G2
  HDN NW4 ... 64 A7
  RSLP HA4 ... 78 A3
  SYD SE26 ... 140 B7
Dartmouth Rw *LEW* SE13 ... 123 J7
Dartmouth St *STJSPK* SW1H ... 17 G2
Dartmouth Ter *GNWCH* SE10 ... 123 K6
Dartnell Rd *CROY/NA* CR0 ... 172 F2
Dart St *MV/WKIL* W9 ... 100 F2
Darville Rd *STNW/STAM* N16 ... 85 M3
Darwell Cl *EHAM* E6 ... 107 G1
Darwin Cl *FBAR/BDGN* N11 ... 48 B5
  ORP BR6 ... 176 D7
Darwin Dr *GFD/PVL* UB6 ... 97 H5
Darwin Gdns *OXHEY* WD19 ... 42 C7
Darwin Rd *BTFD* TW8 ... 116 C3
  WDGN N22 ... 48 D7
  WELL DA16 ... 125 H2
Darwin St *WALW* SE17 ... 19 H5
Daryngton Dr *GFD/PVL* UB6 ... 97 K1
Dashwood Cl *BXLYHS* DA6 ... 145 G2
Dashwood Rd *CEND/HSY/T* N8 ... 66 F7
Dassett Rd *WNWD* SE27 ... 157 H1
Datchelor Pl *CMBW* SE5 ... 121 K6
Datchet Rd *CAT* SE6 ... 140 F7
Date St *WALW* SE17 ... 19 G8
Daubeney Gdns *TOTM* N17 ... 67 J1
Daubeney Rd *CLPT* E5 ... 86 E5
  TOTM N17 ... 67 J1
Dault Rd *WAND/EARL* SW18 ... 137 J3
Davenant Rd *ARCH* N19 ... 84 D2
Davenant St *WCHPL* E1 ... 104 A4
Davenham Av *NTHWD* HA6 ... 41 M6
Davenport Cl *TEDD* TW11 ... 152 A2
Davenport Rd *LEW* SE13 ... 141 H3
  SCUP DA14 ... 144 D6
Daventer Dr *STAN* HA7 ... 61 M1
Daventry Av *WALTH* E17 ... 69 G7
Daventry Gdns *HARH* RM3 ... 56 C7
Daventry Rd *HARH* RM3 ... 56 C7
Daventry St *CAMTN* NW1 ... 9 J2
Davern Cl *GNWCH* SE10 ... 124 C3
Davey Cl *HOLWY* N7 ... 84 F6
Davey Rd *HOM* E9 ... 87 G7
Davey St *PECK* SE15 ... 121 M4
David Av *GFD/PVL* UB6 ... 97 K3
David Dr *HARH* RM3 ... 57 G8
Davidge St *STHWK* SE1 ... 18 C2
David Ms *MHST* W1U ... 9 M2
David Rd *BCTR* RM8 ... 90 B2
Davidson Gdns *VX/NE* SW8 ... 120 E5
Davidson Rd *CROY/NA* CR0 ... 172 E3
Davidson Wy *ROMW/RG* RM7 ... 73 J7
David's Rd *FSTH* SE23 ... 140 C5
David St *SRTFD* E15 ... 87 K6
David's Wy *BARK/HLT* IG6 ... 71 L1
David Twigg Cl *KUTN/CMB* KT2 ... 152 E4
Davies Cl *RAIN* RM13 ... 110 C2
  SNWD SE25 ... 172 F1
Davies La *WAN* E11 ... 87 L2

Davies Ms *MYFR/PKLN* W1K 10 C6
Davies St *MYFR/PKLN* W1K 10 C6
Davies Wk *ISLW* TW7 .... 115 K6 🅸
Davington Gdns *BCTR* RM8 .... 90 B5 🅸
Davington Rd *BCTR* RM8 .... 90 B6
Davinia Cl *WFD* IG8 .... 52 F8
Davis Rd *ACT* W3 .... 99 M7
CHSGTN KT9 .... 168 A6
SOCK/AV RM15 .... 111 K7
Davis St *PLSTW* E13 .... 106 B1
Davisville Rd *SHB* W12 .... 100 A8
Dawes Av *HCH* RM12 .... 92 D3
ISLW TW7 .... 134 A2
Dawes Cl *GRH* DA9 .... 147 M2
HGDN/ICK UB10 .... 94 E1
Dawes Ct *ESH/CLAY* KT10 .... 166 B6
HGDN/ICK UB10 .... 94 E1
Dawes Rd *FUL/PGN* SW6 .... 118 F5
HGDN/ICK UB10 .... 94 E1
Dawes St *WALW* SE17 .... 19 H7
Dawley Av *UX/CGN* UB8 .... 95 H4
Dawley Pde *UX/CGN* UB8 .... 95 J6
Dawley Rd *HYS/HAR* UB3 .... 95 K8
HYS/HAR UB3 .... 113 L2 🅸
Dawlish Av *GFD/PVL* UB6 .... 98 A1
PLMGR N13 .... 48 E6
WAND/EARL SW18 .... 137 H6
Dawlish Dr *GDMY/SEVK* IG3 ..... 89 M4
PIN HA5 .... 60 F6
RSLP HA4 .... 78 A2
Dawlish Rd *CRICK* NW2 .... 82 D6
LEY E10 .... 87 J2
TOTM N17 .... 68 A4
Dawnay Gdns
WAND/EARL SW18 .... 137 K6 🅸
Dawnay Rd *WAND/EARL* SW18 ..... 137 J6
Dawn Cl *HSLWW* TW4 .... 114 E8
Dawpool Rd *CRICK* NW2 .... 81 M2
Daws Hl *CHING* E4 .... 38 C6
Daws La *MLHL* NW7 .... 45 M7
Dawson Av *BARK* IG11 .... 89 M7
STMC/STPC BR5 .... 162 B5
Dawson Cl *HYS/HAR* UB3 .... 95 K4 🅸
WOOL/PLUM SE18 .... 125 J2
Dawson Dr *RAIN* RM13 .... 92 B7 🅸
SWLY BR8 .... 163 L3
Dawson Gdns *BARK* IG11 .... 89 M7
Dawson Pl *BAY/PAD* W2 .... 8 A6
Dawson Rd *CRICK* NW2 .... 82 C5
KUT KT1 .... 152 F6
Dawson St *BETH* E2 .... 7 M6
Dawson Ter *ED* N9 .... 50 C2 🅸
Daybrook Rd *WIM/MER* SW19 ..... 155 H5
Daylesford Av *PUT/ROE* SW15 ... 136 A1
Daylop Dr *CHIG* IG7 .... 54 B5
Daymer Gdns *PIN* HA5 .... 60 C5
Day's Acre *SAND/SEL* CR2 ...... 184 F3
Daysbrook Rd
BRXS/STRHM SW2 .... 138 F5
Days La *BFN/LL* DA15 .... 143 L4
Dayton Dr *ERITH* DA8 .... 128 D3
Dayton Gv *PECK* SE15 .... 122 C6
Deacon Cl *PUR/KEN* CR8 .... 183 L2
Deacon Ms *IS* N1 .... 7 H2
Deacon Rd *CRICK* NW2 .... 82 A6
KUTN/CMB KT2 .... 152 F4
Deacons Cl *BORE* WD6 .... 32 A7
PIN HA5 .... 60 B3
Deacons Hts *BORE* WD6 .... 45 G1
Deacons Hl *OXHEY* WD19 .... 42 C1
Deacon's Hill Rd *BORE* WD6 .... 31 M8
Deacons Leas *ORP* BR6 .... 176 D8
Deacons Wk *HPTN* TW12 .... 133 C8
Deacon Wy *WALW* SE17 .... 18 E5
WFD IG8 .... 70 F1
Deakin Cl *WATW* WD18 .... 41 L2 🅸
Deakins Ter *ORP* BR6 .... 177 G2 🅸
Deal Porters Wy
BERM/RHTH SE16 .... 122 C3 🅸
Deal Rd *TOOT* SW17 .... 156 A2
Deal St *WCHPL* E1 .... 104 A4
Dealtry Rd *PUT/ROE* SW15 ...... 136 C1
Dean Bradley St *WEST* SW1P .... 17 J4 🅸
Dean Cl *HGDN/ICK* UB10 .... 76 F7
Dean Ct *ALP/SUD* HA0 .... 80 B3
Deancross St *WCHPL* E1 .... 104 C5 🅸
Dean Dr *STAN* HA7 .... 62 E3
Deane Av *RSLP* HA4 .... 78 B5
Deane Croft Rd *PIN* HA5 .... 60 C7
Deanery Ms *MYFR/PKLN* W1K ..... 10 B8 🅸
Deanery Rd *SRTFD* E15 .... 87 L6
Deanery St *MYFR/PKLN* W1K 10 B8
Deane Wy *RSLP* HA4 .... 60 B7
Dean Farrar St *STJSPK* SW1H ... 17 H3 🅸
Dean Gdns *WALTH* E17 .... 69 K5
Deanhill Rd *MORT/ESHN* SW14 ... 135 H1
Dean Rd *CRICK* NW2 .... 82 C6
CROY/NA CR0 .... 172 D6
HPTN TW12 .... 151 C1
HSLW TW3 .... 133 H2
THMD SE28 .... 108 A6
Dean Ryle St *WEST* SW1P 17 J4
Deansbrook Cl *EDGW* HA8 .... 63 J1 🅸
Deansbrook Rd *EDGW* HA8 .... 45 K8
Dean's Buildings *WALW* SE17 ... 19 H6
Deans Cl *ABLGY* WD5 .... 20 D5
CHSWK W4 .... 117 H4 🅸
CROY/NA CR0 .... 172 F5
EDGW HA8 .... 45 K2
Dean's Ct *BLKFR* EC4V .... 12 D5 🅸
Deanscroft Av *CDALE/KGS* NW9 .. 81 J2
Dean's Dr *MLHL* NW7 .... 45 K7
PLMGR N13 .... 49 H8
Deans Gate Cl *FSTH* SE23 ...... 140 D7 🅸
Dean's La *EDGW* HA8 .... 45 J8
Dean's Ms *MYFR/PKLN* W1G ...... 10 D4 🅸
Dean's Rd *HNWL* W7 .... 97 M8
SUT SM1 .... 175 G3
Dean Stanley St *WEST* SW1P .... 17 J4 🅸
Dean St *FSTGT* E7 .... 88 A5
SOHO/CST W1F 11 G4
Deansway *ED* N9 .... 49 L5
Deans Wy *EDGW* HA8 .... 45 J7
Deansway *EFNCH* N2 .... 65 K5
Dean Trench St *WEST* SW1P ..... 17 J4 🅸

Dearne Cl *STAN* HA7 .... 44 A7
De'arn Gdns *MTCM* CR4 .... 155 L6
Dearsley Rd *EN* EN1 .... 36 C1
Deason St *SRTFD* E15 .... 87 J8 🅸
Debden Cl *KUTN/CMB* KT2 .... 152 D1 🅸
WFD IG8 .... 70 D1 🅸
De Beauvoir Crs *IS* N1 .... 7 J3
De Beauvoir Rd *IS* N1 .... 7 J2
IS N1 .... 85 L6 🅸
De Beauvoir Sq *IS* N1 .... 7 K2
Debnams Rd
BERM/RHTH SE16 .... 122 C2 🅸
De Bohun Av *STHGT/OAK* N14 .... 48 B1
Deborah Cl *ISLW* TW7 .... 115 L6
De Broome Rd *FELT* TW13 .... 132 C5
Deburgh Rd *WIM/MER* SW19 ...... 155 J3
Decima St *STHWK* SE1 .... 19 J3 🅸
Deck Cl *BERM/RHTH* SE16 .... 104 D7 🅸
Decoy Av *GLDGN* NW11 .... 64 E6
De Crespigny Pk *CMBW* SE5 ..... 121 K7
Dee Cl *UPMR* RM14 .... 75 K7
Deeley Rd *VX/NE* SW8 .... 120 D6
Deena Cl *EA* W5 .... 98 F5
Deepdale *WIM/MER* SW19 .... 136 D8
Deepdale Av *HAYES* BR2 .... 159 M7 🅸
Deepdale Cl *FBAR/BDGN* N11 .... 48 A8
Deepdene *POTB/CUF* EN6 .... 22 D4
Deepdene Av *CROY/NA* CR0 ...... 172 F5
Deepdene Cl *WAN* E11 .... 70 A5
Deepdene Ct *WCHMH* N21 .... 49 H1
Deepdene Gdns
BRXS/STRHM SW2 .... 138 F4
Deepdene Rd *HNHL* SE24 .... 139 J1
WELL DA16 .... 126 A8
Deepwell Cl *ISLW* TW7 .... 116 A6
Deepwood La *GFD/PVL* UB6 ...... 97 K2 🅸
Deerbrook Rd
BRXS/STRHM SW2 .... 139 H5
Deerdale Rd *HNHL* SE24 .... 139 J1
Deere Av *RAIN* RM13 .... 92 A6
Deerhurst Crs *HPTN* TW12 ...... 151 J1 🅸
Deerhurst Rd *KIL/WHAMP* NW6 ... 82 D7
STRHM/NOR SW16 .... 156 F1
Deerings Dr *PIN* HA5 .... 60 A6
Deerleap Gv *CHING* E4 .... 38 B8
Dee Rd *RCH/KEW* TW9 .... 134 F1
Deer Park Cl *KUTN/CMB* KT2 .... 153 L6
Deer Park Gdns *MTCM* CR4 ...... 155 K7 🅸
Deer Park Rd *WIM/MER* SW19 .... 155 L5
Deer Park Wy *WWKM* BR4 .... 174 F4 🅸
Deeside Rd *TOOT* SW17 .... 137 K7
Dee St *POP/IOD* E14 .... 105 J5
Dee Wy *HOR/WEW* KT19 .... 180 E3 🅸
ROM RM1 .... 73 L2
Defiant Wy *WLGTN* SM6 .... 183 L1
Defoe Av *RCH/KEW* TW9 .... 117 G5
Defoe Cl *WIM/MER* SW19 .... 155 J1
BERM/RHTH SE16 .... 104 F8 🅸
STNW/STAM N16 .... 85 L2
Defoe Wy *CRW* RM5 .... 55 G8
De Frene Rd *SYD* SE26 .... 140 D8
Degema Rd *CHST* BR7 .... 161 H1
Dehar Crs *CDALE/KGS* NW9 ...... 63 M8
Dehavilland Cl *NTHLT* UB5 ..... 95 J2
De Havilland Rd *EDGW* HA8 ..... 63 H3
HEST TW5 .... 114 C5 🅸
WLGTN SM6 .... 183 L1
De Havilland Wy *ABLGY* WD5 .... 20 F5 🅸
STWL/WRAY TW19 .... 130 D3
Dekker Rd *DUL* SE21 .... 139 L3
Delacourt Rd
BKHTH/KID SE3 .... 124 B5 🅸
Delafield Rd *CHARL* SE7 .... 124 B3
Delaford Cl *IVER* SL0 .... 94 A5 🅸
Delaford Rd
BERM/RHTH SE16 .... 122 C3 🅸
Delaford St *FUL/PGN* SW6 ...... 118 F5
Delamare Crs *CROY/NA* CR0 ..... 173 J1
Delamere Cl *CHES/WCR* EN8 ..... 26 F2
Delamere Gdns *MLHL* NW7 .... 45 K8
Delamere Rd *BORE* WD6 .... 32 B4
EA W5 .... 98 B8
RYNPK SW20 .... 154 D4 🅸
YEAD UB4 .... 96 D6
Delamere St *BAY/PAD* W2 .... 8 E3 🅸
Delamere Ter *BAY/PAD* W2 ...... 8 D2 🅸
Delancey St *CAMTN* NW1 .... 4 D4
Delaporte Cl *EW* KT17 .... 180 E5 🅸
De Laune St *STMC/STPC* BR5 .... 177 K2
De Laune St *WALW* SE17 .... 18 C4
Delaware Rd *MV/WKIL* W9 .... 2 C1
Delawyk Crs *HNHL* SE24 .... 139 K3
Delcombe Av *WPK* KT4 .... 169 J3
Delhi Rd *EN* EN1 .... 49 M2
Delhi St *IS* N1 .... 5 K4
Delia St *WAND/EARL* SW18 ...... 137 H4
Delius Cl *BORE* WD6 .... 44 C1
Dellbow Rd *EBED/NFELT* TW14 ... 132 B2
Dell Cl *SRTFD* E15 .... 87 K8 🅸
WFD IG8 .... 52 B5
WLGTN SM6 .... 171 J6
Dell Farm Rd *RSLP* HA4 .... 59 K6
Dellfield Cl *BECK* BR3 .... 159 J4
WAT WD17 .... 29 G5
Dellfield Crs *UX/CGN* UB8 ..... 94 C3
Dell La *EW* KT17 .... 169 G7
Dellmeadow *ABLGY* WD5 .... 20 E3
Dellors Cl *BAR* EN5 .... 33 K8
Dellow Gn *GNTH/NBYPK* IG2 ..... 71 K8 🅸
Dellow St *WCHPL* E1 .... 104 B6
Dell Rd *EW* KT17 .... 169 G8
PEND EN3 .... 37 J3
WATN WD24 .... 29 G2
WDR/YW UB7 .... 112 F1
Dells Cl *CHING* E4 .... 51 H2
Dellside *DEN/HRF* UB9 .... 58 C6
Dell Side *WATN* WD24 .... 29 G1
The Dell *ABYW* SE2 .... 126 A3
ALP/SUD HA0 .... 80 B5
BTFD TW8 .... 116 C4 🅸
BXLY DA5 .... 145 L5
EBED/NFELT TW14 .... 132 B4
NRWD SE19 .... 157 M4
NTHWD HA6 .... 41 L4
PIN HA5 .... 60 D3

RAD WD7 .... 31 G1
WFD IG8 .... 52 B5
Dell Wy *NWMAL* KT3 .... 153 L5
Dell Wy *WEA* W13 .... 98 C5
Dellwood Cl *RKW/CH/CXG* WD3 ... 40 B3
Dellwood Gdns *CLAY* IG5 .... 71 G4
Delmey Cl *CROY/NA* CR0 .... 172 F5 🅸
Delme Crs *BKHTH/KID* SE3 ...... 124 B7
Delorme St *HMSMTH* W6 .... 119 G6 🅸
Delta Cl *WPK* KT4 .... 168 E5
Delta Gain *OXHEY* WD19 .... 42 D4
Delta Rd *NTHLT* UB5 .... 96 D2
Delta Rd *WPK* KT4 .... 168 E5
Delta St *BETH* E2 .... 104 A2 🅸
De Luci Rd *ERITH* DA8 .... 127 J3 🅸
De Lucy St *ABYW* SE2 .... 126 B2 🅸
Delvers Md *DAGE* RM10 .... 91 J4 🅸
Delverton Rd *WALW* SE17 .... 18 D7
Delvino Rd *FUL/PGN* SW6 .... 119 G6 🅸
De Mandeville Ga *EN* EN1 ...... 37 G7
Demesne Rd *WLGTN* SM6 .... 171 K6
Demeta Cl *WBLY* HA9 .... 81 J5 🅸
De Montfort Rd
STRHM/NOR SW16 .... 138 D6
De Morgan Rd *FUL/PGN* SW6 ..... 119 H8
Dempster Rd
WAND/EARL SW18 .... 137 J2
Denberry Dr *SCUP* DA14 .... 144 B7
Denbigh Cl *CHST* BR7 .... 160 F2 🅸
EMPK RM11 .... 74 C2
NTGHL W11 .... 100 F6 🅸
STHL UB1 .... 95 F5 🅸
SUT SM1 .... 169 M7 🅸
WLSDN NW10 .... 81 L7
Denbigh Dr *WDR/YW* UB7 .... 95 J8
Denbigh Gdns
RCHPK/HAM TW10 .... 134 F2
Denbigh Pl *PIM* SW1V .... 16 E7 🅸
Denbigh Rd *EHAM* E6 .... 106 D2 🅸
HSLW TW3 .... 115 H7
NTGHL W11 .... 100 F6 🅸
STHL UB1 .... 95 F5 🅸
WEA W13 .... 98 B6
Denbigh St *PIM* SW1V .... 16 F7 🅸
Denbigh Ter *NTGHL* W11 .... 100 F6 🅸
Denbridge Rd *BMLY* BR1 .... 160 F5
Den Cl *BECK* BR3 .... 159 K7
Dendridge Cl *EN* EN1 .... 37 J1
Dendy St *BAL* SW12 .... 138 A3
Dene Av *BFN/LL* DA15 .... 144 B4
HSLW TW3 .... 114 F8
Dene Cl *BROCKY* SE4 .... 122 E8
HAYES BR2 .... 174 F3
RDART DA2 .... 145 L8
WPK KT4 .... 168 F4
Denecroft Crs *HGDN/ICK* UB10 .. 77 H8
Dene Dr *ORP* BR6 .... 177 H5
Denefield Dr *PUR/KEN* CR8 ..... 184 D8
Dene Gdns *STAN* HA7 .... 44 C7
THDIT KT7 .... 167 G4
Denehurst Gdns *ACT* W3 .... 99 H7 🅸
CRICK NW2 .... 64 C7
RCHPK/HAM TW10 .... 135 G1
WFD IG8 .... 52 B6
WHTN TW2 .... 133 K4
Dene Rd *BKHH* IG9 .... 52 E3
DART DA1 .... 146 F4
NTHWD HA6 .... 41 J8
TRDG/WHET N20 .... 47 M3
The Dene *BELMT* SM2 .... 181 M4
CROY/NA CR0 .... 173 K6
WBLY HA9 .... 80 E4
WEA W13 .... 98 B4
WOT/HER KT12 .... 150 F7
Denewood Cl *WAT* WD17 .... 28 F2
Denewood Rd *HGT* N6 .... 65 M7
Dengie Crs *KTTN* NW5 .... 84 A5 🅸
Denham Cl *WELL* DA16 .... 126 F1 🅸
Denham Court Dr *DEN/HRF* UB9 .. 76 B3
Denham Crs *MTCM* CR4 .... 155 M7
Denham Dr *GNTH/NBYPK* IG2 ..... 71 J7
Denham Green Cl *DEN/HRF* UB9 .. 58 A3
Denham Rd *EBED/NFELT* TW14 .... 132 C4
EW KT17 .... 180 F5
TRDG/WHET N20 .... 47 M5
Denham Wy *BARK* IG11 .... 89 L8
BORE WD6 .... 32 C4
DEN/HRF UB9 .... 76 A3
Denholme Rd *MV/WKIL* W9 .... 100 F2 🅸
Denholme Wk *RAIN* RM13 .... 91 M6 🅸
Denison Cl *EFNCH* N2 .... 65 J4
Denison Rd *EA* W5 .... 98 C3
FELT TW13 .... 131 M8
WIM/MER SW19 .... 155 L2
Deniston Av *BXLY* DA5 .... 144 D5
Denleigh Gdns *THDIT* KT7 ...... 166 E1 🅸
WCHMH N21 .... 49 G2
Denman Dr *ASHF* TW15 .... 149 H2
ESH/CLAY KT10 .... 167 G7 🅸
GLDGN NW11 .... 65 G6
Denman Rd *PECK* SE15 .... 121 M6
Denman St *REGST* W1B .... 10 F7 🅸
Denmark Av *WIM/MER* SW19 ...... 154 E3
Denmark Ct *MRDN* SM4 .... 155 G8
Denmark Gdns *CAR* SM5 .... 170 F5
Denmark Gv *IS* N1 .... 6 A5
Denmark Hl *CMBW* SE5 .... 121 K6
HNHL SE24 .... 139 K1
Denmark Hill Dr
CDALE/KGS NW9 .... 63 H5
Denmark Rd *BMLY* BR1 .... 160 B4 🅸
CAR SM5 .... 170 F5
CEND/HSY/T N8 .... 66 F5
CMBW SE5 .... 121 J6
KIL/WHAMP NW6 .... 100 F1 🅸
KUT KT1 .... 152 E6
SNWD SE25 .... 158 A8
WEA W13 .... 98 B6
WHTN TW2 .... 133 K7
WIM/MER SW19 .... 154 D2
Denmark St *LSQ/SEVD* WC2H 11 H5
PLSTW E13 .... 106 A4
TOTM N17 .... 68 B2
WAN E11 .... 87 L3 🅸
WAT WD17 .... 29 H5
Denmead Rd *CROY/NA* CR0 .... 172 B3 🅸

Dennan Rd *SURB* KT6 .... 167 M3
Denner Rd *CHING* E4 .... 51 G4
Denne Ter *HACK* E8 .... 7 M4
Dennett Rd *CROY/NA* CR0 .... 172 A3
Dennett's Gv *NWCR* SE14 .... 122 D7
Dennett's Rd *NWCR* SE14 .... 122 C6
Denning Av *CROY/NA* CR0 .... 172 A7
Denning Cl *HPTN* TW12 .... 150 F1 🅸
STJWD NW8 .... 2 F7
Denning Rd *HAMP* NW3 .... 83 K4
Dennington Park Rd
KIL/WHAMP NW6 .... 83 G6
Dennis Av *WBLY* HA9 .... 80 F5 🅸
Dennises La *UPMR* RM14 .... 93 M7
Dennis Gdns *STAN* HA7 .... 44 C7
Dennis Park Crs *RYNPK* SW20 ... 154 B4
Dennis Reeve Cl *MTCM* CR4 ..... 155 M4
Dennis Rd *E/WMO/HCT* KT8 ...... 151 J7
Dennis Wy *CLAP* SW4 .... 120 D8
Denny Av *WAB* EN9 .... 27 K7
Denny Crs *LBTH* SE11 .... 18 A7
Denny Rd *ED* N9 .... 50 B3
Denny St *LBTH* SE11 .... 18 B7
Den Rd *HAYES* BR2 .... 159 K6
Densham Rd *SRTFD* E15 .... 87 L8
Densole Cl *BECK* BR3 .... 158 E4 🅸
Densworth Gv *ED* N9 .... 50 C4
Denton Av *BAR* EN5 .... 33 J8
Denton Gv *WOT/HER* KT12 .... 165 L4
Denton Rd *BXLY* DA5 .... 145 L5
CEND/HSY/T N8 .... 66 F6
DART DA1 .... 145 L4
TWK TW1 .... 134 D3
UED N18 .... 49 L6
WELL DA16 .... 126 E1
Denton St *WAND/EARL* SW18 ..... 137 H3
Denton Wy *CLPT* E5 .... 86 D3
Dents Rd *BTSEA* SW11 .... 137 M3
Denver Cl *ORP* BR6 .... 176 E1 🅸
Denver Rd *DART* DA1 .... 146 A4
STNW/STAM N16 .... 67 L8
Denver St *CHEL* SW3 .... 15 K5
Denziloe Av *HGDN/ICK* UB10 .... 95 H2
Denzil Rd *WLSDN* NW10 .... 81 H3
Deodar Rd *PUT/ROE* SW15 ...... 136 E1
Deodora Cl *TRDG/WHET* N20 ..... 47 L5 🅸
Depot Ap *CRICK* NW2 .... 82 D4
Depot Rd *EW* KT17 .... 180 E6
HSLW TW3 .... 115 K4
Depot St *CMBW* SE5 .... 121 K4 🅸
Deptford Br *GNWCH* SE10 .... 123 G6 🅸
Deptford Broadway
DEPT SE8 .... 123 G6 🅸
Deptford Church St *DEPT* SE8 .. 123 G4
Deptford Gn *DEPT* SE8 .... 123 G4
Deptford High St *DEPT* SE8 .... 123 G6
Deptford Whf *DEPT* SE8 .... 122 F2 🅸
De Quincey Rd *TOTM* N17 .... 67 K2
Derby Av *KTN/HRWW/W* HA3 ...... 61 J2
NFNCH/WDSP N12 .... 47 J7
ROMW/RG RM7 .... 73 H7
UPMR RM14 .... 92 F3
Derby Ga *WHALL* SW1A 17 J1
Derby Hl *FSTH* SE23 .... 140 C6
Derby Hill Crs *FSTH* SE23 ..... 140 C6
Derby Rd *BRYLDS* KT5 .... 168 A3
CROY/NA CR0 .... 172 B4
FSTGT E7 .... 88 D7
GFD/PVL UB6 .... 79 H8
HOM E9 .... 86 D8 🅸
HSLW TW3 .... 133 H1
MORT/ESHN SW14 .... 135 G3
PEND EN3 .... 37 H8
SUT SM1 .... 169 M8
SWFD E18 .... 69 M2
UED N18 .... 49 L3
UX/CGN UB8 .... 94 C1
WAT WD17 .... 29 J7 🅸
WIM/MER SW19 .... 155 G3 🅸
Derbyshire St *BETH* E2 .... 104 A2 🅸
BETH E2 .... 104 B2 🅸
Derby St *MYFR/PICC* W1J 10 B9
Dereham Pl *SDTCH* EC2A 7 K9
Dereham Rd *BARK* IG11 .... 89 M6
Derek Av *HOR/WEW* KT19 .... 168 A8
WBLY HA9 .... 81 H7
WLGTN SM6 .... 171 H5
Derek Cl *HOR/WEW* KT19 .... 168 B7
Derek Walcott Cl *HNHL* SE24 ... 139 H2 🅸
Derham Gdns *UPMR* RM14 .... 93 J3
Deri Av *RAIN* RM13 .... 110 B3
Dericote St *HACK* E8 .... 86 B8 🅸
Deri Dene Cl
STWL/WRAY TW19 .... 130 E3 🅸
Derifall Cl *EHAM* E6 .... 106 F4 🅸
Dering Pl *CROY/NA* CR0 .... 172 C6 🅸
Dering Rd *CROY/NA* CR0 .... 172 C6 🅸
Dering St *CONDST* W1S 10 C5
Derinton Rd *TOOT* SW17 .... 138 A8
Derley Rd *NWDGN* UB2 .... 114 C1 🅸
Dermody Gdns *LEW* SE13 .... 141 K2 🅸
Dermody Rd *LEW* SE13 .... 141 K2
Deronda Rd *BRXS/STRHM* SW2 .... 139 H5
Deroy Cl *CAR* SM5 .... 170 F8
Derry Ct *CAR* SM5 .... 170 F8
Derrick Av *SAND/SEL* CR2 ...... 187 J8
Derrick Gdns *CHARL* SE7 .... 124 C1
Derrick Rd *BECK* BR3 .... 158 E3
Derry Downs *STMC/STPC* BR5 .... 177 J1
Derry Rd *WLGTN* SM6 .... 171 L5
Derry St *KENS* W8 .... 14 C2
Dersingham Av *MNPK* E12 .... 88 F4
Dersingham Rd *CRICK* NW2 ...... 82 B3
Derwent Av *CDALE/KGS* NW9 ..... 63 L6 🅸
EBAR EN4 .... 47 M1
HGDN/ICK UB10 .... 77 G2
MLHL NW7 .... 45 G2
PIN HA5 .... 42 A2
PUT/ROE SW15 .... 135 G8
UED N18 .... 49 L4
Derwent Cl *DART* DA1 .... 146 B5
EBED/NFELT TW14 .... 131 M5
ESH/CLAY KT10 .... 166 E8
Derwent Crs *BXLYHN* DA7 .... 127 G7 🅸
NFNCH/WDSP N12 .... 47 J5
STAN HA7 .... 62 C2

Derwent Dr *PUR/KEN* CR8 .... 184 D7
STMC/STPC BR5 .... 176 D2
YEAD UB4 .... 95 L4
Derwent Gdns *REDBR* IG4 .... 70 C5
WBLY HA9 .... 62 C8
Derwent Gv *EDUL* SE22 .... 139 M1
Derwent Ri *CDALE/KGS* NW9 ..... 63 L7
Derwent Rd *EA* W5 .... 116 C1
MRDN SM4 .... 169 K1
PGE/AN SE20 .... 158 A5
PLMGR N13 .... 48 F6
STHL UB1 .... 96 F5
WHTN TW2 .... 133 H3
Derwent St *GNWCH* SE10 .... 123 L3 🅸
Derwentwater Rd *ACT* W3 .... 99 J7
Derwent Wy *HCH* RM12 .... 92 B5 🅸
De Salis Rd *HGDN/ICK* UB10 .... 95 J3 🅸
Desborough Cl *SHPTN* TW17 ..... 164 A2 🅸
Desenfans Rd *DUL* SE21 .... 139 L3
Desford Rd *CAN/RD* E16 .... 105 L3
Desford Wy *ASHF* TW15 .... 130 F6 🅸
Desmond Rd *WATN* WD24 .... 28 F1
Desmond St *NWCR* SE14 .... 122 E4 🅸
Despard Rd *ARCH* N19 .... 84 C1
Detling Cl *HCH* RM12 .... 92 C5 🅸
Detling Rd *BMLY* BR1 .... 160 A1
ERITH DA8 .... 127 K5
Detmold Rd *CLPT* E5 .... 86 B2
Devalls Cl *EHAM* E6 .... 107 G6
Devana End *CAR* SM5 .... 170 F5
Devas Rd *RYNPK* SW20 .... 154 E8
Devas St *BOW* E3 .... 105 H3 🅸
Devema Cl *CHST* BR7 .... 161 G4 🅸
Devenay Rd *SRTFD* E15 .... 87 M7 🅸
Devenish Rd *ABYW* SE2 .... 108 A3
De Vere Gdns *IL* IG1 .... 88 F2
KENS W8 .... 14 E2
Deverell St *STHWK* SE1 .... 19 G4
Devereux Dr *WAT* WD17 .... 28 E3
Devereux La *BARN* SW13 .... 118 E5
Devereux Rd *BTSEA* SW11 .... 137 M3
De Vere Wk *WAT* WD17 .... 28 E5
Deveron Wy *ROM* RM1 .... 73 L2
Devey Cl *KUTN/CMB* KT2 .... 153 M3
Devizes St *IS* N1 .... 7 H4 🅸
Devoke Wy *WOT/HER* KT12 .... 165 K4
Devon Av *WHTN* TW2 .... 133 J5
Devon Cl *BKHH* IG9 .... 52 B4
GFD/PVL UB6 .... 80 C8
TOTM N17 .... 67 M4
Devoncroft Gdns *TWK* TW1 ...... 134 M4 🅸
Devon Gdns *FSBYPK* N4 .... 67 H7 🅸
Devonia Gdns *UED* N18 .... 49 H4
Devonia Rd *IS* N1 .... 6 D5
Devonport Gdns *IL* IG1 .... 70 F7
Devonport Rd *SHB* W12 .... 100 B8
Devonport St *WCHPL* E1 .... 104 D5 🅸
WCHPL E1 .... 104 C5 🅸
Devon Ri *EFNCH* N2 .... 65 K5
Devon Rd *BARK* IG11 .... 89 L8
BELMT SM2 .... 181 L2
WATN WD24 .... 29 K4
WOT/HER KT12 .... 165 J6
Devonshire Av *BELMT* SM2 ...... 182 C1
DART DA1 .... 146 B3
Devonshire Cl *CAVSQ/HST* W1G .. 10 C2
SRTFD E15 .... 87 L4
Devonshire Crs *MLHL* NW7 ...... 64 D1
Devonshire Dr *GNWCH* SE10 ..... 123 H5 🅸
SURB KT6 .... 167 K3
Devonshire Gdns *CHSWK* W4 ..... 117 J5
TOTM N17 .... 49 J8
WCHMH N21 .... 49 J2
Devonshire Gv *PECK* SE15 ...... 122 B4
Devonshire Hill La *TOTM* N17 .. 49 J8
Devonshire Ms South
CAVSQ/HST W1G 10 C2
Devonshire Ms West
CAVSQ/HST W1G 10 B1
Devonshire Pl *CAVSQ/HST* W1G .. 10 B1
CRICK NW2 .... 83 G3
KENS W8 .... 14 C4 🅸
Devonshire Place Ms *MHST* W1U . 10 B1
Devonshire Rd *BELMT* SM2 ...... 182 C1
BXLYHS DA6 .... 144 E1
CAN/RD E16 .... 106 B5
CAR SM5 .... 170 F8
CHSWK W4 .... 117 L4 🅸
CROY/NA CR0 .... 172 D2
ED N9 .... 50 C3
ELTH/MOT SE9 .... 142 E6 🅸
FELT TW13 .... 132 E7
FSTH SE23 .... 140 D4
GNTH/NBYPK IG2 .... 71 K8
HCH RM12 .... 92 D2
HRW HA1 .... 61 K7
MLHL NW7 .... 64 D1
ORP BR6 .... 177 G2 🅸
PIN HA5 .... 60 C7
PLMGR N13 .... 48 F6
STHL UB1 .... 97 G4
TOTM N17 .... 49 J8
WALTH E17 .... 69 G7
WEA W13 .... 98 B4
WEY KT13 .... 164 A6 🅸
WIM/MER SW19 .... 155 L3
Devonshire Rw *LVPST* EC2M 13 K3
Devonshire Sq *HAYES* BR2 ...... 160 B7 🅸
LVPST EC2M 13 K4
Devonshire St *CAVSQ/HST* W1G .. 10 C1
CHSWK W4 .... 117 L5
Devonshire Ter *BAY/PAD* W2 .... 8 F5
YEAD UB4 .... 96 B5
Devons Rd *BOW* E3 .... 105 G4
Devon St *PECK* SE15 .... 122 B4
Devon Wy *CHSGTN* KT9 .... 167 G6 🅸
HGDN/ICK UB10 .... 94 F1
HOR/WEW KT19 .... 168 B7 🅸
Devon Waye *HEST* TW5 .... 114 D2
De Walden St
CAVSQ/HST W1G .... 10 B3 🅸
Dewar St *PECK* SE15 .... 122 A8
Dewberry Gdns *EHAM* E6 .... 106 D4 🅸
Dewberry St *POP/IOD* E14 ...... 105 J4 🅸
Dewey Rd *DAGE* RM10 .... 91 H6
IS N1 .... 6 A5
Dewey St *TOOT* SW17 .... 155 M1

Dewgrass Gv CHES/WCR EN8 ... 26 D8 2
Dewhurst Rd CHES/WCR EN8........ 26 C2
HMSMTH W6 .... 118 D1
Dewlands Av RDART DA2 .... 147 H4
Dewsbury Cl PIN HA5 .... 60 E7 1
Dewsbury Gdns HARH RM3 .... 56 D8 2
WPK KT4 .... 169 G5 1
Dewsbury Rd HARH RM3 .... 56 E8 1
WLSDN NW10 .... 82 A5
Dexter Rd BAR EN5 .... 46 D1
DEN/HRF UB9 .... 58 C3
Deyncourt Gdns UPMR RM14 ...... 93 J2
Deyncourt Rd TOTM N17 .... 67 K2 1
Deynecourt Gdns WAN E11 .... 70 C5
D'eynsford Rd CMBW SE5 .... 121 K6
Diamedes Av
STWL/WRAY TW19 .... 130 D4 1
Diameter Rd STMC/STPC BR5 ...... 176 B2
Diamond Cl BCTR RM8 .... 90 C1 4
Diamond Rd RSLP HA4 .... 78 D4
WATN WD24 .... 29 G3
Diamond St PECK SE15 .... 121 L5
Diamond Ter GNWCH SE10 .... 123 J6
Diana Cl DEPT SE8 .... 122 F4 2
SWFD E18 .... 70 B2
Diana Gdns SURB KT6 .... 167 M4
Diana Pl CAMTN NW1 .... 4 D9
Diana Rd WALTH E17 .... 68 F4
Dianne Wy EBAR EN4 .... 34 E7 2
Dianthus Cl ABYW SE2 .... 126 B3 1
Diban Av HCH RM12 .... 92 B4
Dibden St IS N1 .... 6 E3
Dibdin Cl SUT SM1 .... 170 A5
Dibdin Rd SUT SM1 .... 170 A5
Dicey Av CRICK NW2 .... 82 C5
Dickens Av DART DA1 .... 147 G1
FNCH N3 .... 65 J2
UX/CGN UB8 .... 95 H5
Dickens Cl ERITH DA8 .... 127 H5
HYS/HAR UB3 .... 113 L2 2
RCHPK/HAM TW10 .... 134 E6
Dickens Dr CHST BR7 .... 161 J2
Dickens La UED N18 .... 49 L7
Dickenson Rd CEND/HSY/T N8 .... 66 E8
FELT TW13 .... 150 C1
Dickenson's La SNWD SE25 .... 173 G1
Dickenson's Pl SNWD SE25 ...... 173 G1 2
Dickens Ri CHIG IG7 .... 53 G5
Dickens Rd EHAM E6 .... 106 D1
Dickens Sq STHWK SE1 .... 18 F3 1
Dickens St VX/NE SW8 .... 120 B7
Dickens Wy ROM RM1 .... 73 L5
Dickerage Hl NWMAL KT3 .... 153 J5
Dickerage La NWMAL KT3 .... 153 J6
Dickerage Rd KUT KT1 .... 153 J4
NWMAL KT3 .... 153 J5 1
Dickinson Av RKW/CH/CXG WD3 .. 41 G1
Dickinson Sq RKW/CH/CXG WD3 .. 41 H1
Dickson Fold PIN HA5 .... 60 D5
Dickson Rd ELTH/MOT SE9 .... 124 E8
Dick Turpin Wy
EBED/NFELT TW14 .... 131 M1
Didsbury Cl EHAM E6 .... 88 F8
Digby Crs FSBYPK N4 .... 85 J2
Digby Gdns DAGE RM10 .... 91 G8
Digby Pl CROY/NA CR0 .... 172 F5
Digby Rd BARK IG11 .... 89 M7
HOM E9 .... 86 D6
Digby St BETH E2 .... 104 C2 2
Digdens Ri EPSOM KT18 .... 180 C8
Diggon St WCHPL E1 .... 104 D4
Dighton Rd WAND/EARL SW18 .... 137 J2
Dignum St IS N1 .... 6 A5 1
Digswell Cl BORE WD6 .... 32 A3
Digswell St HOLWY N7 .... 85 G6 2
Dilhorne Cl LEE/GVPK SE12 .... 142 B7
Dilke St CHEL SW3 .... 15 M9
Dillwyn Cl SYD SE26 .... 140 E8
Dilston Cl NTHLT UB5 .... 96 D2 3
Dilton Gdns PUT/ROE SW15 .... 136 A5
Dimes Pl HMSMTH W6 .... 118 B2 2
Dimmock Dr NTHLT UB5 .... 79 K5
Dimond Cl FSTGT E7 .... 88 A4
Dimsdale Dr CDALE/KGS NW9 ...... 81 J1
EN EN1 .... 50 A2
Dimson Crs BOW E3 .... 105 G2 1
Dingle Cl BAR EN5 .... 45 M1
Dingle Gdns POP/IOD E14 .... 105 G6 1
Dingle Rd ASHF TW15 .... 149 H1
The Dingle HGDN/ICK UB10 .... 95 H2 2
Dingley La STRHM/NOR SW16 .... 138 D6
Dingley Pl FSBYE EC1V 6 F8
Dingley Rd FSBYE EC1V 6 E8
Dingwall Av CROY/NA CR0 .... 172 C4
Dingwall Gdns GLDGN NW11 .... 65 G7
Dingwall Rd CAR SM5 .... 182 F2
CROY/NA CR0 .... 172 D4
WAND/EARL SW18 .... 137 J4 1
Dinmont St BETH E2 .... 104 B1 4
Dinsdale Gdns BAR EN5 .... 34 B8
SNWD SE25 .... 157 L7
Dinsdale Rd BKHTH/KID SE3 .... 123 M4
Dinsmore Rd BAL SW12 .... 138 B4
Dinton Rd KUTN/CMB KT2 .... 152 F3
WIM/MER SW19 .... 155 K2
Diploma Av EFNCH N2 .... 65 L5 1
Dirdene Cl EW KT17 .... 180 F5 1
Dirdene Gdns EW KT17 .... 180 F5 2
Dirdene Gv EW KT17 .... 180 F5 3
Dirleton Rd SRTFD E15 .... 87 M8
Disbrowe Rd HMSMTH W6 .... 118 E4
Dishforth La CDALE/KGS NW9 ...... 63 L2
Disney Pl STHWK SE1 .... 18 F1 2
Disney St STHWK SE1 .... 18 F1
Dison Cl PEND EN3 .... 37 K4 2
Disraeli Cl THMD SE28 .... 108 B7
Disraeli Rd EA W5 .... 98 D7
FSTGT E7 .... 88 A6
PUT/ROE SW15 .... 136 E1
WLSDN NW10 .... 99 J1
Diss St BETH E2 .... 7 L7
Distaff La BLKFR EC4V 12 E6
Distillery La HMSMTH W6 .... 118 C3
Distillery Rd HMSMTH W6 .... 118 C3
Distin St LBTH SE11 .... 18 A6
District Rd GFD/PVL UB6 .... 80 B5
Ditchburn St POP/IOD E14 .... 105 J6 2
Ditchfield Rd YEAD UB4 .... 96 E3
Dittisham Rd ELTH/MOT SE9 .... 142 E8
Ditton Cl THDIT KT7 .... 167 G2
Dittoncroft Cl CROY/NA CR0 ..... 172 E6 3
Ditton Grange Cl SURB KT6 .... 167 K3
Ditton Grange Dr SURB KT6 .... 167 K3
Ditton Hl SURB KT6 .... 167 J3
Ditton Hill Rd SURB KT6 .... 167 J3
Ditton Lawn THDIT KT7 .... 167 G3
Ditton Reach THDIT KT7 .... 167 H1
Ditton Rd BXLYHS DA6 .... 144 D2
NWDGN UB2 .... 114 F3
SURB KT6 .... 167 L3
Dixon Cl EHAM E6 .... 106 F5
Dixon Pl WWKM BR4 .... 174 B3
Dixon Rd NWCR SE14 .... 122 E6
SNWD SE25 .... 157 L6
Dobbin Cl KTN/HRWW/W HA3 ...... 62 A3
Dobell Rd ELTH/MOT SE9 .... 142 F2
Dobree Av WLSDN NW10 .... 82 B7
Dobson Cl KIL/WHAMP NW6 .... 3 G2
Dockers Tanner Rd
POP/IOD E14 .... 123 G2 5
Dockhead STHWK SE1 .... 19 M2
Dock Hill Av BERM/RHTH SE16 .... 104 D8
Dockland St CAN/RD E16 .... 107 G8
Dockley Rd BERM/RHTH SE16 ...... 122 A1
Dock Rd BTFD TW8 .... 116 D5 3
CAN/RD E16 .... 105 M6
Dockside Rd CAN/RD E16 .... 106 D6
Dock St WCHPL E1 .... 104 A6
Dockwell Cl EBED/NFELT TW14 .. 132 A1
Doctors Cl SYD SE26 .... 158 C1
Dodbrooke Rd WNWD SE27 .... 139 G7 1
Doddington Gv WALW SE17 .... 18 C9
Doddington Pl WALW SE17 .... 18 C9
Dodsley Pl ED N9 .... 50 C5 1
Dodson St STHWK SE1 .... 18 B2
Dod St POP/IOD E14 .... 104 F5
Doebury Wk
WOOL/PLUM SE18 .... 126 A4 1
Doel Cl WIM/MER SW19 .... 155 J3
Doggett Rd CAT SE6 .... 141 G4
Doggetts Ct EBAR EN4 .... 34 E8
Doghurst Av WDR/YW UB7 .... 113 H5
Doghurst Dr WDR/YW UB7 ...... 113 H5 2
Dog Kennel Hl CMBW SE5 .... 121 L8
Dog La WLSDN NW10 .... 81 L4
Dog Rose Ramble NTHLT UB5 ...... 78 A8
Dog Rose Ramble &
Hillingdon Trail YEAD UB4 .... 77 M8
Doherty Rd PLSTW E13 .... 106 A3
Dolben St STHWK SE1 .... 12 D9 1
Dolby Rd FUL/PGN SW6 .... 118 F7 4
Dolis Valley Green Wk FNCH N3 .. 64 E3
GLDGN NW11 .... 64 E5
Dolland St LBTH SE11 .... 17 M8
Dollis Av FNCH N3 .... 64 F2
Dollis Crs RSLP HA4 .... 78 C1
Dollis Hill Av CRICK NW2 .... 82 B3
Dollis Hill La CRICK NW2 .... 81 M4
Dollis Pk FNCH N3 .... 64 F2
Dollis Rd FNCH N3 .... 64 E2
Dollis Valley Green Wk
TRDG/WHET N20 .... 47 H1
Dollis Valley Wy BAR EN5 .... 33 M8
Dolman Rd CHSWK W4 .... 117 K2
Dolman St CLAP SW4 .... 138 F1
Dolphin Ap ROM RM1 .... 73 M5
Dolphin Cl SURB KT6 .... 167 K1
THMD SE28 .... 108 C5
Dolphin Ct
STWL/WRAY TW19 .... 130 A7 2
Dolphin Ct North
STWL/WRAY TW19 .... 130 A7 3
Dolphin La POP/IOD E14 .... 105 H6 1
Dolphin Rd NTHLT UB5 .... 96 F1
Dolphin Sq PIM SW1V 17 G8
Dolphin St KUT KT1 .... 152 E4 3
Dombey St BMSBY WC1N 11 L2
Dome Hill Pk SYD SE26 .... 139 M8
Domett Cl CMBW SE5 .... 139 K1 2
Domingo St FSBYE EC1V 6 E9 1
Dominica Cl EHAM E6 .... 106 D1 1
Dominion Dr CRW RM5 .... 55 H8
Dominion Pde HRW HA1 .... 61 M6 4
Dominion Rd CROY/NA CR0 .... 172 F2
NWDGN UB2 .... 114 E1 1
Dominion St LVPST EC2M 13 H2
Dominion Wy RAIN RM13 .... 110 A2 1
Domonic Dr ELTH/MOT SE9 .... 143 H7
Domville Cl TRDG/WHET N20 .... 47 K4
Donald Dr CHDH RM6 .... 72 C6
Donald Rd CROY/NA CR0 .... 171 M1
PLSTW E13 .... 88 B8
Donaldson Rd
KIL/WHAMP NW6 .... 100 F1 1
WOOL/PLUM SE18 .... 125 G6
Donald Woods Gdns
BRYLDS KT5 .... 168 B4
Doncaster Dr NTHLT UB5 .... 78 F5
Doncaster Gdns FSBYPK N4 .... 67 J7 1
NTHLT UB5 .... 78 F5 1
Doncaster Gn OXHEY WD19 .... 42 C7 4
Doncaster Rd ED N9 .... 50 B2 3
Doncaster Wy UPMR RM14 .... 92 F3
Donegal St IS N1 .... 5 M6
Doneraile St FUL/PGN SW6 .... 118 D7
Dongola Rd PLSTW E13 .... 106 B2
TOTM N17 .... 67 L4
Dongola Rd West
PLSTW E13 .... 106 B2 3
Donington Av BARK/HLT IG6 .... 71 J6
Donkey Aly EDUL SE22 .... 140 A4
Donkey La EN EN1 .... 37 G5
Donnefield Av EDGW HA8 .... 44 E8
Donne Pl CHEL SW3 .... 15 K5
MTCM CR4 .... 156 B7
Donne Rd BCTR RM8 .... 90 C2
Donnington Rd
KTN/HRWW/W HA3 .... 62 D7
WLSDN NW10 .... 82 B8 1
WPK KT4 .... 169 G4
Donnybrook Rd
STRHM/NOR SW16 .... 156 C3
Donovan Av MUSWH N10 .... 66 B3
Donovan Cl HOR/WEW KT19 .... 180 D3
Don Phelan Cl CMBW SE5 .... 121 K6
Don Wy ROM RM1 .... 73 L1
Doone Cl TEDD TW11 .... 152 A2 2
Doon St STHWK SE1 .... 12 A9
Dorado Gdns ORP BR6 .... 177 K5
Doral Wy CAR SM5 .... 170 F7 4
Dorando Cl SHB W12 .... 100 B6 4
Doran Gv WOOL/PLUM SE18 .... 125 L5
Doran Rd WIM/MER SW19 .... 155 G1
Dora St POP/IOD E14 .... 104 F5
Dorchester Av BXLY DA5 .... 144 D5
PLMGR N13 .... 49 J6
RYLN/HDSTN HA2 .... 61 J7
Dorchester Cl DART DA1 .... 146 F4
NTHLT UB5 .... 79 H5
STMC/STPC BR5 .... 162 B3 1
Dorchester Ct CRICK NW2 .... 82 D3
HNHL SE24 .... 139 J2
STHGT/OAK N14 .... 48 B2
Dorchester Dr
EBED/NFELT TW14 .... 131 L3
HNHL SE24 .... 139 J2
Dorchester Gdns CHING E4 .... 51 G6 2
GLDGN NW11 .... 65 G5 1
Dorchester Gv CHSWK W4 .... 117 L4
Dorchester Ms TWK TW1 .... 134 C4 1
Dorchester Rd MRDN SM4 .... 170 B2
NTHLT UB5 .... 79 H5
WEY KT13 .... 164 B5
WPK KT4 .... 169 J3
Dorchester Wy
KTN/HRWW/W HA3 .... 62 F7
Dorchester Waye YEAD UB4 .... 96 C5
Dorcis Av BXLYHN DA7 .... 126 E7
Dordrecht Rd ACT W3 .... 99 L7
Dore Av MNPK E12 .... 89 G5
Doreen Av CDALE/KGS NW9 .... 81 K1
Dore Gdns MRDN SM4 .... 170 B2 1
Dorell Cl STHL UB1 .... 96 F4
Dorian Rd HCH RM12 .... 92 A1
Doria Rd FUL/PGN SW6 .... 118 F7
Doric Wy CAMTN NW1 .... 5 G7
Dorien Rd RYNPK SW20 .... 154 D5
Doris Av BXLYHN DA7 .... 127 J6
Doris Rd ASHF TW15 .... 149 K2
FSTGT E7 .... 88 A7
Dorking Cl DEPT SE8 .... 122 F4 3
WPK KT4 .... 169 K4 2
Dorking Ri HARH RM3 .... 56 D6
Dorking Rd EPSOM KT18 .... 180 B8
HARH RM3 .... 56 D6
Dorking Wk HARH RM3 .... 56 D6
Dorkins Wy UPMR RM14 .... 75 L8
Dorlcote Rd WAND/EARL SW18 .. 137 K4
Dorling Dr EW KT17 .... 180 F5
Dorly Cl SHPTN TW17 .... 149 L7
Dorman Pl ED N9 .... 50 A4 4
Dormans Cl NTHWD HA6 .... 59 K1
Dorman Wy STJWD NW8 .... 3 G3
Dormay St WAND/EARL SW18 ...... 137 H2
Dormer Cl BAR EN5 .... 33 K8
SRTFD E15 .... 87 M6
Dormer's Av STHL UB1 .... 97 G5
Dormers Ri GFD/PVL UB6 .... 97 H5
Dormer's Wells La STHL UB1 .... 97 G5
Dormywood RSLP HA4 .... 59 M6
Dornberg Cl BKHTH/KID SE3 .... 124 A5
Dornberg Rd BKHTH/KID SE3 .. 124 B5 2
Dorncliffe Rd FUL/PGN SW6 .... 118 E7 2
Dorney Gv WEY KT13 .... 164 B4
Dorney Ri STMC/STPC BR5 .... 161 M7
Dorney Wy HSLWW TW4 .... 132 E2
Dornfell St KIL/WHAMP NW6 .... 82 F5 2
Dornton Rd SAND/SEL CR2 .... 172 E7
TOOT SW17 .... 138 B6
Dorothy Av ALP/SUD HA0 .... 80 E7
Dorothy Evans Cl BXLYHN DA7 .. 145 H1
Dorothy Gdns BCTR RM8 .... 90 B4
Dorothy Rd BTSEA SW11 .... 119 M8
Dorrington Gdns HCH RM12 .... 92 D1
Dorrington St HCIRC EC1N 12 A2 2
Dorrit St STHWK SE1 .... 18 F1 3
Dorrit Wy CHST BR7 .... 161 J2
Dorrofield Cl RKW/CH/CXG WD3 .. 28 C8
Dors Cl CDALE/KGS NW9 .... 81 K1
Dorset Av NWDGN UB2 .... 115 G2
ROM RM1 .... 73 K4
WELL DA16 .... 143 M1
YEAD UB4 .... 95 L2
Dorset Buildings EMB EC4Y 12 C5 3
Dorset Cl CAMTN NW1 .... 9 L2
YEAD UB4 .... 95 L2 1
Dorset Dr EDGW HA8 .... 44 F8
Dorset Gdns
STRHM/NOR SW16 .... 156 F7 1
Dorset Ms FNCH N3 .... 65 G2
KTBR SW1X 16 C3
Dorset Pl SRTFD E15 .... 87 K6
Dorset Ri EMB EC4Y 12 C5
Dorset Rd ASHF TW15 .... 130 D7
BECK BR3 .... 158 D6
BELMT SM2 .... 182 A3
EA W5 .... 116 C1
ELTH/MOT SE9 .... 142 E6
HRW HA1 .... 61 J7
MTCM CR4 .... 155 L5
SEVS/STOTM N15 .... 67 K5
VX/NE SW8 .... 120 F5
WDGN N22 .... 66 E2
WIM/MER SW19 .... 155 G4
Dorset Sq CAMTN NW1 .... 9 L1
Dorset St MHST W1U 9 M3
Dorset Wy HGDN/ICK UB10 .... 94 F1
WHTN TW2 .... 133 J5
Dorset Waye HEST TW5 .... 114 F5
Dorville Crs HMSMTH W6 .... 118 B1
Dorville Rd LEE/GVPK SE12 .... 142 A2
Dothill Rd WOOL/PLUM SE18 .... 125 J5
Douai Gv HPTN TW12 .... 151 J4
Doughty Ms BMSBY WC1N 11 L1
Doughty St BMSBY WC1N 5 L9
Douglas Av ALP/SUD HA0 .... 80 E7
HARH RM3 .... 74 E3
NWMAL KT3 .... 154 B7
WALTH E17 .... 69 G2
WATN WD24 .... 29 K2
Douglas Cl STAN HA7 .... 44 A7
WLGTN SM6 .... 171 L8
Douglas Crs YEAD UB4 .... 96 C3
Douglas Dr CROY/NA CR0 .... 174 A5 2
Douglas Ms CRICK NW2 .... 82 E3 1
Douglas Pl POP/IOD E14 .... 123 J3 1
Douglas Rd CAN/RD E16 .... 106 A4
CHING E4 .... 51 L2
ESH/CLAY KT10 .... 166 B4
GDMY/SEVK IG3 .... 72 A8
HSLW TW3 .... 115 H8 2
IS N1 .... 6 E1
KIL/WHAMP NW6 .... 82 F8
KUT KT1 .... 153 H5
ROM RM1 .... 73 M7
STWL/WRAY TW19 .... 130 D3 3
SURB KT6 .... 167 M4
WDGN N22 .... 67 G2
WELL DA16 .... 126 B6
Douglas Rd North IS N1 .... 85 J6 2
Douglas Rd South IS N1 .... 85 J6 3
Douglas St WEST SW1P 17 G6
Douglas Ter WALTH E17 .... 68 F2
Douglas Wy DEPT SE8 .... 122 F5 1
Doulton Ms HAMP NW3 .... 83 H6 1
Dounesforth Gdns
WAND/EARL SW18 .... 137 H5
Douro Pl KENS W8 .... 14 D3 1
Douro St BOW E3 .... 105 G1
Douthwaite Sq WAP E1W 104 A7 4
Dove Ap EHAM E6 .... 106 E4
Dove Cl SAND/SEL CR2 .... 185 K4
YEAD UB4 .... 96 D3 3
Dovecot Cl PIN HA5 .... 60 C6
Dovecote Cl WEY KT13 .... 164 B5 3
Dove Ct LOTH EC2R 13 G5 2
Dovedale Av CLAY IG5 .... 71 G3
KTN/HRWW/W HA3 .... 62 C7
Dovedale Cl DEN/HRF UB9 .... 58 C3
WELL DA16 .... 126 A6
Dovedale Ri MTCM CR4 .... 155 M3 1
Dovedale Rd EDUL SE22 .... 140 B2
RDART DA2 .... 147 J5 1
Dovedon Cl STHGT/OAK N14 .... 48 E4
Dove House Gdns CHING E4 .... 51 G4 2
Dovehouse Md BARK IG11 .... 107 K1 1
Dovehouse St CHEL SW3 .... 15 J8
Dove La POTB/CUF EN6 .... 23 H7
Dove Ms ECT SW5 .... 14 E6
Doveney Cl STMC/STPC BR5 .... 162 D7
Dove Pk PIN HA5 .... 60 F1
Dover Cl ROMW/RG RM7 .... 73 J3
Dovercourt Av THHTH CR7 ...... 157 G7 1
Dovercourt Gdns STAN HA7 .... 44 E7
Dovercourt La SUT SM1 .... 170 C5
Dovercourt Rd EDUL SE22 .... 139 M3
Doverfield CHESW EN7 .... 25 J2
Doverfield Rd
BRXS/STRHM SW2 .... 138 E3
Dover Gdns CAR SM5 .... 170 F5
Dover House Rd
PUT/ROE SW15 .... 136 A1
Doveridge Gdns PLMGR N13 .... 49 H6
Dove Rd IS N1 .... 85 K6
Dove Rw BETH E2 .... 104 A1
Dover Park Dr PUT/ROE SW15 .... 136 B3
Dover Patrol BKHTH/KID SE3 .. 124 B7 2
Dover Rd ED N9 .... 50 C4
MNPK E12 .... 88 C2
NRWD SE19 .... 157 K2 1
WOOL/PLUM SE18 .... 125 H7
Dover St MYFR/PICC W1J 10 D7
Dover Wy RKW/CH/CXG WD3 .... 28 C7
Doves Cl HAYES BR2 .... 175 L4
Doves Yd IS N1 .... 6 A4
Doveton Rd SAND/SEL CR2 ...... 172 D7 5
Doveton St WCHPL E1 .... 104 C3 3
Dowanhill Rd CAT SE6 .... 141 K5
Dowdeswell Cl PUT/ROE SW15 .... 135 L1
Dowding Cl RAIN RM13 .... 92 B7
Dowding Pl STAN HA7 .... 44 A8
Dowding Rd BH/WHM TN16 .... 187 K8
HGDN/ICK UB10 .... 76 F7
Dower Av WLGTN SM6 .... 183 H2
Dowgate Hl CANST EC4R 13 G6
Dowlas St CMBW SE5 .... 121 L5 2
Dowlerville Rd ORP BR6 .... 176 F8
Dowman Cl WIM/MER SW19 ...... 155 H3 1
Downage HDN NW4 .... 64 C4
Downalong BUSH WD23 .... 43 K3
Downbank Av BXLYHN DA7 .... 127 K6
Down Barns Rd RSLP HA4 .... 78 D4
Down Cl NTHLT UB5 .... 96 B2
Downderry Rd BMLY BR1 .... 141 K8 1
Downe Cl WELL DA16 .... 126 C5
Downend WOOL/PLUM SE18 .. 125 H5 1
Downe Rd HAYES BR2 .... 187 L2
MTCM CR4 .... 155 M5
Downer's Cottages
CLAP SW4 .... 138 C1 1
Downes Cl TWK TW1 .... 134 B3 3
Downes Ct WCHMH N21 .... 49 G3
Downfield WPK KT4 .... 168 F3
Downfield Cl MV/WKIL W9 .... 8 C1
Downfield Rd CHES/WCR EN8 .... 26 E4
Down Hall Rd KUTN/CMB KT2 ...... 152 D4
Downham Cl CRW RM5 .... 73 G1
Downham Rd IS N1 .... 7 J2
Downham Wy BMLY BR1 .... 159 L1
Downhills Av TOTM N17 .... 67 K4
Downhills Park Rd TOTM N17 .... 67 J4
Downhills Wy TOTM N17 .... 67 J3
Downhurst Av MLHL NW7 .... 45 K8
Downing Cl RYLN/HDSTN HA2 .... 61 J4
Downing Dr GFD/PVL UB6 .... 79 L8
Downing Rd DAGW RM9 .... 90 F7
Downings EHAM E6 .... 107 G5
Downing St WHALL SW1A 17 J1 1
Downland Cl COUL/CHIP CR5 .... 183 H7
TRDG/WHET N20 .... 47 J3
Downlands WAB EN9 .... 27 L7 1
Downlands Rd PUR/KEN CR8 .... 183 L6
Downleys Cl ELTH/MOT SE9 .... 142 E6
Downman Rd ELTH/MOT SE9 .... 124 E8
Down Pl HMSMTH W6 .... 118 B2
Down Rd TEDD TW11 .... 152 B2
Downs Av CHST BR7 .... 160 F1
DART DA1 .... 147 G4
EPSOM KT18 .... 180 F8
PIN HA5 .... 60 F7
Downs Bridge Rd BECK BR3 .... 159 K4
Downs Court Rd PUR/KEN CR8 .. 184 C6
Downsell Rd WAN E11 .... 87 K4
Downsfield Rd WALTH E17 .... 68 E7
Downshall Av GDMY/SEVK IG3 .... 71 L7
Downs Hl BECK BR3 .... 159 K4
Downs Hill Rd EPSOM KT18 ..... 180 E8 1
Downshire Hl HAMP NW3 .... 83 K4
Downside EPSOM KT18 .... 180 E7
SUN TW16 .... 150 A4
TWK TW1 .... 133 M7
Downside Cl WIM/MER SW19 .... 155 J2
Downside Crs HAMP NW3 .... 83 L5
WEA W13 .... 98 A3
Downside Rd BELMT SM2 .... 170 D8
Downs La CLPT E5 .... 86 B4 2
Downs Park Rd HACK E8 .... 86 A5
Downs Rd BECK BR3 .... 159 H5
BELMT SM2 .... 182 B4
CLPT E5 .... 86 B4 3
EN EN1 .... 36 E7
EPSOM KT18 .... 180 E8
PUR/KEN CR8 .... 184 B4
THHTH CR7 .... 157 J4 1
Downs Side BELMT SM2 .... 181 M4
The Downs RYNPK SW20 .... 154 D3
Down St E/WMO/HCT KT8 .... 151 G8
MYFR/PICC W1J 10 C9
Down Street Ms
MYFR/PICC W1J 16 C1
Downs Vw ISLW TW7 .... 116 A6 3
Downsview Cl SWLY BR8 .... 163 M6 1
Downsview Gdns
NRWD SE19 .... 157 J3 1
Downsview Rd NRWD SE19 .... 157 J3
Downsway ORP BR6 .... 176 E7 1
SAND/SEL CR2 .... 184 E4
The Downsway BELMT SM2 .... 182 C2
Downton Av BRXS/STRHM SW2 .. 138 F6
Downtown Rd
BERM/RHTH SE16 .... 104 E8
Downway NFNCH/WDSP N12 ..... 65 L1 1
Down Wy NTHLT UB5 .... 96 B2
Dowrey St IS N1 .... 6 A3 1
Dowry Wk WAT WD17 .... 28 F3
Dowsett Rd TOTM N17 .... 68 A3
Dowson Cl CMBW SE5 .... 139 K1 3
Doyce St STHWK SE1 .... 18 E1 1
Doyle Cl ERITH DA8 .... 127 L6
Doyle Gdns WLSDN NW10 .... 82 B8
Doyle Rd SNWD SE25 .... 158 A7
D'oyley St KTBR SW1X 16 A5
Doynton St KTTN NW5 .... 84 B2 1
Draco St WALW SE17 .... 18 E9
Dragonfly Cl PLSTW E13 .... 106 B2 4
Dragoon Rd DEPT SE8 .... 122 F3
Dragor Rd WLSDN NW10 .... 99 J3 1
Drake Cl BERM/RHTH SE16 ...... 104 D8 3
Drake Crs THMD SE28 .... 108 C5
Drakefell Rd NWCR SE14 .... 122 D7
Drakefield Rd TOOT SW17 .... 138 A7
Drake Ms RAIN RM13 .... 92 A7 2
Drake Rd BROCKY SE4 .... 123 G8
CHSGTN KT9 .... 168 A7
CROY/NA CR0 .... 171 M2 1
MTCM CR4 .... 171 G1
RYLN/HDSTN HA2 .... 78 F2
Drakes Cl CHES/WCR EN8 .... 26 D1 3
Drakes Ctyd KIL/WHAMP NW6 .. 82 F7 3
Drakes Dr NTHWD HA6 .... 59 H2
Drake St ENC/FH EN2 .... 36 D4
Drakewood Rd
STRHM/NOR SW16 .... 156 D3 2
Draper Cl BELV DA17 .... 126 F2
Drapers Rd ENC/FH EN2 .... 36 B5
SRTFD E15 .... 87 J4
TOTM N17 .... 67 M4 3
Drappers Wy BERM/RHTH SE16 .. 122 A2
Drawell Cl WOOL/PLUM SE18 ... 125 L3 2
Drax Av RYNPK SW20 .... 154 A3
Draxmont WIM/MER SW19 .... 154 E2 1
Draycot Rd SURB KT6 .... 168 A3
WAN E11 .... 70 B7
Draycott Av CHEL SW3 .... 15 K6
KTN/HRWW/W HA3 .... 62 B7 1
Draycott Cl KTN/HRWW/W HA3 .... 62 B7
Draycott Pl CHEL SW3 .... 15 L6
Draycott Ter CHEL SW3 .... 15 L5
Drayford Cl MV/WKIL W9 .... 100 F3 3
Draymans Wy ISLW TW7 .... 115 M8
Drayson Cl WAB EN9 .... 27 K5
Drayson Ms KENS W8 .... 14 B2
Drayton Av LOU IG10 .... 52 F1
ORP BR6 .... 176 B3
POTB/CUF EN6 .... 22 E5
WEA W13 .... 98 A6
Drayton Bridge Rd HNWL W7 .... 97 M6
Drayton Cl HSLWW TW4 .... 132 F2
IL IG1 .... 89 K1
Drayton Gdns WBPTN SW10 .... 14 F7
WCHMH N21 .... 49 H2
WDR/YW UB7 .... 94 D8
WEA W13 .... 98 A6
Drayton Gn WEA W13 .... 98 A6
Drayton Green Rd WEA W13 .... 98 B6
Drayton Gv WEA W13 .... 98 A6
Drayton Pk HBRY N5 .... 85 G5
Drayton Rd BORE WD6 .... 32 A7
CROY/NA CR0 .... 172 B4
TOTM N17 .... 67 L3
WAN E11 .... 87 K1
WEA W13 .... 98 A5
WLSDN NW10 .... 81 M8
Dreadnought St GNWCH SE10 ..... 123 L1
Drenon Sq HYS/HAR UB3 .... 95 M6
Dresden Cl HAMP NW3 .... 83 H6 3
Dresden Rd ARCH N19 .... 84 C1
Dresden Wy WEY KT13 .... 164 C7
Dressington Av BROCKY SE4 .... 141 G3
Drew Av MLHL NW7 .... 46 E8
Drew Gdns GFD/PVL UB6 .... 79 M6
Drew Rd CAN/RD E16 .... 106 E7
Drewstead Rd
STRHM/NOR SW16 .... 138 D6
Driffield Rd BOW E3 .... 104 E1
The Drift HAYES BR2 .... 175 K5
The Driftway BNSTD SM7 .... 181 J8 1
MTCM CR4 .... 156 A4 2
Drinkwater Rd
RYLN/HDSTN HA2 .... 79 H2 1

The Drive ACT W3 ... 99 J5
ASHF TW15 ... 149 K3
BAR EN5 ... 33 L6
BAR EN5 ... 47 J1
BARK IG11 ... 89 M7
BECK BR3 ... 159 G5
BELMT SM2 ... 181 M5
BKHH IG9 ... 52 C2
BXLY DA5 ... 144 D4
CHESW EN7 ... 25 H1
CHESW EN7 ... 26 B1
CHING E4 ... 51 K2
CHST BR7 ... 161 M4
COUL/CHIP CR5 ... 183 L7
CRW RM5 ... 73 K2
EBED/NFELT TW14 ... 132 C4
EDGW HA8 ... 45 G7
ENC/FH EN2 ... 36 D4
ERITH DA8 ... 127 H5
ESH/CLAY KT10 ... 166 C3
FBAR/BDGN N11 ... 48 C8
FNCH N3 ... 65 G1
GLDGN NW11 ... 64 E8
HARH RM3 ... 74 E2
HGDN/ICK UB10 ... 76 E3
HGT N6 ... 65 M6
HOLWY N7 ... 84 F6
HOR/WEW KT19 ... 168 F8
HSLW TW3 ... 115 K7
IL IG1 ... 70 E7
KUTN/CMB KT2 ... 153 J3
LOU IG10 ... 39 L6
MRDN SM4 ... 155 J8
NTHWD HA6 ... 59 L2
ORP BR6 ... 176 F4
POTB/CUF EN6 ... 22 F6
RYLN/HDSTN HA2 ... 61 G8
RYNPK SW20 ... 154 C3
SCUP DA14 ... 144 B7
SWFD E18 ... 70 A4
THHTH CR7 ... 157 K7
WALTH E17 ... 69 H4
WAT WD17 ... 28 D2
WBLY HA9 ... 81 J2
WLGTN SM6 ... 183 J3
WWKM BR4 ... 174 D2
The Driveway POTB/CUF EN6 ... 24 E1
Dr Johnson Av TOOT SW17 ... 138 B7
Droitwich Cl SYD SE26 ... 140 A7
Dromey Gdns
KTN/HRWW/W HA3 ... 61 M1
Dromore Rd PUT/ROE SW15 ... 136 E3
Dronfield Gdns BCTR RM8 ... 90 C5
Droop St NKENS W10 ... 100 E3
Drovers Pl PECK SE15 ... 122 B5
Drovers Rd SAND/SEL CR2 ... 172 D7
Druce Rd DUL SE21 ... 139 L3
Druid St STHWK SE1 ... 19 L1
Druids Wy HAYES BR2 ... 159 K7
Drumaline Rdg WPK KT4 ... 168 E4
Drummond Av
ROMW/RG RM7 ... 73 K5 5
Drummond Cl ERITH DA8 ... 127 L6
Drummond Crs CAMTN NW1 ... 5 G7
Drummond Dr
KTN/HRWW/W HA3 ... 61 M1
Drummond Ga PIM SW1V ... 17 H7 1
Drummond Rd
BERM/RHTH SE16 ... 122 B1
CROY/NA CR0 ... 172 C4 2
ROMW/RG RM7 ... 73 J5
WAN E11 ... 70 B7
Drummonds Pl
RCH/KEW TW9 ... 134 E1 3
Drummond St CAMTN NW1 ... 4 E9
Drum St WCHPL E1 ... 13 M4
Drury Crs CROY/NA CR0 ... 172 A4
Drury La HHOL WC1V ... 11 J4
HOL/ALD WC2B ... 11 K5
Drury Rd HRW HA1 ... 61 J8
Drury Wy WLSDN NW10 ... 81 K5
Dryad St PUT/ROE SW15 ... 118 D8 3
Dryburgh Gdns
CDALE/KGS NW9 ... 63 G4
Dryburgh Rd PUT/ROE SW15 ... 118 B8
Dryden Av HNWL W7 ... 97 M5
Dryden Cl BARK/HLT IG6 ... 53 M8
Dryden Rd EN EN1 ... 49 L1
KTN/HRWW/W HA3 ... 61 M2
WIM/MER SW19 ... 155 J2
WOOL/PLUM SE18 ... 125 M6
Dryden St COVGDN WC2E ... 11 K5
Dryden Wy ORP BR6 ... 177 G3
Dryfield Cl WLSDN NW10 ... 81 J6 1
Dryfield Rd EDGW HA8 ... 45 J8
Dryhill Rd BELV DA17 ... 126 F4
Dryland Av ORP BR6 ... 176 F6
Drylands Rd CEND/HSY/T N8 ... 66 E7
Drynham Pk WEY KT13 ... 164 E5
Drysdale Av CHING E4 ... 51 H1
Drysdale Cl NTHWD HA6 ... 59 L1 3
Drysdale Pl BETH E2 ... 7 K7
Drysdale St IS N1 ... 7 K8
Dublin Av HACK E8 ... 86 A8
Du Burstow Ter HNWL W7 ... 97 L8 3
Ducal St BETH E2 ... 7 M8
Du Cane Rd SHB W12 ... 100 B5
Duchess Cl FBAR/BDGN N11 ... 48 B7
Duchess Ms CAVSQ/HST W1G ... 10 D3 2
Duchess of Bedford's Wk
KENS W8 ... 100 F8
Duchess St REGST W1B ... 10 D3
Duchy Rd EBAR EN4 ... 34 D3
Duchy St STHWK SE1 ... 12 B8
Ducie St CLAP SW4 ... 138 E1
Duckett Rd FSBYPK N4 ... 67 H7
Ducketts Rd DART DA1 ... 145 M2
Duckett St WCHPL E1 ... 104 D4
Ducking Stool Ct ROM RM1 ... 73 L5 2
Duck La SOHO/CST W1F ... 11 G5
Duck Lees La PEND EN3 ... 37 L7
Ducks Hill Rd NTHWD HA6 ... 59 G3
NTHWD HA6 ... 59 H1
Du Cros Dr STAN HA7 ... 44 D8
Du Cros Rd ACT W3 ... 99 L7
Dudden Hill La WLSDN NW10 ... 81 M4
Duddington Cl ELTH/MOT SE9 ... 142 D8
Dudley Av CHES/WCR EN8 ... 26 D5
KTN/HRWW/W HA3 ... 62 C4
Dudley Dr MRDN SM4 ... 169 L3
RSLP HA4 ... 78 B5
Dudley Gdns RYLN/HDSTN HA2 ... 79 K1
WEA W13 ... 98 B8
Dudley Gv EPSOM KT18 ... 180 C7
Dudley Rd ASHF TW15 ... 148 F1
EBED/NFELT TW14 ... 131 K5
FNCH N3 ... 65 H3
HARH RM3 ... 56 D8
IL IG1 ... 89 H4
KIL/WHAMP NW6 ... 100 E1
KUT KT1 ... 152 F6 1
NWDGN UB2 ... 96 D8
RCH/KEW TW9 ... 116 F7
RYLN/HDSTN HA2 ... 79 J2
WALTH E17 ... 69 G3 2
WIM/MER SW19 ... 155 G2
WOT/HER KT12 ... 165 G1
Dudley St BAY/PAD W2 ... 9 G3 1
Dudlington Rd CLPT E5 ... 86 C2 1
Dudmaston Ms CHEL SW3 ... 15 H7
Dudsbury Rd DART DA1 ... 146 B3
Dudset La HEST TW5 ... 114 A6
Dufferin Av STLK EC1Y ... 13 G1 1
Dufferin St STLK EC1Y ... 12 F1
Duffield Cl HRW HA1 ... 61 M6
Duffield Dr SEVS/STOTM N15 ... 67 M5
Duff St POP/IOD E14 ... 105 H5
Dufour's Pl SOHO/CST W1F ... 10 F5 5
Dugdale Hill La POTB/CUF EN6 ... 22 E6
Dugdales RKW/CH/CXG WD3 ... 28 A7
Duke Humphrey Rd
BKHTH/KID SE3 ... 123 L6 1
Duke of Cambridge Cl
WHTN TW2 ... 133 K3
Duke of Edinburgh Rd
SUT SM1 ... 170 D5
Duke of Wellington Pl
WHALL SW1A ... 16 B2
Duke of York St STJS SW1Y ... 10 F8
Duke Rd BARK/HLT IG6 ... 71 K5
CHSWK W4 ... 117 K3
Duke's Av CHSWK W4 ... 117 K3
EDGW HA8 ... 44 F8
FNCH N3 ... 65 H2
HRW HA1 ... 61 L5
HSLWW TW4 ... 132 E1
MUSWH N10 ... 66 C4
NTHLT UB5 ... 78 E7
NWMAL KT3 ... 153 L6
PIN HA5 ... 60 F7
RCHPK/HAM TW10 ... 134 C8
Dukes Cl ASHF TW15 ... 131 J8
HPTN TW12 ... 150 F1
Dukes La KENS W8 ... 14 C1
Duke's Ms MHST W1U ... 10 B4
MUSWH N10 ... 66 B4
Dukes Orch BXLY DA5 ... 145 J5
Duke's Pl HDTCH EC3A ... 13 L5
Dukes Ride HGDN/ICK UB10 ... 76 E4
Dukes Rd ACT W3 ... 99 G3
EHAM E6 ... 89 G8
STPAN WC1H ... 5 H8
WOT/HER KT12 ... 165 K7
Dukesthorpe Rd SYD SE26 ... 140 D8
Duke St MBLAR W1H ... 10 B4
RCH/KEW TW9 ... 134 D2 2
SUT SM1 ... 170 C6
WAT WD17 ... 29 J6
Duke Street Hl STHWK SE1 ... 13 H8
Duke Street St James's
MYFR/PICC W1J ... 10 F8
Dukes Wy WWKM BR4 ... 174 E5
Duke's Yd MYFR/PKLN W1K ... 10 B6 2
Dulas St FSBYPK N4 ... 84 F1 2
Dulford St NTGHL W11 ... 100 E6 4
Dulka Rd BTSEA SW11 ... 137 M2
Dulverton Rd ELTH/MOT SE9 ... 143 J6
HARH RM3 ... 56 D8
RSLP HA4 ... 78 A2
SAND/SEL CR2 ... 185 J3
Dulwich Common DUL SE21 ... 139 M5
The Dulwich Oaks DUL SE21 ... 139 M7 1
Dulwich Rd HNHL SE24 ... 139 G2
Dulwich Village DUL SE21 ... 139 K3
Dulwich Wy RKW/CH/CXG WD3 ... 28 A8
Dulwich Wood Av NRWD SE19 ... 157 L1
Dulwich Wood Pk NRWD SE19 ... 139 L8
Dumbarton Av
CHES/WCR EN8 ... 26 D7 1
Dumbarton Rd
BRXS/STRHM SW2 ... 138 E3
Dumbleton Cl KUT KT1 ... 153 H4 1
Dumbreck Rd ELTH/MOT SE9 ... 143 G1
Dumfries Cl OXHEY WD19 ... 42 A5
Dumont Rd STNW/STAM N16 ... 85 L3
Dumpton Pl CAMTN NW1 ... 4 A2
Dunally Pk SHPTN TW17 ... 164 D2
Dunbar Av BECK BR3 ... 158 E7
DAGE RM10 ... 91 G3
STRHM/NOR SW16 ... 157 G5
Dunbar Cl YEAD UB4 ... 96 A4
Dunbar Ct WOT/HER KT12 ... 165 J4 1
Dunbar Gdns DAGE RM10 ... 91 G5
Dunbar Rd FSTGT E7 ... 88 A6
NWMAL KT3 ... 153 J7
WDGN N22 ... 67 G2
Dunbar St WNWD SE27 ... 139 J7
Dunblane Rd ELTH/MOT SE9 ... 124 E8
Dunboe Pl SHPTN TW17 ... 164 C2 1
Dunboyne Rd HAMP NW3 ... 83 M5 1
Dunbridge St BETH E2 ... 104 A3
Duncan Cl BAR EN5 ... 34 C7
Duncan Gdns STA TW18 ... 148 A2
Duncan Gv ACT W3 ... 99 L5
Duncannon St CHCR WC2N ... 11 J7 4
Duncan Rd HACK E8 ... 86 B8 3
RCH/KEW TW9 ... 134 E1 1
Duncan St IS N1 ... 6 C5
Duncan Ter IS N1 ... 6 C6
Duncan Wy BUSH WD23 ... 29 M5
Dunch St WCHPL E1 ... 104 B5 7
Duncombe Hl FSTH SE23 ... 140 E4
Duncombe Rd ARCH N19 ... 84 D1
Duncrievie Rd LEW SE13 ... 141 K3
Duncroft WOOL/PLUM SE18 ... 125 L5
Dundalk Rd BROCKY SE4 ... 122 E8
Dundas Gdns E/WMO/HCT KT8 ... 151 H6
Dundas Rd PECK SE15 ... 122 C7
Dundee Rd PLSTW E13 ... 106 B1
SNWD SE25 ... 158 B8
Dundee St WAP E1W ... 104 B7 7
Dundee Wy PEND EN3 ... 37 L6
Dundela Gdns WPK KT4 ... 169 H6
Dundonald Cl EHAM E6 ... 106 E5 2
Dundonald Rd WIM/MER SW19 ... 154 F3
WLSDN NW10 ... 82 D8
Dunedin Rd IL IG1 ... 89 J1
LEY E10 ... 87 H3
RAIN RM13 ... 109 M2
Dunedin Wy YEAD UB4 ... 96 C3
Dunelm Gv WNWD SE27 ... 139 J8
Dunelm St WCHPL E1 ... 104 D5 5
Dunfield Rd CAT SE6 ... 159 H1
Dunford Rd HOLWY N7 ... 84 F4
Dungarvan Av PUT/ROE SW15 ... 136 A1
Dunheved Cl THHTH CR7 ... 172 A1 1
Dunheved Rd North
THHTH CR7 ... 172 A1
Dunheved Rd South
THHTH CR7 ... 172 A1
Dunheved Rd West THHTH CR7 ... 172 A1
Dunholme Gn ED N9 ... 49 M5
Dunholme La ED N9 ... 49 M5 2
Dunholme Rd ED N9 ... 49 M5
Dunkeld Rd BCTR RM8 ... 90 B2
SNWD SE25 ... 157 K7 2
Dunkery Rd ELTH/MOT SE9 ... 142 D8
Dunkin Rd DART DA1 ... 147 G1
Dunkirk St WNWD SE27 ... 139 J8 3
Dunlace Rd CLPT E5 ... 86 C5
Dunleary Cl HSLWW TW4 ... 132 F4
Dunley Dr CROY/NA CR0 ... 174 C8
Dunloe Av TOTM N17 ... 67 K4
Dunloe St BETH E2 ... 7 L6
Dunlop Pl BERM/RHTH SE16 ... 19 M4
Dunmail Dr PUR/KEN CR8 ... 184 E6
Dunmore Rd KIL/WHAMP NW6 ... 82 E8
RYNPK SW20 ... 154 C4
Dunmow Cl CHDH RM6 ... 72 C6 2
FELT TW13 ... 132 E8 3
LOU IG10 ... 52 E1
Dunmow Dr RAIN RM13 ... 91 M8
Dunmow Rd SRTFD E15 ... 87 K4
Dunningford Cl HCH RM12 ... 91 M5 1
Dunn Md CDALE/KGS NW9 ... 63 M1
Dunnock Cl BORE WD6 ... 32 A7 2
ED N9 ... 50 D3
Dunnock Rd EHAM E6 ... 106 E5
Dunn St HACK E8 ... 85 M5
Dunnymans Rd BNSTD SM7 ... 181 M8
Dunollie Pl KTTN NW5 ... 84 C5 3
Dunollie Rd KTTN NW5 ... 84 C5
Dunoon Rd FSTH SE23 ... 140 C4
Dunraven Dr ENC/FH EN2 ... 36 A5
Dunraven Rd SHB W12 ... 100 A7
Dunraven St MYFR/PKLN W1K ... 9 M6
Dunsany Rd HMSMTH W6 ... 118 D1
Dunsbury Cl BELMT SM2 ... 182 B2 1
Dunsfold Ri COUL/CHIP CR5 ... 183 K6
Dunsfold Wy CROY/NA CR0 ... 186 C1 1
Dunsmore Cl BUSH WD23 ... 43 K1 1
YEAD UB4 ... 96 D3 4
Dunsmore Rd WOT/HER KT12 ... 150 B8
Dunsmore Wy BUSH WD23 ... 43 J1
Dunsmure Rd STNW/STAM N16 ... 85 L1
Dunspring La CLAY IG5 ... 71 H3
Dunstable Ms
CAVSQ/HST W1G ... 10 B2 3
Dunstable Rd E/WMO/HCT KT8 ... 150 F7
HARH RM3 ... 56 D8
RCH/KEW TW9 ... 134 E1
Dunstall Rd RYNPK SW20 ... 154 B2
Dunstall Wy E/WMO/HCT KT8 ... 151 H6
Dunstan Cl EFNCH N2 ... 65 J4 3
Dunstan Rd GLDGN NW11 ... 82 F1
Dunstan's Gv EDUL SE22 ... 140 B3
Dunstan's Rd EDUL SE22 ... 140 A4
Dunster Av MRDN SM4 ... 169 K3
Dunster Cl BAR EN5 ... 33 K7
DEN/HRF UB9 ... 58 B2
ROMW/RG RM7 ... 73 J3
Dunster Ct FENCHST EC3M ... 13 J6
Dunster Crs UPMR RM14 ... 93 G2
Dunster Dr CDALE/KGS NW9 ... 81 J1
Dunster Gdns KIL/WHAMP NW6 ... 82 F7
Dunster Wy RYLN/HDSTN HA2 ... 78 E3
Dunston Rd BTSEA SW11 ... 120 A8
HACK E8 ... 7 L4
Dunston St HACK E8 ... 7 K3
Dunton Cl SURB KT6 ... 167 L3 1
Dunton Rd LEY E10 ... 69 H8
ROM RM1 ... 73 L5
STHWK SE1 ... 19 L6
Duntshill Rd WAND/EARL SW18 ... 137 H5
Dunvegan Cl
E/WMO/HCT KT8 ... 151 H7 2
Dunvegan Rd ELTH/MOT SE9 ... 142 F1
Dunwich Rd BXLYHN DA7 ... 126 F6
Duplex Ride KTBR SW1X ... 15 M2
Dupont Rd RYNPK SW20 ... 154 D5
Dupont St POP/IOD E14 ... 104 E4 1
Duppas Av CROY/NA CR0 ... 172 B6 1
Duppas Cl SHPTN TW17 ... 149 K8
Duppas Hill Rd CROY/NA CR0 ... 172 A6
Duppas Hill Ter CROY/NA CR0 ... 172 B5
Duppas Rd CROY/NA CR0 ... 172 A5
Dupree Rd CHARL SE7 ... 124 B3
Dura Den Cl BECK BR3 ... 159 H3
Durand Gdns BRXN/ST SW9 ... 120 F6
Durand Wy WLSDN NW10 ... 81 J7
Durants Park Av PEND EN3 ... 37 K7
Durants Rd PEND EN3 ... 37 J7
Durant St BETH E2 ... 104 A1
Durban Gdns DAGE RM10 ... 91 J7 4
Durban Rd BECK BR3 ... 158 F5
GNTH/NBYPK IG2 ... 89 L1
SRTFD E15 ... 105 L2
TOTM N17 ... 49 L8
WALTH E17 ... 68 F2
WNWD SE27 ... 139 J8
Durban Rd East WATW WD18 ... 29 G7
Durban Rd West WATW WD18 ... 29 G7
Durbin Rd CHSGTN KT9 ... 167 L6
Durdans Rd STHL UB1 ... 96 F5
Durell Gdns DAGW RM9 ... 90 D5 2
Durell Rd DAGW RM9 ... 90 D5
Durford Crs PUT/ROE SW15 ... 136 A5
Durham Av GPK RM2 ... 74 C5
HAYES BR2 ... 159 M7
HEST TW5 ... 114 F4
WFD IG8 ... 52 D7
Durham Hl BMLY BR1 ... 141 M8
Durham House St
CHCR WC2N ... 11 K7 2
Durham Pl CHEL SW3 ... 15 L8 1
Durham Ri WOOL/PLUM SE18 ... 125 J3
Durham Rd CAN/RD E16 ... 105 L3
DAGE RM10 ... 91 J5
EA W5 ... 116 D1
EBED/NFELT TW14 ... 132 C4
ED N9 ... 50 A4
EFNCH N2 ... 65 L4
HAYES BR2 ... 160 A7 1
HOLWY N7 ... 84 F2
HRW HA1 ... 61 H6
MNPK E12 ... 88 D4
RYNPK SW20 ... 154 B4
SCUP DA14 ... 162 B1
Durham Rw WCHPL E1 ... 104 E4 2
Durham St LBTH SE11 ... 17 L8
Durham Ter BAY/PAD W2 ... 8 C4
Duriun Wy ERITH DA8 ... 128 B5
Durley Av PIN HA5 ... 60 E7
Durley Gdns ORP BR6 ... 177 H6
Durley Rd STNW/STAM N16 ... 67 L8
Durlston Rd CLPT E5 ... 86 A2
KUTN/CMB KT2 ... 152 E2
Durnford St SEVS/STOTM N15 ... 67 L6 3
Durning Rd NRWD SE19 ... 157 K1
Durnsford Av
WAND/EARL SW18 ... 137 G6
Durnsford Rd FBAR/BDGN N11 ... 66 D2
WAND/EARL SW18 ... 137 G6
WIM/MER SW19 ... 137 G7
Durrants Cl RAIN RM13 ... 110 C1
Durrants Dr RKW/CH/CXG WD3 ... 28 C6
Durrant Wy ORP BR6 ... 176 D7
Durrell Rd FUL/PGN SW6 ... 118 E6
Durrell Wy SHPTN TW17 ... 164 D1
Durrington Av RYNPK SW20 ... 154 C3 1
Durrington Park Rd
RYNPK SW20 ... 154 C4
Durrington Rd CLPT E5 ... 86 E4 1
Dursley Cl BKHTH/KID SE3 ... 124 C7
Dursley Gdns BKHTH/KID SE3 ... 124 D6
Dursley Rd BKHTH/KID SE3 ... 124 C7
Durward St WCHPL E1 ... 104 B4 2
WCHPL E1 ... 104 B4 2
Durweston Ms MHST W1U ... 9 M2 1
Dury Falls Cl EMPK RM11 ... 92 F1 1
Dury Rd BAR EN5 ... 33 M4
Dutch Barn Cl
STWL/WRAY TW19 ... 130 D3
Dutch Gdns KUTN/CMB KT2 ... 153 H2 1
Dutch Yd WAND/EARL SW18 ... 137 G2 7
Duthie St POP/IOD E14 ... 105 J6 3
Dutton St GNWCH SE10 ... 123 J6
Duxford Cl HCH RM12 ... 92 B6
Dwight Rd WATW WD18 ... 41 K2
Dye House La BOW E3 ... 87 G8
Dyers Hall Rd WAN E11 ... 87 L1 3
WAN E11 ... 87 L1 3
Dyer's La PUT/ROE SW15 ... 118 B8
Dyers Wy HARH RM3 ... 74 A1
Dyke Dr STMC/STPC BR5 ... 177 J2
Dykes Wy HAYES BR2 ... 159 M6
Dykewood Cl BXLY DA5 ... 145 K7
Dylan Cl BORE WD6 ... 44 D2 1
Dylan Rd BELV DA17 ... 127 G1
Dylways CMBW SE5 ... 139 K1
Dymchurch Cl CLAY IG5 ... 71 G3
ORP BR6 ... 176 E6 1
Dymock St FUL/PGN SW6 ... 119 H8
Dymoke Rd ROM RM1 ... 73 M8
Dyneley Rd LEE/GVPK SE12 ... 142 C7 3
Dyne Rd KIL/WHAMP NW6 ... 82 F7
Dynevor Rd RCHPK/HAM TW10 ... 134 E2
STNW/STAM N16 ... 85 L3
Dynham Rd KIL/WHAMP NW6 ... 2 A1
Dyott St NOXST/BSQ WC1A ... 11 J4 3
RSQ WC1B ... 11 H3
Dyrham La BAR EN5 ... 33 G1
Dysart Av KUTN/CMB KT2 ... 152 C1
Dysart St SDTCH EC2A ... 13 H1
Dyson Ct ALP/SUD HA0 ... 80 A4
Dyson Rd FSTGT E7 ... 87 M6
WAN E11 ... 69 L7
Dysons Cl CHES/WCR EN8 ... 26 D6
Dyson's Rd UED N18 ... 50 B7

E

Eade Rd FSBYPK N4 ... 67 J8
Eagans Cl EFNCH N2 ... 65 K4 2
Eagle Av CHDH RM6 ... 72 E7
Eagle Cl PEND EN3 ... 37 J7
RAIN RM13 ... 92 B6
WLGTN SM6 ... 171 L8 1
Eagle Ct FARR EC1M ... 12 C2
Eagle Dr CDALE/KGS NW9 ... 63 L3
Eagle Hl NRWD SE19 ... 157 K2
Eagle La WAN E11 ... 70 A5
Eagle Pl WBPTN SW10 ... 14 F7
Eagle Rd ALP/SUD HA0 ... 80 D7
Eaglesfield Rd
WOOL/PLUM SE18 ... 125 H6
Eagle St GINN WC1R ... 11 L3
Eagle Ter WFD IG8 ... 70 B1
Eagle Wharf Rd IS N1 ... 6 F5
Ealdham Sq ELTH/MOT SE9 ... 142 D1 2
Ealing Cl BORE WD6 ... 32 D4
Ealing Gn EA W5 ... 98 D7
Ealing Park Gdns EA W5 ... 116 C2
Ealing Rd ALP/SUD HA0 ... 80 E6
BTFD TW8 ... 116 D2
NTHLT UB5 ... 79 G7
Ealing Village EA W5 ... 98 E5
Eamont Cl RSLP HA4 ... 59 H8 1
Eamont St STJWD NW8 ... 3 J5
Eardemont Cl DART DA1 ... 145 M1
Eardley Crs ECT SW5 ... 14 B7
Eardley Rd BELV DA17 ... 127 G3
STRHM/NOR SW16 ... 156 C2
Earl Cl FBAR/BDGN N11 ... 48 B7
Earldom Rd PUT/ROE SW15 ... 136 C1
Earle Gdns KUTN/CMB KT2 ... 152 E3
Earlham Gv FSTGT E7 ... 87 M5
WDGN N22 ... 66 F1
Earlham St LSQ/SEVD WC2H ... 11 H5
Earl Ri WOOL/PLUM SE18 ... 125 K3
Earl Rd MORT/ESHN SW14 ... 135 J1
Earl's Court Gdns ECT SW5 ... 14 C6
Earl's Court Rd ECT SW5 ... 14 B6
KENS W8 ... 14 A4
Earl's Court Sq ECT SW5 ... 14 C7
Earls Crs HRW HA1 ... 61 L5
Earlsferry Wy IS N1 ... 5 K2
Earlsfield Rd WAND/EARL SW18 ... 137 J5
Earlshall Rd ELTH/MOT SE9 ... 142 F1
Earlsmead RYLN/HDSTN HA2 ... 78 F4
Earlsmead Rd
SEVS/STOTM N15 ... 67 M6 3
WLSDN NW10 ... 100 B2
Earl's Pth LOU IG10 ... 39 J6
Earls Ter KENS W8 ... 14 A4 1
Earlsthorpe Ms BAL SW12 ... 138 A3 1
Earlsthorpe Rd SYD SE26 ... 140 D8
Earlstoke St FSBYE EC1V ... 6 C7 1
Earlston Gv HOM E9 ... 86 B8 3
Earl St SDTCH EC2A ... 13 J2
WAT WD17 ... 29 J6 2
Earls Wk BCTR RM8 ... 90 B4
KENS W8 ... 14 A4
Earlswood Av THHTH CR7 ... 157 G8 1
Earlswood Gdns CLAY IG5 ... 71 G4
Earlswood St GNWCH SE10 ... 123 L3
Early Ms CAMTN NW1 ... 4 D3
Earnshaw St LSQ/SEVD WC2H ... 11 H4 3
Earsby St WKENS W14 ... 118 E2 4
Easby Crs MRDN SM4 ... 170 B1
Easebourne Rd BCTR RM8 ... 90 C5
Easedale Dr HCH RM12 ... 92 B5
East Acton La ACT W3 ... 99 L6 2
East Arbour St WCHPL E1 ... 104 D5
East Av CROY/NA CR0 ... 171 M7
HYS/HAR UB3 ... 95 M8
MNPK E12 ... 88 E7
STHL UB1 ... 96 F6
WALTH E17 ... 69 H5
East Bank STNW/STAM N16 ... 67 L8
Eastbank Rd HPTN TW12 ... 151 J1
East Barnet Rd BAR EN5 ... 34 C7
EBAR EN4 ... 34 D8
Eastbourne Av ACT W3 ... 99 K5
Eastbourne Gdns
MORT/ESHN SW14 ... 117 J8 3
Eastbourne Ms BAY/PAD W2 ... 8 F4
Eastbourne Rd BTFD TW8 ... 116 D3
CHSWK W4 ... 117 J4
EHAM E6 ... 107 G2
FELT TW13 ... 132 D6
SEVS/STOTM N15 ... 67 L7
SRTFD E15 ... 87 L8
TOOT SW17 ... 156 A2
Eastbourne Ter BAY/PAD W2 ... 8 F4
Eastbournia Av ED N9 ... 50 B5
Eastbrook Av DAGE RM10 ... 91 J4
ED N9 ... 50 C2 2
Eastbrook Dr DAGE RM10 ... 91 L3
Eastbrook Rd BKHTH/KID SE3 ... 124 B6
WAB EN9 ... 27 L6
Eastbury Av BARK IG11 ... 89 L8
EN EN1 ... 36 E4
NTHWD HA6 ... 41 L7
Eastbury Gv CHSWK W4 ... 117 L3
Eastbury Rd EHAM E6 ... 107 G3
KUTN/CMB KT2 ... 152 E3
NTHWD HA6 ... 41 L8
OXHEY WD19 ... 42 C2
ROMW/RG RM7 ... 73 K7
STMC/STPC BR5 ... 176 D1
Eastbury Sq BARK IG11 ... 89 M8
Eastbury Ter WCHPL E1 ... 104 D3 5
Eastcastle St GTPST W1W ... 10 E4
Eastcheap BANK EC3V ... 13 H6 1
FENCHST EC3M ... 13 H6
East Churchfield Rd ACT W3 ... 99 K7
Eastchurch Rd HTHAIR TW6 ... 113 L8
East Cl EA W5 ... 99 G3
EBAR EN4 ... 35 G7
GFD/PVL UB6 ... 97 J1
RAIN RM13 ... 110 B3
Eastcombe Av CHARL SE7 ... 124 B4
Eastcote ORP BR6 ... 176 F3
Eastcote Av E/WMO/HCT KT8 ... 150 F8
GFD/PVL UB6 ... 80 A5
RYLN/HDSTN HA2 ... 79 H2
Eastcote La NTHLT UB5 ... 78 F6
RYLN/HDSTN HA2 ... 78 F4
Eastcote La North NTHLT UB5 ... 78 F6
Eastcote Rd PIN HA5 ... 60 D6
RSLP HA4 ... 59 L8
RYLN/HDSTN HA2 ... 79 J3
WELL DA16 ... 125 K7
Eastcote St BRXN/ST SW9 ... 120 F7 2
Eastcote Vw PIN HA5 ... 60 C5
East Ct ALP/SUD HA0 ... 80 C2
East Crs EN EN1 ... 36 E8
TRDG/WHET N20 ... 47 M6
Eastcroft Rd HOR/WEW KT19 ... 180 E1
East Cross Route HOM E9 ... 86 F6
Eastdean Av EPSOM KT18 ... 180 B6
East Dene Dr HARH RM3 ... 56 D7
Eastdown Pk LEW SE13 ... 141 K1
East Dr CAR SM5 ... 182 E2
GSTN WD25 ... 29 H1
NTHWD HA6 ... 41 L4
STMC/STPC BR5 ... 177 H1
East Dulwich Gv EDUL SE22 ... 139 L2
East Dulwich Rd EDUL SE22 ... 139 M1
East End Rd EFNCH N2 ... 65 J4 4
FNCH N3 ... 65 H4
East End Wy PIN HA5 ... 60 E4
East Entrance DAGE RM10 ... 109 H1
Eastern Av CHDH RM6 ... 72 D5
CHERT KT16 ... 148 A6
CHES/WCR EN8 ... 26 F6
GNTH/NBYPK IG2 ... 71 M6

PIN HA5 60 D8
REDBR IG4 70 D7
SOCK/AV RM15 111 J8
WAN E11 70 C7
WTHK RM20 129 M3
Eastern Av East GPK RM2 73 M2
ROM RM1 73 K4
Eastern Av West CHDH RM6 72 E5
ROMW/RG RM7 73 J5
Eastern Perimeter Rd
HTHAIR TW6 113 M8
Eastern Rd BROCKY SE4 141 G1
EFNCH N2 65 M4
PLSTW E13 106 B1
ROM RM1 73 M6
WALTH E17 69 J6
WDGN N22 66 E2
Easternville Gdns
GNTH/NBYPK IG2 71 J7
Eastern Wy ERITHM DA18 109 G8
THMD SE28 108 A8
East Ferry Rd POP/IOD E14 123 J1
Eastfield Av WATN WD24 29 K4
Eastfield Gdns DAGE RM10 91 G4 1
Eastfield Rd CEND/HSY/T N8 66 E4
CHES/WCR EN8 26 F5
DAGE RM10 91 G4
PEND EN3 37 K3
WALTH E17 69 G5
Eastfields PIN HA5 60 C6
Eastfields Rd ACT W3 99 J4
MTCM CR4 156 A5
East Gdns WIM/MER SW19 155 L2
Eastgate BNSTD SM7 181 M7
Eastgate Cl THMD SE28 108 D5
Eastglade NTHWD HA6 41 L7
PIN HA5 60 F4 2
East Hall La RAIN RM13 110 D5
East Hall Rd STMC/STPC BR5 177 L2
Eastham Cl BAR EN5 33 M8
East Ham Manor Wy EHAM E6 107 G5
East Harding St
FLST/FETLN EC4A 12 B4 2
East Heath Rd HAMP NW3 83 K3
East Hl DART DA1 146 F4
SAND/SEL CR2 184 E3
WAND/EARL SW18 137 J2
WBLY HA9 81 G2
East Hill Dr DART DA1 146 F4 1
Eastholm GLDGN NW11 65 H5 2
East Holme ERITH DA8 127 K6
Eastholme HYS/HAR UB3 96 A7 1
East India Dock Rd
POP/IOD E14 105 J5
Eastlake Rd CMBW SE5 121 H7
Eastlands Crs EDUL SE22 139 M3
East La ABLGY WD5 21 G1
ALP/SUD HA0 80 C3
BERM/RHTH SE16 104 A8 3
GSTN WD25 21 H3
KUT KT1 152 D6 1
Eastlea Av GSTN WD25 29 L2
Eastlea Ms CAN/RD E16 105 L3 3
Eastleigh Av RYLN/HDSTN HA2 79 H2
Eastleigh Cl BELMT SM2 182 B1 4
CRICK NW2 81 L3
Eastleigh Rd BXLYHN DA7 127 J7
WALTH E17 68 F3
Eastleigh Wy
EBED/NFELT TW14 132 A5 2
East Lodge La ENC/FH EN2 35 K1
Eastman Rd ACT W3 99 K8
East Md RSLP HA4 78 D3
Eastmead Av GFD/PVL UB6 97 H2
Eastmead Cl BMLY BR1 160 E5
Eastmearn Rd DUL SE21 139 J6
Eastmont Rd ESH/CLAY KT10 166 F4
Eastmoor Pl WOOL/PLUM SE18 124 D1
Eastmoor St CHARL SE7 124 D2 1
East Mount St WCHPL E1 104 B4 3
Eastney Rd CROY/NA CR0 172 B3
Eastney St GNWCH SE10 123 K3
Eastnor Rd ELTH/MOT SE9 143 J5
Easton Gdns BORE WD6 32 E7
Easton St FSBYW WC1X 6 A9
East Park Cl CHDH RM6 72 D6
East Pl WNWD SE27 139 J8
East Poultry Av FARR EC1M 12 C3
East Rp HTHAIR TW6 113 H6
East Ridgeway POTB/CUF EN6 24 D1
East Rd CHDH RM6 72 E6
EBAR EN4 48 A3
EBED/NFELT TW14 131 K4
EDGW HA8 63 H2
EFNCH N2 65 L2
IS N1 7 G8
KUTN/CMB KT2 152 E4
PEND EN3 37 J3
ROMW/RG RM7 73 K8
SRTFD E15 88 A8
WDR/YW UB7 112 F2
WELL DA16 126 B7
WIM/MER SW19 155 J2
East Rochester Wy
BFN/LL DA15 143 L2
DART DA1 145 K4
East Rw NKENS W10 100 E3
WAN E11 70 A7
Eastry Av HAYES BR2 174 F1
Eastry Rd ERITH DA8 127 G5
East Sheen Av
MORT/ESHN SW14 135 K2
Eastside Rd GLDGN NW11 64 F5
East Smithfield WAP E1W 13 M7
East St BARK IG11 89 J7
BMLY BR1 160 A5
BTFD TW8 116 C5
BXLYHN DA7 145 G1
EW KT17 180 E5
WALW SE17 19 H7
East Surrey Gv PECK SE15 121 M5
East Tenter St WCHPL E1 13 M5
East Towers PIN HA5 60 D7
East Vw BAR EN5 33 M5
CHING E4 51 J7
Eastview Av WOOL/PLUM SE18 125 L5
Eastville Av GLDGN NW11 64 F6
East Wk EBAR EN4 48 A3
HYS/HAR UB3 96 A8
East Wy HYS/HAR UB3 96 A7
RSLP HA4 78 A1
WAB EN9 27 K8
CROY/NA CR0 173 L4
Eastway HAYES BR2 175 G2
HOM E9 86 F6
HOR/WEW KT19 180 C5
MRDN SM4 154 D8
SRTFD E15 87 G5
WAN E11 70 B6
WLGTN SM6 171 J6 2
Eastwell Cl BECK BR3 158 E4
Eastwick Rd WOT/HER KT12 165 H8
Eastwood Cl SWFD E18 70 A3 1
TOTM N17 68 B1 2
Eastwood Dr RAIN RM13 110 B5
Eastwood Rd GDMY/SEVK IG3 72 A8
MUSWH N10 66 A3
SWFD E18 70 A3
Eastwood St
STRHM/NOR SW16 156 C2
Eatington Rd LEY E10 69 K6
Eaton Cl BGVA SW1W 16 A6
STAN HA7 44 B6 2
Eaton Dr BRXN/ST SW9 139 H1 4
CRW RM5 73 H1
KUTN/CMB KT2 153 G3
Eaton Gdns DAGW RM9 90 E7
Eaton Ga BGVA SW1W 16 A5
NTHWD HA6 41 J8
Eaton La BGVA SW1W 16 D4
Eaton Ms North KTBR SW1X 16 B4
Eaton Ms South BGVA SW1W 16 B5
Eaton Ms West BGVA SW1W 16 B5
Eaton Park Rd PLMGR N13 49 G4
Eaton Pl KTBR SW1X 16 A4
Eaton Ri EA W5 98 C4
WAN E11 70 C6
Eaton Rd BELMT SM2 170 D8
EN EN1 36 E6
HDN NW4 64 C6
HSLW TW3 133 K1
SCUP DA14 144 D6
UPMR RM14 93 L2
Eaton Rw BGVA SW1W 16 C3
Eatons Md CHING E4 51 G4
Eaton Sq BGVA SW1W 16 B4
Eaton Ter BGVA SW1W 16 A5
Eaton Terrace Ms KTBR SW1X 16 A5 2
Eatonville Rd TOOT SW17 137 M6
Eatonville Vls TOOT SW17 137 M6 2
Ebba's Wy EPSOM KT18 180 B8
Ebbisham Dr VX/NE SW8 17 L9
Ebbisham Rd EPSOM KT18 180 B8
WPK KT4 169 J4
Ebbsfleet Rd CRICK NW2 82 E5
Ebdon Wy BKHTH/KID SE3 124 B8
Ebenezer St IS N1 7 G7 1
Ebenezer Wk MTCM CR4 156 C4
Ebley Cl PECK SE15 121 M4
Ebner St WAND/EARL SW18 137 H2
Ebor St BETH E2 7 L9
Ebrington Rd
KTN/HRWW/W HA3 62 C7
Ebsworth St FSTH SE23 140 D4
Eburne Rd HOLWY N7 84 E3 3
Ebury Ap RKW/CH/CXG WD3 40 D3
Ebury Bridge Rd BGVA SW1W 16 B8
Ebury Cl HAYES BR2 175 L5
NTHWD HA6 41 J7
Ebury Ms BGVA SW1W 16 B5
Ebury Ms East BGVA SW1W 16 C5
Ebury Rd RKW/CH/CXG WD3 40 D3
WAT WD17 29 K6
Ebury Sq BGVA SW1W 16 C6
Ebury St BGVA SW1W 16 B6
Ecclesbourne Cl PLMGR N13 49 G7
Ecclesbourne Gdns PLMGR N13 49 G7
Ecclesbourne Rd IS N1 6 F2
THHTH CR7 157 J8
Eccles Rd BTSEA SW11 137 M1
Eccleston Cl EBAR EN4 34 E8
ORP BR6 176 D3 1
Eccleston Crs CHDH RM6 72 B8
Ecclestone Ct ALP/SUD HA0 80 E5 1
Ecclestone Ms ALP/SUD HA0 80 E5 2
Ecclestone Pl WBLY HA9 80 F5 2
Eccleston Ms KTBR SW1X 16 B4
Eccleston Pl BGVA SW1W 16 C6
Eccleston Rd HNWL W7 98 A6
Eccleston Sq PIM SW1V 16 D6
Eccleston Square Ms PIM SW1V 16 D6
Eccleston St BGVA SW1W 16 B4
Echelforde Dr ASHF TW15 131 G8
Echo Hts CHING E4 51 H3 1
Eckford St IS N1 6 A5
Eckstein Rd BTSEA SW11 137 L1
Eclipse Rd PLSTW E13 106 B4
Ector Rd CAT SE6 141 L6
Edans Ct SHB W12 99 M8
Edbrooke Rd MV/WKIL W9 8 A1
Eddiscombe Rd
FUL/PGN SW6 118 F7 5
Eddy Cl ROMW/RG RM7 73 H7
Eddystone Rd BROCKY SE4 140 E2
Ede Cl HSLWW TW4 114 F8
Edenbridge Cl STMC/STPC BR5 162 D8
Edenbridge Rd EN EN1 49 L1
HOM E9 86 D7 2
Eden Cl ALP/SUD HA0 80 D8
BXLY DA5 145 K8
KENS W8 14 B3
Edencourt Rd
STRHM/NOR SW16 156 B2
Edendale Rd BXLYHN DA7 127 K6
Edenfield Gdns WPK KT4 168 F5
Eden Gv HOLWY N7 84 F5 1
Edenhall Rd HARH RM3 56 C7
Edenham Wy NKENS W10 100 F3
Edenhurst Av FUL/PGN SW6 118 F8
Eden Park Av BECK BR3 158 F7
Eden Rd BECK BR3 158 E7
BXLY DA5 145 J8
CROY/NA CR0 172 D6
WALTH E17 69 H6
WNWD SE27 157 H1
Edensor Rd CHSWK W4 117 L5
Eden St KUT KT1 152 E5
Edenvale Rd MTCM CR4 156 A3
Edenvale St FUL/PGN SW6 119 H7
Eden Wy BECK BR3 159 G8
Ederline Av STRHM/NOR SW16 156 F6
Edgar Cl SWLY BR8 163 M6
Edgar Kail Wy CMBW SE5 121 L8
Edgarley Ter FUL/PGN SW6 118 E6 1
Edgar Rd BOW E3 105 H2
HSLWW TW4 132 F4
SAND/SEL CR2 184 D3
WDR/YW UB7 94 E6
Edgeborough Wy BMLY BR1 160 D4
Edgebury CHST BR7 143 H8
Edgecombe Cl KUTN/CMB KT2 153 K3
Edgecoombe SAND/SEL CR2 185 K2
Edgecote Cl ACT W3 99 J7 2
Edgefield Av BARK IG11 89 M7
Edgefield Cl DART DA1 147 H5 2
Edge Hl WIM/MER SW19 154 D3
WOOL/PLUM SE18 125 H4
Edge Hill Av GLDGN NW11 65 G5
Edgehill Ct WOT/HER KT12 165 J3 3
Edgehill Gdns DAGE RM10 91 G4 2
Edgehill Rd CHST BR7 143 J7
MTCM CR4 156 B5
PUR/KEN CR8 184 A3
WEA W13 98 C5
Edgeley La CLAP SW4 120 D8
Edgeley Rd CLAP SW4 120 D8
Edgel St WAND/EARL SW18 137 H1
Edge St KENS W8 8 B8
Edgewood Dr ORP BR6 176 F7
Edgewood Gn CROY/NA CR0 173 K3
Edgeworth Av HDN NW4 64 A6
Edgeworth Rd EBAR EN4 34 E7
ELTH/MOT SE9 142 C1
Edgington Rd
STRHM/NOR SW16 156 D2 2
Edgington Wy SCUP DA14 162 C3
Edgwarebury Gdns EDGW HA8 45 G7
Edgwarebury La BORE WD6 44 F2
EDGW HA8 44 F3
Edgware Rd BAY/PAD W2 9 G1
CDALE/KGS NW9 63 J4
CDALE/KGS NW9 82 A1
CRICK NW2 82 C3
Edgware Rd Burnt Oak Broadway
EDGW HA8 63 H1
Edgware Rd High St EDGW HA8 45 G8
Edgware Rd the Hyde
CDALE/KGS NW9 63 L5
EDGW HA8 63 J3
Edgware Wy
(Watford By-pass) EDGW HA8 44 F6
EDGW HA8 45 G6 1
Edinburgh Av
RKW/CH/CXG WD3 40 A1
Edinburgh Cl BETH E2 104 C1 3
HGDN/ICK UB10 77 H4
Edinburgh Crs CHES/WCR EN8 26 E6
Edinburgh Dr GSTN WD25 21 G5 1
HGDN/ICK UB10 77 H4
STA TW18 148 D2
Edinburgh Rd HNWL W7 97 M8 3
PLSTW E13 106 B1
SUT SM1 170 C4
UED N18 50 A7 7
WALTH E17 69 G6
Edinburgh's Dr ROMW/RG RM7 73 J5
Edington Rd ABYW SE2 126 B1
PEND EN3 37 J5 6
Edison Av HCH RM12 91 M1
Edison Cl HCH RM12 91 M1
Edison Dr GFD/PVL UB6 97 H5
Edison Gv WOOL/PLUM SE18 125 M5
Edison Rd CEND/HSY/T N8 66 D7
HAYES BR2 160 A5
PEND EN3 37 M5
WELL DA16 125 M6
Edis St CAMTN NW1 4 A3
Edith Gdns BRYLDS KT5 168 B2
Edith Gv WBPTN SW10 119 J4
Edithna St BRXN/ST SW9 120 E8
Edith Rd CHDH RM6 72 D8 2
EHAM E6 88 D7
FBAR/BDGN N11 66 D1
ORP BR6 177 G7
SNWD SE25 157 K8
SRTFD E15 87 K5
WIM/MER SW19 155 H2
WKENS W14 118 E2
Edith Rw FUL/PGN SW6 119 H6 1
Edith St BETH E2 7 M5
Edith Ter WBPTN SW10 119 J5 4
Edith Vls WKENS W14 118 F3
Edlson Cl WALTH E17 69 G6
Edmeston Cl HOM E9 86 E6
Edmund Gv FELT TW13 132 F6 1
Edmund Rd MTCM CR4 155 L6
RAIN RM13 109 L2
STMC/STPC BR5 177 J1
WELL DA16 126 A8
Edmunds Av STMC/STPC BR5 162 D6
Edmunds Cl YEAD UB4 96 C4
Edmund St CMBW SE5 121 K5
Edmunds Wk EFNCH N2 65 L5
Edna Rd RYNPK SW20 154 D5
Edna St BTSEA SW11 119 L6
Edrick Rd EDGW HA8 45 J8
Edrick Wk EDGW HA8 45 J8 1
Edric Rd NWCR SE14 122 D5
Edridge Cl BUSH WD23 30 C8
HCH RM12 92 D5 3
Edridge Rd CROY/NA CR0 172 C5
Edulf Rd BORE WD6 32 B5
Edward Amey Cl GSTN WD25 29 J1
Edward Av CHING E4 51 H7
MRDN SM4 155 K8
Edward Cl ABLGY WD5 20 F5
ED N9 49 M2 2
GPK RM2 74 C4 1
HPTN TW12 151 J1 3
Edward Ct CAN/RD E16 106 A4 2
STA TW18 148 C2
WAB EN9 27 M6
Edwardes Sq KENS W8 14 A4
Edward Gv EBAR EN4 34 D8 2
Edward Ms CAMTN NW1 4 D7 1
Edward Pl DEPT SE8 122 F4
Edward Rd BMLY BR1 160 B3
CHDH RM6 72 E7
CHST BR7 161 H1 2
COUL/CHIP CR5 183 K8
CROY/NA CR0 172 E2
EBAR EN4 34 D8
EBED/NFELT TW14 131 K2
HPTN TW12 151 J1
NTHLT UB5 96 C1
PGE/AN SE20 158 D3
RYLN/HDSTN HA2 61 J4
WALTH E17 68 D5
Edwards Av RSLP HA4 78 C5
Edwards Cl WPK KT4 169 K4 3
Edward's Cottages IS N1 85 H6 4
Edwards Gdns SWLY BR8 163 K7 2
Edward's La STNW/STAM N16 85 K2 1
Edwards Ms IS N1 6 B1
MBLAR W1H 10 A5
Edward Sq IS N1 5 L4
Edwards Rd BELV DA17 127 G2
Edward St DEPT SE8 122 F4
NWCR SE14 122 F5
PLSTW E13 106 A3 5
STBT EC1A 12 E4
Edward Temme Av SRTFD E15 87 M7
Edward Tyler Rd
LEE/GVPK SE12 142 B6
Edward Wy ASHF TW15 130 F6
Edwina Gdns REDBR IG4 70 E6
Edwin Av EHAM E6 107 G1
Edwin Cl BXLYHN DA7 126 F4
RAIN RM13 109 M2
Edwin Petty Pl RDART DA2 147 J4 1
Edwin Rd EDGW HA8 45 K8
RDART DA2 146 B7
WHTN TW2 133 L5
Edwin's Md HOM E9 86 E4 2
Edwin St CAN/RD E16 106 A4
WCHPL E1 104 C3
Edwyn Cl BAR EN5 33 J8
Effie Pl FUL/PGN SW6 119 G5
Effie Rd FUL/PGN SW6 119 G5
Effingham Cl BELMT SM2 182 B1
Effingham Rd CEND/HSY/T N8 67 G6
CROY/NA CR0 171 M2
LEW SE13 141 L2
SURB KT6 167 H2
Effort St TOOT SW17 155 L1
Effra Pde HNHL SE24 139 G2
Effra Rd BRXS/STRHM SW2 138 F1
WIM/MER SW19 155 H2
Egan Wy HYS/HAR UB3 95 L6
Egbert St CAMTN NW1 4 A3
Egerton Av SWLY BR8 163 M4
Egerton Cl DART DA1 146 B5
PIN HA5 60 A5
Egerton Crs CHEL SW3 15 J5
Egerton Dr GNWCH SE10 123 H6
Egerton Gdns CHEL SW3 15 J4
GDMY/SEVK IG3 89 M3
HDN NW4 64 B5
WEA W13 98 B5
WLSDN NW10 82 C8 2
Egerton Gardens Ms
CHEL SW3 15 K4 1
Egerton Pl CHEL SW3 15 K4 2
WEY KT13 164 C8
Egerton Rd ALP/SUD HA0 80 F7
CLPT E5 67 M8 2
NWMAL KT3 153 M7
SNWD SE25 157 L6
WEY KT13 164 C8
WHTN TW2 133 L4
Egerton Ter CHEL SW3 15 K4
Egerton Wy WDR/YW UB7 113 H5
Egham Cl CHEAM SM3 169 L4 1
Egham Crs CHEAM SM3 169 K5
Egham Rd PLSTW E13 106 B4
Eglantine Rd WAND/EARL SW18 137 J2
Egleston Rd MRDN SM4 170 B1
Eglington Rd CHING E4 51 K2
Eglinton Hl WOOL/PLUM SE18 125 H4
Eglinton Rd WOOL/PLUM SE18 125 G4
Egliston Ms PUT/ROE SW15 118 C8
Egliston Rd PUT/ROE SW15 118 C8
Egmont Av SURB KT6 167 M3
Egmont Rd BELMT SM2 182 C1
NWMAL KT3 153 M7
SURB KT6 167 M3
WOT/HER KT12 165 H2
Egmont St NWCR SE14 122 D5
Egremont Rd WNWD SE27 139 G7
Egret Wy YEAD UB4 96 D4
Eider Cl FSTGT E7 87 M5
Eighteenth Rd MTCM CR4 156 E7 1
Eighth Av HYS/HAR UB3 96 A7
MNPK E12 88 F4
Eileen Rd SNWD SE25 157 K8
Eindoven Cl MTCM CR4 171 G3 1
Eisenhower Dr EHAM E6 106 E4
Elaine Gv KTTN NW5 84 A5
Elam Cl CMBW SE5 121 H7
Elam St CMBW SE5 121 H7
Eland Rd BTSEA SW11 119 M8
CROY/NA CR0 172 B5
Elba Pl WALW SE17 18 F5 1
Elberon Av CROY/NA CR0 171 J1 2
Elbe St FUL/PGN SW6 119 J7
Elborough Rd SNWD SE25 158 A8
Elborough St
WAND/EARL SW18 137 G5
Elbury Dr CAN/RD E16 106 A5
Elcho St BTSEA SW11 119 L5
Elcot Av PECK SE15 122 B5
Elder Av CEND/HSY/T N8 66 E6 3
Elderbeck Cl CHESW EN7 26 A1
Elderberry Rd EA W5 98 E8
Elderberry Wy GSTN WD25 21 H8 2
Elder Cl BFN/LL DA15 143 M5
WDR/YW UB7 94 E6 2
Elder Ct BUSH WD23 43 L4
Elderfield Rd CLPT E5 86 D4
Elderfield Wk WAN E11 70 B6 2
Elderflower Wy SRTFD E15 87 L7
Elder Oak Cl PGE/AN SE20 158 B4
Elder Rd WNWD SE27 157 J1
Elderslie Cl BECK BR3 174 A1
Elderslie Rd ELTH/MOT SE9 143 G2
Elder St WCHPL E1 13 L2
Elderton Rd SYD SE26 140 E8
Eldertree Wy MTCM CR4 156 B4
Elder Wk IS N1 6 D3 1
Elder Wy RAIN RM13 110 D2
Eldon Av BORE WD6 32 A5
CROY/NA CR0 173 J4
HEST TW5 115 G5
Eldon Gv HAMP NW3 83 K5
Eldon Pk SNWD SE25 158 B7
Eldon Rd ED N9 50 C3
KENS W8 14 D4
WALTH E17 68 F5
WDGN N22 67 H2
Eldon St LVPST EC2M 13 H3
Eldon Wy WLSDN NW10 99 H1
Eldred Dr STMC/STPC BR5 177 K4
Eldred Gdns UPMR RM14 75 L8
Eldridge Cl EBED/NFELT TW14 132 A5
Eleanor Av HOR/WEW KT19 180 D3
Eleanor Cl TOTM N17 67 M4
Eleanor Crs MLHL NW7 46 D6
Eleanor Cross Rd
CHES/WCR EN8 26 E7
Eleanor Gdns BAR EN5 33 K8 1
Eleanor Gv BARN SW13 117 L8
HGDN/ICK UB10 77 H3
Eleanor Rd CHES/WCR EN8 26 E6
FBAR/BDGN N11 48 E8
HACK E8 86 B6
SRTFD E15 87 M6
Eleanor St BOW E3 105 G2
Eleanor Wy CHES/WCR EN8 26 F7
Electric Av BRXN/ST SW9 139 G1
Electric La BRXN/ST SW9 139 G1 2
Elephant La BERM/RHTH SE16 104 C8
Elephant Rd WALW SE17 18 E5
Elers Rd HYS/HAR UB3 113 J2
WEA W13 98 C8
Eleven Acre Ri LOU IG10 39 M6
Eley Rd UED N18 50 D7
Elfindale Rd HNHL SE24 139 J2
Elfin Gv TEDD TW11 151 M1
Elford Cl ELTH/MOT SE9 142 C1
Elfort Rd HBRY N5 85 G4
Elfrida Crs CAT SE6 141 G8
Elfrida Rd WATW WD18 29 J8
Elf Rw WAP E1W 104 C6
Elfwine Rd HNWL W7 97 L4
Elgal Cl ORP BR6 176 B7
Elgar Av BRYLDS KT5 168 B3
EA W5 98 E8
STRHM/NOR SW16 156 E6
WLSDN NW10 81 K6 2
Elgar Cl BKHH IG9 52 D4
BORE WD6 44 C2
DEPT SE8 123 G5
HGDN/ICK UB10 77 G2
PLSTW E13 106 C1
Elgar St BERM/RHTH SE16 104 E8
Elgin Av ASHF TW15 149 J2
HARH RM3 75 H1
KTN/HRWW/W HA3 62 B3
MV/WKIL W9 8 A1
Elgin Crs HTHAIR TW6 113 L7 1
NTGHL W11 100 F5 7
Elgin Dr NTHWD HA6 59 L1
Elginmeads South
MV/WKIL W9 2 D7 1
Elgin Ms NTGHL W11 100 E5
Elgin Ms North MV/WKIL W9 2 D7
Elgin Rd CHES/WCR EN8 26 C3
CROY/NA CR0 172 F4
GDMY/SEVK IG3 89 L1
SUT SM1 170 C5
WDGN N22 66 C3
WEY KT13 164 A8
WLGTN SM6 171 J8
Elgood Av NTHWD HA6 42 A8
Elham Cl BMLY BR1 160 D3
Elia Ms IS N1 6 C6
Elias Pl LBTH SE11 121 G4
Elia St IS N1 6 C6
Elibank Rd ELTH/MOT SE9 143 G1
Elim St STHWK SE1 19 H3
Elim Wy PLSTW E13 105 M2
Eliot Bank FSTH SE23 140 B6
Eliot Dr RYLN/HDSTN HA2 79 H2
Eliot Gdns PUT/ROE SW15 136 A1
Eliot Hl BKHTH/KID SE3 123 J7
Eliot Pk LEW SE13 123 J7
Eliot Pl BKHTH/KID SE3 123 L7
Eliot Rd DAGW RM9 90 D4
DART DA1 147 H2
Eliot V BKHTH/KID SE3 123 K7
Elizabethan Wy
STWL/WRAY TW19 130 D4
Elizabeth Av ENC/FH EN2 36 B6
IL IG1 89 K2 1
IS N1 6 F2
STA TW18 148 C2
Elizabeth Cl BAR EN5 33 K6
MV/WKIL W9 2 F9 2
ROMW/RG RM7 73 H2
SUT SM1 169 M6 2
Elizabeth Clyde Cl
SEVS/STOTM N15 67 L5 3
Elizabeth Cottages
RCH/KEW TW9 116 F6
Elizabeth Gdns ACT W3 99 M7
STAN HA7 44 C8
SUN TW16 150 C6
Elizabeth Ms HAMP NW3 83 L6
Elizabeth Pl SEVS/STOTM N15 67 K5
Elizabeth Ride ED N9 50 B2
Elizabeth Rd EHAM E6 88 D8
RAIN RM13 110 B4
SEVS/STOTM N15 67 L6 4
Elizabeth Sq POP/IOD E14 104 E6 2
Elizabeth St BGVA SW1W 16 B5
GRH DA9 147 L2
Elizabeth Wy FELT TW13 132 C8
NRWD SE19 157 K3 1
STMC/STPC BR5 162 C8
Elkington Rd PLSTW E13 106 B3

The Elkins *ROM* RM1 ...... 73 L3
Elkstone Rd *NKENS* W10 ...... 100 F4
Ellaline Rd *HMSMTH* W6 ...... 118 D4
Ella Ms *HAMP* NW3 ...... 83 M5 🄯
Ellanby Crs *UED* N18 ...... 50 B7
Elland Rd *PECK* SE15 ...... 140 C1
WOT/HER KT12 ...... 165 K4
Ella Rd *CEND/HSY/T* N8 ...... 66 E8
Element Cl *PIN* HA5 ...... 60 D6
Ellenborough Pl
PUT/ROE SW15 ...... 136 A1 🄯
Ellenborough Rd *SCUP* DA14 ...... 162 D2
WDGN N22 ...... 67 J2
Ellenbridge Wy *SAND/SEL* CR2 ...... 184 E2
Ellenbrook Cl *WATN* WD24 ...... 29 J4 🄯
Ellen Cl *BMLY* BR1 ...... 160 D6
Ellen Ct *ED* N9 ...... 50 C4
Ellen St *WCHPL* E1 ...... 104 A5
Ellen Webb Dr
KTN/HRWW/W HA3 ...... 61 L4
Elleray Rd *TEDD* TW11 ...... 151 M2 🄯
Ellerby St *FUL/PGN* SW6 ...... 118 D6
Ellerdale Rd *HAMP* NW3 ...... 83 J5
Ellerdale St *LEW* SE13 ...... 141 H1
Ellerdine Rd *HSLW* TW3 ...... 133 J1
Ellerker Gdns
RCHPK/HAM TW10 ...... 134 E3
Ellerman Av *WHTN* TW2 ...... 132 F5
Ellerslie Rd *SHB* W12 ...... 100 B7
Ellerton Gdns *DAGW* RM9 ...... 90 C7
Ellerton Rd *BARN* SW13 ...... 118 A6 🄯
DAGW RM9 ...... 90 C7
RYNPK SW20 ...... 154 A3
SURB KT6 ...... 167 M3 🄯
WAND/EARL SW18 ...... 137 K5
Ellery Rd *NRWD* SE19 ...... 157 K3
Ellery St *PECK* SE15 ...... 122 B7
Ellesborough Cl *OXHEY* WD19 ...... 42 C7
Ellesmere Av *BECK* BR3 ...... 159 H5 🄯
MLHL NW7 ...... 45 K5
Ellesmere Cl *RSLP* HA4 ...... 59 J8 🄯
WAN E11 ...... 69 M6
Ellesmere Dr *SAND/SEL* CR2 ...... 185 H7
Ellesmere Gdns *REDBR* IG4 ...... 70 E6
Ellesmere Gv *BAR* EN5 ...... 33 M8 🄯
Ellesmere Rd *BOW* E3 ...... 104 E1
GFD/PVL UB6 ...... 97 J3
TWK TW1 ...... 134 C3
WEY KT13 ...... 164 E8
WLSDN NW10 ...... 82 A5
Ellesmere St *POP/IOD* E14 ...... 105 H5
Ellies Ms *ASHF* TW15 ...... 130 E6
Ellingfort Rd *HACK* E8 ...... 86 B7
Ellingham Rd *CHSGTN* KT9 ...... 167 K8
SHB W12 ...... 100 A8
WAN E11 ...... 87 K4
Ellington Rd *FELT* TW13 ...... 131 M8
HSLW TW3 ...... 115 H7
MUSWH N10 ...... 66 B5
Ellington St *HOLWY* N7 ...... 85 G6
Elliot Cl *SRTFD* E15 ...... 87 L7
WBLY HA9 ...... 80 F3
Elliot Rd *HDN* NW4 ...... 64 B7
Elliott Av *RSLP* HA4 ...... 78 B2 🄯
SHPTN TW17 ...... 149 C7
Elliott Gdns *HARH* RM3 ...... 74 B2
Elliott Rd *BRXN/ST* SW9 ...... 121 H5
CHSWK W4 ...... 117 L2
HAYES BR2 ...... 160 D7
STAN HA7 ...... 44 A8
THHTH CR7 ...... 157 H7
Elliott's Pl *IS* N1 ...... 6 D4
Elliott Sq *HAMP* NW3 ...... 3 K2
Elliott's Rw *LBTH* SE11 ...... 18 D5
Ellis Av *RAIN* RM13 ...... 110 A4
Ellis Cl *ELTH/MOT* SE9 ...... 143 J6
Elliscombe Rd *CHARL* SE7 ...... 124 C3
Ellisfield Dr *PUT/ROE* SW15 ...... 135 M4
Ellison Gdns *NWDGN* UB2 ...... 114 F2
Ellison Rd *BARN* SW13 ...... 117 M7
BFN/LL DA15 ...... 143 K5
STRHM/NOR SW16 ...... 156 D3
Ellis Rd *MTCM* CR4 ...... 170 F1
STHL UB1 ...... 97 J7
Ellis St *KTBR* SW1X 15 M5
Ellis Waterton Cl *SWLY* BR8 ...... 163 K7 🄯
Ellis Wy *DART* DA1 ...... 146 F6 🄯
Ellmore Cl *HARH* RM3 ...... 74 B2
Ellsworth St *BETH* E2 ...... 104 B2 🄯
Elmar Rd *SEVS/STOTM* N15 ...... 67 K5
Elm Av *EA* W5 ...... 98 E7
OXHEY WD19 ...... 42 E2
RSLP HA4 ...... 78 A1
UPMR RM14 ...... 93 H3
Elmbank *WCHMH* N21 ...... 48 E2
Elmbank Av *BAR* EN5 ...... 33 J7
Elmbank Dr *BMLY* BR1 ...... 160 D5
Elm Bank Gdns *BARN* SW13 ...... 117 L7
Elmbank Wy *HNWL* W7 ...... 97 K4
Elmbourne Dr *BELV* DA17 ...... 127 H2
Elmbourne Rd *TOOT* SW17 ...... 138 B7
Elmbridge Av *BRYLDS* KT5 ...... 168 C1
Elmbridge Cl *RSLP* HA4 ...... 60 A7
Elmbridge Dr *RSLP* HA4 ...... 60 A7
Elmbridge Rd *BARK/HLT* IG6 ...... 54 A8
Elmbrook Cl *SUN* TW16 ...... 150 B4
Elmbrook Gdns *ELTH/MOT* SE9 ...... 142 E3
Elmbrook Rd *SUT* SM1 ...... 169 M6 🄯
Elm Cl *BKHH* IG9 ...... 52 C4
BRYLDS KT5 ...... 168 C2
CAR SM5 ...... 170 F3
DART DA1 ...... 146 C5
HDN NW4 ...... 64 D6
HYS/HAR UB3 ...... 96 A5
ROMW/RG RM7 ...... 73 H2
RYLN/HDSTN HA2 ...... 61 H7
RYNPK SW20 ...... 154 C7
SAND/SEL CR2 ...... 172 D8
STWL/WRAY TW19 ...... 130 D5
WAB EN9 ...... 27 K7
WAN E11 ...... 70 B7
WHTN TW2 ...... 133 H6
Elmcote Wy *RKW/CH/CXG* WD3 ...... 40 F1
Elmcourt Rd *WNWD* SE27 ...... 139 H6
Elm Crs *EA* W5 ...... 98 E8
KUTN/CMB KT2 ...... 152 E4
Elmcroft *CEND/HSY/T* N8 ...... 66 F6 🄯
Elmcroft Cl *BFN/LL* DA15 ...... 143 M4
ED N9 ...... 50 B1
GLDGN NW11 ...... 64 F8
WAN E11 ...... 70 B6
Elmcroft Cl *CHSGTN* KT9 ...... 167 L5 🄯
EA W5 ...... 98 D3
EBED/NFELT TW14 ...... 131 M3
Elmcroft Crs *GLDGN* NW11 ...... 64 D8
RYLN/HDSTN HA2 ...... 61 G4
Elmcroft Dr *ASHF* TW15 ...... 149 G1 🄯
CHSGTN KT9 ...... 167 L5
Elmcroft Gdns *CDALE/KGS* NW9 ...... 63 C8
Elmcroft Rd *ORP* BR6 ...... 177 G2
Elmcroft St *CLPT* E5 ...... 86 C4
Elmdale Rd *PLMGR* N13 ...... 48 F7
Elmdene *BRYLDS* KT5 ...... 168 C3
Elmdene Av *EMPK* RM11 ...... 74 F6
Elmdene Rd *WOOL/PLUM* SE18 ...... 125 H3
Elmdon Rd *HEST* TW5 ...... 114 D7
HTHAIR TW6 ...... 113 M8
Elm Dr *CHES/WCR* EN8 ...... 26 E1
RYLN/HDSTN HA2 ...... 61 H7
SUN TW16 ...... 150 C5
SWLY BR8 ...... 163 K5
Elmer Av *ABR/ST* RM4 ...... 55 L5
Elmer Cl *ENC/FH* EN2 ...... 35 M6
RAIN RM13 ...... 92 A7 🄯
Elmer Gdns *EDGW* HA8 ...... 63 H1
ISLW TW7 ...... 115 K8
RAIN RM13 ...... 92 A7
Elmer Rd *CAT* SE6 ...... 141 J4
Elmers Av *SURB* KT6 ...... 152 E8
Elmers End Rd *BECK* BR3 ...... 158 C6
PGE/AN SE20 ...... 158 C5
Elmerside Rd *BECK* BR3 ...... 158 E7 🄯
Elmers Rd *CROY/NA* CR0 ...... 173 G2
Elmfield Av *CEND/HSY/T* N8 ...... 66 E6
MTCM CR4 ...... 156 A4
TEDD TW11 ...... 151 M1
Elmfield Cl *HRW* HA1 ...... 79 L2 🄯
POTB/CUF EN6 ...... 22 E6 🄯
Elmfield Pk *BMLY* BR1 ...... 160 A6
Elmfield Rd *BMLY* BR1 ...... 160 A5
CHING E4 ...... 51 J4
EFNCH N2 ...... 65 K4
NWDGN UB2 ...... 114 E1
POTB/CUF EN6 ...... 22 E6
TOOT SW17 ...... 138 B6
WALTH E17 ...... 68 D7
Elmfield Wy *MV/WKIL* W9 ...... 8 A2
SAND/SEL CR2 ...... 184 F2
Elm Gdns *EFNCH* N2 ...... 65 J4
ENC/FH EN2 ...... 36 D3
ESH/CLAY KT10 ...... 166 F8
MTCM CR4 ...... 156 D7
Elmgate Av *FELT* TW13 ...... 132 B7 🄯
Elmgate Gdns *EDGW* HA8 ...... 45 J7
Elm Gn *ACT* W3 ...... 99 L5
Elmgreen Cl *SRTFD* E15 ...... 87 L8 🄯
Elm Gv *CEND/HSY/T* N8 ...... 66 F7
CRICK NW2 ...... 82 D4
EMPK RM11 ...... 74 F7
EPSOM KT18 ...... 180 C7
ERITH DA8 ...... 127 K5
KUTN/CMB KT2 ...... 152 E4
ORP BR6 ...... 176 F3
PECK SE15 ...... 122 A7
RYLN/HDSTN HA2 ...... 61 L3
SUT SM1 ...... 170 B6
WATN WD24 ...... 29 C2
WDR/YW UB7 ...... 94 F6
WIM/MER SW19 ...... 154 E3
Elmgrove Crs *HRW* HA1 ...... 61 M6
Elmgrove Gdns *HRW* HA1 ...... 62 A6 🄯
Elm Grove Pde *WLGTN* SM6 ...... 171 G5 🄯
Elm Grove Rd *BARN* SW13 ...... 118 A6
Elm Grove Rd *EA* W5 ...... 98 E8
Elmgrove Rd *CROY/NA* CR0 ...... 173 K2
HRW HA1 ...... 61 M6
WEY KT13 ...... 164 A6
Elm Hall Gdns *WAN* E11 ...... 70 B7
Elm Hatch *PIN* HA5 ...... 59 M1
Elmhurst *BELV* DA17 ...... 126 E4 🄯
Elmhurst Av *EFNCH* N2 ...... 65 K4 🄯
MTCM CR4 ...... 156 A3
Elmhurst Dr *EMPK* RM11 ...... 74 C8
SWFD E18 ...... 70 A3
Elmhurst Rd *ELTH/MOT* SE9 ...... 142 E6
FSTGT E7 ...... 88 B7
PEND EN3 ...... 37 J2
TOTM N17 ...... 67 L3
Elmhurst St *CLAP* SW4 ...... 120 D8
Elmhurst Wy *LOU* IG10 ...... 52 F2
Elmington Cl *BXLY* DA5 ...... 145 K4
Elmington Rd *CMBW* SE5 ...... 121 K6
Elmira St *LEW* SE13 ...... 123 H8
Elm La *CAT* SE6 ...... 140 F6
Elm Lawn Cl *UX/CGN* UB8 ...... 76 E7 🄯
Elmlee Cl *CHST* BR7 ...... 160 F2
Elmley Cl *WOOL/PLUM* SE18 ...... 125 K2
Elmley St *WOOL/PLUM* SE18 ...... 125 K2
Elmore Cl *ALP/SUD* HA0 ...... 98 E1
Elmore Rd *LEY* E10 ...... 87 J3
PEND EN3 ...... 37 K4
Elmore St *IS* N1 ...... 7 G1
Elm Pk *BRXS/STRHM* SW2 ...... 138 F5
STAN HA7 ...... 44 B7
Elm Park Av *HCH* RM12 ...... 92 B4
SEVS/STOTM N15 ...... 67 M6
Elm Park Gdns *CHEL* SW3 ...... 15 G8
HDN NW4 ...... 64 D6
Elmpark Gdns *SAND/SEL* CR2 ...... 185 J6
Elm Park La *CHEL* SW3 ...... 15 G8
Elm Park Rd *CHEL* SW3 ...... 15 G9
FNCH N3 ...... 64 E7
LEY E10 ...... 86 E1
PIN HA5 ...... 60 D4
SNWD SE25 ...... 157 M6
WCHMH N21 ...... 49 J2
Elm Pl *SKENS* SW7 ...... 15 G7
Elm Rd *BAR* EN5 ...... 33 M7
BECK BR3 ...... 158 F5
CHSGTN KT9 ...... 167 L6
DART DA1 ...... 146 D5
EBED/NFELT TW14 ...... 131 K5
Elm Rd West *MRDN* SM4 ...... 169 M2
Elm Rw *HAMP* NW3 ...... 83 J5 🄯
Elmroyd Av *POTB/CUF* EN6 ...... 22 F6
Elmroyd Cl *POTB/CUF* EN6 ...... 22 F6
Elms Av *HDN* NW4 ...... 64 C6
MUSWH N10 ...... 66 B4
Elmscott Gdns *WCHMH* N21 ...... 49 J1
Elmscott Rd *BMLY* BR1 ...... 159 L1
Elms Crs *CLAP* SW4 ...... 138 C3
Elmscroft Gdns *POTB/CUF* EN6 ...... 22 F5
Elmsdale Rd *WALTH* E17 ...... 68 F5
Elms Farm Rd *HCH* RM12 ...... 92 C5
Elms Gdns *ALP/SUD* HA0 ...... 80 A4
DAGW RM9 ...... 90 A4
Elmshaw Rd *PUT/ROE* SW15 ...... 136 A2
Elmside *WBLY* HA9 ...... 81 C3
Elms La *ALP/SUD* HA0 ...... 80 A4
Elmsleigh Av
KTN/HRWW/W HA3 ...... 62 B5
Elmsleigh Rd *WHTN* TW2 ...... 133 K6
Elmslie Cl *EPSOM* KT18 ...... 180 C7
WFD IG8 ...... 52 F8
Elms Ms *BAY/PAD* W2 ...... 9 G6
Elms Park Av *ALP/SUD* HA0 ...... 80 A4
Elms Rd *CLAP* SW4 ...... 138 C2
KTN/HRWW/W HA3 ...... 61 L1
Elmstead Av *CHST* BR7 ...... 160 F1
WBLY HA9 ...... 80 E1
Elmstead Cl *HOR/WEW* KT19 ...... 168 E2 🄯
TRDG/WHET N20 ...... 47 G4
Elmstead Gdns *WPK* KT4 ...... 169 C5
Elmstead Gld *CHST* BR7 ...... 160 F2
Elmstead La *CHST* BR7 ...... 160 E3
Elmstead Rd *ERITH* DA8 ...... 127 L6
GDMY/SEVK IG3 ...... 89 L2
Elmsted Crs *WELL* DA16 ...... 126 C4
The Elms *BARN* SW13 ...... 117 M8
Elmstone Rd *FUL/PGN* SW6 ...... 119 C6
Elm St *FSBYW* WC1X 11 M1
Elmsway *ASHF* TW15 ...... 148 F1 🄯
Elmswood *HAYES* BR2 ...... 159 M8 🄯
Elmsworth Av *HSLW* TW3 ...... 115 H7
Elm Ter *CRICK* NW2 ...... 83 G3
ELTH/MOT SE9 ...... 143 G3
KTN/HRWW/W HA3 ...... 61 K1
Elmton Wy *STNW/STAM* N16 ...... 86 A3 🄯
Elm Tree Av *ESH/CLAY* KT10 ...... 166 D2
Elm Tree Cl *ASHF* TW15 ...... 149 H1
NTHLT UB5 ...... 96 F2
STJWD NW8 ...... 3 C8
Elm Tree Rd *STJWD* NW8 ...... 3 C8
Elmtree Rd *TEDD* TW11 ...... 151 L1
Elm Wk *GPK* RM2 ...... 74 A4
HAMP NW3 ...... 83 G2
ORP BR6 ...... 175 M5
RAD WD7 ...... 30 F1
RYNPK SW20 ...... 154 D7
Elm Wy *FBAR/BDGN* N11 ...... 48 A8
HOR/WEW KT19 ...... 168 D7
RKW/CH/CXG WD3 ...... 40 B3
WLSDN NW10 ...... 81 L4
WPK KT4 ...... 169 J5
Elmwood Av *BORE* WD6 ...... 32 B7
FELT TW13 ...... 132 B7
KTN/HRWW/W HA3 ...... 62 A6
PLMGR N13 ...... 48 E4
Elmwood Cl *EW* KT17 ...... 181 C1 🄯
WLGTN SM6 ...... 171 H4
Elmwood Crs *CDALE/KGS* NW9 ...... 63 L6
Elmwood Dr *BXLY* DA5 ...... 144 E4
EW KT17 ...... 181 C1
Elmwood Gdns *HNWL* W7 ...... 97 L5
Elmwood Rd *CHSWK* W4 ...... 117 J4
CROY/NA CR0 ...... 172 B2
HNHL SE24 ...... 139 K2
MTCM CR4 ...... 155 M6
Elmworth Gv *DUL* SE21 ...... 139 K6
Elnathan Ms *MV/WKIL* W9 ...... 8 D1
Elphinstone Rd *WALTH* E17 ...... 68 E1
Elphinstone St *HBRY* N5 ...... 85 H3 🄯
Elrick Cl *ERITH* DA8 ...... 127 L4
Elrington Rd *HACK* E8 ...... 86 A6
WFD IG8 ...... 52 A7 🄯
Elruge Cl *WDR/YW* UB7 ...... 112 D1 🄯
Elsa Cl *WELL* DA16 ...... 126 C7
Elsa Rd *WELL* DA16 ...... 126 D1
Elsa St *WCHPL* E1 ...... 104 E4 🄯
Elsdale St *HOM* E9 ...... 86 C6
Elsden Ms *BETH* E2 ...... 104 C1 🄯
Elsden Rd *TOTM* N17 ...... 67 M2
Elsenham Rd *MNPK* E12 ...... 88 F5
Elsenham St *WIM/MER* SW18 ...... 136 F7
Elsham Rd *WAN* E11 ...... 87 L3
WKENS W14 ...... 100 L8
Elsiedene Rd *WCHMH* N21 ...... 49 J2
Elsie Lane Ct *BAY/PAD* W2 ...... 8 B3
Elsiemaud Rd *BROCKY* SE4 ...... 140 F2
Elsie Rd *EDUL* SE22 ...... 139 M1
Elsinge Rd *EN* EN1 ...... 37 H1
Elsinore Av
STWL/WRAY TW19 ...... 130 E4 🄯
Elsinore Gdns *CRICK* NW2 ...... 82 E3 🄯
Elsinore Rd *FSTH* SE23 ...... 140 E5
Elsinore Wy *RCH/KEW* TW9 ...... 117 H8 🄯
Elsley Rd *BTSEA* SW11 ...... 119 M8
Elspeth Rd *ALP/SUD* HA0 ...... 80 E5
BTSEA SW11 ...... 137 M1
Elsrick Av *MRDN* SM4 ...... 155 C8
Elstan Wy *CROY/NA* CR0 ...... 173 L2
Elsted St *WALW* SE17 ...... 19 H6
Elstow Cl *ELTH/MOT* SE9 ...... 142 F4
RSLP HA4 ...... 60 D8
Elstow Gdns *DAGW* RM9 ...... 90 B8
Elstow Rd *DAGW* RM9 ...... 90 E7
Elstree Gdns *BELV* DA17 ...... 126 E2
ED N9 ...... 50 B3
IL IG1 ...... 89 J5
Elstree HI *BMLY* BR1 ...... 159 L3
Elstree HI North *BORE* WD6 ...... 31 K8
Elstree HI South *BORE* WD6 ...... 44 A1
Elstree Rd *BORE* WD6 ...... 44 A1
BUSH WD23 ...... 43 K3
STAN HA7 ...... 43 M2
Elstree Wy *BORE* WD6 ...... 32 D5
Elswick Rd *LEW* SE13 ...... 123 H8
Elswick St *FUL/PGN* SW6 ...... 119 J7
Elsworth Cl *EBED/NFELT* TW14 ...... 131 L5
Elsworthy *THDIT* KT7 ...... 166 E1
Elsworthy Ri *HAMP* NW3 ...... 3 K2
Elsworthy Rd *HAMP* NW3 ...... 3 J3
Elsworthy Ter *HAMP* NW3 ...... 3 K2
Elsynge Rd *WAND/EARL* SW18 ...... 137 K2
Eltham Green
ELTH/MOT SE9 ...... 142 C2
Eltham Green Road Rd
ELTH/MOT SE9 ...... 142 C2
Eltham High St *ELTH/MOT* SE9 ...... 142 F3
Eltham HI *ELTH/MOT* SE9 ...... 142 D2
Eltham Palace Rd
ELTH/MOT SE9 ...... 142 D3 🄯
Eltham Park Gdns
ELTH/MOT SE9 ...... 143 G1
Eltham Rd *ELTH/MOT* SE9 ...... 142 C2
Elthiron Rd *FUL/PGN* SW6 ...... 119 G6
Elthorne Av *HNWL* W7 ...... 97 M8
Elthorne Ct *FELT* TW13 ...... 132 C5
Elthorne Park Rd *HNWL* W7 ...... 115 M1
Elthorne Rd *ARCH* N19 ...... 84 D7
CDALE/KGS NW9 ...... 63 K8
UX/CGN UB8 ...... 94 D1
Elthorne Wy *CDALE/KGS* NW9 ...... 63 K8
Elthruda Rd *LEW* SE13 ...... 141 K3
Eltisley Rd *IL* IG1 ...... 89 H4
Elton Av *ALP/SUD* HA0 ...... 80 B5
BAR EN5 ...... 33 M8
GFD/PVL UB6 ...... 79 M6
Elton Pl *STNW/STAM* N16 ...... 85 L5
Elton Rd *KUTN/CMB* KT2 ...... 152 F4
PUR/KEN CR8 ...... 183 J5
Eltringham St
WAND/EARL SW18 ...... 137 J1 🄯
Elvaston Ms *SKENS* SW7 ...... 14 E1 🄯
Elvaston Pl *SKENS* SW7 ...... 14 E4
Elveden Pl *WLSDN* NW10 ...... 99 G1
Elveden Rd *WLSDN* NW10 ...... 99 G1
Elvendon Rd *FBAR/BDGN* N11 ...... 48 E8
Elverson Rd *DEPT* SE8 ...... 123 H7
Elverton St *WEST* SW1P ...... 17 C5 🄯
Elvet Av *EMPK* RM11 ...... 74 C5
Elvington Gn *HAYES* BR2 ...... 159 M8 🄯
Elvington La *CDALE/KGS* NW9 ...... 63 L2 🄯
Elvino Rd *SYD* SE26 ...... 158 D1
Elvis Rd *CRICK* NW2 ...... 82 C6
Elwill Wy *BECK* BR3 ...... 159 K7
Elwin St *BETH* E2 ...... 104 A2
Elwood St *HBRY* N5 ...... 85 H3
Elwyn Gdns *LEE/GVPK* SE12 ...... 142 A4 🄯
Ely Cl *ERITH* DA8 ...... 127 M7
NWMAL KT3 ...... 153 M5
Ely Cottages *VX/NE* SW8 ...... 120 F5 🄯
Ely Gdns *BORE* WD6 ...... 32 D8
DACE RM10 ...... 91 J3
Elyne Rd *FSBYPK* N4 ...... 67 G7
Ely Pl *HCIRC* EC1N 12 B3
WFD IG8 ...... 53 G7
Ely Rd *CROY/NA* CR0 ...... 157 K8
HSLWW TW4 ...... 114 C8
HTHAIR TW6 ...... 113 M7 🄯
LEY E10 ...... 69 J7
Elysian Av *STMC/STPC* BR5 ...... 176 E1
Elysium Pl *FUL/PGN* SW6 ...... 118 F7
Elysium St *FUL/PGN* SW6 ...... 118 F7 🄯
Elystan Cl *WLGTN* SM6 ...... 183 J2
Elystan Pl *CHEL* SW3 ...... 15 K6
Elystan St *CHEL* SW3 ...... 15 J5
Elystan Wk *IS* N1 ...... 6 A4 🄯
Emanuel Av *ACT* W3 ...... 99 J5
Embankment *PUT/ROE* SW15 ...... 118 D8
Embankment Gdns *CHEL* SW3 ...... 15 M9
The Embankment *TWK* TW1 ...... 134 A5
Embassey Ct *SCUP* DA14 ...... 144 B7
Emba St *BERM/RHTH* SE16 ...... 104 A8
Ember Farm Av
E/WMO/HCT KT8 ...... 166 D1
Ember Farm Wy
E/WMO/HCT KT8 ...... 151 K8
Ember Gdns *ESH/CLAY* KT10 ...... 166 D2
Ember La *ESH/CLAY* KT10 ...... 166 D3
Embleton Rd *LEW* SE13 ...... 141 H1
OXHEY WD19 ...... 42 A5
Embry Cl *STAN* HA7 ...... 44 A6
Embry Dr *STAN* HA7 ...... 44 A8
Embry Wy *STAN* HA7 ...... 44 A7
Emden Cl *WDR/YW* UB7 ...... 95 G3
Emden St *FUL/PGN* SW6 ...... 119 H6 🄯
Emerald Cl *CAN/RD* E16 ...... 106 E5
Emerald Gdns *BCTR* RM8 ...... 91 C1
Emerald Sq *NWDGN* UB2 ...... 114 D1
Emerald St *BMSBY* WC1N 11 L2
Emerson Dr *EMPK* RM11 ...... 74 D8
Emerson Gdns
KTN/HRWW/W HA3 ...... 62 F7 🄯
Emersons Av *SWLY* BR8 ...... 163 M3
Emerson St *STHWK* SE1 ...... 12 E8
Emerton Cl *BXLYHS* DA6 ...... 144 E1
Emery Hill St *WEST* SW1P ...... 16 F4 🄯
Emery St *STHWK* SE1 ...... 18 B3
Emes Rd *ERITH* DA8 ...... 127 J5
Emilia Cl *PEND* EN3 ...... 37 H8
Emily Pl *HOLWY* N7 ...... 85 G4
Emily St *CAN/RD* E16 ...... 105 M3 🄯
Emlyn Rd *SHB* W12 ...... 99 L8
Emmanuel Rd *BAL* SW12 ...... 138 C5
NTHWD HA6 ...... 59 M1
Emma Rd *PLSTW* E13 ...... 105 M2
Emma St *BETH* E2 ...... 104 B1
Emmaus Wy *CHIG* IG7 ...... 53 C7
Emmott Av *BARK/HLT* IG6 ...... 71 J6
Emmott Cl *WCHPL* E1 ...... 104 E3
Emperor's Ga *SKENS* SW7 ...... 14 E5
Empire Av *UED* N18 ...... 49 J8
Empire Rd *GFD/PVL* UB6 ...... 80 C8
Empire Wy *WBLY* HA9 ...... 80 F3
Empire Wharf Rd *POP/IOD* E14 ...... 123 K2
Empress Av *CHING* E4 ...... 69 G1
IL IG1 ...... 88 F2
MNPK E12 ...... 88 C2
WFD IG8 ...... 69 M1
Empress Dr *CHST* BR7 ...... 161 H2
Empress Pl *ECT* SW5 ...... 14 A8
Empress St *WALW* SE17 ...... 18 F9
Empson St *BOW* E3 ...... 105 H3
Emsworth Cl *ED* N9 ...... 50 C3
Emsworth Rd *BARK/HLT* IG6 ...... 71 H3
Emsworth St
BRXS/STRHM SW2 ...... 138 F6
Emu Rd *VX/NE* SW8 ...... 120 B7
Ena Rd *STRHM/NOR* SW16 ...... 156 E6
Enbrook St *NKENS* W10 ...... 100 D3 🄯
Endale Cl *CAR* SM5 ...... 170 F4
Endeavour Wy *BARK* IG11 ...... 108 A1
CROY/NA CR0 ...... 171 K2
WIM/MER SW19 ...... 137 K5
Endell St *LSQ/SEVD* WC2H 11 J4
Enderby St *GNWCH* SE10 ...... 123 C5
Enderley Rd *KTN/HRWW/W* HA3 ...... 61 K2
Endersby Rd *BAR* EN5 ...... 33 J3
Endersleigh Gdns *HDN* NW4 ...... 64 A5
Enderwick Rd *CHING* E4 ...... 51 J4
Endlebury Rd *CHING* E4 ...... 51 J4
Endlesham Rd *BAL* SW12 ...... 138 A4
Endsleigh Cl *SAND/SEL* CR2 ...... 185 J3
Endsleigh Gdns *IL* IG1 ...... 88 F1
STPAN WC1H 5 C9
SURB KT6 ...... 167 J1
WOT/HER KT12 ...... 165 M5
Endsleigh Pl *STPAN* WC1H ...... 5 H9 🄯
Endsleigh Rd *HNWL* W7 ...... 98 A7
NWDGN UB2 ...... 114 E2
Endsleigh St *STPAN* WC1H ...... 5 H9 🄯
Endway *BRYLDS* KT5 ...... 168 A2
Endwell Rd *BROCKY* SE4 ...... 122 E7
Endymion Rd
BRXS/STRHM SW2 ...... 138 F4
FSBYPK N4 ...... 67 H7
Enfield Cl *UX/CGN* UB8 ...... 94 D1 🄯
Enfield Rd *ACT* W3 ...... 99 H8
BTFD TW8 ...... 116 D3
EBAR EN4 ...... 35 K7
HTHAIR TW6 ...... 113 L7 🄯
IS N1 ...... 7 K2
Enford St *MBLAR* W1H 9 L2
Engadine Cl *CROY/NA* CR0 ...... 172 F5
Engadine St *WAND/EARL* SW18 ...... 136 F5
Engate St *LEW* SE13 ...... 141 J1
Engayne Gdns *UPMR* RM14 ...... 93 H1
Engel Pk *MLHL* NW7 ...... 46 C8
Engineer Cl *WOOL/PLUM* SE18 ...... 125 C6
Engineers Wy *WBLY* HA9 ...... 81 C4
England's La *HAMP* NW3 ...... 83 M6
Englefield Cl *CROY/NA* CR0 ...... 172 C1 🄯
ENC/FH EN2 ...... 36 A3 🄯
STMC/STPC BR5 ...... 161 M7 🄯
Englefield Crs *STMC/STPC* BR5 ...... 162 A8
Englefield Pth
STMC/STPC BR5 ...... 162 A7 🄯
Englefield Rd *IS* N1 ...... 7 H1
Engleheart Dr
EBED/NFELT TW14 ...... 131 M3
Engleheart Rd *CAT* SE6 ...... 141 H4
Englemere Pk *COB* KT11 ...... 178 B7
Englewood Rd *CLAP* SW4 ...... 138 B3
English St *BOW* E3 ...... 104 F3
Enid Cl *LCOL/BKTW* AL2 ...... 21 M4
Enid St *STHWK* SE1 ...... 19 M3
Enmore Gdns *SNWD* SE25 ...... 158 A4
Enmore Gdns
MORT/ESHN SW14 ...... 135 K2
Enmore Rd *PUT/ROE* SW15 ...... 136 C1
SNWD SE25 ...... 158 A8
STHL UB1 ...... 97 C3
Ennerdale Av *HCH* RM12 ...... 92 A5
STAN HA7 ...... 62 C4
Ennerdale Cl
EBED/NFELT TW14 ...... 131 M3 🄯
SUT SM1 ...... 169 M6 🄯
Ennerdale Dr *CDALE/KGS* NW9 ...... 63 L6
Ennerdale Gdns *WBLY* HA9 ...... 80 C1
Ennerdale Rd *BXLYHN* DA7 ...... 127 G6
RCH/KEW TW9 ...... 117 H4
Ennersdale Rd *LEW* SE13 ...... 141 K2
Ennismore Av *CHSWK* W4 ...... 117 M2
GFD/PVL UB6 ...... 79 L6
Ennismore Gdns *SKENS* SW7 ...... 15 H3
Ennismore Gardens Ms
SKENS SW7 ...... 15 H3
Ennismore Ms *SKENS* SW7 ...... 15 J2
Ennismore St *SKENS* SW7 ...... 15 J3
Ennis Rd *FSBYPK* N4 ...... 85 C1
WOOL/PLUM SE18 ...... 125 K4
Ensign Cl *PUR/KEN* CR8 ...... 184 A3
STWL/WRAY TW19 ...... 130 D5
Ensign Dr *PLMGR* N13 ...... 49 J5
Ensign St *WCHPL* E1 ...... 104 A6
Ensign Wy *STWL/WRAY* TW19 ...... 130 D5
Enslin Rd *ELTH/MOT* SE9 ...... 143 G3
Ensor Ms *SKENS* SW7 ...... 15 C7
Enstone Rd *HGDN/ICK* UB10 ...... 76 F3
PEND EN3 ...... 37 L3
Enterprise Cl *CROY/NA* CR0 ...... 172 A3
Enterprise Rw
SEVS/STOTM N15 ...... 67 M6 🄯
Enterprise Wy *TEDD* TW11 ...... 151 M1
WAND/EARL SW18 ...... 137 C1
WLSDN NW10 ...... 99 M2
Enterprize Wy *DEPT* SE8 ...... 122 F2 🄯
Epirus Ms *FUL/PGN* SW6 ...... 119 C5 🄯
Epirus Rd *FUL/PGN* SW6 ...... 118 F5
Epping Cl *POP/IOD* E14 ...... 123 C2 🄯
ROMW/RG RM7 ...... 73 H1
Epping Gld *CHING* E4 ...... 51 J1
Epping New Rd *BKHH* IG9 ...... 52 B2
LOU IG10 ...... 39 K3
Epping Pl *HOLWY* N7 ...... 85 C6 🄯
Epping Wy *CHING* E4 ...... 51 H1
Epple Rd *FUL/PGN* SW6 ...... 118 F6

Epsom Cl BXLYHN DA7 127 H8
NTHLT UB5 78 F5
Epsom Rd CROY/NA CR0 172 A6
EW KT17 180 F4 1
GDMY/SEVK IG3 71 M7
LEY E10 69 J7
MRDN SM4 169 M2 1
Epsom Sq HTHAIR TW6 113 M7 2
Epsom Wy HCH RM12 92 F4
Epstein Rd THMD SE28 108 B7
Epworth Rd ISLW TW7 116 B5
Epworth St SDTCH EC2A 13 H1
Erasmus St WEST SW1P 17 H6
Erconwald St ACT W3 99 M5
Eresby Dr BECK BR3 174 A3
Erica Gdns CROY/NA CR0 174 B6
Erica St SHB W12 100 A6
Eric Clarke La BARK IG11 107 J3
Ericcson Cl WAND/EARL SW18 137 G2
Eric Rd CHDH RM6 72 D8
FSTGT E7 88 A4
WLSDN NW10 81 M6 1
Eric St BOW E3 104 F3
Eridge Green Cl
STMC/STPC BR5 177 J3
Eridge Rd CHSWK W4 117 K1 2
Erin Cl BMLY BR1 159 L3
Erindale WOOL/PLUM SE18 125 K4
Erindale Ter WOOL/PLUM SE18 125 K4
Eriswell Crs WOT/HER KT12 164 F8
Eriswell Rd WOT/HER KT12 164 F8
Erith Ct PUR RM19 129 G2
Erith Crs CRW RM5 73 J2
Erith High St ERITH DA8 127 L3
Erith Rd BELV DA17 127 H3
BXLYHN DA7 127 H8
Erlanger Rd NWCR SE14 122 D6
Erlesmere Gdns HNWL W7 116 A1
Ermine Cl CHESW EN7 26 B4 1
HSLWW TW4 114 C7 3
Ermine Rd LEW SE13 141 H1
SEVS/STOTM N15 67 M7
Ermine Side EN EN1 37 G8
Ermington Rd ELTH/MOT SE9 143 J6
Ernald Av EHAM E6 106 E1
Erncroft Wy TWK TW1 133 M3
Ernest Av WNWD SE27 139 H8
Ernest Cl BECK BR3 159 G8
Ernest Gdns CHSWK W4 117 H4
Ernest Gv BECK BR3 158 F8
Ernest Rd EMPK RM11 74 E7
KUT KT1 153 H5
Ernest St WCHPL E1 104 D3
Ernle Rd RYNPK SW20 154 B3
Ernshaw Pl PUT/ROE SW15 136 E2
Erpingham Rd PUT/ROE SW15 118 C8
Erridge Rd WIM/MER SW19 155 G5
Errington Rd MV/WKIL W9 100 F3 6
Errol Gdns NWMAL KT3 154 A7
YEAD UB4 96 B3
Erroll Rd ROM RM1 73 M5
Errol St STLK EC1Y 12 F1
Erskine Cl SUT SM1 170 E5
Erskine Crs TOTM N17 68 B5
Erskine Hl GLDGN NW11 65 G5
Erskine Rd HAMP NW3 3 M2
SUT SM1 170 D6
WALTH E17 68 F5
Erwood Rd CHARL SE7 124 E3
Esam Wy STRHM/NOR SW16 157 G1
Escot Rd SUN TW16 149 L3
Escot Wy BAR EN5 33 J8
Escreet Gv WOOL/PLUM SE18 125 G2
Esdaile Gdns UPMR RM14 75 K8
Esher Av CHEAM SM3 169 K5
ROMW/RG RM7 73 J7 2
WOT/HER KT12 165 G2
Esher Cl BXLY DA5 144 E5
ESH/CLAY KT10 166 B7
Esher Crs HTHAIR TW6 113 M7
Esher Gn ESH/CLAY KT10 166 B6
Esher Green Dr ESH/CLAY KT10 166 A5
Esher Ms MTCM CR4 156 A6
Esher Park Av ESH/CLAY KT10 166 C7
Esher Place Av ESH/CLAY KT10 166 B6
Esher Rd E/WMO/HCT KT8 151 K8
GDMY/SEVK IG3 89 L3
WOT/HER KT12 165 L6
Eskdale Av NTHLT UB5 78 F8
Eskdale Cl RDART DA2 147 J6
WBLY HA9 80 D2
Eskdale Gdns PUR/KEN CR8 184 D7
Eskdale Rd BXLYHN DA7 127 G7
IVER SL0 94 B1
Eskmont Rdg NRWD SE19 157 L3
Esk Rd PLSTW E13 106 B3
Esk Wy ROM RM1 73 L1
Esmar Crs CDALE/KGS NW9 64 A8
Esmeralda Rd STHWK SE1 122 A2
Esmond Cl RAIN RM13 92 B7 2
Esmond Rd CHSWK W4 117 K1
KIL/WHAMP NW6 82 F8
Esmond St PUT/ROE SW15 136 E1 1
Esparto St
WAND/EARL SW18 137 H4 1
Essenden Rd BELV DA17 127 G3
SAND/SEL CR2 184 E1
Essendine Rd MV/WKIL W9 2 B9
Essex Av ISLW TW7 115 L8
Essex Cl MRDN SM4 169 K2
ROMW/RG RM7 73 H5
RSLP HA4 78 D1
WALTH E17 68 E5
Essex Ct BARN SW13 117 M7 1
Essex Gdns EMPK RM11 75 G6
FSBYPK N4 67 H7 4
Essex Gv NRWD SE19 157 K2
Essex La ABLGY WD5 20 D6
Essex Pk FNCH N3 47 H8
Essex Park Ms ACT W3 99 L7
Essex Pl CHSWK W4 117 J2
Essex Place Sq CHSWK W4 117 K2 5
Essex Rd ACT W3 99 J6
BARK IG11 89 K7
BORE WD6 32 A6
CHDH RM6 90 C1
CHING E4 51 L3
CHSWK W4 117 K2
DAGE RM10 91 J5
DART DA1 146 D3 1
ENC/FH EN2 36 D7
IS N1 6 E2
LEY E10 69 J7
ROMW/RG RM7 73 H5
SWFD E18 70 B3
WALTH E17 68 E7
WAT WD17 29 G5
WLSDN NW10 81 L7
Essex Rd South WAN E11 69 K8
Essex St FSTGT E7 88 A5
TPL/STR WC2R 12 A5
Essex Vls KENS W8 14 A2
Essian St WCHPL E1 104 E4
Essoldo Wy EDGW HA8 62 F4
Estate Wy LEY E10 86 F1
Estcourt Rd FUL/PGN SW6 118 F5
SNWD SE25 173 H1
WAT WD17 29 J6
Estella Av NWMAL KT3 154 B7
Estelle Rd HAMP NW3 83 M4
Esterbrooke St WEST SW1P 17 G6 1
Este Rd BTSEA SW11 119 L8
Esther Cl WCHMH N21 49 G2
Esther Rd WAN E11 69 L8
Estoria Cl BRXS/STRHM SW2 139 G4 1
Estreham Rd
STRHM/NOR SW16 156 D2
Estridge Cl HSLW TW3 133 G1
Estuary Cl BARK IG11 108 B2
Eswyn Rd TOOT SW17 137 M8
Etchingham Park Rd FNCH N3 65 H1
Etchingham Rd SRTFD E15 87 J4 1
Etfield Gv SCUP DA14 162 B1
Ethelbert Cl HAYES BR2 160 A5
Ethelbert Gdns
GNTH/NBYPK IG2 70 F6
Ethelbert Rd BMLY BR1 160 A6
ERITH DA8 127 J5
RYNPK SW20 154 D4
STMC/STPC BR5 162 D6
Ethelbert St BAL SW12 138 B5 1
Ethelbery Rd RDART DA2 146 E8
Ethelburga Rd HARH RM3 74 F2
Ethelburga St BTSEA SW11 119 L6 1
Etheldene Av MUSWH N10 66 C5
Ethelden Rd SHB W12 100 B7
Ethel Rd ASHF TW15 148 E1
CAN/RD E16 106 B6
Ethel St WALW SE17 18 F6 3
Etheridge Rd CRICK NW2 64 C8
Etherley Rd SEVS/STOTM N15 67 J6
Etherow St EDUL SE22 140 A3
Etherstone Rd
STRHM/NOR SW16 138 F8
Ethnard Rd PECK SE15 122 B4
Ethronvi Rd BXLYHN DA7 126 E8
Etloe Rd LEY E10 87 G2
Eton Av ALP/SUD HA0 80 C4
EBAR EN4 47 L1
HAMP NW3 3 H1
HEST TW5 114 F4
NFNCH/WDSP N12 65 J1
NWMAL KT3 153 K8
Eton Cl WAND/EARL SW18 137 H4
Eton College Rd HAMP NW3 83 M6
Eton Garages HAMP NW3 83 L6
Eton Gv CDALE/KGS NW9 63 G4
LEW SE13 123 L8
Eton Rd HAMP NW3 3 M1
HYS/HAR UB3 113 M5
ORP BR6 177 H6
Eton St RCHPK/HAM TW10 134 D2
Eton Vls HAMP NW3 83 M6
Eton Wy DART DA1 146 C1
Etta St DEPT SE8 122 E4
Etton Cl HCH RM12 92 E2
Etton Rd HSLW TW3 133 J2
Ettrick St POP/IOD E14 105 K5 3
Etwell Pl BRYLDS KT5 167 M1
Euclid Wy WTHK RM20 129 M2
Eugene Cl GPK RM2 74 C5
Eugenia Rd BERM/RHTH SE16 122 C3
Eureka Rd KUT KT1 153 G5
Europa Pl FSBYE EC1V 6 E8
Europe Rd WOOL/PLUM SE18 124 F1
Eustace Pl WOOL/PLUM SE18 124 F2 3
Eustace Rd CHDH RM6 72 D8
EHAM E6 106 E2
FUL/PGN SW6 119 G5 3
Euston Av WATW WD18 28 F8
Euston Rd CAMTN NW1 4 E9
CROY/NA CR0 172 A3
Euston Sq CAMTN NW1 5 G8
Euston St CAMTN NW1 4 F9
Evandale Rd BRXN/ST SW9 121 G7
Evangelist Rd KTTN NW5 84 B4 2
Evans Av GSTN WD25 20 F8
Evan's Cl RKW/CH/CXG WD3 28 A8
Evansdale RAIN RM13 109 M2 3
Evans Gv FELT TW13 133 G6
Evans Rd CAT SE6 141 L6
Evanston Av CHING E4 69 J1
Evanston Gdns REDBR IG4 70 E7
Eva Rd CHDH RM6 72 C8
Evelina Rd PECK SE15 122 C8
PGE/AN SE20 158 C3
Eveline Rd MTCM CR4 155 M4
Evelyn Av CDALE/KGS NW9 63 K5
RSLP HA4 59 M8
Evelyn Cl WHTN TW2 133 H4
Evelyn Crs SUN TW16 149 M4
Evelyn Denington Rd EHAM E6 106 E3
Evelyn Dr PIN HA5 60 D1
Evelyn Gdns RCH/KEW TW9 134 E1
WBPTN SW10 14 F8
Evelyn Gv EA W5 98 F7
STHL UB1 96 F5
Evelyn Rd CAN/RD E16 106 A7
CHSWK W4 117 K1 3
EBAR EN4 34 F7
RCH/KEW TW9 116 E8
RCHPK/HAM TW10 134 C7
WALTH E17 69 J5 3
WIM/MER SW19 155 H1
Evelyns Cl UX/CGN UB8 95 G5
Evelyn Sharp Cl GPK RM2 74 D4 1
Evelyn St DEPT SE8 122 F4
Evelyn Ter RCH/KEW TW9 116 E8
Evelyn Wk IS N1 7 G6
Evelyn Wy SUN TW16 149 M4 1
WLGTN SM6 171 K6
Evensyde WATW WD18 41 J1
Evenwood Cl PUT/ROE SW15 136 E2 2
Everard Av HAYES BR2 175 G3
Everard Wy WBLY HA9 80 E3
Everatt Cl WAND/EARL SW18 136 F3 1
Everdon Rd BARN SW13 118 A4
Everest Pl POP/IOD E14 105 J4 3
SWLY BR8 163 K7
Everest Rd ELTH/MOT SE9 142 E2
STWL/WRAY TW19 130 D4
Everett Cl BUSH WD23 43 L3
PIN HA5 59 M4 1
Everglade Strd CDALE/KGS NW9 63 M2
Evergreen Wy HYS/HAR UB3 95 L6 1
STWL/WRAY TW19 130 D4 2
Evering Rd CLPT E5 86 A3
STNW/STAM N16 85 M3
Everington Rd MUSWH N10 65 M3
Everington St HMSMTH W6 118 D4
Everitt Rd WLSDN NW10 99 K2
Everleigh St FSBYPK N4 84 F1 3
Eve Rd ISLW TW7 134 A1
SRTFD E15 87 L4
SRTFD E15 105 L1
TOTM N17 67 L4
Eversfield Gdns EDGW HA8 63 L1
Eversfield Rd RCH/KEW TW9 116 F7
Eversholt St CAMTN NW1 4 F6
Evershot Rd FSBYPK N4 84 F1
Eversleigh Gdns UPMR RM14 93 K1
Eversleigh Rd BAR EN5 34 C8
BTSEA SW11 119 M8
EHAM E6 88 D8
FNCH N3 64 F1
Eversley Av BXLYHN DA7 127 L7
WBLY HA9 81 G2
Eversley Cl WCHMH N21 48 F1
Eversley Crs ISLW TW7 115 K6
RSLP HA4 77 L2
WCHMH N21 48 F1
Eversley Cross BXLYHN DA7 127 L7
Eversley Mt WCHMH N21 48 F1
Eversley Pk WIM/MER SW19 154 B1
Eversley Park Rd WCHMH N21 48 F1
Eversley Rd BRYLDS KT5 152 F7
CHARL SE7 124 B4
NRWD SE19 157 K3
Eversley Wy CROY/NA CR0 174 A5
Everthorpe Rd PECK SE15 121 M8 1
Everton Buildings CAMTN NW1 4 E8
Everton Dr STAN HA7 62 F4
Everton Rd CROY/NA CR0 173 G3
Evesham Av WALTH E17 69 G3
Evesham Cl BELMT SM2 182 A1 3
GFD/PVL UB6 97 H1
Evesham Gn MRDN SM4 170 B1
Evesham Rd FBAR/BDGN N11 48 C7
MRDN SM4 170 B1
SRTFD E15 87 M7
Evesham St NTGHL W11 100 D6 2
Evesham Wk BRXN/ST SW9 121 G7
CMBW SE5 121 K7 3
Evesham Wy BTSEA SW11 120 A8 4
CLAY IG5 71 G4
Evry Rd SCUP DA14 162 C2
Ewald Rd FUL/PGN SW6 118 F7
Ewanrigg Ter WFD IG8 52 C7 1
Ewan Rd HARH RM3 74 D3
Ewart Gv WDGN N22 67 G2
Ewart Pl BOW E3 104 F1 6
Ewart Rd FSTH SE23 140 D4
Ewe Cl HOLWY N7 84 E6
Ewell By-pass EW KT17 181 G1
Ewell Court Av HOR/WEW KT19 168 E7
Ewell Downs Rd EW KT17 181 G4
Ewell House Gv EW KT17 180 F3
Ewellhurst Rd CLAY IG5 70 E3
Ewell Park Gdns EW KT17 181 G1
Ewell Park Wy EW KT17 169 G8
Ewell Rd CHEAM SM3 169 K8
SURB KT6 167 M1
THDIT KT7 167 H2
Ewelme Rd FSTH SE23 140 C5
Ewen Crs BRXS/STRHM SW2 139 G4
Ewer St STHWK SE1 12 E9
Ewhurst Av SAND/SEL CR2 184 F3 1
Ewhurst Cl BELMT SM2 181 J2
Ewhurst Rd BROCKY SE4 140 F3
Exbury Rd CAT SE6 141 G6
Excelsior Cl KUT KT1 153 G5 4
Exchange Rd WATW WD18 29 H7
Exchange St ROM RM1 73 L6
Exeforde Av ASHF TW15 131 G8
Exeter Cl EHAM E6 106 F5
WATN WD24 29 J5
Exeter Gdns IL IG1 88 F1
Exeter Rd CAN/RD E16 106 A4
CRICK NW2 82 E5
CROY/NA CR0 172 E2
DAGE RM10 91 H6
ED N9 50 C4
FELT TW13 132 F7
HTHAIR TW6 113 L8
PEND EN3 37 K6
RYLN/HDSTN HA2 78 E2
STHGT/OAK N14 48 B3
WALTH E17 69 G6 2
WELL DA16 125 M7
Exeter St COVGDN WC2E 11 K6
Exeter Wy HTHAIR TW6 113 L7
NWCR SE14 122 F5 2
Exford Gdns LEE/GVPK SE12 142 B5
Exford Rd LEE/GVPK SE12 142 B6
Exhibition Rd BAY/PAD W2 15 H1
SKENS SW7 15 H5 3
Exit Rd EFNCH N2 65 K3
Exmoor Cl BARK/HLT IG6 71 J2
Exmoor St NKENS W10 100 D3
Exmouth Market CLKNW EC1R 6 A9
Exmouth Ms CAMTN NW1 4 F8 2
Exmouth Pl HACK E8 86 B7 2
Exmouth Rd RSLP HA4 78 C3
WALTH E17 68 F6
WELL DA16 126 C6
YEAD UB4 95 L2
Exmouth St WCHPL E1 104 C5 6
Exning Rd CAN/RD E16 105 M3
Exon St WALW SE17 19 J6
Explorer Av STWL/WRAY TW19 130 E5
Explorer Dr WATW WD18 41 M1
Express Dr GDMY/SEVK IG3 90 B1
Exton Crs WLSDN NW10 81 J7
Exton Gdns BCTR RM8 90 D5
Exton St STHWK SE1 12 A9
Eyhurst Av HCH RM12 92 A3
Eyhurst Cl CRICK NW2 82 A2
Eylewood Rd WNWD SE27 157 J1
Eynella Rd DUL SE21 139 M4
Eynham Rd SHB W12 100 C5
Eynsford Cl STMC/STPC BR5 176 C2
Eynsford Crs SCUP DA14 144 C5
Eynsford Rd GDMY/SEVK IG3 89 L2
Eynsham Dr ABYW SE2 126 B1
Eynswood Dr SCUP DA14 162 B1
Eyot Gdns HMSMTH W6 117 M3
Eyre Cl GPK RM2 74 B5
Eyre Street Hl CLKNW EC1R 12 A1
Eythorne Rd BRXN/ST SW9 121 G6
Ezra St BETH E2 7 M7

F

Faber Gdns HDN NW4 64 A6
Fabian Rd FUL/PGN SW6 118 F5 3
Fabian St EHAM E6 106 F3 1
Factory La CROY/NA CR0 172 A4
TOTM N17 67 M3
Factory Pl POP/IOD E14 123 H3
Factory Rd CAN/RD E16 106 D7
Factory Yd HNWL W7 97 L7
Faesten Wy BXLY DA5 145 L7
Faggs Rd EBED/NFELT TW14 131 M1
EBED/NFELT TW14 132 A1
Fagus Av RAIN RM13 110 D2 1
Faints Cl CHESW EN7 25 L2
Fairacre NWMAL KT3 153 L6
Fair Acres HAYES BR2 160 A8
Fairacres RSLP HA4 59 M8
Fairacres Cl POTB/CUF EN6 22 F6
Fairbairn Cl PUR/KEN CR8 184 A6 1
Fairbank Av ORP BR6 176 B4
Fairbanks Rd TOTM N17 68 A4 5
Fairbourne Rd TOTM N17 67 L4
Fairbridge Rd ARCH N19 84 D2
Fairbrook Cl PLMGR N13 49 G7
Fairburn Cl BORE WD6 32 A4 1
Fairby Rd LEE/GVPK SE12 142 B2
Fairchild Cl BTSEA SW11 119 K7
Fairchildes Av CROY/NA CR0 186 D5
Fairchildes Rd WARL CR6 186 D8
Fairchild Pl SDTCH EC2A 13 K1 1
Fairchild St SDTCH EC2A 13 K1 2
Fair Cl BUSH WD23 43 H2
Fairclough St WCHPL E1 104 A5 4
Faircross Av BARK IG11 89 J6
CRW RM5 73 K1
Fairdale Gdns HYS/HAR UB3 96 A8
PUT/ROE SW15 136 B1 1
Fairey Av HYS/HAR UB3 113 M1
Fairfax Av EW KT17 181 H2
Fairfax Cl WOT/HER KT12 165 H3
Fairfax Gdns BKHTH/KID SE3 124 C6
Fairfax Pl KIL/WHAMP NW6 2 F1
Fairfax Rd CEND/HSY/T N8 67 G5
CHSWK W4 117 L1
KIL/WHAMP NW6 2 F1
TEDD TW11 152 A3
Fairfax Wy MUSWH N10 66 A1 1
Fairfield Av EDGW HA8 45 H8
HDN NW4 64 B7
OXHEY WD19 42 C5
RSLP HA4 59 J8
UPMR RM14 93 J3
WHTN TW2 133 H5
Fairfield Cl BFN/LL DA15 143 M3
HCH RM12 92 A1
HOR/WEW KT19 168 E7
NFNCH/WDSP N12 47 J6
PEND EN3 37 L7 1
RAD WD7 30 E2 1
WIM/MER SW19 155 L3
Fairfield Ct RSLP HA4 77 K1
Fairfield Crs EDGW HA8 45 H8
Fairfield Dr GFD/PVL UB6 80 C8
RYLN/HDSTN HA2 61 J4
WAND/EARL SW18 137 H2
Fairfield East KUT KT1 152 E5
Fairfield Gdns
CEND/HSY/T N8 66 E6 4
Fairfield Gv CHARL SE7 124 D4
Fairfield North KUT KT1 152 E5
Fairfield Pth CROY/NA CR0 172 D5 1
Fairfield Pl KUT KT1 152 E6 2
Fairfield Rd BECK BR3 159 G5
BMLY BR1 160 A3
BOW E3 105 G1
BXLYHN DA7 126 F7
CEND/HSY/T N8 66 E6
CROY/NA CR0 172 D5
IL IG1 89 H6
KUT KT1 152 E5
STHL UB1 96 F5
STMC/STPC BR5 176 D2
UED N18 50 A6
UX/CGN UB8 76 D6
WALTH E17 68 E3
WDR/YW UB7 94 E7
WFD IG8 52 A8
Fairfields Cl CDALE/KGS NW9 63 J6
Fairfields Crs CDALE/KGS NW9 63 J5
Fairfield South KUT KT1 152 E6
Fairfield St WAND/EARL SW18 137 H2
Fairfield Wy BAR EN5 34 A8
COUL/CHIP CR5 183 K7
HOR/WEW KT19 168 E7
Fairfield West KUT KT1 152 E5
Fairfolds GSTN WD25 21 L8
Fairfoot Rd BOW E3 105 G3 1
Fairford Av BXLYHN DA7 127 J6
CROY/NA CR0 158 D8
Fairford Cl CROY/NA CR0 158 D8
HARH RM3 57 H8 2
Fairford Gdns WPK KT4 168 F5
Fairford Wy HARH RM3 57 H8
Fairgreen EBAR EN4 34 F6
Fairgreen Rd THHTH CR7 157 H8 1
Fairhaven Av CROY/NA CR0 173 K1
Fairhaven Crs OXHEY WD19 42 A5
Fairhazel Gdns KIL/WHAMP NW6 2 E1
Fairholme EBED/NFELT TW14 131 K4 1
Fairholme Av GPK RM2 74 A6
Fairholme Cl HDN NW4 64 E5
Fairholme Crs YEAD UB4 95 M3
Fairholme Gdns FNCH N3 64 E4
UPMR RM14 75 M8
Fairholme Rd ASHF TW15 148 E1
CROY/NA CR0 172 A2
HRW HA1 61 L6
IL IG1 70 F8
SUT SM1 169 M8
WKENS W14 118 E3
Fairholt Rd STNW/STAM N16 85 K1
Fairholt St SKENS SW7 15 K3 1
Fairkytes Av EMPK RM11 92 D1
Fairland Rd SRTFD E15 87 M6
Fairlands Av BKHH IG9 52 A4
SUT SM1 170 A4
THHTH CR7 156 F7
Fairlawn CHARL SE7 124 C5
Fairlawn Av CHSWK W4 117 J2
EFNCH N2 65 L5 2
WELL DA16 126 D7
Fairlawn Cl ESH/CLAY KT10 166 F8 2
FELT TW13 132 F8
KUTN/CMB KT2 153 J2
STHGT/OAK N14 48 D1 1
Fairlawn Dr WFD IG8 70 A1
Fairlawn Gdns STHL UB1 96 F6 1
Fairlawn Gv BNSTD SM7 182 D6
CHSWK W4 117 J2
Fairlawn Pk SYD SE26 158 E1
Fairlawn Rd BELMT SM2 182 C4
WIM/MER SW19 154 F3
Fairlawns SUN TW16 150 A6
TWK TW1 134 D3 3
WAT WD17 28 F4
Fairlawns Cl EMPK RM11 74 F8
STA TW18 148 B2 1
Fairlea Pl EA W5 98 C4 2
Fairley Wy CHESW EN7 26 B1
Fairlie Gdns FSTH SE23 140 C4
Fairlight Av CHING E4 51 K4
WFD IG8 52 A8
WLSDN NW10 99 L1 1
Fairlight Cl CHING E4 51 K4 1
WPK KT4 169 J6
Fairlight Dr UX/CGN UB8 76 D6 2
Fairlight Rd TOOT SW17 137 K8
Fairlop Cl HCH RM12 92 B6 3
Fairlop Gdns BARK/HLT IG6 71 J1
Fairlop Rd BARK/HLT IG6 71 J3
WAN E11 69 K8
Fairmark Dr HGDN/ICK UB10 77 G6
Fairmead BMLY BR1 160 F7
BRYLDS KT5 168 B3
Fairmead Cl BMLY BR1 160 F7
HEST TW5 114 D5
NWMAL KT3 153 K6 1
Fairmead Crs EDGW HA8 45 J6
Fairmead Gdns REDBR IG4 70 D6
Fairmead Rd CROY/NA CR0 171 M2 2
HOLWY N7 84 E3
LOU IG10 39 H7
Fairmile Av STRHM/NOR SW16 156 D1
Fairmile Hts COB KT11 178 A6
Fairmont Cl BELV DA17 126 F3
Fairmount Rd
BRXS/STRHM SW2 138 F3
Fair Oak Cl LHD/OX KT22 178 D4
Fairoak Cl PUR/KEN CR8 184 B8
STMC/STPC BR5 176 B2
Fairoak Dr ELTH/MOT SE9 143 K2
Fairoak Gdns ROM RM1 73 L3
Fairoak La LHD/OX KT22 178 E4
Fairoaks Gv PEND EN3 37 K2
Fairseat Cl BUSH WD23 43 L4 1
Fair St HSLW TW3 115 J8 2
STHWK SE1 19 K1
Fairthorn Rd CHARL SE7 124 A3
Fairview ERITH DA8 127 M5 1
EW KT17 181 J4
Fair Vw POTB/CUF EN6 23 H3
Fairview Av ALP/SUD HA0 80 D6
RAIN RM13 110 D1
Fairview Cl CHIG IG7 53 L6
Fair View Cl WALTH E17 68 E2
Fairview Crs RYLN/HDSTN HA2 79 G1
Fairview Dr CHIG IG7 53 L7
ORP BR6 176 D6
SHPTN TW17 148 F8
WAT WD17 28 E1
Fairview Gdns WFD IG8 70 B2
Fairview Pl BRXS/STRHM SW2 138 F4
Fairview Rd CHIG IG7 53 L6
ENC/FH EN2 36 A4
EW KT17 180 F4 2
SEVS/STOTM N15 67 M7
STRHM/NOR SW16 156 F4
SUT SM1 170 D7
Fairview Wy EDGW HA8 45 G6
Fairwater Av WELL DA16 144 A1
Fairway BXLYHS DA6 144 E2
CAR SM5 182 C4
RYNPK SW20 154 C6
STMC/STPC BR5 161 K8
WFD IG8 52 C7
Fairway Av BORE WD6 32 B5 2
CDALE/KGS NW9 63 H4
WDR/YW UB7 94 C7
Fairway Cl CROY/NA CR0 158 E8
GLDGN NW11 65 J8
HOR/WEW KT19 168 C6 3
Fairway Dr GFD/PVL UB6 79 H7
RDART DA2 147 H4
THMD SE28 108 D5
Fairway Gdns BECK BR3 174 D1
IL IG1 89 J5

Fairways *ASHF* TW15 ....149 G2
  STAN HA7 ....62 E3
  TEDD TW11 ....152 D3
The Fairway *ABLGY* WD5 .... 20 D5
  ACT W3 ....99 L5
  ALP/SUD HA0 ....80 B2
  BAR EN5 ....47 H1
  BMLY BR1 ....160 F8
  E/WMO/HCT KT8 ....94 F2
  HGDN/ICK UB10 ....45 K5
  MLHL NW7 ....79 J6
  NTHLT UB5 ....41 L6
  NTHWD HA6 ....41 L6
  NWMAL KT3 ....153 K4
  PLMGR N13 ....49 J5
  RSLP HA4 ....78 C4
  STHGT/OAK N14 ....48 B1
  UPMR RM14 ....75 J8
Fairweather CI
  SEVS/STOTM N15 ....67 L5
Fairweather Rd
  STNW/STAM N16 ....68 A7
Fairwyn Rd *SYD* SE26 ....140 E7
Fakenham CI *MLHL* NW7 ....64 A1
  NTHLT UB5 ....79 G6
Fakruddin St *WCHPL* E1 ....104 A3
Falaize Av *IL* IG1 ....89 H4
Falcon Av *BMLY* BR1 ....160 E6
Falcon CI *CHSWK* W4 ....117 H4
  DART DA1 ....146 F2
  NTHWD HA6 ....59 L1
  STHWK SE1 ....12 D8
Falcon Crs *PEND* EN3 ....37 K8
Falcon Dr *STWL/WRAY* TW19 ...150 D3
Falconer CI *BARK/HLT* IG6 ....54 B7
  BUSH WD23 ....43 G1
Falcon Gv *BTSEA* SW11 ....119 L8
Falconhurst *LHD/OX* KT22 ....178 D8
Falcon La *BTSEA* SW11 ....119 L8
Falcon Rd *BTSEA* SW11 ....119 L8
  HPTN TW12 ....150 F3
  PEND EN3 ....37 K8
Falcon St *PLSTW* E13 ....106 A3
Falcon Ter *BTSEA* SW11 ....119 L8
Falcon Wy *CDALE/KGS* NW9 ....21 L7
  GSTN WD25 ....21 L7
  KTN/HRWW/W HA3 ....62 E6
  SUN TW16 ....149 L5
  WAN E11 ....70 A5
Falconwood Av *WELL* DA16 ....125 K7
Falconwood Pde *WELL* DA16 .....143 M1
Falconwood Rd *CROY/NA* CR0 ...185 M2
Falcourt CI *SUT* SM1 ....170 B7
Falkirk CI *EMPK* RM11 ....93 G1
Falkirk Gdns *OXHEY* WD19 ....42 D7
Falkirk St *IS* N1 ....7 K6
Falkland Av *FBAR/BDGN* N11 .....48 A6
  FNCH N3 ....46 E1
Falkland Park Av *SNWD* SE25 ...157 L6
Falkland Rd *BAR* EN5 ....33 L5
  CEND/HSY/T N8 ....67 G5
  KTTN NW5 ....84 C5
Falling La *WDR/YW* UB7 ....94 E6
Falloden Wy *GLDGN* NW11 ....65 G5
Fallow CI *CHIG* IG7 ....53 M7
Fallow Court Av
  NFNCH/WDSP N12 ....47 J8
Fallowfield *STAN* HA7 ....44 A5
Fallowfield CI *DEN/HRF* UB9 ....58 C2
Fallowfield Ct *STAN* HA7 ....44 A5
Fallow Flds *LOU* IG10 ....52 D2
Fallowfields Dr
  NFNCH/WDSP N12 ....47 L8
Fallows Rd *EFNCH* N2 ....65 J3
Fallsbrook Rd
  STRHM/NOR SW16 ....156 B2
Falman CI *ED* N9 ....50 A3
Falmer Rd *EN* EN1 ....36 E7
  SEVS/STOTM N15 ....67 J6
  WALTH E17 ....69 H4
Falmouth Av *CHING* E4 ....51 K1
Falmouth CI *LEE/GVPK* SE12 ....141 M2
Falmouth Gdns *IL* IG4 ....70 D5
Falmouth Rd *STHWK* SE1 ....18 F4
  WOT/HER KT12 ....165 K2
Falmouth St *SRTFD* E15 ....87 K5
Fambridge CI *SYD* SE26 ....140 F8
Fambridge Rd *BCTR* RM8 ....91 G1
Famet Av *PUR/KEN* CR8 ....184 C6
Famet CI *PUR/KEN* CR8 ....184 C6
Famet Wk *PUR/KEN* CR8 ....184 C6
Fane St *WKENS* W14 ....118 F4
Fanns Ri *PUR* RM19 ....129 G2
Fann St *FARR* EC1M 12 E1
  STLK EC1Y 12 E1
Fanshawe Av *BARK* IG11 ....89 J6
Fanshawe Crs *DAGW* RM9 ....90 E5
  EMPK RM11 ....74 D7
Fanshawe Rd
  RCHPK/HAM TW10 ....134 C8
Fanshaw St *IS* N1 ....7 J7
Fanthorpe St *PUT/ROE* SW15 ....118 C8
Faraday Av *SCUP* DA14 ....144 B6
Faraday CI *HOLWY* N7 ....84 F6
  WATW WD18 ....41 K1
Faraday Rd *ACT* W3 ....99 J6
  E/WMO/HCT KT8 ....151 G7
  GFD/PVL UB6 ....97 H6
  NKENS W10 ....100 D4
  SRTFD E15 ....87 M6
  WELL DA16 ....126 A8
  WIM/MER SW19 ....155 H2
Faraday Wy *STMC/STPC* BR5 ....162 B7
  WOOL/PLUM SE18 ....124 D1
Fareham Rd *EBED/NFELT* TW14 ..132 C4
Fareham St *SOHO/SHAV* W1F 11 G4
Farewell PI *MTCM* CR4 ....155 K4
Faringdon Av *HARH* RM3 ....74 C2
  HAYES BR2 ....176 B1
Faringford CI *POTB/CUF* EN6 ......23 K6
Faringford Rd *SRTFD* E15 ....87 L7
Farjeon Rd *BKHTH/KID* SE3 ....124 D6
Farleigh Av *HAYES* BR2 ....174 F2
Farleigh Court Rd *WARL* CR6 ......185 M7
Farleigh Dean Crs
  CROY/NA CR0 ....186 B4
Farleigh PI *STNW/STAM* N16 ....85 M4
Farleigh Rd *STNW/STAM* N16 ......85 M4

Farleton CI *WEY* KT13 ....164 D8
Farley CI *GDMY/SEVK* IG3 ....89 L1
Farley PI *SNWD* SE25 ....158 A7
Farley Rd *CAT* SE6 ....141 J4
  SAND/SEL CR2 ....185 H1
Farlington PI *PUT/ROE* SW15 ....136 B4
Farlow Rd *PUT/ROE* SW15 ....118 D8
Farlton Rd
  WAND/EARL SW18 ....137 H4
Farm Av *ALP/SUD* HA0 ....80 C6
  CRICK NW2 ....82 E3
  RYLN/HDSTN HA2 ....61 G8
  STRHM/NOR SW16 ....138 E8
  SWLY BR8 ....163 J6
Farmborough CI *HRW* HA1 ....61 K8
Farm CI *BAR* EN5 ....33 H8
  BELMT SM2 ....182 D1
  BKHH IG9 ....52 C5
  BORE WD6 ....31 L3
  CHES/WCR EN8 ....26 C3
  DAGE RM10 ....91 J7
  HGDN/ICK UB10 ....77 H3
  SHPTN TW17 ....164 A2
  STHL UB1 ....97 H6
  WLGTN SM6 ....86 A3
  WWKM BR4 ....174 F5
Farmcote Rd *LEE/GVPK* SE12 ....142 A5
Farmdale Rd *CAR* SM5 ....182 E1
  GNWCH SE10 ....124 A3
Farm Dr *CROY/NA* CR0 ....173 M4
  PUR/KEN CR8 ....183 K5
Farm End *CHING* E4 ....38 E8
Farmer Rd *LEY* E10 ....87 H1
Farmers Rd *CMBW* SE5 ....121 H5
Farmers CI *STGN* WD25 ....21 H6
Farmer St *KENS* W8 ....8 A4
Farmfield Rd *BMLY* BR1 ....159 L1
Farm Flds *SAND/SEL* CR2 ....184 F4
Farm Hill Rd *WAB* EN9 ....27 K7
Farmhouse Rd
  STRHM/NOR SW16 ....156 C3
Farmilo Rd *WALTH* E17 ....69 G8
Farmington Av *SUT* SM1 ....170 D5
Farmlands *ENC/FH* EN2 ....36 A4
  PIN HA5 ....60 A5
The Farmlands *NTHLT* UB5 ....78 F6
Farmland Wk *CHST* BR7 ....161 H1
Farm La *CROY/NA* CR0 ....173 M4
  FUL/PGN SW6 ....119 G4
  PUR/KEN CR8 ....183 J3
  STHGT/OAK N14 ....48 A1
Farmleigh *STHGT/OAK* N14 ....48 C2
Farmleigh Gv *WOT/HER* KT12 ....164 F7
Farm PI *DART* DA1 ....146 A1
  KENS W8 ....8 A4
Farm Rd *BELMT* SM2 ....182 D1
  EDGW HA8 ....45 J7
  ESH/CLAY KT10 ....166 A3
  HSLWW TW4 ....134 C1
  MRDN SM4 ....155 H8
  NTHWD HA6 ....41 J7
  RAIN RM13 ....110 C2
  STA TW18 ....148 B2
  WCHMH N21 ....49 J3
Farmstead Rd *CAT* SE6 ....141 H8
  KTN/HRWW/W HA3 ....61 K2
Farm St *MYFR/PICC* W1J 10 C7
Farm V *BXLY* DA5 ....145 H3
Farmway *BCTR* RM8 ....90 C4
Farm Wy *BKHH* IG9 ....52 C6
  BUSH WD23 ....30 B7
  HCH RM12 ....92 B4
  NTHWD HA6 ....41 L6
  WPK KT4 ....169 J5
Farnaby Rd *BMLY* BR1 ....159 L4
  ELTH/MOT SE9 ....142 C1
Farnan Av *WALTH* E17 ....69 G3
Farnan Rd *STRHM/NOR* SW16 ....156 C1
Farnborough Av
  SAND/SEL CR2 ....185 L1
  WALTH E17 ....69 H2
Farnborough CI *WBLY* HA9 ....81 H2
Farnborough Common
  ORP BR6 ....175 H6
Farnborough Crs *HAYES* BR2 ......174 F3
  SAND/SEL CR2 ....185 L2
Farnborough HI *ORP* BR6 ....176 D7
Farnborough Wy *ORP* BR6 ....176 E8
Farncombe St
  BERM/RHTH SE16 ....104 A8
Farndale Av *PLMGR* N13 ....49 H5
Farndale Crs *GFD/PVL* UB6 ....97 J2
Farnell Ms *ECT* SW5 ....14 C7
Farnell Rd *ISLW* TW7 ....115 K8
  STA TW18 ....130 A7
Farnes Dr *GPK* RM2 ....74 C3
Farnham CI *TRDG/WHET* N20 ......47 J2
Farnham Gdns *RYNPK* SW20 .....154 B5
Farnham PI *STHWK* SE1 ....12 D9
Farnham Rd *GDMY/SEVK* IG3 ......71 M7
  HARH RM3 ....56 D7
  WELL DA16 ....126 C7
Farnham Royal *LBTH* SE11 ....17 M8
Farningham Rd *TOTM* N17 ....68 A1
Farnley *FENCH* E4 ....51 L2
  THHTH CR7 ....157 K7
Farnol Rd *DART* DA1 ....147 G2
Faro CI *BMLY* BR1 ....161 G5
Faroe Rd *WKENS* W14 ....118 D1
Farorna Wk *ENC/FH* EN2 ....36 A4
Farquhar Rd *NRWD* SE19 ....157 M1
  WIM/MER SW19 ....137 G2
Farquharson Rd *CROY/NA* CR0 ...172 C5
Farraline Rd *WATW* WD18 ....29 H8
Farrance Rd *CHDH* RM6 ....72 E7
Farrance St *POP/IOD* E14 ....105 J5
Farrant Av *WDGN* N22 ....67 G3
Farrant Wy *BORE* WD6 ....31 L3
Farr Av *BARK* IG11 ....108 A1
Farrer Ms *CEND/HSY/T* N8 ....66 C5
Farrer Rd *CEND/HSY/T* N8 ....66 C5
  KTN/HRWW/W HA3 ....62 E6
Farrier CI *BMLY* BR1 ....160 D6
  UX/CGN UB8 ....95 G5
Farrier Rd *NTHLT* UB5 ....97 G1
Farriers CI *EW* KT17 ....180 E5
Farriers Rd *EW* KT17 ....180 E5

Farrier St *CAMTN* NW1 ....4 D1
Farriers Wy *BORE* WD6 ....45 K1
Farringdon La *CLKNW* EC1R 12 B1
Farringdon Rd *FARR* EC1M 12 C3
  FSBYW WC1X 6 A9
  HCIRC EC1N 12 C3
Farringdon St
  FLST/FETLN EC4A 12 C4
Farrington Av *STMC/STPC* BR5 ...162 B6
Farrington PI *CHST* BR7 ....161 K3
Farrins Rents
  BERM/RHTH SE16 ....104 E7
Farrow La *PECK* SE15 ....122 C5
Farrow PI *BERM/RHTH* SE16 ......122 E1
Farr Rd *ENC/FH* EN2 ....36 D4
Farthing Aly *STHWK* SE1 ....104 B7
Farthing Flds *WAP* E1W 104 B7
Farthings CI *CHING* E4 ....51 L5
  PIN HA5 ....60 B7
Farthing St *ORP* BR6 ....187 M1
Farwell Rd *SCUP* DA14 ....144 B8
Farwig La *BMLY* BR1 ....160 A4
Fashion St *WCHPL* E1 ....13 L3
Fashoda Rd *HAYES* BR2 ....160 D1
Fassett Rd *HACK* E8 ....86 A6
  KUT KT1 ....152 E7
Fassett Sq *HACK* E8 ....86 A6
Fauconberg Rd *CHSWK* W4 ....117 J4
Faulkner CI *BCTR* RM8 ....72 D8
Faulkner's Rd *WOT/HER* KT12 ....165 J7
Faulkner St *NWCR* SE14 ....122 C6
Fauna CI *CHDH* RM6 ....72 C7
Faunce St *WALW* SE17 ....18 C8
Favart Rd *FUL/PGN* SW6 ....119 L6
Faverolle Gn *CHES/WCR* EN8 ......26 D1
Faversham Av *CHING* E4 ....51 L3
  WCHMH N21 ....49 K1
Faversham Rd *BECK* BR3 ....158 F5
  CAT SE6 ....140 F4
  MRDN SM4 ....170 B1
Fawcett CI *BTSEA* SW11 ....119 G7
  STRHM/NOR SW16 ....139 G8
Fawcett Rd *CROY/NA* CR0 ....172 B5
  WLSDN NW10 ....81 M7
Fawcett St *WBPTN* SW10 ....14 E9
Fawcus CI *ESH/CLAY* KT10 ....166 E8
Fawe Park Rd *PUT/ROE* SW15 ...136 F1
Fawe St *POP/IOD* E14 ....105 H4
Fawkes Av *DART* DA1 ....146 F6
Fawley Rd *KIL/WHAMP* NW6 ....83 H5
Fawnbrake Av *HNHL* SE24 ....139 H2
Fawn Rd *CHIG* IG7 ....53 M7
  PLSTW E13 ....106 C1
Fawns Manor Rd
  EBED/NFELT TW14 ....131 K5
Fawood Av *WLSDN* NW10 ....81 K7
Faygate Crs *BXLYHS* DA6 ....145 G2
Faygate Rd *BRXS/STRHM* SW2 ...138 B7
Fay Gn *ABLGY* WD5 ....20 D6
Fayland Av *STRHM/NOR* SW16 ...156 C1
Fearney Md *RKW/CH/CXG* WD3 ...40 A3
Fearnley Crs *HPTN* TW12 ....150 E1
Fearnley St *WATW* WD18 ....29 H7
  WATW WD18 ....29 H7
Fearon St *GNWCH* SE10 ....124 A3
Featherbed La *CROY/NA* CR0 .....185 M1
  CROY/NA CR0 ....186 B3
Feathers PI *GNWCH* SE10 ....123 K4
Featherstone Av *FSTH* SE23 ......140 C6
Featherstone Gdns *BORE* WD6 ....32 D7
Featherstone Rd *MLHL* NW7 ....46 B8
  NWDGN UB2 ....114 E1
Featherstone St
  STLK EC1Y 7 G9
Featherstone Ter
  NWDGN UB2 ....114 E1
Featley Rd *BRXN/ST* SW9 ....121 H8
Federal Rd *GFD/PVL* UB6 ....98 C1
Federal Wy *WATN* WD24 ....29 J4
Federation Rd *ABYW* SE2 ....126 C2
Fee Farm Rd *ESH/CLAY* KT10 ....178 F1
Felbridge Av *STAN* HA7 ....62 A2
Felbridge CI *BELMT* SM2 ....182 B2
  STRHM/NOR SW16 ....139 G8
Felbrigge Rd *GDMY/SEVK* IG3 .....89 M2
Felcott CI *WOT/HER* KT12 ....165 J5
Felcott Rd *WOT/HER* KT12 ....165 J5
Felday Rd *LEW* SE13 ....141 H3
Felden CI *GSTN* WD25 ....21 K7
Felden St *FUL/PGN* SW6 ....118 F6
Feldman CI *STNW/STAM* N16 ....86 A1
Feldon CI *PIN* HA5 ....60 E1
Felgate Ms *HMSMTH* W6 ....118 E2
Felhampton Rd *ELTH/MOT* SE9 ...143 H7
Felhurst Crs *DAGE* RM10 ....91 J4
Felix Av *CEND/HSY/T* N8 ....66 E7
Felix La *SHPTN* TW17 ....164 F1
Felix Rd *HNWL* W7 ....98 A6
  WOT/HER KT12 ....165 G1
Felixstowe Rd *ABYW* SE2 ....126 B1
  ED N9 ....50 A5
  TOTM N17 ....67 M4
  UED N18 ....50 A6
  WLSDN NW10 ....100 D2
Felix St *BETH* E2 ....104 B1
Fellbrigg Rd *EDUL* SE22 ....139 M2
Fellbrigg St *WCHPL* E1 ....104 B3
Fellbrook *RCHPK/HAM* TW10 .....134 B7
Fellmongers Yd *CROY/NA* CR0 ...174 C4
Fellowes CI *YEAD* UB4 ....96 D3
Fellowes Rd *CAR* SM5 ....170 E5
Fellows Rd *HAMP* NW3 ....3 H1
Fell Rd *CROY/NA* CR0 ....172 C5
Felltram Wy *CHARL* SE7 ....124 A3
Felmersham CI *CLAP* SW4 ....138 E5
Felmingham Rd *PGE/AN* SE20 ....158 E5
Felnex Rd *BRXS/STRHM* SW2 ....138 A8
Fels CI *DAGE* RM10 ....91 K3
Fels Farm Av *DAGE* RM10 ....91 K3
Felsham Rd *PUT/ROE* SW15 ......118 F3
Felspar CI *WOOL/PLUM* SE18 .....125 M3
Felstead Av *CLAY* IG5 ....71 G2
Felstead Rd *CHES/WCR* EN8 ....26 E5
  CRW RM5 ....55 J8
  HOM E9 ....87 G6
  HOR/WEW KT19 ....180 D4
  LOU IG10 ....52 E2
  ORP BR6 ....177 G4

  WAN E11 ....70 A8
Felstead St *HOM* E9 ....86 F6
Felsted Rd *CAN/RD* E16 ....106 D5
Feltham Av *E/WMO/HCT* KT8 .....151 L7
Feltham Rd *ASHF* TW15 ....149 G1
Feltham Hill Rd *ASHF* TW15 ....132 A8
Felthambrook Wy *FELT* TW13 ....132 B7
Felthamhill Rd *FELT* TW13 ....132 B8
Feltham Rd *ASHF* TW15 ....131 H8
  MTCM CR4 ....155 M5
Felton CI *BORE* WD6 ....31 L3
  STMC/STPC BR5 ....176 B1
Felton Lea *SCUP* DA14 ....161 M1
Felton Rd *BARK* IG11 ....107 L1
  WEA W13 ....98 C8
Fencepiece Rd *BARK/HLT* IG6 ......53 J8
  CHIG IG7 ....53 J8
Fenchurch Av *FENCHST* EC3M 13 J5
Fenchurch Buildings
  FENCHST EC3M 13 K6
Fenchurch PI *FENCHST* EC3M 13 K6
Fenchurch St *FENCHST* EC3M 13 J6
Fendall Rd *HOR/WEW* KT19 ......168 C7
Fendall St *STHWK* SE1 ....19 K4
Fendt CI *CAN/RD* E16 ....105 M5
Fendyke Rd *ABYW* SE2 ....126 D2
Fenelon PI *WKENS* W14 ....118 F2
Fen Gv *BFN/LL* DA15 ....143 M3
Fenham Rd *PECK* SE15 ....122 A5
Fenman Ct *TOTM* N17 ....68 B2
Fenman Gdns *GDMY/SEVK* IG3 ...90 B1
Fenn CI *BMLY* BR1 ....160 A2
Fennel CI *CAN/RD* E16 ....105 L3
  CROY/NA CR0 ....173 K5
Fennells Md *HOR/WEW* KT19 ....180 F2
Fennell St *WOOL/PLUM* SE18 .....126 G4
Fenner CI *BERM/RHTH* SE16 ......122 B2
Fenner Sq *BTSEA* SW11 ....119 K8
Fenning St *STHWK* SE1 ....19 J1
Fenn St *HOM* E9 ....86 D5
Fenstanton Av
  NFNCH/WDSP N12 ....47 K7
Fen St *CAN/RD* E16 ....105 M6
Fentiman Rd *VX/NE* SW8 ....120 E4
Fentiman Wy *EMPK* RM11 ....92 E1
Fenton Av *STA* TW18 ....148 C2
Fenton CI *BRXN/ST* SW9 ....120 F7
  CHST BR7 ....160 F1
Fenton Rd *TOTM* N17 ....67 J1
Fenton's Av *PLSTW* E13 ....106 B2
Fenwick Gv *PECK* SE15 ....122 A8
Fenwick PI *BRXN/ST* SW9 ....120 E8
  SAND/SEL CR2 ....184 B1
Fenwick Rd *PECK* SE15 ....122 A8
Ferdinand PI *CAMTN* NW1 ....4 B1
Ferdinand St *CAMTN* NW1 ....4 B1
Ferguson CI *BECK* BR3 ....159 J6
  GPK RM2 ....74 C3
Ferguson Ct *GPK* RM2 ....74 D3
Ferguson Dr *ACT* W3 ....99 K5
Ferguson's CI *POP/IOD* E14 ....123 C2
Fergus Rd *HBRY* N5 ....85 H3
Ferme Park Rd *CEND/HSY/T* N8 ...66 E6
Fermor Rd *FSTH* SE23 ....140 E5
Fermoy Rd *GFD/PVL* UB6 ....97 H3
  MV/WKIL W9 ....100 F3
Fern Av *MTCM* CR4 ....156 D7
Fernbank *BKHH* IG9 ....52 B3
Fernbank Av *ALP/SUD* HA0 ....79 M4
  HCH RM12 ....92 C4
  WOT/HER KT12 ....165 L2
Fernbank Ms *CLAP* SW4 ....138 B3
Fernbrook Dr *RYLN/HDSTN* HA2 ..61 H8
Fernbrook Rd *LEW* SE13 ....141 H3
Ferncliff Rd *HACK* E8 ....86 A5
Fern CI *ERITH* DA8 ....128 B6
Ferncroft Av *HAMP* NW3 ....83 G3
  NFNCH/WDSP N12 ....47 L8
  RSLP HA4 ....78 C2
Ferndale *BMLY* BR1 ....160 C5
Ferndale Av *HSLWW* TW4 ....114 E8
  WALTH E17 ....69 K6
Ferndale CI *BXLYHN* DA7 ....126 E6
Ferndale Crs *UX/CGN* UB8 ....94 C8
Ferndale Rd *ASHF* TW15 ....148 D1
  CLAP SW4 ....138 E1
  CRW RM5 ....73 J5
  FSTGT E7 ....88 B7
  PEND EN3 ....37 L2
  SEVS/STOTM N15 ....67 M7
  SNWD SE25 ....158 B8
  WAN E11 ....87 M2
Ferndale St *EHAM* E6 ....107 H6
Ferndale Ter *HRW* HA1 ....61 M5
Ferndell Av *BXLY* DA5 ....145 K7
Ferndene *LCOL/BKTW* AL2 ....21 M4
Ferndene Rd *HNHL* SE24 ....139 J1
Ferndown *EMPK* RM11 ....75 G7
  NTHWD HA6 ....60 A3
Ferndown Av *ORP* BR6 ....176 D2
Ferndown CI *BELMT* SM2 ....170 D8
  PIN HA5 ....60 E1
Ferndown Rd *ELTH/MOT* SE9 .....142 D4
  OXHEY WD19 ....42 C5
Fernery Meade Wy *ISLW* TW7 ....116 A7
Ferney Rd *EBAR* EN4 ....48 A2
Fern Gv *EBED/NFELT* TW14 ....132 B4
Fernhall Dr *REDBR* IG4 ....70 D6
Fernham Rd *THHTH* CR7 ....157 J6
Fernhead Rd *MV/WKIL* W9 ....100 F2
Fernheath Wy *RDART* DA2 ....163 K1
Fernhill *LHD/OX* KT22 ....178 D7
Fernhill Ct *WALTH* E17 ....69 K3
Fernhill Gdns *KUTN/CMB* KT2 ....152 D1
Fernhills *ABLGY* WD5 ....20 D7
Fernhill St *CAN/RD* E16 ....106 F7
Fernholme Rd *PECK* SE15 ....140 D2
Fernhurst Gdns *EDGW* HA8 ....45 G3
Fernhurst Rd *ASHF* TW15 ....131 J8
  CROY/NA CR0 ....173 G2
  FUL/PGN SW6 ....118 G6
Fern La *NWDGN* UB2 ....114 F3
Fernlea Rd *BAL* SW12 ....138 B5
  MTCM CR4 ....156 A5

Fernleigh CI *CROY/NA* CR0 ....172 A6
  WOT/HER KT12 ....165 H5
Fernleigh Ct *RYLN/HDSTN* HA2 ...80 E1
  WBLY HA9 ....80 E1
Fernleigh Rd *WCHMH* N21 ....49 G4
Fernsbury St *FSBYW* WC1X 6 A8
Ferns CI *PEND* EN3 ....37 L1
  SAND/SEL CR2 ....185 H1
Fernshaw Rd *WBPTN* SW10 ....119 J4
Fernside *BKHH* IG9 ....52 B3
Fernside Av *FELT* TW13 ....132 B8
  MLHL NW7 ....45 K5
Fernside Rd *BAL* SW12 ....137 M5
Fern St *BOW* E3 ....105 G3
Fernthorpe Rd
  STRHM/NOR SW16 ....156 C2
Ferntower Rd *HBRY* N5 ....85 J3
Fern Wk *ASHF* TW15 ....148 D1
Fern Wy *GSTN* WD25 ....21 H8
Fernways *IL* IG1 ....89 H3
Fernwood *CROY/NA* CR0 ....185 L2
Fernwood Av *ALP/SUD* HA0 ....80 C6
  STRHM/NOR SW16 ....138 D8
Fernwood CI *BMLY* BR1 ....160 C5
Fernwood Crs *TRDG/WHET* N20 ...47 M5
Ferny HI *EBAR* EN4 ....34 F3
Ferranti CI *WOOL/PLUM* SE18 ....124 D1
Ferraro CI *HEST* TW5 ....98 C8
Ferrers Av *WDR/YW* UB7 ....94 D8
  WLGTN SM6 ....86 D5
Ferrers Rd *STRHM/NOR* SW16 ...156 D1
Ferrestone Rd
  CEND/HSY/T N8 ....66 F5
Ferriby CI *IS* N1 ....6 A1
Ferrier St *WAND/EARL* SW18 .....137 H1
Ferring CI *RYLN/HDSTN* HA2 ....79 J1
Ferrings *DUL* SE21 ....139 L6
Ferris Av *CROY/NA* CR0 ....185 L2
Ferris Rd *EDUL* SE22 ....140 A1
Ferron Rd *CLPT* E5 ....86 B3
Ferro Rd *RAIN* RM13 ....110 A3
Ferryhills CI *OXHEY* WD19 ....42 C5
Ferry La *BARN* SW13 ....117 M4
  BTFD TW8 ....116 E4
  RAIN RM13 ....109 L5
  RCH/KEW TW9 ....116 F4
  SHPTN TW17 ....164 A3
  STA TW18 ....148 C6
  TOTM N17 ....68 B5
Ferrymead Av *GFD/PVL* UB6 ....97 G1
Ferrymead Dr *GFD/PVL* UB6 ....97 G1
Ferrymead Gdns *GFD/PVL* UB6 ...97 J1
Ferrymoor
  RCHPK/HAM TW10 ....134 B7
Ferry Rd *BARN* SW13 ....118 A5
  E/WMO/HCT KT8 ....151 G6
  TEDD TW11 ....152 B1
  THDIT KT7 ....151 H7
  TWK TW1 ....134 B5
Ferry Sq *BTFD* TW8 ....116 E4
Ferry St *POP/IOD* E14 ....123 J3
Festing Rd *PUT/ROE* SW15 ....118 D8
Festival CI *BXLY* DA5 ....144 D5
  ERITH DA8 ....127 M5
  HGDN/ICK UB10 ....77 H8
Fetherstone CI
  POTB/CUF EN6 ....23 K6
Fetter La *FLST/FETLN* EC4A 12 B4
Ffinch St *DEPT* SE8 ....125 C5
Fiddicroft Av *BNSTD* SM7 ....182 B8
Fidler PI *BUSH* WD23 ....43 H1
Field CI *BKHH* IG9 ....52 C5
  BMLY BR1 ....160 C5
  CHING E4 ....51 H8
  CHSGTN KT9 ....167 J7
  E/WMO/HCT KT8 ....151 H8
  HGDN/ICK UB10 ....77 G2
  HSLWW TW4 ....114 B6
  HYS/HAR UB3 ....94 E6
  RSLP HA4 ....77 J1
  SAND/SEL CR2 ....185 H7
Fieldcommon La
  WOT/HER KT12 ....165 L3
Field End *COUL/CHIP* CR5 ....183 K7
  RSLP HA4 ....78 C6
Fieldend *TEDD* TW11 ....133 M8
Field End CI *OXHEY* WD19 ....42 E2
Field End Rd *PIN* HA5 ....60 B6
  RSLP HA4 ....60 C8
Fieldend Rd *STRHM/NOR* SW16 ..156 C4
Fielders CI *EN* EN1 ....36 C3
  RYLN/HDSTN HA2 ....79 J1
Fieldfare Rd *THMD* SE28 ....108 C3
Fieldgate St *WCHPL* E1 ....104 A3
Fieldhouse CI *SWFD* E18 ....70 B2
Fieldhouse Rd *BAL* SW12 ....138 C5
Fielding Av *WHTN* TW2 ....133 J7
  WKENS W14 ....118 D1
Fieldings Rd *CHES/WCR* EN8 ......26 F2
The Fieldings *FSTH* SE23 ....140 C5
Fielding St *WALW* SE17 ....18 E9
Field La *BTFD* TW8 ....116 C5
  TEDD TW11 ....152 A1
Field Md *CDALE/KGS* NW9 ....63 L1
Field PI *NWMAL* KT3 ....168 F1
Field Rd *EBED/NFELT* TW14 ....132 B3
  FSTGT E7 ....88 A4
  HMSMTH W6 ....118 E3
  OXHEY WD19 ....42 E1
  SOCK/AV RM15 ....111 J7
  TOTM N17 ....67 K4
Fieldsend Rd *CHEAM* SM3 ....169 L7
Fieldside CI *ORP* BR6 ....176 C6
Field St *FSBYW* WC1X 5 L7
Field Vw *BAR* EN5 ....33 H7
  FELT TW13 ....131 K8
Fieldview *WAND/EARL* SW18 .....137 M5
Field View Ri *LCOL/BKTW* AL2 .....21 L2
Field View Rd *POTB/CUF* EN6 ......23 G6
Field Wy *CROY/NA* CR0 ....186 B1
  GFD/PVL UB6 ....79 H8
  RKW/CH/CXG WD3 ....40 B3
  RSLP HA4 ....77 J1
  UX/CGN UB8 ....94 D3
  WLSDN NW10 ....80 F5

Fieldway *BCTR* RM8 .... **90** B4
STMC/STPC BR5 .... **176** D1
Fieldway Crs *HOLWY* N7 .... **85** G5
Fiennes Cl *BCTR* RM8 .... **90** C1
Fiesta Dr *DAGW* RM9 .... **109** J2 2
Fifehead Cl *ASHF* TW15 .... **148** E2
Fife Rd *CAN/RD* E16 .... **106** A4
KUT KT1 .... **152** E5 2
MORT/ESHN SW14 .... **135** J2
WDGN N22 .... **67** H1
Fife Ter *IS* N1 .... **5** M5
Fifield Pth *FSTH* SE23 .... **140** D7
Fifth Av *GSTN* WD25 .... **21** K8
MNPK E12 .... **88** F4
NKENS W10 .... **100** E3
Fifth Cross Rd *WHTN* TW2 .... **133** K6
Fifth Wy *WBLY* HA9 .... **81** H4
Figge's Rd *MTCM* CR4 .... **156** A3
Filby Rd *CHSGTN* KT9 .... **167** M8
Filey Av *STNW/STAM* N16 .... **86** A1
Filey Cl *BELMT* SM2 .... **182** C1 1
Filey Waye *RSLP* HA4 .... **78** A2
Fillebrook Av *EN* EN1 .... **36** E5
Fillebrook Rd *WAN* E11 .... **69** L8
Filmer Rd *FUL/PGN* SW6 .... **118** F6
Finborough Rd *TOOT* SW17 .... **155** M3
WBPTN SW10 .... **14** D9
Finchale Rd *ABYW* SE2 .... **126** A1
Fincham Cl *HGDN/ICK* UB10 .... **77** J3 3
Finch Av *WNWD* SE27 .... **139** K8
Finch Cl *BAR* EN5 .... **34** A8
Finch Dr *EBED/NFELT* TW14 .... **132** D4
Finchingfield Av *WFD* IG8 .... **70** C1
Finch La *BANK* EC3V **13** H5
BUSH WD23 .... **30** A8
Finchley Cl *DART* DA1 .... **147** G3
Finchley La *HDN* NW4 .... **64** D5
Finchley Pk *NFNCH/WDSP* N12 .... **47** J6
Finchley Pl *STJWD* NW8 .... **3** G5 1
Finchley Rd *GLDGN* NW11 .... **64** F6 3
GLDGN NW11 .... **83** G2
HAMP NW3 .... **83** G2
KIL/WHAMP NW6 .... **83** G4
STJWD NW8 .... **3** G4
Finchley Wy *FNCH* N3 .... **47** G8
Finch Ms *PECK* SE15 .... **121** M6 3
Finden Rd *FSTGT* E7 .... **88** B5
Findhorn Av *YEAD* UB4 .... **96** B4
Findhorn St *POP/IOD* E14 .... **105** J5
Findon Cl *RYLN/HDSTN* HA2 .... **79** H3 3
WAND/EARL SW18 .... **137** G3
Findon Gdns *RAIN* RM13 .... **110** A4
Findon Rd *ED* N9 .... **50** B3
SHB W12 .... **100** A8
Fine Bush La *DEN/HRF* UB9 .... **59** H7
Fingal St *GNWCH* SE10 .... **123** M3
Finglesham Cl
STMC/STPC BR5 .... **177** K3 1
Finians Cl *HGDN/ICK* UB10 .... **76** F7 3
Finland Rd *BROCKY* SE4 .... **122** E8
Finland St *BERM/RHTH* SE16 .... **122** E1
Finlays Cl *CHSGTN* KT9 .... **168** A7 1
Finlay St *FUL/PGN* SW6 .... **118** D6
Finnart Cl *WEY* KT13 .... **164** C6 1
Finnis St *BETH* E2 .... **104** B2
Finnymore Rd *DAGW* RM9 .... **90** E7
Finsbury Av *LVPST* EC2M **13** H3 2
Finsbury Circ *LVPST* EC2M **13** H3 3
Finsbury Cottages *WDGN* N22 .. **66** E1 2
Finsbury Market *SDTCH* EC2A **13** J2 2
SDTCH EC2A **13** J1 1
Finsbury Park Av *FSBYPK* N4 .... **67** J7
Finsbury Park Rd *FSBYPK* N4 .... **85** H3 2
Finsbury Pavement
SDTCH EC2A **13** H2
Finsbury Rd *WDGN* N22 .... **66** F2 1
Finsbury Sq *SDTCH* EC2A **13** H1
Finsbury St *STLK* EC1Y **13** G2
Finsbury Wy *BXLY* DA5 .... **144** F3
Finsen Rd *HNHL* SE24 .... **139** J1
Finstock Rd *NKENS* W10 .... **100** D5
Finucane Dr *STMC/STPC* BR5 .... **177** J2
Finucane Gdns *RAIN* RM13 .... **92** A6
Finucane Ri *BUSH* WD23 .... **43** J4
Firbank Cl *CAN/RD* E16 .... **106** D4 1
ENC/FH EN2 .... **36** C7
Firbank Dr *OXHEY* WD19 .... **42** E2
Firbank Rd *CRW* RM5 .... **55** H7
PECK SE15 .... **122** B7 2
Fir Cl *WOT/HER* KT12 .... **165** G2
Fircroft Gdns *HRW* HA1 .... **79** L3
Fircroft Rd *CHSGTN* KT9 .... **167** M6
TOOT SW17 .... **137** M7
Firdene *BRYLDS* KT5 .... **168** C3
Fir Dene *ORP* BR6 .... **175** M5
Fire Bell Aly *SURB* KT6 .... **167** L1
Firebell Ms *SURB* KT6 .... **167** L1 1
Firecrest Dr *HAMP* NW3 .... **83** H3
Firefly Gdns *EHAM* E6 .... **106** E3 1
Fir Grange Av *WEY* KT13 .... **164** B7
Fir Gv *NWMAL* KT3 .... **168** F1
Firham Park Av *HARH* RM3 .... **75** G1 2
Firhill Rd *CAT* SE6 .... **141** G7
Firlands *WEY* KT13 .... **164** E8
Firmin Rd *DART* DA1 .... **146** C2
Fir Rd *CHEAM* SM3 .... **169** M3
FELT TW13 .... **150** D1
Firs Av *FBAR/BDGN* N11 .... **48** A8
MORT/ESHN SW14 .... **135** J1
MUSWH N10 .... **66** A4
Firsby Av *CROY/NA* CR0 .... **173** K3
Firsby Rd *STNW/STAM* N16 .... **85** M1
Firs Cl *ESH/CLAY* KT10 .... **166** E8
FSTH SE23 .... **140** D4
MTCM CR4 .... **156** B5
Firscroft *PLMGR* N13 .... **49** J5
Firs Dr *HEST* TW5 .... **114** B5
Firside Gv *BFN/LL* DA15 .... **143** M5
Firs La *PLMGR* N13 .... **49** J5
POTB/CUF EN6 .... **23** H6
WCHMH N21 .... **49** J2
Firs Park Av *WCHMH* N21 .... **49** K3
Firs Park Gdns *WCHMH* N21 .... **49** K3
Firs Rd *PUR/KEN* CR8 .... **184** B8
First Av *ACT* W3 .... **99** M7
BXLYHN DA7 .... **126** C5
CHDH RM6 .... **72** C6
DAGE RM10 .... **109** H1
E/WMO/HCT KT8 .... **150** F7
EN EN1 .... **36** F8
GSTN WD25 .... **21** J8
HDN NW4 .... **64** C5
HOR/WEW KT19 .... **180** E2
HYS/HAR UB3 .... **95** M7
MNPK E12 .... **88** E4
MORT/ESHN SW14 .... **117** L7
NKENS W10 .... **100** F3
PLSTW E13 .... **106** A2
UED N18 .... **50** C6
WALTH E17 .... **69** G6 3
WBLY HA9 .... **80** D2
WOT/HER KT12 .... **165** H1
First Cl *E/WMO/HCT* KT8 .... **151** J7 1
First Cross Rd *WHTN* TW2 .... **133** L6
The Firs *BXLY* DA5 .... **145** K5
EA W5 .... **98** D4
TRDG/WHET N20 .... **47** K3
First St *CHEL* SW3 .... **15** K5
Firstway *RYNPK* SW20 .... **154** C5
First Wy *WBLY* HA9 .... **81** H4
Firs Wk *NTHWD* HA6 .... **41** K8
WFD IG8 .... **52** A7
Firswood Av *HOR/WEW* KT19 .... **168** E7
Firth Gdns *FUL/PGN* SW6 .... **118** E6
Firtree Av *MTCM* CR4 .... **156** A5
Fir Tree Av *WDR/YW* UB7 .... **113** G1 1
Fir Tree Cl *EA* W5 .... **98** E5 2
ESH/CLAY KT10 .... **166** C7
EW KT17 .... **181** J8
HOR/WEW KT19 .... **168** F6
ORP BR6 .... **176** F7
ROM RM1 .... **73** K4 1
STRHM/NOR SW16 .... **156** C1
Fir Tree Ct *BORE* WD6 .... **31** M7
Fir Tree Gdns *CROY/NA* CR0 .... **174** A6 1
Fir Tree Gv *CAR* SM5 .... **182** F1
Fir Tree Hl *RKW/CH/CXG* WD3 .... **28** A2
Fir Tree Rd *BNSTD* SM7 .... **181** K7
HSLWW TW4 .... **132** E1
Fir Trees Cl *BERM/RHTH* SE16 .... **104** E7
Fir Tree Wk *EN* EN1 .... **36** E6
Fir Wk *EW* KT17 .... **169** K8
Fisher Cl *CROY/NA* CR0 .... **172** F3
GFD/PVL UB6 .... **97** G2 2
KGLGY WD4 .... **20** A2
WOT/HER KT12 .... **165** H6
Fisherdene *ESH/CLAY* KT10 .... **179** G1 1
Fisherman Cl
RCHPK/HAM TW10 .... **134** C8 3
Fishermans Dr
BERM/RHTH SE16 .... **104** D8
Fisher Rd *KTN/HRWW/W* HA3 .... **61** M3
Fishers Cl *CHES/WCR* EN8 .... **27** G7
Fishers Ct *NWCR* SE14 .... **122** D6 1
Fisher's La *CHSWK* W4 .... **117** K2
Fisher St *CAN/RD* E16 .... **106** A4
RSQ WC1B **11** L3
Fisher's Wy *BELV* DA17 .... **109** J7
Fisherton St *STJWD* NW8 .... **9** G1
Fishponds Rd *HAYES* BR2 .... **175** K7
TOOT SW17 .... **137** L8
Fish Street Hl *MON* EC3R **13** H6 2
MON EC3R **13** H7 1
Fisons Rd *CAN/RD* E16 .... **106** A7
Fitzalan Rd *ESH/CLAY* KT10 .... **178** E1
FNCH N3 .... **64** E4
Fitzalan St *LBTH* SE11 .... **17** M5
Fitz-george Av *NWMAL* KT3 .... **153** K4
WKENS W14 .... **118** E2 2
Fitzgerald Av
MORT/ESHN SW14 .... **117** L8
Fitzgerald Rd
MORT/ESHN SW14 .... **117** K8 3
THDIT KT7 .... **167** G1
WAN E11 .... **70** A6 1
Fitzhardinge St *MBLAR* W1H **10** A4
Fitzhugh Gv *WAND/EARL* SW18 .. **137** K3
Fitzilian Av *HARH* RM3 .... **74** F2
Fitzjames Av *CROY/NA* CR0 .... **173** G4
WKENS W14 .... **118** E2 3
Fitzjohn Av *BAR* EN5 .... **33** L8
Fitzjohn's Av *HAMP* NW3 .... **83** K5
Fitzmaurice Pl
MYFR/PICC W1J **10** D8 1
Fitzneal St *ACT* W3 .... **99** M5
Fitzroy Cl *HGT* N6 .... **83** M1
Fitzroy Crs *CHSWK* W4 .... **117** K5 1
Fitzroy Gdns *NRWD* SE19 .... **157** L3
Fitzroy Ms *GTPST* W1W **10** E1 3
Fitzroy Pk *HGT* N6 .... **83** M1
Fitzroy Rd *CAMTN* NW1 .... **4** A3
Fitzroy Sq *FITZ* W1T **10** E1 1
Fitzroy St *CAMTN* NW1 .... **10** E1
FITZ W1T **10** E2
Fitzstephen Rd *BCTR* RM8 .... **90** B5
Fitzwarren Gdns *ARCH* N19 .... **84** C1
Fitzwilliam Av *RCH/KEW* TW9 .... **116** F7
Fitzwilliam Ms *CAN/RD* E16 .... **106** A7
Fitzwilliam Rd *CLAP* SW4 .... **120** C8
Fitz Wygram Cl *HPTN* TW12 .... **151** J1 4
Five Acre *CDALE/KGS* NW9 .... **63** M3
Fiveacre Cl *THHTH* CR7 .... **172** A1
Five Acres Av *LCOL/BKTW* AL2 .... **21** M2
Five Elms Rd *DAGW* RM9 .... **90** F3
HAYES BR2 .... **175** J5
Five Fields Cl *OXHEY* WD19 .... **42** F4
Five Oaks La *CHIG* IG7 .... **54** E8
Five Ways Jct *HDN* NW4 .... **64** A2
Fiveways Rd *BRXN/ST* SW9 .... **121** G7
Fladbury Rd *SEVS/STOTM* N15 .. **67** K7 2
Fladgate Rd *WAN* E11 .... **69** L7
Flag Cl *CROY/NA* CR0 .... **173** K3
Flagstaff Cl *WAB* EN9 .... **27** H6
Flagstaff Rd *WAB* EN9 .... **27** H5
Flag Wk *PIN* HA5 .... **60** A7
Flambard Rd *HRW* HA1 .... **62** A7
Flamborough Rd *RSLP* HA4 .... **78** A3
Flamborough St *POP/IOD* E14 .... **104** E5
Flamingo Wk *RAIN* RM13 .... **92** A7 4
Flamstead End Rd
CHES/WCR EN8 .... **26** B1
Flamstead Gdns *DAGW* RM9 .... **90** C7 2
Flamstead Rd *DAGW* RM9 .... **90** C7
Flamsted Av *WBLY* HA9 .... **81** G6
Flamsteed Rd *CHARL* SE7 .... **124** E3
Flanchford Rd *SHB* W12 .... **117** M1
Flanders Crs *TOOT* SW17 .... **155** M3
Flanders Rd *CHSWK* W4 .... **117** L2
EHAM E6 .... **106** F1
Flanders Wy *HOM* E9 .... **86** D6
Flank St *WCHPL* E1 .... **104** A6 4
Flash La *ENC/FH* EN2 .... **36** C2
Flask Wk *HAMP* NW3 .... **83** J4
Flavell Ms *GNWCH* SE10 .... **123** L3
Flaxen Cl *CHING* E4 .... **51** H5 1
Flaxen Rd *CHING* E4 .... **51** H5
Flaxley Rd *MRDN* SM4 .... **170** B1
Flaxman Rd *CMBW* SE5 .... **121** H7
Flaxman Ter *STPAN* WC1H **5** H8
Flaxton Rd *WOOL/PLUM* SE18 .... **125** K6
Flecker Cl *STAN* HA7 .... **43** M7
Fleece Dr *UED* N18 .... **50** A6 2
Fleece Rd *SURB* KT6 .... **167** J3
Fleece Wk *HOLWY* N7 .... **84** E6 1
Fleeming Cl *WALTH* E17 .... **68** F3 1
Fleeming Rd *WALTH* E17 .... **68** F3
Fleet Av *RDART* DA2 .... **147** J5
UPMR RM14 .... **75** K7
Fleet Cl *E/WMO/HCT* KT8 .... **150** F8
RSLP HA4 .... **59** J7
UPMR RM14 .... **75** K7
Fleet Rd *HAMP* NW3 .... **83** L5
RDART DA2 .... **147** J5
Fleetside *E/WMO/HCT* KT8 .... **150** F8
Fleet Sq *FSBYW* WC1X **5** L8
Fleet St *EMB* EC4Y **12** B5
Fleet Street Hl *BETH* E2 .... **104** A3 5
Fleetwood Cl *CAN/RD* E16 .... **106** D4 2
CHSGTN KT9 .... **179** K1 1
CROY/NA CR0 .... **172** F5
Fleetwood Rd *NWMAL* KT3 .... **153** H6
WLSDN NW10 .... **82** A5
Fleetwood Sq *NWMAL* KT3 .... **153** H6
Fleetwood St
STNW/STAM N16 .... **85** L2 3
Fleetwood Wy *OXHEY* WD19 .... **42** C6
Fleming Ct *CROY/NA* CR0 .... **172** A7 2
Fleming Gdns *HARH* RM3 .... **74** D3 2
Fleming Md *WIM/MER* SW19 .... **155** L3
Fleming Rd *GFD/PVL* UB6 .... **97** H5
WALW SE17 .... **18** D9
Fleming Wy *ISLW* TW7 .... **115** M8
THMD SE28 .... **108** D6
Flemming Av *RSLP* HA4 .... **78** B1
Flempton Rd *LEY* E10 .... **86** E1
Fletcher Cl *EHAM* E6 .... **107** H6 2
Fletcher La *LEY* E10 .... **69** J8
Fletcher Rd *CHIG* IG7 .... **53** M7
CHSWK W4 .... **117** J1
Fletchers Cl *HAYES* BR2 .... **160** B7
Fletcher St *WCHPL* E1 .... **104** A6 5
Fletching Rd *CHARL* SE7 .... **124** D4
CLPT E5 .... **86** C3
Fletton Rd *FBAR/BDGN* N11 .... **66** E1
Fleur De Lis St *WCHPL* E1 .... **13** L1 1
Flexmere Rd *TOTM* N17 .... **67** K2
Flimwell Cl *BMLY* BR1 .... **159** L1
Flint Cl *BNSTD* SM7 .... **182** B7
ORP BR6 .... **176** F8 1
Flint Down Cl
STMC/STPC BR5 .... **162** A4 2
Flintlock Cl *STWL/WRAY* TW19 .... **130** A1
Flintmill Crs *BKHTH/KID* SE3 .... **124** E7
ELTH/MOT SE9 .... **124** E8
Flinton St *WALW* SE17 .... **19** K7 1
Flint St *WALW* SE17 .... **19** H6
Flock Mill Pl *WAND/EARL* SW18 .. **137** H5
Flockton St
BERM/RHTH SE16 .... **104** A8 6
Flodden Rd *CMBW* SE5 .... **121** J6
Flood La *TWK* TW1 .... **134** A5 4
Flood St *CHEL* SW3 .... **15** K8
Flood Wk *CHEL* SW3 .... **15** K9
Flora Cl *POP/IOD* E14 .... **105** H5
Flora Gdns *CHDH* RM6 .... **72** C7
CROY/NA CR0 .... **186** C4
Floral St *COVGDN* WC2E **11** K6
Flora St *BELV* DA17 .... **126** F3 1
Florence Av *ENC/FH* EN2 .... **36** C6
MRDN SM4 .... **155** J8
Florence Cl *GSTN* WD25 .... **21** G8 1
HCH RM12 .... **92** E2 1
WOT/HER KT12 .... **165** H2 2
Florence Ct *WAN* E11 .... **70** B5
Florence Dr *ENC/FH* EN2 .... **36** C6
Florence Gdns *CHSWK* W4 .... **117** J4 1
STA TW18 .... **148** B3
Florence Rd *ABYW* SE2 .... **126** C1
BECK BR3 .... **158** D5
BMLY BR1 .... **160** A4
CHSWK W4 .... **117** K1 4
EA W5 .... **98** E6
EHAM E6 .... **88** C8 1
FELT TW13 .... **132** B5
FSBYPK N4 .... **85** G1
KUTN/CMB KT2 .... **152** F3
NWCR SE14 .... **122** F6
NWDGN UB2 .... **114** D2
PLSTW E13 .... **106** A1
SAND/SEL CR2 .... **184** D2
WIM/MER SW19 .... **155** H2
WOT/HER KT12 .... **165** H2
Florence St *CAN/RD* E16 .... **105** M3
HDN NW4 .... **64** C5
IS N1 .... **6** C2
Florence Ter *NWCR* SE14 .... **122** F6
Florence Wy *BAL* SW12 .... **137** M5
Florfield Rd *HACK* E8 .... **86** B6 2
Florian Av *SUT* SM1 .... **170** D6
Florian Rd *PUT/ROE* SW15 .... **136** E1
Florida Cl *BUSH* WD23 .... **43** K4
Florida Rd *THHTH* CR7 .... **157** H4
Florida St *BETH* E2 .... **104** A2 4
BETH E2 .... **104** B2 7
Florin Ct *UED* N18 .... **49** L6
Floriston Av *HGDN/ICK* UB10 .... **77** J7
Floriston Cl *STAN* HA7 .... **62** B2
Floriston Gdns *STAN* HA7 .... **62** B2
Floss St *PUT/ROE* SW15 .... **118** C7
Flower La *MLHL* NW7 .... **45** M7
Flowers Ms *ARCH* N19 .... **84** C2 1
Floyd Rd *CHARL* SE7 .... **124** C3
Fludyer St *LEW* SE13 .... **141** L1
Foley Ms *ESH/CLAY* KT10 .... **166** E8
Foley Rd *ESH/CLAY* KT10 .... **178** E1
Foley St *GTPST* W1W **10** E3
Folgate St *WCHPL* E1 .... **13** K2
Foliot St *ACT* W3 .... **99** M5
Folkes La *UPMR* RM14 .... **75** M6
Folkestone Rd *EHAM* E6 .... **107** G1
UED N18 .... **50** A6 3
WALTH E17 .... **69** H5
Folkingham La
CDALE/KGS NW9 .... **63** L2 3
Folkington Cnr
NFNCH/WDSP N12 .... **46** F7
Follett Dr *ABLGY* WD5 .... **20** F4
Follett St *POP/IOD* E14 .... **105** J5
Folly Cl *RAD* WD7 .... **30** F1
Follyfield Rd *BNSTD* SM7 .... **182** A7
Folly La *WALTH* E17 .... **68** E2
Folly Wall *POP/IOD* E14 .... **105** J8
Fontaine Rd *STRHM/NOR* SW16 .. **156** F2
Fontarabia Rd *BTSEA* SW11 .... **138** A1
Fontayne Av *CHIG* IG7 .... **53** J6
RAIN RM13 .... **91** L7
ROM RM1 .... **73** L3
Fontenoy Rd *TOOT* SW17 .... **138** B6
Fonteyne Gdns *WFD* IG8 .... **70** D3 1
Fonthill Ms *FSBYPK* N4 .... **85** G2 2
Fonthill Rd *FSBYPK* N4 .... **84** F2
Font Hills *EFNCH* N2 .... **65** J3
Fontley Wy *PUT/ROE* SW15 .... **136** A4
Fontmell Cl *ASHF* TW15 .... **149** G1
Fontmell Pk *ASHF* TW15 .... **149** G1 3
Fontwell Cl *KTN/HRWW/W* HA3 .... **61** L1
NTHLT UB5 .... **79** G6 2
Fontwell Dr *HAYES* BR2 .... **161** G8
Fontwell Park Gdns
HCH RM12 .... **92** E4 1
Foord Cl *RDART* DA2 .... **147** L6
Football La *HRW* HA1 .... **79** M1
Footbury Hill Rd *ORP* BR6 .... **177** G2
The Footpath
PUT/ROE SW15 .... **136** A2 1
Foots Cray High St *SCUP* DA14 .. **162** C2
Foots Cray La *BXLY* DA5 .... **144** C5
Footscray Rd *ELTH/MOT* SE9 .... **143** G3
Forbes Av *POTB/CUF* EN6 .... **23** K6
Forbes Cl *CRICK* NW2 .... **82** A3
HCH RM12 .... **92** B1
Forbes St *WCHPL* E1 .... **104** A5 5
Forbes Wy *RSLP* HA4 .... **78** B2 2
Forburg Rd *STNW/STAM* N16 .... **86** A1
Fordbridge Rd *ASHF* TW15 .... **148** E2
SHPTN TW17 .... **164** E1
SUN TW16 .... **150** A8
Ford Cl *ASHF* TW15 .... **148** E2
BUSH WD23 .... **30** C7 1
HRW HA1 .... **61** K8
RAIN RM13 .... **91** M7
SHPTN TW17 .... **149** G7 3
THHTH CR7 .... **172** B1
Fordcroft Rd *STMC/STPC* BR5 .... **162** B8
Forde Av *BMLY* BR1 .... **160** C6
Fordel Rd *CAT* SE6 .... **141** K5
Ford End *WFD* IG8 .... **52** B8
Fordham Cl *EMPK* RM11 .... **75** G8 1
Fordham Rd *EBAR* EN4 .... **34** D6
Fordham St *WCHPL* E1 .... **104** A5 6
Fordhook Av *ACT* W3 .... **98** F6
Fordingley Rd *MV/WKIL* W9 .... **100** F2
Fordington Rd *HGT* N6 .... **65** M5
Ford La *IVER* SL0 .... **94** A5
RAIN RM13 .... **91** M7
Fordmill Rd *CAT* SE6 .... **141** G6
Ford Rd *ASHF* TW15 .... **130** F8
BOW E3 .... **104** E1
DAGE RM10 .... **91** G7
DAGW RM9 .... **90** F7
Ford's Gv *WCHMH* N21 .... **49** J3
Fords Park Rd *CAN/RD* E16 .... **106** A5
Ford Sq *WCHPL* E1 .... **104** B4 4
Ford St *BOW* E3 .... **86** E8
CAN/RD E16 .... **105** M5
Fordwich Cl *ORP* BR6 .... **176** F2
Fordwych Rd *CRICK* NW2 .... **82** E5
Fordyce Cl *EMPK* RM11 .... **75** G8
Fordyce Rd *LEW* SE13 .... **141** J3
Fordyke Rd *BCTR* RM8 .... **90** E2
Foreland Ct *HDN* NW4 .... **64** E2 1
Foreland St
WOOL/PLUM SE18 .... **125** K2 2
Foremark Cl *BARK/HLT* IG6 .... **53** M7 1
Foreshore *DEPT* SE8 .... **122** F2
Forest Ap *CHING* E4 .... **51** L2
WFD IG8 .... **69** M1
Forest Av *CHIG* IG7 .... **53** G7
CHING E4 .... **51** L2
Forest Cl *CHST* BR7 .... **161** G4
WAB EN9 .... **39** H2
WAN E11 .... **69** M6
WFD IG8 .... **52** B6 1
Forest Ct *CHING* E4 .... **51** M3
WAN E11 .... **69** L5
Forestdale *STHGT/OAK* N14 .... **48** D6
Forest Dr *HAYES* BR2 .... **175** L5 1
MNPK E12 .... **88** D3
SUN TW16 .... **149** M3
WFD IG8 .... **69** K1
Forest Dr East *WAN* E11 .... **69** J8
Forest Dr West *WAN* E11 .... **69** J8
Forest Edge *BKHH* IG9 .... **52** C5
Forester Rd *PECK* SE15 .... **140** B1
Foresters Cl *WLGTN* SM6 .... **183** K1
Foresters Crs *BXLYHN* DA7 .... **145** H1
Foresters Dr *WALTH* E17 .... **69** K5
WLGTN SM6 .... **183** K1
Forest Gdns *TOTM* N17 .... **67** M3
Forest Ga *CDALE/KGS* NW9 .... **63** L5
Forest Gld *CHING* E4 .... **51** L7
WAN E11 .... **69** L7
Forest Gv *HACK* E8 .... **85** M6 3
Forest Hill Rd *EDUL* SE22 .... **140** B3
Forest La *CHIG* IG7 .... **53** G7
FSTGT E7 .... **88** A5
Forest Mount Rd *WFD* IG8 .... **69** K1
Fore St *BARB* EC2Y **13** G3
ED N9 .... **50** A6
PIN HA5 .... **60** A6
Forest Rdg *BECK* BR3 .... **159** G6
HAYES BR2 .... **175** L6
Forest Ri *WALTH* E17 .... **69** K4
Forest Rd *BARK/HLT* IG6 .... **54** B8
CHEAM SM3 .... **170** A3
CHES/WCR EN8 .... **26** D2
ED N9 .... **50** B3
ERITH DA8 .... **128** A6
FELT TW13 .... **132** C7
FSTGT E7 .... **88** A4
GSTN WD25 .... **21** H6
HACK E8 .... **85** M6
LOU IG10 .... **39** K7
PEND EN3 .... **37** L1
RCH/KEW TW9 .... **117** G5
ROMW/RG RM7 .... **73** H4
WALTH E17 .... **68** E5
WAN E11 .... **69** K8
WFD IG8 .... **52** A5
Forest Side *BKHH* IG9 .... **52** B3
CHING E4 .... **51** M2
FSTGT E7 .... **88** B4
WPK KT4 .... **168** F3
Forest St *FSTGT* E7 .... **88** A5
The Forest *WALTH* E17 .... **69** L5
Forest Vw *CHING* E4 .... **51** K2
WAN E11 .... **69** M8
Forest View Av *LEY* E10 .... **69** K6 1
Forest View Rd *MNPK* E12 .... **88** E4
WALTH E17 .... **69** J2
Forest Wy *BFN/LL* DA15 .... **143** K4
LOU IG10 .... **39** L6
STMC/STPC BR5 .... **161** M8
WFD IG8 .... **52** B6
Forfar Rd *BTSEA* SW11 .... **120** A6
WDGN N22 .... **67** H2
Forge Cl *HAYES* BR2 .... **175** G3
Forge Dr *ESH/CLAY* KT10 .... **179** G1
Forge La *BELMT* SM2 .... **181** L1
FELT TW13 .... **150** E1
NTHWD HA6 .... **59** L1
SUN TW16 .... **150** A6
Forman Pl *STNW/STAM* N16 .... **85** M4 2
Formby Av *KTN/HRWW/W* HA3 .... **62** C4
Formosa St *MV/WKIL* W9 .... **8** D1
Formunt Cl *CAN/RD* E16 .... **105** M4 3
Forres Gdns *GLDGN* NW11 .... **65** G7
Forrester Pth *SYD* SE26 .... **140** C8 2
Forrest Gdns
STRHM/NOR SW16 .... **156** F6
Forris Av *HYS/HAR* UB3 .... **95** M7
Forset St *MBLAR* W1H **9** K4
Forstal Cl *HAYES* BR2 .... **160** A6
Forster Rd *BECK* BR3 .... **158** E6
BRXS/STRHM SW2 .... **138** E4
TOTM N17 .... **67** M4
WALTH E17 .... **68** E7 2
Forsters Cl *CHDH* RM6 .... **72** F7
Forston St *IS* N1 .... **6** F5
Forsyte Crs *NRWD* SE19 .... **157** L4
Forsyth Gdns *WALW* SE17 .... **18** D9
Forsythia Cl *IL* IG1 .... **89** H5
Forsyth Pl *EN* EN1 .... **36** E8
Forterie Gdns *GDMY/SEVK* IG3 .... **90** A3
Fortescue Av *WHTN* TW2 .... **133** J7
Fortescue Rd *EDGW* HA8 .... **63** K2
WIM/MER SW19 .... **155** K3
Fortess Gv *KTTN* NW5 .... **84** C5 4
Fortess Rd *KTTN* NW5 .... **84** B5
Fortess Wk *KTTN* NW5 .... **84** B5 2
Forthbridge Rd *BTSEA* SW11 .... **138** A1
Forth Rd *UPMR* RM14 .... **75** K7
Fortis Cl *CAN/RD* E16 .... **106** C5
Fortis Gn *EFNCH* N2 .... **65** M4
Fortis Green Av *EFNCH* N2 .... **66** A4
Fortis Green Rd *MUSWH* N10 .... **66** A4
Fortismere Av *MUSWH* N10 .... **66** A4
Fortnam Rd *ARCH* N19 .... **84** D2
Fortnums Acre *STAN* HA7 .... **43** M8 3
Fort Rd *NTHLT* UB5 .... **79** G7
STHWK SE1 .... **19** M6
Fortrose Gdns
BRXS/STRHM SW2 .... **138** E5
Fort St *CAN/RD* E16 .... **106** B7
WCHPL E1 .... **13** K3 1
Fortunegate Rd *WLSDN* NW10 .... **81** L8
Fortune Green Rd
KIL/WHAMP NW6 .... **83** G5
Fortune La *BORE* WD6 .... **44** D1
Fortunes Md *NTHLT* UB5 .... **78** E6
Fortune St *STLK* EC1Y **12** F1
Fortune Wy *WLSDN* NW10 .... **100** A2 1
Forty Acre La *CAN/RD* E16 .... **106** A4
Forty Av *WBLY* HA9 .... **80** F3
Forty Cl *WBLY* HA9 .... **80** F3
Forty Hl *EN* EN1 .... **36** F2
Forty La *WBLY* HA9 .... **81** H2
Forumside *EDGW* HA8 .... **45** G8
The Forum *E/WMO/HCT* KT8 .... **151** H7 5
Forum Wy *EDGW* HA8 .... **45** G8
Forval Cl *MTCM* CR4 .... **155** M8
Forward Dr *KTN/HRWW/W* HA3 .... **61** M5
Foscote Ms *MV/WKIL* W9 .... **8** B1
Foscote Rd *HDN* NW4 .... **64** B6
Foskett Rd *FUL/PGN* SW6 .... **118** F7
Foss Av *CROY/NA* CR0 .... **172** A7
Fossdene Rd *CHARL* SE7 .... **124** B3
Fossdyke Cl *YEAD* UB4 .... **96** E4 3
Fosse Wy *WEA* W13 .... **98** A4
Fossil Rd *LEW* SE13 .... **123** G8
Fossington Rd *BELV* DA17 .... **126** D2 1
Foss Rd *TOOT* SW17 .... **137** K8
Fossway *BCTR* RM8 .... **90** C2
Foster Cl *CHES/WCR* EN8 .... **26** E3 1
Foster La *CITYW* EC2V **12** E4
Foster Rd *ACT* W3 .... **99** L6
CHSWK W4 .... **117** K3
PLSTW E13 .... **106** A3
Fosters Cl *CHST* BR7 .... **160** F1
SWFD E18 .... **70** B2
Foster St *HDN* NW4 .... **64** C5
Foster Wk *HDN* NW4 .... **64** C5 2
Fothergill Cl *PLSTW* E13 .... **106** A1 2
Fothergill Dr *WCHMH* N21 .... **35** L8 1
Fotheringham Rd *EN* EN1 .... **36** F7
Foulden Rd *STNW/STAM* N16 .... **85** M4
Foulden Ter *STNW/STAM* N16 .. **85** M4 3
Foulis Ter *SKENS* SW7 .... **15** G6
Foulser Rd *TOOT* SW17 .... **137** M7
Foulsham Rd *THHTH* CR7 .... **157** J6

Founders Gdns *NRWD* SE19 ... 157 J3
Foundry Cl
  BERM/RHTH SE16 ... 104 E7
Foundry Ms *CAMTN* NW1 ... 4 F7
Fountain Cl *UX/CGN* UB8 ... 95 J4
Fountain Dr *CAR* SM5 ... 182 F1
  NRWD ... 139 M8
  WAB EN9 ... 27 J7
Fountain Rd *BRXN/ST* SW9 ... 121 G6
  TOOT SW17 ... 155 K1
Fountains Av *FELT* TW13 ... 132 F7
Fountains Cl *FELT* TW13 ... 132 F6
Fountains Crs *STHGT/OAK* N14 ... 48 E2
Fountayne Rd
  SEVS/STOTM N15 ... 68 A5
  STNW/STAM N16 ... 86 A2
Fouracres *PEND* EN3 ... 37 L4
Fourland Wk *EDGW* HA8 ... 45 J8
Fournier St *WCHPL* E1 ... 13 M2
Four Seasons Crs *CHEAM* SM3 ... 169 M4
Fourth Av *GSTN* WD25 ... 21 K8
  HYS/HAR UB3 ... 95 M7
  MNPK E12 ... 88 F4
  NKENS W10 ... 100 E3
  ROMW/RG RM7 ... 91 J1
Fourth Cross Rd *WHTN* TW2 ... 133 K6
Fourth Wy *WBLY* HA9 ... 81 H4
The Four Tubs *BUSH* WD23 ... 43 K2
  BUSH WD23 ... 43 K2
The Four Wents *CHING* E4 ... 51 K4
Fowey Av *REDBR* IG4 ... 70 D6
Fowler Cl *BTSEA* SW11 ... 119 K8
  SCUP DA14 ... 162 E1
Fowler Rd *BARK/HLT* IG6 ... 54 C7
  FSTGT E7 ... 88 A4
  IS N1 ... 6 D3
Fowler's Wk *EA* W5 ... 98 D3
Fowley Cl *CHES/WCR* EN8 ... 26 F7
Fownes St *BTSEA* SW11 ... 119 L8
Fox And Knot St *FARR* EC1M ... 12 D2
Foxberry Rd *BROCKY* SE4 ... 140 E1
Foxborough Gdns *BROCKY* SE4 ... 141 G3
Foxbourne Rd *TOOT* SW17 ... 138 A6
Fox Burrow Rd *CHIG* IG7 ... 54 D6
Foxbury Av *CHST* BR7 ... 161 G2
Foxbury Cl *BMLY* BR1 ... 160 B2
  ORP BR6 ... 177 G7
Foxbury Dr *ORP* BR6 ... 177 G8
Foxbury Rd *BMLY* BR1 ... 160 B2
Fox Cl *BORE* WD6 ... 44 D1
  BUSH WD23 ... 30 B8
  CAN/RD E16 ... 106 A4
  CRW RM5 ... 55 H7
  ORP BR6 ... 177 G7
  WCHPL E1 ... 104 C3
  WEY KT13 ... 164 D7
Foxcroft Rd *WOOL/PLUM* SE18 ... 125 H6
Foxdell *NTHWD* HA6 ... 41 K8
Foxearth Rd *SAND/SEL* CR2 ... 185 J3
Foxearth Sp *SAND/SEL* CR2 ... 185 J2
Foxes Dl *BKHTH/KID* SE3 ... 124 A8
  HAYES BR2 ... 159 K6
Foxes Dr *WAN* E11 ... 70 C5
Foxes La *POTB/CUF* EN6 ... 24 C1
Foxfield Cl *NTHWD* HA6 ... 41 M8
Foxfield Rd *ORP* BR6 ... 176 D4
Foxglove Cl *STHL* UB1 ... 96 E6
  STWL/WRAY TW19 ... 130 D5
Foxglove Dr *WAN* E11 ... 70 C5
Foxglove Gdns *PUR/KEN* CR8 ... 183 L4
Foxglove La *CHSGTN* KT9 ... 168 A6
Foxglove St *ACT* W3 ... 99 M6
Foxglove Wy *MTCM* CR4 ... 171 G2
Fox Gv *WOT/HER* KT12 ... 165 H2
Foxgrove *PLMGR* N13 ... 48 E5
Foxgrove Av *BECK* BR3 ... 159 H3
Foxgrove Pth *OXHEY* WD19 ... 42 D7
Foxgrove Rd *BECK* BR3 ... 159 H3
Foxhall Rd *UPMR* RM14 ... 93 J5
Foxham Rd *ARCH* N19 ... 84 D3
Fox HI *NRWD* SE19 ... 157 M3
Fox Hill Gdns *NRWD* SE19 ... 157 L3
Foxhole Rd *ELTH/MOT* SE9 ... 142 E2
Foxholes *WEY* KT13 ... 164 D7
Fox Hollow Cl
  WOOL/PLUM SE18 ... 125 L3
Fox Hollow Dr *BXLYHS* DA16 ... 126 D8
Foxholt Gdns *WLSDN* NW10 ... 81 J7
Foxhome Cl *CHST* BR7 ... 161 G2
Fox House Rd *BELV* DA17 ... 127 H2
Foxlands Cl *GSTN* WD25 ... 20 F7
Foxlands Crs *DAGE* RM10 ... 91 J5
Foxlands Rd *DAGE* RM10 ... 91 J5
Fox La *EA* W5 ... 98 E4
  HAYES BR2 ... 175 H7
  PLMGR N13 ... 48 F4
Foxlees *ALP/SUD* HA0 ... 80 A4
Foxley Gdns *PUR/KEN* CR8 ... 184 B6
Foxley Hill Rd *PUR/KEN* CR8 ... 184 A5
Foxley La *PUR/KEN* CR8 ... 183 L5
Foxley Rd *CMBW* SE5 ... 121 G5
  PUR/KEN CR8 ... 184 B8
  THHTH CR7 ... 157 H7
Foxleys *OXHEY* WD19 ... 42 E5
Foxmead Cl *ENC/FH* EN2 ... 35 M4
Foxmore St *BTSEA* SW11 ... 119 M6
Fox Rd *CAN/RD* E16 ... 105 M4
Foxton Gv *MTCM* CR4 ... 155 K5
Foxwarren *ESH/CLAY* KT10 ... 178 F2
Foxwell St *BROCKY* SE4 ... 122 E8
Foxwood Cl *FELT* TW13 ... 132 B7
  MLHL NW7 ... 45 L6
Foxwood Green Cl *EN* EN1 ... 49 L1
Foxwood Rd *BKHTH/KID* SE3 ... 141 M1
Foyle Rd *BKHTH/KID* SE3 ... 123 M4
  TOTM N17 ... 68 A2
Framfield Cl *NFNCH/WDSP* N12 ... 47 G6
Framfield Rd *HBRY* N5 ... 85 H5
  HNWL W7 ... 97 M5
  MTCM CR4 ... 156 A3
Framlingham Crs
  ELTH/MOT SE9 ... 142 E8
Frampton Cl *BELMT* SM2 ... 182 A1
Frampton Park Rd *HOM* E9 ... 86 C6
Frampton Rd *HSLWW* TW4 ... 132 E2

  POTB/CUF EN6 ... 23 J3
Frampton St *STJWD* NW8 ... 9 H1
Francemary Rd *LEW* SE13 ... 141 G2
Frances Gdns
  SOCK/AV RM15 ... 111 M5
Frances Rd *CHING* E4 ... 51 G8
Frances St *WOOL/PLUM* SE18 ... 124 F2
Franche Court Rd *TOOT* SW17 ... 137 J7
  FELT TW13 ... 132 A7
  IL IG1 ... 89 K2
Francis Barber Cl
  STRHM/NOR SW16 ... 138 F8
Franciscan Rd *TOOT* SW17 ... 138 A8
Francis Chichester Wy
  BTSEA SW11 ... 120 A6
Francis Cl *HOR/WEW* KT19 ... 168 D6
  SHPTN TW17 ... 149 G7
Francis Gv *WIM/MER* SW19 ... 154 F7
  DART DA1 ... 143 G2
  EFNCH N2 ... 65 M5
  GFD/PVL UB6 ... 98 C1
  HRW HA1 ... 62 A6
  HSLWW TW4 ... 114 D7
  LEY E10 ... 87 J2
  PIN HA5 ... 60 C6
  STMC/STPC BR5 ... 162 D6
  WAN E11 ... 87 K3
  WATW WD18 ... 29 H7
  WLGTN SM6 ... 171 J8
Francis St *SRTFD* E15 ... 87 L5
  WEST SW1P ... 16 F5
Francis Ter *ARCH* N19 ... 84 C3
Francklyn Gdns *EDGW* HA8 ... 45 G5
Francombe Gdns *ROM* RM1 ... 74 A7
Franconia Rd *CLAP* SW4 ... 138 C2
Frank Burton Cl *CHARL* SE7 ... 124 B3
Frank Dixon Cl *DUL* SE21 ... 139 L4
Frank Dixon Wy *DUL* SE21 ... 139 L5
Frankfurt Rd *HNHL* SE24 ... 139 J2
Frankham St *DEPT* SE8 ... 123 G5
Frankland Cl *BERM/RHTH* SE16 ... 122 B1
  RKW/CH/CXG WD3 ... 41 H1
  WFD IG8 ... 52 C7
Frankland Rd *CHING* E4 ... 51 G7
  RKW/CH/CXG WD3 ... 41 H1
Franklin Av *CHESW* EN7 ... 26 A3
Franklin Cl *KUT* KT1 ... 153 G6
  LEW SE13 ... 123 H6
  TRDG/WHET N20 ... 47 J2
  WNWD SE27 ... 139 H7
Franklin Crs *MTCM* CR4 ... 156 C7
Franklin Rd *BXLYHN* DA7 ... 126 E3
  HCH RM12 ... 92 C6
  PGE/AN SE20 ... 158 C3
  WAT WD17 ... 29 H5
  WOT/HER KT12 ... 165 G1
Franklins Ms *RYLN/HDSTN* HA2 ... 79 J2
Franklin Sq *WKENS* W14 ... 118 F3
Franklin's Rw *CHEL* SW3 ... 15 M7
Franklin St *BOW* E3 ... 105 H2
  SEVS/STOTM N15 ... 67 L7
Franklin Wy *CROY/NA* CR0 ... 171 L3
Franklyn Gdns *BARK/HLT* IG6 ... 53 K8
Franklyn Rd *WLSDN* NW10 ... 81 H7
  WOT/HER KT12 ... 165 H1
Frank Martin Ct *CHESW* EN7 ... 26 A3
Franks Av *NWMAL* KT3 ... 153 J7
Franks Wood Av
  STMC/STPC BR5 ... 161 H4
Frankswood Av *WDR/YW* UB7 ... 94 F5
Franlaw Crs *PLMGR* N13 ... 49 J6
Franmil Rd *EMPK* RM11 ... 73 M8
Fransfield Gv *SYD* SE26 ... 140 B7
Frant Cl *PGE/AN* SE20 ... 158 C3
Franthorne Wy *CAT* SE6 ... 141 H6
Frant Rd *THHTH* CR7 ... 157 H8
Fraser Cl *BXLY* DA5 ... 145 J5
Fraser Rd *CHES/WCR* EN8 ... 26 E1
  ED N9 ... 50 B5
  ERITH DA8 ... 127 J3
  GFD/PVL UB6 ... 80 C8
  LEY E10 ... 69 H6
Fraser St *CHSWK* W4 ... 117 L3
Frating Crs *WFD* IG8 ... 52 B8
Frays Av *WDR/YW* UB7 ... 94 D8
Frays Cl *WDR/YW* UB7 ... 112 D1
Frayslea *UX/CGN* UB8 ... 94 C1
Fray's Waye *UX/CGN* UB8 ... 76 C8
Frazer Av *RSLP* HA4 ... 78 C5
Frazer Cl *ROMW/RG* RM7 ... 73 M8
Frazier St *STHWK* SE1 ... 18 A2
Frean St *BERM/RHTH* SE16 ... 122 A1
Freda Corbett Cl *PECK* SE15 ... 122 A5
Frederica Cl *CHING* E4 ... 51 K2
  PEND EN3 ... 37 J5
Frederica Rd *HOLWY* N7 ... 5 L1
Frederick Cl *BAY/PAD* W2 ... 9 K6
  SUT SM1 ... 169 M6
Frederick Gdns *SUT* SM1 ... 169 M7
Frederick Pl *WOOL/PLUM* SE18 ... 125 H3
Frederick Rd *RAIN* RM13 ... 109 K1
  SUT SM1 ... 169 M7
  WALW SE17 ... 18 D8
Frederick's Pl *LOTH* EC2R ... 13 G5
  NFNCH/WDSP N12 ... 47 J6
Frederick Sq *POP/IOD* E14 ... 106 E6
Frederick's Rw *FSBYW* WC1X ... 5 L8
Frederick Ter *HACK* E8 ... 7 L2
Frederic Ms *KTBR* SW1X ... 16 A2
Frederic St *WALTH* E17 ... 68 E6
Fredora Av *YEAD* UB4 ... 95 M3
Freeborne Gdns *RAIN* RM13 ... 92 A6
Freedom Cl *WALTH* E17 ... 68 D5
Freedom Rd *STHGT/OAK* N14 ... 34 ?
Freedom St *BTSEA* SW11 ... 119 M7
Freedown La *BELMT* SM2 ... 182 B6
Freegrove Rd *HOLWY* N7 ... 84 E5
Freeland Pk *HDN* NW4 ... 64 C3
Freeland Rd *EA* W5 ... 98 F6
Freelands Av *SAND/SEL* CR2 ... 185 K2
Freelands Gv *BMLY* BR1 ... 160 B5
Freelands Rd *BMLY* BR1 ... 160 B4
Freeland Wy *ERITH* DA8 ... 128 C6
Freeling St *IS* N1 ... 5 L2
Freeman Cl *NTHLT* UB5 ... 78 E7
  SHPTN TW17 ... 149 J4

Freeman Dr *E/WMO/HCT* KT8 ... 150 F7
Freeman Rd *MRDN* SM4 ... 155 K8
Freemans La *HYS/HAR* UB3 ... 95 L6
Freemantle Av *PEND* EN3 ... 37 K8
Freemantle St *WALW* SE17 ... 19 J7
Freeman Wy *EMPK* RM11 ... 74 E7
Freemasons Rd *CAN/RD* E16 ... 106 B5
  CROY/NA CR0 ... 173 J1
Freesia Cl *ORP* BR6 ... 176 F7
Freethorpe Cl *NRWD* SE19 ... 157 L4
Freezeland Wy *HGDN/ICK* UB10 ... 77 H6
Freke Rd *BTSEA* SW11 ... 120 A8
Fremantle Rd *BARK/HLT* IG6 ... 71 H5
  BELV DA17 ... 127 G2
Fremont St *HOM* E9 ... 86 C8
  HOM E9 ... 86 C8
French Pl *SDTCH* EC2A ... 7 K8
French St *SUN* TW16 ... 150 C5
Frendsbury Rd *BROCKY* SE4 ... 140 E1
Frensham Cl *STHL* UB1 ... 96 F3
Frensham Dr *CROY/NA* CR0 ... 186 C1
  PUT/ROE SW15 ... 136 A7
Frensham Rd *BFN/LL* DA15 ... 143 K6
  PUR/KEN CR8 ... 184 B7
Frensham St *PECK* SE15 ... 122 F6
Frere St *BTSEA* SW11 ... 119 L7
Freshfield Av *HACK* E8 ... 7 L1
Freshfield Cl *LEW* SE13 ... 141 K1
Freshfield Dr *STHGT/OAK* N14 ... 48 B2
Freshfields *CROY/NA* CR0 ... 173 M2
Freshfields Av *UPMR* RM14 ... 93 H5
Freshford St *TOOT* SW17 ... 137 J7
Freshmount Gdns
  HOR/WEW KT19 ... 180 B4
Freshwater Cl *TOOT* SW17 ... 156 A2
Freshwater Rd *BCTR* RM8 ... 90 D1
  TOOT SW17 ... 156 A2
Fresh Wharf Rd *BARK* IG11 ... 89 H8
Freshwood Cl *BECK* BR3 ... 159 H4
Freshwood Wy *WLGTN* SM6 ... 183 J7
Freston Gdns *EBAR* EN4 ... 35 G8
Freston Rd *NKENS* W10 ... 100 D6
Freta Rd *BXLYHS* DA6 ... 144 F2
Frewin Rd *WAND/EARL* SW18 ... 137 K5
Friar Ms *WNWD* SE27 ... 139 H7
Friar Rd *STMC/STPC* BR5 ... 162 A8
  YEAD UB4 ... 96 D3
Friars Av *PUT/ROE* SW15 ... 135 M7
  TRDG/WHET N20 ... 47 L5
Friars Cl *CHING* E4 ... 51 J5
  NTHLT UB5 ... 96 C2
Friars Gdns *ACT* W3 ... 99 K5
Friars Gate Cl *WFD* IG8 ... 52 A6
Friars La *RCH/KEW* TW9 ... 134 D2
Friars Md *POP/IOD* E14 ... 123 J1
Friars Ms *ELTH/MOT* SE9 ... 143 G2
Friars Place La *ACT* W3 ... 99 K6
Friar's Rd *EHAM* E6 ... 88 D7
Friars Stile Rd
  RCHPK/HAM TW10 ... 134 E3
The Friars *CHIG* IG7 ... 53 L6
Friars Wk *ABYW* SE2 ... 126 D3
  STHGT/OAK N14 ... 48 B2
Friars Wy *ACT* W3 ... 99 K5
  BUSH WD23 ... 29 M4
  KGLGY WD4 ... 20 A3
Friary Cl *NFNCH/WDSP* N12 ... 47 L7
Friary La *WFD* IG8 ... 52 A6
Friary Park Ct *ACT* W3 ... 99 J5
Friary Rd *ACT* W3 ... 99 K5
  NFNCH/WDSP N12 ... 47 K6
  PECK SE15 ... 122 A5
Friary Wy *NFNCH/WDSP* N12 ... 47 L6
Friday HI *CHING* E4 ... 51 L5
Friday HI East *CHING* E4 ... 51 L5
Friday HI West *CHING* E4 ... 51 L4
Friday Rd *ERITH* DA8 ... 127 K3
  MTCM CR4 ... 155 M3
Friday St *BLKFR* EC4V ... 12 E6
Frideswide Pl *KTTN* NW5 ... 84 C5
Friendly Pl *LEW* SE13 ... 123 H6
Friendly St *DEPT* SE8 ... 123 G6
Friendly Street Ms *DEPT* SE8 ... 123 G7
Friends Av *CHES/WCR* EN8 ... 26 D5
Friends' Rd *CROY/NA* CR0 ... 182 D5
  PUR/KEN CR8 ... 184 B5
Friend St *FSBYE* EC1V ... 6 C7
Friern Barnet La
  TRDG/WHET N20 ... 47 K5
Friern Barnet Rd
  FBAR/BDGN N11 ... 48 A7
Friern Mount Dr
  TRDG/WHET N20 ... 47 J2
Friern Pk *NFNCH/WDSP* N12 ... 47 H7
Friern Rd *EDUL* SE22 ... 140 A3
Friern Watch Av
  NFNCH/WDSP N12 ... 47 K6
Frigate Ms *DEPT* SE8 ... 123 G4
Frimley Av *EMPK* RM11 ... 93 G1
  WLGTN SM6 ... 171 L7
Frimley Cl *CROY/NA* CR0 ... 186 C1
  WIM/MER SW19 ... 136 E6
Frimley Ct *SCUP* DA14 ... 162 C1
Frimley Crs *CROY/NA* CR0 ... 186 C1
Frimley Gdns *MTCM* CR4 ... 155 L6
Frimley Rd *CHSGTN* KT9 ... 167 K7
  GDMY/SEVK IG3 ... 89 J3
Frimley Wy *WCHPL* E1 ... 104 D3
Fringewood Cl *NTHWD* HA6 ... 59 H2
Frinstead Cl *STMC/STPC* BR5 ... 162 D7
Frinsted Rd *ERITH* DA8 ... 127 K5
Frinton Cl *OXHEY* WD19 ... 42 B4
Frinton Dr *WFD* IG8 ... 69 K1
Frinton Ms *IL* IG1 ... 71 G7
Frinton Rd *CRW* RM5 ... 73 G1
  EHAM E6 ... 106 D2
  SCUP DA14 ... 144 D6
  SEVS/STOTM N15 ... 67 L7
  TOOT SW17 ... 156 A2
Friston St *FUL/PGN* SW6 ... 119 H7
Friswell Pl *BXLYHN* DA7 ... 127 G8
Fritham Cl *NWMAL* KT3 ... 168 E1
Frith Ct *MLHL* NW7 ... 64 E1
Frith Knowle *WOT/HER* KT12 ... 165 H7
Frith La *MLHL* NW7 ... 46 E1
Frith Rd *CROY/NA* CR0 ... 172 C4

  WAN E11 ... 87 J4
Frith St *SOHO/SHAV* W1D ... 11 C5
Frithville Gdns *SHB* W12 ... 100 C7
Frithwood Av *NTHWD* HA6 ... 41 M8
Frizlands La *DAGE* RM10 ... 91 H3
Frobisher Cl *BUSH* WD23 ... 43 G1
  PIN HA5 ... 60 D8
Frobisher Crs
  STWL/WRAY TW19 ... 130 E4
Frobisher Rd *CEND/HSY/T* N8 ... 67 G1
  EHAM E6 ... 106 F5
  ERITH DA8 ... 128 A5
Frog La *DAGW* RM9 ... 109 K4
Frogley Rd *EDUL* SE22 ... 139 M1
Frogmoor La *RKW/CH/CXG* WD3 ... 40 D4
Frogmore *WAND/EARL* SW18 ... 137 G2
Frogmore Av *YEAD* UB4 ... 95 L3
Frogmore Cl *CHEAM* SM3 ... 169 K5
Frogmore Gdns *CHEAM* SM3 ... 169 L6
  YEAD UB4 ... 95 L3
Frognal *HAMP* NW3 ... 83 J4
Frognal Av *HRW* HA1 ... 61 M5
  SCUP DA14 ... 162 A2
Frognal Cl *HAMP* NW3 ... 83 J4
Frognal Gdns *HAMP* NW3 ... 83 H5
Frognal La *HAMP* NW3 ... 83 H5
Frognal Pl *SCUP* DA14 ... 162 A1
Frognal Ri *HAMP* NW3 ... 83 J3
Frognal Wy *HAMP* NW3 ... 83 J3
Froissart Rd *ELTH/MOT* SE9 ... 142 C2
Frome Rd *SEVS/STOTM* N15 ... 67 H4
Frome St *IS* N1 ... 6 E5
Fromondes Rd *CHEAM* SM3 ... 169 L7
Front La *UPMR* RM14 ... 93 L2
Froude St *VX/NE* SW8 ... 120 B7
Frowyke Crs *POTB/CUF* EN6 ... 22 A5
Fruen Rd *EBED/NFELT* TW14 ... 131 M4
Fryatt Rd *TOTM* N17 ... 67 K1
Fry Cl *CRW* RM5 ... 55 G7
Fryent Cl *KTN/HRWW/WS* HA3 ... 63 G7
Fryent Crs *CDALE/KGS* NW9 ... 63 G7
Fryent Flds *CDALE/KGS* NW9 ... 63 L7
Fryent Gv *CDALE/KGS* NW9 ... 63 L7
Fry Rd *EHAM* E6 ... 88 D7
  WLSDN NW10 ... 81 M8
Fryston Av *COUL/CHIP* CR5 ... 183 H8
  CROY/NA CR0 ... 173 G4
Fuchsia Cl *ABYW* SE2 ... 126 B3
Fulbeck Dr *CDALE/KGS* NW9 ... 63 L2
Fulbeck Wy *RYLN/HDSTN* HA2 ... 61 J3
Fulbourne Rd *WALTH* E17 ... 69 J2
Fulbourne St *WCHPL* E1 ... 104 B4
Fulbrook La *SOCK/AV* RM15 ... 111 M6
Fulford Gv *OXHEY* WD19 ... 42 C4
Fulford Rd *HOR/WEW* KT19 ... 180 D1
Fulford St *BERM/RHTH* SE16 ... 104 B8
Fulham Broadway
  FUL/PGN SW6 ... 119 C5
Fulham *UX/CGN* UB8 ... 95 J3
Fulham High St
  FUL/PGN SW6 ... 118 E8
Fulham Palace Rd
  FUL/PGN SW6 ... 118 D5
Fulham Park Gdns
  FUL/PGN SW6 ... 118 F7
Fulham Park Rd *FUL/PGN* SW6 ... 118 F7
Fulham Rd *FUL/PGN* SW6 ... 118 F7
  WBPTN SW10 ... 14 F9
Fullarton Crs *SOCK/AV* RM15 ... 111 M5
Fullbrooks Av *WPK* KT4 ... 168 F3
Fuller Cl *ORP* BR6 ... 177 M7
Fuller Gdns *WATN* WD24 ... 29 H2
  WATN WD24 ... 29 H2
Fuller Rd *BCTR* RM8 ... 90 C3
Fullers Av *SURB* KT6 ... 167 M4
  WFD IG8 ... 69 M1
Fullers Cl *CRW* RM5 ... 73 J1
  WAB EN9 ... 27 M6
Fuller's Rd *SWFD* E18 ... 69 M2
Fuller St *HDN* NW4 ... 64 B2
Fullers Wy North *SURB* KT6 ... 167 M5
Fullers Wy South *CHSGTN* KT9 ... 167 L6
Fuller's Wd *CROY/NA* CR0 ... 174 A7
Fullerton Rd *CAR* SM5 ... 182 E2
  CROY/NA CR0 ... 172 F2
  WAND/EARL SW18 ... 137 J2
Fuller Wy *HYS/HAR* UB3 ... 113 M3
Fullwell Av *CLAY* IG5 ... 71 G2
Fullwood's Ms *IS* N1 ... 7 H7
Fulmar Rd *RAIN* RM13 ... 92 B6
Fulmead St *FUL/PGN* SW6 ... 119 H6
Fulmer Cl *HPTN* TW12 ... 150 E1
Fulmer Rd *CAN/RD* E16 ... 106 D4
Fulmer Wy *WEA* W13 ... 116 D1
Fulready Rd *LEY* E10 ... 69 K6
Fulstone Cl *HSLWW* TW4 ... 132 F1
Fulthorp Rd *BKHTH/KID* SE3 ... 123 M7
Fulton Ms *BAY/PAD* W2 ... 8 F6
Fulton Rd *WBLY* HA9 ... 81 G3
Fulwell Park Av *WHTN* TW2 ... 133 J4
Fulwell Rd *HPTN* TW12 ... 133 K8
Fulwich Rd *DART* DA1 ... 146 F3
Fulwood Av *ALP/SUD* HA0 ... 98 F1
Fulwood Gdns *TWK* TW1 ... 133 M3
Fulwood Wk *WIM/MER* SW19 ... 136 E5
Furber St *HMSMTH* W6 ... 118 D1
Furham Fld *PIN* HA5 ... 61 G1
Furley Rd *PECK* SE15 ... 122 A5
Furlong Cl *MTCM* CR4 ... 171 H3
Furlong Rd *HOLWY* N7 ... 85 G6
Furmage St *WAND/EARL* SW18 ... 137 H4
Furneaux Av *WNWD* SE27 ... 157 H1
Furner Cl *DART* DA1 ... 127 M8
Furness Rd *FUL/PGN* SW6 ... 119 H7
  MRDN SM4 ... 170 B1
  RYLN/HDSTN HA2 ... 61 H8
  WLSDN NW10 ... 100 A1
Furness Wy *HCH* RM12 ... 92 A5
Furnival St *FLST/FETLN* EC4A ... 12 A4
Furrow La *HOM* E9 ... 86 C5
The Furrows *WOT/HER* KT12 ... 165 J4
Fursby Av *FNCH* N3 ... 47 G8
Further Acre *CDALE/KGS* NW9 ... 63 M3
Furtherfield *ABLGY* WD5 ... 20 E5
Furtherfield Cl *CROY/NA* CR0 ... 172 A1
Further Green Rd *CAT* SE6 ... 141 L4

Furze Cl *OXHEY* WD19 ... 42 C5
Furzedown Dr *TOOT* SW17 ... 156 B1
Furzedown Rd *BELMT* SM2 ... 182 C4
  TOOT SW17 ... 156 B1
Furze Farm Cl *CHDH* RM6 ... 72 C3
Furze Fld *LHD/OX* KT22 ... 178 D6
Furzefield Cl *CHST* BR7 ... 161 H2
Furzefield Rd *BKHTH/KID* SE3 ... 124 B4
Furzeground Wy *STKPK* UB11 ... 95 J7
Furzeham Rd *WDR/YW* UB7 ... 94 B8
Furze HI *PUR/KEN* CR8 ... 183 L4
Furzehill Rd *BORE* WD6 ... 32 C8
Furzehill Sq *STMC/STPC* BR5 ... 162 B7
Furze La *PUR/KEN* CR8 ... 183 L4
Furze Rd *THHTH* CR7 ... 157 H3
Furze St *BOW* E3 ... 105 C4
Furzewood *SUN* TW16 ... 150 A4
Fusedale Wy *SOCK/AV* RM15 ... 111 M6
Fyfe Wy *BMLY* BR1 ... 160 A5
Fyfield Cl *BECK* BR3 ... 159 K7
Fyfield Dr *SOCK/AV* RM15 ... 111 M6
Fyfield Rd *BRXN/ST* SW9 ... 121 G8
  EN EN1 ... 36 B6
  RAIN RM13 ... 91 M8
  WALTH E17 ... 69 K4
  WFD IG8 ... 70 C1
Fynes St *WEST* SW1P ... 17 G5

G

Gabion Av *PUR* RM19 ... 129 K2
Gable Cl *ABLGY* WD5 ... 20 E5
  DART DA1 ... 146 A2
  PIN HA5 ... 61 G1
Gable Ct *SYD* SE26 ... 140 B8
Gables Av *ASHF* TW15 ... 148 F1
  BORE WD6 ... 31 M6
Gables Cl *CMBW* SE5 ... 121 L6
  LEE/GVPK SE12 ... 142 A5
The Gables *LHD/OX* KT22 ... 178 C5
  WBLY HA9 ... 80 F3
  WEY KT13 ... 164 C7
Gabriel Cl *CRW* RM5 ... 73 J1
  FELT TW13 ... 132 E8
Gabrielle Cl *WBLY* HA9 ... 80 F3
Gabriel St *FSTH* SE23 ... 140 D4
Gad Cl *PLSTW* E13 ... 106 B2
Gaddesden Av *WBLY* HA9 ... 80 F6
Gaddesden Crs *GSTN* WD25 ... 21 K7
Gade Av *WATW* WD18 ... 28 E7
Gade Bank *RKW/CH/CXG* WD3 ... 28 D7
Gade Cl *HYS/HAR* UB3 ... 96 B7
  WATW WD18 ... 28 E7
Gadesden Rd *HOR/WEW* KT19 ... 168 C5
Gade Valley Cl *KGLGY* WD4 ... 20 A1
Gadsbury Cl *CDALE/KGS* NW9 ... 63 M7
Gadsden Cl *UPMR* RM14 ... 75 L7
Gadwall Cl *CAN/RD* E16 ... 106 B5
Gage Rd *CAN/RD* E16 ... 105 L4
Gainford St *IS* N1 ... 6 A3
Gainsboro Gdns *GFD/PVL* UB6 ... 79 L5
Gainsborough Av *DART* DA1 ... 146 C2
  MNPK E12 ... 89 G5
Gainsborough Cl *BECK* BR3 ... 159 G3
  ESH/CLAY KT10 ... 166 E3
Gainsborough Ct *SHB* W12 ... 100 C8
  WOT/HER KT12 ... 165 H2
Gainsborough Dr
  SAND/SEL CR2 ... 185 G6
Gainsborough Gdns *EDGW* HA8 ... 62 F3
  GLDGN NW11 ... 64 F8
  HAMP NW3 ... 83 M3
  ISLW TW7 ... 133 K2
Gainsborough Rd *BCTR* RM8 ... 90 B3
  CHSWK W4 ... 117 M2
  HOR/WEW KT19 ... 180 C3
  NFNCH/WDSP N12 ... 47 H7
  NWMAL KT3 ... 168 D1
  RAIN RM13 ... 92 A8
  RCH/KEW TW9 ... 116 F7
  SRTFD E15 ... 105 L2
  WAN E11 ... 69 L8
  WFD IG8 ... 52 E3
  YEAD UB4 ... 95 J1
Gainsborough Sq
  BXLYHN DA7 ... 126 D8
Gainsford Rd *WALTH* E17 ... 68 F5
Gainsford St *STHWK* SE1 ... 13 L9
Gairloch Rd *CMBW* SE5 ... 121 L7
Gaisford St *KTTN* NW5 ... 84 C6
Gaitskell Rd *ELTH/MOT* SE9 ... 143 J5
Galahad Rd *BMLY* BR1 ... 142 A7
Galata Rd *BARN* SW13 ... 118 A5
Galatea Sq *PECK* SE15 ... 122 B8
Galbraith St *POP/IOD* E14 ... 123 J1
Galdana Av *BAR* EN5 ... 34 C6
Galeborough Av *WFD* IG8 ... 69 K1
Gale Cl *HPTN* TW12 ... 150 E2
  MTCM CR4 ... 155 K6
Galena Rd *HMSMTH* W6 ... 118 D3
Galen Cl *HOR/WEW* KT19 ... 180 A4
Galesbury Rd
  WAND/EARL SW18 ... 137 J3
Gale St *BOW* E3 ... 105 H4
  CHEL SW3 ... 15 J7
  DAGW RM9 ... 90 B6
Gales Wy *WFD* IG8 ... 70 E1
Galgate Cl *WIM/MER* SW19 ... 136 E5
Gallants Farm Rd *EBAR* EN4 ... 47 L2
Galleon Bvd *GRH* DA9 ... 147 K1
Galleon Cl *BERM/RHTH* SE16 ... 104 C8
  ERITH DA8 ... 127 K2
Gallery Gdns *NTHLT* UB5 ... 96 D1
Gallery Rd *DUL* SE21 ... 139 K5
Galleyhill Rd *WAB* EN9 ... 27 L5
Galley La *BAR* EN5 ... 33 G3
Galleywall Rd
  BERM/RHTH SE16 ... 122 B2
Galleywood Crs *CRW* RM5 ... 55 K8
Galliard Crs *ED* N9 ... 50 A2
Galliard Rd *ED* N9 ... 50 A2
Gallia Rd *HBRY* N5 ... 85 H5
Gallions Cl *BARK* IG11 ... 108 A2
Gallions Rd *CAN/RD* E16 ... 107 H6
  CHARL SE7 ... 124 B2

Gallions View Rd *THMD* SE28 .... 107 L8 ▣
Gallon Cl *CHARL* SE7 .... 124 C2
The Gallop *BELMT* SM2 .... 182 D2
SAND/SEL CR2 .... 185 H1
Gallosson Rd
WOOL/PLUM SE18 .... 125 L2
Galloway Pth *CROY/NA* CR0 .... 172 D6
Galloway Rd *SHB* W12 .... 100 A7
Gallows HI *KGLGY* WD4 .... 20 C4
Gallows Hill La *ABLGY* WD5 .... 20 C5
Gallus Cl *WCHMH* N21 .... 48 F1
Gallus Sq *BKHTH/KID* SE3 .... 124 B8
Galpin's Rd *THHTH* CR7 .... 156 E7
Galsworthy Av *CHDH* RM6 .... 72 B8
Galsworthy Rd *CRICK* NW2 .... 82 E4
KUTN/CMB KT2 .... 153 H4
Galton St *NKENS* W10 .... 100 E3
Galva Cl *EBAR* EN4 .... 35 G7
Galveston Rd *PUT/ROE* SW15 ... 136 F2
Galway St *FSBYE* EC1V 6 F8
Gambetta St *VX/NE* SW8 .... 120 B7 ▣
Gambia St *STHWK* SE1 .... 12 D9
Gambole Rd *TOOT* SW17 .... 137 H5
Games Rd *EBAR* EN4 .... 34 E6
Gamlen Rd *PUT/ROE* SW15 ...... 136 D1
Gammons La *WATN* WD24 .... 29 G2
Gamuel Cl *WALTH* E17 .... 69 G7 ▣
Gander Green Crs *HPTN* TW12 .. 151 L4
Gander Green La *CHEAM* SM3 ... 169 L4
SUT SM1 .... 170 A8
Ganders Ash *GSTN* WD25 .... 21 G6 ▣
Gandhi Cl *WALTH* E17 .... 69 G7
Gandhi Ct *WATN* WD24 .... 29 K5 ▣
Gant Ct *WAB* EN9 .... 27 M7
Ganton St *SOHO/CST* W1F .... 10 F5 ▣
Ganton Wk *OXHEY* WD19 .... 42 E6 ▣
Gantshill Crs *HPTN/NBYPK* IG2 .. 71 G6
Gap Rd *WIM/MER* SW19 .... 155 L5 ▣
Garage Rd *ACT* W3 .... 99 G5
Garbrand Wk *EW* KT17 .... 180 F2
Garbutt Pl *MHST* W1U .... 10 B2 ▣
Garbutt Rd *UPMR* RM14 .... 93 J2 ▣
Garden Av *BXLYHN* DA7 .... 126 F8
MTCM CR4 .... 156 B3
Garden Cl *ASHF* TW15 .... 149 J2 ▣
BAR EN5 .... 33 J7
BNSTD SM7 .... 182 A8
CHING E4 .... 51 G7 ▣
HPTN TW12 .... 150 F1
LEE/GVPK SE12 .... 142 B7
NTHLT UB5 .... 78 E8
PUT/ROE SW15 .... 136 B4
RSLP HA4 .... 77 L2
WAT WD17 .... 28 F5
WLGTN SM6 .... 171 L7
Gardeners Cl *FBAR/BDGN* N11 .. 48 A1 ▣
Gardeners Rd *CROY/NA* CR0 .... 172 B3
Gardenia Rd *EN* EN1 .... 49 L1
Gardenia Wy *WFD* IG8 .... 52 A7 ▣
Garden La *BMLY* BR1 .... 160 C2
BRXS/STRHM SW2 .... 138 F5
Garden Pl *RDART* DA2 .... 146 D7
Garden Rd *ABLGY* WD5 .... 20 E4 ▣
BMLY BR1 .... 160 B3
PGE/AN SE20 .... 158 C4
RCH/KEW TW9 .... 117 G8 ▣
STJWD NW8 .... 2 F7
WOT/HER KT12 .... 165 H1
Garden Rw *STHWK* SE1 .... 18 C4
Garden St *WCHPL* E1 .... 104 D4
Garden Ter *PIM* SW1V 17 G7
Garden Wk *BECK* BR3 .... 158 F4
SDTCH EC2A 7 J9
Garden Wy *WLSDN* NW10 .... 81 J6
Gardiner Av *CRICK* NW2 .... 82 C5 ▣
Gardiner Cl *BCTR* RM8 .... 90 D4 ▣
PEND EN3 .... 50 D1
STMC/STPC BR5 .... 162 C5
Gardner Cl *WAN* E11 .... 70 B7
Gardner Pl
EBED/NFELT TW14 .... 132 B3 ▣
Gardner Rd *PLSTW* E13 .... 106 B3
Gardners La *BLKFR* EC4V 12 E6
Gardnor Rd *HAMP* NW3 .... 83 K4 ▣
Gard St *FSBYE* EC1V 6 D7
Garendon Gdns *MRDN* SM4 ..... 170 B2 ▣
Garendon Rd *MRDN* SM4 .... 170 B2
Gareth Cl *WPK* KT4 .... 169 K4 ▣
Gareth Gv *BMLY* BR1 .... 142 A8
Garfield Rd *BTSEA* SW11 .... 120 A8
CHING E4 .... 51 K3
PEND EN3 .... 37 J7
PLSTW E13 .... 105 M3 ▣
TWK TW1 .... 134 A3
WIM/MER SW19 .... 155 J2
Garfield St *WATN* WD24 .... 29 H3
Garford St *POP/IOD* E14 .... 105 G6 ▣
Garibaldi St *WOOL/PLUM* SE18 . 125 L2
Garland Cl *CHES/WCR* EN8 .... 26 E4 ▣
Garland Dr *STAN* HA7 .... 62 C2
WOOL/PLUM SE18 .... 125 K5
Garland Wy *EMPK* RM11 .... 74 E5
Garlick HI *BLKFR* EC4V 12 F6
Garlies Rd *FSTH* SE23 .... 140 E7
Garlinge Rd *CRICK* NW2 .... 82 E6
Garman Cl *UED* N18 .... 49 K7
Garman Rd *TOTM* N17 .... 50 C8 ▣
TOTM N17 .... 68 C1
Garnault Ms *CLKNW* EC1R .... 6 B8 ▣
Garnault Pl *CLKNW* EC1R 6 B8
Garnault Rd *EN* EN1 .... 36 F3
Garner Rd *WALTH* E17 .... 69 J2
Garner St *BETH* E2 .... 104 A1 ▣
Garnet Rd *THHTH* CR7 .... 157 J7
WLSDN NW10 .... 81 L6
Garnet St *WAP* E1W 104 C6
Garnett Cl *ELTH/MOT* SE9 .... 124 F8
WATN WD24 .... 29 K2
Garnett Dr *LCOL/BKTW* AL2 ...... 21 M2

Garnett Rd *HAMP* NW3 .... 83 M5
Garnham St *STNW/STAM* N16 ... 85 M2 ▣
Garnies Cl *PECK* SE15 .... 121 M5
Garrad's Rd *STRHM/NOR* SW16 . 138 D7
CHST BR7 .... 161 H1 ▣
Garratt Cl *CROY/NA* CR0 .... 171 L6
Garratt La *TOOT* SW17 .... 137 K8
WAND/EARL SW18 .... 137 H4
Garratt Rd *EDGW* HA8 .... 62 B3
Garratts Rd *BUSH* WD23 .... 43 J2
Garratt Ter *TOOT* SW17 .... 137 L8
Garrett St *STLK* EC1Y 6 F9
Garrick Av *GLDGN* NW11 .... 64 E7
Garrick Cl *BTSEA* SW11 .... 137 J1
EA W5 .... 98 E3
RCH/KEW TW9 .... 134 C2
STA TW18 .... 148 A3
WOT/HER KT12 .... 165 H6
Garrick Crs *CROY/NA* CR0 .... 172 E4
Garrick Dr *HDN* NW4 .... 64 C3
WOOL/PLUM SE18 .... 125 K1
Garrick Gdns *E/WMO/HCT* KT8 . 151 G6
Garrick Pk *HDN* NW4 .... 64 C3
GFD/PVL UB6 .... 97 H3
RCH/KEW TW9 .... 117 G7 ▣
Garrick St *COVGDN* WC2E .... 11 J6 ▣
Garrick Wy *HDN* NW4 .... 64 D3
Garrison Cl *HSLWW* TW4 .... 132 F2
WOOL/PLUM SE18 .... 125 G5
Garrison La *CHSGTN* KT9 .... 171 L1 ▣
Garrolds Cl *SWLY* BR8 .... 163 K5
Garry Cl *ROM* RM1 .... 73 L1
Garry Wy *ROM* RM1 .... 73 L1
Garsdale Cl *FBAR/BDGN* N11 .... 48 A8
Garside Cl *HPTN* TW12 .... 151 H3
WOOL/PLUM SE18 .... 125 K1
Garsmouth Wy *GSTN* WD25 ...... 29 K1
Garson Rd *ESH/CLAY* KT10 ..... 165 H7
Garston Crs *GSTN* WD25 .... 21 J7 ▣
Garston Dr *GSTN* WD25 .... 21 J7
Garston La *GSTN* WD25 .... 21 K7
PUR/KEN CR8 .... 184 D8
Garth Cl *KUTN/CMB* KT2 .... 152 F1
MRDN SM4 .... 169 K2
RSLP HA4 .... 78 D1
Garthland Dr *BAR* EN5 .... 33 H8
Garthorne Rd *FSTH* SE23 .... 140 D4
Garth Rd *CHSWK* W4 .... 117 K3
CRICK NW2 .... 82 F2
KUTN/CMB KT2 .... 152 F1
MRDN SM4 .... 169 K3
Garthside *RCHPK/HAM* TW10 .. 152 E1
The Garth *ABLGY* WD5 .... 20 D6
HPTN TW12 .... 151 H2
KTN/HRWW/W HA3 .... 62 F7
Garthway *NFNCH/WDSP* N12 .... 47 L3
Gartlet Rd *WAT* WD17 .... 29 H6
Gartmoor Gdns
WIM/MER SW19 .... 136 F5
Gartmore Rd *GDMY/SEVK* IG3 ... 89 M1
Garton Pl *WAND/EARL* SW18 ... 137 J5
Gartons Cl *PEND* EN3 .... 37 J8
Gartons Wy *BTSEA* SW11 .... 119 J8
Garvary Rd *CAN/RD* E16 .... 106 B5
Garway Rd *BAY/PAD* W2 .... 8 C5
Gascoigne Gdns *WFD* IG8 .... 69 L1
Gascoigne Pl *BETH* E2 .... 7 L7
Gascoigne Rd *BARK* IG11 .... 89 J8
CROY/NA CR0 .... 186 C3
WEY KT13 .... 164 B5 ▣
Gascony Av *KIL/WHAMP* NW6 ..... 2 A2
Gascoyne Av *HARH* RM3 .... 74 D2
Gascoyne Dr *DART* DA1 .... 127 M8
Gascoyne Rd *HOM* E9 .... 86 D7
Gaselee St *POP/IOD* E14 .... 105 J6
Gasholder Pl *LBTH* SE11 .... 17 M8
Gaskarth Rd *BAL* SW12 .... 138 B3
EDGW HA8 .... 63 J2
Gaskell Rd *HGT* N6 .... 65 M7
Gaskell St *CLAP* SW4 .... 120 M7
Gaskin St *IS* N1 .... 6 C3
Gaspar Cl *ECT* SW5 .... 14 D5 ▣
Gaspar Ms *ECT* SW5 .... 14 D5 ▣
Gassiot Rd *TOOT* SW17 .... 137 M8
Gassiot Wy *SUT* SM1 .... 170 D5
Gastein Rd *HMSMTH* W6 .... 118 D4
Gaston Bell Cl
RCH/KEW TW9 .... 116 F8 ▣
Gaston Bridge Rd
SHPTN TW17 .... 149 L8 ▣
SHPTN TW17 .... 164 D1
Gaston Rd *MTCM* CR4 .... 156 A6
Gaston Wy *SHPTN* TW17 .... 149 K8
Gataker St *BERM/RHTH* SE16 .. 122 B1 ▣
Gatcombe Ms *EA* W5 .... 98 F6 ▣
Gatcombe Rd *ARCH* N19 .... 84 D3
Gatcombe Wy *EBAR* EN4 .... 34 F6
Gate Cl *BORE* WD6 .... 32 C4
Gate End *NTHWD* HA6 .... 60 A1
Gateforth St *STJWD* NW8 .... 9 J1
Gatehill Rd *NTHWD* HA6 .... 59 M1
Gatehope Dr *SOCK/AV* RM15 ... 111 M5
Gatehouse Cl *KUTN/CMB* KT2 .. 153 J3
Gateley Rd *BRXN/ST* SW9 .... 120 F8
Gate Ms *SKENS* SW7 .... 15 K2
Gater Dr *ENC/FH* EN2 .... 36 D4
Gates Green Rd *WWKM* BR4 .... 175 L6
Gateshead Rd *BORE* WD6 .... 31 M5
Gatestone Rd *NRWD* SE19 ...... 157 L2
Gate St *HHOL* WC1V 11 L4
HOL/ALD WC2B 11 L4
Gateway *WALW* SE17 .... 18 F9
Gateway Ar *IS* N1 .... 6 C5 ▣
Gateway Cl *NTHWD* HA6 .... 41 J8 ▣
Gateway Ms *HACK* E8 .... 85 M5 ▣
The Gateways *CHESW* EN7 .... 25 K1
Gatfield Gv *FELT* TW13 .... 133 G6
Gathorne Rd *WDGN* N22 .... 49 G5
Gathorne St *BETH* E2 .... 104 D1 ▣
Catley Rd *HOR/WEW* KT19 ...... 168 B7
Catliff Rd *BGVA* SW1W 16 B8
Gatling Rd *ABYW* SE2 .... 126 A3
Gatting Cl *EDGW* HA8 .... 63 J1 ▣

Gatting Wy *HGDN/ICK* UB10 ...... 76 E6
Gatton Cl *BELMT* SM2 .... 182 B2 ▣
Gatton Rd *TOOT* SW17 .... 137 L8
Gattons Wy *SCUP* DA14 .... 144 F8
Gatward Cl *WCHMH* N21 .... 49 H1
Gatward Gn *ED* N9 .... 49 L4
Gatwick Rd *WAND/EARL* SW18 . 136 F1
Gauden Cl *CLAP* SW4 .... 120 D8 ▣
Gauden Rd *CLAP* SW4 .... 120 D8
Gaumont Ap *WATW* WD18 .... 29 H6
Gauntlet Cl *NTHLT* UB5 .... 78 E7
Gauntlett Ct *ALP/SUD* HA0 .... 80 A5
Gauntlett Rd *SUT* SM1 .... 170 D7
Gaunt St *STHWK* SE1 .... 18 D3
Gautrey Rd *PECK* SE15 .... 122 C7
Gavel St *WALW* SE17 .... 19 H5 ▣
Gavenny Pth *SOCK/AV* RM15 ... 111 M5
Gaverick St *POP/IOD* E14 .... 123 G2
Gavestone Crs *LEE/GVPK* SE12 . 142 B4
Gavestone Rd *LEE/GVPK* SE12 . 142 B4
Gavina Cl *MRDN* SM4 .... 155 L8
Gawber St *BETH* E2 .... 104 C2 ▣
Gawsworth Cl *SRTFD* E15 .... 87 M5 ▣
Gawthorne Av *MLHL* NW7 .... 46 E7 ▣
Gay Cl *CRICK* NW2 .... 82 B5
Gaydon La *CDALE/KGS* NW9 ..... 63 L2 ▣
Gayfere Rd *CLAY* IG5 .... 70 F4
EW KT17 .... 169 G7
Gayfere St *WEST* SW1P 17 J4
Gayford Rd *SHB* W12 .... 99 M8
Gay Gdns *DAGE* RM10 .... 91 J4
Gayhurst Rd *HACK* E8 .... 86 A7
Gaylor Rd *NTHLT* UB5 .... 78 F5
Gaynes Ct *UPMR* RM14 .... 110 F1
Gaynesford Rd *CAR* SM5 .... 182 F1
FSTH SE23 .... 140 D6
Gaynes Hill Rd *WFD* IG8 .... 70 E1
Gaynes Park Rd *UPMR* RM14 .... 93 H4
Gaynes Rd *UPMR* RM14 .... 93 H2
Gay Rd *SRTFD* E15 .... 105 K1
Gaysham Av *GNTH/NBYPK* IG2 .. 71 K6
Gayton Crs *HAMP* NW3 .... 83 K4
Gayton Rd *HAMP* NW3 .... 83 K4
HRW HA1 .... 61 M7
Gayville Rd *BTSEA* SW11 .... 137 M3
Gaywood Av *CHES/WCR* EN8 ..... 26 D3
Gaywood Cl *BRXS/STRHM* SW2 . 138 F5
Gaywood Rd *WALTH* E17 .... 69 G4
Gaywood St *STHWK* SE1 .... 18 D4
Gaza St *WALW* SE17 .... 18 C4
Geariesville Gdns *BARK/HLT* IG6 . 71 H5
Geary Rd *WLSDN* NW10 .... 82 A5
Geary St *HOLWY* N7 .... 84 F5
Geddes Pl *BXLYHN* DA7 .... 145 G1
Geddes Rd *BUSH* WD23 .... 30 C7 ▣
Gedeney Rd *TOTM* N17 .... 67 J2
Gedling Pl *STHWK* SE1 .... 19 L3
Geere Rd *SRTFD* E15 .... 87 M8
Gees Ct *W1K* .... 10 C5 ▣
Gee St *FSBYE* EC1V 6 E9
Geffrye St *BETH* E2 .... 7 L5
Geldart Rd *PECK* SE15 .... 122 B5
Geldeston Rd *CLPT* E5 .... 86 A2 ▣
Gellatly Rd *PECK* SE15 .... 122 C7
Gelsthorpe Rd *CRW* RM5 .... 73 L1 ▣
General Gordon Pl
WOOL/PLUM SE18 .... 125 H2 ▣
The Generals Wk *PEND* EN3 ...... 37 L2 ▣
General Wolfe Rd *GNWCH* SE10 . 123 K6
Genesis Cl *STWL/WRAY* TW19 .. 130 F5
Genesta Rd *WOOL/PLUM* SE18 . 125 H4
Geneva Cl *SHPTN* TW17 .... 149 L5 ▣
Geneva Dr *BRXN/ST* SW9 .... 120 F8
Geneva Gdns *CHDH* RM6 .... 72 B6
Geneva Rd *KUT* KT1 .... 152 E7
THHTH CR7 .... 157 J8
Genever Cl *CHING* E4 .... 51 G7
Genista Rd *UED* N18 .... 50 B7 ▣
Genoa Av *PUT/ROE* SW15 .... 136 C2
Genoa Rd *PGE/AN* SE20 .... 158 C4
Genotin Rd *ENC/FH* EN2 .... 36 C6
Gentleman's Rw *ENC/FH* EN2 .... 36 C6
Geoffrey Av *HARH* RM3 .... 57 G8
Geoffrey Cl *CMBW* SE5 .... 121 J7
Geoffrey Gdns *EHAM* E6 .... 106 F1
Geoffrey Rd *BROCKY* SE4 .... 122 F8
George Beard Rd *DEPT* SE8 ...... 122 F2
George Crs *MUSWH* N10 .... 66 A1
George Gange Wy
KTN/HRWW/W HA3 .... 61 L4
George Groves Rd
PGE/AN SE20 .... 158 A4
George La *HAYES* BR2 .... 175 H3
LEW SE13 .... 141 J3
SWFD E18 .... 70 B4
George Mathers Rd
LBTH SE11 .... 18 C5 ▣
George Ms *CAMTN* NW1 .... 4 E8
George Rd *CHING* E4 .... 51 G8
KUTN/CMB KT2 .... 153 H3
NWMAL KT3 .... 153 M7
George Rw *BERM/RHTH* SE16 .. 104 A8
Georges Cl *STMC/STPC* BR5 .... 162 C6
Georges Md *BORE* WD6 .... 44 D7 ▣
George's Rd *HOLWY* N7 .... 84 F5
George St *BARK* IG11 .... 89 J7
CAN/RD E16 .... 105 M5 ▣
CROY/NA CR0 .... 172 C4
HNWL W7 .... 97 L7
HSLW TW3 .... 114 F7
MBLAR W1H 9 M4
MHST W1U 10 A4
NWDGN UB2 .... 114 C2
RCHPK/HAM TW10 .... 134 D2
ROM RM1 .... 73 M7
UX/CGN UB8 .... 76 D7
WATW WD18 .... 29 J7
Georgetown Cl *NRWD* SE19 .... 157 K1 ▣
Georgette Pl *GNWCH* SE10 ...... 123 J5
George V Av *PIN* HA5 .... 61 G5 ▣
Georgeville Gdns *BARK/HLT* IG6 . 71 H5
George V Wy *GFD/PVL* UB6 .... 80 B7
George Wyver Cl
WIM/MER SW19 .... 136 E4 ▣
George Yd *BANK* EC3V 13 H5
MYFR/PKLN W1K 10 B6
Georgiana St *CAMTN* NW1 .... 4 E7
Georgian Cl *HAYES* BR2 .... 175 H3
STA TW18 .... 130 B8

STAN HA7 .... 62 A1
Georgian Ct *WBLY* HA9 .... 81 G6
Georgian Wy *RYLN/HDSTN* HA2 . 79 K2
Geraint Rd *BMLY* BR1 .... 142 A7
Geraldine Rd *CHSWK* W4 .... 117 G4
WAND/EARL SW18 .... 137 J2
Geraldine St *LBTH* SE11 .... 18 C4
Gerald Rd *BCTR* RM8 .... 90 F7
BGVA SW1W 16 B5
CAN/RD E16 .... 105 M3
Gerald's Gv *BNSTD* SM7 .... 181 K7
Gerard Av *HSLWW* TW4 .... 133 G4
Gerard Gdns *RAIN* RM13 .... 109 L1 ▣
Gerard Rd *BARN* SW13 .... 117 M6
HRW HA1 .... 62 A7
Gerards Cl *BERM/RHTH* SE16 .. 122 C4
Gerda Rd *ELTH/MOT* SE9 .... 143 H6
Gerdview Dr *RDART* DA2 .... 146 C8
Germander Wy *SRTFD* E15 ..... 105 L2 ▣
Gernon Rd *RAIN* RM13 .... 110 D1 ▣
Gernon Rd *BOW* E3 .... 104 E1
Geron Wy *CRICK* NW2 .... 82 B2
Gerpins La *UPMR* RM14 .... 110 F1
Gerrard Gdns *PIN* HA5 .... 60 A6
Gerrard Pl *SOHO/SHAV* W1D ..... 11 H6 ▣
Gerrard Rd *IS* N1 .... 6 C5
Gerrards Cl *STHGT/OAK* N14 .... 35 J8
Gerrard St *SOHO/SHAV* W1D ..... 11 G6 ▣
Gerridge St *STHWK* SE1 .... 18 B2
Gertrude Rd *BELV* DA17 .... 127 G2
Gertrude St *WBPTN* SW10 .... 119 J4
Gervase Cl *WBLY* HA9 .... 81 J3 ▣
Gervase Rd *EDGW* HA8 .... 63 J2
Gervase St *PECK* SE15 .... 122 B5
Gew's Cnr *CHES/WCR* EN8 .... 26 D2
Ghent St *CAT* SE6 .... 141 G6
Ghent Wy *HACK* E8 .... 85 M6 ▣
Giant Arches Rd *HNHL* SE24 .... 139 J4
Giant Tree HI *BUSH* WD23 .... 43 K4
Gibbfield Cl *CHDH* RM6 .... 72 E4
Gibbins Rd *SRTFD* E15 .... 87 J7
Gibbon Rd *ACT* W3 .... 99 L6
KUTN/CMB KT2 .... 152 E4
PECK SE15 .... 122 C7
Gibbons Cl *BORE* WD6 .... 31 L4
Gibbons Rd *WLSDN* NW10 .... 81 K6
Gibbon Wk *PUT/ROE* SW15 ..... 136 A1 ▣
Gibbs Av *NRWD* SE19 .... 157 K2
Gibbs Cl *CHES/WCR* EN8 .... 26 D2
NRWD SE19 .... 157 K1 ▣
Gibbs Couch *OXHEY* WD19 .... 42 D5
Gibbs Gn *EDGW* HA8 .... 45 J6
Gibbs Rd *UED* N18 .... 50 C6
Gibbs Sq *NRWD* SE19 .... 157 K1 ▣
Gibraltar Crs *HOR/WEW* KT19 . 180 E3
Gibson Cl *CHSGTN* KT9 .... 167 J7 ▣
ISLW TW7 .... 115 K8
WCHPL E1 .... 104 C3 ▣
Gibson Gdns
STNW/STAM N16 .... 85 M2 ▣
Gibson Pl *STWL/WRAY* TW19 .. 130 C3
Gibson Rd *BCTR* RM8 .... 90 C1
HGDN/ICK UB10 .... 76 F4
LBTH SE11 .... 17 M6
SUT SM1 .... 170 B7
Gibson's HI *STRHM/NOR* SW16 . 157 G2
Gibson Sq *IS* N1 .... 6 B3
Gibson St *GNWCH* SE10 .... 123 L3
Gidea Av *GPK* RM2 .... 74 A1
Gidea Cl *GPK* RM2 .... 74 A1
Gideon Cl *BELV* DA17 .... 127 H2 ▣
Gideon Rd *BTSEA* SW11 .... 120 A8
Giesbach Rd *ARCH* N19 .... 84 C2
Giffard Rd *UED* N18 .... 49 L7
Giffin St *DEPT* SE8 .... 123 G5
Gifford Gdns *HNWL* W7 .... 97 K4
Gifford St *IS* N1 .... 5 K2
Gift La *SRTFD* E15 .... 87 L8
Gilbey Cl *HGDN/ICK* UB10 .... 77 H4
Gilbey Rd *TOOT* SW17 .... 137 J8
Gilbeys Yd *CAMTN* NW1 .... 4 B2
Gilbourne Rd
WOOL/PLUM SE18 .... 125 M4
Gilda Av *PEND* EN3 .... 37 L8
Gilda Crs *STNW/STAM* N16 .... 86 A1
Gildea Cl *PIN* HA5 .... 61 G1
Gildea St *REGST* W1B 10 D3
Gildersome St
WOOL/PLUM SE18 .... 125 G4 ▣
Gilders Rd *CHSGTN* KT9 .... 167 M8
Giles Cl *RAIN* RM13 .... 110 D1
Giles Coppice *NRWD* SE19 ...... 139 M8
Gilfrid Cl *UX/CGN* UB8 .... 95 H5 ▣
Gilham's Av *BNSTD* SM7 .... 181 K5
Gilkes Crs *DUL* SE21 .... 139 L3 ▣
EDUL SE22 .... 139 L3
Gilkes Pl *DUL* SE21 .... 139 L3 ▣
Gillam Wy *RAIN* RM13 .... 93 A6
Gillan Gn *BUSH* WD23 .... 43 J4 ▣
Gillards Ms *WALTH* E17 .... 69 C5 ▣
Gillards Wy *WALTH* E17 .... 69 C5
Gill Av *CAN/RD* E16 .... 106 A5
Gillender St *BOW* E3 .... 105 J3
Gillespie Rd *FSBYPK* N4 .... 85 G3
Gillett Av *EHAM* E6 .... 107 J1
Gillett Pl *STNW/STAM* N16 ...... 85 M5 ▣
Gillett Rd *THHTH* CR7 .... 157 K7
Gillett St *STNW/STAM* N16 .... 85 L5
Gillham Ter *TOTM* N17 .... 50 A8 ▣

Gilliam Gv *PUR/KEN* CR8 .... 184 A3
Gillian Crs *GPK* RM2 .... 74 C3
Gillian Park Rd *CHEAM* SM3 .... 169 M3
Gillian St *LEW* SE13 .... 140 E4
Gilliat Rd *SEVS/STOTM* N15 ..... 141 H2
Gilliam Dr *SRTFD* E15 .... 87 L8
Gillingham Ms *PIM* SW1V 16 D5
Gillingham Rd *CRICK* NW2 .... 82 E3
Gillingham Rw *PIM* SW1V .... 16 E5 ▣
Gillingham St *PIM* SW1V .... 16 E5 ▣
Gillman Dr *SRTFD* E15 .... 87 L8
Gills Hill La *RAD* WD7 .... 30 F1
Gills Hollow *RAD* WD7 .... 30 F1
Gill St *POP/IOD* E14 .... 104 F5
Gillum Cl *EBAR* EN4 .... 47 M3
Gilmore Cl *HGDN/ICK* UB10 ...... 77 G3
Gilmore Crs *ASHF* TW15 .... 149 L3
Gilmore Rd *LEW* SE13 .... 141 K1
Gilmour St *ENC/FH* EN2 .... 26 A3
Gilpin Av *MORT/ESHN* SW14 ... 135 L5 ▣
Gilpin Crs *UED* N18 .... 49 M7
WHTN TW2 .... 133 H4
Gilpin Rd *CLPT* E5 .... 86 E4
Gilpin Wy *HYS/HAR* UB3 .... 113 K5
Gilroy Cl *RAIN* RM13 .... 91 M6 ▣
Gilroy Wy *STMC/STPC* BR5 ..... 177 H2
Gilsland *WAB* EN9 .... 27 L8
Gilsland Rd *THHTH* CR7 .... 157 K7
Gilstead Rd *FUL/PGN* SW6 .... 119 H7
Gilston Rd *WBPTN* SW10 .... 14 E9
Giltspur St *STBT* EC1A 12 E4
Gilwell Cl *CHING* E4 .... 38 B7
Gilwell La *CHING* E4 .... 38 D7
Gippeswyck Cl *PIN* HA5 .... 60 D2 ▣
Gipsy HI *NRWD* SE19 .... 157 L1
Gipsy La *BARN* SW13 .... 118 A8
Gipsy Rd *WELL* DA16 .... 126 D7
WNWD SE27 .... 139 K8
Gipsy Road Gdns *WNWD* SE27 . 139 J8
Giralda Cl *CAN/RD* E16 .... 106 D4
Giraud St *POP/IOD* E14 .... 105 H5
Girdlers Rd *HMSMTH* W6 .... 118 E3
Girdwood Rd
WAND/EARL SW18 .... 136 E4 ▣
Girling Wy *EBED/NFELT* TW14 . 114 A8
Gironde Rd *FUL/PGN* SW6 .... 118 F5
Girtin Rd *BUSH* WD23 .... 30 B8
Girton Av *CDALE/KGS* NW9 ...... 63 G4
Girton Cl *NTHLT* UB5 .... 79 J6
Girton Ct *CHES/WCR* EN8 .... 26 E2
Girton Gdns *CROY/NA* CR0 ..... 174 A5
Girton Rd *NTHLT* UB5 .... 79 J6
SYD SE26 .... 158 D1
Girton Wy *RKW/CH/CXG* WD3 ... 28 C8
Gisborne Gdns *RAIN* RM13 ..... 109 M2 ▣
Gisbourne Cl *WLGTN* SM6 ...... 171 K5 ▣
Gisburne Wy *WATN* SM4 .... 29 G2
Gisburn Rd *CEND/HSY/T* N8 ...... 66 F5
Gittens Cl *BMLY* BR1 .... 141 M8
Glacier Wy *ALP/SUD* HA0 .... 98 D1
Gladbeck Wy *ENC/FH* EN2 .... 36 C7
WCHMH N21 .... 36 B7
Gladding Rd *MNPK* E12 .... 88 D4
Glade Cl *SURB* KT6 .... 167 K4 ▣
Glade Gdns *CROY/NA* CR0 .... 175 L2
Glade La *NWDGN* UB2 .... 97 H8
Gladeside *CROY/NA* CR0 .... 173 K1
WCHMH N21 .... 48 F1
Gladesmore Rd
SEVS/STOTM N15 .... 67 M7
The Glade *BELMT* SM2 .... 181 L2
BMLY BR1 .... 160 D5
CHARL SE7 .... 124 C5
CLAY IG5 .... 70 F2
CROY/NA CR0 .... 158 D8
ENC/FH EN2 .... 36 A6
EW KT17 .... 169 G4
STA TW18 .... 148 F6
UPMR RM14 .... 93 J5
WCHMH N21 .... 48 F1
WFD IG8 .... 52 B5
WWKM BR4 .... 174 B5
The Gladeway *WAB* EN9 .... 27 K6
Gladiator St *FSTH* SE23 .... 140 E3
Glading Ter *STNW/STAM* N16 ... 85 M3 ▣
Gladioli Cl *HPTN* TW12 .... 151 C2 ▣
Gladsdale Dr *PIN* HA5 .... 60 A5
Gladsmuir Rd *WOT/HER* KT12 . 165 J4
Gladsmuir Rd *ARCH* N19 .... 84 C1
BAR EN5 .... 33 L5
Gladstone Av
EBED/NFELT TW14 .... 132 A3
MNPK E12 .... 88 E7
WDGN N22 .... 67 H3
WHTN TW2 .... 133 K4
Gladstone Gdns *HSLW* TW3 .... 115 J6 ▣
Gladstone Ms
KIL/WHAMP NW6 .... 82 F7 ▣
PGE/AN SE20 .... 158 C3 ▣
WDGN N22 .... 67 G3 ▣
Gladstone Park Gdns
CRICK NW2 .... 82 B3
Gladstone Rd *BKHH* IG9 .... 52 C3
CHSWK W4 .... 117 K1 ▣
CROY/NA CR0 .... 172 D2 ▣
DART DA1 .... 146 F3
KUT KT1 .... 153 G6
NWDGN UB2 .... 96 E8 ▣
ORP BR6 .... 176 C5
SURB KT6 .... 167 K4
WAT WD17 .... 29 J6
WIM/MER SW19 .... 155 G3 ▣
Gladstone St *STHWK* SE1 .... 18 C3
Gladstone Ter *VX/NE* SW8 .... 120 B6 ▣
Gladstone Wy
KTN/HRWW/W HA3 .... 61 L4 ▣
Gladwell Rd *BMLY* BR1 .... 160 A2
CEND/HSY/T N8 .... 66 F7
Gladwyn Rd *PUT/ROE* SW15 ... 118 D8
Gladys Rd *KIL/WHAMP* NW6 ...... 2 B1
Glamis Cl *CHESW* EN7 .... 25 M3
Glamis Crs *HYS/HAR* UB3 .... 113 J1
Glamis Dr *EMPK* RM11 .... 92 E1
Glamis Pl *WAP* E1W 104 C6
Glamis Rd *WAP* E1W 104 C6
Glamis Wy *NTHLT* UB5 .... 79 J6
Glamorgan Cl *MTCM* CR4 .... 156 E6 ▣

Glamorgan Rd KUT KT1 152 C3
Glanfield Rd BECK BR3 158 F7
Glanleam Rd STAN HA7 44 D6
Glanville Dr EMPK RM11 92 F1
Glanville Rd BRXS/STRHM SW2 138 E2
HAYES BR2 160 B6
Glasbrook Av WHTN TW2 132 F5
Glasbrook Rd ELTH/MOT SE9 142 D4
Glaserton Rd STNW/STAM N16 67 L8
Glasford St TOOT SW17 155 M2
Glasgow Rd PLSTW E13 106 B1
UED N18 50 B7 5
Glasgow Ter PIM SW1V 16 E8
Glasse Cl WEA W13 98 A6
Glasshill St STHWK SE1 18 D1
Glasshouse Flds WAP E1W 104 D6 5
Glasshouse St REGST W1B 10 F7
Glasshouse Wk LBTH SE11 17 K7
Glasshouse Yd STBT EC1A 12 E1
Glasslyn Rd CEND/HSY/T N8 66 D6
Glassmill La HAYES BR2 159 M5
Glass St BETH E2 104 B3 5
Glass Yd WOOL/PLUM SE18 125 G1
Glastonbury Av WFD IG8 70 D1
Glastonbury Cl STMC/STPC BR5 177 J3
Glastonbury Rd ED N9 50 A3 5
MRDN SM4 170 A2 1
MRDN SM4 170 A1 1
Glastonbury St
KIL/WHAMP NW6 82 F5 5
Glaucus St BOW E3 105 H4
Glazbury Rd WKENS W14 118 E2 7
Glazebrook Cl DUL SE21 139 K6
Glazebrook Rd TEDD TW11 151 M3
Glebe Av ENC/FH EN2 36 B6
HGDN/ICK UB10 77 H3
KTN/HRWW/W HA3 62 E4
MTCM CR4 155 L5
RSLP HA4 78 B6
WFD IG8 52 A8
Glebe Cl HGDN/ICK UB10 77 J4
SAND/SEL CR2 184 F5
Glebe Ct STAN HA7 44 C7
Glebe Crs HDN NW4 64 C5 5
KTN/HRWW/W HA3 62 E4
Glebe Gdns NWMAL KT3 168 E2
Glebe House Dr HAYES BR2 175 H3
Glebe Hyrst SAND/SEL CR2 184 F5
Glebeland Gdns SHPTN TW17 164 C1
Glebelands CHIG IG7 54 B5
DART DA1 145 M1
E/WMO/HCT KT8 151 H8
ESH/CLAY KT10 178 F2
Glebelands Av GNTH/NBYPK IG2 71 K8
SWFD E18 70 A3
Glebelands Rd
EBED/NFELT TW14 132 A4 1
Glebe La BAR EN5 33 G8
KTN/HRWW/W HA3 62 E5
Glebe Pth MTCM CR4 155 M6
Glebe Pl CHEL SW3 15 J9
Glebe Rd BARN SW13 118 A7
BELMT SM2 181 L2
BMLY BR1 160 A4
CAR SM5 170 F8
CEND/HSY/T N8 66 F5
DAGE RM10 91 H6 1
FNCH N3 65 J2
HACK E8 7 L1
RAIN RM13 110 B2
STA TW18 148 B1
STAN HA7 44 C7
UX/CGN UB8 94 C1
WLSDN NW10 82 A6
Glebe Side TWK TW1 133 M3
Glebe St CHSWK W4 117 K3
Glebe Ter BOW E3 105 H2 5
The Glebe BKHTH/KID SE3 123 L8
CHST BR7 161 J4
GSTN WD25 21 J6
KGLGY WD4 20 A2 2
WDR/YW UB7 112 E2
WPK KT4 168 F3
Glebe Wy WWKM BR4 174 C4
EMPK RM11 74 E8
ERITH DA8 127 L4
FELT TW13 133 G7
SAND/SEL CR2 184 F5
Glebeway WFD IG8 52 C7
Gledhow Gdns ECT SW5 14 E6
Gledstanes Rd WKENS W14 118 E3
Gledwood Av YEAD UB4 96 A4
Gledwood Crs YEAD UB4 95 M4
Gledwood Dr YEAD UB4 95 M4
Gledwood Gdns YEAD UB4 96 A4
Gleed Av BUSH WD23 43 K4
Gleeson Dr ORP BR6 176 F7
Glegg Pl PUT/ROE SW15 136 D1 2
Glenaffric Av POP/IOD E14 123 K2 2
Glen Albyn Rd WIM/MER SW19 136 D6
Glenalla Rd RSLP HA4 59 M8
Glenalmond Rd
KTN/HRWW/W HA3 62 E5
Glenalvon Wy CHARL SE7 124 E2 1
Glena Mt SUT SM1 170 C6
Glenarm Rd CLPT E5 86 C4
Glen Av ASHF TW15 131 G8
Glenavon Cl ESH/CLAY KT10 167 G8
Glenavon Rd SRTFD E15 87 L7
Glenbarr Cl ELTH/MOT SE9 125 H8 1
Glenbow Rd BMLY BR1 159 L2
Glenbrook North ENC/FH EN2 35 M7
Glenbrook Rd
KIL/WHAMP NW6 83 G5 1
Glenbrook South ENC/FH EN2 35 M7
Glenbuck Rd SURB KT6 167 K1
Glenburnie Rd TOOT SW17 137 M7
Glencairn Dr EA W5 98 B3
Glencairne Cl CAN/RD E16 106 D4 5
Glencairn Rd
STRHM/NOR SW16 156 E3
Glen Cl SHPTN TW17 149 G7
Glencoe Av GNTH/NBYPK IG2 71 L8
Glencoe Dr DAGE RM10 91 G4
Glencoe Rd BUSH WD23 43 G1
WEY KT13 164 A5 1
YEAD UB4 96 D4 2
Glencorse Gn OXHEY WD19 42 D6 2
Glen Crs WFD IG8 52 B8
Glendale SWLY BR8 163 M8
Glendale Av CHDH RM6 72 C8
EDGW HA8 44 F6
WDGN N22 67 G1
Glendale Cl ELTH/MOT SE9 125 G8 1
Glendale Gdns WBLY HA9 80 D1
Glen Dale Ms BECK BR3 159 H4
Glendale Ri PUR/KEN CR8 184 B8
Glendale Rd ERITH DA8 127 J2
Glendale Wy THMD SE28 108 C7
Glendall St CLAP SW4 138 F1 1
Glendarvon St PUT/ROE SW15 118 D8
Glendish Rd TOTM N17 68 A2
Glendor Gdns MLHL NW7 45 K6
Glendower Crs ORP BR6 177 G1
Glendower Gdns
MORT/ESHN SW14 117 K8 4
Glendower Pl SKENS SW7 15 G5
Glendower Rd CHING E4 51 K3 4
MORT/ESHN SW14 117 K8 4
Glendown Rd ABYW SE2 126 A3
Glendun Rd ACT W3 99 L6
Gleneagle Ms
STRHM/NOR SW16 156 D1 1
Gleneagle Rd
STRHM/NOR SW16 156 D1 2
Gleneagles STAN HA7 44 B8
Gleneagles Cl HARH RM3 74 F1 5
HTHAIR TW6 130 C2
ORP BR6 176 D3
OXHEY WD19 42 D7 5
Gleneldon Ms
STRHM/NOR SW16 138 E8 1
Gleneldon Rd
STRHM/NOR SW16 138 E8
Glenelg Rd BRXS/STRHM SW2 138 E2
Glenesk Rd ELTH/MOT SE9 125 G8
Glenfarg Rd CAT SE6 141 K5
Glenfield Crs RSLP HA4 59 K8
Glenfield Rd ASHF TW15 149 H2
BAL SW12 138 C5
BNSTD SM7 182 B8
WEA W13 98 B8
Glenfinlas Wy CMBW SE5 121 H5
Glenforth St GNWCH SE10 123 M2
Glengall Br POP/IOD E14 123 H1
Glengall Gv POP/IOD E14 123 H1
Glengall Rd BXLYHN DA7 126 E8
EDGW HA8 45 H5
KIL/WHAMP NW6 82 F8
PECK SE15 19 M9
WFD IG8 52 B8
Glengall Ter PECK SE15 19 M9
Glen Gdns CROY/NA CR0 172 A5
Glengarnock Av POP/IOD E14 123 J2
Glengarry Rd EDUL SE22 139 L1
Glenham Dr GNTH/NBYPK IG2 71 H6
Glenhaven Av BORE WD6 32 A6
Glenhead Cl ELTH/MOT SE9 125 H8 2
Glenhill Cl FNCH N3 65 G3
Glenhouse Rd ELTH/MOT SE9 143 G2
Glenhurst Av BXLY DA5 144 F5
KTTN NW5 84 A4
RSLP HA4 59 J8
Glenhurst Ri NRWD SE19 157 J3
Glenhurst Rd BTFD TW8 116 C4
NFNCH/WDSP N12 47 K6
Glenilla Rd HAMP NW3 83 L6
Glenister Park Rd
STRHM/NOR SW16 156 D3
Glenister Rd GNWCH SE10 123 M3
Glenlea Rd ELTH/MOT SE9 143 G2
Glenloch Rd HAMP NW3 83 L6
PEND EN3 37 J5
Glenluge Rd BKHTH/KID SE3 124 A4
Glenlyon Rd ELTH/MOT SE9 143 G2
Glenmere Av MLHL NW7 64 A1
Glenmore Rd HAMP NW3 83 L6
WELL DA16 125 M6
Glenmore Wy BARK IG11 108 A2
Glenn Av PUR/KEN CR8 184 B4
Glennie Rd WNWD SE27 139 G7
Glenny Rd BARK IG11 89 J6
Glenorchy Cl YEAD UB4 96 E4
Glenparke Rd FSTGT E7 88 B6
Glen Ri WFD IG8 52 B8
Glen Rd CHSGTN KT9 167 L5
PLSTW E13 106 C3
WALTH E17 68 F6 5
Glenrosa St FUL/PGN SW6 119 J7
Glenroy St SHB W12 100 C5 2
Glensdale Rd BROCKY SE4 122 F8
Glenshiel Rd ELTH/MOT SE9 143 G2
Glenside CHIG IG7 53 H8
Glentanner Wy TOOT SW17 137 K7 1
Glen Ter POP/IOD E14 105 J8
Glentham Gdns BARN SW13 118 B3
Glentham Rd BARN SW13 118 A4
The Glen CROY/NA CR0 173 K5
ENC/FH EN2 36 B7
HAYES BR2 159 L5
NTHWD HA6 59 K1
NWDGN UB2 114 F3
ORP BR6 175 M5
PIN HA5 60 E8
PIN HA5 60 B6
RAIN RM13 110 C3
WBLY HA9 80 D4
Glenthorne Av CROY/NA CR0 173 J3
Glenthorne Cl CHEAM SM3 170 A3
Glenthorne Gdns BARK/HLT IG6 71 G4
CHEAM SM3 170 A3
Glenthorne Rd FBAR/BDGN N11 47 M7
HMSMTH W6 118 C2 4
KUT KT1 152 F7 1
WALTH E17 68 E6
Glenthorpe Rd MRDN SM4 154 D8
Glenton Cl ROM RM1 73 L1
Glenton Rd LEW SE13 141 L1
Glenton Wy ROM RM1 73 L1
Glentrammon Av ORP BR6 176 F8
Glentrammon Cl ORP BR6 176 F8
Glentrammon Gdns ORP BR6 176 F8
Glentrammon Rd ORP BR6 176 F8
Glentworth St CAMTN NW1 9 M1
Glenure Rd ELTH/MOT SE9 143 G2
Glenview ABYW SE2 126 D4
Glen View Rd BMLY BR1 160 D5
Glenville Av ENC/FH EN2 36 C3
Glenville Gv DEPT SE8 122 F5 5
Glenville Rd KUTN/CMB KT2 153 G4
Glen Wy WAT WD17 28 E3
Glenwood Av CDALE/KGS NW9 81 L1
RAIN RM13 110 A3
Glenwood Cl HRW HA1 61 M6
Glenwood Dr GPK RM2 74 A6
Glenwood Gdns
GNTH/NBYPK IG2 71 G6
Glenwood Gv CDALE/KGS NW9 81 J1
Glenwood Rd CAT SE6 140 F5
EW KT17 169 G8
HSLW TW3 115 K8
MLHL NW7 45 L5
SEVS/STOTM N15 67 H6
Glenwood Wy CROY/NA CR0 173 K1
Glenworth Av POP/IOD E14 123 K2 5
Gliddon Rd WKENS W14 118 E2
Glimpsing Gn ERITH DA18 126 E1
Glisson Rd HGDN/ICK UB10 95 G1
Gload Crs STMC/STPC BR5 177 K4
Globe Pond Rd
BERM/RHTH SE16 104 E7 5
Globe Rd BETH E2 104 C2
EMPK RM11 74 A7
FSTGT E7 87 M5 5
WFD IG8 52 C8
Globe St STHWK SE1 19 G2
Globe Ter BETH E2 104 C2 5
Glossop Rd SAND/SEL CR2 184 D2
Gloster Rd NWMAL KT3 153 L7 5
Gloucester Av BFN/LL DA15 143 L6
CAMTN NW1 4 A2
CHES/WCR EN8 26 E6
EMPK RM11 75 G6
WELL DA16 143 M2
Gloucester Circ GNWCH SE10 123 J5 1
Gloucester Cl THDIT KT7 167 G3 5
WLSDN NW10 81 K7
Gloucester Ct MON EC3R 13 K7
RCH/KEW TW9 117 G5 2
Gloucester Crs CAMTN NW1 4 C3
STA TW18 148 D2
Gloucester Dr FSBYPK N4 85 H2
GLDGN NW11 65 G5
Gloucester Gdns BAY/PAD W2 8 D4
EBAR EN4 35 G7
GLDGN NW11 64 F8
IL IG1 70 E8
SUT SM1 170 B4
Gloucester Ga CAMTN NW1 4 C5
Gloucester Gate Ms CAMTN NW1 4 C5
Gloucester Gv EDGW HA8 63 K2
Gloucester Ms BAY/PAD W2 8 F5
Gloucester Ms West BAY/PAD W2 8 E5
Gloucester Pl CAMTN NW1 9 L1
MHST W1U 9 M3
Gloucester Place Ms MBLAR W1H 9 M3
Gloucester Rd ACT W3 99 J8
BAR EN5 34 B8
BELV DA17 126 F3 2
CROY/NA CR0 172 D2
DART DA1 146 B3
EA W5 98 C8
ENC/FH EN2 36 C3
FELT TW13 132 C5
HPTN TW12 151 H3
HSLWW TW4 132 E1
KUT KT1 153 G5
LEY E10 69 G8
MNPK E12 88 F3
RCH/KEW TW9 117 G5
ROM RM1 73 L7
RYLN/HDSTN HA2 61 H6
SKENS SW7 14 E3
TEDD TW11 151 L1
TOTM N17 67 K4
UED N18 49 M7
WALTH E17 68 D3
WAN E11 70 B6
WHTN TW2 133 J5
Gloucester Sq BAY/PAD W2 9 H5
BETH E2 86 A8 5
Gloucester St PIM SW1V 16 E8
Gloucester Ter BAY/PAD W2 8 D4
Gloucester Wk KENS W8 14 B1
Gloucester Wy CLKNW EC1R 6 B8
Glover Cl ABYW SE2 126 C2
Glover Dr UED N18 50 C8
Glover Rd PIN HA5 60 D7
Glovers Gv RSLP HA4 59 H8
Glycena Rd BTSEA SW11 119 M8
Glyn Av EBAR EN4 34 D7
Glyn Cl EW KT17 181 G2
SNWD SE25 157 L5
Glyndebourne Pk ORP BR6 176 B5
Glynde Ms CHEL SW3 15 K4 5
Glynde Rd BXLYHN DA7 126 E8
Glynde St BROCKY SE4 140 F3
Glyndon Rd WOOL/PLUM SE18 125 J2
Glyn Dr SCUP DA14 144 B8
Glynfield Rd WLSDN NW10 81 L7
Glynne Rd WDGN N22 67 G3 5
Glyn Rd CLPT E5 86 D4
PEND EN3 37 J7 1
WPK KT4 169 K4
Glyn St LBTH SE11 17 L8
Goat La EN EN1 36 F3
Goat Rd MTCM CR4 171 G2
Goatswood La ABR/ST RM4 56 B2
Goat Whf BTFD TW8 116 E4
Gobions Av CRW RM5 73 K1
Godalming Av WLGTN SM6 171 L7
Godalming Rd POP/IOD E14 105 H4 5
Godbold Rd SRTFD E15 105 L3
Goddard Cl SHPTN TW17 148 F6 1
Goddard Pl ARCH N19 84 C3
Goddard Rd BECK BR3 158 D7
Goddington Cha ORP BR6 177 H6
Goddington La ORP BR6 177 J5
Godfrey Av NTHLT UB5 78 E8
WHTN TW2 133 K4
Godfrey Hl WOOL/PLUM SE18 124 E2
Godfrey Rd WOOL/PLUM SE18 124 F2
Godfrey St CHEL SW3 15 K7
SRTFD E15 105 J1
Godfrey Wy HSLWW TW4 132 E4
Goding St LBTH SE11 17 K8
Godley Rd WAND/EARL SW18 137 K5
Godliman St BLKFR EC4V 12 E5 1
Godman Rd PECK SE15 122 B7 5
Godolphin Cl BELMT SM2 181 M4
PLMGR N13 49 H8 1
Godolphin Pl ACT W3 99 K6 1
Godolphin Rd SHB W12 100 B8
WEY KT13 164 D8
Godric Crs CROY/NA CR0 186 D2 1
Godson Rd CROY/NA CR0 172 A5
Godstone Rd PUR/KEN CR8 184 E8
SUT SM1 170 C6
TWK TW1 134 A3
Godstow Rd ABYW SE2 108 C8
Godwin Cl CHING E4 38 C3
HOR/WEW KT19 168 C8
IS N1 6 F5
Godwin Rd FSTGT E7 88 B4
HAYES BR2 160 C6
Goffers Rd BKHTH/KID SE3 123 L6
Goffs Crs CHESW EN7 25 J2
Goff's La CHESW EN7 25 M2
Goff's Oak Av CHESW EN7 25 H1
Goffs Rd ASHF TW15 149 K2
Goidel Cl WLGTN SM6 171 K6 1
Golborne Gdns NKENS W10 100 E3 5
Golborne Ms NKENS W10 100 E4 5
Golborne Rd NKENS W10 100 E4
Golda Cl BAR EN5 46 D1
Goldbeaters Gv EDGW HA8 63 L1 2
Goldcliff Cl MRDN SM4 170 A2
Goldcrest Cl CAN/RD E16 106 D4 5
THMD SE28 108 C6
Goldcrest Wy BUSH WD23 43 J3
CROY/NA CR0 186 D2
PUR/KEN CR8 183 K3
Golden Crs HYS/HAR UB3 95 L7
Golden La STLK EC1Y 6 E9
Golden Mnr HNWL W7 97 L6
Golden Plover Cl CAN/RD E16 106 A5
Golden Sq SOHO/CST W1F 10 F6
Golders Cl EDGW HA8 45 H7
Golders Gdns GLDGN NW11 64 E8
Golders Green Crs GLDGN NW11 64 F8
Golders Green Rd GLDGN NW11 64 E7
Golders Manor Dr GLDGN NW11 64 D7
Golders Park Cl GLDGN NW11 83 G1
Golders Ri HDN NW4 64 D6 5
Golders Wy GLDGN NW11 64 F8
Goldfinch Cl ORP BR6 177 G7
Goldfinch Rd SAND/SEL CR2 185 L3
THMD SE28 125 K1
Goldfinch Wy BORE WD6 32 A7 5
Goldhawk Ms SHB W12 100 B8 2
Goldhawk Rd HMSMTH W6 117 M2
SHB W12 118 B1
Goldhaze Cl WFD IG8 70 D1 2
Gold Hl EDGW HA8 45 K8 1
Goldhurst Ter KIL/WHAMP NW6 2 D2
KIL/WHAMP NW6 83 J6 5
Golding's Hl LOU IG10 39 M3
Golding St WCHPL E1 104 A5 7
Goldington Crs CAMTN NW1 5 G5
Goldington St CAMTN NW1 5 G5
Goldman Cl BETH E2 104 A3 5
Goldney Rd MV/WKIL W9 8 A1
Goldrill Dr FBAR/BDGN N11 48 A4
Goldrings Rd LHD/OX KT22 178 C6
Goldsboro' Rd VX/NE SW8 120 D6
Goldsborough Crs CHING E4 51 J4 5
Goldsdown Cl PEND EN3 37 L5
Goldsdown Rd PEND EN3 37 K5
Goldsel Rd SWLY BR8 163 L7
Goldsmid St WOOL/PLUM SE18 125 L3
Goldsmith Av ACT W3 99 K6
CDALE/KGS NW9 63 L6
MNPK E12 88 E6
ROMW/RG RM7 73 G8
Goldsmith Cl RYLN/HDSTN HA2 79 G1
Goldsmith La CDALE/KGS NW9 63 J5
Goldsmith Rd ACT W3 99 K7
FBAR/BDGN N11 47 M7
LEY E10 87 H1
PECK SE15 122 A6
WALTH E17 68 D3
Goldsmith's Rw BETH E2 86 A8 5
BETH E2 104 A1
Goldsmith St CITYW EC2V 12 F4 5
Goldsworthy Gdns
BERM/RHTH SE16 122 C3 2
Goldwell Rd THHTH CR7 156 F7
Goldwing Cl CAN/RD E16 106 A5
Golf Cl BUSH WD23 29 K6
STAN HA7 62 C1
STRHM/NOR SW16 157 G4
Golf Club Dr KUTN/CMB KT2 153 K3
Golfe Rd IL IG1 89 K3
Golf Ride ENC/FH EN2 25 G8
Golf Rd BMLY BR1 161 G6
EA W5 98 F5 1
Golf Side BELMT SM2 181 L4
WHTN TW2 133 K7 1
Golf Side Cl NWMAL KT3 153 L5
Golfside Cl TRDG/WHET N20 47 L5
Gollogly Ter CHARL SE7 124 C3
Gomer Gdns TEDD TW11 152 A2 5
Gomer Pl TEDD TW11 152 A2
Gomm Rd BERM/RHTH SE16 122 C1
Gomshall Av WLGTN SM6 171 L7
Gomshall Gdns PUR/KEN CR8 184 E8
Gomshall Rd BELMT SM2 181 J3 5
EW KT17 181 J3
Gondar Gdns CRICK NW2 82 F5
Gonson St DEPT SE8 123 H4 1
Gonston Cl WIM/MER SW19 136 E6 2
Gonville Av RKW/CH/CXG WD3 41 H1
Gonville Crs NTHLT UB5 79 H6
Gonville Rd THHTH CR7 156 F8
Gonville St FUL/PGN SW6 118 E8
Goodall Rd WAN E11 87 J3 2
Gooden Ct HRW HA1 79 L3
Goodenough Rd
WIM/MER SW19 154 F3
Goodge Pl FITZ W1T 10 F3
Goodge St FITZ W1T 10 F3
Goodhall St WLSDN NW10 99 M2
Goodhart Wy WWKM BR4 174 E1
Goodhew Rd SNWD SE25 173 G1
Gooding Cl NWMAL KT3 153 J7
Goodinge Rd HOLWY N7 84 E6 2
Goodman Crs
BRXS/STRHM SW2 138 D6 1
BRXS/STRHM SW2 138 E6 5
Goodman Rd LEY E10 69 J8
Goodmans Ct ALP/SUD HA0 80 D4
Goodman's Stile WCHPL E1 104 A5 5
Goodman's Yd WCHPL E1 13 M6 1
Goodmayes Av GDMY/SEVK IG3 90 A1
Goodmayes La GDMY/SEVK IG3 90 A4
Goodmayes Rd GDMY/SEVK IG3 90 A1
Goodmead Rd ORP BR6 177 G2
Goodrich Cl GSTN WD25 21 G8
Goodrich Rd EDUL SE22 139 M3
Goodson Rd WLSDN NW10 81 L7
Goods Wy CAMTN NW1 5 J5
Goodway Gdns POP/IOD E14 105 K5 5
Goodwin Cl BERM/RHTH SE16 19 M4
MTCM CR4 155 K6
Goodwin Ct CHES/WCR EN8 26 E1 5
Goodwin Dr SCUP DA14 144 D6
Goodwin Gdns CROY/NA CR0 172 B8
SAND/SEL CR2 172 B8
Goodwin Rd CROY/NA CR0 172 B7
ED N9 50 C3
SHB W12 100 A8
Goodwin St FSBYPK N4 85 G2
Goodwood Av HCH RM12 92 E3
PEND EN3 37 J2
WATN WD24 20 E8
Goodwood Cl MRDN SM4 155 G7 1
Goodwood Dr NTHLT UB5 79 G6 5
Goodwood Rd NWCR SE14 122 E5
Goodwyn Av MLHL NW7 45 L7
Goodwyn's V MUSWH N10 66 A2
Goodyers Gdns HDN NW4 64 D6 5
Goosander Wy
WOOL/PLUM SE18 125 K1
Gooseacre La
KTN/HRWW/W HA3 62 D6
Goosefields RKW/CH/CXG WD3 40 C1
Goose Green Cl
STMC/STPC BR5 162 A5
Gooseley La EHAM E6 107 G2
Gooshays Dr HARH RM3 56 E8
Gooshays Gdns HARH RM3 56 E8
Goossens Cl SUT SM1 170 C7 5
Gophir La CANST EC4R 13 G6 2
Gopsall St IS N1 7 H4
Goral Md RKW/CH/CXG WD3 40 D3
Gordon Av CHING E4 51 L8
HCH RM12 91 M2
MORT/ESHN SW14 135 L1
PUR/KEN CR8 184 C3
STAN HA7 43 M8
TWK TW1 134 A2
Gordonbrock Rd BROCKY SE4 141 G2
Gordon Cl STA TW18 148 B2
WALTH E17 69 G7 5
Gordon Crs CROY/NA CR0 172 E3
HYS/HAR UB3 114 A2
Gordondale Rd
WIM/MER SW19 137 G6 1
Gordon Dr SHPTN TW17 164 D1 2
Gordon Gdns EDGW HA8 63 H3
Gordon Gv CMBW SE5 121 H7
Gordon Hl ENC/FH EN2 36 C4
Gordon House Rd KTTN NW5 84 A4 1
Gordon Pl KENS W8 14 B1
Gordon Rd ASHF TW15 130 E7
BARK IG11 89 L8
BECK BR3 158 F6
BELV DA17 127 J2
BFN/LL DA15 143 L2
BRYLDS KT5 167 M2
CAR SM5 170 F8
CHDH RM6 72 F7
CHES/WCR EN8 27 G7
CHING E4 51 L2
CHSWK W4 117 H4
DART DA1 146 D4
EA W5 98 C6
ED N9 50 B4
ENC/FH EN2 36 D4
ESH/CLAY KT10 178 E1
FBAR/BDGN N11 66 D1
FNCH N3 64 F1
HSLW TW3 133 J1
IL IG1 89 K3
KTN/HRWW/W HA3 61 L4
KUTN/CMB KT2 152 F4
NWDGN UB2 114 E2
PECK SE15 122 B7
RCH/KEW TW9 116 F7
SHPTN TW17 164 D1
SRTFD E15 87 J4
SWFD E18 70 B2
WAN E11 70 A7
WDR/YW UB7 94 E6
Gordon Sq STPAN WC1H 5 H9
Gordon St PLSTW E13 106 A2
STPAN WC1H 5 G9
Gordon Wy BAR EN5 33 M7
BMLY BR1 160 A4 1
Gorefield Pl KIL/WHAMP NW6 2 A5
Gore Rd HOM E9 86 C8
RDART DA2 147 K6
RYNPK SW20 154 C5
Goresbrook Rd DAGW RM9 90 C8
Gore St SKENS SW7 14 F3
Gorham Pl NTGHL W11 100 E6 5
Goring Cl CRW RM5 73 J2
Goring Gdns BCTR RM8 90 C4
Goring Rd DAGE RM10 91 K6
FBAR/BDGN N11 48 E8 1
Goring St HDTCH EC3A 13 K4 5
Goring Wy GFD/PVL UB6 97 J1
Gorle Cl GSTN WD25 21 G7
Gorleston Rd
SEVS/STOTM N15 67 K6 5
Gorleston St WKENS W14 118 E2 5
Gorman Rd WOOL/PLUM SE18 124 F2
Gorringe Park Av MTCM CR4 155 M3
Gorse Ri TOOT SW17 156 A1
Gorse Rd CROY/NA CR0 174 A5

Gorse Wk WDR/YW UB7 94 E5
Gorseway ROMW/RG RM7 91 L2
Gorst Rd BTSEA SW11 137 M3
WLSDN NW10 99 K3
Gorsuch Pl BETH E2 7 L7
Gorsuch St BETH E2 7 L7
Gosberton Rd BAL SW12 137 M5
Gosbury Hl CHSGTN KT9 167 L6
Gosfield Rd BCTR RM8 91 G1
HOR/WEW KT19 180 D5
Gosfield St GTPST W1W 10 D2
Gosford Gdns REDBR IG4 70 F6
Gosforth La OXHEY WD19 42 A5
Gosforth Pth OXHEY WD19 42 A5
Goshawk Gdns YEAD UB4 95 L2
Goslett Yd SOHO/SHAV W1D 11 H4
Gosling Cl GFD/PVL UB6 97 G2
Gosling Wy BRXN/ST SW9 121 G6
Gospatrick Rd TOTM N17 67 J2
Gosport Dr HCH RM12 92 C6
Gosport Rd WALTH E17 68 F6
Gossage Rd HGDN/ICK UB10 76 F7
WOOL/PLUM SE18 125 K3
The Gossamers GSTN WD25 21 L8
Gosset St BETH E2 104 A2
Gosshill Rd CHST BR7 161 G5
Gossington Cl CHST BR7 143 H8
Gosterwood St DEPT SE8 122 E4
Gostling Rd WHTN TW2 133 G5
Goston Gdns THHTH CR7 157 G6
Goswell Rd FSBYE EC1V 6 D7
Gothic Cl DART DA1 146 D7
Gothic Ct HYS/HAR UB3 113 K4
Gothic Rd WHTN TW2 133 K6
Gottfried Ms KTTN NW5 84 C4
Goudhurst Rd BMLY BR1 159 L1
Gough Rd EN EN1 37 H5
FSTGT E7 87 M4
Gough St FSBYW WC1X 5 M9
Goulding Gdns THHTH CR7 157 J5
Gould Rd EBED/NFELT TW14 131 L4
WHTN TW2 133 L5
Gould's Gn UX/CGN UB8 95 H5
UX/CGN UB8 95 H6
Gould Ter HACK E8 86 B5
Goulston St WCHPL E1 13 L4
Goulton Rd CLPT E5 86 B5
Gourley Pl SEVS/STOTM N15 67 L6
Gourley St SEVS/STOTM N15 67 L6
Gourock Rd ELTH/MOT SE9 143 G2
Govan St BETH E2 86 A8
Government Rw PEND EN3 38 A2
Govett Av SHPTN TW17 149 J8
Govier Cl SRTFD E15 87 L7
Gowan Av FUL/PGN SW6 118 E6
Gowan Rd WLSDN NW10 82 B7
Gowar Fld POTB/CUF EN6 22 A4
Gower Cl BAL SW12 138 C3
Gower Ms GWRST WC1E 11 H3
Gower Pl STPAN WC1H 4 F9
Gower Rd FSTGT E7 88 A6
ISLW TW7 115 M4
WEY KT13 164 D8
Gower St GWRST WC1E 4 F9
Gower's Wk WCHPL E1 104 A5
Gowland Pl BECK BR3 158 F5
Gowlett Rd PECK SE15 122 A8
Gowrie Rd BTSEA SW11 120 A8
Graburn Wy E/WMO/HCT KT8 151 K6
Grace Av BXLYHN DA7 126 F7
Gracechurch St BANK EC3V 13 H6
Grace Cl BARK/HLT IG6 53 M8
BORE WD6 32 D4
EDGW HA8 63 J1
ELTH/MOT SE9 142 D7
Gracedale Rd TOOT SW17 156 B1
Gracefield Gdns
STRHM/NOR SW16 138 E7
Grace Pl BOW E3 105 H2
Grace Rd CROY/NA CR0 172 C1
Grace's Ms CMBW SE5 121 K7
Grace's Rd CMBW SE5 121 L7
Grace St BOW E3 105 H2
The Gradient SYD SE26 140 A8
Graeme Rd EN EN1 36 E5
Graemesdyke Av
MORT/ESHN SW14 117 H8
Grafton Cl HSLWW TW4 132 E5
WEA W13 98 A5
WPK KT4 168 E5
Grafton Crs CAMTN NW1 84 B6
Grafton Gdns BCTR RM8 90 E2
FSBYPK N4 67 J7
Grafton Ms FITZ W1T 10 E1
Grafton Park Rd WPK KT4 168 E4
Grafton Pl CAMTN NW1 5 G8
Grafton Rd ACT W3 99 J6
CROY/NA CR0 172 A3
ENC/FH EN2 35 M6
HRW HA1 61 J6
KTTN NW5 84 A5
NWMAL KT3 153 L7
WPK KT4 168 D5
Grafton Sq CLAP SW4 120 C8
Grafton St MYFR/PICC W1J 10 D7
Grafton Ter KTTN NW5 83 M5
Grafton Wy E/WMO/HCT KT8 150 F7
FITZ W1T 10 F1
GTPST W1W 10 E2
Grafton Yd KTTN NW5 84 B6
Graham Av MTCM CR4 156 A4
WEA W13 98 B8
Graham Cl CROY/NA CR0 174 A4
Grahame Park Wy MLHL NW7 63 M1
Graham Gdns SURB KT6 167 L3
Graham Rd BXLYHN DA7 144 F1
CHSWK W4 117 K1
HACK E8 86 A6
HDN NW4 64 B7
HPTN TW12 133 G8
KTN/HRWW/W HA3 61 L4
MTCM CR4 156 A4
PLSTW E13 106 A3
PUR/KEN CR8 184 A6
SEVS/STOTM N15 67 H4
WIM/MER SW19 154 F3
Graham St IS N1 6 D6
Graham Ter BGVA SW1W 16 B6
Grainger Cl NTHLT UB5 79 J5
Grainger Rd ISLW TW7 115 M7
WDGN N22 67 J2
Gramer Cl WAN E11 87 K2
Grampian Cl HYS/HAR UB3 113 K5
ORP BR6 176 F1
Grampian Gdns CRICK NW2 82 E1
Granada St TOOT SW17 155 M1
Granard Av PUT/ROE SW15 136 B2
Granard Rd BAL SW12 137 M4
The Granaries WAB EN9 27 L6
Granary Cl ED N9 50 C2
Granary Rd WCHPL E1 104 B3
Granary St CAMTN NW1 5 G4
Granby Park Rd CHESW EN7 25 M1
Granby Rd ELTH/MOT SE9 124 F7
Granby St BETH E2 7 M9
BETH E2 104 A3
Granby Ter CAMTN NW1 4 E6
Grand Av BRYLDS KT5 168 B1
FARR EC1M 12 D2
MUSWH N10 66 A5
WBLY HA9 81 G5
Grand Av East WBLY HA9 81 H5
Grand Depot Rd
WOOL/PLUM SE18 125 G3
Grand Dr RYNPK SW20 154 C6
STHL UB1 97 J8
Granden Rd
STRHM/NOR SW16 156 E5
Grandfield Av WAT WD17 28 F4
Grandison Rd BTSEA SW11 137 M2
WPK KT4 169 J4
Grand Union Canal Wk
BAY/PAD W2 8 B2
DEN/HRF UB9 58 B4
HNWL W7 115 L1
NWDGN UB2 114 B1
RKW/CH/CXG WD3 40 A6
STHL UB1 96 F3
STKPK UB11 95 H8
WLSDN NW10 99 H1
Grand Union Crs HACK E8 86 A7
Granfield St BTSEA SW11 119 K6
Grange Av EBAR EN4 47 L3
KTN/HRWW/W HA3 62 B3
NFNCH/WDSP N12 47 J7
SNWD SE25 157 L5
TRDG/WHET N20 46 E2
WHTN TW2 133 L6
Grangecliffe Gdns SNWD SE25 157 L5
Grange Cl BFN/LL DA15 144 A7
E/WMO/HCT KT8 151 H7
HYS/HAR UB3 95 L4
NWDGN UB2 114 F3
WAT WD17 29 G4
WFD IG8 70 A1
Grange Ct NTHLT UB5 96 C1
WAB EN9 27 J7
WOT/HER KT12 165 G4
Grangecourt Rd
STNW/STAM N16 85 L1
Grange Crs CHIG IG7 53 K7
RDART DA2 147 H3
THMD SE28 108 C5
Grangedale Cl NTHWD HA6 59 L2
Grange Dr CHST BR7 160 E2
Grange Farm Cl
RYLN/HDSTN HA2 79 J2
Grange Gdns BNSTD SM7 182 B6
HAMP NW3 83 H3
PIN HA5 60 F5
SNWD SE25 157 L5
STHGT/OAK N14 48 D3
Grange Gv IS N1 85 J6
Grange Hl EDGW HA8 45 J7
SNWD SE25 157 L5
Grangehill Pl ELTH/MOT SE9 124 F8
Grangehill Rd ELTH/MOT SE9 142 F1
Grange La DUL SE21 139 M6
GSTN WD25 30 D4
Grange Meadow BNSTD SM7 182 B6
Grangemill Rd CAT SE6 141 G7
Grangemill Wy CAT SE6 141 G6
Grange Pk EA W5 98 E7
Grange Park Av WCHMH N21 49 H1
Grange Park Pl RYNPK SW20 154 B3
Grange Park Rd LEY E10 87 H1
THHTH CR7 157 K7
Grange Pl STA TW18 148 C5
Grange Rd BARN SW13 118 A6
BELMT SM2 182 A1
BORE WD6 31 M8
BUSH WD23 29 L8
CHSGTN KT9 167 L6
CHSWK W4 117 H3
E/WMO/HCT KT8 151 H7
EA W5 98 D7
EDGW HA8 45 K8
HARH RM3 56 B8
HGT N6 66 A7
HRW HA1 62 A7
HYS/HAR UB3 95 L5
IL IG1 89 J4
KUT KT1 152 E6
LEY E10 87 G1
ORP BR6 176 C4
PLSTW E13 105 M2
RYLN/HDSTN HA2 79 K2
SAND/SEL CR2 184 C3
SNWD SE25 157 K6
SOCK/AV RM15 111 J7
STHL UB1 96 E8
STHWK SE1 19 K4
TOTM N17 50 A8
WALTH E17 68 E6
WLSDN NW10 82 B6
WOT/HER KT12 165 L6
Granger Wy ROMW/RG RM7 74 A7
Grange St IS N1 7 H4
The Grange ALP/SUD HA0 81 G7
CROY/NA CR0 173 M4
HOR/WEW KT19 168 D6
STHWK SE1 19 L3
WIM/MER SW19 154 D2
WOT/HER KT12 165 H4
Grange V BELMT SM2 182 B1
Grangeview Rd
TRDG/WHET N20 47 J3
Grange Wk STHWK SE1 19 K3
Grange Wy ERITH DA8 128 B5
Grangeway KIL/WHAMP NW6 2 A2
NFNCH/WDSP N12 47 H6
WFD IG8 52 C6
Grangeway Gdns REDBR IG4 70 E6
The Grangeway WCHMH N21 49 H1
Grangewood BXLY DA5 144 F5
POTB/CUF EN6 23 H3
Grangewood Av RAIN RM13 110 C3
Grangewood Cl PIN HA5 60 A6
Grangewood La BECK BR3 158 F2
Grange Yd STHWK SE1 19 L4
Granham Gdns ED N9 49 M4
Granite St WOOL/PLUM SE18 125 M3
Granleigh Rd WAN E11 87 L2
Gransden Av HACK E8 86 B7
Gransden Rd SHB W12 99 M8
Grantbridge St IS N1 6 D5
Grantchester Cl HRW HA1 79 M3
Grant Cl SHPTN TW17 164 B1
STHGT/OAK N14 48 C2
Grantham Cl EDGW HA8 44 E5
Grantham Gdns CHDH RM6 72 F7
Grantham Gn BORE WD6 32 C8
Grantham Pl MYFR/PICC W1J 10 C9
Grantham Rd BRXN/ST SW9 120 E8
CHSWK W4 117 L5
MNPK E12 89 G3
Grantley Rd HSLWW TW4 114 C7
Grantley St WCHPL E1 104 D2
Grantock Rd WALTH E17 69 K2
Granton Av HCH RM12 92 F2
Granton Rd GDMY/SEVK IG3 90 A1
SCUP DA14 162 B2
STRHM/NOR SW16 156 C4
Grant Rd BTSEA SW11 119 L8
CROY/NA CR0 172 F3
KTN/HRWW/W HA3 61 L4
Grants Cl MLHL NW7 64 C1
Grant St IS N1 6 A5
PLSTW E13 106 A2
Grantully Rd MV/WKIL W9 2 C8
Grant Wy ISLW TW7 116 A4
Granville Av ED N9 50 C5
FELT TW13 132 A6
HSLWW TW4 133 G2
WEY KT13 164 C8
Granville Cl CROY/NA CR0 172 E4
Granville Gdns ACT W3 98 F7
STRHM/NOR SW16 156 F4
Granville Gv LEW SE13 123 J8
Granville Ms SCUP DA14 144 A8
Granville Pk LEW SE13 123 J8
Granville Pl MBLAR W1H 10 A5
PIN HA5 60 D4
Granville Rd BAR EN5 33 J7
CRICK NW2 82 F2
FSBYPK N4 66 F7
HGDN/ICK UB10 77 H6
HYS/HAR UB3 113 M2
IL IG1 89 H1
KIL/WHAMP NW6 2 A6
LEY E10 69 H7
NFNCH/WDSP N12 65 J1
PLMGR N13 48 F8
SCUP DA14 144 A8
SWFD E18 70 B3
WAND/EARL SW18 136 F4
WATW WD18 29 J7
WDGN N22 67 H2
WELL DA16 126 C8
WEY KT13 164 C8
WIM/MER SW19 155 G3
Granville St FSBYW WC1X 5 M8
Grape St LSQ/SEVD WC2H 11 J4
Grasdene Rd WOOL/PLUM SE18 126 A5
Grasmere Av ACT W3 99 J6
HSLW TW3 133 H3
ORP BR6 176 B5
PUT/ROE SW15 135 K8
RSLP HA4 59 J8
WBLY HA9 62 D8
WIM/MER SW19 155 G6
Grasmere Cl
EBED/NFELT TW14 131 M5
GSTN WD25 21 H5
LOU IG10 39 M5
Grasmere Ct WDGN N22 48 F8
Grasmere Gdns
KTN/HRWW/W HA3 62 A3
ORP BR6 176 B5
REDBR IG4 70 E6
Grasmere Rd BMLY BR1 159 M4
BXLYHN DA7 127 J6
MUSWH N10 66 B2
ORP BR6 176 B5
PLSTW E13 106 A1
PUR/KEN CR8 184 B4
SNWD SE25 173 H1
STRHM/NOR SW16 156 F1
TOTM N17 50 A8
Grassington Cl FBAR/BDGN N11 48 A7
Grassington Rd SCUP DA14 144 A8
Grassmere Rd EMPK RM11 74 F5
Grassmount FSTH SE23 140 B6
WLGTN SM6 183 J3
Grass Pk FNCH N3 64 F2
Grassway WLGTN SM6 171 J6
Grasvenor Av BAR EN5 47 G1
Gratton Rd WKENS W14 118 E1
Gravel Cl CHIG IG7 54 A4
Graveley Av BORE WD6 32 C7
Gravel Hl BXLYHS DA6 145 H2
CROY/NA CR0 173 K8
FNCH N3 64 F3
UX/CGN UB8 76 D5
Gravel Hill Cl BXLY DA5 145 H3
BXLYHS DA6 145 H2
Gravel La CHIG IG7 54 A1
WCHPL E1 13 L4
Gravel Pit Wy ORP BR6 177 G4
Gravel Rd HAYES BR2 175 L4
WHTN TW2 133 L5
Gravelwood Cl CHST BR7 143 J7
Graveney Gv PGE/AN SE20 158 C3
Graveney Rd TOOT SW17 137 L8
Gravesend Rd SHB W12 100 A6
Gray Av BCTR RM8 90 F1
Gray Gdns RAIN RM13 92 A6
Grayham Crs NWMAL KT3 153 K7
Grayham Rd NWMAL KT3 153 K7
Grayland Cl BMLY BR1 160 D4
Grayling Cl CAN/RD E16 105 L3
Grayling Rd STNW/STAM N16 85 K2
The Graylings ABLGY WD5 20 E6
Grayscroft Rd
STRHM/NOR SW16 156 D3
Grays Farm Rd STMC/STPC BR5 162 B4
Grayshott Rd BTSEA SW11 120 A8
Gray's Inn Rd FSBYW WC1X 5 K7
Gray's Inn Sq GINN WC1R 12 A2
Grays La ASHF TW15 131 H8
Gray's Rd HGDN/ICK UB10 76 E7
Gray St STHWK SE1 18 C1
Grayswood Gdns
RYNPK SW20 154 B5
Gray's Yd MHST W1U 10 B5
Graywood Ct
NFNCH/WDSP N12 65 J1
Grazebrook Rd
STNW/STAM N16 85 K2
Grazeley Cl BXLYHS DA6 145 J2
Greasy Cl ABLGY WD5 20 F4
Great Benty WDR/YW UB7 112 E2
Great Brownings DUL SE21 139 M8
Great Bushey Dr
TRDG/WHET N20 47 H3
Great Cambridge Jct
PLMGR N13 49 J7
Great Cambridge Rd
CHES/WCR EN8 26 C7
UED N18 49 K7
Great Castle St REGST W1B 10 E4
Great Central Av RSLP HA4 78 C5
Great Central St CAMTN NW1 9 L2
Great Central Wy WBLY HA9 81 J5
WLSDN NW10 81 L5
Great Chapel St SOHO/CST W1F 11 G4
Great Chertsey Rd CHSWK W4 117 K6
FELT TW13 132 F7
Great Church La HMSMTH W6 118 D3
Great College St WEST SW1P 17 J3
Great Cross Av GNWCH SE10 123 L5
Great Cullings ROMW/RG RM7 91 L2
Great Cumberland Ms
MBLAR W1H 9 L5
Great Cumberland Pl
MBLAR W1H 9 L4
Great Dover St STHWK SE1 19 G3
Greatdown Rd HNWL W7 97 M4
Great Eastern Rd SRTFD E15 87 K7
Great Eastern St SDTCH EC2A 7 J8
Great Elms Rd HAYES BR2 160 C7
Great Fld CDALE/KGS NW9 63 L2
Greatfield Av EHAM E6 106 F3
Greatfield Cl LEW SE13 141 G1
Greatfields Dr UX/CGN UB8 95 G4
Greatfields Rd BARK IG11 89 K8
Great Galley Cl BARK IG11 108 B2
Great Gardens Rd EMPK RM11 74 B7
Great George St STJSPK SW1H 17 H2
Great Gv BUSH WD23 30 B7
Great Groves CHESW EN7 25 L1
Great Guildford St STHWK SE1 12 E9
Greatham Rd BUSH WD23 29 K6
Great Harry Dr ELTH/MOT SE9 143 G7
Great James St BMSBY WC1N 11 L2
Great Marlborough St
SOHO/CST W1F 10 E5
Great Maze Pond STHWK SE1 13 H9
Great Nelmes Cha EMPK RM11 74 F6
Great New St
FLST/FETLN EC4A 12 B4
Great North Rd EFNCH N2 65 L5
Great North Wy (Barnet By-pass)
HDN NW4 64 D4
Great Oaks CHIG IG7 53 J6
Greatorex St WCHPL E1 104 A4
Great Ormond St BMSBY WC1N 11 K2
Great Owl Rd CHIG IG7 53 G5
Great Pk KGLGY WD4 20 A3
Great Percy St FSBYW WC1X 5 M7
Great Peter St WEST SW1P 17 G4
Great Portland St
GTPST W1W 10 D1
Great Pulteney St
SOHO/CST W1F 10 F6
Great Queen St DART DA1 146 F3
HOL/ALD WC2B 11 L4
Great Russell St RSQ WC1B 11 H4
Great St Helen's HDTCH EC3A 13 J4
Great Scotland Yd WHALL SW1A 11 J9
Great Slades POTB/CUF EN6 22 F6
Great Smith St WEST SW1P 17 H3
Great South-west Rd
EBED/NFELT TW14 114 A8
Great Spilmans EDUL SE22 139 L2
Great Strd CDALE/KGS NW9 63 M3
Great Suffolk St STHWK SE1 12 D9
Great Sutton St FSBYE EC1V 12 D1
Great Swan Aly LOTH EC2R 13 G4
Great Thrift STMC/STPC BR5 161 J7
Great Titchfield St GTPST W1W 10 D1
Great Tower St MON EC3R 13 J6
Great Trinity La BLKFR EC4V 12 F6
Great Western Rd MV/WKIL W9 100 F4
Great West Rd CHSWK W4 117 J4
HEST TW5 114 E7
HMSMTH W6 118 B3
ISLW TW7 115 L5
Great West Rd Chiswick
CHSWK W4 117 M4
Great West Rd Ellesmere Rd
CHSWK W4 117 J4
Great West Rd Hogarth La
CHSWK W4 117 K4
Great Winchester St OBST EC2N 13 H4
Great Windmill St
MYFR/PICC W1J 11 G7
SOHO/SHAV W1D 11 G6
Greatwood CHST BR7 161 G3
Great Woodcote Dr
PUR/KEN CR8 183 K3
Great Woodcote Pk
PUR/KEN CR8 183 L3
Greaves Cl BARK IG11 89 K7
Greaves Pl TOOT SW17 137 L8
Grebe Av YEAD UB4 96 D5
Grebe Cl FSTGT E7 87 M5
WALTH E17 68 E1
Grecian Crs NRWD SE19 157 H2
Greek St SOHO/SHAV W1D 11 H5
Greenacre Cl BAR EN5 33 M3
NTHLT UB5 78 F5
SWLY BR8 163 L7
Greenacre Pl WLGTN SM6 171 H4
Greenacres BUSH WD23 43 K4
Green Acres CROY/NA CR0 172 F5
Greenacres ELTH/MOT SE9 143 G3
Greenacres Av HGDN/ICK UB10 76 F3
Greenacres Cl ORP BR6 176 C6
RAIN RM13 110 E2
Greenacres Dr STAN HA7 62 B1
Greenacre Sq
BERM/RHTH SE16 104 D8
Greenacre Wk
STHGT/OAK N14 48 D5
Greenall Cl CHES/WCR EN8 26 E3
Green Arbour Ct STP EC4M 12 C4
Green Av MLHL NW7 45 K6
WEA W13 116 B1
Greenaway Gdns HAMP NW3 83 H4
Greenbank CHESW EN7 26 B1
Green Bank NFNCH/WDSP N12 47 H6
WAP E1W 104 B7
Greenbank Av ALP/SUD HA0 80 A5
Greenbank Cl CHING E4 51 J4
HARH RM3 56 D5
Greenbank Crs HDN NW4 64 E5
Greenbank Rd WAT WD17 28 D1
Greenbanks DART DA1 146 E6
UPMR RM14 93 L2
Greenbay Rd CHARL SE7 124 D5
Greenberry St STJWD NW8 3 J6
Greenbrook Av EBAR EN4 34 C4
Green Chain Wk BECK BR3 159 J3
BMLY BR1 159 K3
CHARL SE7 124 D2
ELTH/MOT SE9 143 H2
SYD SE26 158 D2
THMD SE28 108 C6
Green Cl CAR SM5 170 F4
CDALE/KGS NW9 63 J7
CHES/WCR EN8 26 E5
EFNCH N2 65 J8
FELT TW13 150 E1
HAYES BR2 159 L6
Greencoat Pl WEST SW1P 16 F5
Greencoat Rw WEST SW1P 16 F4
Green Court Av CROY/NA CR0 173 H4
Greencourt Av EDGW HA8 63 G2
Green Court Gdns
CROY/NA CR0 173 H4
Greencourt Rd STMC/STPC BR5 161 L8
Green Court Rd SWLY BR8 163 K8
Greencroft Av RSLP HA4 78 C2
Greencroft Gdns EN EN1 36 E6
KIL/WHAMP NW6 2 E1
Greencroft Rd HEST TW5 114 F6
Green Curve BNSTD SM7 181 M8
Green Dl EDUL SE22 139 L2
Green Dragon La BTFD TW8 116 E3
WCHMH N21 35 M8
Green Dr STHL UB1 97 G7
Greene Fielde End STA TW18 148 D3
Green End CHSGTN KT9 167 K6
WCHMH N21 49 H4
Greenend Rd CHSWK W4 99 L8
Green Farm Cl ORP BR6 176 F7
Greenfield Av BRYLDS KT5 168 B2
OXHEY WD19 42 E4
Greenfield Dr EFNCH N2 65 M5
Greenfield Gdns CRICK NW2 82 E2
DAGW RM9 90 C8
STMC/STPC BR5 176 C2
Greenfield Link COUL/CHIP CR5 183 L8
Greenfield Rd DAGW RM9 90 C8
RDART DA2 163 K1
SEVS/STOTM N15 67 L6
WCHPL E1 104 A5
Greenfields STHL UB1 97 G5
Greenfield St WAB EN9 27 J7
Greenfield Wy RYLN/HDSTN HA2 61 H4
Greenford Av HNWL W7 97 L3
STHL UB1 96 F6
Greenford Gdns GFD/PVL UB6 97 H2
Greenford Rd GFD/PVL UB6 79 L5
GFD/PVL UB6 97 J6
SUT SM1 170 B6
Green Gdns ORP BR6 176 C7
Greengate GFD/PVL UB6 80 B6
Greengate St PLSTW E13 106 B1
Green Glades EMPK RM11 74 F7
Greenhalgh Wk EFNCH N2 65 J5
Greenham Cl STHWK SE1 18 A2
Greenham Crs CHING E4 50 F8
Greenham Rd MUSWH N10 66 A3
Greenhayes Av BNSTD SM7 182 A8
Greenhayes Gdns BNSTD SM7 182 A8
Greenheys Cl NTHWD HA6 59 L2
Greenheys Dr SWFD E18 69 M4
Greenhill BKHH IG9 52 C3
HAMP NW3 83 K4
Green Hl ORP BR6 187 L5
Greenhill SUT SM1 170 C4
WBLY HA9 81 H2
Green Hl WOOL/PLUM SE18 124 F3
Greenhill Crs WATW WD18 41 L1
Greenhill Gdns NTHLT UB5 96 F1
Greenhill Gv MNPK E12 88 E4
Greenhill Pk BAR EN5 34 C8
WLSDN NW10 81 L8
Greenhill Rd HRW HA1 61 L7
WLSDN NW10 81 L8
Greenhill's Rents FARR EC1M 12 C2
Greenhill Wy HRW HA1 61 L7
WBLY HA9 81 H2
Greenhithe Cl ELTH/MOT SE9 143 L4
Greenholm Rd ELTH/MOT SE9 143 H2
Green Hundred Rd PECK SE15 122 A4
Greenhurst Rd WNWD SE27 157 G1

Greening St ABYW SE2 — 126 C2
Greenland Crs NWDGN UB2 — 114 C1
Greenland Ms DEPT SE8 — 122 D3
Greenland Pl CAMTN NW1 — 4 D3
Greenland Quay
  BERM/RHTH SE16 — 122 D2
Greenland Rd BAR EN5 — 46 C1
  CAMTN NW1 —
Greenlands HOR/WEW KT19 — 168 B7
Greenlands Rd STA TW18 — 130 A8
  WEY KT13 — 164 B5
Green La BCTR RM8 — 90 F2
  CHIG IG7 — 53 L5
  CHSGTN KT9 — 179 L2
  E/WMO/HCT KT8 — 151 H8
  EDGW HA8 — 44 F6
  ELTH/MOT SE9 — 143 H8
  FELT TW13 — 142 C1
  HDN NW4 — 64 D6
  HNWL W7 — 97 L8
  HSLWW TW4 — 132 C1
  IL IG1 — 89 K2
  MRDN SM4 — 170 B2
  NTHWD HA6 — 59 K1
  NWMAL KT3 — 153
  OXHEY WD19 — 42 C3
  PGE/AN SE20 — 158 D3
  PUR/KEN CR8 — 183 J4
  SHPTN TW17 — 149 J8
  SHPTN TW17 — 164 C1
  STAN HA7 — 44 B6
  SUN TW16 — 149 M3
  THHTH CR7 — 157 H4
  UX/CGN UB8 — 95 J3
  WOT/HER KT12 — 165 H7
  WPK KT4 — 169 G3
Green Lane Av WOT/HER KT12 — 165 H7
Green Lane Gdns THHTH CR7 — 157 L5
Green La CEND/HSY/T N8 — 67 H4
  FSBYPK N4 — 67 H7
  FSBYPK N4 — 85 J1
  HOR/WEW KT19 — 180 E2
  PLMGR N13 — 48 F7
  WCHMH N21 — 49 H3
Greenlaw Gdns NWMAL KT3 — 168 F2
Green Lawns RSLP HA4 — 78 C1
Greenlaw St WOOL/PLUM SE18 — 125 C1
Green Leaf Av WLGTN SM6 — 171 K6
Greenleafe Dr BARK/HLT IG6 — 71 H4
  WALTH E17 — 68 F4
Green Leas SUN TW16 — 149 M3
Green Leas Cl SUN TW16 — 149 M2
Greenleigh Av STMC/STPC BR5 — 162 B7
Green Man La
  EBED/NFELT TW14 — 132 A1
  WEA W13 — 98 A6
Greenman St IS N1 — 6 E2
Green Mead ESH/CLAY KT10 — 165 M8
Greenmead Cl SNWD SE25 — 158 A8
Green Meadow POTB/CUF EN6 — 23 G3
Greenmoor Rd PEND EN3 — 37 J5
Greenoak Pl EBAR EN4 — 34 F5
Greenoak Wy WIM/MER SW19 — 136 D8
Greenock Rd ACT W3 — 117 H1
  STRHM/NOR SW16 — 156 D4
Greenock Wy ROM RM1 — 73 L1
Greeno Crs SHPTN TW17 — 149 K4
Green Pond Cl WALTH E17 — 68 F2
Green Pond Rd WALTH E17 — 68 E4
Green Ride LOU IG10 — 52 A1
  TRDG/WHET N20 — 47 J5
Greens End
  WOOL/PLUM SE18 — 125 H2
Greenshank Cl WALTH E17 — 68 E1
Greenside BCTR RM8 — 90 C2
  BORE WD6 — 32 A3
  BXLY DA5 — 144 E5
  SWLY BR8 — 163 K5
Greenside Cl CAT SE6 — 141 K6
  TRDG/WHET N20 — 47 K4
Greenside Rd CROY/NA CR0 — 172 A2
  SHB W12 — 118 A1
Greenslade Rd BARK IG11 — 89 K7
Greenstead Av WFD IG8 — 52 C8
Greenstead Gdns
  PUT/ROE SW15 — 136 B2
  WFD IG8 — 52 C8
Greensted Rd LOU IG10 — 52 B8
Greenstone Ms WAN E11 — 70 A7
Green St FSTGT E7 — 88 B5
  MYFR/PKLN W1K — 9 M6
  PEND EN3 — 37 K6
  SUN TW16 — 150 A4
Green Street Green Rd
  DART DA1 — 147 G5
  RDART DA2 — 147 J7
Greensward BUSH WD23 — 43 H1
Green Ter CLKNW EC1R — 6 B8
The Green ACT W3 — 99 L5
  BXLYHN DA7 — 127 G6
  CHES/WCR EN8 — 26 C1
  CROY/NA CR0 — 185 M2
  ED N9 — 50 A4
  EW KT17 — 181 G5
  FELT TW13 — 132 B6
  HAYES BR2 — 175 G2
  HEST TW5 — 115 G4
  HGDN/ICK UB10 — 77 J2
  HRW HA1 — 80 A2
  MRDN SM4 — 154 E7
  NWDGN UB2 — 114 F1
  NWMAL KT3 — 153 J6
  RCH/KEW TW9 — 134 D2
  RDART DA2 — 147 K6
  RKW/CH/CXG WD3 — 40 F1
  SCUP DA14 — 162 A1
  SRTFD E15 — 87 M6
  STHGT/OAK N14 — 48 D4
  STMC/STPC BR5 — 162 B3
  SUT SM1 — 170 D5
  TOTM N17 — 49 J8
  WAN E11 — 70 B7
  WCHMH N21 — 49 G2
  WDR/YW UB7 — 112 D1

WELL DA16 — 143 L1
WHTN TW2 — 133 L5
The Green Wk CHING E4 — 51 K3
Green Wy ELTH/MOT SE9 — 142 D2
  HAYES BR2 — 175 L1
  SUN TW16 — 150 A7
Greenway BCTR RM8 — 90 C2
  CHST BR7 — 161 G1
  HARH RM3 — 57 H3
  KTN/HRWW/W HA3 — 62 E6
  PIN HA5 — 60 B3
  RYNPK SW20 — 154 C2
  STHGT/OAK N14 — 48 E4
  TRDG/WHET N20 — 47 G4
  WLGTN SM6 — 171 J6
  YEAD UB4 — 96 B3
Greenway Av WALTH E17 — 69 K5
Greenway Cl CDALE/KGS NW9 — 63 K3
  FBAR/BDGN N11 — 48 A8
  FSBYPK N4 — 85 J2
  TRDG/WHET N20 — 47 G4
Greenway Ct IL IG1 — 89 C1
Greenway Dr STA TW18 — 148 C4
Greenway Gdns
  CDALE/KGS NW9 — 63 J3
  CROY/NA CR0 — 173 M5
  GFD/PVL UB6 — 97 G2
Green Way Gdns
  KTN/HRWW/W HA3 — 61 L3
Greenways ABLGY WD5 — 20 D4
  BECK BR3 — 159 G5
  CHESW EN7 — 25 H2
  ESH/CLAY KT10 — 166 E6
The Greenway CDALE/KGS NW9 — 63 K3
  EPSOM KT18 — 180 A8
  HGDN/ICK UB10 — 77 H2
  HSLWW TW4 — 132 F1
The Green Wy
  KTN/HRWW/W HA3 — 61 L3
The Greenway PEND EN3 — 26 D8
  PIN HA5 — 60 F7
  POTB/CUF EN6 — 23 G6
  RKW/CH/CXG WD3 — 40 A2
  UX/CGN UB8 — 94 D1
Greenwell St GTPST W1W — 10 D1
Greenwich Church St
  GNWCH SE10 — 123 J4
Greenwich Crs EHAM E6 — 106 E4
Greenwich High Rd
  GNWCH SE10 — 123 H5
Greenwich Park St
  GNWCH SE10 — 123 K4
Greenwich South St
  GNWCH SE10 — 123 H6
Greenwich Vw POP/IOD E14 — 124 E1
Greenwood Av BFN/LL DA15 — 144 A6
  DAGE RM10 — 91 H4
  PEND EN3 — 37 L4
Greenwood Cl BFN/LL DA15 — 144 A6
  CHESW EN7 — 26 B4
  MRDN SM4 — 154 E7
  STMC/STPC BR5 — 176 E1
  THDIT KT7 — 167 G3
Greenwood Dr CHING E4 — 51 K7
  GSTN WD25 — 21 H7
Greenwood Gdns BARK/HLT IG6 — 71 J1
  PLMGR N13 — 49 H5
Greenwood La HPTN TW12 — 151 L1
Greenwood Pk KUTN/CMB KT2 — 153 L3
Greenwood Pl KTTN NW5 — 84 B5
Greenwood Rd BXLY DA5 — 145 K8
  CHIG IG7 — 54 B6
  CROY/NA CR0 — 172 B2
  HACK E8 — 7 M2
  ISLW TW7 — 115 M8
  MTCM CR4 — 156 D6
  PLSTW E13 — 105 M1
  THDIT KT7 — 167 G3
Green Wrythe Crs CAR SM5 — 170 E3
Green Wrythe La CAR SM5 — 170 E3
  MRDN SM4 — 170 D1
Greenyard WAB EN9 — 27 J6
Greer Rd KTN/HRWW/W HA3 — 61 J2
Greet St STHWK SE1 — 12 B9
Greg Cl LEY E10 — 69 J7
Gregor Ms BKHTH/KID SE3 — 124 A5
Gregory Crs ELTH/MOT SE9 — 142 D4
Gregory Pl KENS W8 — 14 C1
Gregory Rd CHDH RM6 — 72 D5
  NWDGN UB2 — 115 G1
Gregson Cl BORE WD6 — 32 C5
Greig Cl CEND/HSY/T N8 — 66 E6
Grenaby Av CROY/NA CR0 — 172 D2
Grenaby Rd CROY/NA CR0 — 172 D2
Grenada Rd CHARL SE7 — 124 C5
Grenade St POP/IOD E14 — 104 F6
Grenadier Pl CAR SM5 — 107 G7
Grenada Gdns RCH/KEW TW9 — 134 F1
Grena Rd RCH/KEW TW9 — 134 F1
Grendon Gdns WBLY HA9 — 81 G2
Grendon St STJWD NW8 — 3 J9
Grenfell Av HCH RM12 — 91 M1
Grenfell Cl BORE WD6 — 32 C4
Grenfell Gdns
  KTN/HRWW/W HA3 — 62 E8
Grenfell Rd NTGHL W11 — 100 D5
  TOOT SW17 — 155 M2
Grennell Cl SUT SM1 — 170 D4
Grennell Rd SUT SM1 — 170 C4
Grenoble Gdns PLMGR N13 — 49 G3
Grenside Rd WEY KT13 — 164 B5
Grenville Cl BRYLDS KT5 — 168 C3
  CHES/WCR EN8 — 26 D1

FNCH N3 — 64 F2
Grenville Gdns WFD IG8 — 70 C1
Grenville Ms HPTN TW12 — 151 H1
  MLHL NW7 — 45 K7
  SKENS SW7 — 14 E5
Grenville Rd ARCH N19 — 84 C1
  CROY/NA CR0 — 186 C3
Grenville St BMSBY WC1N — 11 K1
Gresham Av TRDG/WHET N20 — 47 M6
  ENC/FH EN2 — 36 C6
Gresham Dr CHDH RM6 — 72 B6
Gresham Rd BECK BR3 — 158 E5
  BRXN/ST SW9 — 121 G8
  CAN/RD E16 — 106 B5
  EHAM E6 — 106 F1
  HEST TW5 — 115 J6
  HGDN/ICK UB10 — 95 G1
  HPTN TW12 — 151 G2
  SNWD SE25 — 158 A7
  WLSDN NW10 — 81 K5
Gresham St CITYW EC2V — 12 E4
Gresham Wy WIM/MER SW19 — 137 G7
Gresley Cl SEVS/STOTM N15 — 67 K5
  WALTH E17 — 68 E7
Gresley Rd ARCH N19 — 84 C1
Gressenhall Rd
  WAND/EARL SW18 — 136 F4
Gresse St FITZ W1T — 11 G4
Greswell St SCUP DA14 — 144 A7
Greswell St FUL/PGN SW6 — 118 D6
Gretton Rd TOTM N17 — 67 M1
Greville Av SAND/SEL CR2 — 185 K3
Greville Cl TWK TW1 — 134 B4
Greville Ms KIL/WHAMP NW6 — 2 C4
  RCHPK/HAM TW10 — 134 F3
  WALTH E17 — 69 J5
Greville St HCIRC EC1N — 12 B3
Grey Alders EW KT17 — 181 J7
Greycaine Rd WATN WD24 — 29 K2
Grey Cl EFNCH N2 — 65 J7
Greycoat Pl WEST SW1P — 17 G4
Greycoat St WEST SW1P — 17 G4
Grey Eagle St WCHPL E1 — 13 M2
Greyfell Cl STAN HA7 — 44 B7
Greyfields Cl PUR/KEN CR8 — 184 B6
Greyhound Hl HDN NW4 — 64 A4
Greyhound La POTB/CUF EN6 — 22 A6
  STRHM/NOR SW16 — 156 E2
Greyhound Rd HMSMTH W6 — 118 D4
  SUT SM1 — 170 C7
  TOTM N17 — 67 L4
  WLSDN NW10 — 100 B2
Greyhound Ter
  STRHM/NOR SW16 — 156 C4
Greyhound Wy DART DA1 — 145 L2
Greys Park Cl HAYES BR2 — 175 J7
Greystead Rd FSTH SE23 — 140 C4
Greystoke Av PIN HA5 — 61 G4
Greystoke Dr RSLP HA4 — 59 H8
Greystoke Gdns EA W5 — 98 E3
  ENC/FH EN2 — 35 K7
Greystone Cl SAND/SEL CR2 — 185 J4
Greystone Gdns BARK/HLT IG6 — 71 J3
  KTN/HRWW/W HA3 — 62 C7
Greyswood St
  STRHM/NOR SW16 — 156 B2
Grey Towers Av EMPK RM11 — 92 D1
Grey Towers Gdns
  EMPK RM11 — 74 C8
Grice Av BH/WHM TN16 — 187 H6
Gridiron Pl UPMR RM14 — 93 H2
Grierson Rd FSTH SE23 — 140 E3
Griffin Av UPMR RM14 — 75 L7
Griffin Cl WLSDN NW10 — 81 L3
Griffin Manor Wy THMD SE28 — 125 K1
Griffin Rd TOTM N17 — 67 L1
  WOOL/PLUM SE18 — 125 K3
Griffin Wk DART DA9 — 147 M2
Griffin Wy SUN TW16 — 150 A5
Griffith Cl CHDH RM6 — 72 C8
Griffiths Cl WIM/MER SW19 — 155 G3
Griggs Ap IL IG1 — 89 J2
Griggs Gdns HCH RM12 — 92 C5
Grigg's Pl STHWK SE1 — 19 K4
Griggs Rd LEY E10 — 69 J7
Grimsby St WCHPL E1 — 13 M1
Grimsdyke Crs BAR EN5 — 33 J6
Grimsdyke Rd PIN HA5 — 60 E1
Grimshaw Wy ROM RM1 — 73 M6
Grimston Rd FUL/PGN SW6 — 118 F7
Grimwade Av CROY/NA CR0 — 173 G5
Grimwood Rd TWK TW1 — 133 M4
Grindall St CROY/NA CR0 — 172 B6
Grindleford Av FBAR/BDGN N11 — 48 A4
Grindley Gdns CROY/NA CR0 — 172 F1
Grinling Pl DEPT SE8 — 123 G4
Grinstead Rd DEPT SE8 — 122 E3
Grisedale Cl PUR/KEN CR8 — 184 E7
Grisedale Gdns PUR/KEN CR8 — 184 E7
Grisle Cl ED N9 — 50 B6
Grittleton Av WBLY HA9 — 81 H6
Grittleton Rd MV/WKIL W9 — 2 A9
Grocers' Hall Ct LOTH EC2R — 12 F5
Groombridge Cl WELL DA16 — 144 A2
  WOT/HER KT12 — 165 H7
Groombridge Rd HOM E9 — 86 D7
Groom Crs WAND/EARL SW18 — 137 A4
Groomfield Cl TOOT SW17 — 138 A8
Grooms Dr RSLP HA4 — 60 A6

HGDN/ICK UB10 — 77 H7
KTBR SW1X — 16 B2
Grosvenor Crescent Ms
  KTBR SW1X — 16 A2
Grosvenor Dr EMPK RM11 — 92 C1
  CRICK NW2 — 82 C6
  EHAM E6 — 106 C2
  GLDGN NW11 — 64 F7
  KUTN/CMB KT2 — 152 D2
  MORT/ESHN SW14 — 117 L8
  MUSWH N10 — 66 C4
  UPMR RM14 — 93 K2
  WFD IG8 — 52 A8
  WLGTN SM6 — 183 J1
Grosvenor Gardens Ms East
  BGVA SW1W — 16 D3
Grosvenor Hl MYFR/PKLN W1K — 10 C6
  WIM/MER SW19 — 154 E2
Grosvenor Pk CMBW SE5 — 121 J5
Grosvenor Park Rd WALTH E17 — 69 H6
Grosvenor Pl KTBR SW1X — 16 C4
  WEY KT13 — 164 D5
Grosvenor Ri East WALTH E17 — 69 H6
Grosvenor Rd BCTR RM8 — 90 F1
  BELV DA17 — 126 F4
  BORE WD6 — 32 A6
  BTFD TW8 — 116 D3
  BXLYHS DA6 — 144 D2
  CHSWK W4 — 117 J3
  ED N9 — 50 B3
  EHAM E6 — 88 D8
  FNCH N3 — 64 F1
  FSTGT E7 — 88 B6
  HNWL W7 — 98 A7
  HSLWW TW4 — 114 F8
  IL IG1 — 89 J3
  LEY E10 — 87 J1
  MUSWH N10 — 66 C3
  NTHWD HA6 — 41 M7
  NWDGN UB2 — 114 F1
  PIM SW1V — 16 D9
  RCHPK/HAM TW10 — 134 E2
  ROMW/RG RM7 — 73 K5
  SNWD SE25 — 158 A7
  STA TW18 — 148 A3
  STMC/STPC BR5 — 176 E1
  TWK TW1 — 134 A4
  WAN E11 — 70 B6
  WAT WD17 — 29 J7
  WLGTN SM6 — 171 H8
  WWKM BR4 — 174 B4
Grosvenor Sq MYFR/PKLN W1K — 10 B6
Grosvenor St MYFR/PKLN W1K — 10 B6
Grosvenor Ter CMBW SE5 — 121 J5
Grosvenor V RSLP HA4 — 77 M2
Grosvenor Wy CLPT E5 — 86 C2
Grosvenor Wharf Rd
  POP/IOD E14 — 123 K2
Grote's Buildings
  BKHTH/KID SE3 — 123 L7
Grote's Pl BKHTH/KID SE3 — 123 L7
Groton Rd WAND/EARL SW18 — 137 H6
Grotto Ct STHWK SE1 — 18 E1
Grotto Rd TWK TW1 — 133 M6
  WEY KT13 — 164 C6
Grove Av EW KT17 — 180 E6
  HNWL W7 — 97 L5
  MUSWH N10 — 66 C3
  PIN HA5 — 60 E5
  SUT SM1 — 170 A8
  TWK TW1 — 133 M5
Grove Cl E/WMO/HCT KT8 — 151 K8
  FELT TW13 — 132 E8
  KUT KT1 — 152 E6
  RKW/CH/CXG WD3 — 28 A7
  SWFD E18 — 69 M3
  WOT/HER KT12 — 165 H2
Grove Crescent Rd SRTFD E15 — 87 K6
Grovedale Cl CHESW EN7 — 25 M3
Grovedale Rd ARCH N19 — 84 D2
Grove End KTTN NW5 — 84 B4
  SWFD E18 — 69 M3
Grove End La ESH/CLAY KT10 — 166 D3
Grove End Rd STJWD NW8 — 3 G8
Grove Farm Pk NTHWD HA6 — 41 K7
Grove Gdns DAGE RM10 — 91 J3
  HDN NW4 — 64 A3
  PEND EN3 — 37 K4
  STJWD NW8 — 3 K8
  TEDD TW11 — 134 A8
Grove Green Rd WAN E11 — 87 K1
Grove Hall Rd BUSH WD23 — 29 L7
Groveherst Rd DART DA1 — 128 F8
Grove Hl HRW HA1 — 61 L8
  SWFD E18 — 69 M3
Grove Hill Rd CMBW SE5 — 121 L8
  HRW HA1 — 61 M8
Grove House Rd
  CEND/HSY/T N8 — 66 E5
Groveland Av
  STRHM/NOR SW16 — 156 F3
Groveland Rd BECK BR3 — 158 F6
Grovelands E/WMO/HCT KT8 — 151 G7
Grovelands CMBW SE5 — 121 J5
  RYLN/HDSTN HA2 — 79 H3
Grovelands Rd PLMGR N13 — 49 F7
  PUR/KEN CR8 — 183 M5
  SEVS/STOTM N15 — 68 A2
  STMC/STPC BR5 — 162 A3
Groveland Wy NWMAL KT3 — 153 J8
Grove La CHIG IG7 — 53 M5
  CMBW SE5 — 121 K6
  COUL/CHIP CR5 — 183 H6
  KUT KT1 — 152 E7
  UX/CGN UB8 — 94 F3
Groveley Rd SUN TW16 — 149 M1
Grove Ms HMSMTH W6 — 118 C1

Grove Mill La RKW/CH/CXG WD3 — 28 C3
  CMBW SE5 — 121 J5
  WAN E11 — 70 B6
Grove Park Av CHING E4 — 69 H4
Grove Park Br CHSWK W4 — 117 J5
Grove Park Gdns CHSWK W4 — 117 H5
Grove Park Rd CHSWK W4 — 117 H5
  ELTH/MOT SE9 — 142 E6
  RAIN RM13 — 92 A8
  SEVS/STOTM N15 — 67 L5
Grove Park Ter CHSWK W4 — 117 H5
Grove Pl ACT W3 — 99 J7
  BAL SW12 — 138 B3
  WEY KT13 — 164 C2
Grove Rd ACT W3 — 99 J7
  BARN SW13 — 117 H7
  BELMT SM2 — 170 A8
  BELV DA17 — 126 F4
  BORE WD6 — 32 A7
  BOW E3 — 104 E1
  BTFD TW8 — 116 C3
  BXLYHN DA7 — 145 J1
  CHDH RM6 — 72 C8
  CHING E4 — 51 J5
  CRICK NW2 — 82 C6
  E/WMO/HCT KT8 — 151 K7
  EA W5 — 98 D6
  EBAR EN4 — 34 E6
  EDGW HA8 — 45 C8
  EPSOM KT18 — 180 E6
  FBAR/BDGN N11 — 48 B7
  HOM E9 — 86 B6
  HSLW TW3 — 133 C1
  ISLW TW7 — 115 L6
  LEY E10 — 69 H6
  MTCM CR4 — 156 E5
  NFNCH/WDSP N12 — 47 K7
  NTHWD HA6 — 41 M7
  PIN HA5 — 60 F6
  RCHPK/HAM TW10 — 134 F3
  RKW/CH/CXG WD3 — 40 A4
  SEVS/STOTM N15 — 67 L6
  SHPTN TW17 — 164 C1
  SURB KT6 — 152 D8
  SUT SM1 — 170 B8
  SWFD E18 — 69 M3
  THHTH CR7 — 157 G7
  UX/CGN UB8 — 76 D7
  WAN E11 — 69 M8
  WHTN TW2 — 133 K7
  WIM/MER SW19 — 155 J3
Grove Rd West PEND EN3 — 37 J2
Grover Rd OXHEY WD19 — 42 D1
Groves Cl SOCK/AV RM15 — 111 H6
Groveside Cl ACT W3 — 99 G5
  CAR SM5 — 170 E4
Groveside Rd CHING E4 — 51 L5
Grovestile Waye
  EBED/NFELT TW14 — 131 K4
Grove St BERM/RHTH SE16 — 122 F2
  UED N18 — 49 M8
Grove Ter KTTN NW5 — 84 A3
  TEDD TW11 — 134 A8
The Grove BRW CM14 — 57 M6
  BXLYHS DA6 — 144 D1
  CDALE/KGS NW9 — 63 K6
  CEND/HSY/T N8 — 66 D6
  COUL/CHIP CR5 — 183 K5
  EA W5 — 98 D7
  EDGW HA8 — 45 M4
  ENC/FH EN2 — 36 A5
  EW KT17 — 180 E6
  FNCH N3 — 65 C1
  FSBYPK N4 — 66 F8
  GFD/PVL UB6 — 97 J5
  GLDGN NW11 — 64 E8
  HGDN/ICK UB10 — 77 C5
  HGT N6 — 84 A1
  ISLW TW7 — 115 L6
  PLMGR N13 — 49 G6
  POTB/CUF EN6 — 23 J3
  SCUP DA14 — 144 E8
  SRTFD E15 — 87 L2
  SWLY BR8 — 163 M6
  TEDD TW11 — 134 A8
  UPMR RM14 — 93 G4
  WOT/HER KT12 — 165 H2
  WWKM BR4 — 174 C5
Grove V CHST BR7 — 161 C2
  EDUL SE22 — 139 L1
Groveway BCTR RM8 — 90 D4
  BRXN/ST SW9 — 120 F6
Grove Wy ESH/CLAY KT10 — 166 C3
  UX/CGN UB8 — 76 D7
  WBLY HA9 — 81 L4
Grove Wood Hl COUL/CHIP CR5 — 183 K7
Grovewood Pl WFD IG8 — 53 L2
Grummant Rd PECK SE15 — 121 M6
Grundy St POP/IOD E14 — 105 H5
Gruneisen Rd FNCH N3 — 65 H1
Guardian Cl HCH RM12 — 92 B2
Gubbins La HARH RM3 — 74 F2
Gubyon Av HNHL SE24 — 139 J3
Guernsey Cl HEST TW5 — 115 G6
Guernsey Gv HNHL SE24 — 139 J4
Guernsey Rd IS N1 — 85 J6
  WAN E11 — 87 K1
Guibal Rd LEE/GVPK SE12 — 142 B5
Guildersfield Rd
  STRHM/NOR SW16 — 156 A6
Guildford Av FELT TW13 — 132 A6
Guildford Gv GNWCH SE10 — 123 H6
Guildford Rd CROY/NA CR0 — 172 D1
  EHAM E6 — 106 C5
  GDMY/SEVK IG3 — 89 J2
  HARH RM3 — 56 E8
  VX/NE SW8 — 120 E6
  WALTH E17 — 69 J2
Guildford St STA TW18 — 148 C4
Guildford Wy WLGTN SM6 — 171 L7
Guildhall Buildings CITYW EC2V — 12 F4
Guildhouse St PIM SW1V — 16 E6
Guilford Av BRYLDS KT5 — 152 B5

Guilford Pl BMSBY WC1N 11 L1
Guilford St BMSBY WC1N 11 L1
Guilsborough Cl WLSDN NW10 .. 81 L7 2
Guinevere Gdns
CHES/WCR EN8 .... 26 E3 2
Guinness Cl HOM E9 .... 86 E7 1
HYS/HAR UB3 .... 113 K1
Guinness Sq STHWK SE1 .... 19 J4
Guion Rd FUL/PGN SW6 .... 118 F7
Gulland Cl BUSH WD23 .... 30 C8
Gull Cl WLGTN SM6 .... 183 L1
Gullet Wood Rd GSTN WD25 .... 21 G8
Gulliver Cl NTHLT UB5 .... 78 F8
Gulliver Rd BFN/LL DA15 .... 143 K6
Gulliver St BERM/RHTH SE16 .... 122 F1
Gumleigh Rd EA W5 .... 116 C2
Gumley Gdns ISLW TW7 .... 116 A8 2
Gumping Rd STMC/STPC BR5 .... 176 C4
Gundulph Rd HAYES BR2 .... 160 C6
Gunmakers La HOM E9 .... 86 E8
Gunnell Cl SNWD SE25 .... 172 F1
Gunner La WOOL/PLUM SE18 .... 125 G3
Gunnersbury Av ACT W3 .... 117 G1 1
Gunnersbury Av
(North Circular Road)
ACT W3 .... 117 G1
EA W5 .... 98 F7
Gunnersbury Crs ACT W3 .... 99 G8
Gunnersbury Dr EA W5 .... 98 F8
Gunnersbury Gdns ACT W3 .... 99 G8
Gunnersbury La ACT W3 .... 99 G8
Gunners Gv CHING E4 .... 51 J5
Gunners Rd WAND/EARL SW18 .... 137 K6
Gunning St
WOOL/PLUM SE18 .... 125 L2 2
Gunstor Rd STNW/STAM N16 .... 85 L4 1
Gun St WCHPL E1 .... 13 L3
Gunter Gv EDGW HA8 .... 63 K2
WBPTN SW10 .... 119 J4
Gunterstone Rd WKENS W14 .... 118 E3
Gunthorpe St WCHPL E1 .... 13 M3
Gunton Rd CLPT E5 .... 86 B3
TOOT SW17 .... 156 A2
Gunwhale Cl
BERM/RHTH SE16 .... 104 D7 6
Gurdon Rd CHARL SE7 .... 124 A3
Gurnard Cl WDR/YW UB7 .... 94 D6 1
Gurnell Gv WEA W13 .... 97 M3
Gurney Cl BARK IG11 .... 89 H6
SRTFD E15 .... 87 L5 3
WALTH E17 .... 68 D2
Gurney Crs CROY/NA CR0 .... 171 M3
Gurney Dr EFNCH N2 .... 65 K5
Gurney Rd CAR SM5 .... 171 G6
FUL/PGN SW6 .... 119 J8
NTHLT UB5 .... 96 B2
SRTFD E15 .... 87 L5
Guthrie St CHEL SW3 .... 15 J7
Gutteridge La ABR/ST RM4 .... 55 J1
Gutter La CITYW EC2V 12 E4 1
Guyatt Gdns MTCM CR4 .... 156 A5
Guy Barnett Gv
BKHTH/KID SE3 .... 124 A8 2
Guy Rd WLGTN SM6 .... 171 K5
Guyscliff Rd LEW SE13 .... 141 J2 2
Guysfield Cl RAIN RM13 .... 92 A8 1
Guysfield Dr RAIN RM13 .... 92 A8
Guy St STHWK SE1 .... 19 H1
Gwalior Rd PUT/ROE SW15 .... 118 D8 4
Gwendolen Av PUT/ROE SW15 .... 136 D2
Gwendoline Av PLSTW E13 .... 88 B8
Gwendwr Rd WKENS W14 .... 118 E3
Gwent Cl GSTN WD25 .... 21 K7
Gwillim Cl BFN/LL DA15 .... 144 A3 1
Gwydor Rd BECK BR3 .... 158 D7
Gwydyr Rd HAYES BR2 .... 159 M6
Gwyn Cl FUL/PGN SW6 .... 119 J5
Gwynne Av CROY/NA CR0 .... 173 K2
Gwynne Park Av WFD IG8 .... 52 F8
Gwynne Rd BTSEA SW11 .... 119 K7
Gwynne Whf CHSWK W4 .... 117 M4 1
Gylcote Cl HNHL SE24 .... 139 K1
Gyles Pk STAN HA7 .... 62 C2
Gyllyngdune Gdns
GDMY/SEVK IG3 .... 89 M3
Gypsy La GSTN WD25 .... 20 D8

H

Haarlem Rd HMSMTH W6 .... 118 D1 6
Haberdasher St IS N1 .... 7 H7
Habgood Rd LOU IG10 .... 39 L6
Haccombe Rd WIM/MER SW19 .. 155 J2
Hackbridge Park Gdns
CAR SM5 .... 171 G4 1
Hackbridge Rd CAR SM5 .... 171 G4
Hackford Rd BRXN/ST SW9 .... 120 F6
Hackford Wk BRXN/ST SW9 .... 120 F6
Hackforth Cl BAR EN5 .... 33 H8
Hackington Crs BECK BR3 .... 159 G2
Hackney Cl BORE WD6 .... 32 D8
Hackney Rd BETH E2 .... 7 L7
Hacton Dr HCH RM12 .... 92 E4
Hacton La HCH RM12 .... 92 F2
UPMR RM14 .... 92 F5
Hadden Rd THMD SE28 .... 125 L1
Hadden Wy NTHLT UB5 .... 79 K6
Haddington Rd BMLY BR1 .... 141 K7
Haddon Cl BORE WD6 .... 32 A5
EN EN1 .... 50 A1 1
NWMAL KT3 .... 153 M8
WEY KT13 .... 164 D6 1
Haddon Gv BFN/LL DA15 .... 144 A4
Haddon Rd STMC/STPC BR5 .... 162 C8
SUT SM1 .... 170 B6 3
Haddo St GNWCH SE10 .... 123 H4 2
Hadfield Cl STHL UB1 .... 96 F2 3
Hadfield Rd STWL/WRAY TW19 .... 130 D3
Hadleigh Cl RYNPK SW20 .... 154 F5
Hadleigh Dr BELMT SM2 .... 182 A2
Hadleigh Rd ED N9 .... 50 B2
Hadleigh St BETH E2 .... 104 C3
Hadley Cl BORE WD6 .... 31 M8
WCHMH N21 .... 49 G1
Hadley Gdns CHSWK W4 .... 117 K3
NWDGN UB2 .... 114 F3
Hadley Gn BAR EN5 .... 33 M6
Hadley Green Rd BAR EN5 .... 33 M5
Hadley Gn West BAR EN5 .... 33 L5
Hadley Gv BAR EN5 .... 33 L5
Hadley Highstone BAR EN5 .... 33 M4
Hadley Rdg BAR EN5 .... 33 M6
Hadley Rd BAR EN5 .... 34 B6
BELV DA17 .... 126 F2
EBAR EN4 .... 35 G3
ENC/FH EN2 .... 35 L3
MTCM CR4 .... 156 D7
Hadley St KTTN NW5 .... 84 B6
Hadley Wy WCHMH N21 .... 49 G1
Hadley Wood Ri PUR/KEN CR8 .... 184 B8
Hadley Wood Rd BAR EN5 .... 34 C5
Hadlow Rd SCUP DA14 .... 144 A8
WELL DA16 .... 126 C5
Hadrian Cl STWL/WRAY TW19 .. 130 E4 3
Hadrian's Ride EN EN1 .... 36 F8
Hadrian St GNWCH SE10 .... 123 L3
Hadrian Wy
STWL/WRAY TW19 .... 130 E4 4
Hadyn Park Rd SHB W12 .... 100 A8
Hafer Rd BTSEA SW11 .... 137 M1 1
Hafton Rd CAT SE6 .... 141 L5
Hagden La WATW WD18 .... 28 F7
Haggard Rd TWK TW1 .... 134 B4
Hagger Ct WALTH E17 .... 69 K4 2
Haggerston Rd BORE WD6 .... 31 L3
HACK E8 .... 7 L3
Hague St BETH E2 .... 104 A2 5
Ha-ha Rd WOOL/PLUM SE18 .... 124 F4
Haig Rd STAN HA7 .... 44 C7
UX/CGN UB8 .... 95 H4
Haig Rd East PLSTW E13 .... 106 C2
Haig Rd West PLSTW E13 .... 106 C2
Haigville Gdns BARK/HLT IG6 .... 71 H5
Hailes Cl WIM/MER SW19 .... 155 J2
Haileybury Av EN EN1 .... 49 M1
Haileybury Rd ORP BR6 .... 177 G6
Hailey Rd ERITHM DA18 .... 126 D1
Hailsham Av BRXS/STRHM SW2 .. 138 F6
Hailsham Cl HARH RM3 .... 56 C7
SURB KT6 .... 167 K2
Hailsham Dr HRW HA1 .... 61 K4
Hailsham Rd HARH RM3 .... 56 C7
TOOT SW17 .... 156 A2
Haimo Rd ELTH/MOT SE9 .... 142 D2
Hainault Gore CHDH RM6 .... 72 E6
Hainault Gv CHIG IG7 .... 53 J6
Hainault Rd CHDH RM6 .... 72 B4
CHIG IG7 .... 53 J6
ROMW/RG RM7 .... 73 K4
WAN E11 .... 87 J1
Hainault St ELTH/MOT SE9 .... 143 H5
IL IG1 .... 89 H2
Haines Ct WEY KT13 .... 164 D7
Haines Wk MRDN SM4 .... 170 B2
Haines Wy GSTN WD25 .... 21 G7
Hainford Cl PECK SE15 .... 140 D1
Haining Cl CHSWK W4 .... 117 G3 1
Hainthorpe Rd WNWD SE27 .... 139 H7
Hainton Cl WCHPL E1 .... 104 B5
Halbutt St DAGW RM9 .... 90 F4
Halcomb St IS N1 .... 7 J4
Halcot Av BXLYHS DA6 .... 145 H2
Halcrow St WCHPL E1 .... 104 B4 6
Halcyon Wy EMPK RM11 .... 91 H2
Haldane Cl MUSWH N10 .... 66 B1
Haldane Pl WAND/EARL SW18 .... 137 H5
Haldane Rd EHAM E6 .... 106 D2
FUL/PGN SW6 .... 118 F5
GFD/PVL UB6 .... 97 J6
THMD SE28 .... 108 D6
Haldan Rd CHING E4 .... 51 J8
Haldon Rd WAND/EARL SW18 .... 136 F3
Hale Cl CHING E4 .... 51 J5
EDGW HA8 .... 45 J7
ORP BR6 .... 176 C6
Hale Dr EDGW HA8 .... 45 J8
MLHL NW7 .... 45 K8
Hale End HARH RM3 .... 56 B8
Hale End Cl RSLP HA4 .... 60 A7
Hale End Rd CHING E4 .... 51 K8
WALTH E17 .... 69 K2
WFD IG8 .... 69 K1
Halefield Rd TOTM N17 .... 68 A2
Hale Gdns ACT W3 .... 99 G7
SEVS/STOTM N15 .... 68 A5 4
Hale Grove Gdns MLHL NW7 .... 45 K7
Hale La EDGW HA8 .... 45 J7
MLHL NW7 .... 45 K7
Hale Rd EHAM E6 .... 106 E3
TOTM N17 .... 68 A4
Halesowen Rd MRDN SM4 .... 170 B2
Hales St DEPT SE8 .... 123 G5
Hale St POP/IOD E14 .... 105 H6
Halesworth Cl HARH RM3 .... 56 E8 2
Halesworth Rd HARH RM3 .... 56 E8
LEW SE13 .... 123 H8
The Hale CHING E4 .... 69 K1
SEVS/STOTM N15 .... 68 A4
TOTM N17 .... 68 A4 6
Half Acre BTFD TW8 .... 116 D4
Half Acre Ms BTFD TW8 .... 116 D4 6
Half Acre Rd HNWL W7 .... 97 L7
Halfhides WAB EN9 .... 27 K6
Half Moon Crs IS N1 .... 5 M5 1
Half Moon La HNHL SE24 .... 139 K3
Halfmoon Pas WCHPL E1 .... 13 M5 2
Half Moon St MYFR/PICC W1J .. 10 D9 1
Halford Rd FUL/PGN SW6 .... 119 G4
HGDN/ICK UB10 .... 77 G5
RCHPK/HAM TW10 .... 134 E2
WALTH E17 .... 69 K6
Halfway Ct PUR RM19 .... 129 G2
Halfway Gn WOT/HER KT12 .... 165 H5
Halfway St BFN/LL DA15 .... 143 L5
Haliburton Rd TWK TW1 .... 134 A2
Haliday Wk IS N1 .... 85 K6 5
Halidon Ri HARH RM3 .... 57 H8
Halifax Rd ENC/FH EN2 .... 36 C5
GFD/PVL UB6 .... 79 H8
Halifax St SYD SE26 .... 140 B7
Halifield Dr BELV DA17 .... 126 E1
Haling Gv SAND/SEL CR2 .... 184 C1
Haling Park Gdns
SAND/SEL CR2 .... 172 B8 1
Haling Park Rd SAND/SEL CR2 .... 172 B8
Haling Rd SAND/SEL CR2 .... 172 D8
Halkin Ms KTBR SW1X 16 A3 4
Halkin Pl KTBR SW1X 16 A3 5
Halkin St KTBR SW1X 16 B2
Hallam Cl CHST BR7 .... 160 F1
WATN WD24 .... 29 J5
Hallam Gdns PIN HA5 .... 60 E1
Hallam Rd SEVS/STOTM N15 .... 67 H5 2
Hallam St GTPST W1W 10 D2
Halland Wy NTHWD HA6 .... 41 K8
Hall Av SOCK/AV RM15 .... 111 J7
Hall Cl EA W5 .... 98 E4
RKW/CH/CXG WD3 .... 40 A3
Hall Ct TEDD TW11 .... 151 M1 4
Hall Crs SOCK/AV RM15 .... 111 J8
Hall Dr DEN/HRF UB9 .... 58 C2
SYD SE26 .... 158 C1
Halley Rd FSTGT E7 .... 88 C6
Halley St POP/IOD E14 .... 104 E4 4
Hall Farm Cl STAN HA7 .... 44 B6
Hall Farm Dr WHTN TW2 .... 133 K4
Hallford Wy DART DA1 .... 146 C3
Hall Gdns CHING E4 .... 50 F6
Hall Ga STJWD NW8 .... 2 F8
The Halliards WOT/HER KT12 .. 165 G1 2
Halliday Sq STHL UB1 .... 97 K7
Halliford Cl SHPTN TW17 .... 149 L6
Halliford Rd SHPTN TW17 .... 149 L8
SUN TW16 .... 150 A7
Halliford St IS N1 .... 6 F1
Halliwell Rd BRXS/STRHM SW2 .. 138 F3
Halliwick Rd MUSWH N10 .... 66 A2
Hall La CHING E4 .... 50 F7
HARH RM3 .... 75 J3
HDN NW4 .... 64 A3
HYS/HAR UB3 .... 113 K5
UPMR RM14 .... 75 J6
UPMR RM14 .... 93 J1
Hallmead Rd SUT SM1 .... 170 B5
Hallowell Av CROY/NA CR0 .... 171 L6
Hallowell Cl MTCM CR4 .... 156 A6
Hallowell Rd NTHWD HA6 .... 59 L1
Hallowes Crs OXHEY WD19 .... 42 A5
Hallowfield Wy MTCM CR4 .... 155 K6
Hall Park Rd UPMR RM14 .... 93 J5 1
Hall Pl BAY/PAD W2 .... 9 G1
Hall Place Crs BXLY DA5 .... 145 J2
Hall Place Dr WEY KT13 .... 164 E7
Hall Rd CHDH RM6 .... 72 C7
DART DA1 .... 146 F1
EHAM E6 .... 88 F8
GPK RM2 .... 74 B4
ISLW TW7 .... 133 K2
MV/WKIL W9 .... 2 F8
SOCK/AV RM15 .... 111 J8
WAN E11 .... 87 K4
WLGTN SM6 .... 183 H2
Hallside Rd EN EN1 .... 36 F3
Hall St FSBYE EC1V 6 D7
NFNCH/WDSP N12 .... 47 J7
Hallsville Rd CAN/RD E16 .... 105 M5
Hallswelle Rd GLDGN NW11 .... 64 F6
Hall Ter SOCK/AV RM15 .... 111 K8
The Hall BKHTH/KID SE3 .... 124 A8
Hall Vw ELTH/MOT SE9 .... 142 D6
Hallywell Crs EHAM E6 .... 106 F4
Halons Rd ELTH/MOT SE9 .... 143 G4
Halpin Pl WALW SE17 .... 19 H6
Halsbrook Rd BKHTH/KID SE3 .... 124 C8
Halsbury Cl STAN HA7 .... 44 B7
Halsbury Rd SHB W12 .... 100 B7
Halsbury Rd East NTHLT UB5 .... 79 J4
Halsbury Rd West NTHLT UB5 .... 79 H5
Halsend HYS/HAR UB3 .... 96 B7 1
Halsey Pl WATN WD24 .... 29 H3 2
Halsey Rd WATW WD18 .... 29 H6
Halsey St CHEL SW3 .... 15 L5
Halsham Crs BARK IG11 .... 89 K4
Halsmere Rd CMBW SE5 .... 121 H6
Halstead Cl CROY/NA CR0 .... 172 C5 1
Halstead Gdns WCHMH N21 .... 49 K3
Halstead Hl CHESW EN7 .... 25 L3
Halstead Rd EN EN1 .... 36 E7
ERITH DA8 .... 127 L6
WAN E11 .... 70 B6
WCHMH N21 .... 49 K3
Halstow Rd GNWCH SE10 .... 124 A3
WLSDN NW10 .... 100 D2
Halsway HYS/HAR UB3 .... 96 A7
Halter Cl BORE WD6 .... 32 D8
Halton Cross St IS N1 .... 6 D3 2
Halton Pl IS N1 .... 6 E3 1
Halton Rd IS N1 .... 6 D2
Halt Robin Rd BELV DA17 .... 127 G2
Hambalt Rd CLAP SW4 .... 138 C2
Hamble Cl RSLP HA4 .... 77 L2
Hambledon Cl UX/CGN UB8 .... 95 H3 2
Hambledon Gdns
SNWD SE25 .... 157 M6 1
Hambledon Pl DUL SE21 .... 139 M5
Hambledon Rd
WAND/EARL SW18 .... 136 F4
Hambledown Rd
ELTH/MOT SE9 .... 143 L4 1
Hamble La SOCK/AV RM15 .... 111 M4
Hamble St FUL/PGN SW6 .... 137 K1
Hambleton Cl WPK KT4 .... 169 J4 2
Hambro Av HAYES BR2 .... 175 G3
Hambrook Rd SNWD SE25 .... 158 B6
Hambro Rd STRHM/NOR SW16 .. 156 D2
Hambrough Rd STHL UB1 .... 96 E7
Hamburgh Ct CHES/WCR EN8 .. 26 D1 5
Ham Common
RCHPK/HAM TW10 .... 134 D7
Hamden Crs DAGE RM10 .... 91 H3
Hamel Cl KTN/HRWW/W HA3 .... 62 D5
Hameway EHAM E6 .... 107 G3
Ham Farm Rd
RCHPK/HAM TW10 .... 134 D8
Hamfrith Rd SRTFD E15 .... 87 M6
Ham Gate Av
RCHPK/HAM TW10 .... 134 E8
Hamilton Av BARK/HLT IG6 .... 71 H5
CHEAM SM3 .... 169 L4
ED N9 .... 50 A2 1
ROM RM1 .... 73 K3
SURB KT6 .... 168 A4
Hamilton Cl
BERM/RHTH SE16 .... 104 E8 1
EBAR EN4 .... 34 E7
FELT TW13 .... 149 M1
HOR/WEW KT19 .... 180 C5
POTB/CUF EN6 .... 22 A6
PUR/KEN CR8 .... 184 B5 2
STJWD NW8 .... 3 G8
TOTM N17 .... 67 M4
Hamilton Ct EA W5 .... 98 F6
Hamilton Crs HSLW TW3 .... 133 H2
PLMGR N13 .... 49 G6
RYLN/HDSTN HA2 .... 78 F3
Hamilton Dr EMPK RM11 .... 74 E3
Hamilton Gdns STJWD NW8 .... 2 F7
Hamilton Pk HBRY N5 .... 85 H4
Hamilton Pk West HBRY N5 .... 85 H4
Hamilton Pl MYFR/PKLN W1K 10 B9
SUN TW16 .... 150 B3
Hamilton Rd BFN/LL DA15 .... 144 A8
BTFD TW8 .... 116 D4 7
BXLYHN DA7 .... 126 E7
CHSWK W4 .... 117 L1
EA W5 .... 98 E6
EBAR EN4 .... 34 E7
ED N9 .... 50 A2 2
EFNCH N2 .... 65 J4
FELT TW13 .... 149 L1
GLDGN NW11 .... 64 D8
GPK RM2 .... 74 B6
HRW HA1 .... 61 L6
HYS/HAR UB3 .... 96 B6
IL IG1 .... 89 H4
KGLGY WD4 .... 20 C6
OXHEY WD19 .... 42 B5
SRTFD E15 .... 105 L2
STHL UB1 .... 96 F7
THHTH CR7 .... 157 K6
UX/CGN UB8 .... 94 D3
WALTH E17 .... 68 E3
WHTN TW2 .... 133 L5 1
WIM/MER SW19 .... 155 H3
WLSDN NW10 .... 82 A5
WNWD SE27 .... 139 K8
Hamilton Road Ms
WIM/MER SW19 .... 155 H3 2
Hamilton St DEPT SE8 .... 123 G5
WATW WD18 .... 29 J8 2
Hamilton Ter STJWD NW8 .... 2 E6
Hamilton Wy FNCH N3 .... 47 G8
PLMGR N13 .... 49 H6 2
WLGTN SM6 .... 183 K2
Hamlea Cl BKHTH/KID SE3 .... 142 A2
Hamlet Cl CRW RM5 .... 73 G1
LEW SE13 .... 141 L1
Hamlet Gdns HMSMTH W6 .... 118 A2
Hamlet Rd CRW RM5 .... 73 G1
NRWD SE19 .... 157 M3
Hamlet Sq CRICK NW2 .... 82 E3
Hamlets Wy BOW E3 .... 104 F3 1
Hamlet Wy STHWK SE1 .... 19 H2
Hamlin Crs PIN HA5 .... 60 C6 1
Hamlyn Cl EDGW HA8 .... 44 E5
Hamlyn Gdns NRWD SE19 .... 157 L3
Hammelton Rd BMLY BR1 .... 160 A4
Hammers La MLHL NW7 .... 46 A6
Hammersmith Br HMSMTH W6 .. 118 B3
Hammersmith Bridge Rd
BARN SW13 .... 118 B4
HMSMTH W6 .... 118 C3
Hammersmith Broadway
HMSMTH W6 .... 118 C2 5
Hammersmith F/O
HMSMTH W6 .... 118 C3
Hammersmith Gv
HMSMTH W6 .... 118 C2 6
Hammersmith Rd
HMSMTH W6 .... 118 D2
Hammet Cl YEAD UB4 .... 96 D4
Hammett St TWRH EC3N 13 L6
Hammond Av MTCM CR4 .... 156 B5
Hammond Cl HPTN TW12 .... 151 G4
NTHLT UB5 .... 79 K5 2
Hammond Rd EN EN1 .... 37 H6
NWDGN UB2 .... 114 E1
Hammonds Cl BCTR RM8 .... 90 C3 2
Hammond St KTTN NW5 .... 84 C6 2
Hamond Cl SAND/SEL CR2 .... 184 B2
Hamonde Cl EDGW HA8 .... 45 H4
Hamond Sq IS N1 .... 7 J5
Ham Park Rd FSTGT E7 .... 88 A7
Hampden Av BECK BR3 .... 158 E5
Hampden Crs CHESW EN7 .... 26 B4
Hampden Gurney St
BAY/PAD W2 .... 9 L5 2
Hampden La TOTM N17 .... 67 M2
Hampden Rd ARCH N19 .... 84 D2 3
BECK BR3 .... 158 E5
CEND/HSY/T N8 .... 67 G5
KTN/HRWW/W HA3 .... 61 J2
KUT KT1 .... 153 G6
MUSWH N10 .... 66 A1
TOTM N17 .... 68 A2
Hampden Wy STHGT/OAK N14 .... 48 B3
WAT WD17 .... 28 E1
Hampermill La OXHEY WD19 .... 42 A3
Hampshire Cl UED N18 .... 50 B7 7
Hampshire Hog La
HMSMTH W6 .... 118 B2 4
Hampshire Rd EMPK RM11 .... 75 G5 2
WDGN N22 .... 66 F1 2
Hampshire St KTTN NW5 .... 84 D5 2
Hampson Wy VX/NE SW8 .... 120 F6
Hampstead Cl THMD SE28 .... 108 B7
Hampstead Gdns
GLDGN NW11 .... 65 G7 1
Hampstead Ga HAMP NW3 .... 83 J5
Hampstead Gn HAMP NW3 .... 83 L5 2
Hampstead Gv HAMP NW3 .... 83 J4
Hampstead Hill Gdns
HAMP NW3 .... 83 L4 1
Hampstead La HGT N6 .... 65 M8
Hampstead Rd CAMTN NW1 .... 4 E6
Hampstead Sq HAMP NW3 .... 83 J3 2
Hampstead Wy GLDGN NW11 .... 65 H8
Hampton Cl FBAR/BDGN N11 .... 48 A7
RYNPK SW20 .... 154 C3 2
Hampton Ct IS N1 .... 85 H6 3
Hampton Court Av
E/WMO/HCT KT8 .... 151 L8 1
Hampton Court Rd
E/WMO/HCT KT8 .... 152 A6
HPTN TW12 .... 151 K5
Hampton Court Wy
E/WMO/HCT KT8 .... 151 L7
ESH/CLAY KT10 .... 166 E4
THDIT KT7 .... 166 E2
Hampton Gv EW KT17 .... 180 F4
Hampton La FELT TW13 .... 132 E8
Hampton Ri
KTN/HRWW/W HA3 .... 62 E7 1
Hampton Rd CHING E4 .... 50 F7
CROY/NA CR0 .... 172 C1
FSTGT E7 .... 88 B5
HPTN TW12 .... 151 K1
IL IG1 .... 89 J4
WAN E11 .... 87 K1 3
WHTN TW2 .... 133 K7
WPK KT4 .... 169 G4
Hampton Rd East FELT TW13 .. 132 F8 1
Hampton Rd West FELT TW13 .... 132 E6
Hampton St WALW SE17 .... 18 D6
Ham Ridings
RCHPK/HAM TW10 .... 152 F1
Hamsey Wy SAND/SEL CR2 .... 185 H8
Ham Shades Cl BFN/LL DA15 .... 143 M7
Ham St RCHPK/HAM TW10 .... 134 C6
The Ham BTFD TW8 .... 116 C5
Ham Vw CROY/NA CR0 .... 173 L1
Ham Yd SOHO/SHAV W1D 11 G6 4
Hanameel St CAN/RD E16 .... 106 B7 2
Hanbury Cl CHES/WCR EN8 .... 26 D3
HDN NW4 .... 64 C4
Hanbury Dr BH/WHM TN16 .... 187 H6
WCHMH N21 .... 35 M7
Hanbury Rd ACT W3 .... 99 H8
TOTM N17 .... 68 B3
Hanbury St WCHPL E1 .... 104 A4 7
Hancock Ct BORE WD6 .... 32 C4
Hancock Rd BOW E3 .... 105 J2
NRWD SE19 .... 157 K2
Handcroft Rd CROY/NA CR0 .... 172 B3
Handel Cl EDGW HA8 .... 44 F8
Handel Pl WLSDN NW10 .... 81 K6 5
Handel St BMSBY WC1N 5 J9
Handel Wy EDGW HA8 .... 63 G1
Handen Rd LEW SE13 .... 141 L2
Handforth Rd BRXN/ST SW9 .... 121 G5
IL IG1 .... 89 H3 2
Handley Rd HOM E9 .... 86 C7
Handowe Cl HDN NW4 .... 64 A5
Handside Cl WPK KT4 .... 169 K3 1
Handsworth Av CHING E4 .... 51 K8
Handsworth Cl OXHEY WD19 .... 42 A5
Handsworth Rd TOTM N17 .... 67 K4
Handtrough Wy BARK IG11 .... 107 H1 1
Hanford Cl WAND/EARL SW18 .... 137 G5
Hanford Rd SOCK/AV RM15 .... 111 J7 3
Hangar Ruding OXHEY WD19 .... 42 F5
Hangar View Wy ACT W3 .... 99 G5
Hanger Gn EA W5 .... 99 G3
Hanger Hl WEY KT13 .... 164 B7
Hanger La EA W5 .... 98 F6
Hanger La (North Circular Road)
EA W5 .... 98 E2 1
Hanger Vale La EA W5 .... 98 F5
Hankey Pl STHWK SE1 .... 19 H2
Hankins La MLHL NW7 .... 45 L4
Hanley Gdns FSBYPK N4 .... 84 F1 4
Hanley Pl BECK BR3 .... 159 G3
Hanley Rd FSBYPK N4 .... 84 E1
Hannah Cl BECK BR3 .... 159 H6
Hannan Cl WLSDN NW10 .... 81 J4
Hannards Wy CHIG IG7 .... 54 B7
Hannay La ARCH N19 .... 66 D8
Hannell Rd FUL/PGN SW6 .... 118 E5
Hannen Rd WNWD SE27 .... 139 H7 4
Hannibal Rd
STWL/WRAY TW19 .... 130 E4
WCHPL E1 .... 104 C4
Hannibal Wy CROY/NA CR0 .... 171 M7
Hannington Rd CLAP SW4 .... 120 B8
Hanover Av CAN/RD E16 .... 106 A7
FELT TW13 .... 132 A5
Hanover Cir HYS/HAR UB3 .... 95 J5
Hanover Cl CHEAM SM3 .... 169 L6
RCH/KEW TW9 .... 117 G5 1
Hanover Dr CHST BR7 .... 143 J8
Hanover Gdns BARK/HLT IG6 .... 71 J1
LBTH SE11 .... 121 G4 2
Hanover Pk PECK SE15 .... 122 A6
Hanover Rd SEVS/STOTM N15 .... 67 M5
WIM/MER SW19 .... 155 J3
WLSDN NW10 .... 82 C7
Hanover St CONDST W1S 10 D5
CROY/NA CR0 .... 172 B5 2
Hanover Ter CAMTN NW1 .... 3 K8
Hanover Terrace Ms CAMTN NW1 .. 3 K8
Hanover Wk WEY KT13 .... 164 D5
Hanover Wy BXLYHN DA7 .... 126 D8 2
Hanover Yd IS N1 .... 6 D5 1
Hansard Ms WKENS W14 .... 100 D8
Hansart Wy ENC/FH EN2 .... 36 A4
Hans Crs CHEL SW3 .... 15 L3
Hanselin Cl STAN HA7 .... 43 M7 1
Hansen Dr WCHMH N21 .... 35 M8
Hanshaw Dr EDGW HA8 .... 63 K2 1
Hansler Gv E/WMO/HCT KT8 .... 151 K8
Hansler Rd EDUL SE22 .... 139 M2
Hansol Rd BXLYHS DA6 .... 144 E2
Hanson Cl BAL SW12 .... 138 B4
BECK BR3 .... 159 H2 1
MORT/ESHN SW14 .... 117 J8 1
WDR/YW UB7 .... 112 F1
Hanson Gdns STHL UB1 .... 96 E8
Hanson St GTPST W1W 10 E2
Hans Pl KTBR SW1X 15 L3
Hans Rd CHEL SW3 .... 15 L3
Hans St KTBR SW1X 15 M4
Hanway Pl SOHO/SHAV W1D 11 G4
Hanway Rd HNWL W7 .... 97 K5
Hanway St FITZ W1T 11 G4 2
Hanworth Rd FELT TW13 .... 132 B5
HPTN TW12 .... 132 F8
HSLW TW3 .... 115 H8 3
HSLWW TW4 .... 132 F4

SUN TW16 .... 150 A3
Hanworth Ter HSLW TW3 .... 133 H1
Hanyards La POTB/CUF EN6 .... 24 D1
Hapgood Cl NTHLT UB5 .... 79 K5
Harben Rd KIL/WHAMP NW6 .... 2 F1
Harberson Rd BAL SW12 .... 138 B5
SRTFD E15 .... 87 M8
Harberton Rd ARCH N19 .... 84 C1
Harbet Rd BAY/PAD W2 .... 9 H3
UED N18 .... 50 D7
Harbex Cl BXLY DA5 .... 145 H4
Harbinger Rd POP/IOD E14 .... 123 H2
Harbledown Pl
STMC/STPC BR5 .... 162 C7
Harbledown Rd
FUL/PGN SW6 .... 119 G6
SAND/SEL CR2 .... 185 G4
Harbord Cl CMBW SE5 .... 121 K7
Harbord St FUL/PGN SW6 .... 118 D6
Harborne Cl OXHEY WD19 .... 42 C7
Harborough Av BFN/LL DA15 .... 143 L4
Harborough Rd
STRHM/NOR SW16 .... 138 F8
Harbour Av WBPTN SW10 .... 119 J6
Harbourer Rd BARK/HLT IG6 .... 54 B7
Harbourfield Rd BNSTD SM7 .... 182 B8
Harbour Rd CMBW SE5 .... 121 J8
Harbridge Av PUT/ROE SW15 .... 135 M4
Harbury Rd CAR SM5 .... 182 C2
Harbut Rd BTSEA SW11 .... 137 K1
Harcastle Cl YEAD UB4 .... 96 E3
Harcombe Rd STNW/STAM N16 .... 85 L3
Harcourt Av BFN/LL DA15 .... 144 C3
EDGW HA8 .... 45 J5
MNPK E12 .... 88 F4
WLGTN SM6 .... 171 H6
Harcourt Cl ISLW TW7 .... 116 A8
Harcourt Fld WLGTN SM6 .... 171 H6
Harcourt Ms ROM RM1 .... 73 M6
Harcourt Rd BROCKY SE4 .... 140 F1
BUSH WD23 .... 30 C8
BXLYHS DA6 .... 144 E1
SRTFD E15 .... 105 M1
THHTH CR7 .... 171 M1
WDGN N22 .... 66 D2
WIM/MER SW19 .... 155 C3
WLGTN SM6 .... 171 H6
Harcourt St CAMTN NW1 .... 9 K3
Harcourt Ter WBPTN SW10 .... 14 D8
Hardcastle Cl SNWD SE25 .... 173 L1
Hardcourts Cl WWKM BR4 .... 174 B6
Hardel Wk BRXS/STRHM SW2 .... 139 G4
Hardens Manorway
CHARL SE7 .... 124 D2
WOOL/PLUM SE18 .... 124 D1
Harders Rd PECK SE15 .... 122 B7
Hardess St HNHL SE24 .... 121 J8
Hardie Cl WLSDN NW10 .... 81 K5
Hardie Rd DAGE RM10 .... 91 J3
Harding Cl CROY/NA CR0 .... 172 F5
GSTN WD25 .... 21 J6
KUTN/CMB KT2 .... 152 F4
WALW SE17 .... 18 F3
Hardinge Rd UED N18 .... 49 L8
WLSDN NW10 .... 82 C8
Hardinge St WCHPL E1 .... 104 C5
WCHPL E1 .... 104 C5
Harding Rd BXLYHN DA7 .... 126 F7
Hardings La PGE/AN SE20 .... 158 D2
Hardley Crs EMPK RM11 .... 74 D5
Hardman Rd CHARL SE7 .... 124 B3
KUTN/CMB KT2 .... 152 E5
Hardwick Cl LHD/OX KT22 .... 178 C8
STAN HA7 .... 44 C7
Hardwick Crs DART DA1 .... 147 H3
Hardwicke Av HEST TW5 .... 115 G6
Hardwicke Ms FSBYW WC1X 5 M8
Hardwicke Rd CHSWK W4 .... 117 J2
PLMGR N13 .... 48 E3
RCHPK/HAM TW10 .... 134 C8
Hardwick Gn WEA W13 .... 98 B4
Hardwick St CLKNW EC1R 6 B8
Hardwick's Wy
WAND/EARL SW18 .... 137 G2
Hardwidge St STHWK SE1 .... 19 J1
Hardy Av CAN/RD E16 .... 106 A7
RSLP HA4 .... 78 B5
Hardy Cl BAR EN5 .... 33 L8
BERM/RHTH SE16 .... 104 D8
PIN HA5 .... 60 D8
Hardy Gv DART DA1 .... 147 G1
Hardy Pas WDGN N22 .... 66 F2
Hardy Rd BKHTH/KID SE3 .... 123 M4
WIM/MER SW19 .... 155 H3
Hardy Wy ENC/FH EN2 .... 36 A4
Hare And Billet Rd
BKHTH/KID SE3 .... 123 K6
Harebell Dr EHAM E6 .... 107 G4
Harebell Wy HARH RM3 .... 74 D1
The Harebreaks WATN WD24 .... 29 H2
Harecourt Rd IS N1 .... 85 J6
Hare Crs GSTN WD25 .... 21 G5
Haredale Rd HNHL SE24 .... 139 J1
Haredon Cl FSTH SE23 .... 140 C4
Harefield ESH/CLAY KT10 .... 166 E5
Harefield Av BELMT SM2 .... 181 L2
Harefield Ms BROCKY SE4 .... 122 F8
Harefield Rd BROCKY SE4 .... 122 F8
CEND/HSY/T N8 .... 66 D6
RKW/CH/CXG WD3 .... 40 D4
SCUP DA14 .... 144 D6
STRHM/NOR SW16 .... 156 F3
UX/CGN UB8 .... 76 D6
Hare Hall La GPK RM2 .... 74 B5
Hare La ESH/CLAY KT10 .... 166 E3
Hare Marsh BETH E2 .... 104 A3
Hare Rw BETH E2 .... 104 A1
Haresfield Rd DAGE RM10 .... 91 G6
Hare St WOOL/PLUM SE18 .... 125 G1
Hare Wk IS N1 .... 7 K6
Harewood Av CAMTN NW1 .... 9 K1
NTHLT UB5 .... 77 H6
Harewood Cl NTHLT UB5 .... 78 F7
Harewood Gdns SAND/SEL CR2 .... 185 H8
Harewood Pl CONDST W1S 10 D5

Harewood Rd ISLW TW7 .... 115 M5
OXHEY WD19 .... 42 B4
SAND/SEL CR2 .... 172 E6
WIM/MER SW19 .... 155 L2
Harewood Rw CAMTN NW1 .... 9 K2
Harewood Ter NWDGN UB2 .... 114 F2
Harfield Rd SUN TW16 .... 150 D5
Harford Cl CHING E4 .... 51 H2
Harford Dr WAT WD17 .... 28 E3
Harford Rd CHING E4 .... 51 H2
Harford St WCHPL E1 .... 104 E3
Harford Wk EFNCH N2 .... 65 K5
Harfst Wy SWLY BR8 .... 163 J4
Hargood Cl
KTN/HRWW/W HA3 .... 62 E7
Hargood Rd BKHTH/KID SE3 .... 124 C6
Hargrave Pk KTTN NW5 .... 84 C2
Hargrave Rd ARCH N19 .... 84 C2
Hargreaves Av CHESW EN7 .... 26 B4
Hargreaves Cl CHESW EN7 .... 26 B4
Hargwyne St BRXN/ST SW9 .... 120 F8
Haringey Pk CEND/HSY/T N8 .... 66 E7
Haringey Rd CEND/HSY/T N8 .... 66 E5
Harkett Cl
KTN/HRWW/W HA3 .... 61 M3
Harkness Cl HARH RM3 .... 56 F7
CROY/NA CR0 .... 172 F5
Harland Av BFN/LL DA15 .... 143 K7
Harland Rd LEE/GVPK SE12 .... 142 A5
Harlands Gv ORP BR6 .... 176 B6
Harlech Gdns HEST TW5 .... 114 C4
Harlech Rd ABLGY WD5 .... 21 G4
STHGT/OAK N14 .... 48 E5
Harlequin Av BTFD TW8 .... 116 A4
Harlequin Cl ISLW TW7 .... 133 L2
YEAD UB4 .... 96 B4
Harlequin Rd TEDD TW11 .... 152 B3
Harlescott Rd PECK SE15 .... 140 D1
Harlesden Cl HARH RM3 .... 74 F1
Harlesden Gdns WLSDN NW10 .... 81 M8
Harlesden Rd HARH RM3 .... 56 F8
WLSDN NW10 .... 82 A8
Harley Cl ALP/SUD HA0 .... 80 D6
Harley Crs HRW HA1 .... 61 K5
Harleyford BMLY BR1 .... 160 B4
Harleyford Rd LBTH SE11 .... 17 L9
Harley Gdns ORP BR6 .... 176 E6
WBPTN SW10 .... 14 F8
Harley Gv BOW E3 .... 104 F2
Harley Pl CAVSQ/HST W1G 10 C3
Harley Rd HAMP NW3 .... 3 H2
HRW HA1 .... 61 K5
WLSDN NW10 .... 99 L1
Harley St CAVSQ/HST W1G 10 C1
Harlinger St WOOL/PLUM SE18 .... 124 E1
Harlington Cl HYS/HAR UB3 .... 113 J5
Harlington High St
HYS/HAR UB3 .... 113 K5
Harlington Rd BXLYHN DA7 .... 126 E8
UX/CGN UB8 .... 95 H4
Harlington Rd East
EBED/NFELT TW14 .... 132 B4
Harlington Rd West
EBED/NFELT TW14 .... 132 B3
Harlow Gdns CRW RM5 .... 55 J8
Harlow Rd PLMGR N13 .... 49 K5
RAIN RM13 .... 91 M8
Harlyn Dr PIN HA5 .... 60 B4
Harman Av WFD IG8 .... 69 M1
Harman Cl CHING E4 .... 51 K6
CRICK NW2 .... 82 E3
Harman Dr BFN/LL DA15 .... 143 M3
CRICK NW2 .... 82 E3
Harman Pl PUR/KEN CR8 .... 184 B4
Harman Rd EN EN1 .... 36 F8
Harmondsworth La
WDR/YW UB7 .... 112 C4
Harmondsworth Rd
WDR/YW UB7 .... 112 E1
Harmony Cl GLDGN NW11 .... 64 E1
WLGTN SM6 .... 183 L2
Harmony Wy HAYES BR2 .... 160 A5
HDN NW4 .... 64 C5
Harmood Gv CAMTN NW1 .... 4 C1
Harmood St CAMTN NW1 .... 84 B6
Harmsworth St WALW SE17 .... 18 C8
Harmsworth Wy
TRDG/WHET N20 .... 46 F3
Harness Rd THMD SE28 .... 108 A8
Harold Av BELV DA17 .... 126 F3
HYS/HAR UB3 .... 113 M1
Harold Court Rd HARH RM3 .... 57 H8
Harold Crs WAB EN9 .... 27 J5
Harold Rd CEND/HSY/T N8 .... 66 F6
CHING E4 .... 51 J5
NRWD SE19 .... 157 K3
PLSTW E13 .... 88 B8
RDART DA2 .... 146 F8
SEVS/STOTM N15 .... 67 M6
SUT SM1 .... 170 D6
WAN E11 .... 87 L1
WFD IG8 .... 70 A2
WLSDN NW10 .... 99 K2
Haroldstone Rd WALTH E17 .... 68 D6
Harold Vw HARH RM3 .... 74 F3
Harp Cross La MON EC3R 13 J7
Harpenden Rd MNPK E12 .... 88 C2
Harper Cl STHGT/OAK N14 .... 35 J4
Harper Rd EHAM E6 .... 106 F5
STHWK SE1 .... 18 F3
Harp Island Cl WLSDN NW10 .... 81 K2
Harpley Sq WCHPL E1 .... 104 D3
Harpour Rd BARK IG11 .... 89 J6
Harp Rd HNWL W7 .... 97 M3
Harpsden St BTSEA SW11 .... 120 A6
Harpur St BMSBY WC1N 11 L2
Harraden Rd BKHTH/KID SE3 .... 124 C6
Harrier Cl BRXS/STRHM SW2 .... 139 G4
HACK E8 .... 86 A3
Harrier Gdns CROY/NA CR0 .... 173 G4
Harrier Ms THMD SE28 .... 107 K8
Harrier Wy EHAM E6 .... 106 F4
Harriers Cl EA W5 .... 98 E6
Harriet Cl HACK E8 .... 86 A3
Harriet Gdns CROY/NA CR0 .... 173 G4
Harriet St KTBR SW1X 15 M2

Harriet Wk KTBR SW1X 15 M2
Harriet Wy BUSH WD23 .... 43 K2
Harringay Gdns
CEND/HSY/T N8 .... 67 H5
Harringay Rd CEND/HSY/T N8 .... 67 H6
SEVS/STOTM N15 .... 67 H5
Harrington Cl CROY/NA CR0 .... 171 L4
WLSDN NW10 .... 81 K3
Harrington Gdns SKENS SW7 .... 14 E6
Harrington Hl CLPT E5 .... 86 B1
Harrington Rd SKENS SW7 .... 15 G5
SNWD SE25 .... 158 A7
WAN E11 .... 87 L1
Harrington Sq CAMTN NW1 .... 4 E5
Harrington St CAMTN NW1 .... 4 E7
Harrington Wy
WOOL/PLUM SE18 .... 124 D1
Harriott Cl GNWCH SE10 .... 123 M2
Harris Cl ENC/FH EN2 .... 36 B4
HEST TW5 .... 115 G6
Harrison Cl NTHWD HA6 .... 41 J8
TRDG/WHET N20 .... 47 L3
Harrison Ct SHPTN TW17 .... 149 H8
Harrison Rd DAGE RM10 .... 91 H6
Harrison's Ri CROY/NA CR0 .... 172 B5
Harrison St STPAN WC1H 5 K8
Harrisons Whf PUR RM19 .... 129 G3
Harrison Wk CHES/WCR EN8 .... 27 G2
Harris Rd BXLYHN DA7 .... 126 E6
DAGW RM9 .... 90 F5
GSTN WD25 .... 21 G8
WALTH E17 .... 68 F8
Harris St CMBW SE5 .... 121 K5
WALTH E17 .... 68 F8
Harris Wy SUN TW16 .... 149 L4
Harrogate Rd OXHEY WD19 .... 42 C5
Harrold Rd BCTR RM8 .... 90 B5
Harrow Av EN EN1 .... 49 M1
Harroway Rd BTSEA SW11 .... 119 K7
Harrowby St MBLAR W1H 9 K4
Harrow Cl CHSGTN KT9 .... 179 K1
Harrow Crs HARH RM3 .... 74 B1
Harrowdene Cl ALP/SUD HA0 .... 80 D4
Harrowdene Gdns TEDD TW11 .... 152 A3
Harrowdene Rd ALP/SUD HA0 .... 80 D4
Harrow Dr ED N9 .... 49 M3
EMPK RM11 .... 74 C4
Harrowes Meade EDGW HA8 .... 44 C8
Harrow Fields Gdns HRW HA1 .... 79 L3
Harrow Gdns ORP BR6 .... 177 H6
Harrowgate Rd HOM E9 .... 86 E6
Harrow Gn WAN E11 .... 87 L3
WAN E11 .... 87 L3
Harrow La POP/IOD E14 .... 105 M3
Harrow Manor Wy ABYW SE2 .... 126 C1
THMD SE28 .... 108 C2
Harrow Pk HRW HA1 .... 79 L2
Harrow Pl WCHPL E1 .... 13 K4
Harrow Rd ALP/SUD HA0 .... 80 C6
ASHF TW15 .... 131 G5
CAR SM5 .... 170 E8
IL IG1 .... 89 J4
WAN E11 .... 87 M3
WARL CR6 .... 185 M8
WBLY HA9 .... 80 F5
WLSDN NW10 .... 100 B2
Harrow Road F/O BAY/PAD W2 .... 9 H4
Harrow St CAMTN NW1 .... 9 K2
Harrow Vw HGDN/ICK UB10 .... 95 J2
HYS/HAR UB3 .... 96 A6
RYLN/HDSTN HA2 .... 61 K4
Harrow View Rd EA W5 .... 98 B3
Harrow Wy OXHEY WD19 .... 42 E5
SHPTN TW17 .... 149 J5
Harrow Weald Pk
KTN/HRWW/W HA3 .... 43 K8
Harston Dr PEND EN3 .... 38 A3
Hart Crs CHIG IG7 .... 53 M7
Hart Dyke Rd
STMC/STPC BR5 .... 177 J3
SWLY BR8 .... 163 K6
Harte Rd HSLW TW3 .... 114 F7
Hartfield Cl BORE WD6 .... 32 A7
Hartfield Crs WIM/MER SW19 .... 154 F3
WWKM BR4 .... 175 G5
Hartfield Gv PGE/AN SE20 .... 158 E5
Hartfield Rd CHSGTN KT9 .... 167 K7
WIM/MER SW19 .... 154 F3
WWKM BR4 .... 175 G6
Hartfield Ter BOW E3 .... 105 G1
Hartford Av KTN/HRWW/W HA3 .... 62 A4
Hartforde Rd BORE WD6 .... 32 A5
Hartford Rd BXLY DA5 .... 145 G3
HOR/WEW KT19 .... 168 A8
Hart Gv ACT W3 .... 99 G7
STHL UB1 .... 97 G4
Harthall La KGLGY WD4 .... 20 B1
Hartham Cl HOLWY N7 .... 84 E5
ISLW TW7 .... 116 A6
Hartham Rd HOLWY N7 .... 84 E5
ISLW TW7 .... 115 M6
TOTM N17 .... 67 M3
Harting Rd ELTH/MOT SE9 .... 142 E8
Hartington Cl HRW HA1 .... 79 L4
ORP BR6 .... 176 C7
Hartington Rd CAN/RD E16 .... 106 B5
CHSWK W4 .... 117 H5
NWDGN UB2 .... 96 E8
TWK TW1 .... 134 B4
VX/NE SW8 .... 120 E6
WALTH E17 .... 68 E7
WEA W13 .... 98 B6
Hartismere Rd FUL/PGN SW6 .... 118 F5
Hartlake Rd HOM E9 .... 86 D6
Hartland Cl EDGW HA8 .... 45 G4
WCHMH N21 .... 49 J1
Hartland Dr EDGW HA8 .... 45 G4
RSLP HA4 .... 78 B3
Hartland Rd CAMTN NW1 .... 4 C1
CHES/WCR EN8 .... 26 D3
FBAR/BDGN N11 .... 47 M7
HCH RM12 .... 92 A7
HPTN TW12 .... 133 H8
ISLW TW7 .... 116 A8
KIL/WHAMP NW6 .... 100 F1
MRDN SM4 .... 170 A2
SRTFD E15 .... 87 M7
TOTM N17 .... 67 K4

Hartlands Cl BXLY DA5 .... 144 F3
The Hartlands HEST TW5 .... 114 B4
Hartland Wy CROY/NA CR0 .... 173 L4
MRDN SM4 .... 169 M2
Hartley Av EHAM E6 .... 88 E8
MLHL NW7 .... 45 M7
Hartley Cl BMLY BR1 .... 160 F5
MLHL NW7 .... 45 M7
Hartley Down COUL/CHIP CR5 .... 183 M8
Hartley Farm PUR/KEN CR8 .... 183 M8
Hartley Hl PUR/KEN CR8 .... 183 M8
Hartley Old Rd PUR/KEN CR8 .... 183 M8
Hartley Rd CROY/NA CR0 .... 172 C2
WAN E11 .... 87 M1
WELL DA16 .... 126 C5
Hartley St BETH E2 .... 104 C2
Hartley Wy PUR/KEN CR8 .... 183 M8
Hartmann Rd CAN/RD E16 .... 106 D7
Hartmoor Ms PEND EN3 .... 37 K2
Hartnoll St HOLWY N7 .... 84 F5
Harton Cl BMLY BR1 .... 160 D4
Harton Rd ED N9 .... 50 B4
Harton St DEPT SE8 .... 123 G6
Hartsbourne Av BUSH WD23 .... 43 J4
Hartsbourne Rd BUSH WD23 .... 30 A5
Harts Cl BUSH WD23 .... 30 A5
Harts Gv WFD IG8 .... 52 A7
Hartshill Cl HGDN/ICK UB10 .... 77 G6
Hartshorn Gdns EHAM E6 .... 107 G3
Harts La BARK IG11 .... 89 H7
NWCR SE14 .... 122 C5
Hartslock Dr ABYW SE2 .... 108 D8
Hartsmead Rd ELTH/MOT SE9 .... 142 F6
Hartspring La GSTN WD25 .... 30 B4
Hart St MON EC3R 13 K6
Hartswood Gn BUSH WD23 .... 43 K4
Hartswood Rd SHB W12 .... 99 M8
Hartsworth Cl PLSTW E13 .... 105 M1
Hartville Rd WOOL/PLUM SE18 .... 125 L2
Hartwell Cl BRXS/STRHM SW2 .... 139 G7
Hartwell Dr CHING E4 .... 52 B3
Hartwell St HACK E8 .... 85 M6
Harvard Hl CHSWK W4 .... 117 H4
Harvard Rd CHSWK W4 .... 117 H3
ISLW TW7 .... 115 L6
LEW SE13 .... 141 J2
Harvel Cl STMC/STPC BR5 .... 162 A6
Harvel Crs ABYW SE2 .... 126 D3
Harvest Bank Rd WWKM BR4 .... 175 G5
Harvest End GSTN WD25 .... 29 K1
Harvester Rd HOR/WEW KT19 .... 180 D3
Harvesters Cl ISLW TW7 .... 133 K2
Harvest La LOU IG10 .... 52 D2
THDIT KT7 .... 167 G1
Harvest Rd BUSH WD23 .... 30 B7
FELT TW13 .... 132 A8
Harvey Dr HPTN TW12 .... 151 H4
Harveyfields WAB EN9 .... 27 J7
Harvey Gdns CHARL SE7 .... 124 C3
Harvey Rd CEND/HSY/T N8 .... 66 F6
CMBW SE5 .... 121 K6
HGDN/ICK UB10 .... 95 C1
HSLWW TW4 .... 132 F4
IL IG1 .... 89 H5
NTHLT UB5 .... 78 C7
RKW/CH/CXG WD3 .... 41 G1
WAN E11 .... 87 L1
WOT/HER KT12 .... 165 G2
Harvey's La ROMW/RG RM7 .... 91 K2
Harvey St IS N1 .... 7 H4
Harvill Rd SCUP DA14 .... 162 D1
Harvil Rd DEN/HRF UB9 .... 58 C5
Harvist Rd KIL/WHAMP NW6 .... 100 E1
Harwater Dr LOU IG10 .... 39 M5
Harwell Cl RSLP HA4 .... 77 K1
Harwood Av BMLY BR1 .... 160 B5
EMPK RM11 .... 74 E4
MTCM CR4 .... 155 L6
Harwood Cl ALP/SUD HA0 .... 80 D4
NFNCH/WDSP N12 .... 47 J8
Harwood Dr HGDN/ICK UB10 .... 76 F8
Harwood Hall La UPMR RM14 .... 93 H6
Harwood Rd FUL/PGN SW6 .... 119 C5
WATW WD18 .... 29 C7
Harwood Ter FUL/PGN SW6 .... 119 H6
Haselbury Rd UED N18 .... 49 L6
Haselrigge Rd CLAP SW4 .... 138 D1
Haseltine Rd SYD SE26 .... 140 F8
Haselwood Dr ENC/FH EN2 .... 36 B7
Haskard Rd DAGW RM9 .... 90 D4
Hasker St CHEL SW3 .... 15 K5
Haslam Av CHEAM SM3 .... 169 L3
Haslam Cl HGDN/ICK UB10 .... 77 J2
IS N1 .... 6 B1
Haslam St PECK SE15 .... 121 M6
Haslemere Av EBAR EN4 .... 47 M3
HDN NW4 .... 64 C7
HEST TW5 .... 114 C7
HNWL W7 .... 98 A1
MTCM CR4 .... 155 K5
WAND/EARL SW18 .... 137 H6
Haslemere Cl HPTN TW12 .... 150 F1
WLGTN SM6 .... 171 L7
Haslemere Gdns FNCH N3 .... 64 F4
Haslemere Rd BXLYHN DA7 .... 126 F7
CEND/HSY/T N8 .... 66 D5
GDMY/SEVK IG3 .... 89 M2
THHTH CR7 .... 157 H4
WCHMH N21 .... 49 H4
Hasler Cl THMD SE28 .... 108 B6
Haslett Rd SHPTN TW17 .... 149 L5
Hasluck Gdns BAR EN5 .... 47 J1
Hassard St BETH E2 .... 7 M6
Hassendean Rd BKHTH/KID SE3 .... 124 B4
Hassett Rd HOM E9 .... 86 D6
Hassocks Cl SYD SE26 .... 140 B7
Hassocks Rd
STRHM/NOR SW16 .... 156 D4
Hassock Wd HAYES BR2 .... 175 K6
Hassop Rd CRICK NW2 .... 82 B2
Hasted Rd CHARL SE7 .... 124 D3
Hastings Av BARK/HLT IG6 .... 71 J5
Hastings Cl BAR EN5 .... 34 C7
PECK SE15 .... 121 H6
Hastings Dr SURB KT6 .... 167 J1
Hastings Rd CROY/NA CR0 .... 173 L8
FBAR/BDGN N11 .... 48 C7
GPK RM2 .... 74 B6
HAYES BR2 .... 175 L5
TOTM N17 .... 67 K4

WEA W13 .... 98 B6
Hastings St STPAN WC1H 5 J8
Hastings Wy BUSH WD23 .... 29 L7
RKW/CH/CXG WD3 .... 40 E3
Hastoe Cl YEAD UB4 .... 96 E3
Hatcham Park Ms NWCR SE14 .... 122 C4
Hatcham Park Rd
NWCR SE14 .... 122 C4
Hatcham Rd PECK SE15 .... 122 C4
Hatchard Rd ARCH N19 .... 84 D2
Hatchcroft HDN NW4 .... 64 B4
Hatch Gv CHDH RM6 .... 72 E5
Hatch La CHING E4 .... 51 K6
WDR/YW UB7 .... 112 D5
Hatch Pl RCHPK/HAM TW10 .... 152 F1
Hatch Rd STRHM/NOR SW16 .... 156 E5
Hatch Side CHIG IG7 .... 53 C7
The Hatch PEND EN3 .... 37 K4
Hatchwoods WFD IG8 .... 51 M6
Hatcliffe Cl BKHTH/KID SE3 .... 123 M8
Hatcliffe St GNWCH SE10 .... 123 M3
Hatfield Cl BARK/HLT IG6 .... 71 H4
BELMT SM2 .... 182 B1
HCH RM12 .... 92 D5
MTCM CR4 .... 155 K7
Hatfield Rd CHSWK W4 .... 99 K8
HNWL W7 .... 98 A7
POTB/CUF EN6 .... 23 J4
SRTFD E15 .... 87 L5
WATN WD24 .... 29 H4
Hatfields STHWK SE1 .... 12 B8
Hathaway Cl HAYES BR2 .... 175 M3
RSLP HA4 .... 77 M4
STAN HA7 .... 44 F3
Hathaway Crs MNPK E12 .... 88 F6
Hathaway Gdns CHDH RM6 .... 72 B2
WEA W13 .... 97 M4
Hathaway Rd CROY/NA CR0 .... 172 B2
Hatherleigh Cl CHSGTN KT9 .... 167 K7
MRDN SM4 .... 155 G7
Hatherleigh Gdns
POTB/CUF EN6 .... 23 K5
Hatherleigh Rd RSLP HA4 .... 78 A2
Hatherleigh Wy HARH RM3 .... 74 D2
Hatherley Crs SCUP DA14 .... 144 A6
Hatherley Gdns CEND/HSY/T N8 .... 66 E7
EHAM E6 .... 106 D7
Hatherley Gv BAY/PAD W2 .... 8 C4
Hatherley Rd RCH/KEW TW9 .... 116 F6
SCUP DA14 .... 144 A7
WALTH E17 .... 68 F5
Hatherley St WEST SW1P 16 F6
Hathern Gdns ELTH/MOT SE9 .... 143 G8
Hatherop Rd HPTN TW12 .... 150 F3
Hathorne Cl PECK SE15 .... 122 B7
Hathway St PECK SE15 .... 122 D7
Hatley Av BARK/HLT IG6 .... 71 J5
Hatley Cl FBAR/BDGN N11 .... 47 M7
Hatley Rd HOLWY N7 .... 84 E3
Hatteraick St
BERM/RHTH SE16 .... 104 C8
Hattersfield Cl BELV DA17 .... 126 F4
Hatters La WATW WD18 .... 28 E8
Hatton Cl WOOL/PLUM SE18 .... 125 L5
Hatton Gdn HCIRC EC1N 12 B2
Hatton Gdns MTCM CR4 .... 155 M8
Hatton Gn EBED/NFELT TW14 .... 132 A1
Hatton Gv WDR/YW UB7 .... 94 D8
Hatton Pl HCIRC EC1N 12 B1
Hatton Rd CHES/WCR EN8 .... 26 D2
CROY/NA CR0 .... 172 A3
EBED/NFELT TW14 .... 131 J4
HTHAIR TW6 .... 131 M1
Hatton Rw STJWD NW8 .... 9 H1
Hatton St STJWD NW8 .... 9 H1
Hatton Wall HCIRC EC1N 12 A2
Havana Cl ROM RM1 .... 73 L2
Havana Rd WIM/MER SW19 .... 137 G6
Havannah St POP/IOD E14 .... 105 G8
Havant Rd WALTH E17 .... 69 J4
Havelock Pl HRW HA1 .... 61 L7
Havelock Rd BELV DA17 .... 126 F2
CROY/NA CR0 .... 172 A4
DART DA1 .... 146 B4
HAYES BR2 .... 160 C2
KTN/HRWW/W HA3 .... 61 L4
NWDGN UB2 .... 114 F1
TOTM N17 .... 68 A3
WIM/MER SW19 .... 155 J1
Havelock St IL IG1 .... 89 H2
IS N1 .... 5 K3
Havelock Ter VX/NE SW8 .... 120 B5
Havelock Wk FSTH SE23 .... 140 C5
Haven Cl ELTH/MOT SE9 .... 142 F7
SCUP DA14 .... 162 C2
SWLY BR8 .... 163 M1
WIM/MER SW19 .... 136 D7
YEAD UB4 .... 95 J4
Haven Gn EA W5 .... 98 E5
Havenhurst Ri ENC/FH EN2 .... 36 A5
Haven La EA W5 .... 98 E5
Haven Rd ASHF TW15 .... 131 H8
Haven St CAMTN NW1 .... 4 C2
The Haven RCH/KEW TW9 .... 117 G8
SUN TW16 .... 150 A3
Havenwood WBLY HA9 .... 80 E1
Haverfield Gdns
RCH/KEW TW9 .... 117 G5
Haverfield Rd BOW E3 .... 104 F2
Haverford Wy EDGW HA8 .... 62 F2
Haverhill Rd BAL SW12 .... 138 C5
CHING E4 .... 51 J3
Havering Dr ROM RM1 .... 73 L5
Havering Gdns CHDH RM6 .... 72 C6
Havering Rd CRW RM5 .... 73 K3
ROM RM1 .... 73 K4
Havering St WCHPL E1 .... 104 D5
Havering Wy BARK IG11 .... 108 B2
Havers Av WOT/HER KT12 .... 165 K7
Haversham Cl TWK TW1 .... 134 E6
Haverstock Hl HAMP NW3 .... 83 L6
Haverstock Rd KTTN NW5 .... 84 A5
Haverstock St IS N1 .... 6 D6
Haverthwaite Rd ORP BR6 .... 176 D5
Havil St CMBW SE5 .... 121 L6
Havisham Pl STRHM/NOR SW16 .... 157 H2
Hawarden Gv HNHL SE24 .... 139 J4

Hawarden Hl *CRICK* NW2 82 A3
Hawarden Rd *WALTH* E17 68 D5
Hawbridge Rd *WAN* E11 87 K1
Hawes Cl *NTHWD* HA6 59 M1
Hawes La *WAB* EN9 38 C3
WWKM BR4 174 C3
Hawes Rd *BMLY* BR1 160 B4
UED N18 50 B8
Hawes St *IS* N1 6 D2
Haweswater Dr *GSTN* WD25 21 J7 2
Hawfield Bank *ORP* BR6 177 K5 1
Hawgood St *BOW* E3 105 G4 3
Hawkdene *CHING* E4 51 H1
Hawke Park Rd *WDGN* N22 67 H4 2
Hawke Pl *BERM/RHTH* SE16 104 D8 4
Hawke Rd *NRWD* SE19 157 K2
Hawkesbury Rd
PUT/ROE SW15 136 B2
Hawkesfield Rd *FSTH* SE23 140 E6
Hawkesley Cl *TWK* TW1 134 A8 3
Hawkes Rd *EBED/NFELT* TW14 132 A4
MTCM CR4 155 L4
Hawkesworth Cl *NTHWD* HA6 59 L1 4
Hawkewood Rd *SUN* TW16 150 B6
Hawkhurst *COB* KT11 178 A7
Hawkhurst Gdns *CRW* RM5 55 K8
Hawkhurst Rd
STRHM/NOR SW16 156 D3
Hawkhurst Wy *NWMAL* KT3 153 K8 2
WWKM BR4 174 B4
Hawkinge Wy *HCH* RM12 92 C6 4
Hawkins Cl *BORE* WD6 32 C5 2
EDGW HA8 45 K7 2
HRW HA1 61 K8
Hawkins Rd *TEDD* TW11 152 B2 2
Hawkins Wy *CAT* SE6 159 G1
Hawkley Gdns *WNWD* SE27 139 H6
Hawkridge Cl *CHDH* RM6 72 C7
Hawksbrook La *BECK* BR3 174 B1
Hawkshead Cl *BMLY* BR1 159 L3
Hawkshead La *BRKMPK* AL9 22 E1
Hawkshead Rd *CHSWK* W4 99 L8 2
WLSDN NW10 81 M7 1
Hawkshill Cl *ESH/CLAY* KT10 166 A8
Hawkshill Wy *ESH/CLAY* KT10 165 M8
Hawkslade Rd *PECK* SE15 140 D2
Hawksley Rd *STNW/STAM* N16 85 L3 2
Hawksmead Cl *PEND* EN3 26 D8 4
Hawksmoor Cl *EHAM* E6 106 E5 3
WOOL/PLUM SE18 125 L3 3
Hawksmoor Ms *WCHPL* E1 104 B6 6
Hawksmoor St *HMSMTH* W6 118 D4 2
Hawksmouth *CHING* E4 51 H2
Hawks Rd *KUT* KT1 152 F5
Hawkstone Rd
BERM/RHTH SE16 122 C2
Hawkwood Crs *CHING* E4 51 H1
Hawkwood La *CHST* BR7 161 J4
Hawkwood Mt *CLPT* E5 86 B1
Hawlands Dr *PIN* HA5 60 E8 1
Hawley Cl *HPTN* TW12 150 F2 3
Hawley Crs *CAMTN* NW1 4 D2
Hawley Rd *CAMTN* NW1 4 C1
DART DA1 146 E6
UED N18 50 D7
Hawley St *CAMTN* NW1 4 C2
Hawley Wy *ASHF* TW15 149 H1 1
Hawstead La *ORP* BR6 177 M7
Hawstead Rd *LEW* SE13 141 H3
Hawsted *BKHH* IG9 52 B2 1
Hawthorn Av *PLMGR* N13 48 E7
RAIN RM13 110 B3
THHTH CR7 157 H4
Hawthorn Centre *HRW* HA1 61 M5
Hawthorn Cl *ABLGY* WD5 20 F5
BNSTD SM7 181 L7 1
HEST TW5 114 B5
HPTN TW12 151 G1 1
STMC/STPC BR5 176 D1
WAT WD17 28 F3
Hawthorn Crs *SAND/SEL* CR2 185 J4 1
Hawthornden Cl
NFNCH/WDSP N12 47 L8 2
Hawthorndene Cl
HAYES BR2 174 F4 3
Hawthorndene Rd
HAYES BR2 175 G4 1
Hawthorn Dr *DEN/HRF* UB9 76 C6
RYLN/HDSTN HA2 61 G7
WWKM BR4 174 E6
Hawthorne Av *BH/WHM* TN16 187 K8
CAR SM5 183 G1
CHESW EN7 26 B3
HRW HA1 62 A7
MTCM CR4 155 K5
RSLP HA4 60 B7
Hawthorne Cl *BMLY* BR1 160 F6
CHESW EN7 26 B4
Hawthorne Crs *WDR/YW* UB7 94 F8
Hawthorne Gv
CDALE/KGS NW9 63 J8 1
Hawthorne Pl *EW* KT17 180 E5
Hawthorne Rd *BMLY* BR1 160 F6
UED N18 49 M8
WALTH E17 69 G4 1
Hawthorne Wy *ED* N9 49 M4
Hawthorn Farm Av *NTHLT* UB5 78 E8
Hawthorn Gdns *EA* W5 116 D1
Hawthorn Gv *ENC/FH* EN2 36 D3
PGE/AN SE20 158 B4
Hawthorn Hatch *BTFD* TW8 116 B5
Hawthorn Ms *HDN* NW4 64 E2 2
Hawthorn Pl *ERITH* DA8 127 J3
HYS/HAR UB3 95 M6 2
Hawthorn Rd *BKHH* IG9 52 C6
BTFD TW8 116 B5 2
BXLYHS DA6 144 F1 2
CEND/HSY/T N8 66 E4
DART DA1 146 D6
SUT SM1 170 D7
WLGTN SM6 183 H1
WLSDN NW10 82 A7
Hawthorns *WFD* IG8 52 A5
The Hawthorns *EW* KT17 168 F8
Hawthorn Ter *BFN/LL* DA15 143 M3
Hawthorn Wk *NKENS* W10 100 E3 6
Hawthorn Wy *SHPTN* TW17 149 K7
Hawtrey Av *NTHLT* UB5 96 D1
Hawtrey Dr *RSLP* HA4 60 A8
Hawtrey Rd *HAMP* NW3 3 J2 1
Haxted Rd *BMLY* BR1 160 B4 2
Hayburn Wy *HCH* RM12 91 M1
Hay Cl *BORE* WD6 32 C5
SRTFD E15 87 L7
Haycroft Gdns *WLSDN* NW10 82 A8
Haycroft Rd *BRXS/STRHM* SW2 138 E2
SURB KT6 167 K4
Hay Currie St *POP/IOD* E14 105 H5
Hayday Rd *CAN/RD* E16 106 A4
Haydens Cl *STMC/STPC* BR5 177 J2
Hayden's Pl *NTGHL* W11 100 F5 3
Hayden Wy *CRW* RM5 73 J3
Haydn Av *PUR/KEN* CR8 184 A8
Haydock Av *NTHLT* UB5 79 G6
Haydock Cl *HCH* RM12 92 F4
Haydock Gn *NTHLT* UB5 79 G6
Haydon Cl *CDALE/KGS* NW9 63 J5
EN EN1 49 L1
Haydon Dr *PIN* HA5 60 A5
Haydon Park Rd
WIM/MER SW19 155 G1
Haydon Rd *BCTR* RM8 90 C2
OXHEY WD19 42 E1
Haydon's Rd *WIM/MER* SW19 155 J2
Haydon St *TWRH* EC3N 13 L6
Haydon Wy *BTSEA* SW11 137 J1
Hayes Cha *WWKM* BR4 174 D1
Hayes Cl *HAYES* BR2 175 G4
Hayes Crs *CHEAM* SM3 169 K6
GLDGN NW11 64 F6
Hayes Dr *RAIN* RM13 92 B7
Hayes End Dr *YEAD* UB4 95 K4
Hayes End Rd *YEAD* UB4 95 K3
Hayesford Park Dr *HAYES* BR2 159 M8
Hayes Gdn *HAYES* BR2 175 G4
Hayes Hl *HAYES* BR2 174 E3
Hayes Hill Rd *HAYES* BR2 174 F3
Hayes La *BECK* BR3 159 K6
HAYES BR2 160 B7
Hayes Mead Rd *HAYES* BR2 174 E3
Hayes Pl *CAMTN* NW1 9 K1
Hayes Rd *HAYES* BR2 160 A7
NWDGN UB2 114 C2
RDART DA2 147 L4
Hayes St *HAYES* BR2 175 H3
Hayes Wy *BECK* BR3 159 J7
Hayes Wood Av *HAYES* BR2 175 H3
Hayfield Cl *BUSH* WD23 30 B7
Hayfield Pas *WCHPL* E1 104 C3 6
Hayfield Rd *STMC/STPC* BR5 162 A8
Haygarth Pl *WIM/MER* SW19 154 D1 2
Haygreen Cl *KUTN/CMB* KT2 153 H2
Hay Hl *MYFR/PICC* W1J 10 D7
Hayland Cl *CDALE/KGS* NW9 63 K5
Hay La *CDALE/KGS* NW9 63 K5
Hayles St *LBTH* SE11 18 C5
Hayling Av *FELT* TW13 132 A7
Hayling Rd *OXHEY* WD19 41 M5
Hayman Crs *YEAD* UB4 95 K1
Haymarket *STJS* SW1Y 11 G7
Haymeads Dr *ESH/CLAY* KT10 166 C8
Haymer Gdns *WPK* KT4 169 G5 2
Haymerle Rd *STHWK* SE1 122 A4
Haymill Cl *GFD/PVL* UB6 97 M2
Hayne Rd *BECK* BR3 158 F5
Haynes Cl *FBAR/BDGN* N11 48 A5
LEW SE13 123 L8 1
TOTM N17 68 B1
Haynes La *NRWD* SE19 157 L2
Haynes Rd *ALP/SUD* HA0 80 E7 1
EMPK RM11 74 D6
Hayne St *STBT* EC1A 12 D2
Haynt Wk *RYNPK* SW20 154 E6
Haysleigh Gdns
PGE/AN SE20 158 A5 1
Hay's Ms *MYFR/PICC* W1J 10 C7
Haysoms Cl *ROM* RM1 73 L5
Haystall Cl *YEAD* UB4 95 L1 1
Hay St *BETH* E2 86 A8 8
Hays Wk *BELMT* SM2 181 K3
Hayter Rd *BRXS/STRHM* SW2 138 E2
Hayward Cl *DART* DA1 145 K2
WIM/MER SW19 155 H3
Hayward Gdns *PUT/ROE* SW15 136 C3
Hayward Rd *THDIT* KT7 166 F3
TRDG/WHET N20 47 J4
Haywards Cl *CHDH* RM6 72 C6
Hayward's Pl *CLKNW* EC1R 12 C1 3
Haywood Cl *PIN* HA5 60 D3
Haywood Ri *ORP* BR6 176 E7
Haywood Rd *HAYES* BR2 160 D7
Hayworth Ct *WAB* EN9 27 M7
Hazel Av *WDR/YW* UB7 113 G1
Hazel Bank *BRYLDS* KT5 168 C3
Hazelbank Rd *CAT* SE6 141 K6
Hazelbourne Rd *BAL* SW12 138 B3
Hazelbrouck Gdns *BARK/HLT* IG6 71 K1
Hazelbury Av *ABLGY* WD5 20 C5
Hazelbury Cl *WIM/MER* SW19 155 G5
Hazelbury Gn *UED* N18 49 L5
Hazelbury La *ED* N9 49 L5 1
Hazel Cl *BTFD* TW8 116 B5 3
CROY/NA CR0 173 K2
HCH RM12 92 B3 2
MTCM CR4 156 D7
PLMGR N13 49 K5
WHTN TW2 133 J4
Hazelcroft *PIN* HA5 43 G8
Hazelcroft Cl *HGDN/ICK* UB10 76 F7 4
Hazeldean Rd *WLSDN* NW10 81 K7
Hazeldene *CHES/WCR* EN8 26 E5
Hazeldene Ct *PUR/KEN* CR8 184 D8
Hazeldene Dr *PIN* HA5 60 C4
Hazeldene Gdns *HGDN/ICK* UB10 77 J8
Hazeldene Rd *BCTR* RM8 90 B2
WELL DA16 126 C7
Hazeldon Rd *BROCKY* SE4 140 E2
Hazel Dr *ERITH* DA8 128 A6
Hazeleigh Gdns *WFD* IG8 52 E7
Hazel End *SWLY* BR8 163 L8 1
Hazel Gdns *EDGW* HA8 45 H6
Hazelgreen Cl *WCHMH* N21 49 H3 1
Hazel Gv *ALP/SUD* HA0 80 E8 1
CHDH RM6 72 E4
EN EN1 50 A1 2
GSTN WD25 21 H8
ORP BR6 176 B4
STA TW18 148 B2
SYD SE26 140 D8
Hazelhurst *BECK* BR3 159 K4 1
Hazelhurst Rd *TOOT* SW17 137 J8
Hazell Crs *ROMW/RG* RM7 73 H2
Hazellville Rd *ARCH* N19 66 D8
Hazel Md *BAR* EN5 33 H8
EW KT17 181 G3
Hazelmere Cl
EBED/NFELT TW14 131 K3
NTHLT UB5 96 F1
Hazelmere Dr *NTHLT* UB5 96 F1
Hazelmere Gdns *EMPK* RM11 74 B6
Hazelmere Rd *KIL/WHAMP* NW6 82 F8
NTHLT UB5 96 F1
STMC/STPC BR5 161 J7
Hazelmere Wk *NTHLT* UB5 96 F1
Hazelmere Wy *HAYES* BR2 175 G1
Hazel Ri *EMPK* RM11 74 C7
Hazel Rd *DART* DA1 146 D6
ERITH DA8 128 A6
SRTFD E15 87 L5 4
WLSDN NW10 100 B2
Hazeltree La *NTHLT* UB5 96 E2 3
Hazel Tree Rd *WATN* WD24 29 H2
Hazel Wk *HAYES* BR2 176 A1
Hazel Wy *CHING* E4 50 F8
Hazelwood Av *MRDN* SM4 155 H7
Hazelwood Cl *CLPT* E5 86 E3 1
EA W5 98 E8
RYLN/HDSTN HA2 61 H5
Hazelwood Ct *SURB* KT6 167 L1 2
Hazelwood Crs *PLMGR* N13 49 G6
Hazelwood Dr *PIN* HA5 60 B3
Hazelwood Gv *SAND/SEL* CR2 185 H7
Hazelwood La *ABLGY* WD5 20 D5
PLMGR N13 49 G6
Hazelwood Park Cl
BARK/HLT IG6 53 L7
Hazelwood Rd *EN* EN1 49 M1
RKW/CH/CXG WD3 41 J1
WALTH E17 68 E6
Hazlebury Rd *FUL/PGN* SW6 119 H7
Hazledean Rd *CROY/NA* CR0 172 D5
Hazledene Rd *CHSWK* W4 117 J4
Hazlemere Gdns *WPK* KT4 169 H3 1
Hazlewell Rd *PUT/ROE* SW15 136 C2
Hazlewood Crs *NKENS* W10 100 E3 7
Hazlitt Cl *FELT* TW13 132 E8 3
Hazlitt Rd *WKENS* W14 118 E1
Hazon Wy *HOR/WEW* KT19 180 D5
Heacham Av *HGDN/ICK* UB10 77 J3
Headcorn Rd *BMLY* BR1 159 M1
THHTH CR7 156 F7
TOTM N17 67 M1 3
Headfort Pl *KTBR* SW1X 16 B2
Headington Rd
WAND/EARL SW18 137 J5
Headlam Rd *CLAP* SW4 138 D3
Headlam St *WCHPL* E1 104 B3
Headley Ap *IL* IG1 71 G6
Headley Av *WLGTN* SM6 171 M7
Headley Cl *CHSGTN* KT9 168 A8
Headley Dr *CROY/NA* CR0 186 C1
GNTH/NBYPK IG2 71 H7
Headstone Dr *HRW* HA1 61 L4 3
KTN/HRWW/W HA3 61 L4
Headstone Gdns
RYLN/HDSTN HA2 61 J5
Headstone La
KTN/HRWW/W HA3 61 H2
RYLN/HDSTN HA2 61 H3
Headstone Rd *HRW* HA1 61 L7
Head St *WCHPL* E1 104 D5 10
WCHPL E1 104 D5 10
Headway Cl
RCHPK/HAM TW10 134 C8 4
The Headway *EW* KT17 180 F2
Heald St *NWCR* SE14 122 F6
Healey Rd *WATW* WD18 41 M1
Healey St *KTTN* NW5 84 B6 6
Healy Dr *ORP* BR6 176 F5
Hearne Rd *CHSWK* W4 117 G3
Hearn Ri *NTHLT* UB5 78 D8
Hearn Rd *ROM* RM1 73 M7
Hearn's Buildings *WALW* SE17 19 H6 2
Hearns Cl *STMC/STPC* BR5 162 C7
Hearns Rd *STMC/STPC* BR5 162 C7
Hearn St *SDTCH* EC2A 13 K1
Hearnville Rd *BAL* SW12 138 A5
Heatham Pk *WHTN* TW2 133 M4
Heath Av *BXLYHN* DA7 126 D4
Heathbourne Rd *BUSH* WD23 43 M3
STAN HA7 43 L4
Heath Brow *HAMP* NW3 83 J3
Heath Cl *BNSTD* SM7 182 B7
EA W5 98 F3
GLDGN NW11 65 H8
GPK RM2 74 A4
HYS/HAR UB3 113 K5
POTB/CUF EN6 23 H3
STMC/STPC BR5 177 J1
STWL/WRAY TW19 130 C3
SWLY BR8 163 L5 1
Heathclose Av *DART* DA1 146 B4
Heathclose Rd *DART* DA1 146 A5
Heathcote Av *CLAY* IG5 70 F3
Heathcote Gv *CHING* E4 51 J5
Heathcote Rd *EPSOM* KT18 180 D7
TWK TW1 134 B3
Heathcote St *BMSBY* WC1N 5 L9
Heathcote Wy *WDR/YW* UB7 94 D7 1
Heathcroft *EA* W5 98 F3
Heathcroft Av *SUN* TW16 149 M3
Heathdale Av *HSLWW* TW4 114 E8
Heathdene Dr *BELV* DA17 127 H2
Heathdene Rd
STRHM/NOR SW16 156 F3
WLGTN SM6 183 H1
Heath Dr *BELMT* SM2 182 C2
GPK RM2 74 A2
POTB/CUF EN6 23 G3
RYNPK SW20 154 C7
Heathedge *FSTH* SE23 140 B6 2
Heathend Rd *BXLY* DA5 145 L5
Heather Av *ROM* RM1 73 K3
Heatherbank *CHST* BR7 161 G5
ELTH/MOT SE9 124 F7
Heatherbank Cl *DART* DA1 145 L3
Heather Cl *ABLGY* WD5 21 G5
EHAM E6 107 G5
HPTN TW12 150 F4
ISLW TW7 133 K2 2
LEW SE13 141 K4
ROM RM1 73 K2
UX/CGN UB8 94 F4
VX/NE SW8 120 B8
Heatherdale Cl *KUTN/CMB* KT2 153 G3
Heatherdene Cl *FNCH* N3 65 J1 2
MTCM CR4 155 K7
Heather Dr *DART* DA1 146 A4
ENC/FH EN2 36 B5 1
ROM RM1 73 K3
Heather End *SWLY* BR8 163 K8 1
Heather Gdns *BELMT* SM2 170 A8
GLDGN NW11 64 E7
ROM RM1 73 K3
Heather Gln *ROM* RM1 73 K3
Heatherlands *SUN* TW16 150 A2
Heather La *WDR/YW* UB7 94 E5
Heatherley Dr *CLAY* IG5 70 F4
Heather Park Dr *ALP/SUD* HA0 81 G7
Heather Pl *ESH/CLAY* KT10 166 B6 1
Heather Ri *BUSH* WD23 29 M5
Heather Rd *CHING* E4 50 F8
CRICK NW2 81 M2
LEE/GVPK SE12 142 A6
Heatherset Cl *ESH/CLAY* KT10 166 C7
Heatherset Gdns
STRHM/NOR SW16 156 F3
Heatherside Rd
HOR/WEW KT19 180 D1
SCUP DA14 144 C7
The Heathers
STWL/WRAY TW19 130 F4 1
Heather Wk *EDGW* HA8 45 H7
NKENS W10 100 E3 8
Heather Wy *POTB/CUF* EN6 22 F5
ROM RM1 73 K2
SAND/SEL CR2 185 K2
STAN HA7 43 M8
Heatherwood Cl *MNPK* E12 88 B2
Heatherwood Dr *YEAD* UB4 95 K1 1
Heathfield *CHING* E4 51 J5
CHST BR7 161 J2
COB KT11 178 A7
Heathfield Av
WAND/EARL SW18 137 K4 1
Heathfield Cl *CAN/RD* E16 106 D4 5
HAYES BR2 175 J7 1
POTB/CUF EN6 23 H3
Heathfield Dr *MTCM* CR4 155 L4
WIM/MER SW19 155 L3
Heathfield Gdns *CHSWK* W4 117 J3
GLDGN NW11 64 D7
WAND/EARL SW18 137 K3 1
Heathfield La *CHST* BR7 161 J2
Heathfield North *WHTN* TW2 133 L4
Heathfield Pk *CRICK* NW2 82 C6
Heathfield Park Dr *CHDH* RM6 72 B6
Heathfield Ri *RSLP* HA4 59 J8
Heathfield Rd *ACT* W3 99 H8
BMLY BR1 159 M3
BUSH WD23 29 L7
BXLYHS DA6 144 F1
CROY/NA CR0 172 D7 6
HAYES BR2 175 J7
WAND/EARL SW18 137 J3
WOT/HER KT12 165 L6
Heathfield South *WHTN* TW2 133 M4
Heathfield Sq
WAND/EARL SW18 137 K4
Heathfield Ter *CHSWK* W4 117 J3
WOOL/PLUM SE18 125 L4
Heathfield V *SAND/SEL* CR2 185 K2
Heath Gdns *TWK* TW1 133 M5
Heathgate *GLDGN* NW11 65 H7
Heath Gv *PGE/AN* SE20 158 C3 3
SUN TW16 149 M3
Heathhurst Rd *SAND/SEL* CR2 184 E2
Heathland Rd *STNW/STAM* N16 85 L1
Heathlands Cl *SUN* TW16 150 A5 1
TWK TW1 133 M6
Heathlands Ct *HSLWW* TW4 132 E2 1
Heathlands Ri *DART* DA1 146 B4
Heathlands Wy *HSLWW* TW4 132 E2 2
Heath La *BKHTH/KID* SE3 123 K7
DART DA1 146 B5
Heathlee Rd *BKHTH/KID* SE3 141 M1
DART DA1 145 L3
Heathley End *CHST* BR7 161 J2
Heathman's Rd
FUL/PGN SW6 119 G6 3
Heath Md *WIM/MER* SW19 136 D7 2
Heath Park Dr *BMLY* BR1 160 E6
Heath Park Rd *GPK* RM2 74 A4
Heath Ridge Gn *COB* KT11 178 A6
Heath Ri *HAYES* BR2 175 G1
PUT/ROE SW15 136 D3
Heath Rd *BXLY* DA5 145 J5
CHDH RM6 72 D8
DART DA1 145 M3
HGDN/ICK UB10 95 J3
HRW HA1 61 J8
HSLW TW3 133 J1
LHD/OX KT22 178 C5
OXHEY WD19 42 D2
POTB/CUF EN6 23 H3
THHTH CR7 157 J6
TWK TW1 133 M5
VX/NE SW8 120 B7
WEY KT13 164 A7
Heathrow Cl *WDR/YW* UB7 112 B6
Heath's Cl *EN* EN1 36 D5
Heathside *ESH/CLAY* KT10 166 E5
HAMP NW3 83 K4
HSLWW TW4 132 F4
Heath Side *STMC/STPC* BR5 176 C3
Heathside *WEY* KT13 164 B7
Heathside Av *BXLYHN* DA7 126 E7
Heathside Cl *ESH/CLAY* KT10 166 E5
Heathside Rd *NTHWD* HA6 41 K6
Heathstan Rd *SHB* W12 100 A5
Heath St *DART* DA1 146 D4
HAMP NW3 83 J4
The Heath *HNWL* W7 97 L8 3
Heath Vw *EFNCH* N2 65 J5
Heathview Av *DART* DA1 145 L3
Heath View Cl *EFNCH* N2 65 J5 1
Heathview Crs *DART* DA1 146 A4
Heath View Dr *ABYW* SE2 126 D4 1
Heathview Gdns
PUT/ROE SW15 136 C4
Heathview Rd *THHTH* CR7 157 G7
Heath Vls *WOOL/PLUM* SE18 125 M3
Heathville Rd *ARCH* N19 66 E8
Heathwall St *BTSEA* SW11 119 M8
Heath Wy *ERITH* DA8 127 J6
Heathway *BKHTH/KID* SE3 124 A5
CROY/NA CR0 173 M5
DAGW RM9 90 F4
WFD IG8 52 C6
Heathwood Gdns *CHARL* SE7 124 E2
SWLY BR8 163 J5
Heathwood Wk *BXLY* DA5 145 L5
Heaton Av *HARH* RM3 74 B1
Heaton Cl *CHING* E4 51 J5
HARH RM3 74 C1
Heaton Grange Rd *GPK* RM2 73 M2
Heaton Rd *MTCM* CR4 156 A3
PECK SE15 122 B8
Heaton Wy *HARH* RM3 74 C1
Heaver Rd *BTSEA* SW11 119 K8 4
Heavitree Cl *WOOL/PLUM* SE18 125 K3
Heavitree Rd
WOOL/PLUM SE18 125 K3 2
Hebden Ter *TOTM* N17 49 L8
Hebdon Rd *TOOT* SW17 137 L7
Heber Rd *CRICK* NW2 82 D5
EDUL SE22 139 M3
Hebron Rd *HMSMTH* W6 118 B1
Hecham Cl *WALTH* E17 68 E3
Heckfield Pl *FUL/PGN* SW6 119 G5 3
Heckford St *WAP* E1W 104 D6 4
Hector St *WOOL/PLUM* SE18 125 L2 3
Heddington Gv *HOLWY* N7 84 F5 3
Heddon Cl *ISLW* TW7 134 A1 1
Heddon Court Av *EBAR* EN4 34 F8
Heddon Rd *EBAR* EN4 34 F8 2
Heddon St *CONDST* W1S 10 E7
Hedge Hl *ENC/FH* EN2 36 B4
Hedge La *PLMGR* N13 49 J6
Hedgemans Rd *DAGW* RM9 90 D7
Hedgemans Wy *DAGW* RM9 90 E6
Hedge Place Rd *GRH* DA9 147 L3
Hedgerley Gdns *GFD/PVL* UB6 97 J1 1
Hedger's Gv *HOM* E9 86 E6 3
Hedger St *LBTH* SE11 18 C5
Hedgewood Gdns *CLAY* IG5 71 G5
Hedgley St *LEE/GVPK* SE12 141 M2
Hedingham Cl *IS* N1 6 E2
Hedingham Rd *BCTR* RM8 90 B5
EMPK RM11 93 G1
Hedley Rd *HSLWW* TW4 133 G4 3
Hedley Rw *HBRY* N5 85 K5 2
Hedworth Av *CHES/WCR* EN8 26 D6
Heenan Cl *BARK* IG11 89 J6 3
Heene Rd *ENC/FH* EN2 36 D5
Heidegger Crs *BARN* SW13 118 B5
Heigham Rd *EHAM* E6 88 D7
Heighton Gdns *CROY/NA* CR0 172 B7
Heights Cl *RYNPK* SW20 154 B3
The Heights *CHARL* SE7 124 C3
LOU IG10 39 M5
NTHLT UB5 79 G5
Heiron St *WALW* SE17 121 H4 3
Helby Rd *CLAP* SW4 138 D3
Helder Gv *LEE/GVPK* SE12 141 M4
Helder St *SAND/SEL* CR2 172 D8
Heldmann Cl *ISLW* TW7 133 K1
Helena Cl *EBAR* EN4 34 D3
Helena Pl *HOM* E9 86 B8
Helena Rd *EA* W5 98 D4
PLSTW E13 105 M1
WALTH E17 69 G6
WLSDN NW10 82 B5
Helena Sq *POP/IOD* E14 104 E6 4
Helen Av *EBED/NFELT* TW14 132 B4
Helen Cl *DART* DA1 146 B4
E/WMO/HCT KT8 151 H7
EFNCH N2 65 J4
Helen Rd *EMPK* RM11 74 D4
Helenslea Av *GLDGN* NW11 82 F1
Helen's Pl *BETH* E2 104 C2 10
Helen St *WOOL/PLUM* SE18 125 H2 6
Helford Cl *RSLP* HA4 77 L2 1
Helford Wy *UPMR* RM14 75 K7
Helgiford Gdns *SUN* TW16 149 L3
Helix Gdns *BRXS/STRHM* SW2 138 F3
Helix Rd *BRXS/STRHM* SW2 138 F3
Hellings St *WAP* E1W 104 A7 2
Helme Cl *WIM/MER* SW19 154 F1 2
Helmet Rw *FSBYE* EC1V 6 F9
Helmsdale Cl *ROM* RM1 73 L1
YEAD UB4 96 E3 6
Helmsdale Rd *ROM* RM1 73 L1
STRHM/NOR SW16 156 C4
Helmsley Pl *HACK* E8 86 B7 3
Helmsley St *HACK* E8 86 B7 4
Helsinki Sq *BERM/RHTH* SE16 122 F1
Helston Cl *PIN* HA5 60 F1 2
Helston Pl *ABLGY* WD5 20 F5
Helvetia St *CAT* SE6 140 F6
Hemans St *VX/NE* SW8 120 D5
Hemery Rd *NTHLT* UB5 79 K5 3
Hemingford Rd *CHEAM* SM3 169 J6
IS N1 5 M3
WAT WD17 28 E1
Heming Rd *EDGW* HA8 45 H8
Hemington Av *FBAR/BDGN* N11 47 M7
Hemlock Rd *SHB* W12 99 M6
Hemmen La *HYS/HAR* UB3 95 M6
Hemming Cl *HPTN* TW12 151 G4 1
Hemmings Cl *SCUP* DA14 144 B6
Hemming St *WCHPL* E1 104 A3
Hemming Wy *GSTN* WD25 21 G8
Hemmingway Cl *KTTN* NW5 84 A4 2
Hempstead Cl *BKHH* IG9 52 A4
Hempstead Rd *WALTH* E17 69 K4
WAT WD17 28 D1
Hemsby Rd *CHSGTN* KT9 167 M8
Hemstal Rd *KIL/WHAMP* NW6 2 A1
Hemsted Rd *ERITH* DA8 127 L6

Hemswell Dr CDALE/KGS NW9 63 L2
Hemsworth St IS N1 7 J5
Henbury Wy OXHEY WD19 42 D5
Henchman St SHB W12 99 M5
Hendale Av HDN NW4 64 A4
Henderson Cl WLSDN NW10 81 J6
Henderson Dr DART DA1 147 G1
STJWD NW8 3 G9
Henderson Rd BH/WHM TN16 187 J5
CROY/NA CR0 172 D1
ED N9 50 B3
FSTGT E7 88 C6
WAND/EARL SW18 137 L4
YEAD UB4 96 A2 2
Hendersons Cl HCH RM12 92 B2 2
Hendham Rd TOOT SW17 137 L6
Hendon Av FNCH N3 64 E2
Hendon Gdns CRW RM5 55 J8
Hendon La FNCH N3 64 E4
Hendon Park Rw
GLDGN NW11 64 F7 1
Hendon Rd ED N9 50 A4
Hendon Wy CRICK NW2 82 E1
HDN NW4 64 C7
STWL/WRAY TW19 130 D2
Hendon Wood La MLHL NW7 46 A2
Hendren Cl NTHLT UB5 79 K5
Hendre Rd STHWK SE1 19 K6
Hendrick Av BAL SW12 137 M3
Heneage Crs CROY/NA CR0 186 C3
Heneage La HDTCH EC3A 13 K5 5
Heneage St WCHPL E1 13 M3
Henfield Cl ARCH N19 84 C1
BXLY DA5 145 G3
Henfield Rd WIM/MER SW19 154 F4
Hengelo Gdns MTCM CR4 155 K7
Hengist Rd ERITH DA8 127 J5
LEE/GVPK SE12 142 B4
Hengist Wy HAYES BR2 159 K7
Hengrave Rd FSTH SE23 140 C4
Hengrove Ct BXLY DA5 144 E5 1
Hengrove Crs ASHF TW15 130 D7
Henley Av CHEAM SM3 169 L5
Henley Cl GFD/PVL UB6 97 J1 2
ISLW TW7 115 M6 2
Henley Dr BERM/RHTH SE16 19 M5
KUTN/CMB KT2 153 M3
Henley Gdns CHDH RM6 72 E6
PIN HA5 60 B4
Henley Rd CAN/RD E16 106 F8
IL IG1 89 J4
UED N18 49 L6
WLSDN NW10 82 C8
Henley St BTSEA SW11 120 A7 2
Henley Wy FELT TW13 150 D1 1
Hennel Cl FSTH SE23 140 C7
Henniker Gdns EHAM E6 106 D2
Henniker Ms CHEL SW3 15 G9 1
Henniker Rd SRTFD E15 87 K5
Henningham Rd TOTM N17 67 K2
Henning St BTSEA SW11 119 L6
Henrietta Ms BMSBY WC1N 5 K9
Henrietta Pl CAVSQ/HST W1G 10 C4
MHST W1U 10 C5 2
Henrietta St COVGDN WC2E 11 K6 2
SRTFD E15 87 J5
Henriques St WCHPL E1 104 A5
Henry Cl ENC/FH EN2 36 E3 2
Henry Cooper Wy
LEE/GVPK SE12 142 D7
Henry Darlot Dr MLHL NW7 46 E7
Henry Doulton Dr TOOT SW17 138 A8
Henry Jackson Rd
PUT/ROE SW15 118 D8 5
Henry Peters Dr TEDD TW11 151 L1 2
Henry Rd EBAR EN4 34 D8
EHAM E6 106 E1
FSBYPK N4 85 J1
Henry's Av WFD IG8 51 M7
Henryson Rd BROCKY SE4 141 G2
Henry St BMLY BR1 160 B4
Hensford Gdns SYD SE26 140 B8 4
Henshall St IS N1 85 K6 6
Henshawe Rd BCTR RM8 90 D3
Henshaw St WALW SE17 19 G5
Henslowe Rd EDUL SE22 140 A2
Henson Av CRICK NW2 82 C5 2
Henson Cl ORP BR6 176 B4
Henson Pl NTHLT UB5 78 C8
Henstridge Pl STJWD NW8 3 J5
Hensworth Rd ASHF TW15 148 D2
Henty Cl BTSEA SW11 119 L6 2
Henty Wk PUT/ROE SW15 136 B2
Henville Rd BMLY BR1 160 B4
Henwick Rd ELTH/MOT SE9 124 D8
Henwood Side WFD IG8 52 F8 2
Hepburn Gdns HAYES BR2 174 F3 2
Hepple Cl ISLW TW7 116 B7
Hepscott Rd HOM E9 87 G7 1
Hepworth Gdns BARK IG11 90 A5
Hepworth Rd
STRHM/NOR SW16 156 E3
Hepworth Wy WOT/HER KT12 164 F3
Herald Gdns WLGTN SM6 171 H5
Herald St BETH E2 104 B3 6
Herbal Hl CLKNW EC1R 12 B1
Herbert Crs KTBR SW1X 15 M3
Herbert Gdns CHDH RM6 72 D8
CHSWK W4 117 H4
WLSDN NW10 100 B1
Herbert Pl
WOOL/PLUM SE18 125 H4 1
Herbert Rd BXLYHN DA7 126 E7
CDALE/KGS NW9 64 A7
EMPK RM11 74 E8
FBAR/BDGN N11 66 E1
GDMY/SEVK IG3 89 L2
HAYES BR2 160 D8
KUT KT1 152 F6
MNPK E12 88 E4
SEVS/STOTM N15 67 M6
STHL UB1 96 F7
WALTH E17 68 F8 4
WIM/MER SW19 154 F3
WOOL/PLUM SE18 125 H5
Herbert St KTTN NW5 84 A6
PLSTW E13 106 A1
Herbrand St BMSBY WC1N 11 J1 2
Hercies Rd HGDN/ICK UB10 76 F6
Hercules Pl HOLWY N7 84 E3 4
HOLWY N7 84 E3 4
Hercules Rd STHWK SE1 17 M4
Hercules St HOLWY N7 84 E3 5
Hereford Av EBAR EN4 47 M3
Hereford Cl EPSOM KT18 180 D6
STA TW18 148 B4
Hereford Gdns IL IG1 70 E8
PIN HA5 60 E6
WHTN TW2 133 J5 1
Hereford Ms BAY/PAD W2 8 B4
Hereford Pl NWCR SE14 122 F5 4
Hereford Retreat PECK SE15 122 A5 2
Hereford Rd ACT W3 99 J6
BAY/PAD W2 8 B5
EA W5 116 C1
FELT TW13 132 C5
WAN E11 70 B6
Hereford Sq SKENS SW7 14 F6 1
Hereford St BETH E2 104 A3
Hereford Wy CHSGTN KT9 167 J7
Herent Dr CLAY IG5 70 F4
Hereward Av PUR/KEN CR8 184 A3
Hereward Cl WAB EN9 27 J5 1
Hereward Gdns PLMGR N13 49 G7
Hereward Rd TOOT SW17 137 L8
Herga Ct WAT WD17 29 G5
Herga Rd KTN/HRWW/W HA3 61 M5
Heriot Av CHING E4 51 G4
Heriot Rd HDN NW4 64 C6
Heriots Cl STAN HA7 44 A6
Heritage Cl UX/CGN UB8 94 C3
Heritage Hl HAYES BR2 175 J7
Heritage Vw HRW HA1 79 M3
Herkomer Cl BUSH WD23 43 H1 4
Herkomer Rd BUSH WD23 30 A8
Herlwyn Av RSLP HA4 77 L3
Herlwyn Gdns TOOT SW17 137 M8
Herm Cl ISLW TW7 115 J5
Hermes St IS N1 6 A6 1
Hermes Wy WLGTN SM6 183 K1
Hermiston Av CEND/HSY/T N8 66 E6
Hermitage Cl ENC/FH EN2 36 B5 2
ESH/CLAY KT10 167 G8
SHPTN TW17 149 G7
SWFD E18 69 M5
Hermitage Ct POTB/CUF EN6 23 J6 2
Hermitage Gdns HAMP NW3 83 G3
NRWD SE19 157 J3 3
Hermitage La CRICK NW2 83 G3
CROY/NA CR0 172 F2
STRHM/NOR SW16 156 F3 2
Hermitage Rd FSBYPK N4 67 J8
NRWD SE19 157 K2
Hermitage St BAY/PAD W2 9 G3
The Hermitage BARN SW13 117 M6 1
FSTH SE23 140 C5
RCHPK/HAM TW10 134 E2
UX/CGN UB8 76 D6 3
Hermitage Wk SWFD E18 69 M5
Hermitage Wall WAP E1W 104 A7 6
Hermitage Wy STAN HA7 62 A2
Hermit Rd CAN/RD E16 105 M3
Hermit St FSBYE EC1V 6 C7
Hermon Gv HYS/HAR UB3 96 A7
Hermon Hl WAN E11 70 A5
Herndon Rd WAND/EARL SW18 137 J2
Herne Cl WLSDN NW10 81 K5 3
Herne Hl HNHL SE24 139 J2
Herne Hill Rd HNHL SE24 121 J8
Herne Ms UED N18 50 A6
Herne Pl HNHL SE24 139 H3
Herne Rd BUSH WD23 43 H1
SURB KT6 167 K4
Heron Cl BKHH IG9 52 A3
RKW/CH/CXG WD3 40 D4
UX/CGN UB8 76 D6
WALTH E17 68 F3
WLSDN NW10 81 L6 1
Heron Ct HAYES BR2 160 C7
Heron Crs SCUP DA14 143 L8
Herondale SAND/SEL CR2 185 K2 1
Herondale Av
WAND/EARL SW18 137 K5
Heron Dr FSBYPK N4 85 J2
Heronfield POTB/CUF EN6 23 J3
Heron Flight Av RAIN RM13 92 B7 3
Herongate Rd MNPK E12 88 C2
SWLY BR8 163 L2
Heron Hl BELV DA17 126 F2
Heron Ms IL IG1 89 H2
Heron Quays POP/IOD E14 105 G7
Heron Rd CROY/NA CR0 172 E3 2
HNHL SE24 139 J1
TWK TW1 134 A1
The Heronry WOT/HER KT12 165 G8
Herons Cft WEY KT13 164 C8
Heronsforde WEA W13 98 C5 1
Heronsgate EDGW HA8 45 G7
Heronslea GSTN WD25 29 J1
Heronslea Dr STAN HA7 44 E7
Herons Pl ISLW TW7 116 B8
Herons Ri EBAR EN4 34 E7
Heron Wk NTHWD HA6 41 L6
Heron Wy UPMR RM14 93 L1
Herrick Rd FSBYPK N4 85 J3
Herrick St WEST SW1P 17 H6
Herries St NKENS W10 100 E1 1
Herringham Rd CHARL SE7 124 C1
Herrongate Cl EN EN1 36 E5
Hersant Cl WLSDN NW10 82 A8
Herschell Rd FSTH SE23 140 D4
Hersham Cl PUT/ROE SW15 136 A4
Hersham Gdns
WOT/HER KT12 165 J6 3
Hersham Rd WOT/HER KT12 165 J6
Hertford Av MORT/ESHN SW14 135 K2
Hertford Cl EBAR EN4 34 D6
Hertford Rd BARK IG11 89 H7
EBAR EN4 34 C6
ED N9 50 B3
EFNCH N2 65 L4
GNTH/NBYPK IG2 71 L7
IS N1 7 K3
PEND EN3 26 D8
PEND EN3 37 J3 1
PEND EN3 37 J5 7
Hertford Road High St
PEND EN3 37 J7 2
Hertford St MYFR/PICC W1J 10 C9 2
MYFR/PKLN W1K 10 C9 2
Hertford Wy MTCM CR4 156 E7 2
Hertslet Rd HOLWY N7 84 F3
Hertsmere Rd POP/IOD E14 105 G7
Hervey Cl FNCH N3 65 G2
Hervey Park Rd WALTH E17 68 E5
Hesa Rd HYS/HAR UB3 96 A5
Hesewall Cl VX/NE SW8 120 C7
Hesketh Av RDART DA2 147 H5
Hesketh Pl NTGHL W11 100 E6 6
Hesketh Rd FSTGT E7 88 A3
Heslop Rd BAL SW12 137 M5
Hesper Ms ECT SW5 14 C7
Hesperus Crs POP/IOD E14 123 H2
Hessel Rd WEA W13 98 A8
Hessel St WCHPL E1 104 B5 3
Hesselyn Dr RAIN RM13 92 B7 4
Hessle Gv EW KT17 180 F4
Hestercombe Av FUL/PGN SW6 118 E7
Hesterman Wy CROY/NA CR0 171 L3
Hester Rd BTSEA SW11 119 L5
UED N18 50 A7
Hester Ter RCH/KEW TW9 117 G8
Heston Av HEST TW5 114 E5
Heston Grange La HEST TW5 114 F4
Heston Rd HEST TW5 115 G5
Heston St DEPT SE8 122 F6
Heswell Gn OXHEY WD19 42 A5 3
Hetherington Rd CLAP SW4 138 E1 3
SHPTN TW17 149 J5
Hetherington Wy
HGDN/ICK UB10 76 E4 1
Hetley Rd SHB W12 100 B7
Heton Gdns HDN NW4 64 A5 3
Hevelius Cl GNWCH SE10 123 M3 3
Hever Cft ELTH/MOT SE9 143 G8
Hever Gdns BMLY BR1 161 G5
Heverham Rd
WOOL/PLUM SE18 125 L2
Heversham Rd BXLYHN DA7 127 G7
Hewens Rd HGDN/ICK UB10 95 J2
Hewer St NKENS W10 100 D4
Hewett Cl STAN HA7 44 B6 3
Hewett Pl SWLY BR8 163 K7
Hewett St SDTCH EC2A 13 K1
Hewish Rd UED N18 49 L6
Hewison St BOW E3 104 F1
Hewitt Av WDGN N22 67 H3
Hewitt Cl CROY/NA CR0 174 A5
Hewitt Rd CEND/HSY/T N8 67 G6
Hewlett Rd BOW E3 104 E1
The Hexagon HGT N6 83 M1
Hexal Rd CAT SE6 141 L7
Hexham Gdns ISLW TW7 116 A5
Hexham Rd BAR EN5 34 B7
MRDN SM4 170 B3
WNWD SE27 139 J6
Heybourne Rd TOTM N17 68 B1
Heybridge Av
STRHM/NOR SW16 156 F2
Heybridge Dr BARK/HLT IG6 71 K4
Heybridge Wy LEY E10 68 E8
Heyford Av RYNPK SW20 154 F6
VX/NE SW8 120 E5
Heyford Rd MTCM CR4 155 L5
RAD WD7 30 F2
Heygate St WALW SE17 18 E6
Heynes Rd BCTR RM8 90 C4
Heysham Dr OXHEY WD19 42 C7
Heysham La HAMP NW3 83 H3
Heysham Rd SEVS/STOTM N15 67 K7
Heythorp St WAND/EARL SW18 136 F5
Heythrop Dr HGDN/ICK UB10 76 F4
Heywood Av CDALE/KGS NW9 63 L2
Heyworth Rd CLPT E5 86 B4
FSTGT E7 87 M5
Hibbert Av WATN WD24 29 K3
Hibbert Rd KTN/HRWW/W HA3 61 M3
WALTH E17 68 F8
Hibbert St BTSEA SW11 119 K8 3
Hibbs Cl SWLY BR8 163 K5
Hibernia Gdns HSLW TW3 133 G2
Hibernia Rd HSLW TW3 133 G1
Hichisson Rd PECK SE15 140 C2
Hickin Cl CHARL SE7 124 D2
Hickin St POP/IOD E14 123 J1 1
Hickling Rd IL IG1 89 H5
Hickman Av CHING E4 51 J8
Hickman Cl CAN/RD E16 106 D4 3
Hickman Rd CHDH RM6 72 C8
Hicks Av GFD/PVL UB6 97 K2
Hicks Cl BTSEA SW11 119 L8
Hicks St DEPT SE8 122 E3
Hidcote Gdns RYNPK SW20 154 B6 1
The Hideaway ABLGY WD5 20 F4 1
Hide Pl WEST SW1P 17 G6
Hide Rd HRW HA1 61 K5
High Acres ABLGY WD5 20 D5
Higham Hill Rd WALTH E17 68 E4
Higham Pl WALTH E17 68 E4 3
Higham Rd TOTM N17 67 K4
WFD IG8 52 A8
Higham Station Av CHING E4 51 H8
Higham St WALTH E17 68 E4
Highbanks Cl WELL DA16 126 A5
Highbanks Rd PIN HA5 43 H8
Highbank Wy CEND/HSY/T N8 67 G7 2
Highbarrow Rd CROY/NA CR0 172 F3
High Beech SAND/SEL CR2 184 E1
High Beeches EW KT17 181 K7
ORP BR6 177 G8
SCUP DA14 162 E1
High Beeches Cl
PUR/KEN CR8 183 K3 2
High Beech Rd LOU IG10 39 L7
Highbridge Rd BARK IG11 89 H8
Highbridge St WAB EN9 27 H6
Highbrook Rd BKHTH/KID SE3 124 D8
High Broom Crs WWKM BR4 174 B2
Highbury Av THHTH CR7 157 G5
Highbury Cl NWMAL KT3 153 J7
WWKM BR4 174 B4 2
Highbury Crs HBRY N5 85 H5
Highbury Gdns IL IG1 89 L2
Highbury Gra HBRY N5 85 H4
Highbury Gv HBRY N5 85 H5
Highbury Hl HBRY N5 85 H4
Highbury New Pk HBRY N5 85 J5
Highbury Pk HBRY N5 85 H4 5
Highbury Pl HBRY N5 85 H6
Highbury Qd HBRY N5 85 J3
Highbury Rd WIM/MER SW19 154 E1
Highbury Station Rd IS N1 85 G6 4
Highbury Ter HBRY N5 85 H5
Highbury Terrace Ms HBRY N5 85 H5
High Canons BORE WD6 32 C2
High Cedar Dr RYNPK SW20 154 B3
Highclere Cl PUR/KEN CR8 184 C8
Highclere Rd NWMAL KT3 153 K6
Highclere St SYD SE26 140 E8
Highcliffe Dr PUT/ROE SW15 135 M3
Highcliffe Gdns REDBR IG4 70 E6
Highcombe CHARL SE7 124 B4
High Coombe Pl
KUTN/CMB KT2 153 K3
Highcroft CDALE/KGS NW9 63 L6
Highcroft Av ALP/SUD HA0 80 F7
Highcroft Gdns GLDGN NW11 64 F7 2
Highcroft Rd ARCH N19 66 E8
High Cross GSTN WD25 30 D2
High Cross Rd
SEVS/STOTM N15 68 A4 7
Highdaun Dr
STRHM/NOR SW16 156 F7
Highdown WPK KT4 168 E4
High Down Rd BELMT SM2 182 B4
Highdown Rd PUT/ROE SW15 136 B3
High Dr LHD/OX KT22 178 D7
NWMAL KT3 153 J4
High Elms CHIG IG7 53 L6
UPMR RM14 93 L1
WFD IG8 52 A7 5
High Elms Cl NTHWD HA6 41 J8
High Elms La GSTN WD25 21 H4
Higher Dr BNSTD SM7 181 K6
PUR/KEN CR8 184 A6
Higher Gn EW KT17 181 G6
Highfield OXHEY WD19 42 F5 1
Highfield Av CDALE/KGS NW9 63 J6
ERITH DA8 127 H4 2
GFD/PVL UB6 79 L5
GLDGN NW11 64 D8
ORP BR6 176 F8
PIN HA5 60 F6
WBLY HA9 80 E3
Highfield Cl CDALE/KGS NW9 63 J6 1
CRW RM5 55 J8
LEW SE13 141 K3
LHD/OX KT22 178 D4
NTHWD HA6 59 L2
SURB KT6 167 J3
WDGN N22 67 G2
Highfield Ct STHGT/OAK N14 48 C1
Highfield Crs HCH RM12 92 F2
NTHWD HA6 59 L2
Highfield Dr HAYES BR2 159 L7
HGDN/ICK UB10 76 E3
HOR/WEW KT19 180 F1
WWKM BR4 174 B5
Highfield Gdns GLDGN NW11 64 E7
Highfield Hl NRWD SE19 157 K3
Highfield Link CRW RM5 55 J8
Highfield Rd ACT W3 99 H4
BMLY BR1 160 F7
BRYLDS KT5 168 C2
BUSH WD23 29 L8
BXLYHS DA6 144 F2
CRW RM5 55 J8
DART DA1 146 D4
FELT TW13 132 A5
GLDGN NW11 64 E7 2
HCH RM12 92 F2
ISLW TW7 115 M6
NTHWD HA6 59 L2
PUR/KEN CR8 183 M3
STMC/STPC BR5 161 M6
SUN TW16 149 M8
SUT SM1 170 E7
WCHMH N21 49 H4
WFD IG8 70 E1
WOT/HER KT12 165 G3
Highfield Rd South DART DA1 146 D4
Highfields POTB/CUF EN6 24 E1
Highfields Gv HGT N6 84 A1
Highfield Wy POTB/CUF EN6 23 H4
RKW/CH/CXG WD3 40 B1
High Firs SWLY BR8 163 L7
High Foleys ESH/CLAY KT10 179 H1 1
High Garth ESH/CLAY KT10 166 C8
Highgate Av HGT N6 66 B8
Highgate Cl HGT N6 66 A8
Highgate High St HGT N6 84 A1
Highgate Hl ARCH N19 84 B1
Highgate Rd KTTN NW5 84 A3
Highgate West Hl HGT N6 84 A2
High Gv BMLY BR1 160 C4
WOOL/PLUM SE18 125 K5
Highgrove Cl CHST BR7 160 E4
FBAR/BDGN N11 48 C7
Highgrove Ms CAR SM5 170 F5 1
Highgrove Rd BCTR RM8 90 C5
Highgrove Wy RSLP HA4 60 A7
High Hill Ferry CLPT E5 86 B1
High Holborn HCIRC EC1N 12 A3
HHOL WC1V 11 K4
Highland Av DAGE RM10 91 J3
HNWL W7 97 L5
LOU IG10 52 F1
Highland Cft BECK BR3 159 H1
Highland Dr BUSH WD23 43 H2
Highland Pk FELT TW13 131 M8
Highland Rd BMLY BR1 159 M4
BXLYHS DA6 145 G1 1
NRWD SE19 157 L2
NTHWD HA6 60 A3
PUR/KEN CR8 184 A7
Highlands OXHEY WD19 42 C3
Highlands Av ACT W3 99 J6
WCHMH N21 35 M8
Highlands Cl HSLW TW3 115 H6 1
Highlands Gdns IL IG1 88 E1
Highlands Rd BAR EN5 34 A7
STMC/STPC BR5 177 H2
The Highlands EDGW HA8 63 H3
POTB/CUF EN6 23 J3 1
RKW/CH/CXG WD3 40 B2
High La HNWL W7 97 K5
Highlea Cl CDALE/KGS NW9 63 L2
High Level Dr SYD SE26 140 A8
Highlever Rd NKENS W10 100 C4
High Md WWKM BR4 174 D4
CHIG IG7 53 J4
HRW HA1 61 L6
Highmead WOOL/PLUM SE18 125 M5
Highmead Crs ALP/SUD HA0 80 F7
High Meadow Cl PIN HA5 60 C5 2
High Meadow Crs
CDALE/KGS NW9 63 K6 1
High Mdw CHIG IG7 53 K7
High Meads Rd CAN/RD E16 106 D5
Highmore Rd BKHTH/KID SE3 123 L5
High Oaks ENC/FH EN2 35 M3
High Park Rd RCH/KEW TW9 117 G6
High Pth WIM/MER SW19 155 H4
High Pine Cl WEY KT13 164 C7
High Point ELTH/MOT SE9 143 H7
Highpoint WEY KT13 164 A7
Highridge Cl EPSOM KT18 180 E8 2
High Rd BKHH IG9 52 B4
BUSH WD23 43 K3
CHDH RM6 72 F7
CHIG IG7 53 H5
EFNCH N2 65 K3
FBAR/BDGN N11 48 B7
FNCH N3 65 J2
GDMY/SEVK IG3 90 A1
GSTN WD25 20 F7
IL IG1 89 H3
KTN/HRWW/W HA3 61 L2 1
LEY E10 69 H7
NFNCH/WDSP N12 47 J5 1
NFNCH/WDSP N12 65 J1
RDART DA2 146 C7
SEVS/STOTM N15 67 M6
TOTM N17 67 M3
TRDG/WHET N20 47 J2
UX/CGN UB8 94 C4
WBLY HA9 80 E5
WDGN N22 66 F1
WLSDN NW10 81 L6
High Road Eastcote PIN HA5 60 C5
High Road Great North Rd
EFNCH N2 65 K3
High Road Ickenham
HGDN/ICK UB10 77 J3
HGDN/ICK UB10 77 J3
HGDN/ICK UB10 77 J2
High Road Leyton LEY E10 87 H2
High Road Leytonstone
WAN E11 87 L3
High Road Woodford Gn
SWFD E18 70 A2
WFD IG8 52 A6
Highshore Rd PECK SE15 121 M7 2
High Silver LOU IG10 39 K7
Highstead Crs ERITH DA8 127 L6
Highstone Av WAN E11 70 A7
High St ABLGY WD5 20 F3
ACT W3 99 J7
BAR EN5 33 M7
BARK/HLT IG6 71 J4
BECK BR3 159 G5
BELMT SM2 170 B8
BMLY BR1 160 A6
BNSTD SM7 182 A8
BORE WD6 44 D1
BTFD TW8 116 F4
BUSH WD23 43 G1
CAR SM5 170 F7
CEND/HSY/T N8 66 E5
CHEAM SM3 169 L8
CHES/WCR EN8 26 E7
CROY/NA CR0 172 C5
DART DA1 146 E3
DEN/HRF UB9 58 C3
E/WMO/HCT KT8 151 G7
EA W5 98 D6
EMPK RM11 92 D1
ESH/CLAY KT10 166 F8
ESH/CLAY KT10 166 B6
EW KT17 180 F3
FELT TW13 131 M7
HEST TW5 114 B5
HPTN TW12 151 H4
HRW HA1 79 L2
HSLW TW3 115 H8
HYS/HAR UB3 113 K4
KGLGY WD4 20 A2
KTN/HRWW/W HA3 61 L4
KUT KT1 152 D5
LHD/OX KT22 178 D6
MLHL NW7 46 B7
NTHWD HA6 59 M2
NWMAL KT3 153 L7
ORP BR6 176 C7
ORP BR6 177 G2
PGE/AN SE20 158 C3
PIN HA5 60 E4
POTB/CUF EN6 23 J5
PUR/KEN CR8 184 A4
RKW/CH/CXG WD3 40 D3
ROM RM1 73 K6
RSLP HA4 59 L8
SCUP DA14 144 A8
SHPTN TW17 164 C1 3
SNWD SE25 157 M7
SOCK/AV RM15 111 J7
SRTFD E15 87 K7
STMC/STPC BR5 162 C7
STMC/STPC BR5 177 J1
STWL/WRAY TW19 130 D3
SUT SM1 170 B6
SWLY BR8 163 L6
TEDD TW11 152 A1
THDIT KT7 167 G1
THHTH CR7 157 J7
UX/CGN UB8 76 C7
UX/CGN UB8 94 C3
WAN E11 70 B7
WAT WD17 29 H6
WATW WD18 29 H6

WBLY HA9 .... 80 F4
WDR/YW UB7 .... 94 E7
WDR/YW UB7 .... 112 D4
WEY KT13 .... 164 A6
WHTN TW2 .... 133 J4
WIM/MER SW19 .... 154 D1
WOT/HER KT12 .... 165 G3
WWKM BR4 .... 174 B3
High St Collier's Wd
WIM/MER SW19 .... 155 K3
High St Harlesden
WLSDN NW10 .... 99 M1 🔲
High St Ms *WIM/MER* SW19 .... 154 E1
High St North *EHAM* E6 .... 88 E8
MNPK E12 .... 88 E4
High St South *EHAM* E6 .... 106 F1
High Tor Cl *BMLY* BR1 .... 160 B3
High Trees *BRXS/STRHM* SW2 .... 139 C5
CROY/NA CR0 .... 173 L3
EBAR EN4 .... 34 E8
High Vw *BELMT* SM2 .... 181 M4
PIN HA5 .... 60 C5
WATW WD18 .... 41 M1
Highview Av *EDGW* HA8 .... 45 J6
High View Av *WLGTN* SM6 .... 171 M7
High View Cl *LOU* IG10 .... 39 J8
Highview Cl *POTB/CUF* EN6 .... 23 J6
High View Cl *SNWD* SE25 .... 157 M5
Highview Gdns *EDGW* HA8 .... 45 J7
FBAR/BDGN N11 .... 48 C7
FNCH N3 .... 64 E4
POTB/CUF EN6 .... 23 J6
UPMR RM14 .... 93 H2
High View Rd *SWFD* E18 .... 69 M3
NRWD SE19 .... 157 K2
Highview Rd *SCUP* DA14 .... 144 B8
WEA W13 .... 98 A5
The Highway *BELMT* SM2 .... 182 C2
ORP BR6 .... 177 H7
STAN HA7 .... 61 M2
WAP E1W 104 C6
Highwood Av *BUSH* WD23 .... 29 M4
NFNCH/WDSP N12 .... 47 G6
Highwood Cl *ORP* BR6 .... 176 C4
Highwood Dr *ORP* BR6 .... 176 C4
Highwood Gdns *CLAY* IG5 .... 70 F6
Highwood Gv *MLHL* NW7 .... 45 K7
Highwood Hl *MLHL* NW7 .... 45 M5
Highwood La *LOU* IG10 .... 53 C1
Highwood Rd *ARCH* N19 .... 84 E3
High Worple *RYLN/HDSTN* HA2 .... 78 F3
Highwood Rd *FBAR/BDGN* N11 .... 48 D8
Highworth St *CAMTN* NW1 .... 9 K2 🔲
Hilary Av *MTCM* CR4 .... 156 A6
Hilary Av *FUL/PGN* SW6 .... 119 H5 🔲
HCH RM12 .... 92 D5 🔲
Hilary Rd *ACT* W3 .... 99 H5 🔲
SHB W12 .... 99 M5 🔲
Hilbert Rd *CHEAM* SM3 .... 169 K6
Hilborough Cl *WIM/MER* SW19 .... 155 J3
Hilborough Rd *HACK* E8 .... 7 M2 🔲
Hilborough Wy *ORP* BR6 .... 176 D7
Hilda May Av *SWLY* BR8 .... 163 L6
Hilda Rd *CAN/RD* E16 .... 105 L3 🔲
EHAM E6 .... 88 D7
Hilda Vale Rd *HAYES* BR2 .... 176 A6
Hildenborough Gdns
BMLY BR1 .... 159 L2 🔲
Hilden Dr *ERITH* DA8 .... 128 B5
Hildenlea Pl *HAYES* BR2 .... 159 L5 🔲
Hildreth St *BAL* SW12 .... 138 E3
Hildyard Rd *FUL/PGN* SW6 .... 14 B9
Hiley Rd *WLSDN* NW10 .... 100 C3 🔲
Hilfield La *GSTN* WD25 .... 21 G6
Hilgrove Rd *KIL/WHAMP* NW6 .... 2 F1
Hiliary Gdns *STAN* HA7 .... 62 C3
Hillars Heath Rd
COUL/CHIP CR5 .... 183 L8
Hillary Crs *WOT/HER* KT12 .... 165 J3
Hillary Ri *BAR* EN5 .... 34 A7
Hillary Rd *NWDGN* UB2 .... 115 G1
Hillbarn *SAND/SEL* CR2 .... 184 E4
Hillbeck Cl *PECK* SE15 .... 122 C5 🔲
Hillbeck Wy *GFD/PVL* UB6 .... 79 K8
Hillborne Cl *HYS/HAR* UB3 .... 114 A3
Hillbrook Rd *TOOT* SW17 .... 137 H4
Hill Brow *BMLY* BR1 .... 160 D4
DART DA1 .... 145 M3
Hillbrow *NWMAL* KT3 .... 153 M6
Hillbrow Cl *BXLY* DA5 .... 145 K8
Hillbrow Rd *BMLY* BR1 .... 159 L3
ESH/CLAY KT10 .... 166 C6
Hill Bunker's *BELV* DA17 .... 127 G2
Hill Burgess *CRICK* NW2 .... 83 C4
Hillbury Av *KTN/HRWW/W* HA3 .... 62 B6
Hillbury Rd *TOOT* SW17 .... 138 B7
Hill Cl *BAR* EN5 .... 33 J8
CHST BR7 .... 161 H1
CRICK NW2 .... 82 B3
GLDGN NW11 .... 65 C7
HRW HA1 .... 79 L3
PUR/KEN CR8 .... 184 C5
STAN HA7 .... 44 B6
Hillcote Av *STRHM/NOR* SW16 .... 157 G3
Hillcourt Av *NFNCH/WDSP* N12 .... 47 H6
Hillcourt Rd *EDUL* SE22 .... 140 B3
Hill Crs *BRYLDS* KT5 .... 152 F8
BXLY DA5 .... 145 J5
EMPK RM11 .... 74 C7
HRW HA1 .... 62 A6
TRDG/WHET N20 .... 47 H1
WPK KT4 .... 169 J4
Hill Crest *HGT* N6 .... 66 A8
Hill Crest *POTB/CUF* EN6 .... 23 J7
Hillcrest *WCHMH* N21 .... 49 H2
WEY KT13 .... 164 B6
Hillcrest Av *EDGW* HA8 .... 45 H6
GLDGN NW11 .... 64 E6
PIN HA5 .... 60 D5
Hillcrest Cl *BECK* BR3 .... 173 M1 🔲
EPSOM KT18 .... 180 F8
SYD SE26 .... 140 A8
Hillcrest Gdns *CRICK* NW2 .... 82 A3
Hillcrest Gdns *ESH/CLAY* KT10 .... 166 F5
HDN NW4 .... 64 C5
Hillcrest Rd *ACT* W3 .... 99 C7
BMLY BR1 .... 142 A8

DART DA1 .... 145 L4
EA W5 .... 98 E4
EMPK RM11 .... 74 A8
LOU IG10 .... 52 D1
ORP BR6 .... 177 G4
PUR/KEN CR8 .... 183 M1
SWFD E18 .... 69 M3
WALTH E17 .... 69 K3
Hillside Cl *ABLGY* WD5 .... 20 E5
MRDN SM4 .... 154 E7 🔲
MV/WKIL W9 .... 2 D5
WFD IG8 .... 52 C7 🔲
Hillside Crs *CHES/WCR* EN8 .... 26 D4
ENC/FH EN2 .... 36 D3
NTHWD HA6 .... 60 A2
OXHEY WD19 .... 42 E1 🔲
RYLN/HDSTN HA2 .... 79 J2
Hillside Dr *EDGW* HA8 .... 45 C8
Hillside Gdns *BAR* EN5 .... 33 L7
EDGW HA8 .... 44 F6
HGT N6 .... 66 A7
KTN/HRWW/W HA3 .... 62 E8
NTHWD HA6 .... 60 A1
WLGTN SM6 .... 183 J1
Hillside Gv *MLHL* NW7 .... 64 A1
STHGT/OAK N14 .... 48 D2
Hillside La *HAYES* BR2 .... 175 G4
Hillside Ri *NTHWD* HA6 .... 60 A1
Hillside Rd *BELMT* SM2 .... 181 M1 🔲
BRXS/STRHM SW2 .... 138 F6
BUSH WD23 .... 29 L8
CROY/NA CR0 .... 172 B7
DART DA1 .... 146 A3
EA W5 .... 98 E4
EW KT17 .... 181 J3
HAYES BR2 .... 159 M6
NTHWD HA6 .... 60 A1
PIN HA5 .... 60 B1
SEVS/STOTM N15 .... 67 M7 🔲
STHL UB1 .... 97 G3
STNW/STAM N16 .... 67 L8 🔲
Hills La *NTHWD* HA6 .... 59 L2
Hillsleigh Rd *KENS* W8 .... 100 F7
Hillsgrove Cl *WELL* DA16 .... 126 D1 🔲
Hills Pl *SOHO/CST* W1F 10 E5
Hill's Rd *BKHH* IG9 .... 52 B3
Hillstowe St *CLPT* E5 .... 86 C2
Hill St *MYFR/PICC* W1J 10 C8
Hilltop *GLDGN* NW11 .... 65 H5
MRDN SM4 .... 169 J2
Hilltop Gdns *DART* DA1 .... 146 F2 🔲
ORP BR6 .... 176 E4
Hilltop Rd *KIL/WHAMP* NW6 .... 2 A1
Hill Top Vw *WFD* IG8 .... 52 F8 🔲
Hilltop Wy *STAN* HA7 .... 44 A5
Hillview *RYNPK* SW20 .... 154 B3 🔲
Hillview Av *EMPK* RM11 .... 74 C7
KTN/HRWW/W HA3 .... 62 E6
Hill View Cl *PUR/KEN* CR8 .... 184 B4
Hill View Crs *IL* IG1 .... 70 F7
Hillview Crs *ORP* BR6 .... 176 E3
Hill View Dr *WELL* DA16 .... 125 L7
Hill View Gdns *CDALE/KGS* NW9 .... 63 K6
Hillview Gdns *HDN* NW4 .... 64 D5 🔲
PIN HA5 .... 61 G4
Hill View Rd *ESH/CLAY* KT10 .... 179 G1
ORP BR6 .... 176 F3
TWK TW1 .... 134 A3
Hillway *CDALE/KGS* NW9 .... 81 L1
HGT N6 .... 84 A2
Hillworth Rd *BRXS/STRHM* SW2 .... 139 G4
Hillyard Rd *HNWL* W7 .... 97 L4
Hillyard St *BRXN/ST* SW9 .... 121 G6
Hillyard Rd *WALTH* E17 .... 68 E3
Hilly Fields Crs *BROCKY* SE4 .... 141 G1
Hilsea St *CLPT* E5 .... 86 C4 🔲
Hilton Av *NFNCH/WDSP* N12 .... 47 K7
Hilton Cl *UX/CGN* UB8 .... 94 B1 🔲
Hilton Wy *SAND/SEL* CR2 .... 185 H8
Himalayan Wy *WATW* WD18 .... 41 M1 🔲
Himley Rd *TOOT* SW17 .... 155 L1
Hinchley Cl *ESH/CLAY* KT10 .... 166 F5
Hinchley Dr *ESH/CLAY* KT10 .... 166 F5
Hinchley Wy *ESH/CLAY* KT10 .... 167 G5
Hind Cl *CHIG* IG7 .... 53 M7
Hind Crs *ERITH* DA8 .... 127 J5
Hinde Ms *MHST* W1U .... 10 B4 🔲
Hindes Rd *HRW* HA1 .... 61 M6 🔲
Hinde St *MHST* W1U .... 10 B4 🔲
Hind Gv *POP/IOD* E14 .... 105 C5
Hindhead Cl *UX/CGN* UB8 .... 95 H4 🔲
Hindhead Gn *OXHEY* WD19 .... 42 C7
Hindhead Wy *WLGTN* SM6 .... 171 L7 🔲
Hindmans Rd *EDUL* SE22 .... 140 A2
Hindmans Wy *DAGW* RM9 .... 108 F2
Hindmarsh Cl *WCHPL* E1 .... 104 A6 🔲
Hindrey Rd *CLPT* E5 .... 86 B5
Hindsley's Pl *FSTH* SE23 .... 140 E8
Hinkler Rd *KTN/HRWW/W* HA3 .... 62 D4
Hinkley Cl *DEN/HRF* UB9 .... 58 C5
Hinstock Rd *WOOL/PLUM* SE18 .... 125 J5
Hinton Av *HSLWW* TW4 .... 132 D1
Hinton Cl *ELTH/MOT* SE9 .... 142 E5
Hinton Rd *BRXN/ST* SW9 .... 121 H8
HNHL SE24 .... 121 J8
UED N18 .... 49 L6
UX/CGN UB8 .... 76 C3
Hippodrome Pl *NTGHL* W11 .... 100 E6 🔲
Hitcham Rd *LEY* E10 .... 68 F8
Hitchcock Cl *SHPTN* TW17 .... 148 K6
Hitchin Cl *HARH* RM3 .... 56 C6
Hitherbroom Rd *HYS/HAR* UB3 .... 96 A7
Hitherfield Rd *BCTR* RM8 .... 90 C2
STRHM/NOR SW16 .... 138 F6
Hither Green La *LEW* SE13 .... 141 J2
Hithermoor Rd
STWL/WRAY TW19 .... 130 A3
Hitherwell Dr
KTN/HRWW/W HA3 .... 61 K2 🔲
Hitherwood Dr *HCH* RM12 .... 92 D4 🔲
Hitherwood Dr *DUL* SE21 .... 139 M8
Hive Rd *BUSH* WD23 .... 43 K4
Hoadly Rd *STRHM/NOR* SW16 .... 138 D7

FBAR/BDGN N11 .... 47 M8
PUR/KEN CR8 .... 184 B6
WBLY HA9 .... 80 F4
WFD IG8 .... 52 C7
Hobart Cl *TRDG/WHET* N20 .... 47 L4 🔲
YEAD UB4 .... 96 D3 🔲
Hobart Dr *YEAD* UB4 .... 96 D3 🔲
Hobart Gdns *THHTH* CR7 .... 157 K6 🔲
Hobart La *YEAD* UB4 .... 96 D3 🔲
Hobart Pl *BGVA* SW1W 16 C4
RCHPK/HAM TW10 .... 134 F4
Hobart Rd *DAGW* RM9 .... 90 A4
WPK KT4 .... 169 H5
YEAD UB4 .... 96 D3 🔲
Hobbayne Rd *HNWL* W7 .... 97 K5
Hobbes Wk *PUT/ROE* SW15 .... 136 B2 🔲
Hobbs Cl *CHES/WCR* EN8 .... 26 D2
Hobbs Gn *EFNCH* N2 .... 65 J4
Hobbs Pl *IS* N1 .... 7 J4
Hobbs Rd *WNWD* SE27 .... 139 J8 🔲
Hobday St *POP/IOD* E14 .... 105 H5
Hobury St *WBPTN* SW10 .... 119 K4 🔲
Hockenden La *SWLY* BR8 .... 163 G6
Hocker St *BETH* E2 .... 7 L8 🔲
Hockley Av *EHAM* E6 .... 106 E1
Hockley Dr *GPK* RM2 .... 74 B3
Hockley Ms *BARK* IG11 .... 107 L1
Hocroft Av *CRICK* NW2 .... 82 F3
Hocroft Rd *CRICK* NW2 .... 82 F4
Hocroft Wk *CRICK* NW2 .... 82 F3
Hodder Dr *GFD/PVL* UB6 .... 97 M1
Hoddesdon Rd *BELV* DA17 .... 127 G3
Hodford Rd *GLDGN* NW11 .... 82 E1
Hodges Wy *WATW* WD18 .... 42 A1 🔲
Hodgkins Cl *THMD* SE28 .... 108 D6 🔲
Hodson Cl *RYLN/HDSTN* HA2 .... 78 F3 🔲
Hodson Crs *STMC/STPC* BR5 .... 162 D8 🔲
Hoe La *EN* EN1 .... 37 H3
PEND EN3 .... 37 J3
Hoe St *WALTH* E17 .... 69 G6
The Hoe *OXHEY* WD19 .... 42 D4
Hofland Rd *WKENS* W14 .... 118 E1 🔲
Hogan Ms *BAY/PAD* W2 .... 9 G2
Hogarth Av *ASHF* TW15 .... 149 J2
Hogarth Cl *CAN/RD* E16 .... 106 D4 🔲
EA W5 .... 98 A5 🔲
Hogarth Crs *CROY/NA* CR0 .... 172 C2 🔲
WIM/MER SW19 .... 155 K4
Hogarth Gdns *HEST* TW5 .... 115 C5
Hogarth Hl *GLDGN* NW11 .... 64 F5
Hogarth Reach *LOU* IG10 .... 39 M8
Hogarth Rd *BCTR* RM8 .... 90 B5 🔲
ECT SW5 .... 14 C6
EDGW HA8 .... 63 G3
Hogarth Wy *HPTN* TW12 .... 151 J4
Hogg La *BORE* WD6 .... 31 G7
Hog Hill Rd *CRW* RM5 .... 72 F1
Hogsmill Wy *HOR/WEW* KT19 .... 168 C7
Holbeach Gdns *BFN/LL* DA15 .... 143 L3
Holbeach Rd *CAT* SE6 .... 141 G4
Holbeck Rw *PECK* SE15 .... 122 A5
Holbein Ga *NTHWD* HA6 .... 41 L7
Holbein Ms *BGVA* SW1W 16 A7
Holbein Pl *BGVA* SW1W 16 A6
Holberton Gdns *WLSDN* NW10 .... 100 B2 🔲
Holborn Pl *LINN* WC2A .... 11 L3 🔲
Holborn Rd *PLSTW* E13 .... 106 B4
Holborn Viad *STBT* EC1A 12 C4
Holborn Wy *MTCM* CR4 .... 155 M5 🔲
Holbrook Cl *EN* EN1 .... 36 F4
Holbrook Ct *HOLWY* N7 .... 84 E4 🔲
Holbrook La *CHST* BR7 .... 161 K3
Holbrook Rd *SRTFD* E15 .... 105 M1
Holbrook Wy *HAYES* BR2 .... 175 M1
Holburne Cl *BKHTH/KID* SE3 .... 124 C5
Holburne Gdns *BKHTH/KID* SE3 .... 124 D6
Holburne Rd *BKHTH/KID* SE3 .... 124 C6
Holcombe Hl *MLHL* NW7 .... 46 A5 🔲
Holcombe Rd *TOTM* N17 .... 67 M4 🔲
Holcombe St *HMSMTH* W6 .... 118 B2 🔲
Holcote Cl *BELV* DA17 .... 126 E1 🔲
Holcroft Rd *HOM* E9 .... 86 C7 🔲
Holdbrook Wy *HARH* RM3 .... 74 F3
Holden Av *CDALE/KGS* NW9 .... 81 J1
NFNCH/WDSP N12 .... 47 H7
Holdenby Rd *BROCKY* SE4 .... 140 E2
Holden Cl *BCTR* RM8 .... 89 G2
Holdenhurst Av *FNCH* N3 .... 65 H1
Holden Rd *NFNCH/WDSP* N12 .... 47 H6
Holden St *BTSEA* SW11 .... 120 A7
Holden Wy *UPMR* RM14 .... 93 K1
Holdernesse Rd *ISLW* TW7 .... 116 A6 🔲
TOOT SW17 .... 137 M7
Holderness Wy *WNWD* SE27 .... 157 H1 🔲
Holders Hill Av *HDN* NW4 .... 64 A5
Holders Hill Crs *HDN* NW4 .... 64 A5
Holders Hill Dr *HDN* NW4 .... 64 B6
Holders Hill Gdns *HDN* NW4 .... 64 D3
Holders Hill Rd *HDN* NW4 .... 64 D3
Holecroft *WAB* EN9 .... 27 L7
Holford Rd *HAMP* NW3 .... 83 J3
Holford St *FSBYW* WC1X 6 A1
Holgate Av *BTSEA* SW11 .... 119 K8
Holgate Rd *DACE* RM10 .... 91 G5
Holgate St *CHARL* SE7 .... 124 D1
Holland Av *BELMT* SM2 .... 182 A1
RYNPK SW20 .... 153 M4
Holland Cl *BAR* EN5 .... 47 K2
HAYES BR2 .... 174 F4
ROMW/RG RM7 .... 73 J6 🔲
STAN HA7 .... 44 B7 🔲
Holland Dr *FSTH* SE23 .... 140 E7 🔲
Holland Gdns *GSTN* WD25 .... 21 J8
WATW W14 .... 118 E1 🔲
Holland Gv *BRXN/ST* SW9 .... 121 G5
Holland Pk *KENS* W8 .... 100 F8
NTGHL W11 .... 100 E8
Holland Park Av *GDMY/SEVK* IG3 .... 71 L7
NTGHL W11 .... 100 E7
Holland Park Gdns *WKENS* W14 .... 100 E7
Holland Park Ms *NTGHL* W14 .... 100 E7
Holland Park Rd *WKENS* W14 .... 100 E7
Holland Pl *KENS* W8 .... 14 C1 🔲
Holland Rd *ALP/SUD* HA0 .... 80 D6
EHAM E6 .... 88 F8
SNWD SE25 .... 158 A8
SRTFD E15 .... 105 L2 🔲
WKENS W14 .... 100 D8
WLSDN NW10 .... 81 K1
The Hollands *WPK* KT4 .... 168 F3
Holland St *KENS* W8 .... 14 B2

STHWK SE1 .... 12 D8
Holland Villas Rd *WKENS* W14 .... 100 E8
Holland Wk *STAN* HA7 .... 44 A7
Holland Wy *HAYES* BR2 .... 174 F4
Hollar Rd *STNW/STAM* N16 .... 85 M3 🔲
Hollen St *SOHO/CST* W1F .... 11 G4 🔲
Holles Cl *HPTN* TW12 .... 151 C2
Holles St *CAVSQ/HST* W1G 10 D4
Holley Rd *ACT* W3 .... 99 L3
Hollickwood Av
NFNCH/WDSP N12 .... 47 M8
Holliday Sq *BTSEA* SW11 .... 119 K8 🔲
Hollidge Wy *DACE* RM10 .... 91 H6
Hollies Av *BFN/LL* DA15 .... 143 M6
Hollies Cl *STRHM/NOR* SW16 .... 157 G2
TWK TW1 .... 133 M6
Hollies End *MLHL* NW7 .... 46 B7
Hollies Rd *EA* W5 .... 116 C2
The Hollies *KTN/HRWW/W* HA3 .... 62 A5
Hollies Wy *POTB/CUF* EN6 .... 23 J4
Holligrave Rd *BMLY* BR1 .... 160 A4
Hollingbourne Av *BXLYHN* DA7 .... 126 F6
Hollingbourne Gdns *WEA* W13 .... 98 B4
Hollingbourne Rd *HNHL* SE24 .... 139 J2
Hollingsworth Rd
SAND/SEL CR2 .... 173 H8
Hollington Crs *NWMAL* KT3 .... 168 F1
Hollington Rd *EHAM* E6 .... 106 F2
TOTM N17 .... 68 A3
Hollingworth Cl
E/WMO/HCT KT8 .... 150 F7 🔲
Hollingworth Rd
STMC/STPC BR5 .... 176 B2
Hollman Gdns
STRHM/NOR SW16 .... 157 H2
Holloway La *WDR/YW* UB7 .... 112 E3
Holloway Rd *ARCH* N19 .... 84 D2
EHAM E6 .... 106 F2
HOLWY N7 .... 84 E3
WAN E11 .... 87 K3 🔲
Holloway St *HSLW* TW3 .... 115 H8
The Hollow *WFD* IG8 .... 51 M6 🔲
Holly Av *STAN* HA7 .... 62 E3
WOT/HER KT12 .... 165 K3
Hollybank Cl *HPTN* TW12 .... 151 J4
Hollybrake Cl *CHST* BR7 .... 161 K3 🔲
Hollybush Cl *OXHEY* WD19 .... 42 C2 🔲
WAN E11 .... 70 A6
Hollybush Gdns *BETH* E2 .... 104 B2 🔲
Hollybush HI *WAN* E11 .... 69 M7
Hollybush Pl *BETH* E2 .... 104 B2 🔲
Hollybush Rd *KUTN/CMB* KT2 .... 152 L1
Hollybush St *PLSTW* E13 .... 106 B2
Holly Bush V *HAMP* NW3 .... 83 J4 🔲
Hollybush Wy *CHESW* EN7 .... 26 A1
Holly Cl *BKHH* IG9 .... 52 D5
FELT TW13 .... 150 E1 🔲
WLSDN NW10 .... 81 L7
Holly Crs *BECK* BR3 .... 158 F8
WFD IG8 .... 69 K1
Hollycroft Av *HAMP* NW3 .... 83 G3
WBLY HA9 .... 80 E2
Hollycroft Cl *SAND/SEL* CR2 .... 172 E7
WDR/YW UB7 .... 113 G4
Hollycroft Gdns *WDR/YW* UB7 .... 113 G4
Hollydale Dr *HAYES* BR2 .... 175 M5
Hollydale Rd *PECK* SE15 .... 122 C7
Hollydown Wy *WAN* E11 .... 87 K3
Holly Dr *CHING* E4 .... 51 H2
POTB/CUF EN6 .... 23 H6
Holly Farm Rd *NWDGN* UB2 .... 114 E3
Hollyfield Av *FBAR/BDGN* N11 .... 47 M7
Hollyfield Rd *BRYLDS* KT5 .... 167 M2
Holly Gdns *WDR/YW* UB7 .... 94 F8
Hollygrove *BUSH* WD23 .... 43 K2 🔲
Holly Gv *CDALE/KGS* NW9 .... 63 J8
PECK SE15 .... 122 A7
PIN HA5 .... 60 E2
Hollygrove Cl *HSLWW* TW4 .... 132 F1
Holly Hedge Ter *LEW* SE13 .... 141 J2
Holly HI *HAMP* NW3 .... 83 J4
WCHMH N21 .... 48 F1
Holly Hill Rd *BELV* DA17 .... 127 H3
Holly Lodge Gdns *HGT* N6 .... 84 A2
Hollymead *CAR* SM5 .... 170 F5
Holly Ms *WBPTN* SW10 .... 14 F8
Hollymoor La *HOR/WEW* KT19 .... 180 D3
Holly Mt *HAMP* NW3 .... 83 J4
Hollymount Cl *GNWCH* SE10 .... 123 J6 🔲
Holly Pk *FNCH* N3 .... 64 F4
FSBYPK N4 .... 66 F8 🔲
Holly Park Gdns *FNCH* N3 .... 65 G4
Holly Park Rd *FBAR/BDGN* N11 .... 48 A7
HNWL W7 .... 97 M7
Holly Rd *CHSWK* W4 .... 117 K2 🔲
DART DA1 .... 146 D5
HPTN TW12 .... 151 J2
HSLW TW3 .... 133 H1
PEND EN3 .... 37 K1
TWK TW1 .... 134 A5
Hollytree Av *SWLY* BR8 .... 163 L5
Hollytree Cl *WIM/MER* SW19 .... 136 D5
Hollyview Cl *HDN* NW4 .... 64 A7 🔲
Holly Wy *MTCM* CR4 .... 156 D7
Hollywood Gdns *YEAD* UB4 .... 96 B5
Hollywood Ms *WBPTN* SW10 .... 14 E9 🔲
Hollywood Rd *CHING* E4 .... 50 E7 🔲
WBPTN SW10 .... 14 E9
Hollywood Wy *ERITH* DA8 .... 128 B6
WFD IG8 .... 69 K1
Holman Rd *BTSEA* SW11 .... 119 K7
HOR/WEW KT19 .... 168 C7
Holmbank Dr *SHPTN* TW17 .... 149 L7
Holmbridge Gdns *PEND* EN3 .... 37 K7
Holmbrook Dr *HDN* NW4 .... 64 B8
Holmbury Cl *BUSH* WD23 .... 43 L4 🔲
Holmbury Ct
WIM/MER SW19 .... 155 L3 🔲
Holmbury Gdns
HYS/HAR UB3 .... 95 M7 🔲
Holmbury Pk *CHST* BR7 .... 160 E3
Holmbury Vw *CLPT* E5 .... 86 B1
Holmbush Rd *PUT/ROE* SW15 .... 136 E3
Holmcote Gdns *HBRY* N5 .... 85 J3 🔲
Holmcroft Wy *HAYES* BR2 .... 160 F8

Holmdale Cl BORE WD6 .... 31 M5 3
Holmdale Gdns HDN NW4 .... 64 D6
Holmdale Rd CHST BR7 .... 161 J1
KIL/WHAMP NW6 .... 83 G5
Holmdale Ter
SEVS/STOTM N15 .... 67 L7 4
Holmdene Av HNHL SE24 .... 139 J2
MLHL NW7 .... 46 A8
RYLN/HDSTN HA2 .... 61 H4
Holmdene Cl BECK BR3 .... 159 J5
Holmdene Ct BMLY BR1 .... 160 E6 3
Holmead Rd FUL/PGN SW6 .... 119 H5
Holme Cl CHES/WCR EN8 .... 26 E4 3
Holme Lacey Rd
LEE/GVPK SE12 .... 141 M3
Holme Lea GSTN WD25 .... 21 J7
Holme Pk BORE WD6 .... 31 M5 4
Holme Rd EHAM E6 .... 88 E8
EMPK RM11 .... 93 G1
Holmes Av MLHL NW7 .... 46 E7 3
WALTH E17 .... 68 F4
Holmesdale CHES/WCR EN8 .... 26 C8
Holmesdale Av
MORT/ESHN SW14 .... 117 H8
Holmesdale Cl SNWD SE25 .... 157 M6 2
Holmesdale Rd CROY/NA CR0 .... 157 K8
HGT N6 .... 66 B8
RCH/KEW TW9 .... 116 F6 1
SNWD SE25 .... 157 L7
TEDD TW11 .... 152 C3
WELL DA16 .... 126 D7
Holmesley Rd BROCKY SE4 .... 140 E3
Holmes Rd KTTN NW5 .... 84 B5
TWK TW1 .... 133 M6
WIM/MER SW19 .... 155 J3
Holmes Ter STHWK SE1 .... 18 A1
Holme Wy STAN HA7 .... 43 M8
Holmewood Gdns
BRXS/STRHM SW2 .... 138 F4
Holmewood Rd
BRXS/STRHM SW2 .... 138 E4
SNWD SE25 .... 157 L6
Holmfield Av HDN NW4 .... 64 D6
Holm Gv HGDN/ICK UB10 .... 77 G7
Holmhurst Rd BELV DA17 .... 127 H3
Holmleigh Av DART DA1 .... 146 C1
Holmleigh Rd STNW/STAM N16 .... 85 L1
Holm Oak Cl
WAND/EARL SW18 .... 136 F3 2
Holmsdale Gv BXLYHN DA7 .... 127 L7
Holmshaw Cl SYD SE26 .... 140 E8
Holmshill La BORE WD6 .... 32 F2
Holmside Ri OXHEY WD19 .... 42 B5
Holmside Rd BAL SW12 .... 138 A3
Holmsley Cl NWMAL KT3 .... 168 F1
Holmstall Av EDGW HA8 .... 63 J3
Holmwood Av SAND/SEL CR2 .... 184 F6
Holmwood Cl BELMT SM2 .... 181 K2
NTHLT UB5 .... 79 H6 1
RYLN/HDSTN HA2 .... 61 J4
Holmwood Gdns FNCH N3 .... 65 G3
WLGTN SM6 .... 171 H8
Holmwood Gv MLHL NW7 .... 45 K7
Holmwood Rd BELMT SM2 .... 181 J2
CHSGTN KT9 .... 167 L7
GDMY/SEVK IG3 .... 89 L2
PEND EN3 .... 37 K1
Holne Cha EFNCH N2 .... 65 J7
MRDN SM4 .... 170 A1
Holness Rd SRTFD E15 .... 87 M6
Holroyd Rd ESH/CLAY KT10 .... 178 F2 1
PUT/ROE SW15 .... 136 C1
Holstein Av WEY KT13 .... 164 A6
Holstock Rd IL IG1 .... 89 J2
Holsworth Cl
RYLN/HDSTN HA2 .... 61 J6 1
Holsworthy Wy CHSGTN KT9 .... 167 J7
Holt Cl BORE WD6 .... 31 M7
CHIG IG7 .... 53 M7
MUSWH N10 .... 66 A5
THMD SE28 .... 108 B6
Holton St WCHPL E1 .... 104 D3 7
Holt Rd ALP/SUD HA0 .... 80 B3
CAN/RD E16 .... 106 E7
Holtsmere Cl GSTN WD25 .... 21 J8
The Holt BARK/HLT IG6 .... 53 J8
WLGTN SM6 .... 171 J6
Holt Wy CHIG IG7 .... 53 M7
Holtwhite Av ENC/FH EN2 .... 36 C5
Holtwhite's Hl ENC/FH EN2 .... 36 B4
Holtwood Rd LHD/OX KT22 .... 178 C6
Holwell Pl PIN HA5 .... 60 E5
Holwood Cl WOT/HER KT12 .... 165 J4
Holwood Park Av ORP BR6 .... 175 M6
Holwood Pl CLAP SW4 .... 138 D1 4
Holybourne Av PUT/ROE SW15 .... 136 A4
Holyfield Rd WAB EN9 .... 27 J2
Holyhead Cl BOW E3 .... 105 G2
Holyoake Ct
BERM/RHTH SE16 .... 104 F8 2
Holyoake Wk EA W5 .... 98 C3
EFNCH N2 .... 65 J4
Holyoak Rd LBTH SE11 .... 18 C5
Holyport Rd FUL/PGN SW6 .... 118 C5
Holyrood Av RYLN/HDSTN HA2 .... 78 E4
Holyrood Gdns EDGW HA8 .... 63 H3
Holyrood Rd BAR EN5 .... 47 J1
Holyrood St STHWK SE1 .... 13 J9
Holywell Cl BKHTH/KID SE3 .... 124 A4 2
STWL/WRAY TW19 .... 130 E5
Holywell La SDTCH EC2A 7 K9
Holywell Rd WATW WD18 .... 29 G8
Holywell Rw SDTCH EC2A 13 J1
Holywell Wy STWL/WRAY TW19 .... 130 E5
Home Cl CAR SM5 .... 170 F4
NTHLT UB5 .... 96 F2
Homecroft Rd SYD SE26 .... 158 C1
WDGN N22 .... 67 H2
Home Farm Cl ESH/CLAY KT10 .... 166 B8
SHPTN TW17 .... 149 L7
THDIT KT7 .... 166 F2
Home Farm Gdns
WOT/HER KT12 .... 165 J4
Homefarm Rd HNWL W7 .... 97 L5
Home Farm Rd
RKW/CH/CXG WD3 .... 41 G6
Homefield Av GNTH/NBYPK IG2 .... 71 L6
Homefield Cl
STMC/STPC BR5 .... 162 B7 2
SWLY BR8 .... 163 M6
WLSDN NW10 .... 81 J6 2
YEAD UB4 .... 96 D3 7
Homefield Gdns EFNCH N2 .... 65 K4
WIM/MER SW19 .... 155 J5
Homefield Pk SUT SM1 .... 170 B8
Homefield Ri ORP BR6 .... 177 G3
Homefield Rd ALP/SUD HA0 .... 80 A4
BMLY BR1 .... 160 C4
BUSH WD23 .... 30 A8
CHSWK W4 .... 117 M2
EDGW HA8 .... 45 K8
RAD WD7 .... 30 F2
WIM/MER SW19 .... 154 D2 1
WOT/HER KT12 .... 165 M2
Homefield St IS N1 .... 7 J6 1
Home Gdns DAGE RM10 .... 91 J3 2
DART DA1 .... 146 E3
Home Hl SWLY BR8 .... 163 M3
Homeland Dr BELMT SM2 .... 182 B2
Homelands Dr NRWD SE19 .... 157 L3
Home Lea ORP BR6 .... 176 F7
Homeleigh Ct CHES/WCR EN8 .... 26 B3 1
Homeleigh Rd PECK SE15 .... 140 D2
Home Md STAN HA7 .... 62 C2 1
Homemead Rd CROY/NA CR0 .... 171 J1 3
HAYES BR2 .... 160 F8
Home Park Mill Link Rd
KGLGY WD4 .... 20 B4
Home Park Rd WIM/MER SW19 .... 136 F8
Home Park Wk KUT KT1 .... 152 D7 2
Homer Cl BXLYHN DA7 .... 127 J6
Homer Dr POP/IOD E14 .... 123 G2
Home Rd BTSEA SW11 .... 119 L7
Homer Rd CROY/NA CR0 .... 173 K1
HOM E9 .... 86 E6
Homer Rw CAMTN NW1 .... 9 K3
Homersham Rd KUT KT1 .... 153 G5
Homer St CAMTN NW1 .... 9 K3
Homerton Gv HOM E9 .... 86 D5
Homerton High St HOM E9 .... 86 D5
Homerton Rd HOM E9 .... 86 F5
Homerton Rw HOM E9 .... 86 C5
Homerton Ter HOM E9 .... 86 C6 4
Homesdale Cl WAN E11 .... 70 A6 2
Homesdale Rd HAYES BR2 .... 160 C7
ORP BR6 .... 176 E2
Homesfield GLDGN NW11 .... 65 G6 1
Homestall Rd EDUL SE22 .... 140 C2
Homestead Gdns
ESH/CLAY KT10 .... 166 E7 1
Homestead Paddock
STHGT/OAK N14 .... 35 H8
Homestead Pk CRICK NW2 .... 81 M3
Homestead Rd BCTR RM8 .... 90 F2
FUL/PGN SW6 .... 118 F5
RKW/CH/CXG WD3 .... 40 D2
STA TW18 .... 148 B2
The Homestead DART DA1 .... 146 C3
Homestead Wy CROY/NA CR0 .... 186 C4
Homewaters Av SUN TW16 .... 149 M4
Homeway HARH RM3 .... 57 H8
Homewillow Cl WCHMH N21 .... 49 H1 1
Homewood Cl HPTN TW12 .... 150 F2 4
Homewood Crs CHST BR7 .... 161 L2
Honduras St FSBYE EC1V 6 E9 2
Honeybourne Rd
KIL/WHAMP NW6 .... 83 H5 2
Honeybourne Wy
STMC/STPC BR5 .... 176 C3
Honey Brook WAB EN9 .... 27 L6
Honeybrook Rd BAL SW12 .... 138 C4
Honey Cl DAGE RM10 .... 91 K6
Honeycroft Hl HGDN/ICK UB10 .... 76 E7
Honeyden Rd SCUP DA14 .... 162 E2
Honey Hl HGDN/ICK UB10 .... 76 F7
Honey La CHES/WCR EN8 .... 26 F7
WAB EN9 .... 27 M7
Honeyman Cl CRICK NW2 .... 82 D7
KIL/WHAMP NW6 .... 82 D7
Honeypot Cl
KTN/HRWW/W HA3 .... 62 F5 1
Honeypot La CDALE/KGS NW9 .... 62 F5 2
KTN/HRWW/W HA3 .... 62 F4
STAN HA7 .... 62 E4
Honeysett Rd TOTM N17 .... 67 M3 1
Honeysuckle Cl HARH RM3 .... 56 D8 3
STHL UB1 .... 96 E6 2
Honeysuckle Gdns
CROY/NA CR0 .... 173 K2
Honeywell Rd BTSEA SW11 .... 137 L3
Honeywood Cl POTB/CUF EN6 .... 23 K6
Honeywood Rd ISLW TW7 .... 134 A1 2
WLSDN NW10 .... 99 M1 1
Honeywood Wk CAR SM5 .... 170 F6 2
Honister Cl STAN HA7 .... 62 B2
Honister Gdns STAN HA7 .... 62 B1
Honister Hts PUR/KEN CR8 .... 184 D7
Honister Pl STAN HA7 .... 62 B2
Honiton Rd KIL/WHAMP NW6 .... 100 F1
ROMW/RG RM7 .... 73 K7
WELL DA16 .... 125 M7
Honley Rd CAT SE6 .... 141 H4
Honnor Rd STA TW18 .... 148 D3
Honor Oak Pk FSTH SE23 .... 140 D3
Honor Oak Ri FSTH SE23 .... 140 C3
Honor Oak Rd FSTH SE23 .... 140 C5
Hood Av MORT/ESHN SW14 .... 135 J2
STHGT/OAK N14 .... 48 B1
STMC/STPC BR5 .... 162 B8
Hoodcote Gdns WCHMH N21 .... 49 H2
Hood Rd RAIN RM13 .... 91 L8
RYNPK SW20 .... 153 M3
Hood Wk ROMW/RG RM7 .... 73 H2
Hooker's Rd WALTH E17 .... 68 D4
Hook Farm Rd HAYES BR2 .... 160 D8
Hookfield HOR/WEW KT19 .... 180 C6
Hook Ga EN EN1 .... 37 H2
Hook Green La RDART DA2 .... 145 M7
Hook Hl SAND/SEL CR2 .... 184 E3
Hooking Gn RYLN/HDSTN HA2 .... 61 H6 1
Hook La ABR/ST RM4 .... 54 F1
POTB/CUF EN6 .... 23 M5
WELL DA16 .... 143 M1
Hook Ri North SURB KT6 .... 167 M5
Hook Ri South CHSGTN KT9 .... 167 M5
Hook Rd CHSGTN KT9 .... 167 K6 2
HOR/WEW KT19 .... 180 C3
SURB KT6 .... 167 L4
Hooks Hall Dr DAGE RM10 .... 91 J3 3
Hookstone Wy WFD IG8 .... 70 D1
The Hook BAR EN5 .... 47 K1
Hook Underpass
(Kingston By-pass)
SURB KT6 .... 167 K5
Hook Wk EDGW HA8 .... 45 J8
Hooper Rd CAN/RD E16 .... 106 A5
Hooper's Ms ACT W3 .... 99 J7 3
Hooper St WCHPL E1 .... 104 A6
Hoop La GLDGN NW11 .... 64 F8
Hope Cl BTFD TW8 .... 116 E3 2
CHDH RM6 .... 72 D5
IS N1 .... 85 J6 6
LEE/GVPK SE12 .... 142 B7
SUT SM1 .... 170 C7 4
Hopedale Rd CHARL SE7 .... 124 B4
Hopefield Av KIL/WHAMP NW6 .... 100 E1
Hope Gn GSTN WD25 .... 21 G6
Hope Pk BMLY BR1 .... 159 M3
Hopes Cl HEST TW5 .... 115 G4 1
Hope St BTSEA SW11 .... 119 K8
Hopetown St WCHPL E1 .... 13 M3 1
Hopewell St CMBW SE5 .... 121 K5
Hop Gdns CHCR WC2N 11 J7 5
Hopgood St SHB W12 .... 100 C7 1
Hopkins Cl GPK RM2 .... 74 C4
MUSWH N10 .... 66 A1 2
Hopkins St SOHO/CST W1F 10 F5
Hoppers Rd WCHMH N21 .... 49 G4
Hoppett Rd CHING E4 .... 51 L5
Hopping La IS N1 .... 85 H6 6
Hoppingwood Av NWMAL KT3 .... 153 L6
Hoppner Rd YEAD UB4 .... 95 K1
Hopton Gdns NWMAL KT3 .... 169 G1
Hopton Rd STRHM/NOR SW16 .... 156 E1
Hopton St STHWK SE1 .... 12 D8
Hopwood Cl TOOT SW17 .... 137 J7 2
Hopwood Rd WALW SE17 .... 19 H9
Horace Av ROMW/RG RM7 .... 91 K1
Horace Rd BARK/HLT IG6 .... 71 J4
FSTGT E7 .... 88 B4 2
KUT KT1 .... 152 F6
Horatio Pl POP/IOD E14 .... 105 J8
Horatius Wy CROY/NA CR0 .... 171 M8
Horbeam Cl BORE WD6 .... 32 A4 3
Horbury Crs NTGHL W11 .... 8 A7
Horbury Ms NTGHL W11 .... 100 F6 1
Horder Rd FUL/PGN SW6 .... 118 E6
Hordle Prom North
PECK SE15 .... 121 M5 4
Horley Cl BXLYHS DA6 .... 145 G2 1
Horley Rd ELTH/MOT SE9 .... 142 E8
Hormead Rd NKENS W10 .... 100 F3
Hornbeam Av UPMR RM14 .... 93 G4
Hornbeam Cl IL IG1 .... 89 K5
LBTH SE11 .... 18 A5
NTHLT UB5 .... 78 F5
Hornbeam Crs BTFD TW8 .... 116 B5
Hornbeam Gv CHING E4 .... 51 L5
Hornbeam La CHING E4 .... 38 E8
Hornbeam Rd BKHH IG9 .... 52 D5
YEAD UB4 .... 96 C4
Hornbeams LCOL/BKTW AL2 .... 21 M3
Hornbeams Av EN EN1 .... 26 C8
Hornbeams Ri
FBAR/BDGN N11 .... 48 A8 1
Hornbeam Wy CHESW EN7 .... 25 M2
HAYES BR2 .... 176 A1
Hornbill Cl UX/CGN UB8 .... 94 D5
Hornbuckle Cl
RYLN/HDSTN HA2 .... 79 K2 3
Hornby Cl HAMP NW3 .... 3 H1
Horncastle Cl
LEE/GVPK SE12 .... 142 A4 2
Horncastle Rd LEE/GVPK SE12 .... 142 A4
Hornchurch Cl
KUTN/CMB KT2 .... 152 D1 2
Hornchurch Rd EMPK RM11 .... 92 B1
HCH RM12 .... 92 A1
Horndean Cl PUT/ROE SW15 .... 136 A5 2
Horndon Cl CRW RM5 .... 73 J2
Horndon Gn CRW RM5 .... 73 J2
Horndon Rd CRW RM5 .... 73 J2
Horner La MTCM CR4 .... 155 K5 1
Horne Rd SHPTN TW17 .... 148 F7
The Hornets WATW WD18 .... 29 H7 2
Horne Wy PUT/ROE SW15 .... 118 C7
Hornfair Rd CHARL SE7 .... 124 D4
Hornford Wy ROMW/RG RM7 .... 73 L8
Horniman Dr FSTH SE23 .... 140 B5
Horning Cl ELTH/MOT SE9 .... 142 E8
Horn La ACT W3 .... 99 J7
GNWCH SE10 .... 124 A3 1
WFD IG8 .... 52 A8
Hornminster Gln EMPK RM11 .... 93 G2 1
Horn Park Cl LEE/GVPK SE12 .... 142 B2
Horn Park La LEE/GVPK SE12 .... 142 B2
Horns End Pl PIN HA5 .... 60 C5
Hornsey La ARCH N19 .... 66 C8
Hornsey Lane Gdns HGT N6 .... 66 C8
Hornsey Park Rd
CEND/HSY/T N8 .... 66 F4
Hornsey Ri ARCH N19 .... 66 D8
Hornsey Rise Gdns ARCH N19 .... 66 D8
Hornsey Rd ARCH N19 .... 84 E1
HOLWY N7 .... 84 F5
Hornsey St HOLWY N7 .... 84 F5 1
Hornshay St PECK SE15 .... 122 C4
Horns Rd BARK/HLT IG6 .... 71 J6
Hornton Pl KENS W8 .... 14 B2
Hornton St KENS W8 .... 14 B1
Horsa Rd ERITH DA8 .... 127 J5
LEE/GVPK SE12 .... 142 C4
Horsebridges Cl DAGW RM9 .... 90 E8 2
Horsecroft Cl ORP BR6 .... 177 H3 1
Horsecroft Rd EDGW HA8 .... 63 K1
Horse Fair KUT KT1 .... 152 D5
Horseferry Pl GNWCH SE10 .... 123 J4 5
Horseferry Rd POP/IOD E14 .... 104 E6
WEST SW1P 17 G4
Horse Guards Av WHALL SW1A 11 J9
Horse Guards Rd WHALL SW1A 11 H9
Horse Leaze EHAM E6 .... 107 H5
Horsell Rd HBRY N5 .... 85 G5 3
STMC/STPC BR5 .... 162 A4
Horselydown La STHWK SE1 .... 19 L1
Horseman Side BRW CM14 .... 56 D1
Horsenden Av GFD/PVL UB6 .... 79 L5
Horsenden Crs GFD/PVL UB6 .... 79 M5
Horsenden La North
GFD/PVL UB6 .... 79 L6
Horsenden La South
GFD/PVL UB6 .... 80 A8
Horseshoe Cl CRICK NW2 .... 82 B2
POP/IOD E14 .... 123 J3 2
Horse Shoe Crs NTHLT UB5 .... 97 G1
Horseshoe Dr UX/CGN UB8 .... 95 G5
Horseshoe La ENC/FH EN2 .... 36 C6 4
GSTN WD25 .... 21 H5
TRDG/WHET N20 .... 46 D3
The Horseshoe BNSTD SM7 .... 181 M8
COUL/CHIP CR5 .... 183 K6
Horse Yd IS N1 .... 6 D3
Horsfeld Gdns
ELTH/MOT SE9 .... 142 E2 2
Horsfeld Rd ELTH/MOT SE9 .... 142 D2
Horsfield Cl RDART DA2 .... 147 J4 2
Horsford Rd BRXS/STRHM SW2 .... 138 F2
Horsham Av NFNCH/WDSP N12 .... 47 L7
Horsham Rd BXLYHS DA6 .... 144 F3
EBED/NFELT TW14 .... 131 J3
Horsley Cl HOR/WEW KT19 .... 180 D6
Horsley Dr CROY/NA CR0 .... 186 C1
KUTN/CMB KT2 .... 152 D1 3
Horsley Rd BMLY BR1 .... 160 B4 3
CHING E4 .... 51 J4
Horsley St WALW SE17 .... 19 G9
Horsman St CMBW SE5 .... 121 J4
Horsmonden Cl ORP BR6 .... 176 F2 1
Horsmonden Rd BROCKY SE4 .... 140 F2
Hortensia Rd WBPTN SW10 .... 119 J4
Horticultural Pl CHSWK W4 .... 117 K3 2
Horton Av CRICK NW2 .... 82 E4
Horton Bridge Rd WDR/YW UB7 .... 94 F7
Horton Cl WDR/YW UB7 .... 94 F7
Horton Gdns HOR/WEW KT19 .... 180 C4
Horton Hl HOR/WEW KT19 .... 180 C4
Horton La HOR/WEW KT19 .... 180 A4
Horton Rd HACK E8 .... 86 B6
STWL/WRAY TW19 .... 130 A2
WDR/YW UB7 .... 94 E7
Horton St LEW SE13 .... 123 H8 2
Horton Wy CROY/NA CR0 .... 158 D8
Hortus Rd NWDGN UB2 .... 96 F8
Horvath Cl WEY KT13 .... 164 D6 2
Hosack Rd BAL SW12 .... 137 M6
Hoser Av LEE/GVPK SE12 .... 142 A6
Hosier La STBT EC1A 12 C3
Hoskin's Cl CAN/RD E16 .... 106 C5
HYS/HAR UB3 .... 113 M2 3
Hoskins St GNWCH SE10 .... 123 K3
Hospital Bridge Rd WHTN TW2 .... 133 H5
Hospital Rd HSLW TW3 .... 115 G8
Hospital Wy LEW SE13 .... 141 K3
Hotham Cl E/WMO/HCT KT8 .... 151 G6 3
Hotham Rd PUT/ROE SW15 .... 118 C8
WIM/MER SW19 .... 155 J3
Hotham St SRTFD E15 .... 87 L8 4
Hothfield Pl
BERM/RHTH SE16 .... 122 C1 1
Hotspur Rd NTHLT UB5 .... 97 G1
Hotspur St LBTH SE11 .... 18 A7
Houblon Rd
RCHPK/HAM TW10 .... 134 E2 2
Houghton Cl HPTN TW12 .... 150 E2
Houghton Rd
SEVS/STOTM N15 .... 67 M5 4
Houghton St HOL/ALD WC2B 11 M5 1
Houlder Crs CROY/NA CR0 .... 172 B8
Houndsden Rd WCHMH N21 .... 48 F1
Houndsditch HDTCH EC3A 13 L5 1
Houndsfield Rd ED N9 .... 50 B2
Hounslow Av HSLW TW3 .... 133 H2
Hounslow Gdns HSLW TW3 .... 133 H2
Hounslow Rd
EBED/NFELT TW14 .... 132 B4
FELT TW13 .... 132 D7
HSLW TW3 .... 133 H3
WHTN TW2 .... 133 J3
Houston Rd FSTH SE23 .... 140 E6
Hove Av WALTH E17 .... 68 F6
Hoveden Rd CRICK NW2 .... 82 D5
Hove Gdns SUT SM1 .... 170 B3 1
Hoveton Rd THMD SE28 .... 108 C5
Howard Av BXLY DA5 .... 144 C5
EW KT17 .... 181 G3
Howard Cl ACT W3 .... 99 H5
BUSH WD23 .... 43 L2
CRICK NW2 .... 82 E4 1
FBAR/BDGN N11 .... 48 A4
HPTN TW12 .... 151 J3
SUN TW16 .... 149 M2
WAB EN9 .... 27 K7
WATN WD24 .... 29 G2 3
Howard Dr BORE WD6 .... 32 D7
Howard Rd BARK IG11 .... 89 K8
BMLY BR1 .... 160 A3
BRYLDS KT5 .... 167 M1
COUL/CHIP CR5 .... 183 J8
CRICK NW2 .... 82 D4
DART DA1 .... 147 G3
EHAM E6 .... 106 F1
GFD/PVL UB6 .... 97 H5
IL IG1 .... 89 H4
ISLW TW7 .... 115 M8
NWMAL KT3 .... 153 L6
PGE/AN SE20 .... 158 C4
SEVS/STOTM N15 .... 67 L7 5
SNWD SE25 .... 158 A8
STNW/STAM N16 .... 85 K4
UPMR RM14 .... 93 J2
WALTH E17 .... 69 G4
WAN E11 .... 87 L3 5
Howards Cl PIN HA5 .... 60 B3 1
Howards Crest Cl BECK BR3 .... 159 J5 1
Howard's La PUT/ROE SW15 .... 136 C1
Howard's Rd PLSTW E13 .... 106 A2
Howard St THDIT KT7 .... 167 H2
Howard Wk EFNCH N2 .... 65 J5
Howard Wy BAR EN5 .... 33 K8
Howarth Rd ABYW SE2 .... 126 A3
Howberry Cl EDGW HA8 .... 44 D8
Howberry Rd EDGW HA8 .... 44 D8
THHTH CR7 .... 157 K4
Howbury La ERITH DA8 .... 128 A7
Howbury Rd DART DA1 .... 128 A7
PECK SE15 .... 122 C8
Howcroft Crs FNCH N3 .... 65 G1
Howcroft La GFD/PVL UB6 .... 97 K2 3
Howden Cl THMD SE28 .... 108 C6
Howden Rd SNWD SE25 .... 157 M5
Howden St PECK SE15 .... 122 A8
Howe Cl ROMW/RG RM7 .... 73 G2 1
Howell Cl CHDH RM6 .... 72 D6
Howell Hill Cl EW KT17 .... 181 J4 1
Howell Hill Gv EW KT17 .... 181 J4
Howell Wk WALW SE17 .... 18 D6
Howgate Rd MORT/ESHN SW14 .... 117 K8
Howick Pl WEST SW1P 16 F4
Howie St BTSEA SW11 .... 119 L5
Howitt Rd HAMP NW3 .... 83 L6
Howitts Cl ESH/CLAY KT10 .... 166 A8
Howland Ms East FITZ W1T 10 F2
Howland St FITZ W1T 10 F2
Howland Wy BERM/RHTH SE16 .... 104 E8
Howletts La RSLP HA4 .... 59 J7
Howletts Rd HNHL SE24 .... 139 J3 2
Howley Pl BAY/PAD W2 .... 8 F2
Howley Rd CROY/NA CR0 .... 172 B5
Howsman Rd BARN SW13 .... 118 A4
Howson Rd BROCKY SE4 .... 140 E1
How's Rd UX/CGN UB8 .... 76 C8
How's St BETH E2 .... 7 L5
Howton Pl BUSH WD23 .... 43 K3
Hoxton Market IS N1 .... 7 J8 1
Hoxton Sq IS N1 .... 7 J8
Hoxton St IS N1 .... 7 J4
Hoylake Crs HGDN/ICK UB10 .... 77 G1
Hoylake Gdns HARH RM3 .... 75 G1 3
MTCM CR4 .... 156 C6
OXHEY WD19 .... 42 D6
RSLP HA4 .... 78 B1
Hoylake Rd ACT W3 .... 99 L5 1
Hoyle Rd TOOT SW17 .... 155 L1
Hoy St CAN/RD E16 .... 105 M5 3
Hubbard Dr CHSGTN KT9 .... 167 J8 1
Hubbard Rd WNWD SE27 .... 139 J8
Hubbards Cha EMPK RM11 .... 75 G6
Hubbards Cl EMPK RM11 .... 75 G6
Hubbard St SRTFD E15 .... 87 L8
Hubert Gv BRXN/ST SW9 .... 120 E8
Hubert Rd EHAM E6 .... 106 D2
RAIN RM13 .... 109 M2
Hucknall Cl HARH RM3 .... 56 F8
Huddart St BOW E3 .... 104 F4 3
Huddleston Cl BETH E2 .... 104 C1 5
Huddlestone Rd CRICK NW2 .... 82 B6
FSTGT E7 .... 87 M4
Huddleston Rd ARCH N19 .... 84 C3
Hudson Cl WATN WD24 .... 28 F1
Hudson Pl WOOL/PLUM SE18 .... 125 J3
Hudson Rd BXLYHN DA7 .... 126 F7
HYS/HAR UB3 .... 113 K4
Huggin Hl BLKFR EC4V 12 F6
Huggins Pl
BRXS/STRHM SW2 .... 138 F5 2
Hughan Rd SRTFD E15 .... 87 K5
Hughenden Av
KTN/HRWW/W HA3 .... 62 B6
Hughenden Gdns NTHLT UB5 .... 96 C2
Hughenden Rd WPK KT4 .... 169 G2 1
Hughes Rd ASHF TW15 .... 149 J3
HYS/HAR UB3 .... 96 B6
Hughes Wk CROY/NA CR0 .... 172 C2 2
Hugh Gaitskell Cl
FUL/PGN SW6 .... 118 F4 3
Hugh Ms PIM SW1V 16 D6
Hugh Pl WEST SW1P 17 G5
Hugh St PIM SW1V 16 D6
Hugo Gdns RAIN RM13 .... 91 M6
Hugon Rd FUL/PGN SW6 .... 119 H8
Hugo Rd ARCH N19 .... 84 C4
Huguenot Pl WAND/EARL SW18 .... 137 J2
Hullbridge Ms IS N1 .... 7 G3 1
Hull Cl BERM/RHTH SE16 .... 104 D7 7
Hull St FSBYE EC1V 6 E8 1
Hulse Av BARK IG11 .... 89 K6
ROMW/RG RM7 .... 73 H2
Hulsewood Cl RDART DA2 .... 146 B7
Hulverston Cl BELMT SM2 .... 182 B3
Humber Av SOCK/AV RM15 .... 111 M5
Humber Dr NKENS W10 .... 100 D3 4
UPMR RM14 .... 75 K7
Humber Rd BKHTH/KID SE3 .... 124 A4
CRICK NW2 .... 82 B2
DART DA1 .... 146 D2
Humberstone Rd PLSTW E13 .... 106 C2
Humbolt Rd HMSMTH W6 .... 118 E4
Humes Av HNWL W7 .... 115 M1
Hume Wy RSLP HA4 .... 60 A7
Humphrey Cl CLAY IG5 .... 70 F2 1
Humphrey St STHWK SE1 .... 19 L7
Humphries Cl DAGW RM9 .... 90 F4 1
Hundred Acre CDALE/KGS NW9 .... 63 M3
Hungerdown CHING E4 .... 51 J3
Hungerford Rd HOLWY N7 .... 84 E5 3
Hungerford St WCHPL E1 .... 104 B5 3
Hunsdon Cl DAGW RM9 .... 90 E6
Hunsdon Rd NWCR SE14 .... 122 D5
Hunslett St BETH E2 .... 104 C1 6
Hunston Rd MRDN SM4 .... 170 B3
Hunter Cl BAL SW12 .... 138 A5
BORE WD6 .... 32 C8
POTB/CUF EN6 .... 23 H6
STHWK SE1 .... 19 H4 3
Huntercrombe Gdns
OXHEY WD19 .... 42 C7 6
Hunter Dr HCH RM12 .... 92 C4
Hunter Rd RYNPK SW20 .... 154 C4
THHTH CR7 .... 157 K6
Hunters Cl BXLY DA5 .... 145 L7
HOR/WEW KT19 .... 180 C6 1
Hunters Ct RCH/KEW TW9 .... 134 D2 3
Hunter's Gv CRW RM5 .... 55 H7
HYS/HAR UB3 .... 96 A7
KTN/HRWW/W HA3 .... 62 C5
ORP BR6 .... 176 C6 4
Hunters Hall Rd DAGE RM10 .... 91 G4
Hunters Hl RSLP HA4 .... 78 C3
Hunter's La GSTN WD25 .... 20 F7

Hunters Meadow
NRWD SE19 ... 139 L8 3
Hunters Reach CHESW EN7 ... 25 M2
Hunters Rd CHSGTN KT9 ... 167 L5
IL IG1 ... 89 H5
Hunters Sq DAGE RM10 ... 91 G4
Hunter St BMSBY WC1N ... 5 K9
Hunters Wy CROY/NA CR0 ... 172 E6 4
ENC/FH EN2 ... 36 A4
Hunting Cl ESH/CLAY KT10 ... 166 A6
Huntingdon Cl MTCM CR4 ... 156 E6 4
Huntingdon Gdns
CHSWK W4 ... 117 J5 1
WPK KT4 ... 169 J5 1
Huntingdon Rd ED N9 ... 50 C3 1
EFNCH N2 ... 65 L4
Huntingdon St CAN/RD E16 ... 105 M5
IS N1 ... 5 M1
Huntingfield CROY/NA CR0 ... 185 M1
Huntingfield Rd
PUT/ROE SW15 ... 136 A3
Hunting Gate Cl ENC/FH EN2 ... 36 A6
Hunting Gate Dr CHSGTN KT9 ... 179 L1
Hunting Gate Ms WHTN TW2 ... 133 L5 2
Huntings Rd DAGE RM10 ... 91 G6 2
Huntland Cl RAIN RM13 ... 110 B4 1
Huntley St GWRST WC1E ... 10 F1
Huntley Wy RYNPK SW20 ... 154 A5 1
Huntly Dr FNCH N3 ... 47 G8 1
Huntly Rd SNWD SE25 ... 157 L7
Hunton Bridge Hl KGLGY WD4 ... 20 C6
Hunton St WCHPL E1 ... 104 A3 2
Hunt Rd NWDGN UB2 ... 115 G1
Hunt's La SRTFD E15 ... 105 J1
Huntsman Cl FELT TW13 ... 132 B8 1
Huntsman Rd BARK/HLT IG6 ... 54 B8
Huntsmans Dr UPMR RM14 ... 93 J5
Huntsman St WALW SE17 ... 19 J6
Hunts Md PEND EN3 ... 37 K6
Hunts Mede Cl CHST BR7 ... 160 F3
Huntsmoor Rd HOR/WEW KT19 ... 168 D7
Huntspill St TOOT SW17 ... 137 J7
Hunts Slip Rd DUL SE21 ... 139 L7
Hunt St NTGHL W11 ... 100 D7
Huntsworth Ms CAMTN NW1 ... 3 L9
Hurley Cl WOT/HER KT12 ... 165 H4
Hurley Rd GFD/PVL UB6 ... 97 H4
Hurlfield RDART DA2 ... 146 C7
Hurlingham Gdns
FUL/PGN SW6 ... 118 F8
Hurlingham Rd BXLYHN DA7 ... 126 F5
FUL/PGN SW6 ... 118 F7
Hurlingham Sq
FUL/PGN SW6 ... 119 H8 1
Hurlock St FSBYPK N4 ... 85 H3
Hurlstone Rd SNWD SE25 ... 157 K8
Hurn Court Rd HEST TW5 ... 114 D7 1
Hurnford Cl SAND/SEL CR2 ... 184 E3
Huron Cl ORP BR6 ... 176 F8 2
Huron Rd TOOT SW17 ... 138 A6
Hurren Cl BKHTH/KID SE3 ... 123 L8
Hurricane Wy GSTN WD25 ... 21 G5 2
Hurry Cl SRTFD E15 ... 87 L7
Hursley Rd CHIG IG7 ... 53 M7
Hurst Av CHING E4 ... 51 G5
HGT N6 ... 66 C7
Hurstbourne Gdns BARK IG11 ... 89 K6
Hurstbourne Rd FSTH SE23 ... 140 E5
Hurst Cl CHING E4 ... 51 G5
CHSGTN KT9 ... 168 A7
GLDGN NW11 ... 65 H7
HAYES BR2 ... 174 F3
NTHLT UB5 ... 78 F6
Hurstcourt Rd CHEAM SM3 ... 170 B3
Hurstdene Av HAYES BR2 ... 174 F3
STA TW18 ... 148 B2
Hurstdene Gdns
SEVS/STOTM N15 ... 67 L8
Hurst Dr CHES/WCR EN8 ... 26 D7
Hurstfield HAYES BR2 ... 160 A8 1
Hurstfield Crs YEAD UB4 ... 95 L4
Hurstfield Rd E/WMO/HCT KT8 ... 151 G6
Hurst Gv WOT/HER KT12 ... 164 F3
Hurstlands Cl EMPK RM11 ... 74 C7 2
Hurst La ABYW SE2 ... 126 D3
E/WMO/HCT KT8 ... 151 J7
Hurstleigh Gdns CLAY IG5 ... 70 F2
Hurst Park Av HCH RM12 ... 92 E4 2
Hurst Pl NTHWD HA6 ... 59 H2
Hurst Ri BAR EN5 ... 34 A6
Hurst Rd BFN/LL DA15 ... 144 B6
BKHH IG9 ... 52 D3
BXLY DA5 ... 144 E5
CROY/NA CR0 ... 172 D7
E/WMO/HCT KT8 ... 151 J6
ERITH DA8 ... 127 J5
HOR/WEW KT19 ... 180 D4
WALTH E17 ... 69 H4
WCHMH N21 ... 49 G3
WOT/HER KT12 ... 150 D7
Hurst Springs BXLY DA5 ... 144 E5
Hurst St HNHL SE24 ... 139 H3
Hurst View Rd SAND/SEL CR2 ... 184 E1
Hurst Wy SAND/SEL CR2 ... 172 E8
Hurstwood Av BXLY DA5 ... 144 E5
BXLYHN DA7 ... 127 L6
SWFD E18 ... 70 B5
Hurstwood Dr BMLY BR1 ... 160 F6
Hurstwood Rd GLDGN NW11 ... 64 E5
Hurtwood Rd WOT/HER KT12 ... 165 M2
Huson Cl HAMP NW3 ... 3 J1
Hussars Cl HSLWW TW4 ... 114 E8 1
Husseywell Crs HAYES BR2 ... 175 G3
Hutchingson's Rd
CROY/NA CR0 ... 186 C4 1
Hutching's St POP/IOD E14 ... 105 G8 2
Hutchings Wk GLDGN NW11 ... 65 H5 3
Hutchins Cl HCH RM12 ... 92 E3 2
SRTFD E15 ... 87 J7 1
Hutchinson Ter WBLY HA9 ... 80 D3
Hutchins Rd THMD SE28 ... 108 A6
Hutton Cl NTHLT UB5 ... 79 K5 4
WFD IG8 ... 52 B8
Hutton Gv NFNCH/WDSP N12 ... 47 H7
Hutton La KTN/HRWW/W HA3 ... 61 J1
Hutton Rw EDGW HA8 ... 63 J1 2
Hutton St EMB EC4Y ... 12 C5 4
Hutton Wk KTN/HRWW/W HA3 ... 61 J1
Huxbear St BROCKY SE4 ... 140 F2
Huxley Cl NTHLT UB5 ... 96 E1
Huxley Dr CHDH RM6 ... 72 B8 1
Huxley Gdns WLSDN NW10 ... 98 F2
Huxley Pl PLMGR N13 ... 49 H6
Huxley Rd LEY E10 ... 87 J2
UED N18 ... 49 K6
WELL DA16 ... 125 M8
Huxley St NKENS W10 ... 100 E2
Hyacinth Cl HPTN TW12 ... 151 G2 5
Hyacinth Dr HGDN/ICK UB10 ... 76 E7 2
Hyacinth Rd PUT/ROE SW15 ... 136 A5 3
Hyburn Cl LCOL/BKTW AL2 ... 21 M3
Hycliffe Gdns CHIG IG7 ... 53 J6
Hyde Av POTB/CUF EN6 ... 23 H6
Hyde Cl BAR EN5 ... 33 M6
PLSTW E13 ... 106 A1
Hyde Crs CDALE/KGS NW9 ... 63 L6
Hyde Dr STMC/STPC BR5 ... 162 B7
Hyde Estate Rd CDALE/KGS NW9 ... 63 M6
Hydefield Cl ED N9 ... 49 K3
Hydefield Ct ED N9 ... 49 L4
Hyde La BTSEA SW11 ... 119 L6 3
Hyde Park Av WCHMH N21 ... 49 J4
Hyde Park Crs BAY/PAD W2 ... 9 J5
Hyde Park Gdns BAY/PAD W2 ... 9 H6
WCHMH N21 ... 49 J3
Hyde Park Gardens Ms
BAY/PAD W2 ... 9 H6
Hyde Park Ga KENS W8 ... 14 E2
SKENS SW7 ... 14 F2
Hyde Park Gate Ms
SKENS SW7 ... 14 F2 1
Hyde Park Sq BAY/PAD W2 ... 9 J5
Hyde Park St BAY/PAD W2 ... 9 J6
Hyderabad Wy SRTFD E15 ... 87 L7 2
Hyde Rd BXLYHN DA7 ... 126 F7
IS N1 ... 7 H4
RCHPK/HAM TW10 ... 134 F2 5
SAND/SEL CR2 ... 184 E6
WAT WD17 ... 29 G6 1
Hydeside Gdns ED N9 ... 49 M4
Hyde's Pl IS N1 ... 6 C1
Hyde St DEPT SE8 ... 123 G4
Hyde Ter SUN TW16 ... 149 L2
The Hyde CDALE/KGS NW9 ... 63 L6
Hydethorpe Av ED N9 ... 49 M4
Hydethorpe Rd BAL SW12 ... 138 C5
Hyde V GNWCH SE10 ... 123 J5
Hyde Wk MRDN SM4 ... 170 A2
Hyde Wy ED N9 ... 49 M4
HYS/HAR UB3 ... 113 M2
Hyland Cl EMPK RM11 ... 74 B8
Hylands Ms EPSOM KT18 ... 180 C8
Hylands Rd EPSOM KT18 ... 180 C8
WALTH E17 ... 69 K3
Hyland Wy EMPK RM11 ... 74 B8
Hylton St WOOL/PLUM SE18 ... 125 M2
Hyndman St PECK SE15 ... 122 B4 1
Hynton Rd BCTR RM8 ... 90 C2
Hyperion Pl HOR/WEW KT19 ... 180 D2
Hyson Rd BERM/RHTH SE16 ... 122 B3
Hythe Av BXLYHN DA7 ... 126 E5
Hythe Cl STMC/STPC BR5 ... 162 C7 2
UED N18 ... 50 A6 4
Hythe Rd THHTH CR7 ... 157 K5
WLSDN NW10 ... 99 M2
Hythe St DART DA1 ... 146 E2
Hyver Hl MLHL NW7 ... 45 K1

I

Ibbotson Av CAN/RD E16 ... 105 M5
Iberian Av WLGTN SM6 ... 171 K6
Ibis La CHSWK W4 ... 117 J6
Ibis Wy YEAD UB4 ... 96 D5 2
Ibscott Cl DAGE RM10 ... 91 J6
Ibsley Gdns PUT/ROE SW15 ... 136 A5
Ibsley Wy EBAR EN4 ... 34 E8
Iceland Rd BOW E3 ... 87 G8
Ickburgh Rd CLPT E5 ... 86 B3
Ickenham Cl RSLP HA4 ... 77 K2 2
Ickenham Rd HGDN/ICK UB10 ... 77 J2
RSLP HA4 ... 77 K1
Ickleton Rd ELTH/MOT SE9 ... 142 E8
Icknield Dr GNTH/NBYPK IG2 ... 71 H6
Ickworth Park Rd WALTH E17 ... 68 E5
Ida Rd SEVS/STOTM N15 ... 67 K6
Ida St POP/IOD E14 ... 105 J5
Iden Cl HAYES BR2 ... 159 L6
Idlecombe Rd TOOT SW17 ... 156 A2
Idmiston Rd FSTGT E7 ... 87 M5
WNWD SE27 ... 139 J7
WPK KT4 ... 168 F2
Idmiston Sq WPK KT4 ... 168 F2
Idol La MON EC3R ... 13 J7
Idonia St DEPT SE8 ... 122 F5
Iffley Cl UX/CGN UB8 ... 76 D7
Iffley Rd HMSMTH W6 ... 118 B1
Ifield Rd WBPTN SW10 ... 14 D9
Ightham Rd ERITH DA8 ... 127 G5
Ilbert St NKENS W10 ... 100 E2
Ilchester Gdns BAY/PAD W2 ... 8 C6
Ilchester Pl WKENS W14 ... 118 F1
Ilchester Rd BCTR RM8 ... 90 B5
Ildersly Gv DUL SE21 ... 139 K6
Ilderton Rd BERM/RHTH SE16 ... 122 C4
Ilex Cl SUN TW16 ... 150 C5 1
Ilex Rd WLSDN NW10 ... 81 M6
Ilex Wy STRHM/NOR SW16 ... 157 G1
Ilford Hl IL IG1 ... 89 G3
Ilford La IL IG1 ... 89 H4
Ilfracombe Crs HCH RM12 ... 92 C4
Ilfracombe Gdns CHDH RM6 ... 72 B8 2
Ilfracombe Rd BMLY BR1 ... 141 M7
Iliffe St WALW SE17 ... 18 D7
Iliffe Yd WALW SE17 ... 18 D7
Ilkley Cl NRWD SE19 ... 157 K2 2
Ilkley Rd CAN/RD E16 ... 106 C4
OXHEY WD19 ... 42 D7
Illingworth Cl MTCM CR4 ... 155 K6
Illingworth Wy EN EN1 ... 36 E8 1
Ilmington Rd
KTN/HRWW/W HA3 ... 62 D7
Ilminster Gdns BTSEA SW11 ... 137 L1
Imber Cl STHGT/OAK N14 ... 48 C2
Imber Gv ESH/CLAY KT10 ... 166 D2
Imber Park Rd ESH/CLAY KT10 ... 166 D3
Imber St IS N1 ... 7 G4
Imperial Cl RYLN/HDSTN HA2 ... 61 G7
Imperial College Rd
SKENS SW7 ... 15 H3 1
Imperial Dr RYLN/HDSTN HA2 ... 79 G1
Imperial Gdns MTCM CR4 ... 156 B6
Imperial Pl CHST BR7 ... 161 G4
Imperial Rd EBED/NFELT TW14 ... 131 L4
FUL/PGN SW6 ... 119 H6
WDGN N22 ... 66 E1
Imperial Sq FUL/PGN SW6 ... 119 H6 4
Imperial St BOW E3 ... 105 J2
Imperial Wy CHST BR7 ... 143 J7
CROY/NA CR0 ... 171 M8
KTN/HRWW/W HA3 ... 62 E7
WATN WD24 ... 29 J4
Inca Dr ELTH/MOT SE9 ... 143 H4
Ince Rd WOT/HER KT12 ... 164 E7
Inchmery Rd CAT SE6 ... 141 H6
Inchwood CROY/NA CR0 ... 174 B6
Independents Rd
BKHTH/KID SE3 ... 123 M8 2
Inderwick Rd CEND/HSY/T N8 ... 66 F7
Indescon Ct POP/IOD E14 ... 105 H8 1
India St TWRH EC3N ... 13 L5
India Wy SHB W12 ... 100 B6 5
Indigo Ms STNW/STAM N16 ... 85 K3
Indus Rd CHARL SE7 ... 124 C5
Ingal Rd PLSTW E13 ... 106 A3 7
Ingate Pl VX/NE SW8 ... 120 B6
Ingatestone Rd MNPK E12 ... 88 C1
SNWD SE25 ... 158 B7 3
WFD IG8 ... 70 B1
Ingelow St VX/NE SW8 ... 120 B7
Ingersoll Rd PEND EN3 ... 37 J3
SHB W12 ... 100 B7
Ingestre Pl SOHO/CST W1F ... 10 F5
Ingestre Rd FSTGT E7 ... 88 A4
KTTN NW5 ... 84 B4
Ingham Cl SAND/SEL CR2 ... 185 K2 2
Ingham Rd KIL/WHAMP NW6 ... 83 G4
SAND/SEL CR2 ... 185 J2
Inglebert St CLKNW EC1R ... 6 A7
Ingleboro Dr PUR/KEN CR8 ... 184 D6
Ingleborough St
BRXN/ST SW9 ... 121 G7 2
Ingleby Dr HRW HA1 ... 79 K3
Ingleby Gdns CHIG IG7 ... 54 B5
Ingleby Rd DAGE RM10 ... 91 H6
IL IG1 ... 89 H1
Ingleby Wy CHST BR7 ... 161 G1
WLGTN SM6 ... 183 K2
Ingle Cl PIN HA5 ... 60 F4
Ingledew Rd WOOL/PLUM SE18 ... 125 K3
Inglefield POTB/CUF EN6 ... 23 G3
Ingleglen EMPK RM11 ... 75 G8 2
Inglehurst Gdns REDBR IG4 ... 70 F6
Inglemere Rd FSTH SE23 ... 140 D7
TOOT SW17 ... 155 M3
Ingleside Cl BECK BR3 ... 159 G3
Ingleside Gv BKHTH/KID SE3 ... 123 M4
Inglethorpe St FUL/PGN SW6 ... 118 D6
Ingleton Av WELL DA16 ... 144 A2
Ingleton Rd CAR SM5 ... 182 E2
UED N18 ... 50 A8
Ingleton St BRXN/ST SW9 ... 121 G7
Ingleway NFNCH/WDSP N12 ... 47 K8
Inglewood Cl BARK/HLT IG6 ... 53 M8
HCH RM12 ... 92 D4 3
POP/IOD E14 ... 123 G2
Inglewood Copse BMLY BR1 ... 160 E5
Inglewood Rd BXLYHN DA7 ... 145 K1
KIL/WHAMP NW6 ... 83 G5 2
Inglis Rd CROY/NA CR0 ... 172 F3
EA W5 ... 98 F6
Inglis St CMBW SE5 ... 121 H6
Ingram Av EFNCH N2 ... 65 J8
Ingram Cl LBTH SE11 ... 17 M5
STAN HA7 ... 44 C7 4
Ingram Rd DART DA1 ... 146 E5
EFNCH N2 ... 65 L5
THHTH CR7 ... 157 J4
Ingrams Cl WOT/HER KT12 ... 165 J7
Ingram Wy GFD/PVL UB6 ... 79 K8
Ingrave Rd ROM RM1 ... 73 L5 3
Ingrave St BTSEA SW11 ... 119 K8
Ingrebourne Gdns UPMR RM14 ... 93 J1
Ingrebourne Rd RAIN RM13 ... 110 B3
Ingress St CHSWK W4 ... 117 L3 2
Ingreway HARH RM3 ... 57 H8
Inigo Jones Rd CHARL SE7 ... 124 D5
Inkerman Rd KTTN NW5 ... 84 B6
Inks Gn CHING E4 ... 51 J7
Inkwell Cl NFNCH/WDSP N12 ... 47 J5
Inman Rd WAND/EARL SW18 ... 137 J4
WLSDN NW10 ... 81 L8
Inmans Rw WFD IG8 ... 52 A6
Inner Cir CAMTN NW1 ... 4 A8
Inner Park Rd WIM/MER SW19 ... 136 D6
Innes Cl RYNPK SW20 ... 154 E5
WAND/EARL SW18 ... 137 G4
Innes Gdns PUT/ROE SW15 ... 136 B3
Innes Yd CROY/NA CR0 ... 172 C5 2
Inniskilling Rd PLSTW E13 ... 106 C1
Innovation Cl ALP/SUD HA0 ... 80 E8 2
Inskip Cl LEY E10 ... 87 H2
Inskip Dr EMPK RM11 ... 92 E1 4
Inskip Rd BCTR RM8 ... 90 D1
Institute Pl HACK E8 ... 86 B5 4
Instone Rd DART DA1 ... 146 D4
International Av HEST TW5 ... 114 C3
Inver Ct BAY/PAD W2 ... 8 D5 2
Inveresk Gdns WPK KT4 ... 168 F5
Inverforth Cl HAMP NW3 ... 83 J2
Inverforth Rd FBAR/BDGN N11 ... 48 B7
Inverine Rd CHARL SE7 ... 124 B3
Invermore Pl
WOOL/PLUM SE18 ... 125 J2
Inverness Av EN EN1 ... 36 E4
Inverness Dr BARK/HLT IG6 ... 53 L8
Inverness Gdns KENS W8 ... 8 C9 1
Inverness Ms BAY/PAD W2 ... 8 D6 1
Inverness Pl BAY/PAD W2 ... 8 D6
Inverness Rd HSLW TW3 ... 132 F1
NWDGN UB2 ... 114 E2 2
UED N18 ... 50 B7 3
WPK KT4 ... 169 K3
Inverness St CAMTN NW1 ... 4 C3
Inverness Ter BAY/PAD W2 ... 8 D5
Inverton Rd PECK SE15 ... 140 D1
Invicta Cl CHST BR7 ... 161 G1
EBED/NFELT TW14 ... 131 M5 2
Invicta Gv NTHLT UB5 ... 96 F2
Invicta Plaza STHWK SE1 ... 12 C8
Invicta Rd BKHTH/KID SE3 ... 124 A5
RDART DA2 ... 147 H3
Inville Rd WALW SE17 ... 19 H8
Inwood Av HSLW TW3 ... 115 J8
Inwood Cl CROY/NA CR0 ... 173 L4
Inwood Rd HSLW TW3 ... 133 J1
Inworth St BTSEA SW11 ... 119 L7
Iona Cl CAT SE6 ... 141 G4
Ion Sq BETH E2 ... 104 A1 4
Ipswich Rd TOOT SW17 ... 156 A2
Ireland Cl EHAM E6 ... 106 F4
Ireland Pl WDGN N22 ... 66 E1 3
Irene Rd COB KT11 ... 178 A7
FUL/PGN SW6 ... 119 G6
ORP BR6 ... 176 F2
Ireton Av WEY KT13 ... 164 F4
Ireton Cl MUSWH N10 ... 66 A1 3
Ireton St BOW E3 ... 105 G3 2
Iris Av BXLY DA5 ... 144 E3
Iris Cl CROY/NA CR0 ... 173 K3
EHAM E6 ... 106 E4
SURB KT6 ... 167 M2 2
Iris Crs BXLYHN DA7 ... 126 F4
Iris Rd HOR/WEW KT19 ... 168 B7 2
Iris Wy CHING E4 ... 50 F8
Irkdale Av EN EN1 ... 36 F4
Iron Bridge Cl STHL UB1 ... 97 J7
WLSDN NW10 ... 81 L5 1
Iron Bridge Rd North
WDR/YW UB7 ... 95 G8
Iron Bridge Rd South
WDR/YW UB7 ... 95 G8
Iron Mill La DART DA1 ... 145 M1
Iron Mill Pl DART DA1 ... 145 M1
WAND/EARL SW18 ... 137 H3 1
Iron Mill Rd WAND/EARL SW18 ... 137 H3
Ironmonger La CITYW EC2V ... 13 G5
Ironmonger Rw FSBYE EC1V ... 6 F8
Ironside Cl BERM/RHTH SE16 ... 104 D8 3
Irons Wy CRW RM5 ... 73 J1
Irvine Av KTN/HRWW/W HA3 ... 62 A4
Irvine Cl TRDG/WHET N20 ... 47 L4
Irvine Gdns SOCK/AV RM15 ... 111 M5
Irvine Wy ORP BR6 ... 176 F2
Irving Av NTHLT UB5 ... 78 D8
Irving Gv BRXN/ST SW9 ... 120 F7
Irving Rd WKENS W14 ... 118 D1
Irving St LSQ/SEVD WC2H ... 11 H7
Irving Wy SWLY BR8 ... 163 K5
Irwin Av WOOL/PLUM SE18 ... 125 L5
Irwin Cl HGDN/ICK UB10 ... 77 G3
Irwin Gdns WLSDN NW10 ... 82 B8
Isabella Cl STHGT/OAK N14 ... 48 C2
Isabella Dr ORP BR6 ... 176 C6
Isabella Rd HOM E9 ... 86 C5 2
Isabella St STHWK SE1 ... 12 C9
Isabelle Cl CHESW EN7 ... 25 J2
Isabel St BRXN/ST SW9 ... 120 F6
Isambard Ms POP/IOD E14 ... 123 J1 4
Isambard Pl BERM/RHTH SE16 ... 104 C8
Isham Rd STRHM/NOR SW16 ... 156 E5
Isis Cl RSLP HA4 ... 59 J7
Isis Dr UPMR RM14 ... 75 L7
Isis St WAND/EARL SW18 ... 137 J6
Island Farm Av
E/WMO/HCT KT8 ... 150 F8
Island Farm Rd
E/WMO/HCT KT8 ... 150 F8
Island Rd MTCM CR4 ... 155 M3
Island Rw POP/IOD E14 ... 104 F5 1
Isla Rd WOOL/PLUM SE18 ... 125 J4
Islay Gdns HSLWW TW4 ... 132 D2
Isledon Rd HOLWY N7 ... 85 G3
Islehurst Cl CHST BR7 ... 161 G4
Islington Gn IS N1 ... 6 C4
Islington High St IS N1 ... 6 C5 4
Islington Park Ms IS N1 ... 6 C1 1
Islington Park St IS N1 ... 6 B1
Islip Gdns EDGW HA8 ... 45 K8
NTHLT UB5 ... 78 E7
Islip Manor Rd NTHLT UB5 ... 78 E7
Islip St KTTN NW5 ... 84 C5
Ismailia Rd FSTGT E7 ... 88 B7
Isom Cl PLSTW E13 ... 106 B2
Ivanhoe Cl UX/CGN UB8 ... 94 D4
Ivanhoe Dr KTN/HRWW/W HA3 ... 62 B3
Ivanhoe Rd CMBW SE5 ... 121 M8
HSLWW TW4 ... 114 D8
Ivatt Pl WKENS W14 ... 118 F3
Ivatt Wy SEVS/STOTM N15 ... 67 H4
Iveagh Av WLSDN NW10 ... 99 G1
Iveagh Cl HOM E9 ... 86 D8
NTHWD HA6 ... 59 H2
WLSDN NW10 ... 99 G1 1
Ivedon Rd WELL DA16 ... 126 C7
Ive Farm Cl LEY E10 ... 87 G2
Ive Farm La LEY E10 ... 87 G2
Iveley Rd CLAP SW4 ... 120 C7
Ivere Dr BAR EN5 ... 47 H1
Iverhurst Cl BXLYHS DA6 ... 144 D2
Iver La IVER SL0 ... 94 B4
Iverna Ct KENS W8 ... 14 B3
Iverna Gdns EBED/NFELT TW14 ... 131 K2
KENS W8 ... 14 B3
Iverson Rd KIL/WHAMP NW6 ... 82 F6
Ivers Wy CROY/NA CR0 ... 186 B1
Ives Gdns ROM RM1 ... 73 M5
Ives Rd CAN/RD E16 ... 105 L4
Ives St CHEL SW3 ... 15 K5
Ivimey St BETH E2 ... 104 A2 6
Ivinghoe Cl EN EN1 ... 36 E5
GSTN WD25 ... 21 K8
Ivinghoe Rd BCTR RM8 ... 90 B5
BUSH WD23 ... 43 K1
Ivor Gv ELTH/MOT SE9 ... 143 H5
Ivor Pl CAMTN NW1 ... 9 L1
Ivor St CAMTN NW1 ... 4 E2
Ivory Ct FELT TW13 ... 132 A6 2
Ivorydown BMLY BR1 ... 142 A8
Ivybridge Cl TWK TW1 ... 134 A3
Ivy Bridge Cl UX/CGN UB8 ... 94 E2 2
Ivychurch Cl PGE/AN SE20 ... 158 C3
Ivy Church La STHWK SE1 ... 19 L7 1
Ivy Cl DART DA1 ... 147 G3
PIN HA5 ... 60 C8
RYLN/HDSTN HA2 ... 78 F4
SUN TW16 ... 150 C5
Ivy Crs CHSWK W4 ... 117 J2
Ivydale Rd CAR SM5 ... 170 F4 2
PECK SE15 ... 122 D8
Ivyday Gv STRHM/NOR SW16 ... 138 F7
Ivydene WOT/HER KT12 ... 150 F8
Ivydene Cl SUT SM1 ... 170 C6
Ivy Gdns CEND/HSY/T N8 ... 66 E7 2
MTCM CR4 ... 156 D6
Ivyhouse Rd DAGW RM9 ... 90 D6
HGDN/ICK UB10 ... 77 H3
Ivy La HSLWW TW4 ... 132 F1
Ivy Lea RKW/CH/CXG WD3 ... 40 A3 2
Ivy Lodge La HARH RM3 ... 75 J3
Ivymount Rd WNWD SE27 ... 139 G7
Ivy Rd BROCKY SE4 ... 140 F1
CAN/RD E16 ... 106 A5
CRICK NW2 ... 82 C4
HSLW TW3 ... 133 H1 2
LEY E10 ... 69 G7
STHGT/OAK N14 ... 48 C2
SURB KT6 ... 168 A3 1
TOOT SW17 ... 155 L1 2
Ivy St IS N1 ... 7 J5
Ivy Wk DAGW RM9 ... 90 E6
Ixworth Pl CHEL SW3 ... 15 J6
Izane Rd BXLYHS DA6 ... 144 F1

J

Jacaranda Cl NWMAL KT3 ... 153 L6 1
Jackass La HAYES BR2 ... 175 H8
Jack Clow Rd SRTFD E15 ... 105 L1
Jack Cornwell St MNPK E12 ... 89 G4
Jackets La DEN/HRF UB9 ... 59 G1
Jacketts Fld ABLGY WD5 ... 20 F4
Jackman Ms WLSDN NW10 ... 81 L3
Jackman St HACK E8 ... 86 B8
Jacks La DEN/HRF UB9 ... 58 A2
Jackson Cl EMPK RM11 ... 74 F5 2
EPSOM KT18 ... 180 D7
GRH DA9 ... 147 M2
HOM E9 ... 86 D7 3
Jackson Rd BARK IG11 ... 89 K8
EBAR EN4 ... 47 L1
HAYES BR2 ... 175 M3
HGDN/ICK UB10 ... 76 E7
HOLWY N7 ... 84 F4
Jacksons Dr CHESW EN7 ... 26 A1
Jackson's La HGT N6 ... 66 A8
Jackson's Pl CROY/NA CR0 ... 172 E3 3
Jackson St WOOL/PLUM SE18 ... 125 G4
Jackson's Wy CROY/NA CR0 ... 174 A5
Jack Walker Ct HBRY N5 ... 85 H4 4
Jacobs Av HARH RM3 ... 74 E3
Jacobs Cl DAGE RM10 ... 91 H4
Jacob St STHWK SE1 ... 19 M1
Jacob's Well Ms MHST W1U ... 10 B4 5
Jacqueline Cl NTHLT UB5 ... 78 E8 1
Jade Cl BCTR RM8 ... 90 C1
CAN/RD E16 ... 106 D5
CRICK NW2 ... 64 D8
Jaffe Rd IL IG1 ... 89 J1
Jaffray Rd HAYES BR2 ... 160 D7
Jaggard Wy BAL SW12 ... 137 M4 1
Jagger Cl RDART DA2 ... 147 J4
Jago Cl WOOL/PLUM SE18 ... 125 J4
Jail La BH/WHM TN16 ... 187 K8
Jamaica Rd BERM/RHTH SE16 ... 122 B1
STHWK SE1 ... 19 L2
THHTH CR7 ... 172 B1 1
Jamaica St WCHPL E1 ... 104 C4
James Av BCTR RM8 ... 90 F1
CRICK NW2 ... 82 C5
James Cl BUSH WD23 ... 29 L8
GPK RM2 ... 74 A6
PLSTW E13 ... 106 A1 3
James Gdns WDGN N22 ... 67 J1
James Joyes Wk HNHL SE24 ... 139 H1 1
James La WAN E11 ... 69 J8
James Martin Cl DEN/HRF UB9 ... 58 A7
Jameson St KENS W8 ... 8 B8
James Pl TOTM N17 ... 67 M1
James Rd DART DA1 ... 146 A4
James St BARK IG11 ... 89 J7
COVGDN WC2E ... 11 K6 3
EN EN1 ... 36 F8
HSLW TW3 ... 115 K8
MHST W1U ... 10 B5
Jamestown Rd CAMTN NW1 ... 4 C3
Jamestown Wy POP/IOD E14 ... 105 K6
James Watt Wy ERITH DA8 ... 127 M4
Jane St WCHPL E1 ... 104 B5 10
Janet St POP/IOD E14 ... 123 G1
Janeway Pl
BERM/RHTH SE16 ... 104 B8 1
Janeway St
BERM/RHTH SE16 ... 104 A8
Janson Cl SRTFD E15 ... 87 L5 1
WLSDN NW10 ... 81 K3
Janson Rd SRTFD E15 ... 87 L5
Jansons Rd SEVS/STOTM N15 ... 67 L4
Japan Crs FSBYPK N4 ... 84 F1 5
Japan Rd CHDH RM6 ... 72 D7
Jardine Rd WAP E1W ... 104 D6
Jarrett Cl BRXS/STRHM SW2 ... 139 H5 1
Jarrow Cl MRDN SM4 ... 155 H8
Jarrow Rd BERM/RHTH SE16 ... 122 C2
CHDH RM6 ... 72 C7
TOTM N17 ... 68 B5
Jarrow Wy HOM E9 ... 86 E4
Jarvis Cl BAR EN5 ... 33 K8
Jarvis Rd EDUL SE22 ... 139 L1
SAND/SEL CR2 ... 172 D8
Jarvis Wy HARH RM3 ... 74 E3
Jasmin Cl NTHWD HA6 ... 59 M2
Jasmine Cl HAYES BR2 ... 176 B4
IL IG1 ... 89 H5
STHL UB1 ... 96 E6 3
Jasmine Ct LEE/GVPK SE12 ... 142 A3 1

Jasmine Gdns CROY/NA CR0 174 B5
RYLN/HDSTN HA2 79 G2
Jasmine Gv PGE/AN SE20 158 B4
Jasmine Rd ROMW/RG RM7 91 L2
Jasmine Ter WDR/YW UB7 95 G8
Jasmin Rd HOR/WEW KT19 168 B8
Jason Cl WEY KT13 164 C7
Jasons Cl BRW CM14 57 M6
Jason Wk ELTH/MOT SE9 143 G8
Jasper Cl PEND EN3 37 J3
Jasper Rd CAN/RD E16 106 D5
NRWD SE19 157 M2 2
Javelin Wy NTHLT UB5 96 D2
Jaycroft ENC/FH EN2 36 A4
Jay Gdns CHST BR7 142 F8
Jay Ms SKENS SW7 14 F2
Jebb Av BRXS/STRHM SW2 138 E3
Jebb St BOW E3 105 G1
Jedburgh Rd PLSTW E13 106 C2
Jedburgh St BTSEA SW11 138 A1
Jeddo Rd SHB W12 99 M8
Jefferson Cl GNTH/NBYPK IG2 71 H6
WEA W13 116 B1 2
Jeffrey's Pl CAMTN NW1 4 E1 1
Jeffrey's Rd CLAP SW4 120 E7
PEND EN3 37 M7
Jeffrey's St CAMTN NW1 4 D1
Jeffs Cl HPTN TW12 151 H2 3
Jeffs Rd SUT SM1 169 M6
Jeger Av BETH E2 7 L4
Jeken Rd ELTH/MOT SE9 142 C1
Jelf Rd BRXS/STRHM SW2 139 G2
Jellicoe Gdns STAN HA7 43 M8 4
Jellicoe Rd TOTM N17 67 K1
WATW WD18 42 A1
Jemmett Cl KUTN/CMB KT2 153 H4
Jengar Cl SUT SM1 170 B6
Jenkins Av LCOL/BKTW AL2 21 L3
Jenkins La BARK IG11 107 H1
Jenkins Rd PLSTW E13 106 B3
Jenner Av ACT W3 99 K4
Jenner Rd STNW/STAM N16 85 M2
Jennett Rd CROY/NA CR0 172 A5
Jennifer Rd BMLY BR1 141 M7 1
Jennings Rd EDUL SE22 139 M3
Jennings Wy BAR EN5 33 J6
Jenningtree Rd ERITH DA8 128 B5
Jenningtree Wy BELV DA17 109 J8
Jenny Hammond Cl WAN E11 .. 87 M3 3
Jenson Wy NRWD SE19 157 M3
Jenton Av BXLYHN DA7 126 E6
Jephson Rd FSTGT E7 88 C7
Jephson St CMBW SE5 121 K6 5
Jephtha Rd
WAND/EARL SW18 137 G3 1
Jeppo's La MTCM CR4 155 M7
Jerdan Pl FUL/PGN SW6 119 G5
Jeremiah St POP/IOD E14 105 H5 5
Jeremy's Gn UED N18 50 B6
Jermyn St STJS SW1Y 10 E8
Jernigham Av CLAY IG5 71 H3
Jerningham Rd NWCR SE14 122 E7
Jerome Crs STJWD NW8 3 J9
Jerome St WCHPL E1 13 L2
Jerrard St LEW SE13 123 H8
Jerrold St IS N1 7 K6 1
Jersey Av KTN/HRWW/W HA3 62 B3
Jersey Dr STMC/STPC BR5 176 D1
Jersey Rd CAN/RD E16 106 C4
HEST TW5 115 H6
HNWL W7 98 A8
IL IG1 89 H4
IS N1 85 J6 7
ISLW TW7 115 J5
RAIN RM13 92 A7
TOOT SW17 156 B3
WAN E11 87 K1
Jersey St BETH E2 104 B2 10
Jervis Av PEND EN3 26 E8
Jerviston Gdns
STRHM/NOR SW16 157 G2
Jesmond Av WBLY HA9 80 F6
Jesmond Cl MTCM CR4 156 B6
Jesmond Rd CROY/NA CR0 172 F2
Jesmond Wy STAN HA7 44 E7
Jessam Av STNW/STAM N16 86 B1
Jessamine Pl RDART DA2 147 J4
Jessamine Rd HNWL W7 97 L7
Jessamy Rd WEY KT13 164 A4
Jesse Rd LEY E10 87 J1
Jessett Cl ERITH DA8 127 K2
Jessica Rd WAND/EARL SW18 137 J3
Jessiman Ter SHPTN TW17 149 G8
Jessop Av NWDGN UB2 114 F2 4
Jessops Wy MTCM CR4 171 J1
Jessup Cl WOOL/PLUM SE18 125 J2
Jetstar Wy NTHLT UB5 96 E2 4
Jevington Wy LEE/GVPK SE12 142 B5
Jewel Rd WALTH E17 69 G4
Jewels Hl WARL CR6 187 G5
Jewry St TWRH EC3N 13 L5
Jews Rw WAND/EARL SW18 137 H1
Jews Wk SYD SE26 140 B8
Jeymer Av CRICK NW2 82 B5
Jeymer Dr GFD/PVL UB6 79 J8
Jeypore Rd WAND/EARL SW18 137 J4
Jillian Cl HPTN TW12 151 G3
Jim Bradley Cl
WOOL/PLUM SE18 125 G2 3
Joan Crs ELTH/MOT SE9 142 D4
Joan Gdns BCTR RM8 90 E2
Joan Rd BCTR RM8 90 E2
Joan St STHWK SE1 12 C9
Jocelyn Rd RCH/KEW TW9 116 E8
Jocelyn St PECK SE15 122 A6
Jockey's Flds FSBYW WC1X 11 M2
Jodane Rd DEPT SE8 122 F2
Jodrell Cl ISLW TW7 116 A6 6
Jodrell Rd HOM E9 86 F8
Jodrell Wy WTHK RM20 129 M3
Joel St NTHWD HA6 60 A3
PIN HA5 60 A4
Johanna St STHWK SE1 18 A2 1
John Adam St CHCR WC2N 11 K8
John Aird Ct BAY/PAD W2 8 F2
John Archer Wy
WAND/EARL SW18 137 K3
John Ashby Cl
BRXS/STRHM SW2 138 E3
John Austin Cl
KUTN/CMB KT2 152 F4 4
John Bradshaw Rd
STHGT/OAK N14 48 D3 2
John Burns Dr BARK IG11 89 L8
Johnby Cl PEND EN3 37 L2 4
John Campbell Rd
STNW/STAM N16 85 L5 3
John Carpenter St EMB EC4Y 12 C6
John Felton Rd
BERM/RHTH SE16 104 A8 7
John Fisher St WCHPL E1 104 A6
John Gooch Dr ENC/FH EN2 36 B4
John Islip St WEST SW1P 17 J6
John Lamb Ct
KTN/HRWW/W HA3 61 L2 2
John Maurice Cl WALW SE17 19 G5
John Parker Sq BTSEA SW11 ... 119 K8 2
John Penn St LEW SE13 123 H6
John Perrin Pl
KTN/HRWW/W HA3 62 E8 1
John Prince's St
CAVSQ/HST W1G 10 D4 3
John Roll Wy BERM/RHTH SE16 .. 122 A1
John Ruskin St CMBW SE5 121 H5
John's Av HDN NW4 64 C5
John's Cl ASHF TW15 131 J8 1
John Silkin La DEPT SE8 122 D3
Johns La MRDN SM4 155 J8
John's Ms BMSBY WC1N 11 M1
John Smith Av FUL/PGN SW6 .. 118 F5 5
Johnson Cl HACK E8 86 A8 5
Johnson Rd CROY/NA CR0 172 D2
HAYES BR2 160 D8
HEST TW5 114 C5
Johnson's Cl CAR SM5 170 F5
Johnsons Dr HPTN TW12 151 J4
Johnson's Pl PIM SW1V 16 F8
Johnson St NWDGN UB2 114 C1
WCHPL E1 104 C6 1
Johnsons Wy WLSDN NW10 99 H3
John Spencer Sq IS N1 85 H6 7
John's Ter CROY/NA CR0 172 E3 4
Johnston Cl BRXN/ST SW9 120 F6 1
Johnstone Rd EHAM E6 106 F2
Johnston Rd WFD IG8 52 A7 6
John St BMSBY WC1N 11 M1
EN EN1 36 F8
HSLW TW3 114 E7
SNWD SE25 158 A7
SRTFD E15 87 M8
John Williams Cl PECK SE15 122 D4
John Wilson St
WOOL/PLUM SE18 125 G2 4
John Wooley Cl LEW SE13 141 L1 3
Joiners Arms Yd CMBW SE5 121 K6 6
Joiner St STHWK SE1 13 H9
Joint Rd EFNCH N2 65 L2
Jollys La YEAD UB4 96 D4
Jonathan St LBTH SE11 17 L7
Jones Rd CHESW EN7 25 H3
PLSTW E13 106 B3 1
Jonson Cl MTCM CR4 156 B7
YEAD UB4 96 A4
Jordan Cl GSTN WD25 20 F8
RYLN/HDSTN HA2 78 F3 2
SAND/SEL CR2 184 F4
Jordan Rd GFD/PVL UB6 80 B8
Jordans Cl DAGE RM10 91 H4 1
STWL/WRAY TW19 130 C4
Jordans Ms WHTN TW2 133 L6 1
Jordans Rd RKW/CH/CXG WD3 40 A2
Jordan's Wy LCOL/BKTW AL2 21 L3
RAIN RM13 110 D1
Joseph Av ACT W3 99 K5
Josephine Av
BRXS/STRHM SW2 138 F2
Joseph Locke Wy
ESH/CLAY KT10 166 A4
Joseph Powell Cl BAL SW12 138 C3 2
Joseph Ray Rd WAN E11 87 L2 1
Joseph St BOW E3 105 H4
Joshua St POP/IOD E14 105 J5
Joslin Rd PUR RM19 129 J3
Joslyn Cl PEND EN3 38 A3
Joubert St BTSEA SW11 119 M7
Jowett St PECK SE15 121 M5
Joyce Av UED N18 49 M7
Joyce Ct WAB EN9 27 K7 2
Joyce Green La DART DA1 128 D6
Joyden's Wood Rd BXLY DA5 .. 145 K8 1
Joydon Dr CHDH RM6 72 B7
Joyners Cl DAGW RM9 90 F4
Jubilee Av CHING E4 51 J8
ROMW/RG RM7 73 J6
WHTN TW2 133 J5
Jubilee Cl CDALE/KGS NW9 63 K7 1
PIN HA5 60 C3
ROMW/RG RM7 73 H6
STWL/WRAY TW19 130 C4
Jubilee Crs ED N9 50 A3
Jubilee Dr RSLP HA4 78 D4
Jubilee Gdns STHL UB1 97 G4
Jubilee Pl CHEL SW3 15 K7
Jubilee Rd CHEAM SM3 181 K1
GFD/PVL UB6 80 B8
WATN WD24 29 G3
Jubilee St WCHPL E1 104 C5
Jubilee Wy CHSGTN KT9 168 B5
EBED/NFELT TW14 132 A5
SCUP DA14 144 A6
WIM/MER SW19 155 H4
Judd St CAMTN NW1 5 J7
Jude St CAN/RD E16 105 M5
Judge Heath La UX/CGN UB8 95 J5
Judge's Hl POTB/CUF EN6 23 M2
Judge St WATN WD24 29 H3
Judges' Wk HAMP NW3 83 J3
Judge Wk ESH/CLAY KT10 166 E8
Judith Av CRW RM5 55 H8
Juer St BTSEA SW11 119 L5
Juglans Rd ORP BR6 177 G3
Julia Gdns BARK IG11 108 D1
Juliana Cl EFNCH N2 65 J4
Julian Av ACT W3 99 J6
Julian Cl BAR EN5 34 B6
Julian Hl HRW HA1 79 L2
Julian Pl POP/IOD E14 123 H3
Julian Rd ORP BR6 177 G8
Julien Rd COUL/CHIP CR5 183 J8
EA W5 116 C1
Juliette Rd PLSTW E13 105 M1
Juliette Wy PUR RM19 110 F8
Junction Ap BTSEA SW11 137 L1
LEW SE13 123 J8
Junction Ms BAY/PAD W2 9 J4
Junction Pl BAY/PAD W2 9 H4 1
Junction Rd ARCH N19 84 C3
ASHF TW15 149 J1
DART DA1 146 D3
EA W5 116 C2
ED N9 50 A3
HRW HA1 61 K7 1
PLSTW E13 88 B8
ROM RM1 73 M5
SAND/SEL CR2 172 D8
TOTM N17 68 A4
Junction Rd East CHDH RM6 72 E8 1
Junction Rd West CHDH RM6 72 D8
June Cl COUL/CHIP CR5 183 H7 1
Juniper Cl BAR EN5 33 K8
CHSGTN KT9 167 M8
Juniper Ct CHDH RM6 72 B7
Juniper Gdns MTCM CR4 156 C4 1
SUN TW16 149 M2
Juniper Ga RKW/CH/CXG WD3 40 D4
Juniper Gv WAT WD17 29 G3
Juniper La EHAM E6 106 E4 2
Juniper Rd IL IG1 89 H4 2
Juniper St WCHPL E1 104 C6 2
Juniper Wy HARH RM3 74 E2
HYS/HAR UB3 95 K6
Juno Wy NWCR SE14 122 D4
Jupp Rd SRTFD E15 87 K7
Jupp Rd West SRTFD E15 87 J8
Justice Wk CHEL SW3 119 L4 2
Justin Cl BTFD TW8 116 D5
Justin Rd CHING E4 50 F8
Jute La PEND EN3 37 L5
Jutland Rd CAT SE6 141 J4
PLSTW E13 106 A3
Jutsums Av ROMW/RG RM7 73 H7
Jutsums La ROMW/RG RM7 73 H7
Juxon Cl RYLN/HDSTN HA2 61 H2
Juxon St LBTH SE11 17 M5

K

Kaduna Cl PIN HA5 60 B6 1
Kale Rd ERITH DA18 108 D8
Kambala Rd BTSEA SW11 119 K8 3
Kangley Bridge Rd SYD SE26 158 F1
Kaplan Dr WCHMH N21 35 M8
Karen Cl RAIN RM13 109 L1
Karen Ct BMLY BR1 159 M4 2
Karenza Ct WBLY HA9 62 C8 1
Karina Cl CHIG IG7 53 L7
Kashgar Rd WOOL/PLUM SE18 125 M3
Kashmir Rd CHARL SE7 124 D5
Kassala Rd BTSEA SW11 119 M6
Katharine St CROY/NA CR0 172 C5
Katherine Cl
BERM/RHTH SE16 104 D7 8
Katherine Gdns BARK/HLT IG6 71 J1
ELTH/MOT SE9 142 D1
Katherine Pl ABLGY WD5 21 G5 3
Katherine Rd EHAM E6 88 D7
Kathleen Av ACT W3 99 J4 1
ALP/SUD HA0 80 E7
Kathleen Rd BTSEA SW11 119 M8
Kayemoor Rd BELMT SM2 182 E1
Kay Rd BRXN/ST SW9 120 E7
Kay St BETH E2 104 A1
SRTFD E15 87 K7 5
WELL DA16 126 B6
Kean St HOL/ALD WC2B 11 L5
Keatley Gn CHING E4 50 F8
Keats Av CAN/RD E16 106 B7
HARH RM3 74 B1
Keats Cl CHIG IG7 53 J8
PEND EN3 37 K8
STHWK SE1 19 L6 1
WAN E11 70 B6
WIM/MER SW19 155 K2 2
YEAD UB4 96 A4
Keats Gv HAMP NW3 83 L4
Keats Rd BELV DA17 127 J1
WELL DA16 125 L6
Keats Wy CROY/NA CR0 173 J1
GFD/PVL UB6 97 H4
WDR/YW UB7 112 F2
Keble Cl NTHLT UB5 79 J5
WPK KT4 168 F3 1
Keble Pl BARN SW13 118 B4 1
Keble St TOOT SW17 137 J8
Keble Ter ABLGY WD5 20 F5
Kechill Gdns HAYES BR2 175 G2
Kedleston Dr STMC/STPC BR5 176 F1
Keedonwood Rd BMLY BR1 141 L8
Keel Cl BARK IG11 108 C1
BERM/RHTH SE16 104 D7 9
Keele Cl WATN WD24 29 J5 3
Keeley Rd CROY/NA CR0 172 C4
Keeley St HOL/ALD WC2B 11 L5
Keeling Rd ELTH/MOT SE9 142 D2
Keely Cl EBAR EN4 34 E8
Keens Cl STRHM/NOR SW16 .. 156 D1 3
Keen's Rd CROY/NA CR0 172 C6
Keen's Yd IS N1 85 H6
Keepers Ms TEDD TW11 152 C2
The Keep BKHTH/KID SE3 124 A7
KUTN/CMB KT2 152 F2
Keeton's Rd BERM/RHTH SE16 .. 122 B1
Keevil Dr WIM/MER SW19 136 D4
Keighley Cl HOLWY N7 84 E4 3
Keightley Dr ELTH/MOT SE9 143 J5
Keilder Cl HGDN/ICK UB10 95 G1
Keildon Rd BTSEA SW11 137 M1
Keir Hardie Wy BARK IG11 90 A7
YEAD UB4 96 A2 3
Keith Connor Cl VX/NE SW8 .. 120 B8 2
Keith Gv SHB W12 100 A8
Keith Park Crs BH/WHM TN16 187 J5
Keith Park Rd HGDN/ICK UB10 76 F7
Keith Rd BARK IG11 107 K1
HYS/HAR UB3 113 L1
WALTH E17 68 F2
Keith Wy EMPK RM11 74 E8
Kelbrook Rd BKHTH/KID SE3 124 E7
Kelburn Wy RAIN RM13 110 A2 2
Kelceda Cl CRICK NW2 82 A2
Kelf Gv HYS/HAR UB3 95 M5
Kelfield Gdns NKENS W10 100 D5
Kelland Rd PLSTW E13 106 A3
Kellaway Rd BKHTH/KID SE3 124 C7
Keller Cresent MNPK E12 88 D4
Kellerton Rd LEW SE13 141 L2
Kellett Rd BRXS/STRHM SW2 139 G1
Kelling Gdns CROY/NA CR0 172 B2 1
Kellino St TOOT SW17 137 M8
Kellner Rd THMD SE28 125 M1
Kell St STHWK SE1 18 D3
Kelly Cl BORE WD6 32 D5
SHPTN TW17 149 L5 5
WLSDN NW10 81 K3
Kelly Rd MLHL NW7 46 E8
Kelly St CAMTN NW1 84 B6
Kelly Wy CHDH RM6 72 E6
Kelman Cl CHES/WCR EN8 26 D4 1
CLAP SW4 120 D7
Kelmore Gv EDUL SE22 140 A1
Kelmscott Cl WALTH E17 68 F2 5
WATW WD18 42 A1
Kelmscott Crs WATW WD18 29 G8
Kelmscott Gdns SHB W12 118 A1
Kelmscott Rd BTSEA SW11 137 M2
Kelross Rd HBRY N5 85 H4
Kelsall Cl BKHTH/KID SE3 124 B7 3
Kelsey La BECK BR3 159 G6
Kelsey Park Av BECK BR3 159 H6
Kelsey Park Rd BECK BR3 159 G5
Kelsey Rd STMC/STPC BR5 162 B5
Kelsey Sq BECK BR3 159 G5
Kelsey St BETH E2 104 A3
Kelsey Wy BECK BR3 159 G6
Kelshall GSTN WD25 29 L1
Kelsie Wy BARK/HLT IG6 53 L8
Kelso Pl KENS W8 14 C3
Kelso Rd CAR SM5 170 C2
Kelston Rd BARK/HLT IG6 71 H3
Kelvedon Cl KUTN/CMB KT2 153 G2
Kelvedon Rd FUL/PGN SW6 118 F5
Kelvedon Wy WFD IG8 52 F8 4
Kelvin Av PLMGR N13 48 F8
Kelvinbrook E/WMO/HCT KT8 151 H6
Kelvin Cl HOR/WEW KT19 168 A8 1
Kelvin Crs KTN/HRWW/W HA3 61 L1
Kelvin Dr TWK TW1 134 C3 1
Kelvin Gdns CROY/NA CR0 171 L2
STHL UB1 97 G5
Kelvin Gv SURB KT6 167 L5
SYD SE26 140 B7
Kelvington Cl CROY/NA CR0 173 L2 2
Kelvington Rd PECK SE15 140 D2
Kelvin Pde ORP BR6 176 E3
Kelvin Rd HBRY N5 85 H4
WELL DA16 126 A8
Kember St IS N1 5 L2 2
Kemble Cl POTB/CUF EN6 23 K6
WEY KT13 164 D6
Kemble Dr HAYES BR2 175 L5
Kemble Rd CROY/NA CR0 172 B5
FSTH SE23 140 D5
TOTM N17 68 A2
Kemble St HOL/ALD WC2B 11 L5 1
Kemerton Rd BECK BR3 159 H5
CMBW SE5 121 J8
CROY/NA CR0 172 F2
Kemey's St HOM E9 86 E5 1
Kemnal Rd CHST BR7 161 J2
Kempe Rd EN EN1 37 H1
KIL/WHAMP NW6 100 D1
Kemp Gdns CROY/NA CR0 172 C1 3
Kemplay Rd HAMP NW3 83 K4
Kemp Pl BUSH WD23 43 G1
Kemps Dr NTHWD HA6 59 M1 3
POP/IOD E14 105 G6 3
Kempsford Gdns ECT SW5 14 B8
Kempsford Rd LBTH SE11 18 B6 1
Kempshott Rd
STRHM/NOR SW16 156 E3
Kempson Rd FUL/PGN SW6 119 G5 5
Kempthorne Rd DEPT SE8 122 F2 3
Kempton Av HCH RM12 92 F4
NTHLT UB5 79 G6
SUN TW16 150 B4
Kempton Cl ERITH DA8 127 J4
HGDN/ICK UB10 77 J4 1
Kempton Ct SUN TW16 150 B4
Kempton Rd EHAM E6 88 F8
HPTN TW12 150 F5
Kempton Wk CROY/NA CR0 173 L1
Kempt St WOOL/PLUM SE18 125 G4
Kemsing Cl BXLY DA5 144 E4 1
THHTH CR7 157 J7 2
Kemsing Rd GNWCH SE10 124 A3
Kenbury Cl HGDN/ICK UB10 77 G3
Kenbury St CMBW SE5 121 J7
Kenchester Cl VX/NE SW8 120 E5
Kendal Av ACT W3 99 G4
BARK IG11 89 L8
UED N18 49 K6
Kendal Cl CMBW SE5 121 H5
EBED/NFELT TW14 131 M5 10
WFD IG8 51 M4
YEAD UB4 95 L1
Kendal Ct ACT W3 99 G4
Kendal Cft HCH RM12 92 A5
Kendale Rd BMLY BR1 159 L1
Kendal Gdns SUT SM1 170 C4
UED N18 49 K6 1
Kendall Av BECK BR3 158 E5
SAND/SEL CR2 184 D2
Kendall Av South
SAND/SEL CR2 184 C3
Kendall Pl MHST W1U 10 A3
Kendall Rd BECK BR3 158 E5
ISLW TW7 116 A7
Kendalmere Cl MUSWH N10 66 B2 1
Kendal Pl PUT/ROE SW15 136 F2 2
Kendal Rd WLSDN NW10 82 A4
Kendals Cl RAD WD7 30 E1
Kendal St BAY/PAD W2 9 K5
Kender St NWCR SE14 122 C5
Kendoa Rd CLAP SW4 138 D1 5
Kendon Cl WAN E11 70 B6
Kendor Av HOR/WEW KT19 180 C4
Kendra Hall Rd SAND/SEL CR2 184 B1
Kendrey Gdns WHTN TW2 133 L3
Kendrick Ms SKENS SW7 15 G6
Kendrick Pl SKENS SW7 15 G6 1
Kenelm Cl HRW HA1 80 A3
Kenerne Dr BAR EN5 33 L8
Kenford Cl GSTN WD25 21 H5
Kenilford Rd BAL SW12 138 B4 1
Kenilworth Av COB KT11 178 B7
HARH RM3 57 H7
RYLN/HDSTN HA2 78 F4
WALTH E17 69 G3
WIM/MER SW19 155 G1
Kenilworth Ct WAT WD17 29 G4
Kenilworth Crs EN EN1 36 E4
Kenilworth Dr BORE WD6 32 C6
RKW/CH/CXG WD3 28 B7
WOT/HER KT12 165 K5
Kenilworth Gdns
GDMY/SEVK IG3 89 M2
HCH RM12 92 C3
LOU IG10 52 F1
OXHEY WD19 42 C7 7
STA TW18 148 C1
STHL UB1 96 F2 4
WOOL/PLUM SE18 125 H7
YEAD UB4 95 M4
Kenilworth Rd ASHF TW15 130 D7
BOW E3 104 E1
EA W5 98 E7
EDGW HA8 45 J4
EW KT17 169 G8
KIL/WHAMP NW6 82 F8
PGE/AN SE20 158 D4
STMC/STPC BR5 176 C1
Kenley Av CDALE/KGS NW9 63 L2
Kenley Cl BXLY DA5 145 G4
CHST BR7 161 L6
EBAR EN4 34 E7
Kenley Gdns HCH RM12 92 F2
THHTH CR7 157 H7
Kenley La PUR/KEN CR8 184 C8
Kenley Rd KUT KT1 153 H5
TWK TW1 134 A3
WIM/MER SW19 155 G6
Kenley Wk CHEAM SM3 169 K6
Kenlor Rd TOOT SW17 155 K1
Kenmare Dr MTCM CR4 155 M3 2
Kenmare Gdns PLMGR N13 49 J6
Kenmare Rd THHTH CR7 172 A1 3
Kenmere Gdns ALP/SUD HA0 81 G8
Kenmere Rd WELL DA16 126 C7
Kenmont Gdns
WLSDN NW10 100 B2 3
Kenmore Av KTN/HRWW/W HA3 .. 62 A6
Kenmore Crs YEAD UB4 95 M2
Kenmore Gdns EDGW HA8 63 H3 2
Kenmore Rd KTN/HRWW/W HA3 .. 62 D4
PUR/KEN CR8 184 B7
Kenmure Rd HACK E8 86 B5 5
Kennard Rd FBAR/BDGN N11 47 M7
SRTFD E15 87 K7
Kennard St BTSEA SW11 120 A6
CAN/RD E16 106 F7
Kennedy Av PEND EN3 50 C1
Kennedy Cl CHES/WCR EN8 26 E1
MTCM CR4 156 A4 2
MTCM CR4 156 A5 1
PIN HA5 42 F8
PLSTW E13 106 A1 4
STMC/STPC BR5 176 D3
Kennedy Rd BARK IG11 89 L8
HNWL W7 97 L4
Kennel Wood Crs
CROY/NA CR0 186 D4
Kennet Cl BTSEA SW11 137 K1 1
UPMR RM14 75 L7
Kennet Dr YEAD UB4 96 E4
Kenneth Av IL IG1 89 H4
Kenneth Crs CRICK NW2 82 C5 3
Kenneth Gdns STAN HA7 44 A8
Kenneth Moor Rd IL IG1 89 H3 3
Kenneth Rd BNSTD SM7 182 D8
CHDH RM6 72 E8
Kennet Rd ISLW TW7 115 M8
MV/WKIL W9 100 F3
Kennet St WAP E1W 104 A7
Kennett Wharf La BLKFR EC4V 12 F6
Kenninghall Rd CLPT E5 86 B3
UED N18 50 B7
Kenning St
BERM/RHTH SE16 104 C8 3
Kennings Wy LBTH SE11 18 B7
Kennington Gdns KUT KT1 152 D6 2
Kennington Gv LBTH SE11 17 M9
Kennington La LBTH SE11 17 M8
Kennington Ov LBTH SE11 17 M9
Kennington Park Gdns
LBTH SE11 18 C9
WALW SE17 121 H4 4
Kennington Park Pl WALW SE17 .. 18 B9
Kennington Park Rd
LBTH SE11 121 G4
Kennington Rd LBTH SE11 18 A4
Kennylands Rd BARK/HLT IG6 72 A1
Kenny Rd MLHL NW7 46 E8
Kenrick Pl MHST W1U 10 A2
Kensal Rd NKENS W10 100 E3
Kensington Av MNPK E12 88 F6
THHTH CR7 157 G4
WATW WD18 28 F7
Kensington Church Ct
KENS W8 14 C2 1
Kensington Church St KENS W8 .... 8 B8
Kensington Church Wk
KENS W8 14 C2 2
Kensington Cl
FBAR/BDGN N11 48 A8 2
Kensington Ct KENS W8 14 D2 2
Kensington Court Ms
KENS W8 14 D3 2

Kensington Court Pl KENS W8...... 14 D3
Kensington Dr WFD IG8....... 70 D3
Kensington Gdns IL IG1 ...... 88 F1
Kensington Gardens Sq
  BAY/PAD W2...... 8 C5
Kensington Ga SKENS SW7 ...... 14 C3
Kensington Gore SKENS SW7 ...... 14 C3
Kensington High St KENS W8...... 14 A3
  WKENS W14 ...... 118 E2
Kensington Palace Gdns
  KENS W8 ...... 8 C8
Kensington Park Gdns
  NTGHL W11...... 100 F6
Kensington Park Ms
  NTGHL W11...... 100 F5
Kensington Park Rd
  NTGHL W11...... 100 F5
Kensington Pl KENS W8 ...... 8 A9
Kensington Rd KENS W8...... 14 D2
  NTHLT UB5 ...... 97 C1
  ROMW/RG RM7 ...... 73 J7
  SKENS SW7 ...... 15 J2
Kensington Sq KENS W8 ...... 14 C2
Kensington Ter
  SAND/SEL CR2 ...... 184 D1
Kensington Wy BORE WD6...... 32 D6
Kent Av DAGW RM9...... 109 G3
  WEA W13 ...... 98 B4
  WELL DA16 ...... 143 M2
Kent Cl BORE WD6...... 32 D3
  MTCM CR4 ...... 156 E7
  ORP BR6 ...... 176 E8
  STA TW18 ...... 148 D2
  UX/CGN UB8...... 76 C6
Kent Dr EBAR EN4 ...... 28 D7
  HCH RM12...... 92 D4
  TEDD TW11 ...... 151 L1
Kentford Wy NTHLT UB5 ...... 78 E8
Kent Gdns RSLP HA4 ...... 60 A7
  WEA W13 ...... 98 B4
Kent Gate Wy CROY/NA CRO... 173 M8
Kent House La BECK BR3 ...... 158 E2
Kent House Rd BECK BR3 ...... 158 D3
Kentish Rd BELV DA17 ...... 127 C2
Kentish Town Rd CAMTN NW1... 4 D2
Kentish Wy BMLY BR1 ...... 160 B5
Kentmere Rd
  WOOL/PLUM SE18...... 125 L2
  STHL UB1 ...... 97 G6
  SUN TW16 ...... 150 D5
Kenton Gdns
  KTN/HRWW/W HA3 ...... 62 C6
Kenton La KTN/HRWW/W HA3 ...... 62 C4
Kenton Park Av
  KTN/HRWW/W HA3 ...... 62 D5
Kenton Park Cl
  KTN/HRWW/W HA3 ...... 62 C5
Kenton Park Crs
  KTN/HRWW/W HA3 ...... 62 D5
Kenton Park Rd
  KTN/HRWW/W HA3 ...... 62 C5
Kenton Rd HOM E9 ...... 7 H5
  HRW HA1 ...... 61 M8
  KTN/HRWW/W HA3 ...... 62 E6
Kenton St STPAN WC1H 5 J9
Kenton Wy YEAD UB4 ...... 95 L2
Kent Rd CHSWK W4 ...... 117 J1
  DAGE RM10...... 91 H5
  DART DA1 ...... 146 D3
  E/WMO/HCT KT8 ...... 151 J7
  RCH/KEW TW9 ...... 117 C5
  STMC/STPC BR5 ...... 177 H1
  WCHMN N21...... 49 K3
  WWKM BR4...... 174 B3
Kent St BETH E2 ...... 7 M5
  PLSTW E13 ...... 106 B2
Kent Ter CAMTN NW1 ...... 3 K8
Kent Vw SOCK/AV RM15 ...... 111 J8
Kent View Gdns GDMY/SEVK IG3... 89 L2
Kent Wy SURB KT6 ...... 167 L5
Kentwode Gn BARN SW13...... 118 A5
Kenver Av NFNCH/WDSP N12... 47 K8
Kenward Rd ELTH/MOT SE9 ...... 142 C2
Kenway RAIN RM13 ...... 110 C2
  ROMW/RG RM7 ...... 73 J3
Ken Wy WBLY HA9 ...... 81 J2
Kenway Cl RAIN RM13 ...... 110 C2
Kenway Rd ECT SW5 ...... 14 C6
Kenway Wk RAIN RM13 ...... 110 D2
Kenwood Cl GLDGN NW11 ...... 63 K1
  WDR/YW UB7 ...... 113 G4
Kenwood Dr BECK BR3 ...... 159 J6
  WOT/HER KT12...... 165 H8
Kenwood Gdns CLAY IG5...... 71 G5
  SWFD E18 ...... 70 E1
Kenwood Pk WEY KT13 ...... 164 D8
Kenwood Rd ED N9 ...... 50 A4
  HGT N6 ...... 65 M7
Kenworth Cl CHES/WCR EN8 ...... 26 D6
Kenworthy Rd HOM E9 ...... 86 E5
Kenwyn Dr CRICK NW2 ...... 81 L3
Kenwyn Rd CLAP SW4 ...... 138 C1
  DART DA1 ...... 146 D2
  RYNPK SW20...... 154 C4
Kenya Rd CHARL SE7 ...... 126 C7
Kenyngton Dr SUN TW16 ...... 150 A1
Kenyngton Pl
  KTN/HRWW/W HA3 ...... 62 C6
Kenyon St FUL/PGN SW6...... 118 D6
Keogh Rd SRTFD E15 ...... 87 L6
Kepler Rd CLAP SW4 ...... 138 L1
Keppel Rd DAGW RM9 ...... 90 E4
  EHAM E6 ...... 88 F7
Keppel St GWRST WC1E 11 H2
Kerbela St BETH E2 ...... 104 A3
Kerbey St POP/IOD E14 ...... 105 H5
Kerdistone Cl POTB/CUF EN6 ...... 23 H3
Kerfield Crs CMBW SE5 ...... 121 K6
Kerfield Pl CMBW SE5 ...... 121 K6
Kerri Cl BAR EN5 ...... 33 J7
Kerrison Pl EA W5 ...... 98 D7
Kerrison Rd BTSEA SW11 ...... 119 L8
  EA W5 ...... 98 D7
  SRTFD E15 ...... 87 K8
Kerry Av PUR RM19 ...... 110 F8
  STAN HA7 ...... 44 C6
Kerry Cl CAN/RD E16 ...... 106 B5

PLMGR N13 ...... 48 F4
UPMR RM14 ...... 75 M8
Kerry Ct STAN HA7 ...... 44 D6
Kerry Dr UPMR RM14...... 75 M8
Kerry Pth NWCR SE14 ...... 122 F4
Kerry Rd NWCR SE14 ...... 122 F4
Kersey Dr SAND/SEL CR2...... 185 J5
Kersey Gdns HARH RM3 ...... 74 F1
Kersfield Rd PUT/ROE SW15...... 136 D3
Kershaw Cl EMPK RM11 ...... 74 D8
Kershaw Rd DAGE RM10...... 91 G3
Kersley Ms BTSEA SW11 ...... 119 M6
Kersley Rd STNW/STAM N16... 85 L3
Kersley St BTSEA SW11 ...... 119 M7
Kerstin Cl HYS/HAR UB3 ...... 95 M6
Kerswell Cl SEVS/STOTM N15... 67 L6
Kerwick Cl HOLWY N7 ...... 5 K1
Keslake Rd FUL/PGN NW6...... 100 D1
Kessock Cl WALTH E17 ...... 68 B6
Kesteven Cl BARK/HLT IG6...... 53 M8
Keston Av HAYES BR2 ...... 175 J7
Keston Cl UED N18 ...... 49 K5
  WELL DA16 ...... 126 C5
Keston Gdns HAYES BR2 ...... 175 J6
Keston Ms WAT WD17 ...... 29 H5
Keston Park Cl HAYES BR2 ...... 175 M6
Keston Rd PECK SE15 ...... 122 A8
  THHTH CR7 ...... 171 M1
  TOTM N17 ...... 49 M8
Kestrel Av EHAM E6 ...... 106 E4
  HNHL SE24 ...... 139 H2
Kestrel Cl BARK/HLT IG6 ...... 54 C6
  CDALE/KGS NW9 ...... 63 L3
  GSTN WD25...... 21 L7
  KUTN/CMB KT2 ...... 134 D8
  RAIN RM13 ...... 92 B7
  WLSDN NW10 ...... 81 K5
The Kestrels LCOL/BKTW AL2 ... 21 L4
Kestrel Wy CROY/NA CRO 186 D2
  KUTN/CMB KT2 ...... 153 L1
  SHPTN TW17 ...... 149 L6
  WIM/MER SW19 ...... 155 G5
Keswick Cl SUT SM1 ...... 170 C6
Keswick Dr PEND EN3 ...... 37 J3
Keswick Gdns REDBR IG4 ...... 70 E6
  RSLP HA4 ...... 59 K7
  WBLY HA9 ...... 80 E5
Keswick Ms EA W5 ...... 98 E7
Keswick Rd BXLYHN DA7 ...... 127 G7
  ORP BR6 ...... 176 F3
  PUT/ROE SW15 ...... 136 E2
  WHTN TW2 ...... 133 J3
  WWKM BR4...... 174 E4
Kettering Rd HARH RM3 ...... 74 E1
  PEND EN3 ...... 37 K2
Kettering St STRHM/NOR SW16.. 156 B2
Kettlebaston Rd LEY E10 ...... 86 F1
Kettlewell Cl FBAR/BDGN N11 .. 48 A8
Kettlewell Ct SWLY BR8...... 163 H5
Kevelioc Rd TOTM N17 ...... 67 J2
Kevin Cl HSLWW TW4 ...... 114 D7
Kevington Cl
  STMC/STPC BR5 ...... 161 M7
Kevington Dr CHST BR7 ...... 161 M7
Kew Br RCH/KEW TW9 ...... 117 G4
Kew Bridge Rd BTFD TW8...... 117 G4
Kew Crs CHEAM SM3 ...... 169 M5
Kewferry Dr NTHWD HA6 ...... 41 H7
Kewferry Rd NTHWD HA6 ...... 41 J8
Kew Foot Rd RCH/KEW TW9...... 134 L6
Kew Gardens Rd
  RCH/KEW TW9 ...... 116 F5
Kew Gn RCH/KEW TW9 ...... 116 F4
Kew Meadow Pth
  RCH/KEW TW9 ...... 117 H6
Kew Rd RCH/KEW TW9 ...... 116 F4
  RCH/KEW TW9 ...... 134 L1
Key Cl WCHPL E1 ...... 104 B3
Keyes Rd CRICK NW2 ...... 82 D5
  DART DA1 ...... 147 G1
Keymer Rd BRXS/STRHM SW2 ... 138 F1
Keynes Cl EFNCH N2 ...... 65 M5
Keynsham Av WFD IG8 ...... 51 L6
Keynsham Gdns
  ELTH/MOT SE9 ...... 142 E2
Keynsham Rd ELTH/MOT SE9 ... 142 D2
  MRDN SM4 ...... 170 B3
Keyse Rd STHWK SE1 ...... 7 M9
Keysham Av HEST TW5 ...... 114 A6
Keystone Crs IS N1 ...... 5 K6
Keywood Dr SUN TW16 ...... 150 A2
Keyworth Cl CLPT E5 ...... 86 E4
Keyworth St STHWK SE1 ...... 18 D3
Kezia St DEPT SE8 ...... 122 E3
Khama Rd TOOT SW17 ...... 137 L8
Khartoum Rd IL IG1 ...... 89 H5
  PLSTW E13 ...... 106 B2
  TOOT SW17 ...... 137 K8
Khyber Rd BTSEA SW11 ...... 119 L7
Kibworth St VX/NE SW8 ...... 120 F5
Kidbrooke Gdns
  BKHTH/KID SE3 ...... 124 A7
Kidbrooke La ELTH/MOT SE9 ... 124 A6
Kidbrooke Park Cl
  BKHTH/KID SE3 ...... 124 B6
Kidbrooke Park Rd
  BKHTH/KID SE3 ...... 124 C8
  ELTH/MOT SE9 ...... 142 B2
Kidbrooke Wy BKHTH/KID SE3... 124 B7
Kidderminster Rd
  CROY/NA CRO 172 B3
Kidderpore Av HAMP NW3 ...... 83 G4
Kidderpore Gdns HAMP NW3... 83 G4
Kidd Pl CHARL SE7 ...... 124 E3
Kidlington Wy CDALE/KGS NW9... 63 L3
Kielder Cl BARK/HLT IG6 ...... 53 M8
Kilberry Cl ISLW TW7 ...... 115 K6
Kilburn La NKENS W10 ...... 100 D1
Kilburn Park Rd KIL/WHAMP NW6.. 2 A8
Kilburn Pl KIL/WHAMP NW6 ...... 2 B4
Kilburn Priory KIL/WHAMP NW6 .. 2 C4
Kilburn V KIL/WHAMP NW6...... 2 B4
Kilby Cl GSTN WD25 ...... 21 K8
Kilcorral Cl EW KT17 ...... 181 G7
Kildare Cl RSLP HA4 ...... 78 C1
Kildare Gdns BAY/PAD W2 ...... 8 B4

Kildare Rd CAN/RD E16 ...... 106 A4
Kildare Ter BAY/PAD W2 ...... 8 B4
Kildoran Rd CLAP SW4 ...... 138 E2
Kildowan Rd GDMY/SEVK IG3... 90 A1
Kilgour Rd FSTH SE23 ...... 140 E3
Kilkie St FUL/PGN SW6 ...... 119 J7
Killarney Rd WAND/EARL SW18... 137 J3
Killearn Rd CAT SE6 ...... 141 K5
Killester Gdns EW KT17 ...... 169 H6
Killewarren Wy
  STMC/STPC BR5 ...... 177 J2
Killick St IS N1 ...... 5 L5
Killieser Av BRXS/STRHM SW2... 138 E6
Killip Cl CAN/RD E16 ...... 105 M5
Killowen Av NTHLT UB5 ...... 79 J5
Killowen Rd HOM E9 ...... 86 D7
Killyon Rd VX/NE SW8 ...... 120 C7
Kilmaine Rd FUL/PGN SW6 ...... 119 J4
Kilmarnock Gdns BCTR RM8... 90 C3
Kilmarnock Rd GNWCH SE10 ... 42 D6
Kilmarsh Rd HMSMTH W6 ...... 118 C2
Kilmartin Av STRHM/NOR SW16.. 157 G6
Kilmartin Rd GDMY/SEVK IG3... 90 A2
Kilmartin Wy HCH RM12 ...... 92 B5
Kilmington Rd BARN SW13...... 118 A4
Kilmiston Av SHPTN TW17...... 164 C1
Kilmorey Gdns TWK TW1 ...... 134 B2
Kilmorey Rd TWK TW1 ...... 134 B1
Kilmorie Rd FSTH SE23 ...... 140 E5
Kiln Cl HYS/HAR UB3 ...... 113 K4
Kilner La EW KT17 ...... 180 E4
Kilner St POP/IOD E14 ...... 105 C4
Kiln La EW KT17 ...... 180 E4
Kiln Ms TOOT SW17 ...... 155 K1
Kilnside ESH/CLAY KT10 ...... 179 C1
Kiln Wy NTHWD HA6 ...... 41 L8
Kilpatrick Wy YEAD UB4 ...... 96 A3
Kilravock St NKENS W10 ...... 100 C2
Kilross Rd EBED/NFELT TW14 ... 131 K5
Kilsby Wk BCTR RM8 ...... 89 H3
Kilsha Rd WOT/HER KT12 ...... 165 H1
Kilsmore La CHES/WCR EN8 ... 26 D1
Kimbell Gdns FUL/PGN SW6...... 118 E6
Kimbell Pl ELTH/MOT SE9 ...... 142 C1
Kimberley Av EHAM E6 ...... 106 E1
  GNTH/NBYPK IG2 ...... 71 K8
  PECK SE15 ...... 122 C8
  ROMW/RG RM7 ...... 73 H7
Kimberley Gdns EN EN1 ...... 36 F6
  FSBYPK N4 ...... 67 H6
Kimberley Pl PUR/KEN CR8 ... 184 A4
Kimberley Ride COB KT11 ...... 178 B6
Kimberley Rd BECK BR3 ...... 158 D5
  BRXN/ST SW9 ...... 120 E7
  CAN/RD E16 ...... 105 M3
  CHING E4 ...... 51 L3
  CROY/NA CRO 172 B1
  TOTM N17 ...... 68 A3
  UED N18 ...... 50 B8
  WALTH E17 ...... 68 E2
  WAN E11 ...... 87 K2
Kimberley Wy CHING E4 ...... 51 L3
Kimber Rd WAND/EARL SW18... 137 H4
Kimble Cl WATW WD18 ...... 41 L1
Kimble Crs BUSH WD23 ...... 43 J2
Kimble Rd TOOT SW17 ...... 155 L2
Kimbolton Cl LEE/GVPK SE12... 141 M3
Kimbolton Gn BORE WD6 ...... 32 C7
Kimmeridge Gdns
  ELTH/MOT SE9 ...... 142 E8
Kimmeridge Rd ELTH/MOT SE9 .. 142 E8
Kimpton Pl GSTN WD25 ...... 21 K7
Kimpton Rd CHEAM SM3 ...... 169 M5
  CMBW SE5 ...... 121 K6
Kimptons Cl POTB/CUF EN6 ... 22 D6
Kimptons Md POTB/CUF EN6 ... 22 D6
Kinburn St BERM/RHTH SE16... 104 D8
Kincaid Rd PECK SE15 ...... 122 B5
Kinch Gv WBLY HA9 ...... 62 F8
Kinder Cl THMD SE28 ...... 24 C6
Kindersley Wy ABLGY WD5 ...... 20 C4
Kinder St WCHPL E1 ...... 104 B5
Kinfauns Av EMPK RM11 ...... 74 C7
Kinfauns Rd BRXS/STRHM SW2... 139 G6
  GDMY/SEVK IG3 ...... 90 B1
Kingaby Gdns RAIN RM13 ...... 92 A7
King Alfred Av CAT SE6 ...... 141 C7
King Alfred Rd HARH RM3...... 74 F3
King And Queen Cl
  ELTH/MOT SE9 ...... 142 E8
King And Queen St WALW SE17... 18 F7
King Arthur Cl PECK SE15 ...... 122 C5
King Arthur Crs CHES/WCR EN8 ... 26 E4
King Charles' Rd BRYLDS KT5... 167 M2
King Charles Rd BRYLDS KT5... 167 M1
King Charles St WHALL SW1A... 17 H1
King Charles Wk
  WIM/MER SW19 ...... 136 E5
Kingcup Cl CROY/NA CRO 173 K3
King David La WCHPL E1 ...... 104 D6
Kingdon Rd KIL/WHAMP NW6... 83 G5
King Edward Av DART DA1 ...... 146 D3
  RAIN RM13 ...... 110 D1
King Edward Dr SURB KT6 ...... 167 L5
King Edward Rd BAR EN5 ...... 34 K7
  CHES/WCR EN8 ...... 26 E6
  LEY E10 ...... 87 J1
  OXHEY WD19 ...... 42 E1
  ROM RM1 ...... 73 M7
  WALTH E17 ...... 68 E4
King Edward Wk STHWK SE1 ... 18 B4
King Edward's Gv TEDD TW11... 152 B2
King Edward's Rd BARK IG11... 89 K8
  ED N9 ...... 50 B2
  HACK E8 ...... 86 B8
  PEND EN3 ...... 37 K7
  RSLP HA4 ...... 77 K1
King Edward Wk STHWK SE1 ... 18 B4
Kingfield Rd EA W5 ...... 98 D3
Kingfield St POP/IOD E14 ...... 123 J2

Kingfisher Dr
  RCHPK/HAM TW10 ...... 134 C8
Kingfisher Gdns SAND/SEL CR2... 185 K3
Kingfisher Rd UPMR RM14 ...... 93 M1
Kingfisher St EHAM E6 ...... 107 J3
Kingfisher Wy CROY/NA CRO ... 158 D8
  WLSDN NW10 ...... 81 K5
King Gdns CROY/NA CRO 172 B7
King Garth Ms FSTH SE23 ...... 140 C6
King George Av BUSH WD23...... 43 H1
  CAN/RD E16 ...... 106 D5
  GNTH/NBYPK IG2 ...... 71 K7
  WOT/HER KT12...... 165 K3
King George Cl ROMW/RG RM7 ... 73 J4
  SUN TW16 ...... 149 L1
King George VI Av MTCM CR4... 155 M7
Kingham Cl NTGHL W11 ...... 100 E8
  WAND/EARL SW18 ...... 137 J4
King Harolds Wy BXLYHN DA7... 126 D5
King Henry Ms ORP BR6 ...... 176 F7
King Henry's Dr CROY/NA CRO... 186 C2
King Henry's Ms PEND EN3 ...... 38 A2
King Henry's Rd HAMP NW3...... 3 J2
  KUT KT1 ...... 153 H6
King Henry St STNW/STAM N16... 85 L5
King Henry's Wk IS N1 ...... 85 L6
Kinghorn St STBT EC1A 12 E3
King James Av POTB/CUF EN6... 24 E2
King James St STHWK SE1 ...... 18 D2
King John Ct SDTCH EC2A 7 K9
King John St WCHPL E1 ...... 104 D4
King John's Wk ELTH/MOT SE9... 142 E4
Kinglake St WALW SE17 ...... 19 J8
Kingly Ct REGST W1B 10 E5
Kingly St REGST W1B 10 E5
Kings Arbour NWDGN UB2 ...... 114 E3
King's Arms Yd LOTH EC2R 13 G4
Kingsash Dr YEAD UB4 ...... 96 E3
Kings Av BAL SW12 ...... 138 D5
  BMLY BR1 ...... 160 A2
  CAR SM5 ...... 182 E1
  CHDH RM6 ...... 72 F7
  CLAP SW4 ...... 138 E3
  EA W5 ...... 98 D5
  GFD/PVL UB6 ...... 97 H5
  HSLW TW3 ...... 115 H6
  MUSWH N10 ...... 66 A4
  NWMAL KT3 ...... 153 M7
  SUN TW16 ...... 149 M1
  WATW WD18 ...... 29 G7
  WCHMN N21 ...... 49 H3
  WFD IG8 ...... 52 C7
King's Bench St STHWK SE1 ... 18 D1
Kingsbridge Av EA W5 ...... 98 F8
Kingsbridge Ct POP/IOD E14... 123 G1
Kingsbridge Rd BARK IG11 ...... 107 K1
  HARH RM3 ...... 56 E8
  MRDN SM4 ...... 169 K2
  NKENS W10 ...... 100 C5
  NWDGN UB2 ...... 114 F2
  WOT/HER KT12 ...... 165 H2
Kingsbury Rd
  CDALE/KGS NW9 ...... 63 C6
  IS N1 ...... 85 L6
  STNW/STAM N16 ...... 85 L5
Kingsbury Ter IS N1 ...... 85 L6
Kings Cha E/WMO/HCT KT8 ...... 149 J7
Kingsclere Cl PUT/ROE SW15... 136 A4
Kingscliffe Gdns
  WIM/MER SW19 ...... 136 F5
Kings Cl DART DA1 ...... 145 L1
  HDN NW4 ...... 64 D5
  LEY E10 ...... 69 H8
  NTHWD HA6 ...... 41 M8
  STA TW18 ...... 148 D3
  THDIT KT7 ...... 167 G1
  WATW WD18 ...... 29 J7
  WOT/HER KT12 ...... 165 H3
Kingscote Rd CHSWK W4 ...... 117 K1
  CROY/NA CRO 173 H2
  NWMAL KT3 ...... 153 K6
Kingscote St EMB EC4Y 12 C6
Kings Ct PLSTW E13 ...... 88 B8
  STHWK SE1 ...... 18 D1
Kingscourt Rd
  STRHM/NOR SW16 ...... 138 D7
Kings Crs FSBYPK N4 ...... 85 J3
Kingscroft BNSTD SM7 ...... 182 D8
  CRICK NW2 ...... 82 F6
King's Cross Br FSBYW WC1X ... 5 K7
King's Cross Rd FSBYW WC1X ... 5 M7
Kingsdale Gdns NTGHL W11 ... 100 D7
Kingsdale Rd PGE/AN SE20 ... 158 D3
  WOOL/PLUM SE18 ...... 125 M4
Kingsdown Av ACT W3 ...... 99 G6
  SAND/SEL CR2 ...... 184 C2
  WEA W13 ...... 98 B8
Kingsdown Cl NTGHL W11 ...... 100 D5
Kingsdowne Rd SURB KT6 ...... 167 L7
Kingsdown Rd ARCH N19 ...... 84 E3
  CHEAM SM3 ...... 169 L7
  EW KT17 ...... 181 G6
  WAN E11 ...... 87 L3
Kingsdown Wy HAYES BR2 ...... 175 G1
Kings Dr BRYLDS KT5 ...... 168 A2
  EDGW HA8 ...... 44 F6
  THDIT KT7 ...... 167 H1
  WBLY HA9 ...... 81 H2
Kingsend RSLP HA4 ...... 77 L1
Kings Farm Av
  RCHPK/HAM TW10 ...... 135 G1
Kingsfield Av RYLN/HDSTN HA2... 61 H6
Kingsfield Ct OXHEY WD19 ...... 42 D1
Kingsfield Dr PEND EN3 ...... 26 D8
Kingsfield Rd HRW HA1 ...... 61 K8
  OXHEY WD19 ...... 42 D1
Kingsfield Wy PEND EN3 ...... 26 D8
Kingsford St KTTN NW5 ...... 83 M5
Kingsford Wy EHAM E6 ...... 106 F4
Kingsgate WBLY HA9 ...... 81 J3

UPMR RM14 ...... 75 L8
Kingsgate Av FNCH N3 ...... 65 G4
Kingsgate Cl BXLYHN DA7...... 126 E6
  STMC/STPC BR5 ...... 162 C5
Kingsgate Pl KIL/WHAMP NW6... 2 C1
Kingsgate Rd KIL/WHAMP NW6... 2 C1
  KUT KT1 ...... 152 E4
King's Gn LOU IG10 ...... 39 L6
Kingsground ELTH/MOT SE9 ... 142 D4
Kings Gv PECK SE15 ...... 122 B6
  ROM RM1 ...... 74 A6
Kings Hall Ms LEW SE13 ...... 123 J8
Kings Hall Rd BECK BR3 ...... 158 F3
Kings Head Hl CHING E4 ...... 51 H2
King's Hwy WOOL/PLUM SE18... 125 L4
Kingshill Av CRW RM5 ...... 55 J8
  KTN/HRWW/W HA3 ...... 62 B5
  NTHLT UB5 ...... 96 B2
  WPK KT4 ...... 169 G2
  YEAD UB4 ...... 95 L2
Kingshill Dr KTN/HRWW/W HA3... 62 B4
Kingshold Rd HOM E9 ...... 86 D7
Kingsholm Gdns
  ELTH/MOT SE9 ...... 142 D1
Kingshurst Rd LEE/GVPK SE12... 142 A4
Kingsland Gn HACK E8 ...... 85 L6
Kingsland High St HACK E8 ...... 85 M6
Kingsland Pas HACK E8 ...... 85 L6
Kingsland Rd BETH E2 ...... 7 K6
  HACK E8 ...... 7 L2
  PLSTW E13 ...... 106 C2
King's La SUT SM1 ...... 170 D7
Kingslawn Cl PUT/ROE SW15... 136 D3
Kingsleigh Pl MTCM CR4 ...... 155 K6
Kingsleigh Wk HAYES BR2 ...... 159 M7
Kingsley Av BNSTD SM7 ...... 182 A8
  BORE WD6 ...... 31 M5
  CHES/WCR EN8 ...... 26 B2
  DART DA1 ...... 147 G2
  HSLW TW3 ...... 115 J7
  STHL UB1 ...... 97 G6
  SUT SM1 ...... 170 D6
  WEA W13 ...... 98 A5
Kingsley Cl DAGE RM10 ...... 91 H4
  GLDGN NW11 ...... 65 J8
Kingsley Ct EMPK RM11 ...... 74 B7
Kingsley Dr WPK KT4 ...... 168 F4
Kingsley Gdns CHING E4 ...... 51 C7
  EMPK RM11 ...... 74 D5
Kingsley Ms CHST BR7 ...... 161 H2
Kingsley Pl HGT N6 ...... 66 A8
Kingsley Rd BARK/HLT IG6 ...... 71 J2
  CROY/NA CRO 172 A3
  FSTGT E7 ...... 88 A7
  HSLW TW3 ...... 115 J7
  KIL/WHAMP NW6 ...... 82 F8
  ORP BR6 ...... 176 F8
  PIN HA5 ...... 60 F5
  PLMGR N13 ...... 49 G6
  RYLN/HDSTN HA2 ...... 79 J4
  WALTH E17 ...... 69 J3
  WIM/MER SW19 ...... 155 H1
Kingsley St BTSEA SW11 ...... 119 M8
Kingsley Wy EFNCH N2 ...... 65 J7
Kingsley Wood Dr
  ELTH/MOT SE9 ...... 142 F7
Kingslyn Crs NRWD SE19 ...... 157 L4
Kings Lynn Dr HARH RM3 ...... 56 D8
Kingsman St WOOL/PLUM SE18... 124 F2
Kingsmead BAR EN5 ...... 34 A7
  CHES/WCR EN8 ...... 26 D1
  POTB/CUF EN6 ...... 24 C1
  RCHPK/HAM TW10 ...... 134 F3
Kingsmead Av CDALE/KGS NW9... 63 K8
  ED N9 ...... 50 B3
  MTCM CR4 ...... 156 C6
  ROM RM1 ...... 73 M7
  SUN TW16 ...... 150 C6
  SURB KT6 ...... 168 A4
  WPK KT4 ...... 169 H5
Kingsmead Cl BFN/LL DA15 ... 144 A6
  HOR/WEW KT19 ...... 180 D1
  TEDD TW11 ...... 152 B2
Kingsmead Dr NTHLT UB5 ...... 78 F7
Kings Meadow KGLGY WD4 ...... 20 A1
Kings Mead Pk ESH/CLAY KT10... 178 E1
Kingsmead Rd
  BRXS/STRHM SW2 ...... 139 G2
Kingsmead Wy HOM E9 ...... 86 E4
Kingsmere Cl
  PUT/ROE SW15 ...... 118 D8
Kingsmere Pk CDALE/KGS NW9... 81 J1
Kingsmere Rd WIM/MER SW19... 136 D6
King's Ms BMSBY WC1N 11 M1
Kingsmill Gdns DAGW RM9 ...... 90 F5
Kingsmill Rd DAGW RM9 ...... 90 F5
Kingsmill Ter STJWD NW8 ...... 3 H5
Kingsnympton Pk
  KUTN/CMB KT2 ...... 153 H3
King's Orch ELTH/MOT SE9 ...... 142 E3
King's Paddock HPTN TW12 ... 151 J4
Kingspark Ct SWFD E18 ...... 70 E2
Kings Pl BKHH IG9 ...... 52 C4
  CHSWK W4 ...... 117 J3
  STHWK SE1 ...... 18 E2
Kings Sq FSBYE EC1V 6 E8
Kingsridge Gdns DART DA1 ... 146 D3
Kings Rd BAR EN5 ...... 33 J6
  BARK IG11 ...... 89 J7
  BELMT SM2 ...... 182 A3
  BGVA SW1W 16 B4
  CHES/WCR EN8 ...... 26 E7
  CHING E4 ...... 51 K3
  EA W5 ...... 98 D4
  EHAM E6 ...... 88 C3
  FELT TW13 ...... 132 C5
  FUL/PGN SW6 ...... 119 J5
  KUTN/CMB KT2 ...... 152 E3
  MORT/ESHN SW14 ...... 117 K8
  MTCM CR4 ...... 156 A6
  ORP BR6 ...... 176 F6
  RCHPK/HAM TW10 ...... 134 F2
  ROM RM1 ...... 74 A6
  RYLN/HDSTN HA2 ...... 78 F2
  SNWD SE25 ...... 158 A6
  SURB KT6 ...... 167 J3
  TEDD TW11 ...... 151 K1

TOTM N17 67 M2
TWK TW1 134 B3 7
UED N18 50 A7 8
UX/CGN UB8 94 D1
WAN E11 69 L8
WDGN N22 66 F2
WDR/YW UB7 94 F8
WIM/MER SW19 155 G2
WOT/HER KT12 165 H4
King's Scholars' Pas WEST SW1P 16 E4
King Stairs Cl BERM/RHTH SE16 104 B8
King's Ter CAMTN NW1 4 E4
Kingsthorpe Rd SYD SE26 140 D8
Kingston Av CHEAM SM3 169 L5
EBED/NFELT TW14 131 L3
WDR/YW UB7 94 F6
Kingston By-pass BRYLDS KT5 168 C2
CHSGTN KT9 167 M5
ESH/CLAY KT10 166 E5
Kingston Cl CHDH RM6 72 E4 1
NTHLT UB5 78 F7
Kingston Crs ASHF TW15 148 C1
BECK BR3 158 F4 1
Kingston Gdns CROY/NA CR0 171 L5
Kingston Hall Rd KUT KT1 152 D6
Kingston Hl KUTN/CMB KT2 153 G4
Kingston Hill Av CHDH RM6 72 E4
Kingston Hill Pl KUTN/CMB KT2 135 J8
Kingston La TEDD TW11 152 B2 3
UX/CGN UB8 94 E2
WDR/YW UB7 94 F8
Kingston Ldg NWMAL KT3 153 L7 4
Kingston Rd ASHF TW15 148 E2
BRYLDS KT5 168 B4
EBAR EN4 34 D8
ED N9 50 A4
EW KT17 180 F1
HOR/WEW KT19 168 E7
IL IG1 89 J4
NWDGN UB2 96 F8
NWMAL KT3 153 K7
PUT/ROE SW15 136 B5
ROM RM1 73 M5
RYNPK SW20 154 E5
SHPTN TW17 148 F2
STA TW18 130 A8
TEDD TW11 152 B2
WIM/MER SW19 155 G3
Kingston Sq NRWD SE19 157 K1
Kingston V PUT/ROE SW15 135 K8
Kingstown St CAMTN NW1 4 A3
King St CHSWK W4 117 M2
CITYW EC2V 12 F5
COVGDN WC2E 11 J6
EFNCH N2 65 K3 2
NWDGN UB2 114 E1
PLSTW E13 106 A3
RCH/KEW TW9 134 D2 4
STJS SW1Y 10 F9
TOTM N17 67 M2
TWK TW1 134 A5
WATW WD18 29 J7
Kings Wk SAND/SEL CR2 185 H7
Kingswater Pl BTSEA SW11 119 L5 1
Kings Wy CROY/NA CR0 171 M7
HRW HA1 61 L5
Kingsway HOL/ALD WC2B 11 L4
HYS/HAR UB3 95 J4
MORT/ESHN SW14 117 H8
NWMAL KT3 154 C7
PEND EN3 37 H8
POTB/CUF EN6 24 E3
STMC/STPC BR5 161 K8
STWL/WRAY TW19 130 D5
WBLY HA9 80 E4
WWKM BR4 174 F5
Kingsway Av SAND/SEL CR2 185 J2
Kingsway Crs RYLN/HDSTN HA2 61 J5
Kingsway North Orbital Rd
GSTN WD25 21 G7
Kingsway Rd CHEAM SM3 181 L1 1
The Kingsway EW KT17 180 F3
Kingswear Rd KTTN NW5 84 B3
RSLP HA4 78 A2
Kingswell Ride POTB/CUF EN6 24 E3
Kingswood Av BELV DA17 126 F2
HAYES BR2 159 L6
HEST TW5 114 F7
HPTN TW12 151 H2 4
KIL/WHAMP NW6 82 E8
SAND/SEL CR2 185 H8
SWLY BR8 163 M7
THHTH CR7 157 G8
Kingswood Cl DART DA1 146 C3
EN EN1 36 F8 2
NWMAL KT3 168 F1 2
ORP BR6 176 D2 1
SURB KT6 167 L2 2
TRDG/WHET N20 47 J1
Kingswood Dr BELMT SM2 182 B2 4
CAR SM5 170 F3
NRWD SE19 139 L8
Kingswood La WARL CR6 185 J8
Kingswood Pk FNCH N3 64 F2 1
Kingswood Pl LEW SE13 141 L1 4
Kingswood Rd
BRXS/STRHM SW2 138 E3
CHSWK W4 117 J1
GDMY/SEVK IG3 90 A1
GSTN WD25 21 H7
HAYES BR2 159 L6
PGE/AN SE20 158 C2
WIM/MER SW19 154 F4
Kingswood Ter CHSWK W4 117 J1
Kingswood Wy SAND/SEL CR2 185 K5
WLGTN SM6 171 L7 5
Kingsworth Cl BECK BR3 158 E8 1
Kingsworthy Cl KUT KT1 152 F6 2
Kingthorpe Rd WLSDN NW10 81 K7 2
Kingwell Rd EBAR EN4 34 D3
King William La GNWCH SE10 123 L3 2
King William St CANST EC4R 13 H7
MANHO EC4N 13 H6
King William Wk
GNWCH SE10 123 J4 6
Kingwood Rd FUL/PGN SW6 118 E5
Kinlet Rd WOOL/PLUM SE18 125 J5
Kinloch Dr CDALE/KGS NW9 63 L8
Kinloch St HOLWY N7 84 F3 2
Kinloss Gdns FNCH N3 64 F4
Kinloss Rd CAR SM5 170 C2
Kinnaird Av BMLY BR1 159 M2
CHSWK W4 117 J5
Kinnaird Cl BMLY BR1 159 M2 1
Kinnaird Wy WFD IG8 52 F8
Kinnear Rd SHB W12 99 M8
Kinnerton Pl South
KTBR SW1X 15 M2 1
Kinnerton St KTBR SW1X 15 M2
Kinnerton Yd KTBR SW1X 16 A2 3
Kinnoul Rd HMSMTH W6 118 E4
Kinross Av WPK KT4 169 G4
Kinross Cl KTN/HRWW/W HA3 62 F6
SUN TW16 149 M1
Kinross Dr SUN TW16 149 M1
Kinsale Rd PECK SE15 122 A8
Kintyre Cl STRHM/NOR SW16 156 F5
Kinveachy Gdns CHARL SE7 124 E3
Kinver Rd SYD SE26 140 C8
Kipling Dr TOOT SW17 155 K2
Kipling Rd BXLYHN DA7 126 E6
DART DA1 147 H2 1
Kipling St STHWK SE1 19 H2
Kippington Dr ELTH/MOT SE9 142 D5
Kirby Cl BARK/HLT IG6 53 L8
HARH RM3 57 G7
HOR/WEW KT19 168 F7
LOU IG10 52 E2 2
NTHWD HA6 41 M8
Kirby Gv STHWK SE1 19 J1
Kirby Rd RDART DA2 147 J4
Kirby St HCIRC EC1N 12 B2
Kirchen Rd WEA W13 98 B6
Kirkcaldy Gn OXHEY WD19 42 C5 3
Kirkdale SYD SE26 140 B6
Kirkdale Rd WAN E11 87 L1
Kirkfield Cl WEA W13 98 B7 4
Kirkham Rd EHAM E6 106 E5
Kirkham St WOOL/PLUM SE18 125 L4
Kirkland Av CLAY IG5 71 G3
Kirkland Cl BFN/LL DA15 143 L3
Kirk La WOOL/PLUM SE18 125 J4
Kirkleas Rd SURB KT6 167 L3
Kirklees Rd BCTR RM8 90 C5 1
THHTH CR7 157 G8
Kirkley Rd WIM/MER SW19 155 G4
Kirkly Cl SAND/SEL CR2 184 E2
Kirkmichael Rd POP/IOD E14 105 J5 6
Kirk Rd WALTH E17 68 F7
Kirkside Rd BKHTH/KID SE3 124 A4
Kirk's Pl POP/IOD E14 104 F4 4
Kirkstall Av TOTM N17 67 K5
Kirkstall Gdns
BRXS/STRHM SW2 138 D5
Kirkstall Rd BRXS/STRHM SW2 138 E5
Kirksted Rd MRDN SM4 170 B3
Kirkstone Wy BMLY BR1 159 L3
Kirkton Rd SEVS/STOTM N15 67 L5
Kirkwall Pl BETH E2 104 C2 11
Kirkwood Rd PECK SE15 122 B7
Kirn Rd WEA W13 98 B6 3
Kirrane Cl NWMAL KT3 153 M8
Kirtley Rd SYD SE26 140 E8
Kirtling St VX/NE SW8 120 C5
Kirton Cl CHSWK W4 117 K2 7
HCH RM12 92 C6
Kirton Gdns BETH E2 7 M8
Kirton Rd PLSTW E13 106 C1
Kirton Wk EDGW HA8 63 J1
Kitcat Ter BOW E3 105 G2
Kitchener Rd EFNCH N2 65 L4
FSTGT E7 88 B6
THHTH CR7 157 K6
TOTM N17 67 L4
WALTH E17 69 H2
Kitley Gdns NRWD SE19 157 M4
Kitson Rd BARN SW13 118 A6
CMBW SE5 121 J5
Kittiwake Cl SAND/SEL CR2 185 L3
Kittiwake Rd NTHLT UB5 96 D2
Kittiwake Wy YEAD UB4 96 D4
Kitto Rd NWCR SE14 122 D7
Kitt's End Rd BAR EN5 33 L2
Kiver Rd ARCH N19 84 E2
Klea Av BAL SW12 138 C3
Knapdale Cl FSTH SE23 140 B6
Knapmill Rd CAT SE6 141 G6
Knapmill Wy CAT SE6 141 G6
Knapp Cl WLSDN NW10 81 L6
Knapp Rd ASHF TW15 130 F8 2
BOW E3 105 G3
Knapton Ms TOOT SW17 156 A2 2
Knaresborough Dr
WAND/EARL SW18 137 H5
Knaresborough Pl ECT SW5 14 C5
Knatchbull Rd CMBW SE5 121 H7
WLSDN NW10 81 K8 2
Knebworth Av WALTH E17 69 G2
Knebworth Pth BORE WD6 32 D7 2
Knebworth Rd
STNW/STAM N16 85 L4 2
Knee Hl ABYW SE2 126 C2
Knee Hill Crs ABYW SE2 126 C2
Kneller Gdns ISLW TW7 133 K3
Kneller Rd BROCKY SE4 140 E1
NWMAL KT3 168 E2
WHTN TW2 133 J3
Knighten St WAP E1W 104 B7 9
Knightland Rd CLPT E5 86 B2
Knighton Cl ROMW/RG RM7 73 K7 1
SAND/SEL CR2 184 B2
WFD IG8 52 B6
Knighton Dr WFD IG8 52 B6
Knighton La BKHH IG9 52 B4
Knighton Park Rd SYD SE26 158 D1
Knighton Rd FSTGT E7 88 A3
ROMW/RG RM7 73 J7
Knighton-way La DEN/HRF UB9 76 B5
Knightrider Ct BLKFR EC4V 12 E5 2
Knightrider St BLKFR EC4V 12 D6
Knight's Av EA W5 98 E8
Knightsbridge KTBR SW1X 15 M2
SKENS SW7 15 K2
Knightsbridge Crs STA TW18 148 B2
Knightsbridge Gdns
ROMW/RG RM7 73 K6
Knightsbridge Gn KTBR SW1X 15 L2 1
Knight's Hl WNWD SE27 157 H1
Knight's Hill Sq WNWD SE27 139 H8 3
Knight's La ED N9 50 A5 3
Knights Manor Wy DART DA1 146 F3
Knight's Pk KUT KT1 152 E6
Knights Rdg ORP BR6 177 H7 1
Knights Rd CAN/RD E16 106 A7
STAN HA7 44 C6
Knights Wy BARK/HLT IG6 53 J8
Knightswood Cl EDGW HA8 45 J4 1
Knightwood Crs NWMAL KT3 168 E1
Knivet Rd FUL/PGN SW6 119 G4 3
Knobs Hill Rd SRTFD E15 87 H8
Knockholt Rd ELTH/MOT SE9 142 D2
Knole Cl CROY/NA CR0 173 J1 2
Knole Rd DART DA1 146 A4
The Knole ELTH/MOT SE9 143 G8
Knoll Crs NTHWD HA6 59 L3
Knoll Dr STHGT/OAK N14 48 A2
Knollmead BRYLDS KT5 168 C3
Knoll Ri ORP BR6 176 F3
Knoll Rd BXLY DA5 145 G4
SCUP DA14 162 B1
WAND/EARL SW18 137 J2
Knolls Cl WPK KT4 169 H5
The Knoll BECK BR3 159 H4
COB KT11 178 A6
HAYES BR2 175 G4
WEA W13 98 C4
Knolly's Cl WNWD SE27 139 G7 2
Knolly's Rd STRHM/NOR SW16 139 G7
Knottisford St BETH E2 104 D2 4
Knotts Green Rd LEY E10 69 J7
Knowle Av BXLYHN DA7 126 E5
Knowle Cl BRXN/ST SW9 121 G8 3
Knowle Gn STA TW18 148 A1
Knowle Park Av STA TW18 148 B2
Knowle Rd HAYES BR2 175 L4
WHTN TW2 133 L5 3
Knowles Cl WDR/YW UB7 94 E7
Knowles Ct HRW HA1 61 M7 2
Knowles Hill Crs LEW SE13 141 K2
Knowlton Gn HAYES BR2 159 M8
Knowl Wy BORE WD6 31 M8
Knowsley Av STHL UB1 97 H7
Knowsley Rd BTSEA SW11 119 M7
Knox Rd FSTGT E7 88 A6
Knox St MBLAR W1H 9 L2
Knoyle St NWCR SE14 122 E4
Knutsford Av WATN WD24 29 K3
Kohat Rd WIM/MER SW19 155 H1
Koh-i-noor Av BUSH WD23 43 G1
Koonowla Cl BH/WHM TN16 187 K8
Korda Cl SHPTN TW17 148 F6
Kossuth St GNWCH SE10 123 L3 3
Kramer Ms ECT SW5 14 B8
Kuala Gdns STRHM/NOR SW16 156 F4
Kydbrook Cl STMC/STPC BR5 176 C2
Kylemore Cl EHAM E6 106 D1 2
Kylemore Rd KIL/WHAMP NW6 2 A1
Kymberley Rd HRW HA1 61 L7 2
Kyme Rd ROM RM1 73 M7
Kynance Cl HARH RM3 56 C5
Kynance Gdns STAN HA7 62 C2
Kynance Ms KENS W8 14 D4
Kynance Pl KENS W8 14 E4
Kynaston Av THHTH CR7 157 J8
Kynaston Cl KTN/HRWW/W HA3 61 K1
Kynaston Crs THHTH CR7 157 J8 1
Kynaston Rd BMLY BR1 160 A1
ENC/FH EN2 36 D4
STMC/STPC BR5 177 H2
STNW/STAM N16 85 L3
THHTH CR7 157 J8
Kynaston Wd
KTN/HRWW/W HA3 61 K1
Kynersley Cl CAR SM5 170 F5 2
Kynoch Rd UED N18 50 D6
Kyrle Rd BTSEA SW11 138 A3
Kytes Dr GSTN WD25 21 K6
Kyverdale Rd STNW/STAM N16 67 M8

L

Laburnham Gdns UPMR RM14 75 M8
Laburnum Av DART DA1 146 C5
ED N9 49 L4
HCH RM12 92 A2
SUT SM1 170 E5 1
SWLY BR8 163 K6
TOTM N17 67 K1
WDR/YW UB7 94 F6
Laburnum Cl CHES/WCR EN8 26 D4
CHING E4 50 F8 2
Laburnum Ct STAN HA7 44 C6 1
Laburnum Crs SUN TW16 150 B4 2
Laburnum Gdns CROY/NA CR0 173 K2
Laburnum Gv CDALE/KGS NW9 63 J8
HSLW TW3 132 F1
NWMAL KT3 153 K5
STHL UB1 96 F3
WCHMH N21 49 J4
Laburnum Rd EPSOM KT18 180 E6
HYS/HAR UB3 113 M2
MTCM CR4 156 A5
WIM/MER SW19 155 J3
Laburnum St BETH E2 7 L4
Laburnum Wk HCH RM12 92 C5
Laburnum Wy HAYES BR2 176 A2
STWL/WRAY TW19 130 F5 2
Lacebark Cl BFN/LL DA15 143 M4
Lacey Cl ED N9 50 A4 5
Lacey Dr BCTR RM8 90 C3 4
EDGW HA8 44 E6
HPTN TW12 150 F4
Lackington St SDTCH EC2A 13 H2
Lackmore Rd EN EN1 26 C8 2
Lacock Cl WIM/MER SW19 155 J2
Lacon Rd EDUL SE22 140 A1
Lacy Rd PUT/ROE SW15 136 D1
Ladas Rd WNWD SE27 157 J1
Ladbroke Crs NTGHL W11 100 E5 5
Ladbroke Gdns NTGHL W11 100 F6
Ladbroke Gv NKENS W10 100 E4
Ladbroke Ms NTGHL W11 100 E7 3
Ladbroke Rd EN EN1 49 M1
EPSOM KT18 180 D7
NTGHL W11 100 F7
Ladbroke Sq NTGHL W11 100 F6
Ladbroke Ter NTGHL W11 100 F6 4
Ladbroke Wk NTGHL W11 100 F7
Ladbrook Cl PIN HA5 60 F6
Ladbrooke Cl POTB/CUF EN6 23 G5 1
Ladbrooke Crs SCUP DA14 144 D7
Ladbrooke Dr POTB/CUF EN6 23 G5
Ladbrook Rd SNWD SE25 157 K6
Ladderstile Ride
RCHPK/HAM TW10 153 H1
Ladderswood Wy
FBAR/BDGN N11 48 C7 1
Ladds Wy SWLY BR8 163 K7
Lady Booth Rd KUT KT1 152 E5
Ladycroft Gdns ORP BR6 176 C7 2
Ladycroft Rd LEW SE13 123 H8
Ladycroft Wk STAN HA7 62 D2
Ladycroft Wy ORP BR6 176 C7
Ladygate La RSLP HA4 59 J7
Lady Hay WPK KT4 168 F4
Lady Margaret Rd ARCH N19 84 C4
KTTN NW5 84 C5
STHL UB1 96 F3
Ladymount WLGTN SM6 171 K6 3
Lady's Cl WATW WD18 29 J7
Ladysmith Av EHAM E6 106 E1
GNTH/NBYPK IG2 71 K8
Ladysmith Rd CAN/RD E16 105 M2
ELTH/MOT SE9 143 G3
EN EN1 36 F5
KTN/HRWW/W HA3 61 L3
TOTM N17 68 A3
UED N18 50 B7
Lady Somerset Rd KTTN NW5 84 B4
Ladywell Rd LEW SE13 141 G2
Ladywell St SRTFD E15 87 M8 3
Ladywood Av STMC/STPC BR5 161 L8
Ladywood Rd SURB KT6 168 A4
Lafone Av FELT TW13 132 C6 1
Lafone St STHWK SE1 19 L1
Lagado Ms BERM/RHTH SE16 104 D7
Lagonda Av BARK/HLT IG6 53 M8 2
Lagonda Wy DART DA1 146 C1
Laidlaw Dr WCHMH N21 35 M8
Laing Cl CHIG IG7 53 K8
Laing Dean NTHLT UB5 78 C8
Laings Av MTCM CR4 155 M5
Lainlock Pl HSLW TW3 115 H6 3
Lainson St WAND/EARL SW18 137 G4 3
Lairdale Cl DUL SE21 139 J5
Laitwood Rd BAL SW12 138 B5
Lake Av BMLY BR1 160 A2
RAIN RM13 110 D1
Lakedale Rd WOOL/PLUM SE18 125 L2
Lake Dr BUSH WD23 43 J4
Lakefield Rd WDGN N22 67 H3
Lakefields Cl RAIN RM13 110 D1 3
Lake Gdns DAGE RM10 91 G5
RCHPK/HAM TW10 134 B7
WLGTN SM6 171 H5
Lakehall Gdns THHTH CR7 157 H8
Lakehall Rd THHTH CR7 157 H8
Lake House Rd WAN E11 88 A3
Lakehurst Rd HOR/WEW KT19 168 E7
Lakeland Cl CHIG IG7 54 B6
KTN/HRWW/W HA3 43 K8
Lakenheath STHGT/OAK N14 35 K8
Lake Ri ROM RM1 73 M4
Lake Rd CHDH RM6 72 D5
CROY/NA CR0 173 M4
DAGW RM9 109 H2
WIM/MER SW19 154 F1
Lakeside BECK BR3 159 H6
ENC/FH EN2 35 K7
HOR/WEW KT19 168 E8
RAIN RM13 110 E1
WEA W13 98 C5 2
WEY KT13 164 E4 1
WLGTN SM6 171 H6
Lakeside Av REDBR IG4 70 D5
THMD SE28 108 A7
Lakeside Cl BFN/LL DA15 144 C2
CHIG IG7 53 M6
RSLP HA4 59 J5
SNWD SE25 158 A5 2
Lakeside Crs EBAR EN4 47 M1
Lakeside Dr ESH/CLAY KT10 166 C8
HAYES BR2 175 L5
Lakeside Gra WEY KT13 164 C5
Lakeside Rd CHES/WCR EN8 26 C1
PLMGR N13 48 F6
WKENS W14 118 D1
Lakeside Wy WBLY HA9 81 G4
Lakes Rd HAYES BR2 175 J7
Lakeswood Rd STMC/STPC BR5 176 B1
The Lake BUSH WD23 43 K3
Lake Vw EDGW HA8 44 F7
POTB/CUF EN6 23 J6 3
Lakeview Rd WELL DA16 144 B1
WNWD SE27 157 G1
Lakis Cl HAMP NW3 83 J4 5
Laleham Av MLHL NW7 45 K5
Laleham Cl STA TW18 148 B4
Laleham Rd CAT SE6 141 J4
SHPTN TW17 148 F7
Lalor St FUL/PGN SW6 118 E7
Lambarde Av ELTH/MOT SE9 143 G8
Lamb Cl GSTN WD25 21 J7
Lamberhurst Cl
STMC/STPC BR5 177 K3 2
Lamberhurst Rd BCTR RM8 90 E1
WNWD SE27 139 G8
Lambert Av RCH/KEW TW9 117 G8
Lambert Ct BUSH WD23 29 K7
Lambert Rd BNSTD SM7 182 A7
BRXS/STRHM SW2 138 E2
CAN/RD E16 106 B5
NFNCH/WDSP N12 47 K7
Lambert's Rd SURB KT6 152 E8
Lambert St IS N1 6 A2
Lambert Wy NFNCH/WDSP N12 47 J7
Lambeth Br WEST SW1P 17 K5
Lambeth High St STHWK SE1 17 L6
Lambeth Hl BLKFR EC4V 12 E6
Lambeth Palace Rd STHWK SE1 17 L4
Lambeth Rd CROY/NA CR0 172 A2 1
STHWK SE1 18 A4
Lambeth Wk LBTH SE11 17 M5
Lamb La HACK E8 86 B7
Lamble St KTTN NW5 84 A4 3
Lambley Rd DAGW RM9 90 B6
Lambolle Pl HAMP NW3 83 L6
Lambolle Rd HAMP NW3 83 L6
Lambourn Cha RAD WD7 30 F1 1
Lambourn Cl HNWL W7 97 M8
Lambourne Av WIM/MER SW19 136 F8
Lambourne Cl CHIG IG7 54 B5
Lambourne Ct UX/CGN UB8 76 B8 1
Lambourne Crs CHIG IG7 54 B4
Lambourne Gdns BARK IG11 89 M7 2
CHING E4 51 G4
EN EN1 36 F5
HCH RM12 92 D2
Lambourne Gv KUT KT1 153 H5 1
Lambourne Pl
BKHTH/KID SE3 124 B6 1
Lambourne Rd BARK IG11 89 L7
CHIG IG7 53 M6
GDMY/SEVK IG3 89 L2
WAN E11 69 J8 2
Lambourn Rd CLAP SW4 120 B8
Lambrook Ter FUL/PGN SW6 118 E6
Lambs Cl POTB/CUF EN6 24 F2
Lamb's Conduit St BMSBY WC1N 11 L1
Lambscroft Av LEE/GVPK SE12 142 C7
Lamb's La North RAIN RM13 110 D3
Lamb's La South RAIN RM13 110 C4
Lambs Meadow WFD IG8 70 D3 2
Lamb's Pas STLK EC1Y 13 G1
Lamb St WCHPL E1 13 L2
Lambs Wk ENC/FH EN2 36 C5 3
Lambton Av CHES/WCR EN8 26 D6 1
Lambton Pl NTGHL W11 100 F6 5
Lambton Rd ARCH N19 84 E1 1
RYNPK SW20 154 C5 1
Lamb Wk STHWK SE1 19 J2
Lamerock Rd BMLY BR1 141 M8
Lamerton Rd BARK/HLT IG6 71 H3
Lamerton St DEPT SE8 123 G4 7
Lamford Cl TOTM N17 67 K1
Lamington St HMSMTH W6 118 B2 6
Lamlash St LBTH SE11 18 C5
Lammas Av MTCM CR4 156 A5
Lammas La ESH/CLAY KT10 166 A6
Lammas Park Gdns EA W5 98 C7
Lammas Rd HOM E9 86 D7 5
LEY E10 86 E2
RCHPK/HAM TW10 134 C8
WATW WD18 29 J8 3
Lammermoor Rd BAL SW12 138 B4 2
Lamont Rd WBPTN SW10 119 K4
Lamorbey Cl BFN/LL DA15 143 M6
Lamorna Cl ORP BR6 177 G2 4
WALTH E17 69 J3
Lamorna Gv STAN HA7 62 D2
Lampard Gv STNW/STAM N16 85 M1
Lamplighter Cl WCHPL E1 104 C3 7
Lamplighters Cl DART DA1 146 F3 1
Lampmead Rd LEW SE13 141 L2
Lamport Cl WOOL/PLUM SE18 124 F2
Lampton Av HEST TW5 115 G6
Lampton House Cl
WIM/MER SW19 136 D8 1
Lampton Park Rd HSLW TW3 115 H7 2
Lampton Rd HSLW TW3 115 H7
Lamson Rd RAIN RM13 109 M4
Lanacre Av CDALE/KGS NW9 63 L2
Lanark Cl EA W5 98 C4
Lanark Pl MV/WKIL W9 2 F9
Lanark Rd MV/WKIL W9 2 D6
Lanbury Rd PECK SE15 140 D1
Lancaster Av BARK IG11 89 L7
EBAR EN4 34 D3
MTCM CR4 156 E8
WAN E11 70 B5
WIM/MER SW19 154 D1
WNWD SE27 139 H6
Lancaster Cl CDALE/KGS NW9 63 M1 1
HAYES BR2 159 M7
STWL/WRAY TW19 130 E3 3
TOTM N17 68 A1 1
Lancaster Ct WOT/HER KT12 165 G2
Lancaster Dr HAMP NW3 83 L6
HCH RM12 92 B5
LOU IG10 52 E1
POP/IOD E14 105 J7
Lancaster Gdn KUTN/CMB KT2 152 D1
Lancaster Gdns EFNCH N2 65 K2
WIM/MER SW19 154 E1
Lancaster Ga BAY/PAD W2 8 E7
Lancaster Gv HAMP NW3 83 K6
Lancaster Ms BAY/PAD W2 8 F6
RCHPK/HAM TW10 134 E3 1
WAND/EARL SW18 137 H2 3
Lancaster Pk
RCHPK/HAM TW10 134 E2
Lancaster Pl TWK TW1 134 A4
WIM/MER SW19 154 D1 3
Lancaster Rd UX/CGN UB8 76 D6
EBAR EN4 34 D8
ENC/FH EN2 36 D4
FBAR/BDGN N11 48 D8
FSBYPK N4 67 G8
FSTGT E7 88 A7
NTGHL W11 100 E5 6
NTHLT UB5 79 J6
RYLN/HDSTN HA2 61 G6
SNWD SE25 157 M5
STHL UB1 96 E6
UED N18 49 M7
WALTH E17 68 D3
WAN E11 87 L2
WIM/MER SW19 154 D1
WLSDN NW10 81 M5
Lancaster Stables HAMP NW3 83 L6 1
Lancaster St STHWK SE1 18 C2
Lancaster Ter BAY/PAD W2 9 G6
Lancaster Wk HYS/HAR UB3 95 J5 1
Lancaster Wy ABLGY WD5 20 F4 2
Lancefield St MV/WKIL W9 100 F2
Lancell St STNW/STAM N16 85 L2 4
Lancelot Av ALP/SUD HA0 80 D4
Lancelot Crs ALP/SUD HA0 80 D4

Lancelot Gdns *EBAR* EN4 ...... 48 A2
Lancelot Pl *SKENS* SW7 ...... 15 L2
Lancelot Rd *ALP/SUD* HA0 ...... 80 D4
  BARK/HLT IG6 ...... 53 L8 8
  WELL DA16 ...... 144 A1
Lance Rd *HRW* HA1 ...... 61 J8
Lancey Cl *CHARL* SE7 ...... 124 E2 2
Lanchester Rd *HGT* N6 ...... 65 M6
Lancing Gdns *ED* N9 ...... 49 M3
Lancing Rd *CROY/NA* CR0 ...... 171 M1
  FELT TW13 ...... 131 M6
  GNTH/NBYPK IG2 ...... 71 K7
  HARH RM3 ...... 74 E1
  ORP BR6 ...... 177 H4
  WEA W13 ...... 98 B6 8
Lancing St *CAMTN* NW1 ...... 5 C8
Lancing Wy *RKW/CH/CXG* WD3 ...... 28 B8
Lancresse Ct *UX/CGN* UB8 ...... 76 C6 8
Landale Gdns *DART* DA1 ...... 146 C5
Landau Wy *ERITH* DA8 ...... 128 D3
Landcroft Rd *EDUL* SE22 ...... 139 M3
Landells Rd *EDUL* SE22 ...... 139 M3
Landford Cl *RKW/CH/CXG* WD3 ...... 40 E4
Landford Rd *PUT/ROE* SW15 ...... 118 C8
Landgrove Rd *WIM/MER* SW19 ...... 155 C1
Landmann Wy *NWCR* SE14 ...... 122 D4
Landmead Rd *CHES/WCR* EN8 ...... 26 E2
Landon Pl *KTBR* SW1X 15 L3
Landons Cl *POP/IOD* E14 ...... 105 J7
Landon Wy *ASHF* TW15 ...... 149 H2 2
Landor Rd *BRXN/ST* SW9 ...... 120 E8
Landor Wk *SHB* W12 ...... 100 A8
Landra Gdns *WCHMH* N21 ...... 49 H1
Landridge Rd *FUL/PGN* SW6 ...... 118 E2
Landrock Rd *CEND/HSY/T* N8 ...... 66 E2
Landscape Rd *WFD* IG8 ...... 70 B1
Landseer Av *MNPK* E12 ...... 89 C3
Landseer Cl *EDGW* HA8 ...... 63 C3
  HCH RM12 ...... 92 B1 8
  WIM/MER SW19 ...... 155 K4 8
Landseer Rd *ARCH* N19 ...... 84 E3
  EN EN1 ...... 37 C8
  NWMAL KT3 ...... 168 D2
  SUT SM1 ...... 170 A8
Lands' End *BORE* WD6 ...... 44 D1
Landstead Rd
  WOOL/PLUM SE18 ...... 125 K5
The Landway *STMC/STPC* BR5 ...... 162 C6
Lane Cl *CRICK* NW2 ...... 82 B3
Lane End *BXLYHN* DA7 ...... 127 H8
  EPSOM KT18 ...... 180 B7
Lane Gdns *BUSH* WD23 ...... 43 L3
Lanercost Cl *STHGT/OAK* N14 ...... 48 E1
Lanercost Rd
  BRXS/STRHM SW2 ...... 139 G6
  EDGW HA8 ...... 45 J7
Laneside *CHST* BR7 ...... 161 H1
  EDGW HA8 ...... 45 J7
Laneside Av *BCTR* RM8 ...... 72 B8
The Lane *BKHTH/KID* SE3 ...... 124 A8
  CHERT KT16 ...... 148 A6
Laneway *PUT/ROE* SW15 ...... 136 B2 2
Lanfranc Rd *BOW* E3 ...... 104 E1 2
Lanfrey Pl *WKENS* W14 ...... 118 F3 2
Langbourne Av *HGT* N6 ...... 84 A2
Langbourne Wy
  ESH/CLAY KT10 ...... 166 F8
Langbrook Rd *BKHTH/KID* SE3 ...... 124 D8
Langcroft Cl *CAR* SM5 ...... 170 F5 8
Langdale Av *MTCM* CR4 ...... 155 M6
Langdale Cl *BCTR* RM8 ...... 90 C1
  MORT/ESHN SW14 ...... 135 H1 8
  ORP BR6 ...... 176 B5 8
  WALW SE17 ...... 18 E9 2
Langdale Crs *BXLYHN* DA7 ...... 127 G6
Langdale Dr *YEAD* UB4 ...... 95 L1
Langdale Gdns *HCH* RM12 ...... 92 A5
  PEND EN3 ...... 26 D8
Langdale Rd *GNWCH* SE10 ...... 123 J5
  THHTH CR7 ...... 157 G7
Langdon Ct *WLSDN* NW10 ...... 81 L8 2
Langdon Crs *EHAM* E6 ...... 107 C2
Langdon Dr *CDALE/KGS* NW9 ...... 81 J1
Langdon Park Rd *HGT* N6 ...... 66 B8
Langdon Pl
  MORT/ESHN SW14 ...... 117 J8 2
Langdon Rd *HAYES* BR2 ...... 160 B6
  MRDN SM4 ...... 155 J8
Langdon Shaw *SCUP* DA14 ...... 161 M1
Langdon Wk *MRDN* SM4 ...... 155 J8 2
Langford Cl *HACK* E8 ...... 86 A5 8
  SEVS/STOTM N15 ...... 67 L7 8
Langford Crs *EBAR* EN4 ...... 34 F7
Langford Pl *SCUP* DA14 ...... 144 A7
  STJWD NW8 ...... 2 F6
Langford Rd *EBAR* EN4 ...... 34 F7
  FUL/PGN SW6 ...... 119 H7 2
  WFD IG8 ...... 52 C8 2
Langfords *BKHH* IG9 ...... 52 D4
Langham Av *EMPK* RM11 ...... 74 D8
Langham Dene *PUR/KEN* CR8 ...... 184 B8
Langham Gdns *ALP/SUD* HA0 ...... 80 C2
  EDGW HA8 ...... 63 J1
  RCHPK/HAM TW10 ...... 134 C4
  WCHMH N21 ...... 36 A3
  WEA W13 ...... 98 B6
Langham House Cl
  RCHPK/HAM TW10 ...... 134 D8
Langham Pl *CAVSQ/HST* W1G 10 D3
  CHSWK W4 ...... 117 L5 2
  SEVS/STOTM N15 ...... 67 H4 2
Langham Rd *EDGW* HA8 ...... 45 J8
  RYNPK SW20 ...... 154 C4
  SEVS/STOTM N15 ...... 67 J5
  TEDD TW11 ...... 152 B1
Langham St *GTPST* W1W 10 E3
  REGST W1B 10 D3 2
Langhedge Cl *UED* N18 ...... 49 M8 2
Langhedge La *UED* N18 ...... 49 M7
Langholm Cl *BAL* SW12 ...... 138 D4 2
Langholme *BUSH* WD23 ...... 43 J3
Langhorn Dr *WHTN* TW2 ...... 133 L4
Langhorne Rd *DAGE* RM10 ...... 91 G7
Langland Ct *NTHWD* HA6 ...... 59 J7
Langland Crs *STAN* HA7 ...... 62 D4
Langland Dr *PIN* HA5 ...... 60 L1
Langland Gdns *CROY/NA* CR0 ...... 173 M4
  HAMP NW3 ...... 83 H5

Langlands Ri *HOR/WEW* KT19 ...... 180 C6
Langler Rd *WLSDN* NW10 ...... 100 C1
Langley Av *RSLP* HA4 ...... 78 B2
  SURB KT6 ...... 167 K3
  WPK KT4 ...... 169 K4
Langleybury La *KGLGY* WD4 ...... 20 B1
  WAT WD17 ...... 28 B2
Langley Cl *HARH* RM3 ...... 74 D1 2
  EDGW HA8 ...... 45 J3 2
  HYS/HAR UB3 ...... 113 H6 2
  KGLGY WD4 ...... 20 A3
  WAN E11 ...... 70 B8
Langley Dr *ACT* W3 ...... 99 H8
  WAN E11 ...... 70 B8
Langley Gdns *DAGW* RM9 ...... 90 D7
  STMC/STPC BR5 ...... 176 B1
Langley Gv *NWMAL* KT3 ...... 153 K5
Langley Hill Cl *KGLGY* WD4 ...... 20 A1
Langley La *ABLGY* WD5 ...... 20 F4
  VX/NE SW8 ...... 17 K9
Langley Oaks Av *SAND/SEL* CR2 ...... 185 G3
Langley Pk *EDGW* HA8 ...... 45 L8
Langley Park Rd *BELMT* SM2 ...... 170 C8
Langley Rd *ABLGY* WD5 ...... 20 E4
  BECK BR3 ...... 158 D7
  ISLW TW7 ...... 115 M7
  SAND/SEL CR2 ...... 185 K2 2
  SURB KT6 ...... 167 L2 2
  WAT WD17 ...... 28 F4
  WELL DA16 ...... 126 C4
  WIM/MER SW19 ...... 154 F4
Langley Rw *BAR* EN5 ...... 33 K1
Langley St *LSQ/SEVD* WC2H 11 J5 8
Langley Wy *WAT* WD17 ...... 28 F4
  WWKM BR4 ...... 174 D3
Langmead Dr *BUSH* WD23 ...... 43 K3
Langmead St *WNWD* SE27 ...... 139 J8 8
Langport Ct *WOT/HER* KT12 ...... 165 J3
Langridge Ms *HPTN* TW12 ...... 150 F2 2
Langroyd Rd *TOOT* SW17 ...... 137 M6
Langside Av *PUT/ROE* SW15 ...... 136 A1
Langside Crs *STHGT/OAK* N14 ...... 48 D5
Langston Hughes Cl
  HNHL SE24 ...... 139 H1 8
Lang St *WCHPL* E1 ...... 104 C3
Langthorn Ct *LOTH* EC2R 13 H4 2
Langthorne Rd *WAN* E11 ...... 87 K3
Langthorne St *FUL/PGN* SW6 ...... 118 D6
Langton Av *EHAM* E6 ...... 107 G2
  EW KT17 ...... 180 F4
  TRDG/WHET N20 ...... 47 J2
Langton Cl *FSBYW* WC1X 5 M8
Langton Gv *NTHWD* HA6 ...... 41 J7
Langton Ri *EDUL* SE22 ...... 140 B4
Langton Rd *BRXN/ST* SW9 ...... 121 H5
  CRICK NW2 ...... 82 C3
  E/WMO/HCT KT8 ...... 151 J8
  KTN/HRWW/W HA3 ...... 61 J1
Langton St *WBPTN* SW10 ...... 119 J4
Langton Wy *BKHTH/KID* SE3 ...... 124 A5
  CROY/NA CR0 ...... 172 A6
Langtry Pl *NTHLT* UB5 ...... 96 J1 2
Langtry Rd *KIL/WHAMP* NW6 ...... 2 C4
  NTHLT UB5 ...... 95 H2
Langwood Cha *TEDD* TW11 ...... 152 C2
Langwood Gdns *WAT* WD17 ...... 29 G4 2
Langworth Cl *RDART* DA2 ...... 146 D7
Langworth Dr *YEAD* UB4 ...... 96 B5
Lanhill Rd *MV/WKIL* W9 ...... 2 A9
Lanier Rd *LEW* SE13 ...... 141 J3
Lanigan Dr *HSLW* TW3 ...... 133 H2 2
Lankers Dr *RYLN/HDSTN* HA2 ...... 60 F7
Lankton Cl *BECK* BR3 ...... 159 J4
Lannock Rd *HYS/HAR* UB3 ...... 95 M7
Lannoy Rd *ELTH/MOT* SE9 ...... 143 J5
Lanrick Rd *POP/IOD* E14 ...... 105 K5
Lanridge Rd *ABYW* SE2 ...... 126 D1
Lansbury Av *BARK* IG11 ...... 90 A7
  CHDH RM6 ...... 72 B4
  EBED/NFELT TW14 ...... 132 B3
  UED N18 ...... 49 K7
Lansbury Cl *WLSDN* NW10 ...... 81 J5 2
Lansbury Crs *DART* DA1 ...... 147 G2
Lansbury Dr *YEAD* UB4 ...... 95 M2
Lansbury Gdns *POP/IOD* E14 ...... 105 K5 2
Lansbury Rd *PEND* EN3 ...... 37 K4
Lansbury Wy *UED* N18 ...... 49 L7 2
Lansdell Rd *MTCM* CR4 ...... 156 A5
Lansdown Cl *WOT/HER* KT12 ...... 165 J3 2
Lansdowne Av *BXLYHN* DA7 ...... 126 C5
  ORP BR6 ...... 176 B1
Lansdowne Cl *BRYLDS* KT5 ...... 168 B4 2
  RYNPK SW20 ...... 154 D3 2
  TWK TW1 ...... 133 M5 2
Lansdowne Crs *NTGHL* W11 ...... 100 E6
Lansdowne Dr *HACK* E8 ...... 86 A7
Lansdowne Gdns *VX/NE* SW8 ...... 120 E6
Lansdowne Gv *WLSDN* NW10 ...... 81 L4
Lansdowne Hl *WNWD* SE27 ...... 139 H7
Lansdowne La *CHARL* SE7 ...... 124 C5
Lansdowne Ms *CHARL* SE7 ...... 124 C3
  NTGHL W11 ...... 100 F7 2
Lansdowne Pl *NRWD* SE19 ...... 157 M3
  STHWK SE1 ...... 19 H4 2
Lansdowne Ri *NTGHL* W11 ...... 100 E6
Lansdowne Rd *BMLY* BR1 ...... 160 A3
  CHING E4 ...... 51 G4
  CROY/NA CR0 ...... 172 C4
  FNCH N3 ...... 64 F1
  GDMY/SEVK IG3 ...... 89 M1
  HACK E8 ...... 86 A6
  HOR/WEW KT19 ...... 180 C1
  HSLW TW3 ...... 115 H8 2
  MUSWH N10 ...... 66 C3
  NTGHL W11 ...... 100 F7 2
  PUR/KEN CR8 ...... 184 A5
  RYNPK SW20 ...... 154 C3
  STA TW18 ...... 148 B3
  STAN HA7 ...... 44 C8
  SWFD E18 ...... 70 A4
  TOTM N17 ...... 68 A2
  UX/CGN UB8 ...... 95 H5
  WALTH E17 ...... 69 G7
  WAN E11 ...... 87 M2
Lansdowne Ter *BMSBY* WC1N 11 K1
Lansdowne Wk *NTGHL* W11 ...... 100 E7
Lansdowne Wy *VX/NE* SW8 ...... 120 E6

Lansdowne Wood Cl
  WNWD SE27 ...... 139 H7 2
Lansdown Rd *FSTGT* E7 ...... 88 C7
  SCUP DA14 ...... 144 B7
Lansfield Av *UED* N18 ...... 50 A6 2
Lantern Cl *ALP/SUD* HA0 ...... 80 D5
  PUT/ROE SW15 ...... 136 A1
Lanterns Ct *POP/IOD* E14 ...... 123 C1
Lant St *STHWK* SE1 ...... 18 E1
Lanvanor Rd *PECK* SE15 ...... 122 C7
Lapford Cl *MV/WKIL* W9 ...... 100 F3 7
Lapse Wood Wk *DUL* SE21 ...... 140 B5 8
Lapstone Gdns
  KTN/HRWW/W HA3 ...... 62 C7
Lapwing Cl *CROY/NA* CR0 ...... 185 L3
  ERITH DA8 ...... 128 B5 2
Lapwing Wy *ABLGY* WD5 ...... 21 C4 8
  YEAD UB4 ...... 96 D5 8
Lapworth Cl *ORP* BR6 ...... 177 J4
Lapworth Ct *BAY/PAD* W2 ...... 8 D2
Lara Cl *CHSGTN* KT9 ...... 179 L1 8
  LEW SE13 ...... 141 J5
Larbert Rd *STRHM/NOR* SW16 ...... 156 C4
Larby Pl *EW* KT17 ...... 180 E3 8
Larch Av *ACT* W3 ...... 99 L7
  LCOL/BKTW AL2 ...... 21 L3
Larch Cl *BAL* SW12 ...... 155 L1
  DEPT SE8 ...... 122 F4 8
  FBAR/BDGN N11 ...... 48 A8
Larch Crs *HOR/WEW* KT19 ...... 168 B8
  YEAD UB4 ...... 96 C4
Larch Dene *ORP* BR6 ...... 176 A4
Larches Av *EN* EN1 ...... 37 J1
  MORT/ESHN SW14 ...... 135 K1 8
The Larches *BUSH* WD23 ...... 29 L8
  HGDN/ICK UB10 ...... 95 H1
  PLMGR N13 ...... 49 J5
Larch Rd *CRICK* NW2 ...... 82 C4
  DART DA1 ...... 146 D5
  LEY E10 ...... 87 G2 2
Larch Tree Wy *CROY/NA* CR0 ...... 174 A5
Larchwood Av *CRW* RM5 ...... 55 H8
Larchwood Cl *CRW* RM5 ...... 55 J8
Larchwood Rd *ELTH/MOT* SE9 ...... 143 H6 2
Larcombe Cl *CROY/NA* CR0 ...... 172 F6
Larcom St *WALW* SE17 ...... 18 F6
Larden Rd *ACT* W3 ...... 99 L8
Largewood Av *SURB* KT6 ...... 168 A4
Larissa St *WALW* SE17 ...... 19 H6 8
Larkbere Rd *SYD* SE26 ...... 140 E8
Larkfield *BUSH* WD23 ...... 43 J3
Larken Dr *BUSH* WD23 ...... 43 J3
Larkfield Av *KTN/HRWW/W* HA3 ...... 62 B4
Larkfield Cl *HAYES* BR2 ...... 176 A8
Larkfield Rd *RCH/KEW* TW9 ...... 134 E1 2
  SCUP DA14 ...... 143 M7
Larkhall Cl *WOT/HER* KT12 ...... 165 J8 2
Larkhall La *CLAP* SW4 ...... 120 D7
Larkhall Ri *CLAP* SW4 ...... 120 C8
Larkham Cl *FELT* TW13 ...... 131 L2 2
Lark Rw *BETH* E2 ...... 86 C8 2
Larkshall Crs *CHING* E4 ...... 51 J6
Larkshall Rd *CHING* E4 ...... 51 K8 2
Larkspur Cl *CDALE/KGS* NW9 ...... 63 H6
  ORP BR6 ...... 177 J4 2
  RSLP HA4 ...... 59 H8
Larkspur Gv *EDGW* HA8 ...... 45 J6
Larkspur Wy *HOR/WEW* KT19 ...... 168 C7
Larkswood Cl *ERITH* DA8 ...... 128 A6
Larkswood Ri *PIN* HA5 ...... 60 C5
Larkswood Rd *CHING* E4 ...... 51 G6
Lark Wy *CAR* SM5 ...... 170 E2
Larkway Cl *CDALE/KGS* NW9 ...... 63 K5
Larmans Rd *PEND* EN3 ...... 37 J1 2
Larnach Rd *HMSMTH* W6 ...... 118 C4
Larne Rd *RSLP* HA4 ...... 59 M8
Larner Rd *ERITH* DA8 ...... 127 L5
Larpent Av *PUT/ROE* SW15 ...... 136 C2
Larsen Dr *WAB* EN9 ...... 27 K7 2
Larwood Cl *NTHLT* UB5 ...... 79 K5
Lascelles Av *HRW* HA1 ...... 61 K8
Lascelles Cl *WAN* E11 ...... 87 K2 2
Lascott's Rd *WDGN* N22 ...... 48 F8
Lassa Rd *ELTH/MOT* SE9 ...... 142 E2
Lassell St *GNWCH* SE10 ...... 123 K3
Latchett Rd *SWFD* E18 ...... 70 B2
Latchford Pl *CHIG* IG7 ...... 54 B6
Latchingdon Gdns *WFD* IG8 ...... 52 E8 2
Latchmere Cl
  RCHPK/HAM TW10 ...... 152 L1
Latchmere La *KUTN/CMB* KT2 ...... 152 F2
Latchmere Rd *BTSEA* SW11 ...... 119 M7
  KUTN/CMB KT2 ...... 152 E2
Latchmere St *BTSEA* SW11 ...... 119 M7 2
Lateward Rd *BTFD* TW8 ...... 116 D4
Latham Cl *EHAM* E6 ...... 106 E5
  TWK TW1 ...... 133 M4
Latham Rd *BXLYHS* DA6 ...... 145 G2
  TWK TW1 ...... 133 M4
Latham's Wy *CROY/NA* CR0 ...... 171 M3
Lathkill Cl *EN* EN1 ...... 50 A2
Lathom Rd *EHAM* E6 ...... 88 F7
Latimer Av *EHAM* E6 ...... 88 F7
Latimer Cl *PIN* HA5 ...... 60 C2
  WATW WD18 ...... 41 L2
  WPK KT4 ...... 169 H6
Latimer Dr *HCH* RM12 ...... 92 D3
Latimer Gdns *PIN* HA5 ...... 60 C2
Latimer Pl *NKENS* W10 ...... 100 C5 2
Latimer Rd *BAR* EN5 ...... 34 B6
  CROY/NA CR0 ...... 172 B5 8
  FSTGT E7 ...... 88 B4
  NKENS W10 ...... 100 C4
  SEVS/STOTM N15 ...... 67 J7
  TEDD TW11 ...... 151 M1 2
  WIM/MER SW19 ...... 155 H2
Latona Rd *PECK* SE15 ...... 122 A4
La Tourne Gdns *ORP* BR6 ...... 176 C5 8
Lattimer Pl *CHSWK* W4 ...... 117 L5 2
Latton Cl *ESH/CLAY* KT10 ...... 166 B6
  WOT/HER KT12 ...... 165 M2
Latymer Ct *WEY* KT13 ...... 164 C6
Latymer Rd *ED* N9 ...... 49 M3
Latymer Wy *ED* N9 ...... 49 K4
Lauder Cl *NTHLT* UB5 ...... 96 D1 8
Lauderdale Dr
  RCHPK/HAM TW10 ...... 134 D7

Lauderdale Rd *ABLGY* WD5 ...... 20 C6
  MV/WKIL W9 ...... 2 D8
Laud St *CROY/NA* CR0 ...... 172 C5
  LBTH SE11 ...... 17 L7
Laughton Rd *NTHLT* UB5 ...... 96 D1
Launcelot Rd *BMLY* BR1 ...... 142 A8
Launceston Cl *HARH* RM3 ...... 74 C5
Launceston Gdns *GFD/PVL* UB6 ...... 80 C8
Launceston Pl *KENS* W8 ...... 14 D4
Launceston Rd *GFD/PVL* UB6 ...... 80 C8
Launch St *POP/IOD* E14 ...... 123 J1
Launder's La *RAIN* RM13 ...... 110 E4
Laundry La *ED* N9 ...... 49 M3
Laundry Rd *HMSMTH* W6 ...... 118 E4
Laura Cl *EN* EN1 ...... 36 E8
  WAN E11 ...... 70 C6
Lauradale Rd *EFNCH* N2 ...... 65 M5
Laura Pl *CLPT* E5 ...... 86 C4
Laurel Av *POTB/CUF* EN6 ...... 22 F5
  TWK TW1 ...... 133 M5
Laurel Bank Gdns
  FUL/PGN SW6 ...... 118 F7 7
Laurel Bank Rd *ENC/FH* EN2 ...... 36 C4
Laurel Cl *BARK/HLT* IG6 ...... 53 J8
  DART DA1 ...... 146 C5
  SCUP DA14 ...... 144 A7
  TOOT SW17 ...... 155 L1
Laurel Crs *CROY/NA* CR0 ...... 174 A5
  ROMW/RG RM7 ...... 91 L1
Laurel Dr *WCHMH* N21 ...... 49 G2
Laurel Flds *POTB/CUF* EN6 ...... 22 F4
Laurel Gdns *CHING* E4 ...... 51 H2 8
  HNWL W7 ...... 97 L7
  HSLWW TW4 ...... 132 E1
  MLHL NW7 ...... 45 K5
Laurel Gv *PGE/AN* SE20 ...... 158 B3
  SYD SE26 ...... 158 D1
Laurel La *WDR/YW* UB7 ...... 112 C2 8
Laurel Pk *KTN/HRWW/W* HA3 ...... 61 M1
  HPTN TW12 ...... 151 K1
Laurel Rd *BARN* SW13 ...... 118 A7
  HPTN TW12 ...... 151 K1
  RYNPK SW20 ...... 154 B4
Laurel St *HACK* E8 ...... 85 M6
Laurel Vw *NFNCH/WDSP* N12 ...... 47 H5
Laurel Vw *NFNCH/WDSP* N12 ...... 47 H5
  SWFD E18 ...... 69 M5
Laurence Ms *SHB* W12 ...... 100 A8 8
Laurence Pountney La
  CANST EC4R 13 G7
Laurence Pountney Hl
  CANST EC4R 13 G6 8
Laurie Gv *NWCR* SE14 ...... 122 E6
Laurie Rd *HNWL* W7 ...... 97 L4
Laurier Rd *CROY/NA* CR0 ...... 172 F2
  KTTN NW5 ...... 84 B3
Laurimel Cl *STAN* HA7 ...... 44 B8 8
Laurino Pl *BUSH* WD23 ...... 43 J4
Lauriston Rd *HOM* E9 ...... 86 D7
  WIM/MER SW19 ...... 136 D7 2
Lausanne Rd *CEND/HSY/T* N8 ...... 67 G5
  PECK SE15 ...... 123 L7
Lauser Rd *STWL/WRAY* TW19 ...... 130 C4
Lavell St *STNW/STAM* N16 ...... 85 L3
Lavender Av *CDALE/KGS* NW9 ...... 81 J1
  MTCM CR4 ...... 155 L4
  WPK KT4 ...... 169 J5
Lavender Cl *CAR* SM5 ...... 171 G6
  CHEL SW3 ...... 119 K4 8
  HARH RM3 ...... 74 D1
  HAYES BR2 ...... 175 L1
Lavender Ct
  E/WMO/HCT KT8 ...... 151 H6 2
Lavender Gdns *BTSEA* SW11 ...... 137 H1
  ENC/FH EN2 ...... 36 C3
  KTN/HRWW/W HA3 ...... 43 L8 2
Lavender Gv *HACK* E8 ...... 86 A7
  MTCM CR4 ...... 155 L4
Lavender Hl *BTSEA* SW11 ...... 119 M8
  ENC/FH EN2 ...... 36 C4
  SWLY BR8 ...... 163 K6
Lavender Pl *IL* IG1 ...... 89 H5
Lavender Ri *WDR/YW* UB7 ...... 95 G8
Lavender Rd *BERM/RHTH* SE16 ...... 104 E7
  BTSEA SW11 ...... 119 K8
  CAR SM5 ...... 171 G4
  CROY/NA CR0 ...... 171 M1
  ENC/FH EN2 ...... 36 D4
  HOR/WEW KT19 ...... 168 B7
  SUT SM1 ...... 170 D6 8
  UX/CGN UB8 ...... 94 F4
Lavender Sweep *BTSEA* SW11 ...... 137 H1
Lavender Ter *BTSEA* SW11 ...... 119 L8 2
Lavender V *WLGTN* SM6 ...... 171 K8
Lavender Vw *CROY/NA* CR0 ...... 173 K1
Lavengro Rd *WNWD* SE27 ...... 139 J6
Lavenham Rd
  WAND/EARL SW18 ...... 136 F6
Lavernock Rd *BXLYHN* DA7 ...... 127 G4
Lavers Rd *STNW/STAM* N16 ...... 85 L3
Laverstoke Gdns
  PUT/ROE SW15 ...... 135 M4
Laverton Ms *ECT* SW5 ...... 14 D6 8
Laverton Pl *ECT* SW5 ...... 14 D6
Lavidge Rd *ELTH/MOT* SE9 ...... 142 E6
Lavina Gv *IS* N1 ...... 5 L5
Lavington Rd *CROY/NA* CR0 ...... 171 G1
  WEA W13 ...... 98 B7
Lavington St *STHWK* SE1 ...... 12 D9
Lavinia Av *GSTN* WD25 ...... 21 J7
Lavinia Rd *DART* DA1 ...... 146 F3
Lavrock La *RKW/CH/CXG* WD3 ...... 40 F2
Lawdon Gdns *CROY/NA* CR0 ...... 172 B6 8
Lawford Cl *HCH* RM12 ...... 92 C4 8
  WLGTN SM6 ...... 183 L2
Lawford Rd *CHSWK* W4 ...... 117 J7
  IS N1 ...... 7 J2
  KTTN NW5 ...... 84 C6
Lawless St *POP/IOD* E14 ...... 105 H6 2
Lawley Rd *STHGT/OAK* N14 ...... 48 B2
Lawley St *CLPT* E5 ...... 86 C4 8
Lawn Av *WDR/YW* UB7 ...... 94 C8
Lawn Cl *BMLY* BR1 ...... 160 B3
  EN EN1 ...... 49 M2
  NWMAL KT3 ...... 153 L5
  RSLP HA4 ...... 77 M3
  SWLY BR8 ...... 163 J5
Lawn Crs *RCH/KEW* TW9 ...... 117 G7

Lawn Farm Gv *CHDH* RM6 ...... 72 E5
Lawn Gdns *HNWL* W7 ...... 97 L7
Lawn House Cl *POP/IOD* E14 ...... 105 J8
Lawn La *VX/NE* SW8 ...... 17 K9
Lawn Rd *BECK* BR3 ...... 158 F3
  HAMP NW3 ...... 83 M5
  UX/CGN UB8 ...... 76 C7
The Lawns *BELMT* SM2 ...... 181 L1 2
  CHING E4 ...... 51 G7 8
  NRWD SE19 ...... 157 K4
  PIN HA5 ...... 61 H1
  SCUP DA14 ...... 144 B8 8
Lawns Wy *CRW* RM5 ...... 73 J1
Lawn Ter *BKHTH/KID* SE3 ...... 123 M8
The Lawn *NWDGN* UB2 ...... 115 G3
Lawn V *PIN* HA5 ...... 60 D3
Lawrance Gdns *CHES/WCR* EN8 ...... 26 D1
Lawrence Av *MLHL* NW7 ...... 45 L6
  MNPK E12 ...... 89 G4
  NWMAL KT3 ...... 168 E2
  PLMGR N13 ...... 49 H6 2
  WALTH E17 ...... 68 D2
Lawrence Cl *SEVS/STOTM* N15 ...... 67 L5
  SHB W12 ...... 100 A8
Lawrence Ct *MLHL* NW7 ...... 45 L7
Lawrence Crs *DAGE* RM10 ...... 91 H3
  EDGW HA8 ...... 63 G3
Lawrence Dr *HGDN/ICK* UB10 ...... 77 J4
Lawrence Gdns *MLHL* NW7 ...... 45 M5
Lawrence Hl *CHING* E4 ...... 51 G4
Lawrence Hill Gdns
  DART DA1 ...... 146 C3 8
Lawrence Hill Rd *DART* DA1 ...... 146 C3
Lawrence La *CITYW* EC2V 12 F5 2
Lawrence Rd *EA* W5 ...... 116 C2
  EHAM E6 ...... 88 E8
  ERITH DA8 ...... 127 H5
  GPK RM2 ...... 74 B6
  HPTN TW12 ...... 150 F3
  HSLWW TW4 ...... 132 C1
  PIN HA5 ...... 60 D6
  PLSTW E13 ...... 88 B2 2
  RCHPK/HAM TW10 ...... 134 C8
  SEVS/STOTM N15 ...... 67 L5
  SNWD SE25 ...... 157 M7
  UED N18 ...... 50 B6 2
  WWKM BR4 ...... 175 G6
  YEAD UB4 ...... 95 J1
Lawrence St *CAN/RD* E16 ...... 105 M4 2
  CHEL SW3 ...... 119 L4 8
  MLHL NW7 ...... 45 M6
Lawrence Wy *WLSDN* NW10 ...... 81 J3
Lawrence Yd
  SEVS/STOTM N15 ...... 67 L5 8
Lawrie Park Av *SYD* SE26 ...... 158 A1
Lawrie Park Crs *SYD* SE26 ...... 158 B1
Lawrie Park Gdns *SYD* SE26 ...... 158 B1
Lawrie Park Rd *SYD* SE26 ...... 158 B1
Lawson Cl *CAN/RD* E16 ...... 106 C5 2
  WIM/MER SW19 ...... 136 D7 2
Lawson Gdns *DART* DA1 ...... 146 D2
  PIN HA5 ...... 60 B4
Lawson Rd *DART* DA1 ...... 146 D1
  PEND EN3 ...... 37 J4
  STHL UB1 ...... 96 F3
Law St *STHWK* SE1 ...... 19 H3
Lawton Rd *BOW* E3 ...... 104 E2 2
  EBAR EN4 ...... 34 D6
  LEY E10 ...... 87 J1
Laxcon Cl *WLSDN* NW10 ...... 81 K5
Laxey Rd *ORP* BR6 ...... 176 F8
Laxley Cl *CMBW* SE5 ...... 121 H5
Laxton Pl *CAMTN* NW1 ...... 4 D9 2
Layard Rd *BERM/RHTH* SE16 ...... 122 B2
  EN EN1 ...... 36 F4
  THHTH CR7 ...... 157 K5 2
Laycock St *IS* N1 ...... 85 G6
Layer Gdns *ACT* W3 ...... 99 G6
Layfield Cl *HDN* NW4 ...... 64 B8
Layfield Crs *HDN* NW4 ...... 64 B8
Layfield Rd *HDN* NW4 ...... 64 B8
Layhams Rd *HAYES* BR2 ...... 187 G1
  WWKM BR4 ...... 174 E6
Laymarsh Cl *BELV* DA17 ...... 126 F1
Laymead Cl *NTHLT* UB5 ...... 78 E6
Laystall St *FSBYW* WC1X 12 A1
Layton Ct *WEY* KT13 ...... 164 B6 2
Layton Crs *CROY/NA* CR0 ...... 172 A7
Layton Pl *RCH/KEW* TW9 ...... 117 G6
Layton Rd *BTFD* TW8 ...... 116 D3
  HSLW TW3 ...... 133 H1
  IS N1 ...... 6 B5
Layton's La *SUN* TW16 ...... 149 M5
Layzell Wk *ELTH/MOT* SE9 ...... 142 D5
Leabank Cl *HRW* HA1 ...... 79 L3
Leabank Sq *HOM* E9 ...... 87 G6 2
Leabank Vw
  SEVS/STOTM N15 ...... 68 A7 2
Leabourne Rd *STNW/STAM* N16 ...... 68 A7 2
Lea Bridge Rd *CLPT* E5 ...... 86 D2
  LEY E10 ...... 68 F8
Lea Bushes *GSTN* WD25 ...... 21 L8
Lea Cl *BUSH* WD23 ...... 30 B8 2
Lea Crs *RSLP* HA4 ...... 77 M4
Leacroft *STA* TW18 ...... 148 B1
Leacroft Av *BAL* SW12 ...... 137 M4
Leacroft Cl *STA* TW18 ...... 130 B8
  WDR/YW UB7 ...... 94 E6
Leadale Av *CHING* E4 ...... 51 G4
Leadale Rd *SEVS/STOTM* N15 ...... 68 A7
Leadbeaters Cl
  FBAR/BDGN N11 ...... 47 M7 8
Leadenhall Pl *FENCHST* EC3M 13 J5 8
Leadenhall St *BANK* EC3V 13 J5
Leader Av *MNPK* E12 ...... 89 G5
The Leadings *WBLY* HA9 ...... 81 J3
Leaf Cl *NTHWD* HA6 ...... 59 K1
  THDIT KT7 ...... 151 L8
Leaf Gv *STRHM/NOR* SW16 ...... 157 G1
Leafield Cl *STRHM/NOR* SW16 ...... 157 H2
Leafield La *SCUP* DA14 ...... 144 F2
Leafield Rd *RYNPK* SW20 ...... 154 H6
  SUT SM1 ...... 170 A4
Leaford Crs *WATN* WD24 ...... 28 F2
Leaforis Rd *CHESW* EN7 ...... 26 A1
Leafy Gv *HAYES* BR2 ...... 175 J7
Leafy Oak Rd *LEE/GVPK* SE12 ...... 142 C8
Leafy Wy *CROY/NA* CR0 ...... 172 F4
Lea Gdns *WBLY* HA9 ...... 80 F5

Leagrave St CLPT E5 ... 86 C3
Lea Hall Rd LEY E10 ... 87 G1
Leaholme Waye RSLP HA4 ... 59 H7
Leahurst Rd LEW SE13 ... 141 L3
Leake St STHWK SE1 ... 11 M8
Lealand Rd SEVS/STOTM N15 ... 67 M7
Leamington Av BMLY BR1 ... 160 C1
　MRDN SM4 ... 154 F7
　ORP BR6 ... 176 E6
　WALTH E17 ... 69 C6
Leamington Cl BMLY BR1 ... 142 C8
　HSLW TW3 ... 133 J2
Leamington Crs
　RYLN/HDSTN HA2 ... 78 C3
Leamington Gdns
　GDMY/SEVK IG3 ... 89 M2
Leamington Pk ACT W3 ... 99 K4
Leamington Pl YEAD UB4 ... 95 M3
Leamington Rd HARH RM3 ... 57 G7
　NWDGN UB2 ... 114 D2
Leamington Road Vls
　NTGHL W11 ... 100 F4
Leamore St HMSMTH W6 ... 118 B2
Lea Mt CHESW EN7 ... 25 L1
Leamouth Rd EHAM E6 ... 106 E5
　POP/IOD E14 ... 105 K5
Leander Gdns GSTN WD25 ... 29 L2
Leander Rd BRXS/STRHM SW2 ... 138 F3
　NTHLT UB5 ... 97 G1
　THHTH CR7 ... 156 F7
Learner Dr RYLN/HDSTN HA2 ... 78 A2
Lea Rd BECK BR3 ... 159 G5
　ENC/FH EN2 ... 36 D4
　NWDGN UB2 ... 114 E2
　WAB EN9 ... 27 G7
　WATN WD24 ... 29 H3
Learoyd Gdns EHAM E6 ... 107 G6
Leas Cl CHSGTN KT9 ... 179 M1
Leas Dl ELTH/MOT SE9 ... 143 C7
Leas Gn CHST BR7 ... 161 M2
Leaside Av MUSWH N10 ... 66 A4
Leaside Ct HGDN/ICK UB10 ... 95 H2
Leaside Rd CLPT E5 ... 86 C1
Leasowes Rd LEY E10 ... 87 G1
The Leas BUSH WD23 ... 29 M5
　UPMR RM14 ... 75 K8
Leasway UPMR RM14 ... 93 J3
Leathart Cl HCH RM12 ... 92 B7
Leatherbottle Gn ERITHM DA18... 126 F1
Leather Cl MTCM CR4 ... 156 A5
Leatherdale St WCHPL E1 ... 104 D2
Leatherhead Cl STNW/STAM N16.. 85 L1
Leatherhead Rd CHSGTN KT9 ... 179 H7
　LHD/OX KT22 ... 178 D8
Leather La EMPK RM11 ... 92 D1
　HCIRC EC1N ... 12 A2
Leathermarket St STHWK SE1 ... 19 J2
Leathsale Rd
　RYLN/HDSTN HA2 ... 79 H3
Leathwell Rd DEPT SE8 ... 123 H7
Lea V DART DA1 ... 145 K1
Lea Valley Rd CHING E4 ... 50 F1
Lea Valley Wk CLPT E5 ... 68 B8
　TOTM N17 ... 50 B8
　WAB EN9 ... 27 G6
Leaveland Cl BECK BR3 ... 159 G7
Leaver Gdns GFD/PVL UB6 ... 97 K1
Leavesden Rd STAN HA7 ... 44 A8
　WATN WD24 ... 29 H3
　WEY KT13 ... 164 B7
Leaves Green Crs HAYES BR2 ... 187 J4
Leaves Green Rd HAYES BR2 ... 187 K4
Leaview WAB EN9 ... 27 H6
Lebanon Av FELT TW13 ... 150 D1
Lebanon Cl WAT WD17 ... 28 D1
Lebanon Dr COB KT11 ... 178 A6
Lebanon Gdns
　WAND/EARL SW18 ... 137 G3
Lebanon Pk TWK TW1 ... 134 C4
Lebanon Rd CROY/NA CR0 ... 172 E3
　WAND/EARL SW18 ... 137 G2
Lebrun Sq BKHTH/KID SE3 ... 142 B1
Lechmere Ap WFD IG8 ... 70 D3
Lechmere Av CHIG IG7 ... 53 J7
Lechmere Rd CRICK NW2 ... 82 B6
Leckford Rd WAND/EARL SW18 ... 137 J6
Leckwith Av ABYW SE2 ... 126 E4
Lecky St SKENS SW7 ... 15 G7
Leconfield Av
　PUT/ROE SW15 ... 117 M8
Leconfield Rd HBRY N5 ... 85 K4
Leda Av PEND EN3 ... 37 K4
Leda Rd WOOL/PLUM SE18 ... 124 F1
Ledbury Ms North NTGHL W11... 8 A6
Ledbury Ms West NTGHL W11 ... 8 A6
Ledbury Rd CROY/NA CR0 ... 172 C2
　NTGHL W11 ... 100 F5
Ledbury St PECK SE15 ... 122 A5
Ledrington Rd NRWD SE19 ... 157 M2
Ledway Dr WBLY HA9 ... 62 B8
Lee Av CHDH RM6 ... 72 E7
Leechcroft Av BFN/LL DA15 ... 143 M2
　SWLY BR8 ... 163 M6
Leechcroft Rd WLGTN SM6 ... 171 C5
Lee Church St LEW SE13 ... 141 L1
Lee Cl WALTH E17 ... 68 D2
Lee Conservancy Rd HOM E9 ... 86 F5
Leecroft Rd BAR EN5 ... 33 L8
Leeds Cl ORP BR6 ... 177 K4
Leeds Rd IL IG1 ... 89 K1
Leeds St UED N18 ... 50 A4
Leefe Wy POTB/CUF EN6 ... 24 D1
Lee Gardens Av EMPK RM11 ... 93 C1
Lee Gn STMC/STPC BR5 ... 162 A8
Lee Gv CHIG IG7 ... 53 H4
Lee High Rd LEW SE13 ... 141 K1
Leeke St FSBYW WC1X ... 5 L7
Leeland Rd WEA W13 ... 98 A2
Leeland Ter WEA W13 ... 98 A2
Leeland Wy WLSDN NW10 ... 81 M4
Leeming Rd BORE WD6 ... 31 M4
Lee Navigation CLPT E5 ... 86 C2
Lee Pk BKHTH/KID SE3 ... 141 M1
Lee Park Wy UED N18 ... 50 D7
Lee Rd BKHTH/KID SE3 ... 123 M8
　EN EN1 ... 50 A1
　GFD/PVL UB6 ... 80 C8

MLHL NW7 ... 64 D1
　WIM/MER SW19 ... 155 H4
Lees Av NTHWD HA6 ... 59 M2
Leeside BAR EN5 ... 33 L8
　POTB/CUF EN6 ... 23 K5
Leeside Crs GLDGN NW11 ... 64 C2
Leeside Rd TOTM N17 ... 50 C8
Leeson Rd HNHL SE24 ... 139 D1
Leesons Hl CHST BR7 ... 161 L6
Leesons Wy STMC/STPC BR5 ... 161 M5
Lees Pl MYFR/PKLN W1K ... 10 A6
Lees Rd UX/CGN UB8 ... 95 H3
The Lees CROY/NA CR0 ... 173 M4
Lee Vw ENC/FH EN2 ... 36 B4
Leeward Gdns WIM/MER SW19 ... 154 F2
Leeway DEPT SE8 ... 124 B2
Leewood Cl LEE/GVPK SE12 ... 141 M3
Leewood Pl SWLY BR8 ... 163 K7
Leffern Rd SHB W12 ... 100 A8
Lefroy Rd SHB W12 ... 99 M8
Legard Rd HBRY N5 ... 85 H3
Legatt Rd ELTH/MOT SE9 ... 142 D2
Leggatts Cl WATN WD24 ... 28 F1
Leggatts Ri GSTN WD25 ... 21 G8
Leggatts Wy WATN WD24 ... 29 G1
Leggatts Wood Av WATN WD24 ... 29 H1
Legge St LEW SE13 ... 141 J2
Leghorn Rd WLSDN NW10 ... 100 A1
　WOOL/PLUM SE18 ... 125 K3
Legion Cl IS N1 ... 85 G6
Legion Ter BOW E3 ... 87 G8
Legion Wy NFNCH/WDSP N12 ... 65 L1
Legon Av ROMW/RG RM7 ... 91 J1
Legrace Av HSLWW TW4 ... 114 D7
Leicester Av MTCM CR4 ... 156 E7
Leicester Gdns GDMY/SEVK IG3 ... 71 L8
Leicester Pl LSQ/SEVD WC2H ... 11 H6
Leicester Rd BAR EN5 ... 34 B8
　CROY/NA CR0 ... 172 E2
　EFNCH N2 ... 65 L1
　WAN E11 ... 70 B6
　WLSDN NW10 ... 81 K7
Leicester Sq SOHO/SHAV W1D.... 11 H6
Leigham Av STRHM/NOR SW16 ... 138 E7
Leigham Court Rd
　STRHM/NOR SW16 ... 138 F7
Leigham Dr ISLW TW7 ... 115 L3
Leigham V STRHM/NOR SW16 ... 139 G7
Leigh Av REDBR IG4 ... 70 D5
Leigh Cl NWMAL KT3 ... 153 K7
Leigh Ct BORE WD6 ... 32 D5
　RYLN/HDSTN HA2 ... 79 L1
Leigh Dr HARH RM3 ... 56 D6
Leigh Gdns WLSDN NW10 ... 100 C1
Leigh Hunt Dr STHGT/OAK N14 ... 48 D3
Leigh Orchard Cl
　STRHM/NOR SW16 ... 138 F7
Leigh Pl WELL DA16 ... 126 A7
Leigh Rd EHAM E6 ... 89 G7
　HBRY N5 ... 85 H4
　HSLW TW3 ... 133 K1
　LEY E10 ... 69 J8
Leigh Rodd OXHEY WD19 ... 42 E5
Leigh St STPAN WC1H ... 5 J9
Leighton Av MNPK E12 ... 89 C5
　PIN HA5 ... 60 E4
Leighton Cl EDGW HA8 ... 63 C3
Leighton Crs KTTN NW5 ... 84 C5
Leighton Gdns SAND/SEL CR2 ... 185 H6
　WLSDN NW10 ... 100 C1
Leighton Gv KTTN NW5 ... 84 C5
Leighton Pl KTTN NW5 ... 84 C5
Leighton Rd EN EN1 ... 36 F8
　KTN/HRWW/W HA3 ... 61 K3
　KTTN NW5 ... 84 C5
　WEA W13 ... 98 A8
Leighton St CROY/NA CR0... 172 B3
Leighton Wy EPSOM KT18 ... 180 D7
Leila Parnell Pl CHARL SE7 ... 124 C4
Leinster Av MORT/ESHN SW14 .... 117 J8
Leinster Gdns BAY/PAD W2... 8 E7
Leinster Ms BAY/PAD W2 ... 8 E7
Leinster Pl BAY/PAD W2 ... 8 E5
Leinster Rd MUSWH N10 ... 66 B5
Leinster Sq BAY/PAD W2 ... 8 B6
Leinster Ter BAY/PAD W2 ... 8 E6
Leisure Wy NFNCH/WDSP N12 ... 65 K1
Leith Cl CDALE/KGS NW9 ... 81 K1
Leithcote Gdns
　STRHM/NOR SW16 ... 138 F8
Leithcote Pth
　STRHM/NOR SW16 ... 138 F7
Leith Hl STMC/STPC BR5 ... 162 A4
Leith Rd EW KT17 ... 180 E5
　WDGN N22 ... 67 H2
Lela Av HSLWW TW4 ... 114 C7
Lelitia Cl HACK E8 ... 86 A8
Leman St WCHPL E1 ... 13 M5
Lemark Cl STAN HA7 ... 44 C8
Le May Av LEE/GVPK SE12 ... 142 A1
Lemmon Rd GNWCH SE10 ... 123 L4
Lemna Rd WAN E11 ... 70 B6
Lemon Field Dr GSTN WD25 ... 21 L6
Lemonwell Dr ELTH/MOT SE9 ... 143 H2
Lemsford Cl SEVS/STOTM N15 ... 68 A7
Lemsford Ct BORE WD6 ... 32 C7
Lena Gdns HMSMTH W6 ... 118 C3
Lena Kennedy Cl CHING E4 ... 51 M2
Lendal Ter CLAP SW4 ... 120 E8
Lenelby Rd SURB KT6 ... 168 A3
Len Freeman Pl
　FUL/PGN SW6 ... 118 F4
Lenham Rd BXLYHN DA7 ... 126 F4
　LEW SE13 ... 141 M1
　SUT SM1 ... 170 B6
　THHTH CR7 ... 157 K5
Lennard Av WWKM BR4 ... 174 E4
Lennard Rd CROY/NA CR0 ... 172 C3
　HAYES BR2 ... 175 M3
　PGE/AN SE20 ... 158 D2
　SYD SE26 ... 158 C2

Lennon Rd CRICK NW2 ... 82 C5
Lennox Cl ROM RM1 ... 73 M7
Lennox Gdns CROY/NA CR0 ... 172 B6
　IL IG1 ... 88 F1
　KTBR SW1X ... 15 L4
　WLSDN NW10 ... 81 M4
Lennox Gardens Ms CHEL SW3... 15 L5
Lennox Rd FSBYPK N4 ... 84 F2
　WALTH E17 ... 68 F7
Lenor Cl BXLYHS DA6 ... 144 E1
Lensbury Av CHES/WCR EN8 ... 26 E1
Lensbury Wy ABYW SE2 ... 126 D3
Lens Rd FSTGT E7 ... 88 C7
Lenthall Rd HACK E8 ... 7 M1
Lenthorp Rd GNWCH SE10 ... 123 M3
Lentmead Rd BMLY BR1 ... 141 M7
Lenton Ri RCH/KEW TW9 ... 116 E3
Lenton St WOOL/PLUM SE18 ... 125 K2
Leof Crs CAT SE6 ... 159 H1
Leominster Rd MRDN SM4 ... 170 C1
Leominster Wk MRDN SM4 ... 170 C1
Leonard Av MRDN SM4 ... 155 J8
　ROMW/RG RM7 ... 91 K1
Leonard Ct KENS W8 ... 14 A3
Leonard Pl STNW/STAM N16 ... 85 L4
Leonard Rd CHING E4 ... 51 C8
　ED N9 ... 50 A5
　FSTGT E7 ... 88 A4
　MTCM CR4 ... 156 C4
　NWDGN UB2 ... 114 D1
Leonard St CAN/RD E16 ... 106 E7
　SDTCH EC2A ... 7 H9
Leonard Wy BRW CM14 ... 57 L6
Leontine Cl PECK SE15 ... 122 A5
Leopold Av WIM/MER SW19 ... 154 F1
Leopold Ms HOM E9 ... 86 C8
Leopold Rd EA W5 ... 98 F7
　EFNCH N2 ... 65 K4
　WALTH E17 ... 69 G6
　WIM/MER SW19 ... 136 F8
　WLSDN NW10 ... 81 L7
Leopold St BOW E3 ... 104 F3
Leo St PECK SE15 ... 122 B5
Leppoc Rd CLAP SW4 ... 138 D2
Leroy St STHWK SE1 ... 19 J5
Lescombe Cl FSTH SE23 ... 140 E7
Lescombe Rd FSTH SE23 ... 140 E7
Lesley Cl BXLY DA5 ... 145 H4
　SWLY BR8 ... 163 K6
Leslie Gv CROY/NA CR0 ... 172 D3
Leslie Grove Pl CROY/NA CR0 ... 172 E3
Leslie Park Rd CROY/NA CR0 ... 172 E3
Leslie Rd CAN/RD E16 ... 106 B5
　EFNCH N2 ... 65 K4
　WAN E11 ... 87 K4
Lesney Pk ERITH DA8 ... 127 K4
Lesney Park Rd ERITH DA8 ... 127 K4
Lessar Av CLAP SW4 ... 138 C2
Lessingham Av TOOT SW17 ... 137 M8
Lessing St FSTH SE23 ... 140 E4
Lessington Av ROMW/RG RM7 ... 73 J7
Lessness Av BXLYHN DA7 ... 126 D5
Lessness Pk BELV DA17 ... 126 F3
Lessness Rd MRDN SM4 ... 170 C1
Lester Av SRTFD E15 ... 105 L3
Leston Cl RAIN RM13 ... 110 B2
Leswin Pl STNW/STAM N16 ... 85 M3
Leswin Rd STNW/STAM N16 ... 85 M3
Letchford Gdns
　WLSDN NW10 ... 100 A2
Letchford Ms WLSDN NW10 ... 100 A2
Letchmore Rd RAD WD7 ... 31 G1
Letchworth Av
　EBED/NFELT TW14 ... 131 M4
Letchworth Cl HAYES BR2 ... 160 A8
　OXHEY WD19 ... 42 D7
Letchworth Dr HAYES BR2 ... 160 A8
Letchworth St TOOT SW17 ... 137 M8
Letterstone Rd
　FUL/PGN SW6 ... 118 F5
Lettice St FUL/PGN SW6 ... 118 F7
Lett Rd SRTFD E15 ... 87 K7
Leucha Rd WALTH E17 ... 68 E6
Levana Cl WIM/MER SW19 ... 136 E5
Levehurst Wy CLAP SW4 ... 120 F7
Leven Cl CHES/WCR EN8 ... 26 D6
　OXHEY WD19 ... 42 D7
Levendale Rd FSTH SE23 ... 140 E6
Leven Dr CHES/WCR EN8 ... 26 D6
Leven Rd POP/IOD E14 ... 105 K5
Leven Wy HYS/HAR UB3 ... 95 L5
Leverett Cl CROY/NA CR0 ... 186 D4
　CSTN WD25 ... 21 G7
Leverett St CHEL SW3 ... 15 K5
Leverholme Gdns
　ELTH/MOT SE9 ... 143 G8
Leverson St STRHM/NOR SW16 .. 156 C2
Lever St FSBYE EC1V ... 6 E8
Leverton Pl KTTN NW5 ... 84 C5
Leverton St KTTN NW5 ... 84 C5
Leverton Wy WAB EN9 ... 27 J6
Levett Gdns GDMY/SEVK IG3 ... 89 M4
Levett Rd BARK IG11 ... 89 L6
Levine Gdns BARK IG11 ... 108 D1
Lewes Cl NTHLT UB5 ... 79 G6
Lewesdon Cl
　WIM/MER SW19 ... 136 D5
Lewes Rd BMLY BR1 ... 160 D5
　HARH RM3 ... 56 D6
　NFNCH/WDSP N12 ... 47 L7
Leweston Pl STNW/STAM N16 ... 67 M8
Lewes Wy RKW/CH/CXG WD3 .... 20 B7
Lewgars Av CDALE/KGS NW9 ... 63 J7
Lewing Cl ORP BR6 ... 176 E3
Lewin Rd BXLYHS DA6 ... 144 E1
　MORT/ESHN SW14 ... 117 K3
　STRHM/NOR SW16 ... 156 C2
Lewins Rd EPSOM KT18 ... 180 B7
Lewis Av WALTH E17 ... 51 J8
Lewis Cl DEN/HRF UB9 ... 58 C3
　STHGT/OAK N14 ... 48 C2
Lewis Crs WLSDN NW10 ... 81 K5
Lewis Gdns EFNCH N2 ... 65 K3
Lewis Gv LEW SE13 ... 141 J1
Lewisham High St LEW SE13 ... 141 J1
Lewisham HI LEW SE13 ... 123 J7
Lewisham Pk LEW SE13 ... 141 J2
Lewisham Rd LEW SE13 ... 123 J7

Lewisham Wy BROCKY SE4 ... 122 F7
　NWCR SE14 ... 122 F6
Lewis Rd EMPK RM11 ... 74 C7
　MTCM CR4 ... 155 L5
　RCHPK/HAM TW10 ... 134 D2
　SCUP DA14 ... 144 C2
　STHL UB1 ... 96 E8
　SUT SM1 ... 170 B6
　WELL DA16 ... 126 C8
Lewis St CAMTN NW1 ... 4 D1
Lewis Wy DAGE RM10 ... 91 H6
Lexden Dr CHDH RM6 ... 72 B7
Lexden Rd ACT W3 ... 99 H6
　MTCM CR4 ... 156 D7
Lexham Gdns KENS W8 ... 14 B5
Lexham Ms KENS W8 ... 14 B5
Lexington Cl BORE WD6 ... 32 A6
Lexington Ct PUR/KEN CR8 ... 184 C3
Lexington St SOHO/CST W1F ... 10 F5
Lexington Wy BAR EN5 ... 33 K7
　UPMR RM14 ... 75 L7
Lexton Gdns BAL SW12 ... 138 D5
Leyborne Av WEA W13 ... 98 C5
Leyborne Pk RCH/KEW TW9 ... 117 G6
Leybourne Cl HAYES BR2 ... 175 G1
Leybourne Rd CAMTN NW1 ... 4 D2
　CDALE/KGS NW9 ... 63 G6
　HGDN/ICK UB10 ... 77 J8
　WAN E11 ... 87 M1
Leybourne St CAMTN NW1 ... 4 C2
Leyburn Cl WALTH E17 ... 69 J5
Leyburn Crs HARH RM3 ... 74 E1
Leyburn Gdns CROY/NA CR0 ... 172 E4
Leyburn Gv UED N18 ... 50 C2
Leyburn Rd HARH RM3 ... 74 E1
　UED N18 ... 50 C2
Leycroft Gdns ERITH DA8 ... 128 B6
Leydenhatch La SWLY BR8 ... 163 K4
Leyden St WCHPL E1 ... 13 L3
Leyes Rd CAN/RD E16 ... 106 C6
Leyfield WPK KT4 ... 168 E4
Leyhill Cl SWLY BR8 ... 163 L8
Leyland Av EN EN3 ... 37 L5
Leyland Cl CHES/WCR EN8 ... 26 C1
Leyland Gdns WFD IG8 ... 53 J2
Leyland Rd LEE/GVPK SE12 ... 142 A2
Leys Av DAGE RM10 ... 91 J8
Leys Cl DAGE RM10 ... 91 J7
　DEN/HRF UB9 ... 58 D2
　HRW HA1 ... 61 K5
Leysdown Av BXLYHN DA7 ... 145 J1
Leysdown Rd ELTH/MOT SE9 ... 142 E8
Leysfield Rd SHB W12 ... 100 A8
Leys Gdns EBAR EN4 ... 35 G8
Leyspring Rd WAN E11 ... 87 M1
Leys Rd LHD/OX KT22 ... 178 D5
Leys Rd East PEND EN3 ... 37 L4
Leys The EFNCH N2 ... 65 J5
　KTN/HRWW/W HA3 ... 62 F7
Ley St IL IG1 ... 89 J2
Leyswood Dr GNTH/NBYPK IG2 ... 71 L6
Leythe Rd ACT W3 ... 99 J8
Leyton Cross Rd RDART DA2 ... 145 M7
Leyton Gra LEY E10 ... 69 J7
Leyton Green Rd LEY E10 ... 69 J3
Leyton Park Rd LEY E10 ... 87 J2
Leyton Rd SRTFD E15 ... 87 M7
　WIM/MER SW19 ... 155 J3
Leytonstone Rd SRTFD E15 ... 87 L1
Leyton Wy WAN E11 ... 69 M8
Leywick St SRTFD E15 ... 105 L1
Lezayre Rd ORP BR6 ... 176 F7
Liardet St NWCR SE14 ... 122 E4
Liberia Rd HBRY N5 ... 85 H6
Liberty Av WIM/MER SW19 ... 155 K4
Liberty St BRXN/ST SW9 ... 120 B7
Libra Rd BOW E3 ... 86 F7
　PLSTW E13 ... 106 A1
Library St STHWK SE1 ... 18 D2
Lichfield Cl EBAR EN4 ... 34 F6
Lichfield Gdns
　RCHPK/HAM TW10 ... 134 E2
Lichfield Gv FNCH N3 ... 65 G2
Lichfield Rd BCTR RM8 ... 90 B4
　BOW E3 ... 104 E2
　CRICK NW2 ... 82 E4
　ED N9 ... 50 A4
　EHAM E6 ... 106 D2
　HSLWW TW4 ... 114 C8
　NTHWD HA6 ... 60 A4
　RCH/KEW TW9 ... 116 F6
　WFD IG8 ... 51 L6
Lichfield Ter UPMR RM14 ... 93 L2
　UPMR RM14 ... 93 M2
Lichfield Wy SAND/SEL CR2 ... 185 K3
Lidbury Rd MLHL NW7 ... 46 E8
Liddall Wy WDR/YW UB7 ... 94 F1
Liddell Cl KTN/HRWW/W HA3 ... 62 D4
Liddell Gdns WLSDN NW10 ... 100 C1
Liddell Rd KIL/WHAMP NW6 ... 83 G6
Lidding Rd KTN/HRWW/W HA3 ... 62 D6
Liddington Rd SRTFD E15 ... 87 M8
Liddon Rd BMLY BR1 ... 160 C6
　PLSTW E13 ... 106 B2
Liden Cl LEY E10 ... 68 F8
Lidfield Rd STNW/STAM N16 ... 85 K4
Lidgate Rd PECK SE15 ... 121 M5
Lidiard Rd WAND/EARL SW18 ... 137 L2
Lido Sq TOTM N17 ... 67 K3
Lidyard Rd ARCH N19 ... 84 C1
Lieutenant Ellis Wy CHESW EN7 ... 25 M4
Liffler Rd WOOL/PLUM SE18 ... 125 L3
Lifford St PUT/ROE SW15 ... 136 D1
Lightcliffe Rd PLMGR N13 ... 49 G1
Lighterman Ms WCHPL E1 ... 104 F5
Lighterman's Rd POP/IOD E14 ... 105 G8
Lightfoot Rd CEND/HSY/T N8 ... 66 E6
Ligonier St BETH E2 ... 7 L9
Lilac Cl CHING E4 ... 51 J6
　CHESW EN7 ... 26 A3
Lilac Gdns CROY/NA CR0 ... 174 A5
　EA W5 ... 116 C1
　HYS/HAR UB3 ... 95 L5
　ROMW/RG RM7 ... 91 L1
　SWLY BR8 ... 163 K6
Lilac Pl LBTH SE11 ... 17 L6
　WDR/YW UB7 ... 94 F6

Lilac St SHB W12 ... 100 A6
Lila Pl SWLY BR8 ... 163 L7
Lilburne Gdns ELTH/MOT SE9 ... 142 E2
Lilburne Rd ELTH/MOT SE9 ... 142 E2
Lile Crs HNWL W7 ... 97 L4
Lilestone St CAMTN NW1 ... 3 J7
Lilford Rd BRXN/ST SW9 ... 121 H7
Lilian Barker Cl LEE/GVPK SE12 ... 142 A3
Lilian Board Wy NTHLT UB5 ... 79 K5
Lilian Gdns WFD IG8 ... 70 B2
Lilian Rd MTCM CR4 ... 156 C4
Lillechurch Rd BCTR RM8 ... 90 B6
Lilleshall Rd MRDN SM4 ... 170 D1
Lilley Cl BRW CM14 ... 57 M6
　WAP E1W ... 104 A7
Lillian Av ACT W3 ... 99 G8
Lillian Rd BARN SW13 ... 118 A4
Lillie Rd FUL/PGN SW6 ... 118 F4
Lillieshall Rd CLAP SW4 ... 120 B8
Lillie Yd FUL/PGN SW6 ... 14 A9
Lilliput Av NTHLT UB5 ... 78 E8
Lilliput Rd ROMW/RG RM7 ... 73 K8
Lily Cl HCIRC EC1N ... 12 B2
Lily Gdns ALP/SUD HA0 ... 98 C1
Lily Rd LEY E10 ... 69 G7
Lilyville Rd FUL/PGN SW6 ... 118 F6
Limbourne Av ROMW/RG RM7 ... 72 F6
Limburg Rd BTSEA SW11 ... 137 L1
Lime Av UPMR RM14 ... 93 G4
　WDR/YW UB7 ... 94 F6
Limeburner La STP EC4M ... 12 C4
Lime Cl BKHH IG9 ... 52 D4
　BMLY BR1 ... 160 E7
　KTN/HRWW/W HA3 ... 62 A3
　OXHEY WD19 ... 42 D2
　ROMW/RG RM7 ... 73 J6
　RSLP HA4 ... 59 M4
　WAP E1W ... 104 A7
Lime Crs SUN TW16 ... 150 C5
Limecroft Cl HOR/WEW KT19 ... 180 C1
Limedene Cl PIN HA5 ... 60 D2
Lime Gv BARK/HLT IG6 ... 53 M8
　BFN/LL DA15 ... 143 M3
　HYS/HAR UB3 ... 95 K6
　NWMAL KT3 ... 153 K6
　ORP BR6 ... 176 B4
　RSLP HA4 ... 60 B7
　SHB W12 ... 100 C8
　TRDG/WHET N20 ... 46 E3
　TWK TW1 ... 133 M3
Limeharbour POP/IOD E14 ... 123 H1
Limehouse POP/IOD E14 ... 105 G6
Limehouse Cswy
　POP/IOD E14 ... 104 F6
Limehouse Link POP/IOD E14 ... 104 E6
Limehouse Link (Tunnel)
　POP/IOD E14 ... 104 F6
Lime Kiln Dr CHARL SE7 ... 124 B4
Lime Meadow Av
　SAND/SEL CR2 ... 185 G6
Limerick Cl BAL SW12 ... 138 C4
Limerick Gdns UPMR RM14 ... 75 M4
Lime Rd SWLY BR8 ... 163 K6
Limerston St WBPTN SW10 ... 14 F7
Limes Av BARN SW13 ... 117 M7
　CAR SM5 ... 170 F3
　CHIG IG7 ... 53 J7
　CROY/NA CR0 ... 171 M5
　GLDGN NW11 ... 64 E8
　MLHL NW7 ... 45 L8
　NFNCH/WDSP N12 ... 47 J6
　PGE/AN SE20 ... 158 B5
　WAN E11 ... 70 B5
The Limes FBAR/BDGN N11 ... 48 B7
Limes Cl ASHF TW15 ... 149 G1
　CAR SM5 ... 170 F4
Limesdale Gdns EDGW HA8 ... 63 J3
Limes Field Rd BARN SW13 ... 117 L8
Limesford Rd PECK SE15 ... 140 D1
Limes Gdns WAND/EARL SW18 ... 137 G3
Limes Gv LEW SE13 ... 141 J1
Limes Rd BECK BR3 ... 159 H5
　CHES/WCR EN8 ... 26 D5
　CROY/NA CR0 ... 172 D1
　WEY KT13 ... 164 A6
Limes Rw ORP BR6 ... 176 B7
The Limes PUR RM19 ... 129 G3
Lime St FENCHST EC3M ... 13 J6
　WALTH E17 ... 68 E5
Lime Street Pas BANK EC3V ... 13 J5
Limes Wk EA W5 ... 98 B2
Lime Tree Av THDIT KT7 ... 166 E3

Limetree Cl
　BRXS/STRHM SW2 ... 138 F5
Lime Tree Gv CROY/NA CR0 ... 173 M5
Limetree Pl MTCM CR4 ... 156 A4
Lime Tree Rd HEST TW5 ... 115 H6
Lime Tree Wk BUSH WD23 ... 43 L3
　ENC/FH EN2 ... 36 C3
　WWKM BR4 ... 174 F6
Lime Wk DEN/HRF UB9 ... 76 C5
Limewood Cl WALTH E17 ... 68 F5
　WEA W13 ... 98 B5
Limewood Rd ERITH DA8 ... 127 M5
Limpsfield Av THHTH CR7 ... 156 F8
　WIM/MER SW19 ... 136 D6
Limpsfield Rd SAND/SEL CR2 ... 185 H7
Linacre Rd CRICK NW2 ... 81 M5
Linchmere Rd
　LEE/GVPK SE12 ... 142 A4
Lincln Cl ERITH DA8 ... 127 M5
Lincoln Av ROMW/RG RM7 ... 91 L1
　STHGT/OAK N14 ... 48 C5
　WHTN TW2 ... 133 J6
　WIM/MER SW19 ... 136 D7
Lincoln Cl ERITH DA8 ... 75 G6
　GFD/PVL UB6 ... 79 J8
　RYLN/HDSTN HA2 ... 32 D8
Lincoln Ct BORE WD6 ... 32 D8
Lincoln Crs EN EN1 ... 36 F2
Lincoln Dr OXHEY WD19 ... 42 C5
　RKW/CH/CXG WD3 ... 28 B7
Lincoln Gdns IL IG1 ... 70 E8
Lincoln Green Rd
　STMC/STPC BR5 ... 161 M8
Lincoln Ms KIL/WHAMP NW6 ... 82 F6
Lincoln Rd ALP/SUD HA0 ... 80 D6
　EFNCH N2 ... 65 L1

EN EN1 .... 36 E7
ERITH DA8 .... 127 M7
FELT TW13 .... 132 F7
MTCM CR4 .... 156 E8 ⊟
NTHWD HA6 .... 59 M4
NWMAL KT3 .... 153 J6 ⊟
PLSTW E13 .... 106 B3
RYLN/HDSTN HA2 .... 60 F6
SCUP DA14 .... 162 B1
SNWD SE25 .... 158 B6
SWFD E18 .... 69 M2
WPK KT4 .... 169 H3
Lincoln's Inn Flds LINN WC2A ... 11 L4
Lincolns La BRW CM14 .... 57 J7
The Lincolns MLHL NW7 ..... 45 M5
Lincoln St CHEL SW3 .... 15 L6 ⊟
WAN E11 .... 87 L2
Lincoln Wy EN EN1 .... 37 H8
RKW/CH/CXG WD3 .... 28 B7
SUN TW16 .... 149 L4
Lincombe Rd BMLY BR1 ..... 141 M7
Lindal Crs STHGT/OAK N14 .. 35 L8
The Lindales TOTM N17 ...... 50 A8 ⊟
Lindal Rd BROCKY SE4 .... 140 F2
Lindberg Rd WLGTN SM6 ... 183 L2
Linden Av DART DA1 .... 146 C5
EN EN1 .... 37 G4 ⊟
HSLW TW3 .... 133 H2
RSLP HA4 .... 78 A1
THHTH CR7 .... 157 H7
WBLY HA9 .... 80 F5
WLSDN NW10 .... 100 D1
Linden Cl CHESW EN7 .... 26 B3 ⊟
ORP BR6 .... 177 G7
PUR RM19 .... 129 J4
RSLP HA4 .... 78 A1
STAN HA7 .... 44 B7
STHGT/OAK N14 .... 48 C1
THDIT KT7 .... 167 G2 ⊟
Linden Crs GFD/PVL UB6 ... 79 M6
KUT KT1 .... 152 F5
WFD IG8 .... 52 B8
Lindenfield CHST BR7 .... 161 H5
Linden Gdns BAY/PAD W2 ... 8 B7
CHSWK W4 .... 117 K3
EN EN1 .... 37 G4
Linden Gv NWMAL KT3 .... 153 L6
PECK SE15 .... 122 B8
PGE/AN SE20 .... 158 C2
WOT/HER KT12 .... 164 F4
Linden Lea EFNCH N2 .... 65 J1
GSTN WD25 .... 21 G6
Linden Leas WWKM BR4 ..... 174 D4
Linden Ms BAY/PAD W2 ...... 8 B7
Linden Pl EW KT17 .... 180 E5 ⊟
MTCM CR4 .... 155 L7
Linden Rd FBAR/BDGN N11 ... 47 M4
HPTN TW12 .... 151 L4
MUSWH N10 .... 66 B5
SEVS/STOTM N15 .... 67 J5
The Lindens CHSWK W4 ...... 117 J6 ⊟
LOU IG10 .... 39 M8
Linden St ROMW/RG RM7 ... 73 K5
Linden Wy SHPTN TW17 ..... 149 J8
STHGT/OAK N14 .... 48 C1
WLGTN SM6 .... 183 J3
Lindfield Gdns HAMP NW3 ... 83 J5
Lindfield Rd CROY/NA CR0 ... 172 F1
EA W5 .... 98 C3
HARH RM3 .... 56 E7
Lindfield St POP/IOD E14 .... 105 C5
Lindhill Cl PEND EN3 .... 37 K5 ⊟
Lindisfarne Md HOM E9 ...... 86 E4
Lindisfarne Rd BCTR RM8 ... 90 C3
RYNPK SW20 .... 154 A3
Lindley Pl RCH/KEW TW9 ... 117 G6
Lindley Rd LEY E10 .... 87 J2 ⊟
WOT/HER KT12 .... 165 L5
Lindley St WCHPL E1 .... 104 C4
Lindore Rd BTSEA SW11 .... 137 M1
Lindores Rd CAR SM5 .... 170 C2
Lindo St PECK SE15 .... 122 C7 ⊟
Lindrop St FUL/PGN SW6 .... 119 J7
Lindsay Cl CHSGTN KT9 ..... 179 L1 ⊟
HOR/WEW KT19 .... 180 C6
STWL/WRAY TW19 .... 130 D3
SHPTN TW17 .... 164 D1
Lindsay Dr KTN/HRWW/W HA3 ... 62 E7
Lindsay Pl CHESW EN7 .... 26 B3 ⊟
Lindsay Rd HPTN TW12 .... 133 H8
WPK KT4 .... 169 H4
Lindsay Sq PIM SW1V 17 H7
Lindsell St GNWCH SE10 ..... 123 J6
Lindsey Cl BMLY BR1 .... 160 D6
MTCM CR4 .... 156 E7 ⊟
Lindsey Gdns
EBED/NFELT TW14 .... 131 K4 ⊟
Lindsey Rd BCTR RM8 .... 90 C3
DEN/HRF UB9 .... 76 A3
Lindsey St STBT EC1A 12 D2
Lindsey Wy EMPK RM11 ..... 74 C6 ⊟
Lind St DEPT SE8 .... 123 H7
Lindum Rd TEDD TW11 ...... 152 C3
Lindway WNWD SE27 .... 157 H1
Linfield Cl HDN NW4 .... 64 C4
WOT/HER KT12 .... 165 H7 ⊟
Linford Rd WALTH E17 .... 69 J4
Linford St VX/NE SW8 .... 120 C6
Lingards Rd LEW SE13 .... 141 J1 ⊟
Lingey Cl BFN/LL DA15 .... 143 M6
Lingfield Av BRYLDS KT5 .... 152 F7
RDART DA2 .... 147 H4
UPMR RM14 .... 92 F3
Lingfield Cl EN EN1 .... 49 L1
NTHWD HA6 .... 59 L1
Lingfield Crs ELTH/MOT SE9 ... 143 K1
Lingfield Gdns ED N9 .... 50 B2
Lingfield Rd WIM/MER SW19 ... 136 E8
WPK KT4 .... 169 J5
Lingfield Wy WAT WD17 ...... 28 F3 ⊟
Lingham St BRXN/ST SW9 ... 120 C7
Lingholm Wy BAR EN5 .... 33 K8
Lingmere Cl CHIG IG7 .... 53 J4
Lingmoor Dr GSTN WD25 ... 21 J7
Ling Rd CAN/RD E16 .... 106 F3
ERITH DA8 .... 127 J4
Lingwell Rd TOOT SW17 ..... 137 L7

Lingwood Gdns ISLW TW7 ... 115 L5
Lingwood Rd CLPT E5 .... 68 A8
Linhope St CAMTN NW1 ...... 3 L9
Linkfield E/WMO/HCT KT8 ... 151 L6
Link Fld HAYES BR2 .... 175 G1
Linkfield Rd ISLW TW7 .... 115 M7
Link La WLGTN SM6 .... 171 K8
Link Rd DAGW RM9 .... 109 H1
EBED/NFELT TW14 .... 131 M4
FBAR/BDGN N11 .... 48 A6
MTCM CR4 .... 171 G3
WATN WD24 .... 29 K5
Links Av GPK RM2 .... 74 B3
MRDN SM4 .... 155 G7
Linkscroft Av ASHF TW15 .... 149 H2
Links Dr BORE WD6 .... 31 M7 ⊟
TRDG/WHET N20 .... 47 G3
Links Gdns STRHM/NOR SW16 ... 157 G3
Links Green Wy COB KT11 ... 178 A7
Linkside CHIG IG7 .... 53 J6
NFNCH/WDSP N12 .... 47 G8
NWMAL KT3 .... 153 L6
Linkside Cl ENC/FH EN2 ..... 35 M6
Linkside Gdns ENC/FH EN2 ... 35 M6
Links Rd ACT W3 .... 99 G5
ASHF TW15 .... 148 E1 ⊟
CRICK NW2 .... 81 M2
EW KT17 .... 181 G6
TOOT SW17 .... 156 A2
WFD IG8 .... 52 A7
WWKM BR4 .... 174 C3
Links Side ENC/FH EN2 ...... 35 M6
The Links WALTH E17 .... 68 E5 ⊟
WOT/HER KT12 .... 165 G4
Link St HOM E9 .... 86 C6
Links Vw DART DA1 .... 146 C5
FNCH N3 .... 64 F1
Links View Cl STAN HA7 ..... 44 A8
Links View Rd CROY/NA CR0 ... 174 A5
HPTN TW12 .... 151 J1
Links Wy NTHWD HA6 .... 59 J2
RKW/CH/CXG WD3 .... 28 C6
BECK BR3 .... 174 A1
Linksway HDN NW4 .... 64 D3
NTHWD HA6 .... 59 K2
The Link ACT W3 .... 99 H5
ALP/SUD HA0 .... 80 C1
NTHLT UB5 .... 78 F5 ⊟
PEND EN3 .... 37 L4 ⊟
PIN HA5 .... 60 C7
TEDD TW11 .... 151 M2
Linkway BCTR RM8 .... 90 C4
Link Wy DEN/HRF UB9 .... 58 A7
EMPK RM11 .... 92 E1
Linkway FSBYPK N4 .... 67 J8 ⊟
Link Wy HAYES BR2 .... 175 L2
Linkway PIN HA5 .... 60 D2
Link Wy RCHPK/HAM TW10 ... 134 B6
Linkway RYNPK SW20 .... 154 B6
Link Wy STA TW18 .... 148 B2
Linkway Rd BRW CM14 .... 57 M5
The Linkway BAR EN5 .... 47 G1
BELMT SM2 .... 182 C1
Linley Crs ROMW/RG RM7 ... 73 H4
Linley Rd TOTM N17 .... 67 L3
Linnell Cl GLDGN NW11 ...... 65 H7 ⊟
Linnell Dr GLDGN NW11 ...... 65 H7
Linnell Rd CMBW SE5 .... 121 L7
UED N18 .... 50 A7
Linnet Cl BUSH WD23 .... 43 J3
ED N9 .... 50 D3
SAND/SEL CR2 .... 185 K3
THMD SE28 .... 108 C6
Linnet Ms BAL SW12 .... 138 A4
Linnet Rd ABLGY WD5 .... 21 G4
Linnett Cl CHING E4 .... 51 J6
Linnet Wy PUR RM19 .... 129 J3
Linom Rd BRXS/STRHM SW2 ... 138 E1 ⊟
Linscott Rd CLPT E5 .... 86 C4
Linsdell Rd BARK IG11 .... 89 J8
Linsey St BERM/RHTH SE16 ... 122 A1 ⊟
Linslade Cl HSLWW TW4 ..... 132 E2 ⊟
PIN HA5 .... 60 B4
Linslade Rd ORP BR6 .... 177 G8
Linstead St KIL/WHAMP NW6 ... 2 A1
Linstead Wy WAND/EARL SW18 ... 136 E4
Linster Gv BORE WD6 .... 32 C8
Linthorpe Av ALP/SUD HA0 ... 80 C6
Linthorpe Rd EBAR EN4 ...... 34 E6
STNW/STAM N16 .... 67 L8
Linton Av BORE WD6 .... 31 M4
Linton Cl CAR SM5 .... 170 F2 ⊟
CHARL SE7 .... 124 C3 ⊟
WELL DA16 .... 126 A6
Linton Ct ROM RM1 .... 73 J3
Linton Gdns EHAM E6 .... 106 E5
Linton Gld CROY/NA CR0 ..... 185 L3
Linton Gv WNWD SE27 .... 157 H1
Linton Rd BARK IG11 .... 89 J7
Linton's La EW KT17 .... 180 E5
Linton St IS N1 .... 6 C4
Lintott Ct STWL/WRAY TW19 ... 130 D3
Linver Rd FUL/PGN SW6 ...... 119 F7
Linwood Cl CMBW SE5 .... 121 M7
Linwood Crs EN EN1 .... 37 G4
Linzee Rd CEND/HSY/T N8 ... 66 E5
Lion Av TWK TW1 .... 133 M5
Lion Cl SHPTN TW17 .... 148 E6
Lion Ct BORE WD6 .... 32 C4
Lionel Gdns ELTH/MOT SE9 ... 142 D2
Lionel Ms NKENS W10 .... 100 E4 ⊟
Lionel Rd ELTH/MOT SE9 ..... 142 D2
Lionel Rd North BTFD TW8 ... 116 E1
Lionel Rd South BTFD TW8 ... 116 F2
Lion Gate Gdns RCH/KEW TW9 ... 116 F8
Lion Green Rd COUL/CHIP CR5 ... 183 K8
Lion Park Av CHSGTN KT9 ... 168 A6
Lion Rd BXLYHS DA6 .... 144 E1
CROY/NA CR0 .... 157 J8
ED N9 .... 50 C8
EHAM E6 .... 106 F4
WHTN TW2 .... 133 M5
Lions Cl LEE/GVPK SE12 ..... 142 C7
Lion Wy BTFD TW8 .... 116 D5
Lion Wharf Rd ISLW TW7 ..... 116 C8
Liphook Cl HCH RM12 .... 91 M4 ⊟
Liphook Crs FSTH SE23 .... 140 C4

Liphook Rd OXHEY WD19 .... 42 D6
Lippitts Hl LOU IG10 .... 38 E5
Lipsam Cl BNSTD SM7 .... 182 D6
Lisbon Av WHTN TW2 .... 133 J6
Lisburne Rd HAMP NW3 ...... 83 M4
Lisford St PECK SE15 .... 121 M6
Lisgar Ter WKENS W14 .... 118 F2
Lisle Cl TOOT SW17 .... 138 C1 ⊟
Lisle St SOHO/SHAV W1D .... 11 H6 ⊟
Lismore Cl ISLW TW7 .... 116 A7
Lismore Rd SAND/SEL CR2 ... 172 E8
TOTM N17 .... 67 K4
Lismore Wk IS N1 .... 85 J6 ⊟
Lissenden Gdns KTTN NW5 ... 84 A4
Lisson Gv CAMTN NW1 .... 9 J1
Lisson St CAMTN NW1 .... 9 J2
Lister Av HARH RM3 .... 74 D3
Lister Cl ACT W3 .... 99 G4 ⊟
WIM/MER SW19 .... 155 L4 ⊟
Lister Gdns UED N18 .... 49 J7
Lister Ms HOLWY N7 .... 84 F4
Lister Rd WAN E11 .... 87 L1
Liston Rd CLAP SW4 .... 120 C8
TOTM N17 .... 68 A2
Listowel Cl BRXN/ST SW9 ... 121 C5 ⊟
Listowel Rd DAGE RM10 ...... 91 C3
Listria Pk STNW/STAM N16 ... 85 L2
Litchfield Av MRDN SM4 ...... 169 M2
SRTFD E15 .... 87 L6 ⊟
Litchfield Gdns WLSDN NW10 ... 82 A6
Litchfield Rd SUT SM1 .... 170 C6
Litchfield Wy GLDGN NW11 ... 65 J6
Lithgow's Rd HTHAIR TW6 ... 131 L1
Lithos Rd HAMP NW3 .... 83 H6
Little Acre BECK BR3 .... 159 G6
Little Albany St CAMTN NW1 ... 4 D9
Little Argyll St CONDST W1S ... 10 E5 ⊟
Little Aston Rd HARH RM3 ... 74 F1
Little Benty WDR/YW UB7 ... 112 D3
Little Birches BFN/LL DA15 ... 143 M2
The Little Boltons WBPTN SW10 ... 14 D7
Little Bornes DUL SE21 .... 139 L8
Little Britain STBT EC1A ...... 12 E3 ⊟
Littlebrook Cl CROY/NA CR0 ... 173 K1 ⊟
Littlebrook Gdns
CHES/WCR EN8 .... 26 D3
Littlebrook Manor Wy
DART DA1 .... 147 G2
Littlebury Rd CLAP SW4 ...... 120 D8 ⊟
Little Bury St ED N9 .... 49 L2
Little Bushey La BUSH WD23 ... 30 A6
Little Cedars NFNCH/WDSP N12 ... 47 J6
Little Chester St KTBR SW1X ... 16 C3
Littlecote Cl WIM/MER SW19 ... 136 D4 ⊟
Littlecote Pl PIN HA5 .... 60 F2 ⊟
Little Ct WWKM BR4 .... 174 E4
Littlecroft ELTH/MOT SE9 ... 125 C8
Littledale ABYW SE2 .... 126 A4 ⊟
Little Dimocks BAL SW12 .... 138 B4
Little Dorrit Ct STHWK SE1 ... 18 F1 ⊟
Little Dragons LOU IG10 ...... 39 K7
Little Ealing La EA W5 .... 116 C2
Little Edward St CAMTN NW1 ... 4 D7
Little Elms HYS/HAR UB3 .... 113 K5
Little Essex St TPL/STR WC2R ... 12 A6 ⊟
Little Ferry Rd TWK TW1 ..... 134 B5 ⊟
Littlefield Cl ARCH N19 .... 84 C4
KUT KT1 .... 152 E5 ⊟
Littlefield Rd EDGW HA8 .... 63 J1
Little Friday Rd CHING E4 ... 51 L4 ⊟
Little Gaynes Gdns UPMR RM14 ... 93 H4
Little Gaynes La UPMR RM14 ... 92 F4 ⊟
Little Gearies BARK/HLT IG6 ... 71 H5
Little George St WEST SW1P ... 17 J2
Little Gerpins Rd UPMR RM14 ... 92 F8
Little Graylings ABLGY WD5 ... 20 E6
Little Green La
RKW/CH/CXG WD3 .... 28 B6
Green St KTTN NW5 .... 84 B3 ⊟
Little Gv BUSH WD23 .... 30 B7
Littlegrove EBAR EN4 .... 47 L1
Little Hayes KGLGY WD4 ..... 20 A2 ⊟
Little Heath CHARL SE7 .... 124 E4
CHDH RM6 .... 72 B5
Littleheath La COB KT11 ...... 178 A7
Little Heath Rd BXLYHN DA7 ... 126 F6
Littleheath Rd SAND/SEL CR2 ... 185 H2
Little How Cft ABLGY WD5 ... 20 C4
Little Ilford La MNPK E12 ..... 88 F4
Littlejohn Crs HRW HA1 .... 79 M2
Littlejohn Rd HNWL W7 .... 97 M5
STMC/STPC BR5 .... 177 G1
Little Marlborough St
REGST W1B .... 10 E5 ⊟
Little Martins BUSH WD23 ... 30 B8
Littlemead ESH/CLAY KT10 ... 170 E3
Littlemoor Rd IL IG1 .... 89 K3
Littlemore Rd ABYW SE2 ..... 108 A8
Little Moss La PIN HA5 .... 60 E3
Little Newport St
SOHO/SHAV W1D 11 H6
Little New St
FLST/FETLN EC4A .... 12 B4 ⊟
Little Orchard Cl ABLGY WD5 ... 20 D8
PIN HA5 .... 60 E3 ⊟
Little Orchards EPSOM KT18 ... 180 E7 ⊟
Little Oxhey La OXHEY WD19 ... 42 E7
Little Park Dr FELT TW13 ..... 132 D6
Little Park Gdns ENC/FH EN2 ... 36 C6
Little Piper's Cl CHESW EN7 ... 25 F7
Little Pluckett's Wy BKHH IG9 ... 52 D3
Little Portland St REGST W1B ... 10 D4
Little Potters BUSH WD23 .... 43 K7
Little Queens Rd TEDD TW11 ... 151 M2
Little Queen St DART DA1 .... 146 F4
Little Redlands BMLY BR1 ... 160 E5
Little Roke Av PUR/KEN CR8 ... 184 B7
Little Roke Rd PUR/KEN CR8 ... 184 C7
Little Rownings FSTH SE23 ... 140 B6
Littlers Cl WIM/MER SW19 ... 155 K4 ⊟
Little Russell St
NOXST/BSQ WC1A 11 J3
Little St James's St WHALL SW1A ... 10 E1
Little St Leonards
MORT/ESHN SW14 .... 117 J8

Little Smith St WEST SW1P ... 17 H3
Littlestone Cl BECK BR3 ...... 159 C2 ⊟
Little Strd CDALE/KGS NW9 ... 63 H3
Little Stream Cl NTHWD HA6 ... 41 L7
Little Thrift STMC/STPC BR5 ... 161 J7
Littleton Av CHING E4 .... 51 M3 ⊟
HRW HA1 .... 79 M2
Littleton La SHB W12 .... 137 J6 ⊟
Littleton Rd ASHF TW15 .... 149 J3
Little Trinity La BLKFR EC4V ... 12 F6
Littlewood LEW SE13 .... 141 J2
Little Wood Cl
STMC/STPC BR5 .... 162 A4 ⊟
Littlewood Cl WEA W13 .... 116 B1 ⊟
Little Woodcote La CAR SM5 ... 183 H5
Littleworth Av
ESH/CLAY KT10 .... 166 D7
Littleworth Common Rd
ESH/CLAY KT10 .... 166 D6
Littleworth La ESH/CLAY KT10 ... 166 D5
Littleworth Pl ESH/CLAY KT10 ... 166 D6
Littleworth Rd ESH/CLAY KT10 ... 166 D7
Littit Halliards
WOT/HER KT12 .... 165 G1 ⊟
Livermere Rd HACK E8 .... 7 L3
Liverpool Gv WALW SE17 ..... 19 G8
Liverpool Rd CAN/RD E16 ... 105 L4
EA W5 .... 98 D8
KUTN/CMB KT2 .... 153 G3
LEY E10 .... 69 J7
THHTH CR7 .... 157 J6
WATW WD18 .... 29 H8
Liverpool St LVPST EC2M 13 J3
Livesey Cl KUT KT1 .... 152 F6
Livesey Pl PECK SE15 .... 122 A4
Livingstone Rd BTSEA SW11 ... 119 K8 ⊟
HSLW TW3 .... 133 J1
LEY E10 .... 69 H7
PLMGR N13 .... 48 E8
SRTFD E15 .... 87 J8
STHL UB1 .... 96 D6
THHTH CR7 .... 157 K5
Livonia St SOHO/CST W1F ... 10 F5 ⊟
Lizard St FSBYE EC1V 6 F8
Lizban St BKHTH/KID SE3 ... 124 B5
Llanelly Rd CRICK NW2 .... 82 F2
Llanover Rd WBLY HA9 .... 80 D3
WOOL/PLUM SE18 .... 125 C5
Llanthony Rd MRDN SM4 ... 170 D1
Llanvanor Rd CRICK NW2 ... 82 F2
Llewellyn St
BERM/RHTH SE16 .... 104 A8 ⊟
Lloyd Av COUL/CHIP CR5 .... 183 G7
STRHM/NOR SW16 .... 156 E4
Lloyd Baker St FSBYW WC1X ... 6 A8
Lloyd Ct PIN HA5 .... 60 D6
Lloyd Park Av CROY/NA CR0 ... 172 F6
Lloyd Rd DAGW RM9 .... 90 F6
EHAM E6 .... 88 F8
WALTH E17 .... 68 D5
WPK KT4 .... 169 J5
Lloyd's Av TWRH EC3N 13 K5
Lloyd's Pl BKHTH/KID SE3 ... 123 L7 ⊟
Lloyd Sq FSBYW WC1X 6 A7
Lloyd's Rw CLKNW EC1R 6 B8
Lloyd St FSBYW WC1X 6 A7
Lloyds Wy BECK BR3 .... 158 E8
Lloyd Thomas Ct WDGN N22 ... 66 F1 ⊟
Loampit Hl LEW SE13 .... 123 G7
Loampit V LEW SE13 .... 123 H8
Loates La WAT WD17 .... 29 J6
Loats Rd CLAP SW4 .... 138 C3
Local Board Rd WAT WD17 ... 29 J8 ⊟
Locarno Rd ACT W3 .... 99 J7 ⊟
GFD/PVL UB6 .... 97 J3
Lochaber Rd LEW SE13 .... 141 L1
Lochaline St HMSMTH W6 ... 118 C4
Lochan Cl YEAD UB4 .... 96 E3
Lochinvar St BAL SW12 .... 138 B4
Lochmere Cl ERITH DA8 ...... 127 H4
Lochnagar St POP/IOD E14 ... 105 J4
Lock Cha LEW SE13 .... 123 L8
Lock Cl RAIN RM13 .... 111 M1
Lockesley Dr STMC/STPC BR5 ... 176 F1
Locket Rd KTN/HRWW/W HA3 ... 61 M3
Lockfield Av PEND EN3 .... 37 L5
Lockgate Cl HOM E9 .... 86 F5 ⊟
Lockhart Cl HOLWY N7 .... 84 F6
Lockhart St BOW E3 .... 104 F3 ⊟
Lockhurst St CLPT E5 .... 86 D4
Lockington Rd VX/NE SW8 ... 120 B6 ⊟
Lockmead Rd LEW SE13 ...... 123 J8
SEVS/STOTM N15 .... 68 A7 ⊟
Lock Rd RCHPK/HAM TW10 ... 134 C8
Lock's La MTCM CR4 .... 156 A4
Locksley St POP/IOD E14 .... 104 F4
Locksmeade Rd
RCHPK/HAM TW10 .... 134 B8
Lockwood Cl SYD SE26 .... 140 D8 ⊟
Lockwood Wy CHSGTN KT9 ... 168 A7
WALTH E17 .... 68 C4
Lockyer Rd PUR RM19 .... 129 J3
Lockyer St STHWK SE1 .... 19 H2 ⊟
Loddiges Rd HOM E9 .... 86 C7
Loder Cl PEND EN3 .... 37 L5
Loder St PECK SE15 .... 122 C5
Lodge Av BCTR RM8 .... 90 B5
BORE WD6 .... 31 M8
CROY/NA CR0 .... 171 M5
DAGW RM9 .... 90 B8
DART DA1 .... 146 C3
GPK RM2 .... 74 A6
KTN/HRWW/W HA3 .... 62 C5
Lodge Cl CHIG IG7 .... 54 A5
EDGW HA8 .... 44 F8 ⊟
EW KT17 .... 181 J5 ⊟
ISLW TW7 .... 116 B6
MTCM CR4 .... 171 G3
ORP BR6 .... 177 H3
UED N18 .... 49 J7
UX/CGN UB8 .... 94 B1 ⊟
Lodge Crs CHES/WCR EN8 ... 26 E7 ⊟
ORP BR6 .... 177 H3
Lodge Dr PLMGR N13 .... 49 G6
Lodge End RKW/CH/CXG WD3 ... 28 D7
Lodge Gdns BECK BR3 .... 158 F8

Lodge Hl PUR/KEN CR8 .... 184 A8
WELL DA16 .... 126 B5
Lodgehill Park Cl
RYLN/HDSTN HA2 .... 79 H2 ⊟
Lodge La BXLY DA5 .... 144 D3
CROY/NA CR0 .... 186 B1
CRW RM5 .... 55 G8
NFNCH/WDSP N12 .... 47 J7
WAB EN9 .... 27 K8
Lodge Pl SUT SM1 .... 170 B7
Lodge Rd BMLY BR1 .... 160 C3
CROY/NA CR0 .... 172 B1
HDN NW4 .... 64 C5
RKW/CH/CXG WD3 .... 28 D7
STJWD NW8 .... 3 H8
SUT SM1 .... 170 B7
WLGTN SM6 .... 171 H7
Lodge Vls WFD IG8 .... 69 M1
Lodore Gdns CDALE/KGS NW9 ... 63 L6
Lodore Gn HGDN/ICK UB10 ... 76 E3
Lodore St POP/IOD E14 .... 105 J5
Lofthouse Pl CHSGTN KT9 ... 167 J8
Loftie St BERM/RHTH SE16 ... 104 A8
Lofting Rd IS N1 .... 6 A2
Loftus Rd SHB W12 .... 100 B3
Logan Cl HSLWW TW4 .... 114 F8
PEND EN3 .... 37 K4 ⊟
Logan Ms KENS W8 .... 14 A5 ⊟
Logan Pl KENS W8 .... 14 A5
Logan Rd ED N9 .... 50 B4
WBLY HA9 .... 80 E2
Logs Hl CHST BR7 .... 160 E4
Logs Hill Cl CHST BR7 .... 160 E4
Lois Dr SHPTN TW17 .... 149 H8
Lolesworth Cl WCHPL E1 ..... 13 M3 ⊟
Lollard St LBTH SE11 .... 17 M5
Loman Pth SOCK/AV RM15 ... 111 M5
Loman St STHWK SE1 .... 18 D1
Lomas Cl CROY/NA CR0 .... 186 C1
Lomas St WCHPL E1 .... 104 A4
Lombard Av GDMY/SEVK IG3 ... 89 L1
PEND EN3 .... 37 J4
Lombard Rd BTSEA SW11 ... 119 K7
FBAR/BDGN N11 .... 48 B7
WIM/MER SW19 .... 155 H5
The Lombards EMPK RM11 ... 74 F8
Lombard St BANK EC3V 13 H5
Lombard Wall CHARL SE7 ... 124 C1
Lombardy Pl BAY/PAD W2 ... 8 D7 ⊟
Lombardy Wy BORE WD6 ..... 31 L4
Lomond Cl ALP/SUD HA0 ..... 80 F7
SEVS/STOTM N15 .... 67 L5 ⊟
Lomond Gdns SAND/SEL CR2 ... 185 L3
Lomond Gv CMBW SE5 .... 121 K5
Loncroft Rd CMBW SE5 .... 19 K9
Londesborough Rd
STNW/STAM N16 .... 85 L4
London Br CANST EC4R 13 H7
London Flds HACK E8 .... 86 B7 ⊟
London Fields East Side
HACK E8 .... 86 B7
London Fields West Side
HACK E8 .... 86 A7
London La BMLY BR1 .... 159 M3
HACK E8 .... 86 B7
London Loop BNSTD SM7 ... 181 M6
BORE WD6 .... 45 H1
CROY/NA CR0 .... 173 K5
ENC/FH EN2 .... 35 L2
MLHL NW7 .... 45 J2
PUR/KEN CR8 .... 184 E8
SAND/SEL CR2 .... 185 G8
WWKM BR4 .... 174 D5
London Ms BAY/PAD W2 ...... 9 H5
London Rd BARK IG11 .... 89 H7
BMLY BR1 .... 159 M3
BUSH WD23 .... 42 E1
CHDH RM6 .... 73 G7
CHEAM SM3 .... 169 K4
CROY/NA CR0 .... 172 B3
DART DA1 .... 145 K2
ENC/FH EN2 .... 36 D8
EW KT17 .... 169 H7
FSTH SE23 .... 140 C5
GRH DA9 .... 147 L3
ISLW TW7 .... 115 L7
KUT KT1 .... 152 E5
MRDN SM4 .... 155 L8
MTCM CR4 .... 155 M5
PLSTW E13 .... 106 A1
RDART DA2 .... 147 J4
RKW/CH/CXG WD3 .... 40 C3
ROMW/RG RM7 .... 73 J7
RYLN/HDSTN HA2 .... 79 L2
SOCK/AV RM15 .... 111 G8
STAN HA7 .... 44 C7
STHWK SE1 .... 18 C3
STRHM/NOR SW16 .... 156 F5
STWL/WRAY TW19 .... 130 D6
SWLY BR8 .... 163 L6 ⊟
THHTH CR7 .... 172 A1
TWK TW1 .... 134 A4
WBLY HA9 .... 80 E5
WLGTN SM6 .... 171 H4
London Rd Purfleet PUR RM19 ... 129 H4
London Rd West Thurrock
WTHK RM20 .... 129 M4
Londons Cl UPMR RM14 ...... 93 J5 ⊟
London Stile CHSWK W4 ...... 117 G3 ⊟
London St BAY/PAD W2 .... 9 G5
MON EC3R .... 13 K6 ⊟
London Wall BARB EC2Y 12 F3
OBST EC2N 13 H4
Lonesome Wy MTCM CR4 ... 156 B4
Long Acre COVGDN WC2E ... 11 J5
STMC/STPC BR5 .... 177 K4
Longacre PI CAR SM5 .... 171 G8 ⊟
Longacre Rd WALTH E17 ..... 69 K2
Long Barn Cl GSTN WD25 ... 21 G5
Longbeach Rd BTSEA SW11 ... 119 M8
Longboat Rw STHL UB1 ...... 96 F5
Longbridge Rd BARK IG11 ... 89 H4
BCTR RM8 .... 90 A3
Longbridge Wy LEW SE13 ... 141 J4
UX/CGN UB8 .... 94 B1 ⊟
Longbury Cl STMC/STPC BR5 ... 162 B6

Longbury Dr *STMC/STPC* BR5...... 162 B6
Longcliffe Pth *OXHEY* WD19 ...... 42 A5
Long Ct *PUR* SM1 ...... 129 G2
Longcroft *ELTH/MOT* SE9 ...... 143 G7
Long Cft *OXHEY* WD19 ...... 42 B2
Longcroft Av *BNSTD* SM7 ...... 182 C7
Long Croft Rd *CHES/WCR* EN8 ...... 26 F7
Longdeacon Rd *CHING* E4 ...... 51 L3
Longdon Wd *HAYES* BR2 ...... 175 L6
Longdown La North *EW* KT17 ...... 181 C6
Longdown La South *EW* KT17 ...... 181 C6
Longdown Rd *CAT* SE6 ...... 141 G8
EW KT17 ...... 181 C7
Long Dr *ACT* W3 ...... 99 L5
GFD/PVL UB6 ...... 79 H8
RSLP HA4 ...... 78 C4
Long Elmes *KTN/HRWW/W* HA3 ...... 61 J2
Long Elms *ABLGY* WD5 ...... 20 D6
Long Elms CI *ABLGY* WD5 ...... 20 D6
Longfellow Rd *BOW* E3 ...... 104 E2
WALTH E17 ...... 68 F7
WPK KT4 ...... 169 G3
Longfellow Wy *STHWK* SE1 ...... 19 M6
Longfield *BMLY* BR1 ...... 159 M4
Long Fld *CDALE/KGS* NW9 ...... 63 L1
Longfield *LOU* IG10 ...... 39 J8
Longfield Av *EA* W5 ...... 98 C6
EMPK RM11 ...... 73 M8
MLHL NW7 ...... 64 A1
PEND EN3 ...... 37 J2
WALTH E17 ...... 68 E5
WBLY HA9 ...... 80 E1
WLGTN SM6 ...... 171 G3
Longfield Crs *SYD* SE26 ...... 140 C7
Longfield Dr *MORT/ESHN* SW14 ...... 135 H2
WIM/MER SW19 ...... 155 L4
Longfield La *CHESW* EN7 ...... 26 B1
Longfield Rd *EA* W5 ...... 98 C5
Longfield St *WAND/EARL* SW18 ...... 137 C4
Longford Av *EBED/NFELT* TW14 ...... 131 L3
STHL UB1 ...... 97 G6
STWL/WRAY TW19 ...... 130 E5
Longford CI *HPTN* TW12 ...... 133 C8
YEAD UB4 ...... 96 D6
Longford Ct *HOR/WEW* KT19 ...... 168 C6
Longford Gdns *SUT* SM1 ...... 170 C5
YEAD UB4 ...... 96 D6
Longford Rd *WHTN* TW2 ...... 133 C5
Longford St *CAMTN* NW1 ...... 4 D9
Longford Wy
STWL/WRAY TW19 ...... 130 E5
Long Gn *CHIG* IG7 ...... 53 L6
Long Gv *HARH* RM3 ...... 74 E3
Long Grove Rd *HOR/WEW* KT19 ...... 180 B3
Longhayes Av *CHDH* RM6 ...... 72 D4
Longheath Gdns *CROY/NA* CR0 ...... 158 C8
Longhedge St *BTSEA* SW11 ...... 120 A7
Longhill Rd *CAT* SE6 ...... 141 K6
Longhook Gdns *NTHLT* UB5 ...... 96 A1
Longhope CI *PECK* SE15 ...... 121 L4
Longhurst Rd *CROY/NA* CR0 ...... 173 H1
LEW SE13 ...... 141 L2
Longland Dr *TRDG/WHET* N20 ...... 47 H5
Longlands Av *COUL/CHIP* CR5 ...... 183 H7
Longlands CI *CHES/WCR* EN8 ...... 26 D5
Longlands Crs
BFN/LL DA15 ...... 143 L7
Longlands Rd *BFN/LL* DA15 ...... 143 L7
Long La *BXLYHN* DA7 ...... 126 F7
CROY/NA CR0 ...... 173 J1
EFNCH N2 ...... 65 J4
FNCH N3 ...... 65 J3
HGDN/ICK UB10 ...... 77 H5
HGDN/ICK UB10 ...... 95 C1
STBT EC1A 12 D3
STHWK SE1 ...... 19 H2
STWL/WRAY TW19 ...... 130 F4
Longleat Rd *EN* EN1 ...... 36 E8
Longleat Wy *EBED/NFELT* TW14 ...... 131 J4
Longleigh La *ABYW* SE2 ...... 126 C4
Longley Av *ALP/SUD* HA0 ...... 80 F8
Longley Rd *CROY/NA* CR0 ...... 172 B2
HRW HA1 ...... 61 K6
TOOT SW17 ...... 155 L2
Long Leys *CHING* E4 ...... 51 H8
Longley St *STHWK* SE1 ...... 122 A2
Longley Wy *CRICK* NW2 ...... 82 C3
Long Lodge Dr *WOT/HER* KT12 ...... 156 C5
Long Mark Rd *CAN/RD* E16 ...... 106 D5
Long Md *CDALE/KGS* NW9 ...... 63 M2
Longmead *CHST* BR7 ...... 161 G5
Longmead Dr *SCUP* DA14 ...... 144 D6
Long Meadow *BECK* BR3 ...... 174 C2
Longmeadow Rd *BFN/LL* DA15 ...... 143 L5
Longmead Rd *HOR/WEW* KT19 ...... 180 E3
HYS/HAR UB3 ...... 95 M6
THDIT KT7 ...... 166 E2
TOOT SW17 ...... 155 M1
Long Moor *CHES/WCR* EN8 ...... 26 E2
Longmoore St *PIM* SW1V 16 E6
Longmore Av *BAR* EN5 ...... 47 J1
Longmore Rd *WOT/HER* KT12 ...... 165 L6
Longnor Rd *WCHPL* E1 ...... 104 D2
Long Pond Rd *BKHTH/KID* SE3 ...... 123 L6
Longport CI *BARK/HLT* IG6 ...... 54 A8
Long Reach Rd *BARK* IG11 ...... 107 M3
Longreach Rd *ERITH* DA8 ...... 128 B5
Longridge La *GFD/PVL* UB6 ...... 97 H6
Longridge Rd *ECT* SW5 ...... 14 A6
Long Rd *CLAP* SW4 ...... 138 C1
Longshaw Rd *CHING* E4 ...... 51 K5
Longshore *DEPT* SE8 ...... 122 F2
Longspring *WATN* WD24 ...... 29 H2
Longstaff Crs
WAND/EARL SW18 ...... 137 G3
Longstaff Rd
WAND/EARL SW18 ...... 137 G3
Longstone Av *WLSDN* NW10 ...... 81 M7
Longstone Rd *TOOT* SW17 ...... 156 B1
Long St *BETH* E2 ...... 7 L6
Longthornton Rd
STRHM/NOR SW16 ...... 156 C5
Longton Av *SYD* SE26 ...... 140 C5
Longton Gv *SYD* SE26 ...... 140 D8
Longtown Rd *HARH* RM3 ...... 56 C7
Longview Wy *CRW* RM5 ...... 73 K2
Longville Rd *LBTH* SE11 ...... 18 C5

Long Wk *NWMAL* KT3 ...... 153 J6
STHWK SE1 ...... 19 K3
Longwalk Rd *STKPK* UB11 ...... 95 H7
Longwood CI *UPMR* RM14 ...... 93 J5
Longwood Ct *WPK* KT4 ...... 169 G4
Longwood Dr *PUT/ROE* SW15 ...... 136 A3
Longwood Gdns *CLAY* IG5 ...... 70 F5
Longworth CI *THMD* SE28 ...... 108 D5
Long Yd *BMSBY* WC1N 11 L1
The Loning *CDALE/KGS* NW9 ...... 63 M5
PEND EN3 ...... 37 J3
Lonsdale Av *EHAM* E6 ...... 106 D3
ROMW/RG RM7 ...... 73 J7
WBLY HA9 ...... 80 E5
Lonsdale CI *EHAM* E6 ...... 106 E3
LEE/GVPK SE12 ...... 142 D7
UX/CGN UB8 ...... 95 J5
Lonsdale Crs *GNTH/NBYPK* IG2 ...... 71 H7
RDART DA2 ...... 147 J6
Lonsdale Dr *ENC/FH* EN2 ...... 35 K7
STHGT/OAK N14 ...... 35 L8
Lonsdale Dr North *ENC/FH* EN2 ...... 35 L8
Lonsdale Gdns
STRHM/NOR SW16 ...... 156 F7
Lonsdale Ms *RCH/KEW* TW9 ...... 117 C6
Lonsdale PI *IS* N1 ...... 6 B2
Lonsdale Rd *BARN* SW13 ...... 117 M5
BXLYHN DA7 ...... 126 F7
CHSWK W4 ...... 117 M2
KIL/WHAMP NW6 ...... 100 F1
NTGHL W11 ...... 100 F1 (crossed)
NWDGN UB2 ...... 114 D1
SNWD SE25 ...... 158 B1
WAN E11 ...... 69 M8
Lonsdale Sq *IS* N1 ...... 6 B2
Loobert Rd *SEVS/STOTM* N15 ...... 67 L4
Looe Gdns *BARK/HLT* IG6 ...... 71 H4
Loom La *RAD* WD7 ...... 30 F2
Loom PI *RAD* WD7 ...... 31 G1
Loop Rd *CHST* BR7 ...... 161 J2
WAB EN9 ...... 27 H5
Lopen Rd *UED* N18 ...... 49 L6
Loraine CI *PEND* EN3 ...... 37 J8
Loraine Rd *CHSWK* W4 ...... 117 H4
HOLWY N7 ...... 84 F4
Lord Av *CLAY* IG5 ...... 70 F5
Lord Chancellor Wk
KUTN/CMB KT2 ...... 153 J4
Lord Hills Rd *BAY/PAD* W2 ...... 8 D2
Lord Knyvett CI
STWL/WRAY TW19 ...... 130 D3
Lord Knyvetts Ct
STWL/WRAY TW19 ...... 130 E3
Lord Napier PI *HMSMTH* W6 ...... 118 A3
Lord North St *WEST* SW1P 17 J4
Lord Roberts Ter
WOOL/PLUM SE18 ...... 125 G3
Lordsbury Fld *WLGTN* SM6 ...... 183 J5
Lords CI *DUL* SE21 ...... 139 J6
FELT TW13 ...... 132 E6
Lordship Gv *STNW/STAM* N16 ...... 85 K2
Lordship La *DUL* SE21 ...... 140 A5
EDUL SE22 ...... 139 M3
TOTM N17 ...... 67 J2
WDGN N22 ...... 67 H2
Lordship Pk *STNW/STAM* N16 ...... 85 K2
Lordship Park Ms
STNW/STAM N16 ...... 85 J2
Lordship PI *CHEL* SW3 ...... 119 L4
Lordship Rd *CHESW* EN7 ...... 26 B3
NTHLT UB5 ...... 78 E7
STNW/STAM N16 ...... 85 K1
Lordship Ter *STNW/STAM* N16 ...... 85 K2
Lordsmead Rd *TOTM* N17 ...... 67 L2
Lord St *CAN/RD* E16 ...... 106 E7
WAT WD17 ...... 29 J6
Lords Vw *STJWD* NW8 ...... 3 J8
Lordswood Rd *RDART* DA2 ...... 147 L8
Lord Warwick St
WOOL/PLUM SE18 ...... 124 F1
Loretto Gdns
KTN/HRWW/W HA3 ...... 62 E5
Lorian CI *NFNCH/WDSP* N12 ...... 47 H6
Loring Rd *ISLW* TW7 ...... 115 M7
TRDG/WHET N20 ...... 47 L4
Loris Rd *HMSMTH* W6 ...... 118 C1
Lorn Ct *BRXN/ST* SW9 ...... 121 C7
Lorne Av *CROY/NA* CR0 ...... 173 K2
Lorne CI *STJWD* NW8 ...... 3 K8
Lorne Gdns *CROY/NA* CR0 ...... 173 K2
WAN E11 ...... 70 C5
WKENS W14 ...... 100 E8
Lorne Rd *FSBYPK* N4 ...... 84 F1
FSTGT E7 ...... 88 B4
KTN/HRWW/W HA3 ...... 61 M3
RCHPK/HAM TW10 ...... 134 F2
WALTH E17 ...... 69 G6
Lorn Rd *BRXN/ST* SW9 ...... 120 F7
Lorraine Pk *KTN/HRWW/W* HA3 ...... 61 L1
Lorrimore Rd *WALW* SE17 ...... 121 H4
Lorrimore Sq *WALW* SE17 ...... 18 D9
Loseberry Rd *ESH/CLAY* KT10 ...... 166 D7
Lothair Rd *EA* W5 ...... 98 D8
Lothair Rd North *FSBYPK* N4 ...... 67 H7
Lothair Rd South *FSBYPK* N4 ...... 67 G8
Lothbury *LOTH* EC2R 13 G4
Lothian Av *YEAD* UB4 ...... 96 B4
Lothian CI *ALP/SUD* HA0 ...... 80 A4
Lothian Rd *BRXN/ST* SW9 ...... 121 H6
CMBW SE5 ...... 121 H5
Lothrop St *NKENS* W10 ...... 100 E2
Lots Rd *WBPTN* SW10 ...... 119 J5
Loubet St *TOOT* SW17 ...... 155 M2
Loudoun Av *GNTH/NBYPK* IG2 ...... 71 H6
Loudoun Rd *STJWD* NW8 ...... 2 F1
Loudwater CI *SUN* TW16 ...... 150 A7
Loughborough Pk *HNHL* SE24 ...... 139 H1
Loughborough Rd
BRXN/ST SW9 ...... 121 G7
Loughborough St *LBTH* SE11 ...... 17 M7
Lough Rd *HOLWY* N7 ...... 84 F5
Loughton Wy *BKHH* IG9 ...... 52 D3
Louisa St *WCHPL* E1 ...... 104 D4
Louise Bennett CI
HNHL SE24 ...... 139 H1
Louise Gdns *RAIN* RM13 ...... 109 L2
Louise Rd *SRTFD* E15 ...... 87 L2

Louisville Rd *TOOT* SW17 ...... 138 A7
Louvaine Rd *BTSEA* SW11 ...... 137 K1
Louvain Rd *RDART* DA2 ...... 147 L4
Louvain Wy *GSTN* WD25 ...... 21 H5
Lovage Ap *EHAM* E6 ...... 106 E4
Lovat CI *CRICK* NW2 ...... 81 M3
Lovat La *FENCHST* EC3M 13 J6
Lovatt CI *EDGW* HA8 ...... 45 H8
Lovatt Rd *DEN/HRF* UB9 ...... 28 A7
Loveday Rd *WEA* W13 ...... 98 B7
Lovegrove St *STHWK* SE1 ...... 122 A4
Lovegrove Wk *POP/IOD* E14 ...... 105 J2
Lovekyn CI *KUTN/CMB* KT2 ...... 152 E5
Lovelace Av *HAYES* BR2 ...... 176 A1
Lovelace Gdns *BARK* IG11 ...... 90 A4
SURB KT6 ...... 167 K2
WOT/HER KT12 ...... 165 J7
Lovelace Gn *ELTH/MOT* SE9 ...... 124 F8
Lovelace Rd *DUL* SE21 ...... 139 J6
EBAR EN4 ...... 47 L2
SURB KT6 ...... 167 J2
Love La *ABLGY* WD5 ...... 20 F3
BXLY DA5 ...... 145 G3
CHEAM SM3 ...... 169 L8
CITYW EC2V 12 F4
MRDN SM4 ...... 170 A2
MTCM CR4 ...... 155 L6
PIN HA5 ...... 60 E4
SNWD SE25 ...... 158 B6
SOCK/AV RM15 ...... 111 J8
SURB KT6 ...... 167 K4
TOTM N17 ...... 67 M1
WFD IG8 ...... 52 F8
WOOL/PLUM SE18 ...... 125 G2
Lovel Av *WELL* DA16 ...... 126 A7
Lovelinch CI *PECK* SE15 ...... 122 C4
Lovell PI *BERM/RHTH* SE16 ...... 122 E1
Lovell Rd *EN* EN1 ...... 26 B8
GFD/PVL UB6 ...... 97 H5
RCHPK/HAM TW10 ...... 134 C7
Lovell Wk *RAIN* RM13 ...... 92 A6
Loveridge Rd *KIL/WHAMP* NW6 ...... 82 F6
Lovett Dr *CAR* SM5 ...... 170 C2
Lovett Rd *DEN/HRF* UB9 ...... 58 C4
Lovett Wy *WLSDN* NW10 ...... 81 J5
Love Wk *CMBW* SE5 ...... 121 K7
Lovibonds Av *ORP* BR6 ...... 176 B5
WDR/YW UB7 ...... 94 F5
Lowbrook Rd *IL* IG1 ...... 89 H4
Lowdell CI *WDR/YW* UB7 ...... 94 E5
Lowden Rd *ED* N9 ...... 50 B3
HNHL SE24 ...... 139 H1
STHL UB1 ...... 96 E6
Lowe Av *CAN/RD* E16 ...... 106 A4
Lowe CI *CHIG* IG7 ...... 54 A7
Lowell St *POP/IOD* E14 ...... 104 E5
Lowen Rd *RAIN* RM13 ...... 109 K1
Lower Addiscombe Rd
CROY/NA CR0 ...... 172 D3
Lower Addison Gdns
WKENS W14 ...... 100 E8
Lower Barn Rd *PUR/KEN* CR8 ...... 184 C5
Lower Bedfords Rd *ROM* RM1 ...... 56 A8
Lower Belgrave St *BGVA* SW1W 16 C4
Lower Boston Rd *HNWL* W7 ...... 97 L7
Lower Broad St *DAGE* RM10 ...... 91 G8
Lower Camden *CHST* BR7 ...... 160 F4
Lower Church St
CROY/NA CR0 ...... 172 B4
Lower Clapton Rd *CLPT* E5 ...... 86 B4
Lower Common South
PUT/ROE SW15 ...... 118 B8
Lower Coombe St
CROY/NA CR0 ...... 172 C6
Lower Ct *HOR/WEW* KT19 ...... 180 D4
Lower Court Rd
HOR/WEW KT19 ...... 180 C4
Lower Cft *SWLY* BR8 ...... 163 M7
Lower Derby Rd *WAT* WD17 ...... 29 J7
Lower Downs Rd *RYNPK* SW20 ...... 154 D4
Lower Dunnymans
BNSTD SM7 ...... 181 M7
Lower Gravel Rd *HAYES* BR2 ...... 175 L3
Lower Green Rd
ESH/CLAY KT10 ...... 166 B4
Lower Gn West *MTCM* CR4 ...... 155 L6
Lower Grosvenor PI *KTBR* SW1X 16 C3
Lower Grove Rd
RCHPK/HAM TW10 ...... 134 F3
Lower Hall La *CHING* E4 ...... 50 E7
Lower Hampton Rd *SUN* TW16 ...... 150 D5
Lower Ham Rd *KUTN/CMB* KT2 ...... 152 D2
Lower High St *WAT* WD17 ...... 29 K8
Lower Hill Rd *HOR/WEW* KT19 ...... 180 B5
Lower Island Wy *WAB* EN9 ...... 27 H8
Lower James St
SOHO/CST W1F 10 F6
Lower John St *SOHO/CST* W1F 10 F6
Lower Kenwood Av
STHGT/OAK N14 ...... 35 L8
Lower Lea Crossing
POP/IOD E14 ...... 105 L6
Lower Maidstone Rd
FBAR/BDGN N11 ...... 48 C8
Lower Mardyke Av *RAIN* RM13 ...... 109 J1
Lower Marsh *STHWK* SE1 ...... 18 A2
Lower Marsh La *KUT* KT1 ...... 152 F2
Lower Merton Ri *HAMP* NW3 ...... 3 J2
Lower Morden La *MRDN* SM4 ...... 169 L1
Lower Mortlake Rd
RCH/KEW TW9 ...... 134 E1
Lower Noke CI *BRW* CM14 ...... 56 E4
Lower Northfield
BNSTD SM7 ...... 181 M7
Lower Paddock Rd
OXHEY WD19 ...... 42 E1
Lower Park Rd *BELV* DA17 ...... 127 G1
FBAR/BDGN N11 ...... 48 C7
LOU IG10 ...... 39 K8
Lower Pillory Down *CAR* SM5 ...... 183 G6
Lower Queen's Rd *BKHH* IG9 ...... 52 E4
Lower Richmond Rd
MORT/ESHN SW14 ...... 117 J8
PUT/ROE SW15 ...... 118 C8
RCH/KEW TW9 ...... 117 G8
Lower Rd *BELV* DA17 ...... 127 H1
BERM/RHTH SE16 ...... 104 C8
BERM/RHTH SE16 ...... 122 D2

Lower Sawleywood
BNSTD SM7 ...... 181 M7
Lower Sloane St *BGVA* SW1W 15 M6
Lower Station Rd *DART* DA1 ...... 145 L3
Lower Strd *CDALE/KGS* NW9 ...... 63 M3
Lower Sunbury Rd *HPTN* TW12 ...... 150 F5
Lower Tail *OXHEY* WD19 ...... 42 E5
Lower Teddington Rd *KUT* KT1 ...... 152 D4
Lower Ter *HAMP* NW3 ...... 83 J3
Lower Thames St *MON* EC3R 13 J7
Lower Tub *BUSH* WD23 ...... 43 K2
Lower Wood Rd
ESH/CLAY KT10 ...... 167 G8
Lowestoft Rd *WATN* WD24 ...... 29 H4
WBLY HA9 ...... 80 D2
The Lowe *CHIG* IG7 ...... 54 A7
Lowfield Rd *ACT* W3 ...... 99 J5
KIL/WHAMP NW6 ...... 2 A1
Lowfield St *DART* DA1 ...... 146 E4
Low Hall CI *CHING* E4 ...... 51 C2
Low Hall La *WALTH* E17 ...... 68 E7
Lowick Rd *HRW* HA1 ...... 61 L5
Lowland Gdns *ROMW/RG* RM7 ...... 73 H6
Lowlands Rd *HRW* HA1 ...... 61 L8
PIN HA5 ...... 60 C8
SOCK/AV RM15 ...... 111 J7
STWL/WRAY TW19 ...... 130 C2
Lowman Rd *HOLWY* N7 ...... 84 F4
Lowndes CI *KTBR* SW1X 16 A3
Lowndes PI *KTBR* SW1X 16 A4
Lowndes Sq *KTBR* SW1X 15 M2
Lowndes St *KTBR* SW1X 15 M3
Lowood St *WCHPL* E1 ...... 104 B6
Lowry Crs *MTCM* CR4 ...... 155 L5
Lowry Rd *BCTR* RM8 ...... 90 B5
Lowshoe La *ROMW/RG* RM7 ...... 73 H2
Lowson Gv *OXHEY* WD19 ...... 42 E2
Lowswood CI *NTHWD* HA6 ...... 59 J2
Lowther CI *BORE* WD6 ...... 31 M8
Lowther Dr *ENC/FH* EN2 ...... 35 L7
Lowther HI *FSTH* SE23 ...... 140 E4
Lowther Rd *BARN* SW13 ...... 117 M6
HOLWY N7 ...... 85 G5
KUTN/CMB KT2 ...... 152 F4
STAN HA7 ...... 62 F4
WALTH E17 ...... 68 E5
Lowth Rd *CMBW* SE5 ...... 121 J7
Loxford Av *EHAM* E6 ...... 106 D1
Loxford La *IL* IG1 ...... 89 J5
Loxford Rd *BARK* IG11 ...... 89 H6
Loxham Rd *CHING* E4 ...... 69 H1
Loxham St *STPAN* WC1H 5 K8
Loxley CI *SYD* SE26 ...... 158 D1
Loxley Rd *HPTN* TW12 ...... 132 F8
WAND/EARL SW18 ...... 137 K5
Loxton Rd *FSTH* SE23 ...... 140 D5
Loxwood CI *EBED/NFELT* TW14 ...... 131 K5
STMC/STPC BR5 ...... 177 K4
Loxwood Rd *TOTM* N17 ...... 67 L4
Lubbock Rd *CHST* BR7 ...... 160 F3
Lubbock St *NWCR* SE14 ...... 122 E7
Lucan Dr *STA* TW18 ...... 148 D3
Lucan PI *CHEL* SW3 ...... 15 J4
Lucan Rd *BAR* EN5 ...... 33 L6
Lucas Av *CHING* E4 ...... 51 L8
RYLN/HDSTN HA2 ...... 79 C2
Lucas Rd *PGE/AN* SE20 ...... 158 C2
Lucas St *DEPT* SE8 ...... 123 G7
Lucerne CI *PLMGR* N13 ...... 48 E5
Lucerne Gv *WALTH* E17 ...... 69 K5
Lucerne Ms *KENS* W8 ...... 8 B8
Lucerne Rd *HBRY* N5 ...... 85 H4
ORP BR6 ...... 176 F3
THHTH CR7 ...... 157 H8
Lucerne Wy *HARH* RM3 ...... 56 D8
Lucey Rd *BERM/RHTH* SE16 ...... 122 A1
Lucey Wy *BERM/RHTH* SE16 ...... 122 A1
Lucie Av *ASHF* TW15 ...... 149 H2
Lucien Rd *TOOT* SW17 ...... 138 A4
WAND/EARL SW18 ...... 137 H6
Lucknow St *WOOL/PLUM* SE18 ...... 125 L5
Lucorn CI *LEE/GVPK* SE12 ...... 141 M3
Luctons Av *BKHH* IG9 ...... 52 C3
Ludford CI *CDALE/KGS* NW9 ...... 63 L3
CROY/NA CR0 ...... 172 B6
Ludgate Broadway
BLKFR EC4V 12 D5
Ludgate HI *STP* EC4M 12 C5
Ludgate Sq *BLKFR* EC4V 12 D5
Ludham CI *THMD* SE28 ...... 108 C5
Ludlow CI *HAYES* BR2 ...... 160 A6
RYLN/HDSTN HA2 ...... 78 F4
Ludlow Md *OXHEY* WD19 ...... 42 B5
Ludlow Rd *EA* W5 ...... 98 C3
FELT TW13 ...... 132 A7
Ludlow St *FSBYE* EC1V 6 E9
Ludlow Wy *EFNCH* N2 ...... 65 J5
RKW/CH/CXG WD3 ...... 28 C7
Ludovick Wk *PUT/ROE* SW15 ...... 135 L1
Luffield Rd *ABYW* SE2 ...... 126 B1
Luffman Rd *LEE/GVPK* SE12 ...... 142 B7
Lugard Rd *PECK* SE15 ...... 122 B7
Lugg Ap *MNPK* E12 ...... 89 C3
Luke St *SDTCH* EC2A 7 J9
Lukin Crs *CHING* E4 ...... 51 K5
Lukin St *WCHPL* E1 ...... 104 C5
Lullingstone Av *SWLY* BR8 ...... 163 M6
Lullingstone CI
STMC/STPC BR5 ...... 162 B3
Lullingstone Crs
STMC/STPC BR5 ...... 162 A3
Lullingstone La *LEW* SE13 ...... 141 K3
Lullingstone Rd *BELV* DA17 ...... 126 F4
Lullington Garth *BORE* WD6 ...... 32 B8
MLHL NW7 ...... 46 F7
Lullington Rd *DAGW* RM9 ...... 90 A7
PGE/AN SE20 ...... 158 A3
Lulworth Av *CHESW* EN7 ...... 25 H2
HEST TW5 ...... 115 H6
WBLY HA9 ...... 62 C8

Lulworth Crs *MTCM* CR4 ...... 155 L5
Lulworth Dr *CRW* RM5 ...... 55 H7
PIN HA5 ...... 60 D8
Lulworth Gdns
RYLN/HDSTN HA2 ...... 78 E2
Lulworth Rd *ELTH/MOT* SE9 ...... 142 F5
PECK SE15 ...... 122 B7
WELL DA16 ...... 125 M7
Lulworth Waye *YEAD* UB4 ...... 96 B5
Lumley CI *BELV* DA17 ...... 127 C4
Lumley Gdns *CHEAM* SM3 ...... 169 L7
Lumley Rd *CHEAM* SM3 ...... 169 L8
Lumley St *MYFR/PKLN* W1K 10 B5
Luna Rd *THHTH* CR7 ...... 157 K6
Lundin Wk *OXHEY* WD19 ...... 42 D6
Lundy Dr *HYS/HAR* UB3 ...... 113 L2
Lunedale Rd *RDART* DA2 ...... 147 L5
Lunham Rd *NRWD* SE19 ...... 157 L2
Lupin CI *BRXS/STRHM* SW2 ...... 139 H6
CROY/NA CR0 ...... 173 K3
ROMW/RG RM7 ...... 91 K2
WDR/YW UB7 ...... 112 D3
Lupton CI *LEE/GVPK* SE12 ...... 142 B8
Lupton St *KTTN* NW5 ...... 84 C4
Lupus St *PIM* SW1V 17 G7
Lurgan Av *HMSMTH* W6 ...... 118 D4
Lurline Gdns *BTSEA* SW11 ...... 120 A6
Luscombe Wy *VX/NE* SW8 ...... 120 E5
Lushington Rd *CAT* SE6 ...... 159 H1
WLSDN NW10 ...... 100 B1
Lushington Ter *HACK* E8 ...... 86 A5
Luther CI *EDGW* HA8 ...... 45 J4
Luther King CI *WALTH* E17 ...... 68 E7
Luton PI *GNWCH* SE10 ...... 123 J5
Luton Rd *PLSTW* E13 ...... 106 A3
SCUP DA14 ...... 144 C7
WALTH E17 ...... 68 E4
Luton St *STJWD* NW8 ...... 9 H1
Luttrell Av *PUT/ROE* SW15 ...... 136 B2
Lutwyche Rd *FSTH* SE23 ...... 140 F6
Luxborough La *CHIG* IG7 ...... 52 F6
Luxborough St *MHST* W1U 10 A1
Luxemburg Gdns *HMSMTH* W6 ...... 118 D2
Luxfield Rd *ELTH/MOT* SE9 ...... 142 E5
Luxford St *BERM/RHTH* SE16 ...... 122 D2
Luxmore St *BROCKY* SE4 ...... 122 F6
Luxor St *CMBW* SE5 ...... 121 H7
Lyall Av *DUL* SE21 ...... 139 L8
Lyall Ms *KTBR* SW1X 16 A4
Lyall Ms West *KTBR* SW1X 16 A4
Lyall St *KTBR* SW1X 16 A4
Lyal Rd *BOW* E3 ...... 104 E1
Lycett PI *SHB* W12 ...... 100 A8
Lych Ga *GSTN* WD25 ...... 21 K6
Lych Gate Rd *ORP* BR6 ...... 177 G3
Lych Gate Wk *HYS/HAR* UB3 ...... 95 M6
Lyconby Gdns *CROY/NA* CR0 ...... 173 L2
Lydd CI *BFN/LL* DA15 ...... 143 L7
Lydden Gv *WAND/EARL* SW18 ...... 137 H4
Lydden Rd *WAND/EARL* SW18 ...... 137 H4
Lydd Rd *BXLYHN* DA7 ...... 126 F5
Lydeard Rd *EHAM* E6 ...... 88 F7
Lydford CI *CRICK* NW2 ...... 82 D6
MV/WKIL W9 ...... 100 F3
SEVS/STOTM N15 ...... 67 K6
Lydhurst Av *BRXS/STRHM* SW2 ...... 138 F3
Lydia Rd *ERITH* DA8 ...... 127 M4
Lydney CI *PECK* SE15 ...... 121 L5
WIM/MER SW19 ...... 136 E6
Lydon Rd *CLAP* SW4 ...... 120 C3
Lydstep Rd *CHST* BR7 ...... 143 C8
Lyfield *COB* KT11 ...... 178 B7
Lyford Rd *WAND/EARL* SW18 ...... 137 K4
Lyford St *CHARL* SE7 ...... 124 C7
Lygon PI *BGVA* SW1W 16 C4
Lyham CI *CLAP* SW4 ...... 138 C3
Lyham Rd *BRXS/STRHM* SW2 ...... 138 E2
Lyle CI *MTCM* CR4 ...... 171 G2
Lymbourne CI *BELMT* SM2 ...... 182 A3
Lyme Farm Rd *LEE/GVPK* SE12 ...... 142 A1
Lyme Gv *HOM* E9 ...... 86 C7
Lymer Av *NRWD* SE19 ...... 157 M1
Lyme Rd *WELL* DA16 ...... 126 B6
Lymescote Gdns *SUT* SM1 ...... 170 A4
Lyme St *CAMTN* NW1 ...... 4 E2
Lyminge CI *SCUP* DA14 ...... 143 M8
Lyminge Gdns
WAND/EARL SW18 ...... 137 L3
Lymington Av *WDGN* N22 ...... 67 G3
Lymington CI
STRHM/NOR SW16 ...... 156 D5
Lymington Dr *RSLP* HA4 ...... 77 K2
Lymington Gdns
HOR/WEW KT19 ...... 168 F7
Lymington Rd *BCTR* RM8 ...... 90 D1
KIL/WHAMP NW6 ...... 83 H6
Lynbridge Gdns *PLMGR* N13 ...... 49 H6
Lynbrook CI *PECK* SE15 ...... 121 L5
RAIN RM13 ...... 109 K1
Lynch CI *UX/CGN* UB8 ...... 76 C7
Lynchen CI *HEST* TW5 ...... 114 B6
The Lynch *UX/CGN* UB8 ...... 76 C7
Lyncroft Av *PIN* HA5 ...... 60 D6
Lyncroft Gdns *EW* KT17 ...... 180 F7
HSLW TW3 ...... 133 J2
KIL/WHAMP NW6 ...... 83 G5
WEA W13 ...... 98 C8
Lyndale *CRICK* NW2 ...... 82 D2
Lyndale Av *CRICK* NW2 ...... 82 F3
Lyndale CI *BKHTH/KID* SE3 ...... 123 M4
Lyndale Hampton Court Wy
ESH/CLAY KT10 ...... 166 D2
Lynden Wy *SWLY* BR8 ...... 163 L6
Lyndhurst Av *BRYLDS* KT5 ...... 168 B3
MLHL NW7 ...... 45 L8
NFNCH/WDSP N12 ...... 47 M8
PIN HA5 ...... 60 D2
STHL UB1 ...... 97 H7
STRHM/NOR SW16 ...... 156 D5
SUN TW16 ...... 150 A6
WHTN TW2 ...... 132 F5
Lyndhurst CI *BXLYHN* DA7 ...... 127 H5
CROY/NA CR0 ...... 172 D6
ORP BR6 ...... 176 B6
WLSDN NW10 ...... 81 K3
Lyndhurst Dr *EMPK* RM11 ...... 92 C1
NWMAL KT3 ...... 168 E1
WAN E11 ...... 69 J8

Lyndhurst Gdns *BARK* IG11 ...... 89 L6
 EN EN1 .... 36 E7
 FNCH N3 .... 64 E2
 GNTH/NBYPK IG2 .... 71 K7
 HAMP NW3 .... 83 K5 ⑤
 PIN HA5 .... 60 B2
Lyndhurst Gv *CMBW* SE5 ...... 121 L7
Lyndhurst Ri *CHIG* IG7 .... 53 C6
Lyndhurst Rd *BXLYHN* DA7 .. 127 H8
 CHING E4 .... 69 J1
 GFD/PVL UB6 .... 97 H3
 HAMP NW3 .... 83 K5
 THHTH CR7 .... 157 C7
 UED N18 .... 50 A6
 WDGN N22 .... 49 G8
Lyndhurst Sq *PECK* SE15 ..... 121 M6 ⑤
Lyndhurst Ter *HAMP* NW3 ... 83 K5 ①
Lyndhurst Wy *BELMT* SM2 .. 182 A1 ⑤
 PECK SE15 .... 121 M6
Lyndon Av *BFN/LL* DA15 .... 143 M2
 PIN HA5 .... 42 E8
 WLGTN SM6 .... 171 C5
Lyndon Rd *BELV* DA17 ...... 127 C2
Lyndon Yd *TOOT* SW17 ..... 137 H8
Lyne Crs *WALTH* E17 .... 68 F2
Lynegrove Av *ASHF* TW15 .. 149 J1
Lyneham Wk *CLPT* E5 .... 86 E5 ⑤
Lynette Av *CLAP* SW4 ...... 138 B3
Lynford Cl *EDGW* HA8 ...... 63 J2
Lynford Gdns *EDGW* HA8 ... 45 H5
 GDMY/SEVK IG3 .... 89 M2
Lynhurst Crs *HGDN/ICK* UB10 .. 77 J3
Lynhurst Rd *HGDN/ICK* UB10 .. 77 J7
Lynmere Rd *WELL* DA16 .... 126 B7
Lynmouth Av *EN* EN1 .... 49 M1
 MRDN SM4 .... 169 K2
Lynmouth Dr *RSLP* HA4 .... 78 B2
Lynmouth Gdns *GFD/PVL* UB6 .. 80 B8
 HEST TW5 .... 114 D6
Lynmouth Ri *STMC/STPC* BR5 .. 162 B7
Lynmouth Rd *EFNCH* N2 .... 65 M4
 GFD/PVL UB6 .... 80 B8
 STNW/STAM N16 .... 85 M1
 WALTH E17 .... 68 C7
Lynn Cl *ASHF* TW15 .... 149 K1
 KTN/HRWW/W HA3 ...... 61 K3
Lynne Cl *ORP* BR6 .... 176 F8 ⑤
 SAND/SEL CR2 .... 185 J4
Lynne Wk *ESH/CLAY* KT10 .. 166 C7
Lynne Wy *NTHLT* UB5 .... 96 D1
 WLSDN NW10 .... 81 L7
Lynn Rd *BAL* SW12 .... 138 B4
 GNTH/NBYPK IG2 .... 71 K8
 WAN E11 .... 87 C2
Lynn St *ENC/FH* EN2 .... 36 D4
Lynross Cl *BARH* RM3 ...... 74 E3
Lynscott Wy *SAND/SEL* CR2 .. 184 B2
Lynstead Cl *BMLY* BR1 .... 160 C5
Lynsted Cl *BXLYHS* DA6 ... 145 H2
Lynsted Ct *BECK* BR3 ...... 158 E5 ①
Lynsted Gdns *ELTH/MOT* SE9 .. 142 D1
Lynton Av *ACT* W3 .... 99 J5
 CDALE/KGS NW9 .... 63 H5
 NFNCH/WDSP N12 .... 47 K6
 ROMW/RG RM7 .... 73 J2
 STMC/STPC BR5 .... 162 B7
 WEA W13 .... 98 A5
Lynton Cl *CHSGTN* KT9 .... 167 L6
 ISLW TW7 .... 133 M2
 WLSDN NW10 .... 81 L5
Lynton Crs *GNTH/NBYPK* IG2 .. 71 H7
Lynton Gdns *EN* EN1 .... 49 L2
 FBAR/BDGN N11 .... 48 D8
Lynton Md *TRDG/WHET* N20 .. 47 C5
Lynton Rd *ACT* W3 .... 99 C6
 CEND/HSY/T N8 .... 66 D6
 CHING E4 .... 51 H7
 CROY/NA CR0 .... 172 A1
 KIL/WHAMP NW6 .... 2 D6
 NWMAL KT3 .... 153 K8
 RYLN/HDSTN HA2 .... 78 E2
 STHWK SE1 .... 19 M6
Lynwood Av *COUL/CHIP* CR5 .. 183 H8
 EW KT17 .... 180 F7
Lynwood Dr *CRW* RM5 ..... 73 H1
 NTHWD HA6 .... 59 L2
 WPK KT4 .... 169 C4
Lynwood Gdns *CROY/NA* CR0.. 171 M6
 STHL UB1 .... 96 F5 ⑤
Lynwood Gv *ORP* BR6 ...... 176 E2
 WCHMH N21 .... 49 C3
Lynwood Rd *EA* W5 .... 98 D2
 EW KT17 .... 180 F7
 THDT KT7 .... 166 F4
 TOOT SW17 .... 137 M7
Lyon Meade *STAN* HA7 ..... 62 C2
Lyon Park Av *ALP/SUD* HA0 .. 80 E6
Lyon Rd *HRW* HA1 .... 61 M7
 ROM RM1 .... 73 M8
 WIM/MER SW19 .... 155 J4
 WOT/HER KT12 .... 165 L4
Lyonsdown Av *BAR* EN5 ... 47 J1
Lyonsdown Rd *BAR* EN5 ... 47 J1
Lyons Pl *STJWD* NW8 .... 9 C1
Lyon St *IS* N1 .... 5 L2
Lyons Wk *WKENS* W14 ..... 118 C2
Lyon Wy *GFD/PVL* UB6 ..... 79 L8
Lyoth Rd *STMC/STPC* BR5 .. 176 C4 ①
Lyric Dr *GFD/PVL* UB6 ...... 97 H3
Lyric Ms *SYD* SE26 .... 140 C8
Lyric Rd *BARN* SW13 ...... 117 M6
Lysander Gdns *SURB* KT6 .. 167 M1 ①
Lysander Gv *ARCH* N19 .... 84 D1
Lysander Rd *CROY/NA* CR0 .. 171 M8
 RSLP HA4 .... 77 K2
Lysander Wy *ABLGY* WD5 .. 21 C5 ①
 ORP BR6 .... 176 C5 ②
Lysias Rd *BAL* SW12 .... 138 A3
Lysia St *FUL/PGN* SW6 ..... 118 D5
Lysons Wk *PUT/ROE* SW15 .. 136 A2 ②
Lytchet Rd *BMLY* BR1 ..... 160 A3
Lytchgate Cl *SAND/SEL* CR2 .. 184 L1
Lytcott Dr *E/WMO/HCT* KT8 .. 150 F6 ⑤
Lytcott Gv *EDUL* SE22 ..... 139 M2

Lytham Av *OXHEY* WD19 ... 42 D7
Lytham Gv *EA* W5 .... 98 E2
Lytham St *WALW* SE17 ..... 19 C8
Lyttelton Cl *HAMP* NW3 ..... 3 J2
Lyttelton Rd *EFNCH* N2 .... 65 K6 ①
 LEY E10 .... 87 H3
Lyttleton Cl *HAMP* NW3 ..... 3 J2
Lyttleton Rd *CEND/HSY/T* N8 .. 67 G4 ⑤
Lytton Av *PEND* EN3 .... 37 L3
 PLMGR N13 .... 49 C4
Lytton Cl *EFNCH* N2 .... 65 K6 ②
 NTHLT UB5 .... 78 F7
Lytton Gdns *WLGTN* SM6 ... 171 K6
Lytton Gv *PUT/ROE* SW15 .. 136 D2
Lytton Rd *BAR* EN5 .... 34 C7
 GPK RM2 .... 74 B6
 PIN HA5 .... 60 E1
 WAN E11 .... 69 L8
Lyveden Rd *BKHTH/KID* SE3 .. 124 B5
 WIM/MER SW19 .... 155 L2

M

Mabbutt Cl *LCOL/BKTW* AL2 .. 21 L3
Maberley Crs *NRWD* SE19 .. 158 A3
Maberley Rd *BECK* BR3 .... 158 D6
 NRWD SE19 .... 157 M4
Mabledon Pl *CAMTN* NW1 ... 5 H8
Mablethorpe Rd *FUL/PGN* SW6 .. 118 E5
Mabley St *HOM* E9 .... 86 E5
Macaret Cl *TRDG/WHET* N20 .. 47 H2
Macarthur Cl *FSTGT* E7 .... 88 A6
Macaulay Av *ESH/CLAY* KT10 .. 166 E4
Macaulay Rd *CLAP* SW4 .... 120 B8
 EHAM E6 .... 106 D1
Macbean St *WOOL/PLUM* SE18 .. 125 L1
Macbeth St *HMSMTH* W6 .. 118 B3
Macclesfield Rd *FSBYE* EC1V .. 6 E7
 SNWD SE25 .... 158 B8
Macclesfield St
 SOHO/SHAV W1D .... 11 H6 ④
Macdonald Av *DAGE* RM10 .. 91 H3
 EMPK RM11 .... 74 E5
Macdonald Rd *ARCH* N19 .. 84 C2 ②
 FBAR/BDGN N11 .... 47 M7
 FSTGT E7 .... 88 A4
 WALTH E17 .... 69 J3
Macdonald Wy *EMPK* RM11 .. 74 E5 ②
Macdonnell Gdns *GSTN* WD25 .. 20 F8 ③
Macduff Rd *BTSEA* SW11 ... 120 A6
Mace Gtwy *CAN/RD* E16 ... 106 C6
Mace St *BETH* E2 .... 104 D1 ⑤
 BETH E2 .... 104 D1 ⑤
Macfarlane La *ISLW* TW7 ... 115 M4
Macfarlane Rd *SHB* W12 ... 100 C7
Mac Farren Pl *CAMTN* NW1 .. 10 B1
Macgregor Rd *CAN/RD* E16 .. 106 C4
Machell Rd *PECK* SE15 .... 122 C8
Mackay Rd *CLAP* SW4 ..... 120 B8 ⑤
Mackennal St *STJWD* NW8 ... 3 K6
Mackenzie Rd *BECK* BR3 .. 158 E4 ②
 HOLWY N7 .... 84 F4
Mackeson Rd *HAMP* NW3 .. 83 M4 ②
Mackie Rd *BRXS/STRHM* SW2 .. 139 G4
Mackintosh La *HOM* E9 .... 86 D5 ②
Macklin St *HOL/ALD* WC2B .. 11 K4 ⑤
Macks Rd *BERM/RHTH* SE16 .. 122 A2
Mackworth St *CAMTN* NW1 ... 4 E7
Maclean Rd *FSTH* SE23 .... 140 E3
Maclennan Av *RAIN* RM13 .. 110 D2
Macleod Rd *STHGT/OAK* N14 .. 35 L8 ⑤
 WCHMH N21 .... 35 M8 ⑤
Macleod St *WALW* SE17 .... 18 F8
Maclise Rd *WKENS* W14 ... 118 C1
Macoma Rd *WOOL/PLUM* SE18 .. 125 K4
Macoma Ter *WOOL/PLUM* SE18 .. 125 K4
Maconochies Rd
 POP/IOD E14 .... 123 H3 ①
Macon Wy *UPMR* RM14 .... 75 M7
Macquarie Wy *POP/IOD* E14 .. 123 H2
Macroom Rd *MV/WKIL* W9 .. 100 F2 ③
Mada Rd *ORP* BR6 .... 176 B5
Maddams St *BOW* E3 ...... 105 H3
Maddison Cl *TEDD* TW11 .. 151 M2
Maddox St *MYFR/PKLN* W1K .. 10 D6
Madeira Av *BMLY* BR1 .... 159 L4
Madeira Gv *IL* IG8 .... 52 C8 ③
Madeira Rd *MTCM* CR4 .... 155 M7
 PLMGR N13 .... 49 H6
 STRHM/NOR SW16 ..... 156 E1
 WAN E11 .... 87 K1
Madeira Wk *EPSOM* KT18 .. 180 D5
Madeley Rd *EA* W5 .... 98 E5
Madeline Gv *IL* IG1 .... 89 K5
Madeline Rd *PGE/AN* SE20 .. 158 A3
Madge Gill Wy *EHAM* E6 .. 88 E8
Madison Crs *WELL* DA16 .. 126 C5
Madison Gdns *BXLYHN* DA7 .. 126 C5
Madras Pl *HOLWY* N7 ...... 85 C6
Madras Rd *IL* IG1 .... 89 H4
Madrid Rd *BARN* SW13 .... 118 A6
Madron St *STHWK* SE1 .... 19 K7
Mafeking Rd *BTFD* TW8 ... 116 E4
 EHAM E6 .... 106 D1
 GNTH/NBYPK IG2 .... 71 K8
Mafeking Rd *CAN/RD* E16 .. 105 M3
 EN EN1 .... 36 D1
 TOTM N17 .... 68 A3
Magdala Av *KTTN* NW5 .... 84 C2
Magdala Rd *ISLW* TW7 .... 116 B6
 SAND/SEL CR2 .... 184 D1 ①
Magdalene Gdns *EHAM* E6 .. 107 C3 ②
Magdalene Rd *SHPTN* TW17 .. 148 F6
Magdalen Rd
 WAND/EARL SW18 ...... 137 J5
Magdalen St *STHWK* SE1 .. 13 J9 ②
Magdelan Gv *ORP* BR6 .... 177 H6
Magee St *LBTH* SE11 ...... 18 A9
Magnaville Rd *BUSH* WD23 .. 13 L2
Magnin Cl *HACK* E8 .... 86 A8 ①
Magnolia Av *ABLGY* WD5 ... 20 F5
Magnolia Cl *KUTN/CMB* KT2 .. 153 H2
 LEY E10 .... 87 G2 ③
Magnolia Ct
 KTN/HRWW/W HA3 ..... 62 F8 ①
Magnolia Pl *CLAP* SW4 .... 138 E2 ①

Magnolia Rd *CHSWK* W4 .. 117 H4
Magnolia St *WDR/YW* UB7 .. 112 D2
Magnolia Wy *HOR/WEW* KT19 .. 168 C7
Magnum Cl *RAIN* RM13 .... 110 C3 ③
Magpie Cl *EN* EN1 .... 37 C4
 FSTGT E7 .... 87 M5
Magpie Hall Cl *HAYES* BR2 .. 175 L1
Magpie Hall La *HAYES* BR2 .. 160 F8 ①
Magpie Hall Rd *BUSH* WD23 .. 43 L4
Maguire Dr *RCHPK/HAM* TW10 .. 134 C8
Maguire St *STHWK* SE1 .... 19 M1
 WAP E1W 13 M9
Mahlon Av *RSLP* HA4 ...... 78 B5
Mahogany Cl *BERM/RHTH* SE16 .. 104 E7
Mahon Cl *EN* EN1 .... 36 F4
 CHING E4 .... 51 H2
Maida Rd *BELV* DA17 ...... 127 C1
Maida V *BAY/PAD* W2 ..... 8 F2
 CHING E4 .... 51 H2
Maida V *KIL/WHAMP* NW6 ... 2 D6
 MV/WKIL W9 .... 2 F9
 STJWD NW8 .... 3 C9
Maida Vale Rd *DART* DA1 .. 146 A3
Maida Wy *CHING* E4 .... 51 H2
Maiden Erlegh Av *BXLY* DA5 .. 144 E5
Maiden La *CAMTN* NW1 .... 5 H1
 DART DA1 .... 128 A8
 STHWK SE1 .... 12 F9
Maiden Rd *SRTFD* E15 ..... 87 L7
Maidenshaw Rd
 HOR/WEW KT19 .... 180 D5
Maidenstone HI *GNWCH* SE10 .. 123 J6
Maidstone Av *CRW* RM5 ... 73 J3
Maidstone Rd *FBAR/BDGN* N11 .. 48 D8
 SCUP DA14 .... 162 F3
 SWLY BR8 .... 163 H4
Main Av *EN* EN1 .... 36 F8
 NTHWD HA6 .... 41 J5
Mainridge Rd *CHST* BR7 .. 143 C8
Main Rd *BFN/LL* DA15 ..... 143 L7
 BH/WHM TN16 .... 187 J6
 GPK RM2 .... 74 C3
 ROM RM1 .... 73 M5
 STMC/STPC BR5 .... 162 C6
 SWLY BR8 .... 163 M4
Main St *FELT* TW13 .... 150 D1
Maise Webster Cl
 STWL/WRAY TW19 ..... 130 D4 ③
Maismore St *PECK* SE15 .. 122 A4 ③
Maitland Cl *GNWCH* SE10 .. 123 H5 ③
 HSLWW TW4 .... 114 F8
 WOT/HER KT12 .... 165 L4
Maitland Park Rd *HAMP* NW3 .. 83 M5
Maitland Park Vis *HAMP* NW3 .. 83 M6 ①
Maitland Rd *SRTFD* E15 ... 87 M6 ①
 SYD SE26 .... 157 G2
Majendie Rd *WOOL/PLUM* SE18 .. 125 K3
Major Rd *BERM/RHTH* SE16 .. 122 A1 ⑤
 SRTFD E15 .... 87 K5 ③
Makepeace Av *HGT* N6 ... 84 A2
Makepeace Rd *NTHLT* UB5 .. 96 E1
 WAN E11 .... 70 A5
Makins St *CHEL* SW3 ...... 15 K6
Malabar St *POP/IOD* E14 .. 105 C8
Malam Gdns *POP/IOD* E14 .. 105 H6 ③
Malan Sq *RAIN* RM13 ...... 92 B6
Malbrook Rd *PUT/ROE* SW15 .. 136 B1
Malcolm Ct *STAN* HA7 ..... 44 C7
Malcolm Crs *HDN* NW4 .... 64 A6
Malcolm Dr *SURB* KT6 .... 167 K3
Malcolm Pl *BETH* E2 ...... 104 C3
Malcolm Rd *COUL/CHIP* CR5 .. 183 K8
 HGDN/ICK UB10 .... 76 F4
 PGE/AN SE20 .... 158 C3
 SNWD SE25 .... 173 C1
 WCHPL E1 .... 104 C3
 WIM/MER SW19 .... 154 E2
Malcolm Wy *WAN* E11 .... 70 A6
Malden Av *NTHLT* UB5 .... 79 L6
 SNWD SE25 .... 158 B7
Malden Flds *BUSH* WD23 .. 29 K8
Malden Green Av *WPK* KT4 .. 168 E3
Malden HI *NWMAL* KT3 ... 153 M7
Malden Hill Gdns *NWMAL* KT3 .. 153 M6
Malden Pk *NWMAL* KT3 ... 168 F1
Malden Pl *KTTN* NW5 ...... 84 A3 ③
Malden Rd *BORE* WD6 .... 32 A6
 CHEAM SM3 .... 169 K6
 KTTN NW5 .... 83 M5
 NWMAL KT3 .... 168 F2
 WAT WD17 .... 29 C5 ③
 WPK KT4 .... 168 F2
Malden Wy *NWMAL* KT3 .. 153 M8 ③
Malden Wy (Kingston by Pass)
 NWMAL KT3 .... 153 M8
Maldon Cl *CMBW* SE5 ..... 121 L8 ②
 IS N1 .... 6 E3
Maldon Rd *ACT* W3 .... 99 J6
 ED N9 .... 49 M5
 ROMW/RG RM7 .... 73 J8
 WLGTN SM6 .... 171 H7
Maldon Wk *WFD* IG8 ...... 52 C8
Malet St *GWRST* WC1E 11 H2
Maley Av *WNWD* SE27 ..... 139 H6
Malford Gv *SWFD* E18 ..... 70 A4
Malfort Rd *CMBW* SE5 .... 121 L8
Malham Rd *FSTH* SE23 .... 140 D5
Malins Cl *BAR* EN5 .... 33 J8 ①
Mallams Ms *BRXN/ST* SW9 .. 121 H8 ①
Mallard Cl *BAR* EN5 .... 47 K1 ②
 DART DA1 .... 146 F2
 HSLWW TW4 .... 133 G4 ①
 KIL/WHAMP NW6 .... 2 B4
 UPMR RM14 .... 75 M8 ③
Mallard Pl *TWK* TW1 ...... 134 A7
Mallard Rd *ABLGY* WD5 ... 21 C4
 SAND/SEL CR2 .... 185 K3
Mallard's Reach *WEY* KT13 .. 164 D4
Mallards Rd *WFD* IG8 ..... 70 B1
The Mallards *STA* TW18 ... 148 B5
Mallard Wk *CROY/NA* CR0 .. 158 D8
 WLGTN SM6 .... 183 J2
Mallard Wy *CDALE/KGS* NW9 .. 63 H4
 GSTN WD25 .... 29 L1 ①
 NTHWD HA6 .... 59 J1
 WLGTN SM6 .... 183 J2
Mallet Dr *NTHLT* UB5 ..... 78 F5
Mallet Rd *LEW* SE13 ...... 141 K3

Malling Cl *CROY/NA* CR0 .. 173 J1 ③
Malling Gdns *MRDN* SM4 .. 170 C1 ③
Malling Wy *HAYES* BR2 ... 174 F2
Mallinson Cl *HCH* RM12 ... 92 C5 ③
Mallinson Rd *BTSEA* SW11 .. 137 L2
 WLGTN SM6 .... 171 K5
Mallion Ct *WAB* EN9 ...... 27 M6
Mallord St *CHEL* SW3 ..... 15 H9
Mallory Cl *BROCKY* SE4 ... 140 E5
Mallory Gdns *EBAR* EN4 .. 48 A2
Mallory St *CAMTN* NW1 ... 9 K1
Mallow Cl *CROY/NA* CR0 .. 173 K3 ③
 TOTM N17 .... 51 G6
Mallow Md *MLHL* NW7 .... 64 C1
The Mallows *HGDN/ICK* UB10 .. 77 H3
Mallow St *FSBYE* EC1V 7 C9
Mall Rd *HMSMTH* W6 ...... 118 B3
The Mall *EA* W5 .... 98 E6
 HCH RM12 .... 92 B1
 KTN/HRWW/W HA3 .... 62 F7
 MORT/ESHN SW14 ..... 135 J2
 STHGT/OAK N14 .... 48 E5
 SURB KT6 .... 152 D8
 WHALL SW1A 16 E1
Malmains Cl *BECK* BR3 ... 159 K8
Malmains Wy *BECK* BR3 .. 159 J7
Malm Cl *RKW/CH/CXG* WD3 .. 40 D4
Malmesbury Cl *PIN* HA5 .. 60 A5
Malmesbury Rd *BOW* E3 .. 104 F1
 CAN/RD E16 .... 105 M4
 MRDN SM4 .... 170 C2
 SWFD E18 .... 69 M2
Malmesbury Ter
 CAN/RD E16 .... 105 M4 ③
Malpas Dr *PIN* HA5 .... 60 D6
Malpas Rd *BROCKY* SE4 .. 122 F7
 DAGW RM9 .... 90 D6
 HACK E8 .... 86 B6
Malta Rd *LEY* E10 .... 87 C1
Malta St *FSBYE* EC1V 6 C9
Maltby Cl *ORP* BR6 .... 177 C3
Maltby Dr *EN* EN1 .... 37 H3
Maltby Rd *CHSGTN* KT9 .. 168 A8
Maltby St *STHWK* SE1 ..... 19 L3
Malthouse Dr *FELT* TW13 .. 150 F1
Maltings Pl *FUL/PGN* SW6 .. 119 H6
The Maltings *KGLGY* WD4 .. 20 C6
 ORP BR6 .... 176 F3 ①
 ROMW/RG RM7 .... 73 M8 ②
Malting Wy *ISLW* TW7 .... 115 M8
Malton Ms *NKENS* W10 ... 100 E5 ①
 WOOL/PLUM SE18 ..... 125 L6
Malton Rd *NKENS* W10 ... 100 E5
Malton St *WOOL/PLUM* SE18 .. 125 L6
Maltravers St *TPL/STR* WC2R .. 12 A6 ②
Malt St *STHWK* SE1 .... 122 A4
Malva Cl *WAND/EARL* SW18 .. 137 H2
Malvern Av *BXLYHN* DA7 .. 126 E5
 CHING E4 .... 69 K1
 RYLN/HDSTN HA2 ...... 78 E3
Malvern Cl *BUSH* WD23 ... 30 B1
 MTCM CR4 .... 156 C6
 NKENS W10 .... 100 F4 ②
 SURB KT6 .... 167 L3
Malvern Dr *FELT* TW13 ... 150 D1 ③
 GDMY/SEVK IG3 .... 89 M4
 WFD IG8 .... 52 C7
Malvern Gdns *CRICK* NW2 .. 82 E2
 KTN/HRWW/W HA3 .... 62 E5
 LOU IG10 .... 52 F1
Malvern Ms *KIL/WHAMP* NW6 .. 2 A8
Malvern Pl *MV/WKIL* W9 .. 100 F3 ③
Malvern Rd *CEND/HSY/T* N8 .. 66 F4
 EHAM E6 .... 88 B7 ③
 EMPK RM11 .... 74 A7
 HACK E8 .... 86 A7
 HPTN TW12 .... 151 G4
 HYS/HAR UB3 .... 113 L5
 KIL/WHAMP NW6 .... 100 F1 ②
 ORP BR6 .... 177 H6
 PEND EN3 .... 37 L2
 SURB KT6 .... 167 L4
 THHTH CR7 .... 157 G7
 TOTM N17 .... 68 A4 ③
 WAN E11 .... 87 L2
Malvern Ter *ED* N9 .... 49 M3 ①
 IS N1 .... 6 A3
Malvern Wy *RKW/CH/CXG* WD3 .. 28 B8
 WEA W13 .... 98 B4 ③
Malwood Rd *BAL* SW12 ... 138 B3
Malyons Rd *LEW* SE13 .... 141 H2
 SWLY BR8 .... 163 M3
Malyons Ter *BROCKY* SE4 .. 141 H2
The Malyons *SHPTN* TW17 .. 164 D1 ③
Managers St *POP/IOD* E14 .. 105 J7 ②
Manaton Cl *PECK* SE15 ... 122 B8
Manaton Crs *STHL* UB1 ... 97 G5
Manbey Gv *SRTFD* E15 .... 87 L6
Manbey Park Rd *SRTFD* E15 .. 87 L6 ②
Manbey Rd *SRTFD* E15 .... 87 L6
Manbey St *SRTFD* E15 .... 87 L6
Manbre Rd *HMSMTH* W6 .. 118 C4
Manbrough Av *EHAM* E6 .. 106 F2
Manchester Dr *NKENS* W10 .. 100 E3 ②
Manchester Gv *POP/IOD* E14 .. 123 J5
Manchester Ms *MHST* W1U .. 10 A3 ③
Manchester Rd *POP/IOD* E14 .. 123 J3
 SEVS/STOTM N15 ...... 67 K7 ③
 THHTH CR7 .... 157 J6
Manchester Sq *MHST* W1U .. 10 B4 ③
Manchester St *MHST* W1U .. 10 A3 ③
Manchuria Rd *BTSEA* SW11 .. 138 A3
Manciple St *STHWK* SE1 .. 19 H2
Mandalay Rd *CLAP* SW4 .. 138 C2
Mandarin Wy *YEAD* UB4 .. 96 D5
Mandela Pl *WATN* WD24 .. 29 K5 ③
Mandela Rd *CAN/RD* E16 .. 106 A5
Mandela St *BRXN/ST* SW9 .. 121 C5
 CAMTN NW1 .... 4 E2
Mandela Wy *STHWK* SE1 .. 19 K5
Mandeville Cl
 BKHTH/KID SE3 .... 123 M5 ①
 WAT WD17 .... 28 F3
 WIM/MER SW19 .... 154 E3
Mandeville Dr *SURB* KT6 .. 167 K3
Mandeville Pl *MHST* W1U .. 10 B4 ③
Mandeville Rd *ISLW* TW7 .. 116 A7
 NTHLT UB5 .... 79 G6

PEND EN3 .... 37 L2
 POTB/CUF EN6 .... 23 J5
 SHPTN TW17 .... 149 G8
 STHGT/OAK N14 .... 48 B4
Mandrake Rd *TOOT* SW17 .. 137 M7
Mandrake Wy *SRTFD* E15 .. 87 L7 ③
Mandrell Rd *BRXS/STRHM* SW2 .. 138 E2
Manette St *SOHO/SHAV* W1D .. 11 H5 ③
Manford Cl *CHIG* IG7 ...... 54 B6
Manford Cross *CHIG* IG7 .. 54 A7
Manford Wy *CHIG* IG7 .... 54 A7
Manfred Rd *PUT/ROE* SW15 .. 136 F2
Manger Rd *HOLWY* N7 ..... 84 E6 ③
Manilla St *POP/IOD* E14 ... 105 C8
Manister Rd *ABYW* SE2 .. 126 A1 ①
Manley Ct *STNW/STAM* N16 .. 85 M3
Manley St *CAMTN* NW1 .... 4 A3
Manly Dixon Dr *PEND* EN3 .. 37 L2
Mann Cl *CROY/NA* CR0 .... 172 C5
Manningford Cl *FSBYE* EC1V .. 6 C7 ③
Manning Gdns
 KTN/HRWW/W HA3 .... 62 D8
Manning Pl
 RCHPK/HAM TW10 ..... 134 F3 ③
Manning Rd *DAGE* RM10 .. 91 G7
 STMC/STPC BR5 .... 162 F5
 WALTH E17 .... 68 E6 ③
Manning St *SOCK/AV* RM15 .. 111 J7
Manningtree Cl
 WIM/MER SW19 .... 136 E5
Manningtree Rd *RSLP* HA4 .. 78 B4
Manningtree St *WCHPL* E1 .. 104 A5 ①⑩
Mannin Rd *CHDH* RM6 .... 72 B8
Mannock Rd *DART* DA1 ... 128 B3 ①
 WDGN N22 .... 67 H4
Mann's Cl *ISLW* TW7 ...... 133 M2
Manns Rd *EDGW* HA8 ..... 45 G8
Manoel Rd *WHTN* TW2 .... 133 J6
Manor Av *BROCKY* SE4 .... 122 F7
 EMPK RM11 .... 74 C6
 HSLWW TW4 .... 114 D8
 NTHLT UB5 .... 78 F7
Manorbrook *BKHTH/KID* SE3 .. 142 A1
Manor Cha *WEY* KT13 ..... 164 B7
Manor Cl *BAR* EN5 .... 33 L7
 CDALE/KGS NW9 .... 63 H5
 DAGE RM10 .... 91 K6 ①
 DART DA1 .... 145 K1
 RDART DA2 .... 146 A7
 ROM RM1 .... 74 A6
 RSLP HA4 .... 77 M1
 SOCK/AV RM15 .... 111 J7
 THMD SE28 .... 108 C5
 WPK KT4 .... 168 C5
Manor Cottages *NTHWD* HA6 .. 59 M2 ①
Manor Cottages Ap *EFNCH* N2 .. 65 J3 ①
Manor Ct *DEN/HRF* UB9 .. 58 C3
 EN EN1 .... 37 H1
 RAD WD7 .... 30 F2
 WEY KT13 .... 164 B6
Manor Court Rd *HNWL* W7 .. 97 L6
Manor Crs *BRYLDS* KT5 ... 168 A1
 EMPK RM11 .... 74 C6
Manordene Cl *THDT* KT7 .. 167 G3 ①
Manordene Rd *THMD* SE28 .. 108 C5
Manor Dr *BRYLDS* KT5 .... 168 A1
 ESH/CLAY KT10 .... 166 F5
 FELT TW13 .... 150 D1 ③
 HOR/WEW KT19 .... 168 B8
 MLHL NW7 .... 45 K7
 STHGT/OAK N14 .... 48 B2
 SUN TW16 .... 150 A5
 TRDG/WHET N20 ...... 47 L5
 WBLY HA9 .... 80 F4
Manor Dr North *NWMAL* KT3 .. 168 D2
 WPK KT4 .... 168 E3
The Manor Dr *WPK* KT4 ... 168 E3
Manor Farm Av *SHPTN* TW17 .. 164 B1
Manor Farm Dr *CHING* E4 .. 51 L5
Manor Farm Rd *ALP/SUD* HA0 .. 98 D1
 EN EN1 .... 26 B8
 STRHM/NOR SW16 ..... 157 G5 ③
Manorfields Cl *CHST* BR7 .. 161 M6
Manor Gdns *ACT* W3 ...... 117 G2
 HOLWY N7 .... 84 E3
 HPTN TW12 .... 151 H3
 RCH/KEW TW9 .... 134 F1
 RSLP HA4 .... 78 C5
 RYNPK SW20 .... 154 F5
 SAND/SEL CR2 .... 172 F8
 SUN TW16 .... 150 A4
Manor Ga *NTHLT* UB5 ..... 78 E7
Manorgate Rd *KUTN/CMB* KT2 .. 153 G4
Manor Green Rd
 HOR/WEW KT19 .... 180 C5
Manor Gv *BECK* BR3 ...... 159 H5
 PECK SE15 .... 122 C4
 RCH/KEW TW9 .... 135 G1
Manor Hall Av *HDN* NW4 .. 64 C3
Manor Hall Dr *HDN* NW4 .. 64 D3
Manor Hall Gdns *LEY* E10 .. 87 G1
Manor HI *BNSTD* SM7 ..... 182 F8
Manor House Ct
 EPSOM KT18 .... 180 C6 ③
Manor House Dr
 KIL/WHAMP NW6 .... 82 D7
 NTHWD HA6 .... 59 H1
Manor House Gdns *ABLGY* WD5 .. 20 C4
Manor House Wy *ISLW* TW7 .. 116 B8 ①
Manor La *FELT* TW13 ...... 132 A6
 HYS/HAR UB3 .... 113 K4
 LEW SE13 .... 141 L2
 SUN TW16 .... 150 A5
 SUT SM1 .... 170 C7
Manor Lane Ter *LEW* SE13 .. 141 L1
Manor Ms *KIL/WHAMP* NW6 .. 2 B5
Manor Mt *FSTH* SE23 ..... 140 C5
Manor Pk *CHST* BR7 ...... 161 K5
 LEW SE13 .... 141 K2
 RCH/KEW TW9 .... 134 F1
Manor Park Cl *WWKM* BR4 .. 174 B3
Manor Park Crs *EDGW* HA8 .. 45 G8
Manor Park Dr
 RYLN/HDSTN HA2 ...... 61 H4
Manor Park Gdns *EDGW* HA8 .. 45 G7
Manor Park Rd *CHST* BR7 .. 161 J4
 EFNCH N2 .... 65 J4

MNPK E12 .... 88 D4
SUT SM1 .... 170 C7
WLSDN NW10 .... 81 M8 6
WWKM BR4 .... 174 B3
Manor Pl CHST BR7 .... 161 K5
EBED/NFELT TW14 .... 132 A5
MTCM CR4 .... 156 C6
STA TW18 .... 148 B1
SUT SM1 .... 170 B7
WALW SE17 .... 18 D8
Manor Rd ABR/ST RM4 .... 54 D3
ASHF TW15 .... 148 F1
BAR EN5 .... 33 L7
BECK BR3 .... 159 C5
BELMT SM2 .... 181 M1
BFN/LL DA15 .... 143 M7
BXLY DA5 .... 145 H5
CAN/RD E16 .... 105 L4
CHDH RM6 .... 72 D7
CHIG IG7 .... 53 C8
DAGE RM10 .... 91 J6
DART DA1 .... 145 L1
E/WMO/HCT KT8 .... 151 K7
ENC/FH EN2 .... 36 D5
ERITH DA8 .... 127 M4
HRW HA1 .... 62 A7
HYS/HAR UB3 .... 96 A5
LEY E10 .... 69 G8
LOU IG10 .... 39 H4
LOU IG10 .... 52 B1
MTCM CR4 .... 156 C6
POTB/CUF EN6 .... 22 F4
RCH/KEW TW9 .... 116 F8
ROM RM1 .... 74 A6
RSLP HA4 .... 77 K1
RYNPK SW20 .... 154 F5
SNWD SE25 .... 158 A6
STNW/STAM N16 .... 85 L1
TEDD TW11 .... 152 A1
TOTM N17 .... 27 K6
WAB EN9 .... 27 K6
WALTH E17 .... 68 E3
WAT WD17 .... 29 H4
WDGN N22 .... 48 E8
WEA W13 .... 98 A6
WHTN TW2 .... 133 J6
WLGTN SM6 .... 171 H7
WOT/HER KT12 .... 156 C6
WWKM BR4 .... 174 B4
Manor Rd North
ESH/CLAY KT10 .... 166 F5
WLGTN SM6 .... 171 H6
Manor Rd South
ESH/CLAY KT10 .... 166 E6
Manorside BAR EN5 .... 33 L7
Manor Sq BCTR RM8 .... 90 C2
Manor V BTFD TW8 .... 116 C3 3
Manor Vw FNCH N3 .... 65 H3
Manor Wk WEY KT13 .... 164 B7
Manor Wy WPK KT4 .... 168 E3
BECK BR3 .... 159 C6
BKHTH/KID SE3 .... 142 A1
BORE WD6 .... 32 C7
BXLY DA5 .... 145 G5
BXLYHN DA7 .... 127 K8
CDALE/KGS NW9 .... 63 L5
CHING E4 .... 51 K6
Manorway EN EN1 .... 49 L2
Manor Wy HAYES BR2 .... 175 L1
MTCM CR4 .... 156 C6
NWDGN UB2 .... 114 D2
POTB/CUF EN6 .... 23 C3
PUR/KEN CR8 .... 183 L5
RAIN RM13 .... 109 L4
RKW/CH/CXG WD3 .... 28 A7
RSLP HA4 .... 59 L8
RYLN/HDSTN HA2 .... 61 H5
SAND/SEL CR2 .... 172 E8
STMC/STPC BR5 .... 161 J7
Manorway WFD IG8 .... 52 C7 7
Manor Waye UX/CGN UB8 .... 94 D1
The Manor Wy WLGTN SM6 .... 171 H6
Manor Wood Rd PUR/KEN CR8 .... 183 L6
Manresa Rd CHEL SW3 .... 15 H8
Mansard Beeches TOOT SW17 .... 156 A1
Mansard Cl HCH RM12 .... 92 A2
PIN HA5 .... 60 D4 3
Manse Cl HYS/HAR UB3 .... 113 K4
Mansel Gv WALTH E17 .... 69 G2
Mansell Rd ACT W3 .... 99 K7
GFD/PVL UB6 .... 97 H4
Mansell St TWRH EC3N 13 M7
WCHPL E1 .... 13 M5
Mansel Rd WIM/MER SW19 .... 154 E1
Mansergh Cl WOOL/PLUM SE18 .... 126 E5
Manse Rd STNW/STAM N16 .... 85 M3
Manser Rd RAIN RM13 .... 109 L2
Mansfield Av EBAR EN4 .... 47 M1 6
RSLP HA4 .... 78 B1 3
SEVS/STOTM N15 .... 67 K5
Mansfield Cl ED N9 .... 50 A1
STMC/STPC BR5 .... 177 K2
Mansfield Dr YEAD UB4 .... 95 L3
Mansfield Gdns HCH RM12 .... 92 D2
Mansfield Hl CHING E4 .... 51 H3
Mansfield Ms CAVSO/HST W1G 10 C3 3
Mansfield Pl SAND/SEL CR2 .... 172 D8 6
Mansfield Rd ACT W3 .... 99 H3
CHSGTN KT9 .... 167 J7
HAMP NW3 .... 83 M5
IL IG1 .... 89 G2
SAND/SEL CR2 .... 172 D8
SWLY BR8 .... 163 L1
WALTH E17 .... 68 F5
WAN E11 .... 70 B7
Mansfield St CAVSO/HST W1G 10 C3
Mansford St BETH E2 .... 104 A1
Manship Rd MTCM CR4 .... 156 A4
Mansion House Pl
MANHO EC4N 13 G5 4
Manson Ms SKENS SW7 .... 14 F6
Manson Pl SKENS SW7 .... 15 G6
Manstead Gdns CHDH RM6 .... 71 L7
RAIN RM13 .... 110 B5 1
Manston Av NWDGN UB2 .... 115 G2
Manston Cl CHES/WCR EN8 .... 26 C3 3
PGE/AN SE20 .... 158 C4
Manstone Rd CRICK NW2 .... 82 E5

Manston Gv KUTN/CMB KT2 .... 152 D1
Manston Wy HCH RM12 .... 92 B6
Manthorpe Rd
WOOL/PLUM SE18 .... 125 J3
Mantilla Rd TOOT SW17 .... 138 A3
Mantle Rd BROCKY SE4 .... 122 E8
Mantlet Cl STRHM/NOR SW16 .... 156 C6 3
Mantle Wy SRTFD E15 .... 87 L7 4
Manton Av HNWL W7 .... 97 M8
Manton Cl HYS/HAR UB3 .... 95 L6
Manton Rd ABYW SE2 .... 126 A2
Mantua St BTSEA SW11 .... 119 K8 3
Manus Wy TRDG/WHET N20 .... 47 J4
Manville Gdns TOOT SW17 .... 138 B7 1
Manville Rd TOOT SW17 .... 138 A6
Manwood Rd BROCKY SE4 .... 140 F3
Manwood St CAN/RD E16 .... 106 F7
Manygate La SHPTN TW17 .... 164 C5
Many Gates BAL SW12 .... 138 B6
Mapesbury Rd CRICK NW2 .... 82 E6
Mape St BETH E2 .... 104 B3
Maple Av ACT W3 .... 99 J7
CHING E4 .... 50 F8
RYLN/HDSTN HA2 .... 79 H3
UPMR RM14 .... 93 H3
WDR/YW UB7 .... 94 E6 3
Maple Cl BARK/HLT IG6 .... 53 L7 1
BKHH IG9 .... 52 D5
BUSH WD23 .... 29 L5
CLAP SW4 .... 138 D3
FNCH N3 .... 47 G8 2
HCH RM12 .... 92 B3 3
HPTN TW12 .... 150 F2
MTCM CR4 .... 156 B4
RSLP HA4 .... 60 B7
STMC/STPC BR5 .... 161 K8
STNW/STAM N16 .... 68 A7
SWLY BR8 .... 163 L5 3
YEAD UB4 .... 96 D2 3
Maple Ct NWMAL KT3 .... 153 K6
Maple Crs BFN/LL DA15 .... 144 A3
Maplecroft Cl EHAM E6 .... 106 D5
Mapledale Av CROY/NA CR0 .... 173 H5
Mapledene Rd HACK E8 .... 7 M1
Maple Gdns ASHF TW15 .... 130 E6 5
EDGW HA8 .... 63 L1
Maple Gv BTFD TW8 .... 116 B5
CDALE/KGS NW9 .... 63 J8
EA W5 .... 116 D1
STHL UB1 .... 96 F4
WAT WD17 .... 29 C4 2
Maplehurst Cl KUT KT1 .... 152 E7 2
Maple Leaf Cl ABLGY WD5 .... 21 C5 3
Maple Leaf Dr BFN/LL DA15 .... 143 M5
Mapleleafe Gdns BARK/HLT IG6 .... 71 H4
Maple Leaf Sq
BERM/RHTH SE16 .... 104 D8 7
Maple Ms KIL/WHAMP NW6 .... 2 C5 10
STRHM/NOR SW16 .... 156 F1
Maple Pl EW KT17 .... 181 K7 3
FITZ W1T 10 F2 3
WDR/YW UB7 .... 94 E7
Maple Rd DART DA1 .... 146 C5
PGE/AN SE20 .... 158 B4
SURB KT6 .... 152 E8
WAN E11 .... 69 L7
YEAD UB4 .... 96 C2
Maples Pl WCHPL E1 .... 104 B4 3
Maplestead Rd
BRXS/STRHM SW2 .... 138 F4
DAGW RM9 .... 90 B8
The Maples BNSTD SM7 .... 182 B6
CHESW EN7 .... 25 L1
Maple St FITZ W1T 10 E2
ROMW/RG RM7 .... 73 J5
Maplethorpe Rd THHTH CR7 .... 157 G7
Mapleton Cl HAYES BR2 .... 175 C1 3
Mapleton Crs PEND EN3 .... 37 J3
WAND/EARL SW18 .... 137 H3
Mapleton Rd CHING E4 .... 51 J5
EN EN1 .... 37 H5
WAND/EARL SW18 .... 137 H3
Maple Wk NKENS W10 .... 100 D3 3
Maple Wy FELT TW13 .... 132 A7
Maplin Cl WCHMH N21 .... 48 F1
Maplin Rd CAN/RD E16 .... 106 A5
Maplin St BOW E3 .... 104 F2
Maran Wy ERITH DA18 .... 126 D1
Marban Rd MV/WKIL W9 .... 100 F2
Marble Cl ACT W3 .... 99 H7
Marble Dr CRICK NW2 .... 82 D1
Marble Hill Cl TWK TW1 .... 134 B4 8
Marble Hill Gdns TWK TW1 .... 134 B4
Marbrook Ct LEE/GVPK SE12 .... 142 C7
Marcellina Wy ORP BR6 .... 176 E5
Marcet Rd DART DA1 .... 146 C2
Marchant Rd WAN E11 .... 87 K2
Marchant St NWCR SE14 .... 122 E4 5
Marchbank Rd WKENS W14 .... 118 F4
Marchmont Cl HCH RM12 .... 92 C3 3
Marchmont Rd
RCHPK/HAM TW10 .... 134 F2 3
WLGTN SM6 .... 183 J2
Marchmont St BMSBY WC1N 5 J9
March Rd TWK TW1 .... 134 A4 3
WEY KT13 .... 164 A7
Marchside Cl HEST TW5 .... 114 D6 3
Marchwood Cl CMBW SE5 .... 121 L5 4
Marchwood Crs EA W5 .... 98 C5
Marcia Rd STHWK SE1 .... 19 K6
Marcilly Rd
WAND/EARL SW18 .... 137 K2 3
Marconi Wy GFD/PVL UB6 .... 97 H5
Marcon Pl HACK E8 .... 86 B6
Marcos Rd HMSMTH W6 .... 118 B1
Marcus Garvey Ms EDUL SE22 .... 140 D3 3
Marcus Garvey Wy
HNHL SE24 .... 139 G1 4
Marcus Rd DART DA1 .... 146 A4
Marcus St SRTFD E15 .... 87 L8
WAND/EARL SW18 .... 137 H3
Marcus Ter WAND/EARL SW18 .... 137 H3 1
Mardale Dr CDALE/KGS NW9 .... 63 K6
Mardell Rd CROY/NA CR0 .... 158 D3
Marden Av HAYES BR2 .... 175 G1
Marden Crs BXLY DA5 .... 145 J2

CROY/NA CR0 .... 171 M1
Marden Rd CROY/NA CR0 .... 171 M1
ROM RM1 .... 73 L2 7
TOTM N17 .... 67 L3
Marder Rd WEA W13 .... 98 A3
Marechal Niel Av BFN/LL DA15 .... 143 K7
Maresfield Gdns HAMP NW3 .... 83 J6
Mare St HACK E8 .... 86 B8
Marfleet Cl CAR SM5 .... 170 E4 3
Margaret Av CHING E4 .... 51 H1
Margaret Bondfield Av
BARK IG11 .... 90 A7
Margaret Cl ABLGY WD5 .... 20 F5 3
GPK RM2 .... 74 B6 3
POTB/CUF EN6 .... 23 J6
STA TW18 .... 148 D3
WAB EN9 .... 27 K6 3
Margaret Dr EMPK RM11 .... 92 F1
Margaret Gardner Dr
ELTH/MOT SE9 .... 142 F6 3
Margaret Ingram Cl
FUL/PGN SW6 .... 118 F4 3
Margaret Lockwood Cl
KUT KT1 .... 152 F7 3
Margaret Rd BXLY DA5 .... 144 D3
EBAR EN4 .... 34 D7
GPK RM2 .... 74 B6
STNW/STAM N16 .... 85 M1 3
Margaretta Ter CHEL SW3 .... 15 J9
Margaretting Rd MNPK E12 .... 88 C2
Margaret Wy REDBR IG4 .... 70 E7
Margate Rd CLAP SW4 .... 138 C2
Margeholes OXHEY WD19 .... 42 C4
Margery Rd BCTR RM8 .... 90 D3
Margery St FSBYW WC1X 6 A4
Margherita Pl WAB EN9 .... 27 M7
Margin Dr WIM/MER SW19 .... 153 G4
Margravine Gdns HMSMTH W6 .... 118 D3
Margravine Rd HMSMTH W6 .... 118 D4
Marham Gdns MRDN SM4 .... 170 C1 3
WAND/EARL SW18 .... 137 L5 3
Maria Gdns HCH RM12 .... 92 F2
Marian Cl BARK/HLT IG6 .... 71 K1
YEAD UB4 .... 96 D3
Marian Gdns GSTN WD25 .... 21 H6
Marian Pl BETH E2 .... 104 B1
Marian Rd STRHM/NOR SW16 .... 156 C4
Marian Sq BETH E2 .... 104 A1
Marian St BETH E2 .... 104 B1 3
Marian Wy WLSDN NW10 .... 81 M7
Maria Ter WCHPL E1 .... 104 D4
Maria Theresa Cl NWMAL KT3 .... 153 G5
Maricas Av KTN/HRWW/W HA3 .... 61 K2
Mariette Wy WLGTN SM6 .... 183 L2
Marigold Cl STHL UB1 .... 96 E6 5
Marigold Rd BERM/RHTH SE16 .... 104 B8
Marigold Wy CROY/NA CR0 .... 173 K3
Marina Ap YEAD UB4 .... 96 E4
Marina Av NWMAL KT3 .... 169 H1
Marina Dr DART DA1 .... 147 G5
WELL DA16 .... 125 M5 3
Marina Gdns CHES/WCR EN8 .... 26 C3
ROMW/RG RM7 .... 73 H6
Marina Wy TEDD TW11 .... 152 D3 3
Marine Ct PUR RM19 .... 128 F2
Marine Dr WOOL/PLUM SE18 .... 124 F2
Marinefield Rd FUL/PGN SW6 .... 119 H7
Mariner Gdns
RCHPK/HAM TW10 .... 134 B7
Mariner Rd MNPK E12 .... 89 G4 3
Mariners Ms POP/IOD E14 .... 123 K2
Marine St BERM/RHTH SE16 .... 122 A1
Marion Av SHPTN TW17 .... 149 H8
Marion Cl BUSH WD23 .... 29 M4
Marion Crs STMC/STPC BR5 .... 162 B8
Marion Gv WFD IG8 .... 51 L7
Marion Rd CROY/NA CR0 .... 157 J8
MLHL NW7 .... 46 A7
Marischal Rd LEW SE13 .... 123 K8
Maritime St BOW E3 .... 104 F3 3
Marius Rd TOOT SW17 .... 138 A6
Marjorie Gv BTSEA SW11 .... 137 M1
Mark Av CHING E4 .... 51 H1
Mark Cl BXLYHN DA7 .... 126 E6
HAYES BR2 .... 175 L6
STHL UB1 .... 97 G1 3
Markeston Gn OXHEY WD19 .... 42 D6 3
Market La EDGW HA8 .... 63 J2
Market Link ROM RM1 .... 73 L5
Market Meadow
STMC/STPC BR5 .... 162 C7 3
Market Ms MYFR/PICC W1J 10 C9 3
Market Pl ACT W3 .... 99 J7
BTFD TW8 .... 116 C5
BXLYHS DA6 .... 145 G1
DART DA1 .... 146 E4 1
EFNCH N2 .... 65 K4 3
ROM RM1 .... 73 L6
SOHO/SHAV W1D 10 E4
WATW WD18 .... 29 J7 3
Market Rd HOLWY N7 .... 84 E6
RCH/KEW TW9 .... 117 C8
Market Sq BMLY BR1 .... 160 A5
Market St DART DA1 .... 146 E4
EHAM E6 .... 106 F1
WATW WD18 .... 29 H7
WOOL/PLUM SE18 .... 125 G2
Markfield Gdns CHING E4 .... 51 H2
Markfield Rd SEVS/STOTM N15 .... 68 A5
Markham Pl CHEL SW3 .... 15 L7 3
Markham Sq CHEL SW3 .... 15 L7
Markham St CHEL SW3 .... 15 K7
Markhole Cl HPTN TW12 .... 150 F3 3
Markhouse Av WALTH E17 .... 68 E2
Markhouse Rd WALTH E17 .... 68 F7
Mark La MON EC3R 13 K6
Markmanor Av WALTH E17 .... 68 E8
Mark Rd WDGN N22 .... 67 H3
Marksbury Av RCH/KEW TW9 .... 117 G8
Marks Rd ROMW/RG RM7 .... 73 H1
Mark St SDTCH EC2A 7 J7 3
SRTFD E15 .... 87 L7 3
The Markway SUN TW16 .... 150 C5
Markwell Cl SYD SE26 .... 140 B8 3
Markyate Rd BCTR RM8 .... 90 B5
Marlands Rd CLAY IG5 .... 70 E4

Marlborogh Rd ISLW TW7 .... 116 B5
RSLP HA4 .... 59 J7
STHGT/OAK N14 .... 48 C5 3
Marlborough Av EDGW HA8 .... 45 H5
RSLP HA4 .... 59 J7
STHGT/OAK N14 .... 48 C5 3
TRDG/WHET N20 .... 47 M5 3
UPMR RM14 .... 93 L1 3
WIM/MER SW19 .... 155 L2 3
WOT/HER KT12 .... 156 C6 3
Marlborough Crs CHSWK W4 .... 117 K1
Marlborough Dr CLAY IG5 .... 70 E4
WEY KT13 .... 164 C5
Marlborough Gdns
TRDG/WHET N20 .... 47 M5
UPMR RM14 .... 93 L1
Marlborough Gv STHWK SE1 .... 122 A3
Marlborough Hl HRW HA1 .... 61 L5
STJWD NW8 .... 2 F4
Marlborough La CHARL SE7 .... 124 C4
Marlborough Park Av
BFN/LL DA15 .... 144 A5
Marlborough Pl STJWD NW8 .... 2 E6
Marlborough Rd ARCH N19 .... 84 C3
ASHF TW15 .... 148 E1
BCTR RM8 .... 90 C4
CHING E4 .... 51 H8
CHSWK W4 .... 117 J3
DART DA1 .... 146 C3 3
EA W5 .... 98 D8 3
ED N9 .... 49 M3
FELT TW13 .... 132 D6
FSTGT E7 .... 88 C7
HAYES BR2 .... 160 C7
HGDN/ICK UB10 .... 95 H3
HPTN TW12 .... 151 G2 3
NWDGN UB2 .... 114 C1
RCHPK/HAM TW10 .... 134 C3 5
ROMW/RG RM7 .... 73 G5
SAND/SEL CR2 .... 184 C1 3
SRTFD E15 .... 87 L4 3
SUT SM1 .... 170 A5
SWFD E18 .... 70 A4
WDGN N22 .... 66 F1
WELL DA16 .... 126 D8
WHALL SW1A 10 F9
WIM/MER SW19 .... 155 L2
Marlborough St CHEL SW3 .... 15 J6
Marlborough Yd ARCH N19 .... 84 C2 3
Marle Gdns WAB EN9 .... 27 J5
Marler Rd FSTH SE23 .... 140 F5
Marley Av BXLYHN DA7 .... 126 D4
Marley Cl GFD/PVL UB6 .... 97 C2 3
SEVS/STOTM N15 .... 67 H5
Marlin Cl SUN TW16 .... 149 L2 3
Marlingdene Cl HPTN TW12 .... 151 C2 3
Marlings Cl CHST BR7 .... 161 L1
Marlings Park Av CHST BR7 .... 161 L7
Marlins Cl SUT SM1 .... 170 C7 3
Marlins Meadow WATW WD18 .... 41 K1
Marlin Sq ABLGY WD5 .... 21 C7
The Marlins NTHWD HA6 .... 41 M8
Marloes Cl ALP/SUD HA0 .... 80 D4
Marloes Rd KENS W8 .... 14 C3
Marlow Av PUR RM19 .... 129 C2
Marlow Cl PGE/AN SE20 .... 158 B6
Marlow Ct CDALE/KGS NW9 .... 63 M4
Marlow Crs TWK TW1 .... 133 M3
Marlow Dr CHEAM SM3 .... 169 K5
Marlowe Cl BARK/HLT IG6 .... 71 J2
CHST BR7 .... 161 K2
Marlowe Rd WALTH E17 .... 69 J5
The Marlowes DART DA1 .... 145 K1
STJWD NW8 .... 3 G4
Marlowe Wy CROY/NA CR0 .... 171 L4
Marlow Gdns HYS/HAR UB3 .... 113 K1
Marlow Rd EHAM E6 .... 106 F2
NWDGN UB2 .... 114 F1
PGE/AN SE20 .... 158 B6
Marlow Wy BERM/RHTH SE16 .... 104 D8
Marl Rd WAND/EARL SW18 .... 137 L1
Marlton St GNWCH SE10 .... 123 M3 3
Marlwood Cl BFN/LL DA15 .... 143 L6
Marlyon Rd BARK/HLT IG6 .... 54 B7
Marmadon Rd
WOOL/PLUM SE18 .... 125 M2
Marmion Ap CHING E4 .... 51 G6 3
Marmion Cl CHING E4 .... 50 F6
Marmion Ms BTSEA SW11 .... 120 A8 3
Marmion Rd BTSEA SW11 .... 138 A1
Marmont Rd PECK SE15 .... 122 A6
Marmora Rd EDUL SE22 .... 140 C3
Marmot Rd HSLWW TW4 .... 114 D8
WELL DA16 .... 126 A8
Marne Av FBAR/BDGN N11 .... 48 B6
Marnell Wy HSLWW TW4 .... 114 D8
Marne St NKENS W10 .... 100 E2
Marney Rd BTSEA SW11 .... 138 A1
Marneys Cl EPSOM KT18 .... 180 A8
Marnfield Crs
BRXS/STRHM SW2 .... 138 F5
Marnham Av CRICK NW2 .... 82 A3
Marnham Crs GFD/PVL UB6 .... 97 H2
Marnock Rd BROCKY SE4 .... 140 F2
Maroon St POP/IOD E14 .... 104 E4 3
Maroons Wy CAT SE6 .... 159 G1
Marquess Rd IS N1 .... 85 K6 3
Marquess Rd North IS N1 .... 85 J6
Marquess Rd South IS N1 .... 85 J6 3
Marquis Cl ALP/SUD HA0 .... 80 F7
Marquis Rd CAMTN NW1 .... 84 D6
FSBYPK N4 .... 84 F1
WDGN N22 .... 48 F8 3
Marrabon Cl BFN/LL DA15 .... 144 A5
Marrick Cl PUT/ROE SW15 .... 136 A1
Marrilyne Av PEND EN3 .... 37 M3
Marriot Rd MUSWH N10 .... 65 M2
Marriott Cl EBED/NFELT TW14 .... 131 K3
Marriott Rd BAR EN5 .... 33 K6
DART DA1 .... 147 G4
FSBYPK N4 .... 84 F1
SRTFD E15 .... 87 L8 3
Marriotts Cl CDALE/KGS NW9 .... 63 M7
Marrowells WEY KT13 .... 164 E5
Marryat Pl WIM/MER SW19 .... 136 E8
Marryat Rd EN EN1 .... 26 B2
WIM/MER SW19 .... 154 D1
Marsala Rd LEW SE13 .... 141 H1

Marsden Rd ED N9 .... 50 B4
PECK SE15 .... 121 H8
Marsden St KTTN NW5 .... 84 A6
Marsden Wy ORP BR6 .... 176 F6
Marshall Cl FBAR/BDGN N11 .... 48 B6
HRW HA1 .... 61 K8
HSLWW TW4 .... 132 F2
SAND/SEL CR2 .... 185 C6 3
WAND/EARL SW18 .... 137 L3 3
Marshall Dr YEAD UB4 .... 95 M4
Marshall Rd TOTM N17 .... 67 K2
Marshalls Dr ROM RM1 .... 73 L4
Marshalls Gv WOOL/PLUM SE18 .... 124 E2
Marshalls Rd ROMW/RG RM7 .... 73 K5
SUT SM1 .... 170 B6
Marshall St SOHO/CST W1F 10 F5
Marshalsea Rd STHWK SE1 .... 18 F1
Marsham Cl CHST BR7 .... 161 H1 3
Marsham St WEST SW1P 17 H5
Marsh Av HOR/WEW KT19 .... 180 C3
MTCM CR4 .... 155 K8
Marshbrook Cl
BKHTH/KID SE3 .... 124 D8 3
Marsh Cl CHES/WCR EN8 .... 26 F4
MLHL NW7 .... 45 M5
Marshcroft Dr CHES/WCR EN8 .... 26 E4
Marsh Dr CDALE/KGS NW9 .... 63 M7
Marshe Cl POTB/CUF EN6 .... 23 K5
Marsh Farm Rd WHTN TW2 .... 133 M5
Marshfield St POP/IOD E14 .... 123 J1
Marshgate La SRTFD E15 .... 87 H8
Marsh Green Rd DAGE RM10 .... 91 G8
Marsh Hl HOM E9 .... 86 F5
Marsh La LEY E10 .... 86 F2
MLHL NW7 .... 45 L5
STAN HA7 .... 44 C7
TOTM N17 .... 68 B1
Marsh Rd ALP/SUD HA0 .... 98 D2
PIN HA5 .... 60 B5
Marshside Cl ED N9 .... 50 C3 3
Marsh St DART DA1 .... 129 C8
POP/IOD E14 .... 123 H2 3
Marsh Wall POP/IOD E14 .... 105 C3
Marsh Wy DAGW RM9 .... 109 K3
Marsland Cl WALW SE17 .... 18 D8
Marston HOR/WEW KT19 .... 180 C4
Marston Av CHSGTN KT9 .... 167 L8
DAGE RM10 .... 91 G3
Marston Cl DAGE RM10 .... 91 G3 3
KIL/WHAMP NW6 .... 2 F1
Marston Ct WOT/HER KT12 .... 165 J3 3
Marston Rd CLAY IG5 .... 70 E3
TEDD TW11 .... 152 B1
Marston Wy NRWD SE19 .... 157 H3
Marsworth Av PIN HA5 .... 60 D2
Marsworth Cl WATW WD18 .... 41 L2 3
YEAD UB4 .... 96 E4
Martaban Rd
STNW/STAM N16 .... 85 M2 3
Martello St HACK E8 .... 86 B7
Martell Rd DUL SE21 .... 139 K7
Martel Pl HACK E8 .... 85 M6 3
Marten Rd WALTH E17 .... 69 C3
Martens Av BXLYHN DA7 .... 145 J1
Martens Cl BXLYHN DA7 .... 145 J1
Martham Cl THMD SE28 .... 108 D2 3
Martha Rd SRTFD E15 .... 87 L6 3
Martha St WCHPL E1 .... 104 C5
Marthorne Crs
KTN/HRWW/W HA3 .... 61 K3
Martin Bowes Rd
ELTH/MOT SE9 .... 124 F8
Martin Cl ED N9 .... 50 D3 3
HGDN/ICK UB10 .... 94 E1
SAND/SEL CR2 .... 185 K4
Martin Crs CROY/NA CR0 .... 171 M3
Martindale
MORT/ESHN SW14 .... 135 J2 3
Martindale Av CAN/RD E16 .... 106 A6
ORP BR6 .... 177 G7
Martindale Rd BAL SW12 .... 138 B4
HSLWW TW4 .... 114 E8
Martin Dene BXLYHS DA6 .... 144 F2
Martin Dr NTHLT UB5 .... 78 F5
RAIN RM13 .... 110 B3
Martineau Cl ESH/CLAY KT10 .... 166 D4
Martineau Rd HBRY N5 .... 85 H1
Martineau St WCHPL E1 .... 104 C6 3
Martingale Cl SUN TW16 .... 150 A7
Martingales Cl
RCHPK/HAM TW10 .... 134 D7
Martin Gdns BCTR RM8 .... 90 C4
Martin Gv WIM/MER SW19 .... 155 G6
Martin La CANST EC4R 13 H6
Martin Ri BXLYHS DA6 .... 144 F2
Martin Rd BCTR RM8 .... 90 C4
RDART DA2 .... 146 C2
SOCK/AV RM15 .... 111 K7
Martins Cl RAD WD7 .... 30 E1 3
STMC/STPC BR5 .... 162 D6
WWKM BR4 .... 174 D4
Martins Dr CHES/WCR EN8 .... 26 E1
Martins Mt BAR EN5 .... 34 A7
Martin's Rd HAYES BR2 .... 159 L5
The Martins SYD SE26 .... 158 B3 3
Martins Wk MUSWH N10 .... 66 A2 3
Martin Wy RYNPK SW20 .... 154 E6
Martlesham Cl HCH RM12 .... 92 C5 3
Martlet Gv NTHLT UB5 .... 96 D3 3
Martley Dr IL IG1 .... 71 M2
Martock Cl
KTN/HRWW/W HA3 .... 62 A5 3
Marton Cl CAT SE6 .... 141 G7
Marton Rd STNW/STAM N16 .... 85 L3 3
Marvell Av YEAD UB4 .... 96 A4
Marvels Cl LEE/GVPK SE12 .... 142 B6
Marvels La LEE/GVPK SE12 .... 142 B6
Marville Rd FUL/PGN SW6 .... 118 F5
Marvin St HACK E8 .... 86 B6 3
Marwell Cl ROM RM1 .... 74 A7
WWKM BR4 .... 174 F4 3
Marwood Cl WELL DA16 .... 126 D8
Mary Adelaide Cl
PUT/ROE SW15 .... 135 L8 3
Mary Ann Buildings DEPT SE8 .... 123 C4
Maryatt Av RYLN/HDSTN HA2 .... 79 H2
Marybank WOOL/PLUM SE18 .... 124 F2

Mary Cl *KTN/HRWW/W* HA3 .... 62 F5
Mary Datchelor Cl
CMBW SE5 .... 121 K6 ⊡
Maryfield Cl *BXLY* DA5 .... 145 L7
Maryland Pk *SRTFD* E15 .... 87 L5
Maryland Rd *MV/WKIL* W9 .... 8 B1
SRTFD E15 .... 87 L5
THHTH CR7 .... 157 H4
WDGN N22 .... 49 G8
Maryland Sq *SRTFD* E15 .... 87 L5
Marylands Rd *MV/WKIL* W9 .... 8 B1
Maryland St *SRTFD* E15 .... 87 L5
Maryland Wy *SUN* TW16 .... 150 A5
Mary Lawrenson Pl
BKHTH/KID SE3 .... 123 M5
Marylebone High St *MHST* W1U .. 10 B2
Marylebone La *MHST* W1U 10 B4
Marylebone Ms *CAVSQ/HST* W1G .. 10 B3
Marylebone Pas *GTPST* W1W .. 10 F4 ⊡
Marylebone Rd *CAMTN* NW1 ...... 9 M1 ⊡
Marylebone St *MHST* W1U 10 B3
Marylee Wy *LBTH* SE11 .... 17 M6
Maryon Gv *CHARL* SE7 .... 124 E2
Maryon Ms *HAMP* NW3 .... 83 L4 ⊡
Maryon Rd *CHARL* SE7 .... 124 E2
Mary Peters Dr *NTHLT* UB5 ..... 79 K5
Mary Pl *NTGHL* W11 .... 100 E6
Mary Rose Cl *HPTN* TW12 .... 151 G4 ⊡
Mary Rose Gdns *CHSGTN* KT9 .. 167 L6
Mary Secole Cl *HACK* E8 .... 7 J1
Mary's Ter *TWK* TW1 .... 134 A4 ⊡
Mary St *CAN/RD* E16 .... 105 M4 ⊡
IS N1 .... 6 F4
Mary Ter *CAMTN* NW1 .... 4 D1
Masbro' Rd *WKENS* W14 .... 118 C1
Mascalls Gdns *BRW* CM14 .... 57 M6
Mascalls La *BRW* CM14 .... 57 M6
Mascalls Rd *CHARL* SE7 .... 124 C4
Mascotte Rd *PUT/ROE* SW15 .. 136 D1 ⊡
Mascotts Cl *CRICK* NW2 .... 82 B3
Masefield Av *BORE* WD6 .... 32 B8
STAN HA7 .... 43 M7
STHL UB1 .... 97 G6
Masefield Cl *ERITH* DA8 .... 127 M6
HARH RM3 .... 74 B2
Masefield Crs *GPK* RM2 .... 74 C2
STHGT/OAK N14 .... 35 J3
Masefield Dr *UPMR* RM14 .... 75 J8
Masefield Gdns *EHAM* E6 ...... 107 G3 ⊡
Masefield La *YEAD* UB4 .... 96 B3
Masefield Rd *DART* DA1 .... 147 H2
FELT TW13 .... 132 F8 ⊡
Masefield Vw *ORP* BR6 .... 176 C5
Masefield Wy
STWL/WRAY TW19 .... 130 F5
Mashie Rd *ACT* W3 .... 99 L5
Mashiters Hl *CRW* RM5 .... 73 K2
Mashiters Wk *ROM* RM1 .... 73 L4
Maskell Rd *TOOT* SW17 .... 137 J7
Maskelyne Cl *BTSEA* SW11 ...... 119 L6
Mason Cl *BERM/RHTH* SE16 .... 122 A3
BORE WD6 .... 32 C5
BXLYHN DA7 .... 127 H8
HPTN TW12 .... 150 F4
RYNPK SW20 .... 154 D2 ⊡
Mason Dr *HARH* RM3 .... 74 E3
Mason Rd *WFD* IG8 .... 51 L6 ⊡
Mason's Arms Ms
CONDST W1S .... 10 D5 ⊡
Mason's Av *CROY/NA* CR0 ...... 172 C5
KTN/HRWW/W HA3 .... 61 M1 ⊡
WOOL/PLUM SE18 .... 125 H2 ⊡
Masons Rd *EN* EN1 .... 37 H1
Mason St *WALW* SE17 .... 19 H5
Mason Wy *WAB* EN9 .... 27 L6
Massey Cl *FBAR/BDGN* N11 ..... 48 B7 ⊡
Massie Rd *HACK* E8 .... 86 A6 ⊡
Massingberd Wy *TOOT* SW17 ... 138 B8
Massinger St *WALW* SE17 ...... 19 J6
Massingham St *WCHPL* E1 .... 104 D3 ⊡
Masson Av *RSLP* HA4 .... 78 C6
Masterman Rd *EHAM* E6 ...... 106 E2
Masters Dr *BERM/RHTH* SE16... 122 B3
Master's St *WCHPL* E1 ...... 104 D4 ⊡
Masthead Cl *GRH* DA9 .... 147 J1
Masthouse Ter *POP/IOD* E14 .. 123 G2
Mast House Ter
POP/IOD E14 .... 123 G2 ⊡
Mastmaker Rd *POP/IOD* E14 .. 105 C8
Maswell Park Crs *HSLW* TW3 ... 133 J2
Maswell Park Rd *HSLW* TW3 .. 133 H2 ⊡
Matcham Rd *WAN* E11 .... 87 L3
Matchless Dr
WOOL/PLUM SE18 .... 125 G5
Matfield Cl *HAYES* BR2 .... 160 A8
Matfield Rd *BELV* DA17 ...... 127 G4
Matham Gv *EDUL* SE22 .... 139 M1
Matham Rd *E/WMO/HCT* KT8 ... 151 K8
Matheson Rd *WKENS* W14 .... 118 F2
Mathews Av *EHAM* E6 ...... 107 G1 ⊡
Mathews Park Av *SRTFD* E15.. 87 M5 ⊡
Mathias Cl *EPSOM* KT18 ...... 180 C6 ⊡
Matilda Cl *NRWD* SE19 .... 157 K3
Matilda St *IS* N1 .... 5 M4
Matlock Cl *BAR* EN5 .... 33 K8
OXHEY WD19 .... 42 C5
Matlock Crs *CHEAM* SM3 ...... 169 L6
HCH RM12 .... 92 E3 ⊡
Matlock Gdns *CHEAM* SM3 .... 169 L6
Matlock Pl *SUT* SM1 .... 169 L6 ⊡
Matlock Rd *LEY* E10 .... 69 J7
Matlock St *WCHPL* E1 .... 104 E5
Matlock Wy *NWMAL* KT3 ..... 153 K4
Matthew Arnold Cl
STA TW18 .... 148 C2 ⊡
Matthew Cl *NKENS* W10 ...... 100 D3 ⊡
Matthew Ct *MTCM* CR4 .... 156 D8 ⊡
Matthew's Gdns
CROY/NA CR0 .... 186 D4 ⊡
Matthews Rd *NTHLT* UB5 ..... 79 K5 ⊡
Matthews St *BTSEA* SW11 .... 119 M7 ⊡
Matthias Rd *STNW/STAM* N16 .. 85 K6
Mattingly Wy *PECK* SE15 .... 121 M5 ⊡
Mattison Rd *FSBYPK* N4 ...... 67 G7
Mattock La *WEA* W13 .... 98 C7

Maud Cashmore Wy
WOOL/PLUM SE18 .... 124 F1
Maude Crs *WATN* WD24 .... 29 H2
Maude Rd *CMBW* SE5 .... 121 L7
WALTH E17 .... 68 E6 ⊡
Maudesville Cottages
HNWL W7 .... 97 L7 ⊡
Maude Ter *WALTH* E17 .... 68 E5
Maud Gdns *BARK* IG11 .... 107 M1
PLSTW E13 .... 105 M1 ⊡
Maud Rd *LEY* E10 .... 87 J3
PLSTW E13 .... 87 M8
Maudslay Rd *ELTH/MOT* SE9 .. 124 F8
Maud St *CAN/RD* E16 .... 105 M4
Mauleverer Rd
BRXS/STRHM SW2 .... 138 E2
Maunder Rd *HNWL* W7 .... 97 M7 ⊡
Maunsel St *WEST* SW1P .... 17 G5 ⊡
Maurice Av *WDGN* N22 .... 67 H3
Maurice St *SHB* W12 .... 100 B5 ⊡
Maurice Wk *GLDGN* NW11 ...... 65 J5
Maurier Cl *NTHLT* UB5 .... 78 C8
Mauritius Rd *GNWCH* SE10 ... 123 L2 ⊡
Maury Rd *STNW/STAM* N16 .... 86 A2
Mavelstone Rd *BMLY* BR1 ..... 160 D4
Mavis Av *HOR/WEW* KT19 ..... 168 E7
Mavis Cl *HOR/WEW* KT19 ..... 168 E7
Mavis Gv *HCH* RM12 .... 92 E2
Mawbey Pl *STHWK* SE1 .... 19 M8
Mawbey Rd *STHWK* SE1 ...... 19 M8
Mawbey St *VX/NE* SW8 .... 120 E5
Mawney Cl *ROMW/RG* RM7 .... 73 H3
Mawney Rd *ROMW/RG* RM7 .... 73 H4
Mawson Cl *RYNPK* SW20 ..... 154 E5
Mawson La *CHSWK* W4 ...... 117 M4
Maxey Gdns *DAGW* RM9 ...... 90 E4
Maxey Rd *DAGW* RM9 .... 90 E4
WOOL/PLUM SE18 .... 125 J2
Maxfield Cl *TRDG/WHET* N20 .. 47 J2
Maximfeldt Rd *ERITH* DA8 .... 127 L3
ERITH DA8 .... 127 L3
WCHMH N21 .... 49 G1
Maxted Pk *HRW* HA1 .... 61 L8
Maxted Rd *PECK* SE15 .... 121 M8
Maxwell Cl *CROY/NA* CR0 .... 171 L3
RKW/CH/CXG WD3 .... 40 A4
Maxwell Gdns *ORP* BR6 ..... 176 F5
Maxwell Ri *OXHEY* WD19 ..... 42 E2 ⊡
Maxwell Rd *ASHF* TW15 ...... 149 J2
BORE WD6 .... 32 B6
FUL/PGN SW6 .... 119 H5
NTHWD HA6 .... 59 K1
WDR/YW UB7 .... 112 E2
WELL DA16 .... 144 A1
Maxwelton Av *MLHL* NW7 .... 45 K7
Maxwelton Cl *MLHL* NW7 .... 45 K7
Mayall Rd *HNHL* SE24 .... 139 H2
Maya Rd *EFNCH* N2 .... 65 J5
May Av *STMC/STPC* BR5 ..... 162 B8
Maybank Av *ALP/SUD* HA0 ... 80 A4 ⊡
HCH RM12 .... 92 B5
SWFD E18 .... 70 B3
Maybank Gdns *PIN* HA5 ..... 60 A6
Maybank Rd *SWFD* E18 ...... 70 C2
May Bate Av *KUTN/CMB* KT2 ... 152 E4
Mayberry Pl *BRYLDS* KT5 .... 167 M2 ⊡
Maybrick Rd *EMPK* RM11 .... 74 C6
Maybury Av *CHES/WCR* EN8 ... 26 B1
CHESW EN7 .... 26 B1 ⊡
RDART DA2 .... 147 J3 ⊡
Maybury Cl *STMC/STPC* BR5 .. 161 H8
Maybury Gdns *WLSDN* NW10 .. 82 A7
Maybury Rd *BARK* IG11 ..... 108 A1
PLSTW E13 .... 106 C3
Maybury St *TOOT* SW17 ..... 155 L1
Maybush Rd *EMPK* RM11 .... 74 E8
Maychurch Cl *STAN* HA7 ..... 62 D2 ⊡
May Cl *CHSGTN* KT9 .... 167 M8
Maycock Gv *NTHWD* HA6 .... 41 M8
Maycroft *PIN* HA5 .... 60 B3
Maycross Av *MRDN* SM4 ..... 154 F7
Mayday Gdns *BKHTH/KID* SE3 . 124 E7
Mayday Rd *THHTH* CR7 ...... 172 B1
Maydwell Ldg *BORE* WD6 .... 31 M5
Mayerne Rd *ELTH/MOT* SE9 .. 142 D2
Mayesbrook Rd *BARK* IG11 .. 89 M8
GDMY/SEVK IG3 .... 90 A3
Mayesford Rd *CHDH* RM6 .... 72 C8
Mayes Rd *CEND/HSY/T* N8 ... 67 G4
WDGN N22 .... 66 F3
Mayeswood Rd *LEE/GVPK* SE12.. 142 C8
Mayfair Av *CHDH* RM6 ...... 72 D7
IL IG1 .... 88 F2
WELL DA16 .... 126 D6
WHTN TW2 .... 133 J4
WPK KT4 .... 169 G3
Mayfair Cl *BECK* BR3 .... 159 H4 ⊡
SURB KT6 .... 167 L3
WFD IG8 .... 70 A1
Mayfair Pl *MYFR/PICC* W1J .. 10 D8
Mayfair Rd *DART* DA1 ...... 146 D2
Mayfair Ter *STHGT/OAK* N14 .. 48 D2
Mayfare *RKW/CH/CXG* WD3 .. 28 C8
Mayfield *BXLYHN* DA7 .... 126 F8
Mayfield Av *CHSWK* W4 ..... 117 L2
KTN/HRWW/W HA3 .... 62 B6
NFNCH/WDSP N12 .... 47 J6
ORP BR6 .... 176 F3
STHGT/OAK N14 .... 48 C4
WEA W13 .... 116 B1
WFD IG8 .... 52 A8
Mayfield Cl *ASHF* TW15 .... 149 H2
CLAP SW4 .... 138 Q2
HCDN/ICK UB10 .... 95 H2
THDIT KT7 .... 166 C7
WOT/HER KT12 .... 165 G6
Mayfield Crs *ED* N9 .... 50 B1
THHTH CR7 .... 156 F7
Mayfield Gdns *HDN* NW4 .... 64 D7
HNWL W7 .... 97 K5
WOT/HER KT12 .... 165 G6
Mayfield Rd *ACT* W3 .... 99 H6
BCTR RM8 .... 90 C1

BELMT SM2 .... 170 D8
BELV DA17 .... 127 J2
BMLY BR1 .... 160 E8
CEND/HSY/T N8 .... 66 F7
CHING E4 .... 51 K4
HACK E8 .... 7 K5
PEND EN3 .... 37 K5
PLSTW E13 .... 105 M3 ⊡
SAND/SEL CR2 .... 184 D2
SHB W12 .... 99 L8
WALTH E17 .... 68 E3
WIM/MER SW19 .... 154 F4
WOT/HER KT12 .... 165 G6
Mayfields *WBLY* HA9 .... 81 G2
Mayfields Cl *WBLY* HA9 .... 81 G2
Mayflower Cl
BERM/RHTH SE16 .... 122 D2 ⊡
RSLP HA4 .... 59 J7 ⊡
Mayflower Rd *BRXN/ST* SW9 .. 120 E8
Mayflower St
BERM/RHTH SE16 .... 104 C8 ⊡
Mayfly Cl *PIN* HA5 .... 60 C8
STMC/STPC BR5 .... 162 D7 ⊡
Mayford Cl *BAL* SW12 .... 137 M4 ⊡
BECK BR3 .... 158 B6 ⊡
Mayford Rd *BAL* SW12 ...... 137 M4
May Gdns *BORE* WD6 .... 44 D1
GFD/PVL UB6 .... 98 C1
Maygoods Cl *UX/CGN* UB8 ... 94 D4
Maygoods La *UX/CGN* UB8 ... 94 D4
Maygoods St *IS* N1 .... 5 M5
Maygrove Rd *KIL/WHAMP* NW6.. 82 F6
Mayhew Cl *CHING* E4 .... 51 G5
Mayhill Rd *BAR* EN5 .... 46 E1 ⊡
CHARL SE7 .... 124 B4
Maylands Av *HCH* RM12 ..... 92 B4
Maylands Dr *SCUP* DA14 .... 144 D7
UX/CGN UB8 .... 76 D6
Maylands Rd *OXHEY* WD19 ... 42 C6
Maylands Wy *HARH* RM3 .... 57 J8
Maynard Cl *ERITH* DA8 ..... 127 M5
FUL/PGN SW6 .... 119 H5
SEVS/STOTM N15 .... 67 L2 ⊡
Maynard Pl *POTB/CUF* EN6 .. 24 E2 ⊡
Maynard Rd *WALTH* E17 ..... 69 J6
Maynards *EMPK* RM11 .... 74 E8
Maynooth Gdns *MTCM* CR4 .. 170 F2
Mayo Cl *CHES/WCR* EN8 ..... 26 C1
Mayola Rd *CLPT* E5 .... 86 C4
Mayo Rd *CROY/NA* CR0 ...... 157 K8
WLSDN NW10 .... 81 L6
WOT/HER KT12 .... 165 G2
Mayow Rd *SYD* SE26 .... 140 D8
Maypole Crs *BARK/HLT* IG6 .. 71 K1
ERITH DA8 .... 128 C4
Maypole Dr *CHIG* IG7 .... 54 A5
Maypole Rd *ORP* BR6 .... 177 M8
May Rd *CHING* E4 .... 51 G8
PLSTW E13 .... 106 A1
RDART DA2 .... 146 F8
WHTN TW2 .... 133 L5
Mayroyd Av *SURB* KT6 ...... 168 A4 ⊡
May's Buildings Ms
GNWCH SE10 .... 123 K5 ⊡
May's Hill Rd *HAYES* BR2 .. 159 L5
Mays La *BAR* EN5 .... 46 B2
Maysoule Rd *BTSEA* SW11 ... 137 K1
Mays Rd *HPTN* TW12 .... 151 K1
May St *WKENS* W14 .... 118 F3 ⊡
Mayswood Gdns *DAGE* RM10 .. 91 J6 ⊡
Maythorne Cl *WATW* WD18 .. 28 E7
Maythorne Cottages
LEW SE13 .... 141 K3 ⊡
Mayton St *HOLWY* N7 ...... 84 F3
Maytree Cl *EDGW* HA8 ...... 45 J4
RAIN RM13 .... 109 L1
Maytree Ct *MTCM* CR4 ...... 156 A6
Maytree Crs *WATN* WD24 ... 28 F1
Maytree La *STAN* HA7 ...... 43 M8
Maytrees *RAD* WD7 .... 31 G2
Mayville Rd *IL* IG1 .... 89 H5
WAN E11 .... 87 L3 ⊡
Maywater Cl *SAND/SEL* CR2 .. 184 D4
Maywin Dr *EMPK* RM11 ..... 92 F1
Maze Hl *BKHTH/KID* SE3 .... 123 M5
GNWCH SE10 .... 123 L4
Mazenod Av *KIL/WHAMP* NW6.. 2 B2
Maze Rd *RCH/KEW* TW9 .... 117 G5
Mcadam Dr *ENC/FH* EN2 .... 36 B5 ⊡
Mcauley Cl *ELTH/MOT* SE9 .. 143 G2 ⊡
STHWK SE1 .... 18 A3
Mccall Cl *CLAP* SW4 .... 120 L7
Mc Call Crs *CHARL* SE7 .... 124 F2
Mccarthy Rd *FELT* TW13 .... 150 D1 ⊡
Mccrone Ms *HAMP* NW3 ...... 83 K6 ⊡
Mccudden Rd *DART* DA1 .... 128 F8
Mccullum Rd *BOW* E3 .... 86 F8
Mcdermott Cl *BTSEA* SW11 .. 119 L7
Mcdermott Rd *PECK* SE15 ... 122 A8
Mcdonough Cl *CHSGTN* KT9 .. 167 L6 ⊡
Mcdougall Ct *RCH/KEW* TW9 .. 117 J2
Mcdowall Cl *CAN/RD* E16 ... 106 A4 ⊡
Mcentee Av *WALTH* E17 .... 68 E2
Mcewan Wy *SRTFD* E15 ..... 87 K8 ⊡
Mcgrath Rd *FSTGT* E7 ...... 87 M5
Mcgregor Rd *NTGHL* W11 ... 100 F5
Mcintosh Cl *ROM* RM1 ...... 73 L4 ⊡
WLGTN SM6 .... 183 L1
Mcintosh Rd *ROM* RM1 ..... 73 L4
Mckay Rd *RYNPK* SW20 ..... 154 B3
Mc Kellar Cl *BUSH* WD23 ... 43 J4 ⊡
Mckerrell Rd *PECK* SE15 ... 122 H4
Mcleod Rd *ABYW* SE2 ...... 126 C2
Mcleod's Ms *SKENS* SW7 ... 14 B4
Mcmillan St *DEPT* SE8 ..... 123 G4 ⊡
Mcnair Rd *NWDGN* UB2 .... 97 H8
Mc Neil Rd *CMBW* SE5 ...... 121 L7
Mcnicol Dr *WLSDN* NW10 ... 99 J1
Mcrae La *MTCM* CR4 .... 170 F2 ⊡

HOM E9 .... 86 C6
RKW/CH/CXG WD3 .... 40 B3
Mead Plat *WLSDN* NW10 .... 81 J6
Mead Rd *CHST* BR7 .... 161 J2 ⊡
DART DA1 .... 146 D5
EDGW HA8 .... 63 G1
RCHPK/HAM TW10 .... 134 C7
UX/CGN UB8 .... 76 D6
WOT/HER KT12 .... 165 L6
Mead Rw *STHWK* SE1 .... 18 A3
Meadside Cl *BECK* BR3 .... 158 E4
Meads La *GDMY/SEVK* IG3 ... 71 M8
Meads Rd *PEND* EN3 .... 37 L4
WDGN N22 .... 67 H3
The Meads *CHEAM* SM3 ..... 169 K5
EDGW HA8 .... 45 L8 ⊡
LCOL/BKTW AL2 .... 21 M2
UPMR RM14 .... 93 L2 ⊡
UX/CGN UB8 .... 94 E3
WEY KT13 .... 164 C8
The Mead *BECK* BR3 .... 159 J5
CHES/WCR EN8 .... 26 C2
EFNCH N2 .... 65 J3
HGDN/ICK UB10 .... 77 G2
OXHEY WD19 .... 42 E5
WEA W13 .... 98 B4
WLGTN SM6 .... 171 K8
WWKM BR4 .... 174 D3
Meadvale Rd *CROY/NA* CR0 .. 172 F2
EA W5 .... 98 B3
Mead Wy *BUSH* WD23 ...... 29 L5
CROY/NA CR0 .... 173 L4
HAYES BR2 .... 174 F1
RSLP HA4 .... 59 K7
Meadway *ASHF* TW15 .... 131 G8
BAR EN5 .... 34 A7
BECK BR3 .... 159 J4
BRYLDS KT5 .... 168 C3
ESH/CLAY KT10 .... 178 B2
GDMY/SEVK IG3 .... 89 L4
GLDGN NW11 .... 65 H7
GPK RM2 .... 74 A3
HOR/WEW KT19 .... 180 C6
LHD/OX KT22 .... 178 D7
PEND EN3 .... 37 K1
RYNPK SW20 .... 154 C7
STA TW18 .... 148 A3
STHGT/OAK N14 .... 48 D4
WFD IG8 .... 52 C7 ⊡
WHTN TW2 .... 133 K5
Meadway Cl *GLDGN* NW11 ... 65 H7
PIN HA5 .... 43 H8 ⊡
Meadway Gdns *RSLP* HA4 ... 59 K7
The Meadway *BKHH* IG9 .... 52 D3
BKHTH/KID SE3 .... 123 K7 ⊡
ORP BR6 .... 177 H6
POTB/CUF EN6 .... 24 F1
Meaford Wy *PGE/AN* SE20 .. 158 B3
Meanley Rd *MNPK* E12 ..... 88 E5
Meard St *SOHO/CST* W1F 11 G5
Meath Cl *STMC/STPC* BR5 .. 162 B8
Meath Rd *IL* IG1 .... 89 J3
SRTFD E15 .... 105 M1
Meath St *BTSEA* SW11 ..... 120 B6 ⊡
Mecklenburgh Pl *BMSBY* WC1N . 5 L9
Mecklenburgh Sq *BMSBY* WC1N . 5 L9
Mecklenburgh St *BMSBY* WC1N . 5 L9
Medburn St *CAMTN* NW1 ..... 5 G5
Medcalf Rd *PEND* EN3 ...... 37 M2
Medcroft Gdns
MORT/ESHN SW14 .... 135 J1 ⊡
Medebourne Cl
BKHTH/KID SE3 .... 124 A8 ⊡
Medesenge Wy *PLMGR* N13 .. 49 H8
Medfield St *PUT/ROE* SW15.. 136 A4
Medhurst Cl *BOW* E3 .... 104 F3 ⊡
Median Rd *CLPT* E5 .... 86 C5
Medina Av *ESH/CLAY* KT10 .. 166 B5
Medina Rd *HOLWY* N7 ...... 85 G3
Medlar Cl *NTHLT* UB5 ...... 96 D1 ⊡
Medlar St *CMBW* SE5 .... 121 J6
Medley Rd *KIL/WHAMP* NW6 .. 83 G6 ⊡
Medman Cl *UX/CGN* UB8 .... 94 C1 ⊡
Medora Rd *BRXS/STRHM* SW2 .. 138 F3
ROMW/RG RM7 .... 73 K5
Medusa Rd *LEW* SE13 ...... 141 H3
Medway Cl *CROY/NA* CR0 ... 173 J1 ⊡
GSTN WD25 .... 21 J7
IL IG1 .... 89 J3
Medway Dr *GFD/PVL* UB6 ... 97 M1
Medway Gdns *ALP/SUD* HA0 .. 80 A4
Medway Pde *GFD/PVL* UB6 .. 97 M1 ⊡
Medway Rd *BOW* E3 .... 104 E1
DART DA1 .... 128 A8
Medway St *WEST* SW1P 17 G4
Medwin St *BRXS/STRHM* SW2 . 138 F1
Meek St *WBPTN* SW10 .... 119 J5 ⊡
Meerbrook Rd *ELTH/MOT* SE9 . 124 C8
Meeson Rd *SRTFD* E15 ..... 88 M7
Meeson St *CLPT* E5 .... 86 F2
Meeting Field Pth *HOM* E9 .. 86 C6 ⊡
Meeting House Aly
WAP E1W .... 104 B7 ⊡
Meeting House La *PECK* SE15.. 122 B6
Mehetabel Rd *HACK* E8 .... 86 C6
Meister Cl *IL* IG1 .... 89 K1
Melanda Cl *CHST* BR7 ..... 160 F1
Melanie Cl *BXLYHN* DA7 ... 126 E6
Melaris Ms *KIL/WHAMP* NW6 . 83 G5 ⊡
Melbourne Av *PLMGR* N13 .. 48 F8
RYLN/HDSTN HA2 .... 61 H4
WEA W13 .... 98 A7 ⊡
Melbourne Cl *ORP* BR6 .... 176 E2
WLGTN SM6 .... 171 J7 ⊡
Melbourne Gdns *CHDH* RM6 .. 72 C6
Melbourne Gv *EDUL* SE22 .. 139 M1
Melbourne Ms *BRXN/ST* SW9 . 121 G6 ⊡
CAT SE6 .... 141 J6
Melbourne Pl *HOL/ALD* WC2B . 11 M6 ⊡
Melbourne Rd *BUSH* WD23 .. 30 B8
EHAM E6 .... 89 H1
IL IG1 .... 89 H1
LEY E10 .... 69 H4
TEDD TW11 .... 152 C2
WALTH E17 .... 67 H2
WIM/MER SW19 .... 155 G4
WLGTN SM6 .... 171 H7

Melbourne Sq *BRXN/ST* SW9 ... 121 G6 🖫
Melbourne Wy *EN* EN1 .... 49 M1
Melbury Av *NWDGN* UB2 .... 115 H1
Melbury Cl *CHST* BR7 .... 160 F2
  ESH/CLAY KT10 .... 167 H8
Melbury St *WKENS* W14 .... 118 F1
Melbury Dr *CMBW* SE5 .... 121 L5 🖫
Melbury Gdns *RYNPK* SW20 .... 154 B4
Melbury Rd *KTN/HRWW/W* HA3 .. 62 F6
  WKENS W14 .... 118 F1
Melcombe Gdns
  KTN/HRWW/W HA3 .... 62 F7 🖫
Melcombe Pl *CAMTN* NW1 .... 9 L2
Melcombe St *CAMTN* NW1 .... 9 M1
Meldon Cl *FUL/PGN* SW6 ...... 119 H6 🖫
Meldone Cl *BRYLDS* KT5 .... 168 B1
Meldrum Cl *STMC/STPC* BR5 .. 177 J1 🖫
Meldrum Rd *GDMY/SEVK* IG3 .. 90 A2
Melfield Gdns *CAT* SE6 .... 141 M8
Melford Av *BARK* IG11 .... 89 L6
Melford Cl *CHSGTN* KT9 .... 167 M7 🖫
Melford Rd *DUL* SE21 .... 140 A5
  EHAM E6 .... 106 F3
  IL IG1 .... 89 K2
  WALTH E17 .... 68 E5
  WAN E11 .... 87 L2
Melfort Rd *THHTH* CR7 .... 157 H6
Melgund Rd *HBRY* N5 .... 85 G5
Melina Cl *HYS/HAR* UB3 .... 95 K4
Melina Pl *STJWD* NW8 .... 3 G8
Melina Rd *SHB* W12 .... 100 B8
Melior Pl *STHWK* SE1 .... 19 J1 🖫
Melior St *STHWK* SE1 .... 19 H1
Meliot Rd *CAT* SE6 .... 141 K6
Melksham Cl *HARH* RM3 .... 74 F1 🖫
Melksham Gdns *HARH* RM3 .... 74 E1
Melksham Gn *HARH* RM3 .... 74 E1 🖫
Meller Cl *WLGTN* SM6 .... 171 L5
Melling Dr *EN* EN1 .... 37 G4
Melling St *WOOL/PLUM* SE18 .. 125 L4
Mellison Rd *TOOT* SW17 .... 155 L1
Mellitus St *SHB* W12 .... 99 M5
Mellor Cl *WOT/HER* KT12 ...... 165 M2
Mellow La East *YEAD* UB4 ...... 95 J3
Mellows Rd *CLAY* IG5 .... 70 F4
  WLGTN SM6 .... 171 K7
Mells Crs *ELTH/MOT* SE9 ...... 142 F7
Mell St *GNWCH* SE10 .... 123 L3 🖫
Melody Rd *WAND/EARL* SW18 .. 137 J3
Melon Pl *KENS* W8 .... 14 B1 🖫
Melon Rd *PECK* SE15 .... 122 A6
  WAN E11 .... 87 L3
Melrose Av *BORE* WD6 .... 32 B8
  CRICK NW2 .... 82 C5
  GFD/PVL UB6 .... 97 H1
  MTCM CR4 .... 156 B3
  POTB/CUF EN6 .... 23 H6
  STRHM/NOR SW16 .... 156 F6
  WDGN N22 .... 67 H2
  WHTN TW2 .... 133 H4
  WIM/MER SW19 .... 136 F6
Melrose Cl *GFD/PVL* UB6 .... 97 H1
  LEE/GVPK SE12 .... 142 A5
  YEAD UB4 .... 96 A4
Melrose Crs *ORP* BR6 .... 176 D6
Melrose Dr *STHL* UB1 .... 97 G7
Melrose Gdns *EDGW* HA8 .... 63 H4
  HMSMTH W6 .... 118 C1
  NWMAL KT3 .... 153 K6
  WOT/HER KT12 .... 165 J7
Melrose Pl *WAT* WD17 .... 28 F3
Melrose Rd *BARN* SW13 .... 117 M7 🖫
  COUL/CHIP CR5 .... 183 H8
  RYLN/HDSTN HA2 .... 60 F5
  WAND/EARL SW18 .... 136 F3
  WEY KT13 .... 164 A7
  WIM/MER SW19 .... 155 G5
Melrose Ter *HMSMTH* W6 ...... 100 C8
Melsa Rd *MRDN* SM4 .... 170 C1
Melstock Av *UPMR* RM14 .... 93 J4
Melthorne Dr *RSLP* HA4 .... 78 C3
Melthorpe Gdns
  WOOL/PLUM SE18 .... 124 D6
Melton Cl *RSLP* HA4 .... 78 C1 🖫
Melton Flds *HOR/WEW* KT19 .. 180 D3 🖫
Melton Gdns *ROM* RM1 .... 73 M8
Melton Pl *HOR/WEW* KT19 .... 180 D2
Melton St *CAMTN* NW1 .... 4 F8
Melville Av *GFD/PVL* UB6 ...... 79 M5
  RYNPK SW20 .... 154 A4
  SAND/SEL CR2 .... 172 F7
Melville Cl *HGDN/ICK* UB10 .... 77 K3
Melville Gdns *PLMGR* N13 ...... 49 G7
Melville Rd *BARN* SW13 .... 118 A6
  RAIN RM13 .... 110 A3
  ROMW/RG RM7 .... 73 H2 🖫
  SCUP DA14 .... 144 C6
  WALTH E17 .... 68 F5
  WLSDN NW10 .... 81 K7
Melville Villas Rd *ACT* W3 ..... 99 J7 🖫
Melvin Rd *PGE/AN* SE20 .... 158 C4
Melvyn Cl *CHESW* EN7 .... 25 H1 🖫
Memel St *STLK* EC1Y 12 E1
Memorial Av *SRTFD* E15 .... 105 L2
Memorial Cl *HEST* TW5 .... 114 F4
Memorial Wy *WAT* WD17 .... 29 G6 🖫
Mendip Cl *HYS/HAR* UB3 ..... 113 K5 🖫
  SYD SE26 .... 140 C8
  WPK KT4 .... 169 J4
Mendip Dr *GLDGN* NW11 .... 82 C2
Mendip Rd *BTSEA* SW11 ...... 119 J8
  BUSH WD23 .... 43 J1
  BXLYHN DA7 .... 127 L6
  EMPK RM11 .... 74 A8
  GNTH/NBYPK IG2 .... 71 L6
Mendora Rd *FUL/PGN* SW6 .. 118 C5
Mendoza Cl *EMPK* RM11 .... 74 E6
Menelik Rd *CRICK* NW2 .... 82 E4
Menlo Gdns *NRWD* SE19 .... 157 K3
Menotti St *BETH* E2 .... 104 A3 🖫
Mentmore Cl
  KTN/HRWW/W HA3 .... 62 C7
Mentmore Ter *HACK* E8 .... 86 B7
Meon Rd *ACT* W3 .... 99 J8

Meopham Rd *MTCM* CR4 ...... 156 C4
Meopham Crs *KTN/HRWW/W* HA3 .. 61 J1
Mepham Gdns
  KTN/HRWW/W HA3 .... 61 J1 🖫
Mepham St *STHWK* SE1 .... 12 A3 🖫
Mera Dr *BXLYHN* DA7 .... 147 K3
Merantun Wy *WIM/MER* SW19 .. 155 H4
Merbury Cl *LEW* SE13 .... 141 J2
Merbury Rd *THMD* SE28 ...... 107 L8
Mercator Pl *POP/IOD* E14 .... 123 G3 🖫
Mercator Rd *LEW* SE13 ...... 141 K1
Merceron St *WCHPL* E1 .... 104 B3 🖫
Mercer Pl *PIN* HA5 .... 60 C1
Mercers Cl *GNWCH* SE10 .... 123 M2 🖫
Mercers Pl *HMSMTH* W6 ..... 118 C2 🖫
Mercers Rd *ARCH* N19 .... 84 D3
Mercer St *LSQ/SEVD* WC2H .. 11 J5 🖫
Merchant St *BOW* E3 .... 104 F2 🖫
Merchiston Rd *CAT* SE6 ...... 141 K6
Merchland Rd *ELTH/MOT* SE9 .. 143 J5
Mercia Gv *LEW* SE13 .... 141 J1
Mercier Rd *PUT/ROE* SW15 .. 136 E2
Mercury Gdns *ROM* RM1 .... 73 M6
Mercury Rd *BTFD* TW8 ...... 116 C3 🖫
Mercury Wy *NWCR* SE14 ..... 122 D4
Mercy Ter *LEW* SE13 .... 141 H2 🖫
Merebank La *WLGTN* SM6 .... 171 M7
Mere Cl *ORP* BR6 .... 176 B4
  WIM/MER SW19 .... 136 D4
Meredith Av *CRICK* NW2 .... 82 C5 🖫
Meredith Cl *PIN* HA5 .... 60 D1
Meredith St *CLKNW* EC1R 6 C3
  PLSTW E13 .... 106 A2
Meredyth Rd *BARN* SW13 .... 118 A7 🖫
Mere End *CROY/NA* CR0 .... 173 K2
Mereland Rd *SHPTN* TW17 ... 164 B1 🖫
Mereside *ORP* BR6 .... 176 A4
Meretone Cl *BROCKY* SE4 .... 140 E1 🖫
Merevale Crs *MRDN* SM4 .... 170 C1
Mereway Rd *WHTN* TW2 ...... 133 K5
Merewood Cl *BMLY* BR1 ...... 161 G5
Merewood Rd *BXLYHN* DA7 .. 127 J7
Mereworth Dr
  WOOL/PLUM SE18 .... 125 H5
Mereworth Cl *HAYES* BR2 .... 159 M8 🖫
Meridan Cl *BARK/HLT* IG6 ..... 71 J2
  BMLY BR1 .... 160 D3
Meriden Wy *GSTN* WD25 .... 29 L2
Meridian Rd *CHARL* SE7 ...... 124 D5
Meridian Wy *ED* N9 .... 50 C5
Merifield Rd *ELTH/MOT* SE9 .. 142 C1 🖫
Merino Cl *WAN* E11 .... 70 C5
Merivale Rd *HRW* HA1 .... 61 J8
  PUT/ROE SW15 .... 136 E1
Merle Av *DEN/HRF* UB9 .... 58 C3
Merlewood Dr *CHST* BR7 ..... 160 F4
Merley Ct *CDALE/KGS* NW9 ... 81 J1
Merlin Cl *CROY/NA* CR0 ...... 172 E6
  CRW RM5 .... 55 K8
  MTCM CR4 .... 155 L6
  NTHLT UB5 .... 96 C2 🖫
Merlin Crs *EDGW* HA8 .... 62 F2
Merlin Gdns *CRW* RM5 .... 55 K8 🖫
Merlin Gv *BARK/HLT* IG6 .... 71 H1
  BECK BR3 .... 158 F7
Merlin Rd *CRW* RM5 .... 55 K8
  MNPK E12 .... 88 D2
  WELL DA16 .... 144 A1
Merlin Rd North *WELL* DA16 .. 144 A1
Merlins Av *RYLN/HDSTN* HA2 .. 78 F3
Merlin St *FSBYW* WC1X 6 A8
Mermagen Dr *RAIN* RM13 ...... 92 B7
Mermaid Ct *STHWK* SE1 .... 19 G1
Merredene St
  BRXS/STRHM SW2 .... 138 F3 🖫
Merriam Cl *CHING* E4 .... 51 J7 🖫
Merrick Rd *NWDGN* UB2 ...... 114 F2
Merrick Sq *STHWK* SE1 .... 19 G3
Merridene *WCHMH* N21 .... 49 H1
Merrielands Crs *DAGW* RM9 .. 108 F1
Merrilands Rd *WPK* KT4 .... 169 J3
Merrilees Rd *BFN/LL* DA15 ... 143 L4
Merrilyn Cl *ESH/CLAY* KT10 .. 167 G8
Merriman Rd *BKHTH/KID* SE3 .. 124 B9
Merrington Rd *FUL/PGN* SW6 .. 14 B9
Merrion Av *STAN* HA7 .... 44 D7
Merritt Gdns *CHSGTN* KT9 ... 167 K8 🖫
Merritt Rd *BROCKY* SE4 ...... 140 F2
Merrivale *STHGT/OAK* N14 ..... 35 K8
Merrivale Av *REDBR* IG4 .... 70 D5
Merrow Rd *BELMT* SM2 .... 181 K2
Merrow St *WALW* SE17 .... 19 G8
Merrow Wk *WALW* SE17 .... 19 H7
Merrow Wy *CROY/NA* CR0 .... 174 C8
Merrydown Wy *CHST* BR7 .... 160 E4
Merryfield *BKHTH/KID* SE3 ... 123 M7 🖫
Merryfield Gdns *STAN* HA7 .... 44 C7
Merryfields *UX/CGN* UB8 .... 94 D1 🖫
Merryhill Cl *CHING* E4 .... 51 H2
Merry Hill Mt *BUSH* WD23 ..... 43 H3
Merry Hill Rd *BUSH* WD23 .... 43 G2
Merryhills Dr *ENC/FH* EN2 ...... 35 L7
Merrymeet *BNSTD* SM7 .... 182 F7
Merryweather Cl *DART* DA1 .. 146 F3 🖫
Mersey Av *UPMR* RM14 .... 75 K7
Mersey Rd *WALTH* E17 .... 68 F4 🖫
Mersham Dr *CDALE/KGS* NW9 .. 63 G6
Mersham Pl *PGE/AN* SE20 .... 158 B4 🖫
  THHTH CR7 .... 157 K5 🖫
Mersham Rd *THHTH* CR7 .... 157 K6
Merten Rd *CHDH* RM6 .... 72 E8
Merthyr Ter *BARN* SW13 ...... 118 B4
Merton Av *CHSWK* W4 .... 117 M2
  HGDN/ICK UB10 .... 77 J5
  NTHLT UB5 .... 79 J5
Merton Gdns *STMC/STPC* BR5 .. 161 H8
Merton Hall Gdns *RYNPK* SW20 .. 154 E4
Merton Hall Rd
  WIM/MER SW19 .... 154 C4 🖫
Merton High St
  WIM/MER SW19 .... 155 J3 🖫
Merton La *HGT* N6 .... 83 M2
Merton Ri *HAMP* NW3 .... 3 J1
Merton Rd *BARK* IG11 .... 89 M7
  ENC/FH EN2 .... 36 D3

GDMY/SEVK IG3 .... 71 M8
LEY E10 .... 69 J6
RYLN/HDSTN HA2 .... 79 J1
SNWD SE25 .... 157 M8
WAND/EARL SW18 .... 137 G2 🖫
WATW WD18 .... 29 H7
WIM/MER SW19 .... 155 H3
Merton Wy *E/WMO/HCT* KT8 .. 151 J7
  HGDN/ICK UB10 .... 77 H7 🖫
Merttins Rd *PECK* SE15 ...... 140 D1
Mervan Rd *BRXS/STRHM* SW2 .. 139 G1
Mervyn Av *ELTH/MOT* SE9 .... 143 J7
Mervyn Rd *SHPTN* TW17 .... 164 C2
  WEA W13 .... 116 A1
Messaline Av *ACT* W3 .... 99 J5
Messant Cl *GPK* RM2 .... 74 D3 🖫
Messent Rd *ELTH/MOT* SE9 .. 142 C2
Messeter Pl *ELTH/MOT* SE9 .. 143 G5
Messina Av *KIL/WHAMP* NW6 .. 2 A2
Metcalf Rd *ASHF* TW15 .... 149 H1
Meteor St *BTSEA* SW11 ...... 138 A1
Meteor Wy *WLGTN* SM6 ...... 183 L1 🖫
Methering Wy
  CDALE/KGS NW9 .... 63 L2 🖫
Methley St *LBTH* SE11 .... 18 B8
Methuen Cl *EDGW* HA8 .... 63 G1
Methuen Pk *MUSWH* N10 ...... 66 B3
Methuen Rd *BELV* DA17 ...... 127 H2
  BXLYHS DA6 .... 144 F1
  EDGW HA8 .... 63 G1
Methwold Rd *NKENS* W10 .... 100 D4
Metropolitan Station Ap
  WATW WD18 .... 28 F6
Meux Cl *CHESW* EN7 .... 26 A4
Mews Clare *FUL/PGN* SW6 .. 119 H5 🖫
Mews North *BGVA* SW1W 16 C4
Mews Pl *WFD* IG8 .... 52 A6
Mews South *PIM* SW1V 16 E7
Mews St *WAP* E1W 13 M8
Meynell Av *WAP* E1W .... 104 A7 🖫
Mexfield Rd *PUT/ROE* SW15 .. 136 F2
Meyer Gn *EN* EN1 .... 37 G3
Meyer Rd *ERITH* DA8 .... 127 J4
Meymott St *STHWK* SE1 .... 12 C9
Meynell Crs *HOM* E9 .... 86 D7
Meynell Gdns *HOM* E9 .... 86 D7 🖫
Meynell Rd *HARH* RM3 .... 56 B8
  HOM E9 .... 86 D7
Meyrick Rd *BTSEA* SW11 .... 119 K8
  WLSDN NW10 .... 82 A6 🖫
Mezen Cl *NTHWD* HA6 .... 41 K7
Micawber Av *UX/CGN* UB8 .... 95 G3
Micawber St *IS* N1 .... 6 E7
Michael Adams *CDALE/KGS* NW9 .. [see below]
Michael Gdns *EMPK* RM11 .... 74 D5
Michael Gaynor Cl *HNWL* W7 .. 97 M7
Michaelmas Cl *RYNPK* SW20 .. 154 C6 🖫
Michael Rd *FUL/PGN* SW6 ... 119 H6
  SNWD SE25 .... 157 L6
  WAN E11 .... 87 L1
Michaels Cl *LEW* SE13 .... 141 L1 🖫
Micheldever Rd *LEW* SE13 ... 141 L3
Micheltham Gdns *TWK* TW1 .. 133 M7
Michigan Av *MNPK* E12 .... 88 F4 🖫
Micheltham Down
  NFNCH/WDSP N12 .... 46 F6
Micklefield Wy *BORE* WD6 .... 31 L3 🖫
Mickleham Cl *STMC/STPC* BR5 .. 161 M5
Mickleham Gdns *CHEAM* SM3 .. 169 L8
Mickleham Rd *STMC/STPC* BR5 .. 161 M4
Mickleham Wy *CROY/NA* CR0 .. 186 D1
Micklethwaite Rd
  FUL/PGN SW6 .... 119 G4
Midcroft *RSLP* HA4 .... 77 L1
Middle Cl *EW* KT17 .... 180 E5 🖫
Middle Dene *MLHL* NW7 .... 45 K5
Middlefield *STJWD* NW8 .... 3 G3
Middlefields *WEA* W13 .... 98 B4 🖫
Middle Furlong *BUSH* WD23 ... 30 B7
Middle Green *BRYLDS* KT5 .. 167 M1 🖫
Middleham Gdns *UED* N18 ..... 50 A8
Middleham Rd *UED* N18 .... 50 A8
Middle La *CEND/HSY/T* N8 .... 66 E7 🖫
  EW KT17 .... 180 E5
  TEDD TW11 .... 151 M2 🖫
Middle Lane Ms
  CEND/HSY/T N8 .... 66 E7 🖫
Middle Ope *WATN* WD24 .... 29 H2 🖫
Middle Park Av
  ELTH/MOT SE9 .... 142 D3 🖫
  ELTH/MOT SE9 .... 142 D4 🖫
Middle Rd *EBAR* EN4 .... 47 L1
  PLSTW E13 .... 106 A1
  RYLN/HDSTN HA2 .... 79 K2
  STRHM/NOR SW16 .... 156 C5
  WAB EN9 .... 21 G7
Middle Rw *NKENS* W10 .... 100 E3
Middlesborough Rd *UED* N18 .. 50 A7 🖫
Middlesex Pl *HOM* E9 .... 86 C6 🖫
Middlesex Rd *MTCM* CR4 .... 156 E8
Middlesex St *WCHPL* E1 .... 13 K3
Middle St *CROY/NA* CR0 ...... 172 C5 🖫
  STBT EC1A 12 E2
Middle Temple La
  TPL/STR WC2R 12 A5
Middleton Av *CHING* E4 .... 50 F6
  GFD/PVL UB6 .... 97 K1
  SCUP DA14 .... 162 C2
Middleton Buildings
  GTPST W1W .... 10 E3 🖫
Middleton Cl *CHING* E4 .... 50 F5
Middleton Dr
  BERM/RHTH SE16 .... 104 D7 🖫
  PIN HA5 .... 60 A4
Middleton Gdns
  GNTH/NBYPK IG2 .... 71 H7
Middleton Gv *HOLWY* N7 .... 84 E3 🖫
Middleton Rd *CAR* SM5 .... 170 D2
  GLDGN NW11 .... 65 G8
  HACK E8 .... 7 L2
  HOR/WEW KT19 .... 180 D3 🖫
  HYS/HAR UB3 .... 95 K4
  MRDN SM4 .... 170 C1
  NWMAL KT3 .... 153 J6
  RKW/CH/CXG WD3 .... 40 A3 🖫
Middleton St *BETH* E2 .... 104 B2

Middleton Wy *LEW* SE13 ..... 141 K1
Middle Wy *STRHM/NOR* SW16 .. 156 D5
  WATN WD24 .... 29 H2
Middleway *GLDGN* NW11 .... 65 H6
The Middle Wy
  KTN/HRWW/W HA3 .... 61 M3
Midfield Av *BXLYHN* DA7 ..... 127 J8
Midfield Wy *STMC/STPC* BR5 .. 162 B4
Midford Pl *FITZ* W1T .... 10 F1 🖫
Midholm *GLDGN* NW11 .... 65 H5
  WBLY HA9 .... 81 G1
Midholm Rd *CROY/NA* CR0 .. 173 L5
Midhope St *STPAN* WC1H 5 K8
Midhurst Av *CROY/NA* CR0 .. 172 A2
  MUSWH N10 .... 66 A4
Midhurst Cl *HCH* RM12 .... 92 A4 🖫
Midhurst Gdns *HGDN/ICK* UB10 .. 77 J7
Midhurst Hl *BXLYHS* DA6 .... 145 G2
Midhurst Rd *HNWL* W7 .... 98 A8
Midland Rd *CAMTN* NW1 .... 5 H6
  LEY E10 .... 70 A5
Midland Ter *WLSDN* NW10 .... 99 L3 🖫
Midlothian Rd *BOW* E3 .... 104 F3 🖫
Midmoor Rd *BAL* SW12 ...... 138 C5
  WIM/MER SW19 .... 154 C2
Midship Cl
  BERM/RHTH SE16 .... 104 D7 🖫
Midstrath Rd *WLSDN* NW10 .. 81 L4 🖫
Midsummer Av *HSLWW* TW4 .. 132 F1
Midway *CHEAM* SM3 .... 169 M2
  WOT/HER KT12 .... 165 H4
Midway Av *CHERT* KT16 ...... 148 B6
Midway Cl *STA* TW18 .... 130 B7
Midwinter Cl *WELL* DA16 .... 126 A8 🖫
Mighell Av *REDBR* IG4 .... 70 D6
Milan Rd *STHL* UB1 .... 96 F8
Milborne Gv *WBPTN* SW10 .... 14 F8
Milborne St *HOM* E9 .... 86 C6 🖫
Milborough Crs *LEE/GVPK* SE12 .. 141 L8
Milbourne La *ESH/CLAY* KT10 .. 166 C8
Milbrook *ESH/CLAY* KT10 .... 166 C8
Milburn Dr *WDR/YW* UB7 ...... 94 E6 🖫
Milburn Wk *EPSOM* KT18 .... 180 E8
Milcote St *STHWK* SE1 .... 18 C2
Mildenhall Rd *CLPT* E5 .... 86 C1
Mildmay Av *IS* N1 .... 85 K6 🖫
Mildmay Gv *IS* N1 .... 85 K5
Mildmay Pk *IS* N1 .... 85 K5
Mildmay Rd *IL* IG1 .... 89 H3
  IS N1 .... 85 K5
  ROMW/RG RM7 .... 73 J6
Mildmay St *IS* N1 .... 85 K6
Mildred Av *BORE* WD6 .... 32 A7
  HYS/HAR UB3 .... 113 K2
  NTHLT UB5 .... 79 H5
  WATW WD18 .... 29 G7
Mildred Cl *DART* DA1 .... 147 G3
Mildred Rd *ERITH* DA8 .... 127 L3
Mile Cl *WAB* EN9 .... 21 J6 🖫
Mile End Pl *WCHPL* E1 .... 104 D3
Mile End Rd *BOW* E3 .... 104 F2
  WCHPL E1 .... 104 C4
The Mile End *WALTH* E17 .... 68 D2
Mile Rd *WLGTN* SM6 .... 171 G3
Milespit Hl *MLHL* NW7 .... 46 B7
Miles Rd *CEND/HSY/T* N8 ...... 66 E4
  HOR/WEW KT19 .... 180 D5
  MTCM CR4 .... 155 L6
Miles St *VX/NE* SW8 .... 120 E4
Milestone Cl *BELMT* SM2 .... 170 D8
  ED N9 .... 50 A4
Milestone Rd *NRWD* SE19 ... 157 M2
Mile Stone Rd *RDART* DA2 .. 147 H3
Miles Wy *TRDG/WHET* N20 ... 47 L4
Milfoil St *SHB* W12 .... 100 A6
Milford Cl *ABYW* SE2 .... 126 E4
Milford Gdns *ALP/SUD* HA0 .... 80 D5
  EDGW HA8 .... 63 G1
Milford Gv *SUT* SM1 .... 170 C6
Milford La *TPL/STR* WC2R 12 A6
Milford Ms *STRHM/NOR* SW16 .. 138 F7
Milford Rd *STHL* UB1 .... 97 G6
  WEA W13 .... 98 B7 🖫
Milking La *ORP* BR6 .... 187 L5
Milk St *BMLY* BR1 .... 160 B1
  CAN/RD E16 .... 107 H7
  CITYW EC2V .... 12 F4 🖫
Milkwell Gdns *WFD* IG8 .... 70 B1
Milkwell Yd *CMBW* SE5 .... 121 K6 🖫
Milkwood Rd *HNHL* SE24 .... 139 H2
Milk Yd *WAP* E1W 104 C6
Millais Av *MNPK* E12 .... 89 G5
Millais Gdns *EDGW* HA8 .... 63 G5
Millais Rd *EN* EN1 .... 36 F8
  NWMAL KT3 .... 168 E2
  WAN E11 .... 87 J4
Millais Wy *HOR/WEW* KT19 .. 168 D3
Milland Ct *BORE* WD6 .... 32 D4 🖫
Mill Av *UX/CGN* UB8 .... 94 C1 🖫
Millbank *WEST* SW1P 17 J5
Millbank Wy *LEE/GVPK* SE12 .. 142 A2
Millbourne Rd *FELT* TW13 .... 132 E8
Millbrook *WEY* KT13 .... 164 E6 🖫
Millbrook Av *WELL* DA16 .... 143 K1
Millbrook Gdns *CHDH* RM6 .... 72 E7
  GPK RM2 .... 73 L3
Millbrook Rd *BRXN/ST* SW9 .. 121 H8
  BUSH WD23 .... 29 M4
  ED N9 .... 50 B3
Mill Brook Rd *STMC/STPC* BR5 .. 162 D7
Mill Cl *CAR* SM5 .... 171 G4 🖫
  WDR/YW UB7 .... 112 D1
Mill Cnr *BAR* EN5 .... 33 M4
Millcrest Rd *CHESW* EN7 ...... 25 H1
Millennium Br *BLKFR* EC4V 12 E7
Millennium Whf *POP/IOD* E14 .. 123 K2
Miller Cl *MTCM* CR4 .... 156 C8
  PIN HA5 .... 41 G8
Miller Rd *CROY/NA* CR0 ...... 171 M3 🖫
  WIM/MER SW19 .... 155 L1
Miller's Av *HACK* E8 .... 85 M5 🖫
Millers Cl *CHIG* IG7 .... 54 B4
Miller's La *CHIG* IG7 .... 54 B4
Millers Green Cl *ENC/FH* EN2 .. 36 B5
Miller's Ter *STNW/STAM* N16 .. 85 M5 🖫
Miller St *CAMTN* NW1 .... 4 E5

Miller's Wy *HMSMTH* W6 ..... 100 C8
Millet Rd *GFD/PVL* UB6 .... 97 H2
Mill Farm Av *SUN* TW16 ...... 149 L3
Mill Farm Cl *PIN* HA5 .... 60 C3
Mill Farm Crs *HSLWW* TW4 .. 132 E8
Millfield *SUN* TW16 .... 149 K4
Millfield Av *WALTH* E17 .... 68 E2
Millfield La *HGT* N6 .... 83 M2
Millfield Rd *EDGW* HA8 .... 63 J3
  WHTN TW4 .... 132 E5
Millfields Cl *STMC/STPC* BR5 .. 162 B7
Millfields Rd *CLPT* E5 .... 86 C4
Mill Gdns *SYD* SE26 .... 140 B8
Mill Green Rd *MTCM* CR4 .... 171 G2
Millgrove St *BTSEA* SW11 ... 120 A7 🖫
Millharbour *POP/IOD* E14 .... 123 H1
Millhaven Cl *CHDH* RM6 .... 72 B7
Mill Hl *BARN* SW13 .... 118 A8
Mill Hill Gv *ACT* W3 .... 99 H7 🖫
  BARN SW13 .... 118 B8
Mill Hill Ter *ACT* W3 .... 99 H7
Millhouse Pl *WNWD* SE27 ... 139 H8 🖫
Millicent Rd *LEY* E10 .... 86 F1 🖫
Milligan St *POP/IOD* E14 .... 104 F6
Milling Rd *EDGW* HA8 .... 63 K1
Millington Rd *HYS/HAR* UB3 .. 113 L1
Mill La *CAR* SM5 .... 171 C6
  CHDH RM6 .... 72 E7
  CHES/WCR EN8 .... 26 E1
  CHING E4 .... 38 B6
  CRICK NW2 .... 82 C5
  CROY/NA CR0 .... 172 A5
  DART DA1 .... 146 A1
  EW KT17 .... 180 F2
  KGLGY WD4 .... 20 A2
  WFD IG8 .... 51 M7
  WOOL/PLUM SE18 .... 125 G3
Millman Ms *BMSBY* WC1N .... 11 L1 🖫
Millman St *BMSBY* WC1N 11 L1
Millmark Gv *NWCR* SE14 .... 122 E7
Millmarsh La *PEND* EN3 .... 37 L5
Mill Mead Rd *TOTM* N17 .... 68 B4
Mill Park Av *HCH* RM12 .... 92 E2
Mill Pl *CHST* BR7 .... 161 C4
  DART DA1 .... 146 A1
  KUT KT1 .... 152 F6 🖫
  POP/IOD E14 .... 104 E5 🖫
Mill Plat *ISLW* TW7 .... 116 A7
Mill Plat Av *ISLW* TW7 .... 116 A7
Mill Pond Rd *DART* DA1 .... 146 C3
Mill Rdg *EDGW* HA8 .... 44 F7
Mill Rd *CAN/RD* E16 .... 106 D7
  ERITH DA8 .... 147 L1
  ESH/CLAY KT10 .... 166 A4
  EW KT17 .... 180 F5
  IL IG1 .... 89 G3
  PUR RM19 .... 129 H4
  RDART DA2 .... 146 F8 🖫
  SOCK/AV RM15 .... 111 J6
  WDR/YW UB7 .... 112 D1
  WHTN TW2 .... 133 J6
  WIM/MER SW19 .... 155 J3
Mill Rw *IS* N1 .... 7 K4
Mills Cl *HGDN/ICK* UB10 .... 95 C1
Mills Gv *HDN* NW4 .... 64 C4
  POP/IOD E14 .... 105 J3 🖫
Millshot Cl *FUL/PGN* SW6 ... 118 C6
Millside *CAR* SM5 .... 170 F4
Millside Pl *ISLW* TW7 .... 116 B7
Millsmead Wy *LOU* IG10 .... 39 M5 🖫
Millson Cl *TRDG/WHET* N20 .. 47 K4
Mills Rd *WOT/HER* KT12 ..... 165 J7
Mills Rw *CHSWK* W4 .... 117 K2
Millstream Cl *PLMGR* N13 ..... 49 G7 🖫
Millstream Rd *STHWK* SE1 .... 19 L2
Mill St *CONDST* W1S 10 C6
  KUT KT1 .... 152 F6
  STHWK SE1 .... 19 M2
Mill V *HAYES* BR2 .... 160 A6
Mill View Cl *EW* KT17 .... 180 F1
Mill View Gdns *CROY/NA* CR0 .. 173 K5
Millway Gdns *NTHLT* UB5 ...... 78 F6
Millwell Crs *CHIG* IG7 .... 53 K7
Millwood Rd *HSLW* TW3 ...... 133 J2
  STMC/STPC BR5 .... 162 C6
Millwood St *NKENS* W10 ..... 100 E4 🖫
Milman Cl *PIN* HA5 .... 60 D4
Milman Rd *KIL/WHAMP* NW6 .. 100 D1
Milman's St *WBPTN* SW10 ... 119 K4
Milne Fld *PIN* HA5 .... 61 L1 🖫
Milne Gdns *ELTH/MOT* SE9 .. 142 E2
Milne Pk East *CROY/NA* CR0 .. 186 D4
Milne Pk West *CROY/NA* CR0 .. 186 D4
Milner Cl *GSTN* WD25 .... 21 H7 🖫
Milner Dr *WHTN* TW2 .... 133 K4
Milner Pl *IS* N1 .... 6 B3
Milner Rd *BCTR* RM8 .... 90 C2
  KUT KT1 .... 152 D6
  MRDN SM4 .... 155 K8
  SRTFD E15 .... 105 L2
  THHTH CR7 .... 157 K6
  WIM/MER SW19 .... 155 H4
Milner Sq *IS* N1 .... 6 B2
Milner St *CHEL* SW3 .... 15 L5
Milneway *DEN/HRF* UB9 .... 58 B2
Milnthorpe Rd *CHSWK* W4 .. 117 K4
Milo Rd *EDUL* SE22 .... 139 M3
Milson Rd *WKENS* W14 .... 118 E1
Milton Av *BAR* EN5 .... 33 M8
  CDALE/KGS NW9 .... 63 H4
  CROY/NA CR0 .... 172 C2
  EHAM E6 .... 88 D7
  HCH RM12 .... 91 M2
  HGT N6 .... 66 C8
  SUT SM1 .... 170 D5
  WLSDN NW10 .... 81 K8
Milton Cl *EFNCH* N2 .... 65 J7 🖫
  HYS/HAR UB3 .... 95 J6
  SUT SM1 .... 170 D5
  YEAD UB4 .... 96 A5
Milton Ct *HGDN/ICK* UB10 ..... 77 H3
  WAB EN9 .... 27 J7 🖫

Milton Court Rd *NWCR* SE14 .... 122 E4
Milton Crs *GNTH/NBYPK* IG2 .... 71 J3
Milton Dr *WD6* .... 32 B8 ⑧
  SHPTN TW17 .... 148 E7
Milton Gdns *EPSOM* KT18 .... 180 E7
  STWL/WRAY TW19 .... 130 F5 ⑧
Milton Gv *FBAR/BDGN* N11 .... 48 C7
  STNW/STAM N16 .... 85 K4
Milton Pk *HGT* N6 .... 66 C8
Milton Rd *ACT* W3 .... 99 K7
  BELV DA17 .... 127 G2
  CDALE/KGS NW9 .... 64 A7 ⑧
  CROY/NA CR0 .... 172 D2
  HGDN/ICK UB10 .... 77 H4
  HGT N6 .... 66 C8
  HNHL SE24 .... 139 H2
  HNWL W7 .... 97 H6
  HPTN TW12 .... 151 G3
  HRW HA1 .... 61 L5
  MLHL NW7 .... 46 A7
  MORT/ESHN SW14 .... 117 K8
  ROM RM1 .... 74 A7
  SEVS/STOTM N15 .... 67 H4
  SUT SM1 .... 170 A5
  WALTH E17 .... 69 G5
  WELL DA16 .... 125 M6
  WIM/MER SW19 .... 155 J2
  WLGTN SM6 .... 171 J8
  WOT/HER KT12 .... 165 K5
Milton St *BARB* EC2Y 13 G2
  WATN WD24 .... 29 H4
Milton Wy *WDR/YW* UB7 .... 112 F2
Milverton Dr *HGDN/ICK* UB10 ...... 77 J4
Milverton Gdns *GDMY/SEVK* IG3 ... 89 M2
Milverton Rd *KIL/WHAMP* NW6 ...... 82 C7
Milverton Wy *ELTH/MOT* SE9 .... 143 G8
Milward St *WCHPL* E1 .... 104 B4
Mimms Hall Rd *POTB/CUF* EN6 ..... 22 D4
Mimosa *ORP* BR6 .... 177 J4 ②
Mimosa Rd *YEAD* UB4 .... 96 C4
Mimosa St *FUL/PGN* SW6 .... 118 F6
Minard Rd *CAT* SE6 .... 141 L5
Mina Rd *WALW* SE17 .... 19 K8
  WIM/MER SW19 .... 155 G4
Minchenden Crs
  STHGT/OAK N14 .... 48 D5
Mincing La *MON* EC3R 13 J6
Minden Rd *CHEAM* SM3 .... 169 L4
  PGE/AN SE20 .... 158 B4 ②
Minehead Rd *RYLN/HDSTN* HA2 .... 79 G3
  STRHM/NOR SW16 .... 156 F1
Mineral St *WOOL/PLUM* SE18 ...... 125 L2
Minera Ms *BGVA* SW1W 16 B5
Minerva Cl *BRXN/ST* SW9 .... 121 G5 ⑧
  SCUP DA14 .... 143 L8 ⑧
Minerva Dr *WAT* WD17 .... 28 E1
Minerva Rd *CHING* E4 .... 69 H1 ⑧
  KUT KT1 .... 152 F5
  WLSDN NW10 .... 99 J3
Minerva St *BETH* E2 .... 104 B1 ⑧
Minet Av *WLSDN* NW10 .... 99 L1
Minet Dr *HYS/HAR* UB3 .... 96 A7
Minet Gdns *HYS/HAR* UB3 .... 96 B7
  WLSDN NW10 .... 99 L1 ⑧
Minet Rd *CMBW* SE5 .... 121 H7
Minford Gdns *WKENS* W14 .... 100 D8
Ming St *POP/IOD* E14 .... 105 G6 ⑧
Minimax Cl *EBED/NFELT* TW14 .... 132 A3
Ministry Wy *ELTH/MOT* SE9 .... 142 F6
Mink Cl *HSLWW* TW4 .... 114 C7
Minniedale *BRYLDS* KT5 .... 152 F8
Minorca Rd *WEY* KT13 .... 164 A6 ⑧
Minories *TWRH* EC3N 13 L5
Minshull St *VX/NE* SW8 .... 120 D6 ⑧
Minson Rd *HOM* E9 .... 86 D8 ⑧
Minstead Gdns *PUT/ROE* SW15 ... 135 M4
Minstead Wy *NWMAL* KT3 .... 168 E1
Minster Av *SUT* SM1 .... 170 A4 ②
Minster Dr *CROY/NA* CR0 .... 172 E6
Minster Gdns
  E/WMO/HCT KT8 .... 150 F7 ⑧
Minsterley Av *SHPTN* TW17 .... 149 L1
Minster Rd *BMLY* BR1 .... 160 B3
  CRICK NW2 .... 82 E5
Minster Wy *HYS/HAR* UB3 .... 92 F1
Minstrel Gdns *BRYLDS* KT5 .... 152 F7 ⑧
Mint Cl *HGDN/ICK* UB10 .... 95 H2
Mintern Cl *PLMGR* N13 .... 49 H5 ②
Minterne Av *NWDGN* UB2 .... 115 G2
Minterne Rd
  KTN/HRWW/W HA3 .... 62 F6 ②
Minterne Waye *YEAD* UB4 .... 96 C5
Mintern St *IS* N1 .... 7 H5
Minton Ms *HAMP* NW3 .... 83 H6 ⑧
Mint Rd *WLGTN* SM6 .... 171 H7
Mint St *STHWK* SE1 .... 18 E1
Mint Wk *CROY/NA* CR0 .... 172 C5
Mirabel Rd *FUL/PGN* SW6 .... 118 F5
Miramar Wy *HCH* RM12 .... 92 D5 ⑧
Miranda Cl *WCHPL* E1 .... 104 C4 ②
Miranda Rd *ARCH* N19 .... 84 C1
Mirfield St *CHARL* SE7 .... 124 D1 ②
Miriam Rd *WOOL/PLUM* SE18 ...... 125 L3
Mirren Cl *RYLN/HDSTN* HA2 .... 78 F4
Misbourne Rd *HGDN/ICK* UB10 ..... 95 G1
Miskin Rd *DART* DA1 .... 146 C4
Missenden Cl
  EBED/NFELT TW14 .... 131 M5 ①
Missenden Gdns *MRDN* SM4 .... 170 C1 ⑧
Mission Gv *WALTH* E17 .... 68 F6 ⑧
Mission Pl *PECK* SE15 .... 122 A6 ⑧
Mistletoe Cl *CROY/NA* CR0 .... 173 K3 ①②
Misty's Fld *WOT/HER* KT12 .... 165 J3
Mitcham La *STRHM/NOR* SW16 .... 156 C1
Mitcham Pk *MTCM* CR4 .... 155 M7
Mitcham Rd *CROY/NA* CR0 .... 171 K1
  EHAM E6 .... 106 C2 ⑧
  GDMY/SEVK IG3 .... 71 M8
  TOOT SW17 .... 155 M1
Mitchellbrook Wy *WLSDN* NW10 .. 81 K6
Mitchell Cl *ABLGY* WD5 .... 21 G5 ⑧
  ABYW SE2 .... 126 C3
  BELV DA17 .... 127 J1
  DART DA1 .... 146 E6
  RAIN RM13 .... 110 C1

Mitchell Rd *ORP* BR6 .... 176 F6
  PLMGR N13 .... 49 H7
Mitchell St *FSBYE* EC1V 6 E9
Mitchell Wy *BMLY* BR1 .... 160 A4 ⑧
  WLSDN NW10 .... 81 J6
Mitchison Rd *IS* N1 .... 85 K6
Mitchley Av *PUR/KEN* CR8 .... 184 D6
Mitchley Gv *SAND/SEL* CR2 .... 185 G6
Mitchley Hl *SAND/SEL* CR2 .... 184 F6
Mitchley Rd *TOTM* N17 .... 68 A4
Mitchley Vw *SAND/SEL* CR2 .... 185 G6
Mitford Rd *ARCH* N19 .... 84 E2
Mitre Cl *BELMT* SM2 .... 182 C1
  HAYES BR2 .... 159 M5
  SHPTN TW17 .... 164 D1
Mitre Rd *SRTFD* E15 .... 105 L1
  STHWK SE1 .... 18 B1
Mitre Sq *HDTCH* EC3A 13 K5
Mitre St *HDTCH* EC3A 13 K5
The Mitre *POP/IOD* E14 .... 104 F6 ⑧
Mitre Wy *WLSDN* NW10 .... 100 B4
Mixbury Gv *WEY* KT13 .... 164 D8 ⑧
Mixnams La *CHERT* KT16 .... 148 A6
Moat Cl *BUSH* WD23 .... 30 B8 ②
  ORP BR6 .... 176 F8
Moat Crs *EFNCH* N2 .... 65 H4
Moat Cft *WELL* DA16 .... 126 C8
Moat Dr *HRW* HA1 .... 61 J5
  RSLP HA4 .... 59 L8 ①
Moat Farm Rd *NTHLT* UB5 .... 78 F6
Moatfield Rd *BUSH* WD23 .... 30 B8
Moat La *ERITH* DA8 .... 128 A6
Moat Pl *ACT* W3 .... 99 H5
  BRXN/ST SW9 .... 120 F8
  DEN/HRF UB9 .... 76 B4
Moat Side *FELT* TW13 .... 132 C8
  PEND EN3 .... 37 J7
The Moat *NWMAL* KT3 .... 153 L4
Moberly Rd *CLAP* SW4 .... 138 D4
Modbury Gdns *KTTN* NW5 .... 84 A6 ⑧
Model Farm Cl
  ELTH/MOT SE9 .... 142 E7 ①
Moelyn Ms *HRW* HA1 .... 62 A6
Moffat Rd *PLMGR* N13 .... 48 E8
  THHTH CR7 .... 157 J5
  TOOT SW17 .... 137 L8
Mogden La *ISLW* TW7 .... 133 M2
Mohmmad Khan Rd
  WAN E11 .... 87 M1 ③
Moiety Rd *POP/IOD* E14 .... 105 G8
Moira Cl *TOTM* N17 .... 67 L3
Moira Rd *ELTH/MOT* SE9 .... 142 F1
Moir Cl *SAND/SEL* CR2 .... 185 G2
Molash Rd *STMC/STPC* BR5 .... 162 D7
Mole Abbey Gdns
  E/WMO/HCT KT8 .... 151 G6
Mole Ct *HOR/WEW* KT19 .... 168 C6
Molember Rd *E/WMO/HCT* KT8 ... 151 L8
Mole Rd *WOT/HER* KT12 .... 165 K7
Molescroft *ELTH/MOT* SE9 .... 143 J7
Molesey Av *E/WMO/HCT* KT8 ...... 150 F7
Molesey Cl *WOT/HER* KT12 .... 165 K7
Molesey Dr *CHEAM* SM3 .... 169 L4
Molesey Park Av
  E/WMO/HCT KT8 .... 151 H8
Molesey Park Cl
  E/WMO/HCT KT8 .... 151 J8
Molesey Park Rd
  E/WMO/HCT KT8 .... 151 K8 ②
  WOT/HER KT12 .... 165 K7
Molesford Rd *FUL/PGN* SW6 .... 119 G7 ⑧
Molesham Cl
  E/WMO/HCT KT8 .... 151 H6 ③
Molesham Wy
  E/WMO/HCT KT8 .... 151 H7
Moles HI *LHD/OX* KT22 .... 178 D4
Molesworth St *LEW* SE13 .... 123 J8
Mollison Av *PEND* EN3 .... 26 E8
Mollison Dr *WLGTN* SM6 .... 183 L1
Mollison Wy *EDGW* HA8 .... 62 F3
Molly Huggins Cl *BAL* SW12 .... 138 C4
Molteno Rd *WAT* WD17 .... 29 G4
Molyneux Dr *TOOT* SW17 .... 138 B8 ⑧
Molyneux Rd *WEY* KT13 .... 164 A6
Molyneux St *MBLAR* W1H 9 K3
Monahan Av *PUR/KEN* CR8 .... 183 M5
Monarch Cl *EBED/NFELT* TW14 ... 131 L4
  WWKM BR4 .... 174 F6
Monarch Dr *CAN/RD* E16 .... 106 D4
Monarch Ms *WNWD* SE27 .... 157 L1 ①
Monarch Pl *BKHH* IG9 .... 52 C4
Monarch Rd *BELV* DA17 .... 127 G1
Monarch's Wy
  CHES/WCR EN8 .... 26 D6 ③
  RSLP HA4 .... 77 L1 ①
Mona Rd *PECK* SE15 .... 122 C7
Monastery Gdns *ENC/FH* EN2 ..... 36 D5
Mona St *CAN/RD* E16 .... 105 M4
Monaveen Gdns
  E/WMO/HCT KT8 .... 151 H6 ①
Monck St *WEST* SW1P 17 H4
Monclar Rd *CMBW* SE5 .... 139 K1
Moncorvo Cl *SKENS* SW7 .... 15 J2
Moncrieff St *PECK* SE15 .... 122 A7 ⑧
Mondial Wy *WDR/YW* UB7 .... 113 G9
Monega Rd *FSTGT* E7 .... 88 C6
Money Hill Rd
  RKW/CH/CXG WD3 .... 40 C3
Money La *WDR/YW* UB7 .... 112 D1
Mongers La *EW* KT17 .... 181 G5 ③
Monica Cl *WATN* WD24 .... 29 K5
Monier Rd *BOW* E3 .... 87 C7
Monivea Rd *BECK* BR3 .... 158 F3
Monk Dr *CAN/RD* E16 .... 106 A6
Monkfrith Av *STHGT/OAK* N14 .... 48 B1 ⑧
Monkfrith Wy *STHGT/OAK* N14 ... 48 B2
Monkham's Av *WFD* IG8 .... 52 B7
Monkham's Dr *WFD* IG8 .... 52 B7
Monkham's La *WFD* IG8 .... 52 B7
Monkleigh Rd *MRDN* SM4 .... 154 E6
Monks Av *BAR* EN5 .... 47 J1
  E/WMO/HCT KT8 .... 150 F8
Monks Cl *ABYW* SE2 .... 126 D2
  ENC/FH EN2 .... 36 C5
  RSLP HA4 .... 78 B4 ①
  RYLN/HDSTN HA2 .... 79 H2 ⑧
Monks Crs *WOT/HER* KT12 .... 165 H3

Monksdene Gdns *SUT* SM1 .... 170 B5 ⑧
Monks Dr *ACT* W3 .... 99 G4
Monksmead *BORE* WD6 .... 32 C7
Monks Orch *DART* DA1 .... 146 C6
Monks Orchard Rd *BECK* BR3 ...... 174 A3
Monks Pk *WBLY* HA9 .... 81 J6
Monks Park Gdns *WBLY* HA9 ...... 81 H6
Monks Rd *ENC/FH* EN2 .... 36 B5
Monk St *WOOL/PLUM* SE18 .... 125 G2
Monks Wy *BECK* BR3 .... 174 A1
  STA TW18 .... 148 D3
  STMC/STPC BR5 .... 176 C3
Monkswood Av *WAB* EN9 .... 27 K6
Monkswood Gdns *BORE* WD6 ..... 32 D8
  CLAY IG5 .... 71 G4
Monkton Rd *WELL* DA16 .... 125 M7
Monkton St *LBTH* SE11 .... 18 B5
Monkville Av *GLDGN* NW11 .... 64 F5
Monkwell Sq *BARB* EC2Y .... 12 F3 ⑧
Monkwood Cl *ROM* RM1 .... 74 A6
Monmouth Av *KUT* KT1 .... 152 C3
  SWFD E18 .... 70 A3
Monmouth Cl *CHSWK* W4 .... 117 K1 ⑧
  MTCM CR4 .... 156 F7 ②
  WELL DA16 .... 144 A1
Monmouth Gv *BTFD* TW8 .... 116 E2 ⑧
Monmouth Pl *BAY/PAD* W2 .... 8 B5
Monmouth Rd *BAY/PAD* W2 .... 8 B5 ①
  DAGW RM9 .... 90 F5
  ED N9 .... 50 B4
  EHAM E6 .... 106 F2
  HYS/HAR UB3 .... 113 L2
  WAT WD17 .... 29 H6 ⑧
Monmouth St *LSQ/SEVD* WC2H ... 11 J5
Monnery Rd *ARCH* N19 .... 84 C3
Monnow Rd *SOCK/AV* RM15 .... 111 J6
  STHWK SE1 .... 122 A3
Monoux Gv *WALTH* E17 .... 69 C2
Monroe Cl *EN* EN1 .... 37 H4
Monroe Dr *MORT/ESHN* SW14 .... 135 M2
Monro Gdns *KTN/HRWW/W* HA3 .. 61 L1
Monsell Rd *FSBYPK* N4 .... 85 H3
Monson Rd *NWCR* SE14 .... 122 D5
  WLSDN NW10 .... 100 A1
Mons Wy *HAYES* BR2 .... 175 L1
Montacute Rd *BUSH* WD23 .... 43 L3
  CAT SE6 .... 140 F4
  CROY/NA CR0 .... 186 C2
  MRDN SM4 .... 170 D1
Montagu Av *BROCKY* SE4 .... 140 F1
  HNWL W7 .... 97 M7
  SAND/SEL CR2 .... 184 E5
Montague Av *STHWK* SE1 .... 13 G8
  SWLY BR8 .... 163 M7
  WOT/HER KT12 .... 165 G2 ⑧
Montague Gdns *ACT* W3 .... 99 G6
Montague Hall Pl *BUSH* WD23 .... 43 G1 ①
Montague Pl *GWRST* WC1E 11 H2
Montague Rd *CEND/HSY/T* N8 .... 66 F6
  CROY/NA CR0 .... 172 B3
  HACK E8 .... 86 A5
  HNWL W7 .... 97 M8
  HSLW TW3 .... 115 H8
  NWDGN UB2 .... 114 C2
  RCHPK/HAM TW10 .... 134 E3 ⑧
  SEVS/STOTM N15 .... 68 A5 ⑧
  UX/CGN UB8 .... 76 D7
  WAN E11 .... 87 M2
  WEA W13 .... 98 B5
  WIM/MER SW19 .... 155 H3
Montague Sq *NWCR* SE14 .... 122 C5
Montague St *RSQ* WC1B 11 J2
  STBT EC1A .... 12 E3 ②
Montagu Gdns *UED* N18 .... 50 B6
  WLGTN SM6 .... 171 J6
Montagu Man *MHST* W1U 9 M3
Montagu Ms North
  MBLAR W1H .... 9 M3 ①
Montagu Ms South
  MBLAR W1H .... 9 M4 ③
Montagu Ms West *MBLAR* W1H ... 9 M4
Montagu Pl *MBLAR* W1H 9 L3
Montagu Rd *HDN* NW4 .... 64 A7
  UED N18 .... 50 C6
Montagu Rw *MHST* W1U 9 M3
Montagu Sq *MBLAR* W1H 9 M3
Montagu St *MBLAR* W1H 9 M4
Montalt Rd *WFD* IG8 .... 51 M7
Montana Cl *SAND/SEL* CR2 .... 184 D3
Montana Gdns *CAT* SE6 .... 158 F1 ①
  SUT SM1 .... 170 C7 ②
Montana Rd *RYNPK* SW20 .... 154 C4
  TOOT SW17 .... 138 A7
Montayne Rd *CHES/WCR* EN8 ..... 26 D5
Montbelle Rd *ELTH/MOT* SE9 ...... 143 H7
Montbretia Cl
  STMC/STPC BR5 .... 162 C7 ①
Montcalm Cl *HAYES* BR2 .... 175 C1 ①
  YEAD UB4 .... 96 B2 ②
Montcalm Rd *CHARL* SE7 .... 124 D5
Montclare St *BETH* E2 .... 7 L8
Monteagle Av *BARK* IG11 .... 89 J6
Monteagle Wy *PECK* SE15 .... 122 B8 ②
Montefiore St *VX/NE* SW8 .... 120 B7 ⑧
Monteith Rd *BOW* E3 .... 86 F8
Montem Rd *FSTH* SE23 .... 140 F4
  NWMAL KT3 .... 153 L7
Montem St *FSBYPK* N4 .... 84 F1
Montenotte Rd *CEND/HSY/T* N8 .. 66 C6
Monterey Cl *BXLY* DA5 .... 145 J6
Montford Pl *LBTH* SE11 .... 18 A9
Montford Rd *SUN* TW16 .... 150 A7
Montfort Gdns *BARK/HLT* IG6 ..... 53 J8
Montfort Pl *WIM/MER* SW19 .... 136 D5 ②
Montgomery Av
  ESH/CLAY KT10 .... 166 E4
Montgomery Cl *BFN/LL* DA15 ..... 143 L2 ⑧
  MTCM CR4 .... 156 F7 ⑧
Montgomery Crs *HARH* RM3 .... 56 D7
Montgomery Dr *CHES/WCR* EN8 . 26 E1
Montgomery Rd *CHSWK* W4 .... 117 J2 ⑧
  EDGW HA8 .... 44 F8
Montholme Rd *BTSEA* SW11 .... 137 M3
Monthorpe Rd *WCHPL* E1 .... 104 A4 ①
Montolieu Gdns
  PUT/ROE SW15 .... 136 B2 ⑧
Montpelier Av *BXLY* DA5 .... 144 D4

Montpelier Cl *HGDN/ICK* UB10 .... 77 G8
Montpelier Gdns *CHDH* RM6 .... 72 C8
  EHAM E6 .... 106 D2
Montpelier Gv *KTTN* NW5 .... 84 C5
Montpelier Ms *SKENS* SW7 .... 15 K3 ③
Montpelier Pl *SKENS* SW7 .... 15 K3
  WCHPL E1 .... 104 C5 ⑧
Montpelier Ri *GLDGN* NW11 .... 64 E8
  WBLY HA9 .... 80 D1
Montpelier Rd *EA* W5 .... 98 D4
  FNCH N3 .... 65 J2
  PECK SE15 .... 122 B6
  PUR/KEN CR8 .... 184 B3
  SUT SM1 .... 170 A5
Montpelier Rw *BKHTH/KID* SE3 ... 123 M7
  TWK TW1 .... 134 B4
Montpelier Sq *SKENS* SW7 .... 15 K3 ⑧
Montpelier St *SKENS* SW7 .... 15 K2
Montpelier Ter *SKENS* SW7 .... 15 K2
Montpelier V
  BKHTH/KID SE3 .... 123 M7 ②
Montpelier Wk *SKENS* SW7 .... 15 K2
Montpelier Wy *GLDGN* NW11 ...... 64 E8 ①
Montrave Rd *PGE/AN* SE20 .... 158 C3 ⑧
Montreal Pl *HOL/ALD* WC2B .... 11 L6 ⑧
Montreal Rd *IL* IG1 .... 71 J8
  SEVS/STOTM N15 .... 67 L6 ②
Montrell Rd *BRXS/STRHM* SW2 .. 138 E1
Montrose Av *BFN/LL* DA15 .... 144 A4
  EDGW HA8 .... 63 K3
  GPK RM2 .... 74 C3
  KIL/WHAMP NW6 .... 100 E1
  WELL DA16 .... 125 K8
  WHTN TW2 .... 133 H4
Montrose Cl *ASHF* TW15 .... 149 J2
  WELL DA16 .... 125 M8
  WFD IG8 .... 52 A6
Montrose Crs *ALP/SUD* HA0 .... 80 E6
  NFNCH/WDSP N12 .... 47 H8
Montrose Gdns *LHD/OX* KT22 .... 178 D5
  MTCM CR4 .... 155 M5 ⑧
  SUT SM1 .... 170 B4
Montrose Pl *KTBR* SW1X .... 16 B2 ②
Montrose Rd
  EBED/NFELT TW14 .... 131 K3 ⑧
  KTN/HRWW/W HA3 .... 61 L3
Montrose Wk *WEY* KT13 .... 164 B5 ⑧
Montserrat Av *WFD* IG8 .... 69 K1 ②
Montserrat Cl *NRWD* SE19 .... 157 K1 ②
Montserrat Rd *PUT/ROE* SW15 ... 136 E1 ⑧
Monument Hl *WEY* KT13 .... 164 B6
Monument Rd *WEY* KT13 .... 164 B6
Monument St *MON* EC3R 13 H7
Monument Wy
  SEVS/STOTM N15 .... 67 M4
Monza St *WAP* E1W 104 C6
Moodkee St *BERM/RHTH* SE16 ... 122 C1
Moody St *WCHPL* E1 .... 104 D7 ⑧
Moon La *BAR* EN5 .... 33 M6 ①
Moon St *IS* N1 .... 6 C3
Moorcroft Gdns *HAYES* BR2 .... 160 E8 ①
Moorcroft La *UX/CGN* UB8 .... 95 G4
Moorcroft Rd
  STRHM/NOR SW16 .... 138 E7 ②
Moorcroft Wy *PIN* HA5 .... 59 J4 ①
Moordown *WOOL/PLUM* SE18 .... 125 G6
Moore Cl *MORT/ESHN* SW14 ...... 117 J8 ②
  MTCM CR4 .... 156 B5 ①
  WLGTN SM6 .... 183 L1
Moore Crs *DAGW* RM9 .... 90 B8
Moorefield Rd *TOTM* N17 .... 67 M4
Mooreland Rd *BMLY* BR1 .... 159 M3
Moore Park Rd *FUL/PGN* SW6 .... 119 H5
Moore Rd *NRWD* SE19 .... 157 J2
Moore St *CHEL* SW3 .... 15 L5
Moore Wy *BELMT* SM2 .... 182 A2
Moorey Cl *SRTFD* E15 .... 87 M8 ③
Moorfield Av *EA* W5 .... 98 D5 ①
Moorfield Rd *CHSGTN* KT9 .... 167 L7
  DEN/HRF UB9 .... 58 A7 ①
  ORP BR6 .... 177 G2
  PEND EN3 .... 37 J4
  UX/CGN UB8 .... 94 D5
Moorfields *LVPST* EC2M 13 H3
Moorgate *LOTH* EC2R 13 G4
  LVPST EC2M 13 G3
Moorgate Pl *LOTH* EC2R .... 13 G4 ③
Moorhall Rd *DEN/HRF* UB9 .... 58 B6
Moorhayes Dr *STA* TW18 .... 148 C6
Moorhead Wy *BKHTH/KID* SE3 ... 124 B8
  BKHTH/KID SE3 .... 142 B1
Moorhen Cl *ERITH* DA8 .... 128 B5 ③
Moorhouse Rd *BAY/PAD* W2 .... 8 A4
  KTN/HRWW/W HA3 .... 62 D4
Moorhurst Av *CHESW* EN7 .... 25 H2
Moorland Cl *HSLWW* TW4 .... 133 G4 ③
  ROMW/RG RM7 .... 73 H2 ③
Moorland Rd *BRXN/ST* SW9 .... 139 H1
  WDR/YW UB7 .... 112 C5
Moorlands Av *MLHL* NW7 .... 46 B8
Moor La *BARB* EC2Y 13 G3
  CHSGTN KT9 .... 167 M7
  RKW/CH/CXG WD3 .... 40 C4
  UPMR RM14 .... 93 M1
  WDR/YW UB7 .... 112 C4
Moor Lane Crossing
  WATW WD18 .... 41 J2
Moormead Dr *HOR/WEW* KT19 ... 168 F7
Moor Mead Rd *TWK* TW1 .... 134 A3
Moor Park Gdns
  KUTN/CMB KT2 .... 153 L3
Moor Park Rd *NTHWD* HA6 .... 41 K8
Moorside Rd *BMLY* BR1 .... 141 L8
Moor St *SOHO/SHAV* W1D 11 H5
Moortown Rd *OXHEY* WD19 .... 42 C6
Moor Vw *WATW* WD18 .... 42 A7
Morant Gdns *CRW* RM5 .... 56 C1
Morant Pl *POP/IOD* E14 .... 105 G6 ⑧
Morant Rd *CRICK* NW2 .... 82 C4
Mora St *FSBYE* EC1V 6 F8
Morat St *BRXN/ST* SW9 .... 120 A7
Moravian Pl *WBPTN* SW10 .... 119 K4 ⑧
Moravian St *BETH* E2 .... 104 C2 ③
Moray Av *HYS/HAR* UB3 .... 95 M7
Moray Cl *EDGW* HA8 .... 45 H4 ①
  ROM RM1 .... 73 L1
Moray Ms *HOLWY* N7 .... 84 F2

Moray Rd *HOLWY* N7 .... 84 F2
Moray Wy *ROM* RM1 .... 73 K1
Mordaunt Gdns *DAGW* RM9 .... 90 B5
Mordaunt Rd *WLSDN* NW10 .... 81 K8
Mordaunt St *BRXN/ST* SW9 .... 120 F8
Morden Ct *MRDN* SM4 .... 155 H7
Morden Gdns *GFD/PVL* UB6 ...... 79 M5
  MTCM CR4 .... 155 H6
Morden Hall Rd *MRDN* SM4 .... 155 H6
Morden HI *LEW* SE13 .... 123 J7
Morden La *LEW* SE13 .... 123 J7
Morden Rd *BKHTH/KID* SE3 .... 124 A7
  CHDH RM6 .... 72 B8
  WIM/MER SW19 .... 155 K7
Morden Road Ms
  BKHTH/KID SE3 .... 124 A7
Morden St *LEW* SE13 .... 123 H6
Morden Wy *CHEAM* SM3 .... 170 A2
Morden Wharf Rd
  GNWCH SE10 .... 123 L1
Mordon Rd *GDMY/SEVK* IG3 ...... 71 M8
Mordred Rd *CAT* SE6 .... 141 L6
Morecambe Cl *HCH* RM12 .... 92 B5 ①
  WCHPL E1 .... 104 D4 ⑧
Morecambe Gdns *STAN* HA7 ...... 44 D6 ①
Morecambe St *WALW* SE17 .... 18 F6
More Cl *CAN/RD* E16 .... 105 M5
  PUR/KEN CR8 .... 183 M4
  WKENS W14 .... 118 D2
Morecoombe Cl
  KUTN/CMB KT2 .... 153 H3 ②
Moree Wy *UED* N18 .... 50 A6 ②
Moreland St *FSBYE* EC1V 6 D7
Moreland Wy *CHING* E4 .... 51 H5
More La *ESH/CLAY* KT10 .... 166 B5
Morella Rd *BAL* SW12 .... 137 M4
Morello Av *UX/CGN* UB8 .... 95 H4
Morello Cl *SWLY* BR8 .... 163 K7
Moremead *WAB* EN9 .... 27 K6
Moremead Rd *CAT* SE6 .... 140 F8
Morena St *CAT* SE6 .... 141 H4
Moresby Av *BRYLDS* KT5 .... 168 B2
Moresby Rd *CLPT* E5 .... 86 B1
Moreton Av *ISLW* TW7 .... 115 L6 ③
Moreton Cl *CLPT* E5 .... 86 C1 ②
  MLHL NW7 .... 46 B4
  SEVS/STOTM N15 .... 67 K7 ②
Moreton Cl *DART* DA1 .... 127 K4
Moreton Gdns *WFD* IG8 .... 52 E7
Moreton Pl *PIM* SW1V 16 F7
Moreton Rd *SAND/SEL* CR2 .... 172 D7
  SEVS/STOTM N15 .... 67 K7
  WPK KT4 .... 169 G4
Moreton St *PIM* SW1V 17 G7
Moreton Ter *PIM* SW1V 16 F7
Morford Cl *RSLP* HA4 .... 60 B8
Morford Wy *RSLP* HA4 .... 60 B8
Morgan Av *WALTH* E17 .... 69 K5
Morgan Dr *RDART* DA2 .... 147 L4
Morgan Gdns *GSTN* WD25 .... 30 B3 ③
Morgan Rd *BMLY* BR1 .... 160 A3
  HOLWY N7 .... 85 G5
  NKENS W10 .... 100 F4 ⑧
Morgan's La *HYS/HAR* UB3 .... 95 K4
  STHWK SE1 .... 13 J9
Morgan St *BOW* E3 .... 104 E2
  CAN/RD E16 .... 105 M4
Morgan Wy *RAIN* RM13 .... 110 C2 ①
  WFD IG8 .... 52 E8 ⑧
Moriarty Cl *HOLWY* N7 .... 84 E4
Morie St *WAND/EARL* SW18 .... 137 H1
Morieux Rd *LEY* E10 .... 86 F1
Moring Rd *TOOT* SW17 .... 138 A8
Morkyns Wk *DUL* SE21 .... 139 G8 ②
Morland Av *CROY/NA* CR0 .... 172 E3
  DART DA1 .... 146 B2
Morland Cl *GLDGN* NW11 .... 83 H1
  HPTN TW12 .... 150 F1
  MTCM CR4 .... 155 L6 ⑧
Morland Gdns *STHL* UB1 .... 97 H7
  WLSDN NW10 .... 81 K7
Morland Ms *IS* N1 .... 6 B2
Morland Rd *CROY/NA* CR0 .... 172 F2
  DAGE RM10 .... 91 G7
  IL IG1 .... 89 H2
  KTN/HRWW/W HA3 .... 62 E6
  PGE/AN SE20 .... 158 D3
  SUT SM1 .... 170 C7
  WALTH E17 .... 68 D6
Morland Wy *CHES/WCR* EN8 .... 26 E1
Morley Av *CHING* E4 .... 69 K1
  UED N18 .... 50 A6
  WDGN N22 .... 67 H2
Morley Cl *ORP* BR6 .... 176 B4
Morley Crs *EDGW* HA8 .... 45 J4
  RSLP HA4 .... 78 C2
Morley Crs East *STAN* HA7 .... 62 C4
Morley Crs West *STAN* HA7 .... 62 C4
Morley HI *ENC/FH* EN2 .... 36 D3
Morley Rd *BARK* IG11 .... 89 K8
  CHDH RM6 .... 72 E6
  CHEAM SM3 .... 169 M3
  CHST BR7 .... 161 L4
  LEW SE13 .... 123 J2
  LEY E10 .... 87 J1
  SAND/SEL CR2 .... 184 F3
  SRTFD E15 .... 105 M1
  TWK TW1 .... 134 D3
Morley St *STHWK* SE1 .... 18 B2
Morna Rd *CMBW* SE5 .... 121 J7
Morning La *HOM* E9 .... 86 C6
Morningside Rd *WPK* KT4 .... 169 H4
Mornington Av *BMLY* BR1 .... 160 C6
  IL IG1 .... 71 G8
  WKENS W14 .... 118 F2
Mornington Ct *BXLY* DA5 .... 145 K5
Mornington Crs *CAMTN* NW1 ..... 4 E5
  HEST TW5 .... 114 B6
Mornington Gv *BOW* E3 .... 105 G2 ②
Mornington Ms *CMBW* SE5 .... 121 J6 ③
Mornington Pl *CAMTN* NW1 .... 4 D5
Mornington Rd *ASHF* TW15 .... 149 J1
  CHING E4 .... 51 K2
  DEPT SE8 .... 122 F5
  GFD/PVL UB6 .... 97 H4
  WAN E11 .... 70 C4
Mornington St *CAMTN* NW1 .... 4 D5

Mornington Ter CAMTN NW1 4 D4
Mornington Wk
  RCHPK/HAM TW10 134 C8
Morocco St STHWK SE1 19 J2
Morpeth Av BORE WD6 31 M3
Morpeth Gv HOM E9 86 D8
Morpeth Rd HOM E9 86 D8
Morpeth St BETH E2 104 D2
Morpeth Ter WEST SW1P 16 E4
Morpeth Wk TOTM N17 68 B1
Morrab Gdns GDMY/SEVK IG3 89 M3
Morrel Cl BAR EN5 34 C6
Morris Av MNPK E12 88 F5
Morris Cl CROY/NA CR0 173 L1
  ORP BR6 176 E5
Morris Ct CHING E4 51 H5
  WAB EN9 27 M7
Morris Gdns DART DA1 147 G2
  WAND/EARL SW18 137 G4
Morrish Rd BRXS/STRHM SW2 138 E4
Morrison Av TOTM N17 67 L4
Morrison Rd BARK IG11 108 E1
  YEAD UB4 96 B2
Morrison St BTSEA SW11 120 A8
Morris Pl FSBYPK N4 85 G2
Morris Rd BCTR RM8 90 F2
  HARH RM3 74 B1
  ISLW TW7 115 M8
  POP/IOD E14 105 H4
  WAN E11 87 L4
Morris St WCHPL E1 104 B5
Morriston Cl OXHEY WD19 42 C7
Morse Cl DEN/HRF UB9 58 C3
  PLSTW E13 106 A2
Morshead Rd MV/WKIL W9 2 B8
Morson Rd PEND EN3 50 E1
Mortaine Rd ASHF TW15 130 D7
Morten Gdns DEN/HRF UB9 58 A8
Morteyne Rd TOTM N17 67 K2
Mortham St SRTFD E15 87 L8
Mortimer Cl BAL SW12 138 D6
  BUSH WD23 43 H1
  CRICK NW2 82 F1
Mortimer Crs STJWD NW8 2 C4
  WPK KT4 168 D5
Mortimer Dr WCHMH N21 36 D8
Mortimer Pl KIL/WHAMP NW6 2 C4
Mortimer Rd BH/WHM TN16 187 J8
  EHAM E6 106 F2
  ERITH DA8 127 K4
  IS N1 7 K2
  MTCM CR4 155 M4
  ORP BR6 177 C3
  WEA W13 98 C5
  WLSDN NW10 100 C2
Mortimer Sq NTGHL W11 100 C6
Mortimer St REGST W1B 10 D4
Mortimer Ter KTTN NW5 84 B2
Mortlake Cl CROY/NA CR0 171 L5
Mortlake Dr MTCM CR4 155 L4
Mortlake High St
  MORT/ESHN SW14 117 K8
Mortlake Rd CAN/RD E16 106 B5
  IL IG1 89 J4
  RCH/KEW TW9 117 H7
Morton Crs FBAR/BDGN N11 48 D6
Morton Gdns WLGTN SM6 171 J4
Morton Ms ECT SW5 14 C6
Morton Pl STHWK SE1 18 A4
Morton Rd IS N1 6 F2
  MRDN SM4 155 M8
  SRTFD E15 87 M7
Morton Wy STHGT/OAK N14 48 C5
Morvale Cl BELV DA17 126 F2
Morval Rd BRXS/STRHM SW2 139 G2
Morven Rd POTB/CUF EN6 23 G3
Morven St TOOT SW17 137 M7
Morville St BOW E3 105 L1
Morwell St FITZ W1T 11 G3
Moscow Pl BAY/PAD W2 8 C6
Moscow Rd BAY/PAD W2 8 C6
Moselle Av WDGN N22 67 G3
Moselle Cl CEND/HSY/T N8 66 F4
Moselle St TOTM N17 67 M1
Mospey Crs EW KT17 180 F8
Mossborough Cl
  NFNCH/WDSP N12 47 H8
Mossbury Rd BTSEA SW11 119 L8
Moss Cl PIN HA5 60 F3
  RKW/CH/CXG WD3 40 A6
  WCHPL E1 104 A4
Mossdown Cl BELV DA17 127 G2
Mossendew Cl DEN/HRF UB9 58 D2
Mossford Gn BARK/HLT IG6 71 H4
Mossford La BARK/HLT IG6 71 J3
Mossford St BOW E3 105 H3
Moss Gdns SAND/SEL CR2 185 K1
Moss Hall Crs NFNCH/WDSP N12 47 H8
Moss Hall Gv FNCH N3 47 H8
Moss La PIN HA5 60 F4
  ROM RM1 73 M7
Mosslea Rd HAYES BR2 160 D8
  ORP BR6 176 C5
  PGE/AN SE20 158 C3
Mossop St CHEL SW3 15 K5
Moss Rd DAGE RM10 91 G2
  GSTN WD25 21 H7
Moss Side LCOL/BKTW AL2 21 M3
Mossville Gdns MRDN SM4 154 F6
Moss Wy RDART DA2 147 K8
Moston Cl HYS/HAR UB3 113 M3
Mostyn Av WBLY HA9 80 C3
Mostyn Gdns WLSDN NW10 100 C2
Mostyn Gv BOW E3 105 J1
Mostyn Rd BRXN/ST SW9 121 G6
  BUSH WD23 30 C8
  EDGW HA8 63 K1
  WIM/MER SW19 154 F5
Mosul Wy HAYES BR2 175 L1
Mosyer Dr STMC/STPC BR5 177 K4
Motcomb St KTBR SW1X 16 A3
The Mothers Sq CLPT E5 86 B4
Motley St VX/NE SW8 120 C7
Motspur Pk NWMAL KT3 168 F1
Mottingham Gdns
  ELTH/MOT SE9 142 F7
Mottingham La ELTH/MOT SE9 142 C5
Mottingham Rd ED N9 50 D1

  ELTH/MOT SE9 142 F7
Mottisfont Rd ABYW SE2 126 A1
Mott St CHING E4 38 C4
Mouchotte Ct BH/WHM TN16 187 H5
Moulins Rd HOM E9 86 C7
Moulton Av HEST TW5 114 E7
Moultrie Wy UPMR RM14 75 L8
Moundfield Rd STNW/STAM N16 68 A7
Mountacre Cl SYD SE26 139 M8
Mount Adon Pk DUL SE21 140 A4
Mountague Pl POP/IOD E14 105 J6
Mount Angelus Rd
  PUT/ROE SW15 135 M4
Mount Ararat Rd
  RCHPK/HAM TW10 134 E2
Mount Ash Rd SYD SE26 140 B7
Mount Av CHING E4 51 G5
  EA W5 98 A1
  HARH RM3 57 J8
  STHL UB1 97 G5
Mountbatten Cl NRWD SE19 157 L1
  WOOL/PLUM SE18 125 L4
Mountbatten Ct BKHH IG9 52 D4
Mountbel Rd STAN HA7 62 J2
Mount Cl BMLY BR1 160 E4
  CAR SM5 183 G2
  EBAR EN4 35 G7
Mountcombe Cl SURB KT6 167 L2
Mount Ct WWKM BR4 174 E4
Mount Culver Av SCUP DA14 162 D2
Mount Dr RYLN/HDSTN HA2 60 F6
  WBLY HA9 81 J2
Mountearl Gdns
  STRHM/NOR SW16 138 F7
Mount Echo Av CHING E4 51 H3
Mount Echo Dr CHING E4 51 H3
Mount Ephraim La
  STRHM/NOR SW16 138 D7
Mount Ephraim Rd
  STRHM/NOR SW16 138 D7
Mount Felix WOT/HER KT12 164 F3
Mountfield Cl LEW SE13 141 K4
Mountfield Rd EA W5 98 D5
  EHAM E6 106 F1
  FNCH N3 65 K7
Mountfield Wy STMC/STPC BR5 162 C7
Mountford St WCHPL E1 104 A5
Mountfort Ter IS N1 6 A2
Mount Gdns SYD SE26 140 B6
Mount Grace Rd POTB/CUF EN6 23 C4
Mount Gv EDGW HA8 45 J5
Mountgrove Rd FSBYPK N4 85 J3
Mounthurst Rd HAYES BR2 175 G2
Mountington Park Cl
  KTN/HRWW/W HA3 62 D7
Mountjoy Cl THMD SE28 108 B8
Mount Mills FSBYE EC1V 6 D8
Mount Nod Rd
  STRHM/NOR SW16 138 F7
Mount Pk CAR SM5 183 G2
Mount Park Av
  RYLN/HDSTN HA2 79 K2
  SAND/SEL CR2 184 B2
Mount Park Crs EA W5 98 D5
Mount Park Rd EA W5 98 D4
  PIN HA5 60 A6
  RYLN/HDSTN HA2 79 K2
Mount Pl ACT W3 99 H7
Mount Pleasant ALP/SUD HA0 80 E8
  DEN/HRF UB9 58 A2
  EBAR EN4 34 F7
  EW KT17 180 F3
  FSBYW WC1X 11 M2
  RSLP HA4 78 C3
  WEY KT13 164 A5
  WNWD SE27 139 J8
Mount Pleasant Crs
  FSBYPK N4 66 F8
Mount Pleasant Hl CLPT E5 86 B2
Mount Pleasant La CLPT E5 86 B1
  LCOL/BKTW AL2 21 K3
Mount Pleasant Pl
  WOOL/PLUM SE18 125 K2
Mount Pleasant Rd CHIG IG7 53 K6
  CRW RM5 55 K8
  DART DA1 146 F3
  EA W5 98 C3
  LEW SE13 141 J3
  TOTM N17 67 L3
  WALTH E17 68 E3
  WLSDN NW10 81 M4
Mount Pleasant Vls FSBYPK N4 66 F8
Mount Ri FSTH SE23 140 C6
Mount Rd BCTR RM8 90 F1
  BXLYHS DA6 144 E2
  CHSGTN KT9 167 M7
  CRICK NW2 82 B3
  DART DA1 145 M3
  EBAR EN4 34 E8
  FELT TW13 132 E7
  HDN NW4 64 A7
  HYS/HAR UB3 96 A8
  IL IG1 89 H5
  MTCM CR4 155 K5
  NRWD SE19 157 K2
  NWMAL KT3 153 K6
  WAND/EARL SW18 137 G6
Mount Rw MYFR/PKLN W1K 10 C7
Mountsfield Cl
  STWL/WRAY TW19 130 A2
Mountside KTN/HRWW/W HA3 61 M2
Mounts Pond Rd
  BKHTH/KID SE3 123 K7
Mount Stewart Av
  KTN/HRWW/W HA3 62 D7
Mount St MYFR/PKLN W1K 10 A7
Mount Ter WCHPL E1 104 B4
The Mount COUL/CHIP CR5 183 G8
  EFNCH N2 65 K6
  EW KT17 180 A8
  HAMP NW3 83 J4
  HARH RM3 56 C5
  NWMAL KT3 153 M6
  POTB/CUF EN6 23 H3
  RKW/CH/CXG WD3 40 C1
  TRDG/WHET N20 47 J4
  WBLY HA9 81 J2

  WEY KT13 164 E4
  WPK KT4 169 H6
Mount Vw RKW/CH/CXG WD3 40 B3
  ENC/FH EN2 35 M3
Mountview MLHL NW7 45 K3
Mountview Rd ORP BR6 177 G2
Mount Vis WNWD SE27 139 H7
Mount Wy CAR SM5 183 G2
Mountway POTB/CUF EN6 23 G3
Mountwood E/WMO/HCT KT8 151 H6
Mountwood Cl SAND/SEL CR2 185 H3
Movers La BARK IG11 89 K8
Mowatt Cl ARCH N19 84 D2
Mowbray Rd BAR EN5 34 C7
  EDGW HA8 45 G6
  KIL/WHAMP NW6 82 E7
  NRWD SE19 157 M4
  RCHPK/HAM TW10 134 C7
Mowbrays Cl CRW RM5 73 J2
Mowbrays Rd CRW RM5 73 J3
Mowlem St BETH E2 86 B7
Mowll St BRXN/ST SW9 121 G5
Moxon Av CHES/WCR EN8 26 E3
Moxon Cl PLSTW E13 105 M1
Moxon St BAR EN5 33 M6
  MHST W1U 10 A3
Moyers Rd WAN E11 69 J8
Moylan Rd HMSMTH W6 118 E4
Moyne Pl WLSDN NW10 99 G2
Moynihan Dr STHGT/OAK N14 35 L8
Moys Cl CROY/NA CR0 171 L1
Moyser Rd TOOT SW17 156 B1
Mozart St NKENS W10 100 F2
Muchelney Rd MRDN SM4 170 C1
Muggeridge Cl SAND/SEL CR2 172 D7
Muggeridge Rd DAGE RM10 91 H4
Muirdown Av
  MORT/ESHN SW14 135 J1
Muirfield ACT W3 99 L5
Muirfield Cl POP/IOD E14 123 H1
  OXHEY WD19 42 C7
Muirfield Gn OXHEY WD19 42 C6
Muirfield Rd OXHEY WD19 42 B6
Muirkirk Rd CAT SE6 141 J5
Muir Rd CLPT E5 86 A4
Muir St CAN/RD E16 106 F7
Mulberry Av STWL/WRAY TW19 130 C5
Mulberry Cl CHING E4 51 G4
  EBAR EN4 34 D7
  GPK RM2 74 B5
  HDN NW4 63 M2
  NTHLT UB5 96 E1
  STRHM/NOR SW16 138 C8
  WEY KT13 164 B5
Mulberry Crs BTFD TW8 116 B5
  WDR/YW UB7 95 G8
Mulberry Dr PUR RM19 128 F2
Mulberry La CROY/NA CR0 172 F3
Mulberry Ms NWCR SE14 122 F6
Mulberry Pde WDR/YW UB7 113 G5
Mulberry Pl HMSMTH W6 118 A3
Mulberry Rd HACK E8 7 L2
Mulberry St WCHPL E1 104 A5
Mulberry Wk CHEL SW3 15 H9
Mulberry Wy BARK/HLT IG6 71 J5
  BELV DA17 109 J8
  SWFD E18 70 B3
Mulgrave Rd BELMT SM2 181 M1
  CROY/NA CR0 172 D5
  EA W5 98 D2
  HRW HA1 80 A2
  WKENS W14 118 F4
  WLSDN NW10 81 M4
Mulholland Cl MTCM CR4 156 B5
Mulkern Rd ARCH N19 84 D1
Mullards Cl MTCM CR4 170 F3
Mullet Gdns BETH E2 104 A2
Mullins Pth MORT/ESHN SW14 117 K8
Mullion Cl KTN/HRWW/W HA3 61 H2
Mullion Wk OXHEY WD19 42 D6
Mulready St STJWD NW8 9 J1
Multi Wy ACT W3 99 L8
Multon Rd WAND/EARL SW18 137 K4
Mumford Ct CITYW EC2V 12 F4
Mumford Rd HNHL SE24 139 H2
Muncaster Cl ASHF TW15 131 G8
Muncaster Rd ASHF TW15 149 H1
  BTSEA SW11 137 M1
Muncies Ms CAT SE6 141 J6
Mundania Rd EDUL SE22 140 B3
Munday Rd CAN/RD E16 106 A5
Munden Gv WATN WD24 29 J3
Munden St WKENS W14 118 E2
Mundesly Cl OXHEY WD19 42 C6
Mundford Rd CLPT E5 86 C2
Mundon Gdns IL IG1 89 K1
Mund St WKENS W14 118 F3
Mundy St IS N1 7 J7
Mungo-park Cl BUSH WD23 43 J4
Mungo Park Rd RAIN RM13 92 B7
Mungo Park Wy
  STMC/STPC BR5 177 J2
Munnery Wy ORP BR6 176 A5
Munnings Gdns ISLW TW7 133 K2
Munro Ms NKENS W10 100 E4
Munro Rd BUSH WD23 30 B8
Munster Av HSLWW TW4 132 E1
Munster Gdns PLMGR N13 49 J6
Munster Rd FUL/PGN SW6 118 E5
  TEDD TW11 152 C2
Munster Sq CAMTN NW1 4 D8
Munton Rd WALW SE17 18 F5
Murchison Av BXLY DA5 144 D5
Murchison Rd LEY E10 87 J2
Murdock Cl STA TW18 148 A1
Murdock St PECK SE15 122 B4
Murfett Cl WIM/MER SW19 136 E6
Murfitt Wy UPMR RM14 93 G4
Muriel Av WATW WD18 29 J3
Muriel St IS N1 5 M3

  WEY KT13 164 E4
Murillo Rd LEW SE13 141 K1
Murphy St STHWK SE1 18 A2
Murray Av BMLY BR1 160 B6
  HSLW TW3 133 H2
Murray Crs PIN HA5 60 D2
Murray Gv IS N1 7 G6
Murray Ms CAMTN NW1 5 G1
Murray Rd EA W5 116 C2
  NTHWD HA6 59 L2
  RCHPK/HAM TW10 134 B6
  STMC/STPC BR5 162 B6
  WIM/MER SW19 154 D2
Murray Sq CAN/RD E16 106 A5
Murray St CAMTN NW1 4 F1
Murray Ter HAMP NW3 83 J4
Murtwell Dr CHIG IG7 53 J8
Musard Rd HMSMTH W6 118 E4
Musbury St WCHPL E1 104 C5
Muscatel Pl CMBW SE5 121 L6
Muschamp Rd CAR SM5 170 E4
  PECK SE15 121 M8
Muscovy St TWRH EC3N 13 K7
Museum St NOXST/BSQ WC1A 11 J4
Musgrave Cl EBAR EN4 34 C4
Musgrave Crs FUL/PGN SW6 119 G5
Musgrave Rd ISLW TW7 115 M6
Musgrove Rd NWCR SE14 122 D6
Musjid Rd BTSEA SW11 119 K7
Musquash Wy HSLWW TW4 114 C7
Muston Rd CLPT E5 86 B2
Muswell Av MUSWH N10 66 B3
Muswell Hl MUSWH N10 66 B4
Muswell Hill Broadway
  MUSWH N10 66 B4
Muswell Hill Pl MUSWH N10 66 B5
Muswell Hill Rd HGT N6 66 A7
  MUSWH N10 66 A5
Muswell Ms MUSWH N10 66 B4
Muswell Rd MUSWH N10 66 B3
Mutchetts Cl GSTN WD25 21 L6
Mutton La POTB/CUF EN6 22 D4
Mutrix Rd KIL/WHAMP NW6 2 B3
Mutton Pl CAMTN NW1 4 D1
Muybridge Rd NWMAL KT3 153 G5
Myatt Rd BRXN/ST SW9 121 H6
Mycenae Rd BKHTH/KID SE3 124 A4
Myddelton Av EN EN1 36 E3
Myddelton Gdns WCHMH N21 49 J2
Myddelton Pk TRDG/WHET N20 47 K5
Myddelton Pas CLKNW EC1R 6 B7
Myddelton Rd CEND/HSY/T N8 66 E4
  WDGN N22 66 E1
Myddelton Sq CLKNW EC1R 6 B8
Myddelton St CLKNW EC1R 6 B8
Myddleton Av FSBYPK N4 85 J2
Myddleton Rd UX/CGN UB8 76 C8
  WDGN N22 66 E1
Myers La NWCR SE14 122 D4
Mygrove Cl RAIN RM13 110 D1
Mygrove Gdns RAIN RM13 110 D1
Mygrove Rd RAIN RM13 110 D1
Myles Ct CHESW EN7 25 J2
Mylis Cl SYD SE26 140 B8
Mylne St CLKNW EC1R 6 A6
Mynn's Cl EPSOM KT18 180 B7
Myra St ABYW SE2 126 A3
Myrdle St WCHPL E1 104 A4
Myrna Cl WIM/MER SW19 155 L3
Myron Pl LEW SE13 123 J8
Myrtle Aly WOOL/PLUM SE18 125 G1
Myrtle Av EBED/NFELT TW14 131 L5
  RSLP HA4 60 A8
Myrtle Cl EBAR EN4 47 M3
  ERITH DA8 127 L5
  UX/CGN UB8 94 F4
  WDR/YW UB7 112 F2
Myrtledene Rd ABYW SE2 126 A3
Myrtle Gdns HNWL W7 97 L7
Myrtle Gv ENC/FH EN2 36 D3
  NWMAL KT3 153 J5
  SOCK/AV RM15 111 J8
Myrtle Pl RDART DA2 147 K5
Myrtle Rd ACT W3 99 J7
  CROY/NA CR0 174 A5
  DART DA1 146 D6
  EHAM E6 88 D8
  HARH RM3 56 C8
  HPTN TW12 151 J2
  HSLW TW3 115 J7
  PLMGR N13 49 J5
  SUT SM1 170 C7
  WALTH E17 68 E7
Myrtleside Cl NTHWD HA6 59 K1
Mysore Rd BTSEA SW11 137 M1
Myton Rd DUL SE21 139 K7

N

Nadine St CHARL SE7 124 C3
Naffenton Ri LOU IG10 39 K8
Nagle Cl WALTH E17 69 K3
Nag's Head La UPMR RM14 75 J7
  WELL DA16 126 B8
Nags Head Rd PEND EN3 37 J7
Nairne Gv HNHL SE24 139 K2
Nairn Gn OXHEY WD19 42 A5
Nairn Rd RSLP HA4 78 C6
Nairn St POP/IOD E14 105 J4
Nallhead Rd FELT TW13 150 C1
Namba Roy Cl
  STRHM/NOR SW16 138 F8
Namton Dr
  STRHM/NOR SW16 156 F7
Nan Clark's La MLHL NW7 45 M4
Nancy Downs OXHEY WD19 42 C2
Nankin St POP/IOD E14 105 J5
Nansen Rd BTSEA SW11 137 L4
Nantes Cl WAND/EARL SW18 137 J1
Nant Rd CRICK NW2 82 F2
Nant St BETH E2 104 B2
Naoroji St FSBYW WC1X 6 A8
Napier Av FUL/PGN SW6 118 F8
  POP/IOD E14 123 G3
Napier Cl DEPT SE8 122 F5
  HCH RM12 92 B1
  WDR/YW UB7 112 F1
Napier Ct LEE/GVPK SE12 142 B2
Napier Dr BUSH WD23 29 L7

Napier Gv IS N1 6 F6
Napier Pl WKENS W14 118 F1
Napier Rd ALP/SUD HA0 80 D5
  ASHF TW15 149 K3
  BELV DA17 126 F2
  EHAM E6 89 G8
  HAYES BR2 160 B7
  ISLW TW7 134 A1
  PEND EN3 37 K8
  SAND/SEL CR2 158 B7
  SNWD SE25 158 B7
  SRTFD E15 105 L1
  TOTM N17 67 L4
  WAN E11 87 D3
  WDR/YW UB7 112 D6
  WKENS W14 118 F1
  WLSDN NW10 100 B3
Napier Ter IS N1 6 E3
Napier Wk ASHF TW15 149 K3
Napoleon Rd CLPT E5 86 B3
  TWK TW1 134 B4
The Nap KGLGY WD4 20 A2
Napton Cl YEAD UB4 96 E3
Narbonne Av CLAP SW4 138 C2
Narboro Ct ROM RM1 74 A7
Narborough Cl
  HGDN/ICK UB10 77 J2
Narborough St
  FUL/PGN SW6 119 H7
Narcissus Rd
  KIL/WHAMP NW6 83 G5
Nare Rd SOCK/AV RM15 111 J6
Narford Rd CLPT E5 86 A3
Narrow St ACT W3 99 H7
  POP/IOD E14 104 E6
Narrow Wy HAYES BR2 175 L1
Nascot Pl WAT WD17 29 H5
Nascot Rd WAT WD17 29 H5
Nascot St SHB W12 100 C5
  WAT WD17 29 H5
Nascot Wood Rd WAT WD17 28 F2
Naseby Cl ISLW TW7 115 L6
  KIL/WHAMP NW6 2 F1
Naseby Rd CLAY IG5 70 F2
  DAGE RM10 91 G3
  NRWD SE19 157 K2
Nash Cl CAMTN NW1 4 D1
Nash Gn BMLY BR1 160 A3
Nash La HAYES BR2 175 G8
Nash Rd BROCKY SE4 140 E1
  CHDH RM6 72 C5
  ED N9 50 C4
Nash St CAMTN NW1 4 D7
Nash Wy KTN/HRWW/W HA3 62 B7
Nasmyth St HMSMTH W6 118 E1
Nassau Rd BARN SW13 117 M6
Nassau St GTPST W1W 10 E3
Nassington Rd HAMP NW3 83 L4
Natalie Cl EBED/NFELT TW14 131 K4
Natal Rd FBAR/BDGN N11 48 E8
  IL IG1 89 H4
  STRHM/NOR SW16 156 D2
  THHTH CR7 157 K6
Nathan Cl UPMR RM14 93 L2
Nathaniel Cl WCHPL E1 13 M3
Nathans Rd ALP/SUD HA0 80 C2
Nathan Wy THMD SE28 125 M1
Nation Wy CHING E4 51 J3
Naunton Wy HCH RM12 92 D3
Naval Rw POP/IOD E14 105 J6
Navarino Gv HACK E8 86 A6
Navarino Rd HACK E8 86 A6
Navarre Gdns CRW RM5 55 H8
Navarre Rd EHAM E6 106 E1
Navarre St BETH E2 7 L9
Navestock Cl CHING E4 51 J5
Navestock Crs WFD IG8 70 C2
Navestock Ter WFD IG8 70 C1
Navigator Dr STHL UB1 97 J3
Navy St CLAP SW4 120 D8
Naylor Gv PEND EN3 37 K8
Naylor Rd PECK SE15 122 B5
  TRDG/WHET N20 47 J4
Nazareth Cl PECK SE15 122 B7
Neal Av STHL UB1 96 F3
Neal Cl NTHWD HA6 60 A2
Nealden St BRXN/ST SW9 120 F8
Neale Cl EFNCH N2 65 J4
Neal St LSQ/SEVD WC2H 11 J5
  WATW WD18 29 J5
Neaole Cl BORE WD6 32 C4
Near Acre CDALE/KGS NW9 63 M2
Neasden Cl WLSDN NW10 81 L5
Neasden La WLSDN NW10 81 L3
Neasden La North WLSDN NW10 81 L1
Neasham Rd BCTR RM8 90 B5
Neate St CMBW SE5 121 L4
Neath Gdns MRDN SM4 170 C1
Neathouse Pl PIM SW1V 16 E5
Neats Acre RSLP HA4 59 K8
Neatscourt Rd EHAM E6 106 D4
Neave Crs HARH RM3 74 C2
Nebraska St STHWK SE1 19 G2
Neckinger STHWK SE1 19 M3
Neckinger St STHWK SE1 19 M2
Nectarine Wy LEW SE13 123 H7
Needham Rd NTGHL W11 8 A5
Needleman St
  BERM/RHTH SE16 104 D8
Neela Cl HGDN/ICK UB10 77 H4
Neeld Crs HDN NW4 64 B6
  WBLY HA9 81 G5
Neil Cl ASHF TW15 149 J1
Nelgarde Rd CAT SE6 141 G4
Nella Rd HMSMTH W6 118 D4
Nelldale Rd
  BERM/RHTH SE16 122 C2
Nellgrove Rd UX/CGN UB8 95 H3
Nell Gwynn Av SHPTN TW17 164 D1
Nell Gwynne Cl
  HOR/WEW KT19 180 A2
Nello James Gdns WNWD SE27 139 K8
Nelmes Cl EMPK RM11 74 F6
Nelmes Crs EMPK RM11 74 F6
Nelmes Rd EMPK RM11 74 F6
Nelmes Wy EMPK RM11 74 E5
Nelson Cl EBED/NFELT TW14 131 M5

HGDN/ICK UB10 .... 95 H2
ROMW/RG RM7 .... 73 H2
WOT/HER KT12 .... 165 H3
Nelson Gdns BETH E2 .... 104 A2 🔢
HSLWW TW4 .... 133 G3
Nelson Grove Rd
WIM/MER SW19 .... 155 H4
Nelson La HGDN/ICK UB10 .... 95 H3 🔢
Nelson Mandela Cl MUSWH N10 .. 65 M3
Nelson Mandela Rd
BKHTH/KID SE3 .... 124 C8
Nelson Pl IS N1 .... 6 D6
SCUP DA14 .... 144 A8
Nelson Rd ASHF TW15 .... 148 L1
BELV DA17 .... 126 F3
CEND/HSY/T N8 .... 66 F6
CHING E4 .... 51 H8
DART DA1 .... 146 C3
ED N9 .... 50 B5
GNWCH SE10 .... 123 J4 🔢
HAYES BR2 .... 160 C7
HGDN/ICK UB10 .... 95 H2
HSLWW TW4 .... 133 G3
NWMAL KT3 .... 153 K8
PEND EN3 .... 50 D1
RAIN RM13 .... 109 M1
RYLN/HDSTN HA2 .... 79 K1
SCUP DA14 .... 144 A8 🔢
SEVS/STOTM N15 .... 67 L5 🔢
STAN HA7 .... 44 C8
WAN E11 .... 70 A5
WDR/YW UB7 .... 112 F6
WHTN TW2 .... 133 H4
WIM/MER SW19 .... 155 H3
Nelson Sq STHWK SE1 .... 18 C1
Nelsons Rw CLAP SW4 .... 138 D1
Nelson St CAN/RD E16 .... 105 M6 🔢
EHAM E6 .... 89 G8
WCHPL E1 .... 104 B5
Nelson Ter FSBYE EC1V 6 D6
Nelwyn Av EMPK RM11 .... 74 F4
Nemoure Rd ACT W3 .... 99 J6
Nene Gdns FELT TW13 .... 132 F6
Nene Rd HTHAIR TW6 .... 113 H6
Nepaul Rd BTSEA SW11 .... 119 L7 🔢
Nepean St PUT/ROE SW15 .... 136 A3
Neptune Rd HRW HA1 .... 61 K7
HTHAIR TW6 .... 113 J6 🔢
Neptune St BERM/RHTH SE16 .. 122 C1
Nesbit Cl BKHTH/KID SE3 .... 123 L8 🔢
Nesbit Rd ELTH/MOT SE9 .... 142 D1
Nesham St WAP E1W .... 104 A7 🔢
Ness St BERM/RHTH SE16 .... 122 A1 🔢
Nesta Rd WFD IG8 .... 51 M8
Nestle's Av HYS/HAR UB3 .... 113 M1
Neston Rd WATN WD24 .... 29 J2
Nestor Av WCHMH N21 .... 49 H1
Nethan Dr SOCK/AV RM15 .... 111 J6
Netheravon Rd CHSWK W4 .... 117 M3
HNWL W7 .... 97 M7
Netheravon Rd South
CHSWK W4 .... 117 M4
Netherbury Rd EA W5 .... 116 D1
Netherby Gdns ENC/FH EN2 .... 35 L7
Netherby Pk WEY KT13 .... 164 E7
Netherby Rd FSTH SE23 .... 140 C4
Nether Cl FNCH N3 .... 65 C1
Nethercourt Av FNCH N3 .... 47 G8
Netherfield Gdns BARK IG11 .. 89 K6
Netherfield Rd
NFNCH/WDSP N12 .... 47 H7
TOOT SW17 .... 138 A7 🔢
Netherford Rd CLAP SW4 .... 120 C7
Netherhall Gdns HAMP NW3 .... 83 J6
Netherhall Wy HAMP NW3 .... 83 J5 🔢
Netherlands Rd BAR EN5 .... 47 K1
Netherpark Dr GPK RM2 .... 73 M3
Nether St FNCH N3 .... 65 C1
NFNCH/WDSP N12 .... 47 J7 🔢
Netherton Gv WBPTN SW10 .. 119 J4
Netherton Rd
SEVS/STOTM N15 .... 67 K7 🔢
TWK TW1 .... 134 A2
Netherwood Rd HMSMTH W6 .. 118 D1
Netherwood St
KIL/WHAMP NW6 .... 82 F7
CROY/NA CR0 .... 186 C1
Netley Cl CHEAM SM3 .... 169 K7
Netley Dr WOT/HER KT12 .... 165 M2
Netley Gdns MRDN SM4 .... 170 C2 🔢
Netley Rd BTFD TW8 .... 116 E4
GNTH/NBYPK IG2 .... 71 K6
MRDN SM4 .... 170 C2
WALTH E17 .... 68 F6
Netley St CAMTN NW1 .... 4 E8
Nettlecombe Cl BELMT SM2 .. 182 B2 🔢
Nettleden Av WBLY HA9 .... 81 G6
Nettlefold Pl WNWD SE27 .... 139 H7 🔢
Nettlestead Cl BECK BR3 .... 158 F3 🔢
Nettleton Rd HGDN/ICK UB10 .. 76 F4
HTHAIR TW6 .... 113 H6
NWCR SE14 .... 122 D5
Nettlewood Rd
STRHM/NOR SW16 .... 156 D3 🔢
Neuchatel Rd CAT SE6 .... 140 F6
Nevada Cl NWMAL KT3 .... 153 J7 🔢
Nevada St GNWCH SE10 .... 123 J5
Nevern Pl ECT SW5 .... 14 B6
Nevern Rd ECT SW5 .... 14 A6 🔢
Nevern Sq ECT SW5 .... 14 B7
Nevil Rd NTHWD HA6 .... 41 K7
Neville Av NWMAL KT3 .... 153 K4
Neville Cl ACT W3 .... 99 J8 🔢
BFN/LL DA15 .... 143 M8
BNSTD SM7 .... 182 B7
ESH/CLAY KT10 .... 165 M8
HSLW TW3 .... 115 C2
KIL/WHAMP NW6 .... 100 F1 🔢
PECK SE15 .... 122 A5
POTB/CUF EN6 .... 22 F4
WAN E11 .... 87 M3
Neville Dr EFNCH N2 .... 65 J7
Neville Gdns BCTR RM8 .... 90 D3
Neville Gill Cl WAND/EARL SW18 .. 137 L2 🔢
Neville Pl WDGN N22 .... 66 F2
Neville Rd BARK/HLT IG6 .... 71 J1
BCTR RM8 .... 90 D2
CROY/NA CR0 .... 172 C2

EA W5 .... 98 D3
FSTGT E7 .... 88 A7
KIL/WHAMP NW6 .... 100 F1 🔢
KUT KT1 .... 153 G5
RCHPK/HAM TW10 .... 134 C7
Neville St SKENS SW7 .... 15 G7
Neville Wk CAR SM5 .... 170 E2 🔢
Nevill Av MRDN SM4 .... 29 H4
Nevill Rd STNW/STAM N16 .... 85 L4
Nevill Wy LOU IG10 .... 52 E1
Nevill Wk CAR SM5 .... 170 E2 🔢
Nevin Dr CHING E4 .... 51 H5
Nevinson Cl WAND/EARL SW18 .. 137 K3
Nevis Cl ROM RM1 .... 55 L8
Nevis Rd TOOT SW17 .... 138 A6
Newall Rd HTHAIR TW6 .... 113 J6
Newark Ct WOT/HER KT12 .... 165 J5 🔢
Newark Crs WLSDN NW10 .... 99 K2
Newark Gn BORE WD6 .... 32 E6
Newark Knok EHAM E6 .... 107 G5
Newark Rd SAND/SEL CR2 .. 172 D8
Newark St WCHPL E1 .... 104 B4
New Ash Cl EFNCH N2 .... 65 K4 🔢
New Barn Rd SWLY BR8 .... 163 L4
New Barns Av MTCM CR4 .. 156 D7
New Barn St PLSTW E13 .... 106 A3
New Barns Wy CHIG IG7 .... 53 H5 🔢
New Berry La WOT/HER KT12 .. 165 K8
Newbery Rd ERITH DA8 .... 127 M6
Newbiggin Pth OXHEY WD19 .. 42 C6 🔢
Newbolt Av CHEAM SM3 .... 169 J7
Newbolt Rd STAN HA7 .... 43 M8 🔢
New Bond St MYFR/PICC W1J .. 10 D7 🔢
MYFR/PKLN W1K 10 D5
Newborough Gn NWMAL KT3.. 153 K7
New Brent St HDN NW4 .... 64 C6
New Bridge St STP EC4M 12 C4
New Broad St LVPST EC2M 13 H3
New Broadway EA W5 .... 98 D6
Newburgh Rd ACT W3 .... 99 J7
Newburgh St SOHO/CST W1F .. 10 E5 🔢
New Burlington Ms
CONDST W1S 10 E6
New Burlington Pl CONDST W1S .. 10 E6
New Burlington St
CONDST W1S .... 10 E6 🔢
Newburn St LBTH SE11 .... 17 M7
Newbury Av PEND EN3 .... 37 M2
Newbury Cl HARH RM3 .... 56 C8
NTHLT UB5 .... 78 F6
Newbury Gdns HARH RM3 .... 56 D8
HOR/WEW KT19 .... 168 F6
UPMR RM14 .... 92 F3
Newbury Ms KTTN NW5 .... 84 A6
Newbury Rd CHING E4 .... 51 J8
GNTH/NBYPK IG2 .... 71 K7
HARH RM3 .... 56 C7
HAYES BR2 .... 160 A6
WDR/YW UB7 .... 112 F6
Newbury St STBT EC1A 12 E3
Newbury Wk HARH RM3 .... 56 D7 🔢
New Butt La DEPT SE8 .... 125 G5 🔢
Newby Cl EN EN1 .... 36 E5
Newby Pl POP/IOD E14 .... 105 J6 🔢
Newby St VX/NE SW8 .... 120 B8 🔢
Newcastle Cl STP EC4M .... 12 C4 🔢
New Castle Cl STP EC4M .... 12 C4 🔢
New Cavendish St MHST W1U .. 10 B3
New Change STP EC4M 12 F4
New Charles St FSBYE EC1V.. 6 D7
New Church Rd CMBW SE5 .. 121 J5 🔢
New City Rd PLSTW E13 .... 106 C2
New Cl FELT TW13 .... 150 E1
WIM/MER SW19 .... 155 J6
Newcombe Pk ALP/SUD HA0 .. 80 F8 🔢
MLHL NW7 .... 45 L7
Newcombe Ri WDR/YW UB7 .. 94 E5 🔢
WDR/YW UB7 .... 94 E5 🔢
Newcombe St KENS W8 .... 8 B8 🔢
Newcome Gdns
STRHM/NOR SW16 .... 138 E8 🔢
Newcomen Rd BTSEA SW11 .. 119 K8
WAN E11 .... 87 M3 🔢
Newcomen St STHWK SE1 .... 19 G1
New Compton St
LSQ/SEVD WC2H .... 11 H5 🔢
New Cottages BRKMPK AL9 .. 22 D1
New Ct NTHLT UB5 .... 79 H5 🔢
Newcourt UX/CGN UB8 .... 94 C4 🔢
Newcourt St STJWD NW8 .... 3 J6
Newcroft Cl UX/CGN UB8 .... 94 F4
New Cross Rd NWCR SE14 .. 122 F5
Newdales Cl ED N9 .... 50 A4
Newdene Av NTHLT UB5 .... 96 D1
Newdigate Gn DEN/HRF UB9 .. 58 D2
Newdigate Rd DEN/HRF UB9 .. 58 C2
Newdigate Rd East
DEN/HRF UB9 .... 58 D2
Newell St POP/IOD E14 .... 104 F6
New End HAMP NW3 .... 83 J4
New End Sq HAMP NW3 .... 83 K4
Newent Cl CAR SM5 .... 170 F3
PECK SE15 .... 121 L5
New Farm Av HAYES BR2 .. 160 A7
New Farm La NTHWD HA6 .. 59 J4
New Ferry Ap
WOOL/PLUM SE18 .... 125 G1
New Fetter La
FLST/FETLN EC4A 12 B4
Newfield Cl HPTN TW12 .... 151 L4 🔢
Newfield Ri CRICK NW2 .... 82 A3
New Ford Rd CHES/WCR EN8.. 26 F7
New Forest La CHIG IG7 .... 53 G8
Newgale Gdns EDGW HA8 .. 62 F2 🔢
New Garden Dr WDR/YW UB7 .. 94 E8
Newgate CROY/NA CR0 .... 172 C2 🔢
Newgate Cl FELT TW13 .... 132 E6 🔢
Newgate St CHING E4 .... 51 L5 🔢
STBT EC1A 12 D4
New Goulston St WCHPL E1 .. 13 L4 🔢
New Green Pl NRWD SE19 .. 157 L2 🔢
New Hall Dr HARH RM3 .... 74 E2
Newhall Gdns WOT/HER KT12 .. 165 K8
Newham's Rw STHWK SE1 .... 19 K2
Newham Wy CAN/RD E16 .. 105 M4

Newhaven Cl HYS/HAR UB3 .. 113 M2 🔢
Newhaven Crs ASHF TW15 .. 149 K1
Newhaven Gdns
ELTH/MOT SE9 .... 142 D1
Newhaven La CAN/RD E16 .. 106 A2
PLSTW E13 .... 105 M4
Newhaven Rd SNWD SE25 .. 157 K8
New Heston Rd HEST TW5 .. 114 F5
Newhouse Av CHDH RM6 .... 72 D4
Newhouse Cl NWMAL KT3 .. 168 E2
Newhouse Crs GSTN WD25 .. 21 H6
Newhouse Wk MRDN SM4 .. 170 C2 🔢
Newick Cl BXLY DA5 .... 145 H3
Newick Rd CLPT E5 .... 86 B3
Newing Gn BMLY BR1 .... 160 D3
Newington Barrow Wy
HOLWY N7 .... 84 F3 🔢
Newington Butts LBTH SE11 .. 18 D6
Newington Cswy STHWK SE1 .. 18 E3
Newington Gn
STNW/STAM N16 .... 85 K5 🔢
Newington Green Rd IS N1 .. 85 K5
New Inn Broadway
SDTCH EC2A .... 7 K9 🔢
New Inn Sq SDTCH EC2A .... 7 K9 🔢
New Inn St SDTCH EC2A .... 7 K9 🔢
New Inn Yd SDTCH EC2A 7 K9
New Kelvin Av TEDD TW11 .. 151 L2
New Kent Rd STHWK SE1 .... 18 E5
New Kings Rd FUL/PGN SW6 .. 118 F7
FUL/PGN SW6 .... 119 G7
New King St DEPT SE8 .... 123 G4
Newland Cl PIN HA5 .... 42 E8
Newland Dr EN EN1 .... 37 H4
Newland Gdns HNWL W7 .. 98 A8 🔢
Newland Rd CEND/HSY/T N8 .. 66 E4
Newlands Av ALP/SUD HA0 .. 80 C6
EDGW HA8 .... 44 E5
NWDGN UB2 .... 114 E3 🔢
WOT/HER KT12 .... 165 L6 🔢
Newlands Cl WBLY HA9 .... 81 G2
EDGW HA8 .... 44 A5
NWDGN UB2 .... 114 E3 🔢
Newlands Pk SYD SE26 .... 158 C2
Newlands Pl BAR EN5 .... 33 K8
Newlands Rd
STRHM/NOR SW16 .... 156 E5
WFD IG8 .... 51 M4
The Newlands WLGTN SM6 .. 183 J1
Newland St CAN/RD E16 .. 106 F7
Newlands Wk GSTN WD25 .. 21 K6
Newlands Wy CHSGTN KT9 .. 171 J7
POTB/CUF EN6 .... 23 H3 🔢
Newling Cl EHAM E6 .... 107 K6
New London St MON EC3R .. 13 K6 🔢
New Lydenburg St CHARL SE7 .. 124 C1
Newlyn Cl LCOL/BKTW AL2 .. 21 L3
UX/CGN UB8 .... 95 G4
Newlyn Gdns
RYLN/HDSTN HA2 .... 60 F8 🔢
Newlyn Rd BAR EN5 .... 33 M7 🔢
TOTM N17 .... 67 M2
WELL DA16 .... 125 M7
Newman Cl EMPK RM11 .... 74 E6
Newman Rd BMLY BR1 .... 160 A4 🔢
CROY/NA CR0 .... 171 M2 🔢
HYS/HAR UB3 .... 96 B6 🔢
PLSTW E13 .... 106 B2
WALTH E17 .... 68 D6 🔢
Newman's Rw LINN WC2A .. 11 M3
Newman St FITZ W1T 10 F3
Newman's Wy EBAR EN4 .... 34 C5
Newmarket Av NTHLT UB5 .. 79 G5
Newmarket Wy HCH RM12 .. 92 E4
New Mill Rd STMC/STPC BR5.. 162 C4
Newminster Rd MRDN SM4 .. 170 C1
New Mount St SRTFD E15 .. 87 K7 🔢
Newnham Av RSLP HA4 .... 78 C1
Newnham Cl LOU IG10 .... 52 D1
NTHLT UB5 .... 79 J6
THHTH CR7 .... 157 J5 🔢
Newnham Gdns NTHLT UB5 .. 79 J6
Newnham Rd WDGN N22 .... 66 F2
Newnhams Cl BMLY BR1 .... 160 F6
Newnham Ter STHWK SE1 .. 18 A3
Newnham Wy
KTN/HRWW/W HA3 .... 62 E6
New North Pl SDTCH EC2A 7 J9
New North Rd BARK/HLT IG6 .. 71 K1
IS N1 .... 7 H6 🔢
New North St BMSBY WC1N .. 11 L2
Newnton Cl FSBYPK N4 .... 67 K8
New Oak Rd EFNCH N2 .... 65 J3
New Oxford St
NOXST/BSQ WC1A 11 J4
Newpark Av PLMGR N13 .... 49 J5
New Park Cl NTHLT UB5 .... 78 E6
New Park Est UED N18 .... 50 C7 🔢
New Park Rd ASHF TW15 .. 149 J1
BAL SW12 .... 138 E5
BRXS/STRHM SW2 .... 138 E4
DEN/HRF UB9 .... 58 C2
New Peachey La UX/CGN UB8 .. 94 D5
New Place Gdns UPMR RM14.. 93 K2
New Plaistow Rd SRTFD E15 .. 87 L8
Newport Ct LSQ/SEVD WC2H .. 11 H6 🔢
Newport Cl PEND EN3 .... 37 L2 🔢
Newport Md OXHEY WD19 .. 42 D6 🔢
Newport Pl SOHO/SHAV W1D .. 11 H6 🔢
Newport Rd BARN SW13 .... 118 A6
HTHAIR TW6 .... 113 G6 🔢
WALTH E17 .... 68 E5 🔢
WAN E11 .... 87 K2
YEAD UB4 .... 95 K4
Newport St LBTH SE11 .... 17 L6
Newquay Crs RYLN/HDSTN HA2.. 78 E2
Newquay Gdns OXHEY WD19 .. 42 B4
Newquay Rd CAT SE6 .... 141 H6
New Quebec St MBLAR W1H .. 9 M5
New River Crs PLMGR N13 .. 49 H6
New River Wy FSBYPK N4 .. 67 K8 🔢
New Rd ABR/ST RM4 .... 54 D1
ABYW SE2 .... 126 D2
ALP/SUD HA0 .... 79 M4
BTFD TW8 .... 116 D3 🔢
CEND/HSY/T N8 .... 66 D6
CHING E4 .... 51 H6
DAGW RM9 .... 91 G8
E/WMO/HCT KT8 .... 151 G6

EBED/NFELT TW14 .... 131 K3
EBED/NFELT TW14 .... 132 B5
ED N9 .... 50 A5
ESH/CLAY KT10 .... 166 C6
FELT TW13 .... 150 E1
GDMY/SEVK IG3 .... 89 L2
GSTN WD25 .... 30 E4
HSLW TW3 .... 133 H1
HYS/HAR UB3 .... 113 J5
KUTN/CMB KT2 .... 153 G3
MLHL NW7 .... 64 F1
MTCM CR4 .... 171 G3
ORP BR6 .... 177 G2
POTB/CUF EN6 .... 22 A6
RAD WD7 .... 30 E1
RAIN RM13 .... 109 J2
RCHPK/HAM TW10 .... 134 C8
RKW/CH/CXG WD3 .... 28 A3
SHPTN TW17 .... 149 C6
SWLY BR8 .... 163 M6
UX/CGN UB8 .... 95 J3
WAT WD17 .... 29 J7
WDGN N22 .... 67 J2
WELL DA16 .... 126 B7
WEY KT13 .... 164 C7
New Road Hl HAYES BR2 .. 187 L2 🔢
New Rw TWK TW1 .... 134 A1
Newry Rd TWK TW1 .... 134 A1
Newsam Av SEVS/STOTM N15 .. 67 K6
Newsholme Dr WCHMH N21 .. 35 M8
New Spring Gardens Wk
LBTH SE11 .... 17 K8 🔢
New Sq LINN WC2A 11 M4
Newstead Av ORP BR6 .... 176 D5
Newstead Cl
NFNCH/WDSP N12 .... 47 L8 🔢
Newstead Rd LEE/GVPK SE12.. 141 M4
Newstead Wk MRDN SM4 .. 170 C2
Newstead Wy WIM/MER SW19 .. 136 D8
New St LVPST EC2M 13 K3
STA TW18 .... 130 A8
WATW WD18 .... 29 J7 🔢
New Street Hl BMLY BR1 .. 160 E4
New Street Sq
FLST/FETLN EC4A .... 12 B4 🔢
FLST/FETLN EC4A .... 12 B4 🔢
FLST/FETLN EC4A .... 12 B4 🔢
Newteswell Dr WAB EN9 .... 27 K5
Newton Av ACT W3 .... 99 J8
MUSWH N10 .... 66 A2
Newton Cl RYLN/HDSTN HA2 .. 79 G2
WALTH E17 .... 68 E7 🔢
Newton Crs BORE WD6 .... 32 C7 🔢
Newton Gv CHSWK W4 .... 117 L1
Newton Rd ALP/SUD HA0 .. 80 F7
BAY/PAD W2 .... 8 B5
CRICK NW2 .... 82 C4
ISLW TW7 .... 115 M7
KTN/HRWW/W HA3 .... 61 L2
PUR/KEN CR8 .... 183 J5
SEVS/STOTM N15 .... 67 M6
SRTFD E15 .... 87 K5 🔢
WDR/YW UB7 .... 112 E6
WELL DA16 .... 126 A8
WIM/MER SW19 .... 154 E3
Newtons Cl RAIN RM13 .... 91 J7
Newton's Ct GRH DA9 .... 147 K1
Newton St HOL/ALD WC2B .. 11 K4
Newton's Yd
WAND/EARL SW18 .... 137 G2 🔢
Newton Ter HAYES BR2 .... 175 K1
Newton Wy UED N18 .... 49 J7
Newtown Rd DEN/HRF UB9 .. 76 B6
Newtown St BTSEA SW11 .. 120 B6 🔢
New Trinity Rd EFNCH N2 .. 65 J4
New Union Cl POP/IOD E14 .. 123 J1
New Union St BARB EC2Y .. 13 G3
New Wanstead WAN E11 .... 70 A7
New Way Rd CDALE/KGS NW9 .. 63 L5
New Wharf Rd IS N1 .... 5 K5
Newyears Green La
DEN/HRF UB9 .... 58 F7
New Zealand Av
WOT/HER KT12 .... 164 F3
New Zealand Wy RAIN RM13 .. 109 M2
Niagara Av EA W5 .... 116 C2
Niagara Cl CHES/WCR EN8 .. 26 D2 🔢
IS N1 .... 6 F5
Nibthwaite Rd HRW HA1 .... 61 L6
Nicholas Cl GFD/PVL UB6 .. 97 H1 🔢
WATN WD24 .... 29 H2
Nicholas Gdns EA W5 .... 98 D7
Nicholas La MANHO EC4N .. 13 H6
Nicholas Rd BCTR RM8 .... 90 F2
BORE WD6 .... 44 F1
CROY/NA CR0 .... 171 L6
WCHPL E1 .... 104 C3
Nicholas Wy NTHWD HA6 .. 59 J2
Nicholay Rd ARCH N19 .... 84 D1
Nicholes Rd HSLW TW3 .... 133 G1 🔢
Nichol La BMLY BR1 .... 160 A3
Nicholls Av UX/CGN UB8 .. 95 G5
Nicholl St BETH E2 .... 86 A8 🔢
Nicholson Dr BUSH WD23 .. 43 J3
Nicholson Rd CROY/NA CR0 .. 172 F3
Nicholson St STHWK SE1 .. 12 C9
Nickelby Cl THMD SE28 .... 108 C5
Nickleby Cl UX/CGN UB8 .. 95 H5 🔢
Nicola Cl KTN/HRWW/W HA3 .. 61 K3
SAND/SEL CR2 .... 172 A6
Nicola Ms BARK/HLT IG6 .. 53 H8 🔢
Nicoll Pl HDN NW4 .... 64 B7 🔢
Nicoll Rd WLSDN NW10 .... 81 L8
Nicoll Wy BORE WD6 .... 32 D8
Nicolson Rd STMC/STPC BR5.. 177 L2
Nicosia Rd WAND/EARL SW18 .. 137 L4
Niederwald Rd SYD SE26 .. 140 D8 🔢
Nield Rd HYS/HAR UB3 .... 95 M8 🔢
Nigel Cl NTHLT UB5 .... 78 E3 🔢
Nigel Fisher Wy CHSGTN KT9 .. 179 K1
Nigel Ms IL IG1 .... 89 H4
Nigel Playfair Av HMSMTH W6.. 118 D3
Nigel Rd FSTGT E7 .... 88 C2
PECK SE15 .... 122 A8
Nigeria Rd CHARL SE7 .... 124 C5
Nightingale Av CHING E4 .. 51 L7

UPMR RM14 .... 93 M1
Nightingale Cl ABLGY WD5 .. 21 G4 🔢
BH/WHM TN16 .... 187 J8
CAR SM5 .... 171 G4 🔢
CHING E4 .... 51 L6 🔢
CHSWK W4 .... 117 J4 🔢
HOR/WEW KT19 .... 180 A5 🔢
PIN HA5 .... 60 C6
RAD WD7 .... 30 F1
Nightingale Dr HOR/WEW KT19 .. 168 B8
Nightingale Gv LEW SE13 .. 141 K2
Nightingale La BAL SW12 .. 137 M4
BMLY BR1 .... 160 C5
CEND/HSY/T N8 .... 66 E5
RCHPK/HAM TW10 .... 134 C4
WAN E11 .... 70 B6
Nightingale Pl
RKW/CH/CXG WD3 .... 40 D2 🔢
WBPTN SW10 .... 14 F9
WOOL/PLUM SE18 .... 125 H4
Nightingale Rd BUSH WD23 .. 30 A8
CAR SM5 .... 170 F5
CLPT E5 .... 86 B3
E/WMO/HCT KT8 .... 151 H8
ED N9 .... 50 C2
ESH/CLAY KT10 .... 165 M7
HNWL W7 .... 97 M7
HPTN TW12 .... 151 G2
RKW/CH/CXG WD3 .... 40 C2
SAND/SEL CR2 .... 185 K4
STMC/STPC BR5 .... 176 C1
WDGN N22 .... 66 E2
WLSDN NW10 .... 99 M1 🔢
WOT/HER KT12 .... 165 J2 🔢
Nightingale Sq BAL SW12 .. 138 A4
The Nightingales
STWL/WRAY TW19 .... 130 F5 🔢
Nightingale V
WOOL/PLUM SE18 .... 125 G4
Nightingale Wk BAL SW12 .. 138 B3
Nightingale Wy EHAM E6 .. 106 E4
SWLY BR8 .... 163 L6
Nile Cl STNW/STAM N16 .... 85 M3
Nile Rd PLSTW E13 .... 106 C1 🔢
Nile St IS N1 .... 7 G7
Nile Ter PECK SE15 .... 19 M8
Nimbus Rd HOR/WEW KT19 .. 180 D3
Nimrod Cl NTHLT UB5 .... 96 D2 🔢
Nimrod Pas IS N1 .... 86 B5
Nimrod Rd STRHM/NOR SW16 .. 156 B2
Nina Mackay Cl SRTFD E15 .. 87 L8 🔢
Nine Acres Cl MNPK E12 .. 88 E5
Nine Elms Cl
EBED/NFELT TW14 .... 131 M5 🔢
UX/CGN UB8 .... 94 D4
Nine Elms La VX/NE SW8 .. 120 C5
Ninefields WAB EN9 .... 27 M6
Nine Stiles Cl DEN/HRF UB9 .. 76 B6 🔢
Nineteenth Rd MTCM CR4 .. 156 E7
Ninhams Wd ORP BR6 .... 176 A6
Nithdale Rd WOOL/PLUM SE18 .. 125 H5
Nithsdale Gv HGDN/ICK UB10 .. 77 J3 🔢
Niton Cl BAR EN5 .... 46 D1
Niton Rd RCH/KEW TW9 .. 117 G8 🔢
Niton St FUL/PGN SW6 .... 118 D5
Niven Cl BORE WD6 .... 32 C4 🔢
Noak Hill Rd HARH RM3 .... 56 C6
Nobel Dr HYS/HAR UB3 .... 113 L5
Nobel Rd UED N18 .... 50 C6
Noble St CITYW EC2V 12 E4
Noel Park Rd WDGN N22 .. 67 G3 🔢
Noel Rd ACT W3 .... 99 G5
EHAM E6 .... 106 E3
IS N1 .... 6 D5
Noel St SOHO/CST W1F .... 10 F5 🔢
Nolan Wy CLPT E5 .... 86 A4
Nolton Pl EDGW HA8 .... 62 F2
Nonsuch Cl CHIG IG7 .... 53 H8
Nonsuch Court Av EW KT17 .. 181 H3
Nonsuch Wk BELMT SM2 .. 181 K3
Norbiton Av KUT KT1 .... 153 G5
Norbiton Common Rd
NWMAL KT3 .... 153 H6 🔢
Norbiton Rd POP/IOD E14 .. 104 F5
Norbroke St ACT W3 .... 99 M6
Norburn St NKENS W10 .... 100 E4 🔢
Norbury Av HSLW TW3 .... 133 K2
STRHM/NOR SW16 .... 156 F4
WATN WD24 .... 29 J4
Norbury Cl STRHM/NOR SW16 .. 157 G4
Norbury Court Rd
STRHM/NOR SW16 .... 156 E5
Norbury Crs STRHM/NOR SW16 .. 157 G2
Norbury Cross
STRHM/NOR SW16 .... 156 E6
Norbury Gdns CHDH RM6 .. 72 D6
Norbury Gv MLHL NW7 .... 45 L5
Norbury Hl STRHM/NOR SW16 .. 157 G3
Norbury Ri STRHM/NOR SW16 .. 156 F6
Norbury Rd CHING E4 .... 51 G7
THHTH CR7 .... 157 G3
Norcombe Gdns
KTN/HRWW/W HA3 .... 62 C7
Norcott Rd YEAD UB4 .... 96 C3
Norcott Rd STNW/STAM N16 .. 86 A2
Norcroft Gdns EDUL SE22 .. 140 A4
Norcutt Rd WHTN TW2 .... 133 L5
Nordenfeldt Rd ERITH DA8 .. 127 K3 🔢
Norfield Rd RDART DA2 .... 145 J8
Norfolk Av PLMGR N13 .... 49 H8
SAND/SEL CR2 .... 185 G3
SEVS/STOTM N15 .... 67 M7
WATN WD24 .... 29 J3
Norfolk Cl DART DA1 .... 147 G3
EBAR EN4 .... 35 G7
EFNCH N2 .... 65 L4 🔢
PLMGR N13 .... 49 H8
TWK TW1 .... 134 B3 🔢
Norfolk Crs BAY/PAD W2 .. 9 J4
BFN/LL DA15 .... 143 L4
Norfolk Gdns BORE WD6 .. 32 D7
BXLYHN DA7 .... 126 F6
Norfolk House Rd
STRHM/NOR SW16 .... 138 D7
Norfolk Pl BAY/PAD W2 .... 9 H4
WELL DA16 .... 126 A7
Norfolk Rd BAR EN5 .... 34 A6

BARK IG11 .... 89 L7
DAGE RM10 .... 91 H5
EHAM E6 .... 88 F8
ESH/CLAY KT10 .... 166 E7
FELT TW13 .... 132 C5
GDMY/SEVK IG3 .... 89 L1
HRW HA1 .... 61 H6
PEND EN3 .... 37 H8
RKW/CH/CXG WD3 .... 40 E3
ROMW/RG RM7 .... 73 J7
STJWD NW8 .... 3 H4
THHTH CR7 .... 157 J6
UPMR RM14 .... 93 C3
UX/CGN UB8 .... 76 D6
WALTH E17 .... 68 E2
WIM/MER SW19 .... 155 L3
WLSDN NW10 .... 81 L7
Norfolk Rw STHWK SE1 .... 17 L5
Norfolk Sq BAY/PAD W2 .... 9 H5
Norfolk Square Ms BAY/PAD W2 .... 9 H5
Norfolk St FSTGT E7 .... 88 A5
Norgrove St BAL SW12 .... 138 A5
Norhyrst Av SNWD SE25 .... 157 M6
Nork Gdns BNSTD SM7 .... 181 L7
Nork Wy BNSTD SM7 .... 181 K8
Norland Pl NTGHL W11 .... 100 E7
Norland Rd NTGHL W11 .... 100 D7
Norlands Crs CHST BR7 .... 161 H4
Norlands Wy NTGHL W11 .... 100 E7
Norley V PUT/ROE SW15 .... 136 A5
Norlington Rd LEY E10 .... 87 J1
Norman Av EW KT17 .... 180 F5
FELT TW13 .... 132 E6
SAND/SEL CR2 .... 184 C3
STHL UB1 .... 96 E6
TWK TW1 .... 134 B4
WDGN N22 .... 67 J2
Normanby Cl PUT/ROE SW15 .... 136 F2
Normanby Rd WLSDN NW10 .... 81 M5
Norman Cl ORP BR6 .... 176 C5
ROMW/RG RM7 .... 73 H3
WAB EN9 .... 27 K6
Norman Ct POTB/CUF EN6 .... 23 J3
Norman Crs HEST TW5 .... 114 D5
PIN HA5 .... 60 C2
Normand Ms WKENS W14 .... 118 E4
Normand Rd WKENS W14 .... 118 F4
Normandy Av BAR EN5 .... 33 M8
Normandy Cl SYD SE26 .... 140 E7
Normandy Dr HYS/HAR UB3 .... 95 J3
Normandy Rd BRXN/ST SW9 .... 121 C6
Normandy Ter CAN/RD E16 .... 106 B5
Normandy Wy ERITH DA8 .... 127 L6
Norman Gv BOW E3 .... 104 E1
Normanhurst Av WELL DA16 .... 126 D6
Normanhurst Dr TWK TW1 .... 134 B2
Normanhurst Rd
BRXS/STRHM SW2 .... 138 F6
STMC/STPC BR5 .... 162 B5
WOT/HER KT12 .... 165 K4
Norman Rd ASHF TW15 .... 149 K2
BELV DA17 .... 109 H8
DART DA1 .... 146 E5
EHAM E6 .... 106 F3
EMPK RM11 .... 74 A8
GNWCH SE10 .... 123 H5
IL IG1 .... 89 H5
SEVS/STOTM N15 .... 67 M6
SUT SM1 .... 170 A7
THHTH CR7 .... 157 H8
WAN E11 .... 87 L2
WIM/MER SW19 .... 155 J3
Normans Cl UX/CGN UB8 .... 94 E4
WLSDN NW10 .... 81 K6
Normansfield Av
E/WMO/HCT KT8 .... 152 C3
Normansfield Cl BUSH WD23 .... 43 H2
Normanshire Dr CHING E4 .... 51 L6
Normans Md WLSDN NW10 .... 81 K6
Norman St FSBYE EC1V 6 E4
Normanton Av WIM/MER SW19 .. 137 C6
Normanton Pk CHING E4 .... 51 L5
Normanton Rd SAND/SEL CR2 .. 172 E8
Normanton St FSTH SE23 .... 140 F4
Norman Wy ACT W3 .... 99 H4
STHGT/OAK N14 .... 48 E4
Normington Cl
STRHM/NOR SW16 .... 157 G1
Norrice Lea EFNCH N2 .... 65 K6
Norris St STJS SW1Y 11 G7
Norris Wy DART DA1 .... 127 M8
Norroy Rd PUT/ROE SW15 .... 136 D1
Norrys Cl EBAR EN4 .... 34 F3
Norrys Rd EBAR EN4 .... 34 F2
Norseman Cl GDMY/SEVK IG3 .... 90 B1
Norseman Wy GFD/PVL UB6 .... 79 H8
Norstead Pl PUT/ROE SW15 .... 136 A6
North Access Rd WALTH E17 .... 68 D7
North Acre CDALE/KGS NW9 .... 63 L2
North Acton Rd WLSDN NW10 ..... 99 K1
Northallerton Wy HARH RM3 .... 56 D7
Northall Rd BXLYHN DA7 .... 127 J7
Northampton Gv IS N1 .... 85 J5
Northampton Pk IS N1 .... 85 J6
Northampton Rd CLKNW EC1R 6 B9
CROY/NA CR0 .... 173 G4
PEND EN3 .... 37 L7
Northampton Sq FSBYE EC1V 6 C8
Northampton St IS N1 .... 6 E1
Northanger Rd
STRHM/NOR SW16 .... 156 E2
North Ap GSTN WD25 .... 21 G7
RKW/CH/CXG WD3 .... 41 J4
North Audley St
MYFR/PKLN W1K 10 A5
North Av CAR SM5 .... 183 G1
HYS/HAR UB3 .... 96 A6
RCH/KEW TW9 .... 117 G6
RYLN/HDSTN HA2 .... 61 H7
STHL UB1 .... 96 F6
UED N18 .... 50 A6
WEA W13 .... 98 B5
Northaw Rd West
POTB/CUF EN6 .... 24 A3
North Bank STJWD NW8 .... 3 J8
Northbank Rd WALTH E17 .... 69 J3
North Birkbeck Rd WAN E11 .... 87 K3

Northborough Rd
STRHM/NOR SW16 .... 156 E5
Northbourne HAYES BR2 .... 175 G2
Northbourne Rd CLAP SW4 .... 138 D1
Northbrook Dr NTHWD HA6 .... 59 L2
Northbrook Rd BAR EN5 .... 46 E1
CROY/NA CR0 .... 157 K8
IL IG1 .... 89 G2
LEW SE13 .... 141 K2
WDGN N22 .... 48 E8
Northburgh St FSBYE EC1V 12 D1
North Carriage Dr BAY/PAD W2 ... 9 K6
Northchurch Rd IS N1 .... 7 H1
WBLY HA9 .... 81 G6
North Circular Rd CHING E4 .... 50 E8
CRICK NW2 .... 81 L3
EFNCH N2 .... 65 J3
GLDGN NW11 .... 64 E5
PLMGR N13 .... 49 G7
SWFD E18 .... 70 C4
WALTH E17 .... 69 H2
WLSDN NW10 .... 81 K5
Northcliffe Cl WPK KT4 .... 168 E5
Northcliffe Dr TRDG/WHET N20 .. 46 F3
North Cl BAR EN5 .... 33 J8
BXLYHS DA6 .... 144 D1
CHIG IG7 .... 54 A7
DAGE RM10 .... 91 G8
EBED/NFELT TW14 .... 131 K3
MRDN SM4 .... 154 E7
North Colonnade
POP/IOD E14 .... 105 G7
North Common Rd WEY KT13 .... 164 C6
North Common Rd EA W5 .... 98 E6
UX/CGN UB8 .... 76 D5
Northcote Av BRYLDS KT5 .... 168 A2
EA W5 .... 98 E6
ISLW TW7 .... 134 A2
STHL UB1 .... 96 E6
Northcote Rd BTSEA SW11 .... 137 L1
CROY/NA CR0 .... 172 D1
NWMAL KT3 .... 153 J6
TWK TW1 .... 134 A2
WALTH E17 .... 68 E5
WLSDN NW10 .... 81 L7
Northcott Av WDGN N22 .... 66 E2
North Countess Rd WALTH E17 ... 68 F3
Northcourt
RKW/CH/CXG WD3 .... 40 A3
North Cray Rd BXLY DA5 .... 145 G6
SCUP DA14 .... 162 G2
North Crs CAN/RD E16 .... 105 K3
FITZ W1T 11 G2
FNCH N3 .... 64 F3
Northcroft Rd HOR/WEW KT19 .. 180 E1
WEA W13 .... 98 B8
North Cross Rd BARK/HLT IG6 .... 71 J5
EDUL SE22 .... 139 M2
Northdene CHIG IG7 .... 53 K7
North Dene HEST TW5 .... 115 H6
MLHL NW7 .... 45 K5
Northdene Gdns
SEVS/STOTM N15 .... 67 M7
North Down SAND/SEL CR2 .... 184 E4
Northdown Cl RSLP HA4 .... 77 M3
Northdown Gdns
GNTH/NBYPK IG2 .... 71 L6
Northdown Rd BELMT SM2 .... 182 A3
EMPK RM11 .... 74 B8
WELL DA16 .... 126 B7
North Downs Crs CROY/NA CR0 .. 186 B5
North Downs Rd CROY/NA CR0 .. 186 B5
Northdown St IS N1 .... 5 K5
North Dr GPK RM2 .... 74 C4
HSLW TW3 .... 115 J7
ORP BR6 .... 176 E6
RSLP HA4 .... 59 L8
STRHM/NOR SW16 .... 138 C8
North End BKHH IG9 .... 52 C2
CROY/NA CR0 .... 172 C4
GLDGN NW11 .... 83 J2
North End Av HAMP NW3 .... 83 J2
North End Crs WKENS W14 .... 118 F2
Northend Rd ERITH DA8 .... 127 M6
North End Rd FUL/PGN SW6 .... 119 C5
GLDGN NW11 .... 83 G1
WBLY HA9 .... 81 G3
WKENS W14 .... 118 F4
North End Wy HAMP NW3 .... 83 J2
Northern Av ED N9 .... 49 M4
Northernhay Wk MRDN SM4 .... 154 E7
Northern Perimeter Rd
HTHAIR TW6 .... 113 L6
Northern Perimeter Rd (West)
HTHAIR TW6 .... 112 E6
Northern Relief Rd BARK IG11 ..... 89 J7
Northey Av BELMT SM2 .... 181 K3
North Eyot Gdns
HMSMTH W6 .... 117 M3
Northey St POP/IOD E14 .... 104 E6
North Farm LOU IG10 .... 52 C1
Northfield Av PIN HA5 .... 60 D5
STMC/STPC BR5 .... 177 J1
WEA W13 .... 98 B8
Northfield Cl BMLY BR1 .... 160 E4
HYS/HAR UB3 .... 113 M1
Northfield Ct STA TW18 .... 148 B4
Northfield Crs CHEAM SM3 .... 169 L6
Northfield Gdns WATN WD24 .... 29 J2
Northfield Pk HYS/HAR UB3 .... 113 L1
Northfield Rd BORE WD6 .... 32 B4
CHES/WCR EN8 .... 26 C5
DAGW RM9 .... 90 F4
EBAR EN4 .... 34 E6
EHAM E6 .... 88 F6
HEST TW5 .... 114 D4
PEND EN3 .... 37 H8
STA TW18 .... 148 B4
STNW/STAM N16 .... 67 L8
WEA W13 .... 98 B8
Northfields EW KT17 .... 180 E4
WAND/EARL SW18 .... 137 G1
Northfields Rd ACT W3 .... 99 J4
North Gdns WIM/MER SW19 ..... 155 K3
Northgate NTHWD HA6 .... 59 J8
Northgate Dr CDALE/KGS NW9 .. 63 L7
Northgate Pth BORE WD6 .... 31 M3

North Gower St CAMTN NW1 .... 4 E8
North Gv HGT N6 .... 66 A8
SEVS/STOTM N15 .... 67 K6
North Hatton Rd HTHAIR TW6 ... 113 K6
North Hl HGT N6 .... 65 M7
North Hill Av HGT N6 .... 66 A7
North Hill Dr HARH RM3 .... 56 D6
North Hyde Gdns
HYS/HAR UB3 .... 114 A1
North Hyde La NWDGN UB2 ..... 114 E3
North Hyde Rd HYS/HAR UB3 ... 113 L1
Northiam NFNCH/WDSP N12 .... 47 J7
Northiam St HACK E8 .... 86 B8
Northington St BMSBY WC1N 11 L2
Northlands POTB/CUF EN6 .... 23 K4
Northlands Av ORP BR6 .... 176 E6
Northlands St CMBW SE5 .... 121 J7
North La TEDD TW11 .... 151 M2
North Lodge Cl
PUT/ROE SW15 .... 136 D2
North Ms BMSBY WC1N 11 M1
Northolm EDGW HA8 .... 45 K6
Northolme Gdns EDGW HA8 .... 63 G2
Northolme Ri ORP BR6 .... 176 E4
Northolme Rd HBRY N5 .... 85 H4
Northolt Av RSLP HA4 .... 78 B5
Northolt Gdns GFD/PVL UB6 .... 79 M5
Northolt Rd RYLN/HDSTN HA2 .... 79 H4
WDR/YW UB7 .... 112 D6
Northolt Wy HCH RM12 .... 92 C5
North Orbital Rd
LCOL/BKTW AL2 .... 21 M1
North Orbital Rd St Albans Rd
GSTN WD25 .... 21 K6
Northover BMLY BR1 .... 141 M7
North Pde CHSGTN KT9 .... 167 M7
North Pk ELTH/MOT SE9 .... 142 F3
North Pas
WAND/EARL SW18 .... 137 G2
North Pl TEDD TW11 .... 151 M2
WAB EN9 .... 27 H6
WIM/MER SW19 .... 155 M3
North Pole La HAYES BR2 .... 175 G4
North Pole Rd SHB W12 .... 100 C5
Northport St IS N1 .... 7 H4
North Rd ABR/ST RM4 .... 55 L4
BELV DA17 .... 127 H1
BMLY BR1 .... 160 B4
BTFD TW8 .... 116 E4
CHDH RM6 .... 72 E6
CHES/WCR EN8 .... 26 E6
DART DA1 .... 145 M3
EA W5 .... 116 D1
EBED/NFELT TW14 .... 131 K3
ED N9 .... 50 B3
EDGW HA8 .... 63 H2
EFNCH N2 .... 65 L2
GDMY/SEVK IG3 .... 89 L2
HEST TW5 .... 114 C4
HGT N6 .... 66 A8
HOLWY N7 .... 84 D6
HYS/HAR UB3 .... 95 K4
PUR RM19 .... 129 J2
RCH/KEW TW9 .... 117 G7
STHL UB1 .... 97 G6
SURB KT6 .... 167 K1
TOOT SW17 .... 155 K2
WDR/YW UB7 .... 112 F1
WIM/MER SW19 .... 155 M3
WOOL/PLUM SE18 .... 125 L2
WOT/HER KT12 .... 165 J7
WWKM BR4 .... 174 B3
Northrop Rd HTHAIR TW6 .... 113 L6
North Rw MYFR/PKLN W1K 10 A6
Northrop Rd BMLY BR1 .... 160 A4
North Side Wandsworth Common
WAND/EARL SW18 .... 137 J2
Northspur Rd SUT SM1 .... 170 A5
North Sq GLDGN NW11 .... 65 G6
Northstead Rd
BRXS/STRHM SW2 .... 139 G6
North St BARK IG11 .... 89 H6
BMLY BR1 .... 160 A4
BXLYHN DA7 .... 145 G1
CAR SM5 .... 170 F6
DART DA1 .... 146 D4
EMPK RM11 .... 74 D8
HDN NW4 .... 64 C6
ISLW TW7 .... 116 A8
PLSTW E13 .... 106 B1
ROMW/RG RM7 .... 73 K5
VX/NE SW8 .... 120 B8
North Tenter St WCHPL E1 .... 13 M5
North Ter CHEL SW3 .... 15 J5
Northumberland Aly
TWRH EC3N 13 K5
Northumberland Av
CHCR WC2N 11 H8
EMPK RM11 .... 74 C6
EN EN1 .... 37 H3
ISLW TW7 .... 115 M6
MNPK E12 .... 88 C1
WELL DA16 .... 143 L1
Northumberland Cl
ERITH DA8 .... 127 J5
STWL/WRAY TW19 .... 130 E3
Northumberland Crs
EBED/NFELT TW14 .... 131 L3
Northumberland Gdns
BMLY BR1 .... 161 G7
ED N9 .... 49 M5
MTCM CR4 .... 156 D8
Northumberland Gv TOTM N17 ... 68 B1
Northumberland Pk TOTM N17 ... 68 A1
Northumberland Pl BAY/PAD W2 .. 8 A4
Northumberland Rd BAR EN5 .... 47 J1
EHAM E6 .... 106 A5
RYLN/HDSTN HA2 .... 60 F6
WALTH E17 .... 69 G2
Northumberland Wy
BXLYHN DA7 .... 127 J6
Northumbria St POP/IOD E14 .... 105 C5
North Verbena Gdns
HMSMTH W6 .... 118 A3
North Vw EA W5 .... 98 C3
PIN HA5 .... 60 C8
Northview SWLY BR8 .... 163 L5
North Vw WIM/MER SW19 .... 154 B1

Northview Crs WLSDN NW10 .... 81 M4
Northview Dr WFD IG8 .... 70 D3
North View CEND/HSY/T N8 .... 66 D4
North Vls CAMTN NW1 .... 84 D6
Northway GLDGN NW11 .... 65 H6
RKW/CH/CXG WD3 .... 40 D7
RYNPK SW20 .... 154 E6
WLGTN SM6 .... 171 J6
Northway Crs MLHL NW7 .... 45 L6
CROY/NA CR0 .... 172 F1
Northway Rd CMBW SE5 .... 121 J8
CROY/NA CR0 .... 157 J8
North Weald La KUTN/CMB KT2 .. 152 C1
North Western Av GSTN WD25 .... 21 G8
WATN WD24 .... 20 F8
North Western Av Colne Wy
WATN WD24 .... 29 J1
North Western Av Elton Wy
GSTN WD25 .... 30 B5
North Western Av Gade Side
KGLGY WD4 .... 20 C8
WAT WD17 .... 20 D8
North Western Av Otterspool Wy
GSTN WD25 .... 29 M3
North Western Av (Tylers Way)
BUSH WD23 .... 30 C7
STAN HA7 .... 44 A1
North Western Av (Watford By-pass)
GSTN WD25 .... 44 A1
North Wharf Rd BAY/PAD W2 .... 9 G3
Northwick Av HRW HA1 .... 62 A7
Northwick Cir
KTN/HRWW/W HA3 .... 62 C7
Northwick Cl STJWD NW8 .... 3 C9
Northwick Park Rd HRW HA1 .... 61 M7
Northwick Rd ALP/SUD HA0 .... 80 D8
OXHEY WD19 .... 42 C6
Northwick Ter STJWD NW8 .... 3 C9
Northwold Dr PIN HA5 .... 60 C4
Northwold Rd STNW/STAM N16 .. 85 M2
Northwood Av HCH RM12 .... 92 A4
PUR/KEN CR8 .... 184 A6
Northwood Gdns CLAY IG5 .... 71 C5
GFD/PVL UB6 .... 79 M5
NFNCH/WDSP N12 .... 47 K7
Northwood Pl ERITH DA18 .... 126 F1
Northwood Rd CAR SM5 .... 171 G8
DEN/HRF UB9 .... 58 E2
FSTH SE23 .... 140 F5
HGT N6 .... 66 B8
HTHAIR TW6 .... 112 D6
THHTH CR7 .... 157 J5
Northwood Wy DEN/HRF UB9 ..... 58 D2
NTHWD HA6 .... 60 A2
North Woolwich Rd
CAN/RD E16 .... 106 B7
North Worple Wy
MORT/ESHN SW14 .... 117 K8
Norton Av BRYLDS KT5 .... 168 B2
Norton Cl BORE WD6 .... 32 A4
CHING E4 .... 51 G7
Norton Gdns
STRHM/NOR SW16 .... 156 E5
Norton Rd ALP/SUD HA0 .... 80 D6
DAGE RM10 .... 91 K6
LEY E10 .... 86 F1
UX/CGN UB8 .... 94 D2
Norval Rd ALP/SUD HA0 .... 80 B2
Norway Ga BERM/RHTH SE16 .... 122 E1
Norway Pl POP/IOD E14 .... 104 F5
Norway St GNWCH SE10 .... 123 H4
Norwich Pl BXLYHS DA6 .... 145 G1
Norwich Rd FSTGT E7 .... 88 A5
GFD/PVL UB6 .... 79 H8
PIN HA5 .... 59 M4
THHTH CR7 .... 157 J6
Norwich St FLST/FETLN EC4A 12 A4
Norwich Wk EDGW HA8 .... 63 J1
Norwich Wy RKW/CH/CXG WD3 ... 28 B6
Norwood Av ALP/SUD HA0 .... 80 F8
ROMW/RG RM7 .... 73 K8
Norwood Cl NWDGN UB2 .... 115 C2
WHTN TW2 .... 133 K6
Norwood Crs HTHAIR TW6 .... 113 J6
Norwood Dr RYLN/HDSTN HA2 ... 60 F7
Norwood Gdns NWDGN UB2 .... 114 F2
YEAD UB4 .... 96 C3
Norwood Green Rd
NWDGN UB2 .... 115 G2
Norwood High St WNWD SE27 .. 139 J8
Norwood Park Rd WNWD SE27 .. 157 J1
Norwood Rd CHES/WCR EN8 ..... 26 E5
HNHL SE24 .... 139 H5
NWDGN UB2 .... 114 E1
Notley St CMBW SE5 .... 121 K5
Notson Rd SNWD SE25 .... 158 B7
Notting Barn Rd NKENS W10 .... 100 D3
Nottingham Av CAN/RD E16 .... 106 C4
Nottingham Ct LSQ/SEVD WC2H .. 25 G6
Nottingham Pl MHST W1U 10 A1
Nottingham Rd ISLW TW7 .... 115 M7
LEY E10 .... 69 J7
SAND/SEL CR2 .... 172 C7
TOOT SW17 .... 137 M5
Nottingham St MHST W1U 10 A2
Notting Hill Ga KENS W8 .... 8 B8
Nova Ms MRDN SM4 .... 169 L2
Novar Cl ORP BR6 .... 176 F2
Novar Rd ELTH/MOT SE9 .... 143 J5
Novello St FUL/PGN SW6 .... 119 C6
Novello Wy BORE WD6 .... 32 D4
Nowell Rd BARN SW13 .... 118 A4
Nower Hl PIN HA5 .... 60 B3
Noyna Rd TOOT SW17 .... 137 M7
Nuding Cl LEW SE13 .... 123 G8
Nugent Rd ARCH N19 .... 84 E1
SNWD SE25 .... 157 M6
Nugent's Pk PIN HA5 .... 60 F2
Nugent Ter STJWD NW8 .... 2 F6
Nuneaton Rd DAGW RM9 .... 90 D7
Nunhead Gv PECK SE15 .... 122 B8
Nunhead La PECK SE15 .... 122 B8
Nunnington Cl ELTH/MOT SE9 ... 142 E7
Nunn's Rd ENC/FH EN2 .... 36 C5

Nupton Dr BAR EN5 .... 46 C1
Nursery Av BXLYHN DA7 .... 126 F8
CROY/NA CR0 .... 173 K4
FNCH N3 .... 65 H3
Nursery Cl BROCKY SE4 .... 122 F7
CHDH RM6 .... 72 D7
CROY/NA CR0 .... 173 K4
EBED/NFELT TW14 .... 132 B4
EW KT17 .... 180 E3
ORP BR6 .... 176 F2
PEND EN3 .... 37 K4
RDART DA2 .... 147 J4
SWLY BR8 .... 163 J5
WFD IG8 .... 52 B7
Nursery Gdns CHST BR7 .... 161 H2
HSLWW TW4 .... 132 F2
PEND EN3 .... 37 K4
STA TW18 .... 148 B3
SUN TW16 .... 149 M5
Nursery La BETH E2 .... 7 L4
FSTGT E7 .... 88 A6
NKENS W10 .... 100 C4
Nurserymans Rd
FBAR/BDGN N11 .... 48 A3
Nursery Rd BRXN/ST SW9 .... 138 F1
EFNCH N2 .... 65 K2
HOM E9 .... 86 C6
LOU IG10 .... 39 K7
MTCM CR4 .... 155 L7
PIN HA5 .... 60 C4
STHGT/OAK N14 .... 48 C2
SUN TW16 .... 149 L5
SUT SM1 .... 170 C6
THHTH CR7 .... 157 K7
WIM/MER SW19 .... 154 E5
Nursery St TOTM N17 .... 67 M1
The Nursery ERITH DA8 .... 127 M5
Nursery Wk HDN NW4 .... 64 B4
Nursery Waye UX/CGN UB8 .... 76 D8
Nurstead Rd ERITH DA8 .... 127 G5
Nutbourne St NKENS W10 .... 100 E2
Nutbrook St PECK SE15 .... 121 M8
Nutbrowne Rd DAGW RM9 .... 90 B4
Nutcroft Rd PECK SE15 .... 122 B5
Nutfield Cl CAR SM5 .... 170 C5
UED N18 .... 50 A8
Nutfield Gdns GDMY/SEVK IG3 .... 89 M2
NTHLT UB5 .... 96 C1
Nutfield Rd CRICK NW2 .... 82 A2
EDUL SE22 .... 139 M4
SRTFD E15 .... 87 J4
THHTH CR7 .... 157 H7
Nutfield Wy ORP BR6 .... 176 A4
Nutford Pl BAY/PAD W2 .... 9 K4
Nuthatch Gdns THMD SE28 .... 107 K8
Nuthurst Av BRXS/STRHM SW2 .. 138 F6
Nutley Cl SWLY BR8 .... 163 M4
Nutley Ter HAMP NW3 .... 83 K6
Nutmead Cl BXLY DA5 .... 145 J5
Nutmeg Cl CAN/RD E16 .... 105 L3
Nutmeg La POP/IOD E14 .... 105 K5
Nuttall St IS N1 .... 7 K5
Nutter La WAN E11 .... 70 F1
Nuttfield Cl
RKW/CH/CXG WD3 .... 41 H1
Nutt Gv EDGW HA8 .... 44 D4
Nut Tree Cl ORP BR6 .... 177 K6
Nutt St PECK SE15 .... 121 M5
Nutty La SHPTN TW17 .... 149 J7
Nutwell St TOOT SW17 .... 155 L1
Nuxley Rd BELV DA17 .... 126 F4
Nyanza St WOOL/PLUM SE18 .... 125 K4
Nylands Av RCH/KEW TW9 .... 117 J4
Nymans Gdns RYNPK SW20 ..... 154 B6
Nynehead St NWCR SE14 .... 122 F5
Nyon Gv FSTH SE23 .... 140 F6
Nyssa Cl WFD IG8 .... 52 F8
Nyth Cl UPMR RM14 .... 75 K7

O

Oakapple Cl SAND/SEL CR2 .... 185 H7
Oak Av CEND/HSY/T N8 .... 66 E5
CROY/NA CR0 .... 174 A4
ENC/FH EN2 .... 35 M4
HEST TW5 .... 114 C4
HGDN/ICK UB10 .... 77 H2
HPTN TW12 .... 150 F3
MUSWH N10 .... 66 B1
TOTM N17 .... 67 K1
UPMR RM14 .... 93 H3
WDR/YW UB7 .... 113 G1
Oakbank Av WOT/HER KT12 ..... 165 M2
Oakbank Gv HNHL SE24 .... 139 J1
Oakbrook Cl BMLY BR1 .... 142 B8
Oakbury Rd FUL/PGN SW6 .... 119 H7
Oak Cl DART DA1 .... 145 L4
STHGT/OAK N14 .... 48 B2
WAB EN9 .... 27 K4
Oakcombe Cl NWMAL KT3 .... 153 L4
Oak Cottage Cl CAT SE6 .... 141 M5
Oak Crs CAN/RD E16 .... 105 L4
Oakcroft Cl PIN HA5 .... 60 B3
Oakcroft Rd BKHTH/KID SE3 .... 123 K7
CHSGTN KT9 .... 167 M6
Oakcroft Vls CHSGTN KT9 .... 167 M6
Oakdale STHGT/OAK N14 .... 48 B3
Oakdale Av KTN/HRWW/W HA3 .. 62 C6
NTHWD HA6 .... 60 A3
Oakdale Cl OXHEY WD19 .... 42 C5
Oakdale Gdns CHING E4 .... 51 J7
Oakdale Rd FSBYPK N4 .... 67 J7
FSTGT E7 .... 88 B7
HOR/WEW KT19 .... 180 C5
OXHEY WD19 .... 42 C5
PECK SE15 .... 122 C6
STRHM/NOR SW16 .... 156 E1
SWFD E18 .... 70 B4
WAN E11 .... 87 J1
WEY KT13 .... 164 A5
Oakdale Wy MTCM CR4 .... 171 C2
Oakdene CHES/WCR EN8 .... 26 C4
Oakdene Av CHST BR7 .... 161 G6
ERITH DA8 .... 127 G5
THDIT KT7 .... 167 G3
Oakdene Cl PIN HA5 .... 60 F1

Oak Dene Cl *ROM* RM1 .....74 B7
Oakdene Dr *BRYLDS* KT5 .....168 C3
Oakdene Ms *CHEAM* SM5 .....169 M3
Oakdene Pk *FNCH* N3 .....64 F1
Oakdene Rd *HGDN/ICK* UB10 .....95 H1
  STMC/STPC BR5 .....177 C1
  WATN WD24 .....29 H1
Oakden St *LBTH* SE11 .....18 B5
Oaken Dr *ESH/CLAY* KT10 .....166 F6
Oaken La *ESH/CLAY* KT10 .....166 E6
Oakenshaw Cl *SURB* KT6 .....167 L2
Oakeshott Av *HGT* N6 .....84 A2
Oak Farm *BORE* WD6 .....32 C8
Oakfield *CHING* E4 .....51 H7
  RKW/CH/CXG WD3 .....40 A2
Oakfield Av *KTN/HRWW/W* HA3 .....62 B4
Oakfield Cl *NWMAL* KT3 .....153 M8
  POTB/CUF EN6 .....22 F4
  WEY KT13 .....164 C6
Oakfield Gdns *BECK* BR3 .....159 G8
  CAR SM5 .....170 C3
  GFD/PVL UB6 .....97 K3
  UED N18 .....49 L6
Oakfield Gld *WEY* KT13 .....164 C6
Oakfield La *HAYES* BR2 .....175 J6
  RDART DA2 .....146 A6
Oakfield Park Rd *DART* DA1 .....146 D6
Oakfield Pl *DART* DA1 .....146 D6
Oakfield Rd *ASHF* TW15 .....149 H1
  CROY/NA CR0 .....172 C3
  EHAM E6 .....88 E8
  FNCH N3 .....65 H2
  FSBYPK N4 .....67 C7
  IL IG1 .....89 H3
  PGE/AN SE20 .....158 B4
  STHGT/OAK N14 .....48 E4
  WALTH E17 .....68 E3
  WIM/MER SW19 .....136 D7
Oakfields *WOT/HER* KT12 .....165 G3
Oakfields Rd *GLDGN* NW11 .....64 E7
Oakfield St *WBPTN* SW10 .....14 E9
Oakford Rd *KTTN* NW5 .....84 C4
Oak Gdns *CROY/NA* CR0 .....174 A4
  EDGW HA8 .....63 J3
Oak Gld *NTHWD* HA6 .....59 H2
Oak Gln *EMPK* RM11 .....74 E4
Oak Gn *ABLGY* WD5 .....20 E5
Oak Gv *CRICK* NW2 .....82 D4
  RSLP HA4 .....78 B1
  SUN TW16 .....150 B3
  WWKM BR4 .....174 C4
Oak Grove Rd *PGE/AN* SE20 .....158 C4
Oakhall Dr *SUN* TW16 .....149 M1
Oak Hall Rd *WAN* E11 .....70 B7
Oakham Cl *CAT* SE6 .....140 F6
Oakham Dr *HAYES* BR2 .....160 A7
Oakhampton Rd *MLHL* NW7 .....64 D2
Oakhill *ESH/CLAY* KT10 .....167 G8
Oak Hl *SURB* KT6 .....167 L2
  WFD IG8 .....69 K1
Oakhill Av *HAMP* NW3 .....83 H4
  PIN HA5 .....60 E3
Oak Hill Crs *SURB* KT6 .....167 L2
  WFD IG8 .....69 L1
Oak Hill Gdns *WALTH* E17 .....69 L2
Oakhill Gdns *WEY* KT13 .....164 C6
Oak Hill Gv *SURB* KT6 .....167 L1
Oak Hill Pk *HAMP* NW3 .....83 H4
Oakhill Pl *PUT/ROE* SW15 .....137 G2
Oakhill Rd *ABR/ST* RM4 .....55 K2
  BECK BR3 .....159 J5
  ORP BR6 .....176 F4
  PUR RM19 .....129 H3
  PUT/ROE SW15 .....136 F2
  STRHM/NOR SW16 .....156 K4
Oak Hill Rd *SURB* KT6 .....167 L1
Oakhill Rd *SUT* SM1 .....170 B5
Oak Hill Wy *HAMP* NW3 .....83 H4
Oakhouse Rd *BXLYHS* DA6 .....145 G2
Oakhurst Av *BXLYHN* DA7 .....126 E5
  EBAR EN4 .....47 L2
Oakhurst Cl *BARK/HLT* IG6 .....71 J2
  TEDD TW11 .....151 L1
  WALTH E17 .....69 L5
Oakhurst Gdns *BXLYHN* DA7 .....126 E5
  CHING E4 .....51 M3
  WALTH E17 .....69 L5
Oakhurst Gv *EDUL* SE22 .....140 A1
Oakhurst Pl *CHST* BR7 .....160 F4
Oakhurst Ri *CAR* SM5 .....182 E3
Oakhurst Rd *HOR/WEW* KT19 .....168 C8
  PEND EN3 .....37 K1
Oakington Av *HYS/HAR* UB3 .....113 K2
  RYLN/HDSTN HA2 .....61 G8
  WBLY HA9 .....80 F3
Oakington Dr *SUN* TW16 .....150 C5
Oakington Manor Dr *WBLY* HA9 .....81 G5
Oakington Rd *MV/WKIL* W9 .....2 B9
Oakington Wy
  CEND/HSY/T N8 .....66 E8
Oakland Pl *BKHH* IG9 .....52 A4
Oakland Rd *SRTFD* E15 .....87 L4
Oaklands *PLMGR* N13 .....48 F4
  PUR/KEN CR8 .....184 C7
Oaklands Av *BFN/LL* DA15 .....143 M4
  ED N9 .....50 B1
  ESH/CLAY KT10 .....166 D3
  ISLW TW7 .....115 M4
  OXHEY WD19 .....42 B3
  ROM RM1 .....73 L4
  THHTH CR7 .....157 G7
  WWKM BR4 .....174 B5
Oaklands Cl *ALP/SUD* HA0 .....80 D5
  BXLYHS DA6 .....144 F2
  CHSGTN KT9 .....167 J6
  STMC/STPC BR5 .....176 E1
Oaklands Ct *WAT* WD17 .....29 G4
Oaklands Gdns
  PUR/KEN CR8 .....184 C7
Oaklands Ga *NTHWD* HA6 .....41 L8
Oaklands Gv *SHB* W12 .....100 A7
  BH/WHM TN16 .....187 J8
Oaklands Ms *CRICK* NW2 .....82 D4
Oaklands Park Av *IL* IG1 .....89 J2
Oaklands Pl *CLAP* SW4 .....138 D1
Oaklands Rd *BMLY* BR1 .....159 L3
  BXLYHS DA6 .....144 F1
  CRICK NW2 .....82 D4
  HNWL W7 .....97 M8
  MORT/ESHN SW14 .....117 K8
  RDART DA2 .....147 H5
  TRDG/WHET N20 .....46 F2
Oaklands Wy *WLGTN* SM6 .....183 J1
Oakland Wy *HOR/WEW* KT19 .....168 D8
Oak La *EFNCH* N2 .....65 K3
  FBAR/BDGN N11 .....48 D8
  ISLW TW7 .....133 L1
  POP/IOD E14 .....104 F6
  POTB/CUF EN6 .....24 F1
  TWK TW1 .....134 A2
  WFD IG8 .....51 M6
Oak Leaf Cl *HOR/WEW* KT19 .....180 C5
Oakleafe Gdns *CLAY* IG5 .....71 H4
Oakleigh Av *EDGW* HA8 .....63 H3
  SURB KT6 .....168 A3
  TRDG/WHET N20 .....47 K3
Oakleigh Cl *SWLY* BR8 .....163 L6
  TRDG/WHET N20 .....47 M5
Oakleigh Ct *EDGW* HA8 .....63 J3
  TRDG/WHET N20 .....47 K3
Oakleigh Crs *TRDG/WHET* N20 .....47 L5
Oakleigh Dr *RKW/CH/CXG* WD3 .....41 J1
Oakleigh Gdns *EDGW* HA8 .....44 F7
  ORP BR6 .....176 E6
  TRDG/WHET N20 .....47 J3
Oakleigh Park Av *CHST* BR7 .....161 G5
Oakleigh Pk North
  TRDG/WHET N20 .....47 K3
Oakleigh Pk South
  TRDG/WHET N20 .....47 L3
Oakleigh Rd *HGDN/ICK* UB10 .....77 J7
  PIN HA5 .....42 F8
Oakleigh Rd North
  TRDG/WHET N20 .....47 L4
Oakleigh Rd South
  FBAR/BDGN N11 .....48 A6
Oakleigh Wy *MTCM* CR4 .....156 B4
  SURB KT6 .....168 B3
Oakley Av *ACT* W3 .....99 G6
  BARK IG11 .....89 M6
  CROY/NA CR0 .....173 G2
Oakley Cl *CHING* E4 .....51 J5
  HNWL W7 .....97 L6
  ISLW TW7 .....115 K6
Oakley Crs *FSBYE* EC1V 6 D6
Oakley Dr *BFN/LL* DA15 .....143 K6
  ELTH/MOT SE9 .....143 K5
  HARH RM3 .....57 G7
  HAYES BR2 .....175 L5
  LEW SE13 .....141 K3
Oakley Gdns *BNSTD* SM7 .....182 B8
  CEND/HSY/T N8 .....66 F6
  CHEL SW3 .....15 K9
Oakley Pk *BFN/LL* DA15 .....144 C4
Oakley Pl *STHWK* SE1 .....19 L8
Oakley Rd *HAYES* BR2 .....175 L5
  HRW HA1 .....61 L7
  IS N1 .....7 G1
  SNWD SE25 .....158 B8
Oakley Sq *CAMTN* NW1 .....4 F5
Oakley St *CHEL* SW3 .....15 J9
Oak Lodge Av *CHIG* IG7 .....53 K7
Oak Lodge Cl *STAN* HA7 .....44 C7
  WOT/HER KT12 .....165 J7
Oak Lodge Dr *WWKM* BR4 .....174 B2
Oakmead Av *HAYES* BR2 .....175 C1
Oakmeade *PIN* HA5 .....43 C8
Oakmead Gdns *EDGW* HA8 .....45 K6
Oakmead Gn *EPSOM* KT18 .....180 C8
Oakmead Pl *MTCM* CR4 .....155 L4
Oakmead Rd *BAL* SW12 .....138 B5
  CROY/NA CR0 .....171 K1
Oakmere Av *POTB/CUF* EN6 .....23 J6
Oakmere Cl *POTB/CUF* EN6 .....23 K4
Oakmere La *POTB/CUF* EN6 .....23 J5
Oakmere Rd *ABYW* SE2 .....126 A4
Oakmoor Wy *CHIG* IG7 .....53 L7
Oakmore Gdns *STMC/STPC* BR5 .....162 C7
Oak Park Gdns *WIM/MER* SW19 .....136 D5
Oakridge *LCOL/BKTW* AL2 .....21 M2
Oakridge Dr *EFNCH* N2 .....65 K4
Oakridge Rd *BMLY* BR1 .....141 L8
Oak Ri *BKHH* IG9 .....52 D5
Oak Rd *EA* W5 .....98 D6
  ERITH DA8 .....127 J5
  GRH DA9 .....147 L3
  HARH RM3 .....74 F2
  NWMAL KT3 .....153 K5
Oakroyd Av *POTB/CUF* EN6 .....22 F6
Oakroyd Cl *POTB/CUF* EN6 .....22 F7
Oaks Av *CRW* RM5 .....73 J3
  FELT TW13 .....132 E6
  NRWD SE19 .....157 L1
  WPK KT4 .....169 H6
Oaksford Av *SYD* SE26 .....140 B7
Oaks Gv *CHING* E4 .....51 L4
Oakshade Rd *BMLY* BR1 .....141 K8
  LHD/OX KT22 .....
Oakshaw Rd *WAND/EARL* SW18 .....137 H4
Oakside *LCOL/BKTW* AL2 .....21 M2
Oaks La *CROY/NA* CR0 .....173 J5
  GNTH/NBYPK IG2 .....71 L5
Oaks Rd *CROY/NA* CR0 .....173 H7
  PUR/KEN CR8 .....184 B7
  STWL/WRAY TW19 .....130 D2
Oaks Tr *CAR* SM5 .....183 G3
The Oaks *EPSOM* KT18 .....180 E7
  NFNCH/WDSP N12 .....47 H6
  OXHEY WD19 .....42 C3
  RSLP HA4 .....59 K8
  SURB KT6 .....167 J5
  SWLY BR8 .....163 L5
  WFD IG8 .....69 L1
  WOOL/PLUM SE18 .....125 J5
  YEAD UB4 .....95 J1
Oak Tree Av *GRH* DA9 .....147 M4
Oaktree Av *PLMGR* N13 .....48 G4
Oak Tree Cl *ABLGY* WD5 .....20 D5
  STAN HA7 .....62 C1
  WEA W13 .....98 C5
Oak Tree Ct *BORE* WD6 .....44 D1
Oak Tree Dell *CDALE/KGS* NW9 .....63 J6
Oak Tree Dr *TRDG/WHET* N20 .....47 H3
Oak Tree Gdns *BMLY* BR1 .....160 B1
Oaktree Gv *IL* IG1 .....89 K5
Oak Tree Rd *STJWD* NW8 .....3 H8
Oakview Cl *CHESW* EN7 .....26 B1
Oakview Gdns *EFNCH* N2 .....65 K3
Oakview Gv *CROY/NA* CR0 .....173 L3
Oakview Rd *CAT* SE6 .....159 H1
Oak Village *HAMP* NW3 .....84 A3
  HAMP NW3 .....84 A3
  KTTN NW5 .....84 A4
Oak Wy *ACT* W3 .....99 L7
  STHGT/OAK N14 .....48 A2
  CROY/NA CR0 .....173 K1
  EBED/NFELT TW14 .....131 L5
Oakway *HAYES* BR2 .....159 K5
  RYNPK SW20 .....154 C7
Oakway Cl *BXLY* DA5 .....144 E3
Oakways *ELTH/MOT* SE9 .....143 H3
Oakwell Dr *POTB/CUF* EN6 .....24 B6
Oakwood *WLGTN* SM6 .....183 H4
Oakwood Av *BECK* BR3 .....159 J5
  BORE WD6 .....32 B7
  HAYES BR2 .....160 B6
  MTCM CR4 .....155 K5
  PUR/KEN CR8 .....184 B5
  STHGT/OAK N14 .....48 D2
  STHL UB1 .....97 G6
Oakwood Cha *EMPK* RM11 .....74 F8
Oakwood Cl *CHST* BR7 .....160 F2
  DART DA1 .....147 H5
  STHGT/OAK N14 .....48 C1
  WFD IG8 .....52 E8
Oakwood Ct *WKENS* W14 .....118 F1
Oakwood Crs *GFD/PVL* UB6 .....80 A6
  WCHMH N21 .....48 E1
Oakwood Dr *BXLYHN* DA7 .....145 J1
  EDGW HA8 .....45 J8
  NRWD SE19 .....156 M1
Oakwood Gdns *GDMY/SEVK* IG3 .....89 M2
  ORP BR6 .....176 C4
  SUT SM1 .....170 A4
Oakwood Hl *LOU* IG10 .....53 G1
Oakwood La *WKENS* W14 .....118 F1
Oakwood Park Rd
  STHGT/OAK N14 .....48 E1
Oakwood Pl *CROY/NA* CR0 .....172 A1
Oakwood Rd *CROY/NA* CR0 .....172 A1
  GLDGN NW11 .....65 G6
  LCOL/BKTW AL2 .....21 M2
  ORP BR6 .....176 C4
  PIN HA5 .....60 B3
  RYNPK SW20 .....154 A4
Oakworth Rd *NKENS* W10 .....100 C4
Oarsman Pl *E/WMO/HCT* KT8 .....151 L7
Oast House Wy
  STMC/STPC BR5 .....162 B7
Oates Cl *HAYES* BR2 .....159 K6
Oates Rd *CRW* RM5 .....55 H7
Oatfield Rd *ORP* BR6 .....176 F3
Oatland Ri *WALTH* E17 .....68 E3
Oatlands Av *WEY* KT13 .....164 E3
Oatlands Cha *WEY* KT13 .....164 E5
Oatlands Cl *WEY* KT13 .....164 E3
Oatlands Dr *WEY* KT13 .....164 E3
Oatlands Gn *WEY* KT13 .....164 D5
Oatlands Mere *WEY* KT13 .....164 D5
Oatlands Rd *PEND* EN3 .....37 J4
Oat La *CITYW* EC2V 12 E4
Oban Cl *PLSTW* E13 .....106 C4
Oban Rd *PLSTW* E13 .....106 C2
  SNWD SE25 .....157 K7
Oban St *POP/IOD* E14 .....105 K5
Oberon Cl *BORE* WD6 .....32 C4
Oberon Wy *SHPTN* TW17 .....148 K6
Oberstein Rd *BTSEA* SW11 .....137 K1
Oborne Cl *HNHL* SE24 .....139 H2
Observatory Gdns *KENS* W8 .....14 A1
Observatory Rd
  MORT/ESHN SW14 .....135 J1
  WOOL/PLUM SE18 .....125 H6
Occupation La *EA* W5 .....116 D2
  WOOL/PLUM SE18 .....125 H6
Occupation Rd *WALW* SE17 .....18 E7
  WATW WD18 .....29 H8
  WEA W13 .....98 B8
Ocean St *WCHPL* E1 .....104 D4
Ockendon Rd *IS* N1 .....85 K6
  UPMR RM14 .....93 K6
Ockham Dr *STMC/STPC* BR5 .....162 A3
Ockley Rd *CROY/NA* CR0 .....171 M2
  STRHM/NOR SW16 .....138 E7
Octavia Cl *MTCM* CR4 .....155 L8
Octavia Rd *ISLW* TW7 .....115 M8
Octavia St *BTSEA* SW11 .....119 L6
Octavia Wy *STA* TW18 .....148 A2
Octavius St *DEPT* SE8 .....123 G5
Odard Rd *E/WMO/HCT* KT8 .....151 L7
Odessa Rd *FSTGT* E7 .....87 M4
  WLSDN NW10 .....100 A1
Odessa St *BERM/RHTH* SE16 .....122 F1
Odessey Rd *BORE* WD6 .....32 B4
Odger St *BTSEA* SW11 .....119 M7
Offa's Md *HOM* E9 .....86 F4
Offenham Rd *ELTH/MOT* SE9 .....142 F8
Offerton Rd *CLAP* SW4 .....120 C8
Offham Slope
  NFNCH/WDSP N12 .....46 F7
Offley Rd *BRXN/ST* SW9 .....121 C5
Offord Cl *TOTM* N17 .....68 A1
Offord Rd *IS* N1 .....5 M1
Offord St *HOLWY* N7 .....5 L1
Ogilby St *WOOL/PLUM* SE18 .....124 F2
Oglander Rd *PECK* SE15 .....139 M1
Ogle St *GTPST* W1W 10 E2
Oglethorpe Rd *DAGE* RM10 .....91 C3
Ohio Rd *PLSTW* E13 .....105 M3
Oil Mill La *HMSMTH* W6 .....118 A3
Okeburn Rd *TOOT* SW17 .....156 A1
Okehampton Crs *WELL* DA16 .....126 B6
Okehampton Rd *WLSDN* NW10 .....100 F1
Okehampton Sq *HARH* RM3 .....56 C8
Olaf St *NTGHL* W11 .....100 D6
Old Av *WEY* KT13 .....164 D8
Old Bailey *STP* EC4M 12 D5
Old Barn Cl *BELMT* SM2 .....181 L1
Old Barrack Yd *KTBR* SW1X 16 A1
Oldberry Rd *EDGW* HA8 .....45 K8
Old Bethnal Green Rd *BETH* E2 .....104 B2
Old Bexley La *BXLY* DA5 .....145 K6
Old Bond St *CONDST* W1S 10 E7
Old Brewery Ms *HAMP* NW3 .....83 K4
Old Bridge Cl *NTHLT* UB5 .....97 C1
Old Bridge St *KUT* KT1 .....152 D5
Old Broad St *LVPST* EC2M 13 J4
Old Bromley Rd *BMLY* BR1 .....159 K1
Old Brompton Rd *ECT* SW5 .....14 B8
Old Buildings *LINN* WC2A 11 L4
Old Burlington St *CONDST* W1S 10 E6
Old Castle St *WCHPL* E1 .....13 L4
Old Cavendish St
  CAVSQ/HST W1G 10 C4
Old Charlton Rd *SHPTN* TW17 .....149 J8
Old Chestnut Av
  ESH/CLAY KT10 .....166 A8
Old Church La *CDALE/KGS* NW9 .....81 K2
  GFD/PVL UB6 .....98 A2
  STAN HA7 .....44 B8
Old Church Pth
  ESH/CLAY KT10 .....166 B6
Old Church Rd *CHING* E4 .....51 K3
  ROMW/RG RM7 .....73 L8
Oldchurch Rd *ROMW/RG* RM7 .....73 L7
Old Church St *CHEL* SW3 .....15 H9
Old Claygate La *ESH/CLAY* KT10 .....167 G8
Old Compton St
  SOHO/SHAV W1D 11 G6
Old Cote Dr *HEST* TW5 .....115 G4
Old Court Rd *KENS* W8 .....14 C1
The Old Ctyd *BMLY* BR1 .....160 B4
Old Deer Park Gdns
  RCH/KEW TW9 .....116 E8
Old Devonshire Rd *BAL* SW12 .....138 B4
Old Dock Cl *RCH/KEW* TW9 .....117 G4
Old Dover Rd *BKHTH/KID* SE3 .....124 A5
Olden La *PUR/KEN* CR8 .....184 A5
Old Esher Cl *WOT/HER* KT12 .....165 K7
Old Esher Rd *WOT/HER* KT12 .....165 K7
Old Farleigh Rd *SAND/SEL* CR2 .....185 J3
  WARL CR6 .....185 M8
Old Farm Av *BFN/LL* DA15 .....143 K5
  STHGT/OAK N14 .....48 C2
Old Farm Cl *HSLWW* TW4 .....132 F1
Old Farm Gdns *SWLY* BR8 .....163 M6
Old Farmhouse Dr
  LHD/OX KT22 .....178 D8
Old Farm Rd *EFNCH* N2 .....65 K2
  HPTN TW12 .....150 F2
  WDR/YW UB7 .....94 D8
Old Farm Rd East *BFN/LL* DA15 .....144 A6
Old Farm Rd West
  BFN/LL DA15 .....143 M6
Oldfield Cl *BMLY* BR1 .....160 F7
  NTHLT UB5 .....79 L5
  STAN HA7 .....44 A7
Oldfield Farm Gdns
  GFD/PVL UB6 .....79 K8
Oldfield Gv *DEPT* SE8 .....122 D2
Oldfield La *GFD/PVL* UB6 .....79 K7
Oldfield La North *GFD/PVL* UB6 .....79 K6
Oldfield La South *GFD/PVL* UB6 .....97 J2
Oldfield Ms *HGT* N6 .....66 C8
Oldfield Rd *BMLY* BR1 .....160 F7
  BXLYHN DA7 .....126 E7
  HPTN TW12 .....151 G4
  SHB W12 .....99 M8
  STNW/STAM N16 .....85 L3
  WIM/MER SW19 .....154 E2
  WLSDN NW10 .....81 M7
Oldfields Circ *NTHLT* UB5 .....79 J6
Oldfields Rd *CHEAM* SM3 .....170 A4
Old Fish Street HI *BLKFR* EC4V 12 E6
Old Fleet La *STP* EC4M 12 C4
Old Fold Cl *BAR* EN5 .....33 M4
Old Fold La *BAR* EN5 .....33 M4
Old Fold Vw *BAR* EN5 .....33 J6
Old Ford Rd *BETH* E2 .....104 C1
  BOW E3 .....86 F8
Old Forge Cl *STAN* HA7 .....44 A6
Old Forge Crs *SHPTN* TW17 .....164 B3
Old Forge Rd *EN* EN1 .....36 F3
Old Forge Wy *SCUP* DA14 .....144 B8
Old Gannon Cl *NTHWD* HA6 .....41 J8
Old Gloucester St *BMSBY* WC1N 11 L1
Old Hall Cl *PIN* HA5 .....60 E2
Old Hall Dr *PIN* HA5 .....60 E2
Oldham Ter *ACT* W3 .....99 J7
Old Hl *CHST* BR7 .....161 G4
  ORP BR6 .....176 E6
Oldhill St *STNW/STAM* N16 .....86 A1
Old Homesdale Rd
  HAYES BR2 .....160 C7
Old Hospital Cl *TOOT* SW17 .....137 M5
Old House Cl *EW* KT17 .....180 F3
  WIM/MER SW19 .....154 E1
Old House La *KGLGY* WD4 .....20 A8
Old Howlett's La *RSLP* HA4 .....59 K7
Old Jamaica Rd *STHWK* SE16 .....122 A1
Old Kent Rd *PECK* SE15 .....122 B4
Old Kenton La *CDALE/KGS* NW9 .....62 F4
Old Kingston Rd *WPK* KT4 .....168 C5
Old Lodge La *PUR/KEN* CR8 .....183 M6
Old Lodge Wy *STAN* HA7 .....44 A7
Old Maidstone Rd *SCUP* DA14 .....162 F3
Old Malden La *WPK* KT4 .....168 B4
Old Manor Dr *ISLW* TW7 .....133 J3
Old Manor Wy *BXLYHN* DA7 .....127 K7
  CHST BR7 .....161 G4
Old Marylebone Rd *CAMTN* NW1 .....9 K3
Old Mill Ct *SWFD* E18 .....70 C4
Old Mill La *UX/CGN* UB8 .....94 B4
Old Mill Rd *DEN/HRF* UB9 .....76 A3
  KGLGY WD4 .....20 C7
  WOOL/PLUM SE18 .....125 K7
Old Montague St *WCHPL* E1 .....104 A4
Old Nichol St *BETH* E2 .....7 L9
Old North St *FSBYW* WC1X 11 L2
Old Nursery Pl *ASHF* TW15 .....149 H1
Old Oak Common La *ACT* W3 .....99 L5
  ACT W3 .....99 M6
  WLSDN NW10 .....99 L3
Old Oak La *WLSDN* NW10 .....99 M2
Old Oak Rd *ACT* W3 .....99 M6
Old Oaks *WAB* EN9 .....27 L5
Old Orch *SUN* TW16 .....150 C5
Old Orchard Cl *UX/CGN* UB8 .....95 G5
The Old Orch *HAMP* NW3 .....83 M4
Old Palace Rd *CROY/NA* CR0 .....172 C5
  WEY KT13 .....164 B5
Old Palace Yd *RCH/KEW* TW9 .....134 C2
Old Paradise St *LBTH* SE11 .....17 L5
Old Park Av *BAL* SW12 .....138 A3
  ENC/FH EN2 .....36 C7
Old Park Gv *WCHMH* N21 .....36 C7
Old Park La *MYFR/PICC* W1J 10 B9
Old Park Ms *HEST* TW5 .....114 F5
Oldpark Ride *CHESW* EN7 .....25 K5
Old Park Rd *ABYW* SE2 .....126 A3
  ENC/FH EN2 .....36 B6
  PLMGR N13 .....48 F6
Old Park Rd South *ENC/FH* EN2 .....36 B7
Old Park Vw *ENC/FH* EN2 .....36 A6
Old Perry St *CHST* BR7 .....161 L3
Old Pound Cl *ISLW* TW7 .....116 A6
Old Priory *DEN/HRF* UB9 .....59 H8
Old Pye St *WEST* SW1P 17 G3
Old Quebec St *MBLAR* W1H 9 M5
Old Queen St *STJSPK* SW1H 17 H2
Old Rectory Gdns *EDGW* HA8 .....45 G8
Old Redding *KTN/HRWW/W* HA3 .....43 H7
Old Rd *DART* DA1 .....145 K1
  LEW SE13 .....141 L1
  PEND EN3 .....37 J4
Old Royal Free Sq *IS* N1 .....6 B4
Old Ruislip Rd *NTHLT* UB5 .....96 D1
Old's Ap *WATW* WD18 .....41 J3
Old School Cl *BECK* BR3 .....158 D5
Old School Crs *FSTGT* E7 .....88 A6
Old School Ms *WEY* KT13 .....164 D6
Old Schools La *EW* KT17 .....180 F2
Old's Cl *WATW* WD18 .....41 H3
Old Seacoal La *STP* EC4M 12 C5
Old South Cl *PIN* HA5 .....60 D2
Old Sq *LINN* WC2A 11 M4
Old Station Rd
  HYS/HAR UB3 .....113 M1
  LOU IG10 .....39 L8
Oldstead Rd *BMLY* BR1 .....141 K8
Old St *FSBYE* EC1V 6 E9
  IS N1 .....7 K8
  PLSTW E13 .....106 C1
Old Swan Yd *CAR* SM5 .....170 F6
Old Town *CLAP* SW4 .....120 C8
  CROY/NA CR0 .....172 B5
Old Tramyard
  WOOL/PLUM SE18 .....125 L2
Old Watford Rd *LCOL/BKTW* AL2 .....21 L3
Old Woolwich Rd
  GNWCH SE10 .....123 K4
Old York Rd
  WAND/EARL SW18 .....137 H2
Oleander Cl *ORP* BR6 .....176 D7
Olga St *BOW* E3 .....104 E1
Olinda Rd *STNW/STAM* N16 .....67 M7
Oliphant St *NKENS* W10 .....100 E2
Oliver Av *SNWD* SE25 .....157 M6
Oliver Cl *CHSWK* W4 .....117 H4
  WTHK RM20 .....129 M5
Oliver Gdns *EHAM* E6 .....107 J4
Oliver Gv *SNWD* SE25 .....157 M7
Olive Rd *CRICK* NW2 .....82 C4
  DART DA1 .....146 D5
  EA W5 .....116 D1
  PLSTW E13 .....106 C2
  WIM/MER SW19 .....155 J3
Oliver Rd *LEY* E10 .....87 H2
  NWMAL KT3 .....153 J5
  RAIN RM13 .....91 M8
  SUT SM1 .....170 D6
  SWLY BR8 .....163 K6
  WALTH E17 .....69 J6
  WTHK RM20 .....129 M6
Oliver's Yd *STLK* EC1Y 7 H9
Olive St *ROMW/RG* RM7 .....73 K6
Olivia Gdns *DEN/HRF* UB9 .....58 C2
Ollard's Gv *LOU* IG10 .....39 K7
Ollerton Gn *BOW* E3 .....86 F8
Ollerton Rd *FBAR/BDGN* N11 .....48 D7
Olley Cl *WLGTN* SM6 .....183 L1
Ollgar Cl *ACT* W3 .....99 M7
Olliffe St *POP/IOD* E14 .....123 J1
Olmar St *STHWK* SE1 .....122 A4
Olney Rd *WALW* SE17 .....121 H4
Olron Crs *BXLYHS* DA6 .....144 D2
Olven Rd *WOOL/PLUM* SE18 .....125 J5
Olveston Wk *MRDN* SM4 .....170 D1
Olwen Ms *PIN* HA5 .....60 D3
Olyffe Av *WELL* DA16 .....126 A7
Olyffe Dr *BECK* BR3 .....159 J4
Olympia Wy *WKENS* W14 .....118 E1
Olympic Wy *GFD/PVL* UB6 .....79 H8
  WBLY HA9 .....81 G4
Oman Av *CRICK* NW2 .....82 B2
O'meara St *STHWK* SE1 .....12 F9
Omega Pl *IS* N1 .....5 K6
Omega St *DEPT* SE8 .....123 G6
Ommaney Rd *NWCR* SE14 .....122 D6
Omnibus Wy *WALTH* E17 .....69 J3
Ondine Rd *EDUL* SE22 .....139 M1
Onega Ga *BERM/RHTH* SE16 .....122 F1
One Tree Cl *FSTH* SE23 .....140 C3
Ongar Cl *CHDH* RM6 .....73 J2
Ongar Rd *FUL/PGN* SW6 .....14 B9
  RAIN RM13 .....91 L8
Onra Rd *LEY* E10 .....69 G8
Onslow Av *BELMT* SM2 .....181 M3
  RCHPK/HAM TW10 .....134 E2
Onslow Cl *CHING* E4 .....51 K4
Onslow Crs *CHST* BR7 .....161 H4
Onslow Dr *SCUP* DA14 .....144 D7

Onslow Gdns *MUSWH* N10 ...... 66 B6
 SAND/SEL CR2 ...... 185 G5
 SKENS SW7 ...... 15 G7
 SWFD E18 ...... 70 B4
 THDIT KT7 ...... 166 E3 [8]
 WCHMH N21 ...... 36 A8
 WLGTN SM6 ...... 183 J1
Onslow Ms East *SKENS* SW7 ...... 15 G6
Onslow Ms West *SKENS* SW7 ...... 15 G6
Onslow Rd *CROY/NA* CR0 ...... 172 A2
 NWMAL KT3 ...... 154 A7
 RCHPK/HAM TW10 ...... 134 E3
 WOT/HER KT12 ...... 165 G6
Onslow Sq *SKENS* SW7 ...... 15 H6
Onslow Wy *HCIRC* EC1N ...... 12 B1 [8]
Ontario St *STHWK* SE1 ...... 18 D4
Ontario Wy *POP/IOD* E14 ...... 105 G6
On the Hl *OXHEY* WD19 ...... 42 E4
Opal Cl *CAN/RD* E16 ...... 106 D5 [9]
Opal St *LBTH* SE11 ...... 18 C7
Openshaw Rd *ABYW* SE2 ...... 126 B3
Openview *WAND/EARL* SW18 ...... 137 J5
Ophir Ter *PECK* SE15 ...... 122 A6
Opossum Wy *HSLWW* TW4 ...... 114 C8
Oppenheim Rd *LEW* SE13 ...... 123 J7 [1]
Oppidans Rd *HAMP* NW3 ...... 3 L2
Orange Gv *CHIG* IG7 ...... 53 J8
 WAN E11 ...... 87 L3 [8]
Orange Hill Rd *EDGW* HA8 ...... 63 J7
Orange Pl *BERM/RHTH* SE16 ...... 122 C1 [8]
Orangery La *ELTH/MOT* SE9 ...... 142 F2
The Orangery
 RCHPK/HAM TW10 ...... 134 C6
Orange St *LSQ/SEVD* WC2H ...... 11 H7 [8]
Orange Tree Hl *ROM* RM1 ...... 55 K7
Oratory La *CHEL* SW3 ...... 15 H7 [8]
Orbain Rd *FUL/PGN* SW6 ...... 118 E5
Orbel St *BTSEA* SW11 ...... 119 L6
Orbital Crs *GSTN* WD25 ...... 20 F8
Orb St *WALW* SE17 ...... 19 G6
Orchard *BUSH* WD23 ...... 43 K3
Orchard Av *ASHF* TW15 ...... 149 J2
 BELV DA17 ...... 126 E4
 CROY/NA CR0 ...... 173 L4
 DART DA1 ...... 146 B4
 EBED/NFELT TW14 ...... 131 K2
 FNCH N3 ...... 65 G4
 GSTN WD25 ...... 21 H4
 HEST TW5 ...... 114 E5
 MTCM CR4 ...... 171 C3
 NWMAL KT3 ...... 153 L5
 RAIN RM13 ...... 110 C3
 STHGT/OAK N14 ...... 48 C1
 STHL UB1 ...... 96 E7
 THDIT KT7 ...... 167 G3
 TRDG/WHET N20 ...... 47 K4
Orchard Cl *ALP/SUD* HA0 ...... 80 E8
 ASHF TW15 ...... 149 J2
 BNSTD SM7 ...... 182 B7 [3]
 BORE WD6 ...... 31 M6 [8]
 BXLYHN DA7 ...... 126 E6
 CHING E4 ...... 51 G6
 CRICK NW2 ...... 82 A3
 DEN/HRF UB9 ...... 76 B6
 EDGW HA8 ...... 44 E8
 FSTH SE23 ...... 140 C3 [8]
 HOR/WEW KT19 ...... 168 B3 [8]
 NKENS W10 ...... 100 E4
 POTB/CUF EN6 ...... 24 E1
 RAD WD7 ...... 30 E2
 RSLP HA4 ...... 59 J8
 RYNPK SW20 ...... 154 C7
 WAT WD17 ...... 28 F5
 WOT/HER KT12 ...... 165 H2
Orchard Crs *EDGW* HA8 ...... 45 J7
 EN EN1 ...... 36 F4
Orchard Dr *BKHTH/KID* SE3 ...... 123 L7
 EDGW HA8 ...... 44 F7
 SHPTN TW17 ...... 149 L6
 UX/CGN UB8 ...... 94 D3
 WAT WD17 ...... 28 F4
Orchard End *WEY* KT13 ...... 164 E4
Orchard Gdns *CHSGTN* KT9 ...... 167 L3
 EPSOM KT18 ...... 180 C8 [8]
 WAB EN9 ...... 27 H7
Orchard Ga *CDALE/KGS* NW9 ...... 63 L5 [8]
 ESH/CLAY KT10 ...... 166 D3 [3]
 GFD/PVL UB6 ...... 80 B6
Orchard Gn *ORP* BR6 ...... 176 E4
Orchard Gv *CROY/NA* CR0 ...... 173 L2
 EDGW HA8 ...... 63 G2
 KTN/HRWW/W HA3 ...... 62 F6 [8]
 ORP BR6 ...... 176 F4
 PGE/AN SE20 ...... 158 A4
Orchard Hl *DART* DA1 ...... 145 L2
 LEW SE13 ...... 123 H6 [9]
 LEW SE13 ...... 123 H7 [9]
Orchard La *E/WMO/HCT* KT8 ...... 166 D1
 RYNPK SW20 ...... 154 B4
 WFD IG8 ...... 52 C6
Orchardleigh Av *PEND* EN3 ...... 37 J5
Orchardmede *WCHMH* N21 ...... 49 K1
Orchard Pl *POP/IOD* E14 ...... 105 L6
 TOTM N17 ...... 67 M1
Orchard Ri *CROY/NA* CR0 ...... 173 L3
 KUTN/CMB KT2 ...... 153 J4
 RCHPK/HAM TW10 ...... 135 H1
 RSLP HA4 ...... 59 M4
Orchard Ri East *BFN/LL* DA15 ...... 143 L2
Orchard Ri West *BFN/LL* DA15 ...... 143 L2
Orchard Rd *BAR* EN5 ...... 33 J7
 BELV DA17 ...... 127 G2
 BMLY BR1 ...... 160 C4
 BTFD TW8 ...... 116 C4
 CHSGTN KT9 ...... 167 L6
 DAGE RM10 ...... 91 G8
 HGT N6 ...... 66 B8
 HPTN TW12 ...... 150 F3
 HSLWW TW4 ...... 132 F2
 HYS/HAR UB3 ...... 96 A6
 KUT KT1 ...... 152 E5
 ORP BR6 ...... 176 B7
 PEND EN3 ...... 37 J8
 RCH/KEW TW9 ...... 117 J6
 ROMW/RG RM7 ...... 73 H3
 SAND/SEL CR2 ...... 185 H1 [7]
 SCUP DA14 ...... 143 L8

 SUN TW16 ...... 150 A3
 SUT SM1 ...... 170 A7
 TWK TW1 ...... 134 A2
 WELL DA16 ...... 126 B8
Orchardson St *STJWD* NW8 ...... 9 G1
Orchard St *DART* DA1 ...... 146 E3
 MBLAR W1H 10 A5
 THDIT KT7 ...... 167 H3
 WALTH E17 ...... 68 E5 [6]
The Orchard *BKHTH/KID* SE3 ...... 123 K7
 CHSWK W4 ...... 117 K2
 EW KT17 ...... 180 F1
 GLDGN NW11 ...... 65 G6
 KGLGY WD4 ...... 20 A2
 SWLY BR8 ...... 163 K5 [9]
 WCHMH N21 ...... 49 K1
Orchard Wy *ASHF* TW15 ...... 130 F6
 CHIG IG7 ...... 54 A5
 CROY/NA CR0 ...... 173 L2
 EN EN1 ...... 36 E6 [9]
 ESH/CLAY KT10 ...... 166 C8
 POTB/CUF EN6 ...... 23 H3
 RDART DA2 ...... 146 D7
 RKW/CH/CXG WD3 ...... 40 A2
 SUT SM1 ...... 170 D6
Orchard Waye *UX/CGN* UB8 ...... 94 D1
Orchid Cl *STHL* UB1 ...... 96 E5
Orchid Rd *STHGT/OAK* N14 ...... 48 C2
Orchid St *SHB* W12 ...... 100 A6
Orchis Wy *HARH* RM3 ...... 56 F8
Orde Hall St *BMSBY* WC1N ...... 11 L2 [8]
Ordell Rd *BOW* E3 ...... 104 F1
Ordnance Cl *FELT* TW13 ...... 132 A6 [8]
Ordnance Crs *GNWCH* SE10 ...... 105 L3
Ordnance Hl *STJWD* NW8 ...... 3 H4
Ordnance Ms *STJWD* NW8 ...... 3 H5 [1]
Ordnance Rd *CAN/RD* E16 ...... 105 M4
 PEND EN3 ...... 37 K2
 WOOL/PLUM SE18 ...... 125 G4
Oregano Cl *WDR/YW* UB7 ...... 94 F6 [1]
Oregon Av *MNPK* E12 ...... 88 F2 [3]
Oregon Cl *NWMAL* KT3 ...... 153 J7 [2]
Oregon Sq *ORP* BR6 ...... 176 D3
Oreston Rd *RAIN* RM13 ...... 110 D2
Orford Gdns *TWK* TW1 ...... 133 M6
Orford Rd *CAT* SE6 ...... 141 H7
 SWFD E18 ...... 70 B4
 WALTH E17 ...... 69 G6
Organ Hall Rd *BORE* WD6 ...... 31 L4
Oriel Cl *MTCM* CR4 ...... 156 D7
Oriel Ct *HAMP* NW3 ...... 83 J4 [9]
Oriel Dr *BARN* SW13 ...... 118 C4
Oriel Gdns *CLAY* IG5 ...... 70 F4
Oriel Rd *HOM* E9 ...... 86 D6
Oriel Wy *NTHLT* UB5 ...... 79 H7
Oriental Rd *CAN/RD* E16 ...... 106 D7
Orient St *LBTH* SE11 ...... 18 E5
Orient Wy *CLPT* E5 ...... 86 D3 [8]
Oriole Cl *ABLGY* WD5 ...... 21 G4 [8]
Oriole Wy *THMD* SE28 ...... 108 B6
Orion Rd *MUSWH* N10 ...... 48 A8
Orion Wy *NTHWD* HA6 ...... 41 M6
Orissa Rd *WOOL/PLUM* SE18 ...... 125 L3
Orkney St *BTSEA* SW11 ...... 120 A7
Orlando Gdns
 HOR/WEW KT19 ...... 180 D3 [3]
Orlando Rd *CLAP* SW4 ...... 120 A5
Orleans Rd *NRWD* SE19 ...... 157 K2
 TWK TW1 ...... 134 B4
Orlestone Gdns *ORP* BR6 ...... 177 L7 [1]
Orleston Rd *HOLWY* N7 ...... 85 C6
Orley Farm Rd *HRW* HA1 ...... 79 L3
Ormanton Rd *SYD* SE26 ...... 140 A8
Orme Cl *BAY/PAD* W2 ...... 8 C7
Orme Court Ms *BAY/PAD* W2 ...... 8 D7 [1]
Orme La *BAY/PAD* W2 ...... 8 C7
Ormeley Rd *BAL* SW12 ...... 138 B4
Orme Rd *KUT* KT1 ...... 153 H5
Ormerod Gdns *MTCM* CR4 ...... 156 A5
Ormesby Cl *THMD* SE28 ...... 108 D6 [1]
Ormesby Dr *POTB/CUF* EN6 ...... 22 D5
Ormesby Wy *KTN/HRWW/W* HA3... 62 F7
Ormiston Gv *SHB* W12 ...... 100 B7
Ormiston Rd *GNWCH* SE10 ...... 124 A3
Ormond Av *HPTN* TW12 ...... 151 H4
 ORP BR6 ...... 176 C4
Ormond Cl *BMSBY* WC1N 11 K2
Ormond Crs *HPTN* TW12 ...... 151 J4
Ormond Dr *HPTN* TW12 ...... 151 H3
Ormonde Av *HOR/WEW* KT19 ...... 180 D2
 ORP BR6 ...... 176 F4
Ormonde Ga *CHEL* SW3 ...... 15 L8
Ormonde Pl *BGVA* SW1W ...... 16 B6 [9]
Ormonde Ri *BKHH* IG9 ...... 52 C3
Ormonde Rd
 MORT/ESHN SW14 ...... 117 H8
 NTHWD HA6 ...... 41 K6
Ormonde Ter *STJWD* NW8 ...... 3 L4
Ormond Rd *ARCH* N19 ...... 84 E1
 RCHPK/HAM TW10 ...... 134 D2
Ormond Yd *STJS* SW1Y 10 F8
Ormsby Gdns *GFD/PVL* UB6 ...... 97 J1
Ormsby Pl *STNW/STAM* N16 ...... 85 M3
Ormsby St *BETH* E2 ...... 7 L5
Ormside St *PECK* SE15 ...... 122 C4
Ormskirk Rd *OXHEY* WD19 ...... 42 D6
Ornan Rd *HAMP* NW3 ...... 83 L5
Orphanage Rd *WAT* WD17 ...... 29 J5 [3]
Orpheus St *CMBW* SE5 ...... 121 K6 [9]
Orpington Gdns *UED* N18 ...... 49 L5
Orpington Rd *CHST* BR7 ...... 161 L6
 WCHMH N21 ...... 49 H2 [8]
Orpwood Cl *HPTN* TW12 ...... 150 F2 [8]
Orsett Ms *BAY/PAD* W2 ...... 8 E4
Orsett St *LBTH* SE11 ...... 17 M7
Orsett Ter *BAY/PAD* W2 ...... 8 D4
 WFD IG8 ...... 70 C1 [8]
Orsman Rd *IS* N1 ...... 7 J4
Orton Cl *WAP* E1W ...... 104 F3 [1]
Orville Rd *BTSEA* SW11 ...... 119 K2 [8]
Orwell Cl *HYS/HAR* UB3 ...... 95 L6
 RAIN RM13 ...... 109 M6 [3]
Orwell Ct *WATW* WD18 ...... 29 K5 [3]
Orwell Rd *PLSTW* E13 ...... 106 C1
Osbaldeston Rd
 STNW/STAM N16 ...... 86 A2
Osberton Rd *LEE/GVPK* SE12 ...... 142 A2
Osbert St *WEST* SW1P 17 G6
Osborn Cl *HACK* E8 ...... 86 A8 [8]
Osborne Av *STWL/WRAY* TW19... 130 E5

Osborne Cl *BECK* BR3 ...... 158 E7
 EBAR EN4 ...... 34 F6 [1]
 EMPK RM11 ...... 74 B7 [2]
 FELT TW13 ...... 150 D1
Osborne Gdns *MLHL* NW7 ...... 64 D1
 POTB/CUF EN6 ...... 23 H3 [8]
 THHTH CR7 ...... 157 J5 [9]
Osborne Gv *WALTH* E17 ...... 68 E7 [8]
Osborne Rd *ACT* W3 ...... 99 H8
 BELV DA17 ...... 126 F3
 BKHH IG9 ...... 52 B3
 CRICK NW2 ...... 82 B6
 EMPK RM11 ...... 74 B7
 FSBYPK N4 ...... 85 G1
 FSTGT E7 ...... 88 B5
 GFD/PVL UB6 ...... 97 J5
 HOM E9 ...... 86 F6
 HSLWW TW4 ...... 114 F8
 KUTN/CMB KT2 ...... 152 E3
 LEY E10 ...... 87 H3
 PEND EN3 ...... 37 L5
 PLMGR N13 ...... 49 G5
 POTB/CUF EN6 ...... 23 H3
 THHTH CR7 ...... 157 J5
 WALTH E17 ...... 68 E7
 WAT WD24 ...... 29 J3 [8]
 WOT/HER KT12 ...... 165 G3 [7]
Osborne Sq *DAGW* RM9 ...... 90 F4
Osborn La *FSTH* SE23 ...... 140 F4
Osborn Rd *UX/CGN* UB8 ...... 76 C7
Osborn St *WCHPL* E1 ...... 13 M3
Osborn Ter *BKHTH/KID* SE3 ...... 141 M1 [8]
Osbourne Rd *RDART* DA2 ...... 147 H3
Oscar St *DEPT* SE8 ...... 123 G6
Oseney Crs *KTTN* NW5 ...... 84 C6
Osgood Av *ORP* BR6 ...... 176 F7
Osgood Gdns *ORP* BR6 ...... 176 F7
O'shea Gv *BOW* E3 ...... 86 F8 [3]
Osidge La *STHGT/OAK* N14 ...... 48 A3
Osiers Rd *WAND/EARL* SW18 ...... 137 G1
Osier St *WCHPL* E1 ...... 104 C3
Osier Wy *BNSTD* SM7 ...... 181 L7
 LEY E10 ...... 87 H3
Oslac Rd *CAT* SE6 ...... 159 H1
Osman Rd *ED* N9 ...... 50 A5
 HMSMTH W6 ...... 118 C1 [1]
Osmond Cl *RYLN/HDSTN* HA2 ... 79 J2 [3]
Osmond Gdns *WLGTN* SM6 ...... 171 J7
Osmund St *SHB* W12 ...... 99 M4 [1]
Osnaburgh St *CAMTN* NW1 ...... 10 D1
 GTPST W1W ...... 10 D1 [3]
Osnaburgh Ter *CAMTN* NW1 ...... 4 D9 [3]
Osney Wk *MRDN* SM4 ...... 170 D1
Osprey Cl *EHAM* E6 ...... 106 E4 [3]
 SWFD E18 ...... 70 A5
 WALTH E17 ...... 68 C2 [3]
 WDR/YW UB7 ...... 94 D8
Osprey Gdns *SAND/SEL* CR2 ...... 185 K3
Osprey Ms *PEND* EN3 ...... 37 J5
Ospringe Cl *PGE/AN* SE20 ...... 158 C3 [3]
Ospringe Rd *KTTN* NW5 ...... 84 C4
Ossian Rd *FSBYPK* N4 ...... 66 F8
Ossington Buildings
 MHST W1U ...... 10 A2 [3]
Ossington Cl *BAY/PAD* W2 ...... 8 B7 [1]
Ossington St *BAY/PAD* W2 ...... 8 B6
Ossory Rd *STHWK* SE1 ...... 122 A4
Ossulston St *CAMTN* NW1 ...... 5 H6
Ossulton Wy *EFNCH* N2 ...... 65 J5
Ostade Rd *BRXS/STRHM* SW2 ... 138 F4
Osten Ms *SKENS* SW7 ...... 14 D4
Osterberg Rd *DART* DA1 ...... 146 F1
Osterley Av *ISLW* TW7 ...... 115 K5
Osterley Crs *ISLW* TW7 ...... 115 L6
Osterley Gdns *THHTH* CR7 ...... 157 J5
Osterley La *ISLW* TW7 ...... 115 J2
 NWDGN UB2 ...... 115 H3
Osterley Park Rd
 NWDGN UB2 ...... 114 F1 [3]
Osterley Park View Rd
 HNWL W7 ...... 97 L8
Osterley Rd *ISLW* TW7 ...... 115 L5
 STNW/STAM N16 ...... 85 L4
Ostliffe Rd *PLMGR* N13 ...... 49 H7
Oswald Rd *STHL* UB1 ...... 96 E7
Oswald's Md *CLPT* E5 ...... 86 E4
Oswald St *CLPT* E5 ...... 86 D3
Osward Pl *ED* N9 ...... 50 A4
Osward Rd *BAL* SW12 ...... 137 M6
Oswin St *LBTH* SE11 ...... 18 D5
Oswyth Rd *CMBW* SE5 ...... 121 L7
Otford Cl *BMLY* BR1 ...... 161 G6
 BXLY DA5 ...... 145 H3
 PGE/AN SE20 ...... 158 C4
Otford Crs *BROCKY* SE4 ...... 140 F3
Othello Cl *LBTH* SE11 ...... 18 C7
Otis St *BOW* E3 ...... 105 J2
Otley Dr *GNTH/NBYPK* IG2 ...... 71 H7
Otley Rd *CAN/RD* E16 ...... 106 C5
Otley Ter *CLPT* E5 ...... 86 C2
Otley Wy *OXHEY* WD19 ...... 42 C5
Otlinge Rd *STMC/STPC* BR5 ...... 162 D7 [3]
Ottawa Gdns *DAGE* RM10 ...... 91 K7 [3]
Ottaway St *CLPT* E5 ...... 86 A3 [3]
Otterbourne Rd *CHING* E4 ...... 51 K5 [3]
 CROY/NA CR0 ...... 172 C4 [8]
Otterburn Gdns *ISLW* TW7 ...... 116 A6
Otterburn St *TOOT* SW17 ...... 155 M2 [9]
Otterden Cl *ORP* BR6 ...... 176 E6 [2]
Otterden St *CAT* SE6 ...... 141 G8
Otterfield Rd *WDR/YW* UB7 ...... 94 E6
Otter Rd *GFD/PVL* UB6 ...... 97 J3
Otters Cl *STMC/STPC* BR5 ...... 162 D7 [3]
Otterspool La *GSTN* WD25 ...... 29 M4
Otterspool Wy *GSTN* WD25 ...... 29 M4 [3]
Ottoman Ter *WAT* WD17 ...... 29 J6 [9]
Otto St *WALW* SE17 ...... 121 H4
Otways Cl *POTB/CUF* EN6 ...... 23 H6 [1]
Oulton Crs *BARK* IG11 ...... 89 M6
 POTB/CUF EN6 ...... 22 D5
Oulton Rd *SEVS/STOTM* N15 ...... 67 K6
Oulton Wy *OXHEY* WD19 ...... 42 F6
Oundle Av *BUSH* WD23 ...... 43 J1
Ousden Cl *CHES/WCR* EN8 ...... 26 E3
Ousden Dr *CHES/WCR* EN8 ...... 26 E3
Ouseley Rd *BAL* SW12 ...... 137 M5
Outer Cir *CAMTN* NW1 ...... 3 L9
Outgate Rd *WLSDN* NW10 ...... 81 M7 [1]

Outram Pl *WEY* KT13 ...... 164 C7 [8]
Outram Rd *CROY/NA* CR0 ...... 172 F4
 EHAM E6 ...... 88 E8
 WDGN N22 ...... 66 D2
Outwich St *HDTCH* EC3A ...... 13 K4 [3]
Oval Pl *VX/NE* SW8 ...... 120 F5
Oval Rd *CAMTN* NW1 ...... 4 C3
 CROY/NA CR0 ...... 172 D4
Oval Rd North *DAGE* RM10 ...... 91 H8
Oval Rd South *DAGE* RM10 ...... 109 H1
The Oval *BETH* E2 ...... 104 B1
 BFN/LL DA15 ...... 144 A4
 BNSTD SM7 ...... 182 A7
Oval Wy *LBTH* SE11 ...... 17 M8
Overbrae *BECK* BR3 ...... 159 G2
Overbrook Wk *EDGW* HA8 ...... 63 G1
Overbury Av *BECK* BR3 ...... 159 H6
Overbury Crs *CROY/NA* CR0 ...... 186 C3
Overbury Rd *FSBYPK* N4 ...... 67 K7
Overbury St *CLPT* E5 ...... 86 D4
Overcliff Rd *LEW* SE13 ...... 123 G8
Overcourt Cl *BFN/LL* DA15 ...... 144 B5
Overdale Av *NWMAL* KT3 ...... 153 J5
Overdale Rd *EA* W5 ...... 116 C1
Overdown Rd *CAT* SE6 ...... 141 G8
 PUR/KEN CR8 ...... 184 A2
Overhill Wy *BECK* BR3 ...... 159 K8
Overlea Rd *CLPT* E5 ...... 68 A8
Overmead *ELTH/MOT* SE9 ...... 143 K4
 SWLY BR8 ...... 163 L8 [3]
Overstand Cl *BECK* BR3 ...... 159 G8
Overstone Gdns *CROY/NA* CR0 ... 173 M2
Overstone Rd *HMSMTH* W6 ...... 118 C2
Overton Cl *ISLW* TW7 ...... 115 M6 [3]
 WLSDN NW10 ...... 81 J6 [3]
Overton Dr *CHDH* RM6 ...... 72 C8
 WAN E11 ...... 70 B8
Overton Rd *ABYW* SE2 ...... 126 C4
 BELMT SM2 ...... 170 A8
 BRXN/ST SW9 ...... 121 G7
 LEY E10 ...... 86 E1
 STHGT/OAK N14 ...... 35 L8
Overton's Yd *CROY/NA* CR0 ...... 172 C5
Overy St *DART* DA1 ...... 146 F3
Ovesdon Av *RYLN/HDSTN* HA2 ... 78 F1
Ovett Cl *NRWD* SE19 ...... 157 L2
Ovex Cl *POP/IOD* E14 ...... 123 J1
Ovington Gdns *CHEL* SW3 ...... 15 K4
Ovington Ms *CHEL* SW3 ...... 15 K4
Ovington Sq *CHEL* SW3 ...... 15 K4
Ovington St *CHEL* SW3 ...... 15 K4
Owen Cl *CROY/NA* CR0 ...... 172 D1
 CRW RM5 ...... 55 H8 [8]
 THMD SE28 ...... 108 C7
 YEAD UB4 ...... 96 B2 [8]
Owen Gdns *WFD* IG8 ...... 52 E8
Owenite St *ABYW* SE2 ...... 126 B2 [8]
Owen Rd *PLMGR* N13 ...... 49 J7
 YEAD UB4 ...... 96 B2
Owen's Ct *FSBYE* EC1V 6 C7
Owen's Rw *FSBYE* EC1V 6 C7
Owen St *FSBYE* EC1V ...... 6 C6 [8]
Owens Wy *FSTH* SE23 ...... 140 E4
 RKW/CH/CXG WD3 ...... 28 A8
Owen Wy *WLSDN* NW10 ...... 81 J6
Owgan Cl *CMBW* SE5 ...... 121 K5 [3]
Owl Cl *SAND/SEL* CR2 ...... 185 K3 [1]
Owlets Hall Cl *HARH* RM3 ...... 74 F1 [1]
Ownstead Gdns *SAND/SEL* CR2 ... 184 F4
Ownsted Hl *CROY/NA* CR0 ...... 186 C3
Oxberry Av *FUL/PGN* SW6 ...... 118 F7
Oxdowne Cl *COB* KT11 ...... 178 B7
Oxenden Wood Rd *ORP* BR6 ...... 177 H8
Oxendon St *STJS* SW1Y ...... 11 G7 [3]
Oxenford St *PECK* SE15 ...... 121 M8
Oxenpark Av *WBLY* HA9 ...... 62 B8
Oxestalls Rd *DEPT* SE8 ...... 122 E3
Oxford Av *EMPK* RM11 ...... 75 G5
 HEST TW5 ...... 115 G3 [1]
 HYS/HAR UB3 ...... 113 M5
 RYNPK SW20 ...... 154 E5
Oxford Cl *ASHF* TW15 ...... 149 J3 [3]
 CHES/WCR EN8 ...... 26 C2
 ED N9 ...... 50 B4
 MTCM CR4 ...... 156 C6
 NTHWD HA6 ...... 41 J6
Oxford Crs *NWMAL* KT3 ...... 168 D1 [8]
Oxford Dr *RSLP* HA4 ...... 78 C2
Oxford Gdns *CHSWK* W4 ...... 117 G3 [3]
 DEN/HRF UB9 ...... 76 A3
 NKENS W10 ...... 100 D5
 TRDG/WHET N20 ...... 47 K3
 WCHMH N21 ...... 49 J2
Oxford Ms *BXLY* DA5 ...... 145 G5
Oxford Rd *CAR* SM5 ...... 170 E8
 DEN/HRF UB9 ...... 76 B5
 EA W5 ...... 98 D6
 ED N9 ...... 50 B4
 FSBYPK N4 ...... 85 G1
 HARH RM3 ...... 58 B3
 HPTN TW12 ...... 151 K1
 HRW HA1 ...... 61 J7
 IL IG1 ...... 89 J4
 KIL/WHAMP NW6 ...... 2 A6 [3]
 KTN/HRWW/W HA3 ...... 61 M4
 NRWD SE19 ...... 157 K2
 PEND EN3 ...... 37 H8
 PUT/ROE SW15 ...... 136 E1
 SCUP DA14 ...... 162 B1
 SRTFD E15 ...... 87 K6 [3]
 WFD IG8 ...... 52 D7
 WLGTN SM6 ...... 171 J7 [3]
Oxford Rd North *CHSWK* W4 ...... 117 H5
Oxford Rd South *CHSWK* W4 ...... 117 H5
Oxford Sq *MYFR/PKLN* W1K ...... 10 A5 [7]
Oxford St *MYFR/PKLN* W1K ...... 29 H5 [9]
Oxford Wk *STHL* UB1 ...... 96 F7 [1]
Oxford Wy *FELT* TW13 ...... 132 D8
Oxgate Gdns *CRICK* NW2 ...... 82 B3
Oxgate La *CRICK* NW2 ...... 82 B2
Oxhawth Crs *HAYES* BR2 ...... 161 C8
Oxhey Av *OXHEY* WD19 ...... 42 D2
Oxhey Dr *OXHEY* WD19 ...... 42 B6
Oxhey La *OXHEY* WD19 ...... 42 D2 [8]
 PIN HA5 ...... 43 H8

Oxhey Ridge Cl *OXHEY* WD19 ...... 42 A7
Oxhey Rd *OXHEY* WD19 ...... 42 C2
Oxleas *EHAM* E6 ...... 107 H5
Oxleas Cl *WELL* DA16 ...... 125 K7
Oxleay Rd *RYLN/HDSTN* HA2 ...... 79 G1
Oxleigh Cl *NWMAL* KT3 ...... 153 C8 [2]
Oxley Cl *GPK* RM2 ...... 74 C3 [8]
 STHWK SE1 ...... 19 M7
Oxleys Rd *CRICK* NW2 ...... 82 B3
Oxlow La *DAGE* RM10 ...... 91 G4
 DAGW RM9 ...... 90 F4
Oxonian St *EDUL* SE22 ...... 139 M1 [8]
Oxted Cl *MTCM* CR4 ...... 155 K6
Oxtoby Wy *STRHM/NOR* SW16 ... 156 D4
Oyster Catchers Cl
 CAN/RD E16 ...... 106 B5 [8]
Oyster Rw *WCHPL* E1 ...... 104 C5 [3]
Ozolins Wy *CAN/RD* E16 ...... 105 M5

P

Paceheath Cl *CRW* RM5 ...... 55 K8 [3]
Pace Pl *WCHPL* E1 ...... 104 B5 [1]
Pacific Cl *EBED/NFELT* TW14 ...... 131 M5
Pacific Rd *CAN/RD* E16 ...... 106 A5
Packet Boat La *UX/CGN* UB8 ...... 94 B5
Packington Sq *IS* N1 ...... 6 E4
Packington St *IS* N1 ...... 6 D4
Packmores Rd *ELTH/MOT* SE9 ... 143 K2
Padbury Cl *EBED/NFELT* TW14 ... 131 K5
Padbury Ct *BETH* E2 ...... 7 M8
Padcroft Rd *WDR/YW* UB7 ...... 94 D7
Paddenswick Rd *HMSMTH* W6 ... 118 A1
Paddington Cl *YEAD* UB4 ...... 96 D3
Paddington Gn *BAY/PAD* W2 ...... 9 G2
Paddington St *MHST* W1U 10 A2
Paddock Cl *BKHTH/KID* SE3 ...... 124 A8
 NTHLT UB5 ...... 97 G1
 ORP BR6 ...... 176 B6 [2]
 OXHEY WD19 ...... 42 E1
 SYD SE26 ...... 140 D8
 WPK KT4 ...... 168 E3
Paddock Gdns *NRWD* SE19 ...... 157 L2 [3]
Paddock La *BAR* EN5 ...... 32 E7
Paddock Rd *BXLYHS* DA6 ...... 144 E1
 CRICK NW2 ...... 82 A3
 RSLP HA4 ...... 78 D3 [8]
Paddocks Cl *RYLN/HDSTN* HA2 ... 79 H4
 STMC/STPC BR5 ...... 177 K4
The Paddocks *ABR/ST* RM4 ...... 55 M1
 EBAR EN4 ...... 34 F6 [8]
 WBLY HA9 ...... 81 H7
 WEY KT13 ...... 164 E5
The Paddock *HCDN/ICK* UB10 ...... 77 H4
Paddock Wy *CHST* BR7 ...... 161 K3
Padfield Rd *CMBW* SE5 ...... 121 J8 [9]
Padnall Rd *CHDH* RM6 ...... 72 C5
Padstow Rd *ENC/FH* EN2 ...... 36 B5
Padstow Wk
 EBED/NFELT TW14 ...... 131 K3
Padua Rd *PGE/AN* SE20 ...... 158 C4
Pagden St *VX/NE* SW8 ...... 120 F5
Pageant Crs *BERM/RHTH* SE16 ... 104 F7
Pageant Wk *CROY/NA* CR0 ...... 172 E5
Page Cl *DAGW* RM9 ...... 90 E5
 FELT TW13 ...... 150 C2 [2]
 KTN/HRWW/W HA3 ...... 62 F7
Page Crs *CROY/NA* CR0 ...... 172 B7 [7]
 ERITH DA8 ...... 127 M3
Page Green Rd
 SEVS/STOTM N15 ...... 68 A6 [1]
Page Heath La *BMLY* BR1 ...... 160 D6
Page Heath Vls *BMLY* BR1 ...... 160 D6
Pagehurst Rd *CROY/NA* CR0 ...... 173 G2
Page Meadow *MLHL* NW7 ...... 64 A1 [8]
Page Rd *EBED/NFELT* TW14 ...... 131 K3
Page's Hl *MUSWH* N10 ...... 66 A3
Page's La *MUSWH* N10 ...... 66 A3
 UX/CGN UB8 ...... 76 C6
Page St *MLHL* NW7 ...... 64 A2
 WEST SW1P 17 H5
Page's Wk *STHWK* SE1 ...... 19 L5
Paget Av *SUT* SM1 ...... 170 D5
Paget Cl *HPTN* TW12 ...... 133 K8 [3]
Paget Gdns *CHST* BR7 ...... 161 H4
Paget La *ISLW* TW7 ...... 115 K8
Paget Pl *THDIT* KT7 ...... 166 F3 [3]
Paget Ri *WOOL/PLUM* SE18 ...... 125 H4
 IL IG1 ...... 89 H4
 STNW/STAM N16 ...... 85 K1
Paget St *FSBYE* EC1V 6 C7
Paget Ter *WOOL/PLUM* SE18 ...... 125 H4
Pagitts Gv *EBAR* EN4 ...... 34 B4
Pagnell St *NWCR* SE14 ...... 122 F7
Pagoda Av *RCH/KEW* TW9 ...... 116 F8
Pagoda Gdns
 BKHTH/KID SE3 ...... 123 K7 [2]
Paignton Rd *RSLP* HA4 ...... 78 D3 [8]
 SEVS/STOTM N15 ...... 67 L7 [3]
Paines Brook Wy *HARH* RM3 ...... 56 F7 [2]
Paines Cl *PIN* HA5 ...... 60 E4
Paine's La *PIN* HA5 ...... 60 D3
Pain's Cl *MTCM* CR4 ...... 156 B5 [8]
Painsthorpe Rd
 STNW/STAM N16 ...... 85 L3 [3]
Painters La *PEND* EN3 ...... 26 D3
Painters Rd *GNTH/NBYPK* IG2 ... 72 A4
Paisley Rd *CAR* SM5 ...... 170 D3
 WDGN N22 ...... 49 J5
Pakeman St *HOLWY* N7 ...... 84 F3 [2]
Pakenham Cl *BAL* SW12 ...... 138 A5 [1]
Pakenham St *FSBYW* WC1X 5 M8
Palace Av *KENS* W8 ...... 8 D9
Palace Ct *BAY/PAD* W2 ...... 8 C6
 KTN/HRWW/W HA3 ...... 62 E7
Palace Court Gdns *MUSWH* N10 ... 66 C1
Palace Dr *WEY* KT13 ...... 164 D5
Palace Garden Ms *KENS* W8 ...... 8 B8
Palace Gdns *BKHH* IG9 ...... 52 D8
Palace Gardens Ter *KENS* W8 ...... 8 B7
Palace Gdns West *WEY* KT13 ...... 164 B5 [4]
Palace Ga *KENS* W8 ...... 14 E2
Palace Gates Rd *WDGN* N22 ...... 66 C2
Palace Gn *CROY/NA* CR0 ...... 185 M1
Palace Gv *BMLY* BR1 ...... 160 B4

NRWD SE19 157 M3
Palace Pl WESTW SW1E 16 E3
Palace Rd BMLY BR1 160 B4
BRXS/STRHM SW2 138 F5
CEND/HSY/T N8 66 D6
E/WMO/HCT KT8 151 J6
FBAR/BDGN N11 66 E1
KUT KT1 152 D7
NRWD SE19 157 M3
RSLP HA4 78 E4
Palace Sq NRWD SE19 157 M3
Palace St WESTW SW1E 16 E3
Palace Vw BMLY BR1 160 B6 2
CROY/NA CR0 173 M6
LEE/GVPK SE12 142 A6
Palace View Rd CHING E4 51 H7
Palamos Rd LEY E10 87 G1
Palatine Av STNW/STAM N16 85 L4
Palatine Rd STNW/STAM N16 85 L4
Palermo Rd WLSDN NW10 100 A1
Palestine Gv WIM/MER SW19 155 K4
Palewell Cl STMC/STPC BR5 162 B5
Palewell Common Dr
MORT/ESHN SW14 135 K2
Palewell Pk MORT/ESHN SW14 135 K2
Palfrey Pl BRXN/ST SW9 120 F5
VX/NE SW8 120 F5
Palgrave Av STHL UB1 97 G6
Palgrave Rd SHB W12 117 M1
Palissy St BETH E2 7 L8
Pallant Wy ORP BR6 176 A5
Pallet Wy WOOL/PLUM SE18 124 E6
Palliser Dr RAIN RM13 110 A4
Palliser Rd HMSMTH W6 118 E3
Pall Ml STJS SW1Y 11 G9
Pall Ml East STJS SW1Y 11 H8
Pall Mall Pl STJS SW1Y 10 F9
Palmar Crs BXLYHN DA7 127 G8
Palmar Rd BXLYHN DA7 127 G7
Palmarsh Cl STMC/STPC BR5 162 D7 7
Palm Av SCUP DA14 162 D2
Palm Cl LEY E10 87 H3
Palmeira Rd WELL DA16 126 D8
Palmer Av BUSH WD23 43 H1
CHEAM SM3 169 J6
Palmer Cl HEST TW5 115 G6 2
WWKM BR4 174 D4
Palmer Crs KUT KT1 152 E6
Palmer Gdns BAR EN5 33 K8 2
Palmer Pl HOLWY N7 85 G5 5
Palmer Rd BCTR RM8 90 D1
PLSTW E13 106 B3
Palmers Gv E/WMO/HCT KT8 151 G7
Palmers La PEND EN3 37 J4
Palmer's Moor La IVER SL0 94 A3
Palmers Rd BETH E2 104 D1
BORE WD6 32 C4 4
FBAR/BDGN N11 48 C7
MORT/ESHN SW14 117 J8
STRHM/NOR SW16 156 F5 1
Palmerston Centre
KTN/HRWW/W HA3 61 M4 1
Palmerston Crs PLMGR N13 48 F7
WOOL/PLUM SE18 125 J4
Palmerstone Rd RAIN RM13 110 C1 2
Palmerston Gv
WIM/MER SW19 155 G3 5
Palmerston Rd ACT W3 117 J1
BKHH IG9 52 C4
CAR SM5 170 F6 5
CROY/NA CR0 157 K8 2
FSTGT E7 88 B5
HSLW TW3 115 J6
KIL/WHAMP NW6 82 F7 5
KTN/HRWW/W HA3 61 L4 3
MORT/ESHN SW14 135 J1
ORP BR6 176 C6
SUT SM1 170 C7 7
WALTH E17 68 F5
WDGN N22 66 F1
WHTN TW2 133 L3 2
WHTN TW2 133 M3 5
WIM/MER SW19 155 G3 7
Palmerston Wy VX/NE SW8 120 B5 1
Palmer St STJSPK SW1H 17 G3
Palmers Wy CHES/WCR EN8 26 E2
Palm Gv EA W5 116 E1
Palm Rd ROMW/RG RM7 73 J6
Pamela Gdns PIN HA5 60 B6
Pampisford Rd PUR/KEN CR8 184 A4
Pams Wy HOR/WEW KT19 168 D7
Pancras La MANHO EC4N 12 F5 2
Pancras Rd CAMTN NW1 5 H5
Pandora Rd KIL/WHAMP NW6 83 G6
Panfield Ms GNTH/NBYPK IG2 71 G7 2
Panfield Rd ABYW SE2 108 A8 1
Pangbourne Av NKENS W10 100 C4 1
Pangbourne Dr STAN HA7 44 D7
Panhard Pl GFD/PVL UB6 97 H6
Pank Av BAR EN5 34 D8
Pankhurst Cl ISLW TW7 115 M8 4
Pankhurst Pl WATN WD24 29 K6 1
Pankhurst Rd WOT/HER KT12 165 J2
Panmuir Rd RYNPK SW20 154 B4
Panmure Cl HBRY N5 85 H4
Panmure Rd SYD SE26 140 B7
Pansy Gdns SHB W12 100 A6 1
Panter's SWLY BR8 163 M3
Panther Dr WLSDN NW10 81 K5
Pantile Rd WEY KT13 164 D6
Pantiles Cl PLMGR N13 49 H7
The Pantiles BMLY BR1 160 E6
BUSH WD23 43 K2
BXLYHN DA7 126 F5
Panton St LSQ/SEVD WC2H 11 H7
STJS SW1Y 11 G7 5
Papermill Cl CAR SM5 171 G6
Papillons Wk BKHTH/KID SE3 124 A7
Papworth Wy
BRXS/STRHM SW2 139 G4
Parade Ms
BRXS/STRHM SW2 139 H6 2
The Parade EPSOM KT18 180 D6
ESH/CLAY KT10 166 E8
SUN TW16 149 M3
Paradise Cl CHESW EN7 26 B1
Paradise Rd CLAP SW4 120 E7
RCHPK/HAM TW10 134 E2
WAB EN9 27 J7 4
Paradise Rw BETH E2 104 B2 12
Paradise St BERM/RHTH SE16 104 B8
Paradise Wk CHEL SW3 15 L9
Paragon Cl CAN/RD E16 106 A5 3
Paragon Gv BRYLDS KT5 167 M1
Paragon Ms WALW SE17 19 H5 2
Paragon Pl BKHTH/KID SE3 123 M7
Paragon Rd HACK E8 86 B6
The Paragon BKHTH/KID SE3 124 A7
Parbury Ri CHSGTN KT9 167 L8
Parbury Rd FSTH SE23 140 E3
Parchmore Rd THHTH CR7 157 H5
Parchmore Wy THHTH CR7 157 H5 1
Pardoner St STHWK SE1 19 H3
Pardon St FSBYE EC1V 6 D9 1
Parfett St WCHPL E1 104 A4
Parfrey St HMSMTH W6 118 C4
Parham Dr GNTH/NBYPK IG2 71 H7
Paris Gdn STHWK SE1 12 C8
Parish Cl GSTN WD25 21 J7 3
HCH RM12 92 B2 3
Parish Gate Dr BFN/LL DA15 143 L3
Parish La PGE/AN SE20 158 D3
Parish Whf
WOOL/PLUM SE18 124 E2 4
Park Ap WELL DA16 144 B1
Park Av BARK IG11 89 J6
BMLY BR1 160 A2
BUSH WD23 29 K5
CAR SM5 171 G8
CRICK NW2 82 C6
EHAM E6 89 G8
EN EN1 49 L1
FNCH N3 65 H2
GLDGN NW11 83 H1
HSLW TW3 133 H3
IL IG1 89 G2
MORT/ESHN SW14 135 K1
MTCM CR4 156 B3
ORP BR6 175 M4
PLMGR N13 49 G5
POTB/CUF EN6 23 J6
RSLP HA4 59 L7
SHPTN TW17 149 L6
STHL UB1 96 F8
UED N18 50 A6 3
UPMR RM14 75 L8
WATW WD18 29 G6
WCHMH N21 36 D8
WDGN N22 66 E3
WFD IG8 52 B7
WLSDN NW10 98 F2
WWKM BR4 174 C4
Park Av East EW KT17 169 G8
Park Av North CEND/HSY/T N8 66 D5
WLSDN NW10 82 B5
Park Avenue Rd TOTM N17 68 B1
Park Av South CEND/HSY/T N8 66 D5
Park Av West EW KT17 169 G8
Park Bvd GPK RM2 73 M2
Park Cha WBLY HA9 80 F4
Park Cl BUSH WD23 29 K6
CAR SM5 170 F8
CRICK NW2 82 A3
ESH/CLAY KT10 165 M8
HOM E9 86 C8
HPTN TW12 151 J4
ISLW TW7 133 J2 3
KENS W8 118 F1
KTN/HRWW/W HA3 61 L2
KUTN/CMB KT2 153 G4
RKW/CH/CXG WD3 41 H6
WEY KT13 164 F4
WLSDN NW10 98 F2
Park Ct NWMAL KT3 153 K7
WBLY HA9 80 E5
Park Crs BORE WD6 31 M6
EMPK RM11 74 A8
ENC/FH EN2 36 D7
ERITH DA8 127 K4
FNCH N3 65 H1
KTN/HRWW/W HA3 61 L2
REGST W1B 10 C1
WHTN TW2 133 K5
Park Crescent Ms East
REGST W1B 10 D1
Park Crescent Ms West
CAVSQ/HST W1G 10 C1
Park Cft EDGW HA8 63 J2
Parkcroft Rd LEE/GVPK SE12 141 M4
Parkdale Crs WPK KT4 168 D5
Parkdale Rd WOOL/PLUM SE18 125 L3
Park Dr ACT W3 117 G1
CHARL SE7 124 E3
DAGE RM10 91 J3
GLDGN NW11 83 H1
KTN/HRWW/W HA3 43 K8
MORT/ESHN SW14 135 K2
POTB/CUF EN6 23 H4
ROM RM1 73 K5
RYLN/HDSTN HA2 61 G8
UPMR RM14 93 J4
WCHMH N21 49 J1
WEY KT13 164 B7
Park End BMLY BR1 159 M4
HAMP NW3 83 L4 3
Park End Rd ROM RM1 73 L5
Parker Cl CAN/RD E16 106 E7
Parker Ms HOL/ALD WC2B 11 K4 2
Parke Rd BARN SW13 118 A6
SUN TW16 150 A7
Parker Rd CROY/NA CR0 172 C6
Parker's Rw STHWK SE1 19 M2 1
Parker St CAN/RD E16 106 E7
HOL/ALD WC2B 11 K4
WATN WD24 29 H4
Parkes Rd CHIG IG7 53 M7
Park Farm Cl EFNCH N2 65 J4
Park Farm Rd BMLY BR1 160 D4
KUTN/CMB KT2 152 E3
UPMR RM14 92 F5
Parkfield Av FELT TW13 132 A7 3
HGDN/ICK UB10 95 H2
MORT/ESHN SW14 135 L1
NTHLT UB5 96 D1
RYLN/HDSTN HA2 61 J3
Parkfield Cl EDGW HA8 45 H8
NTHLT UB5 96 E1
Parkfield Crs FELT TW13 132 A7
RSLP HA4 78 E2
RYLN/HDSTN HA2 61 J3
Parkfield Dr NTHLT UB5 96 D1
Parkfield Gdns
RYLN/HDSTN HA2 61 H4
Parkfield Rd FELT TW13 132 A7
HGDN/ICK UB10 77 H2
NTHLT UB5 96 E1
NWCR SE14 122 F6
RYLN/HDSTN HA2 79 J3
WLSDN NW10 82 A7
Parkfields CROY/NA CR0 173 M3
LHD/OX KT22 178 D4
PUT/ROE SW15 136 C1
Parkfields Av CDALE/KGS NW9 81 K1
RYNPK SW20 154 B4
Parkfields Cl CAR SM5 171 G6 4
Parkfields Rd KUTN/CMB KT2 152 F1
Parkfield St IS N1 6 B5
Parkfield Wy HAYES BR2 175 M1
Park Gdns CDALE/KGS NW9 63 H4
ERITH DA8 127 K2
KUTN/CMB KT2 152 F1
Parkgate BKHTH/KID SE3 123 M8
Park Ga EA W5 98 D4 1
EFNCH N2 65 K4
WCHMH N21 48 F2
Parkgate Av EBAR EN4 34 C4
Parkgate Cl KUTN/CMB KT2 153 H2 2
Parkgate Crs EBAR EN4 34 C4
Parkgate Gdns
MORT/ESHN SW14 135 K2
Parkgate Rd BTSEA SW11 119 L5
CAR SM5 171 G7
WATN WD24 29 J2
Park Gv BMLY BR1 160 B4
BXLYHN DA7 145 J1
EDGW HA8 44 F7
FBAR/BDGN N11 66 D1
SRTFD E15 88 A8
Park Grove Rd WAN E11 87 L2
Park Hall Rd DUL SE21 139 K6
EFNCH N2 65 L5
Parkham St BTSEA SW11 119 K6
Park Hl BMLY BR1 160 E7
CAR SM5 170 F8
CLAP SW4 138 D2
EA W5 98 D4
FSTH SE23 140 B6
LOU IG10 39 K8
RCHPK/HAM TW10 134 F3
Park Hill Cl CAR SM5 170 E7 2
Parkhill Cl HCH RM12 92 C2
Park Hill Ri CROY/NA CR0 172 E4
Parkhill Rd BFN/LL DA15 143 L7
BXLY DA5 144 F4
CHING E4 51 J2
Park Hill Rd CROY/NA CR0 172 E4
EW KT17 180 F4
Parkhill Rd HAMP NW3 83 M5
Park Hill Rd HAYES BR2 159 L5
WLGTN SM6 183 H1
Parkholme Rd HACK E8 86 A6
Park House Gdns TWK TW1 134 C2
Parkhouse St CMBW SE5 121 K5
Parkhurst HOR/WEW KT19 180 C3 1
Parkhurst Gdns BXLY DA5 145 G4 1
Parkhurst Rd BXLY DA5 145 G4
FBAR/BDGN N11 48 A6
HOLWY N7 84 E4
MNPK E12 89 G4
SUT SM1 170 D6
TOTM N17 68 A3
WALTH E17 68 E5 5
WDGN N22 66 F1
Parkland Av ROM RM1 73 L3
UPMR RM14 93 H5
Parkland Gv ASHF TW15 131 G8
Parkland Rd ASHF TW15 131 G8
WDGN N22 66 F3
WFD IG8 70 B1
Parklands BRYLDS KT5 152 F8
CHIG IG7 53 J5
HGT N6 66 B8
WAB EN9 27 L5
Parklands Cl EBAR EN4 34 D3
MORT/ESHN SW14 135 J2
Parklands Dr FNCH N3 64 E4
Parklands Rd TOOT SW17 156 B1
Parklands Wy WPK KT4 168 E4 5
Park La CAR SM5 171 G6
CHDH RM6 72 D7
CHEAM SM3 169 L8
CHES/WCR EN8 26 D6
CROY/NA CR0 172 D5
DEN/HRF UB9 58 A2
EMPK RM11 74 A8
HYS/HAR UB3 114 A5
MBLAR W1H 9 M6
MYFR/PICC W1J 16 B1
MYFR/PKLN W1K 10 A7
RAIN RM13 92 B6
RCH/KEW TW9 134 D1 1
RYLN/HDSTN HA2 79 H3
SOCK/AV RM15 111 L4 3
SRTFD E15 87 K8 3
STAN HA7 44 A5
TEDD TW11 151 M2 7
TOTM N17 67 M1 5
UED N18 49 M5
WBLY HA9 80 F4
YEAD UB4 95 L3
Park Lane Cl TOTM N17 68 A1
Parklawn Av EPSOM KT18 180 B6
Park Lawn Rd WEY KT13 164 C6
Parklea Cl CDALE/KGS NW9 63 L2
Parkleigh Rd
WIM/MER SW19 155 H5 1
Parkleys KUTN/CMB KT2 134 D8
Park Md BFN/LL DA15 144 A2
Parkmead PUT/ROE SW15 136 B3
Park Md RYLN/HDSTN HA2 79 H3
Parkmead Gdns MLHL NW7 45 M8
Park Ms CHST BR7 161 H2
NKENS W10 100 E1 2
STWL/WRAY TW19 130 F4
Park Nook Gdns ENC/FH EN2 36 D2
Park Pde WLSDN NW10 99 M1
Park Pl ACT W3 117 G2
EA W5 98 D7
HPTN TW12 151 J2
POP/IOD E14 105 G7
WBLY HA9 80 F4
WHALL SW1A 10 E9
Park Place Vls BAY/PAD W2 8 F2
Park Ridings CEND/HSY/T N8 67 G4
Park Ri KTN/HRWW/W HA3 61 L2
Park Rise Rd FSTH SE23 140 E5
Park Rd ALP/SUD HA0 80 E6
ASHF TW15 149 H1
BAR EN5 33 M7
BECK BR3 158 F3
BMLY BR1 160 B4
BRYLDS KT5 167 M1
BUSH WD23 43 G1
CAMTN NW1 9 M1
CDALE/KGS NW9 63 K8
CEND/HSY/T N8 66 D6
CHEAM SM3 169 L8
CHES/WCR EN8 26 D6 4
CHST BR7 161 H2
CHSWK W4 117 K4
DART DA1 147 G4
E/WMO/HCT KT8 151 J7
E/WMO/HCT KT8 152 C4
EBAR EN4 34 D7
EFNCH N2 65 K4
EHAM E6 88 C8
ESH/CLAY KT10 166 B6
FBAR/BDGN N11 66 D1
FELT TW13 132 D8
HDN NW4 64 B7
HGDN/ICK UB10 76 E6
HNWL W7 97 M6
HPTN TW12 151 J1
HSLW TW3 133 J2
IL IG1 89 K3
ISLW TW7 116 B6
KUT KT1 152 C4
KUTN/CMB KT2 152 F1
KUTN/CMB KT2 153 G4
LEY E10 87 G1
MNPK E12 88 B2
MNPK E12 88 D4 3
NWMAL KT3 153 K7
PEND EN3 37 L1
POTB/CUF EN6 24 A3
PUR/KEN CR8 184 C8
RCHPK/HAM TW10 134 F3
RKW/CH/CXG WD3 40 E2
SEVS/STOTM N15 67 H5 4
SHPTN TW17 164 A3
SNWD SE25 157 L7
SRTFD E15 88 A8
STHGT/OAK N14 48 D2
STJWD NW8 3 K8
STMC/STPC BR5 177 J1
STWL/WRAY TW19 130 B3
SUN TW16 150 B3
SWLY BR8 163 M7
TEDD TW11 151 M3
TWK TW1 134 C3
UED N18 49 M6
UPMR RM14 93 G4 2
UX/CGN UB8 76 D7 2
WALTH E17 68 F6
WAN E11 88 B1
WARL CR6 186 E7
WAT WD17 29 G4
WIM/MER SW19 155 K3
WLGTN SM6 171 H7
WLSDN NW10 81 L8 3
YEAD UB4 95 L4
Park Rd East ACT W3 99 J8
UX/CGN UB8 94 D1
Park Rd North ACT W3 99 H8
CHSWK W4 117 K4
Park Rw GNWCH SE10 123 K4
Park Royal Rd WLSDN NW10 99 J2
Parkshot RCH/KEW TW9 134 D1
Park Side BKHH IG9 52 B4
Parkside CHEAM SM3 169 L8
CHES/WCR EN8 26 E7
Park Side CRICK NW2 82 A3
Parkside FNCH N3 65 H2
HPTN TW12 151 K1
MLHL NW7 46 A8
SCUP DA14 144 B6
WIM/MER SW19 136 D8
WIM/MER SW19 154 D1
Parkside Av BMLY BR1 160 E7
BXLYHN DA7 127 K7
ROM RM1 73 K3
WIM/MER SW19 154 D1
Parkside Cl PGE/AN SE20 158 C3
Parkside Crs BRYLDS KT5 168 C1
HOLWY N7 85 G3
Parkside Cross BXLYHN DA7 127 L7
Parkside Dr EDGW HA8 45 G5
WAT WD17 28 E5
Parkside Gdns EBAR EN4 47 M3
WIM/MER SW19 136 D8
Parkside Rd BELV DA17 127 H2
HSLW TW3 133 H2
NTHWD HA6 41 M7
Parkside St BTSEA SW11 120 A6 2
Parkside Wy RYLN/HDSTN HA2 61 H5
Park Sq East CAMTN NW1 4 C9
Park Square Ms CAMTN NW1 10 C1 1
Parkstead Rd PUT/ROE SW15 136 A2
Parkstone Av EMPK RM11 74 E7
UED N18 49 M7
Parkstone Rd PECK SE15 122 A7 5
Park St CROY/NA CR0 172 C5
MYFR/PKLN W1K 10 A7
STHWK SE1 12 E8
TEDD TW11 151 L2
Park Ter WPK KT4 169 G3
The Park CAR SM5 170 F7
EA W5 98 D7
GLDGN NW11 83 H1
HGT N6 66 A8
SCUP DA14 161 M1
Parkthorne Cl
RYLN/HDSTN HA2 61 H7 1
Parkthorne Dr
RYLN/HDSTN HA2 61 G7
Parkthorne Rd BAL SW12 138 D4
Park Vw ACT W3 99 J4
NWMAL KT3 153 M6
PIN HA5 60 F2
POTB/CUF EN6 23 J6
SOCK/AV RM15 111 K7
WBLY HA9 81 H5
WCHMH N21 48 F2
Park View Crs FBAR/BDGN N11 48 B6
Park View Dr MTCM CR4 155 K5
Park View Gdns HDN NW4 64 C6
Park View Rd CRICK NW2 81 M4
Parkview Rd CROY/NA CR0 173 G3
Park View Rd EA W5 98 E4
ELTH/MOT SE9 143 H5
FNCH N3 65 H2
PIN HA5 42 B8
STHL UB1 97 G7
TOTM N17 68 B3
UX/CGN UB8 95 G5
WDR/YW UB7 94 F5
WELL DA16 126 C8
Park Village East CAMTN NW1 4 C5
Park Village West CAMTN NW1 4 C5
Parkville Rd FUL/PGN SW6 118 F5
Park Vis GNWCH SE10 123 K4
Park Wk WBPTN SW10 14 F9
Park Wy E/WMO/HCT KT8 151 H6
E/WMO/HCT KT8 151 J6
EBED/NFELT TW14 132 B4
EDGW HA8 63 H2
ENC/FH EN2 36 A5
GLDGN NW11 64 E6
RKW/CH/CXG WD3 40 C3
RSLP HA4 78 A1
TRDG/WHET N20 47 M6
BXLY DA5 145 M7
Parkway CAMTN NW1 4 D3
CROY/NA CR0 186 C2
ERITHM DA18 126 E1
GDMY/SEVK IG3 89 M3
GPK RM2 73 M3
HGDN/ICK UB10 77 G7
RAIN RM13 110 A3
RYNPK SW20 154 D7
STHGT/OAK N14 48 E4
WEY KT13 164 D6 5
WFD IG8 52 C7 5
The Parkway HEST TW5 114 A4
NTHLT UB5 96 D2
Park West BAY/PAD W2 9 K4
Park West Pl BAY/PAD W2 9 K4
Parkwood BECK BR3 159 G3
Parkwood Av ESH/CLAY KT10 166 C3
Park Wood Cl BNSTD SM7 181 K8 1
Parkwood Gv SUN TW16 150 A6 1
Parkwood Ms HGT N6 66 B7 1
Park Wood Rd BNSTD SM7 181 K8
Parkwood Rd BXLY DA5 144 F4
ISLW TW7 115 M6
WIM/MER SW19 154 F1
Parliament Hl HAMP NW3 83 L4
Parliament St WHALL SW1A 17 J1
Parma Crs BTSEA SW11 137 M1
Parmiter St BETH E2 104 B1
Parnell Cl ABLGY WD5 20 F3
EDGW HA8 45 J6
Parnell Rd BOW E3 86 F8
HOM E9 86 F8
Parnham St POP/IOD E14 104 E5 5
Parolles Rd ARCH N19 84 C1
Paroma Rd BELV DA17 127 G1
Parr Av EW KT17 181 H2
Parr Cl ED N9 50 B6
Parrotts Cl RKW/CH/CXG WD3 28 A7
Parr Rd EHAM E6 88 D8
STAN HA7 62 D2
Parrs Cl SAND/SEL CR2 184 D2
Parr's Pl HPTN TW12 151 G3
Parr St IS N1 7 G5
Parry Av EHAM E6 106 F5
Parry Cl EW KT17 181 G1
Parry Pl WOOL/PLUM SE18 125 H2
Parry Rd NKENS W10 100 E2
SNWD SE25 157 L6
Parry St VX/NE SW8 17 J9
Parsifal Rd KIL/WHAMP NW6 83 G5 5
Parsloes Av DAGW RM9 90 E5
Parsonage Cl ABLGY WD5 20 E3
HYS/HAR UB3 95 M5 2
Parsonage Gdns ENC/FH EN2 36 C5
Parsonage La ENC/FH EN2 36 D5
SCUP DA14 144 F8
Parsonage Manorway
ERITH DA8 127 G4
Parsonage Rd RAIN RM13 110 C1
RKW/CH/CXG WD3 40 D2
Parsonage St POP/IOD E14 123 J2
Parsonsfield Cl BNSTD SM7 181 K8
Parsons Gn FUL/PGN SW6 119 G6
Parsons Green La
FUL/PGN SW6 119 G6
Parsons Gv EDGW HA8 45 G5
Parsons La RDART DA2 146 B7
Parson's Md CROY/NA CR0 172 B3
E/WMO/HCT KT8 151 J6
Parsons Rd EDGW HA8 45 G5
Parson St HDN NW4 64 C4
Parthenia Rd FUL/PGN SW6 119 G6
Partingdale La MLHL NW7 46 D7
Partridge Cl BAR EN5 46 C1
BUSH WD23 43 J3 2
CAN/RD E16 106 D4 5
STAN HA7 44 E6 1
Partridge Dr ORP BR6 176 C5
Partridge Gn ELTH/MOT SE9 143 G7
Partridge Knoll PUR/KEN CR8 184 B5
Partridge Md BNSTD SM7 181 J8
Partridge Rd HPTN TW12 150 F2
SCUP DA14 143 L7
Partridge Wy WDGN N22 66 E2
Parvills WAB EN9 27 K5
Pasadena Cl HYS/HAR UB3 96 A8 5
Pascal St VX/NE SW8 120 D5

Pascoe Rd LEW SE13 ...... 141 K2
Pasfield Rd WAB EN9 ...... 27 K6 ▣
Pasley Cl WALW SE17 ...... 18 D8
Pasquier Rd WALTH E17 ...... 68 E4
Passey Pl ELTH/MOT SE9 ...... 142 F3
Passfield Dr POP/IOD E14 ...... 105 H4 ▣
Passmore Gdns
  FBAR/BDGN N11 ...... 48 D8
Passmore St BGVA SW1W 16 A6
Pasteur Cl CDALE/KGS NW9 ...... 63 L3
Pasteur Dr HARH RM3 ...... 74 D5
Pasteur Gdns UED N18 ...... 49 J7
Paston Cl WLGTN SM6 ...... 171 J5
Paston Crs LEE/GVPK SE12 ...... 142 B4
Pastor St LBTH SE11 ...... 18 D5 ▣
Pasture Cl ALP/SUD HA0 ...... 80 B3
  BUSH WD23 ...... 43 J2
Pasture Rd ALP/SUD HA0 ...... 80 B2
  CAT SE6 ...... 141 L5
  DAGW RM9 ...... 90 F5
Pastures Md HGDN/ICK UB10 ...... 77 C6
  TRDG/WHET N20 ...... 46 F3
The Pastures OXHEY WD19 ...... 42 C2
Patcham Ter VX/NE SW8 ...... 120 B6 ▣
Patching Wy YEAD UB4 ...... 96 K4
Paternoster Cl WAB EN9 ...... 27 M6
Paternoster HI WAB EN9 ...... 27 M5
Paternoster Rw ABR/ST RM4 ...... 56 C3
  STP EC4M 12 C5
Pater St KENS W8 ...... 14 A4
Pates Manor Dr
  EBED/NFELT TW14 ...... 131 K4
Pathfield Rd
  STRHM/NOR SW16 ...... 156 D2
The Path WIM/MER SW19 ...... 155 H4 ▣
The Pathway OXHEY WD19 ...... 42 D3
  RAD WD7 ...... 30 F1
Patience Rd BTSEA SW11 ...... 119 L7
Patio Cl CLAP SW4 ...... 138 D3
Patmore La WOT/HER KT12 ...... 164 F8
Patmore Rd WAB EN9 ...... 27 L7 ▣
Patmore St VX/NE SW8 ...... 120 C6
Patmore Wy CRW RM5 ...... 55 H7
Patmos Rd BRXN/ST SW9 ...... 121 H5
Paton Cl BOW E3 ...... 105 C2
Patricia Ct WELL DA16 ...... 126 B5
Patricia Dr EMPK RM11 ...... 92 E1
Patrick Rd PLSTW E13 ...... 106 C2
Patrington Cl UX/CGN UB8 ...... 94 C2 ▣
Patriot Sq BETH E2 ...... 104 B1
Patrol Pl CAT SE6 ...... 141 H3
Patshull Pl KTTN NW5 ...... 84 C6 ▣
Patshull Rd KTTN NW5 ...... 84 C6
Pattenden Rd FSTH SE23 ...... 140 F5
Patterdale Cl BMLY BR1 ...... 159 L2 ▣
Patterdale Rd PECK SE15 ...... 122 C5
  RDART DA2 ...... 147 J5
Patterson Rd NRWD SE19 ...... 157 M2
Pattina Wk BERM/RHTH SE16 ...... 104 E7
Pattison Rd CRICK NW2 ...... 83 G3
Paul Cl SRTFD E15 ...... 87 L7
Paulet Rd CMBW SE5 ...... 121 H7
Paul Gdns CROY/NA CR0 ...... 172 F4
Paulhan Rd KTN/HRWW/W HA3 ...... 62 D5
Paulin Dr WCHMH N21 ...... 49 G2
Pauline Crs WHTN TW2 ...... 133 J5
Paulinus Cl STMC/STPC BR5 ...... 162 C5
Paul Julius Cl POP/IOD E14 ...... 105 K6
Paul St SDTCH EC2A 7 J9
  SRTFD E15 ...... 87 L8
Paultons Sq CHEL SW3 ...... 15 H9
Paultons St CHEL SW3 ...... 119 L6
Pauntley St ARCH N19 ...... 84 C1 ▣
Paveley Dr BTSEA SW11 ...... 119 L5 ▣
Paveley St STJWD NW8 ...... 3 K8
The Pavement CLAP SW4 ...... 138 C1
Pavet Cl DAGE RM10 ...... 91 H6
Pavilion Gdns STA TW18 ...... 148 B3
Pavilion Rd IL IG1 ...... 70 E8 ▣
  KTBR SW1X 15 M2
Pavilion St KTBR SW1X ...... 15 M4 ▣
Pavilion Wy EDGW HA8 ...... 63 J1
  RSLP HA4 ...... 78 C2
Pawleyne Cl PGE/AN SE20 ...... 158 C3
Pawsey Cl PLSTW E13 ...... 88 A8
Pawson's Rd CROY/NA CR0 ...... 172 C1
Paxford Rd ALP/SUD HA0 ...... 80 B2
Paxton Cl RCH/KEW TW9 ...... 116 F7 ▣
  WOT/HER KT12 ...... 165 J2 ▣
Paxton Pl WNWD SE27 ...... 139 L8
Paxton Rd BMLY BR1 ...... 160 A3 ▣
  FSTH SE23 ...... 140 E7
  TOTM N17 ...... 68 A1
Paxton Ter PIM SW1V ...... 16 D9 ▣
Paynell Ct BKHTH/KID SE3 ...... 123 L8 ▣
Payne Rd BOW E3 ...... 105 H1
Paynesfield Av
  MORT/ESHN SW14 ...... 117 K8
Paynesfield Rd BUSH WD23 ...... 43 M2
Payne St DEPT SE8 ...... 122 F4
Peabody Cl CROY/NA CR0 ...... 173 J3
Peabody Est HNHL SE24 ...... 139 H4
Peabody Hl DUL SE21 ...... 139 H5
Peace Cl SNWD SE25 ...... 157 L7
  STHGT/OAK N14 ...... 35 H8
Peace Gv WBLY HA9 ...... 81 H3
Peace Prospect WAT WD17 ...... 29 G6 ▣
Peace St WOOL/PLUM SE18 ...... 125 C4
Peaches Cl BELMT SM2 ...... 181 L1
Peachey Cl UX/CGN UB8 ...... 94 B5 ▣
Peachey La UX/CGN UB8 ...... 94 B4 ▣
Peach Rd NKENS W10 ...... 100 D2
Peachum Rd
  BKHTH/KID SE3 ...... 123 M4 ▣
Peacock Av EBED/NFELT TW14 ...... 131 K5
Peacock Cl EMPK RM11 ...... 74 E5 ▣
Peacock Gdns CROY/NA CR0 ...... 185 L3
Peacock St WALW SE17 ...... 18 D6
Peacock Yd WALW SE17 ...... 18 D6
Peaketon Av REDBR IG4 ...... 70 D6
Peak HI SYD SE26 ...... 140 C8
Peak Hill Av SYD SE26 ...... 140 C8
Peak Hill Gdns SYD SE26 ...... 140 C8
Peaks Hi PUR/KEN CR8 ...... 183 L3
Peaks Hill Ri PUR/KEN CR8 ...... 183 L3
The Peak SYD SE26 ...... 140 C7

Peal Gdns WEA W13 ...... 98 A3 ▣
Peall Rd CROY/NA CR0 ...... 171 M1
Pear Av SHPTN TW17 ...... 149 L6 ▣
Pearce Cl MTCM CR4 ...... 156 A5
Pearcefield Av FSTH SE23 ...... 140 C5 ▣
Pear Cl CDALE/KGS NW9 ...... 63 K5
  NWCR SE14 ...... 122 E5
Pearcroft Rd WAN E11 ...... 87 K2
Peardon St VX/NE SW8 ...... 120 B7 ▣
Peareswood Gdns STAN HA7 ...... 62 D7
Peareswood Rd ERITH DA8 ...... 127 M6
Pearfield Rd FSTH SE23 ...... 140 E7
Pearl Cl CRICK NW2 ...... 64 D8
  EHAM E6 ...... 107 G5
Pearl Rd WALTH E17 ...... 69 G4
Pearl St WAP E1W ...... 104 C7 ▣
Pearmain Cl SHPTN TW17 ...... 149 H8 ▣
Pearman St STHWK SE1 ...... 18 B3
Pear Pl STHWK SE1 ...... 18 A1
Pearscroft Ct FUL/PGN SW6 ...... 119 H6 ▣
Pearscroft Rd FUL/PGN SW6 ...... 119 H7 ▣
Pearson's Av DEPT SE8 ...... 123 G6 ▣
Pearson St BETH E2 ...... 7 L5
Pearson Wy DART DA1 ...... 146 F6
Pears Rd HSLW TW3 ...... 115 K8
Pear Tree Av WDR/YW UB7 ...... 94 F5
Pear Tree Cl BXLYHN DA7 ...... 127 K6
  MTCM CR4 ...... 155 M6 ▣
Peartree Cl SAND/SEL CR2 ...... 185 H7 ▣
Pear Tree Ct CLKNW EC1R 12 B1
Peartree Gdns BCTR RM8 ...... 90 B5
  ROMW/RG RM7 ...... 73 H3
Peartree La WAP E1W ...... 104 C6 ▣
Pear Tree Rd ASHF TW15 ...... 149 J1
Peartree Rd EN EN1 ...... 36 E6
Peartree St FSBYE EC1V 6 D9
Peary Pl BETH E2 ...... 104 C2 ▣
Pease Cl HCH RM12 ...... 92 B7 ▣
Peatfield Cl BFN/LL DA15 ...... 143 L7 ▣
Pebworth Rd HRW HA1 ...... 80 A2
Peckarmans Wd DUL SE21 ...... 140 A7
Peckford Pl BRXN/ST SW9 ...... 121 G7 ▣
Peckham High St PECK SE15 ...... 122 A6
Peckham Hill St PECK SE15 ...... 122 A5
Peckham Park Rd PECK SE15 ...... 122 A5
Peckham Rd CMBW SE5 ...... 121 L6
Peckham Rye EDUL SE22 ...... 146 A1
  PECK SE15 ...... 122 A8
Peckwater St KTTN NW5 ...... 84 C5 ▣
Pedley Rd BCTR RM8 ...... 90 C1
Pedley St BETH E2 ...... 104 A3
  WCHPL E1 ...... 13 M1
Pedro St CLPT E5 ...... 86 D3
Peek Crs WIM/MER SW19 ...... 154 D1
Peel Cl CHING E4 ...... 51 H4
  ED N9 ...... 50 A5 ▣
Peel Dr CDALE/KGS NW9 ...... 63 M4
  CLAY IG5 ...... 70 E4
Peel Gv BETH E2 ...... 104 C1
Peel Pas KENS W8 ...... 8 A9 ▣
Peel Pl CLAY IG5 ...... 70 E3
Peel Rd ALP/SUD HA0 ...... 80 C3
  KIL/WHAMP NW6 ...... 2 A7
  KTN/HRWW/W HA3 ...... 61 L4 ▣
  ORP BR6 ...... 176 C6
  SWFD E18 ...... 69 M2
Peel St KENS W8 ...... 8 A9
Peel Wy HARH RM3 ...... 74 F3
  UX/CGN UB8 ...... 94 A4
Peerage Wy EMPK RM11 ...... 74 E8
Peerless Dr DEN/HRF UB9 ...... 58 C6
Peerless St FSBYE EC1V 7 G8
Pegamoid Rd UED N18 ...... 50 C5
Pegasus Cl BTFD TW8 ...... 116 F3 ▣
Pegasus Pl LBTH SE11 ...... 18 A9
Pegasus Rd CROY/NA CR0 ...... 172 A8
Pegasus Wy FBAR/BDGN N11 ...... 48 B8
Pegelm Gdns EMPK RM11 ...... 74 F8
Peggotty Wy UX/CGN UB8 ...... 95 H5
Pegg Rd HEST TW5 ...... 114 D5
Pegley Gdns LEE/GVPK SE12 ...... 142 A6 ▣
Pegmire La GSTN WD25 ...... 30 C4
Pegwell St WOOL/PLUM SE18 ...... 125 L5
Pekin St POP/IOD E14 ...... 105 C5
Pelham Av BARK IG11 ...... 89 M8
Pelham Cl CMBW SE5 ...... 121 L8
Pelham Crs SKENS SW7 ...... 15 J6
Pelham Pl SKENS SW7 ...... 15 J5
Pelham Rd BXLYHN DA7 ...... 127 G8
  IL IG1 ...... 89 K2
  PGE/AN SE20 ...... 158 C5
  SEVS/STOTM N15 ...... 67 M5
  SWFD E18 ...... 70 B4
  WDGN N22 ...... 67 G3
  WIM/MER SW19 ...... 155 G3
Pelhams Cl ESH/CLAY KT10 ...... 166 A6 ▣
The Pelhams GSTN WD25 ...... 21 K8 ▣
Pelham St SKENS SW7 ...... 15 H5
Pelhams Wk ESH/CLAY KT10 ...... 166 A5 ▣
Pelier St WALW SE17 ...... 18 F9
Pelinore Rd CAT SE6 ...... 141 L6
Pellant Rd FUL/PGN SW6 ...... 118 E5
Pellatt Gv WDGN N22 ...... 67 G1
Pellatt Rd EDUL SE22 ...... 139 M2
  WBLY HA9 ...... 62 A7
Pellerin Rd STNW/STAM N16 ...... 85 L5
Pelling St POP/IOD E14 ...... 105 C5
Pellipar Cl PLMGR N13 ...... 49 G5
Pellipar Rd
  WOOL/PLUM SE18 ...... 124 F3 ▣
Pelly Rd PLSTW E13 ...... 88 A8
Pelter St BETH E2 ...... 7 L7
Pelton Rd BELMT SM2 ...... 182 B3
Pelton Rd GNWCH SE10 ...... 123 L3 ▣
Pembar Av WALTH E17 ...... 68 E4 ▣
Pemberley Cha
  HOR/WEW KT19 ...... 168 B7 ▣
Pemberley Cl
  HOR/WEW KT19 ...... 168 B7 ▣
Pember Rd WLSDN NW10 ...... 100 D2
Pemberton Av GPK RM2 ...... 74 B4
Pemberton Gdns ARCH N19 ...... 84 C3
  CHDH RM6 ...... 72 A3
  SWLY BR8 ...... 163 L6 ▣
Pemberton Pl
  ESH/CLAY KT10 ...... 166 C5 ▣
  HACK E8 ...... 86 B7 ▣

Pemberton Rd
  E/WMO/HCT KT8 ...... 151 J7
  FSBYPK N4 ...... 67 G6
Pemberton Rw
  FLST/FETLN EC4A ...... 12 B4 ▣
Pemberton Ter ARCH N19 ...... 84 C3
Pembrey Wy HCH RM12 ...... 92 C6 ▣
Pembridge Av HSLWW TW4 ...... 132 F5
Pembridge Crs NTGHL W11 ...... 100 F6
Pembridge Gdns BAY/PAD W2 ...... 8 A7
Pembridge Ms NTGHL W11 ...... 8 A6
Pembridge Pl BAY/PAD W2 ...... 8 B6
  NTGHL W11 ...... 8 A7
Pembridge Sq BAY/PAD W2 ...... 8 A7
Pembridge Vls NTGHL W11 ...... 8 A6
Pembroke Av BRYLDS KT5 ...... 153 H8
  EN N1 ...... 37 H4
  KTN/HRWW/W HA3 ...... 62 A4
  WOT/HER KT12 ...... 165 J8 ▣
Pembroke Cl EMPK RM11 ...... 75 G5 ▣
  ERITH DA8 ...... 127 K2 ▣
  KTBR SW1X ...... 16 B2 ▣
Pembroke Dr CHESW EN7 ...... 25 H7
Pembroke Gdns DAGE RM10 ...... 91 H3 ▣
  KENS W8 ...... 118 F1 ▣
  WKENS W14 ...... 118 F2 ▣
Pembroke Gardens Cl
  KENS W8 ...... 118 F1 ▣
Pembroke Ms KENS W8 ...... 14 A4 ▣
  MUSWH N10 ...... 66 A2
Pembroke Pl EDGW HA8 ...... 63 G1 ▣
  ISLW TW7 ...... 115 L7 ▣
  KENS W8 ...... 14 A4 ▣
Pembroke Rd BMLY BR1 ...... 160 C1
  CEND/HSY/T N8 ...... 66 E5 ▣
  ECT SW5 ...... 14 A6
  EHAM E6 ...... 106 F4 ▣
  ERITH DA8 ...... 127 J3
  GDMY/SEVK IG3 ...... 89 M1
  GFD/PVL UB6 ...... 97 L8
  MTCM CR4 ...... 156 A5 ▣
  MUSWH N10 ...... 66 A2
  NTHWD HA6 ...... 41 J5
  PLMGR N13 ...... 49 J5
  RSLP HA4 ...... 77 L1
  SEVS/STOTM N15 ...... 67 M6 ▣
  SNWD SE25 ...... 157 L7
  WALTH E17 ...... 69 H6
  WBLY HA9 ...... 80 D3
Pembroke Sq KENS W8 ...... 14 A4
Pembroke St IS N1 ...... 5 K2
Pembroke Vls KENS W8 ...... 14 A4
Pembroke Wk KENS W8 ...... 14 A5
Pembury Av WPK KT4 ...... 169 G2
Pembury Cl COUL/CHIP CR5 ...... 185 G7
  HAYES BR2 ...... 174 F2
Pembury Ct HYS/HAR UB3 ...... 113 K4 ▣
Pembury Crs SCUP DA14 ...... 144 E6
Pembury Rd BXLYHN DA7 ...... 126 E5
  CLPT E5 ...... 86 B5
  SNWD SE25 ...... 158 A7
  TOTM N17 ...... 67 M2
Pemdevon Rd CROY/NA CR0 ...... 172 A2
Pemell Cl WCHPL E1 ...... 104 F3
Pemerich Cl HYS/HAR UB3 ...... 113 M3 ▣
Pempath Pl WBLY HA9 ...... 80 D2 ▣
Penally Pl IS N1 ...... 7 H3
Penang St WAP E1W 104 B7
Penarth St PECK SE15 ...... 122 C4
Penates ESH/CLAY KT10 ...... 166 D6
Penberth Rd CAT SE6 ...... 141 K6
Penbury Rd NWDGN UB2 ...... 114 B1
Pencombe Ms NTGHL W11 ...... 100 F6 ▣
Pencraig Dr DART DA1 ...... 146 C4
Pendall Cl EBAR EN4 ...... 34 E7
Penda Rd ERITH DA8 ...... 127 H5
Pendarves Rd RYNPK SW20 ...... 154 C4
Penda's Md HOM E9 ...... 86 E4 ▣
Pendell Av HYS/HAR UB3 ...... 113 M5
Pendennis Rd ORP BR6 ...... 177 J4
  STRHM/NOR SW16 ...... 138 E8
  TOTM N17 ...... 67 K4
Penderel Rd HSLW TW3 ...... 133 C2
Penderry Ri CAT SE6 ...... 141 K6
Penderyn Wy HOLWY N7 ...... 84 D4
Pendle Rd STRHM/NOR SW16 ...... 156 B2
Pendlestone Rd LEY E10 ...... 69 H6
Pendragon Rd BMLY BR1 ...... 142 A7
Pendrell Rd BROCKY SE4 ...... 122 E8
Pendrell St WOOL/PLUM SE18 ...... 125 K4
Pendula Dr YEAD UB4 ...... 96 D3
Penerley Rd CAT SE6 ...... 141 H5
  RAIN RM13 ...... 110 B4
Penfold Cl CROY/NA CR0 ...... 172 A5 ▣
Penfold Pl BAY/PAD W2 ...... 9 J2
Penfold Rd ED N9 ...... 50 D3
Penfold St STJWD NW8 ...... 9 H1
Penford Gdns ELTH/MOT SE9 ...... 142 D1
Penford St CMBW SE5 ...... 121 H7
Pengarth Rd BXLY DA5 ...... 144 D2
Penge La PGE/AN SE20 ...... 158 C3
Pengelly Cl CHESW EN7 ...... 26 B3 ▣
Penge Rd PLSTW E13 ...... 88 C7
  SNWD SE25 ...... 158 A6
Penhall Rd CHARL SE7 ...... 124 D2
Penhill Rd BXLY DA5 ...... 144 C4
Penhurst Rd BARK/HLT IG6 ...... 71 H1 ▣
Penifather La GFD/PVL UB6 ...... 97 K2
Peninsular Cl
  EBED/NFELT TW14 ...... 131 K3
Peninsular Park Rd CHARL SE7 ...... 124 A3
Penistone Rd
  STRHM/NOR SW16 ...... 156 E3
Penmon Rd ABYW SE2 ...... 126 A1
Pennack Rd PECK SE15 ...... 121 M4 ▣
Pennant Ms KENS W8 ...... 14 C5
Pennant Ter WALTH E17 ...... 68 F3
Pennard Rd SHB W12 ...... 100 C8
The Pennards SUN TW16 ...... 150 C6 ▣
Penn Cl GFD/PVL UB6 ...... 97 H1
  KTN/HRWW/W HA3 ...... 62 C5
  UX/CGN UB8 ...... 94 D3
Penner Cl WIM/MER SW19 ...... 136 E6
Penners Gdns SURB KT6 ...... 167 L2
Pennethorne Cl HOM E9 ...... 86 C8 ▣
Pennethorne Rd PECK SE15 ...... 122 B5
Penney Cl DART DA1 ...... 146 D4
Penn Gdns CHST BR7 ...... 161 H5

  CRW RM5 ...... 73 C1
Pennine Dr CRICK NW2 ...... 82 D2
Pennine La CRICK NW2 ...... 82 E2 ▣
Pennine Wy BXLYHN DA7 ...... 127 L6
  HYS/HAR UB3 ...... 113 K5
Pennington Cl CRW RM5 ...... 55 C8 ▣
Pennington Dr STHGT/OAK N14 ...... 35 L8
Pennington St WAP E1W 104 B6
Pennington Wy LEE/GVPK SE12 ...... 142 B4
Penn La BXLY DA5 ...... 144 D3
Penn Rd HOLWY N7 ...... 84 E5
Penn St IS N1 ...... 7 H4
Penny Cl RAIN RM13 ...... 110 B2
Pennyfields POP/IOD E14 ...... 105 C6
Penny La SHPTN TW17 ...... 164 E2
Pennyroyal Av EHAM E6 ...... 107 G5
Penpoll Rd HACK E8 ...... 86 B6
Penpool La WELL DA16 ...... 126 B8
Penrhyn Av WALTH E17 ...... 69 C2
Penrhyn Crs
  MORT/ESHN SW14 ...... 135 J1 ▣
  WALTH E17 ...... 69 G2
Penrhyn Gv WALTH E17 ...... 69 C2 ▣
Penrhyn Rd KUT KT1 ...... 152 E7
Penrith Cl BECK BR3 ...... 159 H4 ▣
  PUT/ROE SW15 ...... 136 E2
Penrith Pl WNWD SE27 ...... 139 H6
Penrith Rd BARK/HLT IG6 ...... 53 M8
  HARH RM3 ...... 57 C8
  NWMAL KT3 ...... 153 K7
  SEVS/STOTM N15 ...... 67 K6
  THHTH CR7 ...... 157 J5
Penrith St
  STRHM/NOR SW16 ...... 156 C2 ▣
Penrose Av OXHEY WD19 ...... 42 E4
Penrose Gv WALW SE17 ...... 18 E8
Penrose St WALW SE17 ...... 18 E8
Penryn St CAMTN NW1 ...... 5 G5
Penry St STHWK SE1 ...... 19 K6 ▣
Pensbury Pl VX/NE SW8 ...... 120 C7
Pensbury St VX/NE SW8 ...... 120 C7
Penscroft Gdns BORE WD6 ...... 32 D7
Pensford Av RCH/KEW TW9 ...... 117 G7
Penshurst Av BFN/LL DA15 ...... 144 A3
Penshurst Gdns EDGW HA8 ...... 45 H7
Penshurst Gn HAYES BR2 ...... 159 M8
Penshurst Rd BXLYHN DA7 ...... 126 F6
  HOM E9 ...... 86 D7
  POTB/CUF EN6 ...... 23 K4
  THHTH CR7 ...... 157 H8
  TOTM N17 ...... 67 M1
Penshurst Wy BELMT SM2 ...... 182 A1 ▣
  STMC/STPC BR5 ...... 162 C7 ▣
Pensilver Cl EBAR EN4 ...... 34 E7 ▣
Penstemon Cl FNCH N3 ...... 47 C8
Pentelow Gdns
  EBED/NFELT TW14 ...... 132 A3
Pentire Cl UPMR RM14 ...... 75 L7
Pentire Rd WALTH E17 ...... 69 K2
Pentland Av EDGW HA8 ...... 45 H4
  SHPTN TW17 ...... 149 C8
Pentland Cl CRICK NW2 ...... 82 E2 ▣
Pentland Rd BUSH WD23 ...... 43 J1
Pentlands Cl MTCM CR4 ...... 156 A6
Pentland Wy HGDN/ICK UB10 ...... 77 J3
Pentlow St PUT/ROE SW15 ...... 118 C7
Pentlow Wy BKHH IG9 ...... 52 E2
Pentney Rd BAL SW12 ...... 138 C5
  CHING E4 ...... 51 K3 ▣
  RYNPK SW20 ...... 154 E4 ▣
Penton Dr CHES/WCR EN8 ...... 26 D2
Penton Gv IS N1 ...... 6 A6
Penton Hall Dr STA TW18 ...... 148 A4
Penton Hook Rd STA TW18 ...... 148 A4
Penton Pl WALW SE17 ...... 18 E7
Penton Ri FSBYW WC1X 5 M7
Penton St IS N1 ...... 6 A5
Pentonville Rd IS N1 ...... 5 L6
Pentrich Av EN EN1 ...... 37 C1
Pentridge St PECK SE15 ...... 121 M5 ▣
Pentyre Av UED N18 ...... 49 K7
Penwerris Av ISLW TW7 ...... 115 J5
Penwith Rd WAND/EARL SW18 ...... 137 H6
Penwortham Rd
  SAND/SEL CR2 ...... 184 D3
  STRHM/NOR SW16 ...... 156 B2
Penylan Pl EDGW HA8 ...... 63 G1 ▣
Penywern Rd ECT SW5 ...... 14 B7
Penzance Cl DEN/HRF UB9 ...... 58 D3 ▣
Penzance Gdns HARH RM3 ...... 57 G8 ▣
Penzance Pl NTGHL W11 ...... 100 E7
Penzance Rd HARH RM3 ...... 57 C8
Penzance St NTGHL W11 ...... 100 E7
Peony Gdns SHB W12 ...... 100 A6
Peploe Rd KIL/WHAMP NW6 ...... 100 E1
Peplow Cl WDR/YW UB7 ...... 94 D7 ▣
Pepper Cl EHAM E6 ...... 106 F4 ▣
Peppermint Cl CROY/NA CR0 ...... 171 L2 ▣
Pepper St POP/IOD E14 ...... 123 H1
  STHWK SE1 ...... 18 E1
Peppie Cl STNW/STAM N16 ...... 85 L2
Pepys Cl HGDN/ICK UB10 ...... 77 H4
Pepys Crs BAR EN5 ...... 33 J8
Pepys Ri ORP BR6 ...... 176 F3
Pepys Rd NWCR SE14 ...... 122 D7
  RYNPK SW20 ...... 154 C4
Pepys St TWRH EC3N 13 K6
Perceval Av HAMP NW3 ...... 83 L5
Perch St HACK E8 ...... 85 M4
Percival Ct TOTM N17 ...... 67 M1 ▣
Percival Gdns CHDH RM6 ...... 71 J4
Percival Rd EMPK RM11 ...... 74 C7
  EN EN1 ...... 36 F7
  FELT TW13 ...... 131 M6
  MORT/ESHN SW14 ...... 135 J2
  ORP BR6 ...... 176 B4
Percival St FSBYE EC1V 6 D8
Percy Av ASHF TW15 ...... 149 G1
Percy Bryant Rd SUN TW16 ...... 149 L1 ▣
Percy Bush Rd WDR/YW UB7 ...... 112 F1 ▣
Percy Gdns PEND EN3 ...... 37 K8

  WPK KT4 ...... 168 D3
  YEAD UB4 ...... 95 L2
Percy Ms FITZ W1T ...... 11 G3 ▣
Percy Rd BXLYHN DA7 ...... 126 F7
  CAN/RD E16 ...... 105 L4
  GDMY/SEVK IG3 ...... 72 A8
  HPTN TW12 ...... 151 G3
  ISLW TW7 ...... 134 A1
  MTCM CR4 ...... 171 G2
  NFNCH/WDSP N12 ...... 47 J7
  PGE/AN SE20 ...... 158 D4
  ROMW/RG RM7 ...... 73 J4
  SHB W12 ...... 100 A8
  SNWD SE25 ...... 158 A8 ▣
  WAN E11 ...... 69 L8
  WATW WD18 ...... 29 H7 ▣
  WCHMH N21 ...... 49 J2
  WHTN TW2 ...... 133 H5
Percy St FITZ W1T ...... 11 G3 ▣
Percy Wy WHTN TW2 ...... 133 J5 ▣
Peregrine Cl CSTN WD25 ...... 21 L7
  WLSDN NW10 ...... 81 K5 ▣
Peregrine Ct WELL DA16 ...... 125 M6
Peregrine Gdns
  CROY/NA CR0 ...... 173 L4 ▣
Peregrine Rd BARK/HLT IG6 ...... 54 B7
  SUN TW16 ...... 149 L5
Peregrine Wy
  WIM/MER SW19 ...... 154 C3 ▣
Perham Rd WKENS W14 ...... 118 E3
Peridot St EHAM E6 ...... 106 E4
Perifield DUL SE21 ...... 139 J5
Perimeade Rd GFD/PVL UB6 ...... 98 C3
Periton Rd ELTH/MOT SE9 ...... 142 D1
Perivale Gdns GSTN WD25 ...... 21 H7
  WEA W13 ...... 98 B3
Perivale La GFD/PVL UB6 ...... 98 A2
Perkin Cl ALP/SUD HA0 ...... 80 B5
  GRH DA9 ...... 147 M2
Perkin's Rents WEST SW1P 17 G3
Perkins Rd BARK/HLT IG6 ...... 71 K6
Perkins Sq STHWK SE1 ...... 12 F8
Perks Cl BKHTH/KID SE3 ...... 123 L7
Perpins Rd ELTH/MOT SE9 ...... 143 L3
Perran Rd BRXS/STRHM SW2 ...... 139 H6
Perrers Rd HMSMTH W6 ...... 118 B1
Perrin Cl ASHF TW15 ...... 148 F1 ▣
Perrin Rd ALP/SUD HA0 ...... 80 A4
Perrin's Ct HAMP NW3 ...... 83 J4 ▣
Perrin's Wk HAMP NW3 ...... 83 J4
Perry Av ACT W3 ...... 99 K5
Perry Cl RAIN RM13 ...... 109 K1 ▣
  UX/CGN UB8 ...... 95 H5
Perry Ct SEVS/STOTM N15 ...... 67 L7 ▣
Perryfield Wy CDALE/KGS NW9 ...... 63 M7
  RCHPK/HAM TW10 ...... 134 B6
Perry Gdns ED N9 ...... 50 B1
Perry Garth NTHLT UB5 ...... 78 C8
Perry Gv DART DA1 ...... 147 G1
Perry Hall Cl ORP BR6 ...... 177 G2
Perry Hall Rd ORP BR6 ...... 176 F1
Perry Hl CAT SE6 ...... 140 F6
Perry How WPK KT4 ...... 168 F3
Perry Mnr CHST BR7 ...... 161 L2
Perrymans Farm Rd
  GNTH/NBYPK IG2 ...... 71 K7
Perry Md BUSH WD23 ...... 43 J1
  ENC/FH EN2 ...... 24 A2
Perrymead St FUL/PGN SW6 ...... 119 G6
Perryn Rd ACT W3 ...... 99 K6
  BERM/RHTH SE16 ...... 122 B1
Perry Oak Dr HTHAIR TW6 ...... 112 B7
Perry Oaks Dr WDR/YW UB7 ...... 112 B7
Perry Ri FSTH SE23 ...... 140 E7
Perry St CHST BR7 ...... 161 L2
  DART DA1 ...... 127 L8
Perry V FSTH SE23 ...... 140 D6 ▣
Perry Wy SOCK/AV RM15 ...... 111 J6
Persant Rd CAT SE6 ...... 141 L7
Perseverance Pl
  BRXN/ST SW9 ...... 121 G5 ▣
Persfield Rd EW KT17 ...... 181 G3 ▣
Pershore Cl CDALE/KGS NW9 ...... 63 M7
Pershore Gv CAR SM5 ...... 170 D1
Pert Cl MUSWH N10 ...... 66 B1
Perth Av CDALE/KGS NW9 ...... 63 K8
  YEAD UB4 ...... 96 C3
Perth Cl RYNPK SW20 ...... 153 M5
Perth Rd BARK IG11 ...... 107 K1
  BECK BR3 ...... 159 J5
  FSBYPK N4 ...... 85 G1
  GNTH/NBYPK IG2 ...... 71 H7
  LEY E10 ...... 86 E1
  PLSTW E13 ...... 106 B1
  WDGN N22 ...... 67 H2
Perth Ter GNTH/NBYPK IG2 ...... 71 J8
Perwell Av RYLN/HDSTN HA2 ...... 78 F1
Petauel Rd TEDD TW11 ...... 151 L1
Petavel Rd TEDD TW11 ...... 151 L2
Peter Av WLSDN NW10 ...... 82 B7
Peterboat Cl GNWCH SE10 ...... 123 L2
Peterborough Av UPMR RM14 ...... 93 L1
Peterborough Ms
  FUL/PGN SW6 ...... 119 G7 ▣
Peterborough Rd CAR SM5 ...... 170 E1
  FUL/PGN SW6 ...... 119 G7
  HRW HA1 ...... 79 L1
  LEY E10 ...... 69 J6
Peterborough Vls
  FUL/PGN SW6 ...... 119 H6 ▣
Petergate BTSEA SW11 ...... 137 J1
Peters Cl BCTR RM8 ...... 71 K8
  EDGW HA8 ...... 44 D8
  STAN HA7 ...... 44 D8
  WELL DA16 ...... 125 L7
Petersfield Av HARH RM3 ...... 56 E8
  STA TW18 ...... 148 C1
Petersfield Cl HARH RM3 ...... 57 G8
  UED N18 ...... 49 J7
Petersfield Crs COUL/CHIP CR5 ...... 183 J5
Petersfield Ri PUT/ROE SW15 ...... 136 B5
Petersfield Rd ACT W3 ...... 99 J3
  STA TW18 ...... 148 C1
Petersham Cl
  RCHPK/HAM TW10 ...... 134 D6 ▣
  SUT SM1 ...... 169 M7
Petersham Dr STMC/STPC BR5 ...... 161 M5

Petersham Gdns
STMC/STPC BR5 ...... 161 M5
Petersham La *SKENS* SW7 ...... 14 C4
Petersham Ms *SKENS* SW7 ...... 14 C4
Petersham Pl *SKENS* SW7 ...... 14 C4
Petersham Rd
RCHPK/HAM TW10 ...... 134 B5
Peterstone Rd *ABYW* SE2 ...... 108 B8
Peterstow Cl *WIM/MER* SW19 ...... 136 E6
Peter St *SOHO/CST* W1F 11 G6
Peterwood Wy *CROY/NA* CR0 ...... 171 M4
Petherton Rd *HBRY* N5 ...... 85 J5
Petley Rd *HMSMTH* W6 ...... 118 C4
Peto Pl *CAMTN* NW1 ...... 4 D9
Peto St North *CAN/RD* E16 ...... 105 M5
Pett Cl *HCH* 92 B2
Petten Cl *STMC/STPC* BR5 ...... 177 K3
Petten Gv *STMC/STPC* BR5 ...... 177 K3
Pettits Bvd *GPK* RM2 ...... 73 L3
Pettits La *ROM* RM1 ...... 73 L3
Pettits La *ROM* RM1 ...... 73 L4
Pettits La North *ROM* RM1 ...... 73 K2
Pettit's Pl *DAGE* RM10 ...... 91 G5
Pettit's Rd *DAGE* RM10 ...... 91 G5
Pettiward Cl *PUT/ROE* SW15 ...... 136 C1
Pettley Gdns *ROMW/RG* RM7 ...... 73 K6
Pettman Crs *THMD* SE28 ...... 125 K2
Pettsgrove Av *ALP/SUD* HA0 ...... 80 C5
Pett's Hill *NTHLT* UB5 ...... 79 H4
Petts La *SHPTN* TW17 ...... 149 G7
Pett St *CHARL* SE7 ...... 124 E2
Petts Wood Rd
STMC/STPC BR5 ...... 161 K8
Petty France *STJSPK* SW1H 16 F3
Pettys Cl *CHES/WCR* EN8 ...... 26 D2
Petworth Cl *NTHLT* UB5 ...... 78 F7
Petworth Gdns *HGDN/ICK* UB10 ...... 77 J8
RYNPK SW20 ...... 154 B6
Petworth Rd *BXLYHS* DA6 ...... 145 G2
NFNCH/WDSP HA2 ...... 47 L7
Petworth St *BTSEA* SW11 ...... 119 L6
Petworth Wy *HCH* RM12 ...... 91 M4
Petyt Pl *CHEL* SW3 ...... 119 L4
Petyward *CHEL* SW3 ...... 15 K6
Pevensey Av *EN* EN1 ...... 36 C5
FBAR/BDGN N11 ...... 48 D7
Pevensey Cl *ISLW* TW7 ...... 115 J5
Pevensey Rd *FELT* TW13 ...... 132 E5
FSTGT E7 ...... 88 A4
TOOT SW17 ...... 137 K8
Peveril Dr *TEDD* TW11 ...... 151 K1
Pewsey Cl *CHING* E4 ...... 51 G7
Peyton Pl *GNWCH* SE10 ...... 123 J5
Pharaoh Cl *MTCM* CR4 ...... 170 F2
PUR/KEN CR8 ...... 184 B6
Phelp St *WALW* SE17 ...... 19 G8
Phelps Wy *HYS/HAR* UB3 ...... 113 M2
Phene St *CHEL* SW3 ...... 15 K9
Philan Wy *CRW* RM5 ...... 55 K8
Philchurch Pl *WCHPL* E1 ...... 104 A5
Philimore Cl *WOOL/PLUM* SE18 ...... 125 L3
Philip Av *ROMW/RG* RM7 ...... 91 K1
Philip Gdns *CROY/NA* CR0 ...... 173 M4
Philip La *SEVS/STOTM* N15 ...... 67 K5
Philippa Gdns *ELTH/MOT* SE9 ...... 142 D2
Philip Pl *PECK* SE15 ...... 122 A8
RAIN RM13 ...... 109 L2
STA TW18 ...... 148 D2
Philips Cl *MTCM* CR4 ...... 171 G3
Philip St *PLSTW* E13 ...... 106 A3
Philllida Rd *HARH* RM3 ...... 75 G3
Phillimore Gdns *KENS* W8 ...... 14 A2
WLSDN NW10 ...... 82 C8
Phillimore Gardens Cl
KENS W8 ...... 14 A3
Phillimore Pl *KENS* W8 ...... 14 A2
RAD WD7 ...... 30 E1
Phillimore Wk *KENS* W8 ...... 14 A3
Phillip Av *SWLY* BR8 ...... 163 K7
Phillippers *GSTN* WD25 ...... 21 L8
Phillipp St *IS* N1 ...... 7 K4
Phillips Cl *DART* DA1 ...... 146 B3
Philpot La *FENCHS* EC3M 13 J5
Philpots Pl *WDR/YW* UB7 ...... 94 D6
Phineas Pett Road Rd
ELTH/MOT SE9 ...... 124 E8
Phipp's Bridge Rd
MTCM CR4 ...... 155 K6
WIM/MER SW19 ...... 155 J5
Phipps Hatch La *ENC/FH* EN2 ...... 36 C3
Phipp St *SDTCH* EC2A 7 J7
Phoebeth Rd *LEW* SE13 ...... 141 G2
Phoenix Cl *NTHWD* HA6 ...... 41 M6
WWKM BR4 ...... 174 D4
Phoenix Ct *BTFD* TW8 ...... 116 E3
Phoenix Dr *HAYES* BR2 ...... 175 K6
Phoenix Pl *DART* DA1 ...... 146 D4
FSBYW WC1X 5 M9
Phoenix Rd *CAMTN* NW1 ...... 5 C7
PGE/AN SE20 ...... 158 C2
Phoenix St *LSQ/SEVD* WC2H 11 H5
Phoenix Wy *HEST* TW5 ...... 114 D4
Phyllis Av *NWMAL* KT3 ...... 154 B8
Picardy Manorway *BELV* DA17 ...... 109 H8
Picardy Rd *BELV* DA17 ...... 127 G3
Picardy St *BELV* DA17 ...... 127 G1
Piccadilly *MYFR/PICC* W1J 16 B1
Pickard St *FSBYE* EC1V 6 D7
Pickering Av *EHAM* E6 ...... 107 C1
Pickering Gdns *SNWD* SE25 ...... 172 F1
Pickering St *IS* N1 ...... 6 D3
Pickets Cl *BUSH* WD23 ...... 43 K3
Pickets St *BAL* SW12 ...... 138 A4
Pickett Cft *STAN* HA7 ...... 62 D2
Pickett's Lock La *ED* N9 ...... 50 D4
Pickford Cl *BXLYHN* DA7 ...... 126 E7
Pickford La *BXLYHN* DA7 ...... 126 E7
Pickford Rd *BXLYHN* DA7 ...... 126 E8
Pickhurst Gn *HAYES* BR2 ...... 174 F2
Pickhurst La *HAYES* BR2 ...... 159 L8
Pickhurst Md *HAYES* BR2 ...... 174 F1
Pickhurst Ri *WWKM* BR4 ...... 174 D3
Pickwick Cl *HSLWW* TW4 ...... 134 D1
Pickwick Ms *UED* N18 ...... 49 L7
Pickwick Pl *HRW* HA1 ...... 61 L8

Pickwick Rd *DUL* SE21 ...... 139 K4
Pickwick St *STHWK* SE1 ...... 18 E2
Pickwick Wy *CHST* BR7 ...... 161 J2
Picton Pl *MBLAR* W1H 10 B5
Picton St *CMBW* SE5 ...... 121 K5
Piedmont Rd
WOOL/PLUM SE18 ...... 125 K3
Field Heath Av *UX/CGN* UB8 ...... 95 G3
Field Heath Rd *UX/CGN* UB8 ...... 94 F3
Pier Head *WAP* E1W 104 B7
Piermont Pl *BMLY* BR1 ...... 160 D5
Piermont Rd *EDUL* SE22 ...... 140 B2
Pierrepoint Rd *ACT* W3 ...... 99 H6
Pier Rd *CAN/RD* E16 ...... 106 F8
EBED/NFELT TW14 ...... 132 B2
ERITH DA8 ...... 127 L4
Pier St *POP/IOD* E14 ...... 123 J2
Pier Ter *WAND/EARL* SW18 ...... 137 H1
Pier Wy *WOOL/PLUM* SE18 ...... 125 K1
Pigeon La *HPTN* TW12 ...... 133 G8
Pigott St *POP/IOD* E14 ...... 105 G5
Pike Cl *BMLY* BR1 ...... 160 B1
Pike La *UPMR* RM14 ...... 93 M5
Pike Rd *MLHL* NW7 ...... 45 K6
Pike's End *PIN* HA5 ...... 60 B5
Pikestone Cl *YEAD* UB4 ...... 96 E3
Pilgrimage St *STHWK* SE1 ...... 19 G2
Pilgrim Cl *GSTN* WD25 ...... 21 K6
MRDN SM4 ...... 170 B2
Pilgrim Hl *WNWD* SE27 ...... 139 J8
Pilgrims Cl *NTHLT* UB5 ...... 79 J3
PLMGR N13 ...... 48 F6
Pilgrims Ct *DART* DA1 ...... 147 G2
Pilgrim's La *HAMP* NW3 ...... 83 K4
Pilgrims Ms *POP/IOD* E14 ...... 105 K6
Pilgrim's Ri *EBAR* EN4 ...... 34 E3
Pilgrim St *BLKFR* EC4V 12 C5
Pilgrims Wy *ARCH* N19 ...... 84 D1
DART DA1 ...... 147 H5
SAND/SEL CR2 ...... 172 F8
WBLY HA9 ...... 81 H1
Pilkington Rd *ORP* BR6 ...... 176 C5
PECK SE15 ...... 122 B7
Pilot Cl *DEPT* SE8 ...... 122 F4
Pilsden Cl *WIM/MER* SW19 ...... 136 D5
Piltdown Rd *OXHEY* WD19 ...... 42 D6
OXHEY WD19 ...... 42 D7
Pimlico Rd *BGVA* SW1W 16 A7
Pinchbeck Rd *ORP* BR6 ...... 176 F8
Pinchin St *WCHPL* E1 ...... 104 A6
Pincott Pl *BROCKY* SE4 ...... 122 D8
Pincott Rd *BXLYHS* DA6 ...... 145 J5
WIM/MER SW19 ...... 155 J5
Pindar St *SDTCH* EC2A 13 J2
Pindock Ms *MV/WKIL* W9 ...... 8 D1
Pine Apple Ct *WESTW* SW1E 16 E3
Pine Av *SRTFD* E15 ...... 87 K5
WWKM BR4 ...... 174 B3
Pine Cl *CHES/WCR* EN8 ...... 26 C1
NTHWD HA6 ...... 41 L8
PGE/AN SE20 ...... 158 C4
STAN HA7 ...... 44 B6
STHGT/OAK N14 ...... 48 C2
SWLY BR8 ...... 163 M7
Pine Coombe *CROY/NA* CR0 ...... 173 K6
Pine Ct *UPMR* RM14 ...... 93 G4
Pine Crs *CAR* SM5 ...... 182 D4
Pinecrest Gdns *ORP* BR6 ...... 176 B6
Pinecroft *GPK* RM2 ...... 74 C5
KTN/HRWW/W HA3 ...... 62 F6
WELL DA16 ...... 126 A5
Pinecroft Crs *BAR* EN5 ...... 33 L7
Pinefield Cl *POP/IOD* E14 ...... 105 G6
Pine Gdns *BRYLDS* KT5 ...... 168 A1
RSLP HA4 ...... 78 B1
Pine Gld *ORP* BR6 ...... 175 M6
Pine Gv *ARCH* N19 ...... 84 E2
BUSH WD23 ...... 29 M4
LCOL/BKTW AL2 ...... 21 M3
TRDG/WHET N20 ...... 46 F3
WEY KT13 ...... 164 B7
WIM/MER SW19 ...... 154 F1
Pine PI *EW* KT17 ...... 181 K7
Pine Rdg *CAR* SM5 ...... 183 G2
Pine Rd *CRICK* NW2 ...... 82 C4
FBAR/BDGN N11 ...... 48 A4
Pines Av *EN* EN1 ...... 37 J1
Pines Rd *BMLY* BR1 ...... 160 E5
The Pines *BORE* WD6 ...... 31 M5
PUR/KEN CR8 ...... 184 B6
SUN TW16 ...... 150 A6
WFD IG8 ...... 51 M5
Pine St *CLKNW* EC1R 6 A9
Pine Tree Cl *HEST* TW5 ...... 114 B8
Pine Trees Dr *HGDN/ICK* UB10 ...... 76 E4
Pine Wk *BELMT* SM2 ...... 182 D5
BRYLDS KT5 ...... 168 A1
CAR SM5 ...... 182 D3
Pine Wd *SUN* TW16 ...... 150 A4
Pinewood Av *BFN/LL* DA15 ...... 143 L5
PIN HA5 ...... 43 H6
RAIN RM13 ...... 110 B3
UX/CGN UB8 ...... 94 F5
Pinewood Cl *BORE* WD6 ...... 32 D4
CROY/NA CR0 ...... 173 L5
ORP BR6 ...... 176 D3
PIN HA5 ...... 43 H8
WAT WD17 ...... 29 G4
Pinewood Dr *ORP* BR6 ...... 176 E7
POTB/CUF EN6 ...... 22 F4
STA TW18 ...... 148 A1
Pinewood Gv *WEA* W13 ...... 98 C5
Pinewood Ms
STWL/WRAY TW19 ...... 130 D3
Pinewood Rd *ABR/ST* RM4 ...... 55 J6
ABYW SE2 ...... 126 D4
FELT TW13 ...... 132 B7
HAYES BR2 ...... 160 A7
Pinfold Rd *BUSH* WD23 ...... 29 M5
STRHM/NOR SW16 ...... 138 E8
Pinglestone Cl *WDR/YW* UB7 ...... 112 E5
Pinkcoat Cl *FELT* TW13 ...... 132 B7
Pinkham Wy North Circular Rd
MUSWH N10 ...... 65 M1
Pinks Hl *SWLY* BR8 ...... 163 L8

Pinkwell Av *HYS/HAR* UB3 ...... 113 K2
Pinkwell La *HYS/HAR* UB3 ...... 113 J2
Pinley Gdns *DAGW* RM9 ...... 90 B8
Pinnacle Hl *BXLYHN* DA7 ...... 145 H1
Pinnacle Hl North *BXLYHN* DA7 ...... 127 H8
Pinnacles *WAB* EN9 ...... 27 L7
Pinn Cl *UX/CGN* UB8 ...... 94 D5
Pinnell Rd *ELTH/MOT* SE9 ...... 142 D1
Pinner Ct *PIN* HA5 ...... 61 G5
Pinner Gn *PIN* HA5 ...... 60 C3
Pinner Gv *PIN* HA5 ...... 60 E5
Pinner Hl *PIN* HA5 ...... 60 B1
Pinner Hill Rd *PIN* HA5 ...... 60 C2
Pinner Park Av
RYLN/HDSTN HA2 ...... 61 J3
Pinner Park Gdns
RYLN/HDSTN HA2 ...... 61 J3
Pinner Rd *HRW* HA1 ...... 61 H6
NTHWD HA6 ...... 59 M2
OXHEY WD19 ...... 42 D1
PIN HA5 ...... 60 E5
Pinner Vw *RYLN/HDSTN* HA2 ...... 61 J5
Pinn Wy *RSLP* HA4 ...... 59 K8
Pintail Cl *EHAM* E6 ...... 106 E4
Pintail Rd *WFD* IG8 ...... 70 B1
Pintail Wy *YEAD* UB4 ...... 96 D4
Pinto Cl *BORE* WD6 ...... 45 K1
Pinto Wy *BKHTH/KID* SE3 ...... 142 B1
Pioneer Cl *SHB* W12 ...... 100 B5
Pioneer St *PECK* SE15 ...... 122 A6
Pioneer Wy *SHB* W12 ...... 100 C5
SWLY BR8 ...... 163 L6
WATW WD18 ...... 41 M1
Piper Cl *HOLWY* N7 ...... 84 F5
Piper Rd *KUT* KT1 ...... 153 G8
Pipers Gdns *CROY/NA* CR0 ...... 173 L2
Pipers Gn *CDALE/KGS* NW9 ...... 63 J6
Pipers Green La *EDGW* HA8 ...... 44 E5
Pipewell Rd *CAR* SM5 ...... 170 E1
Pippin Cl *CRICK* NW2 ...... 82 A3
CROY/NA CR0 ...... 173 M3
Pippins Cl *WDR/YW* UB7 ...... 112 D1
Pippins Ct *ASHF* TW15 ...... 149 H2
Piquet Rd *PGE/AN* SE20 ...... 158 C5
Pirbright Crs *CROY/NA* CR0 ...... 174 C8
Pirbright Rd *WAND/EARL* SW18 ...... 136 F5
Pirie Cl *CAN/RD* E16 ...... 106 B7
Pitcairn Cl *ROMW/RG* RM7 ...... 73 G5
Pitcairn Rd *MTCM* CR4 ...... 155 M3
Pitchford St *SRTFD* E15 ...... 87 K7
Pitfield Crs *THMD* SE28 ...... 108 A7
Pitfield St *IS* N1 ...... 7 J7
Pitfield Wy *PEND* EN3 ...... 37 J4
WLSDN NW10 ...... 81 J6
Pitfold Rd *LEE/GVPK* SE12 ...... 142 A4
Pitlake *CROY/NA* CR0 ...... 172 B4
Pitman St *CMBW* SE5 ...... 19 H8
Pitsea Pl *WCHPL* E1 ...... 104 D5
Pitsea St *WCHPL* E1 ...... 104 D5
Pitshanger La *EA* W5 ...... 98 B3
Pitt Crs *WIM/MER* SW19 ...... 137 H8
Pittman Gdns *IL* IG1 ...... 89 J5
Pitt Rd *EW* KT17 ...... 180 E7
ORP BR6 ...... 176 C6
RYLN/HDSTN HA2 ...... 79 J2
THHTH CR7 ...... 157 J8
Pitt's Head Ms
MYFR/PICC W1J 10 C9
Pittsmead Av *HAYES* BR2 ...... 175 G2
Pitt St *KENS* W8 ...... 14 B1
Pittville Gdns *SNWD* SE25 ...... 158 A6
Pixley St *POP/IOD* E14 ...... 105 J5
Pixton Wy *CROY/NA* CR0 ...... 185 L2
Place Farm Av *ORP* BR6 ...... 176 D3
Plaistow Gv *BMLY* BR1 ...... 160 B3
SRTFD E15 ...... 87 M8
Plaistow La *BMLY* BR1 ...... 160 A3
Plaistow Park Rd *PLSTW* E13 ...... 106 B1
Plaistow Rd *PLSTW* E13 ...... 106 A1
SRTFD E15 ...... 87 M8
Plaitford Cl *RKW/CH/CXG* WD3 ...... 40 E4
Plane St *SYD* SE26 ...... 140 B7
Plane Tree Crs *FELT* TW13 ...... 132 B7
Plantaganet Pl *WAB* EN9 ...... 27 H6
Plantagenet Cl
HOR/WEW KT19 ...... 168 D6
Plantagenet Gdns *CHDH* RM6 ...... 72 D8
Plantagenet Pl *CHDH* RM6 ...... 72 D8
Plantagenet Rd *BAR* EN5 ...... 34 C7
Plantain Pl *STHWK* SE1 ...... 19 G1
Plantation Dr *STMC/STPC* BR5 ...... 177 K3
Plantation Rd *ERITH* DA8 ...... 128 A6
The Plantation *BKHTH/KID* SE3 ...... 124 A7
Plashet Gv *EHAM* E6 ...... 88 C8
Plashet Rd *PLSTW* E13 ...... 88 A8
Plassy Rd *CAT* SE6 ...... 141 H4
Platford Gn *EMPK* RM11 ...... 74 E2
Platina St *SDTCH* EC2A 7 H9
Plato Rd *CLAP* SW4 ...... 138 C1
Platt's La *HAMP* NW3 ...... 83 G3
Platts Rd *PEND* EN3 ...... 37 J4
Platt St *CAMTN* NW1 ...... 5 G5
Plawsfield Rd *BECK* BR3 ...... 158 D4
Plaxtol Cl *BMLY* BR1 ...... 160 C4
Plaxtol Rd *ERITH* DA8 ...... 127 J6
Playfair St *HMSMTH* W6 ...... 118 C3
Playfield Av *CRW* RM5 ...... 73 J2
Playfield Crs *EDUL* SE22 ...... 139 L2
Playfield Rd *EDGW* HA8 ...... 63 J3
Playford Rd *FSBYPK* N4 ...... 84 F2
FSBYPK N4 ...... 85 G2
Playgreen Wy *CAT* SE6 ...... 141 S8
Playground Cl *BECK* BR3 ...... 158 D5
Playhouse Yd *BLKFR* EC4V 12 C5
Pleasance Rd *PUT/ROE* SW15 ...... 136 B2
STMC/STPC BR5 ...... 162 B5
The Pleasance
PUT/ROE SW15 ...... 136 B1
Pleasant Gv *CROY/NA* CR0 ...... 173 M5
Pleasant Pl *IS* N1 ...... 6 D2
WOT/HER KT12 ...... 165 K8
Pleasant Vw *ERITH* DA8 ...... 127 C7
ORP BR6 ...... 176 C7
Pleasant Wy *ALP/SUD* HA0 ...... 98 C1
Plender St *CAMTN* NW1 ...... 4 E4
Pleshey Rd *HOLWY* N7 ...... 84 D2
Plesman Wy *WLGTN* SM6 ...... 183 L2
Plevna Crs *SEVS/STOTM* N15 ...... 67 J7

Plevna Rd *ED* N9 ...... 50 A5
HPTN TW12 ...... 151 H4
Plevna St *POP/IOD* E14 ...... 123 J1
Pleydell Av *HMSMTH* W6 ...... 117 M1
NRWD SE19 ...... 157 M3
Pleydell St *EMB* EC4Y 12 B5
Plimsoll Cl *POP/IOD* E14 ...... 105 H5
Plimsoll Rd *FSBYPK* N4 ...... 85 H3
Plough Farm Cl *RSLP* HA4 ...... 59 K7
Plough Hl *POTB/CUF* EN6 ...... 24 E2
Plough La *CROY/NA* CR0 ...... 171 L6
DEN/HRF UB9 ...... 40 C8
EDUL SE22 ...... 139 M3
PUR/KEN CR8 ...... 183 M3
WIM/MER SW19 ...... 155 H1
WLGTN SM6 ...... 183 L2
Plough Lane Cl *WLGTN* SM6 ...... 171 L7
Ploughmans Cl *CAMTN* NW1 ...... 5 C1
Ploughmans End *ISLW* TW7 ...... 133 K2
Plough Pl *FLST/FETLN* EC4A 12 B4
Plough Ri *UPMR* RM14 ...... 75 L8
Plough St *WCHPL* E1 ...... 104 A5
Plough Ter *BTSEA* SW11 ...... 137 K1
Plough Wy *BERM/RHTH* SE16 ...... 122 F2
Plough Yd *SDTCH* EC2A 13 K1
Plover Gdns *UPMR* RM14 ...... 93 M1
Plover Wy *BERM/RHTH* SE16 ...... 122 F1
YEAD UB4 ...... 96 D5
Plowman Cl *UED* N18 ...... 49 K7
Plowman Wy *BCTR* RM8 ...... 90 C1
Plumbers Rw *WCHPL* E1 ...... 104 A4
Plumbridge St *GNWCH* SE10 ...... 123 J6
Plum La *WOOL/PLUM* SE18 ...... 125 H5
Plummer La *MTCM* CR4 ...... 155 M4
Plummer Rd *CLAP* SW4 ...... 138 D4
Plumpton Av *HCH* RM12 ...... 92 F3
Plumpton Cl *NTHLT* UB5 ...... 79 G6
Plumpton Wy *CAR* SM5 ...... 170 E5
Plumstead Common Rd
WOOL/PLUM SE18 ...... 125 H4
Plumstead High St
WOOL/PLUM SE18 ...... 125 K2
Plumstead Rd
WOOL/PLUM SE18 ...... 125 J2
Plumtree Cl *DAGE* RM10 ...... 91 J6
Plumtree Ct *FLST/FETLN* EC4A 12 B4
Plymouth Rd *BMLY* BR1 ...... 160 B4
CAN/RD E16 ...... 106 A4
Plymouth Whf *POP/IOD* E14 ...... 123 K2
Plympton Av *KIL/WHAMP* NW6 ...... 82 F7
Plympton Cl *BELV* DA17 ...... 126 E1
Plympton Pl *STJWD* NW8 ...... 9 J1
Plympton Rd *KIL/WHAMP* NW6 ...... 82 F7
Plympton St *STJWD* NW8 ...... 9 J1
Plymstock Rd *WELL* DA16 ...... 126 C5
Pocklington Cl *CDALE/KGS* NW9 ...... 63 L3
Pocock Av *WDR/YW* UB7 ...... 112 F1
Pocock St *STHWK* SE1 ...... 18 C1
Podmore Rd *WAND/EARL* SW18 ...... 137 J1
Poets Ga *CHESW* EN7 ...... 25 K1
Poet's Rd *HBRY* N5 ...... 85 K5
Poets Wy *HRW* HA1 ...... 61 L5
Pointalls Cl *FNCH* N3 ...... 65 J3
Point Cl *GNWCH* SE10 ...... 123 J6
Pointer Cl *THMD* SE28 ...... 108 D5
Pointers Cl *POP/IOD* E14 ...... 123 J3
Point Hl *GNWCH* SE10 ...... 123 J6
Point Pl *WBLY* HA9 ...... 81 H7
Point Pleasant
WAND/EARL SW18 ...... 137 G1
Poland St *SOHO/CST* W1F 10 F4
Polebrook Rd *BKHTH/KID* SE3 ...... 124 C8
Polecroft La *CAT* SE6 ...... 140 F6
Pole Hill Rd *CHING* E4 ...... 51 J2
HGDN/ICK UB10 ...... 95 H3
Polesden Gdns *RYNPK* SW20 ...... 154 B6
Polesworth Rd *DAGW* RM9 ...... 90 D7
Police Station Rd
WOT/HER KT12 ...... 165 J8
Pollard Cl *CAN/RD* E16 ...... 106 A6
CHIG IG7 ...... 54 A7
HOLWY N7 ...... 84 F5
Pollard Rd *MRDN* SM4 ...... 155 K8
TRDG/WHET N20 ...... 47 L4
Pollard Rw *BETH* E2 ...... 104 A2
Pollards Cl *CHESW* EN7 ...... 25 J2
LOU IG10 ...... 39 J8
Pollards Crs *STRHM/NOR* SW16 ...... 156 E6
Pollards Hl East
STRHM/NOR SW16 ...... 156 F6
Pollards Hl North
STRHM/NOR SW16 ...... 156 F6
Pollards Hl South
STRHM/NOR SW16 ...... 156 E6
Pollards Hl West
STRHM/NOR SW16 ...... 156 E6
Pollard St *BETH* E2 ...... 104 A2
Pollards Wood Rd
STRHM/NOR SW16 ...... 156 E5
Pollen St *CONDST* W1S 10 D5
Pollitt Dr *STJWD* NW8 ...... 3 G9
Polperro Cl *ORP* BR6 ...... 161 M6
Polsted Rd *CAT* SE6 ...... 140 F4
Polthorne Gv
WOOL/PLUM SE18 ...... 125 J2
Polworth Rd
STRHM/NOR SW16 ...... 156 E1
Polygon Rd *CAMTN* NW1 ...... 5 G7
The Polygon *CLAP* SW4 ...... 138 C1
Polytechnic St
WOOL/PLUM SE18 ...... 125 G2
Pomell Wy *WCHPL* E1 ...... 13 M4
Pomeroy Crs *WATN* WD24 ...... 29 H1
Pomeroy St *NWCR* SE14 ...... 122 C5
Pomfret Rd *CMBW* SE5 ...... 121 H8
Pomoja La *ARCH* N19 ...... 84 E2
Pond Cl *BKHTH/KID* SE3 ...... 124 A7
DEN/HRF UB9 ...... 58 C3
NFNCH/WDSP N12 ...... 47 L8
WOT/HER KT12 ...... 165 G8
Pond Cottage La *BECK* BR3 ...... 174 A3
Ponder St *HOLWY* N7 ...... 5 L1
Pondfield Rd *DAGE* RM10 ...... 91 L3
HAYES BR2 ...... 174 E3
ORP BR6 ...... 176 B5

Pond Gn *RSLP* HA4 ...... 77 L2
Pond Hill Gdns *CHEAM* SM3 ...... 169 L8
Pond Md *DUL* SE21 ...... 139 K3
Pond Piece *LHD/OX* KT22 ...... 178 B7
Pond Pl *CHEL* SW3 ...... 15 J6
Pond Rd *BKHTH/KID* SE3 ...... 123 M8
SRTFD E15 ...... 105 L1
Pondside Cl *HYS/HAR* UB3 ...... 113 K5
The Ponds *WEY* KT13 ...... 164 D8
Pond St *HAMP* NW3 ...... 83 L5
Pond Wk *UPMR* RM14 ...... 93 L2
Pond Wy *TEDD* TW11 ...... 152 C2
Pondwood Ri *ORP* BR6 ...... 176 C2
Ponler St *WCHPL* E1 ...... 104 B5
Ponsard Rd *WLSDN* NW10 ...... 100 B2
Ponsford St *HOM* E9 ...... 86 C6
Ponsonby Pl *WEST* SW1P 17 H7
Ponsonby Rd
PUT/ROE SW15 ...... 136 D5
Ponsonby Ter *WEST* SW1P 17 H7
Pontefract Rd *BMLY* BR1 ...... 160 A1
Ponton Rd *VX/NE* SW8 ...... 120 D1
Pont St *KTBR* SW1X 15 L4
Pont Street Ms *CHEL* SW1X 15 L4
Pontypool Pl *STHWK* SE1 ...... 18 C1
Pool Cl *BECK* BR3 ...... 159 G1
E/WMO/HCT KT8 ...... 150 F8
Pool Ct *CAT* SE6 ...... 141 G6
Poole Cl *RSLP* HA4 ...... 76 C6
Poole Court Rd *HEST* TW5 ...... 114 E7
Pool End Cl *SHPTN* TW17 ...... 149 G8
Poole Rd *EMPK* RM11 ...... 74 F1
HOM E9 ...... 86 D6
HOR/WEW KT19 ...... 168 D8
Pooles Buildings
FSBYW WC1X 12 A1
Pooles Pk *FSBYPK* N4 ...... 85 G2
Poole St *IS* N1 ...... 7 G4
Poole Wy *YEAD* UB4 ...... 95 L2
Poolmans St *BERM/RHTH* SE16 ...... 104 D8
Pool Rd *E/WMO/HCT* KT8 ...... 150 F8
HRW HA1 ...... 61 K8
Poolsford Rd *CDALE/KGS* NW9 ...... 63 L5
Poonah St *WCHPL* E1 ...... 104 E5
Pope Cl *EBED/NFELT* TW14 ...... 131 M5
WIM/MER SW19 ...... 155 K2
Pope Rd *HAYES* BR2 ...... 160 D8
Pope's Av *WHTN* TW2 ...... 133 L6
Popes Dr *FNCH* N3 ...... 65 G2
Popes Gv *CROY/NA* CR0 ...... 173 M5
WHTN TW2 ...... 133 L6
Pope's La *EA* W5 ...... 116 D1
WATN WD24 ...... 29 H2
Pope's Rd *BRXN/ST* SW9 ...... 138 B2
ABLGY WD5 ...... 20 C4
Pope St *STHWK* SE1 ...... 19 K2
Popham Cl *FELT* TW13 ...... 132 E7
Popham Rd *IS* N1 ...... 6 E3
Popham St *IS* N1 ...... 6 E3
Poplar Av *MTCM* CR4 ...... 155 M4
NWDGN UB2 ...... 115 H1
ORP BR6 ...... 176 B4
WDR/YW UB7 ...... 112 F6
Poplar Bath St *POP/IOD* E14 ...... 105 H6
Poplar Cl *HOM* E9 ...... 86 F5
PIN HA5 ...... 60 D2
Poplar Crs *HMSMTH* W6 ...... 100 C8
HOR/WEW KT19 ...... 168 C8
Poplar Dr *BNSTD* SM7 ...... 181 K7
Poplar Farm Cl *HOR/WEW* KT19 ...... 168 C8
Poplar Gdns *NWMAL* KT3 ...... 153 K5
Poplar Gv *FBAR/BDGN* N11 ...... 48 A8
WBLY HA9 ...... 81 J3
Poplar High St *POP/IOD* E14 ...... 105 H6
Poplar Ms *SHB* W12 ...... 100 C7
Poplar Mt *BELV* DA17 ...... 127 H2
Poplar Pl *BAY/PAD* W2 ...... 8 C6
HYS/HAR UB3 ...... 96 A6
THMD SE28 ...... 108 C6
Poplar Rd *ASHF* TW15 ...... 149 J1
CHEAM SM3 ...... 169 M3
DEN/HRF UB9 ...... 76 C6
HNHL SE24 ...... 139 J1
WIM/MER SW19 ...... 155 C6
Poplar Rd South
WIM/MER SW19 ...... 155 G6
Poplars Cl *GSTN* WD25 ...... 21 H5
RSLP HA4 ...... 77 L1
Poplar Shaw *WAB* EN9 ...... 27 M6
Poplars Rd *LEY* E10 ...... 69 H7
Poplar St *ROMW/RG* RM7 ...... 73 J5
Poplar Wk *CROY/NA* CR0 ...... 172 C4
HNHL SE24 ...... 139 J1
Poplar Wy *BARK/HLT* IG6 ...... 71 J5
FELT TW13 ...... 132 B7
Poppins Ct *FLST/FETLN* EC4A 12 C5
Poppleton Rd *WAN* E11 ...... 69 L7
Poppy Cl *MTCM* CR4 ...... 171 G3
Poppy Gv *CROY/NA* CR0 ...... 173 J2
Poppy Wk *CHESW* EN7 ...... 25 K1
Popular Gv *NWMAL* KT3 ...... 153 K6
Porchester Cl *EMPK* RM11 ...... 74 E7
Porchester Garden Ms
BAY/PAD W2 ...... 8 D5
Porchester Gdns *BAY/PAD* W2 ...... 8 D6
Porchester Md *BECK* BR3 ...... 159 H2
Porchester Pl *BAY/PAD* W2 ...... 9 K5
Porchester Rd *BAY/PAD* W2 ...... 8 D4
KUT KT1 ...... 153 H5
Porchester Sq *BAY/PAD* W2 ...... 8 D4
Porchester Ter *BAY/PAD* W2 ...... 8 E5
Porchester Ter North
BAY/PAD W2 ...... 8 D4
Porchfield Cl *BELMT* SM2 ...... 182 B5
Porch Wy *TRDG/WHET* N20 ...... 47 M5
Porcupine Cl *ELTH/MOT* SE9 ...... 142 E6
Porden Rd *BRXN/ST* SW9 ...... 138 F1
Porlock Av *RYLN/HDSTN* HA2 ...... 79 J1
Porlock Rd *EN* EN1 ...... 49 M2
Porlock St *STHWK* SE1 ...... 19 H1
Porrington Cl *CHST* BR7 ...... 160 F4
Portal Cl *RSLP* HA4 ...... 78 A4
WNWD SE27 ...... 139 G7
Portbury Cl *PECK* SE15 ...... 122 A6
Portchester Cl *CMBW* SE5 ...... 139 J1
Porten Rd *WKENS* W14 ...... 118 E1
Porter Rd *EHAM* E6 ...... 106 F5
Porters Av *DAGW* RM9 ...... 90 B6

Porter St MHST W1U ... 9 M2
STHWK SE1 ... 12 F8
Porters Wy WDR/YW UB7 ... 112 F1
Porteus Rd BAY/PAD W2 ... 8 F3
Portgate CI MV/WKIL W9 ... 100 F3
Porthcawe Rd SYD SE26 ... 140 E8
Porthkerry Av WELL DA16 ... 144 A1
Portia Wy BOW E3 ... 104 F3
Portinscale Rd PUT/ROE SW15 ... 136 E2
Portland Av BFN/LL DA15 ... 144 A3
NWMAL KT3 ... 168 F2
STNW/STAM N16 ... 85 M1
Portland CI CHDH RM6 ... 72 E6
Portland Crs ASHF TW15 ... 131 K8
ELTH/MOT SE9 ... 142 E6
GFD/PVL UB6 ... 97 H3
STAN HA7 ... 62 D3
Portland Crs West STAN HA7 ... 62 D4
Portland Dr CHESW EN7 ... 26 A4
ENC/FH EN2 ... 36 E3
Portland Gdns CHDH RM6 ... 72 D6
FSBYPK N4 ... 67 H7
Portland Gv VX/NE SW8 ... 120 F6
Portland Ms SOHO/CST W1F ... 10 F7
Portland PI CAVSQ/HST W1G ... 10 D3
EW KT17 ... 180 E5
SNWD SE25 ... 158 A7
Portland Ri FSBYPK N4 ... 85 H1
Portland Rd ASHF TW15 ... 130 E7
BMLY BR1 ... 142 C8
ELTH/MOT SE9 ... 142 E6
KUT KT1 ... 152 E6
MTCM CR4 ... 155 L5
NTGHL W11 ... 100 E7
NWDGN UB2 ... 114 F1
SEVS/STOTM N15 ... 67 L5
SNWD SE25 ... 158 B7
YEAD UB4 ... 95 L2
Portland St WALW SE17 ... 19 G8
Portman Av MORT/ESHN SW14 ... 117 K8
Portman CI BXLY DA5 ... 145 L5
BXLYHN DA7 ... 126 E8
MBLAR W1H ... 10 A4
Portman Dr WFD IG8 ... 70 D3
Portman Gdns CDALE/KGS NW9 ... 63 K4
HGDN/ICK UB10 ... 77 G7
Portman Ga CAMTN NW1 ... 9 K1
Portman Ms South MBLAR W1H ... 10 A5
Portman PI BETH E2 ... 104 C2
Portman Sq MBLAR W1H ... 9 M4
Portman St MBLAR W1H ... 10 A5
Portman Towers MBLAR W1H ... 9 M4
Portmeers CI WALTH E17 ... 68 F7
Portmore Gdns CRW RM5 ... 55 G7
Portmore Park Rd WEY KT13 ... 164 A5
Portmore Wy WEY KT13 ... 164 A5
Portnall Rd MV/WKIL W9 ... 100 F2
Portnoi CI ROM RM1 ... 73 K3
Portobello Ms NTGHL W11 ... 8 A7
Portobello Rd NKENS W10 ... 100 E4
NTGHL W11 ... 100 F5
Portpool La FSBYW WC1X ... 12 A2
Portree St POP/IOD E14 ... 105 K5
Portsdown Av GLDGN NW11 ... 64 F7
Portsdown Ms GLDGN NW11 ... 64 F7
Portsea PI BAY/PAD W2 ... 9 K5
Portslade Rd VX/NE SW8 ... 120 C7
Portsmouth Av THDIT KT7 ...
Portsmouth Rd ESH/CLAY KT10 ... 166 C5
KUT KT1 ... 152 D6
PUT/ROE SW15 ... 136 B4
Portsmouth St LINN WC2A ... 11 L3
Portsoken St TWRH EC3N ... 13 L6
Portugal Gdns WHTN TW2 ... 133 J6
Portugal St LINN WC2A ... 11 M5
Portway EW KT17 ... 181 G3
SRTFD E15 ... 87 M8
Portway Crs EW KT17 ... 181 G2
Portway Gdns WOOL/PLUM SE18 ... 124 D6
Postern Gn ENC/FH EN2 ... 36 A5
Post La WHTN TW2 ... 133 K5
Postmill CI CROY/NA CRO ... 173 L5
Post Office Ap FSTGT E7 ... 88 B5
Post Rd NWDGN UB2 ... 115 H1
Postway Ms IL IG1 ... 89 H3
Potier St STHWK SE1 ... 19 H4
Potter CI MTCM CR4 ... 156 B5
Potterne CI WIM/MER SW19 ... 136 E2
Potters CI CROY/NA CRO ... 173 L3
LOU IG10 ... 39 L5
Potters Flds STHWK SE1 ... 13 K9
Potters Gv NWMAL KT3 ... 153 J7
Potters Heights CI PIN HA5 ... 60 B1
Potter's La BAR EN5 ... 34 A7
BORE WD6 ... 32 C4
STRHM/NOR SW16 ... 156 D2
Potter's Rd BAR EN5 ... 34 B7
FUL/PGN SW6 ... 119 J7
Potter St NTHWD HA6 ... 60 A2
Potter Street HI NTHWD HA6 ... 42 B8
Pottery La NTGHL W11 ... 100 E7
BXLY DA5 ...
Pottery St BERM/RHTH SE16 ... 104 B8
Pott St BETH E2 ... 104 B2
Poulett Gdns TWK TW1 ... 133 M6
Poulett Rd EHAM E6 ... 106 F1
Poulters Wd HAYES BR2 ... 175 G5
Poulton Av SUT SM1 ... 170 D5
Poultry LOTH EC2R ... 13 G5
Pound CI ORP BR6 ... 176 D4
SURB KT6 ... 167 J3
Pound Court Dr ORP BR6 ... 176 D4
Pound Fld GSTN WD25 ... 20 F8
Pound La HOR/WEW KT19 ... 180 D4
WLSDN NW10 ... 82 A6
Pound Park Rd CHARL SE7 ... 124 D2
Pound PI ELTH/MOT SE9 ... 143 G3
Pound St CAR SM5 ... 170 F7
Pountney Rd BTSEA SW11 ... 121 G4
Poverest Rd STMC/STPC BR5 ... 161 M8
Powder Mill La DART DA1 ... 146 E6
Powdermill La WAB EN9 ... 27 H6
Powder Mill La WHTN TW2 ... 132 F5
Powdermill Ms WAB EN9 ... 27 H6
Powdermill Wy WAB EN9 ... 27 H5

Powell CI EDGW HA8 ... 44 F8
Powell Gdns DAGE RM10 ... 91 G4
Powell Rd BKHH IG9 ... 52 C2
CLPT E5 ... 86 B3
Power Rd CHSWK W4 ... 117 G2
Powers Ct TWK TW1 ... 134 D4
Powerscroft Rd CLPT E5 ... 86 C4
SCUP DA14 ... 162 C2
Powis Ct POTB/CUF EN6 ... 23 J7
Powis Gdns GLDGN NW11 ... 64 F8
NTGHL W11 ... 100 F5
Powis Ms NTGHL W11 ... 100 F5
Powis PI BMSBY WC1N ... 11 K1
Powis Rd BOW E3 ... 105 H2
Powis Sq NTGHL W11 ... 100 F5
Powis St WOOL/PLUM SE18 ... 125 G3
Powis Ter NTGHL W11 ... 100 F5
Powlett PI CAMTN NW1 ... 4 B1
Pownall Gdns HSLW TW3 ... 133 H1
Pownall Rd HACK E8 ... 86 A3
HSLW TW3 ... 133 H1
Pownsett Ter IL IG1 ... 89 J5
Powster Rd BMLY BR1 ... 160 A1
Powys CI BXLYHN DA7 ... 126 D4
Powys La PLMGR N13 ... 48 E7
Poynders Rd CLAP SW4 ... 138 C4
Poynings Rd ARCH N19 ... 84 C3
Poynings Wy HARH RM3 ... 74 E2
NFNCH/WDSP N12 ... 47 G7
Poyntell Crs CHST BR7 ... 161 K4
Poynter Rd EN EN1 ... 36 F8
Poynton Rd TOTM N17 ... 68 A3
Poyntz Rd BTSEA SW11 ... 119 M7
Poyser St BETH E2 ... 104 E1
Praed Ms BAY/PAD W2 ... 9 H4
Praed St BAY/PAD W2 ... 9 H4
Pragel St PLSTW E13 ... 106 B1
Pragnell Rd LEE/GVPK SE12 ... 142 B6
Prague PI BRXS/STRHM SW2 ... 138 E2
Prah Rd FSBYPK N4 ... 85 G2
Prairie St VX/NE SW8 ... 120 A7
Pratt CI CAMTN NW1 ... 4 E4
Pratts La WOT/HER KT12 ... 165 K6
Pratt St CAMTN NW1 ... 4 F5
Pratt Wk LBTH SE11 ... 17 M5
Prayle Gv CRICK NW2 ... 82 D1
Prebend Gdns CHSWK W4 ... 117 M2
Prebend St IS N1 ... 6 E4
Precinct Rd HYS/HAR UB3 ... 96 A6
Premiere PI POP/IOD E14 ... 105 G6
Premier Park Rd WLSDN NW10 ... 99 H1
Prentis Rd STRHM/NOR SW16 ... 138 D8
Prentiss Ct CHARL SE7 ... 124 D2
Presburg Rd NWMAL KT3 ... 153 L8
Prescelly PI EDGW HA8 ... 62 F2
Prescot St WCHPL E1 ... 13 M6
Prescott Av STMC/STPC BR5 ... 176 B1
Prescott CI HCH RM12 ... 92 B1
Prescott PI CLAP SW4 ... 120 D8
Presentation Ms BRXS/STRHM SW2 ... 138 F5
Presidents Dr WAP E1W ... 104 B7
President St FSBYE EC1V ... 6 F1
Press Rd UX/CGN UB8 ... 76 D7
WLSDN NW10 ... 81 K3
Prestage Wy POP/IOD E14 ... 105 J6
Prestbury Rd FSTGT E7 ... 88 C7
Prestbury Sq ELTH/MOT SE9 ... 142 F4
Prested Rd BTSEA SW11 ... 137 L1
Preston Av CHING E4 ... 51 K8
Preston CI STHWK SE1 ... 19 J5
WHTN TW2 ... 133 L7
Preston Dr BXLYHN DA7 ... 112 E8
HOR/WEW KT19 ... 168 E8
WAN E11 ... 70 E2
WELL DA16 ... 126 D6
Preston Gdns IL IG1 ... 70 E7
PEND EN3 ... 37 L2
WLSDN NW10 ... 81 L6
Preston HI KTN/HRWW/W HA3 ... 62 B8
Preston PI RCHPK/HAM TW10 ... 134 E2
WLSDN NW10 ... 82 A6
Preston Rd HARH RM3 ... 56 D6
KTN/HRWW/W HA3 ... 62 E8
NRWD SE19 ... 157 H2
RYNPK SW20 ... 154 A3
SHPTN TW17 ... 149 G8
WAN E11 ... 69 L7
WBLY HA9 ... 80 E2
Prestons Rd HAYES BR2 ... 175 G5
POP/IOD E14 ... 105 J4
Preston Waye WBLY HA9 ... 80 E1
Prestwick CI NWDGN UB2 ... 114 E3
Prestwick Rd OXHEY WD19 ... 42 D5
Prestwood Av KTN/HRWW/W HA3 ... 62 B5
Prestwood CI KTN/HRWW/W HA3 ... 62 B5
WOOL/PLUM SE18 ... 126 A4
Prestwood Dr CRW RM5 ... 55 J7
Prestwood Gdns CROY/NA CRO ... 172 C2
Prestwood St IS N1 ... 6 F5
Pretoria Av WALTH E17 ... 68 E5
Pretoria Crs CHING E4 ... 51 J3
Pretoria Rd CAN/RD E16 ... 105 M2
CHING E4 ... 51 J3
IL IG1 ... 89 H4
ROMW/RG RM7 ... 73 J5
STRHM/NOR SW16 ... 156 B2
TOTM N17 ... 49 M8
WAN E11 ... 87 K1
WATW WD18 ... 29 G7
Pretoria Rd North UED N18 ... 49 M8
Prevost Rd FBAR/BDGN N11 ... 48 A1
Price CI MLHL NW7 ... 46 C3
TOOT SW17 ... 137 M7
Price Rd CROY/NA CRO ... 172 B7
Price's St STHWK SE1 ... 12 D9
Pricklers HI BAR EN5 ... 34 B8
Prickley Rd HAYES BR2 ... 174 F3
Prideaux PI ACT W3 ... 99 K6
FSBYW WC1X ... 5 M7
Prideaux Rd BRXN/ST SW9 ... 120 E8
Pridham Rd THHTH CR7 ... 157 K7
Priestfield Rd FSTH SE23 ... 140 E7

Priestlands Park Rd BFN/LL DA15 ... 143 M7
Priestley Gdns CHDH RM6 ... 72 B7
Priestley Rd MTCM CR4 ... 156 A5
Priestley Wy CRICK NW2 ... 82 A1
WALTH E17 ... 68 D4
Priest Park Av RYLN/HDSTN HA2 ... 79 G2
Priests Av ROM RM1 ... 73 K3
Priests Br MORT/ESHN SW14 ... 117 L8
Prima Rd BRXN/ST SW9 ... 121 G5
Primrose Av ENC/FH EN2 ... 36 D3
GDMY/SEVK IG3 ... 72 A8
Primrose CI CAT SE6 ... 159 J1
MTCM CR4 ... 171 H3
RYLN/HDSTN HA2 ... 78 F3
Primrose Gdns BUSH WD23 ... 43 H2
HAMP NW3 ... 83 L6
RSLP HA4 ... 78 C5
Primrose Gln EMPK RM11 ... 74 E5
Primrose HI EMB EC4Y ... 12 B5
KGLGY WD4 ... 20 B1
Primrose Hill Rd HAMP NW3 ... 3 L2
Primrose Hill Studios CAMTN NW1 ... 4 A3
Primrose La CROY/NA CRO ... 173 J3
Primrose Pth CHESW EN7 ... 26 A4
Primrose Rd LEY E10 ... 87 H1
SWFD E18 ... 70 B3
WOT/HER KT12 ... 165 J7
Primrose Sq HOM E9 ... 86 C7
Primrose St SDTCH EC2A ... 13 J2
Primrose Wk EW KT17 ... 180 F1
NWCR SE14 ... 122 E5
Primrose Wy ALP/SUD HA0 ... 98 D1
Primula St SHB W12 ... 100 A6
Prince Albert Rd CAMTN NW1 ... 4 A5
STJWD NW8 ... 3 J7
Prince Arthur Rd HAMP NW3 ... 83 K4
Prince Charles Dr HDN NW4 ... 64 C8
Prince Charles Rd BKHTH/KID SE3 ... 123 M6
Prince Consort Dr CHST BR7 ... 161 K4
Prince Consort Rd SKENS SW7 ... 15 G3
Princedale Rd NTGHL W11 ... 100 E7
Prince Edward Rd HOM E9 ... 86 F6
Prince George Av STHGT/OAK N14 ... 35 J8
Prince George Rd STNW/STAM N16 ... 85 L4
Prince George's Av RYNPK SW20 ... 154 C1
Prince Georges Rd WIM/MER SW19 ... 155 K4
Prince Henry Rd WOOL/PLUM SE18 ... 124 D5
Prince Imperial Rd CHST BR7 ... 161 H3
WOOL/PLUM SE18 ... 124 F6
Prince John Rd ELTH/MOT SE9 ... 142 E3
Princelet St WCHPL E1 ... 13 M2
Prince of Orange La GNWCH SE10 ... 123 J5
Prince of Wales CI HDN NW4 ... 64 C5
Prince of Wales Dr BTSEA SW11 ... 120 B5
Prince of Wales Pas CAMTN NW1 ... 4 E8
Prince of Wales Rd BKHTH/KID SE3 ... 123 M6
CAN/RD E16 ... 106 C5
KTTN NW5 ... 84 A4
SUT SM1 ... 170 D4
Prince of Wales Ter CHSWK W4 ... 117 L3
KENS W8 ... 14 E2
Prince Regent La CAN/RD E16 ... 106 C5
PLSTW E13 ... 106 C3
Prince Regent Rd HSLW TW3 ... 115 J8
Prince Rd SNWD SE25 ... 157 L8
Prince Rupert Rd ELTH/MOT SE9 ... 142 F1
Princes Av ACT W3 ... 117 G1
CAR SM5 ... 182 F1
CDALE/KGS NW9 ... 63 G5
FNCH N3 ... 65 H2
MUSWH N10 ... 66 A4
PEND EN3 ... 37 L1
PLMGR N13 ... 49 G7
RDART DA2 ... 147 H5
SAND/SEL CR2 ... 185 H8
STMC/STPC BR5 ... 161 L8
SURB KT6 ... 168 A4
WATW WD18 ... 29 G8
WDGN N22 ... 66 D2
WFD IG8 ... 52 B6
Princes CI CDALE/KGS NW9 ... 63 G5
EDGW HA8 ... 45 G7
HPTN TW12 ... 133 K8
SAND/SEL CR2 ... 185 H8
SCUP DA14 ... 144 D7
Princes Ct WBLY HA9 ... 80 E5
Princes Dr HRW HA1 ... 61 L4
LHD/OX KT22 ... 178 E5
Princes Gdns ACT W3 ... 99 G5
EA W5 ... 98 C3
SKENS SW7 ... 15 H3
Prince's Ga SKENS SW7 ... 15 J2
Princes Gate Ms SKENS SW7 ... 15 H3
Princes La MUSWH N10 ... 66 A4
Prince's Ms BAY/PAD W2 ... 8 B6
Princes Pk RAIN RM13 ... 92 A7
Prince's Pk Av GLDGN NW11 ... 64 D4
HYS/HAR UB3 ... 95 K6
Princes Park Cir HYS/HAR UB3 ... 95 K6
Princes Park CI HYS/HAR UB3 ... 95 K6
Princes Park La HYS/HAR UB3 ... 95 K6
Princes Park Pde HYS/HAR UB3 ... 95 K6
Princes PI NTGHL W11 ... 100 E7
Prince's Pln HAYES BR2 ... 175 L2
Princes Ri LEW SE13 ... 123 J7
Princes Riverside Rd BERM/RHTH SE16 ... 104 D7
Princes Rd ASHF TW15 ... 148 F1
BARK/HLT IG6 ... 71 K5
BKHH IG9 ... 52 C4
DART DA1 ... 146 B4
FELT TW13 ... 131 M7

HPTN TW12 ... 133 K8
KUTN/CMB KT2 ... 153 G4
MORT/ESHN SW14 ... 117 K8
PGE/AN SE20 ... 158 D2
RCH/KEW TW9 ... 116 F6
RCHPK/HAM TW10 ... 134 F2
RDART DA2 ... 147 J5
ROM RM1 ... 74 A6
UED N18 ... 50 C6
WEA W13 ... 98 B7
WEY KT13 ... 164 B7
WIM/MER SW19 ... 155 G2
Princess Av WBLY HA9 ... 80 E2
Princess Crs FSBYPK N4 ... 85 H2
Princess La RSLP HA4 ... 77 L1
Princess May Rd STNW/STAM N16 ... 85 L4
Princess Ms HAMP NW3 ... 83 K5
Prince's Sq BAY/PAD W2 ... 8 B6
Princess Pde CAMTN NW1 ... 4 A3
CROY/NA CRO ... 172 C1
KIL/WHAMP NW6 ... 2 A6
Princess St BXLYHN DA7 ... 126 F8
STHWK SE1 ... 18 D4
Princes St CONDST W1S ... 10 D5
LOTH EC2R ... 13 G5
RCHPK/HAM TW10 ... 134 C2
SUT SM1 ... 170 D6
TOTM N17 ... 49 L8
Prince's Ter PLSTW E13 ... 88 B3
WAT WD17 ... 29 J6
Prince St DEPT SE8 ... 122 F4
WAT WD17 ... 29 J6
Princes Vw DART DA1 ... 147 G5
Princes Wy BKHH IG9 ... 52 C4
CROY/NA CRO ... 171 M7
RSLP HA4 ... 78 E4
WIM/MER SW19 ... 136 D4
Prince's Yd NTGHL W11 ... 100 E7
Princethorpe Rd SYD SE26 ... 140 D8
Princeton St GINN WC1R ... 11 L3
Pringle Gdns PUR/KEN CR8 ... 183 M3
STRHM/NOR SW16 ... 138 C8
Printer St FLST/FETLN EC4A ... 12 B4
Printinghouse La HYS/HAR UB3 ... 95 L8
Printing House Yd BETH E2 ... 7 K8
Priolo Rd CHARL SE7 ... 124 C3
Prior Av BELMT SM2 ... 182 E1
Prior Bolton St IS N1 ... 85 H6
Prioress Rd WNWD SE27 ... 139 H7
Prioress St STHWK SE1 ... 19 H4
Prior Rd IL IG1 ... 89 G3
Priors Cft WALTH E17 ... 68 E3
Priors Fld NTHLT UB5 ... 78 E6
Priorsford Av STMC/STPC BR5 ... 162 A7
Priors Gdns RSLP HA4 ... 78 C5
Priors Md EN EN1 ... 36 E4
Priors Pk HCH RM12 ... 92 C3
Prior St GNWCH SE10 ... 123 J5
Priory Av ALP/SUD HA0 ... 79 M4
CEND/HSY/T N8 ... 66 D5
CHEAM SM3 ... 169 K6
CHING E4 ... 51 F5
CHSWK W4 ... 117 L1
STMC/STPC BR5 ... 176 D1
WALTH E17 ... 68 F4
Priory CI ALP/SUD HA0 ... 79 M4
BECK BR3 ... 158 E6
BMLY BR1 ... 160 F4
CHING E4 ... 50 F5
DART DA1 ... 146 C2
DEN/HRF UB9 ... 58 C5
DEN/HRF UB9 ... 76 A3
HPTN TW12 ... 150 F4
HYS/HAR UB3 ... 96 B6
RSLP HA4 ... 77 M1
STAN HA7 ... 43 M5
STHGT/OAK N14 ... 35 H8
SUN TW16 ... 150 A3
SWFD E18 ... 70 A2
TRDG/WHET N20 ... 46 F8
WOT/HER KT12 ... 165 G5
Priory Ct VX/NE SW8 ... 120 D6
WALTH E17 ... 68 F4
Priory Crs ALP/SUD HA0 ... 80 A3
CHEAM SM3 ... 169 K6
NRWD SE19 ... 157 J3
Priory Dr ABYW SE2 ... 126 D3
STAN HA7 ... 43 M5
Priory Field Dr EDGW HA8 ... 45 H6
Priory Gdns ALP/SUD HA0 ... 80 A4
ASHF TW15 ... 149 K1
BARN SW13 ... 117 M8
CHSWK W4 ... 117 L2
DART DA1 ... 146 D2
DEN/HRF UB9 ... 66 B7
HGT N6 ... 66 B7
HPTN TW12 ... 150 F4
SNWD SE25 ... 157 M7
Priory Gn STA TW18 ... 148 B1
Priory Gv CLAP SW4 ... 120 E6
HARH RM3 ...
Priory HI ALP/SUD HA0 ... 80 A4
DART DA1 ... 146 D3
Priory La E/WMO/HCT KT8 ... 151 G2
PUT/ROE SW15 ... 135 M2
Priory Ms HCH RM12 ... 92 B1
STA TW18 ... 148 B1
Priory Pk BKHTH/KID SE3 ... 123 M8
Priory Park Rd ALP/SUD HA0 ... 80 A4
KIL/WHAMP NW6 ... 82 F8
Priory Pth HARH RM3 ... 56 E5
Priory Rd DART DA1 ... 146 D3
Priory Rd BARK IG11 ... 89 K7
CEND/HSY/T N8 ... 66 D5
CHEAM SM3 ... 169 K6
CHSGTN KT9 ... 167 L5
CHSWK W4 ... 117 K1
CROY/NA CRO ... 172 A2
DART DA1 ... 146 D3
EHAM E6 ... 88 D8
HARH RM3 ... 56 E5
HPTN TW12 ... 150 F3
HSLW TW3 ... 133 J2
KIL/WHAMP NW6 ... 2 C2
LOU IG10 ... 39 L7
MUSWH N10 ... 66 C5
RCH/KEW TW9 ... 117 G4

WIM/MER SW19 ... 155 K3
Priory St BOW E3 ... 105 K2
Priory Ter KIL/WHAMP NW6 ... 2 C3
The Priory BKHTH/KID SE3 ... 123 M8
Priory Vw BUSH WD23 ... 43 L3
Priory Wk WBPTN SW10 ... 14 F8
Priory Wy NWDGN UB2 ... 114 D1
RYLN/HDSTN HA2 ... 61 H5
WDR/YW UB7 ... 112 E4
Pritchard's Rd BETH E2 ... 104 A1
Priter Rd BERM/RHTH SE16 ... 122 A1
Private Rd EN EN1 ... 36 D8
Probert Rd BRXS/STRHM SW2 ... 139 G2
Probyn Rd BRXS/STRHM SW2 ... 139 H6
Procter St BMSBY WC1N ... 11 K3
Proctor CI MTCM CR4 ... 156 A4
Proctors CI EBED/NFELT TW14 ... 132 A5
Profumo Rd WOT/HER KT12 ... 165 K7
Progress Wy CROY/NA CRO ... 171 M4
EN EN1 ... 37 G8
WDGN N22 ... 67 G2
Promenade Approach Rd CHSWK W4 ... 117 L5
Promenade De Verdun PUR/KEN CR8 ... 183 K4
The Promenade CHSWK W4 ... 117 L6
Prospect CI BELV DA17 ... 127 G3
HEST TW5 ... 114 F6
RSLP HA4 ... 60 D8
SYD SE26 ... 140 E8
Prospect Cottages WAND/EARL SW18 ... 137 G1
Prospect Crs WHTN TW2 ... 133 J3
Prospect HI WALTH E17 ... 69 H5
Prospect PI CHSWK W4 ... 117 K3
CRICK NW2 ... 82 F3
CRW RM5 ... 73 J3
DART DA1 ... 146 D4
EFNCH N2 ... 65 K5
EW KT17 ... 180 E6
HAYES BR2 ... 160 B6
RYNPK SW20 ... 154 B3
Prospect Rd BAR EN5 ... 34 A7
CHES/WCR EN8 ... 26 C2
CRICK NW2 ... 82 F3
EMPK RM11 ... 74 F4
SURB KT6 ... 167 J1
WFD IG8 ... 52 C7
Prospect St BERM/RHTH SE16 ... 104 B8
Prospect V CHARL SE7 ... 124 E2
Prospero Rd ARCH N19 ... 84 D1
Prothero Gdns HDN NW4 ... 64 B6
Prothero Rd FUL/PGN SW6 ... 118 C5
Prout Rd CLPT E5 ... 86 B3
Prout Gv WLSDN NW10 ... 81 L4
Providence Ct MYFR/PKLN W1K ... 10 B6
Providence La HYS/HAR UB3 ... 113 K5
Providence PI ROMW/RG RM7 ... 72 F2
Providence Rd WDR/YW UB7 ... 94 E7
Provost Rd HAMP NW3 ... 3 M1
Provost St FSBYE EC1V ... 7 G8
IS N1 ... 7 G6
Prowse Av BUSH WD23 ... 43 J4
Prowse PI CAMTN NW1 ... 4 E1
Prusom St WAP E1W ... 104 B7
Pryor CI ABLGY WD5 ... 20 F5
Pudding La CHIG IG7 ... 53 L1
MON EC3R ... 13 H6
Pudding Mill La SRTFD E15 ... 87 H8
Puddle Dock BLKFR EC4V ... 12 D6
Puddledock La RDART DA2 ... 163 L1
Puffin CI BARK IG11 ...
CRO ... 158 D8
Pulborough Wy HSLWW TW4 ... 132 C1
Pulford Rd SEVS/STOTM N15 ... 67 K7
Pulham Av EFNCH N2 ... 65 J5
Puller Rd BAR EN5 ... 33 K5
Pulleyns Av EHAM E6 ... 106 E2
Pullman Gdns PUT/ROE SW15 ... 136 C3
Pullman PI ELTH/MOT SE9 ... 142 E4
Pullmans PI STA TW18 ... 148 A1
Pulross Rd BRXN/ST SW9 ... 120 F8
Pulteney CI BOW E3 ... 86 F8
Pulteney Rd SWFD E18 ... 70 B1
Pulton PI FUL/PGN SW6 ... 119 C5
Pump Aly BTFD TW8 ... 116 D5
Pump CI NTHLT UB5 ... 97 G1
Pump HI LOU IG10 ... 39 M5
Pumping Station Rd CHSWK W4 ... 117 L5
Pump La HYS/HAR UB3 ... 96 A8
NWCR SE14 ... 122 C5
Punderson's Gdns BETH E2 ... 104 B2
Purbeck Av NWMAL KT3 ... 168 F1
Purbeck Dr CRICK NW2 ... 82 D2
Purbeck Rd EMPK RM11 ... 74 A8
Purberry Gv EW KT17 ... 180 F3
Purbrock Av GSTN WD25 ... 29 J1
Purbrook St STHWK SE1 ... 19 K3
Purcell Ct BORE WD6 ... 31 K4
PUR/KEN CR8 ... 184 C7
Purcell Crs FUL/PGN SW6 ... 118 D5
Purcell Rd GFD/PVL UB6 ... 97 H4
Purcells Av EDGW HA8 ... 45 G7
Purcell St IS N1 ... 7 J5
Purchese St CAMTN NW1 ... 5 G5
Purdy St BOW E3 ... 105 H3
Purfleet By-pass PUR RM19 ... 129 J3
Purfleet Rd SOCK/AV RM15 ... 111 H7
Purland CI BCTR RM8 ... 90 F1
Purland Rd THMD SE28 ... 107 M8
Purleigh Av WFD IG8 ... 52 F6
Purley Av CRICK NW2 ... 82 E2
Purley Bury Av PUR/KEN CR8 ... 184 C4
Purley Bury CI PUR/KEN CR8 ... 184 C4
Purley CI CLAY IG5 ... 71 G3
Purley Downs Rd PUR/KEN CR8 ... 184 C3
Purley HI PUR/KEN CR8 ... 184 B5
Purley Knoll PUR/KEN CR8 ... 183 M4
Purley Oaks Rd SAND/SEL CR2 ... 184 D3
Purley Park Rd PUR/KEN CR8 ... 184 B3
Purley PI IS N1 ... 6 C1
Purley Ri PUR/KEN CR8 ... 183 M5
Purley Rd ED N9 ... 49 K5
SAND/SEL CR2 ... 184 D1
Purley V PUR/KEN CR8 ... 184 B6
Purley Wy CROY/NA CRO ... 171 M2

PUR/KEN CR8 ... 184 A4
Purlings Rd BUSH WD23 ... 30 B8
Purneys Rd ELTH/MOT SE9 ... 142 D1
Purrett Rd WOOL/PLUM SE18 ... 125 M3
Pursers Cross Rd
FUL/PGN SW6 ... 119 G6
Pursewardens CI WEA W13 ... 98 C7
Pursley Gdns BORE WD6 ... 32 A3
Pursley Rd MLHL NW7 ... 64 B1
Purves Rd WLSDN NW10 ... 100 B2
Putney Br PUT/ROE SW15 ... 118 E8
Putney Bridge Ap
PUT/ROE SW15 ... 118 E8
Putney Bridge Rd
PUT/ROE SW15 ... 136 E1
Putney Common
PUT/ROE SW15 ... 118 C8
Putney Heath PUT/ROE SW15 ... 136 B3
Putney Heath La
PUT/ROE SW15 ... 136 D3
Putney High St PUT/ROE SW15 ... 136 E1
Putney Hl PUT/ROE SW15 ... 136 E1
Putney Park Av PUT/ROE SW15.. 136 A1
Putney Park La PUT/ROE SW15... 136 B1
Putney Rd PEND EN3 ... 37 K1
Puttenham CI OXHEY WD19 ... 42 C5
Pycombe Cnr NFNCH/WDSP N12.. 46 F6
Pycroft Wy UED N18 ... 50 A6
Pylbrook Rd SUT SM1 ... 170 A5
Pym CI EBAR EN4 ... 34 D8
Pymers Md DUL SE21 ... 139 J5
Pymmes Brook Trail EBAR EN4 .. 34 E8
EBAR EN4 ... 47 M2
PLMGR N13 ... 48 E6
Pymmes CI PLMGR N13 ... 48 F7
TOTM N17 ... 68 B2
Pymmes Gdns North ED N9 ... 49 M5
Pymmes Gdns South ED N9 ... 49 M5
Pymmes Green Rd
FBAR/BDGN N11 ... 48 B6
Pymmes Rd PLMGR N13 ... 48 E8
Pymms Brook Dr EBAR EN4 ... 34 E7
Pynchester CI HGDN/ICK UB10... 77 G2
Pyne Rd SURB KT6 ... 168 A3
Pynest Green La WAB EN9 ... 39 G2
Pynham CI ABYW SE2 ... 126 A4
Pynnacles CI STAN HA7 ... 44 B7
Pyrcroft La WEY KT13 ... 164 B7
Pyrland Rd HBRY N5 ... 85 K5
RCHPK/HAM TW10 ... 134 F3
Pyrmont Gv WNWD SE27 ... 139 H7
Pyrmont Rd CHSWK W4 ... 117 G4
Pytchley Crs NRWD SE19 ... 157 J2
Pytchley Rd CMBW SE5 ... 121 L8

Q

Quadrant Gv HAMP NW3 ... 83 M5
Quadrant Rd RCH/KEW TW9 ... 134 D1
THHTH CR7 ... 157 H7
The Quadrant BELMT SM2 ... 170 C8
BXLYHN DA7 ... 126 D5
PUR RM19 ... 129 J2
RCH/KEW TW9 ... 134 E1
RYNPK SW20 ... 154 E4
Quaggy Wk BKHTH/KID SE3 ... 142 A1
Quail Gdns CROY/NA CR0 ... 185 L3
Quainton St WLSDN NW10 ... 81 K3
Quaker La NWDGN UB2 ... 115 G2
WAB EN9 ... 27 J7
Quakers Course
CDALE/KGS NW9 ... 63 M2
Quakers La POTB/CUF EN6 ... 23 H3
Quakers PI FSTGT E7 ... 88 D5
Quaker St WCHPL E1 ... 13 L1
Quakers Wk WCHMH N21 ... 49 K1
Quantock CI HYS/HAR UB3 ... 113 K5
Quantock Gdns BXLYHN DA7 ... 127 L7
Quarles CI CRW RM5 ... 73 C1
Quarrendon St FUL/PGN SW6 ... 119 G6
Quarr Rd CAR SM5 ... 170 D1
Quarry Ms PUR RM19 ... 129 J2
Quarry Park Rd SUT SM1 ... 169 M8
Quarry Ri SUT SM1 ... 169 M8
Quarry Rd WAND/EARL SW18 ... 137 J3
Quarry Wy WTHK RM20 ... 129 M4
Quartermile La LEY E10 ... 87 H4
Quebec Ms MBLAR W1 ... 9 M5
Quebec Rd GNTH/NBYPK IG2 ... 71 J8
YEAD UB4 ... 96 C6
Quebec Wy BERM/RHTH SE16 ... 104 D8
Queen Adelaide Rd
PGE/AN SE20 ... 158 C2
Queen Anne Av HAYES BR2 ... 160 A6
Queen Anne Dr ESH/CLAY KT10 .. 178 C4
Queen Anne Ms CAVSQ/HST W1G.. 10 D3
Queen Anne Rd HOM E9 ... 86 F4
Queen Annes CI WHTN TW2 ... 133 K7
Queen Anne's Gdns CHSWK W4 .. 117 L1
EA W5 ... 98 A4
EN EN1 ... 49 L1
MTCM CR4 ... 155 M8
Queen Anne's Ga STJSPK SW1H .. 17 G2
Queen Anne's Gv CHSWK W4 ... 117 L1
EA W5 ... 98 A4
ED N9 ... 49 K2
EN EN1 ... 49 L1
Queen Anne's PI EN EN1 ... 49 L1
Queen Anne St CAVSQ/HST W1G .. 10 C4
Queenborough Gdns CHST BR7.. 161 K2
GNTH/NBYPK IG2 ... 71 C5
Queen Caroline St
HMSMTH W6 ... 118 C4
Queen Elizabeth Gdns
MRDN SM4 ... 155 G7
Queen Elizabeth Ii Br
WTHK RM20 ... 129 L7
Queen Elizabeth Rd
KUTN/CMB KT2 ... 152 F4
WALTH E17 ... 68 E4
Queen Elizabeth's CI
STNW/STAM N16 ... 85 K2
Queen Elizabeth's Dr
CROY/NA CR0 ... 186 D3
STHGT/OAK N14 ... 48 E3

Queen Elizabeth St
STHWK SE1 ... 19 L1
Queen Elizabeth's Wk
STNW/STAM N16 ... 85 K2
WLGTN SM6 ... 171 K6
Queen Elizabeth Wk
BARN SW13 ... 118 A6
Queenhill Rd SAND/SEL CR2 ... 185 H3
Queen Margaret's Gv IS N1 ... 85 L5
Queen Mary Av MRDN SM4 ... 154 D8
Queen Mary CI CHSGTN KT9 ... 168 A5
ROM RM1 ... 73 M7
Queen Mary Rd NRWD SE19 ... 157 H2
SHPTN TW17 ... 149 J5
Queen Mary's Av CAR SM5 ... 182 F1
WATW WD18 ... 28 E7
Queens Acre CHEAM SM3 ... 181 K1
Queens Av FELT TW13 ... 132 C8
FNCH N3 ... 65 J1
GFD/PVL UB6 ... 97 H5
KTN/HRWW/W HA3 ... 62 B4
MUSWH N10 ... 66 A4
TRDG/WHET N20 ... 47 K4
WATW WD18 ... 28 E7
WCHMH N21 ... 49 H3
WFD IG8 ... 52 B7
Queensberry Ms West
SKENS SW7 ... 15 G5
Queensberry PI SKENS SW7 ... 15 G5
Queensberry Wy SKENS SW7 ... 15 G5
Queensborough Ms
BAY/PAD W2 ... 8 E6
Queensborough Pas
BAY/PAD W2 ... 8 E6
Queensborough Ter
BAY/PAD W2 ... 8 D6
Queensbridge Pk ISLW TW7 ... 133 K5
Queensbridge Rd HACK E8 ... 7 M2
HACK E8 ... 85 M6
Queensbury Rd ALP/SUD HA0 ... 98 F1
CDALE/KGS NW9 ... 63 K8
NWDGN UB2 ... 98 F1
Queensbury Station Pde
EDGW HA8 ... 62 F4
Queensbury St IS N1 ... 6 F2
Queen's CI EDGW HA8 ... 45 G7
WLGTN SM6 ... 171 H7
Queen's Club Gdns
WKENS W14 ... 118 E4
Queenscourt WBLY HA9 ... 80 E4
Queen's Ct KEY KT13 ... 164 E8
RCHPK/HAM TW10 ... 134 F2
Queenscroft Rd ELTH/MOT SE9 .. 142 D3
Queensdale Crs NTGHL W11 ... 100 D7
Queensdale PI NTGHL W11 ... 100 E7
Queensdale Rd NTGHL W11 ... 100 E7
Queensdale Wk NTGHL W11 ... 100 E7
Queens Down Rd CLPT E5 ... 86 B4
Queens Dr ABLGY WD5 ... 20 F5
BRYLDS KT5 ... 168 A2
CHES/WCR EN8 ... 27 G7
EA W5 ... 98 F5
LEY E10 ... 69 G8
LHD/OX KT22 ... 178 C4
THDIT KT7 ... 167 G1
Queen's Elm Sq CHEL SW3 ... 15 H8
Queen's Gdns BAY/PAD W2 ... 8 E6
EA W5 ... 98 C4
HEST TW5 ... 114 C6
RAIN RM13 ... 109 K1
RDART DA2 ... 147 H5
UPMR RM14 ... 75 M7
Queen's Ga SKENS SW7 ... 14 F2
Queens Gate Gdns CHST BR7 ... 161 K4
Queen's Gate Gdns SKENS SW7 .. 14 E4
Queen's Gate Ms SKENS SW7 ... 14 E3
Queen's Gate PI SKENS SW7 ... 14 F4
Queen's Gate Place Ms
SKENS SW7 ... 14 F4
Queen's Gate Ter SKENS SW7 ... 14 E3
Queen's Gv STJWD NW8 ... 3 G4
Queen's Grove Rd CHING E4 ... 51 K3
Queen's Head St IS N1 ... 6 D4
Queensland Av UED N18 ... 49 M2
WIM/MER SW19 ... 155 H4
Queensland PI HOLWY N7 ... 85 G4
Queensland Rd HOLWY N7 ... 85 G4
Queensmead La MUSWH N10 ... 66 B4
Queensmead Av EW KT17 ... 181 H3
Queen's Mead Rd HAYES BR2 ... 159 M5
Queensmere CI
WIM/MER SW19 ... 136 D6
Queensmere Rd
WIM/MER SW19 ... 136 D6
Queen's Ms BAY/PAD W2 ... 8 D6
Queensmill Rd FUL/PGN SW6 ... 118 D5
Queens Parade CI
FBAR/BDGN N11 ... 47 M7
Queens Park Gdns
FELT TW13 ... 131 M7
Queens Park Rd HARH RM3 ... 74 E2
Queen's PI MRDN SM4 ... 155 G7
WAT WD17 ... 29 J6
WOT/HER KT12 ... 164 E7
Queen Sq BMSBY WC1N ... 11 K1
Queen's Ride BARN SW13 ... 118 B8
Queen's Ri RCHPK/HAM TW10 ... 134 F3
Queens Rd BAR EN5 ... 33 K6
BARK IG11 ... 89 J7
BECK BR3 ... 158 E5
BELMT SM2 ... 182 A4
BKHH IG9 ... 52 B4
BMLY BR1 ... 160 A5
CHES/WCR EN8 ... 26 E7
CHST BR7 ... 161 H2
CROY/NA CR0 ... 172 B1
EA W5 ... 98 C5
ED N9 ... 50 B4
EN EN1 ... 36 E7
ERITH DA8 ... 127 L4
FBAR/BDGN N11 ... 66 E1
FELT TW13 ... 132 B5
FNCH N3 ... 65 J2

HDN NW4 ... 64 C6
HPTN TW12 ... 133 H8
HSLW TW3 ... 115 H8
HYS/HAR UB3 ... 95 L5
KUTN/CMB KT2 ... 153 G3
LOU IG10 ... 39 M6
MORT/ESHN SW14 ... 117 K8
MRDN SM4 ... 155 G7
NWDGN UB2 ... 96 D8
NWMAL KT3 ... 153 M7
PECK SE15 ... 122 C6
PLSTW E13 ... 88 B8
RCHPK/HAM TW10 ... 134 F3
TEDD TW11 ... 151 M2
THDIT KT7 ... 151 M8
TWK TW1 ... 133 M5
UX/CGN UB8 ... 94 C2
WALTH E17 ... 68 F7
WAN E11 ... 69 L8
WAT WD17 ... 29 J6
WDR/YW UB7 ... 94 F8
WELL DA16 ... 126 B7
WEY KT13 ... 164 D7
WIM/MER SW19 ... 155 H1
WLGTN SM6 ... 171 H7
WOT/HER KT12 ... 164 E6
Queen's Rd West PLSTW E13 ... 106 A1
Queen's Rw WALW SE17 ... 19 G9
Queen's Ter ISLW TW7 ... 134 A1
PLSTW E13 ... 88 B8
STJWD NW8 ... 3 G4
Queensthorpe Rd SYD SE26 ... 140 D8
Queens Town Gdns
RAIN RM13 ... 109 M2
Queenstown Rd VX/NE SW8 ... 120 B4
Queen St BXLYHN DA7 ... 126 F8
CROY/NA CR0 ... 172 C6
ERITH DA8 ... 127 L4
MYFR/PICC W1J ... 10 C8
ROMW/RG RM7 ... 73 K7
TOTM N17 ... 49 M8
Queen Street PI CANST EC4R ... 12 F7
Queensville Rd CLAP SW4 ... 138 D4
Queens Wk ASHF TW15 ... 130 D8
CDALE/KGS NW9 ... 81 J2
CHING E4 ... 51 K3
EA W5 ... 98 C3
HRW HA1 ... 61 L5
RSLP HA4 ... 78 C3
Queens Wy CHES/WCR EN8 ... 26 F7
FELT TW13 ... 132 C8
HDN NW4 ... 64 C6
Queensway BAY/PAD W2 ... 8 D4
CROY/NA CR0 ... 171 M7
PEND EN3 ... 37 J7
STMC/STPC BR5 ... 161 J8
SUN TW16 ... 150 B5
WOT/HER KT12 ... 165 H7
WWKM BR4 ... 175 G6
Queensway North
WOT/HER KT12 ... 165 J6
Queensway South
WOT/HER KT12 ... 165 J7
Queens Well Av
TRDG/WHET N20 ... 47 L6
Queenswood Av HEST TW5 ... 114 F7
HPTN TW12 ... 151 H2
THHTH CR7 ... 157 G8
WALTH E17 ... 69 J2
WLGTN SM6 ... 171 K6
Queenswood Crs GSTN WD25 ... 21 G6
Queenswood Gdns WAN E11 ... 88 A1
Queenswood Pk FNCH N3 ... 64 E3
Queenswood Rd
BFN/LL DA15 ... 143 M3
FSTH SE23 ... 140 E7
Queen's Wood Rd HGT N6 ... 66 B7
Queen's Yd FITZ W1T ... 10 F1
Queen Victoria Av ALP/SUD HA0 .. 80 D7
Queen Victoria St BLKFR EC4V... 12 E6
MANHO EC4N ... 12 F5
Quemerford Rd HOLWY N7 ... 84 F4
Quendon Dr WAB EN9 ... 27 K6
Quentin PI LEW SE13 ... 123 L8
Quentin Rd BKHTH/KID SE3 ... 123 L8
Quernmore CI BMLY BR1 ... 160 A2
Quernmore Rd BMLY BR1 ... 160 A2
FSBYPK N4 ... 67 G7
Querrin St FUL/PGN SW6 ... 119 J7
Quex Rd KIL/WHAMP NW6 ... 2 B3
Quick Rd CHSWK W4 ... 117 L3
Quicks Rd WIM/MER SW19 ... 155 H3
Quick St IS N1 ... 6 D6
Quickswood HAMP NW3 ... 3 K1
Quiet Nook HAYES BR2 ... 175 K5
The Quillot WOT/HER KT12 ... 164 F7
Quill St EA W5 ... 98 E2
FSBYPK N4 ... 85 G3
Quilp St STHWK SE1 ... 18 E1
Quilter Rd STMC/STPC BR5 ... 177 J3
Quilter St BETH E2 ... 104 A2
WOOL/PLUM SE18 ... 125 M3
Quinta Dr BAR EN5 ... 33 H8
Quintin Av RYNPK SW20 ... 154 E4
Quinton CI BECK BR3 ... 159 J6
HEST TW5 ... 114 B5
WLGTN SM6 ... 171 H6
Quinton Rd THDIT KT7 ... 167 G3
Quinton St WAND/EARL SW18 ... 137 J4
Quinton Wy WAB EN9 ... 27 J8
Quixley St POP/IOD E14 ... 105 K6
Quorn Rd EDUL SE22 ... 139 L1

R

Rabbit Rw KENS W8 ... 8 B8
Rabbits Rd MNPK E12 ... 88 E4
Rabournmead Dr RSLP HA4 ... 78 E5
Raby Rd NWMAL KT3 ... 153 K7
Raby St POP/IOD E14 ... 104 E5
Raccoon Wy HSLWW TW4 ... 114 C7
Rachel CI BARK/HLT IG6 ... 71 K4
Rackham CI WELL DA16 ... 126 B7
Rackham Ms
STRHM/NOR SW16 ... 156 C2
Racton Rd FUL/PGN SW6 ... 119 G4

Radbourne Av EA W5 ... 116 C2
Radbourne CI CLPT E5 ... 86 D4
Radbourne Crs WALTH E17 ... 69 K4
Radbourne Rd BAL SW12 ... 138 C4
WLSDN NW10 ... 100 A1
Radcliffe Av ENC/FH EN2 ... 36 C4
WLSDN NW10 ... 100 A1
Radcliffe Gdns CAR SM5 ... 182 E1
Radcliffe Rd CROY/NA CR0 ... 172 F4
KTN/HRWW/W HA3 ... 62 A3
STHWK SE1 ... 19 K3
WCHMH N21 ... 49 H3
Radcliffe Wy NTHLT UB5 ... 96 D2
Radclift Ms HPTN TW12 ... 151 J1
Radcot St LBTH SE11 ... 18 B8
Raddington Rd NKENS W10 ... 100 E4
Radfield Wy ELTH/MOT SE9 ... 143 K4
Radford Rd LEW SE13 ... 141 J3
Radford Wy BARK IG11 ... 107 M2
Radipole Rd FUL/PGN SW6 ... 118 F6
Radland Rd CAN/RD E16 ... 106 A5
Radlet Av FSTH SE23 ... 140 B7
Radlett CI FSTGT E7 ... 87 M6
Radlett PI STJWD NW8 ... 3 J4
WATN WD24 ... 29 K5
Radley Av GDMY/SEVK IG3 ... 89 M4
Radley CI
EBED/NFELT TW14 ... 131 M5
Radley Ct BERM/RHTH SE16 ... 104 D8
Radley Gdns KTN/HRWW/W HA3.. 62 E5
Radley Ms KENS W8 ... 14 B4
Radley Rd TOTM N17 ... 67 L3
Radley's La SWFD E18 ... 70 E3
Radleys Md DAGE RM10 ... 91 H6
Radlix Rd LEY E10 ... 87 C1
Radnor Av HRW HA1 ... 61 L6
WELL DA16 ... 144 B2
Radnor CI CHST BR7 ... 161 L2
MTCM CR4 ... 156 E8
Radnor Crs REDBR IG4 ... 70 F6
WOOL/PLUM SE18 ... 126 A5
Radnor Gdns EN EN1 ... 36 B4
TWK TW1 ... 133 M6
Radnor Ms BAY/PAD W2 ... 9 H5
Radnor PI BAY/PAD W2 ... 9 J5
Radnor Rd HRW HA1 ... 61 K6
KIL/WHAMP NW6 ... 82 E8
PECK SE15 ... 122 A5
TWK TW1 ... 133 M6
WEY KT13 ... 164 A5
Radnor St FSBYE EC1V ... 6 F8
Radnor Ter WKENS W14 ... 118 F2
KUT KT1 ... 152 D3
Radnor Wk CHEL SW3 ... 15 K8
CROY/NA CR0 ... 173 L2
Radnor Wy ACT W3 ... 99 H3
Radstock Av KTN/HRWW/W HA3 .. 62 A4
Radstock CI BTSEA SW11 ... 119 L5
FBAR/BDGN N11 ... 48 A1
Radstock St BTSEA SW11 ... 119 L3
Raebarn Gdns BAR EN5 ... 33 H8
Raeburn Av BRYLDS KT5 ... 168 B1
DART DA1 ... 146 B2
Raeburn CI GLDGN NW11 ... 65 J7
KUT KT1 ... 152 D3
Raeburn Rd BFN/LL DA15 ... 143 L3
EDGW HA8 ... 63 G3
YEAD UB4 ... 95 K1
Raeburn St BRXS/STRHM SW2 .. 138 E1
Rafford Wy BMLY BR1 ... 160 B5
Ragglesswood CHST BR7 ... 161 G4
Raglan Av CHES/WCR EN8 ... 26 D7
Raglan CI HSLWW TW4 ... 132 E2
Raglan Ct SAND/SEL CR2 ... 172 B7
Raglan Gdns OXHEY WD19 ... 42 B3
Raglan Rd BELV DA17 ... 126 F2
EN EN1 ... 49 L2
HAYES BR2 ... 160 C7
WALTH E17 ... 69 J6
WOOL/PLUM SE18 ... 125 J3
Raglan St KTTN NW5 ... 84 B6
Raglan Wy NTHLT UB5 ... 79 J6
Ragley CI ACT W3 ... 99 J8
Raider CI ROMW/RG RM7 ... 73 H2
Railey Ms KTTN NW5 ... 84 C5
Railshead Rd ISLW TW7 ... 134 B1
Railton Rd HNHL SE24 ... 139 G2
Railway Ap KTN/HRWW/W HA3 .. 61 M5
STHWK SE1 ... 13 H8
TWK TW1 ... 134 A4
Railway Ar WDR SM6 ... 171 H7
Railway Av BERM/RHTH SE16 ... 104 C8
Railway Gv NWCR SE14 ... 122 F5
Railway PI BELV DA17 ... 127 G1
Railway Ri EDUL SE22 ... 139 L1
Railway Rd CHES/WCR EN8 ... 26 F8
TEDD TW11 ... 133 L8
Railway Side BARN SW13 ... 117 L8
Railway St BCTR RM8 ... 90 C1
IS N1 ... 5 K6
Railway Ter FELT TW13 ... 132 A5
LEW SE13 ... 141 H2
WALTH E17 ... 69 H2
Rainborough CI WBLY HA9 ... 81 J6
Rainbow Av POP/IOD E14 ... 123 H3
Rainbow Ct OXHEY WD19 ... 42 C1
Rainbow St CMBW SE5 ... 121 L5
Rainer CI CHES/WCR EN8 ... 26 D2
Raine St WAP E1W ... 104 D7
Rainham CI BTSEA SW11 ... 137 L3
ELTH/MOT SE9 ... 143 L3
Rainham Rd RAIN RM13 ... 91 M7
WLSDN NW10 ... 100 C1
Rainham Rd North DAGE RM10 .. 91 H2
Rainham Rd South
DAGE RM10 ... 91 K7
Rainhill Wy BOW E3 ... 105 G2
Rainsborough Av DEPT SE8 ... 122 C2
Rainsford CI STAN HA7 ... 44 B7
Rainsford Rd WLSDN NW10 ... 99 H1
Rainsford St BAY/PAD W2 ... 9 J4
Rainsford Wy HCH RM12 ... 92 A1
Rainton Rd CHARL SE7 ... 124 A3
Rainville Rd HMSMTH W6 ... 118 C4
Raisins HI PIN HA5 ... 60 C4
Raith Av STHGT/OAK N14 ... 48 D5
Raleigh Av WLGTN SM6 ... 171 K6
YEAD UB4 ... 96 B4
Raleigh CI ERITH DA8 ... 127 M4
HDN NW4 ... 64 C6

PIN HA5 ... 60 D8
RSLP HA4 ... 77 M2
Raleigh Ct STA TW18 ... 130 A8
Raleigh Dr BRYLDS KT5 ... 168 C3
ESH/CLAY KT10 ... 166 D7
TRDG/WHET N20 ... 47 L5
Raleigh Gdns MTCM CR4 ... 155 M6
Raleigh Ms ORP BR6 ... 176 F7
CEND/HSY/T N8 ... 67 G5
ENC/FH EN2 ... 36 D7
FELT TW13 ... 131 M6
MUSWH N10 ... 65 L2
NWDGN UB2 ... 114 E3
PGE/AN SE20 ... 158 D3
RCH/KEW TW9 ... 116 F8
Raleigh St IS N1 ... 6 D4
Raleigh Wy FELT TW13 ... 150 C1
STHGT/OAK N14 ... 48 D3
Ralph Perring Ct BECK BR3 ... 159 G7
Ralston St CHEL SW3 ... 15 L8
Ralston Wy OXHEY WD19 ... 42 D4
Rama CI STRHM/NOR SW16 ... 156 E3
Ramac Wy CHARL SE7 ... 124 B2
Rambler CI STRHM/NOR SW16 ... 138 C8
Rame CI TOOT SW17 ... 156 A1
Ramillies CI BRXS/STRHM SW2 .. 138 E3
Ramillies PI SOHO/CST W1F ... 10 E5
Ramillies Rd BFN/LL DA15 ... 144 B3
CHSWK W4 ... 117 K1
MLHL NW7 ... 45 L4
Ramillies St SOHO/CST W1F ... 10 E5
Ramney Dr PEND EN3 ... 37 L1
Ramornie CI WOT/HER KT12 ... 165 M6
Rampart St WCHPL E1 ... 104 B5
Rampayne St PIM SW1V ... 17 G7
Rampton CI CHING E4 ... 51 G5
Ramsay Gdns HARH RM3 ... 74 B2
Ramsay Rd ACT W3 ... 117 J1
FSTGT E7 ... 88 M4
FSTGT E7 ... 88 A3
Ramscroft CI ED N9 ... 49 L2
Ramsdale Rd TOOT SW17 ... 156 A1
Ramsden Dr CRW RM5 ... 73 G1
Ramsden Rd BAL SW12 ... 138 A4
ERITH DA8 ... 127 K5
FBAR/BDGN N11 ... 47 M7
ORP BR6 ... 177 H2
STMC/STPC BR5 ... 181 J3
Ramsey CI CDALE/KGS NW9 ... 63 H7
NTHLT UB5 ... 79 K5
Ramsey Rd THHTH CR7 ... 171 M1
Ramsey St BETH E2 ... 104 A3
Ramsey Wy STHGT/OAK N14 ... 48 C2
Ramsgate St HACK E8 ... 85 M6
Ramsgill Ap GNTH/NBYPK IG2 .. 71 M5
Ramsgill Dr GNTH/NBYPK IG2 ... 71 M6
Rams Gv CHDH RM6 ... 72 E5
Ram St WAND/EARL SW18 ... 137 H2
Ramulis Dr YEAD UB4 ... 96 E3
Ramus Wood Av ORP BR6 ... 176 E7
Rancliffe Gdns ELTH/MOT SE9 .. 142 E1
Rancliffe Rd EHAM E6 ... 106 F1
Randall Av CRICK NW2 ... 81 L2
Randall CI BTSEA SW11 ... 119 L6
ERITH DA8 ... 127 J4
Randall Dr HCH RM12 ... 92 C4
Randall PI GNWCH SE10 ... 123 J4
Randall Rd LBTH SE11 ... 17 L7
Randall Rw LBTH SE11 ... 17 L6
Randell's Rd IS N1 ... 5 K3
Randle Rd RCHPK/HAM TW10 ... 134 C8
Randlesdown Rd CAT SE6 ... 141 G8
Randolph Ap CAN/RD E16 ... 106 C5
Randolph Av KIL/WHAMP NW6 ... 2 E8
MV/WKIL W9 ... 2 C6
Randolph CI BXLYHN DA7 ... 127 J8
COB KT11 ... 178 A8
KUTN/CMB KT2 ... 153 J1
Randolph Crs MV/WKIL W9 ... 8 E1
Randolph Gdns KIL/WHAMP NW6 .. 2 C6
Randolph Ms MV/WKIL W9 ... 8 F1
Randolph Rd EW KT17 ... 180 C7
HAYES BR2 ... 175 M3
MV/WKIL W9 ... 8 E1
STHL UB1 ... 96 D7
WALTH E17 ... 69 H6
Randolph St CAMTN NW1 ... 4 E2
Randon CI PIN HA5 ... 61 H3
Ranelagh Av BARN SW13 ... 118 A7
FUL/PGN SW6 ... 118 E8
Ranelagh CI EDGW HA8 ... 45 G6
Ranelagh Dr EDGW HA8 ... 45 G6
TWK TW1 ... 134 B1
Ranelagh Gdns CHSWK W4 ... 117 J5
FUL/PGN SW6 ... 118 E8
IL IG1 ... 89 G1
WAN E11 ... 70 C6
Ranelagh Gv BCVA SW1W ... 16 B7
Ranelagh PI NWMAL KT3 ... 153 L8
Ranelagh Rd ALP/SUD HA0 ... 80 D5
EA W5 ... 98 D5
EHAM E6 ... 89 G8
PIM SW1V ... 16 F8
SRTFD E15 ... 87 L8
STHL UB1 ... 96 D7
TOTM N17 ... 67 L4
WAN E11 ... 87 L4
WDGN N22 ... 66 F2
WLSDN NW10 ... 99 M1
Ranfurly Rd SUT SM1 ... 170 A4
Rangefield Rd BMLY BR1 ... 160 A2
Rangemoor Rd
SEVS/STOTM N15 ... 67 M6
Range Wy SHPTN TW17 ... 164 A2
Rangeworth PI
BFN/LL DA15 ... 143 M7
Rangoon St TWRH EC3N ... 13 L5
Rankin CI CDALE/KGS NW9 ... 63 L4
Ranleigh Gdns BXLYHN DA7 ... 126 F5
Ranmere St BAL SW12 ... 138 B5
Ranmoor Gdns HRW HA1 ... 61 K5
Ranmoor Av CROY/NA CR0 ... 172 F5
Ranmore Pth STMC/STPC BR5 .. 162 A7
Ranmore Rd BELMT SM2 ... 181 G7
Rannoch CI EDGW HA8 ... 45 H4
Rannoch Rd HMSMTH W6 ... 118 C4
Rannock Av CDALE/KGS NW9 ... 63 G8

Ranskill Rd *BORE* WD6 ....32 A4
Ransom Cl *OXHEY* WD19 ....42 C2
Ransom Rd *CHARL* SE7 ....124 C3
Ranston St *CAMTN* NW1 ....9 J2
Ranulf Rd *CRICK* NW2 ....82 A4
Ranwell Cl *BOW* E3 ....86 F8
Ranworth Rd *ED* N9 ....50 C4
Ranyard Cl *CHSGTN* KT9 ....167 M5
Raphael Av *ROM* RM1 ....73 M4
    WATN WD24 ....29 K5
Raphael Dr *THDIT* KT7 ....166 F2
Raphael St *SKENS* SW7 ....15 L2
Rapier Cl *PUR* RM19 ....128 F2
Rasper Rd *TRDG/WHET* N20 ....47 J4
Rastell Av *BAL* SW12 ....138 D6
Ratcliffe Cl *LEE/GVPK* SE12 ....142 A4
    UX/CGN UB8 ....94 D2
Ratcliffe Cross St
    WCHPL E1 ....104 D5 🔢
Ratcliffe La *POP/IOD* E14 ....104 E5
Ratcliff Rd *FSTGT* E7 ....88 C5
Rathbone Pl *FITZ* W1T 11 G3
Rathbone St *CAN/RD* E16 ....105 M4
    FITZ W1T 10 F3
Rathcoole Av *CEND/HSY/T* N8 ....66 F6
Rathcoole Gdns
    CEND/HSY/T N8 ....66 F6 🔢
Rathfern Rd *FSTH* SE23 ....140 F5
Rathgar Av *WEA* W13 ....98 B7
Rathgar Cl *FNCH* N3 ....64 F3
Rathgar Rd *BRXN/ST* SW9 ....121 H8
Rathmell Dr *CLAP* SW4 ....138 D3
Rathmore Rd *CHARL* SE7 ....124 B3
Rat's La *LOU* IG10 ....39 H3
Rattray Rd *BRXS/STRHM* SW2 ....139 G1
Raveley St *KTTN* NW5 ....84 C4
Ravel Gdns *SOCK/AV* RM15 ....111 J5
Ravel Rd *SOCK/AV* RM15 ....111 K5
Raven Cl *RKW/CH/CXG* WD3 ....40 C2
Ravencroft Crs *ELTH/MOT* SE9 ...142 F7
Ravendale Rd *SUN* TW16 ....149 M5
Ravenet St *BTSEA* SW11 ....120 D6 🔢
Ravenfield Rd *TOOT* SW17 ....137 M7
Ravenhill Rd *PLSTW* E13 ....88 C8
Ravenna Rd *PUT/ROE* SW15 ......136 D2
Ravenoak Wy *CHIG* IG7 ....53 L7
Ravenor Park Rd *GFD/PVL* UB6 ...97 H2
Raven Rd *SWFD* E18 ....70 C3
Raven Rw *WCHPL* E1 ....104 B4
Ravensbourne Av *HAYES* BR2 ....159 K4
    STWL/WRAY TW19 ....133 L6
Ravensbourne Crs *HARH* RM3 .....74 F4
Ravensbourne Gdns *CLAY* IG5 .....71 G2
    WEA W13 ....98 B4
Ravensbourne Pk *BROCKY* SE4 ..141 G4
    CAT SE6 ....140 F4
Ravensbourne Park Crs
    CAT SE6 ....140 F4 🔢
Ravensbourne Pl *DEPT* SE8 ....123 H7 🔢
Ravensbourne Rd *BMLY* BR1 ......160 A6
    DART DA1 ....128 A8
    FSTH SE23 ....140 F4
    TWK TW1 ....134 C3
Ravensbury Av *MRDN* SM4 ....154 B5 🔢
Ravensbury Gv *MTCM* CR4 ....155 K7
Ravensbury La *MTCM* CR4 ....155 K7
Ravensbury Rd
    STMC/STPC BR5 ....161 M7
    WAND/EARL SW18 ....137 H6
Ravensbury Ter
    WAND/EARL SW18 ....137 H5
Ravenscar Rd *BMLY* BR1 ....141 J8
    SURB KT6 ....167 M4
Ravens Cl *CDALE/KGS* NW9 ....63 L3
    EN EN1 ....36 E5
    HAYES BR2 ....159 M5 🔢
Ravenscourt *SUN* TW16 ....149 M4
Ravenscourt Av
    HMSMTH W6 ....118 A2 🔢
Ravenscourt Cl *HCH* RM12 ....92 E3 🔢
    RSLP HA4 ....59 J8
Ravenscourt Dr *HCH* RM12 ....92 E3 🔢
Ravenscourt Gdns
    HMSMTH W6 ....117 M2
Ravenscourt Gv *HCH* RM12 ....92 E2
Ravenscourt Pk *HMSMTH* W6 ....118 A2
Ravenscourt Pl *HMSMTH* W6 ....118 B2 🔢
Ravenscourt Rd *HMSMTH* W6 ....118 A2 🔢
    STMC/STPC BR5 ....162 A6
Ravenscourt Sq *HMSMTH* W6 ....118 A1
Ravenscraig Rd *FBAR/BDGN* N11 ..48 B6
Ravenscroft Av *GLDGN* NW11 .....64 E4
    WBLY HA9 ....80 E1
Ravenscroft Cl *CAN/RD* E16 ....106 A4
Ravenscroft Pk *BAR* EN5 ....25 K4
Ravenscroft Rd *BECK* BR3 ....158 C5
    CAN/RD E16 ....106 A4
    CHSWK W4 ....117 J2 🔢
Ravenscroft St *BETH* E2 ....7 M6
Ravensdale Av
    NFNCH/WDSP N12 ....47 J6
Ravensdale Gdns *NRWD* SE19 ...157 K3
Ravensdale Ms *STA* TW18 ....148 B2 🔢
Ravensdale Rd *HSLWW* TW4 ......114 E8
    STNW/STAM N16 ....67 M8
Ravensdon St *LBTH* SE11 ....18 B8
Ravensfield *DAGW* RM9 ....90 D4
Ravensfield Gdns
    HOR/WEW KT19 ....168 E7
Ravenshaw St
    KIL/WHAMP NW6 ....82 F6 🔢
Ravenshead Cl *SAND/SEL* CR2 ...185 J4
Ravenshill *CHST* BR7 ....161 H4
Ravenshurst Av *HDN* NW4 ....64 C7
Ravenside Cl *UED* N18 ....50 D7
Ravenslea Rd *BAL* SW12 ....138 A5
Ravensmead Rd *HAYES* BR2 ......159 K3
Ravensmede Wy *CHSWK* W4 ......117 M2
Ravenstone Rd
    CDALE/KGS NW9 ....63 M7 🔢
    CEND/HSY/T N8 ....66 F4
Ravenstone St *BAL* SW12 ....138 A5
Ravens Wy *LEE/GVPK* SE12 ....142 A4
Ravens Wold *PUR/KEN* CR8 ....184 C8
Ravenswood *BXLY* DA5 ....144 E5

Ravenswood Av *SURB* KT6 ....167 M4
    WWKM BR4 ....174 C3
Ravenswood Ct *ROM* RM5 ....55 H7
Ravenswood Crs
    RYLN/HDSTN HA2 ....78 F2
    WWKM BR4 ....174 C3
Ravenswood Gdns *ISLW* TW7 ....115 L6 🔢
Ravenswood Rd *BAL* SW12 ....138 B4
    CROY/NA CR0 ....172 B5 🔢
    WALTH E17 ....69 J5 🔢
Ravensworth Rd
    ELTH/MOT SE9 ....142 F8
    WLSDN NW10 ....100 B2 🔢
Ravent Rd *LBTH* SE11 ....17 M6
Ravey St *SDTCH* EC2A 7 J9
Ravine Gv *WOOL/PLUM* SE18 ....125 L4
Rawlings Cl *ORP* BR6 ....176 F7
Rawlings St *CHEL* SW3 ....15 L5
Rawlins Cl *FNCH* N3 ....64 E4
    SAND/SEL CR2 ....185 M1
Rawnsley Av *MTCM* CR4 ....155 K7 🔢
Rawson St *BTSEA* SW11 ....120 A6 🔢
Rawsthorne Cl *CAN/RD* E16 ....106 F7 🔢
Rawstone Pl *FSBYE* EC1V ....6 C7 🔢
Rawstorne St *FSBYE* EC1V 6 C7
Rayburn Rd *EMPK* RM11 ....75 G8
Raydean Rd *BAR* EN5 ....34 A8
Raydons Gdns *DAGW* RM9 ....90 E4
Raydons Rd *DAGW* RM9 ....90 E5
Raydon St *KTTN* NW5 ....84 B2
Rayfield Cl *HAYES* BR2 ....175 L1 🔢
Rayford Av *LEE/GVPK* SE12 ....141 M4
Rayford Cl *DART* DA1 ....146 C2
Ray Gdns *BARK* IG11 ....108 A1
    STAN HA7 ....44 B7
Ray Lamb Wy *ERITH* DA8 ....128 B4
Rayleas Cl *WOOL/PLUM* SE18 ....125 H6
Rayleigh Av *TEDD* TW11 ....151 L2
Rayleigh Cl *PLMGR* N13 ....49 K5 🔢
Rayleigh Ct *KUT* KT1 ....152 F5 🔢
Rayleigh Ri *SAND/SEL* CR2 ....172 E8
Rayleigh Rd *CAN/RD* E16 ....106 B7 🔢
    PLMGR N13 ....49 J5
    WFD IG8 ....70 C1
    WIM/MER SW19 ....154 F4
Ray Lodge Rd *WFD* IG8 ....52 C8
Ray Massey Wy *EHAM* E6 ....88 E3 🔢
Raymead Av *THHTH* CR7 ....157 G8
Raymere Gdns
    WOOL/PLUM SE18 ....125 K5
Raymond Av *HNWL* W7 ....116 A1
    SWFD E18 ....69 M3
Raymond Cl *ABLGY* WD5 ....20 D5 🔢
    SYD SE26 ....158 C1 🔢
Raymond Gdns *CHIG* IG7 ....54 E5
Raymond Rd *BECK* BR3 ....158 E7
    GNTH/NBYPK IG2 ....71 K8
    PLSTW E13 ....88 C7
    WIM/MER SW19 ....154 F2 🔢
Raymond Wy
    ESH/CLAY KT10 ....167 G8 🔢
Raymouth Rd
    BERM/RHTH SE16 ....122 B2
Rayne Ct *SWFD* E18 ....69 M5 🔢
Rayners Cl *ALP/SUD* HA0 ....80 D5
Rayners Gdns *NTHLT* UB5 ....96 B2
Rayners La *PIN* HA5 ....60 F7
    RYLN/HDSTN HA2 ....79 G1
Rayner's Rd *PUT/ROE* SW15 ......136 E2
Raynham Av *UED* N18 ....50 A8
Raynham Rd *HMSMTH* W6 ....118 B2 🔢
    UED N18 ....50 A7
Raynham Ter *UED* N18 ....50 A7
Raynor Cl *STHL* UB1 ....96 F7
Raynor Pl *IS* N1 ....6 F3
Raynton Cl *RYLN/HDSTN* HA2 ......78 L1
    YEAD UB4 ....95 M3
Raynton Dr *YEAD* UB4 ....95 M2
Raynton Rd *PEND* EN3 ....37 K2
Ray Rd *CRW* RM5 ....55 H7
    E/WMO/HCT KT8 ....151 H8
Rays Av *UED* N18 ....50 C6
Rays Rd *UED* N18 ....50 C6
    WWKM BR4 ....174 C2
Ray St *CLKNW* EC1R ....12 B1 🔢
Ray Street Br *CLKNW* EC1R ....12 B1 🔢
Raywood Cl *WDR/YW* UB7 ....113 J5
Reachview Cl *CAMTN* NW1 ....4 F2 🔢
Reading La *HACK* E8 ....86 B6
Reading Rd *NTHLT* UB5 ....79 H5
    SUT SM1 ....170 C7
Reading Wy *MLHL* NW7 ....46 V2
Reads Cl *IL* IG1 ....89 H3 🔢
Reapers Cl *CAMTN* NW1 ....5 G3
Reapers Wy *NTHLT* UB5 ....133 K2 🔢
Reardon Pth *WAP* E1W ....104 B7 🔢
Reardon St *WAP* E1W 104 B7
Reaston St *NWCR* SE14 ....122 C5
Reckitt Rd *CHSWK* W4 ....117 L3
Record St *PECK* SE15 ....122 C4
Recovery St *TOOT* SW17 ....155 L1 🔢
Recreation Av *HARH* RM3 ....74 F3
    ROMW/RG RM7 ....73 J6
Recreation Rd *HAYES* BR2 ....159 M5
    NWDGN UB2 ....114 C2
    SYD SE26 ....140 D8
Recreation Wy *MTCM* CR4 ....156 C6
Rector St *IS* N1 ....6 E4
Rectory Cl *CHING* E4 ....51 G5
    DART DA1 ....145 L1
    FNCH N3 ....64 F2
    RYNPK SW20 ....154 C5
    SCUP DA14 ....144 B8
    SHPTN TW17 ....149 G6
    STAN HA7 ....44 B8
    SURB KT6 ....167 J3
Rectory Field Crs *CHARL* SE7 ....124 B2
Rectory Gdns *CEND/HSY/T* N8 ....66 F5
    NTHLT UB5 ....78 F8
    UPMR RM14 ....93 K2
Rectory Gn *BECK* BR3 ....158 F4
Rectory Gv *CLAP* SW4 ....120 C8
    CROY/NA CR0 ....172 B4
    FELT TW13 ....132 F8
Rectory La *BNSTD* SM7 ....182 F8
    EDGW HA8 ....45 G8

    KGLGY WD4 ....20 A1
    RKW/CH/CXG WD3 ....40 D3
    SCUP DA14 ....144 B8
    STAN HA7 ....44 B7
    SURB KT6 ....167 J3
    TOOT SW17 ....156 A1
    WLGTN SM6 ....171 J6
Rectory Orch *WIM/MER* SW19 ....136 B5
Rectory Pk *SAND/SEL* CR2 ....184 E6
Rectory Park Av *NTHLT* UB5 ....96 F2
Rectory Pl *WOOL/PLUM* SE18 ....125 G2
Rectory Rd *ACT* W3 ....99 H7
    BARN SW13 ....118 A7
    BECK BR3 ....159 G5
    DAGE RM10 ....91 G6
    HAYES BR2 ....187 K1
    HEST TW5 ....114 B7
    HYS/HAR UB3 ....96 A5
    MNPK E12 ....88 F5
    NWDGN UB2 ....114 F1
    RKW/CH/CXG WD3 ....40 D3
    STNW/STAM N16 ....85 M3
    SUT SM1 ....170 A5
    WALTH E17 ....69 H5
Rectory Sq *WCHPL* E1 ....104 D4
Rectory Wy *HGDN/ICK* UB10 ....77 H2
Reculver Ms *UED* N18 ....50 A6 🔢
Reculver Rd *BERM/RHTH* SE16 ...122 C3
Redan Pl *BAY/PAD* W2 ....8 C5
Redan Ter *CMBW* SE5 ....121 F7 🔢
Redbarn Cl *PUR/KEN* CR8 ....184 B4 🔢
Red Barracks Rd
    WOOL/PLUM SE18 ....124 F2 🔢
Redberry Gv *SYD* SE26 ....140 C7
Redbourne Av *FNCH* N3 ....65 G2
Redbridge La East *REDBR* IG4 .....70 D7
Redbridge La West *WAN* E11 ....70 B7
Redburn St *CHEL* SW3 ....15 L9
Redbury Cl *RAIN* RM13 ....110 B3 🔢
Redcar Cl *NTHLT* UB5 ....79 H5
Redcar Rd *HARH* RM3 ....56 F7
Redcar St *CMBW* SE5 ....121 G7 🔢
Redcastle Cl *WCHPL* E1 ....104 C6 🔢
Red Cedars Rd *ORP* BR6 ....176 E2
Redchurch St *BETH* E2 ....7 J9
Redcliffe Ms *WBPTN* SW10 ....14 D8
Redcliffe Pl *WBPTN* SW10 ....119 J4 🔢
Redcliffe Rd *WBPTN* SW10 ....14 D8
Redcliffe Sq *WBPTN* SW10 ....14 D8
Redcliffe St *WBPTN* SW10 ....14 D9
Redclose Av *MRDN* SM4 ....155 G5
Redclyffe Rd *EHAM* E6 ....88 C8
Redcroft Rd *GFD/PVL* UB6 ....97 J6
Redcross Wy *STHWK* SE1 ....18 F1
Redden Court Rd *HARH* RM3 ....74 E4
Reddings Av *BUSH* WD23 ....30 B8
Reddings Cl *MLHL* NW7 ....45 M5
The Reddings *BORE* WD6 ....31 M6 🔢
    MLHL NW7 ....45 M5
Reddington Cl
    SAND/SEL CR2 ....184 D2 🔢
Reddins Rd *PECK* SE15 ....122 A5
Reddons Rd *BECK* BR3 ....158 E3
Reddy Rd *ERITH* DA8 ....127 M4
Rede Pl *BAY/PAD* W2 ....8 C5
Redesdale Gdns *ISLW* TW7 ....116 A5
Redesdale St *CHEL* SW3 ....15 L9
Redfern Av *HSLWW* TW4 ....133 G4
Redfern Cl *UX/CGN* UB8 ....76 C3 🔢
Redfern Gdns *GPK* RM2 ....74 D3
Redfern Rd *CAT* SE6 ....141 J4
    WLSDN NW10 ....81 L7
Redfield La *EC* SW5 ....14 C5
Redford Av *COUL/CHIP* CR5 ....183 H8
    THHTH CR7 ....156 F7
    WLGTN SM6 ....171 L8
Redford Cl *FELT* TW13 ....131 M6
Redford Wy *UX/CGN* UB8 ....76 C7
Redgate Dr *HAYES* BR2 ....175 H4
Redgate Ter *PUT/ROE* SW15 ......136 D3
Redgrave Cl *SNWD* SE25 ....172 F1 🔢
Redgrave Rd *PUT/ROE* SW15 ....136 D1
Redheath Cl *GSTN* WD25 ....20 F8
Red Hi *CHST* BR7 ....161 G1
Redhill Dr *EDGW* HA8 ....63 J3
Redhill St *CAMTN* NW1 ....4 B4
Red House La *BXLYHS* DA6 ....144 D1
    WOT/HER KT12 ....165 G4
Red House Rd *CROY/NA* CR0 .....171 K1
Redington Gdns *HAMP* NW3 ....83 H4
Redington Rd *HAMP* NW3 ....83 H3
Redland Gdns
    E/WMO/HCT KT8 ....150 F7 🔢
Redlands Rd *PEND* EN3 ....37 L4
Redlands Wy
    BRXS/STRHM SW2 ....138 E4
Red La *ESH/CLAY* KT10 ....167 G8
Redleaf Cl *BELV* DA17 ....127 G4
Redleaves Av *ASHF* TW15 ....149 H2
Redlees Cl *ISLW* TW7 ....134 A1
Red Lion Cl *STNC/STPC* BR5 ......177 J1
    STMC/STPC BR5 ....177 J1
    WALW SE17 ....19 G9
Red Lion Hi *EFNCH* N2 ....65 K3 🔢
Red Lion La *WOOL/PLUM* SE18 ..125 G6
Red Lion Pl
    WOOL/PLUM SE18 ....125 G6 🔢
Red Lion Rd *SURB* KT6 ....167 M4
Red Lion Rw *WALW* SE17 ....121 J4
Red Lion Sq *GINN* WC1R ....11 L3 🔢
    RCHPK/HAM TW10 ....134 F3 🔢
Red Lion St *GINN* WC1R ....11 L2 🔢
    RCHPK/HAM TW10 ....134 F3 🔢
Red Lodge Crs *BXLY* DA5 ....145 K7
Red Lodge Rd *BXLY* DA5 ....145 K7
    WWKM BR4 ....174 C5
Redman Cl *NTHLT* UB5 ....96 C1 🔢
Redman's Rd *WCHPL* E1 ....104 E4
Redmead La *WAP* E1W ....104 A7 🔢
Redmead Rd *HYS/HAR* UB3 ....113 L2
Redmore Rd *HMSMTH* W6 ....118 B2 🔢
Red Oak Cl *ORP* BR6 ....176 B5
Red Pl *MYFR/PKLN* W1K ....10 A6 🔢
Red Post Hi *HNHL* SE24 ....139 K2

Redriffe Rd *PLSTW* E13 ....105 M1
Redriff Rd *BERM/RHTH* SE16 .....122 E1
    ROMW/RG RM7 ....73 H3
Red Oak *BORE* WD6 ....31 M6
Redroofs Cl *BECK* BR3 ....159 H4
Redruth Cl *WDGN* N22 ....66 F1
Redruth Rd *HARH* RM3 ....56 F7
    HOM E9 ....86 D8 🔢
Redstart Cl *CROY/NA* CR0 ....186 D3
    EHAM E6 ....106 E4
    NWCR SE14 ....122 E5 🔢
Redston Rd *CEND/HSY/T* N8 ....66 D5
Redvers Rd *WDGN* N22 ....67 G3
Redvers St *IS* N1 ....7 K6
Redwald Rd *CLPT* E5 ....86 D4
Redway Dr *WHTN* TW2 ....133 J4
Redwing Cl *SAND/SEL* CR2 ....185 K4
Redwing Gv *ABLGY* WD5 ....21 G4 🔢
Redwood Cl *BERM/RHTH* SE16 ...104 C3 🔢
    BFN/LL DA15 ....144 A5
    HGDN/ICK UB10 ....95 H1 🔢
    OXHEY WD19 ....42 C6
    PUR/KEN CR8 ....184 C7 🔢
    STHGT/OAK N14 ....48 D2 🔢
Redwood Gdns *CHING* E4 ....51 H1 🔢
Redwood Ms *BAL* SW12 ....33 K8
Redwood Wy *BAR* EN5 ....25 H8
Reece Ms *SKENS* SW7 ....15 G5
Reed Av *ORP* BR6 ....176 E5
Reede Rd *DAGE* RM10 ....91 G6
Reede Wy *DAGE* RM10 ....91 H6
Reedham Cl *TOTM* N17 ....68 B5 🔢
Reedham Dr *PUR/KEN* CR8 ....183 M6
Reedham St *PECK* SE15 ....122 F7 🔢
Reedholm Vls
    STNW/STAM N16 ....85 K4 🔢
Reed Pond Wk *GPK* RM2 ....73 H2 🔢
Reed Rd *TOTM* N17 ....67 M4
Reeds Crs *WATN* WD24 ....29 J5
Reedsfield Cl *ASHF* TW15 ....131 H7 🔢
Reedsfield Rd *ASHF* TW15 ....131 H8 🔢
Reed's Pl *CAMTN* NW1 ....4 E1
Reedworth St *LBTH* SE11 ....18 B6
Reenglass Rd *HARH* RM3 ....44 D6 🔢
Rees Dr *STAN* HA7 ....44 A6
Rees Gdns *CROY/NA* CR0 ....172 F1 🔢
Reesland Cl *MNPK* E12 ....89 G5 🔢
Rees St *IS* N1 ....6 F3
Reets Farm Cl *CDALE/KGS* NW9 ..63 L7
Reeves Av *CDALE/KGS* NW9 ....63 K8
Reeves Cnr *CROY/NA* CR0 ....172 B6 🔢
Reeves Cresent *SWLY* BR8 ....163 K6
Reeves Ms *MYFR/PKLN* W1K 10 A7
Reeves Rd *BOW* E3 ....105 H3
    WOOL/PLUM SE18 ....125 H4 🔢
Reform Rw *TOTM* N17 ....67 M3
Reform St *BTSEA* SW11 ....119 M7
Regal Cl *EA* W5 ....98 D4
    WCHPL E1 ....104 A1 🔢
Regal Ct *MTCM* CR4 ....155 M6 🔢
    UED N18 ....49 M7 🔢
Regal Crs *WLGTN* SM6 ....171 H5 🔢
Regal Dr *FBAR/BDGN* N11 ....48 B7
Regal Wy *KTN/HRWW/W* HA3 ......62 E7
    WATN WD24 ....29 J3
Regan Wy *IS* N1 ....7 J6
Regarder Rd *CHIG* IG7 ....54 E7
Regarth Av *ROM* RM1 ....73 L7
Regency Cl *CHIG* IG7 ....53 J7 🔢
    EA W5 ....98 E5
    HPTN TW12 ....150 F1 🔢
Regency Ct *EN* EN1 ....36 D7
Regency Dr *RSLP* HA4 ....77 L1 🔢
Regency Gdns *EMPK* RM11 ....74 D8
    WOT/HER KT12 ....165 J3 🔢
Regency Ms *BECK* BR3 ....159 J4 🔢
    WLSDN NW10 ....82 A6 🔢
Regency St *WEST* SW1P 17 H6
Regency Wk *CROY/NA* CR0 ....173 L1 🔢
Regent Av *HGDN/ICK* UB10 ....77 H7
Regent Cl *HEST* TW5 ....114 B6
    KGLGY WD4 ....20 A2
    KTN/HRWW/W HA3 ....62 E7
    NFNCH/WDSP N12 ....47 J7
Regent Gdns *GDMY/SEVK* IG3 ....73 G3 🔢
Regent Pl *WIM/MER* SW19 ....155 J1
    WLSDN NW10 ....100 D2 🔢
Regent Rd *BRYLDS* KT5 ....152 F8
    HNHL SE24 ....139 H3
Regents Av *PLMGR* N13 ....49 G7
    YEAD UB4 ....95 M4 🔢
Regents Dr *HAYES* BR2 ....175 M7
Regents Ms *STJWD* NW8 ....2 F5
Regent's Park Rd *CAMTN* NW1 .....3 M3
Regent's Park Ter *CAMTN* NW1 .....4 C3
Regents Pl *LOU* IG10 ....52 D2
Regent Sq *BELV* DA17 ....127 H2
    STPAN WC1H 5 K8
Regents Rw *HACK* E8 ....86 A8
Regent St *CHSWK* W4 ....117 G3
    CONDST W1S 10 E5
    STJS SW1Y 11 G7
    WATN WD24 ....29 H3
    WLSDN NW10 ....100 D2 🔢
Reginald Rd *DEPT* SE8 ....123 C5
    FSTGT E7 ....88 A7
    HARH RM3 ....75 G2
    NTHWD HA6 ....59 M2
Reginald Sq *DEPT* SE8 ....123 C5
Regina Rd *FSBYPK* N4 ....84 F1
    NWDGN UB2 ....114 E2
    SNWD SE25 ....157 J3
    WEA W13 ....98 A7
Regina Ter *WEA* W13 ....98 B7 🔢
Regis Rd *KTTN* NW5 ....84 B5
Regnart Buildings *CAMTN* NW1 .....4 E7 🔢
Reid Cl *PIN* HA5 ....60 A1
Reidhaven Rd
    WOOL/PLUM SE18 ....125 L2
Reigate Av *MRDN* SM4 ....170 B3
Reigate Av *BMLY* BR1 ....142 A8
    EW KT17 ....180 F3
    GDMY/SEVK IG3 ....89 M2

Reigate Wy *WLGTN* SM6 ....171 L7
Reighton Rd *CLPT* E5 ....86 A3
Relay Rd *SHB* W12 ....100 C5
Relf Rd *PECK* SE15 ....122 A8
Relton Ms *SKENS* SW7 ....15 K3 🔢
Rembrandt Cl *BGVA* SW1W ....16 A7 🔢
    POP/IOD E14 ....123 K1
Rembrandt Ct
    HOR/WEW KT19 ....168 F8 🔢
Rembrandt Rd *EDGW* HA8 ....63 G3 🔢
    LEW SE13 ....141 L1
Remington Rd *EHAM* E6 ....106 E5
    SEVS/STOTM N15 ....67 K7 🔢
Remington St *IS* N1 ....6 D6
Remnant St *HOL/ALD* WC2B 11 L4
Remus Rd *BOW* E3 ....87 G7 🔢
Rendle Cl *CROY/NA* CR0 ....157 M8
Rendlesham Av *RAD* WD7 ....30 F2
Rendlesham Rd *CLPT* E5 ....86 A4
    ENC/FH EN2 ....36 B4
Renforth St
    BERM/RHTH SE16 ....104 C8 🔢
Renfrew Wy *SHPTN* TW17 ....164 A2 🔢
Renfrew Cl *EHAM* E6 ....107 G6
Renfrew Rd *HEST* TW5 ....114 D7
    KUTN/CMB KT2 ....153 J3
    LBTH SE11 ....18 C5
Renmuir St *TOOT* SW17 ....156 A3
Rennell St *LEW* SE13 ....123 J8 🔢
Renness Rd *WALTH* E17 ....68 E4
Rennets Cl *ELTH/MOT* SE9 ....143 K2
Rennets Wood Rd
    ELTH/MOT SE9 ....143 K2
Rennie Cl *ASHF* TW15 ....130 D7
Rennie St *STHWK* SE1 ....12 C8
Renown Cl *CROY/NA* CR0 ....172 B3 🔢
    ROMW/RG RM7 ....73 H2 🔢
Rensburg Rd *WALTH* E17 ....68 D6
Renshaw Cl *BELV* DA17 ....126 F4 🔢
Renters Av *HDN* NW4 ....64 C7
Renwick Rd *BARK* IG11 ....108 B3
Repens Wy *YEAD* UB4 ....96 D3 🔢
Rephidim St *STHWK* SE1 ....19 H4
Replingham Rd
    WAND/EARL SW18 ....136 F5
Reporton Rd *FUL/PGN* SW6 ....118 F6
Repository Rd
    WOOL/PLUM SE18 ....124 F4
Repton Av *ALP/SUD* HA0 ....80 C4
    GPK RM2 ....74 A4
    HYS/HAR UB3 ....113 K2
Repton Cl *SUT* SM1 ....169 K5
Repton Ct *BECK* BR3 ....159 H4 🔢
Repton Dr *GPK* RM2 ....74 A5
Repton Gdns *GPK* RM2 ....74 A4
Repton Gv *CLAY* IG5 ....70 F2
    KTN/HRWW/W HA3 ....62 F5
    ORP BR6 ....177 G6
Repton Rd *RKW/CH/CXG* WD3 .....28 A3 🔢
Repton St *POP/IOD* E14 ....104 E5
Repulse Cl *ROMW/RG* RM7 ....73 H2 🔢
Reservoir Rd *BROCKY* SE4 ....122 E7 🔢
    RSLP HA4 ....59 J6
    STHGT/OAK N14 ....35 J5
Restell Cl *BKHTH/KID* SE3 ....123 L4 🔢
Restmor Wy *WLGTN* SM6 ....171 G4 🔢
Reston Cl *BORE* WD6 ....32 A3
Reston Pl *SKENS* SW7 ....14 E2
Restons Crs *ELTH/MOT* SE9 ....143 K3
Retford Cl *BORE* WD6 ....32 A3 🔢
    HARH RM3 ....57 G8
Retford Pth *HARH* RM3 ....57 G8
Retford Rd *HARH* RM3 ....75 G1
Retford St *BETH* E2 ....7 K6 🔢
    BETH E2 ....7 K6 🔢
Retingham Wy *CHING* E4 ....51 H4 🔢
Retreat Cl *KTN/HRWW/W* HA3 .....62 C6
Retreat Pl *HOM* E9 ....86 C6
Retreat Rd *RCH/KEW* TW9 ....134 D2 🔢
The Retreat *BARN* SW13 ....117 L8 🔢
    BRYLDS KT5 ....167 M1
    CDALE/KGS NW9 ....63 K6 🔢
    ORP BR6 ....177 M6
    RYLN/HDSTN HA2 ....61 G8
    THHTH CR7 ....157 K7
    WPK KT4 ....169 H4 🔢
Retreat Wy *CHIG* IG7 ....54 E5
Reveley Sq
    BERM/RHTH SE16 ....104 E8 🔢
Revell Ri *WOOL/PLUM* SE18 ......125 M4
Revell Rd *KUT* KT1 ....153 H5
    SUT SM1 ....169 M8
Revelon Rd *BROCKY* SE4 ....140 E1
Revelstoke Rd *WIM/MER* SW19 ..137 G6
Reventlow Rd *ELTH/MOT* SE9 ....143 J5
Reverdy Rd *STHWK* SE1 ....122 A2
Reverend Cl
    RYLN/HDSTN HA2 ....79 H3 🔢
Revesby Rd *CAR* SM5 ....170 E1
Review Rd *CRICK* NW2 ....81 M2
    DAGE RM10 ....109 H1
Rewell St *FUL/PGN* SW6 ....119 J5 🔢
Rewley Rd *CAR* SM5 ....170 D1
Rex Av *ASHF* TW15 ....149 G2
Rex Pl *MYFR/PKLN* W1K 10 B8
Reydon Av *WAN* E11 ....70 C7
Reynard Cl *BMLY* BR1 ....160 F6
Reynard Dr *NRWD* SE19 ....157 M3 🔢
Reynardson Rd *TOTM* N17 ....67 J3 🔢
Reynard's Wy *LCOL/BKTW* AL2 ...21 M2
Reynolds Av *CHDH* RM6 ....72 C8
    CHSGTN KT9 ....179 L1
    MNPK E12 ....89 C5
Reynolds Cl *CAR* SM5 ....170 F3
    GLDGN NW11 ....65 H8
    WIM/MER SW19 ....155 K4
Reynolds Dr *EDGW* HA8 ....62 E6
Reynolds Pl *BKHTH/KID* SE3 ......124 B3 🔢
    RCHPK/HAM TW10 ....134 F3 🔢
Reynolds Rd *CHSWK* W4 ....117 J1 🔢
    NWMAL KT3 ....168 C2
    PECK SE15 ....140 C2
    YEAD UB4 ....96 C2
Reynolds Wy *CROY/NA* CR0 ......172 E6
Rheidol Ms *IS* N1 ....6 E5
Rheidol Ter *IS* N1 ....6 D5

Rheingold Wy WLGTN SM6 ...... 183 L2
Rheola Cl TOTM N17 ...... 67 M2
Rhoda St BETH E2 ...... 7 M9
Rhodes Av WDGN N22 ...... 66 C2
Rhodesia Rd BRXN/ST SW9 ...... 120 F7
WAN E11 ...... 87 K2
Rhodes St HOLWY N7 ...... 84 F5
Rhodes Wy WATN WD24 ...... 29 K5
Rhodeswell Rd POP/IOD E14 ...... 104 E4
Rhodrons Av CHSGTN KT9 ...... 167 L7
Rhondda Gv BOW E3 ...... 104 E2
Rhyl Rd GFD/PVL UB6 ...... 97 M1
Rhyl St KTTN NW5 ...... 84 A6
Rhys Av FBAR/BDGN N11 ...... 66 D1
Rialto Rd MTCM CR4 ...... 156 A5
Ribble Cl WFD IG8 ...... 52 C8
Ribblesdale Av FBAR/BDGN N11 ...... 47 M8
NTHLT UB5 ...... 79 H6
Ribblesdale Rd CEND/HSY/T N8 ...... 66 F5
RDART DA2 ...... 147 J3
STRHM/NOR SW16 ...... 156 B1
Ribbon Dance Ms
CMBW SE5 ...... 121 K6 [10]
Ribchester Av GFD/PVL UB6 ...... 97 M2
Ribston Cl HAYES BR2 ...... 175 M3
Ricardo Rd POP/IOD E14 ...... 105 H5
Ricards Rd WIM/MER SW19 ...... 154 F1
Richard Cl WOOL/PLUM SE18 ...... 124 E2
Richard House Dr CAN/RD E16 ...... 106 D5
Richards Cl BUSH WD23 ...... 43 K2
HGDN/ICK UB10 ...... 77 C8 [1]
HRW HA1 ...... 62 A6
HYS/HAR UB3 ...... 113 K4
Richards Fld HOR/WEW KT19 ...... 180 D2
Richardson Cl GRH DA9 ...... 147 M2
Richardson Rd SRTFD E15 ...... 106 B1
Richardson's Ms FITZ W1T ...... 10 E1 [3]
Richard's Pl CHEL SW3 ...... 15 K5
WALTH E17 ...... 69 C4 [3]
Richards Rd COB KT11 ...... 178 B7
Richard St WCHPL E1 ...... 104 B5 [16]
WCHPL E1 ...... 104 B5 [16]
Richbell Pl BMSBY WC1N 11 L2
Richborne Ter VX/NE SW8 ...... 120 F5
Richborough Cl
STMC/STPC BR5 ...... 162 D7 [3]
Richborough Rd CRICK NW2 ...... 82 D4
Richens Cl HSLW TW3 ...... 115 K7
Riches Rd IL IG1 ...... 72 C6
Richfield Rd BUSH WD23 ...... 43 K3 [1]
Richford Rd SRTFD E15 ...... 87 M8
Richford St HMSMTH W6 ...... 100 C8
Richland Av COUL/CHIP CR5 ...... 183 C8 [3]
Richlands Av EW KT17 ...... 169 C6
Richmond Av CHING E4 ...... 51 K7
CRICK NW2 ...... 82 C6
EBED/NFELT TW14 ...... 131 L3
HGDN/ICK UB10 ...... 77 H6
IS N1 ...... 6 A3
RYNPK SW20 ...... 154 E4
Richmond Buildings
SOHO/CST W1F ...... 11 C5 [3]
WALTH E17 ...... 68 F7 [3]
Richmond Cl EPSOM KT18 ...... 180 E7 [3]
Richmond Ct POTB/CUF EN6 ...... 23 J4 [3]
Richmond Crs CHING E4 ...... 51 K7
ED N9 ...... 50 A3
IS N1 ...... 5 M3
Richmond Dr SHPTN TW17 ...... 164 C1
WAT WD17 ...... 28 E5
Richmond Gdns HDN NW4 ...... 64 A6
KTN/HRWW/W HA3 ...... 61 M1
Richmond Gn CROY/NA CR0 ...... 171 C5
Richmond Gv IS N1 ...... 6 C2
Richmond Hl
RCHPK/HAM TW10 ...... 134 E3 [3]
Richmond Ms SOHO/CST W1F ...... 11 C5 [3]
Richmond Park Rd
KUTN/CMB KT2 ...... 152 E3
MORT/ESHN SW14 ...... 135 J2
Richmond Pl WOOL/PLUM SE18 ...... 107 J4
Richmond Rd BAR EN5 ...... 34 B8 [1]
CHING E4 ...... 51 K3 [3]
COUL/CHIP CR5 ...... 183 H8
CROY/NA CR0 ...... 171 L5
EA W5 ...... 98 E8
EFNCH N2 ...... 65 J3 [3]
FBAR/BDGN N11 ...... 48 E8 [3]
FSTGT E7 ...... 88 B5
HACK E8 ...... 7 L1
IL IG1 ...... 89 J3
ISLW TW7 ...... 116 A8 [3]
KUTN/CMB KT2 ...... 152 E3
POTB/CUF EN6 ...... 23 J4
ROM RM1 ...... 73 M7 [3]
RYNPK SW20 ...... 154 B4
SEVS/STOTM N15 ...... 67 L7
THHTH CR7 ...... 157 H7
TWK TW1 ...... 134 B4
WAN E11 ...... 87 K2
Richmond St PLSTW E13 ...... 106 A1
Richmond Ter WHALL SW1A 17 J1
Richmond Wy
RKW/CH/CXG WD3 ...... 28 C7
SHB W12 ...... 100 D8
WAN E11 ...... 88 A2
Richmount Gdns
BKHTH/KID SE3 ...... 124 A8 [3]
Rich St POP/IOD E14 ...... 104 F6 [3]
Rickard Cl BRXS/STRHM SW2 ...... 139 C5 [3]
HDN NW4 ...... 64 B5 [3]
WDR/YW UB7 ...... 112 D1 [3]
Rickards Cl SURB KT6 ...... 167 L4
Rickett St FUL/PGN SW6 ...... 14 B9
Rickman St WCHPL E1 ...... 104 C3 [3]
Rickmansworth Rd
DEN/HRF UB9 ...... 58 C2 [3]
NTHWD HA6 ...... 41 M8
PIN HA5 ...... 60 B3
WATW WD18 ...... 28 E7
Rick Roberts Wy SRTFD E15 ...... 87 K8
Rickthorne Rd ARCH N19 ...... 84 C2 [3]
Ridding La GFD/PVL UB6 ...... 79 M5
Riddlesdown Av PUR/KEN CR8 ...... 184 C5 [3]
Riddlesdown Rd
PUR/KEN CR8 ...... 184 C3 [3]
Riddons Rd LEE/GVPK SE12 ...... 142 C7

Rideout St WOOL/PLUM SE18 ...... 124 F2
Rider Cl BFN/LL DA15 ...... 143 L3
The Ride BTFD TW8 ...... 116 B3 [3]
PEND EN3 ...... 37 J6
Ridgdale St BOW E3 ...... 105 G1
Ridge Av DART DA1 ...... 145 M3
WCHMH N21 ...... 49 J2
Ridge Cl CDALE/KGS NW9 ...... 63 K5
HDN NW4 ...... 64 D3 [3]
THMD SE28 ...... 107 K8
Ridge Crest ENC/FH EN2 ...... 35 M4
Ridgecroft Cl BXLY DA5 ...... 145 J5
Ridgefield WAT WD17 ...... 28 E2
Ridge Hl GLDGN NW11 ...... 82 E1
Ridge La WAT WD17 ...... 28 E1
Ridge Langley SAND/SEL CR2 ...... 185 L5
Ridgemont Gdns EDGW HA8 ...... 45 J6 [3]
Ridgemount WEY KT13 ...... 146 K4
Ridgemount Av CROY/NA CR0 ...... 173 K4
Ridgemount Gdns ENC/FH EN2 ...... 36 B6
Ridge Pk WLGTN SM6 ...... 183 K3
Ridge Rd CEND/HSY/T N8 ...... 66 F7
CHEAM SM3 ...... 169 M3
CRICK NW2 ...... 82 F3
MTCM CR4 ...... 156 B3
WCHMH N21 ...... 49 K3
Ridgeview Cl BAR EN5 ...... 46 D1
Ridgeview Rd
NFNCH/WDSP N12 ...... 47 H5
Ridge Wy RKW/CH/CXG WD3 ...... 40 B2
DART DA1 ...... 145 M3
FELT TW13 ...... 132 E7 [3]
Ridgeway HAYES BR2 ...... 175 C4
HOR/WEW KT19 ...... 180 C5
WFD IG8 ...... 52 C6
WOT/HER KT12 ...... 164 F3
Ridgeway Av EBAR EN4 ...... 47 M1
Ridgeway Crs ORP BR6 ...... 176 E5
Ridgeway Crescent Gdns
ORP BR6 ...... 176 E5 [3]
Ridgeway Dr BMLY BR1 ...... 142 B8
Ridgeway East BFN/LL DA15 ...... 143 M2
Ridgeway Gdns REDBR IG4 ...... 70 E6
Ridgeway Pl WIM/MER SW19 ...... 154 C3
Ridgeway North ISLW TW7 ...... 115 L5
The Ridgeway ACT W3 ...... 117 G1
CDALE/KGS NW9 ...... 63 K5
CHING E4 ...... 51 J3
CROY/NA CR0 ...... 171 M5
ENC/FH EN2 ...... 35 J1
FBAR/BDGN N11 ...... 47 M6
FNCH N3 ...... 65 H1
GLDGN NW11 ...... 82 F1
GPK RM2 ...... 74 A5
HARH RM3 ...... 74 E2
KTN/HRWW/W HA3 ...... 62 C7
LHD/OX KT22 ...... 178 C7
MLHL NW7 ...... 46 B6
POTB/CUF EN6 ...... 23 M8
RAD WD7 ...... 30 F2
RSLP HA4 ...... 60 A8
RYLN/HDSTN HA2 ...... 60 F6
The Ridge Wy SAND/SEL CR2 ...... 184 B3
The Ridgeway STAN HA7 ...... 44 C8
STHGT/OAK N14 ...... 48 E4
WAT WD17 ...... 28 E2
Ridgeway West BFN/LL DA15 ...... 143 L2
Ridgewell Cl DAGE RM10 ...... 91 H8 [3]
IS N1 ...... 6 F3
SYD SE26 ...... 140 F8
Ridgmount Gdns GWRST WC1E 11 G2
Ridgmount Rd
WAND/EARL SW18 ...... 137 H2 [3]
Ridgmount St GWRST WC1E 11 G2
Ridgway WIM/MER SW19 ...... 154 C3
Ridgway Gdns WIM/MER SW19 ...... 154 B3
Ridgway Pl WIM/MER SW19 ...... 154 E2
Ridgway Rd BRXN/ST SW9 ...... 121 H8
The Ridgway BELMT SM2 ...... 182 D1
Riding Hl SAND/SEL CR2 ...... 185 G6
Riding House St GTPST W1W ...... 10 E3 [3]
REGST W1B ...... 10 D3 [3]
Ridings Av WCHMH N21 ...... 36 B7
The Ridings BRYLDS KT5 ...... 153 C8
COB KT11 ...... 178 A5
EA W5 ...... 98 F3
EPSOM KT18 ...... 180 E8
EW KT17 ...... 180 E2 [3]
SUN TW16 ...... 150 A4
The Riding GLDGN NW11 ...... 64 F8
Ridler Rd EN EN1 ...... 36 E3
Ridley Av WEA W13 ...... 116 B1
Ridley Cl HARH RM3 ...... 74 B2
Ridley Rd FSTGT E7 ...... 88 C4
HACK E8 ...... 85 M5
HAYES BR2 ...... 159 M6
WELL DA16 ...... 126 B6
WIM/MER SW19 ...... 155 H3
WLSDN NW10 ...... 100 A1
Ridsdale Rd PGE/AN SE20 ...... 158 B4 [3]
Riefield Rd ELTH/MOT SE9 ...... 143 K1 [3]
Riesco Dr CROY/NA CR0 ...... 173 J8
Riffel Rd CRICK NW2 ...... 82 C5
Rifle Ct LBTH SE11 ...... 18 C9
Rifle Pl NTGHL W11 ...... 100 D7 [3]
Rifle Range La HRW HA1 ...... 79 M1
Rifle St POP/IOD E14 ...... 105 H4
Rigault Rd FUL/PGN SW6 ...... 118 E7
Rigby Cl CROY/NA CR0 ...... 172 A5
Rigby La STKPK UB11 ...... 95 J8
Rigby Ms IL IG1 ...... 89 C2 [3]
Rigden St POP/IOD E14 ...... 105 H3 [3]
Rigeley Rd WLSDN NW10 ...... 100 B3 [3]
Rigg Ap LEY E10 ...... 86 D1
Rigge Pl CLAP SW4 ...... 138 D1 [3]
Riggindale Rd
STRHM/NOR SW16 ...... 156 D1
Riley Rd PEND EN3 ...... 37 J3 [3]
STHWK SE1 ...... 19 L3

Riley St WBPTN SW10 ...... 119 K5
Rinaldo Rd BAL SW12 ...... 138 B4
Ring Cl BMLY BR1 ...... 160 B3
Ringcroft St HOLWY N7 ...... 85 G5
Ringer's Rd BMLY BR1 ...... 160 A6
Ringford Rd WAND/EARL SW18 ...... 136 F6
Ringlet Cl CAN/RD E16 ...... 106 B4
Ringmer Av FUL/PGN SW6 ...... 118 E6
Ringmer Pl WCHMH N21 ...... 36 D8
Ringmer Wy BMLY BR1 ...... 160 F8
Ringmore Ri FSTH SE23 ...... 140 B4
Ringmore Rd WOT/HER KT12 ...... 165 J5
Ringshall Rd CHST BR7 ...... 162 A6
Ringslade Rd WDGN N22 ...... 66 F3 [3]
Ringstead Rd CAT SE6 ...... 141 H4
SUT SM1 ...... 170 D6
Ring Wy FBAR/BDGN N11 ...... 48 C8
Ringway NWDGN UB2 ...... 114 E3
Ringwold Cl BECK BR3 ...... 158 E3
Ringwood Av CROY/NA CR0 ...... 171 L2 [3]
EFNCH N2 ...... 65 M4
HCH RM12 ...... 92 D2
Ringwood Cl PIN HA5 ...... 60 C4 [3]
Ringwood Gdns
PUT/ROE SW15 ...... 136 A5 [3]
WCHMH N21 ...... 49 H3 [3]
Ringwood Rd WALTH E17 ...... 68 F7
Ringwood Wy HPTN TW12 ...... 133 G8
WCHMH N21 ...... 49 H3 [3]
Ripley Cl BMLY BR1 ...... 160 F8
CROY/NA CR0 ...... 174 C8
Ripley Gdns MORT/ESHN SW14 ...... 117 K8
Ripley Rd BELV DA17 ...... 127 G2
CAN/RD E16 ...... 106 C5
ENC/FH EN2 ...... 36 C4
GDMY/SEVK IG3 ...... 89 M2
HPTN TW12 ...... 151 G3
Ripley Wy CHESW EN7 ...... 26 B3
Ripon Cl NTHLT UB5 ...... 79 C5
Ripon Gdns CHSGTN KT9 ...... 167 K7
IL IG1 ...... 70 E7
Ripon Rd ED N9 ...... 50 B2 [3]
TOTM N17 ...... 67 K4
WOOL/PLUM SE18 ...... 125 H4
Ripon Wy BORE WD6 ...... 32 C8
Rippersley Rd WELL DA16 ...... 126 A6
Ripple Rd BARK IG11 ...... 89 J7
Ripplevale Gv IS N1 ...... 5 M2
Rippolson Rd
WOOL/PLUM SE18 ...... 125 M3
Ripston Rd ASHF TW15 ...... 149 K1
Risborough Dr WPK KT4 ...... 169 G2
Risborough St STHWK SE1 ...... 18 D1 [3]
Risdon St BERM/RHTH SE16 ...... 104 C3
Risebridge Cha ROM RM1 ...... 73 M1
Risebridge Rd GPK RM2 ...... 73 M3
Risedale Rd BXLYHN DA7 ...... 127 J8
Riseldine Rd FSTH SE23 ...... 140 E3
Rise Park Bvd GPK RM2 ...... 73 M2
Rise Park Pde ROM RM1 ...... 73 L3
The Rise BKHH IG9 ...... 52 D3 [3]
BORE WD6 ...... 31 M8
BXLY DA5 ...... 144 C4
DART DA1 ...... 145 M1
EDGW HA8 ...... 45 H7
EW KT17 ...... 180 F3
GFD/PVL UB6 ...... 80 A5
HGDN/ICK UB10 ...... 94 F1
MLHL NW7 ...... 45 M8
PLMGR N13 ...... 49 G6
SAND/SEL CR2 ...... 185 J2
WAN E11 ...... 70 A6
WLSDN NW10 ...... 81 K3
Rising Gdns IL IG1 ...... 89 K1
Rising Hill Cl NTHWD HA6 ...... 41 J8 [3]
Risinghill St IS N1 ...... 6 A5
Risingholme Cl BUSH WD23 ...... 43 K2
KTN/HRWW/W HA3 ...... 61 L3 [3]
Risingholme Rd
KTN/HRWW/W HA3 ...... 61 L3
The Risings WALTH E17 ...... 69 K5
Risley Av TOTM N17 ...... 67 L2 [3]
Rita Rd VX/NE SW8 ...... 120 E5
Ritches Rd SEVS/STOTM N15 ...... 67 J6
Ritchie Rd CROY/NA CR0 ...... 173 H1
Ritchie St IS N1 ...... 6 B5
Ritchings Av WALTH E17 ...... 68 E5
Ritherdon Rd TOOT SW17 ...... 138 A4
Ritson Rd HACK E8 ...... 85 M6
Ritter St WOOL/PLUM SE18 ...... 125 C4
Ritz Ct POTB/CUF EN6 ...... 23 G4 [3]
Rivaz Pl HOM E9 ...... 86 C6
Rivenhall Gdns SWFD E18 ...... 69 M5
River Av PLMGR N13 ...... 49 H5
THDIT KT7 ...... 167 G2
Riverbank E/WMO/HCT KT8 ...... 151 L6
River Bank THDIT KT7 ...... 151 M4
WCHMH N21 ...... 49 J2 [3]
Riverbank Rd BMLY BR1 ...... 142 A7
Riverbank Wy BTFD TW8 ...... 116 C2
River Barge Cl POP/IOD E14 ...... 105 J8
River Cl CHES/WCR EN8 ...... 27 G7
RAIN RM13 ...... 110 B4 [3]
RSLP HA4 ...... 59 M7
STHL UB1 ...... 97 J8 [3]
WAN E11 ...... 70 C7
Rivercourt Rd HMSMTH W6 ...... 118 E5
Riverdale Dr WAND/EARL SW18 ...... 137 H5
Riverdale Gdns TWK TW1 ...... 134 C2
Riverdale Rd BXLY DA5 ...... 144 F4
ERITH DA8 ...... 127 H3
FELT TW13 ...... 132 E5
TWK TW1 ...... 134 C3
WOOL/PLUM SE18 ...... 125 M3
Riverdene EDGW HA8 ...... 45 J6
Riverdene Rd IL IG1 ...... 89 C3
River Dr UPMR RM14 ...... 75 K7
River Front EN EN1 ...... 36 D6
River Gdns CAR SM5 ...... 171 G4
EBED/NFELT TW14 ...... 132 B2
River Grove Pk BECK BR3 ...... 158 F4
Riverhead Cl WALTH E17 ...... 68 D3 [3]
Riverhead Dr BELMT SM2 ...... 182 B3 [3]
Riverholme Dr HOR/WEW KT19 ...... 180 D2
River La RCHPK/HAM TW10 ...... 134 D5
Rivermead E/WMO/HCT KT8 ...... 151 L6
Rivermead Cl TEDD TW11 ...... 152 B1
River Meads Av WHTN TW2 ...... 133 H7
River Mt WOT/HER KT12 ...... 164 F2

Rivernook Cl WOT/HER KT12 ...... 150 C8
Riverpark Gdns HAYES BR2 ...... 159 K3
River Park Rd WDGN N22 ...... 66 F3
River Park Vw ORP BR6 ...... 177 H2
River Pl IS N1 ...... 6 E2
River Reach TEDD TW11 ...... 152 C2
River Rd BARK IG11 ...... 107 L1
BKHH IG9 ...... 52 E3
BRW CM14 ...... 57 L6
Riversdale Rd CRW RM5 ...... 73 H1
HBRY N5 ...... 85 H3
THDIT KT7 ...... 152 A8
Riversfield Rd EN EN1 ...... 36 E6
Riverside CHARL SE7 ...... 124 B1
HDN NW4 ...... 64 B8
SHPTN TW17 ...... 164 C2
TWK TW1 ...... 134 B5
Riverside Av E/WMO/HCT KT8 ...... 151 K8
Riverside Cl CLPT E5 ...... 86 C1
HNWL W7 ...... 97 J3
KGLGY WD4 ...... 20 B2
KUT KT1 ...... 152 D7
STMC/STPC BR5 ...... 162 C5
WLGTN SM6 ...... 171 H5
Riverside Ct CHING E4 ...... 51 H1 [3]
Riverside Dr CHSWK W4 ...... 117 K5 [3]
ESH/CLAY KT10 ...... 166 A6
MTCM CR4 ...... 155 L8
RCHPK/HAM TW10 ...... 134 B7
RKW/CH/CXG WD3 ...... 40 D3
Riverside Gdns ALP/SUD HA0 ...... 98 E3 [3]
ENC/FH EN2 ...... 36 C5
HMSMTH W6 ...... 118 E3
Riverside Pl STWL/WRAY TW19 ...... 130 D3
Riverside Rd OXHEY WD19 ...... 42 B1
SCUP DA14 ...... 144 E2
SEVS/STOTM N15 ...... 68 A7 [3]
SRTFD E15 ...... 105 J1
STWL/WRAY TW19 ...... 130 D2
TOOT SW17 ...... 137 H8
WOT/HER KT12 ...... 165 K6
Riverside Wk ISLW TW7 ...... 115 L8 [3]
UX/CGN UB8 ...... 76 B8
River St CLKNW EC1R 6 A7
River Ter HMSMTH W6 ...... 118 C5 [3]
Riverview Gdns BARN SW13 ...... 118 B4
River View Gdns TWK TW1 ...... 133 M6
Riverview Pk CAT SE6 ...... 141 G6
Riverview Rd CHSWK W4 ...... 117 H5
HOR/WEW KT19 ...... 168 D7
River Wk FELT TW13 ...... 133 H6
HOR/WEW KT19 ...... 168 D7
LOU IG10 ...... 53 G1
River Wy FELT TW13 ...... 133 H6
Riverway PLMGR N13 ...... 49 G7
STA TW18 ...... 148 B4
Riverwood La CHST BR7 ...... 161 K5
Rivington Av WFD IG8 ...... 70 D3
Rivington Crs CDALE/KGS NW9 ...... 63 L1
Rivington Pl IS N1 ...... 7 K3
Rivington St SDTCH EC2A 7 K3
Rivulet Rd TOTM N17 ...... 67 J3
Rixon St HOLWY N7 ...... 85 G3
Rixsen Rd MNPK E12 ...... 88 E5
Roach Rd HOM E9 ...... 87 G7
Roads Pl ARCH N19 ...... 84 E2
Roan St GNWCH SE10 ...... 123 J4
Roberts Cl PIN HA5 ...... 60 B6 [3]
Roberts Ct STAN HA7 ...... 44 A8
Robert Adam St MBLAR W1H 10 A4
Roberta St BETH E2 ...... 104 A2
Robert Cl CHIG IG7 ...... 53 M7
MV/WKIL W9 ...... 8 F1
POTB/CUF EN6 ...... 22 E6
WOT/HER KT12 ...... 165 H7
Robert Keen Cl PECK SE15 ...... 122 A6 [3]
Robert Lowe Cl NWCR SE14 ...... 122 D5
Roberton Dr BMLY BR1 ...... 160 C4
Robertsbridge Rd CAR SM5 ...... 170 C2
Roberts Cl CHEAM SM3 ...... 181 K1 [3]
CHES/WCR EN8 ...... 26 E3 [3]
ELTH/MOT SE9 ...... 143 K5
HARH RM3 ...... 74 B2
STMC/STPC BR5 ...... 162 C8 [3]
STWL/WRAY TW19 ...... 130 C3
WDR/YW UB7 ...... 94 E7
Roberts Ms KTBR SW1X ...... 16 A4 [3]
Robertson Rd SRTFD E15 ...... 87 J8 [3]
Robertson St VX/NE SW8 ...... 120 B8
Robert's Pl CLKNW EC1R ...... 6 B9 [3]
Roberts Rd BELV DA17 ...... 127 G3
MLHL NW7 ...... 46 E7
WALTH E17 ...... 69 J2
WATW WD18 ...... 29 J8 [3]
Robert St CAMTN NW1 ...... 4 D8
CHCR WC2N ...... 11 K7 [3]
CROY/NA CR0 ...... 172 C5 [3]
WOOL/PLUM SE18 ...... 125 K2
Robeson St BOW E3 ...... 104 F4 [3]
Robeson Wy BORE WD6 ...... 32 C4
Robina Cl BXLYHS DA6 ...... 144 D1 [3]
NTHWD HA6 ...... 59 M3
Robin Cl CRW RM5 ...... 73 G1 [3]
HPTN TW12 ...... 150 E1
MLHL NW7 ...... 45 L5
Robin Gv BTFD TW8 ...... 116 C4
HGT N6 ...... 84 A2
KTN/HRWW/W HA3 ...... 62 F7
Robin Hill Dr CHST BR7 ...... 160 E2
Robinhood Cl MTCM CR4 ...... 156 C6
Robinhood La MTCM CR4 ...... 156 C6
PUT/ROE SW15 ...... 135 L8
SUT SM1 ...... 170 A7
Robin Hood La BXLYHS DA6 ...... 144 E2
Robin Hood La POP/IOD E14 ...... 105 J6
PUT/ROE SW15 ...... 135 L8
Robin Hood Wy GFD/PVL UB6 ...... 79 M6
Robin Hood Wy (Kingston by Pass)
PUT/ROE SW15 ...... 135 L8

Robinia Cl BARK/HLT IG6 ...... 53 L8
Robinia Crs LEY E10 ...... 87 H2
Robins Cl UX/CGN UB8 ...... 94 C4
Robins Gv WWKM BR4 ...... 175 G5
Robinson Av CHESW EN7 ...... 25 H1
Robinson Cl HCH RM12 ...... 92 B7 [3]
Robinson Crs BUSH WD23 ...... 43 J3
Robinson Rd BETH E2 ...... 104 C1
DAGE RM10 ...... 91 G4
WIM/MER SW19 ...... 155 C2
Robinson's Cl WEA W13 ...... 98 A4
Robinson St CHEL SW3 ...... 15 L9
Robinsway WOT/HER KT12 ...... 165 J6
Robin Wy POTB/CUF EN6 ...... 24 E1
STMC/STPC BR5 ...... 162 B6
Robinwood Pl
RCHPK/HAM TW10 ...... 135 K8
Robsart St BRXN/ST SW9 ...... 120 A8
Robson Av WLSDN NW10 ...... 82 A8
Robson Cl EHAM E6 ...... 106 E5
ENC/FH EN2 ...... 36 B5
Robson Rd WNWD SE27 ...... 139 H7
Robsons Cl CHES/WCR EN8 ...... 26 C2 [3]
Roch Av EDGW HA8 ...... 62 F3
Rochdale Rd ABYW SE2 ...... 126 B3
Rochdale Wy DEPT SE8 ...... 123 C5 [3]
Rochester Av BMLY BR1 ...... 160 B5
FELT TW13 ...... 131 M6
PLSTW E13 ...... 88 C8
Rochester Cl BFN/LL DA15 ...... 144 B3 [3]
EN EN1 ...... 36 E4
STRHM/NOR SW16 ...... 156 E3 [3]
Rochester Dr BXLY DA5 ...... 145 G3
GSTN WD25 ...... 21 J8 [3]
PIN HA5 ...... 60 D6
Rochester Gdns
CROY/NA CR0 ...... 172 E5 [3]
IL IG1 ...... 70 F8
Rochester Ms CAMTN NW1 ...... 4 F1
Rochester Pl CAMTN NW1 ...... 84 C6
Rochester Rd CAMTN NW1 ...... 84 C6
CAR SM5 ...... 170 F6 [3]
DART DA1 ...... 147 G4
NTHWD HA6 ...... 59 M4
Rochester Rw WEST SW1P ...... 16 F5 [3]
Rochester Sq CAMTN NW1 ...... 4 F1
Rochester St WEST SW1P ...... 17 G4 [3]
Rochester Ter CAMTN NW1 ...... 84 C6 [3]
Rochester Wk STHWK SE1 ...... 13 G8 [3]
Rochester Wy
BKHTH/KID SE3 ...... 124 C8 [3]
DART DA1 ...... 145 L4
ELTH/MOT SE9 ...... 142 E1 [3]
RKW/CH/CXG WD3 ...... 28 B7
Rochester Wy Relief Rd
ELTH/MOT SE9 ...... 142 E2
Roche Wk MRDN SM4 ...... 170 D1
Rochford Av CHDH RM6 ...... 72 C6
WAB EN9 ...... 27 K7
Rochford Cl EHAM E6 ...... 106 C4 [3]
HCH RM12 ...... 92 B6 [3]
Rochford Wy CROY/NA CR0 ...... 171 L1
Rock Av MORT/ESHN SW14 ...... 117 K8
Rockbourne Av FSTH SE23 ...... 140 D5
Rockchase Gdns EMPK RM11 ...... 74 E7 [3]
Rockcliffe Av KGLGY WD4 ...... 20 B3
Rockell's Pl EDUL SE22 ...... 140 B3
Rockford Av GFD/PVL UB6 ...... 98 B1
Rock Grove Wy
BERM/RHTH SE16 ...... 122 A2
Rockhall Rd CRICK NW2 ...... 82 D4
Rockhampton Rd
SAND/SEL CR2 ...... 172 E8
STRHM/NOR SW16 ...... 139 C8
Rock Hl NRWD SE19 ...... 139 M8
Rockingham Av EMPK RM11 ...... 74 D4
Rockingham Cl
PUT/ROE SW15 ...... 135 M1 [3]
UX/CGN UB8 ...... 76 B3 [3]
Rockingham Pde UX/CGN UB8 ...... 76 C7
Rockingham Rd UX/CGN UB8 ...... 76 B8
Rockingham St STHWK SE1 ...... 18 E4
Rockland Rd PUT/ROE SW15 ...... 136 E1 [3]
Rocklands Dr
KTN/HRWW/W HA3 ...... 62 B3
Rockley Rd SHB W12 ...... 100 D8
Rockmount Rd NRWD SE19 ...... 157 K2
WOOL/PLUM SE18 ...... 125 M3
Rocks La BARN SW13 ...... 118 A8
Rock St FSBYPK N4 ...... 85 G2
Rockware Av GFD/PVL UB6 ...... 79 K8 [3]
Rockways BAR EN5 ...... 45 M1
Rockwell Gdns NRWD SE19 ...... 139 L8 [3]
Rockwell Rd DAGE RM10 ...... 91 H5
Rocliffe St IS N1 ...... 6 D6
Rocombe Crs FSTH SE23 ...... 140 C4 [3]
Rocque La BKHTH/KID SE3 ...... 123 M8
Rodborough Rd GLDGN NW11 ...... 83 G1
Roden Gdns CROY/NA CR0 ...... 172 E5 [3]
Rodenhurst Rd CLAP SW4 ...... 138 C4
Roden St HOLWY N7 ...... 84 F3
IL IG1 ...... 89 G3
Rodeo Cl ERITH DA8 ...... 128 B6
Roderick Rd HAMP NW3 ...... 83 M4
Rodgers Cl BORE WD6 ...... 44 D1
Roding Gdns LOU IG10 ...... 52 E3
Roding La BKHH IG9 ...... 52 E3
CHIG IG7 ...... 53 C3
Roding La North WFD IG8 ...... 70 E3
Roding La South REDBR IG4 ...... 70 D6
Roding Rd CLPT E5 ...... 86 D4
EHAM E6 ...... 107 H4
LOU IG10 ...... 39 M8
The Rodings UPMR RM14 ...... 75 K7
Roding Vw BKHH IG9 ...... 52 D3
Roding Wy RAIN RM13 ...... 110 D1 [3]
Rodmarton St MHST W1U 9 M3
Rodmell Cl YEAD UB4 ...... 96 F3
Rodney Cl NWMAL KT3 ...... 153 L8
PIN HA5 ...... 60 E8

WOT/HER KT12 ....165 J3
Rodney Gdns PIN HA5 ....60 C6
  WWKM BR4 ....175 G6
Rodney Pl STHWK SE1 ....18 F5
  WALTH E17 ....68 E3
  WIM/MER SW19 ....155 J4
Rodney Rd HSLWW TW4 ....133 G3
  HSLWW TW4 ....133 G4
  MTCM CR4 ....155 L5
  NWMAL KT3 ....153 L8
  WALW SE17 ....18 F6
  WAN E11 ....70 B5
  WOT/HER KT12 ....165 H4
Rodney St IS N1 ....5 M5
Rodney Wy ROMW/RG RM7 ....73 L2
Rodway Rd BMLY BR1 ....160 B4
  PUT/ROE SW15 ....136 A4
Rodwell Cl RSLP HA4 ....78 C1
Rodwell Rd EDUL SE22 ....139 M3
Roebuck Cl FELT TW13 ....132 B8
Roebuck La BKHH IG9 ....52 C3
Roebuck Rd BARK/HLT IG6 ....54 B8
  CHSGTN KT9 ....168 A7
Roedean Av PEND EN3 ....37 J4
Roedean Crs ORP BR6 ....177 H6
  PEND EN3 ....37 J4
Roedean Crs PUT/ROE SW15 ....135 L3
Roe End CDALE/KGS NW9 ....63 J5
Roe Gn CDALE/KGS NW9 ....63 J6
Roehampton Cl
  PUT/ROE SW15 ....136 A1
Roehampton Dr CHST BR7 ....161 J2
Roehampton Ga
  PUT/ROE SW15 ....135 L3
Roehampton High St
  PUT/ROE SW15 ....136 A4
Roehampton La
  PUT/ROE SW15 ....136 A2
Roehampton V PUT/ROE SW15 ....135 M7
Roe La CDALE/KGS NW9 ....63 H5
Roe Wy WLGTN SM6 ....171 L8
Rofant Rd NTHWD HA6 ....41 L8
Roffey St POP/IOD E14 ....105 J8
Rogers Gdns DAGE RM10 ....91 C5
Rogers Rd CAN/RD E16 ....105 M5
  DAGE RM10 ....91 C5
  TOOT SW17 ....137 H8
Rogers Ruff NTHWD HA6 ....59 J2
Rojack Rd FSTH SE23 ....140 D5
Rokeby Gdns WFD IG8 ....70 A2
Rokeby Pl RYNPK SW20 ....154 B8
Rokeby Rd BROCKY SE4 ....122 F7
Rokeby St SRTFD E15 ....87 L8
Roke Cl PUR/KEN CR8 ....184 C7
Roke Lodge Rd PUR/KEN CR8 ....184 B6
Roke Rd PUR/KEN CR8 ....184 C8
Roker Park Av HGDN/ICK UB10 ....76 E4
Rokesby Cl WELL DA16 ....125 K7
Rokesby Pl ALP/SUD HA0 ....80 D5
Rokesly Av CEND/HSY/T N8 ....66 E6
Roland Gdns SKENS SW7 ....14 F7
Roland Rd WALTH E17 ....69 K5
Roland Wy WALW SE17 ....19 H8
  WBPTN SW10 ....14 F7
  WPK KT4 ....168 F4
Roles Gv CHDH RM6 ....72 D5
Rolfe Cl EBAR EN4 ....34 E7
Rolinsden Wy HAYES BR2 ....175 K6
Rollesby Rd CHSGTN KT9 ....168 A8
Rollesby Wy THMD SE28 ....108 C6
Rolleston Av STMC/STPC BR5 ....176 B1
Rolleston Cl STMC/STPC BR5 ....176 B2
Rolleston Rd SAND/SEL CR2 ....184 D1
Roll Gdns GNTH/NBYPK IG2 ....71 G4
Rollins St PECK SE15 ....122 C4
Rollit Crs HSLW TW3 ....133 G2
Rollit St HOLWY N7 ....85 G5
Rollo Rd SWLY BR8 ....163 M3
Rolls Buildings FLST/FETLN EC4A 12 A4
Rolls Park Av CHING E4 ....51 G8
Rolls Park Rd CHING E4 ....51 H7
Rolls Rd STHWK SE1 ....19 M7
Rolt St DEPT SE8 ....122 E4
Rolvenden Gdns BMLY BR1 ....160 D4
Rolvenden Pl TOTM N17 ....68 A2
Roman Cl ACT W3 ....99 H8
  EBED/NFELT TW14 ....132 C2
  RAIN RM13 ....109 K1
Romanfield Rd
  BRXS/STRHM SW2 ....138 F4
Roman Gdns KGLGY WD4 ....20 B3
Romanhurst Av HAYES BR2 ....159 L7
Romanhurst Gdns BECK BR3 ....159 L7
Roman Ri NRWD SE19 ....157 K2
Roman Rd BETH E2 ....86 F8
  BOW E3 ....86 F8
  CHSWK W4 ....117 L2
  EHAM E6 ....106 E3
  IL IG1 ....89 H6
  MUSWH N10 ....66 B1
Roman Sq THMD SE28 ....108 A7
Roman Wy CROY/NA CR0 ....172 B4
  DART DA1 ....145 L2
  EN EN1 ....36 F8
  HOLWY N7 ....84 F6
Romany Gdns CHEAM SM3 ....170 A2
Romany Ri STMC/STPC BR5 ....176 C3
Roma Rd WALTH E17 ....68 E4
Romberg Rd TOOT SW17 ....138 A7
Romborough Gdns
  LEW SE13 ....141 J2
Romborough Wy LEW SE13 ....141 J2
Rom Crs ROMW/RG RM7 ....73 L8
Romeland BORE WD6 ....44 D1
  WAB EN9 ....27 J6
Romero Sq ELTH/MOT SE9 ....142 C1
Romeyn Rd STRHM/NOR SW16 ....138 F7
Romford Rd CHDH RM6 ....54 D8
  CHIG IG7 ....54 B6
  CRW RM5 ....72 C1
  FSTGT E7 ....88 A4
  MNPK E12 ....89 C3
  SOCK/AV RM15 ....111 J2
  SRTFD E15 ....87 L7
Romford St WCHPL E1 ....104 A4
Romilly Dr OXHEY WD19 ....42 E6

Romilly Rd FSBYPK N4 ....85 H2
Romilly St SOHO/SHAV W1D 11 H6
Rommany Rd WNWD SE27 ....139 K8
Romney Cha EMPK RM11 ....75 G7
Romney Cl ASHF TW15 ....149 L1
  CHSGTN KT9 ....167 L6
  GLDGN NW11 ....83 H1
  RYLN/HDSTN HA2 ....61 G8
  TOTM N17 ....68 B2
Romney Dr BMLY BR1 ....160 D3
  RYLN/HDSTN HA2 ....61 G8
Romney Rd BXLYHN DA7 ....126 F6
  GNWCH SE10 ....123 H1
  NWMAL KT3 ....168 D1
  YEAD UB4 ....95 K1
Romola Rd BRXS/STRHM SW2 ....139 H5
Romsey Cl ORP BR6 ....176 C6
Romsey Rd DAGW RM9 ....90 B8
  WEA W13 ....98 A3
Rom Valley Wy ROMW/RG RM7 ....73 L7
Ronald Av SRTFD E15 ....105 L2
Ronald Cl BECK BR3 ....158 F8
Ronald Rd HARH RM3 ....75 G2
Ronalds Rd BMLY BR1 ....160 A4
  HBRY N5 ....85 G5
Ronaldstone Rd BFN/LL DA15 ....143 L3
Ronald St WCHPL E1 ....104 D5
Rona Rd HAMP NW3 ....84 A4
Ronart St KTN/HRWW/W HA3 ....61 M1
Rondu Rd CRICK NW2 ....82 C5
Ronelean Rd SURB KT6 ....167 M4
Roneo Cnr ROMW/RG RM7 ....91 M1
Roneo Link HCH RM12 ....91 M1
Ronfearn Av STMC/STPC BR5 ....162 D8
Ronneby Cl WEY KT13 ....164 E5
Ronver Rd LEE/GVPK SE12 ....142 A5
Rood La FENCHST EC3M 13 J6
Rookby Ct WCHMH N21 ....49 H4
Rookeries Cl FELT TW13 ....132 B7
Rookery Dr CHST BR7 ....161 G4
Rookery Gdns WHTN TW2 ....133 K5
Rookery La HAYES BR2 ....175 K1
Rookery Rd CLAP SW4 ....138 C1
  ORP BR6 ....187 M3
  STA TW18 ....148 B1
Rookesley Rd STMC/STPC BR5 ....177 K2
Rookfield Av MUSWH N10 ....66 C5
Rookley Cl BELMT SM2 ....182 B2
  BELMT SM2 ....182 B3
Rooksmead Rd SUN TW16 ....149 M5
Rookstone Rd TOOT SW17 ....155 H8
Rookwood Av NWMAL KT3 ....154 A7
  WLGTN SM6 ....171 K6
Rookwood Gdns CHING E4 ....51 M4
Rookwood Rd STNW/STAM N16 ....67 M7
Roosevelt Wy DAGE RM10 ....91 K6
Rootes St NKENS W10 ....100 D4
Ropemaker Rd
  BERM/RHTH SE16 ....122 E1
Ropemaker's Flds
  POP/IOD E14 ....104 F6
Ropemaker St BARB EC2Y 13 G2
Roper La STHWK SE1 ....19 K2
Ropers Av CHING E4 ....51 J7
Roper St ELTH/MOT SE9 ....142 F2
Roper Wy MTCM CR4 ....156 A5
Ropery St BOW E3 ....104 F3
Rope St BERM/RHTH SE16 ....122 C4
Ropewalk Gdns WCHPL E1 ....104 A5
Rope Yard Rails
  WOOL/PLUM SE18 ....125 H1
Ropley St BETH E2 ....104 A1
Rosa Alba Ms HBRY N5 ....85 J4
Rosa Av ASHF TW15 ....131 G8
Rosaline Rd FUL/PGN SW6 ....118 C5
Rosamond St SYD SE26 ....140 B7
Rosamund Cl SAND/SEL CR2 ....172 D6
Rosary Cl HSLW TW3 ....114 F7
Rosary Ct POTB/CUF EN6 ....23 H3
Rosary Gdns ASHF TW15 ....131 H8
  BUSH WD23 ....43 L2
  SKENS SW7 ....14 F6
Rosaville Rd FUL/PGN SW6 ....118 F5
Roscoe St STLK EC1Y 12 F1
Roscoff Cl EDGW HA8 ....63 H2
Roseacre Cl EMPK RM11 ....92 F1
  SHPTN TW17 ....149 G8
  WEA W13 ....98 B4
Roseacre Rd WELL DA16 ....126 B8
Rose Aly STHWK SE1 ....12 F8
Rose And Crown Yd
  STJS SW1Y 10 F9
Rosary Cl WDR/YW UB7 ....112 D2
Rose Av MRDN SM4 ....155 J8
  MTCM CR4 ....155 M4
  SWFD E18 ....70 B3
Rosebank EPSOM KT18 ....180 C7
  PGE/AN SE20 ....158 B3
  WAB EN9 ....27 L7
Rosebank Av ALP/SUD HA0 ....79 M4
  HCH RM12 ....92 C5
Rose Bank Cl
  NFNCH/WDSP N12 ....47 L7
Rosebank Cl TEDD TW11 ....152 A2
Rosebank Gdns BOW E3 ....104 F1
Rosebank Gv WALTH E17 ....68 F4
Rosebank Rd HNWL W7 ....97 L3
  LEY E10 ....69 H7
Rosebank Wy ACT W3 ....99 K5
Rose Bates Dr
  CDALE/KGS NW9 ....63 G5
Roseberry Cl UPMR RM14 ....75 M7
Roseberry Ct WAT WD17 ....29 G4
Roseberry Gdns DART DA1 ....146 C4
  FSBYPK N4 ....67 H7
  ORP BR6 ....176 E5
  UPMR RM14 ....75 M7
Roseberry Pl HACK E8 ....85 M6
Roseberry St
  BERM/RHTH SE16 ....122 B2
Roseberry Av BFN/LL DA15 ....143 L4
  CLKNW EC1R 6 A9
  EW KT17 ....180 E7
  MNPK E12 ....88 C4
  NWMAL KT3 ....153 M5
  RYLN/HDSTN HA2 ....78 E4
  THHTH CR7 ....157 J5
  TOTM N17 ....68 A3

Rosebery Cl MRDN SM4 ....169 K1
Rosebery Gdns
  CEND/HSY/T N8 ....66 E6
  SUT SM1 ....170 B6
  WEA W13 ....98 A5
Rosebery Rd BUSH WD23 ....43 H3
  CLAP SW4 ....138 C3
  ED N9 ....50 A5
  ISLW TW7 ....133 J2
  KUT KT1 ....153 H5
  MUSWH N10 ....66 C3
  SUT SM1 ....169 M8
Rosebine Av WHTN TW2 ....133 K4
Rosebriars ESH/CLAY KT10 ....166 C7
Rosebriar Wk WATN WD24 ....28 F1
Rosebury Rd FUL/PGN SW6 ....119 H7
Rosebury V RSLP HA4 ....78 A2
Rosecourt Rd CROY/NA CR0 ....171 H1
Rosecroft Av HAMP NW3 ....83 G3
Rosecroft Gdns CRICK NW2 ....82 A3
  WHTN TW2 ....133 K5
Rosecroft Wk ALP/SUD HA0 ....80 D5
  PIN HA5 ....60 D6
Rose Dl ORP BR6 ....176 B4
Rosedale Av CHESW EN7 ....25 M2
  HYS/HAR UB3 ....95 K4
Rosedale Cl ABYW SE2 ....126 B1
  HNWL W7 ....97 M8
  LCOL/BKTW AL2 ....21 L3
  RDART DA2 ....147 H4
  STAN HA7 ....44 B8
Rosedale Gdns DAGW RM9 ....90 B7
Rosedale Rd CRW RM5 ....73 A2
  DAGW RM9 ....90 B7
  EW KT17 ....169 G7
  FSTGT E7 ....88 C5
  RCH/KEW TW9 ....134 E1
Rosedale Wy CHESW EN7 ....26 A2
Rosedene CROY/NA CR0 ....171 M2
  GFD/PVL UB6 ....97 G2
  MRDN SM4 ....155 G8
  STRHM/NOR SW16 ....138 F7
Rosedene Gdns
  GNTH/NBYPK IG2 ....71 G5
Rosedene Ter LEY E10 ....87 H2
Rosedew Rd HMSMTH W6 ....118 D4
Rose End WPK KT4 ....169 K3
Rosefield CAR SM5 ....170 E7
Rosefield Cl CAR SM5 ....170 E7
Rosefield Gdns POP/IOD E14 ....105 G6
  STA TW18 ....130 A8
Rose Garden Cl EDGW HA8 ....44 E8
Rose Gdns EA W5 ....116 D1
  FELT TW13 ....132 A6
  STHL UB1 ....97 G3
  STWL/WRAY TW19 ....130 D4
  WLGTN SM6 ....29 G8
Rose Gln CDALE/KGS NW9 ....63 K5
  ROMW/RG RM7 ....91 L1
Rosehart Ms NTGHL W11 ....8 A5
Rosehatch Av CHDH RM6 ....72 D4
Roseheath Rd HSLWW TW4 ....132 F2
Rosehill ESH/CLAY KT10 ....167 G8
  HPTN TW12 ....151 G4
Rose Hl SUT SM1 ....170 B4
Rosehill Av SUT SM1 ....170 C3
Rosehill Farm Meadow
  BNSTD SM7 ....182 B8
Rosehill Gdns ABLGY WD5 ....20 C5
  GFD/PVL UB6 ....79 M5
  SUT SM1 ....170 B4
Rose Hill Pk West SUT SM1 ....170 C3
Rosehill Rd WAND/EARL SW18 ....137 J3
Roseland Cl TOTM N17 ....67 K1
Rose La CHDH RM6 ....72 C5
Rose Lawn BUSH WD23 ....43 J3
Roseleigh Av HBRY N5 ....85 H4
Roseleigh Cl TWK TW1 ....134 D3
Rosemary Av E/WMO/HCT KT8 ....151 G6
  ED N9 ....50 B3
  ENC/FH EN2 ....36 D4
  FNCH N3 ....65 H3
  HSLWW TW4 ....114 D7
  ROM RM1 ....73 M4
Rosemary Cl CROY/NA CR0 ....171 L2
  UX/CGN UB8 ....95 G4
Rosemary Dr POP/IOD E14 ....105 K5
  REDBR IG4 ....70 D6
Rosemary Gdns BCTR RM8 ....90 A7
Rosemary La
  MORT/ESHN SW14 ....117 J8
Rosemary Rd PECK SE15 ....121 M5
  TOOT SW17 ....137 J7
  WELL DA16 ....125 M6
Rosemead CDALE/KGS NW9 ....63 H8
Rose Md POTB/CUF EN6 ....23 J3
Rosemead Av FELT TW13 ....131 M6
  MTCM CR4 ....156 C6
  WBLY HA9 ....80 E5
Rosemont Av
  NFNCH/WDSP N12 ....47 J8
Rosemont Rd ACT W3 ....99 H6
  BMLY BR1 ....160 F7
  HAMP NW3 ....83 J6
  NWMAL KT3 ....153 J6
  RCHPK/HAM TW10 ....134 C3
Rosemoor St CHEL SW3 ....15 L6
Rosemount Cl WFD IG8 ....52 F8
Rosemount Dr BMLY BR1 ....160 F7
Rosemount Rd WEA W13 ....98 A5
Rosenau Crs BTSEA SW11 ....119 M6
Rosenau Rd BTSEA SW11 ....119 L6
Rosendale Rd DUL SE21 ....139 J6
  HNHL SE24 ....139 J4
Roseneath Av WCHMH N21 ....49 H3
Roseneath Rd BTSEA SW11 ....138 A3
Roseneath Wk EN EN1 ....36 F7
Rosens Wk EDGW HA8 ....45 H5
Rosenthal Rd CAT SE6 ....141 H3
Rosenthorpe Rd PECK SE15 ....140 D2
Roserton St POP/IOD E14 ....105 J8
The Rosery CROY/NA CR0 ....173 K1
Rosethorn Cl BAL SW12 ....138 C4
Roseveare Rd LEE/GVPK SE12 ....142 C8

Roseville Av HSLWW TW4 ....133 C2
Roseville Rd HYS/HAR UB3 ....114 A3
Rose Wk PUR/KEN CR8 ....153 H8
  PUR/KEN CR8 ....183 K4
  WWKM BR4 ....174 D4
The Rose Wk RAD WD7 ....31 H1
Roseway DUL SE21 ....139 K3
  EDGW HA8 ....45 J6
Rose Wy LEE/GVPK SE12 ....142 A2
Rosewell Cl PGE/AN SE20 ....158 B3
Rosewood RDART DA2 ....145 L8
Rosewood Av GFD/PVL UB6 ....80 A5
  HCH RM12 ....92 A5
Rosewood Cl SCUP DA14 ....144 C7
Rosewood Ct
  KUTN/CMB KT2 ....153 G3
  SHPTN TW17 ....148 F8
Rosewood Dr ENC/FH EN2 ....25 C8
Rosewood Gv SUT SM1 ....170 C4
Rosher Cl SRTFD E15 ....87 K7
Rosina St HOM E9 ....86 D5
Roskell Rd PUT/ROE SW15 ....118 D8
Roslin Rd ACT W3 ....117 H1
Roslin Wy BMLY BR1 ....160 A1
Roslyn Cl MTCM CR4 ....155 K5
Roslyn Gdns GPK RM2 ....73 M3
Roslyn Rd SEVS/STOTM N15 ....67 K6
Rosmead Rd NTGHL W11 ....100 E6
Rosoman Pl CLKNW EC1R 6 B9
Rossall Cl EMPK RM11 ....74 A7
Rossall Crs WLSDN NW10 ....98 F2
Ross Av BCTR RM8 ....90 F2
  MLHL NW7 ....46 F7
Ross Cl HYS/HAR UB3 ....113 K2
  KTN/HRWW/W HA3 ....61 J1
Ross Crs GSTN WD25 ....21 G8
Rossdale SUT SM1 ....170 E7
Rossdale Dr CDALE/KGS NW9 ....81 J1
  ED N9 ....50 C1
Rossdale Rd PUT/ROE SW15 ....136 C1
Rosse Ms BKHTH/KID SE3 ....124 B6
Rossendale St CLPT E5 ....86 B2
Rossendale Wy CAMTN NW1 ....4 F2
Rossetti Rd BERM/RHTH SE16 ....122 B3
Rossignol Gdns CAR SM5 ....171 C4
Rossindel Rd HSLW TW3 ....133 C3
Rossington Av BORE WD6 ....31 L3
Rossington Cl EN EN1 ....25 M8
Rossington St CLPT E5 ....86 B2
Rossiter Flds BAR EN5 ....46 E1
Rossiter Rd BAL SW12 ....138 B5
Rossland Cl BXLYHS DA6 ....145 G2
Rosslyn Av BARN SW13 ....117 L8
  BCTR RM8 ....72 F8
  CHING E4 ....51 M4
  EBAR EN4 ....47 L1
  EBED/NFELT TW14 ....132 A3
  HARH RM3 ....74 E3
Rosslyn Cl HYS/HAR UB3 ....95 K4
  SUN TW16 ....149 J2
  WWKM BR4 ....174 F5
Rosslyn Crs HRW HA1 ....61 M5
  WBLY HA9 ....80 E3
Rosslyn Hl HAMP NW3 ....83 K5
Rosslyn Pk WEY KT13 ....146 A6
Rosslyn Park Ms HAMP NW3 ....83 K5
Rosslyn Rd BARK IG11 ....89 K7
  TWK TW1 ....134 C3
  WALTH E17 ....69 L5
  WATW WD18 ....29 H6
Rossmore Rd CAMTN NW1 ....9 K1
Ross Pde WLGTN SM6 ....171 H8
Ross Rd DART DA1 ....146 A3
  SNWD SE25 ....157 L6
  WHTN TW2 ....133 J5
  WLGTN SM6 ....171 J8
Ross Wy ELTH/MOT SE9 ....124 E8
  NTHWD HA6 ....41 M6
Rossway Dr BUSH WD23 ....30 C3
Rosswood Gdns WLGTN SM6 ....171 J8
Rostella Rd TOOT SW17 ....137 K8
Rostrever Gdns HYS/HAR UB3 ....95 L7
Rostrevor Av SEVS/STOTM N15 ....67 M7
Rostrevor Gdns NWDGN UB2 ....114 E3
Rostrevor Rd FUL/PGN SW6 ....118 F6
  WIM/MER SW19 ....155 G1
Rotary St STHWK SE1 ....18 C3
Rothbury Av RAIN RM13 ....110 B4
Rothbury Gdns ISLW TW7 ....116 A5
Rothbury Rd HOM E9 ....87 G7
Rother Cl GSTN WD25 ....21 J7
Rotherfield Rd CAR SM5 ....171 C6
  PEND EN3 ....37 K2
Rotherfield St IS N1 ....6 F2
Rotherhill Av
  STRHM/NOR SW16 ....156 D2
Rotherhithe New Rd
  BERM/RHTH SE16 ....122 B3
Rotherhithe Old Rd
  BERM/RHTH SE16 ....122 D2
Rotherhithe St
  BERM/RHTH SE16 ....104 B8
  BERM/RHTH SE16 ....104 E7
  BERM/RHTH SE16 ....104 E7
Rotherhithe Tnl
  BERM/RHTH SE16 ....104 C8
Rothermere Rd
  CROY/NA CR0 ....171 M7
Rotherwick Hl EA W5 ....98 F3
Rotherwick Rd GLDGN NW11 ....65 G8
Rotherwood Cl RYNPK SW20 ....154 E4
Rotherwood Rd
  PUT/ROE SW15 ....118 D8
Rothery St IS N1 ....6 D3
Rothesay Av NTHLT UB5 ....79 K6
  RCHPK/HAM TW10 ....135 H1
  RYNPK SW20 ....154 E5
Rothesay Rd SNWD SE25 ....157 K7
Rothsay Rd FSTGT E7 ....88 C7
Rothsay St STHWK SE1 ....19 J3
Rothschild Rd CHSWK W4 ....117 J2
Rothschild St WNWD SE27 ....139 H8
Rothwell Gdns DAGW RM9 ....90 C7
Rothwell Rd DAGW RM9 ....90 C8
Rothwell St CAMTN NW1 ....3 M3
Rotterdam Dr POP/IOD E14 ....123 J1
Rouel Rd BERM/RHTH SE16 ....122 A2

Rougemont Av MRDN SM4 ....170 A1
The Roughs NTHWD HA6 ....41 L5
Roughwood Cl WAT WD17 ....28 E3
Roundaway Rd CLAY IG5 ....70 F3
Roundel Cl BROCKY SE4 ....140 F1
Round Gv CROY/NA CR0 ....173 K2
Roundhay Cl FSTH SE23 ....140 D6
Roundhedge Wy
  ENC/FH EN2 ....35 M3
Round Hl FSTH SE23 ....140 B6
Roundhill Dr ENC/FH EN2 ....35 M7
Roundhills WAB EN9 ....27 L7
Roundhill Wy COB KT11 ....178 B4
Roundlyn Gdns
  STMC/STPC BR5 ....162 B7
Roundmoor Dr CHES/WCR EN8 ....26 C2
Roundtable Rd BMLY BR1 ....141 M7
Roundtree Rd ALP/SUD HA0 ....80 B5
Roundways RSLP HA4 ....77 M3
The Roundway ESH/CLAY KT10 ....166 F8
  TOTM N17 ....67 J2
  WATW WD18 ....41 M1
Roundwood CHST BR7 ....161 H5
Roundwood Av WLSDN NW10 ....81 L6
Roundwood Cl RSLP HA4 ....59 K8
Roundwood Rd WLSDN NW10 ....81 J6
Roundwood Vw BNSTD SM7 ....181 K8
Roundwood Wy BNSTD SM7 ....181 K8
Rounton Rd BOW E3 ....105 J3
  WAB EN9 ....27 L1
Roupell Rd BRXS/STRHM SW2 ....138 F5
Roupell St STHWK SE1 ....12 B9
Rousden St CAMTN NW1 ....4 E2
Rouse Gdns DUL SE21 ....139 L8
Rous Rd BKHH IG9 ....52 E3
Routemaster Cl PLSTW E13 ....106 B2
Routh Rd WAND/EARL SW18 ....137 L4
Routh St EHAM E6 ....106 F4
Rover Av BARK/HLT IG6 ....53 M8
Rowallan Rd FUL/PGN SW6 ....118 E5
Rowan Av CHING E4 ....50 F8
Rowan Cl ALP/SUD HA0 ....80 A3
  EA W5 ....98 E8
  IL IG1 ....90 D3
  KTN/HRWW/W HA3 ....43 M8
  NWMAL KT3 ....153 L5
  STRHM/NOR SW16 ....156 C4
Rowan Crs DART DA1 ....146 C5
  STRHM/NOR SW16 ....156 C4
Rowan Dr CDALE/KGS NW9 ....64 A4
Rowan Gdns CROY/NA CR0 ....172 B5
Rowan Gv SOCK/AV RM15 ....111 J3
Rowan Pl HYS/HAR UB3 ....95 M6
Rowan Rd BTFD TW8 ....116 B5
  BXLYHN DA7 ....126 E8
  HMSMTH W6 ....118 D2
  STRHM/NOR SW16 ....156 C5
  SWLY BR8 ....163 K6
  WDR/YW UB7 ....112 D2
The Rowans PLMGR N13 ....49 J5
  SOCK/AV RM15 ....111 J7
  SUN TW16 ....149 M1
Rowans Wy LOU IG10 ....39 M7
Rowantree Cl WCHMH N21 ....49 K3
Rowantree Rd ENC/FH EN2 ....36 B5
  WCHMH N21 ....49 K3
Rowan Wk EFNCH N2 ....65 J7
  EMPK RM11 ....74 D5
  HAYES BR2 ....175 M5
  NKENS W10 ....100 E3
Rowan Wy CHDH RM6 ....72 C4
Rowanwood Av BFN/LL DA15 ....144 A5
Rowben Cl TRDG/WHET N20 ....47 H3
Rowberry Cl FUL/PGN SW6 ....118 C5
Rowcross St STHWK SE1 ....19 L7
Rowdell Rd NTHLT UB5 ....79 G8
Rowden Rd BECK BR3 ....158 E4
  CHING E4 ....51 H8
  HOR/WEW KT19 ....168 C6
Rowditch La BTSEA SW11 ....120 A7
Rowdon Av WLSDN NW10 ....82 B7
Rowdown Crs CROY/NA CR0 ....186 D2
Rowdowns Rd DAGW RM9 ....90 B8
Rowe Gdns BARK IG11 ....107 M1
Rowe La HOM E9 ....86 C5
Rowena Crs BTSEA SW11 ....119 L7
Rowe Wk RYLN/HDSTN HA2 ....79 G3
Rowfant Rd TOOT SW17 ....138 A6
Rowhill Rd CLPT E5 ....86 B4
Rowington Cl BAY/PAD W2 ....8 C2
Rowland Av KTN/HRWW/W HA3 ....62 A2
Rowland Crs CHIG IG7 ....53 L6
Rowland Gv SYD SE26 ....140 B7
  SYD SE26 ....140 B7
Rowland Hill Av TOTM N17 ....67 J1
Rowland Hill St HAMP NW3 ....83 L5
Rowlands Av PIN HA5 ....43 G8
Rowlands Cl CHES/WCR EN8 ....26 D3
  MLHL NW7 ....64 A1
Rowlands Rd BCTR RM8 ....90 F2
Rowland Wy ASHF TW15 ....149 K3
  WIM/MER SW19 ....155 H4
Rowlatt Cl RDART DA2 ....146 C8
Rowley Av BFN/LL DA15 ....144 B4
Rowley Cl ALP/SUD HA0 ....80 C7
  OXHEY WD19 ....42 E1
Rowley Gdns FSBYPK N4 ....67 J8
Rowley Green Rd BAR EN5 ....33 G8
Rowley La BAR EN5 ....32 E7
  BORE WD6 ....32 D4
Rowley Rd SEVS/STOTM N15 ....67 J3
Rowley Wy STJWD NW8 ....2 F3
Rowlheys Pl WDR/YW UB7 ....112 C1
Rowlls Rd KUT KT1 ....152 F6
Rowney Gdns DAGW RM9 ....90 A5
Rowney Rd DAGW RM9 ....90 B6
Rowntree Cl
  KIL/WHAMP NW6 ....83 D3
  PLSTW E13 ....106 B3
Rowntree Rd WHTN TW2 ....133 L6
Rowse Cl SRTFD E15 ....87 J8
Rowsley Av HDN NW4 ....64 C4
Rowstock Gdns HOLWY N7 ....84 D5
Rowton Rd WOOL/PLUM SE18 ....125 J5
Rowzill Rd SWLY BR8 ....163 M2
Roxborough Av HRW HA1 ....61 K8
  ISLW TW7 ....115 M5
Roxborough Pk HRW HA1 ....61 L8

Roxborough Rd HRW HA1 61 K6
Roxbourne Cl NTHLT UB5 78 D6 1
Roxburgh Av UPMR RM14 93 J3
Roxburgh Rd WNWD SE27 157 H1
Roxburn Wy RSLP HA4 77 M3
Roxby Pl FUL/PGN SW6 14 B9
Roxeth Green Av
RYLN/HDSTN HA2 79 H3
Roxeth Gv RYLN/HDSTN HA2 79 H4
Roxeth Hl RYLN/HDSTN HA2 79 K2
Roxford Cl SHPTN TW17 149 L8
Roxley Rd LEW SE13 141 H3
Roxton Gdns CROY/NA CR0 173 M8
Roxwell Rd BARK IG11 108 A1
SHB W12 100 A8
Roxwell Wy WFD IG8 70 C1 2
Roxy Av CHDH RM6 72 C8
Royal Albert Rd EHAM E6 107 G6
Royal Albert Wy CAN/RD E16 106 D6
Royal Av CHEL SW3 15 L7
CHES/WCR EN8 26 E6
WPK KT4 168 E4
Royal Circ WNWD SE27 139 G7
Royal Cl GDMY/SEVK IG3 72 A8
WDR/YW UB7 94 F5
WPK KT4 168 E4
Royal College St CAMTN NW1 4 F2
Royal Crs NTGHL W11 100 D8
RSLP HA4 78 E4
Royal Crescent Ms NTGHL W11 100 D8
Royal Docks Rd EHAM E6 107 H4
Royal Hl GNWCH SE10 123 J5
Royal Hospital Rd CHEL SW3 15 L9
Royal La WDR/YW UB7 94 F5
Royal Ms BAL SW12 138 B4 3
The Royal Ms WHALL SW1A 16 D3
Royal Mint St TWRH EC3N 13 M6
Royal Naval Pl NWCR SE14 122 F5 5
Royal Oak Pl EDUL SE22 140 B3
Royal Oak Rd BXLYHS DA6 144 F2
HACK E8 86 B6 5
Royal Orchard Cl
WAND/EARL SW18 136 E4
Royal Pde BKHTH/KID SE3 123 M7
CHST BR7 161 J3
Royal Pl GNWCH SE10 123 J5 6
Royal Rd CAN/RD E16 106 C5
SCUP DA14 144 D7
TEDD TW11 151 K1
WALW SE17 18 C9
Royal Route WBLY HA9 80 F4
Royal St STHWK SE1 17 M3
Royal Victor Pl BOW E3 104 D1
Roycraft Av BARK IG11 107 M1
Roycroft Cl SWFD E18 70 B2
Roydene Rd WOOL/PLUM SE18 125 L4
Roydon Cl LOU IG10 52 E2
Roydon Ct WOT/HER KT12 165 G6
Roy Gdns GNTH/NBYPK IG2 71 L5
Roy Gv HPTN TW12 151 H2
Royle Cl GPK RM2 74 B6
Royle Crs WEA W13 98 A3
Roy Rd NTHWD HA6 59 M1
Royston Av CHING E4 51 G7
SUT SM1 170 D5
WLGTN SM6 171 K6
Royston Cl HEST TW5 114 B6
WOT/HER KT12 165 G3
Royston Gdns IL IG1 70 D7
Royston Gv PIN HA5 42 F8
Royston Park Rd PIN HA5 42 F8
Royston Rd DART DA1 145 M3
HARH RM3 75 G1
PGE/AN SE20 158 D4
RCHPK/HAM TW10 134 E2 6
The Roystons BRYLDS KT5 153 H8
Royston St BETH E2 104 C1 7
Rozel Rd CLAP SW4 120 C7
Rubastic Rd NWDGN UB2 114 C1
Rubens Rd NTHLT UB5 96 C1
Rubens St CAT SE6 140 F6
Ruby Rd WALTH E17 69 G4
Ruby St PECK SE15 122 B4
Ruby Triangle PECK SE15 122 B4 3
Ruckholt Cl LEY E10 87 H3
Ruckholt Rd LEY E10 87 J3
Rucklidge Av WLSDN NW10 99 M1
Rudall Crs HAMP NW3 83 K4
Ruddington Cl CLPT E5 86 E4 5
Ruddstreet Cl
WOOL/PLUM SE18 125 H2 3
Ruden Wy EW KT17 181 H8
Rudland Rd BXLYHN DA7 127 H8
Rudloe Rd BAL SW12 138 C4
Rudolph Rd BUSH WD23 43 G1
KIL/WHAMP NW6 2 B6
PLSTW E13 105 M1 3
PLSTW E13 106 A1 3
Rudyard Gv EDGW HA8 45 J8
Rue De St Lawrence WAB EN9 27 J7 5
Ruffetts Cl SAND/SEL CR2 185 H1
The Ruffetts SAND/SEL CR2 185 H1
Rufford Cl HRW HA1 62 A7
Rufford St IS N1 5 K3
Rufus Cl RSLP HA4 78 D3
Rufus St IS N1 7 J8
Rugby Av ALP/SUD HA0 80 C4
ED N9 49 M3
NTHLT UB5 79 K6
Rugby Cl HRW HA1 61 L5
Rugby Gdns DAGW RM9 90 C6
Rugby La BELMT SM2 181 K2
Rugby Rd CDALE/KGS NW9 63 G5
CHSWK W4 99 L8 3
DAGW RM9 90 B7
WHTN TW2 133 L3
Rugby St BMSBY WC1N 11 L1
Rugby Wy RKW/CH/CXG WD3 28 B8
Ruggles-brise Rd ASHF TW15 148 D1
Rugg St POP/IOD E14 105 G6 10
Ruislip Cl GFD/PVL UB6 97 H3
Ruislip Rd GFD/PVL UB6 97 H2
NTHLT UB5 78 C8
Ruislip Rd East GFD/PVL UB6 97 J3 1
HNWL W7 97 K3
Ruislip St TOOT SW17 137 M8
Rumbold Rd FUL/PGN SW6 119 H5
Rum Cl WAP E1W 104 C6
Rumsey Cl HPTN TW12 150 F2
Rumsey Rd BRXN/ST SW9 120 F8
Runbury Cir CDALE/KGS NW9 81 K2 2
Runcorn Cl WALTH E17 68 B5 2
Runcorn Pl NTGHL W11 100 E6 3
Rundell Crs HDN NW4 64 B6
Runes Cl MTCM CR4 155 K7
Runnelfield HRW HA1 79 L3
Runnymede WIM/MER SW19 155 K4
Runnymede Cl WHTN TW2 133 H3
Runnymede Crs
STRHM/NOR SW16 156 D4
Runnymede Gdns GFD/PVL UB6 97 K1
WHTN TW2 133 H3
Runnymede Rd WHTN TW2 133 H3
The Runway RSLP HA4 78 B5
Rupack St
BERM/RHTH SE16 104 C8 10
Rupert Av WBLY HA9 80 E5 3
Rupert Gdns BRXN/ST SW9 121 H7
Rupert Rd ARCH N19 84 D3
CHSWK W4 117 L1
KIL/WHAMP NW6 100 F1 3
Rupert St SOHO/SHAV W1D 11 G6 6
Rural Cl HCH RM12 92 B1
Rural Wy STRHM/NOR SW16 156 B3
Ruscoe Rd CAN/RD E16 105 M5
Ruscombe Wy
EBED/NFELT TW14 131 M4 1
Rusham Rd BAL SW12 137 M3
Rushbrook Crs WALTH E17 68 F2 4
Rushbrook Rd
ELTH/MOT SE9 143 J6 1
Rushcroft Rd
BRXS/STRHM SW2 139 G1
CHING E4 69 H1
Rushden Cl NRWD SE19 157 K3 2
Rushdene ABYW SE2 126 C1
Rushdene Av EBAR EN4 47 L2
Rushdene Cl NTHLT UB5 96 C1
Rushdene Crs NTHLT UB5 96 B1
Rushdene Rd PIN HA5 60 C7
Rushden Gdns CLAY IG5 71 G4
MLHL NW7 46 C8
Rushdon Cl ROM RM1 74 A6
Rushes Md UX/CGN UB8 76 C8 4
Rushet Rd STMC/STPC BR5 162 A5
Rushett Cl THDIT KT7 167 H3
Rushett La CHSGTN KT9 179 K5
Rushett Rd THDIT KT7 167 H2
Rushey Cl NWMAL KT3 153 K7
Rushey Gn CAT SE6 141 H4
Rushey Hl ENC/FH EN2 35 M7
Rushey Md BROCKY SE4 141 G2
Rushfield POTB/CUF EN6 22 D6
Rushford Rd BROCKY SE4 140 F3
Rush Green Gdns
ROMW/RG RM7 91 J1
Rush Green Rd ROMW/RG RM7 91 J1
Rushgrove Av CDALE/KGS NW9 63 M5
Rushgrove St
WOOL/PLUM SE18 124 F2 5
Rush Hill Ms BTSEA SW11 120 A8 3
Rush Hill Rd BTSEA SW11 120 A8
Rushleigh Av CHES/WCR EN8 26 D3
Rushley Cl HAYES BR2 175 K6
Rushmead BETH E2 104 B2 14
RCHPK/HAM TW10 134 B7 2
Rushmead Cl CROY/NA CR0 172 F6
Rushmere Av UPMR RM14 93 J3
Rushmere Ct WPK KT4 169 G4 3
Rushmere Pl
WIM/MER SW19 154 D1 4
Rushmoor Cl PIN HA5 60 B5
RKW/CH/CXG WD3 40 D4 1
Rushmore Cl BMLY BR1 160 E6
Rushmore Rd CLPT E5 86 C4
Rusholme Av DAGE RM10 91 G3
Rusholme Gv NRWD SE19 157 L1
Rusholme Rd PUT/ROE SW15 136 D3
Rushout Av KTN/HRWW/W HA3 62 B7
Rushton Av GSTN WD25 21 G8
Rushton St IS N1 7 H5
Rushworth St STHWK SE1 18 D1
Rushy Meadow La CAR SM5 170 E5 2
Ruskin Av EBED/NFELT TW14 131 M4
MNPK E12 88 F6
RCH/KEW TW9 117 G5
UPMR RM14 75 J8
WAB EN9 27 L7
WELL DA16 126 A8
Ruskin Cl GLDGN NW11 65 H7 2
Ruskin Dr ORP BR6 176 E5
WELL DA16 126 A8 2
WPK KT4 169 H4
Ruskin Gdns EA W5 98 D3 2
HARH RM3 74 B2
KTN/HRWW/W HA3 62 F6
Ruskin Gv DART DA1 147 G2
WELL DA16 126 A7 1
Ruskin Rd BELV DA17 127 G2
CAR SM5 171 G7
CROY/NA CR0 172 B4
ISLW TW7 115 M8
STHL UB1 96 E6
TOTM N17 67 M2
Ruskin Wk ED N9 50 A4
HAYES BR2 175 L1
HNHL SE24 139 J2
Ruskin Wy WIM/MER SW19 155 K5
Rusland Av ORP BR6 176 D5
Rusland Park Rd HRW HA1 61 L5
Rusper Cl CRICK NW2 82 C3
STAN HA7 44 C6
Rusper Rd DAGW RM9 90 C6
WDGN N22 67 H3
Russel Cl BECK BR3 159 H6
Russell Av WDGN N22 67 H3
Russell Cl BXLYHN DA7 145 G1
CHARL SE7 124 C5
DART DA1 128 A8
NTHWD HA6 41 J7
RSLP HA4 78 C2
WLSDN NW10 81 J7
Russell Ct WHALL SW1A 10 F9 2
Russell Crs GSTN WD25 20 F8 3
Russell Dr STWL/WRAY TW19 130 D3
Russell Gdns GLDGN NW11 64 E7
RCHPK/HAM TW10 134 C6
TRDG/WHET N20 47 L4
WDR/YW UB7 113 G3
WKENS W14 118 E1 3
Russell Gardens Ms
WKENS W14 100 E8
Russell Green Cl PUR/KEN CR8 184 A3
Russell Gv BRXN/ST SW9 121 G5 3
MLHL NW7 45 L7
Russell Hl PUR/KEN CR8 183 M3
Russell Hill Pl PUR/KEN CR8 184 A4
Russell Hill Rd PUR/KEN CR8 184 A3
Russell Kerr Cl CHSWK W4 117 J5 3
Russell La TRDG/WHET N20 47 M4
WAT WD17 28 D1
Russell Pl HAMP NW3 83 L5 4
Russell Rd BKHH IG9 52 C3
CAN/RD E16 106 A5
CDALE/KGS NW9 63 M7
CEND/HSY/T N8 66 D7
CHING E4 50 F6
EN EN1 36 F3
LEY E10 69 H7
MTCM CR4 155 L6
NTHLT UB5 79 J5
NTHWD HA6 41 J5
SEVS/STOTM N15 67 L6
SHPTN TW17 164 C2
TRDG/WHET N20 47 L4
WALTH E17 68 F4
WDGN N22 48 F8
WHTN TW2 133 M3 4
WIM/MER SW19 155 G3
WKENS W14 118 E1
WOT/HER KT12 165 G1
Russell's Dr CHES/WCR EN8 26 E4 4
Russell Sq GWRST WC1E 11 H2
Russell's Ride CHES/WCR EN8 26 D4
Russell St HOL/ALD WC2B 11 L5 3
Russell Wy OXHEY WD19 42 B2
SUT SM1 170 B7 4
Russet Av SUN TW16 149 L6
Russet Cl UX/CGN UB8 95 J3 4
WOT/HER KT12 165 K5
Russet Dr CROY/NA CR0 173 L3
Russet Wy EMPK RM11 74 E5 4
Russets Cl CHING E4 51 K5
Russett Cl ORP BR6 177 H7
Russett Wy SWLY BR8 163 K5
Russia Dock Rd
BERM/RHTH SE16 104 E7 6
Russia La BETH E2 104 C1
Russia Rw CITYW EC2V 12 F5 3
Russington Rd SHPTN TW17 164 D1
Rusthall Av CHSWK W4 117 K1
Rusthall Cl CROY/NA CR0 173 J1
Rustic Av STRHM/NOR SW16 156 B3
Rustic Cl UPMR RM14 93 L1
Rustic Pl ALP/SUD HA0 80 D4
Rustington Wk MRDN SM4 169 M2
Ruston Av BRYLDS KT5 168 B2
Ruston Ms NTGHL W11 100 E5 3
Ruston Rd WOOL/PLUM SE18 124 E1
Ruston St BOW E3 86 F8
Rust Sq CMBW SE5 121 K5
Rutford Rd STRHM/NOR SW16 156 E1
Ruth Cl KTN/HRWW/W HA3 62 F5
Ruthen Cl EPSOM KT18 180 B7 2
Rutherford Cl BELMT SM2 170 D8
BORE WD6 32 C5
Rutherford St WEST SW1P 17 G5
Rutherford Wy BUSH WD23 43 K3
WBLY HA9 81 G3
Rutherglen Rd ABYW SE2 126 A4
Rutherwyke Cl EW KT17 169 G8
Ruthin Cl CDALE/KGS NW9 63 L7
Ruthin Rd BKHTH/KID SE3 124 A4
Ruthven Av CHES/WCR EN8 26 D6
Ruthven St HOM E9 86 D8 6
Rutland Ap EMPK RM11 75 G6
Rutland Av BFN/LL DA15 144 A4
Rutland Cl BXLY DA5 144 D5 1
DART DA1 146 D4 1
HOR/WEW KT19 180 D3
MORT/ESHN SW14 117 H8
Rutland Ct CHST BR7 161 G4
Rutland Dr EMPK RM11 75 G6
MRDN SM4 170 A2
RCHPK/HAM TW10 134 D5
Rutland Gdns BCTR RM8 90 C5
CROY/NA CR0 172 E6
FSBYPK N4 67 H7
SKENS SW7 15 K2
WEA W13 98 A4 1
Rutland Ga BELV DA17 127 H3
HAYES BR2 159 M7
SKENS SW7 15 J2
Rutland Gate Ms SKENS SW7 15 J2 1
Rutland Gv HMSMTH W6 118 B3 1
Rutland Ms STJWD NW8 2 D4 1
Rutland Ms South SKENS SW7 15 J3 1
Rutland Pk CAT SE6 140 F6
CRICK NW2 82 C6
Rutland Pl FARR EC1M 12 D2 4
Rutland Rd FSTGT E7 88 D7
HOM E9 86 D8
HRW HA1 61 J7
HYS/HAR UB3 113 K2 1
IL IG1 89 H4
STHL UB1 97 G3
WALTH E17 69 G7 5
WAN E11 70 B6
WHTN TW2 133 K6
WIM/MER SW19 155 L3 3
Rutland St SKENS SW7 15 K3
Rutland Wk CAT SE6 140 F6
Rutland Wy STMC/STPC BR5 177 J1
Rutlish Rd WIM/MER SW19 155 G4
Rutter Gdns MTCM CR4 155 K7
Rutters Cl WDR/YW UB7 95 G8
Rutt's Ter NWCR SE14 122 D6
The Rutts BUSH WD23 43 K3
Ruvigny Gdns
PUT/ROE SW15 118 D8 7
Ruxley Cl HOR/WEW KT19 168 B7
SCUP DA14 162 D2
Ruxley Crs ESH/CLAY KT10 179 H1
Ruxley La HOR/WEW KT19 168 B8
Ruxley Ms HOR/WEW KT19 168 B7 4
Ruxley Rdg ESH/CLAY KT10 179 G1
Ruxton Cl SWLY BR8 163 L6
Ruxton Ct SWLY BR8 163 L6 3
Ryall Cl LCOL/BKTW AL2 21 L2
Ryan Cl ELTH/MOT SE9 142 B1
RSLP HA4 78 B1
Ryan Dr BTFD TW8 116 A4
Ryan Wy WATN WD24 29 J4
Ryarsh Crs ORP BR6 176 E6
Rycroft Wy TOTM N17 67 M4 6
Rycuiff Sq BKHTH/KID SE3 123 M7
Rydal Cl HDN NW4 64 E2 3
PUR/KEN CR8 184 D6 2
Rydal Crs GFD/PVL UB6 98 B2
Rydal Dr BXLYHN DA7 127 G6
WWKM BR4 174 E4
Rydal Gdns CDALE/KGS NW9 63 L6
HSLW TW3 133 H3
PUT/ROE SW15 153 L1
WBLY HA9 80 C1
Rydal Rd STRHM/NOR SW16 156 D1
Rydal Wy PEND EN3 50 C1
RSLP HA4 78 C4
Rydens Av WOT/HER KT12 165 J4
Rydens Cl WOT/HER KT12 165 J4
Rydens Gv WOT/HER KT12 165 K6
Rydens Pk WOT/HER KT12 165 K4
Rydens Rd WOT/HER KT12 165 H5
Ryde Pl TWK TW1 134 C3
Ryder Cl BUSH WD23 43 H1 7
Ryder Dr BERM/RHTH SE16 122 B3
Ryder Gdns RAIN RM13 91 M6
Ryder's Ter STJWD NW8 2 E5
Ryder St STJS SW1Y 10 E8
The Ryde STA TW18 148 B4
Ryde Vale Rd BAL SW12 138 B6
Rydon St IS N1 6 F4
Rydston Cl HOLWY N7 5 K1
Rye Cl BXLY DA5 145 H3
HCH RM12 92 C5 6
Ryecotes Md DUL SE21 139 L5
Rye Crs STMC/STPC BR5 177 J3
Ryecroft Av CLAY IG5 71 H3
WHTN TW2 133 H5
Ryecroft Crs BAR EN5 33 H8
Ryecroft Rd LEW SE13 141 J2
STMC/STPC BR5 176 D1
STRHM/NOR SW16 157 G2
Ryecroft St FUL/PGN SW6 119 H6
Ryedale EDUL SE22 140 B3
Ryefield Av HGDN/ICK UB10 77 J8
Ryefield Crs NTHWD HA6 60 A3 2
Ryefield Rd NRWD SE19 157 J2
Rye Hill Pk PECK SE15 140 C1
Ryeland Cl WDR/YW UB7 94 E5
Ryelands Crs LEE/GVPK SE12 142 C3 1
Ryelands Pl WEY KT13 164 E5
Rye La PECK SE15 122 A6
Rye Rd PECK SE15 140 D1
The Rye STHGT/OAK N14 48 C2
Rye Wk PUT/ROE SW15 136 D2
Rye Wy EDGW HA8 44 F8 2
Ryfold Rd WIM/MER SW19 137 G7
Ryland Cl FELT TW13 131 M8
Rylandes Rd CRICK NW2 82 A3
SAND/SEL CR2 185 H2
Ryland Rd KTTN NW5 84 B6 7
Rylett Crs SHB W12 117 M1
Rylett Rd SHB W12 99 M8
Rylston Rd FUL/PGN SW6 118 F4
PLMGR N13 49 K5
Rymer Rd CROY/NA CR0 172 E2
Rymer St HNHL SE24 139 H3
Rymill St CAN/RD E16 107 G7
Rysbrack St CHEL SW3 15 L3
Rythe Ct THDIT KT7 167 G2
Rythe Rd ESH/CLAY KT10 166 D7
The Rythe LHD/OX KT22 178 B3

S

Sabbarton St CAN/RD E16 105 M5 3
Sabine Rd BTSEA SW11 119 M8
Sable Cl HSLWW TW4 114 C8
Sable St IS N1 6 D1
Sach Rd CLPT E5 86 B2
Sackville Av HAYES BR2 175 G3
Sackville Cl HRW HA1 79 K3
Sackville Crs HARH RM3 74 E2
Sackville Gdns IL IG1 88 F1
Sackville Rd BELMT SM2 182 A1
DART DA1 146 D6
Sackville St MYFR/PICC W1J 10 F7
Saddlebrook Pk SUN TW16 149 L3 2
Saddlers Cl BORE WD6 32 D8 2
PIN HA5 43 G7
Saddlescombe Wy
NFNCH/WDSP N12 47 G7
Saddleworth Sq HARH RM3 56 C8 3
Sadler Cl MTCM CR4 155 M5
Sadlers Ride
E/WMO/HCT KT8 151 H6 3
Saffron Av POP/IOD E14 105 K6
Saffron Cl CROY/NA CR0 171 L1
Saffron Hl HCIRC EC1N 12 B2
Saffron Rd CRW RM5 73 K3
Saffron St HCIRC EC1N 12 B2 1
Saffron Wy SURB KT6 167 K3
Sage Cl EHAM E6 106 F4
Sage St WCHPL E1 104 C6 7
Saigasso Cl CAN/RD E16 106 D5
Sail St LBTH SE11 17 M5
Sainfoin Rd TOOT SW17 138 A6
Sainsbury Rd NRWD SE19 157 L1
St Agatha's Dr KUTN/CMB KT2 152 F2
St Agatha's Gv CAR SM5 170 F3 2
St Agnes Cl HOM E9 86 C8 5
St Agnes Pl CMBW SE5 121 H4
St Aidan's Rd EDUL SE22 140 B3
WEA W13 98 B8
St Albans Av CHSWK W4 117 K1
EHAM E6 106 F2
FELT TW13 150 D1
UPMR RM14 75 J8
WEY KT13 164 A5
St Albans Crs WDGN N22 67 G2
St Alban's Gdns TEDD TW11 152 A1
St Alban's Gv CAR SM5 170 E2
KENS W8 14 D3
St Albans La GLDGN NW11 83 G1
St Alban's Ms BAY/PAD W2 9 H2
St Alban's Pl IS N1 6 C4
St Albans Rd BAR EN5 33 L4
DART DA1 146 F3
GDMY/SEVK IG3 89 M1
GSTN WD25 21 K7
KTTN NW5 84 A3
KUTN/CMB KT2 152 E2
POTB/CUF EN6 22 A5
SUT SM1 169 M6
WAT WD17 29 H5
WATN WD24 29 H3
WFD IG8 70 A1
WLSDN NW10 81 L8
St Alban's St STJS SW1Y 11 G7 6
St Alfege Rd CHARL SE7 124 D4
St Alphage Gdn BARB EC2Y 12 F3
St Alphage Wk EDGW HA8 63 J3 3
St Alphege Rd ED N9 50 C2
St Alphonsus Rd CLAP SW4 138 C1
St Amunds Cl CAT SE6 141 G8 1
St Andrews Av ALP/SUD HA0 80 A4
HCH RM12 91 M5
St Andrew's Cl CRICK NW2 82 B3 2
NFNCH/WDSP N12 47 J6 2
RSLP HA4 78 D2
SHPTN TW17 149 K7
STAN HA7 62 C3 1
St Andrew's Ct
WAND/EARL SW18 137 J6 2
St Andrews Dr ORP BR6 177 H1
STAN HA7 62 C2
St Andrew's Gv STNW/STAM N16 85 K1
St Andrew's Hl BLKFR EC4V 12 D6
St Andrew's Ms
STNW/STAM N16 85 L1 1
St Andrew's Pl CAMTN NW1 4 C9
St Andrew's Rd ACT W3 99 L5
CAR SM5 170 E5
CDALE/KGS NW9 81 K1 1
CROY/NA CR0 172 C6 4
ED N9 50 C2
EN EN1 36 D6
GLDGN NW11 64 F7
HGDN/ICK UB10 76 E8
HNWL W7 97 L8 3
IL IG1 70 F8
PLSTW E13 106 B2
ROMW/RG RM7 73 K7
SCUP DA14 144 D7
SURB KT6 167 K1
WALTH E17 68 D3
WAN E11 69 L7 1
WKENS W14 118 E4 3
WLSDN NW10 82 B6
St Andrew's Sq NTGHL W11 100 E5 3
St Andrew St HCIRC EC1N 12 B3
St Andrews Wy BOW E3 105 H3
St Anna Rd BAR EN5 33 K8 3
St Anne's Av
STWL/WRAY TW19 130 D4
St Anne's Cl CHESW EN7 26 A1 2
HGT N6 84 A3
OXHEY WD19 42 C6
St Annes Gdns WLSDN NW10 98 F2
St Anne's Pas POP/IOD E14 104 F5 3
St Anne's Rd ALP/SUD HA0 80 D5
DEN/HRF UB9 58 C4
WAN E11 87 K2
St Anne's Rw POP/IOD E14 104 F5 4
St Anne St POP/IOD E14 104 F5 3
St Ann's BARK IG11 89 J8
St Ann's Crs WAND/EARL SW18 137 H3
St Ann's Gdns KTTN NW5 84 A6 7
St Ann's Hl WAND/EARL SW18 137 H2
St Ann's Park Rd
WAND/EARL SW18 137 J3 3
St Ann's Rd BARK IG11 89 J8 1
BARN SW13 117 M6 2
ED N9 49 M4
HRW HA1 61 L7
NTGHL W11 100 D6
SEVS/STOTM N15 67 L7
St Ann's St WEST SW1P 17 H3
St Ann's Ter STJWD NW8 3 H5
St Ann's Vls NTGHL W11 100 D7
St Ann's Wy CROY/NA CR0 172 B8
St Anselm's Pl
MYFR/PKLN W1K 10 C6 2
St Anselms Rd HYS/HAR UB3 95 M8
St Anthony's Av WFD IG8 52 C8
St Anthonys Cl TOOT SW17 137 L6 1
St Anthony's Ct HAYES BR2 176 B3
St Anthony's Wy
EBED/NFELT TW14 131 M1
St Antony's Rd FSTGT E7 88 B7
St Arvans Cl CROY/NA CR0 172 E5
St Asaph Rd PECK SE15 122 D8
St Aubyn's Av HSLWW TW4 133 G2
WIM/MER SW19 154 F1
St Aubyns Cl ORP BR6 176 F5
St Aubyns Gdns ORP BR6 176 F4
St Aubyn's Rd NRWD SE19 157 M2 3
St Audrey Av BXLYHN DA7 127 G7
St Augustine's Av BMLY BR1 160 E8
EA W5 98 E1
SAND/SEL CR2 184 C1
WBLY HA9 80 E3
St Augustine's Rd BELV DA17 126 F2
CAMTN NW1 5 G1
St Austell Cl EDGW HA8 62 F3
St Austell Rd LEW SE13 123 J7
St Awdry's Rd BARK IG11 89 K7
St Barnabas Cl BECK BR3 159 J5 2
St Barnabas Gdns
E/WMO/HCT KT8 151 G8
St Barnabas Rd MTCM CR4 156 A3
SUT SM1 170 D7
SWFD E18 70 B2
WALTH E17 69 G7
St Barnabas Ter HOM E9 86 D5 3
St Barnabas Vls VX/NE SW8 120 E6 1
St Barnabus St BGVA SW1W 16 B7

St Bartholomew's Cl SYD SE26 .. 140 C8
St Bartholomew's Rd EHAM E6.... 88 E8
St Benedict's Cl TOOT SW17 .... 156 A1 🗓
St Benets Cl TOOT SW17 .... 137 L6 🗓
St Bernards CROY/NA CR0 ...... 172 C5 🗓
St Bernards Rd WNWD SE27 .... 139 K8 🗓
St Bernard's Rd EHAM E6 .... 88 D8
St Blaise Av BMLY BR1 .... 160 B5
St Botolph St HDTCH EC3A ...... 13 L4 🗓
St Bride's Av EDGW HA8 .... 62 F2
St Brides Cl ERITHM DA18 ...... 108 D8
St Bride St FLST/FETLN EC4A 12 C4
St Catherines Cl TOOT SW17 .... 137 L6 🗓
St Catherine's Dr FELT TW13 .... 132 A5 🗓
St Catherine's Dr NWCR SE14.... 122 D7
St Catherines Rd CHING E4...... 51 C4
St Chads Cl SURB KT6........... 167 J2
St Chad's Gdns CHDH RM6 ..... 72 E8
St Chad's Pl FSBYW WC1X 5 K7
St Chad's Rd CHDH RM6 .... 72 E8 🗓
St Chad's St STPAN WC1H 5 K7
St Charles Pl NKENS W10 ...... 100 E4 🗓
St Charles Sq NKENS W10 ...... 100 D4 🗓
St Chads Cl SURB KT6 .... 167 J2
St Christopher's Cl ISLW TW7 ... 115 L6 🗓
St Christophers Dr
HYS/HAR UB3 .... 96 B6 🗓
St Christopher's Ms
WLGTN SM6 .... 171 J7 🗓
St Clair Cl CLAY IG5 .... 70 F3
St Clair Dr WPK KT4 .... 169 H5
St Clair Rd PLSTW E13 .... 106 B2
St Clair's Rd CROY/NA CR0 ..... 172 E4
St Clare St TWRH EC3N 13 L5
St Clement Cl UX/CGN UB8 ..... 94 D5
St Clement's Ct PUR RM19 ...... 129 G2 🗓
St Clement's La LINN WC2A 11 M5
St Clements St IS N1 .... 6 A1 🗓
St Cloud Rd WNWD SE27 .... 139 J8
St Crispins Cl HAMP NW3 ...... 83 L4 🗓
STHL UB1 .... 96 F5
St Cross St HCIRC EC1N 12 B2
St Cuthberts Gdns HNHL SE24 .. 60 F1 🗓
St Cuthbert's Rd CRICK NW2 .... 82 F6
PLMGR N13 .... 49 G8
St Cyprian's St TOOT SW17 .... 137 M8 🗓
St David Cl UX/CGN UB8 .... 94 D4
St Davids Cl WBLY HA9 .... 81 J3
WWKM BR4 .... 174 A2
St David's Dr EDGW HA8 .... 62 F2
St David's Rd SWLY BR8......... 163 M2
St Denis Rd WNWD SE27 .... 139 K8
St Dionis Rd FUL/PGN SW6 ..... 118 F7
St Donatt's Rd NWCR SE14 .... 122 E7
St Dunstan's Av ACT W3 .... 99 K6
St Dunstans Cl HYS/HAR UB3 ... 113 M2
St Dunstan's Gdns ACT W3 .... 99 K6 🗓
St Dunstan's Hl MON EC3R ...... 13 J7 🗓
SUT SM1 .... 169 L6
St Dunstan's La BECK BR3...... 174 C1
MON EC3R .... 13 J7 🗓
St Dunstan's Rd FELT TW13 .... 131 M7
FSTGT E7 .... 88 B6
HEST TW5 .... 114 C7 🗓
HMSMTH W6 .... 118 D3
HNWL W7 .... 97 L8
HSLWW TW4 .... 114 B7 🗓
SNWD SE25 .... 157 M7
St Edmunds Av RSLP HA4 ...... 59 K7
St Edmunds Cl ABYW SE2 ...... 108 D8
STJWD NW8 .... 3 L4
TOOT SW17 .... 137 L6 🗓
St Edmunds Dr STAN HA7 ...... 62 A2
St Edmund's La WHTN TW2 ..... 133 H4 🗓
St Edmunds Rd DART DA1 ...... 146 F1
ED N9 .... 50 A2
IL IG1 .... 70 F7
St Edmund's Ter STJWD NW8 ... 3 K4
St Edwards Cl CROY/NA CR0.... 186 D4
GLDGN NW11 .... 65 C7 🗓
St Edwards Wy ROM RM1....... 73 L5
St Egberts Wy CHING E4 .... 51 J3
St Elizabeth Dr EPSOM KT18 ... 180 C7
St Elmo Rd ACT W3 .... 99 M8
St Elmos Rd BERM/RHTH SE16 .. 104 E8
St Erkenwald Ms BARK IG11 .... 89 K8
St Erkenwald Rd BARK IG11 .... 89 K8
St Ervans Rd NKENS W10 ...... 100 E4 🗓
St Faith's Cl ENC/FH EN2 ...... 36 C4 🗓
St Faith's Rd HNHL SE24 .... 139 H5
St Fidelis' Rd ERITH DA8 .... 127 K2
St Fillans Rd CAT SE6 .... 141 J5
St Francis Cl ORP BR6 .... 176 E1
OXHEY WD19 .... 42 B3
POTB/CUF EN6 .... 23 J6
St Francis Rd EDUL SE22....... 139 L1
St Francis Wy IL IG1 .... 89 K4
St Gabriel's Cl WAN E11........ 88 B1
St Gabriel's Rd CRICK NW2 .... 82 D5
St George's Av CDALE/KGS NW9 63 J5 🗓
EA W5 .... 98 D8 🗓
EMPK RM11 .... 74 F8
FSTGT E7 .... 88 B7
HOLWY N7 .... 84 D4
STHL UB1 .... 96 F6
WEY KT13 .... 164 C8
St Georges Cl ALP/SUD HA0 ... 80 A3
GLDGN NW11 .... 64 F7 🗓
WEY KT13 .... 164 C7 🗓
St George's Dr BCVA SW1W .... 16 C5 🗓
HGDN/ICK UB10 .... 76 F3 🗓
OXHEY WD19 .... 42 E5 🗓
PIM SW1V 16 E7
St George's Gdns EW KT17 .... 180 F7 🗓
SURB KT6 .... 168 B4 🗓
St George's La MON EC3R ...... 13 H6 🗓
St George's Ms HAMP NW3..... 3 M2
St George's Rd BECK BR3 ...... 159 H4
BMLY BR1 ....
CHSWK W4 .... 99 K8 🗓
DAGW RM9 .... 90 E5
ED N9 .... 50 A5 🗓
EN EN1 .... 36 F3
FELT TW13 .... 132 D8

FSTGT E7 .... 88 B7
HNWL W7 .... 97 M7
IL IG1 .... 70 F8
KUTN/CMB KT2 .... 153 G3
LEY E10 .... 87 J3
MTCM CR4 .... 156 B6
PLMGR N13 .... 48 F5
RCH/KEW TW9 .... 116 F8
SCUP DA14 .... 162 D2
STHWK SE1 .... 18 C4
STMC/STPC BR5 .... 176 D1
SWLY BR8 .... 163 M1 🗓
TWK TW1 .... 134 B2
WATN WD24 .... 29 H3 🗓
WATN WD24 .... 29 H2 🗓
WEY KT13 .... 164 D8
WIM/MER SW19 .... 154 F2
WLGTN SM6 .... 171 H7
St Georges Rd West BMLY BR1 . 160 E6 🗓
St Georges's Ct STP EC4M .... 12 C4 🗓
St George's Sq FSTGT E7 ...... 88 B7
PIM SW1V 17 G8
St George's Square Ms
PIM SW1V 17 G8
St George's Ter HAMP NW3 .... 3 M2
St George St CONDST W1S 10 D6
St George's Wk
CROY/NA CR0 .... 172 C5 🗓
St Gerards Cl CLAP SW4 .... 138 C2
St German's Pl BKHTH/KID SE3 . 124 A6
St German's Rd FSTH SE23 .... 140 E5
St Giles Av DAGE RM10........ 91 H7
HGDN/ICK UB10 .... 77 J4
POTB/CUF EN6.................. 22 A6
St Giles Av DAGE RM10........ 91 H7 🗓
ORP BR6 .... 176 D7
St Giles High St LSQ/SEVD WC2H . 11 H4
St Giles Rd CMBW SE5 .... 121 L6
St Gothard Rd WNWD SE27 .... 139 K7
St Gregory Cl RSLP HA4 .... 78 C4 🗓
St Helena Rd BERM/RHTH SE16 . 122 D2
St Helena St FSBYW WC1X .... 6 A8 🗓
St Helen Cl UX/CGN UB8 ...... 94 D5
St Helen's Crs
STRHM/NOR SW16 .... 156 F4 🗓
St Helen's Gdns NKENS W10 ... 100 D4 🗓
NKENS W10 .... 100 D5 🗓
St Helen's Pl OBST EC2N 13 J4
St Helens Rd ERITHM DA18 .... 108 D8
IL IG1 .... 70 F7
STRHM/NOR SW16............. 156 F3
WEA W13 .... 98 C7 🗓
St Helier Av MRDN SM4 .... 170 C2
St Heliers Av HSLWW TW4 .... 133 G2
St Helier's Rd LEY E10 .... 69 J7 🗓
St Hilda's Av ASHF TW15 ...... 148 E1
St Hildas Cl TOOT SW17 ...... 137 L6
St Hilda's Rd BARN SW13 ..... 118 B4
St Hughes Cl TOOT SW17 ..... 137 L6 🗓
St Hugh's Rd PGE/AN SE20 .... 158 B3 🗓
St Ives Cl HARH RM3 .... 74 F1
St Ivians Dr GPK RM2 .... 74 A4
St James Dr EW KT17 .... 180 F4
SUT SM1 .... 170 A7
TRDG/WHET N20............... 47 L5
WEA W13 .... 98 A7 🗓
St James Cl EPSOM KT18 ..... 180 E7
NWMAL KT3 .... 153 M8
RSLP HA4 .... 78 C2
TRDG/WHET N20............... 47 L5
St James' Ct NEWTW SW1E .... 16 F3 🗓
St James' Gdns ALP/SUD HA0.. 80 D7
St James' La RDART DA2 ...... 147 L4
St James Ms POP/IOD E14 .... 123 J1 🗓
WEY KT13 .... 164 B6 🗓
St James Pl DART DA1 .... 146 D5 🗓
St James Rd CAR SM5 .... 170 C5
EBAR EN4 .... 34 C4
ED N9 .... 50 B4
FSTGT E7 .... 87 M5
MTCM CR4 .... 156 A3
PUR/KEN CR8 .... 184 B6
SURB KT6 .... 167 K1
SUT SM1 .... 170 A8
WATW WD18 .... 29 H4
St James's NWCR SE14........ 122 E6
St James's Av BECK BR3 ...... 158 E6
BETH E2 .... 104 C1
HPTN TW12 .... 151 J1
St James's Cl TOOT SW17 .... 137 M6 🗓
WOOL/PLUM SE18 .... 125 J3
St James's Cottages
RCHPK/HAM TW10 .... 134 D2 🗓
St James's Crs BRXN/ST SW9 .. 121 G8
St James's Dr BAL SW12 ...... 137 M5
TOOT SW17 .... 137 M5
St James's Gdns NTGHL W11 .. 100 E7 🗓
St James's Gv BTSEA SW11 ... 119 M7 🗓
St James's La MUSWH N10 .... 66 B5
St James's Ms WALTH E17 .... 68 E6 🗓
St James's Pl WHALL SW1A ... 10 E9
St James Sq SURB KT6 .... 167 J2 🗓
St James's Rd
BERM/RHTH SE16 .... 122 A3
CHESW EN7 .... 25 J1
CROY/NA CR0 .... 172 C2
HPTN TW12 .... 151 H1
KUT KT1 .... 152 D5 🗓
STHWK SE1 .... 122 A3
St James's Sq STJS SW1Y .... 11 G8 🗓
St James St WALTH E17 ...... 68 E6 🗓
WHALL SW1A 10 E8
St James's Terrace Ms
STJWD NW8 .... 3 L4 🗓
St James Wk CLKNW EC1R .... 6 B9 🗓
St Jerome's Gv UX/CGN UB8 ... 95 J5
St Joan's Rd ED N9 .... 49 M4
St John Cl FUL/PGN SW6 ..... 119 C5 🗓
St Johns Av EW KT17 .... 180 F5
FBAR/BDGN N11 .... 47 M7
PUT/ROE SW15 .... 136 D2
St John's Church Rd HOM E9 .. 86 C5 🗓

St John's Cl POTB/CUF EN6 .... 23 J6
RAIN RM13 .... 92 A7 🗓
STHGT/OAK N14 .... 48 C1 🗓
UX/CGN UB8 .... 76 B8 🗓
WBLY HA9 .... 80 E5
St John's Ct BKHH IG9 .... 52 B3
ISLW TW7 .... 115 M7 🗓
St John's Crs BRXN/ST SW9 ... 121 G8
St John's Dr WAND/EARL SW18 . 137 H5
WOT/HER KT12 .... 165 J3
St John's Gdns NTGHL W11 .... 100 E6 🗓
St John's Gv ARCH N19 .... 117 M7 🗓
BARN SW13 .... 117 M7 🗓
RCH/KEW TW9 .... 134 E1 🗓
St John's Hl BTSEA SW11 ..... 137 L1
St John's Hill Gv BTSEA SW11 . 137 K1
St John's La FARR EC1M 12 C1
St John's Pk BKHTH/KID SE3 ... 124 A5
St John's Pl FARR EC1M 12 C1
St John's Rd BARK IG11 ...... 89 L8
BTSEA SW11 .... 137 L1 🗓
CAN/RD E16 .... 106 A5
CAR SM5 .... 170 C5
CHING E4 .... 51 H5
CROY/NA CR0 .... 172 B5 🗓
CRW RM5 .... 55 J7
E/WMO/HCT KT8 .... 151 K7
EHAM E6 .... 88 C8
ERITH DA8 .... 127 K3
FELT TW13 .... 132 F8
GLDGN NW11 .... 64 F7
GNTH/NBYPK IG2 .... 71 L8
HRW HA1 .... 61 M7
ISLW TW7 .... 115 M7 🗓
KUT KT1 .... 152 C5
LOU IG10 .... 39 M5
NWDGN UB2 .... 114 E1 🗓
NWMAL KT3 .... 153 J6
PGE/AN SE20 .... 158 C3
RCH/KEW TW9 .... 134 E1 🗓
RDART DA2 .... 147 J4
SCUP DA14 .... 144 B8
SEVS/STOTM N15 .... 67 L7
STMC/STPC BR5 .... 176 D1
SUT SM1 .... 170 A4 🗓
UX/CGN UB8 .... 76 B8 🗓
WALTH E17 .... 69 H5
WAT WD17 .... 29 H5
WBLY HA9 .... 80 D4
WELL DA16 .... 126 B8
WIM/MER SW19 .... 154 E1
St John's Sq FARR EC1M ...... 12 C1 🗓
FSBYE EC1V 12 C1
St John's Ter ENC/FH EN2 .... 36 D2 🗓
FSTGT E7 .... 88 B6
NKENS W10 .... 100 D3 🗓
WOOL/PLUM SE18 .... 125 J4
St John St FSBYE EC1V........ 6 B6
St John's V BROCKY SE4 ...... 123 G7
St John's Vls ARCH N19 ...... 84 D7
KENS W8 .... 14 D7 🗓
St John's Wy ARCH N19 ...... 84 D1
St John's Wood High St
STJWD NW8 .... 3 H6
St John's Wood Pk STJWD NW8 . 3 G4
St John's Wood Rd STJWD NW8 . 3 C9
St John's Wood Ter STJWD NW8 . 3 J5
St Josephs Cl ORP BR6 .... 176 F6 🗓
St Joseph's Dr STHL UB1 ..... 96 E7
St Josephs Gv HDN NW4 ..... 64 B5 🗓
St Joseph's Rd ED N9 .... 50 B2
St Joseph's V VX/NE SW8 .... 120 B6 🗓
St Joseph's V BKHTH/KID SE3 . 123 L8
St Jude's Rd BETH E2 .... 104 B1 🗓
St Jude St STNW/STAM N16 ... 85 L5 🗓
St Julian's Cl
STRHM/NOR SW16 .... 139 G8 🗓
St Julian's Farm Rd
WNWD SE27 .... 139 G8
St Julian's Rd KIL/WHAMP NW6 . 82 F7
St Justin Cl STMC/STPC BR5 .. 162 D6
St Katharine's Prec
CAMTN NW1 .... 4 C5 🗓
St Katharine's Wy TWRH EC3N . 13 M8
St Katherines Rd ERITHM DA18 . 108 D7 🗓
St Keverne Rd ELTH/MOT SE9 .. 142 E8
St Kilda Rd ORP BR6.......... 176 F5
WEA W13 .... 98 A8 🗓
St Kilda's Rd HRW HA1 .... 61 L7
STNW/STAM N16 .... 85 K1
St Kitts Ter NRWD SE19 ...... 157 L8
St Laurence Cl STMC/STPC BR5 . 162 D6
UX/CGN UB8 .... 94 C4
St Laurence's Cl
KIL/WHAMP NW6 .... 82 D8 🗓
St Lawrence Cl ABLGY WD5.... 20 E3
EDGW HA8 .... 62 F1
St Lawrence Dr PIN HA5 ...... 60 B6
St Lawrence Rd UPMR RM14 .. 93 J2
St Lawrence St POP/IOD E14 .. 105 J7 🗓
St Lawrence Ter NKENS W10 .. 100 E4 🗓
St Lawrence Wy
BRXN/ST SW9 .... 121 G7 🗓
LCOL/BKTW AL2 .... 21 M3
St Leonard's Av CHING E4 .... 51 K8
KTN/HRWW/W HA3 .... 62 C6
St Leonards Cl BUSH WD23.... 29 L7
WELL DA16 .... 126 A8
St Leonard's Gdns HEST TW5 .. 114 E5
IL IG1 .... 89 J5 🗓
St Leonards Ri ORP BR6....... 176 E6
St Leonard's Rd
CROY/NA CR0 .... 172 B5 🗓
ESH/CLAY KT10 .... 166 F8
MORT/ESHN SW14 .... 117 J8
POP/IOD E14 .... 105 J4
SURB KT6 .... 152 D8
THDIT KT7 .... 167 G1
WEA W13 .... 98 C6 🗓
WLSDN NW10 .... 99 K3 🗓
St Leonard's Sq BOW E3 ..... 105 H2 🗓
St Leonard's St BOW E3....... 105 J2
St Loo Av CHEL SW3 .... 15 K9
St Louis Rd WNWD SE27 ..... 139 J8
St Loy's Rd TOTM N17 .... 67 L3

St Lucia Dr SRTFD E15 .... 87 M8
St Luke Cl UX/CGN UB8 ...... 94 D5
St Luke's Av CLAP SW4 .... 138 D1
ENC/FH EN2 .... 36 D1
IL IG1 .... 89 H5
St Luke's Cl SNWD SE25 ..... 173 H1
SWLY BR8 .... 163 K5 🗓
St Luke's Ms NTGHL W11 .... 100 F5
St Luke's Rd HGDN/ICK UB10 . 76 E7 🗓
NTGHL W11 .... 100 F4
St Lukes's Cl FSBYE EC1V 6 F9
St Luke's Sq CAN/RD E16 ... 105 M5 🗓
St Luke's St CHEL SW3 ...... 15 J7
St Malo Av ED N9 .... 50 C5
St Margarets BARK IG11 ..... 89 K8
St Margarets Av ASHF TW15 .. 149 H1
BFN/LL DA15 .... 143 K7
CHEAM SM3 .... 169 L5
RYLN/HDSTN HA2 .... 79 J3
SEVS/STOTM N15 .... 67 H5 🗓
TRDG/WHET N20 .... 47 J3
UX/CGN UB8 .... 94 D5
St Margarets Cl ORP BR6 .... 177 H6 🗓
RDART DA2 .... 147 K6
St Margaret's Crs
PUT/ROE SW15 .... 136 B2 🗓
St Margarets Dr
EPSOM KT18 .... 180 D7 🗓
TWK TW1 .... 134 B2
St Margaret's Gv TWK TW1 ... 134 A3
WAN E11 .... 88 B3 🗓
WOOL/PLUM SE18 .... 125 J4
St Margaret's Rd BROCKY SE4 . 140 F1
EDGW HA8 .... 45 H7
HNWL W7 .... 97 L8
MNPK E12 .... 88 C2
RSLP HA4 .... 59 K7
TOTM N17 .... 67 L3
TWK TW1 .... 134 B1
WLSDN NW10 .... 100 C1
St Margaret's Ter
WOOL/PLUM SE18 .... 125 J3 🗓
St Margaret St WEST SW1P ... 17 J2
St Mark's Crs CAMTN NW1 .... 4 B3
St Marks Ga HOM E9 .... 86 F7 🗓
St Mark's Gv WBPTN SW10 ... 119 H5 🗓
St Mark's HI SURB KT6 .... 167 L1
St Mark's Pl NTGHL W11 ..... 100 E5 🗓
WIM/MER SW19 .... 154 F2 🗓
St Mark's Ri HACK E8 .... 85 M5 🗓
HACK E8 .... 85 M5 🗓
St Mark's Rd EA W5 .... 98 E7
EN EN1 .... 49 M1
HAYES BR2 .... 160 B6 🗓
HNWL W7 .... 97 L8
MTCM CR4 .... 155 M5
NTGHL W11 .... 100 D5
SNWD SE25 .... 158 A7 🗓
TEDD TW11 .... 151 B3
St Mark's Sq CAMTN NW1 .... 4 A3
St Mark St WCHPL E1 .... 13 M5
St Martin Cl UX/CGN UB8 .... 94 D5 🗓
St Martin's Av RSLP HA4 ..... 59 L8
St Martin's Av EHAM E6...... 106 D1
EPSOM KT18 .... 180 E7
St Martin's Cl CAMTN NW1 .... 4 E3
EN EN1 .... 37 H4
ERITHM DA18 .... 108 D8
EW KT17 .... 180 F6 🗓
OXHEY WD19 .... 42 C6 🗓
WDR/YW UB7 .... 112 C1
St Martins Dr WOT/HER KT12 .. 165 J5
St Martin's La CHCR WC2N ... 11 J7 🗓
St Martin's Le Grand STBT EC1A . 12 E4
St Martin's Pl CHCR WC2N ... 11 J7 🗓
St Martin's Rd BRXN/ST SW9 . 120 F7
DART DA1 .... 146 F3
ED N9 .... 50 B4
St Martin's St LSQ/SEVD WC2H . 11 H7 🗓
St Martin's Wy TOOT SW17 ... 137 J6
St Mary Abbot's Pl KENS W8 . 118 F1 🗓
St Mary Abbots Ter
WKENS W14 .... 118 F1 🗓
St Mary At Hl MON EC3R..... 13 J7
St Mary Av WLGTN SM6...... 171 G5
St Mary Axe HDTCH EC3A ... 13 K4
St Marychurch St
BERM/RHTH SE16 .... 104 C8
St Mary Rd WALTH E17 ...... 69 G5
St Marys BARK IG11 .... 107 K1
St Mary's Ap MNPK E12 ..... 88 F5 🗓
St Mary's Av FNCH N3........ 64 E3
HAYES BR2 .... 159 L6
NTHWD HA6 .... 41 L7
NWDGN UB2 .... 115 H2
STWL/WRAY TW19 .... 130 D4
TEDD TW11 .... 151 M2 🗓
WAN E11 .... 70 B8
St Mary's Cl CHSGTN KT9 ... 179 M1
DEN/HRF UB9 .... 58 B4
EW KT17 .... 180 F1
STMC/STPC BR5 .... 162 B5
SUN TW16 .... 150 A7 🗓
TOTM N17 .... 68 A2 🗓
St Mary's Crs HDN NW4 ..... 64 B4
HYS/HAR UB3 .... 95 M6
ISLW TW7 .... 115 K5
STWL/WRAY TW19 .... 130 D4
St Mary's Dr EBED/NFELT TW14 . 131 J4
St Mary's Gdns LBTH SE11 ... 18 B5
St Mary's Gv BARN SW13 .... 118 B8
CHSWK W4 .... 117 H4
IS N1 .... 85 H5
RCH/KEW TW9 .... 134 F1
St Mary's La UPMR RM14 .... 93 G2
St Mary's Man BAY/PAD W2 .. 8 F2
St Mary's Ms KIL/WHAMP NW6 . 2 D1
St Mary's Pth IS N1 .... 6 D3
St Mary's Pl EA W5 .... 98 E7 🗓
KENS W8 .... 14 D3 🗓
St Mary's Rd BXLY DA5 ...... 145 J5
CEND/HSY/T N8 .... 66 E5 🗓
CHES/WCR EN8 .... 26 C2

DEN/HRF UB8 .... 58 B4
E/WMO/HCT KT8 .... 151 K8
EA W5 .... 98 D8
EBAR EN4 .... 47 M2 🗓
ED N9 .... 50 C3
GLDGN NW11 .... 64 E8
GRH DA8 .... 147 L2
HYS/HAR UB3 .... 95 M6 🗓
IL IG1 .... 89 J2
LEY E10 .... 87 J3
PECK SE15 .... 122 C7
PLSTW E13 .... 106 B1
SAND/SEL CR2 .... 184 D3
SNWD SE25 .... 157 L6
SURB KT6 .... 167 J2
SWLY BR8 .... 163 K7
WATW WD18 .... 29 H7
WEY KT13 .... 164 D6
WIM/MER SW19 .... 154 E1
WLSDN NW10 .... 81 L8
WPK KT4 .... 168 E4 🗓
St Mary's Sq BAY/PAD W2 .... 9 G2
EA W5 .... 98 D8 🗓
St Mary's Ter BAY/PAD W2 ... 9 G2
St Mary WOOL/PLUM SE18 ... 124 F2
St Marys Vw KTN/HRWW/W HA3 . 62 C6
St Mary's Wk HYS/HAR UB3 .. 95 M6
LBTH SE11 .... 18 B5
St Marys Wy CHIG IG7 .... 53 G7
St Matthew Cl UX/CGN UB8 .. 94 D5
St Matthew's Av SURB KT6 ... 167 L3
RAIN RM13 .... 92 A7 🗓
St Matthews Cl OXHEY WD19 . 42 D1 🗓
St Matthews Dr BMLY BR1 ... 160 F6
St Matthew's Rd
BRXS/STRHM SW2 .... 138 F2
EA W5 .... 98 E7
St Matthew's Rw BETH E2 ... 104 A2
St Matthew St WEST SW1P ... 17 G3
St Matthias Cl
CDALE/KGS NW9 .... 63 M6 🗓
St Maur Rd FUL/PGN SW6 ... 118 F6
St Merryn Cl
WOOL/PLUM SE18 .... 125 K4 🗓
St Michaels Av ED N9........ 50 C2
WBLY HA9 .... 81 G6
St Michaels Cl BMLY BR1 .... 160 E6
CAN/RD E16 .... 106 D4 🗓
ERITHM DA18 .... 108 D8 🗓
FNCH N3 .... 64 F3 🗓
NFNCH/WDSP N12 .... 47 L7
SOCK/AV RM15 .... 111 J6
WOT/HER KT12 .... 165 J4 🗓
WPK KT4 .... 168 F4
St Michael's Crs PIN HA5 .... 60 E7 🗓
St Michaels Dr GSTN WD25 .. 21 H6
St Michael's Gdns
NKENS W10 .... 100 E4 🗓
St Michaels Rd ASHF TW15 .. 149 G1
BRXN/ST SW9 .... 120 F7
CRICK NW2 .... 82 C4
CROY/NA CR0 .... 172 C3 🗓
WELL DA16 .... 126 B8 🗓
WLGTN SM6 .... 171 J4
St Michael's Ter WDGN N22 .. 66 E2 🗓
St Michaels Wy
POTB/CUF EN6 .... 23 H3 🗓
St Mildred's Ct LOTH EC2R .. 13 G5 🗓
St Mildreds Rd CAT SE6 ..... 141 L4
St Neots Cl BORE WD6 ...... 32 A3 🗓
St Neot's Rd HARH RM3 ..... 74 F1
St Nicholas Av HCH RM12 ... 92 A3
St Nicholas Cl BORE WD6 ... 44 D1
UX/CGN UB8 .... 94 D5
St Nicholas Dr SHPTN TW17 . 164 F4
St Nicholas Glebe
TOOT SW17 .... 156 A2 🗓
St Nicholas Rd SUT SM1 .... 170 B7 🗓
THDIT KT7 .... 166 F1
WOOL/PLUM SE18 .... 125 M3
St Nicholas St DEPT SE8 .... 123 C6 🗓
St Nicholas Wy SUT SM1 .... 170 B6
St Nicolas La CHST BR7 ..... 160 E4
St Norbert Rd BROCKY SE4 .. 140 E1
St Normans Wy EW KT17 .... 181 G3
St Olaf's Rd FUL/PGN SW6 .. 118 E5
St Olave's Rd EHAM E6 ...... 89 G4
St Olave's Wk
STRHM/NOR SW16 .... 156 F6
St Oswald's Pl LBTH SE11 ... 17 L7
St Oswald's Rd
STRHM/NOR SW16 .... 157 H4
St Oswulf St WEST SW1P 17 H4
St Pancras Wy CAMTN NW1 .. 4 F1 🗓
St Paul Cl UX/CGN UB8 ...... 94 D4
St Paul's Av
BERM/RHTH SE16 .... 104 D7 🗓
CRICK NW2 .... 82 B6
KTN/HRWW/W HA3 .... 62 C2
St Paul's Church Yd
BLKFR EC4V .... 12 D5 🗓
St Paul's Cl ASHF TW15 ..... 149 J1 🗓
CAR SM5 .... 170 E2
CHARL SE7 .... 124 D3 🗓
CHSGTN KT9 .... 167 K6 🗓
EA W5 .... 98 F8
EA W5 .... 98 F8
HSLW TW3 .... 114 C7 🗓
HYS/HAR UB3 .... 113 K3
SOCK/AV RM15 .... 111 J6 🗓
St Paul's Cray Rd CHST BR7 . 161 K4
St Pauls Crs CAMTN NW1 .... 5 H1
CAMTN NW1 .... 5 H1
St Paul's Dr SRTFD E15 ..... 87 K5
St Pauls Ms CAMTN NW1 .... 5 H1
St Paul's Pl IS N1 .... 85 K6
SOCK/AV RM15 .... 111 J6 🗓
St Pauls Ri PLMGR N13 ..... 49 H8
St Paul's Rd BARK IG11 ..... 89 L8
BTFD TW8 .... 116 D4
ERITH DA8 .... 127 J5
IS N1 .... 85 H6
RCH/KEW TW9 .... 116 F6
THHTH CR7 .... 157 J4
TOTM N17 .... 68 A1
St Pauls Ter WALW SE17 .... 18 B9

St Paul St IS N1 6 E4
St Paul's Wy FNCH N3 65 H1
POP/IOD E14 104 F4
WAB EN9 27 K6
WATN WD24 29 J5
St Paul's Wood Hl
STMC/STPC BR5 161 L5
St Peter's Av BETH E2 104 A1
UED N18 50 A6
St Petersburgh Ms BAY/PAD W2 8 C6
St Petersburgh Pl BAY/PAD W2 8 C7
St Peter's Cl BAR EN5 33 H8
BETH E2 104 A1
BUSH WD23 43 K3
CHST BR7 161 K3
GNTH/NBYPK IG2 71 L5
RKW/CH/CXG WD3 40 B4
RSLP HA4 78 D2
TOOT SW17 137 L6
St Peters Ct
E/WMO/HCT KT8 151 G7
HDN NW4 64 C6
LEE/GVPK SE12 141 M2
St Peter's Gdns WNWD SE27 139 G7
St Peter's Gv HMSMTH W6 118 A2
St Peter's Pth WALTH E17 69 L5
St Peter's Rd CROY/NA CR0 172 D6
E/WMO/HCT KT8 151 G7
ED N9 50 B3
HMSMTH W6 118 A3
KUT KT1 153 G5
STHL UB1 97 G4
TWK TW1 134 B2
UX/CGN UB8 94 D4
St Peter's Sq BETH E2 104 A1
HMSMTH W6 117 M3
St Peter's St IS N1 6 D4
SAND/SEL CR2 172 D7
St Peter's Ter FUL/PGN SW6 118 F5
St Peter's Vls HMSMTH W6 118 A2
St Peter's Wy EA W5 98 D4
HYS/HAR UB3 113 K3
IS N1 7 K2
St Philip's Av WPK KT4 169 H4
St Philip Sq VX/NE SW8 120 B7
St Philip's Rd HACK E8 86 A6
SURB KT6 167 K1
St Philip St VX/NE SW8 120 B7
St Philip's Wy IS N1 6 F4
St Pinnock Av STA TW18 148 A4
St Quentin Rd WELL DA16 125 M8
St Quintin Av NKENS W10 100 C4
St Quintin Rd PLSTW E13 106 B2
St Raphael's Wy WLSDN NW10 81 J5
St Regis Cl MUSWH N10 66 B3
St Ronans Cl EBAR EN4 34 D3
St Ronans Crs WFD IG8 70 A1
St Rule St VX/NE SW8 120 C7
St Saviour's Rd
BRXS/STRHM SW2 138 F2
CROY/NA CR0 172 C1
Saints Cl WNWD SE27 139 H8
Saints Dr FSTGT E7 88 D5
St Silas Pl KTTN NW5 84 A6
St Simon's Av PUT/ROE SW15 136 C2
St Stephen's Av SHB W12 100 B8
WALTH E17 69 J6
WEA W13 98 B5
St Stephen's Cl STHL UB1 97 G4
WALTH E17 69 H6
St Stephen's Crs BAY/PAD W2 8 B4
THHTH CR7 157 G6
St Stephen's Gdns BAY/PAD W2 8 B4
TWK TW1 134 C3
St Stephen's Gv LEW SE13 123 J8
St Stephen's Ms BAY/PAD W2 8 B3
St Stephens Rd BAR EN5 33 K8
BOW E3 86 E8
EHAM E6 88 C7
HSLW TW3 133 G3
LEY E10 69 H6
PEND EN3 37 K2
WDR/YW UB7 94 D7
WEA W13 98 B5
St Stephen's Ter VX/NE SW8 120 F5
St Swithin's La MANHO EC4N 13 G6
St Swithun's Rd LEW SE13 141 K3
St Theresa Cl EPSOM KT18 180 C7
St Theresa's Rd
EBED/NFELT TW14 131 M1
St Thomas Cl SURB KT6 167 M3
St Thomas Ct BXLY DA5 145 G4
St Thomas' Dr PIN HA5 60 E2
STMC/STPC BR5 176 C3
St Thomas Gdns IL IG1 89 J6
St Thomas Rd BELV DA17 109 J8
CAN/RD E16 106 A5
CHSWK W4 117 J5
STHGT/OAK N14 48 D2
St Thomas's Gdns KTTN NW5 84 A6
St Thomas's Rd FSBYPK N4 85 G2
WLSDN NW10 81 L8
St Thomas's Sq HOM E9 86 C7
St Thomas St STHWK SE1 13 H9
St Thomas's Wy FUL/PGN SW6 118 F5
St Ursula Gv PIN HA5 60 D6
St Ursula Rd STHL UB1 97 G5
St Vincent Cl WNWD SE27 157 H1
St Vincent Rd WHTN TW2 133 J3
WOT/HER KT12 165 H5
St Vincents Rd DART DA1 147 G3
St Vincent St MHST W1U 10 B3
St Vincent's Wy
POTB/CUF EN6 23 J6
St Wilfrid's Cl EBAR EN4 34 E8
St Wilfrid's Rd EBAR EN4 34 D8
St Winefride's Av MNPK E12 88 F5
St Winifred's Cl CHIG IG7 53 J7
St Winifred's Rd TEDD TW11 152 B2
Saladin Dr PUR RM19 129 G2
Salamanca Pl LBTH SE11 17 L6
Salamanca St LBTH SE11 17 L6
Salamander Cl
KUTN/CMB KT2 152 C1
Salamons Wy RAIN RM13 109 L5
Salcombe Dr CHDH RM6 72 F7
MRDN SM4 169 K3
Salcombe Gdns MLHL NW7 46 C8
Salcombe Rd ASHF TW15 130 E8
STNW/STAM N16 85 L5
WALTH E17 68 F8
Salcombe Wy RSLP HA4 78 A2
Salcot Crs CROY/NA CR0 186 C5
Salcott Rd BTSEA SW11 137 L2
CROY/NA CR0 171 L5
Salehurst Cl KTN/HRWW/W HA3 62 E6
Salehurst Rd BROCKY SE4 140 F3
Salem Pl CROY/NA CR0 172 C5
Salem Rd BAY/PAD W2 8 D6
Sale Pl BAY/PAD W2 9 J4
Sale St BETH E2 104 A3
Salford Rd BAL SW12 138 D5
Salisbury Av BARK IG11 89 K7
BELMT SM2 169 M8
FNCH N3 64 F3
Salisbury Cl POTB/CUF EN6 23 J5
WALW SE17 19 G5
WPK KT4 168 F5
Salisbury Ct EMB EC4Y 12 B5
EMB EC4Y 12 C5
Salisbury Crs CHES/WCR EN8 26 D5
Salisbury Gdns
WIM/MER SW19 154 E3
Salisbury Pl MBLAR W1H 9 L2
Salisbury Rd BAR EN5 33 L6
BNSTD SM7 182 B8
BXLY DA5 145 G5
CAR SM5 170 F8
CHING E4 51 G5
CROY/NA CR0 173 G1
DAGE RM10 92 B6
ED N9 50 A5
FELT TW13 132 C5
FSBYPK N4 67 H6
FSTGT E7 88 A6
GDMY/SEVK IG3 89 L2
GPK RM2 74 B6
HAYES BR2 160 E8
HOR/WEW KT19 168 D6
HRW HA1 61 K6
HSLWW TW4 114 C8
LEY E10 87 J2
MNPK E12 88 D5
NWDGN UB2 114 E2
NWMAL KT3 153 K6
PEND EN3 37 M2
PIN HA5 60 A5
RCH/KEW TW9 134 E1
RDART DA2 147 J5
UX/CGN UB8 94 B1
WALTH E17 69 J6
WATN WD24 29 H3
WDGN N22 67 H3
WEA W13 98 B8
WIM/MER SW19 154 E3
Salisbury St ACT W3 99 J8
STJWD NW8 9 J1
Salisbury Ter PECK SE15 122 C8
Salix Cl SUN TW16 150 B3
Salmen Rd PLSTW E13 105 M1
Salmon La POP/IOD E14 104 E5
Salmon Rd BELV DA17 127 G3
DART DA1 128 F8
Salmons Rd CHSGTN KT9 167 L8
ED N9 50 A3
Salmon St CDALE/KGS NW9 63 J7
CDALE/KGS NW9 81 J1
POP/IOD E14 104 F5
WBLY HA9 81 J2
Salomons Rd PLSTW E13 106 C4
Salop Rd WALTH E17 68 D7
Saltash Cl SUT SM1 169 M6
Saltash Rd BARK/HLT IG6 71 K1
WELL DA16 126 C6
Saltbox Hl BH/WHM TN16 187 H6
Saltcoats Rd CHSWK W4 99 L8
Saltcroft Cl WBLY HA9 81 H1
Salter Cl RYLN/HDSTN HA2 78 F4
Salterford Rd TOOT SW17 156 A2
Salter Rd BERM/RHTH SE16 104 E8
Salters Cl RKW/CH/CXG WD3 40 E3
Salters' Hall Ct MANHO EC4N 13 G6
Salter's Hl NRWD SE19 157 K1
Salters Rd NKENS W10 100 D3
WALTH E17 69 K5
Salter St POP/IOD E14 105 G6
WLSDN NW10 100 A2
Salterton Rd HOLWY N7 84 E3
Saltford Cl ERITH DA8 127 L3
Salt Hill Cl UX/CGN UB8 76 D5
Saltley Cl EHAM E6 106 E5
Saltram Crs MV/WKIL W9 100 F2
Saltwell St POP/IOD E14 105 G6
Saltwood Cl ORP BR6 177 J6
Salusbury Rd
KIL/WHAMP NW6 100 F1
Salvador TOOT SW17 155 L1
Salvia Gdns GFD/PVL UB6 98 A1
Salvin Rd PUT/ROE SW15 118 D8
Salway Cl WFD IG8 70 A1
Salway Pl SRTFD E15 87 K6
Salway Rd SRTFD E15 87 K6
Samantha Cl WALTH E17 68 F8
Sam Bartram Cl CHARL SE7 124 C3
Samels Ct HMSMTH W6 118 A3
Samford St STJWD NW8 9 J1
Samos Rd PGE/AN SE20 158 B5
Sampson Av BAR EN5 33 K8
Sampson Cl BELV DA17 126 D2
Sampson St WAP E1W 104 A7
Samson St PLSTW E13 106 C1
Samuel Cl HACK E8 7 M3
NWCR SE14 122 D4
WOOL/PLUM SE18 124 E2
Samuel St WOOL/PLUM SE18 124 F2
Sancroft Cl CRICK NW2 82 B3
Sancroft Rd KTN/HRWW/W HA3 61 M3
Sancroft St LBTH SE11 17 M7
Sanctuary Cl DART DA1 146 C3
DEN/HRF UB9 58 C1
Sanctuary Rd
STWL/WRAY TW19 131 G3
Sanctuary St STHWK SE1 18 F2
The Sanctuary BXLY DA5 144 D3
WEST SW1P 17 H3
Sandall Cl EA W5 98 E3
Sandall Rd EA W5 98 E3
KTTN NW5 84 C6
Sandal Rd NWMAL KT3 153 L7
UED N18 50 A7
Sandal St SRTFD E15 87 L8
Sandalwood Cl WCHPL E1 104 E3
Sandalwood Dr RSLP HA4 59 J8
Sandalwood Rd FELT TW13 132 B7
Sandbach Pl WOOL/PLUM SE18 125 J3
Sandbourne Av
WIM/MER SW19 155 H6
Sandbourne Rd BROCKY SE4 122 E7
Sandbrook Cl MLHL NW7 45 K8
Sandbrook Rd STNW/STAM N16 85 L3
Sandby Gn ELTH/MOT SE9 124 E8
Sandcliff Rd ERITH DA8 127 K2
Sandcroft Cl PLMGR N13 49 H8
Sandell's Av ASHF TW15 131 J8
Sandell St STHWK SE1 18 A1
Sanders Cl HPTN TW12 151 J1
Sandersfield Rd BNSTD SM7 182 A8
Sanders La MLHL NW7 64 C1
Sanderson Cl KTTN NW5 84 B4
Sanderson Rd UX/CGN UB8 76 C6
Sanderstead Av CRICK NW2 82 E2
Sanderstead Cl BAL SW12 138 C4
Sanderstead Court Av
SAND/SEL CR2 185 G6
Sanderstead Hl SAND/SEL CR2 184 E4
Sanderstead Rd LEY E10 86 E1
SAND/SEL CR2 184 D1
STMC/STPC BR5 177 H1
Sandfield Gdns THHTH CR7 157 H6
Sandfield Pl THHTH CR7 157 J6
Sandfield Rd THHTH CR7 157 H6
Sandford Av WDGN N22 67 H2
Sandford Rd BXLYHS DA6 144 E1
EHAM E6 106 F2
HAYES BR2 160 A7
Sandford Rw WALW SE17 19 G7
Sandford St FUL/PGN SW6 119 H5
Sandgate Cl ROMW/RG RM7 73 J8
Sandgate La WAND/EARL SW18 137 L5
Sandgate Rd WELL DA16 126 C5
Sandgate St PECK SE15 122 B4
Sandhills WLGTN SM6 171 K6
Sandhurst Av BRYLDS KT5 168 B2
RYLN/HDSTN HA2 61 H7
Sandhurst Cl CDALE/KGS NW9 63 G4
SAND/SEL CR2 184 E2
Sandhurst Dr GDMY/SEVK IG3 89 M4
Sandhurst Rd BFN/LL DA15 143 M7
BXLY DA5 144 D2
CAT SE6 141 K5
CDALE/KGS NW9 63 G4
ED N9 50 C1
ORP BR6 177 G5
Sandhurst Wy SAND/SEL CR2 184 E1
Sandiford Rd CHEAM SM3 169 M4
Sandiland Crs HAYES BR2 174 F4
Sandilands CROY/NA CR0 173 G5
Sandilands Rd FUL/PGN SW6 119 H6
Sandison St PECK SE15 122 A8
Sandland St GINN WC1R 11 M3
Sandling Ri ELTH/MOT SE9 143 G7
Sandlings Cl PECK SE15 122 B7
Sandmere Rd CLAP SW4 138 E1
Sandon Cl ESH/CLAY KT10 166 D2
Sandon Rd CHES/WCR EN8 26 C3
Sandow Crs HYS/HAR UB3 113 M1
Sandown Av DAGE RM10 91 J6
ESH/CLAY KT10 166 C7
HCH RM12 92 D2
Sandown Cl HEST TW5 114 A6
Sandown Ct DAGE RM10 91 J6
Sandown Dr CAR SM5 183 G2
Sandown Ga ESH/CLAY KT10 166 D4
Sandown Rd ESH/CLAY KT10 166 C6
SNWD SE25 158 B8
WATN WD24 29 J3
Sandown Wy NTHLT UB5 78 E6
Sandpiper Cl
BERM/RHTH SE16 104 F8
WALTH E17 68 D1
Sandpiper Dr ERITH DA8 128 B5
Sandpiper Rd SAND/SEL CR2 185 K4
Sandpiper Wy STMC/STPC BR5 162 D7
Sandpit La BRW CM14 57 M1
Sandpit Pl CHARL SE7 124 E3
Sandpit Rd BMLY BR1 159 L1
Sandpits Rd CROY/NA CR0 173 K6
RCHPK/HAM TW10 134 D6
Sandra Cl HSLW TW3 133 H2
WDGN N22 67 J2
Sandridge Cl HRW HA1 61 L5
Sandringham Av RYNPK SW20 154 E4
Sandringham Cl EN EN1 36 E5
WIM/MER SW19 136 D5
Sandringham Crs
RYLN/HDSTN HA2 79 G3
Sandringham Dr ASHF TW15 130 D8
WELL DA16 125 L7
Sandringham Gdns
BARK/HLT IG6 71 J4
CEND/HSY/T N8 66 E7
HEST TW5 114 A6
NFNCH/WDSP N12 47 K8
Sandringham Rd BARK IG11 89 M6
BMLY BR1 160 A1
CRICK NW2 82 B5
CROY/NA CR0 157 J8
FSTGT E7 88 C5
GLDGN NW11 64 E8
HACK E8 85 M5
LEY E10 69 K8
NTHLT UB5 79 G7
POTB/CUF EN6 23 H3
WATN WD24 29 H2
WDGN N22 67 J4
WPK KT4 169 G5
Sandringham Wy
CHES/WCR EN8 26 C7
Sandrock Pl CROY/NA CR0 173 K6
Sandrock Rd LEW SE13 123 G8
Sandroyd Wy COB KT11 178 A6
Sands End La FUL/PGN SW6 119 H6
Sandstone Rd LEE/GVPK SE12 142 B6
Sands Wy WFD IG8 52 F8
Sandtoft Rd CHARL SE7 124 B4
Sandway Rd STMC/STPC BR5 162 C7
Sandwell Crs
KIL/WHAMP NW6 83 G6
Sandwich St STPAN WC1H 5 J8
Sandwick Cl MLHL NW7 64 A1
Sandy Bury ORP BR6 176 D5
Sandycombe Rd
EBED/NFELT TW14 132 A5
RCH/KEW TW9 117 G7
Sandycoombe Rd TWK TW1 134 C3
Sandycroft ABYW SE2 126 A4
Sandy Cft EW KT17 181 J3
Sandy Dr COB KT11 178 A4
EBED/NFELT TW14 131 L5
Sandy Hill Av
WOOL/PLUM SE18 125 H3
Sandy Hill La
WOOL/PLUM SE18 125 H2
Sandyhill Rd IL IG1 89 H4
Sandy Hill Rd WLGTN SM6 183 J2
WOOL/PLUM SE18 125 H3
Sandy La BELMT SM2 181 L2
BUSH WD23 30 C6
E/WMO/HCT KT8 152 B4
KTN/HRWW/W HA3 62 F7
MTCM CR4 156 A4
NTHWD HA6 41 M4
ORP BR6 177 G2
RCHPK/HAM TW10 134 C6
SOCK/AV RM15 111 G6
STMC/STPC BR5 162 D3
TEDD TW11 152 A3
WOT/HER KT12 165 H1
Sandy La North WLGTN SM6 171 K7
Sandy La South WLGTN SM6 171 K8
Sandy Lodge La NTHWD HA6 41 K4
Sandy Lodge Rd
RKW/CH/CXG WD3 41 H4
Sandy Lodge Wy NTHWD HA6 41 L7
Sandymount Av STAN HA7 44 C7
Sandy Rdg CHST BR7 161 G2
Sandy Rd GLDGN NW11 83 H2
HAMP NW3 83 H2
Sandy's Rw WCHPL E1 13 K3
Sandy Wy COB KT11 178 A5
CROY/NA CR0 173 M5
WOT/HER KT12 164 F3
Sanford La STNW/STAM N16 85 M2
STNW/STAM N16 85 M2
Sanford St NWCR SE14 122 E4
Sanford Ter STNW/STAM N16 85 M3
Sanger Av CHSGTN KT9 167 M7
Sangley Rd CAT SE6 141 H5
SNWD SE25 157 L7
Sangora Rd BTSEA SW11 137 K1
Sansom Rd WAN E11 87 M2
Sansom St CMBW SE5 121 K5
Sans Wk CLKNW EC1R 6 C9
Santers La POTB/CUF EN6 22 E6
Santley St BRXS/STRHM SW2 138 E1
Santos Rd PUT/ROE SW15 137 G2
Saphora Cl ORP BR6 176 D7
Sapphire Cl BCTR RM8 90 C1
Sapphire Rd DEPT SE8 122 E2
Saracen Cl CROY/NA CR0 172 D1
Saracen St POP/IOD E14 105 G5
Sarah St BETH E2 7 K7
Saratoga Rd CLPT E5 86 C4
Sardinia St HOL/ALD WC2B 11 L5
Sargeants Cl UX/CGN UB8 94 D2
Sarita Cl KTN/HRWW/W HA3 61 K3
Sark Cl HEST TW5 115 G5
Sarnesfield Rd ENC/FH EN2 36 D6
Sarre Av HCH RM12 92 C6
Sarre Rd CRICK NW2 82 F5
Sarsen Av HSLW TW3 114 F7
Sarsfeld Rd BAL SW12 137 M5
Sarsfield Rd GFD/PVL UB6 98 B1
Sartor Rd PECK SE15 140 D1
Sarum Gn WEY KT13 164 E5
Satanita Cl CAN/RD E16 106 D5
Satchell Md CDALE/KGS NW9 63 K4
Satchwell Rd BETH E2 104 A2
Sauls Gn WAN E11 87 L3
Saunders Cl CHES/WCR EN8 26 C1
Saunders Ness Rd
POP/IOD E14 123 K2
Saunders Rd HGDN/ICK UB10 76 F7
WOOL/PLUM SE18 125 M3
Saunders St LBTH SE11 18 A5
Saunders Wy DART DA1 146 F6
THMD SE28 108 B6
Saunderton Rd ALP/SUD HA0 80 B5
Saunton Av HYS/HAR UB3 113 M5
Saunton Rd HCH RM12 92 A2
Savage Gdns EHAM E6 106 F5
TWRH EC3N 13 K6
Savay Cl DEN/HRF UB9 58 A8
Savay La DEN/HRF UB9 58 A8
Savernake Rd ED N9 50 A1
HAMP NW3 83 M4
Savile Cl NWMAL KT3 153 L8
THDIT KT7 166 F3
Savile Gdns CROY/NA CR0 172 F4
Savile Rw CONDST W1S 10 E6
Saville Crs ASHF TW15 149 K2
Saville Rd CAN/RD E16 106 E7
CHDH RM6 72 F7
CHSWK W4 117 K1
TWK TW1 133 M5
Saville Rw HAYES BR2 174 F3
Savill Gdns RYNPK SW20 154 A5
Savill Rw WFD IG8 51 M8
Savona Cl WIM/MER SW19 154 D3
Savona St VX/NE SW8 120 C5
Savoy Av HYS/HAR UB3 113 L3
Savoy Cl DEN/HRF UB9 58 D3
EDGW HA8 45 G7
SRTFD E15 87 L8
Savoy Ct TPL/STR WC2R 11 K7
Savoy Hl TPL/STR WC2R 11 L7
Savoy Pl CHCR WC2N 11 K7
Savoy Rd DART DA1 146 C2
Savoy Rw TPL/STR WC2R 11 L6
Savoy Steps TPL/STR WC2R 11 L7
Savoy St TPL/STR WC2R 11 L6
Savoy Wy TPL/STR WC2R 11 L7
Sawbill Cl YEAD UB4 96 D4
Sawkins Cl WIM/MER SW19 136 D6
Sawley Rd SHB W12 100 A7
Sawtry Cl CAR SM5 170 D2
Sawtry Wy BORE WD6 32 A3
Sawyer Cl ED N9 50 A4
Sawyers La POTB/CUF EN6 22 D7
Sawyers Lawn WEA W13 97 M5
Sawyer St STHWK SE1 18 E1
Saxby Rd BRXS/STRHM SW2 138 E4
Saxham Rd BARK IG11 89 L8
Saxlingham Rd CHING E4 51 K5
Saxon Av FELT TW13 132 F6
Saxonbury Av SUN TW16 150 B6
Saxonbury Cl MTCM CR4 155 K6
Saxonbury Gdns SURB KT6 167 J3
Saxon Cl HARH RM3 74 F3
SURB KT6 167 K1
UX/CGN UB8 94 E4
WALTH E17 69 G8
Saxon Ct BORE WD6 31 L4
Saxon Dr ACT W3 99 H5
Saxonfield Cl
BRXS/STRHM SW2 138 F4
Saxon Rd ASHF TW15 149 K2
BMLY BR1 159 M3
BOW E3 104 F1
CROY/NA CR0 157 K8
EHAM E6 106 F3
IL IG1 89 H6
RDART DA2 146 E8
STHL UB1 96 E6
WBLY HA9 81 J3
WDGN N22 67 H2
WOT/HER KT12 165 K5
Saxon Wy STHGT/OAK N14 48 D1
WDR/YW UB7 112 C4
Saxony Pde HYS/HAR UB3 95 J4
Saxton Cl LEW SE13 123 K8
Saxville Rd STMC/STPC BR5 162 B6
Sayes Court Rd
STMC/STPC BR5 162 A6
Sayes Court St DEPT SE8 122 F3
Scadbury Gdns
STMC/STPC BR5 162 A5
Scads Hill Cl ORP BR6 176 F1
Scala St FITZ W1T 10 F2
Scales Rd TOTM N17 67 M4
Scammell Wy WATW WD18 41 M1
Scandrett St WAP E1W 104 B7
Scarborough Cl BELMT SM2 181 M3
Scarborough Rd ED N9 50 C2
FSBYPK N4 67 G8
WAN E11 87 K1
Scarborough St WCHPL E1 13 M5
Scarbrook Rd CROY/NA CR0 172 C5
Scarle Rd ALP/SUD HA0 80 D6
Scarlet Cl STMC/STPC BR5 162 B7
Scarlet Rd CAT SE6 141 L7
Scarsbrook Rd BKHTH/KID SE3 124 D8
Scarsdale Pl KENS W8 14 C3
Scarsdale Rd RYLN/HDSTN HA2 79 J3
Scarsdale Vls KENS W8 14 B4
Scarth Rd BARN SW13 117 M8
Scawen Cl CAR SM5 171 G6
Scawen Rd DEPT SE8 122 E3
Scawfell St BETH E2 7 M6
Scaynes Link
NFNCH/WDSP N12 47 G6
Sceptre Rd BETH E2 104 C2
Scholars Rd BAL SW12 138 C5
CHING E4 51 J3
Scholefield Rd ARCH N19 84 D1
Schonfeld Sq
STNW/STAM N16 85 K1
School Cl DART DA1 145 M1
School House La TEDD TW11 152 B3
Schoolhouse La WAP E1W 104 D6
School La BUSH WD23 43 H2
CHIG IG7 53 M6
KUT KT1 152 C4
LCOL/BKTW AL2 21 M7
PIN HA5 60 E5
SHPTN TW17 164 B1
SURB KT6 167 M3
WELL DA16 126 B8
School Md ABLGY WD5 20 D5
School Pas KUT KT1 152 F5
STHL UB1 96 F7
School Rd ASHF TW15 149 H2
CHST BR7 161 J4
DAGE RM10 91 G8
E/WMO/HCT KT8 151 K7
HPTN TW12 151 J2
HSLW TW3 115 J8
KUT KT1 152 C4
POTB/CUF EN6 23 J3
WDR/YW UB7 112 D4
WLSDN NW10 99 K3
School Road Av HPTN TW12 151 J2
School Wy BCTR RM8 90 B3
Schoolway NFNCH/WDSP N12 47 K8
Schooner Ct GRH DA9 147 J1
Schubert Rd BORE WD6 44 D1
PUT/ROE SW15 136 F2
Sclater St WCHPL E1 7 L9
Scoles Crs BRXS/STRHM SW2 139 G5
Scoresby St STHWK SE1 12 C9
Scorton Av GFD/PVL UB6 98 A1
Scotch Common WEA W13 98 A4
Scot Gv PIN HA5 60 D1
Scotia Rd BRXS/STRHM SW2 139 G4
Scotland Gn TOTM N17 67 M3
Scotland Green Rd PEND EN3 37 K8
Scotland Green Rd North
PEND EN3 37 K7
Scotland Rd BKHH IG9 52 C3
Scots Cl STWL/WRAY TW19 130 D5
Scotsdale Cl BELMT SM2 181 L1
CHST BR7 161 L7
Scotsdale Rd LEE/GVPK SE12 142 B2
Scotshall La WARL CR6 186 C8
Scots Hl RKW/CH/CXG WD3 40 F1
Scots Hill Cl RKW/CH/CXG WD3 40 F1
Scots Mill La RKW/CH/CXG WD3 40 F1
Scotswood St CLKNW EC1R 6 B9
Scott Cl HOR/WEW KT19 168 C7
STRHM/NOR SW16 156 F4

WDR/YW UB7 .... 112 F2
Scott Crs ERITH DA8 ...... 127 M6
  RYLN/HDSTN HA2 .... 79 H1
Scott Ellis Gdns STJWD NW8 .... 3 C8
Scottes La BCTR RM8 .... 90 D1 🗓
Scott Farm Cl THDIT KT7 .... 167 H3
Scott Gdns HEST TW5 ...... 114 D5 🗓
Scott Lidgett Crs
  BERM/RHTH SE16 .... 104 A8
  SUN TW16 .... 149 L3
Scotts Cl HCH RM12 .... 92 C5 🗓
Scotts Dr HPTN TW12 ...... 151 H3
Scotts Farm Rd
  HOR/WEW KT19 .... 168 C8
Scott's La HAYES BR2 ...... 159 K6
Scotts Rd BMLY BR1 .... 160 A3
  LEY E10 .... 87 J1
  NWDGN UB2 .... 114 C1
  SHB W12 .... 100 B8
Scott St WCHPL E1 .... 104 B3
Scotts Wy SUN TW16 ...... 149 L3
Scottswood Cl BUSH WD23 .. 29 L5 🗓
Scottswood Rd BUSH WD23 .. 29 L5
Scott Trimmer Wy HEST .... 114 E7 🗓
Scottwell Dr CDALE/KGS NW9 .. 63 M6
Scoulding Rd CAN/RD E16 .. 105 M5
Scouler St POP/IOD E14 .... 105 K6 🗓
Scout La CLAP SW4 .... 120 C8 🗓
Scovell Rd STHWK SE1 ...... 18 E2
Scratton Ter BARK IG11 .... 108 D1
Scriven St HACK E8 .... 7 M1
Scrooby St CAT SE6 .... 141 H3 🗓
Scrubs La WLSDN NW10 .... 100 B4
Scrutton St SDTCH EC2A 13 J1
Scutari Rd EDUL SE22 ...... 140 B2
Scylla Crs HTHAIR TW6 .... 131 H4
Scylla Rd HTHAIR TW6 ...... 131 H5 🗓
  PECK SE15 .... 122 B8
Seabright St BETH E2 ...... 104 B2 🗓
Seabrook Dr WWKM BR4 .... 174 E4
Seabrook Gdns ROMW/RG RM7.. 73 G8
Seabrook Rd BCTR RM8 .... 90 D3
  KGLGY WD4 .... 20 D1
Seaburn Cl RAIN RM13 .... 109 L2 🗓
Seacole Cl ACT W3 .... 99 K5
Seacourt Rd ABYW SE2 .... 108 D8
Seacroft Gdns OXHEY WD19 .. 42 D5
Seafield Rd FBAR/BDGN N11 .. 48 D6
Seaford Cl RSLP HA4 ...... 77 K1 🗓
Seaford Rd EN EN1 .... 36 E7
  SEVS/STOTM N15 .... 67 K6
  WALTH E17 .... 69 H4
  WEA W13 .... 98 B7
Seaford St STPAN WC1H 5 K8
Seaforth Av NWMAL KT3 .... 154 B8
Seaforth Crs HBRY N5 ...... 85 J5
Seaforth Dr CHES/WCR EN8 .. 26 D7
Seaforth Gdns HOR/WEW KT19.. 168 F6
  WCHMH N21 .... 48 F2
  WFD IG8 .... 52 C7
Seager Pl BOW E3 .... 104 F4 🗓
Seagrave Rd FUL/PGN SW6 .. 14 B9
Seagry Rd WAN E11 .... 70 A7
Sealand Rd HTHAIR TW6 .... 131 G3
Seal St HACK E8 .... 85 M4 🗓
  HACK E8 .... 85 M4 🗓
Searles Cl BTSEA SW11 .... 119 L5
Searles Rd STHWK SE1 ...... 19 H5
Sears St CMBW SE5 .... 121 K5 🗓
Seasprite Cl NTHLT UB5 .... 96 D2 🗓
Seaton Av GDMY/SEVK IG3 .. 89 L5
Seaton Cl PLSTW E13 ...... 106 A3 🗓
  PUT/ROE SW15 .... 136 B4
  WHTN TW2 .... 133 K3
Seaton Dr ASHF TW15 ...... 130 E6
Seaton Rd ALP/SUD HA0 .... 98 E1 🗓
  DART DA1 .... 146 A4
  HYS/HAR UB3 .... 113 K2
  MTCM CR4 .... 155 L5
  WELL DA16 .... 126 C5
  WHTN TW2 .... 133 J3
Seaton St UED N18 .... 50 A7
Sebastian St FSBYE EC1V 6 D8
Sebastopol Rd ED N9 ...... 50 A6
Sebbon St IS N1 .... 6 D2
Sebergham Gv MLHL NW7 .... 64 A1 🗓
Sebert Rd FSTGT E7 .... 88 B5
Sebright Rd BAR EN5 ...... 33 K5
Secker Crs KTN/HRWW/W HA3 .. 61 J2
Secker St STHWK SE1 ...... 12 A9
Second Av ACT W3 .... 99 M7
  CHDH RM6 .... 72 C6
  DAGE RM10 .... 109 H1
  EN EN1 .... 36 F8
  GSTN WD25 .... 21 K8
  HDN NW4 .... 64 D5
  HYS/HAR UB3 .... 95 M7
  MNPK E12 .... 88 E4
  MORT/ESHN SW14 .... 117 L8
  NKENS W10 .... 100 E3
  PLSTW E13 .... 106 A2
  UED N18 .... 50 C6
  WALTH E17 .... 69 G6 🗓
  WBLY HA9 .... 80 D2
  WOT/HER KT12 .... 165 H1
Second Cl E/WMO/HCT KT8 .. 151 H7
Second Cross Rd WHTN TW2 .. 133 K6
Second Wy WBLY HA9 ...... 81 H4
Sedan Wy WALW SE17 ...... 19 J7
Sedcombe Cl SCUP DA14 .... 144 C8 🗓
Sedcote Rd PEND EN3 ...... 37 J8
Sedding St KTBR SW1X 16 A5
Seddon Rd MRDN SM4 ...... 155 K8
Seddon St FSBYW WC1X 5 L8
Sedgebrook Rd
  BKHTH/KID SE3 .... 124 D7
Sedgecombe Av
  KTN/HRWW/W HA3 .... 62 C6
Sedgefield Cl HARH RM3 .... 56 F6
Sedgefield Crs HARH RM3 .. 56 F7
Sedgeford Rd SHB W12 .... 99 M7
Sedgehill Rd CAT SE6 ...... 159 G1
Sedgemere Av EFNCH N2 .... 65 J4
Sedgemere Rd ABYW SE2 .. 126 C1

Sedgemoor Dr DAGE RM10 .. 91 G4
Sedge Rd TOTM N17 .... 68 C1
Sedgeway CAT SE6 .... 141 M5
Sedgewood Cl HAYES BR2 .. 174 F2
Sedgmoor Pl CMBW SE5 .... 121 L5
Sedgwick Av HGDN/ICK UB10.. 77 H7
Sedgwick Rd LEY E10 ...... 87 J2
Sedgwick St HOM E9 .... 86 D5

Serle St LINN WC2A 11 M4
Sermon Dr SWLY BR8 ...... 163 J6
Serpentine Rd BAY/PAD W2 .. 9 J6
The Service Rd POTB/CUF EN6.. 23 G5
Service Route No 1 SRTFD E15.. 87 K7
Service Route No 3
  SRTFD E15 .... 87 K6 🗓
Serviden Dr BMLY BR1 .... 160 D4
Setchell Rd STHWK SE1 .... 19 L5
Seton Gdns DAGW RM9 .... 90 C7
Settle Rd HARH RM3 .... 57 G6
Settles St WCHPL E1 ...... 104 A5 🗓
Settrington Rd FUL/PGN SW6.. 119 H7
Seven Acres CAR SM5 ...... 170 E4 🗓
  NTHWD HA6 .... 42 A8
Seven Kings Rd GDMY/SEVK IG3.. 89 L1
Sevenoaks Cl BELMT SM2 .. 182 A3
  HARH RM3 .... 56 C6
Sevenoaks Rd BROCKY SE4 .. 140 F3
  ORP BR6 .... 176 F6
Sevenoaks Wy STMC/STPC BR5.. 162 C5
Seven Sisters Rd FSBYPK N4.. 85 H1
  HOLWY N7 .... 84 F3
  SEVS/STOTM N15 .... 67 K7
Seventh Av HYS/HAR UB3 .. 95 A7
  MNPK E12 .... 88 F4
Severnake Cl POP/IOD E14 .. 123 G2
Severn Av GPK RM2 .... 74 B4
Severn Dr EN EN1 .... 37 G3
  ESH/CLAY KT10 .... 167 G4
  UPMR RM14 .... 75 K7
  WOT/HER KT12 .... 165 K4 🗓
Severn Rd SOCK/AV RM15 .. 111 J5
Severn Wy GSTN WD25 ...... 21 J7
  WLSDN NW10 .... 81 M5
Severus Rd BTSEA SW11 .... 137 L1
Seville Ms IS N1 .... 7 J2
Seville St KTBR SW1X 15 M2
Sevington Rd HDN NW4 .... 64 B7
Sevington St MV/WKIL W9 .. 8 C1
Seward Rd BECK BR3 ...... 158 D5
  HNWL W7 .... 98 A8
Sewardstone Rd BETH E2 .. 104 C1
  CHING E4 .... 38 B7
  WAB EN9 .... 27 J7
Sewardstone St WAB EN9 .. 27 J7
Sewardstone Wy WAB EN9 .. 38 C1
Seward St FSBYE EC1V 6 D9
Sewdley St CLPT E5 .... 86 D3
Sewell Rd ABYW SE2 ...... 108 A8
  THMD SE28 .... 108 C7
Sewell St PLSTW E13 ...... 106 A2
Sextant Av POP/IOD E14 .... 123 K2
Sexton Cl RAIN RM13 ...... 91 M8 🗓
Seymer Rd ROM RM1 .... 73 K4
Seymour Av EW KT17 ...... 181 H2
  MRDN SM4 .... 169 K2
  TOTM N17 .... 68 A3
Seymour Cl E/WMO/HCT KT8.. 151 J8
  PIN HA5 .... 60 F7
Seymour Dr HAYES BR2 .... 175 M3
Seymour Gdns BROCKY SE4 .. 122 D8
  BRYLDS KT5 .... 152 F8
  FELT TW13 .... 132 B8
  IL IG1 .... 88 F1
  RSLP HA4 .... 78 D1
  TWK TW1 .... 134 B4
Seymour Ms EW KT17 ...... 181 G3 🗓
  MBLAR W1H 10 A4
Seymour Pl MBLAR W1H 9 K3
  SNWD SE25 .... 158 B7 🗓
Seymour Rd CAR SM5 ...... 171 C7 🗓
  CEND/HSY/T N8 .... 67 H6
  CHING E4 .... 51 H3
  CHSWK W4 .... 117 J2 🗓
  E/WMO/HCT KT8 .... 151 J8
  ED N9 .... 50 B4
  EHAM E6 .... 88 D8
  FNCH N3 .... 65 H1
  HPTN TW12 .... 151 J1
  KUT KT1 .... 152 D4
  LEY E10 .... 86 F1
  MTCM CR4 .... 171 G2
  WAND/EARL SW18 .... 136 F4
  WIM/MER SW19 .... 136 D7
Seymour St BAY/PAD W2 .... 9 L5
Seymour St PGE/AN SE20 .. 158 B4
Seymour Vls PGE/AN SE20 .. 158 B4
Seymour Wk WBPTN SW10 .. 14 E9
Seymour Wy SUN TW16 .... 149 L2
Seyssel St POP/IOD E14 .... 123 K2 🗓
Shaa Rd ACT W3 .... 99 K6
Shacklegate La TEDD TW11 .. 133 L8
Shackleton Cl FSTH SE23 .. 140 B6
Shackleton Rd STHL UB1 .. 96 F6
Shackleton Wy ABLGY WD5 .. 21 G5 🗓
Shacklewell La HACK E8 .... 85 M4
Shacklewell Rd
  STNW/STAM N16 .... 85 M4 🗓
Shacklewell Rw HACK E8 .. 85 M4 🗓
Shacklewell St BETH E2 .... 7 M9
Shadbolt Cl WPK KT4 ...... 168 F4
Shadwell Dr NTHLT UB5 .... 96 F2
Shadwell Gdns WCHPL E1 .. 104 C6 🗓
Shadwell Pierhead
  WAP E1W .... 104 C6 🗓
Shady Bush Cl BUSH WD23 .. 43 J2 🗓
Shady La WAT WD17 .... 29 H5 🗓
Shaef Wy TEDD TW11 ...... 152 A3
Shafter Rd DAGE RM10 .... 91 J6
Shaftesbury LOU IG10 ...... 39 K6 🗓
Shaftesbury Av BAR EN5 .. 34 C7
  EBED/NFELT TW14 .... 132 A3
  KTN/HRWW/W HA3 .... 62 D7
  LSQ/SEVD WC2H .... 11 J4 🗓
  NWDGN UB2 .... 115 G2
  PEND EN3 .... 37 K5 🗓
  RYLN/HDSTN HA2 .... 79 H1
Shaftesbury Cir
  RYLN/HDSTN HA2 .... 79 J1 🗓
Shaftesbury Crs STA TW18 .. 148 D3
Shaftesbury Gdns
  WLSDN NW10 .... 99 L3 🗓
Shaftesbury La DART DA1 .. 147 H1
Shaftesbury Ms KENS W8 .. 14 B4 🗓
Shaftesbury Rd ARCH N19 .. 84 E1

BECK BR3 .... 158 F5
  CAR SM5 .... 170 D2
  CHING E4 .... 51 K3 🗓
  FSTGT E7 .... 88 C7
  LEY E10 .... 69 H7 🗓
  LEY E10 .... 87 G1 🗓
  RCH/KEW TW9 .... 116 E8
  ROM RM1 .... 73 M7
  UED N18 .... 49 L8
  WAT WD17 .... 29 J6 🗓
Shaftesburys BARK IG11 .. 107 J1
Shaftesbury St IS N1 ...... 6 F6 🗓
Shaftesbury Wy WHTN TW2 .. 133 K7
Shaftesbury Waye YEAD UB4.. 96 A4
Shafto Ms KTBR SW1X 15 L4
Shafton Rd HOM E9 .... 86 D8
Shakespeare Av
  EBED/NFELT TW14 .... 132 A3
  FBAR/BDGN N11 .... 48 C7
  WLSDN NW10 .... 81 J8
  YEAD UB4 .... 96 B3
Shakespeare Crs MNPK E12.. 88 F7
  WLSDN NW10 .... 81 J8 🗓
Shakespeare Dr
  KTN/HRWW/W HA3 .... 62 F7
Shakespeare Gdns EFNCH N2.. 65 M5
Shakespeare Rd ACT W3 .. 99 J7
  BXLYHN DA7 .... 126 E6
  DART DA1 .... 147 G1
  FNCH N3 .... 65 G2 🗓
  HNHL SE24 .... 139 H2
  HNWL W7 .... 97 M6
  MLHL NW7 .... 45 H3
  ROM RM1 .... 73 M7 🗓
  WALTH E17 .... 68 D3
Shakespeare Sq BARK/HLT IG6.. 53 H8
Shakespeare St WATN WD24.. 29 H3
Shakespeare Wy FELT TW13.. 132 C8
Shakspeare Ms
  STNW/STAM N16 .... 85 L4 🗓
Shakspeare Wk
  STNW/STAM N16 .... 85 L4
Shalcomb St WBPTN SW10 .. 119 J4
Shalcross Dr CHES/WCR EN8.. 26 F3
Shaldon Dr MRDN SM4 .... 154 E8
  RSLP HA4 .... 78 C3
Shaldon Rd EDGW HA8 .... 62 F3
Shaldon Wy WOT/HER KT12.. 165 J5
Shalfleet Dr NKENS W10 .. 100 B9
Shalford Cl ORP BR6 ...... 176 C6
Shalford Ct IS N1 .... 6 C5 🗓
Shalimar Gdns ACT W3 .... 99 J6
Shallons Rd ELTH/MOT SE9.. 143 H8
Shalstone Rd
  MORT/ESHN SW14 .... 117 H8
Shalston Vls SURB KT6 .... 167 M1 🗓
Shamrock Rd CROY/NA CR0.. 171 M1
Shamrock St CLAP SW4 .... 120 D8 🗓
Shamrock Wy STHGT/OAK N14.. 48 B2
Shandon Rd CLAP SW4 .... 138 C3
Shand St STHWK SE1 ...... 19 K1
Shandy St WCHPL E1 ...... 104 D4
Shanklin Cl CHESW EN7 .... 25 M2 🗓
Shanklin Gdns OXHEY WD19.. 42 C6
Shanklin Rd CEND/HSY/T N8.. 66 A5 🗓
  SEVS/STOTM N15 .... 68 A5 🗓
Shannon Cl CRICK NW2 .... 82 D3
  NWDGN UB2 .... 114 C6
Shannon Gv BRXN/ST SW9 .. 138 F1 🗓
Shannon Pl STJWD NW8 .... 3 K5
Shannon Wy BECK BR3 .... 159 H2
  SOCK/AV RM15 .... 111 J5 🗓
Shap Crs CAR SM5 .... 170 F3
Shardcroft Av HNHL SE24 .. 139 H2
Shardeloes Rd BROCKY SE4.. 122 F7
Shard's Sq PECK SE15 .... 122 A4 🗓
Sharland Cl THHTH CR7 .... 172 A1 🗓
Sharman Ct SCUP DA14 .... 144 A8
Sharnbrooke Cl WELL DA16.. 126 C3
Sharon Cl HOR/WEW KT19 .. 180 C6
  SURB KT6 .... 167 J3
Sharon Gdns HOM E9 ...... 86 C8
Sharon Rd CHSWK W4 ...... 117 K3
  PEND EN3 .... 37 L5
Sharples Hall St CAMTN NW1.. 3 M2
Sharps La RSLP HA4 .... 59 K8
Sharp Wy DART DA1 .... 128 F8
Sharratt St PECK SE15 .... 122 C4
Sharsted St WALW SE17 .... 18 C8
Sharvel La NTHLT UB5 ...... 78 A4
Shaw Av BARK IG11 .... 108 F1
Shaw Crs SAND/SEL CR2 .. 184 C5
Shaw Dr WOT/HER KT12 .... 165 J2
Shawbrooke Rd ELTH/MOT SE9.. 142 D1
Shawbury Rd EDUL SE22 .. 139 M2
Shaw Cl BUSH WD23 ...... 43 L4
  CHES/WCR EN8 .... 26 C2
  EW KT17 .... 180 F4
  HCH RM12 .... 92 B1 🗓
  SAND/SEL CR2 .... 184 F5
  THMD SE28 .... 108 B7
Shaw Gdns BARK IG11 .... 108 F1
Shaw Rd BMLY BR1 .... 141 M7
  EDUL SE22 .... 139 L1
  PEND EN3 .... 25 K4
Shaw's Cottages FSTH SE23.. 140 E7 🗓
Shaw Sq WALTH E17 .... 68 E2 🗓
Shaw Wy WLGTN SM6 ...... 183 L1
Shaxton Crs CROY/NA CR0 .. 186 C2
Shearing Dr MRDN SM4 .... 170 C2
Shearling Wy HOLWY N7 .. 84 E6 🗓
Shearman Rd BKHTH/KID SE3.. 141 M1
Shearwater Rd SUT SM1 .. 169 M7
Shearwater Wy YEAD UB4 .. 96 D5 🗓
Shearwood Cresent DART DA1.. 127 M8
Sheath La LHD/OX KT22 .... 178 B6
Sheaveshill Av CDALE/KGS NW9.. 63 L3
Sheen Common Dr
  RCHPK/HAM TW10 .... 135 G5
Sheen Court Rd
  RCHPK/HAM TW10 .... 135 G5
Sheendale Rd RCH/KEW TW9.. 134 F1
Sheenewood SYD SE26 .... 158 M1
Sheen Gate Gdns
  MORT/ESHN SW14 .... 135 M1

Sheen Gv IS N1 .... 6 A3
Sheen La MORT/ESHN SW14.. 135 J1
Sheen Pk RCH/KEW TW9 .. 134 E1
Sheen Rd RCHPK/HAM TW10.. 134 E1
  STMC/STPC BR5 .... 161 M7
Sheen Wy WLGTN SM6 .... 171 M7
Sheen Wd MORT/ESHN SW14.. 135 J2
Sheepbarn La WARL CR6 .. 187 G5
Sheepcot Dr GSTN WD25 .. 21 J7
Sheepcote Cl HEST TW5 .. 114 A5
Sheepcote Gdns
  DEN/HRF UB9 .... 58 A7 🗓
Sheepcote La BTSEA SW11.. 119 M7
  STMC/STPC BR5 .... 163 G7
Sheepcote Rd HRW HA1 .... 61 M7
Sheepcotes Rd CHDH RM6 .. 72 D5
Sheepcot La GSTN WD25 .. 21 H6
Sheephouse Wy NWMAL KT3.. 168 D3
Sheep La HACK E8 .... 86 B8
Sheep Walk Ms
  WIM/MER SW19 .... 154 D2
Sheerwater Rd CAN/RD E16.. 106 D4
Sheffield Dr HARH RM3 .... 57 G7
Sheffield Rd EBED/NFELT TW14.. 131 J3
Sheffield Ter KENS W8 ...... 14 A1
Sheffield Wy HTHAIR TW6 .. 131 K2 🗓
Shefton Ri NTHWD HA6 .... 60 A1
Sheila Rd CRW RM5 .... 73 H1
The Sheilings EMPK RM11 .. 74 F4 🗓
Shelbourne Cl PIN HA5 .... 60 F4 🗓
Shelbourne Rd TOTM N17 .. 68 B2
Shelburne Rd HOLWY N7 .. 84 F4 🗓
Shelbury Cl SCUP DA14 .... 144 A7
Shelbury Rd EDUL SE22 .. 140 B2
Sheldon Av CLAY IG5 ...... 71 H3
  HGT N6 .... 65 M8
Sheldon Cl LEE/GVPK SE12.. 142 B2
  PGE/AN SE20 .... 158 B4 🗓
Sheldon Rd BXLYHN DA7 .. 126 F6
  CRICK NW2 .... 82 A1 🗓
  DAGW RM9 .... 90 E7
  UED N18 .... 49 L6
Sheldon St CROY/NA CR0 .. 172 C5
Sheldrake Cl CAN/RD E16 .. 106 F7 🗓
Sheldrake Pl KENS W8 ...... 98 B3
Sheldrick Cl MTCM CR4 .... 155 K5
Shelduck Cl FSTGT E7 ...... 87 M5
Shelford Pl STNW/STAM N16.. 85 K3
Shelford Ri NRWD SE19 .... 157 L3
Shelford Rd BAR EN5 ...... 46 C1
Shelgate Rd BTSEA SW11 .. 137 M2
Shell Cl HAYES BR2 .... 175 L1
Shelley Av GFD/PVL UB6 .. 97 K2
  HCH RM12 .... 91 M2 🗓
  MNPK E12 .... 88 E6
Shelley Cl EDGW HA8 ...... 45 G6
  GFD/PVL UB6 .... 97 K2
  NTHWD HA6 .... 41 M7
  ORP BR6 .... 176 E5
  YEAD UB4 .... 96 A4
Shelley Crs HEST TW5 .... 114 D6
  STHL UB1 .... 96 F5
Shelley Dr WELL DA16 .... 125 L6
Shelley Gdns ALP/SUD HA0.. 80 C2
Shelley Gv LOU IG10 ...... 39 M7
Shelley La DEN/HRF UB9 .. 58 A1
Shelley Wy TOOT SW17 .. 155 K2 🗓
Shellgrove Rd
  STNW/STAM N16 .... 85 L5 🗓
Shellness Rd CLPT E5 ...... 86 B5
Shell Rd LEW SE13 .... 123 H8
Shellwood Rd BTSEA SW11.. 119 M7
Shelly Cl BNSTD SM7 ...... 181 K8
Shelmerdine Cl BOW E3 .. 105 G4
Shelson Av FELT TW13 .... 131 M7
Shelton Rd WIM/MER SW19.. 155 G4
Shelton St LSQ/SEVD WC2H.. 11 J5 🗓
Shenfield Rd WFD IG8 ...... 70 B1 🗓
Shenfield St IS N1 .... 7 K6
Shenley Av RSLP HA4 ...... 77 M2 🗓
Shenley Rd BORE WD6 .... 32 A6
  DART DA1 .... 147 G3
  HEST TW5 .... 114 E6
Shenstone Gdns HARH RM3.. 74 C2 🗓
Shenwood Ct BORE WD6 .. 32 B2 🗓
  BORE WD6 .... 32 A2 🗓
Shepherdess Pl FSBYE EC1V.. 6 F7 🗓
Shepherdess Wk IS N1 .... 6 F6
Shepherd Market
  MYFR/PICC W1J .... 10 C9 🗓
Shepherd's Bush Gn SHB W12.. 100 C8
Shepherd's Bush Market
  SHB W12 .... 100 C8
Shepherd's Bush Pl
  SHB W12 .... 100 D8 🗓
Shepherd's Bush Rd
  HMSMTH W6 .... 118 C3
Shepherds Cl CHDH RM6 .. 72 D6
  HGT N6 .... 66 B7
  ORP BR6 .... 176 F5 🗓
  SHPTN TW17 .... 164 B1
  UX/CGN UB8 .... 94 C3 🗓
Shepherds Gn CHST BR7 .. 161 K3
Shepherds Hi HARH RM3 .. 75 G3
  HGT N6 .... 66 B7
Shepherds La DART DA1 .. 146 A5
  HOM E9 .... 86 D6 🗓
Shepherds Pl
  MYFR/PKLN W1K .... 10 A6 🗓
Shepherd St MYFR/PICC W1J.. 10 C9
Shepherds Wk BUSH WD23.. 43 K4 🗓
  CRICK NW2 .... 82 A2
  HAMP NW3 .... 83 K5
Shepherds Wy
  RKW/CH/CXG WD3 .... 40 B2 🗓
  SAND/SEL CR2 .... 185 K1
Shepiston La WDR/YW UB7.. 113 H2
Shepley Cl CAR SM5 ...... 171 G5
  HCH RM12 .... 92 D5 🗓
Shepley Ms EN EN3 .... 38 A3
Sheppard Cl EN EN1 ...... 37 H3
  SURB KT6 .... 167 L5
Sheppard Dr BERM/RHTH SE16.. 122 B3
Sheppard St CAN/RD E16 .. 105 M3 🗓
Shepperton Cl BORE WD6 .. 32 D4 🗓

Shepperton Court Dr
SHPTN TW17 .... 149 H8 🄱
Shepperton Rd *IS* N1 .... 6 F3
STA TW18 .... 148 D7
STMC/STPC BR5 .... 176 C1
Sheppey Cl *ERITH* DA8 ...... 128 B5
Sheppey Gdns *DAGW* RM9 ..... 90 C7
Sheppey Rd *DAGW* RM9 ...... 90 B7
Sheppey's La *KGLGY* WD4 ...... 20 E1
Sherard Rd *ELTH/MOT* SE9 .... 142 E2
Sheraton Cl *HOR/WEW* KT19 .. 180 C6
Sheraton Dr *HOR/WEW* KT19 .. 180 C6
Sherborne Av *NWDGN* SB2 ..... 115 G2
PEND EN3 .... 37 J5
Sherborne Cl *YEAD* UB4 ...... 96 C5
Sherborne Crs *CAR* SM5 ...... 170 E2
Sherborne Gdns
CDALE/KGS NW9 .... 63 G4
WEA W13 .... 98 B5
Sherborne La *MANHO* EC4N .. 13 C6
Sherborne Pl *NTHWD* HA6 ..... 41 K8
Sherborne Rd *CHEAM* SM3 ... 170 A4
CHSGTN KT9 .... 167 L7
EBED/NFELT TW14 .... 131 K4 🄱
STMC/STPC BR5 .... 161 M8
Sherborne St *IS* N1 .... 7 G3
Sherborne Wy
RKW/CH/CXG WD3 ...... 28 B7
Sherboro Rd
SEVS/STOTM N15 ...... 67 M7 🄱
Sherbourne Gdns
SHPTN TW17 .... 164 E2 🄱
Sherbrooke Cl *BXLYHN* DA7 .. 145 G1 🄱
Sherbrooke Rd *FUL/PGN* SW6 .. 118 E5
Sherbrook Gdns *WCHMH* N21 .. 49 H2
Shere Av *BELMT* SM2 .... 181 J8
Shere Cl *CHSGTN* KT9 ...... 167 K7
Sheredan Rd *CHING* E4 ...... 51 K7
Sherfield Av *RKW/CH/CXG* WD3 .. 40 D5
Sherfield Gdns *GNTH/NBYPK* IG2 .. 71 C6
Sherfield Gdns *PUT/ROE* SW15 .. 135 M3
Sheridan Av *HARH* RM3 ...... 74 B1
HGDN/ICK UB10 .... 95 J3 🄱
Sheridan Ct *DART* DA1 ...... 147 C1
HSLWW TW4 .... 132 E2
Sheridan Crs *CHST* BR7 ..... 161 H5
Sheridan Gdns
KTN/HRWW/W HA3 ...... 62 D7
Sheridan Pl *HPTN* TW12 ..... 151 H4 🄱
Sheridan Rd *BELV* DA17 ..... 127 G2
BXLYHN DA7 .... 126 E8
FSTGT E7 .... 87 M3
MNPK E12 .... 88 E5
OXHEY WD19 .... 42 D2
RCHPK/HAM TW10 ...... 134 C7
WIM/MER SW19 .... 154 F4
Sheridan St *WCHPL* E1 ...... 104 B5 🄱
Sheridan Wk *GLDGN* NW11 .... 65 C7
Sheridan Wy *BECK* BR3 ..... 158 F4 🄱
Sheriff Wy *GSTN* WD25 ...... 21 C6
Sheringham Av *MNPK* E12 .... 88 F4
ROMW/RG RM7 .... 73 J7
STHCT/OAK N14 .... 35 K8
WHTN TW2 .... 132 F5
Sheringham Dr *BARK* IG11 ... 89 M5
Sheringham Rd *HOLWY* N7 ... 85 G6
PGE/AN SE20 .... 158 B5
Sherington Av *PIN* HA5 ...... 61 G1
Sherington Rd *CHARL* SE7 ... 124 B4
Sherland Rd *TWK* TW1 ...... 133 M5 🄱
Sherlies Av *ORP* BR6 .... 176 E4
Sherlock Ms *MHST* W1U ..... 10 A2 🄱
Sherman Rd *BMLY* BR1 ...... 160 A4
Shernbroke Rd *WAB* EN9 .... 27 M7
WALTH E17 .... 69 J6 🄱
Sherrard Rd *FSTGT* E7 ...... 88 C6
Sherrards Wy *BAR* EN5 ...... 34 A3
Sherrick Green Rd *WLSDN* NW10 .. 82 B5
Sheriff Rd *KIL/WHAMP* NW6 .. 83 G6
Sherringham Av *FELT* TW13 .. 132 A7 🄱
TOTM N17 .... 68 A3
Sherrock Gdns *HDN* NW4 .... 64 A5
Sherry Ms *BARK* IG11 .... 89 K7
Sherwin Rd *NWCR* SE14 .... 122 D6
Sherwood *SURB* KT6 .... 167 K4 🄱
Sherwood Av *GFD/PVL* UB6 .. 79 L6
POTB/CUF EN6 .... 22 E5
RSLP HA4 .... 59 L7
STRHM/NOR SW16 ...... 156 E4
SWFD E18 .... 70 B4
YEAD UB4 .... 96 B3
Sherwood Cl *BXLY* DA5 ...... 144 C3
WEA W13 .... 98 B7
Sherwood Ct *MBLAR* W1H ... 9 L3 🄱
Sherwood Gdns *BARK* IG11 .. 89 K7
POP/IOD E14 .... 123 C2 🄱
STHWK SE1 .... 122 A3 🄱
Sherwood Park Av
BFN/LL DA15 .... 144 A4
Sherwood Park Rd *MTCM* CR4 .. 156 C7
SUT SM1 .... 174 E4
Sherwood Rd *BARK/HLT* IG6 .. 71 K5
CROY/NA CR0 .... 173 H2
HDN NW4 .... 64 C4
HPTN TW12 .... 151 J1
RYLN/HDSTN HA2 ...... 79 J2
WELL DA16 .... 125 L8
WIM/MER SW19 .... 154 F3 🄱
Sherwoods Rd *OXHEY* WD19 .. 42 E2
Sherwood St *REGST* W1B .... 10 F6 🄱
TRDG/WHET N20 .... 47 K5 🄱
Sherwood Ter *TRDG/WHET* N20 .. 47 K5
Sherwood Wy *WWKM* BR4 .... 174 C4
Shetland Cl *BORE* WD6 ...... 45 K1
Shetland Rd *BOW* E3 .... 104 F1 🄱
Shevon Wy *BRW* CM14 .... 11 G7
Shewens Rd *WEY* KT13 ..... 164 D6 🄱
Shield Dr *BTFD* TW8 .... 116 B4
Shieldhall St *ABYW* SE2 .... 126 C2
Shield Rd *ASHF* TW15 ...... 131 J8
Shillibeer Pl *MBLAR* W1H ... 9 K3 🄱
Shillibeer Wk *CHIG* IG7 ..... 53 M5
Shillingford Rd *IS* N1 .... 6 D3 🄱
Shillitoe Av *POTB/CUF* EN6 .. 22 D5
Shinfield St *SHB* W12 ...... 100 C5
Shinglewell Rd *ERITH* DA8 .. 127 C5
Shinners Cl *SNWD* SE25 .... 158 A8

Ship And Mermaid Rw
STHWK SE1 .... 19 H1 🄱
Shipka Rd *BAL* SW12 .... 138 B5
Ship La *MORT/ESHN* SW14 .. 117 J8
SOCK/AV RM15 .... 111 K8
Shipman Rd *CAN/RD* E16 .. 106 B5
FSTH SE23 .... 140 D6
Ship St *DEPT* SE8 .... 123 C6
Shipton Cl *BCTR* RM8 ...... 90 D3
Shipton Rd *HGDN/ICK* UB10 .. 76 F4 🄱
Shipton St *BETH* E2 .... 7 M7
Shipwright Rd
BERM/RHTH SE16 ...... 104 B3
Shipwright Yd *STHWK* SE1 .. 13 J9 🄱
Ship Yd *WEY* KT13 .... 164 A5
Shirburn Cl *FSTH* SE23 ..... 140 E5
Shirbutt St *POP/IOD* E14 ... 105 H6 🄱
Shirebrook Rd *BKHTH/KID* SE3 .. 124 E4
Shirehall Cl *HDN* NW4 ...... 64 D7
Shirehall Gdns *HDN* NW4 ... 64 D7
Shirehall La *HDN* NW4 ...... 64 D7
Shirehall Pk *HDN* NW4 ..... 64 D7 🄱
Shire Horse Wy *ISLW* TW7 .. 115 M8 🄱
Shire La *ORP* BR6 .... 176 E7
Shiremeade *BORE* WD6 ..... 31 M8
The Shires *RCHPK/HAM* TW10 .. 134 E8
Shirland Ms *MV/WKIL* W9 .. 100 F2
Shirland Rd *MV/WKIL* W9 ... 2 B9
Shirley Av *BELMT* SM2 ..... 181 M3
BXLY DA5 .... 144 D4
CROY/NA CR0 .... 173 J3
SUT SM1 .... 170 E6
Shirley Church Rd
CROY/NA CR0 .... 173 K5
Shirley Cl *CHES/WCR* EN8 .. 26 C3
DART DA1 .... 146 C1
HSLW TW3 .... 133 J2
Shirley Crs *BECK* BR3 ..... 158 E7
Shirley Dr *HSLW* TW3 ..... 133 J2
Shirley Gdns *BARK* IG11 .... 89 L6
HCH RM12 .... 92 C2
HNWL W7 .... 97 M7
Shirley Hills Rd *CROY/NA* CR0 .. 173 K7
ED N9 .... 50 C2
Shirley Oaks Rd *CROY/NA* CR0 .. 173 K3
Shirley Park Rd *CROY/NA* CR0 .. 173 H3
Shirley Rd *ABLGY* WD5 ..... 20 F5
BFN/LL DA15 .... 143 L7
CHSWK W4 .... 99 K8 🄱
CROY/NA CR0 .... 173 H3
ENC/FH EN2 .... 36 C5
SRTFD E15 .... 87 L7 🄱
WLGTN SM6 .... 183 J2
Shirley St *CAN/RD* E16 .... 105 M5
Shirley Wy *CROY/NA* CR0 ... 173 M5
Shirlock Rd *HAMP* NW3 ..... 83 M4
Shobden Rd *TOTM* N17 ..... 67 K2
Shobroke Cl *CRICK* NW2 .... 82 C3
Shoebury Rd *EHAM* E6 ...... 88 F7
Shoe La *FLST/FETLN* EC4A .. 12 C3
STBT EC1A 12 C3
Sholden Gdns *STMC/STPC* BR5 .. 162 C8
Shooters Av *KTN/HRWW/W* HA3 .. 62 C5
Shooters Hill *WOOL/PLUM* SE18 .. 124 F6
Shooters Hill Rd
BKHTH/KID SE3 .... 123 L6
CHARL SE7 .... 124 C5
Shooters Rd *ENC/FH* EN2 ... 36 A3
Shoot-up Hl *CRICK* NW2 .... 82 E6
Shore Cl *EBED/NFELT* TW14 .. 132 A4
HPTN TW12 .... 150 F1
Shoredich Cl *HGDN/ICK* UB10 .. 76 F3
Shoreditch High St *BETH* E2 .. 7 K8
WCHPL E1 .... 13 K2
Shore Gv *FELT* TW13 ...... 133 C6
Shoreham Cl *CROY/NA* CR0 .. 173 J1
WAND/EARL SW18 ...... 137 H2 🄱
Shoreham Rd *STMC/STPC* BR5 .. 162 B4
Shoreham Wy *HAYES* BR2 .. 175 G1
Shore Pl *HOM* E9 .... 86 C7
Shore Rd *HOM* E9 .... 86 C7
Shorncliffe Rd *CMBW* SE5 .. 19 L8
STHWK SE1 .... 19 L7
Shorndean St *CAT* SE6 ..... 141 J5
Shorne Cl *BFN/LL* DA15 .... 144 B3
STMC/STPC BR5 .... 162 D7
Shornefield Cl *BMLY* BR1 .. 161 G6 🄱
Shorrolds Rd *FUL/PGN* SW6 .. 119 C5
Shortcroft Rd *EW* KT17 .... 180 F1
Shorter St *WCHPL* E1 ...... 13 L6
Shortgate *NFNCH/WDSP* N12 .. 46 F6
Shortlands *HMSMTH* W6 ... 118 D2
HYS/HAR UB3 .... 113 K4
Shortlands Cl *BELV* DA17 .. 126 F1
UED N18 .... 49 M8
Shortlands Gdns *HAYES* BR2 .. 159 L5 🄱
Shortlands Gv *HAYES* BR2 .. 159 K6
Shortlands Rd *HAYES* BR2 .. 159 K6
KUTN/CMB KT2 .... 152 F3
LEY E10 .... 69 H8
Short La *LCOL/BKTW* AL2 ... 21 L2
STWL/WRAY TW19 ...... 130 F4
Shortmead Dr *CHES/WCR* EN8 .. 26 E4
Short Rd *CHSWK* W4 .... 117 L4
WAN E11 .... 87 L2
Shorts Cft *CDALE/KGS* NW9 .. 63 H5
Shorts Gdns *LSQ/SEVD* WC2H .. 11 K4
Shorts Rd *CAR* SM5 .... 170 G6
Short St *STHWK* SE1 ...... 18 B1 🄱
Shortway *ELTH/MOT* SE9 ... 124 E8
Short Wy *NFNCH/WDSP* N12 .. 47 L8
WHTN TW2 .... 133 J4
Shortwood Av *STA* TW18 ... 130 B7
Shotfield *WLGTN* SM6 ..... 171 H8
Shott Cl *SUT* SM1 .... 170 C7 🄱
Shottendane Rd
FUL/PGN SW6 .... 119 G6 🄱
Shottery Cl *ELTH/MOT* SE9 .. 142 F7
Shottfield Av
MORT/ESHN SW14 ..... 135 L1
Shoulder of Mutton Aly
POP/IOD E14 .... 104 E6 🄱
Shouldham St *MBLAR* W1H .. 9 K3
Showers Wy *HYS/HAR* UB3 .. 96 A7
Shrapnel Cl *WOOL/PLUM* SE18 .. 124 E5
Shrapnel Rd *ELTH/MOT* SE9 .. 124 F8

Shrewsbury Av
KTN/HRWW/W HA3 ...... 62 E5
MORT/ESHN SW14 ..... 135 J1
Shrewsbury Cl *SURB* KT6 ... 167 L4
Shrewsbury Crs *WLSDN* NW10 .. 81 K8 🄱
Shrewsbury La
WOOL/PLUM SE18 ...... 125 H6
Shrewsbury Ms *BAY/PAD* W2 .. 8 A3
Shrewsbury Rd *BAY/PAD* W2 .. 8 A3
BECK BR3 .... 158 E6
CAR SM5 .... 170 E2
EBED/NFELT TW14 ..... 131 J3
FBAR/BDGN N11 .... 48 D8
FSTGT E7 .... 89 M4
MNPK E12 .... 88 D6
Shrewton Rd *TOOT* SW17 .. 155 H8 🄱
Shroffold Rd *BMLY* BR1 .... 141 L8
Shropshire Cl *MTCM* CR4 .. 156 E7 🄱
Shropshire Rd *WDGN* N22 .. 66 F1 🄱
Shroton St *CAMTN* NW1 .... 9 J2
The Shrubberies *CHIG* IG7 .. 53 J7
SWFD E18 .... 70 D1
Shrubbery Gdns *WCHMH* N21 .. 49 H2
Shrubbery Rd *STHL* UB1 ... 97 G7 🄱
STRHM/NOR SW16 ...... 138 E8
The Shrubbery *UPMR* RM14 .. 93 J3
Shrubland Gv *WPK* KT4 ... 169 J5 🄱
Shrubland Rd *HACK* E8 .... 86 A8
LEY E10 .... 69 C8
WALTH E17 .... 69 C8
Shrublands Av *CROY/NA* CR0 .. 174 A6
Shrublands Cl *CHIG* IG7 .... 53 J8
SYD SE26 .... 140 C7 🄱
The Shrublands *POTB/CUF* EN6 .. 22 E6
Shrubsall Cl *ELTH/MOT* SE9 .. 142 E5
Shurland Av *EBAR* EN4 ..... 47 K1
Shurlock Av *SWLY* BR8 ..... 179 K6
Shurlock Dr *ORP* BR6 ...... 176 C6 🄱
Shuttle Cl *BFN/LL* DA15 ... 143 M4
Shuttlemead *BXLY* DA5 .... 144 F4
Shuttle St *WCHPL* E1 ...... 104 A3 🄱
Shuttleworth Rd *BTSEA* SW11 .. 119 H7
Sibella Rd *CLAP* SW4 ...... 120 D7
Sibley Cl *BXLYHS* DA6 ..... 144 E2
Sibley Ct *UX/CGN* UB8 ..... 95 J4
Sibley Gv *MNPK* E12 .... 88 E7
Sibthorpe Rd *LEE/GVPK* SE12 .. 142 C4 🄱
Sibthorp Rd *MTCM* CR4 .... 155 M5 🄱
Sibton Rd *CAR* SM5 .... 170 E2
Sidbury St *FUL/PGN* SW6 .. 118 E6
Sidcup By-pass Rd *SCUP* DA14 .. 143 L8
Sidcup Hl *SCUP* DA14 ...... 162 B1
Sidcup Pl *SCUP* DA14 ...... 162 A1
Sidcup Rd *ELTH/MOT* SE9 .. 142 E5
LEE/GVPK SE12 .... 142 B2
Siddeley Dr *HSLWW* TW4 .. 114 E8
Siddons La *CAMTN* NW1 .... 9 M1
Siddons Rd *CROY/NA* CR0 .. 172 A5
FSTH SE23 .... 140 E6
TOTM N17 .... 68 A2
Side Rd *WALTH* E17 .... 68 F6 🄱
Sidewood Rd *ELTH/MOT* SE9 .. 143 K5
Sidford Pl *STHWK* SE1 ..... 17 M4
The Sidings *STA* TW18 ..... 130 B8
WAN E11 .... 87 J1
Sidmouth Av *ISLW* TW7 .... 115 L7
Sidmouth Cl *OXHEY* WD19 .. 42 B4
Sidmouth Dr *RSLP* HA4 .... 78 A3
Sidmouth Rd *LEY* E10 ..... 87 J3
PECK SE15 .... 121 M6
STMC/STPC BR5 .... 162 B8 🄱
WELL DA16 .... 126 C5
WLSDN NW10 .... 82 C7
Sidmouth St *STPAN* WC1H .. 5 K8
Sidney Av *PLMGR* N13 ..... 48 F8
Sidney Elson Wy *EHAM* E6 .. 107 G1 🄱
Sidney Gdns *BTFD* TW8 .... 116 D4 🄱
Sidney Gv *FSBYE* EC1V 6 C6
Sidney Rd *BECK* BR3 ...... 158 E5
BRXN/ST SW9 .... 120 F7
FSTGT E7 .... 88 A3
RYLN/HDSTN HA2 ...... 61 J4
SNWD SE25 .... 158 A3 🄱
STA TW18 .... 130 A8
TWK TW1 .... 134 A3
WDGN N22 .... 66 F1
WOT/HER KT12 .... 165 H5
Sidney Sq *WCHPL* E1 ...... 104 C4 🄱
Sidney St *WCHPL* E1 ...... 104 C4
Sidworth St *HACK* E8 ..... 86 B7
Siebert Rd *BKHTH/KID* SE3 .. 124 A4
Siemens Rd *WOOL/PLUM* SE18 .. 124 D1
Sierra Dr *DAGW* RM9 ...... 109 H1
Sigdon Rd *HACK* E8 .... 86 A5
The Sigers *RSLP* HA4 ...... 60 B7
Signmakers Yd *CAMTN* NW1 .. 4 D4 🄱
Silbury Av *MTCM* CR4 ..... 155 L4
Silbury St *IS* N1 .... 7 C7 🄱
Silchester Rd *NKENS* W10 .. 100 C5
Silecroft Rd *BXLYHN* DA7 .. 127 G6
Silesia Buildings *HACK* E8 .. 86 B7 🄱
Silex St *STHWK* SE1 ...... 18 D2
Silk Cl *LEE/GVPK* SE12 .... 142 A2
Silkfield Rd *CDALE/KGS* NW9 .. 63 L6
Silk Mill Rd *OXHEY* WD19 .. 42 B2 🄱
Silk Mills Pth *LEW* SE13 ... 123 J8
Silkstream Rd *EDGW* HA8 .. 63 J2
Silk St *BARB* EC2Y 12 F2
Silsoe Rd *WDGN* N22 ...... 66 F3 🄱
Silver Birch Av *CHING* E4 .. 50 F7
Silver Birch Cl *CAT* SE6 ... 140 C8 🄱
FBAR/BDGN N11 .... 48 A8
HGDN/ICK UB10 .... 76 E4
RDART DA2 .... 145 L8
THMD SE28 .... 108 A7
Silver Birch Ms *BARK/HLT* IG6 .. 53 J8 🄱
Silvercliffe Gdns *EBAR* EN4 .. 34 E7
Silver Cl *KTN/HRWW/W* HA3 .. 61 K1
NWCR SE14 .... 122 E5 🄱
Silver Crs *CHSWK* W4 ..... 117 H2
Silverdale *CAMTN* NW1 .... 4 E6
ENC/FH EN2 .... 35 L7
SYD SE26 .... 140 C4
Silverdale Av *LHD/OX* KT22 .. 178 C7
WEY KT13 .... 164 F4
Silverdale Cl *HNWL* W7 .... 97 L7 🄱
NTHLT UB5 .... 78 B3

Silverdale Dr *ELTH/MOT* SE9 .. 142 E6 🄱
HCH RM12 .... 92 B5
SUN TW16 .... 150 B5
Silverdale Gdns *HYS/HAR* UB3 .. 96 A3
Silverdale Rd *BUSH* WD23 .. 29 L8
BXLYHN DA7 .... 127 H7
CHING E4 .... 51 K8
HYS/HAR UB3 .... 96 A3
Silver Dell *WATN* WD24 .... 20 F8
Silverglade *CHSGTN* KT9 ... 179 J5
Silverhall St *ISLW* TW7 .... 116 A8
Silver Hl *BORE* WD6 ...... 32 C1
Silverholme Cl
KTN/HRWW/W HA3 ...... 62 E8
Silver La *PUR/KEN* CR8 .... 183 K5
WWKM BR4 .... 174 D4
Silverleigh Rd *THHTH* CR7 .. 156 F7
Silvermere Av *CRW* RM5 ... 55 H8
Silvermere Rd *LEW* SE13 .. 141 C3
Silver Spring Cl *ERITH* DA8 .. 127 H4
Silverston Wy *STAN* HA7 .. 44 C8
Silver St *CHESW* EN7 ..... 25 K3
ENC/FH EN2 .... 36 D6
UED N18 .... 49 K6
WAB EN9 .... 26 E3
Silverthorne Rd *VX/NE* SW8 .. 120 B7
Silverthorn Gdns *CHING* E4 .. 51 C4
Silverton Rd *HMSMTH* W6 .. 118 D5
Silvertown Wy *CAN/RD* E16 .. 105 L5
Silver Tree Cl *WOT/HER* KT12 .. 165 C6 🄱
Silvertree La *GFD/PVL* UB6 .. 97 K2 🄱
Silver Trees *LCOL/BKTW* AL2 .. 21 M3
Silver Wk *BERM/RHTH* SE16 .. 104 F7 🄱
Silver Wy *HGDN/ICK* UB10 .. 95 H1
ROMW/RG RM7 .... 73 H4
Silverwood Cl *BECK* BR3 .. 159 C3
CROY/NA CR0 .... 185 M2 🄱
NTHWD HA6 .... 59 J2
Silvester Rd *EDUL* SE22 ... 139 M2
Silvester St *SHARK* SE1 ... 19 G2 🄱
Silwood Rd *BERM/RHTH* SE16 .. 122 D3
Simmil Rd *ESH/CLAY* KT10 .. 166 E7
Simmons Ct *TRDG/WHET* N20 .. 47 L3
Simmons La *CHING* E4 ..... 51 K4
Simmons Rd
WOOL/PLUM SE18 ...... 125 H3 🄱
Simmons' Wy *TRDG/WHET* N20 .. 47 L4
Simms Cl *CAR* SM5 .... 170 E4 🄱
Simms Rd *STHWK* SE1 ..... 122 A2
Simnel Rd *LEE/GVPK* SE12 .. 142 B4
Simon Cl *NTGHL* W11 ...... 100 F6
Simonds Rd *LEY* E10 ...... 87 G2 🄱
Simone Cl *BMLY* BR1 ...... 160 D4
Simon Gray Gdns
KUTN/CMB KT2 .... 152 D4
Simons Wk *SRTFD* E15 ..... 87 K5 🄱
SRTFD E15 .... 87 K6 🄱
Simpson Cl *WCHMH* N21 ... 35 L8 🄱
Simpson Dr *ACT* W3 ...... 99 K5 🄱
Simpson Rd *HSLWW* TW4 .. 132 F3
RAIN RM13 .... 91 M3
RCHPK/HAM TW10 ...... 134 C7
Simpson's Rd *HAYES* BR2 .. 160 A6 🄱
POP/IOD E14 .... 105 H6
Simpson St *BTSEA* SW11 .. 119 K7
Simpson Wy *SURB* KT6 .... 167 J1
Sims Cl *ROM* RM1 .... 73 M5
Sinclair Gdns *WKENS* W14 .. 100 D8
Sinclair Gv *GLDGN* NW11 ... 64 D7
Sinclair Rd *CHING* E4 ..... 50 F7
WKENS W14 .... 118 E1
Sinclair Wy *RDART* DA2 ... 147 K8
Sinderby Cl *BORE* WD6 .... 31 L4
Singapore Rd *HNWL* W7 ... 98 A7
Singer St *FSBYE* EC1V ..... 7 H8 🄱
Singleton Cl *CROY/NA* CR0 .. 172 C2 🄱
HCH RM12 .... 91 M4 🄱
WIM/MER SW19 .... 155 M3 🄱
Singleton Rd *DAGW* RM9 .. 90 F5
Singleton Scarp
NFNCH/WDSP N12 ...... 46 G7
Sinnott Rd *WALTH* E17 ..... 68 D2
Sion Rd *TWK* TW1 .... 134 B5
Sipson Cl *WDR/YW* UB7 ... 113 H4
Sipson La *WDR/YW* UB7 ... 113 H4
Sipson Rd *WDR/YW* UB7 ... 113 H2
Sipson Wy *WDR/YW* UB7 ... 113 G5
Sir Alexander Cl *ACT* W3 .. 99 M7
Sir Cyril Black Wy
WIM/MER SW19 .... 155 C3 🄱
Sirdar Rd *MTCM* CR4 ...... 156 A2 🄱
NTGHL W11 .... 100 D6
WDGN N22 .... 67 J3
Sirus Rd *NTHWD* HA6 ..... 42 A7
Sise La *MANHO* EC4N ...... 13 C5 🄱
Siskin Cl *BORE* WD6 ...... 32 A7
BUSH WD23 .... 29 L7 🄱
Sisley Rd *BARK* IG11 ...... 108 E1
Sispara Gdns *WAND/EARL* SW18 .. 136 F3
Sissinghurst Rd
CROY/NA CR0 .... 173 C2 🄱
Sister Mabel's Wy *PECK* SE15 .. 122 A5 🄱
Sisters Av *BTSEA* SW11 .... 137 M1
Sistova Rd *BAL* SW12 ..... 138 B5
Sisulu Pl *BRXN/ST* SW9 ... 121 G8
Sittingbourne Av
WCHMH N21 .... 49 K1 🄱
Sitwell Gv *STAN* HA7 ...... 43 M7
Siverst Cl *NTHLT* UB5 ..... 79 H6 🄱
Siviter Wy *DAGE* RM10 .... 91 H7
Siward Rd *HAYES* BR2 ..... 160 B6
TOOT SW17 .... 137 J2
TOTM N17 .... 67 K3
Sixth Av *GSTN* WD25 ...... 21 K8
HYS/HAR UB3 .... 96 A5
MNPK E12 .... 88 F4
NKENS W10 .... 100 D3
Sixth Cross Rd *WHTN* TW2 .. 133 J7
Skardu Rd *CRICK* NW2 .... 82 C5
Skeena Hl *WIM/MER* SW19 .. 136 E4
Skeet Hill La *STMC/STPC* BR5 .. 177 M4
Skeffington Rd *EHAM* E6 .. 89 K8
Skeffington St
WOOL/PLUM SE18 ...... 125 J3
Skelbrook St *WAND/EARL* SW18 .. 137 H6
Skelgill Rd *PUT/ROE* SW15 .. 136 F1 🄱

Skelley Rd *SRTFD* E15 ..... 87 M7
Skelton Rd *FSTGT* E7 ...... 88 A6
Skelton's La *LEY* E10 ...... 69 H8
Skelwith Rd *HMSMTH* W6 .. 118 C4
Skerne Rd *KUTN/CMB* KT2 .. 152 D4
Sketchley Gdns
BERM/RHTH SE16 ...... 122 D3
Sketty Rd *EN* EN1 .... 36 F6
Skibbs La *ORP* BR6 .... 177 L5
Skid Hill La *WARL* CR6 ..... 186 F8
Skidmore Wy *RKW/CH/CXG* WD3 .. 40 E3
Skiers St *SRTFD* E15 ...... 87 L8
Skiffington Cl
BRXS/STRHM SW2 ...... 139 G5 🄱
Skinner Pl *BGVA* SW1W .... 16 A6 🄱
Skinners La *BLKFR* EC4V ... 12 F6
HEST TW5 .... 115 H6 🄱
Skinner St *FSBYE* EC1V 6 C8
Skipsey Av *EHAM* E6 ...... 107 G3 🄱
Skipton Cl *FBAR/BDGN* N11 .. 48 A8
Skipton Dr *HYS/HAR* UB3 .. 113 J1
Skipworth Rd *HOM* E9 ..... 86 E5
HOM E9 .... 86 E5 🄱
Skyes Dr *STA* TW18 .... 148 B1
Sky Peals Rd *WFD* IG8 .... 69 K2
Skyport Dr *WDR/YW* UB7 .. 112 D5
Sladebrook Rd *BKHTH/KID* SE3 .. 124 D8
Slade Ct *RAD* WD7 .... 31 H1
Sladedale Rd
WOOL/PLUM SE18 ...... 125 L3
Slades Cl *ENC/FH* EN2 .... 127 M6
Slade Green Rd *ERITH* DA8 .. 127 M6
Sladen Pl *CLPT* E5 .... 86 B4 🄱
Slades Dr *CHST* BR7 ...... 143 J8
Slades Gdns *ENC/FH* EN2 .. 36 A5
Slades Hl *ENC/FH* EN2 .... 36 A5
Slades Ri *ENC/FH* EN2 .... 36 A6
The Slade *WOOL/PLUM* SE18 .. 125 L4
Slagrove Pl *BROCKY* SE4 .. 141 G2
Slaidburn St *WBPTN* SW10 .. 119 J4
Slaithwaite Rd *LEW* SE13 .. 141 J1
Slaney Pl *HOLWY* N7 ...... 85 G5 🄱
Slaney Rd *ROM* RM1 .... 73 L6
Slattery Rd *FELT* TW13 .... 132 C5
Sleaford Gn *WDR/YW* WD19 .. 42 D5
Sleaford St *VX/NE* SW8 .... 120 C5
Slewins Cl *EMPK* RM11 .... 74 C6
Slewins La *EMPK* RM11 .... 74 C6
Slievemore Cl *CLAP* SW4 .. 120 D8 🄱
Slingsby Pl *COVGDN* WC2E .. 11 J6
Slippers Pl *BERM/RHTH* SE16 .. 122 B1
Sloane Av *CHEL* SW3 ...... 15 K6
Sloane Ct East *CHEL* SW3 .. 16 A7
Sloane Ct West *CHEL* SW3 .. 16 A7
Sloane Gdns *BGVA* SW1W ... 16 A6
ORP BR6 .... 176 C5 🄱
Sloane Sq *KTBR* SW1X 15 M4
Sloane Ter *KTBR* SW1X 15 M5
Sloane Wk *CROY/NA* CR0 ... 173 M1
Slocum Cl *THMD* SE28 ..... 108 C2 🄱
Slough La *CDALE/KGS* NW9 .. 63 J6
Sly St *WCHPL* E1 .... 104 B5 🄱
Smaldon Cl *WDR/YW* UB7 .. 113 J1
Smallberry Av *ISLW* TW7 .. 115 M7
Smallbrook Ms *BAY/PAD* W2 .. 8 E5
Smalley Cl *STNW/STAM* N16 .. 85 M3 🄱
Smallwood Rd *TOOT* SW17 .. 137 K8
Smarden Cl *BELV* DA17 .... 127 G3
Smart Cl *HARH* RM3 .... 74 B2
Smart's La *LOU* IG10 ...... 39 L7
Smart's Pl *HHOL* WC1V 11 K4
UED N18 .... 50 A1 🄱
Smart St *BETH* E2 .... 104 D2
Smeaton Cl *WAB* EN9 ..... 27 L5 🄱
Smeaton Rd *WAB* EN9 ..... 38 A3
WAND/EARL SW18 ...... 137 G4
WFD IG8 .... 52 F7
Smeaton St *WAP* E1W 104 A7
Smedley St *VX/NE* SW8 .... 120 D7
Smeed Rd *BOW* E3 .... 87 G7
Smiles Pl *LEW* SE13 .... 123 J7
Smitham Bottom La
PUR/KEN CR8 .... 183 K5
Smitham Downs Rd
COUL/CHIP CR5 .... 183 L6
Smith Cl *BERM/RHTH* SE16 .. 104 D7
Smithfield St *STBT* EC1A ... 12 C3
Smithies Rd *ABYW* SE2 .... 126 B2
Smithson Rd *TOTM* N17 ... 67 K2
Smith Rd *BRYLDS* KT5 ..... 15 L7
CHEL SW3 .... 15 L7
WATW WD18 .... 29 J7 🄱
Smith Ter *CHEL* SW3 ...... 15 L8
Smithwood Cl *WIM/MER* SW19 .. 136 E6
Smithy St *WCHPL* E1 ...... 104 C4
Smuggler's Wy
WAND/EARL SW18 ...... 137 H1
Smyrk's Rd *WALW* SE17 .... 19 K8
Smyrna Rd *KIL/WHAMP* NW6 .. 2 A1
Smythe Sт *POP/IOD* E14 .. 105 H6 🄱
Snakes La East *WFD* IG8 .. 52 E6
Snakes La West *WFD* IG8 .. 52 A8
Snaresbrook Dr *STAN* HA7 .. 44 D6
Snaresbrook Rd *WAN* E11 .. 69 L5
Snarsgate St *NKENS* W10 .. 100 C4 🄱
Sneath Av *GLDGN* NW11 ... 64 D8
Snellings Rd *WOT/HER* KT12 .. 165 J7
Snell's Pk *UED* N18 .... 50 B2 🄱
Sneyd Rd *CRICK* NW2 ..... 82 C5
Snipe Cl *ERITH* DA8 ...... 128 B5
Snowbury Rd *FUL/PGN* SW6 .. 119 H7 🄱
Snowden Av *HGDN/ICK* UB10 .. 95 H1
Snowden Dr *CDALE/KGS* NW9 .. 63 L7
Snowden St *SDTCH* EC2A ... 13 J1
Snowdon Crs *HYS/HAR* UB3 .. 113 J1
Snowdon Dr *CDALE/KGS* NW9 .. 63 J2
Snowdown Cl *PGE/AN* SE20 .. 158 C4
Snowdon Rd West *HTHAIR* TW6 .. 133 H3
Snowdrop Cl *HPTN* TW12 .. 151 G2 🄱
Snow Hl *STBT* EC1A 12 C3
Snowsfields *STHWK* SE1 ... 19 H1
Snowshill Rd *MNPK* E12 ... 88 E5
Snowy Fielder Waye *ISLW* TW7 .. 116 B7
Soames St *PECK* SE15 ..... 121 M8
Soames Wk *NWMAL* KT3 .. 153 L4
Soham Rd *PEND* EN3 ...... 37 M2
Soho Sq *SOHO/SHAV* W1D .. 11 G4

Soho St *SOHO/SHAV* W1D 11 G4
Solebay St *WCHPL* E1 .... 104 E3
Solent Ri *PLSTW* E13 .... 106 A2
Solent Rd *KIL/WHAMP* NW6 ... 83 G5 ⑥
Solna Av *PUT/ROE* SW15 .... 136 C2
Solna Rd *WCHMH* N21 .... 49 K3
Solomon Av *UED* N18 .... 50 A6
Solomon's Hl
  RKW/CH/CXG WD3 .... 40 D2 ⑥
Solomon's Pas *PECK* SE15 ..... 140 B1
Solon New Rd *CLAP* SW4 .... 138 E1
Solon Rd *CLAP* SW4 .... 138 E1
Solway Cl *HSLWW* TW4 .... 114 E8
Solway Rd *EDUL* SE22 .... 140 A1
  WDGN N22 .... 67 H2
Somaford Gv *EBAR* EN4 .... 47 K1 ⑥
Somali Rd *CRICK* NW2 .... 82 F4
Somerby Rd *BARK* IG11 .... 89 K7
Somercoates Cl *EBAR* EN4 ...... 34 E6
Somerden Rd *STMC/STPC* BR5 ... 177 K2
Somerfield Cl *FSBYPK* N4 ...... 85 H2 ⑥
Somerford Gv *STNW/STAM* N16 ... 85 M4
  TOTM N17 .... 68 A3
Somerford St *WCHPL* E1 ...... 104 B3 ⑥
Somerford Wy
  BERM/RHTH SE16 .... 104 E8
Somerhill Av *BFN/LL* DA15 ...... 144 A4
Somerhill Rd *WELL* DA16 .... 126 B7
Somerleyton Rd *BRXN/ST* SW9 ... 139 G1
Somersby Gdns *REDBR* IG4 ...... 70 F6
Somers Cl *CAMTN* NW1 .... 5 G5 ⑥
Somers Crs *BAY/PAD* W2 .... 9 J5
Somerset Av *CHSGTN* KT9 ...... 167 K6
  WELL DA16 .... 154 B5
Somerset Cl *HOR/WEW* KT19 .... 180 E2 ⑥
  NWMAL KT3 .... 168 L1
  TOTM N17 .... 67 K3
  WFD IG8 .... 70 B2
Somerset Gdns *EMPK* RM11 ..... 93 G1
  HGT N6 .... 66 A8
  LEW SE13 .... 123 H7 ⑥
  STRHM/NOR SW16 .... 156 E4
  TEDD TW11 .... 151 L1 ⑥
Somerset Rd *BAR* EN5 .... 34 B8
  BTFD TW8 .... 116 C4
  CHSWK W4 .... 117 K1
  DART DA1 .... 146 B3
  HDN NW4 .... 64 C5 ⑥
  HRW HA1 .... 61 J7
  KUT KT1 .... 152 F5
  ORP BR6 .... 177 G2
  PEND EN3 .... 38 A3 ⑥
  STHL UB1 .... 97 G4
  TEDD TW11 .... 151 J1
  TOTM N17 .... 67 M4 ⑥
  UED N18 .... 49 M7
  WALTH E17 .... 69 G6
  WEA W13 .... 98 B7
  WIM/MER SW19 .... 136 D7
Somerset Sq *WKENS* W14 ..... 100 F8 ⑥
Somerset Street Little
  TWRH EC3N 13 L5
Somerset Waye *HEST* TW5 ..... 114 E4
Somersham Rd *BXLYHN* DA7 ... 126 F7
Somers Pl *BRXS/STRHM* SW2 ... 138 F4
Somers Rd *BRXS/STRHM* SW2 ... 138 F3
  WALTH E17 .... 68 F5
Somers Wy *BUSH* WD23 .... 43 J2
Somerton Av *RCH/KEW* TW9 ... 117 H8
Somerton Rd *CRICK* NW2 ...... 82 D3
  PECK SE15 .... 140 B1
Somertrees Av *LEE/GVPK* SE12 ... 142 B6
Somervell Rd *RYLN/HDSTN* HA2... 78 F5
Somerville Rd *CHDH* RM6 ..... 72 C6
  COB KT11 .... 178 A7
  DART DA1 .... 146 F3 ⑥
  PGE/AN SE20 .... 158 D3
Sonderburg Rd *HOLWY* N7 ..... 84 F3 ⑥
Sondes St *WALW* SE17 .... 19 G9
Sonia Cl *OXHEY* WD19 .... 42 C2
Sonia Gdns *CRICK* NW2 .... 81 M4
  HEST TW5 .... 115 G5
  NFNCH/WDSP N12 .... 47 J6 ⑥
Sonning Gdns *HPTN* TW12 ..... 150 E2
Sonning Rd *CROY/NA* CR0 ..... 173 G1
Soper Cl *CHING* E4 .... 50 F7
Soper Ms *PEND* EN3 .... 38 A3 ⑥
Sopers Rd *POTB/CUF* EN6 ..... 24 F2
Sophia Cl *CAN/RD* E16 .... 106 D5
  LEY E10 .... 87 H1
Sophia Sq *POP/IOD* E14 ..... 104 E6 ⑥
Sopwith Av *CHSGTN* KT9 ...... 167 L7
Sopwith Cl *RCHPK/HAM* TW10 ... 152 F1
Sopwith Rd *HEST* TW5 .... 114 C5
Sopwith Wy *KUTN/CMB* KT2 ... 152 E4
  VX/NE SW8 .... 17 K9
Sorbie Cl *WEY* KT13 .... 164 C8 ⑥
Sorrel Cl *THMD* SE28 .... 108 A7
Sorrel Gdns *EHAM* E6 .... 106 E4
Sorrel La *POP/IOD* E14 ...... 105 K5 ⑥
Sorrel Cl *NWCR* SE14 .... 122 C6
Sorrel Wk *ROM* RM1 .... 73 M4
Sorrento Rd *SUT* SM1 .... 170 E6
Sotheby Rd *HBRY* N5 .... 85 J4
Sotheran Cl *HACK* E8 .... 86 A8 ⑥
Sotheron Rd *WAT* WD17 .... 29 J5
Soudan Rd *BTSEA* SW11 ...... 119 M6
Souldern Rd *HMSMTH* W6 ..... 118 D1 ⑦
Souldern St *WATW* WD18 ...... 29 H8
South Access Rd *WALTH* E17 ... 68 E8
South Acre *CDALE/KGS* NW9 ... 63 H3
South Africa Rd *SHB* W12 .... 100 B6
South Ap *NTHWD* HA6 .... 41 K5
South Audley St
  MYFR/PKLN W1K 10 B7
South Av *CAR* SM5 .... 183 C1 ⑥
  CHING E4 .... 51 H2
  RCH/KEW TW9 .... 117 G2 ⑥
  STHL UB1 .... 96 F6
South Avenue Gdns *STHL* UB1 ... 96 F6
South Bank *SURB* KT6 .... 167 L1
Southbank *THDIT* KT7 .... 167 H2
South Bank Ter *SURB* KT6 .... 167 L1 ⑥
South Birkbeck Rd *WAN* E11 ... 87 K3
South Black Lion La
  HMSMTH W6 .... 118 A3 ⑥
South Bolton Gdns
  WBPTN SW10 .... 14 D7
The South Border
  PUR/KEN CR8 .... 183 K4
Southborough Cl *SURB* KT6 ... 167 K3
Southborough La *BMLY* BR1 ... 160 E8
  HAYES BR2 .... 160 F8 ⑥
Southborough Rd *BMLY* BR1 ... 160 E6
  HOM E9 .... 86 C8
  SURB KT6 .... 167 L3
Southborough Rd (The Lane)
  SURB KT6 .... 167 L3 ⑥
Southbourne *HAYES* BR2 ...... 175 G2 ⑥
Southbourne Av
  CDALE/KGS NW9 .... 63 J3
Southbourne Cl *PIN* HA5 ..... 60 E8
Southbourne Crs *HDN* NW4 ... 64 E5
Southbourne Gdns *IL* IG1 .... 89 J5
  LEE/GVPK SE12 .... 142 B2 ⑥
  RSLP HA4 .... 78 B1
Southbridge Pl *CROY/NA* CR0 ... 172 C6
Southbridge Rd *CROY/NA* CR0 ... 172 C6
Southbridge Wy *NWDGN* UB2 ... 96 E8
Southbrook Dr
  CHES/WCR EN8 .... 26 D1 ⑥
Southbrook Rd *LEW* SE13 .... 141 L3
  STRHM/NOR SW16 .... 156 E4
South Bucks Wy *DEN/HRF* UB9 ... 76 A1
Southbury Av *EN* EN1 .... 37 G7
Southbury Cl *RCH* RM12 ...... 92 D5 ⑥
Southbury Rd *EN* EN1 .... 36 F7
South Carriage Dr *KTBR* SW1X ... 15 M1
  SKENS SW7 .... 15 J2
Southchurch Ct *PLMGR* N13 ... 48 F7 ⑥
Southchurch Rd *EHAM* E6 ..... 106 F1
South Cl *BAR* EN5 .... 33 M6
  BXLYHS DA6 .... 144 D1
  DAGE RM10 .... 91 G8
  FELT TW13 .... 133 C7
  HGT N6 .... 66 B7
  PIN HA5 .... 60 F8
  WDR/YW UB7 .... 112 F1
South Colonnade *POP/IOD* E14 ... 105 G7
Southcombe St
  WKENS W14 .... 118 L2 ⑥
Southcote Av *BRYLDS* KT5 .... 168 B2
  FELT TW13 .... 132 K6
Southcote Ri *RSLP* HA4 ...... 59 K8
Southcote Rd *ARCH* N19 ...... 84 C4
  SAND/SEL CR2 .... 184 E3
  SNWD SE25 .... 158 B8
  WALTH E17 .... 69 G6
South Countess Rd *WALTH* E17 ... 68 F4 ⑥
South Crs *CAN/RD* E16 .... 105 K3
Southcroft Av *WELL* DA16 .... 125 L8
  WWKM BR4 .... 174 C4
Southcroft Rd *ORP* BR6 ...... 176 E5
  TOOT SW17 .... 156 A2
South Cross Rd *BARK/HLT* IG6 ... 71 J6
South Croxted Rd *DUL* SE21 ... 139 K7
Southdale *CHIG* IG7 .... 53 K8 ⑥
Southdean Gdns
  WIM/MER SW19 .... 136 F6
South Dene *MLHL* NW7 .... 45 K5
Southdown Av *HNWL* W7 ...... 116 B2
Southdown Crs
  GNTH/NBYPK IG2 .... 71 L6
  RYLN/HDSTN HA2 .... 79 J1
Southdown Dr *RYNPK* SW20 ... 154 D3
Southdown Rd *CAR* SM5 ...... 183 G2 ⑥
  EMPK RM11 .... 74 B8
  RYNPK SW20 .... 154 D4
  WOT/HER KT12 .... 165 L6
South Dr *BELMT* SM2 .... 181 L3
  BNSTD SM7 .... 182 E6
  COUL/CHIP CR5 .... 183 K8
  GPK RM2 .... 74 C4
  ORP BR6 .... 176 E7
  POTB/CUF EN6 .... 24 E3
  RSLP HA4 .... 77 L1
South Ealing Rd *EA* W5 ...... 98 D8
South Eastern Av *ED* N9 ..... 49 M5
South Eden Park Rd *BECK* BR3 ... 159 H8
South Edwardes Sq *KENS* W8 ... 118 F1
South End *CROY/NA* CR0 ...... 172 C6
  KENS W8 .... 14 D3
Southend Arterial Rd
  EMPK RM11 .... 74 E4
Southend Cl *ELTH/MOT* SE9 ... 143 H3
Southend Crs *ELTH/MOT* SE9 ... 143 G3
Southend La *CAT* SE6 .... 140 F8
Southend Rd *BECK* BR3 ...... 159 G4
South End Rd *HAMP* NW3 ..... 83 L4 ⑥
  HAMP NW3 .... 83 L4 ⑥
  RAIN RM13 .... 92 A8
South End Rw *KENS* W8 ...... 14 D3
Southend Rd *REDBR* IG4 ...... 70 F4
Southend Rd
  (North Circular Road)
  SWFD E18 .... 69 M3
  WALTH E17 .... 69 M2
South End Rw *KENS* W8 ...... 14 D3
Southerland Cl *WEY* KT13 .... 164 A1
Southern Av *EBED/NFELT* TW14 ... 132 A5
  SNWD SE25 .... 157 M6
Southern Dr *LOU* IG10 .... 52 F1
Southern Gv *BOW* E3 .... 104 F2 ⑥
Southernhay *LOU* IG10 .... 39 K8 ⑥
Southern Perimeter Rd
  HTHAIR TW6 .... 130 C2
Southern Pl *SWLY* BR8 .... 163 K7 ⑥

Southern Rd *EFNCH* N2 .... 65 M5
  PLSTW E13 .... 106 B1
Southern Rw *NKENS* W10 ..... 100 D3
Southern St *IS* N1 .... 5 L5
Southern Wy *CHDH* RM6 ...... 73 G7
Southerton Rd
  HMSMTH W6 .... 118 C2 ⑩
South Esk Rd *FSTGT* E7 ..... 88 C2
Southey Rd *BRXN/ST* SW9 .... 121 G6
  SEVS/STOTM N15 .... 67 L6
  WIM/MER SW19 .... 155 G3
Southey St *PGE/AN* SE20 .... 158 D3
Southfield *BAR* EN5 .... 46 D1 ⑥
Southfield Av *WATN* WD24 .... 29 J3
Southfield Cl *UX/CGN* UB8 ... 95 G3
Southfield Gdns *TWK* TW1 ... 133 M8 ②
Southfield Pk *RYLN/HDSTN* HA2 ... 61 H5
Southfield Rd *CHES/WCR* EN8 ... 26 C5
  CHST BR7 .... 161 M6
  CHSWK W4 .... 99 K8
  PEND EN3 .... 50 B1
Southfields *E/WMO/HCT* KT8 ... 166 E1
  HDN NW4 .... 64 B4
Southfields Av *ASHF* TW15 ... 149 H2
Southfields Rd
  WAND/EARL SW18 .... 137 G3
Southfleet Rd *ORP* BR6 ..... 176 E5
South Gdns *WIM/MER* SW19 ... 155 K3
South Ga *PUR* RM19 .... 129 J2
South Gate Av *FELT* TW13 ... 131 K8 ⑥
Southgate Gv *IS* N1 .... 7 H2
Southgate Rd *IS* N1 .... 85 L6 ⑥
  POTB/CUF EN6 .... 23 J6
South Gipsy Rd *WELL* DA16 ... 126 D8
South Gv *HGT* N6 .... 84 A1
  SEVS/STOTM N15 .... 67 K6
  WALTH E17 .... 68 F6
South Hall Dr *RAIN* RM13 .... 110 B4
South Hl *CHST* BR7 .... 160 F2
South Hill Av *HRW* HA1 ...... 79 K3
  RYLN/HDSTN HA2 .... 79 J3
South Hill Gv *HRW* HA1 ...... 79 L4
South Hill Pk *HAMP* NW3 .... 83 L4
South Hill Rd *HAYES* BR2 ... 159 L6
Southholme Cl *NRWD* SE19 ... 157 L4 ⑥
Southill La *PIN* HA5 .... 60 A5
Southill Rd *CHST* BR7 ...... 160 D3
Southill St *POP/IOD* E14 .... 105 H5
South Island Pl *BRXN/ST* SW9 ... 120 F5
South Lambeth Pl *LBTH* SE11 ... 17 K8
South Lambeth Rd *VX/NE* SW8 ... 120 E5
Southland Rd
  WOOL/PLUM SE18 .... 125 M5
Southlands Av *ORP* BR6 ..... 176 E6
Southlands Dr *WIM/MER* SW19 ... 136 D6
Southlands Gv *BMLY* BR1 ..... 160 D7
Southlands Rd *HAYES* BR2 ... 160 D7
Southland Wy *ISLW* TW7 ..... 133 C2
South La *KUT* KT1 .... 152 D6
  NWMAL KT3 .... 153 K7
South La West *NWMAL* KT3 ... 153 K7 ⑥
South Lodge Av *MTCM* CR4 ... 156 E7
South Lodge Crs *ENC/FH* EN2 ... 35 K7 ⑥
South Lodge Dr
  STHGT/OAK N14 .... 35 L8 ⑥
South Md *CDALE/KGS* NW9 .... 63 M2
  HOR/WEW KT19 .... 180 F1 ⑥
Southmead Crs *CHES/WCR* EN8... 26 E3
Southmead Rd
  WIM/MER SW19 .... 136 E5
South Molton La
  MYFR/PKLN W1K 10 C5
South Molton Rd *CAN/RD* E16 ... 106 A5
South Molton St
  MYFR/PKLN W1K 10 C5
Southmont Rd *ESH/CLAY* KT10... 166 E4
Southmoor Wy *HOM* E9 .... 86 F6 ⑥
South Norwood Hl *SNWD* SE25 ... 157 L5
South Oak Rd
  STRHM/NOR SW16 .... 139 G8 ⑥
Southold Ri *ELTH/MOT* SE9 .. 143 G7 ⑥
Southolm St *VX/NE* SW8 .... 120 B6 ⑥
South Ordnance Rd *PEND* EN3 ... 38 A2
Southover *BMLY* BR1 .... 160 A1
  NFNCH/WDSP N12 .... 47 G6
South Pde *CHEL* SW3 .... 15 H7
  CHSWK W4 .... 117 K2 ⑥
  IL IG1 .... 89 K3
South Park Crs *CAT* SE6 .... 141 L5
  IL IG1 .... 89 K3
South Park Dr *IL* IG1 ...... 89 J3
South Park Gv *NWMAL* KT3 ... 153 J7
South Park Hill Rd
  SAND/SEL CR2 .... 172 D7
South Park Ms
  FUL/PGN SW6 .... 119 H8 ②
South Park Rd *IL* IG1 ...... 89 K3
  WIM/MER SW19 .... 155 G2
South Park Ter *IL* IG1 ..... 89 K3
South Park Wy *RSLP* HA4 .... 78 C6
South Pl *BRYLDS* KT5 .... 167 M2 ⑥
  LVPST EC2M 13 H3
  PEND EN3 .... 37 J8
South Place Ms *LVPST* EC2M ... 13 H3
Southport Rd
  WOOL/PLUM SE18 .... 125 K2
Southridge Pl *RYNPK* SW20 ... 154 D3 ⑥
South Ri *CAR* SM5 .... 182 E2
South Rd *CHDH* RM6 .... 72 C6
  EA W5 .... 116 D2
  ED N9 .... 50 A3
  EDGW HA8 .... 63 H2
  ERITH DA8 .... 127 M4
  FELT TW13 .... 150 D1
  FSTH SE23 .... 140 D6
  HPTN TW12 .... 150 E2
  STHL UB1 .... 96 F7
  WDR/YW UB7 .... 113 G1
  WEY KT13 .... 164 C7
  WHTN TW2 .... 133 K7
  WIM/MER SW19 .... 155 G2
South Rw *BKHTH/KID* SE3 .... 124 A7
Southsea Av *WATW* WD18 ..... 29 G7
Southsea Rd *KUT* KT1 .... 152 E7
South Sea St *BERM/RHTH* SE16 ... 122 F1
South Side *HMSMTH* W6 ...... 117 M1
Southside Common
  WIM/MER SW19 .... 154 D2
Southspring *ELTH/MOT* SE9 .. 143 K4

South Sq *GINN* WC1R 12 A3
  GLDGN NW11 .... 65 G7
South St *BMLY* BR1 .... 160 A5
  EPSOM KT18 .... 180 D6
  ISLW TW7 .... 116 A8
  MYFR/PKLN W1K 10 B8
  PEND EN3 .... 37 K8
  RAIN RM13 .... 109 J1
  ROM RM1 .... 73 L6
  ROMW/RG RM7 .... 73 L7
South Tenter St *WCHPL* E1 ... 13 M6
South Ter *SKENS* SW7 .... 15 J5
  SURB KT6 .... 167 L1
  WDGN N22 .... 66 E3
Southvale Rd *BKHTH/KID* SE3 ... 123 L7 ③
South Vale *SURB* KT6 .... 167 L4 ⑥
South Vw *BMLY* BR1 .... 160 C5
Southview Av *WLSDN* NW10 ... 81 M5
South View Cl *BXLY* DA5 .... 144 F3
Southview Cl *TOOT* SW17 .... 156 A1 ⑥
South View Crs
  GNTH/NBYPK IG2 .... 71 H7
Southview Dr *SWFD* E18 ..... 70 B4
Southview Gdns *WLGTN* SM6 ... 183 J1
South View Rd *CEND/HSY/T* N8... 66 E4
  LOU IG10 .... 52 F1
  PIN HA5 .... 42 B8
  RDART DA2 .... 146 D7
Southviews *SAND/SEL* CR2 ... 185 K2 ③
South Vils *CAMTN* NW1 ...... 84 D6
Southville *VX/NE* SW8 ...... 120 D6
Southville Cl *EBED/NFELT* TW14... 131 L4
  HOR/WEW KT19 .... 180 D2
Southville Crs
  EBED/NFELT TW14 .... 131 L5
Southville Rd
  EBED/NFELT TW14 .... 131 L5
  THDIT KT7 .... 167 G2
South Wk *WWKM* BR4 .... 174 E5
Southwark Br *BLKFR* EC4V 12 F7
Southwark Bridge Rd
  STHWK SE1 .... 12 F8
Southwark Park Rd
  BERM/RHTH SE16 .... 122 B1
Southwark Pl *BMLY* BR1 ..... 160 F6
Southwark St *STHWK* SE1 .... 12 D8
Southwater Cl *BECK* BR3 .... 159 H3
South Wy *ABLGY* WD5 .... 20 D6
  GSTN WD25 .... 20 E5
  PUR RM19 .... 129 L1
  RYLN/HDSTN HA2 .... 61 G5
  WAB EN9 .... 38 B2
  WBLY HA9 .... 81 G5
  CAR SM5 .... 182 D3
  CROY/NA CR0 .... 173 L5
  FBAR/BDGN N11 .... 48 C8
Southway *GLDGN* NW11 .... 65 H7
  HAYES BR2 .... 175 G2 ⑥
  RYNPK SW20 .... 154 D7
  TRDG/WHET N20 .... 47 G4
  WLGTN SM6 .... 171 J6
South Weald Dr *WAB* EN9 .... 27 K6
Southwell Av *NTHLT* UB5 .... 79 G6
Southwell Gdns *SKENS* SW7 .. 14 E5
Southwell Grove Rd *WAN* E11 ... 87 L2
Southwell Rd *CMBW* SE5 ..... 121 J8
  CROY/NA CR0 .... 172 A1
  KTN/HRWW/W HA3 .... 62 D7
South Western Rd *TWK* TW1 ... 134 B3 ⑥
South West India Dock Entrance
  POP/IOD E14 .... 105 J8
Southwest Rd *WAN* E11 ...... 87 K1
South Wharf Rd *BAY/PAD* W2 ... 9 G2
Southwick Ms *BAY/PAD* W2 ... 9 H4
Southwick Pl *BAY/PAD* W2 ... 9 H5
Southwick St *BAY/PAD* W2 ... 9 J4
Southwold Dr *BARK* IG11 .... 90 A5
Southwold Rd *BXLY* DA5 ..... 145 H3 ⑥
  CLPT E5 .... 86 B2 ⑥
  WATN WD24 .... 29 J2
Southwood Av *COUL/CHIP* CR5... 183 J8
  HGT N6 .... 66 B8
  KUTN/CMB KT2 .... 153 J4
Southwood Cl *BMLY* BR1 ..... 160 F7
Southwood Gdns *BARK/HLT* IG6 ... 71 H5
  ESH/CLAY KT10 .... 167 G5
Southwood La *HGT* N6 .... 66 A8
Southwood Lawn Rd *HGT* N6 ... 66 A8
Southwood Rd *ELTH/MOT* SE9... 143 H6
  THMD SE28 .... 108 B7
South Worple Wy
  MORT/ESHN SW14 .... 117 K8
Sovereign Cl *EA* W5 .... 98 C4 ③
  PUR/KEN CR8 .... 183 M5
  RSLP HA4 .... 77 L1
  WAP E1W 104 F1
Sovereign Ct
  E/WMO/HCT KT8 .... 150 F7 ③
Sovereign Crs *POP/IOD* E14 ... 104 E6
Sovereign Gv *ALP/SUD* HA0 ... 80 D3
Sovereign Rd *BARK* IG11 .... 108 C2
Sowerby Cl *ELTH/MOT* SE9 ... 142 F2 ③
Sowrey Av *RAIN* RM13 .... 91 M6
Space Waye *EBED/NFELT* TW14 ... 132 A2
Spa Cl *NRWD* SE19 .... 157 L2
Spa Dr *EPSOM* KT18 .... 180 A7
Spafield St *CLKNW* EC1R .... 6 A9 ③
Spa Hl *THHTH* CR7 .... 157 K4
Spalding Rd *TOOT* SW17 ..... 156 B1
Spanby Rd *BOW* E3 .... 105 G3
Spaniards Cl *GLDGN* NW11 ... 83 J1
Spaniards End *GLDGN* NW11 ... 83 J1
  HAMP NW3 .... 83 J1
Spaniards Rd *HAMP* NW3 ..... 83 J2
Spanish Pl *MHST* W1U .... 10 B4 ③
Spanish Rd *WAND/EARL* SW18 ... 137 J2
Spareleaze Hl *LOU* IG10 .... 39 M7
Sparkbridge Rd *HRW* HA1 .... 61 L5 ③
Sparks Cl *ACT* W3 .... 99 G5
  BCTR RM8 .... 90 D2 ③
  HPTN TW12 .... 150 E2 ③
Spa Rd *BERM/RHTH* SE16 ..... 19 L4

Sparrow Cl *FELT* TW13 ...... 150 E2 ⑥
Sparrow Dr *STMC/STPC* BR5 ... 176 C3
Sparrow Farm Dr
  EBED/NFELT TW14 .... 132 E4
Sparrow Farm Rd *EW* KT17 ... 174 C5
Sparrow Gn *DAGE* RM10 ..... 91 H3 ⑥
Sparrows Herne *BUSH* WD23 ... 43 H2
Sparrows La *ELTH/MOT* SE9 ... 143 H4
Sparrows Wy *BUSH* WD23 .... 43 J2 ⑥
Sparsholt Rd *ARCH* N19 ..... 84 F1
  BARK IG11 .... 89 L8
Sparta St *LEW* SE13 .... 123 J6
Spearman St
  WOOL/PLUM SE18 .... 125 G4 ②
Spear Ms *ECT* SW5 .... 14 B6
Spears Rd *ARCH* N19 .... 84 E1
Speart La *HEST* TW5 .... 114 E5
Spedan Cl *HAMP* NW3 .... 83 H3
Speedbird Wy *WDR/YW* UB7 ... 112 B5
Speedwell St *DEPT* SE8 ..... 123 G5 ③
Speer Rd *THDIT* KT7 .... 166 F1
Speirs Cl *NWMAL* KT3 .... 168 F1
Spekehill *ELTH/MOT* SE9 .... 142 F7
Speke Rd *THHTH* CR7 .... 157 K5
Speldhurst Cl *HAYES* BR2 ... 159 M8 ③
Speldhurst Rd *CHSWK* W4 .... 117 K1
  HOM E9 .... 86 D7
Spelman St *WCHPL* E1 .... 104 A4 ⑪
Spelthorne Gv *SUN* TW16 .... 149 M3
Spelthorne La *ASHF* TW15 ... 149 J3
Spence Cl *BERM/RHTH* SE16 ... 104 F8 ③
  YEAD UB4 .... 96 A4
Spencer Av *PLMGR* N13 ...... 48 F8
  YEAD UB4 .... 96 A4
Spencer Cl *FNCH* N3 .... 64 F3
  ORP BR6 .... 176 E4
  UX/CGN UB8 .... 94 C2
  WFD IG8 .... 52 C7
  WLSDN NW10 .... 98 F2
Spencer Dr *EFNCH* N2 .... 65 J7
Spencer Gdns
  MORT/ESHN SW14 .... 135 J2 ③
Spencer Hl *WIM/MER* SW19 ... 154 E2
Spencer Hill Rd
  WIM/MER SW19 .... 154 E3
Spencer Ms *DUL* SE21 .... 139 K5 ③
  HMSMTH W6 .... 118 E4
Spencer Pk
  WAND/EARL SW18 .... 137 K2 ③
Spencer Pl *CROY/NA* CR0 .... 172 D2 ③
  WEST SW1E 16 F4
Spencer Ri *KTTN* NW5 .... 84 B4
Spencer Rd *ACT* W3 .... 99 J7
  ALP/SUD HA0 .... 80 C2
  BMLY BR1 .... 159 M3
  BTSEA SW11 .... 137 K1
  CEND/HSY/T N8 .... 66 F6 ③
  CHSWK W4 .... 117 J5
  E/WMO/HCT KT8 .... 151 J7
  EHAM E6 .... 88 D8
  FBAR/BDGN N11 .... 48 B6
  GDMY/SEVK IG3 .... 89 M1
  ISLW TW7 .... 115 K6
  KTN/HRWW/W HA3 .... 61 L3
  MTCM CR4 .... 156 A6
  RAIN RM13 .... 109 K2
  RYNPK SW20 .... 154 B4
  SAND/SEL CR2 .... 172 E7
  TOTM N17 .... 68 A2
  WALTH E17 .... 52 A8
  WHTN TW2 .... 133 L7
Spencer St *FSBYE* EC1V 6 C8
  NWDGN UB2 .... 114 D1
Spencer Wk *PUT/ROE* SW15 ... 136 D1
Spenser Crs *UPMR* RM14 ..... 75 J8
Spenser Gv *STNW/STAM* N16 ... 85 L4 ③
Spenser Rd *HNHL* SE24 ...... 139 H2
Spenser St *WESTW* SW1E ..... 16 F3 ③
Spensley Wk *STNW/STAM* N16... 85 K3
Speranza St *WOOL/PLUM* SE18... 125 M3
Sperling Rd *TOTM* N17 ...... 67 L2
Spert St *POP/IOD* E14 ...... 104 E6 ⑦
Speyside *STHGT/OAK* N14 .... 48 C1
Spey St *POP/IOD* E14 .... 105 J4
Spey Wy *ROM* RM1 .... 73 L1
Spezia Rd *WLSDN* NW10 ...... 100 A1
Spicer Cl *CMBW* SE5 .... 121 H7
  WOT/HER KT12 .... 165 L1
Spicers Fld *LHD/OX* KT22 ... 178 D6
Spices Yd *CROY/NA* CR0 ..... 172 C6
Spielman Rd *DART* DA1 ...... 146 F1
Spigurnell Rd *TOTM* N17 .... 67 K2
Spikes Bridge Rd *STHL* UB1 ... 96 E5
Spilsby Cl *CDALE/KGS* NW9 ... 63 L3 ③
Spilsby Rd *HARH* RM3 .... 74 E1
Spindle Cl *WOOL/PLUM* SE18 ... 124 E1
Spindlewood Gdns
  CROY/NA CR0 .... 172 E6 ③
Spindrift Av *POP/IOD* E14 ... 123 H2
Spinel Cl *WOOL/PLUM* SE18 ... 125 M3
Spingate Cl *HCH* RM12 ...... 92 D5 ③
Spinnells Rd *RYLN/HDSTN* HA2... 78 F1
Spinney Cl *COB* KT11 .... 178 A4
  NWMAL KT3 .... 153 L8
  RAIN RM13 .... 109 L1
  WDR/YW UB7 .... 94 E6 ③
  WPK KT4 .... 168 F5
Spinneycroft *LHD/OX* KT22 ... 178 D8
Spinney Dr *EBED/NFELT* TW14 ... 131 J4
Spinney Gdns *DAGW* RM9 .... 90 B3
  NRWD SE19 .... 157 M1
Spinney Oak *BMLY* BR1 ...... 160 E6
The Spinneys *BMLY* BR1 ..... 160 F5
The Spinney *ALP/SUD* HA0 ... 80 A3
  CHEAM SM3 .... 169 J6
  LHD/OX KT22 .... 178 C4
  POTB/CUF EN6 .... 23 K4 ③
  PUR/KEN CR8 .... 184 D4 ③
  SCUP DA14 .... 162 L1
  STAN HA7 .... 44 A4
  STRHM/NOR SW16 .... 138 D7 ⑥
  SUN TW16 .... 150 A4
  SWLY BR8 .... 163 L5 ③
  WHTN TW2 .... 29 G4
  WCHMH N21 .... 49 G2
The Spires *DART* DA1 .... 146 D6
Spital La *BRW* CM14 .... 57 M5
Spital Sq *WCHPL* E1 .... 13 K2
Spital St *DART* DA1 .... 146 E2

WCHPL E1 .... 104 A3 15
Spital Yd WCHPL E1 .... 13 K2 2
Spitfire Wy HEST TW5 .... 114 C3
Spoonbill Cl YEAD UB4 .... 96 D4
Spondon Rd SEVS/STOTM N15 ... 68 A5
Spooner Wk WLGTN SM6 .... 171 K7 8
Sportsbank St CAT SE6 .... 141 J4
Spottons Gv TOTM N17 .... 67 J2 2
Spout Hl CROY/NA CR0 .... 174 A7
Spout La STWL/WRAY TW19 ..... 130 A2
Spout La North
    STWL/WRAY TW19 .... 130 B1
Spratt Hall Rd WAN E11 .... 70 A7
Spray St WOOL/PLUM SE18 ..... 125 H2
Spreighton Rd
    E/WMO/HCT KT8 .... 151 H7
Sprimont Pl CHEL SW3 .... 15 L7
Springall St PECK SE15 .... 122 B5
Springbank WCHMH N21 .... 48 F1
Springbank Av HCH RM12 .... 92 C5 2
Springbank Rd LEW SE13 .... 141 L3
Springbourne Ct BECK BR3 .... 159 J4
Spring Bridge Rd EA W5 .... 98 D6
Spring Cl BAR EN5 .... 33 K8
    BCTR RM8 .... 90 D1
    BORE WD6 .... 32 A4 8
    DEN/HRF UB9 .... 58 D2
Springclose La CHEAM SM3 .. 169 L8 8
Spring Court Rd ENC/FH EN2 .... 36 A3
Springcroft Av EFNCH N2 .... 65 M4
Spring Crofts BUSH WD23 ...... 30 A8
Springdale Rd STNW/STAM N16.. 85 K4
Spring Dr PIN HA5 .... 60 D4
Springfarm Cl RAIN RM13 ..... 110 D2 8
Springfield BUSH WD23 .... 43 K3
    CLPT E5 .... 86 B1
Springfield Av HPTN TW12 .... 151 H2
    MUSWH N10 .... 66 C4
    RYNPK SW20 .... 154 F6
    SWLY BR8 .... 163 M7 8
Springfield Cl
    NFNCH/WDSP N12 .... 47 H7
    POTB/CUF EN6 .... 23 K4 8
    RKW/CH/CXG WD3 .... 28 B8
    STAN HA7 .... 44 A5
Springfield Dr GNTH/NBYPK IG2.. 71 J3
Springfield Gdns BMLY BR1 ... 160 F7 2
    CDALE/KGS NW9 .... 63 K6
    CLPT E5 .... 86 B1
    RSLP HA4 .... 78 B1
    UPMR RM14 .... 93 J3
    WFD IG8 .... 70 C1
    WWKM BR4 .... 174 B4 8
Springfield Gv CHARL SE7 .... 124 C4
    SUN TW16 .... 150 A4 8
Springfield La KIL/WHAMP NW6 .. 2 C4
    WEY KT13 .... 164 B6
Springfield Mdw WEY KT13 ... 164 B6
Springfield Mt CDALE/KGS NW9.. 63 L6
Springfield Pl NWMAL KT3 .... 153 J7
Springfield Ri SYD SE26 ...... 140 B8
Springfield Rd ASHF TW15 .... 148 F1
    BMLY BR1 .... 160 F7
    BXLYHN DA7 .... 127 H8 8
    CHES/WCR EN8 .... 26 E5
    CHING E4 .... 51 L3
    EHAM E6 .... 88 F7
    EW KT17 .... 181 J3 8
    FBAR/BDGN N11 .... 48 B7
    GSTN WD25 .... 21 H6 2
    HNWL W7 .... 97 L7
    HRW HA1 .... 61 L7
    HYS/HAR UB3 .... 96 C7
    KUT KT1 .... 152 E7
    SEVS/STOTM N15 .... 68 A5
    SRTFD E15 .... 105 L2 8
    STJWD NW8 .... 2 E4
    SYD SE26 .... 158 B1
    TEDD TW11 .... 152 A1 8
    THHTH CR7 .... 157 J4
    WALTH E17 .... 68 F7
    WELL DA16 .... 126 B8
    WHTN TW2 .... 133 C5
    WIM/MER SW19 .... 154 F1 8
    WLGTN SM6 .... 171 H7
Springfield Wk KIL/WHAMP NW6 .. 2 C4
Springfield Wy STMC/STPC BR5.. 162 C6
Spring Gdns E/WMO/HCT KT8 ... 151 J8
    GSTN WD25 .... 21 J8
    HCH RM12 .... 92 B4
    ORP BR6 .... 177 H8 8
    ROMW/RG RM7 .... 73 J6
    WFD IG8 .... 70 C1
    WHALL SW1A 11 J8
    WLGTN SM6 .... 171 J7 8
Spring Gv CHSWK W4 .... 117 C3
    HPTN TW12 .... 151 H4
    LOU IG10 .... 52 D1
    MTCM CR4 .... 156 A4
Spring Grove Crs HEST TW5 ... 115 C3
Spring Grove Rd HSLW TW3 ... 115 J6
    RCHPK/HAM TW10 .... 134 F2
Springhead Rd ERITH DA8 ... 127 M4
Spring Hl CLPT E5 .... 68 A8
    SYD SE26 .... 140 C8
Springhurst Cl CROY/NA CR0.. 173 M6
Spring Lake STAN HA7 .... 44 B6
Spring La CLPT E5 .... 86 B1
    MUSWH N10 .... 66 A4
    SNWD SE25 .... 173 H1
Spring Ms MHST W1U 9 M2 8
Spring Park Av CROY/NA CR0.. 173 K4
Springpark Dr BECK BR3 .... 159 J6
    FSBYPK N4 .... 85 J1
Spring Park Rd CROY/NA CR0.. 173 K4
Spring Pl FNCH N3 .... 65 C3
    KTTN NW5 .... 4 C1
Springpond Rd DAGW RM9 .... 90 E5
Springrice Rd LEW SE13 ...... 141 J3
Spring Rd FELT TW13 .... 131 M7
Spring Shaw Rd
    STMC/STPC BR5 .... 162 A4
Spring St BAY/PAD W2 .... 9 C5
    EW KT17 .... 180 F2
Spring V BXLYHN DA7 .... 145 H1
Springvale Av BTFD TW8 .... 116 D3
Spring Vale Cl SWLY BR8 .... 163 M3
Spring V North DART DA1 ... 146 D3 8

Spring V South DART DA1 .... 146 D4 2
Springvale Ter WKENS W14 .. 118 D1
Spring Villa Rd EDGW HA8 .... 63 G1 8
Springwater Cl
    WOOL/PLUM SE18 .... 125 G6 8
Springwell Av
    RKW/CH/CXG WD3 .... 40 A4
    WLSDN NW10 .... 81 M8
Springwell La RKW/CH/CXG WD3.. 40 A5
Springwell Rd HEST TW5 .... 114 D6
    STRHM/NOR SW16 .... 139 G8
Springwood Cl DEN/HRF UB9 .. 58 D2 8
Springwood Crs EDGW HA8 ... 45 J4
Springwood Wy ROM RM1 ... 74 A6 8
Sprowston Ms FSTGT E7 ..... 88 A6
Sprowston Rd FSTGT E7 ..... 88 A5
Sprucedale Cl SWLY BR8 ..... 163 L5
Sprucedale Gdns CROY/NA CR0.. 173 K6
    PUR/KEN CR8 .... 183 L2
Spruce Hills Rd WALTH E17 ... 69 J3
Sprules Rd BROCKY SE4 ..... 122 E7
Spur Cl ABLGY WD5 .... 20 D6 8
Spurfield E/WMO/HCT KT8 .... 151 H6
Spurgeon Av NRWD SE19 .... 157 K4
Spurgeon Rd NRWD SE19 .... 157 K3
Spurgeon St STHWK SE1 ..... 19 G4
Spurling Rd DAGW RM9 ...... 90 F6
    EDUL SE22 .... 139 M1 8
Spurrell Av RDART DA2 ..... 145 K8
Spur Rd BARK IG11 .... 107 J2
    EBED/NFELT TW14 .... 132 B2
    ISLW TW7 .... 116 A5
    ORP BR6 .... 177 G4
    SEVS/STOTM N15 .... 67 K5 8
    STAN HA7 .... 44 E6
    STHWK SE1 .... 18 A2
Spurstowe Rd HACK E8 ..... 86 B6 8
Spurstowe Ter HACK E8 .... 86 B5 8
The Spur CHES/WCR EN8 .... 26 D1 8
Squadrons Ap HCH RM12 .... 92 C6
The Square CAR SM5 .... 171 G7
    HMSMTH W6 .... 118 C3
    RCHPK/HAM TW10 .... 134 E2
    STKPK UB11 .... 95 K7
    WATN WD24 .... 29 H2
    WDR/YW UB7 .... 112 B6 8
    WFD IG8 .... 52 A7
Squarey St TOOT SW17 .... 137 J7
Squire's Bridge Rd
    SHPTN TW17 .... 148 F7
Squires Ct WIM/MER SW19 .. 137 G8
Squires La FNCH N3 .... 65 H3
Squire's Mt HAMP NW3 ...... 83 K3
Squires Rd SHPTN TW17 ... 148 F7
Squires Wk ASHF TW15 .... 149 K3 8
Squires Wood Dr CHST BR7 .. 160 F3 8
Squirrel Cl HSLWW TW4 .... 114 C8
Squirrel Ms HNWL W7 .... 98 A6 8
Squirrels Cl HGDN/ICK UB10 .. 77 C7
    NFNCH/WDSP N12 .... 47 J6 8
Squirrels Gn WPK KT4 ...... 168 F4 8
Squirrel's Heath Av GPK RM2.. 74 B4
Squirrels Heath La EMPK RM11.. 74 C5
Squirrels Heath Rd HARH RM3.. 74 E3
The Squirrels BUSH WD23 .... 43 K1
    LEW SE13 .... 123 K8 8
    PIN HA5 .... 60 F4
Squirrel's Wy EPSOM KT18 .. 180 D8
Squirries St BETH E2 .... 104 A2
Stable Cl NTHLT UB5 .... 97 G1 8
Stable Ms WNWD SE27 ..... 157 J1
Stables End ORP BR6 .... 176 C5
Stables Wy LBTH SE11 ...... 18 A4
Stable Wy NKENS W10 ..... 100 C5 8
Stable Yard Rd WHALL SW1A .. 10 F9 8
Stacey Av UED N18 .... 50 C6
Stacey Cl LEY E10 .... 69 K6 2
Stacey St HOLWY N7 .... 85 G3 8
    LSO/SEVD WC2H 11 H5 8
Stackhouse St KTBR SW1X .. 15 L3 8
Stadium Rd WOOL/PLUM SE18.. 124 F5
Stadium St WBPTN SW10 .. 119 J5
Stadium Wy DART DA1 ...... 145 L3
    WBLY HA9 .... 80 F4
Staffa Rd LEY E10 .... 86 E1
Stafford Av EMPK RM11 .... 74 D4
Stafford Cl CHEAM SM3 .... 169 L8
    CHES/WCR EN8 .... 26 B2
    GRH DA9 .... 147 M2 8
    KIL/WHAMP NW6 .... 2 A8
    STHGT/OAK N14 .... 35 J8
    WALTH E17 .... 68 F7 2
Stafford Gdns CROY/NA CR0.. 171 M7 2
Stafford Pl RCHPK/HAM TW10.. 134 F4
    CROY/NA CR0 .... 172 A6
    FSTGT E7 .... 88 C7
    KIL/WHAMP NW6 .... 2 A7
    KTN/HRWW/W HA3 .... 61 J1
    NWMAL KT3 .... 153 J6
    RSLP HA4 .... 77 M4
    SCUP DA14 .... 143 L8
    WLGTN SM6 .... 171 J8
Stafford Gdns CROY/NA CR0.. 171 M7 8
Stafford Pl RCHPK/HAM TW10.. 134 F4
Stafford Rd BOW E3 .... 104 F1 8

STA TW18 .... 148 B4
    WHTN TW2 .... 133 J7
Staines Rd East SUN TW16 .. 150 C4
Staines Rd West ASHF TW15.. 149 J3
Stainford Cl ASHF TW15 .... 149 K1
    WALTH E17 .... 69 C5
Staining La CITYW EC2V 12 F4 8
Stainmore Cl CHST BR7 .... 161 K4 8
Stainsbury St BETH E2 ..... 104 C1 8
Stainsby Pl POP/IOD E14 .. 105 G5 2
Stainsby Rd POP/IOD E14 .. 105 G5
Stains Cl CHES/WCR EN8 .... 26 E1
Stainton Rd LEW SE13 ..... 141 K4
    PEND EN3 .... 37 J4
Stalbridge St CAMTN NW1 .... 9 K2 8
Stalham St
    BERM/RHTH SE16 .... 122 B1 8
Stambourne Wy NRWD SE19 .. 157 L3
    WWKM BR4 .... 174 C5
Stamford Brook Av
    HMSMTH W6 .... 117 M1
Stamford Brook Gdns
    HMSMTH W6 .... 117 M1 8
Stamford Brook Rd
    HMSMTH W6 .... 117 M1
Stamford Cl KTN/HRWW/W HA3.. 61 L1
    POTB/CUF EN6 .... 23 K5
    SEVS/STOTM N15 .... 68 A5 8
    STHL UB1 .... 97 G6 8
Stamford Dr HAYES BR2 .... 159 M7
Stamford Gdns DAGW RM9 .. 90 C7
Stamford Green Rd
    EPSOM KT18 .... 180 B6
Stamford Gv East
    STNW/STAM N16 .... 86 A1 8
Stamford Gv West
    STNW/STAM N16 .... 86 A1 8
Stamford Hl STNW/STAM N16.. 85 M1
Stamford Rd DAGW RM9 .... 90 B7
    EHAM E6 .... 88 E8
    IS N1 .... 7 K1
    SEVS/STOTM N15 .... 68 A5 8
    WAT WD17 .... 29 H5
    WOT/HER KT12 .... 165 K5 8
Stamford St STHWK SE1 .... 12 A9
Stamp Pl BETH E2 .... 7 L7
Stanborough Rd HACK E8 .. 85 M6 8
Stanborough Av BORE WD6.. 32 A3
Stanborough Cl HPTN TW12.. 150 F2 2
Stanborough Rd ISLW TW7.. 115 K8 8
Stanbridge Pl WCHMH N21 .. 49 H4 8
Stanbridge Rd
    PUT/ROE SW15 .... 118 C8 8
Stanbrook Rd ABYW SE2 .. 108 B8
Stanbury Av WAT WD17 .... 28 E2
Stanbury Ct HAMP NW3 .... 83 M6 8
Stanbury Rd PECK SE15 .. 122 B6
Stancroft CDALE/KGS NW9 .. 63 L5
Standale Gv RSLP HA4 .... 59 J6
Standard Rd BELV DA17 .. 127 C3
    BXLYHS DA6 .... 144 E1
    HSLWW TW4 .... 114 E8
    PEND EN3 .... 37 L3
    WLSDN NW10 .... 99 J3
Standen Av HCH RM12 .... 92 D3
Standen Rd WAND/EARL SW18.. 137 G4
Standfield ABLGY WD5 .... 20 E4
Standfield Rd DAGE RM10 .. 91 C5
Standish Rd HMSMTH W6 .. 118 A2
Stane Cl WIM/MER SW19 .. 155 H3 8
Stane Wy ISLW TW7 .... 181 G3
    WOOL/PLUM SE18 .... 124 D5
Stanfield Rd BOW E3 ...... 104 E1 8
Stanford Cl HPTN TW12 .. 150 F2 8
    ROMW/RG RM7 .... 73 H7
    RSLP HA4 .... 59 J7
    WFD IG8 .... 53 L2
Stanford Gdns SOCK/AV RM15.. 111 L2
Stanford Pl STHWK SE1 .... 19 J6
Stanford Rd FBAR/BDGN N11.. 47 M7
    KENS W8 .... 14 D4
    STRHM/NOR SW16 .... 156 D1
The Stanfords EW KT17 .. 180 F5 8
Stanford St WEST SW1P 17 G6
Stanford Wy
    STRHM/NOR SW16 .... 156 D5
Stangate Crs BORE WD6 .. 32 E8
Stangate Gdns STAN HA7 .. 44 B6
Stanger Rd SNWD SE25 .. 158 A7
Stanham Pl DART DA1 .... 146 A1
Stanham Rd DART DA1 .... 146 C2
Stanhope Av FNCH N3 .... 64 F4
    HAYES BR2 .... 175 G3
    KTN/HRWW/W HA3 .... 61 K2
Stanhope Cl
    BERM/RHTH SE16 .... 104 D8 8
Stanhope Gdns FSBYPK N4.. 67 H7
    HGT N6 .... 66 B7
    IL IG1 .... 71 M8
    MLHL NW7 .... 45 M7 2
    SKENS SW7 .... 14 F5
Stanhope Ga
    MYFR/PKLN W1K 10 B9
Stanhope Gv BECK BR3 .. 158 F8
Stanhope Heath
    STWL/WRAY TW19 .... 130 C3 8
Stanhope Ms East SKENS SW7.. 14 F5
Stanhope Ms South SKENS SW7.. 14 F6
Stanhope Ms West SKENS SW7 .. 14 F5
Stanhope Park Rd
    GFD/PVL UB6 .... 97 J3 8
Stanhope Pl BAY/PAD W2 .. 9 L5
Stanhope Rd BAR EN5 .... 46 D1
    BCTR RM8 .... 90 F2
    BFN/LL DA15 .... 144 A8
    BXLYHN DA7 .... 126 E7
    CAR SM5 .... 183 G1
    CHES/WCR EN8 .... 26 A5
    CROY/NA CR0 .... 172 E5
    GFD/PVL UB6 .... 97 J4
    HGT N6 .... 66 C7
    NFNCH/WDSP N12 .... 47 J7
    RAIN RM13 .... 110 A1
    WALTH E17 .... 69 H6
Stanhope Rw MYFR/PICC W1J.. 10 C9 8
Stanhope St CAMTN NW1 .... 4 E7
Stanhope Ter BAY/PAD W2 .. 9 H6

Stanhope Wy
    STWL/WRAY TW19 .... 130 C3 8
Stanier Cl ECT SW5 .... 118 F3 8
Stanlake Rd SHB W12 .... 100 C7
Stanlake Vls SHB W12 .... 100 C7
Stanley Av BARK IG11 .... 107 M2
    BCTR RM8 .... 90 F1
    BECK BR3 .... 159 J6
    GFD/PVL UB6 .... 79 J8
    GPK RM2 .... 74 A5
    NWMAL KT3 .... 154 A8
Stanley Cl ALP/SUD HA0 .. 80 E7 8
    GPK RM2 .... 74 A5
    GRH DA9 .... 147 L2
    HCH RM12 .... 92 C2
    UX/CGN UB8 .... 94 D1 8
Stanley Crs NTGHL W11 .. 100 F6
Stanleycroft Cl ISLW TW7 .. 115 L6 8
Stanley Gdns ACT W3 .... 99 J8
    BORE WD6 .... 31 L4
    CRICK NW2 .... 82 C5
    MTCM CR4 .... 156 A2 8
    NTGHL W11 .... 100 F6 8
    SAND/SEL CR2 .... 185 G5 8
    WLGTN SM6 .... 171 J8
    WOT/HER KT12 .... 165 J7
Stanley Gardens Rd
    TEDD TW11 .... 151 L1
Stanley Gv THHTH CR7 .. 172 A1
    VX/NE SW8 .... 120 A7
Stanley Park Dr ALP/SUD HA0.. 80 E7
Stanley Park Rd CAR SM5.. 182 F1
    WLGTN SM6 .... 183 H1
Stanley Rd ACT W3 .... 117 H1
    ASHF TW15 .... 148 F1
    BELMT SM2 .... 170 B8
    CAR SM5 .... 183 C1
    CHING E4 .... 51 K3
    CROY/NA CR0 .... 172 A2
    ED N9 .... 49 M3
    EFNCH N2 .... 65 K5
    EN EN1 .... 36 E6
    FBAR/BDGN N11 .... 48 B7
    HAYES BR2 .... 160 C6
    HCH RM12 .... 92 C2
    HSLW TW3 .... 133 J1
    IL IG1 .... 89 K2
    LEY E10 .... 69 H7
    MNPK E12 .... 88 E5
    MORT/ESHN SW14 .... 135 H1
    MRDN SM4 .... 155 G2
    MTCM CR4 .... 156 A3
    MUSWH N10 .... 66 B1
    NTHWD HA6 .... 60 A2
    ORP BR6 .... 176 F3
    RYLN/HDSTN HA2 .... 60 C8
    SCUP DA14 .... 144 A7
    SEVS/STOTM N15 .... 67 H5
    SRTFD E15 .... 87 K8 8
    STHL UB1 .... 96 E6
    SWFD E18 .... 69 M2
    TEDD TW11 .... 151 L1
    WAT WD17 .... 29 J6 8
    WBLY HA9 .... 80 F6
    WHTN TW2 .... 133 K7
    WIM/MER SW19 .... 155 G3
Stanley Rd North RAIN RM13.. 109 M1
Stanley Rd South RAIN RM13.. 109 M1
Stanley Sq CAR SM5 ...... 182 F2
Stanley St DEPT SE8 ..... 122 F5
Stanley Ter ARCH N19 .... 84 E2 8
Stanley Wy STMC/STPC BR5.. 162 B8
Stanmer St BTSEA SW11 .. 119 L6
Stanmore Gdns
    RCH/KEW TW9 .... 116 F8 8
    SUT SM1 .... 170 C5 8
Stanmore Hl STAN HA7 .... 44 B7 8
Stanmore Rd BELV DA17 .. 127 J2
    RCH/KEW TW9 .... 116 F8
    SEVS/STOTM N15 .... 67 H5
    WAN E11 .... 87 M1
    WATN WD24 .... 29 H4
Stanmore St IS N1 .... 5 L3 8
Stanmore Ter BECK BR3 .. 159 G5 8
Stannard Rd HACK E8 .... 86 A6 8
Stannary St LBTH SE11 .. 18 B9
Stannet Wy WLGTN SM6 .. 171 J6
Stansfeld Rd CAN/RD E16.. 106 D5
Stansfield Rd BRXN/ST SW9.. 120 F8
    HSLWW TW4 .... 114 B7
Stansgate Rd DAGE RM10 .. 91 C2
Stanstead Cl HAYES BR2 .. 174 F1 8
Stanstead Gv FSTH SE23.. 140 F5 8
Stanstead Rd FSTH SE23.. 140 D5
    WAN E11 .... 70 B6
Stansted Cl HCH RM12 .. 92 C6 8
Stansted Crs BXLY DA5 .. 144 F8
Stanswood Gdns CMBW SE5.. 121 L5
Stanthorpe Rd
    STRHM/NOR SW16 .... 156 E1
Stanton Av TEDD TW11 .. 151 L2
Stanton Cl HOR/WEW KT19.. 168 B7
    STMC/STPC BR5 .... 177 J2
    WPK KT4 .... 169 K3 8
Stanton Rd BARN SW13 .. 117 M7
    CROY/NA CR0 .... 172 C2
    RYNPK SW20 .... 154 D5
Stanton Wy SYD SE26 .. 140 F8
Stanway Cl CHIG IG7 .... 53 L7
Stanway Gdns ACT W3 .. 99 G7
    EDGW HA8 .... 45 J8
Stanway St IS N1 .... 7 K5
Stanwell Cl
    STWL/WRAY TW19 .... 130 D3 8
Stanwell Gdns
    STWL/WRAY TW19 .... 130 D3 8
Stanwell Moor Rd
    STWL/WRAY TW19 .... 130 B6
    WDR/YW UB7 .... 112 B6
Stanwell New Rd STA TW18.. 130 B8
Stanwell Rd ASHF TW15 .. 130 E7
    WDR/YW UB7 .... 112 C6
Stanwick Rd WKENS W14 .. 118 F2
Stanworth St STHWK SE1 .. 19 L2 8
Stanwyck Gdns HARH RM3.. 56 B7
Stapenhill Rd ALP/SUD HA0.. 80 B3
Staple Cl BXLY DA5 ...... 145 K7

Staplefield Cl PIN HA5 .... 60 E1
Stapleford Av GNTH/NBYPK IG2.. 71 L6
Stapleford Cl CHING E4 .... 51 J5 8
    KUT KT1 .... 153 G6 8
    WIM/MER SW19 .... 136 E4
Stapleford Rd ALP/SUD HA0.. 80 D7
Stapleford Wy BARK IG11 .. 108 B2 8
Staplehurst Rd CAR SM5 .. 182 E1
    LEW SE13 .... 141 K2
Staples Cl BERM/RHTH SE16.. 104 E7 2
Staples Rd LOU IG10 ...... 39 L6
Staple St STHWK SE1 ...... 19 H2
Stapleton Crs RAIN RM13 .. 110 A1
Stapleton Gdns CROY/NA CR0.. 172 A7
Stapleton Hall Rd FSBYPK N4.. 66 A6
Stapleton Rd BORE WD6 .. 32 A3
    BXLYHN DA7 .... 126 F5
    ORP BR6 .... 176 F5
    TOOT SW17 .... 138 A7
Stapley Rd BELV DA17 .... 127 G3
Staplyton Rd BAR EN5 ... 33 L6
Star And Garter Hl
    RCHPK/HAM TW10 .... 134 C5
Starboard Wy POP/IOD E14.. 123 G1
Starch House La BARK/HLT IG6.. 71 L3
Starcross St CAMTN NW1 .. 4 F8
Starfield Rd SHB W12 .... 100 A8
Star Hl DART DA1 .... 145 L2
Star La CAN/RD E16 ...... 105 L3
    PLSTW E13 .... 105 M3 8
    STMC/STPC BR5 .... 162 D7
Starling Cl BKHH IG9 .... 52 A3
    PIN HA5 .... 60 C4
Starling La POTB/CUF EN6.. 24 F1
Starmans Cl DAGW RM9 .. 90 A6
Star Rd HGDN/ICK UB10 .. 95 J3
    ISLW TW7 .... 115 K7
    WKENS W14 .... 118 F4
Star St BAY/PAD W2 ...... 9 H4
Starts Cl ORP BR6 .... 176 A5
Starts Hill Av ORP BR6 .. 176 B6 8
Starts Hill Rd ORP BR6 .. 176 B5
Starveall Cl WDR/YW UB7.. 112 F1
State Farm Av ORP BR6 .. 176 B6
Staten Gdns TWK TW1 .. 133 M5
Statham Gv STNW/STAM N16.. 85 K3 8
    UED N18 .... 49 L7 2
Station Ap ALP/SUD HA0 .. 80 B6
    ASHF TW15 .... 130 F8 8
    BAR EN5 .... 34 C7
    BECK BR3 .... 159 H5
    BELMT SM2 .... 181 L1 8
    BELMT SM2 .... 182 B3 8
    BKHTH/KID SE3 .... 124 B8
    BXLYHN DA7 .... 126 E7
    BXLYHN DA7 .... 127 J7
    CAT SE6 .... 158 F1
    CHES/WCR EN8 .... 26 E7 8
    CHST BR7 .... 161 G4
    DART DA1 .... 146 E3
    ESH/CLAY KT10 .... 166 F5
    EW KT17 .... 181 H3 8
    FBAR/BDGN N11 .... 48 B7
    FUL/PGN SW6 .... 118 E8 8
    GFD/PVL UB6 .... 79 J7
    HAYES BR2 .... 175 G3
    HOR/WEW KT19 .... 169 G7 8
    HOR/WEW KT19 .... 180 D6
    HPTN TW12 .... 151 G4
    HYS/HAR UB3 .... 113 M1 8
    KUTN/CMB KT2 .... 153 G4 8
    NTHWD HA6 .... 59 L1 8
    ORP BR6 .... 176 F4
    ORP BR6 .... 177 H7
    OXHEY WD19 .... 42 D5 8
    PIN HA5 .... 60 E4
    PUR/KEN CR8 .... 184 A4 8
    RCH/KEW TW9 .... 117 G6 8
    RSLP HA4 .... 77 L1
    RSLP HA4 .... 78 B5
    SAND/SEL CR2 .... 184 D2 8
    SHPTN TW17 .... 149 J8 8
    STA TW18 .... 130 A8 8
    STMC/STPC BR5 .... 162 B7
    STRHM/NOR SW16 .... 156 D1
    SUN TW16 .... 150 A4
    SURB KT6 .... 167 L1 8
    SWLY BR8 .... 163 L7
    WAN E11 .... 70 A6
    WDR/YW UB7 .... 112 C2
    WELL DA16 .... 125 M7 8
    WEY KT13 .... 164 A8
    WLSDN NW10 .... 99 M2 8
    WPK KT4 .... 169 G3 8
Station Approach Rd
    CHSWK W4 .... 117 J5
    COUL/CHIP CR5 .... 183 K8
Station Av HOR/WEW KT19.. 180 E2
    NWMAL KT3 .... 153 L6 8
    WOT/HER KT12 .... 164 F6
Station Cl HPTN TW12 .. 151 H4
    POTB/CUF EN6 .... 22 F4
Station Crs ALP/SUD HA0 .. 80 B6
    ASHF TW15 .... 130 D8
    BKHTH/KID SE3 .... 124 A3
    SEVS/STOTM N15 .... 67 K5
Station Est BECK BR3 ... 158 D7 8
Station Estate Rd
    EBED/NFELT TW14 .... 132 B5
Station Footpath KGLGY WD4.. 20 B3
Station Gdns CHSWK W4 .. 117 J5 8
Station Gv ALP/SUD HA0 .. 80 E6
Station Hl HAYES BR2 ... 175 G8
Station La HCH RM12 .... 92 E2
Station House Ms UED N18.. 50 A6 10
Station Pde BARK IG11 .. 89 J7 8
    CRICK NW2 .... 82 A6
    DEN/HRF UB9 .... 58 A8
    HCH RM12 .... 92 B4 8
    RCH/KEW TW9 .... 117 G6
    STHGT/OAK N14 .... 48 D3 8
Station Pas PECK SE15 .. 122 C6
    SWFD E18 .... 70 B3 8
Station Pl FSBYPK N4 .. 85 G2 8
Station Ri WNWD SE27 .. 139 H6 8
Station Rd ARCH N19 .. 84 C3

ASHF TW15 130 F8
BAR EN5 34 B8
BARK/HLT IG6 71 K4
BARN SW13 117 M7
BCTR RM8 90 D1
BELMT SM2 182 A3
BELV DA17 127 G1
BFN/LL DA15 144 A6
BMLY BR1 160 A4
BORE WD6 32 A7
BXLYHN DA7 126 E8
CAR SM5 170 F6
CHES/WCR EN8 27 G7
CHIG IG7 53 H5
CHING E4 51 K3
CHSGTN KT9 167 L7
CROY/NA CR0 172 C3
DART DA1 145 M3
EA W5 98 F5 2
EDGW HA8 45 G8
ESH/CLAY KT10 166 D7
FBAR/BDGN N11 48 B7
FNCH N3 65 G2
GPK RM2 74 B5
HARH RM3 74 F2 1
HAYES BR2 159 L5
HDN NW4 64 A7
HNWL W7 97 L7
HPTN TW12 151 H4
HRW HA1 61 M7
HSLW TW3 133 H1
HYS/HAR UB3 95 M8
HYS/HAR UB3 113 L2
IL IG1 89 H3
KGLGY WD4 20 B2
KUT KT1 152 D4 1
KUTN/CMB KT2 153 G4 5
LEW SE13 123 J8
LOU IG10 39 L8
MLHL NW7 45 L8
MNPK E12 88 D4
NRWD SE19 158 A2 2
NWMAL KT3 154 B8
ORP BR6 176 F4
PGE/AN SE20 158 C2
POTB/CUF EN6 24 F2
PUR/KEN CR8 184 C7
RKW/CH/CXG WD3 40 D2 4
RYLN/HDSTN HA2 61 H6
SCUP DA14 144 A7
SEVS/STOTM N15 68 A4 9
SHPTN TW17 149 J8
SNWD SE25 157 M7
STMC/STPC BR5 162 C7 6
SUN TW16 150 A3 1
SWLY BR8 163 L7 5
TEDD TW11 152 A2
THDIT KT7 166 F2
TWK TW1 133 M5
UPMR RM14 93 J2
UX/CGN UB8 94 C3 5
WALTH E17 68 E7
WAT WD17 29 H5
WCHMH N21 49 H3
WDGN N22 66 E3 1
WDR/YW UB7 94 E8
WIM/MER SW19 155 J4
WLSDN NW10 99 M1
WWKM BR4 174 C3
Station Rd North BELV DA17 127 H1
Station Sq STMC/STPC BR5 161 J8
Station St SRTFD E15 87 K7
Station Ter CMBW SE5 121 J6
WLSDN NW10 100 C1 1
Station Vw GFD/PVL UB6 79 K8 2
Station Wy BKHH IG9 52 D6
CHEAM SM3 169 L8
Station Yd TWK TW1 134 A4 7
Staunton Rd KUTN/CMB KT2 152 F3
Staunton St DEPT SE8 122 F4
Staveley Cl HOLWY N7 84 E4 6
PECK SE15 122 C6 2
Staveley Gdns CHSWK W4 117 K6
Staveley Rd ASHF TW15 149 K2 4
CHSWK W4 117 K5
Staverton Rd CRICK NW2 82 C7
EMPK RM11 74 D7 1
Stave Yard Rd
BERM/RHTH SE16 104 E7 5
Stavordale Rd CAR SM5 170 C2
HBRY N5 85 G4
Stayner's Rd WCHPL E1 104 D3
Stayton Rd SUT SM1 170 A5
St Catherines Rd RSLP HA4 59 J6
Steadfast Rd KUT KT1 152 D4
Stead St WALW SE17 19 G6
Steam Farm La
EBED/NFELT TW14 131 M1 1
Stean St HACK E8 7 L3
Stebbing Wy BARK IG11 108 A1
Stebondale St POP/IOD E14 123 J3
Stedman Cl BXLY DA5 145 L7
HGDN/ICK UB10 77 G3
Steed Cl HCH RM12 92 B2 4
Steedman St WALW SE17 18 E6 1
Steeds Rd MUSWH N10 65 M2
Steeds Wy LOU IG10 39 L6
Steel Ap BARK IG11 108 B1
Steele Rd CHSWK W4 117 J1 4
ISLW TW7 134 A1
TOTM N17 67 L4
WAN E11 87 L4 5
WLSDN NW10 99 J1
Steele's Ms North HAMP NW3 83 M6 5
Steele's Ms South
HAMP NW3 83 M6 4
Steele's Rd HAMP NW3 83 M6
Steel's La LHD/OX KT22 178 B7
WCHPL E1 104 C5
Steelyard Pas CANST EC4R 13 G7
Steep Cl ORP BR6 176 F8
Steep Hl CROY/NA CR0 172 E6
STRHM/NOR SW16 138 D7
Steeplands BUSH WD23 43 H2
Steeple Cl FUL/PGN SW6 118 E8
WIM/MER SW19 136 E8
Steeplestone Cl UED N18 49 J7
Steerforth St
WAND/EARL SW18 137 H6
Steers Md MTCM CR4 155 M4
Steers Wy BERM/RHTH SE16 104 E8 5
Stella Rd TOOT SW17 155 M2
Stelling Rd ERITH DA8 127 K5
Stellman Cl CLPT E5 86 A3
Stembridge Rd PGE/AN SE20 158 B5
Stephan Cl HACK E8 86 A8 15
Stephen Av RAIN RM13 92 A6
Stephen Cl ORP BR6 176 F5
Stephendale Rd
FUL/PGN SW6 119 H6 8
Stephen Ms FITZ W1T 11 G3
Stephen Pl CLAP SW4 120 C8 4
Stephen Rd BXLYHN DA7 127 J8
Stephens Cl HARH RM3 56 C7
Stephenson Rd HNWL W7 97 M5
HSLWW TW4 133 G4 7
WALTH E17 68 E6 10
Stephenson St CAN/RD E16 105 L4
WLSDN NW10 99 L2
Stephenson Wy BUSH WD23 29 K4
CAMTN NW1 4 F9
Stephen's Rd SRTFD E15 87 M8 5
Stephen St FITZ W1T 11 G3 2
Stepney Cswy WCHPL E1 104 D5 18
Stepney Gn WCHPL E1 104 C4
Stepney High St WCHPL E1 104 D4
Stepney Wy WCHPL E1 104 C4
Sterling Av CHES/WCR EN8 26 D7
EDGW HA8 44 F6
SHPTN TW17 149 L6
Sterling Cl WLSDN NW10 82 A7 2
Sterling Gdns NWCR SE14 122 E4
Sterling Pl BTFD TW8 116 E2
EA W5 116 E2
Sterling Rd ENC/FH EN2 36 D4
Sterling St SKENS SW7 15 K2
Sterling Wy (North Circular Road)
UED N18 49 L7
Stern Cl BARK IG11 108 C1
Sterndale Rd DART DA1 146 F4 2
WKENS W14 118 D1 8
Sterne St SHB W12 100 D8
Sternhall La PECK SE15 122 A8
Sternhold Av
BRXS/STRHM SW2 138 E6
Sterry Crs DAGE RM10 91 G5
Sterry Dr HOR/WEW KT19 168 E6
THDIT KT7 166 E1
Sterry Gdns DAGE RM10 91 G6
Sterry Rd BARK IG11 89 M8
DAGE RM10 91 G4
Sterry St STHWK SE1 19 G2
Steucers La FSTH SE23 140 E5 1
Steve Biko La CAT SE6 141 G8
Steve Biko Rd HOLWY N7 85 G3
Steve Biko Wy HSLW TW3 115 G8
Stevedale Rd WELL DA16 126 C7
Stevedore St WAP E1W 104 B7 16
Stevenage Crs BORE WD6 31 L4
Stevenage Rd EHAM E6 89 G6
FUL/PGN SW6 118 D6
Stevens Av HOM E9 86 C6
Stevens Cl BECK BR3 159 G2 8
BXLY DA5 145 K8
EW KT17 180 E5 7
HPTN TW12 150 F2
PIN HA5 60 C6 2
Stevens Gn BUSH WD23 43 J3 5
Stevens' La ESH/CLAY KT10 179 G1
Stevenson Cl BAR EN5 47 K1
ERITH DA8 128 B5 4
Stevenson Crs
BERM/RHTH SE16 122 A3
Stevens Pl PUR/KEN CR8 184 B6 1
Stevens St STHWK SE1 19 K3
Steventon Rd SHB W12 99 M6
Steward Cl CHES/WCR EN8 26 E3
Steward St WCHPL E1 13 K2
Stewart Av SHPTN TW17 149 G7
UPMR RM14 93 H3
Stewart Cl ABLGY WD5 21 G5
CDALE/KGS NW9 63 J7 5
CHST BR7 143 H8 2
HPTN TW12 150 E2
Stewart Rd WAN E11 87 K4
Stewartsby Cl UED N18 49 J7 1
Stewart's Gv CHEL SW3 15 H7
Stewart's La VX/NE SW8 120 B5 5
Stewart's Rd VX/NE SW8 120 C6
Stewart St POP/IOD E14 105 J8
Stew La BLKFR EC4V 12 E6
Steyne Rd ACT W3 99 J7 5
Steyning Gv ELTH/MOT SE9 142 F8
Steynings Wy
NFNCH/WDSP N12 47 G7
Steyning Wy HSLWW TW4 132 C1
Steynton Av BXLY DA5 144 E6
Sthrathbrook Rd
STRHM/NOR SW16 156 F3
Stickland Rd BELV DA17 127 G2 2
Stickleton Cl GFD/PVL UB6 97 H2
Stifford Rd SOCK/AV RM15 111 M6
Stilecroft Gdns ALP/SUD HA0 80 B3
Stile Hall Gdns CHSWK W4 117 G3
Stile Pth SUN TW16 150 A6 2
Stiles Cl ERITH DA8 127 H3 1
HAYES BR2 175 M1
Stillingfleet Rd BARN SW13 118 A5
Stillington St WEST SW1P 16 F5
Stillness Rd FSTH SE23 140 E3
Stilton Crs WLSDN NW10 81 J7
Stilton Pth BORE WD6 32 A3 5
Stipularis Dr YEAD UB4 96 D3
Stirling Cl RAIN RM13 110 B2
STRHM/NOR SW16 156 C4
UX/CGN UB8 94 C2 1
Stirling Dr ORP BR6 177 H7
Stirling Gv HSLW TW3 115 J7
Stirling Rd ACT W3 117 H1
BRXN/ST SW9 120 E7
HYS/HAR UB3 96 B6
KTN/HRWW/W HA3 61 M4
PLSTW E13 106 B1
TOTM N17 68 A2
WALTH E17 68 E4
WDGN N22 67 H2
WHTN TW2 133 G4
Stirling Wy ABLGY WD5 21 G5
BORE WD6 45 K1
Stiven Crs RYLN/HDSTN HA2 78 F3
Stoats Nest Rd COUL/CHIP CR5 183 L8
Stockbury Rd CROY/NA CR0 173 J1
Stockdale Rd BCTR RM8 90 F2
Stockdove Wy GFD/PVL UB6 97 M2
Stockers Farm Rd
RKW/CH/CXG WD3 40 C5
Stockfield Rd ESH/CLAY KT10 166 E7 5
STRHM/NOR SW16 138 F7
Stockhams Cl SAND/SEL CR2 184 D3 2
Stockholm Rd
BERM/RHTH SE16 122 C3
Stockhurst Cl
PUT/ROE SW15 118 C7 1
Stockingswater La PEND EN3 37 L6
Stockland Rd ROMW/RG RM7 73 K7
Stock La RDART DA2 146 C8
Stockley Cl WDR/YW UB7 95 H8
Stockley Farm Rd
WDR/YW UB7 113 H1
Stockley Rd UX/CGN UB8 95 G5
WDR/YW UB7 95 H8
Stock Orchard Crs HOLWY N7 84 F5 5
Stock Orchard St HOLWY N7 84 F5 9
Stockport Rd
STRHM/NOR SW16 156 D4
Stocksfield Rd WALTH E17 69 K4 4
Stocks Pl POP/IOD E14 104 F6 7
Stock St PLSTW E13 106 A1
Stockton Gdns MLHL NW7 45 K5
TOTM N17 67 J1
Stockton Rd TOTM N17 67 J1
UED N18 50 A8
Stockwell Av BRXN/ST SW9 120 F8
Stockwell Cl BMLY BR1 160 B5
CHESW EN7 26 A1
Stockwell Gdns BRXN/ST SW9 120 F6
Stockwell Gn BRXN/ST SW9 120 F7
Stockwell La BRXN/ST SW9 120 F7 4
Stockwell Park Crs
BRXN/ST SW9 120 F7
Stockwell Park Rd
BRXN/ST SW9 120 F7
Stockwell Park Wk
BRXN/ST SW9 120 F8
Stockwell Rd BRXN/ST SW9 120 F7
Stockwell St GNWCH SE10 123 J4 5
Stockwell Ter BRXN/ST SW9 120 F6 2
Stodart Rd PGE/AN SE20 158 C4
Stofford Cl WIM/MER SW19 136 E5 5
Stoke Av BARK/HLT IG6 54 A8
Stokenchurch St FUL/PGN SW6 119 H6
Stoke Newington Church St
STNW/STAM N16 85 L2 5
Stoke Newington Common
STNW/STAM N16 85 M2 6
Stoke Newington High St
STNW/STAM N16 85 M3
Stoke Newington Rd
STNW/STAM N16 85 M5
Stoke Pl WLSDN NW10 99 M2
Stoke Rd KUTN/CMB KT2 153 J3
RAIN RM13 110 D2 4
WOT/HER KT12 165 J5
Stokesby Rd CHSGTN KT9 167 M8
Stokesheath Rd LHD/OX KT22 178 D4
Stokesley St SHB W12 99 M5
Stokes Rd CROY/NA CR0 173 K1 4
EHAM E6 106 E3
Stoll Cl CRICK NW2 82 C3
Stompond La WOT/HER KT12 165 G4
Stonard Rd BCTR RM8 90 B5
PLMGR N13 49 G5
Stonards Hl LOU IG10 52 F1
Stondon Pk FSTH SE23 140 E4
Stonebanks WOT/HER KT12 165 G2
Stonebridge Pk WLSDN NW10 81 K7
Stonebridge Rd
SEVS/STOTM N15 67 L6
Stonebridge Wy WBLY HA9 81 H6 1
Stone Buildings LINN WC2A 11 M3
Stone Cl BCTR RM8 90 F2
CLAP SW4 120 C7 2
WDR/YW UB7 94 F7
Stonecot Cl MRDN SM4 169 L3
Stonecot Hl CHEAM SM3 169 L3 1
MRDN SM4 169 M2 2
Stone Crs EBED/NFELT TW14 131 M4
Stonecroft Cl BAR EN5 33 H7
Stonecroft Rd ERITH DA8 127 J5
Stonecroft Wy CROY/NA CR0 171 L2
Stonecutter St
FLST/FETLN EC4A 12 C4 6
Stonefield Cl BXLYHN DA7 127 G8
RSLP HA4 78 E5
Stonefield St IS N1 6 B3
Stonefield Wy CHARL SE7 124 D5 1
RSLP HA4 78 D5
Stonegate Cl
STMC/STPC BR5 162 C6 2
Stone Gv EDGW HA8 44 F7
STAN HA7 44 E6
Stonegrove Gdns EDGW HA8 44 F7
Stonehall Av IL IG1 70 E7
Stone Hall Rd WCHMH N21 48 F2
Stoneham Rd FBAR/BDGN N11 48 C7
Stonehill Cl MORT/ESHN SW14 135 K2
Stonehill Rd CHSWK W4 117 G3 5
MORT/ESHN SW14 135 J2
Stonehills Ct DUL SE21 139 L7
Stonehorse Rd PEND EN3 37 J8
Stonehouse La PUR RM19 129 L3
Stoneleigh Av EN EN1 37 H3
WPK KT4 169 G5
Stoneleigh Broadway
EW KT17 169 G7 2
Stoneleigh Cl CHES/WCR EN8 26 D6 5
Stoneleigh Crs HOR/WEW KT19 169 G7
Stoneleigh Pk WEY KT13 164 C8 2
Stoneleigh Park Av
CROY/NA CR0 173 K1
Stoneleigh Park Rd
HOR/WEW KT19 168 F8
Stoneleigh Pl NTGHL W11 100 D6
Stoneleigh Rd CAR SM5 170 E2
CLAY IG5 70 E4
TOTM N17 67 M4
Stoneleigh St NTGHL W11 100 D6 4
Stonemasons Cl
SEVS/STOTM N15 67 K5 5
Stonenest St FSBYPK N4 84 F1 7
Stone Park Av BECK BR3 159 G7
Stone Pl WPK KT4 169 G4
Stone Place Rd GRH DA9 147 L2
Stone Rd HAYES BR2 160 A7
Stones Cross Rd SWLY BR8 163 J8
Stones End St STHWK SE1 18 E2 2
Stone's Rd EW KT17 180 E4
Stone St CROY/NA CR0 172 A7
Stonewall EHAM E6 107 G4
Stonewood Rd ERITH DA8 127 L3 2
Stoney Aly WOOL/PLUM SE18 125 G7
Stoneyard La POP/IOD E14 105 H6 7
Stoneycroft Cl LEE/GVPK SE12 141 M4
Stoneycroft Rd WFD IG8 52 E8
Stoneydown WALTH E17 68 E5
Stoneydown Av WALTH E17 68 E5 6
Stoneyfields Gdns EDGW HA8 45 J6
Stoneyfields La EDGW HA8 45 J7 1
Stoney La HDTCH EC3A 13 K4
NRWD SE19 157 M2 4
Stoney St STHWK SE1 13 G8 5
Stonhouse St CLAP SW4 120 C8
Stonnell's Rd BTSEA SW11 137 M3 1
Stonor Rd WKENS W14 118 F2
Stonycroft Cl PEND EN3 37 L5
Stony Pth LOU IG10 39 M4
Stonyshotts WAB EN9 27 L7
Stopes St PECK SE15 121 M5
Stopford Rd PLSTW E13 88 A8
WALW SE17 18 D8 2
Store Rd CAN/RD E16 107 G8
Storers Quay POP/IOD E14 123 K2
Store St GWRST WC1E 11 G3
SRTFD E15 87 K5
Storey Rd HGT N6 65 M7
WALTH E17 68 F5 3
Storey's Ga WEST SW1P 17 H2
Stories Rd CMBW SE5 121 L8
Stork Rd FSTGT E7 87 M6
Storksmead Rd EDGW HA8 63 L1
Storks Rd BERM/RHTH SE16 122 A1 5
Stormont Rd BTSEA SW11 138 A1
HGT N6 65 M8
Stormont Wy CHSGTN KT9 167 J7
Stormount Dr HYS/HAR UB3 95 J8
Storrington Rd CROY/NA CR0 172 F3
Story St IS N1 5 L2 3
Stothard St WCHPL E1 104 C3 10
Stoughton Av CHEAM SM3 169 K7
Stoughton Cl PUT/ROE SW15 136 A5 6
Stour Av NWDGN UB2 115 G1
Stourcliffe St MBLAR W1H 9 L5 3
Stour Cl HAYES BR2 175 J6
Stourhead Cl
WIM/MER SW19 136 D4 3
Stourhead Gdns
RYNPK SW20 154 A6 1
Stour Rd BOW E3 87 G7
DAGE RM10 91 G2
DART DA1 128 A8
Stourton Av FELT TW13 132 F8
Stour Wy UPMR RM14 75 L7
Stowage DEPT SE8 123 G4
Stow Crs WALTH E17 68 E2
Stowe Crs RSLP HA4 59 H7 1
Stowe Gdns ED N9 49 M3
Stowell Av CROY/NA CR0 186 D3
Stowe Pl SEVS/STOTM N15 67 L4 2
Stowe Rd ORP BR6 177 H6
SHB W12 100 B8
Stowting Rd ORP BR6 176 E6
Stox Md KTN/HRWW/W HA3 61 K2
Stracey Rd WLSDN NW10 81 K8
Strachan Pl RYNPK SW20 154 C2
Stradbroke Dr CHIG IG7 53 H8
Stradbroke Gv BKHH IG9 52 D3
CLAY IG5 70 E4
Stradbroke Pk BARK/HLT IG6 53 H8 2
CHIG IG7 53 H8
Stradbroke Rd HBRY N5 85 J4 5
Stradbrook Cl
RYLN/HDSTN HA2 78 F3 3
Stradella Rd HNHL SE24 139 J3
Strafford Av CLAY IG5 71 G3
Strafford Cl POTB/CUF EN6 23 G5 2
Strafford Ga POTB/CUF EN6 23 G5
Strafford Rd ACT W3 99 J8
BAR EN5 33 L6
HSLW TW3 114 F8
TWK TW1 134 A4 8
Strafford St POP/IOD E14 105 G8
Strahan Rd BOW E3 104 E2
Straight Rd HARH RM3 56 B7
Straightsmouth
GNWCH SE10 123 J5 5
The Straight NWDGN UB2 96 D8
Strait Rd EHAM E6 106 E6
The Straits WAB EN9 27 H5
Straker's Rd EDUL SE22 140 B1
Strand CHCR WC2N 11 J8
TPL/STR WC2R 11 M5
Strandfield Cl
WOOL/PLUM SE18 125 L3
Strand-on-the-green
CHSWK W4 117 G4
Strand Pl UED N18 49 L6
Strangeways WAT WD17 28 E1
Strangways Ter WKENS W14 118 F1 5
Stranraer Wy IS N1 5 L2
Strasburg Rd BTSEA SW11 120 A6
Stratfield Park Cl WCHMH N21 49 H2
Stratfield Rd BORE WD6 31 M6
Stratford Av HGDN/ICK UB10 94 F1 1
Stratford Cl BARK IG11 90 A7
DAGE RM10 91 J7 6
Stratford Ct NWMAL KT3 153 K7 2
Stratford Gv PUT/ROE SW15 136 D1
Stratford House Av BMLY BR1 160 E6
Stratford Pl MHST W1U 10 B5
Stratford Rd KENS W8 14 B4
NWDGN UB2 114 E2
PLSTW E13 88 A8
THHTH CR7 157 G7
WAT WD17 29 G5
YEAD UB4 96 B3
Stratford Vls CAMTN NW1 4 F1
Stratford Wy LCOL/BKTW AL2 21 M2
WAT WD17 28 F5
Strathan Cl WAND/EARL SW18 136 E3
Strathaven Rd LEE/GVPK SE12 142 B3
Strathblaine Rd BTSEA SW11 137 K2
Strathcona Rd WBLY HA9 80 D2
Strathdale STRHM/NOR SW16 156 F1
Strathdon Dr TOOT SW17 137 K7
Strathearn Av HYS/HAR UB3 113 M5 1
WHTN TW2 133 J5
Strathearn Pl BAY/PAD W2 9 J6
Strathearn Rd SUT SM1 170 A7
WIM/MER SW19 155 G1
Stratheden Rd BKHTH/KID SE3 124 A6
Strathfield Gdns BARK IG11 89 K6
Strathleven Rd
BRXS/STRHM SW2 138 E2
Strathmore Gdns EDGW HA8 63 H3 3
FNCH N3 65 H2
HCH RM12 91 M1
Strathmore Rd
CROY/NA CR0 172 D2 4
TEDD TW11 133 L8
WIM/MER SW19 137 G7 2
Strathnairn St STHWK SE1 122 A2 1
Strath Ter BTSEA SW11 137 L1
Strathville Rd
WAND/EARL SW18 137 H6
Strathyre Av
STRHM/NOR SW16 157 G6
Stratton Av ENC/FH EN2 36 D2
WLGTN SM6 183 K2
Stratton Cl BXLYHN DA7 126 E8
EDGW HA8 44 F8
HEST TW5 114 F6
WIM/MER SW19 154 F5
WOT/HER KT12 165 J3 9
Strattondale St POP/IOD E14 123 J1
Stratton Dr BARK IG11 89 L5
Stratton Gdns STHL UB1 96 F5
Stratton Rd BXLYHN DA7 126 E8
HARH RM3 57 G7
SUN TW16 149 M5
WIM/MER SW19 155 G5
Stratton St MYFR/PICC W1J 10 D8
Stratton Wk HARH RM3 57 G7 1
Strauss Rd CHSWK W4 99 K8 6
Strawberry Flds SWLY BR8 163 L5 3
Strawberry Hill Rd TWK TW1 133 M7
Strawberry La CAR SM5 170 F5
Strawberry V EFNCH N2 65 K2
TWK TW1 133 M7
Strayfield Rd ENC/FH EN2 36 A1
Streakes Field Rd CRICK NW2 82 A2
Streamdale ABYW SE2 126 B4
Streamside Cl ED N9 49 M3
HAYES BR2 160 A7
Stream Wy BELV DA17 127 G4
Streatfeild Av EHAM E6 88 F8
Streatfield Rd
KTN/HRWW/W HA3 62 C4
Streatham Common North
STRHM/NOR SW16 156 F1
Streatham Common South
STRHM/NOR SW16 156 E2
Streatham Ct
STRHM/NOR SW16 138 E7
Streatham High Rd
STRHM/NOR SW16 138 E8
Streatham Hl
BRXS/STRHM SW2 138 E5
Streatham Pl
BRXS/STRHM SW2 138 E4
Streatham Rd MTCM CR4 155 M4
Streatham St
NOXST/BSQ WC1A 11 J4 6
Streatham V
STRHM/NOR SW16 156 C4
Streathbourne Rd TOOT SW17 138 A6
Streatley Pl HAMP NW3 83 K4 3
Streatley Rd KIL/WHAMP NW6 82 F7
Streeters La WLGTN SM6 171 K5
Streetfield Ms BKHTH/KID SE3 124 A7
Streimer Rd SRTFD E15 105 J1 3
Strelley Wy ACT W3 99 L6
Stretton Rd CROY/NA CR0 172 E2
RCHPK/HAM TW10 134 C6
Stretton Wy BORE WD6 31 L3
Strickland Av DART DA1 128 F8
Strickland Rw
WAND/EARL SW18 137 K4
Strickland St DEPT SE8 123 G6 3
Strickland Wy ORP BR6 176 F6 2
Stride Rd PLSTW E13 105 M1
Stripling Wy WATW WD18 42 A1
Strode Cl MUSWH N10 66 A1
Strode Rd FSTGT E7 88 A4
FUL/PGN SW6 118 D5
TOTM N17 67 L3
WLSDN NW10 82 A6
Strone Rd FSTGT E7 88 C6
Strone Wy YEAD UB4 96 E3
Strongbow Crs ELTH/MOT SE9 142 F2
Strongbow Rd ELTH/MOT SE9 142 F2
Strongbridge Cl
RYLN/HDSTN HA2 79 G1
Stronsa Rd SHB W12 99 M8
Strood Av ROMW/RG RM7 91 K1
Stroud Crs PUT/ROE SW15 135 M7
Stroudes Cl WPK KT4 168 F2 2
Stroud Fld NTHLT UB5 78 E6
Stroud Ga RYLN/HDSTN HA2 79 H4
Stroud Green Rd FSBYPK N4 84 F1
Stroud Green Wy
CROY/NA CR0 173 J1 5
Stroud Rd SNWD SE25 173 G1
WIM/MER SW19 137 G7
Strouds Cl CHDH RM6 72 B6 1
Stroudwater Pk WEY KT13 164 B8
Stroud Wy ASHF TW15 149 H2
Stroughton Cl LBTH SE11 17 M6 1
Strout's Pl BETH E2 7 L7 3
Strutton Gnd WEST SW1P 17 G3

Strype St WCHPL E1 13 L3 2
Stuart Av CDALE/KGS NW9 64 A8
EA W5 98 F8
HAYES BR2 175 G3
RYLN/HDSTN HA2 78 F3
WOT/HER KT12 165 J3
Stuart Cl HGDN/ICK UB10 77 G6
SWLY BR8 163 M3
Stuart Ct BORE WD6 44 D1 5
Stuart Crs CROY/NA CR0 173 M5
HYS/HAR UB3 95 J5
WDGN N22 66 F2
Stuart Evans Cl WELL DA16 126 C8
Stuart Gv TEDD TW11 151 L1
Stuart Mantle Wy ERITH DA8 127 K5
Stuart Pl MTCM CR4 155 M4
Stuart Rd ACT W3 99 J7
BARK IG11 89 M8
EBAR EN4 47 L2
KIL/WHAMP NW6 2 A8
KTN/HRWW/W HA3 61 M4
PECK SE15 140 C1
RCHPK/HAM TW10 134 B6
THHTH CR7 157 J7
WELL DA16 126 B6
WIM/MER SW19 137 G7
Stuart Wy CHESW EN7 26 B4
STA TW18 148 B2
Stubbers La UPMR RM14 93 L6
Stubbs Dr BERM/RHTH SE16 122 B3 1
Stubbs Wy WIM/MER SW19 155 K4 5
Stucley Pl CAMTN NW1 4 D2
Stucley Rd ISLW TW7 115 J5
Studdridge St FUL/PGN SW6 119 G7
Studd St IS N1 6 C3
Stud Gn GSTN WD25 21 G5
Studholme St PECK SE15 122 B5
Studios Rd SHPTN TW17 148 F6
The Studios BUSH WD23 43 G1 4
Studio Wy BORE WD6 32 C4
Studland Cl BFN/LL DA15 143 M7 2
Studland Rd HNWL W7 97 K5
KUTN/CMB KT2 152 E2
SYD SE26 158 D1
Studland St HMSMTH W6 118 B2
Studley Av CHING E4 69 K1
Studley Cl CLPT E5 86 E5 3
Studley Ct SCUP DA14 162 B1
Studley Dr REDBR IG4 70 D7
Studley Grange Rd HNWL W7 115 L1
Studley Rd CLAP SW4 120 E6
DAGW RM9 90 D7
FSTGT E7 88 B6 1
Stukeley Rd FSTGT E7 88 B7
Stukeley St HOL/ALD WC2B 11 K4
Stumps Hill La BECK BR3 159 G2
Sturdy Rd PECK SE15 122 B7
Sturge Av WALTH E17 69 H2
Sturgeon Rd WALW SE17 18 E8
Sturges Fld CHST BR7 161 K2
Sturgess Av HDN NW4 64 B8
Sturge St STHWK SE1 18 E2
Sturlas Wy CHES/WCR EN8 26 D6
Sturmer Wy HOLWY N7 84 F5 10
Sturminster Cl YEAD UB4 96 C5 1
Sturrock Cl SEVS/STOTM N15 67 K5
Sturry St POP/IOD E14 105 H5
Sturt St IS N1 6 F6
Stutfield St WCHPL E1 104 A5 17
Styles Gdns BRXN/ST SW9 121 H8
Styles Wy BECK BR3 159 J7
Sudbourne Rd
BRXS/STRHM SW2 138 E2
Sudbrooke Rd BAL SW12 137 M3
Sudbrook Gdns
RCHPK/HAM TW10 134 E7
Sudbrook La
RCHPK/HAM TW10 134 E5
Sudbury EHAM E6 107 G5 2
Sudbury Av ALP/SUD HA0 80 C3
Sudbury Court Dr HRW HA1 80 A3
Sudbury Court Rd ALP/SUD HA0 80 A3
Sudbury Crs ALP/SUD HA0 80 B5 2
BMLY BR1 160 A1
Sudbury Cft ALP/SUD HA0 79 M4
Sudbury Gdns CROY/NA CR0 172 E6 5
Sudbury Heights Av
GFD/PVL UB6 79 M5
Sudbury Hl HRW HA1 79 L3
Sudbury Hill Cl ALP/SUD HA0 79 M4
Sudbury Rd BARK IG11 89 M5
Sudeley St IS N1 6 D6
Sudlow Rd WAND/EARL SW18 137 G1
Sudrey St STHWK SE1 18 E2
Suez Av GFD/PVL UB6 97 M1 2
Suez Rd PEND EN3 37 L7
Suffield Cl SAND/SEL CR2 185 K5
Suffield Rd CHING E4 51 H5
PGE/AN SE20 158 C5
SEVS/STOTM N15 67 M6 5
Suffolk Cl BORE WD6 32 D8 5
Suffolk La CANST EC4R 13 G6
Suffolk Park Rd WALTH E17 68 E5 7
Suffolk Rd BARK IG11 89 K7
BARN SW13 117 M5
DAGE RM10 91 H5
DART DA1 146 E3
GDMY/SEVK IG3 71 L7
PEND EN3 37 H8
PLSTW E13 105 M2
POTB/CUF EN6 22 E5
RYLN/HDSTN HA2 60 F7
SCUP DA14 162 C2
SEVS/STOTM N15 67 K7
SNWD SE25 157 M7
WLSDN NW10 81 L7 5
WPK KT4 168 F4
Suffolk St FSTGT E7 88 A5
STJS SW1Y 11 H7
Suffolk Wy EMPK RM11 75 G5 4
Sugar House La SRTFD E15 105 J1
Sugden Rd BTSEA SW11 120 A8
THDIT KT7 167 H3
Sugden Wy BARK IG11 107 M1
Sulgrave Gdns HMSMTH W6 100 C8 3
Sulgrave Rd HMSMTH W6 100 C8
Sulina Rd BRXS/STRHM SW2 138 E4
Sulivan Ct FUL/PGN SW6 119 G7
Sulivan Rd FUL/PGN SW6 119 G8
Sullivan Av CAN/RD E16 106 D4
Sullivan Cl BTSEA SW11 119 L8
DART DA1 146 B3
E/WMO/HCT KT8 151 G6
Sullivan Crs DEN/HRF UB9 58 D3
Sullivan Rd LBTH SE11 18 B5
Sullivans Reach
WOT/HER KT12 164 F2 1
WOT/HER KT12 165 G2 3
Sullivan Wy BORE WD6 44 C1
Sultan Rd WAN E11 70 B5 1
Sultan St BECK BR3 158 D5
CMBW SE5 121 J5
Sumatra Rd KIL/WHAMP NW6 83 G6 4
Sumburgh Rd BAL SW12 138 A3
Summer Av E/WMO/HCT KT8 151 L8
Summercourt Rd WCHPL E1 104 C5
Summerene Cl
STRHM/NOR SW16 156 C3 2
Summerfield Av
KIL/WHAMP NW6 100 E1
NFNCH/WDSP N12 47 L8
Summerfield La SURB KT6 167 K4
Summerfield Rd GSTN WD25 21 G8
LOU IG10 52 D1
WEA W13 98 B3
Summerfield St LEE/GVPK SE12 141 M4
Summer Gdns E/WMO/HCT KT8 151 L8
Summer Gv BORE WD6 44 D1
Summer Hl BORE WD6 32 A8
CHST BR7 161 G5
Summerhill Cl ORP BR6 176 E6
Summerhill Gv EN EN1 49 L1
Summerhill Rd DART DA1 146 D4
SEVS/STOTM N15 67 K5
Summerhill Wy MTCM CR4 156 A4 5
Summerhouse Av HEST TW5 114 E6
Summerhouse Dr RDART DA2 163 K1
Summerhouse La DEN/HRF UB9 58 A1
GSTN WD25 30 C4
WDR/YW UB7 112 D4
Summerhouse Rd
STNW/STAM N16 85 L2 6
Summerhouse Wy
ABLGY WD5 20 F3 1
Summerland Gdns
MUSWH N10 66 B4 4
Summerlands Av ACT W3 99 J6
Summerlee Av EFNCH N2 65 M5
Summerlee Gdns EFNCH N2 65 M5
Summerley St
WAND/EARL SW18 137 H6
Summer Rd E/WMO/HCT KT8 151 K8 3
THDIT KT7 151 M8
Summersby Rd HGT N6 66 B7
Summers Cl BELMT SM2 182 A1
WBLY HA9 81 H1 1
Summers La NFNCH/WDSP N12 65 K1
Summers Rw
NFNCH/WDSP N12 47 L8 4
Summerstown TOOT SW17 137 J7
Summerton Wy THMD SE28 108 D6
Summer Trees SUN TW16 150 B4 3
Summerville Gdns SUT SM1 169 M8
Summerwood Rd TWK TW1 133 M3
Summit Av CDALE/KGS NW9 63 K6
Summit Cl CDALE/KGS NW9 63 K5
EDGW HA8 63 G1
STHGT/OAK N14 48 C4
Summit Dr WFD IG8 70 D3
Summit Rd NTHLT UB5 79 G7
POTB/CUF EN6 22 E3
WALTH E17 69 H5
The Summit LOU IG10 39 M4
Summit Wy NRWD SE19 157 L3
STHGT/OAK N14 48 B4
Sumner Av PECK SE15 121 M6 3
Sumner Cl ORP BR6 176 C6 7
Sumner Gdns CROY/NA CR0 172 A3
Sumner Pl SKENS SW7 15 H6
Sumner Place Ms SKENS SW7 15 H6
Sumner Rd CROY/NA CR0 172 B3
HRW HA1 61 J8
PECK SE15 121 M6 7
PECK SE15 121 M4 2
Sumner Rd South
CROY/NA CR0 172 A3
Sumner St STHWK SE1 12 E8
Sunbeam Crs NKENS W10 100 C3
Sunbeam Rd WLSDN NW10 99 J3
Sunbury Av MLHL NW7 45 K7
MORT/ESHN SW14 135 K1
Sunbury Ct SUN TW16 150 D5
Sunbury Court Rd SUN TW16 150 C5
Sunbury Gdns MLHL NW7 45 K7
Sunbury La BTSEA SW11 119 K6
WOT/HER KT12 165 G1
Sunbury Rd CHEAM SM3 169 K5
FELT TW13 131 M7
Sunbury St WOOL/PLUM SE18 124 F1
Sunbury Wy FELT TW13 150 C1
Sun Ct ERITH DA8 127 M7
Suncroft Pl SYD SE26 140 C7
Sundale Av SAND/SEL CR2 185 J3
Sunderland Rd EA W5 116 D1 2
FSTH SE23 140 D6
Sunderland Ter BAY/PAD W2 8 C4
Sunderland Wy MNPK E12 88 D2
Sundew Av SHB W12 100 A6
Sundial Av SNWD SE25 157 M5
Sundorne Rd CHARL SE7 124 B3
Sundown Av SAND/SEL CR2 184 F4
Sundown Rd ASHF TW15 149 J1 5
Sundridge Av BMLY BR1 160 D4
WELL DA16 125 K7
Sundridge Cl DART DA1 147 G3
Sundridge Rd CROY/NA CR0 172 F3
Sunfields Pl BKHTH/KID SE3 124 B5 5
Sunflower Wy HARH RM3 74 D2
Sunkist Wy WLGTN SM6 183 L2
Sunland Av BXLYHS DA6 144 E1
Sunleigh Rd ALP/SUD HA0 80 E8
Sunley Gdns GFD/PVL UB6 98 A1
Sunlight Cl WIM/MER SW19 155 J2 4
Sunmead Rd SUN TW16 150 A6
Sunna Gdns SUN TW16 150 B5
Sunningdale STHGT/OAK N14 48 D7
Sunningdale Av ACT W3 99 L6
BARK IG11 89 K8
FELT TW13 132 E6
RAIN RM13 110 B3 5
RSLP HA4 78 C1
Sunningdale Cl STAN HA7 62 A1
SURB KT6 167 L4 2
THMD SE28 108 E5 1
Sunningdale Gdns
CDALE/KGS NW9 63 J6 2
Sunningdale Rd HAYES BR2 160 E7
RAIN RM13 92 A7
SUT SM1 169 M5
Sunningfield Rd HDN NW4 64 B4
Sunningfields Crs HDN NW4 64 B3
Sunningfields Rd HDN NW4 64 B3
Sunninghill Rd LEW SE13 123 H7 6
Sunnings La UPMR RM14 93 K6
Sunningvale Av BH/WHM TN16 187 J8
Sunny Bank SNWD SE25 158 A6 2
Sunnybank Rd POTB/CUF EN6 23 G6
Sunny Crs WLSDN NW10 81 J7
Sunnycroft Gdns UPMR RM14 75 M8
Sunnycroft Rd HSLW TW3 115 H7
SNWD SE25 158 A6
STHL UB1 97 G4
Sunnydale ORP BR6 176 A4
Sunnydale Gdns MLHL NW7 45 K8
Sunnydale Rd LEE/GVPK SE12 142 B2
Sunnydene Av CHING E4 51 K7
RSLP HA4 78 A1 1
Sunnydene Cl HARH RM3 74 F1
Sunnydene Gdns
ALP/SUD HA0 80 C6 4
Sunnydene Rd PUR/KEN CR8 184 B6
Sunnydene St SYD SE26 140 E8
Sunnyfield MLHL NW7 45 M6
Sunny Gardens Rd HDN NW4 64 C4
Sunny Hl HDN NW4 64 B4
Sunnyhill Cl CLPT E5 86 E4 5
Sunnyhill Rd
STRHM/NOR SW16 138 E8
Sunnyhurst Cl SUT SM1 170 A5 2
Sunnymead Av MTCM CR4 156 D6 1
Sunnymead Rd CDALE/KGS NW9 63 K8
PUT/ROE SW15 136 B2
Sunnymede CHIG IG7 54 B5
Sunnymede Av CAR SM5 182 D4
HOR/WEW KT19 180 E2
Sunnymede Dr BARK/HLT IG6 71 H5
Sunny Nook Gdns
SAND/SEL CR2 172 D8 3
Sunny Pl HDN NW4 64 C5 7
The Sunny Rd PEND EN3 37 K4
Sunnyside CRICK NW2 82 F3 3
WIM/MER SW19 154 E2
WOT/HER KT12 150 C8
Sunnyside Dr CHING E4 51 J2
Sunnyside Gdns UPMR RM14 93 J3
Sunnyside Rd ARCH N19 66 D8
EA W5 98 D7
IL IG1 89 J3
LEY E10 87 G1
TEDD TW11 133 K8
Sunnyside Rd East ED N9 50 A5
Sunnyside Rd North ED N9 50 A5 7
Sunnyside Rd South ED N9 50 A5 3
Sunny Vw CDALE/KGS NW9 63 K6 3
Sunny Wy NFNCH/WDSP N12 65 L1
Sun Pas BERM/RHTH SE16 122 A1 5
Sunray Av BRYLDS KT5 168 B4
CMBW SE5 139 K1
HAYES BR2 175 L1
HNHL SE24 139 K1 4
WDR/YW UB7 94 D8
Sunrise Av HCH RM12 92 C3 2
Sunrise Cl FELT TW13 132 F7 1
Sun Rd WKENS W14 118 F3
Sunset Av CHING E4 51 H3
WFD IG8 52 A7
Sunset Cl ERITH DA8 128 B5 5
Sunset Gdns SNWD SE25 157 M5 1
Sunset Rd CMBW SE5 139 J1
THMD SE28 108 A8
Sunset Vw BAR EN5 33 L5
Sunshine Wy MTCM CR4 155 M5
Sun St SDTCH EC2A 13 H2
WAB EN9 27 J6
Superior Dr ORP BR6 176 F8 4
Surbiton Crs SURB KT6 152 E7
Surbiton Hall Cl KUT KT1 152 E7 4
Surbiton Hill Pk BRYLDS KT5 152 F8
Surbiton Hill Rd SURB KT6 152 E7
Surbiton Rd KUT KT1 152 D7
Surlingham Cl THMD SE28 108 D6 5
Surma Cl WCHPL E1 104 A3 16
Surrendale Pl MV/WKIL W9 8 B1
Surrey Canal Rd
BERM/RHTH SE16 122 C4
Surrey Crs CHSWK W4 117 G3 5
Surrey Dr EMPK RM11 75 G6
Surrey Gdns FSBYPK N4 67 J7 5
Surrey Gv SUT SM1 170 D5
WALW SE17 19 J8
Surrey La BTSEA SW11 119 L6
Surrey Ms WNWD SE27 139 L8 5
Surrey Quays Rd
BERM/RHTH SE16 122 C1
Surrey Rd BARK IG11 89 L7
DAGE RM10 91 H5
HRW HA1 61 J7
PECK SE15 140 D2
WWKM BR4 174 B3
Surrey Rw STHWK SE1 18 C1
Surrey Sq WALW SE17 19 J7
Surrey St CROY/NA CR0 172 C5
PLSTW E13 106 B2
TPL/STR WC2R 11 M6
Surrey Ter WALW SE17 19 K6
Surrey Water Rd
BERM/RHTH SE16 104 D7
Surridge Cl RAIN RM13 110 C2
Surridge Gdns NRWD SE19 157 K2 4
Surr St HOLWY N7 84 E5
Susan Cl ROMW/RG RM7 73 J4
Susannah St POP/IOD E14 105 J5 5
Susan Rd BKHTH/KID SE3 124 B7
Susan Wd CHST BR7 161 G4
Sussex Av HARH RM3 74 F1
ISLW TW7 115 L8
Sussex Cl NWMAL KT3 153 L7
REDBR IG4 70 F7
TWK TW1 134 B3 10
Sussex Crs NTHLT UB5 79 G6
Sussex Gdns BAY/PAD W2 9 H5
CHSGTN KT9 167 K8
EFNCH N2 65 M6
FSBYPK N4 67 J6 3
Sussex Ms East BAY/PAD W2 9 H6 1
Sussex Ms West BAY/PAD W2 9 H6
Sussex Pl BAY/PAD W2 9 H5
CAMTN NW1 3 L9
HMSMTH W6 118 C3
NWMAL KT3 153 L7
Sussex Rd CAR SM5 170 F8
DART DA1 147 G4
EHAM E6 107 G1
ERITH DA8 127 H5
HGDN/ICK UB10 77 H5
HRW HA1 61 J6
MTCM CR4 156 E8 4
NWDGN UB2 114 D1
NWMAL KT3 153 L7 5
SAND/SEL CR2 172 D8
SCUP DA14 162 B1
STMC/STPC BR5 177 J1
WATN WD24 29 G3
WWKM BR4 174 B3 2
Sussex Sq BAY/PAD W2 9 H6
Sussex St PIM SW1V 16 D8
PLSTW E13 106 B2
Sussex Wy ARCH N19 84 D1
EBAR EN4 35 H8
Sutcliffe Cl BUSH WD23 30 C7
GLDGN NW11 65 H6 1
Sutcliffe Rd WELL DA16 126 C7
WOOL/PLUM SE18 125 L4
Sutherland Av HYS/HAR UB3 114 A2 1
MV/WKIL W9 8 B1
POTB/CUF EN6 24 D1
STMC/STPC BR5 176 F1
SUN TW16 149 M5
WEA W13 98 B5
WELL DA16 143 K1
Sutherland Cl BAR EN5 33 L7
Sutherland Ct CDALE/KGS NW9 63 H5
Sutherland Dr WIM/MER SW19 155 K4
Sutherland Gdns
MORT/ESHN SW14 117 L8 5
SUN TW16 149 M5 1
WPK KT4 169 H3 2
Sutherland Gv TEDD TW11 151 L1
WAND/EARL SW18 136 F4
Sutherland Pl BAY/PAD W2 8 A4
Sutherland Rd BELV DA17 127 G1
BOW E3 104 F1
CHSWK W4 117 L4
CROY/NA CR0 172 A2
ED N9 50 A3
PEND EN3 50 D1
STHL UB1 96 F5 4
TOTM N17 68 A1
WALTH E17 68 E4
WEA W13 98 A5
Sutherland Rw PIM SW1V 16 D7 1
Sutherland Sq WALW SE17 18 E8
Sutherland St PIM SW1V 16 D7
Sutherland Wk WALW SE17 18 F8
Sutherland Wy POTB/CUF EN6 24 D1
Sutlej Rd CHARL SE7 124 C5
Sutterton St HOLWY N7 84 F6
Sutton Cl BECK BR3 159 H4 3
LOU IG10 52 E2
PIN HA5 60 A6
Sutton Common Rd
CHEAM SM3 169 M2
Sutton Ct BELMT SM2 182 C1
Sutton Court Rd BELMT SM2 170 C8
CHSWK W4 117 J4
HGDN/ICK UB10 77 H8
PLSTW E13 106 C2
SUT SM1 170 C8 3
Sutton Crs BAR EN5 33 K8
Sutton Dene HSLW TW3 115 H6
Sutton Gdns CROY/NA CR0 157 M8 1
Sutton Gv SUT SM1 170 D7
Sutton Hall HEST TW5 115 G5
Sutton La BELMT SM2 182 B5
BNSTD SM7 182 B8
CHSWK W4 117 J3
HSLW TW3 114 F7
Sutton La South CHSWK W4 117 J4
Sutton Park Rd SUT SM1 170 B8
Sutton Pl HOM E9 86 C5 5
Sutton Rd BARK IG11 107 L1
HEST TW5 115 G6
MUSWH N10 66 A2
PLSTW E13 105 M3
WALTH E17 68 D2
WAT WD17 29 J6
Sutton Rw SOHO/SHAV W1D 11 H4 5
Suttons Av HCH RM12 92 C3
Suttons Gdns HCH RM12 92 D3
Suttons La HCH RM12 92 D5
Sutton Sq HACK E8 86 C5 6
HEST TW5 114 F6
Sutton St WCHPL E1 104 C5
Sutton Wy HEST TW5 114 F6
NKENS W10 100 C4
Swaby Rd WAND/EARL SW18 137 J6
Swaffield Rd WAND/EARL SW18 137 J4
Swain Cl TOOT SW17 156 B2
Swain Rd THHTH CR7 157 J8
Swains Cl WDR/YW UB7 94 E8 2
Swain's La HGT N6 84 A1
Swainson Rd ACT W3 99 M8 5
Swains Rd MTCM CR4 155 M3
Swaisland Rd DART DA1 146 D2
Swaislands Dr DART DA1 145 M2
Swakeleys Dr HGDN/ICK UB10 77 G4
Swakeleys Rd HGDN/ICK UB10 77 H3
HGDN/ICK UB10 76 F3 1
Swale Cl SOCK/AV RM15 111 J5 2
Swaledale Cl FBAR/BDGN N11 48 A8 4
Swaledale Rd RDART DA2 147 J5
Swale Rd DART DA1 128 A8
Swallands Rd CAT SE6 141 G7
Swallow Cl BUSH WD23 43 H3
BXLYHN DA7 127 L6
GRH DA9 147 M2
NWCR SE14 122 D6 3
RKW/CH/CXG WD3 40 C2 1
Swallowdale SAND/SEL CR2 185 K2
Swallow Dr NTHLT UB5 97 G1
WLSDN NW10 81 K6 4
Swallowfield Rd CHARL SE7 124 B3
Swallowfield Wy HYS/HAR UB3 95 K8
Swallow Gdns
STRHM/NOR SW16 156 D1 4
Swallow Oaks ABLGY WD5 20 F5 3
Swallow Pl CONDST W1S 10 D5 4
Swallow St CONDST W1S 10 F7
EHAM E6 106 E4
Swallowtail Cl
STMC/STPC BR5 162 D7 5
Swanage Rd CHING E4 69 J1
WAND/EARL SW18 137 J3
Swanage Waye YEAD UB4 96 C5
Swan And Pike Rd PEND EN3 38 A3
Swan Ap EHAM E6 106 E4
Swan Av UPMR RM14 93 M1
Swanbourne Dr HCH RM12 92 D4
Swanbridge Rd BXLYHN DA7 127 G6
Swan Cl FELT TW13 132 E8
RKW/CH/CXG WD3 40 D2
STMC/STPC BR5 162 A6
WALTH E17 68 E2 5
Swandon Wy
WAND/EARL SW18 137 H1
Swan Dr CDALE/KGS NW9 63 L3
Swanfield Rd CHES/WCR EN8 26 E6
Swanfield St BETH E2 7 L8
Swanland Rd POTB/CUF EN6 22 B7
Swan La CANST EC4R 13 H7
DART DA1 145 M4
LOU IG10 52 C2
TRDG/WHET N20 47 J5
Swanley Bar La POTB/CUF EN6 23 H1
Swanley Crs POTB/CUF EN6 23 H2
Swanley La SWLY BR8 163 M6
Swanley Rd WELL DA16 126 C6
Swan Md STHWK SE1 19 J4
Swan Ms BRXN/ST SW9 120 F7 5
Swan Pl BARN SW13 117 M7 4
Swan Rd BERM/RHTH SE16 104 C8
FELT TW13 132 E8
GFD/PVL UB6 97 H5
WDR/YW UB7 94 D8
Swanscombe Rd CHSWK W4 117 L3 4
NTGHL W11 100 D7 4
Swansea Rd HTHAIR TW6 131 J3
PEND EN3 37 J7 3
Swans Rd CHES/WCR EN8 26 D7
Swanston Pth OXHEY WD19 42 C5 4
Swan St ISLW TW7 116 B8
STHWK SE1 18 F2
Swanton Gdns
WIM/MER SW19 136 D5 5
Swanton Rd ERITH DA8 127 G5
Swan Wk CHEL SW3 15 L9
SHPTN TW17 164 E2
Swan Wy PEND EN3 37 K5
Swanwick Cl PUT/ROE SW15 135 M4
Swan Yd IS N1 85 H6 5
Sward Rd STMC/STPC BR5 177 G1
Swaton Rd BOW E3 105 G3
Swaylands Rd BELV DA17 127 G4
Swaythling Cl UED N18 50 B6
Sweden Ga
BERM/RHTH SE16 122 E2 1
Sweeney Crs STHWK SE1 19 M2
Sweeps Ditch Cl STA TW18 148 A4
Sweeps La STMC/STPC BR5 162 D8
Sweet Briar Gn UED N18 49 M5
Sweet Briar Gv ED N9 49 M5
Sweet Briar Wk UED N18 49 M6
Sweetcroft La HGDN/ICK UB10 76 F7
Sweetmans Av PIN HA5 60 D4
Sweets Wy TRDG/WHET N20 47 K4
Swete St PLSTW E13 106 A1
Sweyn Pl BKHTH/KID SE3 124 A7
Swift Cl HYS/HAR UB3 95 M5
RYLN/HDSTN HA2 79 H2
UPMR RM14 93 L1 5
WALTH E17 68 E1
Swift Rd FELT TW13 132 D8
NWDGN UB2 114 F1
Swiftsden Wy BMLY BR1 159 L2
Swift St FUL/PGN SW6 118 E6
Swinbrook Rd NKENS W10 100 E4 14
Swinburne Crs CROY/NA CR0 173 J1
Swinburne Rd PUT/ROE SW15 136 A1
Swinderby Rd ALP/SUD HA0 80 E6
Swindon Cl GDMY/SEVK IG3 89 L2
Swindon Gdns HARH RM3 56 F7 1
Swindon La HARH RM3 56 F7
Swindon Rd HTHAIR TW6 131 J3 1
Swindon St SHB W12 100 C7 5
Swinfield Cl FELT TW13 132 E8 5
Swinford Gdns
BRXN/ST SW9 121 H8 5
Swingate La WOOL/PLUM SE18 125 L5
Swinnerton St HOM E9 86 E5 4
Swinton Cl WBLY HA9 81 H1
Swinton Pl FSBYW WC1X 5 L7 1
Swinton St FSBYW WC1X 5 L7
Swires Shaw HAYES BR2 175 K6
Swiss Av WATW WD18 28 E7
Swiss Cl WATW WD18 28 E6
Swithland Gdns ELTH/MOT SE9 142 F8
Swyncombe Av BTFD TW8 116 B2
Swynford Gdns HDN NW4 64 A5 5
Sybil Phoenix Cl DEPT SE8 122 D3 1
Sybourn St WALTH E17 68 F8 5
Sycamore Ap RKW/CH/CXG WD3 28 C8
Sycamore Av BFN/LL DA15 143 M3
EA W5 116 D1 5
HYS/HAR UB3 95 L6
UPMR RM14 93 G3
Sycamore Cl ACT W3 99 L7
BUSH WD23 29 L5 2
CAN/RD E16 105 L3 5
CAR SM5 170 F6
EBAR EN4 47 K1

FELT TW13 .... 132 A7
GSTN WD25 .... 21 H8
NTHLT UB5 .... 78 E8
UED N18 .... 50 A6
WDR/YW UB7 .... 94 F6
Sycamore Ct WEY KT13 .... 164 F5
Sycamore Dr SWLY BR8 .... 163 L6
Sycamore Gdns MTCM CR4 .... 155 K5
  SHB W12 .... 100 B8
Sycamore Gv CAT SE6 .... 141 J3
  CDALE/KGS NW9 .... 63 J6
  NWMAL KT3 .... 153 L6
  PGE/AN SE20 .... 158 A4
Sycamore Hl FBAR/BDGN N11 .... 48 A3
Sycamore Ms CLAP SW4 .... 120 C8
Sycamore Ri BNSTD SM7 .... 181 K7
Sycamore Rd DART DA1 .... 146 D4
  RKW/CH/CXG WD3 .... 28 C8
  WIM/MER SW19 .... 154 C2
Sycamore St FSBYE EC1V 12 E1
Sycamore Wk NKENS W10 .... 100 E8
Sycamore Wy TEDD TW11 .... 152 C2
Sydenham Av SYD SE26 .... 158 B1
  WCHMH N21 .... 35 M8
Sydenham Cl ROM RM1 .... 73 M5
Sydenham Hl EDUL SE22 .... 140 B6
  SYD SE26 .... 140 A7
Sydenham Pk SYD SE26 .... 140 C7
Sydenham Ri FSTH SE23 .... 140 B6
Sydenham Rd CROY/NA CR0 .... 172 C4
  SYD SE26 .... 158 D1
Sydenham Station Ap
  SYD SE26 .... 140 C8
Sydner Rd STNW/STAM N16 .... 85 M4
Sydney Rd PUR/KEN CR8 .... 183 M5
Sydney Cl SKENS SW7 .... 15 H6
Sydney Crs ASHF TW15 .... 149 H2
Sydney Gv HDN NW4 .... 64 C6
Sydney Ms SKENS SW7 .... 15 H6
Sydney Pl SKENS SW7 .... 15 H6
Sydney Rd ABYW SE2 .... 126 D1
  BARK/HLT IG6 .... 71 J3
  BXLYHS DA6 .... 144 D1
  CEND/HSY/T N8 .... 67 G5
  EBED/NFELT TW14 .... 132 A5
  ENC/FH EN2 .... 36 D7
  MUSWH N10 .... 66 B2
  RCH/KEW TW9 .... 134 E1
  RYNPK SW20 .... 154 D5
  SCUP DA14 .... 143 L8
  SUT SM1 .... 170 A6
  TEDD TW11 .... 151 M1
  WAN E11 .... 70 B7
  WATW WD18 .... 28 E8
  WEA W13 .... 98 A7
Sydney St CHEL SW3 .... 15 J7
Sylvana Cl HGDN/ICK UB10 .... 76 F8
Sylvan Av CHDH RM6 .... 72 F7
  EMPK RM11 .... 74 F7
  FNCH N3 .... 65 G3
  MLHL NW7 .... 45 L8
  WDGN N22 .... 67 G1
Sylvan Cl SAND/SEL CR2 .... 185 H3
Sylvan Gdns SURB KT6 .... 167 K2
Sylvan Gv CRICK NW2 .... 82 A4
  PECK SE15 .... 122 B5
Sylvan Hl NRWD SE19 .... 157 L4
Sylvan Rd FSTGT E7 .... 88 A6
  IL IG1 .... 89 J2
  NRWD SE19 .... 157 M4
  WALTH E17 .... 69 G6
  WAN E11 .... 70 A6
Sylvan Wy BCTR RM8 .... 90 B4
  CHIG IG7 .... 54 B5
  WWKM BR4 .... 174 E6
Sylverdale Rd CROY/NA CR0 .... 172 B5
  PUR/KEN CR8 .... 184 B6
Sylvester Av CHST BR7 .... 160 F2
Sylvester Rd ALP/SUD HA0 .... 80 C5
  EFNCH N2 .... 65 J1
  HACK E8 .... 86 B6
  WALTH E17 .... 68 F8
Sylvia Av PIN HA5 .... 42 F8
Sylvia Gdns WBLY HA9 .... 81 H7
Symes Ms CAMTN NW1 .... 4 E5
Symonds Ct CHES/WCR EN8 .... 26 D1
Syon Gate Wy BTFD TW8 .... 116 A5
  ISLW TW7 .... 116 B5
Syon La BTFD TW8 .... 116 B5
  ISLW TW7 .... 115 M4
Syon Park Gdns ISLW TW7 .... 115 M5
Syracuse Av RAIN RM13 .... 110 D2

T

Tabard St STHWK SE1 .... 19 G3
Tabernacle Av PLSTW E13 .... 106 A3
Tabernacle St SDTCH EC2A 13 H1
Tableer Av CLAP SW4 .... 138 C2
Tabley Rd HOLWY N7 .... 84 E4
Tabor Gdns CHEAM SM3 .... 169 L8
Tabor Gv WIM/MER SW19 .... 154 E3
Tabor Rd HMSMTH W6 .... 118 D1
Tabrums Wy UPMR RM14 .... 75 L8
Tachbrook Rd
  EBED/NFELT TW14 .... 131 M4
  NWDGN UB2 .... 114 D2
  UX/CGN UB8 .... 94 C1
Tachbrook St PIM SW1V 16 F6
Tack Ms BROCKY SE4 .... 123 G8
Tadema Rd WBPTN SW10 .... 119 J5
Tadlows Cl UPMR RM14 .... 93 H5
Tadmor Cl SUN TW16 .... 149 M7
Tadmor St SHB W12 .... 100 D7
Tadworth Av NWMAL KT3 .... 153 M8
Tadworth Pde HCH RM12 .... 92 B4
Tadworth Rd CRICK NW2 .... 82 A2
Taeping St POP/IOD E14 .... 123 H2
Taffy's How MTCM CR4 .... 155 L6
Tait Rd CROY/NA CR0 .... 172 E2
Takeley Cl CRW RM5 .... 73 K3
  WAB EN9 .... 27 K6
Talacre Rd KTTN NW5 .... 84 A6 ①⓪
Talbot Av EFNCH N2 .... 65 K4
  OXHEY WD19 .... 42 E2
Talbot Cl SEVS/STOTM N15 .... 67 M5

Talbot Ct BANK EC3V 13 H6
Talbot Crs HDN NW4 .... 64 A6
Talbot Gdns GDMY/SEVK IG3 .... 90 A2
Talbot Pl BKHTH/KID SE3 .... 123 L7
Talbot Rd ALP/SUD HA0 .... 80 D5
  ASHF TW15 .... 148 D1
  BAY/PAD W2 .... 8 B4
  CAR SM5 .... 171 G7
  DAGW RM9 .... 90 F7
  EDUL SE22 .... 139 L1
  EHAM E6 .... 106 F1
  FSTGT E7 .... 88 A4
  HGT N6 .... 66 A7
  ISLW TW7 .... 134 A1
  KTN/HRWW/W HA3 .... 61 M3
  NTGHL W11 .... 100 F5
  NWDGN UB2 .... 114 C2
  RKW/CH/CXG WD3 .... 40 E3
  SEVS/STOTM N15 .... 67 M5
  THHTH CR7 .... 157 K7
  WDGN N22 .... 54 E3
  WEA W13 .... 98 A7
  WHTN TW2 .... 133 M5
Talbot Sq BAY/PAD W2 .... 9 H5
Talbrook BRW CM14 .... 57 M5
Talfourd Pl PECK SE15 .... 121 H6
Talfourd Rd PECK SE15 .... 121 H6
Talgarth Rd HMSMTH W6 .... 118 D3
  WKENS W14 .... 118 E3
Talisman Cl GDMY/SEVK IG3 .... 90 B1
Talisman Sq SYD SE26 .... 140 A8
Talisman Wy WBLY HA9 .... 80 F3
Tallack Rd LEY E10 .... 86 F1
Tall Elms Cl HAYES BR2 .... 159 M8
Tallis Cl CAN/RD E16 .... 106 F5
Tallis Gv CHARL SE7 .... 124 B4
Tallis St EMB EC4Y 12 B6
Tallis Vw WLSDN NW10 .... 81 K6
Tall Trees STRHM/NOR SW16 .... 156 F6
Tall Trees Cl EMPK RM11 .... 74 D7
Talma Gdns WHTN TW2 .... 133 L4
Talmage Cl FSTH SE23 .... 140 C4
Talman Gv STAN HA7 .... 44 D8
Talma Rd BRXS/STRHM SW2 .... 139 G1
Talus Cl PUR RM19 .... 129 K2
Talwin St BOW E3 .... 105 H2
Tamar Cl BOW E3 .... 86 F8
  UPMR RM14 .... 75 L7
Tamar Dr SOCK/AV RM15 .... 111 J5
Tamarisk Sq SHB W12 .... 99 M6
Tamar St CHARL SE7 .... 124 E2
Tamesis Gdns WPK KT4 .... 168 A4
Tamian Wy HSLWW TW4 .... 132 C1
Tamworth Av WFD IG8 .... 51 L8
Tamworth La MTCM CR4 .... 156 B6
Tamworth Pk MTCM CR4 .... 156 B7
Tamworth Pl CROY/NA CR0 .... 172 C4
Tamworth Rd CROY/NA CR0 .... 172 C4
Tamworth St FUL/PGN SW6 .... 14 A9
Tancred Rd FSBYPK N4 .... 67 H7
Tandridge Dr ORP BR6 .... 176 D3
Tandridge Gdns SAND/SEL CR2 .... 184 F6
Tanfield Av CRICK NW2 .... 81 M4
Tanfield Rd CROY/NA CR0 .... 172 C6
Tangent Link HARH RM3 .... 74 D2
Tangent Rd HARH RM3 .... 74 D2
Tangier Rd
  RCHPK/HAM TW10 .... 117 H8
Tangleberry Cl BMLY BR1 .... 160 F7
Tangle Tree Cl EFNCH N2 .... 65 H3
Tanglewood Cl CROY/NA CR0 .... 173 J5
  STAN HA7 .... 43 L4
  UX/CGN UB8 .... 95 G2
Tanglewood Wy FELT TW13 .... 132 B7
Tangley Gv PUT/ROE SW15 .... 135 M4
Tangley Park Rd HPTN TW12 .... 150 F1
Tanglyn Av SHPTN TW17 .... 149 G8
Tangmere Gv
  KUTN/CMB KT2 .... 152 D1
Tangmere Wy CDALE/KGS NW9 .... 63 J3
Tankerton Rd SURB KT6 .... 167 M4
Tankerton St STPAN WC1H 5 K8
Tankerville Rd
  STRHM/NOR SW16 .... 156 D3
Tank Hill Rd PUR RM19 .... 129 G2
Tank La PUR RM19 .... 129 G2
Tankridge Rd CRICK NW2 .... 82 B2
Tanners Cl WOT/HER KT12 .... 165 H1
Tanners End La UED N18 .... 49 L6
Tanners Hl ABLGY WD5 .... 20 F4
  DEPT SE8 .... 123 C6
Tanners La BARK/HLT IG6 .... 71 J4
Tanner St BARK IG11 .... 89 J6
  STHWK SE1 .... 19 K2
Tanners Wood La ABLGY WD5 .... 20 E5
  DAGE RM10 .... 91 H3
Tannery Cl CROY/NA CR0 .... 158 D8
  DAGE RM10 .... 91 H3
Tannsfeld Rd SYD SE26 .... 158 D1
Tanswell St STHWK SE1 .... 18 A2
Tansy Cl EHAM E6 .... 107 G5
  HARH RM3 .... 56 E8
Tantallon Rd BAL SW12 .... 138 A5
Tant Av CAN/RD E16 .... 105 M5
Tantony Gv CHDH RM6 .... 72 D4
Tanworth Cl NTHWD HA6 .... 41 J8
Tanworth Gdns PIN HA5 .... 60 B3
Tan Yard La BXLY DA5 .... 145 G4
Tanza Rd HAMP NW3 .... 83 M4
Tapestry Cl BELMT SM2 .... 182 B1
Taplow NTCM CR4 .... 155 L7
Taplow Ct IS N1 .... 6 F6
Tappesfield Rd PECK SE15 .... 121 L2
Tapping Cl KUTN/CMB KT2 .... 153 G3
Tapp St WCHPL E1 .... 104 B3
Tapster St BAR EN5 .... 33 M6
Tarbert Rd EDUL SE22 .... 139 L2
Target Cl EBED/NFELT TW14 .... 131 L3
Tariff Rd UED N18 .... 50 A8
Tarleton Gdns FSTH SE23 .... 140 B5
Tarling Cl SCUP DA14 .... 144 B7
Tarling Rd CAN/RD E16 .... 105 M5
  EFNCH N2 .... 65 J3
Tarling St WCHPL E1 .... 104 E5
Tarmac Wy WDR/YW UB7 .... 112 B5
Tarnbank STHGT/OAK N14 .... 35 L8 ⑦

Tarn St STHWK SE1 .... 18 E4
Tarnwood Pk ELTH/MOT SE9 .... 142 F5
Tarnworth Rd HARH RM3 .... 57 G7
Tarragon Cl NWCR SE14 .... 122 E6
Tarragon Gv SYD SE26 .... 158 D2
Tarriff Crs DEPT SE8 .... 122 F2
Tarrington Cl
  STRHM/NOR SW16 .... 138 D7
Tarver Rd WALW SE17 .... 18 D8
Tarves Wy GNWCH SE10 .... 123 H5
Tash Pl FBAR/BDGN N11 .... 48 B7
Tasker Cl HYS/HAR UB3 .... 113 J5
Tasker Rd HAMP NW3 .... 83 M5
Tasman Ct UED N18 .... 49 J8
Tasmania Ter UED N18 .... 48 F8
Tasman Rd BRXN/ST SW9 .... 120 E8
Tasso Rd HMSMTH W6 .... 118 E4
Tate Gdns BUSH WD23 .... 43 L2
Tate Rd CAN/RD E16 .... 106 F7
  SUT SM1 .... 170 A7
Tatnell Rd FSTH SE23 .... 140 E3
Tattersall Cl ELTH/MOT SE9 .... 142 E2
Tatton Crs STNW/STAM N16 .... 67 M8
Tatum Rd WLSDN NW10 .... 81 J7
Tatum St WALW SE17 .... 19 H6
Tauber Cl BORE WD6 .... 31 M7
Tauheed Cl FSBYPK N4 .... 85 J2
Taunton Cl BARK/HLT IG6 .... 53 M8
  BXLYHN DA7 .... 127 K8
  CHEAM SM3 .... 170 A3
Taunton Dr EFNCH N2 .... 65 J3
  ENC/FH EN2 .... 36 A6
Taunton Pl CAMTN NW1 .... 9 L1
Taunton Rd GFD/PVL UB6 .... 79 H8
  HARH RM3 .... 56 C6
  LEE/GVPK SE12 .... 141 L2
Taunton Wy STAN HA7 .... 62 E4
Tavern Cl CAR SM5 .... 170 E2
Taverners Wy HACK E9 .... 51 L3
Tavistock Av GFD/PVL UB6 .... 79 J3
  WALTH E17 .... 68 D4
Tavistock Cl HARH RM3 .... 74 D2
  POTB/CUF EN6 .... 23 K4
  STA TW18 .... 148 D3
Tavistock Crs MTCM CR4 .... 156 F7
  NTGHL W11 .... 100 F4
Tavistock Gdns GDMY/SEVK IG3 .... 89 L4
Tavistock Gv CROY/NA CR0 .... 172 D2
Tavistock Ms NTGHL W11 .... 100 F5
Tavistock Pl STHGT/OAK N14 .... 48 B1
  STPAN WC1H 5 H9
Tavistock Rd CAR SM5 .... 170 D3
  CROY/NA CR0 .... 172 D3
  EDGW HA8 .... 62 F2
  FSBYPK N4 .... 67 K7
  FSTGT E7 .... 87 M4
  HAYES BR2 .... 160 A7
  HGDN/ICK UB10 .... 77 K5
  NTGHL W11 .... 100 F4
  SRTFD E15 .... 87 M6
  SWFD E18 .... 70 A4
  WATN WD24 .... 29 K4
  WDR/YW UB7 .... 94 D7
  WELL DA16 .... 126 C6
  WLSDN NW10 .... 99 M1
Tavistock Sq STPAN WC1H 5 H9
Tavistock St COVGDN WC2E 11 K6
  HOL/ALD WC2B 11 L6
Tavistock Ter ARCH N19 .... 84 D3
Taviton St STPAN WC1H 5 G9
Tawney Rd THMD SE28 .... 108 B6
Tawny Av UPMR RM14 .... 93 H5
Tawny Cl FELT TW13 .... 132 A7
  WEA W13 .... 98 B7
Tawny Wy BERM/RHTH SE16 .... 122 D2
Tayben Av WHTN TW2 .... 133 L3
Taybridge Rd BTSEA SW11 .... 120 A8
Tayburn Cl POP/IOD E14 .... 105 J5
Tayfield Cl HGDN/ICK UB10 .... 77 J3
Tayles Hill Dr EW KT17 .... 180 F3
Taylor Av RCH/KEW TW9 .... 117 M7
Taylor Cl CRW RM5 .... 73 G1
  HPTN TW12 .... 151 J1
  HSLW TW3 .... 115 J6
  ORP BR6 .... 176 F6
  TOTM N17 .... 68 A1
Taylor Rd WIM/MER SW19 .... 155 L3
  WLGTN SM6 .... 171 H1
Taylor Rw RDART DA2 .... 146 C7
Taylor's Buildings
  WOOL/PLUM SE18 .... 125 H2
Taylors Cl SCUP DA14 .... 143 H4
Taylors Ct FELT TW13 .... 132 A6
Taylor's Gn ACT W3 .... 99 L5
Taylor's La BAR EN5 .... 33 M4
  SYD SE26 .... 140 B8
  WLSDN NW10 .... 81 L7
Taymount Ri FSTH SE23 .... 140 C6
Tayport Cl IS N1 .... 5 L2
Tayside Dr EDGW HA8 .... 45 H5
Tay Wy ROM RM1 .... 73 M2
Taywood Rd NTHLT UB5 .... 96 F2
Teak Cl BERM/RHTH SE16 .... 104 F7
Teal Av STMC/STPC BR5 .... 162 D7
Teal Cl CAN/RD E16 .... 106 D4
  SAND/SEL CR2 .... 185 K4
Teal Dr NTHWD HA6 .... 59 J1
Teale St BETH E2 .... 104 A1
Tealing Dr HOR/WEW KT19 .... 180 D6
Teasel Cl CROY/NA CR0 .... 173 K3
Teasel Wy SRTFD E15 .... 105 L2
Tebworth Rd TOTM N17 .... 67 M1
Teck Cl ISLW TW7 .... 116 A1
Tedder Cl CHSGTN KT9 .... 167 J7
  HGDN/ICK UB10 .... 76 F7
Tedder Rd SAND/SEL CR2 .... 185 L1
Teddington Pk TEDD TW11 .... 151 M1
Teddington Park Rd
  TEDD TW11 .... 133 M8
Tedworth Gdns CHEL SW3 .... 15 L8
Tedworth Sq CHEL SW3 .... 15 L8
Tees Av GFD/PVL UB6 .... 97 L1
Tees Ct WPTN RM14 .... 75 K8
Teesdale Av ISLW TW7 .... 116 A6
Teesdale Cl BETH E2 .... 104 B1

Teesdale Gdns ISLW TW7 .... 116 A6
  SNWD SE25 .... 157 L5
  WAN E11 .... 69 M7
Teesdale Rd RDART DA2 .... 147 J5
  WAN E11 .... 104 B1
Tees Dr HARH RM3 .... 56 D5
Tees St BETH E2 .... 104 B1
Tees St SE16 .... 122 F2
The Tee ACT W3 .... 99 L5
Teevan Cl CROY/NA CR0 .... 173 G2
Teevan Rd CROY/NA CR0 .... 173 G2
Teignmouth Cl CLAP SW4 .... 138 D1
  EDGW HA8 .... 62 F3
Teignmouth Rd CRICK NW2 .... 82 D5
  WELL DA16 .... 126 C7
Telcote Wy RSLP HA4 .... 60 C8
Telegraph Hl HAMP NW3 .... 83 H3
Telegraph La ESH/CLAY KT10 .... 166 F6
Telegraph Pl POP/IOD E14 .... 123 H2
Telegraph Rd PUT/ROE SW15 .... 136 C2
Telegraph St LOTH EC2R 13 G4
Telegraph Tr WLGTN SM6 .... 183 G4
Telferscot Rd BAL SW12 .... 138 D3
Telford Av BAL SW12 .... 138 D5
  BRXS/STRHM SW2 .... 138 E5
Telford Cl GSTN WD25 .... 21 K8
  NRWD SE19 .... 157 M2
  WALTH E17 .... 68 E8
Telford Dr WOT/HER KT12 .... 165 J1
Telford Rd CDALE/KGS NW9 .... 64 A7
  CHST BR7 .... 143 K6
  GFD/PVL UB6 .... 97 H6
  HSLWW TW4 .... 133 G4
  NKENS W10 .... 100 C4
Telford Rd North Circular Rd
  FBAR/BDGN N11 .... 48 C8
Telford Wy ACT W3 .... 99 L4
  YEAD UB4 .... 96 E4
Telham Rd EHAM E6 .... 107 G1
Tell Gv EDUL SE22 .... 139 M1
Tellisford Rd ESH/CLAY KT10 .... 166 B6
Tellson Av WOOL/PLUM SE18 .... 124 E6
Telscombe Cl ORP BR6 .... 176 E4
Temeraire St BERM/RHTH SE16 .... 104 C8
Tempelhof Av HDN NW4 .... 64 C8
Temperley Rd BAL SW12 .... 138 A4
Tempest Av POTB/CUF EN6 .... 23 J5
Tempest Rd EGH TW20 ....
Tempest Wy RAIN RM13 .... 92 A6
Templar Dr THMD SE28 .... 108 D5
Templar Pl HPTN TW12 .... 151 J3
Templars Av GLDGN NW11 .... 64 E3
Templars Crs FNCH N3 .... 65 G3
Templars Dr
  KTN/HRWW/W HA3 .... 43 K8
Templar St CMBW SE5 .... 121 F7
Temple Av BCTR RM8 .... 91 G1
  CROY/NA CR0 .... 173 M5
  EMB EC4Y 12 B6
  TRDG/WHET N20 .... 47 K2
Temple Cl CHESW EN7 .... 26 A4
  FNCH N3 .... 64 F5
  WAN E11 .... 69 L8
  WAT WD17 .... 28 F5
  WOOL/PLUM SE18 .... 125 J1
Templecombe Rd HOM E9 .... 86 C8
Templecombe Wy MRDN SM4 .... 154 E8
Templecroft ASHF TW15 .... 149 K2
Templedene Av STA TW18 .... 148 B3
Temple Fortune Hl GLDGN NW11 .... 65 G4
Temple Fortune La
  GLDGN NW11 .... 64 F7
Temple Gdns BCTR RM8 .... 90 D3
  GLDGN NW11 .... 64 F7
  RKW/CH/CXG WD3 .... 41 H5
Temple Gv ENC/FH EN2 .... 36 B5
  GLDGN NW11 .... 65 G7
Temple Hl DART DA1 .... 146 F6
Temple Hill Sq DART DA1 .... 146 F2
Temple La EMB EC4Y 12 B5
Templeman Rd HNWL W7 .... 97 M4
Templemead Cl ACT W3 .... 99 L5
Temple Mead Cl STAN HA7 .... 44 B8
Temple Mills La SRTFD E15 .... 87 H7
Temple Mills Rd LEY E10 .... 87 G4
Temple Pk UX/CGN UB8 .... 95 G2
Temple Pl TPL/STR WC2R 11 M6
Temple Rd CEND/HSY/T N8 .... 66 F5
  CHSWK W4 .... 117 J1
  CRICK NW2 .... 82 C4
  EA W5 .... 116 D1
  EHAM E6 .... 88 E8
  HOR/WEW KT19 .... 180 D5
  HSLW TW3 .... 133 H1
  RCH/KEW TW9 .... 116 F7
Temple Sheen Rd
  MORT/ESHN SW14 .... 135 J2
Temple St BETH E2 .... 104 B1
Templeton Av CHING E4 .... 51 C6
Templeton Cl THHTH CR7 .... 157 K4
Templeton Pl ECT SW5 .... 14 B6
Templeton Rd SEVS/STOTM N15 .... 67 K7
Temple Wy SUT SM1 .... 170 D5
Templewood WEA W13 .... 98 B4
Templewood Av HAMP NW3 .... 83 H3
Templewood Gdns HAMP NW3 .... 83 H3
Tempsford Av BORE WD6 .... 32 D7
Tempsford Cl ENC/FH EN2 .... 36 C7 ①
Tempsford Ct RYLN/HDSTN HA2 .... 61 J3
Tenbury Cl FSTGT E7 .... 88 D5
Tenbury Ct BAL SW12 .... 138 D5
Tenby Av KTN/HRWW/W HA3 .... 62 B3
Tenby Cl CHDH RM6 .... 72 E7
Tenby Gdns NTHLT UB5 .... 79 G6
Tenby Rd CHDH RM6 .... 72 E7
  EDGW HA8 .... 62 B2
  PEND EN3 .... 37 J6
  WALTH E17 .... 68 D6
  WELL DA16 .... 126 F1
Tench St WAP E1W 104 D7
Tenda Rd BERM/RHTH SE16 .... 122 B2
Tendring Wy CHDH RM6 .... 72 C6
Tenham Av BRXS/STRHM SW2 .... 138 C8
Tenniel Cl BAY/PAD W2 .... 8 B4
Tennison Av BORE WD6 .... 32 B8
Tennison Rd SNWD SE25 .... 157 M7
Tennis St STHWK SE1 .... 19 G1
Tenniswood Rd EN EN1 .... 36 E4
Tennyson Av CDALE/KGS NW9 .... 63 J4
  MNPK E12 .... 88 E2
  NWMAL KT3 .... 154 B8

TWK TW1 .... 133 M5
WAB EN9 .... 27 L7
WAN E11 .... 70 A8
Tennyson Cl
  EBED/NFELT TW14 .... 132 A3
  PEND EN3 .... 37 K8
  WELL DA16 .... 125 M8
Tennyson Rd ASHF TW15 .... 148 B1
  DART DA1 .... 147 G2
  HARH RM3 .... 74 C1
  HNWL W7 .... 97 M6
  HSLW TW3 .... 115 J7
  KIL/WHAMP NW6 .... 82 F8
  LEY E10 .... 87 H1
  MLHL NW7 .... 45 M7
  PGE/AN SE20 .... 158 D3
  SRTFD E15 .... 87 L7
  WALTH E17 .... 68 F7
  WIM/MER SW19 .... 155 J2
Tennyson St VX/NE SW8 .... 120 B7
Tennyson Wy HCH RM12 .... 91 M1
Tensing Rd NWDGN UB2 .... 115 G3
Tentelow La NWDGN UB2 .... 115 H1
Tenterden Cl ELTH/MOT SE9 .... 142 F8
  HDN NW4 .... 64 D4
Tenterden Dr HDN NW4 .... 64 D4
Tenterden Gdns
  CROY/NA CR0 .... 173 G2
  HDN NW4 .... 64 D4
Tenterden Gv HDN NW4 .... 64 D5
Tenterden Rd BCTR RM8 .... 90 F2
  CROY/NA CR0 .... 173 G2
  TOTM N17 .... 67 M1
Tenterden St CONDST W1S 10 D5
Tenter Gnd WCHPL E1 .... 13 L3
Tent St WCHPL E1 .... 104 B3
Tercel Pth CHIG IG7 .... 54 B6
Teresa Gdns CHES/WCR EN8 .... 26 C7
Terling Cl WAN E11 .... 87 M3
Terling Rd BCTR RM8 .... 91 G2
Terminus Pl PIM SW1V 16 D4
Tern Gdns UPMR RM14 .... 93 L1
Tern Wy BRW CM14 .... 57 L6
Terrace Gdns BARN SW13 .... 117 M7
  WAT WD17 .... 29 H5
Terrace La RCHPK/HAM TW10 .... 134 E3
Terrace Rd HOM E9 .... 86 C7
  PLSTW E13 .... 88 A8
  WOT/HER KT12 .... 165 H2
The Terraces RDART DA2 .... 147 J4
The Terrace BARN SW13 .... 117 J7
  KIL/WHAMP NW6 .... 2 A3
Terrace Wk DAGW RM9 .... 90 E5
Terrapin Rd TOOT SW17 .... 138 B7
Terrick Rd WDGN N22 .... 66 E2
Terrick St SHB W12 .... 100 B5
Terrilands PIN HA5 .... 60 F4
Terront Rd SEVS/STOTM N15 .... 67 J6
Tessa Sanderson Wy
  NTHLT UB5 .... 79 K5 ⑦
Tetcott Rd WBPTN SW10 .... 119 J5
Tetherdown MUSWH N10 .... 66 A4
Tetty Wy HAYES BR2 .... 160 A5
Teversham La VX/NE SW8 .... 120 E6
Teviot Av SOCK/AV RM15 .... 111 J5
Teviot Cl WELL DA16 .... 126 C6
Teviot St POP/IOD E14 .... 105 J4
Tewkesbury Av FSTH SE23 .... 140 B5
  PIN HA5 .... 60 F2
Tewkesbury Gdns
  CDALE/KGS NW9 .... 63 H4
Tewkesbury Rd CAR SM5 .... 170 D3
  FSBYPK N4 .... 67 K8
  WEA W13 .... 98 A7
Tewkesbury Ter
  FBAR/BDGN N11 .... 48 C8
Tewson Rd WOOL/PLUM SE18 .... 125 L3
Teynham Av WCHMH N21 .... 49 K1
Teynham Gn HAYES BR2 .... 160 A8
Teynton Ter TOTM N17 .... 67 J2
Thackeray Cl ISLW TW7 .... 116 A7
  RYLN/HDSTN HA2 .... 79 L1
  UX/CGN UB8 .... 95 H5
  WIM/MER SW19 .... 154 D5
Thackeray Dr CHDH RM6 .... 72 A8
Thackeray Rd EHAM E6 .... 106 D1
  VX/NE SW8 .... 120 B7
Thackeray St KENS W8 .... 14 D3
Thakeham Cl SYD SE26 .... 158 B1
Thalia Cl GNWCH SE10 .... 123 H2
Thame Rd
  BERM/RHTH SE16 .... 104 D8 ⑩
Thames Av CHERT KT16 .... 148 A6
  DAGW RM9 .... 109 J3
  GFD/PVL UB6 .... 97 M1
  WBPTN SW10 .... 119 J9
Thames Bank
  MORT/ESHN SW14 .... 117 J7
Thamesbank Pl THMD SE28 .... 108 C5
Thames Cir POP/IOD E14 .... 123 G2
Thames Cl HPTN TW12 .... 151 H5
  RAIN RM13 .... 110 B5
Thames Down Link
  CHSGTN KT9 .... 168 C6
  EPSOM KT18 .... 179 M7
  WPK KT4 .... 168 D5
Thames Dr RSLP HA4 .... 59 J7
Thamesfield Ct SHPTN TW17 .... 164 C2
Thames Ga DART DA1 .... 147 G2
Thamesgate STA TW18 .... 148 B5
Thamesgate Cl
  RCHPK/HAM TW10 .... 134 B8
Thameside TEDD TW11 .... 152 D3
Thames Md WOT/HER KT12 .... 165 G2
Thames Meadow
  E/WMO/HCT KT8 .... 151 G5
  WOT/HER KT12 .... 164 D3
Thamesmere Dr THMD SE28 .... 108 B6
Thames Pth BERM/RHTH SE16 .... 122 F1
  BOW E3 .... 105 J1
  CHSWK W4 .... 117 M6
  CLPT E5 .... 86 D3
  GNWCH SE10 .... 123 J4
  LBTH SE11 .... 17 K7
  POP/IOD E14 .... 123 G1
  RCH/KEW TW9 .... 116 C7
  STHWK SE1 .... 17 L4

Torridge Gdns PECK SE15 .... 140 C1
Torridge Rd THHTH CR7 .... 157 H8
Torridon Rd CAT SE6 .... 141 K5
LEW SE13 .... 141 K4
Torrington Av
NFNCH/WDSP N12 .... 47 K7 1
Torrington Cl ESH/CLAY KT10 .. 166 E8 2
Torrington Dr POTB/CUF EN6 .... 23 K5
RYLN/HDSTN HA2 .... 79 H4
Torrington Gdns
FBAR/BDGN N11 .... 48 C8
GFD/PVL UB6 .... 80 C8
Torrington Gv
NFNCH/WDSP N12 .... 47 L7 2
Torrington Pk
NFNCH/WDSP N12 .... 47 K6
Torrington Pl FITZ W1T 10 E2
WAP E1W 104 A7 14
Torrington Rd BCTR RM8 .... 90 F1
ESH/CLAY KT10 .... 166 E8
GFD/PVL UB6 .... 80 C8
RSLP HA4 .... 78 A3
Torrington Sq GWRST WC1E 11 H1
Torrington Wy MRDN SM4 .... 170 A2
Tor Rd WELL DA16 .... 126 C6 1
Torr Rd PGE/AN SE20 .... 158 D3
Torver Rd HRW HA1 .... 61 L5
Torver Wy ORP BR6 .... 176 D5
Torwood Rd PUT/ROE SW15 .... 136 A2
Torworth Rd BORE WD6 .... 31 M4
Tothill St STJSPK SW1H 17 G2
Totnes Rd WELL DA16 .... 126 B5
Totnes Wk EFNCH N2 .... 65 K5
Tottenhall Rd PLMGR N13 .... 49 G8
Tottenham Court Rd
CAMTN NW1 .... 4 F9 1
FITZ W1T 10 F1
Tottenham Gn East
SEVS/STOTM N15 .... 67 M5 8
Tottenham La CEND/HSY/T N8 .... 66 E6
Tottenham Ms FITZ W1T 10 F2 2
Tottenham Rd IS N1 .... 85 L6
Tottenham South Side
SEVS/STOTM N15 .... 67 M5 7
Tottenham St FITZ W1T 10 F2 3
Totteridge Common
TRDG/WHET N20 .... 46 A4
Totteridge La TRDG/WHET N20 .... 47 G4
Totteridge Rd PEND EN3 .... 37 K2
Totteridge Village
TRDG/WHET N20 .... 46 F3 1
Totternhoe Cl
KTN/HRWW/W HA3 .... 62 C6
Totton Rd THHTH CR7 .... 157 G6
Toulmin St STHWK SE1 .... 18 E2
Toulon St CMBW SE5 .... 121 J5 4
Tournay Rd FUL/PGN SW6 .... 118 F5
Tovil Cl PGE/AN SE20 .... 158 A5
Towcester Rd BOW E3 .... 105 H3
Tower Br TWRH EC3N 13 L8
Tower Bridge Ap TWRH EC3N 13 L8
Tower Bridge Rd STHWK SE1 .... 19 L1
Tower Cl CHIG IG7 .... 53 H8
ORP BR6 .... 176 F4
PGE/AN SE20 .... 158 B3 5
Tower Gdns ESH/CLAY KT10 .... 179 G1 2
ESH/CLAY KT10 .... 179 H1 2
Tower Gardens Rd TOTM N17 ...... 67 J2
Tower Gv WEY KT13 .... 164 E4
Tower Hamlets Rd FSTGT E7 .... 87 M5
WALTH E17 .... 69 G4
Tower Hl TWRH EC3N 13 K7
Tower Ri RCH/KEW TW9 .... 116 E8
Tower Rd BELV DA17 .... 127 J2
BXLYHN DA7 .... 145 G1
DART DA1 .... 146 C4
ORP BR6 .... 176 F4
WHTN TW2 .... 133 L7
WLSDN NW10 .... 82 A7
Tower Royal MANHO EC4N 12 F6 4
Towers Av HGDN/ICK UB10 .... 95 J3 5
Towers Pl RCHPK/HAM TW10 .. 134 E2 7
Towers Rd PIN HA5 .... 60 E2
STHL UB1 .... 97 G3
The Towers PUR/KEN CR8 .... 184 C8
Tower St LSQ/SEVD WC2H 11 H5 4
Towers Wk WEY KT13 .... 164 B8
Tower Ter WDGN N22 .... 66 F3 6
Tower Vw CROY/NA CR0 .... 173 L3
Towfield Rd FELT TW13 .... 132 F6
Towncourt Crs STMC/STPC BR5 .. 161 J8
Towncourt La STMC/STPC BR5 .... 176 D1
Towncourt Pth FSBYPK N4 .... 85 J1
Towney Md NTHLT UB5 .... 96 F1
Town Farm Wy
STWL/WRAY TW19 .... 130 D4 4
Townfield Rd RKW/CH/CXG WD3 .... 40 C2
Townfield Rd HYS/HAR UB3 .... 95 M7 2
Townfield Sq HYS/HAR UB3 .... 95 M7
Town Field Wy ISLW TW7 .... 116 A7
Town Hall Approach Rd
SEVS/STOTM N15 .... 67 M5
Townhall Av CHSWK W4 .... 117 K3 4
Town Hall Rd BTSEA SW11 ...... 119 M8 1
Townholm Crs HNWL W7 .... 115 M1
Town La STWL/WRAY TW19 .... 130 D4
Townley Ct SRTFD E15 .... 87 M6 5
Townley Rd BXLYHS DA6 .... 144 F2
DUL SE21 .... 139 L2
Townley St WALW SE17 .... 19 G7 1
Town Meadow BTFD TW8 .... 116 D5 4
Townmead Rd FUL/PGN SW6 .... 119 J7
RCH/KEW TW9 .... 117 H7
Town Mead Rd WAB EN9 .... 27 J7
Town Quay BARK IG11 .... 89 H8
STA TW18 .... 148 C6 3
Town Rd ED N9 .... 50 B4
Townsend Av STHGT/OAK N14 .... 48 D6
Townsend La CDALE/KGS NW9 ...... 63 K8
Townsend Rd ASHF TW15 .... 148 E1
SEVS/STOTM N15 .... 67 M6 8
STHL UB1 .... 96 E7
Townsend St WALW SE17 .... 19 H6
Townsend Wy NTHWD HA6 .... 59 M1
Townsend Yd HGT N6 .... 84 B1
Townshead Cl SCUP DA14 .... 162 B2
Townshend Rd CHST BR7 .... 161 H1
RCH/KEW TW9 .... 134 F1
STJWD NW8 .... 3 J4
Townshend Ter RCH/KEW TW9 .. 134 F1
Townson Av NTHLT UB5 .... 96 B1
Townson Wy NTHLT UB5 .... 96 A1 2
Town Tree Rd ASHF TW15 .... 149 G1
Towpath Wy CROY/NA CR0 .... 172 F1
Towton Rd WNWD SE27 .... 139 J6
Toynbec Cl CHST BR7 .... 143 H8 5
Toynbee Rd RYNPK SW20 .... 154 E4
Toynbee St WCHPL E1 .... 13 L3
Toyne Wy HGT N6 .... 65 M7
The Tracery BNSTD SM7 .... 182 B8
Tracey Av CRICK NW2 .... 82 C5 4
Trade Cl PLMGR N13 .... 49 G6
Trader Rd EHAM E6 .... 107 H5
Tradescant Rd VX/NE SW8 .... 120 E5
Trading Estate Rd
WLSDN NW10 .... 99 J3 5
Trafalgar Av PECK SE15 .... 121 M6
STHWK SE1 .... 19 M8
TOTM N17 .... 49 L8 2
WPK KT4 .... 169 K3
Trafalgar Dr WOT/HER KT12 .... 165 H5
Trafalgar Gdns WCHPL E1 .... 104 D4
Trafalgar Gv GNWCH SE10 .... 123 K4
Trafalgar Pl UED N18 .... 50 A7 11
WAN E11 .... 70 A5
Trafalgar Rd DART DA1 .... 146 E6 1
GNWCH SE10 .... 123 L3
RAIN RM13 .... 109 M1
WHTN TW2 .... 133 K6
WIM/MER SW19 .... 155 H3
Trafalgar Sq CHCR WC2N 11 H8
Trafalgar St WALW SE17 .... 19 G7
Trafalgar Wy CROY/NA CR0 .... 171 M4
POP/IOD E14 .... 105 J7
Trafford Cl SRTFD E15 .... 87 H5
Trafford Rd THHTH CR7 .... 156 F8
Tramway Av ED N9 .... 50 B2
SRTFD E15 .... 87 L7 7
Tramway Pth MTCM CR4 .... 155 L7
Tranmere Rd ED N9 .... 49 M2
WAND/EARL SW18 .... 137 J6
WHTN TW2 .... 133 H4
Tranquil Ri ERITH DA8 .... 127 L3
Tranquil V BKHTH/KID SE3 .... 123 M7
Transept St CAMTN NW1 .... 9 K3 2
Transmere Rd STMC/STPC BR5 .. 176 C1
Transom Sq POP/IOD E14 .... 123 H3
Transport Av BTFD TW8 .... 116 B4
Tranton Rd BERM/RHTH SE16 ...... 122 B1
Trap's Hl LOU IG10 .... 39 M7
Traps La NWMAL KT3 .... 153 L5
Travellers Wy HEST TW5 .... 114 C7
Travers Cl WALTH E17 .... 68 D2
Travers Rd HOLWY N7 .... 85 G3 2
Treacy Cl BUSH WD23 .... 43 J4
Treadgold St NTGHL W11 .... 100 D6
Treadway St BETH E2 .... 104 B1 12
Treadwell Rd EPSOM KT18 .... 180 F8
Treaty St IS N1 .... 5 L4
Trebovir Rd ECT SW5 .... 14 B7
Treby St BOW E3 .... 104 F3
Tredegar Rd BOW E3 .... 104 F1
FBAR/BDGN N11 .... 66 D1
RDART DA2 .... 146 A7
Tredegar Sq BOW E3 .... 104 F2
Trederwen Rd HACK E8 .... 86 A8 16
Tredown Rd SYD SE26 .... 158 C1
Tredwell Cl HAYES BR2 .... 160 D7
Tredwell Rd WNWD SE27 .... 139 H8 5
Tree Cl RCHPK/HAM TW10 .... 134 D5 1
Treen Av BARN SW13 .... 117 L8
Tree Rd CAN/RD E16 .... 106 C5
Treeside Cl WDR/YW UB7 .... 112 D2
Treetops Cl ABYW SE2 .... 126 E3
NTHWD HA6 .... 41 K7
Tree View Cl NRWD SE19 .... 157 L4
Treewall Gdns BMLY BR1 .... 142 B8
Trefgarne Rd DAGE RM10 .... 91 G2
Trefoil Rd WAND/EARL SW18 ...... 137 J2
Trefusis Wk WAT WD17 .... 28 E4
Tregaron Av CEND/HSY/T N8 .... 66 E7 5
Tregaron Gdns NWMAL KT3 ...... 153 L7 6
Tregarvon Rd BTSEA SW11 .... 138 A1
Tregenna Av RYLN/HDSTN HA2 .... 79 G4
Tregenna Cl STHGT/OAK N14 ...... 35 J8
Trego Rd HOM E9 .... 87 G7
Tregothnan Rd BRXN/ST SW9 ...... 120 E8
Tregunter Rd WBPTN SW10 .... 14 E9
Trehern Rd BARK/HLT IG6 .... 71 K1
MORT/ESHN SW14 .... 117 K8 6
Trehurst St CLPT E5 .... 86 E5
Trelawney Gv WEY KT13 .... 164 A8
Trelawney Rd BARK/HLT IG6 .... 71 K1
Trelawn Rd BRXS/STRHM SW2 .... 139 G2
LEY E10 .... 87 J3
Trelawny Cl WALTH E17 .... 69 H5 5
Treloar Gdns NRWD SE19 .... 157 K2 5
Tremadoc Rd CLAP SW4 .... 138 D1
Tremaine Rd PGE/AN SE20 .... 158 B5
Tremlett Gv ARCH N19 .... 84 C3
Tremlett Ms ARCH N19 .... 84 C3 1
Trenance Gdns GDMY/SEVK IG3 .... 90 A3
Trenchard Av RSLP HA4 .... 78 B5
Trenchard Cl CDALE/KGS NW9 .... 63 L2 2
STAN HA7 .... 44 B8
WOT/HER KT12 .... 165 J7
Trenchard St GNWCH SE10 .... 123 K3 2
Trenchold St VX/NE SW8 .... 120 E4 2
Trenholme Rd PGE/AN SE20 .... 158 B3
Trenholme Ter PGE/AN SE20 ...... 158 B3 5
Trenmar Gdns WLSDN NW10 .... 100 B2
Trent Av EA W5 .... 116 C1
UPMR RM14 .... 75 K7
Trentbridge Cl BARK/HLT IG6 ...... 53 M8
Trent Ct WAN E11 .... 70 A6 3
Trent Gdns STHGT/OAK N14 .... 48 B1
Trentham Dr STMC/STPC BR5 ...... 162 A7
Trentham St WAND/EARL SW18 .. 137 G5
Trent Rd BKHH IG9 .... 52 B3
BRXS/STRHM SW2 .... 138 F2
Trent Wy WPK KT4 .... 169 J5
YEAD UB4 .... 95 L2 4
Trentwood Side ENC/FH EN2 .... 35 M6
Treport St WAND/EARL SW18 ...... 137 H4
Tresco Cl BMLY BR1 .... 159 L2 5
Trescoe Gdns CRW RM5 .... 55 J7
PIN HA5 .... 60 E8
Tresco Gdns GDMY/SEVK IG3 .... 89 M2
Tresco Rd PECK SE15 .... 140 B1
Tresham Crs STJWD NW8 .... 3 J9
Tresham Rd BARK IG11 .... 89 M7
Tresilian Av WCHMH N21 .... 35 M8
Tressillian Crs BROCKY SE4 .... 123 G8
Tressillian Rd BROCKY SE4 .... 123 G8
Trestis Cl YEAD UB4 .... 96 D3
Treswell Rd DAGW RM9 .... 90 E8
Tretawn Gdns MLHL NW7 .... 45 L6
Tretawn Pk MLHL NW7 .... 45 L6
Trevanion Rd WKENS W14 ...... 118 E2 11
Treve Av HRW HA1 .... 61 J8
Trevellance Wy GSTN WD25 .... 21 K6 2
Trevelyan Av MNPK E12 .... 88 F4
Trevelyan Cl DART DA1 .... 146 F1
Trevelyan Crs
KTN/HRWW/W HA3 .... 62 D8
Trevelyan Gdns WLSDN NW10 .. 82 C8 5
Trevelyan Rd FSTGT E7 .... 87 L4
TOOT SW17 .... 155 L2
Treveris St STHWK SE1 .... 12 D9 2
Treverton St NKENS W10 .... 100 D3 5
Treves Cl WCHMH N21 .... 35 M8
Treville St PUT/ROE SW15 .... 136 B4
Treviso Rd FSTH SE23 .... 140 D6 5
Trevithick Cl
EBED/NFELT TW14 .... 131 M5
Trevithick Dr DART DA1 .... 146 F1
Trevithick St DEPT SE8 .... 123 G4 5
Trevone Gdns PIN HA5 .... 60 E7
Trevor Cl EBAR EN4 .... 47 K1 4
HAYES BR2 .... 174 F2
ISLW TW7 .... 133 M2 1
KTN/HRWW/W HA3 .... 61 M1 4
NTHLT UB5 .... 96 C1
Trevor Crs RSLP HA4 .... 77 M4
Trevor Gdns EDGW HA8 .... 63 K2
Trevor Pl SKENS SW7 .... 15 K2
Trevor Rd EDGW HA8 .... 63 K2
HYS/HAR UB3 .... 95 L8 1
WFD IG8 .... 70 A1
WIM/MER SW19 .... 154 E3
Trevor Sq SKENS SW7 .... 15 K2
Trevor St SKENS SW7 .... 15 K2
Trevose Rd WALTH E17 .... 69 K2
Trevose Wy OXHEY WD19 .... 42 C5
Trewenna Dr CHSGTN KT9 .... 167 K7 5
POTB/CUF EN6 .... 23 K5
Trewince Rd RYNPK SW20 .... 154 C4
Trewint St WAND/EARL SW18 ...... 137 J6
Trewsbury Rd SYD SE26 .... 158 D1
Triandra Wy YEAD UB4 .... 96 D4
Triangle Pl CLAP SW4 .... 138 D1
Triangle Rd HACK E8 .... 86 B8 5
The Triangle NWMAL KT3 .... 153 J5 2
Trident Rd GSTN WD25 .... 20 F7
Trident St BERM/RHTH SE16 .... 122 D2 4
Trident Wy NWDGN UB2 .... 114 B1
Trigon Rd VX/NE SW8 .... 120 F5 4
Trilby Rd FSTH SE23 .... 140 D6
Trim St NWCR SE14 .... 122 F4 5
Trinder Rd ARCH N19 .... 84 E1
BAR EN5 .... 33 J8
Tring Av EA W5 .... 98 F7
STHL UB1 .... 96 F5
WBLY HA9 .... 81 G6
Tring Cl BARK/HLT IG6 .... 71 J6
HARH RM3 .... 56 F6
Tring Gdns HARH RM3 .... 56 E6
Trinidad Gdns DAGE RM10 .... 91 K7
Trinidad St POP/IOD E14 .... 104 F6 5
Trinity Av EFNCH N2 .... 65 K4
EN EN1 .... 49 M1
Trinity Church Rd BARN SW13 .... 118 B4
Trinity Church Sq STHWK SE1 .... 18 E2
Trinity Cl HAYES BR2 .... 175 L3
HSLWW TW4 .... 114 E8
LEW SE13 .... 141 K1
NTHWD HA6 .... 41 L8
SAND/SEL CR2 .... 184 E2
STWL/WRAY TW19 .... 130 C3
WAN E11 .... 87 L2
Trinity Ct ELTH/MOT SE9 .... 143 H3
Trinity Crs TOOT SW17 .... 137 M6
Trinity Gdns BRXN/ST SW9 .... 138 F1
CAN/RD E16 .... 105 M4 7
DART DA1 .... 146 D3
Trinity Gv GNWCH SE10 .... 123 J6 5
Trinity Hall Cl WATN WD24 .... 29 J6 5
Trinity La CHES/WCR EN8 .... 26 E5
Trinity Pl BXLYHS DA6 .... 144 F1
Trinity Ri HNHL SE24 .... 139 H4
Trinity Rd BARK/HLT IG6 .... 71 J4
EFNCH N2 .... 65 K4
RCH/KEW TW9 .... 116 F8 5
STHL UB1 .... 96 E7
TOOT SW17 .... 137 M6
WAND/EARL SW18 .... 137 K3
WDGN N22 .... 66 F2
WIM/MER SW19 .... 155 G2
Trinity Sq TWRH EC3N 13 K7 1
Trinity St CAN/RD E16 .... 105 M4
ENC/FH EN2 .... 36 C5
STHWK SE1 .... 18 F2
Trinity Wy ACT W3 .... 99 L6 4
CHING E4 .... 50 F8
Trio Pl STHWK SE1 .... 18 F2 1
Tristan Sq BKHTH/KID SE3 .... 123 L8
Tristram Cl WALTH E17 .... 69 K4
Tristram Rd BMLY BR1 .... 141 M8
Triton Sq CAMTN NW1 .... 4 E9
Tritton Av CROY/NA CR0 .... 171 L6
Tritton Rd WNWD SE27 .... 139 K7
Triumph Cl HYS/HAR UB3 .... 113 J6
Triumph Rd EHAM E6 .... 106 F5 5
Trojan Wy CROY/NA CR0 .... 171 M5
Trolling Down Hl RDART DA2 .... 147 H6
Troon St WCHPL E1 .... 104 E5 11
Troopers Dr HARH RM3 .... 56 D6
Trosley Rd BELV DA17 .... 127 G4
Trossachs Rd EDUL SE22 .... 139 L2
Trothy Rd STHWK SE1 .... 122 A2
Trotters Bottom BAR EN5 .... 33 G2
Trott Rd MUSWH N10 .... 66 A1
Trott St BTSEA SW11 .... 119 K6
Trotwood CHIG IG7 .... 53 K7
Troughton Rd CHARL SE7 .... 124 B3
Troutbeck Rd NWCR SE14 .... 122 E6
Trout La WDR/YW UB7 .... 94 C6
Trout Rd WDR/YW UB7 .... 94 D7
Trouville Rd BAL SW12 .... 138 C3
Trowbridge Rd HARH RM3 .... 56 D8
HOM E9 .... 86 F6
Trowley Ri ABLGY WD5 .... 20 E4
Trowlock Av TEDD TW11 .... 152 C2
Trowlock Wy TEDD TW11 .... 152 C2
Troy Ct KENS W8 .... 14 A3 4
Troy Rd NRWD SE19 .... 157 K2
Troy Town PECK SE15 .... 122 A8 5
Trueman Cl EDGW HA8 .... 63 H1 5
Truesdale Dr DEN/HRF UB9 .... 58 C5
Trulock Rd TOTM N17 .... 68 A1
Truman's Rd
STNW/STAM N16 .... 85 M5 5
Trumpers Wy HNWL W7 .... 115 M1
Trumpington Rd FSTGT E7 .... 87 M4
Trump St CITYW EC2V 12 F5
Trundlers Wy BUSH WD23 .... 43 L3 1
Trundle St STHWK SE1 .... 18 E1
Trundleys Rd DEPT SE8 .... 122 E4
DEPT SE8 .... 122 D3
Trundley's Ter DEPT SE8 .... 122 D2 5
Truro Gdns IL IG1 .... 70 E8
Truro Rd WALTH E17 .... 68 F5 4
WDGN N22 .... 66 E1
Truro St CAMTN NW1 .... 84 A6 11
Truro Wy YEAD UB4 .... 95 L2 5
Trusedale Rd EHAM E6 .... 106 F5 5
Truslove Rd WNWD SE27 .... 157 G1
Trussley Rd HMSMTH W6 .... 118 C1
Trustons Gdns EMPK RM11 .... 74 A8
Trust Rd CHES/WCR EN8 .... 26 E7 4
Tryfan Cl REDBR IG4 .... 70 D6
Tryon St CHEL SW3 .... 15 L7
Trystings Cl ESH/CLAY KT10 .... 167 G8
Tuam Rd WOOL/PLUM SE18 .... 125 K4
Tubbenden Cl ORP BR6 .... 176 E4
Tubbenden Dr ORP BR6 .... 176 D6
Tubbenden La ORP BR6 .... 176 D6
Tubbenden La South ORP BR6 .... 176 D7
Tubbs Rd WLSDN NW10 .... 99 M1 7
Tucker St WATW WD18 .... 29 J8 5
Tuck Rd RAIN RM13 .... 92 A6
Tudor Av CHESW EN7 .... 26 B4
GPK RM2 .... 74 A4
HPTN TW12 .... 151 G2
WATN WD24 .... 29 K2
WPK KT4 .... 169 H5
Tudor Cl ASHF TW15 .... 130 E8
BNSTD SM7 .... 181 L8
CDALE/KGS NW9 .... 81 J2
CHEAM SM3 .... 169 K7
CHESW EN7 .... 26 B4
CHIG IG7 .... 53 G6
CHSGTN KT9 .... 167 L7
CHST BR7 .... 160 F4
DART DA1 .... 146 B3
HGT N6 .... 66 C8 2
HPTN TW12 .... 151 J1 7
MLHL NW7 .... 46 A8
PIN HA5 .... 60 A6
SAND/SEL CR2 .... 185 H8
WFD IG8 .... 52 B7
WLGTN SM6 .... 183 J1
Tudor Ct BORE WD6 .... 31 L5 1
WALTH E17 .... 68 F8
Tudor Ct North WBLY HA9 .... 81 G5
Tudor Ct South WBLY HA9 .... 81 G5
Tudor Crs BARK/HLT IG6 .... 53 J8
ENC/FH EN2 .... 36 C4
Tudor Dr GPK RM2 .... 74 A5
KUTN/CMB KT2 .... 152 E1
MRDN SM4 .... 169 M2 5
WATN WD24 .... 29 K3
WOT/HER KT12 .... 165 K3
Tudor Gdns ACT W3 .... 99 G5
BARN SW13 .... 117 L8 5
CDALE/KGS NW9 .... 81 J2
GPK RM2 .... 74 A5
TWK TW1 .... 133 M5 5
UPMR RM14 .... 93 J2
WWKM BR4 .... 174 C5
Tudor Gv HOM E9 .... 86 C7
Tudor Manor Gdns GSTN WD25 ...... 21 K5
Tudor Pl WIM/MER SW19 .... 155 L3 4
Tudor Rd ASHF TW15 .... 149 K2
BAR EN5 .... 34 A6
BARK IG11 .... 89 M7
BECK BR3 .... 159 J6
CHING E4 .... 51 H8
ED N9 .... 50 B2
EHAM E6 .... 88 C8
HACK E8 .... 86 B8
HPTN TW12 .... 151 G3
HSLW TW3 .... 133 K1
HYS/HAR UB3 .... 95 K5
KTN/HRWW/W HA3 .... 61 K3
KUTN/CMB KT2 .... 153 G3
NRWD SE19 .... 157 M3
PIN HA5 .... 60 C3
SNWD SE25 .... 158 B8
STHL UB1 .... 96 E6
Tudor Sq HYS/HAR UB3 .... 95 K4
Tudor St EMB EC4Y 12 B6
Tudor Wk WATN WD24 .... 29 K2
Tudor Wy ACT W3 .... 99 G8
HGDN/ICK UB10 .... 77 G6
RKW/CH/CXG WD3 .... 40 A3
STHGT/OAK N14 .... 48 D3 5
STMC/STPC BR5 .... 176 D1
WAB EN9 .... 27 K6
Tudor Well Cl STAN HA7 .... 44 B7
Tudway Rd ELTH/MOT SE9 .... 142 C1
Tufnail Rd DART DA1 .... 146 F3
Tufnell Park Rd HOLWY N7 .... 84 D4
Tufter Rd CHIG IG7 .... 53 M7
Tufton Gdns E/WMO/HCT KT8 .... 151 H5
Tufton Rd CHING E4 .... 51 G6
Tufton St WEST SW1P 17 J4
Tugboat St THMD SE28 .... 107 L8
Tugela Rd CROY/NA CR0 .... 172 D1
Tugela St CAT SE6 .... 140 F6
Tugmutton Cl ORP BR6 .... 176 B6 5
Tulip Cl CROY/NA CR0 .... 173 K3
EHAM E6 .... 106 F4 7
HARH RM3 .... 56 C8
HPTN TW12 .... 150 F2 5
STHL UB1 .... 97 J8 4
Tulip Gdns IL IG1 .... 89 H6
Tull St MTCM CR4 .... 170 F2
Tulse Cl BECK BR3 .... 159 J6
Tulse Hl BRXS/STRHM SW2 .... 139 G4
Tulsemere Rd WNWD SE27 .... 139 J6
Tumbling Bay WOT/HER KT12 .... 165 G1
Tummons Gdns SNWD SE25 .... 157 L5
Tuncombe Rd UED N18 .... 49 L6 1
Tunis Rd SHB W12 .... 100 C7
Tunley Rd BAL SW12 .... 138 A6
WLSDN NW10 .... 81 L8
Tunmarsh La PLSTW E13 .... 106 C2
Tunnan Leys EHAM E6 .... 107 G5
Tunnel Av GNWCH SE10 .... 105 K8
Tunnel Gdns FBAR/BDGN N11 ...... 66 C1
Tunnel Link Rd HTHAIR TW6 .... 131 G2
Tunnel Rd
BERM/RHTH SE16 .... 104 C8 11
Tunnel Rd East HTHAIR TW6 ...... 113 H6
Tunnel Rd West HTHAIR TW6 ...... 113 G7
Tunnel Wood Cl WAT WD17 .... 28 F2
Tunnel Wood Rd WAT WD17 .... 28 F2
WATN WD24 .... 28 F2
Tunstall Av BARK/HLT IG6 .... 54 A8
Tunstall Cl ORP BR6 .... 176 E6
Tunstall Rd BRXN/ST SW9 .... 138 F1
CROY/NA CR0 .... 172 E3
Tunstock Wy BELV DA17 .... 126 E1
Tunworth Cl CDALE/KGS NW9 ...... 63 J7
Tunworth Crs PUT/ROE SW15 .... 135 M3
Tupelo Rd LEY E10 .... 87 H2
Turene Cl BTSEA SW11 .... 137 J1 4
Turin Rd ED N9 .... 50 C2
Turin St BETH E2 .... 104 A2
Turkey Oak Cl NRWD SE19 .... 157 L4
Turkey St EN EN1 .... 37 H2
Turks Cl UX/CGN UB8 .... 95 G2
Turks Rw CHEL SW3 .... 15 M7
Turle Rd FSBYPK N4 .... 84 F2 5
STRHM/NOR SW16 .... 156 E5
Turlewray Cl FSBYPK N4 .... 84 F1 5
Turley Cl SRTFD E15 .... 87 L8 5
Turnagain La STP EC4M 12 C4 7
Turnage Rd BCTR RM8 .... 90 E1
Turnant Rd TOTM N17 .... 67 J2 4
Turnberry Ct OXHEY WD19 .... 42 C5 5
Turnberry Dr LCOL/BKTW AL2 ...... 21 L3
Turnberry Wy ORP BR6 .... 176 D3 4
Turnbull Cl RDART DA2 .... 147 L4
Turnbury Cl THMD SE28 .... 108 D5 1
Turner Av MTCM CR4 .... 155 M4
SEVS/STOTM N15 .... 67 L5
WHTN TW2 .... 133 J7
Turner Cl ALP/SUD HA0 .... 80 D5
CMBW SE5 .... 121 H6
GLDGN NW11 .... 65 H7 5
Turner Ct DART DA1 .... 146 C2
Turner Rd BH/WHM TN16 .... 187 J5
BUSH WD23 .... 30 C7
EDGW HA8 .... 62 E3
NWMAL KT3 .... 168 D2
WALTH E17 .... 69 J5
Turners Cl STA TW18 .... 148 B1 2
Turner's Hl CHES/WCR EN8 .... 26 D3
Turners La WOT/HER KT12 .... 165 H8
Turners Meadow Wy BECK BR3 .. 158 F4
Turner's Rd POP/IOD E14 .... 104 F4
Turner St CAN/RD E16 .... 105 M5 10
WCHPL E1 .... 104 B4
Turners Wy CROY/NA CR0 .... 172 A4
Turner's Wd GLDGN NW11 .... 83 J1
Turneville Rd WKENS W14 .... 118 F4
Turney Rd DUL SE21 .... 139 J4
Turnham Green Ter CHSWK W4 .. 117 L2
Turnham Rd BROCKY SE4 .... 140 E2
Turnmill St FARR EC1M 12 B1
Turnpike Ct DEPT SE8 .... 122 F5 7
Turnpike La CEND/HSY/T N8 .... 67 G5
SUT SM1 .... 170 C7 5
UX/CGN UB8 .... 94 E2
Turnpike Link CROY/NA CR0 .... 172 E4
Turnpike Wy ISLW TW7 .... 116 A6
Turnstone Cl CDALE/KGS NW9 .... 63 L3 5
HGDN/ICK UB10 .... 77 H5 1
PLSTW E13 .... 106 A2
SAND/SEL CR2 .... 185 L3
The Turnstones GSTN WD25 .... 29 L1
Turpentine La PIM SW1V 16 D7
Turpin Av CRW RM5 .... 73 G1
Turpington Cl HAYES BR2 .... 175 L1
Turpington La HAYES BR2 .... 160 E8
Turpin La ERITH DA8 .... 128 A4
Turpin Rd EBED/NFELT TW14 .. 131 M3 1
Turpin's La WFD IG8 .... 52 F7
Turpin Wy WLGTN SM6 .... 183 H1
Turquand St WALW SE17 .... 18 F6 4
Turret Gv CLAP SW4 .... 120 C8
Turton Rd ALP/SUD HA0 .... 80 E5
Turville St BETH E2 .... 7 L9 1
Tuscan Rd WOOL/PLUM SE18 ...... 125 K3
Tuskar St GNWCH SE10 .... 123 L3
Tuxford Cl BORE WD6 .... 31 L3 4
Tweeddale Gv HGDN/ICK UB10 ...... 77 J3
Tweeddale Rd CAR SM5 .... 170 D3
Tweedmouth Rd PLSTW E13 .... 106 B1
Tweed Wy ROM RM1 .... 73 K1
Tweedy Rd BMLY BR1 .... 160 A4
Twelvetrees Crs BOW E3 .... 105 J3
Twentyman Cl WFD IG8 .... 52 A7 7
Twickenham Cl
CROY/NA CR0 .... 171 M5 1
Twickenham Gdns
GFD/PVL UB6 .... 80 A5
KTN/HRWW/W HA3 .... 61 L1
Twickenham Rd FELT TW13 .... 132 F7
ISLW TW7 .... 116 A8
ISLW TW7 .... 134 A1 5
RCH/KEW TW9 .... 134 C2
TEDD TW11 .... 134 A8
WAN E11 .... 87 K2
Twig Folly Cl BOW E3 .... 104 D1
Twigg Cl ERITH DA8 .... 127 L5
Twilley St WAND/EARL SW18 .... 137 H4
Twine Cl BARK IG11 .... 108 B2

Twine Ct *WCHPL* E1 .... 104 C6 🔟
Twineham Gn
  NFNCH/WDSP N12 .... 47 G6
Twining Av *WHTN* TW2 .... 133 J7
Twinn Rd *MLHL* NW7 .... 46 E8
Twinoaks *COB* KT11 .... 178 A6
Twisleton Ct *DART* DA1 .... 146 E3
Twybridge Wy *WLSDN* NW10 .... 81 J7
  WLSDN NW10 .... 98 F2
Twyford Av *ACT* W3 .... 99 G6
  EFNCH N2 .... 65 M4
Twyford Crs *ACT* W3 .... 99 G7
Twyford Rd *CAR* SM5 .... 170 D3
  IL IG1 .... 89 J5
  RYLN/HDSTN HA2 .... 61 H8
Twyford St *IS* N1 .... 5 L3
Tyas Rd *CAN/RD* E16 .... 105 M3
Tybenham Rd *WIM/MER* SW19 ... 155 G6
Tyberry Rd *EN* EN1 .... 37 H6
Tyburn La *HRW* HA1 .... 61 L8
Tycehurst Hl *LOU* IG10 .... 39 M7
Tye La *ORP* BR6 .... 176 C7
Tyers Ga *STHWK* SE1 .... 19 J2
Tyers St *LBTH* SE11 .... 17 L7
Tyers Ter *LBTH* SE11 .... 17 L8
Tyeshurst Cl *ABYW* SE2 .... 128 F4
Tyfield Cl *CHES/WCR* EN8 .... 26 C3 🔟
Tylecroft Rd
  STRHM/NOR SW16 .... 156 E5 🔟
Tyle Gn *EMPK* RM11 .... 74 E6
Tylehurst Gdns *IL* IG1 .... 89 J5
Tyler Cl *BETH* E2 .... 7 L5
Tylers Crs *HCH* RM12 .... 92 C5
Tylersfield *ABLGY* WD5 .... 20 F4
Tylers Ga *KTN/HRWW/W* HA3 ... 62 E7
Tylers St *GNWCH* SE10 .... 123 L3
Tylney Av *NRWD* SE19 .... 157 M1
Tylney Rd *BMLY* BR1 .... 160 D5
  FSTGT E7 .... 89 K3
Tynan Cl *EBED/NFELT* TW14 ...... 132 A5 🔟
Tyndale La *IS* N1 .... 6 C1
Tyndale Ter *IS* N1 .... 6 C1
Tyndall Rd *LEY* E10 .... 87 J2
  WELL DA16 .... 125 M8
Tyne Cl *UPMR* RM14 .... 75 K7
Tynedale Cl *RDART* DA2 .... 147 K5 🔟
Tyne Gdns *SOCK/AV* RM15 .... 111 J6 🔟
Tyneham Rd *BTSEA* SW11 .... 120 A8 🔟
Tynemouth Cl *EHAM* E6 .... 107 H5 🔟
Tynemouth Dr *EN* EN1 .... 37 C3
Tynemouth Rd *MTCM* CR4 .... 156 A3
  SEVS/STOTM N15 .... 67 M5
  WOOL/PLUM SE18 .... 125 L3
Tynemouth St *FUL/PGN* SW6 ... 119 J7
Tyne St *WCHPL* E1 .... 13 M4
Type St *BETH* E2 .... 7 L1
Tyrawley Rd *FUL/PGN* SW6 ...... 119 H6 🔟
Tyrell Cl *HRW* HA1 .... 79 L4
Tyrells Cl *UPMR* RM14 .... 93 H2 🔟
Tyrone Rd *EHAM* E6 .... 106 F1
Tyrrell Av *WELL* DA16 .... 144 A2
Tyrrell Rd *EDUL* SE22 .... 140 A1
Tyrrel Wy *CDALE/KGS* NW9 ...... 63 M8
Tyrwhitt Rd *BROCKY* SE4 .... 123 B3 🔟
Tysea Hl *ABR/ST* RM4 .... 55 M3
Tysoe Av *PEND* EN3 .... 37 M1
Tysoe St *CLKNW* EC1R .... 6 A2 🔟
Tyson Rd *FSTH* SE23 .... 140 C4
Tyssen Rd *STNW/STAM* N16 ... 85 M3 🔟
Tyssen St *HACK* E8 .... 85 M6 🔟
Tytherton Rd *ARCH* N19 .... 84 D3

U

Uamvar St *POP/IOD* E14 .... 105 H4
Uckfield Gv *MTCM* CR4 .... 156 A4
Uckfield Rd *PEND* EN3 .... 37 K2
Udall Gdns *CRW* RM5 .... 55 G8
Udall St *WEST* SW1P 16 F6
Udney Park Rd *TEDD* TW11 ...... 152 A1
Uffington Rd *WLSDN* NW10 ...... 82 A3
  WNWD SE27 .... 139 G8
Ufford Cl *KTN/HRWW/W* HA3 ... 61 H1
Ufford Rd *KTN/HRWW/W* HA3 ... 61 H1
Ufford St *STHWK* SE1 .... 18 B1
Ufton Gv *IS* N1 .... 7 J1
Ufton Rd *IS* N1 .... 7 J2
Ullathorne Rd
  STRHM/NOR SW16 .... 138 C8
Ulleswater Rd *PLMGR* N13 ...... 48 E6
Ullin St *POP/IOD* E14 .... 105 J4 🔟
Ullswater Cl *BMLY* BR1 .... 159 L2
  PUT/ROE SW15 .... 135 K8 🔟
  YEAD UB4 .... 95 L1
Ullswater Crs *PUT/ROE* SW15 ... 135 K8
Ullswater Rd *BARN* SW13 ...... 118 A5
  WNWD SE27 .... 139 H7
Ullswater Wy *HCH* RM12 ...... 92 A5
Ulster Gdns *PLMGR* N13 ...... 49 J6
Ulster Pl *CAMTN* NW1 .... 10 C1
Ulundi Rd *BKHTH/KID* SE3 ...... 123 L4
Ulva Rd *PUT/ROE* SW15 .... 136 D1 🔟
Ulverscroft Rd *EDUL* SE22 ...... 140 A2
Ulverston Rd *WALTH* E17 ...... 69 K3
Ulysses Rd *KIL/WHAMP* NW6 ... 82 E3
Umberston St *WCHPL* E1 ...... 104 B5 🔟🔟
Umbria St *PUT/ROE* SW15 ...... 136 A3 🔟
Umfreville Rd *FSBYPK* N4 ...... 67 H7
Undercliff Rd *LEW* SE13 ...... 123 G8
Underhill *BAR* EN5 .... 34 A8
Underhill Rd *EDUL* SE22 ...... 140 A2
Underhill St *CAMTN* NW1 ...... 4 D4
Undershaft *HDTCH* EC3A 13 J5
Undershaw Rd *BMLY* BR1 ...... 141 L7
Underwood *CHING* E4 .... 51 H7
  WFD IG8 .... 70 D1
Underwood Rd *IS* N1 .... 6 F7 🔟
The Underwood
  ELTH/MOT SE9 .... 142 F6
Undine Rd *POP/IOD* E14 ...... 123 H2
Undine St *TOOT* SW17 .... 155 M1

Uneeda Dr *GFD/PVL* UB6 .... 79 K8
Unicorn Wk *GRH* DA9 .... 147 M2 🔟
Union Ct *CLAP* SW4 .... 120 C7
Union Dr *WCHPL* E1 .... 104 E3 🔟
Union Gv *VX/NE* SW8 .... 120 D7
Union Rd *ALP/SUD* HA0 .... 80 E6
  CLAP SW4 .... 120 D7
  CROY/NA CR0 .... 172 C2
  FBAR/BDGN N11 .... 48 D8
  HAYES BR2 .... 160 D8
  NTHLT UB5 .... 97 G1
Union Sq *IS* N1 .... 6 E4
Union St *BAR* EN5 .... 33 L7
  KUT KT1 .... 152 D5
  SRTFD E15 .... 87 K8 🔟
  STHWK SE1 .... 12 D9
Union Wk *BETH* E2 .... 7 L7
Unity Cl *CROY/NA* CR0 .... 186 B2 🔟
  WLSDN NW10 .... 82 A6
  WNWD SE27 .... 157 J1
Unity Ms *CAMTN* NW1 .... 5 G5
Unity Rd *PEND* EN3 .... 37 J2
Unity Wy *WOOL/PLUM* SE18 ... 124 D1
University Cl *CDALE/KGS* NW9 ... 63 M1 🔟
University Gdns *DART* DA1 ...... 144 F4 🔟
University Rd *WIM/MER* SW19 ... 155 K2
University St *FITZ* W1T 10 F1
University Wy *DART* DA1 ...... 128 D8
Unwin Av *EBED/NFELT* TW14 ... 131 K2
Unwin Cl *PECK* SE15 .... 122 A4
Unwin Rd *ISLW* TW7 .... 115 L8
Upbrook Ms *BAY/PAD* W2 ...... 8 F5
Upcerne Rd *WBPTN* SW10 ...... 119 J5 🔟
Upcroft Av *EDGW* HA8 .... 45 J7
Updale Cl *POTB/CUF* EN6 ...... 22 E6
Updale Rd *SCUP* DA14 .... 143 M8
Upfield *CROY/NA* CR0 .... 173 H4
Upfield Rd *HNWL* W7 .... 97 M3
Uphall Rd *IL* IG1 .... 89 H5
Upham Park Rd *CHSWK* W4 ... 117 L2
Uphill Dr *CDALE/KGS* NW9 ...... 63 J6
  MLHL NW7 .... 45 L7
Uphill Gv *MLHL* NW7 .... 45 L6
Uphill Rd *MLHL* NW7 .... 45 L6
Upland Court Rd *HARH* RM3 ... 74 F3
Upland Rd *BELMT* SM2 .... 182 D1
  BXLYHN DA7 .... 126 F8
  EDUL SE22 .... 140 A4
  PLSTW E13 .... 106 A3 🔟
  SAND/SEL CR2 .... 172 D7
Uplands *BECK* BR3 .... 159 G5
  RKW/CH/CXG WD3 .... 40 F1
Uplands Av *WALTH* E17 .... 68 D2
Uplands Cl
  MORT/ESHN SW14 .... 135 H2 🔟
Uplands Dr *LHD/OX* KT22 ...... 178 D7 🔟
Uplands Park Rd *ENC/FH* EN2 ... 36 A5
Uplands Rd *CEND/HSY/T* N8 ... 66 F6
  CHDH RM6 .... 72 D4
  EBAR EN4 .... 48 A3
  ORP BR6 .... 177 H3
  WFD IG8 .... 70 E1
The Uplands *LCOL/BKTW* AL2 ... 21 L3
  LOU IG10 .... 39 M6
  RSLP HA4 .... 78 A1
Uplands Wy *WCHMH* N21 ...... 36 A8
Upminster Rd *HCH* RM12 ...... 92 F2
Upminster Rd North
  RAIN RM13 .... 110 C2
Upminster Rd South
  RAIN RM13 .... 110 A3
Upney Cl *HCH* RM12 .... 92 D5 🔟
Upney La *BARK* IG11 .... 89 M6
Upnor Wy *WALW* SE17 .... 19 K7
Uppark Dr *GNTH/NBYPK* IG2 ... 71 J7
Upper Abbey Rd *BELV* DA17 ... 126 F2
Upper Addison Gdns
  WKENS W14 .... 100 E8
Upper Belgrave St *KTBR* SW1X ... 16 B3
Upper Berkeley St *BAY/PAD* W2 ... 9 L5
Upper Beulah Hl *NRWD* SE19 ... 157 L4
Upper Brentwood Rd *GPK* RM2... 74 C5
Upper Brockley Rd
  BROCKY SE4 .... 122 F8
Upper Brook St
  MYFR/PKLN W1K 10 A6
Upper Butts *BTFD* TW8 .... 116 C4 🔟
Upper Cheyne Rw *CHEL* SW3 ... 119 L4
Upper Court Rd
  HOR/WEW KT19 .... 180 C4
Upper Dunnymans
  BNSTD SM7 .... 181 M7 🔟
Upper Elmers End Rd
  BECK BR3 .... 158 E7 🔟
  BECK BR3 .... 174 A1 🔟
Upper Farm Rd
  E/WMO/HCT KT8 .... 150 F7
Upper Gn East *MTCM* CR4 ...... 155 M5 🔟
Upper Gn West *MTCM* CR4 ...... 155 M5 🔟
Upper Grosvenor St
  MYFR/PKLN W1K 10 A7
Upper Grotto Rd *TWK* TW1 ... 133 M6 🔟
Upper Gnd *STHWK* SE1 .... 12 A8
Upper Gv *SNWD* SE25 .... 157 L7
Upper Grove Rd *BELV* DA17 ... 126 F4
Upper Halliford Rd
  SHPTN TW17 .... 149 L5
Upper Ham Rd
  RCHPK/HAM TW10 .... 134 D8
Upper Harley St *CAMTN* NW1 ... 10 B1
Upper High St *EW* KT17 .... 180 E6
Upper Hwy *ABLGY* WD5 .... 20 C5
Upper Hill Ri *RKW/CH/CXG* WD3... 40 B1
Upper Hitch *OXHEY* WD19 ...... 42 E3
Upper Holly Hill Rd *BELV* DA17... 127 H5
Upper John St *REGST* W1B 10 F6
Upper MI *HMSMTH* W6 .... 118 A3 🔟
Upper Marsh *STHWK* SE1 ...... 17 M3
Upper Montagu St *MBLAR* W1H... 9 L2
Upper Mulgrave Rd *BELMT* SM2... 181 J6
Upper North St *POP/IOD* E14... 105 H5
Upper Paddock Rd
  OXHEY WD19 .... 42 E1
Upper Pk *LOU* IG10 .... 39 K8
Upper Park Rd *BELV* DA17 ...... 127 H2
  BMLY BR1 .... 160 B4

  FBAR/BDGN N11 .... 48 B7
  HAMP NW3 .... 83 M6
  KUTN/CMB KT2 .... 153 G2
Upper Phillimore Gdns *KENS* W8... 14 A2
Upper Pillory Down *CAR* SM5... 183 G6
Upper Rainham Rd *HCH* RM12... 91 M4
Upper Richmond Rd
  PUT/ROE SW15 .... 136 B1
Upper Richmond Rd West
  RCHPK/HAM TW10 .... 135 G1
  WLGTN SM6 .... 171 K7
Upper Sawleywood
  BNSTD SM7 .... 181 M7 🔟
Upper Selsdon Rd
  SAND/SEL CR2 .... 184 F2
Upper Sheridan Rd
  BELV DA17 .... 127 G2 🔟
Upper Shirley Rd
  CROY/NA CR0 .... 173 J5
Upper Sq *ISLW* TW7 .... 116 A8 🔟
Upper St *IS* N1 .... 6 B6
Upper Sunbury Rd *HPTN* TW12... 150 F4
Upper Sutton La *HEST* TW5 ... 115 G6
Upper Tachbrook St
  PIM SW1V .... 16 F5 🔟
Upper Tail *OXHEY* WD19 ...... 42 E5
Upper Teddington Rd *KUT* KT1 ... 152 F4
Upper Ter *HAMP* NW3 .... 83 J3
Upper Thames St *BLKFR* EC4V... 12 E6
Upper Tollington Pk *FSBYPK* N4... 85 G1
Upperton Rd *SCUP* DA14 ...... 161 M1
Upperton Rd East *PLSTW* E13... 106 C2
Upperton Rd West *PLSTW* E13... 106 C2
Upper Tooting Pk *TOOT* SW17... 137 M6
Upper Tooting Rd *TOOT* SW17... 137 M8
Upper Town Rd *GFD/PVL* UB6... 97 H3
Upper Tulse Hl
  BRXS/STRHM SW2 .... 138 F4
Upper Vernon Rd *SUT* SM1 ...... 170 D7
Upper Walthamstow Rd
  WALTH E17 .... 69 K5 🔟
Upper Wickham La *WELL* DA16... 126 B7
Upper Wimpole St
  CAVSQ/HST W1G 10 B2
Upper Woburn Pl *CAMTN* NW1... 5 H8
Upper Woodcote Village
  PUR/KEN CR8 .... 183 K6
Uppingham Av *STAN* HA7 ...... 62 C4
Upsdell Av *PLMGR* N13 .... 49 G8
Upshire Rd *WAB* EN9 .... 27 M5
Upstall St *CMBW* SE5 .... 121 H6
Upton Av *FSTGT* E7 .... 88 A7
Upton Cl *BXLY* DA5 .... 144 F3
Upton Dene *BELMT* SM2 ...... 182 B1 🔟
Upton Gdns *KTN/HRWW/W* HA3... 62 C7
Upton La *FSTGT* E7 .... 88 B6
Upton Lodge Cl *BUSH* WD23 ... 43 J2 🔟
Upton Park Rd *FSTGT* E7 ...... 88 B7
Upton Rd *BXLYHS* DA6 .... 144 E1
  HSLW TW3 .... 115 G8
  THHTH CR7 .... 157 K5
  UED N18 .... 50 A7
  WATW WD18 .... 29 H7
  WOOL/PLUM SE18 .... 125 J4
Upton Rd South *BXLY* DA5 ...... 144 F3
Upway *NFNCH/WDSP* N12 ...... 65 L1
Upwood Rd *LEE/GVPK* SE12 ... 141 M3
  STRHM/NOR SW16 .... 156 E4
Urban Av *RAIN* RM13 .... 92 C3
Urlwin St *CMBW* SE5 .... 121 J4
Urlwin Wk *BRXN/ST* SW9 ...... 121 G6
Urmston Dr *WIM/MER* SW19 ... 136 E5
Ursula Ms *FSBYPK* N4 .... 85 H1
Ursula St *BTSEA* SW11 .... 119 L6
Urswick Rd *CLPT* E5 .... 86 C5
  DAGW RM9 .... 90 D7
Usher Rd *BOW* E3 .... 87 F8 🔟
Usk Rd *BTSEA* SW11 .... 137 J1
  SOCK/AV RM15 .... 111 J5
Usk St *BETH* E2 .... 7 L2
Uvedale Cl *CROY/NA* CR0 ...... 186 D4 🔟
Uvedale Crs *CROY/NA* CR0 ...... 186 D4
Uvedale Rd *DAGE* RM10 ...... 91 G3
  ENC/FH EN2 .... 36 D8
Uxbridge Rd *FELT* TW13 ...... 132 D6
  HGDN/ICK UB10 .... 95 H3
  HNWL W7 .... 97 L7
  HPTN TW12 .... 133 C8
  RKW/CH/CXG WD3 .... 40 B3
  SHB W12 .... 100 C8
  STHL UB1 .... 97 G7
  SURB KT6 .... 152 D7
  WEA W13 .... 98 B7
  YEAD UB4 .... 95 L4
Uxbridge Rd (Harrow Weald)
  KTN/HRWW/W HA3 .... 43 L8
Uxbridge Rd (Hatch End)
  PIN HA5 .... 60 F1 🔟
Uxbridge Rd High St *STHL* UB1... 96 F7
Uxbridge Rd (Pinner) *PIN* HA5... 60 D3
Uxbridge Rd (Stanmore)
  STAN HA7 .... 43 M8 🔟
Uxbridge Rd the Broadway
  YEAD UB4 .... 96 D6
Uxbridge St *KENS* W8 .... 8 B8 🔟
Uxendon Crs *WBLY* HA9 ...... 80 E1
Uxendon Hl *WBLY* HA9 ...... 80 F1

V

Vaillant Rd *WEY* KT13 .... 164 C6
Valance Av *CHING* E4 .... 51 M3
Valan Leas *HAYES* BR2 .... 159 L6
Vale Av *BORE* WD6 .... 32 B8
Vale Cl *COUL/CHIP* CR5 .... 183 L7 🔟
  EFNCH N2 .... 65 M4
  MV/WKIL W9 .... 2 E8
  ORP BR6 .... 176 A6
  WEY KT13 .... 164 D5
Vale Ct *WEY* KT13 .... 164 D5
Vale Crs *PUT/ROE* SW15 ...... 135 L8
Vale Cft *ESH/CLAY* KT10 ...... 178 F1
  PIN HA5 .... 60 E6
Vale Dr *BAR* EN5 .... 33 M7

Vale End *EDUL* SE22 .... 139 M1
Vale Gv *ACT* W3 .... 99 K7
  FSBYPK N4 .... 67 J8 🔟
Vale La *ACT* W3 .... 99 G4
Valence Av *BCTR* RM8 .... 90 A1
Valence Circ *BCTR* RM8 .... 90 B1
Valence Dr *CHESW* EN7 .... 26 A1
Valence Rd *ERITH* DA8 .... 127 K5
Valence Wood Rd *BCTR* RM8... 90 D3
Valencia Rd *STAN* HA7 .... 44 C6
Valency Cl *NTHWD* HA6 .... 41 M6
Valentia Pl *BRXN/ST* SW9 ...... 139 G1 🔟
Valentine Av *BXLY* DA5 .... 144 E6
Valentine Pl *STHWK* SE1 ...... 18 C1
Valentine Rd *HOM* E9 .... 86 D6 🔟
  RYLN/HDSTN HA2 .... 79 H3 🔟
Valentines Rd *IL* IG1 .... 89 H1
Valentine Wy *SRTFD* E15 ...... 105 L2
Valerian Wy *SRTFD* E15 ...... 105 L2
Vale of Health *HAMP* NW3 ...... 83 J3
Vale Ri *GLDGN* NW11 .... 82 F1
Vale Rd *BMLY* BR1 .... 161 G5
  BUSH WD23 .... 29 L8
  DART DA1 .... 146 B5
  ESH/CLAY KT10 .... 178 E2
  FSBYPK N4 .... 67 J8
  FSTGT E7 .... 88 B6
  HOR/WEW KT19 .... 168 F6
  MTCM CR4 .... 156 D6
  SUT SM1 .... 170 B6
  WEY KT13 .... 164 D5
  WPK KT4 .... 168 F5
Vale Rd North *SURB* KT6 ...... 167 L4
Vale Rd South *SURB* KT6 ...... 167 L4
Vale Royal *HOLWY* N7 .... 5 J2
Vale Ter *FSBYPK* N4 .... 67 J7 🔟
The Vale *ACT* W3 .... 99 K7
  CHEL SW3 .... 15 G9
  COUL/CHIP CR5 .... 183 L7
  CRICK NW2 .... 82 D3
  CROY/NA CR0 .... 175 K4
  EBED/NFELT TW14 .... 132 B3
  GLDGN NW11 .... 82 F1
  HEST TW5 .... 114 E4
  MUSWH N10 .... 66 A2
  RSLP HA4 .... 78 C4
  STHGT/OAK N14 .... 48 E2
  SUN TW16 .... 150 A2 🔟
  WFD IG8 .... 70 A1
Valetta Gv *PLSTW* E13 .... 106 A1
Valetta Rd *ACT* W3 .... 99 L8
Valette St *HOM* E9 .... 86 B6 🔟
Valiant Cl *NTHLT* UB5 .... 96 D2 🔟
  ROMW/RG RM7 .... 73 H3 🔟
Valiant Wy *EHAM* E6 .... 106 F4
Vallance Rd *WCHPL* E1 .... 104 A3
  WDGN N22 .... 66 C3
Vallentin Rd *WALTH* E17 ...... 69 J5
Valley Av *NFNCH/WDSP* N12 ... 47 H5
Valley Cl *DART* DA1 .... 145 M3
  LOU IG10 .... 52 F1
  PIN HA5 .... 60 B3
  WAB EN9 .... 27 J7
Valley Dr *CDALE/KGS* NW9 ...... 63 H6
Valleyfield Rd
  STRHM/NOR SW16 .... 156 F1
Valley Fields Crs *ENC/FH* EN2 ... 36 A5 🔟
Valley Gdns *ALP/SUD* HA0 ...... 80 F7
  WIM/MER SW19 .... 155 K3
Valley Hl *LOU* IG10 .... 52 E2 🔟
Valley Ri *GSTN* WD25 .... 21 H6
Valley Rd *DART* DA1 .... 145 M3
  ERITH DA8 .... 127 J2
  HAYES BR2 .... 159 L5
  HGDN/ICK UB10 .... 94 E1
  PUR/KEN CR8 .... 184 D8
  STMC/STPC BR5 .... 162 B4
  STRHM/NOR SW16 .... 138 F8
Valley Side *CHING* E4 .... 51 G3
Valley Vw *BAR* EN5 .... 46 E1
  CHESW EN7 .... 25 J1
Valley View Gdns
  PUR/KEN CR8 .... 184 E8
Valley Wk *CROY/NA* CR0 ...... 173 J4
  RKW/CH/CXG WD3 .... 28 C8
Valliere Rd *WLSDN* NW10 ...... 100 A2 🔟
Valliers Wood Rd *BFN/LL* DA15... 143 K5
Vallis Wy *CHSGTN* KT9 .... 167 K6
  WEA W13 .... 98 A4
Valmar Rd *CMBW* SE5 .... 121 J6
Valnay St *TOOT* SW17 .... 155 M1
Valognes Av *WALTH* E17 ...... 68 E2
Valonia Gdns
  WAND/EARL SW18 .... 137 H5
Vambery Rd *WOOL/PLUM* SE18... 125 J4
Vanbrough Crs *NTHLT* UB5 ... 96 C1
Vanbrugh Dr *WOT/HER* KT12... 165 J2
Vanbrugh Flds *BKHTH/KID* SE3... 123 M4
Vanbrugh Hl *GNWCH* SE10 ...... 123 L3
Vanbrugh Pk *BKHTH/KID* SE3... 123 M5
Vanbrugh Park Rd
  BKHTH/KID SE3 .... 123 M5
Vanbrugh Park Rd West
  BKHTH/KID SE3 .... 123 M5
Vanbrugh Rd *CHSWK* W4 ...... 117 K1
Vanbrugh Ter *BKHTH/KID* SE3... 123 M6
Vanburgh Cl *CAN/RD* E16 ...... 106 D4 🔟🔟
  ORP BR6 .... 176 E3 🔟
Vancouver Cl *HOR/WEW* KT19... 180 C4
Vancouver Rd *EDGW* HA8 ...... 63 H2
  FSTH SE23 .... 140 E6
  RCHPK/HAM TW10 .... 134 C8 🔟
  YEAD UB4 .... 96 B3

  CROY/NA CR0 .... 172 B3 🔟
  ROMW/RG RM7 .... 73 H3
Vanguard St *DEPT* SE8 .... 123 G6
Vanguard Wy *CROY/NA* CR0... 172 F6
  WARL CR6 .... 185 M6
  WLGTN SM6 .... 183 L1 🔟
Vanneck Sq *PUT/ROE* SW15 ... 136 A2 🔟
Vanoc Gdns *BMLY* BR1 ...... 142 A8
Vansittart Rd *FSTGT* E7 ...... 88 A4
Vansittart St *NWCR* SE14 ...... 122 E5 🔟
Vanston Pl *FUL/PGN* SW6 ...... 119 G5
Vant Rd *TOOT* SW17 .... 155 M1
Varcoe Rd *BERM/RHTH* SE16... 122 B3
Vardens Rd *BTSEA* SW11 ...... 137 K1
Varden St *WCHPL* E1 .... 104 B5
Varley Rd *CAN/RD* E16 ...... 106 B5
Varley Wy *MTCM* CR4 .... 155 K5 🔟
Varna Rd *FUL/PGN* SW6 ...... 118 E5
  HPTN TW12 .... 151 H4 🔟
Varndell St *CAMTN* NW1 ...... 4 E7
Varsity Dr *ISLW* TW7 .... 133 M2 🔟
Varsity Rw *MORT/ESHN* SW14... 117 J7
Vartry Rd *SEVS/STOTM* N15 ... 67 L7
Vassall Rd *BRXN/ST* SW9 ...... 121 G5
Vauban St *BERM/RHTH* SE16... 19 M4
Vaughan Av *HCH* RM12 ...... 92 D4
  HDN NW4 .... 64 A6
  HMSMTH W6 .... 117 M2
Vaughan Gdns *IL* IG1 .... 70 B3
Vaughan Rd *CMBW* SE5 ...... 121 J8 🔟
  HRW HA1 .... 61 J8
  SRTFD E15 .... 87 M6
  THDIT KT7 .... 167 H2
  WELL DA16 .... 125 M7
Vaughan St *BERM/RHTH* SE16... 104 F8
Vaughan Wy *WAP* E1W 104 A6
Vaughan Williams Cl
  DEPT SE8 .... 123 G5 🔟
Vaux Crs *WOT/HER* KT12 ...... 165 H8
Vauxhall Br *LBTH* SE11 ...... 17 J8
Vauxhall Bridge Rd *PIM* SW1V... 16 E4
Vauxhall Gdns *SAND/SEL* CR2... 172 C8
Vauxhall Gv *VX/NE* SW8 ...... 17 K9
Vauxhall Pl *DART* DA1 ...... 146 E4
Vauxhall St *LBTH* SE11 ...... 17 M8
Vauxhall Wk *LBTH* SE11 ...... 17 L7
Vawdrey Cl *WCHPL* E1 ...... 104 C3 🔟
Veals Md *MTCM* CR4 .... 155 L4
Vectis Gdns *TOOT* SW17 ...... 156 B2 🔟
Vectis Rd *TOOT* SW17 ...... 156 B2
Veda Rd *LEW* SE13 .... 141 G1
Vega Crs *NTHWD* HA6 ...... 41 M7
Vega Rd *BUSH* WD23 ...... 43 J2
Veldene Wy *RYLN/HDSTN* HA2... 78 F3
Vellum Dr *CAR* SM5 .... 171 G5 🔟
Venables Cl *DAGE* RM10 ...... 91 H4 🔟
Venables St *STJWD* NW8 ...... 9 H1
Vencourt Pl *HMSMTH* W6 ...... 118 A3
Venetia Rd *EA* W5 .... 98 B3 🔟
  FSBYPK N4 .... 67 H7 🔟
Venetian Rd *CMBW* SE5 ...... 121 J7
Venetia Rd *EA* W5 .... 98 B3 🔟
Venette Cl *RAIN* RM13 ...... 110 B4
Venner Rd *SYD* SE26 ...... 158 C2
Venners Cl *BXLYHN* DA7 ...... 127 L7
Venn St *CLAP* SW4 .... 138 C1 🔟
Ventnor Av *STAN* HA7 ...... 62 B2
Ventnor Dr *NFNCH/WDSP* N12... 47 H5
Ventnor Gdns *BARK* IG11 ...... 89 L6
Ventnor Rd *BELMT* SM2 ...... 182 B1
  NWCR SE14 .... 122 E5
Venture Cl *RAIN* RM13 ...... 144 E4
Venue St *POP/IOD* E14 ...... 105 J4 🔟
Venus Rd *WOOL/PLUM* SE18... 124 F1
Veny Crs *HCH* RM12 ...... 92 D5
Vera Av *WCHMH* N21 ...... 36 A8
Vera Ct *OXHEY* WD19 ...... 42 D2
Vera Lynn Cl *FSTGT* E7 ...... 88 A4 🔟
Vera Rd *FUL/PGN* SW6 ...... 118 E6
Verbena Cl *CAN/RD* E16 ...... 105 L3 🔟
  WDR/YW UB7 .... 112 F3
Verbena Gdns *HMSMTH* W6 ... 118 A3 🔟
Ver-colne Valley Wk *BUSH* WD23... 29 K6
Verdant La *BMLY* BR1 ...... 141 M7
  CAT SE6 .... 141 L5
Verdayne Av *CROY/NA* CR0 ... 173 K3
Verderers Rd *CHIG* IG7 ...... 54 A7
Verdun Rd *BARN* SW13 ...... 118 A4
  WOOL/PLUM SE18 .... 126 A4
Verdure Cl *GSTN* WD25 ...... 21 L5
Vereker Dr *SUN* TW16 ...... 150 A4
Vereker Rd *WKENS* W14 ...... 118 E3 🔟
Vere St *MHST* W1U 10 C5
Vermont Cl *ENC/FH* EN2 ...... 36 B7 🔟
Vermont Rd *NRWD* SE19 ...... 157 K2
  SUT SM1 .... 170 B5
  WAND/EARL SW18 .... 137 H3
Verney Gdns *DAGW* RM9 ...... 90 E4
Verney Rd *BERM/RHTH* SE16... 122 B3
  DAGW RM9 .... 90 E4
Verney St *WLSDN* NW10 ...... 81 K3
Verney Wy *BERM/RHTH* SE16... 122 D5
Vernham Rd *WOOL/PLUM* SE18... 125 J4
Vernon Av *MNPK* E12 ...... 88 F4
  PEND EN3 .... 37 L1
  RYNPK SW20 .... 154 D5
  WFD IG8 .... 52 B8
Vernon Cl *HOR/WEW* KT19 ... 168 C6
  STMC/STPC BR5 .... 162 B6
Vernon Crs *EBAR* EN4 ...... 35 G8
Vernon Dr *DEN/HRF* UB9 ...... 58 C2
  STAN HA7 .... 62 A2
Vernon Ri *FSBYW* WC1X 5 M7
  NTHLT UB5 .... 79 K5
Vernon Rd *BOW* E3 .... 104 F1
  BUSH WD23 .... 29 L8
  CEND/HSY/T N8 .... 67 G4 🔟
  CRW RM5 .... 55 J7
  FELT TW13 .... 131 M6
  GDMY/SEVK IG3 .... 89 M1
  MORT/ESHN SW14 .... 117 K8
  SRTFD E15 .... 87 L7
  SUT SM1 .... 170 C7
  WALTH E17 .... 68 F6 🔟
  WAN E11 .... 87 L1
Vernon Sq *FSBYW* WC1X ...... 5 M7 🔟
Vernon St *WKENS* W14 ...... 118 E2
Vernon Yd *NTGHL* W11 ...... 100 F6 🔟
Veroan Rd *BXLYHN* DA7 ...... 126 E7

Verona Cl *UX/CGN* UB8 ....94 C5
Verona Dr *SURB* KT6 ....167 L4
Veronica Cl *HARH* RM3 ....74 C1
Veronica Gdns *MTCM* CR4 ...156 C4
Veronica Rd *TOOT* SW17 ....138 B7
Veronique Gdns
  GNTH/NBYPK IG2 ....71 J6
Verran Rd *BAL* SW12 ....138 B4 ☐
Versailles Rd *PGE/AN* SE20 ...158 A3
Verulam Av *PUR/KEN* CR8 ......183 J5
  WALTH E17 ....68 F8 ☐
Verulam Rd *GFD/PVL* UB6 ....97 G3
Verulam St *FSBYW* WC1X 12 A2
Verwood Dr *EBAR* EN4 ....34 F6
Verwood Rd *RYLN/HDSTN* HA2 ..61 J3
Veryan Cl *STMC/STPC* BR5 .....162 C7
Vespan Rd *SHB* W12 ....100 A8
Vesta Rd *BROCKY* SE4 ....122 C1
Vestris Rd *FSTH* SE23 ....140 D6
Vestry Rd *CMBW* SE5 ....121 L6
  WALTH E17 ....69 H6
Vestry St *IS* N1 ....7 G7
Vevey St *FSTH* SE23 ....140 F6
Vexil Cl *PUR* RM19 ....129 K2
Viaduct Pl *BETH* E2 ....104 B2 ☐
Viaduct Rd *EFNCH* N2 ....65 K3
Viaduct St *BETH* E2 ....104 B2 ☐
The Viaduct *SWFD* E18 ....70 A3
Vian Av *PEND* EN3 ....26 E8
Vian St *LEW* SE13 ....123 H8
Vibart Gdns *BRXS/STRHM* SW2 .138 F4
Vibia Cl *STWL/WRAY* TW19 ......130 D4
Vicarage Cl *BRW* CM14 ....57 L6
  ERITH DA8 ....127 J4
  NTHLT UB5 ....78 F8
  POTB/CUF EN6 ....23 M3
  RSLP HA4 ....59 K8 ☐
  WPK KT4 ....168 E3
Vicarage Crs *BTSEA* SW11 .....119 K6
Vicarage Dr *BARK* IG11 ....89 J7
  BECK BR3 ....159 C4
  MORT/ESHN SW14 ....135 K2
Vicarage Farm Rd *HEST* TW5 ..114 B6
  HSLWW TW4 ....114 F7
Vicarage Flds *WOT/HER* KT12 ..165 J1
Vicarage Gdns *KENS* W8 ....8 B9 ☐
  MTCM CR4 ....155 L6
Vicarage Ga *KENS* W8 ....8 C9
Vicarage Gv *CMBW* SE5 ....121 K6
Vicarage La *CHIG* IG7 ....53 K5
  EHAM E6 ....106 F2
  IL IG1 ....89 K1
  SRTFD E15 ....87 L6
  STA TW18 ....148 B6
Vicarage Pk *WOOL/PLUM* SE18 .125 J3
  CROY/NA CR0 ....172 A5
  DAGE RM10 ....91 H7
  E/WMO/HCT KT8 ....152 C4
  HCH RM12 ....92 A1
  HDN NW4 ....64 A7
  KUT KT1 ....152 D5
  LEY E10 ....69 H8
  MORT/ESHN SW14 ....135 J2
  SRTFD E15 ....87 M7
  SUN TW16 ....149 M1
  SUT SM1 ....170 A6
  TEDD TW11 ....152 A1
  TOTM N17 ....68 A1
  WATW WD18 ....29 H7
  WATW WD18 ....42 A2
  WFD IG8 ....70 B2
  WHTN TW2 ....133 J3
  WOOL/PLUM SE18 ....125 J3
Vicarage Wk *BTSEA* SW11 .....119 K6 ☐
Vicarage Wy *RYLN/HDSTN* HA2 .61 G8
  WLSDN NW10 ....81 K3
Vicars Bridge Cl *ALP/SUD* HA0 ..98 E1
Vicar's Cl *EN* EN1 ....36 B8
  HACK E8 ....86 C8 ☐
  SRTFD E15 ....88 A8
Vicars Hl *LEW* SE13 ....141 H1
Vicar's Moor La *WCHMH* N21 ....49 G2
Vicars Oak Rd *NRWD* SE19 .....157 L2
Vicar's Rd *KTTN* NW5 ....84 A5
Viceroy Cl *VX/NE* SW8 ....120 L6
Vickers Rd *ERITH* DA8 ....127 K3
Victor Ap *HCH* RM12 ....92 D1
Victor Cl *HCH* RM12 ....92 D1
Victor Gdns *HCH* RM12 ....92 D1
Victor Gv *ALP/SUD* HA0 ....80 E7
Victoria Av *CAR* SM5 ....171 C5
  CRW RM5 ....55 H6
  E/WMO/HCT KT8 ....151 H6
  EHAM E6 ....88 D8
  FNCH N3 ....64 F2
  HGDN/ICK UB10 ....77 H7
  HSLWW TW4 ....133 G2
  SAND/SEL CR2 ....184 C3
  SURB KT6 ....167 K1
  WBLY HA9 ....81 H6
Victoria Cl *E/WMO/HCT* KT8 ...151 C4
  EBAR EN4 ....34 D7
  HYS/HAR UB3 ....95 K5
  RKW/CH/CXG WD3 ....40 D2
  WEY KT13 ....164 D5 ☐
Victoria Cottages
  RCH/KEW TW9 ....116 F6
Victoria Ct *WBLY* HA9 ....81 C6
Victoria Crs *IVER* SL0 ....94 A6
  NRWD SE19 ....157 L1 ☐
  SEVS/STOTM N15 ....67 L6
  WIM/MER SW19 ....154 F3 ☐
Victoria Dock Rd *CAN/RD* E16 .105 L5
Victoria Dr *WIM/MER* SW19 ....136 D4
Victoria Emb *EMB* EC4Y 12 B6
  TPL/STR WC2R 11 L7
  WHALL SW1A 17 K2
Victoria Gdns *BH/WHM* TN16 ...187 J8
  HEST TW5 ....114 E6
  NFNCH/WDSP W11 ....8 C7 ☐
Victoria Grove Ms *NTGHL* W11 ..8 C7 ☐
Victoria Hill Rd *BXLY* DA5 ......163 H4 ☐
Victoria La *HYS/HAR* UB3 ......113 K3
Victoria Ms *KIL/WHAMP* NW6 ....2 A4
  WAND/EARL SW18 ....137 J3 ☐
Victorian Gv *STNW/STAM* N16 ..85 L3

Victorian Rd *STNW/STAM* N16 ...85 L3 ☐
Victoria Park Rd *HOM* E9 ....86 F7
Victoria Park Sq *BETH* E2 .....104 C2 ☐☐
Victoria Pl *EW* KT17 ....180 E5
  RCHPK/HAM TW10 ....134 D2 ☐
Victoria Ri *CLAP* SW4 ....120 B8
Victoria Rd *ACT* W3 ....99 K4
  BARK IG11 ....89 H6
  BFN/LL DA15 ....143 M7
  BKHH IG9 ....52 D4
  BUSH WD23 ....43 H3
  BXLYHS DA6 ....145 G2
  CHING E4 ....51 L3
  CHST BR7 ....161 G1
  COUL/CHIP CR5 ....183 K8
  DAGE RM10 ....91 J5
  DART DA1 ....146 D2
  EBAR EN4 ....34 D7
  ED N9 ....49 M5
  ERITH DA8 ....127 L4
  FELT TW13 ....132 B5
  FSBYPK N4 ....66 F8
  HAYES BR2 ....160 D8
  HDN NW4 ....64 C5
  KENS W8 ....14 E4
  KIL/WHAMP NW6 ....100 F1
  KUT KT1 ....152 F5
  MLHL NW7 ....45 M7
  MORT/ESHN SW14 ....117 K8
  MTCM CR4 ....155 L3
  NWDGN UB2 ....114 F1
  PLSTW E13 ....106 A1
  ROM RM1 ....73 M6
  RSLP HA4 ....76 F8
  SEVS/STOTM N15 ....68 A5 ☐
  SURB KT6 ....167 K1
  SUT SM1 ....170 D7
  SWFD E18 ....70 B4
  TEDD TW11 ....152 A2
  TWK TW1 ....134 B4
  UED N18 ....49 M6
  UX/CGN UB8 ....76 C7
  WAB EN9 ....27 J7
  WALTH E17 ....69 J3
  WAN E11 ....87 K4
  WATN WD24 ....29 H3
  WDGN N22 ....66 C2
  WEA W13 ....98 B4
  WEY KT13 ....164 D5
  WLSDN NW10 ....99 L3
Victoria Sq *BGVA* SW1W ....16 E3 ☐
Victoria St *BELV* DA17 ....126 F3
  SRTFD E15 ....87 L7
  WEST SW1P 16 E4
  WESTW SW1E 16 D4
Victoria Ter *FSBYPK* N4 ....85 G1
  RYLN/HDSTN HA2 ....79 L8 ☐
Victoria Vls *RCH/KEW* TW9 ....116 F8
Victoria Wy *CHARL* SE7 ....124 B3
  WEY KT13 ....164 D5
Victor Rd *PGE/AN* SE20 ....158 D3
  RYLN/HDSTN HA2 ....61 J4
  TEDD TW11 ....151 L1
  WLSDN NW10 ....100 B2
Victors Dr *HPTN* TW12 ....150 E2 ☐
Victors Wy *BAR* EN5 ....33 M6
Victory Av *MRDN* SM4 ....155 J8
Victory Pl *NRWD* SE19 ....157 L2 ☐
  WALW SE17 ....18 F5
Victory Rd *RAIN* RM13 ....110 A1
  WAN E11 ....70 B5
  WIM/MER SW19 ....155 J3
Victory Wy
  BERM/RHTH SE16 ....104 E8 ☐
  GRH DA9 ....147 J1
  ROMW/RG RM7 ....73 H3
Vienna Cl *CLAY* IG5 ....70 D3
View Cl *CHIG* IG7 ....53 K7
  HGT N6 ....65 M8
  HRW HA1 ....61 K5
View Crs *CEND/HSY/T* N8 ....66 D6 ☐
Viewfield Cl *KTN/HRWW/W* HA3 .62 E8 ☐
Viewfield Rd *BFN/LL* DA15 .....144 C5
  WAND/EARL SW18 ....136 F3
Viewland Rd *WOOL/PLUM* SE18 .125 M3
View Rd *HGT* N6 ....65 M8
  POTB/CUF EN6 ....23 J5
The View *ABYW* SE2 ....126 E3
Viga Rd *WCHMH* N21 ....49 G1
Vigilant Cl *SYD* SE26 ....140 A8
Vignoles Rd *ROMW/RG* RM7 .....73 G8
Vigo St *MYFR/PICC* W1J 10 E7
Villacourt Rd *ABYW* SE2 ....126 A4 ☐
Village Cl *CHING* E4 ....51 J7
  WEY KT13 ....164 D5 ☐
Village Gdns *EW* KT17 ....180 E5 ☐
Village Green Rd *DART* DA1 ...146 A1
Village Park Cl *EN* EN1 ....49 L1
Village Rd *DEN/HRF* UB9 ....76 A1
  EN EN1 ....49 K1
  FNCH N3 ....64 E3
Village Rw *BELMT* SM2 ....182 A1
The Village *CHARL* SE7 ....124 C4
Village Wy *ASHF* TW15 ....130 F8
  BECK BR3 ....159 G6
  HNHL SE24 ....139 K3
  PIN HA5 ....60 E8
  SAND/SEL CR2 ....185 G6
  WLSDN NW10 ....81 K3
Village Wy East
  RYLN/HDSTN HA2 ....60 F8
Villa Rd *BRXN/ST* SW9 ....121 G8
Villas Rd *WOOL/PLUM* SE18 ....125 J2
Villa St *WALW* SE17 ....19 H8
Villiers Av *BRYLDS* KT5 ....152 F8
  WHTN TW2 ....132 F5
Villiers Cl *BRYLDS* KT5 ....152 F7
Villiers Gv *BELMT* SM2 ....181 K2
Villiers Rd *BECK* BR3 ....158 D5
  CRICK NW2 ....82 A6
  ISLW TW7 ....115 L7 ☐
  KUT KT1 ....152 F8
  OXHEY WD19 ....42 E1
  STHL UB1 ....96 F7

Villiers St *CHCR* WC2N 11 K8
Villier St *UX/CGN* UB8 ....90 D7
Vincam Cl *WHTN* TW2 ....133 G4
Vincent Av *BRYLDS* KT5 ....168 B3
  CAR SM5 ....182 D4
Vincent Cl *BAR* EN5 ....34 A6
  BFN/LL DA15 ....143 L5
  CHES/WCR EN8 ....26 E1
  ESH/CLAY KT10 ....166 B5
  HAYES BR2 ....160 B7
  WDR/YW UB7 ....113 C4
Vincent Dr *SHPTN* TW17 ....149 L6
Vincent Gdns *CRICK* NW2 ....81 M3
Vincent Rd *ACT* W3 ....117 J1 ☐
  ALP/SUD HA0 ....80 F7 ☐
  CHING E4 ....51 K8 ☐
  CROY/NA CR0 ....172 E2
  DAGW RM9 ....90 E7
  HSLWW TW4 ....114 D8
  ISLW TW7 ....115 K6
  KUT KT1 ....153 G6
  RAIN RM13 ....110 C3
  SEVS/STOTM N15 ....67 J5
  WDGN N22 ....67 C3
  WOOL/PLUM SE18 ....125 H2 ☐☐
Vincent Rw *HPTN* TW12 ....151 J1 ☐
Vincents Cl *BERM/RHTH* SE16 .104 E8
Vincent Sq *BH/WHM* TN16 .....187 J6
  WEST SW1P 16 F5
Vincent St *CAN/RD* E16 ....106 A4 ☐
  WEST SW1P 17 G5
Vincent Ter *IS* N1 ....6 C5
Vince St *FSBYE* EC1V 7 H8
Vine Cl *BRYLDS* KT5 ....167 M1
  STWL/WRAY TW19 ....130 A2
  SUT SM1 ....170 C5
  WDR/YW UB7 ....113 G2
Vine Ct *KTN/HRWW/W* HA3 .....62 E7
  WCHPL E1 ....104 A4 ☐
Vine Gdns *IL* IG1 ....89 J5
Vinegar St *WAP* E1W ....104 B7 ☐☐
Vinegar Yd *STHWK* SE1 ....19 J1 ☐
Vine Gv *HGDN/ICK* UB10 ....76 F7
Vine Hl *CLKNW* EC1R 12 A1
Vine La *HGDN/ICK* UB10 ....76 F8
  STHWK SE1 ....13 K9
Vine Pl *HSLW* TW3 ....133 H1
Vineries Bank *MLHL* NW7 ....46 B7
Vineries Cl *WDR/YW* UB7 ......113 G4
The Vineries *EN* EN1 ....36 E6
  STHGT/OAK N14 ....48 C1
Vine Rd *BARN* SW13 ....117 M8
  E/WMO/HCT KT8 ....151 J7
  ORP BR6 ....176 F8
  SRTFD E15 ....87 M7 ☐
Vines Av *FNCH* N3 ....65 H2
Vine St *CONDST* W1S 10 F7
  HGDN/ICK UB10 ....94 F1
  ROMW/RG RM7 ....73 J6
  TWRH EC3N 13 L5
  UX/CGN UB8 ....76 D8
Vine Street Br *FARR* EC1M ......12 B1 ☐
Vine Street Crs *TWRH* EC3N ...13 L6 ☐
Vine Yd *STHWK* SE1 ....18 F1 ☐
Vineyard Av *MLHL* NW7 ....64 E1
Vineyard Cl *CAT* SE6 ....141 G5
  KUT KT1 ....152 F6 ☐
Vineyard Gv *FNCH* N3 ....65 H2
Vineyard Hill Rd
  WIM/MER SW19 ....137 G8
Vineyard Ms *CLKNW* EC1R ....6 A9 ☐
Vineyard Pth
  MORT/ESHN SW14 ....117 K8
Vineyard Rd *FELT* TW13 ....132 A7
Vineyard Rw *KUT* KT1 ....152 C4 ☐
Vineyards Rd *POTB/CUF* EN6 ...24 B2
The Vineyard
  RCHPK/HAM TW10 ....134 D2
Vineyard Wk *CLKNW* EC1R ....6 A9 ☐
Viney Rd *LEW* SE13 ....123 H8
Vining St *BRXS/STRHM* SW2 ..139 G1 ☐
Vinlake Av *HGDN/ICK* UB10 .....76 F3
Vinson Cl *ORP* BR6 ....177 G3
Vintry Ms *WALTH* E17 ....69 G5 ☐
Viola Av *ABYW* SE2 ....126 B2
  EBED/NFELT TW14 ....132 C3
  STWL/WRAY TW19 ....130 E5
Viola Sq *SHB* W12 ....99 M6
Violet Av *ENC/FH* EN2 ....36 D3 ☐
  UX/CGN UB8 ....94 F4
Violet Cl *CAN/RD* E16 ....105 L3
  DEPT SE8 ....122 F4 ☐
  MTCM CR4 ....171 C3
Violet Gdns *CROY/NA* CR0 .....172 B7
Violet Hl *STJWD* NW8 ....2 E6
Violet La *CROY/NA* CR0 ....172 B7
Violet Rd *BOW* E3 ....105 H3
  LEY E10 ....69 G7
  SWFD E18 ....70 B3
Violet St *BETH* E2 ....104 B3 ☐
Virgil St *STHWK* SE1 ....17 M3
Virginia Cl *CRW* RM5 ....73 J1
  NWMAL KT3 ....153 J7 ☐
  STA TW18 ....148 C6 ☐
  WEY KT13 ....164 D5
Virginia Gdns *BARK/HLT* IG6 ...71 K3 ☐
Virginia Rd *BETH* E2 ....7 L8
  THHTH CR7 ....157 H4
Virginia St *WAP* E1W ....104 A6 ☐
Viscount Cl *FBAR/BDGN* N11 ....48 A7 ☐
Viscount Dr *EHAM* E6 ....106 F4 ☐
Viscount Gv *YEAD* UB4 ....96 D2 ☐
Viscount Rd *STWL/WRAY* TW19 .130 D4
Viscount St *STLK* EC1Y 12 E1
Viscount Wy *HTHAIR* TW6 ......131 L1
Vista Av *PEND* EN3 ....37 K5
Vista Dr *REDBR* IG4 ....70 D6
The Vista *ELTH/MOT* SE9 ......142 D4
Vista Wy *KTN/HRWW/W* HA3 ...62 E7 ☐
Viveash Cl *HYS/HAR* UB3 ......113 H1
Vivian Av *HDN* NW4 ....64 B4
  WBLY HA9 ....81 G6
Vivian Cl *OXHEY* WD19 ....42 A4
Vivian Gdns *OXHEY* WD19 ......42 A3
  WBLY HA9 ....81 G5
Vivian Rd *BOW* E3 ....104 E1

Vivian Sq *PECK* SE15 ....122 B8
Vivian Wy *EFNCH* N2 ....65 K6 ☐
Vivien Cl *CHSGTN* KT9 ....179 L1
Vivienne Cl *TWK* TW1 ....134 D3 ☐
Voce Rd *WOOL/PLUM* SE18 .....125 K5
Voewood Cl *NWMAL* KT3 ....168 F1 ☐
Voltaire Rd *CLAP* SW4 ....120 D8
Volta Wy *CROY/NA* CR0 ....171 M3
Voluntary Pl *WAN* E11 ....70 A7
Vorley Rd *ARCH* N19 ....84 C2
Voss Cst *STRHM/NOR* SW16 ...156 E2
Voss St *BETH* E2 ....104 A2
Voyagers Cl *THMD* SE28 ....108 C5
Vulcan Ga *ENC/FH* EN2 ....36 A5 ☐
Vulcan Rd *BROCKY* SE4 ....122 F2 ☐
Vulcan Ter *BROCKY* SE4 ....122 F2 ☐
Vulcan Wy *CROY/NA* CR0 ......186 E3 ☐
Vyner Rd *ACT* W3 ....99 K6
Vyner St *BETH* E2 ....104 B1
Vyners Wy *HGDN/ICK* UB10 .....77 G5
The Vyne *BXLYHN* DA7 ....127 H8
Vyse Cl *BAR* EN5 ....33 J7

W

Wadding St *WALW* SE17 ....19 G6
Waddington Cl *EN* EN1 ....36 E7
Waddington Rd *SRTFD* E15 ......87 K5
Waddington St *SRTFD* E15 ......87 K6 ☐
Waddington Wy *NRWD* SE19 ...157 J4
Waddon Cl *CROY/NA* CR0 ....177 A5
Waddon Court Rd
  CROY/NA CR0 ....172 A6
Waddon Marsh Wy
  CROY/NA CR0 ....171 M3
Waddon New Rd *CROY/NA* CR0 .172 B5
Waddon Park Av *CROY/NA* CR0 .172 A6
Waddon Rd *CROY/NA* CR0 ......172 B5
Waddon Wy *CROY/NA* CR0 .....172 A8
Wade Av *STMC/STPC* BR5 ......177 K2
Wade Rd *CAN/RD* E16 ....106 C5
Wade's Gv *WCHMH* N21 ....49 G2
Wade's Hl *WCHMH* N21 ....49 G1
Wade's La *TEDD* TW11 ....152 A1
Wadeson St *BETH* E2 ....104 B1
Wade's Pl *POP/IOD* E14 ....105 H6
Wadeville Av *CHDH* RM6 ....72 C7
Wadeville Cl *BELV* DA17 ....127 C3
Wadham Av *CHING* E4 ....69 H1
Wadham Gdns *HAMP* NW3 ....3 J2
  NTHLT UB5 ....79 K6
Wadham Rd *ABLGY* WD5 ....20 F4
  CHING E4 ....69 H7 ☐
  PUT/ROE SW15 ....136 E1
Wadhurst Cl *PGE/AN* SE20 .....158 B5
Wadhurst Rd *CHSWK* W4 ....117 K1
Wadley Rd *WAN* E11 ....69 J8
Wadsworth Cl *GFD/PVL* UB6 ....98 C1 ☐
  PEND EN3 ....37 K8 ☐
Wadsworth Rd *GFD/PVL* UB6 ...98 B1
Wager St *BOW* E3 ....104 F3
Waghorn Rd *KTN/HRWW/W* HA3 .62 D4
  PLSTW E13 ....88 C8
Waghorn St *PECK* SE15 ....122 A8
Wagner St *PECK* SE15 ....122 C5 ☐
Wagon Rd *BAR* EN5 ....23 J4
Wagstaff Gdns *DAGW* RM9 ......90 D7
Wagtail Gdns *SAND/SEL* CR2 ..185 K3
Wagtail Wy *STMC/STPC* BR5 ...162 D7
Waid Cl *DART* DA1 ....146 F1
Waights Ct *KUTN/CMB* KT2 ....152 E4 ☐
Wain Cl *POTB/CUF* EN6 ....23 H2
Wainfleet Av *CRW* RM5 ....73 J3
Wainford Cl *WIM/MER* SW19 ..136 D5 ☐
Wainwright Gv *ISLW* TW7 ......133 K1
Waite Davies Rd
  LEE/GVPK SE12 ....142 A4
Waite St *PECK* SE15 ....19 L9
Wakefield Gdns *IL* IG1 ....70 E7
  NRWD SE19 ....157 L3
Wakefield Rd *FBAR/BDGN* N11 ..48 D7
  RCHPK/HAM TW10 ....134 D2 ☐
  SEVS/STOTM N15 ....67 M6
Wakefield St *BMSBY* WC1N 5 K9
  EHAM E6 ....88 E8
  UED N18 ....50 A7
Wakehams Hl *PIN* HA5 ....60 F4
Wakeham St *IS* N1 ....85 K6 ☐☐
Wakehurst Rd *BTSEA* SW11 ...137 M2
Wakeling Rd *HNWL* W7 ....97 M4 ☐
Wakeling St *WCHPL* E1 ....104 B5 ☐☐
Wakelin Rd *SRTFD* E15 ....105 L1
Wakeman Rd *WLSDN* NW10 ...100 C1
Wakemans Hill Av
  CDALE/KGS NW9 ....63 K6
Wakering Cl *EMPK* RM11 ....74 F5 ☐
Wakering Rd *BARK* IG11 ....89 J7
Wakerly Cl *EHAM* E6 ....106 F5
Wakley St *FSBYE* EC1V 6 C7
Walberswick St *VX/NE* SW8 ...120 E5 ☐
Walbrook *MANHO* EC4N ....13 G6 ☐
Walburgh St *WCHPL* E1 ....104 B5 ☐
Walburton Rd *PUR/KEN* CR8 ...186 J6
Walcorde Av *WALW* SE17 ....18 F6 ☐
Walcot Rd *PEND* EN3 ....37 M5
Walcot Sq *LBTH* SE11 ....18 B5
Walcott St *WEST* SW1P ....16 F5 ☐
Waldeck Gv *WNWD* SE27 ......139 H7
Waldeck Rd *CHSWK* W4 ....117 C4
  DART DA1 ....146 F4
  MORT/ESHN SW14 ....117 J3 ☐
  SEVS/STOTM N15 ....67 H4 ☐
  WEA W13 ....98 B5
Waldegrave Gdns *TWK* TW1 ...133 M6
  UPMR RM14 ....93 H2
Waldegrave Pk *TWK* TW1 ......133 M8
Waldegrave Rd *BMLY* BR1 .....160 E8
  CEND/HSY/T N8 ....67 G4 ☐
  EA W5 ....98 B6
  NRWD SE19 ....157 M3
  TWK TW1 ....133 M8
  WEA W13 ....98 B5
Waldegrove *CROY/NA* CR0 .....172 F5
Waldemar Av *FUL/PGN* SW6 ...118 C4

Waldemar Rd *WIM/MER* SW19 ..155 G1
  PLMGR N13 ....49 G5
  RAIN RM13 ....109 K1
Walden Av *CHST* BR7 ....142 F8
Walden Cl *BELV* DA17 ....126 F3
Walden Gdns *THHTH* CR7 ......156 F7
Waldenhurst Rd
  STMC/STPC BR5 ....177 K2
Walden Rd *CHST* BR7 ....160 F2
  EMPK RM11 ....74 D7
  TOTM N17 ....67 K2 ☐
Waldens Cl *STMC/STPC* BR5 ...177 K2
Waldenshaw Rd *FSTH* SE23 ...140 C5
Waldens Rd *STMC/STPC* BR5 ...177 L1
Walden St *WCHPL* E1 ....104 B5 ☐
Walden Wy *BARK/HLT* IG6 ......71 L1
  EMPK RM11 ....74 D7
  MLHL NW7 ....46 D8
Waldo Cl *CLAP* SW4 ....138 C2
Waldo Pl *WIM/MER* SW19 ....155 L3
Waldorf Cl *SAND/SEL* CR2 .....184 B2
Waldo Rd *BMLY* BR1 ....160 C6
  WLSDN NW10 ....100 A2
Waldram Crs *FSTH* SE23 ....140 F5
Waldram Park Rd *FSTH* SE23 .140 D5
Waldrist Wy *ERITHM* DA18 .....108 F3
Waldron Gdns *HAYES* BR2 .....159 K6
Waldron Rd *RYLN/HDSTN* HA2 .79 L1
  WAND/EARL SW18 ....137 J7
The Waldrons *CROY/NA* CR0 ..172 C6
Waldron's Yd
  RYLN/HDSTN HA2 ....79 K2 ☐
Waldstock Rd *THMD* SE28 .....108 A6
Waleran Cl *STAN* HA7 ....43 M8 ☐
Walerand Rd *LEW* SE13 ....123 J7
Wales Av *CAR* SM5 ....170 F7
Wales Farm Rd *ACT* W3 ....99 K4
Walfield Av *TRDG/WHET* N20 ...47 H2
Walford Rd *STNW/STAM* N16 ...85 M4 ☐
  UX/CGN UB8 ....94 C1
Walfrey Gdns *DAGW* RM9 ......90 A7
Walham Gv *FUL/PGN* SW6 .....119 G5
Walham Ri *WIM/MER* SW19 ....154 E2 ☐
Walham Yd *FUL/PGN* SW6 .....119 G5 ☐
Walkden Rd *CHST* BR7 ....143 G8
Walker Cl *DART* DA1 ....127 M8
  EBED/NFELT TW14 ....131 M4
  FBAR/BDGN N11 ....48 C6
  HNWL W7 ....97 L7
  HPTN TW12 ....150 F2 ☐
  WOOL/PLUM SE18 ....125 J2
Walkerscroft Md *DUL* SE21 ....139 J3
Walker's Pl *PUT/ROE* SW15 ...136 E1 ☐
Walkley Rd *DART* DA1 ....146 B2
The Walks *EFNCH* N2 ....65 K4 ☐
The Walk *EMPK* RM11 ....92 F2
  POTB/CUF EN6 ....23 G5
Wallace Cl *HGDN/ICK* UB10 .....94 E1
  SHPTN TW17 ....149 K7 ☐
  THMD SE28 ....108 D6
Wallace Crs *CAR* SM5 ....170 F7 ☐
Wallace Flds *EW* KT17 ....180 F5
Wallace Rd *IS* N1 ....85 J6 ☐☐
Wallasey Crs *HGDN/ICK* UB10 ..77 G2
Wallbutton Rd *BROCKY* SE4 ...122 C1
Wallcote Av *CRICK* NW2 ....82 D1
Wall End Rd *EHAM* E6 ....89 G7
Wallenger Av *GPK* RM2 ....57 L6
Waller Dr *NTHWD* HA6 ....60 A3 ☐
Waller Rd *NWCR* SE14 ....122 D7
Wallers Cl *DAGW* RM9 ....90 E8 ☐
  WFD IG8 ....52 F8
Waller's Hoppet *LOU* IG10 ......39 M5
Wallflower St *SHB* W12 ....99 M6
Wallgrave Rd *ECT* SW5 ....14 C5
Wallhouse Rd *ERITH* DA8 ....128 C5
Wallingford Av *NKENS* W10 ...100 D4
Wallingford Rd *UX/CGN* UB8 ...94 B1
Wallington Cl *RSLP* HA4 ....59 J7
Wallington Rd *GDMY/SEVK* IG3 .71 J8 ☐
Wallis Cl *BTSEA* SW11 ....119 K8
  HCH RM12 ....92 B1
  RDART DA2 ....146 A7
Wallis Rd *GFD/PVL* UB6 ....97 H5
  HOM E9 ....86 F6
Wallorton Gdns
  MORT/ESHN SW14 ....135 K1
Wall St *IS* N1 ....85 K6
Wallwood Rd *WAN* E11 ....69 K8
Wallwood St *POP/IOD* E14 .....104 F4
  EBAR EN4 ....34 D4
Walmar Cl *EBAR* EN4 ....51 H4
Walm La *CHING* E4 ....176 D6 ☐
  ROMW/RG RM7 ....73 H3
Walmer Gdns *HNWL* W7 ....98 A8
Walmer Rd *NTGHL* W11 ....100 C6
Walmer Ter *WOOL/PLUM* SE18 .125 J2
Walmgate Rd *GFD/PVL* UB6 .....80 B8
Walmington Fold
  NFNCH/WDSP N12 ....47 G3
Walnut Av *WDR/YW* UB7 ....113 G4
Walnut Cl *BARK/HLT* IG6 ....71 J5
  CAR SM5 ....170 F7
  DEPT SE8 ....122 F4 ☐
  EPSOM KT18 ....180 F8
  HYS/HAR UB3 ....95 L6
  WCHMH N21 ....36 D8
Walnut Gn *BUSH* WD23 ....29 K5 ☐
Walnut Ms *BELMT* SM2 ....182 C1
Walnut Rd *LEY* E10 ....87 G2
Walnuts Rd *ORP* BR6 ....177 G3
Walnut Tree Av *DART* DA1 .....146 E6
  MTCM CR4 ....155 L6 ☐
Walnut Tree Cl *BARN* SW13 ...117 M6
  BNSTD SM7 ....181 L5
  CHES/WCR EN8 ....26 D4
  CHST BR7 ....161 J4
Walnut Tree Rd *BCTR* RM8 .....90 D2
  BTFD TW8 ....116 F4 ☐
  ERITH DA8 ....127 L3
  GNWCH SE10 ....125 H4
  HEST TW5 ....114 F4 ☐
  SHPTN TW17 ....149 J4 ☐

Walnut Tree Wk *LBTH* SE11......... 18 A5
Walnut Wy *BKHH* IG9 .... 52 D5
   RSLP HA4 .... 78 C6
   SWLY BR8 .... 163 K5
Walpole Av *RCH/KEW* TW9 ...... 116 F7
Walpole Cl *PIN* HA5 .... 61 G1
   WEA W13 .... 98 C8
Walpole Crs *TEDD* TW11 .... 151 M1 [2]
   WHTN TW2 .... 133 L6
Walpole Gdns *CHSWK* W4 .... 117 J3
Walpole Pl *TEDD* TW11 .... 151 M1 [1]
Walpole Rd *CROY/NA* CR0 .... 172 D4
   EHAM E6 .... 88 C7 [2]
   HAYES BR2 .... 160 D8
   SURB KT6 .... 167 L2
   SWFD E18 .... 69 M2
   TEDD TW11 .... 151 M1
   TOTM N17 .... 67 J3
   WALTH E17 .... 68 E5
   WHTN TW2 .... 133 L6
   WIM/MER SW19 .... 155 K2
Walpole St *CHEL* SW3 .... 15 L7
Walrond Av *WBLY* HA9............. 80 E5
Walsham Cl *STNW/STAM* N16 ... 86 A1
   THMD SE28 .... 108 D8
Walsham Rd *EBED/NFELT* TW14 . 132 B4
   NWCR SE14 .... 122 D7
Walsh Crs *CROY/NA* CR0 .... 186 E5
Walshford Wy *BORE* WD6 .... 32 A3
Walsingham Gdns
   HOR/WEW KT19 .... 168 E6
Walsingham Pk *CHST* BR7 .... 161 K5
Walsingham Rd *BTSEA* SW11 ... 138 A3 [1]
   CLPT E5 .... 86 A3
   CROY/NA CR0 .... 186 C3
   ENC/FH EN2 .... 36 D7
   MTCM CR4 .... 155 M8
   STMC/STPC BR5 .... 162 B4
   WEA W13 .... 98 A7 [2]
Walsingham Wk *BELV* DA17 ... 127 G4
Walter St *BETH* E2 .... 104 D2
   KUTN/CMB KT2 .... 152 E4 [3]
Walters Rd *PEND* EN3 .... 37 J8
   SNWD SE25 .... 157 L7 [2]
Walters Wy *FSTH* SE23 .... 140 D3
Walters Yd *BMLY* BR1 .... 160 A5
Walter Ter *WCHPL* E1 .... 104 D5
Walterton Rd *MV/WKIL* W9 ...... 100 F3
Walter Wk *EDGW* HA8 .... 45 J8
Waltham Av *CDALE/KGS* NW9 ... 63 C7
   HYS/HAR UB3 .... 113 J1
Waltham Cl *DART* DA1 .... 146 A3
   STMC/STPC BR5 .... 177 K3
Waltham Dr *EDGW* HA8 .... 63 C3
Waltham Gdns *PEND* EN3 .... 37 J2 [1]
Waltham Pk *WALTH* E17 .... 69 G1
Waltham Rd *CAR* SM5 .... 170 D3
   NWDGN UB2 .... 114 E1
   WFD IG8 .... 52 E8
Walthamstow Av *CHING* E4 ...... 69 G1
Walthamstow Av (North Circular
   Road) *CHING* E4................... 50 E7
Waltham Wy *CHING* E4 .... 50 F5
Waltheof Av *TOTM* N17 .... 67 K2
Waltheof Gdns *TOTM* N17 .... 67 K2
Walton Av *CHEAM* SM3 .... 169 M5
   NWMAL KT3 .... 153 M7 [3]
   RYLN/HDSTN HA2 .... 78 F5
Walton Bridge Rd
   SHPTN TW17 .... 164 E2 [3]
Walton Cl *CRICK* NW2 .... 82 B2
   HRW HA1 .... 61 K5
   VX/NE SW8 .... 120 E5 [3]
Walton Dr *HRW* HA1................ 61 K5
   WLSDN NW10 .... 81 K6 [2]
Walton Gdns *ACT* W3 .... 99 H4
   FELT TW13.......................... 131 M8
   WAB EN9 .... 27 H6
   WBLY HA9 .... 80 E2
Walton Gn *CROY/NA* CR0......... 186 B2
Walton La *SHPTN* TW17 .... 164 D2
   WEY KT13 .... 164 C4
   WOT/HER KT12 .... 164 C3
Walton Pk *WOT/HER* KT12 ...... 165 K4 [2]
Walton Park La *WOT/HER* KT12 . 165 L4
Walton Pl *CHEL* SW3 .... 15 L3
Walton Rd *BUSH* WD23 .... 29 K7
   CRW RM5 .... 72 F1 [1]
   HRW HA1 .... 61 K5
   MNPK E12 .... 89 G4
   PLSTW E13 .... 106 C1
   SCUP DA14 .... 144 B7
   SEVS/STOTM N15 .... 67 K5 [3]
   WOT/HER KT12 .... 150 D8
Walton St *CHEL* SW3 .... 15 K5
   ENC/FH EN2 .... 36 D4 [3]
Walton Wy *ACT* W3 .... 99 H4
   MTCM CR4 .... 156 C7
Walt Whitman Cl *HNHL* SE24 ... 139 H1 [1]
Walverns Cl *OXHEY* WD19 .... 42 C1 [3]
Walworth Pl *WALW* SE17 .... 18 F8
Walworth Rd *WALW* SE17 .... 18 E5
Walwyn Av *BMLY* BR1 .... 160 D6
Wanborough Dr
   PUT/ROE SW15 .... 136 B5
Wanderer Dr *BARK* IG11 .... 108 B2
Wandle Bank *CROY/NA* CR0 ..... 171 L5
   WIM/MER SW19 .... 155 K2
Wandle Ct *HOR/WEW* KT19 ...... 168 C6
Wandle Court Gdns
   CROY/NA CR0 .... 171 L5 [3]
Wandle Rd *CROY/NA* CR0 .... 171 L5
   MRDN SM4 .... 155 K8
   TOOT SW17 .... 137 L6
   WLGTN SM6 .... 171 H4
Wandle Side *CROY/NA* CR0 ..... 171 M5 [2]
   WLGTN SM6 .... 171 H5 [2]
Wandle Wy *MTCM* CR4 .... 155 M8
   WAND/EARL SW18 .... 137 H5
Wandon Rd *FUL/PGN* SW6 ...... 119 H5
Wandsworth Br
   WAND/EARL SW18 .... 119 J8
Wandsworth Bridge Rd
   FUL/PGN SW6...................... 119 H6
Wandsworth Common West Side
   WAND/EARL SW18 .... 137 J2
Wandsworth High St
   WAND/EARL SW18 .... 137 C2

Wandsworth Rd *CLAP* SW4....... 120 B8
   VX/NE SW8 .... 17 J9
   VX/NE SW8 .... 120 D7 [1]
Wangey Rd *CHDH* RM6 .... 72 D8
Wanless Rd *HNHL* SE24 .... 121 J8
Wanley Rd *CMBW* SE5 .... 139 K1
Wanlip Rd *PLSTW* E13 .... 106 B3
Wannock Gdns *BARK/HLT* IG6... 71 H1
Wansdown Pl *FUL/PGN* SW6 ... 119 H5 [1]
Wansey St *WALW* SE17 .... 18 F6
Wansford Cl *BRW* CM14 .... 57 M5
Wansford Pk *BORE* WD6 .... 32 D7
Wansford Rd *WFD* IG8 .... 70 C2
Wanstead Cl *BMLY* BR1 .... 160 C5
Wanstead La *IL* IG1 .... 70 E7
Wanstead Park Av *MNPK* E12 ... 88 D2
Wanstead Park Rd *IL* IG1 .... 88 E1
Wanstead Pl *WAN* E11 .... 70 A7
Wanstead Rd *BMLY* BR1 .... 160 C5
Wansunt Rd *BXLY* DA5 .... 145 J5
Wantage Rd *LEE/GVPK* SE12 .... 141 M2
Wantz La *RAIN* RM13 .... 110 B3
Wantz Rd *DAGE* RM10.............. 91 H4
Wapping Dock St *WAP* E1W ..... 104 B7 [1]
Wapping High St *WAP* E1W 104 A7
Wapping La *WAP* E1W 104 B6
Wapping Wall *WAP* E1W 104 C7
Warbank Cl *CROY/NA* CR0 .... 186 D7
Warbank Crs *CROY/NA* CR0 ..... 186 E5
Warbank La *KUTN/CMB* KT2 .... 153 M1
Warbeck Rd *SHB* W12 .... 100 B7
Warberry Rd *WDGN* N22 .... 66 F3 [2]
Warboys Ap *KUTN/CMB* KT2 .... 153 H3
Warboys Crs *CHING* E4 .... 51 J7
Warboys Rd *KUTN/CMB* KT2 .... 153 H2
Warburton Cl
   KTN/HRWW/W HA3 .... 43 K8 [2]
   WHTN TW2 .... 133 H5
Warburton Rd *HACK* E8 .... 86 B8 [2]
   WHTN TW2 .... 133 H5
Warburton St *HACK* E8 .... 86 B8 [10]
Warburton Ter *WALTH* E17 ...... 69 H3
Ward Cl *ERITH* DA8 .... 127 K4
   SAND/SEL CR2 .... 172 E7
Wardell Cl *CRW* RM5................ 55 J7
Warden Av *CRW* RM5 .... 55 J7
   RYLN/HDSTN HA2 .... 78 E1
Warden Rd *KTTN* NW5.............. 84 A6
Wardens Gv *STHWK* SE1 .... 12 E2
Wardle St *HOM* E9 .... 86 D5
Wardley St
   WAND/EARL SW18 .... 137 H4 [3]
Wardo Av *FUL/PGN* SW6 .... 118 E6
Wardour Ms *SOHO/CST* W1F .... 10 F5 [3]
Wardour St *SOHO/CST* W1F 10 F4
Ward Rd *ARCH* N19 .... 84 C4
   SRTFD E15 .... 87 K8 [2]
The Wardrobe
   RCH/KEW TW9 .... 134 D2 [3]
Wards Rd *GNTH/NBYPK* IG2 ..... 71 K8
Wareham Cl *HSLW* TW3 .... 133 H1 [3]
Waremead Rd
   GNTH/NBYPK IG2 .... 71 H6 [2]
Warenford Wy *BORE* WD6 .... 32 A4
Warepoint Dr *THMD* SE28 .... 107 K8
Warfield Rd *EBED/NFELT* TW14 . 131 L4
   HPTN TW12 .... 151 H4
   WLSDN NW10 .... 100 D2 [3]
Wargrave Av *SEVS/STOTM* N15 . 67 M7
Wargrave Rd *RYLN/HDSTN* HA2 . 79 J3
Warham Rd *FSBYPK* N4 .... 67 G6
   KTN/HRWW/W HA3 .... 61 J1
   SAND/SEL CR2 .... 172 C7
Warham St *CMBW* SE5 .... 121 H5
Waring Cl *ORP* BR6 .... 176 F8
Waring Dr *ORP* BR6 .... 176 F8
Waring Rd *SCUP* DA14 .... 162 C2
Waring St *WNWD* SE27 .... 139 J8 [3]
Warkworth Gdns *ISLW* TW7 ..... 116 A5
Warkworth Rd *TOTM* N17 .... 67 K1
Warland Rd *WOOL/PLUM* SE18 . 125 K5
Warley Av *ROMW/RG* RM7 .... 72 F8
   YEAD UB4 .... 96 A5
Warley Rd *CLAY* IG5 .... 71 G2 [1]
   ED N9 .... 50 C4
   RBRW/HUT CM13................. 75 L3
   WFD IG8 .... 52 F2
   YEAD UB4 .... 96 A5
Warley St *BETH* E2 .... 104 D2
Warlingham Rd *THHTH* CR7 ..... 157 H7
Warlock Rd *MV/WKIL* W9 .... 100 F3
Warlters Cl *HOLWY* N7 .... 84 E4 [7]
Warlters Rd *HOLWY* N7 .... 84 E4
Warltersville Rd *ARCH* N19 ...... 66 E8
Warming Cl *CLPT* E5 .... 86 D3 [1]
Warmington Rd *HNHL* SE24 ..... 139 J3
Warmington St *PLSTW* E13 ..... 106 A3 [1]
Warminster Rd *SNWD* SE25 ..... 158 A5
Warminster Sq *SNWD* SE25 ..... 158 A5 [1]
Warminster Wy *MTCM* CR4 ...... 156 B4
Warndon St
   BERM/RHTH SE16 .... 122 C2 [3]
Warneford Pl *OXHEY* WD19 ..... 42 E1 [1]
Warneford Rd
   KTN/HRWW/W HA3 .... 62 D4
Warneford St *HOM* E9 .... 86 B8 [3]
Warne Pl *BFN/LL* DA15 .... 144 B3 [3]
Warner Av *CHEAM* SM3 .... 169 L4
Warner Cl *CDALE/KGS* NW9 ..... 63 M8
   HPTN TW12 .... 150 F1 [3]
   HYS/HAR UB3 .... 113 K5 [3]
   SRTFD E15 .... 87 L5 [7]
Warner Pl *BETH* E2 .... 104 A1
Warner Rd *BMLY* BR1 .... 159 M3
   CEND/HSY/T N8 .... 66 D5
   CMBW SE5 .... 121 J6
   WALTH E17 .... 68 E5
Warners Cl *CLKNW* EC1R 12 A1
Warnford Rd *ORP* BR6 .... 177 H7
Warnham Court Rd *CAR* SM5 ... 182 F1
Warnham Rd *NFNCH/WDSP* N12 . 47 K7
Warple Wy *ACT* W3 .... 99 L8
Warren Av *BELMT* SM2 .... 181 M3
   BMLY BR1 .... 160 A7
   ORP BR6 .... 176 F7
   RCHPK/HAM TW10 .... 135 H1
   SAND/SEL CR2 .... 185 K1
   WAN E11 .... 87 K3 [3]

Warren Cl *BXLYHS* DA6............ 145 G2
   ED N9 .... 50 D2
   ESH/CLAY KT10 .... 166 B6
   WBLY HA9 .... 80 D2
   YEAD UB4 .... 96 C3
Warren Ct *CHIG* IG7 .... 53 K6
Warren Crs *ED* N9 .... 49 M2
Warren Cutting *KUTN/CMB* KT2 . 153 K3
Warrender Rd *ARCH* N19 .... 84 C3
Warrender Wy *RSLP* HA4 .... 60 A8
Warren Dr *GFD/PVL* UB6 .... 97 H3
   HCH RM12 .... 92 A3
   ORP BR6 .... 177 H7
   RSLP HA4 .... 60 D8
Warren Dr North *SURB* KT6 ...... 168 B3
Warren Dr South *BRYLDS* KT5 .. 168 C3
The Warren Dr *WAN* E11 .... 70 C8
Warrenfield Cl *CHESW* EN7 ...... 26 A4 [1]
Warren Gdns *ORP* BR6 .... 177 G7
Warrengate La *POTB/CUF* EN6 .. 22 C4
Warrengate Rd *BRKMPK* AL9 .... 22 C1
Warren Gv *BORE* WD6 .... 32 D7
Warren Hl *LOU* IG10 .... 39 J8
Warren La *LHD/OX* KT22 .... 178 C5
   STAN HA7 .... 44 A4
   WOOL/PLUM SE18 .... 125 H1
Warren Md *BNSTD* SM7 .... 181 J8 [1]
Warren Ms *GTPST* W1W .... 10 E1 [2]
Warren Pk *KUTN/CMB* KT2 .... 153 J2
Warren Park Rd *SUT* SM1 .... 170 D6
Warren Pond Rd *CHING* E4 ...... 51 M2
Warren Ri *NWMAL* KT3 .... 153 K4
Warren Rd *ASHF* TW15 .... 149 L3
   BARK/HLT IG6 .... 71 K6
   BNSTD SM7 .... 181 K8
   BUSH WD23 .... 43 J3
   BXLYHS DA6 .... 145 G2
   CHING E4 .... 51 J4
   CRICK NW2 .... 81 M2
   CROY/NA CR0 .... 172 E3
   DART DA1 .... 146 E7
   HAYES BR2 .... 175 G4
   HGDN/ICK UB10 .... 76 A4
   KUTN/CMB KT2 .... 153 J2
   LEY E10 .... 87 J3
   ORP BR6 .... 177 H7
   PUR/KEN CR8 .... 184 B5
   SCUP DA14 .... 144 C7
   WAN E11 .... 70 C7
   WHTN TW2 .... 133 K3
   WIM/MER SW19 .... 155 L2
Warrens Shawe La *EDGW* HA8 .. 45 H4
Warren St *FITZ* W1T 10 E1
The Warren *CAR* SM5 .... 182 D2
   HEST TW5 .... 114 F5
   HOR/WEW KT19 .... 168 D6
   LHD/OX KT22 .... 178 C5
   YEAD UB4 .... 96 A5
Warren Wy *MLHL* NW7 .... 46 B3
   WEY KT13 .... 164 C7 [2]
Warren Wood Cl *HAYES* BR2 .... 175 G4
Warriner Dr *ED* N9 .... 50 A5
Warriner Gdns *BTSEA* SW11 .... 119 M6
Warrington Crs *MV/WKIL* W9 ... 8 E1
Warrington Gdns *EMPK* RM11 .. 74 C7
   MV/WKIL W9 .... 8 E1 [1]
Warrington Pl *POP/IOD* E14 ..... 105 J7 [3]
Warrington Rd *BCTR* RM8 .... 90 D2
   CROY/NA CR0 .... 172 B5
   HRW HA1 .... 61 L6
   RCHPK/HAM TW10 .... 134 D2 [1]
Warrington Sq *BCTR* RM8 .... 90 D2 [3]
Warrior Sq *MNPK* E12 .... 89 C4
Warsaw Cl *RSLP* HA4 .... 78 A1
Warspite Rd *WOOL/PLUM* SE18 . 124 E1
Warton Rd *SRTFD* E15 .... 87 J8
Warwall *EHAM* E6..................... 107 H5
Warwick Av *EDGW* HA8 .... 44 A5
   MV/WKIL W9 .... 8 D1
   RYLN/HDSTN HA2 .... 78 F4
   STA TW18 .... 148 C2
Warwick Cl *BUSH* WD23 .... 43 L2
   BXLY DA5 .... 144 F4
   EBAR EN4 .... 34 D8
   HPTN TW12 .... 151 J3
   ORP BR6 .... 177 G5
Warwick Crs *BAY/PAD* W2....... 8 E2
   YEAD UB4 .... 95 M3
Warwick Dene *EA* W5 .... 98 E7
Warwick Dr *BARN* SW13 .... 118 B8
   CHES/WCR EN8 .... 26 D1
Warwick Gdns *FSBYPK* N4 .... 67 J6
   GPK RM2 .... 74 C4
   IL IG1 .... 89 H1
   THDIT KT7 .... 151 M8
   WKENS W14 .... 119 H1
Warwick Gv *BRYLDS* KT5 .... 167 M2
   CLPT E5 .... 86 B1
Warwick House St *STJS* SW1Y .. 11 H8
   STP EC4M 12 D4
Warwick La *RAIN* RM13 .... 110 F1
   STP EC4M 12 D4
Warwick Pl *EA* W5 .... 98 D8 [1]
   MV/WKIL W9 .... 8 E2
   UX/CGN UB8 .... 76 C7
Warwick Pl North *PIM* SW1V .... 16 E6 [2]
Warwick Rd *ASHF* TW15 .... 148 L1
   BAR EN5 .... 34 B7
   BORE WD6 .... 32 D6
   CHING E4 .... 51 C7
   COUL/CHIP CR5 .... 183 J7
   EA W5 .... 98 E7
   FBAR/BDGN N11 .... 48 D8
   FSTGT E7 .... 87 M6
   HSLWW TW4 .... 114 C8
   KUT KT1 .... 152 C4 [3]
   MNPK E12 .... 88 E3
   NWDGN UB2 .... 114 F1 [3]
   NWMAL KT3 .... 153 J6 [3]
   PEND EN3 .... 37 M2
   PGE/AN SE20 .... 158 B6
   RAIN RM13 .... 110 C3
   SCUP DA14 .... 162 B1
   SUT SM1 .... 170 C7 [3]
   THDIT KT7 .... 151 M8
   THHTH CR7 .... 157 C6
   UED N18 .... 49 L6
   WALTH E17 .... 68 F2

Wan E11 .... 70 B6
   WDR/YW UB7 .... 94 E7
   WELL DA16 .... 126 C8
   WHTN TW2 .... 133 L5
   WKENS W14 .... 118 F2
Warwick Sq *PIM* SW1V 16 E7
   STP EC4M .... 12 D4 [3]
Warwick Square Ms *PIM* SW1V . 16 E6
Warwick St *REGST* W1B 10 F6
Warwick Ter *WOOL/PLUM* SE18 . 125 K4
   WAN E11 .... 70 C7
Warwick Yd *STLK* EC1Y .... 12 F1 [1]
Washington Av *MNPK* E12 .... 88 E4
Washington Cl *BOW* E3 .... 105 H2 [3]
Washington Rd *BARN* SW13 ..... 118 A5
   EHAM E6 .... 88 C7 [3]
   KUT KT1 .... 153 G5
   SWFD E18 .... 69 M3 [3]
   WPK KT4 .... 169 H4
Wash La *BAR* EN5 .... 22 C8
   POTB/CUF EN6 .... 22 C6
Wastdale Rd *FSTH* SE23 .... 140 D5
Watcombe Rd *SNWD* SE25 ...... 158 B8
Waterbank Rd *CAT* SE6 .... 141 H7
Waterbeach Rd *DAGW* RM9 ..... 90 C6
Waterdale Rd *ABYW* SE2 .... 126 A4
Waterden Rd *SRTFD* E15 .... 87 G5
Waterer Ri *WLGTN* SM6 .... 171 K8
Waterfall Cottages
   WIM/MER SW19 .... 155 K2
Waterfall Rd *STHGT/OAK* N14 .. 48 C5 [3]
   WIM/MER SW19 .... 155 K2 [3]
Waterfall Ter *TOOT* SW17 .... 155 L2 [1]
Waterfield Cl *BELV* DA17 .... 127 G1
   THMD SE28 .... 108 B7 [1]
Waterfield Gdns *SNWD* SE25 ... 157 L7 [3]
Waterfields Wy *WAT* WD17 ...... 29 K7
Waterford Rd *FUL/PGN* SW6 .... 119 H5
Water Gdns *STAN* HA7............. 44 H8
Watergate St *DEPT* SE8 .... 123 C4
The Watergate *OXHEY* WD19 ... 42 B1 [1]
Waterhall Av *CHING* E4 .... 51 L6 [3]
Waterhall Cl *WALTH* E17 .... 68 D2
Waterhead Cl *ERITH* DA8 .... 127 L5
Waterhouse Cl *HAMP* NW3 ...... 83 K5
Wateringbury Cl
   STMC/STPC BR5 .... 162 B6
Water La *ED* N9 .... 50 B3
   GDMY/SEVK IG3 .... 89 M3
   KGLGY WD4 .... 20 B2
   KUT KT1 .... 152 D4
   PECK SE15 .... 122 C5
   PUR RM19 .... 129 C2
   RCH/KEW TW9 .... 134 D2
   SCUP DA14 .... 144 F7
   SRTFD E15 .... 87 L6
   TWK TW1 .... 143 A5
   WAT WD17 .... 29 J7 [3]
Water Lily Cl *STHL* UB1 .... 97 J8 [3]
Waterloo Cl *EBED/NFELT* TW14 . 131 M5
Waterloo Gdns *BETH* E2 .... 104 C1 [3]
   ROMW/RG RM7 .... 73 K7
Waterloo Pl *RCH/KEW* TW9 ..... 117 G4 [3]
   STJS SW1Y 11 G8
Waterloo Rd *BARK/HLT* IG6 ..... 71 J3
   CRICK NW2 .... 82 A2
   EHAM E6 .... 88 C7 [3]
   FSTGT E7 .... 87 M5 [3]
   HOR/WEW KT19 .... 180 D5
   LEY E10 .... 69 G8
   ROMW/RG RM7 .... 73 K6
   STHWK SE1 .... 11 M8
   SUT SM1 .... 170 D7
   UX/CGN UB8 .... 76 C8
Waterloo Ter *IS* N1 .... 6 C2
Waterlow Rd *ARCH* N19 .... 84 D1
Waterman St *PUT/ROE* SW15 ... 118 D8
Waterman Wy *WAP* E1W .... 104 B7 [3]
Watermead *EBED/NFELT* TW14 . 131 L5
Watermead La *MTCM* CR4 .... 170 F1
Watermeadow Cl *ERITH* DA8 ... 128 B6 [1]
Watermeadow La
   FUL/PGN SW6...................... 119 J7 [3]
Watermead Rd *CAT* SE6 .... 141 J8
Watermead Wy *TOTM* N17 ...... 68 C2
Water Ms *PECK* SE15 .... 140 C1
Watermill Cl *RCHPK/HAM* TW10 . 134 C7
Watermill La *UED* N18 .... 49 L7
Watermill Rd *FELT* TW13 .... 132 F6
Watermill Wy *WIM/MER* SW19 . 155 J4
Watermint Cl
   STMC/STPC BR5 .... 162 D7 [10]
Watermint Quay *CLPT* E5 .... 68 A8
Water Rd *ALP/SUD* HA0 .... 80 F8
Waters Dr *RKW/CH/CXG* WD3 .. 40 E3 [3]
Watersedge *HOR/WEW* KT19 ... 168 C6
Watersfield Wy *EDGW* HA8 ...... 62 D1
Waterside *DART* DA1 .... 145 L2
   KGLGY WD4 .... 20 A2
   UX/CGN UB8 .... 94 C4 [3]
   WALTH E17 .... 68 C7
Waterside Cl *BARK* IG11 .... 90 A4
   BERM/RHTH SE16 .... 104 A8 [10]
   HARH RM3 .... 75 G1
   HOM E9 .... 86 F8
   NTHLT UB5 .... 96 F2 [3]
   SURB KT6 .... 167 L4 [3]
Waterside Ct *KGLGY* WD4 .... 20 B2 [3]
Waterside Dr *WOT/HER* KT12 .. 150 B8
Waterside Pl *CAMTN* NW1 .... 4 B3 [3]
Waterside Rd *NWDGN* UB2 ..... 115 G1
Waterside Wy *TOOT* SW17 ...... 137 J8
Watersmeet Wy *THMD* SE28 ... 108 D5
Waterson St *BETH* E2 .... 7 K7
Watersplash Cl *KUT* KT1 .... 152 E6 [3]
Watersplash La *HEST* TW5 .... 114 B3
   HYS/HAR UB3 .... 114 A2
Watersplash Rd *SHPTN* TW17 .. 149 G7
Waters Rd *CAT* SE6 .... 141 L7
   KUT KT1 .... 153 H5
Waters Sq *KUT* KT1 .... 153 H6
Water St *TPL/STR* WC2R 12 A6
Water Tower Cl *UX/CGN* UB8 ... 76 E5
Water Tower Hl *CROY/NA* CR0 .. 172 D6
Water Tower Pl *IS* N1 .... 6 B4

Waterworks La *CLPT* E5 .... 86 D2
Waterworks Rd
   BRXS/STRHM SW2 .... 138 E3
Watery La *HYS/HAR* UB3 .... 113 K3 [3]
   NTHLT UB5 .... 96 C1
   RYNPK SW20 .... 154 F5
   SCUP DA14 .... 162 B2
Wates Wy *MTCM* CR4 .... 170 F1
Wateville Rd *TOTM* N17 .... 67 J2
Watford Cl *BTSEA* SW11 .... 173 L1
Watford Field Rd *WAT* WD17 ... 29 J7 [13]
   WATW WD18 .... 29 J8
Watford Heath *OXHEY* WD19 ... 42 D2
Watford Rd *BORE* WD6 .... 44 C1
   CAN/RD E16 .... 106 A4
   HRW HA1 .... 80 A2
   KGLGY WD4 .... 20 A3
   NTHWD HA6 .... 59 M1
   RAD WD7 .... 30 C1
   RKW/CH/CXG WD3 .... 28 D8
Watford Wy *NW4 .... 64 A5
Watford Wy (Barnet By-pass)
   MLHL NW7 .... 45 L6
Watkin Rd *WBLY* HA9 .... 81 H3
Watkinson Rd *HOLWY* N7 .... 84 F6
Watling Av *EDGW* HA8 .... 63 J3
Watlings Cl *CROY/NA* CR0 .... 173 L1
Watling St *BXLYHS* DA6 .... 145 H1
   DART DA1 .... 147 H4
   STP EC4M 12 E5
Watlington Gv *SYD* SE26 .... 158 E1 [1]
Watney Rd *MORT/ESHN* SW14 .. 117 J8
Watneys Rd *MTCM* CR4 .... 156 D8
Watney St *WCHPL* E1 .... 104 B5 [23]
Watson Av *CHEAM* SM3 .... 169 L4
   EHAM E6 .... 89 G7
Watson Cl *STNW/STAM* N16 ..... 85 K5 [3]
   WIM/MER SW19 .... 155 L2 [3]
Watson's Ms *MBLAR* W1H 9 K3
Watsons Rd *WDGN* N22 .... 66 F2
Watson's St *DEPT* SE8 .... 123 G5
Wattisfield Rd *CLPT* E5 .... 86 C3
Watts Cl *SEVS/STOTM* N15 ...... 67 L6 [3]
Watts Crs *PUR* RM19 .... 129 J2
Watts Gv *BOW* E3 .... 105 G4
Watt's La *CHST* BR7 .... 161 H4
   TEDD TW11 .... 152 A1
Watts Rd *THDIT* KT7 .... 167 G2
Watts St *WAP* E1W 104 B7
Wat Tyler Rd *BKHTH/KID* SE3 .. 123 J7
Wauthier Cl *PLMGR* N13 .... 49 H7
Wavell Dr *BFN/LL* DA15 .... 143 L3
Wavel Ms *KIL/WHAMP* NW6 ..... 2 C2
Wavel Pl *NRWD* SE19 .... 139 M4
Wavendon Av *CHSWK* W4 .... 117 K3
Waveney Av *PECK* SE15 .... 140 B1
Waverley Av *BRYLDS* KT5 .... 168 B3
   CHING E4 .... 50 F6
   SUT SM1 .... 170 B4
   WALTH E17 .... 69 K4 [3]
   WBLY HA9 .... 80 F5
   WHTN TW2 .... 133 M2
Waverley Cl *E/WMO/HCT* KT8... 151 G8
   HAYES BR2 .... 160 D8
   HYS/HAR UB3 .... 113 K2 [3]
Waverley Crs *HARH* RM3 .... 56 C5
   WOOL/PLUM SE18 .... 125 K4
Waverley Gdns *BARK* IG11 .... 107 L1
   BARK/HLT IG6 .... 71 J3
   EHAM E6 .... 106 E4 [3]
   NTHWD HA6 .... 60 A2 [3]
Waverley Gv *HDN* NW4 .... 64 D4
Waverley Pl *FSBYPK* N4 .... 85 H1 [3]
   STJWD NW8 .... 3 G5 [3]
Waverley Wy *CAR* SM5 .... 170 E8
Waverton Rd
   WAND/EARL SW18 .... 137 J4
Waverton St *MYFR/PICC* W1J ... 10 B8
   MYFR/PKLN W1K 10 M8
Waxlow Crs *STHL* UB1 .... 97 G5
Waxlow Rd *WLSDN* NW10 .... 99 J1
Waxwell La *PIN* HA5 .... 60 D4
Wayborne Gv *RSLP* HA4 .... 59 J7
Waycross Rd *UPMR* RM14 ...... 75 L2
Waye Av *HEST* TW5 .... 114 A6
Wayfarer Rd *NTHLT* UB5 .... 96 E2
Wayford St *BTSEA* SW11 .... 119 L7
Wayland Av *HACK* E8 .... 86 A5
Waylands *HYS/HAR* UB3 .... 95 K4
   SWLY BR8 .... 163 M7
Waylett Pl *ALP/SUD* HA0 .... 80 A3 [3]
   WNWD SE27 .... 139 H7
Wayne Cl *ORP* BR6 .... 176 F5
Wayneflete Tower Av
   ESH/CLAY KT10 .... 166 A5
Wayneflete Av *CROY/NA* CR0 ... 172 B5 [3]
Wayneflete Sq *NKENS* W10 ...... 100 D6 [3]
Wayneflete St
   WAND/EARL SW18 .... 137 J2
Wayside *CRICK* NW2 .... 82 E1
   MORT/ESHN SW14 .... 135 J1
   POTB/CUF EN6 .... 23 K6 [3]
Wayside Av *BUSH* WD23 .... 43 K1
   HCH RM12 .... 92 D2
Wayside Cl *ROM* RM1 .... 73 M4
   STHGT/OAK N14 .... 48 C1
Wayside Ct *TWK* TW1 .... 134 C3 [3]
Wayside Gdns *DAGE* RM10 ...... 91 G5
Wayside Gv *CHST* BR7 .... 142 F8
Wayside Ms *GNTH/NBYPK* IG2 .. 71 C7
Wayville Rd *DART* DA1 .... 147 H4
Weald Cl *BERM/RHTH* SE16 ..... 122 B3 [3]

HAYES BR2 175 L4
Weald La KTN/HRWW/W HA3 61 K3
Weald Park Wy BRW CM14 57 L5
Weald Ri KTN/HRWW/W HA3 61 M1
Weald Rd BRW CM14 57 G3
HGDN/ICK UB10 95 G1
Wealdstone Rd CHEAM SM3 169 M4
The Weald CHST BR7 160 F2
Weald Wy ROMW/RG RM7 73 H7
YEAD UB4 95 L2
Wealdwood Gdns PIN HA5 43 H8 2
Weale Rd CHING E4 51 K5
Weall Gn GSTN WD25 21 H5
Weardale Av RDART DA2 147 J6
Weardale Gdns ENC/FH EN2 36 D4
Weardale Rd LEW SE13 141 K2
Wear Pl BETH E2 104 B2 17
Wearside Rd LEW SE13 141 H1
Weaver Cl EHAM E6 107 H6 3
Weavers Cl ISLW TW7 133 M1 1
Weaver's La STHWK SE1 13 K9
Weaver St WCHPL E1 104 A3
Weavers Wy CAMTN NW1 5 G3
Weaver Wk WNWD SE27 139 H8 7
Webber Cl BORE WD6 44 D1 7
ERITH DA8 128 B5 3
Webber Rw STHWK SE1 18 B3 1
Webber St STHWK SE1 18 B1
Webb Pl WLSDN NW10 99 M2
Webb Rd BKHTH/KID SE3 123 M4
Webbscroft Rd DAGE RM10 91 H4
Webb's Rd BTSEA SW11 137 M2
YEAD UB4 96 A2
Webb St STHWK SE1 19 J4
Webster Cl COB KT11 178 B7
HCH RM12 92 D3 2
Webster Gdns EA W5 98 D7
Webster Rd BERM/RHTH SE16 122 A1
WAN E11 87 J3 2
Wedderburn Rd BARK IG11 89 K8
HAMP NW3 83 K5
Wedgewood Cl NTHWD HA6 41 J8 4
Wedgwood Wy NRWD SE19 157 J2 1
Wedlake Cl EMPK RM11 92 E1 5
Wedlake St NKENS W10 100 E3 13
Wedmore Av CLAY IG5 71 G2 2
Wedmore Gdns ARCH N19 84 D3
Wedmore Rd GFD/PVL UB6 97 K2
Wedmore St ARCH N19 84 D3
Wednesbury Gdns HARH RM3 74 F1
Wednesbury Gn HARH RM3 74 F1 5
Wednesbury Rd HARH RM3 74 F1
Weech Rd KIL/WHAMP NW6 83 G4
Weedington Rd KTTN NW5 84 A5 5
Weekley Sq BTSEA SW11 119 K8 11
Weigall Rd LEE/GVPK SE12 142 A1
Weighhouse St
MYFR/PKLN W1K 10 B6
Weighton Rd
KTN/HRWW/W HA3 61 K2
PGE/AN SE20 158 B5
Weihurst Gdns SUT SM1 170 D7
Weimar St PUT/ROE SW15 118 E8
Weirdale Av TRDG/WHET N20 47 M4
Weir Hall Av UED N18 49 K8
Weir Hall Gdns UED N18 49 K7
Weir Hall Rd UED N18 49 K7
Weir Rd BAL SW12 138 C5
BXLY DA5 145 H4
WIM/MER SW19 137 H7
WOT/HER KT12 165 G1
Weiss Rd PUT/ROE SW15 118 D8
Welbeck Av BFN/LL DA15 144 A5
BMLY BR1 142 A8
YEAD UB4 96 B3
Welbeck Cl BORE WD6 32 A6 4
EW KT17 181 G1
NWMAL KT3 153 M8 3
Welbeck Rd CAR SM5 170 E2 2
CAR SM5 170 E3 1
EBAR EN4 47 K1
EHAM E6 106 D2
RYLN/HDSTN HA2 79 H1
SUT SM1 170 D4
Welbeck St MHST W1U 10 B3
Welbeck Wy MHST W1U 10 C4 1
Welby St CMBW SE5 121 H6
Welch Pl PIN HA5 60 C2 2
Welcomes Rd PUR/KEN CR8 184 C8
Weldon Cl RSLP HA4 78 B6
Weldon Dr E/WMO/HCT KT8 150 F7 7
Weld Pl FBAR/BDGN N11 48 B7 5
Welfare Rd SRTFD E15 87 L7 3
Welford Cl CLPT E5 86 D3 4
Welford Pl WIM/MER SW19 136 E8
Welham Rd TOOT SW17 156 A1
Welhouse Rd CAR SM5 170 E3
Wellacre Rd KTN/HRWW/W HA3 62 B7
Wellan Cl BFN/LL DA15 144 B2
Welland Gdns GFD/PVL UB6 97 M1
Wellands Cl BMLY BR1 160 F5
Welland St GNWCH SE10 123 J4 3
Well Ap BAR EN5 33 J8 2
Wellbrook Rd ORP BR6 176 A6
Well Cl RSLP HA4 78 E3
STRHM/NOR SW16 138 F8
Wellclose Sq WAP E1W 104 A6 10
WCHPL E1 104 A6 10
Wellclose St WAP E1W 104 A6 11
Wellcome Av DART DA1 146 E1
Well Cottage Cl WAN E11 70 C8 1
Welldon Crs HRW HA1 61 L7
Well End Rd BORE WD6 32 C2
Wellers Ct CAMTN NW1 5 J6
Wellers Gv CHESW EN7 26 A1 3
Weller St STHWK SE1 18 E1
Wellesley Av HMSMTH W6 118 B1 4
NTHWD HA6 41 M7
Wellesley Ct MV/WKIL W9 2 E7
Wellesley Court Rd
CROY/NA CR0 172 D4 1
Wellesley Crs POTB/CUF EN6 22 E6
WHTN TW2 133 L6
Wellesley Gv CROY/NA CR0 172 D4
Wellesley Park Ms
ENC/FH EN2 36 B5 4
Wellesley Pl CAMTN NW1 5 G8 1
KTTN NW5 84 A5 6
Wellesley Rd BELMT SM2 170 C8
CHSWK W4 117 G3
CROY/NA CR0 172 C3
HRW HA1 61 L6
IL IG1 89 H2
KTTN NW5 84 A5
WALTH E17 69 G7
WAN E11 70 A6
WHTN TW2 133 K7
Wellesley St WCHPL E1 104 D4 10
Wellesley Ter IS N1 6 F7
Wellfield Av MUSWH N10 66 B4
Wellfield Gdns CAR SM5 182 E2
Wellfield Rd STRHM/NOR SW16 138 E8
Wellfit St HNHL SE24 121 H8 4
Wellgarth GFD/PVL UB6 80 B6
Wellgarth Rd GLDGN NW11 83 H1
Well Gv TRDG/WHET N20 47 J3
Well Hall Pde ELTH/MOT SE9 142 F1 1
Well Hall Rd ELTH/MOT SE9 124 F8
Wellhouse La BAR EN5 33 J7
Wellhouse Rd BECK BR3 158 F7
Welling High St WELL DA16 126 B8
Wellington Av BFN/LL DA15 144 A3
CHING E4 51 G4
ED N9 50 B5
HSLWW TW4 133 G2
PIN HA5 60 F2 2
SEVS/STOTM N15 68 A7
WPK KT4 169 J5
Wellington Cl DAGE RM10 91 J7 2
NTGHL W11 8 A5
NWCR SE14 122 D6 4
OXHEY WD19 42 E5
WOT/HER KT12 164 F3
Wellington Crs NWMAL KT3 153 J6
Wellington Dr DAGE RM10 91 J7
PUR/KEN CR8 183 M3
Wellington Gdns CHARL SE7 124 C3
HPTN TW12 133 K8
Wellington Gv GNWCH SE10 123 K5 2
Wellington Hl LOU IG10 39 H3
Wellingtonia Av ABR/ST RM4 55 L5
Wellington Pl COB KT11 178 A5
STJWD NW8 3 H7
Wellington Rd ASHF TW15 148 E1
BELV DA17 126 F3
BXLY DA5 144 D3
CROY/NA CR0 172 B2 2
DART DA1 146 C3
EA W5 116 C2
EBED/NFELT TW14 131 L2
EHAM E6 88 F8
EN EN1 36 E8
FSTGT E7 88 A5
HAYES BR2 160 C7
HPTN TW12 133 K8
KTN/HRWW/W HA3 61 L4
LEY E10 86 E1
PIN HA5 60 F2
STJWD NW8 3 H6
STMC/STPC BR5 177 H1
UX/CGN UB8 76 C8
WALTH E17 68 E4
WAN E11 70 A6
WAT WD17 29 H5 5
WIM/MER SW19 137 G6
WLSDN NW10 100 D2 4
Wellington Rd North
HSLWW TW4 114 F8
Wellington Rd South
HSLWW TW4 132 F1
Wellington Rw BETH E2 7 M7
Wellington Sq CHEL SW3 15 L7 2
Wellington St BARK IG11 89 J8
COVGDN WC2E 11 K6
WOOL/PLUM SE18 125 G2
Wellington Ter
RYLN/HDSTN HA2 79 K1 2
Wellington Wy BOW E3 105 G2
Welling Wy ELTH/MOT SE9 125 K8
Well La MORT/ESHN SW14 135 J2
Wellmeadow Rd HNWL W7 116 A2
LEW SE13 141 L3
Well Rd BAR EN5 33 J8
HAMP NW3 83 K3
POTB/CUF EN6 23 L2
Wells Cl NTHLT UB5 96 C2 3
Wells Dr CDALE/KGS NW9 81 K1
Wells Gdns IL IG1 70 E8
RAIN RM13 91 M6
Wells House Rd WLSDN NW10 99 L4
Wellside Cl BAR EN5 33 J7
Wellside Gdns
MORT/ESHN SW14 135 J1 3
Wells Ms FITZ W1T 10 F3 1
Wellsmoor Gdns BMLY BR1 161 G6
Wells Park Rd SYD SE26 140 A7
Wellsprings Crs WBLY HA9 81 H3
Wells Ri STJWD NW8 3 L4
Wells Rd BMLY BR1 160 F5
EPSOM KT18 180 B8
HMSMTH W6 100 C8
Wells St GTPST W1W 10 E3
Wellstead Av ED N9 50 C2
Wellstead Rd EHAM E6 107 G1
Wells Ter FSBYPK N4 85 G2 7
The Wells STHGT/OAK N14 48 D3 4
Wellstones WAT WD17 29 H7 4
Well St HOM E9 86 D6
SRTFD E15 87 L6
Well Wk HAMP NW3 83 K3
Well Wy EPSOM KT18 180 A8
Wellwood Cl COUL/CHIP CR5 183 L7
Wellwood Rd GDMY/SEVK IG3 90 A1
Welsford St STHWK SE1 122 A3
Welsh Cl PLSTW E13 106 A2
Welshpool St HACK E8 86 A8 17
Welstead Wy CHSWK W4 117 M1
Weltje Rd HMSMTH W6 118 A3
Welton Rd WOOL/PLUM SE18 125 L5
Welwyn Av
EBED/NFELT TW14 131 M3 2
Welwyn St BETH E2 104 C2 16
Welwyn Wy YEAD UB4 95 L3 2
Wembley Hill Rd WBLY HA9 80 F5
Wembley Park Dr WBLY HA9 80 F4
Wembley Rd HPTN TW12 151 G4 1
Wembley Wy WBLY HA9 81 H6
Wemborough Rd STAN HA7 62 B2
Wembury Rd HGT N6 66 B8 2
Wemyss Rd BKHTH/KID SE3 123 M7
Wendela Ct HRW HA1 79 L3
Wendell Rd SHB W12 99 M8
Wendling Rd CAR SM5 170 D3
Wendon St BOW E3 86 F8 9
Wendover Cl YEAD UB4 96 D3 9
Wendover Dr NWMAL KT3 168 F1
Wendover Rd ELTH/MOT SE9 124 D8
HAYES BR2 160 B7
WLSDN NW10 99 M1
Wendover Wy BUSH WD23 43 J1
HCH RM12 92 C5 3
ORP BR6 177 G1 2
WELL DA16 144 A2
The Wend COUL/CHIP CR5 183 K7
Wendy Cl EN EN1 49 M1
Wendy Wy ALP/SUD HA0 80 E8
Wenlak Cl DEN/HRF UB9 76 A3 4
Wenlock Gdns HDN NW4 64 A5 5
Wenlock Rd EDGW HA8 45 J8
IS N1 6 E6
Wenlock St IS N1 6 F6
Wennington Gn RAIN RM13 110 E6
Wennington Rd BOW E3 104 D1 5
RAIN RM13 110 B4
Wensley Av WFD IG8 70 A1
Wensley Cl CRW RM5 55 G7
ELTH/MOT SE9 142 F3
Wensleydale Av CLAY IG5 70 E3
Wensleydale Gdns HPTN TW12 151 H3
Wensleydale Rd HPTN TW12 151 G4
Wensley Rd UED N18 50 B8
Wensum Wy RKW/CH/CXG WD3 40 D3
Wentbridge Pth BORE WD6 32 A3 6
Wentland Cl CAT SE6 141 K6 1
Wentland Rd CAT SE6 141 K6
Wentworth Av BORE WD6 31 M8
FNCH N3 65 G1
Wentworth Cl ASHF TW15 131 H8 3
FNCH N3 65 H1 2
HAYES BR2 175 G4 2
MRDN SM4 170 A2 2
ORP BR6 176 E7 2
POTB/CUF EN6 23 G4 2
SURB KT6 167 K4
THMD SE28 108 D5 2
WAT WD17 28 F3
Wentworth Crs HYS/HAR UB3 113 K1
PECK SE15 122 A5 4
Wentworth Dr DART DA1 146 A4
PIN HA5 60 A6
Wentworth Gdns PLMGR N13 49 H5
Wentworth Hl WBLY HA9 80 F1
Wentworth Ms BOW E3 104 E3 3
Wentworth Pk FNCH N3 65 H1 3
Wentworth Pl STAN HA7 44 B8 2
Wentworth Rd BAR EN5 33 K5
CROY/NA CR0 172 A2
GLDGN NW11 64 F7
MNPK E12 88 D4 1
NWDGN UB2 114 C2
Wentworth St WCHPL E1 13 L4
Wentworth Wy PIN HA5 60 D5
RAIN RM13 110 B2
SAND/SEL CR2 185 G8
Wenvoe Av BXLYHN DA7 127 H7
Wernbrook St
WOOL/PLUM SE18 125 J4
Werndee Rd SNWD SE25 158 A7
Werneth Hall Rd CLAY IG5 70 F4
Werrington St CAMTN NW1 4 F6
Werter Rd PUT/ROE SW15 136 E1
Wescott Wy UX/CGN UB8 94 C1
Wesleyan Pl KTTN NW5 84 B4 6
Wesley Av CAN/RD E16 106 A7
HSLW TW3 114 E7
WLSDN NW10 99 K2
Wesley Cl CHESW EN7 25 J1
HOLWY N7 84 F2 6
RYLN/HDSTN HA2 79 J2
STMC/STPC BR5 162 C6
Wesley Rd EFNCH N2 65 L3
HYS/HAR UB3 96 A6
LEY E10 69 J8
WLSDN NW10 81 J8
Wesley St CAVSQ/HST W1G 10 B3 3
Wessex Av WIM/MER SW19 155 G5
Wessex Cl GDMY/SEVK IG3 71 L7
KUT KT1 153 H4 2
Wessex Dr ERITH DA8 127 L7
PIN HA5 60 E1
Wessex Gdns CRICK NW2 82 E1
Wessex La GFD/PVL UB6 97 K1
Wessex Rd HTHAIR TW6 130 C1
Wessex St BETH E2 104 C2 17
Wessex Wy GLDGN NW11 64 E8
Westacott YEAD UB4 95 L4
West Ap STMC/STPC BR5 161 J8
West Arbour St WCHPL E1 104 D5
West Av FNCH N3 47 G8
HDN NW4 64 D6
HYS/HAR UB3 95 M6
PIN HA5 60 F8
STHL UB1 96 F6
WALTH E17 69 H6
WLGTN SM6 171 L7
West Avenue Rd WALTH E17 69 G5
West Bank BARK IG11 89 H8
ENC/FH EN2 36 C6
STNW/STAM N16 67 L8
Westbank Rd HPTN TW12 151 J2
West Barnes La NWMAL KT3 154 A8
RYNPK SW20 154 B6
Westbeech Rd WDGN N22 67 G4
Westbere Dr STAN HA7 44 D7
Westbere Rd CRICK NW2 82 E4
Westbourne Av ACT W3 99 K5
CHEAM SM3 169 L4 2
Westbourne Cl YEAD UB4 96 C3 1
Westbourne Crs BAY/PAD W2 9 G6
Westbourne Dr BRW CM14 57 M6
FSTH SE23 140 D5
Westbourne Gdns
BAY/PAD W2 8 C4 1
Westbourne Gv BAY/PAD W2 8 B5
NTGHL W11 100 F6 9
Westbourne Grove Ms
NTGHL W11 8 A5 2
Westbourne Grove Ter
BAY/PAD W2 8 C4
Westbourne Park Rd
BAY/PAD W2 8 B4
NTGHL W11 100 F5
Westbourne Park Vls
BAY/PAD W2 8 B3
Westbourne Pl ED N9 50 B5 1
Westbourne Rd BXLYHN DA7 126 D5
CROY/NA CR0 172 F1
FELT TW13 131 M7
HOLWY N7 85 G6 3
STA TW18 148 B3 1
SYD SE26 158 D2
UX/CGN UB8 95 H3
Westbourne St BAY/PAD W2 9 G6
Westbourne Ter BAY/PAD W2 8 E3
Westbourne Terrace Rd
BAY/PAD W2 8 E3
Westbridge Cl SHB W12 100 A7 2
Westbridge Rd BTSEA SW11 119 K6
Westbrook Av HPTN TW12 150 F3
Westbrook Cl EBAR EN4 34 D6
Westbrook Crs EBAR EN4 34 D6
Westbrook Dr STMC/STPC BR5 177 K3
Westbrooke Crs WELL DA16 126 C8
Westbrooke Rd BFN/LL DA15 143 K6
WELL DA16 126 C8
Westbrook Rd BKHTH/KID SE3 124 B6
HEST TW5 114 F5
THHTH CR7 157 K4
Westbury CHES/WCR EN8 26 D3 2
Westbury Av ALP/SUD HA0 80 E7
ESH/CLAY KT10 166 F8 3
STHL UB1 97 G3
WDGN N22 67 H4
Westbury Cl RSLP HA4 60 A8
SHPTN TW17 164 B1 5
Westbury Gv FNCH N3 47 G8
Westbury La BKHH IG9 52 C4
Westbury Lodge Cl PIN HA5 60 D4
Westbury Pl BTFD TW8 116 D4 9
Westbury Rd ALP/SUD HA0 80 E7
BARK IG11 89 K8
BECK BR3 158 E6
BKHH IG9 52 C3
BMLY BR1 160 D4
CROY/NA CR0 172 D1
EA W5 98 E5
FBAR/BDGN N11 48 E8
FELT TW13 132 D5
FSTGT E7 88 B5
NFNCH/WDSP N12 47 G8
NTHWD HA6 41 L6
NWMAL KT3 153 K7
PGE/AN SE20 158 D4
WALTH E17 69 G5
WATW WD18 29 H8 4
Westbury Ter FSTGT E7 88 B6 2
UPMR RM14 93 L2
Westcar La WOT/HER KT12 165 H8
West Carriage Dr BAY/PAD W2 9 H7
West Central St
NOXST/BSQ WC1A 11 J4
West Chantry
RYLN/HDSTN HA2 61 H2 1
Westchester Dr HDN NW4 64 D4
West Cl ASHF TW15 130 E8
BAR EN5 33 H8
EBAR EN4 35 G7
ED N9 49 M5
GFD/PVL UB6 97 J1 3
RAIN RM13 110 B3
WBLY HA9 80 F1
Westcombe Av CROY/NA CR0 171 L1
Westcombe Dr BAR EN5 34 A8
Westcombe Hl BKHTH/KID SE3 124 A4
Westcombe Park Rd
BKHTH/KID SE3 124 A5
West Common Rd HAYES BR2 175 G4
UX/CGN UB8 76 D5
Westcoombe Av RYNPK SW20 153 M4
Westcote Ri RSLP HA4 59 J8
Westcote Rd
STRHM/NOR SW16 156 C1
Westcott Cl BMLY BR1 160 E8 3
CROY/NA CR0 186 B2 2
SEVS/STOTM N15 67 M7 5
Westcott Crs HNWL W7 97 L4
Westcott Rd WALW SE17 18 D9
Westcott Wy BELMT SM2 181 J3
West Ct ALP/SUD HA0 80 C2
Westcroft Cl CRICK NW2 82 E4
PEND EN3 37 J3 2
Westcroft Gdns MRDN SM4 154 F6
Westcroft Rd CAR SM5 171 G6
Westcroft Sq HMSMTH W6 118 A2 3
Westcroft Wy CRICK NW2 82 E4
West Cross Route SHB W12 100 D6
West Cross Wy BTFD TW8 116 B4
Westdale Rd WOOL/PLUM SE18 125 H4
Westdean Av LEE/GVPK SE12 142 B5
Westdean Cl
WAND/EARL SW18 137 H3 3
West Dene Dr HARH RM3 56 D7
Westdene Wy WEY KT13 164 E5
Westdown Rd CAT SE6 141 G4
SRTFD E15 87 J4
West Drayton Park Av
WDR/YW UB7 112 E1
West Drayton Rd UX/CGN UB8 95 J4
UX/CGN UB8 95 J4
West Dr BELMT SM2 181 K2
CAR SM5 182 D3
GSTN WD25 29 H1
KTN/HRWW/W HA3 43 K8
TOOT SW17 138 B8
West Drive Gdns
KTN/HRWW/W HA3 43 K8
West Eaton Pl KTBR SW1X 16 A5
West Eaton Place Ms
KTBR SW1X 16 A5 3
West Ella Rd WLSDN NW10 81 L7
West End Av LEY E10 69 J6
PIN HA5 60 D5
West End Gdns ESH/CLAY KT10 165 M7
NTHLT UB5 96 C1
West End La BAR EN5 33 K7
ESH/CLAY KT10 165 M7
HYS/HAR UB3 113 J5
KIL/WHAMP NW6 2 B4
KIL/WHAMP NW6 83 G5 7
PIN HA5 60 D4
West End Rd NTHLT UB5 78 C7
RSLP HA4 77 M3
RSLP HA4 78 B5 2
STHL UB1 96 E7
Westerdale Rd GNWCH SE10 124 A3 2
Westerfield Rd
SEVS/STOTM N15 67 M6 10
Westergate Rd ABYW SE2 126 E4
Westerham Av UED N18 49 K5
Westerham Cl BELMT SM2 182 A3 5
Westerham Dr BFN/LL DA15 144 C3
Westerham Rd HAYES BR2 175 K8
LEY E10 69 H7
Westerley Crs SYD SE26 158 F1 2
Western Av ACT W3 99 J3
CHERT KT16 148 A6
DAGE RM10 91 J6
DEN/HRF UB9 76 C4
EA W5 98 E2
GFD/PVL UB6 97 M2
GLDGN NW11 64 D7
GPK RM2 74 C3
HGDN/ICK UB10 77 H6
RSLP HA4 78 B7
Western Ct FNCH N3 47 G8 3
Western Dr SHPTN TW17 149 K8
Western Gdns ACT W3 99 G6
Western Gtwy CAN/RD E16 106 B6 2
Western La BAL SW12 138 A4
Western Ms MV/WKIL W9 100 F3 3
Western Pde BAR EN5 34 A8
Western Perimeter Rd
STWL/WRAY TW19 130 B1
Western Rd BRXN/ST SW9 121 G8
EA W5 98 D6
EFNCH N2 65 M4
MTCM CR4 155 L4
NWDGN UB2 114 C2
PLSTW E13 88 B8
ROM RM1 73 M6
SUT SM1 170 A7
WALTH E17 69 J6
WDGN N22 66 F3 3
WLSDN NW10 99 J3
Western Vw HYS/HAR UB3 95 M8 2
Westernville Gdns
GNTH/NBYPK IG2 71 J8
Western Wy BAR EN5 47 G1
THMD SE28 107 M8
Westferry Rd POP/IOD E14 105 G8
Westfield Av SAND/SEL CR2 184 D6
WATN WD24 29 K3
Westfield Cl CDALE/KGS NW9 63 J4
CHES/WCR EN8 26 F4
PEND EN3 37 L6
SUT SM1 169 M6 3
Westfield Dr KTN/HRWW/W HA3 62 D6
Westfield Gdns
KTN/HRWW/W HA3 62 D5
Westfield La KTN/HRWW/W HA3 62 D5
Westfield Pk PIN HA5 60 F1
Westfield Park Dr WFD IG8 52 E8
Westfield Rd BECK BR3 158 F5
BXLYHN DA7 127 J8
CROY/NA CR0 172 B4
DAGW RM9 90 E4
MLHL NW7 45 K5
MTCM CR4 155 L5
SURB KT6 152 D8
SUT SM1 169 M6
WEA W13 98 B8
WOT/HER KT12 165 L2
Westfields BARN SW13 117 M8
Westfields Av BARN SW13 117 L8
Westfields Rd ACT W3 99 H4
Westfield St WOOL/PLUM SE18 124 D1
Westfield Wy RSLP HA4 77 L3
WCHPL E1 104 E2
West Gdns EW KT17 180 E3
WAP E1W 104 B6 6
WIM/MER SW19 155 L2
West Ga EA W5 98 E2
Westgate Rd BECK BR3 159 J4
DART DA1 146 D3
SNWD SE25 158 B7
Westgate St HACK E8 86 B8 12
Westgate Ter WBPTN SW10 14 D8
Westglade Ct
KTN/HRWW/W HA3 62 D6 1
West Green Pl GFD/PVL UB6 79 K8 3
West Green Rd
SEVS/STOTM N15 67 K5
West Gv GNWCH SE10 123 J6
WFD IG8 52 C8
WOT/HER KT12 165 H6
Westgrove La GNWCH SE10 123 J6
West Halkin St KTBR SW1X 16 A3
West Hallowes ELTH/MOT SE9 142 D5
West Hall Rd RCH/KEW TW9 117 H6
West Ham La SRTFD E15 87 K7 3
West Hampstead Ms
KIL/WHAMP NW6 83 H6
West Harding St
FLST/FETLN EC4A 12 B4 3
Westharold SWLY BR8 163 K6 1
West Hatch Mnr RSLP HA4 77 M1
Westhay Gdns
MORT/ESHN SW14 135 H2
West Heath Av GLDGN NW11 83 G1
West Heath Cl DART DA1 145 M3 1
HAMP NW3 83 G3
West Heath Dr GLDGN NW11 83 G1
West Heath Gdns HAMP NW3 83 G2
West Heath Rd BXLYHN DA7 126 D4
DART DA1 145 M3
HAMP NW3 83 G3
West Hl DART DA1 146 D3
HGT N6 84 A1
HOR/WEW KT19 180 C6
ORP BR6 187 M5

PUT/ROE SW15 .... 136 D4
RYLN/HDSTN HA2 ...... 79 L2
SAND/SEL CR2 .... 184 E2
WAND/EARL SW18 ...... 137 G2
WBLY HA9 .... 80 F1
West Hill Av HOR/WEW KT19 .... 180 C5
West Hill Dr DART DA1 .... 146 C3
Westhill Rd HGT N6 .... 83 M2
West Hill Ri DART DA1 .... 146 D3
West Hill Rd WAND/EARL SW18 .. 136 F3
West Hill Wy TRDG/WHET N20 ... 47 H3
Westholm GLDGN NW11 .... 65 H5
Westholme ORP BR6 .... 176 E2
Westholme Gdns RSLP HA4 ..... 78 A1
Westhorne Av ELTH/MOT SE9 ... 142 C3
Westhorpe Gdns HDN NW4 ...... 64 C4
Westhorpe Rd PUT/ROE SW15 ... 118 C3
West House CI WIM/MER SW19 .. 136 E5
Westhurst Dr CHST BR7 .... 161 H1
West India Av POP/IOD E14 ... 105 G7
West India Dock Rd
POP/IOD E14 .... 104 F5
Westlake CI PLMGR N13 .... 49 G5
YEAD UB4 .... 96 E3
Westland Av EMPK RM11 .... 92 E1
Westland CI
STWL/WRAY TW19 ...... 130 E3
Westland Dr HAYES BR2 .... 174 F4
Westland PI FSBYE EC1V 7 G8
Westland Rd WAT WD17 .... 29 H5
Westlands Ct EPSOM KT18 ..... 180 C8
Westlands Ter BAL SW12 ...... 138 C3
West La BERM/RHTH SE16 ...... 104 B8
Westlea Av GSTN WD25 .... 29 L2
Westlea Rd HNWL W7 .... 116 A1
Westleigh Av PUT/ROE SW15 ... 136 C2
Westleigh Dr BMLY BR1 .... 160 E5
Westleigh Gdns EDGW HA8 ..... 63 G2
West Links ALP/SUD HA0 ...... 98 D2
Westlinton CI MLHL NW7 ...... 46 E8
West Lodge Av ACT W3 .... 99 G7
Westlyn CI RAIN RM13 .... 110 C3
Westmacott Dr
EBED/NFELT TW14 ...... 132 A5
West MI KENS W8 .... 8 B8
West Malling Av HCH RM12 .... 92 B5
Westmead PUT/ROE SW15 .... 136 B4
West Md RSLP HA4 .... 78 C4
Westmeade CI CHESW EN7 ...... 26 B2
Westmead Rd SUT SM1 .... 170 D6
Westmede Dr MLHL NW7 .... 45 K5
West Ms PIM SW1V 16 D6
Westminster Av THHTH CR7 .... 157 H5
Westminster Br WEST SW1P 17 K2
Westminster Bridge Rd
STHWK SE1 .... 17 L2
Westminster CI
EBED/NFELT TW14 ...... 132 A5
TEDD TW11 .... 152 A1
Westminster Dr PLMGR N13 .... 48 E7
Westminster Gdns BARK IG11 .. 107 L1
BARK/HLT IG6 .... 71 K3
CHING E4 .... 51 L3
Westminster Rd ED N9 .... 50 B3
HNWL W7 .... 97 L7
SUT SM1 .... 170 D4
Westmoat CI BECK BR3 .... 159 J3
Westmont Rd ESH/CLAY KT10 .. 166 E4
Westmoor Gdns PEND EN3 ..... 37 K5
Westmoor Rd PEND EN3 .... 37 K5
Westmoor St CHARL SE7 ...... 124 D2
Westmoreland Av
EMPK RM11 .... 74 C6
WELL DA16 .... 125 L8
Westmoreland Dr
BELMT SM2 .... 182 B1
PIM SW1V 16 D8
Westmoreland PI EA W5 ...... 98 C4
PIM SW1V 16 D8
Westmoreland Rd BARN SW13 .. 117 M6
CDALE/KGS NW9 ...... 62 F5
HAYES BR2 .... 159 L8
WALW SE17 .... 19 G9
Westmoreland St
CAVSQ/HST W1G 10 B3
Westmoreland Ter PIM SW1V .. 16 D7
Westmorland CI
HOR/WEW KT19 ...... 180 E2
MNPK E12 .... 88 D2
TWK TW1 .... 134 B3
Westmorland Rd HRW HA1 ..... 61 H6
LEY E10 .... 69 G7
Westmorland Wy MTCM CR4 .... 156 D7
West Mount St ELTH/MOT SE9 .. 124 F7
West Oak BECK BR3 .... 159 K4
Westoe Rd ED N9 .... 50 D4
Weston Av E/WMO/HCT KT8 .... 150 E7
ESH/CLAY KT10 ...... 166 E2
WTHK RM20 .... 129 M2
Weston CI POTB/CUF EN6 ..... 22 F5
Weston Dr KTN/HRWW/W HA3 ... 62 B2
Weston Gdns ISLW TW7 .... 115 L6
Weston Gn DAGW RM9 .... 90 A4
THDIT KT7 .... 166 E4
Weston Green Rd
ESH/CLAY KT10 ...... 166 D3
THDIT KT7 .... 166 E3
Weston Gv BMLY BR1 .... 159 M4
Weston Pk CEND/HSY/T N8 .... 66 E7
KUT KT1 .... 152 E5
THDIT KT7 .... 166 E4
Weston Park CI THDIT KT7 .... 166 E3
Weston Ri FSBYW WC1X 5 M7
Weston Rd BMLY BR1 .... 159 M4
CHSWK W4 .... 117 J1
DAGW RM9 .... 90 A4
ENC/FH EN2 .... 36 D5
EW KT17 .... 180 E4
THDIT KT7 .... 166 E4
Weston St STHWK SE1 .... 19 H2
Weston Wk HACK E8 .... 86 B7
Westover CI BELMT SM2 ...... 182 B2
Westover HI HAMP NW3 .... 83 G2
Westover Rd WAND/EARL SW18 .. 137 J3
Westow HI NRWD SE19 .... 157 L2

Westow St NRWD SE19 .... 157 L2
West Pk ELTH/MOT SE9 .... 142 E6
West Park Av RCH/KEW TW9 ... 117 C6
West Park CI CHDH RM6 ...... 72 C6
HEST TW5 .... 114 F4
West Park Rd HOR/WEW KT19 .. 179 M5
RCH/KEW TW9 ...... 117 C6
STHL UB1 .... 97 J7
West PI WIM/MER SW19 ...... 154 C1
Westpole Av EBAR EN4 .... 35 H7
Westport Rd PLSTW E13 ...... 106 B3
Westport St WCHPL E1 .... 104 D5
West Poultry Av FARR EC1M ... 12 C3
West Quarters SHB W12 ...... 100 A5
West Quay YEAD UB4 .... 96 E4
West Quay Dr YEAD UB4 ...... 96 E4
West Ridge Gdns
GFD/PVL UB6 .... 97 J1
West Riding LCOL/BKTW AL2 .. 21 M3
West Rd CHDH RM6 .... 72 F7
CHSGTN KT9 .... 179 J4
CLAP SW4 .... 138 D2
EA W5 .... 98 E4
EBAR EN4 .... 48 A3
EBED/NFELT TW14 ...... 131 K4
EFNCH N2 .... 65 K3
KUTN/CMB KT2 ...... 153 J4
ROMW/RG RM7 ...... 73 K8
SRTFD E15 .... 87 M8
TOTM N17 .... 50 B8
WDR/YW UB7 .... 112 F1
West Rw NKENS W10 .... 100 D3
Westrow Dr BARK IG11 ...... 89 M1
Westrow Gdns GDMY/SEVK IG3 .. 89 M2
West Sheen Vw RCH/KEW TW9 .. 134 F1
Westside HDN NW4 .... 64 B3
West Side Common
WIM/MER SW19 ...... 154 C1
West Smithfield STBT EC1A ... 12 D3
West Sq LBTH SE11 .... 18 C4
West St BETH E2 .... 104 B1
BMLY BR1 .... 160 A4
BXLYHN DA7 .... 144 F1
CAR SM5 .... 170 F6
CROY/NA CRO 172 C6
EPSOM KT18 .... 180 C6
ERITH DA8 .... 127 K2
EW KT17 .... 180 E3
HOR/WEW KT19 ...... 180 C6
LEY E10 .... 69 H6
RYLN/HDSTN HA2 ...... 79 K1
SUT SM1 .... 170 B7
WAN E11 .... 87 L3
WAT WD17 .... 29 H5
West Street La CAR SM5 .... 170 F6
West Street PI CROY/NA CRO .. 172 C6
West Temple Sheen
MORT/ESHN SW14 ...... 135 H2
West Tenter St WCHPL E1 .... 13 M5
West Towers PIN HA5 .... 60 D7
West Vw EBED/NFELT TW14 .... 131 J5
Westview HNWL W7 .... 97 L5
West Vw LOU IG10 .... 39 M6
Westview CI RAIN RM13 ...... 110 C2
West View CI WLSDN NW10 .... 81 K4
Westview Ct BORE WD6 ...... 44 D1
Westview Crs ED N9 .... 49 L2
Westview Dr WFD IG8 .... 70 D3
West View Gdns BORE WD6 ... 44 D1
West View Rd DART DA1 ..... 146 F3
Westville Rd SHB W12 ...... 100 A1
THDIT KT7 .... 167 G2
West Wk EBAR EN4 .... 48 A3
HYS/HAR UB3 .... 96 A7
Westward Rd CHING E4 ...... 50 F7
Westward Wy
KTN/HRWW/W HA3 ...... 62 E7
West Warwick PI PIM SW1V ... 16 E6
West Wy PIN HA5 .... 60 D5
RKW/CH/CXG WD3 ...... 40 B3
RSLP HA4 .... 77 M1
SHPTN TW17 .... 164 D1
STMC/STPC BR5 ...... 161 K8
UED N18 .... 49 K6
WAB EN9 .... 38 B2
WLSDN NW10 .... 81 K4
WWKM BR4 .... 174 D1
Westway CI RYNPK SW20 ..... 154 B6
West Way Gdns CROY/NA CRO .. 173 K4
Westways HOR/WEW KT19 ..... 168 F6
Westwell CI STMC/STPC BR5 .. 177 K4
Westwell Rd STRHM/NOR SW16 .. 156 E2
Westwell Road Ap
STRHM/NOR SW16 ...... 156 E2
Westwick Gdns HEST TW4 .... 114 B7
HMSMTH W6 .... 100 D1
Westwick PI WGSTN WD25 .... 21 J7
Westwood Av NRWD SE19 ..... 157 J4
RYLN/HDSTN HA2 ...... 79 H4
Westwood CI BMLY BR1 ...... 160 D6
ESH/CLAY KT10 ...... 166 C5
POTB/CUF EN6 ...... 23 C3
RSLP HA4 .... 59 H7
Westwood Gdns
BARN SW13 .... 117 M8
Westwood HI SYD SE26 ..... 158 A1
Westwood La WELL DA16 ..... 144 A1
Westwood Pk FSTH SE23 ..... 140 B4
Westwood Rd BARN SW13 ..... 117 M8
CAN/RD E16 .... 106 B7
GDMY/SEVK IG3 ...... 89 M1
West Woodside BXLY DA5 .... 144 E5
Wetheral Dr STAN HA7 ...... 62 B2
Wetherby CI NTHLT UB5 ..... 79 H6
Wetherby Gdns ECT SW5 ..... 14 E6
Wetherby Ms ECT SW5 ...... 14 D7
Wetherby PI ECT SW5 .... 14 E6
Wetherby Rd BORE WD6 ..... 31 L4
ENC/FH EN2 .... 36 C4

Wetherby Wy CHSGTN KT9 .... 179 L1
Wetherden St WALTH E17 .... 68 F8
Wetherell Rd HOM E9 .... 86 D8
Wetherill Rd MUSWH N10 .... 66 A2
Wettern CI SAND/SEL CR2 ... 184 E3
Wexford Rd BAL SW12 ...... 137 M4
Wey Av CHERT KT16 .... 148 A6
Weybourne PI SAND/SEL CR2 .. 184 D3
Weybourne St
WAND/EARL SW18 ...... 137 J6
Weybridge Pk WEY KT13 ..... 164 B7
Weybridge Rd THHTH CR7 .... 157 G7
Wey Ct HOR/WEW KT19 ...... 168 C6
Weydown CI WIM/MER SW19 ... 136 E5
Weyhill Rd WCHPL E1 ...... 104 A5
Weylands Pk WEY KT13 ..... 164 D8
Weylond Rd BCTR RM8 ...... 90 F3
Weyman Rd BKHTH/KID SE3 ... 124 C6
Weymouth Av EA W5 .... 116 C1
MLHL NW7 .... 45 L7
Weymouth Ms
CAVSQ/HST W1G 10 C3
Weymouth Rd YEAD UB4 ..... 95 L2
Weymouth St CAVSQ/HST W1G .. 10 B2
Weymouth Ter BETH E2 ..... 7 M5
Weymouth Wk STAN HA7 ..... 44 A8
Whadcoat St FSBYPK N4 ..... 85 G2
Whalebone Av CHDH RM6 .... 72 F7
Whalebone Gv CHDH RM6 .... 72 F7
Whalebone La North CHDH RM6 .. 72 E5
Whalebone La South BCTR RM8 .. 72 F8
Whaley Rd POTB/CUF EN6 .... 23 J6
Wharf Bridge Rd ISLW TW7 ... 116 B8
Wharfdale CI FBAR/BDGN N11 ... 5 K5
Wharfdale Gdns
STRHM/NOR SW16 ...... 156 F7
Wharfedale Rd RDART DA2 ... 147 J5
Wharfedale St WBPTN SW10 ... 14 C8
Wharf La RKW/CH/CXG WD3 ... 40 E2
TWK TW1 .... 134 A5
Wharf PI BETH E2 .... 86 A8
Wharf Rd IS N1 .... 6 E6
PEND EN3 .... 50 E1
SRTFD E15 .... 87 K8
Wharfside Rd CAN/RD E16 ... 105 L5
Wharf St CAN/RD E16 ...... 105 L4
Wharncliffe Dr STHL UB1 ... 97 K7
Wharncliffe Gdns SNWD SE25 .. 157 L5
Wharncliffe Rd SNWD SE25 .. 157 K5
Wharton CI WLSDN NW10 ..... 81 L6
Wharton Rd BMLY BR1 ...... 160 B4
Wharton St FSBYW WC1X 5 M8
Whateley Rd EDUL SE22 ..... 139 M2
PGE/AN SE20 .... 158 D3
Whatley Av RYNPK SW20 ..... 154 D6
Whatman Rd FSTH SE23 ..... 140 D4
Whatmore CI
STWL/WRAY TW19 ...... 130 A3
Wheastone Rd NKENS W10 .... 100 E4
Wheatfields PEND EN3 ...... 37 L4
Wheatfield Wy KUT KT1 ..... 152 E6
Wheathill Rd PGE/AN SE20 ... 158 B5
Wheatlands HEST TW5 ...... 115 G4
Wheatlands Rd TOOT SW17 ... 138 A7
Wheatley CI EMPK RM11 ..... 74 D6
HDN NW4 .... 64 A3
Wheatley Gdns ED N9 ...... 49 L4
Wheatley Rd ISLW TW7 ..... 115 M8
Wheatley St CAVSQ/HST W1G .. 10 B3
Wheatsheaf CI NTHLT UB5 ... 77 H3
Wheatsheaf La
FUL/PGN SW6 .... 118 C5
VX/NE SW8 .... 120 E5
Wheatsheaf Rd ROM RM1 .... 73 M7
Wheatsheaf Ter
FUL/PGN SW6 .... 118 F5
Wheatstone CI WIM/MER SW19 .. 155 K4
Wheeler La WCHPL E1 ...... 13 L2
Wheelers Cross BARK IG11 .. 107 K1
Wheelers Dr RSLP HA4 ..... 59 J7
Wheelers La EPSOM KT18 .... 180 C7
Wheel Farm Dr DAGE RM10 ... 91 J3
Wheelright CI BUSH WD23 ... 43 H1
Wheelwright St HOLWY N7 ... 5 L1
Whelan Wy WLGTN SM6 ...... 171 K5
Wheler St WCHPL E1 .... 13 L1
Whellock Rd CHSWK W4 ..... 117 L1
Whenman Av BXLY DA5 ...... 145 J6
Whetstone CI
TRDG/WHET N20 ...... 47 K4
Whetstone Pk LINN WC2A 11 L4
Whetstone Rd BKHTH/KID SE3 .. 124 C7
Whewell Rd ARCH N19 ...... 84 E2
Whetstone CI
TRDG/WHET N20 ...... 47 K4
Whichcote St STHWK SE1 .... 12 A9
Whidborne CI LEW SE13 .... 123 G7
Whimbrel CI PUR/KEN CR8 ... 184 D4
Whimbrel Wy YEAD UB4 ..... 96 D5
Whinchat Rd THMD SE28 .... 125 K1
Whinfell CI STRHM/NOR SW16 .. 156 D1
Whinyates Rd ELTH/MOT SE9 .. 124 E8
Whippendell CI
STMC/STPC BR5 ...... 162 B4
Whippendell Rd WATW WD18 .. 28 E8
Whippendell Wy
STMC/STPC BR5 ...... 162 B4
Whipps Cross Rd WAN E11 ... 69 L6
Whiskin St CLKNW EC1R 6 C8
Whistler Gdns EDGW HA8 .... 62 F3
Whistlers Av BTSEA SW11 ... 119 K5
Whistler St HBRY N5 ...... 85 H4
Whiston Rd BETH E2 .... 7 L5
Whitakers Wy LOU IG10 .... 39 M4
Whitbread CI TOTM N17 .... 68 A2
Whitbread Rd BROCKY SE4 ... 140 E1
Whitburn Rd LEW SE13 ..... 141 H2
Whitby Gdns
CDALE/KGS NW9 ...... 63 G4
SUT SM1 .... 170 D4
Whitby Rd RSLP HA4 .... 78 B3
RYLN/HDSTN HA2 ...... 79 J3
SUT SM1 .... 170 D4
WOOL/PLUM SE18 ...... 124 F2
Whitby St WCHPL E1 .... 7 L9
Whitcher CI NWCR SE14 .... 122 E4

Whitcher PI CAMTN NW1 ..... 84 C6
Whitchurch Av EDGW HA8 .... 62 F1
Whitchurch CI EDGW HA8 .... 44 F8
Whitchurch Gdns EDGW HA8 .. 62 F1
STAN HA7 .... 100 D6
Whitchurch La EDGW HA8 .... 62 E1
Whitchurch Rd HARH RM3 .... 56 E6
NKENS W10 .... 100 B6
Whitcomb St SOHO/SHAV W1D .. 11 G6
White Acre CDALE/KGS NW9 .. 63 L3
Whitear Wk SRTFD E15 ..... 87 K6
SRTFD E15 .... 87 K6
Whitebarn La DAGE RM10 .... 109 G1
White Bear Yd CLKNW EC1R .. 12 A1
White Bridge Av MTCM CR4 .. 155 K7
White Bridge CI
EBED/NFELT TW14 ...... 131 M3
White Butts Rd RSLP HA4 ... 78 D3
Whitechapel High St WCHPL E1 .. 13 M4
Whitechapel Rd WCHPL E1 ... 104 A5
White Church La WCHPL E1 .. 104 A5
White City CI SHB W12 .... 100 C6
White City Rd SHB W12 .... 100 B6
White Conduit St IS N1 .... 6 B5
Whitecote Rd GFD/PVL UB6 .. 97 H5
White Craig CI PIN HA5 .... 43 G7
Whitecroft SWLY BR8 ...... 163 L5
Whitecroft CI BECK BR3 .... 159 K7
Whitecroft Wy BECK BR3 .... 159 J7
Whitecross St STLK EC1Y ... 6 F9
Whitefield Av CRICK NW2 ... 64 C8
Whitefield CI
STMC/STPC BR5 ...... 162 C6
WAND/EARL SW18 ...... 136 E3
Whitefields Rd CHES/WCR EN8 .. 26 C1
Whitefoot La BMLY BR1 .... 141 J8
Whitefoot Ter BMLY BR1 ... 141 M7
Whitefriars Dr
KTN/HRWW/W HA3 ...... 61 L3
Whitefriars St EMB EC4Y ... 12 B5
White Gate Gdns
KTN/HRWW/W HA3 ...... 61 L1
White Gates HCH RM12 ..... 92 C2
Whitegates CI
RKW/CH/CXG WD3 ...... 28 A7
Whitehall LSQ/SEVD WC2H ... 11 H7
WHALL SW1A 11 J9
Whitehall CI CHIG IG7 .... 54 A5
Whitehall Ct CHSGTN KT9 ... 167 K7
WHALL SW1A 11 J9
Whitehall Gdns ACT W3 .... 99 G7
CHING E4 .... 51 K3
CHSWK W4 .... 117 H4
WHALL SW1A 11 J9
Whitehall La BKHH IG9 .... 52 A4
ERITH DA8 .... 127 M7
Whitehall Pk ARCH N19 .... 84 C7
Whitehall PI CAR SM5 ..... 171 H6
WHALL SW1A 11 J9
Whitehall Rd CHING E4 .... 51 L4
HAYES BR2 .... 160 D8
HNWL W7 .... 98 A8
HRW HA1 .... 61 L8
THHTH CR7 .... 157 C8
UX/CGN UB8 .... 76 D8
Whitehall St TOTM N17 .... 67 M1
White Hart Av BARN SW13 ... 117 L7
ROMW/RG RM7 ...... 73 G2
WDGN N22 .... 67 G2
White Hart Rd ORP BR6 .... 177 G2
WOOL/PLUM SE18 ...... 125 L2
White Hart St LBTH SE11 ... 18 B7
Whitehaven CI HAYES BR2 ... 160 A8
Whitehaven St STJWD NW8 ... 9 J1
Whitehead CI RDART DA2 ... 146 C7
UED N18 .... 49 K7
WAND/EARL SW18 ...... 137 J4
Whitehead's Gv CHEL SW3 ... 15 K7
White Heart Av UX/CGN UB8 .. 95 J4
Whiteheath Av RSLP HA4 ... 59 J8
White Heron Ms TEDD TW11 .. 151 M2
White Hl NTHWD HA6 .... 41 G8
SAND/SEL CR2 .... 184 D3
Whitehill Rd DART DA1 .... 146 A2
Whitehorn PI WDR/YW UB7 ... 94 F7
White Horse Dr EPSOM KT18 .. 180 C8
White Horse HI CHST BR7 ... 143 G8
Whitehorse La SNWD SE25 ... 157 L7
White Horse La WCHPL E1 ... 104 D3
Whitehorse Rd CROY/NA CRO .. 157 K8
White Horse Rd EHAM E6 ... 106 C7
Whitehorse Rd WCHPL E1 ... 104 E4
White Horse St
MYFR/PICC W1J 10 D3
Whitehouse Av BORE WD6 .... 32 B7
White House Dr STAN HA7 ... 44 C6
White House La ENC/FH EN2 .. 36 C4
Whitehouse Wy STHGT/OAK N14 .. 48 B4
White Kennett St WCHPL E1 .. 13 K4
White Ledges WEA W13 ..... 98 C5
White Orchards STAN HA7 ... 44 A7
TRDG/WHET N20 ...... 46 F2
White Post La HOM E9 ..... 86 F7
White Post St PECK SE15 ... 122 C5
White Rd SRTFD E15 ...... 87 L7
Whites Av GNTH/NBYPK IG2 .. 71 L7
Whites Dr HAYES BR2 ...... 174 F2
White's Rw WCHPL E1 ..... 13 L3
White's Sq CLAP SW4 ..... 138 D3
Whitestile Rd BTFD TW8 ... 116 C3
Whitestone La HAMP NW3 ... 83 J3
Whitestone Wk HAMP NW3 ... 83 J3
White St NWDGN UB2 ...... 96 D8

Whitethorn Av COUL/CHIP CR5 .. 183 G8
WDR/YW UB7 .... 94 E6
Whitethorn Gdns
CROY/NA CRO 173 H4
EMPK RM11 .... 74 C7
ENC/FH EN2 .... 36 D8
Whitethorn St BOW E3 ..... 105 C3
Whitewebbs La ENC/FH EN2 .. 25 M8
Whitewebbs Rd ENC/FH EN2 .. 25 H8
Whitewebbs Wy
STMC/STPC BR5 ...... 161 M4
Whitfield PI FITZ W1T 10 E1
Whitfield Rd BXLYHN DA7 ... 126 F5
EHAM E6 .... 88 C7
GNWCH SE10 .... 123 K6
Whitfield St FITZ W1T 10 E1
Whitford Gdns MTCM CR4 ... 155 M6
Whitgift Av SAND/SEL CR2 .. 172 C5
Whitgift St CROY/NA CRO ... 172 C5
LBTH SE11 .... 17 L5
Whit Hern Ct CHES/WCR EN8 .. 26 C3
Whitings Rd BAR EN5 ...... 33 J8
Whitings Wy EHAM E6 ...... 107 G4
Whitland Rd CAR SM5 ...... 170 D3
Whitlars Dr KGLGY WD4 .... 20 A1
Whitley CI ABLGY WD5 ..... 21 C5
STWL/WRAY TW19 ...... 130 E3
Whitley Rd TOTM N17 ..... 67 L3
Whitlock Dr WIM/MER SW19 .. 136 E4
Whitman Rd WCHPL E1 ..... 104 E3
Whitmead CI SAND/SEL CR2 .. 172 D8
Whitmore Av HARH RM3 .... 74 E3
Whitmore CI FBAR/BDGN N11 .. 48 B7
Whitmore Gdns WLSDN NW10 .. 100 C1
Whitmore Rd BECK BR3 .... 158 F6
HRW HA1 .... 61 J8
IS N1 .... 7 J4
Whitmores CI EPSOM KT18 .. 180 C8
Whitnell Wy PUT/ROE SW15 .. 136 C2
Whitney Av REDBR IG4 ..... 70 D5
Whitney Rd LEY E10 ...... 69 G8
Whitney Wk SCUP DA14 .... 162 E2
Whitstable CI BECK BR3 ... 158 F4
Whitstable PI CROY/NA CRO .. 172 C6
Whittaker Av
RCH/KEW TW9 .... 134 D2
Whittaker Rd CHEAM SM3 ... 169 M5
EHAM E6 .... 88 D7
Whittaker St BGVA SW1W ... 16 A6
Whitta Rd MNPK E12 ...... 88 D4
Whittell Gdns SYD SE26 ... 140 C7
Whittingstall Rd FUL/PGN SW6 .. 118 F6
Whittington Av BANK EC3V .. 13 J5
YEAD UB4 .... 95 M4
Whittington Ms
NFNCH/WDSP N12 ...... 47 J6
Whittington Rd WDGN N22 ... 48 F8
Whittington Wy PIN HA5 ... 60 E6
Whittlebury CI CAR SM5 ... 182 F1
Whittle CI GFD/PVL UB6 ... 97 H5
WALTH E17 .... 68 E7
Whittle Rd HEST TW5 ..... 114 C5
NWDGN UB2 .... 97 H8
Whittlesea Rd
KTN/HRWW/W HA3 ...... 61 J1
Whittlesey St STHWK SE1 ... 12 B9
Whitton Av East GFD/PVL UB6 .. 79 H5
Whitton Av West NTHLT UB5 .. 79 H5
Whitton CI GFD/PVL UB6 ... 80 B6
Whitton Dene HSLW TW3 .... 133 H2
WHTN TW2 .... 133 K3
Whitton Dr GFD/PVL UB6 ... 80 A6
Whitton Manor Rd ISLW TW7 .. 133 J3
Whitton Rd HSLW TW3 ..... 133 H1
WHTN TW2 .... 133 L3
Whitton Waye HSLW TW3 .... 133 G3
Whitwell Rd GSTN WD25 .... 21 K8
PLSTW E13 .... 106 A2
Whitworth Rd SNWD SE25 ... 157 L6
WOOL/PLUM SE18 ...... 125 C5
Whitworth St GNWCH SE10 ... 123 L3
Whorlton Rd PECK SE15 .... 122 A8
Whybridge CI RAIN RM13 ... 91 L8
Whymark Av WDGN N22 ..... 67 G4
Whytecliffe Rd North
PUR/KEN CR8 .... 184 B4
Whytecliffe Rd South
PUR/KEN CR8 .... 184 B4
Whytecroft HEST TW5 ..... 114 D5
Whyteville Rd FSTGT E7 ... 88 B6
Wichling CI STMC/STPC BR5 .. 177 K3
Wickersley Rd BTSEA SW11 .. 120 A8
Wicket Rd GFD/PVL UB6 .... 98 A2
The Wickets ASHF TW15 .... 130 E8
Wickets Wy BARK/HLT IG6 .. 53 M8
The Wicket CROY/NA CRO ... 174 A7
Wickford Dr HARH RM3 .... 56 F7
Wickford St WCHPL E1 .... 104 C3
Wickford Wy WALTH E17 ... 68 C5
Wickham Av CHEAM SM3 .... 169 J7
CROY/NA CRO 173 L4
Wickham Cha WWKM BR4 .... 174 D2
Wickham CI DEN/HRF UB9 ... 58 D2
EN EN1 .... 37 H6
NWMAL KT3 .... 153 M8
Wickham Court Rd WWKM BR4 .. 174 C4
Wickham Crs WWKM BR4 .... 174 C4
Wickham Gdns BROCKY SE4 .. 122 F4
Wickham La ABYW SE2 ..... 126 A4
Wickham Rd BECK BR3 ..... 159 H6
BROCKY SE4 .... 122 F8
CHING E4 .... 69 J1
CROY/NA CRO 173 J4
KTN/HRWW/W HA3 ...... 61 K3
Wickham St LBTH SE11 .... 17 L7
WELL DA16 .... 125 J7
Wickham Wy BECK BR3 ..... 159 J7
Wick La BOW E3 .... 105 G1
Wickliffe Av FNCH N3 .... 64 E3
Wickliffe Gdns WBLY HA9 .. 81 G2
Wicklow St FSBYW WC1X 5 L7
Wick Rd HOM E9 .... 86 D6
TEDD TW11 .... 152 B3
Wicks CI LEE/GVPK SE12 ... 142 D8
Wicksteed CI BXLY DA5 ... 145 K7
Wickwood St CMBW SE5 .... 121 H7
Widdenham Rd HOLWY N7 ... 84 F4

Widdicombe Av
RYLN/HDSTN HA2 ... 78 E2
Widdin St SRTFD E15 ... 87 L7 10
Widecombe Cl HARH RM3 ... 74 D2 4
Widecombe Gdns REDBR IG4 ... 70 E5
Widecombe Rd ELTH/MOT SE9 .. 142 E7
Widecombe Wy EFNCH N2 ... 65 K6
Widegate St WCHPL E1 ... 13 K3 2
Widenham Cl PIN HA5 ... 60 C6 5
Wide Wy STRHM/NOR SW16 ... 156 D6
Widgeon Cl CAN/RD E16 ... 106 B5
Widgeon Rd ERITH DA8 ... 128 B5
Widgeon Wy GSTN WD25 ... 29 L1 2
Widley Rd MV/WKIL W9 ... 2 B8
Widmore Lodge Rd BMLY BR1 ... 160 D5
Widmore Rd BMLY BR1 ... 160 B5
UX/CGN UB8 ... 95 H3
Wieland Rd NTHWD HA6 ... 60 A1
Wigeon Wy YEAD UB4 ... 96 D5
Wiggenhall Rd WATW WD18 ... 29 H8
Wiggins Md CDALE/KGS NW9 ... 63 M1
Wigginton Av WBLY HA9 ... 81 G6
Wightman Rd CEND/HSY/T N8 ... 67 G5
Wigley Bush La BRW CM14 ... 57 L4
Wigley Rd FELT TW13 ... 132 D6
Wigmore Pl CAVSQ/HST W1G ... 10 C4 2
Wigmore Rd CAR SM5 ... 170 D4
Wigmore St MBLAR W1H ... 10 B4
Wigram Rd WAN E11 ... 70 C7
Wigram Sq WALTH E17 ... 69 J3
Wigston Cl UED N18 ... 49 L7
Wigston Rd PLSTW E13 ... 106 B3
Wigton Gdns STAN HA7 ... 62 E2
Wigton Pl LBTH SE11 ... 18 B8 1
Wigton Rd HARH RM3 ... 56 E6
WALTH E17 ... 68 F2
Wigton Wy HARH RM3 ... 56 E6
Wilberforce Rd CDALE/KGS NW9 .. 63 M6
FSBYPK N4 ... 85 J3 2
FSBYPK N4 ... 85 H2 3
Wilberforce Wy
WIM/MER SW19 ... 154 D2 2
Wilbraham Pl KTBR SW1X ... 15 M5
Wilbury Av BELMT SM2 ... 181 M3
Wilbury Wy UED N18 ... 49 K7
Wilby Ms NTGHL W11 ... 100 F6
Wilcot Av OXHEY WD19 ... 42 E2
Wilcot Cl OXHEY WD19 ... 42 E2
Wilcox Cl BORE WD6 ... 32 C4
Wilcox Gdns SHPTN TW17 ... 148 F6 2
Wilcox Rd SUT SM1 ... 170 B6 3
TEDD TW11 ... 133 K8
VX/NE SW8 ... 120 E5
Wild Ct HOL/ALD WC2B ... 11 L4 1
Wildcroft Gdns STAN HA7 ... 44 D8 1
Wildcroft Rd PUT/ROE SW15 ... 136 C4
Wilde Cl HACK E8 ... 86 A8 13
Wilde Pl PLMGR N13 ... 49 H8
Wilder Cl RSLP HA4 ... 78 B1
Wilderness Rd CHST BR7 ... 161 H3
The Wilderness
E/WMO/HCT KT8 ... 151 J8
HPTN TW12 ... 133 H8 2
Wilde Rd ERITH DA8 ... 127 H5
Wilderton Rd STNW/STAM N16 ... 67 L8
Wildfell Rd CAT SE6 ... 141 H4
Wild Goose Dr NWCR SE14 ... 122 C6 3
Wild Hatch GLDGN NW11 ... 65 G7
Wild Oaks Cl NTHWD HA6 ... 41 M8
Wild's Rents STHWK SE1 ... 19 J3
Wild St HOL/ALD WC2B ... 11 K5
Wildwood NTHWD HA6 ... 41 K8
Wildwood Av LCOL/BKTW AL2 ... 21 M3
Wildwood Cl LEE/GVPK SE12 ... 141 M4
Wildwood Ct PUR/KEN CR8 ... 184 D8
Wildwood Gv GLDGN NW11 ... 83 J1
Wildwood Ri GLDGN NW11 ... 83 J1
Wildwood Rd GLDGN NW11 ... 65 J8
Wilford Cl ENC/FH EN2 ... 36 D6 3
NTHWD HA6 ... 59 K1
Wilford Rd CROY/NA CR0 ... 172 C2 5
Wilfred Av RAIN RM13 ... 110 A4
Wilfred St WESTW SW1E ... 16 E3
Wilfrid Gdns ACT W3 ... 99 J4
Wilkes Rd BTFD TW8 ... 116 E4 4
Wilkes St WCHPL E1 ... 13 M2
Wilkins Cl HYS/HAR UB3 ... 113 M3
MTCM CR4 ... 155 L4
Wilkinson Rd CAN/RD E16 ... 106 C5
Wilkinson St VX/NE SW8 ... 120 F5
Wilkinson Wy CHSWK W4 ... 99 K8
Wilkin St KTTN NW5 ... 84 A6 12
Wilks Av DART DA1 ... 146 F6
Wilks Gdns CROY/NA CR0 ... 173 L3
Wilks Pl IS N1 ... 7 K6
Willan Rd TOTM N17 ... 67 K3
Willan Wall CAN/RD E16 ... 105 M6 5
Willard St VX/NE SW8 ... 120 B8 5
Willcocks Cl CHSGTN KT9 ... 167 L5
Willcott Rd ACT W3 ... 99 H7
Will Crooks Gdns
ELTH/MOT SE9 ... 142 C1
Willenhall Av BAR EN5 ... 47 J1
Willenhall Dr HYS/HAR UB3 ... 95 L6
Willenhall Rd
WOOL/PLUM SE18 ... 125 H3
Willersley Av BFN/LL DA15 ... 143 M5
ORP BR6 ... 176 D5
Willersley Cl BFN/LL DA15 ... 143 M5
Willesden La KIL/WHAMP NW6 ... 82 D7
Willes Rd KTTN NW5 ... 84 B6 3
Willet Cl NTHLT UB5 ... 96 C2 4
Willett Cl STMC/STPC BR5 ... 176 E1
Willett Rd THHTH CR7 ... 157 G8
Willett Wy STMC/STPC BR5 ... 161 K8
William Barefoot Dr
ELTH/MOT SE9 ... 143 G6
William Booth Rd PGE/AN SE20 .. 158 A4
William Carey Wy HRW HA1 ... 61 L7 3
William Cl CRW RM5 ... 73 J2
EFNCH N2 ... 65 K4
LEW SE13 ... 123 J8 5
STHL UB1 ... 97 J8 5
William Covell Cl ENC/FH EN2 .. 35 M3 3
William Gdns PUT/ROE SW15 ... 136 B2
William Guy Gdns BOW E3 ... 105 H2 7
William Iv St CHCR WC2N ... 11 J7
William Margrie Cl
PECK SE15 ... 122 A7 5
William Ms KTBR SW1X ... 15 M2
William Morley Cl EHAM E6 ... 88 D8
William Morris Cl WALTH E17 ... 68 F4
William Morris Wy
FUL/PGN SW6 ... 119 J8
William Rd CAMTN NW1 ... 4 E8
SUT SM1 ... 170 C7
WIM/MER SW19 ... 154 E3
Williams Av WALTH E17 ... 68 F2
William's Buildings
BETH E2 ... 104 C3 12
Williams Gv WDGN N22 ... 67 G2 2
Williams La MORT/ESHN SW14 ... 117 J8
MRDN SM4 ... 170 C1
Williamson Cl GNWCH SE10 ... 123 M3 6
Williamson Rd FSBYPK N4 ... 67 H7 3
Williamson St HOLWY N7 ... 84 E4 3
Williamson Wy MLHL NW7 ... 46 E8 1
RKW/CH/CXG WD3 ... 40 A3
William Sq POP/IOD E14 ... 104 E6 3
Williams Rd NWDGN UB2 ... 114 E2
WEA W13 ... 98 A7 3
Williams Ter CROY/NA CR0 ... 172 A8
William St BARK IG11 ... 89 J7
BUSH WD23 ... 29 K6
CAR SM5 ... 170 E5
KTBR SW1X ... 15 M2
LEY E10 ... 69 J7
TOTM N17 ... 67 M1
Willifield Wy GLDGN NW11 ... 65 G6
Willingdon Rd WDGN N22 ... 67 H3
Willinghall Cl WAB EN9 ... 27 K5 1
Willingham Ter KTTN NW5 ... 84 C5 5
Willingham Wy KUT KT1 ... 153 G5
Willington Rd BRXN/ST SW9 ... 120 E8
Willis Av BELMT SM2 ... 170 E8
Willis Cl EPSOM KT18 ... 180 B6
Willis Rd CROY/NA CR0 ... 172 C2
ERITH DA8 ... 127 J2
SRTFD E15 ... 105 M1
Willis St POP/IOD E14 ... 105 H5
Willmore End WIM/MER SW19 ... 155 H4
Willoughby Av CROY/NA CR0 ... 171 M6
Willoughby Dr RAIN RM13 ... 91 L7 1
Willoughby Gv TOTM N17 ... 68 B1 4
Willoughby La TOTM N17 ... 68 B1
UED N18 ... 50 B8 1
Willoughby Ms TOTM N17 ... 68 B1 5
Willoughby Park Rd TOTM N17 ... 68 B1
Willoughby Rd CEND/HSY/T N8 ... 67 G4
HAMP NW3 ... 83 K4
KUTN/CMB KT2 ... 152 F4
TWK TW1 ... 134 C2 2
Willoughby Wy CHARL SE7 ... 124 B2
Willow Av BARN SW13 ... 117 M7
BFN/LL DA15 ... 144 A3
DEN/HRF UB9 ... 76 C6
SWLY BR8 ... 163 M7
WDR/YW UB7 ... 94 F6
Willow Bridge Rd IS N1 ... 85 J6 11
Willowbrook Rd NWDGN UB2 ... 114 F1
PECK SE15 ... 121 M4
STWL/WRAY TW19 ... 130 E5
The Willow Centre MTCM CR4 ... 155 M8
Willow Cl BKHH IG9 ... 52 D5
BTFD TW8 ... 116 C4
BXLY DA5 ... 144 F3
HAYES BR2 ... 160 F8
HCH RM12 ... 92 B3 4
STMC/STPC BR5 ... 177 H1
Willowcourt Av
KTN/HRWW/W HA3 ... 62 B6
Willow Crs East DEN/HRF UB9 ... 76 C5
Willow Crs West DEN/HRF UB9 ... 76 C5
Willow Dean PIN HA5 ... 60 D3 2
Willow Dene BUSH WD23 ... 43 L2
PIN HA5 ... 60 D3
Willowdene Cl WHTN TW2 ... 133 J4 1
Willow Dr BAR EN5 ... 33 L7
Willow Edge KGLGY WD4 ... 20 A2 3
Willow End NTHWD HA6 ... 42 A8
TRDG/WHET N20 ... 47 G4
Willow Gdns HEST TW5 ... 115 G6 3
RSLP HA4 ... 77 M2
Willow Gv CHST BR7 ... 161 G2
RSLP HA4 ... 77 M2
Willowhayne Dr
WOT/HER KT12 ... 165 H2
Willowhayne Gdns WPK KT4 ... 169 J6 1
Willow La MTCM CR4 ... 155 M8
WATW WD18 ... 29 G8
Willowmead CHIG IG7 ... 54 A5
STA TW18 ... 148 B4 2
Willowmead Cl EA W5 ... 98 D4 3
Willowmere ESH/CLAY KT10 ... 166 C6
Willow Mt CROY/NA CR0 ... 172 E5 4
Willow Pl WEST SW1P ... 16 F5
Willow Rd CHDH RM6 ... 72 E7
DART DA1 ... 146 C5
EA W5 ... 98 E8
EN EN1 ... 36 E5
ERITH DA8 ... 128 A6
HAMP NW3 ... 83 K4
NWMAL KT3 ... 153 J7
WLGTN SM6 ... 183 H1
Willows Av MRDN SM4 ... 155 H8
Willows Cl PIN HA5 ... 60 C3
Willows Pth EPSOM KT18 ... 180 B7
The Willows ESH/CLAY KT10 ... 166 E8 3
OXHEY WD19 ... 42 B2 3
RKW/CH/CXG WD3 ... 40 A4
WEY KT13 ... 164 A5
Willow St CHING E4 ... 51 K2
ROMW/RG RM7 ... 73 J5
SDTCH EC2A ... 7 J9
Willowtree Cl HGDN/ICK UB10 ... 77 J3
Willow Tree Cl HOM E9 ... 86 E8
WAND/EARL SW18 ... 137 H5 3
YEAD UB4 ... 96 C3
Willow Tree La YEAD UB4 ... 96 C3
Willow Tree Wk BMLY BR1 ... 160 B4 5
Willowtree Wy
STRHM/NOR SW16 ... 157 G4
Willow V CHST BR7 ... 161 G2
SHB W12 ... 100 A7
Willow Vw WIM/MER SW19 ... 155 K4
Willow Wk CHEAM SM3 ... 169 M5
ORP BR6 ... 176 B5
SEVS/STOTM N15 ... 67 H5 6
STHWK SE1 ... 19 K5
UPMR RM14 ... 93 L1
WALTH E17 ... 68 F6
WCHMH N21 ... 48 F1
Willow Wy ALP/SUD HA0 ... 80 A3 1
FNCH N3 ... 65 H1
HARH RM3 ... 57 H8
HOR/WEW KT19 ... 168 D8
POTB/CUF EN6 ... 23 H6
RAD WD7 ... 30 E1
SUN TW16 ... 150 A7
SYD SE26 ... 140 B7
WHTN TW2 ... 133 H6
Willow Wood Crs SNWD SE25 ... 172 E1
Willrose Crs ABYW SE2 ... 126 B3
Wills Crs HSLW TW3 ... 133 H3
Wills Gv MLHL NW7 ... 46 A7
Willshaw St NWCR SE14 ... 123 G6 5
Wilman Gv HACK E8 ... 86 A7
Wilmar Cl UX/CGN UB8 ... 76 D7
YEAD UB4 ... 95 K3
Wilmar Gdns WWKM BR4 ... 174 B3
Wilmer Cl RCHPK/HAM TW10 ... 152 F1
Wilmer Crs RCHPK/HAM TW10 ... 152 F1
Wilmer Gdns IS N1 ... 7 J4
Wilmer Lea Cl SRTFD E15 ... 87 K7 9
Wilmer Pl STNW/STAM N16 ... 85 M2 7
Wilmer Wy STHGT/OAK N14 ... 48 D7
Wilmington Av CHSWK W4 ... 117 K5
ORP BR6 ... 177 J4
Wilmington Court Rd
RDART DA2 ... 146 A7
Wilmington Gdns BARK IG11 ... 89 K7
Wilmington Sq FSBYW WC1X ... 6 A8
Wilmington St FSBYW WC1X ... 6 A8
Wilmot Pl CAMTN NW1 ... 4 E1
HNWL W7 ... 97 L7 4
Wilmot Rd CAR SM5 ... 170 F7 5
DART DA1 ... 146 B2
LEY E10 ... 87 H2
PUR/KEN CR8 ... 184 A5
TOTM N17 ... 67 K4
Wilmot St BETH E2 ... 104 B3
Wilmot Wy BNSTD SM7 ... 182 A8
Wilmount St
WOOL/PLUM SE18 ... 125 H2 11
Wilna Rd WAND/EARL SW18 ... 137 J4
Wilsham St NTGHL W11 ... 100 D7
Wilsmere Dr KTN/HRWW/W HA3 .. 61 L1
NTHLT UB5 ... 78 E6
Wilson Av MTCM CR4 ... 155 L3
Wilson Cl SAND/SEL CR2 ... 172 D7 7
WBLY HA9 ... 62 F8
Wilson Dr WBLY HA9 ... 62 F8
Wilson Gdns HRW HA1 ... 61 J8
Wilson Gv BERM/RHTH SE16 ... 104 B8
Wilson Rd CHSGTN KT9 ... 167 M8
CMBW SE5 ... 121 K6
IL IG1 ... 70 F8
PLSTW E13 ... 106 D2
Wilson's Av TOTM N17 ... 67 M3 2
Wilson's Pl POP/IOD E14 ... 104 F5 7
Wilson's Rd HMSMTH W6 ... 118 D3 1
Wilson St SDTCH EC2A ... 13 H2
WALTH E17 ... 69 J6
WCHMH N21 ... 49 G2
Wilstone Cl YEAD UB4 ... 96 E3 10
Wilthorne Gdns DAGE RM10 ... 91 H7 2
Wilton Av CHSWK W4 ... 117 L3
Wilton Cl WDR/YW UB7 ... 112 D4 1
Wilton Crs KTBR SW1X ... 16 A2
WIM/MER SW19 ... 154 F4
Wilton Dr CRW RM5 ... 73 J1
Wilton Gdns E/WMO/HCT KT8 ... 151 G6
WOT/HER KT12 ... 165 K3 1
Wilton Gv NWMAL KT3 ... 168 F1
WIM/MER SW19 ... 154 F3
Wilton Ms KTBR SW1X ... 16 B3
Wilton Pl KTBR SW1X ... 16 A1
Wilton Rd ABYW SE2 ... 126 C1
EBAR EN4 ... 34 F7
HSLWW TW4 ... 114 D8
MUSWH N10 ... 66 A3
PIM SW1V ... 16 E4
WIM/MER SW19 ... 155 L3
Wilton Rw KTBR SW1X ... 16 A2
Wilton Sq IS N1 ... 7 G3
Wilton St KTBR SW1X ... 16 C3
Wilton Ter KTBR SW1X ... 16 A3
Wilton Vls IS N1 ... 7 G4
Wilton Wy HACK E8 ... 86 A6
Wiltshire Av EMPK RM11 ... 74 F5
Wiltshire Cl MLHL NW7 ... 45 M7 3
RDART DA2 ... 147 K4
Wiltshire Gdns FSBYPK N4 ... 67 J7
WHTN TW2 ... 133 J5
Wiltshire La PIN HA5 ... 60 A5
RSLP HA4 ... 59 M4
Wiltshire Rd BRXN/ST SW9 ... 121 G8
ORP BR6 ... 177 G2
THHTH CR7 ... 157 G6
Wiltshire Rw IS N1 ... 7 G4
Wilverley Crs NWMAL KT3 ... 168 E1
Wimbart Rd
BRXS/STRHM SW2 ... 138 F4 2
Wimbledon Br
WIM/MER SW19 ... 154 F2 4
Wimbledon Hill Rd
WIM/MER SW19 ... 154 E2
Wimbledon Park Rd
WAND/EARL SW18 ... 136 F5
WIM/MER SW19 ... 136 E6
Wimbledon Park Side
WIM/MER SW19 ... 136 D6
Wimbledon Rd TOOT SW17 ... 137 J8
Wimbolt St BETH E2 ... 104 A2
Wimborne Av NWDGN UB2 ... 115 G2
STMC/STPC BR5 ... 161 M6
YEAD UB4 ... 96 B5
Wimborne Cl BKHH IG9 ... 52 C4
EW KT17 ... 180 E6
LEE/GVPK SE12 ... 141 M2
WPK KT4 ... 169 J3 1
Wimborne Dr CDALE/KGS NW9 ... 63 G4
PIN HA5 ... 60 D8
Wimborne Gdns WEA W13 ... 98 B5
Wimborne Gv WAT WD17 ... 28 E2
Wimborne Rd ED N9 ... 50 A4 5
TOTM N17 ... 67 L3
Wimborne Wy BECK BR3 ... 158 D6
Wimbourne St IS N1 ... 7 G5
Wimpole Cl HAYES BR2 ... 160 C7
KUT KT1 ... 153 G5 3
Wimpole Ms CAVSQ/HST W1G ... 10 C2
Wimpole Rd WDR/YW UB7 ... 94 D7
Wimpole St CAVSQ/HST W1G ... 10 C4 3
Wimshurst Cl CROY/NA CR0 ... 171 L3
Winans Wk BRXN/ST SW9 ... 121 G7
Wincanton Crs NTHLT UB5 ... 79 G5
Wincanton Gdns BARK/HLT IG6 ... 71 H4
Wincanton Rd HARH RM3 ... 56 D5
WAND/EARL SW18 ... 136 F4
Winchcombe Rd CAR SM5 ... 170 D2
Winchcomb Gdns
ELTH/MOT SE9 ... 124 E8 2
Winchelsea Av BXLYHN DA7 ... 126 F5
Winchelsea Cl PUT/ROE SW15 ... 136 D2 4
Winchelsea Rd TOTM N17 ... 67 L4
WLSDN NW10 ... 81 K8
Winchelsey Ri SAND/SEL CR2 ... 172 F8
Winchendon Rd FUL/PGN SW6 .. 118 F5
TEDD TW11 ... 133 K8
Winchester Av CDALE/KGS NW9 .. 62 F4
HEST TW5 ... 114 F4
KIL/WHAMP NW6 ... 82 E8
UPMR RM14 ... 93 M1
Winchester Cl EN EN1 ... 36 E8 2
ESH/CLAY KT10 ... 166 A6
HAYES BR2 ... 159 M6 1
KUTN/CMB KT2 ... 153 H3
Winchester Dr PIN HA5 ... 60 D6
Winchester Pk HAYES BR2 ... 159 M6
Winchester Pl HACK E8 ... 85 M5 5
HGT N6 ... 84 B1 2
Winchester Rd CHING E4 ... 69 J1
ED N9 ... 49 M3
FELT TW13 ... 132 F7
HAMP NW3 ... 3 H1
HAYES BR2 ... 159 M6
HGT N6 ... 84 B1
HYS/HAR UB3 ... 113 L5
IL IG1 ... 89 K3
KTN/HRWW/W HA3 ... 62 E5
ORP BR6 ... 177 J6
TWK TW1 ... 134 B3
WELL DA16 ... 126 D7
WOT/HER KT12 ... 165 G3
Winchester Sq STHWK SE1 ... 13 G8 4
Winchester St ACT W3 ... 99 J7
PIM SW1V ... 16 D7
Winchester Wk STHWK SE1 ... 13 G8
Winchester Wy
RKW/CH/CXG WD3 ... 28 B8
Winchfield Cl
KTN/HRWW/W HA3 ... 62 C7
Winchfield Rd SYD SE26 ... 158 E1
Winchfield Wy
RKW/CH/CXG WD3 ... 40 C2
Winchilsea Crs
E/WMO/HCT KT8 ... 151 J5
Winchmore Hill Rd
STHGT/OAK N14 ... 48 E2
Winchstone Cl SHPTN TW17 ... 148 F7
Winckley Cl KTN/HRWW/W HA3 ... 62 F6
Wincott St LBTH SE11 ... 18 B5
Wincrofts Dr ELTH/MOT SE9 ... 143 K1
Windall Cl NRWD SE19 ... 158 A4 2
Windborough Rd CAR SM5 ... 183 G1
Windermere Av FNCH N3 ... 65 G3
HCH RM12 ... 92 A5
KIL/WHAMP NW6 ... 82 E8
RSLP HA4 ... 60 C8
WBLY HA9 ... 62 C8 2
WIM/MER SW19 ... 155 H6
Windermere Cl DART DA1 ... 146 B5
EBED/NFELT TW14 ... 131 M5 16
ORP BR6 ... 176 B5
STWL/WRAY TW19 ... 130 D5 2
Windermere Gdns REDBR IG4 ... 70 E6
Windermere Gv WBLY HA9 ... 80 C1 2
Windermere Rd ARCH N19 ... 84 C2 5
BXLYHN DA7 ... 127 J7
COUL/CHIP CR5 ... 183 L8
CROY/NA CR0 ... 172 F2
EA W5 ... 116 C1
MUSWH N10 ... 66 B2
PUT/ROE SW15 ... 135 L8
STHL UB1 ... 96 F4
STRHM/NOR SW16 ... 156 C4
WWKM BR4 ... 174 E4
Windermere Wy
WDR/YW UB7 ... 94 E7 1
Winders Rd BTSEA SW11 ... 119 L7 7
Windfield Cl SYD SE26 ... 140 D8 2
Windham Av CROY/NA CR0 ... 186 D3
Windham Rd RCH/KEW TW9 ... 116 F8 6
The Windings SAND/SEL CR2 ... 184 F4
Winding Wy BCTR RM8 ... 90 C3
Windlass Pl DEPT SE8 ... 122 E2
Windlesham Gv
WIM/MER SW19 ... 136 D5
Windley Cl FSTH SE23 ... 140 C6 1
Windmill Av EW KT17 ... 180 F4
Windmill Cl EW KT17 ... 180 F5
LEW SE13 ... 123 J7 2
SUN TW16 ... 149 L3
SURB KT6 ... 167 J3
UPMR RM14 ... 93 G2 2
WAB EN9 ... 27 L7
Windmill Dr CLAP SW4 ... 138 B2
HAYES BR2 ... 175 J6
RKW/CH/CXG WD3 ... 40 F1
Windmill End EW KT17 ... 180 F5 5
Windmill Gdns ENC/FH EN2 ... 36 A5
Windmill Gv CROY/NA CR0 ... 172 C2
Windmill Hl ENC/FH EN2 ... 36 B6
RSLP HA4 ... 59 M8
Windmill La BAR EN5 ... 45 M1
BUSH WD23 ... 43 L3
CHES/WCR EN8 ... 26 E3
EW KT17 ... 180 F5
GFD/PVL UB6 ... 97 J4
NWDGN UB2 ... 115 K1
SRTFD E15 ... 87 K6
STHL UB1 ... 97 J8
THDIT KT7 ... 167 H2
Windmill Pas CHSWK W4 ... 117 L2 4
Windmill Ri KUTN/CMB KT2 ... 153 H3
Windmill Rd CHSWK W4 ... 117 L2
CROY/NA CR0 ... 172 C2
EA W5 ... 116 C2
HPTN TW12 ... 151 H1
MTCM CR4 ... 156 C8
SUN TW16 ... 149 L4
UED N18 ... 49 K6
WAND/EARL SW18 ... 137 K3
WIM/MER SW19 ... 154 B1
Windmill Rd West SUN TW16 ... 149 L4 1
Windmill Rw LBTH SE11 ... 18 A8
Windmill St BUSH WD23 ... 43 L3
FITZ W1T ... 11 G3
Windmill Wk STHWK SE1 ... 12 B9 1
Windmill Wy RSLP HA4 ... 77 M1
Windmore Av POTB/CUF EN6 ... 22 C4
Windrose Cl BERM/RHTH SE16 ... 104 D8
Windrush Cl BTSEA SW11 ... 137 K1 5
CHSWK W4 ... 117 J5 5
HGDN/ICK UB10 ... 76 F4
Windrush La FSTH SE23 ... 140 D7
Windsor Av CHEAM SM3 ... 169 L5
E/WMO/HCT KT8 ... 151 G6
EDGW HA8 ... 45 H6
HGDN/ICK UB10 ... 77 H7
NWMAL KT3 ... 153 J8
WALTH E17 ... 68 E3
WIM/MER SW19 ... 155 J4
Windsor Cl CHESW EN7 ... 26 A3
CHST BR7 ... 161 H1
FNCH N3 ... 64 E3 4
NTHWD HA6 ... 60 A3
RYLN/HDSTN HA2 ... 79 G3
WNWD SE27 ... 139 J8 7
Windsor Ct STHGT/OAK N14 ... 48 C2
Windsor Crs RYLN/HDSTN HA2 ... 79 G3
WBLY HA9 ... 81 G3
Windsor Dr ASHF TW15 ... 130 D8
DART DA1 ... 146 A3
EBAR EN4 ... 47 M1
ORP BR6 ... 177 G8
Windsor Gdns CROY/NA CR0 ... 171 L5 4
HYS/HAR UB3 ... 113 K1
MV/WKIL W9 ... 8 A1 1
Windsor Gv WNWD SE27 ... 139 J8 8
Windsor Ms CAT SE6 ... 141 J5 1
Windsor Park Rd HYS/HAR UB3 .. 113 M5
Windsor Rd BAR EN5 ... 46 D1
BCTR RM8 ... 90 E3
BXLYHS DA6 ... 144 E1
CHING E4 ... 51 H6
CRICK NW2 ... 82 B6
EA W5 ... 98 D6
EMPK RM11 ... 74 C8
FNCH N3 ... 64 E3
FSTGT E7 ... 88 B5
HOLWY N7 ... 84 E3
HSLWW TW4 ... 114 B7
IL IG1 ... 89 J4
KTN/HRWW/W HA3 ... 61 J2
KUTN/CMB KT2 ... 152 E3
LEY E10 ... 87 H2
NWDGN UB2 ... 114 F1 7
PEND EN3 ... 37 K1
PLMGR N13 ... 49 G5
RCH/KEW TW9 ... 116 F7
SUN TW16 ... 150 A3
TEDD TW11 ... 151 K1
THHTH CR7 ... 157 H5
TOTM N17 ... 68 A3
WAN E11 ... 88 A1
WATN WD24 ... 29 J3
WPK KT4 ... 169 G4
The Windsors BKHH IG9 ... 52 E4
Windsor St IS N1 ... 6 D4
UX/CGN UB8 ... 76 C8
Windsor Ter IS N1 ... 6 F7
Windsor Wk CMBW SE5 ... 121 K7 7
WEY KT13 ... 164 B7
Windsor Wy HMSMTH W6 ... 118 D2
RKW/CH/CXG WD3 ... 40 A3
Windsor Wd WAB EN9 ... 27 L6 2
Windus Rd STNW/STAM N16 ... 85 M1
Windward Cl PEND EN3 ... 26 D8
Windycroft Cl PUR/KEN CR8 ... 183 K6 1
Windy Rdg BMLY BR1 ... 160 E4
Windy Ridge Cl
WIM/MER SW19 ... 154 D1
Wine Cl WAP E1W ... 104 C6 11
Winery La KUT KT1 ... 152 F6
Winforton St GNWCH SE10 ... 123 J6
Winfrith Rd WAND/EARL SW18 ... 137 J4
Wingate Crs CROY/NA CR0 ... 171 L1
Wingate Rd HMSMTH W6 ... 118 B1
IL IG1 ... 89 H5
SCUP DA14 ... 162 C1
Wingfield Gdns UPMR RM14 ... 75 M7 1
Wingfield Rd KUTN/CMB KT2 ... 152 F2
SRTFD E15 ... 87 L5 8
WALTH E17 ... 69 H6
Wingfield St PECK SE15 ... 122 A8
Wingfield Wy RSLP HA4 ... 78 B6
Wingford Rd CLAP SW4 ... 138 E3
Wingletye La EMPK RM11 ... 92 F1
Wingmore Rd HNHL SE24 ... 121 J8
Wingrave Crs BRW CM14 ... 57 L6 1
Wingrave Rd HMSMTH W6 ... 118 C4 1
Wingrove Rd CAT SE6 ... 141 L6
Wings Cl SUT SM1 ... 170 A6
Winifred Av HCH RM12 ... 92 D4
Winifred Pl NFNCH/WDSP N12 .. 47 J7 2
Winifred Rd BCTR RM8 ... 90 E2
DART DA1 ... 146 B2
ERITH DA8 ... 127 L3
HPTN TW12 ... 133 G8
WIM/MER SW19 ... 155 G4
Winifred St CAN/RD E16 ... 106 F7
Winifred Ter ED N9 ... 49 M2 3
Winkfield Rd WDGN N22 ... 67 G2
Winkley St BETH E2 ... 104 B1 4
Winkworth Rd BNSTD SM7 ... 182 A7
Winlaton Rd BMLY BR1 ... 141 K8
Winmill Rd BCTR RM8 ... 90 F3

Winn Bridge Cl WFD IG8 .... 70 D2
Winn Common Rd
  WOOL/PLUM SE18 .... 125 L4
Winnett St SOHO/SHAV W1D 11 G6 1
Winnington Cl EFNCH N2 .... 65 K7 2
Winnington Rd EFNCH N2 .... 65 K8
  PEND EN3 .... 37 J3
Winnipeg Dr ORP BR6 .... 176 F8
Winnock Rd WDR/YW UB7 .... 94 D7
Winn Rd LEE/GVPK SE12 .... 142 A5
Winns Av WALTH E17 .... 68 F3
Winns Ms SEVS/STOTM N15 .... 67 L5 1
Winns Ter WALTH E17 .... 69 G3
Winsbeach WALTH E17 .... 69 K4
Winscombe Crs EA W5 .... 98 D3 3
Winscombe St KTTN N5 .... 84 B3
Winscombe Wy HA7 .... 44 A7
Winsford Rd CAT SE6 .... 140 F7
Winsham Gv BTSEA SW11 .... 138 A2
Winslade Rd BRXS/STRHM SW2 .... 138 E2
Winsland Ms BAY/PAD W2 .... 9 G4
Winsland St BAY/PAD W2 .... 9 G4
Winsley St GTPST W1W 10 E4
Winslow Cl PIN HA5 .... 60 D7 1
  WLSDN NW10 .... 81 L3 1
Winslow Gv CHING E4 .... 51 L4
Winslow Rd HMSMTH W6 .... 118 C4
Winslow Wy FELT TW13 .... 132 D7
  WOT/HER KT12 .... 165 J5
Winsor Ter EHAM E6 .... 107 G4
Winstanley Rd BTSEA SW11 .... 119 K8 1
Winstead Gdns DAGE RM10 .... 91 J5
Winston Av CDALE/KGS NW9 .... 63 G4
Winston Churchill Wy
  CHES/WCR EN8 .... 26 C6
Winston Cl GRH DA9 .... 147 M3
  KTN/HRWW/W HA3 .... 43 M8
  ROMW/RG RM7 .... 73 H5
Winston Ct PIN HA5 .... 61 H1
Winston Rd STNW/STAM N16 .... 85 K4
Winston Wy IL IG1 .... 89 H3
  POTB/CUF EN6 .... 23 G6 1
Winstre Rd BORE WD6 .... 32 A4
Winter Av EHAM E6 .... 88 E8
Winterborne Av ORP BR6 .... 176 D5
Winterbourne Gv WEY KT13 .... 164 C8
Winterbourne Rd BCTR RM8 .... 90 C2
  FSTH SE23 .... 140 F5
  THHTH CR7 .... 157 G7
Winter Box Wk
  RCHPK/HAM TW10 .... 134 F2 1
Winterbrook Rd HNHL SE24 .... 139 J3
Winterburn Cl
  FBAR/BDGN N11 .... 48 A8 1
Winterdown Gdns
  ESH/CLAY KT10 .... 165 M8 1
Winterdown Rd
  ESH/CLAY KT10 .... 165 L8
Winterfold Cl
  WIM/MER SW19 .... 136 E6 1
Winters Rd THDIT KT7 .... 167 H2 1
Winterstoke Rd CAT SE6 .... 139 L4
Winterton Pl WBPTN SW10 .... 14 F9 1
Winterwell Rd
  BRXS/STRHM SW2 .... 138 E2
Winthorpe Rd PUT/ROE SW15 .... 119 J3
Winthrop St WCHPL E1 .... 104 B4 1
Winton Av RKW/CH/CXG WD3 .... 28 C8
Winton Av FBAR/BDGN N11 .... 66 C1
Winton Cl ED N9 .... 50 D2
Winton Crs RKW/CH/CXG WD3 .... 28 B8
Winton Dr CHES/WCR EN8 .... 26 E2
  RKW/CH/CXG WD3 .... 28 C8
Winton Gdns EDGW HA8 .... 62 F1
Winton Rd ORP BR6 .... 176 B6
Winton Wy STRHM/NOR SW16 .... 157 L1
Wireless Rd BH/WHM TN16 .... 187 K8
Wirral Wood Cl CHST BR7 .... 161 G2
Wisbeach Rd CROY/NA CRO 157 K8
Wisborough Rd SAND/SEL CR2 .... 184 F2
Wisdons Cl DAGE RM10 .... 91 H1
Wise La MLHL NW7 .... 46 A8
  WDR/YW UB7 .... 112 D2
Wiseman Rd LEY E10 .... 87 G2 1
Wise Rd SRTFD E15 .... 87 J8
Wiseton Rd TOOT SW17 .... 137 L5
Wishart Rd BKHTH/KID SE3 .... 124 D6
Wisley Rd BTSEA SW11 .... 137 M2 1
  STMC/STPC BR5 .... 162 A3
Wistaria Cl ORP BR6 .... 176 B4
Wisteria Cl IL IG1 .... 89 H5
Wisteria Gdns SWLY BR8 .... 163 K5
Wisteria Rd LEW SE13 .... 141 K1
Witan St BETH E2 .... 104 B2 1
Witham Cl LOU IG10 .... 52 E1
Witham Rd DAGE RM10 .... 91 G5
  GPK RM2 .... 74 B6
  ISLW TW7 .... 115 K6
  PGE/AN SE20 .... 158 C6
  WEA W13 .... 116 B1
Withens Cl STMC/STPC BR5 .... 162 C7 2
Witherby Cl SAND/SEL CR2 .... 172 E7
The Witherings EMPK RM11 .... 74 E6
Witherington Rd HBRY N5 .... 85 G5 1
Withers Md CDALE/KGS NW9 .... 63 M2
Witherston Wy ELTH/MOT SE9 .... 143 G6
Witheygate Av STA TW18 .... 148 B7
Withy La RSLP HA4 .... 59 J6
Withy Md CHING E4 .... 51 K5
Witley Crs CROY/NA CRO 174 C4
Witley Gdns NWDGN UB2 .... 114 F2
Witley Rd ARCH N19 .... 84 C2
Witney Cl HGDN/ICK UB10 .... 76 F4
  PIN HA5 .... 42 F8
Wittenham Wy CHING E4 .... 51 K5
Wittering Cl KUTN/CMB KT2 .... 152 D1
Wittersham Rd BMLY BR1 .... 159 M1
Wivenhoe Cl PECK SE15 .... 122 A8
Wivenhoe Ct HSLWW TW4 .... 132 F1 1
Wivenhoe Rd BARK IG11 .... 108 A1
Wiverton Rd SYD SE26 .... 158 C2
Wix Rd DAGW RM9 .... 90 D8
Wix's La BTSEA SW11 .... 138 B1
Woburn Pl STPAN WC1H 5 H9

Woburn Rd CAR SM5 .... 170 E3
  CROY/NA CRO 172 C3
Woburn Sq STPAN WC1H 11 H1
Wodehouse Av PECK SE15 .... 121 M6
Wodehouse Rd DART DA1 .... 147 G1
Woffington Cl E/WMO/HCT KT8 .... 152 C4
Woking Cl PUT/ROE SW15 .... 135 M1
Woldham Pl HAYES BR2 .... 160 C7
Woldham Rd HAYES BR2 .... 160 C7
Wolds Dr ORP BR6 .... 176 A6
Wolfe Cl HAYES BR2 .... 175 G1
  YEAD UB4 .... 96 B2
Wolfe Crs CHARL SE7 .... 124 D3
Wolferton Rd MNPK E12 .... 88 F4
Wolfington Rd WNWD SE27 .... 139 H8
Wolfram Cl LEW SE13 .... 141 L2 1
Wolmer Gdns EDGW HA8 .... 45 G5
Wolseley Av WAND/EARL SW18 .... 137 G6
Wolseley Gdns CHSWK W4 .... 117 H4
Wolseley Rd CEND/HSY/T N8 .... 66 D7
  CHSWK W4 .... 117 J2 1
  FSTGT E7 .... 88 F7
  KTN/HRWW/W HA3 .... 61 L4
  MTCM CR4 .... 171 G2
  ROMW/RG RM7 .... 73 K8
  WDGN N22 .... 66 F2
Wolsey Av CHESW EN7 .... 25 M2 1
  EHAM E6 .... 108 A2
  WALTH E17 .... 68 F4 1
Wolsey Cl HSLW TW3 .... 133 J1
  KUTN/CMB KT2 .... 153 H4
  NWDGN UB2 .... 115 J1
  RYNPK SW20 .... 154 B3
  WPK KT4 .... 169 G6
Wolsey Crs CROY/NA CRO 186 C2
  MRDN SM4 .... 169 M2
Wolsey Dr KUTN/CMB KT2 .... 152 E1
  WOT/HER KT12 .... 165 K3
Wolsey Gdns BARK/HLT IG6 .... 53 J8 2
Wolsey Gv EDGW HA8 .... 63 K1
  ESH/CLAY KT10 .... 166 B6 3
Wolsey Ms KTTN NW5 .... 84 C6
  ORP BR6 .... 176 F7
Wolsey Rd ASHF TW15 .... 130 E8
  E/WMO/HCT KT8 .... 151 K7
  EN EN1 .... 37 H5
  ESH/CLAY KT10 .... 166 B6
  HPTN TW12 .... 151 H2
  IS N1 .... 85 K5
  RKW/CH/CXG WD3 .... 41 J4
  SUN TW16 .... 149 M3
Wolsey St WCHPL E1 .... 104 C4
Wolsey Wy CHSGTN KT9 .... 168 A7
Wolsley Cl DART DA1 .... 147 G5
Wolstan Cl DEN/HRF UB9 .... 76 A3 3
Wolstonbury NFNCH/WDSP N12 .... 47 G7
Wolvercote Rd ABYW SE2 .... 108 D8
Wolverley St BETH E2 .... 104 B2 3
Wolverton Av KUTN/CMB KT2 .... 153 G4
Wolverton Gdns EA W5 .... 98 F6
  HMSMTH W6 .... 118 D2
Wolverton Rd STAN HA7 .... 43 H2
Wolverton Wy STHGT/OAK N14 .... 35 J5
Wolves La WDGN N22 .... 49 G4
Womersley Rd CEND/HSY/T N8 .... 66 F7
Wonersh Wy BELMT SM2 .... 181 K2
Wonford Cl NWMAL KT3 .... 153 L4
Wontford Rd PUR/KEN CR8 .... 184 A8
Wontner Rd BAL SW12 .... 138 D8
Wooburn Cl UX/CGN UB8 .... 95 H3 2
Woodall Rd PEND EN3 .... 50 D1
Wood Av PUR RM19 .... 129 J2
Woodbank Rd BMLY BR1 .... 141 M7
Woodbastwick Rd SYD SE26 .... 158 D2
Woodberry Av RYLN/HDSTN HA2 .... 61 J5
  WCHMH N21 .... 49 G4
Woodberry Cl SUN TW16 .... 150 A2
Woodberry Crs MUSWH N10 .... 66 B4 2
Woodberry Down FSBYPK N4 .... 85 J1
Woodberry Gdns
  NFNCH/WDSP N12 .... 47 G5
Woodberry Gv BXLY DA5 .... 145 K7
  FSBYPK N4 .... 67 J8 4
  NFNCH/WDSP N12 .... 47 G5
Woodberry Wy CHING E4 .... 51 J2
  NFNCH/WDSP N12 .... 47 G5
Woodbine Cl WHTN TW2 .... 133 K6 1
Woodbine Gv ENC/FH EN2 .... 36 D3
  PGE/AN SE20 .... 158 B3
Woodbine La WPK KT4 .... 169 H5
Woodbine Pl WAN E11 .... 70 D4
Woodbine Rd BFN/LL DA15 .... 143 L5
Woodbines Av KUT KT1 .... 152 D6
Woodbine Ter HOM E9 .... 86 C6 10
Woodborough Rd
  PUT/ROE SW15 .... 136 B1
Woodbourne Av
  STRHM/NOR SW16 .... 138 D7
Woodbourne Dr
  ESH/CLAY KT10 .... 166 F8
Woodbourne Gdns
  WLGTN SM6 .... 183 H1 1
Woodbridge Cl HARH RM3 .... 56 D6 1
  HOLWY N7 .... 84 F2
Woodbridge La HARH RM3 .... 56 D5
Woodbridge Rd BARK IG11 .... 89 M5
Woodbridge St CLKNW EC1R 6 C9 1
Woodbrook Gdns WAB EN9 .... 27 L6
Woodbrook Rd ABYW SE2 .... 126 B4
Woodburn Cl HDN NW4 .... 64 D6 1
Woodbury Cl CROY/NA CRO 172 F4
  WAN E11 .... 70 D3
Woodbury Dr BELMT SM2 .... 182 C3
Woodbury Hl LOU IG10 .... 39 L5
Woodbury Park Rd WEA W13 .... 98 B3
Woodbury Rd WALTH E17 .... 69 H5
Woodbury St TOOT SW17 .... 155 J1
Woodchester Sq BAY/PAD W2 .... 8 C2
Woodchurch Cl BFN/LL DA15 .... 143 K7
Woodchurch Dr BMLY BR1 .... 160 D3 1
Woodchurch Rd
  KIL/WHAMP NW6 .... 2 B2

Woodclyffe Dr CHST BR7 .... 161 G5
Woodcock Ct
  KTN/HRWW/W HA3 .... 62 E8
Woodcock Dell Av
  KTN/HRWW/W HA3 .... 62 C8
Woodcock Hl
  KTN/HRWW/W HA3 .... 62 C6
  RKW/CH/CXG WD3 .... 40 E7
Woodcocks CAN/RD E16 .... 106 C4
Woodcombe Crs FSTH SE23 .... 140 C5
Woodcote Av HCH RM12 .... 92 A4
  MLHL NW7 .... 46 C8
  THHTH CR7 .... 157 H7
  WLGTN SM6 .... 183 H2
Woodcote Cl CHES/WCR EN8 .... 26 C3
  EPSOM KT18 .... 180 D7
  KUTN/CMB KT2 .... 152 F1
Woodcote Dr ORP BR6 .... 176 D2
Woodcote End EPSOM KT18 .... 180 D8
Woodcote Gn WLGTN SM6 .... 183 J2
Woodcote Grove Rd
  COUL/CHIP CR5 .... 183 K8
Woodcote La PUR/KEN CR8 .... 183 K4
Woodcote Ms LOU IG10 .... 52 D2
Woodcote Park Av
  PUR/KEN CR8 .... 183 J4
Woodcote Pl WNWD SE27 .... 157 H1 3
Woodcote Rd WAN E11 .... 70 A8
  WLGTN SM6 .... 171 H8
Woodcote Side EPSOM KT18 .... 180 B8
Woodcote Valley Rd
  PUR/KEN CR8 .... 183 K6
Woodcroft ELTH/MOT SE9 .... 142 F7
  GFD/PVL UB6 .... 80 A6 1
  WCHMH N21 .... 48 F3
Woodcroft Av MLHL NW7 .... 63 L1
  STAN HA7 .... 62 A2
Woodcroft Crs HGDN/ICK UB10 .... 77 H8
Woodcroft Ms DEPT SE8 .... 122 E2
Woodcroft Rd THHTH CR7 .... 157 H8
Wood Dr CHST BR7 .... 160 E2
Woodedge Cl CHING E4 .... 51 M3
Woodend ESH/CLAY KT10 .... 166 C4
Wood End HYS/HAR UB3 .... 95 L5
Woodend NRWD SE19 .... 157 J2
  SUT SM1 .... 170 C4
Wood End SWLY BR8 .... 163 J1 1
Wood End Av RYLN/HDSTN HA2 .... 79 K4
Wood End Cl NTHLT UB5 .... 79 K5 1
Woodend Gdns ENC/FH EN2 .... 35 L7 4
Wood End Gdns NTHLT UB5 .... 79 J5
Wood End Green Rd
  HYS/HAR UB3 .... 95 K4
  UX/CGN UB8 .... 95 J5 3
Wood End La NTHLT UB5 .... 79 H6
Wood End Rd NTHLT UB5 .... 79 K4
The Wood End WLGTN SM6 .... 183 H2 1
Wooder Gdns FSTGT E7 .... 87 M4
Wooderson Cl SNWD SE25 .... 157 L7
Woodfall Av BAR EN5 .... 33 M8
Woodfall Dr DART DA1 .... 145 M1
Woodfall Rd FSBYPK N4 .... 85 G1
Woodfall St CHEL SW3 .... 15 L8
Woodfarrs CMBW SE5 .... 139 K1
Woodfield Av ALP/SUD HA0 .... 80 C3
  CAR SM5 .... 171 G8
  CDALE/KGS NW9 .... 63 L5
  EA W5 .... 98 C3
  NTHWD HA6 .... 41 L6
  STRHM/NOR SW16 .... 138 D7
Woodfield Cl EN EN1 .... 36 E7 3
  NRWD SE19 .... 157 J3
Woodfield Crs EA W5 .... 98 C3
Woodfield Dr EBAR EN4 .... 48 A3
  GPK RM2 .... 74 A5
Woodfield Gdns NWMAL KT3 .... 153 M8
Woodfield Gv
  STRHM/NOR SW16 .... 138 D7 3
Woodfield Pl MV/WKIL W9 .... 100 F5 10
Woodfield Ri BUSH WD23 .... 43 K2
Woodfield Rd EA W5 .... 98 C3
  ESH/CLAY KT10 .... 166 F4 3
  HSLWW TW4 .... 114 B6 3
  MV/WKIL W9 .... 100 F4
  RAD WD7 .... 31 G1
The Woodfields SAND/SEL CR2 .... 184 F4
Woodfield Wy FBAR/BDGN N11 .... 66 C1
  HCH RM12 .... 92 D1 1
The Woodfines EMPK RM11 .... 74 F6
Woodford Av GNTH/NBYPK IG2 .... 70 F6
  REDBR IG4 .... 70 D4
Woodford Crs PIN HA5 .... 60 B3
Woodford New Rd WALTH E17 .... 69 L5
  WFD IG8 .... 69 M1
Woodford Pl WBLY HA9 .... 80 A1
Woodford Rd FSTGT E7 .... 88 B4
  SWFD E18 .... 70 A5
  WAT WD17 .... 29 H5
Woodgate GSTN WD25 .... 21 H6
Woodgate Av CHSGTN KT9 .... 167 K7
  POTB/CUF EN6 .... 24 B6
Woodgate Crs NTHWD HA6 .... 42 A8
Woodgate Dr
  STRHM/NOR SW16 .... 156 D3
Woodger Rd SHB W12 .... 100 C8 3
Woodgers Gv SWLY BR8 .... 163 M5 10
Woodget Cl EHAM E6 .... 106 E5 10
Woodgrange Av ACT W3 .... 98 F7
  EN EN1 .... 50 A1
  KTN/HRWW/W HA3 .... 62 C6
  NFNCH/WDSP N12 .... 47 K8
Woodgrange Cl
  KTN/HRWW/W HA3 .... 62 D6
Woodgrange Gdns EN EN1 .... 50 A1
Woodhall Av DUL SE21 .... 139 M7
  PIN HA5 .... 60 D2
Woodhall Cl UX/CGN UB8 .... 76 D5
Woodhall Dr DUL SE21 .... 139 M7
  PIN HA5 .... 60 D1
Woodhall Ga PIN HA5 .... 60 D1
Woodhall La OXHEY WD19 .... 42 D5
Woodham Ct SWFD E18 .... 69 M5 1

Woodham Rd CAT SE6 .... 141 J7
Woodhatch Cl EHAM E6 .... 106 E4 3
Woodhayes Rd RYNPK SW20 .... 154 C5
  WIM/MER SW19 .... 154 C2 3
Woodhead Dr ORP BR6 .... 176 E5
Woodheyes Rd WLSDN NW10 .... 81 L5
Woodhill CHARL SE7 .... 126 A4
Woodhill Crs KTN/HRWW/W HA3 .... 62 D7
Woodhouse Av GFD/PVL UB6 .... 97 M1
Woodhouse Cl GFD/PVL UB6 .... 97 M1
  HYS/HAR UB3 .... 95 J1
Woodhouse Eaves
  NTHWD HA6 .... 42 A7 1
Woodhouse Gv MNPK E12 .... 88 E6
Woodhouse Rd
  NFNCH/WDSP N12 .... 47 J2
  WAN E11 .... 87 M3
Woodhurst Av STMC/STPC BR5 .... 176 C1
Woodhurst Rd ABYW SE2 .... 126 A3
  ACT W3 .... 99 J7
Woodhyrst Gdns PUR/KEN CR8 .... 184 B8
Woodington Cl ELTH/MOT SE9 .... 143 H5
Woodison St BOW E3 .... 105 G3 3
Woodknoll Dr CHST BR7 .... 160 F4
Woodland Ap GFD/PVL UB6 .... 80 A6 3
Woodland Cl CDALE/KGS NW9 .... 63 J7
  HGDN/ICK UB10 .... 77 H2 3
  HOR/WEW KT19 .... 168 E3 3
  NRWD SE19 .... 157 L2 3
  WFD IG8 .... 52 B5
Woodland Crs GNWCH SE10 .... 123 L4 3
Woodland Dr WAT WD17 .... 28 F4
Woodland Gdns ISLW TW7 .... 115 L8
  MUSWH N10 .... 66 B6
  SAND/SEL CR2 .... 185 J6
Woodland Gv WEY KT13 .... 164 D6
Woodland Hl NRWD SE19 .... 157 L2
Woodland Ri GFD/PVL UB6 .... 80 A6
  MUSWH N10 .... 66 B5
Woodland Rd CHING E4 .... 51 J3
  LOU IG10 .... 39 L6 3
  NRWD SE19 .... 157 L1
  THHTH CR7 .... 157 H8
Woodlands GLDGN NW11 .... 64 E6
  RYLN/HDSTN HA2 .... 61 G5
  RYNPK SW20 .... 154 D7 3
Woodlands Av ACT W3 .... 99 H7 3
  BFN/LL DA15 .... 143 L5
  CHDH RM6 .... 72 F7
  EMPK RM11 .... 74 D6
  FNCH N3 .... 65 J1
  NWMAL KT3 .... 153 K4
  RSLP HA4 .... 78 C1
  WAN E11 .... 88 B1
  WPK KT4 .... 168 F4
Woodlands Cl BMLY BR1 .... 160 F5
  BORE WD6 .... 32 B7
  ESH/CLAY KT10 .... 178 F1 3
  SWLY BR8 .... 163 M5 3
Woodlands Dr STAN HA7 .... 43 M8
  SUN TW16 .... 150 C5
Woodlands Gv GNWCH SE10 .... 123 L3 3
  ISLW TW7 .... 115 L7
Woodlands Pde ASHF TW15 .... 149 J2 3
Woodlands Pk BXLY DA5 .... 145 K8
Woodlands Park Rd
  BKHTH/KID SE3 .... 123 L4 3
  GNWCH SE10 .... 123 L4
  SEVS/STOTM N15 .... 67 J6
Woodlands Ri SWLY BR8 .... 163 M5 3
Woodlands Rd BARN SW13 .... 117 M8
  BMLY BR1 .... 160 F5
  BUSH WD23 .... 29 L7
  BXLYHN DA7 .... 126 E8
  ED N9 .... 50 C3
  ENC/FH EN2 .... 36 D3
  EPSOM KT18 .... 180 A8
  HARH RM3 .... 75 G2
  HRW HA1 .... 61 M6
  IL IG1 .... 89 J3
  ISLW TW7 .... 115 L8
  ORP BR6 .... 177 G8
  ROM RM1 .... 73 M4
  STHL UB1 .... 96 D7
  SURB KT6 .... 167 K2
  WALTH E17 .... 69 J4
  WAN E11 .... 87 L2 3
Woodlands St LEW SE13 .... 141 K4
The Woodlands ESH/CLAY KT10 .... 166 C4
  ISLW TW7 .... 115 M7
  LEW SE13 .... 141 K4
  NRWD SE19 .... 157 J3
  ORP BR6 .... 177 H8
  STHGT/OAK N14 .... 48 B3
  WLGTN SM6 .... 183 H2 3
Woodland St HACK E8 .... 85 M6 11
Woodlands Wy
  PUT/ROE SW15 .... 136 F2 3
Woodland Ter CHARL SE7 .... 124 C2 3
Woodland Wk HAMP NW3 .... 83 L5 3
  HOR/WEW KT19 .... 168 A8
Woodland Wy ABYW SE2 .... 126 D2
  BRYLDS KT5 .... 168 B4 3
  CHESW EN7 .... 25 H1
  CROY/NA CRO 173 L3
  MLHL NW7 .... 45 L8
  MRDN SM4 .... 154 F7
  MTCM CR4 .... 156 A3
  PUR/KEN CR8 .... 184 A6
  STMC/STPC BR5 .... 161 J7
  WCHMH N21 .... 49 G4
  WEY KT13 .... 164 D7
  WFD IG8 .... 52 B5
  WWKM BR4 .... 174 D2
Wood La CDALE/KGS NW9 .... 63 K8
  DAGE RM10 .... 91 G2
  HCH RM12 .... 92 A5
  HGT N6 .... 66 A6
  ISLW TW7 .... 115 L4
  RDART DA2 .... 147 M7
  RSLP HA4 .... 77 K2
  SHB W12 .... 100 C5
  STAN HA7 .... 44 B5
  WFD IG8 .... 52 A6

Woodlawn Dr FELT TW13 .... 132 D6
Woodlawn Rd FUL/PGN SW6 .... 118 D5
Woodlea Dr HAYES BR2 .... 159 L8
Woodlea Gv NTHWD HA6 .... 41 J8
Woodleigh Av
  NFNCH/WDSP N12 .... 47 L8
Woodleigh Gdns
  STRHM/NOR SW16 .... 138 E7
Woodley Cl TOOT SW17 .... 155 M3 8
Woodley La SUT SM1 .... 170 C5
Woodley Rd ORP BR6 .... 177 J4
Wood Lodge Gdns BMLY BR1 .... 160 E3
Wood Lodge La WWKM BR4 .... 174 C5
Woodman La CHING E4 .... 38 D8
Woodman Pth BARK/HLT IG6 .... 53 L7
Woodman Rd COUL/CHIP CR5 .... 183 J8
Woodmans Gv WLSDN NW10 .... 81 M5 3
Woodmansterne La
  BNSTD SM7 .... 182 B8
  CAR SM5 .... 182 F5
  WLGTN SM6 .... 183 H4
Woodmansterne Rd CAR SM5 .... 182 B3
  COUL/CHIP CR5 .... 183 J8
  STRHM/NOR SW16 .... 156 E4
Woodmansterne St
  BNSTD SM7 .... 182 E8
Woodman St CAN/RD E16 .... 107 G7
Woodmans Yd WAT WD17 .... 29 J1 14
Woodmere ELTH/MOT SE9 .... 142 F4
Woodmere Av CROY/NA CRO 173 K2
  WATN WD24 .... 29 K3
Woodmere Cl CROY/NA CRO 173 K2
Woodmere Gdns CROY/NA CRO 173 K2
Woodmere Wy BECK BR3 .... 159 K8
Woodnook Rd
  STRHM/NOR SW16 .... 156 B1
Wood Peckarmans DUL SE21 .... 140 A7
Woodpecker Cl BUSH WD23 .... 43 J3
  ED N9 .... 50 B1
  KTN/HRWW/W HA3 .... 62 B8
Woodpecker Rd THMD SE28 .... 108 C6 3
Woodquest Av HNHL SE24 .... 139 H2
Wood Ride EBAR EN4 .... 34 D4
  STMC/STPC BR5 .... 161 K7
Woodridge Cl ENC/FH EN2 .... 36 A4 3
Woodridge Wy NTHWD HA6 .... 41 L8
Woodridings Av PIN HA5 .... 60 F2
Woodridings Cl PIN HA5 .... 60 F1
Woodriffe Rd WAN E11 .... 69 K8
Wood Ri PIN HA5 .... 60 A6
Wood Rd SHPTN TW17 .... 149 G7
Woodrow WOOL/PLUM SE18 .... 124 E2
Woodrow Av YEAD UB4 .... 95 M4
Woodrow Cl GFD/PVL UB6 .... 80 B7
Woodrow Ct TOTM N17 .... 68 F1 3
Woodrush Cl NWCR SE14 .... 122 E5 3
Woodrush Wy CHDH RM6 .... 72 D5
Woodseer St WCHPL E1 .... 13 M2
Woodshire Rd DAGE RM10 .... 91 H3
Woodshots Meadow
  WATW WD18 .... 28 D8
Woodside BKHH IG9 .... 52 C4
  BORE WD6 .... 31 M7 3
  CHESW EN7 .... 26 A4
  GLDGN NW11 .... 65 G6
  ORP BR6 .... 177 G7
  WATN WD24 .... 29 G2
  WIM/MER SW19 .... 154 F1
  WOT/HER KT12 .... 165 G3
Woodside Av ALP/SUD HA0 .... 80 E8
  CHST BR7 .... 161 J1
  ESH/CLAY KT10 .... 166 E2
  HGT N6 .... 65 M6
  NFNCH/WDSP N12 .... 47 J6
  SNWD SE25 .... 173 H1
  WOT/HER KT12 .... 165 H6
Woodside Cl ALP/SUD HA0 .... 80 E8
  BRYLDS KT5 .... 168 C2
  BXLYHN DA7 .... 145 K1
  RAIN RM13 .... 110 C3
  RSLP HA4 .... 59 K7 3
  STAN HA7 .... 44 A7
Woodside Court Rd
  CROY/NA CRO 173 G2
Woodside Crs BFN/LL DA15 .... 143 L7
Woodside Dr RDART DA2 .... 145 L8
Woodside End ALP/SUD HA0 .... 80 E8
Woodside Gdns CHING E4 .... 51 H7
  TOTM N17 .... 67 M3
Woodside Grange Rd
  NFNCH/WDSP N12 .... 47 H6
Woodside Gn CROY/NA CRO 173 G2
  SNWD SE25 .... 173 H1
Woodside Gv NFNCH/WDSP N12 .... 47 J5
Woodside La BXLY DA5 .... 144 F3
  NFNCH/WDSP N12 .... 47 H5
Woodside Pk SNWD SE25 .... 173 G1
Woodside Park Av WALTH E17 .... 69 K5
Woodside Park Rd
  NFNCH/WDSP N12 .... 47 H6
Woodside Pl ALP/SUD HA0 .... 80 E8
Woodside Rd BFN/LL DA15 .... 143 L7
  BMLY BR1 .... 160 E8
  BXLYHN DA7 .... 145 K1
  COB KT11 .... 178 A6
  GSTN WD25 .... 21 H4
  KUTN/CMB KT2 .... 153 H7
  LCOL/BKTW AL2 .... 21 M3
  NTHWD HA6 .... 59 M1
  NWMAL KT3 .... 153 K5
  PLSTW E13 .... 107 G3
  PUR/KEN CR8 .... 183 L6
  SNWD SE25 .... 173 H1
  SUT SM1 .... 170 C5
  WDGN N22 .... 67 G1
  WFD IG8 .... 52 A6
Woodside Wy CROY/NA CRO 173 J1 3
  MTCM CR4 .... 156 C4 3
Woods Ms MYFR/PKLN W1K 9 M6
Woods Rd PECK SE15 .... 122 B6
Woodsome Rd KTTN NW5 .... 84 A3
Wood's Pl STHWK SE1 .... 19 K4
Woodspring Rd
  WIM/MER SW19 .... 136 E6
Wood's Rd PECK SE15 .... 122 B6
Woodstead Gv EDGW HA8 .... 44 B8
The Woods HGDN/ICK UB10 .... 77 H4
  NTHWD HA6 .... 42 A7

Woodstock Av *CHEAM* SM3 .... 169 M2
  GLDGN NW11 .... 64 E8
  HARH RM3 .... 57 H7
  HNWL W7 .... 116 A1
  ISLW TW7 .... 134 A2
  STHL UB1 .... 96 F2
Woodstock Cl *BXLY* DA5 .... 144 F5
  STAN HA7 .... 62 E5
Woodstock Crs *ED* N9 .... 50 B1
Woodstock Dr *HGDN/ICK* UB10 .. 76 E4
Woodstock Gdns *BECK* BR3 .... 159 H4
  GDMY/SEVK IG3 .... 90 A2
  YEAD UB4 .... 95 M4
Woodstock Gv *SHB* W12 .... 100 D8
Woodstock La North *SURB* KT6 .. 167 J4
Woodstock La South
  ESH/CLAY KT10 .... 167 H7
Woodstock Ms
  CAVSQ/HST W1G 10 B3
Woodstock Ri *CHEAM* SM3 .... 169 M3
Woodstock Rd *ALP/SUD* HA0 .... 80 F7
  BUSH WD23 .... 43 L2
  CAR SM5 .... 171 G7
  CHSWK W4 .... 117 L2
  CROY/NA CR0 .... 172 D5
  FSBYPK N4 .... 85 G1
  FSTGT E7 .... 88 C7
  GLDGN NW11 .... 64 F8
  WALTH E17 .... 69 K3
Woodstock St *CAN/RD* E16 .. 105 M3
  MYFR/PKLN W1K 10 C5
Woodstock Ter *POP/IOD* E14 .. 105 H6
Woodstock Way *MTCM* CR4 .... 156 C5
Woodstone Av *EW* KT17 .... 169 G7
Wood St *BAR* EN5 .... 33 J7
  BARB EC2Y 12 F3
  CAN/RD E16 .... 106 B6
  CHSWK W4 .... 117 L3
  CITYW EC2V 12 F4
  KUT KT1 .... 152 D5
  MTCM CR4 .... 171 G2
  WALTH E17 .... 69 J4
Woodsway *LHD/OX* KT22 .... 178 E7
Woodsyre *NRWD* SE19 .... 139 M8
Woodthorpe Rd *ASHF* TW15 .. 148 D1
  PUT/ROE SW15 .... 136 B1
Woodtree Cl *HDN* NW4 .... 64 C3
Wood V *EDUL* SE22 .... 140 B5
  MUSWH N10 .... 66 C6
Woodvale Av *SNWD* SE25 .... 157 M6
Woodvale Wy *CRICK* NW2 .... 82 D3
Woodview *CHSGTN* KT9 .... 179 J5
Woodview Av *CHING* E4 .... 51 J6
Woodview Cl *KUTN/CMB* KT2 ..... 135 K8
  SAND/SEL CR2 .... 185 H7
Woodview Rd *SWLY* BR8 .... 163 J5
Woodville Cl *LEE/GVPK* SE12 .. 142 A2
  TEDD TW11 .... 134 A8
Woodville Court Ms
  WAT WD17 .... 29 G5
Woodville Gdns *BARK/HLT* IG6 .. 71 H4
  EA W5 .... 98 E5
  RSLP HA4 .... 59 J8
Woodville Rd *BAR* EN5 .... 33 K3
  EA W5 .... 98 E5
  GLDGN NW11 .... 64 E8
  KIL/WHAMP NW6 .... 100 F1
  MRDN SM4 .... 155 G7
  RCHPK/HAM TW10 .... 134 B7
  STNW/STAM N16 .... 85 L5
  SWFD E18 .... 70 B3
  THHTH CR7 .... 157 J7
  WALTH E17 .... 68 C5
  WAN E11 .... 87 M1
Woodville St *CHARL* SE7 .... 124 E2
Woodward Av *HDN* NW4 .... 64 A6
Woodward Cl *ESH/CLAY* KT10... 166 F8
Woodward Gdns *DAGW* RM9 .... 90 C7
  STAN HA7 .... 61 M1
Woodward Rd *DAGW* RM9 .... 90 B7
Woodward Ter *GRH* DA9 .... 147 L3
Woodway Crs *HRW* HA1 .... 62 A7
Woodwaye *OXHEY* WD19 .... 42 C2
Woodwell St *WAND/EARL* SW18.. 137 J2
Woodyard Cl *KTTN* NW5 .... 84 B5
Woodyard La *DUL* SE21 .... 139 L4
Woodyates Rd *LEE/GVPK* SE12 .. 142 A3
Woolacombe Rd
  BKHTH/KID SE3 .... 124 C7
Woolacombe Wy *HYS/HAR* UB3.. 113 L2
Wooler St *WALW* SE17 .... 19 G8
Woolf Cl *THMD* SE28 .... 108 B7
Woolf Ms *STPAN* WC1H 5 J9
Woolhampton Wy *CHIG* IG7 ..... 54 B5
Woollard St *WAB* EN9 .... 27 H7
Woollaston Rd *FSBYPK* N4 .... 67 H7
Woolmead Av *CDALE/KGS* NW9 ... 64 A8
Woolmer Cl *BORE* WD6 .... 32 A3
Woolmerdine Ct *BUSH* WD23 ..... 29 K6
Woolmer Gdns *UED* N18 .... 50 A8
Woolmer Rd *UED* N18 .... 50 A8
Woolmore St *POP/IOD* E14 .... 105 J6
Woolneigh St *FUL/PGN* SW6 ..... 119 H8
Wool Rd *RYNPK* SW20 .... 154 B2
Woolstaplers Wy
  BERM/RHTH SE16 .... 122 A7
Woolston Cl *WALTH* E17 .... 68 D3
Woolstone Rd *FSTH* SE23 .... 140 E6
Woolwich Church St
  CHARL SE7 .... 124 D2
Woolwich Common
  WOOL/PLUM SE18 .... 125 G4
Woolwich High St
  WOOL/PLUM SE18 .... 125 G1
Woolwich Manorway
  CAN/RD E16 .... 107 H8
Woolwich Manor Wy
  CAN/RD E16 .... 107 H7

EHAM E6 .... 106 F3
Woolwich New Rd
  WOOL/PLUM SE18 .... 125 G3
Woolwich Rd *ABYW* SE2 .... 126 E4
  BELV DA17 .... 126 F3
  BXLYHN DA7 .... 127 G8
  CHARL SE7 .... 124 C2
  GNWCH SE10 .... 124 A3
Wooster Gdns *POP/IOD* E14 .... 105 K5
Wootton Cl *EMPK* RM11 .... 74 D6
Wootton Gv *FNCH* N3 .... 65 G2
Wootton St *STHWK* SE1 .... 18 B1
Worbeck Rd *PGE/AN* SE20 .... 158 B5
Worcester Av *TOTM* N17 .... 68 A1
  UPMR RM14 .... 93 M1
Worcester Cl *CRICK* NW2 .... 82 A3
  CROY/NA CR0 .... 173 M4
  MTCM CR4 .... 156 A5
Worcester Ct *WOT/HER* KT12 .... 165 J4
Worcester Crs *MLHL* NW7 .... 45 L5
  WFD IG8 .... 52 B7
Worcester Dr *ASHF* TW15 .... 149 H1
  CHSWK W4 .... 99 L8
Worcester Gdns *IL* IG1 .... 70 E8
  NTHLT UB5 .... 79 J6
  WPK KT4 .... 168 E5
Worcester Ms *HAMP* NW3 .... 83 H6
Worcester Park Rd *WPK* KT4 ... 168 C5
Worcester Rd *BELMT* SM2... ... 182 A1
  MNPK E12 .... 88 F3
  UX/CGN UB8 .... 94 C4
  WALTH E17 .... 68 D3
  WIM/MER SW19 .... 154 F1
Worcesters Av *EN* EN1 .... 37 G3
Wordsworth Av *GFD/PVL* UB6 ... 97 K1
  MNPK E12 .... 88 E7
  PUR/KEN CR8 .... 184 D8
  SWFD E18 .... 69 M4
Wordsworth Cl *HARH* RM3 .... 74 C2
Wordsworth Dr *CHEAM* SM3 ..... 169 J6
Wordsworth Rd *FELT* TW13 .... 132 F8
  HPTN TW12 .... 132 F8
  PGE/AN SE20 .... 158 D5
  STHWK SE1 .... 19 M6
  STNW/STAM N16 .... 85 L4
  WELL DA16 .... 125 L6
  WLGTN SM6 .... 171 J8
Wordsworth Wk *GLDGN* NW11 ... 64 F5
Wordsworth Wy *DART* DA1 .... 147 G1
  WDR/YW UB7 .... 112 E2
Worfield St *BTSEA* SW11 .... 119 L5
Worgan St *BERM/RHTH* SE16 ... 122 D1
  LBTH SE11 .... 17 L7
Worland Rd *SRTFD* E15 .... 87 L7
World's End La *WCHMH* N21 ..... 35 M8
Worlidge St *HMSMTH* W6 .... 118 C3
Worlingham Rd *EDUL* SE22...... 139 M1
Wormholt Rd *SHB* W12 .... 100 A7
Wormwood St *LVPST* EC2M 13 J4
Wornington Rd *NKENS* W10 ..... 100 E4
Woronzow Rd *STJWD* NW8 .... 3 H4
Worple Av *ISLW* TW7 .... 134 A2
  STA TW18 .... 148 B2
  WIM/MER SW19 .... 153 J2
Worple Cl *RYLN/HDSTN* HA2 .... 78 F1
Worple Rd *EPSOM* KT18 .... 180 D8
  ISLW TW7 .... 134 A1
  PUT/ROE SW15 .... 136 E2
  RYNPK SW20 .... 154 D4
  STA TW18 .... 148 B3
  WIM/MER SW19 .... 154 E3
Worple Road Ms
  WIM/MER SW19 .... 154 F2
Worple St *MORT/ESHN* SW14 ... 117 K8
Worple Wy *RCHPK/HAM* TW10 ... 134 E2
  RYLN/HDSTN HA2 .... 78 F1
Worship St *SDTCH* EC2A 13 H1
Worslade Rd *TOOT* SW17 .... 137 K8
Worsley Bridge Rd *CAT* SE6 ... 158 F1
Worsley Rd *WAN* E11 .... 87 L4
Worsopp Dr *CLAP* SW4 .... 138 C2
Worth Cl *ORP* BR6 .... 176 E6
Worthfield Cl *HOR/WEW* KT19 ... 180 D1
Worthing Cl *SRTFD* E15 .... 87 L8
Worthing Rd *HEST* TW5 .... 114 F4
Worthington Cl *MTCM* CR4 ..... 156 B7
Worthington Rd *SURB* KT6....... 167 M3
Wortley Rd *CROY/NA* CR0 .... 172 A2
  EHAM E6 .... 88 D7
Worton Gdns *ISLW* TW7 .... 115 K7
Worton Rd *ISLW* TW7 .... 115 M8
Worton Wy *ISLW* TW7 .... 115 K7
Wotton Gn *STMC/STPC* BR5 .... 162 D7
Wotton Rd *CRICK* NW2 .... 82 C4
Wotton Wy *BELMT* SM2 .... 181 J3
Wouldham Rd *CAN/RD* E16 .... 105 M5
Wrabness Wy *STA* TW18 .... 148 B4
Wragby Rd *WAN* E11 .... 87 L3
Wrampling Pl *ED* N9 .... 50 A3
Wray Av *CLAY* IG5 .... 71 G4
Wray Cl *HARH* RM11 .... 74 D8
Wray Crs *FSBYPK* N4 .... 84 E2
Wrayfield Rd *CHEAM* SM3 .... 169 K5
Wray Rd *BELMT* SM2 .... 181 M2
Wraysbury Cl *HSLWW* TW4 .... 132 E2
Wrays Wy *YEAD* UB4 .... 95 L4
Wrekin Rd *WOOL/PLUM* SE18..... 125 J5
Wren Av *CRICK* NW2 .... 82 C4
  NWDGN UB2 .... 114 F2
Wren Cl *CAN/RD* E16 .... 105 M5
  ED N9 .... 50 D3
  SAND/SEL CR2 .... 185 K2
  STMC/STPC BR5 .... 162 D6
Wren Crs *BUSH* WD23 .... 43 J3
Wren Dr *WDR/YW* UB7 .... 94 D8
  WDR/YW UB7 .... 112 D1
Wren Gdns *DAGW* RM9 .... 90 D5
  HCH RM12 .... 91 M1
Wren Rd *CMBW* SE5 .... 121 K6
  DAGW RM9 .... 90 D5
  SCUP DA14 .... 144 C7

Wren's Av *ASHF* TW15 .... 149 J1
Wren's Hl *LHD/OX* KT22 .... 178 C8
Wren St *FSBYW* WC1X 5 M9
Wrentham Av *WLSDN* NW10 ..... 100 D1
Wrenthorpe Rd *BMLY* BR1 .... 141 L8
Wrenwood Wy *PIN* HA5 .... 60 B5
Wrexham Rd *BOW* E3 .... 105 G1
  HARH RM3 .... 56 D6
Wricklemarsh Rd
  BKHTH/KID SE3 .... 124 B7
Wrigglesworth St
  NWCR SE14 .... 122 D5
Wright Cl *LEW* SE13 .... 141 K1
Wright Gdns *SHPTN* TW17 .... 149 G8
Wright Rd *HEST* TW5 .... 114 C5
Wrightsbridge Rd *BRW* CM14 ... 56 F3
Wrights Cl *DAGE* RM10 .... 91 H4
Wright's La *KENS* W8 .... 14 C3
Wrights Pl *WLSDN* NW10 .... 81 J6
Wright's Rd *BOW* E3 .... 86 F8
  BOW E3 .... 104 F1
  SNWD SE25 .... 157 L6
Wright's Rw *CAR* SM5 .... 171 H6
Wrotham Rd *BAR* EN5 .... 33 L5
  CAMTN NW1 .... 4 F2
  WEA W13 .... 98 C7
  WELL DA16 .... 126 C6
Wroths Pth *LOU* IG10 .... 39 M4
Wrottesley Rd *WLSDN* NW10 ... 100 B1
  WOOL/PLUM SE18 .... 125 J4
Wroughton Rd *BTSEA* SW11 ... 137 M3
Wroughton Ter *HDN* NW4 .... 64 B5
Wroxall Rd *DAGW* RM9 .... 90 C6
Wroxham Gdns *ENC/FH* EN2 .... 25 G8
  FBAR/BDGN N11 .... 66 C1
  POTB/CUF EN6 .... 22 D4
Wroxham Rd *THMD* SE28 .... 108 D6
Wroxton Rd *PECK* SE15 .... 122 B7
Wrythe Gn *CAR* SM5 .... 170 F5
Wrythe Green Rd *CAR* SM5...... 170 F5
Wrythe La *CAR* SM5 .... 170 D3
Wulfstan St *SHB* W12 .... 99 M5
Wyatt Cl *BUSH* WD23 .... 43 L2
  FELT TW13 .... 132 D5
  YEAD UB4 .... 96 A4
Wyatt Dr *BARN* SW13 .... 118 B4
Wyatt Park Rd
  BRXS/STRHM SW2 .... 138 D7
Wyatt Rd *DART* DA1 .... 127 M8
  FSBYPK N4 .... 85 J3
  FSTGT E7 .... 88 A6
  STA TW18 .... 148 A1
Wyatt's La *WALTH* E17 .... 69 J4
Wybert St *CAMTN* NW1 .... 4 D9
Wyborne Wy *WLSDN* NW10 ..... 81 J7
Wyburn Av *BAR* EN5 .... 33 M6
Wyche Gv *SAND/SEL* CR2 .... 184 C5
Wych Elm Cl *EMPK* RM11 .... 75 G7
Wych Elm Rd *EMPK* RM11 .... 75 G7
Wycherley Cl *BKHTH/KID* SE3 ... 123 M5
Wycherley Crs *BAR* EN5 .... 47 H1
Wychwood Av *EDGW* HA8 .... 44 D8
  THHTH CR7 .... 157 H6
Wychwood Cl *EDGW* HA8 .... 44 D8
  SUN TW16 .... 150 A2
Wychwood End *HGT* N6 .... 66 C8
Wychwood Gdns *CLAY* IG5 .... 70 C5
Wychwood Wy *NTHWD* HA6 ..... 59 M1
Wycliffe Cl *WELL* DA16 .... 125 M6
Wycliffe Rd *BTSEA* SW11 .... 120 A8
  WIM/MER SW19 .... 155 H2
Wyclif St *FSBYE* EC1V 6 C8
Wycombe Gdns *CRICK* NW2 ...... 82 F2
Wycombe Pl
  WAND/EARL SW18 .... 137 J3
Wycombe Rd *ALP/SUD* HA0 ... 81 G8
  GNTH/NBYPK IG2 .... 70 F6
  TOTM N17 .... 68 A2
Wydell Cl *MRDN* SM4 .... 169 J1
Wydehurst Rd *CROY/NA* CR0 ... 173 G2
Wydeville Manor Rd
  LEE/GVPK SE12 .... 142 B8
Wye Cl *ASHF* TW15 .... 131 H8
  ORP BR6 .... 176 F2
  RSLP HA4 .... 59 J7
Wyemead Crs *CHING* E4 .... 51 L4
Wye St *BTSEA* SW11 .... 119 K8
Wyeth's Rd *EW* KT17 .... 180 F6
Wyevale Cl *PIN* HA5 .... 60 A4
Wyfields *CLAY* IG5 .... 71 H2
Wyfold Rd *FUL/PGN* SW6 .... 118 E6
Wyke Cl *ISLW* TW7 .... 115 M4
Wyke Gdns *HNWL* W7 .... 115 M1
Wykeham Av *DAGW* RM9 .... 90 C6
  EMPK RM11 .... 74 D7
Wykeham Gn *DAGW* RM9 .... 90 C6
Wykeham Hl *WBLY* HA9 .... 80 F1
Wykeham Ri *TRDG/WHET* N20 .. 46 E3
Wykeham Rd *HDN* NW4 .... 64 C6
  KTN/HRWW/W HA3 .... 62 B5
Wyke Rd *BOW* E3 .... 87 G7
  RYNPK SW20 .... 154 C5
Wylchin Cl *PIN* HA5 .... 59 M5
Wyldes Cl *GLDGN* NW11 .... 83 J1
Wyldfield Gdns *ED* N9 .... 49 M4
Wyld Wy *WBLY* HA9 .... 81 H6
Wyleu St *FSTH* SE23 .... 140 E4
Wyllen Cl *WCHPL* E1 .... 104 C3
Wyllyotts Pl *POTB/CUF* EN6 .... 22 F5
Wylo Dr *BAR* EN5 .... 46 A1
Wymering Rd *MV/WKIL* W9 ..... 2 B8
Wymond St *PUT/ROE* SW15 ..... 118 C3
Wynan Rd *POP/IOD* E14 .... 123 H3
Wyncham Av *BFN/LL* DA15 ...... 143 K5
Wynchgate *KTN/HRWW/W* HA3... 61 L1
  STHGT/OAK N14 .... 48 D1

Wyncroft Cl *BMLY* BR1 .... 160 F6
Wyndale Av *CDALE/KGS* NW9 ... 63 G7
Wyndcliff Rd *CHARL* SE7 .... 124 B4
Wyndcroft Cl *ENC/FH* EN2 .... 36 B6
Wyndham Cl *BELMT* SM2 .... 182 A1
  ORP BR6 .... 176 C3
Wyndham Crs *HSLWW* TW4 ..... 132 F8
  KTTN NW5 .... 84 C3
Wyndham Ms *MBLAR* W1H 9 L3
Wyndham Pl *MBLAR* W1H 9 L3
  MBLAR W1H 9 L3
  MBLAR W1H 9 L3
Wyndham Rd *CMBW* SE5 .... 121 J5
  EBAR EN4 .... 47 M3
  EHAM E6 .... 88 D7
  KUTN/CMB KT2 .... 152 F3
  WEA W13 .... 116 B1
Wyndham St *MBLAR* W1H....... 9 L2
Wyneham Rd *HNHL* SE24 .... 139 K2
Wynell Rd *FSTH* SE23 .... 140 D7
Wynford Gv *STMC/STPC* BR5 ... 162 B6
Wynford Pl *BELV* DA17 .... 127 G4
Wynford Rd *IS* N1 .... 5 L5
Wynford Wy *ELTH/MOT* SE9 ..... 142 F7
Wynlie Gdns *PIN* HA5 .... 60 B3
Wynndale Rd *SWFD* E18 .... 70 B2
Wynne Rd *BRXN/ST* SW9 .... 121 G7
Wynn's Av *BFN/LL* DA15 .... 144 A2
Wynnstay Gdns *KENS* W8 .... 14 B3
Wynter St *BTSEA* SW11 .... 137 J1
Wynton Gdns *SNWD* SE25 .... 157 L8
Wynton Gv *WOT/HER* KT12 ..... 165 G5
Wynton Pl *ACT* W3 .... 99 H5
Wynyard Ter *LBTH* SE11 .... 17 M7
Wynyatt St *FSBYE* EC1V 6 C7
Wyre Gv *EDGW* HA8 .... 45 J3
  HYS/HAR UB3 .... 114 A2
Wyresdale Crs *GFD/PVL* UB6 ... 97 M2
Wyteleaf Cl *RSLP* HA4 .... 59 J7
Wythburn Pl *MBLAR* W1H....... 9 L5
Wythenshawe Rd *DAGE* RM10... 91 G3
Wythes Cl *BMLY* BR1 .... 160 F5
Wythes Rd *CAN/RD* E16 .... 106 E7
Wythfield Rd *ELTH/MOT* SE9 .... 142 F3
Wyvenhoe Rd
  RYLN/HDSTN HA2 .... 79 J3
Wyvern Cl *DART* DA1 .... 146 C4
  ORP BR6 .... 177 H5
Wyvern Rd *PUR/KEN* CR8 .... 184 A3
Wyvern Wy *UX/CGN* UB8....... 76 B7
Wyvil Rd *VX/NE* SW8 .... 120 E5
Wyvis St *POP/IOD* E14 .... 105 H4

Y

Yabsley St *POP/IOD* E14 .... 105 J7
Yalding Cl *STMC/STPC* BR5 .... 162 D7
Yalding Rd *BERM/RHTH* SE16 ... 122 D1
Yale Cl *HSLWW* TW4 .... 132 F2
Yale Wy *HCH* RM12 .... 92 A4
Yarborough Rd
  WIM/MER SW19 .... 155 K4
Yarbridge Cl *BELMT* SM2 .... 182 B5
Yardley Cl *CHING* E4 .... 38 B8
Yardley La *CHING* E4 .... 38 B8
Yardley St *FSBYW* WC1X 6 A8
  FSBYW WC1X 6 A9
Yarmouth Crs *WALTH* E17 .... 68 B6
Yarmouth Rd *WATN* WD24 .... 29 H3
Yarnton Wy *ERITHM* DA18 ..... 126 F1
Yarrow Crs *EHAM* E6 .... 106 E4
Yateley St *WOOL/PLUM* SE18 ... 124 D1
Yeading Av *RSLP* HA4 .... 78 E2
Yeading Fk *YEAD* UB4 .... 96 C4
Yeading Gdns *YEAD* UB4 .... 96 B4
Yeading La *YEAD* UB4 .... 96 B5
Yeames Cl *WEA* W13 .... 98 A5
Yeate St *IS* N1 .... 7 G2
Yeatman Rd *HGT* N6 .... 65 M7
Yeats Cl *WLSDN* NW10 .... 81 H4
Yeend Cl *E/WMO/HCT* KT8 ..... 151 G7
Yeldham Rd *HMSMTH* W6 .... 119 G7
Yellowpine Wy *CHIG* IG7 .... 54 B6
Yelverton Cl *HARH* RM3 .... 74 C2
Yelverton Rd *BTSEA* SW11 ..... 119 K7
Yenston Cl *MRDN* SM4 .... 167 K5
Yeoman Cl *EHAM* E6 .... 107 H6
  WNWD SE27 .... 138 E2
Yeomanry Cl *EW* KT17 .... 180 F5
Yeomans Acre *RSLP* HA4 .... 60 A7
Yeoman's Rw *CHEL* SW3 .... 15 K4
Yeomans Wy *EN* EN1 .... 37 H5
Yeomen Wy *BARK/HLT* IG6 ..... 53 J8
Yeo St *BOW* E3 .... 105 H4
Yeovil Cl *ORP* BR6 .... 176 E4
Yeovilton Pl *KUTN/CMB* KT2 ... 152 D1
Yerbury Rd *ARCH* N19 .... 84 D3
Yester Dr *CHST* BR7 .... 160 F3
Yester Pk *CHST* BR7 .... 160 F3
Yester Rd *CHST* BR7 .... 160 F3
Yevele Wy *EMPK* RM11 .... 74 E8
Yew Av *WDR/YW* UB7 .... 94 E6
Yewbank Cl *PUR/KEN* CR8 ..... 184 D8
Yew Cl *BKHH* IG9 .... 52 D4
Yewdale Cl *BMLY* BR1 .... 159 L2
Yewfield Rd *WLSDN* NW10 ..... 81 M7
Yew Gv *CRICK* NW2 .... 82 B4
Yewlands Cl *BNSTD* SM7 .... 182 B8
Yews Av *EN* EN1 .... 37 H1
Yew Tree Cl *RYLN/HDSTN* HA2... 61 H5
  WELL DA16 .... 126 A6
  WPK KT4 .... 168 L5
Yew Tree Gdns *CHDH* RM6 ..... 72 C6
  EPSOM KT18 .... 180 C8
  ROMW/RG RM7 .... 73 K6

Yewtree Rd *BECK* BR3 .... 158 F6
Yew Tree Rd *HGDN/ICK* UB10 .. 76 F8
  SHB W12 .... 99 M6
Yew Tree Wk *HSLWW* TW4 .... 132 F2
  PUR/KEN CR8 .... 184 C3
Yew Wk *HRW* HA1 .... 79 L1
Yoakley Rd *STNW/STAM* N16 ... 85 L2
Yoke Cl *HOLWY* N7 .... 84 E6
Yolande Gdns *ELTH/MOT* SE9 .. 142 E2
Yonge Pk *FSBYPK* N4 .... 84 E3
York Av *BFN/LL* DA15 .... 143 L6
  HNWL W7 .... 97 L7
  KTN/HRWW/W HA3 .... 62 B2
  MORT/ESHN SW14 .... 135 J2
  UX/CGN UB8 .... 95 J5
York Br *CAMTN* NW1 .... 4 A9
York Buildings *CHCR* WC2N 11 K7
York Cl *EHAM* E6 .... 106 F5
  HNWL W7 .... 97 L7
  KGLGY WD4 .... 20 A2
  MRDN SM4 .... 155 H7
  LOU IG10 .... 39 L6
York Crs *BORE* WD6 .... 32 D5
  LOU IG10 .... 39 L6
Yorke Ga *WAT* WD17 .... 29 G5
Yorke Rd *RKW/CH/CXG* WD3 ... 41 G1
York Gdns *WOT/HER* KT12 ..... 165 K4
York Ga *CAMTN* NW1 .... 10 B1
  STHGT/OAK N14 .... 48 E2
York Gv *PECK* SE15 .... 122 C6
York Hl *LOU* IG10 .... 39 L6
  STRHM/NOR SW16 .... 139 H7
Yorkland Av *WELL* DA16 .... 143 M1
York Ms *IL* IG1 .... 89 G2
  KTTN NW5 .... 84 B5
York Pl *BTSEA* SW11 .... 119 J8
  IL IG1 .... 89 G2
York Ri *KTTN* NW5 .... 84 B3
  ORP BR6 .... 177 K1
York Rd *ACT* W3 .... 99 J5
  BAR EN5 .... 34 C4
  BELMT SM2 .... 170 A8
  BTFD TW8 .... 116 D3
  BTSEA SW11 .... 119 J8
  CHES/WCR EN8 .... 26 E7
  CHING E4 .... 51 G7
  CROY/NA CR0 .... 172 A2
  DART DA1 .... 146 F4
  EA W5 .... 116 C1
  FBAR/BDGN N11 .... 48 D8
  FSTGT E7 .... 88 A6
  HSLW TW3 .... 115 H8
  IL IG1 .... 89 G3
  KUTN/CMB KT2 .... 152 F5
  LEY E10 .... 87 J3
  NTHWD HA6 .... 60 A3
  RAIN RM13 .... 91 K7
  RCHPK/HAM TW10 .... 134 F2
  SAND/SEL CR2 .... 185 K3
  STHWK SE1 .... 17 M1
  TEDD TW11 .... 133 L8
  UED N18 .... 50 B7
  UX/CGN UB8 .... 76 D7
  WALTH E17 .... 68 D6
  WATW WD18 .... 29 J8
  WCHMH N21 .... 49 K2
  WEY KT13 .... 164 C7
  WIM/MER SW19 .... 155 H2
Yorkshire Cl *STNW/STAM* N16 ... 85 L3
Yorkshire Gdns *UED* N18 .... 50 D7
Yorkshire Grey Yd *WHCLV* ... 11 L3
Yorkshire Rd *MTCM* CR4 .... 156 E8
  POP/IOD E14 .... 104 E5
York Sq *POP/IOD* E14 .... 104 E5
York St *BARK* IG11 .... 89 H8
  MBLAR W1H 9 L3
  MHST W1U 9 M2
  MTCM CR4 .... 171 G2
  TWK TW1 .... 134 A5
York Ter *ENC/FH* EN2 .... 36 C3
  ERITH DA8 .... 127 J6
York Ter East *CAMTN* NW1 ..... 10 B1
York Ter West *CAMTN* NW1 .... 10 A1
Yorkton St *BETH* E2 .... 104 A1
York Wy *CHSGTN* KT9 .... 179 K1
  FELT TW13 .... 132 F7
  GSTN WD25 .... 29 K1
  HOLWY N7 .... 84 D6
  IS N1 .... 5 K5
  TRDG/WHET N20 .... 47 M5
Youngmans Cl *ENC/FH* EN2 ..... 36 C4
Young Rd *CAN/RD* E16 .... 106 C5
Youngs Rd *GNTH/NBYPK* IG2 ... 71 K6
Young St *KENS* W8 .... 14 C2
Yoxley Ap *GNTH/NBYPK* IG2 ... 71 J7
Yoxley Dr *GNTH/NBYPK* IG2 .... 71 J7
Yukon Rd *BAL* SW12 .... 138 B4
Yule Cl *LCOL/BKTW* AL2 .... 21 M3
Yuletide Cl *WLSDN* NW10 .... 81 L6
Yunus Khan Cl *WALTH* E17 ..... 69 G6

Z

Zampa Rd *BERM/RHTH* SE16 ... 122 C3
Zander Ct *BETH* E2 .... 104 A2
Zangwill Rd *BKHTH/KID* SE3 ... 124 D6
Zealand Av *WDR/YW* UB7 .... 112 D5
Zealand Rd *BOW* E3 .... 104 L1
Zelah Rd *STMC/STPC* BR5 .... 177 H2
Zennor Rd *BAL* SW12 .... 138 C5
Zenoria St *EDUL* SE22 .... 139 M1
Zermatt Rd *THHTH* CR7 .... 157 J7
Zetland St *POP/IOD* E14 .... 105 J4
Zion Pl *THHTH* CR7 .... 157 K7
Zion Rd *THHTH* CR7 .... 157 K7
Zoar St *STHWK* SE1 .... 12 E8
Zoffany St *ARCH* N19 .... 84 D2

Aarotya Medical Centre
TOTM N17 .... 67 J5
Abbey Business Centre
VX/NE SW8 .... 120 C6
The Abbey Clinic
BELV DA17 .... 126 F3
Abbey Industrial Estate
ALP/SUD HA0 .... 80 F8
Abbey Industrial Estate
MTCM CR4 .... 155 M8
Abbey Mead Industrial Park
WAB EN9 .... 27 H7
Abbey Medical Centre
STJWD NW8 .... 2 D4
Abbey Park Industrial Estate
BARK IG11 .... 107 H1
Abbey Primary School
ABYW SE2 .... 126 C1
Abbey Road Health Centre
SRTFD E15 .... 87 L8
Abbey Road Surgery
CHES/WCR EN8 .... 26 A1
Abbey Trading Estate
SYD SE26 .... 158 E1
Abbey Wharf Industrial Estate
BARK IG11 .... 107 K2
Abbey Wood Podiatry Clinic
ABYW SE2 .... 126 B2
Abbey Wood Secondary School
ABYW SE2 .... 126 A1
Abbotsbury Primary First School
MRDN SM4 .... 155 L8
Abbotsfield School
HGDN/ICK UB10 .... 95 H1
Abbots Langley Parish Council
ABLGY WD5 .... 20 F4
Abbots School
ABLGY WD5 .... 20 F5
Abbotswood Medical Centre
ABLGY WD5 .... 21 G5
A B C Cinema
BECK BR3 .... 159 G5
A B C Cinema
CAT SE6 .... 141 H5
A B C Cinema
ESH/CLAY KT10 .... 166 B5
A B C Cinema
PUT/ROE SW15 .... 118 E8
A B C Cinema
STRHM/NOR SW16 .... 138 E6
Abc Cinemas
FITZ W1T 11 G5
Abercorn Place School
STJWD NW8 .... 2 F6
Aberglen Industrial Estate
HYS/HAR UB3 .... 95 K3
Acacia Business Centre
WAN E11 .... 87 L3
Aches & Pains Osteopathic Clinic
HOR/WEW KT19 .... 168 D7
Acland Burghley School
KTTN NW5 .... 84 B4
The Acorn Group Practise
TWK TW1 .... 134 A4
Acorn Industrial Park
DART DA1 .... 146 A2
Acorn Medical Centre
HGDN/ICK UB10 .... 77 G8
The Acorn Surgery
PECK SE15 .... 122 B5
Acre Road Health Clinic
KUTN/CMB KT2 .... 152 F3
Acton Business Centre
WLSDN NW10 .... 99 K3
Acton Central Industrial Estate
ACT W3 .... 99 H6
Acton Health Centre
ACT W3 .... 99 J7
Acton High School
ACT W3 .... 99 G8
Acton Hospital
ACT W3 .... 99 G8
Acton Lane Medical Centre
CHSWK W4 .... 99 K8
Acton Park Industrial Estate
ACT W3 .... 99 M7
Acton Park Industrial Estate
CHSWK W4 .... 99 K8
Acton Superbowl
ACT W3 .... 99 G3
Acton Swimming Baths
ACT W3 .... 99 J7
Adams Bridge Business Centre
WBLY HA9 .... 81 H5
Adamsrill Primary School
SYD SE26 .... 140 E7
Addey & Stanhope School
NWCR SE14 .... 122 F6
Addington Business Centre
CROY/NA CR0 .... 186 E3
Addiscombe Cricket Club
CROY/NA CR0 .... 172 F5
Addison Primary School
WKENS W14 .... 118 D1
Adler Industrial Estate
HYS/HAR UB3 .... 95 K4
Admiral Hyson Industrial Estate
BERM/RHTH SE16 .... 122 B2
A D T College
PUT/ROE SW15 .... 136 F2
The Adult College of Barking &
Dagenham
BARK IG11 .... 89 L6
Adult Education Centre
POP/IOD E14 .... 123 J1
Africa Centre
COVGDN WC2E 11 K6
Ailsa Gallery
TWK TW1 .... 134 B3
Ainslie Wood Primary School
CHING E4 .... 51 H7
Airbase Unity Elementary
School
RSLP HA4 .... 77 J2
Airedale Physiotherapy Clinic
CHSWK W4 .... 117 M3
Air Links Industrial Estate
HEST TW5 .... 114 C3

Airport Industrial Estate
BH/WHM TN16 .... 187 K8
Aksaray Sports Club
STNW/STAM N16 .... 85 K4
Akshaya Dance Theatre
GNWCH SE10 .... 123 J5
Alban Wood Infant School
GSTN WD25 .... 21 H5
Albanwood School
GSTN WD25 .... 21 H6
Albany Centre & Theatre
DEPT SE8 .... 122 F5
Albany Clinic
BFN/LL DA15 .... 144 A8
Albany Clinic
WIM/MER SW19 .... 155 H3
The Albany College
HDN NW4 .... 64 C6
Albany School Grant Maintained
PEND EN3 .... 37 K3
The Albany School
HCH RM12 .... 92 B2
Albemarle College
BAY/PAD W2 .... 8 D6
Albemarle Gallery
FUL/PGN SW6 .... 119 H8
Albemarle Primary School
WIM/MER SW19 .... 136 K6
Albion Health Centre
WCHPL E1 .... 104 B4
Albion Junior & Infant School
BERM/RHTH SE16 .... 104 C3
Albion Street Health Centre
BERM/RHTH SE16 .... 104 C8
Albion Surgery
BXLYHS DA6 .... 145 G1
Albright Industrial Estate
RAIN RM13 .... 109 M4
The Alchemy Gallery
CLKNW EC1R 6 A9
Aldenham Parish Council
RAD WD7 .... 31 G1
Aldenham School
BORE WD6 .... 30 F5
Alderbrook Primary School
BAL SW12 .... 138 B4
Aldersbrook County Secondary
School
MNPK E12 .... 88 C1
Aldersbrook Primary School
WAN E11 .... 88 C1
Alderwood Primary School
ELTH/MOT SE9 .... 143 K3
Aldgate Gallery
WCHPL E1 .... 13 L3
Aldwych Theatre
HOL/ALD WC2B 11 L5
Alexander Mcleod
Junior School
ABYW SE2 .... 126 B3
Alexandra Avenue Clinic
RYLN/HDSTN HA2 .... 79 G2
Alexandra Avenue School
RYLN/HDSTN HA2 .... 79 G2
Alexandra Infant School
PGE/AN SE20 .... 158 D3
Alexandra Junior &
Infant School
WDGN N22 .... 66 F3
Alexandra Junior School
HSLW TW3 .... 115 H7
Alexandra Junior School
SYD SE26 .... 158 D2
Alfred Mizen First School
MTCM CR4 .... 156 D6
Alfred Salter Primary School
BERM/RHTH SE16 .... 104 D8
Alfreds Way Industrial Estate
BARK IG11 .... 90 A8
Algerian Embassy
NTGHL W11 .... 100 E7
Allegery Clinc
CAVSQ/HST W1G 10 C4
Allenby Road School
GFD/PVL UB6 .... 97 H5
Allen Edwards Primary School
CLAP SW4 .... 120 L6
The All England Lawn Tennis &
Croquet Club
WIM/MER SW19 .... 136 C7
Allerton Road Surgery
FSBYPK N4 .... 85 J2
Alleyns School
EDUL SE22 .... 139 L2
Allfarthing Junior School
WAND/EARL SW18 .... 137 J3
All Saints Benhilton School
SUT SM1 .... 170 B5
All Saints C of E First School
WIM/MER SW19 .... 155 J3
All Saints C of E Primary School
BKHTH/KID SE3 .... 123 L7
All Saints C of E School
CRICK NW2 .... 82 B7
All Saints C of E School
PUT/ROE SW15 .... 118 C3
All Saints Primary School
TRDG/WHET N20 .... 47 K4
All Saints School
BCTR RM8 .... 91 G1
All Saints School
FUL/PGN SW6 .... 118 C7
All Saints School
NRWD SE19 .... 157 L4
Allum Medical Centre
WAN E11 .... 69 K8
Alma Junior & Infant School
BERM/RHTH SE16 .... 122 A2
The Almanac Gallery Christmas
Collection
BAY/PAD W2 .... 8 F6
The Almanac Gallery
FUL/PGN SW6 .... 118 F7
Alma Road Junior &
Infant School
PEND EN3 .... 37 K8
Almeida Theatre
IS N1 .... 6 C2

Al Muntada Islamic School
FUL/PGN SW6 .... 118 F6
Alperton Community School
ALP/SUD HA0 .... 80 E7
Alperton High School
ALP/SUD HA0 .... 80 D8
Alperton Sports Ground
ALP/SUD HA0 .... 98 D1
Alpha Business Centre
WALTH E17 .... 68 F6
Alternative Health Practice
HAMP NW3 .... 83 G3
Altmore Infant School
EHAM E6 .... 88 F7
Alton Medical Practice
PUT/ROE SW15 .... 136 A4
The Alton School
PUT/ROE SW15 .... 135 M4
Ambassadors Theatre
LSQ/SEVD WC2H 11 H6
Ambler School
FSBYPK N4 .... 85 H3
Ambleside Junior School
WOT/HER KT12 .... 165 J3
A M C Business Centre
WLSDN NW10 .... 99 H2
American Community School
HGDN/ICK UB10 .... 76 F8
Amf Bowling
LEW SE13 .... 123 J8
Amherst Primary School
HACK E8 .... 86 A5
Ampthill Square Medical Centre
CAMTN NW1 .... 4 E6
Amy Johnson Primary School
SCUP DA6 .... 183 L1
Andover Medical Centre
HOLWY N7 .... 84 F3
Andrew Ewing Junior &
Infant School
HEST TW5 .... 114 F5
Andrew Sketchley Theatre
WCHPL E1 .... 104 A4
Andrews Lane Junior &
Infant School
CHESW EN7 .... 26 A1
Anerley Primary School
PGE/AN SE20 .... 158 A4
Anerley Secondary
Boarding School
NRWD SE19 .... 158 A4
Anerley Surgery
PGE/AN SE20 .... 158 B4
Angel Natural Health Practice
IS N1 .... 85 G6
Annandale Primary School
GNWCH SE10 .... 123 M3
The Anna Scher Theatre
IS N1 .... 6 A4
Anne Mount School
EFNCH N2 .... 65 K7
Annunciation RC School
EDGE HA8 .... 63 K2
Anson Primary School
CRICK NW2 .... 82 D5
Ante Natal Clinic
MUSWH N10 .... 66 A4
Antigua & Barbuda High Comm
MHST W1U 10 B4
The Antiques Gallery
BELMT SM2 .... 182 A3
Apex Industrial Estate
WLSDN NW10 .... 99 M3
Apex Retail Park
FELT TW13 .... 132 F7
Apollo Business Centre
DEPT SE8 .... 122 D3
Apollo Theatre
SOHO/SHAV W1D 11 G6
Apollo Victoria Theatre
PIM SW1V 16 E4
Apostolic Nuncio
WIM/MER SW19 .... 136 C7
Applegarth Infant School
CROY/NA CR0 .... 174 B8
Apsley House
BAY/PAD W2 .... 16 A1
Aquarelles Gallery
NTGHL W11 .... 100 F7
Aquarius Business Park
CRICK NW2 .... 82 A1
Arbras Gallery
NTGHL W11 .... 100 F5
The Archbishop Michael Ramsey
School
CMBW SE5 .... 121 H5
Archbishop Sumners
C of E Primary School
LBTH SE11 .... 18 B6
Archbishop Tenisons
C of E School
CROY/NA CR0 .... 172 F5
Archbishop Tenison's School
VX/NE SW8 .... 120 F4
Archdale Business Centre
RYLN/HDSTN HA2 .... 79 J2
Archdeacon Cambridges School
WHTN TW2 .... 133 L6
Arches Business Centre
NWDGN UB2 .... 96 F8
Arches Leisure Centre
GNWCH SE10 .... 123 K4
Archgate Business Centre
NFNCH/WDSP N12 .... 47 J7
Archilton Group Practice
EPSOM KT18 .... 180 C6
Ardleigh Green Junior School
EMPK RM11 .... 74 D4
Arena Estate
FSBYPK N4 .... 67 H7
Argentine Embassy
MYFR/PKLN W1K 10 C6
Argile Gallery
NTGHL W11 .... 100 F5
Argyle Primary School
STPAN WC1H 5 J7
Argyle Surgery
WEA W13 .... 98 A5

Ark College
LBTH SE11 .... 18 C8
Arklow Trading Estate
NWCR SE14 .... 122 E4
Armchair Theatre
LBTH SE11 .... 18 B9
Armourers & Braziers' Hall
CITYW EC2V 13 G3
Army
SKENS SW7 .... 14 F4
Arndale Health Centre
WAND/EARL SW18 .... 137 H2
Arnhem Wharf Primary School
POP/IOD E14 .... 122 F1
Arnold House School
STJWD NW8 .... 3 G5
Arnott Abbey
FARR EC1M 12 C2
Arsenal Football Club
HBRY N5 .... 85 H3
Artbank Gallery
FARR EC1M 12 C1
Art Gallery
LOTH EC2R 13 H5
Art Gallery
RSLP HA4 .... 78 A1
Art Gallery
WLSDN NW10 .... 82 B6
The Art Gallery
CMBW SE5 .... 121 J5
The Art Gallery
RCH/KEW TW9 .... 134 E1
The Artisan Gallery
GRH DA9 .... 147 M4
The Artisan Gallery
WFD IG8 .... 52 B8
Art School
BECK BR3 .... 158 E8
The Art Space School
IS N1 .... 6 E5
Ashbourne Independent
Sixth Form College
KENS W8 .... 14 D1
Ashburnham Primary School
WBPTN SW10 .... 119 K5
Ashburton Primary School
CROY/NA CR0 .... 173 H1
Ashby Mill School
CLAP SW4 .... 138 E2
Ashfield Junior School
BUSH WD23 .... 43 H2
Ashford Clinic
ASHF TW15 .... 130 E7
Ashford C of E School
ASHF TW15 .... 149 H2
Ashford High School
ASHF TW15 .... 130 E7
Ashford Hospital A & E
STWL/WRAY TW19 .... 130 E6
Ashford Sports Club
ASHF TW15 .... 130 D8
Ashford Sports Club
STWL/WRAY TW19 .... 130 F5
Ashgrove College
WALTH E17 .... 69 G4
Ashgrove Estate
BMLY BR1 .... 159 K2
Ashgrove School
BMLY BR1 .... 160 B5
Ashleigh Commercial Estate
CHARL SE7 .... 124 C2
Ashley Centre Surgery
EPSOM KT18 .... 180 D6
Ashley Gallery
HPTN TW12 .... 151 K4
Ashley Infant School
WOT/HER KT12 .... 165 G3
Ashmead Primary School
BROCKY SE4 .... 123 G7
Ashmole Primary School
VX/NE SW8 .... 120 F4
Ashmole School
STHGT/OAK N14 .... 48 C3
Ashmount Junior &
Infant School
ARCH N19 .... 66 C8
Ashton House School
ISLW TW7 .... 115 K6
Ashvale Medical Centre
TOOT SW17 .... 155 M1
Ashville Surgery
FUL/PGN SW6 .... 118 F6
The Ashworth Practice
ORP BR6 .... 177 H2
Aspen House Secondary &
Primary School
BRXS/STRHM SW2 .... 138 E4
Asquith Court School
KTN/HRWW/W HA3 .... 62 B7
Asquith School
PEND EN3 .... 37 J7
Associated Newspapers
BERM/RHTH SE16 .... 122 D1
Aston Clinic
NWMAL KT3 .... 153 L7
Aston House School
EA W5 .... 98 D5
Astoria Theatre
SOHO/SHAV W1D 11 H4
Asylum Medical Centre
CEND/HSY/T N8 .... 67 G4
Athelney Primary School
CAT SE6 .... 141 G7
Athelstan House School
HPTN TW12 .... 151 G4
Athena Medical Centre
CLPT E5 .... 86 C4
Atherton Leisure Centre
FSTGT E7 .... 87 M6
Athlone House Hospital
HGT N6 .... 83 M1
Athlon Industrial Estate
ALP/SUD HA0 .... 98 D1
Atkinson Morley Hospital
RYNPK SW20 .... 154 B3

Atlas Business Centre
CRICK NW2 .... 82 B2
Atlas Transport Estate
BTSEA SW11 .... 119 J7
Atwood Primary School
SAND/SEL CR2 .... 185 G6
Aultone Yard
CAR SM5 .... 170 F5
Auriol Junior School
HOR/WEW KT19 .... 168 F6
Australian High Commission
HOL/ALD WC2B 11 M5
Austrian Embassy
KTBR SW1X 16 A3
Avalon Chinese Medicine Clinic
CHSWK W4 .... 117 J5
Aveley Football Club
SOCK/AV RM15 .... 111 J6
Aveley Primary School
SOCK/AV RM15 .... 111 L7
The Aveley School
SOCK/AV RM15 .... 111 K6
Aveling Park School
WALTH E17 .... 69 G3
Avenue Industrial Estate
CHING E4 .... 50 F8
Avenue Industrial Estate
GPK RM2 .... 74 D3
Avenue Primary School
KIL/WHAMP NW6 .... 82 E7
Avenue Primary School
MNPK E12 .... 88 E2
The Avenue Primary School
BELMT SM2 .... 182 A3
Avigdor High School
STNW/STAM N16 .... 85 K2
Avondale Park Primary School
NTGHL W11 .... 100 D6
Avon House School
WFD IG8 .... 52 A6
Avril Noble Gallery
TPL/STR WC2R 11 K6
Aylands School
PEND EN3 .... 37 J1
Ayloff Primary School
HCH RM12 .... 92 B4
Aylward First & Middle Schools
STAN HA7 .... 44 D7
Aylward School
UED N18 .... 49 K6
Aylwin Secondary School
BERM/RHTH SE16 .... 19 M5
Baa Visitor Centre
HTHAIR TW6 .... 113 J6
Babington House School
CHST BR7 .... 160 F2
Back Care Clinic
WPK KT4 .... 169 G3
Bacons College
BERM/RHTH SE16 .... 104 D8
Bacon's College
BERM/RHTH SE16 .... 104 E7
Baden Powell County
Primary School
CLPT E5 .... 86 B3
Baden Powell House
SKENS SW7 .... 14 F5
Bahamas High Comm
MYFR/PICC W1J 10 B8
Bahram Gallery
IS N1 .... 6 C4
Balaam Leisure Centre
PLSTW E13 .... 106 A3
Balfour Business Centre
NWDGN UB2 .... 114 D1
Balgowan Primary School
BECK BR3 .... 158 E5
Balham Health Centre
BAL SW12 .... 138 B6
Balham Mosque
BAL SW12 .... 138 B4
Ballater Surgery
ORP BR6 .... 176 F2
Baltic Exchange
HDTCH EC3A 13 K4
Bancrofts School
WFD IG8 .... 52 A5
Bandon Hill School
WLGTN SM6 .... 171 K8
Bangabandhu Primary School
BETH E2 .... 104 C2
Bangladesh High Comm
SKENS SW7 .... 14 F3
Bank of England Extension
STP EC4M 12 E5
Bank of England
LOTH EC2R 13 G5
Bankside Gallery
STHWK SE1 .... 12 D7
Bankside Industrial Estate
BARK IG11 .... 108 A2
Bankside Park Industrial Estate
BARK IG11 .... 108 A2
Bannockburn CP School
WOOL/PLUM SE18 .... 125 M2
Banqueting House
WHALL SW1A 11 J9
Banstead Clinic
BNSTD SM7 .... 182 A8
Banstead County Infants School
BNSTD SM7 .... 181 M8
Banstead Village Clinic
BNSTD SM7 .... 182 B8
Barbados High Comm
FITZ W1T 11 H4
Barber Surgeons' Hall
BARB EC2Y 12 F3
The Barbican
STBT EC1A 12 E2
Barbican Theatre
BARB EC2Y 12 F2
Barclay Junior & Infant School
LEY E10 .... 69 K7
Barham Primary School
ALP/SUD HA0 .... 80 C6
Baring Primary School
LEE/GVPK SE12 .... 142 A4

Baring Road Medical Centre
LEE/GVPK SE12 .... 142 A6
Barkantine Clinic
POP/IOD E14 .... 105 G8
Barking Abbey Comprehensive School
BARK IG11 .... 89 K5
Barking Abbey Industrial Estate
BARK IG11 .... 89 H8
Barking College
ROMW/RG RM7 .... 91 K2
Barking & Dagenham Council
DAGW RM9 .... 90 F6
Barking Football Club
BCTR RM8 .... 90 B5
Barking Hospital
BARK IG11 .... 89 M7
Barking Industrial Park
BARK IG11 .... 89 M8
Barking Rugby Union Football Club
DAGW RM9 .... 90 D8
Barkingside Football Club
BARK/HLT IG6 .... 71 K5
Barlby Primary School
NKENS W10 .... 100 D3
Barley Lane Primary School
CHDH RM6 .... 72 B8
Barnabas Medical Centre
NTHLT UB5 .... 79 J6
Barncroft Primary School
WALTH E17 .... 68 E7
Barnehurst Junior School
BXLYHN DA7 .... 127 J6
Barn Elms Water Sports Centre
BARN SW13 .... 118 C7
Barnes Cray Primary School
DART DA1 .... 146 A1
Barnes Hospital
MORT/ESHN SW14 .... 117 L8
Barnes Sports Club
BARN SW13 .... 117 M6
Barnet College
NFNCH/WDSP N12 .... 47 J7
Barnet College of Further Education
BAR EN5 .... 33 M7
Barnet County Court
BAR EN5 .... 34 C7
Barnet County Court
FNCH N3 .... 65 G2
Barnet Football Club
BAR EN5 .... 34 A8
Barnet General Hospital
BAR EN5 .... 33 K7
Barnet Health Centre
BAR EN5 .... 34 A8
Barnet Hill Primary School
BAR EN5 .... 33 M8
Barnet Hospital Chest Clinic
BAR EN5 .... 33 K7
Barnet Magistrates Court
BAR EN5 .... 33 M7
Barnet Synagogue
BAR EN5 .... 34 C8
Barnfield Road School
EDGE HA8 .... 63 J2
Barnhill Community High School
YEAD UB4 .... 96 B2
Barnsbury Gallery
IS N1 .... 6 A2
Barnsbury School for Girls
IS N1 .... 6 A1
The Barn Theatre Club
WOT/HER KT12 .... 165 H6
Barons Court Theatre
WKENS W14 .... 118 E3
Barracuda Swimming Club
POTB/CUF EN6 .... 23 K6
Barratt Industrial Park
BOW E3 .... 105 J3
Barrett Industrial Park
STHL UB1 .... 97 G7
Barrett Way Industrial Estate
HRW HA1 .... 61 K4
Barrington Primary School
WELL DA16 .... 126 D7
Barron Ingrid Gallery
HAMP NW3 .... 83 L4
Barrow Hedges School
CAR SM5 .... 182 E1
Barton House Health Centre
STNW/STAM N16 .... 85 K3
Barwell Business Park
CHSGTN KT9 .... 179 K1
Bashir Gallery
MBLAR W1H 9 M3
Bates Industrial Estate
HARH RM3 .... 75 G1
Bath Factory Estate
HNHL SE24 .... 139 J3
Battersea Business Centre
BTSEA SW11 .... 120 A8
Battersea Fields Practice
VX/NE SW8 .... 120 C6
Battersea Sports Centre
BTSEA SW11 .... 119 K8
Battersea Technology College
BTSEA SW11 .... 119 M6
Battersea Tutorial College
TOOT SW17 .... 138 A6
Baumkotter Gallery
KENS W8 .... 14 B1
BBC
REGST W1B 10 D3
BBC Studios
MV/WKIL W9 .... 2 C1
BBC Television Centre
SHB W12 .... 100 C6
B Day Hospital
BCTR RM8 .... 90 C4
Beacon Hill Industrial Estate
PUR RM19 .... 129 H2
Beacon House School
EA W5 .... 98 F7
Beaconsfield Road First School
STHL UB1 .... 96 E7

Beal High School
REDBR IG4 .... 70 E4
Beam Primary School
DAGE RM10 .... 109 J1
Beatrix Potter Primary School
WAND/EARL SW18 .... 137 J5
Beauclerc County Infant School
SUN TW16 .... 150 C6
Beaumont Primary School
LEY E10 .... 69 H8
Beaumont Primary School
PUR/KEN CR8 .... 183 M7
Beavers Primary School
HSLWW TW4 .... 114 C8
Beaverwood School for Girls
CHST BR7 .... 161 L2
Beckenham Business Centre
BECK BR3 .... 158 E2
Beckenham Cricket Club
BECK BR3 .... 159 H3
Beckenham Hospital
BECK BR3 .... 158 F5
Beckenham Leisure Centre
BECK BR3 .... 158 E4
Beckenham Rugby Football Club
BECK BR3 .... 158 E7
Beckenham Town Football Club
BECK BR3 .... 159 G8
Beckford Primary School
KIL/WHAMP NW6 .... 82 F5
Beckmead School
BECK BR3 .... 174 A3
The Beck Theatre
HYS/HAR UB3 .... 95 M5
Beckton Ski Centre
EHAM E6 .... 107 G3
Beckton Special School
CAN/RD E16 .... 106 D4
Becontree School
BCTR RM8 .... 90 B3
Bective House Clinic
PUT/ROE SW15 .... 136 F1
Beddington Infant School
WLGTN SM6 .... 171 J6
Beddington Infants School
WLGTN SM6 .... 171 J5
Beddington Medical Centre
CROY/NA CR0 .... 171 L6
Beddington Park Primary School
WLGTN SM6 .... 171 L5
Beddington Trading Estate
CROY/NA CR0 .... 171 L3
Bedelsford School
KUT KT1 .... 152 E6
Bedensfield Clinic
SCUP DA14 .... 162 L1
Bedfont Health Clinic
EBED/NFELT TW14 .... 131 L4
Bedfont Junior & Infant School
EBED/NFELT TW14 .... 131 L3
The Bedford Park Surgery
CHSWK W4 .... 117 K2
Bedmond JMI School
ABLGY WD5 .... 20 F1
Bedonwell Clinic
ABYW SE2 .... 126 A4
Bedonwell Medical Centre
BELV DA17 .... 126 F3
Bedonwell Primary Junior & Infant School
BELV DA17 .... 126 C4
Beech Avenue Surgery
UPMR RM14 .... 93 H4
Beechfield Junior Middle & Infant School
WATN WD24 .... 29 G2
Beech House School
SAND/SEL CR2 .... 184 F3
Beecholme Primary School
MTCM CR4 .... 156 B4
Beis Rochel D'satmar Girls School
STNW/STAM N16 .... 67 L8
Beis Yaakov Primary School
CDALE/KGS NW9 .... 63 K5
Belhus Golf Club & Leisure Centre
SOCK/AV RM15 .... 111 L9
Belize High Comm
CAVSQ/HST W1G 10 C1
Bellegrove Surgery
WELL DA16 .... 125 H1
Bellenden Junior & Infant School
PECK SE15 .... 122 A4
Bellenden Road Business Centre
PECK SE15 .... 121 M7
Bellenden Road Group Practice
PECK SE15 .... 121 M7
Belleville School
BTSEA SW11 .... 137 M2
Bell Farm County Middle School
WOT/HER KT12 .... 165 J6
Bell Industrial Estate
CHSWK W4 .... 117 J2
Bellingham Trading Estate
CAT SE6 .... 141 H7
Bell Lane JMI School
HDN NW4 .... 64 D5
Belmont First & Middle School
KTN/HRWW/W HA3 .... 61 M3
Belmont Junior & Infant School
WDGN N22 .... 67 J4
Belmont Medical Centre
UX/CGN UB8 .... 76 D7
Belmont Mill Hill Junior School
MLHL NW7 .... 46 A5
Belmont Primary School
BXLYHN DA7 .... 127 G5
Belmont Road Primary School
CHSWK W4 .... 117 K2
Belmore Primary School
YEAD UB4 .... 96 C2
Belsize Square Synagogue
HAMP NW3 .... 83 K6
Belvedere C of E Trinity School
BELV DA17 .... 127 H2
Belvedere Day Hospital
WLSDN NW10 .... 82 A8

Belvedere Industrial Estate
BELV DA17 .... 109 K7
Belvue Business Centre
NTHLT UB5 .... 79 H7
Belvue School
NTHLT UB5 .... 79 G8
Benhurst JMI School
HCH RM12 .... 92 B3
Ben Jonson Primary School
WCHPL E1 .... 104 E3
Bensham Manor School
THHTH CR7 .... 157 J8
Benson Primary School
CROY/NA CR0 .... 173 L5
Bentalls Shopping Centre
KUT KT1 .... 152 D4
Benthal Primary School
STNW/STAM N16 .... 86 A3
Bentley Wood High School
STAN HA7 .... 43 M7
Bentworth Primary School
SHB W12 .... 100 B5
Beormund Primary School
STHWK SE1 .... 19 G2
Berger Junior & Infant Schools
HOM E9 .... 86 D6
Berkeley Clinic
RKW/CH/CXG WD3 .... 40 C3
Berkeley School
HEST TW5 .... 114 C4
Bermondsey Town Hall
STHWK SE1 .... 19 M4
Bermondsey Trading Estate
BERM/RHTH SE16 .... 122 C3
Berrymede First & Junior School
ACT W3 .... 99 H8
Bertrum House & Little Wandsworth School
TOOT SW17 .... 138 A6
Bessemer Grange Junior & Infant School
CMBW SE5 .... 139 L1
Bethams C of E School
GFD/PVL UB6 .... 97 K2
Bethel Temple
STRHM/NOR SW16 .... 138 D8
Beth Hamedrash Skver Synagogue
STNW/STAM N16 .... 67 M8
The Bethlem & Maudsley NHS Trust
CMBW SE5 .... 121 K7
Bethlem Royal Hospital
BECK BR3 .... 174 A2
Bethnal Green High School
BETH E2 .... 7 M8
Bethnal Green Museum of Childhood
BETH E2 .... 104 B2
Beulah Junior & Infant School
THHTH CR7 .... 157 J5
Beverley County Secondary School for Boys
NWMAL KT3 .... 153 M8
Beverley Primary School
GNWCH SE10 .... 123 H5
Beverley Trading Estate
MRDN SM4 .... 169 K2
Bevington Primary School
NKENS W10 .... 100 E4
Bexley College
ABYW SE2 .... 126 D4
Bexley College
BELV DA17 .... 127 J2
Bexley Cricket Club
BXLY DA5 .... 145 G5
Bexley Erith Technical Boys School
BXLY DA5 .... 145 G3
Bexley Grammar Mixed School
WELL DA16 .... 144 B1
Bexleyheath Centre
BXLYHS DA6 .... 144 E1
Bexleyheath School
BXLYHN DA7 .... 127 G8
Bexley Hospital
BXLY DA5 .... 145 L6
Bexley Rugby Club
BXLY DA5 .... 145 G4
Bickley Park Cricket Club
BMLY BR1 .... 160 E5
Bickley Park School
BMLY BR1 .... 160 E6
Bickley Parva School
BMLY BR1 .... 160 D6
Biggin Hill Business Park
BH/WHM TN16 .... 187 K8
Billingsgate Fish Market
POP/IOD E14 .... 105 H7
Birbeck College
STPAN WC1H 5 G9
Birch Court Colindale Hospital
CDALE/KGS NW9 .... 63 L3
Birchwood County Primary School
SWLY BR8 .... 163 K4
Birkbeck Primary School
SCUP DA14 .... 144 B7
Bishop Challoner RC Secondary School
WCHPL E1 .... 104 C5
Bishop Challoner School
HAYES BR2 .... 159 K5
Bishop Douglass RC High School
EFNCH N2 .... 65 J4
Bishop Gilpin Primary School
WIM/MER SW19 .... 154 F1
Bishophalt School
UX/CGN UB8 .... 94 F2
Bishop John Robinson Primary School
THMD SE28 .... 108 C6
Bishop Perrin School
WHTN TW2 .... 133 H4
Bishop Ramsey C of E School
RSLP HA4 .... 60 A8

Bishop Ramsey C of E School
RSLP HA4 .... 59 M8
Bishopsgate Institute
WCHPL E1 .... 13 K3
Bishop Stopford School
EN EN1 .... 37 H5
Bishops Wood Hospital
RKW/CH/CXG WD3 .... 41 G7
Bishop Thomas Grant RC School
STRHM/NOR SW16 .... 156 F1
Bishop Wand C of E School
SUN TW16 .... 149 M5
Bittacy Business Centre
MLHL NW7 .... 46 E8
Blackburn Trading Estate
STWL/WRAY TW19 .... 130 F3
Blackfen School for Girls
BFN/LL DA15 .... 144 B3
Blackfriars Medical Practice
STHWK SE1 .... 12 B9
The Blackheath Clinic
BKHTH/KID SE3 .... 142 A1
Blackheath High School
BKHTH/KID SE3 .... 124 A5
Blackheath High School Gpdst
BKHTH/KID SE3 .... 123 M7
Blackheath Hospital
BKHTH/KID SE3 .... 123 M8
The Blackheath Practice
BKHTH/KID SE3 .... 124 D6
Blackwall Trading Estate
POP/IOD E14 .... 105 J6
Blaire Peach School
STHL UB1 .... 96 D7
Blanche Neville School
WDGN N22 .... 67 G2
Blenheim Business Centre
MTCM CR4 .... 155 M4
Blenheim High School
HOR/WEW KT19 .... 180 D3
Blenheim Junior & Infant School
ORP BR6 .... 177 J4
Blenheim Shopping Centre
PGE/AN SE20 .... 158 C3
Blessed Dominic RC Primary School
CDALE/KGS NW9 .... 63 L3
Blessed John Roche Secondary School
POP/IOD E14 .... 105 G5
Blessed Sacrament School
IS N1 .... 5 K4
Bloomfield Clinic Guys
STHWK SE1 .... 19 H1
Bloomsbury College
FUL/PGN SW6 .... 119 G5
Bloomsbury Health Authority
CAMTN NW1 .... 4 F7
Bloomsbury Theatre
STPAN WC1H 5 G9
Blossoms Inn Medical Centre
BLKFR EC4V 12 F6
Bluecoat School
STJSPK SW1H 17 G3
The Blue C of E School
ISLW TW7 .... 116 A8
Blue Gate Fields Primary School
WCHPL E1 .... 104 C6
Bnois Jerusalem School
STNW/STAM N16 .... 67 K8
Boathouse Gallery
SHPTN TW17 .... 164 F2
The Bob Hope Theatre
ELTH/MOT SE9 .... 142 E3
Bob Lawrence Gallery
CHEL SW3 .... 15 J8
Bobs Park Surgery
BOW E3 .... 105 H2
Bodywise Natural Health Centre
BETH E2 .... 104 C2
Bolingbroke Hospital
BTSEA SW11 .... 137 L2
Bolingbroke Primary School
BTSEA SW11 .... 119 K6
Bond First School
MTCM CR4 .... 155 M5
Bond Road School
MTCM CR4 .... 155 M5
Bonner Primary School
BETH E2 .... 104 D1
Bonneville Primary School
CLAP SW4 .... 138 C3
Bonneygrove Junior & Infant School
CHESW EN7 .... 26 A3
Bonus Pastor Roman Catholic School
BMLY BR1 .... 141 L8
Boomes Industrial Estate
RAIN RM13 .... 109 M3
Booster Cushion Theatre
WDGN N22 .... 66 F3
Borehamwood Football Club
BORE WD6 .... 32 B5
Borehamwood Industrial Park
BORE WD6 .... 32 D5
Borough Market
STHWK SE1 .... 13 C8
Borough of Broxbourne
CHES/WCR EN8 .... 26 B3
Bosnia Embassy
CAVSQ/HST W1G 10 D4
Boston Business Park
NWDGN UB2 .... 115 L1
Boston University
SKENS SW7 .... 14 E6
Botany Bay Cricket Club
ENC/FH EN2 .... 35 K1
Botswana High Comm
OXSTW W1C 10 C5
Botwell House Primary School
HYS/HAR UB3 .... 95 M8
Bounds Green Health Centre
FBAR/BDGN N11 .... 66 D1
Bounds Green Industrial Estate
FBAR/BDGN N11 .... 48 C8

Bounds Green Junior & Infant School
FBAR/BDGN N11 .... 66 E1
Bourne CP School
RSLP HA4 .... 78 C5
Bourne Hall Health Centre
EW KT17 .... 180 F2
Bournehall Junior & Infant School
BUSH WD23 .... 30 A8
Bourneside Sports Club
STHGT/OAK N14 .... 48 E3
Bousfield Primary School
WBPTN SW10 .... 14 E7
Boutcher C of E Primary School
STHWK SE1 .... 19 L5
Bowater House
SKENS SW7 .... 15 L2
Bow County Court
SRTFD E15 .... 87 M6
Bowden House Clinic
HRW HA1 .... 79 L2
Bower Park School
ROM RM1 .... 55 L8
Bowes Primary School
FBAR/BDGN N11 .... 48 D5
Bowes Road Clinic
FBAR/BDGN N11 .... 48 C7
Bow Industrial Park
SRTFD E15 .... 87 G7
Bowling Alley
BERM/RHTH SE16 .... 122 D1
Bowman Trading Estate
CDALE/KGS NW9 .... 63 G4
Bow Road Surgery
BOW E3 .... 104 F2
Bow Surgery
BOW E3 .... 105 H2
Bow Triangle Business Centre
BOW E3 .... 105 G3
Boxgrove Primary School
ABYW SE2 .... 126 C1
Boyd School
UPMR RM14 .... 93 L2
Brackenbury Health Centre
HMSMTH W6 .... 118 B1
Brackenbury Primary School
HMSMTH W6 .... 118 B1
Brady Primary School
RAIN RM13 .... 110 C4
Brady Recreation Centre
WCHPL E1 .... 104 A4
Braincroft Primary School
CRICK NW2 .... 81 M3
Braintree Road Industrial Estate
RSLP HA4 .... 78 B4
Bramah Tea & Coffee Museum
STHWK SE1 .... 19 M1
Brampton Manor Comprehensive School
PLSTW E13 .... 106 D3
Brampton Primary School
EHAM E6 .... 106 E2
Brampton Primary School
WELL DA16 .... 126 D7
Brandlehow Primary School
PUT/ROE SW15 .... 136 F1
Branfil Junior & Infant School
UPMR RM14 .... 93 G4
Branollys Health Centre
PLSTW E13 .... 106 A3
Breakspeare School
ABLGY WD5 .... 20 E1
Breakspear Junior School
HGDN/ICK UB10 .... 77 L2
Breaside Preparatory School
BMLY BR1 .... 160 D4
Brecknock Primary School
HOLWY N7 .... 84 D4
Bredinghurst School
PECK SE15 .... 140 C1
Brent Adult College
WLSDN NW10 .... 81 K8
Brent Arts Council
CRICK NW2 .... 82 A3
Brent Child & Family Clinic
WLSDN NW10 .... 81 M5
Brent Council
WBLY HA9 .... 80 D3
Brent CP School
RDART DA2 .... 147 J4
Brent Cross Shopping Centre
HDN NW4 .... 64 C2
Brentfield Medical Centre
WLSDN NW10 .... 81 K6
Brentfield Primary School
WLSDN NW10 .... 81 K6
Brentford Business Centre
BTFD TW8 .... 116 C5
The Brentford Clinic
BTFD TW8 .... 116 E4
Brentford County Court
BTFD TW8 .... 116 D5
Brentford Fountain Leisure Centre
CHSWK W4 .... 117 G5
Brentford Health Centre
BTFD TW8 .... 116 C4
Brentford Medical Centre
BTFD TW8 .... 116 D5
Brentford School for Girls
BTFD TW8 .... 116 D4
Brent & Harrow Health Authority
HRW HA1 .... 61 K8
Brent & Harrow Health NHS Trust
HRW HA1 .... 61 L8
Brent Knoll School
SYD SE26 .... 140 F7
Brent Magistrates Court House
WLSDN NW10 .... 81 L7
Brentmead Gardens Surgery
WLSDN NW10 .... 98 F2
Brentside First School
HNWL W7 .... 97 L4
Brentside High School
HNWL W7 .... 97 L3
Brentside Primary School
HNWL W7 .... 97 L3

Brentwaters Business Park
BTFD TW8 .... 116 C5
Brewers' Hall
CITYW EC2V 12 F3
The Bridewell Theatre
EMB EC4Y 12 C5
The Bridge Business Centre
NWDGN UB2 .... 97 G8
Bridge Lane Theatre
BTSEA SW11 .... 119 L6
Brigstock Medical Centre
THHTH CR7 .... 157 H8
Brimsdown Junior & Infant School
PEND EN3 .... 37 K6
Brindishe Primary School
LEE/GVPK SE12 .... 141 M2
Brinkleys Wine Gallery
WBPTN SW10 .... 14 E9
Briset Corner Surgery
ELTH/MOT SE9 .... 142 E1
Britannia Business Centre
CHES/WCR EN8 .... 26 F7
Britannia Business Centre
CRICK NW2 .... 82 D4
Britannia Sports Ground
WALTH E17 .... 69 G1
British Dental Ass
CAVSQ/HST W1G 10 C3
The British Editorial Society
of Bone & Joint Surgery
CHCR WC2N 11 K7
British Friends of Diaspora
Museum
HAMP NW3 .... 83 M6
British Library
CAMTN NW1 .... 5 H1
British Medical Association
STPAN WC1H 5 H1
British Museum
MYFR/PICC W1J 10 C1
British Museum
RSQ WC1B 11 J3
British Telecom Tower
GTPST W1W 10 E2
Brit Performing Arts &
Technology School
SNWD SE25 .... 172 D1
Brittania Business Park
CHES/WCR EN8 .... 26 F7
Brittons School
RAIN RM13 .... 91 H4
Brixton Art Gallery
BRXN/ST SW9 .... 121 G8
Brixton College for Further
Education
BRXS/STRHM SW2 .... 138 C2
Brixton Hill Group Practice
BRXS/STRHM SW2 .... 138 F1
Brixton Mosque
BRXN/ST SW9 .... 121 G8
Brixton Recreation Centre
BRXN/ST SW9 .... 121 G8
Broadfields Infant School
EDGE HA8 .... 45 G4
Broadfields Junior School
EDGE HA8 .... 45 H4
Broadford Primary School
HARH RM3 .... 56 D8
Broadgate
LVPST EC2M 13 H2
Broadhurst School
KIL/WHAMP NW6 .... 2 E1
Broadmead Junior School
CROY/NA CR0 .... 172 D1
Broadwalk Shopping Centre
EDGE HA8 .... 45 H8
Broadwater Farm Junior School
TOTM N17 .... 67 K3
Broadwater Farm Primary
School
TOTM N17 .... 67 K3
Broadwater Junior & Infant
School
TOOT SW17 .... 137 L8
Broadway Clinic
EDGE HA8 .... 63 H1
Broadway Retail Park
CRICK NW2 .... 82 D4
Broadway Shopping Centre
HMSMTH W6 .... 118 C5
Brocklebank Health Centre
WAND/EARL SW18 .... 137 H4
Brocklebank Industrial Estate
GNWCH SE10 .... 124 A2
Brockley Cross Business Centre
BROCKY SE4 .... 122 E8
Brockley Primary School
BROCKY SE4 .... 140 F2
Brockwell Primary School
BRXS/STRHM SW2 .... 139 G3
Bromet School
OXHEY WD19 .... 42 D2
Bromley City Council
BMLY BR1 .... 159 M4
Bromley College of Further &
Higher Education
HAYES BR2 .... 175 K1
Bromley County Court
BMLY BR1 .... 160 A4
Bromley Health Authority
HAYES BR2 .... 175 G3
Bromley High School for Girls
BMLY BR1 .... 161 G7
Bromley Hospital
HAYES BR2 .... 160 B7
Bromley Hospitals NHS Trust
ORP BR6 .... 176 F6
Bromley Hospitals NHS Trust
ORP BR6 .... 176 A6
Bromley Industrial Centre
BMLY BR1 .... 160 D6
Bromley Mall Indoor Market
BMLY BR1 .... 160 A5
Bromley Museum
ORP BR6 .... 177 H2
Bromley Road Infant School
BECK BR3 .... 159 H4

Brompton Medical Centre
WBPTN SW10 .... 14 D7
Bromyard Leisure Centre
ACT W3 .... 99 L7
Brondesbury College for Boys
KIL/WHAMP NW6 .... 82 D7
Brook Business Centre
IVER SL0 .... 94 A1
Brooke Trading Estate
ROM RM1 .... 73 M8
Brook Farm Industrial Estate
ABR/ST RM4 .... 55 K2
Brookfield House School
WFD IG8 .... 51 L8
Brookfield Primary School
ARCH N19 .... 84 B2
Brookfield Primary School
CHEAM SM3 .... 169 L3
Brook Gallery
CHIG IG7 .... 53 H5
Brook General Hospital
WOOL/PLUM SE18 .... 124 E6
Brook House Football Club
YEAD UB4 .... 95 M2
Brookhurst Surgery
ORP BR6 .... 177 G4
Brook Industrial Estate
YEAD UB4 .... 96 D7
Brookland Junior &
Infant School
CHES/WCR EN8 .... 26 E1
Brookland Primary School
GLDGN NW11 .... 65 H5
Brooklands School
BKHTH/KID SE3 .... 124 A8
Brook Lane Business Centre
BTFD TW8 .... 116 D3
Brook Lane Mission Practice
BMLY BR1 .... 160 A2
Brook Lane Mission Practice
ELTH/MOT SE9 .... 142 D8
Brookmarsh Trading Estate
DEPT SE8 .... 123 H5
Brookmead Industrial Estate
MTCM CR4 .... 171 J1
Brookside Junior & Infant
School
HARH RM3 .... 56 E7
Brookside School
YEAD UB4 .... 96 C2
Brookweald Cricket Club
BRW CM14 .... 57 L3
Broomfield House School
RCH/KEW TW9 .... 116 F6
Broomfield School
STHGT/OAK N14 .... 48 D7
Broomsleigh Business Park
CAT SE6 .... 158 F1
Broomwood Hall School
BAL SW12 .... 138 A4
Brownlow Medical Centre
FBAR/BDGN N11 .... 48 E7
Bruce Castle Museum
TOTM N17 .... 67 L2
Bruce Grove Junior School
TOTM N17 .... 67 L3
Brunei Darrusalam High Comm
KTBR SW1X 16 A3
Brunel Engine House
BERM/RHTH SE16 .... 104 C8
Brunel University
ISLW TW7 .... 115 L5
Brunel University
TWK TW1 .... 134 B1
Brunel University
UX/CGN UB8 .... 94 E2
Brunswick Health Centre
FBAR/BDGN N11 .... 48 A4
Brunswick Housing and
Shopping Centre
BMSBY WC1N 5 K9
Brunswick Industrial Park
FBAR/BDGN N11 .... 48 B6
Brunswick Medical Centre
BMSBY WC1N 5 J9
Brunswick Park JMI School
FBAR/BDGN N11 .... 48 A3
Brunswick Park Junior &
Infant School
CMBW SE5 .... 121 K5
BT Centre
STBT EC1A 12 E4
Buckhurst Hill CP School
BKHH IG9 .... 52 E4
Buckhurst Hill Football Club
BKHH IG9 .... 52 E3
Buckhurst Hill Reform
Synagogue
LOU IG10 .... 39 K8
Buckingham College School
HRW HA1 .... 61 L6
Buckingham Palace
WHALL SW1A 16 D2
Buckingham Primary School
HPTN TW12 .... 150 F1
Buckinghamshire Golf Club
DEN/HRF UB9 .... 76 C2
Buckland County Junior &
Infant School
STA TW18 .... 148 D3
Buckland Infant School
CHSGTN KT9 .... 167 H7
Buddhapadipa Temple
WIM/MER SW19 .... 136 D8
Building Centre
GWRST WC1E 11 G3
The Bulgarian Embassy
SKENS SW7 .... 14 F3
Bullers Wood School for Girls
CHST BR7 .... 160 F4
Bullsbridge Industrial Estate
NWDGN UB2 .... 114 B2
The Bull Theatre
BAR EN5 .... 33 M7
Bupa Roding Hospital
REDBR IG4 .... 70 D4
Burbage Junior & Infant School
IS N1 .... 7 J5

Burdett Coutts School
WEST SW1P 17 G4
Burgess Industrial Park
VX/NE SW8 .... 121 K5
Burhill County Infant School
WOT/HER KT12 .... 165 K7
Burleigh Primary School
CHES/WCR EN8 .... 26 D3
Burlington Danes School
SHB W12 .... 100 B5
Burlington Road School
NWMAL KT3 .... 153 M7
Burnham Trading Estate
DART DA1 .... 146 D1
Burnhill Business Centre
BECK BR3 .... 159 G5
Burnley Road Clinic
WLSDN NW10 .... 82 A5
Burnside Industrial Estate
BARK/HLT IG6 .... 54 B7
Burnt Ash Infant School
BMLY BR1 .... 160 A1
Burnt Ash School
BMLY BR1 .... 159 M1
Burnt Oak Primary School
BFN/LL DA15 .... 144 A5
Burntwood School
TOOT SW17 .... 137 K6
Bursted Woodprimary School
BXLYHN DA7 .... 127 H7
Bursted Wood Surgery
BXLYHN DA7 .... 127 H7
Burwell Industrial Estate
LEY E10 .... 86 E1
Burwood Park School & College
WOT/HER KT12 .... 164 F8
Burwood School
ORP BR6 .... 177 K4
Business College
CONDST W1S 10 D5
Bushey & District Synagogue
BUSH WD23 .... 43 J2
Bushey Hall School
BUSH WD23 .... 42 F1
Bushey Hall Swimming Pool
BUSH WD23 .... 29 M8
Bushey Health Centre
BUSH WD23 .... 42 F1
Bushey Heath Primary School
BUSH WD23 .... 43 K3
Bushey Manor School
BUSH WD23 .... 29 L8
Bushey Meads School
BUSH WD23 .... 30 C8
Bushey Middle School
RYNPK SW20 .... 154 B6
Bushey Museum &
Art Gallery
BUSH WD23 .... 43 G1
Bush Hill Park Junior &
Infant School
EN EN1 .... 37 G8
Bush Hill Park Medical Centre
EN EN1 .... 49 M1
Bush House
HOL/ALD WC2B 11 L5
Bush Industrial Estate
ARCH N19 .... 84 C3
Bush Industrial Estate
WLSDN NW10 .... 99 K2
Bush Theatre
SHB W12 .... 100 C8
Business Centre
CHEL SW3 .... 15 K3
Business Centre
BAY/PAD W2 .... 9 J3
Business Centre
HAMP NW3 .... 83 G2
The Business Centre
IL IG1 .... 89 H2
The Business Centre
HARH RM3 .... 74 D1
The Business Centre
IS N1 .... 6 B4
The Business Centre
WDGN N22 .... 66 E3
Business Park
ELTH/MOT SE9 .... 143 G6
Bute House Preparatory
School for Girls
HMSMTH W6 .... 118 C2
Butterfly Sports Club
ELTH/MOT SE9 .... 143 H3
Buxlow Preparatory School
WBLY HA9 .... 80 E3
Buzzard Creek Industrial Estate
BARK IG11 .... 107 M2
Byam Shaw School of Art
ARCH N19 .... 84 C2
Byfleet Industrial Estate
WATW WD18 .... 41 J3
Bygrove Primary School
POP/IOD E14 .... 105 H5
Byron Court Primary School
ALP/SUD HA0 .... 80 C2
Cabinet Gallery
FSBYE EC1V 6 C9
Cabinet War Rooms
WHALL SW1A 17 H1
Cab Mech Theatre
COVGDN WC2E 11 K6
Caledonian Market
STHWK SE1 .... 19 K3
Calvary Temple
CMBW SE5 .... 121 G1
Calverton Primary School
CAN/RD E16 .... 106 D5
Cambell Infant School
DAGW RM9 .... 90 D7
Camberwell Business Centre
CMBW SE5 .... 121 K5
Camberwell College of Arts
CMBW SE5 .... 121 L6
The Camberwell Green Surgery
CMBW SE5 .... 121 J6
Camberwell Trading Estate
CMBW SE5 .... 121 K7

Cambridge Park Bowling &
Sports Club
TWK TW1 .... 134 C3
Cambridge Park Convent
School
WAN E11 .... 70 A7
Cambridge School
HMSMTH W6 .... 118 B2
Cambridge Theatre
LSQ/SEVD WC2H 11 J5
Camden Community Trust Day
Hospital
CAMTN NW1 .... 84 C6
Camden House Clinic
BKHTH/KID SE3 .... 123 L7
Camden Junior School
CAR SM5 .... 170 E6
Camden Peoples Theatre
CAMTN NW1 .... 4 E8
Camden Road Surgery
CAMTN NW1 .... 4 E1
Camden School for Girls
CAMTN NW1 .... 84 C6
Camden Theatre
CAMTN NW1 .... 4 E5
Camden Town Hall
CAMTN NW1 .... 5 J7
Camelot Primary School
PECK SE15 .... 122 B5
Cameron House School
CHEL SW3 .... 15 H9
Camperdown House
WCHPL E1 .... 13 M5
Campion House College
ISLW TW7 .... 115 K5
The Campion School
EMPK RM11 .... 74 F5
Campsbourne Junior School
CEND/HSY/T N8 .... 66 E4
Campshill Surgery
LEW SE13 .... 141 J2
Canada House Business Centre
RSLP HA4 .... 78 C1
Canada Water Retail Park
BERM/RHTH SE16 .... 122 D1
Canadian High Comm
MYFR/PKLN W1K 10 B6
Canal Cafe Theatre
BAY/PAD W2 .... 8 D2
Canary Wharf Tower
POP/IOD E14 .... 105 H7
Canberra Primary School
SHB W12 .... 100 B6
Canbury Business Centre
KUTN/CMB KT2 .... 152 E4
Canbury 2000 Business Park
KUTN/CMB KT2 .... 152 E4
Canbury Medical Centre
KUTN/CMB KT2 .... 152 F4
Canbury School
RCHPK/HAM TW10 .... 153 H2
Cann Hall Primary School
WAN E11 .... 87 M3
The Canning School
KENS W8 .... 14 A1
Cannock House School
ORP BR6 .... 177 M7
Cannon Hill Clinic
STHGT/OAK N14 .... 48 E5
Cannon Lane School
PIN HA5 .... 60 D7
Cannon Sports Club
CANST EC4R 12 F4
Cannon Trading Estate
WBLY HA9 .... 81 H4
Cannon Wharf Business Centre
DEPT SE8 .... 122 E2
Cannon Workshops
POP/IOD E14 .... 105 G6
Canonbury JMI School
IS N1 .... 85 H6
Canon Palmer Catholic School
GDMY/SEVK IG3 .... 89 L1
Canons High School
EDGE HA8 .... 62 F3
Capefield Surgery
ESH/CLAY KT10 .... 166 F8
Capel Manor Primary School
EN EN1 .... 26 A8
Capital Business Centre
ALP/SUD HA0 .... 98 D1
Capital Business Centre
MTCM CR4 .... 155 M8
Capital Business Centre
WATN WD24 .... 29 K1
Capital Industrial Estate
BELV DA17 .... 127 H2
Capital Radio
LSQ/SEVD WC2H 11 H7
Capitol Industrial Park
CDALE/KGS NW9 .... 63 J7
Caplan Estate
MTCM CR4 .... 156 C4
Cardiff Road Industrial Estate
WATW WD18 .... 42 B1
Cardinal Hinsley High RC
School Gm
WLSDN NW10 .... 82 A8
Cardinal Newman RC School
WOT/HER KT12 .... 165 K5
Cardinal Pole RC Secondary Lower
School
HOM E9 .... 86 D7
Cardinal Pole RC Secondary
School Upper
HOM E9 .... 86 E0
Cardinal Road School
FELT TW13 .... 132 B5
Cardinal Vaughan School
WKENS W14 .... 100 B8
Cardinal Wiseman Secondary
School
GFD/PVL UB6 .... 97 J4
Cardwell School
WOOL/PLUM SE18 .... 124 F2
Carew Manor Special School
WLGTN SM6 .... 171 K5

Carlisle Primary School
HPTN TW12 .... 151 H2
Carlton Gate Development
MV/WKIL W9 .... 8 B2
Carlton House
STJS SW1Y 11 G9
Carlton House Surgery
ENC/FH EN2 .... 36 E4
Carlton Primary School
KTTN NW5 .... 84 A5
Carlton Vale Infant School
KIL/WHAMP NW6 .... 100 F1
Carlyle's House
CHEL SW3 .... 119 L4
Carnwath Road Industrial Estate
FUL/PGN SW6 .... 119 H8
Carolyn School Shop
PIN HA5 .... 60 E5
Carpenters' Hall
LVPST EC2M 13 H3
Carpenters Primary School
SRTFD E15 .... 87 J8
The Carpet Gallery
BTSEA SW11 .... 119 L7
The Carpet Gallery
HAMP NW3 .... 83 J4
The Carpet Gallery
HCH RM12 .... 92 B1
The Carpet Gallery
STJWD NW8 .... 9 H1
Carshalton College
CAR SM5 .... 170 F5
Carshalton High
School for Boys
CAR SM5 .... 170 D4
Carshalton High
School for Girls
CAR SM5 .... 170 E5
Carshalton War
Memorial Hospital
CAR SM5 .... 170 F7
Carterhatch School
EN EN1 .... 37 H4
Caryl Thomas Clinic
HRW HA1 .... 61 L5
Cashmere Gallery
SKENS SW7 .... 15 L2
The Cassel Hospital
RCHPK/HAM TW10 .... 134 D8
Cassidy Medical Centre
FUL/PGN SW6 .... 119 G5
Cassio Surgery
WATW WD18 .... 29 H7
Castilion Primary School
THMD SE28 .... 108 C5
Castlebar Special School
WEA W13 .... 98 A4
Castlecombe Primary School
ELTH/MOT SE9 .... 160 E1
Castle Industrial Estate
WALW SE17 .... 18 E5
Castle Road Practice
KTTN NW5 .... 84 B6
Caterham High School
CLAY IG5 .... 70 F3
Catford & Bromley Synagogue
CAT SE6 .... 141 H6
Catford County Girls School
CAT SE6 .... 141 K7
Catford Cricket & Sports Club
CAT SE6 .... 141 H5
Catford Cyphers Cricket Club
CAT SE6 .... 140 F6
Catford Synagogue
CAT SE6 .... 141 H6
Catford Trading Estate
CAT SE6 .... 141 H6
Catford Wanderers Sports Club
CAT SE6 .... 141 J8
Cathall Leisure Centre
WAN E11 .... 87 K3
Cathedral School of St
Saviour & St Mary Overie
STHWK SE1 .... 18 F1
Cator Park School for Girls
BECK BR3 .... 158 E3
Cavendish College
FITZ W1T 11 G3
Cavendish Primary School
CHSWK W4 .... 117 K5
The Cavendish School
CAMTN NW1 .... 4 C3
Cavendish Special School
HNWL W7 .... 97 M5
Caxton Hall
STJSPK SW1H 17 G2
Caxton Trading Estate
HYS/HAR UB3 .... 95 L8
Cayley Primary School
POP/IOD E14 .... 104 E4
Cecil Avenue Surgery
EMPK RM11 .... 74 E4
Cecil Park Clinic
PIN HA5 .... 60 E5
The Cedar School
FSTGT E7 .... 88 C6
Cedars First School
KTN/HRWW/W HA3 .... 61 J3
Cedars Middle School
KTN/HRWW/W HA3 .... 61 J2
The Cedars Primary School
HEST TW5 .... 114 A5
Cedar Way Industrial Estate
CAMTN NW1 .... 5 G2
Centaur Gallery
ARCH N19 .... 66 E8
Centaurs Business Centre
BTFD TW8 .... 116 A4
Centaurs Rugby Football Club
ISLW TW7 .... 115 M4
Central Business Centre
WLSDN NW10 .... 81 L5
Central Criminal Court
STP EC4M 12 C4
Central Estate
E/WMO/HCT KT8 .... 150 F8
Central Foundation Boys School
SDTCH EC2A 7 H9

Central Foundation Girls School
BOW E3..................104 E2
Central Hall
STJSPK SW1H..........17 H2
Central Hendon Clinic
HDN NW4................64 B5
Central London County Court
CAVSQ/HST W1G......10 C1
Central London Markets
STBT EC1A..............12 C3
Central Medical Centre
MRDN SM4...............155 J7
Central Middlesex Hospital
WLSDN NW10............99 J2
Central Park Primary School
EHAM E6................106 D1
Central Park Swimming Pool
HARH RM3................56 E7
Central Primary School
WAT WD17..............29 J7
Central Road Surgery
MRDN SM4...............155 J7
Central St Martins College of
Art & Design
COVGDN WC2E.........11 J6
Central School of Speech &
Drama
HAMP NW3...............3 G1
Central School Speech &
Drama
CAMTN NW1.............5 G4
Central Synagogue
REGST W1B.............10 D2
Central YMCA
ELTH/MOT SE9.........142 D6
Centre Point
LSQ/SEVD WC2H......11 H4
Cen Uni of Iowa
RSQ WC1B...............11 K2
The Chadwell Heath Foundation
School
CHDH RM6..............72 B7
Chadwell Heath Hospital
CHDH RM6..............72 B6
Chadwell Heath Industrial Park
BCTR RM8...............90 E1
Chadwell Heath Luncheon &
Leisure Centre
CHDH RM6..............72 D7
Chafford School
RAIN RM13.............110 C4
Chailey House Chailey Industrial
Estate
HYS/HAR UB3..........96 A8
Chailey Industrial Estate
HYS/HAR UB3..........96 A8
Chalcot School
CAMTN NW1.............4 C1
Chalgrove Primary School
FNCH N3................64 E4
Chalk Farm Gallery
CAMTN NW1.............4 B2
Chalkhill Infant School
WBLY HA9..............81 H3
Chambers Business Park
WDR/YW UB7...........113 C4
Chandlers Field Primary School
E/WMO/HCT KT8........151 G8
Chandos Business Centre
WLGTN SM6.............171 J8
Channing School
HGT N6.................84 B1
Chantry Special School
WDR/YW UB7...........94 E5
Chapel End Infant School
WALTH E17.............69 H2
Chapel End Junior School
WALTH E17.............69 H2
Chapman Park Industrial Estate
WLSDN NW10...........81 M6
Charing Cross Hospital
HMSMTH W6............118 D4
Charles Darwin School
BH/WHM TN16..........187 M8
Charles Edward Brooke Girls
School
CMBW SE5.............121 H6
Charles Edward Brooke School
for Girls
CMBW SE5.............121 H6
Charles Lamb Primary School
IS N1..................6 E3
Charlton Athletic FC
CHARL SE7............124 C3
Charlton House
CHARL SE7............124 D4
Charlton Mosque
CHARL SE7............124 C3
Charlton Park School
CHARL SE7............124 E4
Charlton Rugby Club
ELTH/MOT SE9.........143 H4
Charrington Bowl
SURB KT6..............168 B4
Charville Primary School
YEAD UB4..............95 L1
Charter Clinic
CHEL SW3..............15 L8
Charterhouse School
FARR EC1M.............12 D2
Charterhouse Sutton's Hospital
FARR EC1M.............12 D2
Chartfield School
PUT/ROE SW15.........136 B2
Chartwell Business Centre
BMLY BR1..............160 D6
Chase Bridge School
WHTN TW2.............133 L3
Chase Community School
EN EN1.................36 E4
Chase Farm Hospitals NHS Trust
ENC/FH EN2............36 A3
Chase Lane Junior School
CHING E4...............50 F6
Chase Road Trading Estate
WLSDN NW10...........99 K3
Chase Side Junior & Infant School
ENC/FH EN2............36 C5

Chater Infant School
WATW WD18.............29 G7
Chater Junior School
WATW WD18.............29 G7
Chatsworth Infant School
BFN/LL DA15...........144 A5
Chatsworth Junior &
Infant School
HSLW TW3..............133 J1
Chaucer Clinic
STHL UB1...............97 K8
Cheam Common County Junior School
WPK KT4................169 H4
Cheam Common Infant School
WPK KT4................169 H4
Cheam Family Practice
CHEAM SM3.............169 L8
Cheam Family Practice
SUT SM1................169 M5
Cheam High School
CHEAM SM3.............169 L6
Cheam Leisure Centre
CHEAM SM3.............169 K6
Cheam Park Farm Junior School
CHEAM SM3.............169 L5
Cheam Sports Club
BELMT SM2.............181 K1
Chelsea and Westminster Hotel
WBPTN SW10...........119 J4
Chelsea Barracks
BGVA SW1W............16 B8
Chelsea Bridge Business Centre
BTSEA SW11............120 A5
Chelsea College of Art & Design
CHEL SW3..............15 H8
Chelsea College of Art & Design
FUL/PGN SW6..........119 J7
Chelsea Fields Industrial Estate
WIM/MER SW19.........155 K4
Chelsea Fire Station
CHEL SW3..............15 J8
Chelsea Football Club
FUL/PGN SW6..........119 H5
Chelsea Galleries
WBPTN SW10...........119 J5
Chelsea Gallery
WBPTN SW10...........119 J5
Chelsea Old Town Hall
CHEL SW3..............15 K8
The Chelsea Practice
WBPTN SW10...........14 F9
Chelsea Sports Centre
CHEL SW3..............15 K8
Chelsea Synagogue
CHEL SW3..............15 K8
Chelsfield Park Hospital
ORP BR6................177 M7
Chelsfield Primary School
ORP BR6................177 L7
Chenil Galleries
CHEL SW3..............15 J8
Chennestone County
Middle School
SUN TW16..............150 B5
Cherington House Health
Centre
HNWL W7...............97 M7
Cherry Garden School
BERM/RHTH SE16........122 A2
Cherry Lane Junior School
WDR/YW UB7...........112 F2
Cherry Orchard School
CHARL SE7............124 C5
Cherry Tree JMI School
WATN WD24.............29 G1
Cheshunt Community Hospital
CHES/WCR EN8.........26 C7
Cheshunt Football Club
CHES/WCR EN8.........26 C5
Cheshunt School
CHES/WCR EN8.........26 C3
Cheshunt & Waltham
Cross Council
CHES/WCR EN8.........26 C2
Chessington Community
College
CHSGTN KT9...........179 K1
Chessington Cricket Club
CHSGTN KT9...........179 J1
Chesterfield Junior &
Infant School
PEND EN3..............37 L2
Chesterton Junior Mixed School
BTSEA SW11............120 A6
Cheyne Centre
CHEL SW3..............119 L4
Cheyne Galleries
TWK TW1................134 B3
Chigwell County Primary
School
CHIG IG7...............53 J6
Chigwell & Hainault Synagogue
CHIG IG7...............53 L7
Chigwell Row County
First School
CHIG IG7...............54 C2
Chigwell School
CHIG IG7...............53 J2
Childeric Junior School
NWCR SE14............122 A4
Childrens Hospital Trust Fund
WIM/MER SW19.........136 F8
Childs Hill Clinic
CRICK NW2.............82 E2
Childs Hill School
CRICK NW2.............82 E3
Childs Welfare Clinic
DAGW RM9..............90 C5
Chiltonian Industrial Estate
LEE/GVPK SE12.........141 M3
Chinese Health Centre
BECK BR3..............158 E6
Chinese Health Centre
LEW SE13..............141 K1
Chinese Health Centre
NWCR SE14............122 F5
Chinese Health Centre
PGE/AN SE20..........158 D3

Chinese Medical Centre
BAR EN5................33 L6
Chinese Medical Centre
DART DA1..............146 E3
Chinese Medical Centre
ED N9..................50 B5
Chinese Medical Centre
HCH RM12..............92 E3
Chinese Medical Centre
MHST W1U..............10 A3
Chinese Medical Centre
REGST W1B.............10 E5
Chinese Medical Centre
ROM RM1...............73 L7
Chinese Medical Centre
STNW/STAM N16........85 L2
Chinese Medical Centre
WAND/EARL SW18.......137 G2
Chinese Medical Centre
Watford
WAT WD17.............29 J7
Chinese Medicine Clinic
STRHM/NOR SW16.......138 E8
Chingford C of E Infant School
CHING E4...............51 L3
Chingford C of E Junior School
CHING E4...............51 K3
Chingford Hall Primary School
CHING E4...............50 F8
Chingford Health Centre
CHING E4...............50 F6
Chingford Industrial Centre
CHING E4...............50 E7
Chingford Rugby Football Club
CHING E4...............51 G3
Chingford School
CHING E4...............51 H3
Chiropodist Podiatrist Surgery
WPK KT4................169 G3
Chiropody Surgery
WBLY HA9..............81 G6
Chiropractic Surgery
COUL/CHIP CR5.........183 J7
Chisenhale Primary School
BOW E3.................104 E1
Chislehurst Natural Health
Centre
CHST BR7..............161 H2
Chislehurst & Sidcup
Grammar School
BFN/LL DA15...........144 A6
Chiswick Community School
CHSWK W4.............117 K5
Chiswick House
CHSWK W4.............117 K4
Choir School
WEST SW1P............16 F5
Chrisp Street Health Centre
POP/IOD E14...........105 H5
Christchurch Bentinck
C of E School
CAMTN NW1.............9 J2
Christ Church C of E
Primary School
KIL/WHAMP NW6.........82 E7
Christ Church C E
Primary School
CAMTN NW1.............4 D7
Christ Church C of E
Junior School
NWMAL KT3............153 K6
Christ Church C of E
Middle School
EA W5..................98 D6
Christ Church C of E
Primary School
BAR EN5................33 K5
Christ Church C of E
Primary School
BRXN/ST SW9...........121 G6
Christ Church C of E
Primary School
BRXS/STRHM SW2.......138 F5
Christ Church C of E
Primary School
BRYLDS KT5............168 A1
Christ Church C of E
Primary School
CHEL SW3..............15 L9
Christ Church C of E School
CHEL SW3..............140 D6
Christchurch C of E
Secondary School
NFNCH/WDSP N12.......47 K7
Christchurch Junior &
Infant School
IL IG1..................89 J1
Christ Church Primary School
BTSEA SW11............119 L8
Christ Church Primary School
NWMAL KT3............153 L6
Christ Church Primary School
PUR/KEN CR8...........184 B3
Christchurch Primary School
WCHPL E1..............13 M2
Christchurch School
FSTH SE23.............140 D6
Christchurch Shooters Hill
C of E Primary School
WOOL/PLUM SE18.......125 G6
Christopher Wren School for
Boys
SHB W12...............100 A6
Christs College
BKHTH/KID SE3.........124 A6
Christs College School
EFNCH N2..............65 H4
Christs School
RCHPK/HAM TW10.......134 F2
Christ Temple Ministry
International
HACK E8................86 B5
Christ the King RC First School
STWL/WRAY TW19.......130 D3
Christ the King School
FSBYPK N4.............84 F1
Chrysalis Theatre
BAL SW12..............138 A5

Chrysanthemum Clinic
CHSWK W4.............117 J5
Church Down Adult School
LEE/GVPK SE12.........142 A6
Church End Medical Centre
WLSDN NW10...........81 L6
Church Farm House Museum
HDN NW4...............64 B4
Churchfield Primary School
ED N9..................49 M3
Churchfield School
WOOL/PLUM SE18.......125 M2
Churchfields Junior &
Infant School
SWFD E18..............70 A2
Churchfields Primary School
BECK BR3..............158 D6
Church Hill Junior Middle &
Infant School
EBAR EN4..............47 M2
Churchill Clinic
STHWK SE1.............18 B3
Churchill College
RYNPK SW20...........154 C5
Churchill College
TOOT SW17............137 M6
Churchill Gardens Primary School
PIM SW1V..............16 E8
Churchill Theatre
BMLY BR1..............160 A5
Church Lane Practice
WIM/MER SW19.........154 F4
Church Mead Infant School
LEY E10................87 G1
Church Mead Junior School
LEY E10................87 G1
The Church School
BTFD TW8..............116 E4
Church Trading Estate
ERITH DA8.............128 A5
The Cinema Museum
LBTH SE11..............18 C5
City Business Centre
BERM/RHTH SE16........104 C8
City Business College
FSBYE EC1V............6 D8
City Central Estate
FSBYE EC1V............6 E8
City Gallery
LOTH EC2R.............13 H4
City & Guilds of London Art
School
LBTH SE11..............18 C8
City & Hackney Community
Health Council
BETH E2................7 L4
City & Islington College
FSBYPK N4.............85 H2
City & Islington College
HOLWY N7..............84 E4
City & Islington College
IS N1..................7 G3
City of London Club
OBST EC2N.............13 J4
City of London Magistrates
Court
MANHO EC4N...........13 G5
City of London Polytechnic
Sports Ground
ELTH/MOT SE9.........142 C6
City of London School
BLKFR EC4V............12 D6
City of London School for Girls
BARB EC2Y.............12 E2
City of London Schools
Sports Ground
ELTH/MOT SE9.........142 C7
City of Westminster College
BAY/PAD W2...........9 G2
City of Westminster College
MV/WKIL W9...........100 F2
City of Westminster
Vehicle Pound
BAY/PAD W2...........8 F3
City Temple
STBT EC1A.............12 C3
City University
FSBYE EC1V............6 C7
City University
FSBYE EC1V............6 D8
City University Business School
BARB EC2Y.............12 F2
The City University
FSBYE EC1V............6 C8
Civic Medical Centre
HRW HA1...............61 L6
Civil Service Recreation Centre
WEST SW1P............17 H4
Civil Service Sports Ground
ELTH/MOT SE9.........142 C3
Clapham Common Clinic
CLAP SW4..............138 D1
Clapham Family Practice
CLAP SW4..............138 D1
Clapham Manor Primary School
CLAP SW4..............120 C8
Clapham Manor Street
Public Baths
CLAP SW4..............120 D8
Clapham North Business
Centre 26-32
CLAP SW4..............120 D8
Clapham Park School
CLAP SW4..............138 D2
Clapham Park Surgery
CLAP SW4..............138 D3
Clapham Picture House
CLAP SW4..............138 C1
Clapton Central School
CLPT E5................86 B3
Clapton County Secondary
School
CLPT E5................86 C4
Clapton Jewish Boys School
STNW/STAM N16........67 M8
Clapton Synagogue
CLPT E5................86 C3

Clara Grant Primary School
BOW E3.................105 G3
Clare House Primary School
BECK BR3..............159 J5
Claremont Clinic
FSTGT E7..............88 B5
Claremont Fan Court School
ESH/CLAY KT10.........166 B8
Claremont High School
KTN/HRWW/W HA3.......62 E6
Claremont Way Industrial
Estate
CRICK NW2.............82 C1
Clarence House
WHALL SW1A...........16 F1
Clarendon County Primary School
ASHF TW15.............130 F7
Clarendon School
HPTN TW12............151 H2
Claygate Junior School
ESH/CLAY KT10.........178 E1
Clayhall Clinic
CLAY IG5...............70 E1
Clayponds Hospital
BTFD TW8..............116 E2
Cleeve Park School
SCUP DA14.............144 C4
Clementine Churchill Hospital
HRW HA1...............79 M3
Clerkenwell County Court
IS N1..................6 C5
Clerkenwell Heritage Centre
FARR EC1M.............12 C1
Clerkenwell Parochial C of E Primary
School
FSBYW WC1X...........6 A1
Cleveland Junior & Infant School
IL IG1..................89 H4
Cleves County Junior School
WEY KT13..............164 F6
Cleves Primary School
EHAM E6...............88 D8
Cliff Road Medical Practice
KTTN NW5..............84 D6
Clifton JMI School
NWDGN UB2............114 E2
Clifton Lodge Preparatory
School for Boys
EA W5..................98 D3
Clink Exhibition
STHWK SE1.............13 L8
Clissold Park Natural Health Centre
STNW/STAM N16........85 L2
Clitterhouse Junior School
CRICK NW2.............82 D2
C & L Leisure Centre
NTHLT UB5.............78 B7
Clockhouse Industrial Estate
EBED/NFELT TW14......131 H5
Clockhouse Junior School
CRW RM5...............55 H8
Clock Museum
CITYW EC2V............12 F4
The Clocktower Practice
CEND/HSY/T N8........66 D6
Cloisters Business Centre
VX/NE SW8..............120 B5
Clore Gallery
WEST SW1P............17 J6
Clothworkers' Hall
FENCHST EC3M..........13 K6
Clouster's Green
WAP E1W...............104 A7
Coach House Surgery
WATW WD18.............29 G7
Coates Way School
GSTN WD25.............21 L5
Cobbold Estate
WLSDN NW10...........81 M6
Cobden Hill Infant School
RAD WD7...............31 H3
Cobourg Primary School
CMBW SE5..............19 L9
Cochrane Theatre
GINN WC1R.............11 L3
Cockfosters & N Southgate Synagogue
STHGT/OAK N14........48 C2
Cockfosters Sports Ground
EBAR EN4..............34 F6
The Cockpit Theatre
STJWD NW8.............9 H1
The Coffee Gallery
RSQ WC1B..............11 J3
Coldharbour Sports Ground
ELTH/MOT SE9.........143 G6
Colebrooke Primary School
IS N1..................6 C5
Colegrave Primary School
SRTFD E15.............87 K5
Coleraine Park Junior &
Infant School
TOTM N17..............68 B2
Coleridge Primary School
HGT N6.................66 D8
Colfes School
LEE/GVPK SE12.........142 B3
Colham Manor Junior &
Infant School
UX/CGN UB8............94 A4
Colindale Business Park
CDALE/KGS NW9........63 J4
Colindale Hospital
CDALE/KGS NW9........63 L4
Colindale Primary School
CDALE/KGS NW9........63 M5
The Colin Dove Practice
ROM RM1...............73 M6
Coliseum
CHCR WC2N.............11 J7
College Fields Business Centre
WIM/MER SW19.........155 L4
College of Arms
BLKFR EC4V............12 E5
College of Fuel Technology
HGT N6.................66 A7
The College of Law
GWRST WC1E...........11 G2

The College of Law
LINN WC2A 12 A4
College of North East London
CEND/HSY/T N8 .... 67 K3
College of North East London
FBAR/BDGN N11 .... 66 C2
College of North East London
SEVS/STOTM N15 .... 67 M5
College of North West London
KIL/WHAMP NW6 .... 2 A3
College of North West London
WBLY HA9 .... 81 G3
College of North West London
WLSDN NW10 .... 81 M5
College Park School
BAY/PAD W2 .... 8 B5
College Road Clinic
WBLY HA9 .... 80 D1
Collier Row Clinic
ROMW/RG RM7 .... 73 H2
Collier Row Football Club
ROMW/RG RM7 .... 72 F2
Colliers Wood Surgery
WIM/MER SW19 .... 155 L2
Collingham Sixth Form College
ECT SW5 .... 14 D6
Collingwood Business Centre
ARCH N19 .... 84 E3
Collingwood School
WLGTN SM6 .... 171 H1
Collins Method School
CRICK NW2 .... 82 C6
Collis Primary School
TEDD TW11 .... 152 B2
Coll of Art & Design
NOXST/BSQ WC1A 11 K3
Coll of Law
GWRST WC1E 11 G2
Coll of Organists
FLST/FETLN EC4A 12 B4
Coll of Surgical Sci
LINN WC2A 11 M4
Colnbrook School
OXHEY WD19 .... 42 C4
Colne Bridge Retail Park
WAT WD17 .... 29 K8
Colombian Consulate
GTPST W1W 10 E4
Colonial Business Park
WATN WD24 .... 29 J4
The Colonnades Shopping Centre
BGVA SW1W 16 C5
Colours Sports Club
SUT SM1 .... 170 C7
Columbia Primary School
BETH E2 .... 7 M7
Colville Primary School
NTGHL W11 .... 100 F5
Colyers Lane Medical Centre
BXLYHN DA7 .... 127 K6
Comber Grove Junior &
Infant School
CMBW SE5 .... 121 J5
Comelle House Trading Estate
DEPT SE8 .... 122 E3
Comm for the Rep of Sth Africa
STJS SW1Y 11 H8
Commonwealth Lodge School
PUR/KEN CR8 .... 183 K5
Community Mental Health Cen
BRXN/ST SW9 .... 121 G6
Community Mental Health Centre
GSTN WD25 .... 21 J7
Compass Theatre
HGDN/ICK UB10 .... 77 J3
Complementary Health Centre
LEW SE13 .... 141 L3
The Compton School
NFNCH/WDSP N12 .... 47 L8
Concord Business Centre
ACT W3 .... 99 H4
Concord Shopping Centre
SHB W12 .... 100 D8
Coney Hill School
HAYES BR2 .... 174 F4
Con General of Chile
CAVSO/HST W1G 10 C1
Congress House
RSQ WC1B 11 H3
Connaught Business Centre
CDALE/KGS NW9 .... 63 M6
Connaught Business Centre
CROY/NA CR0 .... 171 M8
Connaught Girls School
WAN E11 .... 87 L1
Consort Clinic
PECK SE15 .... 122 B8
Consulate General of Monaco
SKENS SW7 .... 15 G5
Consulate General of the
Republic of Guinea Bissau
KENS W8 .... 14 E3
The Consulate of the State of
Eritrea
IS N1 .... 6 B5
Contemporary Applied Arts
LSQ/SEVD WC2H 11 J5
Convent of Jesus & Mary
Gm High School
WLSDN NW10 .... 81 M8
Convent of Jesus & Mary Infant
School
CRICK NW2 .... 82 C6
Conway Hall
FSBYW WC1X 11 L2
Conway Junior School
WOOL/PLUM SE18 .... 125 L2
Conway Medical Centre
WOOL/PLUM SE18 .... 125 K3
Coombe Girls School
NWMAL KT3 .... 153 K5
Coombe Hill Junior &
Infant School
NWMAL KT3 .... 153 K4
Coopers' Hall
LVPST EC2M 13 K3
Coopers Lane Primary School
LEE/GVPK SE12 .... 142 A6

Coopers School
CHST BR7 .... 161 J4
Copenhagen Primary School
IS N1 .... 5 K4
Copland Community School &
Technology Centre Gms
WBLY HA9 .... 80 F5
Copperfields Shopping Centre
DART DA1 .... 146 E3
Coppermill Primary School
WALTH E17 .... 68 D6
Coppetts Wood Hospital
MUSWH N10 .... 65 M2
Coppetts Wood School
MUSWH N10 .... 66 A1
Coppice Primary School
CHIG IG7 .... 54 A7
Copthall School
MLHL NW7 .... 46 A8
Coram Gallery
BMSBY WC1N 5 L3
Corbets Tey School
UPMR RM14 .... 93 H5
Cordwainers College
HOM E9 .... 86 C7
Corelli Surgery
WOOL/PLUM SE18 ...... 124 E8
Corinthian Casuals
Football Club
CHSGTN KT9 .... 168 A5
Cornhill Sports Club
BECK BR3 .... 159 G1
Coroners Court
HACK E8 .... 86 C5
Coroners Court
WALTH E17 .... 68 F7
Cosmopolitan College
IS N1 .... 5 L6
Costa Rican Embassy
BAY/PAD W2 .... 8 F6
Coston Secondary Modern Girls
School
GFD/PVL UB6 .... 97 J2
Coteford Infant School
RSLP HA4 .... 60 M4
Cottenham Park C of E Primary
School
RYNPK SW20 .... 154 A4
The Coulsdon Eye Clinic
COUL/CHIP CR5 ...... 183 J1
Coultauld Institute Galleries
HOL/ALD WC2B 11 L5
Council Offices
OXHEY WD19 .... 42 D5
Council Offices
WCHPL E1 .... 104 B6
Council of Mosques
FITZ W1T 10 F3
Counterpoint Theatre
STPAN WC1H 5 K7
County Council Community
Services
RYLN/HDSTN HA2 ..... 79 K2
County Court at the Borough
STHWK SE1 .... 18 D1
Courtfield Medical Centre
ECT SW5 .... 14 D6
Courtland JMI School
MLHL NW7 .... 45 L4
Courtwood Primary School
CROY/NA CR0 ...... 185 M3
The Courtyard Gallery
IS N1 .... 5 K6
The Coventry Gallery
SDTCH EC2A 7 J7
Cowley Business Park
UX/CGN UB8 .... 94 C2
Cowley Hill First School
BORE WD6 .... 32 B4
Cowley Mill Industrial Estate
IVER SL0 .... 94 A1
CPfc Soccer & Sports Centre
BRXN/ST SW9 ..... 120 F8
CP House Business Centre
GSTN WD25 .... 29 M4
Crafts Council
IS N1 .... 6 B6
Crampton Junior & Infant School
WALW SE17 ...... 18 D7
Cranborne Industrial Estate
POTB/CUF EN6 .... 22 E2
Cranborne Primary School
POTB/CUF EN6 .... 22 E4
Cranbrook College
IL IG1 .... 89 G2
Crane School
FELT TW13 ...... 132 F6
Cranford Business Park
HYS/HAR UB3 ... 95 M4
Cranford Community College
HEST TW5 ...... 114 B4
Cranford Infant School
HSLWW TW4 .... 114 A7
Cranford Park Junior School
HYS/HAR UB3 .. 113 M2
Cranford School
HSLWW TW4 ... 114 B7
Cranham Health Centre
UPMR RM14 .... 75 J3
Cranmer Middle School
MTCM CR4 ..... 155 M8
Crauford Business Park
HYS/HAR UB3 .. 113 M1
The Craven Clinic
HMSMTH W6 ... 118 B2
Craven Park Health Centre
WLSDN NW10 .. 81 K6
Craven Park Junior School
SEVS/STOTM N15 . 68 A7
Craven Park Medical Centre
WLSDN NW10 ... 81 K8
Crawford Primary School
CMBW SE5 .... 121 J5
Crayfield Industrial Park
STMC/STPC BR5 . 162 C6
Crayfields Business Park
STMC/STPC BR5 . 162 C8

Crayford Industrial Estate
DART DA1 ...... 145 M2
Crayford Leisure Centre &
Greyhound Stadium
DART DA1 ...... 145 L3
Crayford Medical Centre
DART DA1 ...... 145 M2
Crayside Industrial Estate
DART DA1 ...... 128 A8
Creek Road Health Centre
DEPT SE8 ...... 123 G4
Creek Road Industrial Estate
DEPT SE8 ...... 123 H4
Crescent Surgery
STMC/STPC BR5 . 162 B8
Crewe House
MYFR/PICC W1J . 10 C8
Crews Hill Golf Club
ENC/FH EN2 .... 24 F7
Cricket School Caretaker
FNCH N3 .... 65 H4
Cricklewood Synagogue
CRICK NW2 ..... 82 D5
Cricklewood Trading Estate
CRICK NW2 ..... 82 E3
Crispin Industrial Centre
UED N18 .... 50 C7
Criterion Theatre
STJS SW1Y 11 G7
Crofton Leisure Centre
BROCKY SE4 .... 141 G3
Crofton School
BROCKY SE4 .... 141 G3
Croham Hurst School
SAND/SEL CR2 .. 172 F7
Cromer Road JMI School
BAR EN5 .... 34 B6
Cromwell Business Centre
BARK IG11 ..... 107 L2
Cromwell Hospital
KENS W8 .... 14 C5
Cromwell Industrial Estate
LEY E10 .... 68 E8
Crook Log Baths
BXLYHS DA6 .... 144 D1
Crook Log Primary School
BXLYHS DA6 .... 144 D1
Crook Log Sports Centre
WELL DA16 ..... 126 D8
Cross Deep Surgery
TWK TW1 .... 134 A5
Crosshall Surgery
STMC/STPC BR5 . 162 C2
Cross Street Gallery
IS N1 .... 6 C2
Crouch End Art School
CEND/HSY/T N8 . 66 E6
Crouch End Health Centre
CEND/HSY/T N8 . 66 E6
Crouch Hall Road Surgery
CEND/HSY/T N8 . 66 D7
Crouch Hill Recreation Centre
ARCH N19 ...... 66 E8
Crowland Primary School
SEVS/STOTM N15 . 67 M6
Crowlands Junior &
Infant School
ROMW/RG RM7 ... 73 J7
Crown Business Centre
WDR/YW UB7 .... 94 F7
Crown Close Business Centre
BOW E3 .... 87 G8
Crown Court
ISLW TW7 ...... 115 L6
Crowndale Health Centre
CAMTN NW1 ..... 4 F5
Crownfield School
ROMW/RG RM7 ... 73 G3
Crown Lane Clinic
STHGT/OAK N14 . 48 C3
Crown Lane CP School
WNWD SE27 ..... 157 H1
Crown Plaza Hotel
WDR/YW UB7 .... 113 G1
Crown Prosecution Service
HRW HA1 .... 61 L7
Crown Prosecution Service
SRTFD E15 ..... 87 L6
Crown Road Doctors Surgery
TWK TW1 .... 134 B4
Crown Trading Centre
HYS/HAR UB3 ... 95 L8
Crown Woods Secondary School
ELTH/MOT SE9 .. 143 J2
Croydon Borough Council
CROY/NA CR0 ... 173 H2
Croydon Council
CROY/NA CR0 ... 173 H2
Croydon Football Club
SNWD SE25 ..... 158 C8
Croydon Health Authority
CROY/NA CR0 ... 172 B3
Croydon Health Authority
CROY/NA CR0 ... 173 G6
Croydon High School for Girls
SAND/SEL CR2 .. 185 J4
Croydon Mosque & Islamic
Centre
THHTH CR7 ..... 172 A1
Croydon Road Industrial Estate
SNWD SE25 ..... 158 C7
Crusader Industrial Estate
FSBYPK N4 ..... 67 J7
Crusoe House School
IS N1 .... 7 G7
Crystal Palace Football Club
SNWD SE25 ..... 158 C6
Crystal Palace Museum
NRWD SE19 ..... 157 M3
Crystal Palace National
Sports Centre
NRWD SE19 ..... 158 A2
Cuaco Sports Ground
BECK BR3 ...... 159 G2
Cubitt Town Primary School
POP/IOD E14 ... 123 J1
Cuckoo Hall Lane Junior &
Primary School
ED N9 .... 50 D2

Cuddington CP School
HOR/WEW KT19 .. 168 F5
Cuffley School
POTB/CUF EN6 .. 24 F3
Culloden Primary School
POP/IOD E14 ... 105 K5
Culvers House Primary School
MTCM CR4 ...... 171 G3
Cumberland Business Park
WLSDN NW10 .... 99 H2
Cumberland Comprehensive
School
CAN/RD E16 .... 105 M4
Cumnor House School
SAND/SEL CR2 .. 184 B2
Curwen Primary School
PLSTW E13 ..... 106 A1
Curzon Avenue Surgery
PEND EN3 ...... 37 K8
Curzon Phoenix Theatre
SOHO/SHAV W1D . 11 H5
Custom House
MON EC3R 13 J7
Cutlers' Hall
STP EC4M 12 D4
The Cycle Surgery
HBRY N5 .... 85 G5
Cygnet Clinic Beckton
EHAM E6 .... 107 K5
Cygnus Business Centre
WLSDN NW10 .... 81 M5
Cypress Infant School
SNWD SE25 ..... 157 L5
Cypress Junior School
SNWD SE25 ..... 157 L5
Cyprus College of Art
WNWD SE27 ..... 139 H8
Cyprus High Comm
MYFR/PKLN W1K . 10 A6
Cyprus High Comm Trade Centre
CONDST W1S 10 D5
Cyril Jackson Primary School
POP/IOD E14 ... 104 F6
Dacre Industrial Estate
CHES/WCR EN8 .. 26 E2
Dagenham Chest Clinic
BCTR RM8 ...... 90 F3
Dagenham Civic Centre
DAGE RM10 ..... 91 H2
Dagenham Priory School
DAGE RM10 ..... 91 H7
Dagenham & Redbridge
Football Club
DAGE RM10 ..... 91 H5
Dagenham Superbowl
DAGE RM10 ..... 109 H1
Dagenham Swimming Pool
BCTR RM8 ...... 90 F2
Daily Mirror Off
FLST/FETLN EC4A 12 B3
Daily Telegraph
POP/IOD E14 ... 123 G1
Dalmain Primary School
FSTH SE23 ..... 140 E5
Dalston Practice
HACK E8 .... 86 A6
Dame Alice Owens School
POTB/CUF EN6 .. 22 E6
Dame Tipping School
ABR/YW UB7 .... 55 K5
Danegrove Primary School
EBAR EN4 ...... 47 L1
Dane Junior High School
IL IG1 .... 89 J1
Danesfield Preparatory School
WOT/HER KT12 .. 165 H4
Danes Hill Preparatory School
LHD/OX KT22 ... 178 C7
Danetree School
HOR/WEW KT19 .. 180 C1
Danson Gallery
STMC/STPC BR5 . 161 J8
Danson Primary School
WELL DA16 ..... 144 A1
Darell Junior & Infant School
RCH/KEW TW9 ... 117 G8
Dargent Gallery
STHWK SE1 ..... 12 B7
Darrick Wood Junior &
Primary School
ORP BR6 .... 176 B6
Darrick Wood Swimming Pool
ORP BR6 .... 176 B5
Dartford Borough Council
DART DA1 ...... 146 D5
Dartford County Court
DART DA1 ...... 146 E3
Dartford F C
RDART DA2 ..... 147 H5
Dartford Golf Club
DART DA1 ...... 146 B6
Dartford Grammar School
DART DA1 ...... 146 C3
Dartford Grammar
School for Girls
DART DA1 ...... 146 C4
Dartford Magistrates Court
DART DA1 ...... 146 D3
Dartford Natural Health Centre
DART DA1 ...... 146 E4
Dartford West Boys School
DART DA1 ...... 146 D4
Dartford West Health Centre
DART DA1 ...... 146 C3
Dartford West High School
for Girls
DART DA1 ...... 146 C4
Dashmesh Darbar Sikh Temple
MNPK E12 ...... 88 F6
Datapoint Business Centre
CAN/RD E16 .... 105 K3
Daubeney Primary School
CLPT E5 .... 86 E4
David Curzon Gallery
WIM/MER SW19 .. 154 E1
David Game Tuitorial College
SKENS SW7 ..... 15 G6

David Livingstone School
THHTH CR7 ..... 157 J4
David Lloyd Leisure Centre
SKENS SW7 ..... 14 D5
Davidson Infant & Junior School
CROY/NA CR0 ... 172 F2
Davies Infant School
WAN E11 .... 87 M2
Davies's College
STHWK SE1 ..... 18 F1
Dawlish Primary School
LEY E10 .... 87 J2
Day Hospital
CAMTN NW1 ..... 4 F1
Day Hospital
PUR/KEN CR8 ... 184 A4
Days Lane Primary School
BFN/LL DA15 ... 143 M3
Deanesfield Primary School
RSLP HA4 ...... 78 D4
Deansbrook Junior &
Infant School
MLHL NW7 ...... 45 J8
De Beauvoir School
IS N1 .... 85 L6
De Beauvoir Surgery
IS N1 .... 7 H5
De Bohun School
STHGT/OAK N14 . 35 H8
Decima Gallery
WALW SE17 ..... 18 D8
Delrow School
GSTN WD25 ..... 30 C4
Denmead School
HPTN TW12 ..... 151 G3
Dental Health Centre
CAMTN NW1 ..... 84 D3
The Dental Health Centre
TWK TW1 .... 134 D3
Dentist Surgery
LEE/GVPK SE12 . 142 B5
The Dentist Surgery
OXHEY WD19 .... 42 B7
Department of Health
WHALL SW1A 17 J1
Department of Trade and
Industry
STJSPK SW1H ... 17 H3
Dep of Clinical Haematology
GWRST WC1E 11 G1
Deptford Green School
NWCR SE14 ..... 122 F5
Deptford Park Business Centre
DEPT SE8 ...... 122 F4
Deptford Park Primary School
DEPT SE8 ...... 122 E3
Deptford Trading Estate
DEPT SE8 ...... 122 E3
Dersingham Infant School
MNPK E12 ...... 88 F5
Derwent Water Primary School
ACT W3 .... 99 J7
Descovery Business Park
BERM/RHTH SE16 122 A1
Design Museum
STHWK SE1 ..... 19 M1
Deutsche Schule
RCHPK/HAM TW10 134 D5
Devonshire Hill Junior &
Infant School
TOTM N17 ...... 49 M8
Devonshire Hospital
MHST W1U 10 B2
Devonshire House
Preparatory School
HAMP NW3 ...... 83 J5
Devonshire House School
HAMP NW3 ...... 83 J5
Devonshire School
BELMT SM2 ..... 182 C5
Devons Road Surgery
BOW E3 .... 105 J4
Dewhurst St Mary Junior
Middle & Infant School
CHESW EN7 ..... 26 B2
Diakonos Physical Theatre
PECK SE15 ..... 122 A8
Diamond College
FITZ W1T 11 H4
Diane Matthews Clinic
ROMW/RG RM7 ... 73 K5
Dilkes CP School
SOCK/AV RM15 .. 111 M5
Dilloway Industrial Estate
NWDGN UB2 ..... 96 C5
Discover Bible School
GSTN WD25 ..... 21 J7
Divine Saviour RC JMI School
ABLGY WD5 ..... 20 D5
Docklands Medical Centre
POP/IOD E14 ... 123 G2
Docklands Sailing Centre
POP/IOD E14 ... 123 G1
Docklands Sailing &
Watersports Centre
POP/IOD E14 ... 122 F1
Dockmaster's House
POP/IOD E14 ... 105 G6
Dock Offices
BERM/RHTH SE16 122 C1
Dockyard Industrial Estate
WOOL/PLUM SE18 124 E1
Doctors Chakrabarti Surgery
CRW RM5 .... 73 H1
Doctors Group Practice
BELMT SM2 ..... 182 B3
The Doctors Practice
SKENS SW7 ..... 14 D4
D of Y Theatre
CHCR WC2N 11 J7
Dog Kennel Hill Primary School
CMBW SE5 ...... 121 L8
Dokal Industrial Estate
NWDGN UB2 ..... 96 E8
Dollis County Infant School
MLHL NW7 ...... 64 B1
Dollis Hill Synagogue
CRICK NW2 ..... 82 B4

Dollis Junior School
  MLHL NW7 .... 64 C1
Dolphin School
  BTSEA SW11 .... 137 M2
Dominica High Comm
  ECT SW5 .... 14 D6
The Dominican Rep Embassy
  BAY/PAD W2 .... 8 D5
Dominion Business Park
  ED N9 .... 50 D4
Donmar Warehouse Theatre
  LSQ/SEVD WC2H 11 J5
Donnington Primary School
  WLSDN NW10 .... 82 B7
Dorchester Primary School
  WPK KT4 .... 169 J3
Dormers Wells High School
  GFD/PVL UB6 .... 97 G5
Dormers Wells JMI School
  STHL UB1 .... 97 H6
Dormers Wells Medical Centre
  GFD/PVL UB6 .... 97 G5
Dorothy Barley Infant School
  BCTR RM8 .... 90 B5
Dorset Road Infant School
  ELTH/MOT SE9 .... 142 E6
The Douay Martyrs RC School
  HGDN/ICK UB10 .... 77 H4
Douglas Bader Foundation
  PUT/ROE SW15 .... 136 A3
The Dover House Surgery
  UED N18 .... 49 M7
Dovers Corner Industrial Estate
  RAIN RM13 .... 109 M2
Downderry Primary School
  BMLY BR1 .... 141 L8
Downfield School
  CHES/WCR EN8 .... 26 E4
Downham Health Centre
  BMLY BR1 .... 141 L8
Downhill Junior School
  TOTM N17 .... 67 K5
Down Lane Junior School
  TOTM N17 .... 67 M3
Down Manor Combined
  First & Middle School
  NTHLT UB5 .... 96 B2
Downsell Primary School
  WAN E11 .... 87 K4
Downside Primary School
  CLPT E5 .... 86 A4
Downsview School
  CLPT E5 .... 86 B4
Drapers Sports Ground
  SRTFD E15 .... 87 J4
Drayton Gardens Surgery
  WBPTN SW10 .... 14 E7
Drayton Green Primary School
  WEA W13 .... 98 A6
Drayton Manor High School
  HNWL W7 .... 97 M6
Drayton Park School
  HBRY N5 .... 85 C5
Drca Business Centre
  BTSEA SW11 .... 120 A6
Drew Primary School
  CAN/RD E16 .... 106 E7
Dr Ghosh's Surgery
  SEVS/STOTM N15 .... 67 K7
Drill Hall
  GWRST WC1E 11 G2
Dr Johnson's House
  FLST/FETLN EC4A 12 B4
Dr Samuels Surgery
  WAN E11 .... 87 L3
Dr Sherriff & Partners
  PECK SE15 .... 121 M6
Dr Tripletts School
  HYS/HAR UB3 .... 95 M5
Drury Way Industrial Estate
  WLSDN NW10 .... 81 K4
Dry Ski Slope
  HGDN/ICK UB10 .... 76 F5
Duch Thtr
  COVGDN WC2E 11 L6
Duke of York Column
  STJS SW1Y 11 H9
Duke of York's H.Q.
  CHEL SW3 .... 15 M6
Duke of Yorks Theatre
  SOHO/SHAV W1D 10 F6
Dukes Avenue Practice
  MUSWH N10 .... 66 B4
Dulverton School
  BFN/LL DA15 .... 143 K6
Dulwich College
  DUL SE21 .... 139 L5
Dulwich College Picture Gallery
  DUL SE21 .... 139 K4
Dulwich College Preparatory
  School
  DUL SE21 .... 139 L7
Dulwich Hamlet Football Club
  CMBW SE5 .... 139 L1
Dulwich Hamlet Junior School
  HNHL SE24 .... 139 K3
Dulwich High School for Boys
  HNHL SE24 .... 139 K2
Dulwich Medical Centre
  EDUL SE22 .... 140 A2
Dulwich Village C of E
  Infant School
  DUL SE21 .... 139 L3
Dunbar Wharf
  POP/IOD E14 .... 104 F6
Duncombe Primary School
  ARCH N19 .... 84 E1
Dun Cow Surgery
  STHWK SE1 .... 19 L7
Dundee Wharf
  POP/IOD E14 .... 104 F6
Dundonald Primary School
  WIM/MER SW19 .... 154 F3
Dunningford Primary School
  HCH RM12 .... 91 M5
Dunraven Lower School
  STRHM/NOR SW16 .... 138 F7

Dunraven Upper School
  STRHM/NOR SW16 .... 138 F7
Duppas Primary School
  CROY/NA CR0 .... 172 B7
Durand Primary School
  BRXN/ST SW9 .... 120 F6
Durants School
  EN EN1 .... 37 J4
Durdans Park School
  STHL UB1 .... 96 F4
Durston House School
  EA W5 .... 98 D5
Dycorts School
  HARH RM3 .... 57 G6
Dysart School
  KUTN/CMB KT2 .... 134 D8
Eagle House Surgery
  PEND EN3 .... 37 J7
Eaglesfield Secondary School
  WOOL/PLUM SE18 .... 125 G6
Eagle Trading Estate
  MTCM CR4 .... 170 F1
Ealdham Primary School
  ELTH/MOT SE9 .... 142 C1
Ealing Abbey
  EA W5 .... 98 C5
Ealing Abbey Scriptorium
  WEA W13 .... 98 C5
Ealing & Acton Synagogue
  EA W5 .... 98 D7
Ealing Central Sports Ground
  GFD/PVL UB6 .... 98 A1
Ealing College Upper School
  WEA W13 .... 98 B5
Ealing Cricket Club
  EA W5 .... 98 E5
Ealing Gallery
  EA W5 .... 98 D8
Ealing Hospital NHS Trust
  STHL UB1 .... 97 K8
Ealing Liberal Synagogue
  WEA W13 .... 98 A5
Ealing Northern Sports Centre
  NTHLT UB5 .... 79 K5
Ealing Park Health Centre
  EA W5 .... 116 D2
Ealing Road Trading Estate
  BTFD TW8 .... 116 D3
Ealing Sports Centre
  EA W5 .... 98 E6
Ealing Tertiary College
  EA W5 .... 98 D7
Ealing Tutorial College
  EA W5 .... 98 C6
Eardley Primary School
  STRHM/NOR SW16 .... 156 C2
The Earl Gallery
  POTB/CUF EN6 .... 22 F5
Earlham Junior & Infant School
  WDGN N22 .... 67 G1
Earlham Primary School
  FSTGT E7 .... 87 M5
Earls Court Exhibition Centre
  ECT SW5 .... 14 A8
Earlsfield Primary School
  WAND/EARL SW18 .... 137 J5
Earlsmead Junior &
  Infant School
  SEVS/STOTM N15 .... 67 M6
Earlsmead School
  RYLN/HDSTN HA2 .... 78 F4
Earth Gallery
  SKENS SW7 .... 15 H4
Earthworks Gallery
  HCH RM12 .... 92 E1
East Acton Primary School
  ACT W3 .... 99 L6
East Barking Luncheon &
  Leisure Centre
  BCTR RM8 .... 90 C5
East Barnet Grammar School
  EBAR EN4 .... 47 M1
East Barnet Health Centre
  EBAR EN4 .... 34 D8
East Barnet School
  EBAR EN4 .... 34 D6
Eastbrook Secondary School
  DAGE RM10 .... 91 J4
Eastbury Comprehensive
  School
  BARK IG11 .... 89 K7
Eastbury Infant School
  BARK IG11 .... 89 M7
Eastbury Infant School
  NTHWD HA6 .... 41 M6
Eastcote Cricket Club
  PIN HA5 .... 60 B6
Eastcote Health Centre
  PIN HA5 .... 60 C8
Eastcote Industrial Estate
  RSLP HA4 .... 60 C8
Eastcote Primary School
  ELTH/MOT SE9 .... 125 K8
Eastcote Surgery
  RSLP HA4 .... 60 B7
Eastcourt Independent School
  GDMY/SEVK IG3 .... 90 A1
East Dulwich Baths
  EDUL SE22 .... 139 M1
Eastern Art Gallery
  NOXST/BSQ WC1A 11 J4
Eastfield Primary & Infant
  School
  PEND EN3 .... 37 K3
Eastfields Secondary Modern
  Boys School
  MTCM CR4 .... 156 B5
East Finchley Medical Centre
  EFNCH N2 .... 65 L5
East Greenwich Christ Church
  C of E Primary School
  GNWCH SE10 .... 123 L2
East Ham Industrial Estate
  CAN/RD E16 .... 106 D3
East Ham Memorial Hospital
  FSTGT E7 .... 88 D7
Eastlea Community School
  CAN/RD E16 .... 105 L3

East London Business College
  WAN E11 .... 87 L1
East London Central
  Synagogue
  WCHPL E1 .... 104 C3
East London & City Health
  Authority
  BOW E3 .... 105 G1
East London & City Health
  Authority
  PLSTW E13 .... 106 B3
East London Markazi Mosque
  WCHPL E1 .... 104 A6
East London Mosque
  WCHPL E1 .... 104 A4
East London Rugby Club
  EHAM E6 .... 106 F4
Eastman Dental Hospital
  FSBYW WC1X 5 L9
East Molesey Cricket Club
  E/WMO/HCT KT8 .... 151 J4
East Molesey Infants School
  E/WMO/HCT KT8 .... 151 K8
East Sheen CP Junior School
  MORT/ESHN SW14 .... 135 L1
East West Gallery
  NTGHL W11 .... 100 E5
East Wickham Primary School
  WELL DA16 .... 126 A6
Eaton Manor Rugby Club
  WAN E11 .... 70 C6
Eaton Square Preparatory
  School
  BGVA SW1W 16 C5
Eaton Square School
  PIM SW1V 16 E6
Ebbisham County Infants School
  EPSOM KT18 .... 180 C7
Ebbisham Sports Club
  HOR/WEW KT19 .... 180 C5
Ebury Galleries
  BGVA SW1W 16 B6
Ecclesbourne Junior &
  Infants School
  THHTH CR7 .... 157 J8
Ecclesbourne Primary School
  IS N1 .... 7 G1
Echelford Primary School
  ASHF TW15 .... 149 H1
Eckerd College
  GWRST WC1E 11 G2
Eclipse Estate
  HOR/WEW KT19 .... 180 C6
Ecole De Mime Corporel
  Theatre De Lange Fou
  ARCH N19 .... 84 C2
Eden College
  STHWK SE1 .... 18 D3
Edenham High School
  CROY/NA CR0 .... 173 M2
Eden Medical Centre
  WKENS W14 .... 118 F2
Edenvale Child Health Clinic
  TOOT SW17 .... 156 A3
Edes Business Park
  WLGTN SM6 .... 171 G4
Edgebury Primary School
  CHST BR7 .... 143 J8
Edge Business Centre
  CRICK NW2 .... 82 B2
Edgware Clinic
  EDGE HA8 .... 45 C8
Edgware College
  HAMP NW3 .... 83 J6
Edgware Infant School
  EDGE HA8 .... 45 C8
Edgware Junior School
  EDGE HA8 .... 45 H8
Edgware Reform Synagogue
  EDGE HA8 .... 44 F6
Edgware Secondary School
  EDGE HA8 .... 44 F6
Edgware Town Football Club
  EDGE HA8 .... 63 G1
Edgware United Synagogue
  EDGE HA8 .... 45 H6
Edinburgh Primary School
  WALTH E17 .... 68 F6
Edith Grove Gallery
  WBPTN SW10 .... 119 H4
Edith Neville Primary School
  CAMTN NW1 .... 5 C6
Edmonton County Court
  UED N18 .... 49 M7
Edmonton Leisure Centre
  ED N9 .... 50 A5
Edmonton School
  EN EN1 .... 49 M2
Edmund Waller School
  NWCR SE14 .... 122 D7
Edward Ash Gallery
  ORP BR6 .... 176 A5
Edward Cross Gallery
  WEY KT13 .... 164 D5
Edward Pauling School
  FELT TW13 .... 131 L6
Edward Wilson Primary School
  BAY/PAD W2 .... 8 C2
Edwin Lambert Schooll
  EMPK RM11 .... 74 A7
Effra Primary School
  BRXS/STRHM SW2 .... 139 G2
Eglinton Infant School
  WOOL/PLUM SE18 .... 125 G4
Eglinton Junior School
  WOOL/PLUM SE18 .... 125 G5
Elbourne Trading Estate
  BELV DA17 .... 127 H1
Eldenwall Industrial Estate
  BCTR RM8 .... 90 F1
Eldon JMI School
  ED N9 .... 50 C3
Eleanor Estate
  CHES/WCR EN8 .... 26 F7
Eleanor Palmer Primary School
  KTTN NW5 .... 84 C4
Eleanor Smith Special School
  PLSTW E13 .... 106 A1

Electrical Trades Union College
  ESH/CLAY KT10 .... 166 A6
The Electrolysis Clinic
  BCTR RM8 .... 90 B1
Elephant & Castle
  Shopping Centre
  STHWK SE1 .... 18 D4
Elers Clinic
  HYS/HAR UB3 .... 113 K2
Elfrida Primary School
  CAT SE6 .... 141 H8
Elica Gallery
  NRWD SE19 .... 157 L2
Eliot Bank Primary School
  FSTH SE23 .... 140 B6
Elizabeth Avenue Group
  Practice
  IS N1 .... 6 F3
Elizabeth Garrett
  Anderson School
  IS N1 .... 5 M5
Elizabeth Page Gallery
  FARR EC1 .... 12 D2
Elizabeth Selby Infant School
  BETH E2 .... 104 A2
Elizabeth Trading Estate
  NWCR SE14 .... 122 D4
Ellen Wilkinson High School
  EA W5 .... 98 F5
Ellen Wilkinson Primary School
  EHAM E6 .... 106 D4
Ellerslie Square Industrial Estate
  CLAP SW4 .... 138 E1
Ellingham Primary School
  CHSGTN KT9 .... 179 K1
Elliott Gm School
  PUT/ROE SW15 .... 136 C3
Elmbridge Borough Council
  WOT/HER KT12 .... 165 G2
Elmbridge Leisure Centre
  WOT/HER KT12 .... 150 B8
Elmbridge Museum
  WEY KT13 .... 164 A6
Elmcourt School
  WNWD SE27 .... 139 H6
Elmgrove First & Middle School
  KTN/HRWW/W HA3 .... 62 A5
Elm House Surgery
  BECK BR3 .... 158 F5
Elmhurst Preparatory School
  BECK BR3 .... 158 D7
Elmhurst Primary School
  FSTGT E7 .... 88 B7
Elmhurst School
  CROY/NA CR0 .... 172 D6
Elm Lea Trading Estate
  TOTM N17 .... 68 A1
Elmlodge Surgery
  HNHL SE24 .... 139 J3
The Elms Health Centre
  POTB/CUF EN6 .... 23 J4
Elmwood Junior & Infant School
  CROY/NA CR0 .... 172 B2
Elm Wood Primary School
  WNWD SE27 .... 139 K7
Elsdale Street Health Centre
  HOM E9 .... 86 C7
Elsley Primary School
  BTSEA SW11 .... 120 A8
Elsley Primary School
  WBLY HA9 .... 80 F6
Elstree & Borehamwood
  Town Council
  BORE WD6 .... 32 B6
Elstree Studios
  BORE WD6 .... 32 A6
Elstree Way Clinic
  BORE WD6 .... 32 B5
Eltham Baths
  ELTH/MOT SE9 .... 142 E2
Eltham C of E Primary School
  ELTH/MOT SE9 .... 142 F2
Eltham College
  ELTH/MOT SE9 .... 142 D6
Eltham College Junior School
  ELTH/MOT SE9 .... 142 D5
Eltham Green School
  ELTH/MOT SE9 .... 142 D3
Eltham Health Clinic
  ELTH/MOT SE9 .... 142 E2
Eltham Hill School
  ELTH/MOT SE9 .... 142 E3
Eltham Palace
  ELTH/MOT SE9 .... 142 E4
Elthorne High School
  HNWL W7 .... 115 M1
Elthorne Park Surgery
  HNWL W7 .... 98 A8
Elystan Business Centre
  HYS/HAR UB3 .... 96 C6
Emanuel School
  WAND/EARL SW18 .... 137 K2
Embassy of Afghanistan
  SKENS SW7 .... 15 G2
Embassy of Angola
  MYFR/PKLN W1K 10 A7
Embassy of Bahrain
  SKENS SW7 .... 14 E4
Embassy of Belarus
  KENS W8 .... 14 D2
Embassy of Belgium
  KTBR SW1X 16 B4
Embassy of Bolivia
  KTBR SW1X 16 B4
Embassy of Brazil
  MYFR/PKLN W1K 10 A6
Embassy of Cote d'ivoire
  KTBR SW1X 16 B3
Embassy of Cuba
  HHOL WC1V 11 J4
Embassy of Ecuador
  SKENS SW7 .... 15 L3
Embassy of Ethiopia
  SKENS SW7 .... 15 H2
Embassy of Finland
  KTBR SW1X 16 A3
Embassy of France
  KTBR SW1X 15 M1

Embassy of Greece
  KENS W8 .... 100 F7
Embassy of Guatemala
  WBPTN SW10 .... 14 E9
Embassy of Honduras
  MBLAR W1H 9 M2
Embassy of Iceland
  KTBR SW1X 16 A5
Embassy of Iraq
  SKENS SW7 .... 14 F3
Embassy of Israel
  KENS W8 .... 14 C1
Embassy of Japan
  MYFR/PICC W1J 10 D9
Embassy of Latvia
  CAMTN NW1 .... 10 A1
Embassy of Lebanon
  KENS W8 .... 8 C8
Embassy of Liberia
  BAY/PAD W2 .... 8 B6
Embassy of Mexico
  MYFR/PICC W1J 10 C9
Embassy of Mongolia
  KENS W8 .... 14 D2
Embassy of Morocco
  SKENS SW7 .... 14 E5
Embassy of Nepal
  KENS W8 .... 8 C8
Embassy of Netherlands
  SKENS SW7 .... 14 F2
Embassy of Paraguay
  SKENS SW7 .... 14 D4
Embassy of Portugal
  KTBR SW1X 16 A2
Embassy of Romania
  KENS W8 .... 14 C1
Embassy of Sudan
  WHALL SW1A 10 E9
Embassy of Sweden
  MBLAR W1H 9 J3
Embassy of Switzerland
  MBLAR W1H 9 L3
Embassy of the Arab Rep of Egypt
  MYFR/PICC W1J 10 C8
Embassy of the Democratic Rep of
  the Congo
  KTBR SW1X 15 M4
Embassy of the Federal Rep of
  Germany
  KTBR SW1X 16 A3
Embassy of the Hashemite
  Kingdom of Jordan
  KENS W8 .... 100 F8
Embassy of the Islamic
  Rep of Iran
  SKENS SW7 .... 15 H2
Embassy of the Peoples
  Rep of China
  CAVSQ/HST W1G 10 C2
Embassy of the Rep of Albania
  BCVA SW1W 16 D4
Embassy of the Rep of Croatia
  GTPST W1W 10 D1
Embassy of the Rep of Gabon
  SKENS SW7 .... 14 F4
Embassy of the Rep of Krygyz
  MBLAR W1H 9 L3
Embassy of the Rep of
  Mozambique
  FITZ W1T 10 E1
Embassy of the Rep of Poland
  CAVSQ/HST W1G 10 C2
Embassy of the Rep of Slovenia
  MHST W1U 10 C4
Embassy of the Republic of
  Armenia
  KENS W8 .... 14 C3
Embassy of the Republic of
  Korea
  WESTW SW1E 16 F3
Embassy of the Republic of
  Senegal
  CRICK NW2 .... 82 C7
Embassy of the Russian
  Federation
  KENS W8 .... 8 C9
Embassy of the Slovak Republic
  KENS W8 .... 8 C8
Embassy of the Socialist
  Republic of South Vietnam
  KENS W8 .... 14 D3
Embassy of the State of Qatar
  MYFR/PKLN W1K 10 B9
Embassy of the Syrian Arab Rep
  KTBR SW1X 16 A2
Embassy of the Union of
  Myanmar
  MYFR/PICC W1J 10 C8
Embassy of the United Arab
  Emirates
  SKENS SW7 .... 15 H1
Embassy of Tunisia
  SKENS SW7 .... 15 H2
Embassy of Turkmeistan
  GTPST W1W 10 F3
Embassy of Ukraine
  NTGHL W11 .... 100 E10
Embassy of United Republic of
  Cameroon
  WKENS W14 .... 100 E7
Embassy of Uruguay
  SKENS SW7 .... 15 K3
Embassy of Venezuela
  SKENS SW7 .... 15 H4
Ember Sports Club
  ESH/CLAY KT10 .... 166 C3
Embroidery World Business
  Centre
  WFD IG8 .... 70 D3
Emerson Park School
  EMPK RM11 .... 75 H8
Emmanuel C of E School
  NTHWD HA6 .... 59 M1
Empson & Ewell Bo Co
  EW KT17 .... 180 D6
Endsleigh Industrial Estate
  NWDGN UB2 .... 114 E2

Enfield Business Centre
PEND EN3 .... **37** J5
Enfield Chace Lower School
ENC/FH EN2 .... **36** E3
Enfield College
PEND EN3 .... **37** J5
Enfield Cricket Club
EN EN1 .... **36** E8
Enfield Football Club
ED N9 .... **50** C4
Enfield Football Club
EN EN1 .... **37** G6
Enfield Grammar School
ENC/FH EN2 .... **36** D6
Enfield & Haringey Health
Authority
EBAR EN4 .... **35** C7
Enfield Lower Grammar School
ENC/FH EN2 .... **36** D5
Enfield School of Swimming
FBAR/BDGN N11 .... **48** D7
Engayne Junior School
UPMR RM14 .... **75** L7
English College
SOHO/SHAV W1D **11** G4
English Martyrs RC
Primary School
WALW SE17 .... **19** G6
English Martyrs RC
Primary School
WCHPL E1 .... **13** M5
The English Teaching Theatre
IS N1 .... **7** K2
Enid Lawson Gallery
KENS W8 .... **14** C1
Ennersdale Primary School
LEW SE13 .... **141** K4
Ensham Secondary School
TOOT SW17 .... **155** M1
Enterprise Business Park
POP/IOD E14 .... **105** H8
Enterprise Industrial Estate
BERM/RHTH SE16 .... **122** A3
Epping Forest District Council
CHIG IG7 .... **53** K7
Epsom Business Park
EW KT17 .... **180** E4
Epsom College
EW KT17 .... **181** G7
Epsom County Court
EPSOM KT18 .... **180** D6
Epsom CP School
HOR/WEW KT19 .... **180** D4
Epsom & Ewell High School
HOR/WEW KT19 .... **168** C1
Epsom Ewell & St Hellier
NHS Trust
EPSOM KT18 .... **180** C4
Epsom Ewell & St Helliers
NHS Trust
HOR/WEW KT19 .... **179** M5
Epsom Golf Club
EW KT17 .... **181** G8
Epsom Health Clinic
EPSOM KT18 .... **180** E6
Epsom School of Art & Design
EW KT17 .... **180** E5
Epsom Sports Club
EPSOM KT18 .... **180** C4
Erdos Chinese Medical Centre
RSLP HA4 .... **77** L1
Erith & Belvedere Football Club
BELV DA17 .... **127** H1
Erith & District Hospital
ERITH DA8 .... **127** K4
Erith Health Centre
ERITH DA8 .... **127** L4
Erith Library & Museum
ERITH DA8 .... **127** L3
Erith School
ERITH DA8 .... **127** J5
Erith Small Business Centre
ERITH DA8 .... **127** M4
Erith Theatre Guild
ERITH DA8 .... **127** M3
Ernest Bevin School
TOOT SW17 .... **137** L7
Esher Church School
ESH/CLAY KT10 .... **166** C8
Esher College
THDIT KT7 .... **166** E2
Esher Green Surgery
ESH/CLAY KT10 .... **166** A5
Esher Rugby Club
WOT/HER KT12 .... **165** L4
Essex County Council
BKHH IG9 .... **52** D5
Essex County Council
BRW CM14 .... **57** K3
Essex County Council
CHIG IG7 .... **53** J3
Essex County Council
WAB EN9 .... **27** J4
Essex Galleries
IL IG1 .... **89** G2
Essex House Surgery
BARN SW13 .... **117** M7
Essex Primary School
MNPK E12 .... **88** E6
Estonian Embassy
SKENS SW7 .... **14** F2
Ethelburga Gm School
BTSEA SW11 .... **119** L6
Ethel Davis School
CHDH RM6 .... **72** B6
Euro Link Business Centre
BRXS/STRHM SW2 .... **139** C1
Eurolink Business Centre
BRXS/STRHM SW2 .... **139** G1
Europa Trading Estate
ERITH DA8 .... **127** K3
European School of Economics
KTBR SW1X **16** B2
European Vocational College
HDTCH EC3A **13** L4
Euro Temple
SOHO/CST W1F **10** F5

Euro Way School
CEND/HSY/T N8 .... **67** G4
Euro Way School London
FSBYPK N4 .... **67** H8
Euston Centre
CAMTN NW1 .... **4** E9
Euston Tower
CAMTN NW1 .... **4** E9
Eveline Lowe Primary School
STHWK SE1 .... **122** A3
Evelyns Secondary School
WDR/YW UB7 .... **94** F5
Evendine College
SOHO/SHAV W1D **11** G4
Evendine College
WIM/MER SW19 .... **154** E2
Everest Sports Club
CHES/WCR EN8 .... **26** B2
Eversley Medical Centre
THHTH CR7 .... **172** A1
Eversley Primary School
WCHMH N21 .... **35** L8
Ewell Castle School
EW KT17 .... **181** G2
Ewell Grove Infant School
EW KT17 .... **180** F2
Exhibition Halls
STLK EC1Y **12** F2
Eye Clinic
LSQ/SEVD WC2H **11** J4
The Eye Clinic
IL IG1 .... **89** H4
Eye Clinic
CAVSQ/HST W1G **10** C3
The Eye Practice
HAMP NW3 .... **83** K4
Fairbrook Medical Centre
BORE WD6 .... **32** B5
Faircharm Trading Estate
DEPT SE8 .... **123** H5
Faircharm Trading Estate
IS N1 .... **6** E5
The Faircross Complementary
Medical Centre
BARK IG11 .... **89** L6
Fairfield Clinic
BKHH IG9 .... **52** B3
Fairfield Industrial Estate
KUT KT1 .... **152** F6
Fairfield Pool & Leisure Centre
DART DA1 .... **146** E4
Fairfield Primary School
RAD WD7 .... **30** E1
Fairhill Medical Practice
KUTN/CMB KT2 .... **153** G3
Fairholme Junior &
Infant School
EBED/NFELT TW14 .... **131** K5
Fairlawn Primary School
FSTH SE23 .... **140** C4
Fairley House School
WEST SW1P **17** G6
Fairlop Primary School
BARK/HLT IG6 .... **71** J2
Fairview Industrial Centre
DAGW RM9 .... **109** K5
Fairview Medical Centre
STRHM/NOR SW16 .... **156** E4
Fairway JMI School
MLHL NW7 .... **45** K4
Fairway Primary School
MLHL NW7 .... **45** K4
Fairways Business Park
LEY E10 .... **86** E2
Falconbrook School
BTSEA SW11 .... **119** K7
Falcon Business Centre
BTSEA SW11 .... **137** L1
Falconer School
BUSH WD23 .... **29** M8
Falkland Road Practice
KTTN NW5 .... **84** C5
Family Doctor Unit Surgery
HSLW TW3 .... **115** G3
Fanmakers' Hall
LVPST EC2M **13** J3
Fan Museum
GNWCH SE10 .... **123** J5
Faraday Building
BLKFR EC4V **12** D5
Farleigh Rovers F C
WARL CR6 .... **185** M8
Farley Road Surgery
SAND/SEL CR2 .... **185** H2
Farm Lane Trading Estate
FUL/PGN SW6 .... **119** G4
Farnborough Primary School
ORP BR6 .... **176** D7
Farnell House Medical Centre
HSLW TW3 .... **115** H6
Farnham Green Primary School
GDMY/SEVK IG3 .... **72** A7
Farrington School
CHST BR7 .... **161** L3
Farringtons Girls School
CHST BR7 .... **161** K3
Fashion Gallery
MORT/ESHN SW14 .... **117** J8
Feathers Gallery
HMSMTH W6 .... **118** C1
Featherstone High School
NWDGN UB2 .... **114** D2
Featherstone Industrial Estate
NWDGN UB2 .... **96** E8
Featherstone Infant School
NWDGN UB2 .... **114** E1
Featherstone Junior
Mixed School
NWDGN UB2 .... **114** E1
Featherstone Road Health Clinic
NWDGN UB2 .... **114** E1
Felnex Trading Estate
WLGTN SM6 .... **171** G4
Feltham Airparcs Leisure Centre
FELT TW13 .... **132** D6
Feltham Hill Junior School
FELT TW13 .... **131** M7

Feltham & Hounslow
Boro Football Club
EBED/NFELT TW14 .... **132** A4
The Feltham School
FELT TW13 .... **132** C6
Feltham Superbowl
FELT TW13 .... **132** B6
Fenstanton Junior &
Infant School
BRXS/STRHM SW2 .... **139** G5
Ferndale Surgery
WFD IG8 .... **52** C8
Fern Hill Primary School
KUTN/CMB KT2 .... **152** E2
Ferrier Industrial Estate
WAND/EARL SW18 .... **137** H1
Ferry Lane Industrial Estate
RAIN RM13 .... **110** A4
Ferry Lane Industrial Estate
WALTH E17 .... **68** C4
Ferry Lane Primary School
WALTH E17 .... **68** B5
Ficino Gallery
RYLN/HDSTN HA2 .... **79** K1
Field End Junior School
RSLP HA4 .... **78** D2
Fielding First & Middle School
WEA W13 .... **116** B1
Field Junior School
WATW WD18 .... **29** J8
Fiji High Comm
SKENS SW7 .... **14** E2
Financial Times
STHWK SE1 .... **12** F8
Finborough Theatre Club
WBPTN SW10 .... **14** C9
Finchley Catholic High School
NFNCH/WDSP N12 .... **47** J5
Finchley Central Synagogue
FNCH N3 .... **65** G2
Finchley Cricket Club
FNCH N3 .... **65** H3
The Finchley Industrial Centre
NFNCH/WDSP N12 .... **47** J6
Finchley Memorial Hospital
FNCH N3 .... **65** J1
Finchley Osteopathic Surgery
FNCH N3 .... **65** G1
Finchley Progressive Synagogue
NFNCH/WDSP N12 .... **47** H7
Finchley Reform Synagogue
FNCH N3 .... **65** H1
Finchley Synagogue
FNCH N3 .... **64** F4
Finchley Youth Theatre
EFNCH N2 .... **65** L4
Fine Arts College
HAMP NW3 .... **83** L6
Finsbury Circus Medical Centre
LOTH EC2R **13** G4
Finsbury Health Centre
CLKNW EC1R **6** A9
Finsbury Leisure Complex
FSBYE EC1V **6** E9
Finsbury Park District
Synagogue
FSBYPK N4 .... **85** J1
Finton House School
TOOT SW17 .... **137** M6
Fircroft Primary School
TOOT SW17 .... **137** M6
Fire Brigade Museum
STHWK SE1 .... **18** E1
Fir Road Surgery
FELT TW13 .... **150** E1
Firs Farm Primary School
CLPT E5 .... **49** K5
Fisher Athletic Football Club
BERM/RHTH SE16 .... **104** D7
Fisher Industrial Estate
WATW WD18 .... **29** J8
Fishmonger's Hall
CANST EC4R **13** G7
Fitness Unlimited Leisure Centre
BOW E3 .... **105** G1
Fitzjohns Primary School
HAMP NW3 .... **83** K5
Fitznells Manor Surgery
EW KT17 .... **180** F2
Five Elms School
DAGW RM9 .... **90** F3
Five Ways Business Centre
FELT TW13 .... **132** B7
Flaxman Sports Centre
CMBW SE5 .... **121** J7
Fleecefield Primary School
ED N9 .... **50** A6
Fleetdown Infants School
RDART DA2 .... **147** J5
Fleetdown Junior School
RDART DA2 .... **147** J6
Fleet Primary School
HAMP NW3 .... **83** M5
Fleetway Business Park
GFD/PVL UB6 .... **98** B1
Flora Gardens Primary School
HMSMTH W6 .... **118** B2
Florence Nightingale Museum
STHWK SE1 .... **17** L2
Florence Road Surgery
EA W5 .... **98** E6
The Flower Gallery
KIL/WHAMP NW6 .... **83** G6
Flutters Leisure Centre
FUL/PGN SW6 .... **119** G5
Flying Colours Gallery
CHEL SW3 .... **15** K7
Focus Gallery
NOXST/BSQ WC1A **11** J3
The Focus Gallery
GLDGN NW11 .... **64** F6
Follys End Christian
High School
SNWD SE25 .... **172** E1
Fondu Sports Club
POP RM19 .... **129** J2
The Foot Clinic
WIM/MER SW19 .... **154** E1

The Foot Health Centre
COUL/CHIP CR5 .... **183** K8
Fordbridge Medical Centre
ASHF TW15 .... **130** F8
The Ford College
CONDST W1S **10** D6
Fordview Estate
RAIN RM13 .... **109** K2
Foreign and Commonwealth
Office
WHALL SW1A **17** H1
Foreland Medical Centre
NTGHL W11 .... **100** E6
Forest Business Park
WALTH E17 .... **68** D8
Forestdale Primary School
CROY/NA CR0 .... **185** L2
Foresters Primary School
WLGTN SM6 .... **171** K8
Forest Gate Community School
FSTGT E7 .... **88** A5
Forest Girls School
WALTH E17 .... **69** L5
Forest Healthcare NHS Trust
WALTH E17 .... **69** J4
Forest Healthcare Trust
WALTH E17 .... **68** E6
Forest Healthcare Trust
WAN E11 .... **69** K7
Forest Hill Business Centre
FSTH SE23 .... **140** C6
Forest Hill Industrial Estate
FSTH SE23 .... **140** C6
Forest Hill Secondary School
FSTH SE23 .... **140** D7
Forest House Business Centre
WAN E11 .... **69** M8
Forest Industrial Park
BARK/HLT IG6 .... **71** L1
Forest Medical Centre
LOU IG10 .... **39** L8
Forest Road Medical Centre
WALTH E17 .... **68** F4
Forest Surgery
WALTH E17 .... **69** J3
Forest Trading Estate
WALTH E17 .... **68** D4
Forge Close Clinic
HAYES BR2 .... **175** G3
Forge Lane Junior School
FELT TW13 .... **150** E1
The Former Health Centre
CHARL SE7 .... **124** D2
Forster Park Primary School
CAT SE6 .... **141** L7
Forte Crest Hotel
WDR/YW UB7 .... **113** G3
The Fort House Surgery
WOT/HER KT12 .... **165** C4
Fortismere School North Wing
MUSWH N10 .... **65** M3
Fortismere Secondary School
MUSWH N10 .... **66** A4
Fortune Theatre
HOL/ALD WC2B **11** K5
Forty Hill C of E School
EN EN1 .... **37** G2
Fossdene Primary School
CHARL SE7 .... **124** B3
Fosters Primary School
WELL DA16 .... **126** C7
Foulds Primary School
BAR EN5 .... **33** K6
The Foundling Museum
BMSBY WC1N **5** K9
Fountayne Road Health Centre
CLPT E5 .... **86** J2
The Four Swanns JMI School
CHES/WCR EN8 .... **26** E6
Four Trees Doctors Surgery
KTTN NW5 .... **84** A6
Fox Primary School
KENS W8 .... **8** A9
Framing Gallery
LVPST EC2M **13** K3
Frances Bardsley School
for Girls
ROM RM1 .... **74** A7
Franciscan Primary School
TOOT SW17 .... **138** A8
The Franciscan Surgery
TOOT SW17 .... **137** M8
Francis Combe
Secondary School
GSTN WD25 .... **21** J5
Francis Graham Dixon Gallery
STNW/STAM N16 .... **85** L3
Francis Holland School
BGVA SW1W **16** A6
Frank Barnes School
STJWD NW8 .... **3** H2
Franklin Industrial Estate
PGE/AN SE20 .... **158** C4
Frays College
UX/CGN UB8 .... **76** C6
Freehold Industrial Centre
HSLWW TW4 .... **132** C2
Free Trade Wharf
WAP E1W **104** D6
Fresh Wharf Estate
BARK IG11 .... **89** H8
Freuchen Medical Centre
WLSDN NW10 .... **99** M1
Freud Cafe Bar Gallery
LSQ/SEVD WC2H **11** H5
Freud Museum
HAMP NW3 .... **83** K6
Friars Primary School
STHWK SE1 .... **18** C1
Friends House
CAMTN NW1 .... **5** C8
Friends of Bar Ilan University
GLDGN NW11 .... **83** G1
Friends of Orpington Hospital
ORP BR6 .... **176** E8
Friends of the Hebrew
University
CAMTN NW1 .... **4** C4

Friern Barnet County School
FBAR/BDGN N11 .... **47** M7
Friern Bridge Retail Park
FBAR/BDGN N11 .... **48** B8
Frithwood Primary School
NTHWD HA6 .... **41** M8
Froebel College
PUT/ROE SW15 .... **136** A3
Frogmore Industrial Estate
HYS/HAR UB3 .... **95** L8
Frogmore Industrial Estate
WLSDN NW10 .... **99** J2
Fryent Medical Centre
CDALE/KGS NW9 .... **63** J8
Fryent Primary School
CDALE/KGS NW9 .... **63** J8
Fulham Cross Secondary
School
FUL/PGN SW6 .... **118** D5
Fulham Football Club
FUL/PGN SW6 .... **118** D6
Fulham Medical Centre
FUL/PGN SW6 .... **119** H5
Fulham Palace Chiropractic
& Health Centre
HMSMTH W6 .... **118** D4
Fulham Preparatory School
FUL/PGN SW6 .... **118** E7
Fulham Prep School
FUL/PGN SW6 .... **118** E7
Fulham Primary School
FUL/PGN SW6 .... **119** G4
Fuller Smith & Turner
Sports Club
CHSWK W4 .... **117** L6
Fullwell Cross Health Centre
BARK/HLT IG6 .... **71** J3
Fullwood Primary School
BARK/HLT IG6 .... **71** J5
Fulmar Galleries
WLSDN NW10 .... **81** K5
Furness School
SWLY BR8 .... **163** M2
Furness Swanley Football Club
SWLY BR8 .... **163** K7
The Furniture Gallery
HDN NW4 .... **64** B5
The Furniture Gallery
STHGT/OAK N14 .... **48** C3
Furzedown Primary School
TOOT SW17 .... **156** B2
Furzehill School
BORE WD6 .... **32** A7
Furze Infant School
CHDH RM6 .... **72** E7
Gaflac Sports Ground Pavilion
SUN TW16 .... **150** A4
Gagliardi Gallery
WBPTN SW10 .... **119** J5
Gainsborough Junior &
Infant School
HOM E9 .... **86** F6
Gainsborouh Clinic
PLMGR N13 .... **48** F5
Galleries
BAY/PAD W2 .... **9** J5
Galleries
MYFR/PKLN W1K **10** B7
Gallery
KENS W8 .... **14** E3
Gallery
MYFR/PKLN W1K **10** B7
The Gallery Cafe
NKENS W10 .... **100** E5
The Gallery House
MYFR/PICC W1J **10** D6
Gallery on the Heath
BKHTH/KID SE3 .... **123** L7
The Gallery
CAMTN NW1 .... **4** F2
The Gallery
HNHL SE24 .... **139** H3
The Gallery
IS N1 .... **5** L6
The Gallery
IS N1 .... **6** A6
The Gallery
IS N1 .... **85** L5
The Gallery
ORP BR6 .... **177** G2
The Gallery
SNWD SE25 .... **157** M7
The Gallery
STP EC4M **12** D5
The Gallery
VX/NE SW8 .... **17** K9
The Gallery
WDGN N22 .... **66** F3
Galleywall Primary School
BERM/RHTH SE16 .... **122** B2
Galliard Primary School
ED N9 .... **50** A1
Gallions Mount Primary School
WOOL/PLUM SE18 .... **125** M3
The Gambia High Comm
KENS W8 .... **14** D2
Gants Hill Medical Centre
GNTH/NBYPK IG2 .... **71** G7
Gardener Industrial Estate
BECK BR3 .... **158** E1
Garden Suburb Infant School
GLDGN NW11 .... **64** F6
Garden Vets Surgery
EFNCH N2 .... **65** J4
Garfield First School
WIM/MER SW19 .... **155** J2
Garfield Primary School
FBAR/BDGN N11 .... **48** B7
The Garratt Lane Surgery
WIM/MER SW19 .... **137** H7
Garratt Park School
WAND/EARL SW18 .... **137** J7
Garrick Industrial Centre
CDALE/KGS NW9 .... **63** M6
Garston Clinic
WATN WD24 .... **29** H1

Garston JMI School
GSTN WD25 .... 21 K8
Garston Manor School
GSTN WD25 .... 21 J5
Garston Medical Centre
GSTN WD25 .... 29 J1
Garth Primary School
MRDN SM4 .... 155 K8
Gascoigne Junior & Infant
School
BARK IG11 .... 89 J8
Gatehouse School
BETH E2 .... 104 D1
Gate House Surgery
BRXN/ST SW9 .... 120 F8
The Gatehouse Theatre
HGT N6 .... 66 A8
Gateway Industrial Estate
WLSDN NW10 .... 99 M2
Gateway Primary School
STJWD NW8 .... 3 H9
Gavin Graham Gallery
NTGHL W11 .... 8 A6
Gayhurst Primary School
HACK E8 .... 86 A7
Gaynes School
UPMR RM14 .... 93 J5
Gazelda Industrial Estate
WAT WD17 .... 29 J8
Gearies Infant School
GNTH/NBYPK IG2 .... 71 G6
Gearies Junior School
GNTH/NBYPK IG2 .... 71 H6
Geffrye Museum
BETH E2 .... 7 L6
General Medical Clinics
WCHPL E1 .... 13 L2
General Medical Practice
PECK SE15 .... 122 B6
General Practice
WOOL/PLUM SE18 .... 125 J2
Geoffrey Chaucer
Secondary School
STHWK SE1 .... 19 G4
The Geoffrey Lloyd
Foulkes Clinic
IL IG1 .... 89 G2
Geoffrey Whitworth Theatre
DART DA1 .... 145 M1
George Eliot Junior & Infant
School
STJWD NW8 .... 3 G3
George Green School
POP/IOD E14 .... 123 J2
George Lowe Ct
BAY/PAD W2 .... 8 C2
George Mitchell Comprehensive
School
LEY E10 .... 87 H1
George Mitchell
School Annexe
LEY E10 .... 87 H1
George Spicer
Primary School
EN EN1 .... 36 F6
George Tomlinson
Primary School
WAN E11 .... 87 L1
Georgian Embassy
KENS W8 .... 14 C2
The Ghana Embassy
HGT N6 .... 84 B1
Gibson Business Centre
TOTM N17 .... 49 M8
The Gibson Business Centre
TOTM N17 .... 67 M1
Gidea Park College
GPK RM2 .... 74 A4
Gidea Park Primary School
GPK RM2 .... 73 M1
Gidea Park Sports Ground
GPK RM2 .... 74 C3
The Gielgud Theatre
SOHO/CST W1F 11 C6
Giffin Business Centre
DEPT SE8 .... 123 C6
Gifford Junior & Infant School
NTHLT UB5 .... 96 F1
Giggs Hill Surgery
THDIT KT7 .... 166 F2
Gilbert Colvin School
CLAY IG5 .... 71 G2
Gilbert Scotts Primary School
SAND/SEL CR2 .... 185 L1
Gillespie Primary School
FSBYPK N4 .... 85 H1
Gillian House Surgery
PLMGR N13 .... 49 G5
Girdlers' Hall
CITYW EC2V 12 F5
The Glade Business Centre
WTHK RM20 .... 129 M3
Glade Primary School
CLAY IG5 .... 70 F2
Gladesmore Community
Secondary School
SEVS/STOTM N15 .... 68 A6
Gladstone Court Business
Centre
VX/NE SW8 .... 120 C6
Gladstone Medical Centre
CRICK NW2 .... 81 M4
Gladstone Park Primary School
WLSDN NW10 .... 82 B3
Glaziers/scientific
Instrument Makers Hall
STHWK SE1 .... 13 G8
Glebe First & Middle School
KTN/HRWW/W HA3 .... 62 D5
Glebe Primary School
HGDN/ICK UB10 .... 77 K4
Glebe School
WWKM BR4 .... 174 D3
Gleen Lecky Health Centre
PUT/ROE SW15 .... 136 G1
Glenbrook Junior &
Infant School
CLAP SW4 .... 138 D3

Glencairn Sports Club
FBAR/BDGN N11 .... 66 C1
Glendower School
SKENS SW7 .... 14 F5
Glenham College
IL IG1 .... 89 G2
Glenlyn Medical Centre
E/WMO/HCT KT8 .... 151 J8
Glenthorne High School
CHEAM SM3 .... 170 A3
Globe Theatre
STHWK SE1 .... 12 D7
Globe Town Surgery
BETH E2 .... 104 C2
Globe Wharf
BERM/RHTH SE16 .... 104 D7
Gloucester Primary School
PECK SE15 .... 121 L5
Glyn A D T Technology School
EW KT17 .... 180 F4
Gobions JMI School
CRW RM5 .... 55 K8
Godolphin & Latymer School
HMSMTH W6 .... 118 B2
Godwin Junior School
FSTGT E7 .... 88 B4
Godwin Primary School
DAGW RM9 .... 90 E7
Goffs Oak JMI School
CHESW EN7 .... 25 H1
Goffs School
CHESW EN7 .... 26 A2
Golborne Medical Centre
NKENS W10 .... 100 F3
Goldbeaters School
EDGE HA8 .... 63 K2
Golden Hinde
STHWK SE1 .... 13 G8
Golders Green Beth Hamedrash
Synagogue
GLDGN NW11 .... 64 E8
Golders Green College of
Business Studies
GLDGN NW11 .... 83 G1
Golders Green Health Centre
GLDGN NW11 .... 83 H1
Golders Hill Health Centre
EFNCH N2 .... 65 J7
Goldhawk Industrial Estate
SHB W12 .... 118 B1
Goldsmiths College
BROCKY SE4 .... 122 F8
Goldsmiths College
DEPT SE8 .... 123 G4
Goldsmiths College
LEW SE13 .... 141 L1
Goldsmiths College
NWCR SE14 .... 122 F6
Goldsmiths College
Sports Ground
SCUP DA14 .... 144 F7
Goldsmiths College
University of London
NWCR SE14 .... 122 E6
Goldsmiths Hall
STBT EC1A 12 C4
Golf Centre
STMC/STPC BR5 .... 162 D4
Golf Club Flat
NTHWD HA6 .... 59 K1
Golf Course
RKW/CH/CXG WD3 .... 28 C5
Golf School
KTBR SW1X 15 M2
Gonville School
THHTH CR7 .... 156 F8
The Gooday Gallery
RCHPK/HAM TW10 .... 134 D3
Gooding Health Centre
HOLWY N7 .... 84 E6
Goodrich Junior & Infant School
EDUL SE22 .... 140 A3
The Good Shepherd RC Primary
School
SHB W12 .... 99 M8
Good Shepherd RC School
BMLY BR1 .... 141 M8
Goodwyn School
MLHL NW7 .... 46 A7
Goose Green Trading Estate
EDUL SE22 .... 140 A1
Gordonbrock Primary School
BROCKY SE4 .... 141 G2
Gordon Hospital
WEST SW1P 17 G6
Gordon House Health Centre
WEA W13 .... 98 C7
Gordon Infant School
IL IG1 .... 89 K3
Gordon Primary School
ELTH/MOT SE9 .... 142 F1
Goresbrook Leisure Centre
DAGW RM9 .... 90 D8
Gorringe Park Middle School
MTCM CR4 .... 156 A4
Gosbury Hill Health Centre
CHSGTN KT9 .... 167 L6
Gospel Oak Primary School
HAMP NW3 .... 84 A4
Government Offices
WHALL SW1A 11 J8
Grace Business Centre
MTCM CR4 .... 170 F1
Grace Theatre at the Latchmere
BTSEA SW11 .... 119 M7
Graduate School of Management
TOTM N17 .... 67 M2
Grafton Primary School
BCTR RM8 .... 90 E2
Grafton Primary School
HOLWY N7 .... 84 E3
Grahame Park Health Centre
CDALE/KGS NW9 .... 63 L2
Grahame Park Junior &
Infant School
CDALE/KGS NW9 .... 63 L2
Graham Gallery
IS N1 .... 6 C5

Granard Business Centre
EDGE HA8 .... 45 L8
Granard Primary School
PUT/ROE SW15 .... 136 B3
Granby Sports Club
ELTH/MOT SE9 .... 160 E1
Grand Avenue Infant & Primary
School
BRYLDS KT5 .... 168 C1
Grand Drive Surgery
RYNPK SW20 .... 154 C6
Grande Vitesse Industrial Centre
STHWK SE1 .... 12 D9
Grand Union Industrial Estate
WLSDN NW10 .... 99 H1
Grange First & Middle School
EA W5 .... 98 D8
Grange First & Middle School
RYLN/HDSTN HA2 .... 79 H1
Grange Infant School
CAN/RD E16 .... 105 M2
The Grange Museum
CRICK NW2 .... 81 M4
Grange Park Clinic
YEAD UB4 .... 95 M3
Grange Park Junior School
YEAD UB4 .... 95 M3
Grange Park Preparatory School
WCHMH N21 .... 49 H1
Grange Park Primary School
ENC/FH EN2 .... 36 A7
Grange Park Surgery
LEY E10 .... 87 J2
Grange Primary School
STHWK SE1 .... 19 J4
Grangewood Independent School
FSTGT E7 .... 88 C7
Grangewood Junior School
RSLP HA4 .... 60 A6
Granton Primary School
STRHM/NOR SW16 .... 156 C3
Granville Road Industrial Estate
CRICK NW2 .... 82 F2
Grasmere Primary School
STNW/STAM N16 .... 85 K4
Grasshoppers Rugby Football Club
ISLW TW7 .... 115 M4
Grasvenor Avenue Infant School
BAR EN5 .... 47 G1
Gravel Hill Primary School
BXLYHS DA6 .... 145 H2
Graveney School
TOOT SW17 .... 156 B2
Graves Yard Industrial Estate 96b
WELL DA16 .... 126 A7
Grays Farm Primary School
STMC/STPC BR5 .... 162 B4
Grays Inn Medical Practice
FSBYW WC1X 11 M1
Grazebrook Primary School
STNW/STAM N16 .... 85 L2
Greater London Council
CLAP SW4 .... 138 B2
Greater London Council
HOM E9 .... 86 E4
Great Jubilee Wharf
WAP E1W 104 C7
Great Ormond Street Childrens
Hospital
BMSBY WC1N 11 K1
Great Synagogue
WCHPL E1 .... 104 A4
Greenacres Primary School
ELTH/MOT SE9 .... 143 G6
The Green C of E Primary School
TOTM N17 .... 67 M4
Green Dragon School
BTFD TW8 .... 116 E3
Greenfield Medical Centre
CRICK NW2 .... 82 E3
Greenfield Primary School
OXHEY WD19 .... 42 C7
Greenfields Junior School
SHB W12 .... 99 M6
Greenfields Special School
MUSWH N10 .... 65 M2
Greenford Avenue Medical Centre
HNWL W7 .... 97 L4
Greenford Green Clinic
NTHLT UB5 .... 79 L5
Greenford High School
STHL UB1 .... 97 G2
Greenford Road Medical Centre
GFD/PVL UB6 .... 97 K1
Greenford Synagogue
GFD/PVL UB6 .... 97 J2
Greengate Medical Centre
PLSTW E13 .... 106 B2
Greengrove College
STHGT/OAK N14 .... 48 E4
Green Haven Surgery
ELTH/MOT SE9 .... 143 L4
Greenheath Business Centre
BETH E2 .... 104 B2
Greenhill College
HRW HA1 .... 61 M6
Greenhill College
HRW HA1 .... 61 L8
Greenhill Park Medical Centre
WLSDN NW10 .... 81 L8
Green Lane Primary School
WPK KT4 .... 169 H2
Greenleaf Primary School
WALTH E17 .... 68 F4
Greenmead Primary School
PUT/ROE SW15 .... 136 B2
Greens Antique Galleries
KENS W8 .... 8 B9
The Green School for Girls
ISLW TW7 .... 116 A5
Greenshaw High School
SUT SM1 .... 170 C4
Greenshield Industrial Estate
CAN/RD E16 .... 106 D2
Greenside Primary School
SHB W12 .... 100 A8
Greenslade Primary School
WOOL/PLUM SE18 .... 125 K4

Green Street Primary School
ORP BR6 .... 176 F8
The Green Surgery
WHTN TW2 .... 133 L6
Greenvale Primary School
SAND/SEL CR2 .... 185 K4
Green Waters Surgery
STAN HA7 .... 44 B6
Greenway School
UX/CGN UB8 .... 94 D1
Greenwich Borough Council
GNWCH SE10 .... 123 J4
Greenwich Borough Museum
WOOL/PLUM SE18 .... 125 M3
Greenwich Centre Business Park
DEPT SE8 .... 123 H5
Greenwich College
GNWCH SE10 .... 123 J5
Greenwich Community College
WOOL/PLUM SE18 .... 125 K4
Greenwich Community College
WOOL/PLUM SE18 .... 125 H2
Greenwich Coroners Office
GNWCH SE10 .... 123 H5
Greenwich Council
ELTH/MOT SE9 .... 142 F3
Greenwich District Hospital
BKHTH/KID SE3 .... 123 L4
Greenwich Gallery
GNWCH SE10 .... 123 J5
Greenwich Health Authority
THMD SE28 .... 108 A6
Greenwich Health Authority
WOOL/PLUM SE18 .... 125 G7
Greenwich Healthcare NHS Trust
CHARL SE7 .... 124 E5
Greenwich Healthcare NHS Trust
WOOL/PLUM SE18 .... 125 L3
Greenwich Healthcare NHS Trust
WOOL/PLUM SE18 .... 125 H7
Greenwich Industrial Estate
CHARL SE7 .... 124 B2
Greenwich Natural Health Centre
GNWCH SE10 .... 123 J5
Greenwich Park School
GNWCH SE10 .... 123 J5
Greenwich Theatre & Art Gallery
GNWCH SE10 .... 123 K4
Greenwood First School
MTCM CR4 .... 156 D6
Greenwood Primary School
NTHLT UB5 .... 79 J5
Greenwood School
WOOL/PLUM SE18 .... 125 L6
Greenwood Theatre
STHWK SE1 .... 19 H1
Green Wrythe Primary School
CAR SM5 .... 170 D1
Grenfell Primary School
WCHPL E1 .... 104 B5
Gresham College
FLST/FETLN EC4A 12 A3
Gresham School
SAND/SEL CR2 .... 184 F5
Gresswell Industrial Estate
WIM/MER SW19 .... 137 H7
Gresswell Street School
FUL/PGN SW6 .... 118 D6
Grey Coat Hosp
WESTW SW1E 16 E3
The Greycoat Hospital
WEST SW1P 17 G6
Grey Coat Hospital Upper School
WEST SW1P 17 G4
Grey Court School
RCHPK/HAM TW10 .... 134 C7
Griffen Manor School
WOOL/PLUM SE18 .... 125 L6
Griffin Galleries
PIN HA5 .... 60 C3
Grimsdyke First & Middle School
PIN HA5 .... 42 F8
Grimsdyke Golf Club
PIN HA5 .... 43 G7
Grinling Gibbons Primary School
DEPT SE8 .... 122 F4
Grist Memorial Sports Club
E/WMO/HCT KT8 .... 151 L8
Grocers' Hall
CITYW EC2V 13 G5
Grosvenor Gallery
NTHWD HA6 .... 41 L8
Grosvenor Hospitals
HDN NW4 .... 64 B6
Grosvenor House Surgery
HNWL W7 .... 98 A7
Group Medical Practice
HAMP NW3 .... 3 M2
Grove Health Centre
KENS W8 .... 8 B8
The Grove Health Centre
HMSMTH W6 .... 100 B8
Grove House Primary School
WNWD SE27 .... 139 H6
Grovelands Priory Hospital
STHGT/OAK N14 .... 48 E3
Grovelands School
WOT/HER KT12 .... 165 H1
Grove Medical Centre
DEPT SE8 .... 122 E2
The Grove Medical Centre
ARCH N19 .... 84 C2
The Grove Medical Practice
HMSMTH W6 .... 118 C1
The Grove Medical Practice
NTHLT UB5 .... 79 H5
Grove Park Primary School
CHSWK W4 .... 117 J4
Grove Park School
CDALE/KGS NW9 .... 63 J5
Grove Primary School
CHDH RM6 .... 72 B6
Grove Road Primary School
HSLW TW3 .... 133 G4
The Groves Medical Centre
NWMAL KT3 .... 153 L6
Grove Vale Primary School
EDUL SE22 .... 139 M1

Grove Village Medical Centre
EBED/NFELT TW14 .... 131 L5
Grrck Thtr
LSO/SEVD WC2H 11 H7
Grundy Park Leisure Centre
CHES/WCR EN8 .... 26 E3
Guardian Angels RC Primary
School
BOW E3 .... 104 E3
Guardian Business Centre
HARH RM3 .... 74 D1
Guardian Newspapers
POP/IOD E14 .... 105 H8
Guards' Chapel and Museum
WHALL SW1A 17 G2
Guildhall School of Music &
Drama
BARB EC2Y 12 F2
Guildhall University
WCHPL E1 .... 104 A5
Guinea Consulate
MYFR/PKLN W1K 10 A7
Gumley House Convent School for
Girls
ISLW TW7 .... 116 A8
Gunnersbury Catholic
School for Boys
BTFD TW8 .... 116 C3
Gunnersbury Park Museum
ACT W3 .... 117 G1
Gurnell Leisure Centre
WEA W13 .... 97 M2
Gurnell Middle School
WEA W13 .... 97 M4
Guru Gobind Singh Khalsa College
CHIG IG7 .... 52 F3
Guru Nanak Medical Centre
STHL UB1 .... 96 F1
Guyana High Commission
NTGHL W11 .... 8 A3
Guys Hospital
STHWK SE1 .... 13 H9
Guys & St Thomas Hospital Trust
LBTH SE11 .... 18 C5
Guys & St Thomas Hospital Trust
PECK SE15 .... 122 C5
Gwyn Jones Primary School
WAN E11 .... 69 K8
G X Superbowl
EHAM E6 .... 107 G4
Haberdashers Askes
Hatcham Boys School
NWCR SE14 .... 122 D7
Haberdashers Askes
Hatcham Girls School
NWCR SE14 .... 122 E6
Haberdashers Askes School for Girls
BORE WD6 .... 31 H6
Haberdashers' Hall
CITYW EC2V 12 F4
Haberdashers Rugby Club
BORE WD6 .... 31 M5
Hackbridge Junior School
WLGTN SM6 .... 171 G3
Hackney African Caribbean Disability
Association
HOM E9 .... 86 D5
Hackney Borough Council
CLPT E5 .... 86 A2
Hackney Borough Council
HOM E9 .... 86 C6
Hackney Business Centre
HACK E8 .... 86 B6
Hackney Community College
CLPT E5 .... 86 B3
Hackney Community College
IS N1 .... 7 J6
Hackney Council
BETH E2 .... 7 L6
Hackney Empire Theatre Variety
HACK E8 .... 86 B6
Hackney Hospital
HOM E9 .... 86 E5
The Hackney Museum
HOM E9 .... 86 C6
Hackney Racial Equality Council
HACK E8 .... 85 M6
Hackney Sports Centre
HOM E9 .... 87 G4
Hacton Infant School
HCH RM12 .... 92 E4
Hadley Wood School
EBAR EN4 .... 34 C3
The Haelan Clinic
CEND/HSY/T N8 .... 66 D7
Haggerston School
BETH E2 .... 7 M5
Haggerston Swimming Pool
BETH E2 .... 7 M4
Hague Primary School
BETH E2 .... 104 B3
Haimo Primary School
ELTH/MOT SE9 .... 142 D2
Hainault Forest High School
CHIG IG7 .... 54 A7
Hainault Industrial Estate
BARK/HLT IG6 .... 54 C7
Hakim Qureshi Clinic
NWDGN UB2 .... 96 F8
Hales Gallery
DEPT SE8 .... 123 G5
Haling Manor High School
CROY/NA CR0 .... 184 B1
Halley Primary School
POP/IOD E14 .... 104 E4
Hallfield Clinic NHS
BAY/PAD W2 .... 8 E5
Hallfield Estate
BAY/PAD W2 .... 8 D5
Hallfield Junior & Infant School
BAY/PAD W2 .... 8 D5
Halliford Health Clinic
SHPTN TW17 .... 149 L7
Halliford School
SHPTN TW17 .... 164 C3
The Hall Junior School
HAMP NW3 .... 83 K6

Hallmark Trading Estate
WBLY HA9......................... 81 J4
Hall Mead School
UPMR RM14......................... 75 K8
Halls Business Centre
HYS/HAR UB3......................... 114 A1
Hallsville Primary School
CAN/RD E16......................... 106 A5
Halstow Primary School
GNWCH SE10......................... 123 H3
Hambrough First School
STHL UB1......................... 96 E7
Hamer Indoor Market
BOW E3......................... 104 F1
Ham Health Clinic
RCHPK/HAM TW10......................... 134 C7
Hamlet International
Industrial Estate
ERITH DA8......................... 127 K3
Hammel House Surgery
TOOT SW17......................... 137 L8
The Hammersmith Hospitals NHS
Trust
SHB W12......................... 100 A5
Hammersmith Industrial Estate
HMSMTH W6......................... 118 C4
Hammersmith Physio &
Sportsinjury Clinic
HMSMTH W6......................... 118 C4
Hammersmith & West Kensington
Synagogue
HMSMTH W6......................... 118 D1
Hammersmith & West
London College
WKENS W14......................... 118 E2
Ham & Petersham Cricket Club
RCHPK/HAM TW10......................... 134 D8
Hampstead Cricket Club
KIL/WHAMP NW6......................... 83 H5
Hampstead Garden Suburb
Synagogue
EFNCH N2......................... 65 J6
The Hampstead Group Practice
HAMP NW3......................... 83 L5
Hampstead Medical Centre
HAMP NW3......................... 83 J4
Hampstead School
CRICK NW2......................... 82 E4
Hampstead Synagogue
KIL/WHAMP NW6......................... 83 G6
Hampton Community College
HPTN TW12......................... 151 G1
Hampton Court Palace
E/WMO/HCT KT8......................... 151 M6
Hampton Farm Industrial Estate
FELT TW13......................... 132 E7
Hampton Football Club
HPTN TW12......................... 151 H4
The Hampton Hill Gallery
HPTN TW12......................... 151 J1
Hampton Hill Junior Mixed School
HPTN TW12......................... 151 J1
Hampton Infants School
HPTN TW12......................... 150 F3
Hampton Junior School
HPTN TW12......................... 151 G4
The Hampton Medical Centre
HPTN TW12......................... 151 G3
Hampton School
HPTN TW12......................... 151 G1
Hampton Swimming Baths
HPTN TW12......................... 151 J3
Hampton Wick Infants School
KUT KT1......................... 152 C3
Hampton Wick Surgery
KUT KT1......................... 152 C4
Hamshere Gallery
BARN SW13......................... 117 M7
Ham Surgery
RCHPK/HAM TW10......................... 134 C7
Handsworth Health Clinic
CHING E4......................... 51 K8
Handsworth Primary School
CHING E4......................... 51 K8
Hanover Primary School
IS N1......................... 6 D5
Hanover Trading Estate
HOLWY N7......................... 84 E5
Hanover West Industrial Estate
WLSDN NW10......................... 99 J2
Hanworth Trading Estate
FELT TW13......................... 132 E7
Happy Valley Industrial Estate
KGLGY WD4......................... 20 B1
Harbinger County Primary School
POP/IOD E14......................... 123 G2
Harborough School
ARCH N19......................... 84 C2
Hardware Gallery
HGT N6......................... 66 C8
Harefield Cricket Club
DEN/HRF UB9......................... 58 D3
Harefield Health Centre
DEN/HRF UB9......................... 58 C2
Harefield Hospital
DEN/HRF UB9......................... 58 C2
Harefield Infant School
DEN/HRF UB9......................... 58 B2
Harefield Junior School
DEN/HRF UB9......................... 58 C2
Harenc School
SCUP DA14......................... 162 C1
Hargrave Park Primary School
ARCH N19......................... 84 C2
Haringey Arts Council
ED N9......................... 50 B4
Haringey Community Health Clinic
SEVS/STOTM N15......................... 67 M4
Haringey Council
SEVS/STOTM N15......................... 67 M5
Haringey Health Care NHS Trust
SEVS/STOTM N15......................... 67 M5
Haringey Magistrate Court
HGT N6......................... 66 A7
Harkness Industrial Estate
BORE WD6......................... 32 A7

Harland First School
WIM/MER SW19......................... 155 J5
Harlequin Football Club
WHTN TW2......................... 133 L4
Harlequin Gallery
GNWCH SE10......................... 123 H5
Harlequin Shopping Centre
WAT WD17......................... 29 J7
Harlesden Primary School
WLSDN NW10......................... 99 L1
Harley Medical Centre
CAVSQ/HST W1G......................... 10 C4
The Harley Medical Centre
CANST EC4R......................... 12 F6
The Harley Street Clinic
CAVSQ/HST W1G......................... 10 C2
Harlington Upper School
HYS/HAR UB3......................... 113 K2
Harlyn School
PIN HA5......................... 60 B4
Harold Court School
HARH RM3......................... 75 G1
The Harold Macmillan Medical
Centre
HRW HA1......................... 61 K8
Harold Wood Clinic
HARH RM3......................... 74 F3
Harold Wood JMI School
HARH RM3......................... 75 G4
Harp Business Centre
CRICK NW2......................... 82 A2
Harpley Special School
WCHPL E1......................... 104 C3
Harrington Hill Primary School
CLPT E5......................... 86 B1
Harris City Technology College
NRWD SE19......................... 157 M4
Harrodian School
BARN SW13......................... 117 M5
Harrods Store
CHEL SW3......................... 15 L3
Harrow Borough Football Club
RYLN/HDSTN HA2......................... 79 G4
Harrow Central Mosque
HRW HA1......................... 61 M5
Harrow Cricket Club
HRW HA1......................... 79 L4
Harrow Crown Courts
HRW HA1......................... 61 K4
Harrow Health Authority
RYLN/HDSTN HA2......................... 79 L2
Harrow Heritage Museum
RYLN/HDSTN HA2......................... 61 J4
Harrow High School
HRW HA1......................... 62 A7
Harrow & Hillingdon Health
Authority
STAN HA7......................... 62 D2
Harrow & Hillingdon
Healthcare NHS Trust
KTN/HRWW/W HA3......................... 62 A2
Harrow & Hillingdon
Healthcare NHS Trust
UX/CGN UB8......................... 94 D2
Harrow Leisure Centre
KTN/HRWW/W HA3......................... 61 M4
Harrow Magistrates Court
HRW HA1......................... 61 M5
Harrow Road Health Centre
BAY/PAD W2......................... 8 B2
Harrow Rugby Football Club
STAN HA7......................... 44 B5
Harrow School
HRW HA1......................... 61 L8
Harrow School
HRW HA1......................... 79 L1
Harrow School
RYLN/HDSTN HA2......................... 79 L2
Harrow Superbowl
RYLN/HDSTN HA2......................... 61 H6
Harrow Town Cricket Club
RYLN/HDSTN HA2......................... 79 G1
Hart Gallery
IS N1......................... 6 C3
Hartley Primary School
EHAM E6......................... 88 E8
Hartsbourne JMI School
BUSH WD23......................... 43 K4
Hartspring Industrial Park
GSTN WD25......................... 30 A5
Hartspring Sports Centre
BUSH WD23......................... 30 A5
Harvington School
EA W5......................... 98 C5
Haselbury Junior & Infant School
ED N9......................... 49 L5
Haselrigge School
CLAP SW4......................... 138 D1
Haslemere Business Centre
EN EN1......................... 37 H7
Haslemere Industrial Estate
WAND/EARL SW18......................... 137 H6
Hasmonean Boys High School
HDN NW4......................... 64 D3
Hasmonean High School
Girls Section
MLHL NW7......................... 64 A2
Hasmonean Primary School
HDN NW4......................... 64 D6
Hastings Clinic
BRXS/STRHM SW2......................... 138 F2
Hastingwood Trading Estate
UED N18......................... 50 E8
Hatcham Mews Business Centre
NWCR SE14......................... 122 D5
Hatch End High School
KTN/HRWW/W HA3......................... 61 H1
The Hat Gallery
HACK E8......................... 86 A8
Hatton Medical Practice
EBED/NFELT TW14......................... 131 L3
Hatton School
REDBR IG4......................... 70 D4
Havelock First School
NWDGN UB2......................... 114 F1
Haven Green Clinic
EA W5......................... 98 D5

Haverfield Surgery
KGLGY WD4......................... 20 A2
Havering College of
Further & Higher Education
EMPK RM11......................... 74 E5
Havering College of
Further & Higher Education
EMPK RM11......................... 74 B8
Havering College of
Further & Higher Education
HARH RM3......................... 56 F6
Havering Court Nursing Home
ROM RM1......................... 55 L7
Havering Hospitals NHS Trust
HARH RM3......................... 74 E2
Havering Magistrates Court
ROM RM1......................... 73 L5
Havering Sixth Form College
EMPK RM11......................... 92 F1
Haverstock School
CAMTN NW1......................... 84 A6
Hawes Down Clinic
WWKM BR4......................... 174 D4
Hawes Down Junior &
Infant School
WWKM BR4......................... 174 D3
Hawkedale Gm School
SUN TW16......................... 149 M6
Hawkins Clinic
EW KT17......................... 181 J8
Hawkins Clinic
PUT/ROE SW15......................... 136 D1
Hawkins Clinic
RYNPK SW20......................... 153 M4
Hawksmoor Gm Primary School
THMD SE28......................... 108 B6
Hawkswood School & Centre
ASHF TW15......................... 38 C8
Haydon School
PIN HA5......................... 59 M4
Haydons Medical Practice
WIM/MER SW19......................... 155 H2
Hayes Bridge Middle School
STHL UB1......................... 96 E7
Hayes Bridge Retail Park
HYS/HAR UB3......................... 96 C6
Hayes Cricket Club
HYS/HAR UB3......................... 95 M5
Hayes Football Club
HYS/HAR UB3......................... 95 M6
Hayes Grove Priory Hospital
HAYES BR2......................... 175 G4
Hayes Manor Secondary School
HYS/HAR UB3......................... 95 K5
Hayes Park Junior & Infant School
YEAD UB4......................... 95 M3
Hayes Primary School
HAYES BR2......................... 175 H3
Hayes School
HAYES BR2......................... 175 H4
Hayes Social and Sports Club
HYS/HAR UB3......................... 95 M6
Haymerle School
PECK SE15......................... 122 A4
Hays Galleria
STHWK SE1......................... 13 J8
Hayward Gallery
STHWK SE1......................... 11 M9
Hazeldene Medical Centre
WBLY HA9......................... 81 H6
Hazelhurst School
RYNPK SW20......................... 154 D4
Hazelwood Infant School
PLMGR N13......................... 49 H6
The Health Centre
HARH RM3......................... 56 E7
The Health Clinic
SKENS SW7......................... 15 H5
Health Service Clinic
CHDH RM6......................... 72 C4
Health & Welfare Clinic
BFN/LL DA15......................... 144 A3
Health & Welfare Clinic
BXLY DA5......................... 144 D5
Health & Welfare Clinic
RAIN RM13......................... 92 A4
Health & Welfare Clinic
WELL DA16......................... 126 A7
Healy Medical Centre
CLPT E5......................... 86 B1
The Healy Practice
EFNCH N2......................... 65 M5
Hearnville Primary School
BAL SW12......................... 138 A5
The Heart Hospital
CAVSQ/HST W1G......................... 10 B3
Heathbrook Primary School
VX/NE SW8......................... 120 C7
Heath Business Centre
HSLW TW3......................... 133 J1
Heathcote School
CHING E4......................... 51 L4
Heatherley School of Fine Art
WBPTN SW10......................... 119 J5
Heathfield College
HAYES BR2......................... 175 J8
Heathfield Junior School
WHTN TW2......................... 133 G5
Heathfield School
PIN HA5......................... 60 D7
Heath House Preparatory School
BKHTH/KID SE3......................... 123 M7
Heathland School
HSLWW TW4......................... 132 F3
Heathmere Primary School
PUT/ROE SW15......................... 136 A5
Heathrow Airport
WDR/YW UB7......................... 112 C6
Heathrow International Trading
Estate
HSLWW TW4......................... 114 B8
Heathrow Medical Centre
HYS/HAR UB3......................... 113 K3
Heathrow School
WDR/YW UB7......................... 112 F4
Heathway Medical Centre
DAGW RM9......................... 90 F4

Heavers Farm Primary School
SNWD SE25......................... 157 M8
Heber School
EDUL SE22......................... 139 M3
Heckford Street Business Centre
WAP E1W......................... 104 D6
Hedges & Butler Estate
SRTFD E15......................... 105 J1
Hedgewood School
YEAD UB4......................... 95 L2
Helena Road Clinic NHS
WLSDN NW10......................... 82 B4
Heliport Industrial Estate
BTSEA SW11......................... 119 K7
Hellenic College of London
KTBR SW1X......................... 15 L4
Henderson Hospital
BELMT SM2......................... 182 A2
Hendon College
CDALE/KGS NW9......................... 63 M2
Hendon Football Club
CRICK NW2......................... 82 D2
Hendon Golf Club
HDN NW4......................... 64 C1
Hendon Preparatory School
HDN NW4......................... 64 D4
Hendon Reform Synagogue
HDN NW4......................... 64 D6
Hendon School
HDN NW4......................... 64 B6
Hendon Secretarial College
HDN NW4......................... 64 B6
Hendon United Synagogue
HDN NW4......................... 64 C6
Hendon Youth Sports Centre
CRICK NW2......................... 64 D8
Hengrove CP School
ASHF TW15......................... 130 D8
Henrietta Barnett School
GLDGN NW11......................... 65 H6
Henry Cavendish Junior School
BAL SW12......................... 138 C5
Henry Compton School
FUL/PGN SW6......................... 118 D6
Henry Fawcett Junior School
LBTH SE11......................... 18 A9
Henry Green Primary School
BCTR RM8......................... 90 D1
Henry Maynard Infant School
WALTH E17......................... 69 J6
Henry Maynard Junior School
WALTH E17......................... 69 J6
Henwick Primary School
ELTH/MOT SE9......................... 124 D8
Herbert Morrison Primary School
VX/NE SW8......................... 120 E5
Hereward House School
HAMP NW3......................... 83 L6
Hermitage Primary School
UX/CGN UB8......................... 76 D7
Hermitage Primary School
WAP E1W......................... 104 A7
Herne Hill Group Practice
HNHL SE24......................... 139 J2
Herne Hill Road Medical Practice
CMBW SE5......................... 121 J8
Herne Hill School
HNHL SE24......................... 139 J2
Heron Industrial Estate
SRTFD E15......................... 105 H1
Heronsgate Primary School
THMD SE28......................... 125 K1
Heron Trading Estate
ACT W3......................... 99 H4
Hersham Surgery
WOT/HER KT12......................... 165 K8
Hertfordshire County Council
BUSH WD23......................... 43 K2
Hertfordshire County Council
GSTN WD25......................... 29 J1
Hertfordshire County Council
OXHEY WD19......................... 42 B5
Hertfordshire County Council
POTB/CUF EN6......................... 23 J5
Hertfordshire County Council
RKW/CH/CXG WD3......................... 40 B4
Hertfordshire County Council
WAT WD17......................... 29 G5
Herton Court School
SCUP DA14......................... 144 C8
Hertsmere Borough Council
BORE WD6......................... 32 C5
Hertsmere Council
BORE WD6......................... 32 A5
Hertsmere Jewish Primary School
RAD WD7......................... 31 J3
Hertsmere Progressive Synagogue
BORE WD6......................... 44 D1
Heston Community School
HEST TW5......................... 115 G5
Heston Infants School
HEST TW5......................... 115 G5
Heston Junior School
HEST TW5......................... 115 G4
Heston Park Cricket Club
HEST TW5......................... 114 F4
Heston Swimming Baths
HEST TW5......................... 114 F4
Hextable Comprehensive School
SWLY BR8......................... 163 M4
Hextable CP School
SWLY BR8......................... 163 M2
Hibernia House Surgery
HSLW TW3......................... 133 G1
Higgs Industrial Estate
BRXN/ST SW9......................... 121 H8
Highams Lodge Business Centre
WALTH E17......................... 68 D4
Highams Park Gm School
CHING E4......................... 51 K8
High Beech C of E Primary School
LOU IG10......................... 39 G4
Highbridge Industrial Estate
DEN/HRF UB9......................... 76 C6
Highbury Corner Magistrates Court
HOLWY N7......................... 85 G6
Highbury Fields School
HBRY N5......................... 85 H5

Highbury Grove School
HBRY N5......................... 85 J5
Highbury Park Clinic
HBRY N5......................... 85 H3
Highbury Quadrant Primary School
HBRY N5......................... 85 J4
High Comm for Pakistan
KTBR SW1X......................... 15 M3
High Commission of the Federal
Republic of Nigeria
CHCR WC2N......................... 11 J8
High Comm of Brunei
BAY/PAD W2......................... 9 H4
High Comm of the Republic of
Maldives
MHST W1U......................... 10 A2
High Comm of the Republic of
Namibia
CAVSQ/HST W1G......................... 10 D3
Highfield Infants School
HAYES BR2......................... 159 L7
Highfield Junior & Infant School
WCHMH N21......................... 49 H3
Highfield Junior School
HAYES BR2......................... 159 L7
Highfield School
HGDN/ICK UB10......................... 95 H2
High Firs CP School
SWLY BR8......................... 163 M7
Highgate Group Practice
HGT N6......................... 65 M7
Highgate Junior School
HGT N6......................... 65 M8
Highgate Primary School
HGT N6......................... 65 M7
Highgate Private Hospital
HGT N6......................... 65 M7
Highgate School
HGT N6......................... 66 A8
Highgate Synagogue
HGT N6......................... 66 A8
Highgate Wood Secondary School
CEND/HSY/T N8......................... 66 C6
Highgrove Swimming Pool
RSLP HA4......................... 60 A7
Highlands Junior & Infant School
IL IG1......................... 88 F1
The High Road Surgery
WDGN N22......................... 66 F1
High Road Swimming Baths
IL IG1......................... 89 K2
Highshore School
PECK SE15......................... 121 M6
High View Primary School
BTSEA SW11......................... 137 K1
Highview Primary School
WLGTN SM6......................... 171 L7
Highview Surgery
POTB/CUF EN6......................... 23 J6
The Highways Primary School
ORP BR6......................... 177 J7
The Highway Trading Centre
WAP E1W......................... 104 D6
Highwood Primary School
BUSH WD23......................... 29 L4
Hillbrook Primary School
TOOT SW17......................... 137 M8
Hillcrest Surgery
ACT W3......................... 99 H7
Hillcroft College
SURB KT6......................... 167 L1
Hilldene Junior School
HARH RM3......................... 56 C8
Hille Business Centre
WATN WD24......................... 29 H4
Hillel School
STHGT/OAK N14......................... 48 D1
Hill Farm Industrial Estate
GSTN WD25......................... 20 F6
Hillgate Hill Murugan Temple
HGT N6......................... 66 B8
Hillingdon Area Health Authority
RSLP HA4......................... 59 L8
Hillingdon Borough Football Club
RSLP HA4......................... 59 H6
Hillingdon Health Authority
NTHWD HA6......................... 60 A2
Hillingdon Health Authority
WDR/YW UB7......................... 94 E6
Hillingdon Hospital
UX/CGN UB8......................... 94 F3
Hillingdon Junior & Infant School
UX/CGN UB8......................... 95 G3
Hill Mead Infant School
HNHL SE24......................... 139 H1
Hillsgrove Primary School
WELL DA16......................... 126 C5
Hillside Junior & Infant School
NTHWD HA6......................... 60 A1
Hillside School
BORE WD6......................... 32 C7
Hilly Fields Medical Centre
BROCKY SE4......................... 141 G2
The Hiltongrove Business Centre 12-15
WALTH E17......................... 69 G5
Hinchley Wood Practice
NWMAL KT3......................... 168 F1
Hinchley Wood Secondary School
ESH/CLAY KT10......................... 167 G4
Hindu Temple
STHL UB1......................... 96 F7
Hindu Temple
WLSDN NW10......................... 81 K6
Hippodrm
LSQ/SEVD WC2H......................... 11 H6
Hitherfield Junior School
STRHM/NOR SW16......................... 139 G6
Hither Green Primary School
LEW SE13......................... 141 K3
HM Prison
CLAP SW4......................... 138 E3
HM Prison
WAND/EARL SW18......................... 137 K3
HM Prison Wormwood Scrubs
SHB W12......................... 100 A5
HMS President
EMB EC4Y......................... 12 B6

HM Young Offender Institution
FELT TW13 .... 131 K7
Hobbayne First & Middle School
HNWL W7 .... 97 M5
Hogarth Business Park
CHSWK W4 .... 117 L4
Hogarth Industrial Estate
WLSDN NW10 .... 100 A3
Hogarth Primary School
CHSWK W4 .... 117 L3
Hogarth's Ho
CHSWK W4 .... 117 K4
Holbeach Primary School
CAT SE6 .... 141 G4
Holborn College
WKENS W14 .... 118 E4
Holborn Galleries
HHOL WC1V 11 M3
Holborn Town Hall
HHOL WC1V 11 K4
Holdbrook Junior Middle & Infant School
CHES/WCR EN8 .... 26 F7
Holland & Holland Shooting School
DEN/HRF UB9 .... 59 G3
Holland House School
EDGE HA8 .... 45 G6
Holland Park Secondary School
KENS W8 .... 100 F8
Holland Park Theatre
KENS W8 .... 100 F8
Holland Street Clinic
KENS W8 .... 14 B2
Hollick Wood Primary School
MUSWH N10 .... 66 B1
Holloway School
HOLWY N7 .... 84 D5
Hollydale Primary School
PECK SE15 .... 122 C7
Hollyfield Secondary School
SURB KT6 .... 152 E8
Holly House Private Hospital
BKHH IG9 .... 52 B4
Holly Industrial Park
WATN WD24 .... 29 J4
Hollymount Primary School
RYNPK SW20 .... 154 C4
Holly Park School
FBAR/BDGN N11 .... 48 A6
Hollywood Bowl
BMLY BR1 .... 160 A4
Hollywood Road Gallery
WBPTN SW10 .... 14 E9
Holmesdale Picture Galleries
HAYES BR2 .... 160 C7
The Holme
CAMTN NW1 .... 3 M8
Holmleigh Primary School
STNW/STAM N16 .... 85 M1
Holmshill School
BORE WD6 .... 32 C5
Holmwood Corner Surgery
NWMAL KT3 .... 153 L8
Holy Cross Convent School
NWMAL KT3 .... 153 K7
Holy Cross Preparatory School
KUTN/CMB KT2 .... 153 J3
Holy Cross RC School
CAT SE6 .... 141 J5
Holy Family College
WALTH E17 .... 69 H4
Holy Ghost RC Primary School
BAL SW12 .... 137 M4
Holy Innocents RC Primary School
ORP BR6 .... 176 F5
Holyrood Infant School
WAT WD17 .... 28 D1
Holy Rood Junior School
WAT WD17 .... 28 D1
Holy Trinity C of E First School
WIM/MER SW19 .... 155 G2
Holy Trinity C of E Junior & Infant School
HACK E8 .... 85 M6
Holy Trinity C of E Primary School
BRXS/STRHM SW2 .... 138 F4
Holy Trinity C of E Primary School
CHES/WCR EN8 .... 26 D5
Holy Trinity C of E Primary School
DART DA1 .... 146 C2
Holy Trinity C of E Primary School
EFNCH N2 .... 65 J4
Holy Trinity C of E Primary School
KTBR SW1X 16 A3
Holy Trinity C of E School
RCHPK/HAM TW10 .... 135 G1
Holy Trinity College & Convent Preparatory School
BMLY BR1 .... 160 C4
Holy Trinity Primary School
CAMTN NW1 .... 4 C1
Holy Trinity School
CHEL SW3 .... 15 M5
Holy Trinity School
FSTH SE23 .... 140 C6
Holy Trinity School
NTHWD HA6 .... 41 J8
Holy Trinity School
WLGTN SM6 .... 171 J6
Holywell School
WATW WD18 .... 41 M1
Home Office
STJSPK SW1H 16 F2
Homeopathic Hosp
BMSBY WC1N 11 K2
Home Park Industrial Estate
KGLGY WD4 .... 20 D8
Homerton Hospital Social Services
CLPT E5 .... 86 D5
Homerton House Secondary Boys School
HOM E9 .... 86 C4
Homoeopathic Health Centre
PLSTW E13 .... 106 A3
The Homoeopathic Health Centre
MLHL NW7 .... 45 M7

Honeypot Business Centre
STAN HA7 .... 62 E2
Honeypot Medical Centre
STAN HA7 .... 62 E3
Honeywell Junior & Infant School
BTSEA SW11 .... 137 M3
Hong Kong & Shanghai Sports Club
BECK BR3 .... 158 E2
Honilands Junior & Infant School
EN EN1 .... 37 H1
Honorary Consulate of Burkina Faso
FUL/PGN SW6 .... 119 J8
Honor Oak Gallery
FSTH SE23 .... 140 D3
Honor Oak Health Centre
BROCKY SE4 .... 140 E1
Honourable Artillery Company H.q.
STLK EC1Y 13 G1
Hook Lane Primary School
WELL DA16 .... 126 A8
Hook Rise South Industrial Park
CHSGTN KT9 .... 168 A5
Hook Road Surgery
SURB KT6 .... 167 L5
Horizon Business Centre
ED N9 .... 50 D4
Horizon Industrial Estate
PECK SE15 .... 122 A4
Horizon School
STNW/STAM N16 .... 85 L4
Hornchurch Clinic
EMPK RM11 .... 92 E1
Hornchurch Sports Centre
HCH RM12 .... 92 C2
Horniman Museum
GNWCH SE10 .... 123 L1
The Horniman Museum & Gardens
FSTH SE23 .... 140 B5
Horniman School
FSTH SE23 .... 140 B5
Horn Lane Surgery
ACT W3 .... 99 J6
Hornsey Central Hospital
CEND/HSY/T N8 .... 66 D6
Hornsey Coroners Court & Public Mortuary
CEND/HSY/T N8 .... 66 C5
Hornsey County School
FSBYPK N4 .... 67 H6
Hornsey Rise Health Centre
ARCH N19 .... 66 D8
Hornsey School for Girls
CEND/HSY/T N8 .... 66 C4
Horseferry Road Magistrates Court
WEST SW1P 17 H4
Horse Guards Parade
WHALL SW1A 11 H9
Horsenden Primary School
GFD/PVL UB6 .... 79 L6
Horton Hospital
HOR/WEW KT19 .... 180 C4
Horton Industrial Park
WDR/YW UB7 .... 94 F7
Hospital
MYFR/PKLN W1K 10 A6
Hospital Annexe
DEN/HRF UB9 .... 58 C1
Hospital & Counselling Centre
CAMTN NW1 .... 9 K2
Hospital of St John & St Elizabeth
STJWD NW8 .... 3 G6
Hotham Primary School
PUT/ROE SW15 .... 136 C1
Hotspur Industrial Estate
TOTM N17 .... 50 B8
Houndsfield Primary School
ED N9 .... 50 B2
Hounslow Business Park
HSLW TW3 .... 133 G1
Hounslow College Independent School
FELT TW13 .... 132 D8
Hounslow Cricket Club
HSLW TW3 .... 114 F7
Hounslow Heath Junior School
HSLWW TW4 .... 114 E8
Hounslow Manor School
HSLW TW3 .... 115 H8
Hounslow & Spelthorne Community & Mental Health NHS Trust
STA TW18 .... 148 A1
Hounslow Town Primary School
HSLW TW3 .... 115 H7
House of Detention
CLKNW EC1R 6 B8
Houses of Parliament
WEST SW1P 17 K2
Houston Business Park
YEAD UB4 .... 96 C7
Howard Business Park
WAB EN9 .... 27 K7
Howard School
CROY/NA CR0 .... 172 C6
Hoxton Hall Theatre
IS N1 .... 7 K6
Hqs Wellington
TPL/STR WC2R 12 A6
H R Chinese Medical Centre
WLSDN NW10 .... 99 M1
H & S Community & NHS Trust
STWL/WRAY TW19 .... 130 E6
Hse of St Barnabas
SOHO/SHAV W1D 11 G5
Hughes Fields School
DEPT SE8 .... 123 G4
Hugh Myddelton Primary School
CLKNW EC1R 6 B8
The Humana Wellington Hospital
STJWD NW8 .... 3 H7
Humber Trading Estate
CRICK NW2 .... 82 B2

Hungarian Embassy
KTBR SW1X 16 A4
Hunters Hall School
DAGE RM10 .... 91 H5
Huntsman Sports Club
BKHTH/KID SE3 .... 142 A1
Hurley Clinic
LBTH SE11 .... 18 C6
Hurlingham Business Park
FUL/PGN SW6 .... 119 G8
Hurlingham & Chelsea School
FUL/PGN SW6 .... 119 G8
Huron College
SKENS SW7 .... 14 F5
Huron University
SKENS SW7 .... 15 H3
Hurricane Trading Centre
CDALE/KGS NW9 .... 63 M2
Hurst Drive JMI School
CHES/WCR EN8 .... 26 D7
Hurstmere Secondary School
BFN/LL DA15 .... 144 B5
Hurst Park Primary School
HPTN TW12 .... 151 G5
Hurst Place Surgery
BXLY DA5 .... 144 D5
Hurst Primary School
BXLY DA5 .... 144 D5
Hydeburn School
BAL SW12 .... 138 A5
The Hyde Industrial Estate
CDALE/KGS NW9 .... 63 M6
The Hyde School
CDALE/KGS NW9 .... 63 M6
Hyland House School
WALTH E17 .... 69 K3
Hyleford Leavers Unit School
BARK/HLT IG6 .... 71 K3
Hyleford Special School
IL IG1 .... 89 K5
Ibstock Place School
PUT/ROE SW15 .... 135 L3
Ichthus Primary School
CMBW SE5 .... 121 K5
Ickburgh School
CLPT E5 .... 86 B3
Ickenham Clinic
HGDN/ICK UB10 .... 77 J1
Ifield Gallery
WBPTN SW10 .... 14 D9
Ihlara Sport F C
HBRY N5 .... 85 J4
Ikra Primary School
STNW/STAM N16 .... 85 L4
Ilderton Primary School
BERM/RHTH SE16 .... 122 C4
Ilford County Court
IL IG1 .... 89 K2
Ilford County High School for Boys
BARK/HLT IG6 .... 71 J3
Ilford Jewish Primary School
BARK/HLT IG6 .... 71 K4
Ilford Medical Centre
IL IG1 .... 89 H3
Ilford Preparatory School
GDMY/SEVK IG3 .... 89 M1
Ilford Synagogue
IL IG1 .... 71 G7
Imber Court Trading Estate
E/WMO/HCT KT8 .... 166 D1
Immanuel College
BUSH WD23 .... 43 L2
Immanuel & St Andrew C of E Primary School
STRHM/NOR SW16 .... 156 C2
Immanuel School
ROM RM1 .... 55 L8
Imperial College
PUT/ROE SW15 .... 118 D7
Imperial College
SKENS SW7 .... 15 G8
Imperial College
SKENS SW7 .... 15 G3
Imperial College Athletic Ground
HYS/HAR UB3 .... 113 J4
Imperial College of Science
FUL/PGN SW6 .... 14 A9
Imperial College of Science & Technology
SKENS SW7 .... 15 H2
Imperial College of Science Technology & Medicine
SKENS SW7 .... 14 F3
Imperial College School of Medicine
HMSMTH W6 .... 118 D3
Imperial Trading Estate
RAIN RM13 .... 110 C3
Imperial War Museum
STHWK SE1 .... 18 B4
Independent Industrial Estate
WDR/YW UB7 .... 94 F7
India High Commission
HOL/ALD WC2B 11 L6
Indonesian Embassy
MYFR/PKLN W1K 10 B7
Indoor Market
DEPT SE8 .... 123 G6
Indoor Market
WAT WD17 .... 29 J6
Industrial Cen
STHWK SE1 .... 12 E8
Industrial Estate
CMBW SE5 .... 121 J7
Industrial Estate
DEN/HRF UB9 .... 40 A8
Industrial Estate
GNWCH SE10 .... 123 H5
Industrial Estate
NWCR SE14 .... 122 D4
Industrial Estate
POP/IOD E14 .... 105 G4
Industrial Estate Annexe
RAIN RM13 .... 109 L5
Industrial Health Clinic
UX/CGN UB8 .... 94 B2
Industrial Park
CHES/WCR EN8 .... 27 G7

Infant College
IL IG1 .... 89 G2
The Infirmary Royal Hospital
CHEL SW3 .... 16 A8
Ingrebourne CP School
HARH RM3 .... 56 C6
In House Gallery
KENS W8 .... 8 C9
Inner London Sessions House
STHWK SE1 .... 18 E3
Inner Temple
EMB EC4Y 12 A6
Innholders Hall
CANST EC4R 12 F6
Inns of Court School of Law
GINN WC1R 11 M2
Institut Francais
SKENS SW7 .... 15 G5
International Financial Centre
OBST EC2N 13 J4
International Medical Centre
ECT SW5 .... 14 B6
International School of London
ACT W3 .... 117 G2
International Trading Estate
NWDGN UB2 .... 114 C1
International University
BUSH WD23 .... 29 M7
Invicta Industrial Estate
SRTFD E15 .... 105 J2
Invicta Primary School
BKHTH/KID SE3 .... 124 A4
Invicta Sports Club
DART DA1 .... 146 D2
Inwood Business Centre
HSLW TW3 .... 133 H1
Irish Embassy
KTBR SW1X 16 C2
Ironmongers Hall
STBT EC1A 12 E3
Islamic College
WCHPL E1 .... 104 A5
Islamic College for Advanced Studies
WLSDN NW10 .... 82 B7
Islamic Cultural Centre & London Central Mosque
CAMTN NW1 .... 3 K8
The Islamic Grammar School
WAND/EARL SW18 .... 136 F4
Island Clinic
POP/IOD E14 .... 105 J8
Isleworth Baths
ISLW TW7 .... 133 M1
Isleworth Centre Practice
ISLW TW7 .... 116 A8
Isleworth & Syon School for Boys
ISLW TW7 .... 115 L5
Isleworth Town Primary School
ISLW TW7 .... 115 M7
Islington Business Centre
IS N1 .... 6 E3
Islington Council
HBRY N5 .... 85 H6
Islington Council
IS N1 .... 6 C3
Islington Green Medical Centre
IS N1 .... 6 C3
Islington Green School
IS N1 .... 6 D4
Islington Health Authority
ARCH N19 .... 84 B2
Islington Town Hall
IS N1 .... 6 C1
Ismaili Centre
SKENS SW7 .... 15 H5
Italia Conti Academy of Theatre Arts
BRXN/ST SW9 .... 120 E8
Italia Conti Academy of Theatre Arts
FARR EC1M 12 E1
Italian Embassy
MYFR/PKLN W1K 10 B6
Italian Hospital
WEST SW1P 16 E5
Ithaca College
TWK TW1 .... 14 E6
Ivybridge Primary School
TWK TW1 .... 133 M3
Ivydale Primary School
PECK SE15 .... 140 D1
Jack & Jill School
HPTN TW12 .... 151 G2
Jack Taylor School
STJWD NW8 .... 2 E3
Jaina House Surgery
STHGT/OAK N14 .... 48 D5
Jamahiriya School
CHEL SW3 .... 15 J9
Jamaican High Comm
SKENS SW7 .... 15 G2
James Allens Girls School
HNHL SE24 .... 139 K2
James Dixon Primary School
PGE/AN SE20 .... 158 A3
Jamestown Mental Health Centre
HAMP NW3 .... 3 L1
Jamia Mosque
BARK IG11 .... 89 J1
Jamia Mosque
HSLW TW3 .... 132 F1
Janet Adegoke Leisure Centre
SHB W12 .... 100 A6
Japanese Gallery
IS N1 .... 6 C4
Japanese Gallery
KENS W8 .... 8 B9
Japan Green Medical Centre
ACT W3 .... 99 H7
Jayram Surgery
DEPT SE8 .... 123 G6
Jenner Health Centre
FSTH SE23 .... 140 E5
The Jerdan Gallery
FUL/PGN SW6 .... 119 G5
Jermyn Street Theatre
STJS SW1Y 10 F7

Jessop Primary School
HNHL SE24 .... 139 H1
Jewel Tower
WEST SW1P 17 J3
Jewish Community Theatre
CMBW SE5 .... 121 K8
The Jewish Museum
CAMTN NW1 .... 4 C4
The Jewish Preparatory School
KIL/WHAMP NW6 .... 2 C5
Jews College London
HDN NW4 .... 64 D5
JMI School
SURB KT6 .... 152 D8
Johanna Primary School
STHWK SE1 .... 18 A2
John Ball Primary School
BKHTH/KID SE3 .... 123 L7
John Betts Primary School
HMSMTH W6 .... 118 A1
John Bramston Infant School
BARK/HLT IG6 .... 54 A8
John Busch School
ISLW TW7 .... 116 B6
John Chilton School
NTHLT UB5 .... 78 E7
The John Denham Gallery
CRICK NW2 .... 82 F5
John Dixon Clinic
BERM/RHTH SE16 .... 122 B1
John Donne Primary School
PECK SE15 .... 122 B6
John Fisher School
PUR/KEN CR8 .... 183 L3
John Fisher School
RYLN/HDSTN HA2 .... 61 G5
John F Kennedy Special School
SRTFD E15 .... 87 K8
John Kelly Boys & Girls Technology College
CRICK NW2 .... 81 M3
John Lyon School
RYLN/HDSTN HA2 .... 79 K1
John Milton Primary School
VX/NE SW8 .... 120 C5
John Nightingale School
E/WMO/HCT KT8 .... 150 F6
John Orwell Sports Centre
WAP E1W 104 A7
John Paul Ii School
WIM/MER SW19 .... 136 D4
John Penrose School
DEN/HRF UB9 .... 58 D2
John Perryn Primary School
ACT W3 .... 99 L4
John Perry School
DAGE RM10 .... 91 K6
John Roan Lower School
BKHTH/KID SE3 .... 123 M4
John Roan Secondary School
GNWCH SE10 .... 123 L5
John Ruskin Sixth Form College
SAND/SEL CR2 .... 185 L1
John Scott Health Centre
FSBYPK N4 .... 85 J1
John Scurr Primary School
WCHPL E1 .... 104 C3
John Smith House
WALW SE17 .... 18 E6
Johnsons Industrial Estate
HYS/HAR UB3 .... 114 A1
John Stainer Primary School
BROCKY SE4 .... 122 E8
John the Baptist C of E Junior School
KUT KT1 .... 152 E8
John Vickers Theatre Collection
FUL/PGN SW6 .... 118 F5
Joseph Clarke Special School
CHING E4 .... 51 K8
Joseph Hood Primary & Middle School
RYNPK SW20 .... 154 E5
Joseph Lancaster Primary School
STHWK SE1 .... 18 F4
Joseph Tritton Primary School
BTSEA SW11 .... 119 J8
Joyce Green Hospital
DART DA1 .... 128 F7
Joydens Wood CP School
BXLY DA5 .... 145 L8
Jubilee Market
COVGDN WC2E 11 K6
Jubilee Primary School
STNW/STAM N16 .... 86 A1
Jubilee School
THMD SE28 .... 108 C6
Jubilee Sports Ground
CHING E4 .... 51 K6
Judd Street Gallery
STPAN WC1H 5 J1
Julians Primary School
STRHM/NOR SW16 .... 139 G8
Junior School
KIL/WHAMP NW6 .... 2 A2
Junior School
SAND/SEL CR2 .... 184 D2
Junior & Youth Centre
POP/IOD E14 .... 104 F4
J V C Business Park
CRICK NW2 .... 82 A1
Kangley Business Centre
SYD SE26 .... 158 F2
Karizma Frame Gallery
PLMGR N13 .... 48 F7
Katella Trading Estate
BARK IG11 .... 107 L2
Katherine Road Medical Centre
FSTGT E7 .... 88 C6
The Keats Group Practice
HAMP NW3 .... 83 K4
Keats House Museum
HAMP NW3 .... 83 L4
Keats Surgery
ED N9 .... 49 L4
Keble Preparatory School for Boys
WCHMH N21 .... 49 G2

Keen Students Supplementary School
WCHPL E1.................... 104 A4
The Keet Clinic
COVGDN WC2E................. 11 J5
Keir Hardy Primary School
CAN/RD E16................... 106 A4
Keith Davis Cue Sports Club
DAGW RM9.................... 90 D7
Kelmscott Leisure Centre
WALTH E17.................... 68 F7
Kelmscott School
WALTH E17.................... 68 F7
Kelsey Park School
BECK BR3.................... 159 G6
Kender Primary School
NWCR SE14.................. 122 C6
Kenilworth Primary School
BORE WD6.................... 32 D6
Kenley Sports Club
PUR/KEN CR8................. 184 C7
Kenmont Primary School
WLSDN NW10................. 100 A2
Kenmore Park School
KTN/HRWW/W HA3............. 62 D4
Kenneth More Theatre
IL IG1...................... 89 J3
Kenningtons Primary School
SOCK/AV RM15............... 111 J3
Kensal Rise Primary School
WLSDN NW10................. 100 D1
Kensington and Chelsea Town Hall
KENS W8.................... 14 B2
Kensington Avenue Junior & Infant School
THHTH CR7.................. 157 G4
Kensington & Chelsea College
NKENS W10.................. 100 E4
Kensington & Chelsea College
WBPTN SW10................. 119 J5
Kensington & Chelsea Health Authority
BAY/PAD W2.................. 8 F5
The Kensington Clinic
KENS W8.................... 14 C4
Kensington Market
KENS W8.................... 14 C2
Kensington Palace
KENS W8.................... 14 D1
Kensington Park School
CAVSQ/HST W1G.............. 10 D2
Kensington Preparatory School
FUL/PGN SW6............... 118 F6
Kensington Primary School
MNPK E12................... 88 F6
Kensington School of Business
HCIRC EC1N................. 12 B2
Kensington Sports Centre
NTGHL W11................. 100 D6
Kensit Memorial College
FNCH N3.................... 64 E3
Kent County Council
DART DA1.................. 146 D3
Kent County Council
RDART DA2................. 146 C8
Kentish Town Health Centre
KTTN NW5.................. 84 C6
Kentish Town Industrial Estate
KTTN NW5.................. 84 B5
Kentish Town Primary School
KTTN NW5.................. 84 C5
Kenton Clinic
KTN/HRWW/W HA3............ 62 E6
Kenton Cricket Club
KTN/HRWW/W HA3............ 62 C5
Kenton Synagogue
KTN/HRWW/W HA3............ 62 D6
Kent Park Industrial Estate
PECK SE15................. 122 B4
Kenwood House
HGT N6.................... 83 L1
Kenya High Comm
CAVSQ/HST W1G............. 10 C2
Kenyngton Manor CP School
SUN TW16................. 150 A2
The Kerem School
EFNCH N2.................. 65 K6
Keston C of E Primary School
HAYES BR2................ 175 K7
Keston House Medical Practice
PUR/KEN CR8.............. 183 M5
Kevington CP School
STMC/STPC BR5............ 162 D8
Kew Bridge Steam Museum
BTFD TW8................. 116 F3
Kew College
RCH/KEW TW9.............. 117 G5
Kew Palace
RCH/KEW TW9.............. 116 E5
Keyworth Junior & Infant School
WALW SE17................ 18 C8
Khalsa College London
HRW HA1.................. 61 M7
Kidbrooke Park Primary School
BKHTH/KID SE3............ 124 C7
Kidbrooke School
BKHTH/KID SE3............ 124 D7
Killick Street Medical Centre
IS N1..................... 5 L5
Kilmorie Primary School
FSTH SE23................ 140 E6
Kimberley Industrial Estate
WALTH E17................ 68 F2
Kincade Gallery
GRH DA9................. 147 M4
King Alfred School
GLDGN NW11............... 83 H1
King Athelstan Primary School
KUT KT1................. 152 F6
King Edwards Road Clinic
RSLP HA4................. 77 K1
King Edward Vii Hospital for Officers
MHST W1U................ 10 B2
The Kingfisher Medical Centre
DEPT SE8................ 122 F4
King George Hospital
GDMY/SEVK IG3........... 72 A6

Kingham Industrial Estate
WLSDN NW10............... 99 K2
King Harold Comprehensive School
WAB EN9.................. 27 L6
King & Queen Wharf
WAP E1W................. 104 D6
Kings Acre Primary School
CLAP SW4................ 138 E2
Kings Avenue Medical Centre
GFD/PVL UB6............. 97 J5
Kingsbury Green Primary School
CDALE/KGS NW9........... 63 H6
Kingsbury High School
CDALE/KGS NW9........... 63 H5
Kingsbury Hospital
CDALE/KGS NW9........... 63 G5
Kingsbury Synagogue
CDALE/KGS NW9........... 63 J6
Kingsbury Tamil School
CDALE/KGS NW9........... 63 H4
Kingsbury Trading Estate
CDALE/KGS NW9........... 63 J7
Kings College
LSQ/SEVD WC2H........... 11 K5
Kings College
TPL/STR WC2R............ 11 M6
Kings College Hospital
EDUL SE22.............. 139 L1
Kings College London
CHEL SW3................ 15 J3
Kings College London
CMBW SE5............... 121 K7
Kings College London
HAMP NW3............... 83 G4
Kings College London
KENS W8................ 14 A1
Kings College London
STHWK SE1.............. 12 F4
Kings College London
STHWK SE1.............. 12 D8
Kings College London
STHWK SE1.............. 17 M1
King's College School
WIM/MER SW19........... 154 C1
Kings College School of Medicine & Dentistry
HNHL SE24............. 139 K3
Kings College Sports Ground
RSLP HA4............... 59 L7
Kings Court Gallery
FUL/PGN SW6........... 118 E7
Kingscroft School
STA TW18.............. 148 A2
Kings Cross Practice
STPAN WC1H............. 5 J8
Kingsdale Secondary School
DUL SE21............. 139 L7
Kingsdowne Surgery
SURB KT6............. 167 M3
Kings Estate
HCH RM12............. 92 A4
Kingsgate Business Centre
KUTN/CMB KT2......... 152 E5
Kingsgate Infant School
KIL/WHAMP NW6.......... 2 A1
Kings Head Theatre
IS N1.................. 6 C3
Kings House School
RCHPK/HAM TW10....... 134 F2
Kingsland Health Centre
IS N1.................. 7 K1
Kingsland Secondary School
HACK E8.............. 85 M5
Kingsland Surgery
IS N1.................. 7 K5
Kings Langley Parish Council
KGLGY WD4............. 20 A2
Kingsley Primary School
CROY/NA CR0.......... 171 M3
Kingsmead Junior & Infant School
CLPT E5.............. 86 E4
Kingsmead Medical Centre
CLPT E5.............. 86 E5
Kingsmead School
EN EN1............... 37 G7
The Kings Oak Private Hospital
ENC/FH EN2........... 36 A3
King Solomon High School
BARK/HLT IG6......... 71 K3
Kings Park Industrial Estate
KGLGY WD4............. 20 B2
Kings Private Clinic
GDMY/SEVK IG3........ 89 M1
Kingston Business Centre
CHSGTN KT9.......... 167 L5
Kingston College
KUT KT1............. 152 D6
Kingston Council for Voluntary Service
KUT KT1............. 152 E5
Kingston Crown Court
KUT KT1............. 152 D6
Kingston & District Community NHS Trust
SURB KT6............ 168 A4
Kingston Grammar School
KUT KT1............. 152 F5
Kingston Hospital NHS Trust
KUTN/CMB KT2........ 153 H4
Kingston Hospital NHS Trust
KUTN/CMB KT2........ 153 G4
Kingstonian Football Club
KUT KT1............. 153 H6
Kingston Liberal Synagogue
THDIT KT7........... 167 H2
Kingston Magistrates Court
KUT KT1............. 152 D5
Kingston Museum & Heritage Service
KUT KT1............. 152 D2
Kingston & Richmond Health Authority
BRYLDS KT5.......... 167 M2
Kingston Sport & Recreation Centre
NWMAL KT3........... 153 M7

Kingston University
KUT KT1............. 152 E6
Kingston University
KUTN/CMB KT2........ 153 K4
Kingston University
KUTN/CMB KT2........ 153 K1
King Street College
HMSMTH W6........... 118 C2
Kingsway Business Park
HPTN TW12........... 150 F4
Kingsway College
CLKNW EC1R............ 6 B9
Kingsway College
FSBYW WC1X............ 5 M7
Kingsway College
KTTN NW5............ 84 B6
Kingsway Junior School
STPAN WC1H............ 5 L8
Kingsway Junior School
GSTN WD25........... 21 G7
Kingswood House School
HOR/WEW KT19........ 180 B6
Kingswood Primary School
WNWD SE27.......... 139 K8
Kings Wood School
HARH RM3............ 57 G6
Kisharon Day School
GLDGN NW11.......... 64 F7
Klc School of Design
WBPTN SW10......... 119 J6
Knightland Road Synagogue
CLPT E5.............. 86 B2
Knightsbridge Barracks
SKENS SW7........... 15 K2
Knollmead Primary School
WPK KT4............ 168 C4
Knowledge Point School
HOLWY N7............ 84 F6
Knowle Park County School
STA TW18........... 148 A1
Knutsford Junior & Infant School
WATN WD24........... 29 K3
Kp Estate
RAIN RM13.......... 109 L6
K S Medical Centre
STHL UB1............ 97 H6
Kufa Gallery
BAY/PAD W2........... 8 C5
Kuwait Embassy
KTBR SW1X........... 15 M1
Laburnham Health Centre
DAGE RM10........... 91 G2
Laburnum Junior & Infant School
HACK E8.............. 7 L4
Ladbroke School
POTB/CUF EN6........ 23 H5
Lady Banks Primary School
RSLP HA4............ 78 A2
Lady Edens School
KENS W8............. 14 E3
The Lady Eleanor Holles School
HPTN TW12.......... 151 H1
Lady Margaret Junior Middle & Infant School
STHL UB1............ 96 F4
Lady Margaret Secondary School for Girls
FUL/PGN SW6........ 119 G6
Lady of Holy Rosary School
BFN/LL DA15........ 143 L3
Laharna Trading Estate
WATN WD24........... 29 J3
Laine Theatre Arts
EW KT17............ 180 C4
Laings Sports Ground
BAR EN5............. 32 E7
Lake Business Centre
TOTM N17............ 50 A8
Laker Industrial Estate
BECK BR3............ 158 E1
Lakeside Industrial Estate
DTCH/LGLY SL3...... 112 A4
Laleham C of E Primary School
STA TW18........... 148 C5
Lambeth College
CLAP SW4........... 138 C2
Lambeth College
STHWK SE1............ 13 K9
Lambeth Palace
STHWK SE1............ 17 L4
Lambeth Southwark and Lewisham Health Authority
LEW SE13........... 141 H3
Lambeth Walk Group Practice
LBTH SE11........... 18 A4
Lambs Court
POP/IOD E14........ 104 E6
Lamont Business Centre
CROY/NA CR0........ 171 L2
Lamont Gallery
BETH E2............ 104 C2
Lamorbey Swimming Centre
BFN/LL DA15........ 144 A6
Lampton School
HEST TW5........... 115 G4
The Lanark Medical Centre
MV/WKIL W9........... 2 D7
Lancaster House
WHALL SW1A.......... 16 E1
Lancasterian Junior & Infant School
TOTM N17............ 67 M2
Lancelot Medical Centre
ALP/SUD HA0......... 80 D5
Lanford Obesity Clinic
ED N9.............. 50 B2
Lanfranc Secondary School for Boys
CROY/NA CR0........ 171 L1
Langbourne Primary School
DUL SE21........... 139 L7
Langdon Comprehensive School
EHAM E6............ 107 H1
Langdon Park Secondary School
POP/IOD E14........ 105 H5
Langford Primary School
FUL/PGN SW6........ 119 H7

The Langham School
SEVS/STOTM N15...... 67 J5
Langhedge Lane Industrial Estate
UED N18............. 49 M8
Langley Park School for Boys
BECK BR3........... 174 B1
Langley Park School for Girls
BECK BR3........... 174 B1
Langthorne Health Centre
WAN E11............ 87 K3
Langthorne Hospital
WAN E11............ 87 K4
Langton Galleries
WBPTN SW10......... 119 J5
Langtons Junior & Infant School
EMPK RM11........... 92 E1
Lansdowne School
BRXN/ST SW9........ 120 F8
La Retraite RC Girls School
BAL SW12........... 138 C4
Lark Hall Infants School
CLAP SW4........... 120 D7
Lark Hall Junior School
CLAP SW4........... 120 D7
Larkswood Junior & Infant School
CHING E4............ 51 H6
Larmenier Infant School
HMSMTH W6.......... 118 C1
La Sainte Union Convent School
KTTN NW5............ 84 B3
La Salette RC Primary School
RAIN RM13.......... 110 A2
Laser Clinic
CHESW EN7........... 26 B3
Latchmere Junior School
KUTN/CMB KT2....... 152 F2
Latchmere Leisure Centre
BTSEA SW11......... 119 M7
Lathom Junior School
EHAM E6............. 88 D7
Latimer Industrial Estate 343-453
SHB W12............ 100 C5
Latymer All Saints C of E Primary School
ED N9.............. 49 M4
The Latymer School
ED N9.............. 49 L4
Latymer Upper School for Boys
HMSMTH W6.......... 118 A2
Launcelot Primary School
BMLY BR1........... 142 A8
Laurel Clinic
EA W5.............. 116 C2
Laurence Haines School
WATW WD18........... 42 A1
Lauriston Junior & Infant School
HOM E9............. 86 D8
Lavender Hill Group Practice
BTSEA SW11......... 120 A8
Lavender Junior & Infant School
ENC/FH EN2.......... 36 E3
Lavenders Fields Surgery
MTCM CR4........... 155 L4
Lawrence Trading Estate
GNWCH SE10......... 123 L2
Lawrence University
SKENS SW7........... 14 F6
Lawrence Wharf
BERM/RHTH SE16..... 104 F7
The Lawson Practice
IS N1................ 7 K5
Laycock Primary School
IS N1................ 85 G6
Lazards Sports Club
SUN TW16........... 150 B4
L B H Hayes Swimming Baths
HYS/HAR UB3......... 95 M7
Lea Bridge Industrial Estate
LEY E10............. 86 E1
Leadenhall Market
BANK EC3V........... 13 J5
Lea Farm Junior School
GSTN WD25........... 29 K1
Lea Gallery
IS N1................ 7 J8
Lea Green Special School
LEY E10............. 69 H7
Lea Park Trading Estate
LEY E10............. 68 F8
Leather Gallery
KENS W8............. 14 C1
Leathersellers Sports Ground
ELTH/MOT SE9....... 142 C4
Leathers Hall
HDTCH EC3A.......... 13 J4
Lea Valley High School
PEND EN3............ 26 C8
Lea Valley Ice Centre
LEY E10............. 86 D2
Lea Valley Junior & Infant School
TOTM N17............ 68 A1
Lea Valley Trading Estate
UED N18............. 50 D8
Lea Valley Trading Estate
UED N18............. 50 C6
Leavesden Green Junior Middle & Infant School
GSTN WD25........... 21 G7
Leavesden Hospital
ABLGY WD5........... 21 G4
Lee C of E Primary School
LEW SE13........... 141 L1
Lee Manor Primary School
LEW SE13........... 141 L3
Leeside College
BERM/RHTH SE16..... 104 D7
Leeside Trading Estate
TOTM N17............ 68 C1
Leesons Infant School
STMC/STPC BR5...... 162 A6
Lee Valley Leisure Centre
ED N9.............. 50 E3
Lee Valley Watersports Centre
CHING E4............ 50 E8
Leicester Galleries
IS N1................ 6 D5

Leigh City Technology College
DART DA1........... 147 G5
Leigh Close Industrial Estate
NWMAL KT3.......... 153 K7
Leigh Gallery
STPAN WC1H........... 5 J8
Leighton House Museum & Art Gallery
WKENS W14.......... 118 F1
Leisure Centre
FUL/PGN SW6........ 119 H4
Leisure Centre
KUT KT1............ 152 E5
Lena Gardens Primary School
HMSMTH W6.......... 118 C1
Leopold Primary School
WLSDN NW10.......... 81 M7
Leopold Street Clinic
BOW E3............. 104 F4
Lesney Park Primary School
ERITH DA8.......... 127 K4
Lesotho High Comm
KTBR SW1X........... 16 A3
Lessness Heath CP School
BELV DA17.......... 127 G3
Lewin Mead Community Mental Health Centre
STRHM/NOR SW16..... 156 D2
Lewis Clinic
CAR SM5............ 171 G6
Lewisham Bridge Primary School
LEW SE13........... 123 H8
Lewisham Business Centre
NWCR SE14.......... 122 D4
Lewisham College
BROCKY SE4......... 123 G7
Lewisham College
DEPT SE8........... 123 G6
Lewisham Coroners Office
LEW SE13........... 141 H2
Lewisham Council
CAT SE6............ 141 H7
Lewisham Council
DEPT SE8........... 123 G5
Lewisham & Guys Mental Health NHS Trust
STHWK SE1........... 18 C3
Lewisham Hospital NHS Trust
LEW SE13........... 141 K2
Lewisham Hospital NHS Trust
LEW SE13........... 141 H2
Lewisham & North Southwark Health Authority
CNWCH SE10......... 123 J6
Lewisham & North Southwark Health Authority
LEE/GVPK SE12...... 142 B6
Lewisham Triangle Surgery
LEW SE13........... 141 J1
Lewisham Way Practice
BROCKY SE4......... 123 G7
Leys Infant School
DAGE RM10........... 91 J7
Leyton Business Centre
LEY E10............. 87 G2
Leyton Football Club
LEY E10............. 86 F1
Leyton Foot Clinic
SRTFD E15........... 87 J4
Leyton Orient Football Club
LEY E10............. 87 H3
Leyton Sixth Form College
LEY E10............. 69 K7
Leytonstone Mosque
WAN E11............ 87 M1
Leytonstone School
WAN E11............ 69 L7
Leyton Youth Sports Ground
LEY E10............. 87 H1
Liberal Jewish Synagogue
STJWD NW8............ 3 H8
The Liberty City Clinic
SDTCH EC2A........... 7 J9
Liberty Middle School
MTCM CR4........... 155 L5
Lilian Baylis Theatre
CLKNW EC1R........... 6 B7
Lilian Baylis School
LBTH SE11........... 17 M6
Lilyville Surgery
FUL/PGN SW6........ 118 F6
Limehouse Town Hall
POP/IOD E14........ 104 F5
Limes Farm County Primary & Infant School
CHIG IG7............ 53 K8
Limestone Gallery
VX/NE SW8.......... 120 E4
Lime Tree Surgery
SRTFD E15........... 87 L4
Lincoln Road Clinic
EN EN1............. 37 G8
Linda Blackstone Gallery
PIN HA5............. 60 E4
Linden Bridge School
WPK KT4............ 168 E5
Linden Lodge School
WIM/MER SW19....... 136 E5
Lindon Bennett School
FELT TW13.......... 150 D1
The Link Primary School
CROY/NA CR0........ 171 L6
Links Primary School
TOOT SW17.......... 156 A2
Linley Sambourne House
KENS W8............ 14 A2
Linley Sambourne House
KENS W8............ 118 F1
Linnet House Clinic
STJWD NW8............ 3 J6
Linton Mead Primary School
THMD SE28.......... 108 B6
Lionel Road School
BTFD TW8........... 116 E2
Lion House School
PUT/ROE SW15....... 136 D1

Lismarrine Industrial Park
  BORE WD6 .... 44 B1
Lisson Grove Health Centre
  STJWD NW8 .... 3 J9
Lister Community Secondary School
  PLSTW E13 .... 106 B1
The Lister Hospital
  BCVA SW1W 16 C8
Lister House Clinic
  CAVSQ/HST W1G 10 C4
Little Angel Theatre
  IS N1 .... 6 D3
Littlebrook Business Centre
  DART DA1 .... 129 J8
Little Danson Welfare Clinic
  WELL DA16 .... 144 A1
Little Ealing Primary School
  EA W5 .... 116 C1
Little Furze School
  OXHEY WD19 .... 42 B5
Little Green CP School
  RKW/CH/CXG WD3 .... 28 B6
Little Hands Theatre Co
  HDN NW4 .... 64 C5
Little Heath Junior Mixed School
  POTB/CUF EN6 .... 23 J3
Little Ilford Comprehensive School
  MNPK E12 .... 88 F5
Little Reddings Primary School
  BUSH WD23 .... 30 B8
Little St Helens School
  NTHWD HA6 .... 59 M1
Little Stanmore First & Middle School
  EDGW HA8 .... 62 F2
Littleton C of E Infant School
  SHPTN TW17 .... 149 G6
Livesey Museum
  PECK SE15 .... 122 B6
Livingstone Hospital
  DART DA1 .... 146 F4
Livingstone Primary School
  EBAR EN4 .... 34 D6
Llewelyn Surgery
  WAB EN9 .... 27 K1
Lloyd's
  FENCHST EC3M 13 J5
Lloyds Register Cricket Club
  DUL SE21 .... 139 K5
Lochinver House School
  POTB/CUF EN6 .... 23 H3
Locks View Court
  POP/IOD E14 .... 104 E6
Lockwood Industrial Park
  TOTM N17 .... 68 B4
Lodge Sun Sports Club
  WAT WD17 .... 28 E4
Loggia Gallery
  WESTW SW1E 16 E2
Lombard Business Centre
  BTSEA SW11 .... 119 J1
Lombard Business Park
  CROY/NA CR0 .... 171 M2
Lombard Business Park
  WAND/EARL SW18 .... 137 K3
Lombard Business Park
  WIM/MER SW19 .... 155 L3
Lombard Trading Estate
  CHARL SE7 .... 124 B2
Lombardy Retail Park
  HYS/HAR UB3 .... 96 B6
Lon Brgh of Sthwark
  STHWK SE1 .... 19 L5
London Aquarium
  STHWK SE1 .... 17 K1
London Ballet Theatre
  HAMP NW3 .... 3 H1
London Bible College
  NTHWD HA6 .... 41 K8
London Borough of Bromley
  BMLY BR1 .... 160 B5
London Borough of Camden
  KTTN NW5 .... 84 A5
London Borough of Croydon Council
  CROY/NA CR0 .... 172 C1
London Borough of Hillingdon
  HYS/HAR UB3 .... 95 K1
London Borough of Waltham Forest
  WALTH E17 .... 69 H4
London Bridge City Pier
  STHWK SE1 .... 13 J8
London Bridge Hospital
  STHWK SE1 .... 13 H8
London Bridge Sports Centre
  CANST EC4R 13 C2
London Bubble Theatre
  BERM/RHTH SE16 .... 104 B8
London Canal Museum
  IS N1 .... 5 K5
London Capital College
  CAMTN NW1 .... 4 D3
London City Mission
  STHWK SE1 .... 19 K1
The London Clinic
  MHST W1U 10 B1
London College of Business & Computing
  BETH E2 .... 104 B1
London College of Fashion
  MHST W1U 10 B5
London College of Fashion
  SDTCH EC2A 7 K9
London College of Further Education
  LBTH SE11 .... 18 C6
London College of Higher Education
  CLAP SW4 .... 120 B8
London College of International Business Studies
  NOXST/BSQ WC1A 11 K3
London College of Printing
  STHWK SE1 .... 18 D4

London Commodity Exchange
  WAP E1W 13 M7
London County Courts
  LINN WC2A 12 A4
London Day Surgery Clinic
  NFNCH/WDSP N12 .... 47 J5
London Dungeon
  STHWK SE1 .... 13 H8
London Electronics College
  ECT SW5 .... 14 C7
The London Executive College
  TOOT SW17 .... 138 A7
London Fields Primary School
  HACK E8 .... 86 B8
London Foot Hospital
  FITZ W1T 10 E1
London Fo Temple
  GTPST W1W 10 E4
London Gender Clinic
  HDN NW4 .... 64 C7
London Group Business Park
  CRICK NW2 .... 81 M1
London Guildhall University
  LVPST EC2M 13 H3
London Guildhall University
  TWRH EC3N 13 L5
London Guildhall University Sports Ground
  LEE/GVPK SE12 .... 142 C6
London Guildhall University Sports Ground
  LEE/GVPK SE12 .... 142 C6
London International Festival of Theatre
  FSBYE EC1V 12 D1
London Irish Rugby Football Club
  SUN TW16 .... 150 A4
The London Irish Youth Theatre
  HGT N6 .... 84 B1
London Ladies & Girls Football Club
  CAT SE6 .... 141 K6
London Lane Clinic
  BMLY BR1 .... 159 M3
London Lei Zang Si Temple
  WOOL/PLUM SE18 .... 125 K2
London Living Theatre
  SYD SE26 .... 140 D8
London Nautical School
  STHWK SE1 .... 12 B8
London Open College
  FSBYE EC1V 6 D7
London Oratory School
  FUL/PGN SW6 .... 119 H5
London Pavilion
  REGST W1B 11 G7
London Road Clinic
  ALP/SUD HA0 .... 80 E5
London Road Medical Centre
  THHTH CR7 .... 172 A1
London School of Economics
  LSQ/SEVD WC2H 11 J4
London School of Economics
  STHWK SE1 .... 12 E8
London School of Hygiene & Tropical Medicine
  RSQ WC1B 11 H3
London Silver Vaults
  LINN WC2A 12 A3
London Sri Murugan Temple
  MNPK E12 .... 88 F5
The London Television Centre (Lwt)
  STHWK SE1 .... 12 A8
London Toy & Model Museum
  BAY/PAD W2 .... 8 E6
London Toy & Model Museum
  SHB W12 .... 100 C5
London Underwriting Centre
  MON EC3R 13 K6
London University
  CMBW SE5 .... 121 K7
London Welsh Football Club
  RCH/KEW TW9 .... 116 E8
London Welsh School
  CRICK NW2 .... 82 C6
London Zendo
  CAMTN NW1 .... 4 B1
London Zoo
  CAMTN NW1 .... 4 A5
Lonesome First School
  MTCM CR4 .... 156 B5
The Longcroft Clinic
  BNSTD SM7 .... 182 C8
Long Ditton County Infant School
  SURB KT6 .... 167 J3
Longfield School
  RYLN/HDSTN HA2 .... 61 G7
Longford School
  EBED/NFELT TW14 .... 131 M4
Longlands Primary School
  BFN/LL DA15 .... 143 L7
Long Lane A F C
  BKHTH/KID SE3 .... 124 C7
Longmead Business Centre
  HOR/WEW KT19 .... 180 D4
Longmead Industrial Estate
  HOR/WEW KT19 .... 180 D4
Longmead Junior & Infant School
  WDR/YW UB7 .... 112 D1
Longrove Surgery
  BAR EN5 .... 33 L6
Longshaw Primary School
  CHING E4 .... 51 K5
Lord Chancellors Dep
  RSQ WC1B 11 H3
Lord Chancellors Dep
  WEST SW1P 17 H4
Lord Chancellors Dep
  WESTW SW1E 16 F3
Lord Chancellors Department
  HOL/ALD WC2B 11 L5
Lord Chancellors Department
  LINN WC2A 12 A4

Lord Lister Health Centre
  FSTGT E7 .... 88 A4
Lords Cricket Museum
  STJWD NW8 .... 3 G8
Lordship Lane Clinic
  TOTM N17 .... 67 L3
Lordship Lane Primary School
  WDGN N22 .... 67 J2
Lord Snootys Gallery
  KIL/WHAMP NW6 .... 82 F5
Loughborough Junior & Infant School
  BRXN/ST SW9 .... 121 H7
Loughton Cricket Club
  LOU IG10 .... 39 M6
Loughton Health Centre
  LOU IG10 .... 39 L6
Loughton Mental Health Centre
  LOU IG10 .... 39 L8
Lovelace Primary School
  CHSGTN KT9 .... 167 J7
Lower Clapton Health Centre
  CLPT E5 .... 86 C5
Lower Place Business Centre
  WLSDN NW10 .... 99 J1
Lower Sydenham Industrial Estate
  CAT SE6 .... 158 F1
Lowfield Medical Centre
  DART DA1 .... 146 E4
Low Hall Sports Ground
  WALTH E17 .... 68 D7
Lowther CP School
  BARN SW13 .... 118 A5
Loxford High School
  IL IG1 .... 89 K5
Loyola Preparatory School
  BKHH IG9 .... 52 C3
L P R Sports Club
  BARK/HLT IG6 .... 71 M2
L S E Sports Club
  NWMAL KT3 .... 168 C1
LT Lost Property
  CAMTN NW1 .... 9 M1
Lucas Vale Junior School
  DEPT SE8 .... 123 G6
Lutomer House Business Centre
  POP/IOD E14 .... 105 H7
Luxembourg Embassy
  KTBR SW1X 16 A2
The Lyceum Theatre
  TPL/STR WC2R 11 L6
Lyndean Industrial Estate
  ABYW SE2 .... 126 C1
Lyndhurst Middle School
  BORE WD6 .... 31 M4
Lyndhurst Primary School
  CMBW SE5 .... 121 K7
Lynton Preparatory School
  EW KT17 .... 180 F4
Lyon Business Park
  BARK IG11 .... 107 L1
Lyon Park Junior & Infant School
  ALP/SUD HA0 .... 80 F7
Lyons Industrial Estate
  WDR/YW UB7 .... 94 C5
Lyric Theatre
  SOHO/SHAV W1D 11 G6
Lyric Theatre Hammersmith
  HMSMTH W6 .... 118 C2
Mabwin Supplementary School
  ED N9 .... 50 B4
Macaulay Primary School
  CLAP SW4 .... 138 B1
Madame Tussaud's
  CAMTN NW1 .... 10 A1
Madeira Grove Clinic
  WFD IG8 .... 52 B8
Madison Bowl
  NTHWD HA6 .... 59 L1
Mahatma Gandhi Industrial Estate
  BRXN/ST SW9 .... 121 H6
The Maheswaran Practice
  CRICK NW2 .... 82 F3
Mahieu Osteopathic Surgery
  KENS W8 .... 14 B3
Maida Vale Hospital
  MV/WKIL W9 .... 2 F9
Maida Vale Medical Centre
  MV/WKIL W9 .... 2 C8
Malawi High Comm
  MYFR/PKLN W1K 10 C6
Malayan High Comm
  MBLAR W1H 9 L4
Malaysia High Comm
  KTBR SW1X 16 B2
Malcolm Primary School
  PGE/AN SE20 .... 158 C3
Malden Manor Junior School
  NWMAL KT3 .... 168 E2
Malden Parochial School
  WPK KT4 .... 168 E3
Malden Road Baths
  CHEAM SM3 .... 169 K6
Malham Road Industrial Estate
  FSTH SE23 .... 140 D5
Mall Galleries
  STJS SW1Y 11 H8
The Mall School
  WHTN TW2 .... 133 K7
Malmesbury Middle School
  MRDN SM4 .... 170 C1
Malmesbury Primary School
  BOW E3 .... 104 F2
Malmesbury Primary School
  MRDN SM4 .... 170 C2
Malorees Gm Junior & Infant School
  KIL/WHAMP NW6 .... 82 D7
Malory School
  BMLY BR1 .... 142 A8
Malta High Comm
  MYFR/PICC W1J 10 C7
Malvern Way School
  RKW/CH/CXG WD3 .... 28 C8
Manby Lodge Infant School
  WEY KT13 .... 164 C7

Mandeville Primary School
  CLPT E5 .... 86 E3
Mandeville Special School
  NTHLT UB5 .... 78 F6
Manford Industrial Estate
  ERITH DA8 .... 128 B4
Manford Way Health Centre
  BARK/HLT IG6 .... 53 M8
Manor Brook Medical Centre
  BKHTH/KID SE3 .... 124 B7
Manor Drive Health Centre
  WPK KT4 .... 168 F3
Manorfield Primary School
  POP/IOD E14 .... 105 H4
Manor House Hospital
  GLDGN NW11 .... 83 H1
Manor Junior & Infant School
  BARK IG11 .... 89 M6
Manor Mead School
  SHPTN TW17 .... 149 H8
Manor Park Methodist School
  MNPK E12 .... 88 E4
Manor Park Primary School
  SUT SM1 .... 170 C7
Manor Practice
  WLGTN SM6 .... 171 H7
Manor Practice
  WLGTN SM6 .... 183 L1
Manor Primary School
  SRTFD E15 .... 105 L1
Manor Primary School
  WLSDN NW10 .... 100 C1
The Manor Primary School
  ROM RM1 .... 73 M6
Manor Road Surgery
  DAGE RM10 .... 91 K6
Manorside Primary School
  FNCH N3 .... 65 H2
Manor Way Business Centre
  DAGW RM9 .... 109 K4
Mansion House
  MANHO EC4N 13 C5
Manzoori Clinic
  SWLY BR8 .... 163 M3
Mapledown School
  CRICK NW2 .... 64 C8
Maple Grove Business Centre
  HSLWW TW4 .... 132 C1
Maple Industrial Estate
  FELT TW13 .... 132 A6
Maples Business Centre
  IS N1 .... 6 B3
Marble Arch
  BAY/PAD W2 .... 9 M6
Mardyke Surgery
  PUR RM19 .... 129 G2
Margaret Roper RC Primary School
  PUR/KEN CR8 .... 183 M3
Maria Fidelis Convent Lower School
  CAMTN NW1 .... 4 F8
Maria Fidelis Convent Upper School
  CAMTN NW1 .... 5 G7
Marion Vian Primary School
  BECK BR3 .... 158 D8
Maritime Industrial Estate
  CHARL SE7 .... 124 B2
Maritime Museum
  GNWCH SE10 .... 123 L2
The Marjory Kinnon School
  EBED/NFELT TW14 .... 131 L2
The Market
  COVGDN WC2E 11 K6
Market Trading Estate
  NWDGN UB2 .... 114 B2
Marks Gate Junior School
  CHDH RM6 .... 72 C4
Marlborough Cricket Club
  DUL SE21 .... 140 A5
Marlborough Day Hospital
  STJWD NW8 .... 2 F5
Marlborough Park School
  BFN/LL DA15 .... 144 A5
Marlborough Primary School
  CHEL SW3 .... 15 K6
Marlborough School
  HRW HA1 .... 61 L5
Marlborough School
  ISLW TW7 .... 116 A6
Marlowe Business Centre
  NWCR SE14 .... 122 E5
Marner Primary School
  BOW E3 .... 105 H3
Marshall Gallery
  WKENS W14 .... 118 D1
Marshalls Park School
  ROM RM1 .... 73 L3
Marshalls Park Upper School
  ROM RM1 .... 73 L5
Marshgate Trading Estate
  SRTFD E15 .... 87 H7
Marsh Green School
  DAGE RM10 .... 109 G2
Marston Fine Arts Gallery
  MLHL NW7 .... 45 G7
Martan College
  HOL/ALD WC2B 11 K4
Martinbridge Industrial Estate
  EN EN1 .... 37 G8
Martin Hewitt Practice
  TOOT SW17 .... 137 L5
Martin Primary School
  EFNCH N2 .... 65 L3
Marvels Lane Primary School
  LEE/GVPK SE12 .... 142 C6
Mary Boone School
  WKENS W14 .... 118 C2
Maryland Industrial Estate
  SRTFD E15 .... 87 L1
Maryland Primary School
  SRTFD E15 .... 87 L1
Marylebone Cricket Club
  STJWD NW8 .... 3 H8
Marylebone Mag Ct
  CAMTN NW1 .... 9 K2

Marymount International School
  KUTN/CMB KT2 .... 153 J3
Mary Wallace Theatre
  TWK TW1 .... 134 A5
Masorti Synagogue
  EDGE HA8 .... 45 H7
Maswell Park Health Centre
  HSLW TW3 .... 133 J2
Matilda Marks School
  MLHL NW7 .... 45 K7
Matrix Business Centre
  DART DA1 .... 146 E2
Matthew Arnold County Secondary School
  STA TW18 .... 148 C2
Matts Gallery
  WCHPL E1 .... 104 E4
Maudesley Hospital Day Programme
  CMBW SE5 .... 121 K7
Maudsley Hospital Annexe
  EDUL SE22 .... 139 M1
The Maudsley Hospital
  CMBW SE5 .... 121 J8
Mauritius High Comm
  SKENS SW7 .... 14 F4
Mawbrey Brough Health Centre
  VX/NE SW8 .... 120 E5
Mawney Infant School
  ROMW/RG RM7 .... 73 K6
Mayday Healthcare NHS Trust
  THHTH CR7 .... 172 B1
Mayespark Primary School
  GDMY/SEVK IG3 .... 90 A3
Mayfair Gallery
  KTTN NW5 .... 84 B5
Mayfield High School
  BCTR RM8 .... 90 C1
Mayfield Primary School
  GFD/PVL UB6 .... 97 K5
Mayfield School
  PIN HA5 .... 60 E4
Mayfield Surgery
  PUT/ROE SW15 .... 136 B3
Mayflower Junior & Infant School
  POP/IOD E14 .... 105 G5
Maylands Golf Club
  HARH RM3 .... 57 H7
Mayplace Primary School
  BXLYHN DA7 .... 145 K1
Maypole Community School
  BXLY DA5 .... 145 L4
Maytime School
  IL IG1 .... 89 G3
Mayville Infant School
  WAN E11 .... 87 L3
Mayville Junior School
  WAN E11 .... 87 L2
Maze Hill School
  GNWCH SE10 .... 123 L4
Mazenod RC Primary School
  KIL/WHAMP NW6 .... 2 B2
Mcentee School
  WALTH E17 .... 68 F2
Mckay Trading Estate
  NKENS W10 .... 100 C1
Mcmillan Clinic
  HYS/HAR UB3 .... 95 J6
The Mead County First School
  HOR/WEW KT19 .... 168 F2
Mead Infant School
  HARH RM3 .... 56 F8
Meadlands School
  RCHPK/HAM TW10 .... 134 C8
Meadowgate School
  PECK SE15 .... 122 D8
Meadow School
  UX/CGN UB8 .... 94 E4
Meadow Wood School
  BUSH WD23 .... 30 C8
Mead Road Infant School
  CHST BR7 .... 161 J2
Meanwhile Surgery
  NKENS W10 .... 100 F4
Medical Express Clinic
  CAVSQ/HST W1G 10 C2
The 157 Medical Practice
  FSBYPK N4 .... 84 F1
Mednurs Clinic
  SEVS/STOTM N15 .... 67 K7
Megabowl
  BRXS/STRHM SW2 .... 138 E6
Melcombe Primary School
  HMSMTH W6 .... 118 D4
Mellow Lane School
  HGDN/ICK UB10 .... 95 J3
Melrose School
  MTCM CR4 .... 155 L6
Memorial Hospital
  WOOL/PLUM SE18 .... 125 G7
Menorah Foundation School
  EDGE HA8 .... 63 J1
Menorah Grammar School
  GLDGN NW11 .... 64 E8
Mental Health Trust
  STHWK SE1 .... 13 H9
Mercers' Hall
  CITYW EC2V 12 F5
The Merchant Taylors Hall
  BANK EC3V 13 H5
Merchant Taylors School
  NTHWD HA6 .... 41 L4
Mercury Theatre
  LSQ/SEVD WC2H 11 J5
The Mercury Theatre
  NTGHL W11 .... 8 A7
Meriden Primary School
  GSTN WD25 .... 29 K1
Meridian Clinic
  BRXN/ST SW9 .... 121 H8
Meridian Locality Mental Health Centre
  CHARL SE7 .... 124 C4
Meridian School
  GNWCH SE10 .... 123 K3
Meridian Sports Club
  CHARL SE7 .... 124 C4

Meridian Trading Estate
　CHARL SE7 .... 124 B2
Merlin Primary School
　BMLY BR1 .... 142 A7
Merlin School
　PUT/ROE SW15 .... 136 D2
Mermaid Theatre
　BLKFR EC4V 12 D6
Merryhills Clinic
　ENC/FH EN2 .... 35 M6
Merryhills Primary School
　ENC/FH EN2 .... 35 M6
Merton Abbey Primary School
　WIM/MER SW19 .... 155 H4
Merton Adult College
　RYNPK SW20 .... 154 E6
Merton College
　MRDN SM4 .... 154 F8
Merton Industrial Park
　WIM/MER SW19 .... 155 J4
Merton Park Primary School
　WIM/MER SW19 .... 154 F5
Merton Surgery
　WIM/MER SW19 .... 155 H3
Merton Sutton &
　Wandsworth Health Authority
　MTCM CR4 .... 155 M7
Merton Sutton &
　Wandsworth Health Authority
　SUT SM1 .... 170 C3
Meryfield School
　BORE WD6 .... 31 M4
Metro Business Centre
　SYD SE26 .... 158 F2
Metropolitan Business Centre
　HACK E8 .... 7 K2
Metropolitan Hospital
　STHWK SE1 .... 18 B3
Metropolitan Police
　STJWD NW8 .... 3 J6
Metropolitan Police
　Football Club
　E/WMO/HCT KT8 .... 166 D1
Metropolitan Police Hayes
　Sports Club
　HAYES BR2 .... 174 F5
Metropolitan Tabernacle
　LBTH SE11 .... 18 D4
Metro Trading Centre
　WBLY HA9 .... 81 H4
Meyer Vet Surgery
　FUL/PGN SW6 .... 118 F5
Michael Faraday Primary School
　WALW SE17 .... 19 H9
Michael Manley Industrial
　Estate
　VX/NE SW8 .... 120 C7
Midas Business Centre
　DAGE RM10 .... 91 G4
Midas Industrial Estate
　DAGE RM10 .... 91 G4
Midas Industrial Estate
　UX/CGN UB8 .... 94 B1
Middle Park School
　ELTH/MOT SE9 .... 142 D4
Middlesex Business Centre
　NWDGN UB2 .... 97 G8
Middlesex Guildhall
　WEST SW1P 17 H2
Middlesex Hospital
　GTPST W1W 10 F3
Middlesex Hospital Sports
　Ground
　CHST BR7 .... 161 M1
Middlesex New Synagogue
　HRW HA1 .... 61 K8
Middlesex University
　GLDGN NW11 .... 83 H1
Middlesex University
　TOTM N17 .... 49 L8
Middlesex University
　WDGN N22 .... 66 E3
Middlesex University Business
　School
　HDN NW4 .... 64 B5
Middle Temple
　EMB EC4Y 12 A6
Midfield Primary School
　CHST BR7 .... 162 A3
Mildmay Medical Practice
　HBRY N5 .... 85 K5
Mile End & Bow Business
　Centre
　WCHPL E1 .... 104 B4
Mile End Hospital
　WCHPL E1 .... 104 D2
Milehams Industrial Estate
　PUR RM19 .... 129 G1
Miles Coverdale Primary
　School
　SHB W12 .... 100 C8
Millbank School
　WEST SW1P 17 H6
Millbank Tower
　WEST SW1P 17 J6
Millbourne Lodge Junior
　School
　ESH/CLAY KT10 .... 166 C7
Millbourne Lodge Senior
　School
　ESH/CLAY KT10 .... 166 D8
Millbrook Junior Middle &
　Infant School
　CHES/WCR EN8 .... 26 E2
Millenium Experience
　GNWCH SE10 .... 105 L7
Millenium Harbour
　Development
　BERM/RHTH SE16 .... 104 D4
Millenium Wharf Development
　POP/IOD E14 .... 125 K1
Millennium Balloon
　STHWK SE1 .... 13 K9
The Miller Practice
　HBRY N5 .... 85 J5
Mill Farm Business Park
　HSLWW TW4 .... 132 A4

Millfields Junior & Infant School
　CLPT E5 .... 86 C4
Millfield Theatre
　UED N18 .... 49 K6
Mill Green Business Park
　MTCM CR4 .... 170 F2
Mill Hill County High School
　MLHL NW7 .... 45 L4
The Mill Hill Cricket Club
　MLHL NW7 .... 46 C5
Mill Hill Industrial Estate
　MLHL NW7 .... 45 M8
Mill Hill School
　MLHL NW7 .... 46 B6
Mill Hill Synagogue
　MLHL NW7 .... 45 L8
Mill Lane Medical Centre
　KIL/WHAMP NW6 .... 83 G5
Mill Lane Trading Estate
　CROY/NA CR0 .... 171 M5
Millside Industrial Estate
　DART DA1 .... 146 D1
Mill Street Clinic
　STHWK SE1 .... 19 M1
Millwall Football Club
　BERM/RHTH SE16 .... 122 C3
Millway Medical Practice
　MLHL NW7 .... 45 M7
Milmead Industrial Centre
　TOTM N17 .... 68 B3
Milton Natural Health Centre
　HGT N6 .... 66 C8
Minet Clinic
　HYS/HAR UB3 .... 96 A7
Minet Junior & Infant School
　HYS/HAR UB3 .... 96 B7
Ministry of Agriculture
　WHALL SW1A 11 J9
Ministry of Defence
　WHALL SW1A 11 J9
Mini Town Hall
　WOOL/PLUM SE18 .... 125 M3
Mint Business Park
　CAN/RD E16 .... 106 A4
Mirravale Trading Estate
　BCTR RM8 .... 72 E8
Mitcham Cricket Club
　MTCM CR4 .... 155 L7
Mitcham Industrial Estate
　MTCM CR4 .... 156 A4
Mitcham Parochial Church
　Council
　MTCM CR4 .... 155 L6
Mitcham Road Surgery
　TOOT SW17 .... 156 A2
Mitchell Brook Primary School
　WLSDN NW10 .... 81 K6
Mitchell Junior School
　RKW RM12 .... 92 B6
Mitre Bridge Industrial Park
　WLSDN NW10 .... 100 B3
Moat Bridge School
　ELTH/MOT SE9 .... 142 D3
Mocha Museums
　CAMTN NW1 .... 4 F4
Modern Gallery
　GTPST W1W 10 F3
Modern Tutorial College
　NKENS W10 .... 100 D2
Molesey Hospital
　E/WMO/HCT KT8 .... 151 G8
Mollison Drive Health Centre
　WLGTN SM6 .... 183 L1
Monega Primary School
　MNPK E12 .... 88 D5
Monken Hadley C of E Primary
　School
　EBAR EN4 .... 34 A4
Monkfrith Primary School
　EBAR EN4 .... 48 A2
Monksmead School
　BORE WD6 .... 32 C6
Monks Orchard School
　CROY/NA CR0 .... 158 D8
Monro Industrial Estate
　CHES/WCR EN8 .... 26 E7
Monson Primary School
　NWCR SE14 .... 122 D5
Montbelle Primary School
　ELTH/MOT SE9 .... 143 H7
Monteagle School
　DAGW RM9 .... 90 B8
Montem Junior & Infant School
　HOLWY N7 .... 84 F3
Montpelier Primary School
　EA W5 .... 98 D4
Moorcroft School
　UX/CGN UB8 .... 95 H4
Moorfields Eye Hospital
　FSBYE EC1V 7 G8
Moorfields Primary School
　STLK EC1Y 7 G9
Moor Lane Junior School
　CHSGTN KT9 .... 167 M7
Moor Park Industrial Estate
　WATW WD18 .... 41 J2
Mora Primary School
　CRICK NW2 .... 82 C4
Morden College Homes
　BKHTH/KID SE3 .... 124 A7
Morden First School
　MRDN SM4 .... 155 G8
Morden Hall Medical Centre
　WIM/MER SW19 .... 155 H6
Morden Hill Surgery
　LEW SE13 .... 123 J7
Morden Mount School
　LEW SE13 .... 123 H7
Morden Road Clinic
　WIM/MER SW19 .... 155 H6
Morehouse School
　ISLW TW7 .... 115 L6
Moreland Junior Middle & Infant
　Primary School
　FSBYE EC1V 6 D8
Moreton Bay Industrial Estate
　GPK RM2 .... 74 D3

Moreton Street Gallery
　PIM SW1V 16 F7
Morningside Primary School
　HOM E9 .... 86 C6
Mornington Leisure Centre
　CAMTN NW1 .... 4 D3
Morpeth Secondary School
　BETH E2 .... 104 C2
Morris House Surgery
　TOTM N17 .... 67 K1
Mortimer Road Clinic
　WLSDN NW10 .... 100 C2
Mortimer School
　STRHM/NOR SW16 .... 138 D6
Moselle School
　TOTM N17 .... 67 K3
Mosiah Foundation Supplementary
　School
　STNW/STAM N16 .... 85 L1
Mosque
　BETH E2 .... 7 L4
Mosque
　BETH E2 .... 104 B1
Mosque
　FSTGT E7 .... 88 A6
The Mosque & Islamic Centre
　of Brent
　CRICK NW2 .... 82 D4
The Mosque
　NWDGN UB2 .... 114 F1
Mossford Green Primary School
　BARK/HLT IG6 .... 71 J3
Moss Hall Infant School
　FNCH N3 .... 47 H8
Moss Hall Junior School
　FNCH N3 .... 47 H8
The Mother & Baby Clinic
　HOM E9 .... 86 C6
Motley Thtr
　HOL/ALD WC2B 11 L5
Mottingham Community
　Health Clinic
　ELTH/MOT SE9 .... 142 B8
The Mountfield Surgery
　FNCH N3 .... 65 G4
Mount Grace Gm School
　POTB/CUF EN6 .... 23 H3
The Mount Infant School
　NWMAL KT3 .... 153 H6
Mount Medical Centre
　FELT TW13 .... 132 E6
Mount Pleasant School
　LCOL/BKTW AL2 .... 21 L3
Mount School
　MLHL NW7 .... 46 B7
Mount Stewart School
　KTN/HRWW/W HA3 .... 62 D7
Mount Vernon Hospital
　RKW/CH/CXG WD3 .... 41 H7
Mountview Theatre School
　CEND/HSY/T N8 .... 66 E7
Mountview Theatre School
　WDGN N22 .... 66 F3
The Moving Gallery
　CHSWK W4 .... 117 L1
Mowat Industrial Estate
　WATN WD24 .... 29 J3
Mowlem Junior & Infant School
　BETH E2 .... 104 C1
Mowlem Trading Estate
　TOTM N17 .... 68 C1
Mr Youngs Preview Theatre
　SOHO/CST W1F 10 F5
M S Business Centre
　PIN HA5 .... 60 D4
M S P Business Centre
　WBLY HA9 .... 81 H4
Mudchute City Farm
　POP/IOD E14 .... 123 J2
Mudlands Estate
　RAIN RM13 .... 109 L2
Muhammads Mosque
　SHB W12 .... 100 C8
Mulberry Business Centre
　BERM/RHTH SE16 .... 104 D8
Mulberry House School
　CRICK NW2 .... 82 E5
Mulberry School
　WCHPL E1 .... 104 B5
Mulgrave Jm and I School
　WOOL/PLUM SE18 .... 125 H1
The Multilingual Gallery
　IS N1 .... 85 H6
Murky Puddle Theatre Co/magic
　Fox/panic
　NWMAL KT3 .... 153 M6
Murray Business Centre
　STMC/STPC BR5 .... 162 B6
Museum
　BLKFR EC4V 12 E6
Museum
　BMSBY WC1N 11 M1
Museum
　COVGDN WC2E 11 K6
Museum
　WALW SE17 .... 18 E6
Museum Ass
　CLKNW EC1R 12 B1
Muschamp Junior &
　Infant School
　CAR SM5 .... 170 E4
Museum
　BERM/RHTH E16 .... 104 F7
Museum
　CHEL SW3 .... 16 A8
Museum
　LSQ/SEVD WC2H 11 H4
Museum
　SRTFD E15 .... 87 L6
Museum
　WAB EN9 .... 27 J7
Museum Gallery
　RSQ WC1B 11 J3
Museum in Docklands
　POP/IOD E14 .... 105 G6
Museum & Library
　WALW SE17 .... 18 E6

Moreton Street Gallery

Museum of Artillery
　WOOL/PLUM SE18 .... 124 F3
Museum of Fulham Palace
　FUL/PGN SW6 .... 118 D7
Museum of Garden History
　STHWK SE1 .... 17 K4
Museum of Installation
　LBTH SE11 .... 18 A4
Museum of London
　IS N1 .... 6 F4
Museum of London
　STBT EC1A 12 E3
Museum of Mankind
　CONDST W1S 10 E7
Museum of the Order of St John
　FARR EC1M 12 D1
Museum of Womens Art
　FSBYE EC1V 12 D1
The Museum Practice
　RSQ WC1B 11 H3
The Musical Museum
　BTFD TW8 .... 116 E4
Museum Service
　BARB EC2Y 12 E3
Muswell Hill Bowling Club
　MUSWH N10 .... 66 A4
Muswell Hill Synagogue
　MUSWH N10 .... 66 A4
Myatt Garden Primary School
　BROCKY SE4 .... 122 F7
Myatts Field Clinic
　BRXN/ST SW9 .... 121 H6
Nagi Business Centre
　ALP/SUD HA0 .... 98 D1
Nanjuwany Eye Practice
　FUL/PGN SW6 .... 118 E7
Nascot Wood Junior &
　Infant School
　WAT WD17 .... 29 G3
National Army Museum
　CHEL SW3 .... 15 M9
National Association for Gallery
　Education
　CLKNW EC1R 12 B1
National Film Theatre
　STHWK SE1 .... 11 M8
National Hospital
　RSQ WC1B 11 J2
National Hospital for
　Neurology & Neurosurgery
　RSQ WC1B 11 J1
National Maritime Museum
　GNWCH SE10 .... 123 K4
National Portrait Gallery
　LSQ/SEVD WC2H 11 H7
National Postal Museum
　STBT EC1A 12 D4
National Temperance
　Hospital NHS Trust
　CAMTN NW1 .... 4 E7
National Youth Theatre of Gb
　HOLWY N7 .... 84 E3
The Natural Health Practice
　IS N1 .... 5 L3
Natural History Museum
　SKENS SW7 .... 15 G4
Natural Therapy Clinic
　TOOT SW17 .... 156 B1
Natwest Sports Club
　BECK BR3 .... 158 F2
Navigation College
　MANHO EC4N 12 F6
The Nd Theatre
　NOXST/BSQ WC1A 11 H4
Nelmes Primary &
　Junior Schooll
　EMPK RM11 .... 74 F5
Nelson Dock Museum
　BERM/RHTH E16 .... 104 F7
Nelson Hospital
　WIM/MER SW19 .... 154 F5
Nelson Primary School
　EHAM E6 .... 107 G1
Nelson Primary School
　WHTN TW2 .... 133 H3
Nelson's Colmn
　CHCR WC2N 11 J8
Nelson Trading Estate
　WIM/MER SW19 .... 155 H4
Neo Clinic
　PIM SW1V 16 E7
Netley Primary School
　CAMTN NW1 .... 4 E8
New Addington
　Swimming Pools
　CROY/NA CR0 .... 186 C5
New Amb Theatre
　LSQ/SEVD WC2H 11 H5
The New Aylesbury Medical
　Centre
　WALW SE17 .... 19 H7
Newbury Park Health Centre
　GNTH/NBYPK IG2 .... 71 K7
Newbury Park Primary School
　GNTH/NBYPK IG2 .... 71 K7
Newbury Park Synagogue
　GDMY/SEVK IG3 .... 71 M7
New Caledonian Wharf
　BERM/RHTH SE16 .... 122 F1
New Chiswick Swimming Pool
　CHSWK W4 .... 117 L5
New City Gallery
　STHWK SE1 .... 13 G9
New City Primary School
　PLSTW E13 .... 106 C1
New Connaught Rooms
　HOL/ALD WC2H 11 K4
New Crane Wharf
　WAP E1W 104 C7
New Eltham Galleries
　ELTH/MOT SE9 .... 143 J5
New End Theatre
　HAMP NW3 .... 83 J3
New England Industrial Estate
　BARK IG11 .... 107 H1
Newfield Primary School
　WLSDN NW10 .... 81 M7

The New Furness Primary
　School
　WLSDN NW10 .... 100 A1
New Grafton Gallery
　BARN SW13 .... 117 M7
Newham College of Further
　Education
　EHAM E6 .... 106 F1
Newham College of Further
　Education
　SRTFD E15 .... 87 L7
Newham Community College
　CAN/RD E16 .... 105 L3
Newham General Hospital
　PLSTW E13 .... 106 C3
Newham Leisure Centre
　PLSTW E13 .... 106 C4
Newham Medical Centre
　PLSTW E13 .... 106 C1
Newham Museum Service
　SRTFD E15 .... 87 K7
Newham Sixth Form College
　PLSTW E13 .... 106 B3
New Health Centre
　TOTM N17 .... 67 L2
Newington Court Business
　Centre
　STHWK SE1 .... 18 E4
Newington Green Infant School
　STNW/STAM N16 .... 85 L5
Newington Industrial Estate
　WALW SE17 .... 18 D6
New Kings Primary School
　FUL/PGN SW6 .... 118 F7
Newland House School
　TWK TW1 .... 133 M8
New London Synagogue
　STJWD NW8 .... 2 E5
New London Theatre
　LSQ/SEVD WC2H 11 K4
Newnham Junior & Infant School
　RSLP HA4 .... 78 C1
New Peckham Mosque
　CMBW SE5 .... 19 L9
New Pennyfarthing Galleries
　HNHL SE24 .... 139 H3
Newport Junior & Infant School
　WAN E11 .... 87 J2
New Rush Hall School
　IL IG1 .... 89 J2
New School
　FUL/PGN SW6 .... 118 F6
New Scotland Yard
　STJSPK SW1H 17 G3
News International
　WAP E1W 104 B6
New Southgate Industrial
　Estate
　FBAR/BDGN N11 .... 48 C7
New Southgate Pain Clinic &
　Medical Centre
　FBAR/BDGN N11 .... 48 C7
Newstead Wood School for Girls
　ORP BR6 .... 176 D5
The New Surgery
　CLAP SW4 .... 138 E1
The New Surgery
　KGLGY WD4 .... 20 A2
Newton Farm First & Middle
　School
　RYLN/HDSTN HA2 .... 78 F2
Newton Medical Centre
　BAY/PAD W2 .... 8 B4
Newton Preparatory School
　VX/NE SW8 .... 120 B5
Newtons Primary School
　RAIN RM13 .... 109 K1
New Victoria Hospital
　KUTN/CMB KT2 .... 153 L3
New West End Synagogue
　BAY/PAD W2 .... 8 C7
New Woodlands School
　BMLY BR1 .... 141 L8
New Zealand Comm
　STJS SW1Y 11 H8
Nicholas Hawksmoor School
　BORE WD6 .... 32 B4
Nigeria High Commission
　EMB EC4Y 12 B5
Nightingale Clinic
　PLSTW E13 .... 106 C1
Nightingale House Surgery
　ED N9 .... 50 C1
Nightingale Practice
　CLPT E5 .... 86 A3
Nightingale Primary School
　SWFD E18 .... 70 C5
Nightingale Primary School
　WDGN N22 .... 66 E2
Nightingale Primary School
　WOOL/PLUM SE18 .... 125 H3
Nightingale School
　TOOT SW17 .... 137 L6
The Nightingale School
　STHWK SE1 .... 17 L2
Nineacres School
　WOOL/PLUM SE18 .... 125 K3
Noel Park Junior & Infant School
　WDGN N22 .... 67 G3
Nonsuch High School for Girls
　EW KT17 .... 181 K1
Nonsuch Industrial Estate
　EW KT17 .... 180 E4
Nonsuch Primary School
　EW KT17 .... 169 H7
Norbury Complementary Therapy
　Clinic
　STRHM/NOR SW16 .... 156 F4
Norbury First & Middle School
　HRW HA1 .... 61 L6
Norbury Health Centre
　STRHM/NOR SW16 .... 156 F5
Norbury Manor Primary School
　STRHM/NOR SW16 .... 156 F4
Norbury Manor Secondary Girls
　School
　STRHM/NOR SW16 .... 156 F4

Norbury Trading Estate
STRHM/NOR SW16 .... 156 F5
Norfolk House Preparatory
School
MUSWH N10 .... 66 B3
Norlington School
LEY E10 .... 87 K1
Normand Park Primary School
FUL/PGN SW6 .... 118 A3
Normandy Primary School
BXLYHN DA7 .... 127 K6
Normanhurst School
CHING E4 .... 51 K2
Norman Shaw Building
WHALL SW1A 17 J1
Northaw C of E School
POTB/CUF EN6 .... 24 A2
North Beckton Primary School
EHAM E6 .... 106 F4
North Bridge House School
CAMTN NW1 .... 4 C4
Northbrook C of E Secondary
School
LEW SE13 .... 141 L2
Northbury Junior & Infant School
BARK IG11 .... 89 H6
North Clinic
BMLY BR1 .... 160 A4
Northcote Lodge School
BTSEA SW11 .... 137 L3
North Cray Primary School
SCUP DA14 .... 162 E2
North Croydon Medical Centre
THHTH CR7 .... 172 B1
North Ealing Primary School
WEA W13 .... 98 B3
North East Surrey College of
Technology
EW KT17 .... 181 G4
Northend CP School
ERITH DA8 .... 127 K4
Northfields Industrial Estate
ALP/SUD HA0 .... 81 G8
Northfields Prospect Business
Centre
WAND/EARL SW18 .... 136 F1
Northgate Business Centre
EN EN1 .... 37 H6
Northgate Clinic
CDALE/KGS NW9 .... 63 L7
Northgate Industrial Park
CHDH RM6 .... 72 F2
North Harringay Junior & Infant
School
CEND/HSY/T N8 .... 67 G5
North Havering College of Adult
Education
ROM RM1 .... 73 L2
North Lodge Queens School
BUSH WD23 .... 29 M6
North London Collegiate School
EDGE HA8 .... 44 E8
North London Progressive
Synagogue
FSBYPK N4 .... 67 J7
North London School of
Physiotherapy
ARCH N19 .... 84 C1
North London Tutorial College
HDN NW4 .... 64 C7
North Middlesex Hospital
NHS Trust
UED N18 .... 49 L7
Northolt First & Middle School
NTHLT UB5 .... 78 D7
Northolt High School
NTHLT UB5 .... 78 F6
Northolt Park Infant School
NTHLT UB5 .... 79 H5
Northolt Road Clinic
RYLN/HDSTN HA2 .... 79 J3
North School
STHL UB1 .... 96 F6
Northside Primary School
NFNCH/WDSP N12 .... 47 J7
The North Street Health Centre
CLAP SW4 .... 120 C8
Northumberland Heath Medical
Centre
ERITH DA8 .... 127 K5
Northumberland Heath Primary
School
ERITH DA8 .... 127 H5
Northumberland Park School
TOTM N17 .... 68 A1
Northumbland Park Industrial
Estate
TOTM N17 .... 50 B8
Northview Primary School
WLSDN NW10 .... 81 L5
North Watford Health Clinic
GSTN WD25 .... 21 J7
Northway School
MLHL NW7 .... 45 J5
North West Kent College of
Technology
DART DA1 .... 146 D4
North West London Jewish
Day Gm Primary School
CRICK NW2 .... 82 E7
North West London Medical
Centre
STJWD NW8 .... 2 E7
North Westminster Community
School
BAY/PAD W2 .... 9 H3
North Westminster Community
Secondary School
MV/WKIL W9 .... 2 B9
North Westminster School
STJWD NW8 .... 9 J2
North Weylands Industrial Estate
WOT/HER KT12 .... 165 L4
Northwick Park Hospital & Clinical
Research Centre
HRW HA1 .... 62 B8

Northwold Junior &
Infant School
CLPT E5 .... 86 A2
Northwood College Educational
Foundation
NTHWD HA6 .... 59 K1
Northwood Football Club
NTHWD HA6 .... 59 M3
Northwood & Pinner Community
Hospital
NTHWD HA6 .... 60 A2
Northwood Preparatory School
RKW/CH/CXG WD3 .... 41 J4
Northwood School
NTHWD HA6 .... 60 B2
Northwood Sports Centre
PIN HA5 .... 60 B2
Northwood United Synagogue
NTHWD HA6 .... 59 L1
Norwegien/british Monument
BAY/PAD W2 .... 9 K9
Norwood Green Junior & Infant
School
NWDGN UB2 .... 114 F3
Norwood Park Primary School
WNWD SE27 .... 139 J8
Norwood School
WNWD SE27 .... 157 J1
Norwood Surgery
WNWD SE27 .... 139 H7
Notre Dame RC Girls School
STHWK SE1 .... 18 C3
Notting Hill & Ealing High
School
WEA W13 .... 98 B4
Notting Hill Synagogue
NTGHL W11 .... 100 F5
Novotel Hotel
WDR/YW UB7 .... 113 G2
Nower Hill High School
PIN HA5 .... 61 G5
Now Showing Art Gallery
NTGHL W11 .... 8 A8
N T G B Sports Ground
EHAM E6 .... 89 G6
Nuffield Hospital Midland
Regional Office
SURB KT6 .... 152 D8
Nugent Industrial Park
STMC/STPC BR5 .... 162 C7
The Nunhead Surgery
PECK SE15 .... 122 B8
N W 5 Theatre School
KTTN NW5 .... 84 C5
Oakdale Infant School
SWFD E18 .... 70 B3
Oakdale Junior School
SWFD E18 .... 70 C3
Oak Farm Clinic
HGDN/ICK UB10 .... 77 H7
Oak Farm Junior & Infant School
HGDN/ICK UB10 .... 77 H8
Oakfield CP Junior School
DART DA1 .... 146 D6
Oakfield Preparatory School
DUL SE21 .... 139 K6
Oak Hill College
EBAR EN4 .... 48 A1
Oak Hill Health Centre
SURB KT6 .... 167 L1
Oakington Manor Gm Primary
School
WBLY HA9 .... 81 H5
Oakland CP School
EBAR EN4 .... 47 M1
Oakland School
BNSTD SM7 .... 182 A7
Oaklands College
BORE WD6 .... 32 C5
Oaklands First & Middle School
HNWL W7 .... 97 M8
Oaklands School
ISLW TW7 .... 115 K8
Oaklands School
LOU IG10 .... 39 K8
Oaklands Secondary School
BETH E2 .... 104 A2
Oak Lane Medical Centre
TWK TW1 .... 134 B4
Oakleigh School
TRDG/WHET N20 .... 47 L5
Oak Lodge JMI School
WWKM BR4 .... 174 B2
Oak Lodge Medical Centre
EDGE HA8 .... 63 H1
Oak Lodge School
EFNCH N2 .... 65 J4
Oakmere School
POTB/CUF EN6 .... 23 K5
Oaks Sports Centre
CAR SM5 .... 182 F4
Oakthorpe Junior Mixed School
PLMCR N13 .... 49 J7
Oak Tree Medical Centre
GDMY/SEVK IG3 .... 89 L2
Oakwood Business Park
WLSDN NW10 .... 99 K2
Oakwood Independent School
PUR/KEN CR8 .... 184 B6
Oakwood Medical Centre
STHGT/OAK N14 .... 35 J8
Oasis Sports Centre
LSQ/SEVD WC2H 11 J4
Oatlands Infant School
WEY KT13 .... 164 D6
Objectives Museum Design
KIL/WHAMP NW6 .... 82 F5
Obstetrics Hospital
GWRST WC1E 10 F1
Occupational Health Centre
CROY/NA CR0 .... 172 D5
October Gallery
RSQ WC1B 11 K2
Odeon Cinema
BAR EN5 .... 34 A8

Odeon Cinema
CAMTN NW1 .... 4 D3
Odeon Cinema
ELTH/MOT SE9 .... 142 E1
Odeon Cinema
CNTH/NBYPK IG2 .... 71 G7
Odeon Cinema
HAYES BR2 .... 160 A5
Odeon Cinema
HOLWY N7 .... 84 E3
Odeon Cinema
KENS W8 .... 14 A3
Odeon Cinema
KIL/WHAMP NW6 .... 3 G2
Odeon Cinema
LSQ/SEVD WC2H 11 H7
Odeon Cinema
MUSWH N10 .... 66 A5
Odeon Cinema
RCH/KEW TW9 .... 134 D2
Odeon Cinema
ROM RM1 .... 73 M6
Odeon Cinema
STRHM/NOR SW16 .... 138 E7
Odeon Cinema
UX/CGN UB8 .... 76 C7
Odeon Cinema
WIM/MER SW19 .... 155 G3
Odessa Infant School
FSTGT E7 .... 88 A5
Odhams Industrial Centre
WATN WD24 .... 29 J2
Odhams Trading Estate
WATN WD24 .... 29 G1
Odyssey Business Park
RSLP HA4 .... 78 B5
Oglethorpe County Junior &
Infant School
UPMR RM14 .... 93 M2
Old Actonians Sports Club
EA W5 .... 98 F8
Old Admiralty
WHALL SW1A 11 H9
Old Bancroftians F C
BKHH IG9 .... 52 D6
Old Beckehamian Rugby Football Club
WWKM BR4 .... 174 D5
Old Beligate Wharf Development
POP/IOD E14 .... 122 F1
Old Bexley Business Park
BXLY DA5 .... 145 H4
Old Bexley C of E Primary School
BXLY DA5 .... 144 F5
Old Brockleians Sports Ground
ELTH/MOT SE9 .... 142 C3
Old Bromlians Cricket Club
HAYES BR2 .... 160 B8
Old Chigwellians Sports Club
CHIG IG7 .... 53 H3
Old Church Galleries
CHEL SW3 .... 15 H9
Oldchurch Hospital
ROMW/RG RM7 .... 73 K7
Old Colfeian Sports Club
LEE/GVPK SE12 .... 142 A2
The Old Cottage Hospital
EW KT17 .... 180 F6
Old Curiosity Shop
LINN WC2A 11 L4
Old Elthamians Sports Club
CHST BR7 .... 161 L2
Oldfield Family Practice
GFD/PVL UB6 .... 97 J2
Oldfield House School
HPTN TW12 .... 150 F4
Oldfield Infants School
GFD/PVL UB6 .... 97 K1
Old Fold Manor Golf Club
BAR EN5 .... 33 L4
Old Ford Primary School
BOW E3 .... 104 F1
Old Hall
WEST SW1P 17 G5
Oldhill Medical Centre
STNW/STAM N16 .... 85 M1
Old Lyonian Sports Ground
RYLN/HDSTN HA2 .... 61 J6
Old Merchant Taylors Sports Club
RKW/CH/CXG WD3 .... 28 B7
Old Millnillians Sports Ground
PIN HA5 .... 61 G2
Old Oak Primary School
SHB W12 .... 99 M5
Old Operating Theatre Museum
STHWK SE1 .... 13 G9
Old Owens Sports Ground
TRDG/WHET N20 .... 47 K3
Old Palace Primary School
BOW E3 .... 105 H2
Old Palace School
CROY/NA CR0 .... 172 B5
Old Royel Observatory Greenwich
GNWCH SE10 .... 123 K5
Old Station Museum
CAN/RD E16 .... 107 G4
Old Sun Wharf
POP/IOD E14 .... 104 E6
Old Tiffinians Sports Ground
E/WMO/HCT KT8 .... 151 L8
Old Treasury
WHALL SW1A 17 J1
Old Vic Theatre
STHWK SE1 .... 18 B1
Old War Office
WHALL SW1A 11 J9
Old Wilsonians Sports Club
WWKM BR4 .... 174 E3
Oliver Business Park
WLSDN NW10 .... 99 J1
Oliver Goldsmith Infant & Junior
Schools
CMBW SE5 .... 121 L6
Oliver Goldsmith Primary School
CDALE/KGS NW9 .... 63 K6
Olympia
WKENS W14 .... 118 E1
Olympia Industrial Estate
WDGN N22 .... 66 F3

Olympic Industrial Estate
WBLY HA9 .... 81 H4
Olympic Retail Park
WBLY HA9 .... 81 G4
Olympic Trading Estate
WBLY HA9 .... 81 H4
Omnibus Business Centre
HOLWY N7 .... 84 E5
Omnibus Business Centre
HOLWY N7 .... 84 E5
The One Stanley Medical Centre
ALP/SUD HA0 .... 80 E7
On Sai Clinic
ECT SW5 .... 14 C6
On the Road Tours C C
WAND/EARL SW18 .... 137 J3
Open Air Theatre
CAMTN NW1 .... 4 A8
The Open University
FSBYW WC1X 5 L7
The Open University
KIL/WHAMP NW6 .... 83 G4
Ophaboom Theatre
WLSDN NW10 .... 100 B2
Ophthalmic Hospital
MBLAR W1H 9 K2
The Optical Gallery (hook)
CHSGTN KT9 .... 167 K7
The Optical Gallery
TWK TW1 .... 134 A5
Optimax Laser Eye Clinic
HAMP NW3 .... 83 J4
Optimum Health Services
NHS Trust
CMBW SE5 .... 121 L6
Optimum Health Services
NHS Trust
FSTH SE23 .... 140 E7
Optimum Health Services
NHS Trust
LEE/GVPK SE12 .... 141 M2
Optimum Health Services
NHS Trust
NWCR SE14 .... 122 F5
Optimum Health Services
NHS Trust
STHWK SE1 .... 19 L5
Orange House Action Clinic
BOW E3 .... 104 F1
Orange Tree Theatre
RCH/KEW TW9 .... 134 C1
Oratory School
CHEL SW3 .... 15 J7
Orchard Business Centre
SYD SE26 .... 158 F1
Orchard County Primary School
WATN WD24 .... 28 F1
The Orchard Health Centre
HOM E9 .... 86 C7
Orchard Junior & Infant School
HSLW TW3 .... 133 G1
Orchard School
DART DA1 .... 146 B3
The Orchard Theatre
DART DA1 .... 146 C3
Orchard Way Primary School
CROY/NA CR0 .... 173 L2
Oriel Junior & Infant School
FELT TW13 .... 132 E7
Oriental Medical Centre
ECT SW5 .... 14 C6
Orient Industrial Park
LEY E10 .... 87 G2
Orion Business Centre
BERM/RHTH SE16 .... 122 D3
Orleans House Gallery
TWK TW1 .... 134 B5
Orleans Infant School
TWK TW1 .... 134 B4
Orleans Park School
TWK TW1 .... 134 B4
Orley Farm School
HRW HA1 .... 79 K3
Orpington College of Further
Education
ORP BR6 .... 177 G3
Orpington Mental Health Centre
ORP BR6 .... 176 F5
Orpington Retail Park
STMC/STPC BR5 .... 162 C7
Orpington Sports Centre
ORP BR6 .... 177 G3
Orpington Superbowl
ORP BR6 .... 177 G3
Osbourne Studio Gallery
KTBR SW1X 15 M3
Osidge JMI School
STHGT/OAK N14 .... 48 C3
Osidge Medical Practice
FBAR/BDGN N11 .... 48 A3
Osmani Primary School
WCHPL E1 .... 104 A4
Osterley Rugby Football Club
NWDGN UB2 .... 115 H1
Our Lady Immaculate RC Primary
School
SURB KT6 .... 168 A3
Our Lady of Grace RC JMI School
CHARL SE7 .... 124 B4
Our Lady of Grace RC
Junior School
CRICK NW2 .... 82 B3
Our Lady of Lourdes RC Primary
School
LEW SE13 .... 123 K8
Our Lady of Lourdes RC Primary
School
WAN E11 .... 69 M7
Our Lady of Lourdes School
WLSDN NW10 .... 81 J8
Our Lady of Lourdes School
FNCH N3 .... 46 E6
Our Lady of Muswell RC Infants &
Junior School
MUSWH N10 .... 66 A3
Our Lady of the Rosary School
STA TW18 .... 148 A2

Our Lady of the Sacred Heart
School
HOLWY N7 .... 84 F6
Our Lady Queen of Heaven RC
Primary School
WIM/MER SW19 .... 136 D4
Our Lady RC Primary School
POP/IOD E14 .... 104 C3
Our Lady & St John RC Primary
School
BTFD TW8 .... 116 C3
Our Lady & St Philip Neri RC
Primary School
FSTH SE23 .... 140 D7
Our Ladys Convent High School
STNW/STAM N16 .... 67 J3
Our Ladys RC Primary School
CAMTN NW1 .... 4 C3
Our Ladys RC Primary School
DART DA1 .... 146 C3
Oval Business Centre
LBTH SE11 .... 17 M3
Oval House Theatre
LBTH SE11 .... 121 L6
Oval Primary School
CROY/NA CR0 .... 172 E3
The Oval
LBTH SE11 .... 17 M9
Overton Grange School
BELMT SM2 .... 182 B1
Oxford Gardens Primary School
NKENS W10 .... 100 D5
Oxford House College
SOHO/SHAV W1D 11 G4
Oxhey Infant School
BUSH WD23 .... 29 L8
Oxheywood Junior & Infant
School
OXHEY WD19 .... 42 C6
Oxleas NHS Trust
BXLY DA5 .... 145 L6
Oxleas NHS Trust
ORP BR6 .... 177 H2
Oxleas NHS Trust
WOOL/PLUM SE18 .... 125 L3
Oxo Tower Wharf
STHWK SE1 .... 12 B7
Oxshott Medical Practice
LHD/OX KT22 .... 178 C6
Ozten Zeki Gallery
SKENS SW7 .... 15 J5
Paddington Bowling & Sports
Club
MV/WKIL W9 .... 2 C3
Paddington Green Primary
School
BAY/PAD W2 .... 9 G1
Paddock School
PUT/ROE SW15 .... 135 M1
Pain Relief Clinic
HDN NW4 .... 64 B7
Pakeman Junior School
HOLWY N7 .... 84 F3
Palace Road Surgery
BRXS/STRHM SW2 .... 138 F5
Palace Theatre
WAT WD17 .... 29 H6
Palladium Theatre
REGST W1B 10 E5
Palmer Galleries
RCH/KEW TW9 .... 134 D2
Palmers Green High School
WCHMH N21 .... 49 G4
Palmers Green & Southgate
Synagogue
FBAR/BDGN N11 .... 48 D7
Palmerston Business Centre
SUT SM1 .... 170 C7
Panama Consulate
MYFR/PKLN W1K 10 B3
Papua New Guinea High Comm
STJS SW1Y 10 E3
Paradise Road Practice
RCHPK/HAM TW10 .... 134 E2
Paradise Swimming Pools
MLHL NW7 .... 45 L7
Paramount Industrial Estate
WATN WD24 .... 29 J3
Parayhouse School
WBPTN SW10 .... 119 J5
Parchmore Medical Centre
THHTH CR7 .... 157 J6
Pardes House School
FNCH N3 .... 64 F3
Parent Infant Clinic
HAMP NW3 .... 83 J5
Parish C of E Primary School
BMLY BR1 .... 160 A2
Park Avenue Clinic
WAT WD17 .... 29 G5
Park Business Centre
KIL/WHAMP NW6 .... 2 A8
Parkend Surgery
HAMP NW3 .... 83 L4
The Parker Gallery
BGVA SW1W 16 B6
Parker Industrial Centre
RDART DA2 .... 147 J4
Parkers Row Family Practice
STHWK SE1 .... 19 M2
Parkfield Industrial Estate
BTSEA SW11 .... 120 A7
Parkfield JMI School
HDN NW4 .... 64 B8
Parkfield Medical Centre
POTB/CUF EN6 .... 23 H5
Park Gallery
KUTN/CMB KT2 .... 153 G4
Parkgate Infant School
WATN WD24 .... 29 J2
Parkgate Junior School
WATN WD24 .... 29 J2
Parkgate School
CLAP SW4 .... 138 A1
Park Hall Trading Estate
WNWD SE27 .... 139 J2
Park High School
STAN HA7 .... 62 D3

Parkhill Junior School
CLAY IG5 .... 71 G4
Park Hill Junior School
CROY/NA CR0 .... 172 D5
Park House Medical Centre
KIL/WHAMP NW6 .... 100 E1
Parkhouse Middle School
WIM/MER SW19 .... 136 F8
Park House Rugby Football Club
HAYES BR2 .... 175 J4
Parklands School
ROM RM1 .... 73 K4
Park Lane Primary School
WBLY HA9 .... 80 E4
Park Medical Centre
BERM/RHTH SE16 .... 122 D2
Park Mews Small Business
Centre
HNHL SE24 .... 139 J3
The Park Practice
PGE/AN SE20 .... 158 A3
Park Primary School
SRTFD E15 .... 87 M7
Park Road Clinic
CEND/HSY/T N8 .... 66 D6
Park Road Industrial Estate
SWLY BR8 .... 163 M6
Park Road Surgery
WLGTN SM6 .... 171 H7
Park Royal Business Centre
WLSDN NW10 .... 99 J3
Parks Golf Courses & Sports
Grounds
STA TW18 .... 130 B7
Parkside Clinic
NTGHL W11 .... 100 E5
Parkside First School
BORE WD6 .... 31 M3
Parkside Group Practice
SAND/SEL CR2 .... 184 D2
Parkside Health
NTGHL W11 .... 100 E5
Parkside Health NHS Trust
ALP/SUD HA0 .... 80 D6
Parkside Health NHS Trust
WBLY HA9 .... 81 H2
Parkside Hospital
WIM/MER SW19 .... 136 D7
Park Surgery
WAND/EARL SW18 .... 137 G3
Park Walk Gallery
WBPTN SW10 .... 14 F9
Parkway Primary School
ERITHM DA18 .... 126 E1
Parkway Trading Estate
HEST TW5 .... 114 C4
Parkwood Primary School
FSBYPK N4 .... 85 H2
Parliament Hill School
KTTN NW5 .... 84 A4
Parmiter Industrial Centre
BETH E2 .... 104 B1
Parmiters School
GSTN WD25 .... 21 J4
Parnells Sports Ground
KTN/HRWW/W HA3 ...... 62 F7
The Parochial Church Council of
Goffs Oak St James
CHESW EN7 .... 25 K1
Parsloes Primary School
DAGW RM9 .... 90 F6
Parsonage Farm Infant School
RAIN RM13 .... 110 C2
Parsons Green Health Clinic
FUL/PGN SW6 .... 119 G6
Patent Off
HHOL WC1V 12 A3
Paton Gallery
HACK E8 .... 86 B7
The Patrick Doody Clinic & Health
Centre
WIM/MER SW19 .... 155 G3
Pattinson Clinic
RCHPK/HAM TW10 ...... 134 D2
Paul Mason Gallery
CHEL SW3 .... 15 M5
The Paul Robeson Theatre
HSLW TW3 .... 115 H8
Pavilion Barclays Sports Ground
EA W5 .... 98 E4
Paxton Green Group Practice
DUL SE21 .... 139 L8
Paxton Primary School
NRWD SE19 .... 157 M2
Payne Clinic
EW KT17 .... 181 G6
Peacock Estate
TOTM N17 .... 49 M8
Peacock Industrial Estate
TOTM N17 .... 67 M1
The Peacock Theatre
HOL/ALD WC2B 11 L5
Peak Practice
GINN WC1R 11 L3
Peall Road Industrial Estate
CROY/NA CR0 .... 171 M1
Peckham Park Junior School
PECK SE15 .... 122 A5
The Peckham Pulse
Health & Leisure Centre
PECK SE15 .... 122 A6
Peckham Rye Junior &
Infant School
PECK SE15 .... 122 B8
Peerglow Industrial Estate
WATW WD18 .... 41 H2
Pelham CP School
WIM/MER SW19 .... 155 G3
Pelham Primary School
BXLYHN DA7 .... 127 G8
Pendragon Secondary School
BMLY BR1 .... 142 M4
Penrhyn Avenue Surgery
WALTH E17 .... 68 F2
Pentavia Retail Park
MLHL NW7 .... 63 M1
Penton Primary School
IS N1 .... 6 B5

Penwortham Primary School
STRHM/NOR SW16 ...... 156 B2
Perivale Industrial Park
GFD/PVL UB6 .... 98 A1
Perivale New Business Centre
GFD/PVL UB6 .... 98 C1
Perivale Primary School
GFD/PVL UB6 .... 98 C1
Perrin Road Clinic
ALP/SUD HA0 .... 80 B4
Perrins Art Gallery
HAMP NW3 .... 83 J4
Perry Hall School
ORP BR6 .... 176 F1
Perrymount Primary School
FSTH SE23 .... 140 D6
Peruvian Embassy
KTBR SW1X 15 M3
Peterborough & Queensmill
School
FUL/PGN SW6 .... 119 G7
Peterborough & St
Margarets School for Girls
STAN HA7 .... 43 L5
Peter Hills C of E Primary School
BERM/RHTH SE16 .... 104 D7
Peter James Business Centre
HYS/HAR UB3 .... 96 A4
Peterley Business Centre
BETH E2 .... 104 B1
Peter Pan Statue
BAY/PAD W2 .... 9 G8
Pewterers' Hall
CITYW EC2V 12 F5
Pheonix Court
POP/IOD E14 .... 123 G2
Pheonix Theatre
LSQ/SEVD WC2H 11 H5
Philippine Embassy
KENS W8 .... 8 C9
Phoenix College
MRDN SM4 .... 155 H8
Phoenix College
TOOT SW17 .... 137 L6
Phoenix Industrial Estate
HRW HA1 .... 61 M5
Phoenix Leisure Centre
CAT SE6 .... 141 H4
Phoenix Special School
BOW E3 .... 104 F2
Phoenix Trading Estate
GFD/PVL UB6 .... 80 C8
The Photographers Gallery
LSQ/SEVD WC2H 11 J6
Physical Energy Statue
BAY/PAD W2 .... 9 G9
Piccadilly Theatre
RECST W1B 10 F7
Pickford Land Medical Centre
BXLYHN DA7 .... 126 E6
Pickhurst Junior & Infant School
HAYES BR2 .... 174 F1
Pictorem Gallery
LEY E10 .... 69 H7
The Picture Frame Gallery
ROM RM1 .... 73 K6
Picture Gallery
PUT/ROE SW15 .... 136 D1
Picture Perfect Gallery
CLAY IG5 .... 71 H4
Picture Perfect Gallery
WAN E11 .... 70 B6
Pield Heath House RC School
UX/CGN UB8 .... 94 E3
Piers Feetham Gallery
FUL/PGN SW6 .... 119 H5
Pike Practice
WAND/EARL SW18 ...... 137 K1
Pilgrims Way Junior & Infant
School
PECK SE15 .... 122 C4
Pilton Estate
CROY/NA CR0 .... 172 B4
Pimlico Area Secondary School
PIM SW1V 16 F8
Pinewood Primary School
CRW RM5 .... 55 H7
Pinkwell Junior & Infant School
WDR/YW UB7 .... 113 J2
Pinner & District Synagogue
PIN HA5 .... 60 E5
Pinner Park First School
RYLN/HDSTN HA2 ...... 61 H4
Pinner View Medical Centre
HRW HA1 .... 61 J6
Pinner Wood School
PIN HA5 .... 60 C2
Pinn Medical Centre
PIN HA5 .... 60 E5
Pioneers Industrial Park
CROY/NA CR0 .... 171 L3
Pitfield Street Surgery
IS N1 .... 7 H7
Pitmans College
CAVSO/HST W1G 10 D4
Pitshanger Manor Museum
EA W5 .... 98 C7
The Place Theatre
CAMTN NW1 .... 5 H8
Plaistow Hospital
PLSTW E13 .... 106 B1
Planetarium
CAMTN NW1 .... 10 A1
Plantation House Medical Centre
LOTH EC2R 13 H4
Plashet Comprehensive School
EHAM E6 .... 88 E4
Plashet Road Medical Centre
FSTGT E7 .... 88 B7
Players Theatre
CHCR WC2N 11 J8
Plaza Business Centre
PEND EN3 .... 37 M5
Pleasance Theatre
HOLWY N7 .... 84 E6
Plumcroft Primary School
WOOL/PLUM SE18 ...... 125 J4

Plumstead Manor
Secondary School
WOOL/PLUM SE18 ...... 125 K3
The Pointer School
BKHTH/KID SE3 .... 124 A6
Police Cadet School
WAN E11 .... 88 A1
The Polish Institute & Sikorski
Museum
SKENS SW7 .... 15 H2
Polka Theatre for Children
WIM/MER SW19 .... 155 H2
Pollard Row Surgery
BETH E2 .... 104 A2
The Pompadour Gallery
GPK RM2 .... 74 A5
Ponders End Industrial Estate
PEND EN3 .... 37 M7
Pooles Park Junior School
HOLWY N7 .... 84 F2
Pope John School
SHB W12 .... 100 B6
Pope Paul RC Primary School
POTB/CUF EN6 .... 22 F6
Poplar Business Park
POP/IOD E14 .... 105 J4
Poplar Central Mosque
POP/IOD E14 .... 105 J5
Poplar Coroners Court
POP/IOD E14 .... 105 H6
Poplar First School
WIM/MER SW19 .... 155 G6
Pop Up Theatre
FSBYE EC1V 6 C6
Porchester Leisure Centre
BAY/PAD W2 .... 8 C4
Portland House Medical Centre
GFD/PVL UB6 .... 97 H3
Portland Medical Centre
SNWD SE25 .... 158 B8
The Portman Clinic
HAMP NW3 .... 83 K6
Portobello Gallery
NKENS W10 .... 100 E4
Portobello Medical Centre
NTGHL W11 .... 100 E5
Portway Primary School
SRTFD E15 .... 88 A8
Potters Bar Cricket Club
POTB/CUF EN6 .... 23 H5
Potters Bar Golf Club
POTB/CUF EN6 .... 23 G4
The Pountney Clinic
HSLW TW3 .... 115 G3
Poverest Primary School
STMC/STPC BR5 .... 162 A8
Power Industrial Estate
ERITH DA8 .... 128 A6
The Practice
BKHH IG9 .... 52 C4
The Practice
MBLAR W1H 9 M5
The Practice
SAND/SEL CR2 .... 184 D1
Prassard Surgery
WDGN N22 .... 66 F1
Prendergast School
BROCKY SE4 .... 141 G1
Preparatory School
HAMP NW3 .... 3 H1
Preston Hill Surgery
KTN/HRWW/W HA3 ...... 62 F7
Preston Manor Senior
High School
WBLY HA9 .... 80 F2
Preston Medical Centre
WBLY HA9 .... 80 E3
P R for Schools
SYD SE26 .... 140 C7
Priestmead First &
Middle Schools
KTN/HRWW/W HA3 ...... 62 B4
Primrose Hill Gallery
HAMP NW3 .... 3 L2
Primrose Hill Primary School
CAMTN NW1 .... 4 B3
Prince Charles
SOHO/SHAV W1D 11 H6
Prince Edward Theatre
SOHO/SHAV W1D 11 G5
Prince of Wales Junior &
Infant School
PEND EN3 .... 37 M3
Prince of Wales Road Group
Practice
CAMTN NW1 .... 84 A6
Prince of Wales Theatre
STJS SW1Y 11 G7
Princes Avenue School
MUSWH N10 .... 66 B4
Princes Court Business Centre
WAP E1W 104 B6
Princess Frederica C of E
Primary School
WLSDN NW10 .... 100 B1
Princess Louise Hospital
NKENS W10 .... 100 C4
The Print Room/museum
Books & Prints
BAR EN5 .... 33 L8
Priory Boys & Infant School
ACT W3 .... 99 J8
Priory C of E Middle School
WIM/MER SW19 .... 155 H1
Priory House School
CAT SE6 .... 141 H5
Priory School
BNSTD SM7 .... 181 M8
Priory School
SNWD SE25 .... 157 M7
Priory School
STMC/STPC BR5 .... 177 J3
Private Health Centre
FSTGT E7 .... 88 B6
Privy Council
STJS SW1Y 10 F9
Privy Council Office
WHALL SW1A 17 J1

Progress Business Park
CROY/NA CR0 .... 171 M4
Prospect House School
PUT/ROE SW15 .... 136 D4
Prospect of Whitby
WAP E1W 104 C7
Providence Road School
WDR/YW UB7 .... 94 E7
Provident Industrial Estate
HYS/HAR UB3 .... 96 A8
Pruskin Gallery
KENS W8 .... 14 B1
Public Baths
FSTH SE23 .... 140 C6
Public Swimming Pool
OXHEY WD19 .... 42 E7
Pump House
BERM/RHTH SE16 .... 104 E7
Pump House Theatre
WAT WD17 .... 29 J8
Pumping Station
POP/IOD E14 .... 105 J8
Pump Lane Industrial Estate
HYS/HAR UB3 .... 96 B8
Puppet Theatre Barge
MV/WKIL W9 .... 8 E2
The Purcell School
BUSH WD23 .... 29 M5
The Purcell School
HRW HA1 .... 79 K3
Purdy Hicks Gallery
SKENS SW7 .... 14 E6
Purdy Hicks Gallery
STHWK SE1 .... 12 C8
Purfleet Primary School
PUR RM19 .... 129 G2
Purley Community Health Clinic
PUR/KEN CR8 .... 184 A4
Purley & District War Memorial
Hospital
PUR/KEN CR8 .... 184 A3
Purley Gallery
PUR/KEN CR8 .... 184 A4
Purley Oaks Primary School
SAND/SEL CR2 .... 184 D1
Purley Sports Club
WLGTN SM6 .... 183 K3
Purley Swimming Pool &
Recreation Centre
PUR/KEN CR8 .... 184 B4
Pursuit Centre
WAP E1W 104 C6
Putney High School
PUT/ROE SW15 .... 136 D2
Putney Hospital
PUT/ROE SW15 .... 118 C8
Putney Leisure Centre
PUT/ROE SW15 .... 136 C1
Putneymead Medical Centre
PUT/ROE SW15 .... 136 C1
Putney School of Art
PUT/ROE SW15 .... 136 C1
Putney Surgery
PUT/ROE SW15 .... 136 C1
Pylon Trading Estate
CAN/RD E16 .... 105 K3
Qatar Embassy
MYFR/PKLN W1K 10 B8
Q E Conf Centre
WEST SW1P 17 H2
Quainton Hall School
HRW HA1 .... 61 L6
Quaker Gallery
CHCR WC2N 11 J7
Queen Charlottes &
Chelsea Hospital
HMSMTH W6 .... 118 A1
Queen Elizabeth Hall
STHWK SE1 .... 11 L8
Queen Elizabeth Ii
Jubilee School
MV/WKIL W9 .... 100 F3
Queen Elizabethmilitary
Hospital
CHARL SE7 .... 124 F4
Queen Elizabeth Museum
CHING E4 .... 51 L2
Queen Elizabeths Girls School
BAR EN5 .... 33 M7
Queen Elizabeths School
BAR EN5 .... 33 K6
Queen Marys Hospital
SCUP DA14 .... 162 A1
Queen Marys Hospital for
Children
CAR SM5 .... 182 F2
Queen Marys Sidcup NHS Trust
ABYW SE2 .... 108 D8
Queen Mary & Westfield College
SWFD E18 .... 70 A2
Queen Mary & Westfield College
WCHPL E1 .... 104 D3
Queen Mother Sports Centre
PIM SW1V 16 E5
Queensbridge Group Practice
HACK E8 .... 7 M1
Queensbridge Infant School
HACK E8 .... 7 M2
The Queens C of E Primary
School
RCH/KEW TW9 .... 117 G5
Queens College
CAVSO/HST W1G 10 C3
Queens Ice Skating Club
BAY/PAD W2 .... 8 D7
Queens Manor Primary School
FUL/PGN SW6 .... 118 C5
Queensmead
Comprehensive School
RSLP HA4 .... 78 D4
Queensmead Sports Centre
RSLP HA4 .... 78 A2
Queens Medical Centre
RCHPK/HAM TW10 ...... 134 F2
Queens Park Community School
WLSDN NW10 .... 82 C8
Queens Park Health Centre
NKENS W10 .... 100 E2

Queens Park Primary School
NKENS W10 .... 100 E2
Queens Park Rangers
Football Club
SHB W12 .... 100 B7
Queens Road Practice
NWCR SE14 .... 122 D6
Queens Road Practice
NWCR SE14 .... 122 D6
Queens Road Surgery
WIM/MER SW19 .... 155 G2
Queens Theatre
EMPK RM11 .... 74 D8
Queens Theatre
SOHO/SHAV W1D 11 G6
Queensway Business Centre
PEND EN3 .... 37 J3
Queenswell Infant School
TRDG/WHET N20 .... 47 K4
Queenswood School
BRKMPK AL9 .... 23 K1
The Questors Theatre
EA W5 .... 98 C6
Quicksilver Theatre
IS N1 .... 7 K2
Quintin Kynaston School
STJWD NW8 .... 3 G4
Rabbs Farm Primary School
WDR/YW UB7 .... 94 D6
RADA
GWRST WC1E 11 H1
Radcliffe College
SOHO/CST W1F 10 E5
Radha Krishna Temple
BAL SW12 .... 138 B4
Radlett Cricket Club
RAD WD7 .... 31 H2
Radlett Parochial Church
Council
RAD WD7 .... 31 G1
Radlett Preparatory School
RAD WD7 .... 31 J3
The Rae-smith Gallery
LSQ/SEVD WC2H 11 H7
Ragged School Museum Trust
BOW E3 .... 104 E4
Raglan Infant School
EN EN1 .... 49 L1
Raglan Junior School
EN EN1 .... 49 L2
Raglan Primary School
HAYES BR2 .... 160 C7
Railton Road Clinic
HNHL SE24 .... 139 H2
Rainbow Industrial Estate
RYNPK SW20 .... 154 B5
Rainbow Industrial Estate
WDR/YW UB7 .... 94 D6
Rainbow Quay
BERM/RHTH SE16 .... 122 E1
Rainham Primary School
RAIN RM13 .... 110 A3
Rainham Trading Estate
RAIN RM13 .... 109 M3
Ramgarhia Sikh
Gurdwara Temple
SRTFD E15 .... 88 A7
Rams Episcopal Primary School
HACK E8 .... 86 C5
Randal Cremer Primary School
BETH E2 .... 7 L5
Randolph Surgery
MV/WKIL W9 .... 2 D7
Ranelagh Primary School
SRTFD E15 .... 105 L1
Rangefield Primary School
BMLY BR1 .... 159 L1
Ransomes Dock
Business Centre
BTSEA SW11 .... 119 L5
Raphael School
EMPK RM11 .... 74 A7
Rathfern Primary School
FSTH SE23 .... 140 F5
Ravandos Sikh Temple
MNPK E12 .... 88 E4
Ravenor Primary School
GFD/PVL UB6 .... 97 G2
Ravensbourne College of
Design & Communication
CHST BR7 .... 160 F1
Ravensbourne College of
Design & Communication
CHST BR7 .... 161 K1
Ravensbourne Galleries
BECK BR3 .... 159 J6
Ravensbourne NHS Trust
HAYES BR2 .... 160 C7
Ravensbourne School
HARH RM3 .... 74 D2
The Ravensbourne School
HAYES BR2 .... 160 B7
Ravenscourt Park Preparatory
School
HMSMTH W6 .... 118 A2
Ravenscourt Theatre School
HMSMTH W6 .... 118 B2
Ravenscroft Medical Centre
GLDGN NW11 .... 64 F8
Ravenscroft Primary School
PLSTW E13 .... 106 A3
Ravenscroft School
TRDG/WHET N20 .... 46 F2
Ravenside Retail Park
UED N18 .... 50 D7
Ravensquay Business Centre
STMC/STPC BR5 .... 162 B8
Ravenstone Primary School
BAL SW12 .... 138 A5
Ravenswood Industrial Estate
WALTH E17 .... 69 J5
Ravenswood School for Boys
HAYES BR2 .... 175 K5
Ravin Galleries
FSTH SE23 .... 140 C6
Raw Gallery
WCHPL E1 .... 104 B5

Ray Lodge Junior & Infant School
WFD IG8 .... 52 D8
Raynes Park High School
NWMAL KT3 .... 154 B6
Raynes Park Sports Ground
RYNPK SW20 .... 154 A5
Raynes Park Vale Football Club
RYNPK SW20 .... 154 D8
Raynham Primary School
UED N18 .... 50 A7
R C A Sculpture School
BTSEA SW11 .... 119 K5
Reay Primary School
BRXN/ST SW9 .... 120 F5
Records Office
CLKNW EC1R 6 B9
Recreation Centre
LBTH SE11 .... 18 D5
Rectory Business Centre
SCUP DA14 .... 144 B8
Rectory Paddock School
STMC/STPC BR5 .... 162 C5
Redbridge College
CHDH RM6 .... 72 B6
Redbridge Health Authority
GDMY/SEVK IG3 .... 72 A6
Redbridge Junior & Infant School
REDBR IG4 .... 70 E6
Redbridge Museum Service
IL IG1 .... 89 J2
Redbridge Sports Centre Trust
BARK/HLT IG6 .... 71 K2
Redbridge & Waltham
Forest Health Authority
MNPK E12 .... 89 G3
Redburn Industrial Estate
PEND EN3 .... 50 D1
Redcliffe School
WBPTN SW10 .... 14 D9
Redcliffe Surgery
WBPTN SW10 .... 14 D9
Redden Court School
HARH RM3 .... 74 F4
Reddiford School
PIN HA5 .... 60 E5
Redford Lodge Psychiatric
Hospital
ED N9 .... 50 A4
Redhill Junior School
CHST BR7 .... 161 H1
Red Hill Surgery
CHST BR7 .... 161 H1
Redlands Primary School
WCHPL E1 .... 104 C4
Red Lion Business Park
SURB KT6 .... 167 M4
Redriff Junior & Infants School
BERM/RHTH SE16 .... 104 E8
Red Rose Trading Estate
BAR EN5 .... 34 D2
Reedham Park School
PUR/KEN CR8 .... 184 A7
Reeds School
COB KT11 .... 178 A5
Reed's Wharf Gallery
CLKNW EC1R 12 A1
Refuge Temple
STRHM/NOR SW16 .... 138 E8
Regent Business Centre
HYS/HAR UB3 .... 96 B8
Regent Clinic
CAVSQ/HST W1G 10 C3
Regent's College
CAMTN NW1 .... 4 A7
Regent's Park Barracks
CAMTN NW1 .... 4 C5
The Regina Codi School
CROY/NA CR0 .... 184 B1
Renwick House Surgery
ACT W3 .... 99 G7
Renwick Industrial Estate
BARK IG11 .... 108 B1
Replingham Clinic
WAND/EARL SW18 .... 137 G3
Restaurant and Cafe
BAY/PAD W2 .... 15 J1
The Retail Business Centre
EW KT17 .... 181 G3
Reynolds Health Centre
DART DA1 .... 146 E2
Rhodes Avenue Primary School
FBAR/BDGN N11 .... 66 C2
Rhodes Farm Clinic
MLHL NW7 .... 46 C6
Rhyl Primary School
KTTN NW5 .... 84 A6
RIBA
REGST W1B 10 D2
RIBA Drawings Collection & Heinz
Gallery
MBLAR W1H 9 M4
Ricards Lodge High School
WIM/MER SW19 .... 154 F1
Richard Alibon Infant School
DAGE RM10 .... 91 G5
Richard Atkins School
BRXS/STRHM SW2 .... 138 E4
Richard Cloudesley School
STLK EC1Y 12 E1
Richard Cobden Primary School
CAMTN NW1 .... 4 F4
Richard Tudor Gallery
CHING E4 .... 51 L2
Rich Industrial Estate
PECK SE15 .... 122 B4
Rich Industrial Estate
STHWK SE1 .... 19 M7
Rich Industrial Estate
STHWK SE1 .... 19 K4
Richmond Adult &
Community College
RCH/KEW TW9 .... 134 D1
Richmond Adult &
Community College
TWK TW1 .... 133 M5
The Richmond Clinic
RCHPK/HAM TW10 .... 134 F1

Richmond College
KENS W8 .... 14 C3
Richmond College
RCHPK/HAM TW10 .... 134 E3
Richmond Football Club
RCH/KEW TW9 .... 134 D1
The Richmond Green
Medical Centre
RCH/KEW TW9 .... 134 D2
Richmond House Doctors Surgery
WALW SE17 .... 19 G7
Richmond House School
HPTN TW12 .... 150 A1
Richmond Magistrates Court
RCH/KEW TW9 .... 134 D1
Richmond Road Medical Centre
KUTN/CMB KT2 .... 152 E3
Richmond Synagogue
RCH/KEW TW9 .... 134 E1
Richmond Theatre
RCH/KEW TW9 .... 134 D1
Richmond Twickenham &
Roehampton NHS Trust
HPTN TW12 .... 150 F2
Richmond-upon-Thames
College
WHTN TW2 .... 133 L4
Rickmansworth Public
Golf Course
RKW/CH/CXG WD3 .... 40 F4
Rickmansworth School
RKW/CH/CXG WD3 .... 40 F1
Rickmansworth Sports Club
RKW/CH/CXG WD3 .... 40 E1
Riddlesdown School
SAND/SEL CR2 .... 184 E2
Ridge House Clinic
WCHMH N21 .... 49 K2
Ridgeway Infant School
SAND/SEL CR2 .... 184 E2
The Ridgeway Surgery
RYLN/HDSTN HA2 .... 61 G7
Ripple Junior & Infant School
BARK IG11 .... 89 K8
Rise Park Infant School
ROM RM1 .... 73 K2
Risley Avenue School
TOTM N17 .... 67 L2
River Brent Business Park
NWDGN UB2 .... 115 L1
Riverdene Industrial Estate
WOT/HER KT12 .... 165 K7
River Gardens Business Centre
EBED/NFELT TW14 .... 132 B1
River Place Health Centre
IS N1 .... 6 E2
River Road Business Park
BARK IG11 .... 107 L2
River Road Practice
BKHH IG9 .... 52 E3
Riversdale Primary School
WAND/EARL SW18 .... 137 G5
Riverside Business Centre
WAND/EARL SW18 .... 137 H5
Riverside Business Park
WIM/MER SW19 .... 155 J4
Riverside Community
Health Care
WKENS W14 .... 118 D1
Riverside Health Authority
ECT SW5 .... 14 D6
Riverside Health Authority
PIM SW1V 17 G7
Riverside Health Authority
WBPTN SW10 .... 119 H5
Riverside Industrial Estate
BARK IG11 .... 108 A2
Riverside Industrial Estate
DART DA1 .... 146 E2
Riverside Industrial Estate
ED N9 .... 50 E1
Riverside Primary School
BERM/RHTH SE16 .... 104 A8
Riverside Swimming Centre
ERITH DA8 .... 127 L3
Riverside Wandle Trading Estate
MTCM CR4 .... 170 F2
Riverston School
LEE/GVPK SE12 .... 142 A2
Riverview CP School
HOR/WEW KT19 .... 168 C6
R N I B Sunshine House School
NTHWD HA6 .... 41 K8
Robert Blair Primary School
HOLWY N7 .... 84 E6
Robert Browning Junior & Infant
School
WALW SE17 .... 18 F7
Robert Clack School
BCTR RM8 .... 90 F1
Robin Hood Junior School
SUT SM1 .... 170 B7
Robin Hood Lane Health Centre
SUT SM1 .... 170 A7
Robin Hood Primary School
KUTN/CMB KT2 .... 153 K1
Robinsfield Infant School
STJWD NW8 .... 3 H5
Rochdale Surgery
PLMGR N13 .... 48 F6
The Roche School
WAND/EARL SW18 .... 137 G2
Rockcliffe Manor School
WOOL/PLUM SE18 .... 125 M4
Rockmount School
NRWD SE19 .... 157 J2
Rockware Business Centre
GFD/PVL UB6 .... 79 K8
Rodd Estate
SHPTN TW17 .... 149 J8
Roding Primary School
BCTR RM8 .... 90 C4
Roding Primary School
WFD IG8 .... 70 E1
Roding Valley High School
LOU IG10 .... 39 L8
Roebuck Road Trading Estate
BARK/HLT IG6 .... 54 B8

Roe Green Junior & Infant School
CDALE/KGS NW9 .... 63 H5
Roehampton Church School
PUT/ROE SW15 .... 136 B4
Roehampton Community Council
PUT/ROE SW15 .... 135 M3
Roehampton Institute
PUT/ROE SW15 .... 136 A2
Roehampton Institute
WAND/EARL SW18 .... 136 E3
The Roehampton Priory Hospital
PUT/ROE SW15 .... 135 M1
Roehampton Recreation Centre
PUT/ROE SW15 .... 136 A4
The Roehampton Surgery
PUT/ROE SW15 .... 136 A4
Roger Ascham Primary School
WALTH E17 .... 68 F2
Roger Bannister Sports Ground
KTN/HRWW/W HA3 .... 43 J8
Roger Black Gallery
CROY/NA CR0 .... 172 C4
Rokeby Secondary School
SRTFD E15 .... 87 K7
Roke Primary School
PUR/KEN CR8 .... 184 C7
Rokesly Primary & Junior School
CEND/HSY/T N8 .... 66 E6
Roman Bath
TPL/STR WC2R 11 M6
Roman Industrial Estate
CROY/NA CR0 .... 172 E2
Roman Road Primary School
EHAM E6 .... 106 D3
Roman Wall Remains
BARB EC2Y 12 E3
Romford Clinic
ROM RM1 .... 73 M5
Romford County Court
ROM RM1 .... 73 M5
Romford Ice Rink
ROMW/RG RM7 .... 73 L8
Ronald Rose Primary School
WIM/MER SW19 .... 136 D4
Rood Lane Medical Centre
FENCHST EC3M 13 J6
Rooks Heath High School
RYLN/HDSTN HA2 .... 79 G3
Roosevelt Memorial
MYFR/PKLN W1K 10 B6
Ropery Business Park
CHARL SE7 .... 124 C2
Rosary Priory High School
BUSH WD23 .... 43 L1
Rosary RC Junior School
HEST TW5 .... 114 F4
Roseberry Industrial Park
TOTM N17 .... 68 B3
Rosebery School
EPSOM KT18 .... 180 C7
Rose Bruford College
DEPT SE8 .... 123 G4
Rose Bruford College of
Speech & Drama
BFN/LL DA15 .... 144 B5
Roselands Clinic
NWMAL KT3 .... 153 J7
Rosemary School
NWMAL KT3 .... 153 J7
Rosemary Surgery
CLKNW EC1R 6 C9
Rosemary Surgery
FNCH N3 .... 65 H3
Rose Mcandrew Clinic
BRXN/ST SW9 .... 120 F7
Rosemead Preparatory School
DUL SE21 .... 139 J6
Rosendale Junior &
Infant School
DUL SE21 .... 139 J4
The Rose Street Clinic
LSQ/SEVD WC2H 11 J6
Rose Theatre Exhibition
STHWK SE1 .... 12 F8
Rosetta Primary School
CAN/RD E16 .... 106 B4
Rosewood Medical Centre
HCH RM12 .... 92 B5
Rosh Pinah School
EDGE HA8 .... 45 H4
Rosslyn Park
Rugbyfootball Club
PUT/ROE SW15 .... 135 M1
Rotherhithe Civic Centre
BERM/RHTH SE16 .... 104 C8
Rotherhithe Junior & Infant
School
BERM/RHTH SE16 .... 122 C2
Rotunda Museum
CHARL SE7 .... 124 F3
The Roundhouse Theatre
CAMTN NW1 .... 4 A1
Roundwood Park Medical Centre
WLSDN NW10 .... 82 A7
Rowan High School
CLAP SW4 .... 138 D3
Rowan High School
MTCM CR4 .... 156 C5
Rowans School
RYNPK SW20 .... 154 A3
The Rowans Surgery
STRHM/NOR SW16 .... 156 C4
Rowhill School
RDART DA2 .... 146 C8
Rowley Industrial Park
ACT W3 .... 117 H1
Roxbourne First School
RSLP HA4 .... 78 E2
Roxbourne Medical Centre
RYLN/HDSTN HA2 .... 79 H2
Roxeth First & Middle School
RYLN/HDSTN HA2 .... 79 K2
Roxeth Mead School
RYLN/HDSTN HA2 .... 79 K2
Royal Academy of Arts
CONDST W1S 10 E7
Royal Air Force Museum
CDALE/KGS NW9 .... 64 A3
Royal Albert Hall
SKENS SW7 .... 15 G2

Royal Army Medical College
WEST SW1P 17 H7
Royal Artillery Museums
WOOL/PLUM SE18 .... 125 G5
Royal Borough of Kingston
Upon Thames Health Clinic
NWMAL KT3 .... 153 J6
Royal Brompton & National Heart
Hospitals
CHEL SW3 .... 15 J7
Royal College of Anaesthetists
RSQ WC1B 11 J2
Royal College of Art
SKENS SW7 .... 14 F2
Royal College of Music
SHB W12 .... 118 A1
Royal College of Music
SKENS SW7 .... 15 G3
Royal College of Nursing
CAMTN NW1 .... 4 F9
Royal College of Nursing
IS N1 .... 6 C4
Royal College of Obstetricians &
Gynaecologists
CAMTN NW1 .... 3 L9
Royal College of
Ophthalmologists
CAMTN NW1 .... 10 A1
Royal College of
Paediatrics & Child Health
GTPST W1W 10 D2
The Royal College of Pathology
STJS SW1Y 10 F9
Royal College of Physicians
CAMTN NW1 .... 4 C9
Royal Courts of Justice
LINN WC2A 11 M5
Royal Court Theatre
BGVA SW1W 16 A6
Royal Court Young
Peoples Theatre
NKENS W10 .... 100 E4
Royal Danish Embassy
KTBR SW1X 15 L3
Royal Docks Medical Centre
EHAM E6 .... 107 G5
Royal Embassy of Saudi Arabia
MYFR/PICC W1J 10 C8
Royal Festival Hall
STHWK SE1 .... 11 L8
Royal Free Hampstead NHS Trust
HAMP NW3 .... 83 L5
Royal Free Hospital & School of
Medicine
HAMP NW3 .... 83 L5
Royal Gallery
CHST BR7 .... 161 J3
Royal Geographical Soc
SKENS SW7 .... 15 G2
Royal Horticultural Society
New Hall
WEST SW1P 17 G4
Royal Hospital
RCH/KEW TW9 .... 116 D8
Royal Hospital Chelsea
CHEL SW3 .... 16 A9
Royal Hospital for
Neuro-disability
PUT/ROE SW15 .... 136 E3
Royal Hospital for
Neuro-disability
PUT/ROE SW15 .... 136 B4
Royal Hospital & Home
PUT/ROE SW15 .... 136 B4
The Royal Hospitals NHS Trust
STBT EC1A 12 D4
Royal Institute
MYFR/PICC W1J 10 D7
Royal Kent First & Middle School
LHD/OX KT22 .... 178 C7
Royal Liberty School
GPK RM2 .... 74 C4
The Royal London Estate
TOTM N17 .... 68 B1
Royal London Hospital
NHS Trust
BETH E2 .... 104 C1
The Royal London Hospital
BOW E3 .... 104 F2
The Royal London Hospital
WCHPL E1 .... 104 A5
The Royal London Hospital
A & E
WCHPL E1 .... 104 B4
Royal Marsden Hospital
BELMT SM2 .... 182 C3
Royal Marsden Hospital
CHEL SW3 .... 15 H7
The Royal Masonic School
RKW/CH/CXG WD3 .... 40 D1
The Royal Mews
WHALL SW1A 16 D3
Royal Mint Court
TWRH EC3N 13 M7
Royal National Orthopaedic
STAN HA7 .... 44 C4
Royal National Orthopaedic
Hospital Trust
GTPST W1W 10 D1
Royal National Theatre
BRXN/ST SW9 .... 121 G5
Royal National Theatre
STHWK SE1 .... 12 C8
Royal National Theatre Studio
STHWK SE1 .... 18 B1
Royal National Throat Nose & Ear
Hospital
FSBYW WC1X 5 L7
Royal Naval College
GNWCH SE10 .... 123 K4
Royal Navy
POP/IOD E14 .... 104 C6
Royal Navy & Royal Marines
CHCR WC2N 11 J7
Royal Norwegian Embassy
KTBR SW1X 16 B3
Royal Opera House
COVGDN WC2E 11 K5

Royal Park Primary School
SCUP DA14 .... 144 E7
The Royal School Hampstead
HAMP NW3 .... 83 K4
Royal Society of Arts
CHCR WC2N 11 K7
Royal Society of Medicine
CAVSQ/HST W1G 10 C4
Royal Thai Embassy
SKENS SW7 .... 14 F4
Royal Veterinary College
BRKMPK AL9 .... 22 D1
Royal Victoria Docks
Watersports Centre
CAN/RD E16 .... 106 A6
Royston Primary School
BECK BR3 .... 158 D4
R T R Healthcare Primary Care
PUT/ROE SW15 .... 136 A3
Rudolph Steiner Hall
CAMTN NW1 .... 3 L9
Rufus Business Centre
WAND/EARL SW18 .... 137 H6
Ruislip Manor Football Club
RSLP HA4 .... 77 M2
Ruislip Rugby Football Club
RSLP HA4 .... 77 L2
Rushcroft Secondary School
CHING E4 .... 69 H1
Rushey Green Group Practice
CAT SE6 .... 141 G5
Rush Green School
ROMW/RG RM7 .... 91 K1
Rush Green Surgery
ROMW/RG RM7 .... 91 K2
Rushmore Junior School
CLPT E5 .... 86 D4
Ruskin House School
HNHL SE24 .... 139 J1
The Russell JMI School
RCHPK/HAM TW10 .... 134 D6
The Russell School
RCHPK/HAM TW10 .... 134 D5
Russet House School
EN EN1 .... 37 H4
Russian Arts Gallery
ACT W3 .... 99 G3
Rutland House Surgery
MUSWH N10 .... 66 B3
Rutlish School
RYNPK SW20 .... 154 F1
Ruxley Corner Industrial Estate
SCUP DA14 .... 162 D2
Ruxley Manor School
ELTH/MOT SE9 .... 143 G8
Ryde College
WATW WD18 .... 41 L1
Rydens County Senior School
WOT/HER KT12 .... 165 J6
Ryefield Primary School
HGDN/ICK UB10 .... 77 K8
Ryelands Primary School
SNWD SE25 .... 158 B8
Rylett Road Surgery
SHB W12 .... 117 M1
Saatchi Gallery
KIL/WHAMP NW6 .... 2 D4
Saatchi Synagogue
KIL/WHAMP NW6 .... 2 C5
Sackville Galleries
SAND/SEL CR2 .... 184 C2
Sacred Heart High School
HMSMTH W6 .... 118 C2
Sacred Heart Junior Middle &
Infant School
OXHEY WD19 .... 42 F1
Sacred Heart Junior School
HMSMTH W6 .... 118 D2
The Sacred Heart of Mary RC
School
UPMR RM14 .... 93 J6
Sacred Heart RC Junior & Infant
School
RSLP HA4 .... 77 L2
Sacred Heart RC Junior & Middle
School
BTSEA SW11 .... 119 L8
Sacred Heart RC Primary School
NWMAL KT3 .... 154 A7
Sacred Heart RC School
BTSEA SW11 .... 119 L6
Sacred Heart RC School
KTN/HRWW/W HA3 .... 61 L3
Sacred Heart RC School
TEDD TW11 .... 152 B8
Sacred Heart RC Secondary
School
CMBW SE5 .... 121 J6
Sacred Heart School
HOLWY N7 .... 84 E4
Saddlers Hall
CITYW EC2V 12 E5
Sadlers Wells Theatre
CLKNW EC1R 6 B7
Saffron Green First School
BORE WD6 .... 32 D7
Sai Medical Centre
POP/IOD E14 .... 105 J7
St Agathas RC Primary School
KUTN/CMB KT2 .... 152 E2
St Agnes Primary School
BOW E3 .... 105 G2
St Agnes RC Primary School
CRICK NW2 .... 82 D3
St Aidans Primary School
FSBYPK N4 .... 67 G8
St Aidans RC Primary School
IL IG1 .... 89 K1
St Albans CP School
DART DA1 .... 146 F2
St Albans Health Clinic
KTTN NW5 .... 84 A3
St Albans Junior & Infant RC
School
PECK SE15 .... 121 M6
St Albans Primary School
E/WMO/HCT KT8 .... 151 H2

St Albans RC Church & School
  Presbytery
  HCH RM12 .... 92 A5
St Albans RC School
  RAIN RM13 .... 92 B7
St Albans School
  FSBYW WC1X 12 A2
St Aloysius College
  HGT N6 .... 84 C1
St Aloysius RC Infant School
  CAMTN NW1 .... 5 G7
St Andrews C of E
  Primary School
  BRXN/ST SW9 .... 120 F7
St Andrews C of E
  Primary School
  TRDG/WHET N20 .... 46 F4
St Andrews C of E
  Primary School
  UX/CGN UB8 .... 76 D8
St Andrews C of E School
  EN EN1 .... 36 D5
St Andrews Greek School
  CAMTN NW1 .... 84 B6
St Andrews Hospital
  BOW E3 .... 105 H3
St Andrews Primary School
  STHGT/OAK N14 .... 48 D3
St Andrews RC School
  STRHM/NOR SW16 .... 156 E1
St Andrews School
  CROY/NA CR0 .... 172 B5
St Andrews School
  IS N1 .... 5 M3
St Andrews School
  RYLN/HDSTN HA2 .... 61 H6
St Andrews School
  WLSDN NW10 .... 82 B7
St Angelas RC Secondary School
  FSTGT E7 .... 88 B6
St Angelo Preparatory School
  EA W5 .... 98 D4
St Annes Catholic School for
  Girls
  PLMGR N13 .... 49 G6
St Annes Convent School
  EN EN1 .... 36 D7
St Annes Primary School
  STWL/WRAY TW19 .... 130 E4
St Annes RC Primary School
  LBTH SE11 .... 17 L9
St Annes School
  MRDN SM4 .... 155 H8
St Anns C of E Primary School
  WAND/EARL SW18 .... 137 H2
St Ann's General Hospital
  SEVS/STOTM N15 .... 67 J6
St Anns Primary School
  SEVS/STOTM N15 .... 67 K6
St Anns School
  HNWL W7 .... 97 L7
St Ann's Shopping Centre
  HRW HA1 .... 61 L7
St Anselms RC Primary School
  DART DA1 .... 147 G2
St Anselms RC School
  NWDGN UB2 .... 114 F1
St Anselms School
  HRW HA1 .... 61 L8
St Anslems RC Primary School
  TOOT SW17 .... 138 A7
St Anthony RC School
  PGE/AN SE20 .... 158 B4
St Anthonys Hospital
  WPK KT4 .... 169 K3
St Anthonys RC Junior School
  WATW WD18 .... 28 E8
St Antonys RC Primary School
  FSTGT E7 .... 88 A7
St Antonys RC Primary School
  WFD IG8 .... 52 A6
St Aubyns School
  WFD IG8 .... 69 M1
St Augustine Junior School
  BELV DA17 .... 126 F2
St Augustine Primary School
  BELV DA17 .... 126 F1
St Augustines C of E School
  KIL/WHAMP NW6 .... 2 B6
St Augustines Primary School
  FUL/PGN SW6 .... 118 E4
St Augustines RC Junior School
  GNTH/NBYPK IG2 .... 71 H6
St Augustines R C Primary
  School
  CAT SE6 .... 159 H1
St Barnabas C of E School
  BGVA SW1W 16 B7
St Barnabas & St Philips C of E
  Primary School
  KENS W8 .... 14 A4
St Bartholomews Hospital
  STBT EC1A 12 D3
St Bartholomews Hospital
  SWLY BR8 .... 163 M6
St Bartholomew's Medical
  School
  FARR EC1M 12 D1
St Bartholomews Primary School
  SYD SE26 .... 140 C8
St Bartholomews RC Primary
  School
  SWLY BR8 .... 163 L6
St Bartholomew's the Great
  STBT EC1A 12 D3
St Barts Hospital Sports Ground
  CHST BR7 .... 161 L2
St Bedes Primary School
  BAL SW12 .... 138 D5
St Bedes RC School
  CHDH RM6 .... 72 C6
St Benedicts Junior RC School
  EA W5 .... 98 C4
St Benedicts School
  EA W5 .... 98 D4
St Bernadettes RC First & Middle
  School
  KTN/HRWW/W HA3 .... 62 F5

St Bernadettes RC School
  HGDN/ICK UB10 .... 77 H8
St Bonaventures RC
  Secondary School
  FSTGT E7 .... 88 A7
St Boniface RC School
  TOOT SW17 .... 155 L1
St Catherine of Siena RC School
  GSTN WD25 .... 21 G3
St Catherines RC Girls School
  BXLYHS DA6 .... 145 J6
St Catherines RC Middle School
  NWMAL KT3 .... 154 C5
St Catherines RC Primary School
  WDR/YW UB7 .... 94 B4
St Catherines School
  TWK TW1 .... 133 M6
St Cecilias RC School
  WPK KT4 .... 169 K4
St Chads RC Primary School
  SNWD SE25 .... 157 H1
St Charles Catholic Sixth Form
  College
  NKENS W10 .... 100 D4
St Charles Hospital
  NKENS W10 .... 100 D4
St Charles RC Primary School
  WEY KT13 .... 164 A5
St Christophers School
  BECK BR3 .... 159 J5
St Christophers School
  EPSOM KT18 .... 180 E7
St Christophers School
  WBLY HA9 .... 80 F3
St Christophor House
  STHWK SE1 .... 12 E8
St Clare Business Park
  HPTN TW12 .... 151 J2
St Clements School
  EW KT17 .... 180 F2
St Columbas RC Boys School
  BXLYHS DA6 .... 145 H2
St Cuthbert with St. Mattias
  School
  ECT SW5 .... 14 B7
St Davids College
  WWKM BR4 .... 174 B2
St Davids Group Practise
  FELT TW13 .... 132 A6
St Davids Health Centre
  STWL/WRAY TW19 .... 130 D4
St Davids School
  ASHF TW15 .... 130 F7
St Davids School
  PUR/KEN CR8 .... 183 M4
St Dominics Primary School
  HAMP NW3 .... 83 M5
St Dominics RC Junior &
  Infant School
  HOM E9 .... 86 D6
St Dominics Sixth Form College
  HRW HA1 .... 79 L2
St Dunstans C of E Primary
  School
  CHEAM SM3 .... 181 K1
St Dunstans College
  CAT SE6 .... 140 F4
St Edmunds RC Primary School
  POP/IOD E14 .... 123 G2
St Edmunds RC Primary School
  WHTN TW2 .... 133 H4
St Edmunds RC School
  ED N9 .... 50 B3
St Edwards C of E
  Comprehensive School
  CHDH RM6 .... 73 C7
St Edwards C of E Primary School
  ROM RM1 .... 73 K4
St Edwards RC JMI School
  STJWD NW8 .... 9 J1
St Elizabeths RC School
  RCHPK/HAM TW10 .... 134 F2
St Elpheges RC School
  WLGTN SM6 .... 171 L8
St Faiths C of E School
  WAND/EARL SW18 .... 137 J2
St Fidelis RC Primary School
  ERITH DA8 .... 127 J4
St Francesca Cabrini Primary
  School
  FSTH SE23 .... 140 C3
St Francis Xavier Sixth Form
  College
  BAL SW12 .... 138 B3
St George's Cathedral
  STHWK SE1 .... 18 B3
St Georges C of E Primary School
  VX/NE SW8 .... 120 C5
St Georges College
  HOLWY N7 .... 85 G3
St Georges Elizabethan Theatre
  HOLWY N7 .... 84 D4
St Georges Hospital
  HCH RM12 .... 92 E4
St Georges Hospital
  TOOT SW17 .... 137 K8
St Georges Industrial Estate
  KUTN/CMB KT2 .... 152 D1
St Georges Industrial Estate
  WDGN N22 .... 67 H1
St Georges Medical Centre
  HDN NW4 .... 64 B4
St Georges RC First & Middle
  School
  HRW HA1 .... 79 M3
St Georges RC Primary School
  ENC/FH EN2 .... 36 D5
St Georges RC Primary School
  STHWK SE1 .... 18 C2
St Georges RC Secondary School
  KIL/WHAMP NW6 .... 2 D6
St Georges School
  BMLY BR1 .... 160 C5
St Gildas RC Junior School
  CEND/HSY/T N8 .... 66 E8
St Giles C of E Primary School
  POTB/CUF EN6 .... 22 A5

St Giles C of E Primary School
  POTB/CUF EN6 .... 22 B6
St Giles College London Central
  RSQ WC1B 11 J2
St Giles School
  CROY/NA CR0 .... 172 B8
St Gregorys RC First & Middle
  School
  EA W5 .... 98 D3
St Gregorys RC High School
  KTN/HRWW/W HA3 .... 62 D6
St Helens College
  HGDN/ICK UB10 .... 77 G7
St Helens RC Primary School
  PLSTW E13 .... 105 M3
St Helens School
  BRXN/ST SW9 .... 121 G8
St Helens School
  NTHWD HA6 .... 41 L8
St Ignatius College
  EN EN1 .... 37 G2
St Ignatius Primary School
  SEVS/STOTM N15 .... 67 M7
St Ignatius RC Primary School
  SUN TW16 .... 150 A4
St James C of E Junior School
  FSTGT E7 .... 87 M5
St James C of E Primary School
  PEND EN3 .... 37 J5
St James C of E Primary School
  WEY KT13 .... 164 C5
St James Hatcham C of E School
  NWCR SE14 .... 122 E6
St James Medical Centre
  CROY/NA CR0 .... 172 D2
St James RC Primary School
  HAYES BR2 .... 161 H8
St James School
  MUSWH N10 .... 66 A5
St James's Health Centre
  WALTH E17 .... 68 E6
St James's Palace
  WHALL SW1A 10 F9
St James's School
  WHTN TW2 .... 133 L7
St James the Great School
  THHTH CR7 .... 157 H5
St Joan of Arc RC School
  RKW/CH/CXG WD3 .... 40 E2
St John Baptist School
  BMLY BR1 .... 141 J8
St John Fisher RC Primary
  School
  ERITHM DA18 .... 126 E1
St John Fisher RC Primary
  School
  NWMAL KT3 .... 154 C8
St John Fisher School
  GFD/PVL UB6 .... 98 C2
St John of Jerusalem C of E
  Primary School
  HOM E9 .... 86 C7
St John Rigby School
  WWKM BR4 .... 174 D6
St John & James School
  UED N18 .... 49 M7
St Johns C of E First School
  STAN HA7 .... 44 A6
St Johns C of E Infant School
  HDN NW4 .... 64 B6
St Johns C of E Junior & Infant
  School
  ENC/FH EN2 .... 36 E1
St Johns C of E Middle School
  STAN HA7 .... 44 A6
St Johns C of E Primary School
  ARCH N19 .... 84 D3
St Johns C of E Primary School
  BETH E2 .... 104 B1
St Johns C of E Primary School
  BKHH IG9 .... 52 B3
St Johns C of E Primary School
  FBAR/BDGN N11 .... 47 M6
St John's C of E Primary School
  FUL/PGN SW6 .... 118 E6
St Johns C of E Primary School
  TRDG/WHET N20 .... 47 J4
St Johns C of E School
  CDALE/KGS NW9 .... 63 L6
St John's Concert Hall
  WEST SW1P 17 J4
St John's Hospital
  SOHO/SHAV W1D 11 G6
St John's Hospital Day Centre
  BTSEA SW11 .... 137 K1
St Johns Primary School
  IS N1 .... 7 K4
St Johns Primary School
  KUT KT1 .... 152 E6
St Johns RC Junior Middle &
  Infant School
  RKW/CH/CXG WD3 .... 40 B3
St Johns RC Primary School
  BERM/RHTH SE16 .... 104 E8
St Johns School
  BRXN/ST SW9 .... 121 G7
St Johns School
  ENC/FH EN2 .... 36 A5
St Johns School
  HBRY N5 .... 85 H3
St Johns School
  NTHWD HA6 .... 42 B8
St Johns Special School
  WFD IG8 .... 53 G7
St Johns Way Medical Centre
  ARCH N19 .... 84 D1
St Johns Wood Synagogue
  STJWD NW8 .... 2 F6
St John the Divine Primary School
  CMBW SE5 .... 121 H5
St John Vianney RC School
  SEVS/STOTM N15 .... 67 H5
St Joseph RC School
  DART DA1 .... 145 L1
St Josephs Catholic Primary
  School
  EPSOM KT18 .... 180 C7

St Joseph School
  DAGW RM9 .... 90 F4
St Josephs College
  STRHM/NOR SW16 .... 157 H2
St Josephs Infant School
  CMBW SE5 .... 121 J5
St Josephs Infant School
  HDN NW4 .... 64 B5
St Josephs Infant School
  NRWD SE19 .... 157 J2
St Josephs Junior School
  HDN NW4 .... 64 B5
St Josephs Junior School
  WBLY HA9 .... 80 F5
St Josephs Primary School
  ARCH N19 .... 84 B1
St Josephs Primary School
  BARK IG11 .... 89 J8
St Josephs Primary School
  PUT/ROE SW15 .... 137 G2
St Josephs RC JMI School
  CHES/WCR EN8 .... 26 E6
St Josephs RC Junior School
  LEY E10 .... 87 H1
St Josephs RC Junior School
  NRWD SE19 .... 157 J2
St Josephs RC Primary School
  BERM/RHTH SE16 .... 122 C1
St Josephs RC Primary School
  BMLY BR1 .... 160 C3
St Josephs RC Primary School
  GNWCH SE10 .... 123 L3
St Josephs RC Primary School
  HNWL W7 .... 97 L7
St Josephs RC Primary School
  HOL/ALD WC2B 11 K4
St Josephs RC Primary School
  KUT KT1 .... 152 E5
St Josephs RC Primary School
  MV/WKIL W9 .... 2 E8
St Josephs RC Primary School
  STHWK SE1 .... 18 F1
St Josephs RC School
  DEPT SE8 .... 123 G5
St Josephs RC School
  OXHEY WD19 .... 42 B5
St Josephs RC School
  WBLY HA9 .... 80 F5
St Josephs School
  KTN/HRWW/W HA3 .... 62 A3
St Josephs School
  UPMR RM14 .... 93 H2
St Lawrence Business Centre
  FELT TW13 .... 132 B6
St Lawrence Catholic School
  FELT TW13 .... 132 B5
St Lawrence C of E Junior
  School
  E/WMO/HCT KT8 .... 151 K6
St Lawrence C of E Junior
  School
  UX/CGN UB8 .... 94 C4
St Lawrence C of E Primary
  WAB EN9 .... 27 M6
St Leonards C of E Primary
  School
  STRHM/NOR SW16 .... 156 D1
St Leonards Hospital
  IS N1 .... 7 K5
St Lukes C of E Primary School
  CAN/RD E16 .... 105 M5
St Lukes C of E Primary School
  KUTN/CMB KT2 .... 152 F4
St Lukes C of E Primary School
  MV/WKIL W9 .... 100 F2
St Luke's Health Centre
  CAN/RD E16 .... 105 M5
St Lukes Primary School
  FSBYE EC1V 6 F8
St Lukes Primary School
  POP/IOD E14 .... 123 K2
St Lukes School
  THHTH CR7 .... 157 G7
St Lukes Woodside Hospital
  MUSWH N10 .... 66 A5
St Margaret Clitherow RC Primary
  School
  THMD SE28 .... 108 B7
St Margaret Clitherow RC Primary
  School
  WLSDN NW10 .... 81 K3
St Margarets C of E Primary
  School
  BARK IG11 .... 89 J8
St Margarets Medical Practice
  TWK TW1 .... 134 B2
St Margarets School
  BUSH WD23 .... 43 G2
St Margarets School
  HAMP NW3 .... 83 H4
St Marks C of E School
  LBTH SE11 .... 17 M9
St Marks C of E School
  SNWD SE25 .... 158 A7
St Marks Medical Centre
  WOOL/PLUM SE18 .... 125 H4
St Marks Primary School
  ARCH N19 .... 84 E2
St Marks Primary School
  HAYES BR2 .... 160 A6
St Marks Primary School
  MTCM CR4 .... 155 M5
St Marks Primary School
  STHL UB1 .... 97 L8
St Marks RC School
  HSLW TW3 .... 114 F8
St Marthas Convent
  Senior School
  EBAR EN4 .... 34 A4
St Martin In the Fields
  High School
  BRXS/STRHM SW2 .... 139 H5
St Martin of Porres RC Primary
  School
  FBAR/BDGN N11 .... 48 C8
St Martins C of E Junior School
  EPSOM KT18 .... 180 D8

St Martins Medical Centre
  RSLP HA4 .... 59 L8
St Martins RC Junior School
  EDGE HA8 .... 45 J8
St Martins RC School
  MLHL NW7 .... 45 L7
St Martins School
  NTHWD HA6 .... 41 K7
St Martins School of Art
  SOHO/SHAV W1D 11 H5
St Martins Theatre
  LSQ/SEVD WC2H 11 H6
St Mary Abbots C of E
  Primary School
  KENS W8 .... 14 B2
St Mary Magdalene C of E
  Primary School
  PECK SE15 .... 122 B7
St Mary Magdalene C of E School
  HOLWY N7 .... 85 G6
St Mary Magdalens School
  BROCKY SE4 .... 140 E1
St Mary Magdalens RC Junior
  School
  CRICK NW2 .... 82 B6
St Mary Magdalines Primary
  School
  MV/WKIL W9 .... 8 C1
St Mary Magdelens Primary
  School
  MORT/ESHN SW14 .... 117 K8
St Mary of the Angels RC
  Primary School
  BAY/PAD W2 .... 8 A4
St Marys Abbey
  MLHL NW7 .... 46 A5
St Mary & St Josephs RC School
  SCUP DA14 .... 161 M1
St Mary & St Pancras Primary
  School
  CAMTN NW1 .... 5 G6
St Mary Church of England High
  School
  HDN NW4 .... 64 C4
St Marys C of E JMI School
  EBAR EN4 .... 47 L1
St Marys C of E Junior School
  CEND/HSY/T N8 .... 66 E5
St Marys C of E Primary School
  CHSGTN KT9 .... 167 L8
St Marys C of E Primary School
  IS N1 .... 6 D2
St Marys C of E Primary School
  SWLY BR8 .... 163 L7
St Marys C of E Primary School
  THDIT KT7 .... 167 H3
St Marys C of E Primary School
  WLSDN NW10 .... 81 L6
St Marys C of E School
  LEW SE13 .... 141 H2
St Marys C of E School
  PUT/ROE SW15 .... 118 D8
St Marys C of E School
  TWK TW1 .... 134 A4
St Marys Greek Cathedral
  WDGN N22 .... 66 F2
St Marys Hare Park School
  GPK RM2 .... 74 C4
St Marys High School
  CHESW EN7 .... 26 B3
St Marys Hospital
  BAY/PAD W2 .... 9 H4
St Marys Infant School
  CAR SM5 .... 170 E6
St Mary's Infant School
  SEVS/STOTM N15 .... 67 K6
St Marys Primary School
  BECK BR3 .... 159 J3
St Marys Primary School
  FNCH N3 .... 64 F2
St Marys Primary School
  WKENS W14 .... 118 D1
St Marys Primary School
  WOOL/PLUM SE18 .... 125 G2
St Marys RC Church & School
  HCH RM12 .... 92 A1
St Marys RC Infant School
  CROY/NA CR0 .... 172 D3
St Marys RC Junior School
  CAR SM5 .... 170 F6
St Marys RC Junior School
  SEVS/STOTM N15 .... 67 K7
St Marys RC Junior School
  WALTH E17 .... 69 J4
St Marys RC Primary School
  CHING E4 .... 51 K3
St Marys RC Primary School
  CLAP SW4 .... 138 C2
St Marys RC Primary School
  KIL/WHAMP NW6 .... 2 A5
St Marys RC Primary School
  PEND EN3 .... 37 K7
St Mary's RC Primary School
  VX/NE SW8 .... 120 B6
St Marys RC Primary School
  WIM/MER SW19 .... 155 G3
St Marys RC School
  ELTH/MOT SE9 .... 143 G2
St Marys & St Peters
  C of E Primary School
  TEDD TW11 .... 151 M1
St Marys School
  CEND/HSY/T N8 .... 66 F6
St Marys School
  HAMP NW3 .... 83 J5
St Mary's School
  STNW/STAM N16 .... 85 L2
St Marys School
  UX/CGN UB8 .... 76 C8
St Marys University College
  TWK TW1 .... 133 M7
St Matthews C of E
  Primary School
  PEND EN3 .... 37 J8
St Matthews C of E
  Primary School
  SURB KT6 .... 167 L2

St Matthews C of E
Primary School
WDR/YW UB7 .... 94 D7
St Matthews School
WEST SW1P 17 H4
St Matthias C of E School
STNW/STAM N16 .... 85 L5
St Matthias Primary School
BETH E2 .... 7 M9
St Maurs School
WEY KT13 .... 164 B5
St Meryl Junior Middle &
Infant School
OXHEY WD19 .... 42 E5
St Michael at Bowes C of E
Junior Mixed School
PLMGR N13 .... 49 G8
St Michaels C of E Aided
Primary School Hall
WELL DA16 .... 126 C6
St Michaels C of E Junior &
Infant School
WDGN N22 .... 66 F2
St Michael's C of E School
SYD SE26 .... 140 E8
St Michaels Grammar School
NFNCH/WDSP N12 .... 47 H7
St Michaels Junior & Infant
School
ENC/FH EN2 .... 36 C5
St Michaels RC School
ASHF TW15 .... 149 G1
St Michaels RC School
BERM/RHTH SE16 .... 104 A8
St Michaels RC School
GSTN WD25 .... 21 K5
St Michaels School
HGT N6 .... 66 A8
St Michaels School
HSLWW TW4 .... 114 F8
St Michael's School
WAND/EARL SW18 .... 136 F4
St Monicas RC Primary School
STHGT/OAK N14 .... 48 E5
St Nicholas C of E JMI School
SHPTN TW17 .... 164 B1
St Nicholas School
CHST BR7 .... 161 J3
St Nicholas School
PUR/KEN CR8 .... 183 M6
St Nicks Art Gallery
SUT SM1 .... 170 B7
St Olaves Grammar School
ORP BR6 .... 177 H5
St Olaves Preparatory School
ELTH/MOT SE9 .... 143 H6
St Osmunds RC Primary School
BARN SW13 .... 117 M4
St Pancras Hospital
CAMTN NW1 .... 5 G4
St Pancras International
Youth Hostel
CAMTN NW1 .... 5 H7
St Patricks Church School
STHWK SE1 .... 12 A9
St Patricks Infants School
WAP E1W 104 B7
St Patricks Primary School
KTTN NW5 .... 84 B6
St Patricks RC Junior &
Infant School
WALTH E17 .... 68 C5
St Patricks RC Junior School
WAP E1W 104 B7
St Patricks RC School
WOOL/PLUM SE18 .... 125 K2
St Patricks School
ROMW/RG RM7 .... 73 H2
St Paulinus C of E
Primary School
DART DA1 .... 145 L1
St Pauls Cathedral
STP EC4M 12 C5
St Pauls Catholic School
SUN TW16 .... 150 A4
St Pauls Choir School
STP EC4M 12 C5
St Pauls C of E Junior School
KUTN/CMB KT2 .... 153 G3
St Pauls C of E Primary School
BTFD TW8 .... 116 D4
St Pauls C of E Primary School
FBAR/BDGN N11 .... 48 A7
St Pauls C of E Primary School
HAMP NW3 .... 3 K2
St Pauls C of E Primary School
WALW SE17 .... 18 E8
St Pauls C of E Primary School
WAP E1W 104 A6
St Pauls C of E Primary School
WCHMH N21 .... 49 H2
St Pauls Cray C of E
Primary School
STMC/STPC BR5 .... 162 C6
St Pauls Cray Health Clinic
STMC/STPC BR5 .... 162 A5
St Pauls Girls School
HMSMTH W6 .... 118 D2
St Pauls Primary School
HMSMTH W6 .... 118 C3
St Pauls Primary School
KGLGY WD4 .... 20 C7
St Pauls Primary School
MLHL NW7 .... 46 B6
St Pauls RC Primary School
ESH/CLAY KT10 .... 166 E2
St Pauls RC Primary School
WDGN N22 .... 66 F3
St Pauls RC Secondary School
WOOL/PLUM SE18 .... 125 M4
St Pauls Road Medical Centre
IS N1 .... 85 H6
St Pauls School
BARN SW13 .... 118 A3
St Pauls School
CHSGTN KT9 .... 167 L6
St Pauls Way Community School
BOW E3 .... 105 G4

St Pauls Westminster Cathedral
WEST SW1P 16 E4
St Pauls with St Michaels C of E
Primary School
HACK E8 .... 86 A8
St Paul with St Luke C of E
Primary School
BOW E3 .... 104 F4
St Paul with St Luke C of E
Primary School
POP/IOD E14 .... 104 F4
St Peter Chanel RC School
SCUP DA14 .... 162 C1
St Peter & Paul RC
Primary School
IL IG1 .... 89 K3
St Peter & St Paul RC
Primary School
MTCM CR4 .... 155 M7
St Peter's Church of England
Primary School
HMSMTH W6 .... 118 A3
St Peters C of E Primary School
BRW CM14 .... 57 L4
St Peters C of E Primary School
MV/WKIL W9 .... 8 A1
St Peters C of E Primary School
WALW SE17 .... 19 G8
St Peter's Hospital
COVGDN WC2E 11 K6
St Peters Junior Middle & Infant
School
RKW/CH/CXG WD3 .... 40 B3
St Peters Primary School
WAP E1W 104 C7
St Peters RC Primary School
ROM RM1 .... 73 K4
St Peters RC Primary School
WOOL/PLUM SE18 .... 125 H3
St Peters RC School
DAGW RM9 .... 90 F8
St Peters School
SAND/SEL CR2 .... 172 D8
St Peters Street Medical Practice
IS N1 .... 6 C4
St Philips School
CHSGTN KT9 .... 167 K8
St Philips School
SKENS SW7 .... 14 F6
St Phillips Infant School
SYD SE26 .... 140 B8
St Philomenas RC Primary
School
STMC/STPC BR5 .... 177 J2
St Philomenas School
CAR SM5 .... 170 E7
St Quintins Health Centre
NKENS W10 .... 100 C4
St Raphaels Hospice
WPK KT4 .... 169 K4
St Raphaels School
NTHLT UB5 .... 96 B1
St Raphaels Way Medical Centre
WBLY HA9 .... 81 J5
St Richards with St. Andrews
C of E Primary School
RCHPK/HAM TW10 .... 134 B7
St Robert Southwell RC Primary
School
CDALE/KGS NW9 .... 63 J7
St Saviours Catholic Primary
School
LEW SE13 .... 141 J1
St Saviours C of E Infant School
EA W5 .... 98 D6
St Saviours C of E Primary School
HNHL SE24 .... 121 J8
St Saviours C of E Primary School
MV/WKIL W9 .... 8 D1
St Saviours C of E Primary School
POP/IOD E14 .... 105 H4
St Scholasticas RC Junior Middle &
Infant School
STNW/STAM N16 .... 86 A3
St Stephens C of E Junior School
TWK TW1 .... 134 A3
St Stephens C of E Primary School
BAY/PAD W2 .... 8 B3
St Stephens C of E Primary School
SHB W12 .... 100 B7
St Stephens RC Primary School
WELL DA16 .... 126 A7
St Swithun Wells RC Primary School
RSLP HA4 .... 78 D3
St Teresa RC Primary School
BCTR RM8 .... 90 C4
St Teresas RC School
KTN/HRWW/W HA3 .... 61 J2
St Theresas Primary School
FNCH N3 .... 65 G4
St Thomas Childrens Day Hospital
LBTH SE11 .... 17 M7
St Thomas C of E Primary School
STNW/STAM N16 .... 85 M1
St Thomas Hospital Operation Theatre
STHWK SE1 .... 13 H9
St Thomas More RC Primary School
BXLYHN DA7 .... 126 F7
St Thomas More RC Primary School
ELTH/MOT SE9 .... 124 E8
St Thomas More RC School
ELTH/MOT SE9 .... 143 G3
St Thomas More School
WDGN N22 .... 66 F1
St Thomas of Canterbury RC Middle
School
MTCM CR4 .... 156 A6
St Thomas of Canterbury RC
Primary School
FUL/PGN SW6 .... 118 F5
St Thomas's Hospital
STHWK SE1 .... 17 L3
St Thomas the Apostle College
PECK SE15 .... 122 C6
St Ursulas Convent School
GNWCH SE10 .... 123 K5
St Ursulas Junior School
HARH RM3 .... 56 B8

St Vincents Hospital
RSLP HA4 .... 59 L4
St Vincents Primary School
ELTH/MOT SE9 .... 142 E8
St Vincents RC Primary School
ACT W3 .... 99 H6
St Vincents RC Primary School
BCTR RM8 .... 90 C2
St Vincents RC Primary School
MHST W1U 10 A3
St Vincents RC Primary School
MLHL NW7 .... 46 C6
St Vincent & the Grenadines High
Comm
KENS W8 .... 14 D2
St Walter & St John Sports
Ground
TOOT SW17 .... 137 L5
St William of York School
FSTH SE23 .... 140 E5
St Winifreds Junior School
LEE/GVPK SE12 .... 141 M3
St Winifreds RC School
LEW SE13 .... 141 L2
Salamanca Chenil Galleries
CHEL SW3 .... 15 J8
Salcombe Preparatory School
STHGT/OAK N14 .... 48 D2
Salesian College
BTSEA SW11 .... 119 L6
Salisbury Primary School
MNPK E12 .... 88 D5
Salisbury School
ED N9 .... 50 C3
Salisbury Surgery
FUL/PGN SW6 .... 118 E5
Salters' Hall
BARB EC2Y 13 G3
Salusbury Primary School
KIL/WHAMP NW6 .... 82 E8
Salvatorian College
WAND/EARL SW18 .... 137 H3
Samuel Jones Industrial Estate
PECK SE15 .... 121 L5
Samuel Rhodes School
IS N1 .... 6 A3
The Sanders Draper
Secondary School
HCH RM12 .... 92 C4
Sandgate Trading Estate
BERM/RHTH SE16 .... 122 B3
Sandhurst Junior School
LEW SE13 .... 141 L4
Sandiford Industrial Estate
CHEAM SM3 .... 169 M4
Sandown Industrial Park
ESH/CLAY KT10 .... 166 A4
Sandringham Practice
HACK E8 .... 86 A5
Sandringham Primary School
FSTGT E7 .... 88 C6
Sandys Row Synagogue
WCHPL E1 .... 13 K3
Saracens Rugby Football Club
STHGT/OAK N14 .... 48 A1
Sarah Bonnell
Comprehensive School
SRTFD E15 .... 87 L6
Sarah Devonport Gallery
SKENS SW7 .... 15 J5
Sarum Hall School
HAMP NW3 .... 3 K1
Satay Gallery Restaurant
BRXN/ST SW9 .... 139 G1
Satmer Trust School
STNW/STAM N16 .... 86 A2
Savoy Theatre
TPL/STR WC2R 11 L7
Saxon Business Centre
WIM/MER SW19 .... 155 J5
Saxon CP School
SHPTN TW17 .... 148 F8
Sayer Clinic
CROY/NA CR0 .... 171 M6
Sayer Clinics
MBLAR W1H 9 M5
Scarsdale Place Medical Centre
KENS W8 .... 14 C3
Schiller International University
STHWK SE1 .... 12 A9
School of Econ & Pol Sci
LINN WC2A 11 M5
School of Fine Art
STPAN WC1H 5 H8
School of Hygiene &
Tropical Medicine
STPAN WC1H 5 G9
School of Medicine
FARR EC1M 12 E2
School of Medicine
PIM SW1V 17 G6
School of Music & Drama
BARB EC2Y 12 F3
School of Physiotherapy
FITZ W1T 10 F2
Schoolhouse
ABR/ST RM4 .... 56 D4
School House Aveley School
SOCK/AV RM15 .... 111 L4
School House Grammar School
BFN/LL DA15 .... 144 B6
School of Health
RDART DA2 .... 147 H3
The School of St David &
St. Katharine
CEND/HSY/T N8 .... 66 E5
School of the Good Shepherd
CROY/NA CR0 .... 186 B1
Schopwick Surgery
BORE WD6 .... 44 D1
Science Museum
SKENS SW7 .... 15 G4
The Science Museum Library
SKENS SW7 .... 15 G3
The Scottish Hospital
COVGDN WC2E 11 J6
Scotts Park Primary School
BMLY BR1 .... 160 C4

Scotts Primary School
HCH RM12 .... 92 C5
Scott Wilkie Primary School
CAN/RD E16 .... 106 C5
Screen on Baker Street
MHST W1U 9 M2
Seaton House School
BELMT SM2 .... 182 D3
Sebright Primary School
BETH E2 .... 104 A1
Secombe Theatre
SUT SM1 .... 170 A7
Secretarial College
BECK BR3 .... 158 E4
Sedgehill School
CAT SE6 .... 159 H1
Sedgewick Centre
WCHPL E1 .... 13 M4
S E H A Hindu Temple
WOOL/PLUM SE18 .... 125 H2
Selborne School
GFD/PVL UB6 .... 97 M1
The Selhurst Medical Centre
SNWD SE25 .... 172 D1
Sellincourt School
TOOT SW17 .... 155 M2
Selsdon CP School
SAND/SEL CR2 .... 185 J2
Selsdon High School
SAND/SEL CR2 .... 185 K1
The Selsdon Park
Medical Practice
SAND/SEL CR2 .... 185 H3
Selwyn Infant School
CHING E4 .... 51 H8
Selwyn Junior School
CHING E4 .... 51 J8
Selwyn Primary School
PLSTW E13 .... 88 A8
Sergeant Industrial Estate
WAND/EARL SW18 .... 137 H3
Serpentine Galleries
BAY/PAD W2 .... 9 H9
Servite RC Primary School
WBPTN SW10 .... 14 E9
Seven Islands Leisure Centre
BERM/RHTH SE16 .... 122 C1
Seven Kings Health Centre
GDMY/SEVK IG3 .... 89 L1
Seven Kings High School
GNTH/NBYPK IG2 .... 71 J4
Seven Mills Primary School
POP/IOD E14 .... 105 G8
Sevenoaks Way Industrial
Estate
STMC/STPC BR5 .... 162 C6
Seychelles High Comm
MHST W1U 9 M2
Seymour Gardens Medical
Centre
IL IG1 .... 88 F1
Seymour Leisure Centre
MBLAR W1H 9 L3
Shaare Zedek Medical Centre
GLDGN NW11 .... 64 F7
Shaftesbury Medical Centre
RYLN/HDSTN HA2 .... 79 J1
Shaftesbury Park School
BTSEA SW11 .... 119 M7
Shaftesbury Primary School
FSTGT E7 .... 88 C7
Shaftesbury School
KTN/HRWW/W HA3 .... 61 J2
Shahjalal Medical Centre
WCHPL E1 .... 104 A5
Shakespeare Business Centre
BRXN/ST SW9 .... 121 H8
Shakespeare Globe Exhibition
STHWK SE1 .... 12 E7
Shakespeare Industrial Estate
WATN WD24 .... 29 G3
The Shamrock Sports Club
ACT W3 .... 99 J5
Shanghai Traditional
Chinese Medical Centre
TWK TW1 .... 134 D3
Shannon Corner Retail Park
NWMAL KT3 .... 153 M7
Shapla Junior & Infant School
WCHPL E1 .... 104 A6
Sharp Sports Centre
EDGW HA8 .... 45 G8
Shawcroft School
STMC/STPC BR5 .... 162 E8
Sheen Lane Health Centre
MORT/ESHN SW14 .... 117 J6
Sheen Mount Primary School
RCHPK/HAM TW10 .... 135 H2
Sheen Sports Centre
MORT/ESHN SW14 .... 135 L1
Sheepcot Medical Centre
GSTN WD25 .... 21 J7
Shell Centre
STHWK SE1 .... 11 M9
Shelley School
CLAP SW4 .... 120 C8
Shelley School
LBTH SE11 .... 18 B6
Shene School
MORT/ESHN SW14 .... 135 K1
Shenstone School
DART DA1 .... 145 M4
Shepherds Bush Cricket Club
ACT W3 .... 99 L6
Shepherds Bush Market
MBLAR W1H 9 M4
Shepherds Community
School Y W A M
BROCKY SE4 .... 123 G8
Shepperton Business Park
SHPTN TW17 .... 149 J8
Shepperton Health Centre
SHPTN TW17 .... 149 H8
Sheraton Business Centre
GFD/PVL UB6 .... 98 C1
Sheringdale Primary School
WAND/EARL SW18 .... 136 F5

Sheringham Junior School
MNPK E12 .... 88 F4
Sherington School
CHARL SE7 .... 124 B4
Sherlock Holmes Museum
CAMTN NW1 .... 9 M1
Sherwood First School
MTCM CR4 .... 156 C4
Sherwood Park School
WLGTN SM6 .... 171 K5
Shimmi Shake Dance School
STMC/STPC BR5 .... 176 D1
Shirley Clinic
CROY/NA CR0 .... 173 J3
Shirley High School
CROY/NA CR0 .... 173 K5
Shirley Medical Centre
CROY/NA CR0 .... 173 L4
Shirley Wanderers Rugby
Football Club
WWKM BR4 .... 174 C6
Shomrei Hadath Synagogue
KIL/WHAMP NW6 .... 83 G5
Shooters Hill Golf Club
WOOL/PLUM SE18 .... 125 J3
Shopping Trolley Gallery
BECK BR3 .... 158 F3
Shoreditch Comprehensive
School
IS N1 .... 7 K6
Shoreditch County Court
STLK EC1Y 7 H9
Shortlands Golf Club
HAYES BR2 .... 159 L4
Shortwood County Infant
School
STA TW18 .... 130 B7
Shotfield Health Clinic
WLGTN SM6 .... 171 H8
Shree Ghanapathy Temple
WIM/MER SW19 .... 155 J3
Shree K S Swaminarayan Temple
WOOL/PLUM SE18 .... 125 J3
Shree Swaminarayan Temple
STRHM/NOR SW16 .... 156 E4
Shrewsbury Road Health Centre
FSTGT E7 .... 88 D7
Sidcup Health Centre
SCUP DA14 .... 144 A7
Sidcup Hill Primary School
SCUP DA14 .... 162 B1
Sidcup Sports Club
SCUP DA14 .... 143 M8
Sidney Russell School
DAGW RM9 .... 90 E4
Sierra Leone High Comm
OXSTW W1C 10 E4
Sikh Temple
BELV DA17 .... 127 J1
Sikh Temple
DART DA1 .... 146 D4
Sikh Temple
HYS/HAR UB3 .... 95 L7
Silicon Business Centre
GFD/PVL UB6 .... 98 C1
Silverdale Industrial Estate
HYS/HAR UB3 .... 96 A8
Silverglade Business Park
CHSGTN KT9 .... 179 J3
Silver Street Medical Centre
UED N18 .... 49 L6
Silver Wing Industrial Estate
CROY/NA CR0 .... 171 M8
Simmons Gallery
BMSBY WC1N 11 L2
Simon Marks Primary School
STNW/STAM N16 .... 85 M1
Sinai Primary School
KTN/HRWW/W HA3 .... 63 G7
Sinai Synagogue
GLDGN NW11 .... 64 E8
Singapore High Comm
KTBR SW1X 16 A4
Singapore High Comm
STJS SW1Y 11 G8
Singapore High Comm
WEST SW1P 16 F5
Singh Sabha Temple
BARK IG11 .... 89 H7
Singlegate First School
WIM/MER SW19 .... 155 K3
Sion College
EMB EC4Y 12 B6
Sion Manning RC Secondary
School
NKENS W10 .... 100 D4
Sir Francis Drake School
DEPT SE8 .... 122 E3
Sir George Monoux Sixth Form
College
WALTH E17 .... 69 H3
Sir James Barrie School
VX/NE SW8 .... 120 C6
Sir John Lillie Primary School
HMSMTH W6 .... 118 E4
Sir John Soanes Museum
LINN WC2A 11 L4
Sir Thomas Abney Junior School
STNW/STAM N16 .... 67 K8
Sir Thomas Lipton Memorial
Hospital
STHGT/OAK N14 .... 48 D2
Sir William Burrough Primary
School
POP/IOD E14 .... 104 E5
Six Bridges Trading Estate
STHWK SE1 .... 122 A3
Skidmore Clinic
RKW/CH/CXG WD3 .... 40 E3
Skillion Business Park
BARK IG11 .... 107 M2
Skinners Co Lower Girls School
CLPT E5 .... 86 B1
Skinners Co School for Girls
STNW/STAM N16 .... 67 K8
Ski Slope
STMC/STPC BR5 .... 162 D4

Slade Green Football Club
ERITH DA8 .... 128 B6
Slade Green Infant School
ERITH DA8 .... 128 A5
Slaughter House Art Gallery
FARR EC1M 12 C2
Sleaford Industrial Estate
VX/NE SW8 .... 120 C5
Sloane Hospital
BECK BR3 .... 159 K4
Smallberry Green School
ISLW TW7 .... 116 A7
Smallwood Primary School
TOOT SW17 .... 137 H4
S M A Medical Centre
LEY E10 .... 69 H8
The Smith Gallery
TEDD TW11 .... 152 A1
Smith Village Gallery
STNW/STAM N16 .... 85 K2
Snaresbrook College
SWFD E18 .... 70 A3
Snaresbrook Crown Court
WAN E11 .... 69 M6
Snaresbrook Primary School
SWFD E18 .... 70 A5
Snowsfields Primary School
STHWK SE1 .... 19 J1
Sobell Leisure Centre
HOLWY N7 .... 84 F3
Sobel Medical Centre
HOLWY N7 .... 85 G4
The Soho Theatre
SOHO/SHAV W1D 11 G6
Soho Theatre
SOHO/SHAV W1D 11 G5
Solent Road Health Centre
KIL/WHAMP NW6 .... 83 G6
Somerford Grove Health Centre
STNW/STAM N16 .... 85 M4
Somerford Grove Practice
STNW/STAM N16 .... 85 M4
Somerset House
COVGDN WC2E 11 L4
Somers Town Community Sports Centre
CAMTN NW1 .... 4 F6
Sonic Surgery
IS N1 .... 7 H3
Sophie Hanna Flower School
VX/NE SW8 .... 120 D5
Sorsby Health Centre
CLPT E5 .... 86 D4
South Bank Business Centre
VX/NE SW8 .... 120 D4
Southbank International School
NTGHL W11 .... 8 A7
Southbank University
STHWK SE1 .... 18 C2
Southbank University
VX/NE SW8 .... 120 D6
Southborough Primary School
HAYES BR2 .... 161 G8
Southborough School
SURB KT6 .... 167 L5
Southbury Primary & Infant School
PEND EN3 .... 37 J7
Southbury Primary School
PEND EN3 .... 37 H7
South Camden Community School
CAMTN NW1 .... 4 F5
South Croydon Medical Centre
SAND/SEL CR2 .... 184 C1
South Croydon Medical Practice
SAND/SEL CR2 .... 172 C8
South Croydon Sports Club
SAND/SEL CR2 .... 172 E7
South Dene Surgery
SWFD E18 .... 70 A3
South Eastern University
HOLWY N7 .... 84 F3
Southern Road Infant School
PLSTW E13 .... 106 B1
Southern Road Primary School
PLSTW E13 .... 106 B1
Southfield First & Middle School
CHSWK W4 .... 99 L8
Southfield Medical Centre
CHSWK W4 .... 99 K8
The Southfields Clinic
WAND/EARL SW18 .... 137 G3
Southfields Community College
WAND/EARL SW18 .... 137 G5
Southfields Group Practice
WAND/EARL SW18 .... 137 G6
Southgate College
STHGT/OAK N14 .... 48 C4
Southgate Compton Cricket Club
EBAR EN4 .... 34 F7
Southgate Leisure Centre
STHGT/OAK N14 .... 48 D2
Southgate Road Medical Centre
IS N1 .... 7 H1
Southgate School
EBAR EN4 .... 35 H8
Southgate Surgery
STHGT/OAK N14 .... 48 B1
South Grove Primary School
WALTH E17 .... 68 E7
South Hampstead Cricket Club
CRICK NW2 .... 82 C7
South Hampstead High School
HAMP NW3 .... 83 K6
South Hampstead Synagogue
HAMP NW3 .... 83 M6
South Harringay Junior School
FSBYPK N4 .... 67 G6
South Lambeth Road Practice
VX/NE SW8 .... 120 E6
Southlands College
PUT/ROE SW15 .... 135 M1
Southlands Surgery
ORP BR6 .... 176 E5
South Lewisham Health Centre
CAT SE6 .... 141 J8

South Lodge Queens School
BUSH WD23 .... 30 A6
South London Art Gallery
CMBW SE5 .... 121 L6
South London Liberal Synagogue
STRHM/NOR SW16 .... 138 D7
The South London Natural Health Centre
CLAP SW4 .... 138 C1
South London Tamil School
CROY/NA CR0 .... 172 C2
South London Temple
PECK SE15 .... 122 A8
South London Theatre Centre
WNWD SE27 .... 139 H7
Southmead Primary School
WIM/MER SW19 .... 136 E5
South Norwood Hill Medical Centre
SNWD SE25 .... 157 L5
South Norwood Medical Centre
SNWD SE25 .... 157 L7
South Norwood Primary School
SNWD SE25 .... 158 A7
South Park Business Centre
IL IG1 .... 89 L2
South Park Clinic
IL IG1 .... 89 L4
South Park Junior & Infant School
GDMY/SEVK IG3 .... 89 L3
South Quay Plaza
POP/IOD E14 .... 105 H8
South Rise Junior School
WOOL/PLUM SE18 .... 125 K3
Southside Industrial Estate
VX/NE SW8 .... 120 C5
South Thames College
PUT/ROE SW15 .... 136 D2
South Thames College / Wandsworth Adult College
PUT/ROE SW15 .... 135 M3
South Tottenham District Synagogue
SEVS/STOTM N15 .... 67 M6
Southville Junior School
EBED/NFELT TW14 .... 131 M5
Southwark Cathedral
STHWK SE1 .... 13 G8
Southwark College
BERM/RHTH SE16 .... 122 B1
Southwark College
CMBW SE5 .... 121 L5
Southwark College
STHWK SE1 .... 18 C1
Southwark College
STHWK SE1 .... 19 K3
Southwark Coroners Court
STHWK SE1 .... 19 G1
Southwark Council
PECK SE15 .... 121 M5
Southwark Council
STHWK SE1 .... 18 B4
Southwark Council
STHWK SE1 .... 19 H2
Southwark Council
STHWK SE1 .... 122 A4
Southwark Council for Community Relations
PECK SE15 .... 122 A7
Southwark Crown Court
STHWK SE1 .... 13 J8
Southwark Park Primary School
BERM/RHTH SE16 .... 122 B1
Southwark Sports Ground
DUL SE21 .... 139 M5
South Western Magistrates Court
BTSEA SW11 .... 119 M8
South West Essex Reform Synagogue
GNTH/NBYPK IG2 .... 71 L6
Southwold Primary School
CLPT E5 .... 86 C2
South Woodford Health Centre
SWFD E18 .... 70 A2
Southwood Hospital
HGT N6 .... 66 A8
Sovereign Business Centre
PEND EN3 .... 37 M6
The Space Gallery
NTGHL W11 .... 100 F5
Spanish Embassy
KTBR SW1X 16 A3
Spanish & Portuguese Synagogue
MV/WKIL W9 .... 2 D8
Spanish & Portuguese Synagogue
NTGHL W11 .... 100 E7
The Spare Tyre Theatre Co
KTTN NW5 .... 84 A6
Sparrow Farm County Junior School
EW KT17 .... 169 H7
Sparrow Farm Infant School
EBED/NFELT TW14 .... 132 C4
Sparrow Farm Junior School
EBED/NFELT TW14 .... 132 C4
Speakers Corner
BAY/PAD W2 .... 9 M6
Speedway Industrial Estate
HYS/HAR UB3 .... 95 K8
Speke's Monument
BAY/PAD W2 .... 8 F8
Spelthorne Borough Council
STA TW18 .... 148 A1
Spelthorne Clinic
ASHF TW15 .... 149 L2
Spelthorne College
ASHF TW15 .... 130 C7
Spelthorne County School
ASHF TW15 .... 149 K2
Spelthorne Leisure Centre
STA TW18 .... 148 A1
Spelthorne Sports Club
ASHF TW15 .... 149 K3
Spencer House
WHALL SW1A 10 E9

The Sphinx Theatre Co
STHWK SE1 .... 18 C1
The Spires Shopping Centre
BAR EN5 .... 33 L6
Spiritualist Temple
CAMTN NW1 .... 4 F1
Spitalfields Health Centre
WCHPL E1 .... 13 M3
Spitalfields Market
LEY E10 .... 87 G3
Spitalfields Market
WCHPL E1 .... 13 L2
Sports Centre
BORE WD6 .... 32 C4
Sports Centre
DAGW RM9 .... 90 E8
Sports Centre
ERITH DA8 .... 127 L4
Sports Centre
TOTM N17 .... 67 M2
Sports Centre
WCHPL E1 .... 104 A3
Sports Club
ESH/CLAY KT10 .... 165 M8
Sports Club
LHD/OX KT22 .... 178 C2
Sports Ground
BAR EN5 .... 45 L1
Sports Ground
THHTH CR7 .... 157 H5
Sports Ground
TOOT SW17 .... 137 L7
Sports Ground Pavilion
HGDN/ICK UB10 .... 95 K1
Springfield Hospital
TOOT SW17 .... 137 L7
Springfield Primary School
SUN TW16 .... 149 M4
Springfield Primary School
VX/NE SW8 .... 120 D5
Spring Grove Primary School
ISLW TW7 .... 115 K7
Spring Park School
CROY/NA CR0 .... 174 A5
Springwell Junior School
HEST TW5 .... 114 E5
Spurgeons College
SNWD SE25 .... 157 L5
Squires Lane Medical Practice
FNCH N3 .... 65 J2
Squirrels Heath Junior School
ROM RM1 .... 74 A4
Squirrels Trading Estate
HYS/HAR UB3 .... 113 M1
Sri Lanka High Commission
BAY/PAD W2 .... 9 H6
Sri Saddhatissa International Buddhist Temple
CDALE/KGS NW9 .... 63 J6
The Stables Gallery & Art Centre
CRICK NW2 .... 82 A6
Stadium Business Centre
WBLY HA9 .... 81 H3
Stadium Retail Park
WBLY HA9 .... 81 G3
Stafford Cross Business Park
CROY/NA CR0 .... 171 M7
Stafford Industrial Estate
EMPK RM11 .... 74 D4
Staffords Gallery
SOHO/SHAV W1D 11 H6
Stag Lane Medical Centre
CDALE/KGS NW9 .... 63 J4
Stag Lane School
EDGE HA8 .... 63 G3
Staines County Court
STA TW18 .... 148 A1
Staines Preparatory School
STA TW18 .... 148 A1
Staines Rugby Football Club
FELT TW13 .... 132 A8
Staines Town Football Club
STA TW18 .... 148 A3
Staines Youth Sports Centre
STA TW18 .... 130 A8
Stamford Clinic
HMSMTH W6 .... 118 A2
Stamford Green Primary School
HOR/WEW KT19 .... 180 B5
Stamford Hill Group Practice
CLPT E5 .... 67 M8
Stamford Hill Primary School
SEVS/STOTM N15 .... 67 K7
Stanborough School
GSTN WD25 .... 21 H8
Stanburn First School
STAN HA7 .... 62 C1
Standard Industrial Estate
CAN/RD E16 .... 106 D8
Stanford Middle School
STRHM/NOR SW16 .... 156 D4
Stanhope Junior Mixed School
GFD/PVL UB6 .... 97 J3
The Stanlake Practice
SHB W12 .... 100 C7
Stanley Infant School
TEDD TW11 .... 133 L8
Stanley Junior School
WHTN TW2 .... 133 L8
Stanley Park High School
CAR SM5 .... 171 G8
Stanley Park Infant School
CAR SM5 .... 182 F1
Stanley Technical High School
SNWD SE25 .... 157 M6
Stanmore College
STAN HA7 .... 44 B8
Stanmore Synagogue
STAN HA7 .... 44 D6
Stanton Square Industrial Estate
CAT SE6 .... 140 F8
Staple Inn Buildings
HHOL WC1V 12 A3
Staples Corner Business Park
CRICK NW2 .... 82 B1
Staples Road Junior & Infant School
LOU IG10 .... 39 L6

Star Business Centre
DAGW RM9 .... 109 K4
Stark Gallery
LEE/GVPK SE12 .... 141 M1
Star Primary School
WCHPL E1 .... 105 L3
The Start Gallery
FUL/PGN SW6 .... 118 E7
State Registered Chiropody Practice
CRICK NW2 .... 82 A6
Statham Grove Surgery
STNW/STAM N16 .... 85 K4
Station Approach
WAN E11 .... 87 K4
Stationary Office
GINN WC1R 11 M3
Stationers Hall
STP EC4M 12 C5
Station Road Surgery
HDN NW4 .... 64 A7
Staunton Group Practice
WDGN N22 .... 66 F2
Staverton Surgery
WLSDN NW10 .... 82 C7
Stepney Day Hospital
WCHPL E1 .... 104 C5
Stepney Greencoats Primary School
POP/IOD E14 .... 104 C5
Stepney Green Secondary School
WCHPL E1 .... 104 D4
Stepping Stone School
HAMP NW3 .... 83 K6
Sterling Industrial Estate
DAGE RM10 .... 91 H4
Sterling Way Clinic
UED N18 .... 49 M7
Stewart Fleming School
SNWD SE25 .... 158 C6
Stewart Headlam Primary School
WCHPL E1 .... 104 B3
Stillness Junior & Infant School
BROCKY SE4 .... 140 E3
Stirling Industrial Centre
BORE WD6 .... 32 D8
Stirling Way Industrial Estates
CROY/NA CR0 .... 171 L2
Stockwell Group Practice
BRXN/ST SW9 .... 120 F7
Stockwell Lodge Medical Centre
CHESW EN7 .... 26 A1
Stockwell Park Secondary School
BRXN/ST SW9 .... 120 F6
Stoke Newington School
STNW/STAM N16 .... 85 K3
The Stonebridge Primary School
WLSDN NW10 .... 81 J8
Stonebridge Shopping Centre
WLSDN NW10 .... 81 K8
Stonecot Surgery
MRDN SM4 .... 169 M2
Stonehill Business Centre
UED N18 .... 50 D8
Stonehill Business Park
UED N18 .... 50 D7
Stoneleigh Galleries
EW KT17 .... 169 G7
Storey Primary School
CAN/RD E16 .... 107 G7
Stormont House School
CLPT E5 .... 86 B4
Stormont School
POTB/CUF EN6 .... 23 J4
Stowford College
BELMT SM2 .... 182 C1
Strand on the Green Junior & Infant School
CHSWK W4 .... 117 G4
Strand Theatre
HOL/ALD WC2B 11 L6
Stratford Gm School
FSTGT E7 .... 88 A7
Stratford Magistrates Court
SRTFD E15 .... 87 K7
Strathmore School
RCHPK/HAM TW10 .... 134 D5
Streatham & Croydon Rugby Football Club
THHTH CR7 .... 157 G8
Streatham Hill & Clapham High School
BRXS/STRHM SW2 .... 138 F5
Streatham Hill & Clapham High School
STRHM/NOR SW16 .... 138 C3
Streatham Ice Rink
STRHM/NOR SW16 .... 156 E1
Streatham Modern School
STRHM/NOR SW16 .... 156 E2
Streatham Park Surgery
STRHM/NOR SW16 .... 156 C1
Streatham Swimming Pool
STRHM/NOR SW16 .... 156 E1
Streatham Vale Sports Club
STRHM/NOR SW16 .... 156 C3
Streatham Wells Primary School
BRXS/STRHM SW2 .... 138 F6
Stroud Green Primary School
FSBYPK N4 .... 85 G3
Students Gallery
RYNPK SW20 .... 154 F4
Studholme Medical Centre
ASHF TW15 .... 130 E7
Studio Sienko Gallery
STHWK SE1 .... 18 F2
Study Preparatory School
WIM/MER SW19 .... 154 D1
The Study School
NWMAL KT3 .... 153 L3
Sudbourne Primary School
BRXS/STRHM SW2 .... 138 F2
Sudbury Court Sports Club
ALP/SUD HA0 .... 80 C3

Sudbury Infant School
ALP/SUD HA0 .... 80 B4
Suffolks Junior & Infant School
EN EN1 .... 37 H5
Sulivan Primary School
FUL/PGN SW6 .... 119 G7
Summerside JMI School
NFNCH/WDSP N12 .... 47 K8
Summerswood Primary School
BORE WD6 .... 32 B7
Summit Business Park
SUN TW16 .... 150 A3
Sunbury Business Centre
SUN TW16 .... 149 L4
Sunbury Health Centre
SUN TW16 .... 150 A5
Sunbury Leisure Centre
SUN TW16 .... 149 M4
Sunbury Manor School
SUN TW16 .... 149 M4
Sunderland Estate
KGLGY WD4 .... 20 B2
Sundridge Medical Practice
BMLY BR1 .... 160 A3
Sunnyfield School
HDN NW4 .... 64 C4
Sunnyfields Primary School
HDN NW4 .... 64 B4
Sunnyhill Primary School
STRHM/NOR SW16 .... 138 F8
Sun Strp Thtr
SOHO/CST W1F 11 G5
Super Bowl
BXLYHS DA6 .... 144 F1
Supreme Court Taxing Office
FLST/FETLN EC4A 12 B5
Surbiton Business Centre
SURB KT6 .... 167 K1
Surbiton High School for Girls
KUT KT1 .... 152 E7
Surbiton Hospital
SURB KT6 .... 167 L1
Surbiton Natural Health Centre
SURB KT6 .... 167 L1
Surex Swimming Pools
BH/WHM TN16 .... 187 K8
Surrey County Council
BNSTD SM7 .... 181 M8
Surrey County Council
E/WMO/HCT KT8 .... 151 G7
Surrey County Council
EW KT17 .... 181 G2
Surrey County Council
HOR/WEW KT19 .... 180 E2
Surrey County Council
HOR/WEW KT19 .... 180 D4
Surrey County Council
KUT KT1 .... 152 E6
Surrey County Council
THDIT KT7 .... 167 G1
Surrey County Council
WEY KT13 .... 164 B6
Surrey County Council
WOT/HER KT12 .... 165 H4
Surrey County Cricket Club
LBTH SE11 .... 121 G4
Surrey Docks Farm
BERM/RHTH SE16 .... 104 F8
Surrey Docks Health Centre
BERM/RHTH SE16 .... 104 E8
Surrey Heartlands NHS Trust
HOR/WEW KT19 .... 180 C2
Surrey Quays Leisure Park
BERM/RHTH SE16 .... 122 D1
Surrey Quays Shopping Centre
BERM/RHTH SE16 .... 122 D1
Surrey Square Junior & Infant School
WALW SE17 .... 19 J7
Susan Lawrence Primary School
POP/IOD E14 .... 105 H5
Sussex House School
KTBR SW1X 15 L5
Sutton Alternative Health Centre
SUT SM1 .... 170 C7
Sutton Bowling Club
BELMT SM2 .... 182 A2
Sutton General Hospital
BELMT SM2 .... 182 B3
Sutton Grammar School for Boys
SUT SM1 .... 170 C7
Sutton High School for Girls
SUT SM1 .... 170 B8
Suttons Business Park
RAIN RM13 .... 109 K2
Suttons JMI School
HCH RM12 .... 92 D4
Sutton Station Chiropractic Health Centre
BELMT SM2 .... 170 B8
Sutton Superbowl
SUT SM1 .... 170 B7
Sutton United Football Club
SUT SM1 .... 170 A6
Swaffield Primary School
WAND/EARL SW18 .... 137 J3
Swakeleys School
HGDN/ICK UB10 .... 95 J1
Swaminarayan School
WLSDN NW10 .... 81 K6
Swan Business Centre
CHSWK W4 .... 117 K2
Swan Business Park
DART DA1 .... 146 D1
Swanlea Secondary School
WCHPL E1 .... 104 B3
Swanley School
SWLY BR8 .... 163 K6
Swanley Town Council
SWLY BR8 .... 163 L6
Swanley White Oak County Primary School
SWLY BR8 .... 163 L5
Swansea City A F C
BAY/PAD W2 .... 9 J3
Swansmere School
WOT/HER KT12 .... 165 J3

Swan Wharf Business Centre
UX/CGN UB8...................... 94 B1
Swaziland High Comm
WESTW SW1E....................... 16 E3
Sybil Elgar School
EA W5.............................. 98 E6
Sybil Elgar School
NWDGN UB2........................ 114 F1
Sybourn Infant School
LEY E10............................ 86 E1
Sybourn Junior School
WALTH E17.......................... 68 F8
Sydenham High School
SYD SE26.......................... 158 B1
Sydenham High School
SYD SE26.......................... 140 B8
Sydenham Pre-school
FSTH SE23......................... 140 B6
Sydenham Secondary School
SYD SE26.......................... 140 B7
Sydney Russell School
DAGW RM9.......................... 90 D5
Synagogue
EHAM E6........................... 106 E2
Synagogue
HDN NW4........................... 64 D6
Synagogue
HDTCH EC3A........................ 13 K4
Synagogue
MV/WKIL W9......................... 2 C8
Synagogue
SURB KT6.......................... 152 D8
The Synagogue
E/WMO/HCT KT8.................... 152 D8
The Synagogue
RSLP HA4........................... 78 A1
The Synagogue
SWFD E18........................... 70 A2
The Synagogue
WAN E11............................ 87 K1
Syon House
BTFD TW8.......................... 116 C6
Syracuse University
London Centre
NTGHL W11........................ 100 F6
S Y Thtr Sch
STJWD NW8.......................... 9 J1
Tabard Rugby Club
RAD WD7............................ 31 H2
Tabard Theatre
CHSWK W4......................... 117 L2
Tadema Gallery
IS N1.............................. 6 C5
Tait Road Industrial Estate
CROY/NA CR0...................... 172 D2
Talisman Gallery
WKENS W14........................ 118 F1
Tamworth Manor High School
STRHM/NOR SW16.................. 156 D6
Tanners Wood Junior &
Infant School
ABLGY WD5.......................... 20 E5
Tapling Trading Estate
WDR/YW UB7......................... 94 D6
Tate Gallery
STHWK SE1.......................... 19 K6
Tate Gallery of British Art
WEST SW1P.......................... 17 J6
Tate Gallery of Modern Art
STHWK SE1.......................... 12 D8
Tavistock Clinic
HAMP NW3........................... 83 K6
Tavy Clinic
ABYW SE2.......................... 108 C8
Teddington Business Park
TEDD TW11......................... 151 M1
Teddington Clinic
TEDD TW11......................... 151 L2
Teddington Memorial Hospital
TEDD TW11......................... 151 L2
Teddington School
TEDD TW11......................... 152 D2
Teddington Swimming Pool
TEDD TW11......................... 152 A1
The Teddington Theatre Club
E/WMO/HCT KT8.................... 151 K8
The Teddington Theatre Club
HPTN TW12......................... 151 H3
Telegraph Hill School
BROCKY SE4........................ 122 E7
Telephone Exchange
WATW WD18.......................... 29 H7
Temple
IL IG1............................. 89 H5
Temple
TPL/STR WC2R....................... 12 A6
Temple Hill County Infant &
Primary School
DART DA1.......................... 147 G2
Temple of Bacchus
CMBW SE5.......................... 121 J7
Temple of Mithras
MANHO EC4N......................... 13 G5
The Temple
KENS W8........................... 118 F1
Tenby Road Clinic
EDGE HA8........................... 62 F3
Tenterden Sports Ground
KTN/HRWW/W HA3.................... 62 E8
Thackeray Gallery
KENS W8........................... 14 C2
Thames Ditton County First
School
THDIT KT7......................... 166 F1
Thames Ditton Junior School
THDIT KT7......................... 166 F2
Thames Galleries
EDUL SE22......................... 140 A1
Thames Gateway NHS Trust
RDART DA2......................... 147 J4
Thames House
WEST SW1P.......................... 17 J3
Thameside Industrial Estate
CAN/RD E16........................ 106 D7
Thameslink Healthcare Services NHS
Trust
RDART DA2......................... 147 J3

Thames Magistrates Court
BOW E3............................ 105 G2
Thamesmead Community College
ERITHM DA18....................... 108 E8
Thamesmead County Secondary
School
SHPTN TW17........................ 164 D1
Thames Police Station
TPL/STR WC2R....................... 11 M7
Thames Valley University
EA W5.............................. 98 D7
Thamesview Business Centre
RAIN RM13......................... 109 L4
Thames View Clinic
BARK IG11......................... 107 M1
Thames View Junior & Infant School
BARK IG11......................... 108 A1
20th Century Gallery
FUL/PGN SW6....................... 118 E6
Theatre
CHCR WC2N.......................... 11 J6
Theatre
COVGDN WC2E........................ 11 K7
Theatre
LSQ/SEVD WC2H...................... 11 J4
Theatre
LSQ/SEVD WC2H...................... 11 H7
Theatre De Complicite
HOLWY N7........................... 84 F5
Theatre for Mankind
FSBYPK N4.......................... 84 F1
Theatre Museum
COVGDN WC2E........................ 11 K6
The Theatre Nightclub
WAND/EARL SW18.................... 137 H2
Theatre of the Dispossessed
WIM/MER SW19...................... 136 D5
Theatre Royal
HOL/ALD WC2B....................... 11 L5
Theatre Royal
SRTFD E15.......................... 87 K7
Therapia Trading Estate
CROY/NA CR0....................... 171 K2
Thomas Becket RC Primary School
SNWD SE25......................... 173 G1
Thomas Buxton Primary School
WCHPL E1.......................... 104 A3
Thomas Fairchild Primary School
IS N1.............................. 7 G5
Thomas Gamuel Primary School
WALTH E17.......................... 69 G7
Thomas's Preparatory School
BTSEA SW11........................ 119 K6
Thomas Tallis School
BKHTH/KID SE3..................... 124 B8
Thomas Tallis School
WAB EN9............................ 27 M6
Thorkhill Surgery
THDIT KT7......................... 167 H3
Thornhill Primary School
IS N1.............................. 6 A2
Thornton Heath Baths
THHTH CR7......................... 157 K7
Thornton Heath Health Centre
THHTH CR7......................... 157 J7
Thornton Road Industrial Estate
CROY/NA CR0....................... 171 M1
Thornton Road Surgery
CROY/NA CR0....................... 171 M1
Thorntree School
CHARL SE7......................... 124 D3
Thorpe Hall Primary School
WALTH E17.......................... 69 J2
Three Bridges Primary School
NWDGN UB2......................... 114 D2
Three Bridges Primary School
NWDGN UB2......................... 115 H1
Three Lions Gallery
STJWD NW8........................... 3 J6
Three Rivers District Council
OXHEY WD19......................... 42 C5
Three Rivers District Council
RKW/CH/CXG WD3..................... 40 E2
Thtr Mus Lib & Arc
COVGDN WC2E........................ 11 K6
Thurlow Park School
WNWD SE27......................... 139 H4
Thurrock Business Centre
WTHK RM20......................... 129 M4
Thurrock Council
PUR RM19.......................... 128 F2
Thurston Industrial Estate
LEW SE13.......................... 123 H8
Tidemill Primary School
DEPT SE8.......................... 123 G5
Tideway Industrial Estate
VX/NE SW8......................... 120 C4
Tiffin Girls School
KUTN/CMB KT2...................... 152 E1
Tiffin School
KUTN/CMB KT2...................... 152 F5
Tiller Centre
POP/IOD E14....................... 123 C1
Tiller Leisure Centre
POP/IOD E14....................... 123 G1
Timbercroft Primary School
WOOL/PLUM SE18.................... 125 L5
Timbers Clinic
KTN/HRWW/W HA3..................... 43 K8
Tiverton Road School
SEVS/STOTM N15..................... 67 K7
Tobacco Dock
WAP E1W........................... 104 B6
Toldos School
STNW/STAM N16...................... 85 L1
Tolgate School
CROY/NA CR0....................... 173 H1
Tollgate Primary School
PLSTW E13......................... 106 C3
Tolworth CP School
SURB KT6.......................... 167 M3
Tolworth Recreation Centre
CHSGTN KT9........................ 167 M5
Tolworth Secondary Girls School
SURB KT6.......................... 167 M5
Tom Hood School
WAN E11............................ 87 M3

Tomo Industrial Estate
UX/CGN UB8......................... 94 C5
Tonga High Comm
MBLAR W1H........................... 9 K3
Tonybee Hall & Curtain Theatre
WCHPL E1........................... 13 M3
Tooting Bec Surgery
TOOT SW17......................... 138 A7
Tooting & Mitcham United
Football Club
MTCM CR4.......................... 156 A4
Topcukoy F C
HACK E8............................. 7 L1
Torriano Junior & Infant School
KTTN NW5........................... 84 C5
Torridon Junior & Infant School
CAT SE6........................... 141 K6
Torrington Clinic
NFNCH/WDSP N12..................... 47 J7
Torrington Park Health Centre
NFNCH/WDSP N12..................... 47 J6
Total Health Clinic
SHB W12........................... 100 B8
Tottenhall Infants School
PLMGR N13.......................... 49 G7
Tottenham Hale Retail Park
SEVS/STOTM N15..................... 68 A5
Tottenham Hotspur Football
Club
TOTM N17........................... 67 M1
Totteridge Cricket Club
TRDG/WHET N20...................... 47 G4
The Totteridge Gallery
TRDG/WHET N20...................... 47 J4
Touch Wood Gallery
EN N1.............................. 36 E8
Tourist Board
BCVA SW1W.......................... 16 C3
Tower Bridge Museum
STHWK SE1.......................... 13 K9
Tower Hamlets College
POP/IOD E14....................... 105 H6
Tower Hamlets College
WCHPL E1.......................... 104 C4
Tower House Preparatory
School for Boys
MORT/ESHN SW14.................... 135 J1
Tower Industrial Estate
SNWD SE25......................... 158 A7
Tower Medical Centre
WCHPL E1.......................... 104 A5
Tower of London
TWRH EC3N.......................... 13 L7
Towers Business Park
WBLY HA9........................... 81 H4
Towers Infant School
EMPK RM11.......................... 74 C8
Towers Junior School
EMPK RM11.......................... 74 C8
Tower Theatre
IS N1.............................. 85 H6
Town Farm County
Primary School
STWL/WRAY TW19.................... 130 D4
Townley Grammar
School for Girls
BXLYHS DA6........................ 144 F3
Townmead Business Centre
FUL/PGN SW6....................... 119 J8
Townsend Industrial Estate
WLSDN NW10......................... 81 J8
Townsend Primary School
STHWK SE1.......................... 19 J5
Toy Museum
FITZ W1T........................... 10 F2
Trabzon Spor F C
STNW/STAM N16...................... 85 K4
Trading Estate
BERM/RHTH SE16.................... 122 B2
Trading Estate
HYS/HAR UB3........................ 96 B8
Trafalgar Business Centre
BARK IG11......................... 107 M3
Trafalgar Galleries
WHALL SW1A......................... 10 E8
Trafalgar Junior School
WHTN TW2......................... 133 K6
Trafalgar Trading Estate
PEND EN3........................... 37 M7
Training Schl
IS N1.............................. 6 E3
Tramshed Theatre
WOOL/PLUM SE18.................... 125 H2
Trans Atlantic College
BETH E2............................. 7 L5
Transport House
WEST SW1P.......................... 17 J4
Treasury
WHALL SW1A......................... 17 H2
The Tredegar Practice
BOW E3............................ 104 F1
Trent C of E Primary School
EBAR EN4........................... 34 F7
Triangle Surgery
WAND/EARL SW18.................... 137 G2
Tricor Business Park
CHES/WCR EN8....................... 26 E7
Tricor Trading Estate
CHES/WCR EN8....................... 26 E7
Tricycle Theatre
KIL/WHAMP NW6...................... 82 F7
Trident Business Centre
TOOT SW17......................... 155 M1
Trinidad & Tobago High Comm
KTBR SW1X.......................... 16 A3
Trinity Business Centre
BERM/RHTH SE16.................... 104 F8
Trinity Catholic Lower
High School
WFD IG8............................ 52 A6
Trinity Catholic Upper
High School
WFD IG8............................ 52 A6
Trinity College Centre
CMBW SE5.......................... 121 L5
Trinity College of Music
MHST W1U........................... 10 B3

Trinity Hospital
GNWCH SE10........................ 123 K3
Trinity House
TWRH EC3N.......................... 13 K6
Trinity St Marys C of E
Primary School
BAL SW12.......................... 138 A5
Trinity Surgery
DAGE RM10.......................... 91 G3
The Trinity Surgery
WAND/EARL SW18.................... 137 K4
Trinity Trading Estate
HYS/HAR UB3....................... 114 A1
Triumph Trading Estate
TOTM N17........................... 50 A8
Trocadero Centre
MYFR/PICC W1J...................... 11 G7
Trojan Business Centre
WLSDN NW10......................... 81 M6
Trowbridge Gallery
FUL/PGN SW6....................... 119 J5
Troy Industrial Estate
HRW HA1............................ 61 M6
True Buddha School
IS N1.............................. 5 L4
The T Shirt Gallery
HAMP NW3........................... 83 L6
Tudor Junior Mixed School
STHL UB1........................... 96 E6
Tudor Lodge Health Centre
WIM/MER SW19...................... 136 D4
Tudor Primary School
FNCH N3............................ 65 J2
Tufnell Park Primary School
HOLWY N7........................... 84 D4
Tuke School
PECK SE15......................... 122 B6
Tulloch Clinic
SHB W12........................... 100 D7
Tunnel Avenue Trading Estate
GNWCH SE10........................ 105 K8
Tunnel Industrial Estate
WTHK RM20......................... 129 M2
Turkish Embassy
KTBR SW1X.......................... 16 B2
Turney School
DUL SE21.......................... 139 J4
Turnford School
CHES/WCR EN8....................... 26 E1
Turnham Primary School
BROCKY SE4........................ 140 E1
Tweedale Infant School
CAR SM5........................... 170 D2
Tweeddale Junior School
CAR SM5........................... 170 D2
Twickenham Park Health Centre
TWK TW1.......................... 134 C3
Twickenham Rugby
Football Ground
WHTN TW2......................... 133 L3
Twickenham Trading Estate
TWK TW1.......................... 133 M3
Twin Bridges Business Park
SAND/SEL CR2...................... 172 D8
Twyford C of E High School
ACT W3............................. 99 H7
Tyburn Infant School
STJWD NW8........................... 3 H9
Tyburn School
BRXN/ST SW9....................... 120 F6
The Type Museum Operation
Hannibal
BRXN/ST SW9....................... 120 F6
U C I Cinema
BAY/PAD W2.......................... 8 D5
U C I Cinema
BERM/RHTH SE16.................... 122 D1
U C I Cinema
ED N9............................. 50 D2
U C I Cinema
WTHK RM20......................... 129 M2
UCL
FITZ W1T........................... 10 F2
UCL Hospitals NHS Trust
FITZ W1T........................... 10 F1
Uganda High Commission
STJS SW1Y.......................... 11 H8
Underhill Junior & Infant School
BAR EN5............................ 33 L8
Unicorn School
RCH/KEW TW9....................... 116 F6
Uni of Notre Dame
LSQ/SEVD WC2H...................... 11 H7
Union of Liberal & Progressive
Synagogues
FITZ W1T........................... 10 F1
Fairview Industrial Estate
HYS/HAR UB3........................ 95 M8
Cowley Mill Trading Estate
IVER SL0........................... 94 A1
United Elizabeth Garrett Anderson
Hospital for Women
CAMTN NW1........................... 5 H7
United Services Sports Ground
CHSWK W4.......................... 117 L6
United States Embassy
CAVSQ/HST W1G...................... 10 C4
United Synagogue
CHING E4........................... 51 H8
United Synagogue
CLPT E5............................ 68 A8
Unity College
KTTN NW5........................... 84 B4
Unity Trading Estate
WFD IG8............................ 70 D4
University College
STPAN WC1H.......................... 5 G9
University College Hospital
HAMP NW3........................... 83 K6
University College London
GWRST WC1E......................... 11 G1
University College School
HAMP NW3........................... 83 J4
University of East London
BCTR RM8........................... 90 B4
University of East London
PLSTW E13......................... 106 B2
University of Greenwich
DART DA1.......................... 146 F6

University of Greenwich
DART DA1.......................... 146 C6
University of Greenwich
ELTH/MOT SE9...................... 143 J3
University of Greenwich
GNWCH SE10........................ 123 K3
University of Greenwich
WOOL/PLUM SE18.................... 125 G1
University of Hertfordshire
GSTN WD25.......................... 30 B1
University of London
BAY/PAD W2.......................... 9 G5
University of London
BMSBY WC1N......................... 11 K1
University of London
ENC/FH EN2......................... 37 G1
University of London
GWRST WC1E......................... 11 H2
University of London
NWCR SE14......................... 122 E6
University of London
STPAN WC1H.......................... 5 H9
University of London
TPL/STR WC2R....................... 11 L6
University of Middlesex
EBAR EN4........................... 35 J5
University of Middlesex
PEND EN3........................... 37 H8
University of North London
HOLWY N7........................... 84 F5
University of Westminster
CAMTN NW1........................... 4 E9
University of Westminster
CHSWK W4......................... 117 J6
University of Westminster
GTPST W1W.......................... 10 D2
University of Westminster
HGT N6............................. 84 B1
University of Westminster
HRW HA1............................ 62 A8
University Vandals Rugby
Football Club
WOT/HER KT12...................... 164 D3
Uphall Primary School
IL IG1............................. 89 H5
Upland Junior School
BXLYHN DA7........................ 126 F8
Uplands Business Park
WALTH E17.......................... 68 D3
Upminster Infant School
UPMR RM14.......................... 93 H3
Upminster Primary School
UPMR RM14.......................... 93 J3
Upper Selsdon Road Surgery
SAND/SEL CR2...................... 185 H3
Upper Tooting Independent High
School
TOOT SW17......................... 137 L6
Upton Cross Primary School
PLSTW E13.......................... 88 B8
Upton Day Hospital
BXLYHS DA6........................ 144 E1
Upton Lane Medical Centre
FSTGT E7........................... 88 B6
Upton Primary School
BXLY DA5.......................... 144 E2
Upton Road School
BXLYHS DA6........................ 144 E2
Ursuline High School
IL IG1............................. 89 H2
Ursuline High School
RYNPK SW20........................ 154 D3
US Embassy
MYFR/PKLN W1K...................... 10 A6
US Navy Comm In Chief
MYFR/PKLN W1K...................... 10 B6
Uxbridge College
HGDN/ICK UB10...................... 76 E6
Uxbridge College
HYS/HAR UB3........................ 96 A6
Uxbridge County Court
HYS/HAR UB3........................ 95 L4
Uxbridge County Court
UX/CGN UB8......................... 76 C7
Uxbridge Cricket Club
HGDN/ICK UB10...................... 76 E6
Uxbridge Football Club
WDR/YW UB7......................... 95 G8
Uxbridge Health Centre
UX/CGN UB8......................... 76 D7
Uxbridge Swimming Pool
HGDN/ICK UB10...................... 76 E6
Uxendon Manor School
KTN/HRWW/W HA3..................... 62 E6
Uzbekistan Embassy
NTGHL W11......................... 100 F7
Vale Industrial Estate
WATW WD18.......................... 41 J3
The Vale Medical Centre
FSTH SE23......................... 140 E6
Valence House Museum &
Library
BCTR RM8........................... 90 D7
Valentine High School
IL IG1............................. 71 G7
Valentines High Lower School
GNTH/NBYPK IG2..................... 71 H6
The Vale School
SKENS SW7.......................... 14 E4
Valley Primary School
HAYES BR2......................... 159 M5
Valmar Trading Estate
CMBW SE5.......................... 121 J7
The Vanbrugh Group Practice
GNWCH SE10........................ 123 M3
Vanbrugh Theatre
GWRST WC1E......................... 11 G1
Van & Car Surgery
PEND EN3........................... 37 K7
Vanguard Trading Estate
SRTFD E15.......................... 87 J8
Vaughan Middle School
RYLN/HDSTN HA2..................... 61 J7
Vauxhall Primary School
LBTH SE11.......................... 17 L7
Vernon House School
WLSDN NW10......................... 81 J3

Vestry House Museum
WALTH E17 .... **69** H5
Vestry Medical Practice
CMBW SE5 .... **121** L7
Vicarage Fields Health Clinic
BARK IG11 .... **89** J7
The Vicarage Field
Shopping Centre
BARK IG11 .... **89** J7
Vicarage Primary School
EHAM E6 .... **106** F2
Vicarage School
RCHPK/HAM TW10 .... **134** D3
Vicars Green Primary School
GFD/PVL UB6 .... **98** C1
Victoria & Albert Museum
SKENS SW7 .... **15** H4
Victoria Chiropractic Clinic
CHEL SW3 .... **15** L2
The Victoria Clinic for
Sexual Health
WEST SW1P **17** G5
Victoria Industrial Estate
ACT W3 .... **99** K4
Victoria Junior School
FELT TW13 .... **132** B5
Victoria Medical Centre
PIM SW1V **16** E6
Victoria Palace
WESTW SW1E **16** D4
Victoria Park Industrial Centre
HOM E9 .... **86** F7
Victoria Place Shopping Centre
PIM SW1V **16** D5
Victoria Retail Park
RSLP HA4 .... **78** D5
Victoria Wharf
POP/IOD E14 .... **104** E6
Victoria Wharf Industrial Estate
DEPT SE8 .... **122** F3
Victor Seymour School
CAR SM5 .... **170** F5
Victory Business Centre
ISLW TW7 .... **133** M1
Victory Junior & Infant School
WALW SE17 .... **18** F5
Video Gallery
ARCH N19 .... **84** E1
Vigo Sternberg Galleries
GLDGN NW11 .... **64** F6
Viking Business Centre
ROMW/RG RM7 .... **73** J8
Viking First & Middle School
NTHLT UB5 .... **96** D2
Village Gallery
KENS W8 .... **8** A8
The Village Gallery
PIN HA5 .... **60** E4
Village School
HAMP NW3 .... **83** M6
Village Surgery
NWMAL KT3 .... **153** L7
The Village Surgery
PIN HA5 .... **60** E3
Villiers High School
STHL UB1 .... **97** G7
The Vine Clinic
KUTN/CMB KT2 .... **152** E2
Vine Medical Centre
E/WMO/HCT KT8 .... **151** J6
The Vines School
BTSEA SW11 .... **138** A1
Vineyard Hill Road Surgery
WIM/MER SW19 .... **137** G7
Vinopolis
STHWK SE1 .... **12** F8
Vinters' Hall
BLKFR EC4V **12** F6
V I P Trading Estate
CHARL SE7 .... **124** C2
Virgin Cinema
EA W5 .... **98** D6
Virgin Cinema
WBPTN SW10 .... **14** F8
Virgin Cinemas
CHEL SW3 .... **15** H9
Virgin Cinemas
CRICK NW2 .... **82** B1
Virginia Primary School
BETH E2 .... **7** J3
Virgo Fidelis Convent Schools
NRWD SE19 .... **157** J2
Visitor Cen
STJS SW1Y **11** G8
Vndvl Thtr
COVGDN WC2E **11** K6
The Vogue Gallery
EA W5 .... **98** D6
Vulcan Business Centre
CROY/NA CR0 .... **186** E2
Vyners School
HGDN/ICK UB10 .... **76** F4
Waddon Clinic
CROY/NA CR0 .... **172** A7
Waddon Infant School
CROY/NA CR0 .... **172** A7
Wadham Lodge Sports Centre
WALTH E17 .... **69** H2
Wadsworth Business Centre
GFD/PVL UB6 .... **98** C1
The Waldegrave Clinic
TEDD TW11 .... **151** M1
Waldegrave School
WHTN TW2 .... **133** K7
Waldorf School of S W London
STRHM/NOR SW16 .... **138** C6
Waldorf Steiner School of
S W London
STRHM/NOR SW16 .... **138** D8
Walford Road Synagogue
STNW/STAM N16 .... **85** L4
Walford Secondary School
NTHLT UB5 .... **78** E8
Walker Primary School
STHGT/OAK N14 .... **48** D4
Wallace Collection
MHST W1U **10** A4

Wallace Fields County First School
EW KT17 .... **181** G5
Wallace Fields CP School
EW KT17 .... **181** G5
Wallbrook Business Centre
HSLWW TW4 .... **114** B8
Wallington County Grammar
School
WLGTN SM6 .... **171** H5
Wallington High School for Girls
WLGTN SM6 .... **183** H2
Walmer Road Clinic
NTGHL W11 .... **100** E6
Walm Lane Clinic
CRICK NW2 .... **82** D5
Walm Lane Surgery
CRICK NW2 .... **82** D6
Walnuts Leisure Centre
ORP BR6 .... **177** G3
Walnut Tree Walk Primary School
LBTH SE11 .... **18** A5
Waltham Abbey Swimming Pool
WAB EN9 .... **27** K8
Waltham Forest Black People
Mental Health Authority
WALTH E17 .... **69** G6
Waltham Forest College
WALTH E17 .... **68** D3
Waltham Forest College
WALTH E17 .... **69** H4
Waltham Forest Magistrates
Court
WALTH E17 .... **69** H4
Waltham Forest Theatre
WALTH E17 .... **68** F4
Waltham Holy Cross Council
WAB EN9 .... **27** H6
Waltham Holy Cross Junior
School
WAB EN9 .... **27** K6
Walthamstow Business Centre
WALTH E17 .... **69** J3
Walthamstow School for Girls
WALTH E17 .... **69** H5
Walton Business Centre 44-46
WOT/HER KT12 .... **165** H2
Walton Casuals Football Club
WOT/HER KT12 .... **150** B7
Walton Community Hospital
WOT/HER KT12 .... **165** H4
Walton & Hersham Football Club
WOT/HER KT12 .... **165** G4
Walton Leigh School
WEY KT13 .... **164** F6
Walton-on-thames Cricket Club
WOT/HER KT12 .... **164** F3
Walton Swimming Pool
WOT/HER KT12 .... **165** H3
Walton & Weybridge Urban District
Council
WEY KT13 .... **164** A6
Walworth Lower School
WALW SE17 .... **19** H7
Walworth Town Hall
WALW SE17 .... **18** E6
Walworth Upper
Secondary School
WALW SE17 .... **19** K8
Wandle Primary School
WAND/EARL SW18 .... **137** H5
Wandle Recreation Centre
WAND/EARL SW18 .... **137** H3
Wandsworth Adult College
TOOT SW17 .... **137** L6
Wandsworth Borough Council
TOOT SW17 .... **155** M1
Wandsworth Borough Council
WAND/EARL SW18 .... **137** H4
Wandsworth Borough Council
WAND/EARL SW18 .... **137** H2
Wandsworth Community
Health Trust
TOOT SW17 .... **156** A1
Wandsworth County Court
PUT/ROE SW15 .... **136** E2
Wandsworth Public Baths
TOOT SW17 .... **138** A6
Wandsworth Trading Estate
WAND/EARL SW18 .... **137** H4
Wanstead Church School
WAN E11 .... **70** A6
Wanstead Cricket Club
WAN E11 .... **70** B8
Wanstead High School
WAN E11 .... **70** C7
Wanstead Hospital
WAN E11 .... **70** B5
Wanstead Place Surgery
WAN E11 .... **70** A6
Wapping
WAP E1W **104** C7
Wapping Sports Centre
WAP E1W **104** B7
Warden Lodge Surgery
CHES/WCR EN8 .... **26** D4
Warehouse Theatre
CROY/NA CR0 .... **172** D4
War Memorial Sports Ground
SUT SM1 .... **170** E6
War Museum
STHWK SE1 .... **13** J9
Warner Bros Cinema
ACT W3 .... **99** G3
Warner Bros Cinema
CROY/NA CR0 .... **171** M4
Warnford Industrial Estate
HYS/HAR UB3 .... **95** J3
Warrendell School
OXHEY WD19 .... **42** C5
Warrender School
RSLP HA4 .... **59** M8
Warren Junior School
CHDH RM6 .... **72** F6
Warren Mead Infant School
BNSTD SM7 .... **181** J8
Warren Mead Junior School
BNSTD SM7 .... **181** K8

The Warren Medical Centre
YEAD UB4 .... **96** B5
Warren Road Primary School
ORP BR6 .... **176** F6
Warren School
CHDH RM6 .... **72** F6
Warwick Estate
BAY/PAD W2 .... **8** D3
Warwick Leadlay Gallery
GNWCH SE10 .... **123** J4
Warwick Park Secondary
School
PECK SE15 .... **121** M6
Warwick School for Boys
WALTH E17 .... **69** J5
Wasps Rugby Football Club
ALP/SUD HA0 .... **80** C4
The Watch Gallery
CHEL SW3 .... **15** J6
Watergate School
LEW SE13 .... **141** H1
Waterloo Health Centre
STHWK SE1 .... **18** A2
The Watermans Hall
MON EC3R **13** J7
Watermeads High School
MRDN SM4 .... **170** D1
Watermill Business Centre
PEND EN3 .... **37** M5
Water Rats Theatre
STPAN WC1H **5** K7
Waterside Business Centre
ISLW TW7 .... **134** B1
The Waterside Trading Centre
NWDGN UB2 .... **115** L1
Water Sports Centre
BERM/RHTH SE16 .... **122** E1
Waterways Heritage Museum
RKW/CH/CXG WD3 .... **40** E3
Watford Arches Retail Park
WATW WD18 .... **29** J8
Watford Borough Council
WAT WD17 .... **29** G6
Watford Business Centre
WATW WD18 .... **29** H6
Watford Central Swimming Bath
WAT WD17 .... **29** G5
Watford County Court
WATN WD24 .... **29** H5
Watford Eye Clinic
WATN WD24 .... **29** H3
Watford Football Club
WATW WD18 .... **29** H8
Watford General Hospital
WATW WD18 .... **29** H8
Watford Grammar
School for Boys
WATW WD18 .... **28** F7
Watford Grammar
School for Girls
WATW WD18 .... **29** J8
Watford Museum
WAT WD17 .... **29** J8
Watford Sports & Leisure Centre
GSTN WD25 .... **21** J6
Watford Springs Pool
WATW WD18 .... **29** J8
Watford United Synagogue
WAT WD17 .... **29** H4
Watling Clinic
EDGE HA8 .... **63** K1
Watling Medical Centre
EDGE HA8 .... **63** J2
Waverley Industrial Estate
HRW HA1 .... **61** K4
Waverley Lower Secondary
School
EDUL SE22 .... **140** B2
Waverley School
PEND EN3 .... **37** J7
Waverley Upper Secondary
School
EDUL SE22 .... **140** C2
Waxchandlers' Hall
CITYW EC2V **12** F4
Weald College
KTN/HRWW/W HA3 .... **43** L8
Weald First & Middle School
KTN/HRWW/W HA3 .... **61** M1
Websters Art Gallery
LHD/OX KT22 .... **178** C6
Weekend Arts College
KTTN NW5 .... **84** B6
Welbeck Clinic
CRICK NW2 .... **83** G3
Welfare Clinic
GNWCH SE10 .... **123** J5
Welfare Clinic
HGT N6 .... **66** A7
Wellbourne Junior School
SEVS/STOTM N15 .... **67** M5
Wellcome Institute
CAMTN NW1 .... **5** G9
Welldon Park Middle School
RYLN/HDSTN HA2 .... **79** J4
Wellhouse NHS Trust
EDGE HA8 .... **63** H1
The Welling Clinic
WELL DA16 .... **126** A7
Welling Medical Centre
WELL DA16 .... **143** M1
Welling School
WELL DA16 .... **126** B6
Welling Secondary Girls School
WELL DA16 .... **126** B6
Wellington Barracks
STJSPK SW1H **16** F7
Wellington Primary School
BOW E3 .... **105** G2
Wellington Primary School
HSLW TW3 .... **114** F7
Welling United Football Club
WELL DA16 .... **126** C8
The Wells Park Practice
SYD SE26 .... **140** B7
Wells Park School
CHIG IG7 .... **53** M6

Wells Primary School
WFD IG8 .... **52** B6
The Well Street Surgery
HOM E9 .... **86** C7
Wembley Business Centre
WBLY HA9 .... **81** J3
Wembley Football Club
ALP/SUD HA0 .... **80** B4
Wembley High School
ALP/SUD HA0 .... **80** C3
Wembley Manor Junior School
WBLY HA9 .... **80** E3
Wembley Park Business Centre
WBLY HA9 .... **81** H3
Wembley Station
WBLY HA9 .... **81** G3
Wembley Synagogue
WBLY HA9 .... **80** F3
Wendell Park Primary School
SHB W12 .... **99** M8
Wennington Hall Farm Business
Centre
RAIN RM13 .... **110** E5
The Wenta Business Centre
WATN WD24 .... **29** K2
Wentworth County Infant
School
DART DA1 .... **145** M4
Wentworth CP Junior School
DART DA1 .... **146** A4
Wentworth Tutorial College
GLDGN NW11 .... **64** D7
Wesley's House & Chapel
STLK EC1Y **7** G9
Wessex Gardens Infant School
CRICK NW2 .... **82** E1
West Acton Primary School
ACT W3 .... **99** H5
West Becton Health Centre
CAN/RD E16 .... **106** D5
Westbourne Green Sports
Complex
BAY/PAD W2 .... **8** B2
Westbourne Primary School
SUT SM1 .... **170** A5
Westbridge College
BTSEA SW11 .... **119** L6
Westbrooke School
WELL DA16 .... **126** D8
Westbury Medical Centre
WDGN N22 .... **67** J3
The Westcroft Leisure Centre
CAR SM5 .... **171** G6
West Dene School
PUR/KEN CR8 .... **183** M6
West Drayton Cricket Club
WDR/YW UB7 .... **112** C2
West Drayton Primary School
WDR/YW UB7 .... **94** E8
West Ealing Business Centre
WEA W13 .... **98** A6
West End Great Synagogue
MBLAR W1H **9** L5
Western Hospitality
NWDGN UB2 .... **114** B2
Western Trading Estate
WLSDN NW10 .... **99** J3
West Ewell County Infant School
HOR/WEW KT19 .... **168** D7
Westfield School
WATW WD18 .... **41** M1
Westfields School
BARN SW13 .... **117** M8
Westgate CP School
DART DA1 .... **146** D4
West Grove Primary School
STHGT/OAK N14 .... **48** D2
West Hackney Synagogue
HACK E8 .... **86** A4
West Ham Church Primary
School
SRTFD E15 .... **87** M8
West Ham Lane Clinic
SRTFD E15 .... **87** L8
West Hampstead Clinic
KIL/WHAMP NW6 .... **2** B1
West Ham United Football Club
CHDH RM6 .... **72** F8
West Ham United Football Club
PLSTW E13 .... **106** C1
West Hatch High School
CHIG IG7 .... **52** F7
West Hendon Clinic
CDALE/KGS NW9 .... **63** M7
West Hertfordshire College
WAT WD17 .... **29** G3
West Herts College
BUSH WD23 .... **29** K6
West Hill County Primary School
DART DA1 .... **146** B3
West Hill Hospital
DART DA1 .... **146** D3
West Hill Primary School
WAND/EARL SW18 .... **137** G2
West Lambeth Community Care
NHS Trust
BRXN/ST SW9 .... **120** E8
West Lambeth Health Authority
STRHM/NOR SW16 .... **156** E2
West Lea School
ED N9 .... **49** L5
West Lodge School
BFN/LL DA15 .... **144** A7
West Lodge School
PIN HA5 .... **60** D5
West London County Court
WKENS W14 .... **118** E2
West London Healthcare
NHS Trust
NWDGN UB2 .... **96** F5
West London Healthcare
NHS Trust
NWDGN UB2 .... **114** E1
West London Magistrates Court
HMSMTH W6 .... **118** D3
West London Synagogue of British
Jews
BAY/PAD W2 .... **9** K5

West London Tamil School
WLSDN NW10 .... **99** M1
West Mead Clinic
RSLP HA4 .... **78** C3
West Middlesex Hospital
ISLW TW7 .... **116** A7
Westminster Abbey Choir School
WEST SW1P **17** J3
Westminster Cathedral Primary
School
PIM SW1V **17** H7
Westminster City Council
BAY/PAD W2 .... **8** C3
Westminster City Council
BAY/PAD W2 .... **9** G3
Westminster City Council
BCVA SW1W **16** B7
Westminster City Council
MBLAR W1H **9** L2
Westminster City Council
NKENS W10 .... **100** D3
Westminster City Council
PIM SW1V **16** D8
Westminster City Council
SOHO/CST W1F **10** F5
Westminster City Council
SOHO/SHAV W1D **11** H6
Westminster City Council
STJWD NW8 .... **3** J7
Westminster City Council
STJWD NW8 .... **3** H9
Westminster City Council
STJWD NW8 .... **9** H1
Westminster City Council
WEST SW1P **17** G4
Westminster City Hall
WESTW SW1E **16** F3
Westminster College
BTSEA SW11 .... **120** A6
Westminster Coroners Court
WEST SW1P **17** H5
Westminster Gallery
STJSPK SW1H **17** H2
Westminster School
WEST SW1P **17** G5
Westminster Synagogue
SKENS SW7 .... **15** K2
Westminster Technical College
WEST SW1P **16** F5
Westminster Theatre
WESTW SW1E **16** E3
Westmoor Community Clinic
PUT/ROE SW15 .... **136** A4
West Norwood Clinic
WNWD SE27 .... **139** J6
Weston Park Clinic
CEND/HSY/T N8 .... **66** E6
Weston Park Primary School
CEND/HSY/T N8 .... **66** F6
Westpoint Trading Estate
ACT W3 .... **99** H4
West Ruislip Elementary School
HGDN/ICK UB10 .... **77** J3
West Thames College
ISLW TW7 .... **115** L7
West Thornton Primary School
CROY/NA CR0 .... **171** M2
West Twyford Primary School
WLSDN NW10 .... **99** G1
Westway Business Centre
BAY/PAD W2 .... **8** C3
Westway Sports Centre
NKENS W10 .... **100** D5
West Wickham Swimming Baths
WWKM BR4 .... **174** C3
Westwood High School for Girls
NRWD SE19 .... **157** J3
Westwood Primary
Infant School
WELL DA16 .... **143** L1
Westwood Primary School
WELL DA16 .... **143** K1
Westwood Technology College
WELL DA16 .... **143** L1
Weybridge Cricket Club
WEY KT13 .... **164** E4
Weybridge Hospital &
Primary Care Centre
WEY KT13 .... **164** A6
Whaddon House Clinic
CMBW SE5 .... **121** L8
Whipps Cross Hospital
WAN E11 .... **69** L6
Whiston Road Surgery
BETH E2 .... **7** L4
The White Bridge County
Infant & Junior School
LOU IG10 .... **52** E2
Whitechapel Art Gallery
WCHPL E1 .... **13** M4
White City Child Guidance Unit
SHB W12 .... **100** B6
Whitefield School
CRICK NW2 .... **64** D8
Whitefield Schools & Centre
WALTH E17 .... **69** J3
Whitefriars School
KTN/HRWW/W HA3 .... **61** L3
Whitefriars Trading Estate
KTN/HRWW/W HA3 .... **61** K3
Whitehall Primary School
CHING E4 .... **51** L4
White Hall Primary School
UX/CGN UB8 .... **76** C8
White Hart Lane School
WDGN N22 .... **67** H1
Whiteheath Infant School
RSLP HA4 .... **59** H7
Whiteheath Primary School
RSLP HA4 .... **59** J7
Whitehill House Surgery
DART DA1 .... **146** A2
Whitehorse Manor Junior School
THHTH CR7 .... **157** K7
White House Gallery
WAND/EARL SW18 .... **137** H5
The White House Surgery
CRICK NW2 .... **82** F4

Whitelodge Medical Practice
ENC/FH EN2 .... **36** D6
The Whitewebbs Museum of
Transport & Industry
ENC/FH EN2 .... **25** H8
The Whitgift Galleries
CROY/NA CR0 .... **172** C6
Whitgift School
SAND/SEL CR2 .... **172** C7
Whitmore High School
RYLN/HDSTN HA2 .... **79** J1
Whitmore Junior &
Infant School
IS N1 .... **7** H4
Whittingham Community
Primary School
WALTH E17 .... **68** D2
Whittings Hill School
BAR EN5 .... **33** J8
Whittington Hospital
ARCH N19 .... **84** B2
Whittlesea School
KTN/HRWW/W HA3 .... **61** J1
Whitton Health Centre
WHTN TW2 .... **133** J5
Whitton Health Clinic
WHTN TW2 .... **133** H5
Whitton School
WHTN TW2 .... **133** H6
Wholist Health Centre
SAND/SEL CR2 .... **172** C7
Whybridge Infant School
RAIN RM13 .... **92** A8
Whybridge Junior School
RAIN RM13 .... **91** M8
Whyllotts Council Offices
POTB/CUF EN6 .... **22** F5
Wickham Theatre
WWKM BR4 .... **174** D5
Wide Way Health Clinic
MTCM CR4 .... **156** D6
Wigfall Group Practice
STHWK SE1 .... **12** B9
Wigmore Hall
MHST W1U **10** C4
Wilbury Primary School
UED N18 .... **49** K7
Willesden & Brondesbury
Synagogue
CRICK NW2 .... **82** C6
Willesden Community Hospital
WLSDN NW10 .... **82** A7
Willesden County Court
WLSDN NW10 .... **99** L1
Willesden Green Surgery
WLSDN NW10 .... **82** B6
Willesden High School
WLSDN NW10 .... **82** B8
Willesden Medical Centre
CRICK NW2 .... **82** B6
William Bellamy Junior & Infant
School
DAGE RM10 .... **91** G2
William Byrd School
HYS/HAR UB3 .... **113** J4
William Ellis School
KTTN NW5 .... **84** A3
William Ellis Sports Ground
EDGE HA8 .... **63** G4
William Ford School
DAGE RM10 .... **91** G2
William Morris Gallery
WALTH E17 .... **69** G4
William Morris Middle School
MTCM CR4 .... **156** D6
William Morris School
WALTH E17 .... **68** E2
William Torbitt Junior &
Infant School
GNTH/NBYPK IG2 .... **71** L6
William Tyndale School
IS N1 .... **6** D1

Willington School
WIM/MER SW19 .... **154** F2
Willow Business Centre
MTCM CR4 .... **155** M8
Willow Business Park
SYD SE26 .... **140** C5
Willow Court Colindale Hospital
CDALE/KGS NW9 .... **63** K3
Willowfield Adult Education
Centre
WALTH E17 .... **68** D4
Willowfield School
HNHL SE24 .... **139** J1
Willowfield Secondary School
WALTH E17 .... **68** E4
Willow House Surgery
EN EN1 .... **36** E6
The Willow School
YEAD UB4 .... **96** C3
The Willows Clinic
CHST BR7 .... **161** H1
Willow Tree Primary School
NTHLT UB5 .... **78** E6
Willow Tree Surgery
CDALE/KGS NW9 .... **63** J6
Willow Tree Surgery
YEAD UB4 .... **96** C4
Wilmington Grange Grammar
School for Girls
RDART DA2 .... **146** B6
Wilmington High School
RDART DA2 .... **146** B7
Wilmington Parish Council
DART DA1 .... **146** D6
Wilmington Primary School
RDART DA2 .... **146** B7
Wilsons Grammar School
WLGTN SM6 .... **171** L8
Wimbledon Chase Middle School
RYNPK SW20 .... **154** E4
Wimbledon College for Boys
WIM/MER SW19 .... **154** D3
Wimbledon Common
Preparatory School for Boys
WIM/MER SW19 .... **154** C3
Wimbledon Football Club
SNWD SE25 .... **157** L7
Wimbledon High School for Girls
WIM/MER SW19 .... **154** E2
Wimbledon House School
WIM/MER SW19 .... **155** G4
Wimbledon Magistrates Court
WIM/MER SW19 .... **155** G2
Wimbledon Park First School
WIM/MER SW19 .... **137** H6
Wimbledon Rugby Club
RYNPK SW20 .... **153** M3
Wimbledon School of Art
WIM/MER SW19 .... **154** E4
Wimbledon School of Art
WIM/MER SW19 .... **155** G3
Wimbledon Stadium
Business Centre
WIM/MER SW19 .... **137** H7
Wimbledon Synagogue
WIM/MER SW19 .... **136** D6
Wimbledon Theatre
WIM/MER SW19 .... **155** H3
Winchcombe Business Centre
PECK SE15 .... **121** L4
Winchmore Hill Clinic
WCHMH N21 .... **49** H3
Winchmore Hill Cricket Club
WCHMH N21 .... **49** J3
Winchmore Secondary School
WCHMH N21 .... **49** J4
Windmill Medical Practice
CRICK NW2 .... **82** E5
Windmill School
BRXS/STRHM SW2 .... **138** E2
Windmill Trading Estate
MTCM CR4 .... **156** C8

Winfield House
CAMTN NW1 .... **3** K7
Wingate & Finchley
Football Club
NFNCH/WDSP N12 .... **65** K1
Wingate Trading Estate
TOTM N17 .... **67** M1
Wingfield Primary School
BKHTH/KID SE3 .... **124** A8
Winnington Ingram School
RSLP HA4 .... **59** K8
Winns Primary School
WALTH E17 .... **68** F3
Winsor Primary School
EHAM E6 .... **106** F5
Winston Galleries
RYLN/HDSTN HA2 .... **79** L1
Winton Primary School
IS N1 .... **5** L6
Witley Industrial Estate
NWDGN UB2 .... **114** F2
Witnitz School
STNW/STAM N16 .... **85** M1
Wix School
BTSEA SW11 .... **120** B8
Wolf Fields First School
NWDGN UB2 .... **114** F2
Wolfson Medical Centre
RYNPK SW20 .... **154** A3
Wolsey Business Park
WATW WD18 .... **41** K2
Women & Medical Practice
CEND/HSY/T N8 .... **67** G4
Women's Theatre Workshop
CONDST W1S **10** F7
The Woodberry Clinic
MUSWH N10 .... **66** B4
Woodbridge High School
WFD IG8 .... **70** B1
Woodbridge Surgery
STHL UB1 .... **96** D7
Woodbrook School
BECK BR3 .... **158** F4
Woodcote Group Practice
PUR/KEN CR8 .... **183** M4
Woodcote High School
COUL/CHIP CR5 .... **183** K6
Woodcote Junior & Infant
School
COUL/CHIP CR5 .... **183** J7
Woodcroft Junior School
EDGE HA8 .... **63** K1
Wood End Infant School
NTHLT UB5 .... **79** K5
Wood End Park Junior School
UX/CGN UB8 .... **95** J6
Woodfield School
CDALE/KGS NW9 .... **81** L1
Woodford County High
School for Girls
WFD IG8 .... **51** M8
Woodford Progressive
Synagogue
SWFD E18 .... **70** A4
Woodford Trading Estate
WFD IG8 .... **70** C3
Woodgrange Infant School
FSTGT E7 .... **88** B4
Woodgrange Medical Practice
FSTGT E7 .... **88** B5
Wood Green Crown Court
WDGN N22 .... **67** G2
Wood Green Health Centre
WDGN N22 .... **66** F2
Wood Green Old Boys
Football Club
WDGN N22 .... **67** G1
Woodhill Primary School
CHARL SE7 .... **124** E2
Woodhouse Sixth Form College
NFNCH/WDSP N12 .... **47** K7

Woodlands Infant &
Junior School
IL IG1 .... **89** K5
Woodlands Infant School
BORE WD6 .... **32** A4
Woodlands Park Infant School
SEVS/STOTM N15 .... **67** J6
Woodlands Surgery
BFN/LL DA15 .... **143** L5
Woodland Surgery
GNWCH SE10 .... **123** L3
Wood Lane Medical Centre
RSLP HA4 .... **77** L1
Wood Lane School
FUL/PGN SW6 .... **119** J6
Wood Lane School
SHB W12 .... **100** B5
Wood Lane Sports Centre
BCTR RM8 .... **91** H1
Wood Lane Surgery
HCH RM12 .... **92** A5
Woodmansterne CP School
BNSTD SM7 .... **182** F7
Woodmansterne
Primary School
STRHM/NOR SW16 .... **156** D4
Woodmansterne Sports Club
BNSTD SM7 .... **182** E8
Woodridge Primary School
NFNCH/WDSP N12 .... **46** F5
Woodside Community School
PLSTW E13 .... **106** C3
Woodside Health Centre
SNWD SE25 .... **158** B8
Woodside JMI School
CHESW EN7 .... **25** J2
Woodside Junior School
CROY/NA CR0 .... **173** G2
Woodside Park School
FBAR/BDGN N11 .... **47** M7
Woodside Park School
NFNCH/WDSP N12 .... **47** H6
Woodside Park Synagogue
NFNCH/WDSP N12 .... **47** H7
Woodside School
BELV DA17 .... **127** H2
Wood Street Medical Centre
WALTH E17 .... **69** J4
Wood Wharf
POP/IOD E14 .... **105** H7
Woolmore Primary School
POP/IOD E14 .... **105** J6
Woolwich College
WOOL/PLUM SE18 .... **124** D2
Woolwich College
WOOL/PLUM SE18 .... **125** J2
Woolwich County Court
WOOL/PLUM SE18 .... **125** G1
Woolwich Crown Court
THMD SE28 .... **107** L8
Woolwich Polytechnic School
THMD SE28 .... **108** A7
Worcesters Infant &
Primary School
EN EN1 .... **36** F3
Workers Gallery
SOHO/CST W1F **11** G5
World Business Centre Heathrow
HTHAIR TW6 .... **113** G4
World of Football Hall of Fame
STHWK SE1 .... **17** L2
World Trade Centre
TWRH EC3N **13** M7
World University Service
STLK EC1Y **13** G1
Worlsey Bridge Junior
Mixed School
BECK BR3 .... **159** G3
Wormholt Park Primary School
SHB W12 .... **100** A6

Worple Primary School
ISLW TW7 .... **134** A1
Worton Hall Industrial Estate
ISLW TW7 .... **133** L1
Wroxham JMI School
POTB/CUF EN6 .... **22** H4
The Wrythe Green Surgery
SUT SM1 .... **170** E5
Wyborne Primary Mixed School
ELTH/MOT SE9 .... **143** H5
Wycliffe School
BTSEA SW11 .... **120** A7
Wykeham Junior School
HCH RM12 .... **92** H1
Wykeham Primary School
WLSDN NW10 .... **81** K3
Wyllie Gallery
SKENS SW7 .... **14** E4
Wyvil Primary School
VX/NE SW8 .... **120** E5
Yacob Gallery
KENS W8 .... **8** B8
Yale University Press
HAMP NW3 .... **83** L4
Yardley Primary School
CHING E4 .... **38** B8
Yeading Football Club
HYS/HAR UB3 .... **96** C7
Yeading JMI School
YEAD UB4 .... **96** C4
Yeading Medical Centre
NTHLT UB5 .... **96** C2
Yehudi Gordons Practice
STJWD NW8 .... **3** G5
Yemen Embassy
SKENS SW7 .... **15** G5
Yerbury Primary School
ARCH N19 .... **84** D3
Yeshivo Horomo Talmudical
College
STNW/STAM N16 .... **85** K1
Yeshurun Synagogue
EDGE HA8 .... **45** G8
Yiewsley Health Centre
WDR/YW UB7 .... **94** E7
Yin Yang Chinese Medical Centre
GDMY/SEVK IG3 .... **90** A1
YMCA
ECT SW5 .... **14** C7
York Clinic
STHWK SE1 .... **13** G9
York Galleries
TWK TW1 .... **134** C3
York Road CP School
DART DA1 .... **146** F4
York Water Gate
CHCR WC2N **11** K8
Young England Rugby Club
VX/NE SW8 .... **120** E4
Young Vic Theatre
STHWK SE1 .... **18** B1
Youth Hostel
BERM/RHTH SE16 .... **104** D7
Yth Hostel
BLKFR EC4V **12** D5
Zambia High Comm
SKENS SW7 .... **14** E2
Zebra Two Gallery
HAMP NW3 .... **83** J4
Zella Gallery
WBPTN SW10 .... **14** F9
Zenith Gallery
BAL SW12 .... **138** B4
Zennor Road Industrial Estate
BAL SW12 .... **138** C5
Zimbabwe High Commission
CHCR WC2N **11** J7
Zoo
IL IG1 .... **89** J2

Page 7

H8
1 Bache's St
2 Singer St

J6
1 Homefield St

M9
1 Cygnet St
2 Granby St

Page 9

L5
1 Great Cumberland Ms
2 Hampden Gurney St
3 Stourcliffe St

M4
1 Brunswick Ms
2 Montagu Ms South
3 Portman Towers

Page 10

B3
1 Bulstrode Pl
2 Cross Keys Yd
3 De Walden St
4 Wesley St
5 Wheatley St
6 Woodstock Ms

B5
1 Cray's Yd

E6
1 Coach And Horses Yd
2 New Burlington St

F1
1 Midford Pl

F2
1 Maple St
2 Tottenham Ms
3 Tottenham St

F3
1 Wells Ms

F4
1 Marylebone Pas

C4
1 Berwick St
2 D'arblay St
3 Dufour's Pl
4 Canton St
5 Livonia St
6 Noel St
7 Portland Ms
8 Wardour Ms

F6
1 Lower James St
2 Sherwood St

F7
1 Albany Ctyd

F8
1 Apple Tree Yd

F9
1 Rose And Crown Yd
2 Russell Ct
3 Stable Yard Yd

Page 11

C6
1 Archer St
2 Gerrard St
3 Great Windmill St
4 Ham Yd
5 Old Compton St
6 Rupert St
7 Smith's Ct
8 Winnett St

G8
1 St James's Sq

H3
1 Bedford Sq

H4
1 Andrew Borde St
2 Bainbridge St
3 Earnshaw St
4 Great Russell St
5 Sutton Rw

M6
1 Melbourne Pl

Page 12

B4
1 Bartlett Ct
2 East Harding St
3 Great New St
4 Little New St
5 New Street Sq
6 Pemberton Rw
7 Plough Pl
8 Printer St
9 West Harding St

D6
1 Puddle Dock

E6
1 Lawrence La
2 Pancras La
3 Russia Rw

F6
1 Bread St
2 College Hl
3 Great Trinity La
4 Tower Royal

F9
1 O'meara St

Page 13

C6
1 Allhallows La
2 Gophir La
3 Laurence Poutney Hl
4 Salters' Hall Ct
5 Walbrook

G9
1 Bedale St
2 Borough High St

M6
1 Goodman's Yd

Page 14

C2
1 Kensington Church Ct
2 Kensington Church Wk
3 Kensington Sq

F9
1 Winterton Pl

Page 15

L2
1 Knightsbridge Gn

M2
1 Kinnerton Pl South

M4
1 Pavilion Rd

Page 16

D3
1 Grosvenor Gardens Ms East
2 Victoria Sq

F7
1 Charlwood Cl
2 Denbigh St

Page 18

C5
1 George Mathers Rd
2 Longville Rd

Page 21

E8
1 Beckford Rd

Page 23

G5
1 Edinburgh Dr
2 Hurricane Wy
3 Katherine Pl
4 Lysander Wy
5 Maple Leaf Cl
6 Mitchell Cl
7 Shackleton Wy

L6
1 Chichester Wy
2 Lemon Field Dr

L8
1 Phillipers

Page 26

G6
1 Winston Wy

J6
1 Barnet Rd
2 Hermitage Ct
3 Lake Vw
4 St Vincent's Wy

K6
1 Fetherstone Cl
2 Wayside

B3
1 Homeleigh Ct
2 Linden Cl
3 Lindsay Pl
4 Pengelly Cl

D1
1 Campine Cl
2 The Colonnade
3 Drakes Cl
4 Faverolle Gn
5 Hamburgh Ct
6 Southbrook Dr
7 The Spur
8 Symonds Ct

D6
1 Lambton Av
2 Leven Cl
3 Monarch's Wy
4 Park Rd
5 Stoneleigh Pl

D7
1 Dumbarton Av

D8
1 Abridge Cl
2 Dewgrass Gv
3 The Greenway
4 Hawksmead Cl
5 Kingsfield Wy

E1
1 Bromleigh Cl
2 Cordell Cl
3 Fraser Rd
4 Goodwin Cl
5 Lensbury Ct

E3
1 Foster Cl
2 Guinevere Gdns
3 Roberts Cl
4 Roswell Cl

E4
1 Acton Cl
2 Garland Cl
3 Holme Cl
4 Russell's Dr

E5
1 Burleigh Rd

E6
1 Cross Rd

E7
1 Abbey Rd
2 Lodge Crs
3 Station Ap
4 Trust Rd

F1
1 Fowley Cl
2 Queens Wy

Page 27

H6
1 Bernard Gv
2 North Pl
3 Plantaganet Pl
4 Powdermill Ms

J7
1 Fountain Pl
2 King George Rd
3 Milton Ct
4 Paradise Rd
5 Rue De St Lawrence
6 Silver St

K7
1 Cypress Cl
2 Joyce Ct
3 Larsen Dr

L6
1 The Granaries
2 Windsor Wd

M6
1 Poplar Shaw

Page 29

G4
1 Langwood Gdns
2 Maple Cv
3 Pinewood Cl
4 Roseberry Ct

G6
1 Hyde Rd
2 Memorial Vw
3 Peace Prospect

H3
1 Callowland Cl
2 Halsey Pl
3 Lea Rd
4 St George's Rd

H5
1 Lowestoft Rd

H6
1 Albert Rd South
2 Clarendon Rd
3 Monmouth Rd

H7
1 Fearnley St
2 The Hornets
3 Percy Rd
4 Wellstones

Page 31

H8
1 Aynho St
2 Banbury St
3 Farraline Rd
4 Westbury Rd

F7
1 The Broadway
2 Earl St
3 Lord St
4 Ottoman Ter
5 Queen's Pth
6 Queen's Rd
7 Shaftesbury Rd
8 Stanley Rd
9 Trinity Hall St

J7
1 Cambridge Rd
2 Chapmans Yd
3 Church St
4 The Crescent
5 Derby Rd
6 Granville Rd
7 Kings Cl
8 Lower Derby Rd
9 Market Pl
10 New St
11 Smith St
12 Water La
13 Watford Field Rd
14 Woodmans Yd

J8
1 Cannon Rd
2 Hamilton St
3 Lammas Rd
4 Local Board Rd
5 Roberts Rd
6 Tucker St

L1
1 Beasant House
2 Bevan House
3 Gandhi Ct
4 Mandela Ct
5 Orwell Ct

K6
1 Pankhurst Pl

K8
1 Bridge Pl

L1
1 Mallard Wy
2 Widgeon Wy

L6
1 Leander Gdns

L5
1 Scottswood Cl
2 Sycamore Cl

M5
1 Walnut Gn

Page 31

M5
1 Badgers Cl
2 Chiltern Cl
3 Holmdale Cl
4 Holme Pk
5 The Pines

M7
1 Links Dr
2 Woodside

M8
1 Lowther Cl

Page 32

A3
1 Brampton Ter
2 Pursley Gdns
3 St Neots Cl
4 Sawtry Wy
5 Stilton Pth
6 Wentbridge Pth

A5
1 Badminton Cl

D8
1 Lincoln Cl
2 Saddlers Cl
3 Suffolk Cl
4 Tinwell Wk

Page 36

A5
1 Capstan Ride
2 Englefield Cl
3 Havenhurst Ri
4 Valley Fields Crs
5 Vulcan Ga

B7
1 Haselwood Dr
2 Vermont Cl

C5
1 Christchurch Cl
2 Cricketers Arms Rd
3 Lambs Wk

H6
1 Tempsford Cl

J7
1 Churchbury Cl
2 Churchbury Rd
3 Connaught Ct

J7
1 Fyfield Rd
2 Greencroft Gdns
3 Orchard Wy

K7
1 Fielders Cl
2 Roseneath Wk
3 Woodfield Cl

E8
1 Illingworth Wy
2 Winchester Cl

F4
1 Chinnery Cl
2 Churchbury La

F6
1 Clydach Vw

F8
1 Agricola Pl
2 Kingswood Cl

Page 37

J1
1 Larmans Rd

J6
1 Broadlands Cl

K2
1 Hartmoor Rd

K3
1 Ferns Cl

D3
1 Bourneside Crs
2 John Bradshaw Rd
3 Tudor Wy
4 The Wells

E7
1 Broomfield Rd

E8
1 Goring Rd
2 Hardwicke Rd
3 Richmond Rd

F1
1 Meadowbank

Page 42

M3
1 Arnold Av East

A5
1 Ashburnham Cl
2 Gosforth Pth
3 Hilswell Gn
4 Hillsborough Gn
5 Longcliffe Pth

C5
1 Buxton Pth
2 Harrogate Rd
3 Kirkcaldy Gn
4 Swanston Pth
5 Turnberry Ct

C7
1 Bognor Gdns
2 Bromborough Gn
3 Darwin Gdns
4 Doncaster Gn
5 Harborne Cl
6 Huntercombe Gdns
7 Kemilworth Gdns
8 Morriston Cl
9 Muirfield Cl

D6
1 Crowborough Pth
2 Glencorse Gn
3 Lundin Wk
4 Marketon Gn
5 Mullion Wk
6 Newport Mead
7 Piltdown Rd

E1
1 Avenue Ter
2 Brick Kiln Ct
3 Caroline Pl
4 Hillside Crs
5 Rowley Cl
6 Warneford Pl

E2
1 Field End Cl
2 Maxwell Ri

E6
1 Ganton Wk

E5
1 Highfield

Page 43

H1
1 Baird Cl
2 The Close
3 Fidler Pl
4 Herkomer Cl
5 Meadowcroft
6 Mortimer Cl
7 Ryder Cl
8 Wheelright Cl

J5
1 Langholme
2 Partridge Cl
3 Stevens Gn

J4
1 Gillan Gn
2 Mc Kellar Ct
3 Mungo-park Cl

M8
1 Berwick Cl
2 Coppice Cl
3 Fortnums Acre
4 Jellicoe Gdns
5 Newbolt Rd
6 Rowan Cl
7 Uxbridge Rd (Stanmore)
8 Waleran Cl

Page 44

C8
1 Lemark Cl

D1
1 The Bartons
2 Fox Cl
3 Georges Mead
4 Oak Tree Ct
5 Romeland
6 Stuart Ct
7 Webber Cl
8 Westview Ct
9 Yew Tree Ct

F2
1 Calthorpe Gdns

F8
1 Lodge Cl
2 Rye Wy
3 Whitchurch Cl

Page 45

L7
1 Beechwood Cl
2 Brockenhurst Cl
3 Uphill Dr

L8
1 The Meads

Page 47

J6
1 Cliveden Cl
2 St Andrew's Cl
3 Sonia Gdns
4 Squirrels Cl

K7
1 Rose Bank Cl
2 Torrington Gv

L8
1 Harwood Cl
2 Hawthorden Cl
3 Newstead Cl
4 Summers Rw
5 Thistley Cl

M1
1 Mansfield Cl

M7
1 St Mary's Rd

M5
1 Bruce Gdns
2 Marlborough Cl
3 Porch Wy

F7
1 Leadbeaters Cl

Page 48

B1
1 Monkfrith Av
2 Tavistock Pl

C1
1 St Johns Cl

D3
1 Bourneside Crs
2 John Bradshaw Rd
3 Tudor Wy
4 The Wells

E7
1 Broomfield Rd

E8
1 Goring Rd
2 Hardwicke Rd
3 Richmond Rd

F1
1 Meadowbank

Page 49

H6
1 Connaught Wk
2 Hamilton Wy
3 Lawrence Av

L5
1 Hazelbury La

L6
1 Tuncombe Rd

L7
1 Lansbury Gv
2 Statham Gv

L8
1 Hardinge Rd
2 Trafalgar Av

M1
1 Harrow Av

M2
1 Bury St West
2 Edward Cl
3 Winifred Ter

M3
1 Malvern Ter

M5
1 Briary La
2 Dunholme La
3 Northumberland Av
4 Pymmes Gdns North
5 Pymmes Gdns South

M7
1 College Gdns
2 Regal Ct

M8
1 Bennetts Cl
2 Bradford Cl
3 Castleford Cl
4 Cooperage Cl
5 Langhedge Cl

Page 50

A4
1 Beechwood Ms
2 Cedars Rd
3 Church La
4 Dorman Pl
5 Lacey Cl
6 Lichfield Rd
7 Lion Rd
8 Sawyer Cl
9 Wimborne Rd

A5
1 Balfour Ms
2 Bridge Rd
3 Knight's La
4 Leonard Rd
5 Peel Cl
6 St George's Rd
7 Sunnyside Rd North
8 Sunnyside Rd South

A6
1 Bradwell Ms
2 Fleece Dr
3 Folkestone Rd
4 Hythe Cl
5 Lansfield Av
6 Moree Wy
7 North Av
8 Park Av
9 Reculver Ms
10 Station House Ms

M2
1 Manor Cottages

M4
1 Everett Cl

M5
1 Chippenham Cl

Page 52

A7
1 Butterworth Gdns
2 Colwall Gdns
3 Elrington Rd
4 Gardenia Wy
5 High Elms
6 Johnston Rd
7 Twentyman Cl

C7
1 Ewanrigg Ter
2 Frankland Cl
3 Hillside Cl
4 Manorway
5 Meadway
6 Parkway

C8
1 Gainsborough Rd
2 Green Wk
3 Latchingdon Gdns
4 Morgan Wy
5 Oakwood Cl

F8
1 Chaplemount Rd
2 Henwood Side
3 Hill Top Vw
4 Kelvedon Wy
5 Nyssa Cl
6 Rosemount Cl
7 Sands Wy

Page 51

H1
1 Amesbury Dr
2 Chelwood Cl
3 Redwood Gdns
4 Riverside Ct

J6
1 Retingham Wy

L6
1 Berrybank Cl
2 Conference Cl
3 Goldsborough Crs

J6
1 Woodview Av

K3
1 Cambridge Rd
2 Carbis Cl
3 Cranworth Crs
4 Glendower Rd
5 The Green Wk
6 Pentney Rd
7 Queens Wk

Page 59

F7
1 Broomfield La
2 Southchurch Ct

F8
1 Granville Ct
2 Grasmere Ct
3 Marquis Rd
4 Wynaud Ct

Page 60

G3
1 Barrowdene Cl
2 Burhill Gv
3 Little Orchard Cl

K3
1 School La

A3
1 Moorcroft Wy

A7
1 Dewsbury Rd

E8
1 Hawlands Dr

F1
1 Cherry Croft Gdns
2 Helston Cl
3 St Cuthberts Gdns
4 Thorndyke Ct
5 Uxbridge Rd (Hatch End)

F2
1 Littlecote Pl
2 Wellington Av

F4
1 Beechengrove
2 Eastglade
3 Shelbourne Cl

F7
1 The Gardens
2 The Greenway

F8
1 The Close
2 Newlyn Gdns

Page 61

J3
1 Almond Wy
2 Temsford Cl

K3
1 High Rd
2 John Lamb Ct

L5
1 Badminton Cl
2 Poets Wy
3 Sparkbridge Rd

L6
1 Colton Rd

L7
1 Clarendon Rd
2 Kymberley Rd
3 William Carey Wy

L8
1 Whitehall Rd

M1
1 Caddis Cl
2 Castellane Cl
3 Hill House Av
4 Trevor Cl

M2
1 Broadlawns Cl
2 Woodpecker Cl

Page 62

E8
1 John Perrin Pl

F1
1 Whitchurch Gdns

F2
1 Newgale Gdns

F4
1 Cumberland Rd

F5
1 Friday Hl
2 Newgate St

L6
1 Betoyne Av
2 Brookhouse Gdns
3 Mason Rd
4 Nightingale Cl
5 Waterhall Av

L7
1 Brook Meadow Cl

M3
1 Littleton Av

M4
1 British Legion Rd
2 Rookwood Gdns

M6
1 Hatchwoods
2 The Hollow

Page 63

G3
1 Rembrandt Rd

K7
1 Argyll Gdns
2 Kenmore Gdns
3 Strathmore Gdns

C7
1 Botham Cl
2 Brearley Cl
3 Compton Cl
4 Deansbrook Cl
5 Catting Cl
6 Grace Cl
7 Hutton Rw

J8
1 Hawthorne Gv

E5
1 Blundell Rd
2 Goldbeaters Gv

L2
1 Bovingdon La
2 Elvington La
3 Folkingham La
4 Gaydon La
5 Mathering Wy
6 North Acre
7 Trenchard Cl

L5
1 Kestrel Cl
2 Ludford Cl
3 Solsby Cl
4 Turnstone Cl

L6
1 Orchard Ga

L7
1 Derwent Av

L7
1 Northgate Dr

L4
1 Lancaster Cl
2 University Cl

M6
1 St Matthias Cl

M7
1 Borthwick Rd
2 Ramsey Cl
3 Ravenstone Rd

Page 64

A3
1 Barford Cl

A7
1 Dartmouth Rd
2 Hollview Cl
3 Milton Rd
4 Western Rd

B7
1 Nicoll Pl

C5
1 Brampton Rd
2 Foster Wk
3 Glebe Crs
4 Harmony Wy
5 Prince Of Wales Cl
6 Somerset Rd
7 Sunny Pl

F7
1 The Ap
2 Brent St
3 Danescroft Av
4 Golders Ri
5 Goodyers Gdns
6 Woodburn Cl

E2
1 Foreland Ct
2 Hawthorn Ms
3 Rydal Cl

E3
1 Cumberland Gdns
2 Freeland Pk
3 Queenswood Pk
4 Windsor Cl

E8
1 Beverley Gdns
2 Highfield Rd

F2
1 Montpelier Ms

Page 65

H5
1 Brookland Garth

M4
1 Palmerston Centre

Page 66

B5
1 Beattock Ri
2 Hillfield Park Ms

E2
1 Berkeley Rd
2 The Grove
3 Harefield Rd
4 View Crs

E3
1 Station Rd

E4
1 Campsbourne Rd

E5
1 The Campsbourne
2 Grove House Rd
3 Pembroke Rd
4 St Mary's Rd

M1
1 Chapel Rd
2 Gretton Rd
3 Headcorn Rd
4 Moselle St
5 Park La
6 Percival Ct
7 Tebworth Rd

F2
1 Briston Gv
2 Ivy Gdns
3 Middle La
4 Sandringham Gdns
5 Tregaron Av

J8
1 Linkway
2 Rowley Gdns
3 Vale Gv
4 Woodberry Gv

Page 67

G3
1 Ashley Crs
2 Coombe Rd
3 Gladstone Ms
4 Glynne Rd
5 Noel Park Rd

G5
1 The Mews

H5
1 Alfoxton Av
2 Hallam Rd
3 Hartingay Gdns
4 Park Rd
5 St Margaret's Av
6 Willow Wk

H7
1 Atterbury Rd
2 Cyprus Cl
3 Devon Gdns
4 Essex Gdns
5 Portland Gdns
6 Tancred Rd
7 Venetia Rd
8 Williamson Rd
9 Woollaston Rd

A7
1 Fairweather Rd
2 Leabank Vw
3 Lockmead Rd
4 Riverside Rd

J3
1 Fenman Ct
2 Pymmes Ct
3 Romney Ct

E4
1 Chamberlain Pl
2 Farnborough Cl
3 Higham Ct
4 Pembar Av

Page 68

A2
1 Baronet Gv
2 Burlington Rd
3 Rolvenden Pl
4 St Mary's Cl
5 Whitbread Cl

A4
1 Ashley Rd
2 Burdock Rd
3 Cape Rd
4 The Hale
5 High Cross Rd
6 Malvern Rd
7 Station Rd

A5
1 Bramble Cl
2 Cunningham Rd
3 Fountayne Rd
4 Hale Gdns
5 Montague Rd
6 Shanklin Rd
7 Stamford Rd
8 Victoria Rd

A6
1 Foreland Ct

A7
1 Clare Rd

K8
1 Boscombe Av

L1
1 Bennington Rd

L3
1 St Andrew's Rd

L8
1 Temple Cl

M4
1 Chatham Rd
2 Washington Rd

M5
1 Althorpe Gdns
2 Audley Ct
3 Bradwell Cl
4 Rayne Ct
5 Wooldam Ct

Page 69

G5
1 Boleyn Ct
2 Cairo Rd
3 Cleveland Park Av
4 Cleveland Park Crs
5 Gillards Ms
6 Vintry Ms

G6
1 Connaught Wy
2 Exeter Rd
3 First Av
4 Leamington Av
5 Second Av
6 Sylvan Rd

G8
1 Albany Rd
2 Queens Rd
3 Saxon Cl

H1
1 Minerva Rd
2 Wadham Rd

H5
1 Berry Field Cl
2 Bishop's Cl
3 Bremer Ms
4 Church Rd
5 Trelawny Cl

H7
1 Atkins Rd
2 Rosebank Rd
3 Shaftesbury Rd

J6
1 Comely Bank Rd
2 Elm Rd
3 St Stephen's Rd
4 Shernhall St

J7
1 St Heller's Rd

J8
1 Beaumont Rd
2 Lambourne Rd
3 Moyers Rd

K1
1 Frinton Dr
2 Montserrat Av

K3
1 Fernhill Ct

Page 70

B4
1 Burton Rd
2 Kenwood Gdns

Page 72

C8
1 Well Cottage Cl

D1
1 Debden Cl
2 Coldhaze Cl
3 Underwood Rd

D5
1 Fonteyne Gdns
2 Lambs Meadow

E4
1 Gales Wy

E5
1 Borrowdale Cl

F2
1 Humphrey Cl

F4
1 Crombie Cl

F9
1 Pavilion Rd

Page 73

L6
1 Cherry St
2 Pettley Gdns

L4
1 Mcintosh Cl

L7
1 Brunel Cl
2 Ducking Stool Ct
3 Ingrave Rd

L3
1 Atlanta Bvd
2 Marden Rd

L6
1 Brockton Cl
2 Sydenham Cl

M6
1 Broadfield Cl
2 Grimshaw Wy
3 Harcourt Ms

M7
1 Alexandra Rd
2 King Edward Rd
3 Kingsmead Av
4 Richmond Rd
5 Shakespeare Rd
6 Wheatsheaf Rd

M8
1 Artesian Cl
2 The Maltings

Page 74

D2
1 Buttercup Cl
2 Copperfields Wy
3 Hatherleigh Wy
4 Widecombe Cl

D7
1 Staverton Cl

E1
1 Melksham Cl

E2
1 Aubrietia Cl
2 Camellia Cl
3 Poynings Wy

E5
1 Banyards
2 Macdonald Wy
3 Peacock Cl
4 Russets

E6
1 Ayloffs Cl

E7
1 Porchester Cl
2 Rockchase Gdns

E8
1 Beverley Gdns
2 Dalewood Cl
3 Meadowlands

H1
1 Barnsley Rd
2 Camborne Wy
3 Gleneagles Cl
4 Melksham Cl
5 Wednesbury Gn

H2
1 Station Rd

H3
1 Owlets Hall Cl

H5
1 Grassmere Rd
2 Jackson Cl
3 Wakefield Cl

J6
1 Channing Cl

Page 76

B6
1 Nine Stiles Cl

F4
1 Shipton Rd

K1
1 Beehive Cl
2 Chapter Cl
3 Finians Cl
4 Hazelcroft Cl

Page 78

A3
1 Green Lawns
2 Kildare Ct
3 Melton Cl
4 Rodwell Cl

F3
1 Hodson Cl
2 Jordan Cl
3 Stradbrook Cl

K6
1 Salter Cl

F5
1 Doncaster Gdns
2 The Link

F7
1 Harewood Cl
2 Kingsmead Dr
3 Petworth Cl

Page 79

H2
1 Drinkwater Rd
2 Lodgehill Park Cl
3 Moatfield Rd
4 Thornley Cr

H3
1 Alexandra Cl
2 Beechwood Gdns
3 Findon Cl
4 Grovelands Cl
5 Leathsale Rd
6 Reverend Cl
7 Valentine Rd

H8
1 Norseman Wy

Page 42

A5
1 Ashburnham Cl
2 Gosforth Pth
3 Hilswell Gn
4 Hillsborough Gn
5 Longcliffe Pth

Page 66

M5
1 Ferndale Ter

M6
1 Becket Fold
2 Central Pde
3 Courtfield Av
4 East End Rd
5 Thomas Moore Wy

K4
1 Claybrook Cl
2 Eagans Cl
3 Elmhurst Av
4 Markert Pl
5 New Ash Cl
6 The Walks

K5
1 Ashburnham Cl
2 Cromwell Cl
3 Gorleston Rd
4 Oakview Gdns
5 Prospect Pl

K6
1 Lyttelton Rd
2 Lytton Cl
3 Vivian Wy

K7
1 Byron Dr
2 Winnington Cl

K8
1 Arden Court Gdns

L1
1 Downway

L4
1 Norfolk Cl

L5
1 Diploma Av
2 Stowe Pl

M4
1 Alexandra Ms
2 Annington Rd

M5
1 Francis Rd
2 Keynes Cl

Page 62

K3
1 Lido Sq

K4
1 Hastings Rd

K5
1 Caradon Wy
2 Dagmar Rd
3 Gresley Cl
4 Spur Rd
5 Stonemasons Ct

K6
1 Alexandra Rd
2 Appleby Cl
3 Gorleston Rd
4 Lydford Rd

K7
1 Berkeley Rd
2 Fladbury Rd
3 Manchester Rd
4 Moreton Cl
5 Netherton Rd
6 Remington Rd

K8
1 New River Wy

L1
1 Cemetery Rd

L2
1 All Hallows Rd
2 Risley Av

L5
1 Loobert Rd
2 Stowe Pl

L5
1 Brunswick Rd
2 Clyde Circ
3 Elizabeth Clyde Cl
4 Grove Hart Rd
5 Lawrence Rd
6 Lomond Cl
7 Nelson Rd
8 Winns Ms

L6
1 Ansar Gdns
2 Arkley Crs
3 Arkley Rd
4 Brunner Rd
5 Glen Rd
6 Mission Gv
7 Side Rd
8 Vernon Rd

L7
1 Candler St
2 Chisley Rd
3 Frinton Rd
4 Holmdale Ter
5 Howard Rd
6 Langford Cl
7 Latimer Rd
8 Paignton Rd
9 Perry Ct
10 Thorpe Rd

F7
1 Boundary Av
2 Broomfield
3 Harris St
4 Herbert Rd
5 Samantha Cl
6 Sybourn St
7 Sylvester Rd
8 Verulam Av
9 Wetherden St

K2
1 Ashbourne Av
2 Athena Cl
3 Brickfields
4 Brigade Cl
5 Hornbuckle Cl
6 Waldron's Yd

K5
1 Brasher Cl
2 Hammond Cl
3 Hemery Rd
4 Hutton Cl
5 Matthews Rd
6 Ramsey Cl
7 Tessa Sanderson Wy
8 Wood End Cl

K8
1 Rockware Av
2 Station Vw
3 West Green Pl

L1
1 Leigh Ct
2 Meadow Vw
3 Victoria Ter

L2
1 Elmfield Cl

L3
1 Leabank Cl

L5
1 Oldfield Cl
2 Oldfield La

M4
1 The Boltons

Page 80

D2
1 Loweswater Cl
2 Pempath Pl

E7
1 Haynes Rd
2 Stanley Cl

E8
1 Hazel Gv
2 Innovation Cl
3 Rosemont Rd
4 Woodside Pl

F2
1 Bowling Green Ct

F4
1 Corinium Cl

F5
1 Dennis Av
2 Ecclestone Pl

F6
1 Gaddesden Av

F7
1 Vincent Rd

F8
1 Newcombe Pk

Page 81

J5
1 Buddings Cir
2 Chalalands
3 Demeta Cl
4 Gervase Cl

K1
1 St Andrews Rd

K5
1 Cygnet Cl
2 Hardie Cl
3 Herne Cl
4 Kestrel Cl
5 Kingfisher Wy
6 Peregrine Cl

K7
1 Barrs Rd
2 Kingthorpe Rd

K8
1 Craven Rd
2 Knatchbull Rd
3 Shakespeare Crs
4 Shrewsbury Crs

L4
1 Balnacraig Av
2 Baskerville Gdns
3 Crispian Cl
4 Midstrath Rd

L5
1 Iron Bridge Cl
2 Neasden Cl

L6
1 Heron Cl
2 Preston Gdns
3 Roberts Ct

L7
1 Bishop Wy
2 Guilsborough Cl
3 Norfolk Rd
4 Northcote Rd
5 Suffolk Rd
6 Taylor's La

L8
1 Bolton Rd
2 Charlton Rd
3 Connaught Rd
4 Craven Pk
5 Greenhill Rd
6 Greenhill Rd
7 Langdon Ct
8 Park Rd

M4
1 Leeland Wy
2 Northview Crs

M5
1 Woodmans Gv

M6
1 Eric Rd

M7
1 Hawkshead Rd
2 Outgate Rd

M8
1 Manor Park Rd

Page 82

A7
1 Clare Rd
2 Sterling Cl

C7
1 Brondesbury Pk

E7
1 Bembridge Cl

F5
1 Mortimer Cl
2 Prospect Rd
3 Sunnyside

F5
1 Broomsleigh St
2 Dornfell St
3 Glastonbury St
4 Hillfield Rd

F6
1 Cavendish Cl
2 Kingscroft Rd
3 Ravensmead St

1 Brooklands Cl
2 Clarence Rd
3 Drakes Ctyd
4 Gladstone Ms
5 Palmerston Rd

Page 83

G6
1 Medley Rd
2 Rowntree Cl
3 Sandwell Crs
4 Sumatra St

H6
1 Beswick Ms
2 Crown Cl
3 Doulton Ms
4 Dresden Cl
5 Lymington Rd
6 Minton Ms
7 Worcester Ms

J3
1 Elm Rw
2 Hampstead Sq
3 Whitestone Wk

J5
1 Frognal Cl
2 Netherhall Wy

J8
1 Alexandra Pl
2 Boundary Ms

K4
1 Carlingford Rd
2 Gardnor Rd
3 Old Brewery Ms
4 Prince Arthur Rd
5 Streatley Rd
6 Vane Cl

K6
1 Belsize Court Garages
2 Lyndhurst Gdns
3 Lyndhurst Ter
4 Princess Ms
5 Rosslyn Park Ms

K7
1 Baynes Ms
2 Belsize Ms
3 Belsize Park Ms
4 Belsize Sq
5 Daleham Ms
6 Mccrone Ms

K7
1 Winchester Rd

L1
1 Hampstead Hill Gdns
2 Maryon Ms
3 Park End
4 St Crispins Cl
5 South End Rd

L5
1 Aspern Gv
2 Hampstead Gn
3 Rowland Hill St
4 Russell Pl
5 Woodland Wk

L6
1 Lancaster Stables

L7
1 Briary Cl
2 Brocas Cl
3 Conybeare
4 Elliott Sq
5 Hawtrey Rd
6 Hornby Cl
7 Huson Cl
8 King's College Rd
9 Lyttleton Cl
10 Quickswood
11 Strathray Gdns
12 Tobin St

M4
1 Cressy Rd
2 Mackeson Rd
3 The Old Orch

M5
1 Dunboyne Rd
2 Ella Ms
3 Kingsford Cl
4 Southampton Rd
5 Tasker Rd

M6
1 Maitland Park Vls
2 Stanbury Ct
3 Steele's Ms North
4 Steele's Ms South
5 Thurlow Ter

M7
1 Berkley Rd
2 Chamberlain St
3 Meadowbank
4 Oppidans Rd
5 St George's Ms
6 St George's Ter
7 Sharples Hall St

M8
1 Ormonde Ter
2 St Edmund's Cl
3 St James's Terrace Ms

Page 84

A5
1 Ashdown Crs
2 Dale Rd
3 Dengil Crs
4 Malden Pl
5 Weedington Rd
6 Wellesley Pl

A6
1 Allcroft Rd
2 Baptist Gdns
3 Bassett St
4 Coity Rd
5 Craddock St
6 Modbury Gdns
7 St Ann's Gdns
8 St Thomas's Gdns
9 Talacre Rd
10 Truro St
11 Wilkin St

A7
1 Belmont St
2 Chalcot Sq
3 Dumpton Pl
4 Egbert St
5 Ferdinand Pl
6 Ferdinand St

A8
1 Albert Terrace Ms
2 Kingstown St
3 Manley St
4 Primrose Hill Studios
5 Regal La
6 St Mark's Crs
7 St Mark's Sq

B5
1 Arctic St
2 Fortess Wk
3 Woodyard Cl
4 York Ms

B6
1 Cathcart St
2 Church Av
3 Crown Pl
4 Grafton Crs
5 Grafton Yd
6 Healey St
7 Ryland Rd
8 Willes Rd

B7
1 Albert St
2 Arlington Ms
3 Bayham St
4 Gloucester Gate Br
5 Greenland Pl
6 Greenland Rd
7 Greenland St
8 Inverness St
9 Regent's Park Ter
10 Signmakers Yd
11 Underhill St

B8
1 Ascham St
2 Countess Rd
3 Dunollie Pl
4 Fortess Gv
5 Frideswide Pl
6 Leighton Pl
7 Leverton Pl
8 Peckwater St
9 Willingham Ter

C7
1 Caversham Rd
2 Hammond Cl
3 Patshull Pl
4 Rochester Ter
5 Whitcher Pl

C7
1 Baynes St
2 Farrier St
3 Ivor St
4 Jeffrey's Pl
5 Randolph St
6 Reachview Cl
7 Reed's Pl
8 Rochester Sq
9 Rousden St
10 St Pancras Wy
11 Wrotham Rd

D6
1 Camden Ms
2 Camden Sq
3 Cantelowes Rd

D7
1 Cobham Ms
2 Murray St
3 St Paul's Crs
4 Stratford Vls

D7
1 Buck St
2 Camden Gdns
3 Camden Lock Pl
4 Davey Cl
5 Faraday Cl

D8
1 Bergholt Ms
2 College Gv
3 Ploughmans Cl
4 Reapers Cl
5 Rossendale Wy
6 St Pancras Wy
7 Weavers Wy

E3
1 Bowman's Ms
2 Bowman's Pl
3 Eburne Rd
4 Hercules Pl
5 Hercules St

E5
1 Bardolph Rd
2 Cardwell Rd
3 Chambers Rd
4 Holbrooke Ct
5 Keighley Cl
6 Staveley Cl
7 Warlters Cl
8 Williamson St

E7
1 Broadfield La
2 Bunning Wy

F1
1 Almington St
2 Dulas St
3 Everleigh St
4 Hanley Gdns
5 Japan Crs
6 Lorne Rd
7 Stonenest St
8 Turleway Cl

F2
1 Briset Wy
2 Thistlewood Cl
3 Turle Rd
4 Wesley Cl
5 Woodbridge Cl

F3
1 Annette Rd
2 Kinloch St
3 Newington Barrow Wy
4 Pakeman St
5 Sonderburg Rd

F4
1 Annette Rd
2 Caedmon Rd
3 Crayford Rd

F5
1 Eden Gv
2 Hartnoll St
3 Heddington Gv
4 Lough Rd
5 Pollard St
6 Rhodes St
7 Stock Orchard Crs
8 Stock Orchard St
9 Sturmer Wy

F7
1 Barnsbury Gv
2 Barnsbury Ter
3 Centurion Cl
4 The Courtyard
5 Earlsferry Wy
6 Frederica St
7 Freeling St
8 Kember St
9 Kerwick Cl
10 Lyon St
11 Offord St
12 Ponder St
13 Rydston Cl
14 Thornhill Gv
15 Tilloch St

F8
1 Boadicea St
2 Boxworth Gv
3 Charlotte Ter
4 Edward Sq
5 Muriel St
6 Richmond Av
7 Stanmore St
8 Thornhill Bridge Whf
9 Treaty St

Page 85

G2
1 Coleridge Cl
2 Fonthill Ms
3 Morris Pl
4 Playford Rd
5 Pooles Pk
6 Station Pl
7 Wells Ter
8 Whadcoat St

L1
1 St Andrew's Ms

C5
1 Chillingworth Rd
2 Courtney Rd
3 Horsell Rd
4 Lowther Rd
5 Pollit St
6 Ronalds Rd
7 Slaney Pl
8 Withrington Rd

G5
1 Albion Ms
2 Barnsbury Sq
3 Brayfield Ter
4 Brooksby Ms
5 Carfree Cl
6 College Ms
7 Ferriby Cl
8 Haslam Cl
9 Lonsdale Pl
10 Lonsdale Sq
11 Milner Pl
12 Morland Ms
13 Mountford Crs
14 Mountfort Ter
15 St Clements St

G8
1 Batchelor St
2 Cloudesley Ms
3 Cloudesley Sq
4 Dowrey St
5 Elysan Wk
6 Gibson Sq
7 Malvern Ter
8 Old Royal Free Pl
9 Old Royal Free Sq

H5
1 Fergus Rd
2 Gallia Rd

H7
1 Alwyne La
2 Battishill St
3 Rickthorne Rd
4 Stanley Ter
5 Whewell Rd

H8
1 Assata Ms
2 Calabria Rd
3 Colebeck Ms
4 Edward's Cottages
5 Hampton Cr
6 Hopping La
7 John Spencer Sq
8 Prior Bolton St
9 Swan Yd

J4
1 Alwyne Rd
2 Ashby Gv
3 Douglas Rd
4 Hedingham Cl
5 Northampton St
6 Queensbury St

J5
1 Beresford Ter
2 Holmcote Gdns

J6
1 Alwyne Sq
2 Douglas Rd North
3 Douglas Rd South
4 Guernsey Rd
5 Harecourt Rd
6 Hope Cl
7 Jersey Rd
8 Marquess Rd South
9 Wallace Rd
10 Willow Bridge Rd

J8
1 Arlington Sq
2 Basire St
3 Canon St
4 Pickering St
5 Raynor Pl
6 Rector St
7 Ridgewell Cl
8 St Paul St
9 St Philip's Wy

K1
1 Schofield Sq

K2
1 Edward's La

K3
1 Statham Gv

K4
1 Aden Gv
2 Church Wk
3 Lidfield Rd
4 Reedholm Vls

K5
1 Auriga Ms
2 Hedley Rw
3 Newington Gn
4 Watson Cl

K6
1 Ball's Pond Rd
2 Baxter Rd
3 Bingham St
4 Clapham Rd South
5 Halliday Wk
6 Marquess Rd
7 Mildmay Av
8 Tilney Gdns
9 Wakeham St

L3
1 Ayrsome Rd
2 Hawksley Rd
3 Marton Rd
4 Painsthorpe Rd
5 Victorian Ms

L4
1 Gunstor Rd
2 Knebworth Rd
3 Leonard Pl
4 Shakespeare Ms
5 Spenser Gv
6 Wordsworth Rd

L5
1 Bradbury St
2 Cressington Cl
3 John Campbell Rd
4 Kingsbury Rd
5 St Jude St
6 Selsea Pl
7 Shellgrove Rd

L6
1 Bentley Rd
2 Burder Rd
3 Culford Gv
4 De Beauvoir Rd
5 Kingsbury Ter
6 Kingsland Pas
7 Nimrod Pas
8 Southgate Rd

L7
1 De Beauvoir Ms
2 Ferntower Rd
3 Mortimer Rd
4 Northchurch Rd
5 St Peter's Wy

L8
1 Culford Rd
2 Halcomb St
3 Hertford Rd
4 Hobbs Pl
5 Wilmer Gdns

M1
1 Margaret Rd

M2
1 Belfast Rd
2 Gibson Gdns
3 Martaban Rd
4 Sanford La
5 Stoke Newington Common
6 Wilmer Pl

M3
1 Batley Pl
2 Batley Rd
3 Clading Ms
4 Hollar Rd
5 Leswin Pl
6 Smalley Cl
7 Tyssen Rd

M4
1 Farleigh Pl
2 Forman Pl
3 Foulden Ter
4 Seal St
5 Shacklewell Rw
6 Walford Rd

M5
1 Birkbeck Ms
2 Chester Crs
3 Gateway Ms
4 Miller's Av
5 Miller's Ter
6 St Mark's Ri
7 Truman's Wy
8 Winchester Pl

M6
1 Ashwin St
2 Cumberland Cl
3 Forest Gv
4 Chant St
5 Hartwell St
6 Ramsgate St
7 Stanborough
8 Tyssen St
9 Woodland St

M7
1 Albion Dr
2 Albion Ter
3 Beehive Pl
4 Buxted Rd
5 Frederick Ter
6 Freshfield Av
7 Glebe Rd
8 Hilborough Rd
9 Kingsland Rd
10 Mayfield Cl
11 Mulberry Rd

Page 86

A2
1 Briggeford Cl
2 Geldeston Rd

A5
1 Avebury Ct
2 Baring St
3 Devizes St
4 Grange St
5 Hullbridge Ms
6 Imber St
7 Northport St
8 Wilton Vls

A7
1 Crowland Ter
2 Southgate Gv

A8
1 Benjamin Cl
2 Byron Cl
3 Chester St
4 Gloucester Sq
5 Goldsmith's Rw
6 Govan St
7 Harriet Cl
8 Hay St
9 Johnson Cl
10 Letitia Cl
11 Magnin Cl
12 Nichol St
13 Osborn Cl
14 Stephan Cl
15 Stephan Ct
16 Trederwen Rd
17 Welshpool St
18 Wilde Cl

B2
1 Brampton Cl
2 Charnwood St
3 Comberton Rd
4 Rossington St
5 Southwold Rd

B6
1 Casterton St
2 Florfield Rd
3 Marvin St
4 Penpoll Rd
5 Royal Oak Rd
6 Spurstowe Rd
7 Sylvester Rd
8 Valette St

B7
1 Apprentice Wy
2 Downs La
3 Downs Rd
4 Lower Clapton Rd
5 The Mothers Sq
6 Sladen Pl

B7
1 Bayford St
2 Exmouth Pl
3 Helmsley Pl
4 Helmsley St
5 London Flds
6 Pemberton Pl
7 Sidworth St
8 Silesia Buildings
9 Weston Wk

B8
1 Ada Pl
2 Albert Cl
3 Ash Gv
4 Dericote St
5 Duncan Rd
6 Earlston Gv
7 Mowlem St
8 Triangle Rd
9 Warburton Rd
10 Warburton St
11 Warneford St
12 Westgate St

C2
1 Dudlington Rd
2 Mundford Rd

C4
1 Hilsea St
2 Lawley St

C6
1 Chalgrove Rd
2 Chatham Pl
3 Collent St
4 Homerton Ter
5 Meeting Field Pth
6 Middlesex Pl
7 Milborne St
8 Nursery Rd
9 Ponsford St
10 Woodbine Ter

C6
1 Connor St
2 Derby Rd
3 Minson Rd
4 Morpeth Gv
5 Redruth Rd
6 Well St
7 Worthing Cl

C7
1 Cambridge Pas
2 Holcroft Rd
3 Primrose Sq
4 St Thomas's Sq
5 Terrace Rd

C8
1 Fremont St
2 Lark Rw
3 Leopold Ms
4 Pennethorne Cl
5 St Agnes Cl
6 Skipworth Rd
7 Templecombe Rd
8 Vicar's Cl

D4
1 Baslow Wk
2 Radbourne St

D5
1 Crozier Ter
2 Mackintosh La
3 St Barnabas Ter

D6
1 Anderson Rd
2 Bramshaw Rd
3 Brooksbank St
4 Daley St
5 Shepherd's La
6 Valentine Rd

D7
1 Cassland Rd
2 Edenbridge Rd
3 Jackson Cl
4 Killowen Rd
5 Lammas Rd
6 Meynell Gdns

E3
1 Hazelwood Cl

E4
1 Durrington Rd
2 Edwin's Mead
3 Kingsmead Wy
4 Penda's Mead
5 Ruddington Cl
6 Sunnyhill Cl

E5
1 Kemey's St
2 Lyneham Wk
3 Studley Cl
4 Swinnerton Wy

E6
1 Annis Rd
2 Bartrip St
3 Hedger's Gv

E7
1 Guinness Cl

F1
1 Dagenham Rd
2 Millicent Rd
3 Norton Rd

F4
1 Offa's Mead

K1
1 Schofield Sq

Page 87

F5
1 Crowfoot Cl
2 Lee Conservancy Rd
3 Lockgate Cl
4 Ravenscourt Rd

F6
1 Southmoor Wy

F7
1 Cadogan Cl
2 St Marks Ga

F8
1 Alma Ter
2 Annie Besant Cl
3 O'shea Cl
4 Pulteney Cl
5 Ranwell Cl
6 Roman Rd
7 Tamar Cl
8 Usher Rd
9 Wendon St
10 Wright's Rd

G1
1 Grange Rd
2 Shaftesbury Rd

H3
1 Beaconsfield Rd
2 Goodall Rd
3 Webster Rd
4 York Rd

J4
1 Etchingham Rd

K4
1 Toronto Rd

K5
1 Community Rd
2 Falmouth St
3 Major Rd
4 Newton Rd
5 Simons Wk

K6
1 Alma St
2 Amber St
3 Grove Crescent Rd
4 Oxford Rd
5 Salway Pl
6 Service Route No 3
7 Simons Wk
8 Waddington St
9 Whitear Wk

K7
1 Bryant St
2 Burtons Cl
3 Chant Sq
4 Chopwell Cl
5 Kay St
6 New Mount St
7 Rosher Cl
8 West Ham La
9 Wilmer Lea Cl

K8
1 Dell Cl
2 Mcewan Wy
3 Park La
4 Stanley Rd
5 Union St
6 Ward Rd

L1
1 Burghley Rd
2 Chatham Pl
3 Collent St
4 Dyers Hall Rd
5 Harrington Rd

L2
1 Joseph Ray Rd
2 Woodlands Rd

C7
1 Cambridge Pas
2 Holcroft Rd
3 Primrose Rd
4 St Thomas's Sq
5 Terrace Rd

C8
1 Fremont St
2 Lark Rw
3 Leopold Ms
4 Pennethorne Cl
5 St Agnes Cl
6 Skipworth Rd
7 Templecombe Rd
8 Vicar's Cl

Page 88

E3
1 Anna Neagle Cl
2 Bronte Cl
3 Brownlow Rd
4 Carrington Gdns
5 Vera Lynn Cl

C7
1 Ashley Rd
2 Walpole Rd
3 Washington Rd
4 Waterloo Rd

F4
1 Michigan Av
2 Oregon Av
3 Toronto Av

F5
1 St Mary's Ap

F8
1 Canberra Cl

G2
1 Horminster Cln
2 Windmill

L2
1 Greenbanks
2 Lichfield Ter
3 The Meads
4 Pond Wk

M2
1 Plover Gdns

M8
1 Ada Gdns
2 Cridland Rd
3 Ladwell Cl
4 Mooney Cl
5 Ravenscourt Rd
6 Stephen's Rd

Page 90

C1
1 Asquith Cl
2 Blunden Cl
3 Coulson Cl
4 Diamond Cl
5 Sapphire Cl

F8
1 Butteridges Cl

Page 91

H3
1 Ashbrook Rd
2 Pembroke Gdns

J7
1 Acre Rd
2 Birdbrook Cl
3 Boleyn Gdns
4 Durban Gdns
5 Leys Cl
6 Stratford Cl
7 Wellington St

K7
1 Ottawa Gdns
2 Rainham Rd South
3 York Rd

L1
1 Liphook Cl
2 Singleton Cl

M5
1 Dunningford Cl

M6
1 Denholme Wk
2 Gilroy Cl
3 Locke Cl

M7
1 Theydon Gdns

M8
1 Sexton Cl

Page 92

A6
1 Adnams Wk
2 Beaumont Crs
3 Freeborne Gdns
4 Tempest Wy

A6
1 Apollo Wy
2 Cowley La
3 Denmark St
4 Harrow Gn
5 Howard Rd
6 Mayville Rd
7 Orange Gv
8 Sauls Gn
9 West St
10 Wragby Rd

A7
1 Conway Cl
2 Drake Ms
3 Elmer Cl
4 Flamingo Wk
5 St John's Cl
6 St Matthew's Cl

B1
1 Belton Rd
2 Borthwick Ms
3 Marlborough Rd
4 Morris Rd
5 Steele Rd
6 Thorne Cl

B1
1 Landseer Cl
2 Napier Cl
3 Prescott Cl
4 Priory Ms
5 Shaw Cl

C1
1 Carolina Rd
2 Cherry Tree Rd
3 Gurney Cl
4 Hazel Rd
5 Janson Cl
6 Walnut Gdns
7 Warner Cl
8 Wingfield Rd

C4
1 Canberra Cl
2 Chestnut Cl
3 Lawford Cl

D5
1 Christopher Cl
2 Hitherwood Cl
3 Inglewood Cl

L2
1 Joseph Ray Rd
2 Woodlands Rd

L3
1 Dawson Dr
2 Esmond Cl
3 Heron Flight Av
4 Hesselyn Dr
5 Kestrel Cl
6 Leathart Cl
7 Mungo Park Rd
8 Robinson Rd

L6
1 Litchfield Av
2 Manbey Rd
3 Martha Rd

L7
1 Govier Cl
2 Hyderabad Wy
3 Mandrake Wy
4 Mantle Wy
5 Mark St
6 Shirley Rd
7 Tramway Av
8 Welfare Rd
9 White Rd
10 Widdin St
11 Worland Rd

M1
1 Barfield Rd
2 Dacre Rd

M2
1 Sansom Rd

C6
1 Craword Compton Cl
2 Franklin Rd
3 Gosport Dr
4 Hawkinge Wy
5 Pembrey Wy
6 Sarre Av
7 Stansted Cl

D1
1 Woodfield Wy

D2
1 Barfield Rd
2 Dacre Rd
3 Webster Rd

D4
1 Christopher Cl
2 Griggs Gdns
3 Mallinson Cl
4 Martlesham Cl
5 Rye Cl
6 Scotts Cl
7 Springbank Av
8 Wendover Wy

D6
1 Aylesbury Cl
2 Elm Rd
3 Radlett Cl
4 Townley Ct

Page 93

E3
1 Cumberland Av
2 Hutchins Cl
3 Matlock Gdns
4 Ravenscourt Av

E4
1 Fontwell Park Gdns
2 Hurst Park Av

F1
1 Dury Falls Cl

F3
1 Belmont Av

F5
1 St Mary's Ap

F8
1 Canberra Cl

Page 94

C1
1 Lichfield Ter

C2
1 Buchan Cl
2 Cowley Rd
3 Patrington Cl
4 Stirling Cl

E5
1 Camomile Wy
2 Coltsfoot Dr
3 Tannery Cl

E7
1 Windermere Wy

E8
1 Classon Cl
2 Swains Cl

F1
1 Stratford Rd

F4
1 Myrtle Cl

F5
1 Angelica Cl
2 Frankswood Av

F6
1 Oregano Cl
2 Sycamore Cl

F7
1 Cedar Av

Page 95

G2
1 Brambles Farm Dr
2 Hilliers Av
3 Tanglewood Cl

H4
1 Hindhead Cl

H7
1 Bennetsfield Rd

J3
1 De Salis Rd
2 Fulham Cl
3 Paget Rd
4 Russet Cl
5 Sheridan Cl
6 Towers Av

L2
1 Dorset Cl
2 Kenton Wy
3 Poole Wk
4 Trent Wy
5 Truro Wy

L3
1 Blackpool Gdns
2 Welwyn Wy

L6
1 Evergreen Wy

M2
1 Trevor Cl

M2
1 Adelphi Wy

M4
1 Regents Cl
2 Tithe Cl

M5
1 Church Gn
2 Parsonage Cl

M6
1 Churchfield Cl
2 Hawthorn Rd
3 Rowan Pl

M7
1 Holmbury Gdns
2 Townfield Rd

M8
1 Clarendon Rd
2 Western Vw

Page 96

C3
1 Westbourne Rd

D2
1 Beauvais Ter
2 Brett Cl
3 Dilston Cl
4 Maple Cl
5 Martlet Gv
6 Nimrod Cl
7 Seasprite Cl
8 Valiant Cl
9 Viscount Gv

D4
1 Bourne Rd
2 Courtenay Rd
3 Jenny Hammond Cl
4 Newcomen Rd
5 St Margaret's Gv
6 Tilston Cl

D5
1 Berry Cl
2 Bordington Rd
3 Edridge Cl
4 Hatfield Cl
5 Hilary Cl
6 Miramar Wy
7 Shepley Cl
8 Southbury Cl
9 Repens Wy
10 Upney Cl

D6
1 Bennions Cl

E1
1 Bowden Dr
2 Brendans Cl
3 Chaplaincy Gdns
4 Inskip Dr
5 Wedlake Cl

E2
1 Florence Cl

D6
1 Grebe Av
2 Ibis Wy
3 Lapwing Wy
4 Shearwater Cl

E1
1 Cromwell Cl
2 Riverside Gdns
3 Seaton Rd

Page 97

D6
1 Longford Cl

E1
1 Mulberry Cl

E4
1 Argus Wy
2 Concord Cl
3 Hazeltree La
4 Jetstar Wy

E6
1 Berrydale Rd
2 Blisworth Cl
3 Chirk Cl
4 Coulter Cl
5 Hastoe Cl
6 Helmsdale Cl
7 Kingsash Dr
8 Napton Cl
9 Pikestone Cl
10 Wilstone Cl

E8
1 Gladstone Rd
2 Hartington Rd

F2
1 Abbey Cl
2 Crawford Gdns
3 Hadfield Cl
4 Kenilworth Gdns
5 Waterside Cl
6 Woodstock Rd

F5
1 Frensham Cl

F5
1 Chepstow Gdns
2 Denbigh Cl
3 Lynwood Gdns
4 Sutherland Rd

F6
1 Fairlawn Gdns
2 Meadow Rd

F7
1 Beechcroft Av
2 Cambridge Rd
3 Oxford Wk

F8
1 The Crescent
2 Randolph Rd

H7
1 Lyndhurst Av

J3
1 Ruislip Rd East
2 Stanhope Park Rd

J8
1 Grand Dr
2 Lock Cl
3 River Cl
4 Tulip Cl
5 Water Lily Cl
6 William Cl

K2
1 Carroway La
2 Deepwood La
3 Howcroft La
4 Silvertree La

L7
1 Clairville Gdns
2 Maudesville Cottages
3 Silverdale Cl
4 Wilmot Pl
5 York Cl

L8
1 Bostonthorpe Rd
2 Churchfield Rd
3 Du Burstow Ter
4 The Heath
5 St Andrew's Rd

M1
1 Medway Pde
2 Suez Rd

M4
1 Cheyne Pth
2 Wakeling Rd

M7
1 Burdett Cl
2 Cherrington Rd
3 Maunder Rd

Page 98

A7
1 Brownlow Rd
2 Chignell Pl
3 Hatfield Rd
4 Leeland Rd
5 Melbourne Av
6 Talbot Rd
7 Walsingham Rd
8 William's Rd

B4
1 Clivedon Ct
2 Hardwick Gn
3 Malvern Wy
4 Middlefields
5 Roseacre Cl

B8
1 Burns Rd
2 Chesham Ter
3 Clementine Cl
4 Occupation Rd

C5
1 Pursewardens Cl
2 St Helen's Rd
3 Wrotham Rd

C8
1 Felton Rd

D1
1 Park Ga
2 Westmoreland Pl
3 Willowmead Cl

D5
1 Aston Rd

D7
1 Kerrison Pl

E1
1 Coningsby Cottages
2 Limes Av
3 Marlborough Rd
4 St George's La
5 St Mary's Sq
6 Venetia Rd
7 Warwick Pl

Page 99

E2
1 Hanger La (North Circular Rd)
2 Hogarth Cl

E4
1 Chatsfield Cl
2 Fir Tree Cl

E5
1 Blossom Cl

F3
1 Chatsworth Rd

F5
1 Golf Rd
2 Station Rd

H7
1 Denehurst Gdns
2 Mill Hill Rd
3 Mount Pk
4 Narrow St
5 Woodlands Av

J6
1 Crane Av
2 The Tiltwood

J7
1 Cromwell Rd
2 Edgecote Cl
3 Hooper's Ms
4 Locarno Rd
5 Melville Villas Rd
6 Steyne Rd

K3
1 Gorst Rd
2 St Leonard's Rd

K5
1 Anderson Cl
2 Curtis Cl
3 Ferguson Dr
4 Friars Gdns
5 Simpson Dr

K8
1 Beardsley Wy
2 Bonheur Rd
3 Clovelly Rd
4 St Georges Rd
5 Shirley Rd
6 Strauss Rd

L4
1 Hoylake Rd
2 Muirfield
3 Taylor's Gn
4 The Tee
5 Templemead Cl

L6
1 Beechwood Gv
2 East Acton La
3 Kingsdown Av
4 Trinity Wy

L7
1 Curricle St

L8
1 Bradford Rd
2 Hawkshead Rd
3 Rugby Rd
4 Worcester Dr

M1
1 Caple Rd
2 High Street Harlesden
3 Honeywood Rd
4 Nightingale Rd
5 Ranelagh Rd
6 Tavistock Rd
7 Tubbs Rd

M5
1 Crewe Pl
2 Station Ap

M6
1 Osmund St

M6
1 Bramble Gdns
2 Old Oak Common La
3 Tamarisk Sq
4 Yew Tree Rd

M7
1 Hilary Rd
2 Old Oak Common La

M8
1 Askew Crs
2 Cobbold Ms
3 Cransden Rd
4 Oldfield Rd
5 Swainson Rd

Page 100

A2
1 Fortune Wy
2 Letchford Gdns
3 Letchford Ms
4 Valliere Rd

B2
1 Felixstowe Rd
2 Greyhound Rd
3 Kenmont Gdns
4 Ravensworth Rd
5 Rigeley Rd

B6
1 Bennelong Cl
2 Canada Wy
3 Commonwealth Av
4 Dorando Cl
5 India Wy

C6
1 Batman Cl

C7
1 Hopgood St
2 Poplar Ms
3 Swindon St

C8
1 Astrop Ter
2 Bamborough Gdns
3 Gainsborough Ct
4 Sulgrave Gdns
5 Woodger Rd

D2
1 Bayford Rd
2 Regent St
3 Warfield Rd
4 Wellington Rd

D3
1 Admiral Ms
2 Banbury Gdns
3 Canal Cl
4 Humber Dr
5 Maple Wk
6 Matthew Cl
7 St John's Ter
8 Treverton St

D4
1 Archway Cl
2 Rootes Dr
3 St Charles Sq
4 St Helen's Gdns

D5
1 Bridge Cl
2 Charlotte Ms

D6
1 Blechynden St
2 Evesham St
3 Mortimer Sq
4 Stoneleigh St
5 Waynflete St

A8
1 Bevington St
2 Damsel Ct
3 East La
4 Farncombe St
5 Farthing Alley
6 Flockton St
7 John Felton Rd
8 Llewellyn St
9 Loftie St
10 Waterside Cl

B1
1 Cambridge Crs
2 Canrobert St
3 Corbridge Crs
4 Dinmont St
5 Felix St
6 Hare Rw
7 Marian St
8 Minerva St
9 Poyser St
10 St Jude's Rd
11 Teesdale Cl
12 Treadway St
13 West St
14 Winkley St

B2
1 Ainsley St
2 Birkbeck St
3 Canrobert St
4 Clarkson St
5 Derbyshire St
6 Ellsworth St
7 Florida St
8 Hollybush Gdns
9 Hollybush Pl
10 Jersey St
11 Nant St
12 Paradise Rw
13 Punderson's Gdns
14 Rushmead
15 Seabright St
16 Viaduct Pl
17 Wear Pl
18 Witan St
19 Wolverley St

B3
1 Corfield St
2 Coventry Rd
3 Darling Rw
4 Fellbrigg St
5 Class St
6 Herald St
7 Merceron St
8 Somerford St
9 Tapp St
10 Three Colts La
11 Violet St

B4
1 Court St
2 Durward St
3 East Mount St
4 Ford Sq
5 Fulbourne St
6 Halcrow St
7 Maples Pl
8 Mount Ter
9 Winthrop St

B5
1 Anthony St
2 Barnett St
3 Brinsley St
4 Buross St
5 Burslem St
6 Burwell Cl
7 Dunch St
8 Hessel St
9 Hungerford St
10 Jane St
11 Kinder St
12 Morris St
13 Pace Pl
14 Ponler St
15 Rampart St
16 Richard St
17 Sheridan St
18 Sly St
19 Tillman St
20 Umberston St
21 Walburgh St
22 Walden St
23 Watney St

B6
1 Artichoke Hl
2 Betts St
3 Bewley St
4 Chigwell Hl
5 Cornwall St
6 Hawksmoor Ms
7 Lowood St
8 West Gdns

B7
1 Agatha Cl
2 Brewhouse La
3 Bridewell Pl
4 Chandler St
5 Cinnamon St
6 Clegg St
7 Dundee St
8 Farthing Flds
9 Knighten St
10 Meeting House Alley
11 Pier Head
12 Presidents Dr
13 Raine St
14 Reardon Pth
15 Scandrett St
16 Stevedore St
17 Tench St
18 Vinegar St
19 Wapping Dock St
20 Waterman Wy

B8
1 Janeway Pl
2 Pottery St
3 Rotherhithe St

C1
1 Brierly Gdns
2 Cyprus Pl
3 Edinburgh Cl
4 Elsden Ms
5 Huddleston Cl
6 Hunslett St
7 Royston St
8 Stainsbury St
9 Waterloo Gdns

C2
1 Bacton St
2 Bessy St
3 Braintree St
4 Burnham St
5 Butler St
6 Cornwall Av
7 Digby St
8 Gawber St
9 Globe Ter
10 Helen's Pl
11 Kirkwall Pl
12 Moravian St
13 Peary Pl
14 Portman Pl
15 Victoria Park Sq
16 Welwyn St
17 Wessex St

C3
1 Amiel St
2 Boyton Cl
3 Doveton St
4 Fox Cl
5 Gibson Cl
6 Hayfield Pas
7 Lamplighter Cl
8 Pemell Cl
9 Rickman St
10 Stothard St
11 Vawdrey Cl
12 William's Buildings
13 Wyllen Cl

C4
1 Bardsey Pl
2 Miranda Cl
3 Sidney Sq

C5
1 Aylward St
2 Bromehead St
3 Clearbrook Wy
4 Deancross St
5 Devonport St
6 Exmouth St
7 Hardinge St
8 Montpelier Pl
9 Oyster Rw
10 Poonah St

C6
1 Johnson St
2 Juniper St
3 King David La
4 Martineau St
5 Peartree La
6 Redcastle Cl
7 Sage St
8 Shadwell Gdns
9 Shadwell Pierhead
10 Twine Ct
11 Wine Cl

C7
1 Brunel Rd
2 Clave St
3 Hilliard's Ct
4 Pearl St

C8
1 Canon Beck Rd
2 Clack St
3 Clifton Pl
4 Hatteraick St
5 Kenning St
6 Lower Rd
7 Mayflower St
8 Railway Av
9 Renforth St
10 Rupack St
11 Tunnel Rd

D1
1 Cranbrook St
2 Gathorne St
3 Mace St
4 Type St
5 Wennington Rd

D2
1 Bonner St
2 Bullards Pl
3 Butler St
4 Knottisford St
5 Leatherdale St

D3
1 Beaumont Gv
2 Carlton Sq
3 Colmar Cl
4 Eastbury Ter
5 Frimley Wy
6 Harpley Sq
7 Holton St
8 Massingham St

D4
1 Aylward St
2 Belgrave St
3 Commodore St
4 King John St
5 Master's St
6 Morecambe Cl
7 Ocean St
8 Tinsley Rd
9 Waley St
10 Wellesley St

D5
1 Albert Gdns
2 Arbour Sq
3 Boulcott St
4 Bower St
5 Caroline St
6 Chudleigh St
7 Devonport St
8 Dunelm St
9 Havering St
10 Head St
11 Lighterman Ms
12 Old Church Rd
13 Pitsea Pl
14 Pitsea St
15 Ratcliffe Cross St
16 Ronald St
17 Senrab St
18 Stepney Cswy

D6
1 Bere St
2 Cranford St
3 Glasshouse Flds
4 Heckford St
5 Schoolhouse La

D7
1 Abbotshade Rd
2 Burnside Cl
3 Bury Cl
4 Byelands Cl
5 Deck Cl
6 Gunwhale Cl
7 Hull Cl
8 Katherine Cl
9 Keel Cl
10 Midship Cl
11 Princes Riverside Rd
12 St Paul's Av

D8
1 Clipper Cl
2 Drake Cl
3 Greenacre Sq
4 Hawke Pl
5 Ironside Cl
6 Kinburn St
7 Maple Leaf Sq
8 Middleton Dr
9 Stanhope Cl
10 Thame Rd

E1
1 Bunsen St
2 Chisenhale Rd
3 Conyer St
4 Lanfranc Rd
5 Medhurst Cl
6 Stanfield Rd
7 Thoydon Rd

E2
1 Longfellow Rd

E3
1 Sandalwood Cl
2 Union Dr
3 Wentworth Ms
4 Whitman Rd
5 Woodstock St

E4
1 Dupont St
2 Durham Rw
3 Elsa St
4 Halley St
5 Maroon St
6 Rhodeswell Rd
7 Whitehorse Rd

E5
1 Bekesbourne St
2 Blount St
3 Branch Rd
4 Brenton St
5 Brunton Pl
6 Chaseley St
7 Conder St
8 Mill Pl
9 Parnham St
10 Raby St
11 Troon St
12 Wakeling St
13 York Sq

E6
1 Branch Rd
2 Elizabeth Sq
3 Frederick Sq
4 Helena Sq
5 Shoulder Of Mutton Alley
6 Sophia Sq
7 Spert St
8 William Sq

E7
1 Bevin Cl
2 Farrins Rents
3 Foundry Cl
4 Globe Pond Rd
5 Rotherhithe St
6 Russia Dock Rd
7 Staples Cl
8 Stave Yard Rd

E8
1 Hamilton Cl
2 Reveley Sq
3 Steers Wy
4 Victory Wy

F1
1 Anglo Rd
2 Balmer Rd
3 Beale Pl
4 Centurion La
5 Dane Pl
6 Ewart Pl
7 Rosebank Gdns
8 Shetland Rd
9 Wright's Rd

F2
1 Merchant St

F3
1 Hamlets Wy
2 Lockhart St
3 Maritime St
4 Midlothian Rd
5 Mossford St

F4
1 Baythorne St
2 Callingham Cl
3 Huddart St
4 Kirk's Pl
5 Leopold St
6 Robeson St
7 Seager Pl

F5
1 Island Rw
2 Norway Pl
3 St Anne's Pas
4 St Anne's Rw
5 St Anne St
6 Salmon St
7 Wilson's Pl

F6
1 Bate St
2 Brightlingsea Pl
3 Limehouse Cswy
4 The Mitre
5 Rich St
6 Ropemaker's Flds
7 Stocks Pl
8 Three Colt St
9 Trinidad St

F7
1 Silver Wk

F8
1 Defoe Rd
2 Holyoake Ct
3 Sandpiper Cl
4 Spence Cl

Page 105

G6
1 Dingle Gdns
2 Garford St
3 Kemps Dr
4 Limehouse
5 Ming St
6 Morant St
7 Pinefield Cl
8 Premiere Pl
9 Rosefield
10 Rugg St

G7
1 North Colonnade

G8
1 Chandlers Ms
2 Hutching's St
3 Tobago St

H2
1 Bromley High St
2 Franklin St
3 Glebe Ter
4 Powis Rd
5 St Leonard's St
6 Washington Cl
7 William Guy Gdns

H4
1 Balladier Wk
2 Barchester St
3 Chadbourn St
4 Clutton St
5 Daniel Bolt Cl
6 Godalming Rd
7 Passfield Dr

H6
1 Dolphin La
2 Lawless St
3 Malam Gdns
4 Poplar Bath St
5 Shirbutt St
6 Smythe St
7 Stoneyard La

J5
1 Aberfeldy St
2 Adderley St
3 Athol Sq
4 Byron St
5 Culloden St
6 Kirkmichael Rd
7 Mills Gv
8 Susannah St
9 Tayburn Cl

J6
1 Bullivant St
2 Ditchburn St
3 Duthie St
4 Harrow La
5 Mountague Pl
6 Newby Pl
7 Prestage Wy

J7
1 Bridge House Quay
2 Managers St
3 St Lawrence St
4 Warrington Pl

J8
1 Chipka St
2 Roserton St

K5
1 Ada Gdns
2 Benledi St
3 Ettrick St
4 Goodway Gdns
5 Lansbury Gdns
6 Leven Rd
7 Rosemary Dr
8 Sorrel La
9 Wooster Gdns

K6
1 Quixley St
2 Scouler St

L1
1 Alan Hocken Wy
2 Richardson Rd
3 Tom Nolan Cl

L2
1 Celandine Wy
2 Germander Wy
3 Springfield Rd
4 Teasel Wy

L3
1 Cranberry La
2 Damask Crs
3 Eastlea Ms
4 Fennel Cl
5 Grayling Cl
6 Hilda Rd
7 Nutmeg Cl
8 Sycamore Cl
9 Verbena Cl

L4
1 Birch Cl

M1
1 Maud Gdns
2 Moxon Cl
3 Rudolph Rd

M3
1 Chargeable St
2 Columbia Rd
3 Garfield Rd
4 Mayfield Rd
5 Sheppard St
6 Star La

M4
1 Bernard Cassidy St
2 Cooper St
3 Formunt Cl
4 Lawrence St
5 Malmesbury Ter
6 Mary St
7 Trinity Gdns

M5
1 Burke St
2 Caxton St North
3 Emily St
4 Fendt Cl
5 George St
6 Hoy St
7 Murdock Cl
8 Sabbarton St
9 St Luke's Sq
10 Turner St
11 Woodstock St
12 Wouldham Rd

M6
1 Bowman Av
2 Bray Dr
3 Fen St
4 Nelson St
5 Tidal Basin Rd
6 Willan Wall

Page 106

A2
1 Bob Anker Cl

A3
1 Beatrice Cl
2 Boyce Wy
3 Braemar Rd
4 Clove St
5 Edward St
6 Graham Rd
7 Ingal Rd
8 Seaton Cl
9 Tabernacle Av
10 Upland Rd
11 Warmington St

A4
1 Bothwell Cl
2 Edward Ct
3 Fox Cl
4 Lowe Av
5 Mcdowall Cl
6 Ravenscroft Rd
7 Vincent St

A7
1 Badminton Ms
2 Britannia Ga
3 Charles Flemwell Ms
4 Tom Jenkinson Rd

B3
1 Jones Rd
2 Rowntree Cl

B5
1 Hartington Rd
2 Oyster Catchers Cl
3 Pheasant Cl
4 Throckmorten Rd

B7
1 Beaulieu Av
2 Hanameel St
3 Pirie St
4 Rayleigh Rd
5 Westwood Rd

C5
1 Lawson Cl
2 Randolph Ap

D1
1 Dominica Cl
2 Kylemore Cl

D4
1 Firbank Cl
2 Fleetwood Cl
3 Glencairne Cl
4 Goldcrest Cl
5 Heathfield Cl
6 Hickman Cl
7 Hogarth Cl
8 Meadowsweet Cl
9 Partridge Cl
10 St Michaels Cl
11 Vanburgh Cl

D5
1 Agate Cl
2 Andover Av
3 Long Mark Rd
4 Opal Cl

E3
1 Firefly Gdns
2 Lonsdale Cl

E4
1 Greenwich Crs
2 Juniper La
3 Kestrel Av
4 Osprey Cl
5 Pintail Cl
6 Waverley Gdns
7 Woodhatch Cl

E5
1 Burlington Cl
2 Dundonald Cl
3 Hawksmoor Cl
4 Woodget Cl

E7
1 Constance St

F3
1 Fabian St
2 Saxon Rd

F4
1 Ambassador Gdns
2 Bowyer Cl
3 Derifall Cl
4 Pembroke Rd
5 Pepper Cl
6 Routh St
7 Tulip Cl
8 Viscount Dr

F5
1 Canterbury Cl
2 Chelmsford Cl
3 Clayton Cl
4 Coventry Cl
5 Triumph Rd
6 Trusedale Rd

F7
1 Ben Tillet Cl
2 Muir St
3 Rawsthorne Cl
4 Sheldrake Cl

Page 107

G3
1 Hartshorn Gdns
2 Magdalene Gdns
3 Masefield Gdns
4 Skipsey Av

H6
1 Collier Cl
2 Fletcher Cl
3 Weaver Cl
4 Yeoman Cl

L8
1 Gallions View Rd

Page 108

D6
1 Bernal Cl
2 Hodgkins Cl
3 Martham Cl
4 Ormesby Cl
5 Surlingham Cl

E5
1 Sunningdale Cl

Page 113

J5
1 Harlington Cl

K5
1 Grampian Cl
2 Mendip Cl
3 Pondside Cl
4 Providence La
5 Quantock Cl
6 Warner Cl

M1
1 Black Rod Cl
2 Northfield Cl
3 Old Station Rd
4 Sandow Crs
5 Station Ap

M3
1 Pemerich Cl

M5
1 Strathearn Av

M7
1 Ely Rd
2 Epsom Sq

Page 114

B6
1 Bath Rd
2 Community Cl
3 Lynchen Cl
4 Meadowbank Gdns
5 Pine Tree Cl
6 Woodfield Rd

D1
1 Priory Wy

E1
1 Dominion Rd
2 Featherstone Rd
3 Featherstone Ter
4 St John's Rd

E5
1 Blackberry Farm Cl
2 Blackthorn Ct

E8
1 Hussars Cl

F1
1 Castle Rd
2 Church Rd
3 Grosvenor Rd
4 Osterley Park Rd
5 Portland Rd
6 Warwick Rd
7 Windsor Rd

F2
1 Bixley Cl
2 Bryanston Cl
3 Court Rd
4 Jessop Av
5 Norwood Gdns
6 Wren Av

F4
1 Walnut Tree Rd

F6
1 Burton Gdns

Page 115

H7
1 Concorde Cl
2 Lampton Park Rd

H8
1 Balfour Rd
2 Douglas Rd
3 Hanworth Rd
4 Lansdowne Rd

L6
1 Moreton Av
2 Ravenswood Gdns
3 St Christopher's Cl
4 Stanleycroft Cl
5 Weston Gdns

L7
1 Pembroke Pl
2 Villiers Rd

M7
1 Copper Mill Dr
2 Nottingham Rd
3 St John's Ct

M8
1 Braddock Cl
2 Clydesdale Cl
3 Greenwood Rd
4 Pankhurst Cl

Page 116

A6
1 Cadbury Cl
2 Darcy Rd
3 Downs Vw
4 Hartham Cl
5 Holdernesse Rd
6 Jodrell Cl

A7
1 Ferney Meade Wy
2 Thackeray Cl

A8
1 Carrick Cl
2 Gumley Gdns
3 Harcourt Cl
4 Hartland Rd
5 Richmond Rd
6 Upper Sq

D4
1 Albany Pl
2 Albany Rd
3 Alexandra Rd
4 Brockshot Cl
5 Brook La North
6 Half Acre Ms
7 Hamilton Rd
8 Sidney Gdns
9 Westbury Pl

E2
1 Monmouth Gv

E3
1 Centaur Ct
2 Hope Cl
3 Phoenix Ct

E4
1 Brook Rd South
2 Ferry Sq
3 Walnut Tree Rd
4 Wilkes Rd

F3
1 Pegasus Ct
2 Titan Ct

F5
1 Kew Gardens Rd

F6
1 Holmesdale Rd

F7
1 Paxton Cl

F8
1 Beaumont Av
2 Gaston Bell Cl
3 Stanmore Gdns
4 Topiary Sq
5 Trinity Rd
6 Windham Rd

Page 117

G3
1 Haining Cl
2 London Stile
3 Oxford Gdns
4 Stonehill Rd
5 Surrey Crs

G5
1 Cambridge Rd
2 Gloucester Ct
3 Hanover Cl
4 Haverfield Gdns
5 Kent Rd

H1
1 Greenock Rd

J1
1 Beaulieu Pl
2 Cleveland Rd
3 Reynolds Rd
4 Steele Rd
5 Vincent Rd

J3
1 Beaconsfield Cl
2 Bishops Cl
3 Burlington Rd
4 Kings Pl

J6
1 The Lindens

J8
1 Beechcroft Rd
2 Cromwell Pl
3 Eastbourne Gdns
4 Hanson Cl
5 Langdon Pl
6 Moore Cl
7 Waldeck Rd

K1
1 Bayham Rd
2 Eridge Rd
3 Evelyn Rd
4 Florence Rd
5 Gladstone Rd
6 Monmouth Cl

K2
1 Alfred Cl
2 Belmont Gv
3 Clement Cl
4 Clifton Gdns
5 Essex Place Sq
6 Holly Rd
7 Kirton Cl
8 South Pde

K3
1 Barley Mow Pas
2 Horticultural Pl
3 Prospect Pl
4 Townhall Av

K5
1 Fitzroy Crs
2 Riverside Dr

K8
1 Bulls Alley
2 Chestnut Av
3 Fitzgerald Rd
4 Glendower Gdns
5 Glendower Rd
6 Trehern Rd

L2
1 Chardin Rd
2 Priory Gdns
3 Roman Rd
4 Windmill Pas

L3
1 Alkerden Rd
2 Ingress St
3 Prince Of Wales Ter
4 Swanscombe Rd

L4
1 Bedford Cl
2 Boston Gdns
3 Chiswick Sq
4 Devonshire Rd
5 Langham Pl

L5
1 Anstice Cl
2 Claremont Gv
3 Lattimer Pl

L8
1 Grosvenor Gdns
2 Limes Field Rd
3 Railway Side
4 The Retreat
5 Sutherland Gdns
6 Tudor Gdns

M1
1 Abinger Rd
2 Balmoral Ms
3 Stamford Brook Gdns

M3
1 Airedale Av South
2 Berestede Rd
3 British Grove Pas
4 North Eyot Gdns

M4
1 Gwynne Whf

M5
1 Coniston Cl

M6
1 The Hermitage
2 St Anns Rd

M7
1 Essex Ct
2 Melrose Rd
3 St John's Gv
4 Swan Pl
5 Terrace Gdns

M8
1 Beverley Gdns
2 Leconfield Av
3 Priory Gdns
4 Westwood Gdns

Page 118

A3
1 Lord Napier Pl
2 Mulberry Pl
3 North Verbena Gdns
4 Oil Mill La
5 St Peter's Rd
6 South Black Lion La
7 Theresa Rd
8 Verbena Gdns

B2
1 Argyle Pl
2 Dimes Pl
3 Felgate Ms
4 Hampshire Hog La
5 Holcombe St
6 Lamington St
7 Ravenscourt Pl
8 Raynham Rd
9 Redmore Rd

C2
1 Angel Wk
2 Beadon Rd
3 Bridge Av
4 Glenthorne Rd
5 Hammersmith Broadway
6 Hammersmith Gv
7 Kilmarsh Rd
8 Mercers Pl
9 Overstone Rd
10 Southerton Rd

C3
1 Bridgeview
2 Chancellors St
3 Playfair St
4 River Ter
5 St James St

C7
1 Stockhurst Cl

C8
1 Abbotstone Rd
2 Stanbridge Rd

D1
1 Applegarth Rd
2 Aynhoe Rd
3 Berghem Ms
4 Caithness Rd
5 Fielding Rd
6 Haarlem Rd
7 Souldern Rd
8 Sterndale Rd

D3
1 Wilson's Rd

D4
1 Bothwell St
2 Hawksmoor St

D5
1 Purcell Crs

D7
1 Ashlone Rd

D8
1 Ardshiel Cl
2 Darfur St
3 Dryad St
4 Gwalior Rd
5 Henry Jackson Rd
6 Kingsmere Cl
7 Ruvigny Gdns
8 Thames Pl

E1
1 Beaconsfield Terrace Rd
2 Hofland Rd
3 Holland Gdns
4 Porten Rd
5 Russell Gdns

E2
1 Avonmore Pl
2 Avonmore Rd
3 Bishop King's Rd
4 Earsby St
5 Fitz-george Av
6 Fitzjames Av
7 Glazbury Rd
8 Gorleston St
9 Munden St
10 Southcombe St
11 Trevanion Rd

E3
1 Vereker Rd

E4
1 Bayonne Rd
2 Caroline Wk
3 Crammond Cl
4 Normand Ms
5 St Andrew's Rd

E5
1 Branksea St

E6
1 Edgarley Ter

E7
1 Burlington Pl
2 Dorncliffe Rd

E8
1 Fulham High St
2 Station Ap

F1
1 Napier Pl
2 Oakwood La
3 St Mary Abbot's Pl
4 St Mary Abbots Ter
5 Strangways Ter

F2
1 Addison Bridge Pl
2 Fenelon Pl
3 North End Crs
4 Pembroke Gdns

F3
1 Bellamy Cl
2 Challoner Crs
3 Franklin Sq
4 Lanfrey Pl
5 May St
6 Stanier Cl

F4
1 Chestnut Alley
2 Coomer Ms
3 Hugh Gaitskell Cl
4 Len Freeman Pl
5 Margaret Ingram Cl
6 Mulgrave Rd
7 Tilton St

F5
1 Baths Ap
2 Darlan Rd
3 Fabian Rd
4 Hartismere Rd
5 John Smith Av
6 Letterstone Rd
7 St Peter's Ter
8 Wheatsheaf Ter

F6
1 Beaconsfield Wk
2 Epple Rd

F7
1 Ashington Rd
2 Cortayne Rd
3 Cristowe Rd
4 Dolby Rd
5 Eddiscombe Rd
6 Elysium St
7 Laurel Bank Gdns

Page 119

G1
1 Adam And Eve Ms
2 Cope Pl
3 Earls Ter
4 Eden Cl
5 Iverna Ct
6 Leonard Ct
7 Pater St
8 Pembroke Ms
9 Pembroke Pl
10 Phillimore Gardens Cl
11 Scarsdale Vls
12 Shaftesbury Ms
13 Troy Ct
14 Wynnstay Gdns

G2
1 Child's Pl
2 Child's St
3 Logan Ms
4 Pembroke Vls
5 Pembroke Wk
6 Redfield Ms
7 Templeton Pl

G4
1 Armadale Rd
2 Hildyard Rd
3 Knivet Rd
4 Merrington Rd
5 Rickett St
6 Roxby Pl

G5
1 Argon Ms
2 Epirus Ms
3 Eustace Rd
4 Fulham Broadway
5 Heckfield Pl
6 Kempson Rd
7 North End Rd
8 St John Cl
9 Walham Yd

G7
1 Molesford Rd
2 Peterborough Ms

H1
1 Ansdell St
2 Ansdell Ter
3 Beatrice Pl
4 Blithfield St
5 Chantry Sq
6 Cheniston Gdns
7 Cornwall Gardens Wk
8 Cornwall Ms West
9 Devonshire Pl
10 Kensington Court Ms
11 Kensington Court Pl
12 Lexham Gdns
13 Osten Ms
14 Radley Ms
15 St John's Vls
16 St Margarets La
17 St Mary's Ga
18 St Mary's Pl
19 Scarsdale Pl
20 South End
21 South End Rw
22 Thackeray St
23 Thomas Pl

H2
1 Colbeck Ms
2 Collingham Gdns
3 Courtfield Gdns
4 Earl's Court Gdns
5 Gaspar Ms
6 Laverton Ms
7 Laverton Pl
8 Morton Ms
9 Old Manor Yd
10 Wallgrave Rd

H4
1 Cathcart Rd
2 Redcliffe St
3 Tregunter Rd

H6
1 Edith Rw
2 Emden St
3 Fulmead St
4 Imperial Sq
5 Meldon Cl
6 Pearscroft Ct
7 Peterborough Vls
8 Stephendale Rd
9 Tyrawley Rd

H8
1 Hurlingham Sq
2 South Park Ms

J1
1 Albert Ms
2 Bremner Rd
3 Canning Pl
4 Canning Place Ms
5 Elvaston Ms
6 Elvaston Pl
7 Gore St
8 Grenville Pl
9 Hyde Park Ga
10 Kensington Ga
11 Kynance Pl
12 Petersham La
13 Queen's Gate Gdns
14 Queen's Gate Pl
15 Queen's Gate Place Ms
16 Queen's Gate Ter

J2
1 Ashburn Gdns
2 Ashburn Pl
3 Atherstone Ms
4 Clareville Gv
5 Courtfield Ms
6 Hereford Sq
7 Rosary Gdns
8 Stanhope Gdns
9 Stanhope Ms East
10 Stanhope Ms South

J3
1 The Boltons
2 Boltons Pl
3 Cavaye Pl
4 Eagle Pl
5 Harley Gdns
6 Milborne Gv
7 Priory Wk

J4
1 Hollywood Ms
2 Oakfield St
3 Redcliffe Pl
4 Winterton Pl

J5
1 Ashburnham Rd
2 Cremorne Rd
3 Damer Ter
4 Edith Ter
5 Meek St
6 Rewell St
7 Tadema Rd
8 Thorndike Cl
9 Upcerne Rd
10 Uverdale Rd

J7
1 Charlow Cl
2 Querrin St
3 Watermeadow La

K1
1 Imperial College Rd

K2
1 Barnaby Pl
2 Bute St
3 Cromwell Ms
4 Cromwell Pl
5 Exhibition Rd
6 Glendower Pl
7 Kendrick Ms
8 Kendrick Pl
9 Manson Ms
10 Onslow Ms East
11 Onslow Ms West
12 Queensberry Ms West
13 Queensberry Pl
14 Queensberry Wy
15 Reece Ms
16 Sumner Place Ms
17 Sydney Cl
18 Thurloe Place Ms

K3
1 Chelsea Sq
2 Cranley Gdns
3 Dudmaston Ms
4 Lecky St
5 Manresa Rd
6 Onslow Gdns
7 Oratory La
8 Queen's Elm Sq
9 Selwood Pl
10 Selwood Ter

K4
1 Camera Pl
2 Henniker Ms
3 Hobury St
4 Lavender Cl
5 Moravian Pl

K5
1 Apollo Pl
2 Thorney Crs
3 Whistlers Av

K6
1 Bolingbroke Wk
2 Granfield St
3 Vicarage Wk

K7
1 Musjid Rd
2 Orville Rd

K8
1 Benham Cl
2 Fenner Sq
3 Fowler Cl
4 Heaver Rd
5 Hibbert St
6 Holliday Sq
7 John Parker Sq
8 Kambala Rd
9 Livingstone Rd
10 Mantua St
11 Weekley Sq
12 Winstanley Rd
13 Wye St

L1
1 Egerton Gdns
2 Egerton Gardens Ms
3 Egerton Pl
4 Egerton Ter
5 Ennismore St
6 Fairholt St
7 Glynde Ms
8 Montpelier Ms
9 Montpelier Pl
10 Montpelier Sq
11 Ovington Ms
12 Ovington Sq
13 Relton Ms
14 Rutland Ms South
15 Rutland St
16 Sterling St
17 Trevor Sq

L2
1 Alexander Sq
2 Crescent Pl
3 Leverett St
4 Makins St
5 Marlborough St
6 Pelham Pl

L3
1 Danube St
2 Flood Wk
3 Guthrie St

L4
1 Chelsea Manor Gdns
2 Justice Wk
3 Lawrence St
4 Lordship Pl
5 Petyt Pl
6 Phene St

L5
1 Kingswater Pl
2 Paveley Dr
3 Radstock St

L6
1 Ethelburga St
2 Henty Cl
3 Hyde La

L7
1 Banbury St
2 Colestown St
3 Coppock Cl
4 Crombie Ms
5 Frere St
6 Nepaul Rd
7 Winders Rd

L8
1 Bramlands Cl
2 Falcon Ter
3 Fownes St
4 Grant Rd
5 Lavender Ter
6 Mossbury Rd
7 Wolftencroft Cl

M1
1 Hans Crs
2 Herbert Crs
3 Landon Pl
4 Pavilion Rd
5 Pavilion St
6 Rysbrack St
7 Shafto Ms
8 Stackhouse St

M2
1 Blacklands Ter
2 Lennox Gardens Ms
3 Lincoln St
4 Rosemoor St
5 Sprimont Pl

M3
1 Anderson St
2 Bywater St
3 Cheltenham Ter
4 Coulson St
5 Durham Pl
6 Markham Pl
7 Ormonde Ga
8 Ralston St
9 Redesdale St
10 Tedworth Sq
11 Tryon St
12 Wellington Sq
13 Woodfall St

M4
1 Christchurch Ter
2 Clover Ms
3 Physic Pl
4 Robinson St

M6
1 Beechmore Rd
2 Foxmore St
3 Kersley Ms
4 Rosenau Crs

M7
1 Atherton St
2 Latchmere St
3 Matthews St
4 Poyntz Rd
5 St James's Gv

M8
1 Town Hall Rd

Page 120

A1
1 Belgrave Ms South
2 Chesham Cl
3 Chesham Ms
4 Chesham Pl
5 Groom Pl
6 Halkin Ms
7 Halkin Pl
8 Lowndes Cl
9 Lyall Ms West
10 Lyall St
11 Roberts Ms

A2
1 Boscobel Pl
2 Burton Ms
3 Cundy St
4 Eaton Cl
5 Eaton Ms West
6 Eaton Terrace Ms
7 Gerald Rd
8 Grosvenor Cottages
9 Ormonde Pl
10 Sedding St
11 Skinner Pl
12 Sloane Ter
13 Symons St
14 West Eaton Pl
15 West Eaton Place Ms
16 Whittaker St
17 Wilbraham Pl

A4
1 Chelsea Emb
2 Embankment Gdns

A6
1 Alexandra Av
2 Charlotte Despard Av
3 Chesney St
4 Cupar Rd
5 Francis Chichester Wy
6 Harpsden St
7 Parkside St
8 Rawson St

A8
1 Basnett Rd
2 Brassey Sq
3 Craven Ms
4 Evesham Wy
5 Marmion Ms
6 Rush Hill Ms
7 Tipthorpe Rd
8 Tyneham Rd
9 Wickersley Rd
10 Wycliffe Rd

B1
1 Beeston Pl
2 Chester Ms
3 Chester Square Ms
4 Dorset Ms
5 Eaton La
6 Grosvenor Gardens Ms East
7 Grosvenor Gardens Ms South
8 Little Chester St
9 Lygon Pl
10 Ms North
11 Victoria Sq
12 Warwick Rw
13 Wilton Ms

B2
1 Avery Farm Rw
2 Bridge Pl
3 Hudson's Pl
4 West Warwick Pl

B6
1 Alfreda St
2 Gladstone Ter
3 Lockington Rd
4 Meath St
5 Newtown St
6 Pagden St
7 Patcham Ter
8 Ravenet St
9 St Joseph's St
10 Southolm St

B7
1 Broughton St
2 Coleridge Cl
3 Froude St
4 Gambetta St
5 Montefiore St
6 Peardon St
7 St Philip Sq

B8
1 Daley Thompson Wy
2 Keith Connor Cl
3 Mackay Rd
4 Newby St
5 Willard St

C1
1 Bressenden Pl
2 Buckingham Ms
3 Buckingham Pl
4 Catherine Pl
5 Emery Hill St
6 Greencoat Rw
7 Palace Pl
8 Pine Apple Ct
9 St James' Ct
10 Spencer Pl
11 Vandon St

C2
1 Bloomburg St
2 Charlwood Pl
3 Churton Pl
4 Coburg Cl
5 Dell's Ms
6 Denbigh Ms
7 Denbigh St
8 Eccleston Square Ms
9 Gillingham Ms
10 Gillingham Rw
11 Gillingham St
12 Hatherley St
13 Neathouse Pl
14 Tachbrook Ms
15 Udall St
16 Upper Tachbrook St
17 Vane St
18 Walcott St
19 Warwick Pl North
20 Warwick Square Ms
21 West Ms

C3
1 Denbigh Pl
2 Ms South
3 Moreton Pl
4 Moreton Ter
5 Moreton Terrace Ms North
6 Ranelagh Rd

C5
1 Bradmead

C6
1 Corunna Ter

C7
1 Crichton St
2 Stone Cl

C8
1 Bobbin Cl
2 Charles Barry Cl
3 Scout La
4 Stephen Pl
5 Sycamore Ms

D1
1 Abbey Orchard Street Est
2 Arneway St
3 Artillery Rw
4 Chadwick St
5 Dacre St
6 Dean Farrar St
7 Greycoat Pl
8 Greycoat St
9 Little Smith St
10 Perkin's Rents
11 Rochester St
12 St Ermin's Hl
13 St Matthew St
14 The Sanctuary

D2
1 Bulinca St
2 Esterbrooke St
3 Fynes St
4 Greycoat La
5 Hugh Pl
6 Osbert St
7 Rutherford St
8 St Oswulf St
9 Stanford St
10 Thorndike St

D3
1 Balniel Ga
2 Bessborough St
3 Buonaparte Ms
4 Cureton St
5 Drummond Ga
6 Garden Ter
7 Lupus St
8 Moreton St
9 Ponsonby Pl
10 Ponsonby Ter
11 Rampayne St

D6
1 Blore Cl
2 Cowthorpe Rd
3 Minshull St

D7
1 Wandsworth Rd

D8
1 Gauden Cl
2 Littlebury Rd
3 Shamrock St
4 Slievemore Cl

E1
1 Barton St
2 Cowley St
3 Dean Bradley St
4 Dean Stanley St
5 Dean Trench St
6 Little College St
7 Lord North St
8 Smith Sq

E2
1 Dean Ryle St

E3
1 New Spring Gardens Wk

E4
1 South Lambeth Pl
2 Trenchold St

E5
1 Walberswick St
2 Walton Cl
3 Wheatsheaf La

E6
1 St Barnabas Vls

E7
1 Clarence Wk

E8
1 Cottage Gv
2 Fenwick Pl
3 Lendal Ter

F2
1 Ingram Cl
2 Lilac Pl
3 Randall Rw
4 Salamanca Pl
5 Stroughton Cl

F3
1 Auckland St
2 Brangton Rd
3 Dolland St
4 Casholder Pl
5 Glyn St
6 Loughborough St
7 Wynyard Ter

F4
1 Kennington Gv
2 Meadow Rd

F5
1 Albert Av
2 Ely Cottages
3 St Stephen's Ter
4 Trigon Rd

F6
1 Johnston Cl
2 Stockwell Ter

F7
1 Broomgrove Rd
2 Eastcote St
3 Fenton Cl
4 Stockwell La
5 Swan Ms

F8
1 Bellefields Rd
2 Burgoyne Rd
3 Bythorn St
4 Nealden St

Page 121

G2
1 Hornbeam Cl
2 Kempsford Rd
3 St Mary's Gdns
4 St Mary's Wk
5 Saunders St

G4
1 Brixton Rd
2 Hanover Gdns
3 Pegasus Pl

G5
1 Claylands Pl
2 Cowley Rd
3 Listowel Cl
4 Minerva Cl
5 Perseverance Pl
6 Russell Gv

G7
1 Burton Rd
2 Ingleborough St
3 Peckford Pl
4 St Lawrence Wy

G8
1 Astoria Wk
2 Beehive Pl
3 Knowle Cl
4 Pope's Rd

H1
1 Colnbrook St
2 Gaywood St
3 Geraldine St
4 Gladstone St
5 Princess St
6 Thomas Doyle St

H2
1 Dante Pl
2 Elephant And Castle
3 George Mathers Rd
4 Hedger St
5 Howell Wk
6 Kempsford Rd
7 Longville Rd
8 Pastor St

H3
1 Cottington St
2 Delverton Rd
3 Marsland Cl
4 Stopford Rd

H5
1 Cadman Cl

H8
1 Mallams Ms
2 Pomfret Rd
3 Swinford Gdns
4 Wellfit St

J1
1 Avonmouth St
2 Brockham St
3 Dickens Sq
4 Gaunt St
5 Trinity Church Sq

J3
1 Beckford Pl
2 Borrett Cl
3 Sturgeon Rd
4 Sutherland Sq
5 Sutherland Wk

J4
1 Albany Ms
2 Dartford St
3 Empress St
4 Harding Cl

J5
1 New Church Rd
2 Redcar St
3 Thompson's Av
4 Toulon St

J6
1 Mornington Ms

J8
1 Harbour Rd
2 Hardess St
3 Padfield Rd
4 Vaughan Rd

K1
1 Becket St
2 Black Horse Ct
3 Cardinal Bourne St
4 Hunter Cl
5 Lansdowne Pl
6 Pardoner St
7 Potier St
8 Theobald St

K2
1 Barlow St
2 Beckway St
3 Content St
4 Crosslet St
5 Cavel St
6 Halpin Pl
7 Hearn's Buildings
8 John Maurice Cl
9 Larissa St
10 Paragon Ms
11 Salisbury Cl

K3
1 Blackwood St
2 Brettell St
3 Sandford Rw
4 Townley St

K4
1 Boyson Rd
2 Depot St
3 Horsley St
4 Westmoreland Rd

K5
1 Broome Wy
2 Notley St
3 Owgan Cl
4 Sears St

K6
1 Artichoke Pl
2 Bullace Rw
3 Datchelor Pl
4 Harvey Rd
5 Jephson St
6 Joiners Arms Yd
7 Mary Datchelor Cl
8 Milkwell Yd
9 Orpheus St
10 Ribbon Dance Ms

K7
1 Ashworth Cl
2 Coldharbour Pl
3 Evesham Wk
4 Grace's Ms
5 Harford Cl
6 Selborne Rd
7 Windsor Wk

L1
1 Fendall St
2 Green Wk
3 Grigg's Pl
4 Long Wk
5 Purbrook St
6 Radcliffe Rd
7 Rephidim St
8 Stevens St

L2
1 Aberdour St
2 Guinness Sq
3 Huntsman St
4 Massinger St
5 Penry St
6 Preston Cl
7 Stanford Pl

L3
1 Flinton St

L4
1 Bilbury Cl
2 Brockworth Cl

L5
1 Cottage Gn
2 Dowlas St
3 Lynbrook Cl
4 Marchwood Cl
5 Melbury Dr

L6
1 Brunswick Vls
2 Muscatel Pl
3 Redbridge Gdns

L7
1 Ainsworth Cl
2 Cactus Cl
3 Canning Cross

L8
1 Albrighton Rd
2 Maldon Cl

M1
1 Bridewain St
2 Canon Murnane Rd
3 Gedling Pl
4 Necklanger St

M2
1 Alscot Wy
2 Burnham Cl
3 Buttermere Cl
4 Keats Cl
5 Longfellow Wy
6 Setchell Rd
7 Wordsworth Rd

M3
1 Ivy Church La
2 Mawbey Rd
3 Shorncliffe Rd

M4
1 Pennack Rd
2 Sumner Rd

M5
1 Boathouse Wk
2 Branch St
3 Chandler Wy
4 Hordle Prom North
5 Lidgate Rd
6 Mattingly Wy
7 Tilbury Cl

M6
1 Charles Coveney Rd
2 Crane St
3 Finch Ms
4 Grummant Rd
5 Lyndhurst Sq
6 Sumner Av

M7
1 Azenby Rd
2 Highshore Rd

M8
1 Everthorpe Rd

Page 122

A2
1 Strathnairn St

A3
1 Atwell Rd
2 Moncrieff St
3 Parkstone Rd
4 Reedham St
5 William Margrie Cl

B7
1 Claude Rd
2 Firbank Rd
3 Godman Rd
4 Harders Rd
5 Lulworth Rd
6 Nazareth Cl
7 Sandlings Cl

C1
1 Hothfield Pl
2 Orange Pl

C2
1 Alpine Rd
2 Corbett's La
3 Debnams Rd
4 Nelldale Rd
5 Warndon St

C3
1 Delaford Rd
2 Goldsworthy Gdns

C5
1 Chesterfield Wy
2 Hillbeck Cl
3 King Arthur Cl
4 Wagner St
5 White Post St

C6
1 Faulkner St
2 Staveley Cl
3 Wild Goose Dr

C7
1 Lindo St
2 Senate St

D1
1 Abbotsbury Rd
2 Barset Rd
3 Belvedere Ms
4 Brock St
5 Salisbury Ter

D2
1 Cope St
2 Luxford St
3 Mayflower Cl
4 Trident St
5 Trundley's Ter

D3
1 Sybil Phoenix Cl

D5
1 Wrigglesworth St

D6
1 Fishers Ct
2 Hatcham Park Rd
3 Swallow Cl
4 Wellington Cl

D7
1 Hathway St

E1
1 Lovell Rd
2 Ropemaker Rd

E2
1 Sweden Ga

E4
1 Archer Sq
2 Chubworthy St
3 Desmond St
4 Marchant St
5 Whitcher Cl

E6
1 Alexandra Cottages
2 Batavia Rd
3 Clifton Ri
4 Cottesbrook St
5 Redstart Cl
6 Silver Cl
7 Tarragon Cl
8 Vansittart St
9 Woodrush Cl

F2
1 Deptford Whf
2 Enterprize Wy
3 Kempthorne Rd
4 Tarriff Crs

F4
1 Beech Cl
2 Diana Cl
3 Dorking Cl
4 Kerry Pth
5 Larch Cl
6 Trim St
7 Violet Cl
8 Walnut Cl

F5
1 Douglas Wy
2 Exeter Wy
3 Glenville Gv
4 Hereford Pl
5 Railway Gv
6 Royal Naval Pl
7 Turnpike Cl

F7
1 Rokeby Rd
2 Vulcan Rd
3 Vulcan Ter

F8
1 Beverley Ct

Page 123

G2
1 Britannia St
2 Copeland Dr
3 Crews St
4 Dartmoor Wk
5 Dockers Tanner Rd
6 Epping Cl
7 Mast House Ter
8 Sherwood Gdns
9 Thames Cir

G4
1 Armada St
2 Barque Ms
3 Caravel Ms
4 Carrick Ms
5 Frigate Ms
6 Grinling Pl
7 Lamerton St
8 Mcmillan St
9 Trevithick St

G5
1 Crossfield St
2 Ffinch St
3 New Butt La
4 Octavius St
5 Rochdale Wy
6 Speedwell St
7 Vaughan Williams Cl

G6
1 Cranbrook Rd
2 Deloraine St
3 Deptford Grn
4 Deptford Broadway
5 Omega St
6 Pearson's St
7 St Nicholas St
8 Strickland St
9 Wiltshaw St

H2
1 Ambassador Sq
2 Marsh St

H5
1 Ashburnham Retreat
2 Devonshire Dr
3 Maitland St

H7
1 Coldbath St
2 Nectarine Wy
3 Orchard Hl
4 Ravensbourne Pl
5 Somerset Gdns
6 Sunninghill St

J1
1 Cardale St
2 Friars Mead
3 Hickin St
4 Isambard Ms
5 Olliffe St
6 St James Ms

J3
1 Churchfields
2 Clavell St
3 College Ap
4 Greenwich Church St
5 Horseferry Pl
6 King William Wk
7 Nelson Rd
8 Stockwell St
9 Welland St

J5
1 Gloucester Circ
2 Peyton St
3 Prince of Orange La
4 Royal Pl
5 Straightsmouth

J6
1 Allison Cl
2 Cable Pl
3 Hollymount Cl
4 Plumbridge St
5 Trinity Gv

J7
1 Kings Hall Ms
2 Myron Pl
3 Rennell St
4 St Stephen's Gv
5 William Cl

K2
1 Chichester Wy
2 Glenaffric Av
3 Glenworth Av
4 Seyssel St

K3
1 Collington St
2 Trenchard St

K4
1 Greenwich Park St
2 Old Woolwich Rd
3 Thalia Cl

K5
1 May's Buildings Ms
2 Wellington Gv

K6
1 Clayton Ms
2 Dartmouth Ter

K7
1 The Meadway
2 Pagoda Gdns

K8
1 Biscoe Wy
2 The Squirrels

L3
1 Conley St
2 King William La
3 Kossuth St
4 Mell St
5 Pelton Rd
6 Walnut Tree Wk
7 Woodlands Gv

L4
1 Lemmon Rd
2 Tom Smith Cl
3 Woodland Crs
4 Woodlands Park Rd

L6
1 Duke Humphrey Rd

L7
1 Grote's Buildings
2 Lloyd's Pl
3 Southvale Rd

L8
1 Haynes Cl
2 Nesbit Cl
3 Paynell Ct
4 Quentin Pl

Page 124

B2
1 Brocklebank Rd

D3
1 St Paul's Rd

D7
1 Stonefield Wy

D8
1 Marshbrook Cl

E2
1 Glenalvon Wy
2 Lancey Cl
3 Lyford St
4 Parish Whf
5 Tamar St
6 Woodville St

E3
1 Cannon Pl

E8
1 Sandby Grn
2 Winchcomb Cl

Page 125

G2
1 Bathway
2 Castle Rd
3 Jim Bradley Cl
4 John Wilson St
5 Polytechnic St

H2
1 Anglesea Av
2 Anglesea Rd
3 Ashlar Pl
4 General Gordon Pl
5 Greens End
6 Helen St
7 Masons Hl
8 Ruddstreet Cl
9 Taylor's Buildings
10 Vincent Rd
11 Wilmount St

H3
1 Buttmarsh Cl
2 Sandy Hill Av
3 Simmons Rd

L2
1 Bebbington Rd
2 Gunning St
3 Hector St
4 Old Tramyard

L4
1 Church Hyde
2 Malton Ms

L5
1 Barden St

M3
1 Amardeep Cl
2 Bargate Cl
3 Felspar Cl

M6
1 Tennyson Cl

M7
1 Beliegrove Cl

M8
1 St Quentin Rd

Page 126

K2
1 Doebury Wk
2 Littledale
3 Prestwood Cl
4 Villacourt Rd

D4
1 Heath View Dr

E1
1 Gainsborough Sq
2 Hanover Wy

E3
1 Abbotswood Cl
2 Blakemore Wy
3 Plympton Cl

E4
1 Elmhurst

F1
1 Adams Sq
2 Portman Cl

F1
1 Belvedere Ct

Page 127

H4
1 Camrose Cl
2 Highfield Av

M5
1 Fairview

Page 130

B2
1 Diamedes Av
2 Evergreen Wy
3 Maisie Webster Cl
4 Town Farm Wy

E6
1 Maple Gdns

F5
1 Chesterton Dr
2 Laburnum Wy
3 Milton Gdns
4 The Nightingales

F7
1 College Wy
2 Knapp Rd
3 Station Ap

Page 131

F1
1 Fairholme
2 Lindsey Gdns
3 Sherborne Rd

M5
1 Allcot Cl
2 Ambleside Pl
3 Andover Cl
4 Appleby Gdns
5 Buttermere Cl
6 Churchill Cl
7 Ennerdale Cl
8 Crasmere Cl
9 Invicta Cl
10 Kendal Cl
11 Missenden Cl
12 Nelson Cl
13 Nine Elms Cl
14 Pope Cl
15 Radley Cl
16 Windermere Cl

M7
1 Queens Park Gdns

Page 132

A6
1 Bowsley Ct
2 Ivory Ct
3 Ordnance Cl
4 Taylors Ct

B3
1 Tree Cl

C7
1 Petersham La

D2
1 Heathlands Cl
2 Heathlands Wy
3 Linslade Cl
4 Pickwick Cl

E6
1 Newgate Cl

E7
1 Ridge Wy

E8
1 Burgess Rd
2 Crosby Cl
3 Dunmow Cl
4 Gabriel Cl
5 Hazlitt Cl
6 Swinfield Cl

F1
1 Beverley Av
2 Cobb's Rd
3 The Greenway
4 Wivenhoe Ct

F2
1 Bramley Wy
2 Brompton Cl
3 Crestwood Wy
4 Nursery Gdns

F6
1 Atherley Wy
2 Daniel Cl

F7
1 Edmund Gv

F8
1 Sunrise Cl

F9
1 Hampton Rd East
2 Loxley Rd
3 Masefield Rd

Page 133

G7
1 Sekhon Ter

H4
1 St Edmund's La

K4
1 Rosebine Av

K5
1 College Cl

K6
1 Woodbine Cl

K7
1 Golf Side
2 Queen Annes Cl

K8
1 Paget Cl

L2
1 Chudleigh Rd
2 Palmerston Rd
3 Tayben Av

L5
1 Hamilton Rd
2 Hunting Gate Ms
3 Knowle Rd

L6
1 Jordans Ms

L7
1 Birdwood Cl
2 Clifton Rd

M1
1 Weavers Cl

M2
1 Trevor Cl
2 Varsity Dr

M3
1 Blyth Cl
2 Butterfield Cl
3 Palmerston Rd
4 Russell Rd

M5
1 Lansdowne Cl
2 Talbot Rd
3 Tudor Gdns

M6
1 Chillingworth Gdns

M7
1 Cusack Cl
2 Southfield Gdns

Page 134

A4
1 Cheltenham Pl
2 Devoncroft Gdns
3 Mary's Ter
4 Oak La
5 Railway Ap
6 Station Yd
7 Strafford Rd

A8
1 Chatsworth Pl
2 Clavering Cl
3 Hawkesley Cl
4 Woodville Cl

B3
1 Baronsfield Rd
2 Bridge Rd
3 Bridle La
4 Cumberland Cl
5 Downes Cl
6 King's Rd
7 Norfolk Cl
8 South Western Rd
9 Sussex Cl
10 Westmorland Rd

B4
1 Adelaide Rd
2 All Saints Pas
3 Bush Cottages
4 Carter's Yd
5 Chesterton Cl
6 Church Rw
7 Dutch Yd
8 Merton Rd
9 Newton's Yd
10 North Pas
11 Oakhill Pl

C4
1 Dorchester Ct

C8
1 Cave Rd
2 Fanshawe Rd
3 Fisherman Cl
4 Headway Cl
5 Vancouver Rd

D2
1 Castle Yd
2 Duke St
3 King St
4 Lewis Rd
5 Retreat Rd
6 St James's Cottages
7 Victoria Pl
8 Wakefield Rd
9 The Wardrobe
10 Warrington Rd
11 Whittaker Av

D3
1 Beaulieu Cl
2 Compass Hl
3 Fairlawns
4 Haversham Cl
5 Roseleigh Cl
6 Vivienne Cl

D5
1 Tree Cl

D6
1 Petersham Cl

E2
1 Catherine Dr
2 Clarence St
3 Drummonds Pl
4 Duncan Rd
5 Larkfield Rd
6 The Quadrant
7 St John's Gv
8 St John's Rd
9 Salisbury Rd
10 Sydney Rd

E7
1 Chislehurst Rd
2 Preston Pl
3 Prince's Rd
4 Royston Rd
5 Towers Pl

E3
1 Lancaster Ms
2 Montague Rd
3 Richmond Hl

F1
1 Adelaide Rd
2 Crown Ter

F2
1 Albany Rd
2 Audley Rd
3 Beatrice Rd
4 Connaught Rd
5 Hyde Rd
6 Lorne Rd
7 Marchmont Rd
8 Winter Box Wk
9 York Rd

Page 136

A2
1 The Footpath
2 Lysons Wk

A3
1 Horndean Cl
2 Hyacinth Rd
3 Norley V
4 Ringwood Gdns
5 Stoughton Cl

B4
1 Greenstead Gdns
2 Hobbes Wk
3 Kingslawn Cl
4 Laneway
5 Montolieu Gdns
6 St Margaret's Crs

D1
1 Charlwood Ter
2 Clegg Pl
3 Heath Mead
4 Lawson Cl
5 Ulva Rd

D2
1 Burleigh Rd
2 Chartfield Sq
3 North Lodge Cl

D5
1 Lewesdon Cl
2 Montfort Pl
3 Pilsden Cl
4 Sandringham Cl
5 Swanton Gdns
6 Wainford Cl

D6
1 Chobham Gdns
2 Queensmere Cl

D7
1 Carnegie Pl
2 Heath Mead
3 Lawson Cl

E1
1 Esmond St
2 Rockland Rd
3 Walker's Pl

E2
1 Chepstow Cl
2 Evenwood Cl

E3
1 George Wyver Cl
2 Girdwood Rd

E5
1 Burghley Hall Cl
2 Claudia Pl
3 Galgate Cl
4 King Charles Wk
5 Levana Cl
6 Stoford Cl

F1
1 Brandlehow Rd
2 Skelgill Rd

F2
1 Cavalry Gdns
2 Kendal Pl
3 Woodlands Wy
4 Woodlawn Cl

F3
1 Everatt Cl
2 Holm Oak Cl
3 Sedleigh Rd

Page 137

H2
1 Barchard St
2 Cricketers Ms
3 Lancaster Ms
4 Old York Rd
5 Ridgmount Rd
6 Shoreham Cl
7 Tonsley Pl
8 Tonsley Rd

H3
1 Iron Mill Pl
2 Marcus St
3 Westdean Cl

J3
1 Berisford Ms
2 Dault Rd
3 Galesbury Rd
4 Marshall Cl
5 St Ann's Park Rd
6 Wycombe Pl

K1
1 Beverley Cl
2 Kennet Cl
3 Oberstein Rd
4 Sangora Rd
5 Windrush Cl

L1
1 Abyssinia Cl
2 Abyssinia Rd
3 Barnard St
4 Buckmaster Rd
5 Prested Rd
6 St John's Rd

L2
1 Arundel Cl

L5
1 Cobham Cl

L6
1 St Anthonys Cl
2 St Benets Cl
3 St Catherines Cl
4 St Edmunds Cl
5 St Helens Cl
6 St Peters Cl

M1
1 Hafer Rd

M2
1 Bennerley Rd
2 Berber Rd

M3
1 Stonnell's Rd

M4
1 Jaggard Wy
2 Mayford Cl

M6
1 Old Hospital Cl

M7
1 Morven Rd

M8
1 St Cyprian's St

Page 138

A3
1 Roseneath Rd
2 Walsingham Rd

C1
1 Downer's Cottages
2 The Polygon
3 Venn St

C6
1 Brierley Rd

CB
1 Pringle Gdns

D1
1 Abbeville Ms
2 Carfax Pl
3 Clement Av
4 Holwood Pl
5 Kendoa Rd
6 Oaklands Pl
7 Teignmouth Cl
8 White's Sq

D2
1 Allnutt Wy

E2
1 Bowie Cl
2 Langholm Cl

D6
1 Goodman Crs

D7
1 The Spinney
2 Tarrington Cl
3 Woodfield Rd

D8
1 Babington Rd
2 Campbell Cl

E1
1 Ashmere Gv
2 Felmersham Cl
3 Hetherington Rd
4 Linom Rd
5 Tintern St

F1
1 Magnolia Pl

E6
1 Bowater Cl

E7
1 Brixton Hill Pl
2 Rodmill La

E6
1 Barrhill Rd
2 Broadlands Cl
3 Goodman Crs

E7
1 Blakemore Rd
2 Brancaster Rd
3 Cherry Tree Dr
4 Moorcroft Rd

E8
1 Gleneldon Ms
2 Newcome Gdns

F3
1 Merredene St

F4
1 Saxonfield Cl
2 Wimbart Rd

F5
1 Claremont Cl
2 Huggins Pl
3 Lirmetree Cl
4 Presentation Ms

F6
1 Normanhurst Rd

F7
1 Leigh Orchard Cl
2 Francis Barber Cl

Page 139

G1
1 Brixton Ov
2 Electric La
3 Leeson Rd
4 Marcus Garvey Wy
5 Valentia Pl
6 Vining St

G2
1 Arlingford Rd

H2
1 Chaucer Rd
2 Derek Walcott Cl
3 Mumford Rd
4 Oborne St

H3
1 Heathland Gdns

K2
1 Heathfield Gdns

K3
1 Heathfield Gdns

K4
1 Alice Walker Cl
2 Broughton Dr
3 Cordelia Cl
4 Eaton Dr
5 James Joyes Wk
6 Langston Hughes Cl
7 Louise Bennett Cl
8 Walt Whitman Cl

K4
1 Heathfield Av

K6
1 Dawnay Gdns

K7
1 Glentanner Wy

K8
1 Thurso St

Page 140

A3
1 Alexander Evans Ms
2 Perry V
3 Treviso Rd

C3
1 Orchard Cl

C5
1 Pearcefield Av

D1
1 Montrose Wy

Page 141

J4
1 Melbourne Ms

J5
1 Windsor Ms

K3
1 Lullingstone La
2 Maythorne Cottages
3 St Swithun's Rd

L2
1 Wolfram Cl

L5
1 Leahurst Rd

M1
1 Osborn Ter

M2
1 Falmouth Cl
2 St Peters Ct

M3
1 Burnt Ash Rd
2 Leewood Cl

M5
1 Oak Cottage Cl

M7
1 Jennifer Rd

Page 142

D4
1 Churchbury Rd
2 Kingsground
3 Middle Park Av

E1
1 Rochester Wy
2 Tom Coombs Cl

E7
1 Foxhole Rd
2 Horsfeld Gdns
3 Keynsham Gdns
4 Lilburne Gdns

F1
1 Leigh Orchard Cl

F2
1 Francis Barber Cl

Page 143

G1
1 Kimmeridge Gdns
2 King And Queen Cl

G2
1 Well Hall Pde

G4
1 Sowerby Cl

G5
1 Chaundrye Cl

F6
1 Margaret Gardner Dr

F8
1 Tenterden Gv

J5
1 Brentwood Cl

J2
1 School Road Av

L2
1 Coleshill Rd

H7
1 Bloom Gv
2 Chartham Rd
3 Friar Ms
4 Hannen Rd
5 Lansdowne Wood Cl
6 Nettlefold Pl
7 Pyrmont Gv

K1
1 Basingdon Wy
2 Domett Cl
3 Dowson Cl
4 Sunray Av

K5
1 Spencer Ms

K6
1 Croxted Ms

K8
1 Champness Cl
2 St Bernards Cl

L1
1 Buxted Rd

L2
1 Gilkes Crs

L5
1 Baird Gdns
2 Bell Meadow
3 Hunters Meadow
4 Rockwell Gdns
5 Surrey Ms

M1
1 Frogley Rd
2 Oxonian St
3 Spurling Rd
4 Zenoria St

M7
1 The Dulwich Oaks

Page 145

G4
1 Parkhurst Gdns
2 Tan Yard La

Page 146

C3
1 Hampton Court Av

C5
1 Lawrence Hill Gdns
2 Marlborough Rd

F6
1 Ellis Wy

Page 148

A4
1 Belle Vue Cl

E1
1 Links Rd

F1
1 Albert Rd
2 Badgers Cl
3 Elmsway
4 Perrin Cl

F6
1 Goddard Cl
2 Wilcox Gdns

Page 149

C3
1 Orchard Cl

C5
1 Pearcefield Av

D1
1 Montrose Wy

E1
1 Meretone Cl

E2
1 Cypress Gdns

E4
1 Buckingham La

E5
1 Steucers La

E7
1 Holland Dr
2 Normandy Cl
3 Shaw's Cottages

F4
1 Chilthorne Cl

G1
1 Creeland Gv
2 Stanstead Gv

J1
1 Gaston Bridge Rd

M1
1 Cumbernauld Gdns

M2
1 Bracken Cl
2 Camilla Cl
3 Cavendish Cl
4 Chestnut Cl
5 Green Leas Cl

F7
1 Glenthorne Rd
2 Margaret Lockwood Cl
3 Minstrel Gdns

M4
1 Dale Rd

Page 150

E2
1 Abbott Cl
2 Cheeseman Cl
3 Gale Cl
4 Sparks Cl
5 Sparrow Cl
6 Victors Dr

F2
1 Bramble La
2 Chichester Cl
3 Hawley Cl
4 Homewood Cl
5 Langridge Ms
6 Orpwood Cl
7 Stanborough Cl
8 Stanford Cl
9 Tulip Cl
10 Walker Cl

L2
1 Coombe La West

L6
1 Jacaranda Cl
2 Station Ap

L7
1 Balgowan Cl
2 Cadmer Cl
3 Cloister Rd
4 Kingston Lodge
5 Sussex Rd
6 Tregaron Gdns

Page 151

G1
1 Hawthorn Cl
2 Hollybank Cl

G2
1 Begonia Pl
2 Cyclamen Cl
3 Daffodil Cl
4 Gladioli Cl
5 Hyacinth Cl
6 Marlborough Rd
7 Snowdrop Cl

G5
1 Thames Meadow

J1
1 Salisbury Gdns

J2
1 School Road Av

L2
1 Coleshill Rd

L7
1 Bernard Gdns
2 Helme Cl
3 Springfield Rd

L5
1 Bragg Cl

L7
1 Oarsman Cl

Page 152

A2
1 Blackmore's Gv
2 Chadwick Cl
3 Davenport Cl
4 Doone Cl
5 Gomer Gdns
6 Rosebank Cl
7 Thelma Gv

C4
1 Beverley Rd
2 School La
3 School Rd
4 Vineyard Rw
5 Warwick Rd

D5
1 Bath Pas
2 Bishop's Hall
3 Clarence St
4 St James's Rd

E5
1 Castle St
2 Fife Rd
3 Littlefield Cl
4 Weston Pk

E6
1 Bellevue Rd
2 Fairfield Rd
3 Waltersplash Cl

E7
1 Ardmay Gdns
2 Maplehurst Cl
3 Sheppard Cl
4 Surbiton Hall Cl

E8
1 Ardmay Gdns

F5
1 Cromwell Rd
2 Elm Rd
3 Harding Cl
4 John Austin Cl
5 Queen Elizabeth Rd

F6
1 Camm Gdns
2 Rayleigh Cl

F7
1 Dudley Rd
2 Kingsworthy Cl
3 Vineyard Cl

A4
1 Alice Ms
2 Boucher Cl
3 Bychurch End
4 Hall Lt
5 Latimer Rd
6 Sydney Rd
7 Walpole Crs
8 Walpole Rd

M2
1 Adelaide Rd
2 Bullard Rd
3 The Causeway
4 The Cedars
5 Elleray Rd
6 Middle La
7 Park La
8 St Mary's Av
9 White Heron Ms

Page 153

G4
1 Audric Cl
2 Burnham St
3 Carlisle Cl
4 Station Ap
5 Station Rd

G6
1 Franklin Cl
2 Piper Rd
3 Stapleford Cl

H3
1 Kingsnympton Pk
2 Morecombe Cl

H5
1 Montrose Gdns
2 Sibthorp Rd
3 Upper Grn East
4 Upper Grn West

M6
1 Chatsworth Pl
2 Pear Tree Cl
3 Queen Anne's Gdns
4 Regal Ct

Page 154

C4
1 Cumberland Cl
2 Lansdowne Cl
3 Southridge Pl
4 Thackeray Cl
5 Thaxted Pl

D2
1 Brunswick Ms
2 Edgington Rd
3 Potter's La
4 Rotherhill Av

D3
1 Broadview Rd
2 Drakewood Rd
3 Nettlewood Rd

D6
1 Sunnymead Av

E2
1 Matthew Cl
2 Northumberland Gdns

E3
1 Rochester Cl

E4
1 Croindene Rd

E5
1 Granden Rd
2 Tylecroft Rd

L1
1 Aldis Ms
2 Ivy Rd
3 Recovery St

L2
1 Daniel Cl
2 Defoe Cl
3 Marlborough Cl
4 Waterfall Ter
5 Watson Cl

L3
1 Alphea Cl
2 Holmbury Ct
3 Rutland Rd
4 Tudor Pl

L4
1 Lister Cl
2 Longfield Dr

L5
1 Gilpin Cl
2 Lulworth Crs

L6
1 Benedict Whf
2 Blake Rd
3 Morland Cl
4 Taffy's How
5 Walnut Tree Av

L7
1 Granada Cl

M1
1 Otterburn St

M3
1 Dovedale Ri
2 Kenmare Dr
3 North Pl
4 Shrewton Rd
5 Woodley Cl

M4
1 Camomile Av
2 Mason's Pl

F2
1 Francis Gv
2 Raymond Rd
3 St Mark's Pl
4 Wimbledon Br
5 Worple Road Ms

F3
1 Sherwood Rd
2 Victoria Crs

Page 155

G3
1 Ashbourne Ter
2 Derby Rd
3 Gladstone Rd
4 Granville Rd
5 Harcourt Rd
6 Palmerston Gv
7 Sir Cyril Black Wy

C7
1 Hatherleigh Cl
2 Queen Elizabeth Gdns
3 Queen's Rd
4 Queens Rd

A2
1 Bathurst Av
2 The Path
3 Queensland Av
4 Rowland Wy

A3
1 Norman Rd
2 Olive Rd
3 Pincott Rd

C4
1 Calder Rd
2 Cartmel Gdns
3 Chester Gdns
4 Langdon Wk

D5
1 Landseer Cl
2 Littlers Cl
3 Stubbs Wy
4 Yarborough Rd

D6
1 Horner La
2 Sycamore Gdns
3 Varley Wy

E6
1 Chantry Wy
2 Gale Cl
3 Phipp's Bridge Rd
4 Saxonbury Cl

E7
1 Deer Park Gdns
2 Hatfield Cl
3 Rawnsley Av

Page 156

A2
1 Freshwater Cl
2 Knapton Ms
3 St Nicholas Glebe
4 Sirdar Rd
5 Stanley Gdns

A5
1 Kennedy Cl
2 Leather Cl
3 Pembroke Rd
4 Roper Wy

B5
1 Moyser Rd
2 Pain's Cl
3 Potter Cl
4 Thrupp Cl

E6
1 Caernarvon Cl
2 Cranbourne Cl
3 Glamorgan Cl
4 Huntingdon Cl

E7
1 Eighteenth Wy
2 Hertford Wy
3 Kent Cl
4 Leicester Av
5 Lindsey Cl
6 Monmouth Cl
7 Montgomery Cl
8 Shropshire Cl

E8
1 Buckingham Rd
2 Lincoln Rd
3 Southampton Gdns
4 Sussex Rd

F1
1 Beechcroft Cl

F3
1 Courtland Av
2 Hermitage La

F4
1 Roche Rd
2 St Helen's Crs

F5
1 Palmers Rd

F7
1 Dorset Gdns
2 Namton Dr

Page 157
H5
1 Parchmore Wy

J5
1 Beulah Crs
2 Dairy Cl
3 Goulding Gdns
4 Newnham Cl
5 Osborne Gdns

K2
1 Dover Rd
2 Ilkley Cl
3 Mount Rd
4 Surridge Gdns
5 Treloar Gdns

K3
1 Elizabeth Wy
2 Rushden Cl

K5
1 Layard Rd
2 Mersham Rd

K6
1 Annsworthy Av
2 Hobart Gdns

K7
1 Crowland Rd
2 Dunkeld Rd
3 Oban Rd
4 Zion Pl

K8
1 Alexandra Pl
2 Palmerston Rd

L1
1 Brabourne Cl
2 Bridgetown Cl
3 Thorsden Wy
4 Victoria Crs

L2
1 Childs La
2 New Green Pl
3 Paddock Gdns
4 Victory Pl
5 Woodland Cl

L3
1 Fox Hill Gdns

L4
1 Southholme Cl

L5
1 Teesdale Gdns

L6
1 Cranleigh Gdns

L7
1 Clifton Ms
2 Walter's Rd
3 Waterfield Gdns

M1
1 Burntwood Vw

M2
1 Bowley Cl
2 Jasper Rd
3 St Aubyn's Rd
4 Stoney La
5 Telford Cl

M3
1 Buckleigh Wy
2 Dargate Cl
3 Reynard Dr

M5
1 Sunset Gdns

M6
1 Hambledon Gdns
2 Holmesdale Cl

M8
1 Sutton Gdns

Page 158
A3
1 Bargrove Cl
2 Beaver Cl
3 Brunswick Pl
4 Thicket Gv

A8
1 Greenmead Cl
2 Percy Rd
3 Sidney Rd

B5
1 Bridgewood Cl
2 Chalkenden Cl
3 Limes Av
4 St Hugh's Rd
5 Tower Cl
6 Trenholme Ter

B7
1 Appletree Cl
2 Barfreston Wy
3 Cambridge Av
4 Chartwell Wy
5 Colling Wood Cl
6 Mersham Pl
7 Minden Rd
8 Ridsdale Rd
9 Sheldon Cl

B7
1 Brocklesby Rd
2 Brooklyn Gv
3 Ingatestone Rd
4 Napier Rd
5 Seymour Pl

C4
1 Beeches Cl
2 Challin St

D2
1 Courtenay Rd
2 Hardings La

D3
1 Bycroft St
2 Kingsdale Rd

D4
1 Plawsfield Rd

D5
1 Carlys Cl

D6
1 Mayford Cl

D7
1 Station Est

E1
1 Watlington Gv

E3
1 Station Ap

E4
1 Densole Cl
2 Mackenzie Rd

E5
1 Betts Cl
2 Lynsted Ct

E7
1 Elmerside Rd
2 Upper Elmers End Rd

E8
1 Kingsworth Cl

F1
1 Montana Gdns
2 Westerley Crs

F3
1 Bethersden Cl
2 Nettlestead Cl
3 Sellindge Cl

F4
1 Kingston Crs
2 Sheridan Wy
3 Whitstable Cl

F5
1 Faversham Rd
2 Gowland Pl

F6
1 Yewtree Rd

F8
1 Aviemore Cl
2 Elmdene Cl

Page 159
G5
1 Christ Church Rd
2 Lea Rd
3 Stanmore Ter
4 Thornton Dene

H5
1 Ashdown Cl
2 Ellesmere Av

J5
1 Westmoat Cl

L2
1 Arcus Rd
2 Avondale Rd
3 Hildenborough Gdns
4 Patterdale Cl
5 Tresco Cl
6 Yewdale Cl

M6
1 Winchester Cl

M7
1 Brookwood Cl
2 Chiltern Gdns
3 Deepdale Av
4 Kingsleigh Wk

M8
1 Appledore Cl
2 Bidborough Cl
3 Elvington Gn
4 Mereworth Cl
5 Speldhurst Cl

Page 160
A5
1 Churchill Wy
2 Harmony Wy

A6
1 Cheveney Wk
2 Ludlow Cl
3 Masons Hl
4 Simpson's Rd

B4
1 Denmark Rd
2 Haxted Rd
3 Horsley Rd
4 The Old Ctyd
5 Willow Tree Wk

E4
1 Northfield Cl

E6
1 Armstrong Cl
2 Charlotte Park Av
3 Holmdene Ct

E8
1 Moorcroft Gdns
2 Westcott Cl

F3
1 Squires Wood Dr

F5
1 Beech Copse

F8
1 Magpie Hall La
2 Southborough La

Page 161
H2
1 Furzefield Cl

M7
1 Chequers Cl
2 Englefield Cl
3 Kevington Cl

Page 162
C7
1 Harbledown Pl
2 Hythe Cl
3 Market Meadow
4 Montbretia Cl
5 Penshurst Wy
6 Station Rd
7 Withens Cl

D7
1 Admiral Cl
2 Buttermere Rd
3 Kingfisher Cl
4 Mayfly Cl
5 Otlinge Cl
6 Otters Cl
7 Palmarsh Cl
8 Richborough Cl
9 Swallowtail Cl
10 Watermint Cl
11 Yalding Cl

E1
1 Chantrey Cl

E2
1 Calvert Cl

Page 163
K5
1 Greenside
2 The Orchard
3 Pear Tree Cl
4 St Lukes Cl

K7
1 Apple Orch
2 Edwards Gdns
3 Ellis Waterton Cl
4 Leewood Pl
5 Southern Pl

M6
1 Downsview Cl
2 The Grove
3 Old Farm Gdns

M7
1 Bevan Pl
2 Pine Cl
3 St Georges Rd
4 Springfield Av

Page 164
A6
1 Churchfield Rd
2 Church La
3 Devonshire Rd
4 Minorca Cl

B1
1 Claremont Dr
2 Mere Rd
3 Old Forge Crs
4 School La
5 Westbury Cl

B6
1 Arlington Lodge
2 Castle View Rd
3 Layton Ct

C7
1 Barrington Lodge
2 Outram Pl
3 St George's Cl
4 Warren Wy

D2
1 Mulberry Trees

D5
1 Anderson Rd
2 Cross Rd
3 Grosvenor Rd
4 Mere Rd
5 Oatlands Gn
6 Victoria Cl
7 Village Cl

D6
1 Haddon Cl
2 Horvath Cl
3 Parkway
4 Shewens Rd

D8
1 Kenwood Pk
2 Mixbury Gv

E2
1 Sherbourne Gdns
2 Walton Bridge Rd

E4
1 Lakeside

E5
1 Charlton Kings

E6
1 Ardesley Wd
2 Beechwood Manor
3 Millbrook

F1
1 Queens Ct

F2
1 Sullivans Reach

1 Sycamore Ct

Page 165
G2
1 Harvey Rd
2 Montague Cl
3 Sullivans Reach
4 Thames Mead

J5
1 Cheriton Cl
2 Cottimore La
3 Edgehill Ct
4 Lansdown Cl
5 Marston Ct
6 Newark Ct
7 Regency Gdns
8 Rodney Cl
9 Stratton Cl

K5
1 Wilton Gdns

K4
1 Severn Dr
2 Walton Rd

K5
1 Carrow Rd
2 Marlborough Cl
3 Stamford Rd

K7
1 Old Esher Cl
2 Old Esher Rd
3 Profumo Rd

L6
1 Newlands Cl

L7
1 Kingfisher Cl

M1
1 Brockenhurst

M8
1 Winterdown Gdns

Page 167
G3
1 Brooklands Rd
2 Claygate La
3 Gloucester Cl
4 Manordene Cl
5 Oakdene Av

J4
1 Church Meadow

L2
1 The Close
2 Kingswood Cl
3 Mountcombe Cl
4 Oakenshaw Cl
5 Oak Hill Crs

L3
1 Dunton Cl
2 Southborough Road (the Lane)

L4
1 South Vale Rd
2 Sunningdale Cl
3 Waterside Cl

L6
1 Mcdonough Cl

L8
1 Coutts Av

M1
1 Alfriston Cl
2 Christ Church Rd
3 Lysander Gdns
4 Middle Green Cl
5 Shalston Vls

M2
1 Birchington Rd
2 Iris Cl
3 Mayberry Pl
4 South Pl

M3
1 Ellerton Rd
2 St Thomas Cl

M4
1 Baden Powell Cl
2 Carnegie Cl

M5
1 Beechcroft Rd

M7
1 Melford Cl

M8
1 Clippesby Cl

Page 168
B8
1 Orchard Cl

E7
1 Elmstead Cl

E8
1 Brook Mead
2 Woodland Cl

F1
1 Field Pl
2 Kingswood Cl
3 Voewood Cl

F2
1 Greenlaw Gdns
2 Stroudes Cl

F3
1 Keble Cl

F4
1 Kingsley Dr
2 Squirrels Gn

F5
1 Salisbury Rd

F8
1 Rembrandt Ct

Page 169
H4
1 Cheam Common Rd
2 Dalewood Gdns
3 The Retreat

J3
1 Wimborne Cl

L1
1 Cardinal Cl

L6
1 Frogmore Gdns
2 Matlock Pl
3 Northfield Crs

L7
1 Fieldsend Rd
2 Lumley Gdns

L8
1 Church Farm La
2 Church Rd
3 Dallas Rd
4 Pond Hill Gdns
5 Springclose La

M2
1 Epsom Rd
2 Stonecot Hl
3 Tudor Dr

M5
1 Aldrich Gdns

M6
1 Dale Rd
2 Elizabeth Cl
3 Ennerdale Cl
4 Frederick Cl
5 Westfield Cl

M7
1 Bourne Wy
2 Frederick Gdns

Page 170
B6
1 Belsize Gdns
2 Benhill Av
3 Crown Rd
4 Greenford Rd
5 Haddon Rd
6 Marshall's Rd
7 Rosebery Gdns
8 Willcox Rd

B7
1 Albany Ms
2 Beech Tree Pl
3 Lodge Rd
4 Russell Wy
5 St Nicholas Av
6 Thomas Wall Cl
7 Throwley Rd

C2
1 Lovett Dr
2 Netley Gdns
3 Newhouse Wk
4 St Benet's Gv

C3
1 Chalk Pit Rd
2 Clowser Cl
3 Goossens Cl
4 Hope Ct
5 Marlins Cl
6 Montana Gdns
7 Palmerston Rd
8 Shott Cl
9 Turnpike La
10 Warwick Rd

C8
1 Ambleside Gdns
2 The Quadrant
3 Sutton Court Rd

D1
1 Alphabet Gdns
2 Beadlow Cl
3 Olveston Wk

D4
1 Connaught Cl
2 Whitby Gdns

D6
1 Lavender Rd

D7
1 Betchworth Cl

D8
1 Coniston Gdns

E2
1 Assembly Wk
2 Neville Wk
3 Nevil Wk
4 Thornton Rd
5 Welbeck Rd

E3
1 Welbeck Rd

E4
1 Brooklyn Cl
2 Marfleet Cl
3 Seven Acres
4 Simms Cl

E5
1 Laburnam Av
2 Rushy Meadow La

E7
1 Corrib Dr
2 Park Hill Cl
3 Rosefield Cl

F2
1 Aitken Cl
2 Budge La
3 Chasemore Cl
4 Linton Cl
5 Mcrae La
6 Pharoah Cl

F3
1 Chestnut Cl
2 St Agatha's Gv

F4
1 Cherry Cl
2 Ivydale Rd
3 Limes Cl

F5
1 Highgrove Ms
2 Kynersley Cl
3 Langcroft Cl
4 Wrythe Gn

F6
1 Camden Rd
2 Honeywood Wk
3 Palmerston Rd
4 Rochester Rd

F7
1 Carshalton Park Rd
2 Cator Rd
3 Church Hl
4 Doral Wy
5 Wallace Crs
6 Wilmot Rd

Page 171
G4
1 Hackbridge Park Gdns
2 Mill Cl
3 Nightingale Cl
4 Rossignol Gdns

G7
1 Seymour Rd

H5
1 Bowman's Meadow
2 Caraway Pl
3 Regal Crs
4 Wandle Side

J6
1 Clifford Av
2 Eastway
3 Grassway
4 Greenway

J8
1 Rosswood Gdns

K7
1 Spooner Wk

L2
1 Cinnamon Cl
2 Peppermint Cl

L5
1 Archway Cl
2 Blandford Cl
3 Wandle Court Gdns
4 Windsor Gdns

L6
1 Colliver Rd
2 Plough La

L7
1 Banstead Wy
2 Clouston Cl
3 Haslemere Cl
4 Hindhead Wy
5 Kingswood Wy

L8
1 Eagle Cl

M2
1 Drake Rd
2 Fairmead Rd
3 Newman Rd
4 Rosedene Av

M3
1 Miller Rd

M5
1 Twickenham Cl
2 Wandle Side

M6
1 Bedlow Wy

M7
1 Rothermere Rd
2 Stafford Gdns

Page 172
A2
1 Lambeth Rd

B3
1 Croydon Gv
2 Denmead Rd
3 Renown Cl
4 Vanguard Cl

B4
1 Ainsworth Rd
2 Booth Rd
3 Cairo New Rd
4 Lower Church St
5 Reeves Cnr

B5
1 Arundel Cl
2 Hanover St
3 Latimer Rd
4 Ravenswood Rd
5 St John's Rd
6 St Leonard's Rd
7 Waynflete Av

B7
1 King Gdns
2 Page Crs
3 Thorneloe Gdns

C2
1 Hogarth Crs
2 Hughes Wk
3 Newgate
4 Singleton Cl
5 Wilford Rd

C3
1 Cobblestone Pl
2 St Michael's Rd

C4
1 Charrington Rd
2 Drummond Rd
3 Otterbourne Rd
4 Tamworth Pl

C5
1 Halstead Cl
2 Innes Yd
3 Meadow Stile
4 Middle St
5 Robert St
6 St George's Wk

C6
1 Brafferton Rd
2 Church Rd
3 Dering Pl
4 St Andrew's Rd
5 Thanet Pl
6 West Street Pl

D1
1 Amersham Cl

D2
1 Berney Rd
2 Gladstone Rd
3 Spencer Pl
4 Strathmore Rd

D3
1 Bridge Rw

D4
1 Wellesley Court Rd

D5
1 Fairfield Pth

D6
1 Rosamund Cl

D7
1 Baines Cl
2 Bartlett St
3 Blunt Rd
4 Cliffe Rd
5 Doveton Rd
6 Heathfield Rd
7 Wilson Cl

D8
1 Mansfield Pl
2 Selsdon Av
3 Sunny Nook Gdns

E1
1 Bullrush Cl
2 Roden Gdns

E3
1 Alexandra Cl
2 Heron Rd
3 Jackson's Cl
4 John's Ter

E5
1 Crusader Gdns
2 Rochester Gdns
3 St Bernards
4 Willow Mt

E6
1 Caroline Cl
2 Chichele Gdns
3 Dittoncroft Cl
4 Hunters Wy
5 Spindlewood Gdns
6 Sudbury Gdns
7 Tipton Dr

E8
1 Croham Cl

F1
1 Grindley Gdns
2 Redgrave Cl

F2
1 Amberley Gv
2 Burnham Gdns

F3
1 Anselm Cl
2 Bracewood Gdns
3 Coverdale Gdns
4 Delmey Cl
5 Lyndhurst Cl
6 Rowan Gdns

Page 173
K3
1 Alison Cl
2 Angelica Gdns
3 Basil Gdns
4 Betony Cl
5 Cottongrass Cl
6 Crocus Cl
7 Daffodil Cl
8 Fennel Cl
9 Kingcup Cl
10 Lupin Cl
11 Mallow Cl
12 Mistletoe Cl

L4
1 Peregrine Gdns

M1
1 Hillcrest Cl

Page 175
G4
1 Hawthorndene Rd
2 Wentworth Cl

M3
1 Credenhall Dr
2 Hathaway Cl

Page 176
C1
1 Addison Cl

C6
1 Beeken Dene
2 Brickfield Farm Gdns
3 Greenacres Cl
4 Hunter's Gv
5 Romsey Cl
6 Shurlock Dr
7 Sumner Cl

E4
1 Northolme Ri

E6
1 Cromford Cl
2 Ridgeway Crescent Gdns

E7
1 Downsway
2 Wentworth Cl

F1
1 Cotswold Ri
2 Marlborough Cl

F2
1 Horsmonden Cl
2 Sequoia Cl

F5
1 Ambrose Cl
2 Bishop Butt Cl
3 Shepherds Cl

F6
1 St Josephs Cl
2 Strickland Wy

F7
1 Freesia Cl
2 Raleigh Ms

F8
1 Flint Cl
2 Huron Cl
3 Lynne Cl
4 Superior Dr

Page 177
G2
1 Aynscombe Angle
2 Deakins Ter
3 Devonshire Rd
4 Lamorna Cl

K5
1 Hawfield Bank

L7
1 Orlestone Gdns

Page 180
C7
1 St Theresa Cl

E6
1 Ash Ms
2 Clayton Rd
3 Prospect Pl

E7
1 Little Orchards
2 Richmond Cl

E8
1 Downs Hill Rd
2 Highridge Cl

F1
1 Shire Ct
2 South Mead

F2
1 Chichester Ct
2 The Ridings

F3
1 Curvan Cl
2 Village Gdns

F4
1 Epsom Rd
2 Fairview Rd

F5
1 Dirdene Cl
2 Dirdene Gdns
3 Dirdene Gv
4 The Stanfords
5 Windmill End
6 Yeomanry Cl

F6
1 St Martin's Cl

Page 181
G3
1 Chatsfield
2 Mongers La
3 Persfield Rd
4 Seymour Ms

J3
1 Birchfield Gv
2 Bridleway Cl
3 Gomshall Rd
4 Lodge Cl

K7
1 Acacia Cl
2 Aspen Wy
3 Maple Pl
4 Pine Pl
5 Poplar Av
6 Sycamore Ri

M7
1 Lower Dunnymans
2 Lower Northfield
3 Lower Sawleywood
4 Upper Dunnymans
5 Upper Sawleywood

Page 182
A2
1 Chelmsford Cl

A7
1 Ashley Dr

B1
1 Abbotsleigh Cl
2 Bonchurch Cl
3 Chanctonbury Gdns
4 Eastleigh Cl
5 Grange V
6 Upton Dene
7 Westmoreland Dr

F7
1 Tonbridge Cl

Page 183
H2
1 The Wood End
2 The Woodlands

H7
1 June Cl

J7
1 Ascot Ms
2 Freshwood Wy
3 Sandy Hill Rd
4 Tollhouse La

L1
1 Harmony Cl
2 Plesman Wy
3 Rheingold Wy

L7
1 Bouverie Gdns
2 Mead Dr
3 Vale Cl

M5
1 Sydney Av

Page 184
B4
1 Christchurch Rd
2 Redbarn Cl
3 The Spinney
4 Whytecliffe Rd South

C2
1 Chaseley Dr
2 Stockhams Cl
3 Timberling Gdns
4 White Hl

D1
1 Barn Crs
2 Rydal Cl

D8
1 Ashurst Cl

E1
1 Selsdon Rd

E3
1 Wettern Cl

E4
1 Briton Cl

F3
1 Ewhurst Av

F6
1 Borrowdale Cl

Notes